North Carolina Wills:
A Testator Index, 1665 – 1900

NORTH CAROLINA WILLS:

A Testator Index, 1665 – 1900

Thornton W. Mitchell

Corrected and Revised Edition

In one volume

GENEALOGICAL PUBLISHING Co., Inc

First edition published 1987 in two volumes.
Corrected and revised edition, in one volume,
published by Genealogical Publishing Co., Inc.
Baltimore, 1992, 1996, 2001

Library of Congress Catalogue Card Number 92-72852
International Standard Book Number 0-8063-1361-7
Made in the United States of America

PREFACE TO REVISED EDITION

After initial publication of North Carolina Wills: A Testator Index, 1665-1900, two lists of corrections and additions were sent to those persons who had purchased copies. The first list was dated September 8, 1987, and was also included at the end of each volume in the second printing. The second was dated October 9, 1989. In both instances the master data was corrected to reflect the changes. Additional corrections and additions were entered in the data base two more times; these consisted principally of changing the location of originals because of transfers of wills from several counties to the State Archives. Original wills of Beaufort, Catawba, Union, Pender, Person, and Rowan counties were transferred and their location entry has been changed accordingly.

It should be remembered that the names in the index were taken from the signature line of the original will if it was available or of the recorded copy. This means that alternative spellings should be searched before concluding that a name has not been included.

Many have called attention to errors and corrections and a number of people, particularly the staff of the State Archives Search Room, have noted additions or deletions that needed to be made. This corrected and revised edition could not have been possible without the generous help consistently given by Dr. Arlon K. Kemple, computer manager of the Department of Cultural Resources, Raleigh. To him and to many others, I express my very sincere appreciation.

Thornton W. Mitchell

Spring, 1992

TABLE OF CONTENTS

ACKNOWLEDGMENTS

This index was made possible because of the help received from so many people that I hesitate to name them for fear of omitting someone who made a contribution. My first expression of appreciation must, of course, be to the late William Perry Johnson who first accumulated data for a will index and who made his notes available to me. Although the present index did not develop in the manner in which Johnson apparently projected it, his notes were helpful in its preparation. Since the Johnson notes are now the property of the Friends Historical Collection, Guilford College, Greensboro, North Carolina, I am indebted to the curator of the collection for permission to use them in compiling the index.

Without the availability of computer technology, the preparation of a meaningful index to testators of North Carolina wills would have been an almost endless task. I am deeply indebted to Dr. Arlon K. Kemple, computer manager of the North Carolina Department of Cultural Resources, for his help and guidance in transferring a mass of information into a meaningful data base. Without him and the assistance he gave to a person who knew little about computers, this publication might not have seen the light of day. Barry Weaver, formerly of the Radio Shack Computer Center, Raleigh, and presently of Computer Systems Resources, Sanford, North Carolina, showed a willingness to solve problems that, to me, seemed insoluble. Michael Stroud, Raleigh, generously guided me to a computer program that made this index possible. I am also indebted to Dr. Peter Batke, Edwin A. Camin, Walt Kennedy, and Dr. David Langmeyer, all of whom freely gave technical advice. The expertise and patience of Vicky Boneysteele were invaluable in extricating me from a morass of problems into which I had inadvertently plunged.

Most of the data entry for this index was from microfilm copies of county will registers. That film was made available to me by Lee Albright, Pam Toms, and the staff of the Genealogical Services Branch, North Carolina State Library, Raleigh. This was, however, only one of the ways in which that highly competent staff helped me; I was constantly encouraged--some might call it nagged--to complete the project.

After the data entry and printout, the registered wills were verified from surviving original wills in the State Archives. I cannot praise too highly the quality of the staff of this extraordinary institution and the unfailing courtesy and helpfulness with which they assisted me. In a period of nearly three years, they brought to me about 1,000 archives boxes and many volumes from the Archives stacks, and they did it without complaint. I am deeply indebted to David J. Olson, Frank D. Gatton, George Stevenson, and all of the staff members of the

Reference Unit, Archives and Records Section, Division of Archives and History, which is reponsible for the functioning of the Search Room of the North Carolina State Archives. Without their help, this index could not have been completed.

During the final phases of compilation of data for the index, I visited the offices of clerks of superior court in counties that have retained some or all of their original wills. I was received with unfailing courtesy and willingness to be of assistance. To all of these public officials and the members of their staffs, I express my sincere appreciation.

Many individuals have helped me in many ways--by directing me to wills recorded in unusual places, by calling my attention to errors I had made, by being generally supportive. I must acknowledge the assistance I have received from Ruby Arnold, Jonathan B. Butcher, Lindley S. Butler, Betty J. Camin, Gertrude S. Carraway, James L. Glenn, Weynette P. Haun, Jo White Linn, Ransom McBride, Elizabeth Moore, William S. Price, Jr., George Stevenson, Carl E. Swain, Mary Bondurant Warren, Frances H. Wynne, and Willis Wynne.

Financial assistance in the form of a grant from the Kellenberger Historical Foundation subsidized the project. This assistance is gratefully acknowledged. The Foundation, of course, is not responsible in any way for the contents of the index or for any errors that have been made in it.

My wife, Memory F. Mitchell, put up with my involvement in the will index project for more than three years and joined me at several county courthouses in comparing original wills with the recorded copies. She also helped in the tedious task of checking computer printout to ensure the accuracy of the data entered. She and our sons, James and David, tolerated cheerfully the hours I spent entering, checking, and verifying data. To them, I am particularly grateful and appreciative.

Thornton W. Mitchell

Spring, 1987

INTRODUCTION

In 1963 the late William Perry Johnson began publication of a series which he titled Index to North Carolina Wills, 1663-1900. The research that led to that work was begun at least as early as 1955, and by 1973 lists of recorded wills in twenty-three counties had been published. Johnson's work was not really an index, because he listed only recorded wills, with either the probate or preparation date, in the order in which they were entered in the will books or registers for each county. To locate a specific will from the four volumes that Johnson published, the searcher had to know the county and approximate date of probate.

Johnson began work on his will lists several years before the local records program of the North Carolina Division of Archives and History started in 1959. Because of that program essential county records were microfilmed for security purposes, and valuable records no longer needed in daily operations were removed to the State Archives. It was not until 1971 that local records archivists and microfilm camera operators had visited all counties in the state at least one time, and microfilm copies of recorded wills for all counties were readily available in Raleigh. Neither copies of the county will books nor files of original wills were accessible at a central point at the time Johnson did most of his work. It was necessary, therefore, for him to visit county courthouses to make lists of wills from the will books, and his research was delayed accordingly.

After publishing the fourth volume of his index, which carried the project through Columbus County but did not include Bute County, Johnson discontinued the project, in part, because of poor health. In 1977, after I expressed an interest in continuing and completing the will index, Johnson loaned me his notes which I had microfilmed. Those notes, which are now the property of the Friends Historical Collection, Guilford College, Greensboro, North Carolina, have been useful in preparing the present testator index, and they have been used with the permission of the curator of the collection. It is significant that beginning with Craven County, the next county alphabetically following Columbus, few of the county listings were complete; in some instances the notes were based on the devisor indexes in the county concerned. Although Johnson included some alphabetical listings of the original wills that were in the State Archives, both in his published will indexes and in his notes, he did not compare the recorded and original versions of the same will.

The manner in which wills were proved and probated in North Carolina is described in Helen F. M. Leary and Maurice R. Stirewalt, editors, North Carolina Research: Genealogy and Local History, published by the North Carolina Genealogical Society, in chapters entitled "Wills" by Raymond A. Winslow, Jr., and George Stevenson. Until 1760 wills were proved before the county court of pleas and quarter sessions or before the governor, acting as ordinary, but all were supposed to be filed with the provincial secretary. Not all precincts and, after about 1739, counties followed this practice, however, but kept the original wills. After 1760 wills were proved before the county court, the district superior courts, or the governor. Of the district superior courts, of which there were eventually eight, only Edenton kept a register of wills proved; this is now identified as Chowan County Will Book 1, and surviving original wills proved before the district court have been combined with other surviving original wills of the county. The governor discontinued the practice of proving wills about 1795; those wills were filed with the provincial secretary and later the secretary of state. Because the secretary's office was located in New Bern, some of those original and recorded wills have been intermingled with Craven County records.

Although all county court clerks were supposed to maintain records of wills proved, the manner in which they did so varied considerably. In some instances, a notation in the county court minutes that the will had been proved was considered to meet the requirement for recording, and the original document was then filed in the clerk's office. In some cases, the clerk at a later date copied surviving original wills into a record book which was usually given a number in a different sequence or was identified by a distinctive title such as "Old Will Book." Some counties did not begin to record wills in any other way until relatively late, and files of original wills and notations in the court minutes are the only record. Other county court clerks kept verbatim copies of wills in record books along with all documents submitted to the court except deeds. Those books are variously identified as "recording dockets," "wills and inventories," "record books," or by other titles. Some clerks kept record books containing wills only, but those are a minority. All county court clerks kept files of original wills and of wills that were denied probate. Many of those are missing, however, because of fire or carelessness or because they were loaned but never returned.

Following approval of the code of civil procedure in 1868, the procedure for probating wills changed. The county courts were discontinued, and all of their records were turned over to the county clerks of superior court. The superior court clerk then became responsible for probate and was usually identified as "judge of probate." Beginning in 1868 the probate documents were copied into the will books along with the will, and the original document was filed in the clerk's office. With some exceptions, a new will book was created in each county, although it was numbered in the same sequence as the earlier record volumes. One major distinction, however, was the fact that after 1868 only wills and their probate documents were entered in the will books. The nature of the probate documents varied greatly from one county to another and it was not until about 1875 that they were standardized in all counties. It should be noted in this connection that the probate documents in some counties include a great deal of family history that is not otherwise available.

The first will proved in North Carolina was that of Mary Forsten in 1665, with no county indicated. Only a few of the wills proved before 1700 have survived in the records identified in the State Archives as secretary of state wills. A majority of the counties have transferred all or part of their surviving original wills to the State Archives, but some counties have kept all or part of them. There has been major loss both of recorded and original wills from fire, war, natural disaster, or carelessness as described in Frank D. Gatton, "A History of Local Records in North Carolina, 1665-1959," an unpublished master's thesis at North Carolina State University, Raleigh (1977).

The year 1900 was chosen as the terminal date of this index for several reasons. All but three of North Carolina's 100 counties had been created by that time; and local records at county courthouses seem to be more available in the twentieth century than earlier. In addition, 1900 was a watershed year in the state. Municipalities were developing, and increasing numbers of them were being incorporated by the General Assembly. Industry other than agriculture was growing, and with improvements in transportation the population became increasingly mobile. By 1900 the plantation economy that had played such a major role in antebellum North Carolina had virtually disappeared and wills less and less reflected the passing of real property among members of the same family. Politically, educationally, and economically, North Carolina changed significantly after 1900.

The procedure followed in compiling this index in its first stages was similar to that followed by the late William Perry Johnson in preparing the lists of wills appearing in his four-volume Index to North Carolina Wills: 1663-1900. Wills were first listed as they were recorded in each county, generally in will book order. The data entered for each will is discussed at length in following paragraphs. Data for each county was then printed in alphabetical order by surname and given name of each testator. These printed lists were then compared with surviving original wills in the State Archives and, where necessary, in the courthouses of counties retaining original wills. The disks containing the individual entries were then corrected to reflect errors in name and date of probate appearing in the recorded wills. It must be emphasized that when an original will survived, either in the State Archives or the county, the name appearing in this index has been taken from the _signature_ entry of the original. After correction, the list of names was again printed in alphabetical order and information concerning the wills of that particular county was compiled and printed for preparation of the county directory appearing in these volumes. Upon completion of the entire project, the data was fed into a main-frame computer where it was alphabetized, corrected where necessary, and printed in camera-ready copy for publication.

One exception to this procedure should be noted. Johnson listed wills from the secretary of state records in the State Archives for the counties he completed, using J. Bryan Grimes, _Abstract of North Carolina Wills Compiled from Original and Recorded Wills in the Office of the Secretary of State,_ published initially in Raleigh in 1910. With the exception of Land Grant Book Number Four, which contains wills, the records on which Grimes's _Abstracts_ was based are now in the State Archives. The data from the secretary of state wills entered in this index was taken from those original records, which include another record book which was received from Craven County and identified as one of the long-lost provincial secretary will books. In addition, provincial secretary wills now recorded in Craven County Deed Book Five were also entered, as were wills from Land Grant Book Number Four. Data was not taken from the Grimes _Abstracts_ nor was it taken from Fred A. Olds, _An Abstract of North Carolina Wills from about 1760 to about 1800,_ first published in 1925. In this connection, it should be noted that wills from the secretary of state records and from some of the earliest counties in the state were abstracted in the three-volume _North Carolina Historical and Genealogical Register,_ edited by J. R. B. Hathaway (1900-1902). The Hathaway abstracts have not been cited in this index.

It should also be noted that information about some wills has been taken from the colonial court records (CCR), the surviving records of the district superior courts, and from original case papers of the North Carolina Supreme Court (SC). The wills cited from these sources are copies and were filed in connection with probate or estate appeals. Information about these and other courts is summarized in Leary and Stirewalt, _North Carolina Research,_ in a chapter by George Stevenson entitled "Higher Court Records."

There are five elements for each entry in this index. The first of these is the name of the testator by surname with the first name or initials following. During initial data entry, the given name for each testator was limited to eleven letters which did not permit entry of all middle initials; for some entries, identifications such as "Sr." and "Jr." had to be omitted. The names appearing herein were taken from recorded wills initially and then were verified from originals which have survived. Because of variations in spelling both in originals and recorded copies, the signature of the testator was chosen for the entry in this index, even when the will was signed by a mark. Discrepancies in the spelling of names was great; in one recorded will and probate documents, the given name "Eleanor" was spelled four different ways. In addition, the spelling of the family surname changed from time to time within the same family. The writing of some of the clerks who recorded the wills was not uniformly of high quality and its reproduction on microfilm was occasionally impossible to read. Where an original has survived, or where a copy could be located, the spelling of the last and first name in this index was taken from that original or as it appeared in the copy.

Late in the nineteenth century, some wills were signed by the testators using initials rather than given names. In some instances, the given name could be determined either from the introductory statement of the will or from references to the devisor in the probate papers. In such cases, the given name was substituted for the initials appearing in the signature line of the will.

There are a few exceptions to the way in which names are listed in the index that should be noted. In two cases, one in Mecklenburg County and the other in Randolph County, a will was made by a black woman who used only her given name. The first name appears as a surname, and the will is identified as having been made by a free woman of color (fwc), a phrase used in both wills. Bladen County records include the only will identified as having been made by a slave; the man's name is followed by the phrase, in parentheses, "a slave."

The county in which each will was originally probated is indicated by the three-digit number which has been developed by the State Archives to identify the records of that county. This system has been used because it provides for such discontinued counties as Bute and Tryon, in which wills were proved. If a will was probated in more than one county or in a county other than where filed, the county in which it was initially proved is shown as is the county where it was recorded or where a copy was filed. The three-digit county identifier in which the will was proved has been used even when the will itself indicates that the testator was a resident of another county; this practice was particularly true when a county was divided to form another county or part was attached to an adjoining county.

The inclusion in this index of all wills filed in a particular county has been beneficial in that several wills of burned counties were also proved elsewhere. Wills proved in another state have been identified by use of the two-letter designator used at the present time by the United States Postal Service. Thus, a will originally probated in Virginia is identified by "VA," and the North Carolina county where a copy was recorded and filed is also shown. The practice of recording out-of-state wills varied from county to county and even within a county. Further, a few wills have been included that originally were proved outside the United States (England, West Indies, etc). Those are identified by designators shown in the list of abbreviations. In a few instances, particularly in wills probated during the colonial period, the county could not be identified either from the will or from probate data. Such wills show "N" (none) for the county.

The numerical identification of each county together with comments about each is indicated in a special section appearing at the front of this index.

The date shown is the date of probate of the will if it could be determined either from the original or the recorded will. It should be noted in this respect that frequently probate documents were not dated, even though, if a will was recorded, it was almost universally proved. If the probate date could not be established, the date the will was originally signed is shown and that date is identified by a letter "c" before the date. Throughout the eighteenth and nineteenth centuries, most wills were signed shortly before the death of the testator. In a few instances, long periods of time elapsed between signature and probate; the longest noted in the preparation of this index was sixty years. Note also that until 1868, wills were proved before the county court which met once every three months; there could, therefore, be a lapse of two or three months between the date of death and the proof of the will. In a few instances, neither date could be established, and the date for such wills is indicated as "N. D." (no date).

The location by book and page number of the recorded copy of each will in each of the counties is shown. Will registers were identified by various names; of those "will book" or "record of wills" was the most common. Other designations, such as "recording docket" and "wills and inventories," were also used. The various names of the record books are identified in the list of abbreviations at the beginning of this index.
In addition, original unrecorded wills that have survived were also entered; the entry "Orig. Only" (original only) indicates that the will was not recorded. There were various reasons for failure to record a will. In some instances, particularly in the period before 1868, it was determined that the will was not

authentic; in other cases, probate was never completed because the value of the estate was low. In some counties, recording of wills did not begin until late, and documents for the early period were never formally registered. In a few instances, wills from other counties or states were filed but not recorded; such wills are identified as "copy."

If a will was recorded more than one time in the same county, the duplicate recording was not included in the index. If space was available, however, the page number of the second recording was included. Duplicate recording was not common, but it occurred when a dissent or caveat was filed or when an executor or executrix changed. A will in Rutherford County was originally probated in 1883 and was proved again in 1900 in order to settle the estate. Unless otherwise indicated in the section identifying each county at the beginning of each volume, the record volumes containing the registered wills remain in the custody of the clerk or superior court in the county concerned.

Finally, the location of the original will, if it has survived, is shown. This is either in the State Archives (AR) or in the county (CTY). A three-digit county designator before the symbol showing the location of the original is a key to the county in the records of which that particular will is filed. With only two exceptions (Warren and Tryon counties) the documents probated in one county and again probated or proved in another county are copies. They have been included, however, because some wills originally proved in burned counties were additionally proved elsewhere, and they also show the extent of interests of some of the individuals concerned. Following the symbol locating the original, where appropriate, is the designation "Nunc.," meaning that the will was nuncupative or oral; or the designation that the will is a copy. Additional entries following the location symbol are explained in the list of abbreviations. If an original will or a copy could not be found, there is no entry in this column of the index.

Although other sources for wills were searched, they were limited to public records. Wills or copies of wills were not sought in private papers, principally because of the difficulty of finding them. The large and important repositories at the University of North Carolina, Duke University, and East Carolina University, as well as the private collections in the State Archives undoubtedly contain wills. They were not, however, included within the scope of this present index.

Where it has survived, the original will should be consulted. There were many errors made in transcribing wills prior to the introduction of photocopying, and some names of heirs were omitted or distorted in copying. In one instance, a codicil was not included in a recorded copy, although only it gave the name of the children of the testator, because it devised slaves and the will was probated after emancipation. Recorded copies, particularly after 1868, should not be ignored, because the probate documents in some instances show the names of heirs. It is unfortunate that so many original wills have been lost; it is even more unfortunate that will registers in some counties have been lost or destroyed.

It is frustrating to find a will that devises real or personal property to a wife, husband, or children without naming them. In such cases, the estate papers in the county or in the State Archives should be consulted because they may show the distribution of the estate. In addition, only a small percentage of the people who died in North Carolina before 1901 left wills; many of the remainder did not have property, but if they did there is estate data on those individuals. The State Archives has gathered those papers and filed them alphabetically by name of decedent for each county. Those papers are a valuable source of family information in cases in which the wills contain none.

The names appearing in this index were alphabetized by computer. For this reason, surnames with prefixes such as "Mac" and "Mc" do not appear together or at the beginning of names beginning with "M" as they do in many alphabetical arrangements. Names beginning with the prefix "Mac" are alphabetized with other names beginning with the letters "Ma;" and names with the prefix "Mc" are arranged between names beginning with "Ma" and "Me."

Finally, there are undoubtedly errors and omissions in this index despite my best efforts to avoid them. In the counties where wills were recorded with other estate documents, they were sometimes difficult to spot on microfilm. Some handwriting of nineteenth-century clerks was so difficult to read that I may have listed wills for persons who never actually existed. I regret any errors, but I hope in this case that the pluses will more than offset the minuses.

IDENTIFICATION OF COUNTIES

001--Alamance County

Formed 1849 from Orange County. There has been no significant loss of either recorded or original wills of the county.

002--Albemarle County

Formed about 1664 and consisted, generally, of the northeastern part of the present North Carolina, north of Albemarle Sound and east of the Chowan River. Albemarle County initially included four precincts: Currituck, Pasquotank, Perquimans, and Chowan. There is no indication that Albemarle functioned in the traditional manner of a county, and it disappeared when its precincts were renamed as counties in 1739.

003--Alexander County

Formed 1847 from Iredell, Caldwell, and Wilkes counties. Recording of wills did not begin until 1865, and only a few wills probated before that date have survived. Some records of the county were destroyed by Federal troops in April, 1865.

004--Alleghany County

Formed 1859 from Ashe County. Recording in Will Book A began in 1871, and a few wills for a period 1862-1867 were recorded in a record book for inventories, marriages, and wills which is identified as Will Book 1 and which is now in the State Archives. Only a few original wills for the period prior to 1871 have survived.

005--Anson County

Formed 1750 from Bladen County. Wills in the county apparently were not recorded on a regular basis until about 1822, although surviving original wills probated prior to 1822 were registered much later in Will Books 1 and 2 in rough alphabetical order. In April, 1868, fire destroyed the Anson County courthouse, although will books and original wills survived. In 1906, Will Books 1, A, and B were recopied. Many wills probated after 1760 are recorded in the will books and most of the original wills from which they were copied have survived.

006--Ashe County

Formed 1799 from Wilkes County. Recording of wills on a regular basis apparently began about 1853, although wills proved at earlier dates were later entered into what are now known as Will Books A, B, and C. Some records are believed to have been destroyed in 1865.

007--Avery County
Formed 1911 from Mitchell, Watauga, and Caldwell counties. Not included in this index.

008--Bath County
Formed in 1696 from the territory south of Albemarle Sound. It consisted initially of Archdale (Craven), Pamptecough (Beaufort), and Wickham (Hyde) precincts. Discontinued in 1739 when precincts were renamed counties. There is some indication that there was a county court for Bath, but its records descended to Beaufort County, the court of which continued to sit at Bath Town, the county seat of Bath County.

009--Beaufort County
Created about 1705 as Pamptecough Precinct of Bath County; name changed to Beaufort about 1712. The county court sat at Bath Town and represented both Beaufort and Hyde counties until about 1739 when the precinct system was superseded. The Beaufort County court continued to sit at Bath Town until 1785 when Washington was made the county seat; there are, therefore, some Bath and Hyde county wills and deeds among Beaufort County records. In March, 1808, Beaufort County began a series of court clerk's recording dockets popularly known as Orphan Books (OB). There is some indication that wills probated in the county prior to 1808 were recorded in an "orphan book," but that record volume has not survived. A few early wills were recorded in Deed Book 1; and wills proved prior to 1808 were at a much later date entered into a record book identified as Old Will Book (OWB). Beaufort County discontinued the Orphan Book system in 1868 and initiated Will Book 1 in that year. As of May 1, 1992, original wills of Beaufort County to 1877 were in the State Archives; original wills after 1877 were in the custody of the county clerk of superior court. The orphan books are in the State Archives.

010--Bertie County
Formed 1722 from Chowan County. Recording of wills apparently began in 1760, although surviving original wills contain some indication that they were recorded at a later date. Will Book E (1797-1805) has been copied, and the pagination of the copy does not correspond with the original. Some original wills probated late in the 19th century are missing.

011--Bladen County

Formed 1734 from New Hanover County. Two fires, the most recent in January, 1893, destroyed many court records. A few early wills were recorded in deed books, but wills were not regularly recorded until about 1834. Will Book 1 contains wills recorded from the early 1830s until 1862; Will Book 2 contains wills recorded from 1866 until 1892. Both will books, however, contain wills for the period from 1760 until the early 1830s. In 1958 photostatic copies of 47 wills from the records of the secretary of state in the State Archives were obtained and were recorded at the end of Will Book 2; they have not been included in this index as records of Bladen County because they are indexed with all of the secretary of state wills. The existing Will Books 1 and 2 appear to be copies because they are all in the same handwriting; there is, however, no indication of the date they were made. As of June 1, 1986, the few surviving original wills of Bladen County remained in the custody of the county clerk of superior court.

012--Brunswick County

Formed 1764 from New Hanover and Bladen counties. Recording of wills on a regular basis apparently began about 1869, although Will Book A contains some indication that wills were actually entered at a later date. In 1908 the General Assembly (Ch. 106, Public Laws, 1908 Extra Session) directed that all unrecorded wills of Brunswick County dated before January 1, 1875, that had been proved according to law, were to be recorded and indexed. This was to include all wills that had been recorded in county court minutes or other record books as well as all wills recorded in the register of deeds office. The wills contained in several record books and some original wills previously unrecorded were entered in the volume identified as Will Book B. Some early wills (1764-1783) were recorded in Deed Books A and B.

013--Buncombe County

Formed 1791 from Burke and Rutherford counties. A courthouse fire in 1830 destroyed many court records and many of the surviving records were carried off three years later. In 1848 the Buncombe County courthouse burned again, and in 1865 many records were destroyed when the courthouse burned for the third time. Will books for wills probated after 1830 appear to be complete, but many original wills, particularly for the period before 1865, are missing.

014--Burke County

Formed 1777 from Rowan County. In April, 1865, a detachment

of Union troops from General Stoneman's command threw records from the courthouse and burned them. Will books and original wills were included. Some original wills probated prior to 1865 survived and are in the State Archives; included are copies of wills from other sources such as North Carolina Supreme Court original case papers. As of June 1, 1986, original wills proved after 1868 remained in the custody of the county clerk of superior court.

015--Bute County

Formed 1764 from Granville County; abolished 1779 when the county was divided between Franklin and Warren counties. Wills were recorded in record books that contained inventories, accounts, and other estate data. Bute County Record Book 1 is in the State Archives; Records Books 2 and 3 became Warren County Will Books 1 and 2. Surviving original wills are in the State Archives as records of Bute County. Some original wills probated in Warren County after 1779 are in the Bute County records in the Archives.

016--Cabarrus County

Formed 1792 from Mecklenburg County. Recording of wills in Will Book 1 began in 1843, although wills had been copied into the minutes of the county court of pleas and quarter sessions beginning in 1830. In 1875, a courthouse fire destroyed some records, including most of the original wills. The surviving original wills were principally for testators with surnames beginning with the letters H, M, W, and Y. At a later date, these surviving wills were copied into Will Book A. Many of the original wills are missing.

017--Caldwell County

Formed 1841 from Burke and Wilkes counties. Recording of wills began in 1841, and there appears to have been no significant loss of records.

018--Camden County

Formed 1777 from Pasquotank County. Will Books A and B, covering the period to 1822, are missing; the late William Perry Johnson stated that they were burned during the Civil War but did not indicate the source of his information. The earliest probate date of surviving original wills is 1859. It is known that Union troops moved across Camden County when returning to Currituck Court House after occupying Elizabeth City in December, 1863; there is, however, no indication that Camden County courthouse was burned or that records of the county were destroyed.

019--Carteret County

Formed 1722 from Craven County. Beginning in 1765, wills were recorded in a "Record of Wills and Bonds" by Rob Read, clerk of court. This record book is in the State Archives and is bound into a miscellaneous volume, beginning at leaf 55; the volume has a shelf call number 019.405.1. There is some indication that part of this volume, which is identified as Record Book A, may have been lost. Some of the original wills recorded in what is now identified as Will Book A indicate that they were recorded in Will Book B. The existing Will Book A does not begin until 1830. Wills probated prior to 1830 were recorded in Will Book D and the first several pages of Will Book E in 1908. The court of pleas and quarter sessions of Carteret County was "Suspended by U. S. Martial Law" after February, 1862, and no wills were probated in the county until November term, 1865.

020--Caswell County

Formed 1777 from Orange County. Recording of wills began in 1777 in what are identified as record books (RB). These books were lettered A through T (excluding J); beginning in 1868; the county maintained will books that are identified by letters beginning with A. As of June 1, 1986, original wills of the county for the period after 1867 are in the custody of the Caswell County clerk of superior court.

021--Catawba County

Formed 1842 from Lincoln County. The first wills were recorded in 1843. There has been no significant loss of records of the county.

022--Chatham County

Formed 1771 from Orange County. Recording of wills in the record book identified as Will Book A began in 1798; according to the originals of the first wills registered in the volume, it was initially identified as "Book D." From February court, 1784, until February court, 1794, wills were recorded in a record book identified as "Deeds, Bills of Sale, Inventories of Estates, Wills," which is referred to in entries for Chatham County wills as RB-1. This record volume is now in the State Archives; the shelf call number is 022.801.23. This record book was originally identified as "Book B." "Book C," which includes deeds, bills of sale, inventories of estates, accounts of sale as well as wills for the period 1794-1798, is also in the State Archives and is referred to as RB-2. The volume is identified as "Record of Wills, Book A, Part 1" (shelf number 022.801.18). "Book A," containing recorded copies of wills for the period prior to 1784 has disappeared.

023--Cherokee County

Formed 1839 from Macon County. In 1865, Union troops burned the courthouse, destroying most of the clerk's records. Recording of wills did not resume until 1869.

024--Chowan County

Originally formed as a precinct of Albemarle County, with Edenton serving as seat of the provincial government at various times during the colonial period. Recording of wills on a regular basis appears to have begun in the period 1803-1807 in what was originally identified as Will Book A. At about the same time, however, original wills that had been proved but not registered were copied into two record volumes identified as Will Books A and B. The first Will Book A was then renumbered as Will Book C. The record book identified herein as Chowan County Will Book 1 is actually the register in which wills proved before the Edenton District Superior Court were recorded in the period 1760-1772. Some of the original wills now filed with Chowan County records appear to be strays from the records of the provincial secretary that are now identified as secretary of state wills in the State Archives.

025--Clay County

Formed 1861 from Cherokee County. In May, 1870, the county jail and courthouse burned, destroying all of the court records, including will books and original wills.

026--Cleveland County

Formed 1841 from Rutherford and Lincoln counties. There has been no significant loss of records of the county.

027--Columbus County

Formed 1808 from Brunswick and Bladen counties. Recording of wills in the regular course of business appears to have started about 1852. In 1846 the county court employed a person to transcribe all of the unrecorded wills in the clerk's office; forty-five wills were copied. It is not known if all of the wills offered for probate survived to be recorded at that time.

028--Craven County

Formed 1705 as Archdale Precinct of Bath County; name changed to Craven about 1712. Early records are believed to have been destroyed during the Tuscarora Indian War of 1712. Most, but not all, original wills were filed with the provincial secretary prior to 1760 and thereafter some Craven County wills were filed in the secretary of state records. From 1765 until December term, 1784, wills were not recorded but the originals were filed in the clerk's office. Beginning with December court, 1784, will books were maintained, although part of Will Book C appears to have been lost. After March term, 1862, until September term, 1865, no wills were recorded in Craven County. There is some indication that wills were proved in other counties during that period; at least one is known to have been proved in Lenoir County, the records of which burned in 1878 and 1880.

029--Cumberland County

Formed 1754 from Bladen County. A few wills were recorded in Deed Book 1 about 1760, but regular recording of wills did not begin until 1797 when Will Book A was initiated. Some of the original wills are missing.

030--Currituck County

Originally formed as a precinct of Albemarle County. Recording of wills in the county began in 1772 and will books have survived although Will Book 2 has been severely damaged by water. Most of the surviving original wills were proved after 1853, although there are a few wills probated before that date. No wills were proved in the county between March court, 1862, and September court, 1865, during occupation by the Union army.

031--Dare County

Formed 1870 from Currituck, Tyrrell, and Hyde counties. There has been no significant loss of either recorded or original wills of the county.

032--Davidson County

Formed 1822 from Rowan County. Recording of wills began in 1823. The first two will books were not numbered but they were usually referred to as Will Books 1 and 2; they were so cited at the time the wills were recorded. Although some original wills are missing, there has been no significant loss of records.

033--Davie County

Formed 1836 from Rowan County. Recording of wills began upon the creation of the county. As of June 1, 1986, original wills probated after 1866 were in the custody of the Davie County clerk of superior court. Original wills probated prior to that date were in the State Archives; many of them are illegible because of water damage to the documents.

034--Dobbs County

Formed 1758 from the eastern portion of Johnston County. It was abolished in 1791 when Glasgow (Greene) and Lenoir counties were formed. Lenoir County succeeded to the records of Dobbs County, and they were destroyed when the Lenoir County courthouse burned in 1878 and 1880. The wills cited as from Dobbs County are from the secretary of state wills or certified copies filed in another county.

035--Duplin County

Formed 1750 from New Hanover County. Recording of wills in separate will books began in 1830. The record book containing wills for the period 1835-1845 is missing, although approximately 50 original wills for that period have survived. At a later date, surviving unrecorded wills proved before 1830 and filed in the clerk's office were entered in a record book identified as Will Book A. These generally include wills proved before the county court between about 1760 and 1830, although a few wills probated later than 1830 were included. Some very early wills (1750-1766) were recorded in early registers which remained in Sampson County when it was created from Duplin in 1784; these record books are now identified as Sampson County Deed Books 1, 2, and 3 and are so noted in entries for Duplin County.

036--Durham County

Formed 1881 from Orange and Wake Counties. Recording of wills began immediately, and there has been no significant loss of records. As of April 1, 1986, all original wills were in the custody of the Durham County clerk of superior court.

037--Edgecombe County

Formed 1741 from Bertie County. Recording of wills began in 1760. The original wills for 1884 and 1885 are missing; with this exception, there has been no significant loss of records in the county. Most of the wills that were not recorded (as indicated by "Orig. Only" in the "Recorded Copy" column) were not accepted by the county court and thus were never probated.

038--Forsyth County

Formed 1849 from Stokes County. There has been no significant loss of either recorded or original wills of the county. Many of the wills proved in Stokes County before 1849 were for testators who lived in that portion of the county that became Forsyth.

039--Franklin County

Formed 1779 from Bute County. Although recording of wills appears to have started with formation of the county, neither the registered copy nor the original will, in many instances, show the probate date. Until 1868 wills were recorded with other estate documents such as inventories, reports of sale, and division of real and personal property in registers that are now identified as will books. Will Books O and P were relabeled "Record of Accounts" after they were copied; the originals of these two volumes are in the State Archives in the estates classification of records of the county. Will Book P contains no wills; there is no Will Book T. Although there has been no significant loss of records of the county, some of the original wills are missing.

040--Gaston County

Formed 1846 from Lincoln County. A courthouse fire in December, 1874, resulted in the destruction of some records. The will books appear to be complete, but some of the early original wills are missing.

041--Gates County

Formed 1779 from Chowan, Hertford, and Perquimans counties. Recording of wills began immediately, and there has been no significant loss of either recorded or original wills of the county.

042--Glasgow County

Formed 1791 from Dobbs County. Name changed to Greene County in 1799. No records of Glasgow County are known to have survived.

043--Graham County

Formed 1872 from Cherokee County. Recording of wills appears to have started about 1886, but virtually none of the original wills survived.

044--Granville County

Formed 1746 from Edgecombe County. Surviving will record books date from 1772, although original wills that were probated at an earlier date indicate that they were recorded. After 1772 there has been no significant loss of either recorded or original wills of the county. As of June 1, 1985, all original wills were in the custody of the Granville County clerk of superior court.

045--Greene County

Originally formed as Glasgow County from Dobbs County in 1791; name of the county was changed to Greene in 1799. A courthouse fire in 1876 burned many of the clerk's records, including pre-1868 will books and all original wills probated prior to 1876. Will Book 1, which begins with wills probated in 1868, was originally identified in notations on surviving original wills as "Will Book K."

046--Guilford County

Formed 1771 from Rowan and Orange counties. Recording of wills began with August term, 1816, of the county court. Will Book A, which was started in 1816, was subsequently renumbered as Will Book B, and wills proved before 1816 were entered in a new Will Book A. Some of those probated before 1868 were recorded in county court minute dockets rather than in will books. According to testimony before the Salisbury District Court in 1789, the records of the Guilford County court were destroyed by the British army at the Battle of Guilford Court House in 1781; there does not, however, appear to have been any significant loss of original wills probated prior to that date.

047--Halifax County

Formed 1758 from Edgecombe County. Recording of wills in the county began about 1759. The will books for the county are complete, but many of the original wills probated prior to 1850 are missing. Will Books 1 and 2 in the county are later-day copies of the originals which are in the State Archives.

048--Harnett County

Formed 1855 from Cumberland County. The county courthouse burned in 1892 and again in 1894. Recorded and original wills have survived only from 1892. As of May 1, 1986, all surviving original wills were in the custody of the Harnett County clerk of superior court. Original wills are filed in special proceedings files that are arranged numerically by a number assigned as the transaction occurred. There is an index for wills only that shows the number of the file that includes the original will.

049--Haywood County

Formed 1808 from Buncombe County. Wills appear to have been

recorded irregularly until 1868, although a number of wills were recorded at earlier dates. In 1885 the General Assembly directed the clerk of superior court (Ch. 8, 1885 Public and Private Laws) to record all wills the recording of which had been lost or destroyed but the originals of which were on file in his office. Several wills which initially had been probated earlier were subsequently recorded after 1885. There is some indication on early surviving original wills that another will register had been maintained. The second volume of recorded wills and inventories (WI) is numbered "1/2"; because of computer limitations, this is shown in the "Recorded Copy" column as "WI-1-2," followed by a slant (/) and the page number.

050--Henderson County

Formed 1838 from Buncombe County. Recording of wills did not begin until 1841. As of June 1, 1986, all surviving original wills that were probated in Henderson County were in the custody of the clerk of superior court. A few wills that were not probated are in the State Archives, as are a number of out-of-state wills that appear to have been filed as exhibits in a civil action in Henderson County at a later date.

051--Hertford County

Formed 1759 from Chowan, Bertie, and Northampton counties. In March, 1830, the courthouse burned, destroying most of the clerk's records, including will books and original wills. By Chapter 68, laws of the 1830-1831 General Assembly, filing of copies of wills in Hertford County was allowed; thus some of the wills recorded in Will Book 1, which was started with the next term of court, show a probate date prior to 1830. Chapter 96, laws of 1831-1832 General Assembly, strengthened the authority of the county to replace records destroyed in the fire. In February, 1862, the town of Winton, the county seat, was captured by Union army and naval forces during the course of which the courthouse again burned. Most of the original wills proved between 1830 and 1862 were destroyed, but the will books (of which there were two in 1862) survived.

052--Hoke County

Formed 1911 from Cumberland and Robeson counties. Not included in this index.

053--Hyde County

Formed about 1705 as Wickham Precinct of Bath County; name changed to Hyde about 1712. The county court sat in Bath

Town and represented both Hyde and Beaufort counties until 1739 when the precinct system was superseded. The Beaufort County court continued to sit at Bath Town and succeeded to the records of the combined court. There are, therefore, some Hyde County wills and deeds among Beaufort County records. About 1756 Hyde County court began keeping a record of wills and other estate data which it identified as an orphan book. This record was discontinued about 1764 and is now in the State Archives. In 1765 the county began a series containing wills, inventories, and accounts which it identified as will books. In 1899 and 1900 only the wills from Will Books 1, 2, and 3 were copied into a record that the county identified as Will Book 1 2 3; because of the limitations of space, this transcribed record is identified in the listing of Hyde County wills as "RW-1" (Record of Wills 1). The originals of Will Books 1, 2, and 3 are in the State Archives. After RW-1, the next wills are recorded in Will Book 4, pages 168-201 of which are blank. Entries in Will Book 9 and 10 indicate that many were not recorded until 1868. The first part of Will Book 10 consists of a 1828 and 1829 trial docket of the Hyde County court of pleas and quarter sessions. Many of the original wills for the early period of the county are missing.

054--Iredell County

Formed 1788 from Rowan County. In 1854 fire destroyed most of Statesville, the county seat, but will books and most of the original wills survived. Surviving original wills appear to have been copied into the first 275 pages of Will Book 1 about 1810; thereafter wills appear to have been recorded as they were proved. As of June 1, 1986, surviving original wills proved to 1870 were in the State Archives; original wills after that date were in the custody of the Iredell County clerk of superior court.

055--Jackson County

Formed 1851 from Haywood and Macon counties. The first will was proved in the county in 1853, and until 1868 wills were recorded in a record identified as Inventory Docket (ID). Two wills were copied into the minutes of the county court of pleas and quarter sessions without being otherwise recorded. Beginning in 1869 wills were recorded in will books. None of the original wills of the county have survived, apparently having been lost when the county seat moved from Webster to Sylva in 1913. There was an earlier disasterous fire in Webster, but it is not known if the courthouse was burned.

056--Johnston County

Formed 1746 from Craven County. In 1758 Dobbs County was formed from the eastern portion of Johnston County and the county court moved westward to Hinton's Quarter, leaving its records in Dobbs. The volume was not great, but with the exception of a grantee index to deeds all early records of Johnston County were destroyed when the courthouse in Lenoir, which had succeeded to the records of Dobbs, burned in 1878 and 1880. Although existing Will Book 1 begins in 1787, Johnson began to record wills as early as 1759; in the State Archives a fragment of a record book containing wills has been mounted and bound into Deed Book D. This fragment is in very poor condition and is obviously not complete; it does, however, include four wills not otherwise recorded. Reference to wills bound with Deed Book D is to the leaf (L) on which four pages of the original volume has been mounted. There is some evidence that Will Books 1 and 2 were copied at a later date; an original will recorded in Will Book 1 at page 430 contains a notation that it was recorded in book 10, page 12. Johnston County also maintained record books bearing varying titles but usually referred to as "Record of Estates." These have been indexed by the staff of the State Archives. At least eleven wills not otherwise recorded were entered in these estate books which are cited as "Est" followed by the volume and page number. Only one of the original wills so recorded has survived. Will Book 1 begins with wills proved in 1787; after recording wills proved in 1860, the same volume included wills proved between 1760 and 1770. Will Book 2 includes wills proved from 1860 to 1868, then wills probated in the period 1892-1896, followed by wills proved in the 1770s and later. Except for the early record books of wills, there has been no significant loss of records of the county.

057--Jones County

Formed 1779 from Craven County. The first will was recorded in 1781. In 1862, in a battle between Union and Confederate troops, the Jones County courthouse burned. The record volume in which wills were recorded survived, as did virtually all of the original wills. It should be noted, however, that no wills were recorded in the period 1862-1863 or in 1867.

058--Lee County

Formed 1907 from Moore and Chatham counties. Not included in this index.

059--Lenoir County

Formed 1791 from Dobbs County. In 1878 and again in 1880 the county courthouse burned, destroying most records. A will book that began in 1869 survived, but original wills probated prior to 1878 were destroyed. As of May 1, 1986, all surviving original wills were in the custody of the Lenoir County clerk of superior court.

060--Lincoln County

Formed 1779 from Tryon County, the records of which were turned over to Lincoln. Lincoln County began to record wills in 1824. In 1899, following ratification of an act by the General Assembly requiring the indexing of all wills filed in the clerk's office and an order on June 5, 1899, by the Lincoln County board of commissioners, a cross index of all wills was prepared. Included were all surviving original wills probated prior to September term, 1824, as well as those proved at a later date. A total of 1,201 wills were indexed, including 455 proved through 1824. A few of the pre-1824 wills that were indexed are now missing. Several wills that have been out of public custody have been included in the Lincoln County listing and are indicated by the symbol AR/CRX. Some original wills probated by the Tryon County court are included with the Lincoln County wills in the State Archives.

061--Macon County

Formed 1828 from Haywood County. Recording of wills began in 1830. There is no known loss of records and the will books appear to be complete, but many of the original wills are missing.

062--Madison County

Formed 1851 from Buncombe and Yancey counties. Recording of wills began in 1851 and there has been no significant loss of records.

063--Martin County

Formed 1774 from Halifax and Tyrrell counties. The county courthouse burned in 1885, and although the recorded will books from time of the formation of the county survived, original wills probated before 1885 were destroyed.

064--McDowell County

Formed 1842 from Burke and Rutherford counties. Recording of wills appears to have started upon creation of the county and there has been no substantial loss of records.

065--Mecklenburg County

Formed 1762 from Anson County. About 1850 the county began to record wills as they were proved. With the exception of some pages in Will Book I, beginning in the 1840s, the first nine will books appear to have been copied at a later date. Will Books A-I are in the State Archives. There appears to have been no significant loss of records.

066--Mitchell County

Formed 1861 from Yancey, Watauga, Caldwell, Burke, and McDowell counties. Will record books that have survived date from 1889, although surviving original wills that were probated at an earlier date indicate that wills were recorded in other record volumes that have not survived.

067--Montgomery County

Formed 1779 from Anson County. The courthouse burned in 1843, destroying almost all of the clerk's records including will books and original wills. Beginning with the September, 1843, term of the county court, a new will book was started and identified as Will Book 1. Later, certified copies of wills proved before 1843 were reprobated and were recorded. Another fire in 1886 damaged some of the records but reports of loss appear to have been exaggerated.

068--Moore County

Formed 1785 from Cumberland County. Recording of wills did not begin until 1794. Will Book A also contains court minutes, bonds, and other data; the page numbers in the record volume were assigned at a later date. The book appears to consist of several separate volumes that were combined and bound together. After 1868 original wills were placed in special proceedings files; in September 1889, the courthouse burned and virtually all loose records, including original wills proved prior to 1868 as well as special proceedings files, were destroyed. The will books survived, as did other records in bound form. Surviving original wills after 1889 are in the special proceedings files and may be located by means of a probate docket in the office of the Moore County clerk of superior court. Many of the original wills are missing. A few wills are in the State Archives and some are in the custody of the county clerk of superior court, but virtually none of the original wills probated in Moore County have survived.

069--Nash County

Formed 1777 from Edgecombe County. Recording of wills began in 1778; until about 1873 wills were registered in four volumes identified as "Record of Wills" and numbered 1-4. Later, these four record books were copied into Will Book 1; the wills were numbered as they were copied and the original books were annotated with the will numbers. The four "Record of Wills" volumes are in the State Archives; entries for Nash County, however, are from the recopied Will Book 1.

070--New Hanover County

Formed 1729 from Craven County. Some wills were recorded in deed books as early as 1737, but that practice was discontinued about 1763. Recording in will books began about 1798. In September, 1845, the court of pleas and quarter sessions found that there were in the office of the clerk "a number of wills and partitions of real estate which have not been duly registered." The court ordered that such documents be recorded "forthwith." Those previously unrecorded wills were registered in the first 472 pages of what is now identified as Will Book C. If an original will contained any indication that it had previously been registered, it was not copied at that time. The remainder of Will Book C contains copies of wills probated beginning in 1848. Will Books A and B were subsequently copied into a single record book which is now identified as Will Book AB; the originals of Will Books A and B are now in the State Archives. The New Hanover County courthouse burned in 1840, following earlier fires in 1798 and 1819. Most of the records survived, although some were damaged by fire and water.

071--Northampton County

Formed 1741 from Bertie County. Recording of wills began in 1760; many of the original wills for the early period are missing. Apparently the record book identified as Will Book 1 in the listing for Northampton County wills was copied from an earlier book of records; one original will bears the notation that it was recorded in Book A, page 411, but it is now recorded in Will Book 1, page 392. Other than early original wills for the period 1760 to mid-1770s, there has been no significant loss of records.

072--Onslow County

Formed 1734 from New Hanover County. In 1752 a hurricane destroyed the courthouse and most of the records of the county court were lost. In 1755 the second day of the January term of county court could not be held because a storm had destroyed the place where the court was meeting. Again, in 1786 a tornado blew the courthouse away and many records were lost. Early recorded wills are in two record books, Record of Wills, 1757-1783 (RW) and Wills and Inventories, 1774-1790 (WI). The latter volume does not contain any inventories, but it does have a will index and listing of guardian bonds. Both of the original volumes were dismantled and the pages were individually mounted on sheets which were then bound. Each sheet is numbered in each volume; these sheets are called "leafs (L)" and this sheet number is cited instead of page numbers in these two record books. The page numbers in the Record of Wills (RW) are illegible, and in the Wills and Inventories (WI) several different record books appear to have been mounted and bound within the same covers. It appears that Will Book A was compiled about 1937 from old wills in the clerk's office; additional old wills that were in the State Archives were not included in the compilation. The county began to record wills in the regular course of business about 1827. Despite early losses of records there appears to be no significant number of missing wills.

073--Orange County

Formed 1752 from Johnston, Bladen, and Granville counties. Recording of wills began as early as 1757. According to tradition, when the British army approached Hillsborough in 1781 records of the county were buried in the woods a few miles away. As a result, some were reportedly destroyed. The books in which wills were recorded appear to be complete, although many of the early original wills are missing. As of May 1, 1986, Orange County wills probated through 1855 were in the State Archives; all others probated after 1855 were in the custody of the county clerk of superior court. In a few instances, wills bearing dates after 1855 that were not probated are also in the State Archives.

074--Pamlico County

Formed 1872 from Craven and Beaufort counties. Recording of wills began in 1872 and there has been no significant loss of records.

075--Pasquotank County

Originally formed as a precinct of Albemarle County. Recording of wills began about 1761, and it appears that Will Book I was the first register for wills. In 1798 the county court found that there were a number of wills proved, while Thomas MacKnight was clerk, that had not been recorded; and the current clerk was ordered to record them. It appears that they were recorded in Will Book H. In 1862, after a Union flotilla won a decisive naval victory at the narrows of the Pasquotank River near Elizabeth City, the county court ordered officials to remove public records from the courthouse. The courthouse burned a few days later but there appears to have been no significant loss of records. In December, 1863, Union army forces occupied Elizabeth City, again with no significant loss of records. In 1875 the first three will books were copied into a single volume which is identified as Will Book HIK; it should be noted, however, that they were copied in the order of I H K. The originals of Will Books H, I, and K are now in the State Archives, and entries for Pasquotank County from these volumes were made from the originals. The county also has two will books identified by the letter "M." The first covers the period 1798-1824 and the second 1853-1867, with the latter overlapping, chronologically with the period covered by Will Book N. To distinguish between the two volumes identified as "M," the first is identified as "M1" and the second as "M2" in entries for Pasquotank County.

<u>076--Pender County</u>

Formed 1875 from the New Hanover County. Recording of wills began immediately, and there has been no significant loss of records.

<u>077--Perquimans County</u>

Originally formed as a precinct of Albemarle County. The first recorded will was proved in 1762 and was registered in a record volume identified as Will Book C. Will Book C was copied at a later date, and the copy remains in the county. Fragments of the original Will Book C, with many pages missing, are in the State Archives. Part of it is mounted and bound with pages of the original Deed Book B and identified as "Deeds and Wills;" and parts are in the CRX material for Perquimans County.

<u>078--Person County</u>

Formed 1792 from Caswell County. Recording of wills began in 1792 in record books identified as "Wills, Inventories, Sales of Estates, and Taxables." Except for Book 7, these record books were not numbered; the first fifteen of them are in the State Archives and for internal control purposes they have been numbered. In wills for Person County they are identified by the symbol "WI" and by the control number assigned by the State Archives, as follows:

1792-1797 - WI-1

1797-1801 - WI-2

1801-1804 - WI-3

1805-1807 - WI-4

1807-1811 - WI-5

1811-1815 - WI-6

1815-1817 - WI-7

1817-1820 - WI-8

1820-1823 - WI-9

1823-1827 - WI-10

1827-1830 - WI-11

1831-1835 - WI-12

1835-1837 - WI-13

1837-1841 - WI-14

1841-1843 - WI-15

From December term, 1843, until December term, 1847, there is a gap in the recorded wills of Person County and one record book apparently has been lost. Beginning with December term, 1847, the record books in which wills were recorded were identified as "Record of Wills" and are cited as will books (WB) in the listing for Person County. The record book for the period 1847-1851 is identified as Will Book 13; for 1852-1857, as Will Book 17; and 1857-1867, as Will Book 18. There are no recorded wills from September term, 1867, until December 1868, when Will Book 19 begins. More than half of the wills probated in the county prior to 1901 are missing.

1079--Pitt County

Formed 1760 from Beaufort County. On January 8, 1858, the courthouse burned, destroying virtually all of the clerk's records, including will books and original wills. By legislation ratified January 9, 1959 (Ch. 32, Public Laws of 1858-1859 Session), the General Assembly permitted the filing of copies of documents when the court records had been burned and the filing of oral or written statements of the contents of wills in such instances. Although the legislation was occasioned by the burning of the Pitt County courthouse, it had general applicability throughout the state. In Pitt County, copies of a number of wills were refiled with the clerk and were probated again. There is also some indication that families refiled copies of wills without requesting that they be probated a second time; the will of Elizabeth Tison, for example, bears a notation that it is a copy of "Grandma Tyson's will."

080--Polk County

Formed 1855 from Rutherford and Henderson counties. In an act ratified January 18, 1847, the General Assembly created a Polk County from Rutherford County and that portion of Henderson County that had originally belonged to Rutherford. By action ratified January 16, 1849, the act creating Polk County was repealed. All records of the Polk County court of pleas and quarter sessions were required to be delivered to the clerk of the Rutherford County court of pleas and quarter sessions; none of them have survived, either as records of Polk or of Rutherford County. When Polk County was reestablished in 1855, wills for the period 1855-1867 were recorded in a record identified as a Will Docket (WD). This record is now in the State Archives. In August, 1892, the seventeen wills originally recorded in the Will Docket were copied into Will Book 1 which started in 1868. There has been no signficant loss of records of the county after 1855.

081--Randolph County

Formed 1779 from Guilford County. Recording of wills began in 1784. Some of the original wills are missing, and many of those that have survived appear to have been damaged by water. Some of the water-damaged originals are virtually illegible.

082--Richmond County

Formed 1779 from Anson County. Apparently wills began to be recorded on a regular basis about 1830. In 1835 all surviving unrecorded wills were transcribed into a record book that is now identified as Will Book 1. A fragment of an original record of wills and inventories for the period 1789-1807 has survived and is now in the State Archives. One of the wills recorded in this fragment has not been otherwise recorded and is referred to in the wills for Richmond County by Archives stack number 082.801.1. An additional record book in the State Archives that is identified as "Wills Proved in County Court (1848-1864)" also contains recorded copies of wills. This appears to be another copy of Will Book 4.

083--Robeson County

Formed 1787 from Bladen County. Wills were not recorded on a regular basis until about 1830, when the county court ordered that all unrecorded wills were to be recorded. All of the wills on the first 250 pages of Will Book 1 are in the same handwriting and appear to have been entered at that time. In May term, 1838, the court found "that there still remains a number unrecorded," and James Storm was ordered to record the balance of the wills. Although there has been no major loss of records, some of the original wills are missing.

084--Rockingham County

Formed 1785 from Guilford County. Recording of wills did not begin until 1804, and surviving originals of recorded wills were in the custody of the clerk of superior court as of June 1, 1986. About 1955 a group of unrecorded wills was found in the courthouse; in 1957 photostatic copies of these wills were placed in a record book identified by the title Old Wills Discovered in Office Dated Prior to 1804 (OW). The originals of these unrecorded wills are in the State Archives.

085--Rowan County

Formed 1753 from Anson County. Recording of wills began in 1760, and there has been no significant loss of records. From about 1780 to about 1800, the county appears to have recorded wills in blocks arranged by first letter of the surname but not in alphabetical order. Several of the Rowan County original wills are in German and unless they were translated at the time of probate, the contents were not recorded in the will books. Ute-Ingrid Seidler translated and abstracted German language wills of Rowan County in the State Archives in North Carolina Genealogical Society Journal, Vol. 1, No. 3 (July, 1975), pp. 136-140.

086--Rutherford County

Formed 1779 from Tryon County. Surviving registers of recorded wills date from 1782, probably because the site of the meetings of the county court was not fixed in the early years of the county. Will Books A, B, and C are recording dockets containing powers of attorney, bonds, and estate data. It was not until Will Book D (1822) that only wills were registered in the will books. Until the county court was discontinued in 1868, the probate date of a will was indicated in a caption at the top of each page identifying the term of court at which the action was taken. Typewritten copies of Will Books A-F and G-H were made at a later date; entries for Rutherford County were made from microfilm copies of the original record books which are in the custody of the clerk of superior court. There was a courthouse fire in 1907, but there appears to have been no significant loss of either recorded or original wills.

087--Sampson County

Formed 1784 from Duplin County. Recording of wills on a regular basis began about 1820. At a later date, wills that had been proved prior to 1820 as well as wills that had not been probated were entered into a record book identified as Will Book A. Although a few original wills are missing, there has been no signficant loss of records.

088--Scotland County

Formed 1899 from Richmond County. The first will was probated in January, 1901; Scotland County, therefore, is not included in this index.

089--Stanly County

Formed 1841 from Montgomery County. The first will was recorded in 1841. Although there has been no known loss of records, many of the original wills are missing.

090--Stokes County

Formed 1789 from Surry County. The first will was recorded in 1790. In Will Books 1 and 2, only the left-sided pages are numbered sequentially with the right side pages numbered "1/2." In the listing for Stokes County, only the left-sided page numbers are used. The first twenty-five pages of Will Book 5 consists of an index. There has been no significant loss of records. It should be noted that many of the wills proved in Stokes County prior to 1849 are from the part of the county that subsequently became Forsyth County.

091--Swain County

Formed 1871 from Jackson and Macon counties. Recording of wills began about 1876. As of June 1, 1986, the few surviving original wills of Swain County were in the custody of the county clerk of superior court.

092--Surry County

Formed 1771 from Rowan County. Recording of wills began in 1772, and the will books are complete. Many of the original wills are missing.

093--Transylvania County

Formed 1861 from Henderson and Jackson counties. Recording of wills began in 1862, and there has been no significant loss of either recorded or original wills.

094--Tryon County

Formed 1767 from Mecklenburg County. It was divided into Lincoln and Rutherford counties in 1779 and its records were taken over by Lincoln County. A few wills in the State Archives are filed in miscellaneous records of the county; other surviving original wills probated in Tryon County are in the records of Lincoln County. Tryon County did not record wills other than to indicate probate in the minutes of the county court.

095

This number was not assigned in the State Archives county identification system.

096--Tyrrell County

Formed 1729 from Chowan, Bertie, Currituck, and Pasquotank counties. Although there has been no known disaster that resulted in the destruction of records, some of the early original wills are missing. Recording of wills began in 1750, but many wills that were proved before about 1800 were not recorded, perhaps because the courthouse and the meeting place of the county court moved frequently. Some time before the Historical Records Survey in the 1930s, typewritten copies of the original Will Books 1, 2, and 3 were made; entries for Tyrrell County were made from microfilm copy of the relatively recent typed copy of the will books. The original will books remain in the county.

097--Union County

Formed 1842 from Anson and Mecklenburg counties. The first will was recorded in 1843. There has been no significant loss of records.

098--Vance County

Formed 1881 from Granville, Warren, and Franklin counties. Recording of wills began immediately and there has been no significant loss of records. As of April 1, 1986, surviving original wills were in the custody of the Vance County clerk of superior court. The wills are filed in special proceedings files in numerical order by a number assigned at the time the action was initiated. Wills may be found by consulting an index to special proceedings which gives the case number of the probate transaction.

099--Wake County

Formed 1771 from Johnston, Cumberland, and Orange counties. Recording of wills began with the organization of the county. Wills were entered into record books that were initially identified by letters. By 1836 Book Y was filled and the county then began using double letters to identify will books. By 1875 the identification of will books had reached the double letters of KK. At some time later, the record books were copied and renumbered with numbers 1-35. Record Books B and C were combined into Record Book 2 at the time of copying. After 1875 wills were registered in will books that were identified by letters.

100--Warren County

Formed 1779 from Bute County. Warren County Will Books 1 and 2 were actually created by the Bute County clerk of county court, and wills recorded therein are cited as records of Bute County. Warren County Will Books 45, 46, 47, and 48 contain only inventories, reports of sale, and accounts. About 1856 the county began to separate estate data from wills, and Will Books 49 and 50 contain only wills. There has been no significant loss of records although some of the original wills are missing. A few of the original wills probated in Warren County are in the records of Bute County in the State Archives.

101--Washington County

Formed 1799 from Tyrrell County. The county courthouse was burned in the naval bombardment of Plymouth, the county seat, in 1862. In 1869 fire again destroyed the courthouse, which was rebuilt and burned again in 1873. Surviving recorded wills begin in 1873; original wills with surnames beginning with the letters R through Z apparently have not survived.

102--Watauga County

Formed 1849 from Ashe, Caldwell, Wilkes, and Yancey counties. In 1865 county records were burned when the courthouse was destroyed by units of Union army cavalry. Another devastating fire in 1873 again destroyed the courthouse and all of the records of the county.

103--Wayne County

Formed 1779 from Dobbs County. Surviving recorded wills date from 1782; earlier recorded and original wills were reportedly destroyed by the British army as it marched from Wilmington to Jamestown in 1781 (see will of Thomas Boykin). Recorded wills from 1782 to 1800 are in two record books which also contain inventories of estates, reports of sales of personal property, and other estate data. These volumes are identified in the Wayne County listing as Wills and Inventories (WI) A and B. These two volumes appear originally to have consisted of several separate record books. Recorded wills for 1792 and 1793 are missing. In 1807 the county began a series of recording dockets (RD) that continued until 1868. Recorded wills for the period 1800 to 1808 have not survived, although several of the original wills for the period indicate that they were "recorded." The fourteen volumes of recording dockets contain not only wills but copies of all other documents (except deeds) filed with the county court. The pagination in the first recording docket volume is confused, with each page showing at least two page numbers. The page numbers used were those that were assigned when the county indexed the volume. In 1868 the county began a series of will books (WB); these remain in the county. The volumes of wills and inventories (WI) and recording dockets (RD) are in the State Archives.

104--Wilkes County

Formed 1777 from Rowan County and the District of Washington. Recording of wills began in 1778. Will Book 1, identified as "Wills, Bonds, Inventories, Bills of Sale," is in the State Archives. Because of an error in numbering the pages in Will Book 1, the pages after page 489 repeat numbers beginning with 450.

105--Wilson County

Formed 1855 from Edgecombe, Nash, Johnston, and Wayne counties. Although some of the original wills are missing, there has been no significant loss of records.

106--Yadkin County

Formed 1850 from Surry County. There has been no significant loss of records, although some original wills are missing. Neither the entries in Will Book 1 nor the surviving original wills indicate the date that each will was probated.

107--Yancey County

Formed 1833 from Burke and Buncombe counties. Recording of wills began in 1834, but virtually none of the original wills have survived.

ABBREVIATIONS

The following abbreviations have been used in the preparation of this index:

Ant - Antigua

AR - In the "Original" column: indicates that the original will (or a copy) is in the North Carolina State Archives, Raleigh.

AR/CRX - A record in the State Archives that has been out of legal custody and the provenance of which cannot be proved.

Can - Canada

CCR - Colonial court records. The 3-digit number following the symbol is the State Archives box number

ChM - Chowan County miscellaneous papers. Followed by a volume number, slash (/), and page number. Probate records (estates and wills) in the papers were abstracted by Jonathan B. Butcher in North Carolina Genealogical Society Journal, Volume VII (1981), pp. 18-24, 81-88, 145-150, 203-208.

CTY - Indicates that the original will (or a copy) is in the custody of the county clerk of superior court.

DB - Deed Book. Followed by a book or a volume number, slash (/), and page number.

Deeds - Bound volume in the deeds (500) category in the State Archives. Followed by a period (.), the book number, slash (/), and page number. Used in Craven County only.

EdDSC - Edenton District Superior Court loose papers.

Eng - England

Est - Record of estates. The symbol is followed by a volume or book number, slash (/), and page number. Used in Johnston County only.

(fwc) - Free woman of color.

HaDSC(M) - Halifax District Superior Court minutes. The page number shown is from Weynette P. Haun, Halifax District Superior Court of Law and Equity: 1785-1790 (Bills & Answers); 1797-1805 (Minutes) (Durham, 1982).

HiDSC - Hillsborough District Superior Court loose papers.

ID - Inventory Docket. Used in Jackson County only.

Inc. - An incomplete will.

Jam - Jamaica.

L - Leaf. Some records in the State Archives are mounted in bound volumes in which the pages are numbered by a leaf number. The documents which are mounted on these bound pages usually bear no page number.

LGB - Land Grant Book in the office of the North Carolina secretary of state. The wills in Land Grant Book 4 are numbered, and the digits following the LGB symbol are document numbers.

MD - In the "Recorded Copy" column: Minute docket. The symbol is followed by book or volume number, slash (/), and page number.

N - In the "Co." column: no county was indicated in the will.

NBDSC - New Bern District Superior Court loose papers.

N. D. - In the "Date" column: neither the registered nor original will bore either a probate or signature date.

Nunc. - A nuncupative or oral will.

OB - Orphan Book. In Beaufort County, the symbol is followed by a book or volume number, slash (/), and page number. Also used in Hyde County.

OW - Old Wills Discovered in Office Dated Prior to 1804. Used in Rockingham County only.

OWB - Old Will Book. Used in Beaufort County only.

PQS - Minutes of the county court of pleas and quarter sessions. The symbol is followed by a period (.), a number showing the volume of minutes in the State Archives, slash (/), and page number.

RB - Record Book. The symbol is followed by a book or volume number, slash (/), and page number.

RD - Recording Docket. The symbol is followed by a book or volume number, slash (/), and page number.

RW - Record of wills. The symbol is followed by a book or volume number, slash (/), and page number.

SC - In the "Recorded Copy" column: indicates an original case file of the North Carolina Supreme Court in the State Archives, Raleigh. The symbol is followed by a five-digit number that is the Archives file number for the case.

SCM - Minutes of the county superior court. The symbol is followed by a period (.), a number showing the volume of minutes in the State Archives, slash (/), and page number.

Sco - Scotland

SS - Secretary of state records in the State Archives. The symbol is followed by a 3 or 4-digit number which is the shelf number of a volume in the SS record group, slash (/), and page number.

SS/AR - The secretary of state loose wills in the State Archives.

SS/AR(N) - A nuncupative will in the secretary of state loose wills in the State Archives.

WB - Will book. The symbol is followed by a book or volume number, slash (/), and page number.

WD - Will docket. The symbol is followed by a book or volume number, slash (/), and page number.

WeI - West Indies.

WI - In the "Recorded Copy" column: wills and inventories. The symbol is followed by a book or volume number, slash (/), and page number.

Wills - Bound volume of records in the wills (800) category in the State Archives. Followed by a period (.), a number indicating the book number, slash (/), and page number. Used in Craven County only.

Name	Co.	Date	Recorded Copy	Original
Aaron, Albert G.	047	1891	WB-7/43	AR
Aaron, James M.	FL	1846	047 WB-4/255	Nunc.
Aaron, John T.	047	1852	WB-4/330	
Aaron, Martha	047	1858	WB-5/56	
Aaron, Michael	047	1778	WB-2/78	
Aarond, Frederick	065	1827	WB-A/61	Nunc.
Aarons, Ishmael	028	1850	WB-D/167	AR
Abbington, Littleberry	047	1811	WB-3/517	
Abbot, Sarah	085	1823	WB-H/237	AR
Abbott, Abraham	099	1836	RB-23/496	AR
Abbott, Albert S.	059	1890	WB-B/2	CTY
Abbott, Benjamin	051	1859	WB-B/15	
Abbott, Benjamin	085	1816	WB-G/439	AR
Abbott, Jeremiah	028	1899	WB-F/423	
Abbott, Samuel G.	059	1876	WB-A/114	
Abbott, William	099	1777	RB-1/95	AR
Abbott, William	009	1761	OWB/86	AR
Abbott, William R.	018	1881	WB-E/96	AR
Abendschein, Catharina	016	c1802	WB-A/115	
Abercrombie, Hannah	075	1755	Orig. Only	SS/AR
Abercromby, Robert	073	1779	WB-A/209	
Abernathy, James	040	1881	WB-2/171	AR
Abernathy, Joshua	039	1814	WB-D/119	AR
Abernathy, Marion C.	040	1890	WB-2/354	AR
Abernathy, Marion C.	040	1866	065 WB-M/45	065 AR
Abernathy, Miles	040	1870	WB-2/13	
Abernathy, Nancy	065	1879	WB-K/345	AR
Abernathy, Rachel	014	1871	WB-2/66	
Abernathy, Robert	094	1772	Orig. Only	060 AR
Abernathy, Robert	060	N. D.	Orig. Only	AR
Abernathy, Sidney T.	065	1891	WB-M/24	AR
Abernathy, Starling	040	1873	WB-2/50	AR
Abernethy, A. F.	021	1900	WB-3/294	
Abernethy, Albert	021	1876	WB-2/152	AR
Abernethy, Barbara A.	021	1885	WB-2/324	
Abernethy, David	060	1814	Orig. Only	AR
Abernethy, David	060	1796	Orig. Only	AR
Abernethy, David	021	1870	WB-2/40	
Abernethy, Green D.	060	1886	WB-4/357	AR
Abernethy, Harbert	060	1821	Orig. Only	AR
Abernethy, James	060	1829	WB-1/151	AR
Abernethy, Jane W.	040	1898	WB-3/8	
Abernethy, Joe	021	1897	WB-3/176	AR
Abernethy, John	060	1816	Orig. Only	AR
Abernethy, John	021	1863	WB-1/188	AR
Abernethy, John D.	021	1844	WB-1/13	AR
Abernethy, Mary	039	c1860	WB-Q/698	
Abernethy, Miles	021	1872	WB-2/63	AR
Abernethy, Miles D.	060	1867	WB-3/97	AR
Abernethy, Miles S.	021	1883	WB-2/267	
Abernethy, Miles, Sr.	060	1790	Orig. Only	AR
Abernethy, Robert	021	1872	WB-2/66	AR
Abernethy, Robert	021	1846	WB-1/39	AR
Abernethy, S. Osburn	021	1896	WB-3/133	AR
Abernethy, Samuel	021	1857	WB-1/137	AR
Abernethy, Turner	060	1860	WB-3/26	AR
Abernethy, William	060	1850	WB-2/341	AR
Abington, Hardamon	071	1815	WB-3/142	AR
Abington, James	010	c1772	WB-A/146	AR
Abington, Joseph	030	1735	LGB-4/#10	SS/AR
Abington, Penelope	037	1855	WB-G/114	AR
Abington, Thomas	075	1707	Orig. Only	SS/AR
Able, Arthur	009	1792	OWB/273	AR
Abrams, John	086	1842	WB-E/104	AR
Abrams, John	053	1794	RW-1/240	

Name	Co.	Date	Recorded Copy	Original
Abrams, Mary F.	037	1892	WB-H/241	AR
Abrams, Sarah	037	1869	WB-G/334	AR
Abrams, Sophia	105	1897	WB-3/271	AR
Abshear, William	104	1848	WB-4/345	
Abshear, William	065	c1868	Orig. Only	AR
Abshear, William	104	1842	WB-4/277	AR
Absher, Alfred J.	104	1888	WB-6/317	AR
Abshire, Jeremiah	104	1816	WB-3/118	AR
Abt, Bernhard	099	1889	WB-B/378	AR
Ace, Free	086	1831	WB-D/136	AR
Achender, Johannes	085	1758	WB-A/2	AR
Ackburn, Rachel	009	c1800	OWB/373	
Ackis, John	028	c1778	Orig. Only	AR
Ackis, John	028	1765	Wills.9/211	AR
Ackiss, Mary	075	1811	WB-M1/229	AR
Ackiss, Thomas	075	1811	WB-M1/225	AR
Acock, Francis	015	1766	RB-1/59	
Acock, Richard	100	1789	WB-5/99	AR
Acon, Thomas	024	1766	WB-A/156	AR
Acre, Joshua	100	1847	WB-39/273	AR
Acree, Edward	010	c1791	Orig. Only	AR
Acree, Elizabeth	010	1853	WB-G/492	AR
Acree, Isaac	100	1820	WB-22/294	AR
Acree, John	010	1825	WB-G/134	AR
Acree, John, Sr.	010	1814	WB-F/261	AR
Acree, Ricks	010	1842	WB-G/343	AR
Actor, Andrew	084	1820	WB-A/135	CTY
Acworth, William	009	1817	OB-A/273	AR
Adair, Arminty	086	1900	WB-G/64	AR
Adair, J. H.	086	1896	WB-F/511	AR
Adair, James	011	c1778	WB-1/476	
Adam, Robert	029	1801	WB-A/42	AR
Adaman, Thomas	090	1792	WB-1/31	
Adams, Abednego	026	1858	WB-1/222	AR
Adams, Abraham	008	c1734	SS 876/362	SS/AR
Adams, Abraham	009	c1810	OB-A/112	
Adams, Abraham	009	1791	OWB/255	AR
Adams, Abraham, Sr.	008	1734	SS 876/289	SS/AR
Adams, Alvin G.	056	1889	WB-3/506	AR
Adams, Andrew M.	054	c1837	WB-2/174	AR
Adams, Ann	009	c1760	OWB/75	AR
Adams, Benjamin	047	1811	WB-3/523	
Adams, Bettie A.	001	1893	WB-2/571	AR
Adams, Boaz	001	c1849	WB-1/26	AR
Adams, Charles	028	1757	SS 880/170	SS/AR
Adams, Charles	065	1816	WB-A/51	AR
Adams, Dancy	047	1839	WB-4/181	
Adams, Daniel D.	013	1893	WB-C/245	AR
Adams, David	079	1886	WB-2/372	AR
Adams, David	079	c1846	Orig. Only	AR-Copy
Adams, David C.	099	1899	WB-D/289	AR
Adams, Dempsey	099	1873	RB-35/235	AR
Adams, E. W.	054	1899	WB-6/219	CTY
Adams, Elizabeth	017	1844	WB-A/14	AR-Nunc.
Adams, Elizabeth	054	c1803	WB-1/55	AR
Adams, Elizabeth	083	1835	WB-1/293	AR
Adams, Erastus M.	038	1887	WB-3/29	AR
Adams, George	092	1827	WB-3/175	
Adams, George	084	c1802	WB-A/149	CTY
Adams, George	106	1869	WB-2/24 & 42	AR
Adams, Gibson	104	1833	WB-4/167	AR
Adams, Hardy	056	1823	WB-1/360	AR
Adams, Henry	009	c1809	OB-A/84	AR
Adams, Henry	104	1822	WB-4/26	AR
Adams, Henry	037	1866	WB-G/281	AR

Name	Co.	Date	Recorded Copy	Original
Adams, Hopewell	037	1799	WB-D/86	AR
Adams, Howell	056	1800	WB-1/120	AR
Adams, Isaac	009	1796	OWB/323	AR
Adams, J. Q., Jr.	099	1889	WB-B/351	
Adams, Jacob	054	1873	WB-4/115	CTY
Adams, Jacob	041	1835	WB-2/365	
Adams, Jacob	085	1851	WB-K/127	AR
Adams, James	079	1858	WB-1/18	AR
Adams, James	047	1793	WB-3/213	
Adams, James	037	1820	WB-E/233	AR
Adams, James	009	c1792	OWB/275	AR
Adams, James	009	1759	OWB/58	AR
Adams, James	099	1847	RB-26/289	AR
Adams, James	073	1828	WB-E/156	AR
Adams, James E.	054	1882	WB-4/474	CTY
Adams, James L.	033	1879	WB-2/67	CTY
Adams, James W.	054	1880	WB-4/373	CTY
Adams, Jane	057	1883	WB-C/93	AR
Adams, Jesse	056	1852	WB-1/651	AR
Adams, Jesse	085	1801	WB-C/263	AR
Adams, Jesse	104	1850	WB-5/31	AR
Adams, John	019	1787	RB-A/67	
Adams, John	MA	1750	028 DB-5/120	
Adams, John	060	1813	Orig. Only	AR
Adams, John	008	1734	SS 876/317	SS/AR
Adams, John	047	1798	WB-3/299	
Adams, John	092	c1836	WB-4/109	
Adams, John	009	N. D.	OWB/558	AR
Adams, John	028	1750	Orig. Only	SS/AR
Adams, John	005	1849	WB-C/6	AR
Adams, John	104	1888	WB-6/321	AR
Adams, John	006	1823	WB-A/93	AR
Adams, John	099	1855	RB-29/321	AR
Adams, John	019	1866	WB-B/29	AR
Adams, John	009	1763	OWB/92	AR
Adams, John	085	1828	WB-H/415	AR
Adams, John A.	092	1862	WB-5/60	
Adams, John G.	009	1849	OB-G/194	AR
Adams, John H.	040	1893	WB-2/429	
Adams, John P.	030	1798	WB-2/115	
Adams, John P.	039	1811	WB-C/233	Nunc.
Adams, John P.	001	1870	WB-2/19	AR
Adams, John Q.	009	1878	WB-1/225	CTY
Adams, John, Sr.	019	1811	WB-D/2	AR
Adams, Jonathon	106	c1851	WB-1/4	AR
Adams, Joseph	099	1837	RB-24/93	AR
Adams, Joseph	029	1783	Orig. Only	AR
Adams, Joseph M.	075	1796	WB-L/66	
Adams, Julia	056	1893	WB-2/143	AR
Adams, Julia W.	013	1895	WB-C/372	AR
Adams, Mack	021	c1888	Orig. Only	AR
Adams, Margaret	040	1870	WB-2/12	
Adams, Margaret	001	1874	WB-2/72	AR
Adams, Martha	046	1865	WB-D/256	AR
Adams, Martha A.	070	1894	WB-G/182	AR
Adams, Martha A.	105	1883	WB-2/360	AR
Adams, Martha Ann	046	1842	WB-C/112	AR
Adams, Mary	085	1854	WB-K/173	AR
Adams, Mary	005	1889	WB-D/260	AR
Adams, Mary	060	1829	WB-1/139	AR
Adams, Mary	087	c1808	WB-A/50	AR
Adams, Mary	028	1773	Orig. Only	SS/AR
Adams, Matilda C.	099	1889	WB-B/393	AR
Adams, Matthew	085	c1781	WB-B/99	AR
Adams, Moses	106	c1862	WB-1/95	AR
Adams, Nathan	099	1885	WB-B/222	AR
Adams, Nathan	019	1830	WB-A/2	AR
Adams, Peter	075	1784	WB-K/94	AR
Adams, Peter	024	1746	Orig. Only	SS/AR
Adams, Peter H.	046	1883	WB-E/384	AR
Adams, Phebe	054	1856	WB-3/96	AR
Adams, Phillip	101	1817	063 WB-2/47	
Adams, Reading	037	1808	WB-D/326	AR
Adams, Rebecca C.	054	1892	WB-5/434	CTY
Adams, Richard	082	1782	WB-1/12	AR
Adams, Riddic	056	1878	WB-3/209	AR
Adams, Robert	099	1887	WB-B/222	AR
Adams, Robert T.	026	1877	WB-2/156	AR
Adams, Roderick R.	039	c1818	WB-F/179	AR
Adams, Roger	N	1739	SS 877/146	
Adams, S. D.	068	1894	WB-D/406	
Adams, S. D.	068	1897	WB-D/498	
Adams, Sackfield	069	1780	WB-1/11	AR
Adams, Samuel	060	1830	WB-1/182	AR
Adams, Samuel	054	1841	WB-2/219	AR
Adams, Samuel	009	1807	OWB/448	AR
Adams, Samuel	044	1818	WB-8/124	CTY
Adams, Sarah	079	1867	WB-1/174	AR
Adams, Sidney	056	1890	WB-3/544	AR
Adams, Solomon	081	1861	WB-12/1	
Adams, Squire	102	1877	WB-A/4	AR
Adams, Thomas	038	1843	WB-1/300	
Adams, Thomas	079	1884	WB-2/315	AR
Adams, Thomas M.	009	1870	WB-1/57	AR
Adams, Vine H.	056	1882	WB-3/337	AR
Adams, Wila	104	1893	WB-6/467	AR
Adams, William	046	1835	WB-B/518	AR
Adams, William	040	1862	WB-1/149	
Adams, William	009	1826	OB-A/359	AR-Nunc.
Adams, William	092	1816	WB-3/122	AR
Adams, William	047	1825	WB-4/2	
Adams, William	065	1845	WB-I/6	AR
Adams, William	053	1785	RW-1/127	
Adams, William	106	1899	WB-2/453	
Adams, William	009	1751	SS 879/30	
Adams, William	063	c1803	WB-1/425	
Adams, William B.	009	1822	OB-A/323	AR
Adams, William F.	104	1880	WB-6/181	AR
Adams, William J.	046	1840	WB-C/79	AR
Adams, William J.	009	1897	WB-2/116	CTY
Adamson, George H.	072	1796	WB-A/6	AR
Adcock, Abner	044	1843	WB-15/408	CTY
Adcock, Caleb	044	1893	WB-24/217	CTY
Adcock, David	044	1881	WB-23/432	CTY
Adcock, Edward	044	1799	WB-4/279	CTY
Adcock, Green	100	1896	WB-51/472	AR
Adcock, Henry	005	1802	WB-2/2	AR
Adcock, John	022	1880	WB-E/196	AR
Adcock, John	044	1780	WB-1/258	CTY
Adcock, Joseph J.	044	1882	WB-23/447	CTY
Adcock, Joshua	022	1852	WB-C/314	AR
Adcock, Leonard	044	1798	WB-4/210	CTY
Adcock, Mary	044	1807	WB-6/364	CTY
Adcock, Robert	044	1797	WB-4/157	CTY
Adcock, Susanna	044	1807	WB-6/379	CTY
Adcock, Thomas	005	1823	WB-A/84	AR
Adcock, William H.	044	1858	WB-20/457	CTY
Adcock, William H.	044	1864	WB-22/175	

Name	Co.	Date	Recorded Copy	Original
Adcock, William H.	044	1894	WB-24/247	CTY
Adcoke, Bolen	044	1805	WB-6/168	CTY-Nunc.
Addams, Sarah	072	c1876	WB-4/97	aR
Addams, William	037	1829	WB-F/97	AR
Addcock, Eady	044	1842	WB-15/249	CTY
Adderson, Elijah	030	c1806	WB-2/336	
Adderton, George R.	081	1893	WB-16/271	AR
Adderton, James	032	1888	WB-4/14	
Adderton, Jeremiah	032	1844	WB-1/422	
Adderton, Stephen	032	1878	Orig. Only	AR
Adderton, William	032	1831	WB-1/173	
Addington, Henry	061	1878	WB-2/43	AR
Addison, Richard	024	1724	Orig. Only	SS/AR
Addoms, Mathew	024	1703	Orig. Only	SS/AR
Adear, Charles	046	1786	WB-A/5	AR
Aderholdt, Fredrick	060	1807	Orig. Only	AR
Aderholdt, Jacob	060	1877	WB-4/170	AR
Aderholt, Barbara	040	1890	WB-2/360	AR
Aderholt, David	040	1884	WB-2/220	AR
Aderton, Jeremiah	085	1779	WB-B/63	AR
Adesky, Jacob	038	1893	WB-3/379	AR
Adkins, Benjamin	069	1789	WB-1/55	AR
Adkins, Elizabeth	017	c1869	WB-B/134	AR
Adkins, John	092	c1835	WB-4/81	
Adkins, Nancy	020	c1817	RB-Q/435	AR
Adkins, Wade H.	051	1854	WB-A/366	
Adkins, William	092	1822	WB-3/154	AR
Adkins, William	053	1825	WB-4/160	AR
Adkins, Wilson	089	1898	WB-2/347	AR
Adkinson, James	085	c1798	WB-C/269	AR
Adkinson, James	071	1819	WB-3/217	
Adkinson, James	069	1783	WB-1/33	AR
Adkinson, John	084	c1790	WB-A/203	CTY
Adler, Joseph	065	1867	WB-J/243	AR
Admier, Elizabeth	085	c1823	WB-H/475	AR
Afford, John	053	1818	WB-4/136	
Agender, Elizabeth	085	1813	WB-G/267	AR
Agender, Henry	085	c1790	WB-C/60	AR
Agner, Daniel	085	1861	WB-K/293	AR
Agostini, Maria E.	070	1890	WB-F/356	AR
Ahair, John	057	1795	WB-A/133	AR
Aheir, John	072	1746	SS 877/21	SS/AR
Aiken, Benjamin	084	1852	WB-C/126	CTY
Aiken, David C.	046	1898	WB-G/74	AR
Aiken, Edmonia	084	1865	Orig. Only	CTY
Aiken, James	084	1859	WB-C/294	CTY
Aiken, Sally	072	1830	WB-1/69	Nunc.
Ainsworth, William	029	1760	DB-1/334	
Airs, John	096	c1776	WB-1/100	
Akehurst, Daniel	VA	1700	Copy	024 AR
Aken, Joseph	044	1808	WB-6/407	CTY
Aken, William	046	1799	WB-A/9	AR
Aker, Christian	094	1777	Orig. Only	060 AR
Aker, Peter	060	1799	Orig. Only	AR
Aker, Sally	060	1835	WB-1/329	AR
Akerman, Frederick	028	1772	Orig. Only	AR
Akin, Isham	044	1808	WB-6/430	CTY
Akin, John	013	c1886	Orig. Only	AR
Akin, Joseph	073	1767	WB-A/59	
Akins, James	029	c1789	Orig. Only	AR
Alan, Nathan	073	1820	WB-D/584	AR
Albea, Benjamin	054	c1823	Orig. Only	AR
Albea, Eugene E.	038	1898	WB-4/155	AR
Albea, Rebecca	054	1840	WB-2/217	AR
Albea, Thomas	054	c1843	WB-2/288	AR
Albea, W. W.	038	1898	WB-4/96	AR
Albea, Zacheria	054	1860	WB-3/154	AR
Alberson, Mary	077	1720/1	SS 875/315	SS/AR
Albert, Richard	009	1825	OB-A/348	AR
Albert, William	009	1831	OB-B/145	AR
Albert, William J.	065	1881	WB-K/420	AR
Albertson, Aaron	077	1782	WB-C/245	AR
Albertson, Albert	077	1702	Orig. Only	SS/AR
Albertson, Albert	075	1759	SS 881/179	
Albertson, Anthony B.	077	c1854	WB-F/518	AR
Albertson, Benjamin	077	1800	WB-E/122	AR
Albertson, Benjamin	077	1802	WB-E/174	AR
Albertson, Elihu	077	1789	WB-C/396	AR
Albertson, Francis	077	1816	WB-E/452	AR
Albertson, Henry	075	c1855	WB-M2/34	AR
Albertson, Isaac	075	c1759	Orig. Only	SS/AR
Albertson, John	075	1765	WB-H/70	
Albertson, Joseph	032	1836	WB-1/285	
Albertson, Joseph	077	1826	WB-F/116	AR
Albertson, Joshua	075	1766	WB-I/53	
Albertson, Joshua	077	1753	SS 878/229	SS/AR
Albertson, Joshua	085	c1805	WB-C/267	AR
Albertson, Josiah	077	1800	WB-E/119	AR
Albertson, Kesiah	077	1825	WB-F/90	AR
Albertson, Mary	077	1812	WB-E/372	AR
Albertson, Nathaniel	077	1752	Orig. Only	SS/AR
Albertson, Nathaniel	077	1785	WB-C/324	AR
Albertson, Samuel	035	1824	WB-A/8	AR
Albertson, Thomas	077	1806	WB-E/245	AR
Albertson, William	077	1784	WB-C/278	AR
Albertson, William	075	1851	WB-N/236	AR
Alberty, Elizabeth	092	1860	WB-5/48	
Alberty, Nathan	092	1896	WB-6/424	AR
Albright, Andrew W.	001	1866	WB-1/272	AR
Albright, Anne	001	c1852	WB-1/77	AR
Albright, Daniel	073	1843	WB-F/176	AR
Albright, Daniel	073	1846	WB-F/317	AR
Albright, Elizabeth	046	1852	WB-C/373	AR
Albright, Gabriel	046	1886	Orig. Only	AR
Albright, George	001	c1838	WB 1/51	AR
Albright, George	085	1896	WB-3/132	CTY
Albright, H. C.	022	c1864	WB-D/131	AR
Albright, Henry	085	1844	WB-I/217	AR
Albright, Henry	073	1840	WB-F/59	AR
Albright, Henry	001	1896	WB-3/140	AR
Albright, Jacob	073	1825	WB-E/73	AR
Albright, Jacob	073	c1791	WB-B/156	AR
Albright, James R.	001	1880	WB-2/165	AR
Albright, John	075	1795	WB-L/17	
Albright, John	085	1819	WB-G/544	AR
Albright, John	073	1790	WB-B/108	AR
Albright, John	073	1830	WB-E/231	AR
Albright, John G.	001	1889	WB-2/437	AR
Albright, John P.	001	1890	WB-2/454	
Albright, Joseph	073	c1816	Orig. Only	AR
Albright, Joseph	081	1877	WB-15/237	AR
Albright, Ludwick	073	1811	WB-D/280	AR
Albright, Ludwick	073	1816	WB-D/491	AR
Albright, Ludwick	073	1816	Copy	046 AR
Albright, Mary	054	c1857	WB-3/131	AR
Albright, Mary C.	001	1900	WB-3/355	AR
Albright, Marymagdelin	085	1852	WB-K/141	AR

Name	Co.	Date	Recorded Copy	Original
Albright, Michael	085	1829	WB-H/456	AR
Albright, Nancy J.	001	1895	WB-3/60	AR
Albright, Nicholas	073	1844	WB-F/204	AR
Albright, Peter	085	1885	WB-2/142	
Albright, Peter	085	1892	WB-2/510	CTY
Albright, Peter	085	1832	Orig. Only	AR
Albright, Samuel	085	1831	WB-H/501	AR
Albright, Sarah	085	1896	WB-3/140	CTY
Albright, Solomon	001	1862	WB-1/195	AR
Albright, William	046	1839	WB-C/43	AR
Albright, William	001	1871	WB-2/21	AR
Albright, William	022	1856	WB-C/428	AR
Albright, William	077	1809	WB-E/341	AR
Albritton, Agress	063	1868	WB-2/501	
Albritton, James	045	1882	WB-1/84	AR
Albritton, Josiah	079	c1862	WB-1/79	AR
Albritton, Luke	063	1853	WB-2/397	
Albritton, Noel	059	c1897	Orig. Only	CTY
Albritton, Rachel	059	1891	WB-B/5	CTY
Albritton, Tabitha	079	1865	WB-1/128	AR
Alcock, Solomon	030	1806	WB-2/287	
Alcorn, John	065	c1789	WB-A/38	AR
Alderman, Amariah B.	087	1890	WB-3/445	
Alderman, Daniel	035	1785	WB-A/2	AR
Alderman, Daniel	035	1824	WB-A/7	AR
Alderman, Daniel	070	1857	WB-C/642	AR
Alderman, Daniel W.	087	1892	WB-3/507	AR
Alderman, David	070	1860	WB-D/33	AR
Alderman, John	035	1824	WB-A/3	AR
Alderman, Joseph	035	c1895	Orig. Only	AR
Alderman, Susan Jane	070	c1886	WB-F/14 & 23	AR
Alderson, John	009	1761	OWB/84	AR
Alderson, Levy	053	1786	RW-1/150	
Alderson, Simon	008	c1713	SS 875/80	
Alderson, Simon	009	1740	LGB-4/#131	SS/AR
Alderson, Thomas	009	1814	OWB/467	AR
Aldredge, Susan A.	059	1899	WB-B/238	CTY
Aldridge, Harrison	102	c1898	WB-A/221	AR
Aldridge, Isham	078	1817	WI-7/311	AR
Aldridge, John	008	1706	Orig. Only	SS/AR
Aldridge, John	N	1702	009 DB-1/49	
Aldridge, John S.	028	1870	WB-E/23	
Aldridge, John, Sr.	084	1805	WB-A/23	CTY
Aldridge, Joseph	020	1876	WB-A/226	
Aldridge, Mary	038	1892	WB-3/436	AR
Aldridge, Mary B.	103	1880	WB-1/178	AR
Aldridge, William	059	1870	WB-A/15	
Aldridge, William	092	1803	WB-3/59	AR-Nunc.
Aleen, Hugh	024	c1752	Orig. Only	SS/AR
Alexander, A. C.	016	1889	WB-4/15	AR
Alexander, A. L.	054	1899	WB-6/216	CTY
Alexander, Aaron	065	1772	WB-A/10	AR
Alexander, Aaron	070	1851	WB-C/529	AR
Alexander, Aaron	065	1806	WB-A/50	AR
Alexander, Abigail B.	065	1889	WB-L/387	AR
Alexander, Abner	065	1830	WB-F/51	AR
Alexander, Abner	096	1818	Orig. Only	AR
Alexander, Abner	065	1868	WB-J/255	AR
Alexander, Abner	096	1845	Orig. Only	AR
Alexander, Abraham	054	c1829	WB-2/76	AR
Alexander, Abraham	065	1786	WB-A/1	AR
Alexander, Abram	016	1833	PQS.5/246	
Alexander, Allen	054	c1805	WB-1/62	AR
Alexander, Allen	003	1868	WB-B/1	
Alexander, Allen	096	1867	WB-3/96	AR
Alexander, Allen U.	060	1894	WB-4/527	AR
Alexander, Alphonso	016	1852	WB-1/210	
Alexander, Amos	065	1814	WB-A/63	AR
Alexander, Amos M.	054	1884	WB-4/9	CTY
Alexander, Amos P.	065	1861	WB-J/118	AR
Alexander, Amzi W.	065	1831	WB-E/103	AR
Alexander, Andrew	065	1782	WB-A/37	AR
Alexander, Anthoney	096	1759	WB-1/43	AR
Alexander, Anthony	096	1821	Orig. Only	AR
Alexander, Anthony	096	1784	WB-1/141	AR
Alexander, Anthony	096	1741	Orig. Only	SS/AR
Alexander, Arthur	065	1763	WB-A/9	AR
Alexander, Augustus	065	1846	WB-I/164	AR
Alexander, B. W.	065	c1858	Orig. Only	AR
Alexander, Benjamin	096	1784	WB-1/142	AR
Alexander, Benjamin	016	1862	WB-2/90	
Alexander, C. L.	065	1854	WB-I/232	AR
Alexander, Caroline B.	096	1861	WB-3/69	AR
Alexander, Catharine	065	1775	WB-A/16	AR
Alexander, Charles	065	1802	WB-A/43	AR
Alexander, Charles	065	1834	WB-G/188	AR
Alexander, Charles T.	065	1871	WB-K/59	AR
Alexander, Charles T.	065	1828	Orig. Only	AR
Alexander, Charles W.	016	1837	PQS.5/424	
Alexander, Christain	096	c1760	WB-1/53	
Alexander, Clementine	065	1897	WB-N/98	AR
Alexander, Cornelius	065	1866	WB-J/219	AR
Alexander, Cyrus A.	016	1881	WB-3/315	
Alexander, Dan	065	1863	WB-J/154	AR
Alexander, Daniel	065	1777	WB-A/12	AR
Alexander, David	070	1775	WB-C/6	AR
Alexander, David	065	1796	WB-A/40	AR
Alexander, David	065	1830	WB-F/56	AR
Alexander, Dionisius	016	1864	WB-2/107	
Alexander, Dorcas	065	1800	WB-A/3	AR
Alexander, E. C.	065	1883	WB-K/506	AR
Alexander, Edmund	096	c1830	WB-2/101	AR
Alexander, Elam E.	065	c1864	WB-J/198	
Alexander, Eleanor	065	1823	WB-A/67	AR
Alexander, Eli	065	1834	WB-G/181	AR
Alexander, Elias	065	1826	WB-A/69	AR
Alexander, Elias	086	1818	WB-C/101	AR
Alexander, Elizabeth	065	1878	WB-K/311	
Alexander, Elizabeth	085	1857	WB-K/232	AR
Alexander, Ephraim M.	003	1900	WB-B/405	
Alexander, Esther	072	1790	Orig. Only	AR
Alexander, Ezekell	072	1786	WI/L58	AR
Alexander, Ezekiel	065	1823	WB-A/66	AR
Alexander, Ezekiel	065	1837	WB-E/153	AR
Alexander, Ezekiel	065	1811	WB-A/17	AR
Alexander, Ezra	065	1800	WB-A/14	AR
Alexander, Ezra	065	1821	WB-A/19	AR
Alexander, Francis	070	1760	DB-D/456	AR
Alexander, Gabriel	054	c1804	WB-1/56	AR
Alexander, George	096	1837	WB-2/134	AR
Alexander, George	065	1884	WB-L/45	AR
Alexander, George	081	1780	Orig. Only	AR
Alexander, George	046	1868	WB-D/392	AR
Alexander, George	081	1801	WB-2/90	AR
Alexander, George C.	013	1880	WB-B/229	AR
Alexander, George N.	013	1890	WB-C/55	AR
Alexander, George W.	065	1867	WB-J/233	AR
Alexander, Gideon	096	1840	WB-2/150	AR
Alexander, Harriet	065	1889	WB-L/410	AR
Alexander, Harriet V.	054	1883	WB-5/46	CTY

Name	Co.	Date	Recorded Copy	Original
Alexander, Henry	065	1884	WB-L/42	AR
Alexander, Henry	096	1819	WB-2/74	AR
Alexander, Hezekiah	065	1801	WB-A/20	AR
Alexander, Isaac	096	c1780	WB-1/113	AR
Alexander, Isaac	096	1777	WB-1/96	AR
Alexander, Isaac	096	c1780	WB-1/122	AR
Alexander, Isaac J.	016	1865	WB-2/125	
Alexander, James	065	1841	WB-H/55	AR
Alexander, James	013	1845	WB-A/105	
Alexander, James	065	1784	WB-A/7	AR
Alexander, James	054	1843	WB-2/282	AR
Alexander, James	054	c1824	WB-2/100	AR
Alexander, James C.	013	1867	WB-A/248	AR
Alexander, James Q.	003	1896	WB-B/350	AR
Alexander, James R.	065	1847	WB-I/103	AR
Alexander, James T.	060	1866	WB-3/89	AR
Alexander, James W.	065	1857	WB-J/48	AR
Alexander, Jane	054	c1826	WB-2/169	AR
Alexander, Jane	065	1882	WB-K/521	AR
Alexander, Jediah	065	1815	WB-A/65	AR
Alexander, Joab	065	1828	WB-G/73	AR
Alexander, Joel	065	1864	WB-J/175	AR
Alexander, John	096	1821	WB-2/84	AR
Alexander, John	065	1805	WB-A/49	AR
Alexander, John	010	1799	WB-E/89	AR
Alexander, John	096	1812	WB-2/37	
Alexander, John	022	1779	Orig. Only	AR-Nunc.
Alexander, John A.	065	1888	WB-L/332	AR
Alexander, John G.	096	1853	WB-3/35	AR
Alexander, John H.	016	1833	PQS.5/283	Nunc.
Alexander, John J.	096	1844	WB-3/5	AR
Alexander, John J.	096	1844	Copy	075 AR
Alexander, John M.	065	1848	WB-I/143	AR
Alexander, John M.	065	1817	WB-A/54	AR
Alexander, John M.	016	c1863	Orig. Only	AR-Copy
Alexander, Joseph	096	c1796	Orig. Only	AR
Alexander, Joseph	096	1764	WB-1/57	AR
Alexander, Joseph	072	c1789	Orig. Only	AR
Alexander, Joseph	096	1782	WB-1/130	AR
Alexander, Joseph	014	c1808	086 WB-B/259	
Alexander, Joseph	046	1799	WB-A/7	AR
Alexander, Joseph M.	054	1884	WB-4/7	CTY
Alexander, Joseph McK.	065	1838	WB-H/57	AR
Alexander, Joseph W.	006	1841	WB-A/30	AR
Alexander, Joseph, Sr.	096	c1796	Orig. Only	AR
Alexander, Joshua	096	1796	Orig. Only	AR
Alexander, Josiah	065	1776	WB-A/11	AR
Alexander, Josiah	065	1828	Orig. Only	AR
Alexander, Kezia	065	1819	WB-A/53	AR
Alexander, L. D.	013	1864	WB-A/230	
Alexander, Laird	016	1867	WB-2/148	AR-Copy
Alexander, Lavinia	065	1810	WB-A/62	AR
Alexander, Leander	003	1882	WB-B/136	AR
Alexander, Levi N.	054	c1862	Orig. Only	AR
Alexander, Lucinda	065	1883	WB-L/127	AR
Alexander, Ludford	096	1775	WB-1/89	AR
Alexander, Margaret	065	1882	WB-K/469	AR
Alexander, Margaret	060	1818	Orig. Only	AR
Alexander, Mariah C.	050	1870	WB-1/108	CTY
Alexander, Martha	016	1844	WB-1/40	
Alexander, Martha C.	065	1836	WB-E/140	AR
Alexander, Mary	065	1805	WB-A/47	AR
Alexander, Mary	028	1870	WB-E/40	
Alexander, Mary	065	c1810	WB-A/17	AR
Alexander, Mary	065	c1842	WB-H/99	AR

Name	Co.	Date	Recorded Copy	Original
Alexander, Mary	065	1836	WB-E/148	AR
Alexander, Mary	016	1852	WB-1/209	
Alexander, Mary M.	054	1886	WB-5/110	CTY
Alexander, Mary W.	060	1885	WB-4/323	AR
Alexander, Matthew	065	1865	WB-J/209	AR
Alexander, Micheal	096	1781	WB-1/128	AR
Alexander, Milton	003	1873	WB-B/39	AR
Alexander, Moses	026	1859	WB-1/236	AR
Alexander, Moses	016	1838	PQS.5/529	
Alexander, Moses	065	1859	WB-J/68	AR
Alexander, Moses	003	1871	WB-B/22	AR
Alexander, N. S.	065	1893	WB-M/216	AR
Alexander, Nancy	046	1885	WB-E/422	AR
Alexander, Nancy	065	1847	WB-I/108	AR
Alexander, Nancy	054	c1807	WB-1/64	AR
Alexander, Nathan	096	1863	WB-3/65	AR
Alexander, Nathaniel	065	1892	WB-M/96	AR
Alexander, Nathaniel	065	1808	WB-A/24	AR
Alexander, Nathaniel	065	1808	WB-A/42	AR
Alexander, Noah	040	1899	WB-3/65	AR
Alexander, Obediah F.	070	1871	WB-E/221	AR
Alexander, Penelope	051	1840	WB-A/143	
Alexander, Perry	065	1894	WB-M/289	AR
Alexander, Philander	016	1833	PQS.5/283	
Alexander, Polly	004	1895	WB-A/158	AR
Alexander, R. A.	054	1886	WB-5/89	CTY
Alexander, Reading G.	096	1871	WB-4/20	
Alexander, Rebecca A.	065	1861	WB-J/119	AR
Alexander, Robert	060	1813	Orig. Only	AR
Alexander, Robert D.	065	1863	WB-J/164	AR
Alexander, Robert H.	014	1880	WB-2/202	AR
Alexander, Rodger	100	1896	Orig. Only	AR
Alexander, Rufus L.	065	1877	WB-K/264	AR
Alexander, S. D.	086	1859	WB-E/357	AR
Alexander, Sally	096	1818	Orig. Only	AR
Alexander, Samuel	065	c1784	WB-A/36	AR
Alexander, Samuel P.	065	1900	WB-N/336	AR
Alexander, Sarah	054	c1790	WB-1/12	AR
Alexander, Sarah C.	016	1849	WB-1/165	
Alexander, Sarah D.	065	1865	WB-J/201	AR
Alexander, Sophia	014	1875	WB-2/103	
Alexander, Stephen	016	1831	PQS.5/180	
Alexander, Susan	003	1871	WB-B/17	
Alexander, Susan R.	065	1890	WB-L/441	AR
Alexander, Susanah	065	1856	WB-J/31	AR
Alexander, T. L.	065	1897	WB-N/52	AR
Alexander, Thomas	047	1888	WB-6/486	AR
Alexander, Thomas	065	1845	Orig. Only	AR
Alexander, Thomas	065	1845	WB-I/38	AR
Alexander, Thomas H.	065	1836	WB-G/222	AR
Alexander, Thomas S.	014	1890	WB-2/411	CTY
Alexander, Violet W.	065	1868	WB-J/248	
Alexander, Vira D.	016	1871	WB-3/40	
Alexander, Wallace	060	1802	Orig. Only	AR
Alexander, Washington	003	1896	WB-B/353	
Alexander, William	075	1772	WB-A/6	AR
Alexander, William	065	1837	WB-E/139	AR
Alexander, William	019	1887	WB-B/161	AR
Alexander, William	086	1821	WB-C/164	AR
Alexander, William	065	1805	WB-A/44	AR
Alexander, William	096	1764	WB-1/56	AR
Alexander, William	014	1877	WB-2/149	
Alexander, William	060	1802	Orig. Only	AR
Alexander, William	104	1855	WB-5/124	AR
Alexander, William B.	065	1841	WB-H/162	AR

Name	Co.	Date	Recorded Copy	Original
Alexander, William M.	016	1850	WB-1/175	
Alexander, William S.	065	1858	WB-J/57	AR
Alexander, William S.	016	1827	PQS.4/(Back)	
Alexander, William T.	065	1870	WB-K/36	AR
Alexander, Zebulon	065	1784	WB-A/4	AR
Alexander, Zenas	065	1826	WB-A/71	AR
Alexander, Zilpah	096	c1794	Orig. Only	AR
Alferd, Joseph	002	c1689	Orig. Only	SS/AR
Alfird, Ann	002	1691	Orig. Only	SS/AR
Alford, Bennet H.	039	1857	WB-0/345	AR
Alford, Churchwell	099	1874	RB-35/249	AR
Alford, Elizabeth	056	1883	WB-3/344	AR
Alford, Jaboz	024	1705	SS 874.1/33	SS/AR
Alford, Jacob	083	1861	WB-2/170	AR
Alford, Jacob	083	c1794	WB-1/36	
Alford, Jane	099	1898	WB-D/173	AR
Alford, John W.	083	1875	WB-3/110	AR
Alford, Julius	015	1771	100 WB-1/201	AR
Alford, Kinchen	039	c1848	WB-0/153	AR
Alford, Lockhard	039	c1844	WB-L/253	
Alford, Lodowick	103	c1813	Orig. Only	AR
Alford, Lodwick	099	c1792	Orig. Only	AR-Copy
Alford, Lodwick	099	1820	RB-16/283	AR
Alford, Lodwick	039	1801	WB-B/82	AR
Alford, Medicun A.	039	1849	WB-N/318	AR
Alford, Sion	083	1833	WB-1/269	AR
Alford, Susan	099	1831	RB-22/147	AR
Alford, Susan V.	099	1897	WB-D/14	AR
Alford, Warren	083	1844	WB-1/445	AR
Alford, Warren	075	1814	WB-M1/261	AR
Alford, William	090	1812	WB-2/132	AR
Algea, Francis	065	1794	WB-A/33	AR
Algood, James E.	100	1876	WB-51/108	AR
Alison, James	085	c1760	WB-A/1	AR
Alison, Sarah	085	c1783	WB-B/88	AR
Allan, John	086	1828	WB-D/84	AR
Allan, Mary	029	c1789	Orig. Only	AR
Allan, Thomas	030	1790	WB-1/241	
Allan, Willis J.	064	1897	WB-2/389	AR
Allatt, Louisa	014	1884	WB-2/271	CTY
Allday, Thomas	010	1754	SS 879/161	SS/AR
Alldridge, Elijah	104	1786	WB-1/203	
Allegood, Richard	009	1752	Orig. Only	SS/AR
Allen, Aaron T.	079	1838	WB-2/210	
Allen, Abraham	073	c1818	Orig. Only	AR
Allen, Absabeth	056	1857	WB-1/697	AR
Allen, Absala	079	1900	WB-3/201	AR
Allen, Adeline	070	1875	WB-E/297	AR
Allen, Agnes	065	1791	WB-A/38	AR
Allen, Alexander	073	1836	WB-E/373	AR
Allen, Alexander	065	1825	WB-A/29	AR
Allen, Andrew	028	1762	SS 881/270	SS/AR
Allen, Ann	081	1832	WB-6/265	AR
Allen, Ann	028	1860	WB-D/327	AR
Allen, Ann Eliza	005	1894	WB-D/356	AR
Allen, Antonia	013	1882	WB-B/271	AR
Allen, Archibald	070	1827	WB-C/13	AR
Allen, Arter	069	1785	WB-1/40	AR
Allen, Arthur	024	c1764	WB-A/158	AR
Allen, Bartlett Y.	078	1895	WB-19/378	AR
Allen, Cameron W.	044	1860	WB-21/294	CTY
Allen, Charles	100	1808	WB-14/175	AR
Allen, Charlton Y.	071	1862	WB-5/274	AR
Allen, Chasteen	044	1886	WB-23/553	CTY
Allen, Daniel	084	c1799	OW/22	AR
Allen, Daniel	009	1886	WB-1/386	CTY
Allen, David	065	1869	WB-K/31	AR
Allen, David	078	1828	WI-11/128	AR
Allen, Drury	005	1824	WB-A/107	AR
Allen, Drury	012	1797	WB-B/59	AR
Allen, Drury	078	1803	WI-3/173	AR
Allen, Edmund	100	1878	WB-51/533	AR
Allen, Eleazer	070	c1742	SS 878/11	SS/AR
Allen, Eliza A.	028	1865	WB-D/397	AR
Allen, Elizabeth	071	1862	WB-5/272	AR
Allen, Elizabeth	081	1822	WB-5/55	AR
Allen, Elizabeth	056	1752	SS 880/136	
Allen, Elizabeth	060	1847	WB-2/287	AR
Allen, Elizabeth	046	1891	WB-F/162	AR
Allen, Elkanah	012	1842	WB-B/177	AR
Allen, Elly	084	1856	WB-C/234	CTY
Allen, Enoch E.	023	1885	WB-A/31	AR
Allen, Ephraim	011	1868	WB-2/26	
Allen, Erasmas	044	1884	WB-23/511	CTY
Allen, Erasmus W.	085	c1787	WB-C/259	AR
Allen, Garland	044	1820	WB-8/341	CTY
Allen, George	065	c1770	WB-A/29	AR
Allen, George	100	1805	WB-13/10	AR
Allen, George	050	1859	WB-1/58	CTY
Allen, George	073	1806	WB-D/176	AR
Allen, George	041	1822	WB-2/186	AR
Allen, George B.	099	1884	WB-A/552	AR
Allen, George F.	039	1892	WB-U/565	AR
Allen, George W.	041	c1863	Orig. Only	AR
Allen, George W.	005	1882	WB-D/129	AR
Allen, Gideon	079	1891	WB-2/546	AR
Allen, Henary	035	1795	WB-A/5	AR
Allen, Henry	099	1841	RB-24/508	AR
Allen, Henry	011	1890	WB-2/232	
Allen, Hugh	085	1831	WB-H/523	AR
Allen, Isaac	073	1772	WB-A/156	
Allen, J. E.	009	c1900	Orig. Only	CTY
Allen, J. P.	086	1883	WB-F/200	AR
Allen, J. W.	047	c1900	Orig. Only	AR
Allen, J. W.	064	1897	WB-2/412	AR
Allen, Jacob	073	1806	WB-D/178	AR
Allen, James	030	1799	WB-2/133	
Allen, James	070	1811	WB-AB/167	AR
Allen, James	044	1854	WB-19/457	CTY
Allen, James	099	1864	RB-33/329	AR
Allen, James	067	1782	Orig. Only	SS/AR
Allen, James	106	1898	WB-2/423	
Allen, James	037	1733	SS 876/286	SS/AR
Allen, James	047	1791	WB-3/194	
Allen, James C.	050	1894	WB-2/192	CTY-Nunc.
Allen, James I.	073	1889	WB-H/461	CTY
Allen, James I.	036	1889	WB-A/155	
Allen, James J.	020	1889	WB-B/60	CTY
Allen, Jane	073	1840	WB-F/54	AR
Allen, Jane	092	1806	WB-3/70A	AR
Allen, Jarvis	030	1819	WB-3/111	
Allen, Jeanette	020	1893	WB-B/150	CTY
Allen, Jehu	021	1878	WB-2/195	AR
Allen, Jeremiah	028	1866	WB-D/433	AR
Allen, Jerushia	009	1874	WB-1/133	CTY
Allen, Jesse	053	c1803	RW-1/365	AR
Allen, Jesse	071	1803	WB-2/241	AR
Allen, John	028	1787	WB-A/145	AR
Allen, John	022	1847	WB-C/200	AR

Name	Co.	Date	Recorded Copy	Original
Allen, John	060	1821	Orig. Only	AR
Allen, John	053	c1786	RW-1/195	
Allen, John	053	1782	RW-1/102	AR
Allen, John	009	1801	OWB/389	AR
Allen, John	073	c1812	WB-D/359	AR
Allen, John	099	1820	RB-22/456	AR
Allen, John	011	1884	WB-2/174	
Allen, John	085	c1803	WB-C/266	AR
Allen, John	010	1797	WB-E/24	AR
Allen, John	065	c1778	WB-A/27	AR
Allen, John	092	1801	WB-3/41A	AR-Nunc.
Allen, John	028	1795	WB-A/334	AR
Allen, John	070	1808	WB-AB/117	AR
Allen, John	056	c1796	WB-1/97	
Allen, John	037	1763	WB-A/124	AR
Allen, John	041	1866	WB-3/343	AR
Allen, John	081	1882	WB-15/367	AR
Allen, John	073	1826	WB-E/130	AR
Allen, John	009	1831	OB-B/144	AR
Allen, John	079	1826	Copy	105 AR
Allen, John J.	086	1867	WB-E/479	AR
Allen, John, Sr.	046	1781	WB-A/7	AR
Allen, Joseph	073	c1770	WB-A/122	
Allen, Joseph	081	1847	WB-8/589	AR
Allen, Joseph	028	1800	WB-B/101	AR
Allen, Joseph	078	1821	WI-9/223	AR
Allen, Joseph	011	1864	WB-1/319	
Allen, Joseph	068	1829	WB-B/63	
Allen, Joseph	068	1889	WB-D/298	
Allen, Joseph	084	1846	WB-C/94	CTY
Allen, Joseph B.	044	1854	WB-19/455	CTY
Allen, Joseph T.	005	1900	WB-D/456	AR
Allen, Joshua	005	1875	WB-D/31	AR
Allen, Judith	071	1881	WB-6/339	AR
Allen, Julius	012	c1856	WB-B/6	AR
Allen, L. B.	039	1894	WB-V/31	AR
Allen, L. C.	026	1889	WB-2/376	AR
Allen, M. A.	047	1874	WB-6/133	AR
Allen, Margaret	010	1847	WB-G/423	AR
Allen, Martha	081	1854	WB-10/94	AR
Allen, Mary	099	1852	RB-28/100	AR
Allen, Mary	030	1799	WB-2/135	
Allen, Mary	047	1837	WB-4/155	
Allen, Mary	070	1815	WB-AB/230	AR
Allen, Mary	100	1850	WB-40/310	AR
Allen, Mary Ann	044	1886	WB-23/557	CTY
Allen, Mary H.	044	1857	WB-20/225	CTY
Allen, Mary M.	099	1865	RB-33/480	
Allen, Moody H.	005	1898	WB-D/438	AR
Allen, Moses	054	c1801	WB-1/62	AR
Allen, Moses H.	099	1886	WB-B/132	AR
Allen, Nancy	044	1887	WB-24/23	CTY
Allen, Nancy	054	c1831	WB-2/111	AR
Allen, Nancy	099	1892	WB-C/55	AR
Allen, Narcissa	099	1892	WB-C/109	AR
Allen, Nathaniel	024	1805	WB-B/253	AR
Allen, Nathaniel	071	1856	WB-5/164	AR
Allen, Nathaniel	024	1805	Copy	096 AR
Allen, Paul	005	1835	WB-B/50	AR
Allen, Peter	022	1846	WB-C/191	AR
Allen, Polly	084	1870	WB-E/25	CTY
Allen, Polly	030	1837	WB-4/36	
Allen, Prithiah	084	1821	WB-A/133	CTY-Nunc.
Allen, Rebecca	054	1840	WB-2/217	
Allen, Reubin	078	1851	WB-13/476	AR
Allen, Reynold	099	1881	WB-A/291	AR
Allen, Richard	071	1784	WB-1/455	
Allen, Richard	104	1832	WB-4/157	AR
Allen, Richard	104	1884	WB-6/239	AR
Allen, Robert	020	1784	RB-B/22	AR
Allen, Robert	003	1874	WB-B/43	AR
Allen, Robert	029	c1787	Orig. Only	AR
Allen, Roger	037	1762	WB-A/102	AR
Allen, S. P.	009	c1835	Orig. Only	AR
Allen, Sally	073	1874	WB-H/84	CTY
Allen, Sampson	022	1891	WB-E/469	AR
Allen, Samuel	084	1855	WB-C/203	CTY
Allen, Samuel	044	1813	WB-7/326	CTY
Allen, Samuel	081	1873	WB-15/102	AR
Allen, Samuel	081	1834	WB-6/380	AR
Allen, Samuel	104	1810	WB-2/282	AR
Allen, Samuel Dyer	070	1866	WB-D/191	AR
Allen, Samuel S.	063	1844	WB-2/309	
Allen, Sarah	044	1887	WB-24/25	CTY
Allen, Sarah	070	1761	SS 881/193	SS/AR
Allen, Sarah	041	1794	WB-1/131	AR
Allen, Shadrach	009	1856	OB-K/109	
Allen, Shadrack	028	1780	Orig. Only	AR
Allen, Silas	069	1890	WB-5/302	AR
Allen, Sophonisba	009	1866	OB-M/314	AR
Allen, Susan	028	1865	WB-D/371	AR
Allen, Susan P.	044	1863	WB-22/30	CTY
Allen, Thomas	056	1873	WB-3/106	AR
Allen, Thomas	047	1849	WB-4/278	
Allen, Thomas	104	1892	WB-6/448	AR
Allen, Thomas B.	044	1874	WB-23/120	CTY
Allen, Thomas P.	032	1875	WB-3/131	AR
Allen, Thomas R.	101	c1886	WB-A/252	AR
Allen, Timothy	009	1759	OWB/70	AR
Allen, Titus C.	079	1860	WB-1/45	AR
Allen, Turner	100	1889	WB-51/309	AR
Allen, Unity	039	1882	WB-U/298	AR
Allen, Valentine	084	1826	WB-A/204	CTY
Allen, Valentine	084	1884	WB-E/298	CTY
Allen, Vine	028	c1821	Orig. Only	AR
Allen, Walter P.	057	1843	028 WB-D/75	028 AR
Allen, William	029	1850	WB-C/202	AR
Allen, William	005	c1878	WB-D/92	AR
Allen, William	099	1875	RB-35/292	AR
Allen, William	081	1886	WB-16/20	AR
Allen, William	044	1786	WB-1/516	CTY-Copy
Allen, William	001	c1846	WB-1/38	AR
Allen, William	016	1862	WB-2/89	AR
Allen, William	078	1816	WI-7/125	AR
Allen, William	078	1816	WI-7/123	AR
Allen, William	083	1855	WB-3/231	AR
Allen, William	089	1863	WB-1/248	
Allen, William	022	1787	RB-1/27	AR
Allen, William G.	026	1871	WB-2/62	AR
Allen, William J.	099	1865	RB-33/480	AR
Allen, William L.	044	1871	WB-23/52	CTY
Allen, William M.	054	1851	WB-3/55	AR
Allen, William W.	026	1864	WB-1/354	AR
Allen, Willilam	044	1843	WB-15/410	CTY
Allen, Wincy	005	1880	WB-D/104	
Allen, Young	099	1836	RB-23/545	AR
Allen, Young	099	1774	RB-1/52	AR
Allen, Young H.	005	1851	WB-C/31	AR

Name	Co.	Date	Recorded Copy	Original
Allen, Zachariah	073	1790	WB-B/91	AR
Allen, Zachariah	044	1845	WB-16/244	CTY
Alley, Edmund	020	1806	RB-E/220	AR
Alley, Erasmus	090	1869	WB-6/5	AR
Alley, Howell L.	054	c1859	Orig. Only	AR
Alley, Lewis	054	1886	WB-5/128	CTY
Alley, Martha	104	1880	WB-6/198	AR
Alley, Mary	084	1845	WB-C/23	CTY
Alley, William	090	1884	WB-6/142	AR
Alleyn, George	024	1735	SS 876/387	
Alligood, Allen C.	009	1870	WB-1/60	AR
Alligood, Fannie R.	009	1889	WB-1/459	CTY
Alligood, Francis	009	1851	OB-H/30	AR
Alligood, Francis	009	1816	OB-A/257	AR
Alligood, Hardy	009	1860	OB-L/248	AR
Alligood, John	009	1885	WB-1/358	CTY
Alligood, Mary	009	1843	OB-E/190	AR
Alligood, Nathan	009	1899	WB-2/215	CTY
Alligood, Rebbecca	009	1826	OB-A/369	AR
Alligood, Sarah	009	1843	OB-E/186	AR
Allin, Drewry	086	1814	WB-C/10	AR
Allin, James	047	1781	WB-3/6	
Allin, John	010	1736	LGB-4/#35	SS/AR
Allin, Samuel	037	1763	WB-A/115	AR-Nunc.
Allison, Adam	054	c1809	WB-1/49	AR
Allison, Adam	054	c1802	WB-1/53	AR
Allison, Andrew	085	c1780	WB-C/178	AR
Allison, Andrew	054	1859	WB-3/144	
Allison, Andrew N.	054	1869	WB-4/51	
Allison, Ann	054	1846	WB-3/15	AR
Allison, Anthony	060	1831	WB-1/203	AR
Allison, Archibald	065	1806	WB-A/34	AR
Allison, Augustus	073	1891	WB-H/536	CTY
Allison, Benjamin	024	c1763	WB-A/155	AR
Allison, David	065	1800	WB-A/29	AR
Allison, E. J.	065	1885	WB-L/70	AR
Allison, Eliza Jane	073	1894	WB-I/22	CTY
Allison, George	054	1849	WB-3/32	AR
Allison, James	016	1831	PQS.5/169	
Allison, James	065	1897	WB-M/532	
Allison, James	073	c1838	Orig. Only	AR
Allison, James	073	1884	WB-H/353	CTY
Allison, James	054	1840	WB-2/214	AR
Allison, James W.	038	1900	WB-4/208	AR
Allison, John	073	c1821	Orig. Only	AR
Allison, John	073	c1853	Orig. Only	AR
Allison, John	073	1796	WB-C/75	AR
Allison, Joseph	073	1844	WB-F/206	AR
Allison, Joseph	073	c1789	WB-B/70	AR
Allison, Joseph	073	1861	WB-G/360	CTY
Allison, Joshua	049	c1859	WB-1/30	AR
Allison, Kiziah	054	1861	WB-3/161	AR
Allison, Magdalene	054	1859	WB-3/137	AR
Allison, Magdelin	054	c1794	WB-1/14	AR
Allison, Martha	046	1811	WB-A/5	AR
Allison, Mary	054	1857	WB-3/114	AR
Allison, Mary	054	c1855	WB-3/92	
Allison, Mary	016	1851	WB-1/200	
Allison, Mary	050	1898	WB-2/296	CTY
Allison, Nancy	054	1865	Orig. Only	AR
Allison, R. W.	016	1898	WB-4/309	AR
Allison, Richard	054	c1831	WB-2/112	AR
Allison, Robert	054	1869	WB-4/23	AR
Allison, Robert	044	1797	WB-4/67	CTY
Allison, Robert	016	1844	WB-1/35	
Allison, Robert A.	060	1831	WB-1/213	AR
Allison, S. G.	085	1863	WB-K/308	AR
Allison, S. G.	085	c1862	Copy	016 AR
Allison, Samuel	046	1820	WB-B/95	AR
Allison, Theophilus	085	1896	WB-3/153	CTY
Allison, Theophilus	054	c1815	WB-1/364	AR
Allison, Theophilus	054	c1805	WB-2/44	AR
Allison, Thomas	054	1844	WB-2/290	AR
Allison, Thomas	054	N. D.	WB-2/42	
Allison, Thomas	054	c1793	WB-1/13	
Allison, Thomas	016	1855	WB-1/249	AR
Allison, Thomas	085	c1780	WB-B/119	AR
Allison, Thomas A.	054	1884	WB-4/11	CTY
Allison, William	065	1825	WB-A/69	AR
Allison, William	104	1818	WB-3/170	AR
Allison, William	065	1863	WB-J/159	AR
Allison, William	054	c1814	WB-2/50	AR
Allison, William W.	073	1887	WB-H/435	CTY
Allman, Gideon	049	c1857	WB-1/22	AR
Allman, Margaret	016	1897	WB-4/252	AR
Allman, N. G.	061	1892	WB-2/112	AR
Allmond, Cannaday	099	1823	RB-18/298	AR
Allmond, Mary	036	1887	WB-A/104	CTY
Allmond, Nancy	099	1848	Orig. Only	AR
Allred, Aaron	081	1894	WB-16/295	
Allred, Aley	081	1866	WB-14/41	AR
Allred, Elizabeth	081	1827	WB-5/378	AR
Allred, James B.	092	1885	WB-6/218	AR
Allred, Jesse	081	1899	WB-17/23	AR
Allred, John	081	1792	WB-1/121	AR
Allred, John	081	1844	WB-8/63	AR
Allred, Lewis H.	001	1892	WB-2/525	AR
Allred, Rachel	081	1870	WB-15/36	AR
Allred, Thomas	081	1810	WB-3/188	AR
Allred, William	081	1827	WB-5/194	AR
Allred, William	081	1863	WB-12/475	AR
Allsbrooks, William	063	1857	WB-2/439	
Allsbrooks, William	063	1857	101 WB-A/291	101 AR
Allston, Benjamin	SC	1900	080 WB-1/323	080 AR
Allway, Francis	028	1765	Wills.9/190	AR-Copy
Allways, Bonita	028	1815	WB-C/102	AR
Almand, Perrin	028	1780	Orig. Only	AR
Almon, John P.	082	1859	WB-4/129	AR
Almond, Daniel	089	1862	WB-1/230	
Almond, Edward	067	1841	089 WB-1/202	
Almond, Martin	089	1866	WB-1/303	
Almond, Mary N.	089	1877	WB-2/46	
Almond, Pleasant	089	1858	WB-1/186	
Almond, Sarah	089	1872	WB-2/16	AR
Almond, William	082	c1793	WB-1/39 & 53	AR
Alphin, Absolom	024	c1762	WB-A/154	AR
Alphin, Charles H.	072	1888	WB-4/230	AR
Alphin, Jacob	041	1858	WB-3/233	AR
Alphin, James	041	1858	WB-3/229	AR
Alphin, John	041	1893	WB-4/381	AR
Alphin, John	041	1865	WB-3/322	AR
Alridge, William	081	1789	WB-1/73	AR
Alsbrook, Alice	047	1836	WB-4/130	
Alsbrook, David	047	1879	WB-6/211	AR
Alsobrook, Drury	047	1795	WB-3/255	
Alsobrook, Elizabeth	005	1843	WB-B/152	AR
Alsobrook, Howell	047	1802	WB-3/383	
Alsobrook, John	047	1781	WB-3/23	
Alsobrook, Perthinia	037	1812	WB-E/40	AR
Alsobrook, Samuel	047	1766	WB-1/198	

Name	Co.	Date	Recorded Copy	Original
Alsobrook, William	047	1806	WB-3/457	
Alsobrooks, Willis	097	1867	WB-1/292	AR
Alspaugh, Henry	090	1841	WB-4/91	AR
Alspaugh, John	038	1893	WB-3/422	AR
Alston, Alfred	100	1851	WB-41/127	AR
Alston, Ann E.	022	1896	WB-E/22	AR
Alston, Anna	047	1894	WB-7/128	AR
Alston, Betsy C.	047	1834	WB-4/108	Nunc.
Alston, Edward	100	1856	WB-49/51	AR
Alston, Elizabeth	100	1845	WB-39/455	AR
Alston, Elizabeth	100	1864	WB-50/93	AR
Alston, Elizabeth	044	1854	WB-19/332	CTY
Alston, Elizabeth	100	1835	WB-35/104	AR
Alston, Elizabeth	022	1858	WB-D/4	AR
Alston, Erasmus	047	1835	WB-4/120	
Alston, Eveline	022	1892	WB-E/471	AR
Alston, Francis A.	047	1875	WB-6/138	AR
Alston, George	044	1811	WB-7/191	CTY
Alston, George L.	099	1849	Orig. Only	AR
Alston, George W.	100	1849	WB-40/213	AR
Alston, Gideon	047	1831	WB-4/78	
Alston, Gideon	022	1856	WB-C/408	AR
Alston, J. A.	022	1900	WB-F/157	AR
Alston, James	073	1760	WB-A/13	
Alston, James W.	099	1883	WB-A/394	
Alston, John	047	1784	WB-3/67	
Alston, John	047	1831	WB-4/75	
Alston, John	073	1815	WB-D/440	AR
Alston, John	024	1758	SS 882/128	SS/AR
Alston, John	047	1843	WB-4/226	
Alston, John J.	022	1842	WB-C/134	AR-Nunc.
Alston, John Jones	022	1842	SC/05721	AR-Copy
Alston, Joseph	047	1847	WB-4/256	
Alston, Joseph J.	022	1841	WB-C/120	AR
Alston, Joseph J.	047	1781	WB-3/10	
Alston, Joseph John	022	c1839	Copy	081 AR
Alston, Laura	100	1889	WB-51/295	AR
Alston, Lemuel	073	1818	WB-D/542	AR
Alston, Lucy	100	1839	WB-37/245	AR
Alston, Major W.	047	1851	WB-4/311	
Alston, Martha	100	1830	WB-33/69	AR
Alston, Martha	100	1823	WB-24/232	AR
Alston, Martha	100	1823	Copy	039 AR
Alston, Martha	046	1884	WB-E/389	
Alston, Martha H.	100	1876	WB-51/110	AR
Alston, Martha K.	022	1862	WB-D/89	AR
Alston, Mary	100	1848	WB-40/34	AR
Alston, Mary Jane	100	1900	WB-51/546	AR
Alston, Matthew	046	1884	WB-E/391	AR
Alston, Medicus	100	1810	WB-15/158	AR-Nunc.
Alston, Miriam P.	081	1855	WB-10/195	AR
Alston, Nancy Park	047	1896	WB-7/177	AR
Alston, Nathaniel	022	1856	WB-C/413	AR
Alston, Oran D.	022	1851	WB-C/294	AR
Alston, Oscar F.	099	1881	WB-A/280	AR
Alston, Paddy	047	1882	WB-6/289	AR
Alston, Philip	100	1812	WB-16/311	AR
Alston, Philip	100	1784	WB-4/35	AR
Alston, Philip G.	100	1820	WB-22/518	AR
Alston, Philip G.	100	1852	WB-42/6	AR
Alston, Philip K.	022	1852	WB-C/316	AR
Alston, Richard	039	N. D.	Orig. Only	AR
Alston, Robert F.	SC	1864	Copy	005 AR
Alston, Robert P.	022	1872	WB-E/80	AR
Alston, Salla	100	1814	WB-18/41	AR
Alston, Samuel	099	c1825	RB-19/527	AR
Alston, Samuel	044	1771	Orig. Only	CTY
Alston, Samuel T.	100	1860	WB-49/328	AR
Alston, Samuel W.	TN	1858	Copy	099 AR
Alston, Sarah M.	047	1869	WB-6/25	AR
Alston, Solomon	100	1785	WB-4/70	AR
Alston, Thomas	099	1854	RB-29/128	AR
Alston, Thomas N.F.	100	1872	Copy	039 AR
Alston, Thomas N.F.	100	1873	WB-51/56	AR
Alston, Thomas W.	100	1809	WB-15/118	AR
Alston, W. F. S.	047	1854	WB-4/359	
Alston, Whitmell	100	1824	WB-26/157	AR
Alston, William	047	1816	WB-3/580	
Alston, William	100	1795	WB-8/90	AR
Alston, William	100	1810	WB-16/1	AR
Alston, William	022	1789	RB-1/37	AR
Alston, William F.	100	1828	WB-32/31	AR
Alston, William R.	100	1875	WB-51/78	AR
Alston, Willis	047	1819	WB-3/646	
Alston, Willis	047	1837	WB-4/149	
Altman, Elizabeth	056	1893	WB-2/147	AR
Altman, Nancy	056	1828	WB-1/346	AR
Altman, Nathan	056	1843	WB-1/552	AR
Altstaetter, Henry	OH	1900	Copy	049 AR
Alverson, Elisha	020	1845	RB-P/203	AR
Alves, Gavin	073	1812	WB-D/352	AR
Alway, Mishack	028	1841	WB-D/24	AR
Alway, William W.	028	1835	WB-C/382	AR
Always, Keziah	019	1827	WB-D/7	AR
Always, Obediah	028	1813	WB-C/66	AR
Always, Wealthy	028	1850	WB-D/165	AR
Alyotte, Anne	044	1795	WB-3/187	
Amads, Thomas M.	009	1870	WB-1/57	
Aman, Celia	072	1843	WB-2/45	AR
Aman, Dennis	072	1849	WB-2/104	AR
Aman, Jacob	072	1793	Orig. Only	AR
Aman, Philip	072	1829	WB-1/41	AR
Aman, Zesse	072	1813	WB-A/14	AR-Nunc.
Amason, Delana	037	1841	WB-F/262	AR
Amason, Ellender	037	1832	WB-F/131	AR
Amason, Thomas	037	1792	WB-C/207	AR
Amason, William	037	1797	WB-D/19	AR
Amason, William	037	1811	Orig. Only	AR
Amatis, Nicolas	070	1747	WB-C/1	AR
Ambler, William	077	1745	Orig. Only	SS/AR
Ambros, David	024	1745	Orig. Only	SS/AR
Ambrose, Britton	010	1894	WB-I/398	AR
Ambrose, Daniel	072	1812	WB-A/1	AR
Ambrose, Ellsberry	101	1892	WB-A/206	
Ambrose, John	063	1860	WB-2/469	
Ambrose, John	072	c1784	WI/L24	AR
Ambrose, Mary E.	084	1900	WB-F/187	CTY
Ambrose, Mary Jane	072	c1873	Orig. Only	AR
Ambrose, Sarah	072	1827	WB-1/11	AR
Ambrose, William	072	1764	Orig. Only	AR-Nunc.
Ambrose, William J.	084	1885	WB-E/300	CTY
Ambrose, Wilson	101	1892	WB-A/212	AR
Ambross, William	099	1792	RB-2/376	AR
Ambrous, William	099	1800	RB-5/90	AR
Amburn, John	032	1874	WB-3/126	AR
Amburn, William	085	1811	WB-G/182	AR
Amerson, David W.	105	1865	WB-1/121	AR
Amerson, Elisha	105	1873	WB-2/122	AR
Amerson, Elizabeth	105	1886	WB-2/420	
Amerson, Elizabeth	105	1869	WB-2/7	AR

Name	Co.	Date	Recorded Copy	Original
Ames, Elizabeth	063	c1801	WB-1/385	
Ames, Mary A.	018	1899	WB-E/305	AR
Ames, Thomas	063	1795	WB-1/321	
Amick, Catherine	081	1826	WB-5/298	AR
Amick, George	046	1871	WB-E/56	AR
Amick, John	081	1832	WB-6/264	AR
Amick, Peter	081	1844	WB-8/79	AR
Amick, William	046	1864	WB-D/234	AR
Amick, William	081	1824	WB-5/137	AR
Amis, Elizabeth	CA	1872	100 WB-51/139	100 AR
Amis, James	AR	1853	044 WB-21/373	044 CTY
Amis, John	071	1764	WB-1/101	
Amis, John	044	1897	WB-24/341	CTY
Amis, Joseph	044	1840	WB-14/567	CTY
Amis, Lewis	044	1825	WB-10/55	CTY
Amis, Mary	044	1890	WB-24/131	CTY-Nunc.
Amis, Paulina	044	1885	WB-23/518	CTY
Amis, Thomas	TN	1798	Copy	071 AR
Amis, Thomas	071	1764	WB-1/104	
Amis, Thomas	047	1798	WB-3/302	
Amis, William	071	1824	WB-3/300	AR
Amis, William	044	1857	WB-20/341	CTY
Amit, Peter	057	1798	WB-A/201	AR
Ammons, D. P.	061	1895	WB-2/168	AR
Ammons, E. J.	062	1866	WB-A/35	AR
Ammons, Jesse	103	1826	RD-5/216	AR
Ammons, Joshua	061	1877	WB-2/35	AR
Ammons, Joshua	083	c1806	WB-1/104	AR
Ammons, Thomas	087	c1792	WB-A/21	AR
Amock, Nicholas	081	1798	WB-2/33	AR
Amos, David	086	1868	WB-E/487	AR
Amos, Isham S.	084	1846	WB-C/40	CTY
Amos, Robert	100	1878	WB-51/126	AR
Amyet, Vincent	057	1791	WB-A/152	AR
Amyett, Amos	057	1864	WB-B/256	AR
Amyett, John E.	028	1872	WB-E/67	
Ancrum, John	070	1779	WB-C/7	AR
Anders, Daniel	028	1866	Orig. Only	AR
Anders, James	004	1893	WB-A/147	
Anders, James P.	029	1857	WB-C/368	AR
Anders, John M.	070	1827	WB-C/14	AR
Anders, John, Jr.	011	c1796	WB-1/363	
Anders, Leander	004	1882	WB-A/56	AR
Anders, Maria	011	1897	WB-3/90	CTY
Anders, Nancy C.	087	1873	WB-3/62	AR
Anders, Simon	011	1897	WB-3/90	CTY
Anders, William	004	1877	Orig. Only	AR
Anderson, A. A.	046	1892	WB-F/243	AR
Anderson, Abbey	063	1827	WB-2/132	
Anderson, Alexander	070	1844	WB-AB/417	AR
Anderson, Alexander	073	1884	WB-H/343	CTY
Anderson, Alfred	044	1887	WB-24/27	CTY
Anderson, Ann	024	1788	WB-A/152	AR
Anderson, Archibald	100	1823	WB-25/182	AR
Anderson, Benjamin	046	1854	WB-C/411	AR
Anderson, Carolus	071	1753	SS 879/180	SS/AR
Anderson, Charles	028	1785	WB-A/88	
Anderson, Charles	033	1894	WB-2/167	CTY
Anderson, Charles	085	1831	WB-H/500	AR
Anderson, Daniel	070	1869	WB-E/179	AR
Anderson, David	029	1844	WB-C/64	AR
Anderson, David	073	1822	WB-E/10	AR
Anderson, E. H.	028	1898	WB-F/360	
Anderson, Eady	073	1876	WB-H/154	CTY
Anderson, Eady	036	1892	WB-A/242	CTY
Anderson, Edward	047	1886	WB-6/437	AR
Anderson, Edwin A.	070	1894	WB-G/186	AR
Anderson, Elisabeth	077	1760	Orig. Only	SS/AR
Anderson, Elisabeth	010	1733	SS 876/327	SS/AR
Anderson, Elizabeth	037	1881	WB-G/580	AR
Anderson, Elizabeth	020	1839	RB-N/343	AR
Anderson, Elmore	072	c1772	RW/L39	AR
Anderson, Enoch	028	1859	WB-D/315	AR
Anderson, Enos	104	1896	WB-6/572	AR
Anderson, George	044	1771	Orig. Only	CTY
Anderson, George	044	1758	SS 881/155	SS/AR
Anderson, George	100	1844	WB-38/304	AR
Anderson, H. G.	038	1894	WB-3/476	AR
Anderson, Harriet	051	1866	WB-B/77	
Anderson, Henrietta	046	1896	WB-F/536	AR
Anderson, Henry	037	1802	WB-D/137	AR
Anderson, Isaac	085	1811	Orig. Only	AR
Anderson, J. G.	033	1856	WB-1/127	AR-Nunc.
Anderson, Jacob, Sr.	SC	1824	082 WB-1/255	082 AR
Anderson, James	014	1874	WB-2/86	
Anderson, James	077	1742	Orig. Only	SS/AR
Anderson, James	020	1846	RB-P/299	AR
Anderson, James	046	1815	WB-A/12	AR
Anderson, James	073	1800	WB-D/14	AR
Anderson, James	022	1795	RB-2/35	AR
Anderson, James	001	c1849	WB-1/27	
Anderson, James	047	1817	WB-3/606	
Anderson, James L.	051	1896	WB-C/510	AR
Anderson, James, Sr.	107	c1834	WB-1/1	
Anderson, Jane	073	1900	WB-I/175	CTY
Anderson, Jerry	044	1882	WB-23/445	CTY
Anderson, Jesse	103	1846	RD-9/444	AR
Anderson, John	077	1808	WB-E/315	AR
Anderson, John	084	c1803	WB-A/210	CTY
Anderson, John	077	1744/5	Orig. Only	SS/AR
Anderson, John	020	1822	RB-I/71	
Anderson, John	085	1844	WB-I/215	AR
Anderson, John	079	c1842	Orig. Only	AR-Copy
Anderson, John	073	1806	WB-D/169	AR
Anderson, John	103	1794	WI-A/463	AR
Anderson, John	086	1814	WB-C/11	AR
Anderson, John	033	1896	WB-2/198	CTY
Anderson, John A.	051	1861	WB-B/39	AR
Anderson, Jonas	028	1796	WB-B/1	AR
Anderson, Joseph	077	1751	Orig. Only	SS/AR
Anderson, Joseph	024	1750	Orig. Only	SS/AR
Anderson, Joseph	077	1793	WB-C/461	AR-Copy
Anderson, Joseph	073	1882	WB-H/305	CTY
Anderson, Joseph	073	1847	WB-F/359	AR
Anderson, Joshua	046	c1852	Orig. Only	AR
Anderson, Lewis	044	1805	WB-6/167	CTY
Anderson, Lewis	044	1785	WB-1/439	CTY
Anderson, M. P.	065	1899	WB-N/294	AR
Anderson, Margaret	085	1856	WB-K/210	AR
Anderson, Martha	073	1866	WB-G/492	CTY
Anderson, Martha	044	1834	WB-13/75	CTY
Anderson, Martha	070	1879	WB-E/372	AR
Anderson, Martin	044	c1868	WB-23/13	CTY
Anderson, Mary	070	1879	WB-E/370	AR
Anderson, Mary	028	1885	WB-E/407	AR
Anderson, Mary C.	070	1897	WB-H/75	AR
Anderson, Mary J.	105	1889	WB-2/509	AR

Name	Co.	Date	Recorded Copy	Original
Anderson, Mary Read	070	1845	WB-AB/424	AR
Anderson, Micajah	037	1879	WB-G/545	AR
Anderson, Michael	085	1863	WB-K/322	AR
Anderson, Miles	103	1829	RD-6/78	AR
Anderson, Nancy	044	1866	WB-22/486	CTY
Anderson, Nancy	TN	1851	Copy	065 AR
Anderson, Nathan	062	1857	WB-A/16	AR
Anderson, Nathan	047	1818	WB-3/622	
Anderson, Nathan W.	062	1885	WB-B/80	
Anderson, Patience	044	1844	WB-16/38	CTY
Anderson, Peggy	044	1886	WB-23/547	CTY
Anderson, Peter	069	1801	WB-1/141	AR
Anderson, Rachel	046	1885	WB-E/423	AR
Anderson, Reading	005	1846	WB-B/207	AR
Anderson, Rebecca	105	1899	WB-3/345	AR
Anderson, Richard	033	1857	WB-1/132	AR
Anderson, Richard	085	c1802	WB-D/9	AR
Anderson, Richard	006	1870	WB-D/102	AR
Anderson, Robert	085	1761	WB-A/5	AR-Nunc.
Anderson, Robert	084	1866	WB-D/46	CTY
Anderson, Robert	073	1820	WB-D/572	AR
Anderson, Robert	073	1816	WB-D/458	AR
Anderson, Robert	086	1808	WB-B/216	AR
Anderson, Robert B.	014	1889	WB-2/376	
Anderson, Robert W.	073	1898	WB-I/133	CTY
Anderson, Sally	009	1826	OB-A/357	AR
Anderson, Sally	044	1883	WB-23/466	CTY
Anderson, Samuel	077	1804	WB-E/211	AR
Anderson, Samuel C.	046	1860	WB-D/68	AR
Anderson, Sarah	069	1855	WB-1/546	AR
Anderson, Sarah	097	c1883	WB-2/306	AR
Anderson, Sidney	001	1866	WB-1/278	AR
Anderson, Susan	047	1866	WB-5/140	
Anderson, Tabitha	037	1858	WB-G/153	AR
Anderson, Thomas	103	1812	Orig. Only	AR
Anderson, Thomas	037	1898	WB-H/425	AR
Anderson, Thomas	085	1820	WB-H/55	AR
Anderson, Thomas J.	073	1869	WB-H/12	CTY
Anderson, William	030	1824	WB-3/172	
Anderson, William	070	1851	WB-C/530	AR
Anderson, William	092	c1835	WB-4/80	
Anderson, William	073	1828	WB-E/161	AR
Anderson, William	073	1823	WB-E/36	AR
Anderson, William	013	1857	WB-A/181	AR-Copy
Anderson, William	073	1824	WB-E/49	
Anderson, William	028	1791	WB-A/258	AR
Anderson, William	044	1884	WB-23/489	CTY
Anderson, William	037	1790	WB-C/145	AR
Anderson, William	063	1790	WB-1/154	
Anderson, William F.	085	1840	WB-I/66	AR
Anderson, Winnifred	044	1810	WB-7/108	CTY-Nunc.
Anderton, Julia W.	071	1874	WB-6/137	AR
Andres, B.	011	c1804	WB-1/362	
Andres, Edwin F.	011	c1844	WB-1/106	
Andres, Eliza B.	011	1887	WB-2/220	
Andres, Samuel B.	011	c1837	WB-1/67	
Andres, Sophia	011	1897	WB-3/96	CTY
Andres, William	070	1814	WB-AB/207	AR
Andres, William S.	011	1849	WB-1/173	
Andress, Henry	073	1852	WB-G/20	AR
Andrew, George	084	1806	WB-A/34	CTY
Andrew, Isaac	001	1865	WB-1/250	AR
Andrew, James	054	c1822	WB-2/6	AR
Andrew, James M.	046	1887	WB-F/43	AR
Andrew, Jesse	046	1865	WB-D/253	AR
Andrew, John	022	1891	WB-E/475 & 486	AR
Andrew, Katharine	054	1848	WB-3/27	AR
Andrew, Minerva A.	001	1893	WB-2/564	AR
Andrew, Robert	073	1793	WB-B/241	AR
Andrew, William	016	1869	WB-3/6	AR
Andrews, Abner	010	1762	WB-A/12	AR
Andrews, Abner J.	010	1880	WB-I/122	
Andrews, Abraham	035	1806	WB-A/1	AR
Andrews, Adam	057	1798	WB-A/156	AR
Andrews, Adam	057	1818	WB-B/49	AR
Andrews, Adam	081	1792	WB-1/120	AR
Andrews, Andrew	029	1820	WB-B/40	AR
Andrews, Anna	073	1899	WB-I/164	CTY
Andrews, Archibald	073	1891	WB-H/544	CTY
Andrews, Arden	063	1853	WB-2/393	
Andrews, B. W.	086	1889	WB-F/363	AR
Andrews, Barsheba	063	1839	WB-2/262	
Andrews, Calvin	073	1866	WB-G/501	CTY
Andrews, Catharine	085	1832	WB-H/564	AR
Andrews, Chancy W.	029	1864	WB-D/58	AR
Andrews, David	057	1810	WB-A/322	AR
Andrews, David	099	1827	RB-20/102	AR
Andrews, David	073	1871	WB-H/43	CTY
Andrews, David	085	c1774	WB-A/247	AR
Andrews, David W.	032	1892	WB-4/146	AR
Andrews, Drury	039	c1843	WB-L/131	
Andrews, Elizabeth	044	1867	WB-22/539	CTY
Andrews, Elizabeth	037	1820	WB-E/257	AR
Andrews, Elizabeth	054	1890	WB-5/329	CTY
Andrews, Elizabeth	037	1768	WB-A/160	AR
Andrews, Elizabeth	103	1850	RD-10/403	AR
Andrews, Francis	057	1850	WB-B/204	AR
Andrews, George	085	1844	WB-I/226	AR
Andrews, Hannah	054	1869	WB-4/15	AR
Andrews, Haywood	036	1891	WB-A/188	
Andrews, Henry	073	1881	WB-H/280	CTY
Andrews, Henry	073	1886	WB-H/416	CTY
Andrews, Henry	047	1765	WB-1/174	
Andrews, Hugh	054	1847	WB-3/18	AR
Andrews, James	065	1784	WB-A/28	AR-Nunc.
Andrews, James	085	1821	WB-H/131	AR
Andrews, James	004	c1890	Orig. Only	AR
Andrews, James L.	054	1890	WB-5/333	CTY
Andrews, James M.	011	c1850	WB-1/182	
Andrews, Jeremiah	046	1800	WB-A/8	AR
Andrews, Jesse	037	1772	WB-A/198	AR
Andrews, John	028	1825	WB-C/259	AR
Andrews, John	057	1827	WB-B/97	AR
Andrews, John	085	c1801	WB-C/260	AR
Andrews, John	037	1809	WB-D/352	AR
Andrews, John	085	c1756	SS 880/137	SS/AR
Andrews, John	011	c1850	WB-1/184	
Andrews, John	073	1854	WB-G/80	AR
Andrews, John	057	1846	WB-B/191	AR
Andrews, John N.	054	1889	WB-5/282	CTY
Andrews, Laban	073	1842	WB-F/130	AR
Andrews, Levi	022	1868	WB-E/8	AR
Andrews, Martha	037	1863	WB-G/232	AR
Andrews, Mary	099	1875	RB-35/301	AR
Andrews, Mary	085	1829	WB-H/441	AR
Andrews, Mary	001	1870	WB-2/9	AR

Name	Co.	Date	Recorded Copy	Original
Andrews, Mary	073	1899	WB-I/164	CTY
Andrews, Mary A.	039	1888	WB-U/423	AR
Andrews, Mary A.	037	1884	WB-G/668	AR
Andrews, Nancy	022	1865	WB-D/137	AR
Andrews, Nancy	054	1890	WB-5/327	CTY
Andrews, Nancy	037	1861	WB-G/198	AR
Andrews, Orfa	004	1896	WB-A/176	AR
Andrews, Penelope	057	1828	WB-B/85	AR
Andrews, Peter	028	1767	Orig. Only	AR
Andrews, Peter	087	1844	WB-1/284	AR
Andrews, Petyer	057	1789	WB-A/191	AR
Andrews, Rachel	057	1870	WB-C/8	AR
Andrews, Richard	081	1850	WB-9/219	AR
Andrews, Roland	081	1786	WB-1/32	AR
Andrews, Samuel	086	1805	WB-B/186	AR
Andrews, Samuel A.	103	1853	RD-11/295	AR
Andrews, Sandy	070	1887	WB-F/140	AR
Andrews, Sarah	028	1841	WB-D/41	AR
Andrews, Sarah D.	054	1890	WB-5/331	CTY
Andrews, Thomas	063	1793	WB-1/187	
Andrews, Thomas	022	1779	Orig. Only	AR
Andrews, W. H.	103	1895	WB-2/131	AR
Andrews, Wallace	063	1865	WB-2/533	
Andrews, Warren	096	1774	Orig. Only	SS/AR
Andrews, Warren D.	063	1871	WB-3/17	
Andrews, Whildon	037	1823	WB-E/327	AR
Andrews, William	073	c1820	Orig. Only	AR
Andrews, William	047	1761	WB-1/49	
Andrews, William	073	1826	WB-E/120	AR
Andrews, William	071	1771	WB-1/190	
Andrews, William	099	1828	RB-20/219	
Andrews, William	039	1821	WB-G/16	
Andrews, William D.	039	1896	WB-V/84	AR
Andrews, William E.	039	1844	WB-L/228	AR
Andrews, William R.	099	1869	RB-35/20	AR
Andrews, William W.	063	1868	WB-2/505	
Andrews, Wilson	067	1848	WB-1/47	AR
Andros, Daniel	028	1866	WB-D/429	
Andros, Thomas	010	1737	LGB-4/#135	SS/AR
Andrus, Anny	099	1812	RB-12/316	AR
Andrus, William	075	1765	WB-H/66	AR
Aneline, Peter	N	c1710	Orig. Only	SS/AR
Angel, Alford B.	061	1888	WB-2/92	AR
Angel, Catharine	021	1843	WB-1/5	AR
Angel, Charles	092	1776	WB-1/68	AR
Angel, James	061	1857	WB-1/64	AR
Angel, John	092	1843	WB-4/202	
Angel, Josiah	060	1842	WB-2/142	AR
Angel, Sebe	090	1812	WB-2/137	AR
Angell, Silus	090	1837	WB-4/5	AR
Angell, Uriah	030	1777	WB-1/110	
Angelly, John, Sr.	017	c1853	WB-A/68	AR
Anglin, William	020	1803	RB-E/6	AR
Anmon, Micheal	081	1818	Orig. Only	AR
Annas, Hezekiah	017	1896	WB-B/259	AR
Ansell, Caleb	030	1866	WB-4/257	AR
Ansell, Caleb, Sr.	030	1898	WB-5/266	AR
Ansell, James	030	1740	LGB-4/#110	SS/AR
Ansell, John	N	c1753	Orig. Only	SS/AR
Ansell, John	030	1796	WB-2/68	
Ansell, John	030	1755	Orig. Only	024 AR
Ansell, Malachi	030	1856	WB-4/204	AR
Ansell, Robert	024	1807	WB-B/225	AR
Ansell, William	030	1874	WB-5/38	
Ansley, Asa	024	c1844	Orig. Only	AR
Ansley, John	096	1829	WB-2/99	AR
Ansley, John	096	1799	Orig. Only	AR
Ansley, Joseph	096	1828	WB-2/95	AR
Ansley, Joseph	037	1826	WB-F/56	AR
Ansley, Joseph	096	1800	WB-2/65	AR
Ansley, Nathan, Jr.	096	1819	WB-2/79	AR
Ansley, Solomon	096	1750	Orig. Only	SS/AR
Ansley, William H.	099	1886	WB-B/140	AR
Anstead, Joseph	039	c1856	WB-0/365	AR
Anthony, Catherine	028	1829	WB-C/312	AR
Anthony, Daniel	001	1883	WB-2/205	AR
Anthony, George	060	1847	WB-2/290	AR
Anthony, Henry	046	1818	WB-B/59	AR
Anthony, Henry	001	1862	WB-1/198	AR
Anthony, Jacob	073	c1828	Orig. Only	AR
Anthony, Jacob B.	016	1887	WB-3/518	AR
Anthony, James	046	1799	WB-A/2	
Anthony, James	092	c1836	WB-4/120	
Anthony, John	020	1786	RB-B/136	AR
Anthony, John	047	1812	WB-3/538	
Anthony, John	040	1849	WB-1/24	Nunc.
Anthony, John P.	060	1889	WB-4/402	AR
Anthony, Jonathan	046	1842	WB-C/134	AR
Anthony, Margaret	024	1820	WB-C/90	AR
Anthony, Mary	046	c1881	Orig. Only	AR
Anthony, O. C.	046	1895	WB-F/472	AR
Anthony, Obed	046	1836	WB-A/548	AR
Anthony, Paul	060	1830	WB-1/175	AR
Anthony, Paul	021	1873	WB-2/83	
Anthony, Philip	060	1828	WB-1/86	AR
Anthony, Phillip	060	1797	Orig. Only	AR
Anthony, Thomas	092	1817	WB-3/126	AR
Anthony, Whitmel	047	1851	WB-4/313	
Anthony, William	028	1806	WB-B/233	AR
Antonio, Emanuel	028	1826	WB-C/279	AR
Antwine, Andrew	057	1808	WB-A/303	AR
Apen, Thomas	073	1790	WB-B/82	AR
Aplin, William	063	1812	WB-2/14	
Apperson, Thomas	106	c1853	WB-1/24	AR
Apperson, William W.	092	1826	WB-3/172	AR
Apple, Agnes B.	020	1887	WB-A/522	CTY
Apple, Barbara	046	1843	WB-C/145	AR
Apple, Barbary	046	1841	WB-C/86	AR
Apple, Bingham	046	1857	WB-C/499	AR
Apple, Elisha L.	020	1898	WB-B/339	
Apple, Henry	046	1875	WB-E/139 & 203	AR
Apple, John	046	1869	WB-E/22	AR
Apple, John	046	1864	WB-D/196	AR
Apple, Martha	046	c1873	WB-E/114	AR
Apple, Mary	046	1895	WB-F/387	AR
Appleton, Benjamin	019	1790	Orig. Only	AR
Applewhite, Elisha	103	1835	RD-7/68	AR
Applewhite, Elizabeth	103	1828	RD-5/455	AR
Applewhite, Martha	047	1788	WB-3/158	
Applewhite, Sally	047	1849	WB-4/283	
Applewhite, Thomas	047	1828	WB-4/45	
Applewhite, Thomas	047	1807	WB-3/462	
Archabald, William	085	1764	WB-A/3	AR
Archabold, Ruthy J.	054	1884	WB-5/1	CTY
Archbald, William	085	c1777	WB-A/251	AR
Archbell, Ann	009	1813	OWB/469	AR
Archbell, John	009	c1810	OWB/459	AR
Archbell, John B.	009	1865	OB-M/241	AR
Archbell, John, Sr.	009	1806	OWB/436	AR

Name	Co.	Date	Recorded Copy	Original
Archbell, Joseph P.	009	1899	WB-2/181	CTY
Archbell, Nathan	009	1790	OWB/243	AR
Archbell, Nathan	009	1803	OWB/408	AR
Archbell, Nathan B.	069	1857	WB-1/556	AR
Archbell, Rhoda	069	1876	WB-5/39	AR
Archbell, Richard	009	1807	OB-A/18	AR
Archbell, Samuel	009	1797	OWB/338	AR
Archer, David	046	1835	WB-B/536	AR
Archer, Frusie	037	1891	WB-H/198	AR
Archer, George	100	1806	WB-13/317	AR
Archer, James	046	1799	WB-A/1	AR
Archer, Jesse	073	1855	WB-G/110	AR
Archer, Stephen	065	1842	WB-H/89	AR
Archer, Zachariah	037	1818	WB-E/179	AR
Archibald, E. P.	054	1897	WB-6/124	CTY
Archibald, Nancy	054	1848	WB-3/31	AR
Archibald, Prudence	054	1870	WB-4/69	AR
Archibald, Rachael	054	1852	WB-3/60	AR
Archibald, Thomas	054	c1800	WB-1/57	AR
Archie, Hanna	070	1883	Orig. Only	AR
Archie, Stephen	018	1899	WB-E/300	AR
Ard, James	083	c1785	WB-1/9	AR
Ardle, Mary	030	N. D.	WB-2/324	
Ardorne, John	N	1712	SS 874.1/47	
Ardrey, William A.	065	1862	WB-J/120	AR
Area, Henry A.	016	1866	WB-2/138	AR
Arendell, Bridges	039	c1798	WB-A/126	
Arendell, Bridges	019	1851	WB-A/147	AR
Arendell, James	039	1794	Orig. Only	AR
Arendell, Richard	044	1762	Orig. Only	CTY
Arendell, Sarah	019	1866	WB-B/1	
Arendell, Thomas	039	c1797	WB-B/43	
Arendell, Thomas	039	1821	WB-G/9	
Arendell, William	039	1861	WB-R/120	AR
Arends, Jacob	060	1807	Orig. Only	AR
Arenton, Christopher	024	1753	SS 881/99	SS/AR
Arenton, William	028	c1761	Orig. Only	SS/AR
Arey, Abraham	085	1844	WB-I/200	
Arey, Benjamin	054	1882	WB-4/455	CTY
Arey, Joseph	029	1872	WB-E/51	AR
Arey, Luther	054	1870	WB-4/80	AR-Nunc.
Arey, Peter	085	1841	WB-I/102	AR
Arey, S. R.	085	1889	WB-2/363	CTY
Argo, Kate D.	099	1886	WB-B/163	AR
Arkill, Hannah	077	1821	WB-F/36	AR
Arkill, William	077	1802	WB-E/190	AR
Arledge, Isaac	081	1818	WB-4/608	AR
Arledge, Isaac	086	1820	WB-C/148	AR
Arledge, Isaac	050	1900	WB-2/357	CTY
Arledge, Jonathan	080	1875	WB-1/26	AR
Arlege, Jesse	081	1869	WB-15/30	AR
Arlin, John	024	c1757	WB-A/153	AR
Arline, Jesse	041	1842	WB-3/37	AR
Arlow, James	070	1758	DB-D/318	
Arlow, James	070	1758	SS 882/36	SS/AR
Armfield, David	046	1845	WB-C/233	AR
Armfield, Emsley	046	1879	WB-E/264	AR
Armfield, Isaac	046	1784	WB-A/3	AR
Armfield, Isaac, Sr.	046	1845	WB-C/218	AR
Armfield, Jane	046	1900	WB-G/203	AR
Armfield, Jonathan	046	1801	WB-A/4	AR
Armfield, Solomon	046	1852	WB-C/372	AR
Armfield, William	046	1812	WB-A/10	AR
Armfield, William	046	1833	WB-B/583	AR
Armistead, Alexander	022	1822	WB-B/68	AR
Armistead, Harriet B.	100	1848	WB-39/456	AR
Armistead, Sarah	010	1818	WB-G/42	AR
Armistead, Stark	100	1843	WB-38/208	AR
Armistead, Stark	010	1835	WB-G/246	AR
Armistead, William	010	1791	WB-D/173	AR
Armistead, William	010	1796	WB-D/337	AR
Armor, William	075	1719	SS 875/276	SS/AR
Armour, Arthur	065	1881	WB-K/433	AR
Armour, John	075	1729	Orig. Only	SS/AR
Armour, Joseph	075	1784	WB-K/93	AR
Armour, Martha	075	1792	WB-K/235	AR
Armour, Robert	075	c1768	024 WB-1/25	024 AR
Armour, Robert	075	1762	WB-H/41	AR
Armour, Thomas	075	1764	WB-H/56	AR
Armstead, Lucy	022	1855	WB-C/385	AR
Armstead, Westward	022	1848	WB-C/227	AR
Armstrong, Abel	085	c1799	WB-C/264	AR
Armstrong, Andrew	029	1789	Orig. Only	AR
Armstrong, Ann	029	1800	WB-A/33	AR
Armstrong, Anna	073	1823	WB-E/31	AR
Armstrong, Christopher	029	1764	Orig. Only	AR-Nunc.
Armstrong, Elisabeth	040	1865	WB-1/172	AR
Armstrong, Francis	060	1779	Orig. Only	AR
Armstrong, George	029	1794	Orig. Only	AR
Armstrong, George W.	105	1876	WB-2/194	AR
Armstrong, Gray	037	1867	WB-G/303	AR
Armstrong, Henrietta	105	c1880	WB-2/256	
Armstrong, Holloway	096	1841	WB-2/156	AR
Armstrong, Isaac	082	1821	WB-1/225	AR
Armstrong, Jacob	073	1835	WB-E/338	
Armstrong, James	073	1796	WB-C/88	AR
Armstrong, James	082	1850	WB-4/43 & 102	AR
Armstrong, James	005	1760	WB-1/8	AR
Armstrong, James	030	1755	Orig. Only	SS/AR
Armstrong, James	078	1821	WI-9/322	AR
Armstrong, Jeams	N	1685	Orig. Only	SS/AR
Armstrong, Jennet	029	1842	WB-B/388	AR
Armstrong, Jesse	078	1830	WI-11/242	AR
Armstrong, John	073	1810	WB-D/267	AR
Armstrong, John	073	1791	WB-B/121	AR
Armstrong, John	084	1820	WB-A/134	CTY
Armstrong, John	054	1843	WB-2/269	AR
Armstrong, John M.	040	1891	WB-2/381	AR
Armstrong, Joseph	073	1846	WB-F/271	AR
Armstrong, Joseph	073	1840	WB-F/76	AR
Armstrong, Margaret	085	c1792	WB-B/181	AR
Armstrong, Martha	054	c1844	WB-2/295	AR
Armstrong, Martin	086	1786	WB-A/1	
Armstrong, Mary	040	1857	WB-1/96	AR
Armstrong, Mary M.	060	1895	WB-4/569	AR
Armstrong, Mathew	065	c1779	WB-A/32	AR
Armstrong, Mathew	040	1885	WB-2/240	AR
Armstrong, Matthew	040	1870	WB-2/8	AR
Armstrong, Matthew R.	040	1887	WB-2/291	AR
Armstrong, Nancy H.	096	1880	WB-4/62	
Armstrong, Rachel	073	1827	WB-E/143	AR
Armstrong, Robert	060	1820	Orig. Only	AR
Armstrong, Robert	037	1798	WB-D/65	AR
Armstrong, Russel	096	c1823	Orig. Only	AR
Armstrong, Thomas	029	1765	Orig. Only	AR
Armstrong, Thomas	028	1804	WB-B/208	AR
Armstrong, Thomas	073	1835	WB-E/347	AR
Armstrong, Thomas	029	1802	WB-A/53	AR
Armstrong, Thomas	MA	1735	Copy	CCR 179
Armstrong, Thomas J.	069	c1808	Orig. Only	AR

Name	Co.	Date	Recorded Copy	Original
Armstrong, Visa	040	1887	WB-2/279	AR
Armstrong, Wesley	106	1868	WB-2/1	
Armstrong, William	040	1860	WB-1/120	
Armstrong, William	073	1814	WB-D/416	AR
Armstrong, William	092	1782	WB-1/157	
Armstrong, William	085	c1780	WB-C/177	AR
Armstrong, William	070	1854	WB-C/568	AR
Armstrong, William B.	060	1878	WB-4/136	AR
Armstrong, William J.	105	1857	WB-1/35	AR
Armstrong, Wilson	096	1884	WB-4/104	AR
Arndell, Lorenzo D.	026	1869	WB-2/12	AR
Arnett, James	020	1805	RB-E/179	AR
Arney, Cathriana	017	c1842	Orig. Only	AR
Arney, Christian	060	1834	WB-1/319	AR
Arney, Jacob	060	1782	Orig. Only	AR
Arnhart, John	085	c1795	WB-C/246	AR
Arnold, Daniel	092	1839	WB-4/159	
Arnold, Edward	028	1887	WB-E/451	AR
Arnold, Elizabeth	101	1870	WB-A/228	AR
Arnold, Elizabeth	020	1862	RB-S/550	
Arnold, Henry	013	1892	WB-C/221	AR
Arnold, Henry	068	1864	WB-C/98	
Arnold, Hezekiah	090	1844	WB-4/150	AR
Arnold, James	039	1790	WB-A/70	
Arnold, James W.	020	1899	WB-B/366	CTY
Arnold, John	026	1858	WB-1/235	AR
Arnold, John	077	1735	SS 876/406	SS/AR
Arnold, John	041	1824	WB-2/210	AR
Arnold, John	077	1724	Orig. Only	SS/AR
Arnold, John	071	1764	WB-1/104	
Arnold, Joseph	077	1752	Orig. Only	SS/AR
Arnold, Joseph	096	1801	WB-2/5	AR
Arnold, Lawrence	077	1752	Orig. Only	AR
Arnold, Lawrence	002	1694	SS 874.2/47	SS/AR
Arnold, Mourning	096	1807	WB-2/56	
Arnold, Nancy E.	048	1899	WB-1/93	CTY
Arnold, Nathan	103	1826	RD-5/260	AR
Arnold, Penuel	081	1889	Orig. Only	AR
Arnold, Rachel	020	1883	WB-A/408	CTY
Arnold, Richard	020	1830	RB-L/567	AR
Arnold, Samuel	092	c1829	WB-4/34	
Arnold, Solomon	068	1847	WB-B/168	
Arnold, Thomas	092	1824	WB-3/160	AR
Arnold, William	028	1799	WB-B/74	AR
Arnold, William	077	1774	WB-C/137	AR
Arnold, William	028	1785	WB-A/100	AR
Arnold, William	028	1886	WB-E/431	AR
Arnold, William	077	1794	WB-E/20	
Arnold, Wood	081	1844	WB-8/102	AR
Arnoll, Edward	024	1752	Orig. Only	SS/AR
Arps, Mary	077	1846	WB-F/321	AR
Arrenton, Edward	077	1825	WB-F/93	AR
Arrenton, Ezekiel	077	1809	WB-E/335	AR
Arrenton, Isaac	077	1816	WB-E/444	AR
Arrenton, James B.	077	1834	WB-F/230	AR-Nunc.
Arrenton, Millicent	077	1839	WB-F/288	AR
Arrenton, Perthena	077	1866	WB-H/13	AR
Arrenton, Rebecca	077	1856	WB-F/479	AR
Arrenton, Richard	077	1795	WB-E/31	
Arrenton, William	077	1806	WB-E/235	AR
Arrenton, William	077	1810	WB-E/347	AR
Arrington, Alice A.	071	1894	WB-7/221	AR
Arrington, Archibald	069	1893	WB-5/391	AR
Arrington, Archibald	069	1872	WB-1/614	AR
Arrington, Arthur	069	1795	WB-1/102	AR
Arrington, Arthur	069	1801	WB-1/140	AR
Arrington, Arthur	047	1825	WB-4/3	
Arrington, Barbara	069	1848	WB-1/510	AR
Arrington, Caroline	069	c1895	Orig. Only	AR
Arrington, Carter	047	1838	WB-4/173	
Arrington, Henry	069	1838	WB-1/423	AR
Arrington, Holman	069	1847	WB-1/508	
Arrington, James	100	1810	WB-15/208	AR
Arrington, James	013	1831	WB-A/7	
Arrington, James	100	1851	WB-41/190	AR
Arrington, John	069	1844	WB-1/463	AR
Arrington, John	VA	1878	Copy	047 AR
Arrington, John	005	1835	WB-B/51	AR
Arrington, Joseph	069	1836	WB-1/413	AR
Arrington, Joseph	069	1819	WB-1/300	AR
Arrington, Joseph C.	069	1898	WB-6/32	AR
Arrington, Joseph C.	039	1898	WB-V/210	AR
Arrington, Joseph W.	AL	1860	069 WB-1/571	069 AR
Arrington, Lew	069	1860	WB-1/568	AR
Arrington, Mary	069	1816	WB-1/288A	
Arrington, Mary	069	1805	WB-1/154	AR
Arrington, Mary Jane	039	1878	WB-U/156	AR
Arrington, Milbrey	069	1876	WB-5/52	AR
Arrington, Nicholas	069	1865	WB-1/595	AR
Arrington, Peter	069	1854	WB-1/530	AR
Arrington, Peter	069	1840	WB-1/441	AR
Arrington, Rebeca	069	1856	WB-1/550	AR
Arrington, Rhoda	047	1853	WB-4/355	
Arrington, Richard	069	1839	WB-1/432	AR
Arrington, Ricks	069	1880	WB-5/105	AR
Arrington, Sallie Ann	069	1875	WB-5/31	AR
Arrington, Sarah	069	1826	WB-1/337	AR
Arrington, Temperance	069	c1864	WB-1/587	AR
Arrington, William	071	1752	Orig. Only	SS/AR
Arrington, William	069	1813	WB-1/254	AR
Arrington, William H.	047	1891	WB-7/19	AR
Arrington, William T.	069	1862	WB-1/582	AR
Arrowood, Drury	040	1853	WB-1/44	
Arrowood, Margaret	040	1868	WB-1/201	AR
Arther, John	024	1735	SS 876/415	SS/AR
Arthur, Asa	028	1897	WB-F/293	
Arthur, Jacob	019	1821	WB-D/4	AR
Arthur, James	053	1774	RW-1/47	AR
Arthur, James	028	1790	WB-A/215	AR-Nunc.
Arthur, Jesse, Sr.	072	1897	WB-4/352	AR
Arthur, John	028	1751	DB-5/225	SS/AR
Arthur, John	019	c1777	WB-D/1	AR
Arthur, John	028	1817	WB-C/142	AR
Arthur, John A.	009	1878	WB-1/210	CTY
Arthur, Martha Ann	013	1897	WB-D/5	AR
Arthur, Mary Ann	028	1867	WB-D/443	
Arthur, Mathew	028	1768	Orig. Only	AR
Arthur, Michael	028	1873	WB-E/84	
Arthur, Richard	019	1838	WB-A/79	AR
Arthur, Robert	065	c1780	Copy	085 AR
Arthur, Rosa H.	009	1882	WB-1/320	CTY
Arthur, Samuel	060	1796	Orig. Only	AR
Arthur, Seth	019	1822	WB-D/5	AR
Arthur, William	086	1835	WB-E/14	AR
Artice, Eliza	103	1890	WB-1/524	AR
Artice, George	071	1824	WB-3/296	AR
Artice, Letha Ann	103	1897	WB-2/184	AR
Artis, Clarky	103	1883	WB-1/273	AR
Artis, Zilpha	103	1882	WB-1/245	AR
Artz, William	085	1876	WB-1/329	CTY

Name	Co.	Date	Recorded Copy	Original
Asbill, Elizabeth	010	1880	WB-I/113	
Asbill, John	024	1796	WB-A/291	AR
Asbill, Joseph	010	1827	WB-G/159	AR
Asbill, Mary	081	1860	WB-11/475	AR
Asbill, Solomon	010	1850	WB-G/463	AR
Asbury, Daniel	060	1825	WB-1/21	AR
Asbury, Daniel	065	1883	WB-K/524	AR
Asbury, Henry	060	1874	WB-4/118	AR
Asbury, John R.	060	1898	WB-5/87	AR
Ash, Benjamin	NY	c1879	054 WB-5/403	054 CTY
Ash, Isaac	055	1863	ID/97	
Ash, Jessee	055	1859	ID/44	
Ashbee, Abel C.	031	1887	WB-1/40	AR
Ashbee, Benjamin	031	1895	WB-1/94	AR
Ashbee, Samuel	030	1851	WB-4/161	
Ashbee, Samuel M.	096	c1836	Orig. Only	AR
Ashbee, Solomon	096	c1866	WB-3/85	AR
Ashbee, Solomon	030	c1801	WB-3/33	
Ashborn, John	092	c1835	WB-5/80	
Ashburn, Benjamin	010	1808	WB-F/94	AR
Ashburn, D. L.	092	1875	WB-6/70	AR
Ashburn, Denson	070	1783	WB-C/9	AR
Ashburn, Elisha	010	1801	WB-E/123	AR
Ashburn, Frances	010	1816	WB-G/1	AR
Ashburn, Mary	010	1868	WB-H/213	AR
Ashburn, Thomas	010	1781	WB-C/16	AR
Ashburn, Washington	010	1816	WB-G/4	AR
Ashburn, William	010	1809	WB-F/111	AR
Ashburn, William W.	092	1886	WB-6/245	AR
Ashbury, Joseph	028	1781	Orig. Only	AR
Ashby, Elisabeth	030	1787	WB-1/210	
Ashby, Hallifax	092	1825	WB-3/163	AR
Ashby, John W.	090	1857	WB-4/307	
Ashcraft, Alfred	097	1869	WB-2/22	AR
Ashcroft, Levenia	075	1867	WB-M2/100	AR
Ashe, Amos	055	c1873	WB-A/21	
Ashe, Benjamin	070	1889	Orig. Only	AR
Ashe, Caroline	005	1894	WB-D/344	AR
Ashe, Daniel F.	005	1892	WB-D/312	
Ashe, Edmond	047	1879	WB-6/205	AR
Ashe, Elizabeth	070	1854	WB-C/575	AR
Ashe, John	070	c1774	WB-C/3	AR
Ashe, John	070	1792	WB-C/10	AR
Ashe, John B.	008	1734	SS 876/382	SS/AR
Ashe, Mary	030	c1800	WB-2/354	
Ashe, Samuel	070	1813	WB-AB/188	AR
Ashe, Samuel	070	1820	WB-C/11	AR
Ashe, Samuel	029	1835	WB-B/249	AR
Ashe, Thomas S.	005	1887	WB-D/209	
Ashe, Tinsley	070	1867	WB-D/238	AR
Ashford, Butler	072	1806	WB-A/4	AR
Ashford, Elizabeth	087	1877	WB-3/147	AR
Ashford, Street	011	c1816	WB-2/319	
Ashford, Thomas	087	1865	WB-2/91	AR
Ashford, William	022	1784	RB-1/21	AR
Ashlee, Solomon	030	1774	WB-1/79	
Ashley, James W.	078	1895	WB-19/390	AR
Ashley, Jeremiah	024	1801	WB-A/277	AR
Ashley, John	013	1844	WB-A/96	
Ashley, John	005	c1759	Orig. Only	SS/AR
Ashley, Margaret	024	c1759	WB-A/156	AR
Ashley, Martha	006	1880	WB-E/76	AR
Ashley, Nancy	099	1864	RB-33/260	AR
Ashley, T. M.	106	1891	WB-2/310	AR
Ashley, Thomas	010	1790	WB-D/138	AR
Ashley, William	024	c1782	WB-A/157	AR
Ashley, William	006	1877	WB-E/32	AR
Ashley, William	077	1762	WB-C/21	AR
Ashley, William D.	099	1860	RB-31/432	AR
Ashmore, Walter	065	1798	Orig. Only	AR
Ashworth, Johnson	013	1895	WB-C/384	AR
Askew, Aaron	010	1810	WB-F/133	AR
Askew, Aaron	010	1771	WB-A/135	AR
Askew, Allen	063	1820	WB-2/67	
Askew, Amos	057	1888	WB-C/153	AR
Askew, Andrew J.	010	1874	WB-I/62	AR
Askew, Benjamin	100	1847	WB-39/301	AR
Askew, Cullen	051	1863	WB-B/51	AR
Askew, David	010	1816	WB-F/339	AR
Askew, Elizabeth	051	1886	WB-C/347	AR
Askew, Frances	071	1896	WB-7/336	AR
Askew, Garrison	010	1856	WB-H/31	AR
Askew, George	010	1832	WB-G/220	AR
Askew, George O.	010	1862	WB-H/113	AR
Askew, Harriet B.	010	1866	WB-H/163	AR
Askew, Harriet J.	099	1888	WB-B/237	
Askew, J. D.	047	1900	WB-7/243	AR
Askew, James	062	1852	WB-A/3	AR
Askew, John	100	1890	WB-51/317	AR
Askew, John	010	1829	WB-G/201	AR
Askew, John	100	1857	WB-49/130	AR
Askew, John	051	1846	WB-A/252	
Askew, Josiah	037	1818	WB-E/207	AR
Askew, Lawrence	051	1884	WB-C/318	AR
Askew, Linia	051	1878	WB-C/189	AR
Askew, Lucretia	051	1885	WB-C/338	AR
Askew, Luie	010	1898	WB-I/538	
Askew, Maria C.	010	1894	WB-I/405	AR
Askew, Mary	010	1843	WB-G/349	AR
Askew, Mary	071	1844	WB-4/263	AR
Askew, Mary P.	051	1856	WB-A/387	
Askew, Moses	063	1822	WB-2/77	
Askew, Nathan	072	1813	WB-A/2	AR
Askew, Norfleet	010	1900	WB-K/59	
Askew, Phereby	063	1813	WB-2/19	
Askew, Polly	062	1892	Orig. Only	AR
Askew, Rachel	051	c1889	WB-D/1	
Askew, Rebecca J.	051	1893	WB-C/471	AR
Askew, Sally	072	1830	WB-A/15	AR-Nunc.
Askew, Starkey	051	1868	WB-B/105	AR
Askew, Wiley	039	1900	WB-V/213	AR
Askew, William C.	079	1883	WB-2/267	AR
Askew, William D.	010	1856	WB-H/26	AR
Askew, William F.	099	1888	WB-B/236	AR
Askew, Zadock	057	1818	WB-B/50	AR
Askew, Zephaniah	010	1893	WB-I/386	AR
Askey, Benjamin	057	1821	WB-B/106	AR
Askhart, Joseph	028	1768	Orig. Only	AR
Askin, Alice	028	1845	WB-D/119	AR
Askin, James	028	1853	Orig. Only	AR
Askue, John	VA	c1713	SS 875/31	
Assbell, Christopher	081	1861	WB-12/5	
Asten, William	084	c1796	OW/41	AR
Asten, William	073	1767	WB-A/52	
Aswell, Burcha	045	1893	WB-1/238	AR
Atcheson, William	085	1827	WB-H/373	AR
Atchison, Mary A.	065	1880	WB-K/392	AR
Ates, Richard	104	1827	WB-4/97	AR
Atherey, Sarah	028	1796	WB-A/352	AR
Atherly, Joseph	028	1769	Orig. Only	AR

Name	Co.	Date	Recorded Copy	Original
Atherton, Jepthah	071	1787	WB-1/378	AR
Atherton, Jesse	071	1787	WB-1/2	
Athons, Horatio	106	c1846	WB-1/31	AR
Atkerson, James	047	1786	WB-3/111	
Atkins, A. F.	089	1892	WB-2/247	AR
Atkins, Elizabeth	099	1803	RB-6/108	AR
Atkins, Frances	073	1861	WB-G/377	CTY
Atkins, George B.	029	1842	WB-C/18	AR
Atkins, H. T.	092	1889	WB-6/299	AR
Atkins, Henry A.	036	1899	WB-A/496	CTY
Atkins, Henry G.	099	1863	RB-32/602	AR
Atkins, Ica, Sr.	029	c1796	Orig. Only	AR
Atkins, John	099	1792	RB-2/391	AR
Atkins, John C.	029	1844	WB-C/51	AR
Atkins, John W.	038	1892	WB-3/329	AR
Atkins, John, Jr.	099	1781	RB-1/176	AR
Atkins, Jonathan	104	1871	WB-6/28	AR
Atkins, Josiah	073	1846	WB-F/310	AR
Atkins, Lewis	029	1804	WB-A/64	AR
Atkins, Lewis	092	1863	WB-5/67	AR
Atkins, Marshall C.	092	1888	WB-6/276	AR
Atkins, Richard	029	1814	WB-A/208	AR
Atkins, Samuel	099	1876	RB-35/349	AR
Atkins, Sarah	099	1810	RB-9/178	AR
Atkins, Sarah	083	1827	WB-1/337	AR
Atkins, Sarah A.	099	1851	RB-27/350	AR
Atkins, Silas	083	1807	WB-1/95	AR
Atkins, Thomas	099	1803	RB-6/87	AR
Atkins, Thomas	047	1805	WB-3/442	
Atkins, W. W.	085	1890	WB-2/433	CTY
Atkinson, Aaron	037	1848	WB-F/392	AR
Atkinson, Alfred	085	1886	WB-2/168	
Atkinson, Amos	105	1897	WB-3/252	AR
Atkinson, Braxton	090	1868	WB-5/58	AR
Atkinson, Britton	056	1880	WB-3/249	AR
Atkinson, Cary	056	1843	WB-1/553	AR
Atkinson, Edward	078	1798	WI-2/81	AR
Atkinson, Elijah	069	1817	WB-1/285	AR
Atkinson, Elizabeth	070	1853	WB-C/555	AR
Atkinson, Ephriam	056	1791	WB-1/38	AR
Atkinson, Fannie	071	1881	WB-6/343	AR
Atkinson, Henry	029	1816	Orig. Only	AR
Atkinson, Henry, Sr.	069	1817	WB-1/287	AR
Atkinson, James	071	1819	WB-2/217	AR
Atkinson, James	071	1878	WB-6/261	AR
Atkinson, Joel	047	1837	WB-4/157	
Atkinson, John	035	c1771	WB-A/6	AR
Atkinson, John	070	1811	WB-AB/163	AR
Atkinson, John	070	1772	WB-C/2	AR
Atkinson, John	078	1792	WI-1/30	AR
Atkinson, John	022	1830	WB-B/181	AR
Atkinson, John T.	071	1880	WB-6/333	AR
Atkinson, John, Sr.	056	1847	WB-1/589	AR
Atkinson, Kinchin	083	1879	WB-3/164	AR
Atkinson, Mathew J.	029	1885	WB-E/348	AR
Atkinson, Matthew J.	029	c1880	WB-E/580	
Atkinson, Peyton A.	079	1863	WB-1/154	AR
Atkinson, Phereba	056	1862	WB-2/31	AR
Atkinson, Richard	078	1821	WI-9/321	AR
Atkinson, Robert	020	c1783	RB-B/2	AR
Atkinson, Sally	037	1866	WB-G/272	AR
Atkinson, Samuel	070	1801	WB-AB/52	AR
Atkinson, Sarah	070	c1863	Orig. Only	AR
Atkinson, Thomas	056	1840	WB-1/517	AR
Atkinson, Thomas	070	1881	WB-E/405	AR

Name	Co.	Date	Recorded Copy	Original
Atkinson, Wilie	011	1857	WB-1/260	
Atkinson, William	084	1844	WB-C/5	CTY
Atkinson, William	047	1805	WB-3/439	
Atkison, William	083	1829	WB-1/188	AR
Attkins, James	072	c1785	Orig. Only	AR
Attmore, Nanny	056	1828	Est-15/121	
Attmore, Sarah	028	1843	WB-D/91	
Attwater, Moses	073	1836	WB-E/392	AR
Attwood, Edward	028	1815	WB-C/104	
Atwater, Elizabeth	073	1896	WB-I/101	CTY
Atwater, Julia	073	1896	WB-I/93	CTY
Atwater, Wesley	073	1893	WB-I/7	CTY
Atwell, A. L.	085	1872	WB-1/145	CTY
Atwell, Biner A.	054	1872	WB-4/95	CTY
Atwell, D. F.	054	1898	WB-6/145	CTY
Atwell, Ellen G.	085	c1874	WB-2/372	CTY
Atwell, James	046	1828	WB-B/359	
Atwell, John	054	1865	WB-3/172	AR
Atwell, John H.	054	1852	WB-3/62	
Atwell, John W.	085	1862	WB-K/301	AR
Atwell, Joseph	016	1865	WB-2/126	
Atwell, Lock	085	1844	WB-I/244	
Atwell, Mary E.	085	1862	WB-K/306	AR
Atwell, R. S.	054	1895	WB-5/547	CTY
Atwell, W. M.	054	1894	WB-5/526	CTY
Atwood, John	085	1800	WB-C/258	AR
Aud, Abraham	016	1846	WB-1/112	
Auge, Cullen	063	1874	WB-3/62	
Aughtry, Drury	087	c1808	WB-A/54	AR
Augustus, Solomon	099	1876	RB-35/338	AR
Auld, Ann	082	1822	WB-1/233	AR
Auld, Elizabeth	029	1848	WB-C/124	AR
Auld, James	005	1783	WB-1/43	AR
Auld, Michael	005	c1789	WB-1/61	AR
Auman, Jacob	081	1873	WB-15/132	AR
Auman, Vicy	067	1876	WB-2/68	
Ausband, Allen R.	063	1899	WB-4/248	AR
Ausley, James	022	c1858	WB-D/34	AR
Ausley, Jesse	083	1849	WB-2/6	
Ausley, Jesse A.	083	1881	WB-3/254	AR
Ausley, Mary	022	1890	WB-E/447	AR
Ausley, Merriet	083	1879	WB-3/163	AR
Ausley, Thomas	022	1870	WB-E/49	AR
Aust, Gottfrey	092	1789	WB-2/84	AR
Aust, John George	090	1802	WB-2/25	AR
Aust, Mary	090	1799	WB-1/130	AR
Austill, Moses	106	1881	WB-2/136	
Austin, A. M.	033	1878	WB-2/62	CTY
Austin, Alvin	099	1885	WB-B/67	AR
Austin, Andrew	006	1888	WB-E/173	AR
Austin, Arrison	056	1845	WB-1/533	AR
Austin, Avery	030	c1894	Orig. Only	AR
Austin, Barbra C.	033	1897	WB-2/233	CTY
Austin, Bryant	089	1842	WB-1/13	
Austin, Claiborne	070	1810	WB-AB/136	AR
Austin, Culpepper	097	1893	WB-2/456	AR
Austin, Delha M.	037	1877	WB-G/529	AR
Austin, Dinah	028	1835	WB-C/384	AR
Austin, Elbert	056	1866	WB-2/79	AR
Austin, Elkanah D.	033	1871	WB-2/13	CTY
Austin, Emanuel	014	1880	WB-2/205	
Austin, Henry	037	1845	WB-F/320	AR
Austin, Henry	037	1845	013 WB-C/200	013 AR
Austin, Henry R.	033	1872	WB-2/15	CTY
Austin, Jacob C.	097	c1879	WB-2/169	

Name	Co.	Date	Recorded Copy	Original
Austin, James	056	1864	WB-2/55	AR
Austin, John	030	1805	WB-2/275	
Austin, John	057	c1780	WB-A/193	AR
Austin, John W.	089	1850	WB-1/78	
Austin, Jonathan	097	1886	WB-2/281	AR
Austin, Jonathan L.	097	1886	WB-2/307	AR
Austin, Lydia	037	1853	WB-F/492	AR
Austin, Marquis	097	1883	WB-2/237	AR
Austin, Mary	030	1806	WB-2/290	
Austin, Philip	017	1842	WB-A/9	AR
Austin, Richard	041	1881	WB-4/151	AR
Austin, Robert H.	037	1890	WB-H/169	AR
Austin, Rosanna	102	1885	WB-A/42	AR
Austin, Samuel	017	c1845	WB-A/39	AR
Austin, Samuel	017	1863	Orig. Only	AR
Austin, Samuel J.	089	c1864	WB-1/297	
Austin, Thomas	028	c1778	Orig. Only	AR
Austin, Thomas	028	1821	WB-C/207	AR
Austin, Vernon	097	1897	WB-2/542	AR
Austin, Vernon C.	097	1897	005 WB-D/429	005 AR
Austin, William	030	1824	WB-3/172	
Austin, William	017	c1854	WB-A/109	AR
Austine, John, Sr.	056	1806	WB-1/189	AR
Auston, Alsey	056	1838	Orig. Only	AR
Auston, Arthur	056	1837	Orig. Only	AR
Auston, Richard	041	1812	WB-2/71	AR
Auten, Martha A.	065	1895	WB-M/366	AR
Autrey, Cornelius	029	1829	WB-B/180	AR
Autry, Edney	087	1836	WB-1/176	AR
Autry, George	087	1869	WB-3/4	AR
Autry, Mary	087	1859	WB-1/532	AR
Autry, Maulsey	029	1892	WB-E/578	AR
Autry, Newsom	029	1853	WB-C/352	AR
Autry, Theopilus	029	c1832	WB-B/312	AR
Avant, Isaac W.	048	1900	WB-1/109	CTY
Avant, John	097	1890	WB-2/354	
Avarett, Henry	010	c1771	WB-A/144	AR
Avelin, Peter	024	1712	SS 875/2	
Avendshine, Christian	016	1794	WB-A/112	
Avenshine, Rinehold	016	1802	WB-A/113	
Avent, Esther W.	022	1858	WB-D/5	AR
Avent, Glover	022	1889	WB-E/396	AR
Avent, John	022	1822	WB-B/48	AR
Avent, Judith	022	1869	WB-E/14	AR
Avent, Julyan	022	1828	WB-B/155	AR
Avent, Mary N.	047	1899	WB-7/265	AR
Avent, Peter	071	1779	WB-1/215	
Avent, Sally	047	1844	WB-4/237	
Avent, Thomas	071	1752	Orig. Only	SS/AR
Avent, William	071	1761	WB-1/56	
Avera, Ann Maria	056	1896	WB-2/208	AR
Avera, David B.	056	1900	WB-4/273	AR
Avera, David B.	099	1892	WB-C/88	AR
Avera, David S.	099	1899	WB-D/240	AR
Avera, Florida A.	069	1897	WB-6/26	AR
Avera, H. C.	048	1897	WB-1/60	CTY
Avera, John	056	1803	WB-1/151	AR
Avera, John W.	056	1894	WB-2/171	AR
Avera, Mary Ann	056	1856	WB-1/689	AR
Avera, Mathew	056	1855	WB-1/679	AR
Avera, Rebecca	056	1863	WB-2/38	AR
Avera, Thomas	056	1762	WB-1/755	AR
Avera, Thomas	056	1787	WB-1/5	AR
Avera, William	099	1875	RB-35/307	AR
Avera, William	056	c1795	WB-1/92	AR

Name	Co.	Date	Recorded Copy	Original
Avera, William W.	099	1848	RB-26/368	AR
Avera, Willis H.	056	1888	WB-3/461	AR
Averet, Henry	010	1772	WB-A/166	AR
Averett, Jeduthum	069	1798	WB-1/118	AR
Averett, Thomas R.	044	1896	WB-24/293	CTY
Averit, Benjamin	081	1800	WB-2/59	AR
Averit, Jesse	039	1816	WB-E/67	AR-Nunc.
Averit, Jesse	010	1799	WB-E/81	AR
Averit, Simon	010	1781	WB-C/20	AR
Averitt, Ann	072	1798	Orig. Only	AR
Averitt, Arthur	072	c1795	Orig. Only	AR
Averitt, Benjamin	072	1798	Orig. Only	AR
Averitt, David	079	1808	Orig. Only	AR-Copy
Averitt, David	028	1828	WB-C/297	AR
Averitt, Dempsey	011	1848	WB-1/169	
Averitt, James, Sr.	037	1823	WB-F/4	AR
Averitt, Jenkin	072	1801	WB-A/15	AR
Averitt, John	072	1785	WI/L34	AR
Averitt, John	029	1896	WB-F/74	AR
Averitt, John	070	1830	WB-AB/256	AR
Averitt, Jonathan	029	c1899	Orig. Only	AR
Averitt, Mary	029	1881	WB-E/261	AR
Averitt, Nathaniel	072	1780	RW/L36	AR
Averitt, Nathaniel	072	c1755	SS 880/28	SS/AR
Averitt, Pamela	072	1800	WB-A/5	AR
Averitt, Reuben	070	1822	WB-C/95	AR
Averitt, Richard	072	1800	WB-A/5	AR
Averitt, Starling	079	1868	WB-1/180	
Avery, Adelaide L.	014	1897	WB-3/19	CTY
Avery, Alexander	029	1808	WB-A/134	AR
Avery, Frederick	077	1800	WB-E/117	AR
Avery, Isaac T.	014	1869	WB-2/27	CTY
Avery, John	028	1803	WB-B/179	AR
Avery, John	053	c1740	Orig. Only	SS/AR
Avery, Jonathan	070	1810	WB-AB/154	AR
Avery, Laura S.	014	1890	WB-2/378	CTY
Avery, M. Corrina	014	1897	WB-3/26	CTY
Avery, Marcus	014	1892	WB-2/491	CTY
Avery, Mary	011	1877	WB-2/113	
Avery, Rebecca	028	1822	WB-C/219	AR
Avery, Robert	014	1894	WB-2/534	CTY
Avery, W. W.	014	1864	WB-2/50	AR-Copy
Avery, Waightstill	014	1823	WB-2/356	AR
Avery, Waightstill	014	1823	066 WB-1/58	066 AR
Averyt, Alexander	056	1832	WB-1/474	AR
Avis, Sawyer	010	1790	WB-D/127	AR
Avolin, Peter	024	1710	Orig. Only	AR
Axim, Mary	047	1794	WB-3/236	
Axsom, Andrew	092	1889	WB-6/301	AR
Axsom, Susan	092	1879	WB-6/121	AR
Aycock, Abner	100	1823	WB-25/41	AR
Aycock, Ann	100	1866	WB-50/188	AR
Aycock, Charity	103	1888	WB-1/443	AR
Aycock, Gabriel	103	1864	RD-13/754	AR
Aycock, Isaac	103	1864	RD-13/748	AR
Aycock, J. W.	105	1895	WB-3/154	AR
Aycock, James S.	103	1837	RD-7/252	AR
Aycock, Jesse	103	1823	RD-5/71	AR
Aycock, John	099	1798	RB-4/161	AR
Aycock, John G.	103	1892	WB-1/559	AR
Aycock, Kisiah	103	1865	RD-14/186	AR
Aycock, Mary	056	1879	WB-3/240	AR
Aycock, Mary W. P.	100	1880	WB-51/151	AR
Aycock, Patience	103	1828	RD-5/401	AR
Aycock, Ransom	039	1862	WB-R/309	AR

Name	Co.	Date	Recorded Copy	Original
Aycock, Thomas	103	1808	Orig. Only	AR
Aycock, Timothy	103	1850	RD-10/326	AR
Aycock, Warren	103	1876	WB-1/104	AR
Aydelett, Abner	018	1827	WB-C/90	
Aydelette, John	030	1815	WB-3/73	
Aydelette, Leven	046	1878	WB-E/240	AR
Aydelott, Benjamin	046	1813	WB-A/11	AR
Aydelott, Isaac T.	030	1868	WB-4/269	AR
Aydelott, Tabitha	046	1842	WB-C/130	AR
Aydlotte, Jesse C.	040	c1860	WB-1/113	
Ayer, Henry W.	029	1839	WB-B/305	
Ayers, Edward W.	101	1893	WB-A/243	AR
Ayers, Garlint	013	1831	WB-A/5	
Ayers, Mollie E.	101	1879	WB-A/40	AR
Ayers, Nannie	101	1887	WB-A/158	AR
Ayers, Thomas	065	1776	WB-A/31	AR
Ayres, Analizer	083	1889	WB-3/463	AR
Ayscue, Elizabeth	039	1898	WB-V/121	
Azbill, James	024	1828	WB-C/144	AR
Azwell, Thomas	010	1767	WB-A/80	AR
Babb, John	041	1816	WB-2/111	AR
Babb, John	077	c1753	Orig. Only	AR
Babb, Moses	022	c1799	WB-A/39	AR
Babb, Pleasant	041	1825	WB-2/236	AR
Babb, Sarah	054	1855	WB-3/181	AR
Babb, William	041	1850	WB-3/127	AR
Babb, William	099	1783	RB-1/160	AR
Bacchus, Samuel	051	1883	WB-C/306	AR
Baccus, Thomas	024	1814	WB-C/24	AR
Bachelder, John	035	1851	WB-2/63	AR
Bachop, William	029	1792	Orig. Only	AR
Backet, Samuel	065	1827	WB-A/157	AR
Backhouse, John	019	1785	WB-D/26	AR
Backster, Elijah	033	1839	WB-1/19	AR
Backster, Hannah	033	1848	WB-1/93	AR
Backus, John, Sr.	024	c1767	WB-B/11	AR
Bacon, Edwin Wane	011	1894	WB-3/61	CTY
Bacon, Henry	070	1891	WB-F/430	AR
Bacon, Rebecca	073	1887	WB-H/432	CTY
Badger, George E.	099	1866	RB-34/152	AR
Badger, Thomas	028	1799	WB-B/79	AR
Badget, James	032	1827	WB-1/86	AR
Badget, Roger	044	1781	WB-1/305	CTY
Badget, William	085	1794	WB-D/131	AR
Badgett, John	044	1810	WB-7/138	CTY
Badgett, Martha S.	020	1891	WB-B/53	CTY
Badgett, Presiller	044	1817	WB-8/78	CTY
Badgett, William	020	1858	RB-R/609	AR
Badgett, Wilson	032	1891	WB-4/107	AR
Badham, John	024	1812	WB-C/11	AR
Badham, Mary G.	024	1872	WB-E/29	AR
Badham, Miles	024	1834	WB-C/176	AR
Badham, Will	024	c1781	WB-B/65	AR
Badham, William	024	1736	LGB-4/#136	
Bagby, George K.	019	1898	WB-B/332	AR
Bagby, Helen M.	059	1881	WB-A/318	CTY
Bagby, Thomas	047	1822	WB-3/665	AR
Baget, Nathan	051	1873	WB-C/92	AR
Bagett, Nathan	071	1816	WB-3/184	AR
Bagge, Charles F.	090	1837	032 WB-1/320	032 AR
Bagge, Charles F.	090	1837	WB-4/1 & 42	AR
Bagge, Lucinda F.	038	1872	WB-2/81	AR
Bagge, Traugott	090	1800	WB-1/151	
Baggerly, David	054	c1816	WB-1A/135	AR
Baggerly, Francis	054	c1814	WB-1/345	AR
Baggerly, Lavinia	033	1837	Orig. Only	AR
Bagget, Allen	071	1858	WB-5/207	AR
Bagget, Nicholas	071	1762	WB-1/63	
Baggett, Jonathan	010	1895	WB-I/419	AR
Baggett, Joseph	083	c1789	WB-1/18	AR
Baggett, Nicholas	010	1755	Orig. Only	SS/AR
Baggett, Thomas	063	c1797	WB-1/334	
Baggett, Thomas	063	1793	WB-1/187	
Bagley, D. W.	063	1878	WB-3/139	
Bagley, Henry	022	1802	WB-A/41	AR
Bagley, Jacob	041	1789	WB-1/78	AR
Bagley, James	099	1817	RB-14/108	AR
Bagley, John	077	1807	WB-E/255	AR
Bagley, Nathan	077	1816	WB-E/460	AR
Bagley, Newton T.	103	1894	105 WB-3/399	105 AR
Bagley, Newton T.	103	1894	WB-2/71	AR
Bagley, Sarah E.	070	1888	WB-F/206	AR
Bagley, Thomas	077	1837	WB-F/258	AR
Bagley, Thomas	077	1762	WB-C/11	AR
Bagley, William	077	1827	WB-F/137	AR
Bagley, William	077	c1826	WB-F/188	AR
Bagly, Abner	106	1888	WB-2/247	AR
Bagwell, Berry	099	1884	WB-A/555	AR
Bagwell, Robert	019	1785	WB-D/28	AR
Bagwell, William O.	086	1858	WB-E/351	AR
Bagwell, William S.	099	1888	WB-B/247	AR
Bahnson, Louisa A.	038	1887	WB-3/18	AR
Bahnson, Mattie J.	033	1895	WB-2/184	CTY
Bail, David	044	1786	WB-1/497	CTY
Bailey, Abraham	028	1774	Orig. Only	AR
Bailey, Alexander	054	1878	WB-4/295	CTY
Bailey, Benjamin	079	c1853	Orig. Only	AR-Copy
Bailey, Benjamin	075	1812	WB-M1/231	AR
Bailey, Benjamin	075	1785	WB-K/116	AR
Bailey, Benjamin	075	1764	WB-I/34	AR
Bailey, Bethvel	053	1790	RW-1/199	AR
Bailey, C. T.	099	1895	WB-C/415	AR
Bailey, Daniel W.	063	1877	WB-3/114	
Bailey, David	054	c1837	WB-2/173	AR
Bailey, David	075	1795	WB-L/42	AR
Bailey, David	075	1806	WB-M1/130	AR
Bailey, David	053	1797	RW-1/282	AR
Bailey, David	075	1746	Orig. Only	SS/AR
Bailey, Davis D.	099	1877	RB-35/429	AR
Bailey, Eliza A.	070	1900	WB-H/280	AR
Bailey, Elizabeth	009	1861	OB-L/382	AR
Bailey, F. J.	036	1893	099 WB-C/130	099 AR
Bailey, F. J.	036	1893	WB-A/271	CTY
Bailey, Fabius J.	078	1864	WB-18/353	AR
Bailey, Gabriel	078	1854	WB-17/301	
Bailey, George	075	1824	WB-N/5	AR
Bailey, Giles P.	084	1881	WB-E/216	CTY
Bailey, Hardy	056	1844	WB-1/567	AR
Bailey, Hasey	056	1816	WB-1/257	AR
Bailey, Henry	053	1772	RW-1/38	AR
Bailey, Henry	078	1837	SC/04236	AR-Copy
Bailey, Henry	075	1782	WB-K/77	AR
Bailey, Henry	056	c1789	WB-1/22	AR
Bailey, Henry	078	1837	WI-13/255	AR
Bailey, Isom	056	1816	WB-1/250	AR
Bailey, James	053	1798	RW-1/295	AR
Bailey, James C.	078	1864	WB-18/368	
Bailey, James E.	075	1899	WB-O/480	AR
Bailey, James M.	054	1857	WB-3/116	AR
Bailey, Jean	075	1804	WB-M1/99	AR

Name	Co.	Date	Recorded Copy	Original
Bailey, Jeremiah	044	1830	WB-11/529	CTY
Bailey, Jesse	056	1841	WB-1/526	AR
Bailey, Joacam	030	1806	WB-2/294	
Bailey, John	054	1846	WB-3/8	AR
Bailey, John	075	1774	WB-I/91	AR
Bailey, John	071	1761	WB-1/37	
Bailey, John	078	1871	WB-19/16	AR
Bailey, John	075	1808	WB-M1/172	AR
Bailey, John	081	1806	WB-3/47	AR
Bailey, John	075	1784	WB-K/106	AR
Bailey, John	044	1841	WB-15/16	CTY
Bailey, John	075	1817	WB-M1/302	AR
Bailey, John A.	078	1874	WB-19/56	
Bailey, John A.	054	1862	Orig. Only	AR
Bailey, John C.	070	1880	WB-E/387	AR
Bailey, John P.	099	1870	RB-35/107	
Bailey, John P.	078	1869	WB-19/6	AR
Bailey, John, Sr.	075	1850	WB-N/233	AR
Bailey, John, Sr.	005	1854	WB-C/76	AR
Bailey, Jonathan	028	1822	WB-C/212	AR
Bailey, Jonathan	037	1852	WB-F/470	AR
Bailey, Joseph	075	1784	WB-K/108	AR
Bailey, Joseph	075	1749	Orig. Only	SS/AR
Bailey, Josias	009	1823	OB-A/329	AR
Bailey, Kitturah	078	1855	WB-17/358	AR
Bailey, Leavy	056	1802	WB-1/133	AR
Bailey, Levi	062	1853	WB-A/8	AR
Bailey, Lucretia	044	1834	WB-13/153	CTY
Bailey, Mary	053	1830	WB-4/586	AR
Bailey, Morris	039	1800	WB-A/149	
Bailey, Oden	009	1861	OB-L/282	AR
Bailey, Otway L.	084	1832	WB-B/51	CTY
Bailey, Patrick	065	1764	WB-H/55	
Bailey, Peleg	099	1882	WB-A/312	AR
Bailey, Pennina	056	1861	WB-2/14	AR
Bailey, Prestley	099	c1873	Orig. Only	AR
Bailey, Rebecca	068	1869	WB-D/10	
Bailey, Richmond	033	1891	WB-2/118	CTY
Bailey, Robert	075	1793	WB-K/241	AR
Bailey, Robert	075	1831	WB-N/62	AR
Bailey, Ruffin	056	1864	WB-2/58	AR
Bailey, S. Adaline	099	1879	WB-A/38	AR
Bailey, Samuel	053	1810	RW-1/436	
Bailey, Samuel	069	1832	WB-1/382	AR
Bailey, Sarah	054	1841	WB-2/227	AR
Bailey, Simon	009	c1823	Orig. Only	AR
Bailey, Thomas	053	1789	RW-1/182	AR
Bailey, Thomas	011	c1767	WB-1/467	
Bailey, Thomas	075	1811	WB-M1/222	AR
Bailey, Thomas T.	032	1874	WB-3/121	AR
Bailey, Valentine	047	c1865	WB-5/132	
Bailey, W. H.	033	c1896	Orig. Only	CTY
Bailey, W. L.	063	1899	WB-4/237	AR
Bailey, Warner G.	063	1891	WB-4/70	AR
Bailey, William	060	1846	WB-2/265	AR
Bailey, William	044	1862	WB-21/524	CTY
Bailey, William	107	c1847	WB-1/350	
Bailey, William	044	1828	WB-11/3	CTY
Bailey, William B.	103	1900	WB-2/307	AR
Bailey, William H.	054	1899	WB-6/204	CTY
Bailey, Wilson	069	1863	WB-1/584	AR
Bailey, Yancey	078	1804	WI-3/329	AR
Bailie, John	085	1775	WB-A/219	AR
Bails (Bales), Eden	010	1763	WB-A/71	AR
Baily, Arnold	056	N. D.	Orig. Only	AR-Copy
Baily, Charity	103	1880	WB-1/177	AR
Baily, David	056	1853	WB-1/668	AR
Baily, Fredrick	030	c1809	WB-2/348	
Baily, John	053	1758	SS 879/267	SS/AR
Baily, Joshua	053	1814	RW-1/486	
Baily, William	005	1846	WB-B/205	AR
Bain, Eleanor K.	073	c1881	WB-H/312	AR-Copy
Bain, Frances E.	022	1855	WB-C/392	AR
Bain, Hope	103	1876	WB-1/100	AR
Bain, James M.	073	1899	WB-I/155	CTY
Bain, John	065	1897	WB-M/553	AR
Bain, Keziah	073	1857	WB-G/169	AR
Bain, Rachel	073	1880	WB-H/269	CTY
Bain, Thomas	073	1826	WB-E/127	AR
Baines, A. B.	069	1896	WB-5/516	AR
Baines, Henry J.	039	1880	WB-U/222	AR
Baines, Williamson	037	1814	WB-E/66	
Bains, George	024	1802	WB-B/171	AR
Bains, Inginber	077	1802	WB-E/178	AR
Bains, John C.	024	1827	WB-C/130	AR
Bains, John C.	024	c1772	WB-B/126	AR
Bains, William	010	1840	WB-G/321	AR
Baird, Adam, Sr.	060	c1811	Orig. Only	AR
Baird, Alfred B.	102	1881	WB-A/20	AR
Baird, Bedent	013	1841	WB-A/79	
Baird, Eliza T.	013	1887	WB-B/430	AR
Baird, Francis	060	1789	Orig. Only	AR
Baird, Francis R.	VA	1877	096 WB-4/114	
Baird, Francis R.	VA	1877	031 WB-1/32	031 AR
Baird, Hannah	013	1849	WB-A/134	
Baird, James	060	1808	Orig. Only	AR
Baird, John, Sr.	060	1784	Orig. Only	AR
Baird, Mary	029	1821	WB-B/67	AR
Baird, Mary A.	013	1880	WB-B/260	AR
Baird, Prince	060	1835	WB-1/363	AR
Baird, Rebecca	013	1894	WB-C/302	AR
Baird, Robert	040	1871	WB-2/25	AR
Baird, Thomas H.R.	078	1899	WB-19/470	AR
Baird, William	078	1857	WB-17/474	AR
Baird, Wilson	082	1819	WB-1/200	AR
Baisden, Hugh	072	c1778	RW/L11	AR
Baisden, Jesse	072	1812	WB-A/6	AR
Baity, W. D.	106	1894	WB-2/340	
Baker, A. A.	079	1892	WB-2/586	AR
Baker, A. L.	099	1893	WB-C/142	AR
Baker, Abraham	060	1800	Orig. Only	AR/CRX
Baker, Absolum	085	c1775	WB-A/228	AR
Baker, Agathy	063	1830	WB-2/167	
Baker, Alexander	083	1884	WB-3/304	AR
Baker, Andrew	001	1899	WB-3/254	AR
Baker, Angus S.	083	1883	WB-3/297	AR
Baker, Anna Maria	041	1809	WB-2/47	AR
Baker, Archibald	083	1842	WB-1/412	AR
Baker, Archibald	029	1811	WB-A/173	AR
Baker, Archibald	083	1880	WB-3/176	AR
Baker, Asa	010	1827	WB-G/155	AR
Baker, Avery	084	1889	WB-E/417	
Baker, Basheba	017	c1854	WB-A/75	AR
Baker, Benjamin	047	1837	WB-4/147	AR
Baker, Bettie	051	1894	WB-C/482	AR
Baker, Blake	041	1888	WB-4/264	AR
Baker, Blake	041	1855	WB-3/184	AR
Baker, Blake	037	1890	WB-H/160	AR
Baker, Blake	047	1769	WB-1/250	
Baker, Blake	100	1818	WB-21/266	AR

Name	Co.	Date	Recorded Copy	Original
Baker, Boyakin	039	1827	WB-H/195	
Baker, Catharine	083	1859	WB-2/154	AR
Baker, Catharine	083	1880	WB-3/193	AR
Baker, Catherine	099	1882	WB-A/359	AR
Baker, Charles F.	085	c1899	Copy	049 AR
Baker, Charly R.	099	1891	WB-B/585	AR
Baker, Christian	092	1783	WB-2/4	AR
Baker, Daniel	083	1873	WB-3/60	AR
Baker, Daniel	029	1805	WB-A/83	AR
Baker, David	021	1874	WB-2/120	AR
Baker, David	047	1797	WB-3/291	AR
Baker, David	033	1869	WB-2/5	CTY
Baker, David G.	037	1844	WB-F/313	AR
Baker, David, Sr.	107	c1838	WB-1/30	
Baker, Duncan	069	1861	WB-1/574	AR
Baker, Duncan	083	1875	WB-3/92	AR
Baker, Edmund	083	1884	WB-3/301	AR
Baker, Edward B.	010	1818	WB-G/32	AR
Baker, Edwin	047	1837	WB-4/146	AR
Baker, Elijah	056	1847	WB-1/588	AR
Baker, Elizabeth	017	1856	Orig. Only	AR
Baker, Elizabeth	012	1824	WB-B/132	AR
Baker, Elizabeth	029	1865	WB-D/80	AR
Baker, Eloney	037	1869	WB-G/331	AR
Baker, Emily	100	1888	WB-51/273	AR
Baker, Florence	051	1881	WB-C/262	AR
Baker, G. H.	021	1882	WB-2/249	
Baker, George	073	1845	WB-F/244	
Baker, George	051	1891	WB-C/419	AR
Baker, George	065	1815	WB-A/105	AR
Baker, George B.	099	1872	RB-35/196	AR
Baker, George M.	097	c1883	WB-2/319	AR
Baker, Goslin	003	1876	WB-B/65	AR
Baker, H. N.	051	N. D.	WB-C/520	
Baker, Harrison	041	1867	WB-3/355	AR
Baker, Haywood	056	1882	WB-3/312	AR
Baker, Henry	024	1739	LGB-4/#81	
Baker, Henry	039	1823	WB-G/161	
Baker, Henry	047	1873	WB-6/95	AR
Baker, Henry	009	1821	OB-A/315	AR
Baker, Henry	021	1878	WB-2/192	
Baker, Henry W.	092	1792	WB-3/8	AR
Baker, Henry, Sr.	039	c1859	WB-Q/567	
Baker, Hilary	096	1790	WB-1/163	AR
Baker, Isaac	012	1811	WB-B/98	AR
Baker, Isaac	051	1848	WB-A/291	
Baker, Jacob	060	1786	Orig. Only	AR/CRX
Baker, Jacob	085	1859	WB-K/261	AR
Baker, James	047	1799	WB-3/333	AR
Baker, James	039	1885	WB-U/359	AR
Baker, James	047	1810	WB-3/511	AR
Baker, James B.	041	1897	WB-4/422	AR
Baker, Jesse	037	1788	WB-C/64	AR
Baker, Jesse	105	1891	WB-2/564	
Baker, Joel	010	1831	WB-G/205	AR
Baker, John	051	1869	WB-C/26	AR
Baker, John	051	1880	WB-C/247	AR
Baker, John	010	1756	SS 880/265	SS/AR
Baker, John	006	1855	WB-A/105	
Baker, John	070	1766	WB-C/17	AR
Baker, John	083	1874	WB-3/73	AR
Baker, John	017	c1844	WB-A/41	AR
Baker, John	090	1888	WB-6/185	AR
Baker, John	047	1828	WB-4/42	AR
Baker, John	029	1814	WB-A/205	AR
Baker, John	039	c1853	WB-O/331	AR
Baker, John	028	1799	WB-B/65	AR
Baker, John	068	1822	WB-B/19	
Baker, John B.	041	1838	WB-3/1	AR
Baker, John P.	099	1882	WB-A/373	AR
Baker, John W.	029	1882	WB-E/287	AR
Baker, John, Sr.	068	1836	WB-B/101	
Baker, John, Sr.	054	c1825	WB-2/12	
Baker, Jonathan	010	1785	WB-D/32	AR
Baker, Joseph	051	1894	WB-C/500	AR
Baker, Joseph	085	1857	WB-K/239	AR
Baker, Joseph	073	1831	WB-E/256	AR
Baker, Julia	037	1790	WB-C/148	AR
Baker, Laura	029	1858	WB-C/379	AR
Baker, Lawrence	041	1807	WB-2/1	AR
Baker, Lennie	071	1895	WB-7/228	AR
Baker, Margaret	085	1885	WB-2/137	CTY
Baker, Marmaduke	041	1877	WB-4/91	AR
Baker, Marshall	039	1879	WB-U/214	AR
Baker, Mary	010	1875	WB-I/67	AR
Baker, Mary A.	051	1893	WB-C/457	AR
Baker, Mary W.	009	1845	OB-E/479	AR
Baker, Michael	085	1841	WB-I/95	AR
Baker, Michael	092	1777	WB-1/82	AR
Baker, Moses	037	1786	WB-C/28	AR
Baker, Moses	024	1724	SS 876/21	SS/AR
Baker, Moses	037	1857	WB-G/146	AR
Baker, Nancy	100	1829	WB-32/258	AR
Baker, Nancy	105	1895	WB-3/135	AR
Baker, Nancy	039	1880	WB-U/242	AR
Baker, Nathan	047	1843	WB-4/225	AR
Baker, Philip	021	1863	WB-1/172	AR
Baker, Robeson H.	056	1895	WB-2/200	AR
Baker, Sally	084	1874	WB-E/77	CTY
Baker, Samuel	085	1758	WB-A/20	AR
Baker, Sarah	083	1888	WB-3/430	AR
Baker, Simmons I.	047	1853	WB-4/345	AR
Baker, Simon	039	1884	WB-U/364	AR
Baker, Susanna	073	1846	WB-F/330	AR
Baker, Thomas	010	1798	WB-E/62	AR
Baker, Virginia	099	1895	WB-C/383	AR
Baker, Virginia M.	099	1895	091 WB-1/302	
Baker, William	039	1861	WB-R/159	AR
Baker, William	019	1800	WB-D/87	AR
Baker, William	099	1890	WB-B/455	AR
Baker, William	041	c1803	WB-1/240	AR
Baker, William	069	1824	WB-1/320	AR
Baker, William	015	1777	100 WB-2/103	AR
Baker, William	006	1870	WB-D/98	AR
Baker, William	010	1810	WB-F/164	AR
Baker, William	083	1845	WB-1/451	AR
Baker, William B.	051	1863	WB-B/53	AR
Baker, William H.	010	c1883	WB-I/163	
Baker, William J.	037	1864	WB-G/243	AR
Baker, William S.	037	1862	WB-G/212	AR
Baker, William W.	051	1872	WB-C/75	AR
Balance, John	085	1820	WB-H/65	AR
Balch, John	065	1791	WB-A/86	AR
Balch, Joseph	028	1752	Orig. Only	SS/AR
Baldin, Jonathan	037	1781	WB-B/63	AR
Baldree, Isaac	079	1872	WB-2/63	AR
Baldridge, Alexander	086	1837	WB-E/36	AR
Baldridge, James	073	1803	WB-D/107	AR
Baldridge, John	086	1835	WB-E/10	AR
Baldridge, William	086	1828	WB-D/90	AR

Name	Co.	Date	Recorded Copy	Original
Baldwin, A. L.	106	1897	WB-2/415	
Baldwin, Anna	027	1893	WB-2/106	AR
Baldwin, Charles D.	GA	1900	Copy	027 AR
Baldwin, Elizabeth	046	1840	WB-C/78	AR
Baldwin, Henry	020	1799	RB-C/409	
Baldwin, Hiram	067	1882	WB-2/157	AR
Baldwin, Isaac	070	1806	WB-AB/99	AR
Baldwin, Jacob	006	1856	WB-D/26	AR
Baldwin, Jesse	082	1826	WB-1/276	AR
Baldwin, Jesse A.	082	1881	WB-6/201	AR
Baldwin, Joel	065	1777	WB-A/77	AR
Baldwin, John	046	1824	WB-B/189	AR
Baldwin, John	020	1825	RB-K/98	AR
Baldwin, John R.	036	1900	WB-A/516	CTY
Baldwin, John, Sr.	011	c1791	WB-1/457	
Baldwin, Lucy Ann	027	1853	WB-A/60	AR-Nunc.
Baldwin, Matilda	022	1883	WB-E/265	AR
Baldwin, Nancy L.	040	1896	WB-2/521	AR
Baldwin, Rebecca	067	1890	WB-2/276	AR
Baldwin, Samuel	022	1879	WB-E/191	AR
Baldwin, Samuel	028	1780	Orig. Only	AR
Baldwin, Tabitha	073	1890	WB-H/503	CTY
Baldwin, Terrell	082	1852	Orig. Only	AR-Nunc.
Baldwin, Thomas	027	1886	WB-2/63	AR
Baldwin, Thomas W.	082	1852	WB-4/59	
Baldwin, William	046	1808	WB-A/34	AR
Baldwin, William	073	1859	WB-G/215	CTY
Baldwin, William	011	c1801	WB-1/364	
Baldwin, William M.	006	1898	WB-E/346	AR
Baleman, Jonathan	077	1694/5	SS 874.2/68	
Bales, Caleb	046	1864	WB-D/236	AR
Baley, Abner	054	1890	Orig. Only	AR
Baley, Arniel	053	1760	OB-A/27	AR
Baley, John	024	1716	Orig. Only	SS/AR
Baley, John	069	1781	WB 1/14	AR
Baley, John	056	1831	WB-1/473	AR
Baley, Nancy	072	c1836	WB-1/146	AR
Baley, Richard	047	1762	WB-1/66	
Baley, Samuel	085	1791	WB-B/209	AR
Baley, William	009	1833	OB-B/294	AR
Baley, William	056	1796	WB-1/99	AR
Balfour, Andrew	081	1826	WB-5/250	AR
Balfour, Elizabeth	081	1819	WB-4/691	AR
Balfour, James	015	1775	100 WB-2/61	AR
Balfour, Margaret	081	1818	WB-4/541	AR
Balkcum, Hester	087	1843	WB-1/266	AR
Balkcum, Nancy	087	1854	WB-1/442	AR
Ball, Bathana	009	c1829	OB-B/300	AR
Ball, Daniel	044	1794	WB-3/162	CTY
Ball, Daniel	100	1823	WB-24/187	AR
Ball, David	020	1867	RB-T/207	AR
Ball, Henry	032	c1861	WB-2/211	
Ball, Hosea	030	1833	WB-3/329	
Ball, J. R.	046	1893	WB-F/269	AR
Ball, James	009	c1806	OB-A/176	AR
Ball, James	039	1898	WB-V/147	AR
Ball, James	019	1749	SS 877/280	SS/AR
Ball, James	028	1799	WB-B/73	AR
Ball, Jarius	013	c1862	Orig. Only	AR
Ball, Joel	013	1846	WB-A/121	
Ball, John	057	1847	WB-B/192	AR
Ball, Joseph	072	1854	WB-2/138	AR
Ball, Joshua	030	1834	WB-4/1	
Ball, Lemuel	030	1865	WB-4/256	AR
Ball, Letisha	030	1803	WB-2/223	

Name	Co.	Date	Recorded Copy	Original
Ball, Miles	009	1829	OB-B/15	AR
Ball, Moses	072	1818	WB-A/1	AR
Ball, Nancy G.	100	1875	WB-51/77	AR
Ball, Nathan	019	1788	WB-D/29	AR
Ball, Nicolas	092	1803	WB-3/56A	AR
Ball, Polly	044	1832	WB-12/357	
Ball, Reuben	030	1793	WB-2/17	
Ball, Stephen	072	c1785	WI/L45	AR
Ball, Thomas	024	1722	SS 875/333	SS/AR
Ball, Vinum	044	1839	WB-14/457	CTY
Ball, Warren E.	039	1866	WB-S/291	AR
Ball, William	069	1845	WB-1/483	AR
Ball, William	085	1816	WB-G/438	AR
Ball, William	044	1878	WB-23/305	CTY
Ball, Wilson	009	1861	OB-L/373	AR
Ballance, Aaron	056	1865	WB-2/67	
Ballance, Benjamin	030	1862	WB-4/246	
Ballance, Blackman	056	1874	WB-3/122	
Ballance, Caleb	030	1790	WB-1/246	
Ballance, Caleb S.	053	1890	WB-11/229	AR
Ballance, Demsey	030	1837	WB-4/36	
Ballance, Holloway	051	1862	WB-B/45	AR
Ballance, James C.	053	1873	WB-11/32	AR
Ballance, John	053	c1819	Orig. Only	AR
Ballance, John	030	1825	WB-3/198	
Ballance, Joseph	030	1801	WB-2/198	
Ballance, Laban	053	1856	WB-8/187	AR
Ballance, Mary	030	1829	WB-3/249	
Ballance, Polly	030	1833	WB-3/329	
Ballance, Rebecca	103	1900	WB-2/299	AR
Ballance, Teagle	056	1871	WB-3/49	AR
Ballance, William	056	1834	WB-1/497	AR
Ballance, William	030	1796	WB-2/90	
Ballance, Willoughby	030	1871	WB-5/22	
Ballann, Barbara	030	1805	WB-2/276	
Ballantine, Barbara	030	1835	WB-4/8	
Ballard, Abraham	077	1754	SS 881/96	SS/AR
Ballard, Andrew	092	1818	WB-3/134	
Ballard, Benjamin T.	039	1894	WB-V/17	AR
Ballard, Caleb	056	1851	WB-1/642	AR
Ballard, Caroline	013	1896	WB-C/512	AR
Ballard, Dudley	085	c1807	WB-G/107	AR
Ballard, Edward	069	c1819	Orig. Only	AR
Ballard, Elias	063	1789	WB-1/150	
Ballard, Elias	103	1788	WI-A/133	AR
Ballard, Elisha	063	1824	WB-2/95	
Ballard, Fannie	021	c1891	WB-3/320	AR
Ballard, Fanny B.	063	1864	WB-2/543	
Ballard, James	060	1829	WB-1/114	AR
Ballard, James	072	1824	WB-A/9	AR
Ballard, Jesse	065	1808	WB-A/92	AR
Ballard, Jethro	070	1853	WB-C/562	AR
Ballard, Jethro	041	1802	WB-1/192	AR
Ballard, John	024	1736	LGB-4/#59	SS/AR
Ballard, John	034	1767	Copy	103 AR
Ballard, Jonathan	046	1885	WB-E/407	AR
Ballard, Joseph	096	1773	WB-1/69	AR
Ballard, Joseph Sr.	024	1729	SS 876/198	SS/AR
Ballard, Junius	039	1870	WB-U/23	AR
Ballard, Lewis	060	1797	Orig. Only	AR
Ballard, Martin B.	063	1877	WB-3/123	
Ballard, Nancy	063	1858	WB-2/451	
Ballard, Noah	065	1875	WB-K/188	AR
Ballard, R. H.	050	1880	WB-1/158	CTY
Ballard, Richard H.	041	1851	WB-3/142	AR

Name	Co.	Date	Recorded Copy	Original
Ballard, Robert H.	041	1875	WB-1/57	AR
Ballard, Silas	063	1837	WB-2/226	
Ballard, Silas	063	1826	WB-2/115	
Ballard, Silas E.	063	c1821	WB-2/75	
Ballard, Thomas	090	1804	WB-2/44	AR
Ballard, Walter C.	047	1801	WB-3/347	AR
Ballard, William	062	1859	WB-A/22	AR
Ballard, William	047	1775	WB-2/5	
Ballard, William	046	1821	WB-B/106	AR
Ballard, William	069	1815	WB-1/264	AR
Ballard, William E.	063	1827	WB-2/124	
Ballen, Susan	006	1887	WB-E/147	
Ballence, Ann	030	1843	WB-4/101	
Ballence, Daniel	030	1800	WB-2/158	
Ballence, Keziah	030	1845	WB-4/109	
Ballenger, Edward	056	1773	Orig. Only	AR
Ballentine, Davis	030	1821	WB-3/120	
Ballentine, Edward	063	1801	WB-1/396	
Ballentine, Georg	N	1724	Orig. Only	SS/AR
Ballentine, George W.	011	1866	WB-2/2	
Ballentine, Henry	030	1794	WB-2/26	
Ballentine, Henry	030	c1814	WB-3/38	
Ballentine, J. Seth	099	1882	WB-A/375	AR
Ballentine, James	030	N. D.	WB-2/330	
Ballentine, Joseph	030	c1813	WB-3/20	
Ballentine, Joseph	030	1816	WB-3/89	
Ballentine, Lovey	030	1815	WB-3/71	
Ballentine, Martha	081	1884	WB-15/469	AR
Ballentine, William	069	1863	WB-1/583	AR
Ballew, David	107	1869	WB-2/1	
Ballew, Mary	064	1873	WB-2/38	AR
Ballew, Thomas	064	1861	WB-1/74	AR
Ballinger, Henrey	085	1774	WB-B/105	AR
Ballinger, Henry	085	c1758	WB-A/239	
Ballinger, John	046	1871	WB-E/69	AR
Ballinger, John	056	1792	WB-1/56	AR
Ballow, N. B.	006	1897	WB-E/310	AR
Ballow, Susanna	006	1887	Orig. Only	AR
Balmer, Gray	071	1826	WB-4/17	AR
Balmer, Mary	071	1867	WB-5/350	AR
Balsley, J. B.	046	1891	WB-F/168	AR
Balthrop, Augustin D.	100	1843	WB-38/134	AR
Balthrop, James	100	1780	WB-3/77	
Baly, Thomas	005	1802	WB-2/3	AR
Bame, Edward	085	1897	WB-3/177	CTY
Bame, George	085	1891	WB-2/462	CTY
Bame, Susanna	016	1847	WB-1/133	
Banday, John	021	1846	Orig. Only	AR
Bandy, Christina	060	1830	WB-1/193	AR
Bandy, Christina	021	1873	WB-2/78	
Bandy, George	060	1822	Orig. Only	AR
Bandy, H. M.	060	1885	WB-4/308	AR
Bandy, James	037	1812	WB-E/50	AR
Bandy, Susan	037	1842	WB-F/270	AR
Bandy, William	021	1897	WB-3/188	AR
Bane, James	065	1788	WB-A/114	AR
Bane, John	073	c1881	WB-H/314	AR
Banes, Lilly	020	1863	RB-T/10	CTY
Banes, Wineford	010	1846	WB-G/394	AR
Bangert, Sebastian	028	1886	WB-E/419	AR
Bangle, Cary A.	016	1892	WB-4/143	AR
Bangle, Henry W.	016	1864	WB-2/103	
Bangs, Abiah	028	c1755	DB-8/266	SS/AR
Bangs, Jonathan	028	1743	Wills.6/L66	SS/AR
Banham, Charles	070	1897	WB-G/547	
Banks, A. J. R.	099	1877	RB-35/410	AR
Banks, Adam G.	099	1854	RB-28/586	AR
Banks, Arnst	028	1867	WB-D/447	
Banks, Benjamin L.	075	1854	WB-M2/10	AR
Banks, Clarissa	070	1867	WB-D/216	AR
Banks, David	022	1786	RB-1/25	AR
Banks, Gerard	029	1812	WB-A/176	AR
Banks, Henry H.	013	1878	WB-B/160	AR
Banks, Isom	047	1897	Orig. Only	AR
Banks, James	028	1868	Orig. Only	AR
Banks, James	075	1897	WB-O/436	AR
Banks, James	074	1874	WB-1/37	AR
Banks, John	090	1808	WB-2/96	AR
Banks, John	028	1837	WB-C/400	AR
Banks, John	028	1884	WB-E/350	AR
Banks, Jonathan	075	1790	WB-K/201	AR
Banks, Joseph	075	1831	WB-N/65	AR
Banks, Liza	028	1860	WB-D/343	AR
Banks, Margaret	029	1877	WB-E/167	AR
Banks, Mary	096	1818	Orig. Only	AR
Banks, Mary	099	1848	RB-26/319	AR
Banks, Peter	028	1860	WB-D/340	AR
Banks, Rhoda	071	1841	WB-4/239	AR
Banks, Sally	028	1842	WB-D/63	AR
Banks, Samuel M.	013	1879	WB-B/172	AR
Banks, Sarah	099	1900	WB-D/235	AR
Banks, Sarah	075	1774	WB-I/86	AR
Banks, Susan A.	099	1886	WB-B/99	AR
Banks, Thomas	075	1853	WB-M2/8	AR
Banks, Thomas	037	1829	WB-F/108	AR
Banks, W. M.	107	1887	WB-2/39	
Banks, Walker	037	1877	WB-G/535	AR
Banks, William	009	c1846	OWB/542	AR
Banks, William	028	1772	Orig. Only	SS/AR
Banks, William	075	1809	WB-M1/199	AR
Banks, William	053	1800	RW-1/316	AR
Banks, William C.	075	1826	WB-N/22	AR
Banner, Anna M.	038	1892	WB-3/299	AR
Banner, Benjamin	090	1811	WB-2/125	AR
Banner, Benjamin	090	1840	WB-4/60	AR
Banner, Charles M.	038	1892	WB-3/282	AR
Banner, Henry	090	1790	WB-1/7	AR
Banner, John	092	1888	WB-6/283	AR
Banner, Joseph	090	1838	WB-4/20	AR
Banner, Joseph	038	c1846	WB-1/9	AR
Banner, Lewis B.	102	1887	WB-A/54	AR
Banner, Martha	038	c1854	WB-1/51	AR
Banner, Nancy R.	066	1894	WB-1/130	AR
Banner, Sarah	066	1892	WB-1/117	AR
Banner, Sarah W.	090	1845	WB-4/202	AR
Bannerman, Charles	070	1782	WB-C/29	AR
Bannerman, Charles	070	1838	WB-AB/315	AR
Bannerman, John P.	076	1887	WB-A1/90	AR
Bannerman, Robert	070	1843	WB-AB/396	AR
Bannerman, Robert T.	070	1870	WB-E/198	AR
Bannett, Thomas	063	c1795	WB-1/320	
Banzet, Nicholas	100	1888	WB-51/275	AR
Baptest, Benjamin	024	1752	Orig. Only	SS/AR
Baptist, Edmund	075	1785	WB-K/118	AR
Barba, John	016	1872	WB-3/71	
Barbara, Allen, Sr.	087	1853	WB-1/437	AR
Barbee, Abemalic	022	1879	WB-E/166	AR
Barbee, Ann E.	036	1883	WB-A/102	CTY
Barbee, Benjamin	073	1826	WB-E/122	AR
Barbee, Betsey	022	1831	WB-B/203	AR

Name	Co.	Date	Recorded Copy	Original
Barbee, Christopher	099	1777	RB-1/97	AR
Barbee, Christopher	073	1834	WB-E/321	AR
Barbee, Christopher	N	c1792	HiDSC	AR-Copy
Barbee, Christopher	099	1852	RB-27/399	AR
Barbee, Christopher	073	1792	WB-B/165	AR
Barbee, Dorris	099	1868	RB-35/17	AR
Barbee, Fletcher	073	1881	WB-H/277	CTY
Barbee, Gabriel	073	1867	WB-G/529	CTY
Barbee, Goin	022	1807	WB-A/134	AR
Barbee, Gray	073	1866	WB-G/489	CTY
Barbee, Gray, Sr.	022	1830	WB-B/189	AR
Barbee, James	073	1840	WB-F/43	AR
Barbee, James A.J.	036	1882	WB-A/20	CTY
Barbee, John	073	1797	WB-C/159	AR
Barbee, John	073	1818	WB-D/535	AR
Barbee, Joseph	099	1830	Orig. Only	AR
Barbee, Joseph	073	1802	WB-D/83	AR
Barbee, Josiah	099	1849	RB-26/603	AR
Barbee, Martha	022	1880	WB-E/213	AR
Barbee, Nancy	099	c1835	Orig. Only	AR
Barbee, Patsey	099	1818	RB-14/122	AR
Barbee, Penny D.	046	1899	099 WB-D/358	099 AR
Barbee, Penny D.	046	1899	WB-G/154	AR
Barbee, Phebe	073	1837	WB-E/410	AR
Barbee, Rosey	099	1857	RB-30/218	AR
Barbee, Walter A.	036	1890	WB-A/175	CTY
Barbee, William	099	1895	WB-C/442	AR
Barbee, William	073	1833	WB-E/294	AR
Barbee, William	073	1857	WB-G/177	AR
Barbee, Willis	073	1869	WB-H/3	CTY
Barber, Absalom	072	1837	WB-2/1	AR
Barber, Ann	010	1844	WB-G/368	AR
Barber, B. T.	056	1891	WB-3/561	AR
Barber, Benjamin	016	1893	WB-4/170	AR
Barber, Burrell	056	1851	WB-1/648	AR
Barber, Cassandra	056	1886	WB-3/417	AR
Barber, Catharine	085	1867	WB-L/1	
Barber, Catharine	072	1891	WB-4/255	AR
Barber, David	001	1873	WB-2/60	AR
Barber, Elias	085	1843	WB-I/153	AR
Barber, Elizabeth	072	1811	WB-A/17	AR
Barber, Fanny	089	1880	WB-2/83	AR
Barber, George	056	1837	Orig. Only	AR
Barber, Gideon	056	1866	WB-2/75	AR
Barber, Hester	075	1885	WB-O/234	AR
Barber, Isaac	077	1820	WB-F/29	AR
Barber, J.Marshall	099	1897	WB-D/20	AR
Barber, James	085	1862	WB-K/305	AR
Barber, James D.	001	1875	WB-2/80	AR
Barber, Jane	085	1897	WB-3/186	CTY
Barber, Jerry	068	1875	WB-D/70	
Barber, Joel	077	1808	WB-E/325	AR
Barber, John	086	1799	WB-B/101	AR
Barber, John	072	1811	WB-A/13	AR
Barber, John	075	1693	SS 874.2/170	
Barber, John	030	c1762	Copy	024 AR
Barber, Jonathan	085	1839	WB-I/62	AR
Barber, Jonathan	085	1890	WB-2/429	CTY
Barber, Joseph	085	1894	WB-3/33	CTY
Barber, Joseph	077	1779	WB-C/241	AR
Barber, Joshua	047	1791	WB-3/191	AR
Barber, Luke	085	1869	Orig. Only	CTY
Barber, Margaret	085	1855	WB-K/183	AR
Barber, Martha	077	c1831	WB-F/198	AR
Barber, Mary K.	085	1843	WB-I/183	AR
Barber, Matthew	085	1869	WB-1/33	CTY
Barber, Michel	072	c1766	RW/L40	AR
Barber, Mitchell	072	1845	WB-2/68	AR
Barber, Moses	022	1892	WB-E/499	AR
Barber, Moses	077	1811	WB-E/367	AR
Barber, N. B.	056	1874	WB-3/110	AR
Barber, Penelope	056	1885	WB-3/387	AR
Barber, Plyer	099	1869	RB-35/71	AR
Barber, Richard	072	1792	Orig. Only	AR
Barber, Samuel	077	1835	WB-F/241	AR
Barber, Samuel	069	1790	WB-1/65	AR
Barber, Sarah	060	1830	WB-1/188	AR
Barber, Sarah	077	1851	WB-F/399	AR
Barber, Simeon	056	1890	WB-3/528	AR
Barber, Thomas	085	1887	WB-2/234	CTY
Barber, Thomas	085	1857	WB-K/249	AR
Barber, Thomas	072	c1800	WB-A/14	AR
Barber, Travis	090	1845	WB-4/194	AR
Barber, Walter J.	005	1893	WB-D/329	AR
Barber, William	084	1812	WB-A/91	CTY
Barber, William	085	1855	WB-K/185	AR
Barber, William B.	077	c1835	WB-F/252	
Barber, William J.	056	1870	WB-3/35	AR
Barber, William M.	104	1865	WB-5/411	
Barber, Wilsey	056	1849	WB-1/581	AR
Barberree, Abraham	010	1762	WB-A/14	AR
Barbery, Peter	035	1783	WB-A/35	AR
Barbour, A. P.	056	1886	WB-3/415	AR
Barbree, Peter	096	1771	Orig. Only	AR
Barbrey, A. B.	087	1889	WB-3/414	AR
Barbrick, Elizabeth	016	1841	PQS.6/146	
Barca, Lettia	031	1889	WB-1/65	AR
Barckely, Isaballah	054	c1822	WB-2/135	AR
Barclay, Mildred	048	1863	WB-1/106	
Barclay, William	085	1796	WB-D/127	AR
Barclift, Asa	077	1785	WB-C/320	AR
Barclift, Elizabeth	077	1808	WB-E/308	AR
Barclift, Er	077	1807	WB-E/268	AR
Barclift, George S.	077	1867	WB-H/19	AR
Barclift, James	077	1777	WB-C/206	AR
Barclift, John	077	1759	SS 881/242	SS/AR
Barclift, John	077	1788	WB-C/356	AR
Barclift, Joseph	077	1822	WB-F/41	
Barclift, Joseph	077	1793	WB-C/454	
Barclift, Joshua	077	1756	SS 880/105	SS/AR
Barclift, Martha	077	1871	WB-H/39	AR
Barclift, Noah	077	1784	WB-C/271	AR
Barclift, Noah	077	1797	WB-E/78	
Barclift, Richard	077	1867	WB-H/13	AR
Barclift, Samuel	077	1778	WB-C/309	AR
Barclift, Thomas	077	1750	Orig. Only	SS/AR
Barclift, William	077	1777	WB-C/208	AR
Barclift, William	077	1748	Orig. Only	SS/AR
Barclift, William	077	1733	SS 876/285	SS/AR
Barclift, Winifred	075	1792	WB-K/238	AR
Barco, Bailey	018	1876	WB-E/60	AR
Barcock, William	075	1731	SS 876/237	SS/AR
Barden, Arthur	063	1789	WB-1/147	
Barden, Arthur	103	1844	RD-9/61	AR
Barden, Elizabeth	063	1817	WB-2/44	
Barden, Elizabeth	044	1792	WB-2/317	
Barden, Ephraim	087	1837	WB-1/178	AR
Barden, J. L.	103	1896	WB-2/147	AR
Barden, James	103	1805	Orig. Only	AR
Barden, James W.	103	1892	WB-2/13	AR

Name	Co.	Date	Recorded Copy	Original
Barden, John	035	1856	WB-2/102	AR
Barden, John	063	1869	WB-3/7	
Barden, John	035	1811	WB-A/19	AR
Barden, John	087	1894	WB-3/541	AR
Barden, John L.	063	1881	WB-3/205	
Barden, William	103	1837	RD-7/254	AR
Barden, William	072	c1885	WB-4/187	
Barden, William H.	105	1859	WB-1/56	AR
Barden, Woodard	087	1870	WB-3/52	AR
Bardin, Isaac V.	SC	1900	103 WB-2/277	103 AR
Bardin, Jacob	103	1787	WI-A/113	AR
Bardin, John	103	1823	RD-5/27	AR
Bardin, John C.	103	1852	RD-11/148	AR
Bardin, John P.	105	1899	Copy	103 AR
Bardin, John P.	069	1899	WB-6/48	AR
Bardin, John P.	105	1899	WB-3/357	AR
Bardin, John T.	103	1826	RD-5/262	AR
Bardin, Mary	103	1854	RD-11/542	AR
Bardin, Mary	103	1817	RD-4/34	AR
Bardin, Simon	103	c1785	Orig. Only	AR
Bardin, Woodard	103	1808	RD-1/89	AR
Bare, Elias	006	1881	WB-E/80	AR
Bare, Henry	006	c1895	Orig. Only	AR
Bare, Henry	006	1884	WB-E/181	AR
Bare, Jacob	006	1865	Orig. Only	AR
Barecock, Thomas	075	1721	SS 875/303	SS/AR
Barefoot, Andrew J.	105	1873	WB-2/140	AR
Barefoot, Archie	027	1897	WB-2/142	AR
Barefoot, Bright	087	1899	WB-4/103	
Barefoot, Delila	027	1824	WB-A/17	AR
Barefoot, Elizabeth	056	1868	WB-3/5	AR
Barefoot, Jepthah	037	1805	WB-D/221	AR
Barefoot, Jepthah	037	1800	WB-D/104	AR
Barefoot, John	056	1875	WB-3/127	AR
Barefoot, John	103	1808	WI-B/412	AR
Barefoot, Lucy Ann	027	1899	WB-2/161	AR
Barefoot, Miles	056	1861	WB-1/13	AR
Barefoot, Noah, Sr.	056	1833	WB-1/491	AR
Barefoot, Willey	056	1888	WB-3/470	AR
Bareleft, William B.	041	1796	WB-1/149	AR
Barfield, Allen F.	056	1871	WB-3/38	AR
Barfield, Blake	056	1885	WB-3/399	AR
Barfield, Brian L.	099	1856	RB-29/458	
Barfield, Charles	037	1809	WB-D/349	AR
Barfield, Cornelius	083	1855	WB-2/74	AR
Barfield, Dicey	037	1852	WB-F/468	AR
Barfield, Ephraim	037	1853	WB-F/494	AR
Barfield, George	087	1863	WB-2/42	AR
Barfield, George	087	c1862	Copy	103 AR
Barfield, Granger G.	087	1861	WB-2/34	AR
Barfield, Isaac	035	1862	WB-3/61	AR
Barfield, James	037	c1770	Orig. Only	AR
Barfield, John	072	1742/3	Orig. Only	SS/AR
Barfield, John	103	1849	RD-10/222	AR
Barfield, John	037	1846	WB-F/349	AR
Barfield, John F.	099	1861	Orig. Only	AR
Barfield, Lydia	037	1828	WB-F/95	AR
Barfield, Mary E.	037	1886	WB-H/84	AR
Barfield, Moses	072	1801	WB-A/12	AR
Barfield, Nancy	103	1889	WB-1/493	AR
Barfield, Richard	035	1755	SS 880/10	SS/AR
Barfield, Richard	010	1729	Orig. Only	SS/AR
Barfield, Richard	035	c1754	087 DB-2/237	
Barfield, Richard	011	c1785	WB-1/474	
Barfield, Sarah	056	1866	WB-2/82	AR
Barfield, Solomon	103	1827	RD-5/327	
Barfield, Thomas	010	1770	WB-A/126	AR
Barfield, Turney	083	1845	WB-1/464	AR
Barfield, Willis	083	c1817	WB-1/130	AR
Barfiell, Samuel	010	1775	WB-B/28	AR
Barfoot, Isabel	087	c1797	WB-A/25	AR
Barge, Edward W.	029	1869	WB-E/5	AR
Barge, Elizabeth	083	1832	WB-1/278	AR
Barge, George K.	029	1823	WB-B/108	
Barge, Lewis	083	1830	WB-1/255	AR
Barge, Lewis, Sr.	029	1809	WB-A/137	AR
Barge, Mary	029	1833	WB-B/229	AR
Barge, Rachel	029	1840	WB-B/323	AR
Barger, Catharine	085	1822	WB-H/176	AR
Barger, Charles	085	1793	WB-D/142	AR
Barger, Elizabeth	085	1847	WB-K/56	AR
Barger, George H.	085	1820	WB-H/51	AR
Barger, John	016	1841	PQS.6/121	
Barger, John	021	1863	WB-1/179	AR
Barger, Leah	085	1891	WB-2/458	CTY
Barger, Martin	085	1865	WB-K/364	AR
Barger, Peter	085	1858	WB-K/267	AR
Barger, William	085	1858	WB-K/267	
Barham, Ann	099	1864	RB-33/261	
Barham, Benjamin	099	1832	RB-22/284	AR
Barham, Benjamin	099	1834	RB-23/212	AR
Barham, Jasper	099	1900	WB-D/333	AR
Barham, John	099	1825	RB-19/453	AR
Barham, John	099	c1825	SC/02120	AR-Copy
Barham, Joseph	071	1883	WB-6/409	AR
Barham, Joseph H.	VA	1882	051 WB-C/353	051 AR
Barham, Lavenia F.	071	1895	WB-7/257	AR
Barham, Louisa	071	1880	WB-6/327	AR
Barham, Mary	099	1830	RB-21/382	
Barham, Nathan	046	1856	WB-C/449	AR
Barham, William	099	1864	RB-33/261	AR
Barham, William	099	1807	RB-7/219	AR
Barham, William K.	100	1875	WB-51/79	AR
Barham, William M.	022	1849	WB-C/239	AR
Barham, Willis W.	071	1894	WB-7/217	AR
Baring, Charles	050	1866	WB-1/91	CTY
Baring, Susan	SC	c1830	050 WB-1/14	
Barino, Charles	097	1869	WB-2/15	
Bark, John	071	1835	WB-4/138	
Barker, Burrel	054	c1811	WB-1A/18	AR
Barker, Burrell	099	1844	RB-25/361	AR
Barker, Catey	085	1814	WB-G/329	AR
Barker, Charles J.	044	1885	WB-23/521	CTY
Barker, Clarence	NY	1896	013 WB-C/484	013 AR
Barker, Daniel	046	1892	WB-F/186	AR
Barker, David	020	1840	RB-O/3	
Barker, David C.	020	1847	RB-P/500	
Barker, E. B.	001	1865	WB-1/241	AR
Barker, Edmund	099	1815	RB-12/1	AR
Barker, Enoch	081	1848	WB-9/26	AR
Barker, George	001	1872	WB-2/23	AR
Barker, George	073	c1845	Orig. Only	AR
Barker, George	020	1788	RB-B/251	AR
Barker, Hosea	065	1815	WB-A/141	AR
Barker, Howel	106	c1858	WB-1/67	AR
Barker, Howell, Sr.	054	1847	WB-3/22	AR
Barker, Israel	020	1805	RB-E/205	AR
Barker, Jeremiah	081	1826	WB-5/253	AR
Barker, Jeremiah	092	1851	WB-4/319	
Barker, Joel	099	1779	RB-1/139	AR

Name	Co.	Date	Recorded Copy	Original
Barker, John	001	1866	WB-1/269	AR
Barker, John	044	1840	WB-14/492	CTY
Barker, John	081	1849	WB-9/112	AR
Barker, John	020	1830	RB-L/512	
Barker, John	068	1803	WB-A/225	
Barker, John G.	098	1890	WB-A/118	CTY
Barker, John N.	054	1886	WB-5/98	CTY
Barker, John, Sr.	054	c1808	WB-1/42	AR
Barker, Joseph	070	1855	WB-C/589	AR
Barker, Joshua	047	1792	WB-3/203	AR
Barker, Leander	092	1876	WB-6/78	AR
Barker, Lewis	104	1874	WB-6/97	AR
Barker, Mark	099	1819	RB-15/1	AR
Barker, Mary	077	1807	WB-E/300	AR
Barker, Mary	084	1800	OW/11	AR
Barker, Nicholas	081	1886	WB-16/12	AR
Barker, Nicholas	081	1826	WB-5/279	AR
Barker, Robert	081	1823	WB-5/108	AR
Barker, Robert	081	1854	Orig. Only	AR
Barker, Samuel	081	1808	WB-3/91	
Barker, Stephen	047	1785	WB-3/81	AR
Barker, Thomas	024	1787	WB-B/13	AR
Barker, Thomas	083	c1867	Orig. Only	AR
Barker, William	099	1862	RB-32/123	AR
Barker, William	099	1802	RB-6/6	AR
Barker, Young W.	099	1897	WB-D/65	AR
Barker, Zachariah	099	1861	RB-32/88	AR
Barkley, Allen	071	1845	WB-5/37	AR
Barkley, Archibald	021	1866	WB-1/220	AR
Barkley, Elizabeth	071	1884	WB-6/441	
Barkley, Etheldred	071	1857	WB-5/191	AR
Barkley, George	071	1788	WB-1/457	AR
Barkley, Hendry	085	c1798	WB-F/18	AR
Barkley, Henry P.	071	1835	WB-4/125	AR
Barkley, James	054	c1814	WB-1/327	AR
Barkley, Jesse T.	071	1882	WB-6/402	AR
Barkley, John A.	054	1893	WB-5/470	CTY
Barkley, Joseph G.	069	1896	WB-5/530	AR
Barkley, Moses	054	1871	WB-4/85	CTY
Barkley, Rhodes	071	1846	WB-5/51	AR
Barkley, Robert	085	c1786	WB-C/121	AR
Barkley, Robert	021	1894	WB-3/58	
Barkley, Samuel	085	c1802	WB-F/1	AR
Barkley, Samuel	085	c1804	WB-C/329	AR
Barkly, James	054	1868	WB-4/5	AR
Barks, Joseph	087	c1807	WB-A/49	AR
Barksdale, Cary	047	1788	WB-3/151	AR
Barksdale, Daniel	037	1835	WB-F/179	AR
Barksdale, Sherod	087	1889	WB-3/423	AR
Barksdale, Sherwood	029	1844	WB-C/61	AR
Barley, John	103	1799	WI-B/306	
Barlow, Cloe	075	1846	WB-N/201	AR
Barlow, David	037	1868	WB-G/313	AR
Barlow, David	037	1790	WB-C/130	AR
Barlow, John	017	c1855	WB-A/88	AR
Barlow, Lewis	037	1831	WB-F/127	AR
Barlow, Nancy	072	N. D.	WB-A/1	AR
Barlow, Robert	053	1752	028 DB-5/259	SS/AR
Barlow, William	099	1857	RB-30/351	AR
Barlow, William	073	1874	WB-H/90	CTY
Barlow, William R.	017	1866	WB-A/158	AR
Barnacasel, Beverly	010	1844	WB-G/371	AR
Barnacastle, Catharine	033	1851	WB-1/104	AR
Barnard, Andrew	025	1868	WB-A/11	
Barnard, Andrew J.	025	1886	WB-A/58	AR
Barnard, Benjamin	046	1792	WB-A/16	AR
Barnard, Benoni	009	1790	028 WB-A/230	028 AR
Barnard, Carter	075	1841	WB-N/166	AR
Barnard, Edmond	018	1856	WB-D/29	
Barnard, Edmund	030	1827	WB-3/221	
Barnard, Goram	046	1847	WB-C/284	AR
Barnard, Grandy	030	1852	WB-4/165	
Barnard, Grandy	030	1839	WB-4/62	
Barnard, Hulda	075	1769	WB-H/87	AR
Barnard, Jesse	018	1828	WB-C/105	
Barnard, Jesse	030	1829	WB-3/244	
Barnard, John	054	1893	WB-5/454	CTY
Barnard, Libni	046	1828	WB-B/362	AR
Barnard, Luke	030	c1810	WB-3/1	
Barnard, Mava	030	1843	WB-4/102	
Barnard, Nancy	030	1837	WB-4/26	
Barnard, Saml.	030	1774	WB-1/76	
Barnard, Samuel	030	1792	WB-1/251	
Barnard, Samuel	018	1848	WB-C/332	
Barnard, Samuel	030	1802	WB-2/199	
Barnard, Tristram	090	1807	WB-2/75	AR
Barnehill, Jane	003	c1864	Orig. Only	AR
Barner, Martha	090	1833	WB-3/260	AR
Barnes, A. Jackson	041	1860	WB-3/251	AR
Barnes, Aaron	003	1895	WB-B/334	AR
Barnes, Abraham	083	c1794	WB-1/35	AR
Barnes, Absalom	037	1792	WB-C/186	AR
Barnes, Alexander	032	1872	WB-3/57	AR
Barnes, Allen	028	1892	WB-F/23	
Barnes, Amelia E.	051	1896	WB-C/513	AR
Barnes, America	071	1816	WB-3/169	AR
Barnes, Archelaus	037	1807	WB-D/264	AR
Barnes, Aziel	037	1805	WB-D/230	AR
Barnes, B. J.	105	1893	WB-3/114	AR
Barnes, Barsha	069	1840	WB-1/438	AR
Barnes, Benjamin	069	1794	WB-1/91	AR
Barnes, Benjamin	041	1809	WB-2/48	AR
Barnes, Bennet	069	1859	WB-1/561	AR
Barnes, Bennett	103	1889	WB-1/482	AR
Barnes, Breton	037	1818	WB-E/191	AR
Barnes, Brice	072	1858	Orig. Only	AR
Barnes, Brinsley	003	1855	Orig. Only	AR
Barnes, Brittain	083	1827	WB-1/344	AR
Barnes, Britton	083	1824	WB-1/215	AR
Barnes, Bryan	037	1839	WB-F/236	AR
Barnes, Bryant L.	105	1868	WB-2/5	AR
Barnes, Burwell W.	037	1881	WB-G/592	AR
Barnes, Charity	103	1856	RD-12/135	AR
Barnes, Charity	069	1805	WB-1/161	AR
Barnes, Charles	037	1841	WB-F/252	AR
Barnes, Chesley	084	1840	WB-B/248	CTY
Barnes, Christian	041	1856	WB-3/202	AR
Barnes, Collin W.	071	1855	WB-5/131	AR
Barnes, Daniel	051	1892	WB-C/433	AR
Barnes, David A.	051	1892	WB-C/438	AR
Barnes, Dempsey	037	1807	WB-D/283	AR
Barnes, Dolly	103	1888	WB-1/449	
Barnes, Drewry	103	1816	RD-4/195	AR
Barnes, E. G.	098	1898	WB-A/300	CTY
Barnes, E. P.	084	1881	WB-E/219	CTY
Barnes, Edith	037	1849	WB-F/435	AR
Barnes, Edward	037	1762	WB-A/91	AR
Barnes, Edward B.	046	1891	WB-F/129	AR
Barnes, Edwin	037	1843	Orig. Only	AR-Nunc.
Barnes, Edwin	037	1807	WB-D/298	AR

Name	Co.	Date	Recorded Copy	Original
Barnes, Elias	105	1856	WB-1/30	AR
Barnes, Elias	056	1868	WB-2/114	AR
Barnes, Elizabeth	037	1794	WB-C/275	AR
Barnes, Elizabeth	041	1826	WB-2/245	AR
Barnes, Elizabeth	069	1828	WB-1/360	AR
Barnes, Elizabeth	056	1849	WB-1/618	AR
Barnes, Ephraim	105	1879	WB-2/240	AR
Barnes, Fanny	032	1874	WB-3/110	AR
Barnes, George	070	1774	WB-C/25	AR
Barnes, George B.	VA	1894	051 WB-C/474	051 AR
Barnes, George B.	VA	1894	071 WB-7/211	071 AR
Barnes, George W.	100	1848	WB-40/54	AR
Barnes, Hardy F.	105	1889	WB-2/511	AR
Barnes, Haywood W.	009	1900	WB-2/222	CTY
Barnes, Henry	010	1813	WB-F/233	AR
Barnes, Henry	071	1821	WB-3/256	AR
Barnes, Henry	056	1827	WB-1/342	AR
Barnes, Henry	056	1885	WB-3/392	AR
Barnes, Hezekiah	072	1798	Orig. Only	AR
Barnes, Hilman H.	044	1881	WB-23/395	CTY
Barnes, Jacob	083	c1822	WB-1/364	AR
Barnes, Jacob	105	1867	WB-1/73 & 132	AR
Barnes, Jacob	083	c1803	WB-1/184	AR
Barnes, Jacob	069	1846	WB-1/487	AR
Barnes, Jacob	099	1811	RB-10/1	AR
Barnes, Jacob	037	1764	WB-A/128	AR
Barnes, Jacob	069	1781	WB-1/21	AR
Barnes, Jacob J.	105	1900	WB-3/396	AR
Barnes, Jacob S.	105	1863	WB-1/92	AR
Barnes, James	029	1770	Orig. Only	AR
Barnes, James	037	1805	WB-D/223	AR
Barnes, James	051	1869	WB-C/11	AR
Barnes, James	041	1811	WB-2/67	AR
Barnes, James	069	1826	WB-1/333	AR
Barnes, James	047	1822	WB-3/679	AR
Barnes, James	047	1775	WB-2/20	Nunc.
Barnes, James A.	037	1849	WB-F/425	AR
Barnes, James D.	105	1877	WB-2/217	AR
Barnes, James R.	056	1888	WB-3/490	AR
Barnes, James S.	105	1873	WB-2/152	AR
Barnes, James T.	069	1866	WB-1/622	
Barnes, James W.	037	1845	WB-F/324	AR
Barnes, Jane C.	105	1892	WB-3/36	AR
Barnes, Jane E.	041	1891	WB-4/309	AR
Barnes, Jeremiah	104	1895	WB-6/543	AR
Barnes, Jesse	037	1843	WB-F/296	AR
Barnes, Jesse	103	c1804	WI-B/414	AR
Barnes, Jesse	051	1863	WB-B/52	AR
Barnes, Jesse D.	105	1866	WB-1/116	AR
Barnes, Jesse S.	105	1863	WB-1/96	AR
Barnes, Jethro	103	1816	RD-3/382	AR
Barnes, Jethro W.	051	1899	WB-C/564	AR
Barnes, Joel	069	1885	WB-5/222	AR
Barnes, John	103	1857	RD-12/245	AR
Barnes, John	037	1823	WB-E/342	AR
Barnes, John	103	1791	WI-A/224	AR
Barnes, John	047	1822	WB-3/675	AR
Barnes, John	069	1828	WB-1/358	AR
Barnes, John	003	1881	WB-B/130	AR
Barnes, John	010	1784	WB-C/75	AR
Barnes, John	046	1802	WB-A/33	AR
Barnes, John	069	1875	WB-5/28	AR
Barnes, John	104	1822	WB-4/21	AR
Barnes, John C.	075	1849	WB-N/226	AR
Barnes, John H.	071	1900	WB-7/468	AR

Name	Co.	Date	Recorded Copy	Original
Barnes, John J.	056	1886	WB-3/420	AR
Barnes, John J.	056	1898	WB-4/109	AR
Barnes, John M.	044	1872	WB-23/71	CTY
Barnes, John, Sr.	010	1778	WB-B/120	AR
Barnes, Johnathan	106	c1862	WB-1/86	AR
Barnes, Jonathan	030	1796	WB-2/67	
Barnes, Jordan	037	1822	WB-E/309	AR
Barnes, Joseph	037	1824	WB-F/21	AR
Barnes, Joseph	103	1828	RD-5/434	AR
Barnes, Josiah	083	1866	WB-2/234	AR
Barnes, Josiah	071	1836	WB-4/142	AR
Barnes, Josiah	083	c1806	WB-1/103	AR
Barnes, Julon	037	1824	WB-F/20	AR
Barnes, Lewis	051	1888	WB-C/366	AR
Barnes, Louisa	071	1866	WB-5/325	AR
Barnes, Lydia W.	051	1878	WB-C/205	AR
Barnes, Mahala	105	1873	WB-2/131	AR
Barnes, Martha	105	1856	WB-1/29	
Barnes, Mary	044	1824	WB-9/348	CTY
Barnes, Mary	069	1871	WB-1/609	AR
Barnes, Mary	105	1886	WB-2/386	AR
Barnes, Mary	103	1856	RD-12/208	AR
Barnes, Mary	069	1807	WB-1/172	AR
Barnes, Maryman	044	1810	WB-7/113	CTY
Barnes, Marzilla	105	1888	WB-2/462	AR
Barnes, Meredith	083	1891	Orig. Only	AR
Barnes, Michael	083	c1809	WB-1/115 & 134	AR
Barnes, Milbry	105	1885	WB-2/350	AR
Barnes, Milicent	105	1862	WB-1/82	AR
Barnes, Nancy	037	1835	WB-F/178	AR
Barnes, Nathan	037	1777	WB-A/247	AR
Barnes, Ned	105	1885	WB-2/357	AR
Barnes, Olivia	105	1894	Orig. Only	AR
Barnes, Patience	037	1818	WB-E/202	AR
Barnes, Patsey	105	1880	WB-2/265	AR
Barnes, Peggey	037	1816	WB-E/143	AR
Barnes, Peter	003	c1865	Orig. Only	AR
Barnes, Piety	069	1844	WB-1/461	AR
Barnes, Polly	037	1845	WB-F/327	AR
Barnes, Polly	069	1815	WB-1/270	AR
Barnes, Polly	037	1848	WB-F/397	AR
Barnes, Polly	037	c1843	Copy	105 AR
Barnes, Polly	103	1888	WB-1/449	AR
Barnes, Pricilla	105	1872	WB-2/104	AR
Barnes, Reddick	037	1835	WB-F/181	AR
Barnes, Richard	032	1854	WB-2/101	AR
Barnes, Sally	105	1872	WB-2/94	AR
Barnes, Samuel	103	1819	RD-4/246	AR
Barnes, Samuel	084	1863	WB-C/385	CTY
Barnes, Samuel	105	1857	WB-1/41	AR
Barnes, Samuel	103	1825	RD-5/201	AR
Barnes, Samuel J.	105	1873	WB-2/119	AR
Barnes, Sarah	037	1834	WB-F/161	AR
Barnes, Sarah	103	1831	RD-6/279	AR
Barnes, Sarah	037	1854	WB-G/56	AR
Barnes, Sarah	010	1854	WB-H/6	AR
Barnes, Sherard	105	1891	WB-2/570	AR-Copy
Barnes, Simon	103	1826	RD-5/218	AR
Barnes, Simon	103	1810	RD-1/250	
Barnes, Solomon	104	1807	WB-2/193	AR
Barnes, Solomon	104	1830	WB-4/144	
Barnes, Stephen	037	1823	WB-E/340	AR
Barnes, Susan Ann	103	1900	WB-2/315	AR
Barnes, Temperance	047	1841	WB-4/194	AR

Name	Co.	Date	Recorded Copy	Original
Barnes, Thomas	041	1782	WB-1/29	AR
Barnes, Thomas	041	1815	WB-2/95	AR
Barnes, Thomas	037	1761	WB-A/42	AR
Barnes, Thomas	075	1796	WB-L/74	AR
Barnes, William	047	c1779	WB-2/107	
Barnes, William	077	1826	WB-N/25	AR
Barnes, William	084	1861	WB-C/358	
Barnes, William	035	c1769	WB-A/55	AR
Barnes, William	105	1869	WB-2/10	AR
Barnes, William	105	1890	WB-2/560	AR
Barnes, William	105	1858	WB-1/52	AR
Barnes, William	069	1826	WB-1/334	AR
Barnes, William	044	1824	WB-9/303	CTY
Barnes, William	103	1851	RD-10/476	AR
Barnes, William	044	1850	WB-18/177	CTY
Barnes, William	032	1892	WB-4/175	AR
Barnes, William G.	105	1880	WB-2/246	AR
Barnes, William H.	065	1896	WB-M/529	AR
Barnes, Williamson	037	1814	WB-E/66	AR
Barnes, Willis	083	1855	WB-2/63	AR
Barnes, Winnifred	099	1826	RB-20/43	AR
Barnes, Wright	037	1857	Orig. Only	AR
Barnet, Hugh	065	1786	WB-A/137	AR
Barnet, Margaret	065	1834	WB-G/155	AR
Barnet, Robert	020	1777	RB-A/3	AR
Barnet, William	065	c1778	WB-A/131	AR
Barnett, A. F.	060	1889	WB-4/409	AR
Barnett, Able	065	1839	WB-E/226	AR
Barnett, Absalom	060	1873	WB-4/107	AR
Barnett, Currie	078	1854	WB-17/249	AR
Barnett, D. W.	065	1898	WB-N/169	AR
Barnett, David	026	1858	WB-1/233	AR
Barnett, Elijah	044	1846	WB-17/3	CTY
Barnett, George W.	001	1892	WB-2/550	AR
Barnett, Hezekiah	053	1866	WB-10/6	AR
Barnett, Hugh	065	1799	WB-A/130	AR
Barnett, Hugh	078	1796	WI-1/235	AR
Barnett, Hugh	078	1797	WI-2/20	AR
Barnett, James	078	1850	WB-13/341	AR
Barnett, James M.	078	1888	WB-19/231	AR
Barnett, James, Sr.	020	1804	RB-E/134	AR
Barnett, Jarrett	010	1894	WB-3/32	AR
Barnett, Jean	046	1805	WB-A/33	AR
Barnett, John	044	1857	WB-20/319	CTY
Barnett, John	065	1807	WB-A/92	AR
Barnett, John	078	1816	WI-7/80	AR
Barnett, John	065	1804	WB-A/83	AR
Barnett, John	084	1833	WB-B/82	CTY
Barnett, John	065	1829	WB-E/74	AR
Barnett, John	046	1781	WB-A/19	AR
Barnett, John S.	065	1832	WB-G/77	AR
Barnett, Joseph	060	1900	WB-5/145	AR
Barnett, Joseph	073	1773	WB-A/166	
Barnett, Joseph	044	1829	WB-11/83	CTY
Barnett, Joseph G.	044	1857	WB-20/338	CTY
Barnett, Luther R.	065	1900	WB-N/368	AR
Barnett, M. A.	065	1897	WB-N/49	AR
Barnett, Marcus	017	1896	WB-B/277	AR
Barnett, Margaret	065	1838	WB-E/201	AR
Barnett, Margaret	104	1872	WB-6/59	AR
Barnett, Mary	044	1863	WB-22/29	CTY
Barnett, Mary	044	1825	WB-10/78	CTY
Barnett, Mary A.	001	1898	WB-3/209	AR
Barnett, Matilda	044	1839	WB-14/460	CTY
Barnett, Moses	065	1798	WB-A/136	AR
Barnett, Nancy	086	1877	WB-F/92	AR
Barnett, Oliver N.	031	1893	WB-1/80	AR
Barnett, Robert	065	1830	WB-E/81	AR
Barnett, Robert C.	065	1864	WB-J/175	AR
Barnett, Samuel	060	1794	Orig. Only	AR
Barnett, Samuel C.	078	1883	WB-19/139	AR
Barnett, Sarah C.	044	1814	WB-7/366	CTY
Barnett, Thomas	065	1848	WB-I/127	AR
Barnett, Thomas	060	1885	WB-4/306	AR
Barnett, Thomas	078	1800	WI-2/257	AR
Barnett, Thomas	044	1780	WB-1/273	CTY
Barnett, Thomas	026	1866	WB-1/404	
Barnett, Thomas G.	065	1872	WB-K/87	AR
Barnett, William	044	1845	WB-16/336	CTY
Barnett, William	065	1823	WB-A/149	AR
Barnett, William	057	1796	WB-A/146	AR
Barnett, William	065	1785	WB-A/133	AR
Barnett, William	084	1831	WB-B/38	CTY
Barnett, William P.	065	1864	WB-J/188	AR
Barney, James	028	1824	WB-C/253	AR
Barney, Joseph S.	053	1832	WB-5/89	
Barneycastle, Pleasant	033	1878	WB-2/63	CTY
Barnhardt, Adam	016	1855	WB-1/248	
Barnhardt, George	016	1883	WB-3/410	AR
Barnhardt, George H.	016	1892	WB-4/123	AR
Barnhardt, George M.	085	1885	WB-2/111	CTY
Barnhardt, J. C.	016	1896	085 WB-3/199	085 CTY
Barnhardt, Jacob C.	065	1896	WB-M/487	AR
Barnhardt, Jacob C.	016	1896	WB-4/232	AR
Barnhardt, Jane A.	065	1899	WB-N/222	AR
Barnhart, Charles	016	1846	WB-1/97	
Barnhart, George	016	1833	PQS.5/259	
Barnhart, James E.H.	016	1882	WB-3/360	AR
Barnhart, John F.	016	1883	WB-3/380	AR
Barnhart, Philip	016	1838	PQS.5/510	
Barnhart, Polly	016	1871	WB-3/57	
Barnheart, Danl.	016	1879	WB-3/256	AR
Barnheart, Henry	016	1864	WB-2/112	
Barnhill, A. J.	011	1883	WB-2/159	
Barnhill, Catharine	011	1878	WB-2/105	
Barnhill, Daniel	079	1875	WB-2/119	AR
Barnhill, James H.	079	c1862	WB-1/155	AR
Barnhill, Jesse G.	047	c1862	WB-5/105	
Barnhill, John	079	c1864	WB-1/116	
Barnhill, Marina	079	1860	WB-1/47	AR
Barnhill, Martha	079	1892	WB-3/6	AR
Barnhill, Mary Ann	040	1885	WB-2/244	AR
Barnhill, Robert	073	1797	WB-C/100	AR
Barnhill, Robert W.	065	1863	WB-J/172	AR
Barnhill, Samuel	063	1842	WB-2/292	
Barnhill, Sarah A.	065	1868	WB-J/245	AR
Barnhill, Turner E.	063	1866	WB-2/540	
Barnhill, William	046	1791	WB-A/19	AR
Barns, Elizabeth	077	1777	WB-C/198	AR
Barns, George	049	c1825	WI-A/23	AR
Barns, John, Sr.	060	1794	Orig. Only	AR
Barns, Joseph	072	1755	Orig. Only	SS/AR
Barns, Joseph	071	1751	Orig. Only	SS/AR
Barns, Levira	071	1857	WB-5/195	
Barns, Selena	021	1861	WB-1/162	AR
Barns, Stephen	075	1808	WB-M1/174	AR
Barns, William	075	1774	WB-I/67	AR
Barnsfield, Anne	075	1721	SS 875/319	SS/AR
Barnwell, J. S.	020	1896	WB-B/267	CTY
Barnwell, James	073	1825	WB-E/82	AR

Name	Co.	Date	Recorded Copy	Original
Barnwell, Minnie L.	001	1900	WB-3/357	AR
Barnwell, R. I.	050	1891	WB-2/91	
Barnwell, Susan	001	1879	WB-1/117	AR
Barnwell, Susanah	001	c1853	WB-1/117	AR
Barnwell, William	050	1889	WB-2/53	CTY
Baros, Moses	008	1733/4	SS 876/269	SS/AR
Barr, David	065	1811	WB-A/140	AR
Barr, David	084	1856	WB-C/239	CTY
Barr, Isaac	090	1833	WB-3/247	
Barr, James	085	c1785	WB-C/102	AR
Barr, James S.	060	1872	WB-4/90	AR
Barr, John	092	1796	WB-3/20A	AR
Barr, John	085	c1804	WB-C/323	AR
Barr, John	085	1844	WB-I/238	AR
Barr, John C.	065	1868	WB-J/246	AR
Barr, John, Sr.	085	1831	WB-H/519	AR
Barr, Margaret	065	1822	WB-B/14	AR
Barr, Martha C.	065	1897	WB-N/44	AR
Barr, Robert	084	1838	WB-B/189	CTY
Barr, Robert D.	009	1852	Orig. Only	AR
Barr, Stephen	097	1846	WB-1/36	AR
Barr, William	085	c1789	WB-D/149	AR
Barr, William	085	1767	WB-A/10	AR
Barr, William	085	1842	WB-I/122	AR
Barr, William	041	1823	WB-2/199	AR
Barradalle, Joseph	010	1762	WB-A/15	AR
Barren, James	018	1859	WB-D/48	
Barret, Margaret	075	1838	WB-N/145	AR
Barret, Thomas	057	1809	WB-A/319	AR
Barrett, Davis G.	069	1872	WB-1/613	AR
Barrett, Dominick	005	1840	WB-B/114	AR
Barrett, Jane E.	005	1891	WB-D/303	AR
Barrett, John	010	1803	WB-E/198	AR
Barrett, Jonathan	032	1840	WB-1/354	AR
Barrett, Margaret	005	1879	WB-D/76	AR
Barrett, Mary	026	1874	WB-2/106	AR
Barrett, Mary	051	1850	WB-A/312	
Barrett, Nancy	069	1859	WB-1/564	AR
Barrett, Perry	068	1896	WB-D/459	
Barrett, Thomas	005	1887	WB-D/233	AR
Barrett, Thomas	005	1823	WB-2/4	AR
Barrett, Thomas	071	1800	WB-2/197	AR
Barrett, William A.	005	1887	WB-D/227	Nunc.
Barrier, Caleb	016	1862	WB-2/88	
Barrier, Daniel	016	1887	WB-3/531	AR
Barrier, David	016	1866	WB-2/139	
Barrier, Edmond B.	016	1863	WB-2/99	
Barrier, Edmund	016	1870	WB-3/22	
Barrier, George H.	016	1862	WB-2/91	
Barrier, John	016	1889	WB-4/48	AR
Barrier, Mathias	016	1873	WB-3/91	AR
Barrier, Millie	016	1891	WB-4/78	AR
Barrier, Moses	016	1882	WB-3/347	AR
Barrier, Nelson	016	1864	WB-2/109	
Barrier, Philip	032	1853	WB-2/91	AR
Barrier, Rufus A.	016	1876	WB-3/175	AR
Barrier, Sophy	016	1884	WB-3/428	AR
Barrier, Susanna	032	1826	WB-1/50	
Barrier, W. A.	065	1890	WB-L/495	AR
Barringer, Catharine	016	1848	WB-1/144	
Barringer, Catharine	085	1855	WB-K/190	AR
Barringer, Christina	085	1863	WB-K/311	AR
Barringer, David	021	1884	WB-2/283	
Barringer, David	085	1895	WB-3/95	CTY
Barringer, E. G. L.	067	1890	WB-2/279	AR
Barringer, H. A.	021	1863	WB-1/171	AR
Barringer, John	016	1888	WB-3/575	AR
Barringer, John	016	1834	PQS.5/270	
Barringer, John	054	1859	WB-3/141	AR
Barringer, Margaret	016	1858	WB-2/40	
Barringer, Margarett	099	1879	WB-A/87	AR
Barringer, Mary M.	054	1873	WB-4/113	CTY
Barringer, Matthew	089	1853	WB-1/104	
Barringer, Moses	085	1874	WB-1/243	CTY
Barringer, Nelson	089	1883	WB-2/104	AR
Barringer, Nicholas	085	1841	WB-I/97	AR
Barringer, Noah	021	1896	WB-3/116	AR
Barringer, P.	016	1844	WB-1/47	
Barringer, Paul	016	1845	WB-1/59	
Barringer, Peter	085	1827	WB-H/390	AR
Barringer, Rufus	065	1895	WB-M/336	AR
Barrington, John	028	1807	WB-B/294	AR
Barrington, Martha	028	1840	WB-D/22	
Barriot, John	030	1801	WB-2/183	
Barron, Barnaby	069	1793	WB-1/81	AR
Barron, David	028	1778	Orig. Only	AR
Barron, James	037	1848	Orig. Only	AR
Barron, Thomas	037	1777	WB-A/252	AR
Barronton, Nathan	019	1786	WB-D/76	AR
Barrott, John	030	1795	WB-2/53	
Barrott, William	030	1793	WB-2/16	
Barroud, Francis	063	1821	WB-2/77	
Barrow, Abraham	072	c1799	WB-A/8	AR
Barrow, Abraham	072	1798	Orig. Only	AR
Barrow, Alfred S.	077	1842	WB-F/304	AR
Barrow, Ann	053	1812	RW-1/459	AR
Barrow, Arodi	077	1808	WB-E/284	AR
Barrow, Bezer	053	1802	RW-1/347	AR
Barrow, Daniel	100	1797	WB-9/104	AR
Barrow, Edmund	071	1758	SS 882/33	SS/AR
Barrow, Elizabeth	009	c1811	OB-A/177	AR
Barrow, Eri	077	1832	WB-F/209	AR
Barrow, Frederic	009	1827	OB-A/384	AR
Barrow, Fredrick	009	1841	OB-D/137	AR/CRX
Barrow, George	053	1801	RW-1/329	
Barrow, George	053	c1788	RW-1/180	
Barrow, George W.	009	1870	WB-1/63	AR
Barrow, Jacob	047	1790	WB-3/179	AR
Barrow, Jaemina	077	1900	WB-H/336	AR
Barrow, James	024	1719	SS 875/151	SS/AR
Barrow, James	039	1817	WB-E/132	AR
Barrow, John	053	1748	SS 877/258	SS/AR
Barrow, John	077	1718	Orig. Only	AR
Barrow, John	077	1719	SS 875/146	SS/AR
Barrow, John	077	1742	Orig. Only	SS/AR
Barrow, John	009	1781	OWB/167	AR
Barrow, John, Jr.	077	1807	WB-E/274	AR
Barrow, John, Sr.	077	1718	SS 875/174	SS/AR
Barrow, Joseph	009	1752	028 DB-5/272	SS/AR
Barrow, Joseph	077	1755	Orig. Only	SS/AR
Barrow, Joseph N.	077	1837	WB-F/261	AR
Barrow, Joseph W.	077	1856	WB-F/476	AR
Barrow, Joseph, Jr.	077	1753	SS 881/32	SS/AR
Barrow, Martha	009	1790	OWB/244	AR
Barrow, Mary J.	038	1889	WB-3/118	AR
Barrow, Moses	090	1840	WB-4/65	AR
Barrow, Moses	038	1877	WB-2/318	AR
Barrow, Phillip	038	1872	WB-2/71	AR
Barrow, Rebekah	077	1722	Orig. Only	SS/AR
Barrow, Senus	072	1831	WB-1/88	AR

Name	Co.	Date	Recorded Copy	Original
Barrow, Susan E.	009	1896	WB-2/101	CTY
Barrow, T. A.	010	1893	WB-I/384	AR
Barrow, Theophilus	077	1826	WB-F/113	AR
Barrow, Thomas	072	1839	WB-2/18	AR
Barrow, Thomas	056	1810	WB-1/218	AR
Barrow, Thomas	072	c1761	RW/L55	AR
Barrow, Thomas	009	1806	OWB/435	AR
Barrow, Thomas	053	1762	OB-A/54	AR
Barrow, William	053	1717	SS 875/115	SS/AR
Barrow, William	037	1758	SS 881/221	SS/AR
Barrow, William	053	c1802	RW-1/412	
Barrow, William	009	1793	OWB/292	AR
Barrow, William	053	1746	SS 877/344	SS/AR
Barrow, William	075	1797	WB-L/107	AR
Barrow, William	047	1787	WB-3/118	AR
Barrow, William M.	024	1841	WB-C/228	AR
Barrow, William T.	009	1835	OB-B/532	AR
Barrow, Z. W.	053	1848	WB-7/177	AR
Barrow, Zachariah	072	1799	WB-A/12	AR
Barrow, Zachariah	053	1796	RW-1/269	AR
Barrus, Eliza A.	057	1879	WB-C/70	AR
Barrus, Roscoe	057	1871	WB-C/11	AR
Barry, Albert	028	1794	WB-A/307	AR
Barry, Amey	030	1784	WB-1/196	
Barry, Andrew	065	c1844	WB-H/168	AR
Barry, Andrew	060	1839	WB-2/18	AR
Barry, Ann	065	1842	WB-H/80	AR
Barry, Buckner	072	1852	WB-2/119	AR
Barry, Daniel	028	1779	Orig. Only	AR
Barry, Esther	072	1844	WB-2/55	AR
Barry, Hugh	065	1837	WB-E/204	AR
Barry, Jane	065	1864	WB-J/190	AR
Barry, John	VA	1788	024 WB-B/30	024 AR
Barry, Mary	065	1869	WB-K/3	AR
Barry, Mary S.	065	1876	WB-K/232	AR
Barry, Thomas	010	1795	WB-D/298	AR
Barry, William	008	1721	SS 875/338	SS/AR
Bart, Elizabeth	085	1821	Orig. Only	AR-Nunc.
Bart, William	047	1805	WB-3/445	
Bartee, William	077	1799	WB-E/107	AR
Bartee, William B.	077	c1832	WB-F/252	AR
Bartelitt, William	100	1807	WB-14/114	AR
Bartholomew, Lewis	039	1889	WB-U/482	AR
Bartholomew, Samuel	070	1779	WB-C/28	AR
Bartholomew, William	085	1771	WB-A/18	AR
Bartie, Anthony	024	c1792	WB-A/81	AR
Bartie, Robert	096	1838	WB-2/141	AR
Bartleson, Elizabeth	059	1885	WB-A/422	CTY
Bartleson, Richard	085	c1778	WB-D/134	AR
Bartlett, C. B.	046	1821	WB-B/139	AR
Bartlett, Hasten	020	1837	RB-N/13	AR
Bartlett, James	065	1871	WB-K/112	AR
Bartlett, Mary	018	1862	WB-D/66	AR
Bartlett, Sarah	103	1836	RD-7/197	AR
Bartlett, William	077	1698	Copy	024 AR
Bartlett, William	028	1799	WB-B/70	AR
Bartlett, William	077	1698	SS 874.2/97	SS/AR
Bartlett, William	018	1852	WB-C/366	
Bartley, Mary	046	1886	WB-E/449	AR
Bartley, Sarah	090	1820	WB-3/54	
Bartley, William	092	1816	WB-3/119	AR
Barton, Charles	020	1785	RB-B/88	AR
Barton, Eleanor	073	1857	WB-G/166	AR
Barton, Elizabeth	081	1818	WB-4/602	AR
Barton, Elizabeth	020	1835	RB-M/498	
Barton, Hetty	073	1896	WB-I/81	CTY
Barton, John	081	1795	WB-2/12	AR
Barton, Lewis	020	1831	RB-M/15	AR
Barton, Lewis	084	1849	WB-C/91	CTY
Barton, Temperance	073	1873	WB-H/77	CTY
Barton, Thomas	073	1847	WB-F/366	AR
Barton, Vallentin	002	1686	Orig. Only	SS/AR
Barton, William	081	1787	WB-1/39	AR
Barton, William	073	1888	WB-H/453	CTY
Barton, William	073	1804	WB-D/120	
Bartram, Elizabeth	011	1772	SS 881/306	SS/AR
Barwick, Alexander	059	1894	WB-B/84	CTY
Barwick, Craven T.	059	1885	WB-A/429	CTY
Barwick, Edith	059	1884	WB-A/379	CTY
Barwick, William	070	1779	WB-C/26	AR
Basden, Cordil	072	c1800	WB-A/17	AR
Basden, Richard	072	1853	WB-2/130	AR
Basden, Rilley	072	1863	Orig. Only	AR
Basden, Sally	072	1848	WB-2/91	AR
Basden, William	072	c1885	WB-4/197	AR
Baseman, J. B.	047	c1898	WB-7/208	
Bashford, Alexander	037	1791	WB-C/161	AR
Bashford, Thomas	099	1881	WB-A/262	AR
Bashier, Conrad	085	1846	WB-K/35	
Basinger, Elizabeth	065	1900	WB-N/356	AR
Baskerville, George D.	100	1862	WB-49/426	AR
Baskerville, George T.	044	1863	WB-22/75	CTY
Basket, Elizabeth	100	1796	WB-8/316	AR
Basket, Joseph	098	1888	WB-A/94	CTY
Basket, Mary E.	098	1892	WB-A/140	CTY
Basket, Pleasant	100	1837	WB-36/167	
Basket, Rebecca	100	1848	WB-40/48	AR
Baskett, James	100	1789	WB-5/25	AR
Baskett, John	073	c1771	WB-A/135	
Baskett, William	073	1767	WB-A/72	
Basnett, Josiah	030	1785	WB-1/199	
Basnett, Willoughby	030	1822	WB-3/134	
Basnight, B. S.	096	1871	WB-4/16	
Basnight, Dorkis	096	1833	Orig. Only	AR
Basnight, Jacob	096	1800	WB-2/66	
Basnight, James	096	1814	WB-2/60	AR
Basnight, Jonathan	096	1838	WB-2/140	AR
Basnight, Joseph	101	1885	WB-A/147	AR
Basnight, Lemuel	096	1839	WB-2/145	AR
Basnight, Thomas	096	1873	WB-4/29	
Bason, Henry	001	1858	WB-1/148	AR
Bason, Isaac	046	1847	WB-C/261	
Bason, Joseph	001	1849	WB-1/8	AR
Bason, Joseph R.	001	1885	WB-2/263	AR
Bason, William F.	001	1889	WB-2/440	AR
Bass, Abraham	069	1805	WB-1/157	AR
Bass, Absalom	103	1827	RD-5/391	
Bass, Andrew	087	1786	WB-A/19	
Bass, Andrew	103	1791	WI-A/241	AR
Bass, Andrew	028	1770	Orig. Only	AR
Bass, Anna	039	1817	WB-F/43	AR
Bass, Arthur	103	1824	RD-5/78	AR
Bass, Bardin	105	1863	WB-1/91	AR
Bass, Becky Ann	069	1899	WB-6/69	AR
Bass, Benjamin	047	1877	WB-6/170	AR
Bass, Boyakin	039	1827	WB-H/195	AR
Bass, Burgess	071	1794	WB-2/47	AR
Bass, Cader	010	1791	WB-D/155	AR
Bass, Cader	024	1847	WB-C/280	AR
Bass, Council	071	1830	WB-4/74	AR

Name	Co.	Date	Recorded Copy	Original
Bass, Darling	044	1845	WB-16/334	
Bass, David	069	1896	WB-6/4	AR
Bass, Dempsey	044	1828	WB-10/405	CTY
Bass, Dennis	047	1818	WB-3/624	AR
Bass, Drewry	071	1866	WB-5/320	AR
Bass, E.	054	1888	WB-5/203	CTY
Bass, Edward	071	1751	Orig. Only	SS/AR
Bass, Edward	006	1845	WB-A/68	AR
Bass, Edward	044	1800	WB-5/116	CTY
Bass, Ephraim	103	1828	RD-5/454	AR
Bass, Felix	087	1835	WB-1/172	AR
Bass, Isaac	069	1801	WB-1/136	AR
Bass, Isaac	047	1825	WB-4/9	AR
Bass, Jacob	010	1810	WB-F/150	AR
Bass, Jacob	103	1865	RD-14/237	AR
Bass, Jacob	024	1855	WB-C/383	AR
Bass, James	083	1888	WB-3/416	AR
Bass, James R.	075	1879	WB-0/100	AR
Bass, Jesse	069	1822	WB-1/323	AR
Bass, Jesse	105	1887	WB-2/434	
Bass, Jethro	071	1795	WB-2/73	AR
Bass, John	087	1887	WB-3/358	AR
Bass, John	071	1828	WB-4/40	AR
Bass, John	047	1786	WB-3/116	AR
Bass, John	010	1732	SS 876/305	SS/AR
Bass, John	071	1777	WB-1/292	
Bass, John C.	097	1890	WB-2/345	AR
Bass, Jordan	081	1808	WB-3/90	AR
Bass, Joshua	087	1829	WB-1/98	AR
Bass, Julian	103	1853	RD-11/355	AR
Bass, Lewis	018	1899	WB-E/302	AR
Bass, Lewis G.	035	1886	WB-4/281	AR
Bass, Lucy	069	1872	WB-1/613	AR
Bass, Mahala	020	1882	WB-A/387	CTY
Bass, Manerva	069	1895	WB-5/513	AR
Bass, Mary	083	1869	WB-3/7	AR
Bass, Mildred	069	1845	WB-1/473	AR
Bass, Mordecai	105	1900	WB-3/403	AR
Bass, Mourning	069	1875	WB-5/18	AR
Bass, Nancy	069	1812	WB-1/224	AR
Bass, Nancy	103	1814	RD-3/180	AR
Bass, Nathan	044	1837	WB-14/20	CTY
Bass, Penelope	105	1876	WB-2/179	
Bass, Perry	105	1896	WB-3/220	AR
Bass, Rhoda	087	1853	WB-1/424	AR
Bass, Richard	035	1781	WB-A/31	AR
Bass, Richard	097	1866	WB-1/276	
Bass, Sallie T.	083	1898	WB-4/209	AR
Bass, Samuel	071	1790	WB-1/408	AR
Bass, Simon	047	1825	WB-4/15	AR
Bass, Stephen	056	1874	WB-3/119	AR
Bass, Terissa	054	1865	WB-3/175	AR
Bass, Thomas	105	1896	WB-3/181	AR
Bass, Thomas	010	1766	WB-A/68	AR
Bass, Thomas	105	1896	103 WB-7/227	103 AR
Bass, Turner	047	1873	WB-6/93	AR
Bass, W. S.	054	1863	Orig. Only	AR
Bass, Warren	039	1806	WB-C/43	
Bass, William	087	1853	WB-1/429	AR
Bass, William	087	c1802	WB-A/33	AR
Bass, William	103	1874	WB-1/73	AR
Bass, William	103	1858	RD-12/493	AR
Bass, William	103	1888	WB-1/428	AR
Bass, William A.	056	1890	WB-3/535	AR
Bass, William R.	070	1872	WB-E/274	AR
Bass, Wright	103	1850	RD-10/398	AR
Bastable, William	077	1728	SS 876/123	SS/AR
Batchelder, James	053	1780	RW-1/98	
Batcheler, Edward	N	c1706	Orig. Only	SS/AR
Batcheler, Stephen	039	c1801	WB-B/81	
Batchelor, Abel	069	1899	WB-6/80	AR
Batchelor, Charlotte	069	1872	WB-1/612	AR
Batchelor, Cullen	069	1849	WB-1/515	AR
Batchelor, Drury	069	1864	WB-1/589	AR
Batchelor, Edith	069	1862	Orig. Only	AR
Batchelor, Edward	028	1777	Orig. Only	SS/AR
Batchelor, James	069	1820	Orig. Only	AR
Batchelor, James W.	047	1850	WB-4/296	AR
Batchelor, John	069	1849	WB-1/517	AR
Batchelor, John A.	069	1896	WB-5/534	AR
Batchelor, Louisa W.	039	1874	WB-U/91	AR
Batchelor, Mary Ann	069	1892	WB-5/388	AR
Batchelor, Mary C.	099	1900	WB-D/424	AR
Batchelor, Nancy P.	069	1892	WB-5/381	AR
Batchelor, Nathan W.	069	1894	WB-5/451	AR
Batchelor, Samuel	069	1827	WB-1/347	AR
Batchelor, Samuel	069	1866	WB-1/599	AR
Batchelor, Samuel Mc.	069	1864	WB-1/590	AR
Batchelor, Solomon	039	1869	WB-U/15	AR
Batchelor, Stephen	069	1806	WB-1/165	AR
Batchelor, William	069	1805	WB-1/153	AR
Batchelor, William J.	069	1865	WB-1/593	AR
Batchelor, Wright S.	069	1845	WB-1/493	AR
Bate, Henry L.	N	1740	LGB-4/#113	SS/AR
Bate, Margery	070	1894	WB-G/192	AR
Bateman, Benjamin	077	c1780	Orig. Only	AR
Bateman, Benjamin	096	1818	Orig. Only	AR
Bateman, Daniel H.	096	1841	WB-3/1	
Bateman, Henry	096	1859	WB-3/58	AR
Bateman, Hopkins	028	1803	Orig. Only	AR
Bateman, Isaac B.	101	1881	WB-A/55	AR
Bateman, James	084	c1816	WB-A/151	CTY
Bateman, Jasper	101	1890	Orig. Only	AR
Bateman, John	037	1803	WB-D/186	AR
Bateman, John	024	1818	WB-C/66	AR
Bateman, John	077	1750	Orig. Only	SS/AR
Bateman, John	096	c1812	WB-2/30	
Bateman, John, Jr.	096	1783	WB-1/134	AR
Bateman, Jonathan	002	1695	Orig. Only	SS/AR
Bateman, Jonathan	096	1761	WB-1/20	AR
Bateman, Jonathan	077	1802	WB-E/160	AR
Bateman, Joseph	096	1844	WB-3/9	
Bateman, Levi	101	1820	WB-A/226	AR
Bateman, Levi	096	1820	WB-2/82	AR
Bateman, Lloyd	101	1885	WB-A/132	AR
Bateman, Lois	096	1849	WB-3/22	AR
Bateman, Mary	101	1875	WB-A/15	AR
Bateman, Nancy E.	101	1898	WB-A/314	AR
Bateman, Nathan	096	1815	WB-2/58	AR
Bateman, Nathan	096	1790	WB-1/170	AR
Bateman, Nehemiah	024	1785	WB-A/126	AR
Bateman, Pattie E.	024	1893	WB-E/211	AR
Bateman, Thomas	077	1766	WB-C/60	AR
Bateman, William	077	1773	WB-C/126	AR
Bateman, William	030	1704	Orig. Only	SS/AR
Bateman, William	024	c1780	WB-A/108	AR
Bateman, Wilson H.	096	1886	WB-4/128	AR
Bates, Andrew	030	1823	WB-3/162	
Bates, Daniel	072	1777	RW/L18	AR
Bates, Daniel	085	c1765	WB-A/14	AR

Name	Co.	Date	Recorded Copy	Original
Bates, Dempsey B.	037	1885	WB-H/18	
Bates, Henry G.	028	1890	WB-E/554	AR
Bates, John	030	1792	WB-1/255	
Bates, Larkin A.	017	1846	WB-A/36	
Bates, Samuel	084	c1803	WB-A/146	CTY
Bates, William	105	1898	WB-3/315	
Batey, Rebecca	040	1848	WB-1/6	
Batman, Stephen	063	1849	WB-2/346	
Batmon, Thomas	028	1779	Orig. Only	AR
Batson, Batt	070	1839	WB-C/42	AR
Batson, Emma P.	076	1892	WB-A1/172	AR
Batson, John	070	1848	WB-C/482	AR
Batt, John	070	1803	WB-C/37	AR
Batten, Abraham	056	1860	WB-1/737	
Batten, Daniel	027	1899	WB-2/149	AR
Batten, James	067	1882	WB-2/150	AR
Batten, James	067	1855	WB-1/69	AR
Batten, James H.	056	1874	WB-3/115	AR
Batten, John	056	1857	WB-1/699	AR
Batten, Jorg	030	1800	WB-2/159	
Batten, Pleasant	056	1865	WB-2/62	AR
Batten, W. H.	056	1888	WB-3/487	AR
Batters, Thomas	008	1734	SS 876/339	SS/AR
Battle, Abner	072	c1801	WB-A/7	AR
Battle, Allen	037	1872	WB-G/374	AR
Battle, Benjamin	069	1858	WB-1/557	AR
Battle, Dempsey	037	1815	WB-E/91	AR
Battle, Dossey	037	1900	WB-H/466	AR
Battle, Elisha	037	1799	WB-D/90	AR
Battle, Ephraim	072	1798	Orig. Only	AR
Battle, Ephraim	072	c1798	Copy	028 AR
Battle, Frances	037	1806	WB-D/253	AR
Battle, George C.	037	1891	WB-H/193	AR
Battle, Iva I. S.	069	1895	WB-5/477	AR
Battle, Jacob	037	1815	WB-E/96	AR
Battle, James	069	1803	WB-1/255	AR
Battle, James	051	1832	WB-A/178	
Battle, James	051	c1826	WB-A/123	
Battle, James L.	037	1884	WB-G/640	
Battle, James S.	100	1894	WB-51/360	
Battle, James S.	037	1854	WB-G/71	AR
Battle, James, Sr.	029	1812	WB-A/184	AR
Battle, James, Sr.	099	1852	RB-28/90	AR
Battle, Jane	099	1852	RB-28/85	AR
Battle, Jason	069	1878	WB-5/75	AR
Battle, John	037	1774	WB-A/211	AR
Battle, John	010	1740	LGB-4/#127	SS/AR
Battle, John	037	1796	WB-C/358	AR
Battle, Joseph J.	037	1889	WB-H/140	AR
Battle, Joseph S.	037	1847	WB-F/366	AR
Battle, Josiah	099	1815	RB-12/225	AR
Battle, Martha	069	1870	Copy	039 AR
Battle, Mary	099	1831	RB-21/383	AR
Battle, Mary P.	073	1866	WB-G/495	CTY
Battle, Pene	028	1897	WB-F/261	
Battle, Randolph	022	1837	WB-C/61	AR
Battle, Richard H.	099	1882	WB-A/377	AR
Battle, T. W.	037	1895	WB-H/330	AR
Battle, Thomas	072	1788	WI/L6	AR
Battle, Thomas	072	c1769	RW/L51	AR
Battle, W. H.	005	1893	WB-D/332	AR
Battle, William	051	1779	WB-A/42	
Battle, William H.	073	1879	WB-H/200	CTY
Battle, William L.	069	1859	WB-1/562	AR
Batton, David	056	1885	WB-3/372	AR

Name	Co.	Date	Recorded Copy	Original
Batton, Hardy	056	1815	WB-1/239	AR
Batts, Bailey	105	c1840	WB-1/27	AR
Batts, Benjamin	037	1807	WB-D/290	AR
Batts, Benjamin	037	1860	WB-G/188	AR
Batts, David	105	c1855	WB-1/22	AR-Copy
Batts, Demce	076	1888	WB-A1/93	AR
Batts, Jeremiah	105	1886	WB-2/417	AR
Batts, Jesse	035	1868	WB-3/127	AR
Batts, John	105	1858	WB-1/45	AR
Batts, John	105	1872	WB-2/64	AR
Batts, John	076	1898	WB-A1/228	AR
Batts, John B.	069	1897	WB-6/13	AR
Batts, Joseph	037	1807	WB-D/292	AR
Batts, Lewis	035	1862	WB-3/47	AR
Batts, Lucy	037	1867	WB-G/309	AR
Batts, Marry	105	1888	WB-2/480	AR
Batts, Nathaniel	035	1896	WB-4/478	AR
Batts, Polly	105	c1861	WB-1/112	
Batts, Thomas R.	105	1886	WB-2/408	
Batts, William	037	1806	WB-D/255	AR
Batts, William	105	1856	WB-1/31	AR
Batts, William	105	1898	WB-3/317	AR
Battson, Peter	070	1822	WB-C/41	AR
Baty, Elizabeth	065	1828	WB-A/228	AR
Baucom, Don	005	1899	WB-D/451	AR
Baucom, John	099	1834	Orig. Only	AR
Baucom, John	099	1800	RB-5/93	AR
Baucom, John	099	1898	WB-D/158	AR
Baucom, Maria A.	099	1898	WB-D/160	
Baucom, Sallie	056	1898	WB-4/125	AR
Baucom, Sanders	097	1870	WB-2/35	AR
Baucom, Troy	099	1899	WB-D/269	AR
Baucom, Urias	056	1879	WB-3/230	AR
Baucom, Wiley	099	1891	WB-B/579	AR
Baucom, Willis	005	1880	WB-D/102	AR
Baucum, Alfred	005	1882	WB-D/132	AR
Baucum, Sarah Ann	099	1852	RB-27/399	
Baucum, Willie	005	1839	WB-B/95	AR
Baugert, Francis W.	028	1893	WB-F/90	
Baugess, Richard	104	1822	WB-4/25	AR
Baugh, Madison	099	1886	WB-B/105	AR
Baugham, Elisha	071	1860	WB-5/232	AR
Baughcomb, Thomas	056	1762	DB-D/L104	
Baughn, William R.	084	1899	WB-F/150	CTY
Baughn, Zairiah	078	1792	WI-1/24	AR
Baum, Abraham	030	1888	WB-5/158	AR
Baum, Abram	053	1896	WB-11/325	AR
Baum, Anna	030	1867	WB-4/265	AR
Baum, Joseph	030	1854	WB-4/186	AR
Baum, Joseph	030	1861	WB-4/244	AR
Baum, Maurice	030	1784	WB-1/172	
Baum, Maurice	030	1805	WB-2/263	
Baum, Mauris	030	1840	WB-4/70	
Baum, Peter	075	1807	WB-M1/152	AR
Baum, Robert	071	1844	WB-5/8	AR
Baum, Sally	030	1837	WB-4/24	
Baum, Thomas	053	1876	WB-11/56	AR
Baumann, A.	099	1892	WB-C/86	AR
Bawcomb, Nicholes	056	c1762	Orig. Only	AR
Bawstick, Mary	009	1831	OB-B/89	AR
Baxly, William	083	1831	WB-1/257	AR
Baxter, Andrew	065	c1775	WB-A/96	AR
Baxter, Bernard	070	1862	WB-D/101	AR
Baxter, Isaac	030	1860	WB-4/234	AR
Baxter, J. J.	030	1889	WB-5/167	AR

Name	Co.	Date	Recorded Copy	Original
Baxter, Joseph	030	1879	WB-5/60	
Baxter, Joseph	030	1822	WB-3/130	
Baxter, Joseph W.	028	1882	WB-E/315	
Baxter, Joshua	030	1786	WB-1/204	
Baxter, Mary	030	1858	WB-4/226	
Baxter, Nathaniel	100	1816	WB-20/126	AR
Baxter, Oscar F.	075	1895	WB-O/409	AR
Baxter, Oscar F.	075	1895	018 WB-E/273	018 AR
Baxter, P. F.	060	1897	WB-5/50	AR
Baxter, Peter	060	1808	Orig. Only	AR
Baxter, Samuel	085	c1828	WB-H/433	AR
Baxter, Sarah	030	1843	WB-4/93 & 99	
Baxter, Thomas	020	1790	RB-B/324	AR
Baxter, Thomas F.	030	1891	WB-5/186	AR
Baxter, William	086	1853	WB-E/232	AR
Baxter, William	086	1838	SC/06863	AR-Copy
Baxter, William	086	1838	WB-E/53	AR
Bay, J. R.	055	1898	WB-A/147	
Bayard, John	024	1716	Orig. Only	SS/AR
Bayer, Edward	024	1696	SS 874.2/89	SS/AR
Bayers, George	044	1785	WB-1/426	CTY
Bayles, Joseph A.	014	1894	WB-2/536	
Bayley, John	024	1716	SS 875/108	
Bayley, Thomas	010	c1785	WB-D/46	AR
Bayley, Thomas	077	1727	Orig. Only	SS/AR
Baylis, John	047	1768	WB-1/230	
Bayly, Ann	010	1870	WB-I/73	AR
Bayly, Miles	010	1893	WB-I/368	AR
Bayne, William H.	029	1851	WB-C/195	AR
Bayner, Alfred	009	1828	OB-A/505	AR
Bayner, Wiley	009	1832	OB-B/226	AR
Baynes, Barbara H.	020	2897	WB-B/292	CTY
Baynes, James	046	1877	WB-E/210	AR
Baynor, Eli	009	1887	WB-1/439	CTY
Baynor, Emeline	009	1892	WB-1/540	CTY
Baynor, Louisa	009	1858	OB-K/402	CTY
Baynor, Virginia	101	1893	WB-A/241	AR
Bazemore, Alden	010	1900	WB-K/27	
Bazemore, Amelia	010	1846	WB-G/406	AR
Bazemore, James	010	1805	WB-E/250 & 271	
Bazemore, James N.	010	1897	WB-I/510	AR
Bazemore, Jesse	010	1809	WB-F/96	AR
Bazemore, Jesse	010	c1800	Orig. Only	AR
Bazemore, Jesse, Jr.	010	1807	WB-F/42	AR
Bazemore, John	010	1790	WB-D/129	AR
Bazemore, Mary A.	010	1896	WB-I/476	AR
Bazemore, Reddin	010	1878	WB-I/97	
Bazemore, Stephen	010	1867	WB-H/192	AR
Beach, Benjamin	017	c1848	WB-A/45	
Beach, Rebecca	027	1879	WB-2/38	AR
Beach, Silas C.	070	1849	WB-C/494	AR
Beach, Thomas	063	1794	WB-1/203	
Beach, William	017	1889	WB-B/162	AR
Beacham, Jesse	009	1833	OB-B/282	
Beacham, John	030	1832	WB-3/311	
Beacham, Julia	009	1825	OB-A/345	AR
Beacham, William	053	1798	RW-1/301	AR
Beacom, J. E.	098	1897	WB-A/275	CTY
Beacom, Mary	098	1900	WB-A/383	CTY
Beacom, Robert	098	1900	WB-A/379	CTY
Beacom, Robert J.	098	1891	WB-A/138	CTY
Beacom, Thomas	098	1894	WB-A/197	CTY
Beaker, John	054	c1825	Orig. Only	AR
Beal, Britton	022	c1853	Orig. Only	AR
Beal, Charles	060	1890	WB-4/436	AR
Beal, Cherry	VA	1836	Copy	071 AR
Beal, Drewry	071	1870	WB-6/65	AR
Beal, John	060	1810	Orig. Only	AR
Beal, John	056	1835	Orig. Only	AR
Beal, Joseph	085	1826	WB-H/369	AR
Beal, Peter S.	060	1899	WB-5/130	AR
Beal, Peter S.	060	1899	085 WB-3/315	085 CTY
Beal, Reason	104	1848	WB-4/342	
Beal, Thomas	022	1823	Orig. Only	AR
Beal, Thomas	022	1884	WB-E/284	AR
Beale, Riddick E.	051	1891	WB-C/416	
Bealk, John	060	1804	Orig. Only	AR
Beall, Burgess L.	032	1853	WB-2/84 & 92	AR
Beall, David	054	c1806	WB-1/230	
Beall, Horatio	054	1849	WB-3/36	AR
Beall, James O.	054	1842	WB-2/250	AR
Beall, Robert	054	c1794	WB-1/227	
Beall, Zadoch	054	c1795	WB-1/233	
Bealmear, Jacob F.	MD	1874	091 WB-1/55	
Beals, Jesse	046	1811	WB-A/18	AR
Beals, John	046	1809	WB-A/15	AR
Beals, Margaret	018	1845	WB-C/294	
Beam, Adam	026	1863	WB-1/328	AR
Beam, D. M.	026	1889	WB-2/363	AR
Beam, David	086	1858	WB-E/338	AR
Beam, David, Sr.	060	1836	WB-1/382	AR
Beam, Jacob	085	c1801	WB-D/117	AR-Nunc.
Beam, Jacob M.	060	1893	WB-4/507	AR
Beam, John	026	1851	WB-1/127	AR
Beam, John T.	026	1874	WB-2/114	AR
Beam, John, Sr.	060	1870	WB-4/68	AR
Beam, Joshua	060	1869	WB-4/6	AR
Beam, Lee Anna	026	1897	WB-2/548	AR
Beam, Martin	026	1886	WB-2/292	AR
Beam, Mary N.	026	1875	WB-2/134	AR
Beam, Michel	085	c1791	WB-B/215	AR
Beaman, Allen W.	041	1899	WB-4/502	AR
Beaman, David	103	1805	Orig. Only	AR
Beaman, G. W. G.	045	1893	WB-1/282	AR
Beaman, Gennia	041	1883	WB-4/188	AR
Beaman, J. R.	087	1892	WB-3/503	AR
Beaman, John	085	1819	Orig. Only	AR
Beaman, John	041	1832	WB-2/309	AR
Beaman, Noah	045	1881	WB-1/65	AR
Beaman, Rhoda	045	1895	WB-1/383	AR
Beamer, Andrew	092	1899	WB-6/503	AR
Beamer, Frost	092	1880	WB-6/138	AR
Beamer, Henry	092	1858	WB-5/40	
Beamer, Jacob	092	1895	WB-6/411	AR
Beamer, Rebecca	092	1879	WB-6/18	AR
Bean, Alexander	032	1877	WB-3/211	AR
Bean, Allen H.	067	1866	WB-1/134a	AR
Bean, Mumford	033	1865	WB-1/192	AR
Bean, Peter	081	1881	WB-15/356	AR
Bean, Richard	085	1815	WB-G/353	AR
Bean, Ruth	032	1852	WB-2/65	AR
Bean, Sarah Ann	017	1870	WB-B/24	AR
Bean, Thomas	085	c1800	WB-F/2	AR
Bean, William	085	c1807	Orig. Only	AR
Beaner, Richard	009	1795	OWB/313	AR
Beannock, William	073	1832	WB-E/272	
Beans, Lucy J.	069	1886	WB-5/220	AR
Bear, Jacob	006	1865	WB-C/19	
Bear, Marcus	070	1887	WB-F/128	AR

Name	Co.	Date	Recorded Copy	Original
Beard (Baird), Richard	N	1692	Orig. Only	SS/AR
Beard, A. P.	054	1876	WB-4/200	CTY
Beard, Agnes	046	1841	WB-C/102	AR
Beard, Catharine	011	1875	WB-2/82	
Beard, Catherine	065	1838	WB-E/172	AR
Beard, David	085	c1785	WB-B/51	AR
Beard, David	054	c1822	WB-2/91	AR
Beard, Elam	046	1874	WB-E/119	AR
Beard, Elizabeth	011	1872	WB-2/61	
Beard, Horace H.	085	1858	WB-K/263	AR
Beard, James	029	1801	WB-A/39	AR
Beard, James B.	021	1899	WB-3/223	AR
Beard, James C.	040	1862	WB-1/145	
Beard, James W.	038	1897	WB-4/66	AR
Beard, John	011	c1835	WB-1/27	
Beard, John	029	1800	WB-A/30	AR
Beard, John	081	1809	WB-3/150	AR
Beard, John	005	1837	WB-B/75	AR
Beard, John Lewis	085	c1788	WB-C/129	AR
Beard, John, Sr.	085	1845	WB-K/7	AR
Beard, John, Sr.	060	1808	Orig. Only	AR
Beard, Lewis	085	1821	WB-H/78	AR
Beard, Margaret	085	1819	WB-G/539	AR
Beard, Michael	005	1841	WB-B/127	AR
Beard, Nancy	029	1897	WB-F/112	AR
Beard, Neill	011	c1772	WB-1/492	
Beard, Rachel	029	1808	WB-A/123	AR
Beard, Richard C.	065	1893	WB-M/198	AR
Beard, Robert	065	1892	WB-M/79	AR
Beard, Ruben	046	1841	Orig. Only	AR
Beard, Susana	085	1840	WB-I/73	AR
Beard, Thomas	103	1887	WB-1/419	AR
Beard, Thomas	054	c1816	WB-2/8	AR
Beard, Thomas J.	032	1900	WB-4/460	AR
Beard, William	046	1795	WB-A/20	AR
Beard, William	054	c1793	WB-1/67	AR
Beard, William	086	1791	Orig. Only	AR
Beard, William	065	c1843	WB-H/174A	AR
Beard, William	046	c1839	Orig. Only	AR
Beard, William L.	065	1873	WB-K/137	AR
Beard, William S.	046	1888	WB-E/511	AR
Bearden, Benjamin	044	1822	WB-9/70	CTY
Beardsley, Lambert P.	079	1885	WB-2/336	AR
Beardsley, Nancy R.	079	1881	WB-2/225	AR
Bears, Moses	028	1823	WB-C/225	AR
Beasely, Frederic	099	1794	Orig. Only	AR
Beasely, John	099	1794	RB-3/40	AR
Beasley, Abel	030	1849	WB-4/145	
Beasley, Bass	035	1881	WB-4/187	AR
Beasley, C. W.	030	1882	WB-5/88	AR
Beasley, Caleb	030	1834	WB-4/2	
Beasley, Caroline	030	1877	WB-5/35	AR
Beasley, Daniel	099	1853	RB-28/201	AR
Beasley, Daniel	082	c1829	Orig. Only	AR
Beasley, Daniel J.	035	1891	WB-4/397	AR
Beasley, Edny	030	1819	WB-3/108	
Beasley, Elizabeth	101	1881	WB-A/79	AR
Beasley, Fielding	099	1847	RB-26/265	AR
Beasley, Francis	024	1719	SS 875/172	SS/AR
Beasley, George	024	1810	WB-B/299	AR
Beasley, Henry	099	1821	RB-17/222	AR
Beasley, Henry	030	1824	WB-3/174	
Beasley, Isaac	081	1796	WB-2/12	AR
Beasley, Jacob	030	1788	WB-1/222	
Beasley, James	044	1850	WB-18/42	CTY
Beasley, James	024	1720	SS 875/239	
Beasley, Jeames	010	1758	Orig. Only	SS/AR
Beasley, John	024	1801	WB-B/166	AR
Beasley, John	090	1893	WB-6/304	AR
Beasley, John	024	1814	WB-C/26	AR
Beasley, John B.	024	1790	WB-B/87	AR
Beasley, John M.	029	1889	WB-E/460	AR
Beasley, John M.	101	1900	WB-A/320	AR
Beasley, John Pitts	100	1792	WB-6/97	AR
Beasley, Joseph	024	1801	WB-B/174	AR
Beasley, Joseph W.	010	1890	WB-I/306	AR
Beasley, Kindrect	056	1879	WB-3/217	AR
Beasley, Malachi	030	1841	WB-4/81	
Beasley, Malachi	030	1858	WB-4/225	
Beasley, Mark	099	1823	RB-18/252	AR
Beasley, Martha	024	1809	WB-B/241	AR
Beasley, Mary	099	1855	RB-29/230	AR
Beasley, Mary	009	c1799	OWB/350	AR
Beasley, Mary A.	044	c1869	WB-23/17	CTY
Beasley, Rebecca L.	100	1871	WB-51/37	AR
Beasley, Richard	090	1804	WB-2/55	AR
Beasley, Robert	011	c1808	WB-1/445	
Beasley, Robert	024	c1766	WB-A/222	AR
Beasley, Rosalie	028	1881	WB-E/300	AR
Beasley, Samuel	N	1736	LGB-4/#27	SS/AR
Beasley, Simon	028	c1759	Orig. Only	AR-Copy
Beasley, Solomon	070	1803	WB-C/36	
Beasley, Stephen	044	1857	WB-20/340	CTY
Beasley, Thomas	082	1886	WB-6/338	AR
Beasley, Thomas	010	1875	WB-I/81	AR
Beasley, Thomas	009	1792	OWB/277	AR
Beasley, Valentine	024	1833	WB-C/166	AR
Beasley, William	030	1822	WB-3/126	
Beasley, William	030	1832	WB-3/315	
Beasley, William	030	1791	WB-1/248	
Beasley, William	099	1825	RB-19/456	AR
Beasly, Alfred B.	009	1842	OB-D/278	AR
Beasly, Henry	022	1795	RB-2/36	AR
Beasly, John	097	1864	WB-1/231	AR
Beason, Isaac	046	1847	WB-C/261	AR
Beason, Jacob	073	1800	WB-D/15	AR
Beason, William	090	1830	WB-3/217	
Beastall, William E.	024	1808	WB-B/214	AR
Beatey, Francis	065	1773	WB-G/81	AR
Beatey, Francis M.	065	1844	WB-H/178	AR
Beathune, David	083	c1812	WB-1/127	AR
Beathune, Flora	083	c1821	WB-1/331	AR
Beatie, Esther	040	1860	WB-1/114	AR
Beattie, Francis	040	1879	WB-2/138	AR
Beattie, Franklin	021	c1883	WB-2/277	
Beattie, James O.	040	1890	WB-2/364	AR
Beattie, Martha	026	1873	WB-2/76	AR
Beatty, Ann	065	c1843	WB-I/40	AR
Beatty, Charles	065	1767	WB-A/96	AR
Beatty, Charles	021	1864	Orig. Only	AR
Beatty, Francis	060	1830	WB-1/194	AR
Beatty, Henry B.	029	1841	WB-B/352	AR
Beatty, Isabella	060	1842	WB-2/160	AR
Beatty, James M.	065	1889	WB-L/412	AR
Beatty, John	094	1774	Orig. Only	060 AR
Beatty, John	026	1865	WB-1/379	AR
Beatty, John	011	c1774	WB-1/471	
Beatty, John D.	011	1849	WB-1/170	
Beatty, Lucien T.	011	1899	WB-3/105	CTY
Beatty, Samuel	040	1869	WB-2/5	AR

Name	Co.	Date	Recorded Copy	Original
Beatty, Smith	040	1864	WB-1/168	AR-Copy
Beatty, Thomas	060	1787	Orig. Only	AR
Beatty, Thomas	060	1831	WB-1/233	AR
Beatty, Thomas	021	c1881	WB-2/260	
Beatty, William	065	1867	WB-J/237	AR
Beatty, William	065	c1866	Copy	040 AR
Beatty, William G.	070	c1825	WB-AB/290	AR
Beatty, Wm. Henry	011	1853	WB-1/222	
Beaty, Beeson	054	1895	WB-5/557	CTY
Beaty, Charles	065	c1764	085 WB-F/44	085 AR
Beaty, Francis	054	c1843	WB-2/283	AR
Beaty, Isabella	065	1878	WB-K/328	AR
Beaty, Isabella	065	1825	WB-A/228	
Beaty, Isabella	054	1854	WB-3/83	AR
Beaty, James	054	c1790	WB-1/74	AR
Beaty, James	049	1828	WB-2/232	AR
Beaty, James S.	054	1889	WB-5/280	CTY
Beaty, Jemima	054	1853	WB-3/67	AR
Beaty, John	065	1818	WB-A/123	AR
Beaty, John	065	1805	WB-A/91	AR
Beaty, John	085	c1792	WB-B/184	AR
Beaty, John, Sr.	065	1809	WB-A/122	AR
Beaty, Mary	065	1843	WB-H/116	AR
Beaty, Mary J.	054	1895	WB-5/555	CTY
Beaty, Milton	054	1869	WB-4/31	AR
Beaty, Moses	065	c1827	WB-H/166	AR
Beaty, Robert	065	1821	WB-A/110	AR
Beaty, Samuel	065	1825	WB-A/94	AR
Beaty, Thomas	054	c1825	WB-2/57	AR
Beaty, William	065	1816	WB-A/145	AR
Beaty, William C.	065	1860	WB-J/101	AR
Beaublossom, Frederick	032	1872	WB-3/65	AR
Beauchamp, James	033	1863	WB-1/178	
Beauchamp, John	085	c1800	WB-D/123	AR
Beauchamp, John	033	1887	WB-2/96	CTY
Beauchamp, Sarah L.	033	1888	WB-2/101	CTY
Beauchamp, Stephen	033	1847	WB-1/87	AR
Beavans, John	047	1894	WB-7/133	AR
Beavens, Mary	053	1754	SS 879/71	
Beaver, Catherine	016	1840	PQS.6/101	
Beaver, Catherine	085	1884	WB-2/109	CTY
Beaver, Christopher	016	1833	PQS.5/257	
Beaver, Daniel	085	c1867	WB-L/29	CTY
Beaver, Daniel	085	1888	WB-2/301	CTY
Beaver, David	085	1854	WB-K/162	AR
Beaver, Eli Martin	085	1865	WB-K/370	AR
Beaver, Elizabeth	085	1892	WB-2/539	CTY
Beaver, George	085	1882	WB-2/17	CTY
Beaver, Henry	085	1880	WB-1/519	CTY
Beaver, Henry	085	1845	WB-I/262	AR
Beaver, Isaac	016	1879	WB-3/264	AR
Beaver, Jacob	085	1843	WB-I/175	AR
Beaver, Jacob	085	1891	WB-2/451	CTY
Beaver, Jeremiah	085	1864	WB-K/324	AR
Beaver, Jesse	085	1875	WB-1/288	CTY
Beaver, John A.	085	1857	WB-K/248	AR
Beaver, Mary	085	1898	WB-3/220	CTY
Beaver, Mary C.	085	c1868	WB-L/36	AR
Beaver, Michael	085	1834	WB-H/612	AR
Beaver, Moses	054	1865	WB-3/178	AR
Beaver, Nicholas	085	1826	WB-H/344	AR
Beaver, Peter	054	1892	WB-5/439	CTY
Beaver, William	065	1889	WB-L/358	AR
Beaverly, Benjamin	047	1834	WB-4/115	AR
Beavers, Abigail	092	1803	WB-3/59A	AR
Beavers, Julia A.	078	1900	WB-19/492	AR
Beavers, William	084	c1788	OW/85	AR
Beazley, Charles	090	1819	WB-3/31	AR
Beazley, Jeremiah	090	1824	WB-3/124	AR
Beazley, Robert	090	1811	WB-2/118	AR
Bebber, Isaac	003	1878	WB-B/124	
Bechtel, John	085	1865	WB-K/362	AR
Bechtler, Christopher	086	1844	WB-E/122	AR
Beck, David	032	1875	WB-3/138	AR
Beck, Frederic	016	1830	PQS.5/136	
Beck, Frederick	044	1800	WB-5/54	CTY
Beck, Frederick	032	1847	WB-2/4	AR
Beck, George	085	1817	WB-G/485	AR
Beck, George W.	032	1875	WB-3/127	AR
Beck, H. J.	091	1900	WB-1/172	
Beck, I. P.	014	1878	WB-2/161	
Beck, Jacob	085	c1775	WB-A/237	AR
Beck, Jacob	032	1844	WB-1/440	AR
Beck, Jacob	032	1869	WB-3/11	AR
Beck, James	033	1846	WB-1/78	AR
Beck, Jeffery	081	1780	WB-1/57	AR
Beck, John	047	1761	WB-1/19	
Beck, John	035	1790	WB-A/20	AR
Beck, John, Sr.	090	1819	WB-3/38	AR
Beck, John, Sr.	032	1844	WB-1/432	AR
Beck, Leah	032	1889	WB-4/45	AR
Beck, Levi	032	1891	WB-3/102	AR
Beck, Moses	047	1760	WB-1/10	
Beck, N. P.	014	1899	WB-3/53	CTY
Beck, Nancy	009	1837	OB-B/473	AR/CRX
Beck, Philip	085	1817	WB-G/473	AR
Beck, Posey H.	014	1893	WB-2/511	CTY
Beck, Sarah	032	1896	WB-4/292	AR
Beck, Sentleger	085	1822	WB-H/148	AR
Beck, Solomon	032	1871	WB-3/35	AR
Beck, Thomas	070	1883	WB-E/506	AR
Beck, William	035	1814	SC/02833	AR-Copy
Beck, William	035	1814	WB-A/41	AR
Beck, William	038	1891	WB-3/215	AR
Beck, William	035	1814	WB-A/37	AR
Beck, William H.	038	1866	WB-1/270	AR
Beckel, Barbara	090	c1816	Orig. Only	AR
Beckerdite, Bethel	081	1864	Orig. Only	AR
Beckerdite, Ezra	081	1863	WB-12/413	AR
Beckerdite, John, Sr.	032	1863	WB-2/253	AR
Beckerdite, Oliver C.	081	1864	WB-13/105	AR
Becket, Elizabeth	085	1848	WB-K/71	AR
Becket, John	085	1843	WB-I/186	AR
Beckham, John	100	1780	WB-3/40	AR
Beckham, Lemuel	003	1867	WB-A/19	
Beckham, Stephen	073	1821	WB-D/606	AR
Beckham, William	044	1777	WB-1/153	CTY
Beckwith, Amos	069	1818	WB-1/297	AR
Beckwith, Anelizar	022	1900	WB-F/132	AR
Beckwith, Dempsey	069	1854	WB-1/540	AR
Beckwith, Green	099	1880	WB-A/200	AR
Beckwith, Henry	069	1796	WB-1/109	AR
Beckwith, Isaack	099	1863	RB-32/620	AR
Beckwith, John B.	056	1894	WB-2/167	AR
Beckwith, L. P.	022	1889	WB-E/400	AR
Beckwith, Malvina D.	099	1871	RB-35/156	
Beckwith, Nathaniel	053	1886	WB-11/184	AR
Beckwith, S. T.	009	1897	056 WB-4/65	056 AR
Beckwith, S. T.	009	1897	WB-2/110	CTY
Beckwith, Sion	099	1883	WB-A/416	AR

Name	Co.	Date	Recorded Copy	Original
Beckwith, Thomas	069	1826	WB-1/336	AR
Beckwith, Virginia B.	065	1880	WB-K/365	AR
Beckwith, William H.	099	1896	WB-C/523	AR
Becton, Charles	103	1889	WB-1/484	AR
Becton, Cora A.	059	1885	035 WB-4/268	035 AR
Becton, Cora A.	059	1885	WB-A/415	CTY
Becton, Ephraim	028	1875	WB-E/125	AR
Becton, Fred I.	103	1892	WB-1/567	AR
Becton, Frederick	028	N. D.	Orig. Only	AR-Copy
Becton, Frederick	028	1775	Orig. Only	AR
Becton, Frederick	057	1843	WB-B/162	AR
Becton, Fredk. Ed.	103	1813	RD-3/78	
Becton, John	028	1753	Orig. Only	SS/AR
Becton, John	057	1814	WB-B/14	AR
Becton, Joseph	028	1892	WB-F/19	
Becton, Mary	057	c1802	WB-B/26	AR
Becton, Mary Ann	019	1872	WB-B/69	AR
Becton, Michael	057	1799	WB-A/224	AR
Becton, Nancy M.	059	1869	WB-A/3	
Becton, Richard	009	1759	OWB/62	AR
Becton, Simon S.	019	1860	WB-A/244	AR
Becton, Susanah	057	1824	WB-B/83	AR
Becton, William B.	057	1890	WB-C/171	AR
Becton, William M.	057	1820	WB-B/55	AR
Beddingfield, John	056	c1857	WB-1/720	AR
Beddingfield, William	099	1775	RB-1/58	AR
Bedford, Council	103	1877	WB-1/122	AR
Bedford, Jonas	086	1823	WB-D/10	AR
Bedford, Jonas	086	1869	WB-F/9	AR
Bedingfield, Sarah	071	1807	WB-2/346	AR
Bedingfield, Thomas	071	1779	WB-1/216	
Bedscott, John	028	1798	WB-B/40	AR
Bedscott, Mary	028	1762	Orig. Only	AR
Bedsole, William	029	1890	WB-E/518	AR
Beebe, Asa	029	1842	WB-B/384	AR
Beebe, Betty	029	1879	WB-E/188	AR
Beecham, Edmon	030	1792	WB-1/252	
Beefle, Paul	085	c1764	WB-A/240	AR
Beeker, Henry	032	1839	WB-1/326	AR
Beels, Jacob	075	1746	Orig. Only	SS/AR
Beels, James	075	1722	SS 875/336	SS/AR
Beels, Malachi	018	1836	WB-C/196	
Beeman, Abraham	041	1832	WB-2/299	AR
Beeman, David	041	1810	WB-2/52	AR
Beeman, Samuel	033	1844	WB-1/56	AR
Been, Jacob	084	c1797	OW/88	AR
Beenblosom, Christian	085	1788	WB-C/81	AR
Beery, Daniel	012	N. D.	WB-B/63	AR
Beery, Samuel	070	1853	WB-C/547	AR
Beesley, Abraham	070	1803	WB-AB/81	AR
Beesley, Austin	035	1823	WB-A/9	AR
Beesley, James	028	1834	WB-C/371	
Beesley, Mordecia	030	1801	WB-2/186	
Beesley, Simon	028	c1759	Orig. Only	AR
Beesley, Solomon	028	1791	Orig. Only	AR
Beesley, Solomon	070	1803	WB-C/36	AR
Beesley, William	090	1804	WB-2/58	AR
Beeson, Benjamin	081	1794	WB-2/5	AR
Beeson, Benjamin	046	1835	WB-B/539	AR
Beeson, Isaac	046	1802	WB-A/32	AR
Beeson, Isaac	081	1811	WB-3/307	AR
Beeson, Jehu	046	1820	WB-B/93	AR
Beeson, Joel	046	1831	WB-B/443	AR
Beeson, Kinney C.	032	1876	WB-3/192	AR-Nunc.
Beeson, Louisa	046	1867	WB-D/360	AR
Beeson, Polly	046	1855	WB-C/437	AR
Beeson, Richard	046	1854	WB-C/424	AR
Beeson, Richard	081	1782	WB-1/58	AR
Beeson, Richard	081	1815	WB-4/511	AR
Beeson, Seth	081	1816	WB-4/359	AR
Beeson, William	090	1830	WB-3/217	AR
Beezly, Thomas	N	1733	LGB-4/#17	SS/AR
Befret, Benjamin	035	1753	SS 878/79	SS/AR
Beggarly, Alpheus	054	1842	WB-2/258	AR
Beggarly, Benjamin	054	c1807	WB-1/286	AR
Beggarly, Charles	054	c1819	WB-1A/71	AR
Beggerly, Levina	033	1837	WB-1/6	
Beggs, James	029	1837	WB-B/286	AR
Beggs, Samuel	083	1830	WB-1/277	
Beimus, John	028	1801	WB-B/117	
Beine, Eliza H.	099	1880	WB-A/192	AR
Beine, Maud A.	099	1897	WB-D/88	AR
Beine, Maud A.	099	1897	071 WB-7/366	071 AR
Beinghaus, Elizabeth	038	1854	WB-1/50	
Beissener, John Henry	060	1847	WB-2/289	AR
Belange, Elisha	096	N. D.	WB-2/46	
Belch, Elisha	051	N. D.	WB-A/123 & 183	
Belch, Lewis	010	1823	WB-G/121	AR
Belch, Ryan	010	1855	WB-H/15	AR
Belch, Willis	083	1829	WB-1/326	AR
Belcher, Benjamin	079	1862	WB-1/140	AR
Belcher, Beverley	037	1821	WB-E/283	AR
Belcher, Elizabeth	079	c1863	WB-1/143	AR
Belcher, George	037	1757	SS 879/232	Nunc.
Belcher, Henry	037	1861	WB-G/218	AR
Belcher, Martha	079	1892	WB-3/21	AR
Belcher, Mary A.	099	1900	WB-D/378	AR
Belcher, Moses	079	1859	WB-1/21	AR
Belden, Daniel	029	1807	WB-A/93	AR
Belden, Emily E.	029	1836	WB-B/266	AR
Belden, Simeon	029	1831	WB-B/206	AR
Belew, Isaac	020	1795	RB-C/134	AR
Belk, Elizabeth	097	1882	WB-2/213	
Belk, James P.	097	1869	WB-2/16	AR
Belk, Jennie P.	065	1900	WB-N/383	AR
Belk, John	065	c1804	WB-A/104	AR
Bell, Abigail	019	1805	WB-D/53	AR
Bell, Abner	019	1815	WB-D/93	AR
Bell, Abner	019	1832	WB-A/24	
Bell, Abraham	053	1788	RW-1/176	AR
Bell, Alfred	054	1881	Orig. Only	AR
Bell, Alfred L.	053	1854	WB-8/67	AR
Bell, Alvania	037	c1880	Orig. Only	AR
Bell, Alvania	047	1885	WB-6/414	AR
Bell, Amy	100	1815	WB-19/125	AR
Bell, Andrew	028	1790	WB-A/224	AR
Bell, Ann	047	1772	WB-1/325	
Bell, Ann	075	1852	WB-N/239	AR
Bell, Ann	028	1843	WB-D/88	AR
Bell, Anna	039	1900	WB-V/209	AR
Bell, Archbell	035	1779	WB-A/59	AR
Bell, Arthur	069	1779	WB-1/5	AR
Bell, Arthur	047	1818	WB-3/621	AR
Bell, Arthur	047	1775	WB-2/22	
Bell, Bathania	037	1845	Orig. Only	AR
Bell, Benjamin	067	1843	WB-1/1	AR
Bell, Benjamin	047	1814	WB-3/558	AR
Bell, Benjamin	047	1775	WB-2/18	
Bell, Benjamin	039	1789	WB-A/39	

Name	Co.	Date	Recorded Copy	Original
Bell, Benjamin	075	1765	WB-I/38	AR
Bell, Betsy	053	c1859	Orig. Only	AR
Bell, Branson	030	1816	WB-3/77	
Bell, Branson C.	030	1886	WB-5/134	
Bell, Brickhouse	018	1822	WB-C/4	
Bell, Burrel	099	1824	RB-19/71	AR
Bell, Burrel	099	1884	WB-A/569	AR
Bell, Bythal	037	1802	WB-D/154	AR
Bell, C. G.	021	1880	WB-2/216	
Bell, Caleb	018	1838	WB-C/238	
Bell, Caleb	019	1811	WB-D/90	AR
Bell, Candis	081	1860	WB-11/488	AR
Bell, Catherine	024	c1809	WB-C/21	AR
Bell, Chlora	018	1871	WB-E/31	AR
Bell, Cornelius	009	1730	Orig. Only	SS/AR
Bell, David	019	1817	WB-D/95	AR
Bell, David	019	1784	WB-D/23	AR
Bell, David	056	1799	Est-3/284	
Bell, David W.	019	1898	WB-C/7	AR
Bell, Dixon	053	1805	RW-1/379	AR
Bell, Dolly	047	1887	WB-6/465	AR
Bell, Duke, Sr.	030	1825	WB-3/199	
Bell, Eadey	030	1800	WB-2/163	
Bell, Ebenezer	053	1817	RW-1/525	AR
Bell, Edney	030	1846	WB-4/122	
Bell, Edwin S.	030	1853	WB-4/177	AR
Bell, Eelnsy	047	1851	037 WB-F/453	037 AR
Bell, Elijah	019	1809	WB-D/88	AR
Bell, Elijah	022	1849	WB-C/245	AR
Bell, Elisha	047	1791	WB-3/198	AR
Bell, Elizabeth	054	1854	WB-3/78	AR
Bell, Elizabeth	003	1891	WB-B/289	AR
Bell, Elizabeth	096	1750	SS 879/6	SS/AR
Bell, Elizabeth	022	1882	WB-E/259	AR
Bell, Ella R.	047	1898	WB-7/193	
Bell, Etheldred	056	1861	WB-2/10	AR
Bell, Fletcher A.	076	1891	WB-A1/138	
Bell, Frances Ann	053	1847	WB-7/100	AR
Bell, Frank M.	053	1899	WB-11/351	AR
Bell, Frederick	037	1846	WB-F/337	AR
Bell, Frederick	037	1803	WB-D/157	AR
Bell, George	037	1755	Orig. Only	SS/AR
Bell, George	053	1791	RW-1/214	AR
Bell, George	075	1735	Orig. Only	AR
Bell, George	019	1794	WB-D/36	AR
Bell, George	037	1752	Orig. Only	SS/AR
Bell, George	047	1762	WB-1/61	
Bell, George	019	1812	WB-D/54	AR
Bell, George	039	1819	WB-F/180	AR
Bell, George, Jr.	053	1791	Orig. Only	AR-Nunc.
Bell, Haman, Sr.	018	1853	WB-C/369	
Bell, Haywood S.	018	1845	WB-C/293	
Bell, Henrietta	070	1889	WB-F/318	AR
Bell, Horace	100	1817	WB-20/245	AR-Nunc.
Bell, Hutson	047	1862	WB-5/103	
Bell, J. B.	AL	1877	022 WB-E/149	022 AR
Bell, J. R.	003	1877	WB-B/90	AR
Bell, James	019	1801	WB-D/77	AR
Bell, James	054	c1835	WB-2/128	AR
Bell, James	071	1798	WB-2/170	
Bell, James	019	c1780	Orig. Only	AR
Bell, James	065	1820	WB-A/108	AR
Bell, James	VA	1778	HiDSC	AR-Copy
Bell, James	019	1823	WB-D/98	AR
Bell, James	047	1813	WB-3/536	AR
Bell, James F.	054	1871	WB-4/87	CTY
Bell, James J.	047	1884	WB-6/346	AR
Bell, James M.	039	1888	WB-U/433	AR
Bell, James, Sr.	012	1797	WB-B/56	AR
Bell, Jane	085	1819	Orig. Only	AR
Bell, Jane A.	060	1836	WB-1/370	AR
Bell, Jeannie S.	019	1894	WB-B/257	AR
Bell, Jesse	100	1805	WB-13/96	
Bell, Jesse	018	1844	WB-C/292	
Bell, Jesse C.	018	1881	WB-E/102	AR
Bell, Joab	018	1855	WB-D/21	
Bell, John	075	1827	WB-N/32	AR
Bell, John	030	c1813	WB-3/21	
Bell, John	083	c1788	WB-1/16	
Bell, John	030	1848	WB-4/138	
Bell, John	075	1721	SS 875/316	SS/AR
Bell, John	053	1848	WB-7/188	AR
Bell, John	040	c1851	WB-1/50	
Bell, John	053	1841	WB-6/182	AR
Bell, John	030	1806	WB-2/284	
Bell, John	065	1817	WB-A/146	AR
Bell, John	035	1783	WB-A/18	AR
Bell, John	012	1789	Orig. Only	AR
Bell, John	029	1882	WB-E/285	AR
Bell, John	037	1794	WB-C/263	AR
Bell, John	030	c1706	Orig. Only	ChM-1/33
Bell, John C.	054	c1847	003 WB-A/22	003 AR
Bell, John M.	065	1875	WB-K/205	AR
Bell, John P.	065	1837	WB-E/163	AR
Bell, Joseph	019	1793	WB-D/42	AR
Bell, Joseph	019	1813	WB-D/64	AR
Bell, Joseph	030	1831	WB-3/263	
Bell, Joseph	019	1745	SS 877/350	SS/AR
Bell, Joseph	019	1777	RB-A/53	AR
Bell, Joseph H.	053	1843	WB-6/215	AR
Bell, Joseph J.	047	1884	071 WB-6/487	071 AR
Bell, Joshua	037	1793	WB-C/242	AR
Bell, Joshua	009	1830	OB-B/86	AR
Bell, Joshua	047	1784	WB-3/59	
Bell, Joshua	053	1811	RW-1/452	
Bell, Joshua L.	063	1895	WB-4/161	AR
Bell, Josiah	019	1843	WB-A/103	AR
Bell, Josiah	030	1816	WB-3/83	
Bell, Lancelot	075	1781	WB-K/54	AR
Bell, Levi	075	1776	WB-I/152	AR
Bell, Levi	019	1869	WB-B/51	AR
Bell, Littleton	053	1821	WB-4/202	AR
Bell, Littleton	053	1832	WB-5/100	
Bell, Malachi	019	1804	WB-D/47	AR
Bell, Malvina	099	1871	Orig. Only	AR
Bell, Marmaduke	047	1797	WB-3/284	AR
Bell, Marmaduke	037	1830	WB-F/111	AR
Bell, Martha	018	1860	WB-D/61	
Bell, Martha	053	1888	WB-11/212	AR
Bell, Marthew	081	c1816	Orig. Only	AR
Bell, Mary	053	1837	WB-5/448	AR
Bell, Mary	018	1825	WB-C/58	
Bell, Mary	075	1773	WB-I/135	AR
Bell, Mary	083	1826	Copy	087 AR
Bell, Mary	083	c1804	WB-1/88	AR
Bell, Mary	022	1840	WB-C/107	AR
Bell, Mary	056	1827	WB-1/344	AR
Bell, Mary E.	101	1885	WB-A/140	AR
Bell, Mary M.	054	1880	WB-4/366	CTY

Name	Co.	Date	Recorded Copy	Original
Bell, Michael	087	1831	WB-1/121	AR
Bell, Miles H.	019	1822	WB-D/96	AR
Bell, Nancy	079	1899	WB-3/195	AR
Bell, Nancy	037	1822	WB-E/293	AR
Bell, Nathan	019	1829	WB-D/55	AR
Bell, Nathan	018	1853	WB-C/373	
Bell, Nuel, Sr.	019	1793	WB-D/41	AR-Nunc.
Bell, Nuell	019	1782	WB-D/30	AR
Bell, Penelope	030	1867	WB-4/267	AR
Bell, Peter H.	047	1898	WB-7/194	AR
Bell, Phebe	018	1866	WB-D/80	AR
Bell, Priscilla	099	c1831	Orig. Only	AR
Bell, Rachel	065	1840	WB-H/8	AR
Bell, Ralph E.	065	1883	WB-K/537	AR
Bell, Ralpheus	019	1872	WB-B/70	AR
Bell, Richard	037	1790	WB-C/140	AR
Bell, Robert	065	1891	WB-P/286	AR
Bell, Robert	087	c1816	WB-1/13	AR
Bell, Robert	030	1815	WB-3/63	
Bell, Robert	085	c1784	WB-B/70	AR
Bell, Robert Mc.	060	1864	WB-3/72	AR
Bell, Ross	030	1727	SS 876/149	SS/AR
Bell, Rufus	019	1887	WB-B/154	AR
Bell, Sally	046	1830	WB-B/431	AR
Bell, Sally G.	037	1825	WB-F/47	AR
Bell, Samuel	012	1811	WB-B/96	AR
Bell, Sarah	023	1891	WB-A/98	AR
Bell, Sarah	019	1859	WB-A/240	AR
Bell, Sarah	019	1837	WB-A/76	AR
Bell, Sarah Ann	030	1869	WB-5/1	
Bell, Sarah E.	070	1890	WB-F/405	AR
Bell, Sarah F.	030	1883	WB-5/95	AR
Bell, Sarah L.	079	1898	WB-3/144	AR
Bell, Sarah V.	065	1867	WB-J/236	AR
Bell, Seth	019	1827	WB-C/92	
Bell, Solomon	019	1780	WB-D/85	AR
Bell, Susan	040	1884	WB-2/223	AR
Bell, Susan B.	019	1888	WB-D/9	AR
Bell, Susan I.	046	1889	WB-F/17	AR
Bell, Susie M.	047	1879	WB-6/220	AR
Bell, T. A.	054	1867	WB-3/196	AR
Bell, T. Smith	054	1888	WB-5/211	CTY
Bell, Thomas	022	1830	WB-B/196	AR
Bell, Thomas	037	1763	WB-A/121	AR
Bell, Thomas	060	1830	WB-1/190	AR
Bell, Thomas	013	1886	WB-B/372	AR
Bell, Thomas	044	1761	Orig. Only	CTY
Bell, Thomas	024	1733	SS 876/276	SS/AR
Bell, Thomas	085	c1792	WB-D/147	AR
Bell, Thomas	054	1825	WB-2/30	AR
Bell, Thomas	022	1861	WB-D/79	AR
Bell, Thomas	100	1782	WB-3/159	AR
Bell, Thomas	054	c1824	WB-2/15	AR
Bell, Thomas	024	1751	Orig. Only	SS/AR
Bell, Thomas A.	072	1829	WB-1/55	AR
Bell, Thomas O.	019	1845	WB-A/127	AR
Bell, Thomas S.	104	1892	WB-6/453	AR
Bell, Thomas,Sr.	013	1834	WB-A/30	
Bell, Tully	030	1843	WB-4/101	
Bell, W. H.	039	1895	WB-V/67	AR
Bell, Walter	054	c1794	WB-1/226	
Bell, Walter R.	035	1885	WB-4/253	AR
Bell, Whitmell	037	1824	WB-F/26	AR
Bell, William	071	1801	WB-2/213	AR
Bell, William	029	1865	WB-D/83	AR
Bell, William	019	1845	WB-A/120	AR
Bell, William	030	1721	SS 876/48	SS/AR (N)
Bell, William	075	1771	WB-H/127	AR
Bell, William	030	1806	WB-2/281	
Bell, William	053	1775	RW-1/71	AR
Bell, William	100	1852	WB-42/64	AR
Bell, William	100	1784	WB-4/44	AR
Bell, William	053	1800	RW-1/314	
Bell, William	085	1819	WB-G/543	AR
Bell, William	037	1754	SS 881/107	SS/AR
Bell, William	044	1772	Orig. Only	CTY
Bell, William B.	019	1876	WB-B/87	AR
Bell, William C.	019	1851	WB-A/150	AR
Bell, William F.	019	1868	WB-B/40	AR
Bell, William F.	053	1831	WB-5/58	AR
Bell, William H.	053	1875	WB-11/53	AR
Bell, William T.	071	1863	WB-5/278	AR
Bell, William W.	087	1885	WB-3/300	AR
Bell, Willie	079	1872	WB-2/73	AR
Bell, Wilson	053	1815	RW-1/494	
Bell, Winifred	037	c1837	WB-F/235	AR
Bell, Zadok	099	1827	RB-20/100	AR
Bell, Zechonias	053	1815	RW-1/284	AR
Bellamy, John	037	1797	WB-D/31	AR
Bellamy, John D.	070	1896	WB-G/531	AR
Bellamy, John D.	070	1896	012 WB-B/342	
Bellamy, John F.	069	1846	WB-1/485	AR
Bellamy, Mary E.	037	1884	WB-G/659	
Bellamy, Nelly N.	037	1881	WB-G/619 & 626	AR
Bellamy, William	037	1780	WB-B/60	AR
Bellamy, William	069	1847	WB-1/494	AR
Bellamy, William E.	047	1896	WB-7/166	AR
Belle, William	081	1821	WB-5/44	
Bellen, John	070	1796	Orig. Only	AR-Nunc.
Beller, Peter	090	c1790	Orig. Only	AR
Belleraphant, Sallie	084	1861	WB-C/351	CTY
Belletter, Alexander	090	1825	WB-3/136	
Bellings, Anna	024	1837	WB-C/205	AR
Bellins, Maria	090	1822	WB-3/85	AR
Bellknap, Elisha	028	1762	SS 882/446	
Bellknap, Elisha	028	1762	Wills.8/446	AR
Bellman, John	075	1706/7	Orig. Only	SS/AR
Bellmann, John	077	1740	LGB-4/#133	SS/AR
Belloat, Margaret	070	1797	WB-AB/39	AR
Bellsire, Mary	046	1843	WB-C/167	AR
Belo, J. Levin	038	1899	WB-4/156	AR
Belo, Lewis	038	c1863	WB-1/229	AR
Beloat, Abbet	053	1775	RW-1/67	
Beloat, Augustus	070	1795	WB-C/34	AR-Nunc.
Belote, Amele	010	1797	WB-E/37	AR
Belote, Catherine	010	1798	WB-E/47	AR
Belote, Hillery	009	1763	OWB/91	AR
Belote, John	010	1796	WB-D/352	AR
Belote, Milly	010	1816	WB-G/2	AR
Belote, Silas	010	1794	WB-D/237	AR
Belote, William	010	1771	WB-A/143	AR
Belt, Amelia M.	054	1890	WB-5/314	CTY
Belt, Richard	054	1890	WB-5/339	CTY
Belt, Thomas	054	c1810	WB-1/123	AR
Belt, Thomas	054	1829	WB-2/81	AR
Belton, James	084	1826	WB-A/207	CTY
Belton, Martha Ann	084	1878	WB-E/140	CTY
Belvat, Thomas	053	1786	RW-1/147	

Name	Co.	Date	Recorded Copy	Original
Belven, Robert	099	1782	RB-1/179	AR
Belvin, Lacy H.	099	1900	WB-D/374	AR
Belvin, Nancy C.	036	1895	WB-A/356	CTY
Belvin, William	073	1797	WB-C/93	AR
Belyew, Katherine	005	c1819	WB-2/5	AR
Bemis, Susan W.	092	1879	WB-6/129	AR
Benbow, Benjamin	046	1829	WB-B/378	
Benbow, CHarles	046	1868	WB-D/383	AR
Benbow, Charles	011	c1774	WB-1/470	
Benbow, Evan	106	1894	WB-2/349	
Benbow, Gershon	011	c1751	SS 878/15	
Benbow, Mary E.	046	1896	WB-F/499	AR
Benbow, Thomas	046	1825	WB-B/205	AR
Benbow, Thomas J.	046	1899	WB-G/156	AR
Benbow, W. E.	106	1900	WB-2/483	AR
Benbury, Cain	024	1895	WB-E/239	AR
Benbury, Charles	024	1777	WB-A/210	AR
Benbury, James E.	041	1863	WB-3/330	AR
Benbury, John	024	1774	WB-B/162	AR
Benbury, John A.	024	1865	WB-D/37	AR
Benbury, Joseph C.	024	1837	WB-C/207	AR
Benbury, Joseph R.	024	1858	WB-C/430	AR
Benbury, Lawrence	024	1897	WB-E/275	AR
Benbury, Richard	024	1807	WB-B/296	AR
Benbury, Richard B.	FL	1844	024 WB-C/254	024 AR
Benbury, Robert	024	1766	WB-1/24	
Benbury, Ruth	024	c1793	WB-B/71	AR
Benbury, Samuel	024	c1766	Orig. Only	AR
Benbury, Sarah	024	c1838	WB-C/249	AR
Benbury, Thomas	024	1857	WB-C/417	AR
Benbury, Thomas	024	c1793	WB-A/114	AR
Benbury, William	024	c1709	SS 875/39	
Benbury, William	024	1755	SS 880/73	SS/AR
Benbury, William	024	c1778	WB-A/105	AR
Bender, Brice	072	1816	WB-A/16	AR
Bender, John	072	1832	WB-1/108	AR
Bender, John	028	1815	WB-C/113	
Bender, John	057	1842	WB-B/150	AR
Bender, Martin	028	1750	DB-5/136	SS/AR
Benders, Laner	028	1842	WB-D/63	AR
Benedict, Charles B.	FL	1898	013 WB-D/207	013 AR
Benfield, Andrew	017	1896	WB-B/286	AR-Nunc.
Benfield, E. Amy	003	1899	WB-B/380	AR
Benfield, Jane E.	017	1900	WB-B/323	AR
Benfield, Joseph	014	1885	WB-2/274	CTY
Benfield, Marcus	003	1874	WB-B/50	AR
Benge, James	104	1818	WB-3/174	AR
Benge, Thomas	104	1811	WB-2/328	AR
Bengel, Henry	060	1829	WB-1/123	AR
Benham, Catharine	070	1882	WB-E/452	
Benick, Henry	060	0863	WB-3/57	AR
Benick, Philip	060	1808	Orig. Only	AR
Benjamin, Mary	063	1856	WB-2/422	
Benn, Dorothy	071	1840	WB-4/224	AR
Benn, George	071	1825	WB-3/331	AR
Benn, George W.	071	1839	WB-4/199	AR
Benn, John T.	071	1839	WB-4/202	AR
Bennatte, Richard	020	1811	RB-F/197	AR
Bennehan, Richard	073	1826	WB-E/96	AR
Bennehan, Richard	073	1826	Copy	099 AR
Bennehan, Thomas D.	073	1847	WB-F/375	AR
Bennehan, Thomas D.	073	1847	Copy	099 AR
Benners, Francis S.	028	1855	WB-D/242	
Benners, J. N.	049	1895	WB-2/342	AR
Benners, John	028	1801	Orig. Only	AR
Benners, Lucas J.	028	1819	WB-C/178	AR
Bennet, Carter	030	1799	WB-2/144	
Bennet, Euphan	030	c1806	WB-2/328	
Bennet, John	030	c1710	SS 875/49	
Bennet, John	013	1835	107 WB-1/5	
Bennet, Luke	009	1787	OWB/222	AR
Bennet, Mary	100	1808	WB-14/215	AR-Nunc.
Bennet, Nehemiah	030	1753	SS 879/87	SS/AR
Bennet, Solomon	030	1755	Orig. Only	SS/AR
Bennet, William	072	1793	Orig. Only	AR
Bennet, William	047	1784	WB-3/71	AR
Bennett, Alexander	100	1898	WB-51/502	
Bennett, Alvy D.	009	1895	WB-2/67	CTY
Bennett, Amey	063	c1802	WB-1/409	
Bennett, Anderson	090	1897	WB-6/425	AR
Bennett, Archelaus	005	1882	WB-D/146	AR
Bennett, Artaxetes	081	1819	Orig. Only	AR-Copy
Bennett, Betsy	028	1882	WB-E/317	AR
Bennett, C. E.	039	1897	WB-V/112	AR
Bennett, Catherine	005	1881	WB-D/111	AR
Bennett, Charley	090	1899	WB-6/523	AR
Bennett, Clary	071	1813	WB-3/97	AR
Bennett, David	001	c1844	WB-1/41	
Bennett, David A.	107	1896	WB-2/94	
Bennett, E. J.	035	1898	WB-4/526	AR
Bennett, Elisha	046	1835	WB-B/534	AR
Bennett, Eliza Ann	005	1896	WB-D/397	AR
Bennett, Elizabeth	099	1816	RB-13/50	AR
Bennett, Ellender	044	1825	WB-10/14	CTY
Bennett, Fleet S.	087	1864	WB-2/77	AR
Bennett, George S.	003	1866	WB-A/6	AR
Bennett, Hardy	087	1870	WB-3/22	AR
Bennett, Henry T.	RI	1892	028 WB-F/165	
Bennett, Isham	100	1872	WB-51/75	AR
Bennett, James	022	1808	WB-A/153	AR
Bennett, James	063	1819	WB-2/60	
Bennett, James	063	1839	WB-2/253	
Bennett, James	087	1870	WB-3/27	AR
Bennett, James	005	c1793	WB-A/24	AR
Bennett, Jane M.	SC	1883	050 WB-1/237B	
Bennett, Jessee	030	1795	WB-2/35	
Bennett, John	028	1817	Orig. Only	AR
Bennett, John	099	1810	RB-9/343	AR
Bennett, John	085	c1807	WB-G/98	AR
Bennett, John	026	1852	WB-1/131	AR
Bennett, John B.	077	1808	Orig. Only	AR
Bennett, John W.	100	1900	WB-51/535	
Bennett, John W.	005	1899	WB-D/443	AR
Bennett, Josephus	009	1880	WB-1/253	CTY
Bennett, Julius D.	099	1808	RB-8/13	AR
Bennett, Lemuel D.	005	1878	WB-D/66	AR
Bennett, Lewis	044	1825	WB-10/75	CTY
Bennett, Lydia	024	c1807	WB-B/289	AR
Bennett, Milner	020	1814	RB-G/6	AR
Bennett, Moses	100	1824	WB-25/175	AR
Bennett, Moses	030	1787	WB-1/211	
Bennett, Moses D.	054	1885	WB-5/44	CTY
Bennett, Nancy C.	063	1882	WB-3/232	
Bennett, Nevel, Sr.	005	1820	WB-2/6	AR
Bennett, R. H.	005	1888	WB-D/241	AR
Bennett, Reading	097	1855	WB-1/110	AR
Bennett, Reuben	090	1877	WB-6/79	AR
Bennett, Reubin	100	1793	WB-7/9	AR
Bennett, Richard	044	1786	WB-1/468	CTY
Bennett, Richard	100	1823	WB-25/84	AR

Name	Co.	Date	Recorded Copy	Original
Bennett, Richard	054	c1837	WB-2/179	AR
Bennett, Robert	030	1806	WB-2/284	
Bennett, Sampson	087	1863	WB-2/40	AR
Bennett, Sarah B.	099	1892	WB-C/96	AR
Bennett, Sebron L.	035	1881	WB-4/166	AR
Bennett, Susannah	005	1847	WB-B/233	AR
Bennett, Thomas	020	1831	RB-M/23	AR
Bennett, Thomas	035	1816	WB-A/45	AR
Bennett, Wiley	009	1871	WB-1/69	AR
Bennett, William	107	c1854	WB-1/42	
Bennett, William	071	1765	WB-1/112	
Bennett, William	071	1805	WB-2/282	AR
Bennett, William	005	1840	WB-B/117	AR
Bennett, William	035	1804	WB-A/49	AR
Bennett, William	082	1795	WB-1/44	AR
Bennett, William	063	c1801	WB-1/421	
Bennett, William H.	MS	1882	005 WB-D/160	005 AR
Bennett, William M.	084	1885	WB-E/323	CTY
Bennette, S. W.	083	1898	WB-4/192	AR
Benning, Jacob	085	1829	WB-H/467	AR
Bennit, Joseph	030	1723	Orig. Only	SS/AR
Bennitt, Joel	063	1817	WB-2/52	
Bennitt, Richard	015	1764	RB-1/3	AR
Bennitt, William	063	1817	WB-2/46	
Benoit, John	024	1813	WB-C/19	AR
Benson, Anne	010	1818	WB-G/35	AR
Benson, David	011	c1831	WB-1/37	
Benson, Elizabeth	028	1856	WB-D/263	AR
Benson, John	046	1793	WB-A/22	AR
Benson, John	053	1811	RW-1/455	
Benson, John	070	1744	DB-C/64	AR
Benson, Martha	073	1846	WB-F/305	AR
Benson, Mary	053	1756	OB-A/7	
Benson, Reuben	053	1828	WB-4/344	AR
Benson, Reuben	046	1825	WB-B/204	AR
Benson, Robert	085	1816	WB-G/413	AR
Benson, Robert P.	016	1872	WB-3/74	
Benson, Samuel S.	085	1899	WB-3/260	CTY
Benson, Spencer	085	1855	WB-K/207	AR
Benson, Thomas	072	1839	WB-2/18	
Benson, W. L. D.	016	1889	WB-4/18	AR
Benson, William	010	1802	WB-E/168	AR
Benthall, John	051	1831	WB-A/27	
Benthall, John, Sr.	019	c1773	WB-D/19	AR
Benthall, Joseph	071	1798	WB-2/176	AR
Benthall, Reubin	019	1782	WB-D/21	AR
Benthall, Susanna	071	1828	WB-4/46	AR
Bentley, Isaac	063	1774	WB-1/446	
Bentley, John	003	1887	WB-B/216	AR
Bentley, John	010	1754	SS 879/165	SS/AR
Bentley, John	096	1754	SS 880/102	SS/AR
Bentley, John	010	1802	WB-E/151	AR
Bentley, Martha	010	1795	WB-D/270	AR
Bentley, Martha	037	1808	WB-D/328	AR
Bentley, Sally	009	1820	OB-A/304	AR
Bentley, Sarah	003	1856	Orig. Only	AR
Bentley, William	010	1804	WB-E/240	AR
Bently, John	077	1695	Orig. Only	SS/AR
Bently, John	N	1741	Orig. Only	SS/AR
Bently, Joshua	037	1799	WB-D/98	AR
Bently, Richard	N	1697	Orig. Only	SS/AR
Benton, Absalom	037	1806	WB-D/241	AR
Benton, Alexander	087	1838	WB-1/201	AR
Benton, Alexander	038	1881	WB-2/410	AR
Benton, Charity	037	1818	WB-E/200	AR
Benton, Cinthia	041	1888	WB-4/286	AR
Benton, David	041	1840	WB-3/24	AR
Benton, Elisha	041	1799	WB-1/164	AR
Benton, Henry	041	1863	WB-3/303	AR
Benton, Isaac	041	1791	WB-1/91	AR
Benton, Jacob	041	1823	WB-2/204	AR
Benton, James	104	1883	WB-6/230	AR
Benton, James	037	1821	WB-E/263	AR
Benton, Jeremiah	005	1838	WB-B/80	AR
Benton, Jesse	073	1791	WB-B/144	AR
Benton, Jethro	037	1775	WB-A/229	AR
Benton, John	099	1797	RB-3/270	AR
Benton, John	041	1785	WB-1/47	AR
Benton, John	056	1875	WB-3/138	AR
Benton, John	024	1750	Orig. Only	SS/Ar
Benton, John	041	1801	WB-1/182	AR
Benton, John, Jr.	041	1781	WB-1/22	AR
Benton, Joseph	084	1843	WB-B/304	CTY
Benton, Martha	041	1882	WB-4/176	AR
Benton, Mary	041	1847	WB-3/81	AR
Benton, Mary	041	1828	WB-2/277	AR
Benton, Meriam	075	1825	WB-N/17	AR
Benton, Miles	041	1805	WB-1/224	AR
Benton, Moses	041	1793	WB-1/114	AR
Benton, Moses	012	c1860	WB-B/28	AR
Benton, Nancy	041	1892	WB-4/326	AR
Benton, Polly	099	1815	RB-12/212	AR
Benton, Robert F.	041	1797	WB-1/151	AR-Nunc.
Benton, S. E.	038	1896	WB-3/599	AR
Benton, Samuel	044	1770	Orig. Only	CTY
Benton, Samuel	044	1770	Copy	073 AR
Benton, Samuel	073	1810	WB-D/276	AR
Benton, Seth	041	1889	WB-4/293	AR
Benton, Seth	041	1832	WB-2/303	AR
Benton, Thomas	044	1766	Orig. Only	CTY
Benton, William	041	1845	WB-3/71	AR
Benton, William	005	1828	WB-A/146	AR
Benton, William A.	005	1864	WB-C/202	AR
Benzein, Christian	090	1811	WB-2/126	AR
Benzein, Wm. Lewis	090	1832	WB-3/241	
Berger, Joseph B.	103	1893	WB-2/41	AR
Bergerom, G. T.	079	1887	WB-2/408	AR
Bergerom, Harriet	079	1888	WB-2/420	AR
Bergeron, Judeth	009	1742	LGB-4/#150	SS/AR
Bergeron, William B.	069	1870	WB-1/607	AR
Bergerson, Barzilla	079	1886	WB-2/370	AR
Bergman, William R.	068	1855	WB-C/44	
Berkley, Aylworth	019	1769	RB-A/35	AR
Bernard, Joseph	030	1780	WB-1/149	
Bernard, Robert	030	1801	WB-2/188	
Bernard, William	030	1803	WB-2/212	
Bernard, William	030	1782	WB-1/156	
Bernett, Edward	N	c1687	Orig. Only	SS/AR
Bernhardt, Martin A.	085	1864	WB-K/344	AR
Bernheim, C. H.	021	c1900	WB-3/318	
Bernie, William	070	1752	DB-C/353	
Beroth, Henry	085	c1799	WB-D/152	AR
Beroths, Jacob	090	c1801	Orig. Only	AR
Berrier, Andrew	032	1894	Orig. Only	AR
Berrier, Antonette	032	1882	WB-3/362	AR
Berrier, Henderson	032	1862	WB-2/229	AR
Berrier, Henry	032	1864	WB-2/279	AR
Berrier, Jacob	032	1879	WB-3/294	AR
Berrier, Jacob	032	c1856	WB-2/143	AR
Berrier, Sarah	032	1894	Orig. Only	AR

Name	Co.	Date	Recorded Copy	Original
Berriman, Benjamin	041	1791	WB-1/89	AR
Berriman, Edward	041	1800	WB-1/176	AR
Berriman, William	041	1827	WB-2/266	AR
Berry, (Not shown)	030	c1813	WB-3/23	
Berry, Balson	018	1834	WB-C/161	
Berry, Barbara	030	1888	WB-5/152	AR
Berry, Bartlett	014	1900	WB-3/108	CTY
Berry, Bartlett	014	1897	WB-3/3	CTY
Berry, Charles	024	1766	WB-1/21	AR
Berry, Curnealus	030	1752	Orig. Only	SS/AR
Berry, Edwin M.	040	1881	WB-2/175	AR
Berry, Elisha	020	1839	RB-N/379	
Berry, Elizabeth	078	1816	WI-7/127	AR
Berry, Henry	073	1858	WB-G/199	AR
Berry, J. W.	014	1900	WB-3/120	CTY
Berry, John	060	1833	WB-1/283	AR-Copy
Berry, John	073	1870	WB-H/29	CTY
Berry, John	053	1899	WB-11/340	AR
Berry, John A.	077	1871	WB-H/38	AR
Berry, John H.	073	1894	WB-I/47	CTY
Berry, Lancelot	028	1775	Orig. Only	AR
Berry, Mary	030	1802	WB-2/203	
Berry, Michel	073	1782	WB-A/272	AR
Berry, Richard	018	1842	WB-C/274	
Berry, Robert	060	1835	WB-1/346	
Berry, Robert	073	1814	WB-D/408	AR
Berry, Robert	060	1835	Orig. Only	AR/CRX
Berry, Ruth	065	1852	Orig. Only	AR
Berry, Sarah	018	1827	WB-C/89	
Berry, Thomas	073	1761	WB-A/19	
Berry, Thomas	070	c1742	WB-C/15	AR
Berry, Thomas B.	018	1870	WB-E/23	AR
Berry, William	030	1832	WB-3/326	
Berry, William A.	070	1875	WB-E/299 & 486	AR
Berry, William G.	060	1835	WB-1/328	AR
Berryhill, Elisabeth	065	1806	WB-A/93	AR
Berryhill, Harriet	065	1879	WB-K/337	AR
Berryhill, John	065	1820	WB-A/147	AR
Berryhill, Joseph	065	1781	WB-A/79	AR
Berryhill, Samuel	065	1879	WB-K/318	AR
Berryhill, Samuel	065	1778	WB-A/120	AR
Berryhill, Thomas	065	1799	WB-A/98	AR
Berryhill, William M.	065	1869	WB-K/17	AR
Berryman, A. C.	068	1887	WB-D/252	
Berryman, Benjamin	072	1831	WB-1/74	AR
Berryman, Jelsin	085	1834	WB-H/635	AR
Berryman, John	047	1794	WB-3/234	AR
Berryman, Joseph	072	1793	Orig. Only	AR
Berryman, Josiah	047	1790	WB-3/178	AR
Bertie, Eli	024	1829	WB-C/148	AR-Nunc.
Bertoli, Joseph S.	KY	1889	025 WB-A/117	025 AR
Bery, James	019	1788	WB-D/81	AR
Bescherer, Sophia	085	1889	WB-2/343	CTY
Beseley, Elisha	028	1809	WB-B/338	AR
Besely, John	030	1772	WB-1/74	
Bess, Boston	060	1869	WB-4/44	AR
Bess, Hiram	060	1847	WB-2/284	AR
Bess, Mary Ann	028	1860	WB-D/326	AR
Bess, Peter	060	1899	WB-5/134	AR
Bess, Peter	060	c1832	Orig. Only	AR
Bessell, Mary	024	1836	WB-C/203	
Bessent, Ransom P.	033	1892	016 WB-4/277	016 AR
Bessent, Ransom P.	033	1892	WB-2/129	CTY
Bessent, Rebecca	033	1879	WB-2/70	CTY
Best, Allen	103	1891	WB-1/557	AR
Best, B. J.	045	1899	WB-1/394	AR
Best, Benjamin	100	1866	WB-50/171	AR
Best, Bosten	060	1809	Orig. Only	AR
Best, Bostian	065	1761	WB-A/127	AR
Best, Calvin C.	103	1882	WB-1/253	AR
Best, Catherine	035	1818	WB-A/63	AR
Best, Charles	103	1889	WB-1/484	
Best, David R.	051	1889	WB-C/394	AR
Best, Edward W.	039	1889	WB-U/480	AR
Best, Eliza	009	1898	WB-2/141	CTY
Best, Elizabeth	051	1872	WB-C/67	AR
Best, Elizabeth	045	1900	WB-1/402	
Best, Francis J.	063	1885	WB-3/290	AR
Best, George S.	035	1863	WB-3/62	AR
Best, Henry	035	1851	WB-2/62	AR
Best, Henry	051	1845	WB-A/241	
Best, Hinton J.	103	1890	WB-1/528	AR
Best, Howel	035	1839	Orig. Only	AR
Best, Howel	035	1864	WB-3/89	AR
Best, Howel	035	1864	Copy	087 AR
Best, J. J.	051	1865	WB-B/73	AR
Best, James	096	1787	WB-1/155	AR
Best, James	085	1762	WB-A/9	AR
Best, John	051	1845	WB-A/240	
Best, John	063	1887	WB-4/17	AR
Best, John	035	1799	WB-A/13	AR
Best, John W.	100	1800	WB-11/25	AR
Best, Kedar	015	1775	100 WB-2/75	AR
Best, Marietta	009	1893	WB-1/591	CTY
Best, Mary A.	103	1881	WB-1/225	AR
Best, Nancy	103	1871	WB-1/35	AR
Best, Nancy	051	1874	WB-C/127	AR
Best, Patience	083	c1808	WB-1/110	AR
Best, Permelia A.	051	1894	WB-C/491	AR
Best, Prudence	035	1867	WB-3/120	AR
Best, Rachel	103	1859	RD-13/37	AR
Best, Redden	035	1857	WB-2/115	AR
Best, Rigdon	103	c1839	Orig. Only	AR
Best, Rufus E.	045	c1879	Orig. Only	AR
Best, Samuel	040	1891	WB-2/399	
Best, Sarah	070	1842	WB-AB/370	AR
Best, Theophilus	103	1831	RD-6/228	AR
Best, Thomas	030	c1814	WB-3/48	
Best, Thomas	030	1818	WB-3/102	
Best, Thomas	072	c1784	WI/L48	AR
Best, Thomas	051	1822	WB-A/203	
Best, Thomas	063	1791	WB-1/170	
Best, Thomas T.	038	1896	WB-3/572	AR
Best, W. R.	105	1899	WB-3/324	AR
Best, William	035	1791	WB-A/44	AR
Best, William	030	c1810	WB-3/2	
Bestow, Marcus P.	NY	c1882	Copy	064 AR
Betcham, Thomas	030	1793	WB-2/13	
Bethea, Jennet	048	1900	WB-1/116	CTY
Bethell, Mary	084	1873	WB-E/52	CTY
Bethell, W. D.	084	1888	WB-E/388	CTY
Bethell, William	084	c1804	WB-A/4	CTY
Bethell, William	020	1838	RB-N/150	
Bethey, James	041	1797	WB-1/152	AR
Bethey, John	041	1799	WB-1/170	AR
Bethune, Allen	068	1844	WB-B/145	
Bethune, Christian	083	1868	WB-2/241	AR
Bethune, Colin	029	1820	WB-B/35	
Bethune, Elizabeth	082	1827	WB-1/288	AR

Name	Co.	Date	Recorded Copy	Original
Bethune, Flora	083	1850	WB-2/13	AR
Bethune, Flora Jane	083	1860	WB-2/165	AR
Bethune, John	083	1854	WB-2/101	
Bethune, John	082	c1856	WB-6/127	AR
Bethune, Kate M.	083	1875	WB-3/87	AR
Bethune, Lauchlin	029	1874	WB-E/131	AR
Bethune, Malcolm	082	1827	WB-1/286	AR
Bethune, Sarah	067	c1883	Orig. Only	AR
Bettencourt, Emanuel	070	1854	WB-C/569	AR
Bettencourt, Mary Isabel	070	1893	WB-G/142	AR
Bettencourt, William C.	070	1863	WB-D/118	AR
Bettencourt, William C.	070	1863	Copy	012 AR
Betterley, Thomas	024	c1729	Orig. Only	AR
Bettis, Elisha	029	1767	Orig. Only	AR
Bettis, Elisha	068	1804	WB-A/233	
Betts, A. W.	099	1862	RB-32/259	AR
Betts, Barzilla	099	1833	RB-22/528	AR
Betts, Charles	012	1809	WB-B/83	AR
Betts, Joseph	099	1806	RB-7/114	AR
Betty, George	100	1809	WB-15/17	AR
Betz, George	085	1817	WB-G/456	AR
Bevans, Richard	053	c1744	SS 878/124	SS/AR
Bevel, Joseph	044	1800	WB-5/49	CTY
Bevens, Mary	053	1754	Orig. Only	SS/AR
Bever, David	085	1815	WB-G/345	AR
Bever, Peter	085	1817	WB-G/457	AR
Beveret, Benjamin	035	1750	087 DB-2/84	
Beverley, John, Sr.	010	1737	Orig. Only	SS/AR
Beverly, Allen	051	1876	WB-C/168	AR
Beverly, George W.	051	1894	WB-C/486	AR
Beverly, John	005	1843	Orig. Only	AR
Beverly, Mary L.	037	1886	WB-H/67	
Beverly, Rebecca	041	1842	WB-A/149	
Beverly, William H.	037	1865	WB-G/269	AR
Bevers, Thomas	099	1853	RB-28/321	AR
Beves, Stanford D.	039	1867	WB-S/427	
Beves, Zachariah	099	1810	RB-9/222	AR
Bevill, Francis	078	1812	WI-6/94	
Bevill, Hezekiah	046	1828	Orig. Only	AR
Bevill, Phillip	046	1860	WB-D/57	AR
Bevill, Pleasant	046	1830	WB-B/430	AR
Bevill, Spencer G.	046	1881	WB-E/294	AR
Bevill, William	046	1821	WB-B/122	AR
Bevis, Christopher	070	c1750	DB-D/51	AR
Bexley, Cristopher	028	1838	WB-C/412	AR
Bexley, William	N	1745	SS 877/32	SS/AR (N)
Bexton, Harriett	029	1870	WB-E/19	
Bezwell, Mary Ann	046	1829	WB-B/400	AR
Bibb, Margaret	097	1884	WB-2/256	AR
Bibb, William	097	1875	WB-2/84	
Bibighaus, Christina	090	1828	WB-3/189	AR
Bibighouse, George	090	1806	WB-2/71	AR-Nunc.
Bichop, John M.	047	1857	WB-5/35	
Bickett, Thoms W.	097	1882	WB-2/215	
Bickle, Tobias	085	c1807	WB-F/4	AR
Bicknell, Samuel	104	1820	WB-3/214	AR
Bicknell, Thomas	104	1781	WB-1/54	AR
Biddel, Isaac	072	c1760	RW/L56	AR
Bidding, Isaac	032	1899	WB-4/397	AR
Biddle, Alonzo	028	1885	WB-E/390	AR
Biddle, Jacob	072	1758	SS 879/261	SS/AR
Biddle, Jacob	072	1790	Orig. Only	AR
Biddle, Samuel S.	028	1872	WB-E/71	AR
Biddle, William P.	028	1853	WB-D/208	
Bigelow, Roderick	020	1819	RB-H/284	
Bigelow, Thomas	020	1873	WB-A/113	CTY
Biggam, Alexander	028	1792	WB-A/272	AR
Bigger, Joseph	085	1835	WB-H/654	AR
Biggers, Garrison	097	1900	WB-3/19	AR
Biggers, Norris	097	1892	WB-2/429	AR
Biggers, Robert	016	1846	WB-1/119	
Biggers, W. D.	032	1899	WB-4/419	AR
Biggerstaff, Benjamin	086	1900	WB-G/75	AR
Biggerstaff, Kinchen N.	086	1887	WB-F/316	AR
Biggerstaff, Noah	086	1882	WB-F/179	AR
Biggerstaff, Samuel	086	1850	WB-E/195	AR
Biggerstaff, Samuel	065	1764	WB-A/117	AR
Biggleston, Ann C.	028	1796	WB-A/341	AR
Biggleston, James	028	1786	WB-A/148	AR
Biggs, Alfred	083	1857	WB-2/120	AR
Biggs, Asa	VA	1878	010 WB-I/237	010 AR
Biggs, Benjamin	006	1893	WB-E/244	AR
Biggs, Catherine	063	1895	WB-4/183	AR
Biggs, Daniel	063	1834	WB-2/198	
Biggs, Eli C.	047	1894	WB-7/126	AR
Biggs, Henry C.	063	1877	WB-3/129	
Biggs, James	083	1826	WB-1/319	AR
Biggs, James	063	1789	WB-1/152	
Biggs, John	028	1812	WB-C/61	AR
Biggs, John	037	1789	WB-C/114	AR
Biggs, John	028	1769	Orig. Only	AR
Biggs, Joseph	063	1844	WB-2/308	
Biggs, Joseph	063	c1798	WB-1/352	
Biggs, Kader	063	1888	WB-4/26	
Biggs, Kader	VA	1884	047 WB-6/337	047 AR
Biggs, Kader	VA	1884	010 WB-I/241	010 AR
Biggs, Lydia	006	1893	WB-E/244	AR
Biggs, Martha E.	063	1885	WB-3/272	AR
Biggs, Samuel	083	1830	Orig. Only	AR
Biggs, Thedar	063	1815	WB-2/25	
Biggs, Warren	063	1866	WB-2/550	
Biggs, Wiley	063	1846	WB-2/322	
Biggs, William	028	1792	WB-A/282	AR
Biggs, William	063	1817	WB-2/45	
Biggs, William	028	1810	WB-C/10	AR
Biggs, William G.	063	1862	WB-2/508	
Bigham, Andrew	065	1788	WB-A/125	AR
Bigham, James	065	c1845	WB-I/37	AR
Bigham, James	065	1875	WB-K/190	
Bigham, John	065	1792	WB-A/138	AR
Bigham, John	065	1826	WB-A/151	AR
Bigham, John	065	1839	WB-E/230	AR
Bigham, Joseph H.	016	1866	WB-2/137	
Bigham, Martha	065	1849	WB-I/153	AR
Bigham, Robert	065	1815	WB-A/144	AR
Bigham, Samuel	065	1823	WB-B/15	AR
Bigham, William	065	1866	WB-J/222	AR
Bigham, William	065	1824	WB-A/150	AR
Bignall, Edward	100	1811	WB-16/36	AR
Bignall, Elizabeth	037	1795	WB-C/318	AR
Bignall, Robert	037	1793	WB-C/225	AR
Bignall, Robert	037	1787	WB-C/51	AR
Bilbery, Duel	037	1837	WB-F/200	AR
Bilbery, Nathaniel	037	1836	WB-F/191	AR
Bilbo, John	073	1836	Orig. Only	AR
Bilbre, Marget	037	1787	WB-C/45	AR
Bilbro, Berryman	069	1816	WB-1/283	AR
Bilbro, Sarah P.	099	1881	WB-A/225	AR
Bilbry, James, Sr.	037	1861	WB-G/209	AR

Name	Co.	Date	Recorded Copy	Original
Bilbry, Nancy	037	1843	WB-F/288	AR
Biles, Alexander	089	1882	WB-2/91	AR
Biles, Daniel	085	1835	WB-H/666	
Biles, Daniel	089	1875	WB-2/165	AR
Biles, Deborah	085	c1804	WB-D/115	AR
Biles, Elizabeth	085	c1792	WB-D/166	AR
Biles, Franklin	089	1863	WB-1/246	
Biles, Thomas	085	c1781	WB-D/163	AR
Biles, Thomas	089	1845	WB-1/39	AR
Biles, William	089	1896	WB-2/326	
Bill, Avery A.	070	1811	WB-AB/166	AR
Bill, Francis	070	1893	WB-G/161	AR
Billet, John	075	1720	SS 875/223	
Billing, John, Sr.	085	c1799	WB-F/23	AR
Billing, Juliana	085	c1803	WB-C/301	AR
Billings, Benjamin	032	1851	Orig. Only	AR
Billings, Elisha	104	1875	WB-6/251	AR
Billings, Frederick	032	1831	WB-1/166	AR
Billings, Henry	032	1883	WB-3/408	AR
Billings, James	084	1893	WB-E/539	CTY
Billings, John	032	1827	WB-1/72	AR
Billings, John L.	004	1893	WB-A/143	AR
Billings, Phebe	032	1873	WB-3/71	AR
Billings, Sarah	032	1881	WB-3/325	AR
Billings, Sarah	104	1888	WB-6/309	AR
Billingsby, Amos S.	054	1897	WB-6/115	CTY
Billingsby, David P.	005	1851	WB-C/36	AR
Billingsby, James	046	1776	WB-A/27	AR
Billingsly, Elizabeth	081	c1782	Orig. Only	AR
Billingsly, Hezekiah	082	1795	WB-1/59	AR
Billingsly, Lorenzo D.	084	1850	WB-C/110	CTY
Billitter, Zebadee	090	1814	WB-2/152	AR
Billue, Robert S.	097	1884	WB-2/261	AR
Billue, Stephen	065	1838	WB-E/203	AR
Billups, Georgiana	077	1889	WB-H/186	AR
Billups, Isabel	037	1850	WB-F/437	AR
Billups, James M.	077	1880	WB-H/98	AR
Billups, Langly	077	1832	WB-F/199	AR
Billups, Robert L.	041	1887	WB-4/260	AR
Binford, James	071	1824	WB-3/302	AR
Binford, James R.	047	1844	WB-4/228	AR
Binford, John	078	1798	WB-2/175	AR
Bing, John	100	1856	WB-49/82	AR
Bingham, Amy	022	1859	WB-D/35	AR
Bingham, Eliza A.	073	1885	WB-H/374	CTY
Bingham, Jason L.	081	1900	WB-17/88	
Bingham, John M.	104	1888	WB-6/337	AR
Bingham, Lourania	081	1897	WB-16/409	AR
Bingham, Mabel	029	1859	WB-C/407	AR
Bingham, Thomas	081	1816	WB-4/361	AR
Bingham, William	073	1873	WB-H/65	AR-Copy
Bingham, William J.	073	1866	WB-G/482	CTY
Bingman, Eli	092	1880	WB-6/143	AR
Bingman, J. A.	092	1895	WB-6/400	
Bingman, John	092	1858	WB-5/32	
Binkley, John	092	1844	WB-4/218	
Binkly, Peter	090	1793	WB-1/42	AR
Binnarger, William	090	1813	WB-2/146	AR
Biram, John	010	1799	WB-E/78	AR
Birce, James	039	c1794	WB-A/113	
Birch, Mary	046	1872	WB-E/77	AR
Birchett, Ann E.	086	1844	WB-E/134	
Birckhead, Linggurn	081	1872	WB-15/90	AR
Birckhead, M. B.	081	1863	WB-12/515	
Bird, Ann	092	1847	WB-4/260	

Name	Co.	Date	Recorded Copy	Original
Bird, Benjamin	064	1892	WB-2/285	AR
Bird, Clara W.	001	1874	WB-2/103	AR
Bird, Empson	073	1831	WB-E/237	AR
Bird, Francis A.	013	1898	WB-D/196	AR
Bird, Henry	085	1826	WB-H/356	AR
Bird, Isaac	083	1842	WB-1/404	AR
Bird, J. C.	061	1892	WB-2/117	AR
Bird, James	073	1805	WB-D/155	AR
Bird, Jehu	020	1894	WB-B/173	CTY
Bird, Joab	099	1782	RB-1/156	AR
Bird, John	015	1778	100 WB-2/265	AR
Bird, John	085	c1801	WB-E/8	AR
Bird, Joseph	092	c1832	WB-4/44	
Bird, Levi	010	1846	WB-G/395	AR
Bird, Marinah	105	1864	WB-1/109	AR
Bird, Mary	073	1815	WB-D/429	AR
Bird, Mealy	085	1823	WB-H/238	AR
Bird, Nancy	001	1858	WB-1/129	AR
Bird, Peter	047	1784	WB-3/72	AR
Bird, Rebecka	073	1837	WB-E/509	AR
Bird, Richard	073	1829	WB-E/202	AR
Bird, Richard	064	1856	WB-1/47	AR
Bird, Richard	047	1835	WB-4/122	AR
Bird, Richard	064	c1900	Orig. Only	AR
Bird, Robert	035	1802	WB-A/32	AR
Bird, Susanna	085	1816	WB-G/403	AR
Bird, Thomas	073	1835	WB-E/362	AR
Bird, Thomas	010	1742	Orig. Only	SS/AR
Bird, Wiley	069	1833	WB-1/393	AR
Bird, William	096	1791	063 WB-1/183	
Bird, William	020	1850	RB-Q/368	AR
Birdseye, Ezekiel	CT	1861	062 WB-B/45	
Birdseye, Ezekiel	CT	1861	049 WB-1/270	
Birdseye, Mary M.	CT	1878	049 WB-1/280	
Birdseye, Mary M.	CT	1878	062 WB-B/53	
Birkhead, Margaret	085	c1868	WB-L/35	AR
Birmingham, George W.	005	1888	WB-D/269	AR
Birmingham, Stephen	005	1837	Copy	097 AR
Birnie, William	070	1752	Orig. Only	SS/AR
Birote, Peter	024	1743	Orig. Only	SS/AR
Birum, Briand	024	c1772	WB-B/18	AR
Birum, Isaac	024	1834	WB-C/177	AR
Birvighaus, Elizabeth	038	c1854	WB-1/50	AR
Biscoe, Anna D.	014	1890	WB-2/421	CTY
Biscoe, Mary	030	1788	WB-1/221	
Bishier, Conrod	085	1846	WB-K/35	AR
Bishind, Jacob	073	1774	WB-A/172	
Bishop, Anderson	086	1896	WB-F/503	AR
Bishop, Avis	104	1784	WB-1/127	AR
Bishop, Benjamin	022	1801	Orig. Only	AR
Bishop, Bolin	047	1844	WB-4/230	AR
Bishop, Burage	053	1872	WB-11/28	AR
Bishop, Charles	070	1787	WB-C/30	AR
Bishop, George	072	1744	SS 878/24	SS/AR
Bishop, George	072	1744	070 DB-C/35	070 AR
Bishop, George	071	1900	WB-7/471	AR
Bishop, James	028	1854	WB-D/223	
Bishop, James	044	1798	WB-4/222	CTY
Bishop, James	103	1816	RD-4/7	AR
Bishop, James	047	1854	WB-4/358	AR
Bishop, Jesse	072	1865	WB-3/7	AR
Bishop, John	053	1824	Orig. Only	AR
Bishop, John	047	1819	WB-3/636	AR
Bishop, John	028	1781	Orig. Only	AR
Bishop, John	028	1801	WB-B/114	AR

Name	Co.	Date	Recorded Copy	Original
Bishop, John J.	047	1890	WB-6/575	AR
Bishop, John M.	047	1857	WB-5/35	
Bishop, John, Sr.	028	1772	Orig. Only	AR
Bishop, Jonathan	047	1802	WB-3/371	AR
Bishop, Joseph	028	1798	WB-B/61	AR
Bishop, Marcus	047	1833	WB-4/97	AR
Bishop, Rebecca	028	1790	WB-A/231	AR
Bishop, Thomas H.	031	1887	096 WB-4/134	
Bishop, William	072	1851	WB-2/109	AR
Bishop, William	053	1812	RW-1/470	
Bishop, William	047	1783	WB-3/47	AR
Bishop, William J.	010	1889	WB-I/271	AR
Bissell, Edward H.	065	1886	WB-L/187	AR
Bissell, Edward H.	040	1886	WB-2/254	AR
Bissell, J. H.	065	1845	WB-I/24	
Bissell, Mary	024	1836	WB-C/203	AR
Bissell, Nathl. C.	024	1834	WB-C/175	AR
Bissell, Thomas	028	1812	WB-C/49	AR
Bisset, David	069	1806	WB-1/166	AR
Bisset, John	069	1838	WB-1/431	AR
Bissit, Judith	069	1827	WB-1/343	AR
Bitting, Anthony	090	1804	WB-2/56	AR
Bitting, Anthony	038	1876	WB-2/269	AR
Bitting, Elizabeth	090	1828	WB-3/186	AR
Bitting, John H.	090	1847	WB-4/235	AR
Bitting, John L.	090	1851	WB-4/267	AR
Bitting, Julia E.	TX	c1885	Copy	106 AR
Bitting, Martha	090	1875	WB-6/72	AR
Bittle, Jesse	005	1818	WB-2/7	AR
Bittle, John	071	1787	WB-1/377	AR
Bivens, Daniel	073	1880	WB-H/259	CTY
Bivens, James	097	1865	WB-1/251	AR
Bivens, John	065	1818	WB-A/124	AR
Bivens, Nathaniel	005	1818	WB-2/8	AR
Bivens, Stephen	001	1889	WB-2/426	AR
Bizwell, Benjamin	046	1820	WB-B/105	AR
Bizwell, Mary A.	046	1829	WB-B/377	AR
Bizzell, A. F.	082	1896	WB-6/535	AR
Bizzell, A. F.	082	1896	011 WB-3/93	011 CTY
Bizzell, David	103	1817	RD-4/99	AR
Bizzell, George W.	103	1898	WB-2/219	AR
Bizzell, James	035	1822	WB-A/50	AR
Bizzell, James A.	087	1878	WB-3/173	AR
Bizzell, John	051	1866	WB-B/90	
Bizzell, John	103	c1797	Orig. Only	AR-Copy
Bizzell, John	103	1819	RD-4/294	AR-Nunc.
Bizzell, John S.	103	c1895	Orig. Only	AR-Copy
Bizzell, M. H.	103	1895	WB-2/141	AR
Bizzell, Mary	035	1829	WB-A/12	AR
Bizzell, Repsy	087	1872	WB-3/42	AR
Bizzell, Rueben	065	1836	Orig. Only	AR-Copy
Bizzell, Samuel	056	1871	WB-3/59	AR
Bizzell, Simon	051	c1887	WB-C/519	AR
Bizzell, William	035	1800	WB-A/14	AR
Black, Absalum	065	1858	WB-J/54	AR
Black, Adam	085	c1789	WB-D/156	AR
Black, Ame	065	1837	WB-E/162	AR
Black, Andrew	032	1896	WB-4/273	AR
Black, Archibald	068	c1834	WB-B/118	
Black, Archibald	029	1792	Orig. Only	AR
Black, Daniel	029	1889	Orig. Only	AR
Black, Daniel B.	068	1850	WB-B/211	
Black, David	054	c1803	WB-1/77	AR
Black, David	001	1886	WB-2/293	AR
Black, David	029	1890	WB-E/500	
Black, Donald	029	1810	WB-A/161	AR
Black, Elizabeth	084	1821	WB-A/136	CTY
Black, Ephriam	060	1843	WB-2/184	AR
Black, Ezekiel	065	1837	WB-H/22	AR
Black, F. H.	099	1891	WB-B/561	AR
Black, Frances	024	1788	WB-B/161	AR
Black, George	032	1884	WB-3/440	AR
Black, George	078	1801	WI-2/331	AR
Black, George	081	1817	WB-4/412	AR
Black, Henry	020	1789	RB-B/255	
Black, Henry	085	c1804	WB-F/61	AR
Black, Henry	028	1831	WB-C/334	AR
Black, Henry	046	1881	Orig. Only	AR
Black, Hugh	068	1820	WB-B/6	
Black, Hugh	068	1882	WB-D/142	AR
Black, Isaac	070	1754	SS 879/176	SS/AR
Black, Isaac	070	1754	DB-D/120	
Black, Jacob	085	1821	WB-H/135	AR
Black, James	065	1842	WB-H/101	AR
Black, James	029	1801	WB-A/40	AR
Black, James G.	065	1858	WB-J/56	AR
Black, Jane	065	1840	WB-H/7	AR
Black, Jefferson	026	1899	WB-3/35	AR
Black, John	065	1829	WB-E/66	AR
Black, John	078	1795	WI-1/211	AR
Black, John	004	1871	WB-A/3	AR
Black, John	068	1833	WB-B/82	
Black, John	065	1809	WB-A/142	AR
Black, John	070	1866	WB-D/186	AR
Black, John C.	065	1837	WB-E/160	AR
Black, John M.	016	1877	WB-3/220	AR
Black, John, Sr.	054	c1823	Orig. Only	AR
Black, Joseph M.	016	1877	WB-3/216	AR
Black, Josiah	099	1788	RB-2/184	AR
Black, Kitty	028	1881	WB-E/280	AR
Black, Martin	019	1821	WB-D/57	AR
Black, Maryann	065	1848	WB-I/124	AR
Black, Matilda E.	084	1894	WB-E/578	CTY
Black, Michael	028	1760	Orig. Only	SS/AR
Black, Nancy A.	065	1881	WB-K/477	AR
Black, Pleasant	084	1881	WB-E/200	CTY
Black, Rebekah	054	c1808	WB-1/125	AR
Black, Robert	020	1781	RB-A/169	AR
Black, Sallie	029	1900	WB-F/209	AR
Black, Samuel	070	1851	WB-C/523	AR
Black, Samuel	024	c1782	WB-B/36	AR
Black, Samuel	065	1875	WB-K/174	AR
Black, Samuel	065	1831	WB-E/102	AR
Black, Samuel	070	1851	Copy	012 AR
Black, Samuel J.	065	1899	WB-N/314	AR
Black, Samuel N.	016	1856	WB-1/277	
Black, Stephen	040	c1853	WB-1/67	AR
Black, Thomas	065	1845	WB-I/23	AR
Black, Thomas	065	1772	WB-A/76	AR
Black, Thomas	078	1793	WI-1/108	AR
Black, Thomas N.	016	1848	WB-1/150	
Black, Thomas O.	065	1844	WB-H/146	AR
Black, Thomas P.	060	1873	WB-4/100	AR
Black, Vincent	040	1889	WB-2/346	AR
Black, William	065	1764	WB-A/115	AR
Black, William	065	1852	WB-I/193	AR
Black, William	065	1826	WB-A/151	AR
Black, William	054	c1792	WB-1/79	AR
Black, William	065	1776	WB-A/77	AR
Black, William S.	100	1897	WB-51/474	

Name	Co.	Date	Recorded Copy	Original
Black, William W.	054	c1812	WB-1/299	AR
Blackall, Abraham	024	1749	Orig. Only	SS/AR
Blackall, Sarah	024	1754	SS 881/92	SS/AR
Blackborn, William	035	1762	WB-A/24	AR
Blackburn, Bryson	090	1840	WB-4/55	AR
Blackburn, Burrell	087	1892	WB-3/510	AR
Blackburn, Elizabeth	006	1804	WB-A/39	AR
Blackburn, Gabriel W.	090	1843	WB-4/132	AR
Blackburn, Hamilton	006	1892	WB-E/222	AR
Blackburn, Hiram	087	1858	WB-1/524	AR
Blackburn, James	060	1808	Orig. Only	AR
Blackburn, Jane	046	1899	WB-G/168	AR
Blackburn, John	047	1778	WB-2/88	
Blackburn, John	024	c1785	WB-A/104	AR
Blackburn, John T.	090	1844	WB-4/160	AR
Blackburn, John, Sr.	084	1834	WB-B/90	CTY
Blackburn, Lavina	084	1875	WB-E/106	CTY
Blackburn, Martha T.	060	1900	WB-5/162	AR
Blackburn, Mary	047	1854	WB-4/368	
Blackburn, Mary	047	1830	WB-4/67	AR
Blackburn, Mary M.	092	1876	WB-6/73	AR
Blackburn, Newman	092	1772	WB-1/2	AR
Blackburn, Robert	032	1842	WB-1/403	AR
Blackburn, Robert	060	1879	WB-4/212	AR
Blackburn, S. A. R.	060	c1898	Orig. Only	AR
Blackburn, William	037	1804	WB-D/190	AR
Blackburn, William	060	1882	WB-4/253	AR
Blackburn, William	087	1822	WB-1/39	AR
Blackburn, Winifred	090	1843	WB-4/131	AR
Blackburn, Younger	090	1817	WB-3/2	AR
Blackford, Samuel	005	1785	WB-1/46	
Blackledge, Ann	028	1807	WB-B/277	AR
Blackledge, Benjamin	028	1783	Orig. Only	AR
Blackledge, Benjamin	009	c1806	OWB/436	AR
Blackledge, Louisa	037	1789	WB-C/49	AR
Blackledge, Richard	028	1777	Orig. Only	SS/AR
Blackledge, Susanna	047	1818	WB-3/628	AR
Blackledge, William S.	028	1856	WB-D/273	AR
Blackley, James	044	1803	WB-5/337	CTY
Blackley, Rebecca	065	1838	WB-E/183	AR
Blackman, Abigail	087	1876	WB-3/139	AR
Blackman, Ann	103	1818	RD-4/120	AR
Blackman, Arthur	028	1768	Orig. Only	AR
Blackman, Barzilla C.	056	1865	WB-2/66	
Blackman, Barzillai	056	1806	WB-1/183	AR
Blackman, Bennett	056	c1765	Orig. Only	AR
Blackman, Druzilla	056	1842	WB-1/544	AR
Blackman, Joab	087	c1819	Orig. Only	AR
Blackman, John	010	1736	Orig. Only	SS/AR
Blackman, John	056	1760	Orig. Only	AR
Blackman, John	056	1810	WB-1/228	AR
Blackman, Joseph	056	c1780	Orig. Only	AR
Blackman, Joseph	056	1815	WB-1/247	AR
Blackman, Joshua	035	c1768	WB-A/48	AR
Blackman, Josiah	056	1871	WB-3/55	AR
Blackman, Mary	056	1815	WB-1/237	AR
Blackman, Moore	056	1840	WB-1/519	AR
Blackman, Nicholas	010	1730	Orig. Only	SS/AR
Blackman, Ruth	056	1899	WB-4/189	AR
Blackman, Susannah	087	1839	WB-1/216	AR
Blackman, Unity J.	056	1900	WB-4/233	AR
Blackman, William	087	c1818	WB-A/92	AR
Blackman, William	087	1841	WB-1/238	AR
Blackmer, E. G.	085	1868	WB-1/3	CTY
Blackmer, Luke	085	1889	WB-2/322	CTY

Name	Co.	Date	Recorded Copy	Original
Blackmon, Cullen A.	103	1836	RD-7/155	AR
Blackmon, Herrall	035	1781	WB-A/22	
Blackmon, Loverd	029	1872	WB-E/69	AR
Blacknall, Elizabeth	073	1848	WB-F/400	AR
Blacknall, Louisa A.	044	1895	WB-24/289	CTY
Blacknall, Thomas	039	1864	WB-R/750	AR
Blacknall, Thomas	044	1837	WB-14/18	CTY
Blacknall, William J.	039	1834	WB-K/27	
Blackshear, Agness	057	1793	WB-A/78	AR
Blackshear, Alexander	057	1786	WB-A/61	AR
Blackshear, Elisha	057	1810	WB-A/326	AR
Blackshear, James	057	1788	WB-A/175	AR
Blackstock, John	075	1787	WB-K/153	AR
Blackstock, William	065	1831	WB-G/70	AR
Blackwelder, Alexander	016	1892	WB-4/131	AR
Blackwelder, Allen M.	033	1872	WB-2/25	CTY
Blackwelder, Archibald	016	1872	WB-3/52	
Blackwelder, Christian	085	1862	WB-K/302	AR
Blackwelder, Daniel	016	1829	PQS.5/48	AR
Blackwelder, Elizabeth	016	1886	WB-3/498	AR
Blackwelder, Hiram	085	1866	WB-K/387	AR
Blackwelder, Isaac	016	1844	WB-1/29	
Blackwelder, Martin A.	016	1872	WB-3/54	AR
Blackwelder, Melinda	016	1890	WB-4/59	AR
Blackwelder, Rue Ann	016	1889	WB-4/20	AR
Blackwelder, Wiley	016	1891	WB-4/76	AR
Blackwelder, Willie	016	1864	WB-2/109	AR-Copy
Blackwell, Alexander	078	c1886	WB-19/324	AR
Blackwell, C. C.	005	1875	WB-D/46	
Blackwell, David A.	013	1898	WB-D/180	AR
Blackwell, Elendor	085	1848	WB-K/66	AR
Blackwell, Elizabeth	011	1864	WB-1/321	
Blackwell, Garland	020	1855	RB-R/298	AR
Blackwell, George	037	1767	WB-A/156	AR
Blackwell, George H.	080	1874	WB-1/18	AR
Blackwell, Isaiah	086	1810	WB-B/243	AR
Blackwell, James	085	1844	WB-I/206	AR
Blackwell, James	086	1853	WB-E/251	AR
Blackwell, James L.	036	1893	WB-A/291	CTY
Blackwell, James S.	020	1892	WB-B/92	CTY
Blackwell, Joel	086	1817	WB-C/156	AR
Blackwell, John	085	1846	WB-K/45	AR
Blackwell, John	020	1879	WB-A/259	CTY
Blackwell, John	044	1818	WB-8/105	CTY
Blackwell, John B.	020	1881	WB-A/328	CTY
Blackwell, John P.	078	1858	WB-18/6	AR
Blackwell, Joseph S.	090	1886	WB-6/164	AR
Blackwell, Josiah V.	014	1893	WB-2/516	CTY
Blackwell, Mary	078	1838	Orig. Only	AR
Blackwell, Micajah	010	1771	WB-A/136	AR
Blackwell, Milton G.	020	1879	WB-A/273	CTY
Blackwell, Rachael	078	1849	WB-13/230	AR
Blackwell, Robert	033	1897	WB-2/215	CTY
Blackwell, Robert	020	1813	RB-F/346	AR
Blackwell, Robert	020	1816	RB-G/128	
Blackwell, Robert M.	NY	1869	009 WB-1/17	009 AR
Blackwell, Rosey	044	1872	WB-23/63	CTY
Blackwell, Sally J.	100	1851	WB-41/189	AR
Blackwell, Susan	078	1877	WB-19/69	AR
Blackwell, Temperance	044	1840	WB-14/532	CTY
Blackwell, Thomas	084	1856	WB-C/223	CTY
Blackwell, William	054	1850	WB-3/37	AR
Blackwell, William M.	044	1894	WB-24/251	CTY
Blackwell, Zillah	020	1823	RB-I/241	AR
Blackwill, Nathan	069	1846	WB-1/479	AR

Name	Co.	Date	Recorded Copy	Original
Blackwood, Ann	040	1880	WB-2/165	AR
Blackwood, David K.	073	1859	WB-G/226	CTY
Blackwood, Elizabeth	040	1883	WB-2/208	AR
Blackwood, Gideon	040	1874	WB-2/70	AR
Blackwood, James	060	1810	Orig. Only	AR
Blackwood, Jane	040	1889	WB-2/341	AR
Blackwood, John	085	1819	WB-G/542	AR
Blackwood, John	073	1843	WB-F/174	AR
Blackwood, Joseph	040	1864	WB-1/167	
Blackwood, Joseph	060	c1780	Orig. Only	AR
Blackwood, Joseph	065	N. D.	WB-E/127	AR
Blackwood, Joseph	040	1865	WB-1/182	AR
Blackwood, Joseph L.	065	1853	WB-I/229	AR
Blackwood, Leander W.	040	1887	WB-2/277	AR
Blackwood, Margaret	040	1896	WB-2/518	AR
Blackwood, Robert	073	1850	WB-F/451	AR
Blackwood, Samuel	060	1832	WB-1/250	AR
Blackwood, Thomas	065	1793	WB-A/94	AR
Blackwood, William	073	c1772	WB-A/129	
Blackwood, William	073	1830	WB-E/229	AR
Blades, Abraham	041	1847	WB-3/82	AR
Blades, Tilman	085	1826	WB-H/358	AR
Blair, Arminta J.	065	1882	WB-K/460	AR
Blair, Cynthia J.	081	1899	WB-16/548	
Blair, Enos	081	1834	WB-6/376	AR
Blair, Eunice	081	1899	WB-17/3	AR
Blair, Florence	065	1883	WB-K/578	AR
Blair, George	024	1772	WB-1/51	AR
Blair, Hugh	092	1783	WB-2/13	AR
Blair, J. Milikan	081	1896	WB-16/398	AR
Blair, James	046	1776	WB-A/28	AR
Blair, James	065	1838	WB-E/217	AR
Blair, James	017	1868	WB-B/4	AR
Blair, James	085	c1800	WB-D/150	AR
Blair, James G.	065	1856	WB-J/25	AR
Blair, James S.	016	1880	WB-3/286	AR
Blair, Jane	024	1789	WB-B/128	AR
Blair, Jesse	081	1864	WB-13/105	AR
Blair, Jesse C.	081	1866	WB-13/437	AR
Blair, John	046	1772	WB-A/27	AR
Blair, John	046	1778	WB-A/13	AR
Blair, John, Sr.	017	c1844	WB-A/33	AR
Blair, Jordan	024	1893	WB-E/218	AR
Blair, Margaret	065	1865	WB-J/207	AR
Blair, Maryan	017	1887	WB-B/145	
Blair, Morgan	017	c1885	Orig. Only	AR
Blair, Samuel	065	1836	WB-E/169	
Blair, Sarah	081	1890	WB-16/187	AR
Blair, Smith	085	1824	WB-H/292	AR
Blair, Thomas	046	1825	WB-B/206	AR
Blair, William	077	1813	WB-E/376	AR
Blake, Ann	070	1794	Orig. Only	AR-Nunc.
Blake, Anna	099	1861	RB-32/87	AR
Blake, Asa	099	1850	RB-27/65	AR
Blake, Benjamin	073	1783	WB-A/275	AR
Blake, Craty	099	1896	WB-C/548	AR
Blake, Daniel	050	1873	WB-1/132	CTY
Blake, David	030	1714/5	Orig. Only	SS/AR
Blake, Demsey	099	1819	RB-15/158	AR
Blake, Elizabeth	099	1861	RB-31/558	AR
Blake, Isham, Sr.	029	1836	WB-B/256	AR
Blake, James	010	1783	WB-C/53	AR
Blake, John	090	1824	WB-3/117	AR
Blake, Joseph	067	1849	WB-1/48	AR
Blake, Joshua	035	1834	WB-1/59	AR

Name	Co.	Date	Recorded Copy	Original
Blake, Marenva	099	1895	WB-C/470	AR
Blake, Mary M.	029	1844	WB-C/73	AR
Blake, Nancy	037	1825	WB-F/47	AR
Blake, Reddick	099	1869	RB-35/43	AR
Blake, Robert	028	1766	Orig. Only	AR
Blake, Samuel	099	1807	RB-7/284	AR
Blake, Susan	099	1841	RB-24/496	AR
Blake, Susan O. R.	083	1887	WB-3/394	AR
Blake, William Z.	099	c1892	WB-C/145	AR
Blakely, James	065	1873	WB-K/114	AR
Blakeney, Albert	097	1856	WB-1/130	AR
Blalock, Barnett	078	1867	WB-18/472	AR
Blalock, Charles	029	c1790	Orig. Only	AR
Blalock, David	089	1868	WB-2/1	Nunc.
Blalock, Green	078	1837	WI-13/254	AR
Blalock, Hasten	078	1860	WB-18/119	
Blalock, Jeremiah	026	1886	WB-2/297	
Blalock, Rebecca	044	1851	WB-18/392	CTY
Blalock, Richard	029	1805	Orig. Only	AR
Blalock, William P.	078	c1891	Orig. Only	AR
Blancett, William G.	090	1890	WB-6/242	
Blanchard, Absley	041	1829	WB-2/253	AR
Blanchard, Benjamin	VA	c1719	Copy	SS/AR
Blanchard, Easton	041	1890	WB-4/307	AR
Blanchard, Elender	001	1886	WB-2/307	AR
Blanchard, Ephraim	024	1749	Orig. Only	SS/AR
Blanchard, Ephraim	071	1823	WB-3/287	AR
Blanchard, Frederick	001	c1851	WB-1/79	AR
Blanchard, John N. L.	035	1891	WB-4/385	AR
Blanchard, Josiah	071	1824	WB-3/297	AR
Blanchard, Micajah	024	1867	WB-D/54	AR
Blanchard, Millenton	024	1815	WB-C/39	AR
Blanchard, Nancy	071	1853	WB-5/111	AR
Blanchard, Palatiah	041	1820	WB-2/164	AR
Blanchard, Reuben	035	1844	Orig. Only	AR
Blanchard, Robert	041	1873	WB-4/37	AR
Blanchard, Thomas L.	065	1895	WB-M/425	AR
Blanchard, William	041	c1842	Orig. Only	AR
Blanchard, William	024	1841	WB-C/229	AR
Blanchett, Micajah	024	1798	WB-A/341	AR
Blanchett, Thomas	100	1806	WB-13/285	AR
Bland, Barnes	079	1888	WB-2/429	AR
Bland, Charles	046	1841	WB-C/93	AR
Bland, D. W.	087	1897	WB-4/61	AR
Bland, Daniel	035	1871	WB-4/41	AR
Bland, Gabriel	035	1893	Orig. Only	AR
Bland, Isaac	087	c1873	Orig. Only	AR
Bland, Isaac N.	087	1876	WB-3/120	AR
Bland, J. C.	086	1899	WB-G/8	AR
Bland, James	022	1850	WB-C/280	AR
Bland, James	070	1774	WB-C/23	AR
Bland, James	035	1863	WB-3/67	AR
Bland, John	036	1891	WB-A/193	CTY
Bland, John	022	1827	WB-B/137	AR
Bland, Joseph J.	079	c1863	WB-1/95	AR
Bland, Moses	081	1800	WB-2/60	AR
Bland, Oliver	022	1868	WB-D/176	AR
Bland, Theophilus	047	1881	WB-6/256	AR
Bland, Thomas	047	c1772	063 WB-1/70	
Bland, Thomas	063	1791	WB-1/169	
Bland, William	086	1868	WB-F/4	AR
Bland, William	035	1775	WB-A/25	AR
Bland, William	035	1854	WB-2/88	AR
Blaney, Benjamin	012	1817	WB-B/113	
Blaney, George	012	1835	WB-B/171	

Name	Co.	Date	Recorded Copy	Original
Blango, Isaac	009	1842	OB-D/281	AR
Blaning, Hugh	011	1752	Orig. Only	SS/AR
Blankenship, Elias P.	065	1878	WB-K/293	AR
Blankenship, Fore	054	c1817	WB-2/2	AR
Blankenship, Hezekiah	086	1862	WB-E/398	AR
Blankenship, Hezekiah	086	1842	WB-E/100	AR
Blankenship, John F.	054	1879	WB-4/313	CTY
Blankenship, Sarah M.	003	1887	WB-B/225	AR
Blanks, Niccolas	072	1792	Orig. Only	AR-Nunc.
Blanks, Richard	044	1831	WB-12/97	CTY
Blanks, Samuel	044	1846	WB-16/462	CTY
Blanks, William	098	1893	WB-A/177	CTY
Blanshard, Aaron	041	1779	WB-1/1	AR
Blanshard, Aaron	024	1773	WB-A/227	AR
Blanshard, Absolom	041	1785	WB-1/44	AR
Blanshard, Benjamin	024	c1762	WB-A/212	AR
Blanshard, Jesse	103	1821	RD-4/380	AR
Blanshard, Mary	035	1848	WB-2/26	AR
Blanshard, Micajah	024	c1764	WB-A/213	AR
Blanshard, Sarah	041	1782	WB-1/25	AR
Blanton, Abraham	035	1874	WB-4/90	AR
Blanton, B. S.	086	1858	WB-E/342	AR
Blanton, B., Sr.	026	1887	WB-2/317	AR
Blanton, Burrel W.	026	1864	WB-1/356	AR
Blanton, Burwell	026	1863	WB-1/320	AR
Blanton, Charles	026	1866	WB-1/394	AR
Blanton, Elijah	086	1884	WB-F/228	AR
Blanton, George	086	1835	WB-E/15	AR
Blanton, George	086	1802	WB-B/144	AR
Blanton, Grandison	026	1862	WB-1/297	AR
Blanton, Guilford E.	086	1863	WB-E/416	AR
Blanton, John	026	1862	WB-1/291	AR
Blanton, John	063	1790	WB-1/165	
Blanton, John W.	026	1880	WB-2/203	AR
Blanton, Malinda	026	1897	WB-2/537	AR
Blanton, Rachel	026	1893	WB-2/461	AR
Blanton, Richard	035	1821	WB-A/12	AR
Blanton, Rubin	026	1889	WB-2/366	AR
Blare, Hugh	081	1840	WB-7/304	AR
Blatchford, John C.	009	1840	OB-C2/358	AR
Blaylock, John A.	054	1883	WB-4/490	CTY
Blaylock, John M.	046	1898	WB-G/54	AR
Bleadsoe, Kinchen	039	1863	WB-R/519	AR
Bledso, George	015	1777	100 WB-2/107	AR
Bledsoe, Abraham	044	1753	Orig. Only	CTY
Bledsoe, Addie A.	099	1896	WB-C/540	AR
Bledsoe, Isaac	056	1761	WB-1/750	AR
Bledsoe, Jacob	099	1817	RB-13/358	AR
Bledsoe, Jacob	099	1877	RB-35/373	AR
Bledsoe, James A.	039	1895	WB-V/44	AR
Bledsoe, John	099	1829	RB-21/140	AR
Bledsoe, Lewis	099	1853	RB-28/276	AR
Bledsoe, Mary	099	1861	RB-32/54	AR
Bledsoe, Patrick W.	039	1831	WB-J/120	AR
Bledsoe, Salley	099	1837	RB-24/48	AR
Bledsoe, Sallie	099	1885	WB-B/16	AR
Bledsoe, Solomon	099	1843	RB-25/344	AR
Bledsoe, Solomon H.	099	1873	RB-35/225	AR
Bledsoe, Ufame	039	1846	WB-M/124	AR
Blessing, John	032	1835	WB-1/258	AR
Bleu, Peter	009	c1783	OWB/179	AR
Blevins, Armstrong	006	c1868	Orig. Only	AR
Blevins, Daniel	006	1885	WB-E/106	AR
Blevins, Jehu	006	1899	WB-E/396	AR
Blevins, John	104	1891	WB-6/408	AR

Name	Co.	Date	Recorded Copy	Original
Blevins, Nancy B.	092	1900	WB-6/555	AR
Blevins, Sarah E.	090	1893	WB-6/307	AR
Blevins, Wells, Sr.	006	1840	WB-A/22	AR
Blevins, Wiley	066	c1875	Orig. Only	AR
Blewets, William	005	c1790	WB-A/34	AR
Blick, Robert	047	1825	WB-4/14	AR
Blickenden, Thomas	077	1745	Orig. Only	SS/AR
Blickensdoerfer, Catherine	038	1871	WB-2/68	AR
Blin, Daniel	009	1753	SS 879/117	SS/AR
Blinson, James R.	099	1890	WB-B/405	AR
Blish, John	075	1718	Orig. Only	SS/AR
Bliss, Daniel	009	1753	SS 877/340	
Blocker, John	029	c1796	Orig. Only	AR
Blocker, Michal	029	1761	Orig. Only	AR
Blockledge, William S.	028	1856	019 WB-E/79	
Bloodworth, Adam	070	1846	WB-AB/444	AR
Bloodworth, James, Sr.	070	1799	WB-AB/26	AR
Bloodworth, Leah	070	1858	WB-D/1	AR
Bloodworth, Martha	070	1847	WB-AB/474	AR
Bloodworth, Mary	070	1848	WB-C/481	AR
Bloodworth, Robert	070	1789	WB-C/32	AR
Bloodworth, William	037	1794	WB-C/271	AR
Bloom, Herman H.	070	1896	WB-G/538	AR
Bloom, John F.	070	1897	WB-H/78	AR
Bloom, John G.	065	1884	WB-L/18	AR
Bloss, Penelope	047	1826	WB-4/19	AR
Blossom, Frances E.	070	1898	WB-H/141	AR
Blount, Abraham	075	1847	WB-N/213	AR
Blount, Ann	024	1843	WB-C/238	AR
Blount, Benjamin	009	N. D.	Orig. Only	AR-Nunc.
Blount, Benjamin	096	1740	LGB-4/#114	SS/AR
Blount, Benjamin	096	1788	WB-1/158	AR
Blount, Bryan	009	c1807	OB-A/20	AR
Blount, Charles	077	1784	WB-C/275	AR
Blount, Charles W.	077	1807	WB-E/257	AR
Blount, Charles W.	075	1852	WB-N/240	AR
Blount, Charlotte	075	1884	WB-0/192	AR
Blount, Edmund	024	c1792	WB-A/151	AR
Blount, Edmund	096	1794	Orig. Only	AR
Blount, Edmund	096	1754	SS 882/90	
Blount, Edmund C.	075	1848	WB-N/220	AR
Blount, Eleanor	035	1862	WB-3/53	AR
Blount, Elizabeth	009	1807	OWB/451	AR
Blount, Elizabeth	024	1732/3	Orig. Only	SS/AR
Blount, Elizabeth	024	1723/4	SS 876/307	
Blount, Esther J.	079	1864	WB-1/110	AR
Blount, Evelina S.	079	1867	WB-1/173	AR-Copy
Blount, Francis	057	c1786	NBDSC	AR-Copy
Blount, Francis	057	c1786	WB-A/186	AR
Blount, Frederick	028	1824	WB-C/242	AR
Blount, George W.	105	1895	WB-3/165	AR
Blount, Henry	009	1842	OB-D/355	AR
Blount, J. H.	079	1897	WB-3/110	AR
Blount, Jacob	083	1846	WB-1/474	AR
Blount, Jacob	096	1794	Orig. Only	AR
Blount, Jacob	083	c1801	WB-1/72	
Blount, Jacob	096	1767	Orig. Only	AR
Blount, Jacob, Sr.	096	1766	WB-1/37	AR
Blount, James	101	1881	WB-A/71	AR
Blount, James	024	1686	SS 874.2/120	
Blount, James	024	1717	SS 875/113	SS/AR
Blount, James H.	009	1849	OB-G/138	AR
Blount, James S.	009	1845	OB-E/408	AR
Blount, Jesse	009	c1808	OWB/452	AR

Name	Co.	Date	Recorded Copy	Original
Blount, John	087	1830	WB-1/107	AR
Blount, John	096	1766	WB-1/61	AR
Blount, John	024	c1753	Orig. Only	AR-Copy
Blount, John	024	1836	WB-C/194	AR
Blount, John	024	1726	SS 876/43	SS/AR
Blount, John	009	1765	Orig. Only	AR
Blount, John	024	1754	Orig. Only	SS/AR
Blount, John	097	1856	WB-1/121	AR
Blount, John	083	c1790	WB-1/22	AR
Blount, John G.	037	1828	WB-F/95	
Blount, John Gray	009	1833	107 WB-2/142	
Blount, John Gray	009	1833	019 WB-B/254	019 AR
Blount, John Gray	009	1833	093 WB-2/16	
Blount, John Gray	009	1833	OB-B/223	AR
Blount, John Gray	009	1833	049 WB-2/406	049 AR
Blount, John Gray	009	1833	Copy	096 AR
Blount, John Gray	009	1833	013 WB-C/95	
Blount, John Gray	009	1833	062 WB-B/115	
Blount, John H.	077	1838	WB-F/270	AR
Blount, John W.	087	1884	WB-3/292	AR
Blount, Joseph	009	c1779	OWB/142	AR
Blount, Joseph	099	1823	RB-18/293	AR
Blount, Joseph	024	c1792	WB-A/295	AR
Blount, Joseph	073	1864	WB-G/438	CTY
Blount, Joseph	024	1777	WB-B/119	AR
Blount, Joseph W.	101	1898	WB-A/307	AR
Blount, Lewis	053	1805	RW-1/389	AR
Blount, Lewis	009	1824	OB-A/343	AR
Blount, Lucy	009	1818	OB-A/280	AR
Blount, Lucy C.	VA	1837	100 WB-36/162	100 AR
Blount, M. C.	087	c1866	WB-2/104	AR
Blount, M. Delia	105	1886	WB-2/393	AR
Blount, Martha	024	1762	Orig. Only	AR
Blount, Mary	009	1828	OB-A/466	AR
Blount, Mary	024	1811	WB-C/3	AR
Blount, Mary A.	009	1884	WB-1/354	CTY
Blount, Mary J.	079	1883	WB-2/277	AR
Blount, Mary L.	101	1893	WB-A/239	
Blount, Mary S.	037	1823	WB-E/319	AR
Blount, Nathan G.	059	c1849	SC/06397	AR-Copy
Blount, Patsy B.	009	1886	WB-1/371	CTY
Blount, Penelope	087	1838	WB-1/211	AR
Blount, Philip	083	c1801	WB-1/69	AR
Blount, Rachel	028	1842	WB-D/68	AR
Blount, Reading	009	1776	OWB/128	AR
Blount, Samuel	065	1883	WB-K/569	AR
Blount, Samuel	096	1779	WB-1/106	AR
Blount, Sarah	024	1770	WB-A/144	AR
Blount, Sarah	009	c1820	OWB/477	AR
Blount, Sarah E.	105	1880	WB-2/259	AR
Blount, Sarah E.	079	1899	WB-3/181	AR
Blount, Thomas	002	1701	Orig. Only	SS/AR
Blount, Thomas	002	1706	SS 874.1/7	SS/AR
Blount, Thomas	037	1812	WB-E/33 & 133	AR
Blount, Thomas	009	1793	OWB/290	AR
Blount, Thomas H.	009	1850	OB-G/226	AR
Blount, W. A.	SC	1895	Copy	050 CTY
Blount, Warren	035	1823	WB-A/47	AR
Blount, William	024	1819	WB-C/77	AR
Blount, William A.	099	1867	RB-34/449	AR
Blount, Willie	009	1840	OB-C2/269	AR
Blount, Winnifred	059	1872	WB-A/47	
Blow, Nancy	103	1829	RD-6/41	AR-Nunc.
Blow, William J.	079	1864	WB-1/133	AR
Bloxom, Severan	019	1799	WB-D/44	AR
Bloxsom, Richard	037	1828	WB-F/94	AR
Bloyse, Mary	047	1814	WB-3/554	AR
Blue, Angus	082	1890	WB-6/410	AR
Blue, Angus	068	1827	WB-B/55	
Blue, Catherine	011	1863	WB-1/304	
Blue, Daniel	082	1844	WB-3/21	AR
Blue, Daniel	083	1858	WB-2/124	AR
Blue, Daniel	082	1900	WB-7/42	AR
Blue, Daniel	029	1845	WB-C/79	AR
Blue, Duncan	068	1815	WB-A/290	
Blue, Duncan	029	1775	Orig. Only	AR
Blue, Duncan M.	068	c1879	WB-D/163	
Blue, Effy	082	1854	WB-4/70	AR
Blue, John	082	1831	WB-2/16	AR
Blue, Malcolm	085	c1783	WB-D/138	AR
Blue, Malcolm	082	1806	WB-1/111	AR
Blue, Malcom	029	1806	WB-A/86	AR
Blue, Malcom	029	1766	Orig. Only	AR
Blue, Mary	082	1833	WB-2/27	AR
Blue, Neill R.	029	1892	WB-E/562	AR
Blum, Anna M.	038	1875	WB-2/234	AR
Blum, Catharina	090	1839	WB-4/49	AR
Blum, David	038	c1860	WB-1/161	AR
Blum, Dorothea	038	1865	WB-1/252	AR
Blum, Edmond	038	1884	WB-2/522	AR
Blum, Elizabeth	038	1869	WB-2/17	AR
Blum, Henry	090	1824	WB-3/111	AR
Blum, John Henry	038	1866	WB-1/274	AR
Blume, G. C.	016	1887	WB-3/569	AR
Blume, Jacob	090	1802	WB-2/30	AR
Blumenthal, Gustave M.	GA	1898	023 WB-A/144	023 AR
Blunt, Chloe	047	1800	WB-3/336	AR
Blunt, Robert	047	1811	WB-3/512	AR
Blute, Mary	068	1882	WB-D/152	AR
Blye, William	010	1749	Orig. Only	SS/AR
Blythe, John	071	1826	WB-4/1	AR
Blythe, Robert W.	065	1896	WB-M/583	AR
Blythe, Samuel	065	1796	WB-A/99	AR
Boak, John	084	c1823	WB-A/332	
Boak, Robert	084	1826	WB-A/201	CTY
Boal, Thomas	065	N. D.	WB-A/128	AR
Boals, Robert	068	1803	WB-A/237	
Boam, Jean	030	1772	WB-1/69	
Boardman, Jonathan	072	1792	Orig. Only	AR
Boast, John	065	1778	WB-A/118	AR
Bobbett, Elizabeth	039	1833	WB-J/243	AR
Bobbett, Elizabeth	039	1852	WB-N/306	AR
Bobbit, John	100	1791	WB-6/54	AR
Bobbit, John	010	1736	Orig. Only	SS/AR
Bobbitt, Allen	044	1848	WB-17/184	CTY
Bobbitt, C. J.	098	1896	WB-A/268	CTY
Bobbitt, Durell E.	044	1887	WB-23/584	CTY
Bobbitt, Green	036	1897	WB-A/407	CTY
Bobbitt, Harriet B.	099	1880	WB-A/178	AR
Bobbitt, Harris	100	1847	WB-39/355	AR
Bobbitt, James B.	099	1896	WB-C/535	AR
Bobbitt, John	044	1858	WB-20/554	CTY
Bobbitt, John B.	099	1860	RB-31/488	AR
Bobbitt, John R.	100	1888	WB-51/287	AR
Bobbitt, Kinchen	100	1880	WB-51/147	AR
Bobbitt, Lewis	100	1818	WB-21/192	AR
Bobbitt, Lewis	044	1862	WB-21/569	CTY
Bobbitt, Lewis C.	039	1836	WB-K/75	AR
Bobbitt, Louisa E.	047	1896	WB-7/160	AR
Bobbitt, Martha	039	1887	WB-U/410	AR

Name	Co.	Date	Recorded Copy	Original
Bobbitt, Martha	022	1880	WB-E/195	AR
Bobbitt, Martha D.	100	1870	WB-51/35	AR
Bobbitt, Miles	100	1861	WB-49/383	AR
Bobbitt, Patrick H.	044	1875	WB-23/204	CTY
Bobbitt, Richard E.	100	1888	WB-51/261	
Bobbitt, Sherrod	047	1827	WB-4/39	AR
Bobbitt, Stephen	100	1824	WB-26/259	AR
Bobbitt, Thomas V.	044	1860	WB-21/286	CTY
Bobbitt, Washington	036	1898	WB-A/458	CTY
Boddie, Elijah	071	1761	WB-1/61	
Boddie, George	037	1830	WB-F/111	
Boddie, George	069	1843	WB-1/465	AR
Boddie, Mary A. E.	069	1892	WB-5/365	AR
Boddie, N. W.	069	1894	WB-5/456	AR
Boddie, Nathan	069	1798	WB-1/117	AR
Boddie, Patty	069	1839	WB-1/436	AR
Boddie, W. W.	069	1843	WB-1/460	AR
Boddie, William	069	1817	WB-1/286	AR
Boddie, William W.	069	1870	WB-1/606	AR
Boddie, Willie	071	1814	WB-3/132	AR
Bodenhamer, Christian	032	1871	WB-3/22	AR
Bodenhamer, John	085	1820	WB-H/68	AR
Bodenhamer, John B.	032	1894	WB-4/221	AR
Bodenhamer, Katharine	032	1826	WB-1/57	AR
Bodenhamer, R.	038	1899	WB-4/189	AR
Bodenhamer, William	032	1839	WB-1/331 & 359	AR
Bodenhamer, William	032	1891	WB-4/117	AR
Bodley, Joshua	024	c1775	WB-A/133	AR
Bodridge, Elizabeth	099	1854	RB-28/585	AR
Boee, Jacob	033	c1842	Orig. Only	AR-Copy
Boehlo, Frederick	090	1827	WB-3/167	AR
Bogart, Anne	103	1869	WB-1/5	AR
Boge, Josiah	077	1753	Orig. Only	SS/AR
Boge, William	077	1721	SS 875/318	SS/AR
Boger, Allen	016	1897	WB-4/279	AR
Boger, Daniel	016	1860	WB-2/66	
Boger, Daniel N.	016	1864	WB-2/111	
Boger, Eda	085	1874	WB-1/230	CTY
Boger, George	054	1894	WB-5/508	CTY
Boger, George Sr.	016	1865	WB-2/121	
Boger, Jacob	016	1832	PQS.5/202	
Boger, John E.	060	1899	WB-5/108	AR
Boger, Laird	016	1867	WB-2/154	
Boggan, Abner	005	1870	WB-D/12	AR
Boggan, Jane C.	005	1858	WB-C/131	AR
Boggan, Martha	005	1851	WB-C/26	AR
Boggan, Mary	005	1831	WB-B/9	AR
Boggan, Norfleet	005	1855	WB-C/92	AR
Boggan, Patrick	005	1883	WB-D/156	AR
Boggan, Patrick	005	1817	WB-2/9	AR
Boggs, Charity	001	1890	WB-2/481	AR
Boggs, David	060	1842	WB-2/145	AR
Boggs, James	026	1843	WB-1/16	AR
Boggs, John D.	026	1883	WB-2/253	AR
Boggs, Rebecca	060	1822	Orig. Only	AR
Boggs, Sarah	026	1882	WB-2/235	AR
Boggs, Simpson	032	1897	WB-4/324	AR
Boggs, Thomas H.	001	1895	WB-3/80	AR
Boggs, William	060	1842	WB-2/154	AR
Boghart, Daniel	010	1796	WB-D/351	AR
Bogle, Matilda	003	1887	WB-B/204	AR
Bogle, Robert	054	1802	WB-1/75	AR
Bogue, Elizabeth	077	1785	WB-C/313	AR
Bogue, Jesse	103	1847	RD-9/462	AR
Bogue, Job	077	1788	WB-C/380	AR
Bogue, Joseph	077	1803	WB-E/200	AR
Bogue, Mark	057	1798	WB-A/205	AR
Bogue, Martha	103	1870	WB-1/12	AR
Bogue, Robert	057	1788	WB-A/74	AR
Bogue, William	077	1745	Orig. Only	SS/AR
Bohaman, John Anna	009	1893	WB-1/566	CTY
Bohanan, James	092	1774	WB-1/27	
Bohannan, James	090	1808	WB-2/95	AR
Bohannan, John, Sr.	092	1789	WB-2/51A	AR
Bohannon, Duncan	073	1760	WB-A/5	
Bohannon, Neal	106	c1861	WB-1/87	AR
Bohannon, Robert	099	1784	RB-1/186	AR
Bohanon, John	029	1800	Orig. Only	AR-Nunc.
Bohanon, John	090	1858	WB-4/317	AR
Boice, Christopher	024	c1758	WB-B/110	AR
Boing, A. H.	098	1895	WB-A/218	CTY
Boing, Tabitha	044	1879	WB-23/337	
Bolch, Abraham	003	1873	WB-B/34	AR
Bolch, Adam	060	1794	Orig. Only	AR
Bolch, Adam	021	1848	WB-1/66	AR
Bolch, Andrew	021	1881	WB-2/234	
Bolch, Daniel	021	1888	WB-2/413	AR
Bolch, Sally	021	1894	WB-3/40	AR
Bolch, Sebastian	060	1822	Orig. Only	AR
Bolejack, Joseph	090	1846	WB-4/225	AR
Boles, Aaron	073	1816	WB-D/494	AR
Boles, Alexander	090	1824	WB-3/122	AR
Boles, Benjamin	067	c1842	WB-1/15	AR
Boles, Benjamin	090	1852	WB-4/276	AR
Boles, Edward	090	1888	WB-6/197	AR
Boles, James	090	1828	WB-3/173	AR
Boles, Joseph	090	1876	WB-6/77	AR
Boley, Elizabeth	020	1846	RB-P/362	AR
Bolicheck, Joseph	090	1801	WB-2/1	AR
Bolick, Godfrey	060	c1823	Orig. Only	AR
Bolick, Jacob	060	1826	WB-1/30	AR
Bolick, Mary Ann	021	1898	WB-3/207	AR
Bolick, Rebecca	021	1890	WB-2/520	AR
Bolick, Salina	021	1890	WB-2/498	AR
Bolin, James	029	1843	WB-C/33	AR
Bolin, William	029	c1794	Orig. Only	AR
Boling, Christopher	068	1876	022 WB-E/122	AR
Boling, Lewiza	081	1892	WB-16/213	AR
Boling, Taply	022	1877	WB-E/146	AR
Bolling, A. J.	046	1896	WB-F/497	AR
Bollinger, Henry	060	1804	Orig. Only	AR
Bollinger, John D. M.	060	1876	WB-4/154	AR
Bollinger, Legion	021	1858	WB-1/139	AR
Bollins, John	085	1795	WB-F/14	AR
Bolls, Adaline	073	1862	WB-G/386	AR
Bolton, Bartholomew	086	1836	WB-E/27	AR
Bolton, James	099	1813	RB-11/166	AR
Bolton, Richard	028	1768	Orig. Only	AR
Bolton, Richard	037	1820	WB-E/241	AR
Bolton, Richard	037	1789	WB-C/78	AR
Bolton, Robert	020	1846	RB-P/361	AR
Bolton, Woodson	099	1883	WB-A/448	AR
Bolyn, Guion	086	1847	WB-E/173	AR
Boman, Royal	020	1791	RB-B/407	
Bond, Ann	041	1845	WB-3/64	AR
Bond, Annie D.	024	1893	WB-E/215	AR
Bond, Charles	092	1775	WB-1/43	AR
Bond, David	056	1772	Orig. Only	AR
Bond, Demsey	041	1788	WB-1/74	AR

Name	Co.	Date	Recorded Copy	Original
Bond, Edmund	024	1826	WB-C/126	AR-Nunc.
Bond, Elizabeth	024	1802	WB-B/196	AR
Bond, Elizabeth	024	1892	WB-E/205	AR
Bond, Ezbon	028	1802	WB-B/174	AR
Bond, Francis	028	1795	WB-A/323	AR
Bond, Francis L.	037	1890	WB-H/172	AR
Bond, George	024	1883	WB-E/120	AR
Bond, Henry	024	1817	WB-C/52	AR
Bond, Henry	037	1761	WB-A/36	AR
Bond, Henry	041	1848	WB-3/99	AR
Bond, Henry A.	024	1891	WB-E/187	AR
Bond, James	009	1769	OWB/103	AR
Bond, John	024	1812	WB-C/14	AR
Bond, John	009	1749	SS 877/147	SS/AR
Bond, John	010	1800	WB-E/108	AR
Bond, John	024	1820	WB-C/83	AR
Bond, John	024	1883	WB-E/126	AR
Bond, John	010	1793	WB-D/232	AR
Bond, John	009	c1808	OB-A/32	AR
Bond, John T.	010	1876	WB-I/76	AR
Bond, Lewis	010	1851	WB-G/474	AR
Bond, Lewis	010	c1849	SC/06231	AR-Copy
Bond, Lewis	024	1753	SS 881/103	SS/AR
Bond, Louis	016	1898	WB-4/295	AR
Bond, Margaret	010	1829	WB-G/190	AR
Bond, Mary	024	1823	WB-C/100	AR
Bond, Penelope	024	1866	WB-D/43	AR
Bond, Pheriby	009	c1809	OB-A/32	AR
Bond, R. H. L.	041	1867	WB-3/356	AR
Bond, Richard	024	c1826	Orig. Only	AR
Bond, Richard	041	1825	WB-2/226	AR
Bond, Richard	VA	1727	Copy	024 AR
Bond, Richard	N	1727/8	Orig. Only	SS/AR
Bond, Richard	041	1795	WB-1/134	AR
Bond, Robert	028	1738	LGB-4/#71	SS/AR
Bond, Robert	009	1802	OWB/394	AR
Bond, Samuel	077	1723	SS 876/15	SS/AR
Bond, Samuel	090	1812	WB-2/131	AR
Bond, Samuel	077	1767	WB-C/73	AR
Bond, Sarah	028	1800	WB-B/98	AR
Bond, Sarah	028	1752	DB-5/280	SS/AR
Bond, Sarah F.	024	1882	WB-E/114	AR
Bond, Sarah P.	024	1879	WB-E/78	AR
Bond, Sarah R.	075	1894	WB-0/398	AR
Bond, Sarah R.	024	1894	WB-E/257	AR
Bond, Southey	099	1826	RB-19/522	AR
Bond, Sweeting	070	1818	WB-C/39	AR
Bond, Thomas	010	c1767	WB-A/98	AR
Bond, Thomas	041	1819	WB-2/155	AR
Bond, Thomas	010	1795	WB-D/282	AR
Bond, Thomas	010	1854	WB-H/6	AR
Bond, Vinyard	009	1762	SS 881/263	SS/AR
Bond, William	009	1757	SS 882/29	SS/AR
Bond, William	077	1791	WB-C/421	AR
Bond, William	024	c1772	WB-A/305	AR
Bonden, John	072	1832	WB-1/108	
Bondfield, Charles	024	c1781	WB-B/84	AR
Bondfield, John	024	c1786	Orig. Only	AR
Bone, John	069	1829	WB-1/362	AR
Bone, Wilie	069	c1848	Orig. Only	AR
Bone, William	054	c1826	WB-2/70	AR
Bone, William	054	c1787	WB-1/73	AR
Boner, Benigna	TN	1854	038 WB-1/97	038 AR
Boner, William	038	1891	WB-3/188	AR
Boner, William	085	c1785	WB-C/74	AR

Name	Co.	Date	Recorded Copy	Original
Boney, Barbra C.	035	1894	WB-4/450	AR
Boney, Daniel	035	1860	WB-3/33	AR
Boney, Daniel W.	035	1895	WB-4/462	AR
Boney, Festus	076	c1894	Orig. Only	AR
Boney, Isham	076	1892	WB-A1/164	AR
Boney, Jacob	035	c1761	WB-A/61	AR
Boney, James W.	035	1885	WB-4/262	AR
Boney, John	035	1831	WB-1/18	AR
Boney, John A.	035	1871	WB-4/32	AR
Boney, William	035	1849	WB-2/46	AR
Boney, William	035	1854	WB-2/82	AR
Boney, Wright	035	1857	WB-2/108	AR
Bonham, Catharine	070	1882	WB-E/452	AR
Bonham, Charles M.	070	1897	WB-G/547	AR
Bonham, Hezekiah	070	1821	WB-C/40	AR
Bonham, Samuel	070	1771	WB-C/20	AR
Bonner, Anthony	009	1877	WB-1/206	CTY
Bonner, Benjamin F.	053	1881	WB-11/115	AR
Bonner, Elizabeth	039	c1843	WB-L/190	AR
Bonner, George	009	1796	OWB/326	AR
Bonner, Henry	024	1738	LGB-4/#162	SS/AR
Bonner, Henry	024	c1766	WB-1/38	
Bonner, Henry	009	1779	OWB/145	AR
Bonner, Henry	024	1797	WB-A/330	AR
Bonner, James	063	c1783	WB-1/99	
Bonner, James	009	1791	OWB/263	AR
Bonner, James	009	1782	OWB/177	AR
Bonner, John	009	1787	OWB/220	AR
Bonner, John	024	1754	Orig. Only	SS/AR
Bonner, John	024	1832	WB-C/200	AR
Bonner, John B.	009	1871	WB-1/78	CTY
Bonner, John G.	009	1846	OB-F/116	AR
Bonner, Joseph	009	1805	OWB/432	AR
Bonner, Joseph	009	1876	WB-1/164	CTY
Bonner, Luten	037	1819	WB-E/213	AR
Bonner, Mary	024	1750	Orig. Only	SS/AR
Bonner, Mary	024	1789	WB-A/134	AR
Bonner, Mary E.	009	1879	WB-1/248	CTY
Bonner, Moses	044	1827	Orig. Only	CTY
Bonner, Norfleet	024	1837	WB-C/206	AR
Bonner, Patience	103	1878	WB-1/129	AR
Bonner, Thomas	044	1819	WB-8/227	CTY
Bonner, Thomas	009	1764	OWB/566	AR
Bonner, Thomas	010	1756	SS 880/252	
Bonner, Thomas	024	c1785	WB-A/227	AR
Bonner, William	010	1775	WB-B/43	AR
Bonner, William	096	1759	WB-1/42	AR
Bonner, William S.	103	1854	RD-11/556	AR
Bonney, Catharne	021	1891	WB-2/533	
Bonney, Jonathan	030	1792	WB-2/10	
Bonney, William	030	1831	WB-3/268	
Bonniwell, James	021	1894	WB-3/42	
Bonnor, Thomas	N	1685	Orig. Only	SS/AR
Bonny, William	030	1837	WB-4/26	
Booe, George	033	1838	WB-1/14	
Booe, Jacob	085	1812	WB-G/213	AR
Booe, Jacob	033	c1851	WB-1/103	
Booe, Phillip	033	c1837	WB-1/10	
Booker, Benjamin	092	1872	WB-6/39	
Booker, Daniell	022	1783	Orig. Only	AR
Booker, Dilly	099	1885	WB-B/6	AR
Booker, Gaston	099	1887	WB-B/226	AR
Booker, Henry	046	1887	WB-E/475	AR
Booker, James	022	1819	WB-B/18	AR
Booker, John	022	1799	WB-A/11	AR

Name	Co.	Date	Recorded Copy	Original
Booker, John	073	1761	WB-A/23	
Booker, Phebe	022	1843	WB-C/142	AR
Bookout, Joseph	081	1806	WB-3/56	AR
Boomar, John	075	1761	WB-H/23	AR
Boomer, Abram	053	1864	WB-10/11	AR
Boomer, Cassandra	053	1843	WB-6/211	AR
Boomer, Henry Jones	053	1885	WB-11/152	AR
Boomer, Jones	053	1866	WB-10/2	AR
Boomer, Nathan	053	1807	RW-1/407	
Boomer, William	053	1842	WB-6/216	AR
Boomer, William	053	1794	RW-1/246	AR
Boon, Ann	001	1860	WB-1/172	AR
Boon, Benjamin	071	1815	WB-3/159	AR
Boon, Deborah	071	1826	WB-3/335	AR
Boon, Edwin	071	1845	WB-5/25	AR
Boon, Henry	071	1826	WB-4/11	AR
Boon, Henry	071	1873	WB-6/130	AR
Boon, Jacob	071	1790	WB-1/409	AR
Boon, Jacob	046	1859	WB-D/32	AR
Boon, Jacob	046	1796	WB-A/25	AR
Boon, James	071	1829	WB-4/50	AR
Boon, James	099	1858	RB-30/639	AR
Boon, James	039	1807	WB-C/89	
Boon, James W.	039	1833	WB-J/246	AR
Boon, Jane	051	1882	WB-C/298	AR
Boon, Jehu P.	022	1898	WB-F/77	AR
Boon, Jesse	071	1832	WB-4/89	AR
Boon, John	056	1874	WB-3/113	AR
Boon, John	046	c1836	WB-B/562	AR
Boon, Joseph	071	1794	WB-2/59	AR
Boon, Joseph	N	c1728	Orig. Only	SS/AR
Boon, Joseph	056	1836	Orig. Only	AR
Boon, Joyner	071	1848	WB-5/67	AR
Boon, Levina	071	1857	WB-5/195	AR
Boon, Nancy	071	1875	WB-6/162	AR
Boon, Nasa	022	1883	WB-E/275	AR
Boon, Nicholas	071	1807	WB-2/352	AR-Nunc.
Boon, Nicolas	N	N. D.	Orig. Only	SS/AR
Boon, Philemon	069	1879	WB-5/77	AR
Boon, Raiford	022	1835	WB-C/20	AR
Boon, Raiford	069	1854	WB-1/537	AR
Boon, Ratliff	092	1787	WB-2/77A	AR
Boon, Rebecca	085	1822	WB-H/169	AR
Boon, Samuel	011	1891	WB-2/241	
Boon, Sarah	039	c1796	WB-B/50	AR
Boon, Sina	022	1900	WB-F/139	AR
Boon, Solomon	047	1865	WB-5/130	AR-Copy
Boon, Susanna	071	1806	WB-2/320	AR
Boon, Thomas	071	1796	WB-2/114	AR
Boon, Thomas	071	1800	WB-2/193	AR
Boon, W. S.	056	1897	WB-4/53	AR
Boon, Warren	051	1888	WB-C/374	AR-Nunc.
Boon, William	039	1799	WB-A/137	
Boon, William	071	1795	WB-2/82	AR
Boon, William	071	1805	WB-2/280	AR
Boon, William	069	1899	WB-6/67	AR
Boon, William	046	1881	WB-E/299	AR
Boon, William	051	1839	WB-A/138	
Boon, William	071	1857	WB-5/186	AR
Boon, William H.	047	1880	WB-6/234	AR
Boon, Willis	039	1840	WB-L/3	AR
Boonacker, Michael	085	1778	WB-A/257	AR
Boone, Elizabeth	071	1900	WB-7/461	AR
Boone, James	010	1735	SS 876/379	SS/AR
Boone, Mary	069	1886	WB-5/242	AR
Boone, Sam Bell	071	1885	WB-6/509	AR
Boone, W. J. M.	039	1899	WB-V/175	AR
Booswell, John N.	044	1824	WB-9/378	CTY
Booth, Bartholomew	099	1841	RB-24/498	AR
Booth, Daniel	073	1802	WB-D/78	AR
Booth, Elizabeth	037	1849	WB-F/411	AR
Booth, Fox	068	1877	WB-D/98	
Booth, George	030	1730	LGB-4/#2	SS/AR
Booth, James	N	1737/8	SS 877/217	SS/AR
Booth, James	037	1808	WB-D/303	AR
Booth, John	098	1888	WB-A/100	CTY
Booth, John	019	1752	028 DB-5/259	SS/AR (N)
Booth, Moses	022	1819	WB-A/310	AR
Booth, Phillip	063	c1780	WB-1/72	
Booth, Solomon	073	1811	WB-D/316	AR
Booth, Thomas	037	1786	WB-C/37	AR
Boothe, Alfred	073	1871	WB-H/42	CTY
Boothe, Benjamin	022	1887	WB-E/358	AR
Boothe, Daniel	073	1850	WB-F/472	AR
Boothe, James	041	1842	WB-3/31	AR
Boothe, John Wesley	099	1899	WB-D/304	AR
Boothe, Joseph	099	1867	RB-34/385	AR
Boothe, Joseph	073	1825	WB-E/86	AR
Boothe, Mary H.	099	1891	WB-C/21	AR
Boothe, Nancy	099	1844	RB-25/432	AR
Boothe, Sarah	041	1867	WB-3/357	AR
Boothe, William L.	041	1860	WB-3/255	AR
Boothe, Williams	099	1872	RB-35/184	AR
Boovy, Mathias	060	1829	WB-1/139	AR
Boozman, James	037	1796	WB-C/354	AR
Boozman, Ralph	077	1750	Orig. Only	SS/AR
Boozman, William	082	1825	WB-1/260	AR-Nunc.
Bordeaux, William W.	087	1875	WB-3/92	AR
Borden, Benjamin	028	1841	019 WB-D/99	019 AR
Borden, Benjamin	028	1886	WB-E/404	AR
Borden, Benjamin	028	1841	WB-D/35	AR
Borden, Eliza Hope	028	1872	WB-E/64	AR
Borden, Joseph	075	1769	WB-H/91	
Borden, Joseph	019	1825	053 WB-11/276	053 AR
Borden, Joseph	054	c1803	WB-1/65	AR
Borden, Joseph	019	1825	WB-A/26	AR
Borden, Maria A.	103	1884	WB-1/321	AR
Borden, S. M.	026	1881	Copy	086 AR
Borden, William	019	1799	WB-D/38	AR
Borden, William	019	1749	WB-D/12	SS/AR
Borders, Hugh	026	c1879	WB-2/372	AR
Borders, John	026	1894	WB-2/477	AR
Borders, John	060	1800	Orig. Only	AR
Borders, Mary	026	1898	WB-3/4	AR
Borders, Michal	026	1850	WB-1/104	AR
Borders, S. M.	026	1880	WB-2/204	AR
Bordin, Mary	086	1828	WB-D/92	AR
Boring, John	073	1775	WB-A/187	
Boring, William	073	1768	WB-A/93	
Borland, Alexander	073	1821	WB-D/602	AR
Borland, James	085	c1796	WB-F/13	AR
Borland, John	060	1793	Orig. Only	AR
Borland, Mary E.	073	1867	WB-G/532	CTY
Borland, Rachel	073	1875	WB-H/126	CTY
Borland, Thomas	051	1832	WB-A/32	
Boroughs, Atlas J.	022	1890	WB-E/431	AR
Boroughs, Bryant	022	1897	WB-F/46	AR
Boroughs, James H.	081	1900	WB-17/56	
Boroughs, John	067	1891	WB-2/298	AR

Name	Co.	Date	Recorded Copy	Original
Boroughs, Reuben	022	1899	WB-F/106	AR
Boroughs, Zacheus	022	c1858	WB-D/63	AR
Borrin, Joseph	073	1775	WB-A/188	
Borritz, James	024	1827	WB-C/129	AR
Borritz, William	024	1803	WB-B/170	AR
Bortals, Christin	014	1843	Orig. Only	AR
Borton, Richard	046	1801	WB-A/23	AR
Boseman, J. D.	047	1898	Orig. Only	AR
Boseman, William	047	1864	WB-5/121	
Bosher, William	070	1765	012 DB-A/16	012 AR
Bosman, Micajah	071	1823	WB-3/276	AR
Bosney, John	073	1761	WB-A/27	
Boss, Mary	032	1843	WB-1/416	AR
Boss, Philip	085	1807	WB-F/7	AR
Bost, Adaline	054	1892	WB-5/412	CTY
Bost, Adolphus T.	021	1864	WB-1/205	AR
Bost, Bostian	065	1761	WB-A/127	
Bost, Daniel M.	016	1864	WB-2/102	
Bost, Danl. L.	016	1895	WB-4/199	AR
Bost, David A.	085	1862	WB-K/297	AR
Bost, Dorcas E.	085	1893	WB-2/551	CTY
Bost, Elizabeth	085	1892	WB-2/536	CTY
Bost, George	085	1853	WB-K/154	AR
Bost, Henry C.	085	1887	WB-2/227	CTY
Bost, Jacob, Sr.	016	1830	PQS.5/135	
Bost, Jemima	016	1876	WB-3/157	AR
Bost, Jesse	021	1892	WB-3/4	AR
Bost, John	016	1858	WB-2/37	
Bost, John	085	1835	WB-H/663	AR
Bost, John M.	016	1858	WB-2/37	
Bost, Jonas	021	1871	WB-2/54	
Bost, Jonathan	021	1867	WB-1/240	AR
Bost, Joseph	021	1881	WB-2/236	
Bost, Joseph	021	c1880	WB-2/268	
Bost, Joseph	021	1883	WB-2/256	
Bost, L. E.	021	1867	WB-1/250	AR
Bost, Levi	054	1897	WB-6/74	CTY
Bost, Lodemia C.	016	1896	WB-4/245	AR
Bost, Mary	016	1864	WB-2/112	
Bost, Mary S.	054	1890	WB-5/348	CTY
Bost, Paul	016	1864	WB-2/101	
Bost, Silas	054	1883	WB-4/494	
Bost, Simon	016	1862	WB-2/92	
Bost, W. R. D.	021	1862	WB-1/169	AR
Bost, William	016	1891	WB-4/150	AR
Bost, William	060	c1811	Orig. Only	AR-Copy
Bost, William W.	016	1888	WB-3/584	AR
Bostian, Aaron	085	1885	WB-2/154	CTY
Bostian, Alexander	085	1882	WB-2/19	CTY
Bostian, Andrew	085	1877	WB-1/376	CTY
Bostian, Andrew	085	1837	WB-I/10	AR
Bostian, David	085	1889	WB-2/327	CTY
Bostian, David	003	1870	WB-B/11	AR
Bostian, George W.	085	1864	WB-K/341	AR
Bostian, Jacob	054	c1838	Copy	085 AR
Bostian, Jacob	054	1898	WB-6/159	CTY
Bostian, Jacob	003	1847	Orig. Only	AR
Bostian, Jacob	085	1874	WB-1/262	CTY
Bostian, Jacob	054	1854	WB-3/85	AR
Bostian, John	054	1876	WB-4/208	CTY
Bostian, Lydia	085	1872	WB-1/99	CTY
Bostian, Michael	016	1865	WB-2/124	
Bostian, Michael	085	1850	WB-K/110	AR
Bostian, Michael	085	1850	WB-K/116	AR
Bostian, Nancy	085	1873	WB-1/160	CTY
Bostian, Peter	085	1846	WB-K/37	AR
Bostian, Philip	085	1831	WB-H/521	AR
Bostick, Absolom	090	1803	WB-2/37	AR
Bostick, Boswell	086	1874	WB-F/46	AR
Bostick, Charles	086	1814	WB-C/5	AR
Bostick, Elisha	082	1843	WB-3/4	AR
Bostick, Ferdinand	090	1825	WB-3/132	AR-Nunc.
Bostick, James	082	1824	WB-1/248	AR
Bostick, John	082	1799	WB-1/71	AR
Bostick, John, Sr.	035	1848	WB-2/30	AR
Bostick, Mary	009	1831	OB-B/89	AR
Bostick, Solomon	082	1884	WB-6/279	AR
Bostick, Tristram	082	1876	WB-6/138	AR
Bostick, William	082	1829	WB-1/311	AR
Bostick, William	078	1792	WI-1/47	
Bostion, David	085	1833	WB-H/587	AR
Bostion, David	085	1844	WB-I/203	AR
Bostion, Jonas	085	c1799	WB-D/116	AR
Boston, Abram	017	1889	WB-B/161	AR
Boston, James	072	1782	RW/L40	AR
Boston, Sally	054	1858	WB-3/132	AR
Boswell, Ann N.	044	1846	WB-17/1	CTY
Boswell, Antiochus	020	1885	WB-A/445	CTY
Boswell, Bedford A.	020	1876	WB-A/212	CTY
Boswell, Benjamin	103	1846	RD-9/445	AR
Boswell, Edward	073	1830	WB-E/223	AR
Boswell, George	077	1785	Orig. Only	AR
Boswell, George	077	1741	LGB-4/#156	SS/AR
Boswell, Goldsberry	027	1867	WB-A/112	AR
Boswell, Hezekiah	020	1829	RB-L/364	AR
Boswell, Ichabod	077	1761	Orig. Only	AR
Boswell, James	044	1843	WB-15/413	CTY
Boswell, John	077	1816	WB-E/458	AR
Boswell, John	020	1854	RB-R/175	AR
Boswell, Joseph	103	1858	RD-12/405	AR
Boswell, Joshua	077	1762	WB-C/25	AR
Boswell, L. F.	011	1888	WB-2/224	
Boswell, Mary A.	044	1817	WB-8/77	CTY
Boswell, Pruellia	106	c1857	Orig. Only	AR
Boswell, Rachel	054	1840	WB-2/206	
Boswell, Ransom	020	1887	WB-A/510	CTY
Boswell, Ransom	020	1836	RB-M/538	
Boswell, Rebecca	103	1853	RD-11/226	AR
Boswell, Simon	103	1812	RD-2/206	AR
Boswell, Thomas	010	1818	WB-G/39	AR
Boswell, Verlindo	090	1829	WB-3/204	AR
Boswell, William	077	1734	SS 876/368	SS/AR
Boswell, William	077	1834	WB-F/232	AR
Bosworth, Joseph	019	1735	Orig. Only	SS/AR
Bosworth, Stewart	056	1825	WB-1/457	AR-Nunc.
Boteright, Richard	099	1810	RB-9/180	AR
Botson, Mary	053	1785	RW-1/129	
Bottom, William	071	1842	WB-4/253	AR
Bottom, William B.	071	1869	WB-6/36	AR
Bottoms, John L.	069	c1816	Orig. Only	AR
Bottoms, Samuel L.	069	1796	WB-1/98	AR
Bottoms, Sarah Long	069	1805	WB-1/156	AR
Bottoms, Thomas L.	044	1793	WB-3/29	CTY
Boucher, Joseph	028	c1765	Orig. Only	AR
Boude, John	010	1738	LGB-4/#87	SS/AR
Boudger, Benjamin	085	1762	WB-A/11	AR
Boudinot, Elias	PA	c1878	062 WB-B/15	
Boudinot, Elias	PA	c1821	049 WB-2/35	
Boudreaux, William F.	070	1856	WB-C/618	
Bould, George	028	1745	SS 878/119	SS/AR

Name	Co.	Date	Recorded Copy	Original
Bouldin, Ephraim	090	1863	WB-4/362	AR
Bouldin, George T.	020	1849	RB-Q/244	
Boulton, Charles	020	1803	RB-E/27	AR
Boulton, James	099	1813	RB-11/166	
Boulton, Thomas	020	1808	RB-F/2	AR
Bounds, George	094	1772	Orig. Only	060 AR
Bounds, Richard	077	1721	SS 875/298	SS/AR
Bourdeaux, Anthony	070	1769	WB-C/18	AR
Bourdeaux, Anthony	070	1853	WB-C/551	AR
Bourdeaux, Daniel	070	1815	WB-AB/235	AR
Bourdeaux, Daniel	070	1856	WB-C/624	
Bourdeaux, James	070	1860	WB-D/29	AR
Bourdeaux, Priscilla	070	1847	WB-AB/471	AR
Bourdeaux, Richard L.	076	1894	WB-A1/180	AR
Bourdeaux, William T.	070	1856	WB-C/618	AR
Bourden, Clarissa	035	1898	WB-4/528	AR
Bourden, Samuel	103	1841	RD-8/150	AR
Bourdon, Jane L.	013	1842	WB-A/85	
Bouren, Edmund	030	c1711	SS 875/42	
Bourke, John	029	1857	WB-C/367	AR
Boushell, Adaline J.	010	1868	WB-I/4	AR
Boushell, Malachi W.	018	1834	WB-C/153	AR
Boutley, John	077	1695	SS 874.2/61	
Boutwell, Samuel	009	1779	OWB/147	AR
Bovender, George W.	106	c1862	WB-1/81	AR
Bovender, John	106	c1867	WB-2/7	AR
Bovey, William	021	1855	WB-1/115	AR
Bow, William	029	1888	WB-E/433	AR
Bowden, Arthur	030	1832	WB-3/326	
Bowden, Bacor	070	1790	WB-C/33	AR
Bowden, Dempsey N.	039	1881	WB-U/264	AR
Bowden, Fanny	039	1863	WB-R/397	
Bowden, Hiram	069	1863	WB-1/584	AR
Bowden, James	030	1886	WB-5/131	AR
Bowden, John	100	1826	WB-30/41	AR
Bowden, John	039	1830	WB-J/40	AR
Bowden, John	082	1849	WB-4/30	AR
Bowden, Jordan J.	039	1827	WB-H/183	AR
Bowden, Judith	100	1828	WB-31/149	AR
Bowden, M. B.	039	1898	WB-V/126	AR
Bowden, Martha	070	1792	WB-C/34	AR
Bowden, Mary	039	1857	WB-O/386	AR
Bowden, Reddick	082	1894	WB-6/503	AR
Bowden, Richard	070	1848	WB-C/480	
Bowden, Sarah C.	070	1893	WB-G/134	AR
Bowden, William	039	1819	WB-F/172	AR
Bowden, Wilson	035	1892	WB-4/407	AR
Bowdin, Ezey	028	1805	WB-B/220	AR
Bowdish, Asa	070	1800	Orig. Only	AR-Nunc.
Bowdish, Sarah	070	1841	WB-AB/347	AR
Bowdoin, Josiah	081	1885	WB-15/521	
Bowdon, William	044	1774	WB-1/51	CTY
Bowe, Amy Ann	020	1888	WB-A/554	CTY
Bowe, Tully	075	1828	WB-N/45	AR
Bowell, Lewis	029	1795	Orig. Only	AR
Bowen, Arthur	037	1763	Orig. Only	AR
Bowen, David	086	1882	WB-F/180	AR
Bowen, Dianah E.	009	1884	WB-1/342	CTY
Bowen, Edward	028	1845	WB-D/113	AR
Bowen, Edward J.	074	1876	WB-1/31	AR
Bowen, Elias	083	1898	WB-4/222	AR
Bowen, Fannie M.	078	1895	Orig. Only	AR
Bowen, Fanny M.	073	1899	WB-I/163	
Bowen, Henry C.	010	1898	WB-I/541	
Bowen, James C.	101	1881	WB-A/58	AR

Name	Co.	Date	Recorded Copy	Original
Bowen, John	076	1895	WB-A1/193	AR
Bowen, Joseph	086	1825	WB-D/44	AR
Bowen, Nelson	050	1882	WB-1/177	
Bowen, Orpah	009	1899	WB-2/198	CTY
Bowen, Orpah	105	1899	WB-3/374	AR
Bowen, Rhoda	009	1886	WB-1/379	CTY
Bowen, Tennert	009	1802	OWB/399	AR
Bowen, Thomas	092	1800	WB-3/38A	AR
Bowen, Thomas	009	1820	OB-A/297	AR
Bowen, William	101	1874	WB-A/28	AR
Bowen, William	082	1800	WB-1/76	AR
Bowen, William	022	1856	WB-C/410	AR
Bowens, Mary	028	1876	WB-E/149	AR
Bower, Absolam	006	1857	WB-D/15	
Bower, George	006	c1850	WB-D/56	
Bower, George	073	c1770	WB-A/128	
Bower, George	006	1899	WB-E/387	AR
Bower, John	006	c1838	WB-B/103	AR
Bowers, Annie	105	1894	WB-3/89	AR
Bowers, Barbarah	039	1805	WB-C/37	
Bowers, Canen	073	1880	WB-H/235	CTY
Bowers, George	032	1889	WB-4/47	AR
Bowers, George	032	1844	WB-1/447	AR
Bowers, Giles, Sr.	039	1800	WB-A/148	
Bowers, Henrietta	047	1890	WB-6/567	AR
Bowers, John	020	1824	RB-I/301	AR
Bowers, Joseph	030	1786	WB-1/205	
Bowers, Lewelling	063	1838	WB-2/247	
Bowers, Martha K.	047	1864	WB-5/115	
Bowers, Peter	006	c1836	WB-B/70	AR
Bowers, Robert	104	1884	WB-6/243	AR
Bowers, Robert D.	047	1884	WB-6/353	AR
Bowers, Simeon C.	073	1882	WB-H/322	CTY
Bowin, Goodin	070	c1799	011 WB-1/367	
Bowin, Joseph	073	1775	WB-A/188	
Bowin, Nathan	010	1810	WB-F/132	AR
Bowles, Benjamin	092	1780	WB-1/139	AR
Bowles, Joseph	090	1876	WB-6/77	AR
Bowles, Lavinia	003	1895	WB-B/336	
Bowles, Sarah	020	1784	RB-B/32	AR
Bowles, Stephen	VA	1851	Copy	084 AR
Bowles, Thomas	073	1847	WB-F/344	AR
Bowles, William	073	1849	WB-F/449	AR
Bowles, William	092	1849	WB-4/273	
Bowling, Christiana	044	1896	Copy	078 AR
Bowling, Christiana	044	1896	WB-24/313	CTY
Bowling, Elizabeth	084	1866	WB-D/70	CTY
Bowling, Jane	073	c1789	WB-B/57	AR
Bowling, Jarrett	084	1850	WB-C/106	CTY
Bowling, Priestly	036	1887	WB-A/110	CTY
Bowls, Nancy	073	1856	WB-G/143	CTY
Bowls, Thomas	073	c1789	Orig. Only	AR
Bowman, Andrew	065	1779	WB-A/129	AR
Bowman, Andrew	090	1845	WB-4/184	
Bowman, Archibald	046	1857	WB-C/470	AR
Bowman, Daniel	046	1866	WB-D/319	AR
Bowman, Daniel	046	1898	WB-G/94	AR
Bowman, Daniel	060	1812	Orig. Only	AR
Bowman, David	003	1864	Orig. Only	AR
Bowman, David	003	1852	Orig. Only	AR
Bowman, E.	003	1897	WB-B/365	
Bowman, Edmond	090	1794	WB-1/53	AR
Bowman, George	090	1868	WB-5/50	AR
Bowman, George	003	1876	WB-B/70	AR
Bowman, George W.	046	1883	WB-E/371	AR

Name	Co.	Date	Recorded Copy	Original
Bowman, Henry	046	1898	WB-G/91	AR
Bowman, Hugh	054	c1791	WB-1/68	AR
Bowman, Jesse	003	1887	WB-B/222	AR
Bowman, John	014	1787	Orig. Only	AR-Copy
Bowman, John	005	1857	WB-C/113	AR
Bowman, Jonas	003	1886	WB-B/174	AR
Bowman, Joseph	003	1863	Orig. Only	AR
Bowman, Lavina	017	1891	WB-B/202	AR
Bowman, Lydia	003	1885	WB-B/158	AR
Bowman, Margaret	065	1777	WB-A/78	AR
Bowman, Nancy E.	017	c1897	Orig. Only	AR
Bowman, Paul	003	1879	WB-B/122	AR
Bowman, Rebecca	017	1891	WB-B/202	AR
Bowman, Teracy	046	1876	WB-E/174	AR
Bowman, William	085	c1792	WB-D/144	AR
Bowren, Edmond	030	1778	WB-1/129	
Bowzer, Emanual	035	1801	WB-A/29	AR
Bowzer, Mary	035	1810	WB-A/46	AR
Boyar, David	047	1760	WB-1/4	
Boyce, Benjamin	024	1866	WB-D/38	AR
Boyce, Hardy	010	1816	WB-F/307	AR
Boyce, Healy	024	1862	WB-D/12	AR
Boyce, Isaac	077	1751	Orig. Only	SS/AR
Boyce, Jacob	024	1779	WB-B/94	AR
Boyce, Jacob D.	024	1897	WB-E/270	AR
Boyce, James	024	1864	WB-D/23	AR
Boyce, Jemimah	077	1833	WB-F/213	AR
Boyce, Job	024	c1779	WB-A/219	AR
Boyce, John	077	1823	WB-F/62	AR
Boyce, John	077	1749	Orig. Only	SS/AR
Boyce, John L.	075	1798	WB-M1/12	AR
Boyce, Joseph	024	1817	WB-C/54	AR
Boyce, Lemuel H.	071	1888	WB-7/36	AR
Boyce, Margaret	065	1886	WB-L/148	AR
Boyce, Margaret	071	1876	WB-6/200	AR
Boyce, Milecent	077	1828	WB-F/159	AR
Boyce, Moses	077	1811	WB-E/364	AR
Boyce, Moses	077	1855	WB-F/466	AR
Boyce, Nancy	010	1829	WB-G/189	AR
Boyce, Samuel A.	065	1880	WB-K/411	AR
Boyce, Sarah	071	1843	WB-4/273	AR
Boyce, Sion	071	1819	WB-3/210	AR
Boyce, William	077	1703	SS 874.1/26 &19	SS/AR
Boyce, William	002	1693	SS 874.2/169	SS/AR
Boyce, William	010	1795	WB-D/277	AR
Boyce, William	077	1877	WB-H/77	AR
Boyce. Epaproditus	024	1755	Orig. Only	AR
Boyd, A. J.	084	1893	WB-E/553	CTY
Boyd, Andrew	084	1815	WB-A/125	CTY
Boyd, Ann	067	c1859	Orig. Only	AR
Boyd, Archibald	071	1842	WB-4/256	AR
Boyd, Armistead	VA	1886	100 WB-51/242	100 AR
Boyd, C. S.	098	1895	WB-A/216	
Boyd, Catharine	046	1783	WB-A/24	AR
Boyd, Charles	084	1894	WB-E/569	CTY
Boyd, Deborah	067	1858	WB-1/87	AR
Boyd, E. V.	049	1895	WB-2/337	AR
Boyd, George	009	1843	OB-E/132	AR
Boyd, Hannah	054	c1830	WB-2/98	AR
Boyd, James	013	1853	WB-A/156	
Boyd, James	044	1772	Orig. Only	CTY
Boyd, James	044	1814	WB-7/417	CTY
Boyd, Jennie	079	1898	WB-3/169	AR
Boyd, John	060	1822	Orig. Only	AR
Boyd, John	021	1874	WB-2/109	AR
Boyd, John	024	1738	LGB-4/#86	SS/AR
Boyd, John	075	1814	WB-M1/256	AR
Boyd, John	075	1742	LGB-4/#168	SS/AR
Boyd, John H.	009	1828	OWB/494	AR
Boyd, John J.	065	1880	WB-K/409	AR
Boyd, John S.	009	1852	OB-H/82	AR
Boyd, John T.	028	1866	WB-D/418	AR
Boyd, M. C.	016	1883	WB-3/387	AR
Boyd, Martha	010	1790	WB-D/115	AR
Boyd, Mary	070	1798	WB-AB/13	AR
Boyd, Mary	020	1807	RB-E/360	AR
Boyd, Miriam	024	c1790	WB-A/71	AR
Boyd, Richard	100	1860	WB-49/366	AR
Boyd, Richard G.	100	1894	WB-51/374	AR
Boyd, Robert	054	c1818	Orig. Only	AR
Boyd, Robert	009	1775	053 RW-1/69	053 AR
Boyd, Robert	044	1782	WB-1/331	CTY
Boyd, Robert	060	1835	WB-1/357	AR
Boyd, Robert	054	1882	WB-4/458	CTY
Boyd, Robert	054	c1806	WB-1/76	AR
Boyd, Robert	071	1780	WB-1/228	
Boyd, Robert M.	040	1881	WB-2/180	AR
Boyd, Robert W.	067	1854	WB-1/72	AR
Boyd, Samuel	029	1772	Orig. Only	AR
Boyd, Sarah	009	1843	OB-E/191	AR
Boyd, Thomas	008	1726	SS 876/95	SS/AR
Boyd, Thomas	009	1785	OWB/201	AR
Boyd, Thomas	075	1793	WB-L/8	AR
Boyd, Thomas	075	1782	WB-K/74	AR
Boyd, Thomas	009	1822	OB-A/325	AR
Boyd, W. B.	028	1896	WB-F/224	
Boyd, William	075	1771	WB-H/139	AR
Boyd, William	009	1797	OWB/333	AR
Boyd, William	024	c1778	WB-B/139	AR
Boyd, William	081	1831	WB-6/162	AR
Boyd, William	020	1799	RB-C/358	
Boyd, William	009	c1809	OWB/458	AR
Boyd, William	009	1830	OB-B/47	AR
Boyd, William	024	1785	WB-B/122	AR
Boyd, William	075	1792	WB-K/244	AR
Boyd, William C.	016	1898	WB-4/314	AR
Boyd, William H.	098	1894	WB-A/200	CTY
Boyd, William P.	009	1894	WB-2/44	CTY
Boyd, Winefred	075	1720	SS 875/242	
Boyd, Zachariah	009	1873	WB-1/116	AR
Boyden, Jane C.	085	1885	WB-2/181	CTY
Boyden, Nathaniel	085	1873	Copy	006 AR
Boyden, Nathaniel	085	1873	WB-1/207	
Boyer, Anna	090	1843	WB-4/114	AR
Boyer, Benjamin	010	c1789	024 WB-A/224	
Boyer, Henry	090	1796	WB-1/84	AR
Boyer, Junius	038	1889	WB-3/109	AR
Boyer, William	090	1845	WB-4/202	AR
Boyes, Anna M.	065	1848	WB-I/137	AR
Boyes, James	065	1803	WB-A/90	AR
Boyet, Joseph	056	1841	WB-1/538	AR
Boyet, Martha	041	1816	WB-2/127	AR
Boyet, Samuel	035	1791	WB-A/30	AR
Boyet, Shadrach	103	1807	Orig. Only	AR
Boyet, Thomas	063	c1823	WB-2/85	
Boyet, Thomas	103	1787	WI-A/85	AR
Boyett, Isaac	105	1872	WB-2/76	AR
Boyett, Martha	035	1840	Orig. Only	AR
Boyett, Moses	035	1780	WB-A/61	AR

Name	Co.	Date	Recorded Copy	Original
Boyett, Stephen	005	1891	WB-D/289	AR
Boyette, Baalam	035	1891	WB-4/382	AR
Boyette, George	056	1852	WB-1/659	AR
Boyette, John	087	1882	WB-3/242	AR
Boyette, Katie H.	051	1896	WB-C/515	AR
Boyette, Mary J.	087	1888	WB-3/397	AR
Boyette, Susan A.	035	1897	WB-4/499	AR
Boyette, Zilla	105	1885	WB-2/338	
Boyintone, Joseph	024	1738	SS 877/74	SS/AR
Boykin, Abraham	071	1891	WB-7/87	AR
Boykin, Arthur	071	1837	WB-4/149	AR
Boykin, Blount	047	1814	WB-3/556	AR
Boykin, Burwell	071	1795	WB-2/77	AR
Boykin, Byers	087	c1812	WB-A/73	AR
Boykin, Edward	071	c1743	Orig. Only	SS/AR
Boykin, Francis	071	1761	WB-1/58	
Boykin, Hardy	069	1837	WB-1/419	AR
Boykin, Hilliard	105	1894	WB-3/99	
Boykin, Husted	056	1900	WB-4/213	AR
Boykin, John	071	1777	WB-1/294	
Boykin, John	071	1836	WB-4/144	AR
Boykin, John	047	1762	WB-1/60	
Boykin, Jonathan	069	1832	WB-1/383	AR
Boykin, Joseph	035	1766	WB-A/58	AR
Boykin, Joseph	087	c1806	WB-A/46	AR
Boykin, L. W.	071	1861	WB-5/256	AR
Boykin, Martha	071	1810	WB-3/38	AR
Boykin, Mattie	087	1898	WB-4/87	AR
Boykin, Nancy	105	1886	WB-2/397	AR
Boykin, Nancy L.	010	1860	WB-H/98	AR
Boykin, Sarah	105	c1868	WB-1/134	AR
Boykin, Sarah	087	1865	WB-2/84	AR
Boykin, Solomon	056	c1790	WB-1/36	AR
Boykin, Sterling	071	1829	WB-4/47	AR
Boykin, Thomas	103	1781	WI-A/104	AR
Boykin, Thomas, Sr.	071	1750	Orig. Only	SS/AR
Boykin, William	087	c1803	WB-A/43	AR
Boykin, William	103	1816	RD-3/379	AR
Boykin, William S.	071	1844	WB-4/164	AR
Boylan, Catharine	099	1895	WB-C/445	AR
Boylan, Jane	099	1871	RB-35/139	AR
Boylan, Jerry	022	1890	WB-E/442 & 449	AR
Boylan, John H.	099	1870	RB-35/105	AR
Boylan, William	099	1861	SC/08587	AR-Copy
Boylan, William	099	1861	RB-32/78	AR
Boylan, William	099	1861	056 WB-2/239	056 AR
Boylan, William M.	099	1899	WB-D/445	AR
Boyle, Ann	073	1816	WB-D/484	AR
Boyle, John	073	1815	WB-D/443	AR
Boyle, John	073	1796	WB-C/90	AR
Boyle, John McC.	063	c1862	WB-2/488	
Boyle, William	073	1815	WB-D/441	AR
Boyles, Alexander	090	1896	WB-6/410	AR
Boyles, Alexander	092	1874	WB-6/56	
Boyles, Charles B.	065	1893	WB-M/169	AR
Boyles, D.	090	1895	WB-6/367	AR
Boyles, Daniel	084	1851	WB-C/117	CTY
Boyles, Drucilla	065	1888	WB-L/317	
Boyles, Harmon	090	1885	WB-6/153	AR
Boyles, John	090	1887	WB-6/178	AR
Boyles, John	026	1891	WB-2/428	AR
Boyles, John, Sr.	021	1846	WB-1/42	AR
Boyles, Mary	060	1882	WB-4/267	AR
Boyles, Noah	090	1890	WB-6/236	AR
Boyles, William	090	1831	WB-3/229	AR
Boynes, Elizabeth	020	1890	WB-B/21	CTY
Boyse, James	065	1794	WB-A/88	AR
Boyte, Amos	103	1826	RD-5/261	AR
Boyte, Joseph B.	103	1816	RD-3/341	AR
Boyte, Martha	097	1896	WB-2/538	AR
Boyte, Polly	103	1838	RD-7/336	AR
Boyte, Thomas	103	1817	RD-4/33	AR
Bozman, Chloe	024	c1845	WB-C/279	AR
Bozman, Frances	024	1854	WB-C/359	AR
Bozman, John	010	1812	WB-F/196	AR
Bozman, Mary	010	1839	WB-G/310	AR
Bozman, Samuel	082	1835	WB-2/51	AR
Bozzell, Reuben	065	1836	WB-E/152	AR
Brabball, John	030	c1806	WB-2/320	
Brabble, William	030	1780	WB-1/139	
Braboy, David	083	c1787	WB-1/10	AR
Bracewell, Henry	022	1785	RB-1/23	AR
Bracewell, Richard	037	1807	WB-D/267	AR
Brack, George	072	1751	028 DB-5/159	SS/AR
Brack, Richard	100	1815	WB-19/124	AR
Brack, William	072	1776	RW/L14	AR
Bracken, John	073	1822	WB-E/10	AR
Brackett, Elizabeth	064	1860	WB-1/70	AR
Brackin, Joseph	020	1846	RB-P/338	AR
Brackin, Nancy	020	1852	RB-Q/585	AR-Copy
Brackin, Samuel	020	1812	RB-F/268	AR
Brackin, Samuel E.	020	1886	WB-A/492	CTY
Brackins, Samuel	004	1892	WB-A/139	AR
Bracy, Solomon	071	1893	WB-7/197	AR
Bradberry, Charlotta	IN	1890	103 WB-1/504	
Bradberry, George	103	1820	RD-4/364	
Bradbury, George	103	1836	RD-7/194	AR
Bradbury, James	103	1787	WI-A/86	AR
Braddick, Ayers	028	1873	WB-E/86	AR
Braddock, David	028	1816	WB-C/122	AR
Braddy, Benjamin	009	1822	OB-A/320	AR
Braddy, Benjamin	009	1900	WB-2/227	CTY
Braddy, Elizabeth	056	1896	WB-4/37	AR
Braddy, Estelle A.	037	1898	WB-H/428	AR
Braddy, James	079	c1845	WB-1/11	AR-Copy
Braddy, James	024	1750	Orig. Only	SS/AR
Braddy, Joseph	079	1862	WB-1/113	AR
Braddy, Joseph	037	1804	WB-D/211	AR
Braddy, Lewis	009	1882	WB-1/314	CTY
Braddy, Patric	037	1782	WB-B/98	AR
Braddy, Willie	012	1841	WB-B/176	AR
Bradford, D. L.	054	1897	WB-6/97	
Bradford, David	044	1800	WB-5/52	CTY
Bradford, David	065	1779	WB-A/84	AR
Bradford, David	016	1845	WB-1/65	
Bradford, David	001	1864	WB-1/231	AR
Bradford, Henry	047	1833	WB-4/100	AR
Bradford, John	044	1865	WB-22/376	CTY
Bradford, John	044	1829	WB-11/218	CTY
Bradford, John	047	1787	WB-3/140	AR
Bradford, Nathanall	037	1757	SS 879/203	SS/AR
Bradford, Philemon	044	1804	WB-6/107	CTY
Bradford, Richard	044	1757	Orig. Only	CTY
Bradford, Thomas	044	1786	WB-1/484	CTY
Bradford, Thomas	071	1762	WB-1/75	
Bradford, W. B.	016	1875	WB-3/162	AR
Bradford, W. M.	044	1898	WB-24/399	CTY
Bradford, William	047	1824	WB-3/705	AR
Bradford, William	073	1822	WB-E/27	AR

Name	Co.	Date	Recorded Copy	Original
Bradley, Agy	037	1820	WB-E/248	AR
Bradley, Albert	040	1894	WB-2/471	AR
Bradley, Alexander	040	1885	WB-2/246	AR
Bradley, Ann	047	1866	WB-5/148	
Bradley, Ann	011	c1809	WB-2/299	
Bradley, Benjamin	047	1782	WB-3/29	AR
Bradley, Benjamin	100	1811	WB-16/192	AR
Bradley, Benjamin	037	1854	WB-G/76	AR
Bradley, Burrel	037	1838	WB-F/221	AR
Bradley, Charles	030	c1809	WB-2/357	
Bradley, Charles	CT	1889	070 WB-F/346	070 AR
Bradley, Charles W.	070	1899	WB-H/172	AR
Bradley, David	037	1852	WB-F/477	AR
Bradley, David	037	c1848	Orig. Only	AR
Bradley, Dolley	037	1868	WB-G/318	AR
Bradley, Drury	080	1886	WB-1/122	AR
Bradley, Eleanor	047	1790	WB-3/188	AR
Bradley, Elias	050	1900	WB-2/347	CTY
Bradley, Eliza C.	070	1854	WB-C/572	AR
Bradley, Enoch	073	1800	WB-D/11	AR
Bradley, Francis	039	c1792	WB-A/106	
Bradley, Gee	099	1804	RB-6/251	AR
Bradley, George S.	017	c1851	WB-A/65	AR
Bradley, George W.	080	1864	WB-1/185	AR
Bradley, Hardy	037	1872	WB-G/377	AR
Bradley, Henry	047	1764	WB-1/141	
Bradley, Increase	019	1829	WB-D/8	AR
Bradley, J. B.	100	1887	WB-51/230	AR
Bradley, James	047	1820	WB-3/649	AR
Bradley, James	020	1787	RB-B/178	AR
Bradley, James	069	1789	WB-1/54	AR
Bradley, James	011	c1804	WB-1/450	
Bradley, James	047	1816	WB-3/582	AR
Bradley, James	011	c1804	WB-2/320	
Bradley, James, Sr.	011	c1807	WB-1/363	
Bradley, Jesse	085	1802	WB-C/328	AR
Bradley, John	047	1788	WB-3/156	AR
Bradley, John	070	1811	WB-AB/166	
Bradley, John	037	1772	WB-A/194	AR
Bradley, John	030	1789	WB-1/236	
Bradley, John	094	1778	Orig. Only	060 AR
Bradley, Jonas	065	1779	WB-A/117	AR
Bradley, Jonathan	037	1844	WB-F/312	AR
Bradley, Joseph	047	1774	WB-1/338	
Bradley, Joseph W.	040	1880	WB-2/148	
Bradley, Joshua	026	1875	WB-2/130	AR
Bradley, Julia A.	071	1885	WB-6/462	AR
Bradley, Lawrence	037	1874	WB-G/437	AR
Bradley, Malinda	064	1894	WB-2/322	AR
Bradley, Malvina	047	1882	WB-6/280	AR
Bradley, Margarit	011	c1816	WB-2/330	
Bradley, Martha	021	1886	WB-2/357	
Bradley, Mary	047	1817	WB-3/608	AR
Bradley, Mary	037	1866	WB-G/285	AR
Bradley, Mitchell	SC	1873	040 WB-2/252	040 AR
Bradley, Nancy	047	1841	WB-4/192	AR
Bradley, Nancy	037	1854	WB-G/94	AR
Bradley, Nelson	086	1898	WB-F/583	AR
Bradley, Penelope	037	1847	WB-F/372	AR
Bradley, Priscilla	037	1842	WB-F/267	AR
Bradley, Rachael	012	1767	DB-A/39	AR
Bradley, Rebecca	040	1877	WB-2/113	AR
Bradley, Richard	037	1827	WB-F/75	AR
Bradley, Richard	030	1756	SS 880/208	SS/AR
Bradley, Richard	070	1834	WB-AB/291	AR
Bradley, S. B.	047	1900	WB-7/236	AR
Bradley, Sally	037	1847	WB-F/356	AR
Bradley, Sarah	080	1891	WB-1/162	AR
Bradley, Sarah Jane	070	1898	WB-H/152	AR
Bradley, Stephen	037	1830	WB-F/112	AR
Bradley, Stephen	037	1861	WB-G/207	AR
Bradley, T. C.	062	1892	100 WB-51/346	
Bradley, T. C.	062	1892	WB-B/153	AR
Bradley, Terry	092	1785	WB-2/60	AR
Bradley, Wiley	037	1884	WB-G/661	AR
Bradley, William	009	1839	OB-C2/119	AR
Bradley, William	012	1764	DB-A/1	
Bradley, William D.	060	1835	WB-1/361	AR
Bradley, Wilson	086	1897	WB-F/540	AR
Bradly, John	028	1753	SS 881/1	SS/AR
Bradly, Joseph	049	c1827	WI-A/27	AR
Bradly, Susan Ann	070	1895	WB-G/377	AR
Bradly, Uriah	056	1881	WB-3/272	AR
Bradly, William	017	c1849	WB-A/47	AR
Bradshaw, A. M.	046	1893	WB-F/262	AR
Bradshaw, Benjamin	060	1815	Orig. Only	AR
Bradshaw, Carter	016	1896	WB-4/226	AR
Bradshaw, Charles	060	1800	Orig. Only	AR
Bradshaw, David	016	1842	PQS.6/188	
Bradshaw, Elijah	014	1887	WB-2/345	CTY
Bradshaw, Elizabeth	033	1839	WB-1/22	AR
Bradshaw, Elizabeth	001	1870	WB-2/5	AR
Bradshaw, Field	060	1788	Orig. Only	AR
Bradshaw, Field	060	1803	Orig. Only	AR
Bradshaw, George W.	036	1898	WB-A/441 & 479	CTY
Bradshaw, Guy	085	1873	WB-1/179	CTY
Bradshaw, H. R.	016	1865	WB-2/119	Nunc.
Bradshaw, Isabella	046	1899	WB-G/163	AR
Bradshaw, James	017	c1852	WB-A/116	AR
Bradshaw, Jesse	087	c1821	WB-1/6	AR
Bradshaw, John	078	1808	WI-5/10	
Bradshaw, John	087	1829	WB-1/94	AR
Bradshaw, Jonas	060	1885	WB-4/325	AR
Bradshaw, Judith	060	1820	Orig. Only	AR
Bradshaw, Letitia	001	1877	WB-2/98	AR
Bradshaw, Mary Ann	001	1859	WB-1/163	AR
Bradshaw, Nancy	017	1868	WB-A/181	AR
Bradshaw, Robert	085	1832	WB-H/547	AR
Bradshaw, Samuel	035	1886	WB-4/284	AR
Bradshaw, Seth	MO	c1856	Copy	017 AR
Bradshaw, T. F.	001	1866	WB-1/271	AR
Bradshaw, Thomas	028	c1778	Orig. Only	AR
Bradshaw, Thomas	087	1880	WB-3/204	AR
Bradshaw, W. L.	001	1898	WB-3/215	AR
Bradshaw, W. S.	032	1892	WB-4/169	AR
Bradshaw, William	014	c1864	WB-1/11	AR
Bradshaw, William	014	1881	WB-2/209	
Bradsher, Abner	078	1858	WB-18/38	AR
Bradsher, Addison	044	1894	WB-24/249	CTY
Bradsher, Eliza	046	1897	WB-F/567	AR
Bradsher, Elizabeth	078	1894	WB-19/361	AR
Bradsher, George M.	078	1893	WB-19/352	AR
Bradsher, James O.	078	1897	WB-19/428	AR
Bradsher, John	078	1876	WB-19/60	AR
Bradsher, John	078	c1802	Orig. Only	AR
Bradsher, John	078	c1883	WB-19/194	
Bradsher, Martha	020	1840	RB-O/123	
Bradsher, Martha	078	1894	WB-19/361	AR
Bradsher, Moses, Sr.	020	1820	RB-H/384	AR

Name	Co.	Date	Recorded Copy	Original
Bradsher, Sarah	078	1848	WB-13/111	AR
Bradsher, Zackery T.	020	1877	WB-A/230	CTY
Bradwell, Daniel	054	1881	WB-4/425	CTY
Brady, Archibald	054	c1824	WB-2/93	AR
Brady, Blake	041	1852	WB-3/147	AR
Brady, Disey A.	081	1894	WB-16/302	
Brady, Elbert	021	1889	WB-2/488	AR
Brady, George A.	021	1895	WB-3/81	AR
Brady, James	041	1794	WB-1/125	AR
Brady, John	047	1800	WB-3/340	AR
Brady, John	085	1882	WB-2/41	CTY
Brady, John	009	c1810	OWB/556	AR
Brady, John	056	1794	WB-1/80	AR
Brady, John	041	1859	WB-3/246	AR
Brady, Joseph	024	1753	Orig. Only	SS/AR
Brady, Joshua	070	1808	WB-AB/110	AR
Brady, Joshua	072	1785	WI/L35	AR
Brady, Levi H.	056	1898	WB-4/138	AR
Brady, Marcy	009	1815	OB-A/238	AR
Brady, Sallie Ann	037	1894	WB-H/284	AR
Bragaw, Anna T.	NY	1880	009 WB-2/177	009 CTY
Bragg, Caleb	OH	1894	Copy	023 AR
Bragg, Caleb S.	OH	1894	091 WB-1/196	
Bragg, Hugh	044	1834	WB-13/142	CTY
Bragg, Isabella	099	1877	RB-35/392	AR
Bragg, Joel	044	1872	WB-23/83	CTY
Bragg, John	028	1816	WB-C/114	AR
Bragg, Maley	044	1874	WB-23/149	CTY
Bragg, Mary	028	1820	WB-C/191	AR
Bragg, Thomas	099	1872	RB-35/162	AR
Bragg, Thomas W.	039	1896	WB-V/87	AR
Bragg, Thomas, Sr.	071	1851	WB-5/94	AR
Braithwaite, William	030	1894	WB-5/217	AR
Brake, Jacob	037	1830	WB-F/118	AR
Brake, Patience	037	1854	WB-G/93	AR
Brake, William	037	1882	WB-G/632	AR
Braley, Noel	054	c1832	WB-2/150	
Brall, Zachariah	054	c1817	WB-1/406	
Braly, Hugh	085	1825	WB-H/321	AR
Braly, John	085	c1797	WB-F/10	AR
Braly, Mary	054	c1830	WB-2/192	AR
Braly, Sarah	085	c1800	WB-D/125	AR
Braly, Thomas	085	1765	WB-A/5	AR
Braly, William	085	c1789	WB-D/132	AR
Braman, Anson	080	1886	WB-1/114	AR
Bramble, Edward	029	1888	Orig. Only	AR
Bramble, William W.	029	1885	WB-E/405	AR
Brame, Dickey	044	1816	WB-7/586	CTY
Brame, Dillie J.	098	1894	WB-A/209	CTY
Brame, Elizabeth	044	1878	WB-23/316	CTY
Brame, James W.	098	1895	WB-A/227	CTY
Brame, John T.	028	1819	WB-C/187	AR
Brame, Marcus G.	AL	1845	Copy	100 AR
Brame, Nancy	044	1861	WB-21/461	CTY
Brame, Nancy J.	044	1874	WB-23/151	CTY
Brame, Nelson	044	1865	WB-22/330	CTY
Brame, Sally	044	1873	WB-23/130	CTY
Brame, Sarah P.	028	1847	WB-D/137	AR
Brame, William	098	1882	WB-A/14	
Branch, Alpheus	105	1893	WB-3/43	AR
Branch, Archibald	035	1819	WB-A/28	AR
Branch, Archilus	035	1865	WB-3/97	AR
Branch, Arthur	099	1852	RB-28/85	AR
Branch, Benjamin	071	1803	WB-2/242	AR
Branch, Burrel	035	1833	DB-4/265	

Name	Co.	Date	Recorded Copy	Original
Branch, Clabourne	014	1878	WB-2/165	
Branch, Edelph	035	1815	WB-A/26	AR
Branch, Elizabeth	039	1859	WB-0/396	AR
Branch, Francis	071	1800	WB-2/191	AR
Branch, Francis	N	1739	LGB-4/#123	SS/AR
Branch, George	029	1863	WB-C/446	AR
Branch, Issacher	077	1802	WB-E/139	AR
Branch, James	047	1807	WB-3/468	AR
Branch, James G.	035	1873	WB-4/70	AR
Branch, Jesse	047	1842	WB-4/214	AR
Branch, Jessee	087	1856	WB-1/494	AR
Branch, Job	077	1802	WB-E/161	AR
Branch, John	047	1863	WB-5/103	
Branch, John	071	1790	WB-1/406	AR
Branch, John R.	047	1882	WB-6/272	AR
Branch, John T.	071	1866	WB-5/334	AR
Branch, John, Sr.	047	1806	WB-3/453	AR
Branch, Martha A.	039	1883	WB-U/325	AR
Branch, Mary	071	1803	WB-2/237	AR
Branch, Mary	071	1811	WB-3/45	AR
Branch, Matthew	029	1846	WB-C/96	AR
Branch, Norman	071	1836	WB-4/140	AR
Branch, Olive	014	1890	WB-2/401	AR-Copy
Branch, R. C.	099	1894	WB-C/254	AR
Branch, Sallie	099	1887	WB-B/201	AR
Branch, Samuel W.	047	1864	WB-5/118	
Branch, Thomas	071	1847	WB-5/59	AR
Branch, William	024	1721	SS 875/294	SS/AR
Branch, William	024	1727	Orig. Only	AR
Branch, William	083	1853	WB-2/88	AR
Branch, William	047	1808	WB-3/482	AR
Branch, William	047	1794	WB-3/218	AR
Branch, William H.	099	1867	RB-34/480	AR
Branch, Wm. Jordan	013	1892	WB-C/190	AR
Brand, Isabella	N	1758	Orig. Only	SS/AR
Brand, Jane E.	103	1899	WB-2/266	AR
Brand, Xaver	013	1887	WB-B/428	AR
Brandon, Alexander	085	1855	WB-K/180	AR
Brandon, Christopher	085	c1806	WB-F/5	AR
Brandon, David	054	1892	WB-5/410	CTY
Brandon, Elizabeth	085	1810	WB-G/154	AR
Brandon, Esther	085	1822	WB-H/142	AR
Brandon, George	085	1772	WB-A/6	AR
Brandon, James	085	c1790	WB-B/49	AR
Brandon, John	085	1827	WB-F/386	AR
Brandon, John	085	c1801	WB-D/3	AR
Brandon, Margaret	085	1831	WB-H/512	AR
Brandon, Mary	085	c1797	WB-D/161	AR
Brandon, Matthew	085	1819	Orig. Only	AR
Brandon, Minervia	065	1866	WB-J/227	AR
Brandon, Richard	085	c1790	WB-C/14	AR
Brandon, Sophia G.	085	1847	WB-K/49	AR
Brandon, Thomas	085	c1783	WB-B/107	AR
Brandon, Thomas	090	1834	WB-3/265	AR
Brandon, William	038	1869	WB-2/17	AR
Brandon, William	085	c1755	SS 880/133	AR
Braner, Lezebeth	077	c1817	WB-F/1	AR
Braner, Michel	077	1777	WB-C/243	AR
Braner, Sarah	077	1808	WB-E/319	AR
Branham, Benjamin	104	1805	WB-2/157	AR
Branham, John R.	056	1881	WB-3/294	AR
Brank, Joseph R.	013	1875	WB-B/103	
Brank, Letta R.	062	1888	WB-B/90	AR
Brann, Catherine	078	1817	WI-8/30	AR
Brann, John	078	1855	WB-17/372	AR

Name	Co.	Date	Recorded Copy	Original
Brann, John	084	1856	WB-C/231	CTY
Brann, Paulina	106	1896	WB-2/383	
Brann, Vincent	084	1863	WB-C/382	CTY
Brannan, Leroy	056	1808	WB-1/213	AR
Brannan, Thomas	056	1804	WB-1/166	AR
Brannock, Alexander	020	1886	WB-A/479	CTY
Brannock, Ann	072	c1774	Orig. Only	AR
Brannock, Edmund	001	1860	WB-1/174	AR
Brannock, Henry	073	1841	WB-F/97	AR
Brannock, William	073	c1830	Orig. Only	AR
Brannon, George	040	1847	WB-1/1	
Branock, John	001	1899	WB-3/276	AR
Branock, William	001	1866	WB-1/281	AR
Branson, Eli	081	1888	WB-16/99	AR
Branson, Henry	029	1871	WB-E/32	AR
Branson, John	081	1867	WB-14/187	AR
Branson, Joseph	022	1827	WB-B/138	AR
Branson, Levi	022	1824	WB-B/113	AR
Branson, Luke L.	062	c1873	Orig. Only	AR
Branson, Mary E. J.	090	1891	WB-6/265	AR
Branson, Thomas	081	1879	WB-15/310	AR
Branson, Thomas A.	081	1864	WB-13/183	AR
Branson, William	081	1894	WB-16/281	
Branson, Zachariah	090	1825	WB-3/138	AR
Brantley, Edward	048	1805	WB-3/435	AR
Brantley, Edward	047	1768	WB-1/218	
Brantley, Edward	010	1837	WB-G/290	AR
Brantley, James H.	071	1864	WB-5/289	AR
Brantley, Jincy	071	1826	WB-3/334	AR
Brantley, John	069	1786	WB-1/41	AR
Brantley, Lewis	047	1799	WB-3/324	AR
Brantley, Margaret	054	1894	WB-5/501	CTY
Brantley, Philip	047	1775	WB-2/9	
Brantley, Richard A.	054	1890	WB-5/351	CTY
Brantley, Robert	047	1795	WB-3/238	AR
Brantley, Robert R.	047	1803	WB-3/385	AR
Brantley, Thomas	071	1777	WB-1/16	AR
Brantley, William	047	1807	WB-3/470	AR
Brantly, Elizabeth	022	1829	WB-B/126	AR
Brantly, Henry	079	1867	WB-1/170	AR
Brantly, James	051	1881	WB-C/275	AR
Brantly, John	022	1782	Orig. Only	AR
Brantly, John	022	1812	WB-A/221	AR
Brantly, Joseph	022	1807	WB-A/133	AR
Brantly, Penelope	047	1864	WB-5/109	
Brantly, William	022	1823	WB-B/106	AR
Branton, Moses	041	1854	WB-3/171	AR
Branton, William	026	1878	WB-2/167	AR
Branton, William	022	1828	WB-B/151	AR
Brasfield, Elijah	099	1796	RB-3/216	AR
Brasfield, George	044	1809	WB-7/11	CTY
Brasfield, George	099	1823	RB-17/435	AR
Brasfield, George	044	1771	WB-2/155	CTY
Brasfield, Hannah	099	1841	RB-24/501	AR
Brasfield, John	099	1788	RB-2/206	AR
Brasfield, John, Sr.	099	1844	RB-25/458	AR
Brasfield, Sarah	099	1857	RB-30/299	AR
Brasher, Asa	084	1818	WB-A/138	CTY
Brasher, Jemima	084	1828	WB-A/329	CTY
Brasington, James T.	005	1898	WB-D/440	AR
Brasington, Joseph	022	1810	WB-A/185	AR
Brask, Larance	075	1687	Orig. Only	SS/AR
Brassel, William	069	1796	WB-1/104	AR
Brassell, Abner	037	1807	WB-D/279	AR
Brassfield, Simeon S.	099	1892	WB-C/50	AR
Brassfield, William	099	1796	RB-3/271	AR
Brasswell, Jacob, Sr.	069	1823	WB-1/313	AR
Brasswell, Richard	085	1761	WB-A/16	
Braswell, Aquilla	097	1891	WB-2/398	AR
Braswell, Arthur	083	c1819	WB-1/354	AR
Braswell, Benjamin	005	1865	WB-C/206	AR
Braswell, Benjamin	037	1792	WB-C/194	AR
Braswell, Benjamin	069	1827	WB-1/344	AR
Braswell, Boston	105	1875	WB-2/173	AR
Braswell, Bythal	037	1842	WB-F/266	AR
Braswell, Crissey	037	1853	WB-F/497	AR
Braswell, Cullen	097	1869	WB-2/13	
Braswell, David	047	1837	WB-4/148	AR
Braswell, Drew	047	1899	WB-7/241	AR
Braswell, Eliabeth	105	1894	WB-3/106	
Braswell, Emmeliza	037	1900	WB-H/481	AR
Braswell, Exum	069	1900	WB-6/124	AR
Braswell, George W.	056	1882	WB-3/315	AR
Braswell, Irvin	005	1845	WB-B/200	AR
Braswell, Isaac	037	1873	WB-G/424	AR
Braswell, J. N.	099	1899	WB-D/217	AR
Braswell, James	037	1783	WB-B/126	AR
Braswell, James	047	1840	WB-4/185	AR
Braswell, James	037	1765	WB-A/142	AR
Braswell, James	037	1824	WB-F/18	AR
Braswell, James	039	1871	WB-U/28	AR
Braswell, James P.	069	1898	WB-6/30	AR
Braswell, Jeremiah	069	1857	WB-1/554	AR
Braswell, Jesse	069	1865	WB-1/592	AR
Braswell, John	069	1860	WB-1/621	AR
Braswell, Martha Ann	105	1899	WB-3/322	AR
Braswell, Mary	037	1895	WB-H/316	AR
Braswell, Mary	069	c1855	WB-1/551	AR
Braswell, Mary P.	037	1890	WB-H/167	AR
Braswell, Matilda	039	1874	WB-U/100	AR
Braswell, Nathan	083	1801	WB-1/70	AR-Nunc.
Braswell, Norfleet	099	1887	WB-B/220	AR
Braswell, Permenter	037	1830	WB-F/119	AR
Braswell, Polly	037	1863	WB-G/230	AR
Braswell, Richard	037	1772	WB-A/193	AR
Braswell, Robert	010	1736	Orig. Only	SS/AR
Braswell, Robert R.	037	1848	WB-F/402	AR
Braswell, Samuel	069	1795	WB-1/94	AR
Braswell, Shadrick	103	1820	RD-4/350	AR
Braswell, Stephen	103	1855	RD-12/37	AR
Braswell, Valintine	099	1797	RB-3/67	AR
Braswell, Whitmill	047	1861	WB-5/94	
Braswell, William	069	c1785	Orig. Only	AR
Braswell, William	069	1779	WB-1/6	AR
Braswell, Winnifred	037	1897	WB-H/384	AR
Braswell, Zadoc	037	1852	WB-F/472	AR
Bratcher, Roger	028	1784	WB-D/202	AR
Bratcher, Susan A.	028	1866	WB-D/431	AR
Bratcher, Thomas	028	1805	WB-B/216	AR
Brattain, John	081	1784	WB-1/18	AR-Nunc.
Bratten, Edward	077	1849	WB-F/371	AR
Bratten, John	077	1782	WB-C/246	AR
Bratten, Nathaniel	077	1804	WB-E/219	AR
Bratten, Nathaniel	077	1841	WB-F/297	
Bratten, Thomas	077	1845	WB-F/314	AR
Bratton, Claiborn	065	1898	WB-0/393	AR
Brawley, Cornelius	054	1873	WB-4/109	CTY
Brawley, D. J.	054	1898	WB-6/181	CTY
Brawley, Esther T.	054	1900	WB-6/324	CTY
Brawley, Finley S.	054	1879	WB-4/360	CTY

Name	Co.	Date	Recorded Copy	Original
Brawley, John	054	1852	WB-3/57	AR
Brawley, John	054	c1823	Orig. Only	AR
Brawley, Mary A.	054	1897	WB-6/109	CTY
Brawley, Mary Ann	054	1856	WB-3/95	AR
Brawley, Nancy	054	1890	WB-5/343	CTY
Brawley, Robert M.	054	c1861	Orig. Only	AR
Brawley, W. J.	054	1889	WB-5/272	CTY
Brawly, Daniel	054	1861	WB-3/158	AR
Brawn, Luke	030	1820	WB-3/291	
Brawton, John	020	1841	RB-0/196	AR
Braxton, Council	079	1861	WB-1/71	AR
Braxton, Elisha	001	1865	WB-1/238	AR
Braxton, Felix	079	1886	WB-2/364	AR
Braxton, John	022	1860	WB-D/60	AR
Braxton, John H.	001	1895	WB-3/72 & 87	AR
Braxton, Jonathan	001	1900	WB-3/305	AR
Braxton, Joseph	022	1814	WB-A/256	
Braxton, Thomas	022	1814	WB-A/256	
Braxton, William	022	1773	Orig. Only	AR
Bray, Andrew	030	1825	WB-3/208	
Bray, Andrew	030	1872	WB-5/25	
Bray, Christopher	075	1762	WB-I/19	AR
Bray, Eli	081	1856	WB-10/298	AR
Bray, Elizabeth	022	c1858	Orig. Only	AR
Bray, Hanan	092	1843	WB-4/206	
Bray, Harmon	022	1853	WB-C/382	AR
Bray, Henry	081	1874	WB-15/150	AR
Bray, Henry	022	1794	RB-2/5	AR
Bray, Henry	022	1812	WB-A/198	AR
Bray, Henry	075	1758	SS 881/176	SS/AR
Bray, Henry M.	022	1885	WB-E/315	AR
Bray, Henry, Jr.	018	1827	WB-C/91	
Bray, Henry, Sr.	018	1833	WB-C/136	
Bray, Henry, Sr.	022	1855	WB-C/386	AR
Bray, Hessey	057	1867	Orig. Only	AR
Bray, James	030	1799	WB-2/140	
Bray, James	022	1857	WB-C/452	AR
Bray, James	030	1823	WB-3/138	
Bray, Jesse	081	c1845	Orig. Only	AR
Bray, John	081	1822	WB-5/73	AR
Bray, John	030	1844	WB-4/103	
Bray, John	075	1805	WB-M1/109	AR
Bray, Joseph	092	c1847	WB-4/268	
Bray, Joseph	018	1844	WB-C/290	
Bray, L. W.	092	1898	WB-6/478	AR
Bray, Lemuel	018	1890	WB-E/180	AR
Bray, Linner	030	c1814	WB-3/50	
Bray, Mathias	081	1825	WB-5/238	AR
Bray, Nancy	030	c1810	WB-2/355	
Bray, Nathan B.	022	1896	WB-F/38	
Bray, Ortha	092	1867	WB-5/88	
Bray, Rebecca	081	1878	WB-15/293	AR
Bray, Thomas W.	075	N. D.	WB-M2/57	AR
Bray, William	022	1846	WB-C/187	AR
Bray, William	018	1848	WB-C/331	
Bray, William	075	1774	WB-I/72	AR
Bray, William	030	1789	WB-1/237	
Bray, William	075	1725	SS 876/130	SS/AR
Bray, William P.	075	1875	WB-O/61	AR
Bray, Willis	030	1816	WB-3/81	
Brazier, James	029	1790	Orig. Only	AR
Brazier, William	092	1815	WB-3/113	AR
Brazill, Ridley	046	1830	WB-B/409	AR
Bready, Robert M.	054	1865	WB-3/179	AR
Breazier, Thomas	073	1784	WB-A/286	AR
Breckill, Benjamin A.	039	1841	WB-L/30	
Breden, Alexander	046	1793	WB-A/14	AR
Breden, Robert	046	1777	WB-A/17	AR
Breece, Cornelious	072	1818	WB-A/10	AR
Breece, Frederick	029	1858	Orig. Only	AR
Breece, Ross	019	1802	WB-D/45	AR
Breece, Samson F.	029	1895	WB-F/40	AR
Breece, Sarah A.	029	1872	WB-E/60	AR
Breeden, Catherine	SC	1886	082 WB-6/367	082 AR
Breedlove, Emanuel	098	1882	WB-A/16	CTY
Breedlove, Henry	046	1900	WB-G/229	AR
Breedlove, Levi	081	1873	WB-15/110	AR
Brees, Henry	019	c1787	WB-D/33	AR
Brees, William	019	1793	WB-D/84	AR
Breese, Thomas	073	1784	WB-A/297	AR
Breeze, John	073	1820	WB-D/583	AR
Brehon, James G.	100	1819	WB-22/88	AR
Brehon, James G.	100	1839	WB-37/267	AR
Brem, Adelaide M.	065	1893	WB-M/163	AR
Brem, H. N.	065	1874	WB-K/145	AR
Brem, Thomas H.	065	1876	WB-K/230	AR
Bremer, John M.	070	1897	WB-H/59	AR
Brendle, Abram	032	1834	WB-1/248	AR
Brendle, Daniel	032	1843	WB-1/421	AR
Brendle, David	021	1862	WB-1/164	AR
Brendle, E. D.	055	1886	WB-A/76	
Brendle, John D.	023	1891	WB-A/100	AR
Brendle, Tony	038	1898	WB-4/111	AR
Brenn, William	037	1792	WB-C/184	
Brent, James	047	1820	WB-3/649	AR
Brent, James	030	1753	SS 879/146	SS/AR
Brent, Peter	047	1834	WB-4/111	AR
Brent, Thomas	030	c1713	SS 875/25	
Brent, Thomas	030	1727	SS 876/103	SS/AR
Brentle, James	020	1831	RB-M/3	AR
Bretsch, Mary E.	099	1891	WB-B/541	AR
Bretson, Mary E.	099	1891	WB-B/541	
Brett, Clifton L.	051	1894	WB-C/478	AR
Brett, Elias	051	1850	WB-A/320	
Brett, Elisha D.	051	1876	WB-C/172	AR
Brett, George A.	051	1871	WB-C/49	
Brett, Priscilla	051	1871	WB-C/49	AR
Brevard, Alexander	060	1830	WB-1/166	AR
Brevard, Ephraim	065	1781	WB-A/113	AR
Brevard, Ephraim J.	065	1885	WB-L/78	AR
Brevard, Ephriam A.	060	1854	WB-2/390	
Brevard, James	013	1847	WB-A/126	
Brevard, John F.	054	c1827	WB-2/47	AR
Brevard, Joseph M.	060	1843	WB-2/176	
Brevard, R. A.	060	1879	WB-4/209	AR
Brevard, Robert	054	c1797	WB-1/70	AR
Brevard, Sarah	054	c1801	WB-1/72	AR
Brew, Moses	071	1804	WB-2/254 & 263	
Brewer, Ambrose	022	c1860	WB-D/67	AR
Brewer, Ann	100	1782	WB-3/138	AR
Brewer, Asberry	022	1882	WB-E/258	AR
Brewer, Biddy	073	1858	WB-G/191	AR
Brewer, Elizabeth	073	1830	WB-E/220	AR
Brewer, Ervin	083	1898	WB-4/232	AR
Brewer, Fisk P.	IA	1890	Copy	099 AR
Brewer, George	099	1817	RB-14/40	AR
Brewer, George	071	1757	Orig. Only	SS/AR
Brewer, Henry	087	1840	WB-1/228	AR
Brewer, Henry	022	1779	Orig. Only	AR

Name	Co.	Date	Recorded Copy	Original
Brewer, Isaac	063	1835	WB-2/203	
Brewer, Jacob P.	056	c1783	WB-1/779 & 794	AR
Brewer, James	069	1879	WB-5/83	AR
Brewer, Jane	070	1739	SS 877/120	SS/AR
Brewer, Jesse	047	1818	WB-3/629	AR
Brewer, Jesse	103	1852	RD-11/197	AR
Brewer, John	039	1892	WB-U/557	AR
Brewer, John	005	1877	WB-D/54	AR
Brewer, John	099	1822	RB-17/384	AR
Brewer, John	022	1849	WB-C/240	AR
Brewer, Joseph	100	1782	WB-3/125	AR
Brewer, Katey	073	1801	WB-D/30	AR
Brewer, Letty	022	1877	WB-E/118	AR
Brewer, Manley M.	073	1894	WB-I/18	CTY
Brewer, Martha	073	1822	WB-E/27	AR
Brewer, Mary	063	1827	WB-2/133	
Brewer, Mary Ann	083	1900	WB-4/264	AR
Brewer, Moses	103	1813	RD-3/8	AR
Brewer, Nathan	022	1838	WB-C/89	AR
Brewer, Oliver	022	1792	RB-1/45	AR
Brewer, Rebecca	079	1858	WB-1/15	AR
Brewer, Sackfield	073	1813	WB-D/384	AR
Brewer, Sally	047	1845	WB-4/248	AR
Brewer, Samuel	022	1831	WB-B/201	AR
Brewer, Samuel C.	099	1856	RB-29/516	AR
Brewer, Solomon	022	1824	WB-B/79	AR
Brewer, Stephen	103	1889	WB-1/488	AR
Brewer, Thomas	073	1844	WB-F/224	AR
Brewer, Turner	047	1847	WB-4/260	AR
Brewer, W. T.	105	1871	WB-2/50	AR
Brewer, William	073	1833	WB-E/303	AR
Brewer, William	009	1783	OWB/184	AR
Brewer, William	073	1875	WB-H/128	CTY
Brewer, William	071	1816	WB-3/181	AR
Brewer, William	039	1856	WB-O/344	AR
Brewer, Zachariah	044	1853	WB-19/292	CTY
Brewster, Delia S.	099	1892	WB-C/63	AR
Brewster, John C.	099	1894	WB-C/288	AR
Briant, Elizabeth	022	1798	WB-A/3	AR
Briant, James A.	026	1862	WB-1/293	AR
Briant, Samuel	024	1717	Orig. Only	SS/AR
Brice (Bryce), Maggie	065	1899	WB-N/236	AR
Brice, Francis	035	1881	WB-4/196	AR
Brice, Francis	082	1780	WB-1/2	AR
Brice, Francis	035	1881	Copy	076 AR
Brice, George	035	1831	WB-1/11	AR
Brice, John	085	1791	WB-B/183	AR
Brice, Joseph	035	1829	WB-A/40	AR
Brice, Margaret	035	c1899	Orig. Only	AR
Brice, Martha	073	1836	WB-E/377	
Brice, Martha	035	1849	WB-2/51	AR
Brice, William	019	1719	SS 875/226	
Brice, William	019	1719	WB-E/42	
Brice, William	N	1753	028 DB-5/287	SS/AR
Brice, William	019	1753	WB-E/44	
Brickel, Sarah	079	1852	WB-1/60	AR
Brickell, Benjamin	039	1812	WB-C/282	AR
Brickell, James	009	1746	SS 878/61	SS/AR
Brickell, John	047	1789	WB-3/167	AR
Brickell, Jonathan	051	1856	WB-A/391	
Brickell, Martha	099	1852	RB-28/101	AR
Brickell, Rebecca W.	047	1887	WB-6/448	AR
Brickell, Susanah	009	1836	OWB/531	AR
Brickell, William W.	047	1878	WB-6/189	AR

Name	Co.	Date	Recorded Copy	Original
Brickhouse, Affey	096	1878	WB-4/46	
Brickhouse, Annis	096	1899	WB-4/171	AR
Brickhouse, Benjamin	096	1868	WB-3/87	
Brickhouse, Benjamin	030	1816	WB-3/76	
Brickhouse, Elizabeth	096	1832	WB-2/110	AR
Brickhouse, James	096	1882	WB-4/71	
Brickhouse, Jesse	096	1858	WB-3/75	AR
Brickhouse, John	096	1837	Orig. Only	AR
Brickhouse, John	096	1886	WB-4/122	
Brickhouse, John M.	096	1861	WB-3/74	AR
Brickhouse, Mathew	096	1814	WB-2/64	AR
Brickhouse, Matthew	096	1857	WB-3/52	AR
Brickhouse, Nathan E.	070	1869	WB-E/181	AR
Brickhouse, Nathaniel	096	1889	WB-4/143	AR
Brickhouse, Peter	096	1764	WB-1/27	AR
Brickhouse, Sarah	096	1837	WB-2/137	AR
Brickhouse, Simeon	096	1853	Orig. Only	AR
Brickhouse, William	096	c1821	Orig. Only	AR
Brickhouse, William	096	1825	Orig. Only	AR
Brickhouse, William	096	1818	WB-2/97	
Brickle, Nathaniel	100	1896	WB-51/438	AR
Bridgeman, Thomas	053	1858	WB-8/324	AR
Bridgen, Edward	028	1815	Orig. Only	AR
Bridgen, Samuel	070	1758	SS 882/44	SS/AR
Bridgen, Samuel	070	1758	DB-D/323	
Bridger, Elizabeth	071	1814	WB-3/125	AR
Bridger, Josiah	051	c1820	WB-A/16	
Bridger, Patience	010	1803	WB-E/196	AR
Bridgers, Benjamin	039	1822	WB-G/99	AR
Bridgers, Benjamin	056	1797	WB-1/109	AR
Bridgers, Briton	037	1795	WB-C/345	AR
Bridgers, Catherine	105	1896	WB-3/172	
Bridgers, Delany	039	1852	WB-N/306	AR
Bridgers, Etheldred	056	c1796	WB-1/102	AR
Bridgers, Frances I.	099	c1863	RB-32/425	AR
Bridgers, James T.	056	1888	WB-3/485	AR
Bridgers, John	071	1764	WB-1/97	
Bridgers, John L.	037	1884	WB-G/651	
Bridgers, John T.	105	1890	WB-2/558	AR
Bridgers, Joseph	071	1810	WB-3/39	AR
Bridgers, Joseph	071	1808	WB-3/13	AR
Bridgers, Mary	105	1889	WB-2/519	AR
Bridgers, Rachel	071	1764	WB-1/99	
Bridgers, Robert R.	070	1888	WB-F/244	AR
Bridgers, Sampson	083	1831	WB-1/219	AR
Bridgers, T. B.	099	1893	WB-C/171	AR
Bridgers, Turner	071	1804	WB-2/262	AR
Bridgers, William	010	1730	Orig. Only	SS/AR
Bridgers, William	010	1729	Orig. Only	SS/AR
Bridgers, William	071	1899	WB-7/438	AR
Bridgers, William	069	1805	WB-1/162	AR
Bridgers, William	056	c1789	WB-1/20	AR
Bridgers, William	071	1763	WB-1/81	
Bridgers, William B.	039	1833	WB-J/253	AR
Bridgers, Willis	071	1802	WB-2/235	AR
Bridgers, Young	056	1834	WB-1/505	AR
Bridges, Aaron	026	1887	WB-2/330	AR
Bridges, Alfred	021	1885	WB-2/314	
Bridges, Amanda	021	c1896	Orig. Only	AR
Bridges, Cornelia	022	1895	WB-F/5	AR
Bridges, Cynthia	026	1900	WB-3/59	AR
Bridges, David	060	1807	Orig. Only	AR
Bridges, E. L.	021	1866	WB-1/233	AR
Bridges, Edwin	071	1783	WB-1/265	
Bridges, Elisha	060	1803	Orig. Only	AR

Name	Co.	Date	Recorded Copy	Original
Bridges, Elizabeth	086	1846	WB-E/157	AR
Bridges, Henry B.	044	1863	WB-22/78	CTY
Bridges, J. M.	082	1898	WB-7/5	AR
Bridges, James	086	1883	WB-F/181	AR
Bridges, James W.	026	1862	WB-1/291	AR
Bridges, John	060	1791	Orig. Only	AR
Bridges, John	026	1848	WB-1/86	AR
Bridges, John	026	1862	WB-1/292	AR
Bridges, Joseph	085	c1785	WB-D/136	
Bridges, Joseph	022	1837	WB-C/50	AR
Bridges, Joseph	039	1805	WB-C/35	
Bridges, Josiah	039	1841	WB-L/39	
Bridges, Killis	026	1873	WB-2/101	
Bridges, Lewis	022	1883	WB-E/283	AR
Bridges, Rebecca	086	1884	WB-F/254	AR
Bridges, S. J.	026	1865	WB-1/363	AR
Bridges, Samuel	086	1891	WB-F/416	AR
Bridges, Sarah	022	1863	WB-D/107	AR
Bridges, Tabitha	047	1852	WB-4/329	AR
Bridges, Thomas S.	026	1894	WB-2/481	AR
Bridges, W. A.	086	1889	WB-F/366	AR
Bridges, Wiley	086	1891	WB-F/418	AR
Bridges, William	044	1762	Orig. Only	CTY
Bridgess, Samuel	071	1756	SS 880/46	SS/AR
Brient, John	060	1864	WB-3/68	AR
Brietz, Antoniette	038	1849	WB-1/1	AR
Brietz, Levin R.	038	1880	WB-2/389	AR
Brietz, Sophia M.	038	1897	WB-4/22	AR
Brigers, Etheldred	071	1869	WB-6/17	AR
Brigers, William	056	1751	028 DB-5/263	SS/AR
Briggs, Allen	041	1888	WB-4/277	AR
Briggs, Andrew	041	1864	WB-3/317	AR
Briggs, Benjamin	041	1823	WB-2/208	AR
Briggs, Duncan	073	1815	WB-D/457	AR
Briggs, Edward	041	1885	WB-4/232	AR
Briggs, Elmira A.	078	c1881	WB-19/254	AR
Briggs, Fannie J.	078	1888	WB-19/218	
Briggs, Federick	103	1790	Orig. Only	AR
Briggs, George	078	1856	WB-17/420	AR
Briggs, Henry	038	1851	WB-1/109	AR
Briggs, Henry	041	1835	WB-2/364	AR
Briggs, Jesse	092	1877	WB-6/98	AR
Briggs, Joel	037	1783	WB-B/116	AR
Briggs, Josiah	041	1838	WB-3/2	AR
Briggs, Judah E.	078	1899	WB-19/465	AR
Briggs, Moses	041	1826	WB-2/258	AR
Briggs, Rebecca H.	036	1897	WB-A/400	CTY
Briggs, Richard	024	1754	Orig. Only	SS/AR
Briggs, Richard	041	1840	WB-3/22	AR
Briggs, Samuel H.	078	1870	WB-19/9	AR
Briggs, Sarah J.	085	1883	WB-2/49	CTY
Briggs, Solomon	041	1817	WB-2/140	AR
Briggs, Thamer	041	1822	WB-2/183	AR
Briggs, Thomas	107	c1844	WB-1/340	
Briggs, Thomas H.	078	1900	WB-19/489	AR
Briggs, Thomas H.	099	1886	WB-B/143	AR
Bright, Aaron	030	1816	WB-3/78	
Bright, Alna	064	1865	WB-1/93	AR
Bright, Churchill	009	1890	WB-1/485	CTY
Bright, Cornelius	022	1870	WB-E/44	AR
Bright, Debbie C.	059	1882	WB-A/251	CTY
Bright, Elizabeth	077	1881	WB-H/105	AR
Bright, Henery	075	1739	LGB-4/#134	SS/AR
Bright, Henry	030	1749	Orig. Only	SS/AR
Bright, Henry	030	1801	WB-2/178	
Bright, Henry	030	1836	WB-4/16	
Bright, Hester	022	1870	WB-E/56	AR
Bright, Isaac	030	c1812	WB-3/14	
Bright, James	053	1735	SS 876/401	SS/AR
Bright, James G.	009	1894	WB-2/47	CTY
Bright, John	064	1864	WB-1/92	AR
Bright, John	009	1833	OB-B/234	AR
Bright, John	053	c1720	009 OWB/1	009 AR
Bright, John	030	1780	WB-1/145	
Bright, John R.	030	1851	WB-4/163	
Bright, Nathen	030	1841	WB-4/85	
Bright, Polly	064	c1888	Orig. Only	AR
Bright, Polly	022	1880	WB-E/211	AR
Bright, Richard	030	1735	SS 876/425	SS/AR
Bright, Richard	009	1731/2	OWB/11	AR
Bright, Richard	030	1740	LGB-4/#111	SS/AR
Bright, Richard	099	1876	RB-35/351	AR
Bright, Robert	011	c1829	WB-1/47	
Bright, Samuel	027	1890	WB-2/80	AR
Bright, Samuel F.	027	1864	WB-A/87	AR
Bright, Sarah	075	1893	WB-0/394	AR
Bright, Sarah	030	c1810	WB-2/355	
Bright, Sidney	028	1846	WB-D/124	AR
Bright, Silas	030	1796	WB-2/74	
Bright, Simon	034	1777	Orig. Only	SS/AR
Bright, Simon	022	c1835	WB-C/34	AR
Bright, Simon	011	c1797	WB-1/373	
Bright, Solomon	030	1755	SS 880/63	SS/AR
Bright, Solomon	030	c1815	WB-3/57	
Bright, Stockwell	028	1791	WB-A/256	AR
Bright, Thomas	030	1807	WB-2/305	
Bright, William	028	1754	SS 879/119	SS/AR
Bright, William	035	1762	WB-A/62	AR
Bright, William	099	1895	WB-C/428	AR
Bright, Willis	030	1801	WB-2/171	
Brighte, Joseph	075	1819	Orig. Only	AR
Brightman, James	028	1784	WB-A/300	AR
Brightwell, Ronald	044	1781	WB-1/319	CTY
Brigman, Adaline	083	1898	WB-4/206	AR
Brile, Conrad	081	1784	WB-1/12	AR
Briles, Annis	081	1889	WB-16/131	AR
Briles, Elizabeth	081	1877	WB-15/241	AR
Briles, Noah	081	1861	WB-12/8	
Briley, Benjamin	079	1855	WB-1/50	
Briley, Daniel	009	1885	WB-1/351	CTY
Briley, George	005	1818	WB-2/11	AR
Briley, Jesse	079	1891	WB-2/565	AR
Briley, John J.	079	1893	WB-3/31	AR
Briley, Rebecca	079	1865	WB-1/117	AR
Brill, Jacob	035	1866	WB-3/108	AR
Brily, Benjamin	079	c1853	SC/05071	AR-Copy
Brim, Brinze	084	1868	WB-D/98	CTY
Brim, Conrad	054	c1816	WB-1/412	AR
Brim, Richins	084	1851	WB-C/115	CTY
Brim, Sarah	077	1872	WB-H/43	AR
Brim, William	092	1888	WB-6/271	AR
Brimage, Elizabeth	010	1816	WB-F/334	AR
Brimage, Sophia	028	1897	WB-F/297	
Brimage, William	010	1799	WB-E/94	AR
Brimer, Samuel	060	1827	WB-1/70	AR
Brincefield, Anderson	084	1864	WB-C/390	CTY
Brincefield, John	046	1829	WB-B/384	AR
Brincefield, Sally	046	1899	WB-G/137	AR
Brincefield, Thomas	046	c1878	WB-E/212	AR
Brindel, Henry	092	1873	WB-6/44	

Name	Co.	Date	Recorded Copy	Original
Brindle, Daniel	092	1844	WB-4/213	
Brindle, Elizabeth	021	1892	WB-2/574	AR
Brindle, Joseph	086	1863	WB-E/422	AR
Brindle, William T.	021	1864	WB-1/202	
Brinegar, Paul	106	c1856	WB-1/55	AR
Bringle, Casper	032	1839	WB-1/328	AR
Bringle, John	085	1884	WB-2/95	CTY
Bringle, Lawrence	085	1876	WB-1/348	CTY
Brininger, Adam	085	1767	WB-A/8	AR
Brinkley, Owen	041	1876	WB-4/79	AR
Brinkley, Abraham	037	1838	WB-F/218	AR
Brinkley, Agatha	077	1829	WB-F/163	AR
Brinkley, B. R.	105	1895	WB-3/120	AR
Brinkley, Calvin R.	024	1872	WB-E/31	AR
Brinkley, Crosley	090	1841	WB-4/75	AR
Brinkley, Daniel	032	1893	WB-4/180	AR
Brinkley, David	041	1877	WB-4/89	AR
Brinkley, Edmund	024	1854	WB-C/365	AR
Brinkley, Esther	077	1834	WB-F/231	AR
Brinkley, Frances	032	1829	WB-1/119	AR
Brinkley, Griffin	077	1869	WB-H/29	AR
Brinkley, H. L.	066	1895	WB-1/144	AR
Brinkley, James	077	1792	WB-C/441	AR
Brinkley, James	041	1842	WB-3/34	AR
Brinkley, Jeremiah	047	1840	WB-4/190	AR
Brinkley, Jeremiah	047	1870	WB-6/43	AR
Brinkley, Jeremiah	047	1803	WB-3/418	
Brinkley, John	041	1786	WB-1/54	AR
Brinkley, John	077	1781	Orig. Only	AR
Brinkley, John	041	1886	WB-4/253	AR
Brinkley, John, Sr.	065	1835	WB-G/231	AR
Brinkley, Joseph	041	1801	WB-1/185	AR
Brinkley, Josiah	047	1831	WB-4/77	AR
Brinkley, Judith	047	1860	WB-5/77	
Brinkley, Judith	047	1799	WB-3/332	AR
Brinkley, Judith	047	c1860	Orig. Only	AR
Brinkley, Levinia	041	1839	WB-3/20	AR
Brinkley, Malvina E.	027	1880	WB-2/40	AR
Brinkley, Mary	041	1781	WB-1/9	AR
Brinkley, Mary	032	1890	WB-4/82	AR
Brinkley, Nancy	041	1877	WB-4/89	AR
Brinkley, Peter	077	1771	WB-C/102	AR
Brinkley, Richard	041	1885	WB-4/210	AR
Brinkley, Sally	041	1817	WB-2/147	AR
Brinkley, Simeon	041	1828	WB-2/274	AR
Brinkley, Thomas	024	c1790	WB-A/206	AR
Brinkley, William	047	1796	WB-3/270	AR
Brinkley, William	041	1816	WB-2/130	AR
Brinkley, William	047	1797	WB-3/284	AR
Brinkley, William T.	024	1875	WB-E/53	AR
Brinkly, Albert	041	1891	WB-4/321	AR
Brinkly, Pennie	041	1887	WB-4/262	AR
Brinkly, William	012	c1848	WB-B/1	AR
Brinn, James	024	1820	WB-C/89	AR
Brinn, Jesse	024	c1776	WB-A/107	AR
Brinn, John	024	1802	WB-B/190	AR
Brinn, Joseph	024	1776	WB-A/217	AR
Brinn, Nicholas	053	c1807	RW-1/409	
Brinn, Reading J.	009	1851	OB-H/7	AR
Brinn, Richard	053	1808	RW-1/421	AR
Brinn, Sarah	024	1811	WB-C/4	AR
Brinsen, Assa	028	1836	WB-C/396	AR
Brinson, Adam	072	c1769	RW/L33	AR
Brinson, Ann	028	1853	WB-D/211	AR
Brinson, Benj.	028	1839	WB-C/428	AR
Brinson, Cason	028	1777	Orig. Only	AR
Brinson, Cason	028	c1765	Orig. Only	AR
Brinson, Cason	028	1803	WB-B/192	AR
Brinson, Elizabeth	072	1812	WB-A/11	AR
Brinson, Gorge	072	1799	Orig. Only	AR
Brinson, Hiram	057	1856	WB-B/231	AR
Brinson, James	030	1883	WB-5/98	
Brinson, John	072	1805	WB-A/10	AR
Brinson, Josephus	028	1878	WB-E/189	AR
Brinson, S. R.	028	1884	WB-E/353	AR
Brinson, Sally	074	1875	WB-1/39	AR
Brinson, String	072	1778	RW/L4	AR
Brinson, W. G.	028	1896	WB-F/223	
Brintle, James M.	020	1864	RB-T/77	AR
Brintle, Sally	092	1879	WB-6/125	AR
Brintle, William	020	1846	RB-P/336	
Brintle, William	020	1860	RB-S/352	AR
Brion, Nathan	019	1789	WB-D/35	AR
Brisco, Edward	024	1767	WB-A/307	AR
Brisco, Elizabeth	086	1820	WB-C/133	AR
Brisco, Lafayette	086	1869	WB-F/1	AR
Brisco, Nancy C.	086	1875	WB-F/80	AR
Briscoe, Elizabeth	041	1863	WB-3/331	AR
Briscoe, Nathan	086	1807	WB-B/207	AR
Brisendine, Henry	060	1892	WB-4/498	AR
Brisendine, Philip	084	1848	WB-C/97	CTY
Brison, John	040	1847	WB-1/2	
Brister, Mary	071	1815	WB-3/164	aR
Bristol, George W.	TN	1892	025 WB-A/158	025 AR
Bristow, Catherine	071	1805	WB-2/288	AR
Bristow, George	044	1783	WB-1/370	CTY
Bristow, James	071	1800	WB-2/192	AR
Bristow, William	081	1847	WB-8/366	AR
Britain, Catherine	028	1817	WB-C/149	AR
Brite, Ammon	018	c1865	WB-D/76	
Brite, Anson H.	074	1892	WB-1/126	AR
Brite, Charles	018	1847	WB-C/324	
Brite, Elizabeth	018	1835	WB-C/184	
Brite, Elizabeth	018	1870	WB-E/18	AR
Brite, Ephraim	075	1836	WB-N/130	AR
Brite, Ephraim	075	1876	WB-0/64	AR
Brite, Hezekiah	018	1823	WB-C/16	
Brite, Hollowell	075	1897	WB-0/454	AR
Brite, Isaac	075	1837	WB-N/137	AR
Brite, Jesse	075	1824	WB-M1/405	AR
Brite, John R.	018	1843	WB-C/285	
Brite, John, Sr.	018	1845	WB-C/307	
Brite, Jonathan	075	c1855	WB-M2/33	AR
Brite, Jonathan	075	1852	WB-N/241	AR
Brite, Malachi	018	1832	WB-C/136	
Brite, Martha	018	1825	WB-C/53	
Brite, Nathan	075	1819	WB-M1/331	AR
Brite, Nathan	075	1826	WB-N/23	AR
Brite, Olly	018	1880	WB-E/71	AR
Brite, Richard	075	1790	WB-K/185	AR
Brite, Richard	018	1834	WB-C/163	
Brite, Sarah	018	1846	WB-C/312	
Brite, Shadrach	018	1879	WB-E/69	AR
Brite, Shadrack	018	1834	WB-C/150	
Brite, Sophia	018	1837	WB-C/200	
Brite, Willis	075	c1832	Orig. Only	AR
Britt, Alexander	083	1850	WB-2/13	AR
Britt, Alexander	051	1868	WB-C/10	AR
Britt, Ann	010	1804	WB-E/234	AR
Britt, Arthur L.	075	1847	WB-N/218	AR

Name	Co.	Date	Recorded Copy	Original
Britt, B. W., Sr.	059	1891	WB-B/25	CTY
Britt, Benjamin	051	1833	WB-A/53A	
Britt, Benjamin	083	1836	WB-1/300	AR
Britt, Benjamin	068	1810	WB-A/269	
Britt, Benjamin L.	083	1874	WB-3/352	AR
Britt, Brittian	083	1852	WB-2/132	AR
Britt, Cyprian	051	1838	WB-A/131	
Britt, Elijah	071	1870	WB-6/50	AR
Britt, Elizabeth	099	c1892	Orig. Only	AR
Britt, Elizabeth	051	1834	WB-A/66	
Britt, Everett	083	1868	WB-2/245	AR
Britt, Graves	103	1836	RD-7/196	AR
Britt, Hardy	051	1831	WB-A/173	
Britt, Henry	103	1830	RD-6/183	AR
Britt, J. L.	099	1874	RB-35/255	
Britt, James	087	1891	WB-3/488	AR
Britt, James	083	c1896	Orig. Only	AR
Britt, James E.	051	1829	WB-A/6	
Britt, James P.	045	1888	WB-1/162	AR
Britt, Jesse	010	1808	WB-F/83	AR
Britt, Jesse	056	1805	WB-1/171	AR
Britt, John	083	1830	WB-1/276	AR
Britt, Kenneth	083	1891	WB-3/555	AR
Britt, Kinchen	103	1820	RD-4/332	AR
Britt, Kinchen	103	1884	WB-1/315	AR
Britt, Lula A.	059	c1897	103 WB-2/337	103 AR
Britt, Lula A.	059	1897	WB-B/171	CTY
Britt, Lyddia	071	1823	WB-3/295	AR-Nunc.
Britt, M. D.	099	1887	WB-B/231	AR
Britt, Manalcha	027	1891	WB-2/95	AR
Britt, Mariah	024	1891	WB-E/201	AR
Britt, Mary	051	1837	WB-A/96	
Britt, Melvin L.	027	1889	WB-2/78	AR
Britt, Rebecca	027	1891	WB-2/95	AR
Britt, Samuel	083	c1795	WB-1/41	AR
Britt, Samuel	071	1868	WB-5/355	AR
Britt, Sarah A.	087	1881	WB-3/224	AR
Britt, Sarah Ann	087	1884	WB-3/283	AR
Britt, Sealy	083	1890	WB-3/489	AR
Britt, Thomas	056	1862	WB-2/21	
Britt, W. P.	103	1895	WB-2/116	AR
Britt, William	067	1866	WB-1/130	AR
Britt, William	083	1881	WB-3/251	AR
Britt, William W.	045	1890	WB-1/279	AR
Britt, Williston	N	c1711	SS 875/34	
Britt, Wilmoth	056	1894	WB-2/174	AR
Brittain, Christina	014	1887	WB-2/343	CTY
Brittain, Daniel	010	1831	WB-G/215	AR
Brittain, George W.	013	1886	WB-B/407	AR
Brittain, John	010	1803	WB-E/199	AR
Brittain, John	046	1887	Orig. Only	AR
Brittain, John	092	1850	WB-4/305	AR
Brittain, Joseph	085	1774	WB-A/183	AR
Brittain, Joseph	028	1830	WB-C/330	AR
Brittain, Joseph	028	1789	WB-A/190	AR
Brittain, Joseph W.	028	1844	WB-D/104	AR
Brittain, William	013	1889	WB-B/540	AR
Brittain, William	046	1794	WB-A/30	AR
Brittain, William L.	014	c1863	WB-1/3	AR
Brittan, Frances	010	1810	WB-F/173	AR
Brittan, Judith	010	1811	WB-F/186	AR
Britte, Marinda	051	1882	WB-C/296	AR
Brittian, W. E.	014	1899	WB-3/87	CTY
Brittle, Brittain	071	1782	WB-1/252	
Brittle, Exum	071	1809	WB-3/23	AR
Brittle, Jesse	071	1791	WB-1/435	AR
Brittle, John	071	1780	WB-1/222	
Brittle, John, Jr.	071	1777	WB-1/10	AR
Brittle, Sarah	071	1806	WB-2/330	AR
Britton, Charles	071	1897	WB-7/345	AR
Britton, Charles	069	1793	WB-1/124	AR
Britton, Eli	071	1850	WB-5/90	AR
Britton, Elizabeth	071	1857	WB-5/196	AR
Britton, George	009	1888	WB-1/446	CTY
Britton, James	041	1854	WB-3/175	AR
Britton, Jesse	071	1841	WB-4/233	AR
Britton, John	071	1851	WB-5/97	AR
Britton, John L.	010	1878	WB-I/100	
Britton, Margaret	010	1866	WB-H/165	AR
Britton, Mary	051	1867	WB-B/98	AR
Britton, Miles	079	1843	WB-1/171	
Britton, Nathan	071	1844	WB-4/279	AR
Britton, Thomas	035	1779	WB-A/54	AR
Britton, William P.	051	1867	WB-B/110	
Broach, James	078	c1844	Orig. Only	AR
Broach, Nathaniel	078	1898	WB-19/446	AR
Broach, Richard	078	1870	WB-19/13	AR
Broach, Zilphia	078	1890	WB-19/274	AR
Broadaway, John	005	1871	WB-D/15	AR
Broadaway, Whiten	040	1893	WB-2/434	
Broadfoot, Andrew	029	1810	WB-A/151	AR
Broadfoot, Francis R.	029	1892	WB-E/534	AR
Broadfoot, Thomas W.	029	1890	WB-E/484	AR
Broadnax, Edward T.	084	1874	WB-E/73	
Broadribbs, Thomas	037	1794	WB-C/274	AR
Broadstreet, James	103	c1809	RD-1/194	
Broadstreet, Nancy	056	1841	WB-1/527	AR
Broadway, John	085	1885	WB-2/115	CTY
Broadway, Nancy	032	1879	WB-3/267	AR
Broadway, Sarah	032	1876	WB-3/177	AR
Broadway, Sophia	033	1897	WB-2/207	CTY
Broadway, Thomas W.	032	1869	WB-3/1	AR
Broadway, William	032	1873	WB-3/114	AR
Broadwell, Harrison	099	1895	WB-C/486	AR
Broadwell, Ruffin	099	1865	RB-33/479	AR
Broadwell, William	099	1825	RB-19/450	AR
Brobbell, Tatem	030	1827	WB-3/233	
Brock, Barbara	059	1872	WB-A/27	
Brock, Benjamin	057	1886	WB-C/146	AR
Brock, Christopher	028	1843	WB-D/86	
Brock, James N.	033	1886	WB-2/86	CTY
Brock, John	035	1848	WB-2/36	AR
Brock, John J.	028	1832	WB-C/346	AR
Brock, John M. F.	072	1897	WB-4/348	AR
Brock, Joseph	057	1809	WB-A/321	AR
Brock, Joseph	072	1860	WB-2/179	AR
Brock, Lavina J.	035	1895	WB-4/464	AR
Brock, Lewis	035	1839	Orig. Only	AR
Brock, Losson	009	1836	OWB/487	AR
Brock, Louizer	087	1885	WB-3/323	AR
Brock, Nathaniel	085	1818	WB-G/513	AR
Brock, Noah	038	1892	WB-3/334	AR
Brock, Richard E.	033	1889	WB-2/103	CTY
Brock, Sarah	057	1897	WB-C/224	
Brock, William B.	033	1874	WB-2/38	CTY
Brockett, Benjamin	028	1758	SS 881/145	SS/AR
Brockett, Elizabeth	030	1855	WB-4/201	AR
Brockett, Elizabeth	070	c1874	WB-E/273	AR
Brockett, John B.	075	1900	WB-O/498	AR
Brockett, Kezziah	075	1886	WB-O/296	AR

Name	Co.	Date	Recorded Copy	Original
Brockman, A. J.	046	1898	WB-G/48	AR
Brockman, Major	020	1825	RB-K/100	AR
Brodes, Michael	084	1818	WB-A/144	
Brodess, Peter	011	1777	WB-1/496	
Brodie, Alexander	044	1802	WB-5/278	CTY
Brodie, E. G.	098	1892	WB-A/152	CTY
Brodie, Edmund G.	044	1853	WB-19/243	CTY
Brodie, Elizabeth	098	1896	WB-A/243	CTY
Brodie, John	100	1851	WB-41/191	AR
Brodie, Thomas	044	1865	WB-22/379	CTY
Brodnax, Rebecca A.	VA	1842	071 WB-5/4	071 AR
Brodnax, Robert	084	1854	WB-C/183	CTY
Brodrick, Thomas	070	1770	Orig. Only	SS/AR
Broesing, Christina	038	1867	WB-1/279	AR
Brogden, Aaron	010	1825	WB-G/129	AR
Brogden, Benjamin	036	1888	WB-A/124	CTY
Brogden, David	044	1882	Orig. Only	CTY
Brogden, David	010	1762	WB-A/56	AR
Brogden, George	099	1884	WB-A/529	AR
Brogden, Iverson	099	1888	WB-B/268	AR
Brogden, James	046	1810	WB-A/35	AR
Brogden, John	010	1774	WB-B/17	AR
Brogden, John	010	1795	WB-D/268	AR
Brogden, Mary	010	c1777	WB-B/117	AR
Brogden, Mary	044	1891	WB-24/186	CTY
Brogden, Pierce	103	1854	RD-11/544	AR
Brogden, Timothy	063	1815	WB-2/24	
Brogdon, George	044	1817	WB-8/20	CTY
Bromley, George	010	1728	SS 876/131	SS/AR
Bronson, Alice S.	100	1900	WB-51/537	
Bronson, Arthur	NY	1885	Copy	050 AR
Bronson, Frederic	NY	1868	Copy	050 AR
Bronson, Frederic	NY	1900	Copy	050 AR
Bronson, Isaac	NY	1838	097 WB 3/282	097 AR
Bronson, Oliver	NY	1875	Copy	050 AR
Bronson, Theodore	NY	1882	Copy	050 AR
Brook, Andrew	073	1812	WB-D/328	AR
Brook, Horatio	009	c1778	OWB/136	AR
Brookbank, Henry T.	038	1887	WB-3/23	AR
Brookbank, William	046	1870	WB-E/27	AR
Brookes, George	038	1868	WB-1/297	AR
Brookes, Richard	020	1790	RB-B/321	AR
Brooks, A. G.	105	1888	WB-2/495	AR
Brooks, Ann	020	1808	RB-E/379	AR
Brooks, Asa	078	1876	WB-19/63	AR
Brooks, Bettie F.	099	1890	WB-B/419	AR
Brooks, Charles B.	020	1816	RB-G/134	
Brooks, Christopher	020	1840	RB-O/126	
Brooks, Christopher	039	1813	WB-D/1	AR
Brooks, David	090	1815	WB-2/161	AR
Brooks, David	089	1842	WB-1/12	AR
Brooks, David	006	c1873	Orig. Only	AR
Brooks, Dempsey	078	1880	WB-19/105	AR
Brooks, Elizabeth	022	1876	WB-E/112	AR
Brooks, Francis	041	1837	WB-2/382	AR
Brooks, George W.	075	1882	WB-O/137	AR
Brooks, Isaac	022	1825	WB-B/97	AR
Brooks, Jacob	056	1827	WB-1/450	AR
Brooks, James	079	1889	WB-2/476	AR
Brooks, Jeremiah	078	1871	WB-19/15	AR
Brooks, Joab	022	1843	WB-C/144	
Brooks, Joell	073	1764	WB-A/34	
Brooks, John	030	1708	Orig. Only	SS/AR
Brooks, John	078	1885	WB-19/181	AR
Brooks, John	089	1875	WB-2/39	AR

Name	Co.	Date	Recorded Copy	Original
Brooks, John	086	1885	WB-F/257	AR
Brooks, John	104	1842	WB-4/282	AR
Brooks, John	VA	1840	Copy	078 AR
Brooks, John	019	1833	WB-A/35	AR
Brooks, John C.	078	1897	WB-19/413	AR
Brooks, Jonas	040	1869	WB-2/3	AR
Brooks, Joseph	028	1795	WB-A/337	AR
Brooks, Joseph	041	1853	WB-3/167	AR
Brooks, Joseph H.	086	1897	WB-F/534	AR
Brooks, Joseph S.	074	1874	WB-1/63	AR
Brooks, Larkin	022	1837	WB-C/79	AR
Brooks, Larkin	078	1884	WB-19/165	
Brooks, Lydia	019	1826	WB-D/78	AR
Brooks, Martha	079	1894	WB-3/54	AR
Brooks, Martha B.	022	1897	WB-F/55	AR
Brooks, Mary	097	1852	WB-1/79	AR
Brooks, Mary A.	019	1887	WB-B/158	AR
Brooks, Mary Ann	022	1899	WB-F/103	AR
Brooks, Matthew	078	1885	WB-19/183	AR
Brooks, Nancy D.	022	1879	WB-D/155	AR
Brooks, Polly	006	1874	WB-E/9	AR
Brooks, Richard	022	1852	WB-C/339	AR
Brooks, Robert	078	1842	Orig. Only	AR
Brooks, Sarah	078	1842	WI-15/63	AR
Brooks, Sentleger	006	1896	WB-E/303	AR
Brooks, Stephen	053	1797	RW-1/290	AR
Brooks, Susanah	022	1890	WB-E/446	AR
Brooks, Susannah	022	1858	WB-D/17	AR
Brooks, Thomas	006	c1861	WB-D/60	AR
Brooks, Thomas	073	1810	Orig. Only	AR
Brooks, Thomas	020	1855	RB-R/280	AR
Brooks, Thomas	022	1796	RB-2/69	AR
Brooks, Thomas	022	1812	WB-A/217	AR
Brooks, Thomas A.	022	1892	WB-E/493	AR
Brooks, Thomas D.	022	c1863	WB-D/127	AR
Brooks, William	071	1768	WB-1/165	
Brooks, William	028	1790	WB-A/220	AR
Brooks, William	026	1844	WB-1/21	AR
Brooks, William	053	1838	WB-6/53	AR
Brooks, William	041	1837	WB-2/383	AR
Brooks, William F.	065	1898	WB-N/91	AR
Brooks, William T.	099	1883	WB-A/410	AR
Brooks, Willoughby	030	1795	WB-2/37	
Brooks, Yancy	078	1834	WI-12/275	AR
Brooks, Yong N.	104	1886	WB-6/278	AR
Brookshear, Thomas	046	1835	WB-B/538	AR
Brookshire, Benjamin	081	1863	WB-12/476	AR
Brookshire, Lula M.	013	1889	WB-B/521	AR
Brookshire, Nancy	032	1825	WB-1/38	AR
Brookshire, William	104	1882	WB-6/211	AR
Broom, Burrel	097	1871	WB-2/56	AR
Broom, Haly	047	1823	WB-3/692	AR
Broom, John	065	1795	WB-A/121	AR
Broom, John	096	1772	WB-1/80	AR
Broom, Levi E.	097	1869	WB-2/25	AR
Broom, Walker	065	1840	WB-H/47	AR
Broom, William	065	1840	WB-E/239	AR
Brophy, James T.	101	1889	WB-A/169	AR
Brosher, Elisabeth	075	1836	WB-N/126	AR
Brosher, John	075	1774	WB-I/108	AR
Brosher, John L.	075	1807	WB-M1/161	AR
Brothers, Andrew	075	1794	WB-L/15	AR
Brothers, Anne	046	1858	WB-C/529	AR
Brothers, David	075	1812	WB-M1/232	AR
Brothers, Elias	075	1839	WB-N/147	AR

Name	Co.	Date	Recorded Copy	Original
Brothers, Job	075	1800	WB-M1/42	AR
Brothers, John	075	1783	WB-K/87	AR
Brothers, John	028	1788	WB-A/176	AR
Brothers, John	075	1762	WB-I/14	AR
Brothers, John	075	1735	SS 876/391	SS/AR
Brothers, John	075	1825	WB-N/18	AR
Brothers, Jonathan	075	1798	WB-M1/15	AR
Brothers, Joseph	028	1815	WB-C/107	AR
Brothers, Judy	028	1847	WB-D/134	AR
Brothers, Martha	041	1873	WB-4/29	AR
Brothers, Martha R.	046	1898	WB-G/101	AR
Brothers, Mary	075	c1890	Orig. Only	AR
Brothers, Mary Ann	027	1885	WB-2/59	AR
Brothers, Miles	075	1848	WB-N/221	AR
Brothers, Miles	075	c1867	Orig. Only	AR
Brothers, Mrs. M. E.	065	1887	WB-L/223	AR
Brothers, Nathaniel	054	c1833	WB-2/144	AR
Brothers, Richard	075	1795	WB-L/24	AR
Brothers, Richard	075	1816	WB-M1/282	AR
Brothers, Rufus S.	041	1861	WB-3/276	AR
Brothers, Samuel	028	1826	WB-C/277	AR
Brothers, Sarah	075	1844	WB-N/186	AR
Brothers, Susan	075	1872	WB-0/40	AR
Brothers, Thomas	075	1815	WB-M1/275	AR
Brothers, William	075	c1711	Orig. Only	SS/AR
Brothers, William	075	1793	WB-L/14	AR
Brothers, William	075	1765	WB-H/60	AR
Brothertin, James	104	1843	WB-4/293	AR
Brothertin, John M. C.	104	1864	WB-5/397	
Brotherton, George	054	1846	WB-3/9	AR
Brotherton, James	060	1857	WB-3/5	AR
Brotherton, William B.	054	1857	WB-3/115	AR
Broughton, Abel	028	1814	WB-C/89	AR
Broughton, Adam	019	1832	WB-A/12	AR
Broughton, John	099	1889	WB-B/375	AR
Broughton, Matilda	099	1878	WB-A/6	AR
Broun, William	085	c1772	WB-D/118	
Browder, Abram	001	1899	WB-3/268	
Browder, Edmund	022	1785	RB-1/24	AR
Browder, Isham	084	1833	WB-B/84	CTY
Browder, Talitha	084	1828	WB-B/26	CTY
Brower, Alfred	081	1887	WB-16/46	AR
Brower, Christain	081	1819	WB-4/693	AR
Brower, Eli	081	1863	WB-12/414	AR
Brower, John	081	1814	WB-4/79	AR
Brower, Lewis	073	1801	WB-D/47	AR
Brower, Margaret	081	1857	WB-11/141	AR-Copy
Brower, Williiam	028	1840	WB-D/21	AR
Brown, Aaron	104	1893	WB-6/489	AR
Brown, Abner	022	1797	RB-2/127	AR
Brown, Abner	063	1822	WB-2/78	
Brown, Abraham	085	c1795	WB-F/15	AR
Brown, Abram	083	1857	WB-2/110	
Brown, Adaline	065	1887	WB-L/254	AR
Brown, Adam	081	1882	WB-15/371	AR
Brown, Adam	085	1864	WB-K/337	AR
Brown, Adeline E.	035	1899	WB-4/551	AR
Brown, Adelphia	017	1878	WB-B/74	AR
Brown, Alan	035	1863	WB-3/65	AR
Brown, Albert	054	1881	WB-4/429	CTY
Brown, Alexander	084	c1815	WB-A/123	CTY
Brown, Alexander	075	1796	WB-L/87	AR
Brown, Alexander	085	1892	WB-2/524	CTY
Brown, Alexander	063	1889	WB-4/45	AR
Brown, Alexander	085	1880	WB-1/530	CTY

Name	Co.	Date	Recorded Copy	Original
Brown, Alfred	016	1854	WB-1/243	
Brown, Allen H.	065	1898	WB-N/172	AR
Brown, Anderson	021	1897	WB-3/170	AR
Brown, Andrew	085	c1804	WB-C/325	AR
Brown, Andrew	085	1834	WB-H/624	AR
Brown, Angus	083	c1820	WB-1/213	AR
Brown, Angus	083	1826	WB-1/335	AR
Brown, Ann	060	1808	Orig. Only	AR
Brown, Ann E.	065	1891	WB-L/544	AR
Brown, Anna	038	1896	WB-3/580	AR
Brown, Archibald	100	1839	WB-37/193	AR
Brown, Archibald	022	1796	RB-2/81	AR
Brown, Argent	059	1871	WB-A/22	
Brown, Arthur	010	1785	WB-D/13	AR
Brown, Arthur	087	1830	WB-1/110	AR
Brown, Arthur	099	1818	RB-14/121	AR
Brown, Asa A.	070	1865	WB-D/168	AR
Brown, Asey	073	1815	WB-D/439	AR
Brown, Barbara	085	1845	WB-K/1	AR
Brown, Basel	085	1812	WB-G/220	AR
Brown, Becky	069	1893	WB-5/397	AR
Brown, Bedford	020	1871	WB-A/67	CTY
Brown, Benjamin	010	1869	WB-I/8	AR
Brown, Benjamin	065	c1801	WB-A/101	AR
Brown, Benjamin	024	1806	WB-B/237	AR
Brown, Benjamin	099	1879	WB-A/72	AR
Brown, Benjamin	065	1795	WB-A/87	AR
Brown, Benjamin	035	1841	Orig. Only	AR
Brown, Betsey	069	1894	WB-5/463	AR
Brown, Bettie	011	1887	WB-2/211	
Brown, Bryan	076	1887	WB-A1/88	
Brown, Burt	099	1875	RB-35/284	AR
Brown, Calvin	022	1859	WB-D/38	AR
Brown, Calvin	021	1898	WB-3/194	AR
Brown, Caroline	037	1894	WB-H/302	AR
Brown, Catherine	076	1896	WB-A1/199	AR
Brown, Charles	012	1800	Orig. Only	AR-Nunc.
Brown, Charles W.	099	1892	WB-C/68	AR
Brown, Christian	041	1799	WB-1/168	AR
Brown, Christina	065	1878	WB-K/296	AR
Brown, Cintha	051	1836	WB-A/89	
Brown, Clayton	080	1881	WB-1/68	AR
Brown, Collins	039	c1777	WB-A/50	
Brown, Conrad	046	1864	WB-D/248	AR
Brown, Council	070	1876	Orig. Only	AR
Brown, Crossley	038	1899	WB-4/184	AR
Brown, Cynthia	099	1888	WB-B/260	AR
Brown, Cyrus	057	1887	WB-C/148	AR
Brown, Cythia	085	1851	WB-K/134	AR
Brown, Daniel	081	1791	WB-1/104	AR
Brown, Daniel	022	c1807	WB-A/132	AR
Brown, Daniel	083	1816	WB-1/227	AR
Brown, Daniel	013	1893	WB-C/258	AR
Brown, Daniel	047	1803	WB-3/410	AR
Brown, Daniel H.	033	1863	WB-1/176	AR
Brown, David	086	1855	WB-E/301	AR
Brown, David	065	1797	WB-A/111	AR
Brown, David	070	1765	DB-E/206	AR
Brown, David	051	1879	WB-C/210	
Brown, David	085	1855	WB-K/208	AR
Brown, Delphine	038	1889	WB-3/128	AR
Brown, Denson	037	1860	WB-G/197	AR
Brown, Dorothy	009	1780	OWB/154	AR
Brown, Dorothy	009	1849	OB-G/124	AR
Brown, Duncan	073	1899	WB-I/154	CTY

Name	Co.	Date	Recorded Copy	Original
Brown, Duncan	083	c1797	WB-1/49	AR
Brown, Duncan	029	1761	Orig. Only	AR
Brown, Ebenezer	022	1834	WB-C/11	AR
Brown, Edward	057	1798	WB-A/203	AR
Brown, Edward	028	1874	WB-E/112	AR
Brown, Edward	035	1784	WB-A/16	AR
Brown, Edwin	017	c1891	Orig. Only	AR
Brown, Eleanor W.	013	1900	WB-D/436	AR
Brown, Elenor	085	1817	WB-G/461	AR
Brown, Elias	047	1815	WB-3/576	AR
Brown, Elizabeth	065	1867	WB-J/236	AR
Brown, Elizabeth	009	1894	WB-2/35	CTY
Brown, Elizabeth	099	1893	WB-C/118	AR
Brown, Elizabeth	090	1807	WB-2/82	
Brown, Elizabeth	092	1867	WB-5/93	
Brown, Elizabeth	038	1879	WB-2/345	AR
Brown, Elizabeth	054	1893	WB-5/448	CTY
Brown, Elizabeth	054	1880	WB-4/393	CTY
Brown, Elizabeth	070	1894	WB-G/263	AR
Brown, Elizabeth	070	1788	WB-C/31	AR
Brown, Elizabeth	035	1847	WB-2/18	AR
Brown, Ellen	106	c1866	WB-1/109	
Brown, Ellen J.	050	1900	WB-2/360	CTY
Brown, Ephram	078	1876	WB-19/46	AR
Brown, Ezekiel	032	c1846	WB-2/40	AR
Brown, Frances	063	1864	WB-2/519	
Brown, Francis	051	c1828	WB-A/127	
Brown, Francis	010	1750	SS 879/3	SS/AR
Brown, George	061	1830	WB-1/1	AR
Brown, George	011	c1782	WB-1/472	
Brown, George	104	1805	WB-2/146	AR
Brown, George L.	027	1888	WB-2/73	AR
Brown, George W.	MO	1874	Copy	032 AR
Brown, George W.	104	1892	WB-6/458	AR
Brown, H. A.	106	c1876	Orig. Only	AR
Brown, Haley	046	1866	WB-D/307	AR
Brown, Hamilton	104	1870	WB-6/21	AR
Brown, Hannah	070	1870	WB-E/245	AR
Brown, Hardy	047	1774	063 WB-1/445	
Brown, Harriet E.	064	1898	WB-2/427	AR
Brown, Henrietta	010	1869	WB-I/12	AR
Brown, Henry	063	1858	WB-2/450	
Brown, Henry	054	1887	WB-5/175	CTY
Brown, Henry	099	1849	RB-26/568	AR
Brown, Henry	085	1829	WB-H/457	AR
Brown, Henry James	104	1897	106 WB-2/391	
Brown, Hugh	083	c1789	WB-1/19	AR
Brown, Hugh	083	1858	WB-2/124	AR
Brown, Hugh	049	1858	WB-1/23	AR
Brown, Isaac	035	1879	WB-4/143	AR
Brown, Isaac	010	1880	WB-I/115	
Brown, Isaac	057	1840	WB-B/145	AR
Brown, J. A.	105	1899	WB-3/347	AR
Brown, J. C.	036	1897	WB-A/405	CTY
Brown, J. G.	048	1897	WB-1/66	CTY
Brown, Jacob	035	1812	WB-A/52	AR
Brown, Jacob	106	1899	WB-2/462	
Brown, Jacob	009	c1805	OWB/434	AR
Brown, Jacob	054	c1806	WB-1/356	AR
Brown, James	041	1842	WB-3/33	AR
Brown, James	063	1818	WB-2/50	
Brown, James	085	1840	WB-I/86	AR
Brown, James	006	1850	WB-A/69	AR
Brown, James	084	c1774	OW/89	AR
Brown, James	037	1797	WB-D/24	AR

Name	Co.	Date	Recorded Copy	Original
Brown, James	009	1750	SS 877/269	SS/AR
Brown, James	054	1887	WB-5/142	CTY
Brown, James	081	1809	WB-3/154	AR
Brown, James	104	1805	WB-2/158	
Brown, James	063	1879	WB-3/160	
Brown, James	104	1814	WB-3/88	AR-Nunc.
Brown, James	076	1890	WB-A1/125	AR
Brown, James	106	1896	WB-2/389	
Brown, James	037	c1744	Orig. Only	SS/AR
Brown, James	021	1894	WB-3/63	
Brown, James	085	c1778	WB-A/264	AR
Brown, James	030	1721	SS 875/284	SS/AR
Brown, James	071	1827	WB-4/34	AR
Brown, James F.	073	1883	WB-H/327	CTY
Brown, James H.	065	1893	WB-M/150	AR
Brown, James R.	073	1854	WB-G/72	AR
Brown, James, Sr.	020	1827	RB-L/196	AR
Brown, James, Sr.	063	1855	WB-2/411	
Brown, James, Sr.	046	1818	WB-B/60	AR
Brown, Jane	065	1871	WB-K/77	AR
Brown, Jane	081	1871	WB-15/52 & 191	AR
Brown, Jane	054	1880	WB-4/404	CTY
Brown, Jane M.	079	1899	WB-3/191	AR
Brown, Jenny	010	1762	WB-A/7	AR
Brown, Jeremiah	072	c1780	RW/L34	AR
Brown, Jeremiah	069	1785	WB-1/39	AR
Brown, Jesse	099	1829	RB-21/1	AR
Brown, Jesse	070	1858	WB-C/660	AR
Brown, Jesse	056	1808	WB-1/215	AR
Brown, Jesse	056	1883	WB-3/340	AR
Brown, Jesse	041	1847	WB-3/83	AR
Brown, Jesse	092	1834	Orig. Only	AR-Nunc.
Brown, Jethro	020	1829	RB-L/337	AR
Brown, Joab	103	1821	RD-4/461	AR
Brown, John	056	1846	WB-1/580	AR
Brown, John	083	1849	WB-2/9	
Brown, John	090	1858	WB-4/312	AR
Brown, John	083	c1794	WB-1/33	AR
Brown, John	085	1818	WB-G/493	AR
Brown, John	009	1846	OB-F/252	AR
Brown, John	020	1799	RB-C/353	
Brown, John	026	1888	WB-2/346	AR
Brown, John	071	1890	WB-7/58	AR
Brown, John	011	c1812	WB-2/402	
Brown, John	099	1807	RB-7/305	AR
Brown, John	092	c1830	WB-4/26	AR
Brown, John	057	1804	WB-A/271	AR
Brown, John	020	1817	RB-G/347	AR
Brown, John	104	1834	WB-4/178	AR
Brown, John	069	1852	WB-1/532	AR
Brown, John	019	1788	WB-D/34	AR
Brown, John	047	1878	WB-6/176	AR
Brown, John	104	1810	WB-2/319	AR-Nunc.
Brown, John	075	1815	WB-M1/278	AR
Brown, John	067	1885	WB-2/234	AR
Brown, John	079	1874	WB-2/165	AR
Brown, John	029	1892	WB-E/540	AR
Brown, John	029	1761	Orig. Only	AR
Brown, John	070	1871	WB-E/234	AR
Brown, John	100	1782	WB-3/125a	015 AR
Brown, John	054	c1795	WB-1/231	
Brown, John	022	1776	Orig. Only	AR
Brown, John	104	1785	WB-1/159	AR
Brown, John	035	1801	WB-A/42	AR

Name	Co.	Date	Recorded Copy	Original
Brown, John	047	1759	SS 881/206	SS/AR
Brown, John	104	1812	WB-3/28	AR
Brown, John A.	054	1897	WB-6/67	CTY
Brown, John B.	011	1848	WB-1/166	
Brown, John D.	055	1867	ID/164	
Brown, John H.	063	1897	WB-4/205	AR
Brown, John L.	073	1864	WB-G/419	AR
Brown, John L.	065	1893	WB-M/226	AR
Brown, John L.	071	1839	WB-4/203	AR
Brown, John M.	VA	1900	090 WB-6/562	090 AR
Brown, John M.	104	1893	WB-6/464	AR
Brown, John R.	070	c1878	Orig. Only	AR
Brown, John T.	079	c1864	WB-1/124	AR
Brown, John W.	010	1892	WB-I/345	AR
Brown, John W.	064	1891	WB-2/297	AR
Brown, Jonas	071	1743	Orig. Only	SS/AR
Brown, Joseph	046	1844	WB-C/171	AR
Brown, Joseph	022	1812	WB-A/213	AR
Brown, Joseph	073	1862	WB-G/380	CTY
Brown, Joseph	018	1848	WB-C/343	
Brown, Joseph	099	1815	RB-12/231	AR
Brown, Joseph	021	1847	WB-1/48	AR
Brown, Joseph	010	1830	WB-G/196	AR
Brown, Joseph	104	1842	WB-4/273	AR
Brown, Joseph	027	1891	WB-2/98	AR
Brown, Joseph	092	1825	WB-3/162	AR
Brown, Joseph	006	c1830	WB-B/26	AR
Brown, Joseph H.	081	1841	WB-7/387	AR
Brown, Joseph H.	081	1867	WB-14/170	AR
Brown, Joshua	010	1856	WB-H/30	AR
Brown, Josiah	071	1884	WB-6/449	AR
Brown, Josiah	099	1798	RB-4/253	AR
Brown, Josiah	029	1820	WB-B/52	AR
Brown, Kannon	085	c1826	WB-H/505	AR
Brown, Kate	070	1897	WB-H/63	AR
Brown, Letita	085	1887	WB-2/242	CTY
Brown, Lettia	030	1807	WB-2/306	
Brown, Levi	001	1892	WB-2/507	AR
Brown, Lewis	073	1801	WB-D/47	
Brown, Livingston	020	1896	WB-B/234	CTY
Brown, Louis S. F.	070	1894	WB-G/301	AR
Brown, Lucy	070	1843	WB-AB/402	AR
Brown, Lucy Ann	MS	1871	011 WB-2/55	
Brown, Luke	030	1827	WB-3/222	
Brown, Luther	022	c1861	Orig. Only	AR
Brown, Lydia J.	099	1898	WB-D/211	AR
Brown, M. L.	060	1876	WB-4/150	AR
Brown, Macon B.	009	1893	WB-1/587	CTY
Brown, Marcie	056	1890	WB-3/558	AR
Brown, Margaret	054	c1804	WB-1/234	
Brown, Margaret	041	1881	WB-4/141	AR
Brown, Margret	072	c1864	Orig. Only	AR
Brown, Martha	051	1886	WB-C/342	AR
Brown, Martha	100	1849	WB-40/172	AR
Brown, Martha	056	1827	WB-1/335	AR
Brown, Martha J.	041	1880	WB-4/136	AR
Brown, Mary	083	1865	WB-2/217	AR
Brown, Mary	085	1857	WB-K/231	
Brown, Mary	100	1863	WB-50/57	AR
Brown, Mary	085	1874	WB-1/282	CTY
Brown, Mary	085	1852	WB-K/144	AR
Brown, Mary	051	1797	WB-1/153	AR
Brown, Mary	068	1839	WB-B/123	
Brown, Mary Ann	022	1895	WB-E/579	AR
Brown, Mary B.	101	1887	096 WB-4/130	096 AR

Name	Co.	Date	Recorded Copy	Original
Brown, Mary D.	100	1852	WB-42/4	AR
Brown, Mary E.	011	1898	WB-3/102	CTY
Brown, Mary M.	016	1895	WB-4/222	AR
Brown, Mary T.	013	1893	WB-C/361	AR
Brown, Mary V.	106	1894	WB-2/427	
Brown, Matthew	046	c1787	WB-A/31	AR
Brown, Mattie E.	085	1897	WB-3/213	CTY
Brown, Michael	085	c1807	WB-D/17	AR
Brown, Michael L.	085	1878	WB-1/436	CTY
Brown, Nancy	009	1816	OB-A/264	AR
Brown, Nancy	057	1852	WB-B/214	AR
Brown, Nancy	035	1836	Orig. Only	AR
Brown, Nancy	022	1839	WB-C/100	AR
Brown, Nancy	084	1858	WB-C/279	CTY
Brown, Nancy	022	1809	WB-A/176	AR
Brown, Nathan	009	1845	OB-F/84	AR
Brown, Nathan	013	1886	WB-B/389	
Brown, Nathan	090	1858	WB-4/322	AR
Brown, Nathan	009	1845	OB-F/57	AR
Brown, Nathaniel	046	1790	WB-A/22	AR
Brown, Nathaniel	028	1825	WB-C/267	AR
Brown, Nathaniel	081	1900	WB-17/133	
Brown, Nathaniel	013	1889	WB-B/513	AR
Brown, Neill	083	1819	WB-1/208	AR
Brown, Neill	083	1836	WB-1/291	AR
Brown, Neill B.	083	1846	WB-1/472	AR
Brown, Noah	104	1886	WB-6/271	AR
Brown, Parson W.	009	1874	WB-1/126	CTY
Brown, Parthenia	078	1838	WI-14/19	AR
Brown, Patrick	051	1842	WB-A/208	
Brown, Patrick	065	1804	WB-A/103	AR
Brown, Perneter	011	c1899	Orig. Only	CTY
Brown, Peter	085	1813	WB-G/270	AR
Brown, Peter A.	085	1865	WB-K/367	AR
Brown, Peterson	071	1823	WB-3/294	AR
Brown, Philip	010	1725	Orig. Only	SS/AR
Brown, Philip	085	1841	WB-I/93	AR
Brown, Philip	085	1813	WB-G/290	AR
Brown, Polly	006	c1838	WB-B/101	AR
Brown, R. B.	016	1866	WB-2/131	
Brown, Rachel	072	c1797	Orig. Only	AR
Brown, Rachel	049	c1835	WI-1-2/6	AR
Brown, Rebecca	065	1891	WB-L/526	AR
Brown, Rice	090	1833	WB-3/248	
Brown, Richard	010	1736	LGB-4/#41	SS/AR
Brown, Richard	104	1801	WB-2/58	AR
Brown, Robert	065	1795	WB-A/89	AR
Brown, Robert	065	1772	WB-A/116	AR
Brown, Robert	054	c1797	WB-1/232	
Brown, Robert	054	c1818	WB-2/3	AR
Brown, Robert	054	1853	WB-3/63	AR
Brown, Robert	084	1844	WB-C/17	CTY
Brown, Robert	060	1843	WB-2/170	AR
Brown, Robert	084	1881	WB-E/204	CTY
Brown, Robert F.	070	1865	WB-D/158	AR
Brown, Robert O.	054	1885	WB-5/82	CTY
Brown, Robert W.	070	1856	WB-C/626	AR
Brown, Ruffin R.	100	1872	Orig. Only	AR-Copy
Brown, Rufus D.	038	1893	WB-3/409	AR
Brown, Sallie	014	1894	WB-2/530	CTY
Brown, Samuel	106	c1840	WB-1/14	AR
Brown, Samuel	082	c1804	WB-1/102	AR
Brown, Samuel	065	1772	WB-A/75	AR
Brown, Samuel	047	1764	WB-1/138	
Brown, Samuel	065	1815	WB-A/107	AR

Name	Co.	Date	Recorded Copy	Original
Brown, Samuel	057	c1813	WB-B/4	AR
Brown, Sandy	065	1882	WB-K/499	AR
Brown, Sarah	018	1830	WB-C/113	
Brown, Sarah	009	c1802	OWB/406	AR
Brown, Sarah	035	1833	WB-1/47	AR
Brown, Sarah H.	104	1889	WB-6/349	AR
Brown, Senie	056	1889	WB-3/514	AR
Brown, Shelley	084	1886	WB-E/354	CTY
Brown, Solomon	022	1876	WB-E/108	AR
Brown, Solomon	099	1892	WB-C/34	AR
Brown, Stephen	071	1826	WB-4/19	AR
Brown, Susan	085	1867	WB-L/15	
Brown, Susan O.	079	1898	WB-3/149	AR
Brown, Susan O.	079	1898	045 WB-1/350	
Brown, Temperance	009	1860	OB-L/66 & 142	AR
Brown, Thaddeus	053	1866	WB-10/4	AR
Brown, Thomas	090	1850	WB-4/265	AR
Brown, Thomas	001	1862	WB-1/199	AR
Brown, Thomas	054	1867	WB-3/198	
Brown, Thomas	006	c1833	WB-B/68	AR
Brown, Thomas	099	1803	RB-6/114	AR
Brown, Thomas	085	1815	WB-G/356	AR
Brown, Thomas	061	1835	WB-1/13	AR
Brown, Thomas	020	1855	RB-R/344	AR
Brown, Thomas	100	1862	WB-49/423	AR
Brown, Thomas	078	1813	WI-6/128	
Brown, Thomas	030	c1814	WB-3/39	
Brown, Thomas	092	c1822	WB-3/177	AR
Brown, Thomas	011	c1813	WB-2/407	
Brown, Thomas	024	1718	SS 875/158	SS/AR
Brown, Thomas	070	1749	SS 878/1	SS/AR
Brown, Thomas D.	071	1829	WB-4/54	AR
Brown, Thomas E.	013	1900	WB-D/431	AR
Brown, Thomas W.	070	1872	WB-E/251	AR
Brown, Thompson	021	1864	WB-1/199	
Brown, Tobias	054	1866	WB-3/192	AR
Brown, Virgil	029	1892	WB-E/542	AR
Brown, W. J.	099	1869	RB-35/54	AR
Brown, W. L.	038	1899	WB-4/169	AR
Brown, W. W.	099	1875	RB-35/321	AR
Brown, Walter	049	1890	WB-2/258	AR
Brown, Warren	084	1887	WB-E/367	CTY
Brown, Wiley	051	1880	WB-C/245	AR
Brown, William	057	1807	WB-A/296	AR
Brown, William	100	1779	WB-3/12	015 AR
Brown, William	104	1806	WB-2/182	
Brown, William	063	c1779	WB-1/95	
Brown, William	006	1885	WB-E/134	
Brown, William	022	1843	WB-C/147	AR
Brown, William	081	1877	WB-15/269	AR
Brown, William	046	1826	WB-B/344	AR
Brown, William	009	1751	028 DB-5/239	SS/AR
Brown, William	082	1848	WB-3/46	AR
Brown, William	047	1797	WB-3/280	AR
Brown, William	051	1884	WB-C/321	AR
Brown, William	065	1851	WB-I/176	AR
Brown, William	054	1843	WB-2/271	AR
Brown, William	099	1833	RB-22/529	AR
Brown, William	006	1800	WB-A/102	AR
Brown, William	020	1807	RB-E/350	AR
Brown, William	039	1837	WB-K/133	AR
Brown, William	054	1858	WB-3/130	AR
Brown, William	085	1772	WB-A/19	AR
Brown, William	006	1876	WB-E/20	AR
Brown, William	055	c1868	ID/173	
Brown, William	046	1817	WB-B/44	AR
Brown, William	073	1839	WB-F/26	AR
Brown, William	071	1896	WB-7/309	AR
Brown, William	046	1795	WB-A/29	AR
Brown, William	100	1862	WB-49/424	AR
Brown, William	051	1849	WB-A/295	
Brown, William	063	1817	WB-2/42	
Brown, William	073	1764	WB-A/31	
Brown, William	065	1795	WB-A/112	AR
Brown, William	006	c1873	Orig. Only	AR
Brown, William	099	1795	RB-3/151	AR
Brown, William	003	1876	WB-B/72	AR
Brown, William	104	1836	WB-4/208	AR
Brown, William	024	1719	SS 875/152	SS/AR
Brown, William	073	1800	WB-C/109	AR
Brown, William	083	c1824	WB-1/334	AR
Brown, William	085	c1787	WB-D/154	AR
Brown, William	078	1828	WI-11/64	AR
Brown, William	056	1807	WB-1/199	AR
Brown, William A.	046	1899	WB-G/141	AR
Brown, William C.	033	1862	WB-1/175	AR
Brown, William H.	013	1886	WB-B/362	AR
Brown, William H.	104	1896	WB-6/556	AR
Brown, William H.	073	1866	WB-G/487	CTY
Brown, William H.	099	1900	WB-D/386	AR
Brown, William H.	054	1866	WB-3/182	AR
Brown, William H.	083	1883	WB-3/289	AR
Brown, William H.	013	1886	091 WB-1/109	
Brown, William M.	090	1862	WB-4/351	AR
Brown, William M.	085	1867	WB-L/7	AR
Brown, William P.	020	1863	RB-S/620	CTY
Brown, William R.	063	1841	WB-2/280	
Brown, William S.	035	1891	WB-4/376	AR
Brown, William W.	075	1883	WB-O/166	AR
Brown, William W.	003	1896	WB-B/346	AR
Brown, Willie	079	1867	WB-1/167	
Brown, Wilson	073	1898	WB-I/130	CTY
Brown, Winaford R.	079	1869	Orig. Only	AR
Brown, Winneford	063	1846	WB-2/323	
Brown, Zaccheus	028	1899	WB-F/411	
Brown, Zada	053	1869	WB-11/13	AR
Browne, J. F.	100	1884	WB-51/197	AR
Browne, John	024	1718	SS 875/300	SS/AR
Browne, John	075	1699	Orig. Only	SS/AR
Browne, Mary B.	101	1887	WB-A/150	AR
Browne, Mary L.	100	1883	WB-51/174	AR
Browne, Ridley	100	1887	WB-51/250	AR
Browne, Walter	010	1735	Orig. Only	SS/AR
Browne, William	010	1735	LGB-4/#54	
Brownen, Richard	071	1771	WB-1/191	
Browning, E. D.	070	1888	WB-F/145	AR
Browning, E. D.	047	1888	WB-6/471	AR
Browning, Edmond	020	1807	RB-E/347	AR
Browning, Feribee	047	1876	WB-6/146	AR
Browning, Jane S.	046	1893	WB-F/289	AR
Browning, Jefferson	073	1863	WB-G/407	AR
Browning, John	073	c1820	Orig. Only	AR
Browning, John	002	1733	SS 876/280	SS/AR
Browning, Levi	047	1839	WB-4/176	
Browning, Nicholas	020	1787	RB-B/166	AR
Browning, Redick	045	1885	WB-1/208	AR
Browning, Robert	020	1843	RB-P/18	
Browning, Sanders W.	020	1868	RB-T/344	CTY
Browning, Tippo M.	047	1870	WB-6/41	AR
Browning, William	049	c1865	WB-1/2	AR

Name	Co.	Date	Recorded Copy	Original
Browning, William	047	1858	WB-5/54	
Brownrigg, George	037	1784	WB-B/134	AR
Brownrigg, John	024	1790	Orig. Only	AR-Copy
Brownrigg, Obedience	037	1840	WB-F/242	AR
Brownrigg, Richard	024	c1771	WB-B/135	AR
Brownrigg, Thomas	024	1826	WB-C/121	AR
Bruce, Amy	044	1795	WB-3/186	CTY
Bruce, Charles	047	1832	WB-B/447	AR
Bruce, Frederick	029	1858	WB-C/390	
Bruce, George	044	1787	WB-2/39	CTY
Bruce, George	037	1807	WB-D/278	AR
Bruce, James	028	1801	WB-B/131	AR
Bruce, Jane	106	1896	WB-2/381	
Bruce, John	104	1816	WB-3/127	AR
Bruce, John D.	092	1842	WB-4/189	
Bruce, Margaret	068	1855	WB-C/27	
Bruce, Miles	071	1826	WB-4/14	AR
Bruce, Moses	071	1804	Orig. Only	AR
Bruce, Peter	054	1803	WB-1/78	AR
Bruce, Peter	047	1762	WB-1/69	
Bruce, Robert	020	1795	RB-C/137	AR
Bruce, S. C.	068	c1866	WB-C/160	
Bruce, William	047	1795	WB-3/243	
Bruffet, Patsey A.	009	1870	WB-1/53	CTY
Brumble, Eli	083	1892	Orig. Only	AR
Brumel, Jacob	085	c1789	WB-D/129	AR
Brumit, Mary	020	1851	RB-Q/590	CTY
Brummell, Jacob	032	1841	WB-1/371	AR
Brummell, Susannah	032	1859	WB-2/166	AR
Brummett, William L.	044	1881	WB-23/418	CTY
Brummit, Edmund	020	1884	WB-A/422	CTY
Brummit, Thomas	020	1884	WB-A/424	CTY
Brummit, William	020	1826	RB-L/76	AR
Brummitt, Nimrod	044	1823	WB-9/235	CTY
Brummitt, Samuel B.	044	1877	WB-23/291	CTY
Brumsey, Julia	030	1872	WB-5/23	
Bruner, Barbara	085	c1793	WB-D/135	AR
Bruner, George	085	c1787	WB-D/155	AR
Bruner, Henry	085	c1803	WB-C/330	AR
Bruner, Henry	085	1770	WB-A/16	AR
Bruner, John J.	085	1890	WB-2/414	CTY
Brunit, Marcey	020	1884	WB-A/420	
Bruns, J. H.	021	1898	WB-3/203	AR
Brunt, Richard	030	1794	WB-2/22	
Bruton, David	AR	1876	067 WB-2/215	067 AR
Bruton, J. J.	067	1874	WB-2/55	AR
Bruton, James	067	1873	WB-2/32	AR
Bruton, William	067	1849	WB-1/51	AR
Brutz, Christian	090	1845	WB-4/185	
Bryan, Aaron	022	1839	WB-C/96	AR
Bryan, Abram M.	004	1877	WB-A/26	AR
Bryan, Alexander	028	1885	WB-E/372	AR
Bryan, Alse	071	1781	WB-1/244	
Bryan, Andrew	035	1864	WB-3/88	AR
Bryan, Ann	028	1769	Orig. Only	AR
Bryan, Ann	028	1868	WB-D/458	AR
Bryan, Ann Cady	028	N. D.	Orig. Only	AR
Bryan, Anne	028	1773	Orig. Only	SS/AR
Bryan, Armalyn	012	1847	WB-B/186	
Bryan, Asa	072	1826	Orig. Only	AR
Bryan, B. L. C.	063	1891	WB-4/67	AR
Bryan, Bartholomew	037	1865	WB-G/261	AR
Bryan, Battley	085	1811	WB-G/173	AR
Bryan, Benjamin	071	1796	WB-2/131	AR
Bryan, Benjamin	071	1789	WB-1/393	AR

Name	Co.	Date	Recorded Copy	Original
Bryan, Bennett	103	1850	RD-10/457	AR
Bryan, Blake	071	1847	WB-5/63	AR
Bryan, Blount	037	1875	044 WB-23/164	044 CTY
Bryan, Bythan	056	1849	WB-1/617	AR
Bryan, C. J.	009	1825	OB-A/353	AR
Bryan, Caroline	011	1862	WB-1/275	
Bryan, Clarinda	009	1885	WB-1/369	
Bryan, Clarissa	009	1898	WB-2/161	CTY
Bryan, Cuzza	103	1885	WB-1/346	AR
Bryan, David	076	1885	WB-A1/52	AR
Bryan, David	010	1777	WB-B/103	AR
Bryan, Delphia	104	1858	WB-5/203	
Bryan, Dempsey	037	1847	WB-F/352	AR
Bryan, Drewry	037	1843	WB-F/277	AR
Bryan, Edward	010	1799	WB-E/69	AR
Bryan, Edward	N	1746	SS 878/36	SS/AR
Bryan, Edward	028	c1762	Orig. Only	AR
Bryan, Edward	010	1762	WB-A/8	AR
Bryan, Elias	037	1821	WB-E/276	AR
Bryan, Elizabeth	010	1839	WB-G/309	AR
Bryan, Elizabeth	072	1780	Orig. Only	AR
Bryan, Elizabeth	071	1856	WB-5/154	AR
Bryan, Elizabeth	010	1841	WB-G/327	AR
Bryan, Elizabeth	077	1798	WB-E/99	AR
Bryan, Elizabeth M. B.	009	1860	OB-L/231	AR
Bryan, Fletcher	099	1890	WB-B/401	AR
Bryan, Frances L.	010	1852	WB-G/490	AR
Bryan, Frederick	057	1801	WB-A/252	AR
Bryan, Frederick	028	1816	WB-C/129	AR
Bryan, G. H.	006	c1860	Orig. Only	AR
Bryan, George	028	1815	WB-C/109	AR
Bryan, George	028	1849	WB-D/159	AR
Bryan, George W.	011	1856	WB-1/257	
Bryan, Gideon	092	c1878	Orig. Only	AR
Bryan, Hardy	028	1781	Orig. Only	AR-Copy
Bryan, Hardy	028	c1760	Orig. Only	AR
Bryan, Hardy	028	1808	WB-B/327	
Bryan, Hardy	069	1889	WB-5/274	AR
Bryan, Hardy	028	1760	Orig. Only	SS/AR
Bryan, Hardy B.	028	1790	WB-A/233	AR
Bryan, Harriet	062	1899	WB-B/215	AR
Bryan, Isaac	028	1794	WB-A/309	AR
Bryan, James	010	1734	SS 876/297	
Bryan, James	079	1895	WB-3/78	AR
Bryan, James	028	c1794	Orig. Only	AR
Bryan, James	060	1881	WB-4/236	AR
Bryan, James	047	1786	WB-3/108	AR
Bryan, James B.	071	1819	WB-3/222	AR
Bryan, James H. C.	057	1878	WB-C/60	AR
Bryan, James L.	010	1856	WB-H/39	AR
Bryan, James R.	063	1867	WB-2/495	
Bryan, James W.	028	1865	WB-D/377	AR
Bryan, Jesse	063	1786	WB-1/123	
Bryan, John	085	1800	WB-D/1	AR
Bryan, John	028	c1781	Orig. Only	AR
Bryan, John	011	c1774	WB-1/463	
Bryan, John	087	1840	WB-1/223	AR
Bryan, John	028	1796	WB-B/6	
Bryan, John	028	1741	Deeds.21/L8	Nunc.
Bryan, John	104	1842	WB-4/220	AR
Bryan, John	037	1803	WB-D/166	AR
Bryan, John	028	c1763	DB-8/177	AR
Bryan, John C.	028	1807	WB-B/268	AR
Bryan, John H.	099	1870	RB-35/77	AR
Bryan, John M.	071	1791	WB-1/430	AR

Name	Co.	Date	Recorded Copy	Original
Bryan, John S.	099	1848	RB-27/93	AR
Bryan, John S.	010	1848	WB-G/433	AR
Bryan, Joseph	028	1770	Orig. Only	AR
Bryan, Julia C.	056	1866	WB-2/81	AR
Bryan, Kitt	028	1896	WB-F/217	
Bryan, Larry O.	009	1893	WB-1/589	CTY
Bryan, Lewis	028	1815	WB-C/96	AR
Bryan, Lewis	071	c1848	Orig. Only	AR
Bryan, Lewis	056	1818	WB-1/278	AR
Bryan, Lewis	063	1830	WB-2/160	
Bryan, Lewis	057	1796	WB-A/123	AR
Bryan, Lovard	103	c1797	Orig. Only	AR-Copy
Bryan, Loverd	056	1798	WB-1/111	AR
Bryan, Martha	071	1812	WB-3/78	AR
Bryan, Martha	010	1777	WB-B/109	AR
Bryan, Martha	010	1802	WB-E/175	AR
Bryan, Mary	010	1810	WB-F/165	AR
Bryan, Mary	009	1824	OB-A/334	AR
Bryan, Mary H.	028	1896	WB-F/243	
Bryan, Mary L.	047	1889	WB-6/529	AR
Bryan, Mary S.	028	1892	WB-F/17	
Bryan, Mary W.	099	1881	WB-A/256	AR
Bryan, Mathias	071	1866	WB-5/317	AR
Bryan, Michael	010	1794	WB-D/247	AR
Bryan, Morgan	004	1882	WB-A/52	AR
Bryan, Morgan	085	1763	WB-A/13	AR
Bryan, N. R.	068	1885	WB-D/201	
Bryan, Nancy	001	1866	WB-1/260	AR
Bryan, Nathan	057	1798	WB-A/212	
Bryan, Nathan	011	1884	WB-2/173	
Bryan, Nedom	063	c1797	WB-1/343	
Bryan, Needam	028	1798	WB-B/41	AR
Bryan, Needham	099	1863	RB-32/623	AR
Bryan, Needham	056	1787	WB-1/3	AR
Bryan, Needham	056	1815	WB-1/249	AR
Bryan, Needham	035	1861	WB-3/40	AR
Bryan, Needham	010	1770	WB-A/124	AR
Bryan, Needham	011	1894	WB-3/66	CTY
Bryan, Needham G.	056	1837	Orig. Only	AR
Bryan, P. A. E.	037	1891	WB-H/184	AR
Bryan, Polly	071	1860	WB-5/236	AR
Bryan, Rachel	027	1835	WB-A/33	AR
Bryan, Reddin	022	1850	WB-C/283	AR
Bryan, Riddick	071	1888	WB-7/24	AR
Bryan, Rigdon	035	1793	WB-A/11	AR
Bryan, Robert	047	1774	063 WB-1/444	
Bryan, Robert B.	104	1890	WB-6/379	AR
Bryan, Rosa	037	1850	Orig. Only	AR
Bryan, Samuel	085	c1798	WB-D/121	AR
Bryan, Samuel	056	1807	WB-1/195	AR
Bryan, Sarah	028	1796	WB-B/12	AR
Bryan, Shadrach	004	1883	WB-A/60	AR
Bryan, Simon	010	1753	SS 878/207	SS/AR
Bryan, Smith	037	1811	WB-E/14	AR
Bryan, Susan	037	1858	WB-G/156	AR
Bryan, Susanna	022	1897	WB-F/48	AR
Bryan, Susanna	087	1865	WB-2/88	AR
Bryan, Thomas	072	c1779	RW/L10	AR
Bryan, Thomas	010	1789	WB-D/98	AR
Bryan, Thomas	071	1794	WB-2/44	AR
Bryan, Thomas	N	c1760	Orig. Only	SS/AR
Bryan, Thomas	011	c1786	WB-1/456	
Bryan, Thomas	104	1863	WB-5/353	
Bryan, Thomas	028	1760	Orig. Only	AR
Bryan, Thomas	037	1785	WB-C/16	AR
Bryan, Thomas	011	1767	DB-36/303	
Bryan, Ursilla	017	1891	WB-B/201	AR
Bryan, W. R., Sr.	045	1893	WB-1/274	AR
Bryan, Wealthy	057	1855	WB-B/227	AR
Bryan, Wilie	071	1895	WB-7/289	AR
Bryan, William	028	1791	WB-A/242	AR
Bryan, William	056	1821	WB-1/439	AR
Bryan, William	028	1771	Orig. Only	AR
Bryan, William	012	c1867	WB-B/22	AR
Bryan, William	071	1770	WB-1/187	
Bryan, William	063	1775	WB-1/19	
Bryan, William	037	1797	WB-D/33	AR
Bryan, William	028	1747	SS 877/27	SS/AR
Bryan, William	028	1811	WB-C/31	AR
Bryan, William	085	c1780	WB-B/36	AR
Bryan, William	LA	1846	Copy	071 AR
Bryan, William	012	1833	WB-B/163	AR
Bryan, William	056	c1780	Orig. Only	AR
Bryan, William A.	071	1892	WB-7/159	AR
Bryan, William C.	074	1879	103 WB-2/160	103 AR
Bryan, William C.	074	1879	WB-1/55	AR
Bryan, William G.	028	1888	WB-E/467	AR
Bryan, William P.	079	c1872	Orig. Only	AR
Bryan, William S.	010	c1858	WB-H/108	AR
Bryan, Zeporah	063	c1792	WB-1/204	
Bryant, Arthur	103	1811	RD-1/337	AR
Bryant, Beneter	070	1852	WB-C/540	AR
Bryant, Benjamin	072	c1823	WB-A/3	AR
Bryant, Berry	082	1900	WB-7/53	AR
Bryant, Clarky	071	1793	WB-2/24	AR-Nunc.
Bryant, Elizabeth	005	1894	WB-D/351	AR
Bryant, Eveline	032	1891	WB-4/111	AR
Bryant, Evin	037	1810	WB-E/1	AR
Bryant, Faithey	037	1804	WB-D/210	AR
Bryant, Gale	037	1793	WB-C/240	AR
Bryant, George A.	106	1881	WB-2/156	
Bryant, H. W.	076	1894	WB-A1/177	AR
Bryant, Harriet	065	1900	WB-N/376	AR
Bryant, Henry T.	035	1897	WB-4/506	AR
Bryant, Jacob	083	1871	WB-3/31	AR
Bryant, Jacob	035	1828	WB-A/34	AR
Bryant, James	010	1734	Orig. Only	SS/AR
Bryant, James S.	047	1894	WB-7/136	AR
Bryant, Jesse	010	1775	WB-B/42	AR
Bryant, John	030	1803	WB-2/222	
Bryant, John	081	1791	WB-1/107	
Bryant, John	037	1735	LGB-4/#4	SS/AR
Bryant, John	071	1788	WB-1/382	AR
Bryant, John B.	099	1888	WB-B/256	AR
Bryant, Joseph	063	1898	WB-4/221	AR
Bryant, Mary McLean	100	1858	WB-49/169	AR
Bryant, Miles	051	1900	WB-C/567	AR
Bryant, Nedom	047	1785	WB-3/89	AR
Bryant, Nicholas	019	1766	RB-A/22	AR
Bryant, Obediah	022	1800	WB-A/31	
Bryant, Peter	092	1804	WB-3/64	AR
Bryant, Ransom A.	089	1875	WB-2/27	AR
Bryant, Richard	071	1855	WB-5/136	AR
Bryant, Robert	056	c1760	WB-1/767	AR
Bryant, Rowland	044	1843	WB-15/485	CTY
Bryant, Ruffin L.	099	1865	RB-33/482	AR
Bryant, Samuel	069	c1791	WB-1/236	AR
Bryant, Susan	069	1865	WB-1/593	AR
Bryant, Thomas	096	1860	WB-3/59	AR
Bryant, Thomas	069	c1848	WB-1/531	AR

Name	Co.	Date	Recorded Copy	Original
Bryant, William	047	1762	WB-1/79	
Bryant, William	037	1749	Orig. Only	SS/AR
Bryant, William	056	1789	WB-1/18	AR
Bryant, William	037	1761	WB-A/77	AR
Bryant, William	071	1785	WB-1/350	AR
Bryant, William	011	1855	WB-1/246	
Bryant, William	069	1826	WB-1/340	AR
Bryant, William	037	1763	WB-A/114	AR
Bryant, William B.	069	1861	WB-1/571	AR
Bryant, William J.	069	1872	WB-1/616	AR
Bryant, William S.	037	1887	WB-H/100	AR
Bryce (Brice), Maggie	065	1899	WB-N/236	AR
Bryce, Marie L.	065	1900	WB-M/326	AR
Bryce, Peter	AL	1892	028 WB-F/432	
Bryer, Benjamin	010	1789	024 WB-A/224	024 AR
Bryson, A. S.	061	1900	WB-2/267	AR
Bryson, A. S.	061	1900	Copy	049 AR
Bryson, Andrew	055	1884	WB-A/66	
Bryson, Ann J.	065	1864	WB-J/186	AR
Bryson, Daniel G.	055	1900	WB-A/182	
Bryson, Hugh	065	1835	WB-G/224	AR
Bryson, Jane A.	040	1894	WB-2/461	AR
Bryson, John	092	1808	WB-3/84	AR
Bryson, Mary	073	1853	WB-G/37	AR
Bryson, Robert	055	1887	WB-A/79	
Bryson, Thaddeus D.	091	1890	WB-1/122	
Bryson, William	013	c1817	050 WB-1/15	
Buchanan, Andrew	078	1826	WI-10/250	AR
Buchanan, Arthur	066	1864	Orig. Only	AR
Buchanan, Duncan	082	1836	WB-2/61	AR
Buchanan, Effy	082	1846	WB-3/39	AR
Buchanan, Elizabeth	022	1832	WB-B/224	AR
Buchanan, Hector R.	029	1807	WB-A/94	AR
Buchanan, Henry	005	1845	WB-B/193	AR
Buchanan, Isabella	065	1899	WB-N/179	AR
Buchanan, James	044	c1815	Orig. Only	CTY
Buchanan, James	092	1774	WB-1/27	AR
Buchanan, James C.	082	1864	WB-4/176	AR
Buchanan, Jane	066	1898	WB-1/161	AR
Buchanan, Jennette	082	1892	WB-6/452	AR
Buchanan, John	082	1867	WB-5/17	AR
Buchanan, John C. D.	005	1885	WB-D/184	AR
Buchanan, Mary	070	1895	WB-G/345	AR
Buchanan, Noah	029	1854	WB-C/285	AR
Buchanan, Richmond	005	1876	WB-D/53	AR
Buchanan, Sally	009	1889	WB-1/465	CTY
Buchanan, Samuel	087	c1791	WB-A/20	AR
Buchanan, Stephen	066	c1896	Orig. Only	AR
Buchanan, Thomas	005	1900	WB-D/464	AR
Buchanan, Thomas	046	1899	WB-G/131	AR
Buchanan, Thomas	022	1884	WB-E/293	AR
Buchanan, Thomas	060	1807	Orig. Only	AR
Buchanan, Wesley	022	1883	WB-E/254	AR
Buchanan, William	082	1818	WB-1/199	AR
Buchanan, William	070	1900	WB-H/331	AR
Buchanan, William A.	013	1871	WB-B/50	AR
Buchanan, William R.	055	1881	WB-A/44	
Buchannan, Robert	065	1811	WB-A/143	AR
Buchannan, Susannah	068	c1789	WB-A/238	
Buchannon, John	029	1800	WB-A/32	Nunc.
Buchannon, William J.	068	1881	WB-D/137	
Buchanon, James B.	078	1854	WB-17/237	AR
Buchanon, Riley	068	1878	WB-D/113	
Buchanon, Sarah	022	c1819	WB-B/11	
Buck, Allen	009	1895	WB-2/59	
Buck, Dudley	FL	1897	061 WB-2/200	061 AR
Buck, Francis	019	1803	WB-D/43	AR
Buck, Isaac, Jr.	009	1844	OB-E/206	AR
Buck, John	N	1711/2	SS 874.1/44	
Buck, John	047	1803	WB-3/409	AR
Buck, John H.	079	1883	WB-2/294	AR
Buck, Marshall	079	1877	WB-2/133	AR
Buck, Penelope	009	1875	WB-1/142	CTY
Buck, Richard	009	1832	OB-B/148	AR
Buck, Sarah	057	c1897	WB-C/224	AR
Buck, Thomas	028	1900	WB-F/480	
Buckanan, William	044	1789	WB-2/111	CTY
Buckhanan, Frederick	005	1863	WB-C/194	AR
Buckhanan, Mary	044	1838	WB-14/248	CTY
Buckhannon, Benjamin	005	1798	WB-2/12	AR
Buckhannon, Jane	065	c1844	Orig. Only	AR
Buckingham, Joseph	073	1795	WB-C/61	AR
Buckingham, Lucy	020	1843	RB-O/21	
Buckingham, Stephen	009	c1760	OWB/80	
Buckingham, W. J.	029	1895	WB-F/52	AR
Buckler, Morris	024	1789	WB-A/122	AR
Buckley, Elenor	075	1705	Orig. Only	SS/AR
Buckley, Elizabeth	028	1839	WB-C/438	AR
Buckley, John	029	c1796	Orig. Only	AR
Buckley, Michael	065	1792	WB-A/135	AR-Nunc.
Buckley, Richard	024	1801	WB-B/167	AR
Buckley, Thomas F.	028	1806	WB-B/235	AR
Buckman, Guy E.	035	1854	WB-2/90	AR
Bucknall, George P.	090	1885	WB-6/161	AR
Buckner, Able	061	1891	WB-2/103	AR
Buckner, Betsy	022	1887	WB-E/349	AR
Buckner, Jesse	022	1826	WB-B/122	AR
Buckner, Jesse	022	c1863	WB-D/139	AR
Buckner, John T.	022	1876	WB-E/120	AR
Buckner, Martha M.	062	c1881	WB-B/69	
Budd, Margaret	013	1892	WB-C/204	AR
Budgate, David	077	1770	WB-C/89	AR
Budget, Mary	024	1789	WB-A/112	AR
Bueler, Michael	085	c1807	WB-C/319	AR
Buff, Catherine	026	1891	WB-2/434	AR
Buff, Joseph	014	c1878	Copy	026 AR
Buff, Joseph	014	1878	WB-2/170	
Buff, Martin	049	c1829	WI-1-2/1	AR
Buff, William	014	1890	WB-2/382	CTY
Buffaloe, Henry W.	099	1869	RB-35/21	AR
Buffaloe, Mary	099	c1868	RB-34/504	AR
Buffaloe, Nancy	099	1851	RB-27/302	AR
Buffaloe, William	071	1858	WB-5/197	AR
Buffalow, William	071	1765	WB-1/116	
Buffelow, Samuel	039	1814	WB-D/107	AR
Bufferlow, Mathew	071	1820	WB-3/242	AR
Buffet, Josiah	096	1786	WB-1/152	AR
Buffkin, M. W.	075	1900	WB-O/510	AR
Buffkin, Margaret J.	075	c1889	Orig. Only	AR
Buffkin, Pinckney	027	1899	WB-2/154	AR
Bufkin, Rachel	077	1875	WB-H/66	AR
Bufkin, Sarah	024	1794	WB-A/93	AR
Buford, Henry	070	1816	WB-AB/240	AR
Buford, Rebecca	070	1812	WB-AB/168	AR
Bugg, William	049	1829	WB-2/235	AR
Bugnion, Ralph	070	1754	Orig. Only	SS/AR
Bugnion, Ralph	070	1752	Orig. Only	AR
Buie, Alexander	068	1818	WB-A/298	
Buie, Allen	068	1900	WB-E/25	
Buie, Archibald	029	1782	Orig. Only	AR

Name	Co.	Date	Recorded Copy	Original
Buie, Archibald	029	1775	Orig. Only	AR
Buie, Archibald	029	1806	WB-A/92	AR
Buie, Archibald	029	1811	WB-A/162	AR
Buie, Archibald	083	1812	WB-1/140	AR
Buie, Archibald	083	c1887	WB-3/407	AR
Buie, Archibald	029	1889	WB-E/464	AR
Buie, Catharine	068	1849	WB-B/192	
Buie, Daniel	068	1795	WB-A/182	
Buie, Duncan	029	1820	WB-B/39	AR
Buie, Duncan	068	1822	WB-B/28	
Buie, Duncan	083	c1807	WB-1/106	
Buie, Effy	083	1877	WB-3/138	AR
Buie, Flora	083	1860	WB-2/155	AR
Buie, Gilbert	029	1799	WB-A/29	AR
Buie, John	029	1881	WB-E/263	AR
Buie, John	029	1823	WB-B/105	AR
Buie, John A.	032	1900	WB-4/453	AR
Buie, Malcom	029	1826	WB-B/141	AR
Buie, Margaret	029	1834	WB-B/233	AR
Buie, McPherson	083	1900	WB-4/298	AR
Buie, Neil	029	1761	Orig. Only	AR
Buie, Neil	011	1880	WB-2/130	
Buie, Neill	083	1880	WB-3/172	AR
Buie, Neill	083	1839	WB-1/381	AR
Buie, Nevin C.	032	1863	WB-2/258	AR
Buie, Sarah	029	1837	WB-B/279	AR
Buis, Thomas	085	1759	WB-A/5	
Buis, William	085	1763	WB-A/12	AR
Bulkley, Charles H.	OH	1896	Copy	070 AR
Bull, Ambrose	028	c1789	Orig. Only	AR
Bull, Elizabeth	078	1831	WI-12/82	AR
Bull, Thomas	047	1794	WB-3/219	AR
Bull, Thomas	047	1763	WB-1/103	
Bulla, Thomas	081	1809	WB-3/121	AR
Bullard, Duncan	029	1891	WB-E/512	
Bullard, Emma J.	083	1891	WB-3/513	AR
Bullard, James	087	1886	WB-3/336	AR
Bullard, James	083	1832	WB-1/280	AR
Bullard, James	022	1801	WB-A/57	AR
Bullard, Jeremiah	087	1798	Orig. Only	AR-Nunc.
Bullard, Joel	082	1879	WB-6/179	AR
Bullard, John	083	c1782	WB-1/18	
Bullard, Owen	029	1890	WB-E/498	AR
Bullard, Walter G.	038	1897	WB-4/49	AR
Bullard, William	087	1887	WB-3/342	AR
Bullen, Conrad	085	c1805	WB-D/158	AR
Bullin, William	092	1875	WB-6/69	AR
Bullinger, Henry	085	c1774	WB-B/105	
Bullins, John	085	c1795	WB-F/14	
Bullock, Charles	083	1826	WB-1/344	AR
Bullock, Charles	044	1841	WB-15/172	CTY
Bullock, David	037	1782	WB-B/100	AR
Bullock, David, Jr.	037	1815	WB-E/100	AR
Bullock, Durant L.	044	c1867	WB-23/6	CTY
Bullock, Edward	046	1813	WB-A/36	AR
Bullock, Edward	044	1862	WB-21/558	CTY
Bullock, Eli	083	1881	WB-3/242	AR
Bullock, Elizabeth	044	1816	WB-7/664	CTY
Bullock, Fanny	024	1824	WB-C/108	AR
Bullock, Frank	100	1894	WB-51/357	
Bullock, George	044	1866	WB-22/551	CTY
Bullock, Henry	083	1872	WB-3/50 & 348	AR
Bullock, James	029	1795	Orig. Only	AR
Bullock, James	044	1783	WB-1/358	CTY
Bullock, James	100	1825	WB-28/235	AR
Bullock, James M.	044	1864	WB-22/246	CTY
Bullock, Jency	099	1899	WB-D/257	AR-Copy
Bullock, Jeremiah	044	1815	WB-7/505	CTY
Bullock, John	024	1812	WB-C/5	AR
Bullock, John	044	1866	WB-22/484	CTY
Bullock, John	071	1789	WB-1/390	AR
Bullock, John	044	1774	WB-1/36	CTY
Bullock, John H.	100	1884	WB-51/194	AR
Bullock, John P.	044	1900	WB-24/484	CTY
Bullock, Joshua	044	1815	WB-7/553	CTY
Bullock, Joshua R.	037	1867	WB-G/295	AR
Bullock, Kemp P.	100	1856	WB-49/11	AR
Bullock, Lemuel	083	1850	WB-2/17	AR
Bullock, Len H.	100	1868	WB-50/261	AR
Bullock, Len Henley	100	1798	WB-9/294	AR
Bullock, Lucy	044	1842	WB-15/340	CTY
Bullock, Martha A.	044	c1866	WB-23/13	CTY
Bullock, Mary	077	1786	WB-C/335	AR
Bullock, Mary H.	100	1889	WB-51/296	AR
Bullock, Micajah	044	1828	WB-11/2	CTY
Bullock, Mollie C.	047	1883	WB-6/297	AR
Bullock, Obediah	063	1828	WB-2/145	
Bullock, Philip P.	044	1855	WB-19/543	CTY
Bullock, Reubin	044	1875	WB-23/177	CTY
Bullock, Richard	044	1766	Orig. Only	CTY
Bullock, Sarah	098	1894	WB-A/203	CTY
Bullock, Sarah D.	044	1894	WB-24/255	CTY
Bullock, Sophia	044	1889	WB-24/71	CTY
Bullock, Susan M.	044	1876	WB-23/212	CTY
Bullock, Thomas	063	1850	WB-2/353	
Bullock, Thomas	071	1828	WB-4/43	AR
Bullock, W. A.	063	1895	WB-4/153	AR
Bullock, W. B.	069	1900	WB-6/96	AR
Bullock, W. G.	044	1892	WB-24/184	CTY
Bullock, W. J.	105	1895	WB-3/163	AR
Bullock, William	024	1839	WB-C/221	AR
Bullock, William	044	1829	WB-11/253	CTY
Bullock, William	044	1796	WB-3/245	CTY
Bullock, William E.	044	1898	WB-24/381	CTY
Bullon, Phillip	085	c1794	WB-D/159	AR-Nunc.
Bulls, Henry	056	1780	DB L/126	AR
Bulls, Henry	056	1787	WB-1/10	AR
Bulluck, Martha	077	1787	WB-C/342	AR
Bully, William	092	c1819	WB-3/142	AR
Bumgarner, A. P.	040	1873	WB-2/63	AR
Bumgarner, Amos	104	1884	WB-6/245	AR
Bumgarner, Eliza	003	c1884	WB-B/280	AR
Bumgarner, Hosea	055	c1877	WB-A/41	
Bumgarner, John	060	1820	Orig. Only	AR
Bumgarner, John	026	1890	WB-2/412	AR
Bumgarner, Leah H.	014	1900	WB-3/104	CTY
Bumgarner, Nancy	104	1835	WB-4/107	AR
Bumgarner, Thomas	017	1890	WB-B/183	AR
Bumingham, Joshua	005	1815	WB-2/13	
Bump, Elizabeth	057	1793	WB-A/91	AR
Bump, Jabes	057	1793	WB-A/119	AR
Bumpas, Job	056	1746	SS 877/56	SS/AR
Bumpas, William	073	1776	WB-A/201	
Bumpass, Edward	020	1777	RB-A/1	AR
Bumpass, H. L.	078	1880	WB-19/111	AR
Bumpass, John	037	1855	WB-G/115	AR
Bumpass, John	078	1813	WI-6/179	AR
Bumpass, John	078	1839	WI-14/113	
Bumpass, Nancy A.	078	1892	WB-19/330	
Bumpass, Robert	020	1777	RB-A/4	AR

Name	Co.	Date	Recorded Copy	Original
Bumpass, Robert	029	1798	WB-A/12	AR
Bumpass, S. D.	046	1852	WB-C/369	AR
Bumpass, Samuel	020	1777	RB-A/6	AR
Bumpass, Samuel	073	1851	WB-G/2	AR
Bumpass, Vina	081	1897	WB-16/402	
Bumps, Jesse	092	1808	WB-3/88	AR
Bun, Barnaba	071	1825	WB-3/322	AR
Bun, John	010	1727	Orig. Only	SS/AR
Bunce, Charity	087	1863	WB-2/50	AR
Bunch, Absley	010	1841	WB-G/328	AR
Bunch, Achsah	024	1874	WB-E/48	AR
Bunch, Collen	024	1818	WB-C/70	AR
Bunch, Cullen	024	1860	WB-D/4	AR
Bunch, Elijah	010	1857	WB-H/56	AR
Bunch, Elizabeth	010	1832	WB-G/216	AR
Bunch, Embrey	010	1789	WB-D/99	AR
Bunch, Ervin	099	1829	RB-21/150	AR
Bunch, Frederick	010	1810	WB-F/162	AR
Bunch, Henry	010	1775	WB-B/34	AR
Bunch, James, Sr.	024	1896	WB-E/265	AR
Bunch, Jeremiah	010	1863	WB-H/127	AR
Bunch, Jeremiah	010	1798	WB-E/48	AR
Bunch, Jesse	099	1888	WB-B/240	AR
Bunch, John	010	1814	WB-F/267	AR
Bunch, Joshua	077	1796	WB-E/67	
Bunch, Joshua	010	1822	WB-G/88	AR
Bunch, Julius	024	c1789	WB-A/223	AR
Bunch, King S.	024	1892	WB-E/204	AR
Bunch, Micajah	024	c1783	WB-B/62	AR
Bunch, Narcissa	010	1897	WB-I/500	AR
Bunch, Nehemiah	010	1815	WB-F/278	AR
Bunch, Paul	099	1771	RB-1/1	AR
Bunch, Paul	N	1726	SS 876/138	
Bunch, Rhoda	024	1840	WB-C/225	AR
Bunch, Samuel J.	099	1885	WB-B/34	AR
Bunch, Shadrack	024	1790	WB-A/73	AR
Bunch, Thompson	099	1803	RB-6/88	AR
Bunch, William	046	1832	WB-B/463	AR
Bunch, William H.	010	1887	WB-I/233	AR
Bunch, William N.	024	1861	WB-D/9	AR
Bunch, Willis	041	1848	WB-3/101	AR
Bunch, Zadock	010	1801	EB-E/125	AR
Buncombe, Edward	096	N. D.	024 WB-A/263	024 AR
Bundy, Anna	075	1744	Orig. Only	SS/AR
Bundy, Benjamin	075	1728	SS 876/129	SS/AR
Bundy, Caleb	075	1785	WB-K/128	
Bundy, Caleb	046	1816	WB-B/12	AR
Bundy, Caleb	075	c1721	SS 875/328	SS/AR
Bundy, Caleb, Jr.	075	c1722	SS 875/322	SS/AR
Bundy, Camilla	056	1893	WB-2/149	AR
Bundy, David	077	1750	Orig. Only	SS/AR
Bundy, Demsey	103	1798	WI-B/195	AR
Bundy, Elizabeth	075	1814	Orig. Only	AR
Bundy, Joseph	075	1809	WB-M1/200	AR
Bundy, Joseph	075	c1762	WB-I/30	
Bundy, Joseph W.	075	c1857	WB-M2/44	AR
Bundy, Josiah	075	1797	WB-L/115	
Bundy, Josiah	077	1761	Orig. Only	AR
Bundy, Moses	103	1782	WI-A/12	AR
Bundy, Noah	079	1870	WB-2/46	AR
Bundy, Samuel	075	1802	WB-M1/62	AR
Bundy, Samuel	075	1740	LGB-4/#122	SS/AR
Bundy, Sarah	046	1816	WB-B/13	AR
Bundy, William	077	1749	Orig. Only	SS/AR
Bunker, Chang	092	1874	WB-6/47	

Name	Co.	Date	Recorded Copy	Original
Bunker, Eng	092	1874	WB-6/45	AR-Copy
Bunker, Nancy A.	092	1874	WB-6/61	
Bunn, Benjamin	069	1815	WB-1/263	AR
Bunn, Benjamin	099	1820	RB-16/5	AR
Bunn, Benjamin	069	1805	WB-1/155	AR
Bunn, David, Sr.	069	1785	WB-1/28	AR
Bunn, Edwin	017	1891	WB-B/204	
Bunn, Hester Ann	070	1869	WB-E/176	AR
Bunn, J. B.	039	1891	WB-U/519	AR
Bunn, J. T.	039	1898	WB-V/144	AR
Bunn, James	039	c1795	WB-B/19	
Bunn, Jesse	099	1816	RB-12/384	
Bunn, Joel	069	1808	WB-1/185	AR
Bunn, Joel D.	069	1848	WB-1/509	AR
Bunn, John	037	1760	WB-A/3	AR
Bunn, John J.	069	1885	WB-5/212	AR
Bunn, Joseph	029	1848	WB-C/126	AR
Bunn, Lewis	099	1815	RB-12/145	AR
Bunn, Margret	039	1900	WB-V/207	AR
Bunn, Mary Anna	070	1892	WB-F/531	AR
Bunn, Nancy	099	1885	WB-B/57	AR
Bunn, Nancy J.	069	1897	WB-6/28	AR
Bunn, Rachel	069	1840	WB-1/447	AR
Bunn, Redmun	069	1826	WB-1/337	AR
Bunn, Sally	069	1866	WB-1/600	AR
Bunn, Sarah E. A.	037	1895	047 WB-7/261	
Bunn, Sarah E. A.	037	1895	WB-H/318	AR
Bunn, Vina	045	1888	WB-1/176	AR
Bunn, Wesley	099	1900	WB-D/414	AR
Bunn, William	099	1897	WB-D/40	AR
Bunn, William H.	105	1865	WB-1/117	AR
Bunn, Willie	069	1831	WB-1/377	AR
Bunnell, Edward	030	1825	WB-3/181	
Bunnell, Embly	030	1803	WB-2/211	
Bunnell, John B.	030	1829	WB-3/243	
Buntan, Lyda	103	1825	RD-5/203	AR
Buntin, James	103	1805	Orig. Only	AR
Bunting, Benjamin	069	1847	WB-1/509	AR
Bunting, David	087	1828	WB-1/90	AR
Bunting, Julia A.	103	1857	RD-12/248	AR
Bunting, Sally	069	1860	WB-1/569	AR
Bunting, Samuel	075	1768	WB-H/80	AR
Bunting, William	069	1835	WB-1/405	AR
Bunton, Jacob	022	1872	WB-E/82	AR
Bunton, John	037	1846	WB-F/348	AR
Bunyard, James Beal	006	1817	WB-A/103	AR
Burbage, John S.	009	1881	WB-1/271	CTY
Burbbagge, John	009	c1786	OWB/211	AR
Burch, Dudley	073	1886	WB-H/408	CTY
Burch, Ephraim	020	1880	WB-A/337	CTY
Burch, Frances	020	1900	WB-B/392	CTY
Burch, Henry	078	1816	WI-7/87	AR
Burch, Jacob	028	1858	WB-D/300	AR
Burch, James	070	1852	WB-C/541	AR
Burch, James	073	1795	WB-C/53	AR
Burch, John	092	1793	WB-3/9A	Nunc.
Burch, John	092	1801	WB-3/47	AR
Burch, John	AL	1823	020 RB-I/283	020 AR
Burch, Joseph	035	c1765	WB-A/56	AR
Burch, Joseph	012	1822	WB-B/126	AR
Burch, Mary	046	1872	WB-E/77	
Burch, Nicholass	078	1821	WI-9/247	AR
Burch, Norman J.	VA	1899	070 WB-H/251	070 AR
Burch, O. L.	099	1878	RB-35/421	AR
Burch, Phillip	078	1819	WI-8/246	AR

Name	Co.	Date	Recorded Copy	Original
Burch, R. E.	060	1877	WB-4/176	AR
Burch, Robert	056	1788	WB-1/14	AR
Burch, Thomas	104	1828	WB-4/115	AR
Burch, William	020	1900	WB-B/386	CTY
Burch, William M.	092	1834	Orig. Only	AR-Nunc.
Burcham, Henry	090	1815	WB-2/167	
Burcham, John	104	1881	WB-6/207	AR
Burcham, John	092	1813	WB-3/105	AR
Burcham, William E.	036	1882	WB-A/32	CTY
Burchard, Elizabeth	022	c1836	WB-C/33	AR
Burchard, Jedediah	022	1835	WB-C/25	AR
Burcher, Robert H.	075	1829	WB-N/58	AR
Burchett, Daniel	100	1861	WB-49/357	AR
Burchett, Emily J.	044	1896	WB-24/321	CTY
Burchett, Joseph	100	1795	WB-8/168	AR
Burchett, Theodorick	026	1845	WB-1/37	AR
Burd, Edmon	099	1781	RB-1/175	AR
Burdee, John	028	1815	Orig. Only	AR
Burden, Elizabeth	044	1792	WB-2/317	CTY
Burden, John L.	010	1890	WB-I/294	AR
Burden, Thomas	044	1789	WB-2/134	CTY
Burdin, William	010	1827	WB-G/161	AR
Burdine, Gabril	054	c1827	WB-2/53	AR
Burfoot, Alif	018	1843	WB-C/284	
Burfoot, Ambrose	018	1824	WB-C/29	
Burfoot, John D.	018	1893	WB-E/225	AR
Burford, Milton M.	018	1884	WB-E/126	AR
Burge, Alexander	090	1814	WB-2/149	AR
Burge, John	086	1865	WB-E/451	AR
Burge, John	086	1859	WB-E/371	AR
Burge, Nelson	086	1879	WB-F/141	AR
Burge, Priscilla	086	1863	WB-E/419	
Burge, William	092	1865	WB-5/74	
Burges, Elizabeth	041	1821	WB-2/177	AR
Burges, James	029	1787	Orig. Only	AR
Burges, Malachi	053	1793	RW-1/226	AR
Burges, Sarah	053	1796	Orig. Only	AR
Burges, Stephen	N	1730	SS 876/200	SS/AR
Burges, Stephen	075	1736	LGB-4/#44	SS/AR
Burges, Thomas	047	1836	WB-4/132	AR
Burges, Thomas	047	1794	WB-3/223	AR
Burges, Thomas A.	047	1884	WB-6/324	AR
Burgess, Albert	100	1879	WB-51/137	AR
Burgess, Amanda	030	1866	WB-4/259	
Burgess, Andrew	081	1850	WB-9/146	AR
Burgess, Ann	075	1822	WB-M1/356	AR
Burgess, Charity A.	047	1883	WB-6/303	AR
Burgess, Elizabeth	075	1764	WB-I/37	AR
Burgess, Gilly	099	1889	WB-B/350	AR
Burgess, Hugh L.	006	1898	WB-E/352	AR
Burgess, James	039	c1856	WB-0/365	
Burgess, John	022	1834	WB-C/16	AR
Burgess, John	081	1877	WB-15/260	AR
Burgess, John	075	1763	WB-H/50	AR
Burgess, John	073	1775	WB-A/185	
Burgess, John, Sr.	018	1838	WB-C/229	
Burgess, Joseph	018	1837	WB-C/216	
Burgess, Mary	099	1878	WB-A/13	AR
Burgess, Mordecai	020	1807	RB-E/342	AR
Burgess, Nicholas	018	1861	WB-D/63	
Burgess, Pamela	SC	1893	050 WB-2/167	050 CTY
Burgess, Reuben	085	1820	WB-H/60	AR
Burgess, Robert	071	1799	WB-2/181	AR
Burgess, Sanders	006	1886	WB-E/136	AR
Burgess, Simon	018	1850	WB-C/350	
Burgess, Timothy	053	1841	WB-6/132	AR
Burgess, William	099	1887	WB-B/183	AR
Burgess, William	047	1781	WB-3/25	AR
Burgess, William	075	1761	WB-H/18	AR
Burgess, William H.	003	1878	WB-B/92	AR
Burgess, Wilson	018	1846	WB-C/316	
Burgin, Alney	064	1899	WB-2/457	AR
Burgin, Benjamin	064	1875	WB-2/41	AR
Burgin, Jesse	064	1864	WB-1/91	AR
Burgin, Leah	064	1860	WB-1/73	AR
Burgin, Mary H.	036	1892	WB-A/264	CTY
Burgin, Mary H.	064	1892	WB-2/294	AR
Burgin, R. L.	064	1900	WB-2/502	AR
Burgin, Robert	064	1884	WB-2/145	AR
Burgin, Rosamond	064	c1878	WB-2/203	AR
Burgwin, Hill	PA	1898	070 WB-H/168	070 AR
Burgwin, John	070	1804	WB-AB/76	AR
Burgwyn, Collinson	071	1842	WB-4/254	AR
Burgwyn, J. A.	071	1898	WB-7/397	AR
Burgwyn, J. A.	071	1898	098 WB-A/306	098 CTY
Burgwyn, John F.	099	1864	RB-33/287	AR
Buris, Christopher	070	c1750	DB-D/48	
Burk, Arnold S.	024	c1805	WB-B/274	AR
Burk, Edward	032	1825	WB-1/43	AR
Burk, Edward	032	1872	WB-2/67	AR
Burk, John	084	c1801	WB-A/142	CTY
Burk, John	071	1835	WB-4/138	AR
Burk, Nancy	024	1851	WB-C/323	AR
Burk, Naomi C.	022	1873	WB-E/86	AR
Burk, Sarah	072	1809	WB-A/7	AR
Burk, William	071	1761	WB-1/62	
Burke, Alfred S.	077	c1858	WB-F/496	AR
Burke, Charlotte	024	1893	WB-E/220	AR
Burke, Elisha	024	1889	WB-E/173	AR
Burke, Harvey	024	1895	WB-E/244	AR
Burke, Henry C.	085	1832	WB-H/573	AR
Burke, Henry T.	054	1894	WB-5/499	CTY
Burke, James	092	1783	WB-2/1	AR
Burke, James C.	022	c1864	WB-D/145	AR
Burke, John	022	c1866	WB-D/165	AR
Burke, John R.	022	1868	WB-E/20	AR
Burke, Mary	022	1824	WB-B/73	AR
Burke, Moses	077	c1858	WB-F/493	AR
Burke, Robert D.	022	1862	WB-D/92	AR
Burke, Sarah I.	020	1893	WB-B/155	CTY
Burke, Thomas	073	1784	WB-A/283	AR
Burke, W. H.	022	1892	WB-E/504	AR
Burke, Wiley	020	1864	RB-T/61	CTY
Burke, William	071	1793	WB-2/25	AR
Burke, William	085	1843	WB-I/189	AR
Burket, Christian	006	1854	WB-D/4	AR
Burket, Christopher	077	1847	WB-F/340	AR
Burkett, Catherine	006	1888	WB-E/161	AR
Burkett, John, Sr.	077	1728	SS 876/172	SS/AR
Burkett, Lemuel	071	1807	WB-2/345	AR
Burkhard, John C.	090	1846	WB-4/214	AR
Burkhard, John, Sr.	032	1841	WB-1/365	AR
Burkhard, Molly	032	1824	WB-1/29	AR
Burkhart, Daniel	085	1816	WB-G/409	AR
Burkhart, George	085	1814	WB-G/301	AR
Burkhart, George	085	1814	Copy	032 AR
Burkhead, J. W.	016	1895	WB-4/211	AR
Burkhead, S. F.	054	1900	WB-6/300	CTY
Burkitt, Prudence	010	1808	WB-F/87	AR
Burkitt, Thomas	024	1798	WB-A/336	AR

Name	Co.	Date	Recorded Copy	Original
Burkitt, William	024	c1792	WB-B/38	AR
Burleigh, Robert	070	1757	DB-D/292	SS/AR
Burleson, J. O.	066	1883	Orig. Only	AR
Burleson, Martha E.	066	1898	WB-1/179	
Burleson, Thomas	066	N. D.	WB-1/181	
Burleyson, Absolom	089	1898	WB-2/334	AR
Burleyson, Jonathan	097	1858	WB-1/138	AR
Burleyson, William	089	1898	WB-2/313	
Burlingham, William	039	1834	WB-K/13	AR
Burlington, Jonathan	092	1864	WB-5/70	
Burlison, Edward	013	1841	WB-A/72	
Burly, Solomon	028	1791	WB-A/240	
Burmingham, Stephen	005	1837	WB-B/74	
Burn, Andrew	010	1781	WB-C/14	AR
Burn, Andrew	010	1788	WB-D/62	AR
Burn, Elizabeth	010	1812	WB-F/200	AR
Burn, Frederick	103	1837	RD-7/251	AR
Burn, Jesse	099	1816	RB-12/384	AR
Burn, Jesse	103	1791	WI-A/234	AR
Burn, John	010	1774	WB-B/1	AR
Burn, Lewis	099	1815	RB-12/145	
Burn, Michail	037	1780	WB-B/35	AR
Burn, Owing	071	1795	WB-2/83	AR
Burn, William	071	1794	WB-2/43	AR
Burnap, Eben	072	1837	WB-1/158	AR
Burnap, Isaac	072	1799	Orig. Only	AR
Burnap, John	072	1744	SS 878/31	SS/AR
Burnby, John	075	1707	SS 875/46	SS/AR
Burnby, Thomas	075	1687	Orig. Only	SS/AR
Burnell, William W.	PA	1877	Copy	067 AR
Burnes, Jane W.	022	1866	WB-D/147	AR
Burnes, Thomas	046	1889	WB-F/1	AR
Burnet, George	010	1753	SS 879/143	SS/AR
Burnet, John	057	1808	WB-A/304	AR
Burnet, John	075	1703/4	Orig. Only	SS/AR
Burnett, Abigil	063	1865	WB-2/538	
Burnett, Alexander	022	1805	WB-A/120	AR
Burnett, Alice	009	1900	WB-2/251	CTY
Burnett, Archable	039	1896	WB-V/69	AR
Burnett, Benjamin	047	1857	WB-5/34	
Burnett, Berry	064	1843	WB-1/1	AR
Burnett, C. E.	039	1897	WB-V/112	
Burnett, Carter	086	1889	WB-F/367	AR
Burnett, Charity	063	1851	WB-1/373	
Burnett, David	029	1884	WB-E/311	AR
Burnett, David	039	1830	WB-J/113	
Burnett, Eldrige	013	1880	WB-B/217	AR
Burnett, Elizabeth	047	1860	WB-5/84	
Burnett, Elizabeth	047	1853	WB-4/337	AR
Burnett, Godfrey	005	1823	WB-A/86	AR
Burnett, Green	039	1872	WB-U/47	
Burnett, Hannah J.	013	1899	WB-D/272	AR
Burnett, Isaiah	022	1848	WB-C/213	AR
Burnett, J. S.	GA	1894	013 WB-D/17	013 AR
Burnett, James	063	1847	WB-2/332	
Burnett, James M.	TN	1881	013 WB-B/244	013 AR
Burnett, James, Sr.	063	1823	WB-2/88	
Burnett, John	072	1811	WB-A/14	AR-Nunc.
Burnett, John	097	1851	WB-1/71	AR
Burnett, John B.	077	1808	WB-E/312	
Burnett, Joseph	063	1854	WB-2/407	
Burnett, Julia F.	070	1889	WB-F/257	AR
Burnett, Mary E.	071	1895	WB-7/274	AR
Burnett, Matthew	063	c1790	WB-1/216	
Burnett, Matthew	039	1843	WB-L/158	
Burnett, P. L.	105	1885	WB-2/347	AR
Burnett, P. M.	065	1894	WB-M/310	AR
Burnett, Rebecca	064	1859	WB-1/62	AR
Burnett, Regnal	039	c1872	WB-U/171	AR
Burnett, Richard B.	070	1880	WB-E/383	AR
Burnett, Robert J.	071	1898	WB-7/370	AR
Burnett, Sikes	022	1890	WB-E/443	AR
Burnett, Simmons B.	063	1854	WB-2/402	
Burnett, Swan P.	064	1881	WB-2/98	AR
Burnett, Thomas	070	1763	DB-E/127	AR
Burney, John	028	1854	WB-D/231	AR
Burney, John	046	1848	WB-C/303	AR
Burney, John	046	1794	WB-A/26	AR
Burney, John N.	011	1884	WB-2/176	
Burney, Joseph	VA	1864	028 WB-D/462	028 AR
Burney, Joseph	028	1847	WB-D/131	AR
Burney, Lydia	046	1871	WB-E/45	AR
Burney, Mary L.	ME	1884	012 WB-A/63	012 AR
Burney, Reuben	053	1828	WB-4/443	
Burney, Robert	028	c1779	Orig. Only	AR
Burney, Robert S.	028	1871	WB-E/59	AR
Burney, Sarah	028	1794	WB-A/322	AR
Burney, William	046	1824	WB-B/176	AR
Burney, William	028	1794	WB-A/266	AR
Burney, William	027	c1824	WB-A/5	AR
Burney, William	011	c1783	WB-1/468	
Burney, William C.	027	1880	WB-2/42	AR
Burney, Yancy	046	1891	WB-F/135	AR
Burnham, Benjamin	075	1762	WB-I/16	AR
Burnham, Esebel	030	1751	Orig. Only	SS/AR
Burnham, Gabriel	075	1799	WB-M1/31	AR
Burnham, Hiram B.	NY	1887	013 WB-B/441	013 AR
Burnham, Isaac	018	1839	WB-C/249	
Burnham, James	030	1772	WB-1/69	
Burnham, John	075	1765	WB-I/44	AR
Burnham, Mary Ann	077	1885	WB-H/151	AR
Burnham, Nancy	018	1840	WB-C/256	
Burnham, Samuel	018	c1808	Orig. Only	AR-Copy
Burnham, Samuel	030	1799	WB-2/138	
Burnham, Timothy	075	1799	WB-M1/21	AR
Burnham, William	077	1846	WB-F/325	AR
Burns, Alexander	081	1884	WB-15/475	AR
Burns, Andrew	073	1837	WB-E/513	AR
Burns, Anne	096	c1793	Orig. Only	AR
Burns, Birdsong	022	1854	WB-C/364	AR
Burns, Brice	072	1858	WB-2/164	AR
Burns, Daniel	014	1893	WB-2/514	
Burns, Eli	021	1898	WB-3/217	AR
Burns, Francis	072	1824	WB-A/9	AR
Burns, Francis	072	1792	Orig. Only	AR
Burns, George	044	1843	WB-15/506	CTY
Burns, Hiram	022	1860	WB-D/69	AR
Burns, Jacob	071	1805	WB-2/285	AR
Burns, James	072	1790	Orig. Only	AR
Burns, James	022	1845	WB-C/184	AR
Burns, James	022	c1837	WB-C/47	
Burns, Joanna	057	c1814	WB-B/37	AR
Burns, John	022	1848	WB-C/230	AR
Burns, John	017	1881	WB-B/97	AR
Burns, John B.	022	c1877	WB-E/414	AR
Burns, John, Sr.	022	1812	WB-A/215	AR
Burns, Luanda R.	099	1897	WB-D/46	
Burns, Mary	081	1887	WB-16/26	AR
Burns, Mary	046	1864	WB-D/229	AR
Burns, Mary Ann	022	1858	WB-D/12	AR

Name	Co.	Date	Recorded Copy	Original
Burns, Nathan G.	099	1897	WB-D/27	AR
Burns, Pattie A.	022	1886	WB-E/342	AR
Burns, Philip	021	1889	WB-2/469	AR
Burns, Solomon	067	c1824	089 WB-1/92a	089 AR
Burns, Thomas	022	1833	WB-B/245	AR
Burns, William	022	1819	WB-B/20	AR
Burns, William	022	c1860	WB-D/94	AR
Burns, William M.	022	c1864	WB-D/133	AR
Burnside, Benjamin	046	1854	WB-C/412	AR
Burnside, James	092	1821	WB-3/146	AR
Burnside, James	029	c1794	Orig. Only	AR
Burnside, John	073	1862	WB-G/387	AR
Burnside, Margaret	029	1818	WB-B/16	AR
Burnside, Robert	073	1806	WB-D/170	AR
Burnside, Sarah	046	1858	WB-C/520	AR
Burnsides, James	073	1856	WB-G/147	CTY
Burr, Samuel	044	1875	WB-23/163	CTY
Burrease, Sallie C.	055	1897	WB-A/140	
Burrig, William	030	c1810	WB-2/358	
Burrington, George	N	c1750	SS 885/177	Abstract
Burrington, Martha	028	1840	Orig. Only	AR
Burris, Allen	089	1899	WB-2/349	AR
Burris, Joshua A.	089	1897	WB-2/289	AR
Burris, Judeth	089	1847	WB-1/62	AR
Burris, Solomon	089	1845	WB-1/43	
Burriss, Hardy	045	c1895	Orig. Only	AR
Burriss, Solomon	024	c1828	WB-C/147	AR
Burrough, Eliza C.	085	1840	WB-I/76	AR
Burroughs, Allen	085	1843	WB-I/184	AR
Burroughs, Harriet	100	1884	WB-51/188	AR
Burroughs, Jonathan	085	1819	WB-G/533	AR
Burroughs, Sarah H.	030	1825	WB-3/196	
Burroughs, Townsen	085	1822	WB-H/171	AR
Burrow, Henry	032	1865	WB-2/298	AR
Burrow, John	VA	1778	Copy	073 AR
Burrow, Lucy	081	1837	WB-7/93	AR
Burrow, Philip	VA	1778	Copy	073 AR
Burrow, Susan Jane	081	1885	WB-15/538	AR
Burrow, William	100	1820	WB-22/410	AR
Burrows, David	092	1835	WB-4/85	
Burrows, James W.	100	1861	WB-49/386	AR
Burrows, Martha A.	039	1883	WB-U/317	AR
Burrus, Allen	053	1881	WB-11/111	AR
Burrus, Allen	053	1866	WB-10/8	AR
Burrus, George S.	053	1860	WB-9/24	AR
Burrus, Levin	053	1857	WB-8/247	AR
Burrus, Reuben	053	1828	Orig. Only	AR
Burrus, Robbard	030	1792	WB-2/7	
Burrus, Robert	030	1816	WB-3/82	
Burrus, Virginia	053	1888	WB-11/210	AR
Burrus, Zechariah	053	1842	WB-6/197	AR
Burruss, E. E.	070	1887	WB-F/95	AR
Burruss, Elizabeth	070	1887	WB-F/118	AR
Burston, Angeline	105	1896	WB-3/189	AR
Burt, Elizabeth	069	1852	WB-1/531	AR
Burt, Emily	100	1896	WB-51/417	
Burt, Etta M.	048	1897	WB-1/64	CTY
Burt, Etta M.	048	c1896	022 WB-G/48	022 AR
Burt, Hilliard	047	1868	WB-5/171	AR
Burt, Ida M.	099	1894	WB-C/248	AR
Burt, Jacob	100	1834	WB-34/491	AR
Burt, John	099	1824	RB-20/44	AR
Burt, John	022	1780	Orig. Only	AR
Burt, John A.	100	1846	WB-39/175	AR
Burt, Joseph	047	1788	WB-3/152	AR
Burt, Mary	010	1724	Orig. Only	SS/AR
Burt, Nancy	100	1817	WB-21/44	AR-Nunc.
Burt, Richard	022	1792	RB-1/41	AR
Burt, Richard	047	1805	WB-3/437	AR
Burt, Salumith	100	1841	WB-38/11	AR
Burt, Stephen	047	1793	WB-3/214	AR-Nunc.
Burt, William	100	1823	WB-25/178	AR
Burt, William	047	1824	WB-3/695	AR
Burt, William	047	1805	WB-3/445	
Burt, Young	029	1847	WB-C/138	AR
Burtenshall, Richard	096	1743	Orig. Only	SS/AR
Burtenshell, Jacob	010	1817	WB-G/19	AR
Burton, Abner	020	1814	RB-G/23	AR
Burton, Agatha	044	1831	WB-12/103	CTY
Burton, Alfred M.	060	1857	WB-3/10	
Burton, Allen	020	1841	RB-O/224	
Burton, Bazel	032	c1851	WB-2/259	AR
Burton, Charles	020	1785	RB-B/88	
Burton, Charles H.	078	1797	WI-2/23	AR
Burton, Charlotte	035	1890	WB-4/337	AR
Burton, Charlotte	024	1881	WB-E/101	AR
Burton, Conway H.	MA	1857	037 WB-G/159	037 AR
Burton, Culbirth	073	1821	WB-D/601	AR
Burton, David	090	1872	WB-6/31	
Burton, Edward	054	c1826	WB-2/147	AR
Burton, Edward	054	c1826	WB-2/147	
Burton, Eli G.	032	1879	WB-3/264	AR
Burton, Elizabeth	106	c1863	WB-1/88	AR
Burton, Elizabeth	060	1872	WB-4/83	AR
Burton, Elizabeth	073	1847	WB-F/351	AR
Burton, Francis C.	060	1896	WB-5/27	AR
Burton, Francis C.	060	1896	016 WB-4/228	016 AR
Burton, Francis C.	065	1896	WB-M/484	AR
Burton, Franklin	020	1848	RB-Q/85	AR
Burton, Henry W.	060	c1897	Orig. Only	AR
Burton, Hilary	030	1788	WB-1/228	
Burton, Horace A.	044	1866	WB-22/411	CTY
Burton, James M.	033	1864	WB-1/185	AR
Burton, Jesse	046	c1850	WB-C/333	AR
Burton, John	046	1855	WB-C/434	AR
Burton, John	030	1800	WB-2/157	Nunc.
Burton, Jones W.	084	1888	WB-E/399	CTY
Burton, Mary A.	084	1891	WB-E/507	CTY
Burton, Priscilla	073	1774	WB-A/143	
Burton, Richard	046	1817	WB-B/36	AR
Burton, Richard	046	1801	WB-A/23	
Burton, Robert	044	1825	WB-10/47	CTY
Burton, Robert H.	060	1842	WB-2/132	AR
Burton, Robert O.	047	1892	WB-7/32	AR
Burton, Sarah	046	1817	WB-B/37	AR
Burton, Sarah	020	1857	RB-R/507	AR
Burton, Susanna	051	1844	WB-A/213	
Burton, Thomas	078	1854	WB-17/246	AR
Burton, Thomas	070	1798	WB-AB/21	AR
Burton, William	078	1892	WB-19/328	AR
Burton, William	065	1842	WB-H/88	AR
Burton, William B.	020	1805	RB-E/178	AR
Burton, William H.	099	1847	RB-26/255	AR
Burttin, Halley	099	1873	RB-35/201	AR
Burus, John	030	1799	WB-2/149	
Burwell, Armistead	044	1868	WB-22/718	CTY
Burwell, Blair	044	1848	WB-17/191	CTY
Burwell, Edmond S.	065	1887	WB-L/206	AR
Burwell, George W.	VA	1873	044 WB-23/221	044 CTY
Burwell, Mary E.	039	1875	WB-U/118	AR

Name	Co.	Date	Recorded Copy	Original
Burwell, Spotswood	044	1855	WB-19/544	CTY
Burwell, Susan C.	098	1897	WB-A/286	CTY
Busbee, Jerusha	099	1824	RB-19/113	AR
Busbee, Thomas	099	1815	RB-12/227	AR
Busbee, Washington	099	1890	WB-B/470	AR
Busbee, Winifred	099	1816	RB-15/242	AR
Busbey, Cateran	010	1738	SS 877/184	SS/AR
Busbey, Thomas	010	1738	SS 877/236	
Bush, Hardy	028	c1758	Orig. Only	AR
Bush, John	015	1771	100 WB-1/173	AR
Bush, John	024	c1768	WB-A/106	AR
Bush, John	017	c1845	WB-A/71	
Bush, John J.	024	c1862	Orig. Only	AR
Bush, Joseph	020	1809	RB-F/85	AR
Bush, Richard	017	1894	WB-B/247	AR
Bush, William	057	c1797	WB-A/229	AR
Bush, William	028	1784	Orig. Only	AR
Bush, William	024	c1716	Orig. Only	SS/AR
Bush, William	051	1838	WB-A/186	
Bush, William J.	011	1886	WB-2/210	
Bushee, Consider	029	1846	WB-C/98	AR
Bushnell, Henry	020	1861	RB-S/419	AR
Busick, David W.	046	c1885	WB-N/204	
Busick, Durant H.	046	1881	WB-E/324	AR
Busick, Green L.	046	1878	WB-E/244	AR
Busick, James	057	1794	WB-A/89	AR
Busick, Mitchel	057	1794	WB-A/177	AR
Busick, William	073	1808	WB-D/228	AR
Busick, William Y.	020	1898	WB-B/325	CTY
Bustin, Martha	047	1825	WB-4/4	AR
Bustin, Thomas	047	1841	WB-4/202	AR
Bustle, Henry	054	1845	WB-2/321	AR
Bustle, John	054	c1832	WB-2/134	AR
Butcher, James	092	1842	WB-4/184	
Butcher, Thomas	083	c1810	WB-1/118	AR
Bute, Samuel	071	1868	WB-5/355	
Butlar, Robert	087	c1802	WB-1/83	AR
Butler, Alexander	044	1867	WB-22/704	CTY
Butler, Aron	061	1831	WB-1/5	AR
Butler, Arthur	028	1823	WB-C/237	AR
Butler, Charles	087	c1811	WB-A/70	AR
Butler, Charles	028	1862	WB-D/360	AR
Butler, David	024	1749	Orig. Only	SS/AR
Butler, David L.	012	1887	WB-A/67 & 74	AR
Butler, Dolly	010	1824	WB-G/112	AR
Butler, Elizabeth	039	1822	WB-G/92	AR
Butler, Elizabeth	044	c1848	WB-23/15	CTY
Butler, Gabriel	087	1828	WB-1/87	AR
Butler, Hartwell	087	1838	WB-1/196	AR
Butler, Hartwell	087	1900	WB-4/133	AR
Butler, Horace	077	1876	WB-H/64	AR
Butler, Isaac	044	1809	WB-7/67	CTY
Butler, Jacob	024	1745	Orig. Only	SS/AR
Butler, Jacob	024	c1789	WB-B/90	AR
Butler, James	096	1765	WB-1/34	AR
Butler, James	099	1798	RB-4/251	AR
Butler, James	099	1792	RB-2/338	AR
Butler, James M.	010	1892	WB-I/356	AR
Butler, John	011	c1875	WB-2/207	
Butler, John	044	1809	WB-7/53	CTY
Butler, John	046	1872	WB-E/88	AR
Butler, John	039	N. D.	WB-A/158	
Butler, John	096	1773	Orig. Only	SS/AR
Butler, John	099	1838	RB-24/128	AR
Butler, John	085	c1785	073 WB-B/1	073 AR
Butler, John	028	1800	WB-B/105	AR
Butler, John	010	1857	WB-H/44	AR
Butler, John	010	1896	WB-I/486	AR
Butler, John P.	010	1856	WB-H/32	AR
Butler, John T.	065	1891	091 WB-1/127	
Butler, John T.	065	1890	WB-L/510	AR
Butler, John W.	083	1880	WB-3/306	AR
Butler, John, Sr.	010	1807	WB-F/66	AR
Butler, Joseph	047	1763	WB-1/101	
Butler, Joseph	065	1892	WB-M/52	AR
Butler, Joshua	020	1875	WB-A/191	CTY
Butler, Kenneth L.	010	1900	WB-K/11	
Butler, Linsey	044	1842	WB-15/302	
Butler, Martha	010	1844	WB-G/367	AR
Butler, Mary	087	1895	WB-3/560	AR
Butler, Mary J.	044	1872	WB-23/49	CTY
Butler, Mary M.	075	1833	WB-N/88	AR
Butler, Micajah	099	1810	RB-9/344	AR
Butler, Moses	055	1855	ID/11	
Butler, Nancy	044	c1848	WB-23/15	CTY
Butler, Othnial	086	1877	WB-F/108	AR
Butler, Pelham	065	1894	WB-M/281	AR
Butler, Polly	060	1833	WB-1/265	AR
Butler, Reden	087	c1849	Copy	AR
Butler, Richard H.	086	1880	WB-F/153	AR
Butler, Robert	039	c1787	WB-A/160	
Butler, Robert	087	c1802	WB-A/31	AR
Butler, Robert	087	c1857	WB-2/111	AR
Butler, Robert	027	1832	WB-A/32	AR
Butler, Ryan	010	1855	WB-H/18	AR
Butler, Samuel	024	1812	WB-B/256	AR
Butler, Sarah	033	1845	WB-1/68	AR
Butler, Sarah Ann	029	1863	WB-D/55	AR
Butler, Stephen	087	1830	WB-1/105	AR
Butler, Susan A.	083	1898	WB-4/182	AR
Butler, Susan Jane	020	1892	WB-B/117	CTY
Butler, Thomas	039	1807	WB-C/90	
Butler, Tobias	010	1791	WB-D/194	AR
Butler, Travis	087	1859	WB-1/544	
Butler, Wiley	087	1885	WB-3/309	AR
Butler, William	085	1818	WB-G/518	AR
Butler, William	067	1866	WB-1/136	
Butler, Zachariah	029	1815	WB-A/216	AR
Butner, Christopher	090	1808	WB-2/99	AR
Butner, David	085	1821	WB-H/10	AR
Butner, Edward S.	092	1882	WB-6/168	AR
Butner, Eliza R.	038	1896	WB-3/557	AR
Butner, Elizabeth	038	1850	WB-1/20	AR
Butner, Harmon	090	1845	WB-4/193	AR
Butner, Herman	085	c1795	WB-D/160	AR
Butner, Jemima	085	c1801	WB-C/321	AR
Butner, John	038	c1856	WB-1/102	AR
Butner, Joseph	038	1872	WB-2/110	AR
Butner, Lewis	038	c1867	WB-1/293	AR-Copy
Butner, Susana	085	1826	WB-H/372	AR
Butner, Thomas	090	1833	WB-3/250	
Butner, Thomas	085	c1781	WB-B/1	AR
Butner, Thomas	090	1838	WB-4/22	AR
Butt, Cornelius	030	1801	WB-2/172	
Butt, John W.	077	1865	WB-H/26	AR
Butt, Joseph	075	1871	WB-O/24	AR
Butt, Mary A.	065	1899	WB-N/228	AR
Butt, Moses	047	1803	WB-3/419	AR
Butterfield, John C.	IL	1887	Copy	097 AR
Butterfield, Sarah H.	IL	1892	Copy	097 AR

Name	Co.	Date	Recorded Copy	Original
Butterton, Celia M.	010	1887	WB-I/236	AR
Butterton, James	010	1876	WB-I/80	AR
Butterton, Joseph	010	c1762	WB-A/34	AR
Butterton, Robert	010	1785	WB-D/10	AR
Buttery, James R.	101	1877	WB-A/34	AR
Buttery, Silvanus	063	1794	WB-1/202	
Buttler, Mical	029	1794	Orig. Only	AR
Butts, Eli	047	1868	WB-5/169	
Butts, Jesse	047	1803	WB-3/399	AR
Butts, John	060	1863	WB-3/52	AR
Buxton, Harriet	029	1870	Orig. Only	AR
Buxton, John W.	071	1900	WB-7/448	AR
Buxton, Ralph P.	029	1900	WB-F/221	AR
Buxton, Samuel	071	1743	Orig. Only	SS/AR
Buxton, Samuel N.	071	1896	WB-7/297	AR
Buxton, William F.	054	1882	WB-4/464	CTY
Byars, James	044	1799	WB-4/344	CTY
Byars, John	100	1853	WB-42/256	AR
Byars, Thomas	065	c1845	Copy	054 AR
Byars, William	044	1832	WB-12/188 & 227	CTY
Byasee, John	078	1820	WI-8/334	AR
Byerley, David	032	1823	WB-1/1	AR
Byerly, Francis	032	1896	WB-4/295	AR
Byerly, Jacob	032	1848	WB-2/34	AR
Byerly, Jacob	085	1822	WB-H/180	AR
Byerly, Lucy	032	1844	WB-1/445	AR
Byerly, Martin	032	1866	WB-2/331	AR
Byerly, Peter	032	c1847	WB-2/75	AR
Byers, B. B.	086	1898	WB-F/580	AR
Byers, Catherine	065	1894	WB-M/308	AR
Byers, F. L.	054	1900	WB-6/322	CTY
Byers, Francis	049	1894	WB-2/235	AR
Byers, G. B.	026	1865	WB-1/365	AR
Byers, James S.	054	1863	Copy	003 AR
Byers, James S.	054	1863	WB-4/49	AR
Byers, Joseph	054	c1819	WB-2/67	AR
Byers, Joseph	054	c1844	WB-2/296	AR
Byers, Margaret	065	1857	WB-J/45	AR
Byers, Robert	054	c1833	WB-2/132	AR
Byers, Thomas	065	1846	WB-I/62	AR
Byers, Thomas	065	1846	Copy	060 AR
Byers, Thomas S.	054	1899	WB-6/265	CTY
Byery, Martin	085	c1794	WB-D/140	AR
Byford, William	046	1796	WB-A/328	AR
Byhan, Gotleib	038	1862	WB-1/195	AR
Bylerly, Philip	081	1800	WB-2/63	AR
Bynam, James	047	1763	WB-1/98	
Bynum, Arthur	060	1813	Orig. Only	AR
Bynum, Carney	022	1877	WB-E/139	AR
Bynum, Catherine	037	1872	WB-G/376	AR
Bynum, Cordall	071	1816	WB-3/166	AR
Bynum, Elizabeth	071	1848	WB-5/66	AR
Bynum, Elmina	022	1883	WB-E/320	AR
Bynum, Fanny	028	1806	WB-B/249	AR
Bynum, George	021	1894	WB-3/76	AR
Bynum, Gray	090	1814	WB-2/150	
Bynum, Hampton	090	1861	WB-4/337	
Bynum, J. F.	060	1876	WB-4/148	AR
Bynum, James	037	1886	WB-H/71	
Bynum, James	022	1842	WB-C/131	AR
Bynum, John B.	071	1857	WB-5/170	AR
Bynum, Joseph	037	1841	WB-F/259	AR
Bynum, Luke	022	1810	WB-A/182	AR
Bynum, Mark	022	1893	WB-E/536	AR
Bynum, R. A.	079	1888	WB-2/442	AR
Bynum, Robert	105	1868	WB-2/1	AR
Bynum, Samuel	060	1802	Orig. Only	AR
Bynum, Samuel V.	037	1848	WB-F/408	AR
Bynum, Thomas	037	1837	WB-F/207	AR
Bynum, Turner	105	c1858	WB-1/130	AR
Bynum, Turner	022	1864	WB-D/119	AR
Byrd, A. W.	059	1887	WB-A/481	CTY
Byrd, Archibell	083	c1795	WB-1/42	AR
Byrd, Carney	022	1877	WB-E/144	AR
Byrd, Charles	029	1898	Orig. Only	AR
Byrd, Hudson	066	1892	WB-1/107	AR
Byrd, Iley	083	1875	WB-3/104	AR
Byrd, James	073	1829	WB-E/178	
Byrd, James	104	1897	WB-7/22	AR
Byrd, James	104	1870	WB-6/18	AR
Byrd, James	001	1867	WB-1/292	AR
Byrd, James	067	1888	WB-2/255	
Byrd, Jethro	099	1858	RB-31/53	AR
Byrd, John	104	1814	WB-3/74	AR
Byrd, John	035	c1761	087 DB-3/163	AR
Byrd, Lemuel	056	1896	WB-2/225	AR
Byrd, Mitchell	066	1900	Orig. Only	AR
Byrd, Moses	071	1808	WB-2/362	AR
Byrd, Philip	071	1808	WB-2/363	AR
Byrd, Richard	103	1832	RD-6/368	AR
Byrd, Richard	056	1818	WB-1/293	AR
Byrd, Robert	087	1845	WB-1/301	AR
Byrd, Samuel	073	1829	Orig. Only	AR
Byrd, Susanah	104	1896	WB-6/553	AR
Byrd, Sutton	056	1857	WB-1/708	AR
Byrd, Thomas	085	c1803	WB-C/325	AR
Byrd, Thomas K.	087	1899	WB-4/107	AR
Byrd, William	048	1897	WB-1/73	CTY
Byrd, William	083	c1800	WB-1/61	
Byrd, William	022	1775	Orig. Only	AR
Byrd, William	083	1841	WB-1/393	AR
Byrly, Mikeal	032	1856	Orig. Only	AR
Byrn, Charles	085	c1797	WB-D/128	AR
Byrn, James K.	073	1797	WB-C/97	AR
Byrne, Alexander	011	c1787	WB-1/465	
Byrne, Ceazar	029	c1896	Orig. Only	AR
Byrne, John M.	011	1858	WB-1/263	
Byrne, Mary	011	1853	WB-1/214	
Byrne, Matthew	011	c1837	WB-1/84	
Byrns, John	070	1810	WB-AB/135	AR
Byrom, Thomas	075	c1710	Orig. Only	SS/AR
Byron, Diantha A.	054	1882	WB-4/469	CTY
Byrum, Cary	010	1892	WB-I/367	AR
Byrum, Edwin	024	1884	WB-E/134	AR
Byrum, Elizabeth	010	1876	WB-I/82	AR
Byrum, H. A.	010	1885	WB-I/205	
Byrum, Henry	010	1833	WB-G/230	AR
Byrum, Isaac	024	1815	WB-C/38	AR
Byrum, Isaac	024	1895	WB-E/251	AR
Byrum, James	010	1806	WB-F/2	AR
Byrum, James I.	024	1895	WB-E/246	AR
Byrum, Josiah	024	1899	WB-E/302	AR
Byrum, Mary	010	1891	WB-I/324	AR
Byrum, Ransom	099	1876	RB-35/356	AR
Byrum, Starky	010	1868	WB-H/203	AR
Byrum, William	010	1891	WB-I/332	AR
Bysiner, Catherine	060	1849	WB-2/327	AR
Cabaniss, A. A.	026	1899	WB-3/46	AR
Cabaniss, A. M.	026	1900	WB-3/65	AR

Name	Co.	Date	Recorded Copy	Original
Cabaniss, F. W.	026	1865	WB-1/379	AR
Cabaniss, F. W.	026	1869	WB-2/23	AR
Cabaniss, George	026	1846	WB-1/48	AR
Cabaniss, J. B.	026	1882	WB-2/225	AR-Nunc.
Cabaniss, James W.	026	1863	WB-1/323	AR
Cabaniss, John	026	1893	Orig. Only	AR
Cabarrus, Stephen	024	c1807	SC/02272	AR-Copy
Cabarrus, Stephen	024	1808	WB-B/262	AR
Cabe, J. M.	061	1894	WB-2/145	AR
Cabe, Jamima	073	1845	WB-F/248	AR
Cabe, John	049	c1810	WI-A/3	AR
Cable, John	073	1845	WB-F/240	AR
Cabral, Jobe	029	1806	005 WB-2/20	005 AR
Caddell, Sallie J.	083	1892	WB-4/8	AR
Cade, Barbara	083	1854	WB-2/60	
Cade, John	083	c1788	WB-1/14	AR
Cade, William	029	1882	Orig. Only	AR
Cador, James	030	1796	WB-2/77	
Cadwell, Robert	011	1750	028 DB-5/210	
Caffee, Jesse M.	030	1825	WB-3/197	
Caffee, John	046	c1783	WB-A/41	AR
Caffey, George	030	1799	WB-2/141	
Caffey, Michael	084	1810	WB-A/35	CTY
Caffey, William	009	c1779	OWB/151	AR
Cagle, Benjamin	089	1843	WB-1/16	
Cagle, Elisha	068	1895	WB-D/444	
Cagle, George	068	1865	WB-C/119	
Cagle, George	089	1888	WB-2/176	AR
Cagle, George	089	1851	WB-1/83	
Cagle, Henry	068	1802	WB-A/224	
Cagle, John	068	1799	WB-A/199	
Cagle, John	050	1854	WB-1/37	
Cagle, John	068	c1867	WB-D/14	
Cagle, Roda	067	1876	WB-2/73	
Cagle, Sarah	067	1882	WB-2/154	AR
Cagle, Tillithia	089	1898	WB-2/336	
Cahoon, Abel	096	1847	WB-3/12	AR
Cahoon, Alexander	053	1828	WB-4/363	AR
Cahoon, Alice	053	1889	WB-11/221	AR
Cahoon, Ashberry	096	1878	WB-4/43	
Cahoon, Daniel	072	1822	WB-A/20	AR
Cahoon, Dudley	028	1824	WB-C/240	AR
Cahoon, Emma J.	101	1885	WB-A/144	AR
Cahoon, John	057	1783	WB-A/22	AR
Cahoon, Mary	072	1828	WB-1/21	AR
Cahoon, William	053	1802	RW-1/343	
Cail, Henry	077	1825	WB-F/149	AR
Caila, Jaila S.	009	1884	WB-1/344	CTY
Caila, John M.	009	1854	OB-I/271	AR
Cain, Archibald	047	1864	WB-5/120	
Cain, Daniel	033	1859	WB-1/169	AR
Cain, Edward J.	011	1896	WB-3/74	
Cain, Fanny O.	063	1833	WB-2/175	
Cain, Hardy	037	1755	Orig. Only	SS/AR
Cain, Hardy	037	1774	WB-A/224	AR
Cain, Hugh	073	1781	WB-A/235	AR
Cain, Jacob	073	1779	WB-A/208	
Cain, James	047	1814	WB-3/549	
Cain, James	037	1761	WB-A/70	AR
Cain, James W.	011	1847	WB-1/160	
Cain, James, Sr.	011	c1826	WB-2/368	
Cain, Jeremiah	047	1828	WB-4/42	
Cain, John	037	1757	SS 879/218	SS/AR
Cain, Joseph	011	c1798	WB-1/35	
Cain, Lewis	073	1884	WB-H/355	CTY
Cain, Margaret	073	1864	WB-G/452	CTY
Cain, Mary	073	1851	WB-G/5	AR
Cain, Olive	083	c1797	WB-1/46	AR
Cain, Peter	085	c1791	WB-C/235	AR
Cain, Richard S.	029	1855	WB-C/322	AR
Cain, Samuel	011	c1830	WB-1/13	
Cain, Samuel	011	1871	WB-2/59	
Cain, Thomas	033	1838	WB-1/11	AR
Cain, Thomas H.	085	1832	WB-H/556	AR
Cain, William	073	1834	WB-E/324	AR
Cain, William	011	1781	DB-37/295	
Cain, William	033	1894	WB-2/157	
Cain, William	073	1857	WB-G/182	AR
Cain, William	010	1734	SS 876/302	SS/AR
Cain, William	047	1762	WB-1/88	
Cain, William	073	c1827	Orig. Only	AR
Cains, Lydia	012	1825	WB-B/135	AR
Cains, Mary	012	1772	DB-A/143	AR
Caison, Jacob	087	1895	WB-3/558	AR
Cake, John	010	1771	WB-A/139	AR
Cake, John	010	1796	WB-D/329	AR
Cake, Mary	063	1788	WB-1/140	
Cake, Robert	063	c1781	WB-1/115	
Calaway, B. C.	106	1897	WB-2/401	
Caldcleugh, Alexander	032	1833	WB-1/204	AR-Copy
Caldcleugh, Andrew	085	1822	WB-H/163	AR
Calder, Duncan	065	1883	WB-K/525	AR
Calder, Phila C.	070	1888	WB-F/210	AR
Calder, Robert E.	070	1888	WB-F/155	AR
Caldwell, Agnes	065	1832	WB-G/92	AR
Caldwell, Andrew	054	1865	WB-3/169	AR
Caldwell, Andrew	054	c1822	WB-2/7	AR
Caldwell, C. A.	016	1889	WB-4/31	AR
Caldwell, Charles	065	1792	WB-A/184	AR
Caldwell, Cyrus	065	1884	WB-K/572	
Caldwell, D. F.	085	1867	WB-L/8	AR
Caldwell, D. S.	016	1887	WB-3/542	AR
Caldwell, David	054	c1808	WB-1/26	
Caldwell, David	065	1781	WB-A/185	AR
Caldwell, David	046	1857	WB-C/476	AR
Caldwell, David	046	1824	WB-B/184	AR
Caldwell, David F.	046	1899	WB-G/104	AR
Caldwell, David T.	065	1862	WB-J/132	AR
Caldwell, Elizabeth	040	c1867	WB-1/205	
Caldwell, F.	021	c1888	WB-2/460	AR
Caldwell, Henderson	021	1873	WB-2/76	AR
Caldwell, Isabella	065	1858	WB-I/96	AR
Caldwell, J. W.	065	1862	WB-J/141	AR
Caldwell, Jacob V.	099	1856	RB-29/465	AR
Caldwell, James	054	c1810	WB-1/228	AR
Caldwell, James	065	1840	Orig. Only	AR
Caldwell, James	054	1839	WB-2/198	AR
Caldwell, John	014	1857	WB-2/90	
Caldwell, John	021	1856	WB-1/126	AR
Caldwell, John	016	1875	WB-3/140	AR
Caldwell, John H.	016	1872	WB-3/68	
Caldwell, John H.	083	1891	WB-3/537	
Caldwell, John N.	065	1875	WB-K/178	AR
Caldwell, John, Sr.	021	1843	Orig. Only	AR
Caldwell, Joseph	073	1835	Orig. Only	AR
Caldwell, Letitia C.	046	1864	WB-D/209	AR
Caldwell, M. S.	065	1894	WB-M/313	AR
Caldwell, Martha	054	c1815	WB-1/381	AR
Caldwell, Mary C.	097	1900	WB-3/49	AR
Caldwell, Mary M.	046	1894	WB-F/355	AR

Name	Co.	Date	Recorded Copy	Original
Caldwell, Minerva R.	014	1890	WB-2/398	CTY
Caldwell, November	073	1874	WB-H/89	CTY
Caldwell, Rebecca M.	085	1856	WB-K/211	AR
Caldwell, Richard A.	089	1883	WB-2/110	AR
Caldwell, Robert	011	1750	028 DB-5/143	SS/AR
Caldwell, Robert	065	1832	WB-G/93	AR
Caldwell, Robert	065	1847	WB-I/96	AR
Caldwell, Robert	065	1896	016 WB-4/235	016 AR
Caldwell, Robert C.	046	1878	WB-E/236	AR
Caldwell, Robert C.	016	1881	WB-3/327	AR
Caldwell, Sarah	065	1842	WB-H/87	AR
Caldwell, Silas	065	1868	WB-J/253	AR
Caldwell, Susan	046	1865	WB-D/280	AR
Caldwell, Thomas G.	054	1840	WB-2/215	AR
Caldwell, Thomas J.	054	1891	WB-5/383	CTY
Caldwell, William	021	1888	WB-2/398	AR
Caldwell, William	065	1838	WB-E/211	AR
Caldwell, William	065	1801	WB-A/165	AR
Cale, Chancy	106	1861	WB-1/78	AR-Nunc.
Cale, Charney	010	1860	WB-H/95	AR
Cale, John	077	1806	WB-E/233	AR
Cale, Joseph	077	1806	WB-E/247	AR
Cale, Judith	106	1883	WB-2/168	AR
Cale, Nathaniel	077	1821	WB-F/32	AR
Cale, Thomas	028	1785	Orig. Only	AR
Cale, Thomas A.	051	1900	WB-C/581	AR
Calhoon, Andrew A.	037	1849	WB-F/428	AR
Calhoon, Hardy G.L.	037	1847	WB-F/375	AR
Calhoon, James	046	1795	WB-A/48	AR
Calhoon, Jeney	046	1805	WB-A/78	AR
Calhoon, John W.	037	1847	WB-F/374	AR
Calhoon, Pharaba	037	1845	WB-F/326	AR
Calhoon, Polly	037	1888	WB-H/109	AR
Calhorda, John	070	1831	WB-AB/283	
Calhorda, Zilpha	070	1848	WB-C/483	AR
Calhoun, Christian	082	1858	WB-4/117	AR
Calhoun, Daniel C.	082	1838	WB-2/80	AR
Calhoun, Mary	082	1842	WB-2/533	AR
Calicot, James	067	1861	WB-1/96	AR
Califor, Emily R.	044	c1888	Orig. Only	CTY
Call, Daniel	085	1822	WB-H/149	AR
Call, Daniel	104	1860	WB-5/255	
Call, David	033	1838	WB-1/12	AR
Call, David D.	104	1847	WB-4/332	AR
Call, Elizabeth	033	1883	WB-2/84	CTY
Call, Henry	085	c1828	WB-H/430	AR
Call, Henry	033	1879	WB-2/66	CTY
Call, I. S.	104	1893	WB-6/496	AR
Call, William	085	c1778	WB-C/156	AR
Call, William W.	104	1875	WB-6/122	AR
Callaghahan, Martin	028	1827	WB-C/290	AR
Callahan, Darby	084	c1787	OW/79	AR
Callahan, James	060	1806	Orig. Only	AR
Callahan, James, Sr.	054	c1824	WB-2/28	AR
Callahan, William	054	1839	WB-2/197	AR
Calland, Booker S.	084	c1826	WB-A/194	
Callard, John	063	1816	WB-2/39	
Callaway, Caleb	077	1706	Orig. Only	SS/AR
Callaway, John	077	1772	WB-C/103	AR
Callaway, Joshua	077	1742	Orig. Only	SS/AR
Callaway, Reuben	028	1835	WB-C/379	AR
Callaway, Thomas	006	1885	WB-E/126	AR
Callaway, Zebulon	077	1791	WB-C/428	AR
Callen, John	065	1825	WB-A/227	AR
Callendine, Anna	099	1891	WB-B/546	AR
Callendine, Martin B.	099	1883	WB-A/444	AR
Caller, Charles	100	1781	WB-3/122	AR
Caller, Robert	100	1805	WB-13/9	AR
Callett, John	014	1884	WB-2/266	
Calley (Kalley), Mathew	002	1699	Orig. Only	SS/AR
Calley (Kelley), John	030	1764	024 WB-1/14	024 AR
Calley, Smith	N	1734	SS 876/294	Nunc.
Callicott, Beverly	081	1824	WB-5/161	AR
Callicott, P. C.	067	1895	WB-2/339	AR
Callicutt, Eli	068	1819	WB-B/3	
Callio, Joseph	N	1719	SS 875/217	
Callis, John	030	1780	WB-1/138	
Calloway, A. J.	004	1900	WB-A/239	AR
Calloway, Annie P.	104	1890	WB-6/396	AR
Calloway, Benjamin C.	104	1886	WB-6/269	AR
Calloway, Elijah	006	1843	WB-A/56	
Calloway, Elijah P.	009	1854	OB-I/174	AR
Calloway, George H.	089	1898	WB-2/342	AR
Calloway, James	104	1897	102 WB-A/134	102 AR
Calloway, James	104	1878	WB-6/164	AR
Calloway, Job	067	1858	089 WB-1/191	
Calloway, Nancy R.	009	1868	OB-M/286	AR
Calloway, Samuel	092	1837	WB-4/166	
Calloway, Sarah Ann	013	1886	WB-B/418	AR
Calloway, Thomas S.	006	1889	WB-E/192	AR
Callum, Hezekiah	010	1793	WB-D/220	AR-Nunc.
Callum, Mary	010	1799	WB-E/31	AR
Callum, Willis	010	1816	WB-F/330	AR
Calton, John K.	086	1873	WB-F/44	AR
Calton, Susanah	086	1873	WB-F/44	AR
Calton, Thomas B.	086	1897	WB-F/537	AR
Calvert, Matt	071	1839	WB-4/204	AR
Calvert, Samuel	071	1882	WB-6/377	AR
Calvin, Satira	076	1896	WB-A1/204	
Camble, William	009	1743	Orig. Only	SS/AR
Cambridge, Francis	VA	c1710	SS 875/36	
Cambrill, Alexander	024	1726	SS 876/50	SS/AR
Cambrill, Anne	024	1726	Orig. Only	SS/AR
Camdell, Buckner	085	1823	WB-H/695	
Camel, Samuel	011	1853	WB-1/216	
Camerlen, Daniell	071	1752	Orig. Only	SS/AR
Cameron, Absalom	032	1840	WB 1/340	
Cameron, Alexander	029	c1791	Orig. Only	AR
Cameron, Allen, Sr.	029	1842	WB-B/372	AR
Cameron, Ann	073	1897	WB-I/107	CTY
Cameron, Anna	073	c1892	Copy	099 AR
Cameron, Anne	073	1856	WB-G/148	AR
Cameron, Catharine	068	c1827	WB-B/131	
Cameron, Duncan	099	1853	RB-28/224	AR
Cameron, Duncan	036	1886	WB-A/98	CTY
Cameron, Francis H.	099	1900	WB-D/395	AR
Cameron, James	070	1798	WB-AB/15	AR-Nunc.
Cameron, James	032	c1861	WB-2/205	
Cameron, James W.R.	032	1862	WB-2/257	AR
Cameron, John	029	1842	WB-C/25	AR
Cameron, John	068	1814	WB-A/282	
Cameron, John	068	1823	WB-B/32	
Cameron, John	082	1844	WB-3/17	AR
Cameron, Julia	032	1892	WB-4/140	AR
Cameron, Mary	029	1834	WB-B/239	AR
Cameron, Norman	029	1844	WB-C/69	AR
Cameron, Paul C.	073	1891	078 WB-19/288	
Cameron, Paul C.	073	1891	071 WB-7/96	071 AR
Cameron, Paul C.	073	1891	093 WB-2/82	093 AR
Cameron, Paul C.	073	1891	099 WB-B/519	099 AR

Name	Co.	Date	Recorded Copy	Original
Cameron, Paul C.	073	1891	065 WB-L/567	065 AR
Cameron, Paul C.	073	1891	036 WB-A/202	036 CTY
Cameron, Paul C.	073	1891	013 WB-C/130	013 AR
Cameron, Paul C.	073	1891	WB-H/512	CTY
Cameron, Paul C.	073	1891	050 WB-2/109	050 CTY
Cameron, Paul C.	073	1891	044 WB-24/153	044 CTY
Cameron, Sarah	082	1853	WB-4/67	AR
Cameron, Tabitha	054	1846	WB-3/15	AR
Cammack, William	075	1824	WB-M1/406	AR
Camp, Cranshaw	086	1808	WB-B/220	AR
Camp, Humphrey	047	1856	WB-5/17	
Camp, J. G.	086	1872	WB-F/62	AR
Camp, John T.	086	1897	WB-F/542	AR
Camp, Joseph	026	1876	WB-2/152	AR
Camp, Joshua	086	1849	WB-E/181	AR
Camp, Lawrence S.	060	1882	WB-4/250	AR
Camp, M. E.	047	1881	WB-6/241	AR
Camp, Martha	047	1854	WB-4/363	
Camp, Stephen	086	1846	WB-E/153	AR
Camp, Thomas	086	1798	Orig. Only	AR
Camp, William	086	1855	WB-E/285	AR
Camp, William F.	014	1900	WB-3/102	CTY
Campain, Joseph	009	1775	OWB/121	AR
Campbell, Adam	054	1863	Orig. Only	AR
Campbell, Adelaide	032	1891	WB-4/130	AR
Campbell, Alexander	065	1804	WB-A/196	AR
Campbell, Alexander	029	1824	WB-B/113	AR
Campbell, Alexander	082	c1818	WB-1/198	AR
Campbell, Alexander	029	1779	Orig. Only	AR
Campbell, Allen	049	c1840	Orig. Only	AR
Campbell, Allen C.	020	1880	WB-A/294	CTY
Campbell, Americus	070	1883	WB-E/493	AR
Campbell, Anaka	070	1882	WB-E/488	AR
Campbell, Angus	083	c1822	WB-1/359	AR
Campbell, Angus	082	1840	WB-2/95	AR
Campbell, Archibald	082	1820	Orig. Only	AR
Campbell, Archibald	011	1856	WB-1/250	
Campbell, Archibald	029	1853	WB-C/253	AR
Campbell, Archibald	065	1797	WB-A/176	AR
Campbell, C.	061	1882	WB-2/47	AR
Campbell, Cassandra	070	1805	WB-AB/90	AR
Campbell, Catharine	083	1860	WB-2/157	AR
Campbell, Catharine	083	1862	WB-2/189	AR
Campbell, Catherine	070	1816	WB-AB/239	AR
Campbell, Catlett	073	1845	WB-F/245	AR
Campbell, Charles	068	1799	WB-A/205	
Campbell, Christian	011	c1819	WB-2/329	
Campbell, Colin	029	1804	WB-A/67	AR
Campbell, Collan, Sr.	054	c1808	WB-1/25	AR
Campbell, Cornelius	010	1763	WB-A/61	AR
Campbell, Cyntha D.	068	1882	WB-D/187	
Campbell, D. R.	068	1898	WB-E/1	CTY
Campbell, Daniel	085	c1781	WB-B/21	AR
Campbell, Daniel	009	1825	OB-A/350	AR
Campbell, Daniel	029	1800	WB-A/28	AR
Campbell, Daniel D.	027	1871	WB-2/5	AR
Campbell, David	081	1862	WB-12/287	AR
Campbell, Donald	029	1798	Orig. Only	AR
Campbell, Donald	029	c1784	Orig. Only	AR
Campbell, Donald	099	1885	WB-B/95	AR
Campbell, Dugald	083	1891	WB-3/509	AR
Campbell, Duncan	083	1881	WB-3/261	AR
Campbell, Duncan	029	1843	WB-C/29	AR
Campbell, Duncan	083	c1790	WB-1/23	AR
Campbell, Effy	083	c1855	Orig. Only	AR
Campbell, Elizabeth	054	1869	WB-4/29	AR
Campbell, Elizabeth	GA	c1875	029 WB-E/424	
Campbell, Elizabeth	065	1855	WB-J/13	AR
Campbell, Elizabeth	028	1817	WB-C/145	AR
Campbell, Eneas	054	c1824	WB-2/72	AR
Campbell, Ferquhard	029	1808	WB-A/124	AR
Campbell, Findley	068	1900	WB-E/78	
Campbell, Flora J.	048	1897	WB-1/81	
Campbell, Friason	054	1888	WB-5/191	CTY
Campbell, Hannah	054	1889	WB-5/269	CTY
Campbell, Henrietta	029	1851	WB-C/172	AR
Campbell, Hugh	029	1846	WB-C/112	
Campbell, Hugh	020	1869	WB-A/24	CTY
Campbell, Hugh	070	1796	Orig. Only	AR
Campbell, Hugh	N	1737	SS 877/187	SS/AR
Campbell, Isabella	029	1856	WB-C/349	AR
Campbell, Isabella	029	1846	WB-C/129	AR
Campbell, Israel	071	1771	WB-1/197	
Campbell, James	070	1759	SS 881/186	SS/AR
Campbell, James	065	1784	WB-A/189	AR
Campbell, James	010	1798	HiDSC	AR-Copy
Campbell, James	085	1859	WB-K/271	AR
Campbell, James	026	1853	WB-1/162	AR
Campbell, James	047	1814	WB-3/555	
Campbell, James	011	c1842	WB-1/63	
Campbell, James	010	1798	WB-E/50	AR
Campbell, Janett	083	1881	WB-3/224	AR
Campbell, Jannett	029	1843	WB-C/41	AR
Campbell, Jeane	029	1766	Orig. Only	AR
Campbell, Jennet	065	1799	WB-A/200	AR
Campbell, John	047	1866	WB-5/145	
Campbell, John	081	1825	WB-5/235	AR
Campbell, John	021	1865	WB-1/213	AR
Campbell, John	083	c1806	WB-1/102	AR
Campbell, John	083	1871	WB-3/29	AR
Campbell, John	029	1757	DB-1/180	AR
Campbell, John	010	1781	WB-C/6	AR
Campbell, John	070	1796	Orig. Only	AR
Campbell, John	065	1851	WB-I/170	AR
Campbell, John	020	1828	RB-L/297	AR
Campbell, John	070	1770	Orig. Only	SS/AR
Campbell, John	010	1781	HiDSC	AR-Copy
Campbell, John	073	1775	WB-A/189	
Campbell, John	083	1850	WB-2/19	AR
Campbell, John	085	1838	WB-I/43	AR
Campbell, John	028	1748	SS 877/316	
Campbell, John	063	c1833	WB-2/187	
Campbell, John A.	065	1869	WB-K/24	AR
Campbell, John D.	021	1890	WB-2/522	AR
Campbell, John W.	054	c1862	Orig. Only	AR
Campbell, Joseph	028	1812	WB-C/54	AR
Campbell, Joseph	085	c1805	WB-E/271	AR
Campbell, Joshua	030	1776	WB-1/109	
Campbell, Katharine	083	1823	WB-1/231	AR
Campbell, L. A.	054	1898	WB-6/186	CTY
Campbell, Lauchlin	029	1829	WB-B/175	AR
Campbell, Laughlin	081	1791	WB-1/95	AR
Campbell, Malcom	029	1813	WB-A/191	AR
Campbell, Malcom	081	1834	WB-6/337	AR
Campbell, Margaret	068	1830	WB-B/74	
Campbell, Margaret	011	1862	WB-1/299	
Campbell, Maria	100	1854	WB-43/10	AR
Campbell, Martha	081	1861	WB-12/121	AR
Campbell, Mary	046	1841	WB-C/87	AR
Campbell, Mary	083	1885	WB-3/331	AR

Name	Co.	Date	Recorded Copy	Original
Campbell, Mary	046	1806	WB-A/65	AR
Campbell, Mary	103	1894	WB-2/69	AR
Campbell, Mary A.	083	1891	WB-3/509	
Campbell, Mary M.	068	1863	WB-C/96	
Campbell, Mary P.	020	1852	RB-Q/648	AR
Campbell, Millie G.	013	1897	WB-D/76	AR
Campbell, Minerva	065	1899	WB-N/277	AR
Campbell, Montesquieu	070	1850	WB-C/510	AR
Campbell, Moses	046	c1782	WB-A/38	AR
Campbell, Murdock	029	1863	WB-C/444	AR
Campbell, Nancy	054	1862	WB-3/168	AR
Campbell, Nancy	083	1891	WB-3/509	
Campbell, Neill	029	1857	WB-C/361	AR
Campbell, Neill	029	1825	WB-B/129	AR
Campbell, Niel	068	1809	WB-A/244	
Campbell, Patrick	029	1775	Orig. Only	AR
Campbell, Penny	029	1829	WB-B/175	AR
Campbell, Perciphall	054	1854	WB-3/87	
Campbell, Peter	104	1817	WB-3/159	AR
Campbell, Richard	030	1774	WB-1/95	
Campbell, Robert	065	1795	WB-B/22	AR
Campbell, Robert	029	1827	WB-B/151	AR
Campbell, Robert	082	1831	WB-2/19	AR
Campbell, Robert	086	1806	WB-B/191	AR
Campbell, Robert M.	071	1871	WB-6/71	AR
Campbell, S. B.	003	1896	WB-B/347	AR
Campbell, Sallie M.	027	1878	WB-2/31	AR
Campbell, Sarah	022	1870	WB-E/40	AR
Campbell, Sarah	083	1829	WB-1/349	AR
Campbell, Solomon	030	1780	WB-1/141	
Campbell, Susanna	047	1819	WB-3/645	
Campbell, Thomas	060	1784	Orig. Only	AR
Campbell, Thomas	030	1785	WB-1/200	
Campbell, Thomas	054	1845	WB-2/319	AR
Campbell, Thomas S.	032	1889	WB-4/41	AR
Campbell, Vineyard	009	1839	OB-C2/220	AR
Campbell, Vineyard	053	1832	WB-5/137	AR
Campbell, William	082	1808	WB-1/121	AR
Campbell, William	029	1787	Orig. Only	AR
Campbell, William	053	1783	RW-1/104	
Campbell, William	029	1776	Orig. Only	AR
Campbell, William	070	1812	WB-AB/174	AR
Campbell, William	038	1899	WB-4/150	AR
Campen, Benjamin	009	1819	OB-A/293	AR
Campen, David	009	1841	OB-D/136	AR
Campen, Henry	009	1842	OB-D/280	AR
Campen, James	009	1851	OB-H/6	AR
Campen, James	009	1762	OWB/82	AR
Campen, Jane	009	N. D.	OWB/560	AR
Campen, Joram	009	c1771	OWB/108	AR
Campen, Joseph	009	1832	OB-B/217	AR
Campen, Joseph, Sr.	009	1815	OB-A/246	AR
Campen, Robert	009	c1785	OWB/202	AR
Campen, Robert	009	c1790	OWB/253	AR
Campen, Robert	009	c1795	OWB/307	AR
Campen, Robert	009	c1785	OWB/204	AR
Campen, Thomas	009	c1802	OWB/401	AR
Camplin, Henry	046	1805	WB-A/63	AR
Camplin, Jacob	090	1820	WB-3/47	
Canaday, C. D.	072	1880	WB-4/192	AR
Canaday, Cornelias	019	c1774	Orig. Only	AR
Canaday, Elijah	019	1841	WB-A/93	AR
Canaday, Frances	019	1877	WB-B/98	AR
Canaday, John	046	1845	WB-C/231	AR
Canaday, Joseph	035	1794	Orig. Only	AR-Nunc.
Canaday, Patrick	035	1761	WB-A/87	AR
Canaday, Richard	019	1824	WB-D/114	AR
Canaday, Samuel	N	c1728	Orig. Only	SS/AR
Canaday, Thomas	019	1795	WB-D/104	AR
Canaday, Wagstaff	099	1812	RB-10/317	AR
Canaday, William J.	029	1885	WB-E/366	AR
Canady, Alexander	075	1775	WB-I/133	AR
Canady, Benjamin	045	1873	WB-1/23	
Canady, C. W.	039	1899	WB-V/168	AR
Canady, Henry	045	1876	Orig. Only	AR
Canady, Jacob	047	1836	WB-4/125	
Canady, James L.	059	1882	WB-A/238	
Canady, Lewis	072	1844	WB-2/57	AR
Canady, Micajah	070	1881	WB-E/440	AR
Canady, Penelope	045	1879	WB-1/47	AR
Canady, Richard	028	1767	Orig. Only	AR
Canady, Richard	096	1746/7	Orig. Only	SS/AR
Canady, Uriah	072	1837	WB-1/161	AR
Canady, Willet	070	1842	WB-AB/354	AR
Candler, Zachairah	013	1845	WB-A/116	
Candy, Miles	009	1869	WB-1/34	CTY
Candy, Sarah	064	1890	Orig. Only	AR
Cane, Hudson M.	073	1866	WB-G/485	CTY
Cane, Nathaniel	077	1800	WB-E/114	AR
Cane, William	037	1761	WB-A/59	AR
Caneday, Elizabeth	078	1886	WB-19/187	
Canlape, Michaell	028	1743	Wills.6/L66	SS/AR
Cann, Cela	075	1885	WB-O/243	
Cannaday, Absalom	084	1899	WB-F/154	CTY
Cannaday, John	096	1791	Orig. Only	AR
Cannaday, Patrick	087	1811	WB-1/11	AR
Cannady, Abigail	046	1819	WB-B/72	AR
Cannady, Dorris	099	1845	RB-25/585	AR
Cannady, I. G.	036	1885	WB-A/74	CTY
Cannady, John F.	044	1896	WB-24/298	CTY
Cannady, Mary S.	099	1861	RB-31/559	AR
Cannady, Nathaniel	044	1894	WB-24/257	CTY
Cannady, Samuel H.	044	1888	WB-24/29	CTY
Cannady, William E.	044	1862	WB-21/567	CTY
Cannady, Wyatt	044	1855	WB-19/602	CTY
Cannady, Wyatt M.	044	1863	WB-21/746	CTY
Cannings, Joseph	002	1729	SS 876/197	SS/AR
Cannon, Ann	016	1851	WB-1/189	
Cannon, Caltern C.	024	1864	WB-D/26	AR
Cannon, Dennis	012	1874	WB-A/23	AR
Cannon, Edward	008	1729	Orig. Only	SS/AR
Cannon, Edward J.	VA	1893	098 WB-A/186	098 CTY
Cannon, Elizabeth	100	1835	WB-35/177	AR
Cannon, Ellis B.	SC	1897	080 WB-1/283	080 AR
Cannon, Emma J.	085	1887	WB-2/238	CTY
Cannon, Emma J.	054	1893	WB-5/483	CTY
Cannon, Henry	035	1781	WB-A/89	AR
Cannon, Henry	028	1767	Orig. Only	AR
Cannon, Jacob	077	1832	WB-F/204	AR
Cannon, James	016	1838	PQS.5/470	
Cannon, Jeremiah	057	1857	WB-B/238	AR
Cannon, Jeremiah	024	c1779	WB-B/132	AR
Cannon, Joel	020	1832	RB-M/225	AR
Cannon, John	099	1783	RB-1/188	AR
Cannon, John	028	1806	WB-B/259	AR
Cannon, John	057	1871	WB-C/41	AR
Cannon, Joseph A.	016	1887	WB-3/558	AR
Cannon, Joseph S.	VA	1882	077 WB-H/124	077 AR
Cannon, Joseph S.	VA	1882	Copy	100 AR
Cannon, Joseph S.	VA	1882	Copy	024 AR

Name	Co.	Date	Recorded Copy	Original
Cannon, Mary E.	079	1861	WB-1/72	AR
Cannon, Nancy	079	1865	WB-1/132	AR
Cannon, Rachel	077	c1781	Orig. Only	AR
Cannon, Sarah	009	c1733	OWB/14	AR
Cannon, Sarah E.	070	1877	WB-E/315	AR
Cannon, Theophilus	016	1884	WB-3/408	AR
Cannon, William F.	040	1892	WB-2/422	AR
Cannun, Joseph	024	1785	WB-B/82	AR
Canon, Edward	065	c1844	Orig. Only	AR
Canon, Job	065	1842	WB-H/105	AR
Canon, John	065	1794	WB-A/204	AR
Canon, Margaret	065	1802	WB-A/197	AR
Cansler, Alexander	060	1890	WB-4/419	AR
Cansler, John	021	1892	WB-2/569	
Cansler, Matilda	060	1893	WB-4/511	AR
Cansler, Peter	040	1873	WB-2/56	AR
Cansler, Philip	060	1854	Copy	040 AR
Cansler, Phillip	060	1854	WB-2/377	AR
Cansler, Phillip	060	1805	Orig. Only	AR
Cansler, William M.	060	c1891	Orig. Only	AR
Canter, James M.	104	1874	WB-6/92	AR
Canter, Jonathan	104	1896	WB-6/582	AR
Canter, Jones	022	1891	WB-E/449	AR
Cantrell, Fielding	SC	1898	050 WB-2/279	050 CTY
Cantrell, Isaac	073	1838	WB-F/13	AR
Cantrell, Jacob	073	1790	WB-B/102	AR
Cantrell, Joseph	073	1804	WB-D/127	AR
Cantrell, Nancy	084	1840	WB-B/245	CTY
Cantrell, W. H.	050	1889	WB-2/44	CTY
Cantrell, William	020	1837	RB-N/50	AR
Cantrill, Isaac, Sr.	020	1831	RB-L/628	AR
Canup (Knupp), Louisa C.	085	1899	WB-3/345	CTY
Canup, John	085	1862	WB-K/306	AR
Capall, Joseph	078	c1851	Orig. Only	AR
Capehart, Alanson	071	1893	WB-7/178	AR
Capehart, Celia	010	1889	WB-I/285	AR
Capehart, Celia	010	1832	WB-G/218	AR
Capehart, Cullen	010	1867	WB-H/185	AR
Capehart, George	010	1804	WB-E/227	AR
Capehart, George	010	1810	WB-F/170	AR
Capehart, George W.	010	1885	WB-I/192	
Capehart, Harry	101	1889	WB-A/182	AR
Capehart, Michael	010	1838	WB-G/311	AR
Capehart, Michael	010	1811	WB-F/179	AR
Capehart, Tristram	051	1849	WB-A/296	
Capehart, William	101	1897	WB-A/288	AR
Capehart, William J.	071	1898	WB-7/379	AR
Capehart, William J.	010	1895	WB-I/428 & 464	AR
Capel, Pleasant	082	1900	WB-7/45	AR
Capel, Thomas	071	1810	WB-3/27	AR
Capel, Thomas	086	1833	WB-D/162	AR
Capel, Thomas C.	005	1895	WB-D/363	AR
Capel, Tom	071	1881	WB-6/365	AR
Capel, William C.	082	1872	WB-6/94	AR
Capell, Ava	059	1887	WB-A/476	CTY
Caphart, Michael	010	1785	WB-D/18	AR
Caple, Edward	071	1795	WB-2/92	AR
Capper, Thomas	073	1780	WB-A/215	AR
Capps, Amy	046	1826	WB-B/368	AR
Capps, Caleb	030	1823	WB-3/155	
Capps, Caleb M.	030	1894	WB-5/216	AR
Capps, Caleb, Sr.	030	1823	WB-3/158	
Capps, Cason	073	1833	WB-E/308	AR
Capps, Dennis	030	1749	Orig. Only	SS/AR
Capps, Dennis	030	1803	WB-2/220	
Capps, Dennis	030	1839	WB-4/61	
Capps, Eliza	030	1882	WB-5/90	AR
Capps, Elizabeth	030	1841	WB-4/84	
Capps, Gideon	070	1867	WB-D/237	AR
Capps, Hillary	100	1841	WB-37/413	AR
Capps, James	053	1796	RW-1/276	AR
Capps, Jesse	030	1819	WB-3/115	
Capps, Joel	030	1831	WB-3/266	
Capps, John	065	1856	Orig. Only	AR
Capps, John	030	1795	WB-2/39	
Capps, John	100	1804	WB-12/164	AR
Capps, John, Sr.	009	c1803	OWB/414	AR
Capps, Joshua	100	1805	WB-13/94	AR
Capps, Malachi	030	1803	WB-2/232	
Capps, Mathew	056	1850	WB-1/639	AR
Capps, Polly	030	1831	WB-3/266	
Capps, Polly	001	c1851	WB-1/54	AR
Capps, R. M.	065	1893	WB-M/136	AR
Capps, Robert R.	001	1891	WB-2/486	AR
Capps, Shadrach	009	1842	OB-D/197	AR
Capps, Thomas	072	1823	WB-A/21	AR
Capps, Tully	030	1882	WB-5/91	AR
Capps, William	001	1898	WB-3/238	AR
Capts, Franky	018	1827	WB-C/78	
Capts, Moses	030	1815	WB-3/61	
Car, Patrick	010	1742	Orig. Only	SS/AR
Carawan, B. B.	074	1898	WB-1/146	AR
Caraway, Arche	005	1835	WB-B/54	AR
Caraway, Bedreadon	087	1844	WB-1/294	
Caraway, Charlotte	063	1850	WB-2/369	
Caraway, Susanah	103	1835	RD-7/70	AR
Carbrey, Thomas	NY	1830	046 WB-B/419	046 AR
Card, Benson, Sr.	099	1821	RB-22/457	AR
Card, Elizabeth	020	1792	WB-2/1	
Carden, Elizabeth	036	1892	WB-A/256	CTY
Carden, John	073	1896	WB-I/102	CTY
Cardin, Susan M.	046	1899	WB-G/170	AR
Cardwell, Edmund M.	084	1896	WB-F/71	CTY
Cardwell, Elizabeth	084	1865	WB-D/37	CTY
Cardwell, Joseph N.	084	1862	WB-C/368	CTY
Cardwell, Margaret	084	1850	WB-C/109	CTY
Cardwell, Maria	084	1860	WB-C/342	CTY
Cardwell, Peter A.	084	1847	WB-C/55	CTY
Cardwell, Thomas	044	1800	WB-5/48	CTY
Carell, John	087	c1814	WB-A/76	AR
Carely, William	104	1796	WB-1/452	
Carey, Elizabeth	035	1848	WB-2/35	AR
Carey, Matthew	072	c1767	Orig. Only	AR
Cargile, William	104	1846	WB-4/323	
Cargill, Elizabeth	044	1891	WB-24/173	CTY
Carington, John	073	1803	WB-D/110	
Carington, L. A.	070	1899	WB-H/197	
Carithers, John	085	1823	WB-H/206	AR
Carkeet, Benjamin	010	1808	WB-F/77	AR
Carl, Jacob	085	1858	WB-K/258	AR
Carleton, Arthur	024	1719	Orig. Only	SS/AR
Carley, Abslum	003	1878	WB-B/110	AR
Carley, Sarah	071	1809	WB-3/16	AR
Carlile, Atlas	083	1863	WB-2/201	AR
Carlile, Dennis	083	1865	WB-2/213	AR
Carlile, Edward	039	c1794	WB-A/156	
Carlile, James	083	1861	WB-2/168	AR
Carlile, Nancy	039	c1784	Orig. Only	AR
Carlile, Robert	037	1786	WB-C/36	AR

Name	Co.	Date	Recorded Copy	Original
Carlile, Robert	037	1815	WB-E/81	AR
Carlile, Sarah	037	1776	WB-A/245	AR
Carlile, William	083	1842	WB-1/410	AR
Carlile, William	037	1769	Orig. Only	AR
Carlilse, Thomas M.	047	1888	WB-6/504	AR
Carlisle, Cary	037	1831	WB-F/130	AR
Carlisle, Chloe	047	1883	WB-6/295	AR
Carlisle, Elizabeth	047	1881	WB-6/252	AR
Carlisle, Hardy	047	1871	WB-6/60	AR
Carlisle, Nathaniel	047	1812	WB-3/534	
Carlisle, Penelope	047	1878	WB-6/194	AR
Carlisle, Penny F.	037	1892	WB-H/217	AR
Carlisle, Sanders	083	c1822	WB-1/210	AR
Carlon, Richard	020	1782	RB-A/184	AR
Carlos, Archelus	020	1799	RB-C/357	
Carlton, A. M.	036	1887	WB-A/115	CTY
Carlton, A. W.	035	1898	087 WB-4/117	087 AR
Carlton, A. W.	035	1898	WB-4/520	AR
Carlton, Daniel	073	1856	WB-G/139	AR
Carlton, Elizabeth	104	1878	WB-6/162	AR
Carlton, Elizabeth	106	1873	WB-2/34	AR
Carlton, John	104	1855	WB-5/122	
Carlton, John	028	1829	WB-C/313	AR
Carlton, John L.	035	1884	WB-4/228	AR
Carlton, Lewis	104	1827	WB-4/101	AR
Carlton, Nathan	036	1892	WB-A/250	CTY
Carlton, Peter	035	c1840	WB-2/19	AR
Carlton, Pickens	017	1892	WB-B/209	AR
Carlton, Richard	028	1792	WB-A/284	AR
Carlton, Richard	028	1842	WB-D/66	AR
Carlton, Tearcey	028	1873	WB-E/90	
Carlton, Theroyal	035	1898	WB-4/523	AR
Carlton, Thomas	028	1837	WB-C/398	AR
Carlton, Thomas	104	1877	WB-6/137	AR
Carlton, Thomas	035	1795	WB-A/69	AR
Carlton, Thomas	014	1867	WB-1/24	CTY
Carlton, Thomas	104	1844	WB-4/300	AR
Carlyle, Ervin	083	1886	WB-3/449	AR
Carman, Joshua	029	1802	WB-A/56	AR
Carman, Malinda	029	1857	WB-C/387	AR
Carman, William	N	1727	SS 876/137	SS/AR
Carman, William R.	029	1867	WB-D/92	AR
Carmechal, Archibald	092	c1827	WB-4/15	
Carmichael, Catharine	082	1850	WB-4/34	AR
Carmichael, Catherine	082	1880	WB-6/191	AR
Carmichael, Daniel	082	1822	WB-1/231	AR
Carmichael, Daniel	082	1825	WB-1/261	AR
Carmichael, Effy	082	1869	WB-6/29	AR
Carmichael, Gilbert	029	1833	WB-B/221	AR
Carmichael, Hugh	082	1806	WB-1/112	AR
Carmichael, Jennet	082	1862	WB-4/158	AR
Carmichael, John	082	1837	WB-2/64	AR
Carmichael, John	085	1759	WB-A/38	
Carmichael, John B.	029	1838	WB-B/288	AR
Carmichael, Margaret	082	1806	WB-1/112	AR
Carmichael, Mary	082	1829	WB-1/303	AR
Carmichael, Thomas	073	1819	WB-D/559	AR
Carmichiel, Andrew	046	1831	WB-B/434	AR
Carmicle, Gracy	068	c1821	WB-B/15	
Carmon, Burton	028	c1853	Orig. Only	AR
Carmon, Mary G.	028	1893	WB-F/99	
Carmott, James	075	1812	WB-M1/237	AR
Carmott, John	072	c1791	Orig. Only	AR
Carn, John A.	090	1895	WB-6/371	
Carnal, Margaret	044	1834	WB-13/121	CTY
Carnal, Mary	078	1793	WI-1/79	AR
Carnal, Moses	044	1818	WB-8/155	CTY
Carnal, Patrick	020	1789	RB-B/273	
Carnal, Richard	078	1827	WI-10/325	
Carnal, Thomas	063	c1795	WB-1/328	
Carney, James	028	1807	WB-B/260	AR
Carney, Jane	028	1842	WB-D/58	AR
Carney, Jinny	079	1860	WB-1/52	AR
Carney, John	028	1765	Wills.9/232	AR
Carney, John	028	1796	WB-B/11	AR
Carney, Mary A.	037	1892	WB-H/204	AR
Carney, Rachel	070	1883	WB-E/491	AR
Carney, Richard	079	1881	WB-2/240	AR
Carney, Richard	047	1793	WB-3/210	
Carney, Stephen	037	1867	WB-G/308	AR
Carney, Stephen W.	047	1812	WB-3/527	
Carney, William	072	1858	WB-2/161	AR
Carns, Alexander	065	1815	WB-A/221	AR
Caroon, James	030	1845	WB-4/110	
Caroon, John	096	c1791	Orig. Only	AR
Caroon, Joseph	096	1863	WB-3/68	AR
Caroon, Thomas	096	1860	WB-3/62	AR
Caroon, Thomas	096	1856	Orig. Only	AR
Carothers, David	065	1865	WB-J/210	AR
Carothers, Hugh	065	1782	WB-A/207	AR
Carothers, Jane C.	065	1879	WB-K/342	AR
Carothers, John	065	1838	WB-E/175	AR
Carothers, Sarah	065	1798	WB-A/208	AR
Carpenter, A. W.	040	1884	WB-2/222	
Carpenter, Allen	005	1859	WB-C/146	AR
Carpenter, Alpheus	099	1887	WB-B/175	AR
Carpenter, Amelia	060	1859	WB-3/23	AR
Carpenter, Ann Sophia	040	1899	WB-3/36	AR
Carpenter, Caleb	060	1864	WB-3/74	AR
Carpenter, Christian	060	1800	Orig. Only	AR
Carpenter, Christopher	026	1867	WB-1/408	AR
Carpenter, D. W.	021	1899	WB-3/232	AR
Carpenter, Daniel	026	1877	WB-2/157	AR
Carpenter, Daniel	040	1853	WB-1/46	AR
Carpenter, David	060	1849	WB-2/323	AR
Carpenter, E. M.	086	1889	WB-F/356	AR
Carpenter, Elizabeth	060	1840	WB-2/27	AR
Carpenter, Elizabeth	060	1890	WB-4/434	AR
Carpenter, Elizabeth	086	1856	WB-E/316	AR
Carpenter, Emanuel	040	1898	WB-3/18	AR
Carpenter, Frederick	060	1848	WB-2/41	AR
Carpenter, G. B.	061	1893	WB-2/119	AR
Carpenter, Harriet	013	1897	Orig. Only	AR
Carpenter, Henry	060	1838	WB-1/417	AR
Carpenter, J. Wesley	060	1885	WB-4/300	AR
Carpenter, Jacob	026	1899	WB-3/26	AR
Carpenter, Jacob	060	1840	WB-2/31	AR
Carpenter, Jacob	060	1821	Orig. Only	AR
Carpenter, Jacob	021	c1899	WB-3/327	AR
Carpenter, Jacob	060	c1803	Orig. Only	AR
Carpenter, Jacob	060	1830	WB-1/185	AR
Carpenter, Jacob	107	c1849	WB-1/111	
Carpenter, Jacob J.	060	1863	WB-3/60	AR
Carpenter, Jacob L.	014	1896	WB-2/569	CTY
Carpenter, James H.	086	1889	WB-F/350	AR
Carpenter, John	060	1875	WB-4/140	AR
Carpenter, John	060	1809	Orig. Only	AR
Carpenter, John	060	1846	Orig. Only	AR
Carpenter, John	013	1895	WB-C/379	AR
Carpenter, John	026	1890	Orig. Only	AR

Name	Co.	Date	Recorded Copy	Original	Name	Co.	Date	Recorded Copy	Original
Carpenter, John, Sr.	040	1871	WB-2/23		Carraway, Charles	028	1837	WB-C/402	AR
Carpenter, Joseph	086	1853	WB-E/253	AR	Carraway, David	063	c1800	WB-B/362	
Carpenter, Joseph	026	c1863	Copy	021 AR	Carraway, Edward	028	1819	WB-C/181	AR
Carpenter, Joseph	026	1866	WB-1/388	AR	Carraway, Francis	028	1811	WB-C/22	AR
Carpenter, Joseph	021	1867	WB-1/247	AR	Carraway, Frederick	028	1852	WB-D/186	AR
Carpenter, Marcus M.	026	1864	WB-1/351	AR	Carraway, George P.	028	1847	WB-D/133	AR
Carpenter, Michael	060	1874	WB-4/120	AR	Carraway, Gideon	028	1777	Orig. Only	AR
Carpenter, Michael	060	1880	WB-4/233	AR	Carraway, H. J.	047	1895	WB-7/147	AR
Carpenter, Michael	026	1892	WB-2/445	AR	Carraway, Henry	028	1824	WB-C/243	AR
Carpenter, Moses	060	1858	WB-3/19	AR	Carraway, Henry	103	1784	Orig. Only	AR
Carpenter, Nancy	099	1893	WB-C/122	AR	Carraway, James	028	1773	Orig. Only	SS/AR
Carpenter, Peter	026	1866	WB-1/389	AR	Carraway, John	029	1795	Orig. Only	AR
Carpenter, Peter	070	1810	WB-AB/155		Carraway, John	028	1789	WB-A/194	AR
Carpenter, Peter	060	1845	WB-2/235	AR	Carraway, Jonathan	063	c1830	WB-2/178	
Carpenter, Peter	060	1817	Orig. Only	AR	Carraway, Joseph	028	1807	WB-B/297	AR
Carpenter, Peter	026	1874	WB-2/116	AR	Carraway, Joseph G.	063	1888	WB-4/24	AR
Carpenter, Sally	040	1875	WB-2/80	AR	Carraway, Joseph G.	063	1817	WB-2/43	
Carpenter, Samuel	046	1870	WB-E/25	AR	Carraway, Joshua	028	1839	WB-C/437	AR
Carpenter, Seth M.	074	1881	WB-1/58	AR	Carraway, Margaret	029	1808	WB-A/120	AR
Carpenter, Solomon	060	1894	WB-4/553	AR	Carraway, Mary	009	1827	OB-A/380	AR
Carpenter, Solomon	026	1862	WB-1/290	AR	Carraway, Mary	028	1856	WB-D/247	AR
Carpenter, Stephen	024	c1805	WB-B/39	AR	Carraway, Nathan	028	1803	WB-B/168	AR
Carpenter, William	092	1860	WB-5/46		Carraway, Nathaniel	028	1795	WB-A/325	AR
Carpenter, William	061	c1836	WB-1/14	AR	Carraway, Patience	028	1818	WB-C/161	AR
Carpenter, William L.	005	1883	WB-D/149		Carraway, Peter F.	019	1893	WB-B/235	AR
Carpenter, William L.	005	c1867	WB-D/6		Carraway, Sarah	028	1810	WB-C/14	AR
Carpenter, William T.	097	1897	WB-2/529	AR	Carraway, Sarah	009	1864	OB-L/443	AR
Carr, A. M.	059	1894	WB-B/92	CTY	Carraway, Sarah	009	c1855	028 WB-E/105	
Carr, Barbara	065	1858	WB-J/51	AR	Carraway, Snoad B.	059	1888	WB-A/540	CTY
Carr, Celia	037	1840	WB-F/246	AR	Carraway, Temperance	103	1886	WB-1/368	AR
Carr, Elias	039	1823	WB-G/159		Carraway, Thomas	028	1842	WB-D/42	AR
Carr, Elias	037	1822	WB-E/289	AR	Carraway, Thomas	028	1769	Orig. Only	AR
Carr, Elias	037	1900	WB-H/486	AR	Carraway, Warren	009	1895	WB-2/78	CTY
Carr, J. S.	009	1882	WB-1/306	CTY	Carraway, William	103	1865	RD-14/244	AR
Carr, Jacob W.	035	1898	WB-4/518	AR	Carraway, William	028	1783	Orig. Only	AR
Carr, James	035	1796	WB-A/65	AR	Carrawon, Frances	053	c1808	WB-4/94	
Carr, James	024	c1783	WB-A/143	AR	Carrawon, Green	009	1832	OB-B/185	AR
Carr, James	035	1882	WB-4/201	AR	Carrel, Jesse	087	c1802	WB-A/34	AR
Carr, Jane	090	1857	WB-4/303	AR	Carrel, Stephen	073	1828	WB-E/173	AR
Carr, John	035	1879	WB-4/149	AR	Carrel, Sterling	022	1813	WB-A/239	AR
Carr, John	035	1823	WB-A/90	AR	Carrell, Alexander	087	c1827	WB-A/125	AR
Carr, Jonas J.	037	1843	WB-F/289	AR	Carrell, Eli	032	1846	WB-1/493	
Carr, Joseph	035	1856	WB-2/106	AR	Carrell, Henry	084	1835	WB-B/137	CTY
Carr, Joseph	035	1781	WB-A/73	AR	Carrell, James	073	1842	WB-F/136	AR
Carr, Linda	035	1885	WB-4/241	AR	Carrell, John	056	1817	WB-1/275	AR
Carr, Mathew W.	059	1870	WB-A/11		Carrell, Sarah	056	1812	WB-1/388	AR
Carr, Matthew L.	045	1889	WB-1/166	AR	Carrell, Sarah	087	1855	WB-1/476	AR
Carr, Moses	039	1841	WB-L/16	AR	Carrell, William	044	1782	WB-1/355	CTY
Carr, Ozborn	035	1869	WB-4/18	AR	Carrell, William	056	1812	WB-1/391	AR
Carr, Patience	087	c1818	WB-A/86	AR	Carrender, Lewis	106	1896	WB-2/386	
Carr, Patrick	087	c1825	WB-A/118	AR	Carrick, James	085	1818	WB-G/494	AR
Carr, Rachel	065	1858	WB-J/52	AR	Carrier, Harvey D.	086	1890	WB-F/387	AR
Carr, Robert	065	1784	WB-D/129	AR	Carrigan, Adeline E.	085	1891	WB-2/473	CTY
Carr, Samuel	056	1822	WB-1/279	AR	Carrigan, Edward	073	1783	WB-A/261	AR
Carr, Susannah	081	1859	WB-11/302	AR	Carrigan, Hugh	065	1795	WB-A/170	AR
Carr, Thomas	087	c1798	WB-A/27	AR	Carrigan, James	016	1840	PQS.6/78	
Carr, William	037	1827	WB-F/77	AR	Carrigan, James E.	001	1866	WB-1/261	AR
Carr, William	005	1823	WB-A/92	AR	Carrigan, John	073	1831	WB-E/240	AR
Carr, William	035	c1753	087 DB-2/236		Carrigan, John	085	1822	WB-H/157	AR
Carr, William	035	1846	WB-2/3	AR	Carrigan, Lemuel	054	1900	WB-6/291	CTY
Carr, William	035	1754	SS 879/66	SS/AR	Carrigan, Robert	016	1874	WB-3/101	AR
Carr, William B.	100	1871	WB-51/39	AR	Carrigan, William	073	1782	WB-A/247	AR
Carr, William B.	100	c1863	Copy	103 AR	Carrigan, William	016	1845	WB-1/57	
Carr, William E.	012	1874	WB-A/26	AR	Carriker, John	016	1863	WB-2/98	
Carraway, Asa	028	1811	WB-C/27	AR	Carriker, Philip	085	1873	WB-1/196	CTY

Name	Co.	Date	Recorded Copy	Original
Carriker, William P.	016	1866	WB-2/134	
Carrill, John	035	c1761	087 DB-3/124	AR
Carringer, George	068	1804	WB-A/232	
Carrington, Duncan	073	1874	WB-H/92	CTY
Carrington, Ephraim	073	1822	WB-E/17	AR
Carrington, James	073	1816	WB-D/485	AR
Carrington, John	073	1803	WB-D/110	AR
Carrington, John B.	VA	1864	047 WB-6/97	
Carrington, John C.	073	1864	WB-G/457	CTY
Carrington, Nathaniel	073	1831	WB-E/241	AR
Carrington, Nathaniel	073	1856	WB-G/133	AR
Carrington, Priscilla	073	1844	WB-F/190	AR
Carrington, Thomas R.	044	c1864	WB-24/308	CTY
Carrington, William	073	1851	WB-F/476	AR
Carrol, John	044	1814	WB-7/468	CTY
Carroll, Benjamin	073	1846	WB-F/274	AR
Carroll, Calvin J.	090	1899	WB-6/496	AR
Carroll, E. I.	040	1900	WB-3/70	AR
Carroll, James	029	1890	WB-E/485	AR
Carroll, James	100	1834	WB-34/382	AR
Carroll, James G.	035	1864	WB-3/89	AR
Carroll, John	071	1760	WB-1/1	
Carroll, John	068	1822	WB-B/21	
Carroll, John	079	1897	WB-3/121	AR
Carroll, John D.	035	1885	WB-4/247	AR
Carroll, John L.	013	1895	WB-C/458	AR
Carroll, John L.	084	1895	WB-F/31	CTY
Carroll, Katharine	032	1880	WB-3/302	AR
Carroll, L. R.	087	c1885	Copy	035 AR
Carroll, Lewis	087	1872	WB-3/55	AR
Carroll, Margaret	040	1876	WB-2/109	AR
Carroll, Mary	030	1831	WB-3/269	
Carroll, Milbrough	015	1774	100 WB-1/275	AR
Carroll, Raiford	087	1848	WB-A/169	AR
Carroll, S. M.	040	1900	WB-3/71	AR
Carroll, Thomas	063	c1787	WB-1/135	
Carroll, Thomas	100	1813	WB-17/143	AR
Carroll, William	099	1856	RB-30/79	AR
Carroll, William	100	1828	WB-31/148	AR
Carroll, William C.	035	1884	WB-4/236	AR
Carron, James	096	c1763	WB-1/45	AR
Carrow, John	009	1879	WB-1/237	CTY
Carrow, John, Sr.	009	1849	OB-F/13	AR
Carrow, Joseph	028	1869	WB-E/20	
Carrow, Nelly Jane	009	1868	OB-M/312	AR
Carrow, Samuel F.	009	1887	WB-1/417	
Carrow, Sophia	009	1867	OB-M/219	AR
Carrowan, Frances	053	c1808	RW-1/502	
Carrowan, John	053	1791	RW-1/209	
Carrowon, John	053	1771	RW-1/19	AR
Carrowon, John	053	1836	WB-5/376	AR
Carrowon, William	053	1804	RW-1/374	AR
Carruth, Adam	060	1782	Orig. Only	AR
Carruth, Alexander	085	N. D.	WB-C/137	AR
Carruth, Ephraim	086	1842	WB-E/98	AR
Carruth, George	065	1829	WB-E/63	AR
Carruth, James	065	1776	WB-A/199	AR
Carruth, Margaret	086	1823	WB-C/16	AR
Carruth, Robert	086	1817	WB-C/63	AR
Carruth, Walter	085	1769	WB-A/46	AR
Carruth, Warren H.	080	1878	WB-1/42	AR
Carruthers, Alexander	028	1816	WB-C/135	AR
Carruthers, Clayton	028	1811	WB-C/37	AR
Carruthers, Eunice	028	1786	WB-A/139	AR
Carruthers, John	028	1752	DB-5/264	SS/AR
Carruthers, John	028	1756	SS 880/62	
Carruthers, John, Sr.	028	1811	WB-C/29	AR
Carruthers, Nathaniel	077	1750	Orig. Only	SS/AR
Carruthers, Robert	028	1758	SS 881/135	SS/AR
Carruthers, William	028	1772	Orig. Only	AR
Carson, Abel	085	1816	WB-G/421	AR
Carson, Alexander	073	1791	WB-B/137	AR
Carson, Andrew	054	1841	WB-2/222	AR
Carson, Andrew	060	1799	Orig. Only	AR
Carson, Anne	004	c1864	WB-1/12	AR
Carson, Bettie	004	1900	WB-A/236	AR
Carson, Caswell	079	1900	WB-3/206	AR
Carson, David	073	1799	WB-C/127	AR
Carson, George M.	064	1863	WB-1/87	AR
Carson, George S.	085	1887	WB-2/284	CTY
Carson, George S.	085	1887	Copy	064 AR
Carson, Harriet	064	1900	WB-2/496	AR
Carson, James	073	1808	WB-D/219	AR
Carson, James	085	c1773	WB-C/158	AR
Carson, James	085	c1774	WB-A/186	
Carson, James M.	040	1893	WB-2/458	AR
Carson, John	065	1819	WB-A/172	AR
Carson, John	037	1858	WB-G/157	AR
Carson, John	086	1846	WB-E/165	AR
Carson, John	085	1816	WB-G/418	AR
Carson, John	065	1812	WB-A/219	AR
Carson, John	085	1896	WB-3/114	CTY
Carson, John	086	1790	Orig. Only	AR
Carson, John	060	1789	Orig. Only	AR
Carson, John	085	c1803	WB-E/228	AR
Carson, John	014	1841	064 WB-2/301	064 AR
Carson, John C.	050	1886	WB-1/265	CTY
Carson, John M.	080	1890	WB-1/154	AR
Carson, John M.	006	1898	WB-E/357	AR
Carson, John S.	085	1863	WB-K/321	AR
Carson, Joseph McD.	080	1866	WB-1/194	AR
Carson, Joseph W.	040	1869	WB-2/7	AR
Carson, Lemuel	073	1896	WB-I/103	CTY
Carson, Margaret	073	1802	WB-D/61	AR
Carson, Martha	079	1882	WB-2/260	AR
Carson, Nancy	079	1900	WB-3/206	AR
Carson, Retta	085	1879	WB-1/494	CTY
Carson, Richard R.	039	1872	WB-U/41	AR
Carson, Richardine	065	1887	054 WB-5/165	054 CTY
Carson, Robert	054	1866	WB-3/184	AR
Carson, Robert	054	c1832	WB-2/147	AR
Carson, Robert	040	1896	WB-2/524	AR
Carson, Robert	054	c1798	WB-1/87	AR
Carson, Robert	VA	1892	004 WB-A/226	004 AR
Carson, Sarah	065	1830	WB-E/80	
Carson, Sarah	065	c1830	SC/02266	AR-Copy
Carson, Sarah	037	1851	WB-F/452	AR
Carson, Thomas	085	c1804	WB-F/45	AR
Carson, William	085	1759	WB-A/49	AR
Carson, William	055	1870	WB-A/5	
Carson, William	065	1847	WB-I/78	AR
Carson, William	065	c1846	004 WB-A/189	
Carson, William	090	1801	WB-1/175	AR
Carson, William	054	c1827	WB-2/90	AR
Carson, William M.	064	1863	WB-1/83	AR
Carstarphan, Martha	047	1819	WB-3/636	
Carstarphen, Exum	VA	1887	063 WB-3/292	063 AR
Carstarphen, James	047	1815	WB-3/570	
Carstarphen, William	071	1880	WB-6/315	AR
Carstarphen, William H.	063	1894	WB-4/141	AR

Name	Co.	Date	Recorded Copy	Original
Cartee, John	050	1893	WB-2/180	CTY
Carter, Abraham	029	1817	Orig. Only	AR
Carter, Alexander	028	1852	WB-D/189	AR
Carter, Alexander	029	1818	WB-A/251	
Carter, Alexander	041	1824	WB-2/219	AR
Carter, Anderson	090	1859	WB-4/330	AR
Carter, Ann	028	1826	WB-C/273	AR
Carter, Ann	072	1770	RW/L21	AR
Carter, Ann	072	1770	Orig. Only	SS/AR
Carter, B. H.	089	1896	WB-2/301	AR
Carter, Barney	104	1834	WB-4/183	AR
Carter, Benjamin	047	1796	WB-3/270	
Carter, Benjamin	020	1832	RB-M/159	AR
Carter, Benjamin H.	020	1879	WB-A/261	CTY
Carter, Bram	029	1882	WB-E/282	AR
Carter, Braxton	020	1848	RB-Q/3	
Carter, Charles	047	1810	WB-3/510	
Carter, Charles	028	1834	WB-C/365	AR
Carter, Cornelius	047	1776	WB-2/30	
Carter, Cox	029	1841	WB-B/355	AR
Carter, Cullen	010	1804	WB-E/233	AR
Carter, Daniel	084	1815	WB-A/121	CTY
Carter, David	053	1829	WB-4/608	AR
Carter, E. B.	084	1878	WB-E/147	CTY
Carter, Edward	070	1736	SS 877/142	
Carter, Elizabeth	090	1859	WB-4/331	AR
Carter, Elizabeth	028	1819	WB-C/179	AR-Nunc.
Carter, Elizabeth	075	1832	WB-N/73	AR
Carter, Elizabeth	029	1889	WB-E/450	AR
Carter, Elizabeth	022	c1860	WB-D/70	AR
Carter, Elizabeth	046	1819	WB-B/73	AR
Carter, Elizabeth	047	1777	WB-2/57	
Carter, Emma	041	1892	WB-4/332	AR
Carter, George	090	1835	WB-3/290	
Carter, George	084	1854	WB-C/193	CTY
Carter, George	028	1820	WB-C/191	AR
Carter, Giles	100	1790	WB-5/184	AR
Carter, Harden	084	1885	WB-E/304	CTY
Carter, Hattie L.	038	1885	WB-2/549	AR
Carter, Henry	053	1735	LGB-4/#33	SS/AR
Carter, Henry	029	1857	Orig. Only	AR
Carter, Henry	090	1843	WB-4/111	AR
Carter, Henry Clay	084	1896	WB-F/53	CTY
Carter, Isaac	051	1844	WB-A/214	
Carter, Isaac	092	1802	WB-3/53	AR
Carter, Isaiah S.	053	1891	WB-11/242	AR
Carter, Jacob	047	1798	WB-3/310	
Carter, James	073	1847	WB-F/355	AR
Carter, James	047	1776	WB-2/29	
Carter, James	085	1765	WB-A/43	
Carter, James	041	1884	WB-4/207	AR
Carter, James C.	106	1885	WB-2/194	
Carter, Jane	071	1764	WB-1/88	
Carter, Jane	046	1886	WB-E/452	AR
Carter, Jarret	089	1883	WB-2/114	AR
Carter, Jeremiah	071	1887	WB-6/559	AR
Carter, Jesse	020	1816	RB-G/126	
Carter, Jesse	028	1811	WB-A/163	AR
Carter, Jesse	037	1779	WB-B/11	AR
Carter, Jesse	084	1890	WB-E/454 & 470	CTY
Carter, Jesse	013	1838	WB-A/56	
Carter, John	022	1844	WB-C/169	AR
Carter, John	029	c1784	Orig. Only	AR
Carter, John	092	1846	WB-4/258	
Carter, John	087	1860	WB-1/561	AR
Carter, John	035	1783	WB-A/86	AR
Carter, John	056	1854	WB-1/680	AR
Carter, John	077	1801	WB-E/142	AR
Carter, John J.	037	1834	WB-F/155	AR
Carter, John S.	020	1893	WB-B/158	CTY
Carter, John, Sr.	047	1848	WB-4/268	
Carter, Joseph	028	1798	Orig. Only	AR
Carter, Joseph	047	1795	WB-3/238	
Carter, Joseph	092	c1832	WB-4/179	
Carter, Joshua	092	1846	WB-4/246	
Carter, Julia A.M.	099	1854	RB-28/540	AR
Carter, Kindred	037	1777	WB-A/260	AR
Carter, Landon	090	1838	Orig. Only	AR
Carter, Lemuel	020	1861	RB-S/434	AR
Carter, Lethia	005	1882	WB-D/126	AR
Carter, Littleton	104	1863	WB-5/361	
Carter, Louisa A.	044	1858	WB-20/459	CTY
Carter, Margaret	010	1836	WB-G/259	AR
Carter, Margaret	106	c1863	WB-1/88	AR
Carter, Martha A.	020	1871	WB-A/61	
Carter, Mary	069	1837	WB-1/417	AR
Carter, Mary M.	068	1895	WB-D/441	
Carter, Matthew	056	1793	WB-1/70	AR
Carter, Melvin E.	013	1895	WB-C/365	AR
Carter, Mial	046	1839	WB-C/35	AR
Carter, Minnie B.	071	1899	WB-7/443	AR
Carter, Moore	041	1805	WB-1/218	AR
Carter, Moses	053	1842	WB-6/196	AR
Carter, Naaman	087	c1810	WB-A/60	AR
Carter, Nathaniel	073	1822	WB-E/13	AR
Carter, Nathaniel	022	1782	Orig. Only	AR
Carter, Nelson	029	1842	WB-B/381	AR
Carter, Nicholas	046	1841	WB-C/89	AR
Carter, Peter	053	c1766	Orig. Only	AR
Carter, Phebe	032	1889	WB-4/56	AR
Carter, Phoebe	038	1898	WB-4/138	AR
Carter, Priscilla	051	1869	WB-C/28	AR
Carter, R. T.	020	1885	WB-A/432	CTY
Carter, Rebecca	071	1822	WB-3/264	AR
Carter, Rebecca	062	1899	WB-B/211	AR
Carter, Richard	089	1875	WB-2/29	AR
Carter, Richard	028	1818	WB-C/166	AR
Carter, Richard	071	1851	WB-5/98	AR
Carter, Robert	010	1784	WB-D/5	AR
Carter, Robert	047	1798	WB-3/307	
Carter, Ruth	099	1828	RB-20/351	AR
Carter, Samuel	092	1815	WB-3/115	AR
Carter, Samuel	022	1804	WB-A/44	AR
Carter, Samuel	046	1841	WB-C/88	AR
Carter, Sarah	081	1834	WB-6/360	AR
Carter, Sarah	028	1837	WB-C/405	AR
Carter, Sarah	047	1799	WB-3/331	
Carter, Sarah	084	1892	WB-E/519	CTY
Carter, Sarah	009	1815	OB-A/242	AR
Carter, Sarah	028	1836	WB-C/387	AR
Carter, Sarah B.	033	1857	WB-1/131	AR
Carter, Sarah H.	011	1875	WB-2/87	
Carter, Solomon	013	1873	WB-B/74	AR
Carter, Stephen	081	1827	WB-5/353	AR
Carter, Stephen	028	1803	WB-B/169	AR
Carter, Stephen D.	053	1869	WB-11/5	AR
Carter, Temperance	010	1836	WB-G/257	AR
Carter, Theodorick	084	c1833	WB-B/147	CTY
Carter, Thomas	084	1888	WB-E/402	CTY

Name	Co.	Date	Recorded Copy	Original
Carter, Thomas	016	1851	WB-1/196	
Carter, Thomas	084	1862	WB-C/369	CTY
Carter, Thomas	084	c1832	OW/14	AR
Carter, Turner	010	1835	WB-G/250	AR
Carter, Tyre	038	1872	WB-2/118	AR
Carter, W. B.	090	1888	WB-6/193	AR
Carter, Wilford	084	1869	WB-E/9	CTY
Carter, Wilie	071	1806	WB-2/310	AR
Carter, William	081	1827	WB-5/327	AR
Carter, William	041	1824	WB-2/214	AR
Carter, William	075	1819	WB-M1/329	AR
Carter, William	047	1810	WB-3/500	
Carter, William	026	1886	WB-2/302	AR
Carter, William C.	010	1826	WB-G/148	AR
Carter, William F.	084	1856	WB-C/238	CTY
Carter, William R.	069	1894	WB-5/436	AR
Carter, William W.	047	1868	WB-6/2	AR
Carter, William W.	047	1886	WB-6/438	AR
Carter, Willie B.	051	1850	WB-A/314	
Cartland, Herbert H.	046	1899	WB-G/129	AR
Cartner, Fredrick	085	1886	WB-2/161	CTY
Cartner, William	085	1841	WB-I/101	AR
Cartright, William	075	1734	SS 876/354	SS/AR
Cartwright, Abram	075	1763	WB-H/53	AR
Cartwright, Ahaz	075	1796	WB-L/76	AR
Cartwright, Albert	053	1892	WB-11/245	AR
Cartwright, Asa	018	1823	WB-C/23	
Cartwright, Benjamin	075	1801	WB-M1/46	AR-Nunc.
Cartwright, Benoni	075	1824	WB-M1/394	AR
Cartwright, Benoni	075	1882	WB-0/161	AR
Cartwright, Caleb	075	1891	WB-0/325	AR
Cartwright, Caleb	075	1797	WB-L/103	AR
Cartwright, Chloe	018	1857	WB-D/37	
Cartwright, Christopher	075	1760	WB-H/9	AR
Cartwright, Daniel	018	1822	WB-C/2	
Cartwright, Darius	075	1793	WB-L/1	AR
Cartwright, Davis	075	1866	WB-M2/90	AR
Cartwright, Deborah	018	1835	WB-C/178	
Cartwright, Eva	075	1899	WB-0/482	AR
Cartwright, Gideon	018	1837	WB-C/202	
Cartwright, Grace	075	1729	Orig. Only	SS/AR
Cartwright, Hezekiah	075	1793	WB-L/6	AR
Cartwright, Isaac	075	1826	WB-N/24	AR
Cartwright, Isaac	075	1776	WB-I/149	
Cartwright, Isaac E.	018	1854	WB-D/6	
Cartwright, James	075	1828	WB-N/42	AR
Cartwright, James	075	1824	WB-N/3	AR
Cartwright, James	075	1842	WB-N/174	AR
Cartwright, Jesse	075	1844	WB-N/189	AR
Cartwright, Jesse	075	1777	WB-I/113	AR
Cartwright, Jesse	075	1798	WB-M1/20	AR
Cartwright, Job	075	1776	WB-I/150	AR
Cartwright, John	075	1804	WB-M1/103	AR
Cartwright, John	037	1780	WB-B/54	AR
Cartwright, John	075	c1714	Orig. Only	SS/AR
Cartwright, John	075	1884	WB-0/184	AR
Cartwright, John	075	1790	WB-K/203	AR
Cartwright, John	075	1845	WB-N/195	AR
Cartwright, John	075	1835	WB-N/111	AR
Cartwright, John	075	1813	WB-M1/250	AR
Cartwright, John	075	1778	WB-K/13	AR
Cartwright, Joseph	018	1837	WB-C/224	
Cartwright, L. J.	106	1899	WB-2/455	
Cartwright, Lemuel	053	1839	WB-6/74	AR
Cartwright, Martin L.	018	1898	WB-E/293	AR

Name	Co.	Date	Recorded Copy	Original
Cartwright, Matthias	075	1807	WB-M1/151	AR
Cartwright, Olley	075	1893	WB-0/388	AR
Cartwright, Peter	018	N. D.	Extract	AR
Cartwright, Polly	018	1839	WB-C/245	
Cartwright, Rebecca	075	1840	WB-N/155	AR
Cartwright, Robert	075	1746	Orig. Only	SS/AR
Cartwright, Theophilus	018	1897	WB-E/282	AR
Cartwright, Thomas	075	1772	Orig. Only	AR
Cartwright, Thomas	075	1805	WB-M1/113	AR
Cartwright, Thomas	075	1707	Orig. Only	SS/AR
Cartwright, Thomas	075	c1751	Orig. Only	AR
Cartwright, Thomas	075	1777	Orig. Only	AR
Cartwright, Thomas	075	1762	WB-I/11	AR
Cartwright, Timothy	018	1818	Orig. Only	AR-Copy
Cartwright, William	075	1831	WB-N/66	AR
Cartwright, William	075	1806	WB-M1/117	
Cartwright, William	024	1730	Orig. Only	SS/AR
Cartwright, William	075	1732	SS 876/260	
Caruth, Mary	050	1850	WB-1/27	CTY
Caruthers, George	077	1821	WB-F/32	AR
Caruthers, John	085	1823	WB-H/696	
Caruthers, John	077	1752	Orig. Only	SS/AR
Caruthers, Samuel	073	1819	WB-D/565	AR
Caruthers, Stephen	077	c1857	WB-F/495	AR
Carver, David	029	1852	WB-C/219	AR
Carver, Elizabeth	029	c1832	WB-B/277	AR
Carver, Elizabeth	062	1900	Orig. Only	AR
Carver, Evergan	075	1856	WB-M2/37	AR
Carver, George	090	c1813	Orig. Only	AR
Carver, Isham	029	1860	WB-D/49	AR
Carver, James	011	c1778	WB-1/480	
Carver, James	075	1816	WB-M1/284	
Carver, James	011	1753	SS 877/93	SS/AR
Carver, James B.	AR	1889	Copy	029 AR
Carver, James, Sr.	011	1739	SS 877/233	SS/AR
Carver, Jesse	029	1806	WB-A/89	AR
Carver, Jobe	075	1799	WB-M1/25	AR
Carver, John B.	089	1857	WB-1/178	
Carver, Joseph	013	1857	WB-A/167	
Carver, Josiah	078	1857	WB-17/483	AR
Carver, Landrum	078	1842	WI-15/61	
Carver, Lazer	078	1838	WI-14/1	
Carver, Margaret	077	c1843	Orig. Only	AR
Carver, Mary	029	1841	WB-B/336	AR
Carver, Robert	029	1767	Orig. Only	AR
Carver, Robert	029	1852	WB-C/243	AR
Carver, Robert	029	1797	Orig. Only	AR
Carver, Samuel	011	1758	Orig. Only	SS/AR
Carver, Sidney	029	1860	WB-C/424	AR
Carver, William	078	1888	WB-19/225	
Carver, William	029	1767	Orig. Only	AR
Carver, William	078	c1819	Orig. Only	AR
Carver, William J.	075	1894	WB-0/411	AR
Cary, Jephthah	072	1840	WB-2/22	AR
Cary, John	072	1822	WB-A/18	AR
Cary, Jordan	073	1883	WB-H/332	CTY
Cary, Matthew	072	1794	RW/L42	AR
Cary, Richard	028	1816	WB-C/136	AR
Cary, Richard	074	1875	WB-1/75	AR
Cary, Samuel	073	1819	Orig. Only	AR
Cary, Sarah	028	1822	WB-C/218	AR
Cary, Shadrach	072	1823	WB-A/29	AR
Cary, Thomas	072	1812	WB-A/19	AR
Caryl, Joseph	065	1790	WB-A/211	AR
Caryl, Samuel	065	1771	WB-A/180	AR

Name	Co.	Date	Recorded Copy	Original
Case, C. Maggie	046	1882	WB-E/323	AR
Case, E. F.	050	1884	WB-1/253	CTY
Case, Ezekiel	046	1883	WB-E/355	AR
Case, Francis	086	1852	WB-E/226	
Case, John	030	1793	WB-2/11	
Case, John	013	1854	WB-A/160	
Case, Nannie	020	1900	WB-B/399	CTY
Case, William	046	1834	WB-B/500	AR
Casey, Cullen	103	1872	WB-1/44	AR
Casey, David	033	1844	WB-1/56	AR
Casey, Dempsey	030	c1814	WB-3/39	
Casey, Frederick	075	1834	WB-N/96	AR
Casey, J. Y.	106	1879	WB-2/113	AR
Casey, Jeremiah M.	082	1811	WB-1/145	AR
Casey, John, Sr.	019	1828	WB-D/113	AR
Casey, Mary Lyon	028	1801	WB-B/110	AR
Casey, Mary, Sr.	103	1860	RD-13/224	AR
Casey, Matthew	103	1891	WB-1/553	AR
Casey, Micajah	074	1880	WB-1/65	AR
Casey, Richard	103	1889	WB-1/459	AR
Casey, Richard	103	1855	RD-12/20	AR
Casey, Samuel	085	1826	WB-H/333	AR
Casey, Sarah	033	1839	WB-1/20	AR
Casey, Thomas	019	1767	Orig. Only	AR-Nunc.
Casey, William	033	1857	WB-1/161	AR
Casey, William	103	1900	WB-2/329	AR
Casey, Willis	075	1825	WB-N/10	AR
Casey, Willis	075	1897	WB-O/437	AR
Casey, Wright	103	1875	WB-1/91	AR
Cash, Briant	044	1831	WB-12/158	CTY
Cash, Bryant	044	1890	WB-24/141	CTY
Cash, John	070	1898	WB-H/128	AR
Cash, John, Sr.	078	1810	WI-5/201	AR
Cash, Joseph	044	1780	WB-1/288	CTY
Cash, Joseph	044	1878	WB-23/303	CTY
Cash, Mary	106	c1855	WB-1/26	AR
Cash, Moses	078	1860	WB-18/114	
Cash, Peter	044	1846	WB-17/4	CTY
Cash, Valentine	044	1891	WB-24/143	CTY
Cashatt, Jacob	081	1829	WB-6/23	AR
Cashatt, John	022	1813	WB-A/240	AR
Cashaw, Robert	024	1772	WB-1/55	AR
Cashin, Burrel	065	1829	WB-H/164	AR
Cashion, Mary	060	1864	WB-3/68	AR
Cashion, Susanna	085	1897	WB-3/195	CTY
Cashion, Wilmoth	054	1856	WB-3/96	AR
Cashon, Thomas	065	1835	WB-G/201	AR
Cashwell, Herring	087	1878	WB-3/180	AR
Cashwell, Hugh J.	029	1896	WB-F/83	AR
Cashwell, John N.	029	1897	WB-F/99	AR
Cashwell, John, Sr.	011	1882	WB-2/148	
Cashwell, John, Sr.	011	c1823	WB-2/349	
Caskat, John	032	c1847	WB-2/50	
Casner (Kasner), Andon	090	1817	WB-3/10	AR
Cason, Cannon	087	1847	WB-1/331	AR
Cason, Charity	087	c1808	Orig. Only	AR
Cason, Elijah	030	c1813	WB-3/25	
Cason, James	072	1788	WI/L57	AR
Cason, James F.	097	1865	WB-1/253	AR
Cason, John	005	1834	WB-B/38	AR
Cason, Polly	030	1865	WB-4/252	
Casper, Adam	085	1846	WB-K/19	AR
Casper, Alexander	085	1900	WB-3/379	CTY
Casper, Andrew	085	1874	WB-1/246	CTY
Casper, Cullen	010	1870	WB-I/23	AR
Casper, Henry	085	1832	WB-H/577	AR
Casper, Mary	010	1889	WB-I/268	AR
Casper, Peter	085	c1786	WB-C/139	AR
Casper, Thomas	010	c1870	WB-I/51	AR
Casper, Thomas	010	1828	WB-G/177	AR
Casper, Thomas D.	010	1897	WB-I/501	AR
Casper, William	010	1876	WB-I/78	AR
Cass, Ezekiel	054	c1829	WB-2/96	AR
Cass, James	104	1827	WB-4/98	AR
Cass, John	104	1814	WB-3/73	AR
Cass, Leander H.	104	1892	WB-6/443	AR
Cassadey, John	081	1851	WB-9/282	AR
Cassady, William	081	1881	WB-15/349	AR
Casse, Arthur	075	1795	WB-L/36	AR
Casse, Dorcas	075	1795	WB-L/38	AR
Casse, Enoch	075	1821	WB-M1/335	AR
Casse, James	075	1778	WB-K/10	AR
Casse, John	075	1824	WB-N/6	AR
Casse, John	075	1790	WB-K/205	AR
Casse, Thomas	075	1780	WB-K/45	AR
Cassel, John	085	1822	WB-H/152	
Cassel, Wesley	016	1897	WB-4/281	AR
Cassidey, James	070	1867	WB-D/218	AR
Cast, James	054	c1816	WB-1A/12	AR
Casteen, Jeremiah	070	1874	WB-E/278	AR
Casteen, Kizziah	076	1899	Orig. Only	AR
Castellaw, Levi	010	1883	WB-I/158	
Castellaw, William	010	1749	Orig. Only	SS/AR
Castellow, John	010	1868	WB-H/215	AR
Castellow, John	010	1816	WB-F/336	AR
Castephens, Thomas	104	1803	WB-2/101	AR
Caster, Jacob	085	1809	Orig. Only	AR
Casterem, John	092	1841	WB-4/167	
Castevens, John	092	1811	WB-3/97	
Castleberry, Rosanna	073	1860	WB-G/241	CTY
Castlebury, David	073	1847	WB-F/368	AR
Castlebury, J. Ruffin	099	1886	WB-B/136	AR
Castlebury, Sarah	099	1887	WB-B/199	AR
Castlen, John	GA	c1858	Copy	018 AR
Castner, Larrance	086	1831	WB-D/141	AR
Caswell, Harriet M.	028	1886	WB-E/401	
Caswell, Matthew	096	1754	SS 879/133	SS/AR
Caswell, Matthew	096	1771	WB-1/74	AR
Caswell, Matthew	096	1754	Orig. Only	AR-Copy
Caswell, Richard	034	1790	Copy	028 AR
Caswell, Richard	034	1790	Copy	SS/AR
Caswell, Samuel	010	1818	WB-G/44	AR
Caswell, Samuel	096	c1808	WB-2/26	AR
Catchey, John, Jr.	085	1815	WB-G/351	AR
Cate, Barnard	073	1826	WB-E/134	AR
Cate, Benjamin	073	1799	WB-C/136	AR
Cate, John, Jr.	020	1785	RB-B/84	AR
Cate, Joseph	073	1794	WB-C/28	AR
Cate, Lazarus	073	1803	WB-D/89	AR
Cate, Neverson C.	073	1883	WB-H/324	CTY
Cate, Ransom	073	1885	WB-H/399	CTY
Cate, Richard	073	1794	WB-B/259	AR
Cate, Richard	073	1806	WB-D/304	AR
Cate, Richard	022	1815	WB-A/253	AR
Cate, Richard	022	1831	WB-B/204	AR
Cate, Robert	073	1765	WB-A/66	
Cate, Solomon	073	1844	WB-F/216	AR
Cate, Thomas	073	c1811	WB-D/369	AR
Cate, Thomas	073	1816	WB-D/490	AR
Caten, Alicia	009	1855	OB-K/20	AR

Name	Co.	Date	Recorded Copy	Original
Caten, Liddie	009	1877	WB-1/186	CTY-Nunc.
Cater, George	103	1795	WI-B/72	AR
Cates, Elizabeth	078	1860	WB-18/146	AR
Cates, Huldah	073	1894	WB-I/35	CTY
Cates, Isaiah	078	1879	WB-19/89	AR
Cates, Jane	001	1892	WB-2/549	AR
Cates, John	078	1816	WI-7/88	AR
Cates, John D.	078	1881	WB-19/123	
Cates, John M.	078	1884	WB-19/157	AR
Cates, Joshua	078	1890	WB-19/276	AR
Cates, Lazarus	073	1855	WB-G/108	AR
Cates, Martha A.	078	c1900	WB-19/572	AR-Copy
Cates, Mary	020	1837	RB-N/114	
Cates, Mary B.	073	1897	WB-I/125	
Cates, Mary E.	036	1894	WB-A/336	CTY
Cates, Matthias	078	1815	WI-7/1	AR
Cates, Robert	078	c1816	Orig. Only	AR-Copy
Cates, Sarah	073	1896	WB-I/104	CTY
Cates, Sarah	078	1864	WB-18/371	AR
Cates, Solomon	073	1876	WB-H/140	CTY
Cates, Thomas	073	1863	WB-G/411	CTY
Cates, Wilson	020	1824	RB-I/313	
Cathcart, Gabriel	071	1768	WB-1/160	
Cathcart, John	065	1818	WB-A/177	AR
Cathcart, John	065	1856	WB-J/33	AR
Cathcart, William	PA	1806	066 WB-1/69	
Cathcart, William	PA	1806	075 WB-M1/324	075 AR
Cathcart, William	PA	1806	093 WB-2/54	
Cathcart, William	PA	1806	013 WB-C/352	
Cathey, Alexander	085	1766	WB-A/39	AR
Cathey, Andrew	065	1786	WB-A/181	AR
Cathey, Archibald	065	1811	WB-A/177	AR
Cathey, Barbara E.	013	1897	WB-D/97	AR
Cathey, Barbara E.	013	1897	049 WB-2/393	049 AR
Cathey, Eliza	065	1888	040 WB-2/351	040 AR
Cathey, Eliza	065	1888	WB-L/324	AR
Cathey, Faney	065	1838	WB-E/196	AR
Cathey, Fannie G.	040	1893	WB-2/452	AR
Cathey, G. C.	065	1896	WB-M/526	AR
Cathey, George	065	1802	WB-A/168	AR
Cathey, George	049	c1828	WI-A/29	AR
Cathey, George	060	1825	WB-1/17	AR
Cathey, George	065	1877	WB-K/271	AR
Cathey, Henry A.	065	1873	WB-K/123	AR
Cathey, Henry A.	065	c1871	054 WB-6/253	054 AR
Cathey, James	060	1781	Orig. Only	AR
Cathey, James	085	1757	WB-A/50	AR
Cathey, James A.	065	1854	WB-I/252	AR
Cathey, Jane	065	1826	WB-B/17	AR
Cathey, Jeane	065	1777	WB-A/202	AR
Cathey, John	060	1837	WB-1/398	AR
Cathey, John	065	1788	WB-A/186	AR
Cathey, John	046	1845	WB-C/222	AR
Cathey, Malinda	065	1882	WB-K/473	AR
Cathey, Margaret	065	1842	WB-H/99	AR
Cathey, Mary	065	1803	WB-B/19	AR
Cathey, Morris	040	1898	WB-3/26	AR
Cathey, Nancy H.	065	1883	WB-K/519	AR
Cathey, Sarah	065	1841	WB-H/65	AR
Catholic, Daniel	072	c1771	RW/L12	AR
Cathy, Alexander	065	c1844	Orig. Only	AR
Cathy, John	085	1764	WB-A/51	AR
Catlet, Clark	044	1849	WB-17/448	CTY
Catlett, Rebecca	039	1885	WB-U/350	AR
Catlett, Thomas A.	039	1878	WB-U/180	AR
Caton, Charles	085	1815	WB-G/389	AR
Caton, Jesse	009	1898	WB-2/133	CTY
Caton, John	085	c1830	Copy	033 AR
Caton, John	085	1830	WB-H/492	AR
Caton, John, Sr.	030	1880	WB-5/71	AR
Caton, Prudence	028	1866	WB-D/416	
Caton, Stephen	054	c1799	Orig. Only	AR
Caton, William Z.	009	1900	WB-2/220	CTY
Catton, John	078	1809	WI-5/159	AR
Catz, Youst	085	1798	WB-E/223	AR
Cauble, George	085	1850	WB-K/121	AR
Cauble, Henry	060	c1841	Orig. Only	AR
Cauble, Jacob	013	1891	WB-C/170	
Cauble, James H.	085	1891	WB-2/471	CTY
Cauble, John	085	1888	WB-2/313	CTY
Cauble, John	085	1822	WB-H/159	AR
Cauble, Michael	085	1821	WB-H/138	AR
Cauble, Peter	085	c1829	WB-H/478	
Cauble, Peter	085	1813	WB-G/278	AR
Cauble, Peter	085	1836	WB-H/679	AR
Caudill, Biddie	004	1891	WB-A/121	AR
Caudill, J. P.	004	1891	WB-A/126	AR
Caudill, James R.	004	1887	WB-A/85	AR
Caudle, Catharine	033	1866	WB-1/200	AR
Caudle, Celia	092	c1874	WB-6/57	
Caudle, Sampson	106	1888	WB-2/251	
Cauley, Samuel	026	1899	WB-3/33	AR
Caulk, Hannah	046	1847	WB-C/265	AR
Causett, Jane	020	1825	RB-I/344	
Causey, Ann	028	1804	WB-B/193	AR
Causey, Greenbury	037	1863	WB-G/235	AR
Causey, Hollon	028	1837	WB-C/408	AR
Causey, Hugh W.	081	1837	WB-7/93	AR
Causey, Isaac	081	1837	WB-7/79	AR
Causey, John	028	1779	Orig. Only	AR
Causey, Leavin	037	1793	WB-C/251	AR
Causey, Philip	037	1825	WB-F/35	AR
Causey, Zebulon	046	1809	Orig. Only	AR
Causway, Elizabeth	079	1859	WB-1/25	AR
Caven, Jane	054	1848	WB-3/29	
Cavena, Charles	037	1757	SS 879/208	SS/AR
Cavenagh, Ananias	019	1768	RB-A/14	AR
Cavenagh, Mary	019	1768	RB-A/27	AR
Cavenah, Mary M.	037	1794	WB-C/256	AR
Cavenaugh, James	035	1899	WB-4/533	AR
Cavenaugh, Silvester	035	1799	WB-A/63	AR
Cavender, Fanny	044	1849	WB-17/451	CTY
Cavender, Sally	030	c1815	WB-3/62	
Cavendish, George	044	1796	WB-3/250	CTY
Caveness, Henry	081	1824	WB-5/138	AR
Caveness, Matthew	022	1828	WB-B/143	AR
Caveness, Matthew	022	1808	WB-A/131	AR
Cavenner, Bryant	044	1827	WB-10/330	CTY
Caves, Cornelius	030	1801	WB-2/166	
Cavin, Arabella	054	1841	WB-2/226	AR
Cavin, John	054	1899	WB-6/268	CTY
Cavin, John	054	c1838	WB-2/196	AR
Cavin, John H.	054	1865	WB-3/171	AR
Cavin, Sarah	054	1862	WB-3/166	AR
Caviness, Elizabeth	081	1853	Orig. Only	AR
Caviness, Hannah	081	1873	WB-15/96	
Cavness, Isaac F.	081	1847	Orig. Only	AR
Cawdell, Buckner	085	1823	WB-H/191	AR
Cawdrey, Thomas	028	1748	SS 877/61	SS/AR

Name	Co.	Date	Recorded Copy	Original
Cawley, Penelope	047	1847	WB-4/257	
Cawthon, William	044	1811	WB-7/168	CTY
Cawthorn, Henry	100	1851	WB-41/45	AR
Cawthorn, James S.	100	1886	WB-51/218	AR
Cawthorn, John	100	1796	WB-7/197	AR
Cawthorn, John V.	100	1869	WB-51/80	AR
Caywood, Elizabeth	026	1846	WB-1/54	AR
Ceake, John	010	1796	WB-D/329	
Ceareley, Larkin	104	1841	WB-4/266	AR
Cearsey, Thomas	010	1731	SS 876/273	SS/AR
Cecil, Daniel J.	032	1845	WB-1/460	
Cecil, J. W.	032	1899	WB-4/407	AR
Cecil, Rachel	032	1839	WB-1/337	
Cecil, S. A.	032	1896	WB-4/301	AR
Cecil, Samuel	032	1875	WB-3/140	AR
Cecil, Solomon	046	1897	WB-G/32	AR
Cecil, William	032	1845	WB-1/471	
Cecil, Wilson L.	032	c1899	Orig. Only	AR
Cellars, Duncan	068	1809	WB-A/263	
Celley (Kelley), Grigry	056	1762	WB-1/782	AR
Celley (Kelley), John	056	1791	WB-2/271	AR
Celley (Kelley), Smith	077	1734	Orig. Only	SS/AR
Cerbey (Kirby), Absalom	056	1795	WB-1/90	AR
Cersey, Agnus	071	1824	WB-3/296	AR
Certain, Margaret	100	1808	WB-14/179	AR
Chadbourn, George	070	1891	WB-F/471	AR
Chadwell, William	084	1815	WB-A/122	CTY
Chadwick, Amelia	019	1813	WB-D/112	AR
Chadwick, Anson	019	1862	WB-A/261	AR
Chadwick, Barnabas	019	1835	WB-A/50	AR
Chadwick, David	028	1843	WB-D/82	AR
Chadwick, David	019	1774	WB-D/103	AR
Chadwick, David W.	028	1843	WB-D/90	AR
Chadwick, Gear	019	1803	WB-D/120	AR
Chadwick, Hubert S.	065	1899	WB-N/194	AR
Chadwick, James	019	1826	WB-D/115	AR
Chadwick, James	019	1895	WB-B/268	AR
Chadwick, James	072	1834	WB-1/128	AR
Chadwick, John	044	1805	WB-6/151	CTY
Chadwick, John	028	1859	WB-D/319	
Chadwick, John	028	1805	WB-B/215	AR
Chadwick, Margaret	046	1878	WB-E/222	AR
Chadwick, Margret	046	1845	WB-C/221	AR
Chadwick, Martin	019	1843	WB-A/106	AR
Chadwick, Mary	028	1884	WB-E/357	AR
Chadwick, Mary	019	1860	WB-A/242	AR
Chadwick, Noah	069	1781	WB-1/19	AR
Chadwick, Oliver	019	1876	WB-B/90	AR
Chadwick, Oliver	019	1830	WB-A/6	AR
Chadwick, Samll.	019	1749	SS 877/308	SS/AR
Chadwick, Samuel	019	1826	WB-D/108	AR
Chadwick, Solomon	019	1838	WB-A/80	AR
Chadwick, Thaddeus	019	1844	WB-A/111	AR
Chadwick, Thomas	019	1802	Orig. Only	AR
Chaffin, Joseph	033	1845	WB-1/67	AR
Chaffin, Nathan	033	1841	WB-1/33	AR
Chaffin, Nathan	085	1823	WB-H/698	AR
Chaffin, P.	085	1815	WB-G/364	AR
Chaffin, Stanley	085	1824	WB-H/295	AR
Chaffin, Washington	068	1896	WB-D/453	
Chafin, Elisabeth	090	1893	WB-6/301	AR
Chainey, James	085	1823	WB-H/225	AR
Chaires, John	SC	c1781	012 WB-B/70	012 AR
Chaires, Nathaniel	082	1795	WB-1/61	AR
Chairs, Samuel	082	1802	WB-1/92	AR
Chalk, Benjamin	040	1879	WB-2/144	AR-Nunc.
Chalk, William	075	1808	WB-M1/176	AR
Chalkhill, John	070	1758	DB-D/322	
Chalkill, John	N	1758	SS 882/4	SS/AR
Challes, Martha	084	1804	WB-A/3	CTY
Challis, Hugh	084	c1786	OW/80	AR
Chalmers, Charlott	068	c1858	WB-C/66	
Chalmers, John A.	068	c1858	WB-C/64	
Chamberlain, Barnett	032	1873	WB-3/86	AR
Chamberlain, Charles	018	18834	WB-C/151	
Chamberlain, James	075	1813	WB-M1/245	AR
Chamberlain, Joseph	018	1827	WB-C/86	
Chamberlain, Lewis	037	1887	WB-H/104	AR
Chamberlain, Milly	092	1849	WB-4/309	
Chamberlain, Nelson	018	1882	WB-E/107 & 110	AR
Chamberlain, Rebecca	075	1821	WB-M1/333	AR
Chamberlain, Samuel	059	1897	WB-B/187	CTY
Chamberlen, John	075	1753	Orig. Only	SS/AR
Chamberlin, Henry C.	018	18853	WB-C/377	
Chamberlin, Lewis T.	106	1869	WB-2/23	AR
Chamberlin, Robert	075	1765	WB-I/48	AR
Chambers, Alfred F.	009	1853	OB-I/126	AR
Chambers, Arthur	054	c1816	Orig. Only	AR
Chambers, Caleb	009	1824	OB-A/337	AR
Chambers, Charles	035	1862	WB-3/44	AR
Chambers, David	065	c1852	SC/08526	AR-Copy
Chambers, David	085	1835	WB-H/652	AR
Chambers, David	065	1859	WB-J/60	AR
Chambers, Edmond	075	1693	Orig. Only	SS/AR
Chambers, Edward	085	1816	WB-G/419	AR
Chambers, Edward J.	MS	1859	051 WB-B/23	
Chambers, Edward W.	016	1848	WB-1/145	
Chambers, Elenor	046	c1781	WB-A/39	AR
Chambers, Ezekiel	053	1787	RW-1/158	AR
Chambers, Ezekiel	009	1826	OB-A/368	AR
Chambers, Francis	072	1832	WB-1/91	AR
Chambers, Henry	054	1866	WB-3/185	AR
Chambers, Henry	006	1812	WB-A/26	AR
Chambers, Henry	054	c1802	WB-2/32	AR
Chambers, Henry	029	1796	Orig. Only	AR
Chambers, Henry	085	1817	WB-G/463	AR
Chambers, Jesse	078	1887	WB-19/215	
Chambers, John	013	1844	WB-A/94	
Chambers, John	053	1762	OB-A/53	
Chambers, John	009	1822	OWB/476	AR
Chambers, John	046	1800	WB-A/76	AR
Chambers, John	053	1806	RW-1/393	
Chambers, John	035	1875	WB-4/95	AR
Chambers, John C.	013	1896	WB-C/560	AR
Chambers, John W.	090	1863	WB-4/354	AR
Chambers, Joseph	016	1890	WB-4/51	AR
Chambers, Joseph	085	1818	WB-G/523	AR
Chambers, Joseph	054	1848	WB-3/25	AR
Chambers, Josiah	104	1844	WB-4/297	AR
Chambers, Mary	054	1854	WB-3/84	AR
Chambers, Mary A.	067	1882	WB-2/141	AR
Chambers, Maxwell	085	1855	WB-K/191	AR
Chambers, Maxwell	085	c1809	WB-G/133	AR
Chambers, Maxwell	085	1817	WB-G/488	AR
Chambers, Moses	078	c1858	Orig. Only	AR
Chambers, Nancy	104	1850	WB-5/1	AR
Chambers, Otho	085	c1830	WB-H/499	AR
Chambers, Panthea	085	1822	WB-H/685	AR
Chambers, Pinkney	084	1876	WB-E/120	CTY

Name	Co.	Date	Recorded Copy	Original
Chambers, Robert A.	067	1867	WB-1/143	AR
Chambers, Robert C.	054	1874	WB-4/149	CTY
Chambers, Ruth W.	054	1868	WB-3/204	AR
Chambers, Samuel	073	1809	WB-D/251	AR
Chambers, Samuel	085	1824	WB-H/269	AR
Chambers, Seth	104	1871	WB-6/26	AR
Chambers, Thomas	085	1824	WB-H/273	AR
Chambers, Thomas	085	1828	WB-H/532	AR
Chambers, William	085	1847	WB-K/47	AR
Chambers, William	078	1801	WI-2/326	AR
Chambers, William	013	1877	WB-B/149	AR
Chambers, William M.	078	1887	WB-19/201	
Chambers, Wilson	005	1866	WB-C/250	AR
Chamblain, Hardy	099	1805	RB-7/62	AR
Chamblee, Alfred	073	1853	WB-G/38	AR
Chamblee, John	099	1850	RB-27/116	AR
Chamblee, Rayford	099	1880	WB-A/204	AR
Chamblee, W. B.	099	1895	WB-C/484	AR
Chamblee, William	073	1851	WB-F/480	AR
Chambliss, Joel	044	1817	Copy	073 AR
Chambliss, Joel	044	1817	WB-8/84	CTY
Chamlee, Robert	099	1820	RB-16/3	AR
Chamly, Martha J.	051	1885	WB-C/333	AR
Chamness, Anthony	081	1858	WB-11/205	AR
Chamness, Anthony	022	1783	Orig. Only	AR
Chamness, Joseph	081	1818	WB-4/607	AR
Chamness, Joshua	022	1844	WB-C/153	AR
Chamness, Stephaness	022	1858	WB-D/27	AR
Chamness, William	081	1873	WB-15/119	AR
Champen, John	024	1751	Orig. Only	SS/AR
Champin, Richard	039	1858	WB-0/366	AR
Champion, Benjamin	047	1785	WB-3/94	
Champion, Benjamin	047	1769	WB-1/246	
Champion, Charles	044	1791	WB-2/244	CTY
Champion, Edward	024	1718	Orig. Only	SS/AR
Champion, Elizabeth	099	1825	RB-19/385	AR
Champion, Helen M.	026	1854	WB-1/169	AR
Champion, Henry	024	c1794	WB-A/299	AR
Champion, John	044	1787	WB-2/40	CTY
Champion, John	047	1774	WB-1/341	
Champion, John	086	1823	WB-D/8	AR
Champion, Joseph	044	1795	WB-3/200	CTY
Champion, Joseph	024	c1794	WB-B/115	AR
Champion, Orlando	024	1744	Orig. Only	SS/AR
Champion, R. C.	026	1890	WB-2/417	AR
Champion, Richard	026	1852	WB-2/144	AR
Champion, Susannah	024	1803	WB-B/216	AR
Champion, Tempea	086	1827	WB-D/77	AR
Champlain, Hannah	033	1893	WB-2/137	CTY
Champlin, Mary A.	072	1898	082 WB-6/581	082 AR
Champlin, Mary A.	072	1898	WB-4/384	
Chance, Elijah	082	1885	WB-6/306	AR
Chance, Elizabeth	029	1897	WB-F/114	AR
Chance, John	028	1782	Orig. Only	AR
Chance, Rebeka	057	1793	WB-A/122	AR
Chance, William	028	1767	Orig. Only	AR
Chancey, Edmund	075	1754	SS 881/55	SS/AR
Chancey, Sarah	009	1864	OB-L/439	AR
Chancy, Edmond	075	1803	WB-M1/83	AR
Chancy, Edmund	075	1778	WB-K/24	AR
Chancy, Martha	075	1887	WB-O/260	AR
Chancy, Martha S.	075	1887	WB-O/260	
Chancy, Neill	011	1882	WB-2/146	
Chancy, Samuel	027	c1848	WB-A/79	AR
Chandler, Daniel J.	078	1867	WB-18/479	AR
Chandler, David	044	1838	WB-14/279	CTY
Chandler, Elizabeth	064	1858	WB-1/59	AR
Chandler, Elize	020	1857	RB-R/532	AR
Chandler, George W.	020	1885	WB-A/487	CTY
Chandler, Henry R.	044	1791	WB-2/249	CTY
Chandler, Hosea A.	020	1864	RB-T/60	CTY
Chandler, J. H.	078	1891	WB-19/280	
Chandler, James W.	020	1889	WB-A/586	CTY
Chandler, Jane R.	044	1883	WB-23/472	CTY
Chandler, Jemima	046	1866	WB-D/314	AR
Chandler, Joel	044	1800	WB-5/107	CTY
Chandler, John	072	1782	RW/L31	AR
Chandler, John J.	020	1893	WB-B/129	CTY
Chandler, Joseph	020	1806	RB-E/229	AR
Chandler, Kindrick	067	1899	WB-2/391	AR
Chandler, Larkin	062	1867	WB-A/48	AR
Chandler, McVay	099	1862	RB-32/125	AR
Chandler, Nancy	020	1857	RB-R/532	AR
Chandler, Peggy	062	1881	WB-B/61	
Chandler, Samuel	084	1862	Orig. Only	CTY
Chandler, Stephen J.	078	1850	WB-13/340	AR
Chandler, Timothy	060	1834	WB-1/318	AR
Chandler, William	030	1801	WB-2/192	
Chandler, William	020	1844	Orig. Only	AR
Chandler, William	090	1795	WB-1/69	AR
Chandler, William D.	049	1891	WB-2/275	AR
Chaney, Abraham	092	1878	WB-6/146	AR
Chaney, Henry	097	1846	WB-1/28	AR
Chaney, James	065	1823	WB-A/225	AR
Chaney, Noah	097	1866	WB-1/272	AR
Chaney, William	N	1736	LGB-4/#30	SS/AR
Chaney, William	075	1749	Orig. Only	SS/AR
Chanler, Isaac	092	1797	WB-3/26A	AR
Chantrell, John	024	c1774	WB-A/114	AR
Chany, John	047	1760	WB-1/7	
Chapel, Mahaly	106	1884	WB-2/179	AR
Chapell, Thomas	071	1764	WB-1/84	
Chaplain, John	030	1831	WB-3/279	
Chaplain, Spence	030	1827	WB-3/225	
Chaplain, William	030	1831	WB-3/270	
Chaplain, William J.	030	1844	WB-4/106	
Chaplin, Caleb	030	1821	WB-3/118	
Chaplin, Caleb	030	1789	WB-1/235	Nunc.
Chaplin, David	081	1794	WB-2/4	AR
Chaplin, Edmund S.	030	1835	WB-4/6	
Chaplin, George	024	1784	WB-B/158	AR-Nunc.
Chaplin, James	030	1795	WB-2/54	
Chaplin, Jasper	030	1871	WB-5/16	
Chapman, Allen	SC	1823	005 WB-A/99	
Chapman, Belinda	028	1845	WB-D/112	
Chapman, Charles	071	1753	SS 880/23	SS/AR
Chapman, David	079	1872	WB-2/82	AR
Chapman, David, Sr.	022	1780	Orig. Only	AR
Chapman, David, Sr.	022	1815	WB-A/270	AR
Chapman, Dorcas	009	1822	OB-A/322	AR
Chapman, Elizabeth	044	1855	WB-19/612	CTY
Chapman, George	044	c1827	Orig. Only	CTY
Chapman, Harriet	024	1881	WB-E/97	AR
Chapman, Helen B.	037	1885	WB-H/6	
Chapman, Henry Lee	028	1808	WB-B/323	AR
Chapman, Jane	046	1863	WB-D/192	AR
Chapman, Jasper	096	1779	WB-1/105	AR
Chapman, Jesse	079	1862	WB-1/79	AR
Chapman, Jesse	028	1825	WB-C/261	AR
Chapman, John	028	1784	WB-A/77	AR

Name	Co.	Date	Recorded Copy	Original
Chapman, John	104	1837	Copy	003 AR
Chapman, John	019	1770	Orig. Only	SS/AR
Chapman, John	047	1768	WB-1/229	
Chapman, John	104	1837	WB-4/216	AR
Chapman, Joshua	019	c1771	WB-D/106	AR
Chapman, Lucy	059	1897	WB-B/199	CTY
Chapman, Lydia	044	1878	WB-23/321	CTY
Chapman, Mary	077	1788	WB-C/376	AR
Chapman, Mary	075	1729	SS 876/207	SS/AR
Chapman, Nancy	044	1846	WB-16/529	CTY
Chapman, Nancy M.	021	1868	WB-2/1	
Chapman, Richard	096	1792	Orig. Only	AR
Chapman, Robert	044	1874	WB-23/132	CTY
Chapman, Russell	037	1874	WB-G/456	AR
Chapman, Samuel	028	1807	WB-B/266	AR
Chapman, Sarah	028	1835	WB-C/385	AR
Chapman, Seth	028	1833	WB-C/363	AR
Chapman, Verina S.	013	1890	WB-C/12	AR
Chapman, W. L.	021	1885	WB-2/336	
Chapman, Weeks	028	1812	WB-C/43	AR
Chapman, William C.	046	1820	WB-B/85	AR
Chappel, Andrew J.	044	1884	WB-23/515	CTY
Chappel, George	030	N. D.	WB-3/60	
Chappel, Hannah	024	c1808	WB-C/25	AR
Chappel, Henry	077	1829	WB-F/162	AR
Chappel, Isaac	024	1817	WB-C/53	AR
Chappel, James	024	c1814	WB-C/23	AR
Chappel, James	024	1836	WB-C/192	AR
Chappel, Jonathan	077	c1860	WB-F/532	AR
Chappel, Josiah	024	1806	WB-B/242	AR
Chappel, Malachi	077	1775	WB-C/185	AR
Chappel, Marachi	063	1812	WB-2/12	
Chappel, Mary	077	1853	WB-F/434	AR
Chappel, Mary	071	c1799	WB-2/153	AR
Chappel, Richard	024	1735	LGB-4/#11	SS/AR
Chappel, Robert	077	1774	WB-C/135	AR
Chappel, Ruth	046	1885	WB-E/411	AR
Chappel, William T.	010	1882	WB-I/137	
Chappell, Darling A.	044	1893	WB-24/224	CTY
Chappell, Edward	099	1881	WB-A/241	AR
Chappell, Exum	077	1893	WB-H/247	AR
Chappell, Francis	077	1898	WB-H/310	AR
Chappell, Gideon	077	1811	WB-E/366	AR
Chappell, Gideon	077	1873	WB-H/52	AR
Chappell, Henry R.	077	1899	WB-H/315	AR
Chappell, James R.	106	c1863	WB-1/107	
Chappell, John	077	1802	WB-E/171	AR
Chappell, John W.	044	1895	WB-24/266	CTY
Chappell, Joseph	077	1803	WB-E/198	AR
Chappell, Marcy	077	1803	WB-E/205	AR
Chappell, Margaret	077	1894	WB-H/254	AR
Chappell, Mark	077	1824	WB-F/77	AR
Chappell, Martha	010	1898	WB-I/556	
Chappell, Mary	030	1825	WB-3/204	
Chappell, Mary	071	1797	WB-2/161	AR-Nunc.
Chappell, Rainer	077	1825	WB-F/101	AR
Chappell, Richard	044	1847	WB-17/138	CTY
Chappell, Robert	077	1807	WB-E/267	AR
Chappell, Ruth	106	c1856	WB-1/54	AR
Chappell, Sabrah C.	024	1895	WB-E/238	AR
Chappell, Samuel	077	1825	WB-F/103	AR
Chappell, Sherrel	106	c1862	WB-1/83	AR
Chappell, Squires	077	c1855	WB-F/492	AR
Chapple, Ambrose	046	1824	WB-B/181	AR
Chapple, Judith R.	005	1829	WB-B/1	AR
Chapple, Micajah	024	1801	WB-B/239	AR
Chapple, Richard	024	1766	WB-A/110	AR
Charles, Benjamin H.	075	c1839	Orig. Only	AR
Charles, Daniell	N	c1687	Orig. Only	SS/AR
Charles, Davidson	038	1896	WB-3/570	AR
Charles, Elisha	046	1875	WB-E/144	AR
Charles, Elizabeth	046	1831	WB-B/440	AR
Charles, Francis M.	037	1881	WB-G/599	AR
Charles, George W.	075	1877	WB-O/82	AR
Charles, Hannah	077	1752	Orig. Only	SS/AR
Charles, James	092	1781	WB-1/145	AR
Charles, James G.	076	1898	WB-A1/230	AR
Charles, Jeane	077	c1688	Orig. Only	SS/AR
Charles, John	103	1823	RD-5/72	AR
Charles, John	077	1780	WB-C/434	AR
Charles, John	N	N. D.	Orig. Only	SS/AR
Charles, John W.	099	1829	RB-20/143	AR
Charles, Levin	032	1833	WB-1/226	
Charles, Millicent	075	1882	WB-O/149	AR
Charles, Samuel	077	1774	WB-C/145	AR
Charles, Samuel	077	1728	SS 876/186	SS/AR
Charles, Stephen	075	1843	WB-N/183	AR
Charles, Stephen	075	1837	WB-N/133	AR
Charles, William	077	1771	WB-C/94	AR
Charles, William	N	1687	Orig. Only	SS/AR
Charles, William	046	1796	WB-A/50	AR
Charlescraft, Thomas	046	1795	WB-A/45	AR
Charlet, John	028	1798	WB-B/41	AR-Nunc.
Charlotte, Eliza Jane	028	1879	WB-E/195	
Charlton, Celatha	028	1844	WB-D/102	AR
Charlton, Jasper	010	1797	WB-E/12	AR
Charlton, Jasper	010	1782	WB-C/43	AR
Charlton, Job	024	c1804	WB-B/186	AR
Charlton, Job	024	1898	WB-E/278	AR
Charlton, John	024	c1768	WB-A/110	AR
Charlton, John	024	1792	WB-A/70	AR
Charlton, John	024	1736	LGB-4/#50	SS/AR
Charlton, Thomas J.	024	1848	WB-C/287	AR
Charlton, William	024	c1772	WB-A/116	AR
Charlton, William	024	c1795	WB-B/116	AR
Charters, John	084	1827	WB-A/197	
Charters, John	084	c1826	SC/06308	AR-Copy
Chason, Joseph	029	1815	WB-A/225	AR-Nunc.
Chason, Richard	035	1788	WB-A/67	AR-Nunc.
Chasten, J. M.	070	1892	WB-G/61	AR
Chasten, Joseph	035	1867	WB-3/114	AR
Chasten, Mary	035	1888	WB-4/331	AR
Chasten, Richard	035	1868	WB-3/129	AR
Chasten, Richard	077	1715	Orig. Only	SS/AR
Chatham, Benjamin	047	1787	WB-3/138	
Chatterton, Thomas	NY	1898	Copy	029 AR
Chatwin, Joseph	072	1779	Orig. Only	AR
Chauncey, Susan	009	1897	WB-2/123	CTY
Chauncy, Walley	009	1764	OWB/92	AR
Chavis, Gibia	044	1777	WB-1/143	CTY
Chavis, J. B.	051	1898	WB-C/540	
Chavis, Sallie	081	1857	WB-10/498	
Chavis, William	044	1854	WB-19/334	CTY
Chavise, Thomas	081	1874	WB-15/146	
Chears, Vachel T.	097	1867	WB-1/289	AR
Cheatham, Asenath F.	098	1887	WB-A/78	CTY
Cheatham, Isham	044	1871	WB-23/43	CTY
Cheatham, Isham J.	039	c1899	WB-V/238	
Cheatham, James	100	1797	WB-9/138	AR
Cheatham, James F.	099	1886	WB-B/155	

Name	Co.	Date	Recorded Copy	Original
Cheatham, James F.	099	1890	WB-B/422	AR
Cheatham, John A.	099	1886	WB-B/154	AR
Cheatham, Kinchin	104	1834	WB-4/174	AR
Cheatham, Thomas G.	044	1897	WB-24/372	CTY
Cheatham, Thomas G.	044	1897	Copy	099 AR
Cheaves, Mary	099	1793	RB-2/486	AR
Cheek, Aaron W.	104	1891	WB-6/404	AR
Cheek, Anderson	099	1880	WB-A/158	AR
Cheek, Charles C.	022	1900	WB-F/153	AR
Cheek, Cylus	065	c1808	WB-A/92	AR-Copy
Cheek, Edward	039	1866	WB-S/330	AR
Cheek, Elbert A.	100	1873	WB-51/67	AR
Cheek, Elcy	103	c1846	Orig. Only	AR
Cheek, Elizabeth	001	1886	WB-2/315	AR
Cheek, F. J.	047	1896	WB-7/178	
Cheek, Fritz A.	098	1892	WB-A/154	CTY
Cheek, Goodin	081	1892	WB-16/219	AR
Cheek, H. A.	001	1899	WB-3/278	AR
Cheek, Henderson	004	1897	WB-A/180	AR
Cheek, J. W.	073	1875	WB-H/111	CTY
Cheek, James A.	100	1863	WB-50/76	AR
Cheek, James B.	068	1855	WB-C/36	
Cheek, Joab	068	1827	WB-B/49	
Cheek, John	022	1892	WB-E/480	AR
Cheek, John	073	1889	WB-H/467	CTY
Cheek, John S.	100	1880	WB-51/152	AR
Cheek, Josiah	081	1874	WB-15/153	AR
Cheek, Josiah	081	1874	Copy	022 AR
Cheek, Louisa F.	047	1896	WB-7/179	AR
Cheek, Mary H.	100	1864	WB-50/114	AR
Cheek, Masting	073	1847	WB-F/331	AR
Cheek, Merrett	073	1899	WB-I/145	CTY
Cheek, R. T.	100	1841	WB-37/480	AR
Cheek, Richard	004	1866	WB-1/19	AR
Cheek, Richard	068	1837	WB-B/103	
Cheek, Richard	073	1868	WB-G/555	CTY
Cheek, Richard	009	1745	SS 878/144	SS/AR
Cheek, Robert	001	1865	WB-1/248	AR
Cheek, Sarah	065	1868	WB-J/245	AR
Cheek, Tony	047	1884	WB-6/331	AR
Cheek, W. H.	098	1892	WB-A/153	CTY
Cheek, Wade H.	098	1899	WB-A/336	CTY
Cheek, William	104	1896	WB-6/578	AR
Cheek, William	100	1800	WB-10/213	AR
Cheek, William	092	1802	WB-3/54A	AR
Cheek, William A.	MS	1897	100 WB-51/539	
Cheek, William N.	001	1867	WB-1/294	
Cheeke, Thomas L.	028	1815	WB-C/111	AR
Cheesborough, Emeline F.	013	1897	WB-D/55	AR
Chelpen, Leaven	005	1819	WB-2/16	AR
Cheney, Benjamin	053	1813	RW-1/475	AR
Cherry, Aaron	037	1835	WB-F/182	AR
Cherry, Addison P.	018	1886	WB-E/147	
Cherry, Arter	010	1871	WB-I/37	AR
Cherry, Bernice	009	1896	WB-2/89	CTY
Cherry, Brister	037	1869	WB-G/330	AR
Cherry, Caesar	010	1885	WB-I/203	
Cherry, Caroline	037	1866	WB-G/283	AR
Cherry, Charles	009	1812	OB-A/525	AR
Cherry, David	060	1800	Orig. Only	AR
Cherry, David	037	1833	WB-F/145	AR
Cherry, David	065	1865	WB-J/106	AR
Cherry, Eli	063	1860	WB-2/465	
Cherry, Elizabeth	037	1841	WB-F/250	AR
Cherry, Elizabeth	079	1862	WB-1/101	AR
Cherry, Erastus	037	1891	WB-H/196 & 206	AR
Cherry, Faithfull	063	1788	WB-1/145	
Cherry, Felisha	063	1898	WB-4/232	AR
Cherry, Frances	010	1871	WB-I/37	
Cherry, Henry R.	037	1867	WB-G/299	AR
Cherry, Irene	009	1844	OB-E/209	AR
Cherry, Isaac	063	1789	WB-1/151	
Cherry, James	010	1826	WB-G/150	AR
Cherry, James	063	c1785	WB-1/356	
Cherry, James	030	1801	WB-2/181	Nunc.
Cherry, James	086	1856	WB-E/307	AR
Cherry, James	010	1854	WB-G/511	AR
Cherry, Jenney	063	c1822	WB-2/85	
Cherry, Jeremiah	009	1845	OB-F/38	AR
Cherry, Jesse	063	1823	WB-2/89	
Cherry, Job	063	1814	WB-2/22	
Cherry, Joel	063	1818	WB-2/51	
Cherry, Joel	097	1848	WB-1/52	AR
Cherry, John	010	1808	WB-F/92	AR
Cherry, John	096	c1766	WB-1/40	
Cherry, John	009	1839	OB-C2/98	AR
Cherry, John	009	c1858	Orig. Only	CTY
Cherry, John, Sr.	009	1870	WB-1/38	AR
Cherry, Jonah	030	1805	WB-2/271	
Cherry, Jonathan	063	1818	WB-2/58	
Cherry, Joseph B.	010	1882	WB-I/155	
Cherry, Joseph O.	010	1887	WB-I/224	AR
Cherry, Julia	037	1868	WB-G/316	AR
Cherry, Julius A.	009	1864	OB-L/447	AR
Cherry, Lemuel	009	1754	SS 879/94	SS/AR
Cherry, Luke	063	1811	WB-2/5	
Cherry, Mary	009	1865	OB-L/471	AR
Cherry, Mary	037	1886	WB-H/39	
Cherry, Mary F.	074	1885	WB-1/80	
Cherry, Mercer	009	1838	OB-C2/82	AR
Cherry, Peggy	079	1892	WB-3/1	AR
Cherry, R. C.	009	1860	OWB/541	AR
Cherry, Robert	086	1826	WB-D/54	AR
Cherry, Robert	037	1820	WB-E/254	AR
Cherry, Samuel	037	1815	WB-E/110	
Cherry, Samuel	037	1816	WB-E/126	AR
Cherry, Samuel	063	1847	WB-2/336	
Cherry, Sarah	030	1807	WB-2/302	
Cherry, Solomon	037	1808	WB-D/340	AR
Cherry, Solomon	010	1777	WB-B/111	AR
Cherry, Susanna	010	1814	WB-F/254	AR
Cherry, T. A.	079	1891	WB-2/543	AR
Cherry, Thomas	010	1812	WB-F/217	AR
Cherry, Tillman R.	079	1890	WB-2/479	AR
Cherry, Wiley	047	1896	WB-7/171	AR
Cherry, William	010	1803	WB-E/188	AR
Cherry, William G.	063	1881	WB-3/218	
Cherry, William J.	065	1891	WB-M/6	AR
Cherry, William W.	010	1845	WB-G/387	AR
Cherry, Willis W.	035	1801	WB-A/79	AR
Cheshen, John	010	1728	Orig. Only	SS/AR
Cheshier, John	085	1832	WB-H/549	AR
Cheshire, Alexander	024	1858	WB-C/428	AR
Cheshire, Alexander	024	1860	WB-D/2	AR
Cheshire, Elizabeth	037	1870	024 WB-E/159	
Cheshire, Elizabeth	037	1870	WB-G/342	AR
Cheshire, Jinny	085	1817	WB-G/482	AR
Cheshire, Jonathan	054	1888	WB-5/250	CTY

Name	Co.	Date	Recorded Copy	Original
Cheshire, Joseph B.	037	1900	WB-H/478	AR
Cheshire, Richard	011	c1842	WB-1/191	
Cheshire, Tennison	033	1854	WB-1/112	AR
Cheshire, Theo. P.	037	1893	WB-H/248	AR
Chesnut, John R.	028	1838	WB-C/410	AR
Chesnut, Owen	028	1862	WB-D/364	AR
Chesnutt, Daniel	087	c1889	Orig. Only	AR
Chesnutt, David	087	1846	WB-1/319	AR
Chesnutt, David	087	1831	WB-1/119	AR
Chesnutt, Driver	087	1830	WB-1/112	AR
Chesnutt, Eleanor C.	035	1895	WB-4/469	AR
Chesnutt, Elizabeth	087	1857	WB-1/500	AR
Chesnutt, J. P.	056	1887	WB-3/432	AR
Chesnutt, Jacob	087	c1805	Orig. Only	AR
Chesnutt, Jacob	087	c1826	Orig. Only	AR
Chesnutt, Joshua	087	1850	WB-1/372	AR
Chesnutt, Joshua J.	087	1851	WB-1/399	AR
Chesnutt, Nicholas	087	1887	WB-3/338	AR
Chesnutt, Robert	087	1868	WB-3/3	AR
Chesnutt, William C.	035	1895	WB-4/467	
Chesnutt, William K.	087	1898	Copy	035 AR
Chesnutt, William K.	087	1898	WB-4/79	AR
Cheson, Abraham	092	1791	WB-3/4A	
Cheson, James	077	1727	SS 876/105	SS/AR
Chesson, A. L.	101	1891	WB-A/194	AR
Chesson, Anne	077	1727	SS 876/127	SS/AR
Chesson, Elizabeth	096	1814	WB-2/57	AR
Chesson, Friley F.	101	1897	WB-A/292	AR
Chesson, James	101	1884	WB-A/125	AR
Chesson, John	024	1807	WB-B/225	AR
Chesson, John	096	c1766	WB-1/67	AR
Chesson, Mollie	101	1891	WB-A/199	AR
Chesson, Samuel	101	1807	SC/05731	AR-Copy
Chester, John	N	c1733	SS 876/328	SS/AR
Chester, Samuel	070	1758	DB-D/359	SS/AR
Chester, William	053	1886	WB-11/179	AR
Chestney, C. M.	TN	1894	049 WB-2/306	049 AR
Chestnutt, Anna B.	087	1887	WB-3/361	AR
Chestnutt, Charles	087	1838	WB-1/192	AR
Chestnutt, Gavin L.	035	1856	WB-2/97	AR
Cheston, Martha	009	1797	OWB/331	AR
Chevallier, Urbain	070	1792	Orig. Only	AR
Chevens, Nathaniel	002	1719/0	SS 875/218	
Cheves, John	039	1810	WB-C/169	AR
Cheves, Margaret	039	1889	WB-U/493	AR
Cheves, Thomas	099	1772	RB-1/10	AR
Chew, Henry	019	1758	SS 882/125	SS/AR
Chew, James	077	c1767	Orig. Only	AR
Chew, Mary	024	c1794	WB-B/67	AR
Chewning, George	005	1803	WB-2/17	AR
Chewning, Susannah	005	1875	WB-D/45	AR
Chewning, Thomas	005	1897	WB-D/411	AR
Cheyney, William S.	103	1900	WB-2/319	AR
Chilcutt, Elijah	046	1874	WB-E/134	AR
Child, Francis	073	1792	WB-B/204	AR
Child, Francis	TN	1823	073 WB-E/271	073 AR
Child, James	011	1855	WB-1/244	
Child, Wilson	073	1811	WB-D/277	AR
Childers, Alfred	060	1898	WB-5/81	AR
Childers, Ausburn	092	1878	WB-6/120	AR
Childers, George P.	060	1864	WB-3/73	AR
Childers, Hiram	006	1893	WB-E/266	AR
Childers, Keltury	092	1861	WB-5/52	
Childers, Robert	060	c1787	Orig. Only	AR
Childers, Zelpha	003	1879	Orig. Only	AR

Name	Co.	Date	Recorded Copy	Original
Childres, William	092	1861	WB-5/54	
Childress, Mary	078	1896	WB-19/407	AR
Childress, Miles	021	1888	WB-2/438	AR
Childress, Sarah	092	1891	WB-6/332	AR
Childress, William	090	1822	WB-3/84	AR
Childress, Willis	104	1898	WB-7/285	AR
Childs, Alvira	060	1880	WB-4/214	AR
Chiles, John	082	1786	WB-1/51	AR
Chiles, Sarah	005	1827	WB-A/132	AR
Chiles, Thomas	005	1820	WB-2/19	AR
Chilson, Arnold W.	001	1865	WB-1/236	AR
Chilson, Asa	085	1871	WB-1/90	CTY
Chilton, John	020	1806	RB-E/291	AR
Chilton, Olive	092	c1871	Orig. Only	AR
Chilton, Raleigh	092	1869	WB-6/8	
Chilton, Stephen A.	092	1900	WB-6/564	AR
Chilton, Tabbitha	092	1889	WB-6/291	AR
Chinn, Jesse	092	1830	WB-4/25	
Chinn, Perry	092	1848	WB-4/287	
Chipman, John	046	1835	WB-B/516	AR
Chipman, Mary	046	1874	WB-E/125	AR
Chipman, Paris	046	1801	WB-A/71	AR
Chisenhall, Davis	073	1877	WB-H/171	CTY
Chisholm, Alexander	083	1891	WB-3/516	AR
Chisholm, Alexander	083	c1880	068 WB-D/432	
Chisholm, Daniel	068	1864	WB-C/111	
Chisholm, Malcom	067	1844	WB-1/10	AR
Chisholm, Mary	067	1850	WB-1/57	AR
Chisniel, Peter	030	c1811	WB-3/9	
Chitmore, Jesse	086	1856	WB-E/309	AR
Chittem, John	030	1829	WB-3/246	
Chittim, John	060	1819	Orig. Only	AR
Chitton, Winney	030	1832	WB-3/290	
Chittum, Peter	030	1824	WB-3/166	
Chittum, Polly	030	1819	WB-3/116	
Chittum, Sarah	030	1785	WB-1/194	
Chitty, Charles	090	1836	WB-3/308	
Chitty, W. T. A.	051	1897	WB-C/518	Nunc.
Chitwood, J. M.	086	1863	WB-E/412	AR
Chivers, Edward	070	1772	WB-C/43	AR
Chizenall, Alexander	073	1796	WB-C/78	AR
Choat, Sabret	006	1821	WB-A/42	AR
Choat, Sallie	004	1897	WB-A/193	AR
Choate, Enock	VA	1833	Copy	018 AR
Choate, Josiah M.	065	1870	WB-K/49	AR
Chocke, George	077	1779	WB-C/233	AR
Chrisman, Elizabeth	046	1851	WB-C/342	
Chrisman, George	046	1841	WB-C/314	AR
Chrisman, Henry	046	1847	WB-C/316	AR
Chrisman, Jacob	001	1876	WB-2/78	AR
Chrisman, Jacob	086	1804	Orig. Only	AR
Chrisman, Joseph	046	1825	WB-B/208	AR
Chrismon, Catherine	046	1842	WB-C/106	AR
Chrisp, William	063	c1783	WB-1/107	
Chrispin, Daniel	057	1877	WB-C/57	AR
Christ, Philip	070	1895	WB-G/351	AR
Christ, Rudolph	090	1833	WB-3/258	AR
Christain, Christopher	067	1783	Orig. Only	SS/AR
Christenberry, William	047	1806	WB-3/460	
Christenbury, Calep	065	1863	WB-J/169	AR
Christenbury, James	065	1846	Orig. Only	AR
Christenbury, Nicholas	065	1814	WB-A/221	AR
Christian, Charles B.	090	1882	WB-6/7	AR
Christian, Drury	100	1785	WB-4/135	AR
Christian, Eliza	067	1892	WB-2/311	

Name	Co.	Date	Recorded Copy	Original
Christian, John	067	1831	WB-1/20	
Christian, Maryan	024	1823	WB-C/104	AR
Christian, Thomas	073	1852	WB-G/23	AR
Christiansen, Georgia	GA	1890	013 WB-C/563	013 AR
Christie, Jesse	047	1810	WB-3/507	
Christman, Balthasar	090	1797	WB-1/97	AR
Christman, Christina	038	1866	WB-1/263	AR
Christman, Daniel	090	1818	WB-3/24	AR
Christman, Elizabeth	090	1848	WB-4/253	AR
Christman, Jacob	046	1779	WB-A/40	AR
Christman, John	046	1853	WB-C/409	AR
Christman, John Daniel	090	1822	WB-3/83	
Christmas, Charles	073	1812	WB-D/322	AR
Christmas, Henry	100	1793	WB-6/247	AR
Christmas, Jane Y.	100	1820	WB-22/287	AR
Christmas, John	100	1784	WB-4/42	AR
Christmas, John	073	1783	WB-A/264	AR
Christmas, John	015	1777	100 WB-2/128	AR
Christmas, Lewis Y.	100	1862	WB-49/414	AR
Christmas, Mary L.	100	1821	WB-23/218	AR
Christmas, Mary W.	001	c1856	WB-1/97	AR
Christmas, Richard	073	1833	WB-E/300	AR
Christmas, Thomas	100	1816	WB-20/70	AR
Christmas, Thomas	VA	1769	100 WB-1/105	
Christopher, Jane	049	1885	WB-2/126	AR
Christopher, John	073	1840	WB-F/56	AR
Christopher, John	084	1830	WB-B/31	CTY
Christopher, John	003	1888	WB-B/246	AR
Christopher, Rebecca	003	1898	WB-B/376	
Christopher, Simon	046	1812	WB-A/80	AR
Christophers, Frank C.	099	1880	WB-A/169	AR
Christy, Rachael	020	1831	RB-L/627	
Chronicle, William	060	1786	Orig. Only	AR
Chunn, Joseph	013	1876	WB B/137	AR
Chunn, Robert	085	1850	WB-K/119	AR
Chunn, Thomas	085	1823	WB-H/216	AR
Chunn, William	085	1845	WB-K/8	AR
Church, Amos	104	1863	WB-5/364	
Church, Constant	RI	c1782	019 WB-D/107	019 AR
Church, Elijah	104	c1854	Orig. Only	AR
Church, John	030	1819	WB-3/109	
Church, John, Sr.	104	1875	WB-6/110	AR
Church, Joseph	024	1723	Orig. Only	AR
Church, Joseph	030	1723	SS 876/1	SS/AR
Church, Thomas	010	1804	WB-E/235	AR
Church, Thomas	077	1807	WB-E/275	AR
Church, Wiley	006	1897	WB-E/328	AR
Church, William	044	1814	WB-7/429	CTY
Church, William	010	1800	WB-E/101	AR
Church, William F.	104	1895	WB-6/524	AR
Churchhill, Larry	045	1881	WB-1/72	AR
Churchill, Benjamin	028	1880	WB-E/221	
Churchill, Lewis F.	086	1899	WB-G/10	AR
Churchwell, Chapple H.	045	1897	WB-1/269	AR
Churchwell, James	010	1789	WB-D/113	AR
Churchwell, Mary	037	1846	WB-F/333	AR
Churchwell, Sally	010	1855	WB-H/14	AR
Churton, William	024	c1768	WB-A/120	AR
Cimbrew, Cathorine	020	1855	RB-R/343	AR
Cimmins, Robert	046	1837	WB-B/574	AR
Cimmins, Samuel	046	1826	WB-B/224	AR
Civil, William	028	1781	Orig. Only	AR
Clack, Francis E.	050	1900	WB-2/335	CTY
Clack, Frederick	044	1852	WB-19/68	CTY
Claghorn, Shuball	063	1793	WB-1/196	
Claghorn, Shubell	063	1787	WB-1/136	
Claghorn, Timothy	063	1789	WB-1/149	
Clagon, Smith M.	101	1889	WB-A/172	AR
Clamens, John	009	1801	OWB/385	AR
Claments, Peyton	044	1775	WB-1/100	CTY
Clampet, George	006	c1835	WB-A/2	AR
Clampet, William	090	1843	WB-4/133	AR
Clampitt, Richard	090	1820	WB-3/55	
Clancy, George	073	1813	WB-D/396	AR
Clancy, Phoebe	073	1873	WB-H/71	CTY
Clandance, George	072	c1787	WI/L9	AR
Clandance, Mary Ann	072	c1789	Orig. Only	AR
Clanton, Dudley	047	1853	WB-4/353	
Clanton, Dudley	100	1817	WB-20/174	AR
Clanton, Edward	100	1784	WB-4/19	AR
Clanton, Jesse R.	047	1851	WB-4/315	
Clanton, Martha W.	100	1848	WB-39/454	AR
Clanton, William	100	1789	WB-5/79	AR
Clanton, William	015	1774	100 WB-1/266	AR
Clanton, William C.	100	1862	WB-49/538	AR
Clap, Barney	073	1844	WB-F/229	AR
Clap, Judy	073	1826	WB-E/99	AR
Clapham, Joseph	010	1733	SS 876/315	SS/AR
Clapp, Abraham	046	1884	WB-E/326	AR
Clapp, Alfred	022	1899	WB-F/109 & 113	AR
Ciapp, Daniel	PA	1882	Copy	075 AR
Clapp, Daniel	046	1848	WB-C/294	AR
Clapp, Daniel F.	046	1885	WB-E/417	AR
Clapp, Emmanuel	073	1846	WB-F/327	AR
Clapp, George	046	1846	WB-C/254	AR
Clapp, George	046	1866	WB-D/301	AR
Clapp, Henry	081	1890	WB-16/190	AR
Clapp, Isaac	046	1832	WB B/470	AR
Clapp, J. Henry	046	1839	WB-C/45	AR
Clapp, Jacob	046	1846	WB-C/256	AR
Clapp, Jacob, Sr.	046	1832	WB-B/444	AR
Clapp, John	046	1866	WB-D/322	AR
Clapp, John	084	1882	WB-E/257	CTY
Clapp, John J.	046	1882	WB-E/326	AR
Clapp, John P.	046	1798	WB-A/51	AR
Clapp, Joseph W.	013	1900	WB-D/380	AR
Clapp, Joshua	046	c1884	Orig. Only	AR
Clapp, Loderick	073	1778	WB-A/203	
Clapp, Martha E.	MA	1897	013 WB-D/184	013 AR
Clapp, Riley	046	1864	WB-D/228	AR
Clapp, Tobias	046	1800	WB-A/64	AR
Clardy, Elizabeth	044	1811	WB-7/148	CTY
Clardy, James	011	c1793	WB-1/484	
Clardy, John, Sr.	044	1855	WB-19/669	CTY
Clare, Hannah	077	1727	SS 876/118	SS/AR
Clark, A. M.	079	1896	WB-3/90	AR
Clark, Absolom	064	1883	WB-2/151	AR
Clark, Alexander	060	1842	WB-2/136	AR
Clark, Alexander	054	1869	WB-4/34	AR
Clark, Alexander	029	1826	WB-B/150	AR
Clark, Anna M.	099	1899	WB-D/248	AR
Clark, Arabella	037	1860	WB-G/192	AR
Clark, Archibald	035	c1770	WB-A/76	AR
Clark, Archibald	029	c1793	Orig. Only	AR
Clark, Archibald	VA	1829	044 WB-11/311	044 CTY
Clark, Archibald	068	1824	WB-B/38	
Clark, Archibald	029	1765	Orig. Only	AR
Clark, Bella	070	1808	WB-C/58	AR
Clark, Benjamin	011	c1783	WB-1/489	

Name	Co.	Date	Recorded Copy	Original
Clark, Benjamin	099	1883	WB-A/432	AR
Clark, Beverly	005	1797	WB-A/55	AR
Clark, Burrell	097	1843	WB-1/5	AR
Clark, Caroline	081	1894	WB-16/285	AR
Clark, Catherine	029	1832	WB-B/212	AR
Clark, Cathren	029	1816	WB-A/235	AR
Clark, Charles A.	009	c1859	Copy	AR/CRX
Clark, Charlott	005	1863	WB-C/186	AR
Clark, Christopher	005	1790	WB-A/1	AR
Clark, Christopher	054	1890	WB-5/320	CTY
Clark, Christr.	010	1803	WB-E/216	AR
Clark, Colin M.	047	1868	WB-6/3	AR
Clark, Corina	047	1885	WB-6/412	AR
Clark, Cornelius	060	1789	Orig. Only	AR
Clark, Cornelius	060	1823	Orig. Only	AR
Clark, Cornelius	005	1797	WB-2/15	AR-Nunc.
Clark, Daniel	081	1813	WB-4/28	AR
Clark, Daniel	011	c1854	WB-1/240	
Clark, David	011	c1798	WB-1/376	
Clark, David	072	c1777	RW/L8	AR
Clark, David	047	1829	WB-4/55	
Clark, Deliverance	028	1844	WB-D/97	AR
Clark, Diana	035	1828	WB-A/90	AR
Clark, Dougan	046	1855	WB-C/439	AR
Clark, Dugand	011	1807	DB-34/160	
Clark, Duncan	070	1850	WB-C/515	AR
Clark, E. M. Ann	053	1814	RW-1/487	
Clark, E. McDaniel	049	1897	WB-2/374	AR
Clark, Edmond B.	032	c1863	WB-2/261	AR
Clark, Edward	053	1900	WB-11/354	AR
Clark, Eleanor	065	1803	WB-A/214	AR
Clark, Elijah	001	1864	WB-1/223	AR
Clark, Elizabeth	060	1900	WB-5/160	AR
Clark, Elsy	092	1827	WB-4/1	AR
Clark, Francis	054	1889	WB-5/288	CTY
Clark, G. W.	060	1888	WB-4/391	AR
Clark, George	030	1784	WB-1/176	
Clark, George	009	c1793	OWB/294	AR
Clark, George	010	1724	SS 876/8	SS/AR
Clark, Gilbert	029	1798	WB-A/14	AR
Clark, Gilbert	029	1819	WB-B/28	AR
Clark, Hance	046	1791	WB-A/50	AR
Clark, Hannah	081	1799	WB-2/52	AR
Clark, Harriet	005	1844	WB-B/180	AR
Clark, Harriet C.	065	1886	WB-L/135	AR
Clark, Henry	037	1788	WB-C/76	AR
Clark, Henry	037	1785	WB-C/8	AR
Clark, Henry	009	1825	OB-A/347	AR
Clark, Henry S.	079	1869	WB-2/25	AR
Clark, Henry T.	037	1874	WB-G/451	AR
Clark, Ickhebud	075	1790	WB-K/191	AR
Clark, J. Adger	013	1891	WB-C/75	AR
Clark, Jacob	VA	1858	090 WB-4/324	090 AR
Clark, James	079	1877	WB-2/158	AR
Clark, James	060	1795	Orig. Only	AR
Clark, James	065	1807	WB-A/216	AR
Clark, James	100	1857	WB-49/96	AR
Clark, James	073	1844	WB-F/191	AR
Clark, James	060	1815	Orig. Only	AR
Clark, James	022	1896	WB-F/24	AR
Clark, James	051	1834	WB-A/67	
Clark, James	028	1806	WB-B/254	AR
Clark, James	073	1854	WB-G/46	AR
Clark, James	065	1824	WB-B/15	AR
Clark, James	029	1807	WB-A/95	AR
Clark, James	073	1796	WB-C/71	AR
Clark, James	071	1782	WB-1/262	AR
Clark, James A.	065	1863	WB-J/171	AR
Clark, James B.	046	1888	WB-E/506	AR
Clark, James E.	105	1894	WB-3/102	AR
Clark, James F.	009	1865	OB-L/478	AR
Clark, James M.	040	1890	WB-2/409	AR
Clark, James S.	079	1862	WB-1/83	AR
Clark, James W.	037	1844	WB-F/302	AR
Clark, James W.	073	1860	WB-G/245	AR
Clark, James, Sr.	N	c1757	Orig. Only	SS/AR
Clark, Jesse	013	1871	WB-B/44	AR
Clark, John	073	1880	WB-H/236	CTY
Clark, John	009	c1809	OB-A/142	AR
Clark, John	046	1888	WB-E/512	AR
Clark, John	046	1883	WB-E/352	AR
Clark, John	029	1818	WB-A/248	AR
Clark, John	037	1867	WB-G/300	AR
Clark, John	046	1790	WB-A/55	AR
Clark, John	039	1833	WB-J/244	AR
Clark, John	100	1815	WB-19/119	AR
Clark, John	053	1826	WB-4/334	AR
Clark, John	022	c1864	WB-D/141	AR
Clark, John	035	1767	WB-A/82	
Clark, John	100	1850	WB-41/30	AR
Clark, John	065	1782	WB-B/26	AR
Clark, John	063	1845	WB-2/318	
Clark, John	077	1717	SS 875/137	SS/AR
Clark, John	028	1808	WB-B/325	AR
Clark, John	065	1783	WB-A/202	AR
Clark, John	029	c1802	WB-A/82	AR
Clark, John B.	097	1863	WB-1/221	AR
Clark, John E.	071	1861	WB-5/241	AR
Clark, John N.	073	1886	WB-H/417	CTY
Clark, John W.	011	1887	WB-2/222	
Clark, Joseph	046	1844	WB-C/193	AR
Clark, Joseph	044	1899	WB-24/446	CTY
Clark, Joseph	028	1799	WB-B/87	AR
Clark, Joseph B.	028	1897	WB-F/321	
Clark, Joseph M.	009	1870	WB-1/46	CTY
Clark, Joseph N.	090	1889	WB-6/220	AR
Clark, Levi	049	1880	WB-2/89	AR
Clark, Luke	029	1807	WB-A/96	AR
Clark, Major	053	1786	RW-1/141	
Clark, Major John	009	1850	OB-G/257	AR
Clark, Malcolm	029	1794	Orig. Only	AR
Clark, Malcom	029	1810	WB-A/159	AR
Clark, Margaret	029	1844	WB-C/67	AR
Clark, Margaret	029	1807	WB-A/113	AR
Clark, Martha	046	1819	WB-B/76	AR
Clark, Martha	099	1898	WB-D/116	AR
Clark, Martha A.	047	1885	WB-6/385	AR
Clark, Mary	005	1822	WB-A/71	AR
Clark, Mary	022	1897	WB-F/62	AR
Clark, Mary	065	1890	WB-L/472	AR
Clark, Mary	029	1799	WB-A/23	AR
Clark, Mary	075	1848	WB-N/225	AR
Clark, Mary	029	1808	WB-A/121	AR
Clark, Mary	053	c1786	Orig. Only	AR
Clark, Mary	075	1798	WB-M1/14	AR
Clark, Mary	047	1815	WB-3/568	
Clark, Mary	075	1783	WB-K/92	AR
Clark, Mary C.	045	1886	WB-1/153	AR
Clark, Mary W.	037	1896	WB-H/364	AR
Clark, Miles	075	1841	WB-N/166	AR

Name	Co.	Date	Recorded Copy	Original
Clark, Moses	009	1892	WB-2/31	CTY
Clark, Moses	090	1887	WB-6/184	AR
Clark, Nancy	022	1858	WB-D/16	AR
Clark, Nancy	090	1898	WB-6/483	AR
Clark, Nancy E.	VA	1875	044 WB-23/245	044 CTY
Clark, Nancy P.	046	1880	WB-E/273	AR
Clark, Nathaniel	028	1850	WB-D/167	AR
Clark, Nathaniel	046	1803	WB-A/61	AR
Clark, Nicholas	082	1809	WB-1/132	AR
Clark, Peaty	103	1892	WB-2/10	AR
Clark, Penelope	063	1844	WB-2/311	
Clark, Peter	073	1836	WB-E/372	AR
Clark, Reuben	044	1851	WB-18/284	CTY
Clark, Robert	037	1753	SS 881/45	SS/AR
Clark, Ruth	046	1857	WB-C/496	AR
Clark, Sallie W.	082	1897	WB-6/552	AR
Clark, Samuel	081	1817	WB-4/513	AR
Clark, Samuel	090	c1843	Orig. Only	AR
Clark, Samuel	009	1845	OB-E/406	AR
Clark, Samuel	081	1783	WB-1/5	AR
Clark, Sarah	075	1870	WB-0/1	AR
Clark, Sarah	009	1842	OB-D/361	AR
Clark, Sarah	029	1814	WB-A/207	AR
Clark, Sarah	029	1881	WB-E/259	AR
Clark, Sarah	067	c1853	WB-1/74	AR
Clark, Sarah J.	067	1883	WB-2/170	AR
Clark, Scyntha	016	1899	WB-4/332	AR
Clark, Sidney P.	105	1896	WB-3/190	AR
Clark, Silvanus	075	1789	WB-K/181	AR
Clark, Stephen	073	1854	WB-G/73	AR
Clark, Susan M.	105	1886	WB-2/411	AR
Clark, Susannah	064	1861	WB-1/75	AR
Clark, Susannah	022	1871	WB-E/47	AR
Clark, Sylvanus	075	1837	WB-N/135	AR
Clark, Tamah	063	1857	WB-2/430	
Clark, Thomas	081	1788	WB-1/52	AR
Clark, Thomas	082	1789	WB-1/32	AR
Clark, Thomas	073	1781	WB-A/226	AR
Clark, Thomas	081	c1862	022 WB-D/151	022 AR
Clark, Thomas	053	1806	RW-1/391	AR
Clark, W. H.	065	1881	WB-K/424	AR
Clark, Weeks H.	079	1893	WB-3/30	AR
Clark, Wesley	049	1884	WB-2/117	AR
Clark, Wiley	009	1895	WB-2/72	CTY
Clark, William	028	1796	WB-B/4	AR
Clark, William	065	1772	WB-A/206	AR
Clark, William	073	1829	WB-E/192	
Clark, William	065	1872	WB-K/103	AR
Clark, William	022	1795	RB-2/59	AR
Clark, William	022	1852	WB-C/307	AR
Clark, William	100	1810	WB-15/159	AR
Clark, William	065	1794	WB-A/209	AR
Clark, William	044	1852	WB-19/96	CTY
Clark, William	040	1884	WB-2/218	AR
Clark, William	100	1838	WB-36/229	AR
Clark, William	084	c1784	OW/90	AR
Clark, William	081	1836	WB-7/29	AR
Clark, William	073	1782	WB-A/243	AR
Clark, William	073	1858	WB-G/204	CTY
Clark, William	053	1814	WB-6/8	AR
Clark, William C.	033	1893	WB-2/142	CTY
Clark, William F.	028	c1817	Orig. Only	AR
Clark, William M.	010	1837	WB-G/269	AR
Clark, William R.	047	1860	WB-5/93	
Clark, William W.	100	1869	WB-51/8	AR
Clark, Willie	071	1812	WB-3/68	AR
Clark, Winafred	100	1856	WB-49/48	AR
Clarke, Archabiel	029	1761	Orig. Only	AR-Nunc.
Clarke, Barnes G.	VA	1872	071 WB-6/97	071 AR
Clarke, C. W.	017	1878	WB-B/78	
Clarke, Charles	044	1822	WB-9/121	CTY
Clarke, Edward L.	071	1886	WB-6/524	AR
Clarke, Edwin T.	071	1888	047 WB-6/496	047 AR
Clarke, Edwin T.	071	1888	WB-1/13	AR
Clarke, Gabriel	MD	1792	085 WB-G/226	085 AR
Clarke, George	057	1782	WB-A/9	AR
Clarke, John	002	c1689	Orig. Only	SS/AR
Clarke, Mary B.	028	1886	WB-E/413	
Clarke, Thomas	010	c1728	Orig. Only	SS/AR
Clarke, Thomas	024	1719	SS 875/149	
Clarke, William	073	c1789	WB-B/72	
Clarke, William H.	047	1865	WB-5/127	
Clarkson, Samuel R.	010	1810	WB-F/142	AR
Clary, Ann	085	1846	WB-K/34	AR
Clary, Charles W.	081	1888	WB-16/105	AR
Clary, Daniel	085	1832	WB-H/553	AR
Clary, E. D. N.	071	1852	WB-5/104	AR
Clary, Elizabeth	085	1850	WB-K/118	AR
Clary, John	077	1825	WB-F/109	AR
Clary, John	077	1828	WB-F/151	AR
Clary, John	033	1840	WB-1/30	AR
Clary, Martha	071	1855	WB-5/146	AR
Clary, Paul	098	1899	WB-A/326	CTY
Clary, Sally	100	1847	WB-39/356	AR
Clary, Sarah A.	081	1898	WB-16/482	AR
Clary, Willie G.	010	1854	WB-H/9	AR
Clasby, Charles	090	c1790	054 WB-1/282	054 AR
Clauder, Charles G.	090	1843	WB-4/134	AR
Claver, John	085	c1794	WB-E/199	AR
Clawson, Asey	006	1837	WB-A/32	AR
Clay, Allen	044	1860	WB-21/203	CTY
Clay, Charles	044	1834	WB-13/17	CTY
Clay, Edward	078	1820	WI-9/23	AR
Clay, Elizabeth	021	1866	WB-1/230	AR
Clay, Joseph	060	1840	WB-2/47	AR
Clay, Permelia	044	1898	WB-24/406	CTY
Clay, Peter	044	1831	WB-12/42	CTY
Clay, Rowan R.	044	1897	WB-24/366	CTY
Clay, Samuel	044	1809	WB-7/52	CTY
Claybrook, Josiah	084	1825	WB-A/199	CTY
Clayland, Nathan C.	065	1854	WB-I/249	AR
Claypoole, William	070	1797	WB-AB/10	AR
Clayton, Arta E.	055	1899	WB-A/172	
Clayton, Asher	077	1801	WB-E/132	AR
Clayton, Brittain	090	1799	WB-1/126	AR
Clayton, Calvin C.	078	1898	WB-19/453	AR
Clayton, Coleman	078	1839	WI-14/115	
Clayton, David	096	1857	WB-3/49	AR
Clayton, Elizabeth	077	1737	SS 877/176	SS/AR
Clayton, Elizabeth	078	1864	WB-18/359	AR
Clayton, Eveline	101	1882	WB-A/87	AR
Clayton, Francis	070	1790	WB-AB/3	AR
Clayton, G. E.	038	1864	WB-1/245	AR
Clayton, G. T.	038	1864	WB-1/236	AR
Clayton, George	085	1786	WB-C/95	AR
Clayton, George	054	c1814	WB-1/329	
Clayton, Henderson	078	1865	WB-18/399	AR
Clayton, Henry	024	1725/6	SS 876/40	SS/AR
Clayton, James	028	1783	Orig. Only	AR
Clayton, Jane	078	1860	WB-18/215	AR

Name	Co.	Date	Recorded Copy	Original
Clayton, Jesse C.	078	1891	WB-19/315	AR
Clayton, John	038	1863	WB-1/215	AR
Clayton, John	047	1810	WB-3/504	
Clayton, John	093	c1867	WB-1/82	
Clayton, John	077	1770	WB-C/87	AR
Clayton, John	053	1786	RW-1/163	
Clayton, John	090	1801	WB-2/7	AR-Nunc.
Clayton, John D.	078	1893	WB-19/341	AR
Clayton, Joseph	044	1899	WB-24/449	CTY
Clayton, L. T.	099	1864	RB-33/285	AR
Clayton, Margred	032	1825	WB-1/46	
Clayton, Mary	028	1795	WB-A/344	AR
Clayton, Mary E.	092	1894	WB-6/379	AR
Clayton, Mary J.	093	1897	WB-2/154	AR
Clayton, Philip	092	1784	WB-1/163	
Clayton, Richard	077	1781	WB-C/308	AR
Clayton, Sarah	054	c1800	WB-1/80	AR
Clayton, Sarah E.P.	024	1887	WB-E/161	AR
Clayton, Sarah T.	078	1895	WB-19/393	AR
Clayton, Solomon J.	061	1847	WB-1/38	AR
Clayton, Thomas	070	1793	WB-AB/6	AR
Clayton, Thomas	078	1859	WB-18/89	
Clayton, William	078	1840	WI-14/224	
Clayton, William	092	1781	Orig. Only	AR-Nunc.
Clayton, William L.	050	1898	WB-2/288	CTY
Claywell, Peter	054	1842	WB-2/246	AR
Claywell, Sarah	054	1865	Orig. Only	AR
Claywell, Shadrach	054	1868	WB-3/205	AR
Clear, Mary	028	c1775	Orig. Only	AR-Copy
Clear, Peter	024	1765	WB-A/108	AR
Clear, Peter	028	1763	DB-8/93	
Cleare, Timothy	077	1724	Orig. Only	SS/AR
Cleaton, William B.	010	1896	WB-I/470	AR
Cleaveland, William B.	061	1894	WB-2/138	AR
Cleaves, Emanual	053	1718	009 DB-1/285	
Cleeves, Hosea	053	1812	RW-1/469	AR
Cleeves, James	053	c1818	RW-1/508	AR
Cleeves, James	053	1795	RW-1/260	AR
Cleeves, John	053	1803	RW-1/353	AR
Cleeves, John	053	1774	RW-1/51	AR
Cleeves, Thomas	053	c1793	RW-1/229	AR
Clegg, Araminta	099	1885	WB-B/64	AR
Clegg, Eliza	022	1869	WB-E/36	AR
Clegg, Peter	029	c1895	Orig. Only	AR
Clegg, Richard	022	1887	WB-E/361	AR
Clegg, Sallie A.	022	1877	WB-E/125	AR
Clegg, Samuel	072	1787	WI/L44	AR-Copy
Clegg, Thomas C.	022	1887	WB-E/365	AR
Clegg, Thomas J.	068	1862	WB-C/91	
Clegg, William	084	1789	OW/97	AR-Nunc.
Cleghorn, William	094	1775	Orig. Only	060 AR
Cleland, Rebecca	030	1798	WB-2/120	
Clemens, Georg	010	1730	Orig. Only	SS/AR
Clement, Adam	VA	1813	Copy	090 AR
Clement, Henry	085	c1807	WB-E/225	AR
Clement, Jesse A.	033	1877	WB-2/59	CTY
Clement, John	VA	1749	Copy	044 CTY
Clement, Johnson	092	1851	WB-4/312	
Clement, Laurence	085	1834	WB-H/632	AR
Clement, Margaret	032	c1847	WB-2/45	
Clement, Simon	044	1838	WB-14/249	CTY
Clement, Thomas	009	c1765	OWB/98	AR
Clement, W. B.	033	1896	WB-2/187	CTY
Clement, William	044	1889	WB-24/69	CTY
Clements, Anderson	099	1837	RB-24/94	AR
Clements, Andrew	086	1863	WB-E/414	AR
Clements, Andrew	064	1845	WB-1/12	AR
Clements, Benjamin	090	1835	WB-3/292	AR
Clements, Cornelius	086	1860	WB-E/383	AR
Clements, Elizabeth	033	1846	WB-1/80	AR
Clements, George	010	1794	WB-D/244	AR
Clements, Hardy	063	c1832	WB-2/176	
Clements, John	028	1785	WB-A/83	AR-Copy
Clements, John	085	c1777	WB-A/247	AR
Clements, Matthew	005	1783	WB-1/38	
Clements, Samuel	099	1897	WB-D/76	AR
Clements, Simon	044	1800	WB-5/117	CTY
Clements, Thomas	028	1796	WB-A/359	AR
Clements, William	071	1816	WB-3/172	AR
Clements, Woodson	099	1837	RB-24/94	AR
Clemet, John	010	1734	SS 876/347	SS/AR
Clemmer, Levi	040	1888	WB-2/311	AR
Clemmer, Mary	040	1899	WB-3/66	AR
Clemmons, A. D.	062	1900	WB-B/232	
Clemmons, E. T.	013	1897	WB-C/579	AR
Clemmons, Esther	046	1857	WB-C/462	AR
Clemmons, James	046	1835	WB-B/524	AR
Clemmons, Peter	085	1815	WB-G/372	AR
Clemons, Leonard	099	1873	RB-35/208	AR
Clendenin, Fisher	001	1897	WB-3/190	AR
Clendenin, Fisher	073	1815	WB-D/453	AR
Clendenin, Isabell	073	1848	WB-F/394	AR
Clendenin, William	073	1801	WB-D/25	AR
Clendenin, William	073	1844	WB-F/179	AR
Clendenin, William G.	073	c1835	Orig. Only	AR
Clendening, Mathew	054	c1801	WB-1/88	AR
Cleneay, Samuel	073	1795	WB-C/68	AR
Cleve, William	028	1897	WB-F/267	
Cleveland, Amelia	104	1879	WB-6/178	AR
Cleveland, John	KY	1853	070 WB-C/635	070 AR
Cleveland, Robert	104	1812	WB-3/35	AR
Cleven, Timothy	029	c1757	DB-1/212	AR
Clever, Jacob	085	c1786	WB-C/124	AR
Clewis, George	012	1816	WB-B/109	AR
Cliborn, William	083	1825	WB-1/320	AR
Click, Anginette	033	1878	WB-2/61	CTY
Click, Daniel	033	1846	WB-1/72	AR
Click, J. G.	054	1883	WB-4/581	CTY
Click, John N.	033	1880	WB-2/71	CTY
Click, Magdalene	033	1895	WB-2/173	CTY
Click, Nicholas	033	1862	WB-1/173	AR
Click, Nicholas	085	1832	WB-H/567	AR
Click, Susannah	033	1864	WB-1/182	AR
Clifford, James	009	c1789	OWB/231	AR
Clifford, James G.	033	1900	WB-2/258	CTY
Clifford, John	085	1826	WB-H/370	AR
Clifford, Mary	070	1763	DB-E/31	
Clifford, Michel	085	c1784	WB-C/72	AR
Clifford, Thomas	070	1735	SS 877/125	SS/AR
Clifford, William	009	c1800	OWB/372	AR
Cliftin, H. A.	056	1877	WB-3/177	AR
Clifton, A. P.	056	1877	WB-3/175	AR
Clifton, Benjamin	071	1797	WB-2/150	AR
Clifton, Cloyd	071	1813	WB-3/102	AR
Clifton, Ezekiel	057	1792	WB-A/160	AR
Clifton, Gervas	010	1812	WB-F/208	AR
Clifton, Joel	099	1850	RB-27/91	AR
Clifton, John	099	1806	RB-7/136	AR
Clifton, Josiah	073	1828	WB-E/155	AR
Clifton, Sarah	057	1812	WB-A/330	AR

Name	Co.	Date	Recorded Copy	Original
Climer, John	046	1826	WB-B/350	AR
Climer, Noah M.	046	1866	WB-D/289	AR
Climer, William	046	1867	WB-D/324	AR
Climer, William G.	046	1879	WB-E/268	AR
Clinard, Charles	032	1890	WB-4/75	AR
Clinard, Charles	038	c1862	WB-1/203	AR-Copy
Clinard, John W.	032	1879	WB-3/278	AR
Clinard, Philip	085	c1802	WB-E/214	AR
Clinard, Sally	032	1874	WB-3/108	AR
Clinard, William	032	1877	WB-3/244	AR
Clinch, Edward	069	1779	WB-1/7	AR
Clinch, Joseph J.	069	1795	WB-1/100	AR
Cline, Anna Mary	021	1898	WB-3/199	AR
Cline, Barbara	021	1859	WB-1/148	AR
Cline, Barnet	021	1866	WB-1/231	AR
Cline, Bostian	060	1792	Orig. Only	AR
Cline, David	021	1845	WB-1/29	AR
Cline, David	026	1894	WB-2/486	AR
Cline, Dinah R.	021	1900	WB-3/264	AR
Cline, Ephraim	021	1878	WB-2/197	
Cline, George	021	1899	WB-3/255	AR
Cline, Gertrout	060	1822	Orig. Only	AR
Cline, H. B.	016	1865	WB-2/127	
Cline, Henry	021	1877	WB-2/178	AR
Cline, Henry	016	1853	WB-1/229	
Cline, Jacob	016	1866	WB-2/144	
Cline, James	016	1891	WB-4/111	AR
Cline, John	060	1857	WB-3/7	AR
Cline, John, Sr.	060	1842	WB-2/45	AR
Cline, Joseph	016	1869	WB-3/10	
Cline, Leah	016	1873	WB-3/83	AR
Cline, Lucy A.	091	1888	WB-1/106	
Cline, Michael	060	1840	WB-2/33	AR
Cline, Noah	054	1858	WB-3/127	AR-Copy
Cline, Susanah	021	1867	WB-1/242	AR
Cline, William	021	1884	WB-2/293	
Clingerman, Alexander	085	c1803	WB-E/234	AR
Clingman, Peter	092	1845	WB-4/237	
Clinton, Elizabeth	073	1844	WB-F/213	AR
Clinton, Penelope	083	1814	WB-1/138	AR
Clinton, Robert	086	1790	Orig. Only	AR
Clitherall, Sally Ann	AL	1885	028 WB-E/392	
Clixby, John	078	1818	WI-8/203	AR
Cloase, George	070	1760	SS 881/149	SS/AR
Clodfelter, Daniel	038	1898	WB-4/72	AR
Clodfelter, Daniel A.	032	1886	WB-3/494	AR
Clodfelter, David	032	1895	WB-4/239	AR
Clodfelter, David C.	032	1864	WB-2/272	AR
Clodfelter, Elias	032	1846	WB-1/487	
Clodfelter, Felix	085	1845	WB-I/258	AR
Clodfelter, Felix	085	1814	WB-G/306	AR
Clodfelter, George	085	1837	WB-I/29	AR
Clodfelter, George	085	1847	WB-K/47	AR
Clodfelter, George	054	1863	Orig. Only	AR
Clodfelter, George A.	085	1865	WB-K/363	AR
Clodfelter, J. A.	085	1891	WB-2/457	CTY
Clodfelter, Jacob	032	1866	WB-2/334	AR
Clodfelter, Jacob	032	1842	WB-1/383	
Clodfelter, Jacob	032	1837	WB-1/288	
Clodfelter, Jacob L.	032	1900	WB-4/476	AR
Clodfelter, Jacob L.	032	1900	085 WB-3/397	085 CTY
Clodfelter, John	032	1826	WB-1/61	
Clodfelter, Joseph	032	1874	WB-3/104	AR
Clodfelter, Peter	032	1843	WB-1/419	
Clodfeltor, Joseph	085	1844	WB-I/219	AR
Cloer, Nicholas	054	1839	WB-2/202	AR
Cloman, Lavina	063	1857	Copy	037 AR
Cloman, Lavina	063	1857	WB-2/445	
Cloman, Mary L.	047	1864	WB-5/118	
Cloman, Samuel T.	063	1858	WB-2/447	
Clomon, Zodia	009	1884	WB-1/352	CTY
Cloninger, Adam	060	1818	Orig. Only	AR
Cloninger, Adam	040	c1851	WB-1/41	
Cloninger, David	040	1874	WB-2/65	
Cloninger, Fanny	040	1871	WB-2/22	AR
Cloninger, Jonas	040	1870	WB-2/18	
Cloninger, Mary	060	1839	WB-2/9	AR
Cloninger, Michael	060	1829	WB-1/122	
Cloninger, Moses	040	1888	WB-2/326	AR
Cloninger, Noah	021	1897	WB-3/174	AR
Cloninger, Thomas	021	1871	WB-2/47	AR
Clonts, Adam	097	1898	WB-2/567	AR
Clopton, Elizabeth	039	1880	WB-U/220	AR
Clopton, Richard	039	1807	WB-C/64 & 76	
Close, Jordan	075	1898	WB-O/473	AR
Close, Joseph	046	1837	WB-B/565	AR
Close, Susanah	046	1859	WB-D/25	AR
Cloud, Daniel	073	1812	WB-D/327	AR
Cloud, Joel	080	1855	WB-1/172	
Cloud, Mary F.	SC	1892	065 WB-M/319	065 AR
Cloud, Nancy	073	1837	WB-E/411	AR
Cloud, Nancy	073	1867	WB-G/531	CTY
Clouse, Joseph	032	1862	WB-2/223	AR
Cloutz, Jeremiah	065	1841	WB-H/28	AR
Cloyn, Peter	085	c1791	WB-B/175	AR
Clubb, Peter	060	1787	Orig. Only	AR
Clubb, Peter	060	1802	Orig. Only	AR
Cluff, Mathew	075	1845	WB-N/191	AR
Clutz, Jacob	085	1814	WB-G/305	AR
Clyburn, John	083	1824	WB-1/224	AR
Clyde, Thomas	PA	1885	028 WB-F/132	
Coakley, Mildred	009	c1812	OB-A/220	AR
Coakley, Sally	009	c1804	OWB/425	AR
Coale, William	019	c1775	WB-D/110	AR
Coaleman, Elias	103	1795	WI-B/71	AR
Coalman, James P.	025	1874	WB-A/18	AR
Coalman, William H.	025	1876	WB-A/28	AR
Coase, Fleet M.	022	1873	WB-E/90	AR
Coats, Alvin	056	1883	WB-3/347	AR
Coats, Benjamin	054	c1803	WB-1/82	AR
Coats, Gabriel G.	062	1866	WB-A/37	AR
Coats, Josiah	056	1872	WB-3/65	AR
Coats, Miranda B.	032	1892	WB-4/159	AR
Coats, William	056	1856	WB-1/695	AR
Coats, Willis	032	1880	WB-3/296	AR
Cobb, A. V.	010	1880	WB-I/119	
Cobb, Absalom	071	1797	WB-2/156	AR
Cobb, Amariah B.	037	1861	WB-G/208	AR
Cobb, Ambrose	060	1797	Orig. Only	AR
Cobb, Archey	020	1884	WB-A/406	CTY
Cobb, Catharine	010	1858	WB-H/59	AR
Cobb, Catharine	046	1881	WB-E/293	AR
Cobb, Clisby G.	017	c1861	WB-A/131	AR
Cobb, David	010	1884	WB-I/178	AR
Cobb, David	103	1791	WI-A/221	AR
Cobb, Deveroux	045	1883	WB-1/104	AR
Cobb, Eaton	037	1862	Orig. Only	AR
Cobb, Ebenezer	020	1864	RB-T/44	
Cobb, Edward	037	1817	WB-E/167	AR
Cobb, Elizabeth	020	1860	RB-S/271	AR

Name	Co.	Date	Recorded Copy	Original
Cobb, Elizabeth	075	1818	WB-M1/321	AR-Nunc.
Cobb, Elizabeth	037	1856	WB-G/135	AR
Cobb, Enoch	083	1866	WB-2/231	AR
Cobb, Ephraim E.	037	1869	WB-G/340	AR
Cobb, Fannie H.	073	1897	WB-I/128	CTY
Cobb, Gaston D.	001	1885	WB-2/249	AR
Cobb, Gray	105	c1891	Orig. Only	AR
Cobb, Gray	083	1851	WB-2/41	AR
Cobb, Hannah	071	1848	WB-5/70	AR
Cobb, Hardy	071	1833	WB-4/98	AR
Cobb, Henry	020	1861	RB-S/441	AR
Cobb, Henry	010	1763	WB-A/28	AR
Cobb, Henry	046	1893	WB-F/273	AR
Cobb, Henry	046	1844	WB-C/199	AR
Cobb, Henry W.	020	1876	WB-A/208	CTY
Cobb, J. C.	060	1895	WB-4/586	AR
Cobb, James	010	1792	WB-D/205	AR
Cobb, James	020	1853	RB-R/87	AR
Cobb, James	103	1795	WI-A/534	
Cobb, James	010	1859	Orig. Only	AR
Cobb, James A.	079	1883	WB-2/292	AR
Cobb, James H.	045	1899	WB-1/369	AR
Cobb, Jennie	059	1900	WB-B/267	CTY
Cobb, John	037	1837	WB-F/198	AR
Cobb, John	020	1864	RB-T/59	CTY
Cobb, John	010	1809	WB-F/120	AR
Cobb, John	046	1846	WB-C/252	AR
Cobb, John	059	1834	WB-B/394	CTY-Copy
Cobb, John D.	084	1850	WB-C/108	CTY
Cobb, John E.	037	1864	WB-G/250	AR
Cobb, John P.	028	1891	WB-E/572	
Cobb, Jonas G.	037	1900	WB-H/470	AR
Cobb, Jonas G.	037	1896	WB-H/347	AR
Cobb, Jordan H.	083	1885	WB-3/339	AR
Cobb, Joseph	010	1821	WB-G/80	AR
Cobb, Kenneth	047	1884	WB-6/344	AR
Cobb, M. E.	060	1897	WB-5/46	AR
Cobb, Margaret	040	1865	WB-1/173	
Cobb, Mark	075	1836	WB-N/128	AR
Cobb, Mary	037	1884	WB-G/656	
Cobb, Mary E.	041	1875	WB-4/55	AR
Cobb, Nancy W.	038	1879	103 WB-1/182	103 AR
Cobb, Nathan	010	1812	Orig. Only	AR
Cobb, Nephtha	084	1891	WB-E/501	CTY
Cobb, Noah	020	1808	RB-F/3	AR
Cobb, Noah	020	1857	RB-R/538	AR
Cobb, Ollen	079	1875	WB-2/106	AR
Cobb, Orren	069	1878	WB-5/70	AR
Cobb, Reubin	037	1872	WB-G/379	AR
Cobb, Robert	071	1767	WB-1/157	
Cobb, Robert B.	051	1882	WB-C/288	AR
Cobb, Robert L.	084	1892	WB-E/517	CTY
Cobb, Rutha	010	1864	WB-H/142	AR
Cobb, Salley	071	1809	WB-3/14	AR
Cobb, Sally	037	1881	WB-G/623	AR
Cobb, Samuel	046	1857	WB-C/479	AR
Cobb, Stephen	103	1824	RD-5/95	AR
Cobb, Susan V.	028	1888	WB-E/470	AR
Cobb, Suthy	064	c1781	WB-1/77	
Cobb, Thomas	010	1860	WB-H/96	AR
Cobb, Thomas N.	037	1829	WB-F/98	AR
Cobb, William	079	c1863	WB-1/96	AR
Cobb, William	020	1835	RB-M/462	
Cobb, William C.	010	1875	WB-I/63	AR

Name	Co.	Date	Recorded Copy	Original
Cobb, Willie M.	083	1845	WB-1/462	AR
Cobbis, Bolser	085	c1780	WB-C/216	AR
Cobbs, Annie E.	020	1885	WB-A/475	CTY
Cobbs, John, Sr.	020	1838	RB-N/202	
Cobel, John	081	1801	WB-2/86	AR
Coble, Abraham	046	1847	WB-C/263	AR
Coble, Adam	085	c1794	WB-E/217	AR
Coble, Anthony	046	1793	WB-A/44	AR
Coble, Anthony	046	1793	Copy	081 AR
Coble, Barbary	046	1870	WB-E/38	AR
Coble, Catharine	001	c1843	WB-1/89	AR
Coble, Daniel	081	1880	WB-15/334	AR
Coble, David	001	c1855	WB-1/96	AR
Coble, David	046	1888	WB-E/492	AR
Coble, David	073	1827	WB-E/151	AR
Coble, David	089	1842	WB-1/4	AR
Coble, Eli	081	1843	WB-8/28	AR
Coble, Elias	046	1865	WB-D/268	AR
Coble, Elizabeth	022	1877	WB-E/121	AR
Coble, George	073	1815	WB-D/432	AR
Coble, George	073	1793	WB-B/257	
Coble, George	046	1816	WB-B/14	AR
Coble, George P.	046	1855	WB-C/441	AR
Coble, Henderson	046	1869	WB-E/3	AR
Coble, Henry	073	1826	WB-E/125	AR
Coble, Jacob	046	1847	WB-C/283	AR
Coble, Jacob	046	1832	WB-B/459	AR
Coble, Jacob	046	1816	WB-B/28	AR
Coble, Jacob	089	1854	WB-1/121	
Coble, John	073	1815	WB-D/447	AR
Coble, John	001	1878	WB-2/126	AR
Coble, John	046	1815	WB-A/84	AR
Coble, John	081	1835	WB-6/462	AR
Coble, John	001	1874	WB-2/94	AR
Coble, John A.	081	1852	WB-11/416	AR
Coble, Ludwick	046	1809	WB-A/60	AR
Coble, Manly	081	1894	WB-16/329	AR
Coble, Martha	089	1848	WB-1/70	AR
Coble, Martin	073	1847	WB-F/331	AR
Coble, Mary	046	1863	WB-D/169	AR
Coble, Michael	046	1855	WB-C/422	AR
Coble, Milton	001	1896	WB-3/145	AR
Coble, Murphy	022	1864	WB-D/122	AR
Coble, Oliver	046	1861	WB-D/119	AR
Coble, P. N.	082	1898	WB-7/2	AR
Coble, Paul	046	1852	WB-C/378	AR
Coble, Peter	046	1816	Orig. Only	AR
Coble, Peter	001	c1851	WB-1/50	AR
Coble, Philip	046	1842	WB-C/107	AR
Coble, Samuel	001	1894	WB-3/25	AR
Coble, Sarah	001	1875	WB-2/97	AR
Coble, Sarah	001	1887	WB-2/330	AR
Cobler, Nicholas	084	1860	WB-C/324	CTY
Coburn, Abner S.	063	1877	WB-3/151	
Coburn, Brown	063	1859	WB-2/463	
Coburn, Charlotte	063	1853	WB-2/396	
Coburn, Courtney	063	1900	WB-4/257	AR
Coburn, Courtney	063	c1893	101 WB-A/323	101 AR
Coburn, Elizabeth	063	1886	WB-3/288	AR
Coburn, Ellen	063	1856	WB-2/428	
Coburn, Francis	005	1813	WB-2/21	AR
Coburn, George	063	c1798	WB-1/359	
Coburn, John	005	c1754	WB-1/4	
Coburn, John	063	1828	WB-2/134	
Coburn, Lucinda	063	1883	WB-3/244	

Name	Co.	Date	Recorded Copy	Original
Coburn, Tilitha	063	1891	WB-4/55	AR
Coburn, William	063	1849	WB-2/350	
Coche, Joseph	013	1848	WB-A/130	
Cochran, Adam	047	1889	WB-6/544	AR
Cochran, Addison	078	1821	WI-9/228	AR
Cochran, Ann Maria	029	1849	Orig. Only	AR
Cochran, Dolly	030	1819	WB-3/116	
Cochran, H. G.	065	1855	WB-J/7	AR
Cochran, Harriet	013	1868	WB-B/4	AR
Cochran, Henry	086	1871	WB-F/35	
Cochran, J. L.	065	1864	WB-J/177	AR
Cochran, James	016	1854	WB-1/236	
Cochran, James M.	016	1846	WB-1/116	
Cochran, Jane	016	1846	WB-1/98	
Cochran, John	028	1781	Orig. Only	AR
Cochran, John	060	1794	Orig. Only	AR
Cochran, John Q.	065	1854	WB-I/253	AR
Cochran, John, Sr.	020	1807	RB-C/293	AR
Cochran, Joseph	016	1890	WB-4/62	AR
Cochran, Joseph	085	c1808	WB-G/110	
Cochran, Robert	016	1846	WB-1/95	
Cochran, Robert	085	c1806	WB-G/49	AR
Cochran, Robert	086	1851	WB-E/206	AR
Cochran, Robert C.	016	1846	WB-1/88	
Cochran, Robert L.	016	1853	WB-1/227	
Cochran, Robert, Sr.	016	1837	PQS.5/453	
Cochran, Samuel	085	c1772	WB-A/226	AR
Cochran, Sarah	085	c1776	WB-A/227	AR
Cochran, Sarah L.	016	1858	WB-2/39	
Cochran, Sarah M.	016	1846	WB-1/99	
Cochran, Thomas	010	1798	WB-E/57	AR
Cochran, Thomas	065	1794	WB-A/190	AR
Cochran, William	013	1841	WB-A/71	
Cochran, William C.	065	1862	WB-J/136	AR
Cochran, William J.	047	1864	WB-5/108	
Cochrane, Thomas	024	1871	WB-E/23	AR
Cock, Odom	005	1828	WB-A/151	AR
Cockburn, Azariah	065	1838	WB-E/166	AR
Cockburn, Elizabeth	063	c1785	WB-1/121	
Cockburn, George	063	c1779	WB-1/111	
Cockburn, George	037	1799	WB-D/83	AR
Cockburn, John	005	c1808	WB-2/22	AR
Cockburn, Mary	063	1815	WB-2/32	
Cockburn, Nancy	063	1844	WB-2/302	
Cocke, Benjamin	044	1815	WB-7/494	CTY
Cocke, Minnie L.	013	1897	WB-D/50	AR
Cocke, Rebeccah	044	1797	WB-4/69	CTY-Nunc.
Cocke, William	044	1796	WB-4/50	CTY
Cockerham, Alfred N.	055	1889	WB-A/91	
Cockerham, Daniel C.	092	1877	WB-6/93	AR
Cockerham, David	092	1842	WB-4/188	AR
Cockerham, Moses	092	1817	WB-3/124	AR
Cockerham, P. C.	092	1893	WB-6/365	AR
Cockerham, Pleasant B.	092	1854	WB-5/8	AR
Cockerham, William	055	1861	ID/140	
Cockran, Aniss	078	1821	WI-9/252	AR
Cockran, Robert	070	1794	WB-C/54	AR-Nunc.
Cockrell, Elisha H.	069	1900	WB-6/115	AR
Cockrell, Jacob	069	1792	WB-1/80	AR
Cockrell, John	069	1809	WB-1/199	AR
Cockrell, Samuel	056	1811	WB-1/382	AR
Cockrell, Stephen	056	1816	WB-1/265	AR
Cocks, Martha	100	1821	WB-23/51	AR
Cocks, Robert	077	1768	WB-C/82	AR
Cockton, John	030	1789	WB-1/233	
Cody, Lucreecy	062	1872	WB-B/6	
Cody, Thomas	032	1853	WB-2/83	AR
Cody, W. A. J.	084	1875	WB-E/93	CTY
Coe, Isaiah	092	c1836	Copy	106 AR
Coe, Jemima	106	c1847	WB-1/15	AR
Coe, John	092	1806	WB-3/70	AR
Coe, John	046	1852	WB-C/382	AR
Coe, John	046	1807	WB-A/73	AR
Coe, Josiah	092	1836	WB-4/168	
Coe, Nancy	081	1866	WB-14/3	AR
Coen, Daniel	075	c1747	Orig. Only	AR
Cofer, James	038	c1857	WB-1/124	AR
Cofer, James	090	1816	WB-2/176	
Coffee, Joshua	046	1798	WB-A/59	AR
Coffey, James	104	1786	WB-1/202	
Coffey, James	017	c1841	WB-A/48	AR
Coffey, James M.	065	1893	WB-M/230	AR
Coffey, Joel	104	1789	WB-1/260	AR
Coffey, John	104	1826	WB-4/82	AR
Coffey, John	104	1812	WB-3/21	AR
Coffey, Joshua T.	104	1891	WB-6/401	AR
Coffey, Mary	061	1900	WB-2/269	AR
Coffey, Thomas	104	1825	WB-4/75	AR
Coffey, William	053	c1806	RW-1/413	
Coffey, William	014	1839	Orig. Only	AR-Copy
Coffield, Benjamin	010	1857	WB-H/55	AR
Coffield, Benjamin	024	1802	WB-B/186	AR-Nunc.
Coffield, Benjamin	037	1770	WB-A/182	AR
Coffield, Benjamin	037	1838	WB-F/220	AR
Coffield, Benjamin	024	1812	WB-C/10	AR
Coffield, David	037	1818	WB-E/180	AR
Coffield, David	010	1805	WB-E/255	AR
Coffield, Elizabeth	010	1830	WB-G/197	AR
Coffield, Elizabeth	037	1835	WB-F/170	AR
Coffield, Frederick	024	1829	WB-C/146	AR
Coffield, Henrietta	099	1889	WB-B/398	AR
Coffield, Isaac	010	1812	WB-F/211	AR
Coffield, James	024	1843	WB-C/239	AR
Coffield, Jethro	010	1825	WB-G/138	AR
Coffield, John	024	1818	WB-C/63	AR
Coffield, John, Sr.	024	c1789	WB-B/52	AR
Coffield, Luke A.	010	1880	WB-I/114	
Coffield, Mary	010	1814	WB-F/248	AR
Coffield, Noah	010	1799	WB-E/92	AR
Coffield, Olive	010	1840	WB-G/322	AR
Coffield, Speir	037	1771	WB-A/188	AR
Coffield, Spier W.	037	1825	WB-F/46	AR
Coffield, Thomas	037	1812	WB-E/45	AR
Coffield, West	037	1781	WB-B/86	AR
Coffield, William	024	1878	WB-E/61	AR
Coffield, William	029	1825	WB-B/135	AR
Coffield, William	010	1812	WB-F/204	AR
Coffin, Abel	046	1861	WB-D/113	AR
Coffin, Abijah	046	1793	WB-A/46	AR
Coffin, Abner	046	1880	WB-E/292	AR
Coffin, Agnes	046	1875	WB-E/163	AR
Coffin, Barnabas	046	1815	WB-A/78	AR
Coffin, Benjamin	046	1790	WB-A/47	AR
Coffin, Benjamin	081	1898	WB-16/491	
Coffin, Elihu	046	1857	WB-C/468	AR
Coffin, Isaac G.	MD	1892	075 WB-0/379	075 AR
Coffin, Peter	046	1818	WB-A/60	AR
Coffin, Samuel	046	1799	WB-A/57	AR
Coffin, William	046	1796	WB-A/52	AR

Name	Co.	Date	Recorded Copy	Original
Coffin, William	046	1803	WB-A/71	AR
Coffine, Mary	077	1707	Orig. Only	SS/AR
Cofield, Caroline	010	1887	WB-I/232	AR
Cofield, Thomas H.	063	1821	WB-2/72	
Cogdall, Thomas	026	1882	WB-2/262	AR
Cogdell, Daniel	103	1892	WB-2/28	AR
Cogdell, George	034	1761	Copy	103 AR
Cogdell, Margaret	034	1784	Copy	103 AR
Cogdell, Richard	028	1787	WB-A/218	AR
Coggens, John	085	c1793	WB-E/209	AR
Coggin, Abram	067	1870	WB-2/14	
Coggin, B. T.	067	1896	WB-2/342	AR
Coggin, Daniel	032	c1850	WB-2/53	
Coggin, Eliza	032	c1851	WB-2/58	
Coggin, Elizabeth	010	1870	WB-I/30	AR
Coggin, George F.	073	1857	WB-G/179	CTY
Coggin, Jackie	069	1899	WB-6/70	AR
Coggin, Jarret	085	1835	WB-H/656	AR
Coggin, Jeremiah	032	1839	WB-1/335	
Coggin, Mary J.	039	1898	WB-V/136	AR
Coggin, William	067	1870	WB-2/17	AR
Coggin, William B.	067	1871	WB-2/23	AR
Coggin, Zachariah	032	1840	WB-1/353	
Coggins, Brantley	032	c1847	WB-2/14	
Coggins, Frances E.	010	1875	WB-I/74	AR
Coggins, Henry	071	1870	WB-6/63	AR
Coggins, Nancy C.	067	1882	WB-2/126	
Coggins, Thomas	087	c1797	WB-A/26	AR
Coghill, Henderson	044	1890	WB-24/121	CTY
Coghill, James O.	098	1891	WB-A/126	CTY
Coghill, Ruben	100	1838	WB-37/17	AR
Coghill, Thomas	044	1842	WB-15/291	CTY
Cogwell, Henry	077	1719	SS 875/150	SS/AR
Cogwell, Israem	039	1829	WB-J/61	
Cogwell, Isrom	100	1811	WB-15/349	AR
Cogwell, Vincent	044	1890	WB-24/119	CTY
Coharon, Alexander	073	1776	WB-A/199	
Cohen, Hannah	NY	1887	028 WB-E/443	
Cohen, Jonas	065	1826	WB-A/225	AR
Cohen, Samuel	065	1895	WB-M/363	AR
Cohn, Adolph	028	1899	WB-F/449	
Cohoon, Alexander	053	1828	WB-4/364	
Cohoon, Ann	096	1793	Orig. Only	AR
Cohoon, John	011	c1781	WB-1/482	
Cohoon, John	037	1789	WB-C/82	AR
Cohoon, Joseph	096	1817	Orig. Only	AR
Cohoon, Ludford	075	1881	WB-O/125	AR
Cohoon, William	037	1790	WB-C/121	AR
Cohoon, Wilson G.	096	1866	WB-3/70	AR
Coile, Elizabeth	020	1832	RB-M/82	AR
Coin, Benjamin	075	1734	SS 876/375	SS/AR
Coiner, Amos	081	1823	WB-5/121	
Coit, Mehitable	085	c1792	WB-E/212	AR
Coite, Eliza A.	054	1891	WB-5/368	CTY
Coker, Brumble	085	1818	WB-G/495	AR
Coker, Caleb	037	1785	WB-C/25	AR
Coker, Caleb	037	1748	SS 878/205	SS/AR
Coker, Henry	037	1896	WB-H/360	AR
Coker, James	037	1848	WB-F/409	AR
Coker, James, Jr.	037	1830	WB-F/117	AR
Coker, James, Sr.	037	1796	WB-D/14	AR
Coker, John	037	1877	WB-G/540	AR
Coker, John	071	1778	WB-1/310	
Coker, John	071	1839	WB-4/184	AR
Coker, Olive	037	1855	WB-G/108	AR

Name	Co.	Date	Recorded Copy	Original
Coker, Richard	009	1756	SS 879/258	SS/AR
Coker, Richard	037	1808	WB-D/305	AR
Coker, William	037	1798	WB-D/40	AR
Coker, William R.	037	1866	WB-G/278	AR
Colbraith, Neven	029	1783	Orig. Only	AR
Colbreath, Angus	029	1787	Orig. Only	AR
Colbreath, Daniel	086	1836	WB-E/31	AR
Colbreath, Duncan	029	1802	WB-A/58	AR
Colby, Isaac	057	1894	WB-C/200	AR
Colclough, James	100	c1822	Orig. Only	AR
Colclough, John	100	1803	WB-12/61	AR
Colclough, Mary	100	1794	WB-7/121	AR
Colclough, William	100	1783	WB-4/12	AR
Colclough, William	044	1779	WB-1/250	CTY
Coldison, George	085	c1803	WB-E/229	
Coldwell, Samuel Lee	040	1866	WB-1/189	
Cole, Andrew	068	1808	WB-A/261	
Cole, Ann	010	1847	WB-G/425	AR
Cole, Anthony	073	1889	WB-H/477	CTY
Cole, Clerkey	035	1889	WB-4/336	AR
Cole, Daniel	100	1870	WB-51/16	
Cole, Edward	009	1828	OB-A/510	AR
Cole, Edward	024	c1783	WB-A/104	AR
Cole, Elizabeth	022	1833	WB-B/260	AR
Cole, Elizabeth	082	1824	WB-1/242	AR
Cole, Florence	040	1898	WB-3/6	AR
Cole, Francis	082	1818	WB-1/197	AR
Cole, George	099	1829	RB-21/168	AR
Cole, Henry	099	1790	RB-2/299	AR
Cole, James	046	1848	WB-C/292	AR
Cole, James C.	028	1865	WB-D/382	AR
Cole, Jesse	013	1839	WB-A/61	
Cole, Joel	013	1886	WB-B/394	AR
Cole, John	082	1781	WB-1/9	AR
Cole, John	036	1886	WB-A/89	CTY
Cole, John	068	1808	WB-A/262	
Cole, John	086	1871	WB-F/36	AR
Cole, John	082	1804	WB-1/90	AR
Cole, John	073	1869	WB-H/10	CTY
Cole, John D.	013	1893	WB-C/243	AR
Cole, John D.	100	1893	WB-51/344	
Cole, John W.	082	1896	WB-6/541	AR
Cole, John, Sr.	082	c1802	WB-1/90	AR
Cole, John, Sr.	099	1806	RB-7/200	AR
Cole, Joseph	013	1832	WB-A/11	
Cole, Joseph	068	1875	WB-D/77	
Cole, Joseph	068	1817	WB-A/295	
Cole, Joshua	047	1839	WB-4/178	
Cole, Patience	081	1827	Orig. Only	AR
Cole, Rachel	068	1857	WB-C/46	
Cole, Richard	077	1795	WB-E/36	
Cole, Richard	009	1815	OB-A/241	AR
Cole, Richard M.	068	1889	WB-D/306	
Cole, Robert	086	1794	Orig. Only	AR
Cole, Robert	046	1816	Orig. Only	AR
Cole, Robert	100	1825	WB-28/134	AR
Cole, Robert	035	1829	WB-A/75	AR
Cole, S. W.	085	1889	WB-2/369	CTY
Cole, S. W.	085	1889	005 WB-D/271	005 AR
Cole, Samuel	073	1876	WB-H/147	CTY
Cole, Stephen	081	1798	WB-2/37	AR
Cole, Stephen	082	c1855	WB-5/8	
Cole, Stephen	081	1842	WB-7/412	AR
Cole, Stephen E.	022	1892	WB-E/502	AR
Cole, Susan A.	084	1900	WB-F/172	CTY

Name	Co.	Date	Recorded Copy	Original
Cole, Thomas	022	1829	WB-B/168	AR
Cole, Thomas	028	1785	WB-A/85	
Cole, Thomas	029	c1778	Orig. Only	AR
Cole, Thomas	068	1817	WB-A/297	
Cole, Thomas	073	1881	WB-H/290	CTY
Cole, Thomas	068	1890	WB-D/386	
Cole, Thomas	035	1841	Orig. Only	AR
Cole, Thomas	065	1820	WB-A/224	AR
Cole, Wesley	073	1900	WB-I/171	CTY
Cole, William	073	1881	WB-H/301	CTY
Cole, William	081	1883	WB-15/429	AR
Cole, William	022	1824	WB-B/70	AR
Cole, William	047	1873	WB-6/94	AR
Cole, William	087	c1807	WB-A/44	AR
Cole, William	077	1825	WB-F/82	
Cole, William C.	090	1840	WB-4/67	AR
Cole, Willis	056	1832	WB-1/486	
Coleman, Aaron	037	1800	WB-D/106	AR
Coleman, Amelia	SC	1892	055 WB-A/110	
Coleman, Amos	027	1860	WB-A/74	AR
Coleman, Ann	009	1829	OB-B/4	AR
Coleman, Asa	027	c1834	WB-A/19	AR
Coleman, Carter	100	1843	WB-38/210	AR
Coleman, Celia	103	1852	RD-11/149	AR
Coleman, Charles	037	1761	WB-A/61	AR
Coleman, Charles	037	1761	WB-A/46	AR
Coleman, Daniel	047	1849	WB-4/272	
Coleman, Daniel	015	1777	100 WB-2/164	AR
Coleman, Dempsey	027	1823	WB-A/48	AR
Coleman, Ebenizer	100	1871	WB-51/55	AR
Coleman, Edwin S.	020	1879	WB-A/278	CTY
Coleman, Elijah	103	1849	RD-10/455	AR
Coleman, Elijah	103	1832	RD-6/349	AR
Coleman, Ellar	023	1897	Orig. Only	AR
Coleman, Hardee	037	1807	WB-D/294	AR
Coleman, Henry	105	1870	WB-2/107	AR
Coleman, Hezekiah	100	1838	WB-36/197	AR
Coleman, Jacob B.	085	1864	WB-K/328	AR
Coleman, John C.	001	1866	WB-1/268	AR
Coleman, John T.	SC	1892	055 WB-A/101	
Coleman, Jones W.	055	1892	WB-A/106	
Coleman, Joseph	078	1862	WB-18/247	AR
Coleman, Josiah	105	1894	WB-3/93	AR
Coleman, Juley Ann	063	1835	WB-2/204	
Coleman, Levi P.	100	1863	WB-50/119	AR
Coleman, Littleton	100	1824	WB-26/257	AR
Coleman, Mark	049	c1817	WI-A/10	AR
Coleman, Mary	104	1835	WB-4/196	AR
Coleman, Mary	105	1877	WB-2/201	AR
Coleman, Moses	011	c1799	WB-1/377	
Coleman, Moses	037	1760	WB-A/5	AR
Coleman, Noel	020	1808	RB-F/2	AR
Coleman, Peter	065	1800	WB-A/212	AR
Coleman, Phillip	085	1830	WB-H/483	AR
Coleman, Rachel	103	1851	RD-11/2	AR
Coleman, Richard	086	1791	Orig. Only	AR
Coleman, Richard	078	1813	WI-6/156	
Coleman, Robert	008	1721	SS 875/346	SS/AR
Coleman, Robert	037	1795	WB-C/313	AR
Coleman, Robert	037	1807	WB-D/276	AR
Coleman, Robert	037	1761	WB-A/29	AR
Coleman, Spillsby	020	1807	RB-E/319	AR
Coleman, Stephen	037	1803	WB-D/169	AR
Coleman, Theophilas	027	1844	WB-A/23	AR
Coleman, Thomas	028	1791	WB-A/252	AR
Coleman, W. D.	020	1895	WB-B/215	CTY
Coleman, W. J.	027	1892	WB-2/103	AR
Coleman, William	037	1752	Orig. Only	SS/AR
Coleman, William	005	1750	SS 877/270	SS/AR
Coleman, William	013	1889	WB-B/535	AR
Coleman, William H.	100	1854	WB-43/229	AR-Nunc.
Coleman, William R.	100	1876	WB-51/89	AR
Coles, James	077	1713	SS 875/22	SS/AR
Coles, William T.	085	1777	WB-A/221	AR
Coleson, Etheldred	051	1883	WB-C/311	AR
Coleson, William	010	1736	Orig. Only	SS/AR
Colewell, Andrew	073	1766	WB-A/44	
Coley, Benjamin	047	1889	WB-6/524	AR
Coley, Charles	047	1808	WB-3/479	
Coley, David	044	1858	WB-20/451	CTY
Coley, E. A.	099	1897	WB-D/267	AR
Coley, Elizabeth	044	1857	WB-20/234	CTY
Coley, Freeman	103	1888	WB-1/431	AR
Coley, Gabriel	103	1815	RD-3/216	AR
Coley, Gilford E.	069	1887	WB-5/253	AR
Coley, John	044	1855	WB-20/13	CTY-Nunc.
Coley, Lovet	039	1884	WB-U/344	AR
Coley, Milly	089	1863	WB-1/283	
Coley, Orren	039	1890	WB-U/501	
Coley, Rachel	027	1834	WB-A/27	AR-Nunc.
Coley, Richard H.	044	1856	WB-20/189	CTY
Coley, Robert	047	1785	WB-3/096	
Coley, Sally	103	1839	RD-7/400	AR
Coley, Weldon	047	1890	WB-6/571	AR
Coley, William	089	1893	WB-2/254	AR
Coley, William	089	c1848	WB-1/72	AR
Colgrove, David D.	028	1873	WB-E/73	
Collard, Elizabeth	063	1823	WB-2/91	
Collens, Abiga	053	1869	Orig. Only	AR
Collens, John	065	1825	WB-A/227	
Coller, Cornelious	009	1741	Orig. Only	SS/AR
Coller, Joseph	090	1837	WB-3/325	
Colles, Thomas	075	1719	SS 875/217	
Collett, Charles	017	c1852	WB-A/85	AR
Collett, James	081	1807	WB-3/66	AR
Collett, John	014	1884	WB-2/266	CTY
Collett, John	032	1898	WB-4/350	AR
Collett, Samuel	081	1851	WB-9/280	AR
Collett, Thomas A.	039	1878	WB-U/180	
Colley, John	039	1834	WB-K/30	AR
Colley, Joseph	085	1877	WB-1/421	CTY
Colley, Robert	028	1744	Wills.6/L82	SS/AR
Collier, Also	071	1793	WB-2/37	AR
Collier, Ann	070	c1784	Orig. Only	AR
Collier, Charles	073	1800	WB-D/265	AR
Collier, Drury	060	1809	Orig. Only	AR
Collier, Elizabeth	026	1845	WB-1/41	AR
Collier, Jesse	071	1814	WB-3/112	AR
Collier, John	022	1810	WB-A/187	AR
Collier, Joseph	071	1769	WB-1/173	
Collier, Joshua	071	1807	WB-2/347	AR
Collier, Morris G.	056	1891	WB-3/572	AR
Collier, Robert	103	1835	RD-7/30	AR
Collier, Thomas	028	1791	WB-A/254	AR
Collier, Thomas	071	1807	WB-2/351	AR
Collier, Zachariah	075	1769	WB-H/86	AR
Collings, Watson	086	1824	WB-D/30	AR
Collings, William	075	1709	Orig. Only	SS/AR
Collins, Abel R.	041	c1857	WB-3/224	AR

Name	Co.	Date	Recorded Copy	Original
Collins, Allen	073	1890	WB-H/509	CTY
Collins, Andrew	077	1777	WB-C/186	AR
Collins, Andrew	099	1791	RB-2/265	AR
Collins, Anthony	092	1884	WB-6/197	AR
Collins, Benjamin	057	1812	WB-A/333	AR
Collins, Brice	020	1849	RB-Q/283	AR
Collins, Cader	099	1824	RB-19/524	AR
Collins, Calvin	069	1885	WB-5/189	AR
Collins, Caroline	103	1897	WB-2/197	AR
Collins, Catharine	073	1882	WB-H/311	AR
Collins, Charles	028	1738	SS 877/79	SS/AR
Collins, Christopher	077	1761	WB-C/7	AR
Collins, Christopher	077	1795	WB-E/8	
Collins, Clary	079	1840	WB-1/31	AR-Copy
Collins, Daniel	060	1815	Orig. Only	AR
Collins, Davis	097	1865	WB-1/248	AR
Collins, Dennis	099	1785	RB-2/72	AR
Collins, Elizabeth	099	1884	WB-A/565	AR
Collins, Ephraim	063	c1801	WB-1/396	
Collins, Gideon	099	1872	RB-35/191	AR
Collins, Henry	053	c1791	RW-1/207	
Collins, Henry	047	1764	WB-1/150	
Collins, Hollon	028	1824	WB-C/246	AR
Collins, Hulda	020	1872	WB-A/91	CTY
Collins, Isaac	022	1779	Orig. Only	AR
Collins, Isaac	026	1871	WB-2/54	AR
Collins, Isham	099	1888	WB-B/278	AR
Collins, James	060	1799	Orig. Only	AR
Collins, James	039	c1815	WB-F/222	AR
Collins, James	077	1730	SS 876/192	SS/AR
Collins, James	047	1824	WB-3/700	
Collins, James	073	1762	WB-A/27	
Collins, James	039	1827	WB-H/167	AR
Collins, James T.	039	c1891	WB-V/165	AR
Collins, Jesse	039	1824	WB-H/29	AR
Collins, Jesse	070	1838	WB-AB/314	AR
Collins, John	094	c1774	Orig. Only	060 AR
Collins, John	070	1808	WB-C/57	AR
Collins, John	086	1842	WB-E/85	AR
Collins, John	063	c1802	WB-1/410	
Collins, John	010	1752	SS 879/52	SS/AR
Collins, John	086	1816	WB-C/46	AR
Collins, John	VA	1871	004 WB-A/7	004 AR
Collins, John	028	1750	DB-5/154	SS/AR
Collins, John	100	1874	WB-51/31	AR
Collins, John	028	1899	WB-F/435	
Collins, John	073	1762	WB-A/27	
Collins, John Henry	029	1893	WB-E/568	AR
Collins, Joseph	060	1815	Orig. Only	AR
Collins, Joseph	010	1802	WB-E/161	AR
Collins, Josiah	039	1866	WB-S/158	AR
Collins, Josiah	101	c1849	WB-A/224	
Collins, Josiah	024	1819	Copy	096 AR
Collins, Josiah	024	1819	WB-C/73	AR
Collins, Josiah	024	c1819	Copy	009 CTY
Collins, Lewis	044	1785	WB-1/436	CTY
Collins, Lucee	N	1730	Orig. Only	SS/AR
Collins, Luke	010	1802	WB-E/153	AR
Collins, Martha	039	1871	WB-U/29	
Collins, Martha	057	1858	WB-B/251	AR
Collins, Mary	086	1810	WB-B/235	AR
Collins, Mary	086	1822	WB-C/169	AR
Collins, Mary E.	010	1880	WB-I/123	
Collins, Merab	005	c1862	WB-D/7	
Collins, Michael	100	1857	WB-49/98	AR

Name	Co.	Date	Recorded Copy	Original
Collins, Morris C.	076	1891	WB-A1/248	AR
Collins, Nicholas	024	c1767	WB-A/205	AR
Collins, Obediah	092	1830	WB-4/22	AR
Collins, Oliver T.	005	1866	WB-C/237	AR
Collins, Patrick	009	1859	OB-L/67	AR
Collins, Peter	039	1817	WB-E/175	
Collins, Richard	072	1794	Orig. Only	AR
Collins, Richard	009	c1701	SS 874.1/13	SS/AR
Collins, Richard	072	1847	WB-2/80	AR
Collins, Richard F.	047	1818	WB-3/630	
Collins, Riddick	013	1842	WB-A/83	
Collins, Sally R.	073	1893	WB-I/56	CTY
Collins, Samuel	060	1831	WB-1/204	AR
Collins, Samuel	060	1790	Orig. Only	AR
Collins, Samuel	060	1836	WB-1/365	AR
Collins, Samuel	009	1866	OB-M/269	AR
Collins, Sarah	053	1795	RW-1/261	
Collins, Shadrach	037	1814	WB-E/68	AR
Collins, Thomas	010	1800	WB-E/112	AR
Collins, Thomas	085	1812	WB-G/218	AR
Collins, Thomas L.	100	1890	WB-51/328	
Collins, Uriah	053	1752	028 DB-5/235	SS/AR
Collins, Whitmell	039	1844	WB-L/197	AR
Collins, William	070	1895	WB-G/322	AR
Collins, William	097	1878	WB-2/152	
Collins, William	022	1791	RB-2/39	AR
Collins, William	039	c1821	WB-G/69	AR
Collins, William	086	1832	WB-D/148	AR
Collins, William C.	099	1879	WB-A/78	AR
Collis, John	107	c1843	WB-1/334	
Collson, John	010	1736	LGB-4/#138	SS/AR
Collson, John	005	1791	WB-2/23	AR
Collum, Dennis	011	c1780	WB-1/481	
Collum, Richard	011	c1791	WB-1/462	
Collum, Sion	011	1875	WB-2/118	
Colly, Isaac	057	1894	WB-C/200	AR
Colman, James	054	1848	WB-3/25	AR
Colquhoun, Charles	082	1834	WB-2/40	AR
Colquhoun, Duncan	082	1828	WB-1/289	AR
Colquhoun, John	050	1880	WB-1/156	CTY
Colquhoun, Laughlin	029	1828	WB-B/158	AR
Colson, Anna J.	054	1900	WB-6/318	CTY
Colson, Jacob	005	1808	WB-2/27	AR
Colson, James	070	1784	WB-C/52	AR
Colson, John	077	1787	WB-C/343	AR
Colson, Joseph	005	c1788	WB-1/59	AR
Colson, Kirby B.	005	1825	WB-A/113	AR
Colson, Mildred	005	1845	WB-B/195	AR
Colson, T. K.	089	1875	WB-2/37	AR
Colston, William	069	1880	WB-5/111	AR
Colter, Andrew	086	1807	WB-B/210	AR
Coltharp, H. T.	065	1892	WB-M/131	AR
Colton, Jesse	010	1803	SC/02761	AR-Copy
Colton, John	075	1692	Orig. Only	SS/AR
Colton, Simeon	081	1869	WB-15/7	AR
Coltrain, John	063	1843	WB-2/300	
Coltrain, Washington	063	1879	WB-3/162	
Coltrane, Abner	081	1869	WB-15/20	
Coltrane, Daniel W.	081	1885	WB-15/492	
Coltrane, David	081	1892	WB-16/249	AR
Coltrane, Elizabeth	081	1892	WB-16/227	AR
Coltrane, J. H.	038	1865	WB-1/256	AR
Coltrane, Jacob	081	1840	WB-7/340	AR
Coltrane, Joseph	046	1878	WB-E/242	AR
Coltrane, Kelly	046	1859	WB-C/532	AR

Name	Co.	Date	Recorded Copy	Original
Coltrane, Lindsay	046	1896	WB-F/512	AR
Coltrane, Mary	081	1891	WB-16/201	AR
Coltrane, William	081	1815	WB-4/110	AR
Coltrane, William	081	1858	WB-11/219	AR
Coltrane, William	081	1880	WB-15/331	AR
Coltson, Mary	N	1734	SS 876/298	SS/AR
Colvard, B. G.	106	1899	WB-2/457	
Colvard, Thomas	039	1846	WB-M/110	AR
Colvard, William	104	1824	WB-4/53	AR
Colvard, William	023	1885	WB-A/34	AR
Colver, Johanna E.	090	1797	WB-1/95	AR
Colvett, John	057	1816	WB-B/39	AR
Colvett, John	057	1788	WB-A/66	AR
Colvill, Maturin	011	c1776	WB-1/453	
Colvin, Alexander	070	1776	WB-C/45	AR
Colvin, Ann	029	1826	WB-B/140	AR
Colvin, Annie M.	013	1900	Orig. Only	AR
Colvin, Charles	011	1869	WB-2/41	
Colvin, Christina	013	1900	WB-D/363	AR
Colvin, James	029	1865	WB-D/99	AR
Colvin, James	029	1815	WB-A/223	AR
Colvin, John	070	1776	WB-C/47	AR
Colvin, John	070	1839	WB-C/63	AR
Colvin, John Ann	029	1885	WB-E/369	AR
Colvin, Satira	076	1896	WB-A1/204	AR
Colvin, William	029	1797	Orig. Only	AR
Colvin, William B.	070	1836	WB-C/62	AR
Colwell, Elizabeth	087	1838	WB-1/208	AR
Colwell, James	062	1892	WB-B/146	AR
Colwell, John	037	1762	WB-A/96	AR
Colwell, John	087	1829	WB-1/103	AR
Colwell, John, Sr.	021	1843	WB-1/1	AR
Colwell, Richard	087	1863	WB-2/48	AR
Colyar, Ann	103	1840	RD-8/30	AR
Colyar, John	103	1875	WB-1/84	AR
Colyar, Samuel	103	1809	RD-1/170	AR
Colyar, Zachariah	103	1834	RD-7/7	
Colyer, Zacariah	029	1898	WB-F/149	
Comander, Joseph M.	N	1698	SS 874.2/75	SS/AR
Comb, William	073	1791	WB-B/141	AR
Combast, David	040	1881	WB-2/173	AR
Combo, Britton	071	1899	WB-7/410	AR
Combs, Bennett	103	1889	WB-1/456	AR
Combs, C. W.	054	1897	WB-6/103	CTY
Combs, E. E.	003	1900	WB-B/409	
Combs, Elizabeth	054	1881	WB-4/453	CTY
Combs, Gatsey	103	1894	WB-2/79	AR
Combs, George	104	1843	WB-4/294	AR
Combs, Jeremiah	096	1771	Orig. Only	AR
Combs, John	096	1840	Orig. Only	AR
Combs, John, Sr.	096	1840	WB-2/152	
Combs, Malvina	004	1900	WB-A/234	AR
Combs, Needham	103	1877	WB-1/109	AR
Combs, Thomas	096	c1780	WB-1/120	
Combs, William	096	1775	WB-1/93	AR
Combs, William	104	1876	WB-6/132	AR
Combs, William	054	1870	WB-4/71	AR
Combs, Winnifitt	096	1750	Orig. Only	SS/AR
Combs, Zachariah	104	1866	WB-5/441	AR
Comer, Henry C.	084	1883	WB-E/278	CTY
Comer, James	081	1823	Orig. Only	AR
Comer, Margaret	020	1825	RB-K/103	AR
Comer, Nathaniel	020	1829	RB-L/336	AR
Comer, Nathaniel	020	1817	RB-H/83	AR
Comer, Nathaniel	033	1873	WB-2/33	CTY

Name	Co.	Date	Recorded Copy	Original
Comes, Thomas	096	1753	WB-1/2	AR
Comes, Tobitha	004	1892	WB-A/138	AR
Cominfort, Richard	030	1720	SS 875/249	
Commander, Alethia	075	1882	WB-O/146	AR
Commander, Aylesberry	075	1803	WB-M1/82	AR
Commander, John	075	1774	WB-I/103	AR
Commander, John	075	1808	WB-M1/183	AR
Commander, John S.	075	c1851	WB-M2/11	AR
Commander, Joseph	075	1763	WB-H/42	AR
Commander, Joseph	075	1796	WB-L/85	AR
Commander, Sarah	075	1810	WB-M1/215	AR
Commander, Thomas	075	1739	Orig. Only	SS/AR
Commander, Thomas	075	1827	WB-N/33	AR
Commander, Thomas	075	1742	Orig. Only	SS/AR
Commander, William	075	1830	WB-N/59	AR
Comminfort, Kendrick	030	c1712	SS 875/44	
Commins, Thomas	072	c1790	Orig. Only	AR
Commons, Isaac	081	1842	WB-7/434	AR
Commons, Mat	049	c1866	WB-1/1	AR
Compton, Aquilla	073	1883	WB-H/334	CTY
Compton, Hezekiah	104	1821	WB-4/14	AR
Compton, John F.	073	1890	WB-H/500	CTY
Compton, John L.	020	1896	WB-B/240	CTY
Conaway, Edward	092	1783	WB-2/11A	AR
Conaway, James	028	c1745	SS 877/26	
Conaway, Stephen	056	1864	WB-2/61	AR
Conder, John	097	1875	WB-2/95	
Conder, Lewis	097	c1862	WB-2/36	AR
Conder, Philip	097	1861	WB-1/188	AR
Condry, Sarah	064	1890	WB-2/218	
Cone, Adaline	069	1890	WB-5/331	AR
Cone, Burkley	069	c1882	105 WB-3/510	105 AR
Cone, Burkley	069	1892	WB-5/371	AR
Cone, Burtis	069	1880	WB-5/114	AR
Cone, Gilford	069	1856	WB-1/548	AR
Cone, John	009	1813	OB-A/232	AR
Cone, John	047	1784	WB-3/61	
Cone, Mary E.	045	1869	WB-1/5	
Cone, Neel	063	c1782	WB-1/113	
Cone, Sabry	009	c1832	OWB/500	AR
Cone, Stapleton	063	1852	WB-2/384	
Cone, William	063	c1795	WB-1/217	
Cone, William	069	1850	WB-1/522	AR
Conely, Michal	029	1770	Orig. Only	AR
Coner, John	075	1774	WB-I/79	AR
Conerly, John	035	1839	Orig. Only	AR
Conger, John	085	c1784	WB-B/78	AR
Congilton, William	009	1755	SS 879/242	SS/AR
Congleton, Allen	009	1869	WB-1/22	CTY
Congleton, Daniel C.	009	1826	OB-A/375	AR
Congleton, David	009	1779	OWB/137	AR
Congleton, Henry	009	1776	Orig. Only	AR
Congleton, Henry	079	1876	WB-2/130	AR
Congleton, James	009	1815	OB-A/243	AR
Congleton, James D.	009	1881	WB-1/282	CTY
Congleton, James R.	079	1858	WB-1/8	AR
Congleton, Jane	009	1816	OB-A/262	AR
Congleton, Luther O.	009	1879	WB-1/235	CTY
Congleton, Major	009	1890	WB-1/481	CTY
Congleton, Thomas	009	1855	OB-K/45	AR
Congleton, William S.	009	1900	WB-2/210	CTY
Conigland, Andrew	047	1879	WB-6/213	AR
Conigland, Nancy	047	1880	WB-6/236	AR
Conklin, Augustus	024	1899	075 WB-O/491	075 AR
Conklin, Augustus	024	1899	WB-E/304	AR

Name	Co.	Date	Recorded Copy	Original
Conley, Albert	064	1885	WB-2/179	AR
Conley, Allen	064	1883	WB-2/130	AR
Conley, Allen	014	c1859	WB-2/299	
Conley, Amos	014	1892	WB-2/493	CTY
Conley, Elizabeth	038	1896	WB-4/1	AR
Conley, Hugh	014	1875	WB-2/98	
Conley, Isaac	014	1876	WB-2/122	
Conley, Israel P.	017	1882	WB-B/104	AR
Conley, J. W.	014	1892	WB-2/499	CTY
Conley, James M.	066	1887	WB-1/27	AR
Conley, John	013	1882	WB-B/268	AR
Conley, John	014	1868	WB-1/44	AR
Conley, Joseph	064	1871	WB-2/20	AR
Conley, Lucy	014	1877	WB-2/127	
Conley, Nancy	014	1885	WB-2/309	CTY
Conley, Thomas	014	1890	WB-2/492	
Conley, William C.	061	c1862	WB-1/90	AR
Conly, Duncan	029	1855	WB-C/337	AR
Conn, Alexander	065	1895	WB-M/374	AR
Conn, Cila	075	1885	WB-0/243	
Connally, George	020	1819	RB-H/237	
Connally, Thomas	VA	1829	020 RB-L/391	020 AR
Connel (Hardt), Sarah	040	1885	WB-2/242	AR
Connell, John	090	1821	WB-3/69	AR
Connell, Mary Ellen	040	1892	WB-2/417	
Connell, Michael	047	1760	WB-1/14	
Connell, Robert	040	1874	WB-2/75	
Connell, Thomas	037	c1769	Orig. Only	AR
Connelly, Anny	071	1814	WB-3/126	AR
Connelly, Bryant	061	c1857	WB-1/60	AR
Connelly, W. W.	014	1892	WB-2/486	CTY
Connelly, William	039	1816	WB-E/122	AR
Conner, Abrams	028	1892	WB-F/52	
Conner, Albert W.	010	1896	WB-I/469	AR
Conner, Andrew	009	1754	SS 878/178	SS/AR
Conner, Ann	053	1812	RW-1/456	AR
Conner, Asa	019	1865	WB-A/279	AR
Conner, Cader	075	1785	WB-K/137	AR
Conner, Charles	065	1804	WB-A/173	AR
Conner, Cornelius	021	1847	WB-1/60	AR
Conner, Demsey	075	1790	WB-K/197	AR-Nunc.
Conner, Demsey	075	1754	SS 881/83	SS/AR
Conner, Edward	029	1760	DB-1/1760	AR
Conner, Elenor	054	1845	WB-2/315	AR
Conner, Elizabeth	047	1812	WB-3/529	
Conner, Elizabeth	021	1896	WB-3/102	AR
Conner, Elizabeth	026	1865	WB-1/383	AR
Conner, George	019	1832	WB-A/13	AR
Conner, George A.L.	075	1807	WB-M1/160	AR
Conner, Jacob	053	1800	RW-1/320	
Conner, Jacob	053	c1780	RW-1/93	
Conner, Jacob	026	1844	WB-1/31	AR
Conner, Jacob	009	1834	OB-B/300	AR
Conner, James	096	1761	WB-1/14	AR
Conner, James	065	1835	WB-G/206	AR
Conner, James	047	1802	WB-3/370	
Conner, Jesse R.	010	1885	WB-I/207	
Conner, John	084	1797	OW/100	AR
Conner, John	065	1832	WB-G/88	AR
Conner, John	073	1792	WB-B/180	AR
Conner, John	057	1798	WB-A/223	AR
Conner, John	075	1753	SS 881/119	SS/AR
Conner, John M.	081	1900	WB-17/90	
Conner, Michael	057	1852	WB-B/213	AR
Conner, Noah	010	1858	WB-H/71	AR
Conner, Phillip	053	1731	009 OWB/8	009 AR
Conner, Rachel	057	1857	WB-B/237	AR
Conner, Thomas	084	c1801	WB-A/208	CTY
Conner, William	010	1818	WB-G/25	AR
Conner, William	026	1870	WB-2/46	AR
Conner, William	047	1807	WB-3/467	
Conner, William	084	1857	WB-C/241	CTY
Conner, William H.	054	1875	WB-4/198	CTY
Connerly, Cullin	035	1812	WB-A/70	AR
Connerly, John	056	1751	028 DB-5/270	SS/AR
Connerly, William	028	1807	WB-B/282	AR-Copy
Connolly, William	017	c1852	Orig. Only	AR
Connor, Elizabeth	084	c1790	OW/99	AR
Connor, Henry W.	065	1873	WB-K/129	AR
Connor, John	065	1832	WB-G/88	
Connor, Joseph W.	081	1885	WB-15/570	AR
Connor, Lilly	065	1844	WB-H/183	AR
Connor, Mary L.	060	1900	WB-5/142	AR
Conoly, James	083	1872	WB-3/42	AR
Conoly, Peter	083	1873	WB-3/61	AR
Conoly, Thomas J.	083	1877	WB-3/132	AR
Conoway, Francis	018	1864	WB-D/67	AR
Conrad, Elizabeth	038	c1858	WB-1/140	AR
Conrad, Henry	032	1834	WB-1/242	
Conrad, Jacob	090	1848	WB-4/251	AR
Conrad, John	038	1850	WB-1/22	AR
Conrad, John	090	1802	WB-2/27	AR
Conrad, John	090	1841	WB-4/86	AR
Conrad, John J.	106	1873	WB-2/37	AR
Conrad, Joseph C.	038	1889	WB-3/135	AR
Conrad, Leonard	038	c1865	WB-1/261	AR
Conrad, Peter	038	1850	WB-1/13	AR
Conrad, Solomon	090	1845	WB-4/204	AR
Conrad, Timothy	038	1884	WB-2/513	AR
Conrad, William A.	038	1864	WB-1/247	AR
Conrow, Thornton	PA	1882	075 WB-0/169	075 AR
Contipi, Michael	028	1743	SS 878/14	
Conway, D. W.	017	1891	WB-B/206	AR
Conway, Jeames	028	1770	Orig. Only	AR
Conway, John	072	1799	Orig. Only	AR
Conway, John J.	017	c1887	WB-B/227	AR
Conway, Margaret	072	c1862	Orig. Only	AR
Conway, Margaret	064	1861	WB-1/78	AR
Conway, Mary	028	1774	Orig. Only	SS/AR
Conway, William	028	1813	WB-C/65	AR
Conwell, William	071	1880	WB-6/312	AR
Conyers, Ephraim	039	1844	WB-M/33	AR
Conyers, Francis	039	c1858	WB-0/372	AR
Conyers, John	039	c1844	WB-L/252	
Conyers, Richard	039	1881	WB-U/262	AR
Conyers, William	039	1804	WB-C/15	
Cook, Abraham	046	1793	WB-A/56	AR
Cook, Abraham	022	1814	WB-A/251	AR
Cook, Abraham	054	1801	WB-1/390	AR
Cook, Abraham	104	1801	WB-2/57	AR
Cook, Abram	022	1880	WB-E/204	AR
Cook, Adam	006	1817	WB-A/28	AR
Cook, Allen	046	1846	WB-C/244	AR
Cook, Alston	051	1888	WB-C/369	AR
Cook, Amy	039	1824	WB-H/2	AR
Cook, Arthur	103	1809	RD-1/167	AR
Cook, Arthur	099	1797	RB-3/20	AR
Cook, Benjamin	103	1796	WI-B/92	
Cook, Benjamin	039	1816	WB-E/37	AR
Cook, Catherine	009	1898	WB-2/143	CTY

Name	Co.	Date	Recorded Copy	Original
Cook, Charles	005	1818	WB-2/25	AR
Cook, Charles	065	1821	WB-A/223	AR
Cook, Christanna	047	1895	WB-7/146	
Cook, Delilah	039	1860	WB-Q/566	AR
Cook, Delphia	102	1897	WB-A/131	AR
Cook, Edward	026	1843	WB-1/18	AR
Cook, Elisha	021	1843	WB-1/6	AR
Cook, Eliza Jane	075	1884	WB-O/189	AR
Cook, Elizabeth	092	1824	WB-3/159	AR
Cook, Emily	075	1879	WB-O/102	AR
Cook, Ephraim	104	1873	WB-6/64	AR
Cook, Fanny	028	1826	WB-C/273	AR
Cook, Frances	073	1848	WB-F/433	AR
Cook, Francis	086	c1882	Orig. Only	AR
Cook, G. A.	065	1894	WB-M/248	AR
Cook, G. L.	069	1891	WB-5/361	AR
Cook, George	085	1822	WB-H/187	AR
Cook, Harriet C.	028	1851	WB-D/173	AR
Cook, Harrison	033	1894	WB-2/158	CTY
Cook, Havana L.	100	1878	WB-51/26	AR
Cook, Henry	035	1843	Orig. Only	AR
Cook, Henry	022	1806	WB-A/130	AR
Cook, Henry	073	c1799	Orig. Only	AR
Cook, Henry	090	1822	Orig. Only	AR
Cook, Isaac	075	1798	WB-M1/5	AR
Cook, Isaac	046	1843	WB-C/161	AR
Cook, Isaac W.	046	1861	WB-D/97	AR
Cook, Jacob	028	1819	WB-C/176	AR
Cook, Jacob	103	1830	RD-6/181	AR
Cook, Jacob W.	072	1846	WB-2/75	AR-Nunc.
Cook, James	092	1880	WB-6/140	AR
Cook, James	087	1786	WB-A/17	AR
Cook, James	092	1829	WB-4/21	
Cook, James M	046	1869	WB-E/9	AR
Cook, Jane	054	1896	WB-5/568	CTY
Cook, John	060	1796	Orig. Only	AR
Cook, John	022	1777	Orig. Only	AR
Cook, John	090	1807	WB-2/81	AR
Cook, John	104	1785	WB-1/170	AR
Cook, John	026	1852	WB-1/147	AR
Cook, John	035	1799	WB-A/85	AR
Cook, John	073	1812	WB-D/278	AR
Cook, John	073	1844	WB-F/184	AR
Cook, John	075	1697	SS 874.2/80	SS/AR
Cook, John	103	1817	RD-4/99	AR
Cook, John	071	1812	WB-3/90	AR
Cook, John	092	1804	WB-3/62A	AR
Cook, John	028	1772	Orig. Only	AR
Cook, John	010	1745	Orig. Only	SS/AR
Cook, John	035	1788	WB-A/77	AR
Cook, John	067	1890	WB-2/283	AR
Cook, John	028	1785	WB-A/101	
Cook, John	046	1821	Orig. Only	AR
Cook, John A.	085	1889	WB-2/354	CTY
Cook, John F.	046	1900	WB-F/243	AR
Cook, John F.	054	1875	WB-4/182	CTY
Cook, John Lett	022	1803	WB-A/42	AR
Cook, John M.	092	1888	WB-6/278	AR
Cook, John R.	099	1817	RB-13/208	AR
Cook, Jones	103	1783	WI-A/26	AR
Cook, Joseph	016	1897	WB-4/256	AR
Cook, Joseph F.	099	1862	RB-32/254	AR
Cook, Laura	054	1887	WB-5/168	CTY
Cook, Lazarus	069	1854	WB-1/538	AR
Cook, Lemuel	099	1864	RB-33/172	AR
Cook, Margaret	085	c1870	Orig. Only	CTY
Cook, Margaret	021	1864	WB-1/204	AR
Cook, Margaret	046	1817	Orig. Only	AR-Nunc.
Cook, Mary	022	1834	WB-C/6	AR
Cook, Mary T.	085	1877	WB-1/400	CTY
Cook, Michael	006	1844	WB-A/65	AR
Cook, N. Caroline	102	1893	WB-A/92	AR
Cook, Nancy	099	1840	RB-24/420	AR
Cook, Nancy	056	1892	WB-3/581	AR
Cook, Nathan	046	1852	WB-C/363	AR
Cook, Patsey	092	c1832	WB-4/43	
Cook, Perigreen	087	1852	WB-1/420	
Cook, Polly	021	1899	WB-3/240	AR
Cook, R. G.	046	1894	WB-F/351	AR
Cook, Ransom	032	1832	WB-1/178	
Cook, Richard	054	c1800	WB-1/89	AR
Cook, Richard J.	104	1853	WB-5/94	
Cook, Robert	087	1896	WB-4/15	AR
Cook, Robert	092	1780	WB-1/138	AR
Cook, Robert	065	1832	WB-G/97	AR
Cook, Robert F.	054	1889	WB-5/297	CTY
Cook, Samuel	028	1822	WB-C/211	AR
Cook, Samuel	010	1757	SS 880/240	SS/AR
Cook, Sarah	075	1794	WB-L/22	AR-Nunc.
Cook, Sarah	039	1875	WB-S/126	AR
Cook, Sarah J.	027	1898	WB-2/146	AR
Cook, Sarah J.	051	1898	WB-C/551	AR
Cook, Seaser	010	1791	WB-D/185	AR
Cook, Shem	044	1796	WB-4/41	CTY
Cook, Sophia	021	1895	WB-3/96	AR
Cook, Thomas	028	1784	WB-A/78	AR
Cook, Thomas	028	1798	WB-B/38	AR
Cook, Thomas	046	1805	WB-A/66	AR
Cook, Thomas	100	1794	WB-7/244	AR
Cook, Thomas	039	c1798	WB-B/71	
Cook, Thomas	009	c1781	OWB/164	AR
Cook, Thomas	104	1819	WB-3/195	AR
Cook, Thomas	090	1823	Copy	092 AR
Cook, Thomas	054	c1807	WB-1/52	AR
Cook, Thomas	024	1734	SS 876/344	
Cook, Thomas	054	c1791	WB-1/85	AR
Cook, Thomas	090	1823	WB-3/96	AR
Cook, Thomas B.	039	1861	WB-R/195	
Cook, Thomas C.	001	1886	WB-2/323	AR
Cook, Thomas E.	046	1897	WB-G/44	AR
Cook, Tobias	103	1817	RD-4/80	AR
Cook, Vincent	039	1874	WB-U/105	AR
Cook, W. John	090	1837	WB-3/324	AR
Cook, W. L.	065	1875	WB-K/203	AR
Cook, William	071	1874	WB-6/142	AR
Cook, William	010	1785	WB-D/35	AR
Cook, William	092	1812	WB-3/100	AR
Cook, William	010	1838	WB-G/300	AR
Cook, William	071	1758	Orig. Only	SS/AR
Cook, William	090	1825	WB-3/132	AR
Cook, William	063	1792	WB-1/184	
Cook, William	065	1841	WB-H/43	AR
Cook, William	092	1801	WB-3/44	AR
Cook, William T.	084	1896	WB-F/46	CTY
Cooke, Albert M.	001	c1884	Orig. Only	AR
Cooke, Benjamin	010	1806	WB-F/1	AR
Cooke, Charles W.	RI	1895	006 WB-E/291	006 AR
Cooke, Dorsey	051	1855	WB-A/373	
Cooke, Eleanor A.	068	1898	WB-D/558	
Cooke, Esther	019	1816	WB-D/117	AR

Name	Co.	Date	Recorded Copy	Original
Cooke, J. A.	039	1881	WB-U/256	AR
Cooke, Jackey B.	071	1887	WB-6/564	AR
Cooke, John	039	1900	WB-V/193	AR
Cooke, John	099	1814	RB-11/238	AR
Cooke, John	035	c1774	Orig. Only	AR
Cooke, John	028	1785	Orig. Only	AR
Cooke, Margaret	099	1819	RB-15/316	
Cooke, Margaret	054	c1802	WB-1/86	AR
Cooke, Mary M.	044	1827	WB-10/329	CTY
Cooke, Patience	039	1891	WB-U/525	AR
Cooke, Richard	044	1815	WB-7/510	CTY
Cooke, Richard	044	1785	WB-1/437	CTY-Nunc.
Cooke, Richard D.	044	1811	WB-7/205	CTY
Cooke, Roland A.	073	1881	WB-H/275	CTY
Cooke, Sarah E.	039	1900	WB-V/205	AR
Cooke, William	054	1802	WB-1/84	AR
Cooker, Benjamin	071	1806	WB-2/316	AR
Cooker, John	022	c1781	Orig. Only	AR
Cooley, G. M.	069	1899	WB-6/77	AR
Cooley, John	047	1769	WB-1/245	
Cooley, Obedience	099	1870	RB-35/102	AR
Cooliron, Jacob	085	1817	WB-G/460	AR
Coon, George	060	1844	WB-2/223	AR
Coon, George	060	1887	WB-4/359	AR
Coon, Jacob	033	1843	WB-1/53	AR
Coon, Jacob	085	1872	WB-1/148	CTY
Coon, Michal	085	1765	WB-A/36	AR
Coon, William	060	1842	WB-2/141	AR
Coone, W. P.	054	1897	WB-6/82	CTY
Coonrod, Peter	081	1795	WB-2/23	AR
Coons, Adam	021	1872	WB-2/72	AR
Coop, John	073	1844	WB-F/184	
Coope, Nicholas	085	c1785	WB-C/175	
Cooper, Alexander	065	1863	WB-J/158	AR
Cooper, Alexander	044	1880	WB-23/361	CTY
Cooper, Barnit	085	1818	WB-G/509	AR
Cooper, Benjamin	075	1784	WB-K/109	AR
Cooper, Benjamin	030	c1815	WB-3/51	
Cooper, Benjamin	044	1761	Orig. Only	CTY
Cooper, Benjamin	035	1848	WB-2/33	AR
Cooper, Benjamin	015	1777	100 WB-2/106	AR
Cooper, Benjamin	011	c1784	WB-1/464	
Cooper, Blount	037	1854	WB-G/49	AR
Cooper, Bluford	054	1889	WB-5/295	CTY
Cooper, Charity	028	1881	WB-E/286	
Cooper, Charles	038	1866	WB-1/269	AR
Cooper, Daniel W.	010	1895	WB-I/433	AR
Cooper, David	046	1792	WB-A/49	AR
Cooper, Dianah	013	1900	WB-D/446	AR
Cooper, Dina	060	1800	Orig. Only	AR
Cooper, Elizabeth	001	1852	WB-1/61	AR
Cooper, Elizabeth	069	1827	WB-1/348	AR
Cooper, Elizabeth	013	c1858	Orig. Only	AR
Cooper, Elizabeth	063	c1783	WB-1/97	
Cooper, Fanny W.	020	1889	WB-A/547	
Cooper, Fleet	087	1828	WB-1/81	
Cooper, Fleet, Sr.	087	c1795	Orig. Only	AR
Cooper, George	028	1865	WB-D/410	
Cooper, George	069	1845	Orig. Only	AR
Cooper, George	035	1793	Orig. Only	AR-Nunc.
Cooper, H. M.	020	1889	WB-A/502	CTY
Cooper, Henderson	044	c1867	WB-23/14	
Cooper, Henry	099	1810	RB-9/341	AR
Cooper, Isaac	060	1789	Orig. Only	AR
Cooper, J. W.	023	1899	Copy	061 AR
Cooper, J. W.	023	1899	WB-A/176	AR
Cooper, Jacob	039	c1794	Orig. Only	AR
Cooper, James	022	1848	WB-C/223	AR
Cooper, James	096	1874	WB-4/26	
Cooper, James	044	1867	WB-22/641	CTY
Cooper, James E.	063	1872	WB-2/22	
Cooper, James G.	054	1899	WB-6/250	CTY
Cooper, Jesse	063	1859	WB-2/458	
Cooper, Jesse	072	1854	WB-2/136	AR
Cooper, John	035	1867	WB-3/117	AR
Cooper, John	069	1785	WB-1/33	AR
Cooper, John	099	1866	RB-33/571	AR
Cooper, John	047	1794	WB-3/233	
Cooper, John	054	c1794	WB-1/81	AR
Cooper, John	069	1798	WB-1/119	AR
Cooper, John S.	087	1866	WB-2/99	AR
Cooper, John, Sr.	072	1791	Orig. Only	AR
Cooper, Jonathan	010	1831	WB-G/207	AR
Cooper, Joseph	011	c1779	WB-1/493	
Cooper, Joseph	075	1754	SS 881/82	SS/AR
Cooper, Kannon	039	c1794	WB-A/167	AR
Cooper, Luerany	077	1839	WB-F/281	AR
Cooper, Marcom	069	1811	WB-1/215	AR
Cooper, Mary H. E.	009	1897	WB-2/121	CTY
Cooper, N. W.	069	1884	WB-5/200	AR
Cooper, Nancy	010	1869	WB-I/6	AR
Cooper, Richard	001	1885	WB-2/264	AR
Cooper, Samuel	009	c1734	OWB/20	AR
Cooper, Samuel	085	1793	WB-E/209	AR
Cooper, Samuel	085	c1777	WB-B/75	AR
Cooper, Starling	081	1843	WB-8/30	AR
Cooper, Tempe	069	1880	WB-5/99	AR
Cooper, Thomas	047	1794	WB-3/218	
Cooper, Thomas	092	1807	WB-3/79	
Cooper, William	085	1811	WB-G/170	AR
Cooper, William	039	c1801	WB-B/72	
Cooper, William	069	1850	WB-1/510	AR
Cooper, William	065	1834	WB-G/185	AR
Cooper, William A.	069	1875	WB-5/12	AR
Cooper, Willis	096	1809	WB-2/47	AR
Cooper, Wilson	030	1870	WB-5/6	AR
Coopper, Edmond	099	1836	RB-23/547	AR
Coor, Anna M.	103	1885	WB-1/420	AR
Coor, Calvin	103	1857	RD-12/252	
Coor, Dorcas	103	1840	RD-7/575	AR
Coor, Edmund	103	1895	WB-2/93	AR
Coor, Fleet	103	1808	RD-1/91	AR
Coor, Hilary	103	1843	Orig. Only	AR
Coor, James	028	1797	WB-B/14	AR
Coor, Newton C.	103	1887	WB-1/421	AR
Coor, Thomas	103	1794	WI-A/510	AR
Coorel, James	028	1897	WB-F/259	
Coornetzar, Catharine	085	1833	WB-H/589	AR
Coots, James	046	1820	Orig. Only	AR
Cope, Andrew	085	1845	WB-I/254	AR
Cope, Catharine	085	1815	WB-G/384	AR
Cope, Elizabeth	085	1834	WB-H/640	AR
Cope, Elizabeth	033	1844	WB-1/55	AR
Cope, Jacob	085	1845	WB-K/2	AR
Cope, John	033	1846	WB-1/85	AR
Cope, Nicholas	085	c1785	Orig. Only	AR
Cope, Philip	085	1835	WB-H/657	AR
Cope, Yost	085	c1785	WB-C/66	AR
Copelain, Fruza	010	1847	WB-G/424	AR

Name	Co.	Date	Recorded Copy	Original
Copeland, Abner	073	1884	WB-H/348	CTY
Copeland, Ann	071	1887	WB-6/553	AR
Copeland, Anna	022	1890	WB-E/423	AR
Copeland, Anthony	010	1818	WB-G/40	AR
Copeland, Benjamin	051	1839	WB-A/189	
Copeland, Benjamin	071	1898	WB-7/387	AR
Copeland, C. B.	105	1876	WB-2/198	AR
Copeland, Charity	071	1858	Orig. Only	AR
Copeland, Charles	024	1786	WB-B/75	AR
Copeland, David	073	1800	WB-C/163	AR
Copeland, David	051	1862	WB-B/46	AR
Copeland, Dempsey	024	1871	WB-E/17	AR
Copeland, Eli	051	1831	WB-A/100	
Copeland, Elisha	024	1818	WB-C/64	AR
Copeland, Eliza	010	1884	WB-I/173	
Copeland, Elizabeth	103	1855	RD-12/115	AR
Copeland, Emily A.	077	1855	WB-F/465	AR
Copeland, Henry	071	1876	WB-6/195	AR
Copeland, Henry	077	1819	WB-F/26	AR
Copeland, Isaac	092	1852	WB-4/320	AR
Copeland, Isaac	092	1808	WB-3/89	AR
Copeland, James	083	1817	WB-1/340	
Copeland, James	022	1809	WB-A/39	AR
Copeland, James	024	c1752	Orig. Only	SS/AR
Copeland, James	024	1883	WB-E/123	AR
Copeland, Jesse	024	c1785	WB-A/117	AR
Copeland, John	024	c1773	WB-A/128	AR
Copeland, John	083	c1799	WB-1/58	
Copeland, Jordan	041	1824	WB-2/225	AR
Copeland, Joseph	024	1891	WB-E/192	AR
Copeland, Joseph	024	1800	Orig. Only	AR-Nunc.
Copeland, Josiah	024	1827	WB-C/129	AR
Copeland, Judith	071	1828	WB-4/40	AR
Copeland, Kindred	051	1860	WB-B/21	
Copeland, Mark	022	1822	WB-B/66	AR
Copeland, Martha Ann	051	1874	WB-C/116	AR
Copeland, Nancy	092	1860	WB-5/47	
Copeland, Robert	103	1862	RD-13/464	AR
Copeland, Roderic C.	022	1862	WB-D/87	AR
Copeland, Sally	051	1880	WB-C/244	AR
Copeland, Sarah	024	c1809	Orig. Only	AR
Copeland, Sarah	092	1814	WB-3/111	AR-Nunc.
Copeland, Theny	075	1824	WB-M1/398	AR
Copeland, Thomas	024	1852	WB-C/334	AR
Copeland, Timothy	024	1874	WB-E/49	AR
Copeland, William	022	1792	RB-1/43	AR
Copeland, William	N	1724	SS 876/14	SS/AR
Copeland, William	024	1753	Orig. Only	SS/AR
Copelen, Elizabeth	099	1877	RB-35/385	AR
Copes, Peter S.	075	c1858	WB-M2/57	AR
Copes, Thomas	099	1847	RB-26/441	AR
Copland, David	022	1859	WB-D/31	AR
Copley, Alexander	036	1884	WB-A/59	CTY
Copley, George	036	1891	WB-A/220	CTY
Copley, John	073	1825	WB-D/581	AR
Copp, Henry	046	1812	WB-A/82	AR
Coppage, William	077	1814	WB-E/403	AR
Coppedge, Charles B.	005	1880	WB-D/103	
Coppedge, Clarra	039	1898	WB-V/139	AR
Coppedge, Franky	069	1896	WB-5/527	AR
Coppedge, Henry	039	1880	WB-S/270	AR
Coppedge, Jesse	069	1870	WB-1/604	AR
Coppedge, Perry	039	1899	WB-V/171	AR
Coppedge, W. D.	039	1887	WB-U/389	AR
Copper, Gustavus	028	1788	WB-A/169	AR
Copper, John	075	1825	WB-N/16	AR
Coppersmith, John	075	c1796	WB-L/72	AR
Coppersmith, Lowry	075	1840	WB-N/162	AR
Coppersmith, Martha	075	N. D.	WB-M2/99	AR
Coppidge, Augusten	003	1793	WB-C/227	AR
Copple, Nicholas	085	c1807	WB-G/111	AR
Coram, Richard	084	1864	WB-D/19	CTY
Coram, Robert	065	1795	WB-B/18	AR
Corbell, Temperance	047	1873	WB-6/96	AR
Corbet, Johnston	103	1830	RD-6/351	AR
Corbett, Jacob H.	070	1899	Copy	012 AR
Corbett, Jacob H.	070	1899	WB-H/292	AR
Corbett, James	027	1821	WB-A/40	
Corbett, James R.	011	1892	WB-2/253	
Corbett, John	056	1892	WB-2/128	AR
Corbett, John	070	1822	WB-C/59	AR
Corbett, John M.	070	1857	WB-C/654	AR
Corbett, Joseph	041	1888	WB-4/269	AR
Corbett, Nancy	020	1850	RB-Q/453	AR
Corbett, Robert J.	041	1900	WB-4/520	AR
Corbett, S. Wallace	076	1895	WB-A1/186	AR
Corbett, Solomon	020	1881	WB-A/305	CTY
Corbett, Sophia	076	1884	WB-A1/34	AR
Corbett, Thomas	070	1863	WB-D/143	AR
Corbett, Thomas	002	1693	Orig. Only	SS/AR
Corbett, William	020	1881	WB-A/325	CTY
Corbett, William R.	070	1851	WB-C/531	AR
Corbin, Edmund	070	1782	WB-C/49	AR
Corbin, Jean	070	1775	Orig. Only	SS/AR
Corbit, John	037	1807	WB-D/270 & 290	AR
Corbit, Thomas	010	1848	WB-G/431	AR
Corbitt, Catherine	079	1892	WB-2/583	AR
Corbitt, David	070	1752	DB-D/49	
Corbitt, James M.	079	1898	WB-3/159	AR
Corbitt, Lewis	026	1851	WB-1/126	AR
Corbitt, Pleasant	020	1866	RB-T/204	AR
Corbitt, Thomas	070	c1792	Orig. Only	AR
Corbitt, W. S.	079	1892	WB-2/581	AR
Corbitt, W. S.	026	1869	WB-2/17	
Cordemann, Barnard	057	1798	WB-A/218	AR
Corder, William	020	1782	RB-A/213	
Cording, Mary	009	1840	OB-C2/370	AR
Cording, Thomas	009	c1798	OWB/346	AR
Cording, William	053	1785	RW-1/136	
Cordon, William	053	1813	RW-1/479	AR-Copy
Core, Thomas	071	1752	Orig. Only	SS/AR
Corey, Jesse	063	1869	WB-3/8	
Corey, John, Sr.	075	1757	Orig. Only	SS/AR
Corey, Smith	063	c1893	Orig. Only	AR
Corl, Daniel	085	1870	WB-1/55	
Corl, Mary	085	1891	WB-2/491	CTY
Corl, Peter	085	1842	WB-I/130	AR
Corlew, John	047	1785	WB-3/201	
Corlew, Lemuel	047	1809	WB-3/489	
Corlew, Martha	047	1820	WB-3/660	
Corlew, Sarah	047	1800	WB-3/344	
Corlin, John	047	1762	WB-1/54	
Cormack, Ellen	065	1895	WB-M/406	AR
Corn, Annie	073	1887	WB-H/437	CTY
Corn, Dickerson	001	1881	WB-2/184	AR
Corn, Dickson	001	1886	WB-2/304	AR
Corn, Eveline	001	1887	WB-2/340	AR
Corn, H. P.	013	1900	WB-D/460	AR
Corn, John A.	090	1895	WB-6/371	AR

Name	Co.	Date	Recorded Copy	Original
Corn, John P.	050	1846	Orig. Only	CTY
Corn, John P.	013	c1831	050 WB-1/19	
Corn, Richerson	001	1878	WB-2/131	AR
Corn, Robert	099	1816	RB-13/47	AR
Cornatzer, Daniel	033	1856	WB-1/125	AR
Cornatzer, John	033	1837	WB-1/4	AR
Cornealson, Jonathan	067	1874	WB-2/58	AR
Cornelius, Austin	021	1871	WB-2/56	
Cornelius, James	021	c1859	WB-1/158	AR
Cornelius, William	060	1800	Orig. Only	AR
Cornell, Katura H.	009	1876	WB-1/154	CTY
Corner, John	068	1828	WB-B/59	
Cornick, Endymion	VA	1812	030 WB-5/248	030 AR
Cornick, Henry, Sr.	VA	1855	030 WB-5/251	030 AR
Cornick, William	030	1860	WB-4/233	AR
Cornish, Jacob	038	1898	WB-4/124	AR
Cornish, Temperance	105	1868	WB-1/138	AR
Cornish, William	032	1844	WB-1/437	
Cornwell, Edieth	084	1846	WB-C/38	CTY
Cornwell, Elias	084	1853	WB-C/153	CTY
Cornwell, Grace	084	1854	WB-C/197	CTY
Cornwell, Marlin B.	026	1897	WB-2/538	AR
Cornwell, Micajah	026	1849	WB-1/94	AR
Cornwell, Sarah	026	1893	WB-2/460	AR
Cornwell, W. E.	026	1896	WB-2/519	AR
Corofton, Henry	009	1757	SS 879/254	
Corp, Elinor	075	1720	SS 875/221	
Corp, John	N	1718/9	SS 875/178	SS/AR
Corp, John	075	1753	SS 881/81	SS/AR
Corpening, C. L. S.	064	1877	WB-2/58	AR
Corpening, Calvin	017	c1883	Orig. Only	AR
Corpening, Caroline	017	1884	WB-B/107	
Corpening, Elizabeth	017	c1863	WB-A/152	AR
Corpening, George	014	1856	WB-2/108	
Corpening, George	014	c1856	Copy	050 AR
Corpening, Jacob H.	014	1875	WB-2/124	
Corpening, John	014	c1834	Copy	017 AR
Corpenning, Albert G.	021	1894	WB-3/67	
Corprew, Jonathan	096	1795	Orig. Only	AR
Corprew, Matthew	096	1787	WB-1/155	AR
Corprew, Thomas	009	c1809	OB-A/79	AR
Corprew, Thomas	024	1749	Orig. Only	SS/AR
Corprew, Wilson	030	1854	WB-4/189	AR
Corree, James	010	1754	Orig. Only	SS/AR
Correl, John	085	1822	Orig. Only	AR
Correll, Adam	085	c1803	WB-E/227	AR
Correll, Christian	085	1880	WB-1/526	CTY
Correll, David	085	1848	WB-K/74	AR
Correll, John A.	085	1843	WB-I/194	AR
Correll, John, Sr.	054	c1829	WB-2/89	
Correll, Philip	085	1843	WB-I/147	AR
Correll, Terrissa	016	1843	WB-1/3	
Corriher, Jacob	085	1830	WB-H/487	AR
Corriker, Catharine	085	1881	WB-1/558	CTY
Corriker, Daniel	085	1883	WB-2/52	CTY
Corriker, George	085	1898	WB-3/257	CTY
Corriker, Henry	085	1851	WB-K/135	AR
Corriker, John F.	085	1897	WB-3/191	CTY
Corriker, Octavia	085	1888	WB-2/230	CTY
Corsbie, Hans	046	1822	WB-B/147	AR
Corsbie, Mariah	046	1898	WB-G/97	AR
Cortheran, Thomas	104	1881	WB-6/205	AR
Cortland, Herbert H.	046	1899	WB-G/124	
Cortland, Mary C.	013	1891	WB-C/102	AR
Cortland, Mary C.	013	1891	050 WB-2/92	050 CTY
Cortney, John	005	1799	WB-2/30	AR
Corum, William	065	1794	WB-A/167	AR
Cory, Elizabeth	075	1807	WB-M1/143	AR
Cory, Hepsabeth	063	1892	WB-4/92	AR
Cory, John, Sr.	063	c1802	WB-1/400	
Cory, Joseph	063	1879	WB-3/167	
Cory, Milly A.	063	1893	WB-4/109	AR
Cory, Samuel	079	1893	WB-3/25	AR
Corzin, John	065	1777	WB-A/192	AR
Corzine, Levi	085	1825	WB-H/305	AR
Corzine, Nicholas	065	1769	WB-A/200	AR
Corzine, Noah	016	1854	WB-1/240	
Corzine, R. F.	085	1871	WB-1/93	CTY
Cosand, Aaron	077	1793	WB-C/463	AR-Copy
Cosand, Gabriel	077	1810	WB-E/350	AR
Cosand, John	077	1825	WB-F/94	AR
Cosby, Dabney	099	1862	RB-32/338	AR
Cosens, Cornelius	046	1875	WB-E/152	AR
Cosens, Richard	009	1871	WB-1/96	CTY
Cossens, Richard	009	1830	OB-B/49	AR
Coste, Ephriam	N	1719	SS 875/332	SS/AR
Costen, Benjamin	041	1816	WB-2/110	AR
Costen, Christian	041	c1800	WB-1/239	AR
Costen, David	041	1835	WB-2/366	AR
Costen, Demsey	041	1782	WB-1/33	AR
Costen, Demsy	041	1820	WB-2/172	AR
Costen, Elizabeth	041	1819	WB-2/159	AR
Costen, Francis	072	1799	Orig. Only	AR
Costen, George	041	1866	WB-3/345	AR
Costen, Henry	041	1848	WB-3/103	AR
Costen, Isaac	041	1819	WB-2/156	AR
Costen, James	024	c1768	WB-A/119	AR
Costen, James	041	1847	WB-3/87	AR
Costen, James	041	1812	WB-2/76	AR
Costen, James K.	041	1863	WB-3/302 & 354	AR
Costen, James, Sr.	041	1791	WB-1/95	AR
Costen, John	072	c1771	Orig. Only	AR
Costen, Matthias	072	c1785	WI/L47	AR
Costen, Thomas	041	1809	WB-2/40	AR
Costephens, Margaret	017	c1854	WB-A/66	AR
Costillo, Michael	005	1798	WB-2/29	AR
Costner, Catharine	040	1871	WB-2/19	AR
Costner, Daniel	026	1882	WB-2/226	AR
Costner, J. D.	026	1864	WB-1/338	AR
Costner, Jacob	060	1820	Copy	040 AR
Costner, Jacob	040	1862	WB-1/139	
Costner, Jonas	060	1832	Copy	040 AR
Costner, Jonas	060	1832	WB-1/257	AR
Costner, Joseph	026	1873	WB-2/110	AR
Costner, Lizzie K.	060	1897	WB-5/42	AR
Costner, Simon P.	040	1886	WB-2/274	AR
Coston, Ellen	024	1874	WB-E/51	AR
Coston, Erasmus H.	072	1873	WB-4/56	AR
Coston, James, Sr.	072	1853	WB-2/127	AR
Coston, John	070	1803	WB-AB/83	AR
Coston, Thomas	072	c1814	WB-A/28	AR
Coteral, William	024	c1767	WB-B/10	AR
Cothran, James	078	1842	WI-15/157	
Cothran, Jesse	078	1837	WI-13/181	
Cothran, John	078	1834	WI-12/325	
Cothran, William	078	1862	WB-18/269	AR
Cotner, Rosannah	073	1826	WB-E/107	AR
Cotten, Alexander	037	1826	WB-F/56	AR
Cotten, Allen	071	1795	WB-2/90	AR

Name	Co.	Date	Recorded Copy	Original
Cotten, Amos	037	1781	WB-B/70	AR
Cotten, Ann W.	022	1846	WB-C/192	AR
Cotten, Arthur S.	063	1861	WB-2/507	
Cotten, Fanny	037	1818	WB-E/193	AR
Cotten, Frederick	037	1815	WB-E/102	AR
Cotten, Godwin	037	1837	WB-F/201	AR
Cotten, Green	037	c1885	WB-H/45	
Cotten, Henry J.	022	1858	WB-D/28	AR-Nunc.
Cotten, James	071	1797	WB-2/153	AR
Cotten, James	010	1758	SS 882/59	SS/AR
Cotten, Jesse	056	1822	WB-1/432	AR
Cotten, Jessee	010	1803	WB-E/191	AR
Cotten, Joab	047	1796	WB-3/261	
Cotten, John W.	099	1848	RB-26/49	AR
Cotten, Lewis	010	1882	WB-I/139	
Cotten, Lydia	071	1783	WB-1/267	AR
Cotten, Margaret	099	1856	RB-29/517	AR
Cotten, Primus	073	1886	WB-H/418	CTY
Cotten, Randolph	037	1852	WB-F/482	AR
Cotten, Rhoderick	022	1827	WB-B/135	AR
Cotten, Samuel	071	1774	Orig. Only	SS/AR
Cotten, Seth	022	1815	WB-A/266	AR
Cotten, Stephen W.	022	1877	WB-E/147	AR
Cotten, Susan	073	1891	WB-H/549	CTY
Cotten, William	071	1794	WB-2/42	
Cotten, Willie	037	1807	WB-D/269	AR
Cotter, Timothy	075	1812	WB-M1/254	AR
Cottle, Robert	035	1817	WB-A/68	AR
Cotton, Augustus	051	1886	WB-C/342	AR
Cotton, Benjamin	037	1789	WB-C/105	AR-Nunc.
Cotton, Charles	071	1763	WB-1/83	AR
Cotton, Dolly M.	047	1849	WB-4/279	
Cotton, Godwin	051	1830	WB-A/5	
Cotton, Henry	047	1785	WB-3/90	
Cotton, James W.	047	c1865	WB-5/129	
Cotton, John	071	1790	WB-1/458	
Cotton, John	010	1728	SS 876/141	SS/AR
Cotton, John	071	1761	WB-1/53	
Cotton, John	071	1742	Orig. Only	SS/AR (N)
Cotton, Joseph	047	1772	WB-1/314	AR
Cotton, Letitia	AL	1849	071 WB-5/81	071 AR
Cotton, Martha	103	1888	WB-1/448	AR
Cotton, Martha	047	1895	WB-7/245	AR
Cotton, Mary	071	1783	WB-1/276	
Cotton, Mary	047	1844	WB-4/229	AR-Copy
Cotton, Nancy	051	c1858	WB-B/17	
Cotton, Sally	051	1833	WB-A/53A	
Cotton, Sarah	071	1754	Orig. Only	SS/AR
Cotton, Sarah	071	c1753	Copy	073 AR
Cotton, William	047	1797	WB-3/287	
Cotton, William	044	1890	WB-24/101	CTY
Cottrell, Allen J.	054	1894	WB-5/519	CTY
Cottrell, Samuel	044	1843	WB-15/502	CTY
Cottrell, Solomon	044	1864	WB-22/177	CTY
Cottrell, Thomas	104	1828	WB-4/118	AR
Cottrell, William	017	c1847	WB-A/145	AR
Cottrell, William	017	1885	WB-B/122	AR
Couch, Elijah	073	1864	WB-G/449	CTY
Couch, George W.	046	1864	WB-D/232	AR
Couch, John	073	1877	WB-H/385	CTY
Couch, John	046	1866	WB-D/302	AR
Couch, Joshua	104	1860	WB-5/246	
Couch, Meshach	046	1824	WB-B/187	AR
Couch, Nathan	073	1874	WB-H/85	CTY
Couch, Thomas	073	1845	WB-F/265	AR
Couch, Thomas	073	c1829	Orig. Only	AR
Couch, Thomas	036	1892	WB-A/268	CTY
Couch, William	073	1891	WB-H/541	CTY
Coudert, Charles	NY	1898	050 WB-2/299	050 CTY
Coughanour, Christian	085	c1808	WB-G/103	AR
Coulson, William	N	c1712	SS 875/53	
Coulter, Elcana P.	021	1874	WB-2/106	AR
Coulter, Elvira	060	1890	WB-4/411	AR
Coulter, Henson	073	1832	WB-E/280	AR
Coulter, John	060	1866	WB-3/78	AR
Coulter, Martin	021	1847	WB-1/59	AR
Coulter, S. M.	060	1896	WB-5/31	AR
Council, Addison	099	1893	WB-C/161	AR
Council, Ann E.	029	1870	WB-E/23	AR
Council, Arthur	011	c1819	WB-2/331	
Council, Charles	083	1819	WB-1/205	AR
Council, Ensley	022	1881	WB-E/225	AR
Council, Isam	083	c1826	WB-1/339	AR
Council, J. E.	099	1895	WB-C/379	AR
Council, Josiah	037	1887	WB-H/87	AR
Council, Kimbro	022	c1843	Orig. Only	AR
Council, Kinchin K.	011	1887	WB-2/212	
Council, Mary	011	c1822	WB-2/351	
Council, Mathew	083	c1817	WB-1/217	AR
Council, Nancy	083	1820	WB-1/216	AR
Council, Robert	022	1862	WB-D/88	AR
Council, Robert C.	022	1887	WB-E/352	AR
Council, Syman	011	1885	WB-2/195	
Councill, Jordan	006	1838	WB-A/14	AR
Councilman, George C.	068	1888	WB-D/278	
Counsel, Claresa	069	1849	WB-1/518	AR
Counsel, Nathan	047	1787	WB-3/123	
Counsell, Hardy	063	1780	WB-1/68	
Counsell, Joshua	037	1774	WB-A/214	AR
Counsil, Charles	037	1805	WB-D/236	AR
Countz, Nicholas	060	1798	Orig. Only	AR
Couplan, Samuel	047	1786	WB-3/106	
Coupland, William	047	1782	WB-3/28	
Courtney, Joseph	073	1822	WB-E/25	AR
Courtney, Joseph	073	1800	WB-C/161	AR
Courtney, Robert	072	1751	028 DB-5/156	SS/AR
Courts, George	084	1847	WB-C/58	CTY
Courts, Martha	099	1862	RB-32/248	AR
Cousins, Agnes	044	1889	WB-24/230	CTY
Cousins, William	044	1852	WB-19/107	CTY
Coutanike, Michael	009	1761	OWB/54	AR
Coventon, Josiah	086	1818	WB-C/97	AR
Coventon, William	086	1818	WB-C/91	AR
Covey, Mary	046	1807	WB-A/76	AR
Covey, Noble	085	c1790	WB-C/28	AR
Covington, Alexander	083	1883	WB-6/253	AR
Covington, Benjamin	005	1863	WB-C/190	AR
Covington, Benjamin C.	082	c1850	Copy	097 AR
Covington, Benjamin C.	082	1855	WB-4/96	AR
Covington, David A.	097	1898	WB-2/532	AR
Covington, David A.	097	1870	WB-2/31	AR
Covington, Diza C.	082	1879	Orig. Only	AR
Covington, Edmond	084	1863	WB-C/376	CTY
Covington, Elevetta	082	1889	WB-6/431	AR
Covington, Ellen W.	082	1895	WB-6/520	AR
Covington, Henry	082	1866	WB-5/12	AR
Covington, Henry A.	082	1886	WB-6/341	AR
Covington, Henry C.	071	1862	WB-5/266	AR
Covington, Isaac	028	1795	WB-A/344	AR

Name	Co.	Date	Recorded Copy	Original
Covington, James H.	082	1888	WB-6/358	AR
Covington, James M.	090	1888	WB-6/189	AR
Covington, John	084	1818	WB-A/153	CTY
Covington, John	082	1809	WB-1/134	AR
Covington, John	082	1862	WB-4/156	AR
Covington, John Wall	082	1809	WB-1/130	AR
Covington, L. A.	070	1899	WB-H/197	AR
Covington, Levin	028	1781	Orig. Only	AR
Covington, Rebecca	082	1863	WB-4/159	AR
Covington, Salathiel	082	1826	WB-1/273	AR
Covington, Stephen W.	082	1879	WB-6/182	AR
Covington, Susan A.	097	1897	WB-2/584	AR
Covington, Thomas P.	082	1899	WB-7/20	AR
Covington, Thomas T.	082	1872	WB-6/83	AR
Covington, Wesley	082	1895	WB-6/523	AR
Covington, William	082	1858	WB-4/126	AR
Covington, William	005	1829	WB-A/163	AR
Covington, William	082	1794	WB-1/40	AR
Covington, William	026	1861	WB-1/262	AR
Covington, William H.	082	1900	WB-7/57	AR
Covington, William L.	082	1864	WB-4/186	AR
Covington, William P.	005	1894	WB-D/359	AR
Covington, Wyatt	078	1889	WB-19/259	AR
Cowan, Aaron	085	c1801	WB-E/200	AR
Cowan, Aaron V.	085	1850	WB-K/106	AR
Cowan, Abel	085	1843	WB-I/144	AR
Cowan, Ann	085	1859	Orig. Only	AR
Cowan, Benjamin	085	1829	WB-H/449	AR
Cowan, Daniel	085	1879	WB-1/514	CTY
Cowan, David	085	1837	WB-I/26	AR
Cowan, David	065	c1809	WB-B/16	AR
Cowan, David	085	c1802	WB-E/236	AR
Cowan, Elizabeth	085	1858	PQS.18/460	
Cowan, Elmira R.	085	1893	WB-2/554	CTY
Cowan, George	085	c1802	WB-E/200	AR
Cowan, Henry	085	c1799	WB-E/204	AR
Cowan, Isaac	085	1853	WB-K/160	AR
Cowan, Isaac	085	1851	WB-K/131	AR
Cowan, Isabella	070	1836	WB-AB/307	AR
Cowan, James	085	1819	WB-G/535	AR
Cowan, Jean	085	c1801	WB-E/202	AR
Cowan, Jincy	085	1867	WB-L/2	AR
Cowan, John	085	c1789	WB-E/207	AR
Cowan, John	085	c1789	WB-G/117	
Cowan, John	011	c1807	WB-2/302	
Cowan, John	085	1827	WB-H/408	AR
Cowan, John	070	1815	WB-AB/227	AR
Cowan, John	070	1827	WB-C/60	AR
Cowan, John	085	1846	WB-K/13	AR
Cowan, John	085	1827	WB-H/388	AR
Cowan, John A.	051	1898	WB-C/542	AR
Cowan, John M.	085	1887	WB-2/261	CTY
Cowan, Mary	085	1890	WB-2/407	CTY
Cowan, Mary	085	1836	WB-H/708	AR
Cowan, Mary	085	c1802	WB-E/220	AR
Cowan, Mary S.	085	1854	WB-K/169	AR
Cowan, Nenian	085	1844	WB-I/228	AR
Cowan, Robert	085	1833	WB-H/594	AR
Cowan, Robert H.	070	1845	WB-AB/428	AR
Cowan, Robert H.	070	1872	WB-E/253	AR
Cowan, Samuel	085	1815	WB-G/365	AR
Cowan, Sarah	070	1874	WB-E/282	AR
Cowan, Sarah E.	076	1899	WB-A1/245	AR
Cowan, Thomas	085	1818	WB-G/505	AR
Cowan, Thomas	070	1831	WB-AB/274	AR
Cowan, Thomas L.	085	1856	WB-K/218	AR
Cowan, William	085	c1806	WB-E/237	AR
Cowan, William	085	1834	Orig. Only	AR
Cowan, William	085	c1789	WB-B/196	AR
Cowan, William	085	1840	WB-I/69	AR
Cowan, William F.	054	1880	WB-4/386	CTY
Cowan, William J.	011	1864	WB-1/314	
Coward, John	024	c1771	WB-A/204	AR
Coward, Nathan	010	1836	WB-G/258	AR
Coward, Starkey	010	1900	WB-K/25	
Coward, Starky	010	1898	WB-I/562	
Coward, William	010	1843	WB-G/356	AR
Coward, Wineford	010	1842	WB-G/339	AR
Coward, Chloe B.	009	1866	OB-M/240	AR
Coward, Fanny	081	1884	WB-15/476	AR
Coward, John	010	1737	Orig. Only	SS/AR
Coward, John H.	059	1878	WB-A/144	CTY
Coward, William	045	1896	WB-1/375	AR
Cowart, Stephen	080	1868	WB-1/1	AR
Cowden, Benjamin	085	c1780	WB-C/212	AR
Cowden, John	085	1777	WB-A/250	AR
Cowden, Robert	065	1782	WB-A/201	AR
Cowden, Samuel	065	1782	WB-A/168	AR
Cowel, Benjamin	072	c1831	WB-1/146	AR
Cowell, Benjamin	030	1756	Copy	028 AR
Cowell, Benjamin	030	1756	SS 880/67	SS/AR
Cowell, Bernard	037	1829	WB-F/96	AR
Cowell, Elizabeth	030	1861	WB-4/243	
Cowell, Henry G.	009	1828	OB-A/467	AR
Cowell, Mary E.	018	1860	WB-D/60	
Cowell, William	096	1795	Orig. Only	AR
Cowell, William	009	c1811	OWB/462	AR
Cowen, Elias	046	1816	Orig. Only	AR
Cowen, Esther	060	1824	Orig. Only	AR
Cowen, Garrett	002	1721	SS 875/303	SS/AR
Cowen, James	060	1822	Orig. Only	AR
Cowen, John	065	1776	WB-A/179	AR
Cowen, John	064	1870	WB-2/9	AR
Cowen, Texas G.	086	1890	WB-F/386	AR
Cowen, William	065	1785	WB-B/27	AR
Cowey, Charles	063	1842	WB-2/288	
Cowey, Mary L.	063	1850	WB-2/355	
Cowin, Susannah	064	1875	WB-2/49	AR
Cowles, Josiah	106	c1858	WB-1/64	AR
Cowper, Annis	051	1890	WB-C/412	AR
Cowper, Caleb	077	1832	WB-F/209	AR
Cowper, Louisa	041	1804	WB-1/204	AR
Cowper, Richard G.	051	1873	WB-C/97	AR
Cowper, William F.	041	1849	WB-3/131	AR
Cox, Aaron	049	c1841	WI-1-2/17	AR
Cox, Aaron	081	1854	WB-10/104	
Cox, Aaron	079	c1856	WB-1/79	AR
Cox, Abel	081	1881	WB-15/360	
Cox, Abel	081	1880	WB-15/328	AR
Cox, Abel	081	1887	WB-16/33	AR
Cox, Abel	081	1854	WB-10/90	AR
Cox, Abraham	009	1797	OWB/335	AR
Cox, Abram	053	1826	WB-4/334	AR
Cox, Abram	079	1898	WB-3/135	AR
Cox, Abram R.	081	1883	WB-15/445	AR
Cox, Alexander	030	1859	WB-4/233	AR
Cox, Amy	081	1865	WB-13/239	AR
Cox, Andrew	057	1818	WB-B/46	AR
Cox, B. R.	071	1899	WB-7/446	AR
Cox, Benjamin	081	1817	WB-4/392	AR

Name	Co.	Date	Recorded Copy	Original
Cox, Benjamin	010	1804	WB-E/229	AR
Cox, Benjamin	081	1847	WB-8/455	AR
Cox, Caleb	077	1824	WB-F/76	AR
Cox, Catharine	081	1848	WB-9/14	AR
Cox, Charity	079	1872	WB-2/64	AR
Cox, Charity B.	103	1888	WB-1/441	AR
Cox, Charles	035	1759	SS 882/168	SS/AR
Cox, Charles	081	1855	WB-11/411	AR-Copy
Cox, Charles	073	1860	WB-G/338	AR
Cox, Charles	072	c1771	RW/L36	AR
Cox, Charles	081	1840	WB-7/319	AR
Cox, Charles	072	1891	WB-4/252	AR
Cox, Charlotte	010	1874	WB-I/55	AR
Cox, Cranford	081	1887	WB-16/60	AR
Cox, Daniel	081	1835	WB-6/500	AR
Cox, David	006	1862	004 WB-1/8	004 AR
Cox, Dennis	081	1897	WB-16/449	AR
Cox, Diana	103	1900	WB-2/290	AR
Cox, Drucilla	083	1896	Orig. Only	AR
Cox, Durant	072	c1865	Orig. Only	AR
Cox, Edward	030	1751	Orig. Only	SS/AR
Cox, Elany	057	1826	WB-B/96	AR
Cox, Eleazer	081	1895	WB-16/340	AR
Cox, Eli	072	1829	WB-1/49	AR
Cox, Elisha	081	1845	WB-8/203	AR
Cox, Elisha	057	1785	WB-A/51	AR
Cox, Elizabeth	072	1794	Orig. Only	AR-Nunc.
Cox, Elizabeth	081	1876	WB-15/219	
Cox, Elkanah	009	c1804	OWB/423	AR
Cox, G. H.	080	1890	WB-1/146	AR
Cox, Gilbert	083	c1810	WB-1/119	
Cox, Gilbert	083	1865	WB-2/222	AR
Cox, Hannah	081	1897	WB-16/447	AR
Cox, Harman	081	1889	WB-16/120	AR
Cox, Harmon	022	1880	WB-E/202	AR
Cox, Henry	068	1835	WB-B/95	
Cox, Hermon	081	1812	WB-3/322	AR
Cox, Isaac	081	1797	WB-2/29	AR
Cox, Isham	081	1894	WB-16/333	AR
Cox, Israel	085	c1778	WB-B/134	AR
Cox, Jacob	018	1871	WB-E/35	AR
Cox, Jacob	075	1819	WB-M1/327	AR
Cox, Jacob	081	1838	WB-7/148	AR
Cox, James	089	1843	WB-1/21	AR
Cox, James A.	087	1887	WB-3/354	AR
Cox, Jemima	103	1831	RD-6/231	AR
Cox, Jesse	053	1801	RW-1/334	
Cox, Joanna V.	046	1890	WB-F/21	AR
Cox, John	103	1863	RD-13/621	AR
Cox, John	024	1856	WB-C/392	AR
Cox, John	081	1803	WB-2/115	AR-Copy
Cox, John	081	1843	Orig. Only	AR
Cox, John	077	1807	WB-E/298	AR
Cox, John	005	1836	WB-B/68	AR
Cox, John	047	1784	WB-3/74	
Cox, John	072	1743	LGB-4/#141	SS/AR
Cox, John D.	030	1854	WB-4/183	AR
Cox, John H.	001	1898	WB-3/232	AR
Cox, John H.	057	1860	WB-B/252	AR
Cox, John M.	068	1873	WB-D/50	
Cox, John R.	004	1898	WB-A/204	AR
Cox, Joseph	077	1813	WB-E/378	AR
Cox, Joseph	037	1825	WB-F/31	AR
Cox, Joseph	053	1772	RW-1/40	AR
Cox, Joseph B.	080	1896	WB-1/276	AR
Cox, Joseph M.	038	1897	WB-4/42	AR
Cox, Joseph M.	077	1863	WB-F/539	AR
Cox, Joshua	081	1847	WB-8/529	AR
Cox, Joshua	090	1836	WB-3/305	AR
Cox, Josiah	072	c1810	WB-A/22	AR
Cox, Josiah	103	1819	RD-4/219	AR
Cox, July	018	1891	WB-E/194	AR
Cox, Kinsey	103	1814	RD-3/154	AR
Cox, Levi	103	1832	RD-6/369	AR
Cox, Levinah	057	1837	WB-B/130	AR
Cox, Lidia	081	1844	WB-8/103	AR
Cox, Longfield	028	1783	Orig. Only	AR
Cox, Lydia P.	103	1883	WB-1/281	AR
Cox, M. W.	077	1891	WB-H/204	AR
Cox, Mahlon	081	1826	WB-5/252	AR
Cox, Marmaduke	057	1808	WB-A/317	AR
Cox, Marmaduke	030	1806	WB-2/292	
Cox, Martha	072	1851	WB-2/115	AR
Cox, Mary	072	1873	WB-4/59	AR
Cox, Mary	081	1877	WB-15/271	AR
Cox, Mary	077	c1827	WB-F/145	AR
Cox, Mary	107	1836	WB-1/22	
Cox, Mary	081	1880	WB-15/336	AR
Cox, Mary	072	1885	WB-4/171	
Cox, Mary	010	1822	WB-G/95	AR
Cox, Mary	090	1837	WB-3/317	AR
Cox, Mary Susan	072	1884	WB-4/155	AR
Cox, Matthew	104	1804	WB-2/131	AR
Cox, Micajah	103	1839	RD-7/445	AR
Cox, Micajah	103	1808	RD-1/89	AR
Cox, Mildred	090	1827	WB-3/163	AR
Cox, Mildred	090	1822	WB-3/91	AR
Cox, Miriam	103	1859	RD-13/40	AR
Cox, Missouri	084	1846	WB-C/38	CTY
Cox, Moses	085	c1778	WB-A/261	AR
Cox, Moses	087	1857	WB-1/502	AR
Cox, Moses	072	1776	RW/L26	AR
Cox, Nancy	077	1856	WB-F/481	AR
Cox, Nancy	028	1858	WB-D/311	
Cox, Naomi	053	1830	WB-5/30	AR
Cox, Nathan	081	1878	WB-15/285	AR
Cox, Nathan	081	1042	WB-7/432	AR
Cox, Nathan T.	081	1893	WB-16/265	
Cox, Neri	081	1888	WB-16/82	AR
Cox, Owen B.	057	1844	WB-B/170	AR
Cox, Peter	016	1888	WB-4/1	AR
Cox, Phebe	081	1815	WB-4/107	AR
Cox, Rachel L.	081	1873	WB-15/114	AR
Cox, Reuben	081	1888	WB-16/102	AR
Cox, Richard	053	1829	WB-4/610	AR
Cox, Richard	103	1785	Orig. Only	AR
Cox, Richard	090	1810	WB-2/106	AR
Cox, Richard	103	1809	RD-1/166	AR
Cox, Robert	103	1795	WI-A/565	AR
Cox, Rosa	103	1884	WB-1/302	AR
Cox, Sampson D.	066	1890	WB-1/86	AR
Cox, Samuel	010	1869	WB-I/5	AR
Cox, Samuel	065	1848	WB-I/140	AR
Cox, Samuel	103	1800	Orig. Only	AR
Cox, Sanders P.	045	1882	WB-1/87	AR
Cox, Sarah	047	1824	WB-3/703	
Cox, Serena	087	1856	WB-1/487	AR
Cox, Silas	103	1863	RD-13/532	AR
Cox, Simpson	103	1839	RD-7/445	
Cox, Smithson	103	1828	RD-5/433	AR

Name	Co.	Date	Recorded Copy	Original
Cox, Solomon	081	1848	WB-9/42	AR
Cox, Stanton	103	1857	RD-12/322	AR
Cox, Stephen	081	1837	WB-7/116	AR
Cox, Susan	020	1878	WB-A/241	CTY
Cox, Susan	059	1894	WB-B/96	CTY
Cox, Theodosia	010	1886	WB-I/213	
Cox, Thomas	030	1743	LGB-4/#143	SS/AR
Cox, Thomas	046	1771	WB-A/37	AR
Cox, Thomas	081	1871	WB-15/68	AR
Cox, Thomas	103	1818	RD-4/184	AR
Cox, Thomas	030	1825	WB-3/190	
Cox, Thomas	103	1810	RD-1/217	
Cox, Thomas	092	1824	WB-3/159	AR
Cox, Thomas	081	1872	WB-15/77	
Cox, Thomas	081	1875	WB-15/175	AR
Cox, Thomas	030	1840	WB-4/77	
Cox, Thomas	081	1822	WB-5/69	AR
Cox, Thomas	030	1838	WB-4/48	
Cox, Thomas	010	1894	WB-I/400	AR
Cox, Thomas	047	1836	WB-4/127	
Cox, Thomas	081	1873	WB-15/128	
Cox, Thomas	068	c1860	WB-C/145	AR-Copy
Cox, Thomas L.	081	1897	WB-16/416	AR
Cox, Thomas S.	073	1842	WB-F/115	
Cox, Thos., Jr.	030	1850	WB-4/157	
Cox, William	073	1767	WB-A/53	
Cox, William	081	1845	WB-8/121	AR
Cox, William	087	1835	WB-1/163	AR
Cox, William	053	1785	RW-1/126	AR
Cox, William	006	1878	WB-E/38	AR
Cox, William	032	1869	WB-3/7	AR
Cox, William	071	1814	WB-3/131	AR
Cox, William	056	1886	WB-3/412	AR
Cox, William	022	1818	WB-A/294 & 313	
Cox, William	028	1802	WB-B/148	AR
Cox, William	081	1896	WB-16/369	AR
Cox, William	081	1856	WB-11/186	AR
Cox, William	047	1803	WB-3/384	
Cox, William	079	1870	009 WB-1/69	009 AR
Cox, William	047	1772	WB-1/309	
Cox, William	103	1854	RD-11/546	AR
Cox, William H.	005	1885	WB-D/182	AR
Cox, William J.	005	1896	WB-D/390	AR
Cox, William K.	084	1870	WB-E/22	CTY
Cox, William T.	081	1890	WB-16/176	AR
Cox, Zilpha J.	045	1892	WB-1/228	AR
Cox, Zimri	081	1866	WB-13/444	AR
Coxe, Francis S.	086	1852	WB-E/226	AR
Coxe, Robert	024	1730	Orig. Only	SS/AR
Coxe, Tench C.	PA	1877	086 WB-F/99	086 AR
Coxetter, Esther	070	1850	WB-C/511	AR
Coxsey, John	086	1791	Orig. Only	AR
Coyler, Cornelius	009	c1741	OWB/32	AR
Cozart, Adeline	036	1898	WB-A/428	CTY
Cozart, Anthony	044	1781	WB-1/301	CTY
Cozart, Anthony	073	c1800	Orig. Only	AR
Cozart, Brodie	044	1887	WB-23/581	CTY
Cozart, Calvin	044	1887	WB-24/4	CTY
Cozart, Catharine	078	1880	WB-19/113	AR
Cozart, Elizabeth	078	1861	WB-18/203	AR
Cozart, Isabella	044	1900	WB-24/469	CTY
Cozart, Jacob	078	1858	WB-18/28	AR
Cozart, James	099	1865	RB-33/423	AR
Cozart, James	073	1806	WB-D/165	AR
Cozart, Joshua	078	1854	WB-17/300	AR
Cozart, Mary	044	1849	WB-18/2	CTY
Cozart, Mary A.	044	1893	078 WB-19/372	078 AR
Cozart, Mary A.	044	1893	WB-24/213	CTY
Cozart, Sarah	044	1893	WB-24/232	CTY
Cozart, Simeon	044	1838	WB-14/254	CTY
Cozart, Thomas S.	099	1888	WB-B/275	AR
Cozart, W. D.	044	c1890	WB-24/234	CTY
Cozens, Martha	099	1811	RB-10/159	AR
Cozort, David	078	1810	WI-5/200	AR
Cozort, Thomas	078	1851	WB-13/477	AR
Cozort, William C.	017	c1883	Orig. Only	AR
Crabtree, Abraham	073	1876	WB-H/133	CTY
Crabtree, Charles F.	073	1898	WB-I/139	CTY
Crabtree, Dicey	036	1886	WB-A/94 & 120	
Crabtree, Elizabeth	073	1871	WB-H/50	CTY
Crabtree, Elizabeth	073	1868	WB-G/535	CTY
Crabtree, Elizabeth	044	1880	WB-23/368	CTY
Crabtree, H. M.	073	1900	WB-I/186	CTY
Crabtree, James	073	1832	WB-E/282	AR
Crabtree, John L.	044	1870	WB-23/32	CTY
Crabtree, Lurany	073	1853	WB-G/40	AR
Crabtree, Mahala	073	1884	WB-H/361	CTY
Crabtree, N. M.	073	c1900	WB-I/186	
Crabtree, Richard	073	1849	WB-F/433	AR
Crabtree, S. W.	059	1898	WB-B/209	CTY
Crabtree, Sarah	036	1889	WB-A/148	CTY
Crabtree, Susanna	073	1855	WB-G/106	AR
Crabtree, Thomas	073	1833	WB-E/291	AR
Crabtree, Thomas	073	1774	WB-A/177	
Crabtree, William	073	1868	WB-G/543	CTY
Crabtree, William	073	1812	WB-D/333	AR
Crabtree, William H.	022	1885	WB-E/311	AR
Crabtree, William M.	073	1894	WB-I/27	CTY
Craddock, Civel	087	1891	WB-3/490	AR
Craddock, James F.	031	1898	Orig. Only	AR
Craddock, Thomas	103	1803	Orig. Only	AR
Cradock, Mary A.	063	1860	WB-2/475	
Cradock, Richard	075	c1685	Orig. Only	SS/AR
Crafford, James	041	1808	WB-2/32	AR
Crafford, William, Jr.	041	1814	WB-2/90	AR
Crafford, William, Sr.	041	1814	WB-2/88	AR
Craft, Anthony C.	072	1791	Orig. Only	AR
Craft, Archibald	072	1840	WB-2/23	AR
Craft, David	060	1863	WB-3/60	AR
Craft, Isaac	072	c1817	WB-A/18	AR
Craft, J. P.	040	1894	WB-2/463	AR
Craft, Joel	101	1875	WB-A/13	AR
Craft, John	010	1762	WB-A/63	AR
Craft, Margaret	106	c1854	WB-1/51	AR
Craft, Michael	040	1865	WB-1/186	
Craft, Stephen C.	072	1792	Orig. Only	AR
Craft, Thomas	044	1789	WB-2/104	CTY
Craft, Thomas	038	1869	WB-2/9	AR
Crafton, Thomas	009	c1784	OWB/192	AR
Crag, Thadeus	072	1827	WB-1/6	AR
Crage, Aaron	026	1860	WB-1/258	AR
Crage, Crozier	085	c1776	WB-C/172	AR
Craig, A. M.	010	1874	WB-I/59	AR
Craig, Abram	073	c1818	WB-D/552	AR
Craig, Alexander	073	1855	WB-G/113	AR
Craig, Charles	072	1896	WB-4/404	AR
Craig, David	073	1862	WB-G/397	AR
Craig, David	073	c1785	WB-A/361	AR
Craig, Elizabeth	097	1857	WB-1/134	AR

Name	Co.	Date	Recorded Copy	Original
Craig, Elmer H.	WI	1898	Copy	013 AR
Craig, Emily Jane	MD	1893	040 WB-3/13	040 AR
Craig, Henrietta	073	1892	WB-H/566	CTY
Craig, Hugh B.	097	1863	WB-2/26	
Craig, Huldah	097	1849	WB-1/61	AR
Craig, Isaac	073	1859	WB-G/219	CTY
Craig, James	073	1821	WB-D/603	AR
Craig, James	073	1827	WB-E/146	AR
Craig, James A.	001	1849	WB-1/18	AR
Craig, John W.	001	1888	WB-2/358	AR
Craig, Josiah	097	1863	WB-1/220	AR
Craig, Martha	065	1827	WB-B/5	AR
Craig, Martha	065	1841	WB-H/51	AR
Craig, Martha O.	065	1825	WB-B/18	AR
Craig, Mary	073	1826	WB-E/103	AR
Craig, Mary A.	070	1869	WB-E/154	AR
Craig, Mary A.	010	1855	WB-H/13	AR
Craig, Matilda	097	1877	WB-2/127	AR
Craig, Moses	065	1801	WB-A/213	AR
Craig, Richard	N	1696	SS 874.2/88	SS/AR
Craig, Robert H.	040	1875	WB-2/90	AR
Craig, Ruth Ann	070	1888	WB-F/190	AR
Craig, Samuel	073	1791	WB-B/112	AR
Craig, Samuel	017	1842	WB-A/1	AR
Craig, Susanah	017	1866	WB-A/169	AR
Craig, Thomas	070	1881	WB-E/426	AR
Craig, Vernon H.	WI	1900	013 WB-D/412	
Craig, William	090	1823	WB-3/107	AR
Craig, William	065	1830	WB-F/57	AR
Craige, Alfred	049	1898	WB-2/400	AR
Craige, Elizabeth	085	1881	WB-1/568	CTY
Craige, John	017	c1854	WB-A/77	AR
Craige, John	073	1817	WB-D/552	AR
Craige, Robert N.	085	c1857	Orig. Only	AR
Craige, William	073	1785	WB-A/329	AR
Craighead, Alexander	065	c1765	WB-A/167	AR
Craiglow, Leonard	085	1822	WB-H/177	AR
Craike, Thomas	070	1792	WB-C/53	AR
Crain, Thomas	096	1821	WB-2/83	AR
Crain, William	086	1837	WB-E/38	AR
Crandal, Lydia	012	c1775	DB-B/54	
Crandall, Christopher	009	1882	WB-1/308	CTY
Crandall, R. C.	079	1897	WB-3/114	AR
Crandell, James	009	1824	OB-A/331	AR
Crandell, Matthias	009	1828	OB-B/1	AR
Crane, Forrester	065	1890	WB-L/460	AR
Crane, Hiram	026	1863	WB-1/304	AR
Crane, Mary Ann	OH	c1884	013 WB-B/398	
Crane, Philemon	104	1786	WB-1/191	AR
Cranfield, Hezekiah	085	c1795	WB-E/222	AR
Cranfill, Jonathan	033	1847	WB-1/91	AR
Cranford, Absaly	081	1883	WB-15/434	AR
Cranford, Burgess	085	1885	WB-2/157	CTY
Cranford, Elias L.	085	1873	WB-1/167	CTY
Cranford, John	072	c1785	Orig. Only	AR
Cranford, John	035	1818	WB-A/78	AR
Cranford, Nelly	081	1850	Orig. Only	AR
Cranford, Sawney	081	1848	Orig. Only	AR
Cranford, Seth	081	1884	WB-15/441	AR
Cranford, Temple	081	1871	WB-15/73	AR
Cranford, William	072	1745	SS 878/58	SS/AR
Cranford, Wilson	021	1889	WB-2/471 & 497	AR
Crank, Caleb T.	030	1880	WB-5/76	AR
Crank, John	030	1825	WB-3/193	
Cranor, Sarah	046	1801	WB-A/68	AR
Cranor, Thomas	046	1796	WB-A/54	AR
Cransett, Jane	020	1825	RB-B/344	AR
Cratch, Caroline	009	1891	WB-1/518	CTY
Cratch, Richard	028	1811	WB-C/23	AR
Cratch, Sally Ann	028	1828	WB-C/298	AR
Crater, John	038	1884	WB-2/475	AR
Crause, George H.	090	1899	WB-6/514	AR
Craven, Anderson	081	1872	WB-15/83	AR
Craven, B.	081	1882	WB-15/405	AR
Craven, Daniel	032	1888	WB-4/24	AR
Craven, Elizabeth	081	1848	Orig. Only	AR-Copy
Craven, Emma	099	1896	WB-C/529	AR
Craven, Enoch	081	1893	WB-16/252	
Craven, Henry	081	1843	WB-8/15	AR
Craven, James	024	1755	SS 880/12	SS/AR
Craven, John	081	1850	WB-11/414	
Craven, John	099	1808	RB-8/383	AR
Craven, John	081	1846	WB-8/338	AR
Craven, John	024	1766	WB-1/20	AR
Craven, John	081	1832	WB-6/227	AR
Craven, John A.	081	1850	WB-9/217	AR
Craven, John A.	032	1887	WB-3/568	AR
Craven, John R.	081	1858	WB-11/225	AR
Craven, Joshua	081	1847	WB-8/528	AR
Craven, Lydia	081	1885	WB-15/490	
Craven, Lydia	081	1900	WB-17/111	
Craven, Margaret	099	1813	RB-11/22	AR
Craven, Margaret	063	1813	WB-2/15	
Craven, Martha	081	1882	WB-15/393	
Craven, Orren A.	032	1898	WB-4/384	AR
Craven, Peter	081	1830	WB-6/110	AR
Craven, Rebecca	081	1900	WB-17/97	
Craven, Samuel	081	1849	WB-9/117	AR
Craven, Samuel	032	1872	WB-3/63	AR
Craven, W. O.	081	1895	WB-16/346	AR
Craver, John	032	1898	WB-4/340	AR
Craver, Sarah A.	038	1900	WB-4/248	AR
Craver, Thomas	081	1817	WB-4/431	AR
Cravers, Philip	085	1820	WB-H/74	AR
Cravey, James	071	c1758	Orig. Only	037 AR
Crawford, Abraham	041	1876	WB-4/77	AR
Crawford, Allison	016	1844	WB-1/51	
Crawford, Ann	009	c1798	OWB/342	AR
Crawford, Anna Maria	005	1896	WB-D/392	AR
Crawford, Archibald	029	1763	Orig. Only	AR
Crawford, Charles D.	009	c1807	OWB/444	AR
Crawford, Cotesworth	097	1844	WB-1/11	AR
Crawford, David	054	c1814	WB-1/330	AR
Crawford, David	005	1832	WB-B/20	AR
Crawford, David M.	086	1885	WB-F/265	AR
Crawford, Duncan	083	1817	WB-1/182	
Crawford, Elizabeth	054	c1825	WB-2/4	AR
Crawford, G. W.	055	1890	WB-A/94	
Crawford, Harriet	075	1843	WB-N/175	AR
Crawford, Harriett	028	1899	WB-F/377	
Crawford, Hugh	073	1803	WB-D/85	AR
Crawford, Hugh A.	005	1893	WB-D/331	AR
Crawford, James	050	1872	WB-1/116	CTY
Crawford, James	064	1860	WB-1/72	AR
Crawford, James	025	1896	WB-A/188	AR
Crawford, James	073	1812	WB-D/326	AR
Crawford, James	016	1832	PQS.5/236	
Crawford, James	081	1789	WB-1/37	AR
Crawford, James L.	040	1864	WB-1/166	AR

Name	Co.	Date	Recorded Copy	Original
Crawford, John	073	1867	WB-G/512	CTY
Crawford, John	075	1779	WB-K/31	AR
Crawford, John	001	1874	WB-2/73	AR
Crawford, Johnson	084	1867	WB-D/81	CTY
Crawford, Joseph	016	1843	WB-1/19	
Crawford, Letty	073	1888	WB-H/445	CTY
Crawford, Margaret	011	c1768	WB-1/461	
Crawford, Margaret	001	1883	WB-2/209	AR
Crawford, Margaret M.	054	1896	WB-6/20	CTY
Crawford, Mary L.	054	1887	WB-5/152	
Crawford, Mary M.	040	1898	WB-3/20	AR
Crawford, Neill	083	1840	WB-1/389	AR
Crawford, Neill	083	1855	WB-2/109	AR
Crawford, Phillip	005	1881	WB-D/108	AR
Crawford, Phillip	001	1886	WB-2/286	AR
Crawford, Robert	103	1820	RD-4/364	AR
Crawford, Robert N.	SC	1865	026 WB-1/371	026 AR
Crawford, Samuel	073	1900	WB-I/189	CTY
Crawford, Samuel	001	1900	WB-3/339	AR
Crawford, Samuel J.	001	1899	WB-3/290	AR
Crawford, Sarah	073	1879	WB-H/203	CTY
Crawford, Thomas	082	1789	WB-1/29	AR
Crawford, Thomas	040	1862	WB-1/144	
Crawford, Thomas A.	061	1898	WB-2/223	AR
Crawford, Virgil	028	1815	WB-C/95	AR
Crawford, Virgil A.	028	1897	WB-F/300	
Crawford, W. R.	055	1883	WB-A/62	
Crawford, William	067	1843	WB-1/6	AR
Crawford, William	024	1735	LGB-4/#140	SS/AR
Crawford, William	075	c1858	WB-M2/53	AR
Crawford, William	085	c1807	WB-E/233	AR-Nunc.
Crawford, William	040	1862	WB-1/137	AR
Crawford, William R.	055	1883	WB-A/38 & 62	
Crawley, Ann Eliot	044	1795	WB-3/187	CTY
Crawley, B. J.	081	1875	WB-15/180	AR
Crawley, David	047	1777	WB-2/42	
Crawley, David	047	1828	WB-4/41	
Crawley, Mary A.	009	1895	WB-2/83	CTY
Crawley, Thomas	046	1778	WB-A/38	AR
Crawmer, John E.	038	1865	WB-1/254	AR
Cray, John	070	1778	WB-C/48	AR
Cray, William	072	1779	WI/L50	AR
Crayton, Samuel	SC	c1828	Copy	060 AR
Creamer, James	009	1833	OB-B/235	AR
Crean, William	029	c1793	Orig. Only	AR
Creasey, Levi	077	1734	SS 876/330	SS/AR
Creasman, Abraham	013	1898	WB-D/188	AR
Creasy, Walter R.	070	1899	WB-H/241	AR
Creath, Samuel	100	1813	WB-17/77	AR
Crech, Henry	002	c1709	SS 875/28	
Credle, Eliza L.	053	1885	WB-11/154	AR
Credle, James	053	1829	WB-4/438	AR
Credle, John	053	1866	WB-10/12	AR
Credle, Kate	053	1889	WB-11/223	AR
Credle, Matthias	053	1873	WB-11/27	AR
Credle, Nathaniel	053	1850	WB-7/434	AR
Credle, Sallie D.	053	1888	WB-11/205	AR
Credle, Tilman F.	053	1873	WB-11/35	AR
Credle, William	053	1820	WB-4/140	
Credle, William M.	053	1890	WB-11/232	AR
Creech, Agrippa	103	1879	WB-1/162	AR
Creech, Barney	056	1896	WB-4/41	AR
Creech, Bennett	056	1871	WB-3/46	AR
Creech, Elizabeth	056	1890	WB-3/550	AR
Creech, Elizabeth	045	c1857	Orig. Only	AR
Creech, Ezekiel	056	1862	WB-2/35	AR
Creech, Fannie A.	056	1882	WB-3/328	AR
Creech, Jesse	056	1896	WB-4/29	AR
Creech, John	045	1877	Orig. Only	AR
Creech, John	099	1866	RB-34/529	AR
Creech, Joshua	056	1841	WB-1/539	AR
Creech, Joshua	056	1835	Orig. Only	AR
Creech, Joshua	056	1866	WB-2/74	AR
Creech, Levi P.	056	1896	WB-4/5	AR
Creech, Margret	056	c1849	Orig. Only	AR
Creech, Nasro	056	1877	WB-3/185	AR
Creech, Richard	029	c1775	Orig. Only	AR
Creech, Robert G.	045	1880	WB-1/57	AR
Creech, Stanford	056	1893	WB-2/135	AR
Creech, William H.	056	1897	WB-4/45	AR
Creecy, Frederick	024	1820	WB-C/88	AR
Creecy, Jeremiah	024	c1878	WB-E/72	AR
Creecy, John	077	1777	WB-C/204	AR
Creecy, Joseph	024	c1785	WB-A/303	AR
Creecy, Joshua S.	024	1817	WB-C/60	AR
Creecy, Lemuel	024	1816	WB-C/43	AR
Creecy, Lemuel, Sr.	024	1816	WB-C/41	AR
Creecy, Levi	024	1771	WB-1/47	AR
Creecy, Martha A.	024	1894	WB-E/232	AR
Creecy, Nathan	024	1818	WB-C/68	AR
Creecy, William	077	1816	WB-E/464	AR
Creed, Bennett	092	1817	WB-3/125	AR
Creed, Enoch	092	1897	WB-6/455	AR
Creed, Henry	030	1797	WB-2/105	
Creed, John	092	c1852	Orig. Only	AR
Creedle, Chloe	001	1877	WB-2/112	AR
Creef, Lydia	030	1795	WB-2/44	
Creef, Truxton	031	1879	WB-1/15	AR
Creef, William	030	1792	WB-1/254	
Creekman, Samuel	030	1817	WB-3/98	
Creekmeer, Leonidas	009	1864	OB-L/461	AR
Creekmore, Ellet	018	1898	WB-E/291	AR
Creekmore, Francis	069	c1854	WB-1/541	AR
Creekmore, Seth	030	1844	WB-4/107	
Creekmore, Timothy	069	1834	WB-1/400	AR
Creekmore, Uriah	069	1881	WB-5/138	AR
Creel, Thomas	005	1804	WB-2/18	AR
Creeson, Charles W.	081	1860	WB-11/371	AR
Crenshaw, Mary	099	1822	RB-18/2	AR
Crenshaw, Susan A.	099	1898	WB-D/216	AR
Crenshaw, William	099	1861	RB-32/72	AR
Crenshaw, William	VA	1787	Copy	054 AR
Cresemore, Henry	060	1841	WB-2/103	AR
Cresemore, Jacob	060	1805	Orig. Only	AR
Cresimon, Bettie Ann	021	c1885	WB-2/356	
Creson, James	090	1896	WB-6/418 & 422	AR
Cress, Aaron	016	1891	WB-4/254	AR
Cress, Daniel	085	1822	WB-H/688	AR
Cress, Daniel	016	1843	WB-1/2	
Cress, Daniel H.	085	1846	WB-K/31	AR
Cress, Darcus	016	1848	WB-1/152	
Cress, Henry	016	1847	WB-1/129	
Cress, John	085	1867	WB-L/20	AR
Cress, Leah	085	1890	WB-2/445	CTY
Cress, Nicholas	085	1843	WB-I/171	AR
Cress, Thomas	085	1862	WB-K/305	AR
Cress, Tobias, Sr.	016	1845	WB-1/75	
Cressman, Moses	092	c1841	WB-4/186	
Cresson, Nicholass	085	c1799	WB-E/211	AR

Name	Co.	Date	Recorded Copy	Original
Cresson, Samuel	085	1824	WB-H/257	AR
Cresswell, Isaac	085	1772	WB-A/47	AR
Creswell, David	054	1883	WB-4/488	CTY
Creswell, Elizabeth	065	1894	054 WB-5/542	054 CTY
Creswell, Elizabeth	054	1857	WB-3/113	AR
Creswell, Elizabeth	065	1894	WB-M/236	AR
Creswell, John	073	1810	WB-D/306	AR
Creswell, Margaret	054	c1805	WB-1/303	AR
Creswell, William	054	c1803	WB-1/83	AR
Crew, Andrew	071	1830	WB-4/67	AR
Crew, David	090	1821	WB-3/59	AR
Crew, Henry	071	1825	WB-3/324	AR
Crew, Jonathan	071	1817	WB-3/190	AR
Crews, Arthur	070	1796	Orig. Only	AR
Crews, Ashley	106	c1853	WB-1/45	AR
Crews, Benjamin	044	1877	WB-23/240	CTY
Crews, Caleb	044	1814	WB-7/355	CTY
Crews, Edward	044	1887	WB-23/579	CTY
Crews, Edward	090	1846	WB-4/216	AR
Crews, Edward N.	044	1899	WB-24/456	CTY
Crews, Fuel	090	1846	WB-4/208	AR
Crews, Gideon	044	1815	WB-7/554	CTY
Crews, Gideon	044	1859	WB-21/106	CTY
Crews, Iverson H.	038	c1856	WB-1/79	AR
Crews, James	044	1875	WB-23/200	CTY
Crews, James	090	1831	WB-3/236	AR
Crews, James A.	044	1892	WB-24/201	CTY
Crews, James C.	038	1895	WB-3/531	AR
Crews, James W.	038	1883	WB-2/449	AR
Crews, Jemima	044	1826	WB-10/98	CTY
Crews, John	070	1828	WB-C/60	AR
Crews, Joseph	038	1874	WB-2/181	AR
Crews, Mary	003	c1869	Orig. Only	AR
Crews, Matthew	038	1857	WB-1/101	AR
Crews, Meredith	044	c1869	WB-23/20	CTY
Crews, Reuben	038	c1847	WB-1/111	AR
Crews, Thomas	090	1846	WB-4/228	AR
Crews, Thomas	038	1851	WB-1/34	AR
Crews, Thomas	090	1841	WB-4/73	AR
Crewse, Augustain	090	1844	WB-4/173	AR
Crichlow, John	010	1867	WB-H/195	AR
Cricket, John	010	1755	Orig. Only	SS/AR
Crickett, Lucretia	010	1809	WB-F/106	AR
Crickmore, Thomas F.	069	1890	WB-5/295	AR
Crim, Jacob	090	1829	WB-3/205	AR
Criminger, Frederick	016	1859	WB-2/54	
Crimminger, Christopher	016	1858	WB-2/42	
Crimminger, R. A.	016	1895	WB-4/188	AR
Crismon, Elizabeth	046	1851	Orig. Only	AR
Crisp, Benjamin	037	1898	WB-H/409	AR
Crisp, Francis	063	1813	WB-2/20	
Crisp, Hiram	017	1867	WB-A/175	AR
Crisp, Jesse	037	1837	WB-F/205	AR
Crisp, Jesse	037	1895	WB-H/327	AR
Crisp, Jesse, Sr.	037	1831	WB-F/129	AR
Crisp, John	020	1850	RB-Q/343	
Crisp, Lucy	079	1871	WB-2/61	AR
Crisp, Merrill B.	043	1899	WB-1/67	
Crisp, Nicholas	024	1727	SS 876/93	SS/AR
Crisp, Samuel	037	1829	WB-F/103	AR
Crisp, Thomas	037	1825	WB-F/39	AR
Crisp, Thomas J.	037	1884	WB-G/688	
Crisp, William	037	1819	WB-E/230	AR
Crispin, Joseph	028	1774	Orig. Only	AR
Crispin, Mary	028	1807	WB-B/274	AR
Criss, Daniel	085	1823	WB-H/210	
Crissman, Charles L.	092	c1833	WB-4/112	
Crissman, George	090	1811	WB-2/119	AR
Crissman, Moses	092	1842	PQS.16/(90)	
Crissman, Susanah	092	1851	WB-4/336	
Cristey, Rachel	020	1831	RB-L/627	AR
Criswell, James	046	1823	WB-B/165	AR
Criswell, Jean	046	1801	WB-A/67	AR
Criswell, William	046	1819	WB-B/71	AR
Criswell, William	073	1830	WB-E/233	AR
Criswick, Jemima	100	1807	WB-14/117	AR
Critcher, Albert J.	044	1897	WB-24/347	CTY
Critcher, Anson	044	1882	WB-23/438	CTY
Critcher, Thomas	044	1779	WB-1/207	CTY
Critchfield, Nancy	092	1889	WB-6/288	AR-Nunc.
Critchfield, Richard	092	1881	WB-6/164	AR
Critchit, John	010	1788	WB-D/89	AR
Critendon, Chrisanna	090	1834	WB-3/282	AR
Crittenden, Henry	071	1783	WB-1/264	
Crittenden, Henry	071	1803	WB-2/246	AR
Crittenden, Robert	071	1801	WB-2/211	AR
Critz, Evaline	092	1897	WB-6/452	AR
Crockat, William	037	1852	WB-F/475	AR
Crocker, Arthur	047	1772	WB-1/312	
Crocker, Charity	071	1845	WB-5/14	AR
Crocker, Drewry	037	1779	WB-B/30	AR
Crocker, Harry	056	1894	WB-2/166	AR
Crocker, Henry	071	1826	WB-3/337	AR
Crocker, Jacob	039	c1790	WB-A/94	
Crocker, James H.	071	1889	WB-7/52	AR
Crocker, John	099	1853	RB-28/317	AR
Crocker, John	075	1803	WB-M1/80	AR
Crocker, Nathan J.	071	1880	WB-6/323	AR
Crocker, Peter	037	1753	SS 881/34	SS/AR
Crocker, W. L.	099	1899	WB-D/233	AR
Crocker, William M.	071	1868	WB-5/357	AR
Crocket, Archibald	065	1804	WB-A/215	AR
Croft, Frances	063	1886	WB-3/284	
Croft, Sarah Ann	SC	1896	050 WB-2/240	050 CTY
Croft, Sarah Ann	SC	1896	013 WB-C/530	013 AR
Croft, Thomas C.	046	1795	WB-A/45	
Crofton, George H.	063	1870	WB-3/15	
Crofton, Henry	009	1757	Orig. Only	SS/AR
Croker, Antony	044	1754	Orig. Only	SS/AR
Cromarte, A.	011	c1838	WB-1/55	
Cromartie, Calvin	011	1849	WB-1/175	
Cromartie, George	011	1892	WB-2/245	
Cromartie, Henry A.	087	1900	WB-4/143	AR
Cromartie, James	011	1846	WB-1/125	
Cromartie, John	011	c1850	WB-1/189	
Cromartie, Patrick L.	011	1897	WB-3/93	
Cromartie, Patrick L.	087	1897	Orig. Only	AR-Copy
Cromartie, Peter	011	c1861	Orig. Only	CTY
Cromartie, Rhenny	011	c1813	WB-2/318	
Cromartie, William	011	c1806	WB-1/370	
Cromen, Martin	010	1733	SS 876/320	SS/AR
Cromer, William	038	1894	WB-3/479	AR
Crompton, Henery	010	1735	LGB-4/#56	SS/AR
Cromwell, Alexander	037	1788	WB-C/66	AR
Cromwell, Elizabeth	037	1840	WB-F/239	AR
Cromwell, Epinetus	037	1861	WB-G/202	AR
Cromwell, Thomas	037	1795	WB-C/347	AR
Croney, Dinnis	075	1735	LGB-4/#13	SS/AR
Cronkleton, James	021	1886	WB-2/350	
Crook, James	090	1793	WB-1/47	

Name	Co.	Date	Recorded Copy	Original
Crooks, Andrew	086	1814	WB-C/14	AR
Crooks, Catherine	060	1890	WB-4/425	AR
Crooks, David	060	1859	WB-3/21	AR
Croom, Charles	103	1840	RD-7/574	AR
Croom, Charles S.	059	1876	WB-A/108	
Croom, Elijah	103	1838	RD-7/337	AR
Croom, Elizabeth	090	1843	WB-4/115	AR
Croom, Hardy	070	1862	WB-D/83	AR
Croom, Hillory	070	1859	WB-D/17	AR
Croom, Jesse	103	1812	RD-2/179	AR
Croom, John M.	038	1889	WB-3/125	AR
Croom, Lott	076	1884	WB-A1/45	AR
Croom, Lott	070	1859	WB-D/3	AR
Croom, Lucy	059	1889	WB-A/566	CTY
Croom, Major T.	070	1862	WB-D/76	AR
Croom, Margaret	039	1849	WB-1/12	AR
Croom, Mary	103	1824	RD-5/118	AR
Croom, Richard	103	1805	Orig. Only	AR
Croom, Simon	090	1837	WB-3/326	AR
Croom, William	070	1864	WB-D/149	AR
Croon, William	030	1857	WB-4/218	
Crop, Harriet	063	c1889	Orig. Only	AR
Cropley, John	002	1686	Orig. Only	SS/AR
Cropley, Vines	024	1719	Orig. Only	SS/AR
Crosby, Asenith	085	1877	WB-1/368	CTY
Crosby, Henry C.	099	1897	WB-D/92	AR
Crosby, Margaret	029	1853	WB-C/245	AR
Crosby, Mary G.	085	1894	WB-3/47	CTY
Crosby, Mary J.	054	1886	WB-5/91	CTY
Croset, John	020	1796	RB-C/171	AR
Croset, Sarah	065	1894	WB-M/595	AR
Crosland, Elizabeth	024	1694	SS 874.2/42	SS/AR
Croslon, John	024	1694	SS 874.2/43	SS/AR
Cross, Abraham	041	1830	WB-2/286	AR
Cross, Asel	104	1820	WB-3/215	AR
Cross, Charity	041	1884	WB-4/196	AR
Cross, Christian	041	1828	WB-2/276	AR
Cross, Cyprian	041	1810	WB-2/53	AR
Cross, David	041	1823	WB-2/285	AR
Cross, David	041	1823	WB-2/206	AR
Cross, David	032	1878	WB-3/251	AR
Cross, Elizabeth	083	c1803	WB-1/85	AR
Cross, Emily	041	1863	WB-3/299	AR
Cross, Etheldred	041	1854	WB-3/179	AR
Cross, George	032	1860	WB-2/181	AR
Cross, Hardy	041	1816	WB-2/118	AR
Cross, Hardy	041	1884	WB-4/202	AR
Cross, Isabel	032	c1864	WB-2/266	AR
Cross, Jacob	085	c1803	WB-E/197	AR
Cross, James	009	1832	OB-B/225	AR
Cross, Jesse R.	071	1823	WB-3/293	AR
Cross, John	032	1873	WB-3/69	AR
Cross, Lemuel L.	071	1845	WB-5/12	AR
Cross, Leonard	032	1865	WB-2/319	AR
Cross, M. M.	016	1887	WB-3/521	AR
Cross, Mary	041	1793	WB-1/112	AR
Cross, Mary	032	1885	WB-3/456	AR
Cross, Matilda R.	NY	1883	Copy	050 AR
Cross, Nancy	022	1884	WB-E/294	AR
Cross, Parrish	022	1837	WB-C/80	AR
Cross, Peter, Sr.	032	c1848	WB-2/95	
Cross, Riddick	041	1866	WB-3/351	AR
Cross, Sarah	041	1853	WB-3/163	AR
Cross, Square	022	1899	WB-F/89	AR
Cross, William	099	1814	RB-11/312	AR
Cross, Willis	041	1859	WB-3/236	AR
Crossett, Hetty B.	073	1895	WB-I/69	CTY
Crossland, Edward	047	1778	WB-2/79	
Crossot, Joseph	019	1728	SS 876/191	SS/AR
Crots, Jacob	085	c1800	WB-E/203	AR
Crotts, Valintine	026	1856	WB-1/209	AR
Crouch, Eliphalet	003	1887	WB-B/218	
Crouch, Jacob	003	1893	WB-B/307	
Crouch, John	104	1828	WB-4/120	AR
Crouch, John	082	1869	WB-6/10	AR
Crouch, John B.	082	1863	WB-4/164	AR
Crouch, Samuel	082	1864	WB-4/172	AR
Crouch, Wm. Calvin	003	1900	WB-B/396	
Crouse, Ann	060	1839	WB-2/14	AR
Crouse, Charles	004	1883	WB-A/61	AR
Crouse, David	060	1870	WB-4/48	AR
Crouse, Elizabeth	060	1811	Orig. Only	AR
Crouse, Isaac W.	092	1898	WB-6/482	AR
Crouse, Jane	004	1892	WB-A/136	
Crouse, John	060	1835	WB-1/332	AR
Crouse, John	060	1817	Orig. Only	AR
Crouse, Sarah A.	004	1898	WB-A/207	AR
Crouse, Sary	060	1835	WB-1/349	AR
Crouse, William L.	060	1900	WB-5/150	AR
Crow, James	046	1859	WB-C/537	AR
Crow, James	022	1795	RB-2/37	AR
Crow, John	040	1894	WB-2/466	AR
Crow, John	026	1869	WB-2/1	AR
Crow, John	029	1857	WB-C/363	AR
Crow, John	022	c1815	WB-A/267	AR
Crow, Moses	103	1883	WB-1/293	AR
Crow, Nannie B.	099	1895	WB-C/461	AR
Crow, Peter	065	c1763	Orig. Only	AR
Crow, Robert	071	1796	WB-2/106	AR
Crow, Theophilus	035	1865	WB-3/101	AR
Crow, Thomas	060	1838	WB-2/3	AR
Crow, Thomas	103	1810	RD-1/320	AR
Crow, William H.	099	1885	WB-B/48	AR
Crowder, Abram	026	1873	WB-2/97	AR
Crowder, Bartlett	026	1883	WB-2/223	AR
Crowder, Batt	039	c1788	WB-A/51	
Crowder, Calvin	005	1899	WB-D/446	AR
Crowder, Daniel P.	026	1856	WB-1/200	AR
Crowder, Elizabeth	099	1854	RB-28/586	AR
Crowder, Elizabeth	005	1893	WB-D/334	AR
Crowder, George	099	1848	RB-26/7	AR
Crowder, Hillkier	044	1789	WB-2/91	CTY
Crowder, Jaremier	046	1795	WB-A/42	AR
Crowder, Jarrel	026	1858	WB-1/234	AR
Crowder, Mary	044	1850	WB-18/173	CTY
Crowder, Nancy	071	1812	WB-3/67	AR
Crowder, Nathaniel	038	1898	WB-4/135	AR
Crowder, P. P.	026	1866	WB-1/387	AR
Crowder, R. W.	026	1863	WB-1/311	AR
Crowder, Richard	005	1840	WB-B/104	AR-Nunc.
Crowder, Robert	086	1820	WB-C/139	AR
Crowder, Robert	026	1857	WB-1/220	AR
Crowder, Thomas	099	1842	RB-25/110	AR
Crowder, William	086	1839	WB-E/59	AR
Crowell, A. S.	097	1895	WB-2/483	AR
Crowell, Asbury	047	1870	WB-6/39	AR
Crowell, Benjamin	047	1828	WB-4/43	
Crowell, Edward	047	1878	WB-6/181	AR
Crowell, Edward	047	1792	WB-3/206	
Crowell, Edward	047	1827	WB-4/31	

Name	Co.	Date	Recorded Copy	Original
Crowell, George	089	1863	WB-1/242	
Crowell, George W.	089	1865	WB-1/282	
Crowell, George W.	089	1889	WB-2/192	AR
Crowell, James B.	069	1855	WB-1/543	AR
Crowell, Joel	089	c1863	WB-1/295	
Crowell, John	097	1865	WB-1/255	AR
Crowell, John	047	1761	WB-1/23	
Crowell, John	047	1836	WB-4/129	
Crowell, John W.	097	1864	WB-1/244	AR
Crowell, Joseph	069	1787	WB-1/44	AR
Crowell, Martha	047	1817	WB-3/608	
Crowell, Michael	097	1865	WB-1/250	AR
Crowell, Robert S.	089	1898	Orig. Only	AR
Crowell, Samuel	047	1826	WB-4/23	
Crowell, Thomas	047	1793	WB-3/212	
Crowell, Thomas M.	047	1880	WB-6/225	
Crowell, William	047	1826	WB-4/28	
Crowley, Abigail	047	1837	WB-4/158	
Crowley, Benjamin	047	1841	WB-4/198	
Crowley, Wade S.	047	1851	WB-4/309	
Crows, Daniel	004	1866	WB-1/23	AR
Crows, Frainey	085	1815	WB-G/387	AR
Crows, James	004	1891	WB-A/134	AR
Crows, John	006	1858	WB-D/50	AR
Crowson, Henry H.	082	1879	WB-6/162	AR
Crowson, John	082	1813	WB-1/157	AR
Croxton, Arthur	077	1765	WB-C/46	AR
Crudup, Edward A.	039	1876	WB-U/124	AR
Crudup, George	047	1764	WB-1/232	
Crudup, Hannah	039	1897	WB-V/114	AR
Crudup, J. B.	098	1899	WB-A/312	CTY
Crudup, Josiah	044	1872	WB-23/67	CTY
Crudup, Mary	047	1761	WB-1/23	
Crudup, Paladora	039	1880	WB-U/224	AR
Crum, Godfred	085	1812	WB-G/219	AR
Crum, Mary	085	1815	WB-G/399	AR
Crump, Charles	071	1819	WB-3/214	AR
Crump, Charles	071	1825	WB-3/333	AR
Crump, Daniel	089	1852	WB-1/85	
Crump, James R.	071	1838	WB-4/172	AR
Crump, Joseph	022	1796	RB-2/88	AR
Crump, Joseph	071	1759	Orig. Only	SS/AR
Crump, Josias	071	1812	WB-3/82	AR
Crump, Martha	022	1835	WB-C/22	AR
Crump, Richard	071	1832	WB-4/94	AR
Crump, Roland	033	1852	WB-1/106	AR
Crumpler, Alexander	029	1889	WB-E/454	AR
Crumpler, Bashaba	103	1896	WB-2/169	AR
Crumpler, Charity	105	1889	WB-2/547	AR
Crumpler, Edmon	056	c1813	WB-1/235	AR
Crumpler, J. M.	038	1897	WB-4/18	AR
Crumpler, Jacob	087	c1817	WB-A/83	AR
Crumpler, John	087	1782	WB-A/8	AR
Crumpler, John	035	1782	WB-A/81	AR
Crumpler, Kinchen	105	1878	WB-2/236	AR
Crumpler, Thomas	103	1874	WB-1/78	AR
Crumpler, Wiley	103	1885	WB-1/353	AR
Crumpler, William	103	1891	WB-1/552	AR
Crumpley, Benjamin	069	1825	WB-1/331	AR
Crumpton, Thomas	035	1808	Orig. Only	AR
Cruse, Jacob A.	016	1884	WB-3/434	AR
Cruse, John	086	1838	WB-E/45	AR
Cruse, Joseph A.	016	1899	WB-4/334	AR
Cruse, Lawrence	002	c1690	Orig. Only	SS/AR
Cruse, Nancy C.	085	1891	WB-2/466	CTY
Cruse, Paul	016	1879	WB-3/261	AR
Cruse, Peter	016	1887	WB-3/549	AR
Cruse, Philip	085	c1804	WB-E/216	AR
Cruse, Sarah A.	016	1897	WB-4/249	AR
Crusenberry, Ann F.	103	c1881	Orig. Only	AR
Crutch, George D.	075	1842	WB-N/170	AR
Crutchfield, Ann	057	1805	WB-A/274	AR
Crutchfield, Benjamin	022	1854	Orig. Only	AR
Crutchfield, Enoch	081	1885	WB-15/544	AR
Crutchfield, Henry	022	1787	RB-1/28	AR
Crutchfield, James	073	1807	WB-D/206	AR
Crutchfield, James H.	073	1896	WB-I/92	CTY
Crutchfield, Jane	073	1852	WB-G/22	AR
Crutchfield, Joseph H.	022	1894	WB-E/562	AR
Crutchfield, Mariah	022	1897	Orig. Only	AR
Crutchfield, Mary	022	1878	WB-E/163	AR
Crutchfield, Nancy	073	1846	WB-F/273	AR
Crutchfield, Samuel	100	1795	WB-8/179	AR
Crutchfield, Thomas	022	1844	WB-C/160	AR
Crutchfield, William H.	022	1864	WB-D/138	AR
Cruthes, John	081	1831	WB-6/139	AR
Cruthis, Margaret	081	1851	WB-9/307	
Cry, James	065	1803	WB-B/23	AR
Cry, John	065	1808	WB-A/218	AR
Crye, Samuel	065	1804	WB-B/25	AR
Cryer, John	084	1849	WB-C/100	CTY
Cryer, Sampson L.	084	1848	WB-C/68	CTY
Cryer, Samuel	071	1800	WB-2/196	AR
Crysel, Venie	006	1900	WB-E/409	AR
Crytz, Henry J.	040	1863	WB-1/159	
Cude, Eleanor	046	1860	WB-D/71	AR
Cude, Timothy	081	1813	WB-4/26	AR
Cude, Timothy	046	1856	WB-C/446	AR
Cudworth, John	030	c1807	WB-2/327	
Cuff, Kezah	041	1845	WB-3/70	AR
Cuff, Nisum	041	1870	WB-4/12	AR
Culberhouse, John	085	c1802	WB-G/92	AR
Culberson, Andrew	022	c1802	WB-A/45	AR
Culberson, Anne E.	073	1816	WB-D/482	AR
Culberson, John	022	1851	WB-C/301	AR
Culberson, Margaret	022	1858	WB-D/9	AR
Culberson, Samuel	022	1817	WB-A/306	AR
Culberson, William	020	1825	RB-K/64	AR
Culbertson, Daniel	085	1856	WB-K/216	AR
Culbertson, Gillaspie	085	1845	WB-K/6	AR
Culbertson, John G.	085	1890	WB-2/411	CTY
Culbertson, Samuel	085	1843	WB-I/157	AR
Culbraith, Archibald	011	c1844	WB-1/103	
Culbreath, Camp	083	1856	WB-2/68	AR
Culbreath, Edward	086	1844	WB-E/124	AR
Culbreath, John	029	1813	WB-A/197	AR
Culbreath, Peter	029	1810	WB-A/156	AR
Culbreth, Angus	083	1822	WB-1/223	AR
Culbreth, John	029	1890	WB-E/469	AR
Culbreth, John J.	011	1894	WB-3/59	CTY
Cullen, Edmund	028	1765	Wills.9/212	AR
Cullen, Jonathan	041	1799	WB-1/167	AR
Cullen, Jonathan	028	1757	DB-8/165	AR
Cullen, Nehemiah	028	1795	WB-A/331	AR
Culler, David	092	1896	WB-6/426	AR
Culler, Solomon	092	1891	WB-6/331	AR
Culley, John	056	c1791	WB-1/52	
Culley, Thomas	019	1802	WB-D/111	AR
Cullifer, Marcus	010	1893	WB-I/391	AR
Cullifer, Nathaniel	010	1837	WB-G/276	AR

Name	Co.	Date	Recorded Copy	Original
Cullifer, Thomas	063	1884	WB-3/251	
Cullins, Nathan	041	1833	WB-2/327	AR
Cullipher, James	010	1866	WB-H/157	AR
Cullipher, Judah	024	1882	WB-E/113	AR
Cullum, Elizabeth	NY	1884	047 WB-6/374	047 AR
Cullum, Jeremiah	047	1816	WB-3/595	
Cullum, William	047	1822	WB-3/675	
Cully, Francis	028	1814	WB-C/77	AR
Cully, George D.	099	1893	WB-C/169	AR
Cully, John	028	1822	WB-C/209	AR
Culnor, Cornelius	075	1774	Orig. Only	AR
Culp, David	016	1864	WB-2/104	
Culp, George	016	1841	PQS.6/157	
Culp, Peter	016	1846	WB-1/114	
Culpeper, Benjamin	037	1772	WB-A/197	AR
Culpeper, Henry	063	1781	WB-1/76	Nunc.
Culpepper, Arthur	030	1846	WB-4/122	
Culpepper, Elizabeth	069	1789	WB-1/56	AR
Culpepper, Henry	030	1815	WB-3/70	
Culpepper, James	069	1799	WB-1/127	AR
Culpepper, James M.	039	1891	WB-U/521	AR
Culpepper, Jeremiah	069	1801	WB-1/137	AR
Culpepper, Peter	018	1825	WB-C/54	
Culpepper, William	069	1871	WB-1/611	AR
Culpepper, Zion	075	1849	WB-N/231	AR
Culverhouse, Hugh	085	1877	WB-1/365	CTY
Culverhouse, Nancy	044	1821	WB-9/39	CTY
Culverhouse, Thomas W.	044	1789	WB-2/136	CTY
Cumbo, Cannon	083	1823	WB-1/204	AR
Cumbo, Giby	083	N. D.	WB-1/327	AR-Nunc.
Cumbo, John	083	1814	WB-1/153	AR-Nunc.
Cumings, Charity	077	1774	WB-C/134	AR
Cumins, Robert	072	c1774	RW/L18	AR
Cumming, F. F.	011	1890	WB-2/234	
Cumming, Francis E.	011	1891	WB-2/236	
Cumming, Naomi	070	1860	WB-D/32	AR
Cumming, William	024	c1796	WB-A/349	AR
Cummings, Anson W.	NY	1895	013 WB-C/435	
Cummings, Anson W.	NY	1895	050 WB-2/207	
Cummings, Bartlett Y.	084	1864	WB-D/16	CTY
Cummings, E. F.	046	1890	WB-F/30	AR
Cummings, Ednie	046	1876	WB-E/176	AR
Cummings, Jesse W.	092	1871	WB-6/24	
Cummings, John	028	1816	WB-C/136	AR
Cummings, Robert	046	1837	WB-B/574	
Cummings, Sarah	084	1848	WB-C/67	CTY
Cummings, Staton	037	1897	WB-H/394	AR
Cummings, William M.	046	1896	WB-F/488	AR
Cummins, Benjamin	028	1818	WB-C/165	AR
Cummins, Charles	065	1777	WB-A/182	AR
Cummins, Daniel	044	1874	WB-23/128	CTY
Cummins, Francis	046	1800	WB-A/69	AR
Cummins, George	046	1808	WB-A/75	AR
Cummins, Jane	054	c1805	WB-2/104	AR
Cummins, John	054	1809	WB-1/46	AR
Cummins, Rachel	046	1816	Orig. Only	AR
Cummins, Thomas	035	1798	WB-A/75	AR
Cummins, Thomas	046	1813	WB-A/81	AR
Cummins, Thomas	072	c1761	RW/L51	AR
Cummins, William	020	1784	RB-B/38	AR
Cummins, William R.	046	1895	WB-F/442	AR
Cummons, Thomas	046	1816	WB-A/62	AR
Cunengain, Morris	N	1696	Orig. Only	SS/AR
Cuniffe, John	010	1771	WB-A/141	AR
Cuninggim, Margaret	059	1885	WB-A/433	CTY
Cuninggim, W. H.	099	1895	WB-C/438	AR
Cuningham, Henry	059	1878	WB-A/147	CTY
Cuningham, Patsey M.	078	1868	WB-19/1	AR
Cunninggim, Jesse A.	046	1899	WB-G/112	AR
Cunninggim, William H.	045	c1874	Orig. Only	AR
Cunningham, Enoch H.	013	1879	WB-B/186	AR
Cunningham, Hugh	085	1817	WB-G/486	AR
Cunningham, James	046	1821	WB-B/124	AR
Cunningham, James	024	1816	WB-C/50	AR
Cunningham, James	046	c1791	WB-A/43	AR
Cunningham, James	090	1864	WB-4/369	
Cunningham, James	065	1833	WB-G/133	AR
Cunningham, James	060	1821	Orig. Only	AR
Cunningham, Jane	065	1866	WB-J/228	AR
Cunningham, Jeremiah	046	1836	WB-B/546	AR
Cunningham, John	085	1825	WB-H/311	AR
Cunningham, John	085	1762	WB-A/41	AR
Cunningham, John	084	c1801	WB-A/145	CTY
Cunningham, John	046	1821	WB-B/107	AR
Cunningham, John	024	c1778	WB-A/229	AR
Cunningham, John	024	c1799	WB-A/325	AR
Cunningham, John W.	078	1887	WB-19/211	AR
Cunningham, John W.	078	1900	021 WB-3/287	021 AR
Cunningham, John W.	078	1887	013 WB-B/479	
Cunningham, Joseph	085	c1801	WB-E/219	AR
Cunningham, Joseph	085	c1803	WB-D/11	AR
Cunningham, Joseph	084	c1793	OW/148	AR
Cunningham, Letitia	065	1857	WB-J/46	AR
Cunningham, Margaret	085	1866	WB-K/386	AR
Cunningham, Mary	065	1848	WB-I/141	AR
Cunningham, Nathaniel	065	1831	WB-E/99	AR
Cunningham, R. M.	054	1888	WB-5/216	CTY
Cunningham, Robert	065	1863	WB-J/169	AR
Cunningham, Roger	065	1808	WB-A/171	AR
Cunningham, Sarah G.	070	1853	WB-C/550	AR
Cunningham, Susan	046	1900	WB-G/218	AR
Cunningham, Thomas	070	1797	WB-C/54	
Cunningham, William	046	1837	WB-B/586	AR
Cunningham, William	065	1843	WB-H/144	AR
Cunningham, William	092	1826	WB-3/171	AR
Cunningham, William	092	1829	WB-4/20	AR
Cunyard, Richard	039	1792	WB-A/100	
Cupplus, William	085	c1800	WB-E/230	AR
Cureton, Eliza R.	SC	c1861	097 WB-2/5	097 AR
Cureton, Jeremiah	097	1847	WB-1/44	AR
Cureton, John	010	1789	WB-D/96	AR
Cureton, Richard	047	1760	WB-1/11	
Cureton, William J.	SC	1863	097 WB-1/214	097 AR
Curl, Andrew	022	1889	WB-E/413	AR
Curl, Elizabeth	069	1821	Orig. Only	AR
Curl, Jethro	051	1837	WB-A/92	
Curl, Peggie	051	1889	WB-C/390	AR
Curl, Sarah	037	1820	WB-E/231	AR
Curl, Sophia	069	1815	WB-1/266	AR
Curl, Thomas	037	1854	WB-G/86	AR
Curl, William	022	1818	WB-B/13	AR
Curl, Willis	037	1811	WB-E/5	AR
Curle, Sarah	037	1865	WB-G/262	AR
Curlee, Clement B.	097	1885	WB-2/270	AR
Curlee, John	005	1847	WB-B/215	AR
Curlee, Jolly	005	1893	WB-D/337	AR
Curlee, Mariner	005	1879	WB-D/83	AR
Curlee, Obediah	097	1858	WB-1/143	AR
Curlee, Sarah M.	097	1893	WB-2/442	AR
Curlee, William	097	1880	WB-2/175	

Name	Co.	Date	Recorded Copy	Original
Curlee, William R.	089	1853	WB-1/96	
Curling, John	030	1777	WB-1/121	
Curran, Mary	065	N. D.	WB-A/188	AR
Currell, Susanna	063	c1780	WB-1/73	
Currell, William	096	1775	WB-1/89	AR
Current, Alfred	054	1896	WB-6/12	CTY
Current, John	054	1865	WB-5/534	CTY
Currer, John	N	1683	Orig. Only	SS/AR
Currey, James	065	1805	WB-A/215	AR
Currey, James	047	1884	WB-6/321	AR
Currey, James	073	1804	WB-D/137	AR
Currie, Adam	083	1889	WB-3/460	AR
Currie, Alexander	083	1889	WB-3/446	AR
Currie, Angus	068	1888	WB-D/258	
Currie, Angus	083	1843	WB-1/420	AR
Currie, Archibal	068	1822	WB-B/30	
Currie, Blunt	083	1888	WB-3/472	AR
Currie, Catherine	082	1898	WB-6/572	AR
Currie, Catherine	020	1817	RB-H/2	AR
Currie, Daniel	011	1899	WB-3/110	CTY
Currie, Daniel C.	029	1880	WB-E/247	AR
Currie, Duncan B.	068	1885	WB-D/232	
Currie, Edward	083	1847	WB-1/501	AR
Currie, Eliza	020	1871	WB-A/63	CTY
Currie, Francis S.	083	1875	WB-3/89	AR
Currie, Hector	083	1852	WB-2/57	
Currie, Hugh	073	1851	WB-F/491	AR
Currie, Isabella	083	1846	WB-1/495	
Currie, James	084	1855	WB-C/208	CTY
Currie, John	083	1821	WB-1/338	AR
Currie, John	020	1790	RB-B/308	AR
Currie, John W.	083	1894	WB-4/92	AR
Currie, Malcom	029	1892	WB-E/547	AR
Currie, Malcom	068	1866	WB-C/136	
Currie, Mary	083	1877	WB-3/134	AR
Currie, Maryan	073	1759	WB-A/11	
Currie, Nancy	083	1861	WB-2/174	AR
Currie, Nelly	083	1850	WB-2/20	AR
Currie, Randal	083	1843	WB-1/425	AR
Curries, Archibald	068	1879	WB-D/126	
Currin, Elizabeth	044	c1865	Orig. Only	CTY
Currin, Fleming B.	044	1861	WB-21/484	CTY
Currin, G. M.	044	1864	WB-22/250	
Currin, Hugh	044	1823	WB-9/247	CTY
Currin, Hugh	044	1780	WB-1/278	CTY
Currin, James	044	1866	WB-22/413	CTY
Currin, James	044	1781	WB-1/318	CTY
Currin, Lemuel	044	1844	WB-16/39	CTY
Currin, Mitchell	044	1890	WB-24/112	CTY
Currin, Nancy	044	1863	WB-21/742	CTY
Curry, Angus	082	1813	WB-1/161	AR
Curry, Catharine	054	1886	WB-5/86	CTY
Curry, Catharine	054	1871	WB-4/92	CTY
Curry, Catharine	068	1875	WB-D/74	
Curry, Daniel	046	1825	WB-B/211	AR
Curry, David	032	c1856	WB-2/194	AR
Curry, Donald	082	1799	WB-1/73	AR
Curry, Elam A. M.	060	1890	WB-4/416	AR
Curry, George	104	1855	WB-5/127	
Curry, James	024	1814	WB-C/20	AR
Curry, James	010	1849	WB-G/446	AR
Curry, James S.	032	1900	WB-4/467	AR
Curry, John	084	N. D.	OW/37	AR
Curry, John	104	1877	WB-6/140	AR
Curry, Judith	010	1866	WB-H/157	AR
Curry, Laughlin	068	1833	WB-B/87	
Curry, Malachi	010	1845	WB-G/390	AR
Curry, Malcom	090	1813	WB-2/140	AR
Curry, Martha W.	047	1869	WB-6/29	AR
Curry, Mary	082	1788	WB-1/25	AR
Curry, Nathaniel	085	1770	WB-A/44	AR
Curry, Samuel	104	c1864	Orig. Only	AR
Curry, Sarah	054	1886	WB-5/86	CTY
Curry, Sarah	054	1869	WB-4/47	AR
Curry, Shepard	032	1891	WB-4/120	
Curry, William	085	c1802	WB-E/221	AR
Curry, William	104	1855	WB-5/115	
Cursey, William	100	1836	WB-35/309	AR
Curtes, Claiborne	046	1803	WB-A/73	AR
Curtice, Michael	099	1786	RB-2/99	AR
Curtice, Samuel	104	1853	WB-5/87	
Curtis, Abner	005	1868	WB-C/264	AR
Curtis, Benjamin	013	1870	WB-B/24	AR
Curtis, Benjamine	013	1864	WB-A/225	
Curtis, C. C.	001	1889	WB-2/452	AR
Curtis, Charles	046	c1781	WB-A/41	AR
Curtis, Clarissa	039	1869	WB-U/13	AR
Curtis, Clement C.	001	1882	WB-2/194	AR
Curtis, Delilah	013	1864	WB-A/235	
Curtis, Elijah	005	1818	WB-2/31	AR
Curtis, Frances	005	1792	WB-A/17	AR
Curtis, Francis R.	NY	1892	Copy	013 AR
Curtis, Francis R.	NY	1892	Copy	093 AR
Curtis, George T.	070	1870	WB-E/195	AR
Curtis, Hiram	081	1874	WB-13/102	AR
Curtis, J. A.	061	c1853	WB-1/95	AR
Curtis, James	081	1795	WB-2/14	AR
Curtis, Jim	098	c1900	WB-A/349	CTY
Curtis, John	009	c1791	OWB/262	AR
Curtis, John	099	1816	RB-13/99	AR
Curtis, Margrey	084	c1792	OW/103	AR
Curtis, Moses	064	1853	WB-1/34	AR
Curtis, Nancy	005	c1824	WB-A/153	
Curtis, Nelly	070	1874	WB-E/265	AR
Curtis, Peter	028	1842	WB-D/54	AR
Curtis, Robert H.	100	1864	WB-50/120	AR
Curtis, Sigley	072	1829	WB-1/37	AR
Curtis, Tempy	001	1900	WB-3/351	AR
Curtis, Tilda	072	c1877	Orig. Only	AR
Curtis, William E.	100	1862	WB-50/69	AR
Cushing, Martha	063	1868	WB-2/524	
Cushion, Edward	010	c1769	WB-A/106	AR
Cushman, Sirus	047	1820	WB-3/651	
Cusick, William	046	1817	WB-B/34	AR
Custis, Ann	009	c1780	OWB/157	AR
Custis, E. Y. W.	028	1892	WB-F/35	
Custis, George W.	028	1860	WB-D/312	
Custis, Julia	028	1842	WB-D/48	AR
Cutchin, Eli	037	1856	WB-G/137	AR
Cutchin, Humphrey	037	1774	WB-A/225	AR
Cutchin, Josiah	037	1871	WB-G/358	AR
Cutchin, Norfleet	037	1889	WB-H/149	AR
Cutchin, Norfleet	037	c1889	Copy	047 AR
Cutchin, Thomas	037	1827	WB-F/64	AR
Cutchins, Thomas	037	1781	WB-B/87	AR
Cuterel, Peter	053	1785	RW-1/128	
Cuthbert, James G.	028	1831	WB-C/333	AR
Cuthbert, Rachel	028	1858	WB-D/296	AR
Cuthbertson, Jason W.	TN	c1894	091 WB-1/361	
Cuthbertson, John	065	1899	WB-N/226	AR

Name	Co.	Date	Recorded Copy	Original
Cuthbertson, John D.	097	1869	Orig. Only	AR
Cuthbertson, Josiah	097	1854	WB-1/99	AR
Cuthbertson, Margaret	097	1880	WB-2/173	
Cuthbertson, Moses W.	097	1865	WB-1/249	AR
Cuthbertson, W. F.	065	1887	WB-L/214	AR
Cutherell, Charles	053	1791	RW-1/213	AR
Cuthrell, James	028	1838	WB-C/424	AR
Cuthrell, Joshua	028	1781	Orig. Only	AR
Cuthrell, Thomas	028	1784	Orig. Only	AR
Cutlar, Ann	070	1815	WB-AB/220	AR
Cutlar, Ann	070	1899	WB-H/234	
Cutlar, DuBrutz	070	1898	WB-H/147	AR
Cutlar, Elizabeth	070	1850	WB-C/514	AR
Cutlar, Euphemia	070	1850	WB-C/502	AR
Cutlar, Louisa B.	070	1899	WB-H/213	AR
Cutlar, Lucy	070	1843	WB-AB/405	AR
Cutlar, Roger	070	1805	WB-C/56	AR
Cutlar, Sylvester	027	1884	WB-2/57	AR
Cutlar, William	070	1815	WB-AB/216	AR
Cutler, Aaron	009	1842	OB-D/315	AR
Cutler, Abner N.	009	1898	WB-2/128	CTY
Cutler, Elizabeth	009	1837	OB-C2/28	AR
Cutler, George B.	009	1889	WB-1/454	CTY
Cutler, John, Jr.	009	1849	OB-G/6	AR
Cutler, John, Sr.	009	1815	OB-A/237	AR
Cutler, John, Sr.	009	1844	OB-E/353	AR
Cutler, Mary	009	1833	OB-B/296	AR
Cutler, Moses	009	1829	OB-B/29	AR
Cutler, Moses, Sr.	009	1820	OB-A/302	AR
Cutler, Nathan C.	009	1896	WB-2/149	CTY
Cutler, Penelope	009	1883	WB-1/326	CTY
Cutler, Robert, Sr.	009	1821	OB-A/313	AR
Cutler, Robert, Sr.	009	1856	OB-K/55	AR
Cutler, Samuel F.	086	1821	WB-C/166	AR
Cutler, Stephen C.	009	1836	OWB/535	AR
Cutler, Wilson	009	1876	WB-1/152	CTY
Cutrell, Joseph	053	c1818	RW-1/510	
Cutting, James	028	1800	WB-B/93	AR
Cutts, Mary Ann	098	1886	WB-A/59	CTY
Cutts, William M.	044	1864	WB-22/179	CTY
Cyrus, Frederick	100	1827	WB-30/161	
D'Allinges, Eugene	013	1895	WB-C/471	AR
D'Berry, Elizabeth	047	1884	WB-6/326	AR
D'Berry, Lemuel	047	1884	WB-6/328	AR
Dabbs, Penelope	005	1844	WB-B/178	
Dabbs, William	005	1835	WB-B/58	
Dabney, John A.	047	1879	WB-6/200	AR
Dacons, Azel	054	1876	WB-4/212	CTY
Dade, Barney	081	1811	WB-3/291	
Dade, John	081	c1808	WB-3/94	AR
Daffin, George	047	1797	WB-3/279	AR
Daffin, Henry	071	1788	WB-1/467	AR
Daffin, John	047	1803	WB-3/388	AR
Dagenhart, Henry	003	1876	WB-B/68	AR
Dagenhart, Peter	003	1882	WB-B/134	AR
Daggett, William T.	070	1893	WB-G/154	AR
Dagus, Moses	030	c1849	WB-4/153	
Dahmer, John Peter	070	1868	WB-E/3	AR
Dahnhardt, Delia	070	1894	WB-G/285	AR
Dahnhardt, Lucy H.	NY	1899	070 WB-H/315	070 AR
Daiken, David	047	1764	WB-1/140	
Dail, Abel	035	1821	WB-A/105	AR
Dail, Curtis	035	1865	WB-3/100	AR
Dail, Elizabeth	035	1824	WB-A/125	AR
Dail, Henery	077	1828	Orig. Only	AR
Dail, Julas B.	024	1856	WB-C/390	AR
Dail, Mary E.	077	1900	WB-H/331	AR
Dail, Nathan P.	077	1892	WB-H/217	AR
Dail, Sarah Ann	077	1856	WB-F/467	AR
Dail, William	024	1828	WB-C/142	AR
Dail, William A.	077	1897	WB-H/306	AR
Dailey, Jesse	075	1823	WB-M1/372	AR
Dailey, Samuel	053	1789	RW-1/183	AR
Dailey, William	053	1812	RW-1/465	AR
Daily, Bartlett	046	1864	WB-D/237	AR
Daily, Gatsey	105	1876	WB-2/183	AR
Daily, John	086	1865	WB-E/463	AR
Daily, Lawson S.	060	1886	WB-4/348	AR
Daily, Thomas	053	1791	RW-1/203	
Daingerfield, Matilda W.	029	1900	WB-F/224	AR
Dake, John	030	1895	WB-5/221	AR
Dalby, James W.	044	1880	WB-23/366	CTY
Dale, George	014	1805	Orig. Only	AR
Dale, Isaac	073	1819	WB-D/555	AR
Dale, Richard	PA	1826	093 WB-2/59	
Dale, Richard	PA	1826	013 WB-A/204	013 AR
Dale, Richard	PA	1826	066 WB-1/80	
Dale, Samuel	064	1895	WB-2/359	AR
Daley, Enoch P.	018	1853	WB-C/380	
Dalez, Sally	039	1868	WB-U/6	AR
Dallas, Charlotte	083	1893	WB-4/53	AR
Dalrymple, Alexander	028	1818	WB-C/164	
Dalrymple, Ann	028	1841	WB-D/33	
Dalrymple, Archibald	068	1885	WB-D/199	
Dalrymple, James	068	1829	WB-B/71	
Dalrymple, John	068	1879	WB-D/122	
Dalrymple, John	070	c1752	DB-D/32	
Dalrymple, John	068	1822	WB-B/24	
Dalrymple, John	070	1752	DB-B/32	
Dalrymple, Martha	012	c1768	DB-A/126	
Dalrymple, William	068	c1855	WB-C/24	
Dalrymple, William	068	c1850	WB-C/21	
Dalton, Arena	092	1898	WB-6/480	AR
Dalton, Christina	090	1863	WB-4/361	AR
Dalton, David	090	1847	Orig. Only	AR
Dalton, David	090	1820	WB-3/44	AR-Copy
Dalton, Isaac	090	1824	WB-3/118	AR
Dalton, John A. B.	090	1879	WB-6/104	AR
Dalton, John Fox	090	1893	WB-6/318	AR
Dalton, Jubal L.	090	1845	WB-4/186	AR
Dalton, Maggie Reed	084	1891	WB-E/492	CTY
Dalton, Nicholas	084	1838	WB-B/186	CTY
Dalton, P. H.	033	1896	WB-2/196	CTY
Dalton, Rebecca	086	1849	WB-E/187	AR
Dalton, Robert J.	084	1862	WB-C/363	CTY
Dalton, Samuel	090	1807	WB-2/72	AR
Dalton, T. J.	064	1881	WB-2/102	AR
Dalton, Thomas	084	1864	WB-C/392	CTY
Dalton, Thomas	080	1890	WB-1/144	AR
Daly, John	075	1774	WB-I/109	AR
Dalyrymple, John	070	1767	SS 881/300	SS/AR
Dalzell, Mary	028	1785	WB-A/90	AR
Dalzinwurts, Louis	009	c1790	OWB/251	AR
Damerell, John	024	1704	Orig. Only	SS/AR
Dameron, Bartholomew	020	1809	RB-F/20	AR
Dameron, Christopher	020	1808	RB-E/381	AR
Dameron, James H.	020	1885	WB-A/469	CTY
Dameron, John	047	1778	WB-2/82	
Dameron, John	020	c1804	Orig. Only	AR
Dameron, John	040	1882	WB-2/184	AR

Name	Co.	Date	Recorded Copy	Original
Dameron, Joseph	020	1818	RB-H/168	AR
Dameron, Thomas	060	1837	WB-1/410	AR
Damron, John D.	026	1871	WB-2/64	AR
Dan, Dannel	075	1756	Orig. Only	AR
Dana, Miles W.	071	1817	WB-3/195	AR
Danbe, Daniel	037	1750	SS 881/40	SS/AR
Dancey, Benjamin	044	1807	WB-6/404	CTY-Nunc.
Dancey, Isham	104	1860	WB-5/263	
Dancy, A. B.	104	1884	WB-6/249	AR
Dancy, Archibald	037	1800	WB-D/117	AR
Dancy, Charlotte	037	1872	WB-G/393	AR
Dancy, Francis	071	1806	WB-2/318	AR
Dancy, Francis L.	037	1848	WB-F/404	AR
Dancy, James	071	1790	WB-1/403	AR
Dancy, Lucy	037	1820	WB-E/249	AR
Dancy, Lucy	037	1858	WB-G/153	AR
Dancy, William	037	1840	WB-F/247	AR
Dancy, William	037	1807	WB-D/299	AR
Dancy, William	085	1837	WB-I/9	AR
Danelly, Duncan	083	1804	WB-1/89	AR-Nunc.
Daniel, A. N.	105	1895	WB-3/144	AR
Daniel, Aaron	037	1761	WB-A/79	AR-Nunc.
Daniel, Alexander	085	1830	WB-H/493	AR
Daniel, Alvis	084	1868	WB-E/3	CTY
Daniel, Ambros	047	1795	WB-3/251	AR
Daniel, Anne H.	044	1883	WB-23/474	CTY
Daniel, Annie A.	078	1892	Orig. Onmlly	AR
Daniel, Arch	105	1877	WB-2/214	AR
Daniel, Archabel	030	1843	WB-4/97	
Daniel, Asa	037	1813	WB-E/61	AR
Daniel, Barna	103	1893	WB-2/30	AR
Daniel, Belcher	051	1832	WB = A/40	
Daniel, Beverly	099	1822	RB-24/439	
Daniel, Britton	047	1816	WB-3/579	AR
Daniel, Chesley	044	1812	WB-7/258	CTY
Daniel, Chesley	044	1814	WB-7/469	CTY
Daniel, Chesly	VA	1822	Copy	044 CTY
Daniel, David	069	1825	WB-1/327	AR
Daniel, Edward Van	009	c1807	OB-A/28	AR
Daniel, Eli	010	1891	WB-I/309	AR
Daniel, Elisabeth	096	1752	Orig. Only	SS/AR
Daniel, Elizabeth	103	1887	WB-1/415	
Daniel, Emma E.	105	1886	WB-2/405	AR
Daniel, Ephraim	037	1819	WB-E/211	
Daniel, Ephraim	103	1822	RD-5/19	AR
Daniel, G. T.	105	1894	WB-3/91	AR
Daniel, George	078	1891	WB-19/317	AR
Daniel, Gidion	030	1803	WB-2/235	
Daniel, Green	078	1898	WB-19/444	AR
Daniel, Harriet W.	047	1881	WB-6/260	AR
Daniel, Henry M.	071	1847	WB-5/58	AR
Daniel, Isaac	103	1809	RD-1/169	AR
Daniel, Isaiah	073	1891	WB-H/552	CTY
Daniel, J. J.	047	1848	WB-4/262	AR
Daniel, Jacob	105	1880	WB-2/253	AR
Daniel, James	044	1785	WB-1/452	CTY
Daniel, James	047	1789	WB-3/173	AR
Daniel, James	009	1834	OWB/509	AR
Daniel, James E.	044	1882	WB-23/461	CTY
Daniel, James R.	009	1878	WB-1/208	CTY
Daniel, James W.	075	1780	WB-K/51	
Daniel, Jane E.	044	1880	WB-23/356	CTY
Daniel, John	103	1836	RD-7/157	AR
Daniel, John	100	1847	WB-39/297	AR
Daniel, John	047	1782	WB-3/26	AR
Daniel, John	012	1808	WB-B/83	
Daniel, John	086	1803	WB-B/147	AR
Daniel, John	071	1755	SS 880/41	SS/AR
Daniel, John	044	1779	WB-1/235	CTY
Daniel, John	073	1837	WB-E/422	AR
Daniel, John	044	1762	Orig. Only	CTY
Daniel, John	030	1829	WB-3/248	
Daniel, John	044	1779	HiDSC	AR-Copy
Daniel, John G.	044	1848	WB-17/351	CTY
Daniel, John H.	071	1824	WB-3/298	AR
Daniel, John H.	037	1864	WB-G/252	AR
Daniel, John H.	037	1873	WB-G/413	AR
Daniel, John S.	079	1870	WB-2/29	AR
Daniel, John W.	100	1809	WB-15/116	AR
Daniel, Jonathan	087	c1811	WB-A/70	AR
Daniel, Joseph	030	1821	WB-3/295	
Daniel, Joseph	079	c1861	WB-1/158	AR
Daniel, Joseph	044	1819	WB-8/224	CTY
Daniel, Joseph	037	1800	WB-D/118	AR
Daniel, Joseph A.	030	1860	WB-4/237	AR
Daniel, Josiah	044	1811	WB-7/182	CTY
Daniel, Judiath	037	1837	WB-F/208	AR
Daniel, Junius	047	1870	WB-6/36	AR
Daniel, Kennith	063	1865	WB-2/537	
Daniel, Lemuel	037	1822	WB-E/286	AR
Daniel, Leonard	086	1852	WB-E/229	AR
Daniel, Margaret	047	1849	WB-4/280	
Daniel, Martha	105	1863	WB-1/96	AR
Daniel, Mary	103	1823	RD-5/45	AR
Daniel, Mary L.	086	1880	WB-F/157	AR
Daniel, Mathew	VA	1825	Copy	078 AR
Daniel, Matilda	047	1843	WB-4/221	AR
Daniel, Moore	046	1842	WB-C/109	AR
Daniel, Nancy	082	1829	WB-1/302	AR
Daniel, Nathaniel	044	1853	WB-19/302	
Daniel, Nelly	044	1838	WB-14/253	CTY
Daniel, Nicholas	030	1807	WB-2/312	
Daniel, Overton	011	N. D.	WB-1/366	
Daniel, Owin	024	1701	SS 874.1/5	SS/AR
Daniel, Parrot F.M.	103	1865	RD-14/187	AR
Daniel, Patty	085	c1800	WB-E/251	AR
Daniel, Peter	085	c1791	WB-C/30	AR
Daniel, Rhoda	069	1831	WB-1/373	AR
Daniel, Richard	065	1823	WB-C/46	AR-Nunc.
Daniel, Richard V.	044	1859	WB-21/198	CTY
Daniel, Robert	063	1781	WB-1/80	Nunc.
Daniel, Robert	063	c1786	WB-1/127	
Daniel, Rosy	047	1871	WB-6/58	AR
Daniel, Samuel H.	071	1845	WB-5/21	AR
Daniel, Sarah	105	c1863	WB-1/111	
Daniel, Sarah	031	1879	WB-1/13	AR
Daniel, Sarah	012	1797	WB-B/55	AR
Daniel, Simon	037	1763	WB-A/117	AR
Daniel, Spencer	051	1858	WB-B/11	
Daniel, Spencer A.	063	1864	WB-2/541	
Daniel, Susan E.	033	1887	WB-2/94	CTY
Daniel, Sydney	079	1861	WB-1/73	AR
Daniel, T. H.	032	1897	WB-4/316	AR
Daniel, Thomas	096	1749	SS 877/102	SS/AR
Daniel, Thomas	044	1831	WB-12/192	CTY
Daniel, Thomas	028	1822	WB-C/216	AR
Daniel, Thomas M.	078	1883	WB-19/142	
Daniel, Travers	032	1852	WB-2/67	AR
Daniel, Trury	103	1832	RD-6/367	AR

Name	Co.	Date	Recorded Copy	Original
Daniel, W. H.	103	1900	WB-2/317	AR
Daniel, William	078	1818	WI-8/166	AR
Daniel, William	047	1800	WB-3/337	AR
Daniel, William	100	1794	WB-7/221	Nunc.
Daniel, William	054	1879	WB-4/357	CTY
Daniel, William	063	1881	WB-3/215	
Daniel, William	063	c1830	WB-2/177	
Daniel, William H.	047	1817	WB-3/596	AR
Daniel, William W.	047	1885	WB-6/399	AR
Daniel, Willie	105	1897	WB-3/275	
Daniel, Willie	105	1897	103 WB-5/190	103 AR
Daniel, Willis	047	1828	WB-4/46	AR
Daniel, Willis	044	1886	WB-23/577	CTY
Daniel, Woodson	099	1791	RB-2/306	AR
Daniel, Yearby	003	1866	WB-A/12	AR
Daniel, Zadok	099	1850	RB-27/203	AR
Daniel, Zilpha	105	c1862	WB-1/87	AR
Danieley, Henson	001	1897	WB-3/168	AR
Danieley, John	001	c1854	WB-1/110	AR
Danieley, John W.	001	1875	WB-2/96	AR
Daniell, John	070	c1763	012 DB-A/88	
Daniell, John	012	1771	DB-A/131	AR
Daniell, William	009	1740	Orig. Only	SS/AR
Daniels, Alex E.	032	1887	WB-3/565	AR
Daniels, Brian	019	1879	WB-B/110	AR
Daniels, Crissie	031	1895	WB-1/92	AR
Daniels, Ester E.	085	1892	WB-2/556	CTY
Daniels, Jacob	028	1823	WB-C/234	
Daniels, James	028	1856	WB-D/246	
Daniels, John B.	046	1883	WB-E/382	AR
Daniels, Josiah	019	1882	WB-B/135	AR
Daniels, Milley M.	065	1895	WB-M/398	AR
Daniels, Nelson G.	032	1885	WB-3/460	AR
Daniels, Sophia	053	1785	RW-1/139	
Daniels, William	054	1879	Copy	003 AR
Danley, Elizabeth	001	1876	WB-2/83	AR
Danley, Polly M.	001	c1877	WB-2/528	AR
Dann, John	009	1807	OWB/445	AR
Dann, John, Sr.	N	1697	SS 874.2/82	SS/AR
Dannelly, John	073	1834	WB-E/311	AR
Danner, Alexander	021	1885	WB-2/308	
Danner, Jacob	085	c1795	WB-E/244	
Dap, John D.	028	1764	Wills.9/72	AR
Darby, James	070	1878	WB-E/362	AR
Darden, Abraham	071	1831	WB-4/81	AR
Darden, Billy, Sr.	087	c1818	WB-A/90	AR
Darden, Charles	035	1801	WB-A/106	AR
Darden, Jane S.	051	1897	WB-C/529	
Darden, Jet R.	051	1883	WB-C/304	
Darden, Jethro	051	1834	WB-A/73	
Darden, Jethro	070	1812	WB-AB/173	AR
Darden, John	070	1817	WB-AB/253	AR
Darden, John	041	c1796	Orig. Only	AR
Darden, Joseph	010	1733	SS 876/326	SS/AR
Darden, Joseph	087	1874	WB-3/84	AR
Darden, Josiah	051	1837	WB-A/98	
Darden, Levina	051	1873	WB-C/94	AR
Darden, Lydia	051	1839	WB-A/141	
Darden, Martha B.	047	1806	WB-3/458	AR
Darden, Martha J.	077	1885	WB-H/156	AR
Darden, Reddick	071	1822	WB-3/275	AR
Darden, Sarah	071	1837	WB-4/165	AR
Darden, Titus	051	1834	WB-A/71	
Darden, William S.	045	1887	WB-1/136	AR
Dargan, Ellen A.	005	1875	WB-D/37	AR
Dargan, Jeremiah	010	1787	WB-D/74	AR
Dark, Aaron B.	022	1883	WB-E/268	AR
Dark, Joseph	022	1814	WB-A/259	AR
Dark, Nancy	022	1861	WB-D/75	AR
Dark, Susannah	022	1847	WB-C/205	AR
Dark, William	022	1880	WB-E/210	AR
Dark, Willis	022	1858	WB-D/18	AR
Darlet, William	063	1826	WB-2/116	
Darling, Richard	024	1702	SS 874.1/16	SS/AR
Darnall, Ann	030	1721/2	Orig. Only	SS/AR
Darnall, Joseph	065	1812	WB-C/41	AR
Darnall, William	065	1799	WB-C/17	AR
Darnall, Winefred	065	1829	WB-E/69	AR
Daroald, Dwelly	100	1870	WB-51/34	AR
Darr, Andrew	032	c1856	WB-2/348	AR
Darr, Elizabeth	032	1856	WB-2/118	AR
Darr, Henry	085	1816	WB-G/434	AR
Darr, Henry C.	032	1888	WB-4/35	AR
Darr, John	032	1836	WB-1/278	AR
Darr, Lorenz	060	1794	Orig. Only	AR
Darr, Melcher	032	1862	WB-2/220	AR
Darr, Melker	032	1834	WB-1/240	AR
Darr, Samuel	032	1896	WB-4/280	AR
Darr, Solomon	032	1885	WB-3/450	AR
Darroch, Alexander	029	1880	WB-E/240	AR
Dashiell, Phillip R.	OH	1885	075 WB-0/255	075 AR
Dauge, Angelia	030	1788	WB-1/227	
Dauge, Benjamin	030	1788	WB-1/222	
Dauge, Benjamin	030	1790	WB-1/245	
Dauge, Dory	030	1831	WB-3/276	
Dauge, Griffith	030	1802	WB-2/201	
Dauge, James	030	1782	WB-1/151	
Dauge, Peter	030	1799	WB-2/153	
Dauge, Tulley	030	1799	WB-2/150	
Dauge, Willis	030	1806	WB-2/295	
Dauge, Willis	030	1823	WB-3/165	
Dauge, Willoughby	030	1804	WB-2/248	
Daugherty, Daniel	046	1786	WB-A/91	AR
Daugherty, Daniel	028	1794	WB-A/314	AR
Daugherty, Esther	073	1855	WB-G/107	AR
Daugherty, Jane L.	028	1897	WB-F/319	
Daugherty, John	013	1865	WB-A/236	
Daugherty, John	013	1865	Copy	064 AR
Daugherty, Lemuel	013	1884	WB-B/342	AR
Daugherty, Owen	028	1786	WB-A/138	AR
Daugherty, Robert	046	1804	WB-A/102	AR
Daughety, Absalum	083	1824	WB-1/210	AR
Daughety, James F.	059	1887	WB-A/505	CTY
Daughfin, Isom Swain	010	1808	WB-F/71	AR
Daughterey, Thomas	071	1757	SS 882/46	SS/AR
Daughtery, Elizabeth	037	1817	WB-E/170	AR
Daughtery, Henry A.	103	1851	RD-11/1	AR
Daughtery, John	056	1762	WB-1/774	AR
Daughtery, Samuel	037	1787	WB-C/47	AR
Daughtie, Edward	041	1791	WB-1/88	AR
Daughtrey, Jesse	071	1796	WB-2/111	aR
Daughtrey, Lewis	071	1804	WB-2/266	AR
Daughtry, Ally	087	1882	Orig. Only	AR
Daughtry, Arthur	103	1828	RD-5/453	AR
Daughtry, Bryan	087	1863	WB-2/54	AR
Daughtry, Bryan	071	1788	WB-1/469	AR
Daughtry, Elijah W.	071	1892	WB-7/146	AR
Daughtry, Hardy	087	1856	WB-1/482	AR
Daughtry, Jacob	056	1826	WB-1/460	AR
Daughtry, Jacob	056	1876	WB-3/157	AR

Name	Co.	Date	Recorded Copy	Original
Daughtry, Jeremiah	071	1814	WB-3/127	AR
Daughtry, Joshua	071	1784	WB-1/328	AR
Daughtry, Lavinia	041	1854	WB-3/173	AR
Daughtry, Lawrence	071	1809	WB-3/17	AR
Daughtry, Lydda	087	c1813	WB-A/75	
Daughtry, Mandow	071	1793	WB-2/32	AR
Daughtry, Redin	037	1880	WB-G/562	AR
Daughtry, Rhoda	071	1808	WB-3/4	AR
Daughtry, S. R.	087	1893	WB-3/537	AR
Daughtry, Samuel	037	1805	WB-D/222	AR
Daughtry, William G.	041	1852	WB-3/148	AR
Daughtry, William M.	051	c1819	WB-A/122 & 179	
Daughty, Dempsy	037	1788	WB-C/70	AR
Daunery, Elizabeth	Eng	1899	100 WB-51/527	
Davbis, Nancy	100	1822	WB-24/123	AR
Davenport, A. W.	040	1885	WB-2/250	AR
Davenport, Ann C.	101	1881	WB-A/74	AR
Davenport, Augustine	085	c1799	WB-E/238	AR
Davenport, B. A.	079	1894	WB-3/56	AR
Davenport, Charles	086	1883	WB-4/99	AR
Davenport, Charlotte	079	1885	WB-2/345	AR
Davenport, David F.	069	1893	WB-5/410	AR
Davenport, Donnel	069	1785	WB-1/34	AR
Davenport, E. S.	101	1874	WB-A/9	AR
Davenport, Elizabeth	096	c1843	WB-3/7	
Davenport, Ephraim	024	1852	WB-C/339	AR
Davenport, Frederick	096	1838	WB-2/143	AR
Davenport, George W.	096	1851	WB-3/30	AR
Davenport, Hugh	096	1836	WB-2/132	
Davenport, Isaac	072	1815	WB-A/23	AR
Davenport, Isaac H.	096	1881	WB-4/64	
Davenport, Jacob	096	1746	Orig. Only	SS/AR
Davenport, James, Sr.	096	1790	WB-1/174	AR
Davenport, Jeston	101	1888	WB-A/159	AR
Davenport, Joanna	096	1841	WB-2/153	AR
Davenport, Joannah	096	1795	Orig. Only	AR
Davenport, John	096	1818	Orig. Only	AR
Davenport, John	096	c1823	Orig. Only	AR
Davenport, John	086	1864	WB-E/444	AR
Davenport, Jordan	096	1857	WB-3/46	AR
Davenport, Joseph	096	1792	Orig. Only	AR
Davenport, Joseph B.	101	1893	WB-A/237	AR
Davenport, Joshua B.	101	1892	WB-A/203	AR
Davenport, Lewis	096	1881	WB-4/70	AR
Davenport, Luraney	096	1802	WB-2/10	AR
Davenport, Mary	060	1840	WB-2/28	AR
Davenport, Patsey	096	1812	WB-2/36	AR
Davenport, Penelope	101	1875	WB-A/17	AR
Davenport, Redden	101	1894	WB-A/259	AR
Davenport, Richard	096	1866	WB-3/72	AR
Davenport, Richard	096	1774	WB-1/84	AR
Davenport, Robason	101	1869	Orig. Only	AR
Davenport, Sallie Ann	101	1889	WB-A/183	AR
Davenport, Sarah E.	096	1858	WB-3/53	AR
Davenport, Silas	096	1853	WB-3/35	AR
Davenport, Stephen A.	101	1887	WB-A/154	AR
Davenport, Thomas	096	c1824	Orig. Only	AR
Davenport, Thomas T.	078	1875	WB-19/42	AR
Davenport, W. C.	063	1890	WB-4/51	AR
Davenport, Warren W.	096	1859	WB-3/57	AR
Davenport, William	085	1822	WB-H/184	AR
Davenport, William	096	1785	WB-1/146	AR
Davenport, William	101	1857	SC/08283	AR-Copy
Daves, Alice DeR.	070	1897	WB-H/104	
Daves, Aughter	N	1735	SS 877/164	
Daves, Bartlett	013	1844	WB-A/93	
Daves, Edward G.	MD	1894	028 WB-F/148	
Daves, Elizabeth	028	1885	WB-E/377	AR
Daves, James A.	026	1891	WB-2/449	AR
Daves, John P.	028	1838	WB-C/417	AR
Daves, Joshua	030	1841	WB-4/86	
Daves, Mathias	030	1840	WB-4/79	
Daves, Samuel	030	1840	WB-4/80	
Daves, Thomas	061	1859	WB-1/71	AR
Davey, Gabril	078	1792	WI-1/25	AR
Davey, James	078	1797	WI-1/306	AR
Davey, Walter	009	1734	Orig. Only	SS/AR
Davey, William	078	1813	WI-6/180	AR
Davice, Thomas	008	1714	Orig. Only	SS/AR
David, Aaron	016	1847	WB-1/134	
David, Benjamin	078	1877	WB-19/74	
David, Philip	070	1747	DB-C/172	
David, Philip	070	1747	028 DB-5/198	SS/AR
David, Solomon	003	1894	WB-B/323	
David, Willis J.	029	1818	WB-B/31	
Davidson, A. Brevard	065	1897	040 WB-2/565	040 AR
Davidson, A. Brevard	065	1896	WB-M/473	AR
Davidson, Barttel M.	063	c1781	WB-1/84	
Davidson, Daniel R.	PA	1884	085 WB-3/317	085 CTY
Davidson, Edward W.	065	1895	WB-M/385	AR
Davidson, Elizabeth	010	1827	WB-G/158	AR
Davidson, Ephraim	054	1842	WB-2/239	AR
Davidson, Gatchy	103	1893	WB-2/23	AR
Davidson, George	054	c1814	WB-1/337	AR
Davidson, Hugh H.	025	1889	WB-A/88	AR
Davidson, J. H.	064	1895	WB-2/344	AR
Davidson, James	081	1794	WB-2/3	AR
Davidson, James	081	c1851	Orig. Only	AR
Davidson, James L.	065	1853	WB-I/203	AR
Davidson, John	084	1808	WB-A/82	CTY
Davidson, John	010	1779	WB-B/135	AR
Davidson, John	065	c1778	WB-C/14	AR
Davidson, John	065	1832	WB-G/74	AR
Davidson, John	054	1886	WB-5/95	CTY
Davidson, John	065	c1793	WB-C/28	AR
Davidson, John	049	1849	WI-1-2/21	AR
Davidson, John	049	c1844	SC/06569	AR-Copy
Davidson, John T.	051	1843	WB-A/158	
Davidson, Joseph	054	1859	WB-3/143	AR
Davidson, M. E.	086	1898	WB-F/574	AR
Davidson, Margaret	065	1864	WB-J/180	AR
Davidson, Mary	010	1900	WB-K/53	
Davidson, Mary	081	1897	WB-16/434	AR
Davidson, Mary E.	065	1897	WB-M/543	AR
Davidson, Robert	065	1853	WB-I/214	AR
Davidson, Samuel W.	013	1859	WB-A/199	
Davidson, Sarah F.	065	1889	WB-L/366	AR
Davidson, Sophronia	013	1865	WB-A/239	
Davidson, Thomas	065	1800	WB-C/23	AR
Davidson, Thomas	047	1770	Orig. Only	024 AR
Davidson, Walton	064	1882	Orig. Only	AR
Davidson, William	065	1781	WB-C/15	AR
Davidson, William	054	1803	WB-1/91	AR
Davidson, William L.	085	c1780	WB-B/11	AR
Davie, Ashburn	078	1806	WI-4/175	AR
Davies, Francis	070	1753	Orig. Only	SS/AR
Davies, George	065	1807	WB-C/35	AR
Davies, James	085	1765	WB-A/33	AR
Davies, John N.	065	c1844	WB-H/176	AR

Name	Co.	Date	Recorded Copy	Original
Davies, Robert	065	1774	WB-C/12	AR
Davieson, John	024	c1772	WB-A/238	AR
Davis (Tuten), Elizabeth	009	1835	OWB/523	AR
Davis, Aaron	072	c1826	WB-A/17	AR
Davis, Aaron	076	1888	WB-A1/95	AR
Davis, Aaron	076	1888	070 WB-I/149	070 AR
Davis, Abram	024	1846	WB-C/273	AR
Davis, Abram B.	019	1889	WB-B/189	AR
Davis, Absalom	083	1851	WB-2/33	AR
Davis, Adaline	010	1866	WB-H/155	AR
Davis, Adam C.	103	1900	WB-2/301	AR
Davis, Alexander	065	1843	WB-H/117	AR
Davis, Alexander	019	1892	WB-B/214	AR
Davis, Alfred	081	1875	WB-15/211	
Davis, Alfred	079	1860	WB-1/46	AR
Davis, Alfred H.	071	1861	WB-5/242	AR
Davis, Allen	060	1809	Orig. Only	AR
Davis, Allen	022	c1850	WB-D/155	AR
Davis, Allen J.	022	c1862	WB-D/125	AR
Davis, Allen W.	099	1820	RB-16/230	AR
Davis, Amanda	100	1885	Orig. Only	AR
Davis, Amor	081	1834	WB-6/397	AR
Davis, Andrew	016	1853	WB-1/217	
Davis, Andrew	085	1800	WB-E/243	AR
Davis, Andrew O.	097	1863	WB-1/222	AR
Davis, Ann	047	1803	WB-3/401	AR
Davis, Ann	100	1844	WB-38/250	AR
Davis, Ann	029	c1820	WB-B/30	
Davis, Annie	053	1890	WB-11/224	AR
Davis, Anthony	075	1799	WB-M1/27	AR
Davis, Anthony	059	1894	WB-B/112	CTY
Davis, Archibald	039	c1854	WB-O/350	AR
Davis, Archibald	039	1821	WB-G/59	
Davis, Arthur	N	1735	Orig. Only	SS/AR
Davis, Arthur	071	1848	WB-5/72	AR
Davis, Arthur	056	1794	WB-1/81	AR
Davis, Arthur	029	c1774	Orig. Only	AR
Davis, Arthur	075	1807	WB-M1/154	AR
Davis, Arthur	047	1790	WB-3/184	AR
Davis, Arthur	100	1881	WB-51/156	AR
Davis, Arthur	071	1880	WB-6/306	AR
Davis, Asbury	013	1889	WB-B/500	AR
Davis, Bailey	075	1823	WB-M1/390	AR
Davis, Barbara	032	1876	WB-3/184	AR
Davis, Barbara	032	1854	WB-2/97	AR
Davis, Basheba	037	1882	WB-G/633	AR
Davis, Baxter	073	1877	WB-H/176	CTY
Davis, Benjamin	009	1830	OB-B/80	AR
Davis, Benjamin	099	1802	RB-6/74	AR
Davis, Benjamin	027	1872	WB-2/11	AR-Nunc.
Davis, Benjamin	009	1843	OB-E/189	AR
Davis, Benjamin	047	1850	WB-4/291	AR
Davis, Benjamin	079	1849	WB-1/25	AR
Davis, Benjamin	075	1816	WB-M1/297	
Davis, Benjamin	075	1836	WB-N/118	AR
Davis, Benjamin	047	1838	WB-4/170	AR
Davis, Benjamin	071	1770	WB-1/179	
Davis, Benjamin	019	1814	WB-E/41	AR
Davis, Benjamine	078	1877	WB-18/74	AR
Davis, Bethany	106	c1860	WB-1/83	AR
Davis, Betsy	075	1831	WB-N/64	AR-Nunc.
Davis, Briscoe	028	1792	WB-A/280	AR
Davis, Buckner	100	1820	WB-22/436	AR
Davis, Burwell	100	1846	WB-39/183	AR
Davis, Calvin J.	019	1896	WB-B/298	AR
Davis, Celah	009	1831	OB-B/92	AR
Davis, Charity E.	019	1887	WB-B/170	AR
Davis, Charles	075	1873	WB-O/53	AR
Davis, Charles	081	1850	WB-9/183	
Davis, Charlotte	012	1875	WB-A/30	AR
Davis, Christian	081	1877	WB-15/277	AR
Davis, Christopher	005	1786	WB-1/51	
Davis, Conrad	085	c1789	WB-E/250	AR
Davis, D. A.	085	1881	WB-1/585	CTY
Davis, D. F.	062	1881	WB-B/65	
Davis, Dafren	081	1826	WB-5/310	AR
Davis, David	065	1832	WB-G/98	AR
Davis, David	081	1885	WB-15/486	AR
Davis, David	053	1809	RW-1/433	AR
Davis, David	065	1833	WB-G/106	AR
Davis, David	073	1894	WB-I/31	CTY
Davis, David	092	1783	WB-2/12A	AR
Davis, David	092	1806	WB-3/72	AR
Davis, David	011	1741/2	Orig. Only	SS/AR
Davis, David	081	1900	WB-17/107	
Davis, David	035	1824	WB-A/126	AR
Davis, David	020	1818	RB-H/168	AR
Davis, David	049	c1835	WI-1-2/5	AR
Davis, David	092	1869	WB-6/65	
Davis, David	065	1777	WB-C/17	AR
Davis, David	085	c1784	WB-B/102	AR
Davis, Dennis	071	1892	WB-7/171	AR
Davis, Devotion	068	1875	WB-D/67	AR-Copy
Davis, Devotion	075	1800	WB-M1/36	AR
Davis, Dinah	085	1893	WB-2/568	CTY
Davis, Dixon, Sr.	056	1857	WB-1/706	AR
Davis, Dolithy	041	1817	WB-2/142	AR
Davis, Dorças	053	1797	RW-1/289	AR
Davis, Drewry	071	1845	WB-5/18	AR
Davis, Duke	070	1886	WB-F/11	AR
Davis, E. H.	032	1890	WB-4/72	AR
Davis, E. Harvey	016	1900	WB-4/360	AR
Davis, Easter	096	1882	WB-4/82	AR
Davis, Edmond	011	c1839	WB-1/81	
Davis, Edward	071	1803	WB-2/244	AR
Davis, Edward	100	1895	Orig. Only	AR
Davis, Edward	011	c1780	WB-1/485	
Davis, Edward	100	1796	Orig. Only	AR
Davis, Edward G.	027	c1835	WB-A/42	AR
Davis, Edward H.	047	1849	WB-4/288	AR
Davis, Edward M.	PA	1887	017 WB-B/169	017 AR
Davis, Edward M.	PA	1887	102 WB-A/67	102 AR
Davis, Eemory	037	c1795	WB-D/1	AR
Davis, Elijah A.	073	1894	WB-I/33	CTY
Davis, Elisha	105	1867	WB-1/126	AR
Davis, Elisha	096	1815	Orig. Only	AR
Davis, Eliza	065	1887	WB-L/211	AR
Davis, Elizabeth	100	1840	WB-37/297	AR
Davis, Elizabeth	016	1871	WB-3/42	
Davis, Elizabeth	100	1821	WB-23/232	AR
Davis, Elizabeth	053	c1814	RW-1/504	
Davis, Elizabeth	085	1821	WB-H/133	AR
Davis, Elizabeth	075	1817	WB-M1/309	AR
Davis, Elizabeth	046	1844	WB-C/178	AR
Davis, Elva	103	1895	WB-2/136	AR
Davis, Emma J.	019	1892	WB-B/217	AR
Davis, Enoch	073	1792	WB-B/168	AR
Davis, Enoch	057	1821	WB-B/61	AR
Davis, Eupham	030	1775	WB-1/98	
Davis, Evan	092	1892	WB-6/347	AR

Name	Co.	Date	Recorded Copy	Original
Davis, Eveline	101	1871	Orig. Only	AR
Davis, Fannie	059	1883	WB-A/368	CTY
Davis, Fanny	100	1896	WB-51/451	
Davis, Frances B.	044	1886	WB-23/570	CTY
Davis, Francis	047	1781	WB-3/16	AR
Davis, Frank	044	1879	WB-23/330	CTY
Davis, Franky P.	046	1869	WB-E/7	AR
Davis, Frederick	018	1825	WB-C/63	
Davis, Garrett	041	1782	WB-1/24	AR
Davis, George	012	1814	WB-B/107	AR
Davis, George	070	1896	WB-G/467	AR
Davis, George	010	1797	WB-E/30	AR
Davis, George	086	1876	WB-F/84	AR
Davis, George W.	020	1893	WB-B/136	CTY
Davis, Giles	100	1809	WB-15/113	AR
Davis, Goodde	100	1815	WB-19/123	AR
Davis, Goodoram	047	1809	WB-3/484	AR
Davis, Hannah	081	1834	WB-6/357	AR
Davis, Hannah	100	1821	WB-29/63	AR
Davis, Hannah	028	1849	WB-D/157	AR
Davis, Henrietta	073	1894	WB-I/29	CTY
Davis, Henrietta	009	1897	WB-2/119	CTY
Davis, Henrietta	054	1899	WB-6/263	CTY
Davis, Henry	070	1881	WB-E/421	AR
Davis, Henry	090	1805	WB-2/61	AR
Davis, Henry	020	1799	RB-C/410	
Davis, Henry	009	1873	WB-1/121	CTY
Davis, Henry	081	1891	WB-16/545	
Davis, Henry	046	1891	WB-F/117	AR
Davis, Henry	011	c1832	WB-1/6	
Davis, Henry C.	105	1897	WB-3/254	AR
Davis, Henry H.	103	1885	WB-1/352	AR
Davis, Hillery	071	1845	WB-5/17	AR
Davis, Hugh	N	1724	SS 876/36	SS/AR
Davis, Hugh J.	100	1865	WB-50/166	AR
Davis, Huldah	103	1796	WI-B/182	AR
Davis, Humphrey	099	1790	RB-2/304	AR
Davis, Ichabod	083	1835	WB-1/298	AR
Davis, Irene	010	1897	WB-I/531	AR
Davis, Isaac	044	1884	100 WB-51/283	100 AR
Davis, Isaac	092	1828	WB-3/172	AR
Davis, Isaac	012	1818	Orig. Only	AR
Davis, Isaac	003	c1851	Orig. Only	AR
Davis, Isaac	030	1743	LGB-4/#146	SS/AR
Davis, Isaac H.	044	1884	078 WB-19/166	078 AR
Davis, Isaac H.	044	1884	WB-23/496 & 572	CTY
Davis, Isaac H.	044	1884	074 WB-1/77	074 AR
Davis, Isaac M.	019	1881	WB-B/129	AR
Davis, Isabella	011	c1824	WB-1/16	
Davis, Isham	100	1830	WB-33/143	AR
Davis, J. B.	030	1899	WB-5/280	
Davis, Jacob	103	1831	RD-6/261	AR
Davis, Jacob	043	c1869	WB-1/22	AR
Davis, Jacob	085	c1795	WB-E/241	AR
Davis, Jacob	092	c1838	WB-4/155	
Davis, James	079	c1857	WB-1/2	AR
Davis, James	056	1800	WB-1/122	AR
Davis, James	071	1873	WB-6/104	AR
Davis, James	071	1838	WB-4/180	AR
Davis, James	090	1872	WB-6/38	AR
Davis, James	081	1805	WB-3/18	AR
Davis, James	047	1817	WB-3/598	AR
Davis, James	046	1837	WB-B/568	AR
Davis, James	028	1785	WB-A/82	AR

Name	Co.	Date	Recorded Copy	Original
Davis, James	017	1869	WB-B/10	AR
Davis, James	011	1886	WB-2/205	
Davis, James	028	1797	WB-B/31	AR
Davis, James	065	1806	WB-C/31	AR
Davis, James	059	1879	WB-A/188	CTY
Davis, James	019	1844	WB-A/114	AR
Davis, James	069	1893	WB-5/400	AR
Davis, James	065	1837	WB-E/177	AR
Davis, James	041	1797	WB-1/154	AR
Davis, James	090	1844	WB-4/163	AR
Davis, James	073	1827	WB-E/140	AR
Davis, James	071	1791	WB-1/425	AR
Davis, James A.	100	1895	WB-51/403	
Davis, James A.	009	1865	OB-M/272	AR
Davis, James B.	100	1878	WB-51/163	AR
Davis, James C.	068	1869	WB-D/5	
Davis, James C.	097	1865	WB-1/258	AR
Davis, James K.	059	1889	WB-A/578	CTY
Davis, James P.	083	1891	WB-3/519	AR
Davis, James, Sr.	040	1861	WB-1/125	AR
Davis, Jeams	N	1718	SS 875/179	SS/AR
Davis, Jehu	070	1788	WB-C/80	AR
Davis, Jehu, Jr.	070	1771	012 DB-A/138	
Davis, Jehue	012	c1765	DB-A/37	
Davis, Jemima	078	1818	WI-8/75	AR
Davis, Jeremiah	072	1808	WB-A/22	AR
Davis, Jesse	081	1829	WB-6/20	AR
Davis, Jesse	009	1822	OB-A/324	AR
Davis, Jesse	092	1872	WB-6/41	
Davis, Job	081	1825	Orig. Only	AR
Davis, Job	089	1853	WB-1/94	
Davis, Joel	032	1860	WB-2/198	AR
Davis, John	060	1830	WB-1/162	AR
Davis, John	013	1843	WB-A/91	
Davis, John	032	1835	WB-1/267	AR
Davis, John	012	c1853	WB-B/44	AR
Davis, John	035	1761	087 DB-3/122	AR
Davis, John	085	c1775	WB-A/232	AR
Davis, John	047	1761	WB-1/26	
Davis, John	063	1790	WB-1/160	
Davis, John	071	1834	WB-4/110	AR
Davis, John	075	1753	SS 881/18	SS/AR
Davis, John	012	c1765	DB-A/28	
Davis, John	084	c1797	OW/104	AR
Davis, John	028	1855	WB-D/238	AR
Davis, John	069	c1817	Orig. Only	AR
Davis, John	020	1841	RB-O/253	AR
Davis, John	006	1888	WB-E/166	AR
Davis, John	103	1841	RD-8/102	AR
Davis, John	061	c1867	WB-2/24	AR
Davis, John	022	1807	WB-A/142	AR
Davis, John	103	1831	RD-6/260	AR
Davis, John	065	1777	WB-C/10	AR
Davis, John	032	1841	WB-1/367	AR
Davis, John	053	1797	RW-1/280	AR
Davis, John	009	1833	OB-B/227	AR
Davis, John	056	c1779	Orig. Only	AR
Davis, John	041	1793	WB-1/108	AR
Davis, John	037	1799	WB-D/69	AR
Davis, John	008	c1726	009 OWB/5	009 AR
Davis, John	092	1850	WB-4/332	
Davis, John	053	1752	028 DB-5/214	SS/AR
Davis, John	030	c1812	WB-3/31	
Davis, John	103	1850	RD-10/461	AR
Davis, John	037	1824	WB-F/15	AR

Name	Co.	Date	Recorded Copy	Original
Davis, John	073	1825	WB-E/92	AR
Davis, John	075	1808	WB-M1/192	AR
Davis, John	VA	1728	Copy	024 AR
Davis, John	056	1880	WB-3/251	AR
Davis, John	090	1807	WB-2/82	AR
Davis, John	026	1844	WB-1/20	AR
Davis, John	002	1688	Orig. Only	SS/AR
Davis, John	028	1804	WB-B/205	
Davis, John	075	1754	Orig. Only	SS/AR
Davis, John	071	1852	WB-5/106	AR
Davis, John	075	1784	WB-K/99	AR
Davis, John	054	1858	WB-3/129	AR
Davis, John A.	020	1847	RB-P/501	
Davis, John A.	016	1899	WB-4/326	AR
Davis, John B.	064	1898	WB-2/431	AR
Davis, John B.	065	c1845	WB-I/9	AR
Davis, John D.	009	1869	WB-1/24	CTY
Davis, John D.	019	1899	WB-C/12	AR
Davis, John E.	092	1822	WB-3/152	AR
Davis, John H.	016	1891	WB-4/120	AR
Davis, John M.	059	1887	WB-A/472	CTY
Davis, John P.	GA	1890	059 WB-B/10	059 CTY
Davis, John P. C.	019	1866	WB-A/289	AR
Davis, John R.	009	1844	OB-E/383	
Davis, John S.	053	1844	WB-6/285	AR
Davis, John S.	100	1874	WB-51/102	AR
Davis, John S.	019	1880	WB-B/117	AR
Davis, John T.	053	1848	WB-7/178	AR
Davis, John W.	103	1869	WB-1/10	AR
Davis, John W.	055	1862	PQS.2/462	
Davis, John W.	075	1887	WB-O/278	AR
Davis, John, Sr.	085	1821	WB-H/123	AR
Davis, John, Sr.	009	1826	OB-A/371	
Davis, Jonathan	044	1832	WB-12/381	CTY
Davis, Jonathan	082	1859	WB-4/138	AR
Davis, Jonathan	073	1823	WB-E/47	AR
Davis, Jonathan	096	1779	WB-1/110	AR
Davis, Jonathan	099	1819	RB-15/165	AR
Davis, Jonathan	044	1900	WB-24/487	CTY
Davis, Jonathan	039	1842	WB-L/64	AR
Davis, Jonathan	096	1750	WB-1/1	AR
Davis, Joseph	075	1836	WB-N/121	AR
Davis, Joseph	012	1868	Orig. Only	AR
Davis, Joseph	075	1804	WB-M1/102	AR
Davis, Joseph	032	1826	WB-1/52	AR
Davis, Joseph	028	1843	WB-D/83	AR
Davis, Joseph	099	1790	RB-2/249	AR
Davis, Joseph	075	1772	WB-I/60	AR
Davis, Joseph	019	1792	WB-D/118	AR
Davis, Joseph	037	1799	WB-D/75	AR
Davis, Joseph	075	1778	WB-K/28	AR
Davis, Joseph J.	019	1877	WB-B/97	AR
Davis, Joseph P.	044	1812	WB-7/232	CTY
Davis, Joseph P.	044	1872	WB-23/86	CTY
Davis, Joseph W.	019	1826	WB-D/143	
Davis, Joshua	100	1800	WB-10/294	AR
Davis, Joshua	103	1813	RD-3/13	AR
Davis, Joshua	075	1886	WB-O/246	AR
Davis, Joshua	075	1787	WB-K/146	AR
Davis, Joshua	103	1789	WI-A/138	AR
Davis, Joshua A.	100	1845	WB-38/347	AR
Davis, Josiah	030	1788	WB-1/219	
Davis, Josiah	066	c1897	Orig. Only	AR
Davis, Judith	020	1834	RB-M/409	
Davis, Junius	012	c1861	WB-B/39	AR

Name	Co.	Date	Recorded Copy	Original
Davis, Lawson W.	028	1865	WB-D/408	AR
Davis, Lewis	069	1780	WB-1/13	AR
Davis, Lewis	099	1816	RB-12/275	AR
Davis, Lewis	047	1760	WB-1/16	
Davis, Lewis	071	1826	WB-3/338	AR
Davis, Littleton	028	1786	WB-A/141	AR
Davis, Lou	062	1894	WB-B/173	AR
Davis, Louis	100	c1797	039 WB-A/210	
Davis, Louisa	044	1899	WB-24/431	CTY
Davis, Lucretia	099	1893	WB-C/133	AR
Davis, Lucy	044	1878	WB-23/317	CTY
Davis, Lucy T.	022	1862	WB-D/91	AR
Davis, Lula E.	039	1888	WB-U/457	AR
Davis, Mabel	075	1827	WB-N/39	AR
Davis, Major	078	1860	WB-18/153	AR
Davis, Margaret	047	1873	WB-6/86	AR
Davis, Margaret	065	1862	WB-J/123	AR
Davis, Margaret	070	1832	WB-AB/287	AR
Davis, Margaret S.	053	1849	WB-7/245	AR
Davis, Margerett	013	1848	WB-A/131	
Davis, Maria	103	1900	WB-2/294	AR
Davis, Marmaduke	077	1778	Orig. Only	AR
Davis, Martha	039	c1844	WB-M/30	AR
Davis, Martha	071	1856	WB-5/153	AR
Davis, Martha	085	c1811	WB-G/198	AR
Davis, Martha	047	1829	WB-4/49	AR
Davis, Martha	016	1832	PQS.5/216	
Davis, Martha	047	1760	WB-1/17	
Davis, Martha V.	099	1894	WB-C/332	AR
Davis, Mary	100	1863	WB-50/50	AR
Davis, Mary	005	1831	WB-B/12	AR
Davis, Mary	039	1851	WB-N/338	AR
Davis, Mary	029	1898	Orig. Only	AR
Davis, Mary	019	1866	WB-B/9	AR
Davis, Mary	071	1839	WB-4/204	AR
Davis, Mary	047	1815	WB-3/573	AR
Davis, Mary L.	086	1890	WB-F/390	AR
Davis, Mary P.	020	c1872	WB-B/270	CTY
Davis, Matthew	100	1827	WB-30/158	AR
Davis, Matthew	081	1857	WB-10/496	AR
Davis, Matthew	092	1836	WB-4/209	
Davis, Matthew	081	1875	WB-15/172	AR
Davis, Micajah	011	c1827	WB-2/375	
Davis, Micajah	039	c1802	WB-B/71	AR-Copy
Davis, Milton	102	1870	WB-A/6	
Davis, Myrick	085	c1808	WB-G/105	AR
Davis, N. D.	026	1896	WB-2/518	AR
Davis, Nancy	032	1892	WB-4/141	AR
Davis, Nancy	103	1887	WB-1/391	AR
Davis, Nancy	071	1863	WB-5/284	AR
Davis, Naney	075	1789	WB-K/175	AR
Davis, Nannie E.	059	1883	WB-A/322	CTY
Davis, Nathan	019	1808	WB-D/150	AR
Davis, Nathaniel	053	1764	OB-A/73	
Davis, Nathaniel	062	1872	WB-B/4	AR
Davis, Nathaniel	099	1816	RB-12/386	AR
Davis, Nathaniel	053	1881	Orig. Only	AR
Davis, Newton	054	1869	WB-4/21	AR
Davis, Oroondates	047	1781	WB-3/21	AR
Davis, Osker	039	1900	WB-V/190	AR
Davis, P. R.	086	c1876	Orig. Only	AR
Davis, Penelope	099	1866	RB-34/288	AR
Davis, Peter	010	1723	SS 876/104	SS/AR
Davis, Peter	100	1804	WB-12/192	AR
Davis, Peter	046	1887	WB-E/484	AR

Name	Co.	Date	Recorded Copy	Original
Davis, Peter E.	100	1878	WB-51/133	AR
Davis, Peter M.	100	1822	WB-23/223	
Davis, Peter R.	100	1836	WB-40/297	AR
Davis, Philip	086	1830	WB-D/126	AR
Davis, Phillip	026	1873	WB-2/107	AR
Davis, Polly	053	c1839	Orig. Only	AR
Davis, Polly	105	1888	WB-2/497	AR
Davis, Pressilla	039	1842	WB-L/90	AR
Davis, Prudence	105	1862	WB-1/81	AR
Davis, R. A.	065	1898	WB-N/492	
Davis, Rachel	035	1836	WB-A/129	AR
Davis, Rachel	103	1852	RD-11/83	AR
Davis, Rachel	037	1800	WB-D/116	AR
Davis, Ralph	068	1811	WB-A/271	
Davis, Ransom	039	c1794	WB-A/157	
Davis, Rebecca	073	1847	WB-F/373	AR
Davis, Reuben	075	1798	WB-M1/4	AR
Davis, Richard	103	1809	RD-1/134	AR
Davis, Richard	044	1761	Orig. Only	CTY
Davis, Richard	077	1737	LGB-4/#67	SS/AR
Davis, Richard	012	1896	WB-A/114	AR
Davis, Richard	100	1839	WB-37/155	AR
Davis, Richard	009	1830	OB-B/77	AR
Davis, Richard	009	1842	OB-D/362	AR
Davis, Richard	073	1831	WB-E/239	AR
Davis, Richard	096	1822	WB-2/86	AR
Davis, Richard B.	079	1861	WB-1/76	AR
Davis, Richard L.	019	1850	WB-A/141	AR
Davis, Robert	065	1837	WB-E/149	AR
Davis, Robert	MS	1845	Copy	103 AR
Davis, Robert	075	1750	Orig. Only	SS/AR
Davis, Robert	016	1842	PQS.6/187	
Davis, Robert	092	1847	WB-4/264	
Davis, Robert	020	1819	RB-H/284	
Davis, Robert	077	1799	WB-E/104	AR
Davis, Robert N.	060	1871	WB-4/77	AR
Davis, Robert W.	012	1880	WB-A/46	AR
Davis, Roenah	005	1887	WB-D/213	AR
Davis, Ruth	081	1861	WB-12/2	
Davis, Sallie	012	1898	WB-A/131	AR
Davis, Sally	009	1825	OB-A/353	AR
Davis, Samuel	082	1782	WB-1/10	AR
Davis, Samuel	035	1838	Orig. Only	AR
Davis, Samuel	002	c1688	Orig. Only	SS/AR
Davis, Samuel	053	1802	RW-1/339	AR
Davis, Samuel	092	1848	WB-4/281	
Davis, Samuel	072	1851	WB-2/110	AR
Davis, Samuel	077	1900	WB-H/338	AR
Davis, Samuel	075	1788	WB-K/166	AR
Davis, Samuel	075	1769	WB-H/96	AR
Davis, Samuel	100	1892	WB-51/326	AR
Davis, Samuel	009	1871	WB-1/87	CTY
Davis, Samuel	053	1795	RW-1/262	AR
Davis, Samuel C.	019	1860	WB-A/250	AR
Davis, Sanford	075	1801	WB-M1/55	AR
Davis, Sara	103	1885	WB-1/356	AR
Davis, Sarah	103	1822	RD-4/472	AR
Davis, Sarah	089	1856	WB-1/155	
Davis, Sarah	026	1866	WB-1/399	AR
Davis, Sarah	024	1820	WB-C/79	AR
Davis, Sarah	071	1858	WB-5/279	AR
Davis, Sarah	024	N. D.	WB-A/246	AR
Davis, Sarah	012	1805	WB-B/80	AR
Davis, Sarah	090	1807	WB-2/79	AR
Davis, Sarah	103	c1868	WB-1/64	AR
Davis, Sarah	077	1817	WB-E/473	AR
Davis, Sarah A.	019	1885	WB-B/148	AR
Davis, Sarah P.	026	c1874	Orig. Only	AR
Davis, Senas	059	1876	WB-A/127	
Davis, Senas	059	1876	028 WB-E/136	028 AR
Davis, Shadrach	075	1836	WB-N/125	AR
Davis, Shadrick	075	1814	WB-M1/259	AR
Davis, Silvanus	075	N. D.	WB-M2/27	AR
Davis, Simon	035	1800	WB-A/104	AR
Davis, Simpson	097	1889	WB-2/340	AR
Davis, Solomon	104	1831	WB-4/150	AR
Davis, Solomon	019	1827	WB-D/152	AR
Davis, Solomon	044	1809	WB-7/460	CTY
Davis, Solomon	075	1739	LGB-4/#100	SS/AR
Davis, Solomon W.	019	1794	WB-D/132	AR
Davis, Sophia	046	1848	WB-C/288	AR
Davis, Squire B.	092	1813	WB-3/108	AR
Davis, Stephen	022	1898	WB-F/69	AR
Davis, Stephen	100	1857	WB-49/128	AR
Davis, Sugar S.	047	c1849	WB-4/276	
Davis, Sumner	100	1898	WB-51/509	
Davis, Susanna	019	1827	WB-D/141	AR
Davis, Sutton	009	1897	WB-2/119	
Davis, Tabitha	071	1833	WB-4/100	AR
Davis, Theophilus	100	1899	WB-51/525	
Davis, Thomas	077	1746	Orig. Only	SS/AR
Davis, Thomas	030	1754	SS 878/166	
Davis, Thomas	106	1898	WB-2/440	
Davis, Thomas	072	1798	Orig. Only	AR
Davis, Thomas	020	1822	RB-I/91	
Davis, Thomas	047	1770	WB-1/256	
Davis, Thomas	075	1798	WB-M1/13	AR
Davis, Thomas	083	1815	WB-1/159	AR
Davis, Thomas	039	1862	WB-R/347	AR
Davis, Thomas	070	1865	022 WB-D/129	022 AR
Davis, Thomas	075	1781	WB-K/70	AR
Davis, Thomas	047	1765	WB-1/153	
Davis, Thomas	096	c1762	WB-1/51	
Davis, Thomas	092	1887	WB-6/264	AR
Davis, Thomas	046	c1780	WB-A/89	AR
Davis, Thomas	075	1791	WB-K/210	AR
Davis, Thomas	029	1822	WB-B/96	AR
Davis, Thomas	075	1817	WB-M1/303	AR
Davis, Thomas	011	1770	Orig. Only	SS/AR
Davis, Thomas	070	1796	WB-C/82	AR-Nunc.
Davis, Thomas	047	1803	WB-3/411	AR
Davis, Thomas	044	1860	WB-21/289	
Davis, Thomas	103	1812	RD-2/178	AR
Davis, Thomas	044	1758	SS 881/161	SS/AR
Davis, Thomas	072	c1774	RW/L41	AR
Davis, Thomas	085	c1789	WB-E/239	AR
Davis, Thomas H.	065	1853	WB-I/228	AR
Davis, Thomas H.	100	1845	WB-38/338	AR
Davis, Thomas H.	085	1820	WB-H/31	AR
Davis, Thomas J.	106	1881	WB-2/142	
Davis, Thomas O.	070	1825	WB-C/86	AR
Davis, Thomas T.	100	1851	WB-41/106	AR
Davis, Turner	071	1885	WB-6/514	AR
Davis, Turner	011	c1794	WB-1/487	
Davis, Tyra H.	091	1889	WB-1/115	
Davis, Wallace	070	1895	WB-G/381	AR
Davis, Walter	065	1839	WB-E/223	AR
Davis, Walter	065	1800	WB-C/32	AR
Davis, Whittington	019	c1867	WB-D/142	AR
Davis, Wiatt	073	1877	WB-H/180	CTY

Name	Co.	Date	Recorded Copy	Original
Davis, William	019	1822	WB-D/149	AR
Davis, William	011	c1790	WB-1/452	
Davis, William	092	1822	WB-3/152	AR
Davis, William	044	1892	WB-24/189	CTY
Davis, William	019	1836	WB-A/61	AR
Davis, William	070	1809	WB-AB/124	AR
Davis, William	083	1860	WB-2/163	AR
Davis, William	011	c1817	WB-2/353	
Davis, William	013	1846	WB-A/120	
Davis, William	092	1795	WB-3/19	AR
Davis, William	063	c1797	WB-1/331	
Davis, William	086	1807	WB-B/193	AR
Davis, William	107	c1836	WB-1/353	
Davis, William	053	1803	RW-1/357	AR
Davis, William	092	1852	WB-4/324	AR
Davis, William	065	1800	WB-C/19	AR
Davis, William	024	1719	SS 875/151	
Davis, William	019	1756	SS 880/186	SS/AR
Davis, William	086	1854	WB-E/282	AR
Davis, William	068	c1788	WB-A/235	
Davis, William	053	1774	RW-1/43	AR
Davis, William	028	1802	WB-B/153	AR-Nunc.
Davis, William	106	c1853	WB-1/40	AR
Davis, William	100	1854	WB-43/52	AR
Davis, William	075	1781	WB-K/69	AR
Davis, William	011	c1859	WB-1/292	
Davis, William	092	1803	WB-3/58	AR
Davis, William	063	1810	WB-2/2	
Davis, William	090	1815	WB-2/165	AR
Davis, William	075	1808	WB-M1/194	AR
Davis, William	073	1858	WB-G/209	AR
Davis, William	092	1883	WB-6/185	AR
Davis, William	043	c1874	WB-1/27	AR-Copy
Davis, William	085	c1799	WB-E/247	AR
Davis, William	090	1879	WB-6/106	AR
Davis, William A.	071	1897	WB-7/355	AR
Davis, William F.	030	1837	WB-4/32	
Davis, William F.	020	c1841	RB-O/377	AR
Davis, William H.	075	1853	WB-M2/5	AR
Davis, William H.	075	1882	WB-O/147	AR
Davis, William U.	047	1764	WB-1/118	
Davis, Willie	029	1820	Orig. Only	AR
Davis, Winifred	100	1866	WB-50/172	AR
Davis, Winifred	100	1848	WB-39/457	AR
Davis, Winniferd	103	1861	RD-13/336	
Davis, Zilphia	019	1859	WB-A/237	AR
Davison, George	085	1760	WB-A/35	AR
Davison, James	047	1794	WB-3/229	AR
Davison, John	010	1772	WB-A/148	AR
Davison, John	024	1773	Orig. Only	SS/AR
Davison, John	010	1756	SS 880/261	SS/AR
Davison, John	081	1825	WB-5/237	AR
Davison, Joseph	054	c1795	WB-1/92	AR
Davison, R.	100	1845	WB-38/394	AR
Davison, Thomas H.	MD	1892	091 WB-1/343	
Davison, William	MD	1881	091 WB-1/349	
Davolt, David T.	046	1898	WB-G/79	AR
Davy, Elisabeth	078	1842	WI-15/160	AR
Daw, Nicholas	053	1717	009 DB-1/282	
Dawe, William	009	1745	SS 877/35	SS/AR
Dawell, Phillip	104	1823	WB-4/35	AR
Dawkins, Drucilla	082	1844	WB-3/16	AR
Dawkins, Eli	082	1884	WB-6/286	AR
Dawkins, George	024	1764	WB-A/243	AR
Dawkins, John	082	1822	WB-1/220	AR
Dawkins, Samuel	082	1850	WB-4/35	AR
Dawly, Jacob	030	1859	WB-4/232	AR
Daws, William	024	1719	Orig. Only	SS/AR
Dawson, Abner	057	1895	WB-C/216	AR
Dawson, Benjamin	079	1895	WB-3/82	AR
Dawson, Charity	071	1764	WB-1/94	
Dawson, Christopher	028	1766	Orig. Only	AR
Dawson, Cristopher	028	1774	Orig. Only	AR
Dawson, David	087	1844	WB-1/288	AR
Dawson, Dempsey	069	c1797	WB-1/252	AR
Dawson, Edith	105	1857	WB-1/34	AR
Dawson, Eliza	059	1897	WB-B/196	CTY
Dawson, Elizabeth	090	1830	WB-3/219	AR
Dawson, Francis	028	1775	Orig. Only	AR
Dawson, Francis	028	1760	WB-B/261	AR
Dawson, Francis	028	1782	Orig. Only	AR
Dawson, George F.	038	c1863	WB-1/222	AR
Dawson, Henry	071	1770	WB-1/188	
Dawson, Henry	047	1800	WB-3/338	AR
Dawson, Henry	047	1824	WB-3/702	AR
Dawson, Isaac	099	1787	RB-2/142	AR
Dawson, James	070	1882	WB-E/461	AR
Dawson, Jerry	029	1894	WB-F/15	AR
Dawson, Jesse A.	047	1840	WB-4/187	AR
Dawson, John	071	1762	WB-1/69	
Dawson, John	037	1749	Orig. Only	SS/AR
Dawson, John	047	1797	WB-3/288	AR
Dawson, John	090	1815	WB-2/170	AR
Dawson, John K.	047	1864	WB-5/117	
Dawson, John, Sr.	072	c1862	Orig. Only	AR
Dawson, Joseph	103	1784	Orig. Only	AR
Dawson, Joseph	087	1837	WB-1/184	AR
Dawson, Joshua	015	1772	100 WB-1/212	AR
Dawson, Lemuel	045	1893	WB-1/303	AR
Dawson, Levi	028	1812	WB-C/59	AR
Dawson, Louisa J.	029	c1892	Orig. Only	AR
Dawson, Mary	047	1816	WB-3/578	AR
Dawson, Missouri	NY	1888	070 WB-F/167	070 AR
Dawson, Naomy	090	1835	WB-3/298	AR
Dawson, Newton C.	038	1872	WB-2/86	AR
Dawson, Rachel	081	1818	WB-4/589	AR
Dawson, Richard	010	1796	WB-D/334	AR
Dawson, Sarah	029	1851	WB-C/209	AR
Dawson, Sophia J.	VA	1887	070 WB-F/111	070 AR
Dawson, William	099	1795	RB-3/84	AR
Dawson, William	081	1873	WB-15/105	
Day, Abraham	016	1865	WB-2/122	
Day, David	054	1865	WB-3/178	AR
Day, David	047	1829	WB-4/54	
Day, Edmon	071	c1784	WB-1/346	AR
Day, Edward M.	017	1869	WB-B/18	AR
Day, Eliza R.	078	1882	WB-19/131	AR
Day, Eve	032	1824	WB-1/31	AR
Day, Francis	078	1816	WI-7/126	
Day, Francis	020	1848	RB-Q/85	AR
Day, Francis J.	078	1887	WB-19/206	
Day, James	014	1827	Orig. Only	AR
Day, John	071	1768	WB-1/170	
Day, John	078	1864	WB-18/368	
Day, John	063	c1795	WB-1/335	
Day, John	078	1841	WI-14/296	AR
Day, Julia A.	009	1892	WB-1/537	CTY
Day, L. D.	038	1891	WB-3/241	AR
Day, Lucinda	102	1900	WB-A/177	AR
Day, Lucy	078	1860	WB-18/146	AR

Name	Co.	Date	Recorded Copy	Original
Day, Malinda	054	1851	WB-3/50	AR
Day, Margaret G.	020	1870	WB-A/54	CTY
Day, Michael	032	1828	WB-1/90	AR
Day, Nannie	078	1895	WB-19/382	AR
Day, Nicholas	014	1815	Orig. Only	AR
Day, Richard	046	1826	WB-B/231	AR
Day, Rufus	025	1899	WB-A/234	AR
Day, Samuel	044	1893	WB-24/222	CTY
Day, Thomas J.	047	1810	WB-3/502	AR
Day, Valentine	085	1821	WB-H/103	AR
Day, William	009	1869	WB-1/26	CTY
Day, William	104	1863	WB-5/332	
Day, William	078	1876	WB-19/48	AR
Day, William P.	078	1899	WB-19/478	AR
Dayvault, Jacob	016	1822	WB-A/116	
Daywalt, Solomon M.	033	1865	WB-1/188	
De Choiseul, Beatrix	SC	1898	050 WB-2/290	050 CTY
De Choiseul, Charles	LA	1865	050 WB-2/88	050 CTY
De Lestiez, Calmetz	024	1796	Orig. Only	AR
De Schweinitz, Emil A.	038	1879	WB-2/359	AR
De St. Leger, Duryvault	028	1792	WB-A/280	AR
DeAraman, James	065	1880	WB-K/384	AR
DeArmon, R. L.	065	1892	WB-M/77	AR
DeBerry, Benjamin	067	1876	WB-2/63	AR
DeBerry, Henry W.	005	1881	WB-D/115	AR
DeBerry, Margret	067	1877	WB-2/82	AR
DeBerry, William G.	067	1890	WB-2/294	AR
DeBrule, Susannah	013	1890	WB-B/564	AR
DeCornis, Tullie A.	030	c1877	WB-5/36	AR
DeForest, Abigail T.	062	1876	WB-B/10	AR
DeLaney, Terrence	009	1827	OB-A/391	AR
DeRosset, Armand J.	070	1897	WB-H/107	AR
DeRosset, Armand John	070	1859	WB-D/6	AR
DeRosset, Elizabeth	070	1888	WB-F/218	AR
DeRosset, Elizabeth	070	c1778	Orig. Only	AR
DeRosset, John	070	1768	Orig. Only	SS/AR
DeRosset, Lewis Henry	070	1786	WB-C/77	AR
DeRosset, Moses J.	070	1826	WB-C/86	AR
DeRosset, Sallie E.	070	1863	WB-D/124	AR
DeSchweintz, Emil A.	038	1879	WB-2/359	
DeVeaux, Thomas L.	070	1877	WB-E/321	AR
Deacon, Mary	011	c1770	WB-1/478	
Deacons, Richard	054	1842	WB-2/238	AR
Deadman, Edmund	033	1849	WB-1/99	
Deadman, Elizabeth	033	1855	WB-1/123	
Deadman, George	033	1872	WB-2/23	CTY
Deadman, Tatum	033	1857	WB-1/160	
Deadman, William	033	1837	WB-1/8	
Deal, Abel	035	1867	WB-3/123	AR
Deal, Bennet	037	1865	WB-G/263	AR
Deal, Eliza A.	017	1890	WB-B/180	AR
Deal, Elizabeth	003	1900	WB-B/402	
Deal, Elizabeth	085	1896	WB-3/144	CTY
Deal, Henry	085	1857	WB-K/241	AR
Deal, Jacob	085	1865	WB-K/363	AR
Deal, Jacob	085	1899	WB-3/286	CTY
Deal, Jacob	003	1891	WB-B/296	AR
Deal, John	021	1846	WB-1/37	AR
Deal, John E.	003	1876	WB-B/62	AR
Deal, John, Sr.	085	1871	WB-1/75	CTY
Deal, Jonos	021	1882	WB-2/244	
Deal, Joseph P.	077	1873	WB-H/46	AR
Deal, Joshua	024	1774	WB-A/241	AR
Deal, Levi	085	1883	WB-2/59	
Deal, Levi A.	085	1893	WB-2/565	CTY
Deal, Margaret	085	1895	WB-3/112	CTY
Deal, Margrate	085	1845	WB-I/260	AR
Deal, Mary	037	1834	WB-F/155	AR
Deal, Mary A.	054	c1888	Orig. Only	AR
Deal, Mary Ann	085	1898	WB-3/236	CTY
Deal, Miles H.	021	1864	WB-1/204	AR
Deal, Nancy	018	1835	WB-C/189	
Deal, Peter	060	1828	WB-1/81	AR
Deal, Peter	085	1865	WB-K/360	AR
Deal, Peter	085	1827	WB-H/383	AR
Deal, Sidney	017	1896	WB-B/284	AR
Deal, Sylvanus	014	1899	WB-3/78	CTY
Deal, William	017	1870	WB-B/27	AR
Deal, William S.	021	1865	WB-1/210	AR
Deale, Thomas	009	1822	OB-A/316	AR
Dealy, Mary	085	1820	WB-H/37	AR-Nunc.
Dean, Archibald	038	c1858	WB-1/197	AR
Dean, Cooper	039	1842	WB-L/63	AR
Dean, Daniel	044	1868	WB-22/767	CTY
Dean, Eliza	028	1875	WB-E/119	AR
Dean, Francis	044	1839	WB-14/440	CTY
Dean, Frederick	046	1778	WB-A/95	AR
Dean, Hardy	099	1823	RB-18/19	AR
Dean, John	030	1800	WB-2/164	
Dean, Joseph	070	1804	WB-AB/87	AR
Dean, Kezia	092	1787	WB-2/81	AR
Dean, L. D.	044	1899	WB-24/459	CTY
Dean, Lydia	046	1861	WB-D/98	AR
Dean, Mary	099	1849	RB-26/590	AR
Dean, Moses	009	1788	OWB/223	AR
Dean, Moses C.	044	1895	WB-24/268	CTY
Dean, Polly	005	1879	WB-D/85	AR
Dean, R. C.	078	1889	WB-19/242	
Dean, Thomas	028	1761	Orig. Only	AR
Dean, Thomas	039	1883	WB-U/310	AR
Dean, William	056	1761	WB-1/757	AR
Deanes, Daniel	103	1789	Orig. Only	AR
Deanes, James	026	1888	WB-2/343	AR
Deanes, Kisire	103	1859	RD-12/672	AR
Deanes, Thomas	051	1838	WB-A/232	
Deanes, Thomas	051	1830	Copy	071 AR
Deanes, Thomas	051	1830	WB-A/3 & 101	
Deange, Michael	090	1799	WB-1/128	AR
Deans, Bartley	105	1862	WB-1/75	AR
Deans, Caroline	069	1898	WB-6/40	AR
Deans, Daniel	046	1850	WB-C/326	AR
Deans, Daniel C.	046	1897	WB-G/18	AR
Deans, George	103	1824	RD-5/123	AR
Deans, James	103	1812	RD-2/112	AR
Deans, John	069	1847	WB-1/496	AR
Deans, Rachel	024	1870	WB-E/15	AR
Deans, Robert D.	069	1893	WB-5/415	AR
Deans, Thomas	069	1797	WB-1/114	AR
Dear, Joseph	024	c1762	WB-A/315	AR
Dearden, Ann	100	1788	WB-5/7	AR
Dearman, James	084	1848	WB-C/399	CTY
Dearman, James	084	1848	Copy	090 AR
Dearman, Nancy M.	054	1900	WB-6/284	CTY
Dearmond, Jennet L.	065	1862	WB-J/122	AR
Dearmond, John	065	1848	WB-I/132	AR
Deatherage, Bird	084	1815	WB-A/131	
Deatherage, Braxton	085	c1806	WB-E/240	AR
Deatherage, Elizabeth	084	1824	WB-B/46	CTY
Deatherage, George	090	1807	WB-2/73	AR
Deatherage, Philemon	046	1778	WB-A/88	AR

Name	Co.	Date	Recorded Copy	Original
Deatherage, Robert	084	c1817	WB-A/168	CTY
Deaton, Cecelia	054	1887	WB-5/187	CTY
Deaton, Dison	067	1895	WB-2/333	AR
Deaton, E. M. C.	054	1886	WB-5/106	CTY
Deaton, Hiram	016	1875	WB-3/118	AR
Deaton, James	022	1806	WB-A/127	AR
Deaton, James K.	016	1898	WB-4/312	AR
Deaton, Laban	054	1865	WB-3/172	AR
Deaton, Thomas	054	c1838	WB-2/187	AR
Deaver, Edward	059	1880	Orig. Only	CTY
Deaver, Elijah	049	1859	WB-1/26	AR
Deaver, James	059	1881	WB-A/388	CTY
Deaver, John	084	1790	OW/232	AR
Deaver, Thomas	037	1805	WB-D/227	AR
Deberry, Absalom	071	1795	WB-2/80	AR
Deberry, Benjamin	071	1804	WB-2/259	AR
Deberry, Drury	071	1794	WB-2/48	AR
Deberry, Drury	071	1808	WB-3/6	
Deberry, Edmond	067	1874	WB-2/35	AR
Deberry, Elizabeth	071	1804	WB-2/270	AR
Deberry, Henry	071	1806	WB-2/311	AR
Deberry, Henry	071	1844	WB-4/274	AR
Deberry, Holland	071	1836	WB-4/142	AR
Deberry, James Henry	071	1866	WB-5/318	AR
Deberry, John	067	1864	WB-1/116	AR
Deberry, John	071	1763	WB-1/76	
Deberry, Lemuel	071	1812	WB-3/88	AR
Deberry, Peter	071	1796	WB-2/113	AR
Deberry, Thomas	071	1815	WB-3/155	AR
Debery, Abner	071	1856	WB-5/152	AR
Debery, Clary	071	1818	WB-3/201	AR
Deblaugham, John	028	1788	WB-A/182	AR
Debley, Jacob	073	1791	WB-B/126	AR
Debnam, B. Y.	039	1873	WB-U/74	AR
Debnam, Damsel V.	044	1864	WB-22/107	CTY
Debnam, Elizabeth	099	1888	WB-B/284	AR
Debnam, Peter F.	039	1870	WB-U/27	AR
Debnam, Priscilla	039	1885	WB-U/354	
Debnam, Priscilla	099	1878	WB-A/8	AR
Debnam, Robert	039	1823	WB-G/158	
Debnam, Thomas C.	098	1897	WB-A/298	CTY
Debnam, Thomas R.	099	1872	RB-35/224	AR
Debnill, Francis	028	1857	WB-D/293	
Debord, Benjamin	006	1897	WB-E/324	AR
Debord, Benjamin	006	1853	WB-D/1	AR
Debow, John	073	1783	WB-A/259	AR
Debrule, Edward C.	047	1879	WB-6/203	AR
Debrule, Edward C.	057	1857	WB-B/240	AR
Debrule, Joel	028	1873	WB-E/93	AR
Debruler, Anny	073	1850	WB-F/474	AR
Decker, Christopher	060	1808	Orig. Only	AR
Decrow (Derrow), Sarah	077	1795	Copy	024 AR
Decrow, Sarah	077	1795	WB-E/50	
Dedman, Edmond	085	1813	WB-G/287	AR
Dedman, Thomas G.	033	1845	WB-1/66	CTY
Dedmon, Thomas J.	033	1893	WB-2/149	
Deeds, Jacob	038	1856	WB-1/75	AR
Deen, Frederick	046	1839	WB-C/38	AR
Deen, Solomon	090	1844	WB-4/144	AR
Deen, Thomas	047	1778	WB-2/92	
Deens, Jeremiah	069	1788	WB-1/48	AR
Deens, Nancy	046	1867	WB-D/339	AR
Deer, Charles	046	1811	WB-A/106	AR
Dees, Emanuel	056	1770	WB-1/785	AR
Dees, Penniah	103	1874	WB-1/76	AR

Name	Co.	Date	Recorded Copy	Original
Deese, Allen, Sr.	089	1887	WB-2/139	AR
Deese, Caleb	097	1899	WB-3/7	AR
Deese, Edmond	097	1844	WB-1/17	AR
Deese, Mary	089	1897	WB-2/286	AR
Deford, William H.	018	1854	WB-C/382	
Defreece, John	086	1798	Orig. Only	AR
Degraffinreidt, Thomas H.E.	068	1823	WB-B/31	
Deiptt, John	028	1724	SS 876/4	SS/AR
Deirs, John	028	c1754	SS 878/180	
Deitz, Christian	021	1866	WB-1/218	AR
Deitz, Elizabeth	060	1841	WB-2/115	AR
Deitz, Jacob	055	1861	ID/71	
Deitz, Lazareth	021	1894	WB-3/61	
Delahuide, William	028	1738	SS 877/204	SS/AR (N)
Delamar, Francis	009	1741	LGB-4/#161	SS/AR
Delamar, Francis	028	1799	WB-B/76	AR
Delamar, Smith	028	1842	WB-D/59	AR
Delamar, Stephen	028	1814	WB-C/80	AR
Delamar, Thomas	028	1789	WB-A/160	AR
Delamothe, Francis A.	089	1845	WB-1/38	AR
Delamothe, Henry	067	1839	WB-1/32	AR
Delaney, Mary S.	079	1888	WB-2/450	AR
Delano, Ichabod	077	1774	WB-C/153	AR
Delap, Alexander	032	1887	WB-3/570	AR
Delap, Amos	032	1886	WB-3/508	AR
Delap, Elizabeth	032	1878	WB-3/249	AR
Delap, Valentine	032	1864	WB-2/276	AR
Delap, William	029	1770	Orig. Only	AR
Delapp, Daniel	032	1823	WB-1/17	AR
Delapp, John, Sr.	032	1840	WB-1/350	AR
Delastatus, Rebecca	028	1815	WB-C/103	
Delemare, Stephen	075	1732	SS 876/254	SS/AR
Deley, William	073	1803	WB-D/105	AR
Delgado, F. R.	084	1900	WB-F/181	CTY
Delinger, Valentine	065	c1766	WB-C/18	AR
Delislle, Emanuel	024	1789	Orig. Only	AR
Delk, Joseph	081	1857	WB-11/139	
Dellahunt, Alice	057	1861	WB-B/255	AR
Dellinger, Adam	060	1866	WB-3/91	AR
Dellinger, Andrew	060	1863	WB-3/59	AR
Dellinger, Barbara	021	1853	WB-1/108	AR
Dellinger, David	060	1833	WB-1/291	AR
Dellinger, G. H.	040	1890	WB-2/362	AR
Dellinger, Harriet R.	014	1900	WB-3/106	CTY
Dellinger, John	060	1829	WB-1/142	AR
Dellinger, John P.	014	1894	WB-2/542	CTY
Dellinger, Joseph	060	1826	WB-1/36	AR
Dellinger, Lewis	060	1885	WB-4/330	AR
Dellinger, Matthias	066	1894	WB-1/133	AR
Dellinger, Michael	060	1825	WB-1/15	AR
Dellinger, P. F.	026	1893	WB-2/464	AR
Dellinger, Peter	060	1848	WB-2/315	AR
Dellinger, Peter	040	1865	WB-1/165	
Dellinger, Samuel	060	1865	WB-3/82	AR
Dellinger, Susan J.	060	1898	WB-5/90	AR
Dellinger, Tempy	040	1874	WB-2/73	AR
Deloach, Britton	099	1823	RB-18/18	AR
Deloach, Francis	071	1770	WB-1/185	
Deloach, James	039	1840	WB-K/235	
Deloach, Mary	037	1774	WB-A/205	AR
Deloach, Nancy	071	1837	WB-4/167	AR
Deloach, Samuel	056	1805	WB-1/180	AR
Deloach, Samuell	037	1764	WB-A/134	AR

Name	Co.	Date	Recorded Copy	Original
Deloach, Solomon	071	1800	WB-2/208	AR
Deloach, William J.	047	1788	WB-3/153	AR
Deloatch, Charlotte	071	1835	WB-4/136	AR
Deloatch, Dawsey	071	1858	WB-5/204	AR
Deloatch, Elizabeth	071	1835	WB-4/129	AR
Deloatch, Francis	071	1814	WB-3/134	AR
Deloatch, Jesse	071	1878	WB-6/277	AR
Deloatch, Jesse	071	1844	WB-5/3	AR
Deloatch, John	071	1869	WB-6/22	AR
Deloatch, Kezia	071	1885	WB-6/504	AR
Deloatch, Madison E.	071	1864	WB-5/292	AR
Deloatch, Moody	071	1866	WB-5/319	AR
Deloatch, Noah	071	1863	WB-5/276	
Deloatch, Rebecha T.	071	1863	WB-4/272	AR
Deloatch, Robert H.	071	1897	WB-7/349	AR
Deloatch, Salley	071	1823	WB-3/283	AR
Deloatch, Soloman	071	1887	WB-6/582	AR
Deloatch, Thomas L.	071	1860	WB-5/230	AR
Delon, Charles	075	1798	WB-M1/11	AR
Delon, Harvey	075	1877	WB-0/72	AR
Delon, Mark	075	1808	WB-M1/186	AR
Delong, Francis	075	1784	WB-K/110	AR
Delow, Michael H.	085	1805	WB-E/268	AR
Delp, Stephen C.	004	1865	WB-1/11	AR
Demarcus, Solomon	016	1839	PQS.6/49	
Dement, Harriett	044	1889	WB-24/74	CTY
Dement, John	044	1818	WB-8/154	CTY
Dement, Peter J.	039	1892	WB-U/572	AR-Nunc.
Dement, Wilson W.	044	1876	WB-23/207	CTY
Demill, Thomas A.	NY	1877	009 WB-1/192	009 CTY
Deming, Gordon	029	1864	WB-D/68	AR
Demmick, John	VA	1741	028 Wills.6/L34	028 AR
Demmitt, James	085	1774	WB-A/185	AR
Dempsey, George	071	1788	WB-1/399	AR-Nunc.
Dempsey, Patience	010	1764	WB-A/58	AR
Dempsey, Wealthy	010	1860	WB-H/97	AR
Dempster, John	099	1779	RB-1/154	AR
Demsey, Richard	077	1849	WB-F/375	AR
Denby, Elijah	039	1812	WB-C/298	
Denby, James	039	c1795	WB-B/67	
Denby, Samuel B.	009	1870	WB-1/59	AR
Deneham, Elisabeth	009	1716	Orig. Only	SS/AR
Denison, Philinda	053	1801	RW-1/335	
Denke, Christian	090	1838	WB-4/16	AR
Denke, Mary	038	1868	WB-2/4	AR
Denkins, John	065	1811	WB-C/37	AR
Denkins, Mary	065	1827	WB-B/6	AR
Dennes, Joshua	019	1800	WB-D/119	AR
Denney, James	104	1812	WB-3/20	
Denney, Stephen	106	c1878	WB-2/104	AR
Denning, George W.	087	1888	WB-3/376	AR
Denning, George W.	056	1889	WB-3/498	AR
Denning, James	087	c1894	Copy	056 AR
Denning, James	087	1895	Orig. Only	AR
Denning, Jonas	087	1862	WB-2/36	AR
Denning, Margaret	070	1785	WB-C/72	AR
Denning, Nancy	087	1871	WB-3/49	AR
Denning, Nathan	087	1898	WB-4/93	AR
Denning, Robert	087	1861	WB-2/32	AR
Denning, Stephen	012	1781	DB-B/152	
Dennis, Anderson	022	1829	WB-B/164	AR
Dennis, Catharine	092	1836	WB-4/94	
Dennis, Daniel	046	1846	WB-C/259	AR
Dennis, Elisha	099	1859	RB-31/219	AR
Dennis, Francis	019	1826	WB-D/162	AR
Dennis, H. J.	068	1896	WB-D/455	
Dennis, John C.	065	1875	WB-K/209	AR
Dennis, John C.	099	1883	WB-A/405	AR
Dennis, John Henry	070	1891	WB-F/411	AR
Dennis, John S.	092	1898	WB-6/490	AR
Dennis, Joseph	022	1795	RB-2/58	
Dennis, Joseph H.	046	1842	WB-C/139	AR
Dennis, Joshua	019	1836	WB-A/58	AR
Dennis, Nathaniel	099	1800	RB-5/67	AR
Dennis, Phillis	029	1848	WB-C/148	AR
Dennis, Reuben	019	1825	WB-D/159	AR
Dennis, Skilton	079	1900	WB-3/226	AR
Dennis, Susanna	072	1857	WB-2/152	AR
Dennis, Thomas	046	1775	WB-A/90	AR
Dennis, Thomas	081	1803	WB-2/116	AR
Dennis, William	099	1797	RB-3/44	AR
Dennis, William	019	1800	WB-D/153	AR
Dennis, William	046	1890	WB-F/55	AR
Dennis, William	065	1896	WB-M/568	AR
Dennis, William	046	1846	WB-C/260	AR
Dennis, William	046	1791	WB-A/100	AR
Dennis, William	019	1802	WB-D/121	AR
Dennis, William N.	019	1895	WB-B/284	AR
Denniss, Thomas	081	c1795	WB-2/116	AR
Dennum, Hugh	092	1789	WB-2/94	AR
Denny, Allen	092	1878	WB-6/116	AR
Denny, Benjamin C.	078	1870	Orig. Only	AR
Denny, Edmund	104	1801	WB-2/39	AR
Denny, Eli	046	1876	WB-E/160	AR
Denny, Elijah	046	1881	WB-E/296	AR
Denny, Eliza	046	1888	WB-E/542	AR
Denny, Elizabeth	046	1885	WB-E/412	AR
Denny, George	046	1816	WB-A/110	AR
Denny, Iley	106	c1853	WB-1/18	AR
Denny, James	046	1816	Orig. Only	AR
Denny, James	046	1774	WB-A/87	AR
Denny, James	046	1795	WB-A/94	AR
Denny, James L.	020	1868	RB-T/345	CTY
Denny, Jennette	046	1841	WB-C/86	AR
Denny, Joel	092	1896	WB-6/419	AR
Denny, John C.	085	1898	WB-3/239	CTY
Denny, Margaret	046	1896	WB-F/490	AR
Denny, Margaret	046	1895	WB-F/433	AR
Denny, Mary A.	046	1900	WB-G/240	AR
Denny, Mary M.	092	1893	WB-6/355	AR
Denny, Nancy R.	046	1892	WB-F/212	AR
Denny, Robert W.	046	1886	WB-E/444	AR
Denny, Samuel	046	1885	WB-E/419	AR
Denny, Simon	020	1833	RB-M/318	
Denny, Thomas	078	1860	WB-18/216	AR
Denny, Walter	084	1805	WB-A/28	CTY
Denny, William	046	1826	WB-B/347	AR
Denny, William	085	1770	WB-A/31	AR
Denny, William	046	1825	WB-B/199	AR
Denny, William	092	1892	WB-6/342	AR
Denny, William R.	001	1867	WB-1/291	AR
Denson, Benjamin	069	1781	WB-1/20	AR
Denson, James	072	c1756	SS 880/55	SS/AR
Denson, Masee	069	1818	WB-1/294	AR
Denson, Right	069	1876	WB-5/43	AR
Denson, Sarah	068	c1842	WB-B/135	
Denson, Susan	039	c1855	WB-0/342	AR
Dent, Ann	085	1838	Orig. Only	AR
Dent, John	039	1836	WB-K/111	AR
Dent, John	039	c1812	WB-F/178	AR

Name	Co.	Date	Recorded Copy	Original
Dent, L. W.	099	1895	WB-C/431	AR
Dent, Mary	100	1790	WB-5/153	AR
Dent, Michael	039	1829	WB-J/37	AR
Dent, Rebeckah	100	1790	WB-5/154	AR
Dent, Sarah	039	1824	WB-H/50	AR
Dent, Tabitha	100	1793	WB-7/11	AR-Nunc.
Dent, Thomas H.	085	1817	WB-G/465	AR
Dent, William T.	039	1884	WB-U/334	AR
Denton, A. H.	069	1895	WB-5/472	AR
Denton, Anderson	014	1883	WB-2/262	CTY
Denton, Ann	039	1816	WB-E/37	AR
Denton, Boykin	069	1882	WB-5/130	AR
Denton, Cynthia	039	c1890	Orig. Only	AR
Denton, Drewry	039	c1857	WB-O/384	AR
Denton, Elizabeth	037	1867	WB-G/292	AR
Denton, James H.	039	1867	WB-S/433	AR
Denton, John	086	1850	WB-E/199	AR
Denton, Milley E.	084	1888	WB-E/385	CTY
Denton, Peter	014	1879	WB-2/197	
Denton, Simon P.	069	1896	WB-5/581	AR
Denton, William	039	1793	WB-A/111	
Denton, William	046	1828	WB-B/370	AR
Depriest, R. M.	086	1899	WB-G/12	AR
Depriest, W. C.	086	1899	WB-G/12	AR
Dept, Penelope	N	1735	SS 876/377	SS/AR
Derby, William	N	1688	Orig. Only	SS/AR
Derbyshire, Alex. Jas.	PA	1879	022 WB-E/180	022 AR
Dereham, Elizabeth	009	1717	DB-1/276	
Derham, Elizabeth	008	c1716	SS 875/125	
Dering, John	069	1847	WB-1/500	AR
Derr, Jonas W.	060	1881	WB-4/243	AR
Derr, Mary A.	060	1862	WB-3/45	AR
Derr, Moses A.	060	1848	WB-2/309	AR
Derr, Rufus M.	060	1848	WB-2/301	AR
Derr, Silvy G.	040	1888	WB-2/296	AR
Derreberry, Mary B.	014	c1877	Orig. Only	CTY
Derring, Margaret	069	1881	WB-5/124	AR
Desern, Anna J.	022	1890	WB-E/441	AR
Desern, John	022	c1893	WB-E/524	AR
Deshazo, Richard	078	1814	WI-6/243	AR
Deshazo, Robert	078	c1845	Orig. Only	AR
Desmukes, Richard T.	084	1852	WB-C/150	CTY
Detter, Albert W.	060	1898	WB-5/89	AR
Detter, Christian	021	1884	WB-2/291	
Detter, George	060	1896	WB-5/25	AR
Detter, John	060	1870	WB-4/62	AR
Deumelandt, Christine	070	1896	WB-G/479	AR
Devan, Jeremiah	010	1812	WB-F/220	AR
Devan, Margaret	010	1835	WB-G/251	AR
Devan, Sarah	010	1803	WB-E/214	AR
Devane, Duncan J.	070	1884	WB-E/525	AR
Devane, Eliza A.	087	1876	WB-3/125	AR
Devane, George	087	c1810	WB-A/63	AR
Devane, Helen	070	1845	WB-AB/426	AR
Devane, John	011	c1783	WB-1/374	
Devane, Milton K.	035	1888	087 WB-3/403	087 AR
Devane, Milton K.	035	1888	WB-4/323	AR
Devane, R. M.	093	1900	WB-2/186	AR
Devane, Thomas	070	1805	WB-AB/93	AR
Devane, Thomas	070	1774	WB-C/67	AR
Devane, Thomas	070	1831	WB-AB/266	AR
Devane, Thomas	070	1818	WB-AB/266	AR
Devane, Thomas	070	1847	WB-AB/479	AR
Devaney, Samuel	046	1835	WB-B/522	AR
Devany, Jinkins	039	1804	WB-B/182	AR

Name	Co.	Date	Recorded Copy	Original
Devaul, William	072	c1772	RW/L47	AR
Devault, Gideon	046	1889	WB-F/19	AR
Devenish, Elizabeth	075	1823	WB-M1/369	AR-Nunc.
Devepaugh, Phillip	060	1825	WB-1/19	AR
Devereux, Frances	099	1852	RB-28/124	AR
Devereux, George P.	010	1837	WB-G/281	AR
Devereux, John	099	1893	WB-C/167	AR
Devereux, John	099	1844	RB-25/492	AR
Devereux, Thomas P.	047	1869	WB-6/18	AR
Devine, Hugh	100	1893	WB-51/342	
Devine, James	014	1794	Orig. Only	AR
Deviney, Ann	046	1840	WB-C/61	AR
Deviney, Elbert	046	1891	WB-F/113	AR
Deviney, J. G	026	1889	WB-2/391	AR
Devinna, Hannah	046	c1849	Orig. Only	AR
Devinna, Jemima	046	c1849	Orig. Only	AR
Devis, John	028	1754	Orig. Only	SS/AR
Dew, Arthur	037	1816	WB-E/149	AR
Dew, C. C.	083	1900	WB-4/325	
Dew, Chanie	069	1887	WB-5/261	AR
Dew, David, Jr.	105	1864	WB-1/114	AR
Dew, David, Sr.	105	1863	WB-1/83	AR
Dew, Dennis	069	1891	WB-5/362	AR
Dew, Duncan	069	1805	WB-1/160	AR
Dew, John	069	1791	WB-1/71	AR
Dew, John	047	1836	WB-4/140	AR
Dew, John	071	1744	Orig. Only	SS/AR
Dew, John	037	1760	WB-A/1	AR
Dew, Larry	105	1862	WB-1/80	AR
Dew, Mary	037	1801	WB-D/122	AR
Dew, Milicent	037	1786	WB-C/31	AR
Dew, Thomas	047	1803	WB-3/381	AR
Dew, William	037	c1802	Orig. Only	AR
Deweese, Jonathan	020	1777	RB-A/22	AR
Dewese, Barnette	016	1873	WB-3/84	AR
Dewese, Ezekiel	046	1821	WB-B/114	AR
Dewese, Garrett	013	1840	WB-A/63	
Dewese, Isaiah	016	1892	WB-4/133	
Dewese, Isaiah	016	1844	WB-1/36	
Dewese, Rachel	065	1860	WB-J/72	AR
Dewese, Rebecca	016	1847	WB-1/140	
Dewese, Walter B.	016	1900	WB-4/368	AR
Dewese, William	065	1859	WB-J/73	
Dewey, Adeline	028	1882	WB-E/310	
Dewey, Charles	099	1880	WB-A/206	
Dewey, Charles	099	1880	065 WB-M/193	065 AR
Dewey, Euphena	011	c1796	WB-1/382	
Dewey, James	011	c1842	WB-1/90	
Dewey, Julia A.	099	1886	WB-B/119	AR
Dewey, Mahala C.	103	1900	WB-2/309	AR
Dewry, Phineas S.	065	1837	WB-E/134	
Dews, John	047	1772	WB-1/308	
Dews, Thomas	060	1851	WB-2/356	AR
Dews, Thomas, Jr.	086	1838	WB-E/51	AR
Dexter, Hope	072	1746	SS 878/27	SS/AR
Dezern, John	036	1900	WB-A/514	CTY
Dial, John	075	1818	WB-M1/319	
Dial, Peter	083	1872	WB-3/39	AR
Dial, Robert	085	c1793	WB-E/245	AR
Diamond, John	084	1867	WB-D/86	CTY
Diamond, Margaret	084	1818	WB-A/162	CTY
Diamond, Patrick	046	c1790	WB-A/101	AR
Diamond, Stewart	084	c1792	OW/160	AR
Dias, Henry	008	1737	LGB-4/#76	SS/AR
Dias, Wilson	057	1788	WB-A/70	AR

Name	Co.	Date	Recorded Copy	Original
Dick, Charles	075	1805	WB-M1/115	AR
Dick, Eliza	070	1821	WB-C/85	AR
Dick, Hiram C.	046	1891	WB-F/93	AR
Dick, Isabella	046	1893	WB-E/552	AR
Dick, James	046	1830	WB-B/429	AR
Dick, James	046	1826	WB-B/232	AR
Dick, John D. A.	083	1888	WB-3/421	AR
Dick, John M.	046	1861	WB-D/102	AR
Dick, John W.	046	1822	Orig. Only	AR-Nunc.
Dick, P. P.	046	1882	WB-E/321	AR
Dick, Robert P.	046	1898	WB-G/82	AR
Dick, Thomas	046	1821	WB-B/103	AR
Dick, Viney	046	1887	WB-E/460	AR
Dick, William	046	1810	WB-A/109	AR
Dicken, Benjamin	037	1851	WB-F/464	AR
Dicken, Benjamin	037	1794	WB-C/276	AR
Dicken, Benjamin	047	1794	WB-3/225	AR
Dicken, Bennett	047	1842	WB-4/213	AR
Dicken, Christopher	037	1860	WB-G/173	AR
Dicken, Christopher	037	1779	WB-B/32	AR
Dicken, Ephraim	037	1845	WB-F/323	AR
Dicken, Ephraim	037	1791	WB-C/159	AR
Dicken, Henry	047	1807	WB-3/469	AR
Dicken, James	047	1814	WB-3/547	AR
Dicken, Joseph	047	1802	WB-3/379	AR
Dicken, Joseph	047	1806	WB-3/450	AR
Dicken, Kenelen	037	1880	WB-G/566	AR
Dicken, Lunsford	047	1883	WB-6/312	AR
Dicken, Martha	047	1803	WB-3/406	AR
Dicken, Merritt	022	1858	WB-D/24	AR
Dicken, Thomas	022	1852	WB-C/322	AR
Dicken, William	047	1830	WB-4/68	AR
Dicken, William	037	1852	WB-F/488	AR
Dickens, Albert	092	1886	WB-6/258	AR
Dickens, Andrew	092	1899	WB-6/510	AR
Dickens, Christopher	047	1889	WB-6/563	AR
Dickens, Dudley	092	1862	WB-5/63	AR
Dickens, Enoch D.	047	1892	WB-7/66	AR
Dickens, Ephraim H.	047	1877	WB-6/159	AR
Dickens, Felix G.	047	1874	WB-6/118	AR
Dickens, Harriet	078	1863	WB-18/322	AR
Dickens, John	PA	1798	047 WB-3/341	047 AR
Dickens, William	047	1836	WB-4/138	AR
Dickenson, Liven	028	1809	WB-B/337	AR
Dickenson, William	103	1843	RD-8/502	AR
Dickerson, Alfonso	106	1897	WB-2/405	AR
Dickerson, David	019	1865	WB-A/272	AR
Dickerson, Garland	086	1859	WB-E/364	AR
Dickerson, Griffith	092	1788	WB-2/128	AR
Dickerson, Isam	104	1837	WB-4/218	AR
Dickerson, Louisa P.	044	1896	WB-24/311	CTY
Dickerson, Samuel W.	044	1896	WB-24/326	CTY
Dickerson, Wiley	106	c1847	WB-1/8	AR
Dickerson, William	044	1819	WB-8/303	CTY
Dickey, Andrew J.	040	1865	WB-1/174	
Dickey, David	054	c1830	WB-2/167	AR
Dickey, George W.	023	1886	WB-A/58	AR
Dickey, J. M.	023	1896	WB-A/117	AR
Dickey, James	086	1793	Orig. Only	AR
Dickey, James	085	c1796	WB-E/260	AR
Dickey, James	001	c1845	WB-1/36	AR
Dickey, James	085	c1796	Copy	054 AR
Dickey, John	085	1817	WB-G/466	AR
Dickey, John	054	c1808	WB-1/30	AR
Dickey, John	020	1802	RB-D/108	
Dickey, Mary	054	c1803	Orig. Only	AR-Copy
Dickey, Mary	085	c1803	WB-E/257	AR
Dickey, Mary	046	1828	WB-B/367	AR
Dickey, Mary A.	001	1887	WB-2/339	AR
Dickey, Sarah	085	c1829	WB-H/463	AR
Dickey, Thomas	085	1806	WB-E/255	AR
Dickey, William	046	1824	WB-B/180	AR
Dickey, William L.	001	1894	WB-3/19	AR
Dickie, James	073	1804	WB-D/123	AR
Dickie, Laura M.	073	1890	WB-H/504	CTY
Dickie, Mary	073	1835	WB-E/343	AR
Dickin, Obediah G.	039	1886	WB-U/384	AR
Dickins, Jesse	078	1838	WI-14/31	AR
Dickins, Robert	078	1804	WI-3/248	AR
Dickins, Stephen M.	078	1857	WB-17/468	AR
Dickinson, Alice H.	070	1881	WB-E/426	AR
Dickinson, Ava	037	1838	WB-F/213	AR
Dickinson, Daniel	019	1857	WB-A/212	AR
Dickinson, David	071	1783	WB-1/279	
Dickinson, Davy	024	1852	WB-C/337	AR
Dickinson, Francis M.	028	1856	WB-D/271	
Dickinson, Isaac	071	1767	WB-1/143	
Dickinson, James	019	1806	WB-D/138	AR
Dickinson, James	071	1787	WB-1/384	AR
Dickinson, Joel	103	1793	Orig. Only	AR
Dickinson, John	037	1780	WB-B/43	AR
Dickinson, John	071	1749	Orig. Only	SS/AR
Dickinson, John	071	1787	WB-1/384	AR
Dickinson, John	019	1803	WB-D/137	AR
Dickinson, John R.	071	1844	WB-4/276	AR
Dickinson, John S.	MD	1891	028 WB-F/281	
Dickinson, John S.	MD	1891	Copy	063 AR
Dickinson, Joseph F.	051	1822	WB-A/194	
Dickinson, Marshall	079	1870	WB-2/15	AR
Dickinson, Mary	071	1753	SS 879/191	SS/AR
Dickinson, Mary Ann	028	1900	WB-F/457	
Dickinson, Miriam	103	1815	RD-3/290	AR
Dickinson, Platt K.	070	1867	WB-D/226	AR
Dickinson, Rebeckah	071	1753	SS 879/184	SS/AR
Dickinson, Robert	029	1759	DB-1/384	AR
Dickinson, Samuel	024	c1802	WB-B/277	AR
Dickinson, Shadrack	103	1819	RD-4/218	AR
Dickinson, Turner	037	1836	WB-F/183	AR
Dickinson, Wallace	019	1874	WB-B/76	AR
Dickinson, William	103	1822	RD-4/471	AR
Dicks, Cornelius	081	1894	WB-16/299	
Dicks, John	024	1706	Orig. Only	SS/AR
Dicks, Nathan	085	1766	WB-A/29	AR
Dicks, Peter	046	1796	WB-A/98	AR
Dicks, U. S.	081	1896	WB-16/378	
Dickson, A. C.	040	1899	WB-3/31	AR
Dickson, Alexander	035	1814	WB-A/95	AR
Dickson, Benadick	035	1838	WB-A/97	AR
Dickson, Calvin J.	011	1862	WB-1/277	
Dickson, Daniel	006	1856	WB-D/19	AR
Dickson, Daniel	057	1844	WB-B/172	AR
Dickson, David	006	1888	WB-E/170	AR
Dickson, G.	026	1885	WB-2/275	AR
Dickson, James	073	c1789	WB-B/78	AR
Dickson, James	035	1882	WB-4/180	AR
Dickson, James	035	1812	WB-A/118	AR
Dickson, James	028	1815	WB-C/100	AR
Dickson, James G.	035	1867	WB-3/122	AR
Dickson, James H.	070	1862	WB-D/91	AR
Dickson, John	034	c1769	Orig. Only	SS/AR

Name	Co.	Date	Recorded Copy	Original
Dickson, John	060	1804	Orig. Only	AR
Dickson, John	060	1840	WB-2/72	AR
Dickson, John	078	1849	WB-13/229	AR
Dickson, Joseph	073	1834	WB-E/319	AR
Dickson, Joseph L.	085	1839	WB-I/59	AR
Dickson, Josiah	078	1804	WI-3/273	
Dickson, Lewis	036	1888	WB-A/121	CTY
Dickson, Lewis	035	1815	WB-A/130	AR
Dickson, Margaret	070	1894	WB-G/203	AR
Dickson, Margaretta	085	1862	WB-K/300	AR
Dickson, Mary	082	1880	WB-6/198	AR
Dickson, Mary C.	035	1871	WB-4/50	AR
Dickson, Milley S.	047	1835	WB-4/119	AR
Dickson, Morris	035	1803	WB-A/120	AR
Dickson, Moses	006	1857	WB-D/42	
Dickson, Ritison	037	1779	WB-B/22	AR
Dickson, Robert	035	1790	WB-A/101	AR
Dickson, Robert	035	1815	WB-A/100	AR
Dickson, Robert	026	1856	WB-1/202	AR
Dickson, Robert D.	082	1896	WB-6/533	AR
Dickson, S. F.	011	1898	WB-3/100	CTY
Dickson, Samuel	035	1829	WB-A/135	
Dickson, Samuel A.	036	1895	WB-A/345	CTY
Dickson, Sarah	029	1822	WB-B/87	AR
Dickson, Solomon B.	085	1827	WB-H/405	AR
Dickson, Susan	035	1852	WB-2/72	AR
Dickson, Thomas	026	1844	WB-1/27	AR
Dickson, W. F. A.	040	1872	WB-2/48	AR-Nunc.
Dickson, William	035	1817	WB-A/109	AR
Dickson, William	026	1879	WB-2/194	AR
Dickson, William	017	c1855	WB-A/86	AR
Dickson, William	046	1817	WB-B/33	AR
Dickson, William S.	040	1870	WB-2/14	AR
Dickson, Zilpha	035	1860	WB-3/16	AR
Dietz, Daniel	054	1888	WB-5/209	CTY
Diffee, John	054	c1871	Copy	081 AR
Diffee, John	054	1883	WB-4/501	CTY
Diffee, Moses	081	1803	WB-2/122	AR
Diffy, William	081	1790	WB-1/96	AR
Digby, James	077	1796	WB-E/71	
Diggs, Dixon D.	005	1856	WB-C/111	AR
Diggs, Henry	005	1860	WB-C/168	AR
Diggs, Marshall	005	1831	WB-B/10	AR
Diggs, Marshall	005	1854	WB-C/72	AR
Diggs, Nancy	005	1855	WB-C/110	AR
Diggs, Robert	037	1789	WB-C/119	AR
Diggs, Thomas	005	1878	WB-D/69	AR
Diggs, Washington	005	1896	WB-D/404	
Dike, James	046	1886	WB-E/450	AR
Dilday, Benjamin	079	1880	WB-2/193	AR
Dilday, John R.	051	1888	WB-C/381	AR
Dilday, Joseph	051	1841	WB-A/190	
Dilday, W. S.	051	1899	WB-C/568	AR
Dildy, Warren	105	1871	WB-2/61	AR
Dill, Edward	019	c1797	WB-D/139	AR-Copy
Dill, George W.	019	1878	WB-B/102	AR
Dill, Harriet T.	079	1881	WB-2/223	AR
Dill, Stephen	062	1892	WB-B/129	AR
Dillard, Calvin H.	099	1881	WB-A/236	AR
Dillard, Caroline C.	084	1864	WB-C/389	CTY
Dillard, Drury C.	084	1860	WB-C/338	CTY
Dillard, Elizabeth	037	1817	WB-E/172	AR
Dillard, Elizabeth	051	1879	WB-C/225	AR
Dillard, George	010	1780	WB-B/164	AR
Dillard, Hilman P.	044	1897	WB-24/356	CTY
Dillard, James	037	c1789	Orig. Only	AR
Dillard, James	084	1859	WB-C/289	CTY
Dillard, James P.	084	1899	WB-F/131	CTY
Dillard, John	037	1780	WB-B/42	AR
Dillard, John H.	046	1896	WB-F/546	AR
Dillard, M. L.	084	1883	WB-E/276	CTY
Dillen, Nancy S.	097	1871	WB-2/51	
Dilliard, James H.	039	1881	WB-U/280	AR
Dilliard, Josiah	099	1822	RB-20/100	AR
Dilliard, Lydia	073	1831	WB-E/250	AR
Dilliard, Mamie B.	049	1900	WB-2/449	AR
Dilliard, William	044	1854	WB-19/492	CTY
Dillin, Benjamin	096	1807	WB-2/50	AR
Dillin, Sally	096	1849	WB-3/21	AR
Dillingham, Absolom	013	1838	WB-A/55	
Dillingham, Rebeca	013	1847	WB-A/127	
Dillon, Catharine	085	1869	WB-1/23	
Dillon, Charity	046	1811	WB-A/110	AR
Dillon, Daniel	046	1806	WB-A/105	AR
Dillon, Elizabeth	021	1852	WB-1/95	AR
Dillon, John	060	1805	Orig. Only	AR
Dillon, Mary	018	1884	075 WB-O/199	075 AR
Dillon, Nathan	046	1820	WB-B/86	AR
Dillon, Nina	103	1882	WB-1/231	AR
Dillon, Peter	046	1796	WB-A/97	AR
Dillon, Prudence	038	1873	WB-2/124	AR
Dillow, Jacob	085	1822	WB-H/168	AR
Dills, Bartlett D.	055	c1872	WB-A/17	
Dills, Petter	086	1787	WB-A/9	AR
Dills, William	061	c1860	WB-1/72	
Dillworth, Thomas	046	1830	WB-B/411	AR
Dilsworth, Thomas	084	c1792	OW/220	
Dilworth, Abram	084	1857	WB-C/261	CTY
Dilworth, Benjamin	084	1829	WB-A/324	CTY
Dilworth, Benjamin	084	1830	WB-B/7	CTY
Dilworth, George	084	1829	WB-A/328	CTY
Dilworth, John	084	1808	WB-A/74	CTY
Dilworth, Richard	084	c1829	WB-B/8	CTY
Dilworth, Thomas	084	c1792	OW/220	AR
Dimock, Edwin	073	1895	WB-I/76	CTY
Dimond, Ira	084	1856	WB-C/227	CTY
Dimsdale, William	080	1872	WB-1/12	AR
Dinkins, Ada	028	1896	WB-F/234	
Dinkins, Dionecious	100	1794	WB-7/195	AR
Dinkins, James	065	1829	WB-B/147	AR
Dinkins, John	065	1805	WB-C/20	AR
Dinkins, John	092	1844	WB-4/217	
Dinkins, Joseph J.	087	c1810	WB-A/58	AR
Dinkins, Obedience	065	1838	WB-E/191	AR
Dinning, David	073	c1802	Orig. Only	AR
Discorah, Thomas	077	1726/7	SS 876/38	SS/AR
Dishman, James	054	1854	WB-3/82	AR
Dishman, Lewis	104	1864	WB-5/399	
Dishman, Nancy	003	c1879	Orig. Only	AR
Dismuke, Richard T.	084	c1852	WB-C/150	CTY
Dismukes, George	022	1827	WB-B/133	AR
Dismukes, John	033	1855	WB-1/122	
Dismukes, S. N.	022	c1860	WB-D/167	AR
Dispain, Samuel	100	1783	WB-3/184	AR
Ditchburn, Bartholomew	024	c1784	WB-A/240	AR
Ditson, Oliver	MA	1889	022 WB-E/403	022 AR
Diveny, Aaron	086	1843	WB-E/96	AR
Divers, John G.	018	c1866	WB-D/83	
Divine, Elizabeth	026	1890	WB-2/407	AR
Diviney, Sophia	081	1889	WB-16/128	AR

Name	Co.	Date	Recorded Copy	Original
Divoux, Frederick	028	1825	WB-C/259	AR
Dix, George W.	084	1881	WB-E/214	CTY
Dix, James H.	092	1896	WB-6/422	AR
Dix, John W. K.	070	1862	WB-D/90	AR
Dix, Martha L.	084	1899	WB-F/157	CTY
Dixon, Anderson	001	1863	WB-1/209	AR
Dixon, Benjamin	022	1839	WB-C/94	AR
Dixon, Bettie	069	1899	WB-6/75	AR
Dixon, Burrell	072	1832	WB-1/93	AR
Dixon, C. H.	026	1865	WB-1/364	
Dixon, Charles	020	1806	RB-E/221	AR
Dixon, Cofield	037	1838	WB-F/223	AR
Dixon, Cornelius	028	1859	WB-D/314	AR
Dixon, David	001	1858	WB-1/138	AR
Dixon, Edmund	078	1835	WI-13/58	AR
Dixon, Eleazer	028	1821	WB-C/207	AR
Dixon, Elijah	028	1811	WB-C/22	AR
Dixon, Elisha	047	1798	WB-3/311	AR
Dixon, Elizabeth	065	1867	WB-J/234	AR
Dixon, F. W.	045	1882	WB-1/81	
Dixon, Gatsey	045	1880	WB-1/60	AR
Dixon, George	028	1801	WB-B/114	AR
Dixon, George	022	1821	WB-B/33	AR
Dixon, George	001	1895	WB-3/57	AR
Dixon, Green	037	1809	WB-D/343	AR
Dixon, Henry	020	1795	RB-C/135	AR
Dixon, Henry A.	045	1868	WB-1/3	
Dixon, Henry, Jr.	020	1782	RB-A/211	
Dixon, Jacob	078	1855	WB-17/336	AR
Dixon, James	019	1813	WB-D/163	AR
Dixon, John	053	1786	RW-1/152	
Dixon, John	010	1773	Orig. Only	SS/AR
Dixon, John	001	1874	WB-2/67	AR
Dixon, John	028	1817	WB-C/152	
Dixon, John	019	1802	WB-D/146	AR
Dixon, John	065	1856	WB-J/20	AR
Dixon, John C.	045	1886	WB-1/129	AR
Dixon, John S.	079	1887	WB-2/391	AR
Dixon, John, Sr.	072	1896	WB-4/329	AR
Dixon, John, Sr.	056	1851	WB-1/649	AR
Dixon, Jonathan	072	1811	WB-A/22	AR
Dixon, Kittura	028	1854	WB-D/228	
Dixon, Lafayette	045	1897	WB-1/260	AR
Dixon, Lemuel	056	1878	WB-3/192	AR
Dixon, Margaret	065	1878	WB-K/284	AR
Dixon, Matilda	074	1893	WB-1/116	AR
Dixon, Matilda	074	1897	WB-1/141	AR
Dixon, Miller	028	1832	WB-C/351	AR-Copy
Dixon, Moses	004	1857	Orig. Only	AR
Dixon, Moses	004	1890	WB-A/113	
Dixon, Nancy	045	1882	WB-1/99	AR
Dixon, Nancy A.	028	1891	WB-F/8	
Dixon, Nancy A.	038	1891	028 WB-F/502	
Dixon, Nancy A.	074	1891	WB-1/111	
Dixon, Nathan	022	1827	WB-B/127	AR
Dixon, Noah	009	1860	OB-L/206	AR
Dixon, Pattie L.	045	1889	WB-1/165	AR
Dixon, Piercy Ann	074	1899	WB-1/150	AR
Dixon, Priscilla	105	1895	WB-3/226	AR
Dixon, Priscilla	045	1895	WB-1/246 & 293	AR
Dixon, R. D. S.	MS	1862	Copy	045 AR
Dixon, Richard W.	022	1888	WB-E/391	AR
Dixon, Robert	001	1878	WB-2/129	AR
Dixon, Robert	047	1887	WB-6/446	AR
Dixon, Sallie	026	1898	WB-2/5	AR
Dixon, Samuel A.	078	1881	WB-19/339	AR
Dixon, Samuel B.	061	1887	WB-2/90	AR
Dixon, Sarah	022	1830	WB-B/173	AR
Dixon, Silvanus	019	1813	WB-D/140	AR
Dixon, Solomon	022	1827	WB-B/131	AR
Dixon, Solomon	028	1826	WB-C/282	AR
Dixon, Stephen	072	1873	WB-4/54	AR-Nunc.
Dixon, Stewart	073	1835	WB-E/335	AR
Dixon, Thomas	022	1824	WB-B/76	AR
Dixon, Thomas	009	c1780	OWB/155	AR-Nunc.
Dixon, Thomas	072	c1769	RW/L44	AR
Dixon, Thomas	001	1865	WB-1/227	AR
Dixon, Thomas	037	1790	WB-C/154	AR
Dixon, Thomas C.	081	1899	WB-17/39	
Dixon, Thomas C.	001	1899	WB-3/263	AR
Dixon, Walter	009	c1812	OB-A/222	AR
Dixon, Wesley	004	1886	WB-A/80	AR
Dixon, William	070	1765	DB-E/193	AR
Dixon, William	037	1800	WB-D/113	AR
Dixson, George	022	c1780	Orig. Only	AR
Dixson, James	009	1838	OB-B/528	AR
Dixson, Robert	010	1727	SS 876/128	SS/AR
Doak, Dejoina P.	046	1861	WB-D/116	AR
Doak, Hannah	046	1856	WB-C/452	AR
Doak, James	046	1806	WB-A/108	AR
Doak, James W.	046	1850	WB-C/320	AR
Doak, Robert	046	1796	WB-A/99	AR
Doak, William	046	1845	WB-C/229	AR
Doak, William	046	1807	WB-A/103	AR
Doan, John	022	c1801	WB-A/43	AR
Doane, George	024	c1700	SS 874.2/121	
Doaye, William	047	1855	WB-5/14	
Dobbin, Alexander	020	1778	RB-A/57	AR
Dobbin, Elizabeth	085	1846	WB-K/40	AR
Dobbin, Hugh	MD	1799	Copy	020 AR
Dobbin, James	085	c1788	WB-C/76	AR
Dobbin, James C.	029	1857	WB-C/355	AR
Dobbin, Joseph	085	1842	WB-I/124	AR
Dobbin, Nancy	085	1849	WB-K/92	AR
Dobbin, Rachel	020	1798	RB-C/264	AR
Dobbins, Alexander	020	1778	RB-A/57	
Dobbins, Alexander	085	1829	WB-H/447	AR
Dobbins, Alexander	085	1799	WB-E/263	AR
Dobbins, Bowler	100	1854	WB-43/351	AR
Dobbins, Elizabeth	106	1885	WB-2/190	AR
Dobbins, Hannah	086	1848	WB-E/176	AR
Dobbins, Hugh	085	1811	WB-G/196	AR
Dobbins, Hugh	TN	1800	020 RB-C/454	
Dobbins, Jacob	106	c1863	WB-1/90	AR
Dobbins, Jacob	092	1798	WB-3/28	AR
Dobbins, John	085	1818	WB-G/498	AR
Dobbins, John	106	c1856	WB-1/77	AR
Dobbins, John	054	1818	WB-1/93	AR
Dobbins, John M.	029	1837	WB-B/281	AR
Dobbins, Lamira	054	1897	WB-6/112	CTY
Dobbins, Mary	013	1894	WB-C/432	AR
Dobbins, Mary	013	1894	080 WB-1/244	080 AR
Dobbins, Mary	085	1866	WB-K/380	AR
Dobbins, William J.	TN	c1864	106 WB-1/108	
Dobbs, Arthur	070	1765	SS 881/290	SS/AR
Dobbs, Arthur	070	c1763	Copy	028 AR
Dobings, Hugh	020	1781	RB-A/175	AR
Dobins, John	020	1814	RB-F/409	AR
Dobins, John	054	c1820	WB-1A/106	

Name	Co.	Date	Recorded Copy	Original
Dobson, Archibald	092	1900	WB-6/543	AR
Dobson, Benjamin	054	c1810	WB-1/186	AR
Dobson, Elizabeth	035	1845	Orig. Only	AR
Dobson, Ester	054	1856	WB-3/101	
Dobson, G. W.	064	1897	WB-2/401	AR
Dobson, Hannah	035	1840	Orig. Only	AR
Dobson, Henry H.	092	1865	WB-5/76	
Dobson, Hiram	054	c1863	Orig. Only	AR
Dobson, John	035	1871	WB-4/34	AR
Dobson, John	064	1873	WB-2/26	AR
Dobson, John	054	c1859	WB-3/146	AR
Dobson, Leander H.	092	c1875	WB-6/107	AR
Dobson, Lewis	035	1826	WB-A/124	AR
Dobson, Margaret	054	1880	WB-4/431	CTY
Dobson, Mary	092	1874	WB-6/50	
Dobson, Perry H.	035	1891	WB-4/392	AR
Dobson, Robert	054	c1810	WB-1/190	AR
Dobson, William	032	1833	WB-1/237	AR
Dobson, William	024	1690	Orig. Only	SS/AR
Dobson, William	090	1822	WB-3/88	AR
Dobyns, Thomas M.	VA	1872	004 WB-A/109	004 AR
Dockery, Alfred	082	1873	WB-6/111	
Dockery, Elisha	017	1869	WB-B/7	AR
Dockery, Fannie S.	082	1894	WB-6/495	AR
Dockery, Thomas	082	1854	WB-4/76	AR
Dockery, Thomas	082	1798	WB-1/Front	AR
Dockings, Samuel	082	1821	WB-1/223	AR
Dockrey, Robert	073	1826	WB-E/106	AR
Dockrey, William	099	1793	RB-2/463	AR
Docton, Jacob	077	1764	WB-C/34	AR
Docton, Thomas	077	1754	Copy	024 AR
Dodd, Allen	084	1801	OW/92	AR
Dodd, Benjamin	022	1836	WB-C/37	AR
Dodd, David	087	c1813	WB-2/127	AR
Dodd, Dempsey	056	c1851	WB-2/289	AR-Copy
Dodd, Elizabeth	056	1814	WB-1/234	AR
Dodd, Emily	056	1896	WB-4/13	AR
Dodd, Gaston H.	056	1892	WB-2/126	AR
Dodd, Harriet C.	029	1897	WB-F/108	AR
Dodd, Herbert H.	022	1841	WB-C/116	
Dodd, Isaac	029	1878	WB-E/181	AR
Dodd, James	022	c1835	WB-C/27	AR
Dodd, James	099	1896	WB-C/551	AR
Dodd, James S.	022	c1864	WB-D/142	AR
Dodd, John	056	1795	WB-1/794	AR
Dodd, Phereby	056	1860	WB-1/736	AR
Dodd, Reubin	056	1820	WB-1/309	AR
Dodd, Theophilus	039	1878	WB-U/162	AR
Dodd, William	056	1813	WB-1/334	AR
Dodd, William	022	1825	WB-B/205	AR
Dodd, Willis	056	1865	WB-2/69	AR
Dodge, Angelica	075	1843	WB-N/181	AR
Dodge, Daniel D.	NH	1886	070 WB-F/73	070 AR
Dodge, Edward	NY	c1873	016 WB-3/296	016 AR
Dodson, Alsey	084	1819	WB-A/164	CTY
Dodson, Charles	044	1799	WB-4/282	CTY
Dodson, Francis	044	1796	WB-3/247	CTY
Dodson, George C.	032	1859	WB-2/175	AR
Dodson, John	073	1895	WB-I/60	CTY
Dodson, John T.	046	1872	WB-E/81	AR
Dodson, Mary	046	1833	WB-B/475	AR
Dodson, Richard	046	1829	WB-B/398	AR
Dodson, Rubin	090	1804	WB-2/58	AR-Nunc.
Dodson, Ruffin C.	073	1890	WB-H/507	CTY
Dodson, Stephen	020	1852	RB-Q/651	AR
Dodson, William	044	1791	WB-2/234	CTY
Dodson, William	073	1887	WB-H/439	CTY
Doe, Edward	009	c1751	OWB/41	AR
Doe, Elisabeth	047	1794	WB-3/232	AR
Doerner, Powel	085	1799	WB-E/33	AR
Doggett, Ann	086	1840	WB-E/62	AR
Doggett, B. R.	086	1881	WB-F/162	AR
Doggett, Coalman	026	1853	WB-1/158	AR
Doggett, George	086	c1863	Orig. Only	AR
Doggett, Henry	047	1853	Copy	086 AR
Doggett, Henry	047	1853	WB-4/341	AR
Doggett, James P.	026	1852	WB-1/141	AR
Doggett, Jeremiah	047	1818	WB-3/627	AR
Doggett, John	046	1899	084 WB-F/128	084 CTY
Doggett, John	046	1895	WB-F/423	AR
Doggett, John R.	060	1840	WB-2/29	AR
Doggett, Richard	047	1832	WB-4/91	AR
Doggett, Sally	046	1900	WB-G/196	AR
Doggett, William	047	1835	WB-4/121	AR
Doggette, Bushrod	086	1829	WB-D/108	AR
Doggette, George	086	1814	WB-C/17	AR
Dogles, Rosana	073	1855	WB-G/89	AR
Doherty, Daniel	065	1823	WB-C/47	AR
Doherty, Daniel, Jr.	065	1819	WB-C/36	AR
Doherty, David	065	1835	WB-G/214	AR
Doherty, George	073	1793	WB-B/236	AR
Doherty, M. C.	070	1890	WB-F/376	AR
Doherty, Mary W.	065	1844	WB-H/174	AR
Doherty, Samuel	084	1820	WB-A/191	CTY
Dohonossier, Ahix	075	1711	SS 874.1/37	Nunc.
Doick, William	046	1810	WB-A/109	
Doik, Elizabeth	041	1865	WB-3/321	AR
Dolby, Elizabeth	029	1828	WB-B/169	AR
Dolby, John	044	1821	WB-8/430	CTY
Dolby, Stephen	024	1858	WB-C/424	AR
Doleer, Gyles	002	1689	Orig. Only	SS/AR
Doles, Arthur J.	071	1834	WB-4/109	AR
Doles, Benjamin	071	1812	WB-3/87	AR
Doles, Benjamin	VA	1801	071 WB-3/123	
Doles, Benjamin	047	1801	WB-3/348	AR
Doles, Bettie V.	047	1880	WB-6/223	AR
Doles, Elizabeth	071	1877	WB-6/236	AR
Doles, Francis	071	1805	WB-2/294	AR
Doles, Jesse	071	1817	WB-3/189	AR
Doles, Mariah	069	1890	WB-5/328	AR
Doles, Rebekah	047	1815	WB-3/565	AR
Doles, Robert	071	1884	WB-6/452	AR
Doles, Sarah	047	1791	WB-3/192	AR
Doles, Thomas	071	1800	WB-2/201	AR
Doles, William	071	1829	WB-4/65	AR-Nunc.
Doll, Jacob	084	1878	WB-E/145	
Doll, Nicholas	090	1813	WB-2/146	AR
Dollar, Hampton W.	036	1882	WB-A/27	CTY
Dollar, Henry	073	1843	WB-F/167	AR
Dollar, James	022	c1852	Orig. Only	AR
Dollar, Jonas	086	1810	WB-B/237	
Dollar, Jonathan	073	1835	WB-E/330	AR
Dollar, Jonathan	073	1864	WB-G/431	AR
Dollar, Rebecca	073	1845	WB-F/268	AR
Dollar, Sallie	022	1880	WB-E/219	AR
Dollen, John	090	1802	WB-2/14	AR
Dollerhide, Mary	020	1824	RB-I/328	
Dolton, John A. B.	090	1879	WB-6/104	
Donaho, Hiram	085	1852	WB-K/147	AR
Donahue, Ann	104	1837	WB-4/213	

Name	Co.	Date	Recorded Copy	Original
Donahue, Anna	104	N. D.	Orig. Only	014 AR
Donald, Adolphus	046	c1898	Orig. Only	AR
Donaldson, Alexander	085	c1797	WB-E/265	AR
Donaldson, Andrew	077	1768	WB-C/78	AR
Donaldson, Arthur	065	1777	WB-C/13	AR
Donaldson, Hannah	020	1780	RB-B/307	AR
Donaldson, Humphrey	020	1781	RB-A/144	AR
Donaldson, John	082	1781	WB-1/8	AR
Donaldson, John	077	1795	WB-E/40	
Donaldson, John	077	1784	WB-C/254	AR
Donaldson, John	085	1827	WB-H/404	AR
Donaldson, John J.	MD	1866	Copy	066 AR
Donaldson, Joseph	061	c1860	WB-1/81	AR
Donaldson, Martha P.	061	1883	WB-2/51	AR
Donaldson, Marthew	085	1833	WB-H/603	AR
Donaldson, Robert	029	1808	WB-A/132	AR
Donaldson, Robert	037	1804	WB-D/189	AR
Donaldson, Thomas	086	1792	Orig. Only	AR-Nunc.
Donaldson, William	054	c1817	WB-1A/49	AR
Donaldson, William	037	1819	WB-E/214	AR
Donaldsonn, Robert	NY	1873	029 WB-E/113	
Donalson, Robert	073	1770	WB-A/106	
Donalson, Spencer	077	1824	WB-F/73	AR
Donathan, Jacob	092	1859	WB-5/45	AR
Done, Esther	011	c1799	WB-1/460	
Done, Henry	077	1785	WB-C/314	AR
Donelly, Henry	053	1809	RW-1/422	AR
Donelson, Hannah	053	c1807	RW-1/420	
Donelson, Margaret	TN	1871	Copy	047 AR
Donly, John	023	1884	WB-A/29	
Donnell, Andrew	046	1836	WB-B/542	AR
Donnell, Benjamin W.	053	1887	WB-11/195	AR
Donnell, Charlotte	046	1845	WB-C/226	AR
Donnell, Daniel	046	1888	WB-E/508	AR
Donnell, Edmund	046	1871	WB-E/68	AR
Donnell, Elizabeth	046	1847	WB-C/272	AR
Donnell, Elizabeth	046	1802	WB-A/106	AR
Donnell, Erwin	046	1845	WB-C/227	AR
Donnell, George	046	1842	WB-C/136	AR
Donnell, John	046	1822	WB-B/153	AR
Donnell, John R.	099	1864	RB-33/325	AR
Donnell, John S.	MD	1872	046 WB-H/477	
Donnell, John S.	MD	1891	016 WB-4/81	016 AR
Donnell, Latham	046	1829	WB-B/392	AR
Donnell, Nancy	046	1836	WB-C/34	AR
Donnell, Nancy P.	084	1866	WB-D/66	CTY
Donnell, Robert	046	1847	WB-C/274	AR
Donnell, Robert	046	1816	Orig. Only	AR
Donnell, Robert C.	046	1872	WB-E/79	AR
Donnell, Thomas	046	1845	WB-C/225	AR
Donnell, William	046	1823	WB-B/160	AR
Donnell, William	046	1860	WB-D/37	AR
Donnock, Kartherine	077	1764	Orig. Only	AR-Nunc.
Donoho, Charles	020	1828	RB-L/319	AR
Donoho, Dixon	020	1828	RB-L/319	
Donoho, John	070	1743	LGB-4/#149	SS/AR
Donoho, Keziah	020	1844	RB-P/73	
Donoho, Thomas	020	1825	RB-K/58	AR
Donohoe, Ann	104	c1822	Copy	014 AR
Dooles, Thomas	037	1757	SS 879/216	SS/AR
Dooling, John	092	1798	WB-3/27	
Doozier, Chloe	018	1833	WB-C/139	
Dorch, Young	073	1846	WB-F/315	AR
Doremyer, Andrew	085	1811	WB-G/186	AR
Dorland, Luke	062	1898	WB-B/206	AR
Dormady, William	024	1777	WB-A/242	AR
Dorman, Mary	037	1801	WB-D/125	AR
Dorran, Daniel	078	1814	WI-6/244	AR
Dorsett, Ezra	081	1894	WB-16/338	AR
Dorsett, Francis	022	1864	WB-D/134	AR
Dorsett, Francis	022	1813	WB-A/225	AR
Dorsett, Henry	081	1860	WB-11/488	AR
Dorsett, Henry	022	1900	WB-F/161	AR
Dorsett, Hesekiah	022	1877	WB-E/129	AR
Dorsett, Hezekiah	081	1899	WB-17/12	AR
Dorsett, John	022	1851	WB-C/305	AR
Dorsett, John D.	022	1900	WB-F/183	AR
Dorsett, Robert	022	1882	WB-E/249	AR
Dorsett, Soloman	022	1848	WB-C/221	AR
Dorsett, Soloman	022	1858	WB-D/25	AR
Dorsey, Endymon	085	c1777	WB-A/258	AR
Dorsey, Thomas A.	014	1890	WB-2/415	CTY
Dorsey, William	005	1852	WB-C/56	AR
Dortch, Anney	069	1790	WB-1/62	AR
Dortch, William T.	103	1889	WB-1/491	AR
Dorton, James C.	016	1848	WB-1/154	
Dortsch, Lewis	069	c1838	Copy	037 AR
Dorumn, Mary	039	1864	WB-S/1	AR
Doscher, E. W.	070	1888	WB-F/186	AR
Doscher, Metta Maria	070	1893	WB-G/137	AR
Dosher, Frank	012	1898	WB-A/139	AR
Doson, Robert	072	1786	WI/L40	AR
Doss, Martin	090	1879	WB-6/101	AR
Doss, Sarah	092	1880	WB-6/133	
Doss, Thomas J.	092	1892	WB-6/337	AR
Doss, William	092	1845	WB-4/230	
Dosset, Phillip	073	1784	WB-A/298	AR
Dossey, James	046	1847	WB-C/264	AR
Dossey, Mary W.	046	1852	WB-C/370	AR
Dossey, Solomon	039	c1818	WB-F/157	AR
Dosson, Jane	072	c1784	WI/L27	AR
Dosson, Robert	072	1827	WB-1/7	AR
Doster, H. Milas	097	1890	WB-2/380	AR
Doster, James	065	1818	WB-C/39	AR
Doster, James W.	097	1879	WB-2/160	
Doster, Mary	097	1900	WB-3/24	AR
Doster, Sampson	097	1857	WB-1/132	AR
Dotson, A. S.	102	1888	WB-A/56	
Dotson, Jacob K.	049	1876	WB-2/25	AR
Doty, Benejah	072	c1780	RW/L39	AR
Doty, Edward	070	1780	WB-C/69	AR
Doub, J. W.	038	1879	WB-2/352	AR
Doub, Jacob	090	1837	WB-4/6	AR
Doub, John B.	038	1891	WB-3/227	
Doub, Joseph	038	1869	WB-2/15	AR
Doub, Joseph C.	038	1900	WB-4/257	AR
Doub, Mary E.	038	1874	WB-2/177	AR
Doub, Mary Eve	090	1835	WB-3/291	AR
Doub, Michael	038	1876	WB-2/285	AR
Doub, Will C.	046	1885	WB-E/415	AR
Doub, William	038	1863	WB-1/221	AR
Doub, William B.	036	1896	WB-A/389	CTY
Doubleday, Ulysses	NY	1893	080 WB-1/210	080 AR
Doud, Michael	065	1823	WB-C/45	AR
Douday, Caleb	030	1793	WB-2/14	
Doudge, Even	030	c1814	WB-3/49	
Doudge, Nathan	092	1827	Orig. Only	AR
Dougan, Thomas	081	1795	WB-2/16	AR
Dougan, William	081	1869	WB-15/23	AR
Douge, James	030	c1810	WB-3/12	

Name	Co.	Date	Recorded Copy	Original
Douge, Peter	030	1824	WB-3/175	
Douge, Peter	030	1778	WB-1/132	
Douge, Tull	030	1746	Orig. Only	SS/AR
Dough, Abiah	030	1846	WB-4/119	
Dough, Benjamin	030	1816	WB-3/87	
Dough, George	030	1792	WB-1/253	
Dough, Richard	030	1825	WB-3/186	
Dough, Thomas	030	1801	WB-2/174	
Dougharty, George	082	1807	WB-1/113	AR
Dougherty, Agnes	065	1808	WB-C/84	AR
Dougherty, John	065	1790	WB-C/21	AR
Dougherty, John	065	1817	WB-C/45	AR
Dougherty, John	084	1838	WB-B/195	CTY
Dougherty, Sally	073	1859	WB-G/217	CTY
Doughten, Clarke	006	1857	WB-D/18	AR
Doughter, Winiford	051	1842	WB-A/154	
Doughtie, Daniel	041	1793	WB-1/113	AR
Doughtie, John	051	1855	WB-A/382	
Doughtie, Leah	041	1816	WB-2/127	AR
Doughtie, William	041	1824	WB-2/222	AR
Doughty, Fanny	009	c1849	OB-G/6	AR
Doughty, John	070	1749	SS 877/298	SS/AR
Doughty, John	070	1749	DB-C/197	
Douglas, Adam W.	073	1884	WB-H/341	CTY
Douglas, Alexander	024	1781	WB-A/239	AR
Douglas, Archibald	068	1854	WB-C/18	
Douglas, Benjamin	005	1858	WB-C/136	AR
Douglas, Clarissa M.	106	1883	WB-2/177	AR
Douglas, Daniel	082	1816	WB-1/175	AR
Douglas, Frances C.	065	1885	WB-L/72	AR
Douglas, James	030	1833	WB-3/324	
Douglas, James	030	1791	WB-1/248	
Douglas, James	085	c1778	WB-B/80	AR
Douglas, Jane	083	1893	Orig. Only	AR
Douglas, Jilson B.	005	1855	WB-C/106	AR
Douglas, John	073	1816	WB-D/481	AR
Douglas, John	065	1880	WB-K/387	AR
Douglas, John F.	075	1892	WB-0/365	AR
Douglas, Julius P.	054	1885	WB-5/71	CTY
Douglas, Selah M.	053	1888	WB-11/214	AR
Douglas, T. C.	004	1899	WB-A/215	AR
Douglas, William	085	1773	WB-A/188	AR
Douglass, Alexander	092	1806	WB-3/77	AR
Douglass, Anthony	030	1844	WB-4/103	
Douglass, Catharine	054	1857	WB-3/123	AR
Douglass, Christian	083	1861	WB-2/169	AR
Douglass, Daniel	068	1877	WB-D/103	
Douglass, David	071	1753	Orig. Only	SS/AR
Douglass, Isaac	077	c1849	WB-F/490	AR
Douglass, James	010	1752	SS 879/61	SS/AR
Douglass, James	044	1821	WB-9/49	CTY
Douglass, James W.	029	1837	WB-B/285	AR
Douglass, John	022	1800	WB-A/30	AR
Douglass, Joseph	016	1872	WB-3/51	
Douglass, Margaret	065	1818	WB-C/44	AR
Douglass, Mark	022	1881	WB-E/238	AR
Douglass, Nathan	048	1893	WB-1/13	CTY
Douglass, Sollomon	054	1816	WB-1/396	AR
Douglass, Thomas	092	c1837	WB-4/157	
Douglass, Thomas	016	1850	WB-1/177	
Dougles, Abel	030	1788	WB-1/230	
Douglis, William	047	1766	WB-1/193	
Douthet, Pheby	032	c1851	WB-2/54	AR
Douthit, Abraham	032	1828	WB-1/98	AR
Douthit, Catherine	033	1855	WB-1/118	
Douthit, Henry	033	1900	WB-2/248	CTY
Douthit, Isaac	090	1823	WB-3/98	AR
Douthit, John	085	1784	WB-C/148	AR
Douthit, Mary	085	c1790	WB-E/254	AR
Douthit, Rebecca	032	1853	WB-2/88	AR
Douthit, Thomas	085	1819	WB-G/538	AR
Douthit, William	085	1799	WB-E/245	AR
Douty, Eliseah	009	c1792	OWB/268	AR
Douty, John	009	1825	OB-A/349	AR
Dove, Caleb	016	1835	PQS.5/343	
Dover, D. T.	026	1899	WB-3/50	AR
Dover, John	SC	1889	026 WB-2/401	026 AR
Dow, John	065	1828	WB-B/1	AR
Dow, William	009	c1792	OWB/269	AR
Doway, Robert	011	1758	Orig. Only	SS/AR
Dowd, Clement	065	1898	WB-N/135	AR
Dowd, Emanuel	035	1779	WB-A/107	AR
Dowd, Judith	022	1803	WB-A/88	AR
Dowd, Mary	068	c1889	WB-D/337	
Dowd, Richard	022	1856	WB-C/426	AR
Dowd, Samuel	022	1852	WB-C/319	AR
Dowd, Thomas S.	022	1883	WB-E/286	AR
Dowd, William	030	1804	WB-2/246	
Dowd, William	028	1808	WB-B/320	
Dowday, Jacob	030	c1806	WB-2/322	
Dowday, Jesse	028	1818	WB-C/169	AR
Dowday, William	028	1803	WB-B/169	AR
Dowden, William	028	1808	Orig. Only	AR
Dowdle, Samuel W.	061	1871	WB-2/11	AR
Dowdy, Charlotte	030	1866	WB-4/263	
Dowdy, Daniel	051	1831	WB-A/175	
Dowdy, Daniel	051	c1819	WB-A/120	
Dowdy, Elijah	028	1826	WB-C/268	
Dowdy, Elizabeth	022	1888	WB-E/395	AR
Dowdy, Ivy	030	c1875	WB-5/33	AR
Dowdy, James	028	1816	WB-C/131	AR
Dowdy, John	N	c1828	Orig. Only	028 AR
Dowdy, John	022	1884	WB-E/295	AR
Dowdy, John	022	1895	WB-E/12	AR
Dowdy, John	028	1834	WB-C/368	AR
Dowdy, John	030	1824	WB-3/178	
Dowdy, John	028	1804	WB-B/200	AR
Dowdy, John	030	1844	WB-4/104	
Dowdy, John A.	028	1850	WB-D/169	
Dowdy, Josiah	030	1828	WB-3/238	
Dowdy, Josiah	030	1818	WB-3/105	
Dowdy, Manual	009	1818	OB-A/290	AR
Dowdy, Margaret	030	1886	WB-5/133	AR
Dowdy, Sally	022	1868	WB-D/119	AR
Dowdy, Samuel	030	1893	WB-5/206	AR
Dowdy, Samuel	030	1838	WB-4/48	
Dowdy, Thomas	022	1859	WB-D/42	AR
Dowdy, Thomas	022	1815	WB-A/273	AR
Dowdy, William	096	c1811	WB-2/54	
Dowdy, Willoughby	030	1854	WB-4/185	AR
Dowe, John A.	080	1893	WB-1/216	AR
Dowell, James	054	1858	WB-3/130	AR
Dowell, Mary	107	c1849	WB-1/388	
Dowell, Peter	085	c1802	WB-E/258	AR
Dowell, Priscilla	104	1863	WB-5/330	
Dowell, William	054	c1824	WB-2/7	AR
Dowey, James	011	c1811	WB-2/308	
Dowling, Frances	100	1866	WB-50/185	
Dowling, John	092	1798	WB-3/27	AR
Dowling, Susanah	092	c1830	WB-4/31	

Name	Co.	Date	Recorded Copy	Original
Dowling, William	092	c1829	WB-4/18	AR
Down, Richard	068	1888	WB-D/283	
Downer, Francis	005	1870	WB-D/13	AR
Downer, Joseph W.	005	1887	WB-D/217	AR
Downer, Ursula	005	1899	WB-D/449	AR
Downer, William	070	1745	SS 877/294	SS/AR
Downer, William	070	1745	DB-C/92	
Downes, William	047	1793	WB-3/216	AR
Downey, Isaiah	044	1885	WB-23/541	CTY
Downey, Robert	044	1809	WB-7/45	CTY
Downey, Samuel S.	044	1851	WB-18/281	CTY
Downie, Alexander	035	1799	WB-A/127	AR
Downing, Ann	012	1846	Orig. Only	AR
Downing, George	011	c1837	WB-1/57	
Downing, Henry	101	1873	WB-A/3	AR
Downing, Henry	096	1781	WB-1/125	AR
Downing, Henry A.	101	1883	WB-A/107	AR
Downing, James, Sr.	037	1808	WB-D/322	AR
Downing, John	051	1850	WB-A/322	
Downing, Joseph	029	1871	WB-E/37	AR
Downing, Marcus L.	028	c1868	WB-D/465	
Downing, Turner	051	1886	WB-C/345	AR
Downing, Valentine	029	1887	WB-E/420	AR
Downing, William	096	1748/9	Orig. Only	SS/AR
Downing, William	N	1739	LGB-4/#92	SS/AR
Downmon, Richard A.	085	1865	WB-K/353	AR
Downs, Alexander	061	1895	WB-2/158	AR
Downs, Daniel D.	009	1889	WB-1/466	CTY
Downs, Edward	028	1880	WB-E/239	
Downs, Frederick	009	1866	OB-M/247	AR
Downs, Fredrick	009	1838	OB-C2/59	AR
Downs, Henry	065	1798	WB-C/22	AR
Downs, J. Smith	017	1880	WB-B/94	AR
Downs, Joanna	009	1898	WB-2/165	CTY
Downs, Kinion	079	1890	WB-2/526	AR
Downs, Robert	026	1876	WB-2/141	AR
Downs, Susan	009	1898	WB-2/163	CTY
Downs, Thomas	065	1840	WB-H/21	AR
Downum, Speakman	016	1852	WB-1/205	
Downy, Iley	106	c1853	WB-1/18	
Dowthit, John F.	104	1844	WB-4/298	AR
Dowtin, David D. W.	100	1850	WB-40/259	AR
Dowtin, John	100	1846	WB-39/191	AR
Dowtin, Mary H.	105	1876	WB-51/111	AR
Dowtin, William A.	100	1862	WB-49/534	AR
Dowty, Teagle	009	1866	OB-M/238	AR
Doxey, Aby	030	1835	WB-4/4	
Doxey, Alex. A.	030	1881	WB-5/82	AR
Doxey, Dempsey	030	1840	WB-4/80	
Doxey, Henry	030	1859	WB-4/228	
Doxey, John	030	1824	WB-3/173	AR
Doxey, John	030	1884	WB-5/112	
Doxey, Susan	030	1893	WB-5/210	AR
Doxey, William	030	1834	WB-3/333	
Doyle, Edward	019	1896	WB-B/308	AR
Doyle, Margaret	070	1784	WB-C/71	AR
Dozier, Abner	018	1834	WB-C/170	
Dozier, Alfred	030	1898	WB-5/268	AR
Dozier, Allen	075	1878	WB-0/95	AR
Dozier, Ann	069	1825	WB-1/330	AR
Dozier, C. H.	037	1883	WB-G/665	
Dozier, Caleb	018	1832	WB-C/127	
Dozier, Cyntha	030	1832	WB-3/311	
Dozier, Edmund L.	018	1870	WB-E/20	AR
Dozier, Edmund S.	030	1821	WB-3/287	
Dozier, Elias	030	1827	WB-3/232	
Dozier, Evan	018	1826	WB-C/70	
Dozier, Fred	069	1887	WB-5/271	AR
Dozier, Isaac E.	018	1834	WB-C/143	
Dozier, James	018	1875	WB-E/49	AR
Dozier, Jesse D.	018	1900	WB-E/310	AR
Dozier, Joab	030	1844	WB-4/106	
Dozier, John	096	1791	Orig. Only	AR
Dozier, John	069	1884	WB-5/204	AR
Dozier, Joseph	018	1837	WB-C/205	
Dozier, Margaret	018	c1843	WB-D/53	
Dozier, Mary	018	1839	WB-C/252	
Dozier, Mary	018	1845	WB-C/298	
Dozier, Peter	030	1858	WB-4/222	
Dozier, Peter	018	1830	WB-C/115	
Dozier, Polly	018	1855	WB-D/17	
Dozier, Richard	069	1829	WB-1/364	AR
Dozier, Samuel B.	059	1882	WB-A/263	CTY
Dozier, Sarah	018	1827	WB-C/81	
Dozier, Sarah	018	1841	WB-C/262	
Dozier, Thomas	069	1847	WB-1/501	AR
Dozier, Thomas	018	1834	WB-C/154	
Dozier, Tully B.	030	1852	WB-4/168	
Dozier, Tully B.	018	1832	WB-C/131	
Dozier, William	018	1887	WB-E/171	AR
Dozier, William	069	1782	WB-1/123	AR
Dozier, Willoughby	030	1818	WB-3/102	
Drake, Archibald	099	1864	RB-35/437	AR
Drake, Augustin	069	1842	WB-1/464	AR
Drake, Benton	068	1825	WB-B/42	
Drake, Charity	069	1899	WB-6/55	AR
Drake, Edmund	069	1803	WB-1/142	AR
Drake, Edwin	069	1841	WB-1/453	AR
Drake, Edwin B.	100	1863	WB-50/28	AR
Drake, Elizabeth	069	1853	WB-1/534	AR
Drake, Elsey	029	1875	WB-E/144	AR
Drake, Ethelbert	075	1849	WB-N/230	AR
Drake, Francis	069	1838	WB-1/426	AR
Drake, George A.	037	1892	WB-H/232	AR
Drake, Harriet A.	069	1846	WB-1/492	AR
Drake, Hartwell	069	1796	WB-1/109	AR
Drake, Henry	037	1858	WB-G/160	AR
Drake, Hines	069	1831	WB-1/378	AR
Drake, Isabella	050	1893	WB-2/164	CTY
Drake, James	VA	1791	069 WB-1/249	069 AR
Drake, Jesse	037	1796	WB-D/4	AR
Drake, Jesse H.	069	1879	WB-5/92	AR
Drake, John	010	1729	Orig. Only	SS/AR
Drake, John	083	1863	WB-2/198	AR
Drake, Jonas	069	1816	WB-1/274	AR
Drake, Joseph A.	100	1886	WB-51/202	AR
Drake, Lazarus	037	1785	WB-C/3	AR
Drake, M. M.	100	1865	WB-50/149	AR
Drake, Mary	047	1833	WB-4/104	AR
Drake, Mary Ann	037	1892	WB-H/219	AR
Drake, Matthew	069	1810	WB-1/205	AR
Drake, Matthew	069	1816	WB-1/282	AR
Drake, Mourning	069	1867	WB-1/623	AR
Drake, Nathaniel	069	1810	WB-1/204	AR
Drake, Nicholas	047	1831	WB-4/72	AR
Drake, Oliver P.	050	1887	WB-2/15	CTY
Drake, Rebecca M.	100	1869	WB-51/20	AR
Drake, Richard	022	1834	WB-C/26	AR
Drake, Sally M.	022	1837	WB-C/75	AR
Drake, Sarah	037	1804	WB-D/208	AR

Name	Co.	Date	Recorded Copy	Original
Drake, William	069	1838	WB-1/428	
Drake, William	037	1827	WB-F/69	AR
Drake, William	022	1837	WB-C/44	AR
Drane, Catharine	024	1885	WB-E/142	AR
Drane, Robert B.	070	1862	WB-D/95	AR
Draper, Hannah	077	c1774	Orig. Only	AR
Draper, Joseph	077	1811	WB-E/358	AR
Draper, Peter	077	1764	WB-C/45	AR
Draper, Samuel	077	1829	WB-F/165	AR
Draper, Silas	077	1794	WB-E/6	
Draper, Solomon	078	1829	WI-11/156	AR
Draper, Solomon	078	1807	WI-4/248	AR
Draper, William	047	1883	WB-6/310	AR
Draper, William	071	1834	WB-4/115	AR
Draughan, Wells	037	1872	WB-G/385	AR
Draughn, Ashley	092	1899	WB-6/509	AR
Draughn, Isaac	017	1874	WB-B/46	AR
Draughn, Matilda	105	1896	WB-3/218	AR
Draughon, Elizabeth	087	c1856	WB-1/498	AR
Draughon, George	087	1866	WB-2/100	AR
Draughon, George	029	1816	WB-A/226	AR
Draughon, Robert	029	1816	WB-A/227	AR
Draughon, Robert	044	1760	Orig. Only	CTY
Draughon, William	092	1876	WB-6/82	AR
Draughon, William	037	1835	WB-F/175	AR
Draughon, William F.	037	1900	WB-H/464	AR
Drayton, John G.	SC	1891	050 WB-2/133	050 CTY
Dreding, John	028	1758	SS 882/174	SS/AR
Dresser, Joseph	075	1799	WB-M1/32	AR
Drevale, Alvin S.	092	c1826	WB-3/175	
Drew, Alcy	087	c1825	WB-A/122	AR
Drew, Eddie	071	1891	WB-7/135	AR
Drew, Hardaway	100	1858	WB-49/182	AR
Drew, Jesse B.	071	1846	WB-5/54	AR
Drew, John	085	1791	028 WB-A/261	028 AR
Drew, John	005	1816	WB-2/33	AR
Drew, John	100	1827	WB-31/50	AR
Drew, John	087	1886	WB-3/329	AR
Drew, Joshua	047	1841	WB-4/196	AR
Drew, Mary E.	010	1892	WB-I/344	AR
Drew, Mary L. W.	037	1898	WB-H/432	AR
Drew, Thomas	047	1812	WB-3/525	AR
Drew, William	047	1827	WB-4/31	AR
Drew, Winnifred	071	1846	WB-5/52	AR
Drewit, Fanny	071	1829	WB-4/60	AR
Drewry, Darling	071	1810	WB-3/27	AR
Drewry, Mary W.	071	1885	WB-6/485	AR
Drewry, William	046	1826	WB-B/347	
Dring, Pearcival	030	c1807	WB-3/37	
Drinkwater, John	008	1718	009 DB-1/287	SS/AR
Driskell, John	086	1811	WB-B/253	AR
Driver, Giles	039	1852	WB-N/335	AR-Nunc.
Driver, John W.	105	1861	WB-1/65	AR
Driver, Nancy A.	036	1896	WB-A/386	CTY
Driver, Shaw	039	1873	WB-U/65	AR
Driver, William D.	087	1895	WB-3/585	AR
Driver, Zachariah	069	1881	WB-5/117	AR
Driver, Zaney	039	1887	WB-U/392	AR
Drizzle, John	010	1836	WB-G/265	AR
Drizzle, Mary	010	1838	WB-G/280	AR
Drock, Nathaniel	033	1873	WB-2/29	
Droughan, Walter	010	1766	WB-A/74	AR
Drum, Barbary	021	c1884	WB-2/383	
Drum, John	021	1844	WB-1/18	AR
Drum, John J.	021	1875	WB-2/138	AR
Drum, Joseph	003	1879	WB-B/114	AR
Drum, Joshua L.	021	1891	WB-2/547	AR
Drum, Mary L.	021	c1882	WB-2/258	
Drum, Melissa M.	003	1892	WB-B/298	AR
Drum, Peter	021	c1849	Orig. Only	AR
Drum, Philip	054	c1835	Copy	003 AR
Drum, Philip	054	c1835	WB-2/188	AR
Drum, S. Peter	021	c1897	WB-3/316	AR
Drummons, Thomas	037	1815	WB-E/89	AR
Drumright, Elizabeth	078	1889	WB-19/246	AR
Drury, Charles	047	1760	WB-1/3	
Drury, Ellis	044	1779	WB-1/233	CTY
Drury, Henry	039	1834	WB-K/4	AR
Drury, Samuel	010	1782	WB-C/41	AR
Dry, Daniel	016	1855	WB-1/246	
Dry, David	016	1879	WB-3/253	AR
Dry, Elizabeth	089	1892	Orig. Only	AR
Dry, Ellen	070	1871	WB-E/224	AR
Dry, Esther	016	1878	WB-3/242	AR
Dry, George	089	1857	WB-1/161	
Dry, John B.	016	1855	WB-1/267	
Dry, Martin	016	1837	PQS.5/405	
Dry, Moses	016	1864	WB-2/110	
Dry, Owen	016	1840	PQS.6/78	
Dry, Peter	016	1855	WB-1/253	
Dry, Rebecca	070	1752	DB-D/47	AR
Dry, William	012	1783	DB-B/162 & 181	AR-Copy
Dryman, Elizabeth	061	c1864	WB-1/89	AR
Dryman, Mary Eliza	061	1886	WB-2/74	AR
Dryman, William J.	061	1900	WB-2/258	AR
Drysdale, Robert H.	079	1862	WB-1/97	AR
DuBois, John	070	1768	Orig. Only	SS/AR
Duach, Magdalene	087	c1785	WB-A/13	AR
Duacks, William	035	1782	WB-A/132	AR
Dubberley, John	028	1796	WB-B/18	AR
Dubberley, Sacker	028	1837	Orig. Only	AR
Dubberley, Sacker	028	1837	WB-C/401	AR
Dubberley, William	028	1781	Orig. Only	AR
Dubberly, Annabella	028	1803	WB-B/182	AR
Duberry, Joiles	047	1789	WB-3/164	AR
Dubois, Abraham	PA	1807	083 WB-2/47	083 AR
Dubose, Anthony	070	c1769	WB-C/65	AR
Dubrutz, Deborah	022	1825	Orig. Only	AR
Dubrutz, Gabriel	029	1824	WB-B/116	AR
Duck, Jacob	056	1796	WB-1/104	AR
Duckenfield, Nathaniel	010	1756	SS 880/144	
Duckenfield, William	024	1721	SS 875/312	SS/AR
Duckett, Margaret	013	1893	WB-C/239	AR
Duckett, Mary A.	013	1899	WB-D/251	AR
Duckett, Mary A.	050	1900	WB-2/340	CTY
Ducksworth, Hannah	068	c1828	WB-B/65	
Ducksworth, Joseph	068	1818	WB-A/365	
Duckworth, Alexander	014	1879	WB-2/192	
Duckworth, Elizabeth	065	1861	WB-J/105	AR
Duckworth, James A.	014	1882	WB-2/225	
Duckworth, John M.	SC	1887	093 WB-2/40	
Duckworth, Rocinda	065	1889	WB-L/423	AR
Dudley, Abraham	057	1802	WB-A/260	AR
Dudley, Alfred	070	1858	WB-C/661	AR
Dudley, Bishop	072	c1787	WI/L8	AR
Dudley, Catherine	070	1852	WB-C/536	AR
Dudley, Christopher	019	c1774	WB-D/135	AR
Dudley, Christopher	072	1745	SS 878/29	SS/AR
Dudley, Christopher	070	1840	WB-AB/345	AR
Dudley, Christopher	070	1764	WB-C/64	AR

Name	Co.	Date	Recorded Copy	Original
Dudley, Christopher	072	1829	WB-1/43	AR
Dudley, Christopher	047	1781	WB-3/2	
Dudley, Creed H.	028	1828	WB-C/301	AR
Dudley, David	072	c1766	RW/L32	AR
Dudley, David W.	028	1859	WB-D/311	AR
Dudley, Edward	072	1800	WB-A/29	AR
Dudley, Edward	028	1745	SS 877/347	SS/AR
Dudley, Edward B.	070	1855	WB-C/605	AR
Dudley, Edward O.	028	1872	WB-E/63	AR
Dudley, Elijah	019	1763	WB-D/147	AR
Dudley, Elijah M.	019	1867	WB-B/37	AR
Dudley, Elizabeth	030	1900	WB-5/290	AR
Dudley, Elizabeth	019	1824	WB-D/145	AR
Dudley, Elizabeth	072	c1770	RW/L46	AR
Dudley, George A.	070	1861	WB-D/61	AR
Dudley, Jacob	028	1824	WB-C/247	AR
Dudley, Jacob	019	1766	RB-A/12	AR
Dudley, Jenny	028	1898	WB-F/340	AR
Dudley, John	072	1751	028 DB-5/161	
Dudley, John	056	1762	WB-1/753	AR
Dudley, Labon	087	1861	WB-2/31	AR
Dudley, Leah	070	1841	WB-AB/348	AR
Dudley, Levi	087	c1808	WB-A/62	AR
Dudley, Malachi	030	1833	WB-3/309	
Dudley, Malachi	030	1820	WB-3/117	
Dudley, Mary	099	1844	RB-25/431	AR
Dudley, Meddy	030	1884	WB-5/108	AR
Dudley, Nathaniel	030	1867	WB-4/266	AR
Dudley, Robert	092	1834	Orig. Only	AR-Nunc.
Dudley, Samuel	028	1877	WB-E/179	AR
Dudley, Sarah J.	099	1881	WB-A/299	AR
Dudley, Stephen	019	1867	WB-B/32	AR
Dudley, Susan J.	028	1893	WB-F/65	
Dudley, Thomas	019	1753	SS 877/95	SS/AR
Dudley, Thomas	099	1801	RB-5/211	AR
Dudley, Thomas	072	1812	WB-A/24	AR
Dudley, Thomas	030	1865	WB-4/252	
Dudley, Thomas	030	1865	WB-4/252	AR
Dudley, Thomas	030	1857	WB-4/217	
Dudley, Thomas	030	1757	Orig. Only	SS/AR
Dudley, Thomas	057	1806	WB-A/288	AR
Dudley, Violet	070	1888	WB-F/143	
Dudley, Virginia	028	1873	WB-E/91	
Dudley, Virginia	028	1886	WB-E/426	AR
Dudley, William	072	1773	RW/L57	AR
Dudley, William	028	1831	WB-C/342	AR
Dudley, William	030	c1849	WB-4/152	
Duer, Leonard	051	1840	WB-A/144	
Duers, Anne	010	1817	WB-G/17	AR
Duers, James S.	010	1853	WB-G/499	AR
Duers, John	010	1815	WB-F/272	
Duff, Abram	046	1791	WB-A/96	AR
Duff, James G.	Eng	1791	Copy	028 AR
Duffell, William	SC	1813	Copy	029 AR
Duffey, John	060	1846	WB-2/270	
Duffey, Margaret	103	c1875	WB-1/94	AR
Duffield, Charles B.	013	1887	WB-B/445	AR
Duffy, Charles	072	1893	WB-4/305	AR
Duffy, Elizabeth	028	1898	WB-F/352	
Duffy, Frances S.	028	1885	WB-E/369	
Duffy, Henry B.	028	1900	WB-F/464	
Duffy, James E.	072	1841	WB-2/34	AR
Duffy, Nancy	072	1893	WB-4/305	AR
Duffy, Patrick	099	1812	RB-10/232	AR
Duffy, R. N.	028	1895	WB-F/163	
Duffy, William	022	1810	WB-A/155	AR
Dugan, Thomas	092	1784	WB-2/28	AR
Duggan, John	096	1763	WB-1/55	AR
Duggan, John, Jr.	096	1763	WB-1/26	AR
Duggan, Lanier	096	1763	WB-1/29	AR
Duggan, Sally	063	1828	WB-2/137	
Duggan, Stanley	063	1876	WB-3/112	AR-Copy
Duggan, Thomas	096	1754	SS 881/110	SS/AR
Duggin, Aaron	063	c1797	WB-1/349	
Duggin, William	063	c1798	WB-1/351	
Duggins, John	090	1826	WB-3/144	AR
Duglass, John	073	1808	WB-D/224	AR
Dugliss, William	047	1761	WB-1/33	
Duke, Albert E.	100	1864	WB-50/71	AR
Duke, Andrew	030	1825	WB-3/182	
Duke, Britton	039	c1800	WB-A/203	
Duke, Burwell	039	1866	WB-S/159	AR
Duke, Burwell	100	1824	WB-26/174	AR
Duke, Dolly	100	1855	WB-43/392	AR
Duke, Frances	100	1829	WB-32/257	AR
Duke, Francis	100	1821	WB-23/253	AR
Duke, George	053	1790	RW-1/178	AR
Duke, Green, Sr.	100	1811	WB-16/31	AR
Duke, Hardeman	073	1839	WB-F/35	AR
Duke, James	071	1790	WB-1/390	AR-Nunc.
Duke, James	041	1808	WB-2/22	AR
Duke, Jessee	099	1884	WB-A/519	AR
Duke, John	100	1787	WB-4/256	AR
Duke, John	085	1815	WB-G/363	AR
Duke, John	073	1880	WB-H/233	CTY
Duke, John	071	1787	WB-1/464	AR
Duke, Joseph	100	1779	WB-3/15	
Duke, Joseph	100	1779	WB-3/13	015 AR
Duke, Lewis S.	100	1864	WB-50/121	AR
Duke, Lititia	100	1871	WB-51/58	AR
Duke, Louise N.	065	1891	WB-L/592	AR
Duke, Mark C.	100	1889	WB-51/235	
Duke, Mary	100	1789	WB-5/100	AR
Duke, Matthew	100	1819	WB-22/12	AR
Duke, Peter, Sr.	028	1771	Orig. Only	AR
Duke, Richard	100	1853	WB-42/151	AR
Duke, Robert	071	1767	WB-1/150	
Duke, Samuel	100	1868	WB-50/260	AR
Duke, Sherrod	100	1782	WB-3/142	AR
Duke, T. J.	018	1894	WB-E/227	AR
Duke, Tabitha	100	1871	WB-51/46	AR
Duke, Temperance	039	c1860	WB-Q/697	AR
Duke, Thomas K.	039	c1857	WB-Q/705	
Duke, Thomas S.	100	1896	WB-51/466	
Duke, William	100	1793	WB-8/278	AR-Nunc.
Duke, William	073	1842	WB-F/139	AR
Duke, William	073	1854	WB-G/44	AR
Duke, William G.	100	1868	WB-50/270	AR
Duke, William J.	036	1883	WB-A/51	CTY
Dukeminier, John	029	1787	Orig. Only	AR
Dukes, Ephraim	037	1845	WB-F/323	
Dukes, J. C.	051	1895	WB-C/506	AR
Dula, Alfred	017	1884	WB-B/108	AR
Dula, Bennett	104	1822	WB-4/29	AR
Dula, Elizabeth	017	c1856	WB-A/156	AR
Dula, Thomas B.	013	1885	WB-B/357	
Dula, William	104	1835	WB-4/185	AR
Dulany, Thomas	072	1815	WB-A/23	AR
Dulin, Ambrose	065	1900	WB-N/380	AR
Dulin, Rice	057	1794	WB-A/132	AR

Name	Co.	Date	Recorded Copy	Original
Dulin, Thomas	057	1792	WB-A/188	AR
Dull, John	038	1885	WB-2/535	AR
Dumas, Benjamin	082	1840	WB-2/91	AR
Dumas, Sally	082	1844	WB-3/18	AR
Dun, Francis	104	1825	WB-4/61	
Dunagan, Anderson	092	1890	WB-6/310	
Dunaway, Abraham	078	1819	WI-8/212	AR
Dunbar, Dun	009	1747	SS 877/37	SS/AR
Dunbar, Franklin	053	1891	WB-11/237	AR
Dunbar, John	096	c1866	WB-3/80	AR
Dunbar, John	081	1863	WB-12/471	AR
Dunbar, Mary	009	c1763	OWB/91	AR-Nunc.
Dunbar, Thomas	075	c1856	WB-M2/43	AR
Dunbar, Thomas	096	1844	WB-3/7	AR
Dunbar, William	096	1883	WB-4/101	
Dunbibin, Daniel	070	1767	WB-C/66	AR
Dunbibin, Jonathan	070	1785	WB-C/73	AR
Dunbibin, Jonathan	070	1783	WB-C/73	AR
Duncan, Abraham	009	1751	028 DB-5/183	SS/AR
Duncan, Absolom	060	1851	WB-2/365	AR
Duncan, Alexander	070	1768	SS 881/302	SS/AR
Duncan, Alexander	056	1869	WB-3/13	AR
Duncan, Alexander	054	1844	WB-2/295	AR
Duncan, Alfred	087	1883	WB-3/275	
Duncan, Ambrose H.	044	1828	WB-10/443	CTY
Duncan, Anderson	044	1841	WB-15/108	
Duncan, Annie B.	056	1881	WB-3/278	AR
Duncan, Benjamin F.	090	1867	WB-5/44	AR
Duncan, Betsy	100	1873	WB-51/52	AR
Duncan, Charles R.	044	1876	WB-23/233	
Duncan, Edmund	035	1799	WB-A/108	AR
Duncan, Elizabeth	054	1803	WB-1/90	AR
Duncan, Elizabeth	044	1873	WB-23/102	CTY
Duncan, George	047	1834	WB-4/110	AR
Duncan, George	078	1899	WB-19/472	AR
Duncan, George	070	1817	WB-C/84	AR-Nunc.
Duncan, George	078	c1841	Orig. Only	AR
Duncan, Howell	044	1874	WB-23/173	CTY
Duncan, Isaac	035	1793	WB-A/127	AR
Duncan, Isaac	044	1845	Orig. Only	CTY
Duncan, J. W.	004	1884	WB-A/65	AR
Duncan, Jacob	083	1864	WB-2/211	AR
Duncan, James	100	1854	WB-43/56	AR
Duncan, James	100	1884	WB-51/191	AR
Duncan, John	066	1862	Orig. Only	AR
Duncan, Louisa	076	1896	WB-A1/202	AR
Duncan, Margaret J.	100	1877	WB-51/114	AR
Duncan, Marshal	092	1777	WB-1/73	AR
Duncan, Mary	078	1796	WI-1/268	CTY
Duncan, Pearson	100	1867	WB-50/243	AR
Duncan, Priscilla	073	1831	WB-E/243	AR
Duncan, Rachael	104	1882	WB-6/219	AR
Duncan, Rebecca	044	1856	WB-20/54	CTY
Duncan, Stanford	044	1888	WB-24/59	CTY
Duncan, Thomas	100	1869	WB-51/33	AR
Duncan, Thomas	019	1880	WB-B/119	AR
Duncan, W. W.	097	1897	WB-2/549	AR
Duncan, William	047	1766	WB-1/196	
Duncan, William	047	1810	WB-3/508	AR
Duncan, William	022	1883	WB-E/290	AR
Duncan, Wilson	018	1881	WB-E/90	AR
Duncan, Z. H.	078	1894	WB-19/365	AR
Duncom, Thomas	090	1836	WB-3/311	
Dundas, John	046	1892	WB-F/229	AR
Dunford, Philip	037	1829	WB-F/99	AR
Dunford, Thomas	037	1842	WB-F/264	AR
Dunford, William	037	1807	WB-D/288	AR
Dunford, William P.	037	1874	WB-G/462	AR
Dunham, James S.	011	c1879	WB-2/200	
Dunham, Joseph	005	1796	WB-A/40	AR
Dunham, William J.	011	1861	WB-1/326	
Dunham, William R.	011	c1827	WB-2/382	
Duning, Samuel	010	1802	WB-E/173	AR
Dunivant, Lucy A.	020	1860	RB-S/215	AR
Dunivent, Elizabeth	020	1855	RB-R/346	AR
Dunkan, William	035	1806	WB-A/121	AR
Dunkin, George	022	1784	RB-1/19	AR
Dunkin, Jacob	035	1812	WB-A/133	AR
Dunkin, Mary	014	1833	Orig. Only	AR
Dunkin, Peter	022	1782	Orig. Only	AR-Nunc.
Dunkin, Thomas	030	1801	WB-2/197	
Dunlap, Alexander	054	c1830	WB-2/112	AR
Dunlap, Bryan G.	068	c1867	WB-C/158	
Dunlap, David R.	065	1859	WB-J/130	AR
Dunlap, Fanny	068	1871	WB-D/21	
Dunlap, Franklin	090	1895	WB-6/374	AR
Dunlap, George	005	1860	WB-C/159	AR
Dunlap, George	090	1900	WB-6/550	AR
Dunlap, Hannah P.	005	1865	WB-C/219	AR
Dunlap, James	068	1849	WB-B/193	
Dunlap, John	046	1805	WB-A/104	AR
Dunlap, Joseph P.	005	1884	WB-D/164	AR
Dunlap, Sarah	068	1837	WB-B/106	
Dunlap, Sarah J.	097	1876	WB-2/103	
Dunlap, William A.	054	1886	WB-5/123	CTY
Dunmire, Adam	014	1825	Orig. Only	AR
Dunn, Andrew	065	1816	WB-C/43	AR
Dunn, Andrew	065	c1803	Copy	085 AR
Dunn, Andrew	065	1791	WB-C/24	AR
Dunn, Andrew J.	065	1863	WB-J/150	AR
Dunn, Andrew, Sr.	065	1805	WB-C/25	AR
Dunn, Ann	039	1845	WB-M/18	AR
Dunn, Ann	037	1809	WB-D/351	AR
Dunn, Benjamin	099	1852	RB-28/141	
Dunn, Benjamin	069	1865	WB-1/596	AR
Dunn, Bennet R.	VA	1894	070 WB-G/226	070 AR
Dunn, Bolling	099	1825	RB-19/523	AR
Dunn, Burrell	047	1854	WB-4/365	AR
Dunn, Cynthia	059	1887	WB-A/460	CTY
Dunn, David	073	1809	WB-D/256	AR
Dunn, David	028	1785	Orig. Only	AR
Dunn, David	028	1768	Orig. Only	AR
Dunn, Demcy	028	c1763	DB-11/196	AR
Dunn, Dilly	037	1853	WB-F/508	AR
Dunn, Drury	099	1799	RB-5/3	AR
Dunn, Eliza J.	059	1886	WB-A/449	CTY
Dunn, Francis	104	1853	WB-5/89	
Dunn, George W.	099	1898	WB-D/214	AR
Dunn, Gray	037	1900	WB-H/462	AR
Dunn, Hardyman	099	1829	RB-21/91	AR
Dunn, Hardyman	099	1823	RB-18/15	AR
Dunn, James	065	1813	WB-C/42	AR
Dunn, James	103	1859	RD-12/673	AR
Dunn, James	065	1800	WB-C/30	AR
Dunn, James	005	1873	WB-D/26	AR
Dunn, James A.	097	c1860	WB-1/167	
Dunn, James R.	065	1888	WB-L/263	AR
Dunn, Jane	065	1842	WB-H/91	AR
Dunn, Jeremiah	099	1854	RB-28/587	AR
Dunn, Jerry	105	1890	WB-2/536	AR

Name	Co.	Date	Recorded Copy	Original
Dunn, John	099	1784	RB-1/168	AR
Dunn, John	028	1783	Orig. Only	AR
Dunn, John	039	1791	WB-A/75	
Dunn, John	037	1793	WB-C/233	AR
Dunn, John	028	1817	WB-C/154	AR
Dunn, Juriah	067	1882	WB-2/128	AR
Dunn, Lawrence	103	1821	RD-4/379	AR
Dunn, Lucy	099	1826	RB-20/46	AR
Dunn, Margaret	065	1870	WB-K/73	AR
Dunn, Margaret	047	1873	WB-6/84	AR
Dunn, Mary	037	1875	WB-G/469	
Dunn, Mary	099	1868	Orig. Only	AR
Dunn, Mary	065	1835	WB-G/194	AR
Dunn, Mary	005	1862	WB-C/179	AR
Dunn, Mary	037	1862	WB-G/222	AR
Dunn, Milbry	039	1864	WB-R/752	AR
Dunn, Penny	037	1847	WB-F/371	AR
Dunn, Polly E.E.	037	1899	WB-H/457	AR
Dunn, Richard	037	1867	WB-G/291	AR
Dunn, Robert	065	1824	WB-C/46	AR
Dunn, Ruth	068	1799	WB-A/203	
Dunn, Samuel	035	1829	WB-A/135	AR
Dunn, Samuel H.	099	1891	WB-C/99	AR
Dunn, Sarah	041	1786	WB-1/55	AR
Dunn, Sidney M.	099	1891	WB-B/495	AR
Dunn, Thomas	065	1839	WB-E/220	AR
Dunn, Walter	028	1800	WB-B/96	AR
Dunn, William	099	1883	WB-A/452	AR
Dunn, William	065	1809	WB-C/36	AR
Dunn, William	033	1893	WB-2/152	CTY
Dunnagan, Anderson	092	1890	WB-6/310	AR
Dunnagan, Lorenzo	073	1864	WB-G/423	CTY
Dunnagan, Sherid	073	1800	WB-D/22	AR
Dunnagan, Tyre	092	1865	WB-5/73	AR
Dunnagan, William	073	1799	WB-C/135	AR
Dunnahoe, Henry	092	1777	WB-1/69	AR
Dunngan, Ruben	092	1865	WB-5/75	
Dunning, Charles	010	1796	WB-D/348	AR
Dunning, Exum	071	1818	WB-3/204	AR
Dunning, John	010	1858	WB-H/79	AR
Dunscomb, Samuel	024	c1776	WB-A/308	AR
Dunscomb, Sarah	024	N. D.	WB-B/48	AR
Dunston, B. H.	099	1898	WB-D/106	AR
Dunston, Edmond F.	051	1857	WB-B/3	
Dunston, Edmund	010	1814	WB-F/264	AR
Dunston, John	024	1726	SS 876/107	
Dunton, David	030	1867	WB-4/263	
Dunton, Dennis W.	030	1854	WB-4/192	AR
Dunton, Leven	030	1832	WB-3/319	
Dunton, Polly	030	1833	WB-3/310	
Dunton, Sandford	030	1885	WB-5/118	AR
Dunweddee, Henry	073	1795	WB-B/292	AR
Dupee, Elias	028	1754	SS 878/190	SS/AR
Dupree, David	099	1900	WB-D/427	AR
Dupree, Furney G.	059	1877	WB-A/142	
Dupree, Haley	099	1830	RB-21/192	AR
Dupree, J. Q.	103	1897	WB-2/180	AR
Dupree, Jacob	071	1815	WB-3/163	AR
Dupree, James B.	047	1856	WB-5/22	
Dupree, James W.	079	1887	WB-2/412	AR
Dupree, Jesse	047	1822	WB-3/678	AR
Dupree, Keziah	071	1814	WB-3/115	AR
Dupree, Lewis	099	1880	WB-A/211	AR
Dupree, Lewis H.	099	1885	WB-B/31	AR
Dupree, Louis Bird	079	1884	WB-2/304	AR
Dupree, Madison	047	1858	WB-5/53	
Dupree, Mary	071	1863	WB-5/285	AR
Dupree, Mary	071	1828	WB-4/45	AR
Dupree, Mourning	037	1882	WB-G/624	AR
Dupree, Obediah	099	1883	WB-A/486	AR
Dupree, Redmond R.	037	1877	WB-G/506	AR
Dupree, S. G.	099	1874	RB-35/241	AR
Dupree, Sarah D.	099	1886	WB-B/147	AR
Dupree, Tabitha	071	1846	WB-5/45	AR
Dupree, William	099	1851	RB-27/205	AR
Dupree, Willie Ann	099	1874	RB-35/241	
Dupree, Willis	037	1849	WB-F/430	AR
Duprer, Amelia	011	c1796	WB-1/460	
Dupuy, John J.	065	1898	WB-N/154	AR
Durand, John L.	028	1854	WB-D/221	
Durant, Ann	002	1694	Orig. Only	SS/AR
Durant, George	002	1693/4	Orig. Only	SS/AR
Durant, George	002	1730	024 WB-A/146	SS/AR
Durant, Thomas	077	1734	SS 876/302	SS/AR
Durant, Thomas A.	012	1896	WB-A/104	AR
Durden, David	053	1796	RW-1/268	AR
Durden, Elizabeth	078	1887	WB-19/207	AR
Durden, Jacob	053	1790	RW-1/194	AR
Durden, Jacob	009	1816	OB-A/253	AR
Durden, James	078	1867	WB-18/465	AR
Durden, Samuel J.	009	1824	OB-A/338	AR
Durfey, Patrick	085	c1781	WB-B/40	AR
Durfey, Peleg	019	1774	WB-D/164	AR
Durham, Alexander	022	1879	WB-E/173	AR
Durham, Alvis	073	1881	WB-H/283	CTY
Durham, C. C.	026	1897	WB-2/549	AR
Durham, Elbert S.	022	1859	WB-D/41	AR
Durham, Gregory	020	1816	RB-G/154	
Durham, Harry	056	1893	WB-2/153	AR
Durham, Isaac	020	1823	RB-I/235	AR
Durham, James	056	1769	WB-1/784	AR
Durham, James	104	1818	WB-3/186	AR
Durham, James	104	1897	WB-7/56	AR
Durham, James W.	073	1866	WB-G/507	CTY
Durham, Jesse	073	1876	WB-H/152	CTY
Durham, John	014	1803	Orig. Only	AR
Durham, John	020	1866	RB T/149	AR
Durham, John	104	1863	WB-5/351	
Durham, Josiah	086	1840	WB-E/68	AR
Durham, Lou Della	056	1886	WB-3/404	AR
Durham, Lysias	073	1838	WB-F/3	AR
Durham, Martha	073	1888	WB-H/452	CTY
Durham, Matthew	073	1796	WB-C/69	AR
Durham, Nancy	056	1892	WB-3/584	AR
Durham, Sallie J.	026	1873	WB-2/99	AR
Durham, Sarah	073	1848	WB-F/422	AR
Durham, Susana	073	1799	WB-C/137	AR
Durham, Thomas	073	1803	WB-D/103	AR
Durham, Thomas L.	001	1885	WB-2/273	AR
Durham, Walter A.	036	1899	WB-A/476	CTY
Durham, William	100	1793	WB-6/249	AR
Durham, William	073	1839	WB-F/34	AR
Durham, William	056	1803	WB-1/142	AR
Durham, William	056	1879	WB-3/220	AR
Durley, Mary	037	1835	Orig. Only	AR-Nunc.
Durrance, Samuel	096	1756	SS 879/222	SS/AR
Dusenbery, Henry R.	032	c1852	WB-2/69	AR
Dusenbery, Mary Bowie	016	1881	WB-3/339	AR
Dusenbery, Samuel	032	1829	WB-1/125	
Duskin, William	073	1872	WB-H/58	CTY

Name	Co.	Date	Recorded Copy	Original
Duston, John	024	1726	Copy	AR
Dutcher, Samuel	030	1888	WB-5/162	AR
Dutton, James	NY	1879	028 WB-F/418	
Dutton, Zachariah	044	1829	WB-11/209	CTY
Duttrow, Balser	085	c1801	WB-E/252	AR
Duty, James R.	044	1879	WB-23/350	CTY
Duty, Lucy	044	1865	WB-22/383	CTY
Duty, Matthew	020	1782	RB-A/215	
Duty, Richard	044	1795	WB-3/181	CTY
Duty, William	022	1815	WB-A/262	AR
Duvall, Alvin S.	092	1827	WB-3/175	AR
Duvall, James W.	050	1882	WB-1/191	CTY
Duvall, John R.	061	c1862	WB-1/79	AR
Duvall, Thomas	006	c1885	WB-E/114	AR
Duvall, Thomas I.	061	1900	WB-2/255	AR
Duvals, Kisin	096	1884	WB-4/118	
Dweight, Matthew	024	1738	LGB-4/#70	SS/AR
Dweyer, Darbey	065	1787	WB-C/16	AR
Dwiggins, John B.	046	1897	WB-F/562	AR
Dwiggins, John, Sr.	085	1815	WB-G/362	AR
Dwiggins, Robert	046	1789	WB-A/92	AR
Dwiggins, Sally	046	1870	WB-E/35	AR
Dwiggins, Samuel	046	1862	WB-D/124	AR
Dwiggins, Ursely	033	1867	WB-1/205	
Dwyar, James	SC	1873	065 WB-K/119	065 AR
Dwyer, Dennis	010	1790	WB-D/151	AR
Dwyer, Elizabeth	010	1795	WB-D/304	AR
Dwyer, Morgan	010	1787	WB-D/71	AR
Dwyer, Patrick	047	1809	WB-3/486	AR
Dyar, James	047	1771	WB-1/289	
Dyarnett, Mumford	005	1823	WB-A/91	AR
Dycus, William	086	1868	WB-E/486	AR
Dye, M. E.	029	1891	WB-E/510	AR
Dye, Nancy	068	1797	WB-A/196	
Dye, Reuben	100	1806	WB-13/337	AR-Nunc.
Dyer, Jane B.	075	1882	WB-0/154	AR
Dyer, Jeremiah	060	1805	Orig. Only	AR
Dyer, Samuel	020	1791	RB-B/427	
Dyers, Caleb	104	1821	WB-4/1	
Dysart, Samuel	014	1825	Orig. Only	AR
Dysart, William	014	1837	Orig. Only	AR
Dysert, James Y.S.	064	1848	WB-1/22	AR
Dyson, Barton	054	1835	WB-2/154	AR
Dyson, Thomas	046	c1872	WB-E/86	AR
Eacock, Jesse	065	1823	WB-A/68	AR
Eadens, Ann	069	1831	WB-1/371	AR
Eader, Winston	090	1900	WB-6/537	AR
Eades, Gilpin	054	1885	WB-5/69	CTY
Eades, William	029	1882	WB-E/272	
Eadey, Henrey	075	1750	Orig. Only	SS/AR
Eads, Andrew	092	1881	WB-6/162	AR
Eads, Isaac	090	1817	WB-3/13	AR
Eads, William	092	1888	WB-6/287	AR
Eady, Conrad	089	1855	WB-1/136	
Eady, Samuel	030	1832	WB-3/318	
Eagan, Elizabeth	070	1789	WB-C/93	AR
Eagerton, James	072	1801	WB-A/27	AR
Eagle, George A.	085	1893	WB-3/21	CTY
Eagle, Sarah	065	1894	WB-M/296	AR
Eagle, Solomon	085	1877	WB-1/371	CTY
Eagle, Thomas J.	016	1887	WB-3/561	AR
Eagles, Joseph	070	1827	WB-C/96	AR
Eagles, Richard	070	1811	WB-AB/159	AR
Eagles, Richard	012	1769	Orig. Only	SS/AR
Eagles, Richard	070	1756	Orig. Only	SS/AR
Eagon, James	011	1738	SS 877/160	SS/AR
Eaker, Christian	040	1875	WB-2/87	AR
Eaker, Christian	060	1831	WB-1/223	AR-Copy
Eaker, Daniel	040	c1849	WB-1/53	
Eaker, David	040	1873	WB-2/325	
Eaker, John	026	1885	WB-2/287	AR
Eaker, Michael	060	1816	Orig. Only	AR
Eaker, Peter	060	1846	WB-2/263	AR
Eakes, Woodson	044	1877	WB-23/289	CTY
Eakes, Zachariah	044	1889	WB-24/76	CTY
Eakins, Daniel H.	051	1897	WB-C/539	
Eakins, Joseph	086	1825	WB-D/45	AR
Eakle, Henry	085	1816	WB-G/448	AR
Ealey, Catherine	009	c1803	OWB/416	AR
Ealland, Thomas	070	1762	DB-E/17	AR
Earhart, Abraham	060	1813	Orig. Only	AR
Earl, Abel	026	1889	WB-2/396	AR
Earl, Ann	024	1796	WB-B/7	AR
Earl, Daniel	024	c1785	WB-A/65	AR
Earl, John	044	1797	WB-4/154	CTY
Earl, W. D.	039	1895	WB-V/59	AR
Earl, Zibeah	044	1819	WB-8/288	CTY
Earle, Lizzie	013	1898	Orig. Only	AR
Earle, Obediah	100	1832	WB-33/372	AR
Earle, Richard	070	1777	WB-C/91	AR
Earles, Plesant	086	1860	WB-E/376	AR
Earles, William	086	1803	WB-B/151	AR
Earls, Joshua	086	1890	WB-F/392	AR
Early, Andrew	010	1897	WB-I/505	AR
Early, Asa	090	1833	WB-3/249	
Early, Asa F.	010	1886	WB-I/210	
Early, Benjamin	010	1815	WB-F/276	AR
Early, Christian	010	1856	WB-H/36	AR
Early, Hetty	051	1872	WB-C/77	AR
Early, Jacob W.	051	1892	WB-C/428	AR
Early, James	010	1786	WB-D/59	AR
Early, Jason	010	1881	WB-I/130	
Early, John	010	1740	Orig. Only	SS/AR
Early, John	NY	1891	Copy	029 AR
Early, John	010	1884	WB-I/177	
Early, Justin	010	1819	WB-G/55	AR
Early, Shadrach	010	1798	WB-E/53	AR
Early, Thomas	086	1810	WB-B/242	AR
Early, William	089	1881	WB-2/84	
Early. Elionor	010	1734	SS 876/296	SS/AR
Earnest, Barbara	033	1854	WB-1/115	
Earnest, M. Maria	017	1890	WB-B/178	AR
Earney, John	021	1847	WB-1/56	AR
Earnhardt, George	089	1860	WB-1/214	
Earnhart, George	085	1826	WB-H/348	AR
Earnhart, James	085	1856	WB-K/214	AR
Earnhart, John A.	016	1871	WB-3/32	
Earnhart, Peter	085	1864	WB-K/348	AR
Earnhart, Philip	085	c1797	WB-C/251	AR
Earnheart, Ann E.	085	1884	WB-2/101	CTY
Earnheart, John	085	1900	WB-3/394	CTY
Earnheart, John	085	1869	WB-1/40	CTY
Earnheart, Mary A.	085	1899	WB-3/269	CTY
Earp, Abednego	104	1845	WB-4/304	
Earp, Alice	071	1797	WB-2/133	AR
Earp, Alsey	056	1846	WB-1/271	AR
Earp, Edward	056	1825	WB-1/379	AR
Earp, Edward	099	1784	RB-1/170	AR
Earp, Littleberry	099	1876	RB-35/335	AR
Earp, Patience	056	1888	WB-3/469	AR

Name	Co.	Date	Recorded Copy	Original
Earp, Shearod	056	1818	WB-1/284	AR
Earp, Welthay	056	1860	WB-1/738	AR
Earp, William	056	1863	WB-2/39	AR
Earp, Wyatt	056	1893	WB-2/150	AR
Eary, Zachariah	085	1815	WB-G/346	AR
Easley, Charles B.	VA	1889	078 WB-19/264	
Easley, James	047	1799	WB-3/328	
Easley, Lucy	047	1875	WB-6/131	AR
Easley, Rhoderick	047	1768	WB-1/221	
Easley, Susan	089	c1864	WB-1/266	
Easley, William	092	c1833	WB-4/75	
Easman, Benjamin	081	1799	WB-2/53	AR
Eason, Abner	010	1815	WB-F/282	AR
Eason, Abner	037	1819	WB-E/223	AR
Eason, Abner	010	1794	WB-D/241	AR
Eason, Agatha	041	1857	WB-3/216	AR
Eason, Augustus	018	1883	WB-E/114	AR
Eason, Bethena	090	1851	WB-4/269	AR
Eason, Betsey	056	1892	WB-2/133	AR
Eason, Coburn	037	1803	WB-D/183	AR
Eason, Dempsey	069	1780	WB-1/10	AR
Eason, Dempsey	105	1874	WB-2/159	AR
Eason, Elizabeth	105	1887	WB-2/431	
Eason, Elizabeth	056	1890	WB-3/551	AR
Eason, Eunice	069	1806	WB-1/170	AR
Eason, Francis	056	1846	WB-2/287	AR
Eason, George	077	1774	WB-C/151	AR
Eason, George	041	1802	WB-1/199	AR
Eason, Jacob	070	1823	WB-C/96	AR
Eason, Jacob, Sr.	041	1831	WB-2/291	AR
Eason, Jacquea E.	037	1892	WB-H/214	AR
Eason, James	075	1887	WB-O/274	
Eason, Jesse	041	1788	WB-1/72	AR
Eason, Jesse	018	1858	WB-D/44	
Eason, John	056	1816	WB-1/252	AR
Eason, Jonathan	063	1863	WB-2/499 & 517	
Eason, Joseph	010	1816	WB-F/302	AR
Eason, Levi	041	1805	WB-1/222	AR
Eason, Lydia	037	1857	WB-G/145	
Eason, Martha	041	1886	WB-4/236	AR
Eason, Milla	063	1827	WB-2/130	
Eason, Nathan R.	037	1861	WB-G/210	AR
Eason, Rachel	024	1845	WB-C/269	AR
Eason, Rena	041	1890	WB-4/301	AR
Eason, Reuben	063	c1780	WB-1/74	
Eason, Reuben	063	1857	WB-2/436	
Eason, Ruben	009	c1780	OWB/158	AR
Eason, Sally	056	1839	WB-1/534	AR
Eason, Samuel	069	1801	WB-1/139	AR
Eason, Samuel	069	1794	WB-1/90	AR
Eason, Sanders	056	1821	WB-1/325	AR
Eason, Sarah	056	1795	Orig. Only	AR
Eason, Solomon	010	1818	WB-G/13	AR
Eason, Solomon	041	1834	WB-2/348	AR
Eason, Stephen	005	1874	WB-D/30	AR
Eason, Susan A.	070	1856	WB-C/613	AR
Eason, William	041	1781	WB-1/14	AR
Eason, William	010	1736	Orig. Only	SS/AR
Eason, William	069	c1783	WB-1/246	AR
Eason, Zilpha	037	1881	WB-G/603	AR
East, Thomas	090	1808	WB-2/97	AR
Easteb, Thomas	085	c1805	WB-G/28	AR
Eastep, Jacob	104	1869	WB-6/16	AR
Eastep, Shadrack	006	1801	WB-A/66	AR

Name	Co.	Date	Recorded Copy	Original
Easter, Abraham	053	1751	028 DB-5/213	SS/AR
Easter, Harriot	053	1829	WB-4/464	AR
Easter, Henry	032	1898	WB-4/344	AR
Easter, John	053	1732/3	SS 876/272	SS/AR
Easter, John	053	1752	028 DB-5/215	SS/AR
Easter, John	053	1802	RW-1/346	AR
Easter, Levi	032	1891	WB-4/113	AR
Easter, Mary	053	1751	028 DB-5/216	SS/AR
Easter, Michael	032	1892	WB-4/173	AR
Easter, Michael	032	1823	WB-1/14	AR-Copy
Easter, Thomas	053	1804	RW-1/372	AR
Easters, Eliza B.	028	1845	WB-D/119	AR
Eastham, George	047	1774	WB-1/376	
Eastin, Samuel N.	070	1799	WB-AB/33	
Eastlane, Mary Ann	022	c1862	WB-D/86	AR
Easton, David	053	1804	RW-1/369	
Easton, John	019	1802	WB-D/167	AR
Easton, Thomas	053	c1804	RW-1/407	AR
Easton, W. Oscar	065	1890	WB-L/438	AR
Eastwood, Israel	053	1831	WB-5/31	AR
Eastwood, Israel	044	1794	WB-3/94	
Eastwood, John	044	1837	WB-13/495	CTY
Eastwood, Margaret	029	1845	WB-C/83	AR
Eastwood, Mary	044	1811	WB-7/172	CTY
Eastwood, Mary	054	1866	WB-3/193	AR
Eastwood, Thomas	096	1767	Orig. Only	AR
Eatman, Alsey	099	1868	RB-35/30	AR
Eatman, Chacey	105	1873	WB-2/128	AR
Eatman, Martha	069	1881	WB-5/133	AR
Eatman, Mrs. K. C.	099	1889	WB-B/357	AR
Eatman, Theophilus	069	1851	WB-1/524	AR
Eatman, Thomas	056	1844	WB-1/563	AR
Eatman, Wiley	069	1853	WB-1/535	AR
Eatmon, Martha	105	1897	WB-3/291	AR
Eatmon, Milly	105	1893	WB-3/85	
Eatmon, Ruffin	069	1826	WB-1/339	AR
Eatmon, Zillah	105	1895	WB-3/150	AR
Eaton, B. F.	085	1893	WB-3/1	CTY
Eaton, Benjamin	019	1891	WB-B/206	
Eaton, Charles R.	044	1873	WB-23/99	CTY
Eaton, Charles R.	044	1822	WB-9/141	CTY
Eaton, George	085	c1797	WB-C/276	AR
Eaton, Henry W.	100	1888	WB-51/267	AR
Eaton, James	024	1729	SS 876/209	SS/AR
Eaton, John	047	1812	WB-3/526	
Eaton, John	085	c1775	WB-C/16	AR
Eaton, John	033	1840	WB-1/26	
Eaton, John H.	038	1867	WB-1/284	AR
Eaton, John R.	044	1830	WB-11/502	CTY
Eaton, John S.	044	1853	WB-19/299	CTY
Eaton, John W.	090	1884	WB-6/144	AR
Eaton, Lucy F.	100	1864	WB-50/91	AR
Eaton, Martha	100	c1875	Copy	047 AR
Eaton, Martha	069	1870	WB-3/12	
Eaton, Martha P.	100	1880	WB-51/148	
Eaton, Mary	100	1856	WB-49/75	AR
Eaton, Peter	092	1817	WB-3/128	AR
Eaton, Sarah H.	033	1895	WB-2/175	CTY
Eaton, Susan	044	1842	WB-15/294	CTY
Eaton, Susan	090	1849	WB-4/260	
Eaton, Thomas	047	1809	WB-3/485	
Eaton, Thomas	100	1809	WB-15/85	AR
Eaton, Thomas	098	1900	WB-A/366	CTY
Eaton, William	060	1803	Orig. Only	AR
Eaton, William	100	1881	WB-51/162	AR

Name	Co.	Date	Recorded Copy	Original
Eaton, William	044	1759	SS 881/156	SS/AR
Eaton, William	071	1789	WB-1/391	AR
Eaton, William	071	1776	WB-1/452	AR
Eaton, William	100	1869	WB-51/11	AR
Eaton, William A.	039	1869	WB-U/18	
Eaton, William A.	047	1818	WB-3/620	
Eaton, William A.	100	1841	WB-37/414	AR
Eaves, A. R.	086	1896	WB-F/513	AR
Eaves, Andrew	086	1861	WB-E/385	AR
Eaves, Benjamin	039	c1800	WB-A/204	AR
Eaves, John B.	086	1900	WB-G/56	AR
Eaves, Nancy L.	086	1889	WB-F/342	AR
Eaves, Richard	019	1779	WB-D/166	AR
Eaves, Sarah Jane	086	1875	WB-F/74	AR
Eaves, Spencer	086	1883	WB-F/207	AR
Eavins, John A.	039	1871	WB-U/49	AR
Eavis, S. C.	039	1878	WB-U/160	AR
Ebert, Christian	038	1884	WB-2/489	AR
Ebert, Eva Barbara	090	1801	WB-1/174	
Ebert, Martin	090	1808	WB-2/89	AR
Ebert, Martin	090	1792	WB-1/25	AR
Ebert, Sarah	038	1897	WB-4/47	AR
Eborn, Ann	053	c1769	RW-1/11	AR
Eborn, Ann W.	009	1850	OB-G/348	AR
Eborn, Anna	009	1820	OB-A/300	AR
Eborn, Arcadah	009	1839	OB-C2/152	AR
Eborn, Edmond	053	1809	RW-1/426	AR
Eborn, Enoch	053	1799	RW-1/307	
Eborn, Ephraim	053	1789	RW-1/181	AR
Eborn, Henry	053	1789	RW-1/184	
Eborn, Henry	053	1732	SS 876/310	SS/AR
Eborn, James	053	1797	RW-1/283	AR
Eborn, James	009	c1823	OB-A/341	AR
Eborn, John	053	1796	RW-1/274	AR
Eborn, John	053	1809	RW-1/429	
Eborn, John B.	009	1830	OB-B/50	AR
Eborn, Lewis Z.	063	1875	WB-3/97	
Eborn, Littleton	053	1758	SS 882/104	SS/AR
Eborn, Littleton	053	1760	OB-A/25	AR
Eborn, Luther S.	009	1842	OB-D/360	AR
Eborn, Margaret	009	1825	OB-A/354	AR
Eborn, Mary Ann	009	1867	OB-M/142	AR
Eborn, Nancy	028	1855	WB-D/239	AR
Eborn, Nathaniel	053	1754	SS 879/108	SS/AR
Eborn, Rebecah	053	1758	SS 882/102	SS/AR
Eborn, Rebecah	053	1794	RW-1/236	
Eborn, Samuel	054	c1809	RW-1/439	
Eborn, Samuel C.	009	1856	OB-K/107	AR
Eborn, Sarah	009	1879	WB-1/244	CTY
Eborn, William	009	1821	OB-A/312	AR
Eborn, William	053	1885	WB-11/160	AR
Eborn, William S.	009	1879	WB-1/246	CTY
Eborn, Wyriott	009	1856	OB-K/220	AR
Eborn, Zachariah	009	1842	OB-D/365	AR
Eborne, Aaron	053	1785	RW-1/133	
Eborne, William	053	1784	RW-1/119	
Eburn, Elizabeth	053	1751	028 DB-5/180	SS/AR
Eccles, Gilbert	029	c1826	WB-B/208	AR
Eccles, Henry	032	1863	WB-2/263	AR
Eccles, Henry	032	c1859	Copy	106 AR
Eccles, John	029	1833	WB-B/227	AR
Eccles, John	073	1820	WB-D/567	AR
Eccles, Sarah	001	1887	WB-2/333	AR
Eccleston, Thomas	024	c1773	WB-A/60	AR
Echard, Barbary	021	1870	WB-2/43	
Eckard, Eli	021	1864	WB-1/194	AR
Eckerd, George	003	1872	WB-B/26	AR
Eckert, Adam	060	1803	Orig. Only	AR
Eckles, William	001	1852	WB-1/73	AR
Ecklin, Joshua	009	1824	OB-A/339	AR
Ecklin, Sarah	009	c1827	OWB/490	AR
Ecklin, William C.	009	1900	WB-2/257	CTY
Eckols, George	009	c1797	OWB/337	AR
Eckols, John	009	1750	OWB/39	AR
Eckols, Joses	009	c1792	OWB/271	AR
Eckols, Joss	009	c1797	OWB/341	AR
Eclin, Charles	028	1785	WB-A/186	AR
Ector, Hugh	001	1859	WB-1/165	AR
Ector, James	073	1847	WB-F/348	AR
Ector, Jane	001	1862	WB-1/203	AR
Ector, John A.	001	1865	WB-1/233	AR
Ector, Joseph	001	1858	WB-1/135	AR
Ector, Samuel	073	1811	WB-D/314	AR
Ector, Thomas S.	020	1863	RB-S/612	AR
Ector, William	073	1848	WB-F/416	AR
Eddings, Spencer	026	1865	WB-1/375	AR
Eddleman, John	016	1864	WB-2/113	
Eddleman, Peter	106	c1865	Orig. Only	AR
Eddleman, William P.	040	1863	WB-1/159	
Eddmonds, Richard	071	1750	Orig. Only	SS/AR
Edelmon, Peter	092	1789	WB-2/87A	AR
Eden, Charles	N	1722	SS 875/299	
Edengance, John	047	1804	WB-3/427	
Edens, Edward	072	1893	WB-4/287	AR
Edens, Ezekel	072	1896	WB-4/333	AR
Edens, Ezekiel	072	1832	WB-1/105	AR
Edens, Florence W.	083	1896	WB-4/125	AR
Edens, Jacob	070	1835	WB-C/98	AR
Edens, John	056	1760	WB-1/781	AR
Edens, Margaret	070	c1859	WB-D/141	AR
Edens, Mary	069	1833	WB-1/392	AR
Edens, Richard	069	1808	WB-1/187	AR
Edens, Thomas	072	1881	WB-4/142	AR
Edeon, Elizabeth	009	c1770	OWB/109	
Edge, Allen	011	1874	WB-2/77	
Edge, Eliza M.	011	1881	WB-2/142	
Edge, J. G.	107	1892	WB-2/74	
Edge, Jordan	075	1843	WB-N/176	AR
Edge, William	010	1857	WB-H/54	AR
Edgerton, Apsilla	103	1865	RD-13/764	
Edgerton, Rosa Lee	056	1894	WB-2/161	AR
Edgerton, Thomas	103	1863	RD-13/534	AR
Edgerton, Thomas	103	1794	WI-A/513	AR
Edgerton, William	103	1857	RD-12/360	AR
Edgeworth, Richard	005	1797	WB-A/49	
Edleman, Peter	040	1847	WB-1/3	
Edmands, Samuell	024	1721	SS 875/310	SS/AR
Edmend, John	054	c1807	WB-1/97	AR
Edmiston, Sary	014	1835	Orig. Only	AR
Edmonds, Howard	071	1891	WB-7/142	AR
Edmonds, Polly	047	1820	WB-3/652	
Edmonds, William	047	1786	WB-3/103	
Edmondson, Ann	037	1822	WB-E/307	AR
Edmondson, Bryant	047	1795	WB-3/240	
Edmondson, Calvin	103	1900	WB-2/283	AR
Edmondson, Danford	047	1894	WB-7/119	AR
Edmondson, Edward	028	1797	WB-B/20	AR
Edmondson, Garry	105	1890	WB-2/541	AR
Edmondson, Henderson	037	1869	WB-G/341	AR
Edmondson, Jane	046	1891	WB-F/142	AR

Name	Co.	Date	Recorded Copy	Original
Edmondson, Joseph	028	1744	Wills.6/L78	
Edmondson, Joseph	028	1743	SS 878/111	SS/AR
Edmondson, Pollard	037	1892	WB-H/236	AR
Edmondson, Pollard	037	1892	047 WB-7/68	047 AR
Edmondson, Rufus W.	105	1884	WB-2/325	AR
Edmondson, Simeon	028	1799	WB-B/88	AR
Edmondson, Smithy	103	c1863	RD-14/424	
Edmondson, Susan	105	1872	WB-2/86	
Edmondson, William	037	1804	WB-D/201	AR
Edmondson, William A.	047	1860	WB-5/88	
Edmondson, William B.	103	1868	RD-14/649	AR
Edmondston, Catherine	047	c1874	Copy	099 AR
Edmondston, Catherine	047	1875	WB-6/128	AR
Edmons, Elizabeth	013	1837	WB-A/46	
Edmonson, Bryan	028	1831	WB-C/344	AR
Edmonson, Milly	016	1844	WB-1/27	
Edmonson, Penny	063	c1799	WB-1/408	
Edmonson, Reuben	063	c1797	WB-1/347	
Edmonson, William	047	1845	WB-4/247	
Edmonston, Bazil B.	055	1882	WB-A/55	
Edmonston, James	104	1793	WB-1/372	AR
Edmonston, Margaret	054	c1807	WB-1/95	AR
Edmonston, N.	049	c1867	WB-1/3	AR
Edmonston, Rufus A.	055	1863	ID/144	
Edmund, John	070	1762	DB-E/17	AR
Edmund, Robert A.	083	1888	WB-4/45	AR
Edmunds, Augustus	047	1866	WB-5/149	
Edmunds, Benjamin	047	1857	WB-5/37	
Edmunds, Carter	071	1829	WB-4/52	AR
Edmunds, Charles	047	1828	WB-4/45	
Edmunds, Elizabeth	071	1822	WB-3/274	AR
Edmunds, Howell	071	1810	WB-3/30	AR
Edmunds, Howell	071	1814	WB-3/116	AR
Edmunds, Jane	071	1798	WB-2/166	AR
Edmunds, John	071	1788	WB-1/392	AR
Edmunds, Joseph N.	VA	1894	014 WB-2/524	014 CTY
Edmunds, Nathaniel	071	1896	WB-7/301	AR
Edmunds, Nicholas	071	1840	WB-4/210	AR
Edmunds, Nicholas	071	1796	WB-2/127	AR
Edmunds, Sarah E.	098	1893	WB-A/180	Nunc.
Edmundson, Bryan	028	1794	WB-A/321	AR
Edmundson, Bryant	072	c1769	RW/L53	AR
Edmundson, Burwell	103	1894	WB-2/67	AR
Edmundson, James	079	1865	WB-1/129	
Edmundson, James	103	1799	WI-B/273	AR
Edmundson, Joseph	028	1788	WB-A/166	AR
Edmundson, Mary W.	103	1894	WB-2/64	AR
Edmundson, Rufus	103	1888	WB-1/433	AR
Edmundson, Thomas	063	1790	WB-1/160	
Edmundson, Thomas	047	1792	WB-3/205	
Edmundson, Thomas	063	c1792	WB-1/191	
Edmundson, Zilla	105	1895	WB-3/150	AR
Edney, James M.	NY	1866	013 WB-B/449	013 AR
Edney, Joseph	075	1797	WB-M1/1	AR
Edney, Rufus	050	1897	WB-2/277	CTY
Edny, Asa	050	1850	WB-1/29	CTY-Copy
Edny, Robert	075	1758	SS 882/162	SS/AR
Edward, Cullen	047	1784	WB-3/70	
Edward, John	065	1775	WB-C/52	AR
Edwards, Abner	079	1891	WB-2/539	AR
Edwards, Alfred	046	1889	WB-F/8	AR
Edwards, Allen	011	1881	WB-2/138	
Edwards, Allen	009	1875	WB-1/140	CTY
Edwards, Amanda	105	1898	WB-3/29	AR

Name	Co.	Date	Recorded Copy	Original
Edwards, Amanda	004	1895	WB-A/161	AR
Edwards, Amos	026	1880	WB-2/210	AR
Edwards, Ann	092	1820	WB-3/146	AR
Edwards, Ann H.	039	1893	WB-U/581	
Edwards, Arabella	078	1860	WB-18/154	AR
Edwards, Augustus R.	039	1863	WB-R/524	
Edwards, Axum	071	1847	WB-5/59	AR
Edwards, Barbara	060	1876	WB-4/143	AR
Edwards, Benjamen	071	c1800	Orig. Only	AR
Edwards, Benjamin	105	1873	WB-2/144	AR
Edwards, Benjamin	083	1813	WB-1/147	AR
Edwards, Berry	004	1879	WB-A/37	AR
Edwards, Berry, Sr.	004	1871	WB-A/1	AR
Edwards, Betsy, Sr.	037	1818	WB-E/177	AR
Edwards, Briggs S.	039	1845	WB-M/44	AR
Edwards, Britain	037	1817	WB-E/165	AR
Edwards, Britton	009	1844	OB-E/298	AR
Edwards, Catherine	011	1755	Orig. Only	SS/AR
Edwards, Charity	071	1788	WB-1/380	AR
Edwards, Charity	037	1896	WB-H/366	AR
Edwards, Charles	044	1815	WB-7/551	CTY
Edwards, Charles	011	c1811	WB-2/309	
Edwards, Daniel	005	1800	WB-2/34	AR
Edwards, Daniel	039	1849	WB-N/315	
Edwards, Daniel	039	1812	WB-C/299	AR
Edwards, David	009	1829	OB-B/31	AR
Edwards, David	103	1839	RD-7/441	AR
Edwards, David	009	1821	OB-A/307	AR
Edwards, David	022	1849	WB-C/247	AR
Edwards, David, Sr.	013	1845	WB-A/99	
Edwards, Dempsey	071	1823	WB-3/292	AR
Edwards, Dempsy	071	1853	WB-5/110	AR
Edwards, Dolley	070	1886	WB-F/26	AR
Edwards, Edward	022	1790	RB-1/39	AR
Edwards, Edward	090	1844	WB-4/174	AR
Edwards, Edward	071	1758	SS 882/32	SS/AR
Edwards, Edward	020	1868	WB-A/10	CTY
Edwards, Edward	022	1868	WB-E/19	AR
Edwards, Edward H.	090	1863	WB-4/357	AR
Edwards, Eliza Ann	005	1897	WB-D/418	AR
Edwards, Elizabeth	045	1881	WB-1/70	AR
Edwards, Elizabeth	035	1880	WB-4/205	AR
Edwards, Elizabeth	072	1792	Orig. Only	AR
Edwards, Emanuel	009	1828	OB-A/507	AR
Edwards, Francis C.	044	1897	WB-24/360	CTY
Edwards, Frederick	035	1863	WB-3/75	AR
Edwards, George	069	1815	WB-1/269	AR
Edwards, George	086	1862	WB-E/394	AR
Edwards, George M.	086	1891	WB-F/410	AR
Edwards, George R.	084	1829	WB-B/11	CTY
Edwards, Gideon	092	1810	WB-2/57A	AR
Edwards, Gray	039	1855	WB-O/326	AR
Edwards, Hallon	045	1881	WB-1/67	
Edwards, Hannah	022	1854	WB-C/375	AR
Edwards, Hanuel	085	1769	WB-A/23	AR
Edwards, Helen M.	MA	1884	013 WB-B/330	013 AR
Edwards, Henry	037	1758	Orig. Only	SS/AR
Edwards, Henry	073	1850	WB-F/466	AR
Edwards, Henry	069	1850	WB-1/519	AR
Edwards, Hester	069	1898	WB-6/36	AR
Edwards, Hugh	022	1849	WB-C/233	AR
Edwards, Isaac	103	1863	RD-13/686	AR
Edwards, Isaac	022	1848	WB-C/226	AR
Edwards, Isaac	071	1759	Orig. Only	SS/AR
Edwards, Isaac	071	1822	WB-3/272	AR

Name	Co.	Date	Recorded Copy	Original
Edwards, Isham	013	1847	WB-A/125	
Edwards, J. S.	060	1887	WB-4/378	AR
Edwards, Jacob	056	1885	WB-3/367	AR
Edwards, James	005	1879	WB-D/79	AR
Edwards, James	046	c1817	Orig. Only	AR
Edwards, James	046	1868	WB-D/388	AR
Edwards, James	009	1874	WB-1/128	CTY
Edwards, James	022	c1817	WB-C/1	AR
Edwards, James	071	1864	WB-5/295	AR
Edwards, James E.	079	1889	WB-2/465	AR
Edwards, James F.	004	1890	WB-A/116	AR
Edwards, James F. R.	100	1872	WB-51/63	AR
Edwards, James L.	021	1892	WB-3/16	
Edwards, Jane	105	1885	WB-2/371	AR
Edwards, Jane	006	1847	WB-A/23	AR
Edwards, Jesse	047	1797	WB-3/286	
Edwards, Joel	022	1851	WB-C/299	AR
Edwards, Joel	071	1857	WB-5/192	AR
Edwards, Joel	037	1890	WB-H/179	AR
Edwards, John	073	1801	WB-D/56	AR
Edwards, John	097	1877	WB-2/129	AR
Edwards, John	073	1818	WB-D/520	AR
Edwards, John	071	1765	WB-1/119 & 122	
Edwards, John	080	1886	WB-1/119	AR
Edwards, John	070	1744	SS 877/16	SS/AR
Edwards, John	103	1810	RD-1/306	AR
Edwards, John	044	1792	WB-2/286	CTY-Nunc.
Edwards, John	086	1862	WB-E/395	AR
Edwards, John	021	1860	WB-1/156	AR
Edwards, John	015	1765	RB-1/32	AR
Edwards, John	071	1829	WB-4/51	AR
Edwards, John	071	1760	WB-1/36	
Edwards, John	005	1855	WB-C/104	AR
Edwards, John C.	004	c1890	WB-A/104	AR
Edwards, John D.	071	1888	WB-7/1	AR
Edwards, John M.	071	1849	WB-5/76	AR
Edwards, John M.	071	1819	WB-3/216	AR
Edwards, John W.	021	1865	WB-1/209	AR
Edwards, John W.	044	1858	WB-20/622	CTY
Edwards, John, Sr.	005	1814	WB-2/35	AR
Edwards, Joseph	099	1796	Orig. Only	029 AR
Edwards, Joseph	056	1890	WB-3/548	
Edwards, Joseph	047	1794	WB-3/228	
Edwards, Joseph B.	046	1871	WB-E/156	AR
Edwards, Joshua	046	1829	WB-B/399	AR
Edwards, Joshua	022	1824	WB-B/83	AR
Edwards, Judith	044	1802	WB-5/190	CTY
Edwards, Kinchen	037	1851	Orig. Only	AR
Edwards, Letticca	071	1889	WB-7/44	AR
Edwards, Lewis	060	1866	WB-3/87	AR
Edwards, Littleton	044	1826	WB-10/239	CTY
Edwards, Lucretia	045	1897	WB-1/389	AR
Edwards, Lucy	100	1845	WB-38/397	AR
Edwards, Lucy N.	054	1877	WB-4/165	CTY
Edwards, M. B.	065	1892	WB-M/42	AR
Edwards, Mahala T.	105	1896	WB-3/174	AR
Edwards, Malcom M.	080	c1862	Orig. Only	AR
Edwards, Margaret	078	1854	WB-17/229	AR
Edwards, Maria	059	1885	WB-A/419	CTY
Edwards, Mark	071	1811	WB-3/53	AR
Edwards, Martha	069	1828	WB-1/356	AR
Edwards, Martha	047	1793	WB-3/216	
Edwards, Martha Ann	062	1887	WB-B/83	AR

Name	Co.	Date	Recorded Copy	Original
Edwards, Mary	071	1855	WB-5/137	AR
Edwards, Mary	035	1878	WB-4/130	AR
Edwards, Mary Ann	071	1890	WB-7/76	AR
Edwards, Mary Ann	099	1888	WB-B/258	AR
Edwards, Mary Jane	099	1889	WB-B/353	AR
Edwards, Maryan	071	1813	WB-3/105	AR
Edwards, Matilda	106	1889	WB-2/288	AR
Edwards, Matthew	069	1875	WB-5/33	AR
Edwards, Matthew	035	1817	WB-A/143	AR
Edwards, Matthew A.	065	1869	WB-K/26	AR
Edwards, Matthew G.	097	1874	WB-2/73	AR-Nunc.
Edwards, Micajah	037	1796	WB-C/352	AR
Edwards, Micajah	056	1816	WB-1/256	AR
Edwards, Micajah	071	1857	WB-5/183	AR
Edwards, Milley	069	1853	WB-1/533	AR
Edwards, Milton S.	046	1866	WB-D/284	AR
Edwards, Moses	029	1822	WB-B/89	AR
Edwards, Nancy	037	1855	WB-G/99	AR
Edwards, Nancy	029	1816	WB-A/238	AR
Edwards, Nancy	071	1858	WB-5/203	AR
Edwards, Nathan	037	1814	WB-E/75	AR
Edwards, Nathan	045	c1875	Orig. Only	AR-Copy
Edwards, Nathaniel	005	c1793	WB-A/31	AR
Edwards, Nathaniel	071	1814	WB-3/122	AR
Edwards, P. W.	049	1887	WB-2/143	AR
Edwards, Pomfret	044	1842	WB-15/303	CTY
Edwards, R. V.	039	1888	WB-U/435	AR
Edwards, Raiford	056	1894	WB-2/189	AR
Edwards, Rial	009	1819	OB-A/295	AR
Edwards, Rice	071	1767	WB-1/149	
Edwards, Richard	004	1875	WB-A/29	AR
Edwards, Richard	056	1762	DB-D/L105	AR
Edwards, Robert	060	1899	WB-5/124	AR
Edwards, Robert	029	1803	WB-A/62	AR
Edwards, Robert J.	011	1895	WB-3/71	
Edwards, Robert P.	021	1891	WB-3/8	AR
Edwards, Sallie F.	045	1900	WB-1/411	
Edwards, Sally	037	1861	WB-G/204	AR
Edwards, Sally	098	1886	WB-A/51	CTY
Edwards, Sampson	103	1881	WB-1/221	AR
Edwards, Samuel	071	1790	WB-1/398	AR
Edwards, Samuel	044	1877	WB-23/287	CTY
Edwards, Samuel	047	1764	WB-1/131	
Edwards, Samuel J.	071	1868	WB-5/257	AR
Edwards, Samuel S.	046	1880	WB-E/284	AR
Edwards, Samuel T.	100	1875	WB-51/86	AR
Edwards, Sarah	056	1894	WB-2/170	AR
Edwards, Seth	099	1888	WB-B/270	AR
Edwards, Shepherd	005	1894	WB-D/339	AR
Edwards, Silas	079	1884	WB-2/297	AR
Edwards, Siley	037	1843	WB-F/299	AR
Edwards, Simon	005	1827	WB-A/129	AR
Edwards, Simon	009	c1876	Orig. Only	CTY
Edwards, Simon	057	1781	WB-A/5	AR
Edwards, Solomon	069	1823	WB-1/315	AR
Edwards, Sopha	056	1898	WB-4/105	AR
Edwards, Stephen	011	1884	WB-2/182	
Edwards, Stokes	022	c1838	WB-C/90	AR
Edwards, Stourton	037	1784	WB-B/130	AR
Edwards, Susan	083	1843	WB-1/415	AR
Edwards, Temperance	071	1860	WB-5/226	AR
Edwards, Thomas	044	1792	WB-2/289	CTY
Edwards, Thomas	009	1877	WB-1/182	CTY
Edwards, Thomas A.	046	1855	WB-C/435	AR
Edwards, Titus	039	1848	WB-N/312	AR

Name	Co.	Date	Recorded Copy	Original
Edwards, Titus	039	c1842	WB-0/340	
Edwards, Titus	010	1785	WB-D/43	AR
Edwards, W. F.	045	1899	WB-1/362	AR
Edwards, Walker	009	c1805	OWB/431	AR
Edwards, Weldon N.	100	1873	WB-51/97	AR
Edwards, William	092	1862	WB-5/62	AR
Edwards, William	081	1846	WB-8/345	AR
Edwards, William	071	1811	WB-3/50	AR
Edwards, William	022	1810	WB-A/179	AR
Edwards, William	056	1787	WB-1/1	AR
Edwards, William	010	1785	WB-D/45	AR
Edwards, William	073	1784	WB-A/300	AR
Edwards, William	040	c1864	WB-1/200	
Edwards, William	071	1777	WB-1/5	AR
Edwards, William	054	1857	WB-3/119	AR
Edwards, William	009	1900	WB-2/263	CTY
Edwards, William	086	1811	WB-B/252	AR
Edwards, William B.	009	1817	OB-A/276	AR
Edwards, William H.	069	1860	WB-1/566	AR
Edwards, William H.	079	1886	WB-2/366	AR
Edwards, William J.	100	1879	WB-51/145	AR
Edwards, William W.	106	c1860	WB-1/74	AR
Edwards, William W.	037	1882	WB-G/630	AR
Edwards, Winnie W.	080	1888	WB-1/134	AR
Edwards, Zachariah	044	c1868	WB-23/19	CTY
Edway, Thomas	030	1803	WB-2/228	
Edwell, Sally	020	1887	WB-A/519	CTY
Edy, John	N	1727	SS 876/107	SS/AR (N)
Edy, Samuel	030	c1807	WB-2/350	
Eelbanck, Elizabeth	047	1800	WB-3/335	
Eelbeck, Dorothea	047	1827	WB-4/37	
Eelbeck, Henry	047	1785	WB-3/83	
Eelbeck, John D.	047	1820	WB-3/652	
Eelbeck, Montfort	047	1790	WB-3/180	
Eelbeck, Montfort	047	1818	WB-3/625	
Eells, Christian	070	1886	WB-E/569	AR
Effler, Henry	107	1896	WB-2/90	
Efird, Jacob	089	1845	WB-1/31	AR
Efird, John Jacob	089	1897	WB-2/292	AR
Efird, Margaret	089	1852	WB-1/87	
Efird, Martha	089	c1900	Orig. Only	AR
Efland, John	046	1870	WB-E/39	AR
Efland, Peter	073	1793	WB-B/234	AR
Egan, Robert	024	1796	WB-A/300	AR
Egender, Henry	085	c1798	WB-C/271	AR
Egerton, C. J.	039	1880	WB-U/230	AR
Egerton, Gilbert G.	100	1847	WB-39/270	AR
Egerton, James	100	1786	WB-4/153	AR
Egerton, James N.	086	1851	WB-E/214	AR
Egerton, John	100	1851	WB-41/184	AR
Egerton, Martha	100	1811	WB-16/195	AR
Egerton, Mary E.	100	1866	WB-50/186	AR
Egerton, Nancy J.	100	1895	WB-51/411	
Egerton, Priscilla	100	1830	WB-33/296	
Egerton, Thomas	080	1892	WB-1/164	AR
Egerton, Thomas J.	100	1881	WB-51/157	AR
Egerton, William H.	100	1862	WB-49/422	AR
Egerton, Wilmot	100	1815	WB-19/225	AR
Eggers, Brazilla	102	1889	WB-A/62	AR
Eggers, Landrine	102	1884	WB-A/39	AR
Eggers, Landrine	006	1837	WB-A/41	AR
Eggerton, James	077	1750	Orig. Only	SS/AR
Eggleston, Benjamin	028	1785	WB-A/93	AR
Eggleston, Elizabeth	028	1785	WB-A/108	AR

Name	Co.	Date	Recorded Copy	Original
Eggleston, Jacob	029	1813	WB-A/194	AR
Egle, John	085	1858	WB-K/255	AR
Egleton, Margaret	009	c1823	OWB/482	AR
Egner, Margaret	085	c1819	Orig. Only	AR
Ehringhaus, John C.	075	1865	WB-N/255	AR
Eidson, Edward	054	1843	WB-2/273	AR
Eidson, Joseph	054	1857	WB-3/117	AR
Eilers, Herman B.	070	1886	WB-F/64	AR
Eilers, Mary D. A.	070	1891	WB-F/493	AR
Eisenhour, John	060	1821	Orig. Only	AR
Eivens, Richard	077	1693	SS 875/327	
Ekard, Solomon	021	1885	WB-2/303	
Ekels, James	009	1777	OWB/131	AR
Eken, William	046	1799	WB-A/9	
Ekman, Adam	022	1792	RB-1/42	AR
Elam, Barkley	020	1800	RB-C/457	AR
Elam, John	054	1875	WB-4/180	CTY
Elam, Letty	026	1882	WB-2/228	AR
Elam, Thomas	020	1819	RB-H/290	
Elam, William D.	100	1887	WB-51/226	AR
Elbeck, Henry John	024	1803	WB-B/215	AR
Elbeck, William	024	1799	WB-B/189	AR
Elbuss, Braswell	029	1846	WB-C/106	AR
Elder, John	081	1887	WB-16/29	AR
Elder, John	054	c1822	WB-2/115	AR
Elder, John, Sr.	081	1834	WB-6/358	AR
Elder, Peter	092	1804	WB-3/63	
Eldreth, Jane	004	c1882	Orig..Only	AR
Eldridge, Drury	106	1881	WB-2/140	
Eldridge, J. E.	056	1885	WB-3/369	AR
Eldridge, John	056	1880	WB-3/264	AR
Eldridge, John B.	092	1878	WB-6/114	AR
Eldridge, John T.	051	1900	WB-C/579	AR
Eldridge, Samuel	056	1778	WB 2/286	AR
Eldridge, William	056	1857	WB-1/711	AR
Eldridge, William	005	1866	WB-C/234	AR
Eldrige, Elizabeth	IN	1840	090 WB-4/121	
Eldrige, William	071	1751	Orig. Only	SS/AR
Elems, John	064	1863	WB-1/80	
Elender, Mary	104	1859	WB-5/220	
Eley, Josiah	039	1803	WB-B/173	AR
Eley, Margaret	051	1897	WB-C/537	AR
Eley, Peter	051	1884	WB-C/322	AR
Elias, K.	061	c1897	091 WB-1/385	
Eliot, John, Sr.	103	1850	RD-10/400	AR
Eliot, Moses	077	1756	SS 880/121	SS/AR
Eliot, William	035	1784	WB-A/136	AR
Elixon, Joseph J.	044	1886	WB-23/551	CTY
Elixson, Alexander	078	1872	WB-19/24	AR
Elixson, William	044	1831	WB-12/156	CTY
Elkins, Benjamin	054	1887	WB-5/143	CTY
Elkins, Fredrick	029	c1796	Orig. Only	AR
Elkins, John	107	1889	WB-2/54	
Elks, Charles	009	1887	WB-1/426	CTY
Elks, Elizabeth	009	1850	OB-G/262	AR
Elks, John	N	c1708	Orig. Only	SS/AR
Elks, Richard	002	c1687	Orig. Only	SS/AR
Elledge, John	104	1845	WB-4/309	AR
Elledge, Joseph	104	1797	WB-1/466	AR
Ellegood, Matthias	075	1774	Orig. Only	SS/AR
Ellen, Absellam	039	1875	WB-U/115	AR
Ellen, C. N. F.	069	1896	WB-5/537	AR
Ellen, Howell F.	069	1805	WB-1/161	AR
Ellen, James B.	041	1898	WB-4/455	AR
Ellen, Massey	047	1831	WB-4/76	

Name	Co.	Date	Recorded Copy	Original
Ellen, Micajah	056	1861	WB-2/9	AR
Ellen, William J.	041	1894	WB-4/385	AR
Elleott, George	075	1728	SS 876/132	SS/AR
Elleott, James	073	1803	WB-D/292	AR
Eller, Adam	013	1870	WB-B/37	AR
Eller, Alexander	054	1880	WB-4/395	CTY
Eller, Andrew	085	1846	WB-K/14	AR
Eller, Benjamin	054	1842	WB-2/244	AR
Eller, Catharine	085	1877	WB-1/407	CTY
Eller, Christian	085	c1804	WB-C/277	AR
Eller, David	054	1880	WB-4/383	CTY
Eller, Francis	104	c1894	Orig. Only	AR
Eller, George	032	1869	WB-3/16	AR
Eller, Jacob	006	1899	WB-E/393	AR
Eller, Jacob	085	c1782	WB-B/145	AR
Eller, Jane	085	1877	WB-1/409	CTY
Eller, Jeremiah	021	1890	WB-2/494	AR
Eller, John	085	1820	WB-H/45	AR
Eller, John M.	085	1841	WB-I/90	AR
Eller, Joseph P.	013	1892	WB-C/212	AR
Eller, Mary	085	1877	WB-1/411	CTY
Eller, Mary	013	1837	WB-A/48	
Eller, Mary C.	085	1897	WB-3/208	CTY
Eller, Simeon	104	1850	WB-5/40	AR
Eller, William J.	013	1889	WB-B/554	AR
Ellerbe, Helen M.	082	1892	WB-6/450	AR
Ellerbee, Elizabeth	083	1853	WB-2/105	AR
Ellery, William	012	c1772	DB-B/7	
Elles, Unity	037	1818	WB-E/176	AR
Ellett, Michael	073	1757	WB-A/1	
Elliner, James	037	1845	WB-F/319	AR
Ellington, Creed F.	084	1894	WB-F/4	CTY
Ellington, Daniel	084	1817	WB-A/167	CTY
Ellington, Daniel	084	1813	WB-A/99	CTY
Ellington, Edward M.	100	1863	WB-50/51	AR
Ellington, George W.	098	1897	WB-A/280	CTY
Ellington, Guilford	044	1855	WB-20/10	
Ellington, Jesse	056	1864	WB-2/49	AR
Ellington, Jesse	056	1820	WB-1/314	AR
Ellington, John	100	1873	WB-51/53	AR
Ellington, John M.	084	1894	WB-E/562	CTY
Ellington, John T.	084	1897	WB-F/84	CTY
Ellington, John W.	084	1886	WB-E/359	CTY
Ellington, Marshall	001	1875	WB-2/106	AR
Ellington, Marthy	056	1830	WB-1/415	AR
Ellington, Meredeth	044	1872	WB-23/58	CTY
Ellington, Paschal	084	1844	WB-C/6	CTY
Ellington, Richard A.	084	c1883	037 WB-H/92	037 AR
Ellington, Richard A.	084	1884	WB-E/285	CTY
Ellington, Sarah	084	1837	WB-B/172	CTY
Ellington, William	044	1809	WB-7/17	CTY
Ellington, William W.	084	1885	WB-E/302	CTY
Ellinor, Francis	037	1769	WB-A/173	AR
Ellinor, William	037	1798	WB-D/55	AR
Elliot, Abraham	081	1808	WB-3/95	AR
Elliot, Benjamin	081	1842	WB-7/405	
Elliot, George	029	1807	WB-A/100	AR
Elliot, Henry	029	1855	WB-C/341	AR
Elliot, Isabella	029	1876	WB-E/160	AR
Elliot, Jacob	081	1806	WB-3/42	AR
Elliot, James	067	1843	WB-1/4	AR
Elliot, James	075	c1790	Orig. Only	AR
Elliot, James	065	1772	WB-C/49	AR
Elliot, John	081	1796	WB-2/20	AR
Elliot, Joseph	081	1819	WB-4/664	AR
Elliot, Joseph	065	c1779	WB-C/52	AR
Elliot, Joseph	081	1852	WB-9/376	AR
Elliot, Joseph B.	019	1832	WB-A/17	
Elliot, Robert	054	1839	WB-2/201	AR
Elliot, Samuel	081	1834	WB-6/358	AR
Elliot, Thomas	077	1729	SS 876/203	SS/AR
Elliot, W. H.	029	1892	WB-E/524	AR
Elliott, A. L.	086	1870	WB-F/19	AR
Elliott, Abraham	077	1813	WB-E/383	AR
Elliott, Abraham	077	1825	WB-F/99	AR
Elliott, Adam H. F.	026	1887	WB-2/319	AR
Elliott, Alexander	029	1864	WB-D/67	AR
Elliott, Allen W.	032	1883	WB-3/389	AR
Elliott, Andrew J.	026	1893	WB-2/470	AR
Elliott, Ann	092	1777	WB-1/82	AR
Elliott, Anthony B.	077	1858	WB-F/491	AR
Elliott, Augustus	086	1898	WB-F/577	AR
Elliott, Axey	077	1848	WB-F/363	AR
Elliott, Benjamin	077	1774	WB-C/141	AR
Elliott, Benjamin	077	c1779	Orig. Only	AR
Elliott, Caleb	077	1820	WB-F/27	AR
Elliott, Caleb	077	1777	WB-C/196	AR
Elliott, Charles	047	1757	Orig. Only	SS/AR
Elliott, Charles	089	1879	WB-2/78	AR
Elliott, Christian	054	1842	WB-2/249	AR
Elliott, Doctrine	077	c1862	WB-F/537	AR
Elliott, E. O.	021	1900	065 WB-0/118	065 AR
Elliott, E. O.	021	1900	WB-3/303	AR
Elliott, Elcana	054	1873	WB-4/136	CTY
Elliott, Elisabeth	077	1816	WB-E/444	AR
Elliott, Emma P.	026	1888	WB-2/348	AR
Elliott, Ephraim	077	1802	WB-E/151	AR
Elliott, Exum	077	1866	WB-H/12	AR
Elliott, Francis	053	1761	OB-A/35	
Elliott, Gabriel	077	c1861	WB-F/533	AR
Elliott, George	078	1818	WI-8/79	AR
Elliott, George	020	1827	RB-L/241	AR
Elliott, George	085	1805	Orig. Only	AR
Elliott, George	065	1873	WB-K/131	AR
Elliott, Handsel	032	1865	WB-2/313	AR
Elliott, Harvey W.	075	1827	WB-N/31	AR
Elliott, Henry	064	1851	WB-1/27	AR
Elliott, Hugh	077	1876	WB-H/62	AR
Elliott, Humphrey	077	1841	WB-F/302	AR
Elliott, Huskai	077	1815	WB-E/413	AR
Elliott, Isaac	077	1789	WB-C/391	AR
Elliott, James	019	1832	WB-A/17	AR
Elliott, James	032	c1855	WB-2/128	AR-Copy
Elliott, James	046	1847	WB-C/265	AR
Elliott, James	067	c1861	Orig. Only	AR
Elliott, James	077	1831	WB-F/184	AR
Elliott, James	077	1791	WB-C/418	AR
Elliott, John	077	1823	WB-F/58	AR
Elliott, John	085	1850	WB-K/123	AR
Elliott, John G.	064	1899	WB-2/474	AR
Elliott, John P.	026	1873	WB-2/97	AR
Elliott, Jonathan	086	1863	WB-E/414	AR
Elliott, Jonathan	086	1878	WB-F/127	AR
Elliott, Jonathan	077	1856	WB-F/473	AR
Elliott, Joseph	077	1812	WB-E/370	AR
Elliott, Joseph	077	c1831	WB-F/185	AR
Elliott, Joseph	036	1893	WB-A/303	CTY
Elliott, Joseph	077	1788	WB-C/374	AR
Elliott, Joseph	075	1835	WB-N/109	AR
Elliott, Joseph P.	MD	1898	079 WB-3/154	079 AR

Name	Co.	Date	Recorded Copy	Original
Elliott, Joshua	077	1840	WB-F/293	
Elliott, Josiah	077	1806	WB-E/242	AR
Elliott, K. Caroline	086	1888	WB-F/333	AR
Elliott, Lillie A.	064	1897	WB-2/405	AR
Elliott, Lydia	077	1823	WB-F/52	AR
Elliott, Margaret S.	085	1899	WB-3/266	CTY
Elliott, Martin J.	086	1831	WB-D/137	AR
Elliott, Mary	077	1866	WB-H/8	AR
Elliott, Mary	077	1854	WB-F/453	AR
Elliott, Mary Eliza	077	1881	WB-H/111	AR
Elliott, Miriam	077	1803	WB-E/187	AR
Elliott, Mordecai	077	1816	WB-E/467	AR
Elliott, Mordecai M.	075	1892	WB-O/347	AR
Elliott, Moses, Sr.	046	1827	WB-B/355	AR
Elliott, Nanna	077	1810	WB-E/346	AR
Elliott, Nelson	067	1868	WB-1/164	AR
Elliott, Nimrod	064	1857	WB-1/53	AR
Elliott, Osborne S.	032	1896	WB-4/306	AR
Elliott, Pritlow	077	1787	WB-C/354	AR
Elliott, Quinton	077	1839	WB-F/281	AR
Elliott, Richard W.	065	1899	WB-N/257	AR
Elliott, Robert	065	1806	WB-C/53	AR
Elliott, Robinson	077	1819	WB-F/20	AR
Elliott, Ruth	077	1839	WB-F/282	AR
Elliott, S. D.	046	1891	WB-F/126	AR
Elliott, S. H.	065	1876	WB-K/212	AR
Elliott, Sarah	071	1828	WB-4/42	AR
Elliott, Sarah	085	1853	WB-K/150	AR
Elliott, Solomon	065	1774	WB-C/50	AR
Elliott, Solomon	024	1816	WB-C/49	AR
Elliott, Stephen	077	1825	WB-F/95	AR
Elliott, Tempy S.	089	1886	WB-2/131	AR
Elliott, Thomas	064	1889	WB-2/197	AR
Elliott, Thomas	046	1821	WB-B/141	AR
Elliott, Thomas F.	026	1847	WB-1/84	AR
Elliott, Thomas F.	026	1873	WB-2/84	AR
Elliott, Thomas P.	071	1878	WB-6/273	AR
Elliott, Wilburn	006	1898	WB-E/340	AR
Elliott, William	086	1863	WB-E/408	AR
Elliott, William	046	1857	WB-C/494	AR
Elliott, William	092	1802	WB-3/55	
Elliott, William	085	c1791	WB-B/214	AR
Elliott, Willis	077	1838	WB-F/271	AR
Elliott, Willis	077	1830	WB-F/178	AR-Nunc.
Elliotte, Nathan	081	1824	WB-5/169	AR
Ellis, A. D.	039	1893	WB-V/6	AR
Ellis, Abraham	022	1774	Orig. Only	AR
Ellis, Absalom	103	1828	RD-5/435	AR
Ellis, Allen	068	1875	WB-D/64	
Ellis, Allen	022	1877	WB-E/150	AR
Ellis, Altony A.	056	1881	WB-3/283	AR
Ellis, Amanda	033	1875	WB-2/55	CTY
Ellis, Anderson	085	c1832	Copy	032 AR
Ellis, Anderson	085	1832	WB-H/714	AR
Ellis, Arita S.	028	1865	WB-D/390	
Ellis, Batt	071	1794	WB-2/53	AR
Ellis, Benjamin	053	1809	RW-1/429	AR
Ellis, Benjamin	100	1796	WB-8/346	AR
Ellis, Benjamin	071	1845	WB-5/20	AR
Ellis, Cathrine	010	1779	WB-B/143	AR
Ellis, Charles D.	024	1885	WB-E/145	AR
Ellis, Charles D.	024	1885	070 WB-E/579	070 AR
Ellis, Charles H.	026	1873	WB-2/88	AR
Ellis, Christipher	054	c1820	WB-1A/45	AR
Ellis, Cofield	037	1854	WB-G/51	AR
Ellis, Daniel L.	071	1886	WB-6/521	AR
Ellis, David R.	026	1857	WB-1/210	AR
Ellis, Delilah	071	1817	WB-3/194	AR
Ellis, Dollie A.	028	1898	WB-F/344	
Ellis, Edmund	037	1808	WB-D/320	AR
Ellis, Edward	100	1784	WB-4/34	AR
Ellis, Elias	071	1814	WB-3/132	AR
Ellis, Elijah	028	1884	WB-E/334	
Ellis, Elijah W.	028	1884	WB-E/234	AR
Ellis, Elisha	037	1824	WB-F/25	AR
Ellis, Elizabeth	105	1895	WB-3/167	AR
Ellis, Etheldred	054	1853	Orig. Only	AR
Ellis, Etheldred	054	1853	003 WB-B/98	003 AR
Ellis, Evan	085	c1796	WB-C/281	AR
Ellis, Evan	085	1826	WB-H/329	AR
Ellis, Evan	011	N. D.	WB-1/454	
Ellis, Farley	085	1877	WB-1/405	CTY
Ellis, Ferdinand	099	1894	WB-C/319	AR
Ellis, Freeman	019	1803	WB-D/169	AR
Ellis, Gearman	087	1837	WB-1/183	AR
Ellis, George	075	1721	SS 875/295	SS/AR
Ellis, George W.	028	1871	WB-E/47	
Ellis, Harrison	041	1882	WB-4/164	AR
Ellis, Hilliard	105	1900	WB-3/405	
Ellis, Ira	073	1864	WB-G/426	CTY
Ellis, Isaac	085	1833	WB-H/579	AR
Ellis, James	032	1843	WB-1/410	AR
Ellis, James H.	096	1827	WB-2/95	AR
Ellis, James R.	021	1891	WB-2/528	
Ellis, Jean	037	1815	WB-E/118	AR
Ellis, John	073	c1819	Orig. Only	AR
Ellis, John	047	1774	WB-1/343	
Ellis, John	056	1841	WB-1/528	AR
Ellis, John	085	1834	Orig. Only	AR
Ellis, John	039	1896	WB-V/100	AR
Ellis, John	011	c1795	WB-1/372	
Ellis, John	041	1811	WB-2/62	AR
Ellis, John	011	c1818	WB-2/325	
Ellis, John	029	1874	WB-E/128	
Ellis, John C.	029	1879	WB-E/192	AR
Ellis, John Wiley	085	1837	WB-I/1	AR
Ellis, Joseph	037	1803	WB-D/164	AR
Ellis, Joseph M.	019	1891	WB-B/252	
Ellis, Joseph N.	099	1894	WB-C/222	AR
Ellis, Joshua	103	c1871	WB-1/80	AR
Ellis, Joshua	100	1783	WB-3/183	AR
Ellis, Joshua	054	c1828	WB-2/79	AR
Ellis, Katie	099	1886	WB-B/129	AR
Ellis, Lecy	056	1875	WB-3/125	AR
Ellis, Lemuel	022	1890	WB-E/429	AR
Ellis, Levin	073	1879	WB-H/216	CTY
Ellis, Margaret	036	1890	WB-A/179	CTY
Ellis, Martha	100	1850	WB-41/25	AR
Ellis, Mary	041	1799	WB-1/163	AR
Ellis, Mary	019	1874	WB-B/78	
Ellis, Mary	032	1898	WB-4/338	AR
Ellis, Mary	029	1886	WB-E/394	AR
Ellis, Mathew	073	c1863	Orig. Only	AR
Ellis, Matthew	030	1806	WB-2/282	
Ellis, Michael	028	1834	WB-C/367	
Ellis, Rianah	078	1895	WB-19/388	AR
Ellis, Richard	032	1872	WB-3/61	AR
Ellis, Richard E.	029	1900	WB-F/231	
Ellis, Robert	071	1810	WB-3/34	AR
Ellis, S. B.	003	1895	WB-B/331	AR

Name	Co.	Date	Recorded Copy	Original
Ellis, Samuel	054	c1798	WB-1/98	AR
Ellis, Sarah	028	1838	WB-C/411	
Ellis, Sarah	024	c1775	WB-A/63	AR
Ellis, Stephen	085	c1806	WB-C/273	AR
Ellis, Stephen J.	044	1849	WB-17/594	CTY
Ellis, Thomas	024	1820	WB-C/90	AR
Ellis, Thomas	071	1838	WB-4/173	AR
Ellis, Thomas C.	073	1890	WB-H/487	CTY
Ellis, Turner	072	1886	WB-4/209	AR
Ellis, W. G.	105	1889	WB-2/516	
Ellis, W. H.	067	1887	WB-2/253	
Ellis, West	072	1847	WB-2/82	AR
Ellis, Wiley	035	1838	Orig. Only	AR
Ellis, William	036	1894	WB-A/325	CTY
Ellis, William	041	1799	WB-1/165	AR
Ellis, William	071	1816	WB-3/187	AR
Ellis, William	063	1812	WB-2/10	
Ellis, William	037	1813	WB-E/51	AR
Ellis, William H.	073	1863	WB-G/406	CTY
Ellis, Willie	033	1844	WB-1/59	
Ellis, Willis	104	1852	WB-5/64	AR
Ellis, Willis	085	1816	WB-G/437	AR
Ellis, Zephania	054	c1829	WB-2/86	AR
Ellise, Mary	N	c1689	Orig. Only	SS/AR
Ellison, Allman	081	1897	WB-16/461	AR
Ellison, Elizabeth	028	1895	WB-F/201	
Ellison, Henry A.	105	1864	WB-1/102	AR
Ellison, James B.	009	1838	OB-C2/81	AR
Ellison, James, Sr.	009	1865	OB-L/467	AR
Ellison, Jesse	035	1804	WB-A/137	AR
Ellison, John	086	1836	WB-E/26	AR
Ellison, Joseph A.	046	1886	WB-E/441	AR
Ellison, Mathew	028	1892	WB-F/45	
Ellison, Nancy N.	009	1842	OB-D/279	AR
Ellison, Sarah J.	009	1855	Orig. Only	AR
Ellison, Thomas	009	1834	OWB/515	AR
Ellison, Thomas	053	c1780	RW-1/91	
Ellison, Thomas	028	1811	WB-C/41	AR
Ellison, William	070	1737	SS 877/178	SS/AR
Ellison, William H.	028	1892	WB-F/48	
Ellison, William John	009	1862	OB-L/393	AR
Elliss, Elizabeth	044	1828	WB-11/4	CTY
Elliss, John	071	1788	WB-1/381	AR
Ellius, Robert	010	1743	Orig. Only	SS/AR
Ellot, Nancy	059	1873	WB-A/62	
Ellott, Michael	073	1757	SS 880/194	SS/AR
Elmo, John	064	1863	Orig. Only	AR
Elmore, Ann	015	1772	100 WB-1/210	AR
Elmore, Atha	092	1821	WB-3/150	AR
Elmore, J. J.	103	1886	WB-1/360	AR
Elmore, John	020	1830	RB-L/441	AR
Elmore, John	022	1863	WB-D/116	AR
Elmore, John	103	1821	RD-4/418	AR
Elmore, Martha	103	1827	RD-5/326	
Elmore, Thomas	104	1810	WB-2/289	
Elmore, W. K.	060	1890	WB-4/431	AR
Elmore, William	022	c1861	WB-D/82	AR
Elmore, William S.	103	1883	WB-1/278	AR
Elms, Charles	065	1835	WB-G/226	
Elms, Dicy	047	1862	WB-5/101	
Elms, James	065	1848	WB-I/125	AR
Elms, James A.	065	c1862	WB-J/148	AR
Elms, John	065	1869	WB-K/8	AR
Elms, John	086	1873	Orig. Only	AR
Eloris, John	086	1813	WB-B/271	

Name	Co.	Date	Recorded Copy	Original
Elrod, Adam	085	1813	WB-G/253	AR
Elrod, Adam	085	1817	WB-G/459	AR
Elrod, Benton C.	085	1890	WB-2/402	CTY
Elrod, Christopher	032	1827	WB-1/82	
Elrod, Christopher	085	1785	WB-C/82 & 270	AR
Elrod, Maria	090	1819	WB-3/39	
Elsbro, John	053	1770	RW-1/12	AR
Elton, Zachariah	077	1752	Orig. Only	SS/AR
Elwich, Darwin	044	1764	Orig. Only	CTY
Elwood, John	086	1873	WB-F/42	
Elwood, Margaret	065	1870	WB-K/35	AR
Ely, David J.	NY	1877	020 WB-A/363	020 CTY
Emberson, George	085	1833	WB-H/607	AR
Embler, Joseph	013	1889	WB-B/516	AR
Embler, Mary	085	1816	WB-G/416	AR
Embry, Martha	099	1830	RB-21/353	AR
Embry, William	099	1802	RB-6/76	AR
Emenson, Sarah	033	1845	WB-1/68	
Emerson, Ann	065	1816	WB-C/55	AR
Emerson, Eli	022	1853	WB-C/341	AR
Emerson, Harry, Jr.	065	1812	WB-C/54	AR-Nunc.
Emerson, John	100	1788	WB-5/12	AR
Emerson, John M.	022	c1864	WB-D/154	AR
Emerson, John R.	022	1863	WB-D/112	AR
Emerson, Margit	022	1813	WB-A/224	AR
Emerson, Nancy	065	1846	WB-I/63	AR
Emerson, Richard	085	1834	WB-H/629	AR
Emerson, William	054	1851	WB-3/51	AR
Emerson, William T.	065	1814	WB-C/54	AR-Copy
Emery, Edmund	044	1825	WB-10/51	CTY
Emery, Elizabeth	028	1837	WB-C/408	
Emery, Ephraim	044	1799	WB-5/15	
Emery, James P.	028	1852	WB-D/187	
Emery, Laura A.	059	1883	WB-A/186	CTY
Emler, John	032	1845	WB-1/454	
Emmenson, Amey	033	c1845	WB-1/69	
Emmerson, George	085	1825	WB-H/324	AR
Emmerson, Jane	065	1833	WB-G/128	AR
Emmerson, Phendle	085	1829	WB-H/469	AR
Emmerson, Susannah	065	1826	WB-C/57	AR
Emmery, Shadrack	019	1818	WB-D/168	AR
Emmet, James	029	1787	Orig. Only	AR
Emmett, John W.	029	1892	WB-E/536	AR
Emmit, Margaret	029	1806	WB-A/85	AR
Emmory, Stephen	053	c1777	RW-1/84	
Emory, Edward	047	1792	WB-3/207	
Emory, John	053	1869	WB-11/1	AR
Emory, John	044	1881	WB-23/414	CTY
Emory, Wyatt	099	1865	RB-33/352	AR
Empie, Adam	VA	1860	070 WB-D/35	070 AR
Emry, Daniel	089	1871	WB-2/11	
Emry, Green	047	1764	WB-1/126	
Endsley, Abraham	046	c1808	WB-A/112	AR
Endsley, Andrew	090	1817	WB-3/3	AR
Endsley, John	060	1827	WB-1/75	AR
Endsley, John	060	1832	WB-1/245	AR
Endy, John W.	054	1897	WB-6/106	CTY
Engel, Peter	024	1722	SS 876/22	SS/AR
England, Daniel	014	1819	Orig. Only	AR
England, Isaac W.	NJ	1885	066 WB-1/7	066 AR
England, James G.	064	1862	WB-1/79	AR
England, John	014	1795	Orig. Only	AR
England, John	SC	1842	RB-31/502	
England, Thomas	014	1821	Orig. Only	AR
England, William	014	1832	Orig. Only	AR

Name	Co.	Date	Recorded Copy	Original
England, William H.	064	1888	WB-2/176	AR
English, John, Sr.	081	1840	WB-7/335	AR
English, Joseph	009	1744	Orig. Only	SS/AR
English, Nathan	071	1798	WB-2/174	AR
English, Thomas	019	1808	WB-D/170	
English, Thomas	081	1891	WB-16/196	AR
English, Thomas	076	1885	WB-A1/55	AR
English, William	064	1881	WB-2/90	AR
Enloe, Abram	049	c1841	WI-1-2/19	AR
Enloe, Mary	055	1899	WB-A/167	
Enloe, W. H.	055	1900	WB-A/204	
Enlors, Abraham	053	1775	RW-1/65	
Ennet, Edmond	072	1735	SS 877/156	SS/AR
Ennett, Caty	072	1819	WB-A/28	AR
Ennett, Joseph	072	c1806	Orig. Only	AR
Ennett, Lucretia	072	1887	WB-4/225	AR
Ennett, Thomas	072	1846	WB-2/71	AR
Ennis, Elizabeth	076	1889	WB-A1/103	AR
Ennis, William	056	1877	WB-3/182	AR
Enoch, Benjamin	020	1792	RB-C/1	AR
Enoch, John S.	020	1857	RB-R/565	AR
Enoch, Rees	020	c1824	Orig. Only	AR-Copy
Enoch, Samuel	020	1806	RB-E/220	AR
Enochs, David	085	c1781	WB-B/34	AR
Enochs, David	038	1890	WB-3/149	AR
Enochs, Enoch	085	c1787	WB-C/99	AR
Enochs, John	085	1765	WB-A/24	AR
Enochs, John H.	038	1892	WB-3/312	AR
Enochs, Martha O.	IL	1882	Copy	087 AR
Enochs, Molcy M.	IL	1876	Copy	087 AR
Ensley, Anderson	032	c1855	Orig. Only	AR
Ensley, Elisabeth	053	1853	WB-8/5	AR
Ensley, Ella	053	1874	WB-11/42	AR
Ensley, James	013	1875	WB-B/109	AR
Ensley, John	055	1898	WB-A/157	
Ensley, John, Sr.	053	1802	RW-1/342	
Ensley, Mary Ann	032	1886	WB-3/545	AR
Ensley, Robert	053	1874	WB-11/44	AR
Ensley, Solomon	032	1831	WB-1/170	
Ensly, Andrew	049	c1835	WI-1-2/8	AR
Epes, Thomas G.	020	1891	WB-B/49	CTY
Ephland, Cathrine	046	1866	WB-D/312	AR
Ephland, Elizabeth	081	1866	WB-14/44	
Ephland, Peter	081	1846	WB-8/341	AR
Epley, Brozey	029	1765	Orig. Only	AR
Epley, John F.	014	1898	WB-3/46	CTY
Epley, Peter	014	1877	WB-2/139	
Epperson, John	078	1850	WB-13/339	AR
Epperson, Lucy	078	1889	WB-19/249	AR
Eppes, Harriett	047	1836	WB-4/139	
Eppes, Isham	044	1834	WB-13/125	CTY
Eppes, Martha B.	VA	1864	047 WB-5/110	
Eppes, Richard	047	1827	WB-4/36	
Epply, Andrew	014	1885	WB-2/313	CTY
Epps, Peter	078	1861	WB-18/223	AR
Epps, William	071	1821	WB-3/255	AR
Erenhart, Catherine	085	1798	WB-C/278	AR-Nunc.
Erenhart, Henry	085	1805	WB-C/247	AR
Erenhart, Henry	085	1813	WB-G/262	AR
Erexson, Jonathan	072	1801	WB-A/26	AR
Ernhart, Philip	085	1829	WB-H/440	AR
Ernst, Anna C.	090	1816	WB-2/178	AR
Ernul, Aaron	028	1799	WB-B/70	AR
Ernul, Major F.	028	1849	WB-D/157	AR
Ernul, Margaret	028	1861	WB-D/354	AR

Name	Co.	Date	Recorded Copy	Original
Erp, Joseph	069	1819	WB-1/304	AR
Erson, Eric	060	1872	WB-4/96	AR
Ervin, Adolphus	054	1886	WB-5/116	CTY
Ervin, Edward	072	1852	WB-2/123	AR
Ervin, George	054	1866	WB-3/186	AR
Ervin, James	054	1879	WB-4/352	CTY
Ervin, John B.	021	1892	WB-2/584	
Ervin, R. F.	085	1874	WB-1/268	CTY
Ervin, Richard	059	1853	WB-B/13	CTY
Ervin, Thomas	054	c1792	WB-1/99	AR
Ervin, William	081	1814	WB-4/64	AR
Ervin, William	054	c1829	WB-2/156	AR
Erwen, Edward	065	1790	WB-D/94	AR
Erwin, Abraham	054	c1794	WB-1/131	AR
Erwin, Adelade	SC	1885	097 WB-2/284	097 AR
Erwin, Agnes	085	1803	WB-C/273	AR
Erwin, Alexander	014	1877	WB-2/153	
Erwin, Alexander	014	1829	Orig. Only	AR
Erwin, Ann E.	014	1890	WB-2/387	CTY
Erwin, Arthur	014	1821	Orig. Only	AR
Erwin, Cecelia M.	014	1894	WB-2/532	CTY
Erwin, Charles H.	016	1885	WB-3/476	AR
Erwin, Edward J.	014	1871	WB-2/63	
Erwin, Francis	070	1760	DB-D/457	
Erwin, George	085	c1783	WB-B/142	AR
Erwin, James	014	c1842	Orig. Only	AR
Erwin, James	085	1770	WB-A/25	AR
Erwin, James	054	c1811	WB-1/275	
Erwin, James	054	c1794	WB-1/275	AR
Erwin, James M.	065	1895	WB-M/416	AR
Erwin, James M.	085	1887	WB-2/270	
Erwin, James S.	016	1860	WB-2/63	
Erwin, Jane	054	1872	WB-4/97	CTY
Erwin, John	070	1802	WB-AB/152	AR
Erwin, John	054	c1813	WB-1/310	AR
Erwin, Joseph	085	c1793	WB-C/279	AR
Erwin, Mary	054	1850	WB-3/42	AR
Erwin, Matilda	014	1843	Orig. Only	AR
Erwin, Robert	046	1796	WB-A/111	AR
Erwin, Shadrach	057	1836	WB-B/137	AR
Erwin, Thomas	050	c1844	WB-1/20	CTY
Erwin, Ulysses	014	1835	Orig. Only	AR
Erwin, William	085	1815	WB-G/385	AR
Erwin, William A.	014	c1846	Orig. Only	AR
Erwin, William A.	013	1869	WB-B/22	AR
Erwin, William W.	014	1837	Orig. Only	AR
Eshenbrener, Urban	060	c1795	Orig. Only	AR
Eshon, Samuel	024	1892	WB-E/209	AR
Eskridge, Elijah	026	1868	WB-1/421	AR
Eskridge, Mary G.	026	1898	WB-3/13	AR
Eskridge, Richard	020	1816	RB-G/124	
Eskridge, Richard	086	1832	WB-D/142	AR
Esleven, William	085	1763	WB-A/28	AR
Eslick, Francis	072	1816	WB-A/27	AR
Eson, William	077	1719	SS 875/147	SS/AR
Espey, Samuel	060	1839	WB-2/8	AR
Espy, James	070	1739	SS 877/141	SS/AR
Espy, Mary L.	014	1836	Orig. Only	AR
Espy, Thomas	085	1833	WB-H/589	AR
Espy, Usher	012	c1767	DB-A/50	
Essex, Jacob	032	1900	WB-4/440	AR
Essex, Jacob	032	1898	WB-4/342	
Essick, Jacob	032	c1849	WB-2/73	
Esson, Thomas	070	1790	WB-C/94	AR
Ester, Michel	085	1793	WB-C/282	AR

Name	Co.	Date	Recorded Copy	Original
Ester, William	053	c1765	RW-1/7	
Esterline, Ann Mary	090	1799	WB-1/129	AR
Esterline, Matthew	090	1798	WB-1/110	
Estes, Bartlett	084	1841	WB-B/250	CTY
Estes, Delphi	014	1818	Orig. Only	AR
Estes, Eliza	073	c1844	Orig. Only	AR
Estes, Eliza	073	c1844	Copy	056 AR
Estes, Elizabeth	017	c1859	Orig. Only	AR
Estes, Elizabeth	073	1845	WB-F/249	AR
Estes, Frances	017	c1843	WB-A/92	AR
Estes, James	017	1887	WB-B/137	AR
Estes, John	073	1799	WB-C/153	AR
Estes, John	044	1809	WB-7/11	CTY
Estes, Laban	014	1817	Orig. Only	AR
Estes, Langston	017	1852	WB-A/61	AR
Estes, Larkin	017	c1845	Orig. Only	AR
Estes, Louisa A.	044	1877	WB-23/250	CTY
Estes, Martha	092	1889	WB-6/289	AR
Estes, Matilda	068	1899	WB-E/4	
Estes, Reuben	014	1811	Orig. Only	AR
Estes, Richard	020	1802	RB-D/121	
Estes, Robert	VA	1775	090 WB-3/164	090 AR
Estes, W. A.	090	1894	WB-6/348	AR
Estes, Wiley	068	1884	WB-D/176	
Estis, Elizabeth	044	1857	WB-20/197	CTY
Estis, Mary	022	1822	WB-B/100	AR
Estis, William	044	1828	WB-10/406	CTY
Estridge, Ephraim	044	1784	WB-1/399	CTY-Copy
Estridge, Sarah	016	1890	WB-4/69	AR
Etcheson, Edmund	033	c1843	WB-1/71	
Etchison, Caswell H.	033	1875	WB-2/53	CTY
Etherage, Richard	030	1794	WB-2/27	
Etheredge, Elizabeth	024	1852	WB-C/342	AR
Etheredge, Henry	030	1743	LGB-4/#147	SS/AR
Ethergain, James	047	1865	WB-5/122	
Etheridge, Aaron	047	1786	WB-3/114	
Etheridge, Adam D.	030	1869	WB-5/2	AR
Etheridge, Amos	030	1792	WB-1/268	
Etheridge, Amos	030	1784	WB-1/182	
Etheridge, Andrew J.	030	1896	WB-5/232	AR
Etheridge, Asa	096	1817	Orig. Only	AR
Etheridge, Bertheney	018	1871	WB-E/27	AR
Etheridge, Caleb	030	1784	WB-1/168	
Etheridge, Caleb	037	1826	WB-F/63	AR
Etheridge, Caleb, Sr.	030	1880	WB-5/69	AR
Etheridge, Dorcas	030	1855	WB-4/199	
Etheridge, Edith	030	1838	WB-4/56	
Etheridge, Elizabeth	030	1898	WB-5/275	AR
Etheridge, Elmer	030	1780	WB-1/148	
Etheridge, Emmaline	031	1883	WB-1/23	AR
Etheridge, Ephraim	096	1793	Orig. Only	AR
Etheridge, Henry	020	1792	WB-1/257	
Etheridge, Hollowell	018	1859	WB-D/49	
Etheridge, James	030	1804	WB-2/253	
Etheridge, James	030	1782	WB-1/157	
Etheridge, Jasper	072	c1853	WB-4/92	AR
Etheridge, Jefferson	030	1885	WB-5/122	AR
Etheridge, Jeremiah	069	1809	WB-1/242	AR-Nunc.
Etheridge, Jeremiah	030	1858	WB-4/227	
Etheridge, Jesse	031	1896	WB-1/101	AR
Etheridge, Joel	030	1838	WB-4/44	
Etheridge, John	030	1789	WB-1/235	
Etheridge, John	030	1783	WB-1/167	
Etheridge, John	030	1744	Orig. Only	SS/AR
Etheridge, John F.	030	1888	WB-5/160	AR
Etheridge, Josiah	030	1840	WB-4/71	
Etheridge, Mable	030	1849	WB-4/144	
Etheridge, Margaret	030	1831	WB-3/282	
Etheridge, Marian	063	1813	WB-2/15	Nunc.
Etheridge, Marmaduke	030	1735	SS 876/423	SS/AR
Etheridge, Mathias	030	1846	WB-4/125	
Etheridge, Mathias	030	1798	WB-2/121	
Etheridge, Mourning	047	1843	WB-4/222	
Etheridge, Peter	069	c1820	Orig. Only	AR
Etheridge, Polly A.	030	1868	WB-4/271	AR
Etheridge, Reuben	030	1820	WB-3/294	
Etheridge, Richard	030	1750	Orig. Only	SS/AR
Etheridge, Robert	030	1828	WB-3/240	
Etheridge, Salley	030	1842	WB-4/91	
Etheridge, Sampson	030	1824	WB-3/169	
Etheridge, Samson	030	1793	WB-2/19	
Etheridge, Samuel	030	1889	WB-5/169	AR
Etheridge, Sarah	024	1812	WB-C/6	AR
Etheridge, Solomon	030	1749	Orig. Only	SS/AR
Etheridge, Tart	030	1825	WB-3/195	
Etheridge, Thomas	018	1824	WB-C/40	
Etheridge, Thomas	030	1897	WB-5/246	AR
Etheridge, Timothy	030	1798	WB-2/117	
Etheridge, Unity	047	1795	WB-3/258	
Etheridge, William	103	1879	WB-1/164	AR
Etheridge, William	047	1795	WB-3/257	
Etheridge, William	010	1837	WB-G/267	AR
Etheridge, William	030	1847	WB-4/126	
Etheridge, William B.	075	c1854	WB-M2/19	AR
Etheridge, William E.	031	1884	WB-1/27	AR
Etheridge, William S.	030	1838	WB-4/50	
Etheridge, Winney	096	1845	WB-3/11	AR
Ethredge, Luke	030	1735	SS 876/424	SS/AR
Ethridge, Adam	030	c1812	WB-3/24	
Ethridge, Cader	037	1825	WB-F/37	
Ethridge, Demcy	030	c1813	WB-3/22 & 30	
Ethridge, John	053	1803	RW-1/359	
Ethridge, Martha	069	1849	WB-1/519	AR
Ethridge, Mary	069	1893	WB-5/412	AR
Ethridge, Sampson	030	1815	WB-3/71	
Ethridge, Samuel	053	c1780	RW-1/94	
Ethridge, Thomas	083	c1799	WB-1/207	AR
Ethridge, Willis	018	1833	WB-C/142	
Ethridge, Willis	030	c1806	WB-3/8	
Etters, Andrew	026	1886	WB-2/294	AR
Eubank, Allen G.	028	1877	WB-E/171	AR
Eubank, George	078	1798	WI-2/133	AR"K
Eubank, George	010	1732	SS 876/233	SS/AR
Eubank, Isaac W.	028	1899	WB-F/365	
Eubank, Thomas	078	1818	WI-8/54	AR
Eubanks, Barsheba	054	1854	WB-3/79	AR
Eubanks, Elisha	072	1826	Orig. Only	AR
Eubanks, Elisha A.	072	1882	WB-4/134	AR
Eubanks, Hester	054	1854	WB-3/79	AR
Eubanks, John	057	1817	WB-B/44	AR
Eubanks, John	046	1813	WB-A/113	AR
Eubanks, Lot	057	1857	WB-B/235	AR
Eubanks, Sarah	054	1854	WB-3/79	AR
Eubanks, Sidney	022	c1862	WB-G/25	AR
Eubanks, Thomas	057	c1776	WB-A/196	AR
Eubanks, Thomas	072	1808	WB-A/25	AR
Eubanks, William	054	c1816	WB-2/26	
Eudaily, E. J.	104	1894	WB-6/504	AR
Eudy, David	016	1884	WB-3/430	AR

Name	Co.	Date	Recorded Copy	Original
Eudy, John	016	1872	WB-3/98	AR
Eudy, John	046	1897	WB-F/586	AR
Eudy, William	089	1881	WB-2/84	AR
Eudy, William R.	089	1896	WB-2/323	AR
Euless, Eli	073	1846	WB-F/304	AR
Euless, John	073	1846	WB-F/322	AR
Eulice, Philip	073	c1812	WB-D/346	AR
Eulis, Henry	073	1845	WB-F/242	AR
Euliss, Rosannah	001	1873	WB-2/59	AR
Eure, Benjamin	041	1847	Orig. Only	AR
Eure, Celia	041	1884	WB-4/200	AR
Eure, Charles	041	1816	WB-2/122	AR
Eure, Elisha	047	1836	WB-4/142	
Eure, Harriet	041	1889	WB-4/288	AR
Eure, Jethro	041	1856	WB-3/207	AR
Eure, Judith	041	1823	WB-2/198	AR
Eure, Levi	051	1844	WB-A/217	
Eure, Luton	041	1889	WB-4/280	AR
Eure, Mary	041	1888	WB-4/274	AR
Eure, Mary	041	1844	WB-3/58	AR
Eure, Mary	041	1869	WB-4/2	AR
Eure, Mills	041	1834	Orig. Only	AR
Eure, Mills	041	c1823	Orig. Only	AR
Eure, Nancy	041	1842	WB-3/42	AR
Eure, Reddick	041	1886	WB-4/245	AR
Eure, Selia	041	1818	WB-2/150	AR
Eure, Stephen	041	1817	WB-2/146	AR
Eure, Uriah	041	1837	WB-2/394	AR
Eury, David	089	1872	Orig. Only	AR
Evans, Aaron	022	1829	WB-B/156	AR
Evans, Abernall	N	N.D.	SS 880/205	Inc.
Evans, Abner	079	1887	WB-2/389	AR
Evans, Abraham	037	1762	WB-A/95	AR
Evans, Albert	SC	1886	097 WB-2/386	097 AR
Evans, Alice	029	1897	WB-F/90	AR
Evans, Amos	079	1888	WB-2/458	AR
Evans, Angus	083	1888	WB-3/434	AR
Evans, Anne	103	1864	RD-13/734	AR
Evans, Anne	103	1864	079 WB-2/77	
Evans, Anthony	022	1835	WB-C/24	AR
Evans, Arthur A.	070	1843	WB-AB/389	AR
Evans, Augusta J.	047	1886	WB-6/430	AR
Evans, Barbary W.	020	1861	RB-S/381	
Evans, Barnabas	006	1851	WB-A/90	AR
Evans, Beneter	072	1845	WB-2/65	AR
Evans, Benjamin	070	1765	DB-E/132	AR
Evans, Benjamin	030	1777	WB-1/113	
Evans, Benjamin	075	1808	WB-M1/195	AR
Evans, Benjamin	079	1889	WB-2/493	AR
Evans, Berwell	009	1756	SS 879/238	SS/AR
Evans, Caleb	072	1779	RW/L11	AR
Evans, California	030	1872	WB-5/30	AR
Evans, Calvin	079	1883	WB-2/285	AR
Evans, Catharine	029	1880	WB-E/232	AR
Evans, Chalkey	077	1832	WB-F/201	AR
Evans, Charles	037	1759	SS 881/225	SS/AR
Evans, Charlotte	070	1888	WB-F/150	AR
Evans, Daniel B.	012	c1866	WB-B/20	AR
Evans, David	026	1888	WB-2/360	AR
Evans, David	085	c1808	WB-G/123	AR
Evans, David	035	1863	WB-3/77	AR
Evans, David H.	020	1880	WB-A/297	CTY
Evans, David L.	029	1815	WB-A/209	AR
Evans, David L.	044	1821	WB-9/47	CTY
Evans, Duncan	027	1896	WB-2/129	AR
Evans, Edward	090	1800	WB-1/145	AR
Evans, Elias	024	1785	WB-B/158	AR-Nunc.
Evans, Elizabeth	077	1845	WB-F/320	AR
Evans, Elizabeth	079	c1851	WB-1/37	AR-Copy
Evans, Elizabeth	024	1827	WB-C/140	AR
Evans, Enoch	099	1874	RB-35/274	AR
Evans, Enoch	036	1888	WB-A/126	CTY
Evans, Erasmus H.	029	1879	WB-E/202	AR
Evans, Evilina M.	047	1881	WB-6/238	AR
Evans, Francis K.	051	1892	WB-C/422	AR
Evans, Freeman	051	1872	WB-C/60	AR
Evans, George	010	1854	WB-H/11	AR
Evans, George	029	1774	Orig. Only	AR
Evans, George W.	020	1885	WB-A/459	CTY
Evans, George W.	106	1878	WB-2/106	AR
Evans, Gilbert	099	1827	RB-20/100	AR
Evans, Granderson	022	1881	WB-E/233	AR
Evans, Henderson	054	1876	WB-4/219	CTY
Evans, Henry	073	1815	WB-D/427	AR
Evans, Henry	029	1811	WB-A/165	AR
Evans, Henry	030	1785	WB-1/200	
Evans, Henry C.	070	1896	WB-G/487	AR
Evans, Hilbert	105	1896	WB-3/209	AR
Evans, Horace B.	038	1900	WB-4/266	AR
Evans, Hunt	075	1729/0	Orig. Only	SS/AR
Evans, Isabella	068	1883	Orig. Only	CTY
Evans, Isham	103	1815	RD-3/217	AR
Evans, Jacob	012	1885	Orig. Only	AR
Evans, James	072	c1789	Orig. Only	AR
Evans, James	029	1869	WB-E/10	
Evans, James	085	1820	WB-H/38	AR
Evans, James	004	1894	WB-A/149	AR
Evans, James	072	c1774	RW/L25	AR
Evans, James	032	1840	WB-1/347	
Evans, James	024	c1818	WB-C/71	AR
Evans, James	035	1802	WB-A/138	AR
Evans, James M.	044	1893	WB-24/208	CTY
Evans, Jesse	046	1839	WB-C/30	AR
Evans, Jesse	086	1827	WB-D/69	AR
Evans, Jesse	078	1879	WB-19/84	AR
Evans, Joel	099	1881	WB-A/282	AR
Evans, John	029	1815	WB-A/212	AR
Evans, John	072	1837	WB-1/163	AR
Evans, John	072	c1781	WI/L21	AR
Evans, John	024	1739	Orig. Only	SS/AR
Evans, John	069	1806	WB-1/164	AR
Evans, John	024	1770	WB-A/59	AR
Evans, John, Sr.	012	1823	WB-B/129	AR
Evans, Jonah	051	1841	WB-A/147	
Evans, Jonathan	029	1859	WB-C/400	AR
Evans, Jonathan	070	1770	WB-C/89	AR
Evans, Joseph	077	1827	WB-F/134	AR
Evans, Joseph	024	c1783	WB-A/57	AR
Evans, Joseph	050	1869	WB-1/105	CTY
Evans, Joseph W.	099	1854	RB-28/585	AR
Evans, Joshua	056	1805	WB-1/174	AR
Evans, Joshua	029	1896	WB-F/67	AR
Evans, Josiah	029	1842	WB-C/58	AR-Copy
Evans, Josiah	105	1871	WB-2/57	AR
Evans, Leathy Ann	039	1874	WB-U/99	AR
Evans, Lemuel	051	1871	WB-C/55	AR
Evans, Lilly	020	1893	WB-B/153	CTY
Evans, Lucinda	069	1887	WB-5/269	AR
Evans, Lydia	018	1838	WB-C/240	
Evans, Margaret	070	1836	WB-AB/311	AR

Name	Co.	Date	Recorded Copy	Original
Evans, Margaret	079	1842	047 WB-4/212	
Evans, Mariah	047	1883	WB-6/315	AR
Evans, Martha	087	1848	WB-1/336	AR
Evans, Martha	039	1874	WB-U/111	AR
Evans, Martha C.	038	1887	WB-3/55	AR
Evans, Mary	079	1878	WB-2/167	AR
Evans, Mary	010	1870	WB-I/29	AR
Evans, Mary	077	1723	Orig. Only	SS/AR
Evans, Mary	032	1843	WB-1/417	
Evans, Mary	018	1870	WB-E/26	AR
Evans, Mary	020	1882	WB-A/379	CTY
Evans, Medy	010	1843	WB-G/347	AR
Evans, Michael	032	1895	WB-4/248	AR
Evans, Michael C.	010	1796	WB-D/332	AR
Evans, Moses	038	1864	WB-1/242	AR-Copy
Evans, Mrs. A. E.	065	1876	WB-K/248	AR
Evans, Nancy	020	1890	WB-B/39	CTY
Evans, Nancy	069	1896	WB-6/59	AR
Evans, Nancy	020	1879	WB-A/286	CTY
Evans, Nancy	041	1855	WB-3/190	AR
Evans, Nicholas	:92	1774	WB-1/23	AR
Evans, Oran S.	022	1864	WB-D/123	AR
Evans, Penelope	028	1872	WB-E/66	AR
Evans, Peter	047	1853	WB-4/334	
Evans, Peter G.	046	1863	WB-D/185	AR
Evans, Peter S.	100	1850	WB-41/34	AR
Evans, Phineas	Eng	c1759	Copy	010 AR
Evans, Preston L.	024	1872	WB-E/42	AR
Evans, Richard	077	1693	Orig. Only	SS/AR
Evans, Richard	022	1855	WB-C/409	AR
Evans, Richard	009	1753	SS 879/106	SS/AR
Evans, Richard	079	1863	WB-1/107	AR
Evans, Robert	077	1797	WB-E/74	
Evans, Robert	077	1758	SS 880/213	SS/AR
Evans, Rufus G.	020	1870	WB-A/27	CTY
Evans, Ruth	022	c1802	WB-A/43	AR
Evans, Sally	069	1866	WB-1/598	AR
Evans, Samuel	072	1834	WB-1/124	AR
Evans, Sarah	029	1852	WB-C/242	
Evans, Sherwood	039	1842	WB-L/77	AR
Evans, Shubal G.	081	1858	WB-11/224	
Evans, Starkey	010	1898	WB-I/532	
Evans, Starkey B.	024	1899	WB-E/293	AR
Evans, Starkey R.	051	1881	WB-C/263	AR
Evans, Susanna	037	1807	WB-D/296	AR
Evans, Telitha	059	1873	WB-A/105	
Evans, Theophilus	029	1822	WB-B/70	AR
Evans, Theophilus	079	c1864	WB-1/131	AR
Evans, Thomas	090	1790	WB-1/11	AR
Evans, Thomas	024	1732	SS 876/258	SS/AR
Evans, Thomas	096	1745	Orig. Only	SS/AR
Evans, Thomas	020	1801	RB-D/75	AR
Evans, Thomas	028	1805	WB-B/214	AR
Evans, Thomas P.	010	1888	WB-I/258	AR
Evans, William	099	1823	RB-18/300	AR
Evans, William	073	1801	WB-D/33	AR
Evans, William	070	1769	WB-C/87	AR
Evans, William B.	044	c1868	WB-23/1	CTY
Evans, William J.	079	1872	WB-2/71	AR
Evans, Yancey	010	1900	WB-K/61	
Evans, Zachariah	024	1856	WB-C/388	AR
Evans, Zachariah	024	1857	WB-C/420	AR
Evath, William	071	1758	SS 881/29	SS/AR
Eve, John G.	KY	1883	061 WB-2/54	061 AR
Eve, John G.	KY	1883	091 WB-1/290	

Name	Co.	Date	Recorded Copy	Original
Eve, John G.	KY	1883	Copy	023 AR
Eveans, Thomas	077	1825	WB-F/96	AR
Even, Elizabeth	047	1801	WB-3/363	
Evens, John	071	1805	WB-2/307	AR
Evens, John	056	1760	WB-1/780	
Evens, Joseph	030	1796	WB-2/96	
Evens, Sarah D.	010	1891	WB-I/330	AR
Evens, Thomas	022	1795	RB-2/61	
Eventon, William	075	1786	WB-K/140	AR
Everanton, William	028	1840	WB-D/6	
Everett, Ann H.	082	1892	WB-6/447	AR
Everett, Calvin A.	082	1873	WB-6/100	AR
Everett, Charity	063	1887	WB-4/8	AR
Everett, Charlotta	063	1854	WB-2/406	
Everett, Charlotte	063	1890	WB-4/53	AR
Everett, Daniel	020	1891	WB-B/87	CTY
Everett, Elisha	063	c1890	Orig. Only	AR-Copy
Everett, Hardy	101	1871	Orig. Only	AR
Everett, James	096	1770	Orig. Only	AR
Everett, James A.	063	1874	WB-3/66	AR
Everett, James H.	103	1868	RD = 14/650	AR
Everett, Jesse	047	1797	WB-3/277	
Everett, John	096	1754	SS 880/86	SS/AR
Everett, John	020	1858	RB-S/39	AR
Everett, John	063	1794	WB-1/206	
Everett, John C.	082	1871	WB-6/67	AR
Everett, John Lewis	VA	1878	051 WB-C/197	051 AR
Everett, Joseph J.	063	1876	WB-3/93	
Everett, Joshua	101	1874	Orig. Only	AR
Everett, Joshua	096	c1765	WB-1/49	AR
Everett, Julia A.	070	1900	WB-H/295	AR
Everett, Kenneth	069	1895	WB-5/496	AR
Everett, Laurence	082	1844	WB-3/19	AR
Everett, Lawrence T.	082	1889	WB-6/390	AR
Everett, Louis F.	VA	1893	047 WB-7/186	047 AR
Everett, Louis F.	MD	1893	009 WB-2/97	009 CTY
Everett, Lucinda	105	1899	WB-3/390	AR
Everett, Marcella L.	079	1878	WB-2/170	AR
Everett, Mary E.	041	1893	WB-4/378	AR
Everett, Matthew	103	1819	RD-4/296	AR
Everett, Nathaniel	063	c1796	WB-1/332	
Everett, Rebecca	037	1865	WB-G/254	AR
Everett, Reubin	063	1897	WB-4/197	AR
Everett, Samuel H.	038	1900	WB-4/225	AR
Everett, Samuel T.	063	c1780	WB-1/78	
Everett, Simon	063	1826	WB-2/121	
Everett, Susan	037	1884	WB-G/671	
Everett, Wade H.	063	1875	WB-3/82	
Everett, William	063	c1793	WB-1/338	
Everett, William C.	009	1891	WB-1/516	CTY
Everette, Laurence	082	c1800	WB-1/78	AR
Everette, Simon B.	047	1881	WB-6/243	AR
Everette, Thomas	063	1858	WB-2/456	
Everhart, Eli	032	1896	WB-4/275	AR
Everhart, George	032	1877	WB-3/235	AR
Everhart, Mary	032	1888	WB-4/11	AR
Everhart, Peter	032	1836	WB-1/286	
Everington, John	028	1846	WB-D/122	AR
Everitt, Eadith	037	1837	WB-F/204	AR
Everitt, Elizabeth	051	1879	WB-C/232	AR
Everitt, Hollan	070	c1832	WB-AB/284	AR
Everitt, James	009	c1800	OB-A/85	AR
Everitt, John	051	1831	WB-A/12	
Everitt, Joseph	103	1836	RD-7/190	AR
Everitt, Keton	037	1823	WB-E/326	AR

Name	Co.	Date	Recorded Copy	Original
Everitt, Martha	037	1884	WB-G/680	
Everitt, Mary	051	1856	WB-A/392	
Everitt, Nancy	037	1884	WB-G/680	
Everitt, Nathan	096	c1781	WB-1/127	AR
Everitt, Nathaniel	096	c1782	WB-1/121	
Everitt, Nathaniel	096	1749	Orig. Only	SS/AR
Everitt, Reuben	070	1884	WB-E/545	AR
Everitt, Rolin	009	c1807	OB-A/81	AR
Everitt, Samuel	070	1885	WB-E/577	AR
Everitt, Sarah	037	1884	WB-G/680	
Everitt, Silas	037	1840	WB-F/240	AR
Everitt, Sterling	012	c1855	WB-B/3	AR
Everitt, Turner	063	1846	WB-2/325	
Everitt, William	063	1848	WB-3/337	
Everitt, William	047	1762	WB-1/74	
Evers, James	011	1862	WB-1/271	
Everton, Elizabeth	030	1848	WB-4/139	
Everton, Jeremiah	075	1740	LGB-4/#164	SS/AR
Everton, Mager	030	1885	WB-5/120	AR
Everton, Thomas	092	1819	WB-3/140	AR
Evett, Moses	009	1859	OB-L/71	AR
Evington, John C. T.	053	1853	WB-7/555	AR
Evins, Clement	029	c1806	WB-A/91	AR
Evins, Elizabeth	037	1766	WB-A/154	AR
Evins, Henry	030	1830	WB-3/259	
Evins, Mary	106	1897	WB-2/419	
Evins, Thomas	029	c1784	Orig. Only	AR
Evitt, John B.	009	1865	OB-M/248	AR
Evitt, John, Sr.	009	1820	OB-A/296	AR
Evitt, Thomas	009	1832	OB-B/187	AR
Evitt, Walter	009	1775	OWB/123	AR
Evitts, Joseph	009	c1779	OWB/152	AR
Ewart, Joseph	065	1863	WB-J/160	AR
Ewart, Margaret	060	1805	Orig. Only	AR
Ewart, Robert	065	c1830	WB-H/60	AR
Ewart, Robert	060	1781	Orig. Only	AR
Ewart, Robert	065	c1764	WB-C/48	AR
Ewell, Francis	063	1899	WB-4/246	AR
Ewell, James	028	1886	WB-E/398	
Ewell, Sally C.	071	1779	WB-1/327	
Ewell, Thomas	028	1857	WB-D/285	
Ewin, John	082	1804	WB-1/103	AR
Ewing, Alexander	054	c1816	WB-1/404	AR
Ewing, David	097	1865	WB-1/264	AR
Ewing, Gustavus	037	1778	WB-A/264	AR
Ewing, Hugh	040	1869	WB-2/1	AR
Ewing, Jabes	040	1856	WB-1/84	AR
Ewing, James W.	067	1890	WB-2/286	AR
Ewing, John	067	1877	WB-2/79	AR
Ewing, W. M.	065	1897	WB-N/61	AR
Exum, Anne	071	1792	WB-1/445	AR
Exum, Barneby	037	1796	WB-D/12	AR
Exum, Etheldred	037	1779	WB-B/23	AR
Exum, James	071	1827	WB-4/24	AR
Exum, James	071	c1772	Orig. Only	AR
Exum, James L.	071	1830	WB-4/73	AR
Exum, John	037	1806	WB-D/239	AR
Exum, John	037	1775	WB-A/236	AR
Exum, Joseph	071	1790	WB-1/414	AR
Exum, L. Esther	071	1845	WB-5/34	AR
Exum, Matthew	071	1777	WB-1/396	AR
Exum, Micajah	037	1785	WB-C/23	AR
Exum, Sarah	103	1843	RD-8/389	AR
Exum, William	071	1788	WB-1/388	AR
Exum, William	037	1795	WB-C/316	AR

Name	Co.	Date	Recorded Copy	Original
Exum, William J.	103	1885	WB-1/342	AR
Exum, William T.	071	1828	WB-4/38	AR
Exum, Williamson	037	1803	WB-D/161	AR
Eyeres, Richard	N	1685	Orig. Only	SS/AR
Ezard, William	070	1775	WB-C/90	AR
Ezel, Miel	047	1809	WB-3/489	
Ezell, Asenith	099	1808	RB-8/3	AR
Ezell, Frederick	065	1825	WB-C/55	AR
Ezell, John	099	1800	RB-5/94	AR
Ezell, Mikel	035	1800	WB-A/141	AR
Ezell, Reuben	035	1830	WB-1/1	AR
Ezzel, Willie	051	1879	WB-C/222	AR
Ezzell, Alexander	087	1864	Orig. Only	AR
Ezzell, Fannie M.	035	1899	WB-4/548	AR
Ezzell, Fedrick	097	c1858	WB-1/295	AR
Ezzell, John	035	1890	WB-4/349	AR
Ezzell, John R.	087	1879	WB-3/185	AR
Ezzell, Patrick	035	1847	WB-2/16	AR
Fabbin, Andrew J.	070	1762	DB-E/17	AR
Faddis, John	073	1829	WB-E/201	AR
Fadyen, John	082	1863	WB-4/167	
Fadyeon, Finlay M.	068	1865	WB-C/117	
Fagan, Bedford	096	1778	WB-1/101	AR
Fagan, Enoch	096	1777	Orig. Only	SS/AR
Fagan, Harriet	063	1821	WB-2/75	
Fagan, Levi	063	1839	WB-2/263	
Fagan, Richard	096	c1773	WB-1/87	AR
Fagan, Sarah	096	1783	WB-1/133	AR
Fagan, Stephen	063	1813	WB-2/16	
Fagan, Thomas	096	c1779	WB-1/115	AR
Fagg, Marcellus	013	1894	046 WB-I/480	
Fagg, Marcellus	013	1894	WB-C/278	AR
Fagg, William	013	1844	WB-A/97	
Faggart, David	016	1859	WB-2/60	
Faggart, Eli	016	1846	WB-1/120	
Faggart, J. M.	016	1900	WB-4/374	AR
Faggart, Mary I.	016	1893	WB-4/159	AR
Faggart, Solomon	016	1857	WB-2/32	
Faggart, Valentine	016	1830	PQS.5/120	
Faicen, Edward	047	1803	WB-3/415	Nunc.
Fail, Needham	056	1845	WB-1/570	AR
Fain (Fane), Nancy	100	1816	WB-20/111	AR-Nunc.
Fain, Daniel	100	1807	WB-14/47	AR
Fain, Joel	100	1780	WB-3/33	AR
Fain, John	100	1787	WB-4/219	
Fain, John D.	100	1856	WB-49/50	AR
Fain, John D.	044	1866	WB-22/487	CTY
Fain, Nancy	100	1842	WB-38/105	AR
Fain, Sally	044	1854	WB-19/513	CTY
Fain, Susan M.	098	1881	WB-A/3	CTY
Fair, Arabella	009	1855	OB-I/378	AR
Fair, Barnabas	092	1787	WB-2/79A	AR
Fair, Joseph	014	1818	Orig. Only	AR
Fair, Mary Ann	090	1823	WB-3/101	AR
Fair, Michael	090	1820	WB-3/52	AR
Fairbairn, Thomas	028	1857	WB-D/291	AR
Fairbanks, William	046	1797	WB-A/118	AR
Fairchild, Mary M.	070	1857	WB-C/639	AR
Fairchild, Wilson F.	104	1894	WB-6/502	AR
Faircloth, Greenville	029	1884	WB-E/323	AR
Faircloth, Isaac	018	1829	WB-C/111	
Faircloth, James	029	1877	WB-E/172	AR
Faircloth, Lucy	087	1898	WB-4/63	AR
Faircloth, Newsom	037	1831	WB-F/123	AR
Faircloth, Samuel	087	c1807	Orig. Only	AR

Name	Co.	Date	Recorded Copy	Original
Faircloth, Thomas	051	c1823	WB-A/79	
Faircloth, William	045	1882	WB-1/95	AR
Faircloth, William R.	087	1896	WB-4/28	AR
Faircloth, Wilson	029	1864	WB-D/69	AR
Faires, James	065	1808	WB-C/81	AR
Faires, John	099	1819	RB-15/136	AR
Faires, Mary	099	1822	RB-17/364	AR
Fairley, Alexander	082	1828	WB-1/281	AR
Fairley, Angus	082	1864	WB-4/171	AR
Fairley, Effy	083	1845	WB-1/468	AR
Fairley, John	082	1872	WB-6/90	AR
Fairley, Margaret	082	1794	Orig. Only	AR-Nunc.
Fairley, Robert N.	082	1891	WB-6/434	AR
Fairly, John	083	1899	WB-4/238	AR
Fairly, Robert	083	1844	WB-1/443	AR
Faison , Elias	087	1867	WB-2/116	AR
Faison, Amelia A.	083	1862	WB-2/172	AR
Faison, Claiborne	071	1899	WB-7/441	AR
Faison, Elias	071	1800	WB-2/194	AR
Faison, Elias	035	1871	WB-4/37	AR
Faison, Elias K.	035	1859	WB-3/1	AR
Faison, Henry	071	1817	WB-3/199	AR
Faison, Henry	035	1788	WB-A/147	
Faison, Henry W.	035	1886	WB-4/270	AR
Faison, Herod	071	1815	WB-3/160	AR
Faison, Herod	071	1865	WB-5/307	AR
Faison, Isham	035	1831	WB-1/15	AR
Faison, James	087	1838	WB-1/199	AR
Faison, John L.	071	1855	WB-5/142	AR
Faison, Killbee	087	1848	WB-1/338	AR
Faison, Mary A.	087	1882	WB-3/248	AR
Faison, Mary E.	035	1876	WB-4/111	AR
Faison, Nancy	083	1866	WB-2/240	AR
Faison, Patsy	035	1843	Orig. Only	AR
Faison, Paul F.	099	1896	WB-C/507	AR
Faison, Solomon J.	087	1880	WB-3/206	AR
Faison, Thomas	071	1824	WB-3/302	AR
Faison, Thomas J.	087	1860	WB-2/14	AR
Faison, Virginia	035	1899	WB-4/558	AR
Faison, W. L.	087	1891	WB-3/482	
Faison, Wesley J.	071	c1868	WB-6/5	AR
Faison, William	071	1806	WB-2/331	AR
Faison, William	087	1857	WB-1/512	AR
Faison, William H.	087	1890	WB-3/452	AR
Faithful, David	037	1865	WB-G/256	AR
Faithful, William	037	1885	WB-H/11	
Falconar, John	024	1741	Orig. Only	SS/AR
Falconar, Thomas	024	1756	SS 880/109	SS/AR
Falconer, Alexander	039	1818	WB-F/104	
Falconer, Thomas	099	1818	RB-14/250	AR
Falk, Richard	024	N. D.	SS 875/27	
Falkener, A. M.	100	1891	WB-51/324	AR
Falkener, Elizabeth	100	1819	WB-22/104	AR
Falkener, Oliver E.	100	1887	WB-51/232	AR
Falkener, William	100	1842	WB-38/122	AR
Falkner, Benjamin	005	c1783	WB-A/15	AR
Falkner, James H.	098	1888	WB-A/102	CTY
Falkner, Joseph W.	005	1859	WB-C/140	AR
Fallin, John	009	1784	OWB/194	AR
Fallow, William	024	N. D.	WB-B/209	AR
Falls, Andrew	060	1798	Orig. Only	AR
Falls, Andrew	040	1850	WB-1/29	
Falls, Andrew	060	1840	WB-2/62	AR
Falls, Elizabeth	060	1832	WB-1/262	AR
Falls, Ellison	040	1848	WB-1/12	
Falls, Esther	060	1837	WB-1/406	AR
Falls, George	060	1836	WB-1/364	AR
Falls, J. Z.	026	1895	WB-2/510	AR
Falls, James	060	1822	Orig. Only	AR
Falls, John	060	1828	WB-1/84	AR
Falls, Mary	060	1832	WB-1/263	AR
Falls, Mary R.	040	1865	WB-1/179	
Falls, Robert	026	1879	WB-2/185	AR
Falls, T. D.	026	1871	WB-2/58	AR
Falls, Theophilus	054	1850	WB-3/44	
Falls, William	026	1892	WB-2/453	AR
Falls, William	060	1828	WB-1/97	AR
Falls, William	054	c1832	WB-2/167	AR
Fananders, Mary	092	1819	WB-3/140	AR
Fane (Fain), Nancy	100	1816	WB-20/111	AR-Nunc.
Fane, Jacob	044	1838	WB-14/135	CTY
Fann, John	073	1798	WB-C/107	AR
Fann, Rachel	022	1833	WB-B/255	AR
Fann, Willibe	100	1782	WB-3/157	AR
Fanning, Emily J.	070	1895	WB-G/339	AR
Fanning, James	028	1827	WB-C/297	AR
Fanshau, Tully B.	030	1849	WB-4/146	
Fanshaw, Moses	030	1780	WB-1/139	
Fanshaw, Thomas	030	1840	WB-4/68	
Farabee, Benjamin	032	1836	WB-1/284	
Farabee, E. C.	046	1893	WB-F/252	AR
Farabee, Joseph	032	1866	WB-2/328	AR
Farabee, Joseph C.	032	c1863	WB-2/277	
Farabough, William	044	1859	WB-21/50	CTY
Farabow, William S.	044	1889	WB-24/78	CTY
Fare, John	090	1795	WB-1/73	AR
Fare, Martha G.	038	1889	WB-3/132	AR
Farguson, John	083	1826	WB-1/342	AR
Faribault, Joseph F.	024	1841	WB-C/227 & 250	AR
Faribault, Thomas F.	024	1843	WB-C/242	AR
Faris, Sarah	070	1782	WB-C/101	AR
Faris, William	070	1757	DB-D/248	AR
Farish, Frances	020	1864	RB-T/78	AR
Farish, Thomas	020	1863	RB-S/614	AR
Farlee, James	024	1750	Orig. Only	SS/AR
Farlee, James	024	1727	SS 876/97	SS/AR
Farless, Julia	069	1878	WB-5/69	AR
Farley, August	040	1899	WB-3/50	
Farley, George	020	1799	RB-C/355	
Farley, Isakiah	020	1808	RB-E/428	AR
Farley, Janette S.	040	1900	WB-3/85	AR
Farley, John	082	1806	WB-1/110	AR
Farley, Joseph	020	1811	RB-F/244	AR
Farley, Moses	073	1776	WB-A/196	
Farley, Nathaniel	020	1788	RB-B/294	
Farley, Stewart	020	1799	RB-C/416	
Farlow, Clarissa	081	1882	WB-15/390	
Farlow, Enoch	081	1892	WB-16/215	AR
Farlow, George	081	1883	WB-15/431	AR
Farlow, George	081	1850	WB-9/147	AR
Farlow, Isaac	081	1860	WB-11/443	AR
Farlow, J. C.	081	1880	WB-15/321	
Farlow, James	081	1898	WB-16/488	
Farlow, Mary	067	c1856	WB-1/81	AR
Farlow, Michael	081	1842	WB-7/434	AR
Farlow, Nathan	081	1832	WB-6/190	AR
Farlow, Samuel	081	1897	WB-16/436	AR
Farlow, Sewell	046	1878	WB-E/215	AR
Farmer, Adelphia	105	1898	WB-3/362	AR

Name	Co.	Date	Recorded Copy	Original
Farmer, Asa	056	1851	WB-1/646	AR
Farmer, Barnard	090	1841	WB-4/76	AR
Farmer, Benjah	103	1805	Orig. Only	AR
Farmer, Benjamin	105	1886	WB-2/384	AR
Farmer, Benjamin	037	1827	WB-F/65	AR
Farmer, Braswell	TN	1827	037 WB-F/511	037 AR
Farmer, Catherine	105	1899	WB-3/365	AR
Farmer, Ceburn	105	1884	WB-2/328	AR
Farmer, Christian	046	1836	WB-B/552	AR
Farmer, Elisha	102	N. D.	Orig. Only	AR
Farmer, Elizabeth	105	1891	WB-3/17	AR
Farmer, Elizabeth	105	1896	WB-3/224	AR
Farmer, Elizabeth	037	1852	WB-F/490	AR
Farmer, Everlina	070	1899	WB-H/189	AR
Farmer, Fredrick	081	1818	WB-4/532	AR
Farmer, Gabriel B.	029	1883	WB-E/292	AR
Farmer, Henry	020	1873	WB-A/97	CTY
Farmer, Iredell B.	105	1885	WB-2/335	AR
Farmer, Isaac	105	1885	WB-2/344	AR
Farmer, Isaac	037	1805	WB-D/220	AR
Farmer, Isaac B.	105	1892	WB-3/111	AR
Farmer, James	056	1761	WB-1/758	
Farmer, Jesse	037	1812	WB-E/38	AR
Farmer, Job	073	c1786	WB-B/13	AR
Farmer, Jobe	073	1786	WB-A/372	
Farmer, John	056	1761	WB-1/760	AR
Farmer, John B.	056	1863	WB-2/44	AR
Farmer, John W.	105	1888	WB-2/493	
Farmer, Joseph	010	1796	WB-D/362	AR
Farmer, Joseph	105	1892	WB-3/20	AR
Farmer, Joseph	081	1802	WB-2/93	AR
Farmer, Larry D.	105	1887	WB-2/441	AR
Farmer, Moses	037	1844	WB-F/317	AR
Farmer, Nancy	105	1865	WB-1/118	AR
Farmer, Rachel	013	c1875	Orig. Only	AR
Farmer, Sallie	105	1894	WB-3/97	
Farmer, Samuel	020	1783	RB-A/234	AR
Farmer, Samuel	037	1817	WB-E/158	AR
Farmer, Thomas	024	c1760	WB-A/272	AR
Farmer, Thomas	054	c1815	WB-1/385	AR
Farmer, Thomas	037	1785	WB-C/10	AR
Farmer, Treesey	105	1874	WB-2/161	AR
Farnel, Benjamin	072	1811	WB-A/30	AR
Farnell, Aaron F.	072	1898	WB-4/379	AR
Farnell, Benjamin	072	1831	WB-1/86	AR
Farnell, Dexter	072	1822	WB-A/32	AR
Farnell, John E.	072	1837	WB-1/152	AR
Farnsworth, David	062	1860	WB-A/31	AR
Faron, William	039	1809	WB-C/148	
Farquhar, James	078	1814	WI-6/206	AR
Farqurharson, Cosmas	070	1756	DB-D/209	AR
Farr, Ephraim	065	1783	WB-C/66	AR
Farr, Henry	016	1844	WB-1/42	
Farr, Joseph	017	c1860	WB-A/130	AR
Farr, Mary	016	1846	WB-1/122	
Farr, Richard	072	1758	RW/L58	AR
Farr, Richd. Sr.	072	1758	SS 882/72	SS/AR
Farr, Samuel	016	1844	WB-1/41	
Farr, Samuel	065	1809	WB-C/82	AR
Farr, Titus Green	072	1762	RW/L55	AR
Farrabee, John T.	032	1895	WB-4/1895	
Farrah, Powell	022	1848	WB-C/220	AR
Farrar, Alcy	022	1863	WB-D/113	AR
Farrar, Alice A.	MD	1868	061 WB-2/1	061 AR
Farrar, Allis A.	MD	1869	055 WB-A/1	

Name	Co.	Date	Recorded Copy	Original
Farrar, Frank	044	1900	WB-24/480	CTY
Farrar, Gaston	022	1889	WB-E/415	AR
Farrar, John	022	1800	WB-A/38	AR
Farrar, John	073	1833	WB-E/290	AR
Farrar, John	099	1808	RB-7/320	AR
Farrar, Mary H.	044	1854	WB-19/451	CTY
Farrar, Milley	022	1811	WB-A/190	AR
Farrar, Nathaniel	065	1840	WB-H/18	AR
Farrar, O. C.	037	1891	WB-H/190	AR
Farrar, Obadiah	044	1825	WB-9/395	CTY
Farrar, Peter	022	1802	WB-A/67	AR
Farrar, Peter	022	1826	WB-B/121	AR
Farrar, Thomas	022	1858	WB-D/1	AR
Farrar, W. B.	046	1898	WB-G/59	AR
Farrar, William	081	1826	WB-5/252	AR
Farrar, William	022	1822	WB-B/52	AR
Farrel, John, Sr.	054	c1826	WB-2/43	AR
Farrell, Charles	020	1788	RB-B/218	AR
Farrell, Francis	022	1887	WB-E/347	AR
Farrell, Martha H.	105	1900	WB-3/408	AR
Farrell, William	103	1837	RD-7/287	AR
Farrell, William S.	022	1882	WB-E/239	AR
Farrer, Alice A.	MD	1868	091 WB-1/282	
Farrill, John	103	1802	Orig. Only	AR
Farrington, Susan	065	1888	WB-L/303	AR
Farrior, Hettie	035	1894	WB-4/452	AR
Farrior, Hettie	035	1894	076 WB-A1/268	
Farrior, Hugh	035	1884	WB-4/239	AR
Farrior, John	035	1851	WB-2/57	AR
Farrior, John, Sr.	035	1812	WB-A/146	AR
Farrior, Margret	035	1779	WB-A/143	AR
Farrior, Martha	035	1823	WB-A/191	AR
Farrior, Nicholas	035	1896	WB-4/485	AR
Farrior, William H.	065	1888	WB-L/270	AR
Farris, Thomas P.G.	065	1869	WB-K/18	AR-Nunc.
Farris, William	009	1812	OWB/468	AR
Farror, Henry	065	c1769	WB-C/57	AR
Farror, William	044	1788	WB-2/68	CTY
Farrow, Abram	044	1894	WB-24/239	CTY
Farrow, Asena	053	1875	WB-11/55	AR
Farrow, Benjamin	070	1843	WB-AB/387	AR
Farrow, Christopher	030	1807	WB-2/311	
Farrow, Ellen	053	1900	WB-11/356	AR
Farrow, Elvina	105	1883	WB-2/311	AR
Farrow, Elvina A.	009	c1870	Orig. Only	CTY
Farrow, Francis	030	1722/3	SS 876/11	SS/AR
Farrow, Hezekiah	053	1851	WB-7/489	AR
Farrow, Hezekiah	030	c1811	WB-3/4	
Farrow, Hezekiah	030	1798	WB-2/128	
Farrow, Isaac L.	053	1843	WB-6/219	AR
Farrow, Jacob	030	1785	WB-1/186	
Farrow, Jacob	030	1789	WB-1/239	
Farrow, Jeremiah	053	1830	WB-5/24	AR
Farrow, John	053	1797	RW-1/285	AR
Farrow, John	030	1820	WB-3/292	
Farrow, John	078	1812	WI-6/79	AR
Farrow, Joseph	078	1863	WB-18/295	AR
Farrow, Joseph	053	1822	Orig. Only	AR
Farrow, Lorenzo B.	053	1869	WB-11/17	AR
Farrow, Mary E.	065	1891	WB-L/595	AR
Farrow, Nathaniel	024	c1799	WB-A/324	AR
Farrow, Pharaoh	053	1847	WB-7/127	AR
Farrow, Susan P. A.	009	c1876	WB-1/331	CTY
Farrow, Thomas	030	c1815	WB-3/64	
Farrow, Thomas M.	SC	1860	065 WB-J/102	065 AR

Name	Co.	Date	Recorded Copy	Original
Farrow, Tilmon	053	1880	WB-11/101	AR
Farrow, William	044	1792	WB-2/318	CTY
Farrow, William C.	070	1892	WB-G/52	AR
Farrow, Zacheas	019	c1851	Orig. Only	AR
Farson, John	065	1828	WB-A/229	AR
Farthing, Abner C.	102	1896	WB-A/117	AR
Farthing, Dudley	102	1878	Orig. Only	AR
Farthing, Joanna	073	1839	WB-F/25	AR
Farthing, John A.	102	1887	WB-A/50	AR
Farthing, Stephen J.	102	1882	WB-A/23	AR
Farthing, Thomas B.	036	1896	WB-A/372	CTY
Farthing, W. B.	017	1886	WB-B/132	AR
Farthing, William	036	1895	WB-A/350	CTY
Farthing, William W.	006	1827	WB-A/91	AR
Fasnach, Edward	099	1897	WB-D/30	AR
Fason, Elizabeth	071	1778	WB-1/301	
Fatheree, Hillyard	009	c1780	OWB/156	AR
Fatherer, Jane	028	1806	WB-B/251	AR-Nunc.
Faucett, Abisha	073	1873	WB-H/69	CTY
Faucett, Eli V.	001	1857	WB-1/117	AR
Faucett, Elizabeth	073	1831	WB-E/235	AR
Faucett, George	073	1827	WB-E/141	AR
Faucett, James	073	1811	WB-D/309	AR
Faucett, Jane	001	1877	WB-2/119	AR
Faucett, John	073	1797	WB-C/94	AR
Faucett, John	073	1806	WB-D/179	AR
Faucett, John R.	001	c1857	WB-1/113	AR
Faucett, John, Sr.	001	1864	WB-1/224	AR
Faucett, Joseph	073	1869	WB-H/22	CTY
Faucett, Josephine	047	1890	WB-6/553	AR
Faucett, Martha	001	1863	WB-1/212	AR
Faucett, Mary	020	1856	RB-R/368	AR
Faucett, Ralph	073	1837	WB-E/510	AR
Faucett, Rebecca	073	1853	WB-G/41	AR
Faucett, Richard	073	1828	WB-E/163	AR
Faucett, Robert	073	1827	WB-E/137	AR
Faucett, Robert	001	c1850	WB-1/35	AR
Faucett, Robert A.	073	1835	WB-E/332	AR
Faucett, Samuel	073	1847	Orig. Only	AR
Faucett, Thomas B.	001	1885	WB-2/238	AR
Faucett, Thomas D.	073	1863	WB-G/403	AR
Faucett, Thomas U.	001	1888	WB-2/395	AR
Faucett, William	001	1857	WB-1/115	AR
Faucett, William E.	001	1875	WB-2/88	AR
Faucett, William F.	046	1860	WB-D/42	AR
Faucette, George A.	073	1886	WB-H/419	CTY
Faucette, Henry C.	022	1883	WB-E/274	AR
Faucette, James R.	022	1869	WB-E/34	AR
Faucette, Mary	073	1886	WB-H/406	CTY
Faucette, Robert	073	1890	WB-H/496	CTY
Faucette, Sallie A.	022	1882	WB-E/256	AR
Faucette, William C.	022	1883	WB-E/277	AR
Faulcon, Fannie M.	047	1878	WB-6/190	AR
Faulcon, Isaac N.	047	1879	WB-6/197	AR
Faulcon, Jacob	100	1838	WB-36/254	AR
Faulcon, Jessee N.	047	1843	WB-4/217	
Faulcon, John	100	1812	WB-16/344	AR
Faulcon, Rosanna C.	047	1853	WB-4/336	
Faulk, Harriett	039	1895	WB-V/47	AR
Faulk, James	056	1882	WB-3/319	AR
Faulk, Joel	027	1856	WB-A/70	AR
Faulk, Joel	027	c1834	WB-A/18	AR
Faulk, Richard	027	c1808	WB-A/15	AR
Faulk, William	027	1858	WB-A/71	AR
Faulkener, Sarah	003	c1867	Orig. Only	AR
Faulkner, Hattie A.	098	1894	WB-A/190	CTY
Faulkner, James	081	1887	WB-16/133	AR
Faulkner, Thomas	054	c1835	WB-2/172	AR
Fausett, William	073	1816	WB-D/465	AR
Faust, Elleanor	085	1838	WB-I/32	AR
Faw, Amos	038	1883	WB-2/433	AR
Faw, Daniel	090	c1844	WB-4/151	AR
Faw, Jacob	038	1887	WB-3/46	AR
Faw, John	006	1867	WB-D/70	AR
Faw, William	090	1845	WB-4/195	AR
Fawcet, James	047	1787	WB-3/139	
Fawl, John	028	1769	Orig. Only	AR
Fawn, Elizabeth	039	1850	WB-N/314	AR
Feagan, Henry	086	1839	Orig. Only	AR
Feagans, John H.	080	c1863	WB-1/188	AR
Feagans, Matilda	080	1875	WB-1/22	AR
Feagans, William	080	1880	WB-1/63	AR
Feagin, Burgess	047	1818	WB-3/619	
Feare, Obadiah	075	c1719	Orig. Only	SS/AR
Fearing, Isaiah	075	1858	WB-M2/61	AR
Fearington, Fant	022	1900	WB-F/175	AR
Fearn, Sarah	057	1799	WB-A/156	AR
Fearrington, Bithany	022	1900	WB-F/163	AR
Fearrington, E. P.	022	1879	WB-E/168	AR
Feaser, Nicholas	085	1765	WB-A/55	AR
Featherston, Ambrose M.	050	c1846	WB-1/17	CTY
Featherston, Merrimon	050	1884	WB-1/248	CTY
Feazer, George	085	1815	WB-G/366	AR
Fedler, Godfrey	090	1814	WB-2/155	
Fee, Lizzie J.	013	1899	WB-D/268	AR
Feezor, George	032	c1858	WB-2/164	
Feezor, Henry	032	1865	WB-2/327	AR
Feezor, Jacob	032	1871	WB-3/32	AR
Feild, Richard	072	1744	Orig. Only	SS/AR
Feilds, James	077	1751	Orig. Only	SS/AR
Feimster, Jerusha	054	c1859	Orig. Only	AR
Feimster, John	054	c1837	WB-2/178	AR
Feimster, Margaret	054	1863	Orig. Only	AR
Feimster, William	054	1842	WB-2/259	AR
Feinster, S. E.	054	1899	WB-6/238	CTY
Feinster, William R.	054	1888	WB-5/219	CTY
Felker, Elizabeth	085	1841	WB-I/101	AR
Felker, Michael	060	1803	Orig. Only	AR
Felker, Samuel	085	1880	WB-1/509	
Felker, Susan	085	1891	WB-2/454	
Fellows, James	090	1883	WB-6/139	AR
Fellows, Robert	103	1819	RD-4/221	AR-Nunc.
Felmet, Sarah	026	1852	WB-2/146	AR
Felps, James	024	c1768	WB-B/1	AR
Felps, Jonathan	096	c1795	Orig. Only	AR
Felps, Thomas	085	c1794	WB-C/317	AR
Felthen, James	010	1726	SS 876/132	SS/AR
Felton, Cader	077	1837	WB-F/265	AR
Felton, David F.	041	1865	WB-3/326	AR
Felton, Elisha	105	1858	WB-1/55	
Felton, Elizabeth	099	1883	WB-A/436	AR
Felton, Elizabeth	077	1847	WB-F/337	AR
Felton, Jane	041	1850	WB-3/138	AR
Felton, John	077	1868	WB-H/24	AR
Felton, John	024	1844	WB-C/247	AR
Felton, Marey	041	1785	WB-1/53	AR
Felton, Mary A. E.	024	1886	WB-E/153	AR
Felton, Pennina	041	1859	WB-3/234	AR
Felton, Polly	105	1893	WB-3/83	AR
Felton, Richard	024	c1776	WB-A/344	AR

Name	Co.	Date	Recorded Copy	Original	Name	Co.	Date	Recorded Copy	Original
Felton, Robert R.	024	1879	WB-E/80	AR	Ferebee, James	096	c1826	Orig. Only	AR
Felton, Rosanna M.	019	1892	WB-B/226	AR	Ferebee, James	030	1789	WB-1/234	
Felton, Thomas	077	1822	WB-F/50	AR	Ferebee, James	018	1893	WB-E/221	AR
Felton, Trizina	037	1899	WB-H/440	AR	Ferebee, James M.	030	c1874	WB-5/64	AR
Felton, William	105	1871	WB-2/79		Ferebee, James W.	018	1865	WB-D/74	AR
Felton, William	024	1817	WB-C/56	AR	Ferebee, Jean	030	1787	WB-1/217	
Felton, William	077	1825	WB-F/107	AR	Ferebee, Joseph	030	1821	WB-3/303	
Felts, Edward	100	1883	WB-51/192	AR	Ferebee, Peter	030	1786	WB-1/201	
Felts, Harison C.	106	1880	WB-2/118	AR	Ferebee, Robert	030	1793	WB-2/15	
Felts, Humphry	077	1726	SS 876/38	SS/AR	Ferebee, S. W.	018	1856	WB-D/27	
Felts, John	099	1802	RB-6/42	AR	Ferebee, Samuel	030	1845	WB-4/115	
Felts, Mary	100	1818	WB-21/229	AR	Ferebee, Sarah M.	018	1886	WB-E/151	AR
Felts, Molley	099	1828	RB-20/295	AR	Ferebee, Thomas	030	1802	WB-2/207	
Felts, Nathaniel	100	1798	WB-9/349	AR	Ferebee, William	030	1792	WB-1/263	
Felts, Nathaniel	100	1852	WB-42/71	AR	Ferebee, William	030	1783	WB-1/164	
Felts, Randolph	100	1799	WB-10/146	AR	Ferebee, William	030	1870	WB-5/9	AR
Felts, William	104	1843	WB-4/294	AR	Fergeson, Adam	028	1715	PQS.1/98	SS/AR
Felts, William	045	1854	037 WB-G/92		Fergeson, Ellon	001	1852	WB-1/63	AR
Fendall, John	077	1696	SS 874.2/81	SS/AR	Fergeson, Murdoch	068	1830	WB-B/73	
Fendall, Robert	077	1711/2	Orig. Only	SS/AR	Fergueson, Daniel C.	068	c1869	WB-D/16	
Fender, Christian	092	1800	WB-3/34A	AR	Fergurson, Norman	068	1864	WB-C/106	
Fender, Isham	107	c1885	Orig. Only	AR	Fergus, John	070	1802	WB-AB/57	AR
Fender, John	006	1857	WB-D/14	AR	Ferguson, Alexander	046	1819	WB-B/75	AR
Fenderson, Boston	028	1839	WB-C/434	AR	Ferguson, Andrew	060	1811	Orig. Only	AR
Feney, Jenet	085	c1777	WB-A/246	AR	Ferguson, Andrew	085	c1797	WB-E/163	AR
Feney, John	065	c1805	Orig. Only	AR-Copy	Ferguson, Andrew R.	026	1874	WB-2/111	AR
Fenn, Mary	073	1846	WB-F/296	AR	Ferguson, Archibald	022	1848	WB-C/218	AR
Fennel, Franey	085	1836	WB-H/717	AR	Ferguson, Charles	029	1819	WB-B/18	AR
Fennel, Joseph	073	1838	WB-F/10	AR	Ferguson, Daniel	070	1798	WB-C/108	AR
Fennel, Lemuel	071	1782	WB-1/258		Ferguson, David	005	1761	WB-1/11	
Fennel, Margaret	087	1854	WB-1/455	AR	Ferguson, Eli	017	c1846	WB-A/40	AR
Fennell, Anny	071	1856	WB-5/149	AR	Ferguson, Elizabeth	026	1860	WB-1/260	AR
Fennell, George	070	1859	WB-D/4	AR	Ferguson, Elizabeth	049	1869	WB-2/3	AR
Fennell, George E.	070	1868	WB-D/242	AR	Ferguson, Elizabeth	060	1845	WB-2/238	AR
Fennell, George E.	070	1859	WB-D/4	AR	Ferguson, Elvira	104	1894	WB-6/527	AR
Fennell, Hardy L.	070	1863	WB-D/126	AR	Ferguson, Hannah	028	1819	WB-C/175	AR
Fennell, James	071	1839	WB-4/201	AR	Ferguson, Isaac	037	1764	WB-A/138	AR
Fennell, Jesse W.	070	1853	WB-C/552		Ferguson, James	104	1837	WB-4/222	AR
Fennell, John	071	1827	WB-4/22	AR	Ferguson, James	017	1872	WB-B/35	AR
Fennell, Joseph	071	1824	WB-3/313	AR	Ferguson, James	083	c1820	WB-1/347	AR
Fennell, Mary	MD	1853	029 WB-C/239	029 AR	Ferguson, James	037	1769	WB-A/168	AR
Fennell, Mary	071	1856	WB-5/149		Ferguson, James	040	1895	WB-2/494	AR
Fennell, Nicholas	070	1792	WB-C/106	AR	Ferguson, James	040	1854	WB-1/58	AR
Fennell, Penelope	035	1855	WB-2/95	AR	Ferguson, James	040	1883	WB-2/233	AR
Fenner, Ann	028	1777	Orig. Only	AR	Ferguson, John	029	1803	WB-A/61	AR
Fenner, John	028	1822	WB-C/213	AR	Ferguson, John	029	1845	WB-C/82	AR
Fenner, John H.	047	1871	WB-6/63	AR	Ferguson, John	083	1827	WB-1/340	AR
Fenner, Mary	047	1831	WB-4/74		Ferguson, John	104	1835	WB-4/108	AR
Fenner, Robert	047	1816	WB-3/593		Ferguson, John B.	104	1860	WB-5/247	
Fenner, Sally	070	c1885	Orig. Only	AR	Ferguson, John H.	099	1900	WB-D/371	AR
Fenner, Thomas	VA	1853	047 WB-4/340		Ferguson, Laura J.	049	1883	WB-2/105	AR
Fenner, William E.	047	c1894	Orig. Only	AR	Ferguson, Lewis B.	065	1885	WB-L/66	AR
Fenton, Richard	030	1780	WB-1/141		Ferguson, Mark	028	1751	DB-5/190	SS/AR
Fenton, Thomas	030	1773	WB-1/75		Ferguson, Mary	060	1827	WB-1/64	AR
Fentres, Horatio	075	1760	Orig. Only	AR	Ferguson, Mary	104	1894	WB-6/534	AR
Fentress, Dinah	030	1842	WB-4/88		Ferguson, Mary	017	1876	WB-B/57	AR
Fentress, Pharoah	081	1811	WB-3/309	AR	Ferguson, Mary G.	044	1859	WB-20/709	CTY
Fentress, William	030	c1809	WB-2/350		Ferguson, Mary J.	104	1889	WB-6/357	AR
Fentriss, William	092	1859	WB-5/43	AR	Ferguson, Murdock	068	1855	WB-C/28	
Feran, Henry	083	1832	WB-1/277	AR	Ferguson, Nathan J.	049	c1869	WB-1/6	AR
Ferebee, Courtney	018	1857	WB-D/38		Ferguson, Neil	083	1835	WB-1/295	AR
Ferebee, Dennis D.	018	1884	WB-E/121	AR	Ferguson, Priscilla	104	1894	WB-6/530	AR
Ferebee, Elizabeth	030	1796	WB-2/70		Ferguson, Robert	060	1795	Orig. Only	AR
Ferebee, Enoch D.	VA	1876	018 WB-E/52	018 AR	Ferguson, Robert	049	c1825	WI-A/25	AR
Ferebee, Hester C.	044	1882	WB-23/455	CTY	Ferguson, Robert	060	1815	Orig. Only	AR

Name	Co.	Date	Recorded Copy	Original
Ferguson, Samuel	065	c1786	Copy	085 AR
Ferguson, Sarah	083	1837	WB-1/305	AR
Ferguson, Slocomb	028	1807	Orig. Only	AR
Ferguson, Smith	017	1878	WB-B/77	AR
Ferguson, T. M.	099	1890	WB-B/486	AR
Ferguson, Thomas	028	1793	WB-A/304	AR
Ferguson, Thomas	065	1795	WB-C/70	AR
Ferguson, Thomas	040	1866	WB-1/190	
Ferguson, W. I.	049	c1861	WB-1/17	AR
Ferguson, William	065	1817	WB-C/85	AR
Ferguson, William	047	1764	WB-1/130	
Ferguson, William M.	040	1865	WB-1/185	AR
Feriel, Richard	075	1740	LGB-4/#124	SS/AR
Fern, Thomas	057	1790	WB-A/206	AR
Fernsler, Fredrick	090	1803	WB-2/38	AR
Ferrall, Michael	047	1862	WB-5/95	
Ferrall, Thomas	047	1856	WB-5/28	
Ferrand, Joseph B.	028	1900	WB-F/466	
Ferrand, Stephen L.	085	1831	WB-H/510	AR
Ferrand, William	072	c1813	WB-A/37	AR
Ferrand, William P.	072	1847	WB-2/87	
Ferre, John H.	081	1898	WB-16/467	AR
Ferrebee, James M.	018	1874	WB-E/46	
Ferrebee, John	018	1778	Orig. Only	AR/CRX
Ferree, Joseph D.	014	1875	WB-2/120	
Ferree, Milton M.	081	1898	WB-16/485	
Ferree, Priscilla	IN	1850	Copy	073 AR
Ferrel, Gabriel	065	1841	WB-I/21	AR
Ferrell, Allen	073	1854	WB-G/56	AR
Ferrell, Ann K.	039	1882	WB-U/329	
Ferrell, Bryant	039	1793	WB-A/110	
Ferrell, Burton	099	1898	WB-D/225	AR
Ferrell, Charles	020	1788	RB-B/218	
Ferrell, Christian	099	1802	RB-5/354	AR
Ferrell, Delacy	105	1897	WB-3/287	AR
Ferrell, Elizabeth	099	1844	RB-25/360	AR
Ferrell, Elizabeth	105	1880	WB-2/261	AR
Ferrell, Elizabeth	069	1862	WB-1/581	AR
Ferrell, Fielding	073	1868	WB-G/545	CTY
Ferrell, Frances A.	036	1889	WB-A/151	CTY
Ferrell, G. W.	044	1891	Copy	045 AR
Ferrell, Henry	099	1879	Orig. Only	AR
Ferrell, Hezekiah	099	1815	RB-12/3	AR
Ferrell, J. H.	020	1892	WB-B/95	CTY
Ferrell, Jacob	099	1823	RB-18/117	AR
Ferrell, James	069	1850	WB-1/521	AR
Ferrell, James D.	099	1892	WB-C/104	AR
Ferrell, James J.	099	1865	RB-33/427	AR
Ferrell, James L.	099	1899	WB-D/328	AR
Ferrell, John	105	c1862	WB-1/88	
Ferrell, John	039	c1786	WB-B/12	AR
Ferrell, Jonas	105	1877	WB-2/207	AR
Ferrell, Joseph	105	1886	WB-2/400	AR
Ferrell, Lucy	056	1872	WB-3/75	AR
Ferrell, Lydia	105	1894	WB-3/104	AR
Ferrell, Martha	099	1891	WB-C/18	AR
Ferrell, Martha	073	1878	WB-H/191	CTY
Ferrell, Mourning	103	1815	RD-3/272	AR
Ferrell, Noel	105	1871	WB-2/90	AR
Ferrell, Paul	099	1838	RB-24/171	AR
Ferrell, Presley C.	099	1894	WB-C/231	AR
Ferrell, Rachel M.	099	1891	WB-C/1	AR
Ferrell, Sarah J.	036	1889	WB-A/153	CTY
Ferrell, Thomas	099	1839	RB-24/299	AR
Ferrell, William	099	1824	RB-18/356	AR
Ferrell, William	069	1842	WB-1/475	AR
Ferrer, Lorenzo	040	1875	WB-2/83	AR
Ferril, William	030	1742/3	Orig. Only	SS/AR
Ferrill, G. W.	044	1891	WB-24/165	CTY
Ferrill, Hutchings	084	1872	WB-E/35	CTY
Ferrill, Thomas	047	1786	WB-3/111	
Ferrill, Thomas	018	1823	WB-C/17	
Ferris, Owen	070	1785	WB-C/105	AR
Fesler, Andrew	090	1811	WB-2/121	AR
Fesperman, Barbara	085	1878	WB-1/445	CTY
Fesperman, Henry	065	1791	WB-C/63	AR
Fesperman, John	085	1870	WB-1/70	CTY
Fesperman, Simeon G.	085	1888	WB-2/307	CTY
Fessenden, Frank	101	1899	WB-A/316	AR
Fessenden, Julia Ann	101	1875	WB-A/11	AR
Festerman, Michael	065	1859	WB-J/75	
Fevely, A. T.	038	1872	WB-2/495	AR
Few, James	073	1787	WB-B/32	AR
Fewax, James	N	1711/2	Orig. Only	SS/AR
Fiddler, William	038	1886	WB-2/566	AR
Fidler, Godfrey	090	c1814	WB-2/187	AR
Fidler, John Peter	090	1829	WB-3/196	AR
Field, Jeremiah	081	1830	WB-6/41	AR
Field, John	046	c1787	WB-A/116	AR
Field, Mills R.	041	1834	WB-2/343	AR
Fielder, Benjamin	020	c1826	RB-L/174	AR
Fielder, Samuel	084	1804	WB-A/19	CTY
Fields, Absalom	046	c1868	WB-E/105	AR
Fields, Alvis	022	1889	WB-E/399	AR
Fields, Benjamin	046	1844	WB-C/170	
Fields, Bennet	045	1883	WB-1/100	AR
Fields, Henry	022	1799	WB-A/4	AR
Fields, Henry	022	1871	WB-E/62	AR
Fields, Jacob	072	1823	WB-A/36	AR
Fields, James	072	1803	WB-A/37	AR
Fields, James	022	1832	WB-B/231	AR
Fields, Jehu	022	1891	WB-E/496	AR
Fields, Jeremiah	046	1821	WB-B/116	AR
Fields, John	073	1766	WB-A/56	
Fields, John	084	1832	WB-B/133	CTY
Fields, John	022	1880	WB-E/208	AR
Fields, John	010	1783	WB-C/65	AR
Fields, Lemuel	019	1867	WB-B/31	AR
Fields, Mary	084	1838	WB-B/199	CTY
Fields, Mathew	045	1889	WB-1/199	AR
Fields, Moses	072	c1816	WB-A/35	AR
Fields, Patsy	092	1850	WB-4/297	
Fields, Peter	046	1816	WB-B/16	AR
Fields, Rebekah	072	c1819	WB-A/35	AR
Fields, Richard	057	1784	WB-A/28	AR
Fields, Roddy	046	1866	WB-D/287	AR
Fields, Samuel	072	c1782	WI/L28	AR
Fields, Smith	005	1799	WB-2/37	AR
Fields, Thommas	104	1807	WB-2/194	AR
Fields, W. A.	079	1899	WB-3/184	AR
Fields, William	046	1815	WB-A/126	AR
Fields, William	081	1805	WB-3/31	AR
Fields, William	081	1798	WB-2/38	AR
Fields, William D.	081	1886	WB-16/15	AR
Fields, Zachariah	072	c1796	Orig. Only	AR
Fife, Lewis	028	1861	WB-D/347	
Fife, William W.	032	1882	WB-3/364	AR
Figg, Alsey	041	1816	WB-2/126	AR
Figg, John	041	1852	WB-3/159	AR
Figg, Joseph	041	1795	WB-1/132	AR

Name	Co.	Date	Recorded Copy	Original
Figg, Prissillia	041	1859	WB-3/248	AR
Fight, Henry	085	1843	WB-I/167	AR
Figures, Bartholomew	071	1758	SS 882/18	SS/AR
Figures, Bartholomew	071	1775	WB-1/27	AR
Figures, Elizabeth	051	1832	WB-A/53	
Figures, John	071	1766	WB-1/130	
Fike, Horace	022	1882	WB-E/237	AR
Fike, Isaac H.	022	1880	WB-E/197	AR
Fike, Lydia	022	1808	WB-A/114	AR
Fike, Mary J.	022	1870	WB-E/57	AR
Fike, Nancy	022	1880	WB-E/193	AR
Fike, Thomas	022	1894	WB-E/568	AR
File, Sarah	085	1896	WB-3/142	CTY
File, Tobias	085	1884	WB-2/97	CTY
Filgo, Anthony	010	1777	WB-B/99	AR
Filgo, David	099	1794	RB-3/61	AR
Filhauer, John N.	085	c1815	WB-H/443	AR
Fillingham, Benjamin	028	1803	Orig. Only	AR
Fillingham, John, Sr.	079	1773	Orig. Only	SS/AR
Fillingim, Robert	028	1799	Orig. Only	AR
Fillman, William	084	1899	WB-F/141	CTY
Fillyan, John	028	1747/8	SS 877/42	SS/AR
Fillyaw, Elizabeth	070	1843	WB-AB/399	AR
Fillyaw, Emily A.	076	1897	WB-A1/221	AR
Fillyaw, John	070	1784	WB-C/103	AR
Fillyaw, Julia G.	070	1898	WB-H/163	AR
Fillyaw, Owen L.	070	1862	WB-D/86	AR
Fillyaw, Stephen	070	1839	WB-C/116	AR
Filyaw, Susan M.	076	1897	WB-A1/220	AR
Fincannon, John	017	1841	WB-A/2	AR
Fincannon, Julia	054	1883	WB-5/15	CTY
Fincannon, Peter	017	c1846	WB-A/73	AR
Finch, Caswell	039	1852	WB-N/344	AR
Finch, E. A.	100	1891	WB-51/399	
Finch, Edward	022	1885	WB-E/309	AR
Finch, G. M. L.	039	1863	WB-R/616	
Finch, H. H.	056	1899	WB-4/141	AR
Finch, Henry	099	1820	RB-16/9	AR
Finch, Irvin	069	1880	WB-5/101	AR
Finch, John	054	c1815	WB-1/370	AR
Finch, John	044	1822	WB-9/122	CTY
Finch, John	039	1793	WB-A/110	
Finch, Samuel J.	MO	c1850	Copy	081 AR
Finch, Susan S.	065	1887	WB-L/203	AR
Finch, Temperance	039	1853	WB-N/334	AR
Finch, Thomas A.	081	1887	WB-16/67	AR
Finch, William G.	099	1856	RB-30/81	AR
Finch, William M.	026	1862	WB-1/283	AR
Fincher, Jonathan	073	1757	WB-A/3	
Fincher, Lydia	097	1846	WB-1/37	AR
Fincher, Silas	097	1847	WB-1/47	
Findley, Ann	073	1884	WB-H/354	CTY
Findley, Archibald	073	1834	WB-E/312	AR
Findley, Donald	029	1802	WB-A/57	AR
Findley, George	046	1833	WB-B/476	AR
Findley, John	065	c1839	WB-H/58	AR
Findley, William	013	1900	WB-D/443	AR
Fineash, Thomas	077	1841	WB-F/296	
Finey, John	065	1805	WB-C/75	AR
Finger, Daniel	021	1859	WB-1/144	AR
Finger, Daniel	060	1833	WB-1/275	AR
Finger, Daniel	021	1888	WB-2/440	AR
Finger, J. F.	021	1897	WB-3/153	AR
Finger, Jacob	060	1831	WB-1/201	AR
Finger, Jonas	060	1827	WB-1/53	AR
Finger, Michael	060	1877	WB-4/162	AR
Finger, Peter	060	1792	Orig. Only	AR
Finger, Sidney M.	021	1897	WB-3/136	AR
Finger, Solomon	060	1871	WB-4/81	AR
Fink, Ann	016	1899	WB-4/343	AR
Fink, Daniel	054	1887	WB-5/145	CTY
Fink, Israel	065	1876	WB-K/207	AR
Fink, John	085	1883	WB-2/63	CTY
Fink, John	016	1887	WB-3/515	AR
Fink, John W.	016	1895	WB-4/207	AR
Fink, Levi	016	1900	WB-4/372	AR
Fink, Mary L.	016	1881	WB-3/336	AR
Fink, Sarah	016	1875	WB-3/125	AR
Finland, Joseph	073	1848	WB-F/406	
Finley, Alexander	064	1872	WB-2/6	AR
Finley, Ann M.	040	1884	WB-2/216	AR
Finley, Charles	064	1852	WB-1/28	AR
Finley, Charles	014	1829	Orig. Only	AR
Finley, Isabel	060	1802	Orig. Only	AR
Finley, James	046	1835	WB-B/520	
Finley, James	065	1808	WB-C/79	AR
Finley, John	046	1846	WB-C/248	AR
Finley, John	104	1866	WB-5/428	AR
Finley, Josiah	046	c1801	WB-A/125	AR
Finley, Malissa J.	040	1879	WB-2/142	AR
Finley, Nancy	046	c1868	WB-E/19	AR
Finley, R. J. J.	086	1895	WB-F/491	AR
Finley, Robert	060	1791	Orig. Only	AR
Finley, William W.	104	1874	WB-6/86	AR
Finn, Peter	012	c1854	WB-B/2	AR
Finney, Eleanor	065	1800	WB-C/73	AR
Finney, Erwin	065	1885	WB-L/96	AR
Finney, Joseph	092	1800	WB-3/35A	AR
Finney, William H.	051	1825	WB-A/14	
Finnie, William	071	1808	WB-3/10	AR
Finny, Thomas	005	1791	WB-A/14	
Fipes, William	009	1754	SS 879/101	SS/AR
Fipps, Josiah	028	1777	Orig. Only	AR
Fireshiett, J. C.	020	1892	WB-B/123	CTY
Fischesser, Joseph	038	1894	WB-3/465	AR
Fish, Bryant	021	1866	WB-1/232	AR
Fish, Sidney	021	1876	WB-2/165	AR
Fish, Susan	021	1888	WB-2/420	AR
Fish, William	060	1837	WB-1/411	AR
Fish, William	037	1751	Orig. Only	SS/AR
Fish, William	056	1791	WB-1/45	AR
Fish, William D.	099	1881	WB-A/218	AR
Fishblate, Laura	070	1882	WB-E/465	AR
Fishcus, Fredrick	092	1772	WB-1/4	AR
Fishel, Jacob	090	1836	WB-3/310	
Fishel, John Adam	090	1843	WB-4/129	AR
Fishel, John, Sr.	032	1845	WB-1/461	
Fishel, Nathaniel	032	1895	WB-4/188	AR
Fishel, Sophia S.	032	1898	WB-4/379	AR
Fishel, Thomas	038	1896	WB-3/594	AR
Fisher, Albert	054	1871	WB-4/99	CTY
Fisher, Ann	085	c1803	WB-E/169	AR
Fisher, Anna	021	1882	WB-2/243	
Fisher, Caleb A.	016	1900	WB-4/349	AR
Fisher, Charity	019	1824	WB-D/179	AR
Fisher, Charles	065	1817	WB-C/83	AR
Fisher, Daniel	046	1798	WB-A/119	AR
Fisher, Daniel	028	1866	WB-D/466	Nunc.
Fisher, Daniel	016	1892	WB-4/139	AR
Fisher, Daniel	089	1891	WB-2/214	AR

Name	Co.	Date	Recorded Copy	Original
Fisher, Elijah	029	1888	WB-E/426	AR
Fisher, Elizabeth	065	1892	WB-M/74	AR
Fisher, Elizabeth	054	1870	WB-4/79	AR
Fisher, Frederick	085	c1796	WB-E/170	AR
Fisher, George	028	1785	WB-A/86	AR
Fisher, George	090	1832	WB-3/232	AR
Fisher, George	030	1803	WB-2/212	
Fisher, George S.	028	1892	WB-F/40	
Fisher, Harmon	085	1837	WB-I/19	AR
Fisher, Jacob	085	c1803	WB-E/174	AR
Fisher, Jacob	085	1865	WB-K/356	AR
Fisher, Jacob	085	1824	WB-H/270	AR
Fisher, James	085	1796	WB-E/164	AR
Fisher, James	N	c1702	SS 874.1/25	
Fisher, James R.	053	1878	WB-11/77	AR
Fisher, Jefferson	038	1894	WB-3/500	AR
Fisher, John	030	1832	WB-3/322	
Fisher, John	087	1830	WB-1/113	AR
Fisher, John	060	c1803	Orig. Only	AR
Fisher, John	060	1836	WB-1/385	AR
Fisher, John	072	1804	WB-A/32	AR
Fisher, John	060	1803	Orig. Only	AR
Fisher, John	016	1871	WB-3/36	AR
Fisher, Joseph	021	1869	WB-2/27	AR
Fisher, Lawson A.	085	1891	WB-2/481	CTY
Fisher, Lucy	028	1890	WB-E/528	
Fisher, Malkim	028	1758	Orig. Only	AR
Fisher, Marshall	029	1875	WB-E/145	AR
Fisher, Martin	085	c1781	WB-E/161	AR
Fisher, Mary B.	036	1896	WB-A/384	CTY
Fisher, Michael N.	028	c1855	Orig. Only	AR
Fisher, Paul	065	1804	WB-C/74	AR
Fisher, Peter	046	1883	WB-E/340	AR
Fisher, Philip	065	1890	WB-L/453	AR
Fisher, Raiford	011	1873	WB-2/70	
Fisher, Randolph	028	1751	DB-5/171	SS/AR
Fisher, Robinson	053	1786	RW-1/146	AR
Fisher, Roboson	053	1835	WB-5/326	AR
Fisher, Sarah	085	1879	WB-1/498	CTY
Fisher, Sarah	046	1865	WB-D/244	AR
Fisher, Simpson	021	1900	WB-3/280	AR
Fisher, Solomon	021	1883	WB-2/266	
Fisher, Solomon	016	1884	WB-3/440	AR
Fisher, Stephen	060	1785	Orig. Only	AR
Fisher, Stephen	054	1855	WB-3/93	AR
Fisher, Thomas	060	1819	Orig. Only	AR
Fisher, Thomas	092	1779	WB-1/124	AR
Fisher, Thomas	087	1861	WB-2/29	AR
Fisher, Timothy	053	1896	WB-11/320	AR
Fisher, W. J.	063	1885	WB-3/266	AR
Fisher, William	019	1822	WB-A/203	AR
Fisher, William G.	028	1862	WB-D/363	
Fitch, Lydia	020	1890	WB-B/46	CTY
Fitch, Mary	046	1878	WB-E/223	AR
Fitch, Mary	001	1862	WB-1/202	AR
Fitch, Thomas	073	1835	WB-E/365	AR
Fitch, William W.	020	1897	WB-B/316	CTY
Fitchett, William H.	101	1894	024 WB-E/228	024 AR
Fitchett, William H.	101	1894	WB-A/250	AR
Fitchpartrick, Brayen	024	c1709	SS 875/64	
Fite, David	040	1848	WB-1/11	
Fite, Peter	060	1818	Orig. Only	AR
Fitsgarell, Elizabeth	085	1799	WB-E/155	AR
Fitsgarrell, Garrot	085	1798	WB-E/157	AR
Fittingin, Robert	028	1799	WB-B/66	

Name	Co.	Date	Recorded Copy	Original
Fitts, Clara	078	1877	Orig. Only	AR"K
Fitts, Henry	100	1804	WB-12/281	AR
Fitts, Henry	100	1847	WB-39/291	AR-Copy
Fitts, James H.	VA	1862	100 WB-49/432	100 AR
Fitts, Oliver D.	100	1854	WB-43/47	AR
Fitzgarrell, John	056	1751	028 DB-5/194	SS/AR
Fitzgerald, Catharine	070	1891	WB-F/498	AR
Fitzgerald, David	054	1847	WB-3/22	AR
Fitzgerald, H. W.	020	1890	WB-B/29	CTY
Fitzgerald, James W.	001	1898	WB-3/222	AR
Fitzgerald, John B.	020	1895	WB-B/181	CTY
Fitzgerald, Nancy S.	032	c1860	WB-2/176	AR
Fitzgerald, Thomas	070	1806	WB-C/109	AR
Fitzgerald, Thomas J.	VA	1900	013 WB-D/371	013 AR
Fitzgerald, William	054	c1823	WB-2/13	AR
Fitzgerald, William H.	097	1899	WB-3/1	AR
Fitzharris, Catherine	029	1862	WB-C/435	AR
Fitzmaurice, John R.	Eng	c1867	Copy	046 AR
Fitzpatrick, Cornelass	002	1722	SS 875/307	SS/AR
Fitzpatrick, Thomas	VA	c1798	Copy	092 AR
Fitzrandolph, Benjamin	011	c1841	WB-1/82	
Fitzrandolph, Benjamin	011	c1818	WB-2/327	
Fivash, Millender	056	1839	WB-1/509	AR
Flack, Andrew	046	1845	WB-C/241	AR
Flack, Elisha	046	1802	WB-A/121	AR
Flack, George	086	1860	WB-E/380	AR
Flack, Jane	046	1802	WB-A/122	AR
Flack, Jane	084	1867	WB-D/83	CTY
Flack, John	086	1883	WB-F/198	AR
Flack, John J.	086	1890	WB-F/402	AR
Flack, Michael	054	c1824	WB-2/9	AR
Flake, Ephrom	089	1899	WB-2/352	AR
Flake, Flarel B.	005	1891	WB-D/306	AR
Flake, John	079	1879	WB-2/181	AR
Flake, Jurdan	005	1843	WB-B/163	AR
Flake, Mancel	079	1858	WB-1/2	AR
Flake, Samuel	005	c1802	WB-2/36	
Flake, Tempy	079	c1858	Orig. Only	AR
Flake, Thomas G.	005	1850	WB-C/23	AR
Flake, William C.	005	1857	WB-C/114	AR
Flanagan, Elizabeth	100	1881	Orig. Only	AR
Flanagan, Jacob	060	1869	WB-4/1	AR
Flanagin, John	037	1793	WB-C/231	AR
Flanakin, Richard	009	1741	Orig. Only	SS/AR
Flanekin, A. H.	079	1887	WB-2/382	AR
Flanekin, William	079	1872	WB-2/67	AR
Flanigan, J. O.	065	1849	WB-I/150	AR
Flaniken, Mary	065	1847	WB-I/114	AR
Flanken, Elezebeth	009	c1798	OWB/346	AR
Flannagan, John	060	1814	Orig. Only	AR
Flannakin, Elizabeth	SC	c1798	Copy	028 AR
Flannakin, James	009	1752	OWB/47	AR
Flanner, Bennet	070	1868	WB-D/241	AR
Flanner, John D.	028	1873	WB-E/79	
Flanner, Lizzie	028	1893	Copy	065 AR
Flanner, Lizzie H.	028	1893	WB-F/101	
Flanner, Macy E.	019	1895	WB-B/292	AR
Flanner, Susan A.	070	1890	WB-F/399	AR
Flannigan, David G.	065	1863	WB-J/152	AR
Flanniken, William	065	1833	WB-G/121	AR
Flatt, John	060	c1798	Orig. Only	AR
Flavell, William	070	1737/8	DB-AB/141	
Flavell, William	070	1737	SS 877/190	SS/AR
Fleetwood, Edmund	010	1819	WB-G/49	AR
Fleetwood, George B.	077	1888	WB-H/182	AR

Name	Co.	Date	Recorded Copy	Original
Fleetwood, Henry	010	1774	WB-B/14	AR
Fleetwood, William	010	c1769	WB-A/108	AR
Fleetwood, William	010	1799	WB-E/64	AR
Fleetwood, Winifred	010	1840	WB-G/315	AR
Fleming, A.	054	1855	WB-3/98	
Fleming, Alexander	044	1867	WB-22/603	CTY
Fleming, Alexander	087	1824	WB-1/54	AR
Fleming, Allison	085	1837	WB-I/1	AR
Fleming, Archibald	060	1826	WB-1/40	AR
Fleming, Benjamin	079	1866	WB-2/34	AR
Fleming, Benjamin	079	1882	WB-2/249	AR
Fleming, Benjamin O.	079	1895	WB-3/70	AR
Fleming, Charles	037	1829	WB-F/105	AR
Fleming, Cyrus	054	1866	WB-3/190	AR
Fleming, David J.	106	1878	WB-2/100	
Fleming, David S.	079	1884	WB-2/312	AR
Fleming, Eleana	079	1897	WB-3/119	AR
Fleming, Elizabeth	044	1874	WB-23/159	CTY
Fleming, Elizabeth	100	1854	WB-43/187	AR
Fleming, Elizabeth	106	1900	WB-2/480	
Fleming, Elizabeth	014	1842	Orig. Only	AR
Fleming, F. T.	106	1889	WB-2/275	
Fleming, Georg	075	1694	Orig. Only	SS/AR
Fleming, George	085	c1784	WB-C/189	AR
Fleming, George	100	1850	WB-40/289	AR
Fleming, George	086	1811	WB-B/248	AR
Fleming, Henrietta	079	1889	WB-2/473	AR
Fleming, Ivy	079	1890	WB-2/519	AR
Fleming, J. Q.	106	1884	WB-2/183	
Fleming, Jacob D.	100	1873	WB-51/68	AR
Fleming, James	014	1831	Orig. Only	AR
Fleming, James	024	1804	WB-B/219	AR
Fleming, James L.	079	c1862	WB-1/114	AR
Fleming, James S.	085	1878	WB-1/479	CTY
Fleming, Jane	016	1871	WB-3/33	
Fleming, Jane L.	070	1866	WB-D/195	AR
Fleming, John	098	1892	WB-A/142	CTY
Fleming, John	087	1840	WB-1/234	AR
Fleming, John	060	1820	Orig. Only	AR
Fleming, John	044	1895	WB-24/270	CTY
Fleming, John	092	1794	WB-3/15A	AR
Fleming, John C.	046	1864	WB-D/198	AR
Fleming, John H.	100	1887	WB-51/255	AR
Fleming, John L.	079	1879	WB-2/173	AR
Fleming, John, Sr.	100	1793	WB-6/184	AR
Fleming, L. E.	079	1900	WB-3/222	AR
Fleming, Little B.	079	1881	WB-2/238	AR
Fleming, Littleton	106	c1858	WB-1/63	AR
Fleming, Lucinda	054	1873	WB-4/133	CTY
Fleming, Luke	079	1899	WB-3/179	AR
Fleming, Mary	070	1831	WB-AB/271	AR
Fleming, Mary A.	079	1900	WB-3/229	AR
Fleming, Mordecai	092	1893	WB-6/373	AR
Fleming, Nancy A.	063	1892	WB-4/94	AR
Fleming, Nathan N.	085	1864	WB-K/341	AR
Fleming, Peter	100	1816	WB-20/67	AR
Fleming, Peter	079	1887	WB-2/406	AR
Fleming, R. D.	100	1898	WB-51/496	
Fleming, R. H.	044	1895	WB-24/287	CTY
Fleming, Rebecca M.	021	1896	WB-3/147	
Fleming, Robert	046	1806	WB-A/123	AR
Fleming, Robert	017	1873	WB-B/43	AR
Fleming, Robert	046	1831	WB-B/432	AR
Fleming, Robert	099	1795	RB-3/112	AR
Fleming, Robert	014	1823	Orig. Only	AR
Fleming, Robert A.	GA	1890	050 WB-2/76	
Fleming, Rosannah	077	1758	SS 882/109	SS/AR
Fleming, Sarah	037	1873	WB-G/435	AR
Fleming, Simon	100	1878	WB-51/134	AR
Fleming, Syfax	079	1897	WB-3/107	AR
Fleming, T. A.	016	1900	WB-4/353	AR
Fleming, Thomas	100	1830	WB-33/66	AR
Fleming, Thomas	100	1860	WB-49/329	AR
Fleming, Thomas B.	044	1861	WB-21/489	CTY
Fleming, William	084	c1793	OW/105	AR
Fleming, William	017	c1854	WB-A/114	AR
Fleming, William B.	079	c1862	WB-1/114	AR
Fleming, Willis	037	1855	WB-G/96	AR
Flemings, Frederick	037	1855	WB-G/116	AR
Flemming, Anna	084	1854	WB-C/196	CTY
Flemming, Fannie R.	021	1897	WB-3/192	AR
Flemming, Samuel H.	064	1887	WB-2/170	AR
Flemming, William	016	1858	WB-2/47	
Flemon, Peter	085	1763	WB-A/54	AR
Fleniken, Martha	065	1828	WB-A/228	AR
Flenniken, Jane	065	1792	WB-C/62	AR
Flere, Thomas	046	1781	WB-A/115	AR
Fletcher, Aaron	075	1831	WB-N/67	AR
Fletcher, Abner W.	036	1899	WB-A/467	CTY
Fletcher, Clayborn	099	1900	WB-D/338	AR
Fletcher, Curtis	N	1679	Orig. Only	SS/AR
Fletcher, Eliabeth	075	1855	WB-M2/41	AR
Fletcher, Francis	075	1743	Orig. Only	SS/AR
Fletcher, Francis	075	1807	WB-M1/138	AR
Fletcher, Frederick	077	1838	WB-F/275	AR
Fletcher, Frederick	077	1844	WB-F/311	AR
Fletcher, Isaac	106	1884	WB-2/188	
Fletcher, James	106	1871	WB-2/35	AR
Fletcher, James	092	1824	WB-3/159	AR
Fletcher, James	054	1888	WB-5/240	CTY
Fletcher, James	104	1805	WB-2/154	AR
Fletcher, James	020	1786	RB-B/100	AR
Fletcher, James H.	077	1830	WB-F/172	AR
Fletcher, Job	028	1887	WB-E/509	
Fletcher, John	VA	1822	Copy	071 AR
Fletcher, John	092	1802	WB-3/54	AR
Fletcher, Joseph	039	1806	WB-C/52	AR
Fletcher, Joshua	099	1825	RB-19/197	AR
Fletcher, Joshua	103	1785	Orig. Only	AR
Fletcher, Peggy	030	1795	WB-2/36	
Fletcher, Priscilla	036	1881	WB-A/5	CTY
Fletcher, Ralph	077	1728	Orig. Only	SS/AR
Fletcher, Ralph	078	1826	Orig. Only	AR
Fletcher, Ralph	077	1752	Orig. Only	SS/AR
Fletcher, Ralph	077	1785	WB-C/295	AR
Fletcher, Rebecca	029	1824	WB-B/119	AR
Fletcher, Reubin	054	c1810	WB-1/198	AR
Fletcher, Sarah	104	1840	WB-4/253	AR
Fletcher, Susan	050	1885	WB-1/257	CTY
Fletcher, Theodore C.	075	1880	WB-O/116	AR
Fletcher, Thomas	104	1835	WB-4/189	AR
Fletcher, Thomas	024	1734	SS 876/423	SS/AR
Fletcher, Wiley C.	099	1893	WB-C/153	AR
Fletcher, Wiley C.	099	1893	036 WB-A/283	036 CTY
Fletcher, William	077	1827	WB-F/126	AR
Fletcher, William E.	047	1899	WB-7/276	AR
Fleuellen, Richard	047	1798	WB-3/307	
Flibus, John	028	1775	Orig. Only	AR
Flin, Nicholas	065	c1785	WB-C/60	AR
Flinchum, Mary	090	c1888	092 WB-6/366	092 AR

Name	Co.	Date	Recorded Copy	Original
Flinchum, Mary	090	1893	WB-6/293	AR
Flinchum, William	090	1888	WB-6/208	AR
Flinn, Alfred	038	1886	WB-3/8	AR
Flinn, Benjamin	053	c1805	RW-1/395	
Flinn, Daniel	011	c1785	WB-1/537	
Flinn, Enoch	009	1837	OWB/506	AR
Flinn, Mary K.	084	1889	WB-E/424	CTY
Flinn, Patrick	020	1784	RB-B/35	AR
Flinn, William	065	1840	WB-H/16	
Flint, Thomas	073	c1837	Orig. Only	AR
Flintham, John	073	1825	WB-E/88	AR
Flintoff, William	073	1826	WB-E/125	
Flippen, John C.	090	c1864	WB-6/347	
Flippin, Josiah	092	1848	WB-4/285	
Flippin, Raleigh W.	092	1899	WB-6/497	AR
Flippin, Samuel	090	1852	WB-4/278	AR
Flippin, Samuel M.	090	1894	WB-6/357	AR
Flood, James	070	1736	SS 877/162	SS/AR
Flood, James	024	1750	Orig. Only	SS/AR
Flora, Aaron	030	c1814	WB-3/51	
Flora, Andrew	018	1861	WB-D/62	
Flora, Larsus	030	1778	WB-1/124	
Flora, Susan	018	1881	WB-E/81	AR
Florance, Louis	020	1898	WB-B/347	CTY
Florance, Toliver	020	1875	WB-A/177	CTY
Flory, John	030	1827	WB-3/223	
Flory, Lazarus	037	1799	WB-D/88	AR
Flory, William	030	c1811	WB-3/9	
Flournoy, John	005	1827	WB-A/139	AR
Flow, D. W.	065	1894	WB-M/239	AR
Flow, David	065	1869	WB-K/7	AR
Flow, W. M.	016	1891	WB-4/107 & 117	AR
Flowe, James	065	1878	WB-K/291	
Flowe, John M.	065	1885	WB-L/80	AR
Flowe, Jonathan	065	1893	WB-M/157	AR
Flower, Ransford	071	1789	WB-1/392	AR
Flowers, Adam	003	1880	WB-B/128	AR
Flowers, Annie E.	029	1898	WB-F/144	AR
Flowers, Beniamin	069	c1782	WB-1/31	AR
Flowers, Benjamin	069	c1852	WB-1/549	AR
Flowers, Christopher	053	1857	WB-8/220	AR
Flowers, Christopher	053	1850	WB-7/437	AR
Flowers, David F.	011	1899	WB-3/112	CTY
Flowers, Edward	037	1778	WB-A/267	AR
Flowers, Elizabeth	054	1853	WB-3/74	AR
Flowers, Elkanah	017	1887	WB-B/143	AR
Flowers, George	103	1877	WB-1/110	AR
Flowers, George	054	1854	Orig. Only	AR
Flowers, Henry	069	1792	WB-1/74	AR
Flowers, Hugh	083	1871	WB-3/32	AR
Flowers, Ignatius	011	c1793	WB-1/359	
Flowers, Jacob	037	1766	WB-A/161	AR
Flowers, Jacob, Sr.	056	1856	WB-1/692	AR
Flowers, James	012	1826	WB-B/141	AR
Flowers, Jesse	105	1885	WB-2/368	AR
Flowers, Jessee	083	1896	WB-4/216	
Flowers, Job	070	c1748	SS 882/7	
Flowers, John	083	1813	WB-1/137	AR
Flowers, John	054	c1829	WB-2/84	AR
Flowers, John	048	1893	WB-1/26	CTY
Flowers, John	083	1890	WB-3/506	AR
Flowers, John N.	105	1885	WB-2/354	AR
Flowers, Joseph	021	1864	WB-1/192	AR
Flowers, Michael	005	1850	WB-C/21	AR
Flowers, Nancy	099	N. D.	Orig. Only	AR
Flowers, Phereby	056	1868	WB-2/103	AR
Flowers, Samuel	103	1862	RD-13/371	AR
Flowers, Sarah	029	1847	WB-C/144	AR
Flowers, Thomas	069	c1858	Orig. Only	AR
Flowers, Thomas	070	1821	WB-C/111	AR
Flowers, Thomas	070	1794	WB-C/107	AR
Flowers, Thomas	103	1818	RD-4/120	AR
Floyd, Amos	069	1807	WB-1/173	AR
Floyd, Ann	039	c1795	WB-B/13	AR
Floyd, Ann	009	1818	OB-A/289	AR
Floyd, B. M.	083	1890	WB-3/475	
Floyd, Belle H.	VA	1899	013 WB-D/350	013 AR
Floyd, Catherine	010	1862	WB-H/120	AR
Floyd, Cullin	069	1888	WB-5/309	AR
Floyd, Elizabeth W.	009	1827	OB-A/390	AR
Floyd, Francis	085	1816	WB-G/447	AR
Floyd, Francis	037	1761	WB-A/32	AR
Floyd, Francis	027	1886	WB-2/66	AR
Floyd, George	044	1844	WB-16/79	CTY
Floyd, George	044	N. D.	WB-23/20	
Floyd, George W.	081	1898	WB-16/507	AR
Floyd, Griffin	009	1762	OWB/56	AR
Floyd, Grissom	009	1822	Orig. Only	AR
Floyd, Halsy	077	1832	WB-F/200	AR
Floyd, Henry	044	1832	WB-12/226	CTY
Floyd, Ivey	009	1826	OB-A/370	AR
Floyd, James	072	1828	WB-1/16	
Floyd, James T.	098	1900	WB-A/373	CTY
Floyd, John	071	1756	Orig. Only	SS/AR
Floyd, John	071	1779	WB-1/214	
Floyd, Mary	010	1856	WB-H/28	AR
Floyd, Morris	071	1792	WB-2/13	AR
Floyd, Nancy D.	069	1890	WB-5/311	AR
Floyd, Peter	009	c1790	OWB/244	AR
Floyd, Pleasant	044	1858	WB-20/632	CTY
Floyd, Rachel	010	1859	WB-H/88	AR
Floyd, Randal	010	1818	WB-G/24	AR
Floyd, Simeon	009	c1793	OWB/281	AR
Floyd, Thomas	009	1820	OB-A/299	AR
Floyd, Uriah	009	c1790	OWB/247	AR
Floyd, William	044	1826	WB-10/96	CTY
Floyd, William	044	1838	WB-14/47	CTY
Floyd, William	044	1881	WB-23/412	CTY
Floyd, William S.	083	1880	WB-3/197	AR
Floyed, John	010	1831	WB-G/203	AR
Fluelton, William	047	1786	WB-3/112	
Fly, Emilus	071	1831	WB-4/85	AR
Flybus, John S.	028	1842	WB-D/46	AR
Flyn, Collumb	008	1737	SS 877/72	SS/AR
Flynn, Cornelius	009	1858	OB-K/404	AR
Flynn, George P.	009	1887	WB-1/412	CTY
Flynn, Langley R.	009	1842	OB-D/275	AR
Flynn, Thomas	009	c1861	Orig. Only	AR
Flynt, David	099	1775	RB-1/66	AR
Flynt, Elisabeth	090	1842	WB-4/94	AR
Flynt, Haston	090	1804	WB-2/59	AR
Flynt, John	090	c1821	Orig. Only	AR
Flynt, Nancy P.	038	1869	WB-2/11	AR
Flynt, Richard	090	1840	WB-4/61	AR
Flynt, Thomas	090	1825	WB-3/137	AR
Flynt, William H.	SC	1876	090 WB-6/82	090 AR
Flythe, Jesse	071	1898	047 WB-7/189	
Flythe, Jesse	071	1898	WB-7/425	AR
Flythe, John	071	1876	WB-6/207	AR

Name	Co.	Date	Recorded Copy	Original
Foard, John	065	1798	WB-C/72	AR
Foard, John C.	033	1892	WB-2/125	CTY
Foard, John C.	033	1892	085 WB-2/519	085 CTY
Foard, Nancy	078	1855	WB-17/344	AR
Foard, Sarah E.	046	1891	WB-F/98	AR
Foard, William F.	046	1891	WB-F/156	AR
Foard, Wyatt	085	1816	WB-G/429	AR
Foard, Zebulon	065	1807	WB-C/76	AR
Fockel, Maria R.	090	1833	WB-3/252	AR
Foddery, Thomas	053	1842	WB-6/198	AR
Foddral, Samuel	090	1835	WB-3/296	AR
Foddrill, William	090	1894	WB-6/337	AR
Fogg, John	090	1890	WB-6/224	AR
Fogg, Moses	028	1751	DB-5/223	SS/AR
Fogle, Anna P.	038	1890	WB-3/156	AR
Fogle, Antoinette	038	1900	WB-4/242	AR
Fogle, Augustus	038	1897	WB-4/35	AR
Fogle, Charles A.	038	1893	WB-3/344	AR
Fogle, Christian	038	1898	WB-4/101	AR
Fogle, Samuel G.	038	1897	WB-4/63	AR
Fogleman, George	073	1847	WB-F/380	AR
Fogleman, George	073	1785	WB-A/323	AR
Fogleman, James	001	1884	WB-2/220	AR
Fogleman, William	073	1849	WB-F/428	AR
Fogler, Lawrence	092	1779	WB-1/131	AR
Foil, Alexander	016	1889	WB-4/12	AR
Foil, Ellen	016	18777	WB-3/234	AR
Foil, Philip	016	1852	WB-1/210	
Foister, Mary	092	c1872	Orig. Only	AR
Folk, Andrew	090	1790	WB-1/14	AR
Folk, Edmund D.	037	1876	WB-G/477	
Folk, George N.	017	1896	WB-B/264	AR
Folk, Sally	010	1835	WB-G/249	AR
Folk, Samuel	063	1828	WB-2/142	
Folk, William K.	010	1867	WB-H/181	AR
Folkner, Ephraim	029	1792	Orig. Only	AR
Folks, Martha	071	1821	WB-3/258	AR
Folsom, Ebenezer	029	1792	Orig. Only	AR
Folsom, Edith	056	1793	WB-1/66	AR
Foltz, Anna C.	038	1862	WB-1/193	AR
Foltz, Elizabeth	PA	1896	085 WB-3/322	085 CTY
Foltz, Jacob	090	1845	WB-4/205	AR
Foltz, Lewis	038	1894	WB-3/462	AR
Foltz, Louisa	038	1896	WB-4/134	AR
Foltz, Louise	032	1896	WB-4/309	AR
Foltz, Peter	090	1806	WB-2/69	AR
Fondall, Robert	077	1711/2	SS 874.1/38	
Fones, John	063	c1792	WB-1/375	
Fones, Thomas	063	c1798	WB-1/374	
Fontaine, William	VA	1810	Copy	041 AR
Fonviele, John	028	1741	Deeds.1/L106	
Fonvielle, David	028	1770	Orig. Only	AR
Fonvielle, Francis	028	1799	WB-B/68	AR
Fonvielle, Frederick	028	1785	WB-A/107	AR
Fonvielle, Jeremiah	028	1852	WB-D/192	AR
Fonvielle, John	028	1773	Orig. Only	SS/AR
Fonvielle, John	028	1794	WB-A/318	AR
Fonvielle, L. O.	072	1900	103 WB-3/321	103 AR
Fonvielle, Lewis	028	1807	WB-B/291	AR
Fonvielle, Mary B.	028	1853	WB-D/219	AR
Fonvielle, Richard	028	1836	WB-C/393	AR
Fonvielle, Richard G.	028	1843	WB-D/83	AR
Fonvielle, Sidney	028	1830	WB-C/316	AR
Fonvielle, Stephen	072	1775	RW/L14	AR
Fonvielle, William	028	1788	WB-A/172	AR
Fonvielle, Wm. Brice	028	1780	Orig. Only	AR
Fonville, Brice	028	1835	WB-C/385	AR
Fonville, Brice F.	001	1900	WB-3/296	AR
Fonville, Frederick	073	1835	WB-E/350	AR
Fonville, James B.	001	1863	WB-1/211	AR
Fonville, James R.	001	1880	WB-2/178	AR
Fonville, John, Sr.	028	c1741	Copy	024 AR
Fonville, L. O.	103	1900	072 WB-4/431	072 AR
Fonville, Mary E.	059	1900	WB-B/257	CTY
Fonville, Mary E.	001	1890	WB-2/467	
Fookes, John	028	1776	Orig. Only	AR
Fookes, Joseph	028	1802	Orig. Only	AR
Fooks, John	028	1812	WB-C/46	AR
Foops, Joseph	N	c1755	SS 880/135	
Foort, Elias	047	1812	WB-3/527	
Foort, Elizabeth	037	1817	WB-E/155	AR
Foort, George	037	1761	WB-A/84	AR
Foort, John, Jr.	047	1803	WB-3/402	
Foorte, Willis	047	1795	WB-3/242	
Fooshee, Catharine	022	1853	WB-C/350	AR
Fooshee, Charles	001	1865	WB-1/245	AR
Fooshee, Everett	022	1871	WB-E/71	AR
Fooshee, Happy	022	1824	WB-B/85	AR
Fooshee, John	022	1843	WB-C/143	AR
Fooshee, Joseph	022	1818	WB-A/309	AR
Fooshee, Joseph	022	1820	WB-B/27	AR
Fooshee, Joseph	022	c1813	Orig. Only	AR
Fooshee, Martha A.	022	1885	WB-E/323	AR
Fooshee, Mary	022	1854	WB-C/361	AR
Fooshee, Nelly	022	1838	WB-C/87	AR
Fooshee, Simon	022	c1800	WB-A/37	AR
Fooshee, Simon	022	c1835	WB-C/21	AR
Fooshee, William	022	1854	WB-C/362	AR
Foot, William	092	1834	WB-4/98	AR-Copy
Foote, George A.	100	1899	WB-52/5	AR
Foote, Henry	015	1776	100 WB-2/82	AR
Foote, Henry A.	100	1863	WB-50/9	
Foote, L. R.	033	1898	WB-2/243	CTY
Foote, Mary	100	1852	WB-42/92	AR
Foote, William	054	c1829	WB-2/141	AR
Foox, Hugh	014	1828	Orig. Only	AR
Foraster, James	073	1755	SS 880/56	SS/AR
Forbas, Ralph	046	c1869	WB-E/20	AR
Forbes, Abner	018	1844	WB-C/291	
Forbes, Bale	075	1774	WB-I/80	AR
Forbes, Bathsheba	018	1834	WB-C/172	
Forbes, Bettie	037	1900	WB-H/488	AR
Forbes, Brittania	018	1844	WB-C/301	
Forbes, Caleb	018	c1829	WB-C/175	
Forbes, David	070	1780	WB-C/100	AR
Forbes, Demcy	030	1816	WB-3/88	
Forbes, Edward M.	019	1893	WB-B/239	AR
Forbes, Edward M.	019	1893	028 WB-F/109	
Forbes, Elizabeth	018	1832	WB-C/131	
Forbes, Elizabeth	018	1852	WB-C/365	
Forbes, Enoch S.	030	1823	WB-3/160	
Forbes, Etheridge	018	1879	WB-E/67	AR
Forbes, Hyrum	105	1862	WB-1/68	AR
Forbes, Irena	079	1889	WB-2/468	AR
Forbes, James	075	1888	WB-0/298	AR
Forbes, John	030	1854	WB-4/180	AR
Forbes, John F.	075	1837	WB-N/138	AR
Forbes, John S.	026	1843	WB-1/10	AR
Forbes, John, Sr.	075	1750	Orig. Only	SS/AR
Forbes, Joseph W.	105	1883	WB-2/306	AR

Name	Co.	Date	Recorded Copy	Original
Forbes, Penelope	028	1818	WB-C/168	AR
Forbes, Peter D.	030	1884	WB-5/100	
Forbes, Rebecca	075	1848	WB-N/223a	AR
Forbes, Richard	028	1811	WB-C/26	AR
Forbes, Robert	079	c1845	WB-1/17	AR-Copy
Forbes, Samuel W.	018	1886	WB-E/153	AR
Forbes, Sarah	030	1888	WB-5/156	AR
Forbes, Sarah	018	1826	WB-C/75	
Forbes, Silas	018	1840	WB-C/258	
Forbes, Southy	018	1822	WB-C/1	
Forbes, William	072	1834	WB-1/136	
Forbes, William	070	1751	DB-C/344	AR
Forbes, William	073	1764	WB-A/32	
Forbes, William	075	1854	WB-M2/16	AR
Forbes, William	030	1802	WB-2/205	
Forbes, William H.	070	1886	WB-F/21	AR
Forbis, Ann	046	1896	WB-F/524	AR
Forbis, Arthur	046	1790	WB-A/117	AR
Forbis, Arthur	046	c1780	WB-A/115	AR
Forbis, David, Sr.	046	c1873	WB-E/195	AR
Forbis, George	085	1769	WB-A/58	AR
Forbis, Hugh	046	1816	Orig. Only	AR
Forbis, John	046	1806	WB-A/124	AR
Forbis, Joseph	086	1834	WB-E/1	AR
Forbis, Sarah R.	026	1900	Orig. Only	AR
Forbis, Sarah R.	065	1900	WB-N/379	AR
Forbis, William	046	1772	WB-A/114	AR
Forbs, Jacob	018	1857	WB-D/39	
Forbus, Elizabeth	040	c1857	WB-1/98	
Ford, George	082	1810	WB-1/143	AR
Ford, Gerrel	085	1836	WB-H/678	AR-Nunc.
Ford, Hardy	099	1872	RB-35/181	AR
Ford, Hendry	065	1788	WB-C/61	AR
Ford, John	078	1865	WB-18/394	AR
Ford, John	033	1866	WB-1/193	
Ford, John T.	049	c1833	WI-1-2/3	AR
Ford, Joseph P.	049	1897	WB-2/383	AR
Ford, Joshua	086	1892	WB-F/442	AR
Ford, Lilly W.	084	1882	WB-E/243	CTY
Ford, Lilly W.	084	1882	016 WB-4/126	016 AR
Ford, Marcus	070	1768	WB-C/99	AR
Ford, Mary	060	1805	Orig. Only	AR
Ford, Nancy	099	1897	WB-D/43	AR
Ford, Nathan	060	1821	Orig. Only	AR/CRX
Ford, Rebecca	044	1828	Orig. Only	CTY-Nunc.
Ford, Samuel	099	1823	RB-18/299	AR
Ford, Sarah	087	1842	WB-1/256	AR
Ford, Sarah S.	040	1865	WB-1/184	
Ford, T. W.	VA	1878	098 WB-A/328	098 CTY
Ford, Thaddeus	032	1899	WB-4/391	AR
Ford, William	024	1837	WB-C/199	AR
Ford, William M.	085	1841	WB-I/109	AR
Fordham, Alice	028	1785	WB-A/91	AR
Fordham, Benjamin	028	c1777	Orig. Only	AR
Fordham, C. C.	057	1900	WB-C/261	AR
Fordham, John	057	1845	WB-B/175	AR
Fore, S. G.	062	1867	WB-A/50	
Foreham, Cornelius	075	1728	Orig. Only	SS/AR
Forehand, David	046	1802	WB-A/121	AR
Forehand, David	069	1838	WB-1/430	AR
Forehand, James	103	1860	RD-13/222	AR
Forehand, Joel	024	1878	WB-E/67	AR
Forehand, Joseph	075	1807	WB-M1/168	AR
Forehand, Lemuel	075	1808	WB-M1/196	AR
Forehand, Levi	103	c1865	RD-14/185	AR
Forehand, Mary	018	1852	WB-C/360	
Forehand, Needham	103	1862	RD-13/536	AR
Forehand, Pennina	024	1878	WB-E/75	AR
Forehand, Sally	103	1861	RD-13/335	
Forehand, Solomon	037	1802	WB-D/146	AR
Forehand, William	035	1883	WB-4/216	AR
Foreman, Amelia	047	1824	WB-3/704	
Foreman, Benjamin	053	1815	RW-1/497	
Foreman, Benjamin	022	1796	RB-2/70	AR
Foreman, Benjamin	047	1811	WB-3/513	
Foreman, Caleb	053	1826	WB-4/333	AR
Foreman, Caleb	053	1790	RW-1/192	AR
Foreman, Charles A.	070	1899	WB-H/246	AR
Foreman, George	037	1803	WB-D/180	AR
Foreman, John	053	1744	Orig. Only	SS/AR
Foreman, John	085	c1807	WB-E/176	AR
Foreman, John T.	053	1758	SS 882/112	SS/AR
Foreman, Joseph	053	1785	RW-1/140	
Foreman, Lazarus	053	1796	RW-1/272	AR
Foreman, Lazarus	053	1771	RW-1/18	AR
Foreman, Lovey	053	1830	WB-5/23	AR
Foreman, Martha	079	1892	WB-3/3	
Foreman, Martin	053	c1779	RW-1/85	
Foreman, Olive	009	1827	OB-A/378	AR
Foreman, William	047	1766	WB-1/185	
Foreman, William	009	1752	OWB/44	AR
Forester, Arthur C.	104	1862	WB-5/329	
Forester, John	104	1827	WB-4/105	AR
Forester, Thomas	092	1778	WB-1/89	AR
Forgerson, Jack	090	1806	WB-2/68	AR
Forgey, Samuel	085	1770	WB-A/56	AR
Forguson, Samuel	065	1787	WB-C/68	AR
Forguson, Sarah	060	1819	Orig. Only	AR
Forkner, Deborah	092	1894	WB-6/385	AR
Forkner, Emanual	054	c1797	WB-1/99	AR
Forkner, James	092	1858	WB-5/33	
Forkner, James A.	092	1893	WB-6/367	AR
Forkner, Joseph	092	c1836	WB-4/105	
Forkner, William	092	1892	WB-6/348	AR
Forkner, William	092	1807	WB-3/80	
Forksey, Philip	075	1727	SS 876/106	
Forlaw, Elizabeth	035	1856	WB-2/99	AR
Forlaw, John H.	019	1858	WB-A/215	AR
Forlaw, Nancy	028	1837	WB-C/407	AR
Forman, Caleb	053	1774	RW-1/49	
Forman, Charles G.	019	1868	WB-B/43	AR
Forman, Cornelius	069	1864	WB-1/588	AR
Forman, John	VA	c1724	024 WB-B/77	024 AR
Forman, Joshua	053	1776	RW-1/78	
Forman, Quincy A.	005	1872	WB-D/21	AR
Forman, William	019	c1872	Orig. Only	AR
Formes, John	028	1842	WB-D/56	
Fornes, Jerusha	028	1838	WB-C/426	AR
Fornes, John	028	1842	Orig. Only	AR
Forney, A. E.	060	1887	WB-4/368	AR
Forney, Albert G.	086	1851	WB-E/210	AR
Forney, E. M.	086	1900	WB-G/40	AR
Forney, Flora	085	1891	WB-2/469	CTY
Forney, H. A.	021	1897	060 WB-5/59	060 AR
Forney, H. A.	021	1897	WB-3/190	AR
Forney, Jacob	014	c1840	Copy	026 AR
Forney, Jacob	014	1841	Orig. Only	AR
Forney, Jacob, Sr.	060	1806	WB-1/307	AR
Forney, Peter	060	1834	WB-1/307	AR

Name	Co.	Date	Recorded Copy	Original
Forney, Peter B.	014	1867	WB-1/20	AR
Forney, Robert	086	1884	WB-F/247	AR
Forraus, Alexander	028	1807	WB-B/280	
Forraus, Richard N.	028	1830	WB-C/325	
Forraus, Samuel	028	1812	WB-C/50	
Forrest, Francis H.	099	1887	WB-B/181	AR
Forrest, Isaac	073	1798	WB-C/113	AR
Forrest, William	089	c1865	Orig. Only	AR
Forrest, William	073	1778	WB-A/207	
Forrest, Winefred	103	1835	RD-7/93	AR
Forrester, Benjamin	073	1801	WB-D/23	AR
Forrester, David	022	1869	WB-E/30	AR
Forrester, James	092	c1837	WB-4/129	AR
Forrester, Samuel C.	022	1890	WB-E/426	AR
Forster, Anthony	064	1891	WB-2/220	AR
Forster, Margaret	071	1781	WB-1/243	
Forsyth, Henderson	054	1848	Orig. Only	AR
Forsyth, James	044	1831	WB-12/189	CTY
Forsyth, John A.	054	1839	WB-2/202	AR
Forsyth, William	073	1819	WB-D/560	AR
Fort, Ann	047	1785	WB-3/76	
Fort, Chloe	099	1848	RB-26/1848	AR
Fort, David	099	1864	RB-33/283	AR
Fort, Elias	047	1774	WB-1/354	
Fort, Elias	037	1761	WB-A/27	AR
Fort, Elias	047	1766	WB-1/208	
Fort, Elizabeth	099	c1853	Orig. Only	AR
Fort, Elizabeth	099	1849	RB-26/591	AR
Fort, Foster	099	1843	RB-25/372	AR
Fort, Frances C.	099	1876	RB-35/325	
Fort, Franky	099	1839	RB-24/259	AR
Fort, Frederick	099	1819	RB-15/239	AR
Fort, George	002	1719	SS 875/154	SS/AR
Fort, Ibell	047	1793	WB-3/216	
Fort, James	099	1838	RB-24/193	AR
Fort, Jane	037	1822	WB-E/314	AR
Fort, John	037	1761	WB-A/17	AR
Fort, John	028	1745/6	SS 878/76	SS/AR
Fort, John	037	1780	WB-B/49	AR
Fort, John	056	1748	SS 877/254	SS/AR
Fort, John	099	1825	RB-19/451	AR
Fort, John	011	1853	WB-1/217	
Fort, John F.	099	1882	WB-A/361	AR
Fort, John T.	087	1882	WB-3/244	AR
Fort, Joseph	083	c1797	WB-1/47	AR
Fort, Joseph	037	1791	WB-C/163	AR
Fort, Junius W.	099	1876	RB-35/325	AR
Fort, Mary	037	1782	WB-B/104	AR
Fort, Micaja	037	1799	WB-D/70	AR
Fort, Milly	087	1866	WB-2/110	AR
Fort, Pheriba A.	039	1888	WB-U/456	AR
Fort, Phillis	065	1781	WB-C/65	AR
Fort, Richard	028	1746	SS 877/104	SS/AR
Fort, Thomas W.	029	1864	WB-D/70	AR
Fort, Turner	005	1850	WB-C/25	AR
Fort, W. S.	099	1865	RB-33/480	
Fort, William	099	1843	RB-25/320	AR
Fort, William	103	1791	WI-A/239	AR
Forte, Elizabeth	005	1855	WB-C/90	AR
Forte, Nanney	103	1811	RD-2/37	AR
Forte, William L.	099	1871	RB-35/148	AR
Fortescue, Bill	053	1775	RW-1/56	
Fortescue, Edmund A.	053	1893	WB-11/302	AR
Fortescue, Hiram B.	053	1897	WB-11/334	AR
Fortescue, James H.	009	1880	Orig. Only	CTY
Fortescue, John	053	1806	RW-1/394	AR
Fortescue, Moses	053	c1819	WB-4/8	AR
Fortescue, William	053	1760	OB-A/23	
Fortescue, William H.	053	1887	WB-11/199	AR
Fortescue, Zachariah	053	1829	WB-4/434	AR
Fortescue, Zacheus	053	1848	WB-7/165	AR
Fortesque, Simon	053	1765	RW-1/2	Nunc.
Fortiscue, Elizabeth	009	1853	OB-I/109	AR
Fortner, Aaron	003	1890	WB-B/282	AR
Fortner, James	008	c1729	009 OWB/8	AR
Fortner, John E.	087	1855	WB-1/478	AR
Fortner, John E.	087	1896	WB-4/12	AR
Fortsen, Mary	N	1665	Orig. Only	SS/AR
Fortune, Jesse	054	c1813	WB-1/317	AR
Fortune, John	013	1856	WB-A/170	
Fortune, Lavender	014	1839	Orig. Only	AR
Fortune, Pleasant	086	1897	WB-F/521	aR
Fortune, Pleasant	086	1846	WB-E/169	AR
Foscue, Ann	028	1842	WB-D/60	AR
Foscue, Benjamin	028	1797	WB-B/23	AR
Foscue, Elizabeth	028	1841	WB-D/29	AR
Foscue, Frederick	057	1835	WB-B/123	AR
Foscue, John	053	1752	028 DB-5/227	SS/AR
Foscue, John E.	057	1849	WB-B/199	AR
Foscue, Lewis	028	1865	WB-D/405	
Foscue, Richard	028	1784	Orig. Only.	AR
Foscue, Simon	053	1751	028 DB-5/208	SS/AR
Foscue, Simon	057	1831	WB-B/108	AR
Foscue, Simon	057	1814	WB-B/35	AR
Foscue, Susan H.	057	1858	WB-B/250	AR
Fosett, Robert	073	c1785	WB-A/362	AR
Foshee, Charles	073	1759	WB-A/62	
Foshee, Charles	073	1757	WB-A/2	
Fossett, William	073	1785	WB-A/339	AR
Fosskey, Thomas	009	1830	OB-B/78	AR
Foster, Abigail	054	1894	WB-5/496	CTY
Foster, Ambrose	VA	1802	Copy	020 AR
Foster, Anderson	085	c1834	Copy	033 AR
Foster, Anderson	085	1836	WB-H/677	AR
Foster, Ann	077	1818	WB-F/13	AR
Foster, Augustus	039	1873	WB-U/86	AR
Foster, Barsheba	046	1840	WB-C/52	AR
Foster, Brisco	001	1887	WB-2/343	AR
Foster, Catharine	033	1848	WB-1/94	
Foster, Catharine	070	1874	WB-E/341	AR
Foster, Charlotte	031	1874	WB-1/7	AR
Foster, Christopher	015	1775	100 WB-2/65	AR
Foster, Daniel	039	1817	WB-E/133	AR
Foster, David	085	1828	WB-H/420	AR
Foster, David C.	054	1868	WB-3/204	
Foster, Edmond S.	013	1842	WB-A/86	
Foster, Elizabeth	039	1863	WB-R/615	
Foster, Elsey	024	N. D.	Orig. Only	AR
Foster, Francis	077	1761	WB-C/8	AR
Foster, Francis	077	1819	WB-F/18	AR
Foster, Francis	077	1847	WB-F/338	AR
Foster, Frederick	077	1784	WB-C/255	AR
Foster, George	073	1848	WB-F/404	AR
Foster, George	014	1817	Orig. Only	AR
Foster, Hannah	077	1728	SS 876/131	SS/AR
Foster, James	N	1727	SS 876/107	SS/AR
Foster, James	085	1811	WB-G/195	AR
Foster, James	033	1867	WB-1/206	
Foster, James I.	039	1864	WB-R/795	AR
Foster, Jesse A.	033	c1873	WB-2/37	CTY

Name	Co.	Date	Recorded Copy	Original
Foster, Jesse L.	085	1844	WB-I/231	AR
Foster, John	020	1846	RB-P/343	AR
Foster, John	046	1839	WB-C/39	AR
Foster, John	065	1821	WB-C/86	AR
Foster, John	046	1845	WB-C/232	AR
Foster, John	028	1754	SS 879/124	SS/AR
Foster, John	104	1824	WB-4/44	AR
Foster, John H.	077	1848	WB-F/365	AR
Foster, John, Sr.	039	c1803	WB-B/151	
Foster, John, Sr.	104	1860	WB-5/256	
Foster, Jordan H.	100	1867	WB-50/242	AR
Foster, Joseph	085	1811	WB-G/207	AR
Foster, Kerr B.	085	1833	WB-H/602	AR
Foster, Lettice	020	1837	RB-N/56	AR
Foster, Levin C.	077	1841	WB-F/300	AR
Foster, Louizer E.	085	1899	WB-3/284	CTY
Foster, Lucy	104	1834	WB-4/180	AR
Foster, Lucy E.	098	1886	WB-A/75	CTY
Foster, Margarett	018	1845	WB-C/305	
Foster, Martha Ann	100	1884	WB-51/198	AR
Foster, Martha D.	020	1896	WB-D/283	CTY
Foster, Mary	085	1818	WB-G/520	AR
Foster, Mary	015	1768	100 WB-1/49	AR
Foster, Mary	077	1806	WB-E/249	AR
Foster, Mary	033	1897	WB-2/209	CTY
Foster, Mary	013	1864	WB-A/229	
Foster, Mary	100	1884	WB-51/198	AR
Foster, Nancy	024	1783	WB-B/38	AR-Nunc.
Foster, Nathaniel	006	1896	WB-E/294	AR
Foster, Patsy	100	1856	WB-49/73	AR
Foster, Peter	039	c1840	WB-L/230	AR-Copy
Foster, Richard	085	1814	WB-G/303	AR
Foster, Richard	099	1810	RB-9/179	AR
Foster, Richard M.	078	1883	WB-19/134	AR
Foster, Robert	085	1818	WB-G/496	AR
Foster, Robert	010	1740	LGB-4/#128	SS/AR
Foster, Sally	020	1856	RB-R/408	AR
Foster, Samuel P.	001	c1854	WB-1/82	AR
Foster, Sarah	033	1879	WB-2/65	CTY
Foster, Silas	096	1792	Orig. Only	AR
Foster, T. H.	104	1891	WB-6/419	AR
Foster, Thomas	013	1839	WB-A/60	
Foster, Thomas	104	1888	WB-6/313	AR
Foster, Thomas	020	1861	RB-S/418	AR
Foster, Thomas	085	c1781	WB-B/81	AR
Foster, Thomas	013	1859	WB-A/196	
Foster, Tilmon	085	1854	WB-K/164	AR
Foster, Weldon G.	033	1865	WB-1/190	
Foster, William	N	c1687	Orig. Only	SS/AR
Foster, William	077	1833	WB-F/223	AR
Foster, William	078	1895	WB-19/380	AR
Foster, William	072	1805	WB-A/31	AR
Fotts, Barbara	090	1845	WB-4/187	
Foulkes, John A.	046	1853	WB-C/392	AR
Foulkes, Mary B.	046	1867	WB-D/353	AR
Fountain, Henry	037	1797	WB-D/18	AR
Fountain, James	037	1824	WB-F/19	AR
Fountain, Jane	090	1827	WB-3/162	AR
Fountain, Joab	035	1800	WB-A/144	AR
Fountain, Loderick	037	1850	Orig. Only	AR
Fountain, Noah	070	1828	WB-C/115	AR
Fountain, Samuel	046	1825	WB-B/210	AR
Fountain, Stephen	090	1810	WB-2/105	AR
Fountain, Timothy	037	1860	WB-G/187	AR
Fountaine, Isabella	070	1828	WB-C/114	AR
Fountaine, J. R.	090	1871	WB-6/18	AR
Fourhand, Daniel	077	1783	WB-C/249	AR
Fourre, John	075	1732	SS 876/242	SS/AR
Fourre, Peter	002	1697	Orig. Only	SS/AR
Foushee, Annie J.	068	1897	WB-D/525	
Foushee, Jonathon	073	1757	WB-A/2	
Foushee, Mary Eliz.	022	c1876	WB-E/453	AR
Foushee, William F.	022	1893	WB-E/530	AR
Foust, Christian	046	1871	WB-E/63	AR
Foust, Daniel	032	1887	WB-4/1	AR
Foust, Daniel	046	1882	WB-E/360	AR
Foust, Daniel	073	1826	WB-E/124	AR
Foust, Gemima	001	1900	WB-3/294	AR
Foust, George	073	1836	WB-E/382	AR
Foust, George	001	1861	WB-1/189	AR
Foust, Henry	073	1840	WB-F/53	AR
Foust, Henry M.	081	1867	WB-14/155	
Foust, Jacob	081	1863	WB-12/367	
Foust, Jacob	081	1796	WB-2/21	AR
Foust, John	073	1790	WB-B/79	AR
Foust, John, Sr.	046	1835	WB-B/532	AR
Foust, Maria D.	001	1882	WB-2/191	AR
Foust, Mary	001	1852	WB-1/57	AR
Foust, Melinda	046	1896	WB-F/521	AR
Foust, Peter	073	1808	WB-D/239	AR
Foust, Peter	001	1888	WB-2/403	AR
Foust, Peter	001	c1854	WB-1/94	AR
Foust, Peter Z.	001	1863	WB-1/216	AR
Foust, William	073	1846	WB-F/308	AR
Fouts, Andrew	081	1834	WB-6/398	AR
Fouts, Daniel	032	1863	WB-2/236	AR
Fouts, Jacob	081	1835	WB-6/460	AR
Fowle, Daniel G.	099	1891	WB-B/513	AR
Fowle, Mary E.	099	1886	WB-B/126	AR
Fowle, Samuel R.	009	1877	WB-1/175	CTY
Fowler, Aaron	080	1864	WB-1/189	AR
Fowler, Amanda A.	044	1897	WB-24/352	CTY
Fowler, Ann	012	1772	DB-A/161	AR
Fowler, Cassa	087	1885	WB-3/315	AR
Fowler, Elizabeth	086	1892	WB-F/427	AR
Fowler, Elizabeth	073	1862	WB-G/385	CTY
Fowler, Elizabeth	087	1885	WB-3/303	AR
Fowler, Elvira	080	1884	WB-1/75	AR
Fowler, Henry	044	1796	WB-4/43	CTY
Fowler, John H.	038	1882	WB-2/414	AR
Fowler, John W.	054	1899	WB-6/232	CTY
Fowler, Joseph	099	1859	RB-31/150	
Fowler, Joseph	099	1794	RB-3/68	AR-Nunc.
Fowler, Joseph	099	1793	RB-2/405	AR
Fowler, Joseph	039	1883	WB-U/314	AR
Fowler, Lewis	074	1875	WB-1/53	AR
Fowler, Marvin	071	1846	WB-5/49	AR
Fowler, Mary	099	1822	RB-18/1	AR
Fowler, Minerva	036	1894	WB-A/322	CTY
Fowler, Moody	044	1863	WB-21/669	CTY
Fowler, Nathaniel	070	1884	WB-E/521	AR
Fowler, Owen C.	033	1864	WB-1/183	
Fowler, Richard	044	1771	Orig. Only	CTY
Fowler, Richard	044	1771	Copy	020 AR
Fowler, Sarah	038	1888	WB-3/99	AR
Fowler, Thomas B.	055	1899	WB-A/161	
Fowler, Thomas J.	073	1879	WB-H/226	CTY
Fowler, William	099	1814	RB-11/298	AR
Fowler, William A.	099	1799	RB-5/32	AR
Fowler, William B.	099	1828	RB-20/293	AR

Name	Co.	Date	Recorded Copy	Original
Fowler, William G.	070	1896	WB-G/465	AR
Fox, A. J.	060	1884	WB-4/291	AR
Fox, A. M.	016	1893	WB-4/166	AR
Fox, Aaron	072	c1780	RW/L30	AR
Fox, Andrew	022	1868	WB-E/2	AR
Fox, Charles J.	065	1876	WB-K/222	AR
Fox, David	022	1857	WB-C/434	AR
Fox, David	021	1891	WB-2/544	
Fox, Eliza	022	1884	WB-E/300	AR
Fox, George	022	1858	Orig. Only	AR-Nunc.
Fox, Hugh	054	c1826	WB-2/37	AR
Fox, Isham	039	1822	WB-G/98	AR
Fox, J. A.	085	1865	WB-K/371	AR
Fox, Jacob	039	1807	WB-C/74	AR
Fox, Jacob	069	1861	WB-1/573	AR
Fox, James	096	1755	SS 880/180	SS/AR
Fox, James	054	c1830	WB-2/136	AR
Fox, James T.	014	1892	WB-2/497	CTY
Fox, John	065	1814	WB-C/83	AR
Fox, John	022	1844	WB-C/164	AR
Fox, John	028	1799	WB-B/77	AR
Fox, John	022	c1866	WB-D/159	AR
Fox, John	022	1860	WB-D/59	AR
Fox, John S.	065	1826	WB-C/87	AR
Fox, John W.	Can	1889	031 WB-1/74	031 AR
Fox, Leonard	081	1876	WB-15/227	AR
Fox, Margaret	081	1868	WB-15/3	AR
Fox, Mary K.	069	1873	Orig. Only	AR
Fox, Moses	021	1855	WB-1/119	AR
Fox, Moses	072	c1780	RW/L34	AR
Fox, Nathan	078	1889	WB-19/267	AR
Fox, Nicholas	070	1744	DB-C/26	
Fox, Philip	085	c1792	WB-E/167	AR
Fox, Robert	071	1812	WB-3/63	AR
Fox, Sarah	003	1892	WB-B/302	AR
Fox, Solomon S.	022	1891	WB-E/472	AR
Fox, Stephen	065	1843	WB-H/150	AR
Fox, Stephen	065	c1842	SC/05728	AR-Copy
Fox, Thomas	081	1807	WB-3/80	AR
Fox, Thomas	085	c1783	WB-C/138	AR
Fox, William	098	1886	WB-A/67	CTY
Fox, William	071	1832	WB-4/96	AR
Fox, William J.	098	1888	WB A/90	
Foxhall, John	037	1794	WB-C/262	AR
Foxhall, Martha	037	1856	WB-G/122	AR
Foxhall, Sarah E.	037	1872	WB-G/401	AR
Foxhall, Thomas	037	1792	WB-C/198	AR
Foxhall, Thomas	037	1798	WB-D/42	AR
Foxwell, Mary C.	024	1860	WB-D/2	AR
Foy, Benjamin	084	1876	WB-E/116	CTY
Foy, Christian	072	1847	WB-2/89	AR
Foy, Damsel	024	c1762	WB-A/271	AR
Foy, Enoch	057	1842	WB-B/152	AR
Foy, Frederick	028	1815	Copy	057 AR
Foy, Frederick	072	1833	WB-1/114	AR
Foy, Frederick	028	1815	WB-C/105	AR
Foy, Henrietta	070	1840	WB-AB/333	AR
Foy, Jacob	057	1786	WB-A/58	AR
Foy, James	070	1889	WB-F/292	AR
Foy, James	070	1823	WB-C/112	AR
Foy, James, Sr.	072	1823	WB-A/33	AR
Foy, Joseph M.	070	1861	WB-D/46	AR
Foy, Joshua	072	1852	WB-2/120	AR
Foy, Julia	099	1894	WB-C/233	AR
Foy, Mark	085	1774	WB-A/184	AR
Foy, N. B.	057	1895	WB-C/206	AR
Foy, Thomas	057	1789	WB-A/85	AR
Foy, Thomas	057	1800	WB-A/247	AR
Foy, William	028	1891	WB-E/569	AR
Foyle, James	072	1828	Orig. Only	AR
Foyle, James	072	c1771	RW/L66	AR
Foyles, Martha	070	1859	WB-D/18	AR
Foyles, Moses	072	1820	WB-A/34	AR
Fracheir, David	064	1894	WB-2/320	AR
Frady, Henry	086	1896	WB-F/507	AR
Frady, J. A.	013	1894	WB-C/327	AR
Frady, John	013	1895	WB-C/368	AR
Fraim, John	010	1845	WB-G/385	AR
Fraiser, Duncan	028	1773	Orig. Only	SS/AR
Fraizar, Houston R.	087	1887	WB-3/371	AR
Fraizer, Ephraim	044	1839	WB-14/458	CTY
Fraizer, Samuel	028	1772	Orig. Only	SS/AR
Fraizer, Samuel	085	1809	WB-G/145	AR
Fraizer, William	044	1827	Orig. Only	CTY
Fraley, Benjamin	085	1886	WB-2/167	CTY
Fraley, Daniel	085	1892	WB-2/516	CTY-Nunc.
Fraley, David	085	1849	WB-K/100	AR
Fraley, Elizabeth	085	1857	WB-K/235	AR
Fraley, George	085	1817	WB-G/472	AR
Fraley, George	085	1843	WB-I/150	AR
Fraley, Henry	085	1831	WB-H/522	AR
Fraley, John	085	1849	WB-K/84	AR
Fraley, John	085	1823	WB-H/213	AR
Fraley, M. S.	085	1897	WB-3/189	CTY
Fraley, W. R.	085	1890	WB-2/398	CTY-Nunc.
Fraley, William A.	085	1899	WB-3/313	CTY
Frame, James	MD	1877	091 WB-1/278	
Frances, Delilah	010	1868	WB-H/210	AR
Frances, Elizabeth	010	1844	WB-G/368	AR
Frances, James H.	010	1866	WB-H/175	AR
Frances, Micagah	090	1832	WB-3/239	AR
Francis, B. F.	049	1866	WB-2/239	AR
Francis, Howel	071	1866	WB-5/331	AR
Francis, Hubert R.	011	1890	WB-2/229	
Francis, James	051	1864	WB-B/58	AR
Francis, John, Sr.	090	1864	WB-4/371	AR
Francis, Joseph	090	1879	WB-6/110	AR
Francis, Lucy	051	1880	WB-C/240	AR
Francis, Mahala	006	1900	WB-E/405	AR
Francis, Margaret	049	1897	WB-2/380	AR
Francis, Mary	054	c1816	WB-1/395	AR
Francis, Reuben	026	1886	WB-2/293	AR
Francis, Robert	MD	1718	009 DB-1/286	
Francis, Sarah	FL	1849	090 WB-4/270	
Francis, William	049	1894	WB-2/324	AR
Franck, Elijah L.	072	1897	WB-4/376	AR
Franck, John	028	1768	Orig. Only	AR
Franck, John M.	028	1745	SS 877/371	SS/AR
Franck, John M.	103	1868	WB-1/2	AR
Francks, E. S.	057	1886	WB-C/142	AR
Francks, Edward L.	057	1828	WB-B/90	AR
Francks, Maria	057	1873	WB-C/36	AR
Francks, Sarah A.	057	1893	WB-C/128	AR
Francks, William W.	057	1850	WB-B/207	AR
Frank, Christian	032	1888	WB-4/31	AR
Frank, John	013	1869	WB-B/17	AR
Frank, Peter, Sr.	032	c1856	WB-2/120	
Frank, Theophilus	032	1884	WB-3/436	AR

Name	Co.	Date	Recorded Copy	Original
Frank, William	032	c1847	WB-2/113	
Frank, William	085	c1799	WB-E/153	AR
Frankes, William	009	c1844	OWB/544	AR
Frankfort, Lewis	103	1856	RD-12/221	AR
Franklin, Ailsey	092	c1851	Orig. Only	AR
Franklin, Barnard	092	c1820	WB-4/10	AR
Franklin, Charity C.	092	1886	WB-6/235	AR
Franklin, George	062	1877	WB-B/58	AR
Franklin, Hettie	028	1897	WB-F/307	
Franklin, James	092	1819	WB-3/138	AR
Franklin, James	065	c1764	WB-C/59	AR
Franklin, Jason	041	1839	WB-3/16	AR
Franklin, Jesse	092	1823	WB-3/158	
Franklin, John	014	1837	Orig. Only	AR
Franklin, John, Sr.	014	1819	Orig. Only	AR
Franklin, Jonas	041	1826	WB-2/264	AR
Franklin, Martha M.	078	1887	WB-19/209	
Franklin, Medean	092	1862	WB-5/56	
Franklin, Mildred	092	1843	WB-4/200	
Franklin, Mishack	092	1840	WB-4/161	
Franklin, Peter	041	1890	WB-4/296	AR
Franklin, William	099	1839	RB-24/259	AR
Franks, Anthony	099	1871	RB-35/152	AR
Franks, Barbary	013	1890	WB-C/43	AR
Franks, Edward	057	c1813	WB-B/30	
Franks, J. D.	061	1893	WB-2/134	AR
Franks, Lewis	099	1849	RB-26/592	AR
Franks, Lorenzo	099	1879	WB-A/67	AR
Franks, M. V.	028	1899	WB-F/409	
Franks, Wickliff	057	1791	WB-A/190	AR
Fraser, David	024	1729	SS 876/228	SS/AR
Fraser, Donald	014	1888	WB-2/367	
Fraser, H. Y.	021	1866	WB-1/225	AR
Fraser, James	051	1826	WB-A/237	
Fraser, James	065	1787	WB-C/69	AR
Fraser, James	085	c1794	WB-E/166	AR
Fraser, John H.	051	1820	WB-A/45	
Fraser, Judith	051	1832	WB-A/104	
Fraser, Pleasant	067	1879	WB-2/105	AR
Frasier, Jeremiah	024	c1798	WB-A/331	AR
Frasier, Richard G.	022	1890	WB-E/423	AR
Frasier, Robert B.	071	1841	WB-4/243	AR
Frasier, Thomas	044	1829	WB-11/261	CTY-Nunc.
Frat, Joseph	053	1748	SS 878/8	
Frater, David D.	028	1848	WB-D/152	AR
Fray, John J.	099	1884	WB-B/1	AR
Frazar, James	072	1844	WB-2/61	AR
Frazar, James	072	1783	RW/L59	AR
Frazar, John	087	1848	WB-1/333	AR
Frazar, Mary	057	1809	WB-A/318	AR
Frazar, Micajah	057	1792	WB-A/178	AR
Frazar, Urban	057	1805	WB-A/275	AR
Frazer, Alexander	069	1816	WB-1/284	AR
Frazer, John	038	1866	WB-1/268	AR
Frazer, Josiah	068	1799	WB-A/202	
Frazer, Stephen	090	1811	WB-2/122	AR
Frazer, Thomas	024	c1772	WB-B/2	AR
Frazer, William	044	1793	WB-3/14	CTY
Frazier, Aaron	054	1882	WB-4/460	CTY
Frazier, Abel	046	1818	WB-B/62	AR
Frazier, David L.	046	1897	WB-F/593	AR
Frazier, Elizabeth	044	1861	WB-21/491	CTY
Frazier, Hugh	021	1871	WB-2/52	
Frazier, Isaac	081	1867	WB-14/186	
Frazier, Israel	085	1856	WB-K/212	AR
Frazier, Israel	085	1856	Copy	054 AR
Frazier, James	046	1817	WB-B/46	AR
Frazier, James M.	044	1864	WB-22/207	CTY
Frazier, Jane C.	016	c1871	WB-3/82	AR
Frazier, John	046	1862	WB-D/130	AR
Frazier, John	019	1744	Orig. Only	AR-Copy
Frazier, John	019	1744	SS 878/133	019 AR
Frazier, John C.	065	1873	WB-K/133	AR
Frazier, John V.	081	1881	WB-15/353	
Frazier, Joseph A.	045	1897	WB-1/357	AR
Frazier, Lavinia	028	1898	WB-F/356	
Frazier, Malachi	044	1784	WB-1/412	CTY
Frazier, Margaret	065	1897	WB-N/24	AR
Frazier, Martha	046	c1825	WB-B/582	AR
Frazier, Robert J.	065	1899	WB-N/254	AR
Frazier, Sally	069	1825	WB-1/331	AR
Frazier, Stephen	044	1864	WB-22/251	
Frazier, William	045	1881	WB-1/62	AR
Freck, A.	013	1900	WB-D/405	AR
Frederick, James	087	1821	WB-1/4	AR
Frederick, Nickolas	065	1856	WB-G/18	AR
Frederick, Norris	035	1868	WB-3/131	AR
Frederick, William	035	1830	WB-1/5	AR
Frederick, William C.	005	1875	WB-D/32	AR
Fredrick, Felix	035	1832	WB-1/28	AR
Fredrick, John	029	1757	DB-1/180	AR
Free, Christian	072	1781	RW/L40	AR
Free, Daniel	081	1804	WB-2/130	AR
Free, Milton M.	081	1898	WB-16/485	AR
Freear, Elizabeth	071	1812	WB-3/77	AR
Freear, Richard	071	1814	WB-3/121	AR
Freear, Richard	047	1774	WB-1/371	
Freear, Richard W.	071	1809	WB-3/24 & 32	AR
Freear, Robert	047	1794	WB-3/230	
Freedle, John	032	1837	WB-1/300	
Freedle, Lewis	090	1884	WB-6/147	AR
Freedle, William E.	032	1895	WB-4/245	AR
Freeland, Agness	054	1855	WB-3/106	AR
Freeland, Alexander	054	1850	WB-3/42	AR
Freeland, Amy	001	1882	WB-2/196	AR
Freeland, Andrew	054	1807	WB-1/20	AR
Freeland, George J.	065	1882	WB-K/487	AR
Freeland, Green	073	1897	WB-I/138	CTY
Freeland, James	054	c1828	WB-2/74	AR
Freeland, James	073	1807	WB-D/199	AR
Freeland, John	073	1844	WB-F/200	AR
Freeland, John D.	001	1885	WB-2/239	AR
Freeland, Joseph	073	1837	WB-E/409	AR
Freeland, Joseph	001	1866	WB-1/257	AR
Freeland, Joseph	073	1848	WB-E/406	AR
Freeland, Mary	054	1867	WB-3/203	AR
Freeland, Nancy	073	1852	WB-G/21	AR
Freeland, Samuel	073	c1802	Orig. Only	AR
Freeland, Sophia	070	1895	WB-G/343	AR
Freeland, Thomas	054	c1817	WB-1/408	AR
Freeland, Thomas	073	1835	WB-E/341	AR
Freeland, Thomas	073	1894	WB-I/52	CTY
Freeland, William	054	1854	WB-3/79	AR
Freeland, William A.	054	1871	WB-4/83	CTY
Freeman, A. B.	099	1891	WB-B/503	AR
Freeman, Abraham	082	1788	WB-1/17	AR
Freeman, Alexander	070	1859	WB-D/40	AR
Freeman, Alexander	092	1858	WB-5/26	
Freeman, Allen	099	1867	RB-34/476	AR

Name	Co.	Date	Recorded Copy	Original
Freeman, Allen	065	1807	WB-C/78	AR
Freeman, Amy	067	1884	WB-2/184	AR
Freeman, Arthur	037	1857	WB-G/144	AR
Freeman, Benjamin	083	c1819	WB-1/196	AR
Freeman, Celia	010	1873	WB-I/48	AR
Freeman, Celia	010	1838	WB-G/298	AR
Freeman, Christian	010	1854	WB-G/518	AR
Freeman, Daniel	089	1877	WB-2/47	AR
Freeman, Daniel E.	062	1873	WB-B/7	
Freeman, David	041	c1828	Copy	077 AR
Freeman, David	065	1808	WB-C/80	AR
Freeman, Deborah	037	1884	WB-H/64	
Freeman, Dugger	086	1897	WB-F/523	AR
Freeman, Edmond	044	1817	WB-8/79	CTY
Freeman, Edmund B.	099	1868	RB-35/4	AR
Freeman, Edward	039	c1811	WB-C/240	
Freeman, Elisha	072	1793	Orig. Only	AR
Freeman, Eliza	037	1858	WB-G/163	AR
Freeman, Elizabeth	099	1850	RB-27/92	AR
Freeman, Elizabeth	044	1881	WB-23/397	
Freeman, Evan E.	044	1854	WB-19/459	CTY
Freeman, Ewell	099	1879	WB-A/55	AR
Freeman, Ewell	036	1880	WB-B/96	
Freeman, George	082	1783	WB-1/16	AR
Freeman, George	082	1783	Orig. Only	SS/AR
Freeman, Hanson	044	1826	WB-10/258	CTY
Freeman, Isabella	070	1895	WB-G/385	AR
Freeman, J. H.	050	1898	Copy	086 AR
Freeman, J. H.	050	1898	WB-2/292	CTY
Freeman, J. T.	050	1891	WB-2/89	CTY
Freeman, James	104	1797	WB-1/477	AR
Freeman, James	099	1845	RB-26/39	AR
Freeman, James	101	1882	WB-A/89	AR
Freeman, James	012	1824	WB-B/133	AR
Freeman, James T.	041	1843	WB-3/47	AR
Freeman, Jay W.	050	1900	WB-2/367	CTY
Freeman, Jeremiah	010	1810	WB-F/136	AR
Freeman, John	099	1800	RB-5/164	AR
Freeman, John	024	1732	SS 876/243	SS/AR
Freeman, John	009	1753	SS 877/250	SS/AR
Freeman, John	010	1793	WB-D/227	AR
Freeman, John	010	1896	WB-I/488	AR
Freeman, John	072	1857	WB-2/162	AR
Freeman, John	VA	1865	051 WB-B/74	
Freeman, John	090	1834	WB-3/278	AR
Freeman, John	069	1805	WB-1/157	AR
Freeman, John	010	1785	WB-D/27	AR
Freeman, John C.	039	1891	WB-U/533	AR
Freeman, John H.	045	1885	WB-1/130	AR
Freeman, John, Sr.	024	1777	WB-A/269	AR
Freeman, Joseph	041	1842	WB-3/36	AR
Freeman, Joshua	010	1794	WB-D/252	AR
Freeman, Josiah	037	1839	WB-F/229	AR
Freeman, King	010	1793	WB-D/217	AR
Freeman, Lewis	022	1845	WB-C/181	AR
Freeman, M. D.	039	c1879	Orig. Only	AR
Freeman, Martha	010	1818	WB-G/29	AR
Freeman, Martha	041	1888	WB-4/267	AR
Freeman, Martha	010	1867	WB-H/201	AR
Freeman, Mary	009	1876	WB-1/170	CTY
Freeman, Mary	044	1885	WB-23/219 & 534	CTY
Freeman, Mary W.	070	1894	WB-G/275	AR
Freeman, Merideth	050	1869	WB-1/103	CTY
Freeman, Michael B.	086	1886	WB-F/279	AR
Freeman, Nancy	010	1873	WB-I/48	AR
Freeman, Nicy	010	1848	WB-G/430	AR
Freeman, Penelope	010	1873	WB-I/48	AR
Freeman, Peter	086	1858	WB-E/355	AR
Freeman, Rebecca J.	039	c1884	Orig. Only	AR
Freeman, Rederick	017	1873	WB-B/42	AR
Freeman, Richard	024	1761	WB-A/267	AR
Freeman, Richard P.	010	1867	WB-H/180	AR
Freeman, Robert	039	1856	WB-0/387	AR
Freeman, Robert	039	1821	WB-G/65	AR
Freeman, Rudolph	075	1881	WB-0/128	AR
Freeman, Sally	010	1873	WB-I/48	AR
Freeman, Samuel	092	1796	WB-3/19A	AR
Freeman, Samuel A.	092	1876	WB-6/85	AR
Freeman, Sarah	010	1807	WB-F/53	AR
Freeman, Sarah	073	1840	WB-F/82	
Freeman, Sarah L.J.	010	1885	WB-I/184	
Freeman, Solomon	010	1788	WB-D/90	AR
Freeman, T. A.	090	1899	WB-6/500	AR
Freeman, Tabitha	100	1797	Copy	073 AR
Freeman, Tabitha	100	1797	WB-9/156	AR
Freeman, Thomas	099	1841	RB-24/491	AR
Freeman, Timothy	010	1827	WB-G/173	AR
Freeman, Walter W.	029	1899	WB-F/176	AR
Freeman, William	024	1739	Orig. Only	SS/AR
Freeman, William	092	1802	WB-3/48A	
Freeman, William	010	1782	WB-C/33	AR
Freeman, William	010	1831	WB-G/199	AR
Freeman, William	010	1781	Copy	073 AR
Freeman, William	039	1824	WB-H/53	AR
Freeman, William	041	1781	WB-1/20	AR
Freeman, William	073	1801	WB-D/43	AR
Freeman, William C.	070	1866	WB-D/204	AR
Freeman, William E.	070	1879	WB-E/365	AR
Freeman, William G.	069	1854	WB-1/540	AR
Freeman, William H.	039	1894	WB-V/41	AR
Freeman, William J.	010	1884	WB-I/174	
Freeman, Wyatt	099	1866	RB-33/490	AR
Freemon, Agga	085	c1809	WB-G/132	AR
Freer, Carolina	013	1883	WB-B/297	AR
Freet, William H.	001	1870	WB-2/12	AR
Freeze, Aaron	016	1849	WB-1/160	
Freeze, Absalom	085	1867	WB-L/22	AR
Freeze, Andrew	016	1874	WB-3/100	AR
Freeze, Caleb	085	1888	WB-2/303	CTY
Freeze, Catharine	085	1872	WB-1/124	CTY
Freeze, J. M.	085	1896	WB-3/135	CTY
Freeze, John	085	1877	WB-1/391	CTY
Freeze, John	054	1886	WB-5/133	CTY
Freeze, Molly	085	1872	WB-1/127	CTY
Freeze, Noah	085	1866	WB-K/378	AR
Freeze, Peter	054	1878	WB-4/305	CTY
Freeze, Peter	085	1848	WB-K/76	AR
Fremont, S. L.	070	1886	Orig. Only	AR
French, Abigail	072	1779	RW/L32	AR
French, George R.	070	1889	WB-F/282	AR
French, Joseph	072	1775	RW/L4	AR
French, Junius B.	065	1863	WB-J/171	AR
French, Richard	077	1716	SS 875/104	SS/AR
French, William	072	1824	WB-A/30	AR
French, William	090	1801	WB-2/3a	AR
Freshour, M. F.	062	1888	WB-B/86	AR
Freshour, Rebecca	062	1889	Orig. Only	AR
Freshwater, Anna	075	1821	WB-M1/348	AR
Freshwater, Frances	075	1830	WB-N/60	AR

Name	Co.	Date	Recorded Copy	Original
Freshwater, John	075	1753	SS 881/88	SS/AR
Freshwater, John A.	072	1897	WB-4/343	AR
Freshwater, Thaddeus	075	1814	WB-M1/263	AR
Freshwater, Thaddeus	075	1827	WB-N/31	AR
Freshwater, William	019	c1781	Orig. Only	AR
Freshwater, William	073	1808	WB-D/301	AR
Freshwater, William A.	001	1886	WB-2/296	AR
Freshwater, William W.	075	1837	WB-N/138	AR
Frew, Archibald	075	1818	WB-M1/323	AR
Frewhill, Levi	028	1812	WB-C/53	
Frey, Lucy	038	1886	WB-2/572	AR
Frey, Valentine	090	1814	WB-2/154	AR
Friar, Sion	010	1795	WB-D/275	AR-Nunc.
Frick, Charles	089	c1854	WB-1/234	
Frick, Daniel	085	1889	WB-2/329	CTY
Frick, Levi	085	1895	WB-3/80	CTY
Frick, Mathias	085	1833	WB-H/592	AR
Friday, Andrew	040	1848	WB-1/7	
Friday, David	040	1883	WB-2/204	AR
Friday, Elizabeth	040	1869	WB-2/4	
Friday, Ephraim	040	1893	WB-2/440	AR
Friday, John N.	040	1882	WB-2/193	AR
Friday, Jonas	060	1812	Orig. Only	AR
Friday, Martin	060	1817	Orig. Only	AR
Friday, Nicholas	060	1790	Orig. Only	AR
Friday, William	040	1849	WB-1/26	
Friddle, George	073	1805	WB-D/158	AR
Friel, C. J.	099	1885	WB-B/61	AR
Fries, Francis	038	1863	WB-1/223	AR
Fries, William	038	1866	WB-1/265	AR
Frilick, Joseph	028	1800	WB-B/92	
Frillick, Mary	056	1828	WB-1/350	AR
Frink, Jabesh	012	1896	WB-A/109	AR
Frink, Lorenzo	012	1889	WB-A/70	AR
Frink, Lorenzo	012	c1879	Copy	070 AR
Frink, Martha	012	1795	WB-B/54	AR
Frink, Samuel	012	1862	Copy	070 AR
Frink, Samuel	012	1795	WB-B/53	AR
Frink, Samuel	012	c1856	WB-B/41	
Frink, Samuel R.	FL	1900	070 WB-H/651	070 AR
Frink, Sarah	012	1791	Orig. Only	AR
Frink, Sarah J.	070	1898	WB-H/118	AR
Frink, William	012	c1857	WB-B/16	AR
Frion, Abram	020	1890	WB-B/27	CTY
Frion, Jarvis	020	1896	WB-B/272	CTY
Frisbee, William	013	1884	WB-B/316	AR
Fritts, Amos	032	1885	WB-3/454	AR
Fritts, George	032	1845	WB-1/462	
Fritts, John	029	c1792	Orig. Only	AR
Fritts, Rebecca	032	c1846	WB-2/157	
Fritts, William	032	1863	WB-2/240	AR
Frizzle, John J.	079	1897	WB-3/125	AR
Frizzle, Margaret	009	1880	WB-1/260	CTY
Frizzle, William R.	079	c1861	WB-1/98	AR
Frock, Conrad	085	c1785	WB-E/162	AR
Froelich, Charles	047	1893	WB-7/76	AR
Froelich, Cornelia	047	1895	WB-7/139	AR
Frohock, John	085	1772	WB-C/224	AR
Frohock, Thomas	085	c1794	WB-G/547	AR
Frohock, William	085	1781	HaDSC(M)/167	
Frolich, Henry	085	c1793	WB-E/158	AR
Fromm, Charles C.	026	1891	WB-2/435	AR
Fromm, Rosa	026	1896	WB-2/520	AR
Fronebarger, David	060	1842	WB-2/174	AR
Fronebarger, Jacob	060	1822	Orig. Only	AR
Froneberger, Elizabeth	040	1893	WB-2/432	AR
Froneberger, Jane	040	1888	WB-2/319	
Froneberger, John	040	1873	WB-2/54	AR
Froneberger, Philip	040	1892	WB-2/414	AR
Froneryberg, William	060	1805	Orig. Only	AR
Frontis, Stephen	085	1867	WB-L/10	AR
Frost, Charles L.	061	1893	WB-2/125	
Frost, Elizabeth	085	1825	WB-H/323	AR
Frost, Elizabeth	090	1841	WB-4/71	AR
Frost, Hannah	085	1824	WB-H/263	AR
Frost, Henry H.	MD	1897	028 WB-F/324	
Frost, J. F.	030	1900	WB-5/294	AR
Frost, James B.	090	1836	WB-3/304	AR
Frost, Sarah R.	033	1857	WB-1/135	
Frost, William	002	1718	SS 875/156	SS/AR
Fruit, James	073	1800	WB-D/10	AR
Fruit, John	081	1824	WB-5/160	AR
Fruit, Susanna	081	1860	WB-11/371	AR
Fry, Abel	021	1897	WB-3/161	AR
Fry, Catharine	021	1844	WB-1/26	AR
Fry, Catharine	085	1822	WB-H/145	AR
Fry, Catherine	085	1815	WB-G/388	AR
Fry, Cethring	010	1782	WB-C/39	AR
Fry, Christian	085	c1799	WB-E/159	AR
Fry, David W.	003	1885	WB-B/154	AR
Fry, George	060	1823	Orig. Only	AR
Fry, George	085	1813	WB-G/269	AR
Fry, Green	023	1873	WB-A/7	AR
Fry, Jacob	021	1896	WB-3/130	
Fry, Jacob	060	1834	WB-1/325	AR
Fry, Jacob	060	1801	Orig. Only	AR
Fry, Jesse	090	1850	WB-4/261	AR
Fry, John	090	1890	WB-6/229	AR
Fry, John	090	1825	WB-3/135	
Fry, John	021	1856	WB-1/128	AR
Fry, Johnson	081	1864	WB-13/4	
Fry, Lawson	021	1871	WB-2/61	
Fry, Lockhart	068	1853	WB-C/3	
Fry, Lockhart	068	1869	WB-D/100	
Fry, Lucretia	089	1846	WB-1/45	
Fry, Lucy	038	1886	WB-2/572	
Fry, Lydia	068	1869	WB-D/12	
Fry, Marcus	021	1871	WB-2/59	AR
Fry, Marcus L.	021	1897	WB-3/164	AR
Fry, Massy	090	1858	WB-4/319	AR
Fry, Michael	090	1815	WB-2/164	
Fry, Moses	021	1874	WB-2/99	AR
Fry, Nicholas	060	1784	Orig. Only	AR
Fry, Peter	085	1810	WB-G/157	AR
Fry, Peter, Sr.	085	1767	WB-A/53	AR
Fry, Philip	060	1826	WB-1/29	AR
Fry, Solomon	021	1879	WB-2/201	
Fry, Thomas	008	1726	SS 876/101	SS/AR
Fry, Thomas	068	1821	WB-B/16	
Fry, Thomas	068	1863	WB-C/93	
Fry, Tobias	068	c1827	WB-B/70	
Fry, Valentine	090	1798	WB-1/113	AR
Fry, Wesley	032	1894	WB-4/219	AR
Fryar, Henry	035	1899	WB-4/556	AR
Fryar, John	087	1884	WB-3/285	AR
Fryar, Mary A.	087	1897	WB-4/55	AR
Fryar, William	087	1883	WB-3/255	AR
Frye, M. M.	068	1897	WB-D/488	
Frye, Thomas	038	1864	WB-1/237	AR
Fryer, Jacob	087	1785	WB-A/14	AR

Name	Co.	Date	Recorded Copy	Original
Fryer, Jonathan	087	1820	WB-1/1	AR
Fryer, R. W.	037	1899	WB-H/444	AR
Fryer, Robert	046	1873	WB-E/116	AR
Fryer, Willis	010	1816	WB-F/314	AR
Fryly, William	096	1737	SS 877/194	SS/AR
Fryout, Sarah	070	1796	WB-C/107	AR
Fugett, Mary H.	MD	1878	039 WB-U/206	039 AR
Fugit, John	104	1786	WB-1/181	AR
Fukes, William	028	1775	Orig. Only	AR
Fulbright, Catharin	021	1877	WB-2/161	AR
Fulbright, Daniel	060	1892	WB-4/483	AR
Fulbright, Elizabeth	021	1898	WB-3/214	AR
Fulbright, Elizabeth	021	1864	WB-1/193	AR
Fulbright, John	021	c1871	Orig. Only	AR
Fulbright, Joseph	021	1887	WB-2/380	
Fulbright, William	060	1808	Orig. Only	AR
Fulcher, Burgess	078	1867	Orig. Only	AR
Fulcher, Dicy	061	c1867	WB-1/94	AR
Fulcher, Eliza	078	1862	WB-18/275	AR
Fulcher, Fanny	028	1900	WB-F/452	
Fulcher, Francis	074	1899	WB-1/151	AR
Fulcher, Harriet J.	061	1899	WB-2/234	AR
Fulcher, John	028	1766	Orig. Only	AR
Fulcher, John	019	1871	WB-B/63	AR
Fulcher, Wallas L.	019	1889	WB = B/178	AR
Fulenwider, Elenor	085	1815	WB-G/402	AR
Fulenwider, John	060	1826	WB-1/46	AR-Copy
Fulford, Abigail	019	1824	WB-D/182	AR-Nunc.
Fulford, Benjamin B.	053	1892	WB-11/266	AR
Fulford, Benjamin B.	053	1874	WB-11/49	AR
Fulford, Charles	030	1844	WB-4/105	
Fulford, Charlotte	033	1876	WB-2/56	CTY
Fulford, Hannah	019	1836	WB-A/64	AR
Fulford, Henrietta	053	1887	WB-11/191	AR
Fulford, John J.	053	1880	WB-11/96	AR
Fulford, John J.	053	1837	WB-6/3	AR
Fulford, Joseph	019	1775	RB-A/49	
Fulford, Matthew	033	1896	WB-2/191	CTY
Fulford, N. S.	009	1897	WB-2/104	CTY
Fulford, Nancy	028	1821	WB-C/205	AR
Fulford, Rodney	009	1849	OB-G/138	AR
Fulford, Sarah	079	1859	WB-1/26	AR
Fulford, Stephen	019	1834	WB-A/44	AR
Fulford, Thomas	084	c1796	OW/20	AR
Fulford, Uriah	019	1825	Orig. Only	AR
Fulford, William	019	1806	WB-D/173	AR
Fulgam, John	047	1833	WB-4/96	
Fulgam, Michal	071	1802	WB-2/238	AR
Fulghum, John	103	1825	RD-5/205	AR
Fulghum, Mikel	103	1804	Orig. Only	AR
Fulghum, Molly	103	1805	Orig. Only	AR
Fulinton, Andrew	009	1764	OWB/97	AR
Fulk, Adam	090	1899	Orig. Only	AR
Fulk, Daniel A.	038	1899	WB-4/176	AR
Fulk, Wilson	092	1896	WB-6/438	AR
Fulkerson, Sarah A.	038	1884	WB-2/539	AR
Fulks, William	071	1795	WB-2/94	AR
Fullbright, Regina	054	1885	WB-5/51	CTY
Fuller, Alex M.	020	1885	WB-A/451	CTY
Fuller, Barnaba	070	1805	WB-AB/92	AR
Fuller, Bartholomew	039	1829	WB-J/62	AR
Fuller, Belcher	019	1828	WB-D/180	AR
Fuller, Britain	081	1805	WB-3/17	AR
Fuller, David	044	1831	WB-12/191	CTY
Fuller, David	053	1849	WB-7/244	AR

Name	Co.	Date	Recorded Copy	Original
Fuller, Edward	019	1768	RB-A/31	AR
Fuller, Edwin W.	039	1876	WB-U/125	AR
Fuller, Elizabeth	081	1827	WB-5/381	AR
Fuller, Emma James	039	1897	WB-V/117	AR
Fuller, Ezekiel	044	1811	WB-7/169	CTY
Fuller, Ezekiel	044	1762	Orig. Only	CTY
Fuller, Ezekiel	081	1801	WB-2/79	AR
Fuller, Francis T.	099	1894	WB-C/298	AR
Fuller, Henry	044	1800	WB-5/103	CTY
Fuller, Henry	020	1838	RB-N/147	
Fuller, Henry, Sr.	020	1790	RB-B/341	AR
Fuller, Isaih	078	1824	Orig. Only	AR
Fuller, Jacob	078	1824	WI-10/84	
Fuller, James	020	1831	RB-L/630	AR
Fuller, James B.	024	1820	WB-C/87	AR
Fuller, James N.	044	1897	WB-24/333	CTY
Fuller, James T.	046	1873	WB-E/103	AR
Fuller, James W.	039	1890	WB-U/507	
Fuller, Jane A.	NY	1896	061 WB-2/173	061 AR
Fuller, Jesse	020	1882	WB-A/361	CTY
Fuller, John	044	1873	WB-23/107	CTY
Fuller, John H.	020	1881	WB-A/340	CTY
Fuller, Jones	039	1815	WB-D/137	AR
Fuller, Joseph	056	1893	WB-2/157	AR
Fuller, Murcy	044	1822	WB-9/120	CTY
Fuller, Nathan	019	1801	WB-D/175	AR
Fuller, Peter	078	1796	WI-1/234	AR
Fuller, Plen	070	1797	WB-AB/24	AR
Fuller, Ratzeman	083	1846	WB-1/480	AR
Fuller, Robert	071	1803	WB-2/248	AR
Fuller, S. T.	044	1895	WB-24/260	CTY
Fuller, Samuel	044	1793	WB-3/9	CTY
Fuller, Sarah	039	1859	WB-0/382	AR
Fuller, Sarah	044	1814	WB-7/354	CTY
Fuller, Sarah P.	024	1837	WB-C/197	AR
Fuller, W. Thompson	039	1894	WB-V/23	AR
Fuller, William D.	044	1866	WB-22/489	CTY
Fullerton, Robert	024	1750	Orig. Only	SS/AR
Fullerton, William	014	1798	Orig. Only	AR
Fullerton, William	009	1787	OWB/219	AR
Fullilove, Susanah	044	1774	WB-1/52	CTY
Fullington, James G.	020	1888	WB-A/542 & 557	CTY
Fullington, Nelly	009	1826	OB-A/361	AR
Fullington, Thomas	041	1785	WB-1/48	AR
Fullshire, Levy	028	c1834	Orig. Only	AR
Fullwood, Andrew	072	c1796	Orig. Only	AR
Fullwood, John M.	065	1843	WB-H/140	AR
Fullwood, William	072	1788	Orig. Only	AR-Nunc.
Fullwood, William	014	c1850	Orig. Only	AR
Fulmore, Anthony	083	1887	Orig. Only	AR
Fulmore, Elizabeth	028	1775	Orig. Only	AR
Fulmore, John	027	1850	Orig. Only	AR
Fulp, George	038	c1851	WB-1/39	AR-Copy
Fulp, George V.	038	1877	WB-2/297	AR
Fulp, Isabel	038	1869	WB-2/20	AR
Fulp, Jacob L.	092	1855	WB-5/12	
Fulp, James M.	038	1878	WB-2/329	AR
Fulp, Joseph	090	1888	WB-6/212	AR
Fulp, Sarah	003	1889	WB-B/250 & 261	AR
Fulp, Thomas	090	1886	WB-6/176	AR
Fulps, George	092	1786	WB-2/71	
Fulsher, Benjaman	028	1809	WB-B/343	AR
Fulsher, Cason	028	1821	WB-C/195	AR

Name	Co.	Date	Recorded Copy	Original
Fulsher, Jesse	028	1795	WB-A/342	AR
Fulsher, Joseph	028	1845	Orig. Only	AR
Fulsher, Joshua	028	1796	WB-B/16	AR
Fulsher, Levi	028	1805	WB-B/229	AR
Fulsher, Maxmillion	009	1784	OWB/190	AR
Fulsher, Peregrin	028	1811	WB-C/33	AR
Fulsher, Shadrack	028	1790	WB-A/212	AR
Fulsher, Thomas	028	c1744	Orig. Only	AR
Fulsher, William	028	1778	Orig. Only	AR
Fulshire, Ephraim	028	1810	WB-C/1	AR
Fulshire, Levi	028	1857	WB-D/292	AR
Fulshire, Mary	028	1844	WB-D/109	AR
Fulshire, William	028	1818	WB-C/160	AR
Fultin, Francis	090	1849	WB-4/257	AR
Fulton, Ellen M.	085	1867	WB-L/3	AR
Fulton, Francis	090	1877	WB-6/86	AR
Fulton, George	046	1846	WB-C/251	AR
Fulton, James	073	c1806	WB-D/430	AR
Fulton, James	070	1865	WB-D/171	AR
Fulton, Mary	046	1857	WB-C/501	AR
Fulton, Mary	013	1895	WB-C/389	AR
Fulton, Samuel	046	1821	WB-B/142	AR
Fulton, Susanah	073	1817	WB-D/506	AR
Fulwood, Charles	012	1837	Orig. Only	AR
Fuqua, William	047	1763	WB-1/99	
Fuquay, David C.	099	1885	WB-B/43	AR
Fuquay, Sarah	099	1881	WB-A/296	AR
Fuquay, William	099	1814	RB-11/237	AR
Furbish, Thomas	075	1732	SS 876/341	SS/AR
Furches, John M.	054	1875	WB-4/192	CTY
Furches, Tobias	085	1824	WB-H/256	AR
Furgason, Levi	071	1837	WB-4/159	AR
Furgeson, Andrew	001	1852	WB-1/62	AR
Furgison, Orpha	022	c1892	WB-E/487	AR
Furguson, Thomas T.	084	1857	WB-C/265	CTY
Furlough, John M.	101	1883	WB-A/120	AR
Furniss, William P.	NY	1875	016 WB-3/130	
Furr, Allen	016	1873	WB-3/94	AR
Furr, Catherine	016	1858	WB-2/39	
Furr, Henry	016	1852	WB-1/201	
Furr, Israel L.	016	1882	WB-3/363	AR
Furr, John	089	1888	WB-2/220	AR
Furr, Mary	016	1843	WB-1/22	
Furr, Matthias	089	1860	WB-1/216	
Furr, Paul P.	089	1876	WB-2/42	AR
Furror, Henry	065	1769	WB-C/57	
Furror, Paul, Sr.	016	1840	PQS.6/76	AR-Copy
Fussel, Thomas	010	c1735	Orig. Only	SS/AR
Fussell, Aaron	100	1812	WB-16/348	AR
Fussell, Aaron	100	1783	WB-4/1	015 AR
Fussell, Benjamin	035	1784	WB-A/146	AR
Fussell, Elizabeth	035	1860	WB-3/14	AR
Futch, David K.	070	1875	WB-E/292	AR
Futch, John	070	1828	WB-C/113	AR
Futch, Martin	028	1767	Orig. Only	AR-Nunc.
Futch, Onesimus	070	1782	WB-C/102	AR-Nunc.
Futral, Noah	072	c1864	Orig. Only	AR
Futrall, Benjamin	071	1790	WB-1/394	AR
Futrall, John	071	1788	WB-1/471	AR
Futrell, B. G.	071	1898	WB-7/421	AR
Futrell, Charlotte	051	1897	WB-C/527	AR
Futrell, David	071	1795	WB-2/97	AR
Futrell, Dempsey	071	1811	WB-3/40	AR
Futrell, Elizabeth	071	1821	WB-3/243	AR
Futrell, Elliott	071	1837	WB-4/154	AR
Futrell, Enos	071	1838	WB-4/182	AR
Futrell, Hosea	071	1841	WB-4/235	AR
Futrell, Jefferson	071	1900	WB-7/466	AR
Futrell, Jesse	071	1867	WB-5/349	AR
Futrell, Jesse	071	1780	WB-1/231	
Futrell, John	071	1835	WB-4/127	AR
Futrell, Lemuel	071	1842	WB-4/256	AR
Futrell, Noah	071	1844	WB-5/10	AR
Futrell, Patience	071	1865	WB-5/315	AR
Futrell, Prissilla	071	1846	WB-5/55	AR
Futrell, Randolph	071	1859	WB-5/218	AR
Futrell, Rebecca	071	1900	WB-7/466	AR
Futrell, Sallie J.	051	1888	WB-C/367	AR
Futrell, Sampson	071	1811	WB-3/58	AR
Futrell, Sanders	071	1804	WB-2/272	AR
Futrell, Sarah E.	071	1859	WB-5/211	AR
Futrell, Solimon	056	1837	Est-18/187	
Futrell, Thomas	071	1770	WB-1/180	
Futril, Thomas	071	1796	WB-2/139	AR
Futrill, Joseph	071	1799	WB-2/188	AR
Futterlow, Benjamin	073	c1833	Orig. Only	AR
Fye, Jacob	060	1801	Orig. Only	AR
Fye, Jonas A.	021	1866	WB-1/226	AR
Fyffe, Samuel	104	1835	WB-4/195	AR
Gabie, John M.	070	1815	WB-AB/231	AR
Gabie, Robert	065	c1766	WB-C/112	AR
Gabourel, Philip	070	1756	DB-D/234	AR
Gabriel, Benjamin	019	1866	WB-B/10	AR
Gabriel, Benjamin	019	1807	WB-D/195	AR
Gabriel, Henry C.	009	1887	WB-1/419	CTY
Gabriel, J. M.	021	1893	WB-3/27	AR
Gabriel, Richard	019	c1775	Orig. Only	AR
Gabriel, Samuel W.	019	1890	WB-B/191	AR
Gabriel, Sarah M.	019	1896	WB-B/295	AR
Gad, Elizabeth	N	1720	SS 875/230	
Gad, James	075	1701	Orig. Only	SS/AR
Gadd, Elizabeth	067	1857	SCM.2/58	
Gaddis, John, Sr.	081	1836	WB-6/512	AR
Gaddy, Clement	005	1878	WB-D/74	AR
Gaddy, James	083	1869	WB-3/14	AR
Gaddy, Jane	097	1863	WB-1/226	AR
Gaddy, Joel	005	1887	WB-D/199	
Gaddy, Meridith	083	1896	WB-4/139	AR
Gaddy, Nancy	005	1854	WB-C/71	AR
Gaddy, Nancy	005	1863	WB-C/182	AR
Gaddy, Pleasant	097	1853	WB-1/94	AR
Gaddy, Thomas	005	1815	WB-2/38	AR
Gaddy, Thomas	005	1855	WB-C/93	AR
Gaddy, Thomas	037	1788	WB-C/73	AR
Gaddy, Thomas J.	005	1865	WB-C/226	AR
Gadsby, Henry Clay	029	1892	WB-E/558	AR
Gaffin, John	047	1832	WB-4/84	
Gage, A. D.	054	1885	WB-5/24	CTY
Gailard, Benjamin	009	c1803	OWB/415	AR
Gailey, Robert N.	080	1878	Orig. Only	AR
Gainer, Ann	047	1802	WB-3/378	
Gainer, Arthur	063	c1780	WB-1/89	
Gainer, Benjamin	096	1771	Orig. Only	AR
Gainer, James	063	c1786	WB-1/120	
Gainer, Joseph	009	1793	OWB/288	AR
Gainer, Mary	037	1751	Orig. Only	SS/AR
Gainer, Samuel	096	1752	SS 879/81	SS/AR
Gainer, William	037	1750	Orig. Only	SS/AR
Gaines, Edward	073	1799	WB-C/142	AR
Gaines, James	067	1855	WB-1/67	AR

Name	Co.	Date	Recorded Copy	Original
Gaines, James L.	067	1863	WB-1/97	AR
Gaines, John C.	067	1864	WB-1/124	AR
Gaines, Samuel	047	1763	WB-1/90	
Gaines, Thomas	090	1811	WB-2/120	AR
Gaines, William	047	1771	WB-1/283	
Gainey, Bartholomew	087	c1818	WB-1/15	AR
Gainey, Martha	087	1894	WB-3/551	AR
Gainey, Thaddeus	087	1895	WB-3/565	AR
Gainey, William G.	087	1883	WB-3/270	AR
Gainey, William H.	029	1885	WB-E/339	AR
Gainus, Reubin	045	1884	WB-1/118	AR
Gaither, A. F.	054	1883	WB-4/583	CTY
Gaither, Basil	085	1803	WB-G/61	AR
Gaither, Bazzel	054	1844	WB-2/286	AR
Gaither, Benjamin	085	1803	WB-G/55	AR
Gaither, Benjamin	085	c1788	WB-C/101	AR
Gaither, Burgess	033	1887	WB-2/99	CTY
Gaither, Burgess	054	c1819	Orig. Only	AR
Gaither, Burgess S.	014	1892	WB-2/488	CTY
Gaither, Carrie	026	1864	WB-1/358	AR
Gaither, Eleanor	054	1850	WB-3/48	AR
Gaither, Eli	085	c1809	WB-G/126	AR
Gaither, Emily	033	1890	WB-2/108	CTY
Gaither, Enos	054	1877	WB-4/253	CTY
Gaither, Greenbury	054	1860	WB-3/150	AR
Gaither, J. L.	021	1863	WB-1/177	AR
Gaither, John, Sr.	054	1844	WB-2/302	AR
Gaither, John, Sr.	054	c1809	WB-1/274	AR
Gaither, Julia M.	014	1882	WB-2/219	
Gaither, Lebitious	054	1860	WB-3/149	AR
Gaither, Mary M.	033	1891	WB-2/116	CTY
Gaither, Nancy Jane	033	1886	WB-2/88	CTY
Gaither, Nicholas	054	c1793	WB-1/105	AR
Gaither, Sarah	054	c1792	WB-1/106	AR
Gaither, Sarah H.	033	1887	WB-2/92	CTY
Gaither, Wilee	033	1865	WB-1/191	
Gaither, Zacariah	033	1843	WB-1/51	
Galaspy, Alexander	020	1777	RB-A/7	AR
Galbraith, Christian	083	1859	WB-2/152	AR
Galbraith, Flora	083	1889	WB-3/432	AR
Galbraith, Malcolm	083	1840	WB-1/393	AR
Galbraith, Malcom	083	1865	WB-2/215	AR
Galbraith, Margaret	083	1884	Orig. Only	AR
Galbreath, Catherine	029	1815	WB-A/212	AR
Galbreath, Joseph	065	1795	WB-C/110	AR
Galbreath, Margret	083	1813	WB-1/146	AR
Galbreath, Sarah	086	1883	WB-F/205	AR
Galbreath, William	073	1800	WB-D/18	AR
Galbreth, Donald	083	1817	WB-1/178	AR
Galbreth, John	083	c1822	WB-1/198	AR
Gale, Christopher	024	1734	SS 876/394	SS/AR
Gale, Delona	010	1830	WB-G/195	AR
Gale, Edmund	024	1738	LGB-4/#69	SS/AR
Gale, John D.	010	1826	WB-G/151	AR
Gale, Miles	024	c1761	WB-A/273	AR
Gales, Joseph	099	1841	RB-24/537	AR
Gales, Nathan	100	1894	WB-51/377	AR
Galey, Thomas	065	1791	WB-C/107	AR
Galin, James	028	1801	WB-B/116	
Galispie, William	029	1794	Orig. Only	AR
Gall, Christian	021	1898	WB-3/209	AR
Gall, John	075	1804	WB-M1/94	AR
Gallagher, Charles K.	009	1893	WB-1/559	CTY
Gallagher, Frederick	009	1892	WB-1/527	CTY
Gallagher, John	009	1832	OB-B/214	AR
Galland, Mary	070	1766	SS 881/288	
Gallaway, Alexander	092	1897	WB-6/441	AR
Gallaway, James	012	1879	WB-A/41	AR
Gallaway, Mary S.	084	1852	WB-C/151	CTY
Gallaway, Robert	084	c1831	WB-B/55	CTY
Gallaway, Robert, Jr.	084	1834	WB-B/95	CTY
Gallemore, William	032	1830	WB-1/130	AR
Gallent, Daniel	065	1827	WB-A/154	AR-Nunc.
Galley, John	075	1729	SS 876/203	SS/AR
Gallimore, Owen	032	1865	WB-2/294	AR
Gallion, Jacob	092	1813	WB-3/104	AR
Gallop, Abel	075	1766	WB-I/54	AR
Gallop, Courtney	018	c1878	WB-E/64	AR
Gallop, Elihu	018	1881	WB-E/84	AR
Gallop, Hodges	030	1878	WB-5/39	AR
Gallop, Josiah, Sr.	018	1834	WB-C/147	AR-Copy
Gallop, Padrick	018	1836	WB-C/197	
Gallop, Shadrach	030	1802	WB-2/204	
Gallop, Willis	030	c1814	WB-3/40	
Gallop, Willis	030	1848	WB-4/132	
Galloway, Abraham	053	1798	RW-1/304	AR
Galloway, Agnes	065	1825	WB-C/130	AR
Galloway, Alexander	012	1896	WB-A/137	AR
Galloway, C. W.	092	1884	WB-6/195	
Galloway, Cornelius	012	1848	Orig. Only	AR
Galloway, Cornelius	012	1871	WB-A/19	AR
Galloway, Daniel	065	1853	WB-I/236	AR
Galloway, Edney	079	1892	WB-3/8	AR
Galloway, Francis M.	012	1900	WB-A/157	AR
Galloway, James W.	065	1833	WB-G/125	AR
Galloway, Jesse	105	1893	WB-3/67	AR
Galloway, John	012	1795	WB-B/52	AR
Galloway, John	054	1844	WB-2/286	AR
Galloway, John	079	1883	WB-2/282	AR
Galloway, Lewis	012	1826	WB-B/140	AR-Nunc.
Galloway, Mary S.	090	1886	WB-6/166	AR
Galloway, Nancy S.	084	1852	Copy	090 AR
Galloway, Noah	009	1892	WB-1/545	CTY
Galloway, Noah, Sr.	009	1849	OB-G/172	AR
Galloway, Robert	084	1832	Copy	090 AR
Galloway, Sarah C.	103	1896	WB-2/149	AR
Galloway, Susan S.	084	1868	WB-D/92	CTY
Galloway, Thomas H.	093	c1874	WB-1/173	
Galloway, Thomas S.	084	1879	WB-E/153	CTY
Galloway, William	009	c1808	OB-A/54	AR
Gallway, Thomas	024	1753	SS 881/94	SS/AR
Gally, Ann	070	1895	Orig. Only	AR
Galt, Robert	064	1889	WB-2/191 & 437	AR
Galyean, Bennett	092	1893	WB-6/357	AR
Galyean, Elizabeth	092	1892	WB-6/353	AR
Galyean, James C.	092	1892	WB-6/333	AR
Galyean, Samuel	092	1880	WB-6/149	AR
Gambell, Adam	N	1694	SS 874.2/55	SS/AR
Gambil, James	077	1835	WB-F/237	AR
Gambill, J. J.	004	1893	WB-A/144 & 153	AR
Gambill, James	006	1893	WB-E/249	AR
Gambill, John	104	1891	WB-6/411	AR
Gambill, John	049	1884	WB-2/115	AR
Gambill, John	104	1858	WB-5/224	AR
Gambill, John, Sr.	004	1879	WB-A/35	AR
Gambill, Martin	006	1812	WB-A/27	
Gambill, Robert	004	1885	WB-A/76	AR
Gambill, William	104	1779	WB-1/25	AR

Name	Co.	Date	Recorded Copy	Original
Gamble, Andrew M.	038	1871	WB-2/60	AR
Gamble, Ann R.	040	1897	WB-2/540	AR
Gamble, Elizabeth	020	1847	RB-P/387	
Gamble, John B.	046	1862	WB-D/163	AR
Gamble, Joseph	040	1887	WB-2/289	AR
Gamblin, Joshua	018	1807	Copy	075 AR
Gambling, Lazarus	075	1818	WB-M1/320	AR
Gambold, Anna Maria	038	1854	WB-1/64	AR
Gambold, John	090	1828	WB-3/191	AR
Gambrel, John A.	MD	1878	075 WB-0/269	075 AR
Gamewell, Bridgett	030	1806	WB-2/283	
Gamewell, James	030	1787	WB-1/214	
Gamil, Joshua	030	1821	WB-3/119	
Gammey, John	060	1826	WB-1/35	AR
Gammey, Mary	060	1827	WB-1/63	AR
Gammidge, Francis	030	1737	Orig. Only	SS/AR
Gammill, James	090	1794	WB-1/56	AR
Gammon, James	047	1838	WB-4/168	
Gammon, Joshua	047	1810	WB-3/503	
Gammon, Josiah	030	1873	WB-5/44	AR
Gammon, Richard	047	1858	WB-5/62	
Gandley, John	073	1802	WB-D/62	AR
Gandy, Edward	069	1817	WB-1/291	AR
Gandy, Tamsy	103	1842	RD-8/309	AR
Ganey, Edmund	087	c1791	Orig. Only	AR
Gann, Bethel	090	1866	WB-5/32	
Gann, Mary	084	1897	WB-F/87	CTY
Gann, Samuel	084	1885	WB-E/329	CTY
Gann, Samuel	084	1843	WB-B/289	CTY
Gannon, Rebecca	046	1877	WB-E/229	AR
Gant, A. J.	040	1895	WB-2/488	AR
Gant, Albert	020	1894	WB-B/171	CTY
Gant, Charles	039	1816	WB-E/38	AR
Gant, Edward	073	1783	WB-A/279	AR
Gant, Henry	046	1863	WB-D/191	AR
Gant, Isham	073	1807	WB-D/183	AR
Gant, J. A.	001	1870	WB-2/18	AR
Gant, J. M.	046	1896	WB-F/492	AR
Gant, James	039	c1797	WB-A/209	
Gant, Jesse, Sr.	021	1875	WB-2/133	AR
Gant, John	073	1801	WB-D/30	AR
Gant, Jonathan	001	1858	WB-1/149	AR
Gant, Lizzie	084	1890	WB-E/437	
Gant, Sally	021	c1877	WB-2/300	
Gant, Samuel	046	1895	WB-F/412	AR
Gantt, Evan	021	1896	WB-3/100	AR
Gantt, Theophilus	021	1863	WB-1/176	AR
Gantt, Tira T.	026	c1876	Orig. Only	AR
Garawood, Sarah	033	1855	WB-1/120	
Gard, David	028	1783	Orig. Only	AR
Garden, Mary E.	064	1867	Orig. Only	AR
Gardiner, John	085	1831	WB-H/506	AR
Gardiner, John	085	1871	WB-1/69	CTY
Gardiner, Minnie L.	035	1891	WB-4/381	AR
Gardiner, Minnie L.	035	1891	076 WB-A1/143	076 AR
Gardiner, Samuel	085	1863	WB-K/313	
Gardner, Abel	046	1894	WB-F/348	AR
Gardner, Ambrose	075	1835	WB-N/115	AR
Gardner, Ann	046	1873	WB-E/94	AR
Gardner, Asa	079	1870	WB-2/55	AR
Gardner, B. F.	099	1898	WB-D/154	AR
Gardner, Barbary	009	1841	OB-D/170	AR
Gardner, Barzilla	046	1829	WB-B/401	AR
Gardner, Caroline	028	1893	WB-F/93	
Gardner, Charlotte	046	1898	WB-G/70	AR

Name	Co.	Date	Recorded Copy	Original
Gardner, Christian	064	1888	WB-2/173	AR
Gardner, Daniel	056	1869	WB-3/21	AR
Gardner, Daniel A.	092	1888	WB-6/277	AR
Gardner, Dosson	037	1900	WB-I/34	AR
Gardner, Edward	054	1884	WB-4/574	CTY
Gardner, Edward	063	1857	WB-2/442	
Gardner, Elias	082	1836	WB-2/60	AR
Gardner, Eliza	079	1870	WB-2/256	AR
Gardner, Elizabeth	063	1777	WB-1/36	
Gardner, George	069	1819	WB-1/302	AR
Gardner, George	037	1789	WB-C/96	AR
Gardner, Henry	024	1816	WB-C/45	AR
Gardner, Henry Bell	103	1891	WB-1/544	AR
Gardner, Hezekiah	046	1819	WB-B/81	AR
Gardner, Isaac	010	1827	WB-G/155	AR
Gardner, Isaac	063	c1801	WB-1/418	
Gardner, J. M.	026	1864	WB-1/349	AR
Gardner, James	010	1790	WB-D/141	AR
Gardner, James	070	1787	WB-C/128	AR
Gardner, James	085	c1803	WB-G/58	AR
Gardner, James T.	103	1878	WB-1/137	AR
Gardner, Jemima	046	1842	WB-C/110	AR
Gardner, Jesse	097	1872	WB-2/60	AR
Gardner, Jesse D.	071	1882	WB-6/386	
Gardner, John	085	c1791	WB-G/77	AR
Gardner, John	096	1749	Orig. Only	SS/AR
Gardner, John	085	1847	WB-K/61	AR
Gardner, John	079	1877	WB-2/155	AR
Gardner, John L.	028	1869	WB-E/21	AR-Nunc.
Gardner, John W.	100	1837	WB-35/375	
Gardner, Jonathan	046	1843	WB-C/165	AR
Gardner, Joseph	099	1809	RB-9/73	AR
Gardner, Josiah	029	1850	WB-C/174	AR
Gardner, Josiah	103	1865	RD-14/235	AR
Gardner, Josiah W.	103	1896	WB-2/173	AR
Gardner, Lettisha	009	1824	OWB/479	AR
Gardner, Lidia	046	c1900	Orig. Only	AR
Gardner, Lucy	037	1896	WB-H/345	AR
Gardner, Maranza	083	1893	WB-4/11	AR
Gardner, Margaret	038	1873	WB-2/139	AR
Gardner, Margaret	037	1877	WB-G/538	AR
Gardner, Margaret	063	1849	WB-2/349	
Gardner, Margaret	037	1839	WB-F/237	AR
Gardner, Martha	056	1899	WB-4/145	AR
Gardner, Martin	010	1784	WB-C/83	AR
Gardner, Martin	037	1894	WB-H/290	AR
Gardner, Martin	010	1760	SS 881/211	SS/AR
Gardner, Mary	065	1821	WB-C/128	AR
Gardner, Miriam	046	1852	WB-C/378	AR
Gardner, Nathan H.	046	1854	WB-C/415	AR
Gardner, O. P.	026	1900	WB-3/81	AR
Gardner, Patty	099	1883	WB-A/382	AR
Gardner, Randolph	051	1887	WB-C/357	AR
Gardner, Richard	046	1818	WB-B/63	AR
Gardner, Richard W.	085	1892	WB-2/544	CTY
Gardner, Samuel	063	c1798	WB-1/368	
Gardner, Samuel	063	1815	WB-2/27	
Gardner, Samuel W.	067	1889	Orig. Only	AR
Gardner, Sarah	046	1874	WB-E/122	AR
Gardner, Silvanus	046	1844	WB-C/204	AR
Gardner, Stephen	046	1830	WB-B/421	AR
Gardner, Susannah	063	1835	WB-2/296	
Gardner, Thaddeus	046	1851	WB-C/355	AR
Gardner, Thomas	107	c1857	WB-1A/1	
Gardner, Thomas	100	1827	WB-31/117	AR

Name	Co.	Date	Recorded Copy	Original
Gardner, Thomas	063	1885	WB-3/279	AR
Gardner, Thomas	047	1777	WB-2/51	
Gardner, Thomas J.	105	1888	WB-2/465	AR
Gardner, Thomas M.	070	1892	WB-H/777	AR
Gardner, Thomas S.	026	1867	WB-1/412	AR
Gardner, William	097	1889	WB-2/338	AR
Gardner, William	105	1884	WB-2/323	AR
Gardner, William	046	1817	WB-B/49	AR
Gardner, William	090	1846	WB-4/209	AR
Gardner, William	096	1754	SS 880/102	SS/AR
Gardner, William	028	1810	WB-C/17	AR
Garfort, Gregory	077	1704	SS 874.1/23	SS/AR
Garibaldi, Angelo	047	1892	086 WB-F/444	086 AR
Garibaldi, Angelo	047	1892	WB-7/63	AR
Garinger, Catherin	085	c1797	WB-G/39	AR
Garish, Simon H.	053	1848	WB-7/187	AR-Nunc.
Gariwood, Hannah	033	1866	WB-1/201	
Garland, Henry	020	1890	WB-B/43	CTY
Garland, James G.	020	1872	WB-A/87	CTY
Garland, John T.	020	1874	WB-A/168	CTY
Garland, John W.	TN	1887	107 WB-2/48	
Garland, Lizzie	100	1897	WB-51/486	AR
Garland, Mary E.	105	1887	WB-2/503	AR
Garland, Nelson	020	1891	WB-B/63	CTY
Garland, Patrick	047	1783	WB-3/49	
Garland, Stephen	066	1894	WB-1/126	
Garland, William	047	c1778	WB-2/100	
Garlant, James	029	c1787	Orig. Only	AR
Garlard, Henry W.	009	1873	WB-1/118	
Garman, George Sr.	016	1850	WB-1/181	
Garman, John	005	1822	WB-A/72	
Garmen, John	016	1843	WB-1/15	
Garmon, George	065	1784	WB-C/120	
Garmon, Michael	016	1839	PQS.6/29	
Garmon, Michael	016	1885	WB-3/455	AR
Garmon, Michael A.	016	1893	WB-4/155	AR
Garmon, William H.	013	c1854	WB-A/163	
Garner, A. W.	071	1879	WB-6/286	
Garner, Absolom	037	1798	WB-D/57	AR
Garner, Barbara	085	1864	WB-K/338	AR
Garner, Catherine	056	1893	WB-2/155	AR
Garner, Dexter G.	019	1888	WB-B/167	AR
Garner, Eli	056	1876	WB-3/168	AR
Garner, Elijah	019	1865	WB-A/283	AR
Garner, Elizabeth	056	1885	WB-3/374	AR
Garner, Elizabeth	085	1875	WB-1/302	CTY
Garner, Elizabeth	056	1845	WB-1/572	AR
Garner, Elizabeth	103	1847	RD-9/514	AR
Garner, Enoch	081	1900	WB-17/51	
Garner, Francis	019	1879	WB-B/113	AR
Garner, Francis	019	1769	WB-A/34	AR
Garner, Francis	019	1825	WB-D/211	AR
Garner, Harrison T.	071	1861	WB-5/240	AR
Garner, Henderson	056	1893	WB-2/159	AR
Garner, Henry	071	1876	WB-6/203	AR
Garner, Henry	035	1900	WB-4/569	AR
Garner, Henry	032	1885	WB-3/475	AR
Garner, Hillary T.	104	1863	WB-5/352	
Garner, Honar	032	1846	WB-1/492	AR
Garner, J. H.	047	1891	WB-6/583	AR
Garner, Jacob	092	1818	WB-3/135	AR
Garner, Jeremiah	060	1819	Orig. Only	AR
Garner, Joel	056	1866	WB-2/80	AR
Garner, John	085	1819	WB-H/21	AR
Garner, John	092	1850	WB-4/308	
Garner, John	071	1755	SS 880/48	SS/AR
Garner, John	099	1868	Orig. Only	AR
Garner, John	085	1825	WB-H/303	AR
Garner, John	029	1809	WB-A/145	AR
Garner, John	019	1794	WB-D/189	AR
Garner, John, Sr.	037	1760	WB-A/13	AR
Garner, Joseph	056	1772	WB-2/282	AR
Garner, Margaret	085	1851	WB-K/130	AR
Garner, Mary	071	1863	WB-5/276	AR
Garner, Mary	056	1824	WB-1/363	AR
Garner, Mason	071	1877	Orig. Only	AR
Garner, Mathias	085	1831	WB-H/525	AR
Garner, Nancy	099	1877	RB-35/382	AR
Garner, Nathan	035	1861	WB-3/29	AR
Garner, Philip	032	1844	WB-1/433	AR
Garner, Phillip	085	1814	WB-G/314	AR
Garner, Presley K.	071	1861	WB-5/254	AR
Garner, Sabra	037	1801	WB-D/123	AR
Garner, Salley	071	1815	WB-3/142	AR
Garner, Samuel	019	1836	WB-A/60	AR
Garner, Samuel	022	1827	WB-B/130	AR
Garner, Samuel	019	1865	WB-A/275	AR
Garner, Samuel	019	1765	RB-A/15	AR-Nunc.
Garner, Samuel C.	019	1892	WB-B/220	AR
Garner, Stephen	081	1800	WB-2/57	AR
Garner, Susan D.	071	1886	WB-6/530	AR
Garner, Thomas	071	1837	WB-4/160	AR
Garner, W. B.	068	1899	WB-E/7	
Garner, William	092	1805	WB-3/67A	AR
Garner, William	071	1835	WB-4/134	AR
Garner, William	019	1830	WB-A/1	AR
Garner, William	071	1824	WB-3/307	AR
Garner, William L.	022	1844	WB-C/159	AR
Garner, William L.	019	1835	WB-A/48	AR
Garner, Willis	103	1838	RD-7/334	AR
Garner, Wyatt N.	071	1893	WB-7/192	AR
Garnes, John	018	1851	WB-C/358	
Garnes, Nancy Ann	028	1877	WB-E/185	AR
Garnor, Ralfe	075	1695	SS 874.2/84	
Garrak, John	029	1792	Orig. Only	AR
Garrard, James	073	1845	WB-F/258	AR
Garrard, James Γ.	073	1881	WB-H/281	CTY
Garrard, John	073	1859	WB-G/234	AR
Garrard, Mildred	073	1816	WB-D/477	AR
Garrard, Samuel	073	1828	Orig. Only	AR
Garrard, Thomas	073	1828	WB-E/158	
Garrard, Tyre	073	1829	Orig. Only	AR
Garrard, William F.	073	1875	WB-H/108	CTY
Garrason, James	076	1884	WB-A1/38	AR
Garrason, Thomas	012	1897	WB-A/116	AR
Garratt, Henry	001	1866	WB-1/254	AR
Garrell, John	030	1816	WB-3/88	
Garren, David	013	1894	WB-C/312	AR
Garren, James	050	1894	WB-2/188	CTY
Garren, John	013	1843	WB-A/90	
Garren, Marian	013	1890	WB-B/581	AR
Garren, Silas	093	1891	WB-2/97	AR
Garret, Humphry	082	1835	WB-2/53	AR
Garret, John	072	1835	WB-1/141	
Garret, John	085	c1793	WB-G/79	AR
Garret, Mary	077	1796	WB-E/70	
Garrett, Alfred F.	101	1885	WB-A/142	AR
Garrett, Amos	044	1854	WB-19/449	CTY
Garrett, Ann M.	047	1878	WB-6/182	AR
Garrett, Benjamin	009	1818	OB-A/287	AR

Name	Co.	Date	Recorded Copy	Original
Garrett, Celia	086	1857	WB-E/332	AR
Garrett, Cicero S.	047	1854	WB-4/359	
Garrett, Daniel	096	1761	WB-1/19	AR
Garrett, Elizabeth	030	1828	WB-3/237	
Garrett, H. H.	078	1891	WB-19/305	AR
Garrett, Harrett	GA	1875	084 WB-E/129	084 CTY
Garrett, James F.	010	1862	WB-H/121	AR
Garrett, James M.	086	1857	WB-E/332	AR
Garrett, James, Sr.	041	1781	WB-1/18	AR
Garrett, Jemima	096	c1825	Orig. Only	AR
Garrett, Jesse	010	1797	WB-E/18	AR
Garrett, John	085	1757	WB-A/59	AR
Garrett, John	024	c1784	WB-B/93	AR
Garrett, John	046	1897	WB-G/16	AR
Garrett, John	096	1791	Orig. Only	AR
Garrett, John H.	024	1888	WB-E/167	AR
Garrett, John W.	039	1900	098 WB-A/346	098 CTY
Garrett, John W.	020	1897	WB-B/307	CTY
Garrett, Malvina	069	1890	040 WB-2/371	040 AR
Garrett, Malvina	069	1890	026 WB-2/415	026 AR
Garrett, Malvina	069	1890	WB-5/280	AR
Garrett, Margret H.	062	1867	WB-A/51	
Garrett, Mary	010	1823	WB-G/122	AR
Garrett, Meddy	018	1868	WB-D/86	AR
Garrett, N. A.	091	1880	WB-1/7	
Garrett, Stephen	020	1885	Copy	078 AR
Garrett, Stephen	020	1885	WB-A/442	CTY
Garrett, Thomas	030	1816	WB-3/75	
Garrett, Thomas	024	1735	SS 876/419	SS/AR
Garrett, Thomas	024	1783	WB-A/314	AR
Garrett, Thomas M.	010	1864	WB-H/147	AR
Garrett, William	002	1735	SS 876/378	SS/AR
Garrett, William B.	091	1876	WB-1/1	
Garrett, William E.	037	1891	WB-H/211	AR
Garrett, Wilson	073	1870	WB-H/40	CTY
Garringer, Andrew	046	1829	Orig. Only	AR
Garriott, Jesse	044	1818	WB-8/175	CTY
Garris, Bedford	065	1835	WB-G/195	AR
Garris, Hannah	071	1802	WB-2/234	AR
Garris, James	047	1879	WB-6/199	AR
Garris, James	005	1849	WB-C/1	AR
Garris, John	071	1800	WB-2/198	AR
Garris, Joseph	071	1833	WB-4/106	AR
Garris, Nehemiah	079	1862	WB-1/137	AR
Garrish, Edward	077	1827	WB-F/133	AR
Garrish, Eliza J.	NM	c1894	064 WB-2/364	064 AR
Garrison, David	065	1794	WB-C/122	AR
Garrison, Eleanor	073	1844	WB-F/236	AR
Garrison, Eliza J.	084	1896	WB-F/68	CTY
Garrison, Ephraim	035	1793	WB-A/175	AR
Garrison, Garrett	073	1829	WB-E/186	AR
Garrison, Garrett	001	1863	WB-1/220	AR
Garrison, George	073	1822	WB-E/11	AR
Garrison, Hannah	104	1818	WB-3/179	AR
Garrison, Isabella	001	1894	WB-3/5	AR
Garrison, J. Thomas	065	1886	WB-L/144	AR
Garrison, Jacob	073	1832	WB-E/275	AR
Garrison, James M.	065	1891	WB-M/15	AR
Garrison, John	080	1899	WB-1/318	AR
Garrison, Joseph L.	001	1866	WB-1/277	AR
Garrison, Levi	001	1893	WB-2/578	AR
Garrison, Mary	001	c1845	WB-1/83	AR
Garrison, Richard	086	1814	WB-C/7	AR
Garrison, Sarah	065	1810	WB-C/102	AR
Garrison, Thomas	085	c1805	WB-G/52	AR
Garrison, William	001	1865	WB-1/246	AR
Garriss, Etheldred	071	1862	WB-5/259	AR
Garriss, Flora	076	1883	WB-A1/29	AR
Garriss, Gray C.	103	1887	WB-1/396	AR
Garriss, Isaac	071	1872	WB-6/84	AR
Garriss, Joshua	103	1840	RD-8/85	AR
Garriss, Julia J. V.	103	1887	WB-1/395	AR
Garriss, Wade	051	1871	WB-C/51	AR
Garrit, Jonathan	075	1764	WB-H/58	AR
Garrot, Stephen	073	1831	WB-E/243	AR
Garrott, Easter	082	1826	WB-1/278	AR
Garrott, Thomas	063	1819	WB-2/59	
Garrott, Thomas	099	1815	RB-12/213	AR
Garrte, John	030	1735	Orig. Only	SS/AR
Garth, Thomas	VA	1834	090 WB-4/52	090 AR
Garvan, Ann	011	c1836	WB-1/39	
Garvey, A. J.	037	1891	WB-H/181	AR
Garvey, Anne	035	1872	WB-4/59	AR
Garvey, James	006	1899	WB-E/365	AR
Garvin, Sarah C.	SC	1859	040 WB-2/58	040 AR
Gary, Caroline	047	1859	WB-5/68	
Gary, George W.	047	1857	WB-5/41	
Gary, John	047	1830	WB-4/66	
Gary, Mary N.	047	1864	WB-5/106	
Gary, Richard H.	071	1857	WB-5/185	AR
Gary, Roderick B.	071	1856	WB-5/158	AR
Gary, Sarah J.	047	1875	WB-6/122	AR
Gary, Susan I.	047	1853	WB-4/339	
Gary, William	047	1830	WB-4/60	
Gash, B. S.	013	1891	WB-C/62	AR
Gash, Ellen C.	013	1882	Orig. Only	AR
Gash, John	013	1858	WB-A/190	
Gash, Leander S.	050	1872	WB-1/113	CTY
Gash, Leander S.	050	1872	093 WB-2/47	
Gaskill, Anson C.	019	1850	WB-A/143	AR
Gaskill, Benjamin	009	1859	OB-K/516	AR
Gaskill, Elizabeth	073	1844	WB-F/210	AR
Gaskill, Esther	019	1844	WB-A/112	AR
Gaskill, Isaac	019	1882	WB-B/134	AR
Gaskill, Jacob	053	1877	WB-11/70	AR
Gaskill, Jacob	053	1820	WB-4/139	
Gaskill, John	019	1819	WB-D/205	AR
Gaskill, John A.	019	1854	WB-A/176	AR
Gaskill, Joseph	019	1826	WB-D/208	AR
Gaskill, Joseph W.	009	1889	WB-1/452	CTY
Gaskill, Lowry	053	1835	WB-5/258	AR
Gaskill, Martha M.	009	1900	WB-2/249	CTY
Gaskill, Mellie H.	037	1894	WB-H/293	AR
Gaskill, Noah	028	1867	WB-D/452	AR
Gaskill, Olivia C.	028	1883	WB-E/330	AR
Gaskill, Pleasant	019	1862	WB-A/258	AR
Gaskill, Richard M.	009	1859	OB-L/62	AR
Gaskill, Thomas	009	1844	OB-E/207	AR
Gaskill, William	019	1814	WB-D/201	AR
Gaskill, William	019	1770	RB-A/37	AR
Gaskill, William	075	1703	Orig. Only	SS/AR
Gaskill, William G.	009	1870	WB-1/40	CTY
Gaskill, William S.	053	1873	WB-11/40	AR
Gaskins, Alexander	009	1871	WB-1/72	CTY
Gaskins, Amiticus	FL	1847	010 WB-G/459	010 AR
Gaskins, Ann	053	1803	RW-1/362	
Gaskins, Asa	028	1875	WB-E/128	AR
Gaskins, Asa A.	028	1882	WB-E/302	AR
Gaskins, Benjamin	010	1840	WB-G/314	AR
Gaskins, Catrin	075	1755	Orig. Only	SS/AR

Name	Co.	Date	Recorded Copy	Original
Gaskins, David	010	1843	WB-G/453	AR
Gaskins, David	028	c1900	WB-F/485	
Gaskins, David	010	1881	WB-I/133	
Gaskins, David	028	1860	WB-D/328	AR
Gaskins, David	010	1806	WB-F/15	AR
Gaskins, Elizabeth	028	1841	WB-D/39	AR
Gaskins, Fisher	028	1758	Orig. Only	SS/AR
Gaskins, Harman	028	1816	WB-C/122	AR
Gaskins, James	028	1812	WB-C/52	AR
Gaskins, James W.	028	1853	WB-D/204	AR
Gaskins, Jane M.	028	1882	WB-E/312	AR
Gaskins, John	010	1858	WB-H/72	AR
Gaskins, John	028	1804	WB-B/198	
Gaskins, John S.	028	1885	WB-E/405	AR
Gaskins, Joseph	028	1800	WB-B/124	Nunc.
Gaskins, Julia F.	047	1882	WB-6/274	AR
Gaskins, Levi	028	c1818	Orig. Only	AR
Gaskins, Lewis	028	1853	WB-D/212	
Gaskins, Lorenzo D.	010	1840	WB-G/323	AR
Gaskins, Mary	010	1866	WB-H/162	AR
Gaskins, Mary	028	1846	WB-D/128	
Gaskins, Mary E.	037	1897	WB-H/396	AR
Gaskins, Mary R. P.	024	1871	WB-E/24	AR
Gaskins, Patsy Ann	028	1897	WB-F/247	
Gaskins, Seth	079	1880	WB-2/183	AR
Gaskins, Starkey	010	1843	WB-G/357	AR
Gaskins, Thomas	028	1791	Orig. Only	AR
Gaskins, Thomas	075	1865	WB-N/252	
Gaskins, Thomas	075	c1865	WB-M2/82	
Gaskins, Thomas	075	1805	WB-M1/111	AR
Gaskins, William	028	1814	WB-C/81	AR
Gaskins, William	075	c1711	Orig. Only	SS/AR
Gaskins, William	028	1839	WB-C/427	AR
Gaskins, William A.	075	1847	WB-N/212	AR
Gaston, John	040	c1862	WB-1/156	
Gaston, Margaret	028	1812	WB-C/48	AR
Gaston, P. C.	061	1891	WB-2/106	AR
Gaston, Thomas L.	013	1854	WB-A/159	
Gaston, William	028	1844	WB-D/93	AR
Gateley, William	078	1799	WI-2/195	AR
Gater, Samuel	037	1820	WB-E/236	AR
Gates, Burgwin M.	028	1887	WB-E/440	
Gates, Edward	085	c1799	WB-G/69	AR
Gates, Jean	011	c1799	WB-1/357	
Gates, John	073	1850	WB-F/452	AR
Gates, John	037	1851	WB-F/457	AR
Gates, Lovit	044	1789	WB-2/92	CTY
Gates, Mary Jane	036	1889	WB-A/163	CTY
Gates, Peter	011	c1789	WB-1/503	
Gates, Rhoda	070	1854	WB-C/577	AR
Gates, William F.	073	1881	WB-H/304	CTY
Gates, Willie P.	036	1886	WB-A/81	CTY
Gatewood, Ambrose	020	1781	RB-A/137	AR
Gatewood, Dudley	090	1836	WB-3/307	
Gatewood, Griffin	005	1831	WB-B/13	AR
Gatewood, James M.	020	1899	WB-B/349	CTY
Gatewood, Rebecca	020	1857	RB-R/540	AR
Gatewood, Robert	005	1790	WB-A/4	AR
Gatewood, Robert A.	020	1871	WB-A/77	CTY
Gatewood, William H.	020	1900	WB-B/396	CTY
Gatewood, William T.	005	1863	WB-C/183	AR
Gathings, Jane	097	1876	WB-2/118	AR
Gatlin, Bethel	081	1900	WB-17/93	
Gatlin, David	028	1814	WB-C/90	
Gatlin, Edward	028	1781	Orig. Only	AR
Gatlin, Edward	028	1725/6	SS 876/54	SS/AR
Gatlin, Elizabeth	028	1806	WB-B/258	AR
Gatlin, John	028	1766	Orig. Only	AR
Gatlin, Shadrack	028	1833	WB-C/352	AR
Gatlin, Thomas	028	1793	WB-A/305	AR
Gatlin, William	028	1793	WB-A/277	AR-Nunc.
Gatlin, William	028	1823	WB-C/233	AR
Gatling, Ann	041	1852	WB-3/161	AR
Gatling, Ann	037	1814	WB-E/65	AR
Gatling, Charles	072	1828	WB-1/29	
Gatling, David	051	1852	WB-A/338	
Gatling, David	051	1831	WB-A/116	
Gatling, Elizabeth	041	1874	WB-4/42	AR
Gatling, Etheldred	041	1826	WB2/247	AR
Gatling, James	051	c1822	WB-A/118	
Gatling, James	077	1882	WB-H/119	AR
Gatling, Jordan	051	1848	WB-A/289	
Gatling, Joseph	041	1879	WB-4/114	AR
Gatling, Mary	041	1826	WB-2/263	AR
Gatling, Mary E.	041	1862	WB-3/284	AR
Gatling, Richard B.	TX	c1889	051 WB-C/459	051 AR
Gatling, Robert R.	099	1899	WB-D/260	AR
Gatling, Sallie A.	041	1897	WB-4/429	AR
Gatling, Sally L.	099	1891	WB-B/491	AR
Gatling, Sarah	071	1782	WB-1/259	AR
Gatling, Susan	071	1863	WB-5/286	AR
Gatling, Thomas B.	071	1857	WB-5/181	AR
Gatling, William	041	1791	WB-1/92	AR
Gatling, William	041	1808	WB-2/23	AR
Gatling, William J.	051	1899	WB-C/553	AR
Gattis, Alexander	073	1843	WB-F/153	AR
Gattis, James R.	036	1896	WB-A/380	CTY
Gattis, John	073	1810	WB-D/269	AR
Gattis, John W.	036	1892	WB-A/260	CTY
Gattis, Pattie B.	099	1894	WB-C/274	AR
Gattis, Rebecca	001	1883	WB-2/212	AR
Gattis, William	073	1844	WB-F/212	AR
Gattis, William	073	1854	WB-G/55	AR
Gatton, Azariah	054	c1807	WB-1/19	AR
Gault, Sarah B.	065	1888	WB-L/506	AR
Gause, Benjamin	012	c1826	WB-B/145	AR
Gause, Charles	012	1808	WB-B/81	AR
Gause, Jane	070	1871	WB-E/230	AR
Gause, John	012	1783	DB-B/166	AR
Gause, John J.	012	1836	WB-B/171	AR
Gause, Kate S.	070	1900	WB-H/267	AR
Gause, Louisa F.	070	1895	WB-G/410	AR
Gause, Needham	011	c1792	WB-1/505	
Gause, Needham	012	c1794	WB-B/65	AR
Gause, Peter	012	c1823	WB-B/131	
Gause, Samuel	012	1811	WB-B/100	AR
Gause, William	012	c1801	WB-B/71	AR
Gause, William	012	c1858	WB-B/30	AR-Copy
Gause, Wm. James	012	1824	WB-B/134	AR
Gautier, Anna Bella	070	1823	WB-C/133	AR
Gautier, Joseph R.	070	1816	WB-AB/244	AR
Gauzy, Henderson	059	1892	WB-B/48	CTY
Gavin, Edward C.	087	1850	WB-1/374	
Gavin, Samuel	087	c1807	WB-A/47	AR
Gavin, Samuel	035	1762	WB-A/155	AR
Gavvan, Richard	011	c1827	WB-2/370	
Gay, Bashaba	051	1832	WB-A/41	
Gay, Benjamin	044	1799	WB-4/300	
Gay, Burrel	069	1877	WB-5/67	AR
Gay, Charles	051	1830	WB-A/1	

Name	Co.	Date	Recorded Copy	Original
Gay, Dempsey	037	1840	WB-F/251	AR
Gay, Elias	039	1811	WB-C/232	AR
Gay, Elizabeth	071	1883	WB-6/424	
Gay, Eunicy	039	c1893	WB-V/9	
Gay, Franklin	054	1883	WB-4/483	CTY
Gay, Gatsy T.	009	1895	WB-2/69	CTY
Gay, Green	071	1878	WB-6/257	AR
Gay, Henry	037	1792	WB-C/204	AR
Gay, Henry	037	1871	WB-G/363	AR
Gay, Henry	071	1851	WB-5/96	AR
Gay, James	054	c1818	WB-1A/137	AR
Gay, James	039	1853	WB-N/345	AR
Gay, John	039	c1794	WB-B/19	
Gay, John	069	1883	WB-5/176	AR
Gay, John	037	1761	WB-A/88	AR
Gay, John	054	1844	WB-2/301	AR
Gay, John	082	1854	WB-4/84	AR
Gay, John	069	1808	WB-1/196	AR
Gay, John	037	1761	WB-A/57	AR
Gay, John	071	c1783	WB-1/285	AR
Gay, John D.	105	1898	WB-3/370	AR
Gay, Johnathan	071	1892	WB-7/165	AR
Gay, Jonathan	071	1822	WB-3/269	AR
Gay, Jonathan	081	1810	WB-3/289	AR
Gay, Joshua	085	1827	WB-H/396	AR
Gay, Josiah	056	1878	WB-3/194	AR
Gay, Kinchen	037	1870	WB-G/353	AR
Gay, Levin	037	1888	WB-H/111	AR
Gay, Lydia	037	1865	WB-G/265	AR
Gay, Martha	069	c1883	Orig. Only	AR
Gay, Mary	085	1838	WB-I/44	AR
Gay, Nathaniel	037	1894	WB-H/297	AR
Gay, Redden	079	1861	WB-1/69	AR
Gay, Thomas	039	c1841	WB-L/254	
Gay, Thomas	039	1839	WB-K/217	AR
Gay, Thomas	039	1803	WB-B/94 & 166	
Gay, W. H.	039	1880	WB-U/234	AR
Gay, William	085	1842	WB-I/136	AR
Gay, William	039	1878	WB-U/176	AR
Gay, William	037	1798	WB-D/47	AR
Gay, Willis	056	1825	WB-1/380	AR
Gay, Wilson	039	1893	WB-V/12	AR
Gaye, Peter	072	c1779	RW/L12	AR
Gaye, Vines	073	1836	WB-E/385	
Gaylard, Henry W.	009	1873	WB-1/118	CTY
Gaylard, Jeremiah	009	1823	OB-A/329	AR
Gaylard, John T.	009	1897	WB-2/126	CTY
Gaylard, Mary H.	009	1853	OB-H/249	AR
Gaylard, Matilda	009	1868	OB-M/311	AR
Gayle, J. B.	099	1874	RB-35/247	
Gaylord, Asa O.	101	1876	WB-A/20	AR
Gaylord, E. W.	009	1898	WB-2/157	
Gaylord, Ebenezer	009	1890	WB-1/478	CTY
Gaylord, Elmy	053	1832	WB-5/137	AR
Gaylord, John	053	c1809	RW-1/437	
Gaylord, John W.	101	1895	WB-A/279	AR
Gaylord, Rosanah	053	1794	RW-1/237	AR
Gaylord, Seth	009	1883	WB-1/333	CTY
Gaylord, Stephen	030	1819	WB-3/111	
Gaylord, Thomas	053	c1784	RW-1/200	AR
Gaylord, Winfield	053	1791	RW-1/212	AR
Gaynor, Hardy	063	1893	WB-4/106	AR
Gaynor, Mary W.	103	1849	RD-10/307	AR
Gaynor, William R.	063	1852	WB-2/385	
Geans, Parham	039	1885	WB-U/346	AR
Geddie, Cary	029	1895	WB-F/44	AR
Geddy, Elizabeth	099	1843	RB-25/319	AR
Gee, Arabell	020	1889	WB-A/581	CTY
Gee, Charles	047	1810	WB-3/509	
Gee, David	029	1868	WB-D/101	AR
Gee, Drury	071	1786	WB-1/367	AR
Gee, Eliza A.	022	1885	WB-E/319	AR
Gee, George	029	1863	Orig. Only	AR
Gee, George	022	1848	WB-C/217	AR
Gee, Guilford	047	1881	WB-6/250	AR
Gee, Hannah	100	1847	WB-39/298	AR
Gee, Howell	071	1788	WB-1/399	AR
Gee, James	047	1783	WB-3/44	
Gee, Mary	071	1826	WB-4/15	AR
Gee, Sterling	047	1866	WB-5/151	
Geekie, James	070	1793	WB-C/130	AR
Geer, Frederick	099	1848	RB-26/429	AR
Geer, Frederick	099	1840	RB-24/418	AR
Geer, John	073	1770	WB-A/105	
Geffroy, William V.	019	1878	WB-B/109	AR
Geiger, Adam	090	1827	WB-3/155	AR
Genkins, David	028	1714	PQS.1/57	
Genkins, Thomas	087	c1809	WB-A/55	
Gennans, John	056	1762	WB-2/272	AR
Gentle, George	085	c1795	WB-G/45	AR
Gentrey, Allen	104	1825	WB-4/59	
Gentrey, Levi	006	1865	WB-C/18	AR
Gentry, Abednego	078	1839	WI-14/103	AR
Gentry, Agnes	092	1826	WB-3/169	AR
Gentry, Alice A.	004	1889	WB-A/98	AR
Gentry, Allen	004	1863	WB-1/3	AR
Gentry, James	084	c1783	OW/114	
Gentry, James	006	1875	WB-E/3	AR
Gentry, John N.	013	1850	WB-A/141	
Gentry, Jonathan	104	1871	WB-6/30	AR
Gentry, Jonathan	104	1852	WB-5/66	AR
Gentry, Joseph	092	1813	WB-3/107	AR
Gentry, Mildred	092	1850	WB-4/303	AR
Gentry, Priscilla	037	1846	WB-F/339	
Gentry, Richard	092	1812	WB-3/100	AR
Gentry, Richard	084	1893	WB-E/555	CTY
Gentry, Richard	090	1831	WB-3/228	AR
Gentry, Shadrach	106	c1853	WB-1/22	AR
Gentry, Shelton	092	c1830	WB-4/68	
Gentry, Simon	078	1868	WB-19/3	
Gentry, Wiley	092	1878	Orig. Only	AR
George, Allen	022	1795	Orig. Only	AR
George, Asa	065	1887	WB-L/218	AR
George, Asa	100	1859	WB-49/234	AR
George, Barbary	070	1846	WB-AB/447	AR
George, David	028	1760	Orig. Only	AR
George, David	056	1821	WB-1/427	AR
George, David	075	1748	Orig. Only	SS/AR
George, David E.	076	1885	WB-A1/73	AR
George, Elcy	027	1883	WB-2/48	AR
George, Elias	037	1771	WB-A/191	AR
George, Elias	056	c1780	WB-2/283	AR
George, Elizabeth	037	1833	WB-F/152	AR
George, Forney K.	027	1865	WB-A/98	AR
George, Harris	022	1798	RB-2/134	AR
George, Henry	N	c1711	SS 875/34	
George, Jane	046	1895	WB-F/439	AR
George, John	062	1860	WB-A/24	
George, John	037	1816	WB-E/131	AR
George, John	099	1832	RB-22/284	AR

Name	Co.	Date	Recorded Copy	Original
George, Joseph	073	c1770	WB-A/126	
George, Kitsey	056	1900	WB-4/205	AR
George, Mathew	084	c1793	OW/116	AR
George, Michael	037	1823	WB-F/6	AR
George, Peter	028	1763	DB-8/220	AR
George, Presley	099	1824	RB-19/111	AR
George, Prestly	090	1867	WB-5/40	AR
George, Previlly	028	1847	WB-D/133	AR
George, Selah	037	1808	WB-D/308	AR
George, Timothy T.	070	1873	WB-E/256	AR
George, William	022	1800	WB-A/30	AR
Georgeson, Christian	028	1822	WB-C/223	AR
Gerald, C. F.	056	1879	WB-3/227	AR
Gerald, Isaac	056	1815	WB-1/253	AR
Gerald, John	056	1832	WB-1/487	AR
Gerald, John, Sr.	056	1811	WB-1/383	AR
Gerard, William T.	009	1877	WB-1/189	CTY
Gerber, Michael	092	1783	WB-2/2	AR
Gerganes, Alfred	070	1862	WB-D/106	AR
Gerganes, Zachray	009	c1807	OWB/451	AR
Gerkins, Charles	096	1794	Orig. Only	AR
German, George	065	1785	WB-C/120	AR
German, Hubbard	104	1892	WB-6/426	AR
German, Lewis	017	1896	WB-B/262	AR
German, Nancy C.	017	1898	WB-B/296	AR
German, Wilborn	017	1896	WB-B/279	
Gerner, Lizia	046	1889	WB-F/15	AR
Gerrard, Charles	037	1797	WB-D/36	AR
Gerrard, Forbes	009	c1786	OWB/210	AR
Gerringer, Andrew	046	1851	WB-C/353	AR
Gerringer, Boston	046	1844	WB-C/175	AR
Gerringer, Catharine	046	1864	WB-D/225	AR
Gerringer, Jesse	001	1863	WB-217	AR
Gerringer, Lewis	001	1888	WB-2/388	AR
Gerringer, Margaret	046	1884	WB-E/391	AR
Gerringer, Sarah	046	1887	WB-E/481	AR
Gerver, Leonard	065	1786	WB-C/106	AR
Getchen, Christina	085	c1790	WB-G/48	
Getchey, John	085	1774	WB-A/172	AR
Getsinger, John C.	063	1891	WB-4/57	AR
Gettis, Mary R.	097	1845	WB-1/21	AR
Gettys, A.	086	1888	WB-F/338	AR
Gettys, James	086	1876	WB-F/83	AR
Gettys, James	086	1868	WB-E/488	AR
Gettys, John	086	1861	WB-E/387	AR
Gettys, Mary I.	086	1886	WB-F/282	AR
Gettys, R. C.	026	1892	Orig. Only	AR
Gettys, Robert	086	1867	WB-E/478	AR
Gettys, William	086	1813	WB-C/1	AR
Gettys, William C.	086	1872	WB-F/64	AR
Geurin, Nathan	084	c1819	WB-A/165	CTY
Gevins, John	075	1735	SS 876/403	
Gewin, Christopher	037	1749	Orig. Only	SS/AR
Gewin, Christopher	005	1808	WB-2/40	AR
Gheen, George H.	085	1887	WB-2/217	CTY
Gheen, James, Sr.	085	c1796	WB-G/71	AR
Gheen, John H.	085	1895	WB-3/106	CTY-Nunc.
Gheen, Margaret	085	c1867	Orig. Only	AR
Gheen, Milos A.	085	1865	WB-K/356	AR
Gheen, Thomas	085	1867	WB-L/20	AR
Gheen, Thomas	085	c1827	WB-H/428	
Gheen, Warren	060	1883	WB-4/270	AR
Gholson, Joseph	100	1873	WB-51/61	AR
Gholson, Lucy	039	1811	WB-C/233	AR
Gholson, Mollie B.	100	1896	WB-51/445	AR
Gibbens, John	024	c1782	WB-A/190	AR
Gibbens, John C.	090	1841	WB-4/74	AR
Gibbens, Sally	030	1840	WB-4/69	
Gibbens, William	030	1783	WB-1/160	
Gibble, Dederick	019	1754	SS 879/63	SS/AR
Gibble, Frederick	037	1781	WB-B/73	AR
Gibble, Frederick	019	1833	WB-A/36	AR
Gibble, James E.	019	1861	WB-A/255	AR
Gibble, John B.	019	1840	WB-A/85	AR
Gibbon, Catherine	065	1875	WB-K/183	AR
Gibbon, Robert	065	1898	WB-N/143	AR
Gibbons, Celia	103	c1866	RD-14/369	
Gibbons, Jesse K.	026	1886	WB-2/303	AR
Gibbons, Joshua	030	1824	WB-3/170	
Gibbons, M. D.	026	1866	WB-1/402	AR
Gibbs, Affa	053	1882	WB-11/131	AR
Gibbs, Ambrose	053	1849	WB-7/226	AR
Gibbs, Anson	053	c1817	RW-1/509	
Gibbs, Anson E.	053	1862	WB-9/142	AR
Gibbs, Barbara S.	053	1844	WB-6/309	AR
Gibbs, Barsheba	035	1835	WB-1/68	AR
Gibbs, Benjamin	053	1820	WB-4/142	
Gibbs, Benjamin	053	c1807	RW-1/418	
Gibbs, Benjamin	053	c1813	WB-4/141	
Gibbs, Benjamin	053	1859	WB-8/441	AR
Gibbs, C. J.	074	1898	WB-1/143	AR
Gibbs, Cason	053	1826	WB-4/151	AR
Gibbs, Cason	053	1887	WB-11/193	AR
Gibbs, Cornelius	053	1894	WB-11/189	AR
Gibbs, Debitha	053	1824	Orig. Only	AR
Gibbs, Elisabeth	053	1815	RW-1/496	AR
Gibbs, Francis M.	014	1900	WB-3/122	CTY
Gibbs, George	011	c1778	WB-1/501	
Gibbs, George M.	064	1885	WB-2/159	AR-Copy
Gibbs, Giels	030	1801	WB-2/180	
Gibbs, Henry	053	1763	OB-A/74	AR
Gibbs, Henry	053	1876	WB-11/61	AR
Gibbs, Henry	053	1836	WB-5/313	AR
Gibbs, Henry H.	080	1892	WB-1/202	AR
Gibbs, Henry W.	053	1843	WB-6/252	AR
Gibbs, Henry, Sr.	053	1777	RW-1/82	
Gibbs, Ivey	053	1864	WB-10/13	AR
Gibbs, Jerry	028	1818	WB-C/165	AR
Gibbs, Jesse	054	1854	WB-8/15	AR
Gibbs, Jesse	053	1850	WB-7/392	
Gibbs, Jesse	053	1824	WB-4/264	AR
Gibbs, John	080	1885	WB-1/99	AR
Gibbs, John	039	1815	WB-D/140	AR
Gibbs, John	011	1771	WB-1/497	
Gibbs, John, Sr.	035	1810	WB-A/164	AR
Gibbs, Joseph	053	c1819	WB-4/155	AR
Gibbs, Joseph, Jr.	053	1805	RW-1/375	AR
Gibbs, Louiza	053	1874	WB-11/46	AR
Gibbs, Mary Ann	053	1877	WB-11/84	AR
Gibbs, Mary J.	039	1885	044 WB-23/536	044 CTY
Gibbs, Mary J.	039	1885	WB-U/360	AR
Gibbs, Matthias	053	1844	WB-6/260	AR
Gibbs, Nathaniel	009	c1803	OWB/410	AR
Gibbs, Polly S.	053	1885	WB-11/164	AR
Gibbs, Rabon	100	1814	WB-19/57	AR
Gibbs, Rebecca	053	1853	WB-7/554	AR
Gibbs, Richard	100	1874	WB-51/71	AR
Gibbs, Robert	053	1794	RW-1/230	AR
Gibbs, Robert	070	1847	WB-AB/458	AR

Name	Co.	Date	Recorded	Copy	Original
Gibbs, Robert	053	1801	RW-1/327		
Gibbs, Robert W.	070	1861	WB-D/42		AR
Gibbs, Ruthy	053	c1823	WB-4/162		AR
Gibbs, Sallie A.	072	1876	WB-4/79		AR
Gibbs, Sarah L.	053	1874	WB-11/48		AR
Gibbs, Sarah R.	053	1865	WB-10/15		AR
Gibbs, Selby	053	1807	RW-1/405		
Gibbs, Seth	053	1844	WB-6/263		AR
Gibbs, Seth	053	1888	WB-11/208		AR
Gibbs, Silvester	053	1834	WB-5/195		AR
Gibbs, Stafford	065	1844	WB-H/180		AR
Gibbs, Stephen	053	1837	WB-6/1		AR
Gibbs, Theresa J.	009	1890	WB-1/499		CTY
Gibbs, Thomas	053	1862	WB-9/128		AR
Gibbs, Thomas	053	1807	RW-1/414		AR
Gibbs, Thomas R.	053	1855	WB-8/90		AR
Gibbs, Washington	053	1860	WB-9/44		AR
Gibbs, Watson	053	1826	WB-4/35		AR
Gibbs, William	100	1794	WB-7/228		AR
Gibbs, William	053	1812	RW-1/467		
Gibbs, William	053	c1780	RW-1/89		
Gibbs, William	106	1896	WB-2/378		
Gibbs, William	060	1831	WB-1/220		AR
Gibbs, William M.	053	1846	WB-7/30		AR
Gibbs, Wilson	053	1857	WB-8/211		AR
Gibbs, Wismington	053	1826	Orig. Only		AR
Gibbs, Zachariah	053	1856	WB-8/142		AR
Gibins, William	081	1789	WB-1/71		
Gible, Dederith	075	1720	SS 875/236		SS/AR
Giblin, Sarah	010	1805	WB-E/267		AR
Giblin, Sarah	047	1807	WB-3/465		
Gibney, Alexander	065	1853	WB-I/204		AR
Gibson, Alexander	085	1775	WB-A/200		AR
Gibson, Andrew	046	1823	WB-B/172		AR
Gibson, Archey	028	1819	WB-C/175		AR
Gibson, Benjamin	084	c1792	OW/75		AR
Gibson, Charles	038	1881	WB-2/400		AR
Gibson, Charlotte	046	1887	WB-E/486		AR
Gibson, David	081	1808	WB-3/87		
Gibson, Dempsey	082	1890	WB-6/422		AR
Gibson, Dexter	028	1837	WB-C/406		AR
Gibson, Elisha	082	1816	WB-1/183		AR
Gibson, Elizabeth	028	1856	WB-D/262		
Gibson, George	085	1821	WB-H/121		AR
Gibson, George	081	1810	WB-3/199		AR
Gibson, George	073	1776	WB-A/194		
Gibson, George	065	1878	WB-K/286		AR
Gibson, Harriette	054	1898	WB-6/143		CTY
Gibson, Henry	030	N. D.	WB-3/3		
Gibson, Henry	096	1862	WB-3/64		AR
Gibson, Henry	082	1837	WB-2/66		AR
Gibson, Hugh	054	1880	WB-4/399		CTY
Gibson, Hugh	085	1765	WB-A/58		AR
Gibson, Hugh	060	1841	WB-2/76		AR
Gibson, Isaac	072	1790	Orig. Only		AR
Gibson, J. E.	065	1899	WB-N/187		AR
Gibson, J. F.	091	1886	WB-1/87		
Gibson, James	020	1803	RB-D/174		AR
Gibson, James	077	1766	WB-C/74		AR
Gibson, James B.	085	1885	WB-2/150		CTY
Gibson, James C.	016	1900	WB-4/377		AR
Gibson, Jane	026	1841	WB-1/1		AR
Gibson, Jeptha	082	1894	WB-6/499		AR
Gibson, Jeremiah	090	1849	WB-4/259		
Gibson, John	067	1859	Orig. Only		AR

Name	Co.	Date	Recorded	Copy	Original
Gibson, John B.	065	1892	WB-M/119		AR
Gibson, Jonathan	024	c1772	WB-A/274		AR
Gibson, Joseph	046	1857	WB-C/466		AR
Gibson, Joseph	084	c1790	OW/76		
Gibson, Levi	054	1881	WB-4/436		CTY
Gibson, Lucrecy	100	1783	WB-4/8		AR
Gibson, Luke	082	1854	WB-4/83		AR
Gibson, Martha	053	1894	WB-11/318		AR
Gibson, Mathew	060	1813	Orig. Only		AR
Gibson, N. B.	090	1891	WB-6/252		AR
Gibson, Nathaniel	082	1878	WB-6/153		
Gibson, Nathaniel	082	1875	WB-6/131		AR
Gibson, Nelson	082	1842	WB-3/1		AR
Gibson, Nelson	082	1823	WB-1/238		AR
Gibson, Nelson	082	1879	WB-6/156		
Gibson, Rachel	072	1791	Orig. Only		AR
Gibson, Rachel	082	1873	WB-6/105		AR
Gibson, Robert	024	c1770	WB-B/22		AR
Gibson, Robert	030	1795	WB-2/34		
Gibson, Samuel	082	1893	WB-6/474		AR
Gibson, Samuel	082	1864	WB-4/187		AR
Gibson, Samuel	077	1803	WB-E/189		AR
Gibson, Samuel J.	082	1877	WB-6/144		AR
Gibson, Sarah	090	1863	WB-4/352		AR
Gibson, Sarah L.	082	1883	WB-6/260		AR
Gibson, Starling F.	082	1881	WB-6/219		AR
Gibson, Thomas	082	1872	WB-6/88		AR
Gibson, Thomas	060	1832	WB-1/246		AR
Gibson, Thomas	029	1762	Orig. Only		SS/AR (N)
Gibson, Thomas	072	1803	WB-A/42		AR
Gibson, Thomas	081	1804	WB-1/99		AR
Gibson, Walter	070	1783	WB-C/125		AR
Gibson, William	029	1802	WB-A/59		AR
Gibson, William	072	1815	WB-A/44		AR
Gibson, William	063	c1785	WB-1/121		
Gibson, William	054	1853	WB-3/66		AR
Gibson, William	082	1882	WB-6/230		AR
Gibson, William	085	1842	WB-I/128		AR
Gibson, Willilam	072	c1784	WI/L60		AR
Gibson, Yancy	046	1880	Orig. Only		AR
Gibson, Ziba	082	1870	WB-6/58		AR
Giddens, Abraham	072	1808	WB-A/42		AR
Giddens, Isaac	072	1779	RW/L22		AR
Giddens, Moses	009	1829	OB-B/16		AR
Giddins, Jacob	072	c1774	RW/L45		AR
Giddins, Thomas	056	1747	SS 878/67		SS/AR
Gideon, James	073	c1782	Orig. Only		AR
Gideons, Margareth	090	1816	WB-2/186		AR
Gidings, William	053	1758	SS 879/269		SS/AR
Gidney, J. C.	026	1889	WB-2/392		AR
Gidney, Phoebe	086	1879	WB-F/144		AR
Gidney, Robert E.	026	1854	WB-1/182		AR
Gidney, Samuel S.	026	1848	WB-1/92		AR
Gifford, Jonathan	046	1793	WB-A/129		AR
Gilaspe, Ann	020	1796	RB-C/147		
Gilberd, Thomas	024	1720	Orig. Only		SS/AR
Gilbert, America	063	c1859	WB-2/547		
Gilbert, Andrew	021	1879	WB-2/241		
Gilbert, Atlas J.	022	1893	WB-E/529		AR
Gilbert, B. F.	062	1891	WB-B/113		AR
Gilbert, Benjamin	057	1782	WB-A/12		AR
Gilbert, Conrad	060	1807	Orig. Only		AR
Gilbert, David W.	028	1874	WB-E/100		AR
Gilbert, Dorcas	057	1869	WB-C/6		AR

Name	Co.	Date	Recorded Copy	Original
Gilbert, Francis	008	1726	SS 876/38	SS/AR
Gilbert, Henery	075	1762	WB-H/34	AR
Gilbert, James	077	1857	WB-F/489	
Gilbert, James	028	1882	Orig. Only	AR
Gilbert, John	072	1853	WB-2/132	AR
Gilbert, John A.	063	1860	WB-2/474	
Gilbert, John F.	070	1890	WB-F/384	AR
Gilbert, John M.	018	1854	WB-D/15	
Gilbert, John, Sr.	063	c1803	WB-1/424	
Gilbert, Joseph	057	1784	WB-A/30	AR
Gilbert, Joseph	077	1806	WB-E/240	AR
Gilbert, Joseph	057	c1807	WB-B/13	AR
Gilbert, Martha	077	1816	WB-E/436	AR
Gilbert, Martin	080	1887	WB-1/130	AR
Gilbert, Nathan	069	1808	WB-1/192	AR
Gilbert, Oliver F.	024	1889	WB-E/175	AR
Gilbert, Paul	013	1833	WB-A/26	
Gilbert, Perulla	077	1799	WB-E/106	AR
Gilbert, Robert D.	080	1884	WB-1/89	AR
Gilbert, Thomas	028	1857	WB-D/294	
Gilbert, Thomas	075	1774	WB-I/99	AR
Gilbert, William	028	1783	Orig. Only	AR
Gilbert, William	057	1781	WB-A/1	AR
Gilbert, William	085	c1787	WB-G/46	AR
Gilbirt, Josiah	077	1760	Orig. Only	SS/AR
Gilbreath, Catharine	046	1854	WB-C/416	AR
Gilbreath, John	104	1803	WB-2/83	AR
Gilbreath, Joseph	046	1853	WB-C/385	AR
Gilbreath, Robert	046	1832	WB-B/450	AR
Gilbreath, William	046	1862	WB-D/159	AR
Gilchrist, Adam	029	1861	WB-C/428	AR
Gilchrist, Angus	082	1835	WB-2/47	AR
Gilchrist, Charles	068	1871	WB-D/28	
Gilchrist, David D.	032	1883	WB-3/394	AR
Gilchrist, Elizabeth	AL	1850	083 WB-2/139	
Gilchrist, John	083	c1802	WB-1/75	AR
Gilchrist, John	046	1825	WB-B/213	AR
Gilchrist, Martha	047	1801	WB-3/348	
Gilchrist, Moses	046	1868	WB-D/368	AR
Gilchrist, Polly	046	1850	WB-C/334	AR
Gilchrist, Robert	046	1848	WB-C/295	AR
Gilchrist, Samuel	046	1816	WB-A/146	AR
Gilchrist, Sarah	083	1864	WB-2/206	AR
Gilchrist, Thomas	037	1789	WB-C/109	AR
Gilchrist, William	083	1834	WB-1/284	AR
Gilchrist, William	046	1835	WB-B/529	AR
Gilder, Henry	022	1856	WB-C/402	AR
Giles, Almeria	070	1887	WB-F/100	AR
Giles, Edward S.F.	072	1868	WB-4/19	AR
Giles, Henry	085	c1806	WB-G/49	
Giles, Jeremiah	086	1838	WB-E/46	AR
Giles, John	053	1837	WB-5/442	AR
Giles, John	044	1855	WB-19/667	CTY
Giles, John	065	1778	WB-C/92	AR
Giles, John	005	c1766	WB-1/21	
Giles, John	080	1874	Orig. Only	AR
Giles, John, Sr.	057	1807	WB-A/291	AR
Giles, Mary	085	c1800	WB-D/13	AR
Giles, Mathias	024	c1713	SS 875/14	024 AR
Giles, Milas	065	c1827	WB-A/163	AR
Giles, Nathaniel	056	c1790	WB-1/34	AR
Giles, Reuben	081	1865	WB-13/354	AR
Giles, Susan	085	1867	WB-L/4	AR
Giles, Thomas	081	1801	WB-2/74	AR
Giles, Thomas	084	1847	WB-C/50	CTY
Giles, William	085	1800	Orig. Only	AR
Gilford, John	075	1753	Orig. Only	SS/AR
Gilham, Sallie	046	1878	Orig. Only	AR
Giliam, David	046	1840	WB-C/62	AR
Gilkey, J. H.	064	1892	WB-2/291	AR
Gilkey, Robert	086	1813	WB-B/278	AR
Gilkey, William	060	1790	Orig. Only	AR
Gill, Andrew J.	013	1899	Orig. Only	AR
Gill, Catherine	028	1803	WB-B/178	AR
Gill, David	099	1788	RB-2/188	AR
Gill, Drury	VA	1870	100 WB-51/93	100 AR
Gill, Elvius E.	099	1885	WB-B/26	AR
Gill, Frances	028	1866	WB-D/442	AR
Gill, Gideon E.	044	1838	WB-14/278	CTY
Gill, Henry F.	044	1894	WB-24/253	CTY
Gill, Ida L.	099	1884	Orig. Only	AR
Gill, Isaac	099	1831	RB-22/58	AR
Gill, James	010	1856	WB-H/33	AR
Gill, John	085	1796	WB-G/91	AR-Nunc.
Gill, John	028	1804	WB-B/209	AR
Gill, John C. B.	039	1843	WB-L/163	AR
Gill, John D.	100	1808	WB-14/252	AR
Gill, Joseph	044	1830	WB-11/308	CTY
Gill, Levi	028	1785	WB-A/87	AR
Gill, Nelson G.	070	1850	WB-C/519	AR
Gill, Phillip P.	100	1864	WB-50/70	AR
Gill, Rebecca	013	1851	WB-A/151	
Gill, Robert F.	039	1899	WB-V/163	AR
Gill, Rowlett J.	070	1878	WB-E/352	AR
Gill, Sarah	010	1839	WB-G/311	AR
Gill, Susanna	054	c1828	WB-2/92	AR
Gill, Taylor	037	1793	WB-C/223	AR
Gill, Thomas	047	1788	WB-3/154	
Gill, William	037	1794	WB-C/288	AR
Gill, William	054	c1797	WB-1/103	AR
Gillam, Allen	010	1893	WB-I/377	AR
Gillam, Burrill	071	1800	WB-2/207	AR
Gillam, Charles	044	1784	WB-1/394	
Gillam, Elizabeth	010	1892	WB-I/350	AR
Gillam, Francis	010	c1879	WB-I/138	
Gillam, John B.	010	1900	WB-K/49	
Gillam, Moses	010	1877	WB-I/93	
Gillam, Moses	010	1824	WB-G/114	AR
Gillam, Thomas	010	1893	WB-I/381	AR
Gillam, Thomas	010	1844	WB-G/363	AR
Gillam, William	010	1827	WB-G/172	AR
Gillam, William	022	1822	WB-B/45	AR
Gillam, William	097	1847	WB-1/43	AR
Gillaspie, Alexander	020	1854	RB-R/166	AR
Gillaspie, Elijah	092	1862	WB-5/55	
Gillaspie, Elizabeth	092	1872	WB-6/35	
Gillaspie, James	092	1862	WB-5/64	
Gillaspie, John	046	1806	WB-A/135	AR
Gillaspie, Mary	050	1872	WB-2/127	CTY
Gillaspie, Riley Jones	092	1874	WB-6/62	
Gillaspie, William	050	1851	WB-1/33	CTY
Gillaspie, Wilson	092	1874	WB-6/51	
Gillaspy, James	020	c1821	RB-L/78	AR
Gilleland, Alexander	060	1796	Orig. Only	AR
Gilleland, Esther L.	003	1886	WB-B/186	AR
Gilleland, R. K.	054	1890	WB-5/362	CTY
Gilleland, Thomas	060	1824	WB-1/5	AR
Gilleland, Thomas	021	1888	WB-2/415	AR
Gillen, William N.	016	1867	WB-2/153	
Gilles, Norman	068	1831	WB-B/81	

Name	Co.	Date	Recorded Copy	Original
Gillespie, Agness	085	1837	WB-I/3	AR
Gillespie, Alexander	065	1834	WB-G/170	AR
Gillespie, Aley C.	054	1861	WB-3/162	AR
Gillespie, Amy	085	1880	WB-1/538	CTY
Gillespie, Archibald	072	c1776	WB-A/46	AR
Gillespie, C. A.	046	1854	WB-C/420	AR
Gillespie, Catherine	028	1848	WB-D/144	AR
Gillespie, Daniel	046	1829	WB-B/380	AR
Gillespie, Daniel	046	1833	WB-B/487	AR
Gillespie, David	064	1860	WB-1/71	AR
Gillespie, David	011	c1820	WB-2/388	
Gillespie, Francis S.	013	1848	WB-A/128	
Gillespie, J. H.	050	1891	WB-2/152	CTY
Gillespie, J. L.	092	c1900	Orig. Only	AR
Gillespie, James	011	1847	WB-1/162	
Gillespie, Jason R.	093	1889	WB-2/51	
Gillespie, Jean	085	1823	WB-H/243	AR
Gillespie, John	060	1790	Orig. Only	AR
Gillespie, John	061	1890	WB-2/99	AR
Gillespie, Joseph	035	1837	Orig. Only	AR
Gillespie, Joseph	065	1800	WB-C/123	AR
Gillespie, Joseph G.	085	1840	WB-I/78	AR
Gillespie, Lucressa	046	1844	WB-C/191	AR
Gillespie, Mattie A.	054	1878	WB-4/293	CTY
Gillespie, Nancy	046	1852	WB-C/367	AR
Gillespie, Richard	085	1831	WB-H/534	AR
Gillespie, Richard S.	011	1879	WB-2/116	
Gillespie, Robert	085	1843	WB-I/152	AR
Gillespie, Robert	044	1823	WB-9/187	CTY
Gillespie, Ruth	065	1811	WB-C/126	AR
Gillespie, Sarah	028	1833	WB-C/358	AR
Gillespie, Silas	085	1896	WB-3/161	CTY
Gillespie, Thomas	085	1797	WB-G/2	AR
Gillespie, Thomas C.	085	1849	WB-K/86	AR
Gillespie, Tyre	092	1870	WB-6/9	
Gillespie, W. W.	064	1881	WB-2/94	AR
Gillespie, William	064	1855	WB-1/42	AR
Gillespy, William	049	1811	WI-A/6	AR
Gillet, Anderson	072	c1784	WI/L55	AR
Gillet, Seth	057	1812	WB-A/336	AR
Gillet, Thomas	057	1853	WB-B/217	AR
Gillett, Ann	028	1861	WB-D/359	AR
Gillett, Jacob	019	1873	WB-B/72	AR
Gillett, Jasper	099	1827	RB-20/103	AR
Gillett, John	019	1756	SS 880/176	SS/AR
Gillett, John	028	1749	SS 877/329	SS/AR
Gillett, Sarah R.	039	1832	WB-J/200	AR
Gilliam, Edmund	073	1816	WB-D/489	AR
Gilliam, Ephraim	039	1830	WB-J/100	
Gilliam, Henry	041	1843	WB-3/44	AR
Gilliam, Hinsha	077	1801	WB-E/138	AR
Gilliam, Hobson	084	1844	WB-C/11	CTY
Gilliam, Isly	039	1898	WB-V/156	AR
Gilliam, James	039	1889	WB-U/475	AR
Gilliam, James	104	1866	WB-5/427	AR
Gilliam, John	104	1899	WB-7/77	AR
Gilliam, Julia A.	105	1889	WB-2/538	
Gilliam, Martha	098	1891	WB-A/135	CTY
Gilliam, Martha	001	1892	WB-2/500	AR
Gilliam, Maynard	064	1883	WB-2/134	AR
Gilliam, Sarah	064	1857	WB-1/52	AR
Gilliam, William	104	1831	WB-4/149	AR
Gilliam, William	016	1850	WB-1/176	
Gilliam, William	044	1781	WB-1/300	CTY
Gilliam, William	044	1804	WB-6/52	CTY
Gilliam, William H.	044	1864	WB-22/103	CTY
Gilliam, William W.	001	1889	WB-2/419	AR
Gillian, Abraham	085	c1804	WB-G/57	AR
Gillian, Ann	085	1877	WB-1/402	CTY
Gillies, Malcolm	029	1815	WB-A/222	AR
Gilligan, Picket	030	1890	WB-5/180	AR
Gilliher, James	054	c1834	WB-2/192	AR
Gillikin, Alexander	019	1808	WB-D/196	AR
Gillikin, Anson	019	1873	WB-B/73	AR
Gillikin, Asa	019	1866	WB-B/19	AR
Gillikin, George	019	1831	WB-A/9	AR
Gillikin, James	019	1826	WB-D/207	AR
Gillikin, Rebecca	019	1884	WB-B/146	AR
Gillikin, Thomas	019	c1778	WB-D/187	AR
Gillikin, Thomas	019	1812	WB-D/199	AR
Gillikin, Uriah	019	c1841	Orig. Only	AR
Gilliland, James	022	1870	WB-E/41	AR
Gilliland, Rebecca	017	1899	WB-B/318	
Gillis, Anguish	067	1853	WB-1/62	AR
Gillis, David	029	1873	WB-E/96	AR
Gillis, John	082	1864	WB-4/175	AR
Gillis, John, Sr.	029	1853	WB-C/345	AR
Gillis, Kenneth	044	1862	WB-21/572	CTY
Gillis, Malcom	082	1810	WB-1/142	AR-Nunc.
Gillis, Malcom	082	1853	WB-4/54	AR
Gillis, Martin	067	1899	WB-2/394	AR
Gillis, Mary	029	c1867	Orig. Only	AR
Gillis, Rebecca	029	1830	WB-B/191	AR
Gillis, Roderick	029	1872	WB-E/62	AR
Gillis, William A.	078	1894	WB-19/363	AR
Gillispie, James	035	1805	WB-A/178	AR
Gillispie, Shadrack	035	1862	WB-3/59	AR
Gillispie, Silas	107	c1842	Copy	062 AR
Gillispie, Silas	107	c1842	WB-1/373	
Gillmore, Samuel	022	1807	WB-A/146	AR
Gillon, Jane	016	1856	WB-1/272	
Gillon, John	016	1833	PQS.5/281	
Gillon, Penelope	016	1882	WB-3/367	AR
Gillum, Harris	099	1807	RB-6/170	AR
Gillum, William	104	1853	WB-5/85	
Gillyam, Thomas	N	c1702	Orig. Only	SS/AR
Gilman, John	070	1835	WB-AB/302	AR
Gilmer, Anna	046	1862	WB-D/151	AR
Gilmer, Augustus	046	1900	WB-G/205	AR
Gilmer, Elizabeth	092	1899	WB-6/516	AR
Gilmer, James C.	092	1878	WB-6/118	AR
Gilmer, John A.	046	1892	WB-F/200	AR
Gilmer, John A.	046	1868	WB-D/372	AR
Gilmer, Julia	046	c1875	WB-E/159	AR
Gilmer, Millie A.D.	046	c1897	Orig. Only	AR
Gilmer, Robert	046	N. D.	Orig. Only	AR
Gilmer, William V.	046	1892	WB-F/239	AR
Gilmore, Hasten	022	1887	WB-E/346	AR
Gilmore, Hugh	029	1859	WB-C/408	AR
Gilmore, J. J.	068	c1880	WB-D/134	AR
Gilmore, John	065	1773	WB-C/93	AR
Gilmore, John	029	c1789	Orig. Only	AR
Gilmore, John	022	1868	WB-E/4	AR
Gilmore, John T.	029	1864	WB-D/64	AR
Gilmore, Nancy	081	1845	WB-8/123	AR
Gilmore, Robert	029	1890	WB-E/496	AR
Gilmore, Stephen	022	1849	WB-C/251	
Gilmore, Stephin	029	1816	WB-A/229	AR
Gilmore, Thomas	029	1820	WB-B/45	AR
Gilmour, John	047	1793	WB-3/211	

Name	Co.	Date	Recorded Copy	Original
Gilreath, Alexander	104	1854	WB-5/101	
Gilreath, George A.	104	1864	WB-5/374	
Gilreath, Henry	104	1843	WB-4/288	AR
Gilreath, Hiram	104	1826	WB-4/95	AR
Gilreath, Jeremiah	104	1862	WB-5/296	
Gilreath, Noah	104	1854	WB-5/101	
Gilreath, William	104	1836	WB-4/202	AR
Gilstrap, Peter	028	1796	WB-A/361	AR
Gingles, Dorcas	040	1870	WB-2/14	AR
Gingles, Eliz. B.H.	016	1885	WB-3/453	AR
Gingles, John	065	1831	WB-E/125	AR
Gingles, Samuel	040	1857	WB-1/87	AR
Gingles, Samuel	065	1776	WB-C/96	AR
Ginn, Harriett	103	1877	WB-1/108	AR
Ginnans, John	056	c1762	DB-D/L103	
Ginnings, Lydia	104	1890	WB-6/386	AR
Gipson, John	072	1802	WB-A/44	AR
Gipson, Mahala	017	1882	WB-B/100	AR
Gittens, Richard	092	1801	WB-2/55A	AR
Given, James	029	1771	Orig. Only	AR
Givens, Agnass	054	c1789	WB-1/101	AR
Givens, Edward	065	1792	WB-C/94	AR
Givens, Edward	065	1784	WB-C/114	AR
Givens, Jane	014	c1830	Copy	064 AR
Givens, Jane	097	1899	WB-2/573	AR
Givens, M. F.	097	1900	WB-3/53	AR
Givens, Samuel	097	1846	SC/03724	AR-Copy
Givens, Samuel	097	1846	WB-1/26	AR
Givens, William	065	1798	WB-C/100	AR
Givin, Ann	078	1813	WI-6/157	
Gladden, Hosea M.	026	1864	WB-1/335	AR
Gladden, James A.	026	c1884	Orig. Only	AR
Gladin, John	009	c1783	OWB/185	AR
Gladin, Moses	060	1824	WB-1/8	AR
Gladson, Nathan	046	1810	WB-A/137	AR
Gladson, Rebecca J.	085	1895	WB-3/99	CTY
Gladson, Sallie B.	038	1893	WB-3/374	AR
Gladstains, George	N	c1712	SS 875/44	
Gladville, Candyce	099	1896	WB-C/558	AR
Glair, Peter	028	1763	Wills.4/191	AR
Glair, Stephen	083	c1794	WB-1/34	AR
Glaister, Joseph	075	1718/9	SS 875/142	SS/AR
Glaister, Mary	075	1740	Orig. Only	SS/AR
Glancy, Rebecca	019	1895	WB-B/271	AR
Glanden, Stephen	085	c1795	WB-G/44	AR
Glasco, Robert	024	1690	Orig. Only	SS/AR
Glascock, Gregory	085	1790	WB-B/177	AR
Glascock, Julius	068	1848	WB-B/177	
Glascock, Peter	085	c1783	WB-C/208	AR
Glascock, Scarlet	054	c1843	WB-2/281	AR
Glascow, Ava	045	1882	WB-1/78	AR
Glasgow, Caleb	075	1808	WB-M1/177	AR
Glasgow, Isaac	047	1893	WB-7/79	AR
Glasgow, John	013	1900	WB-D/450	AR
Glasgow, Thomas	030	1803	WB-2/222	
Glasgow, William	030	1747	Orig. Only	SS/AR
Glass, David	064	1856	WB-1/44	AR
Glass, Dudley	VA	1827	Copy	020 AR
Glass, Ellen H.	005	1898	WB-D/435	AR
Glass, Eve	046	1849	WB-C/311	AR
Glass, Iverson M.	020	c1895	Orig. Only	AR-Copy
Glass, James	065	1800	WB-C/119	AR
Glass, John	046	1868	WB-D/381	AR
Glass, Josiah	022	1824	WB-B/88	AR
Glass, Lettie	046	1895	WB-F/419	AR

Name	Co.	Date	Recorded Copy	Original
Glass, Levy	011	c1779	WB-1/528	
Glass, Mary	046	1858	WB-C/526	AR
Glass, Pall	046	1816	WB-B/24	AR
Glass, Peter	016	1898	WB-4/306	AR
Glass, Robert	065	1824	WB-C/104	AR
Glass, Robert	065	1794	WB-C/122	AR
Glass, Stephen	073	1847	WB-F/362	AR
Glass, Thomas	022	1796	RB-2/69	AR
Glass, Tirzah	065	1849	WB-I/151	AR
Glass, W. L.	017	1880	WB-B/92	AR
Glass, William	022	c1804	WB-B/61	AR
Glassco, Hendy	026	1895	Orig. Only	AR
Glasscock, David	026	1876	WB-2/147	AR
Glasscock, James	054	1863	Orig. Only	AR
Glasscock, Thomas	026	1848	WB-1/89	AR
Glaze, Benjamin	044	1782	WB-1/345	CTY
Glazebrook, James	092	1816	WB-3/118	AR
Glazebrook, Larkin W.	099	1869	RB-35/27	AR
Glazener, George	093	1874	WB-1/171	AR
Glazner, Giles	093	1887	WB-2/42	AR
Glazner, Joseph	093	1886	WB-2/36	AR
Glen, Elizabeth	106	1895	WB-2/376	AR
Glen, James	092	1781	WB-1/154	AR
Glen, Jeremiah	092	1846	Orig. Only	AR
Glen, Thomas	106	1876	WB-2/73	AR
Glen, Tyre	106	1875	WB-2/51	AR
Glen, Tyree	092	1775	WB-1/36	AR
Glen, Worsham	073	1810	WB-D/262	AR
Glendinning, William	099	1816	RB-13/43	AR
Glenn, Clarissa	073	1867	WB-G/513	CTY
Glenn, Daniel	084	1831	WB-B/36	CTY
Glenn, Dunking	073	1873	WB-H/67	CTY
Glenn, E. L.	040	1894	WB-2/476	AR
Glenn, Eliza	078	1890	WB-19/270	AR
Glenn, Elizabeth	097	1881	WB-2/205	
Glenn, Elizabeth	106	1890	WB-2/292	
Glenn, George, Sr.	078	1852	WB-17/23	AR
Glenn, Gideon	039	1808	WB-C/127	
Glenn, Gideon	039	1848	WB-N/308	AR
Glenn, Hugh	072	c1776	RW/L16	AR
Glenn, James R.	TN	c1878	039 WB-U/300	
Glenn, Jeremiah	073	1816	WB-D/475	AR
Glenn, John	060	1828	WB-1/115	AR
Glenn, John	078	1818	WI-8/164	AR
Glenn, John	060	1858	WB-3/17	AR
Glenn, John	060	1794	Orig. Only	AR
Glenn, John, Sr.	084	c1794	OW/78	AR
Glenn, Margaret	072	c1797	Orig. Only	AR
Glenn, Martin	073	1869	WB-H/1	CTY
Glenn, Mary	060	1837	WB-1/402	AR
Glenn, Mary B.	046	1897	WB-F/584	AR
Glenn, Robert	081	1840	WB-7/339	AR
Glenn, Sarah	106	1885	WB-2/198	AR
Glenn, Stephen W.	078	1889	WB-19/237	AR
Glenn, Thomas	072	1812	WB-A/40	AR
Glenn, Thomas H.	036	1900	WB-A/518	CTY
Glenn, Thomas K.	078	1898	WB-19/456	AR
Glenn, Wiseley B.	099	1867	RB-34/388	AR
Gless, Crisley	046	1772	WB-A/146	AR
Gless, Philip	046	1774	WB-A/140	AR
Glesson, Bryan	035	1824	WB-A/182	AR
Glidewell, John L.	090	1863	WB-4/370	AR
Glidwell, Zachariah	090	1877	WB-6/88	AR
Glin, Richard	024	1728	Orig. Only	SS/AR
Glishan, John	010	c1734	SS 876/286	SS/AR

Name	Co.	Date	Recorded Copy	Original
Glisson, Daniel	035	1880	WB-4/203	AR
Glisson, Harry J.	035	1888	WB-4/315	AR
Glisson, Jacob	035	1806	WB-A/166	AR
Glisson, Leah	047	1827	WB-4/40	
Gliston, Ann	010	1795	WB-D/295	AR
Gliston, Daniel	010	1790	WB-D/137	AR
Gliston, James	010	1781	WB-C/30	AR
Gliston, Sarah	010	1784	WB-C/89	AR
Glossen, Jasper	022	1889	WB-E/412	AR
Glosson, Joseph	022	1812	WB-A/243	AR
Glosson, William	022	1869	WB-E/38	AR
Glover, Absalom D.	044	1824	WB-9/284	CTY
Glover, Allen	071	1790	WB-1/398	AR
Glover, Allen J.	071	1815	WB-3/165	AR
Glover, B. N. R.	086	1893	WB-F/469	AR
Glover, Benjamin	022	1798	WB-A/1	AR
Glover, Benjamin	071	1764	WB-1/93	
Glover, C. H.	105	1891	WB-2/567	AR
Glover, Charles	085	1840	WB-I/68	AR
Glover, Claborn H.	069	1885	WB-5/206	AR
Glover, Daniel	044	1818	WB-8/108	CTY
Glover, Elizabeth	083	1876	WB-3/115	AR
Glover, Elizabeth	085	1865	WB-K/371	AR
Glover, Francis H.	065	1888	WB-L/310	AR
Glover, George	037	1768	WB-A/167	AR
Glover, George W.	070	1844	WB-AB/412	AR
Glover, Henry H.	065	1840	WB-H/3	AR
Glover, John	071	1804	WB-2/269	AR
Glover, John B.	071	1833	WB-4/102	AR
Glover, John, Sr.	069	1836	Orig. Only	AR
Glover, Jones	071	1828	WB-4/37	AR
Glover, Joseph	083	1872	WB-3/49	AR
Glover, Joseph	044	1786	WB-1/469	
Glover, Joseph B.	044	1826	WB-10/182	CTY
Glover, Mary	071	1764	WB-1/86	
Glover, Mary A.	044	1851	WB-18/373	CTY
Glover, Nathaniel	047	1810	WB-3/503	
Glover, Squire	086	1897	WB-F/529	AR
Glover, Susannah	016	1854	WB-1/242	
Glover, Thomas	022	1800	WB-A/25	AR
Glover, Thomas	071	1789	WB-1/389	AR
Glover, Wilam	071	1754	Orig. Only	SS/AR
Glover, William	075	1858	WB-M2/52	AR
Glover, William	028	c1761	Orig. Only	AR
Glover, William	071	1802	WB-2/229	AR
Glover, William	083	1854	WB-2/121	AR
Glover, William H.	037	1869	WB-G/322	AR
Goarner, John	085	1847	WB-K/54	
Gobble, Addison	032	1881	WB-3/307	AR
Gobble, Anderson	032	1882	WB-3/381	AR
Gobble, David	032	c1853	WB-2/90	
Gobble, Jacob	032	c1863	WB-2/269	
Gobble, Jacob	032	1850	WB-2/49	AR
Gobble, John	032	1855	WB-2/106	AR
Gobble, Susan	032	1875	WB-3/129	AR
Gobel, Corbin	054	1840	WB-2/203	AR
Gober, George	044	1786	WB-1/466	CTY
Goble, Corban	003	1885	WB-B/160	AR
Goble, George	073	1794	WB-C/269	AR
Goble, Jacob	085	1827	WB-H/403	AR
Goble, John	003	1865	WB-A/3	AR
Goble, Lewis	021	1880	WB-2/224	
Godbey, George	085	1835	WB-H/665	AR
Godby, Cary	072	1759	Orig. Only	SS/AR
Goddard, George	063	1826	WB-2/108	

Name	Co.	Date	Recorded Copy	Original
Goddin, Ann R.	099	1898	047 WB-7/273	047 AR
Goddin, Ann R.	099	1894	WB-C/322	AR
Godet, William	028	1816	Orig. Only	AR
Godett, George	028	1803	WB-B/188	AR
Godett, George	028	1827	WB-C/293	AR
Godett, William	028	1807	WB-B/280	AR
Godfrey, Dempsey S.	096	N. D.	WB-3/28	AR
Godfrey, Francis	002	1675	Orig. Only	SS/AR
Godfrey, G. W.	075	1829	WB-N/55	AR
Godfrey, Hesta	018	1844	WB-C/287	
Godfrey, James	065	1835	WB-G/237	AR
Godfrey, Joseph	077	1831	WB-F/189	AR
Godfrey, Joseph	077	c1859	WB-F/501	AR
Godfrey, Malachi	018	1824	WB-C/33	
Godfrey, Mathew	028	1796	WB-B/4	
Godfrey, Matthew	028	1747	SS 878/50	SS/AR
Godfrey, Nancy	097	c1852	WB-1/146	AR
Godfrey, Susan	075	1869	WB-0/2	AR
Godfrey, Susana	077	1830	WB-F/174	AR
Godfrey, Tamer	018	1822	WB-C/9	
Godfrey, Thomas	097	1844	WB-1/15	AR
Godfrey, Thomas	077	1749	Orig. Only	SS/AR
Godfrey, Thomas	077	1774	WB-C/139	AR
Godfrey, Tully	077	1845	WB-F/326	AR
Godfrey, William	072	1792	Orig. Only	AR
Godley, John	009	c1793	OWB/287	AR
Godley, Joseph W.	009	1841	OB-D/120	AR
Godley, Nathan	009	c1791	OWB/265	AR
Godley, Robert	009	c1827	OWB/490	AR
Godley, Thomas	009	1860	OB-L/143	AR
Godley, Thomas	009	1854	OB-I/176	AR
Godly, John	010	1732	SS 876/255	SS/AR
Godly, John L.	009	1898	WB-2/134	CTY
Godsey, Bird	084	1888	WB-E/379	CTY
Godsey, Edward	084	1842	WB-B/281	CTY
Godsy, Amy	084	1894	WB-E/571	CTY
Godward, George	063	1790	WB-1/167	
Godwin, Albert J.	051	1886	WB-C/348	AR
Godwin, Anthony	051	1888	WB-C/382	AR
Godwin, Archibald	048	1899	WB-1/95	CTY
Godwin, Benjamin	056	1873	WB-3/99	AR
Godwin, Calvin	010	1887	WB-I/229	AR
Godwin, Edmund	056	1797	WB-1/108	AR
Godwin, Elizabeth	087	1869	WB-3/13	AR
Godwin, Elizabeth	056	1895	WB-2/196	AR
Godwin, James	019	c1858	Copy	057 AR
Godwin, James	056	1855	WB-1/675	AR
Godwin, James L.	051	1900	WB-C/569	AR
Godwin, James, Sr.	019	1858	WB-A/217	AR
Godwin, Jarret	029	1888	WB-E/438	AR
Godwin, Jesse	027	1821	WB-A/8	AR
Godwin, John	087	1873	WB-3/71	AR
Godwin, John	027	1830	WB-A/30	AR
Godwin, John S.	051	1872	WB-C/64	AR
Godwin, Joseph	028	1885	WB-E/383	
Godwin, Minton M.	105	1887	WB-2/427	AR
Godwin, Nathan	087	1882	WB-3/253	
Godwin, Nathan	009	1752	Orig. Only	SS/AR
Godwin, Nathan	087	1823	WB-1/34	AR
Godwin, Patience	097	1885	WB-2/264	AR
Godwin, Peter	056	1898	WB-4/93	AR
Godwin, Pierce	027	c1845	WB-A/55	AR
Godwin, Polly	056	1884	WB-3/352	AR
Godwin, Samuel	056	1807	WB-1/196	AR
Godwin, Simon	097	1878	WB-2/144	AR

Name	Co.	Date	Recorded Copy	Original
Godwin, T.	010	1885	WB-I/197	
Godwin, Thomas	056	1807	WB-1/201	AR
Godwin, Tobias	056	1845	WB-1/573	AR
Godwin, W. B.	038	1891	WB-3/247	AR
Godwin, William	010	1753	SS 878/199	SS/AR
Godwin, William	037	1783	WB-B/118	AR
Goepfert, George	090	1798	WB-1/107	
Goff, John	035	1810	WB-A/168	AR
Goffe, Arthur	024	1737	LGB-4/#74	SS/AR
Goforth, George	026	1857	WB-1/217	AR
Goforth, George	026	1869	WB-2/24	AR
Goforth, John E.	064	1892	WB-2/281	AR
Goforth, Mildred	104	1855	WB-5/131	
Goforth, Preston	086	1855	WB-E/298	AR
Gofourth, William	026	1868	WB-2/3	AR
Going, Thomas	081	1797	WB-2/37	AR
Gola, Lotta	046	c1837	WB-B/585	AR
Gold, Daniel	026	1846	WB-1/52	AR
Gold, Ephraim	020	1778	RB-A/36	AR
Gold, Joseph	078	1804	WI-3/326	AR
Gold, Milton	026	1887	WB-2/314	AR
Gold, W. M.	026	1862	WB-1/282	AR
Golden, Abraham	070	1815	WB-AB/234	AR
Golden, Jacob	072	1830	WB-1/59	AR
Golden, James	060	1795	Orig. Only	AR
Golding, Algias	092	1850	WB-4/310	
Golding, Isaac	090	1880	WB-6/111	AR
Golding, James	092	c1874	Orig. Only	AR
Golding, Mary B.	038	1885	WB-2/532	AR
Golding, Rubin	092	1856	WB-5/21	AR
Golding, Thomas	092	c1833	WB-4/49	
Goldman, Henry	065	1785	WB-C/116	AR
Goldston, A. J.	022	1893	WB-E/545	AR
Goldston, Annie E.	022	1899	WB-F/85	AR
Goldston, Elizabeth	022	c1867	WB-D/166	AR
Goldston, G. W.	022	1863	WB-D/114	AR
Goldston, Thomas	081	1840	WB-7/336	AR
Goldston, William	022	1808	WB-A/151	AR
Goldwin, Joseph	012	1770	DB-A/106	AR
Golger, Samuel	092	1880	WB-6/149	
Golson, John	039	c1799	WB-C/156	
Gomer, Elizabeth	020	1885	WB-A/455 & 495	CTY
Gomer, John W.	020	1881	WB-A/320	CTY
Gomm, John	096	1754	SS 879/97	SS/AR
Gonsolvo, Lawrance	077	1698	SS 874.2/95	SS/AR
Gooch, Abner	020	1845	RB-P/232	AR
Gooch, Amos	044	1822	WB-9/118	CTY
Gooch, Benjamin	020	c1898	Orig. Only	AR
Gooch, Daniel	044	1837	WB-14/49	CTY
Gooch, Francis	020	1855	RB-R/345	AR
Gooch, Gideon	044	1800	WB-5/105	CTY
Gooch, Hannah A.	044	1890	WB-24/115	CTY
Gooch, Henry S.	044	1887	WB-24/32	CTY
Gooch, John	044	1793	WB-3/66	CTY
Gooch, John C.	020	1804	RB-E/79	AR
Gooch, Judith	078	1819	WI-8/211	
Gooch, Louisa	099	1894	WB-C/295	AR
Gooch, Martha	020	1851	RB-Q/549	AR
Gooch, Nathaniel	020	1870	WB-A/41	CTY
Gooch, Pumfret	099	1820	RB-16/292	AR
Gooch, R. L.	073	1900	WB-I/167	CTY
Gooch, Rowland	099	1899	WB-D/221	AR
Gooch, Rowland	044	1822	WB-9/68	CTY
Gooch, Sally	044	1815	WB-7/509	CTY
Gooch, Sarah	044	1846	WB-16/463	CTY
Gooch, William	020	1832	RB-M/83	AR
Gooch, William	020	1803	RB-D/130	AR
Good, Benjamin	028	1827	WB-C/289	AR
Good, Joseph	028	1795	WB-A/329	AR
Good, Thomas	047	1789	WB-3/161	
Good, William	028	1820	WB-C/194	AR
Goodale, Gilbert	002	c1712	SS 875/47	
Goodbread, John	086	1814	WB-C/15	AR
Goodby, Cary	072	1759	SS 882/43	
Goodding, Ann	041	1805	WB-1/216	AR
Goode, Abraham	086	1860	WB-E/376	AR
Goode, Edward	086	1798	WB-B/98	AR
Goode, John T.	026	1892	WB-2/454	AR
Goode, John W.	086	1900	WB-G/80	AR
Goode, Joseph	086	1827	WB-D/78	AR
Goode, N. A. G.	026	1887	WB-2/324	AR
Goode, Richard	104	1819	WB-3/205	AR
Goode, Samuel	068	1899	WB-E/15	CTY
Goode, Sarah H.	026	1872	WB-2/73	AR
Goode, Thomas	026	1861	WB-1/272	AR
Goode, Thomas	092	1789	WB-2/92	AR
Goode, Thomas	090	1834	WB-3/267	AR
Goode, W. T.	026	1900	WB-3/63	AR
Goode, William	086	1862	WB-E/401	AR
Gooden, Aaron	057	c1787	WB-A/177	AR
Gooden, Isham	054	1858	WB-3/134	AR
Gooden, Z. B.	054	1884	WB-5/16	CTY
Goodin, B. G.	054	1889	WB-5/311	CTY
Goodin, Federick	099	1887	WB-B/192	AR
Goodin, Gideon	003	1867	WB-A/7	AR
Goodin, Lucy	054	1890	WB-5/322	CTY
Gooding, Council	057	1865	WB-B/263	AR
Gooding, Elizabeth	086	1817	WB-C/68	AR
Gooding, Elizabeth	070	1882	WB-E/442	
Gooding, Elizabeth	028	1874	WB-E/110	AR
Gooding, Frederick	057	c1793	WB-B/23	AR
Gooding, Furnifold	057	1881	WB-C/77	AR
Gooding, Furnifold	028	1798	WB-B/37	AR
Gooding, Isaac	057	1900	WB-C/250	AR
Gooding, James M.	028	1853	WB-D/199	
Gooding, John	099	1793	RB-2/427	AR
Gooding, John	028	1811	WB-C/35	AR
Gooding, Mary	057	1833	WB-B/117	AR
Gooding, Matthew R.	019	1866	WB-B/6	
Gooding, Moses	057	1803	WB-A/267	AR
Gooding, Moses	057	1869	WB-C/1	AR
Gooding, Narcissa A.	074	1892	WB-1/114	AR
Gooding, Rachael	019	1852	WB-A/155	AR
Gooding, Sarah E.	WA	1882	046 WB-E/527	046 AR
Gooding, Stephen	059	1895	WB-B/135	CTY
Gooding, William	057	1858	WB-B/249	AR
Gooding, Willis	099	1842	RB-25/92	AR
Goodlake, Thomas	013	1867	WB-A/246	AR
Goodlatt, Alexander	N	1713	SS 875/4	
Goodloe, Garrett	039	c1802	WB-B/70	
Goodloe, Henry	039	1824	WB-H/22	AR
Goodloe, John	044	1767	Orig. Only	CTY
Goodloe, Robert	044	1797	WB-4/71	CTY
Goodman, Agdalena	071	1853	WB-5/112	AR
Goodman, Alfred N.	085	1871	WB-1/104	CTY
Goodman, Ame	012	1801	WB-B/68	AR
Goodman, Barnes	041	1863	WB-3/305	AR
Goodman, Bartholomew	054	c1799	WB-1/104	AR
Goodman, Caroline	085	1876	WB-1/334	CTY

Name	Co.	Date	Recorded Copy	Original
Goodman, Daniel	016	1881	WB-3/322	AR
Goodman, Daniel	016	1862	WB-2/88	
Goodman, David	085	c1873	Orig. Only	CTY
Goodman, Elizabeth	016	1874	WB-3/106	AR
Goodman, Elizabeth	085	1854	WB-K/170	AR
Goodman, Elizabeth	077	1837	WB-F/267	AR
Goodman, Ellen	085	1889	WB-2/361	CTY
Goodman, G. C.	016	1900	WB-4/379	AR
Goodman, George	016	1838	PQS.5/470	
Goodman, George	016	1842	PQS.6/182	
Goodman, Henry	054	1878	WB-4/283	CTY
Goodman, Henry	041	1783	WB-1/35	AR
Goodman, Henry	041	1818	WB-2/124	AR
Goodman, Isaac	006	1898	WB-E/344	AR
Goodman, J. J.	006	1893	Orig. Only	AR
Goodman, Jacob	016	1842	PQS.6/225	
Goodman, Jacob	085	1869	WB-1/44	CTY
Goodman, Jacob C.	085	1871	WB-1/65	CTY
Goodman, Jacob F.	054	1875	WB-4/178	CTY
Goodman, Jacob M.	085	1899	WB-3/347	CTY
Goodman, Jacob, Sr.	006	1871	WB-E/78	AR
Goodman, Joel	041	1795	WB-1/133	AR
Goodman, Joel	041	1786	WB-1/60	AR
Goodman, John	085	1842	WB-I/132	AR
Goodman, John	054	1867	WB-3/200	AR
Goodman, John	083	1832	WB-1/263	AR
Goodman, John T.	085	1898	WB-3/226	CTY
Goodman, Lucretia J.	041	1878	WB-4/104	AR
Goodman, Luke	012	c1859	WB-B/25	AR
Goodman, Mary	041	1847	WB-3/94	AR
Goodman, Mary	041	1823	WB-2/205	AR
Goodman, Michael	065	1777	WB-C/95	AR
Goodman, Nancy	016	1858	WB-2/44	
Goodman, Nancy M.	016	1895	WB-4/218	AR
Goodman, Nellie	085	1889	WB-2/359	CTY
Goodman, Peter	006	1811	WB-A/55	AR
Goodman, Rosiana	016	1843	WB-1/11	
Goodman, Sam	029	1892	WB-E/561	AR
Goodman, Sarah	054	1877	WB-4/258	CTY
Goodman, Thomas	016	1846	WB-1/80	
Goodman, Tobias	016	1844	WB-1/28	
Goodman, Tobias	085	1880	WB-1/547	CTY
Goodman, William	041	1782	WB-1/26	AR
Goodman, William	012	1794	WB-B/46	AR
Goodman, William	041	1841	WB-3/27	AR
Goodman, William H.	006	1882	WB-E/95	AR
Goodman, William H.	041	1900	WB-4/516	AR
Goodnight, Henry	016	1855	WB-1/254	
Goodram, Maria	013	1893	WB-C/266	AR
Goodrum, John	100	1852	WB-42/50	AR
Goodrum, Martha W.	100	1856	WB-49/18	AR
Goodson, Abner	060	1837	WB-1/412	AR
Goodson, Abner	060	1899	WB-5/137	AR
Goodson, Disey	071	1834	WB-4/116	AR
Goodson, Edward	071	1782	WB-1/258	AR
Goodson, James	039	1869	WB-U/7	AR
Goodson, John F.	060	1890	WB-4/445	AR
Goodson, Lucy	020	1865	RB-T/107	AR
Goodson, Miles	021	1870	WB-2/45	AR
Goodson, Thomas	037	1762	WB-A/101	AR
Goodson, Thomas	053	c1758	OB-A/37	
Goodson, William	039	1888	WB-U/449	AR
Goodwin, Axum	024	1832	WB-C/158	AR
Goodwin, Caleb	077	c1819	Copy	024 AR
Goodwin, Caleb	077	1819	WB-F/21	AR
Goodwin, Calvin	077	1885	WB-H/143	AR
Goodwin, Charles	077	1827	WB-F/130	AR
Goodwin, Drury	072	1804	WB-A/43	AR
Goodwin, Elizabeth	024	1900	WB-E/321	AR
Goodwin, George	047	1764	WB-1/136	
Goodwin, Henry M.	022	1851	WB-C/304	AR
Goodwin, Jacob	077	1803	WB-E/195	AR
Goodwin, James	022	1863	WB-D/106	AR
Goodwin, James M.	077	1855	WB-F/462	AR
Goodwin, Jesse	047	1804	WB-3/432	
Goodwin, John	099	1793	RB-2/397	
Goodwin, John	077	1815	WB-E/421	AR
Goodwin, John	024	1823	WB-C/102	AR
Goodwin, John L.	019	1896	WB-B/304	AR
Goodwin, Joseph	024	1762	WB-B/97	AR
Goodwin, Kendrick	099	1896	WB-C/524	AR
Goodwin, Lucresha	019	1798	WB-D/192	AR
Goodwin, Miles	099	1893	WB-C/241	AR
Goodwin, Nancy	024	c1845	Orig. Only	AR
Goodwin, Nancy B.	099	1896	WB-C/569	AR
Goodwin, Oliver	019	1819	WB-D/204	AR
Goodwin, Pheriby	022	1872	WB-E/76	AR
Goodwin, Richard	077	1781	Orig. Only	AR
Goodwin, Ruffin	099	1900	WB-D/360	AR
Goodwin, Samuel	044	1775	WB-1/103	CTY
Goodwin, Thomas	009	1872	WB-1/106	CTY
Goodwin, Thomas	024	1865	WB-D/35	AR
Goodwin, Thomas	019	1803	WB-D/193	AR
Goodwin, Thomas	019	c1783	Orig. Only	AR
Goodwin, William	077	1825	WB-F/83	AR
Goodwin, William	060	1795	Orig. Only	AR
Goodwin, William	099	1856	RB-30/78	AR
Goodwin, William	037	1781	WB-B/81	AR
Goodwin, Wright	019	1855	WB-A/181	AR
Goodyear, Charles	NY	1896	049 WB-2/460	
Goolsby, Fleming	084	1857	WB-C/251	CTY
Goomer, William	041	1870	WB-4/18	AR
Goose, John, Sr.	085	1816	WB-G/446	AR
Goostree, Absalom	084	1801	OW/51	AR
Gordan, Alexander	078	1849	WB-13/214	
Gordan, James J.	046	1874	WB-E/129	AR
Gordan, John	063	1795	WB-1/215	
Gorden, Frances	090	1843	WB-4/135	AR
Gorden, George	077	1748	Orig. Only	SS/AR
Gorden, Howel	044	1893	WB-24/218	CTY
Gorden, James, Sr.	032	1837	WB-1/298	AR
Gorden, Joseph	032	1844	WB-1/441	AR
Gorden, Plura	065	1864	WB-J/178	AR
Gordet, William	028	1816	WB-C/117	
Gordin, Dudly	028	1715	PQS.1/92	
Gordin, Jean	060	1797	Orig. Only	AR
Gordon, Abraham	075	1836	WB-N/119	AR
Gordon, Alexander	082	1807	WB-1/116	AR
Gordon, Branch	046	1853	WB-C/391	AR
Gordon, Carolina F.	041	1861	WB-3/278	AR
Gordon, Charles	104	1811	WB-3/14	AR
Gordon, Charles	104	1799	WB-1/514	AR
Gordon, Daniel	077	1813	WB-E/373	AR
Gordon, David D.	073	1891	WB-H/553	CTY
Gordon, Elizabeth	077	1887	WB-H/163	AR
Gordon, Fanny	018	1854	WB-D/3	
Gordon, Felitia W.	020	1889	WB-B/18	CTY
Gordon, Frances	030	1881	WB-5/80	AR
Gordon, G. B.	104	1864	WB-5/388	
Gordon, George	104	1800	WB-2/26	AR

Name	Co.	Date	Recorded Copy	Original
Gordon, George	024	c1762	WB-B/106	AR
Gordon, George W.	009	1861	OB-L/383	AR
Gordon, J. M.	092	1896	WB-6/433	AR
Gordon, Jacob	041	1820	WB-2/165	AR
Gordon, James	094	1776	Orig. Only	060 AR
Gordon, James B.	SC	1887	050 WB-2/1	050 CTY
Gordon, John	039	c1794	WB-A/159	
Gordon, John	077	1758	SS 880/227	SS/AR
Gordon, John	032	1900	WB-4/438	AR
Gordon, John	041	1793	WB-1/118	AR
Gordon, John	065	1810	WB-C/124	AR
Gordon, John C.	041	1861	WB-3/273	AR
Gordon, Maria L.	077	1854	WB-F/444	AR
Gordon, Mary Duff	028	1784	Orig. Only	AR
Gordon, Nathaniel	077	1756	SS 880/118	SS/AR
Gordon, Nathaniel	104	1829	WB-4/123	AR
Gordon, Nathaniel	077	1824	WB-F/70	AR
Gordon, Patrick	028	1773	Orig. Only	SS/AR
Gordon, Rebecca L.	097	1881	WB-2/207	
Gordon, Robert	054	c1805	WB-1/102	AR
Gordon, Robert A.	077	1850	WB-F/385	AR
Gordon, Ross	MD	1800	037 WB-D/103	037 AR
Gordon, Sarah	104	1842	WB-4/273	AR
Gordon, Sarah	075	1807	WB-M1/169	AR
Gordon, Seth C.	106	c1858	WB-1/58	AR
Gordon, Thomas	018	1827	WB-C/79	
Gordon, Thomas	082	1799	WB-1/72	AR
Gordon, Thomas	092	1803	WB-3/58	AR-Nunc.
Gordon, William	085	1812	WB-G/223	AR
Gordon, William	092	1873	WB-6/58	
Gordon, William	020	1820	RB-H/377	AR
Gordon, William	078	1816	WI-7/191	AR
Gordon, William	029	1792	Orig. Only	AR
Gordon, William	075	1778	WB-K/19	AR
Gordon, William	070	1791	WB-C/130	AR
Gordon, William	009	1841	OB-D/1	AR
Gordon, William H.	044	1893	WB-24/228	CTY
Gordon, Wilson	046	1867	WB-D/338	AR
Gordy, Bailey	090	1891	WB-6/262	AR
Gordy, Isaac	032	1840	WB-1/342	AR
Gordy, Moses	046	1802	WB-A/144	AR
Gore, John, Sr.	035	1822	WB-A/160	AR
Gore, Richard	037	1779	WB-B/16	AR
Gore, William	012	1883	WB-A/162	AR
Goreham, John	024	1718	SS 875/159	SS/AR
Gorham, George F.	079	c1844	WB-1/172	AR-Copy
Gorman, A. M.	099	1865	RB-33/354	AR
Gorman, Henry	099	1840	RB-24/444	AR
Gormark, Patrick	N	1708	SS 874.1/35	SS/AR
Gorner, Jacob	060	c1799	Orig. Only	AR
Gornto, David R.	070	1866	WB-D/203	
Gornto, Elizabeth	072	1874	WB-4/62	AR
Gornto, John	072	1835	WB-1/141	AR
Gorrell, David	046	1848	WB-C/299	AR
Gorrell, Euphema	046	1850	WB-C/336	AR
Gorrell, F. L.	038	1866	WB-1/275	AR
Gorrell, Ralph	046	1816	WB-A/141	AR
Gorrell, Ralph	046	1875	WB-E/149	AR
Gorrell, Rebecca	046	1842	WB-C/142	AR
Gorrell, Robert G.	046	1893	WB-F/293	AR
Gorrell, Sophia	038	1866	WB-1/266	AR
Gorrell, Thomas	046	1888	WB-F/28	AR
Gorrell, William	046	1816	WB-B/18	AR
Gorrie, John	028	1823	WB-C/227	AR
Gorrie, Joseph	070	1830	WB-AB/259	AR
Gosa, Sally	086	1888	WB-F/340	AR
Gosbe, John	N	1693	Orig. Only	SS/AR
Goslen, William	038	1888	WB-3/93	AR
Goslin, Elizabeth	090	1802	WB-2/22	AR
Goslin, Peter	080	1892	WB-2/382	AR
Gosney, John	037	1770	WB-A/181	AR
Goss, Ephraim	085	c1801	WB-G/73	AR
Goss, Ephram	032	1848	WB-2/13	AR
Goss, Frederick	085	c1804	WB-G/20	AR
Goss, Frederick	032	1833	WB-1/239	AR
Goss, George W.	032	1864	WB-2/274	AR
Goss, Jacob	032	1834	WB-1/255	AR
Goss, John	044	1894	WB-24/235	CTY
Goss, John	044	1825	WB-10/50	CTY
Goss, Joseph	085	c1777	WB-A/245	AR
Goss, Joseph	032	c1850	WB-2/59	
Goss, Leonard	032	c1858	WB-2/179	AR
Goss, Rahab	044	1833	WB-12/447	CTY
Goss, Rowland	044	1886	WB-23/574	CTY
Goss, Shearmon	099	1830	RB-21/194	AR
Goss, Thomas	044	1816	WB-7/638	CTY
Gossett, Abraham	046	1822	Orig. Only	AR
Gossett, Thomas	046	1858	WB-C/529	AR
Gossett, Thomas	046	1832	WB-B/446	AR
Gossett, Thomas	081	1887	WB-16/54	
Goswick, George	039	1812	WB-C/278	
Goswick, Jason	039	c1854	WB-O/330	
Goswick, Jefrey	039	1875	WB-U/130	AR
Goswick, Mary	039	c1875	WB-U/167	AR
Goswick, William H.	039	1889	WB-U/485	AR
Gott, Richard	073	1821	WB-D/601	AR
Gouge, Edmund	066	1893	WB-1/124	AR
Gouger, Henry	085	1859	WB-K/275	AR
Gough, Catharine	092	1843	WB-4/205	
Gough, James	106	c1871	WB-2/108	AR
Gough, James	092	c1831	WB-4/123	AR
Gough, John	010	1762	WB-A/19	AR
Gough, Thomas	077	1695	SS 874.2/64	SS/AR
Gough, Thomas S.	106	c1852	WB-1/23	AR
Goughf, Stephen	046	1799	WB-A/133	AR
Gould, C.Nutcombe	GA	1890	023 WB-A/94	023 AR
Gould, Daniel	005	1829	WB-A/162	AR
Gould, Elizabeth	010	1764	024 WB-1/12	024 AR
Gould, George	010	1749	Orig. Only	AR
Gould, Isaac	028	1741	Deeds.21/L7	
Gould, Sarah E.	ME	c1888	080 WB-1/247	080 AR
Goulding, Thomas	019	1793	WB-D/190	AR
Gourley, John	072	1747	SS 877/101	SS/AR
Goutier, J. R.	011	c1800	WB-1/352	
Govenlock, Agnes	098	1891	WB-A/133	CTY
Govenlock, John	044	1881	WB-23/402	CTY
Gowan, Elias	027	c1880	WB-2/45	
Gowan, Richard	033	1844	WB-1/63	
Gowdy, James	046	1810	WB-A/136	AR
Gowdy, William	046	c1786	WB-A/128	AR
Gowen, John	083	c1800	WB-1/60	
Gower, Cary	056	1858	WB-1/723	AR
Gower, Gideon	056	1876	WB-3/161	AR
Gower, James H.	053	1877	WB-11/73	AR
Gower, John K.	099	1859	RB-31/222	AR
Gowing, James	071	1836	WB-4/147	AR
Grabs, Lewis E.	090	1892	WB-6/268	AR
Grace, John	005	1843	WB-B/171	AR
Grace, Thomas	019	1837	WB-A/75	
Gracie, Henry S.	028	1894	WB-F/119	

Name	Co.	Date	Recorded Copy	Original
Graddy, John	035	1787	WB-A/152	AR
Grady, Alexander	035	1881	WB-4/161	AR
Grady, Alexander	035	1825	WB-A/178	AR
Grady, Alexander	035	1867	WB-3/118	
Grady, Alexr, Jr.	035	1854	WB-2/83	AR
Grady, Ann Maria	103	1890	WB-1/536	AR
Grady, B. S.	059	1887	WB-A/457	CTY
Grady, Barbara	035	1893	WB-4/428	AR
Grady, Christian	073	N. D.	WB-B/32	
Grady, Curtis	029	1832	WB-B/213	AR
Grady, Dennis	099	1832	RB-22/311	AR
Grady, Dennis	005	1853	WB-C/57	AR
Grady, Henry	035	1834	WB-1/56	AR
Grady, Henry G.	035	1870	WB-4/27	AR
Grady, James	099	1851	RB-27/352	AR
Grady, John	035	1899	WB-4/536	AR
Grady, Mark	099	1848	RB-26/377	AR
Grady, Patrick	083	1889	WB-3/451	AR
Grady, Putsy	035	1891	WB-4/378	AR
Grady, Robert	099	1801	RB-5/243	AR
Grady, Sallie	VA	1893	059 WB-B/63	059 CTY
Grady, Samuel	009	1892	WB-1/530	CTY
Grady, Sary	099	1819	RB-15/166	AR
Grady, Susan	029	1860	WB-C/416	AR
Grady, T. J.	099	1897	WB-D/90	AR
Grady, Thomas	035	1865	WB-3/99	AR
Grady, Thomas M.	035	1881	WB-4/162	AR
Grady, Thomas N.	035	1887	WB-4/301	AR
Grady, Whitfield	059	1880	WB-A/211	CTY
Grady, Winifred	035	1890	WB-4/368	AR
Graff, Justine	090	1823	WB-3/106	AR
Grafflin, Christopher	070	1887	WB-F/125	AR
Gragg, Benjamin	017	c1844	WB-A/23	AR
Gragg, William	107	c1847	WB-1/348	
Gragg, William	066	c1847	WB-1/50	AR
Gragg, William A.	013	1898	Orig. Only	AR
Graham, Abel	085	1844	WB-I/223	AR
Graham, Agnes	085	c1786	WB-C/46	AR
Graham, Alexander	029	1846	WB-C/90	AR
Graham, Alexander	029	1844	WB-C/56	AR
Graham, Alexander	083	1873	WB-3/67	AR
Graham, Andrew	068	c1853	WB-C/7	
Graham, Ann	068	1858	WB-C/68	
Graham, Ann	085	1857	WB-K/234	AR
Graham, Archibald	SC	1888	Copy	013 AR
Graham, Archibald	029	1812	WB-A/179	AR
Graham, Archibald	060	1803	Orig. Only	AR
Graham, Arthur	060	1805	Orig. Only	AR
Graham, Calvin	083	1892	WB-3/561	AR
Graham, Catharine	083	1890	WB-3/468	AR
Graham, Christian	093	1894	WB-2/132	AR
Graham, Daniel	083	1860	WB-2/156	AR
Graham, Daniel	029	1854	WB-C/314	AR
Graham, Daniel	029	1852	WB-C/234	AR
Graham, Daniel	082	1801	WB-1/85	AR
Graham, Donald	029	1801	WB-A/52	AR
Graham, Donald	029	1799	WB-A/26	AR
Graham, Donald	068	1800	WB-A/212	
Graham, Dugald	083	1830	WB-1/250	AR
Graham, Dugald	083	1875	WB-6/141	
Graham, Duncan	083	1856	WB-2/77	AR
Graham, Ebenezer	041	1809	WB-2/46	AR
Graham, Edward	028	1833	WB-C/354	
Graham, Edward	029	1806	WB-A/88	AR
Graham, Edward E.	028	1865	WB-D/384	AR

Name	Co.	Date	Recorded Copy	Original
Graham, Effia	029	1837	WB-B/284	AR
Graham, Eliza A.	079	1861	WB-1/106	AR
Graham, Ellonar	085	c1782	WB-G/75	AR
Graham, Fergus	085	1822	WB-H/155	AR
Graham, Flora Maria	085	1892	WB-2/504	CTY
Graham, George	060	1815	Orig. Only	AR
Graham, George	065	1826	WB-C/105	AR
Graham, George	082	1856	WB-4/106	AR
Graham, Henry P.	082	1862	WB-4/156	AR
Graham, Hugh	085	1785	WB-B/151	AR
Graham, Hugh	083	1824	WB-1/212	AR
Graham, Isabella	083	1892	WB-3/576	AR
Graham, Jackson	082	1889	WB-6/394	AR
Graham, James	001	c1856	WB-1/111	AR
Graham, James	060	1851	WB-2/352	AR
Graham, James	085	c1779	WB-B/89	AR
Graham, James	085	c1788	WB-G/67	AR
Graham, James	085	1856	WB-K/228	AR
Graham, James	054	1854	WB-3/77	AR
Graham, James	085	1840	WB-I/76	AR
Graham, James	085	1834	WB-H/701	AR
Graham, James D.	085	1849	WB-K/101	AR
Graham, James G.	085	1863	WB-K/319	AR
Graham, James P.	079	1813	Orig. Only	AR-Copy
Graham, Jane	085	1803	WB-G/53	AR
Graham, Jane	054	c1844	WB-3/146	AR
Graham, Jane Cowan	085	1843	WB-I/170	AR
Graham, Jane G.	085	1867	WB-L/3	AR
Graham, Jane T.	085	1870	WB-1/61	CTY
Graham, Jiles	006	1897	WB-E/315	AR
Graham, Jincy	085	1863	WB-K/309	AR
Graham, John	085	c1795	WB-G/66	AR
Graham, John	073	1810	WB-D/259	AR
Graham, John	029	1800	WB-A/27	AR
Graham, John	083	1841	WB-1/403	AR
Graham, John	060	1831	WB-1/206	AR
Graham, John	054	1839	WB-2/200	AR
Graham, John	085	1791	WB-B/206	AR
Graham, John	082	1835	WB-2/52	AR
Graham, John	085	1844	WB-I/236	AR
Graham, John B.	054	c1857	Orig. Only	AR
Graham, John D.	060	1847	WB-2/275	AR
Graham, John L.	085	1866	WB-K/373	AR
Graham, John W.	083	1862	WB-2/183	AR
Graham, John, Sr.	054	c1811	WB-1/363	
Graham, John, Sr.	029	1797	WB-A/7	AR
Graham, Joseph	085	1849	WB-K/81	AR
Graham, Joseph	060	1837	WB-1/395	AR-Copy
Graham, Joseph	065	1830	WB-F/51	AR
Graham, Malcom	082	1876	Orig. Only	AR
Graham, Margaret	SC	1859	Copy	013 AR
Graham, Martha	054	1870	WB-4/65	AR
Graham, Mary	083	1886	WB-3/376	AR
Graham, Mary	073	1841	WB-F/94	AR
Graham, Mary K.	085	1873	WB-1/170	CTY
Graham, Micheal	081	1788	WB-1/50	AR
Graham, Moses	085	1848	WB-K/73	AR
Graham, Nahan	068	1889	WB-D/285	
Graham, Neill	083	1875	WB-3/102	AR
Graham, Neill	083	1837	Orig. Only	AR
Graham, Patrick	054	c1809	WB-1/304	AR
Graham, Rachael	001	1890	WB-2/478	
Graham, Richard	054	c1819	WB-2/133	AR
Graham, Richard	085	1779	WB-B/27	AR
Graham, Richard	085	1843	WB-I/172	AR

Name	Co.	Date	Recorded Copy	Original
Graham, Richard	085	1830	WB-H/484	AR
Graham, Richard L.	085	1873	Orig. Only	CTY
Graham, Robert	083	1864	WB-2/209	AR
Graham, Robert	083	1885	WB-3/354	AR
Graham, Sally	035	1854	WB-2/80	AR/CRX
Graham, Sarah	029	1854	WB-C/290	AR
Graham, Stephen	051	1825	WB-A/20	
Graham, Stephen	021	1881	WB-2/235	
Graham, Stephen	035	1835	WB-1/61	AR
Graham, Susan W.	073	1890	WB-H/491	CTY
Graham, Thomas	001	1866	WB-1/274	AR
Graham, William	065	1767	WB-C/105	AR
Graham, William	085	c1787	WB-G/86	AR
Graham, William	082	1852	WB-4/60	AR
Graham, William	085	1865	WB-K/357	AR
Graham, William	065	1818	WB-C/109	AR
Graham, William	085	1849	WB-K/94	AR
Graham, William	020	1809	RB-F/70	AR
Graham, William	083	1894	WB-4/196	AR
Graham, William A.	073	1875	WB-H/113	CTY
Graham, William A.	060	1883	WB-4/276	
Graham, William B.	085	1818	WB-G/511	AR
Graham, William P.	085	1870	WB-1/53	CTY
Grainger, Caleb	070	1786	WB-C/126	AR
Grainger, Caleb	070	1765	Orig. Only	SS/AR
Grainger, John	084	c1799	OW/119	AR
Grainger, Joshua	070	1763	DB-E/130	AR
Grainger, Joshua	070	c1741	SS 878/86	SS/AR
Grainger, William	028	1788	WB-A/165	AR
Gramling, D. H.	026	1894	WB-2/488	AR
Granade, John	057	1791	WB-A/98	AR
Granade, Joseph	057	1800	WB-A/230	AR
Granade, Joseph	057	1799	WB-A/246	AR
Granade, Martin	005	1802	WB-2/39	AR
Granberry, James	071	1816	WB-3/167	AR
Granberry, Josiah T.	077	1865	WB-H/2	AR
Granberry, Pherebe	077	1857	WB-F/483	AR
Granberry, Samuel	010	1774	WB-B/16	AR-Nunc.
Granberry, Sarah A.	077	1879	WB-H/87	AR
Granberry, William	071	1790	WB-1/390	AR
Granberry, William	071	1808	WB-3/7	AR
Granbery, James	024	1804	WB-B/183	AR
Granbery, Mary	024	c1833	WB-C/166	AR
Granbery, Nancy	041	1836	WB-2/371	AR
Granbery, Samuell	028	c1760	Orig. Only	SS/AR
Grandy, C. W.	VA	1874	018 WB-E/215	018 AR
Grandy, C. W., Sr.	VA	1875	063 WB-3/78	
Grandy, Carey D.	044	1883	WB-23/483	CTY
Grandy, Demsey	018	1835	WB-C/176	
Grandy, John D.	018	1843	WB-C/288	
Grandy, Lydia	018	1822	WB-C/12	
Grandy, Miriam	018	1838	WB-C/233	
Grandy, Patsy	018	1881	WB-E/93	AR
Grandy, Susan	018	1834	WB-C/145	
Grandy, Thomas	075	1761	WB-I/4	AR
Grange, John	012	1788	Orig. Only	AR
Grange, John	012	1816	WB-B/108	AR
Grange, John	011	1740	SS 877/132	SS/AR
Grange, John, Sr.	012	c1791	Orig. Only	AR
Granger, John	045	1873	WB-1/26	
Grant, Adam	060	1822	Orig. Only	AR
Grant, Alexander	072	1738	SS 877/245	SS/AR
Grant, Alexander	072	c1767	Orig. Only	AR
Grant, Alexander	072	1809	WB-A/41	AR
Grant, Ann	020	1808	RB-E/427	AR
Grant, Asa	084	1808	WB-A/79	CTY
Grant, Catherine	054	1898	WB-6/155	CTY
Grant, Cornelia	070	1894	WB-G/212	AR
Grant, Deborah	020	1851	RB-Q/578	AR
Grant, Edmon	103	1874	WB-1/103 & 570	AR
Grant, Eliza M.	054	1883	WB-4/485	CTY
Grant, Elizabeth	047	1851	WB-4/310	
Grant, Ephraim	103	1864	RD-13/745	AR
Grant, Henry	103	1886	WB-1/378	AR
Grant, Huldy	071	1840	WB-4/211	AR
Grant, Ichabod	059	1894	WB-B/106	
Grant, Ichabod	103	1892	WB-2/5	AR
Grant, James	071	1767	WB-1/147	
Grant, James	071	c1842	Orig. Only	AR
Grant, James	IA	1891	047 WB-7/59	047 AR
Grant, James	051	1876	WB-C/174	AR
Grant, James	047	1792	WB-3/203	
Grant, James H.	071	1837	WB-4/156	AR
Grant, James, Sr.	020	1804	RB-E/177	AR
Grant, Jane	072	1760	Orig. Only	AR
Grant, Jesse B.	071	1899	WB-7/432	AR
Grant, John	071	1804	WB-2/268	AR
Grant, John	044	1844	WB-2/289	AR
Grant, Joseph	020	1899	WB-B/352	CTY
Grant, Marina A.	009	1885	WB-1/363	CTY
Grant, Martha	071	1864	WB-5/298	AR
Grant, Martha A.	071	1892	WB-7/154	AR
Grant, Newit	071	1892	WB-7/149	AR
Grant, Newit	071	1846	WB-5/44	AR
Grant, Reuben	072	1793	WB-A/41	AR
Grant, Richard	071	1851	WB-5/101	AR
Grant, Richard	071	1824	WB-3/312	AR
Grant, Sarah	064	1879	WB-2/82	AR
Grant, Shadrach	071	1875	WB-6/150	AR
Grant, Solomon	072	c1771	RW/L24	AR
Grant, Solomon E.	070	1853	WB-C/554	AR
Grant, Stephen	072	1778	RW/L21	AR
Grant, Temperance	071	1836	WB-4/141	AR
Grant, Thomas	044	1774	WB-1/59	CTY
Grant, William	034	1773	Orig. Only	SS/AR
Grant, William	086	1795	Orig. Only	AR
Grant, William	103	1887	WB-1/408	
Grant, William	071	1830	WB-4/71	AR
Grant, William	064	1854	WB-1/36	AR
Grant, William	071	1895	WB-7/238	AR
Grant, William P.	071	1843	WB-4/261	AR
Grantham, David J.	103	1896	WB-2/145	AR
Grantham, Frederick	056	1839	WB-1/530	AR
Grantham, Joshua	083	c1820	WB-1/225	AR
Grantham, Needham	087	1879	WB-3/195	AR
Grantham, Richard	083	1817	WB-1/236	AR
Grantham, Sarah	103	1896	WB-2/176	AR
Grantham, Sarah A.	103	1881	WB-1/201	AR
Grantham, Sarah G.	045	1885	WB-1/114	AR
Grantham, Solomon	103	1844	RD-9/113	AR
Grantham, Stephen	083	1858	WB-2/136	AR
Grantham, Thomas	103	1782	WI-A/2	AR
Grantland, Graham	029	1770	Orig. Only	AR
Graves, Ann L.	020	1858	RB-R/606	AR
Graves, Azariah	020	1837	RB-N/59	AR
Graves, Azariah	020	1850	RB-Q/373	AR
Graves, Barzillai	020	1827	RB-L/244	
Graves, Benjamin	067	1871	WB-2/20	AR
Graves, Betsy B.	073	1833	WB-E/310	AR

Name	Co.	Date	Recorded Copy	Original
Graves, Calvin	081	1872	WB-15/99	AR
Graves, Conrad	085	1822	WB-H/161	AR
Graves, David	046	c1870	Orig. Only	AR
Graves, Elijah	020	1856	RB-R/360	AR
Graves, Francis	071	1764	WB-1/98	
Graves, Hannah	020	1802	RB-D/123	
Graves, Henry	044	1797	WB-4/136	CTY
Graves, Henry L.	044	1829	WB-11/251	CTY
Graves, J. F.	092	1895	WB-6/404	AR
Graves, Jacob	073	1819	WB-D/575	AR
Graves, James	020	1790	RB-B/311	AR
Graves, James L.	020	1853	RB-R/79	
Graves, Jeremiah	020	1868	WB-A/16	CTY
Graves, John	081	1862	WB-12/158	AR
Graves, John	081	1811	WB-3/311	AR
Graves, John	020	1830	RB-L/462	AR
Graves, John A.	020	1864	RB-T/45	
Graves, John W.	044	1789	WB-2/110	CTY
Graves, Joseph	092	1774	WB-1/25	AR
Graves, Mary M.	001	1894	WB-3/34	AR
Graves, Milly	046	1871	WB-E/62	AR
Graves, Ralph	044	1825	WB-10/77	CTY
Graves, Ralph	073	1889	WB-H/474	CTY
Graves, Richard	028	1774	Orig. Only	AR-Copy
Graves, Richard	081	1876	WB-15/213	AR
Graves, Richard	028	1774	Orig. Only	SS/AR
Graves, Richd.	028	1730	Deeds.1/36	SS/AR
Graves, Solomon	GA	1830	Copy	020 AR
Graves, Solomon	092	1862	WB-5/57	
Graves, Theresa L.	056	1894	WB-2/162	AR
Graves, Thomas	028	1767	Orig. Only	AR
Graves, Thomas	028	1770	WB-C/137	AR
Graves, Thomas	078	1812	WI-6/62	AR
Graves, William	044	1786	WB-1/492	CTY
Graves, William	020	c1833	RB-P/283	AR
Graves, William	081	1792	WB-1/111	
Gravitt, Martha Ann	090	1896	WB-6/414	AR
Gravitt, Martin	078	1877	WB-19/71	AR
Gravitt, Mitchell	078	1878	WB-19/78	AR
Gray, A.	033	1858	WB-1/163	
Gray, Abram	011	c1793	WB-1/358	
Gray, Alexander	081	1864	WB-13/143	
Gray, Alexander	046	1832	WB-B/445	AR
Gray, Alexander	081	1803	WB-2/110	AR
Gray, Alexander	046	1861	WB-D/94	AR
Gray, Alexander	056	1783	WB-2/284	AR
Gray, Allen	072	1755	SS 880/17	SS/AR
Gray, Andrew	054	1883	WB-4/499	CTY
Gray, Andrew	078	1857	WB-17/469	
Gray, Ann	075	1732	SS 876/239	SS/AR
Gray, Anthony	075	1804	WB-M1/91	AR
Gray, B. S.	016	1889	WB-4/40	AR
Gray, Benjamin	037	1817	WB-E/168	AR
Gray, Beverly	016	1847	WB-1/141	
Gray, Caleb	018	1823	WB-C/25	
Gray, Charles	037	1811	WB-E/21	AR
Gray, Chauncey	059	1890	WB-A/582	CTY
Gray, Constantine	104	1872	WB-6/58	AR
Gray, David	086	1870	WB-F/76	AR
Gray, David	005	1832	WB-B/22	AR
Gray, Elisha	075	c1855	WB-M2/34	AR
Gray, Elizabeth	046	1827	WB-B/356	AR
Gray, Elizabeth	065	1843	WB-H/118	AR
Gray, Ellen B.	054	1864	Orig. Only	AR
Gray, Emma M.	046	1896	WB-F/478	AR
Gray, Etheldred	037	1790	WB-C/124	AR
Gray, Etheldred	037	1846	WB-F/341	AR
Gray, George	085	c1805	WB-G/38	AR
Gray, George	104	1850	WB-5/47	
Gray, George	010	1806	WB-F/17	AR
Gray, George	073	1775	WB-A/182	
Gray, George	024	c1785	WB-B/60	AR
Gray, George A.	054	1875	WB-4/193	CTY
Gray, Godfrey	096	1792	Orig. Only	AR
Gray, Grier	081	1874	WB-15/162	AR
Gray, Grifen	N	1684	Orig. Only	SS/AR
Gray, Griffith	030	c1805	WB-2/269	
Gray, Griffith	075	1765	WB-I/45	AR
Gray, Hanner	075	1824	WB-N/1	AR
Gray, Henry	096	1763	WB-1/30	AR
Gray, Henry	063	c1865	WB-2/487	
Gray, Hugh	054	c1826	WB-2/95	AR
Gray, Hugh M.	054	1886	WB-5/121	CTY
Gray, Isabella	085	1887	WB-2/274	CTY
Gray, Israel	057	1796	WB-A/79	AR
Gray, James	085	c1801	WB-G/89	AR
Gray, James	072	1758	SS 882/122	SS/AR
Gray, James	047	1797	WB-3/275	
Gray, James	104	1815	WB-3/102	AR
Gray, James	037	1797	WB-D/35	AR
Gray, James	104	1847	WB-4/330	AR
Gray, James	046	1892	WB-F/203	AR
Gray, James	086	1836	WB-E/30	AR
Gray, James	033	1873	WB-2/34	CTY
Gray, James	104	1881	WB-6/203	AR
Gray, James W.	006	1873	Orig. Only	AR
Gray, Jane	104	1873	WB-6/62	AR
Gray, Jennet	081	1835	WB-6/460	AR
Gray, John	037	1777	Orig. Only	AR
Gray, John	010	1750	SS 879/1	SS/AR
Gray, John	081	1792	WB-1/119	AR
Gray, John	035	1781	WB-A/153	AR
Gray, John A.	047	1811	WB-3/515	
Gray, John G.	078	1861	WB-18/242	AR
Gray, Joseph	032	1900	WB-4/447	AR
Gray, Joseph	047	1797	WB-3/274	
Gray, Joseph	075	1800	WB-M1/38	AR
Gray, Joseph	030	1806	WB-2/296	
Gray, Joseph Cox	057	1798	WB-A/220	AR
Gray, Joshua	030	1794	WB-2/30	
Gray, Judy B.	073	1896	WB-I/95	CTY
Gray, Laban	018	1832	WB-C/132	
Gray, Louiza	047	1876	WB-6/158	AR
Gray, M. M.	009	c1885	Orig. Only	CTY
Gray, Margaret	046	1884	WB-E/393	AR
Gray, Margaret	016	1877	WB-3/231	AR
Gray, Martha	065	1830	WB-F/54	AR
Gray, Martha D.	037	1868	WB-G/311	AR
Gray, Mary	046	1865	WB-D/251	AR
Gray, Mary	079	1883	WB-2/275	AR
Gray, Mary	005	1833	WB-B/23	AR
Gray, Mary	030	c1811	WB-3/11	
Gray, Mary	047	1841	WB-4/201	
Gray, Mary	075	1799	WB-M1/26	AR
Gray, Mary A.	037	1885	WB-G/706	
Gray, Mary R.	099	1895	WB-C/402	AR
Gray, Nancy	054	1887	WB-5/183	CTY
Gray, Nathan	022	1896	WB-F/38	
Gray, Olive	065	1846	WB-I/94	AR
Gray, Penelope	010	1859	WB-H/80	AR

Name	Co.	Date	Recorded Copy	Original
Gray, Ransom A.	065	1866	WB-J/228	AR
Gray, Richard	075	1729	SS 876/209	SS/AR
Gray, Robert	037	1781	WB-B/64	AR
Gray, Robert	075	1813	WB-M1/251	AR
Gray, Robert	054	c1799	WB-1/106	AR
Gray, Robert B.	085	1877	WB-1/425	CTY
Gray, Robert H.	081	1863	WB-12/416	AR
Gray, Robin	054	1885	Orig. Only	AR
Gray, Sampson	065	1793	WB-C/113	AR
Gray, Samuel	094	1775	Orig. Only	060 AR
Gray, Samuel	030	1784	WB-1/170	
Gray, Samuel	047	1777	WB-2/47	
Gray, Sarah	081	1858	WB-11/230	AR
Gray, Sarah	054	c1809	WB-1/305	AR
Gray, Stephen	030	1804	WB-2/254	
Gray, Stevens	010	1796	WB-D/305	AR
Gray, T. C.	104	1900	WB-7/111	AR
Gray, Thomas	054	c1810	WB-1/271	AR
Gray, Thomas	075	1770	WB-H/104	AR
Gray, Thomas	104	1887	WB-6/284	AR
Gray, Thomas	015	1774	100 WB-1/265	AR
Gray, Thomas	047	1801	WB-3/352	
Gray, Thomas	030	1826	WB-3/210	
Gray, Thomas B.	018	1832	WB-C/134	
Gray, Thornton	075	1776	WB-I/158	AR
Gray, W. L.	063	1893	WB-4/108	AR
Gray, Wesley	028	1867	WB-D/456	AR
Gray, William	046	1794	WB-A/131	AR
Gray, William	065	1820	WB-C/103	AR
Gray, William	063	1879	WB-3/165	
Gray, William	010	1801	WB-E/128	AR
Gray, William	085	1854	WB-K/174	AR
Gray, William	104	1870	WB-6/43	AR
Gray, William	018	1823	WB-C/24	
Gray, William	028	1784	Orig. Only	AR
Gray, William	046	1900	WB-G/172	AR
Gray, William	072	c1766	RW/L43	AR
Gray, William	081	1900	WB-17/103	
Gray, William	063	1879	Copy	101 AR
Gray, William F.	037	c1872	WB-G/628	
Gray, William G.	057	1806	WB-A/281	AR
Gray, William G.	065	1899	WB-N/261	AR
Gray, William H.	071	1886	WB-6/545	AR
Gray, William J.	063	1893	WB-4/117	AR
Gray, William J.	073	1888	WB-H/448	CTY
Gray, William R.	064	1894	WB-2/325	AR
Gray, Wm. Lee	010	1846	WB-G/392	AR
Graybeal, David	006	1873	WB-E/4	AR
Graybeal, Eli	006	1885	WB-E/111	AR
Graybeal, Jacob	006	1900	WB-E/420	AR
Graybeal, John	006	1884	WB-E/98	AR
Graybeal, Joseph	006	1890	WB-E/208	
Graybeal, Peter	006	1868	WB-D/76	AR
Graybeal, Rachel	006	1900	WB-E/422	AR
Grayson, Rachel	086	1828	WB-D/96	AR
Grayson, William	086	1841	WB-E/77	AR
Greacen, John	NY	c1747	LGB-10/323	
Greason, Isaac	073	1768	WB-A/89	
Greaves, Mathew	072	c1807	WB-A/39	AR
Greaves, Olly	075	1831	WB-N/66	AR
Green (Kroehn), Elizabeth	090	1834	WB-3/269	AR
Green, A. J.	089	c1864	WB-1/288	
Green, Abraham	041	1822	WB-2/181	AR
Green, Adam, Sr.	102	1891	WB-A/87	AR
Green, Annie	036	1892	WB-A/266	CTY
Green, Archibald	047	1825	WB-4/16	
Green, Arthur	047	1830	WB-4/62	
Green, Beedy A.	097	1875	WB-2/79	
Green, Benjamin	081	c1781	Orig. Only	AR
Green, Benjamin	028	1873	WB-E/87	AR
Green, Benjamin T.	039	1885	WB-U/352	AR
Green, Bowen	030	1815	WB-3/69	
Green, Caldony	039	1896	WB-V/104	AR
Green, Charles	046	1798	WB-A/133	AR
Green, Charles P.	100	1843	WB-38/211	
Green, Conrad	090	1826	WB-3/149	AR
Green, Cornelius	026	1896	WB-2/525	AR
Green, Daniel	028	1895	WB-F/192	
Green, Daniel	102	1880	WB-A/18	AR
Green, Daniel	073	1850	WB-F/455	AR
Green, David	057	1881	WB-C/73	AR
Green, David	053	1784	RW-1/120	
Green, David	089	1843	WB-1/24	AR
Green, David H.	026	1863	WB-1/323	AR
Green, David J.	057	1875	WB-C/45	AR
Green, E. E.	039	1898	WB-V/125	AR
Green, E. H.	056	1887	WB-3/434	AR
Green, Edward	099	1786	RB-2/95	AR
Green, Edward	046	1835	WB-B/537	AR
Green, Elenor	047	1841	WB-4/200	
Green, Elijah	102	1882	WB-A/27	AR
Green, Elijah	044	1856	WB-20/119	CTY
Green, Elisha	019	c1808	WB-D/197	AR
Green, Elisha	096	c1779	WB-1/109	AR
Green, Elizabeth	028	1897	WB-F/309 & 331	AR
Green, Elizabeth	027	1881	WB-2/44	AR
Green, Elizabeth	005	1813	WB-2/41	AR
Green, Elizabeth	063	1881	WB-3/214	
Green, Elizabeth	073	c1858	Orig. Only	AR
Green, Elizabeth	028	1804	WB-B/202	AR
Green, Elizabeth	063	1885	WB-3/255	AR
Green, Elizabeth	044	1836	WB-13/337	CTY
Green, Esther	041	1843	WB-3/53	AR
Green, Etheldred	039	1877	WB-U/149	AR
Green, Fanny	100	1853	WB-42/120	AR
Green, Farnifold	028	1774	Orig. Only	AR
Green, Farnifold	028	1763	DB-8/94	
Green, Farnifold	028	1759	Orig. Only	AR
Green, Farnifold	008	c1711	SS 875/10	
Green, Furnifold	039	1807	WB-C/83	
Green, Furnifold	028	1804	WB-B/196	AR
Green, G. M.	026	1889	WB-2/389	AR
Green, Gaston	073	1894	WB-I/50	CTY
Green, George	028	1892	WB-F/54	
Green, George	047	1848	WB-4/266	
Green, Gracie M.	028	1881	WB-E/264	AR
Green, Hannah	103	1805	Orig. Only	AR
Green, Hannah	012	1811	WB-B/95	AR
Green, Hannah	012	1831	WB-B/157	AR
Green, Henry	044	1810	WB-7/102	
Green, Henry	047	1801	WB-3/368	
Green, Isaac	041	1836	WB-2/380	AR
Green, Jackson	067	1884	WB-2/194	AR
Green, Jacob	024	1752	Orig. Only	SS/AR
Green, James	100	1798	WB-9/280	AR
Green, James	035	c1784	WB-A/155	AR
Green, James	049	1891	WB-2/268	AR
Green, James	027	1810	WB-A/24	AR-Nunc.
Green, James	030	c1812	WB-3/12	

Name	Co.	Date	Recorded Copy	Original
Green, James	028	1788	WB-A/183	AR
Green, James	005	1837	WB-B/69	AR
Green, James	057	1801	WB-A/255	AR
Green, James	026	1845	WB-1/46	AR
Green, James K.	103	1861	RD-13/333	
Green, James L.	097	1894	WB-2/464	AR
Green, James L.	026	1866	WB-1/389	AR
Green, James M.	067	1880	WB-2/111	AR
Green, James N.	022	1891	WB-E/470	AR
Green, James S.	092	1893	WB-6/369	AR
Green, James West	047	1787	WB-3/136	
Green, Jane	100	1845	WB-38/356	AR
Green, Jefferson	073	1875	WB-H/104	CTY
Green, Jeremiah	049	1846	WB-2/208	AR
Green, Jeremiah	013	1844	WB-A/98	
Green, Jerry	026	1890	WB-2/408	AR
Green, Joel	067	1863	WB-1/106	AR
Green, John	039	1792	WB-A/82	AR
Green, John	085	c1781	WB-B/26	AR
Green, John	054	c1793	WB-1/100	AR
Green, John	065	1794	WB-C/98	AR
Green, John	069	1824	WB-1/323	AR
Green, John	011	1749	SS 877/100	SS/AR
Green, John	024	c1779	WB-A/318	AR
Green, John	039	1868	WB-U/1	
Green, John	086	1858	WB-E/350	AR
Green, John	035	1807	WB-A/176	AR
Green, John	039	c1803	WB-B/181	AR
Green, John	028	1865	WB-D/372	AR
Green, John	028	1781	Orig. Only	AR
Green, John	028	1791	WB-A/234	AR
Green, John	022	1873	WB-D/111	AR
Green, John	006	1826	WB-A/51	AR
Green, John	080	1888	WB-1/132	AR
Green, John	056	1810	WB-1/219	AR
Green, John	100	1825	WB-27/261	AR
Green, John B.	003	1888	WB-B/240	AR
Green, John B.	044	1886	WB-23/549	CTY
Green, John R.	073	1869	WB-H/14	CTY
Green, John, Jr.	028	1787	WB-A/162	AR
Green, Joseph	028	1791	WB-A/251	AR
Green, Joseph	086	1847	WB-E/171	AR
Green, Joseph	094	1772	Orig. Only	060 AR
Green, Joseph	100	1824	WB-25/214	AR
Green, Joseph	015	1775	100 WB-2/57	AR
Green, Joseph	086	1838	WB-E/41	AR
Green, Joseph	026	1864	WB-1/359	AR
Green, Joseph	028	1824	WB-C/250	AR
Green, Joseph	099	c1804	Orig. Only	AR-Copy
Green, Joseph	047	1854	WB-4/367	
Green, Joseph	050	1900	WB-2/349	CTY
Green, Joseph A.	036	1889	WB-A/150	CTY
Green, Katharine	013	1872	WB-B/63	AR
Green, Kinchen	022	1887	WB-E/353	AR
Green, Lott	035	1829	WB-A/170	AR
Green, Louisa	080	1900	WB-1/337	AR
Green, Lucretia	047	1886	WB-6/416	AR
Green, Luke	041	1862	WB-3/296	AR
Green, Manerva A.	020	1863	RB-T/10	
Green, Margaret	046	1840	WB-C/67	AR
Green, Martha	041	1804	WB-1/210	AR
Green, Martha B.	086	1900	WB-G/62	AR
Green, Mary	106	1881	WB-2/134	AR
Green, Mary	086	1863	WB-E/411	AR
Green, Mary	069	1846	WB-1/488	AR

Name	Co.	Date	Recorded Copy	Original
Green, Mary	027	c1884	WB-2/53	
Green, Mary	100	1825	WB-27/79	AR
Green, Mary	041	1820	WB-2/170	AR
Green, Mary	070	1815	WB-AB/215	AR
Green, Mary	100	1799	Orig. Only	AR
Green, Mary	011	c1792	WB-1/532	
Green, Mary Ann	032	1889	WB-4/70	AR
Green, Michael J.	073	1879	WB-H/213	CTY
Green, Monty	099	1891	WB-C/325	AR
Green, Nancy	046	1855	WB-C/432	AR
Green, Nathan	070	1855	WB-C/593	AR
Green, Nathan	016	1862	WB-2/84	
Green, Nathan P.	039	1863	WB-R/524	AR
Green, Nicholas	082	1796	WB-1/69	AR
Green, Parthenia	100	1832	WB-34/7	AR
Green, Perceda	021	1900	WB-3/313	AR
Green, Peter	067	1882	WB-2/149	AR-Nunc.
Green, Peter	080	1892	WB-1/168	AR
Green, Phillip	090	1818	WB-3/22	AR
Green, Phoebe	009	1900	WB-2/231	CTY
Green, Priscilla	100	1815	WB-19/184	AR
Green, Rebecca J.	032	1880	WB-3/322	AR
Green, Reddick	041	1844	WB-3/54	AR
Green, Richard	028	1804	WB-B/213	AR
Green, Richard	024	1742	Orig. Only	SS/AR
Green, Richard	012	1818	WB-B/118	AR
Green, Richard F.	059	1872	WB-A/36	
Green, Robert	086	1886	WB-F/286	AR
Green, Robert	067	1848	WB-1/43	
Green, Robert	017	1885	WB-B/131	AR
Green, Robert N.	022	1897	WB-F/41	AR
Green, Sally	069	1833	WB-1/392	AR
Green, Samuel	019	1792	WB-D/188	AR
Green, Samuel	067	1884	WB-2/191	AR
Green, Samuel	032	1855	WB-2/111	AR
Green, Samuel	041	1850	WB-3/135	AR
Green, Samuel	041	1782	WB-1/27	AR
Green, Samuel	041	1816	WB-2/125	AR
Green, Samuel	070	1771	WB-C/117	AR
Green, Samuel	073	1859	WB-G/228	AR
Green, Sarah	039	1883	WB-U/304	AR
Green, Sarah A.	047	1871	WB-6/55	AR
Green, Shadrach	026	1846	WB-1/55	AR
Green, Simon	039	1833	WB-J/255	AR
Green, Simon	027	c1824	WB-A/12	AR
Green, Solomon	100	1829	WB-32/260	AR
Green, Susan	056	1892	WB-2/145	AR
Green, Susannah	008	1735	LGB-4/#18	SS/AR
Green, Susannah	090	1837	WB-3/321	AR
Green, Thomas	073	1895	WB-I/65	CTY
Green, Thomas	029	1785	Orig. Only	AR
Green, Thomas	100	1850	WB-41/36	AR
Green, Thomas	046	1839	WB-C/41	
Green, Thomas	071	1760	WB-1/33	
Green, Thomas	047	1772	WB-1/301	
Green, Thomas	104	1815	WB-3/105	
Green, Thomas	DE	1755	Copy	075 AR
Green, Thomas	104	1867	WB-5/518	AR
Green, Thomas	010	1762	WB-A/21	AR
Green, Thomas	044	1888	WB-24/34	CTY
Green, Thomas	080	1882	WB-1/72	AR
Green, Thomas	049	1893	WB-2/296	AR
Green, Thomas D.	005	1849	WB-C/14	AR
Green, Thomas E.	100	1864	WWB-51/81	AR
Green, Thomas J.	100	1864	WB-50/79	AR

Name	Co.	Date	Recorded Copy	Original
Green, Tilmon	097	1871	WB-2/54	AR
Green, W. W.	026	1897	WB-2/551	AR
Green, William	067	1853	WB-1/60	
Green, William	044	1815	WB-7/498	CTY
Green, William	098	1893	WB-A/173	CTY
Green, William	049	1837	WB-2/237	AR
Green, William	028	1824	WB-C/248	AR
Green, William	099	1808	RB-8/15	AR
Green, William	086	1832	WB-D/159	AR
Green, William	044	1814	WB-7/467	CTY
Green, William	104	1865	WB-5/414	
Green, William	099	1786	RB-2/100	AR
Green, William	100	1799	WB-10/168	015 AR
Green, William	046	1867	WB-D/357	AR
Green, William	100	1824	WB-26/40	AR
Green, William	047	1761	WB-1/22	
Greene, Albert	026	1898	WB-3/2	AR
Greene, Ann Hunt	047	1797	WB-3/281	
Greene, J. E.	097	1898	WB-2/551	AR
Greene, John	089	1893	WB-2/270	AR
Greene, Julia C.	022	c1864	WB-D/144	AR
Greene, Matthew	081	1877	WB-15/269	AR
Greene, Rebecca	102	1895	WB-A/98	AR
Greene, Rhoda	102	1888	WB-A/59	AR
Greene, Shadrach	020	1789	RB-B/276	
Greene, Silas	099	1850	RB-27/140	AR
Greene, Simeon	066	1888	WB-1/37	AR
Greene, Zeno H.	069	1895	WB-5/492	AR
Greenhill, Philip	060	1868	WB-3/104	AR
Greenlee, David W.	064	1865	WB-1/95	AR
Greenlee, David W.	064	1897	WB-2/398	AR
Greenlee, Ephraim M.	064	1863	WB-1/81	AR
Greenlee, James M.	064	1891	Orig. Only	AR
Greenlee, James M.	014	1891	WB-2/431	CTY
Greenlee, John H.	014	c1841	Copy	064 AR
Greenlee, Marcus	064	1895	WB-2/341	AR
Greenlee, Martha M.	064	1898	WB-2/420	AR
Greenlee, Mary A.	064	1891	WB-2/231	
Greenway, Thomas	086	1850	WB-E/197	ar
Greenwell, Elias	104	1852	WB-5/69	
Greenwood, B.	105	1893	WB-3/73	AR
Greenwood, Frederick	024	1855	WB-C/378	AR
Greenwood, James	092	1882	WB-6/173	
Greenwood, John	104	1896	WB-6/560	AR
Greenwood, Joseph S.	092	1900	WB-6/551	AR
Greenwood, Nancey	104	1859	WB-5/239	
Greenwood, William	092	1874	WB-6/53	AR
Greer, Andrew	009	1800	OWB/347	AR
Greer, Annanias	084	c1824	WB-A/174	CTY
Greer, Aquilla	006	c1838	WB-B/104	AR
Greer, Benjamin	017	1892	WB-B/219	AR
Greer, Daniel	106	1889	WB-2/295	AR
Greer, E. D.	VA	c1884	Orig. Only	006 AR
Greer, George W.	032	1888	WB-4/29	AR
Greer, Hiram L.	017	1893	WB-B/225	AR
Greer, James	065	1833	WB-G/145	AR
Greer, James	065	1808	WB-C/88	AR
Greer, John	072	c1752	028 DB-5/277	
Greer, John F.	006	1897	WB-E/330	AR
Greer, John, Sr.	104	1782	WB-1/78	AR
Greer, Robert	081	1784	WB-1/11	AR
Greer, Thomas	046	1839	WB-C/41	AR
Greer, Thomas	065	1828	WB-A/161	AR
Greer, Thomas	029	1783	Orig. Only	AR
Greer, William	065	1790	WB-C/118	AR
Greeson, David	073	1821	WB-D/610	AR
Greeson, Gideon	046	1865	WB-D/263	AR
Greeson, Jacob	046	1854	WB-C/418	AR
Greeves, James	075	1765	WB-I/47	AR
Greggory, Thomas	092	1800	WB-3/39	AR
Gregorie, Mary	024	c1761	WB-A/278	AR
Gregory, Alex	048	1898	WB-1/86	CTY
Gregory, Alexander	029	1793	Orig. Only	AR
Gregory, Arthur	018	1838	WB-C/244	
Gregory, Arthur B.	072	c1806	Orig. Only	AR
Gregory, Asa	087	1861	WB-2/27	AR
Gregory, Benjamin	024	1799	WB-A/322	AR
Gregory, Benjamin	024	1770	WB-B/27	AR
Gregory, Catherine	029	1796	Orig. Only	AR
Gregory, Charles	071	1800	WB-2/195	AR
Gregory, Charles	071	1767	WB-1/146	
Gregory, Charles	072	1859	WB-2/175	AR
Gregory, Cornelius	030	1807	WB-2/313	
Gregory, David L.	010	1869	WB-I/7	AR
Gregory, Elijah	087	1844	WB-1/278	AR
Gregory, Elisha	087	1878	WB-3/170	AR
Gregory, Eliza	030	1861	WB-4/240	
Gregory, Elizabeth	018	1823	WB-C/18	
Gregory, Ellener	024	1798	WB-A/343	AR
Gregory, Enoch	030	1806	WB-2/291	
Gregory, Fanny W.	047	1876	WB-6/145	AR
Gregory, Frances	030	1823	WB-3/145	
Gregory, Francis R.	044	1854	WB-19/458	CTY
Gregory, George N.	009	1853	OB-I/95	AR
Gregory, Griffith	030	1790	WB-1/242	
Gregory, Griffith	030	1797	WB-2/106	
Gregory, Hardy	072	c1790	Orig. Only	AR
Gregory, Henry	024	c1862	Orig. Only	AR
Gregory, Herbert	044	1891	WB-24/172	CTY
Gregory, Isaac	077	1824	WB-F/69	AR
Gregory, Isaac	018	1830	WB-C/112	
Gregory, Jaan	024	1811	WB-B/316	AR
Gregory, James	024	c1810	WB-B/313	AR
Gregory, James	075	1777	WB-I/155	
Gregory, Jane	087	1871	WB-3/40	AR
Gregory, Jane	018	1842	WB-C/272	
Grcgory, Jesse	072	c1792	Orig. Only	AR
Gregory, Jesse	030	1798	WB-2/123	
Gregory, John	041	1784	WB-1/39	AR
Gregory, John	099	1844	RB-25/499	AR
Gregory, John	077	1816	WB-E/441	AR
Gregory, John W.	098	1894	WB-A/201	CTY
Gregory, Joseph	030	1806	WB-2/288	
Gregory, Joseph L.	010	1877	WB-I/86	
Gregory, Judith	075	1754	Orig. Only	SS/AR
Gregory, Julia A.E.	018	1894	WB-E/219	AR
Gregory, Lemuel	010	1846	WB-G/396	AR
Gregory, Leonard	030	1836	WB-4/22	
Gregory, Lucy F.	044	1852	WB-19/157	CTY
Gregory, Luke	024	1799	WB-A/311	AR
Gregory, Luke	030	1827	WB-3/220	
Gregory, Lydia	018	1866	WB-D/79	AR
Gregory, Mackey	024	1832	WB-C/173	AR
Gregory, Mahala	018	1892	Orig. Only	AR
Gregory, Major	018	1864	WB-D/68	AR
Gregory, Major P.	018	1858	WB-D/42	
Gregory, Margaret	075	1753	Copy	024 AR
Gregory, Margaret	075	1753	SS 881/13	SS/AR
Gregory, Mark	018	1837	WB-C/222	
Gregory, Mark D.	018	1886	Orig. Only	AR

Name	Co.	Date	Recorded Copy	Original
Gregory, Martha	024	1871	WB-E/25	AR
Gregory, Martha H.	065	1891	WB-L/550	AR
Gregory, Martha H.	065	1891	050 WB-2/102	050 CTY
Gregory, Mary	037	1858	WB-G/164	AR
Gregory, Mary	018	1838	WB-C/232	
Gregory, Mary	024	1894	WB-E/234	AR
Gregory, Mary C.	075	1852	WB-N/243	AR
Gregory, Miles	018	1869	WB-E/10	AR
Gregory, Noah	018	1833	WB-C/140	
Gregory, Pheby	018	1837	WB-C/204	
Gregory, Priscilla	056	1803	WB-1/143	AR
Gregory, R. B.	083	1890	WB-3/485	AR
Gregory, Rachel	030	c1812	WB-3/19	
Gregory, Rebecca M.	056	1876	WB-3/155	AR
Gregory, Richard	075	1720	SS 875/235	
Gregory, Richard	030	1758	SS 881/166	SS/AR
Gregory, Richard	085	1819	Orig. Only	AR-Nunc.
Gregory, Richard B.	041	1825	WB-2/242	AR
Gregory, Samuel	024	1774	WB-B/19	AR
Gregory, Samuel	024	1825	WB-C/115	AR
Gregory, Samuel T.	018	1896	WB-E/247	AR
Gregory, Sarah	018	1887	WB-E/168	AR
Gregory, Sarah	075	1761	WB-I/3	AR
Gregory, Sarah	024	1839	WB-C/221	AR
Gregory, Susan	018	1824	WB-C/30	
Gregory, Sylvia	071	1783	WB-1/271	
Gregory, Tabithe	009	c1809	OWB/456	AR
Gregory, Thomas	048	1895	WB-1/45	
Gregory, Thomas	030	1836	WB-4/23	
Gregory, Thomas	030	1845	WB-4/111	
Gregory, Thomas	075	1740	LGB-4/#106	SS/AR
Gregory, Thomas	024	1850	WB-C/298	AR
Gregory, Tilman N.	077	1856	WB-F/477	AR
Gregory, Tully	030	1818	WB-3/101	
Gregory, W. S.	075	1880	WB-O/120	AR
Gregory, William	075	1752	Orig. Only	SS/AR
Gregory, William	024	1804	WB-B/286	AR
Gregory, William	030	1866	WB-4/262	
Gregory, William	070	1778	WB-C/124	AR-Nunc.
Gregory, William	075	1753	SS 881/20	SS/AR
Gregory, William D.	VA	1858	044 WB-21/290	044 CTY
Gregory, William O.	044	1886	WB-23/564	CTY
Gregory, Wright	087	1892	WB-3/512	AR
Gregpry, Mark R.	018	1886	WB-E/156	
Gresham, David J.	073	1881	WB-H/276	CTY
Gresson, Daniel	046	1821	WB-B/118	AR
Gretter, David B.	046	1849	WB-C/313	AR
Gretter, John A.	046	1853	WB-D/387	AR
Gretter, Martha J.	046	1851	WB-C/341	AR
Greves, Mathew D.	075	1788	WB-K/165	AR
Grey, Hugh A.	065	1898	WB-N/146	AR
Grey, John	035	1863	Orig. Only	AR
Grey, William	065	1823	WB-C/129	AR
Grey, William B.	092	c1836	WB-4/106	
Greyham, James	020	1782	RB-A/214	
Gribble, Elizabeth	046	1886	WB-E/436	AR
Gribble, James	065	1836	WB-E/159	AR
Gribble, William	065	1859	WB-J/67	AR
Gribble, William	046	1880	WB-E/386	AR
Grice, Francis	056	1750	028 DB-5/196	SS/AR
Grice, Francis	075	1808	WB-M1/190	AR
Grice, Jacob	069	1818	WB-1/291	AR
Grice, James	021	1850	WB-1/86	AR
Grice, John	047	1764	WB-1/149	
Grice, Lewis	056	1810	WB-1/221	AR
Grice, Mary	075	1840	WB-N/156	AR
Grice, Theophilus	069	1823	WB-1/316	AR
Grider, Martin	064	c1871	Orig. Only	AR
Grider, Sarah	060	1841	WB-2/92	AR
Grier, Andrew	065	1850	Orig. Only	AR
Grier, E. W.	065	1897	WB-N/32	AR
Grier, Isaac	065	1862	WB-J/138	AR
Grier, Isaac, Sr.	065	c1843	WB-H/156	AR
Grier, J. Laban	065	1863	WB-J/146	AR
Grier, John	065	c1841	WB-H/183	AR
Grier, John S.	040	c1862	WB-1/154	
Grier, Joshua	104	1796	WB-1/450	
Grier, Margaret	065	1825	WB-C/130	AR
Grier, Margaret	065	1888	WB-L/277	AR
Grier, Margaret	065	1899	WB-N/251	AR
Grier, Margaret	016	1897	WB-4/289	AR
Grier, Margaret	020	1817	RB-H/87	AR
Grier, Margaret	040	1894	WB-2/485	AR
Grier, Mary	AL	1854	WB-1/238	
Grier, Mary Ann	065	1892	WB-M/31	AR
Grier, Mathew	046	1802	WB-A/145	AR
Grier, R. A.	065	1899	WB-N/297	AR
Grier, Robert	AL	1822	Copy	065 AR
Grier, Sarah L.	065	1900	WB-N/344	AR
Grier, Susannah	065	1853	WB-I/225	AR
Grier, Thomas J.	065	1872	WB-K/89	AR-Copy
Grier, Thomas P.	065	1892	WB-M/109	AR
Grier, Thomas P.	065	1867	WB-J/235	AR
Griffen, Armiza	009	1844	OB-E/382	AR
Griffen, Benjamin	028	1777	Orig. Only	AR
Griffen, Epenetus	096	1756	SS 880/178	SS/AR
Griffen, John	063	c1801	WB-1/358	
Griffen, Solomon	028	1766	Orig. Only	AR
Griffen, Thomas	005	1807	WB-2/44	AR
Griffen, William	063	c1800	WB-1/357	
Griffeth, John	010	1727	SS 876/135	SS/AR
Griffey, J. A.	062	1890	WB-B/97	AR
Griffice, Mary A.	099	1889	WB-B/308	AR
Griffice, William I.	099	1874	RB-35/431	AR
Griffin, A. Hurley	097	1892	WB-2/428	AR
Griffin, Alexander	063	1823	WB-2/87	
Griffin, Allen	027	1894	WB-2/110	AR
Griffin, Amos	077	1805	Orig. Only	AR
Griffin, Andrew	085	N. D.	WB-G/74	AR
Griffin, Asa	063	1817	WB-2/40	
Griffin, Benjamin	028	1811	WB-C/33	AR
Griffin, Benjamin J.	039	1900	WB-V/199	AR
Griffin, Brinkley	047	1800	WB-3/343	
Griffin, Bryan H.	053	1854	WB-8/54	AR
Griffin, C. M.	059	1893	WB-B/66	CTY
Griffin, Calvin	063	1895	WB-4/171	AR
Griffin, Chancey	075	1857	WB-M2/49	AR
Griffin, Charity	077	1843	WB-F/308	AR
Griffin, Charles P.	005	1896	WB-D/401	AR
Griffin, David	005	1816	WB-2/43	AR
Griffin, Edmund	071	1771	WB-1/200	
Griffin, Edward	096	1754	SS 881/113	SS/AR
Griffin, Edward	010	1790	WB-D/136	AR
Griffin, Edward	063	1857	WB-2/441	
Griffin, Egbert	065	1882	WB-K/492	AR
Griffin, Egbert	065	1882	097 WB-2/276	
Griffin, Elizabeth	010	1825	WB-G/128	AR
Griffin, Elizabeth	037	1859	WB-G/168	AR
Griffin, Elizabeth	077	1896	WB-H/288	AR
Griffin, Enoch	097	1859	WB-1/153	AR

Name	Co.	Date	Recorded Copy	Original
Griffin, Enoch H.	097	1856	WB-1/114	AR
Griffin, Epenetus	063	1791	WB-1/179	
Griffin, Esther	024	1878	WB-E/73	AR
Griffin, Ezbell	047	1787	WB-3/125	
Griffin, Ezekiel	085	1832	WB-H/542	AR
Griffin, George H.	105	1881	WB-2/277	AR
Griffin, Hannah	077	1789	WB-C/385	AR
Griffin, Harvey D.	039	1863	WB-R/395	AR
Griffin, Henry, Sr.	037	1819	WB-E/220	AR
Griffin, Henry, Sr.	063	1857	WB-2/438	
Griffin, Isaac	075	1829	WB-N/53	AR
Griffin, Isaac	075	1781	WB-K/60	AR
Griffin, Jacob	069	1865	WB-1/591	AR
Griffin, James	024	c1748	Orig. Only	SS/AR
Griffin, James	077	1839	WB-F/287	AR
Griffin, James	069	1795	WB-1/100	AR
Griffin, James	028	1859	WB-D/279	AR
Griffin, James C.	097	1887	WB-2/302	AR
Griffin, Jesse	077	1807	WB-E/295	AR
Griffin, Jesse	063	1885	WB-3/277	AR
Griffin, Jesse C.	097	1878	WB-2/148	
Griffin, John	037	1761	WB-A/74	AR
Griffin, John	063	1873	WB-3/45	Nunc.
Griffin, John	039	1872	WB-U/38	
Griffin, John	070	1815	WB-AB/213	AR-Nunc.
Griffin, John	063	c1781	WB-1/81	
Griffin, John	077	1774	WB-C/146	AR
Griffin, John	083	1865	WB-2/222	AR
Griffin, John	097	c1863	Orig. Only	AR
Griffin, John	077	1772	WB-C/113	AR
Griffin, John A.	063	1892	WB-4/79	AR
Griffin, John C.	023	1893	WB-A/106	AR
Griffin, John G.	033	1857	WB-1/137	
Griffin, John R.	039	c1887	WB-U/409	AR
Griffin, John W.	097	1853	WB-1/96	AR
Griffin, John, Jr.	063	1827	WB-2/127	
Griffin, Jonas	063	1898	WB-4/218	AR
Griffin, Joseph	069	1785	WB-1/36	AR
Griffin, Joseph	027	1829	WB-A/37	AR
Griffin, Joseph	077	1828	WB-F/160	AR
Griffin, Joseph B.	063	1900	WB-4/269	AR
Griffin, Joshua	063	1883	WB-3/240	
Griffin, Josiah	077	1807	WB-E/291	AR
Griffin, Lewis	028	1832	WB-C/350	AR
Griffin, Lewis	044	1877	WB-23/274	CTY
Griffin, Louis	081	1897	WB-16/405	AR
Griffin, Louisa	037	1889	WB-H/147	AR
Griffin, M. A.	039	1892	WB-U/541	AR
Griffin, Martha	075	1816	WB-M1/291	AR
Griffin, Martin	063	c1796	WB-1/324	
Griffin, Mary Jane	065	1895	WB-M/369	AR
Griffin, Matthew	063	1778	WB-1/48	
Griffin, Matthew	063	1835	WB-2/201	
Griffin, Michael	060	1873	WB-4/109	AR
Griffin, Milley R.	069	1896	WB-5/562	AR
Griffin, Moses	028	1816	WB-C/132	AR
Griffin, Nancy	063	1828	WB-2/146	
Griffin, Nancy S.	069	1875	WB-5/22	AR
Griffin, Noah	077	1867	WB-H/21	AR
Griffin, Noah	063	1863	WB-2/546	
Griffin, Oen	028	1802	WB-B/152	AR
Griffin, Oliver S.	057	1860	WB-B/252	AR
Griffin, Patsy	063	1839	WB-2/264	
Griffin, Pleasant	038	1883	WB-2/456	AR
Griffin, Reuben	077	c1780	Orig. Only	AR
Griffin, Robert	103	1832	RD-6/348	AR
Griffin, Ruffin B.	069	1882	WB-5/135	AR
Griffin, Sallie A.	069	1890	WB-5/330	AR
Griffin, Sallie E.	010	1895	WB-I/436	AR
Griffin, Sarah	097	1855	WB-1/112	AR
Griffin, Sarah	071	1823	WB-3/282	AR
Griffin, Seth	071	1815	WB-3/154	AR
Griffin, Silvia	077	1824	WB-F/74	AR-Nunc.
Griffin, Simeon	024	1846	WB-C/275	AR
Griffin, Simon	063	1855	WB-2/425	
Griffin, Susan	037	1855	WB-G/116	AR
Griffin, Theophilus	083	c1827	WB-1/356	AR
Griffin, Thomas	097	1866	WB-1/267	AR
Griffin, Thomas	073	1844	WB-F/178	AR
Griffin, Thomas E.	069	1891	WB-5/343	AR
Griffin, Thomas J.	097	1881	WB-2/203	
Griffin, Turner H.	039	1899	WB-V/177	AR
Griffin, W. W.	075	1898	WB-O/458	AR
Griffin, William	100	1822	WB-24/44	AR
Griffin, William	097	1896	WB-2/502	AR
Griffin, William	037	1813	WB-E/57	AR
Griffin, William	028	1853	WB-D/203	AR
Griffin, William	077	c1779	Orig. Only	AR
Griffin, William	028	1809	WB-B/339	AR
Griffin, William	063	1790	WB-1/157	
Griffin, William	077	1846	WB-F/327	AR
Griffin, William	010	1735	LGB-4/#36	SS/AR
Griffin, William A.	097	1889	WB-2/383	AR-Nunc.
Griffin, William B.	028	1890	WB-E/540	
Griffin, William E.	044	1849	WB-17/447	CTY
Griffin, William J.	075	1897	WB-O/447	AR
Griffin, William S.	022	1890	WB-E/430	AR
Griffin, Willis	024	1817	WB-C/62	AR
Griffin, Zacheriah	037	c1837	WB-F/233	AR
Griffis, Abel	TX	1892	001 WB-2/516	001 AR
Griffis, Ann	047	1798	WB-3/311	
Griffis, Benjamin	037	1808	WB-D/318	AR
Griffis, John	037	1799	WB-D/100	AR
Griffis, Joshua	099	1808	RB-8/122	AR
Griffis, Peggy	099	1821	RB-17/218	AR
Griffith, A. R.	038	1900	WB-4/259	AR
Griffith, Aaron	065	1815	WB-C/126	AR
Griffith, Ann E.	099	1887	WB-B/215	AR
Griffith, Charles F.	065	1886	WB-L/141	AR
Griffith, Daniel	057	c1778	WB-A/194	AR
Griffith, Daniel	033	1869	WB-2/4	CTY
Griffith, Edward	054	c1817	WB-1/413	AR
Griffith, Edward	028	c1806	WB-B/271	AR
Griffith, Elizabeth	051	1868	WB-B/98	AR
Griffith, George R.	022	1887	WB-E/362	AR
Griffith, Hannah	071	1778	WB-1/303	
Griffith, Hartwell	051	1831	WB-A/11	
Griffith, Henry	051	1874	WB-C/112	AR
Griffith, Isaac	001	c1849	WB-1/112	AR
Griffith, Isaac	075	1763	WB-H/54	AR
Griffith, J. H.	065	1867	WB-J/230	AR
Griffith, James	046	1884	WB-E/446	AR
Griffith, James B.	065	1866	WB-J/212	AR
Griffith, Jane G.	065	1893	WB-M/145	AR
Griffith, Jeremiah	070	c1749	DB-C/248	AR
Griffith, John	006	1896	WB-E/297	AR
Griffith, Joseph	084	c1817	WB-A/173	CTY
Griffith, Louisa R.	022	1900	WB-F/151	AR
Griffith, Mary	033	1880	WB-2/73	CTY
Griffith, Roger	022	1796	RB-2/80	AR

Name	Co.	Date	Recorded Copy	Original
Griffith, Thomas	051	1848	WB-A/282	
Griffith, W. A.	038	1891	WB-3/202	AR
Griffith, William	090	1845	WB-4/196	AR
Griffith, Zadock	085	1844	WB-I/224	AR
Griffith, Zadock	084	c1821	WB-A/171	CTY
Griffiths, William	004	1875	WB-A/15	AR
Griffon, William	030	1681	Orig. Only	SS/AR
Grifon, Martin	024	1718	SS 875/165	SS/AR
Grifon, Richard	024	1702/3	Orig. Only	SS/AR
Grigg, Berry P.	060	1850	WB-2/344	AR
Grigg, Burrell	026	1877	WB-2/162	AR
Grigg, E. J.	026	1868	WB-1/422	AR
Grigg, P. H.	026	1900	WB-3/93	AR
Grigg, P. H.	026	1900	086 WB-G/77	086 AR
Grigg, P. T.	026	1860	WB-1/249	AR
Grigg, Spencer M.	026	1894	WB-2/489	AR
Grigg, Thomas H.	090	1848	WB-4/248	Nunc.
Griggs, Alexander	038	c1861	WB-1/173	AR
Griggs, Charles	030	c1838	WB-4/47	
Griggs, George	030	1820	WB-3/288	
Griggs, John	071	1771	WB-1/202	
Griggs, John	005	1811	WB-2/46	AR
Griggs, Lydia	030	1830	WB-3/252	
Griggs, Menus	044	1761	Orig. Only	CTY
Griggs, Samuel	NY	1750	SS 877/273	
Grigory, Lott	087	1824	WB-1/10 & 57	AR
Grigory, Lott	087	c1811	WB-A/65	AR
Grigory, Samuel	024	1747	Orig. Only	SS/AR
Grills, Richard	N	1720	SS 875/221	
Grimes, Absollom	075	1759	SS 882/132	SS/AR
Grimes, Ann	073	1849	WB-F/447	AR
Grimes, Benjamin	056	1893	WB-2/137	AR
Grimes, Bryan	079	1860	WB-1/40	AR
Grimes, Charles	032	1830	WB-1/136	AR
Grimes, Chloe	063	1844	WB-2/305	
Grimes, Elizabeth	073	1856	WB-G/154	CTY
Grimes, Godlieb	032	c1846	WB-2/35	
Grimes, Hugh	035	1781	WB-A/161	AR
Grimes, James	011	1866	WB-2/1	
Grimes, Joseph	035	1790	WB-A/158	AR
Grimes, Lydia	073	1855	WB-G/96	AR
Grimes, Phebe	073	1836	WB-E/370	AR
Grimes, Phebe	073	1801	WB-D/52	AR
Grimes, Robert	057	1791	WB-A/156	AR
Grimes, Sampson	035	1828	WB-A/169	AR
Grimes, Samuel	010	1783	WB-C/62	AR
Grimes, Thomas	037	1797	WB-D/28	AR
Grimes, Thomas	037	1885	WB-H/8 & 52	
Grimes, Wesley	006	1900	WB-E/407	AR
Grimes, William	099	1884	WB-A/575	AR
Grimes, William	099	c1884	079 WB-3/52	
Grimes, William	037	1850	WB-F/450	AR
Grimes, William	032	1892	WB-4/161	AR
Grimmer, John	047	1801	WB-3/351	
Grimmer, Robert	047	1837	WB-4/156	
Grimmer, Thomas	047	1803	WB-3/407	
Grimmer, Viletta	079	1899	WB-3/197	AR
Grimmer, William	047	1800	WB-3/344	
Grimshawe, Thomas	055	1893	Copy	093 AR
Grimshawe, Thomas	055	1893	WB-A/115	
Grimsley, Irvin	083	1850	WB-2/25	AR
Grimsley, James	035	1834	WB-1/50	AR
Grimsley, Sarah A.	045	1899	WB-1/372	AR
Grimsley, William	044	1790	WB-2/161	CTY
Grimstead, Gideon	030	1891	WB-5/188	AR

Name	Co.	Date	Recorded Copy	Original
Grinnan, John	056	1762	WB-1/773	
Grise, Moses	083	c1789	WB-1/17	AR
Grisett, George	027	c1853	WB-A/65	
Grisham, George	073	1822	WB-E/20	AR
Grisham, Thomas	035	1881	WB-4/173	AR
Grissett, John G.	012	1870	WB-A/17	AR
Grissett, William	012	1833	WB-B/162	AR
Grissim, Barnabus	064	1846	WB-1/15	AR
Grissom, Candice D.	099	1883	WB-A/496	AR
Grissom, Charles W.	044	1890	WB-24/107	CTY
Grissom, Christopher	046	1827	WB-B/357	AR
Grissom, Drury	060	1829	WB-1/121	AR
Grissom, Elizabeth	005	1841	WB-B/124	AR
Grissom, Gerome B.	044	1871	WB-23/36	CTY
Grissom, James D.	044	1895	WB-24/277	CTY
Grissom, Jane	097	1865	WB-1/245	AR
Grissom, L. T.	099	1893	WB-C/140	AR
Grissom, L. T.	099	1893	098 WB-A/169	098 CTY
Grissom, Lucilla	098	1894	WB-A/196	CTY
Grissom, N.	067	1888	WB-2/264	AR
Grissom, Polly	098	1894	WB-A/194	CTY
Grissom, Sarah E.	012	1885	Orig. Only	AR
Grissom, Wiley H.	044	1867	WB-22/604	CTY
Grissom, William J.	012	c1888	Orig. Only	AR
Grist, Apsley	009	1870	WB-1/42	CTY
Grist, Benjamin	009	c1795	OWB/312	AR
Grist, Elizabeth	009	1843	OB-E/135	AR
Grist, Isaac	032	1841	WB-1/377	AR
Grist, John	009	c1786	OWB/208	AR
Grist, John W.	009	1860	OB-L/246	AR
Grist, Penelope	009	1870	WB-1/36	CTY
Grist, Reading	009	1847	OB-F/330	AR
Grist, Richard	009	c1789	OWB/237	AR
Grist, Richard	009	1753	028 DB-5/287	SS/AR
Grist, William T.	032	1888	WB-4/20	AR
Griswold, Susan A.	103	1865	RD-14/241	AR
Grizard, Henry	071	1857	WB-5/174	AR
Grizzard, Hulon	071	1826	WB-4/3	AR
Grizzell, William	069	1806	WB-1/168	AR
Grobs, William	090	1823	WB-3/134	
Groce, Hezekiah	022	1864	WB-D/132	AR
Groce, Isaac	106	N. D.	WB-1/79	AR
Groce, Jacob	092	1836	Copy	106 AR
Groce, Peter	092	1818	WB-3/134	
Groce, Simon	092	c1819	WB-3/142	AR
Groce, Simon	092	1844	WB-4/208	
Groesbeck, Anna B.	PA	1894	013 WB-C/317	013 AR
Groeter, Jacob	092	1789	WB-2/84	AR
Groff, Martha L.	065	1856	WB-J/14	AR
Grogan, Bartholomew	084	1893	WB-E/544	CTY
Grogan, Constantine	084	1897	WB-F/93	CTY
Grogan, Francis	084	c1847	WB-C/88	CTY
Grogan, John	084	1853	WB-C/164	CTY
Grogan, Samuel	084	1882	WB-E/229	CTY
Grogan, Susan Ann	084	1874	WB-E/71	CTY
Grogan, Thomas	084	1898	WB-F/107	CTY
Groom, John	084	1888	WB-E/407	CTY
Gross, Adam	021	1866	WB-1/234	AR
Gross, Anna	021	1869	WB-2/24	
Gross, Eli	086	c1863	Orig. Only	AR
Gross, Henry	106	c1871	WB-2/31	
Gross, Hoile U.	086	1891	WB-F/408	AR
Gross, Jacob	092	1836	WB-4/101	
Gross, Philip	086	1864	WB-E/433	AR
Gross, Sarah	106	1870	WB-2/28	AR

Name	Co.	Date	Recorded Copy	Original
Grossvenor, William	077	1721	SS 875/322	SS/AR
Grove, Polly	029	1857	Orig. Only	AR-Copy
Grover, Absylla	010	1831	WB-G/203	AR
Grover, Edward M.	068	1898	WB-D/565	CTY
Grover, Elizabeth	028	1856	WB-D/248	AR
Grover, George H.	028	1880	WB-E/223	AR
Grover, James S.	010	1807	WB-F/32	AR
Grover, James S.	010	1818	WB-G/23	AR
Grover, John	028	1838	WB-C/411	AR
Grover, Louisa	028	1868	WB-D/460	AR
Grover, Mary	028	1844	WB-D/98	
Groves, Amanda W.	MD	1895	010 WB-I/452	010 AR
Groves, George	086	1855	WB-E/289	AR
Groves, N. E.	040	1897	WB-2/547	AR
Groves, Samuel	060	1830	WB-1/189	AR
Groves, Thomas	040	1861	WB-1/124	AR
Groves, William	060	1805	Orig. Only	AR
Groves, William	009	c1792	OWB/274	AR
Groves, William U.	086	1827	WB-D/71	AR
Grub, George	085	1807	WB-G/1	AR
Grubb, David	032	c1854	WB-2/204	
Grubb, James	023	c1858	Orig. Only	AR-Copy
Grubb, John	102	1891	WB-A/77	AR
Grubb, John	032	1846	WB-1/476	AR
Grubbs, Daniel	038	1884	WB-2/472	AR
Grubbs, Endsley	038	1888	WB-3/91	AR
Grubbs, John	090	1872	WB-6/27	
Grubbs, Patcy	038	1862	WB-1/175 & 192	AR
Grubbs, Thomas	090	1807	WB-2/84	AR
Grund, Adam	060	1822	Orig. Only	AR
Gryder, Elizabeth	003	1848	Orig. Only	AR
Gryder, J. H.	102	1897	WB-A/139	AR
Gryder, Nancy	003	1878	WB-B/108	AR
Grymes, Johannes	085	1798	WB-G/81	AR
Guard, James	030	1852	WB-4/166	
Guard, William	030	1856	WB-4/205	AR
Guardner, Moses	056	1839	WB-1/513	AR
Gudger, J. J.	062	1890	WB-B/98	AR
Gudger, Joseph	013	c1863	Orig. Only	AR
Gudger, Montraville	TN	1896	062 WB-B/197	
Gudger, William	013	1833	WB-A/25	
Guerard, John	070	1789	WB-C/129	AR
Guerin, Edward F.	038	1893	WB-3/396	AR
Guerrant, Magdaline	084	1858	WB-C/278	CTY
Guerrant, Malinda A.	084	1868	WB-E/1	CTY
Guess, Moses	073	1847	WB-F/337	AR
Guess, William	073	1833	WB-E/293	AR
Guffey, Cynthia R.	086	1897	WB-F/525	AR
Guffey, Eli	086	1859	WB-E/362	AR
Guffey, Ephriam	015	1778	100 WB-2/215	AR
Guffey, Henry	085	c1794	WB-G/83	AR
Guffey, James	086	1832	WB-D/155	AR
Guffey, John	086	1856	WB-E/313	
Guffey, John	086	1819	WB-C/117	AR
Guffey, William	086	1880	WB-F/150	AR
Guffey, William	086	1834	WB-E/9	AR
Gufford, Andrew	035	1805	WB-A/170	AR
Gufford, James	070	1801	WB-AB/50	AR
Guffy, Marget	085	1811	WB-G/200	AR
Guice, Starlen	050	N. D.	Orig. Only	CTY
Guice, Thomas	050	1889	WB-2/50	CTY
Guilbert, Edward	046	1782	WB-A/128	AR
Guilford, Joseph	009	1840	OB-C2/361	AR
Guilford, Stephen	018	1826	WB-C/74	
Guilford, William	018	1830	WB-C/116	
Guilliams, George	024	1747	Orig. Only	SS/AR
Guin, Henry	056	1881	WB-3/280	AR
Guin, Joseph	092	1815	WB-3/116	AR
Guin, Peter	104	1798	WB-1/491	AR
Guin, Samuel	092	1785	WB-2/60A	AR
Guinn, Almand	090	1800	WB-1/170	AR
Guinn, David B.	090	1841	WB-4/85	AR
Guinn, Thomas	073	c1822	Orig. Only	AR
Guinn, Thornton P.	090	1833	WB-3/243	AR
Guins, Abraham	029	1891	WB-E/520	AR
Guion, Ellen P.	011	1897	WB-3/86	CTY
Guion, George B.	028	1885	WB-E/409	
Guion, Hannah	085	1899	WB-3/279	CTY
Guion, Hannah	065	1899	WB-N/214	AR
Guion, Haywood W.	065	1883	WB-K/563	AR
Guion, Isaac	028	1803	WB-B/175	AR
Guion, John W.	028	1840	WB-D/19	
Guion, Mary	028	1856	WB-D/272	
Guion, Sarah	037	1828	WB-F/83	AR
Guion, Thomas	037	1822	WB-E/315	AR
Guiss, Lucy	029	1795	Orig. Only	AR
Gulick, Laura McK.	099	1879	WB-A/98	AR
Gulledge, James R.	005	1896	WB-D/388	
Gulledge, Rebecca	005	1853	WB-C/65	AR
Gulledge, Thomas	005	1894	WB-D/342	AR
Gullet, Andrew J.	085	1899	WB-3/290	CTY
Gullet, Daniel	104	1815	WB-3/98	
Gullett, George	046	1796	WB-A/132	AR
Gullett, Joshua	046	1844	WB-C/203	AR
Gulley, John	099	1834	RB-23/189	AR
Gulley, Mead	056	1803	WB-1/149	AR
Gulley, Needham G.	056	1899	WB-4/161	AR
Gulley, Ransom	099	1897	WB-D/6	AR
Gulley, Robert	056	1816	WB-1/261	AR
Gulley, Robert N.	056	1871	WB-3/40	AR
Gulley, William	035	1822	WB-A/157	AR
Gulley, William	035	1802	Orig. Only	AR
Gulley, Zilpha	056	1839	WB-1/535	AR
Gullick, Jonathan	060	1831	WB-1/210	AR
Gullick, Milton H.	040	1866	WB-1/188	
Gully, George	056	1823	WB-1/356	AR
Gully, Jesse	029	1841	WB-B/347	AR
Gumbs, Abraham	071	1806	WB-2/322	AR
Gumbs, Matthew	024	1754	Orig. Only	SS/AR
Gumbs, Nathan	071	1813	WB-3/92	AR
Gumbs, Susanah	071	1820	WB-3/236	AR
Gums, Abram	071	1813	WB-3/101	AR
Gums, Esther	071	1844	WB-4/281	AR
Gums, Humphrey	071	1861	WB-5/249	
Gums, Leah	071	1846	WB-5/47	AR
Gun, John	020	1780	RB-A/110	AR
Gun, Thomas	078	1796	WI-1/264	AR
Gunn, Allen	020	1884	WB-A/410	CTY
Gunn, Daniel	020	1857	RB-R/562	AR
Gunn, Griffin	020	c1825	RB-L/77	AR
Gunn, Huldah	020	1865	RB-T/108	AR
Gunn, John, Sr.	020	1863	RB-S/619	
Gunn, Starling	020	1852	RB-Q/662	AR
Gunn, Thomas	020	1801	RB-D/21	AR-Copy
Gunn, William	044	1814	WB-7/467	
Gunn, Willis	030	1802	WB-2/206	
Gunter, Abner	022	1865	WB-D/130	AR
Gunter, Andrew	047	1881	WB-6/245	AR
Gunter, Asa B.	036	1890	WB-A/171	CTY

Name	Co.	Date	Recorded Copy	Original
Gunter, Charles	030	N. D.	WB-2/320	
Gunter, Elsey	024	N. D.	WB-C/22	
Gunter, Harriet	047	1881	WB-6/258	AR
Gunter, Isham	022	1834	WB-C/8	AR
Gunter, James B.	022	1892	WB-E/491	AR
Gunter, Joab	037	1826	WB-F/53	AR
Gunter, John	022	1857	WB-C/441	AR
Gunter, John	068	1804	WB-A/234	
Gunter, John	057	1784	WB-A/26	AR
Gunter, John	008	1725	SS 876/36	SS/AR
Gunter, John W.	022	1858	WB-D/6	AR
Gunter, Judy	047	1819	WB-3/646	
Gunter, Margaret	047	1894	WB-7/110	AR
Gunter, Matilda	068	1881	WB-D/155	
Gunter, Neal	022	1871	WB-E/72	AR
Gunter, Priscilla	037	1846	WB-F/339	AR
Gunter, Richard	057	c1779	WB-A/197	AR
Gunter, Richard	022	1831	WB-B/213	AR
Gunter, William	049	1853	WB-2/186	AR
Gunter, Willis	022	1855	WB-C/390	AR
Gupton, Francis	039	1867	WB-S/458	AR
Gupton, James	039	1807	WB-C/88	
Gupton, James	039	c1845	WB-N/360	AR
Gupton, James A.	039	1885	WB-U/358	AR-Nunc.
Gupton, John	039	c1844	WB-M/10	AR
Gupton, Stephen	039	1816	WB-E/65	AR
Gupton, William B.	039	1888	WB-U/417	AR
Gurganas, Uriah	035	1789	WB-A/175	AR
Gurganious, John	009	1881	WB-1/273	CTY
Gurganious, Timothy	076	1894	WB-A1/183	AR
Gurganus, Aaron	009	1849	OB-G/91	AR
Gurganus, Aaron	009	1822	OB-A/325	AR
Gurganus, Aaron	053	1812	RW-1/462	AR
Gurganus, Clemmy	063	1884	WB-3/257	AR
Gurganus, David	053	1772	RW-1/32	AR
Gurganus, Jesse	072	1822	WB-A/38	AR
Gurganus, John M.	101	1879	WB-A/39	AR
Gurganus, Jonathan	053	1798	RW-1/297	AR
Gurganus, Margaret	009	1835	OWB/522	AR
Gurganus, Mary	009	1836	OWB/499	AR
Gurganus, Molsey	072	1823	WB-A/39	AR
Gurganus, Robert	009	1869	WB-1/23	CTY
Gurganus, Sarah Ann	063	1882	WB-3/226	
Gurganus, Swinson	070	1849	WB-C/490	AR
Gurganus, Thomas	070	1871	WB-E/237 & 270	AR
Gurganus, William	053	1794	RW-1/245	AR
Gurganus, William	009	1823	OB-A/327	AR
Gurganus, William	030	1806	WB-2/279	
Gurganus, Zachariah	072	1882	WB-4/140	AR
Gurganus, Zachariah	072	1820	WB-A/46	AR
Gurkin, Benjamin	009	1831	OB-B/87	AR
Gurkin, Benjamin	009	c1800	OWB/370	AR
Gurkin, Henry A.	063	1885	WB-3/259	AR
Gurkin, Horace	063	1885	WB-3/262	AR
Gurkin, Martha E.	101	1897	WB-A/298	
Gurkin, Martha E.	063	1897	WB-4/211	AR
Gurley, Apsilla	103	1893	WB-2/59	AR
Gurley, Arthur	056	1761	WB-1/764	AR
Gurley, Benjamin	070	1771	WB-C/123	AR
Gurley, Charles	010	1895	WB-I/441	AR
Gurley, Edwards	056	1795	WB-1/86	AR
Gurley, Ezekiel	097	1871	WB-2/46	
Gurley, Hugh	013	1833	WB-A/19	
Gurley, Jacob	005	c1820	WB-2/49	AR
Gurley, John	056	c1794	WB-1/88	AR
Gurley, John	056	1760	Orig. Only	AR
Gurley, John G.	056	1899	WB-4/185	AR
Gurley, Mary	056	1792	WB-1/62	AR
Gurley, Nathan	056	1777	WB-1/765	AR
Gurley, Richard	103	1889	WB-1/453	AR
Gurley, William	005	1804	WB-2/47	AR
Gurley, William P.	010	1880	WB-I/106	
Gurley, William P.	010	1887	WB-I/234	AR
Gusum, William	024	1870	Orig. Only	AR-Nunc.
Gutan, Joseph	009	c1770	Orig. Only	SS/AR
Guthery, Charles	072	1828	WB-A/39	AR
Guthrie, Anne J.	070	1865	WB-D/160 & 180	AR
Guthrie, Claburn	022	1831	WB-B/223	AR
Guthrie, Elijah F.	019	1882	WB-B/128	AR
Guthrie, Frederick	019	1858	WB-A/226	AR
Guthrie, James	073	1801	WB-D/40	AR
Guthrie, John	075	1750	Orig. Only	SS/AR
Guthrie, John B.	001	1895	WB-3/82	AR
Guthrie, John D.	019	1889	WB-B/182	AR
Guthrie, John W.	019	1899	WB-C/21	AR
Guthrie, Lydia	009	1843	OB-E/187	AR
Guthrie, Margaret	001	1896	WB-3/157	AR
Guthrie, Nancy	054	1878	WB-4/307	CTY
Guthrie, Susan G.	028	1897	WB-F/314	
Guthrie, Thomas	078	1864	WB-18/379	AR
Guthrie, William	022	1810	WB-A/177	AR
Guthrie, William	022	c1840	WB-C/269	AR
Guthrie, William	019	1842	WB-A/101	AR
Guttery, Reuben	086	1809	WB-B/228	AR-Nunc.
Guttry, Benjamin	028	1761	Wills.7/261	AR
Guttry, Benjamin	028	1761	SS 882/261	
Guttry, Ebenezer	028	1785	WB-A/95	AR
Guy, Alexander	054	c1819	WB-2/116	
Guy, Benjamin	044	1798	WB-4/300	CTY
Guy, Hiram	054	1850	WB-3/39	
Guy, James	054	c1818	WB-1/419	
Guy, James	029	1872	WB-E/49	AR
Guy, James	054	c1813	WB-1/308	AR
Guy, James	054	c1834	WB-2/139	AR
Guy, John	035	1863	WB-3/77	
Guy, Lemuel	035	1794	WB-A/171	AR
Guy, Lemuel	035	1858	WB-2/126	AR
Guy, Lettisha	009	c1797	OWB/324	AR
Guy, Sarah E.	035	1891	WB-4/374	AR
Guy, Thomas	054	c1857	WB-3/122	AR
Guy, William	075	1806	WB-M1/134	AR
Guy, William	056	1815	WB-1/412	AR
Guy, William	087	1847	WB-1/325	AR
Guy, William	035	1820	WB-A/162	AR
Guy, William	077	1754	Orig. Only	SS/AR
Guy, William	009	c1790	OWB/248	AR
Guy, William H.	056	1844	WB-1/557	AR
Guye, Vines	073	1836	Orig. Only	AR
Guyer, Andrew C.	092	1879	WB-6/123	AR
Guyer, Cicero H.	092	1894	WB-6/391	AR
Guyer, Jacob	046	1887	WB-E/464	AR
Guyer, John	077	1803	WB-E/215	AR
Guyer, Joseph	077	1790	WB-C/411	AR
Guyer, Phillip	061	1854	WB-1/54	AR
Guyott, Mary	009	c1823	OWB/481	AR
Guyther, John	063	1815	WB-2/33	
Guyther, Robert J.	063	1826	WB-2/120	
Gwaltney, Louisa	003	1894	Orig. Only	AR

Name	Co.	Date	Recorded Copy	Original
Gwaltney, Lucy	003	1887	WB-B/196	AR
Gwaltney, Mary A.	028	1893	WB-F/80	
Gwaltney, Nathan	060	1827	WB-1/57	AR
Gwaltney, Thomas	028	1783	Orig. Only	AR
Gwathmey, William W.	VA	1898	Copy	069 AR
Gwenk, George	085	1867	Orig. Only	AR
Gwin, Daniel	037	1796	WB-D/6	AR
Gwin, Henry	019	1814	WB-D/202	AR
Gwin, Mordecai	073	1785	WB-A/320	AR
Gwin, Moses	073	1782	WB-A/250	AR
Gwin, Robert	046	1772	WB-A/138	AR
Gwin, William	060	1817	Orig. Only	AR
Gwinn, Elizabeth	041	1879	WB-4/130	AR
Gwinn, John	078	1816	WI-7/176	AR
Gwinn, John	041	1843	WB-3/50	AR
Gwinn, John W.	041	1896	WB-4/407	AR
Gwinn, William	041	1781	WB-1/8	AR
Gwyn, Daniel	020	1833	RB-M/342	
Gwyn, Hugh M.	020	1892	WB-B/126	CTY
Gwyn, James	104	1889	WB-6/367	AR
Gwyn, James, Sr.	104	1850	WB-5/27	AR
Gwyn, John	020	1895	WB-B/209	CTY
Gwyn, Littleton	020	1853	RB-R/85	AR
Gwyn, Martha	104	1829	WB-4/133	AR
Gwyn, Mary Jane	104	1887	076 WB-B/116	076 AR
Gwyn, Mary Jane	104	1887	WB-6/298	AR
Gwyn, R. R.	092	1894	WB-6/393	AR
Gwyn, Richard	092	1881	WB-6/160	AR
Gwyn, Robert	046	1801	WB-A/134	AR
Gwyn, William R.	020	1890	WB-B/25	CTY
Gwyn, Zera	020	1840	RB-0/125	
Gwynn, Rice	020	1873	WB-A/93	CTY
Gwynn, Richard	020	1862	RB-S/579	
Gyn, Moses	022	1782	Orig. Only	AR
Haar, Henry	070	1898	WB-H/160	AR
Haas, John	017	c1862	WB-A/168	AR
Habourn, John	009	1881	WB-1/287	CTY
Hackburn, Joseph H.	028	1859	WB-D/351	AR
Hackburn, Rachel	009	c1800	Orig. Only	AR
Hacket, Mary	046	1826	WB-B/342	AR
Hackett, Florence	104	1893	WB-6/476	AR
Hackett, James	104	1845	WB-4/311	
Hackett, Leven	046	1871	WB-E/72	AR
Hackett, M. H.	104	1867	WB-5/510	AR
Hacklefield, John	024	1741	Orig. Only	SS/AR
Hackler, Griggs	004	1884	WB-A/68	AR
Hackney, Daniel	022	1885	WB-E/301	AR
Hackney, James	022	c1863	WB-D/121	AR
Hackney, Jennings	047	1765	WB-1/158	
Hackney, John	022	1861	WB-D/77	AR
Hackney, John A.	022	1867	WB-D/170	AR
Hackney, Joseph	022	1853	WB-C/356	AR
Hackney, Joseph	022	1803	WB-A/62	AR
Hackney, Joseph	022	1839	WB-C/92	AR
Hackney, Joseph J.	022	c1862	WB-D/94	AR
Hackney, Joshua W.	022	1892	WB-E/500	AR
Hackney, L. M.	022	1882	WB-E/244	AR
Hackney, Rachel	069	c1788	WB-1/244	AR
Hackney, Robert	022	1837	WB-C/76	AR
Hackney, Samuel	071	1762	WB-1/68	
Hackney, William	022	1868	WB-E/12	AR
Hackney, William	069	c1787	WB-1/241	AR
Hackney, William	022	1822	WB-B/54	AR
Hackney, Willis N.	105	1887	WB-2/456	AR
Hadden, David	050	1851	WB-1/31	CTY

Name	Co.	Date	Recorded Copy	Original
Haddock, John B.	020	1866	RB-T/163	AR
Haddock, Rebecca	020	1889	WB-A/579	CTY
Haddock, Shadrach	037	c1817	Orig. Only	AR
Haddock, Stephen	020	1837	RB-N/47	AR
Haddock, William	079	1866	WB-1/157	AR
Haddock, William A.	063	1866	WB-2/531	
Haddock, Zachariah	063	1875	WB-3/91	
Haden, George	032	1832	WB-1/195	
Haden, Heneritta	033	1846	WB-1/84	
Haden, Joseph	085	c1802	WB-D/197	AR
Haden, Joseph	085	1821	WB-H/92	AR
Haden, William	085	c1789	WB-D/170	AR
Haden, William	033	1846	WB-1/77	
Haden, William	032	1836	WB-1/283	AR-Copy
Haden, William H.	032	c1855	WB-2/108	
Haden, Willie	032	1826	WB-1/48	
Hadley, Edward	053	1743	Orig. Only	SS/AR
Hadley, Jacob	022	1849	WB-C/249	AR
Hadley, Jane	022	c1832	Copy	081 AR
Hadley, Jane	022	1833	WB-B/258	AR
Hadley, Jeremiah	022	c1786	RB-1/26	AR
Hadley, Jonathan	046	1826	WB-B/236	AR
Hadley, Joseph	047	1793	WB-3/215	
Hadley, Joseph	047	1817	WB-3/604	
Hadley, Joshua	073	1760	WB-A/7	
Hadley, Joshua	016	1805	WB-A/75	AR
Hadley, Joshua	022	1815	WB-A/271	AR
Hadley, Lydia	047	1819	WB-3/641	
Hadley, Mary	081	1836	WB-6/512	AR
Hadley, Sarah J.	103	1883	WB-1/259	AR
Hadley, Simon	092	c1827	WB-4/37	
Hadley, Simon	092	1803	WB-3/57	
Hadley, Thomas	029	1873	WB-E/93	AR
Hadley, Thomas	092	1822	WB-3/155	AR
Hadley, William	047	1801	WB-3/362	
Hadley, William	082	1824	WB-1/243	AR
Hadley, William P.	022	1896	WB-F/31	AR
Hadley, Willis	022	1873	WB-E/83	AR
Hadly, Bridget	092	1808	WB-3/85	AR
Hadly, Isbel	016	1830	PQS.5/119	AR
Hadly, James	016	c1823	WB-A/17	AR
Hadnot, Rachel	072	1777	RW/L14	AR
Hadnot, Seth	072	1831	WB-1/82	AR
Hadnot, West	072	1789	Orig. Only	AR
Hadnot, Western	070	1810	WB-AB/134	AR
Hadnot, Whitehurst	072	1786	Orig. Only	AR-Nunc.
Hadnot, William	072	c1761	RW/L69	AR
Hafer, John	003	1865	WB-A/4	AR
Haffner, John	021	1873	WB-2/80	
Hafner, Jacob	060	1834	WB-1/324	AR
Haga, Jacob	060	1806	Orig. Only	AR
Hagaman, John	006	c1880	WB-E/231	AR
Hagaman, Lizzie S.	TN	1894	062 WB-B/167	062 AR
Hagaman, Sallie	102	1887	WB-A/52	AR
Hagan, Adam	046	1895	WB-F/460	AR
Hagan, Christopher	009	1824	OB-A/335	AR
Hagan, John	010	1803	WB-E/209	AR
Hagans, Harriett	047	1888	WB-6/502	AR
Hagans, William	065	1790	WB-D/51	AR
Hage, George F.	038	1891	WB-3/191	
Hage, Jacob	032	1842	WB-1/400	
Hage, Valentine	032	c1852	WB-2/126	
Hagemeyer, George	NY	1892	091 WB-1/259	
Hagen, Augusta M.	038	1895	WB-3/524	AR
Hagen, John J.	090	1844	WB-4/152	AR

Name	Co.	Date	Recorded Copy	Original
Hager, Barbara	060	1881	WB-4/239	AR
Hager, Christopher	060	1827	WB-1/55	
Hager, David F.	060	1896	WB-5/18	AR
Hager, James	060	1864	WB-3/72	AR
Hager, John B.	060	1867	WB-3/96	AR
Hager, John, Sr.	060	1842	WB-2/139	AR
Hager, Jonathan	060	1827	WB-1/69	AR
Hager, Lawson S.	040	1888	WB-2/309	AR
Hager, M.Elizabeth	060	1886	WB-4/343	AR
Hager, Margaret	065	1891	WB-M/18	AR
Hager, Margaret	026	1898	WB-3/19	AR
Hager, S. C.	060	1887	WB-4/365	AR
Hager, Samuel C.	054	1893	WB-5/488	CTY
Hager, Simon	060	1844	Orig. Only	AR
Hager, Simon	060	1835	WB-1/338	AR
Hager, Simon S.	060	1888	WB-4/380	AR
Hager, Solomon	060	1842	WB-2/143	AR
Hager, Susan	060	1886	WB-4/341	AR
Hager, William	060	1841	WB-2/101	AR
Hager, William	021	1864	WB-1/205	AR
Hager, William E.	040	1896	WB-2/529	AR
Hager, William M.	060	1870	WB-4/55	AR
Hagerty, Margaret	040	1897	WB-2/544	AR
Haggard, Benjamin	084	c1798	OW/73	AR
Haggard, Elliott W.	SC	1896	013 WB-C/571	
Haggard, James B.	029	1866	WB-D/86	
Haggett, Amanda	070	1890	WB-F/391	AR
Hagin, Derby	009	c1812	OB-A/192	AR
Hagin, John	085	1816	WB-G/425	
Hagin, Mary	085	1837	WB-I/20	AR
Hagins, Goldman	004	1887	WB-A/86	AR
Hagins, Napoleon	103	1896	WB-2/171	AR
Hagler, Caroline	097	1899	WB-2/578	AR
Hagler, Charles	097	1877	WB-2/142	AR
Hagler, John	104	1816	WB-3/141	AR
Hagler, John, Sr.	016	1811	WB-A/93	AR
Hagler, Sarah	016	1883	WB-3/389	AR
Hagler, Skelton W.	017	c1875	Orig. Only	AR
Hagler, William	017	c1856	WB-A/90	AR
Hagley, Penelope	077	1882	WB-H/129	AR
Hagood, Betsy	100	1855	WB-43/196	AR
Hagood, Burwell	020	1848	RB-Q/87	AR
Hagood, Cynthia Ann	100	1886	WB-51/213	AR
Hagood, Franklin	SC	1895	Copy	013 AR
Hagood, Howel	100	1852	WB-42/52	AR
Hagood, John	100	1864	WB-50/92	AR
Hagood, John	100	1808	WB-14/207	AR
Hagood, Lucy	100	1821	WB-23/216	
Hagood, Martha	100	1859	WB-49/249	AR
Hagood, Pherby	100	1783	Orig. Only	AR
Hagood, Susan	100	1858	WB-49/155	AR
Hagood, William	100	1855	WB-43/393	AR
Hagor, Catharine	040	1888	WB-2/300	AR
Hagwood, Harriet	099	1885	WB-B/71	AR
Hagwood, James	099	1887	WB-B/186	AR
Hahn, Absolum	089	c1863	WB-1/295	AR
Hahn, Henry	016	1822	WB-A/82	AR
Haig, Mary	075	1718	SS 875/169	SS/AR
Haig, William	075	1718/9	SS 875/167	SS/AR
Haig, William	075	1735	LGB-4/#3	SS/AR
Haigh, Charles T.	029	1868	WB-D/103	AR
Haigh, Sarah	029	1873	WB-E/98	AR
Haigler, Skelton W.	017	1878	WB-B/70	
Hail, Aris	047	1795	WB-3/239	
Hail, Jonas	071	1804	WB-2/265	AR-Nunc.
Hail, Lewis	047	1794	WB-3/236	Nunc.
Hail, Robert	047	1797	WB-3/278	
Hailey, Ezekiel	073	1854	WB-G/91	AR
Hailey, Henry	044	1897	WB-24/364	CTY
Hailey, John W.	005	1880	WB-D/98	AR
Hailey, Jonathan	082	1855	WB-4/91	AR
Hailey, Richard	073	1894	WB-I/58	CTY
Haily, Alfred	071	1887	WB-6/569	AR
Haine, Penelipe	010	1792	WB-D/198	AR
Haines, Amah	084	c1796	OW/33	AR
Haines, John	032	1882	WB-3/352	AR
Haines, Robert	090	1815	WB-2/163	AR-Nunc.
Hainey, Anny	064	1843	WB-1/4	AR
Hainline, John	085	1775	WB-A/211	AR
Hair, Daniel	054	c1789	WB-1/7	AR
Hair, Esther	054	c1814	WB-1/341	AR
Hair, John	087	c1809	WB-A/53	AR
Hair, Nancy	051	1861	WB-B/44	AR
Hair, Tabitha	051	1893	WB-C/454	AR
Hair, William	087	c1825	WB-A/120	AR
Haire, David	054	1849	WB-3/31	AR
Hairston, Mary A.	038	1894	WB-3/482	AR
Hairston, Peter	090	c1832	SC/07274	AR-Copy
Hairston, Peter	090	1832	WB-3/241	AR
Hairston, Peter W.	085	1886	WB-2/173	CTY
Hairston, Robert	VA	c1841	SC/07274	AR-Copy
Hairston, Robert	MS	1852	SC/07274	AR-Copy
Hairston, Ruth S.	VA	1869	090 WB-6/1	090 AR
Haisley, John	090	1815	WB-2/170	AR
Haith, Smith	046	1816	WB-A/182	AR
Haithcock, Eaton	021	1895	098 WB-A/228	
Haithcock, Eaton	021	1895	WB-3/85	AR
Haithcock, Lucy A.	099	1876	RB-35/359	AR
Hakins, Daniell	028	c1732	Deeds.1/156	
Hakony, John	002	1673	Orig. Only	SS/AR
Halaway, Daniel	006	1869	WB-D/89	AR
Halbert, John	086	1821	WB-C/162	AR
Halbridge, William	029	1809	WB-A/143	AR
Halcome, John	092	1781	WB-1/144	
Hale, Ann C.	012	1845	WB-B/185	AR
Hale, Dolly	081	1809	WB-3/119	
Hale, George	099	1816	RB-13/31	AR
Hale, Harlen B.	081	1853	WB-9/520	AR
Hale, John	010	1736	Orig. Only	SS/AR
Hale, Lewis	047	c1852	WB-5/128	
Hale, Louisa W.	NY	1880	028 WB-E/251	028 AR
Hale, Nancy	037	1874	WB-G/458	AR
Hale, Nancy Ann	009	1852	OB-H/201	AR
Hale, Peyton G.	VA	1889	004 WB-A/95	
Hale, Sarah	047	1867	WB-5/165	
Hale, Willie	047	1883	WB-6/308	AR
Hales, Daniel	065	1835	WB-G/223	AR
Hales, Gilford	056	1887	WB-3/451	AR
Hales, Gillis	056	1890	WB-3/546	
Hales, Henry H.	056	1891	WB-3/574	AR
Hales, Ivy	056	1858	WB-1/722	AR
Hales, Samuel	103	1883	WB-1/262	AR
Haley, George	082	1837	WB-2/69	AR
Haley, Holliday	071	1815	WB-3/136	AR
Haley, James	073	1847	WB-F/378	AR
Haley, John	046	1813	WB-A/179	
Haley, John	082	1834	WB-2/38	AR
Haley, Randol	082	1806	WB-1/108	AR
Hall, A. A.	104	c1859	WB-5/219	
Hall, A. N.	078	1900	WB-19/494	AR

Name	Co.	Date	Recorded Copy	Original
Hall, Abraham	033	1839	WB-1/21	
Hall, Albert G.	076	1875	WB-A1/1	AR
Hall, Alexander	100	1851	WB-41/182	AR
Hall, Alexander	106	1879	WB-2/116	
Hall, Alexander	054	c1828	WB-2/151	AR
Hall, Alfred	035	1899	WB-4/540	AR
Hall, Anderson	073	1846	WB-F/291	AR
Hall, Ann	077	1741	LGB-4/#163	SS/AR
Hall, Anne C.	029	1873	WB-E/111	AR
Hall, Archibald	065	1856	WB-J/24	AR
Hall, Armager	087	c1811	WB-A/67	AR
Hall, Avon E.	013	1873	WB-B/86	AR
Hall, Bembury	051	1873	WB-C/105	AR
Hall, Benjamin	028	1839	WB-C/436	AR
Hall, Benjamin	012	1823	WB-B/130	AR
Hall, Calton	087	1899	WB-4/91	AR
Hall, Caroline	NJ	1897	Copy	026 AR
Hall, Carrie G.	047	1896	WB-7/176	AR
Hall, Charity	063	1811	WB-2/3	
Hall, Charles	037	1791	WB-C/177	AR
Hall, Clement	075	1770	WB-H/107	AR
Hall, David	020	1786	RB-B/119	AR
Hall, David	073	1808	WB-D/233	AR
Hall, David	019	1801	WB-D/232	AR
Hall, David	018	1835	WB-C/190	
Hall, David	090	1886	WB-6/174	AR
Hall, Director	030	1796	WB-2/89	
Hall, Drury	035	1849	WB-2/42	AR
Hall, Duran	028	1813	WB-C/71	AR
Hall, Durham	073	1861	WB-G/359	AR
Hall, Edward	037	1823	WB-F/11	AR
Hall, Edward	070	1799	WB-AB/33	Nunc.
Hall, Edward	077	1790	WB-C/400	AR
Hall, Edward	100	1877	WB-51/122	AR
Hall, Edward P.	070	1863	WB-D/109	AR
Hall, Elbert	055	1885	WB-A/71	
Hall, Eli W.	070	1881	WB-E/412	AR
Hall, Elihu	030	1834	WB-4/1	
Hall, Elisabeth	075	1788	WB-K/168	AR
Hall, Elisabeth	087	1864	WB-2/64	AR
Hall, Eliza	022	1881	WB-E/231	AR
Hall, Elizabeth	054	c1801	WB-1/117	AR
Hall, Elizabeth	073	1831	WB-E/255	AR
Hall, Elizabeth	085	c1795	WB-D/180	AR
Hall, Elizabeth	073	1852	WB-G/25	AR
Hall, Elizabeth	054	c1830	WB-2/136	AR
Hall, Elizabeth	012	1780	DB-B/152	AR
Hall, Emaline	054	1891	WB-5/399	CTY
Hall, Emanuel	028	1843	WB-D/88	
Hall, Emily	028	1838	WB-C/422	AR
Hall, Emma	054	1891	WB-5/401	CTY
Hall, Enoch	049	1874	WB-1/260	AR
Hall, Esther	054	1890	WB-5/390	CTY
Hall, Gatsy	076	1897	WB-A1/212	AR
Hall, George	049	c1835	WI-1-2/9	AR
Hall, George A.	028	1831	WB-C/336	AR
Hall, George C.	029	1834	WB-B/241	AR
Hall, George S.	065	1899	WB-N/299	AR
Hall, Halbert	065	c1782	WB-D/47	AR
Hall, Henry	087	1872	WB-3/197	AR
Hall, Henry	077	1792	WB-C/439	AR
Hall, Henry	077	1774	WB-C/143	AR
Hall, Hezekiah	019	1734	SS 876/292	SS/AR
Hall, Hugh	054	c1816	WB-1/410	AR
Hall, Hugh R.	054	1856	WB-3/103	AR

Name	Co.	Date	Recorded Copy	Original
Hall, Ignatious	047	1783	WB-3/50	
Hall, Isaac	077	1826	WB-F/114	AR
Hall, Isaac	022	1858	WB-D/13	
Hall, Isaac	054	1844	WB-2/285	AR
Hall, Isaac A.	085	1840	WB-I/84	AR
Hall, J. F.	065	1893	WB-M/133	AR
Hall, Jacob	077	1785	WB-C/328	AR
Hall, James	038	1870	WB-2/21	AR
Hall, James	053	c1806	RW-1/505	
Hall, James	073	1796	WB-C/82	AR
Hall, James	070	1787	WB-C/152	AR
Hall, James	037	1772	WB-A/200	AR
Hall, James	090	1887	WB-6/181	AR
Hall, James	035	1870	WB-4/21	AR
Hall, James	065	1827	WB-D/88	AR
Hall, James	071	1764	WB-1/108	
Hall, James	029	1898	WB-F/136	AR
Hall, James D.	040	1893	WB-2/427	AR
Hall, James E.	035	1863	WB-3/72	AR
Hall, James G.	030	1827	WB-3/221	
Hall, James M.	064	1887	WB-2/165	AR
Hall, James M.	064	1882	WB-2/110	AR
Hall, James W.	010	1881	WB-I/135	
Hall, James, Sr.	054	c1800	WB-1/121	AR
Hall, James, Sr.	054	c1821	WB-2/45	AR
Hall, Janet	100	1842	WB-38/122	AR
Hall, Jean	073	1792	WB-B/174	
Hall, Jehu	030	1777	WB-1/116	
Hall, Jehue	001	c1855	WB-1/105	AR
Hall, Jenet	029	1878	WB-E/179	AR
Hall, John	085	1766	WB-A/68	AR
Hall, John	085	1834	WB-I/213	AR
Hall, John	054	c1835	WB-2/165	AR
Hall, John	024	c1785	WB-A/1	AR
Hall, John	053	c1776	RW-1/81	
Hall, John	016	1821	WB-A/63	AR
Hall, John	012	c1801	WB-B/67	AR
Hall, John	PA	1801	Copy	096 AR
Hall, John	033	1872	WB-2/20	CTY
Hall, John	073	1785	WB-A/319	AR
Hall, John	057	1794	WB-A/118	AR
Hall, John	100	1833	WB-34/50	AR
Hall, John	106	1887	WB-2/229	AR
Hall, John	037	1783	WB-B/109	AR
Hall, John	046	1816	WB-A/187	AR
Hall, John	099	1780	RB-1/165	AR
Hall, John	015	1765	RB-1/42	AR
Hall, John	049	1875	WB-1/257	AR
Hall, John	PA	1854	028 WB-D/225	AR
Hall, John	028	1830	WB-C/323	AR
Hall, John G.	012	c1867	WB-B/24	
Hall, John H.	029	1867	WB-D/94	AR
Hall, John W.	027	1887	WB-2/69	AR
Hall, Jonathan	011	c1837	WB-1/100	
Hall, Joseph	065	1880	WB-K/368	AR
Hall, Joseph	103	1808	RD-1/90	AR
Hall, Joseph	033	1850	WB-1/101	
Hall, Joseph	072	1748	SS 878/7	SS/AR
Hall, Joseph	028	1787	WB-A/159	AR
Hall, Joseph	028	1807	WB-B/295	AR
Hall, Joseph	071	1891	WB-7/119	AR
Hall, Joseph	078	1803	WI-3/234	AR
Hall, Joseph	CT	1874	089 WB-2/106	089 AR
Hall, Joseph	090	1888	WB-6/192	AR
Hall, Joseph, Sr.	028	1807	WB-B/284	AR

Name	Co.	Date	Recorded Copy	Original
Hall, Josephus	028	1843	WB-D/76	AR
Hall, Joshua	061	1852	WB-1/49	AR
Hall, Joshua	061	1847	WB-1/32	AR
Hall, Judith	020	1839	RB-N/377	
Hall, Judith	024	c1791	WB-A/90	AR
Hall, Junia	001	c1846	WB-1/49	AR
Hall, L. C.	055	1892	Copy	013 AR
Hall, L. C.	055	1892	WB-A/98	
Hall, Lemuel	075	c1820	Orig. Only	AR
Hall, Levi	073	1868	WB-G/534	CTY
Hall, Love	028	1848	WB-D/147	AR
Hall, M. A.	092	1893	WB-6/370	AR
Hall, M. Etta	006	1895	WB-E/287	AR
Hall, Margaret	027	1899	WB-2/158	AR
Hall, Martha	047	1889	WB-6/526	AR
Hall, Mary	047	1799	WB-3/322	
Hall, Mary	073	1828	WB-E/157	AR
Hall, Mary	028	1814	WB-C/87	AR
Hall, Mary	035	1857	WB-2/123	AR
Hall, Mary	100	1851	WB-41/186	AR
Hall, Mary	077	1792	WB-C/437	AR
Hall, Mary	085	1882	WB-2/37	CTY
Hall, Mary	016	c1824	WB-A/18	AR
Hall, Mary A.	NY	1864	Copy	053 AR
Hall, Mary A.	NY	1864	Copy	096 AR
Hall, Mary W.	029	1888	WB-E/440	AR
Hall, Micajah	064	1892	WB-2/276	AR
Hall, Millun	104	1803	WB-2/92	AR
Hall, Morgan	016	1822	WB-A/87	AR
Hall, Moses	071	1762	WB-1/65	
Hall, Moses	071	1850	WB-5/84	AR
Hall, Nathan	030	1801	WB-2/195	
Hall, Nathaniel	075	1734	SS 876/370	SS/AR
Hall, Nicholas	035	1862	WB-3/45	AR
Hall, Orpha	019	c1882	Orig. Only	AR
Hall, Penelope	024	1844	WB-C/246	AR
Hall, Phillip	078	1806	WI-4/175	AR
Hall, Polly	053	1843	WB-6/230	AR
Hall, R. D.	104	1888	WB-6/345	AR
Hall, Rachel	077	1810	WB-E/352	AR
Hall, Rachel Ann	076	1892	WB-A1/160	AR
Hall, Rebecca	046	1844	WB-C/196	AR
Hall, Rebecca	028	1894	WB-F/129	
Hall, Richard	054	1853	WB-3/65	
Hall, Richard S.	019	1880	WB-B/124	AR
Hall, Robart	099	1822	RB-17/394	AR
Hall, Robert	075	1787	WB-K/150	AR
Hall, Robert	073	1858	WB-G/194	AR
Hall, Robert	075	1783	WB-K/85	AR
Hall, Robert	099	1893	WB-C/138	AR
Hall, Robert	073	1864	WB-G/433	CTY
Hall, Robert	104	1845	WB-4/304	
Hall, Robert P.	012	1826	WB-B/148	AR
Hall, Sally	073	1859	WB-G/218	CTY
Hall, Salmon	028	1840	WB-D/8	AR
Hall, Samuel	019	1795	Orig. Only	AR
Hall, Samuel	085	c1793	WB-E/127	AR
Hall, Samuel	012	1826	WB-B/142	AR
Hall, Samuel	085	1839	WB-I/58	AR
Hall, Samuel	054	c1829	WB-2/72	AR
Hall, Sarah	039	1821	Copy	099 AR
Hall, Sarah	035	1789	WB-A/193	AR
Hall, Sarah E.	001	1885	WB-2/271	AR
Hall, Sary	039	1821	WB-G/68	AR
Hall, Shadrich	072	1791	Orig. Only	AR
Hall, Solomon	085	1861	WB-K/285	AR
Hall, Spence	030	c1807	WB-2/330	
Hall, Spence, Sr.	030	1792	WB-2/5	
Hall, Stephen	075	1762	WB-H/24	AR
Hall, Susan P.	036	1900	WB-A/508	CTY
Hall, Theoderick	047	1799	WB-3/334	
Hall, Thomas	035	c1764	WB-A/193	AR
Hall, Thomas	028	1789	WB-A/210	AR
Hall, Thomas	037	1819	WB-E/212	AR
Hall, Thomas	036	1882	WB-A/17	CTY
Hall, Thomas	012	c1772	DB-B/40	AR
Hall, Thomas	086	1824	WB-D/20	AR
Hall, Thomas	065	1777	WB-C/133	AR
Hall, Thomas	054	c1800	WB-1/118	AR
Hall, Thomas H.	037	1853	WB-F/506	AR
Hall, Thomas M.	012	1820	WB-B/122	AR
Hall, William	073	1827	WB-E/149	
Hall, William	054	c1801	WB-1/117	AR
Hall, William	067	1847	WB-1/38	AR
Hall, William	085	1844	WB-I/227	AR
Hall, William	035	1826	WB-A/192	AR
Hall, William	099	1809	RB-9/132	AR
Hall, William	054	c1828	WB-2/87	AR
Hall, William	101	1888	WB-A/165	AR
Hall, William	011	1765	Orig. Only	SS/AR
Hall, William	072	c1783	WI/L54	
Hall, William	012	1820	WB-B/121	
Hall, William H.	038	1897	WB-4/51	AR
Hall, William W.	073	1825	WB-E/86	AR
Hall, William W.	024	1863	WB-D/18	AR
Hall, Willis	103	1857	RD-12/249	AR
Hall, Willis	103	c1857	Copy	081 AR
Hall, Wilsher	090	1863	WB-4/360	AR
Hallaway, William	085	1816	WB-G/414	AR
Halleck, Henry W.	NY	1882	047 WB-6/365	047 AR
Hallett, Benjamin	NY	1866	070 WB-E/32	
Hallett, James R.	070	1785	WB-C/151	AR
Halliburton, Benjamin	078	c1845	Orig. Only	AR
Halliburton, David	073	1767	WB-A/68	
Halliburton, John	078	1843	WI-15/288	AR
Halliburton, Luvicie	078	1866	WB-18/413	AR
Halliburton, Mary F.	099	1872	RB-35/433	AR
Halliburton, Robert	078	1808	WI-5/27	AR
Halliburton, Thomas	078	1843	WI-15/226	AR
Halliday, Robert	029	1816	WB-A/239	AR
Halling, Eunice	028	1795	WB-A/332	AR
Halling, Sarah	070	1810	WB-AB/133	AR
Hallman, Anthony	060	1833	WB-1/286	AR
Hallman, Barbara	060	1874	WB-4/116	AR
Hallman, Daniel	060	1891	WB-4/450	AR
Hallman, Daniel	060	c1888	Orig. Only	AR
Hallman, Henry	060	1820	Orig. Only	AR
Hallman, Jacob	060	1851	WB-2/349	AR
Hallman, Wiley	060	1870	WB-4/58	AR
Hallom, Jeremiah	010	1784	WB-D/3	AR
Hallom, John	010	1804	WB-E/243	AR
Hallowell, Joseph	053	1771	RW-1/22	
Hallowell, Mary	009	1848	OB-G/124	
Hallsell, Robert	060	1879	WB-4/203	AR
Hallum, John, Sr.	085	1765	WB-A/60	AR
Hallyburton, Jacob H.	014	1894	WB-2/520	CTY
Halsey, Daniel	024	c1781	WB-A/24	AR
Halsey, Daniel	024	1719	SS 875/222	
Halsey, Daniel	024	1800	WB-B/188	AR
Halsey, Edmund	077	1806	WB-E/237	AR

Name	Co.	Date	Recorded Copy	Original
Halsey, Elizabeth	024	1824	WB-C/113	AR
Halsey, James	024	c1792	WB-A/290	AR
Halsey, Jeremiah	024	c1771	WB-1/37	AR
Halsey, John	024	1805	WB-B/206	AR
Halsey, John	024	1762	WB-1/6	AR
Halsey, Joseph B.	077	1836	WB-F/250	AR
Halsey, Josiah	004	c1860	Orig. Only	AR-Copy
Halsey, L. B.	077	1864	WB-F/545	AR
Halsey, Lavinia	024	1866	WB-D/51	AR
Halsey, Lotty	024	c1857	WB-C/415	AR
Halsey, Louisa Ann	075	1897	WB-0/456	AR
Halsey, Martha	077	c1760	Orig. Only	AR
Halsey, Mary R.	096	1854	WB-3/39	AR
Halsey, Miles	024	1846	WB-C/266	AR
Halsey, R. F.	004	1899	WB-A/213	AR
Halsey, Rhoda	070	1877	WB-E/343	AR
Halsey, Saml.	024	1780	WB-A/23	AR
Halsey, Thomas	077	1774	WB-C/165	AR
Halsey, William	024	1802	WB-B/169	AR
Halstead, Benjamin	075	1816	WB-M1/295	AR
Halstead, Drew	075	1783	WB-K/82	AR
Halstead, Elisabeth	075	1837	WB-N/134	
Halstead, John	NY	1899	067 WB-2/399	067 AR
Halstead, John	075	1791	WB-K/211	AR
Halstead, Millicent	075	1803	WB-M1/85	AR
Halstead, Samuel	075	1832	WB-N/77	
Halstead, Seth	030	1799	WB-2/143	
Halstead, Tully	030	1872	WB-5/26	AR
Halstead, Unice	030	1830	WB-3/258	
Haltom, Alson C.	032	1898	WB-4/372	AR
Haltom, Tamer	067	1891	WB-2/305	AR
Halton, Robert	024	1749	Orig. Only	SS/AR
Haly, William	082	1782	WB-1/7	AR
Ham, Amy	100	1849	WB-40/214	AR
Ham, Angelina	045	1890	WB-1/210	AR
Ham, Ben B.	SC	1863	103 WB-1/218	103 AR
Ham, Callie E.	103	1882	WB-1/249	AR
Ham, Catherine	029	1855	WB-C/325	AR
Ham, Dicey	103	1822	RD-5/20	AR
Ham, Elisha	039	1824	WB-H/18	AR
Ham, Erastus	103	1893	WB-2/53	AR
Ham, H. J.	103	1900	WB-2/302	AR
Ham, Haywood	103	1859	RD-13/19	AR
Ham, Henry B.	103	1879	WB-1/150	AR
Ham, John	054	1847	WB-3/21	AR
Ham, John	085	1814	WB-G/309	AR
Ham, Joseph	090	1795	WB-1/64	AR
Ham, Joseph B.	039	c1860	WB-S/3	
Ham, Matthew J.	103	1893	WB-2/25	AR
Ham, Nancy	103	1893	WB-2/44	AR
Ham, Nathan	039	1864	WB-S/2	
Ham, Philip	046	1814	WB-A/180	AR
Ham, Prucy A.	103	1877	WB-1/113	AR
Ham, Richard	039	1794	WB-A/159	
Ham, Richard	103	1817	RD-4/79	AR
Ham, Silas S.	054	1890	WB-5/341	CTY
Ham, William	103	1898	WB-2/222	AR
Haman, Adam	038	c1856	WB-1/105	AR
Haman, Mary	096	1804	Orig. Only	AR
Haman, Rebecca	038	1873	WB-2/145	AR
Haman, Thomas	075	1721	SS 875/320	SS/AR
Haman, Willis	083	1862	WB-2/187	AR
Haman, Willis	083	1829	WB-1/346	AR
Hamblet, William	022	1822	WB-B/63	AR
Hambleton, Archibald	073	1791	WB-B/34	AR

Name	Co.	Date	Recorded Copy	Original
Hambleton, Emily	010	1849	WB-G/462	AR
Hambleton, James	028	1791	WB-A/250	AR
Hambleton, James	053	1774	RW-1/55	
Hambleton, Jane	096	1734	SS 876/293	SS/AR
Hambleton, John	VA	1711	SS 876/174	SS/AR
Hambleton, John	070	1835	WB-C/182	AR
Hambleton, John	009	1843	OB-E/63	AR
Hambleton, Joseph	N	1737	SS 877/183	SS/AR
Hambleton, Kesiah	099	1801	RB-5/272	AR
Hambleton, Susan	103	1853	RD-11/338	AR
Hambleton, William	099	1788	RB-2/182	AR
Hamblett, Richard	020	1794	RB-C/99	AR
Hamblin, Peter	092	1804	WB-3/63A	AR
Hamblin, Stephen	020	1782	RB-A/210	
Hamblin, Thomas	075	1758	SS 882/148	SS/AR
Hambright, Christopher	026	1864	WB-1/337	AR
Hambright, Jefferson	SC	1851	026 WB-1/117	026 AR
Hames, William	026	1870	WB-2/42	AR
Hamilton, Asia	099	c1855	RB-19/350	
Hamilton, Audley	086	1838	WB-E/49	AR
Hamilton, Barnaba	103	1830	RD-6/141	AR
Hamilton, Blanch	085	1821	WB-H/125	AR
Hamilton, Bonita	028	1837	WB-C/397	AR
Hamilton, Christian	053	1855	WB-8/122	AR
Hamilton, Claudius S.	103	1864	RD-13/743	AR
Hamilton, David	057	1783	WB-A/25	AR
Hamilton, Edward	086	1845	WB-E/147	AR
Hamilton, Elijah N.	019	1869	WB-B/47	AR
Hamilton, Emily	038	1899	WB-4/173	AR
Hamilton, George H.	006	1879	WB-E/59	AR
Hamilton, Griffin S.	097	1891	WB-2/400	AR
Hamilton, Guy	103	1791	WI-A/218	AR
Hamilton, H. C.	021	1899	WB-3/238	AR
Hamilton, Horatio	090	1840	WB-4/56	AR
Hamilton, Ira J.	067	1897	WB-2/350	AR
Hamilton, J. M.	080	1894	WB-1/232	AR
Hamilton, J. W.	097	1886	WB-2/291	AR-Nunc.
Hamilton, James	053	1872	WB-11/29	AR
Hamilton, Jane	086	1854	WB-E/255	AR
Hamilton, John	046	1819	Orig. Only	AR
Hamilton, John	053	1836	WB-5/379	AR
Hamilton, John	011	1765	Orig. Only	SS/AR
Hamilton, John	005	c1757	Orig. Only	SS/AR
Hamilton, John	084	c1797	OW/34	AR
Hamilton, John, Sr.	028	1812	WB-C/55	AR
Hamilton, Joseph	086	1824	WB-D/28	AR
Hamilton, Joseph	073	1818	WB-D/540	AR
Hamilton, Julia	086	1899	WB-G/18	AR
Hamilton, Malatiah	070	1797	WB-AB/8	AR
Hamilton, Mark	028	1809	WB-B/333	AR
Hamilton, Martha E.	065	1894	WB-M/305	AR
Hamilton, Mary	016	1875	WB-3/164	AR
Hamilton, Mary	028	1829	WB-C/303	AR
Hamilton, Nancy C.	103	1883	WB-1/285	AR
Hamilton, Robert	086	1819	WB-C/124	AR
Hamilton, Robert	019	1827	WB-D/262	AR
Hamilton, Robert S.	090	1807	WB-2/75	AR
Hamilton, S. W.	017	1899	WB-B/307	AR
Hamilton, Samuel G.	046	1851	WB-C/359	AR
Hamilton, Sarah	086	1881	WB-F/164	AR
Hamilton, Thomas	046	1829	WB-B/394	AR
Hamilton, W. H.	099	1889	Orig. Only	AR
Hamilton, Wesley	046	1852	WB-C/381	AR
Hamilton, William	065	1824	WB-D/83	AR
Hamilton, William	028	1816	WB-C/119	AR

Name	Co.	Date	Recorded Copy	Original
Hamilton, William	073	1793	WB-B/149	AR
Hamilton, William	046	c1785	WB-A/156	AR
Hamilton, William	067	1874	WB-2/47	AR
Hamilton, Z. A.	056	1900	WB-4/241	AR
Hamlet, Richard	047	1831	WB-4/82	
Hamlett, Francis	078	1821	WI-9/232	AR
Hamlett, Jane	078	1849	WB-13/137	AR
Hamlett, Margaret	078	1876	WB-19/49	AR
Hamlett, Martha Ann	078	1893	WB-19/350	AR
Hamlett, William H.	078	1890	WB-19/279	AR
Hamlin, Charles	047	1789	WB-3/176	
Hamlin, Fanny	047	1838	WB-4/165	
Hamlin, Kitty	051	1892	WB-C/445	AR
Hamlin, Lucy	084	1899	WB-F/138	CTY
Hamlin, Richmond	084	1900	WB-F/184	CTY
Hamlin, Thomas	084	1859	WB-C/309	CTY
Hamlin, Willis	084	1900	WB-F/189	CTY
Hamlin, Wood Jones	047	1838	WB-4/163	
Hammack, John, Sr.	044	1777	WB-1/148	CTY
Hammer, Abraham	081	1851	Orig. Only	AR
Hammerskold, Hedwig M.	060	1869	WB-4/9	
Hammock, John A.	022	1890	WB-E/437	AR
Hammock, Robert	092	c1823	Orig. Only	AR
Hammond, Aaron	081	1885	WB-15/561	AR
Hammond, Albert	029	1884	WB-E/318	AR
Hammond, Alfred F.	057	1885	WB-C/108	AR
Hammond, Archelaus	072	c1773	RW/L42	AR
Hammond, Boaz	053	1795	RW-1/257	AR
Hammond, Covington	009	1875	WB-1/148	CTY
Hammond, Edward	072	1815	Orig. Only	AR
Hammond, Elizabeth Ann	009	1855	OB-I/463	AR
Hammond, Ezra	081	1876	WB-15/214	AR
Hammond, George	005	1840	WB-B/108	AR
Hammond, Hampton B.	065	1883	Copy	005 AR
Hammond, Hampton B.	065	1883	WB-K/556	AR
Hammond, Harriet	083	1883	WB-3/322	AR
Hammond, John	030	1804	WB-2/240	
Hammond, John	009	c1800	OWB/377	AR
Hammond, John	072	1823	WB-A/52	AR
Hammond, John	009	c1802	OWB/396	AR
Hammond, John B.	009	c1809	OB-A/63	AR
Hammond, John H.	009	1884	Orig. Only	AR-Copy
Hammond, Joshua	072	1819	Orig. Only	AR
Hammond, Julia Ann	009	c1883	Orig. Only	CTY
Hammond, Leroy	072	c1846	Orig. Only	AR
Hammond, Levi	009	c1803	OWB/419	AR
Hammond, Martin	072	1801	WB-A/47	AR
Hammond, Nell	009	c1802	OWB/392	AR
Hammond, Peter	085	c1788	WB-C/97	AR
Hammond, William	005	1855	WB-C/98	AR
Hammond, William	081	1864	WB-13/183	AR
Hammond, William H.	023	1896	WB-A/124	AR
Hammonds, Dicey	029	1852	WB-C/229	AR
Hammonds, Jesse	039	1814	WB-D/73	AR
Hammons, Charity	069	1872	Orig. Only	AR
Hammons, Deborah	083	1832	WB-1/266	AR
Hammons, Eaton	069	1821	Orig. Only	AR
Hammons, Elsa	029	1838	WB-B/290	AR
Hammons, Isaac	081	1866	WB-14/4	AR
Hammons, Jesse	069	1822	WB-1/308	AR
Hammons, John	083	c1811	WB-1/125	AR
Hammons, Samuel	083	1815	WB-1/158	
Hammons, Shadrach	037	1828	WB-F/92	AR
Hammons, William	027	1865	WB-A/95	AR
Hammons, William	104	1800	WB-2/10	AR
Hammons, Willie	069	1815	WB-1/268	AR
Hammontree, Enoch	028	1834	WB-C/372	AR
Hammontree, Griffin	028	1797	WB-B/21	AR
Hamon, Ambrose	104	1794	WB-1/395	AR
Hamon, James	024	1788	WB-A/43	AR
Hampleton, John	009	c1801	OWB/391	AR
Hampton, Alfred	106	1892	WB-2/325	
Hampton, Anderson	085	1894	WB-3/28	CTY
Hampton, Andrew	086	1805	WB-B/184	AR
Hampton, Celeste B.	040	1896	WB-2/508	AR
Hampton, Collins	092	1804	WB-3/65A	AR
Hampton, Cynthia	065	1895	WB-M/412	AR
Hampton, Cyrus A.	040	1899	WB-3/40	AR
Hampton, David	085	1758	WB-A/62	AR
Hampton, Eliza P.	038	1900	WB-4/251	AR
Hampton, Ephraim	085	1814	WB-G/322	AR
Hampton, Ezekiel	107	c1848	WB-1/351	
Hampton, Florence	030	1900	WB-5/286	
Hampton, Frances	104	1871	WB-6/46	AR
Hampton, G. M. F.	WV	1895	107 WB-2/80	
Hampton, George W.	023	1889	WB-A/92	AR
Hampton, Harry R.	065	1899	WB-M/239	AR
Hampton, Henry	092	c1831	WB-4/40	
Hampton, Henry C.	092	1899	WB-6/511	AR
Hampton, James	090	1801	WB-2/3b	AR
Hampton, James B.	085	1833	WB-H/687	AR
Hampton, James H.H.	030	1836	WB-4/14	
Hampton, James J.	086	1875	WB-F/71	AR
Hampton, Joel	104	1847	WB-4/339	
Hampton, John	085	1816	WB-G/432	AR
Hampton, John	085	1834	WB-H/627	AR
Hampton, John	028	c1801	Orig. Only	AR
Hampton, John	106	c1869	WB-2/46	AR
Hampton, John T.	030	1831	WB-3/273	
Hampton, John T.	030	1884	WB-5/110	AR
Hampton, John, Sr.	085	1819	WB-H/17	AR-Nunc.
Hampton, Levi	013	1872	WB-B/52	AR
Hampton, Milly	085	1816	WB-G/430	AR-Nunc.
Hampton, Pattie P.	036	1895	WB-A/343	CTY
Hampton, Samuel	090	1803	WB-2/34	AR-Nunc.
Hampton, T. J.	106	1893	WB-2/337	
Hampton, Thomas	060	1850	WB-2/339	AR
Hampton, Thomas	104	1817	WB-3/152	AR
Hampton, Thomas	019	c1766	RB-A/19	AR-Nunc.
Hampton, Turner	104	1834	WB-4/181	AR
Hampton, William	085	1813	WB-G/285	AR
Hampton, William	085	1814	WB-G/320	AR
Hampton, William	028	1802	WB-B/150	
Hampton, William W.	030	1900	WB-5/284	
Hamrick, Albert	026	c1894	Orig. Only	AR
Hamrick, Allen	026	1891	WB-2/441	AR
Hamrick, Catherine	026	1888	WB-2/367	AR
Hamrick, D. M.	026	1894	WB-2/475	AR
Hamrick, David	026	1869	WB-2/36	AR
Hamrick, David	026	1892	WB-2/450	AR
Hamrick, David	026	1863	WB-1/327	AR
Hamrick, Elijah	026	1864	WB-1/348	AR
Hamrick, Elijah	026	1863	WB-1/313	AR
Hamrick, George	086	1882	WB-F/177	AR
Hamrick, George	026	1847	WB-1/59	AR
Hamrick, J. W.	026	1862	WB-1/288	AR
Hamrick, James	026	1895	WB-2/492	AR
Hamrick, James	026	1888	WB-2/349	AR
Hamrick, Jane	026	1887	WB-2/316	AR

Name	Co.	Date	Recorded Copy	Original
Hamrick, John	026	1860	WB-1/255	AR
Hamrick, Jonathan	026	1884	WB-2/260	AR
Hamrick, L. Dow	026	1887	WB-2/321	AR
Hamrick, M. A.	026	1894	WB-2/483	AR
Hamrick, Nancy	086	1889	WB-F/373	AR
Hamrick, Nathan	026	1887	WB-2/315	AR
Hamrick, Nathan	086	1825	WB-D/35	AR
Hamrick, P. M.	026	1886	WB-2/304	AR
Hamrick, Price	026	1888	WB-2/362	AR
Hamrick, Price	086	1817	WB-C/79	AR
Hamrick, Pricilla	086	1808	WB-B/209	AR
Hamrick, Reuben	026	1863	WB-1/322	AR
Hamrick, Richard	026	1859	WB-1/241	AR
Hamrick, Samuel	026	1862	WB-1/289	AR
Hamrick, William	026	1849	WB-1/102	AR-Nunc.
Hamrick, William M.	026	1884	WB-2/277	AR
Hamrie, Bengamin	106	1871	WB-2/43	AR
Hamton, Abraham	102	1885	WB-A/44	AR
Hamton, David	054	1855	WB-3/90	AR
Hanby, John	077	1752	Orig. Only	SS/AR
Hanchey, Marten	035	1811	WB-A/203	AR
Hancock, Anna	081	1887	WB-16/37	AR
Hancock, Evachael	067	1869	WB-2/6	AR
Hancock, Everett	010	1866	WB-H/156	AR
Hancock, Grace	051	1834	WB-A/68	
Hancock, Hector	019	1752	028 DB-5/256	SS/AR
Hancock, Henry	047	1798	WB-3/304	
Hancock, Henry	019	1782	WB-D/222	AR
Hancock, James	047	1765	WB-1/161	
Hancock, James	019	1858	WB-A/219	AR
Hancock, James	073	1816	WB-D/478	AR
Hancock, James E.	047	1884	WB-6/332	AR
Hancock, Jehu	046	1833	WB-B/477	AR
Hancock, Jehu	046	1841	Orig. Only	AR-Nunc.
Hancock, John	092	1897	WB-6/445	AR
Hancock, John	029	1772	Orig. Only	AR
Hancock, John	019	1820	WB-D/254	AR
Hancock, John	047	1872	WB-6/79	AR
Hancock, Lewis W.	028	1900	WB-F/483	
Hancock, Margaret	001	1895	WB-3/43	AR
Hancock, Martha	071	1874	WB-6/132	AR
Hancock, Roger	073	1818	WB-D/531	AR
Hancock, Sarah	025	1893	WB-A/111	AR
Hancock, William	068	1797	WB-A/194	
Hancock, William	068	1848	WB-B/179	
Hancock, William	096	1794	Orig. Only	AR
Hancock, William H.	047	1880	WB-6/228	AR
Hancock, William W.	025	1870	WB-A/5	AR
Hancock, Zebedee	072	1824	WB-A/54	AR
Hand, Jonathan	065	1863	WB-J/165	AR
Hand, Joseph	028	1888	WB-E/492	AR
Hand, Margaret	070	1858	WB-C/664	AR
Hand, Peter	028	1730/1	Deeds.1/64	SS/AR
Hand, Sarah	029	1825	WB-B/132	AR
Handcock, James	028	1781	Orig. Only	AR
Handcock, John	081	1788	WB-1/51	AR
Handcock, Mary	028	1834	WB-C/373	AR
Handcock, Nathan	073	1816	WB-D/480	AR
Handcock, Nathaniel	072	1802	Orig. Only	AR
Handcock, William	028	1730/1	Deeds.1/61	SS/AR
Handcock, William	028	1770	Orig. Only	AR
Handcock, William	028	1854	WB-D/224	AR
Handcock, William	028	1746	SS 878/69	
Handley, James	103	1823	RD-5/46	AR
Handley, William	103	1839	RD-7/444	AR

Name	Co.	Date	Recorded Copy	Original
Handock, Elizabeth	028	1744	Wills.6/L87	SS/AR
Handrick, Richard	077	1712	SS 875/13	
Handworker, Daniel	077	1730	SS 876/213	SS/AR
Handy, John, Sr.	104	1857	WB-5/174	AR
Handy, Matthias	056	1803	WB-1/147	AR
Handy, Thomas	104	1865	WB-5/419	
Haneline, David	085	1900	WB-3/386	CTY
Haneline, Jacob	085	1813	WB-G/256	
Haneline, Jacob	085	1813	Copy	033 AR
Hanes, C. L.	038	1900	WB-4/207	AR
Hanes, David	032	1874	WB-3/147	AR
Hanes, Elizabeth	045	1871	WB-1/16	
Hanes, Ellis	003	1886	WB-B/188	AR
Hanes, George	090	1828	WB-3/193	AR
Hanes, Jacob	026	1876	WB-2/145	AR
Hanes, Johanna S.	032	1845	WB-1/465	
Hanes, John	032	1862	WB-2/235	AR
Hanes, Joshua	046	1813	WB-A/184	AR
Hanes, Lewis	032	1882	WB-3/350	AR
Hanes, Mahala	106	c1857	WB-1/69	AR
Hanes, Mourning	086	1843	WB-E/111	AR
Hanes, Nancy	026	1885	WB-2/285	AR
Hanes, Naomi	003	1893	WB-B/309	AR
Hanes, Phillip	085	1820	WB-H/41	AR
Hanes, Sally	085	1823	WB-H/220	AR
Hanes, Solomon	032	c1847	WB-2/6	
Hanes, Susanna	032	1834	WB-1/247	
Haney, John	086	1868	WB-E/485	AR
Haney, Judge G.	026	1868	WB-1/424	AR
Haney, Labin	081	1874	WB-15/166	AR
Haney, Sarah	087	c1814	WB-A/78	AR
Haney, Serena	072	1883	WB-4/238	AR
Haney, Thomas	069	1788	WB-1/24	AR
Haney, William S.	097	1884	WB-2/260	AR
Hanford, Randolph	024	c1780	WB-A/221	AR
Hanigan, Dennis	065	1817	WB-D/76	AR
Hankins, Dennis	012	c1781	WB-B/47	AR
Hankins, Flora	012	1900	WB-A/152	AR
Hankins, Hiram H.	070	1887	WB-F/98	AR
Hankins, James	012	1897	WB-A/127	AR
Hankins, Masters M.	070	1897	WB-H/89	AR
Hankins, Thomas	024	1807	WB-B/208	AR
Hanks, Argyle H.	044	c1867	WB-23/5	CTY
Hanks, Elijah	044	1798	WB-4/236	CTY
Hanks, Elizabeth	040	1875	WB-2/95	AR
Hanks, Fanny	044	1829	WB-11/207	CTY
Hanks, Henry	022	c1897	Orig. Only	AR
Hanks, John	022	1839	WB-C/99	AR
Hanks, John D.	044	1865	WB-22/335	CTY
Hanks, Martin	022	1878	WB-E/154	AR
Hanks, Thomas	040	1851	WB-1/37	
Hanks, William	044	1795	WB-3/191	
Hanks, William	044	1787	WB-2/38	CTY
Hanks, Willis M.	044	1817	WB-8/42	CTY
Hanland, Sarah	019	1842	WB-A/99	AR
Hanley, Daniel	073	1794	WB-B/262	AR
Hann, Elijah M.	086	1830	WB-D/115	
Hanna, John	065	c1765	WB-D/39	AR
Hanna, John	092	1794	WB-3/13	AR
Hanna, Nina C.	065	1891	WB-M/9	AR
Hanna, Robert	005	1875	WB-D/36	AR
Hanna, Thomas	040	1851	WB-1/34	AR
Hanna, Thomas M.	040	1900	WB-3/68	AR
Hanna, William	081	1824	WB-5/162	AR
Hannah, Catherine	032	1890	WB-4/78	AR

Name	Co.	Date	Recorded Copy	Original
Hannah, Fathy	005	1841	WB-B/139	AR
Hannah, John	081	1860	WB-11/422	AR
Hannah, John	094	c1767	Orig. Only	060 AR
Hannah, Joseph	085	c1797	WB-D/178	AR
Hannah, Nelly P.	073	1875	WB-H/102	CTY
Hannah, Solomon	032	1871	WB-3/44	AR
Hannah, Susan	032	1896	WB-4/298	AR
Hannah, William	073	c1785	Orig. Only	AR
Hannay, John	028	1768	Orig. Only	AR
Hanner, Alexander	046	1881	WB-E/317	AR
Hanner, Allen A.	046	1886	WB-E/453	AR
Hanner, Ann	046	1858	WB-C/506	AR
Hanner, Elmina R.	001	1891	WB-2/490	AR
Hanner, Mary E.	046	1898	WB-G/50	AR
Hanner, Robert	046	1819	WB-B/77	AR
Hanner, Roddy	046	1829	WB-B/387	AR
Hanner, Roddy E.	046	1886	WB-E/442	AR
Hanner, Samuel	092	1795	WB-3/17A	AR
Hanner, Sarah	046	1845	WB-C/239	AR
Hannis, Joseph	028	1745	Orig. Only	SS/AR
Hannon, Elizabeth	080	1855	WB-1/170	AR
Hannon, William	086	c1849	Copy	080 AR
Hannon, William	086	1854	WB-E/268	AR
Hannum, Levi T.	103	1848	RD-10/301	AR
Hanrahan, James A.	079	1891	WB-2/556	AR
Hanrahan, Walter	009	1823	OB-A/328	AR
Hanrahan, William K.	009	1838	OB-C2/59	AR
Hansbrick, Price	086	1817	WB-C/79	
Hansen, Albertina	099	1874	RB-35/239	AR
Hansen, George C.	MD	1888	025 WB-A/236	025 AR
Hansen, Henry	070	1879	WB-E/392	AR
Hansill, James	060	1848	WB-2/312	AR
Hansley, E.	056	1877	WB-3/187	AR
Hansley, Hopsy	072	1865	WB-3/8	AR
Hansley, John	072	1814	WB-A/49	AR
Hansley, William	070	1822	WB-C/174	AR
Hanson, George C.	MD	1889	061 WB-2/94	061 AR
Hanson, Jesse	037	1863	WB-G/233	AR
Hanson, John	037	1849	WB-F/417	AR
Hanson, John W.	MD	1897	025 WB-A/238	025 AR
Happoldt, Sarah A.	014	1881	WB-2/215	
Haralson, Paul	078	1805	WI-4/1	AR
Harbert, Ignatus	053	1798	RW-1/298	
Harbin, Edward	085	c1803	WB-D/193	AR
Harbin, James F.	054	1884	WB-4/570	CTY
Harbin, James F.	054	1870	WB-4/75	AR
Harbin, Julia E.	102	1897	Orig. Only	AR
Harbin, Robert	028	c1761	Orig. Only	AR
Harbison, William	060	1794	Orig. Only	AR
Harbour, Harrison	001	1883	WB-2/199	AR
Harbour, Thomas	090	1870	WB-6/10	AR
Harbrett, Edward	028	1754	SS 879/78	SS/AR
Hardaway, Jane	037	1821	WB-E/261	AR
Hardcastle, Elizabeth	036	1882	WB-A/24	CTY
Hardcastle, John	056	1780	Orig. Only	AR
Hardcastle, Mary	036	1896	WB-A/473	CTY
Hardcastle, Nancy Jane	073	1892	WB-H/568	CTY
Hardcastle, Temperance	099	1858	RB-30/535	AR
Hardcastle, William	056	1777	WB-2/285	AR
Hardee, Anna B.	059	1883	WB-A/349	CTY
Hardee, Betsey	079	1881	WB-2/218	AR
Hardee, Cordee C.	071	1877	WB-6/221	AR
Hardee, David	073	1824	WB-E/57	AR
Hardee, David C.	071	1898	WB-7/400	AR
Hardee, Guilford	047	1885	WB-6/359	AR

Name	Co.	Date	Recorded Copy	Original
Hardee, Louisa	079	1885	WB-2/320	AR
Hardee, Louise Y.	073	1864	WB-G/428	CTY
Hardee, Major	056	1849	WB-1/615	AR
Hardee, Margaret	047	1890	WB-6/574	AR
Hardee, Mariah	079	1894	WB-3/45	AR
Hardee, Pinckney	059	1873	WB-A/51	
Hardee, Thomas	039	1824	WB-H/54	AR
Hardee, Whitmel	045	1897	WB-1/387	AR
Hardee, William H.	071	1862	WB-5/262	AR
Hardee, Willie	079	1874	WB-2/91	AR
Hardee, Winney	073	1833	WB-E/298	AR
Harden, Abel	086	1830	WB-D/131	AR
Harden, David	086	1811	WB-B/260	AR
Harden, Edmund	073	c1769	WB-A/124	
Harden, George	084	1843	WB-B/297	CTY
Harden, H. L. B.	010	1893	WB-I/389	AR
Harden, James	047	1791	WB-3/193	
Harden, Mark	084	1839	WB-B/213	CTY
Harden, Nancy	069	1817	WB-1/288	AR
Harden, Peggy	084	1840	WB-B/235	CTY
Harden, Peter	084	c1819	WB-A/179	CTY
Harden, Robert	085	c1785	WB-C/126	AR
Harden, Sarah	073	1814	WB-D/418	AR
Harden, Thomas	010	1813	WB-F/230	AR
Harden, Thomas	010	1861	WB-H/106	AR
Harden, Thomas	084	c1809	WB-A/86	CTY
Harden, William	047	1791	WB-3/196	Nunc.
Harder, Austin W.	001	1863	WB-1/219	AR
Harder, Joseph	001	1874	WB-2/68	AR
Hardester, Asbery	081	1878	WB-15/286	AR
Hardesty, Benjamin	019	1833	WB-A/31	AR
Hardesty, Burton	019	1865	WB-A/265	AR
Hardesty, Joseph	019	1882	WB-B/132	AR
Hardesty, Joseph	019	1805	WB-D/241	AR
Hardesty, Thomas	019	1758	SS 882/180	SS/AR
Hardesty, William	019	1895	WB-B/276	AR
Hardie, Curtis	047	c1778	WB-2/85	
Hardie, Mary Ann	029	1895	WB-F/64	AR
Hardiman, John	046	c1774	Orig. Only	AR
Hardin, Abigail	068	1849	WB-B/206	
Hardin, Agelois	054	c1832	WB-2/145	AR
Hardin, Benjamin	026	1850	WB-1/107	AR
Hardin, Charles	046	1807	WB-A/172	AR
Hardin, Charles	046	c1853	Orig. Only	AR
Hardin, D. D.	026	1886	WB-2/332	AR
Hardin, David B.	046	1864	WB-D/197	AR
Hardin, Henry	006	1856	WB-D/22	AR
Hardin, Henry	006	1856	Copy	017 AR
Hardin, John	073	1808	WB-D/235	AR
Hardin, Mark	081	1797	WB-2/25	AR
Hardin, Mark	006	1885	WB-E/131	AR
Hardin, Mary Ann	006	1887	Orig. Only	AR
Hardin, R. T.	006	1890	WB-E/204	AR
Hardin, William	030	1748	Orig. Only	SS/AR
Hardin, William	084	c1794	OW/35	AR
Harding, Bernard A.	099	1897	WB-D/70	AR
Harding, Fanny J.	009	1866	OB-M/235	AR
Harding, Frederick	079	1892	WB-3/14	AR
Harding, George	VA	1871	071 WB-6/82	071 AR
Harding, Henry	009	1853	OB-H/249	AR
Harding, Israel	009	1824	OB-A/332	AR
Harding, James B.	071	1884	WB-6/427	AR
Harding, Jesse B.	028	1897	WB-F/272	
Harding, John	071	1816	WB-3/175	AR
Harding, Josiah	071	1756	Orig. Only	SS/AR

Name	Co.	Date	Recorded Copy	Original
Harding, Lavinia	009	1818	OB-A/289	AR
Harding, Mary	077	1744	Orig. Only	SS/AR
Harding, Nathaniel	009	1865	OB-M/271	AR
Harding, Nehemiah	020	1849	RB-Q/186	AR
Harding, Richard	077	1741	Orig. Only	SS/AR
Harding, Squire B.	106	1888	WB-2/263	
Harding, Stephen	009	c1802	OWB/403	AR
Harding, Susanna	071	1842	WB-4/248	AR
Harding, Thomas	084	1844	WB-C/16	CTY
Harding, William B.	VA	1845	071 WB-5/13	
Harding, Wyatt	071	1829	WB-4/58	AR
Hardison, Ann M.	009	1859	OB-L/70	AR
Hardison, Asa M.	028	1856	WB-D/256	AR
Hardison, Benjamin	063	c1785	WB-1/118	
Hardison, Charles	028	1807	WB-B/293	AR
Hardison, David	063	1817	WB-2/48	
Hardison, Elizabeth	009	1876	WB-1/156	CTY
Hardison, Elzy S.	072	1867	WB-3/14	AR
Hardison, Esther	063	1823	WB-2/92	
Hardison, Gabriel	028	1884	WB-E/360	
Hardison, Hannah	063	1815	WB-2/26	
Hardison, Isaac	053	1805	RW-1/384	AR
Hardison, Jasper	002	1733	SS 876/279	SS/AR
Hardison, Jasper	028	1866	WB-D/432	AR
Hardison, Jesse	070	1858	WB-C/667	AR
Hardison, Jesse	063	1859	WB-2/457	
Hardison, Jesse	072	1827	WB-1/12	AR
Hardison, John	072	c1785	WI/L52	AR
Hardison, John	063	1780	WB-1/61	
Hardison, John B.	009	1857	OB-K/274	AR
Hardison, Joseph	063	1788	WB-1/143	
Hardison, Lemuel	053	1806	RW-1/392	AR
Hardison, Martha	009	1844	OB-E/354	AR
Hardison, Noah	063	1878	WB-3/136	
Hardison, Sarah D.	072	1898	WB-4/387	AR
Hardison, Stephen F.	028	1853	WB-D/218	AR
Hardison, William	063	c1797	WB-1/326	
Hardister, Elijah	081	1888	WB-16/73	AR
Hardister, Elisha	081	1868	WB-14/208	AR
Hardister, Ezekiel	067	1868	WB-2/2	AR
Hardister, William L.	039	1889	WB-U/465	AR
Hardman, Mary	085	c1806	WB-E/121	AR
Hardman, Peter	032	c1839	WB-2/28	
Hardt (Connel), Sarah	040	1885	WB-2/242	AR
Hardwick, Aaron	015	1765	RB-1/28	AR
Hardwick, George	009	c1785	OWB/200	AR
Hardy, Agnes	024	1782	WB-B/160	AR
Hardy, Allen	045	1871	WB-1/13	
Hardy, Benjamin	105	1885	WB-2/379	AR
Hardy, Benjamin	099	1775	RB-1/75	AR
Hardy, Benjamin	010	1821	WB-G/87	AR
Hardy, Caroline	047	1888	WB-6/494	AR
Hardy, Charles	010	c1816	Orig. Only	AR
Hardy, Charles	010	c1816	Orig. Only	AR
Hardy, Charles	010	c1817	Copy	037 AR
Hardy, Charles	010	1818	WB-G/43	AR
Hardy, Curtis	100	1858	WB-49/158	AR
Hardy, Edward	047	1896	WB-7/163	AR
Hardy, Edward	030	1837	WB-4/37	
Hardy, Eleanor	010	1852	WB-G/487	AR
Hardy, Elizabeth	047	1877	WB-6/163	AR
Hardy, Ella E.	010	1880	WB-I/124	
Hardy, Francis M.	047	1867	WB-5/164	
Hardy, Henry	047	1825	WB-4/15	
Hardy, Hugh	047	1763	WB-1/95	
Hardy, Humphrey	010	1861	WB-H/100	AR
Hardy, Humphrey	010	1810	WB-F/139	AR
Hardy, James M.	LA	1900	010 WB-K/38	
Hardy, Jesse	069	1895	WB-5/505	AR
Hardy, John	056	1854	WB-1/682	AR
Hardy, John	047	1774	WB-1/345	
Hardy, John	024	1719	SS 875/233	SS/AR
Hardy, John H.	010	1885	WB-I/183	
Hardy, John Sutton	059	1883	WB-A/364	CTY
Hardy, Joseph	010	1897	WB-I/508	AR
Hardy, Lamb	010	1797	WB-E/9	AR
Hardy, Lemuel	045	1846	Orig. Only	AR-Copy
Hardy, Levi S.	059	1881	WB-A/220	CTY
Hardy, Lydia	030	1853	WB-4/178	AR
Hardy, Martha	010	1813	WB-F/242	AR
Hardy, Martha T.	010	1869	WB-I/15	AR
Hardy, Mary	047	1846	WB-4/250	
Hardy, Mary Ann	059	1869	WB-A/6	
Hardy, Phineas	035	1897	WB-4/500	
Hardy, Pinckney	079	1891	WB-2/573	AR
Hardy, Rebecca	100	1884	WB-51/182	AR
Hardy, Richard	070	1758	SS 882/41	SS/AR
Hardy, Richard	070	1758	WB-C/135	AR-Copy
Hardy, Robert	024	1781	WB-B/159	AR-Nunc.
Hardy, Robert	024	1779	WB-A/26	AR
Hardy, Robert	037	1820	WB-E/239	AR
Hardy, Rosa	059	1881	WB-A/259	CTY
Hardy, Samuel	100	1859	WB-49/232	AR
Hardy, Sarah	010	1809	WB-F/118	AR
Hardy, Thomas A.	VA	1876	044 WB-23/261	044 CTY
Hardy, Thomas B.	010	1860	WB-H/94	AR
Hardy, Thomas E.	071	1889	WB-7/41	AR
Hardy, William	010	1784	WB-C/70	AR
Hardy, William I.	010	1841	WB-G/332	AR
Hare, Brian	041	1879	WB-4/122	AR
Hare, Edward	051	1777	Orig. Only	SS/AR
Hare, Edward	024	1757	Orig. Only	SS/AR
Hare, Elisha	041	1808	WB-2/5	AR
Hare, Jackson B.	051	1900	WB-C/573	
Hare, Jackson B.	051	1900	Copy	041 AR
Hare, Jacob	010	1858	WB-H/58	AR
Hare, Jesse	037	1774	WB-A/219	AR
Hare, John	041	1819	WB-2/157	AR
Hare, John	056	c1855	WB-1/690	AR
Hare, John	044	1821	WB-9/5	CTY
Hare, John Porter	009	c1784	OWB/186	AR
Hare, Joseph	041	1825	WB-2/233	AR
Hare, Martha	105	1858	WB-1/43	
Hare, Mary	041	1788	WB-1/75	AR
Hare, Mary	041	1894	WB-4/388	AR
Hare, Mary	041	1895	WB-4/399	AR
Hare, Moses	041	1794	WB-1/127	AR
Hare, Moses, Jr.	041	1794	WB-1/122	AR
Hare, Priscilla	069	1850	037 WB-F/462	037 AR
Hare, Reddin	087	1898	WB-4/65	AR
Hare, Thomas	010	1786	WB-D/47	AR
Hare, Thomas E.	010	1815	Orig. Only	AR
Haren, Margaret	092	1789	WB-2/81	AR
Harfoot, Robert	009	1759	OWB/61	AR
Harford, Mark	028	1774	Orig. Only	AR
Harford, Nicholas	085	1762	WB-A/67	AR
Harford, Wateman	028	1868	WB-D/464	AR
Harget, Abner	028	1817	WB-C/152	AR
Harget, Elizabeth	028	1834	WB-C/377	AR
Harget, Frederick	028	1810	WB-C/2	AR

Name	Co.	Date	Recorded Copy	Original
Harget, Lucy	028	1857	WB-D/283	AR
Harget, Peter	057	1841	WB-B/149	AR
Hargett, A. J.	097	1895	WB-2/536	AR
Hargett, Abner	057	1882	WB-C/85	AR
Hargett, David	097	1886	WB-2/285	AR
Hargett, Elisabeth	097	1889	WB-2/337	AR
Hargett, Henry	065	1827	WB-D/90	AR
Hargett, Henry	065	1803	WB-C/147	AR
Hargett, James C.	097	1897	WB-2/510	
Hargett, John	097	1881	WB-2/196	
Hargett, Joseph	097	1844	WB-1/12	AR
Hargett, Joseph C.	059	1900	WB-B/289	CTY
Hargett, Peter	057	1797	WB-A/198	AR
Hargett, Rebecca C.	097	1885	WB-2/274	AR
Hargis, Abraham	078	1827	WI-11/50	AR
Hargis, Elizabeth	078	1851	WB-13/440	AR
Hargis, Lavira	078	1893	WB-19/359	AR
Hargis, Lawrence P.	078	1842	WI-15/159	
Hargis, Martha	078	1851	WB-13/523	AR
Hargis, O. V.	078	1888	WB-19/233	
Hargis, Richard	078	1800	WI-2/260	AR
Hargis, Romulus	078	1893	WB-19/343	AR
Hargis, Shadrack	078	1816	WI-7/85	
Hargis, Susanna	078	1884	WB-19/163	
Hargis, Thomas	078	1888	WB-19/221	AR
Hargrave, Alfred	070	1898	WB-H/132	AR
Hargrave, Hal	032	1885	WB-3/481	AR
Hargrave, Jennie	032	1891	WB-4/92	AR
Hargrave, Jesse	073	1854	WB-G/61	AR
Hargrave, Kate D.	065	1897	WB-N/12	AR
Hargrave, Lemuel H.	071	1866	WB-5/332	AR
Hargrave, Margaret	073	1863	WB-G/404	AR
Hargrave, Mary L.	071	1875	WB-6/173	AR
Hargrave, Naomi	046	1799	WB-A/165	AR
Hargrave, Sarah F.	071	1880	WB-6/330	AR
Hargrave, Walter C.	032	1885	WB-3/487	AR
Hargraves, J. C.	054	1884	WB-4/504	CTY
Hargraves, Richard	044	1766	Orig. Only	CTY
Hargrove, Ann W.	087	1871	WB-3/57	AR
Hargrove, Arthur	087	c1815	WB-A/80	AR
Hargrove, Carr	029	1853	WB-C/247	AR
Hargrove, Charles M.	098	1886	WB-A/56	CTY
Hargrove, Duncan	037	1871	WB-G/368	AR
Hargrove, Hartwell	098	1891	WB-A/136	CTY
Hargrove, Israel W.	044	1867	WB-22/650	CTY
Hargrove, James B.	037	1864	WB-G/253	AR
Hargrove, Jesse	032	1830	WB-1/139	
Hargrove, John	044	1792	WB-2/326	CTY
Hargrove, John	065	1795	WB-D/56	AR
Hargrove, John	098	1900	WB-A/350	CTY
Hargrove, John	035	1811	WB-A/215	AR
Hargrove, Mary A.	044	1842	WB-15/338	CTY
Hargrove, Sallie	087	1887	WB-3/356	AR
Hargrove, Samuel H.	037	1874	WB-G/444	AR
Hargrove, Tazwell L.	044	1889	WB-24/98	CTY
Hargrove, Tazwell L.	044	1889	078 WB-19/354	078 AR
Hargrove, William	044	1848	WB-17/412	CTY
Hargrove, William	047	1777	WB-2/34	
Harison, J. W.	071	1830	WB-4/73	
Harison, John	024	1694	SS 874.2/43	
Hariss, Roe	047	1790	WB-3/190	
Harkel, George	028	1746	SS 878/103	SS/AR
Harker, Clarissa	019	1836	WB-A/65	AR
Harker, Eben	019	1803	WB-D/234	AR
Harker, Ebenezer	019	1765	RB-A/4	AR
Harker, Elisebeth	019	1777	Orig. Only	SS/AR
Harker, James	019	1814	WB-D/245	AR
Harker, John	019	1867	WB-B/36	AR
Harker, Ruth	019	1827	WB-D/261	AR
Harker, William	028	1822	WB-C/221	AR
Harker, Zachariah	019	1824	WB-E/38	
Harkey, Daniel	097	1868	WB-1/294	AR
Harkey, J. F.	097	1884	WB-2/247	AR
Harkey, John	065	1821	WB-D/79	AR
Harkey, John	097	1883	WB-2/225	AR
Harkey, John M.	016	1886	WB-3/506	AR
Harkey, Mary	085	1826	WB-H/359	AR
Harkey, Peter	065	1870	WB-K/43	AR
Harkey, Soloman	065	1886	WB-L/156	AR
Harkill, Sarah	019	1846	WB-A/129	AR
Harkness, George	065	1809	WB-C/153	AR
Harky, George	016	1828	WB-A/23	AR
Harlan, Abigail	081	1885	WB-15/483	AR
Harlan, Elizabeth	081	1875	WB-15/202	AR
Harlan, Jonathan	081	1875	WB-15/198	
Harlan, Mary	081	1886	WB-16/7	AR
Harle, Sarah	010	1779	WB-B/146	AR
Harlen, Enoch	081	1897	WB-16/420	AR
Harleston, John, Jr.	SC	1783	012 DB-B/286	
Harlow, Enoch	081	1863	WB-12/473	
Harlow, Stephen	081	1830	WB-6/77	AR
Harlowe, John	024	c1762	Orig. Only	AR
Harman, Abraham	051	1831	WB-A/170	
Harman, Abraham	051	1823	WB-A/113	
Harman, Adam	032	c1859	WB-2/284	AR
Harman, Adam	032	c1847	WB-2/18	
Harman, Caleb	077	1774	Orig. Only	SS/AR
Harman, David	060	1828	WB-1/80	AR
Harman, Eli	006	1829	Orig. Only	AR
Harman, George	022	1853	WB-C/354	AR
Harman, Hezekiah	022	1873	WB-E/107	AR
Harman, James H.	022	1892	WB-E/497	AR
Harman, John	094	1774	Orig. Only	060 AR
Harman, John	077	1758	SS 882/113	
Harman, Parker	010	1877	WB-I/87	
Harman, Peter	060	1794	Orig. Only	AR
Harman, Robert	077	1758	Orig. Only	SS/AR
Harman, Robert	077	1729	SS 875/269	
Harman, Robert	N	1715	SS 875/102	
Harmon, Andrew	086	1863	WB-E/409	AR
Harmon, Christian	010	1868	WB-I/2	AR
Harmon, George, Jr.	021	1850	Orig. Only	AR
Harmon, Henry	026	1855	WB-1/187	AR
Harmon, Jacob	081	c1822	Orig. Only	AR
Harmon, John	026	1876	WB-2/148	AR
Harmon, Julia A.	060	c1884	Orig. Only	AR
Harmon, Nicholas	010	1802	WB-E/157	AR
Harmon, Phebe	032	1892	WB-4/151	AR
Harmon, Rachel	060	1841	WB-2/75	AR
Harmon, Richard	060	1839	WB-2/11	AR
Harmon, Richard T.	010	1871	WB-I/32	AR
Harmon, Riddick H.	010	1889	WB-I/262	AR
Harmon, William	060	1813	Orig. Only	AR
Harmons, Lewis	099	1812	RB-10/231	AR
Harnett, Cornelius	070	1782	WB-AB/484	
Harnett, Mary	NY	1792	070 WB-AB/486	070 AR
Harp, B. F.	099	1895	WB-C/398	
Harp, Elizabeth	077	1825	WB-F/93	
Harp, John	099	1862	RB-32/336	AR
Harp, N. S.	099	1884	WB-A/509	AR

Name	Co.	Date	Recorded Copy	Original
Harp, Raford	026	1855	WB-1/184	AR
Harp, Valentine	077	1781	Orig. Only	AR
Harper, Ambrose	047	1815	WB-3/576	
Harper, Andrew J.	047	1881	WB-6/271	AR
Harper, Ann	028	1815	WB-C/110	AR
Harper, Banister	056	1860	WB-1/740	AR
Harper, Bartley	056	1885	WB-3/396	AR
Harper, Blany, Jr.	045	1825	WB-1/145	
Harper, Charlotte	059	1879	WB-A/173	CTY
Harper, Daniel	035	1871	WB-4/44	AR
Harper, Elizabeth	038	c1857	WB-1/174	AR
Harper, Elizabeth	069	1894	WB-5/454	AR
Harper, F. M.	050	1888	WB-2/33	
Harper, George W.	047	1862	WB-5/107	
Harper, Henry	047	1766	WB-1/200	
Harper, J. R. M.	045	1866	WB-1/49	
Harper, James	017	1879	WB-B/84	AR
Harper, James	039	c1848	WB-O/336	AR
Harper, Jane	090	1828	WB-3/194	Nunc.
Harper, Jeduthon	081	1820	Orig. Only	AR
Harper, Jesse	081	1851	WB-9/271	AR
Harper, Jesse	044	1787	WB-2/5	CTY
Harper, John	056	1897	WB-4/57	
Harper, John	019	c1762	WB-D/215	AR
Harper, John	056	1860	WB-1/734	AR
Harper, John	081	1828	WB-5/453	AR
Harper, John, Sr.	056	1834	WB-1/503	AR
Harper, Joseph	039	1898	WB-V/128	AR
Harper, Joseph J.	039	1876	WB-U/154	AR
Harper, Joseph K.	069	1881	WB-5/119	AR
Harper, Judith	038	1895	WB-3/538	AR
Harper, Katy	017	1879	WB-B/89	AR
Harper, Lott	013	1866	WB-A/244	AR
Harper, Margaret	047	1833	WB-4/95	
Harper, Martha	022	1877	WB-E/160	AR
Harper, Martha A.	079	1900	WB-3/209	AR
Harper, Mary	022	1875	WB-E/104	AR
Harper, Mary	105	1895	WB-3/137	AR
Harper, Mary S.	067	1884	WB-2/209	AR
Harper, Peter	028	1816	WB-C/138	AR
Harper, Reddick	056	1864	WB-2/60	AR
Harper, Samuel	100	1818	WB-21/167	AR
Harper, Sarah	065	c1804	WB-C/148	AR
Harper, Sarah	037	1862	WB-G/223	AR
Harper, Stephen	037	1863	WB-G/233	AR
Harper, Susan	037	1874	WB-G/459	AR
Harper, W. B.	037	1877	WB-G/549	AR
Harper, William	047	1849	WB-4/272	
Harper, William	085	c1793	WB-D/174	AR
Harper, William A.	038	1894	WB-3/491	AR
Harper, William G.	047	1892	WB-7/56	AR
Harper, William H.	069	1884	WB-5/203	AR
Harper, Williamson	069	1849	WB-1/516	AR
Harper, Winnifred	059	1895	WB-B/148	CTY
Harper, Zephaniah	090	1830	WB-3/210	AR
Harrawood, John	085	1813	WB-G/260	AR
Harrel, Elizabeth	063	1816	WB-2/36	
Harrel, Jacob	063	1815	WB-2/28	
Harrel, John	066	1874	Orig. Only	AR
Harrel, Samuel	103	1793	Orig. Only	AR
Harrel, Wilson	072	c1816	WB-A/50	
Harrell, A. G.	026	1881	WB-2/216	
Harrell, Abner	051	1865	WB-B/66	AR
Harrell, Abraham	010	1755	Orig. Only	SS/AR
Harrell, Abraham	041	1810	WB-2/59	AR

Name	Co.	Date	Recorded Copy	Original
Harrell, Absolem	024	1789	WB-A/39	AR
Harrell, Agatha	041	1878	WB-4/110	AR
Harrell, Alice	024	N. D.	Orig. Only	AR
Harrell, Amos	010	1806	WB-F/11	AR
Harrell, Angee	063	1858	WB-2/455	
Harrell, Anne	103	c1806	WI-B/415	AR
Harrell, Arthur	010	1850	WB-G/468	AR
Harrell, Benjamin	010	1809	WB-F/127	AR
Harrell, Benjamin	010	1775	WB-B/40	AR
Harrell, Burr H.	103	1859	RD-13/37	AR
Harrell, Christopher	010	1772	WB-A/155	AR-Nunc.
Harrell, Christopher	037	1844	WB-F/306	AR
Harrell, Cristian	041	1795	WB-1/239	AR
Harrell, D. C.	010	1898	WB-I/569	
Harrell, Daniel	083	1889	WB-3/456	AR
Harrell, David	010	1779	WB-B/140	AR
Harrell, David	075	1826	WB-N/30	AR
Harrell, David	046	1821	WB-B/126	AR
Harrell, David	046	1824	WB-B/182	AR
Harrell, David	010	1768	WB-A/96	AR
Harrell, Dempsey H.	051	1868	WB-B/107	AR
Harrell, Demsey	041	1812	WB-2/74	AR
Harrell, Dorsey	010	1889	WB-I/281	AR
Harrell, Edward	010	1754	SS 879/170	SS/AR
Harrell, Edward	063	1877	WB-3/118	
Harrell, Elijah	010	1795	WB-D/301	AR
Harrell, Elisha	041	1840	WB-3/23	AR
Harrell, Elisha	037	1867	WB-G/306	AR
Harrell, Elisha	083	1823	WB-1/221	AR
Harrell, Elizabeth	046	1830	WB-B/428	AR
Harrell, Elizabeth	063	1860	WB-2/465	
Harrell, Emily A.	063	1872	WB-3/28	
Harrell, Ewen	055	1899	WB-A/164	
Harrell, Ezekiel	010	1764	WB-A/45	AR
Harrell, F. D. M.	037	1882	WB-G/629	AR
Harrell, Francis	010	1763	WB-A/26	AR
Harrell, Hardy	083	1869	WB-3/7	AR
Harrell, Henry	010	1777	WB-B/66	AR
Harrell, Hezekiah	063	1816	WB-2/39	
Harrell, Hezekiah	010	1801	WB-E/134	AR
Harrell, Hugh W.	083	1892	WB-3/578	AR
Harrell, Isaac	041	1806	WB-1/234	AR
Harrell, Isaac	041	1805	WB-1/221	AR
Harrell, Isaac S.	041	1862	WB-3/290	AR
Harrell, Isaac, Sr.	010	1815	WB-F/288	AR
Harrell, Israel H.	010	1783	WB-C/59	AR
Harrell, Jacob	022	1803	WB-A/85	AR
Harrell, Jacob	035	1878	WB-4/137	AR
Harrell, James	010	1785	WB-D/8	AR
Harrell, James	010	1864	WB-H/150	AR
Harrell, James	010	1810	WB-F/169	AR
Harrell, James	010	1878	WB-I/95	
Harrell, James J.	047	1876	WB-6/139	AR
Harrell, Jarrett N.	051	1892	WB-C/446	Nunc.
Harrell, Jeconiah	010	1866	WB-H/176	AR
Harrell, Jemima	010	1826	WB-G/152	AR
Harrell, Jesse	063	1841	WB-2/283	
Harrell, Jesse	010	1788	WB-D/82	AR
Harrell, Jesse	041	1837	WB-2/390	AR
Harrell, Jesse	105	1898	Copy	037 AR
Harrell, Jesse	105	1898	WB-3/299	AR
Harrell, Jesse	083	c1810	WB-1/202	AR
Harrell, Jethro	041	1784	WB-1/36	AR
Harrell, Jethro	041	1847	WB-3/90	AR
Harrell, John	051	1846	WB-A/235	

Name	Co.	Date	Recorded Copy	Original
Harrell, John	010	1769	WB-A/121	AR
Harrell, John	010	1777	WB-B/92	AR
Harrell, John	010	1814	WB-F/270	AR
Harrell, John	010	1759	SS 881/180	SS/AR
Harrell, John	010	1781	WB-C/25	AR
Harrell, John A.	010	1896	WB-I/490	AR
Harrell, John P.	010	1885	WB-I/186	
Harrell, John R.	063	c1858	WB-2/513	
Harrell, John T.	051	1846	WB-A/253	
Harrell, John W.	051	1894	WB-C/493	AR
Harrell, John, Jr.	010	1756	SS 880/164	SS/AR
Harrell, Joshua	010	1789	WB-D/107	AR
Harrell, Joshua	063	1856	WB-2/427	
Harrell, Joshua	010	1810	WB-F/167	AR
Harrell, Joshua	010	1885	WB-I/199	
Harrell, Josiah	010	1773	Orig. Only	SS/AR
Harrell, Josiah	010	1783	WB-C/67	AR
Harrell, Josiah	041	1825	WB-2/230	AR
Harrell, Judith	041	1833	WB-2/319	AR
Harrell, Kader	010	1781	WB-C/23	AR
Harrell, Lamuell	010	1781	WB-C/2	AR
Harrell, Lelah	010	1783	WB-C/68	AR
Harrell, Linda E.	035	1891	WB-4/394	AR
Harrell, Louisa F.	070	1899	WB-H/175	AR
Harrell, Lucretia	069	1838	WB-1/422	AR
Harrell, Luke	063	1857	WB-2/440	
Harrell, M. W.	010	1891	WB-I/320	AR
Harrell, Margaret	084	1869	WB-E/7	CTY
Harrell, Margret	010	1803	WB-E/197	AR
Harrell, Mary	063	1895	WB-4/181	AR
Harrell, Mary	041	1834	WB-2/341	AR
Harrell, Mary	075	1840	WB-N/157	AR
Harrell, Mary	010	1840	WB-G/325	AR
Harrell, Mary E.	041	1898	WB-4/440	AR
Harrell, Mary F.	063	1872	WB-3/27	
Harrell, Mary J.	041	1891	WB-4/312	AR
Harrell, Mills	005	c1820	WB-2/52	AR
Harrell, Mingen	041	1875	WB-4/67	AR
Harrell, Nancy	041	1858	WB-3/232	AR
Harrell, Nathan	041	1860	WB-3/257	AR
Harrell, Noah	041	1847	WB-3/107	AR
Harrell, Penelope	076	1895	WB-A1/196	AR
Harrell, Penelope	010	1853	WB-G/502	AR
Harrell, Penelope	041	1842	WB-3/32	AR
Harrell, Peter	041	1802	WB-1/194	AR
Harrell, Powell	010	1837	WB-G/279	AR
Harrell, Rebecca	072	1855	WB-2/148	AR
Harrell, Rebecca A.	010	1898	WB-I/567	
Harrell, Reuben	005	1819	WB-2/51	AR
Harrell, Riddick	010	1873	WB-I/49	AR
Harrell, Rutha	079	1896	WB-3/94	AR
Harrell, Samuel	041	1811	WB-2/64	AR
Harrell, Samuel	024	c1761	WB-A/14	AR
Harrell, Samuel	063	c1801	WB-1/405	
Harrell, Samuel	037	1825	WB-F/32	AR
Harrell, Samuel R.	063	1884	WB-3/248	
Harrell, Samuel R.	041	1864	WB-3/314	AR
Harrell, Sarah	056	1807	WB-1/206	AR
Harrell, Selah	010	1783	WB-C/68	
Harrell, Sophia	084	1855	WB-C/207	CTY
Harrell, Susan	037	1887	WB-H/95	AR
Harrell, Susana	051	1865	WB-B/59	
Harrell, Thomas	077	1831	WB-F/151	
Harrell, Thomas	010	1791	WB-D/186	AR
Harrell, Thomas	037	1763	WB-A/119	AR
Harrell, Thomas	041	1824	WB-2/217	AR
Harrell, Thomas	041	1808	WB-2/26	AR
Harrell, U. G.	103	1864	RD-13/737	AR
Harrell, Virginia	077	1896	WB-H/286 & 296	AR
Harrell, Virginia	077	c1895	010 WB-I/513	010 AR
Harrell, William	010	1807	WB-F/35	AR
Harrell, William	024	c1762	WB-A/5	AR
Harrell, William	041	1834	WB-2/352	AR
Harrell, William	066	1898	WB-1/165	AR
Harrell, William H.	041	1877	WB-4/84	AR
Harrell, Willis W.	041	1858	WB-3/225	AR
Harrell, Wilson	072	c1816	WB-A/50	AR
Harrell, Winnefrid	010	1793	WB-D/234	AR
Harrelson, Elkanah	020	1781	RB-A/134	AR
Harrelson, Ezekiel	020	1779	RB-A/85	AR
Harrelson, Isabella	020	1892	WB-B/118	CTY
Harrelson, James F.	040	1891	WB-2/390	AR
Harrelson, James M.	020	1867	RB-T/241	AR
Harrelson, John L.	020	1884	WB-A/463	AR-Copy
Harrelson, Martha	020	1837	RB-N/48	AR
Harrelson, Mary J.	020	c1869	WB-A/496	CTY
Harrelson, Nathaniel	020	1781	RB-A/133	AR
Harrelson, Parthenia	020	1896	WB-B/274	CTY
Harrelson, William	040	1877	WB-2/111	AR
Harrelson, William E.	020	1866	RB-T/202	AR
Harrelson, Williamson	020	1889	WB-B/11	CTY
Harriet, Thomas	077	c1831	WB-F/191	
Harriett, Eliza W.	057	1877	WB-C/50	AR
Harriett, James	057	1877	WB-C/53	AR
Harrill, A. M.	086	1878	WB-F/133	AR
Harrill, A. S.	086	1886	WB-F/284	AR
Harrill, Abram G.	060	1900	WB-5/147	AR
Harrill, Drury	026	1862	WB-1/275	AR
Harrill, Howard	086	1809	WB-B/229	
Harrill, Howsen	026	1887	WB-2/323	AR
Harrill, J. B.	086	1890	WB-F/395	AR
Harrill, John H.	026	1874	WB-2/104	AR
Harrill, N. S.	026	1880	WB-2/213	AR
Harrill, Richard	077	1762	WB-C/18	AR
Harrill, Samuel	086	1871	WB-F/21	AR
Harrill, Samuel	010	1772	WB-A/162	AR
Harrill, Samuel C.	086	1862	WB-E/393	AR
Harrill, William	086	1881	WB-F/160	AR
Harrill, William	086	1886	WB-F/269	AR
Harrill, William A.	026	1863	WB-1/316	AR
Harrilson, Burges	073	c1772	WB-A/152	
Harrington, Austin B.	048	1899	WB-1/104	
Harrington, Charles	005	1796	WB-A/42	
Harrington, Charles G.	022	1881	WB-E/229	AR
Harrington, Eugenia	068	1889	WB-D/303	
Harrington, Henry W.	082	1868	WB-5/23	AR
Harrington, Henry W.	082	1809	WB-1/137	AR
Harrington, Humphrey	077	c1713	SS 875/18	
Harrington, Isaac	018	1823	WB-C/27	
Harrington, John	022	1879	WB-E/192	AR
Harrington, John, Sr.	005	1863	WB-C/197	AR
Harrington, Mary	048	1897	WB-1/68	CTY
Harrington, Phillamon	022	1803	WB-A/83	AR
Harrington, Rosana	005	1829	WB-A/164	AR
Harrington, Sion	068	1830	WB-B/75	
Harrington, Tabitha	079	1887	WB-2/379	AR
Harrington, Thomas	068	1852	WB-B/249	
Harrington, Thomas	086	1790	Orig. Only	AR
Harrington, Thomas	068	1889	WB-D/324	

Name	Co.	Date	Recorded Copy	Original
Harrington, William D.	068	1888	WB-D/272	
Harris, Abby	016	1856	WB-1/274	AR
Harris, Agness	100	1855	WB-44/108	AR
Harris, Alexander	054	1870	WB-4/60	AR
Harris, Alexander	065	1897	WB-M/589	AR
Harris, Alice	047	1825	WB-4/17	
Harris, Amos	010	1824	WB-G/120	
Harris, Anderson	078	1889	WB-19/244	AR
Harris, Ann Eliza	053	1898	WB-11/338	AR
Harris, Archelaus	005	1894	WB-D/353	AR
Harris, Arlos	073	1847	WB-F/390	AR
Harris, Arthur	037	1784	WB-B/137	AR
Harris, Augustus	044	1852	WB-19/105	CTY
Harris, Bansey	067	1884	WB-2/186	
Harris, Benjamin	022	1821	WB-B/39	AR
Harris, Benjamin	047	1821	WB-3/661	
Harris, Benjamin	055	c1872	WB-A/7	
Harris, Benjamin	022	1867	WB-D/160	AR
Harris, Benjamin C.	071	1887	WB-6/580	AR
Harris, Betsy	100	1864	WB-50/134	AR
Harris, C. F.	046	1896	WB-F/506	
Harris, Caroline	070	1891	WB-F/484	AR
Harris, Catharine	078	1885	WB-19/188	
Harris, Catharine	070	1854	WB-C/567	AR
Harris, Catherine	016	1843	WB-1/8	AR
Harris, Cecelia	065	1822	WB-D/79	
Harris, Charity	024	1852	WB-C/336	AR
Harris, Charles	044	1811	WB-7/176	CTY
Harris, Charles	075	1887	WB-O/265	AR
Harris, Charles	016	1825	WB-A/99	AR
Harris, Charles	065	1777	WB-D/41	AR
Harris, Charles B.	046	1867	WB-D/363	AR
Harris, Charles H.	056	1872	WB-3/78	AR
Harris, Charles W.	005	1804	WB-2/54	AR
Harris, Charles W.	084	1866	WB-D/55	CTY
Harris, Charlton	024	1881	WB-E/94	AR
Harris, Churchill	099	1891	WB-B/558	AR
Harris, Cicero F.	046	1896	WB-E/506	AR
Harris, Cornelius	071	1871	WB-6/68	AR
Harris, Daniel	084	1804	WB-A/13	CTY
Harris, Daniel	099	1780	RB-1/148	AR
Harris, Daniel	086	1821	WB-C/163	
Harris, David	046	1800	WB-A/168	AR
Harris, Dempsey	075	1893	WB-O/404	AR
Harris, Dicey	073	1836	WB-E/386	AR
Harris, Drury A.	078	1874	WB-19/37	AR
Harris, E. D. C.	054	1875	WB-4/170	CTY
Harris, Easter	075	1778	WB-K/30	AR
Harris, Ebenezer	053	1806	RW-1/390	AR
Harris, Edmund	096	c1800	WB-2/2	
Harris, Edmund E.	099	1875	RB-35/316	AR
Harris, Edney M.	044	1897	WB-24/379	CTY
Harris, Edward	044	1807	WB-6/370	CTY
Harris, Edward	073	1801	WB-D/36	AR
Harris, Edward W.	032	1863	WB-2/239	AR
Harris, Edwin R.	016	1869	WB-3/8	AR
Harris, Eleanor	065	1825	WB-D/85	AR
Harris, Eli	032	c1857	WB-2/155	
Harris, Elias	047	1788	WB-3/156	
Harris, Eliza	100	1892	WB-51/339	AR
Harris, Eliza	071	1881	WB-6/351	AR
Harris, Eliza J.	039	1889	WB-U/470	AR
Harris, Elizabeth	067	1843	WB-1/3	AR
Harris, Elizabeth	100	1856	WB-49/64	AR
Harris, Elizabeth	097	1876	WB-2/99	

Name	Co.	Date	Recorded Copy	Original
Harris, Elizabeth	021	1872	WB-2/70	AR
Harris, Elizabeth	016	1835	PQS.5/343	AR
Harris, Elizabeth	016	1813	WB-A/42	AR
Harris, Elizabeth	021	1885	WB-2/312	
Harris, Ellenor	053	1837	WB-6/2	AR
Harris, Emeline B.	044	1892	036 WB-A/241	036 CTY
Harris, Emeline B.	044	1892	WB-24/188	CTY
Harris, Ephraim	075	1871	WB-O/20	
Harris, Ephraim D.	016	1816	WB-A/43	AR
Harris, Faithy	VA	c1855	099 WB-A/297	099 AR
Harris, Fannie L.	098	c1895	WB-A/239	
Harris, Fealman	046	1838	WB-B/595	AR
Harris, Feilman	046	1838	WB-B/596	AR
Harris, Frances	099	1841	RB-24/500	AR
Harris, Francis	071	1881	WB-6/346	AR
Harris, Franklin	084	1878	WB-E/142	
Harris, George	044	1820	WB-8/360	CTY
Harris, George A.	044	1874	WB-23/144	CTY
Harris, George R.	053	1886	WB-11/166	AR
Harris, George W.	099	1893	WB-C/180	AR
Harris, Gideon	047	1788	WB-3/145	
Harris, Gideon	100	1844	WB-38/305	AR
Harris, Grace	065	1803	WB-D/66	AR
Harris, Grizzle	016	1831	PQS.5/192	AR
Harris, Harbert H.	039	c1853	WB-O/332	AR
Harris, Hardy	044	1832	WB-12/350	CTY
Harris, Henderson	004	1890	WB-A/107	AR
Harris, Henry	075	1864	WB-N/250	AR
Harris, Henry	022	1879	WB-D/178	AR
Harris, Henry	100	1838	WB-37/88	AR
Harris, Henry	100	1876	WB-51/118	AR
Harris, Henry H.	028	1800	WB-B/108	AR
Harris, Henry N.	100	1838	WB-37/88	
Harris, Herbert	064	c1860	Orig. Only	AR
Harris, Hope	046	1880	WB-E/286	AR
Harris, Howell	039	1864	WB-R/798	
Harris, Hugh	SC	c1855	Copy	065 AR
Harris, Hugh	065	1824	WB-D/86	AR
Harris, Isaac	075	1819	WB-M1/328	AR
Harris, Isabella	099	1876	RB-35/360	AR
Harris, Isabella M.	098	1898	044 WB-24/475	044 CTY
Harris, Isabella M.	098	1898	WB-A/302	CTY
Harris, Isham	044	1824	WB-9/351	CTY
Harris, Ivey	044	1872	WB-23/70	CTY
Harris, J. A.	086	1880	Orig. Only	AR
Harris, Jabez K.	053	1859	WB-9/1	AR
Harris, Jacob	029	1847	WB-C/146	AR
Harris, Jacob	009	c1787	OWB/216	AR
Harris, James	044	1897	WB-24/377	CTY
Harris, James	039	1876	WB-U/138	AR
Harris, James	100	1890	WB-51/364	AR
Harris, James	085	1811	WB-G/177	AR
Harris, James	047	1828	WB-4/47	
Harris, James	037	1749	Orig. Only	SS/AR
Harris, James	046	1842	WB-C/132	AR
Harris, James	044	1896	WB-24/317	CTY
Harris, James	065	c1796	Orig. Only	AR
Harris, James	016	1843	WB-1/1	AR
Harris, James	086	1830	WB-D/114	AR
Harris, James	073	1785	WB-A/337	AR
Harris, James	065	1779	WB-C/136	AR
Harris, James	075	1861	WB-M2/77	AR
Harris, James	024	c1766	WB-A/41	AR
Harris, James	099	1794	RB-3/13	AR
Harris, James	016	1794	WB-A/73	AR

Name	Co.	Date	Recorded Copy	Original
Harris, James	099	1820	RB-16/304	AR
Harris, James	047	1828	100 WB-51/364	100 AR
Harris, James H.	099	c1888	Orig. Only	AR
Harris, James H.	078	1871	WB-19/18	AR
Harris, James P.	100	1875	WB-51/87	AR
Harris, James, Jr.	100	1800	WB-11/44	AR
Harris, Jane	046	1875	WB-E/153	AR
Harris, Jane C.	100	1854	WB-43/59	AR
Harris, Jane W.	084	1879	WB-E/183	CTY
Harris, Jean	015	1770	100 WB-1/125	AR
Harris, Jennetta	053	1866	WB-9/285	AR
Harris, Jesse	032	1833	WB-1/227	
Harris, Jesse C.	017	c1863	WB-A/171	
Harris, Joel	046	1824	Orig. Only	AR
Harris, Joel	039	1850	WB-N/302	AR
Harris, Joel	047	1857	WB-5/43	
Harris, John	075	1846	WB-N/203	AR
Harris, John	085	1813	WB-G/276	AR
Harris, John	078	1825	WI-10/171	AR
Harris, John	024	c1711	SS 875/48	
Harris, John	028	1801	WB-B/132	AR
Harris, John	078	1872	WB-19/22	AR
Harris, John	024	1713	WB-A/54	AR
Harris, John	053	N. D.	RW-1/515	
Harris, John	103	1824	RD-5/124	AH
Harris, John	028	1749	SS 877/322	SS/AR
Harris, John	100	1790	WB-5/143	AR
Harris, John	075	1762	WB-I/26	AR
Harris, John	075	1821	WB-M1/344	
Harris, John	086	1798	WB-B/99	AR
Harris, John	081	1822	WB-5/74	AR
Harris, John	071	1848	WB-5/68	AR
Harris, John	054	1849	WB-3/32	AR
Harris, John	009	1824	OB-A/336	AR
Harris, John	GA	c1863	Copy	090 AR
Harris, John	044	1892	WB-244/191	CTY
Harris, John	078	1847	WB-13/6	AR
Harris, John A.	075	1872	WB-0/34	AR
Harris, John G.	044	1885	WB-23/530	CTY
Harris, John H.	044	1866	WB-22/576	CTY
Harris, John H.	069	1892	WB-5/368	AR
Harris, John W.	086	1859	WB-E/358	AR
Harris, John W.	099	1872	RB-35/175	AR
Harris, John W.	084	1895	WB-F/37	CTY
Harris, Jonathan	065	1829	WB-E/76	AR
Harris, Jonathan	053	1851	WB-7/458	AR
Harris, Jonathan	082	c1813	WB-1/162	AR
Harris, Joseph	100	1797	WB-9/97	AR
Harris, Joseph	075	1860	WB-M2/67	AR
Harris, Joseph	028	1745	SS 877/337	
Harris, Joseph	075	1808	WB-M1/191	AR
Harris, Joseph	046	1879	WB-E/246	AR
Harris, Joseph	053	1834	WB-5/251	AR
Harris, Joseph B.	085	c1862	Copy	067 AR
Harris, Joseph B.	085	1863	WB-K/308	AR
Harris, Joshua	016	1859	WB-2/60	AR
Harris, Josiah	053	1868	WB-10/33	AR
Harris, Josiah	075	1826	WB-N/26	AR
Harris, Josiah	075	1815	WB-M1/274	AR
Harris, Judith H.	020	1868	WB-A/13	CTY
Harris, Katherine	016	1816	WB-A/74	AR
Harris, Kiah P.	016	1869	WB-3/11	AR
Harris, Kinion	079	1882	WB-2/245	AR
Harris, Leah E.	100	1898	Orig. Only	AR
Harris, Lelia L.	047	1897	WB-7/281	AR
Harris, Leonard	100	1858	WB-49/189	AR
Harris, Leonora J.	016	1897	WB-4/272	
Harris, Levin	084	1834	WB-B/101	CTY
Harris, Lovick	028	1848	WB-D/148	AR
Harris, Marcus	073	1877	WB-H/173	CTY
Harris, Margaret	016	1830	PQS.5/134	AR-Copy
Harris, Margaret	063	1864	WB-2/549	
Harris, Margaret	065	c1789	WB-D/49	AR
Harris, Margaret	003	1875	WB-B/52	AR
Harris, Margaret	032	1863	WB-2/259	AR
Harris, Margaret E.	085	1899	WB-3/351	CTY
Harris, Margarett	071	1881	WB-6/354	AR
Harris, Margret	016	1870	WB-3/29	
Harris, Martha	099	1825	WB-19/448	AR
Harris, Martha	039	1834	WB-K/28	
Harris, Martha	065	1834	WB-G/157	AR
Harris, Martha A.	065	1878	WB-K/282	AR
Harris, Martin	084	1849	WB-C/86	CTY
Harris, Mary	065	1849	WB-I/154	AR
Harris, Mary	028	1831	WB-C/344	AR
Harris, Mary	067	1890	WB-2/290	AR
Harris, Mary	054	c1829	Orig. Only	AR
Harris, Mary L.	044	1900	WB-24/489	CTY
Harris, Matilda	019	1890	WB-B/197	AR
Harris, Maximillian	075	1840	WB-N/148	AR
Harris, Michael	071	1840	WB-4/217	AR
Harris, Michal	100	1794	WB-7/158	AR
Harris, Mildred	071	1844	WB-5/9	AR
Harris, Mildridge	100	1892	Orig. Only	AR
Harris, Miles	075	1856	WB-M2/42	AR
Harris, Minerva F.	038	1896	WB-4/54	AR
Harris, Minyard	017	1882	WB-B/101	AR
Harris, Moses	029	1886	WB-E/377	AR
Harris, Moses	039	c1785	WB-A/4	
Harris, Moses	083	1855	WB-2/83	
Harris, Nancy	089	1861	WB-1/227	
Harris, Nathan	071	1806	WB-2/325	AR
Harris, Nathan	071	1811	WB-3/42	AR
Harris, Nathan	060	1809	Orig. Only	AR
Harris, Nathaniel	084	1803	OW/39	AR
Harris, Nathaniel	073	1849	WB-F/430	AR
Harris, Nathaniel	071	1837	WB-4/162	AR
Harris, Nehemiah	070	ca872	WB-E/242	AR
Harris, Newitt	100	1811	WB-16/8	AR
Harris, P. Edna	044	1885	WB-23/546	
Harris, Peledg	053	1837	WB-5/445	AR
Harris, Peter	053	1786	RW-1/153	
Harris, Peter	046	1790	WB-A/158	AR
Harris, Peter	046	c1868	Orig. Only	AR
Harris, Polly	075	1882	WB-0/141	AR
Harris, Polly	073	1845	WB-F/256	AR
Harris, Polly	078	1864	WB-18/353	AR
Harris, Presley W.	100	1900	WB-51/369	AR
Harris, Priscilla	071	1830	WB-4/66	AR
Harris, Priscilla	039	1887	WB-U/405	AR
Harris, Priscilla	047	1835	WB-4/117	
Harris, R. C.	078	1866	WB-18/451	AR
Harris, Ransom	100	1831	WB-33/337	AR
Harris, Ransom	032	1841	WB-1/369	
Harris, Ransom W.	046	1886	WB-E/427	AR
Harris, Rebea E.	103	1886	WB-1/361	AR
Harris, Rebecca	065	1831	WB-E/100	AR
Harris, Rhoda	039	1840	WB-L/1	AR
Harris, Richard	075	1854	WB-M2/18	AR
Harris, Richard	044	1815	WB-7/512	CTY

Name	Co.	Date	Recorded Copy	Original
Harris, Richard	078	1875	WB-19/45	AR
Harris, Richard	044	1787	WB-2/11	CTY
Harris, Richard	085	1884	WB-2/91	CTY
Harris, Richard	079	1836	WB-2/104	AR-Copy
Harris, Richard A.	017	1892	WB-B/220	
Harris, Richard W.	098	1892	WB-A/148	CTY
Harris, Riley	086	1893	WB-F/463	AR
Harris, Robert	078	c1842	Orig. Only	AR
Harris, Robert	016	1798	WB-A/1	AR
Harris, Robert	092	1809	WB-3/93	AR
Harris, Robert	029	1880	WB-E/243	AR
Harris, Robert	065	1795	WB-C/144	AR
Harris, Robert	078	1855	WB-17/357	AR
Harris, Robert	092	1816	WB-3/120	AR
Harris, Robert	078	1847	SC/08044	AR-Copy
Harris, Robert	044	1786	WB-1/519	
Harris, Robert	079	1893	WB-3/31	AR
Harris, Robert	016	1804	WB-A/85	AR
Harris, Robert	100	1843	WB-38/214	AR
Harris, Robert	073	1831	WB-E/259	AR
Harris, Robert	016	1834	PQS.5/303	AR
Harris, Robert A.	039	1864	WB-R/718	AR
Harris, Robert E.	099	1899	WB-D/293	AR
Harris, Robert W.	016	1846	WB-1/113	AR
Harris, Robert, Sr.	016	1817	WB-A/69	AR
Harris, Sallie	079	1889	WB-2/471	AR
Harris, Sally	079	c1853	WB-1/30	AR-Copy
Harris, Samuel	099	1794	RB-3/9	AR
Harris, Samuel	054	c1796	WB-1/9	AR
Harris, Samuel	065	1825	WB-D/23	AR
Harris, Samuel	039	1873	WB-U/67	AR
Harris, Samuel	078	1803	WI-3/172	AR
Harris, Samuel	044	1825	WB-10/55	CTY
Harris, Samuel C.	016	1869	WB-3/3	AR
Harris, Samuel L.	065	c1798	WB-D/14	AR
Harris, Samuel S.	065	c1844	WB-H/159	AR
Harris, Sarah	053	c1816	RW-1/529	AR
Harris, Sarah	044	1786	WB-1/510	
Harris, Sarah A.	065	1842	WB-H/95	AR
Harris, Satatheel	097	1879	WB-2/150	
Harris, Shade	009	1880	WB-1/262	CTY
Harris, Sherrod	005	1805	WB-2/53	AR
Harris, Sherwood	044	1763	Orig. Only	CTY
Harris, Simon	096	1818	WB-2/71	AR
Harris, Sollomon	065	1837	WB-E/180	AR
Harris, Solomon	016	1885	WB-3/467	AR
Harris, Spencer	079	1895	WB-3/80	AR
Harris, Stephen	028	1813	WB-C/68	AR
Harris, Stephen F.	074	1896	WB-1/135	
Harris, Sterling	073	1813	WB-D/387	AR
Harris, Susan	005	1847	WB-B/219	AR
Harris, Susan	053	1882	WB-11/127	AR
Harris, Tandy	090	1890	WB-6/232	AR
Harris, Thomas	044	1841	WB-15/17	CTY-Nunc.
Harris, Thomas	065	c1776	WB-C/132	AR
Harris, Thomas	009	1854	OB-I/173	AR
Harris, Thomas	019	1814	WB-D/246	AR
Harris, Thomas	054	1869	Orig. Only	AR
Harris, Thomas	028	1784	Orig. Only	AR
Harris, Thomas	047	1841	WB-4/193	
Harris, Thomas	054	c1826	WB-2/108	
Harris, Thomas	015	1770	100 WB-1/136	AR
Harris, Thomas	030	1749	Orig. Only	SS/AR
Harris, Thomas	075	1814	WB-M1/265	AR

Name	Co.	Date	Recorded Copy	Original
Harris, Thomas	N	c1665	Copy	CCR 187
Harris, Thomas	030	1804	WB-2/244	
Harris, Thomas	071	1814	WB-3/119	AR
Harris, Thomas	SC	1887	026 WB-2/368	026 AR
Harris, Thomas	037	1787	WB-C/40	AR
Harris, Thomas	086	1865	WB-E/464	AR
Harris, Thomas B.	022	1874	WB-E/98	AR
Harris, Thomas C.	016	1872	WB-3/77	AR
Harris, Thomas E.	019	1897	WB-B/321	AR
Harris, Thomas P.	071	1874	WB-6/147	AR
Harris, Thomas, Jr.	053	1775	RW-1/70	AR
Harris, Thompson	046	1775	WB-A/152	AR
Harris, Turner	032	1876	WB-3/171	AR
Harris, Tyree	020	1787	RB-B/162	AR
Harris, W. G.	022	1893	WB-E/526	AR
Harris, W. T.	067	1887	WB-2/239	AR
Harris, Warren	047	1835	WB-4/123	
Harris, William	016	1833	PQS.5/282	AR
Harris, William	047	1772	WB-1/317	
Harris, William	053	1772	RW-1/26	AR
Harris, William	009	c1795	OWB/315	AR
Harris, William	016	c1839	WB-A/74	
Harris, William	104	1849	WB-5/7	AR
Harris, William	039	c1894	Orig. Only	AR
Harris, William	053	1810	RW-1/442	AR
Harris, William	070	1892	WB-G/87	AR
Harris, William	028	1803	WB-B/176	AR
Harris, William	100	1829	WB-32/262	AR
Harris, William	009	1832	OB-B/188	AR
Harris, William	016	1828	WB-A/45	AR
Harris, William A.	098	1883	WB-A/23	CTY
Harris, William F.	098	1898	WB-A/310	CTY
Harris, William G.	GA	1855	Copy	016 AR
Harris, William H.	078	1869	WB-19/5	AR
Harris, William R.	044	1876	WB-23/231	CTY
Harris, William S.	074	1885	WB-1/34	AR
Harris, William S.	016	1876	WB-3/188	AR
Harris, William T.	070	1893	WB-G/169	AR
Harris, Willie	067	1879	WB-2/102	AR
Harris, Willis	030	1881	WB-5/79	AR
Harris, Zephaniah	085	c1798	WB-D/183	AR
Harris, Zeremiah	057	1793	WB-A/153	AR
Harrison, A.	106	1900	WB-2/488	
Harrison, Aaron	101	c1849	WB-A/254	
Harrison, Abraham	081	1804	Orig. Only	AR-Nunc.
Harrison, Andrew	020	1832	RB-M/164	AR
Harrison, Andrew	073	1774	WB-A/140	
Harrison, Ann	069	1844	WB-1/476	
Harrison, Ann L.	069	1875	WB-5/26	AR
Harrison, Archibald	081	1823	WB-5/129	AR
Harrison, Asa	101	1880	WB-A/43	AR
Harrison, Asa H.	101	1883	WB-A/101	AR
Harrison, B. S.	099	1889	WB-B/342	AR
Harrison, Benjamin	044	1774	WB-1/37	CTY
Harrison, Brittany	063	1900	WB-4/276	AR
Harrison, Cassandra	028	1861	WB-D/353	AR
Harrison, Charles	071	1812	WB-3/79	AR
Harrison, Clifton	071	1802	WB-2/233	AR
Harrison, Daniel	057	1881	WB-C/79	AR
Harrison, Daniel	024	c1726	SS 876/143	SS/AR
Harrison, Daniel	057	1795	WB-A/149	AR
Harrison, David	030	1839	WB-4/64	
Harrison, Davis B.	063	1886	WB-4/4	AR
Harrison, Dempsey	018	1824	WB-C/42	
Harrison, Edmond	101	1872	WB-A/116	AR

Name	Co.	Date	Recorded Copy	Original
Harrison, Edmond	086	1871	WB-F/60	AR-Nunc.
Harrison, Effy	083	1857	WB-2/113	
Harrison, Eliza	063	1900	WB-4/271	AR
Harrison, Elizabeth	032	1898	WB-4/375	AR
Harrison, Emilius	069	c1853	Orig. Only	AR
Harrison, Emma S.	101	1887	WB-A/152	AR
Harrison, Fanny	018	c1858	WB-D/50	
Harrison, George	044	1816	WB-7/589	CTY
Harrison, Harmon	101	1892	WB-A/210	AR
Harrison, Henry	069	1854	WB-1/537	AR
Harrison, Henry	046	1834	WB-B/505	AR
Harrison, Henry W.	101	1895	WB-A/265	
Harrison, Hezekiah	085	1839	WB-I/60	AR
Harrison, Isaac	028	1893	WB-F/89	
Harrison, Isaac	018	1834	WB-C/1834	
Harrison, J. P.	061	1887	WB-2/83	AR
Harrison, James	063	1840	WB-2/268	
Harrison, James	069	1877	WB-5/54	AR
Harrison, James	084	c1800	OW/61a	AR
Harrison, James A.	056	1867	WB-2/88	AR
Harrison, James C.	028	1893	WB-F/97	
Harrison, James C.	071	1823	WB-3/288	AR
Harrison, James N.	020	1876	WB-A/210	CTY
Harrison, James, Sr.	057	1792	WB-A/181	AR
Harrison, Jesse	063	1848	WB-2/339	
Harrison, Jethro	069	1811	WB-1/216	AR
Harrison, Joel	092	1887	WB-6/261	AR
Harrison, John	057	1828	WB-B/93	AR
Harrison, John	063	1825	WB-2/104	
Harrison, John	040	1883	WB-2/210	AR
Harrison, John	099	1829	RB-21/170	AR
Harrison, John	086	1859	WB-E/368	
Harrison, John	099	1879	WB-A/74	AR
Harrison, John	096	1766	WB-1/36	AR
Harrison, John	056	1821	WB-1/438	AR
Harrison, John	011	1785	WB-1/518	
Harrison, John	057	c1788	WB-A/184	AR
Harrison, John	069	1870	WB-1/603	AR
Harrison, John	030	c1832	WB-3/312	
Harrison, John	069	1827	WB-1/347	AR
Harrison, John	N	c1710	SS 875/32	
Harrison, John F.	071	1886	WB-6/518	AR
Harrison, John L.	020	1883	WB-A/389	CTY
Harrison, John P.	020	1849	RB-Q/240	
Harrison, John W.	045	c1860	WB-1/398	AR-Copy
Harrison, John W.	071	1830	WB-4/69	AR
Harrison, Joshua	096	1794	Orig. Only	AR
Harrison, Josiah	065	1812	WB-D/73	AR
Harrison, Judeth	018	1838	WB-C/242	
Harrison, Kenelm	085	1845	WB-K/5	AR
Harrison, King	063	1837	WB-2/228	
Harrison, Levina	099	1807	RB-7/256	AR
Harrison, Lewis A.	071	1843	WB-4/260	AR
Harrison, Louisa M.	020	1889	WB-B/6	CTY
Harrison, Margaret	018	1890	WB-E/185	AR
Harrison, Margaret F.	039	1898	WB-V/132	AR
Harrison, Maria	099	1899	WB-D/228	AR
Harrison, Maria M.	028	1847	WB-D/139	AR
Harrison, Mary	057	1882	WB-C/88	AR
Harrison, Maryann	037	1792	WB-C/208	AR
Harrison, Nancy	069	1845	WB-1/478	AR
Harrison, Nathaniel	073	1774	WB-A/146	
Harrison, Nathaniel	069	1866	WB-1/597	AR
Harrison, Nathaniel	071	1803	WB-2/245	AR
Harrison, Nehemiah	065	1863	WB-J/170	AR
Harrison, Penny	099	1893	WB-C/203	AR
Harrison, Phillip	086	1885	WB-F/260	
Harrison, R. B.	066	1889	Orig. Only	AR
Harrison, Ransom	099	1878	WB-A/1	AR
Harrison, Redmond	063	1877	WB-3/116	
Harrison, Rhody	069	c1855	WB-1/549	AR
Harrison, Richard	028	1827	WB-C/291	AR
Harrison, Richard	037	1856	WB-G/125	AR
Harrison, Richard	099	1814	RB-11/312	AR
Harrison, Richard	057	1819	WB-B/52	AR
Harrison, Robert	N	c1713	Orig. Only	SS/AR
Harrison, Robert	044	1861	WB-21/366	CTY
Harrison, Sally	037	1835	WB-F/170	AR
Harrison, Samuel	020	1789	RB-B/256	
Harrison, Sarah	085	1838	WB-I/39	AR
Harrison, Simons	047	1778	WB-2/68	
Harrison, Thomas	029	1823	WB-B/111	AR
Harrison, Thomas	057	1885	WB-C/113	AR
Harrison, Thomas	009	1774	OWB/115	AR
Harrison, Thomas	020	1790	RB-B/344	AR
Harrison, Thomas	020	1799	RB-C/352	
Harrison, Thomas D.	084	1865	WB-D/20	CTY
Harrison, Vines	024	1738	LGB-4/#78	SS/AR
Harrison, Virginia	099	1889	WB-B/346	
Harrison, William	057	1837	WB-B/133	AR
Harrison, William	084	1829	WB-A/323	CTY
Harrison, William	057	1812	WB-A/334	AR
Harrison, William	039	1829	WB-J/42	AR
Harrison, William	028	1770	Orig. Only	AR
Harrison, William	071	1786	WB-1/360	AR
Harrison, William	057	c1796	WB-A/228	AR
Harrison, William B.	101	1877	WB-A/33	AR
Harrison, William K.	020	1816	RB-G/307	
Harrison, Willie	099	1860	RB-31/672	AR
Harrison, Winiford	010	1844	WB-G/372	AR
Harrison, Zorabable	030	c1810	WB-3/15	
Harriss, Able	013	1863	WB-A/219	
Harriss, Amelia	024	1809	WB-B/297	AR
Harriss, Benjamin	005	1878	WB-D/64	AR
Harriss, Dawson	051	1846	WB-A/249	
Harriss, Della	079	1893	WB-3/36	AR
Harriss, Drewry	071	1860	WB-5/233	AR
Harriss, Drury	047	1799	WB-3/335	
Harriss, Edith	039	1818	WB-F/123	
Harriss, Edward	071	1793	WB-2/24	AR
Harriss, Eliy	047	1807	WB-3/471	
Harriss, Elizabeth	099	1805	RB-7/90	AR
Harriss, Ichabod	079	1848	WB-1/32	AR-Copy
Harriss, Isaac	047	1808	WB-3/476	
Harriss, Jacky E.	069	1871	Orig. Only	AR
Harriss, James	079	1879	WB-2/179	AR
Harriss, Jesse	084	1851	WB-C/124	CTY
Harriss, Joel	100	1790	WB-5/135	AR
Harriss, John	020	1782	RB-A/217	Nunc.
Harriss, Joseph	100	1785	WB-4/84	AR
Harriss, Lafayette	100	1890	WB-51/313	AR
Harriss, Lewis	064	1845	WB-1/14	AR
Harriss, Lucretia	100	1847	WB-39/276	AR
Harriss, Martha H.	047	1891	WB-6/578	AR
Harriss, Mary Ann	105	1900	WB-3/460	
Harriss, Nathan	037	1810	WB-D/360	AR
Harriss, Rachel	100	1823	WB-24/260	AR
Harriss, Randolph	069	1827	WB-1/349	AR
Harriss, Tabitha	100	1852	WB-42/35	
Harriss, Tabitha	100	1847	WB-39/382	AR

Name	Co.	Date	Recorded Copy	Original
Harriss, Temperance	047	1783	WB-3/43	
Harriss, Thomas	047	1795	WB-3/249	
Harriss, Thomas	044	1780	WB-1/277	
Harriss, Thomas	047	1891	WB-7/2	AR
Harriss, Tyree	020	1787	RB-B/162	
Harriss, Unity	060	1852	WB-2/372	AR
Harriss, William H.	100	1854	WB-43/186	AR
Harrisson, Josiah	030	1792	WB-2/1	
Harrisson, Thomas	096	1798	Orig. Only	AR
Harrisson, Thomas	096	1792	Orig. Only	AR
Harritage, William	028	1808	WB-B/315	
Harrocks, Thomas	070	1789	WB-C/154	AR
Harrold, Alice	038	1898	WB-4/82	AR
Harrold, Hansan	086	1809	WB-B/229	AR
Harron, Joseph	024	c1743	WB-A/50	AR
Harron, Lydia	024	1766	WB-1/17	AR
Harry, John B.	026	1866	WB-1/396	AR
Harry, John B.	026	1863	WB-1/308	AR
Harry, Washington	026	1889	WB-2/386	AR
Harshaw, Abram	023	1857	Orig. Only	AR
Harshaw, Fannie	065	1899	WB-N/199	AR-Copy
Harshaw, Jacob	014	1868	066 WB-1/92	
Harshaw, Jacob	014	1868	WB-2/10	AR
Harshaw, Sidney S.	GA	1876	014 WB-2/143	014 AR
Hart, Absolem	072	N. D.	RW/L37	
Hart, Anney	090	1817	WB-3/7	AR
Hart, Archibald	020	1803	RB-D/132	AR
Hart, Arthur	071	1788	WB-1/473	AR
Hart, Arthur	071	1785	WB-1/355	AR
Hart, Benjamin	071	1777	WB-1/6	AR
Hart, David	054	1876	WB-4/210	CTY
Hart, Elisha B.	069	1850	WB-1/519	AR
Hart, Elizabeth	054	1846	WB-3/2	AR
Hart, Elizabeth	071	1794	WB-2/61	AR
Hart, Harry	071	1800	WB-2/209	AR
Hart, Haslet S.	054	1846	WB-3/3	AR
Hart, Henry	038	1879	WB-2/338	AR
Hart, Henry	037	1785	WB-C/5	AR
Hart, Henry P.	044	1782	WB-1/333	
Hart, Jacob	014	1891	WB-2/466	CTY
Hart, James	029	1840	WB-B/314	AR
Hart, James	054	c1812	WB-1/290	AR
Hart, James	073	1839	WB-F/29	AR
Hart, James, Sr.	044	1839	WB-14/461	CTY
Hart, John	022	1848	WB-C/209	AR
Hart, John	071	1746	Orig. Only	SS/AR
Hart, Joseph	083	c1797	WB-1/47	
Hart, Joseph	044	1829	WB-11/73	CTY
Hart, Levi A.	070	1882	WB-E/457	AR
Hart, Mary	071	1751	Orig. Only	SS/AR
Hart, Mary	071	1782	WB-1/246	
Hart, Mary	071	1761	WB-1/47	
Hart, Mary D.	071	1835	WB-4/131	AR
Hart, Nancy	044	1849	WB-17/506	CTY
Hart, Nancy	044	1875	WB-23/170	CTY
Hart, Pleasant	044	1851	WB-18/279	CTY
Hart, Priscilla	037	1798	WB-D/61	AR
Hart, Rebecca	073	1856	WB-G/153	AR
Hart, Richard	103	1794	WI-A/448	
Hart, Sallie	022	1863	WB-D/98	AR
Hart, Samuel B.	065	1839	WB-H/19	AR
Hart, Spencer L.	037	1853	WB-F/513	AR
Hart, Thomas	069	1794	WB-1/90	AR
Hart, Thomas	073	1830	WB-E/222	AR
Hart, Thomas	071	1761	WB-1/51	
Hart, Thomas	071	1751	Orig. Only	SS/AR
Hart, Thomas A.	054	1854	WB-3/82	AR
Hart, W. L.	069	1891	WB-5/354	AR
Hart, Warren	071	1812	WB-3/61	AR
Hart, William	MD	1827	065 WB-C/1	065 AR
Hart, William	065	1803	WB-C/147	AR
Hart, William	071	1833	WB-4/98	AR
Hart, Wright	071	1789	WB-1/474	
Harte, O. L.	084	1872	WB-E/39	CTY
Hartgrove, Clarissa	065	1892	WB-M/90	AR
Hartgrove, Eliza H.	065	1891	WB-M/87	AR
Hartgrove, Jean	065	1836	WB-E/141	AR
Hartgrove, John	065	1847	WB-I/83	AR
Hartgrove, Thompson	065	c1827	WB-D/9	AR
Harth, Mary Y.	SC	1895	Copy	013 AR
Hartley, Abner	028	1847	Copy	009 AR
Hartley, Abner	028	1847	WB-D/140	AR
Hartley, Francis	046	c1788	WB-A/158	AR
Hartley, Francis	002	1692	Orig. Only	SS/AR
Hartley, Jesse	017	c1864	WB-A/162	AR
Hartley, John	028	1817	WB-C/140	AR
Hartley, Joseph	082	1803	WB-1/94	AR
Hartley, Joseph	028	1806	WB-B/237	AR
Hartley, Mahala	017	c1860	WB-A/121	AR
Hartley, Richard	085	1808	Orig. Only	AR-Nunc.
Hartley, Thomas	032	1842	WB-1/404	
Hartline, George	085	1794	WB-E/125	AR
Hartly, Ann	028	1831	WB-C/332	AR
Hartly, George	017	1876	WB-B/54	AR
Hartman, Catharine	085	1885	WB-2/135	CTY
Hartman, Catharine	021	1896	WB-3/110	AR
Hartman, George	016	c1811	WB-A/5	AR
Hartman, George	033	1855	WB-1/118	
Hartman, George	016	1822	WB-A/48	AR
Hartman, George	085	c1788	WB-C/107	AR
Hartman, Harman	038	c1860	WB-1/171 & 184	AR
Hartman, Jesse	032	1895	WB-4/265	AR
Hartman, John	085	1858	WB-K/256	AR
Hartman, John	085	1852	WB-K/140	AR
Hartman, John	085	1843	WB-I/168	AR
Hartman, John	085	1845	WB-K/10	AR
Hartman, John	090	1822	WB-3/82	
Hartman, Michael	085	1812	WB-G/243	AR
Hartman, Peter	085	1857	WB-K/242	AR
Hartman, Polly	085	1883	WB-2/75	CTY
Hartman, Rebecca	090	1839	WB-4/38	AR
Hartman, Susan	038	1897	WB-4/33	AR
Hartmus, Francis C.	024	1842	WB-C/236	AR
Hartness, Nathaniel	054	c1796	Orig. Only	AR
Hartness, Robert	003	1862	Orig. Only	AR
Hartness, Silas	003	1884	WB-B/146	AR
Harton, Harbert	086	1867	WB-E/480	AR
Harton, Hardy	005	1839	WB-B/90	AR
Harton, Thomas	100	1795	WB-8/26	AR
Hartsel, George	016	1833	PQS.5/269	AR
Hartsel, Rosanah	016	1845	WB-1/69	AR
Hartsell, Andrew	097	1873	WB-2/68	
Hartsell, John	089	1848	WB-1/69	AR
Hartsell, Joshua	016	1871	WB-3/31	AR
Hartsell, Nimrod	016	1864	WB-2/106	AR
Hartsell, Tilmon	089	1897	WB-2/307	AR
Hartsell, Wilson	089	1886	WB-2/133	AR
Hartsfield, Andrew	056	1762	WB-1/772	AR
Hartsfield, Andrew	099	1823	RB-18/123	AR

Name	Co.	Date	Recorded Copy	Original
Hartsfield, John	099	1821	RB-17/148	AR
Hartsfield, Thomas L.	059	1889	WB-A/570	CTY
Hartsoe, Abel	014	1875	WB-2/114	
Hartsoe, Isaac	022	1853	WB-C/345	AR
Hartt, David	065	1812	WB-C/156	AR
Hartt, David M.	065	1830	WB-F/174	AR
Hartt, Dinah	065	1823	WB-D/81	AR
Hartt, Henry	090	1834	WB-3/268	AR
Harty, Elizabeth	065	1877	WB-K/252	AR
Harty, Patrick	065	1854	WB-I/256	AR
Hartzog, John	021	1883	WB-2/275	
Harvell, Helen P.	035	1882	Orig. Only	AR
Harvey, Abram	073	1898	WB-I/141	CTY
Harvey, Allderson	009	1837	OB-C2/26	AR
Harvey, Allen	039	c1816	WB-F/221	AR
Harvey, Anne	037	1805	WB-D/231	AR
Harvey, Eleanor	001	1886	WB-2/302	AR
Harvey, Eliza	077	c1830	Orig. Only	AR
Harvey, Elizabeth	024	c1801	Orig. Only	AR-Copy
Harvey, Elizabeth	085	c1804	WB-D/182	AR
Harvey, Francis	070	1784	WB-C/149	AR
Harvey, George A.	041	1824	WB-2/213	AR
Harvey, Henry	009	1827	OB-A/377	AR
Harvey, Isaac	073	1802	WB-D/63	AR
Harvey, James	028	c1777	Orig. Only	AR-Copy
Harvey, James H.	NY	1834	Copy	024 AR
Harvey, John	077	1784	WB-C/291	AR
Harvey, John	047	1826	WB-4/18	
Harvey, John	085	1826	WB-H/361	AR
Harvey, John	009	1845	OB-E/412	AR
Harvey, John	073	1800	WB-D/16	AR
Harvey, John	009	c1801	OWB/383	AR
Harvey, John	053	1759	SS 882/156	SS/AR
Harvey, John	077	1775	WB-C/173	AR
Harvey, John F.	046	1875	WB-E/135	AR
Harvey, Joseph	047	1816	WB-3/580	
Harvey, Julia	001	1898	WB-3/218	AR
Harvey, Lillie	009	1899	WB-2/185	
Harvey, Martha B.	024	1852	WB-C/325	AR
Harvey, Mary	028	1840	WB-D/12	AR
Harvey, Mary	044	1802	WB-5/280	CTY
Harvey, Mary C.	028	1866	WB-D/422	AR
Harvey, Michael	081	1805	WB-3/24	AR
Harvey, Miles	077	1785	WB-C/302	AR
Harvey, Miles	077	1777	WB-C/211	AR-Copy
Harvey, Miles	077	1785	WB-C/281	AR
Harvey, Moses	073	1833	WB-E/306	AR
Harvey, Nancy	063	1873	WB-3/47	
Harvey, Nathan	073	1837	WB-E/416	AR
Harvey, Nathan	053	c1802.	RW-1/350	AR
Harvey, Pennie	024	1886	WB-E/154	AR
Harvey, Peter	053	1769	RW-1/10	AR
Harvey, Priscilla	011	1861	WB-1/270	
Harvey, Richard	N	1733	SS 876/278	SS/AR
Harvey, Richard	053	1800	RW-1/322	
Harvey, Richard	028	1786	WB-A/141	AR
Harvey, Robert	011	c1839	WB-1/76	
Harvey, Robert	085	c1781	WB-B/86	AR
Harvey, Sarah	041	1816	WB-2/128	AR
Harvey, Somerset	024	1875	WB-E/52	AR
Harvey, Susan M.	020	1865	RB-T/107	AR
Harvey, Thomas	077	1729	SS 876/214	SS/AR
Harvey, Thomas	002	1699	Orig. Only	SS/AR
Harvey, Thomas	077	1748	Orig. Only	SS/AR
Harvey, Thomas	077	1788	WB-C/364	AR

Name	Co.	Date	Recorded Copy	Original
Harvey, Thomas	047	1814	WB-3/548	
Harvey, Thomas	075	1805	WB-M1/116	AR
Harvey, Thomas	075	1844	WB-N/184	AR
Harvey, Thomas	073	1863	WB-G/415	AR
Harvey, Travis W.	011	c1805	WB-1/353	
Harvey, William	101	1874	WB-A/8	AR
Harvey, William	047	1803	WB-3/394	Nunc.
Harvey, William	001	1863	WB-1/221	AR
Harvey, William	009	1812	OWB/466	AR
Harvey, William	070	1775	WB-C/145	AR
Harvey, William	046	1828	WB-B/358	AR
Harvey, William	047	1825	WB-4/5	
Harvey, William M.	041	1827	WB-2/269	AR
Harvey, William W.	011	c1850	WB-1/180	
Harvie, Alexander	070	1762	DB-E/128	AR
Harvile, John	029	1767	Orig. Only	AR
Harvill, Nancy H.	020	1833	RB-M/345	
Harvill, Tyre	106	1891	WB-2/308	AR
Harvill, William	035	1791	WB-A/196	AR
Harvy, Dorothy	075	1682	SS 875/332	SS/AR
Harvy, John	046	1811	WB-A/176	AR
Harvy, Mary	069	1898	WB-6/37	AR
Harward, Elizabeth	099	1891	WB-B/537	AR
Harward, James	099	1840	RB-24/441	AR
Harward, James	089	1887	WB-2/141	AR
Harward, John	099	1845	RB-26/8	AR
Harward, John	099	1832	RB-22/309	AR
Harward, L. M.	036	1895	WB-A/353	CTY
Harward, Lewis H.	022	1890	WB-E/434	AR
Harward, Polly	022	1864	WB-D/120	AR
Harward, William	022	1852	WB-C/318	AR
Harwell, Ambrose	054	c1802	WB-1/112	AR
Harwell, Elisabeth	047	1823	WB-3/687	
Harwell, Elsey H.	021	1886	WB-2/345	
Harwell, James	021	c1863	WB-2/347	
Harwell, Lemuel	054	c1805	WB-1/113	AR
Harwell, Lucy	047	1819	WB-3/631	
Harwell, Peggy	054	1805	Orig. Only	AR-Nunc.
Harwell, Samuel	060	1794	Orig. Only	AR
Harwell, Starling	047	1806	WB-3/451	
Harwood, Celia	089	1886	WB-2/137	AR
Harwood, Edward	072	1737	Orig. Only	SS/AR
Harwood, Emsley B.	089	1897	WB-2/310	AR
Harwood, George	009	1868	WB-1/1	AR
Harwood, Howell	089	1870	WB-2/3	AR
Harwood, John	085	c1805	WB-D/189	AR
Harwood, John	085	1812	WB-G/249	AR
Harwood, Joseph	037	1770	WB-A/176	AR
Harwood, Mary	089	1855	WB-1/135	AR
Harwood, Milly	022	c1862	WB-D/140	AR
Harwood, Myrick	089	1866	WB-1/305	
Harwood, Susan	089	1887	WB-2/137	
Harwood, Zachariah	085	c1805	WB-E/117	AR
Hase, Catharine	010	1869	WB-I/5	AR
Hase, Elizabeth	063	c1779	WB-1/113	
Hase, John	063	1774	WB-1/448	
Haselette, Fletcher	041	1838	WB-3/3	AR
Hasell, James	070	1785	Copy	SS/AR
Hasell, James, Sr.	070	1785	WB-C/150	AR
Haselrig, James	044	1778	WB-1/203	CTY
Hash, James	006	1882	WB-E/84	AR
Hashagen, Henry C.	070	1878	WB-E/354	AR
Haskall, Deodatus	NY	1867	037 WB-G/296	037 AR
Haskell, Henry F.	028	1825	WB-C/265	AR
Hasket, Aaron	028	1865	WB-D/412	AR

Name	Co.	Date	Recorded Copy	Original
Hasket, Abraham	081	1818	WB-4/539	AR
Hasket, Joseph	081	1826	Orig. Only	AR
Hasket, Joshua	077	1814	WB-E/401	AR
Hasket, Joshua	077	1776	WB-C/182	AR
Hasket, William	077	c1828	WB-F/153	AR
Haskett, Elizabeth	077	1879	WB-H/78	AR
Haskett, John	077	1819	WB-F/17	AR
Haskett, Joseph	081	1834	WB-6/360	AR
Haskett, Matilda	075	1889	WB-0/305	AR
Haskett, Nathan	077	1832	WB-F/203	AR
Haskett, Silas	077	1835	WB-F/236	AR
Haskett, William F.	075	1892	WB-0/352	AR
Haskill, William H.	074	1894	WB-1/133	AR
Haskins, Ann	044	1837	WB-13/497	CTY
Haskins, Augustus	057	1895	WB-C/212	AR
Haskins, Benjamin	069	1860	WB-1/564	AR
Haskins, Benjamin	072	1828	WB-1/19	AR
Haskins, Ezekel	072	1816	WB-A/49	AR
Haskins, George	044	1847	WB-17/177	CTY
Haskins, Hanniball	N	c1698	Orig. Only	SS/AR
Haskins, James	044	1834	WB-13/152	CTY
Haskins, Martha	077	1888	WB-H/171	AR
Haskit, Alice	077	1797	WB-E/82	
Haskit, Mary	077	1785	WB-C/300	AR
Haskit, William	077	1772	WB-C/122	AR
Haskitt, Borden	019	1866	WB-B/27	AR
Haskitt, John	077	1837	WB-F/266	AR
Haskitt, Joseph	077	c1831	WB-F/190	AR
Haskitt, Keziah	077	1835	WB-F/235	AR
Haskitt, Michael F.	019	1859	WB-A/230	AR
Haslen, Elizabeth	028	1833	044 WB-12/512	044 CTY
Haslen, Margaret	028	1812	WB-C/47	AR
Haslen, Thomas	028	1797	WB-B/19	AR
Haslen, Thomas	028	1782	Orig. Only	AR
Haslep, Andrew	060	1782	Orig. Only	AR
Haslett, John W.	041	1856	WB-3/192	AR
Haslett, Sidney	041	1881	WB-4/155	AR
Hass, Robert M.	021	1864	WB-1/200	AR
Hassel, Abraham	096	1771	Orig. Only	AR
Hassel, Benjamin	096	c1781	WB-1/118	AR
Hassel, James	024	1796	WB-A/298	AR
Hasselberger, John	060	1807	Orig. Only	AR
Hassell, Abraham	024	1803	WB-B/307	AR
Hassell, Benjamin	101	1873	Orig. Only	AR
Hassell, Benjamin	046	1880	WB-E/271	AR
Hassell, Cushing B.	063	1880	WB-3/179	
Hassell, Edward	096	1810	WB-2/48	AR
Hassell, Edward	096	c1798	Orig. Only	AR
Hassell, Edward	096	1774	WB-1/81	AR
Hassell, Edward	096	1795	Orig. Only	AR
Hassell, George	101	1889	WB-A/175	AR
Hassell, Isaac	096	1766	WB-1/65	AR
Hassell, Jabes	096	1762	WB-1/24	AR
Hassell, James	096	1823	Orig. Only	AR
Hassell, Jesse	046	1838	WB-B/592	AR
Hassell, Jesse	096	1857	WB-3/47	AR
Hassell, John	096	1754	WB-1/91	AR-Copy
Hassell, John	096	1754	SS 879/128	SS/AR
Hassell, Joseph	096	c1816	Orig. Only	AR
Hassell, Joseph	096	1783	WB-1/136	AR
Hassell, Martha	063	1861	WB-2/482	
Hassell, Mary	096	1884	WB-4/106	
Hassell, Miles	024	1819	WB-C/78	AR
Hassell, Priscilla	096	1777	WB-1/94	AR
Hassell, Rachel	096	c1778	WB-1/105	
Hassell, Richard D.	096	1843	WB-3/5	AR
Hassell, Solomon	096	1817	Orig. Only	AR
Hassell, Solomon	096	1811	WB-2/38	AR
Hassell, Stark	096	1846	WB-3/15	AR
Hassell, Thomas S.	101	1881	WB-A/49	AR
Hassell, William	096	1784	WB-1/140	AR
Hassell, Zebedee	096	1807	WB-2/18	AR
Hassey, Simeon	072	c1781	WI/L29	
Hassold, Thomas	N	c1696	Nunc. Copy	CCR 187
Hassom, Margaret	099	1839	RB-24/297	AR
Haste, Charlton	024	1831	WB-C/157	AR
Haste, Hariet	024	1844	WB-C/257	AR
Hasten, John	038	1887	WB-3/32	AR
Hasten, William	020	1863	RB-T/20	CTY
Hastey, Samuel	071	1805	WB-2/284	AR
Hastin, Henry C.	026	1877	WB-2/150	AR
Hastin, Sarah C.	026	1878	WB-2/170	AR
Hasting, John	020	1828	RB-L/277	AR
Hasting, Zachariah	020	1835	RB-M/529	AR
Hastings, Curtis	103	1895	WB-2/114	AR
Hastings, Elizabeth	103	1852	RD-11/185	AR
Hastings, Henry	073	1812	WB-D/339	AR
Hastings, James	073	1822	WB-E/29	AR
Hastings, Joshua	103	1829	RD-6/5	AR
Hastings, Pennina	056	1886	WB-3/422	AR
Hastings, Robert	073	1859	WB-G/231	AR
Hastings, Wilie	056	1886	WB-3/406	AR
Hastings, Wilie	056	c1883	103 WB-2/89	103 AR
Hastings, William	026	1847	WB-1/63	
Hasty, Christian	082	1859	WB-4/135	
Hasty, Henry	071	1898	WB-7/407	AR
Hasty, James	097	1854	WB-1/105	AR
Hasty, James	082	1843	WB-3/6	AR
Hasty, Jesse	097	1889	WB-2/324	AR
Hasty, Lydda	063	1813	WB-2/17	
Hasty, Matthew	063	c1803	WB-1/411	
Hasty, Pebles	097	1860	WB-1/163	AR
Hasty, Rachel	097	1872	WB-2/69	
Hasty, Samuel	082	1885	WB-6/305	AR
Hasty, Stephen	097	1847	WB-1/57	AR
Hasty, Stephen G.	097	1876	WB-2/102	
Haswell, Edward	044	1879	WB-23/343	CTY
Haswell, Nathan	044	1841	WB-15/18	CTY
Hatch, Alexander	073	1850	WB-F/456	AR
Hatch, Anthony	077	1744	Orig. Only	SS/AR
Hatch, Anthony	077	1726	SS 876/57	SS/AR
Hatch, Anthony	057	1810	WB-A/324	AR
Hatch, Charles	028	1806	WB-B/239	AR
Hatch, Chelly	103	1897	WB-2/210	AR
Hatch, Durant	028	1830	WB-C/317	AR
Hatch, Edmund	028	1770	Orig. Only	AR
Hatch, Edmund	028	1821	WB-C/201	AR
Hatch, Edmund	057	1789	WB-A/168	AR
Hatch, Edmund B.	057	1839	WB-B/136	AR
Hatch, Eliza	028	1874	WB-E/101	AR
Hatch, Elizabeth	028	1847	WB-D/134	AR
Hatch, Joseph	057	1819	WB-B/54	AR
Hatch, Lemuel	057	1790	WB-A/122	AR
Hatch, Lemuel	057	1807	WB-A/293	AR
Hatch, Lemuel	028	1777	Orig. Only	SS/AR
Hatch, R. Clarissa	103	1862	RD-13/504	AR
Hatch, William H.	022	1899	WB-F/91	AR
Hatch, William M.	022	1881	WB-E/217	AR
Hatchell, Green	072	1867	WB-3/16	AR
Hatchell, Susan	019	1899	WB-C/10	AR

Name	Co.	Date	Recorded Copy	Original
Hatchell, William W.	029	1864	WB-D/61	AR
Hatcher, Alladdin	029	1892	WB-E/572	AR
Hatcher, Austin	056	1863	WB-2/43	AR
Hatcher, Benjamin	078	1800	WI-2/271	AR
Hatcher, Benjamin	056	1843	WB-1/556	AR
Hatcher, Charles	056	1843	WB-1/551	
Hatcher, James	056	1890	WB-3/525	AR
Hatcher, John	056	1857	WB-1/710	AR
Hatcher, John	037	1766	WB-A/153	AR
Hatcher, John	044	1787	WB-2/15	
Hatcher, John T.	056	1881	WB-3/274	AR
Hatcher, Sallie	056	1890	WB-3/540	
Hatcher, Timothy	070	1838	WB-AB/319	AR
Hatcher, William	056	1863	WB-2/47	AR
Hatcher, William	056	c1784	WB-1/306	AR
Hatcher, William	056	1820	WB-1/306	AR
Hatchett, Bartlett	020	1814	RB-F/389	AR
Hatchett, Thomas H.	020	1897	WB-B/312	CTY
Hatchett, Thomas R.	020	1897	WB-B/295	CTY
Hatchett, William	054	1888	WB-5/226	CTY
Hatchett, William	020	1861	RB-S/472	AR
Hatchett, William S.	020	1891	WB-B/83	CTY
Hatfield, Benjamin	071	1791	WB-1/437	AR
Hatfield, Charles	096	1848	WB-3/18	AR
Hatfield, Elizabeth	077	1885	WB-H/153	AR
Hatfield, George	077	1775	WB-C/170	AR
Hatfield, Jesse	096	c1804	WB-2/19	AR
Hatfield, John	071	1811	WB-3/49	AR
Hatfield, Richard	077	1809	WB-E/329	AR
Hatfield, Richard	077	1800	WB-E/121	AR
Hath, Nehemiah	030	1750	Orig. Only	SS/AR
Hathaway, Anna	079	1879	WB-2/177	AR
Hathaway, Burton W.	024	c1855	WB-C/398	AR
Hathaway, Cyrena	079	1897	WB-3/123	AR
Hathaway, Ivy	037	1897	WB-H/388	AR
Hathaway, John	MA	1859	070 WB-D/20	070 AR
Hathaway, Nathan H.	079	1898	WB-3/142	AR
Hathaway, Sarah	018	1822	WB-B/10	
Hathaway, Thomas N.	077	1896	WB-H/284	AR
Hathaway, William B.	047	1853	WB-4/342	
Hathaway, Zachariah	079	1872	WB-2/70	AR
Hathcock, Ira	089	1883	WB-2/99	
Hathcock, Nancy	022	1796	RB-2/69	AR
Hathcock, Patrick	022	1857	WB-C/460	AR
Hathway, Isaac	057	1793	WB-A/211	AR
Hatley, Abner	022	1838	WB-C/83	AR
Hatley, Alfred	089	c1862	WB-1/265	
Hatley, Green	089	1897	WB-2/295	AR
Hatley, John	022	c1801	WB-A/76	AR
Hatley, Josiah	017	1882	WB-B/99	AR
Hatley, Richard	085	c1801	WB-E/106	AR
Hatley, Tilman	089	1891	WB-2/216	AR
Hatley, Uriah	022	1834	WB-C/18	AR
Hatley, William	089	1847	WB-1/60	AR
Hatley, William	022	c1836	Orig. Only	AR
Hatley, William S.	089	1888	WB-2/160	AR
Hatly, William	089	1866	WB-1/301	
Hatmaker, Malichiset	073	c1823	Orig. Only	AR-Copy
Hatmaker, Molly	001	c1851	WB-1/102	
Hatrick, Elizabeth	046	1849	WB-C/309	AR
Hatrick, Robert	046	1838	WB-C/23	AR
Hatrick, Sarah	046	1866	WB-D/303	AR
Hatsell, Armstead	019	1824	WB-D/256	AR
Hatsell, William	019	1817	WB-D/252	AR
Hatsell, William	019	c1797	WB-D/226	AR
Hattan, Charles	102	1875	WB-A/2	AR
Hattaway, William	047	1795	WB-3/245	AR-Copy
Hatton, Charles	054	c1819	Orig. Only	AR
Hatton, Francis	037	1828	WB-F/86	AR
Hatton, John	075	1698	Orig. Only	SS/AR
Hatton, William	085	1811	WB-G/184	AR
Hattridge, Anne Blount	070	1842	WB-AB/368	AR
Hatwood, Thomas	073	1817	WB-D/501	AR
Hauckle, Christian	SC	1882	050 WB-1/164	
Haughton, Adeline	022	1872	WB-E/78	AR
Haughton, Charles	024	1840	WB-C/222	AR
Haughton, Charles	024	1756	SS 880/89	SS/AR
Haughton, Charles	024	1805	WB-B/281	AR
Haughton, Deborah	024	1836	WB-C/202	AR
Haughton, Edward	024	1818	WB-C/65	AR
Haughton, Eliza A.	024	1850	WB-C/301	AR
Haughton, Eliza B.	024	c1871	096 WB-4/174	096 AR
Haughton, Eliza B.	024	1873	WB-E/43	
Haughton, Henrietta	024	1872	WB-E/28	AR
Haughton, Henry	075	1775	WB-I/131	AR
Haughton, Henry	024	1816	WB-C/46	AR
Haughton, Jeremiah	024	1801	WB-B/177	AR
Haughton, John	022	1850	WB-C/253	AR
Haughton, Jonathan	024	1817	WB-C/57	AR
Haughton, Jonathan	024	1835	WB-C/188	AR
Haughton, Josiah	024	1823	WB-C/102	AR
Haughton, L. J.	022	1898	WB-F/70	AR
Haughton, Lemuel	024	1816	WB-C/40	AR
Haughton, Malachi	024	c1847	WB-C/282	AR
Haughton, Margaret	101	1869	Orig. Only	AR
Haughton, Mary R.	022	c1860	WB-D/135	AR
Haughton, Richard	024	c1748	Orig. Only	SS/AR
Haughton, Richard	077	c1785	Orig. Only	AR
Haughton, Samuel G.	024	1822	WB-C/98	AR
Haughton, Thomas	024	1809	WB-B/220	AR
Haughton, William	024	1752	Orig. Only	SS/AR
Haul, John	071	1838	WB-4/179	AR
Haun, Margaret	092	1789	WB-2/91	
Hause, Henry	060	1860	WB-3/35	AR
Hauser, Abraham	090	1820	WB-3/42	
Hauser, Benjamin	038	c1857	WB-1/120	AR
Hauser, C. S.	038	1896	WB-4/4	AR
Hauser, C. T.	038	1874	WB-2/169	AR
Hauser, Catharina	090	1818	WB-3/18	AR
Hauser, Clark	038	1892	WB-3/285	AR
Hauser, Fredric	090	1807	WB-2/80	AR
Hauser, George	090	1801	WB-1/178	
Hauser, George P.	090	1802	WB-2/20	AR
Hauser, Heinrich	090	1821	WB-3/70	AR
Hauser, Hermina E.	038	1898	WB-4/106	AR
Hauser, Jacob	090	1806	WB-2/66	AR
Hauser, John	092	1784	Copy	090 AR
Hauser, John	092	1886	WB-6/237	AR
Hauser, John	092	1784	WB-2/21A	AR
Hauser, John L.	090	1828	WB-3/184	AR
Hauser, John W.	032	c1869	WB-3/5	
Hauser, Martin	090	1814	WB-2/158	AR
Hauser, Mary C.	038	1875	WB-2/210	AR
Hauser, Mary E.	038	1890	WB-3/183	AR
Hauser, Michael	092	1789	WB-2/85A	AR
Hauser, Samuel	092	1882	WB-6/169	AR
Hauser, Solomon	090	1839	WB-4/47	AR
Hauser, T. C.	106	1887	WB-2/226	AR
Hauser, Wilson	038	1887	WB-3/20	AR
Hausington, Benidictus	028	1730	Orig. Only	SS/AR

Name	Co.	Date	Recorded Copy	Original
Hauss, Peter	060	1850	WB-2/330	AR
Havard, Joseph	030	c1811	WB-3/8	
Havens, B. F.	009	1880	WB-1/256	CTY
Havens, Jonathan	009	1828	OB-A/491	AR
Havens, Mary E.	009	1896	WB-2/91	CTY
Havens, Mary W.	028	1895	WB-F/157	
Havens, Sally M.	009	1856	OB-K/197	AR
Havens, Sydney C.	009	1857	OB-K/255	CTY
Hawes, Edmond A.	070	1874	WB-E/275	AR
Hawes, Elias	028	1841	WB-D/31	AR
Hawes, Samuel	070	1816	WB-AB/241	AR
Hawes, Sarah	028	1815	Orig. Only	AR
Hawkes, Johnston	078	1888	WB-19/229	
Hawkings, John	024	1717	SS 875/111	SS/AR
Hawkins, Allen T.	050	1900	WB-2/352	CTY
Hawkins, Ann	047	1824	WB-3/705	
Hawkins, Basil H.	072	1887	WB-4/222	AR
Hawkins, Bazel	072	1836	WB-1/150	AR
Hawkins, Benjamin	009	c1784	OWB/191	AR
Hawkins, Benjamin	009	c1791	OWB/258	AR
Hawkins, Benjamin	047	1895	WB-7/141	AR
Hawkins, C. E.	VA	1894	084 WB-E/575	084 CTY
Hawkins, Catherine	033	1883	WB-2/82	CTY
Hawkins, Charles S.	026	c1870	Orig. Only	AR
Hawkins, Dolly	047	1833	WB-4/98	
Hawkins, Dolly	099	1827	RB-20/129	
Hawkins, Edward	026	1859	WB-1/239	AR
Hawkins, Edward	010	1777	WB-B/72	AR
Hawkins, Edward	028	1893	WB-F/84	
Hawkins, Eli	082	1884	WB-6/287	
Hawkins, Elizabeth	057	1854	WB-B/223	AR
Hawkins, Elmyra	047	1858	WB-5/55	Nunc.
Hawkins, Elsa	037	1837	WB-F/206	AR
Hawkins, Ezeriah	072	1829	WB-1/53	AR
Hawkins, Frank	100	1851	WB-41/80	AR
Hawkins, Hannah	026	1893	WB-2/466	AR
Hawkins, Hardy	028	1812	WB-C/57	
Hawkins, Howell	047	1852	WB-4/332	Nunc.
Hawkins, Isham	047	1817	WB-3/610	
Hawkins, J. B.	026	1890	WB-2/404	
Hawkins, J. H.	016	1860	WB-2/72	AR
Hawkins, J. R.	060	1878	WB-4/190	AR
Hawkins, Jacobina	039	1881	WB-U/284	AR
Hawkins, James L.	057	1891	WB-C/174	
Hawkins, Jane A.	099	1898	WB-D/185	AR
Hawkins, John	002	1688	Orig. Only	SS/AR
Hawkins, John	035	c1756	087 DB-2/391	
Hawkins, John	078	c1880	WB-19/161	
Hawkins, John	059	1873	WB-A/57	
Hawkins, John	002	1720	SS 875/227	
Hawkins, John	077	1744	Orig. Only	SS/AR
Hawkins, John	100	1805	WB-12/106	AR
Hawkins, John D.	039	c1858	WB-O/389	AR
Hawkins, John H.	100	1855	WB-44/34	AR
Hawkins, Johnathan	072	c1856	WB-4/40	AR
Hawkins, Joseph	047	1818	WB-3/611	
Hawkins, Joseph	100	1786	WB-4/167	AR
Hawkins, Joseph	099	1827	RB-20/127	AR
Hawkins, Joseph	072	1791	Orig. Only	AR
Hawkins, Joseph A.	085	1878	WB-1/428	CTY
Hawkins, Joseph W.	100	1842	WB-38/89	AR
Hawkins, Littleton	009	c1852	OWB/548	AR
Hawkins, Major	009	c1810	OWB/460	AR
Hawkins, Major	009	1824	OB-A/333	AR
Hawkins, Maria	099	1883	WB-A/460	AR
Hawkins, Maria E.	100	c1883	Orig. Only	AR
Hawkins, Mary A.	100	1851	WB-41/210	AR
Hawkins, Mary A.	057	1899	WB-C/244	AR
Hawkins, Mary A.	099	1895	WB-C/382	AR
Hawkins, Mary F.	100	1876	WB-38/13	AR
Hawkins, Mathew	100	1856	WB-49/12	AR
Hawkins, Micajah T.	100	1859	WB-49/211	AR
Hawkins, Nancy R.	047	1839	WB-4/176	
Hawkins, Obediah	072	1801	WB-A/55	AR
Hawkins, P.	039	c1857	WB-O/378	AR
Hawkins, Patsy	047	1864	WB-5/122	
Hawkins, Peter	047	1893	WB-7/91	AR
Hawkins, Peter B.	047	1889	WB-6/522	AR
Hawkins, Philemon	100	1818	WB-21/104	AR
Hawkins, Philemon	100	1833	WB-34/45	AR
Hawkins, Philemon	100	1802	WB-11/226	AR
Hawkins, Philomon B.	039	1891	WB-U/512	AR
Hawkins, R. C.	047	1880	WB-6/229	AR
Hawkins, Rachel	013	1834	WB-A/27	
Hawkins, Rachel	009	1827	OB-A/388	AR
Hawkins, Sarah	075	1722	SS 875/340	SS/AR
Hawkins, Sarah	072	1886	WB-4/212	AR
Hawkins, Solomon	047	1816	WB-3/589	
Hawkins, Stephen	072	c1799	Orig. Only	AR
Hawkins, Thomas	096	1732	SS 876/268	SS/AR
Hawkins, Thomas	026	1881	WB-2/219	AR
Hawkins, Thomas	010	1793	WB-D/214	AR
Hawkins, William	086	1786	WB-A/8	AR
Hawkins, William	057	1812	WB-A/331	AR
Hawkins, William	090	1804	WB-2/49	Nunc.
Hawkins, William	044	1820	WB-8/352	CTY
Hawkins, William J.	099	1894	WB-C/312 & 356	AR
Hawkins, William J.	099	1894	Copy	068 AR
Hawkins, William J.	099	1894	Copy	070 AR
Hawkins, Winifred	100	1863	WB-50/63	AR
Hawks, Benjamin	100	1841	WB-38/13	AR
Hawks, Benjamin	100	1897	WB-51/492	AR
Hawks, Elizabeth	078	1846	Orig. Only	AR
Hawks, Francis	028	1832	WB-C/349	AR
Hawks, Jeremon	100	1864	WB-50/116	AR
Hawks, John	100	1848	WB-39/403	AR
Hawks, Mary E.	009	1873	WB-1/119	CTY
Hawley, Ann	103	1783	WI-A/39	AR
Hawley, Benjamin	071	1805	WB-2/276	AR
Hawley, Burton	028	1840	WB-D/20	AR
Hawley, Daniel	073	1794	WB-B/262	
Hawley, Eleanor	029	1844	WB-C/71	AR
Hawley, Jerutha	029	1879	WB-E/196	AR
Hawley, Josiah	028	1801	WB-B/120	AR
Hawley, Levi	013	1881	WB-B/234	AR
Hawley, Matilda	105	1877	WB-2/224	AR
Hawley, Mikell	071	1752	Orig. Only	SS/AR
Hawley, Nathan	044	1884	WB-23/504	CTY
Hawley, Samuel T.	029	1883	WB-E/327	AR
Hawn, Amzi A.	021	1864	WB-1/195	AR
Hawn, Anna Mary	021	1854	WB-1/114	AR
Hawn, Anna P.	021	1899	WB-3/226	AR
Hawn, Daniel	021	1897	WB-3/168	AR
Hawn, David	021	1887	WB-2/377	
Hawn, David	060	1838	WB-1/424	AR
Hawn, Frederick	085	c1801	WB-D/173	AR
Hawn, Frederick	021	1857	WB-1/133	AR
Hawn, Henry	021	1891	WB-2/511	
Hawn, Jesse	021	c1891	WB-3/312	AR

Name	Co.	Date	Recorded Copy	Original
Hawn, John	060	1793	Orig. Only	AR
Hawn, John	021	1848	WB-1/63	AR
Hawn, John, Jr.	060	1801	Orig. Only	AR
Hawn, John, Sr.	021	1898	WB-3/220	AR
Hawn, Jonas	021	c1898	WB-3/326	AR
Hawn, Jonas F.	021	c1891	WB-3/12	AR
Hawn, Moses	021	1885	WB-2/333	
Haworth, John	085	1814	WB-G/318	AR
Haworth, Mary	032	1834	WB-1/251	
Haworth, Mary M.	064	1898	WB-2/442	AR
Haworth, Micajah	085	1823	WB-H/227	AR
Haws, Henry	047	1761	WB-1/43	
Haws, John	072	1798	Orig. Only	AR
Haws, Joseph	072	1794	Orig. Only	AR
Haws, Sarah	028	1815	WB-C/112	
Hawthorn, A. S.	004	1900	WB-A/245	AR
Hawthorn, Andrew	006	1878	WB-E/46	AR
Hawthorn, John	006	1858	WB-D/55	AR-Nunc.
Hawthorn, John T.	004	1885	WB-A/71	AR
Hay, Charles	087	1784	WB-A/16	AR
Hay, Charles	057	1802	WB-A/262	AR
Hay, Charles	072	1765	RW/L47	AR
Hay, George	086	1882	WB-F/175	AR
Hay, Hannah	019	1777	WB-D/219	AR
Hay, James	070	1775	WB-C/144	AR
Hay, James E.	057	1895	WB-C/209	AR
Hay, Joseph	057	1866	WB-B/258	AR
Hay, Lorenzo D.	057	1894	WB-C/202	AR
Hay, Mary	057	1813	WB-B/29	AR
Hay, Reuben	065	1817	WB-D/4	AR
Hay, Robert	028	1851	WB-D/171	AR
Hay, Thomas	057	1796	WB-A/140	AR
Hayer, Hugh	016	1847	WB-1/127	AR
Hayes, Abram	065	1824	WB-D/83	AR
Hayes, Ann	099	1833	RB-22/494	AR
Hayes, Arthur	084	1834	WB-B/106	CTY
Hayes, Bartholomew	078	1820	WI-9/195	AR
Hayes, Belle	039	1893	WB-U/579	AR
Hayes, Catharine	065	1859	WB-J/62	AR
Hayes, Chrissie	041	1873	WB-4/35	AR
Hayes, David	073	1897	WB-I/132	CTY
Hayes, Dempsy	099	1797	RB-4/35	AR-Nunc.
Hayes, Docton	041	1881	WB-4/138	AR
Hayes, Elizabeth	099	1882	WB-A/349	AR
Hayes, Emma E.	041	1869	WB-4/8	AR
Hayes, Hardy	010	1784	WB-C/86	AR
Hayes, Hardy	010	1845	WB-G/383	AR
Hayes, Hugh	100	1814	WB-19/18	AR
Hayes, James	060	1845	WB-2/232	AR
Hayes, James H.	039	1857	WB-O/381	AR
Hayes, John	071	1795	WB-2/66	AR
Hayes, John	084	c1792	OW/62	AR
Hayes, John	099	1841	RB-24/472	AR
Hayes, John	039	1822	WB-G/113	AR
Hayes, John	060	1847	WB-2/271	AR
Hayes, Joseph	044	1793	WB-3/13	CTY
Hayes, Joshua	044	1797	WB-4/132	CTY
Hayes, Mahala	099	1862	RB-32/248	AR
Hayes, Martha	065	1824	WB-D/8	AR
Hayes, Mary A.	100	1887	WB-51/290	AR
Hayes, Mary M.	039	c1856	WB-O/369	AR
Hayes, Moses	065	1809	WB-D/68	AR
Hayes, Peter	044	1889	WB-24/93	CTY
Hayes, Robert	065	1796	WB-D/57	AR
Hayes, Ruthe	010	1818	WB-G/27	AR
Hayes, Samuel	010	1831	WB-G/206	AR
Hayes, Sarah	071	1795	WB-2/76	AR
Hayes, Silvy	010	1851	WB-G/480	AR
Hayes, Tabitha	070	1897	WB-H/110	AR
Hayes, Willis R.	041	1899	WB-4/469	AR
Haygler, John	065	c1771	WB-D/40	AR
Haygood, Benjamin	056	c1781	Orig. Only	AR
Haygood, James	073	1768	WB-A/83	
Haygood, Lucy	100	1821	WB-23/216	AR
Hayles, John, Sr.	056	1804	WB-1/163	AR
Hayley, Holliday	071	1865	WB-5/310	AR
Hayley, Hudson	071	1815	WB-3/138	AR
Hayley, Julia	071	1882	WB-6/390	AR
Hayman, Henery	002	c1709	Orig. Only	SS/AR
Hayman, Henry	075	1727	SS 876/122	SS/AR
Hayman, Tedrick	096	1878	WB-4/35	
Hayman, Thomas	030	1788	WB-1/220	
Haymes, John	005	1781	WB-1/32	AR
Haymond, Esther A.	013	1899	WB-D/280	AR
Haymore, Daniel	092	1900	WB-6/537	AR
Haymore, Hasten	092	1900	WB-6/533	AR
Haymore, Jermon	092	1897	WB-6/460	AR
Haymore, John	092	1825	WB-3/164	AR
Haynes, Amey	030	1827	WB-3/224	
Haynes, Bartholomew	065	1815	WB-D/3	AR
Haynes, Bethel	105	1866	WB-1/115	AR
Haynes, Christopher	047	1787	WB-3/127	
Haynes, Daniel	086	1821	Orig. Only	AR
Haynes, Eaton	071	1812	WB-3/74	AR
Haynes, Elizabeth	086	1836	WB-E/32	AR
Haynes, H. P.	049	1894	WB-2/330	AR
Haynes, Harbert	100	1793	WB-6/239	AR
Haynes, Herbert	022	1832	Orig. Only	AR
Haynes, Jesse K.	105	1898	WB-3/312	
Haynes, John	106	1870	WB-2/25	AR
Haynes, Joshua	011	c1794	WB-1/499	Nunc.
Haynes, Lucy	046	1818	WB-B/53	AR
Haynes, Margaret	071	1821	WB-3/245	AR
Haynes, Margaret	070	1770	WB-C/136	AR
Haynes, Mary	049	1857	WB-2/200	AR
Haynes, Nancy	083	1862	WB-2/190	AR
Haynes, Susan	090	1899	WB-6/512	AR
Haynes, Thomas	047	1796	WB-3/267	
Haynes, Wilkerson	086	1869	WB-F/6	AR
Haynes, William	092	c1837	WB-4/122	AR
Haynes, William	049	1853	WB-2/194	AR
Haynes, William	105	c1888	WB-1/129	AR
Haynes, William	105	1893	WB-3/87	AR
Haynes, William	086	1788	Orig. Only	AR
Haynes, William H.	054	c1863	Orig. Only	AR
Haynes, William H.	026	1892	WB-2/437	AR
Haynes, William M.	090	1866	WB-5/34	
Haynie, Benjamin	072	1784	WI/L19	AR
Hayns, James	054	c1788	WB-1/8	AR
Hayns, Patsy	100	1790	WB-5/190	AR-Nunc.
Hayns, Sarah	065	1839	WB-E/225	AR
Hayr, Margaret	016	1853	WB-1/221	AR
Hays, Andrew	085	c1806	WB-E/109	AR
Hays, Barnard C.	073	1866	WB-G/508	CTY
Hays, Bartrey	010	1891	WB-I/318	AR
Hays, Benjamin	041	1833	WB-2/320	AR
Hays, Bennet J.	083	1870	WB-3/22	AR
Hays, Darkis	073	1810	WB-D/261	AR
Hays, David	065	c1778	WB-D/12	AR
Hays, Edmund	081	1856	WB-11/188	AR

Name	Co.	Date	Recorded Copy	Original
Hays, Elizabeth	011	N. D.	WB-1/342	
Hays, Elizabeth	077	1825	Orig. Only	AR
Hays, George	086	1843	WB-E/95	AR
Hays, George W.	023	1870	Orig. Only	AR
Hays, Gideon	009	1881	WB-1/292	CTY
Hays, Greenbury	054	1845	WB-2/322	AR
Hays, Jacob	041	1808	WB-2/8	AR
Hays, Jacob	039	1874	WB-U/107	AR
Hays, James	041	1808	WB-2/31	AR
Hays, John	071	1783	WB-1/283	
Hays, John	056	c1781	WB-1/796	AR
Hays, John	041	1836	WB-2/376	AR
Hays, John	097	1878	WB-2/146	AR
Hays, John W.	041	1878	WB-4/100	AR
Hays, Joseph	085	c1793	WB-E/99	AR
Hays, Joseph R.	041	1866	WB-3/352	AR
Hays, Levi C.	083	1888	WB-3/437	AR
Hays, Levi M.	105	1882	WB-2/286	AR
Hays, Malinda J.	046	1889	WB-F/10	AR
Hays, Martha	086	1859	WB-E/370	AR
Hays, Mary	071	1854	WB-5/121	AR
Hays, Mary	099	1863	RB-32/604	AR
Hays, Mary	071	1800	WB-2/198	AR
Hays, Maxey	041	1878	WB-4/107	AR
Hays, Nancy	071	1885	WB-6/498	AR
Hays, Noah	054	1865	WB-3/180	AR
Hays, Oliver P.	081	1894	WB-16/314	AR
Hays, Patrick	046	1792	WB-A/159	AR
Hays, Peter	047	1761	WB-1/24	
Hays, R. A.	051	1890	WB-C/410	
Hays, Reuben	103	1829	RD-6/42	AR
Hays, Richard	041	1837	WB-2/381	AR
Hays, Richard	010	1786	WB-D/68	AR
Hays, Ruben	103	1831	RD-6/263	AR
Hays, S. A.	054	1892	WB-5/419	CTY
Hays, Samson	071	1789	WB-1/385	AR
Hays, Samuel	071	1796	WB-2/129	AR
Hays, Samuel	033	1840	WB-1/27	
Hays, Samuel	054	c1830	WB-2/101	AR
Hays, Samuel	071	1761	WB-1/54	
Hays, Samuel	054	1892	WB-5/423	CTY
Hays, Sarah	061	1885	WB-2/70	AR
Hays, Solomon	071	1801	WB-2/217	AR
Hays, Southy	011	c1805	WB-1/341	
Hays, Susan	010	1845	WB-G/384	AR
Hays, W. R.	105	c1870	WB-2/75	
Hays, William	104	1896	WB-6/568	AR
Hays, William	104	1864	WB-5/387	
Hays, William	041	1784	WB-1/40	AR
Hays, William	051	1877	WB-C/184	AR
Hays, William	031	1886	WB-1/37	AR
Hays, William G.	053	1844	WB-6/267	AR
Hays, William M.	031	1878	WB-1/11	AR
Hays, William W.	054	1896	WB-5/572	CTY
Hays, Willie D.	010	1889	WB-I/267	AR
Hayse, Cornelius	071	1825	WB-3/325	AR
Hayse, Joshua	010	1800	WB-E/110	AR
Haysell, Rogger	070	c1866	WB-E/244	AR
Haywood, Ann	099	1866	RB-33/490	AR
Haywood, E. Burke	099	1894	WB-C/212	AR
Haywood, Egbert	047	1801	WB-3/365	
Haywood, Eleanor	099	1856	RB-29/459	AR
Haywood, Eliza E.	099	1877	RB-35/387	AR
Haywood, Elizabeth	099	1832	RB-22/347	AR
Haywood, Fanny	069	1889	WB-5/321	
Haywood, Frances A.	099	1883	WB-A/502	AR
Haywood, George W.	099	1890	WB-B/429	AR
Haywood, James M.	097	1896	WB-2/496	AR
Haywood, Jane F.	099	1876	RB-35/363	AR
Haywood, John	037	1758	SS 882/63	
Haywood, John	099	1827	RB-20/145	AR
Haywood, John	037	1758	SS 881/223	SS/AR
Haywood, John	039	1826	WB-H/154	AR
Haywood, John, Jr.	037	1758	SS 882/84	SS/AR
Haywood, M. W.	039	1872	WB-U/43	
Haywood, Philemon	099	1852	RB-28/99	AR
Haywood, Richard B.	099	1891	WB-B/544	AR
Haywood, Sally	100	c1815	Orig. Only	AR
Haywood, Sherwood	099	1830	RB-21/226	AR
Haywood, Sherwood	037	1780	WB-B/45	AR
Haywood, Stephen	099	1823	RB-19/387	AR
Haywood, Stephen	099	1824	RB-19/521	AR
Haywood, V. A.	029	1897	WB-F/102	AR
Haywood, William	067	1888	WB-2/258	AR
Haywood, William	037	1780	WB-B/37	AR
Haywood, William H.	099	1852	RB-28/184	AR
Haywood, William H.	099	1857	RB-30/298	AR
Hayworth, Clemmons	081	1874	WB-15/140	AR
Hayworth, D. H.	081	1898	WB-16/518	AR
Hayworth, Eli	046	1866	WB-D/316	AR
Hayworth, Elizabeth	046	1861	WB-D/76	AR
Hayworth, George	046	1842	WB-C/137	AR
Hayworth, James L.	046	1899	WB-G/147	AR
Hayworth, M. M.	081	1894	046 WB-J/79	
Hayworth, M. M.	081	1894	WB-16/310	
Hayworth, Mary M.	081	1900	WB-17/139	
Hayworth, Rachel	046	1859	WB-D/31	AR
Hayworth, Richard	046	1838	WB-B/597	AR
Hayworth, Stephanus	046	1804	WB-A/169	AR
Hayworth, Wilmot	046	1864	WB-D/206	AR
Hazard, George	072	1822	WB-2/2	AR
Hazard, Nancy	028	1828	WB-C/299	AR
Hazel, Sarah	070	1872	Orig. Only	AR
Hazell, Duncan	001	1893	WB-2/568 & 574	AR
Hazell, Henry S.	103	1893	WB-2/38	AR
Hazell, Nancy E.	001	1895	WB-3/41	AR
Hazelton, Benja	079	1864	WB-1/147	AR
Hazelwood, George	100	1788	WB-5/15	AR
Hazelwood, Randolph	100	1797	WB-9/204	AR
Hazelwood, Warrick	100	1820	WB-22/293	AR
Hazelwood, Worwick	039	1879	WB-U/188	AR
Hazlett, John	085	c1788	WB-C/105	AR
Hazlett, Robert	090	1802	WB-2/26	AR
Hazzard, Elliott W.	SC	1896	Copy	013 AR
Head, Alexander	099	1798	RB-4/167	AR
Head, Anna C.	090	1896	WB-6/396	AR
Head, Henry	099	1804	RB-6/320	AR
Head, James	054	c1829	WB-2/123	AR
Head, William	092	c1836	WB-4/163	
Headen, Aaron D.	022	1859	WB-D/30	AR
Headen, Benjamin	022	1894	WB-E/552	AR
Headen, Dolly	022	1852	WB-C/323	AR
Headen, Elizabeth	022	1855	Orig. Only	AR
Headen, Isaac	022	1845	WB-C/171	AR
Headen, Isaac B.	022	1852	WB-C/326	AR
Headen, John	022	c1859	WB-D/152	AR
Headen, John	022	1779	Orig. Only	AR
Headen, John	022	1805	WB-A/105	AR
Headen, John B.	022	c1881	WB-E/484	

Name	Co.	Date	Recorded Copy	Original
Headen, Josiah	022	1859	WB-D/37	AR
Headen, Martha L.	022	1898	WB-F/73	AR
Headen, Sarah	022	1795	RB-2/62	AR
Headen, Susanah	022	1874	WB-E/93	AR
Headen, Temperance	022	1877	WB-E/130	AR
Headen, William	022	1869	WB-E/23	AR
Headen, William	022	1865	WB-D/143	AR
Headrick, George	032	1844	WB-1/446	
Headrick, Margaret	085	c1800	WB-E/113	AR
Headrick, Solomon	032	c1851	WB-2/154	
Heady, Daniel	019	1804	WB-D/236	AR
Heafner, George H.	060	1894	WB-4/550	AR
Heafner, John	060	1837	WB-1/400	
Heafner, Levi	060	1860	WB-3/27	
Healy, John	046	1813	WB-A/179	AR
Heannon, William	060	1824	Orig. Only	AR
Heareson, John	002	1694	Orig. Only	SS/AR
Hearick, Jesse	035	1789	WB-A/206	AR
Hearn, Abraham	022	1783	Orig. Only	AR
Hearn, George	065	1896	WB-M/448	AR
Hearn, Hasten H.	022	1892	WB-E/494	AR
Hearn, James	009	1752	Orig. Only	SS/AR
Hearn, James	037	1783	WB-B/129	
Hearn, John	105	1861	WB-1/66	
Hearn, John	079	1861	WB-1/153	AR
Hearn, John T.	022	1886	WB-E/325	AR
Hearn, Mary	016	1900	WB-4/365	AR
Hearn, Mary M.	079	1880	WB-2/190	AR
Hearn, Mason	056	1810	WB-1/229	AR
Hearn, Michael	037	1788	WB-C/59	AR
Hearn, S. W.	005	1890	WB-D/277	AR
Hearne, A. J.	069	1897	WB-5/584	AR
Hearne, George	065	1790	WB-C/141	AR
Hearne, Parham	089	1895	Orig. Only	AR
Hearne, Selby	067	1878	Orig. Only	AR-Copy
Heart, Abraham	072	c1781	Orig. Only	AR
Heartsfield, Andrew	099	1862	RB-32/428	AR
Heartsfield, Jacob	039	1814	WB-D/120	AR
Heartsfield, Wesley	099	1880	WB-A/183	AR
Heartt, Caroline	073	1884	WB-H/351	CTY
Heartt, Henrietta	073	1884	WB-H/349	CTY
Heartt, Susan	073	1864	WB-G/445	CTY
Heath, Amos	057	1858	WB-B/243	AR
Heath, Argent	057	1866	WB-B/265	AR
Heath, Delilah	075	1885	WB-O/226	AR
Heath, Eliza A.	046	1887	WB-E/489	AR
Heath, Frederick	028	1819	WB-C/177	AR
Heath, Henry	028	1798	WB-B/51	AR
Heath, Jacob	046	1816	WB-A/189	AR
Heath, James	035	1832	WB-1/27	AR
Heath, James J. M.	097	1893	WB-2/445	AR
Heath, Jeremiah	028	1798	WB-B/52	AR
Heath, Jeremiah	028	1867	WB-D/444	
Heath, John	047	1765	WB-1/168	
Heath, John	057	1848	WB-B/195	AR
Heath, John	046	1816	WB-A/188	AR
Heath, John	090	1820	WB-3/41	AR
Heath, John	028	1771	Orig. Only	AR
Heath, John	047	1795	WB-3/258	
Heath, Julian	030	c1809	WB-2/356	
Heath, Levina	057	1882	WB-C/86	AR
Heath, Mary	028	1804	WB-B/201	AR
Heath, Mary	028	1794	WB-A/312	Nunc.
Heath, Nancy	057	1866	WB-B/259	AR
Heath, Presly	084	1882	WB-E/241	CTY
Heath, Reuben	028	1798	WB-B/55	AR
Heath, Rigdon	028	1799	WB-B/65	AR
Heath, Robert	030	1795	WB-2/40	
Heath, Samuel	046	1816	WB-A/189	AR
Heath, Shadrack	028	1816	Orig. Only	AR
Heath, Smith	046	1897	WB-F/565	AR
Heath, Theophilus	047	1844	WB-4/241	Nunc.
Heath, Thomas	028	1796	WB-A/353	AR
Heath, Thomas	090	1804	WB-2/48	AR
Heath, Thomas	030	1802	WB-2/209	
Heath, Thomas	047	1773	WB-1/331	
Heath, Thomas	030	c1813	WB-3/29	
Heath, Thomas B.	035	1876	WB-4/113	AR
Heath, Thomas C.	075	1884	WB-O/196	AR
Heath, William	046	1876	WB-E/170	AR
Heath, William	028	1782	Orig. Only	AR
Heath, William	046	1816	WB-A/183	AR
Heath, William	028	1781	Orig. Only	AR
Heath, William	054	1885	WB-5/78	CTY
Heather, William	084	1827	WB-A/211	CTY
Heathman, Hezekiah	085	1852	WB-K/147	AR
Heathman, William	085	1855	WB-K/188	AR
Heaton, David	028	1870	Orig. Only	AR
Heavener, Christena	014	1872	WB-2/73	
Heavner, Abraham	060	1876	WB-4/157	AR
Heavner, Daniel M.	060	1862	WB-3/44	AR
Heavner, Henry	060	1882	WB-4/242	AR
Heavner, Martin	060	1844	WB-2/221	AR
Heck, Eugene Gray	046	1898	099 WB-D/166	
Heck, Eugene Gray	046	1898	WB-G/52	AR
Heck, Eugene Gray	046	1898	100 WB-51/564	100 AR
Heck, Jonathan M.	099	1894	WB-C/224	AR
Heck, Jonathan M.	099	1894	090 WB-6/457	090 AR
Heckedorn, Catherine	038	c1857	WB-1/126	AR
Heckelfield, John	077	1721	SS 875/305	SS/AR
Hecker, George	060	1784	Orig. Only	AR
Heckstall, Joseph	010	1898	WB-I/536	
Heckstall, Sallie E.	010	1898	WB-I/544	
Heckstall, William H.	010	1848	WB-G/427	AR
Hedgcock, John P.	038	1885	WB-2/556	AR
Hedgcock, William	090	1824	WB-3/129	AR
Hedgecock, Alfred A.	046	1874	WB-E/127	AR
Hedgecock, Barnitt	032	1891	WB-4/115	AR
Hédgecock, Emmet L.	032	1899	WB-4/425	AR
Hedgecock, John	046	1870	WB-E/34	AR
Hedgecock, Joseph	046	1848	WB-C/290	AR
Hedgecock, Joshua	046	1895	WB-F/448	AR
Hedgecock, Joshua	046	1860	WB-D/53	AR
Hedgecock, Joshua	032	1895	WB-4/267	AR
Hedgecock, Joshua M.	046	1865	WB-D/277	AR
Hedgecock, Margaret	046	1896	WB-F/526	AR
Hedgeman, Lewis	070	1822	WB-C/173	AR
Hedgepeth, Abram	069	1845	WB-1/479	AR
Hedgepeth, Hannah	069	1893	WB-5/421	
Hedgepeth, Harriet	069	1886	WB-5/243	AR
Hedgepeth, Henry	069	1855	WB-1/548	AR
Hedgepeth, J. C.	069	1897	WB-6/19	AR
Hedgepeth, John M.	044	1889	WB-24/91	CTY
Hedgepeth, Martha Ann	069	1900	WB-6/109	AR
Hedgepeth, Pater	069	1893	WB-5/418	AR
Hedgepeth, Sarah	044	1840	WB-14/533	CTY
Hedgepeth, W. G.	044	1895	WB-24/279	CTY
Hedges, Thomas	070	1746	SS 877/31	SS/AR
Hedgpeth, Charity	083	c1805	WB-1/94	
Hedgpeth, Daniel	103	1808	WI-B/405	AR

Name	Co.	Date	Recorded Copy	Original
Hedgpeth, James	098	1896	WB-A/245	CTY
Hedgpeth, John	037	1823	WB-E/337	AR
Hedgpeth, John H.	071	1900	WB-7/464	AR
Hedgpeth, Patsey	047	1886	WB-6/418	AR
Hedgpeth, Taylor	039	c1856	WB-0/328	AR
Hedrick, Adam	032	1826	WB-1/65	
Hedrick, Adam	032	1842	WB-1/390	
Hedrick, Adam	085	1815	Orig. Only	AR
Hedrick, Andrew	060	1813	Orig. Only	AR
Hedrick, Caspar	032	1899	WB-4/414	AR
Hedrick, Francis	032	1831	WB-1/160	
Hedrick, George	032	1885	WB-3/469	AR
Hedrick, George	032	c1841	WB-2/29	
Hedrick, Jacob	032	1838	WB-1/316	
Hedrick, Jacob	032	1896	WB-4/282	AR
Hedrick, Jacob	032	1832	WB-1/193	
Hedrick, Jacob	032	c1852	WB-2/94	AR-Copy
Hedrick, Jesse	032	1895	WB-4/262	AR
Hedrick, John	032	1898	WB-4/382	AR
Hedrick, John L.	085	1899	WB-3/331	CTY
Hedrick, Joseph	032	1874	WB-3/119	AR
Hedrick, Mariah B.	032	1899	WB-4/414	
Hedrick, Michael	032	1884	WB-3/431	AR
Hedrick, Minnie L.	032	1895	WB-4/252	AR
Hedrick, Peter	032	1846	WB-1/497	
Hedrick, Philip	085	1814	WB-G/324	AR
Hedrick, Samuel	032	1867	WB-2/354	AR
Hedrick, Valentine	032	1865	WB-2/343	AR
Heffner, Jacob	054	1893	WB-5/459	CTY
Heffner, William	021	1881	WB-2/233	
Heflin, Benjamin	044	1858	WB-20/469	CTY
Heflin, Charles	099	1804	RB-6/249	AR
Heflin, Charles	044	1841	WB-15/21	
Hefner, Daniel	021	c1897	WB-3/325	AR
Hefner, Henry	021	1855	WB-1/118	AR
Hefner, Jacob	021	1865	WB-1/211	AR
Hefner, Solomon	021	1883	WB-2/273	
Hege, Christian	038	1874	WB-2/162	AR
Hege, Elizabeth	032	1866	WB-2/333	AR
Hege, Eve	090	1844	WB-4/152	AR
Hege, George	038	1891	WB-3/222	AR
Hege, George F.	038	1891	WB-3/191	AR
Hege, Henry	085	1819	WB-G/540	AR
Hege, Henry	032	1865	WB-2/316	AR
Hege, John	033	1882	WB-2/77	
Hege, John	032	1874	Orig. Only	AR
Hege, Lazarus	085	1817	WB-G/468	AR
Hege, Mary C.	038	1898	WB-4/80	AR
Hege, Sallie	032	1877	WB-3/242	AR
Hege, Valentine	032	1873	WB-3/92	AR
Hegey, George	032	1824	WB-1/26	
Hegge, Jacob	038	1882	WB-2/423	AR
Heggie, William	084	1867	WB-D/85	CTY
Heggons, Jepteth	011	c1768	WB-1/500	
Heide, Rudolph E.	070	1895	WB-G/369	AR
Heidelberg, John	072	1789	WI/L7	AR
Heigan, Irvin	039	1885	WB-U/368	AR
Heigens, Ryalus	104	1869	WB-6/9	AR
Heighe, James	075	1761	WB-H/17	AR
Heighe, Samuel	075	c1754	Orig. Only	AR
Heileg, J. S.	016	1885	WB-3/474	AR
Heileg, Paul N.	085	1892	WB-2/529	CTY
Heileig, Michael G.	085	1861	WB-K/295	AR
Heilig, Charles H.	016	1897	WB-4/268	AR
Heilig, George	085	1845	WB-K/3	AR

Name	Co.	Date	Recorded Copy	Original
Heilig, George H.	085	1897	WB-3/206	CTY
Heilig, George M.	085	1828	Orig. Only	AR
Heilig, James M.	016	1900	WB-4/370	AR
Heilig, L. G.	016	1889	WB-4/24	AR
Heilig, Salome	085	1859	WB-K/272	AR
Hein, Catherine	038	1855	WB-1/95	AR
Hein, John Jacob	090	c1795	Orig. Only	AR-Copy
Hein, Juliana	090	1821	WB-3/62	AR
Hein, Juliana C.	090	1836	WB-3/303	AR
Heins, Ralph	054	c1808	WB-1/108	AR
Heinsaman, William	016	1821	WB-A/91	AR
Heinsberger, Margaret	070	1890	WB-F/372	AR
Heinsley, Alfred	022	c1893	WB-E/540	
Heinze, Christian	090	1824	WB-3/116	AR
Heisler, Anna Lydia	038	1886	WB-3/15	AR
Heisler, Maria A.	038	c1861	WB-1/177	AR
Heitman, John A.	032	1893	WB-4/184	AR
Helderman, Frances	021	1898	WB-3/213	AR
Helderman, George C.	021	1844	WB-1/22	AR
Helderman, John F.	021	c1897	Orig. Only	AR
Helderman, Mary M.	060	1899	WB-5/115	AR
Helderman, Valentine	060	c1880	Orig. Only	AR
Helfer, Catherine	033	1842	WB-1/44	
Helfer, Jacob	085	1814	WB-G/325	AR
Hellard, Henry	085	1836	WB-H/713	AR
Hellard, James	085	1888	WB-2/318	CTY
Hellard, Jesse	085	1845	WB-I/259	AR
Hellen, Jonathan	019	1791	WB-D/223	AR
Hellen, Sidney	079	1888	WB-2/446	AR
Hellior, Richard	070	1757	DB-D/249	AR
Hellmund, Bell	106	1898	WB-2/434	
Helmes, John	065	1829	WB-E/68	AR
Helms, Abel	097	1900	WB-3/21 & 33	AR
Helms, Asa M.	097	1892	WB-2/424	AR
Helms, Copelan	097	1879	WB-2/153	
Helms, E. Pinkney	065	1897	WB-N/57	AR
Helms, Emanuel	097	1874	WB-2/75	
Helms, Gabriel	097	1856	WB-1/120	AR
Helms, George	065	1838	WB-H/2	AR
Helms, Giles	097	1864	WB-1/235	AR
Helms, H. J.	097	1877	WB-2/107	AR
Helms, Hannah	097	1852	WB-1/77	AR
Helms, Isaac H.	097	1847	WB-1/41	AR
Helms, Isam	097	1878	WB-2/141	AR
Helms, Israel L.	097	1881	WB-2/186	
Helms, Jacob	097	1860	WB-1/180	AR
Helms, Jane D.	097	1887	WB-2/334	AR
Helms, Joel	097	1862	WB-1/191	AR
Helms, Michael	097	1892	WB-2/426	AR
Helms, Moses	097	1864	WB-1/243	AR
Helms, Russell	097	1899	WB-3/5	AR
Helms, Samson	097	1888	WB-2/321	AR
Helms, William	097	1900	WB-3/17	AR
Helmstetler, John	032	1873	WB-3/74	
Helmstetter, Christian	032	c1833	WB-2/98	
Helmstetter, John Adam	085	c1807	WB-E/26	AR
Helper, Jacob	085	1808	Copy	033 AR
Helsabeck, Isaac Edwin	090	1892	WB-6/280	AR
Helsabeck, John F.	038	c1865	WB-1/253	AR
Helsly, Jacob	085	c1794	WB-E/124	AR
Helton, Joseph	100	1786	WB-4/182	AR
Helton, Joseph G.	014	1882	WB-2/230	AR
Helton, Peter	073	1803	WB-D/93	AR
Hemby, Amos	065	1887	WB-L/266	AR
Hemby, Amos	097	1887	WB-2/299	AR

Name	Co.	Date	Recorded Copy	Original
Hemby, Eli	097	1891	WB-2/407	AR
Hemby, Elizabeth	005	1819	WB-2/57	AR
Hemby, Joab	079	1898	WB-3/146	AR
Hemby, Margaret E.	097	1898	WB-2/554	AR
Hemby, Mary	079	1874	WB-2/93	AR
Hemby, Thomas	097	1887	WB-2/309	AR
Hemingway, Mary	012	1843	WB-B/179	AR
Hemly, Eli	097	c1890	WB-2/368	
Hemmingway, David M.	MS	1890	050 WB-2/86	050 CTY
Hemphill, David	078	c1849	Orig. Only	AR
Hemphill, Eliza A.	014	c1885	Orig. Only	CTY
Hemphill, James	085	c1784	WB-C/117	AR
Hemphill, John	086	1884	WB-F/232	AR
Hemphill, Matthew	065	1829	WB-E/65	AR
Hemphill, Thomas	014	c1824	Orig. Only	AR-Copy
Hemphill, Thomas	064	1893	WB-2/303	AR
Hemphill, William	013	1892	107 WB-2/240	
Henby, Dennis	005	1806	WB-2/58	AR
Henby, John	077	c1775	Orig. Only	AR
Henby, Joseph	077	1752	Orig. Only	SS/AR
Henby, Nathan	077	1825	WB-F/106	AR
Henby, Sylvanus	077	1767	WB-C/69	AR
Henby, Thomas	077	1807	WB-E/294	AR
Henderson, Adam S.	029	1813	WB-A/190	AR
Henderson, Alexander	018	c1857	WB-D/40	
Henderson, Alexander	022	1894	WB-E/564	AR
Henderson, Alexander	072	1839	WB-2/15	AR
Henderson, Alfred	022	1879	WB-E/162	AR
Henderson, Allen	086	1814	WB-C/17	AR
Henderson, Andrew	065	1837	WB-E/187	AR
Henderson, Anne	046	1884	WB-E/401	AR
Henderson, Archibald	044	1853	WB-19/242	CTY
Henderson, Archibald	065	1797	WB-D/48	AR
Henderson, Argalus	022	1806	WB-A/106	AR-Copy
Henderson, Barnabas, Jr.	072	1803	WB-A/53	AR
Henderson, Barnabas, Sr.	072	c1799	WB-A/52	AR
Henderson, C. C.	021	1869	WB-2/13	
Henderson, C. C.	021	1869	Copy	060 AR
Henderson, Carns	065	1845	WB-I/1	AR
Henderson, Caroline	070	1894	WB-G/234	AR
Henderson, David	013	1890	WB-B/559	AR
Henderson, David	010	1735	SS 876/377	SS/AR
Henderson, David	065	1879	WB-K/354	AR
Henderson, David R.	065	1846	WB-I/42	AR
Henderson, Duncan	070	1852	WB-C/543	AR
Henderson, Elizabeth	065	1828	WB-D/19	AR
Henderson, Elizabeth	084	c1790	OW/65	AR
Henderson, Elizabeth	044	1792	WB-2/282	CTY-Nunc.
Henderson, Frances	044	1845	WB-16/416	CTY
Henderson, George	010	1736	LGB-4/#64	SS/AR
Henderson, Griswold	065	1881	WB-K/439	AR
Henderson, Hattie P.	044	1874	WB-23/146	CTY
Henderson, Herman	MA	1728	Orig. Only	SS/AR
Henderson, Hezekiah	022	1877	WB-E/142	AR
Henderson, Hiram	020	1874	WB-A/145	CTY
Henderson, Isaac	080	1886	WB-1/125	AR
Henderson, Isaac S.	065	1862	WB-J/128	AR
Henderson, Jacob	020	1846	RB-P/341	AR
Henderson, James	065	1863	WB-J/157	AR
Henderson, James	072	c1770	RW/L37	AR
Henderson, James	022	1885	WB-E/308	AR
Henderson, James	104	1825	WB-4/71	
Henderson, James	060	1795	Orig. Only	AR
Henderson, James A.	040	1888	WB-2/306	AR
Henderson, James P.	065	1868	WB-J/256	AR
Henderson, Jeremiah	054	1889	WB-5/276	CTY
Henderson, John	073	c1838	WB-F/80	AR
Henderson, John	065	1809	WB-D/69	AR
Henderson, John	085	c1783	WB-C/167	AR
Henderson, John	053	1809	RW-1/430	AR
Henderson, John	022	1825	WB-B/89	AR
Henderson, John	065	c1793	WB-D/43	AR
Henderson, John	046	1800	WB-A/168	AR
Henderson, John C.	060	1834	WB-1/294	AR
Henderson, John L.	016	1884	WB-3/414	AR
Henderson, John L.	044	1848	WB-17/181	CTY
Henderson, John M.	070	1892	WB-G/56	AR
Henderson, Joseph	020	1837	RB-N/43	
Henderson, Josiah	072	1844	WB-2/50	AR
Henderson, Julius	085	1898	WB-3/233	CTY
Henderson, L. D.	013	1876	WB-B/142	AR
Henderson, Lawson	060	1843	WB-2/196	AR
Henderson, Lawson, Jr.	AR	1839	060 WB-2/24	060 AR
Henderson, Lemuel	072	1898	WB-4/390	AR
Henderson, Lemuel	072	1867	WB-3/3	AR
Henderson, Leonard	044	1833	WB-12/520	CTY
Henderson, Lydia	072	1882	WB-4/145	AR
Henderson, Margaret	065	1854	WB-I/241	AR
Henderson, Margaret	065	1878	WB-K/354	AR
Henderson, Mary	065	1825	WB-D/84	AR
Henderson, Mary	065	1818	WB-D/78	AR
Henderson, Mary Y.	065	1882	WB-K/495	AR
Henderson, Moses	086	1832	WB-D/157	AR
Henderson, Nancy B.	065	1856	WB-J/17	AR
Henderson, Nat. S.	020	1885	WB-A/440 & 477	CTY
Henderson, Norman	085	1877	WB-1/396	CTY
Henderson, Phillip	080	1896	WB-1/268	AR
Henderson, Richard	084	c1814	WB-A/190	CTY
Henderson, Richard	044	1786	WB-1/471	CTY
Henderson, Robert	065	1863	WB-J/161	AR
Henderson, Robert	065	1874	WB-K/167	AR
Henderson, Robert	065	1788	WB-D/13	AR
Henderson, Samuel	044	1783	WB-1/369	CTY
Henderson, Samuel	020	1819	RB-H/257	
Henderson, Sarah	085	1836	WB-H/708	AR
Henderson, T. C.	065	1888	WB-L/307	AR
Henderson, Thomas	070	1788	WB-C/153	AR
Henderson, Thomas	072	1870	WB-4/29	AR
Henderson, Thomas	028	1875	085 WB-3/452	085 CTY
Henderson, Thomas	028	1875	WB-E/115	AR
Henderson, Thomas	084	1821	WB-A/175	CTY
Henderson, Thomas S.	016	1850	WB-1/169	AR
Henderson, W. B.	040	1892	WB-2/420	AR
Henderson, Wallace	MS	1852	Copy	060 AR
Henderson, William	086	1853	080 WB-1/176	080 AR
Henderson, William	AR	1860	040 WB-1/117	
Henderson, William	065	1819	WB-D/6	AR
Henderson, William	086	1853	WB-E/245	
Henderson, William	065	c1794	WB-D/55	AR
Henderson, William	072	1849	WB-2/100	AR
Henderson, William	065	1777	WB-D/11	AR
Henderson, William	065	c1818	SC/01722	AR-Copy
Henderson, William A.	040	1890	WB-2/356	AR
Henderson, William L.	065	1871	WB-K/67	AR
Henderson, Wilson	084	1843	WB-B/307	CTY
Hendley, Edmund	078	1792	WI-1/59	AR
Hendley, Henry	044	1853	WB-19/222	CTY
Hendley, John	054	c1802	WB-1/110	AR

Name	Co.	Date	Recorded Copy	Original
Hendley, Thomas	005	1863	WB-C/184	AR
Hendly, William	082	1808	WB-1/126	AR
Hendon, Isham	099	1804	RB-6/225	AR
Hendon, James	099	1792	RB-2/340	AR
Hendon, Josiah	011	c1830	WB-2/393	
Hendon, William	011	c1778	WB-1/522	
Hendren, Drusilla	003	1897	WB-B/373	AR
Hendren, George	104	1831	WB-4/146	AR
Hendren, Jabez	104	1888	WB-6/329	AR
Hendren, Jesse	104	1866	WB-5/426	AR
Hendren, Richard	054	1894	WB-5/520	CTY
Hendren, Stephen	104	1876	WB-6/127	AR
Hendren, William	104	1838	WB-4/231	AR
Hendren, William	104	1868	WB-5/529	
Hendrick, Chapel	026	1889	WB-2/355	AR
Hendrick, E.	026	1899	WB-3/24	AR
Hendrick, Francis	075	c1714	Orig. Only	SS/AR
Hendrick, Francis	028	1734	SS 877/163	SS/AR
Hendrick, Frederick	092	1833	WB-4/60	AR
Hendrick, George	026	1862	WB-1/287	AR
Hendrick, Gustavus	005	1810	WB-2/55	AR
Hendrick, Jeremiah	077	1756	SS 880/123	SS/AR
Hendrick, Mary	026	1851	WB-1/120	AR
Hendrick, Mourning	069	1887	WB-5/256	AR
Hendrick, Nathaniel	090	1834	WB-3/281	AR
Hendrick, Simon	069	c1868	Orig. Only	AR
Hendrick, Stephen	044	1848	WB-17/182	CTY
Hendrick, Temperance	069	1854	WB-1/539	AR
Hendrick, William	069	1841	WB-1/454	AR
Hendrick, William	099	1787	RB-2/115	AR
Hendrick, William	037	1767	WB-A/151	AR
Hendrick, William	100	1857	WB-49/144	AR
Hendricks, Daniel	010	c1768	WB-A/101	AR
Hendricks, David	085	1821	WB-H/76	AR
Hendricks, Henry	046	1841	WB-C/92	AR
Hendricks, Isaac	085	1821	WB-H/132	AR
Hendricks, Job	077	1788	WB-C/368	AR
Hendricks, Joseph	081	1795	WB-2/15	AR
Hendricks, Joshua	065	1856	WB-J/16	AR
Hendricks, Margaret	085	1801	WB-E/108	AR
Hendricks, Peter	073	1788	WB-B/41	AR
Hendricks, Sarah	077	1768	WB-C/6	AR
Hendricks, Solomen	077	c1744	Orig. Only	SS/AR
Hendricks, Solomon	077	1833	WB-F/223	AR
Hendricks, Thomas	033	1848	WB-1/97	
Hendricks, Tobias	081	1847	WB-8/532	AR/CRX
Hendrickson, Elizabeth	010	1855	WB-H/22	AR
Hendrickson, Isaac	010	1840	WB-G/316	AR
Hendrickson, John	019	1803	WB-D/235	AR
Hendrix, Abel	077	1828	WB-F/160	AR
Hendrix, David	038	1884	WB-2/505	AR
Hendrix, George W.	104	1888	WB-6/305	AR
Hendrix, Henry	085	1786	WB-C/100	AR
Hendrix, Isaac	010	1889	WB-I/277	AR
Hendron, Arania	085	1803	WB-D/192	AR
Hendron, John	085	c1788	WB-E/111	AR
Hendron, Solomon	003	1872	WB-B/24	AR
Hendry, Alexander	070	1820	WB-C/171	AR
Hendry, John	060	1779	Orig. Only	AR
Hendry, Moses	060	1781	Orig. Only	AR
Hendry, Theodore	PA	1893	013 WB-C/422	013 AR
Hendry, Thomas	022	c1779	Orig. Only	AR
Heneley, John	072	1747/8	SS 877/45	SS/AR
Henesey, John	070	1757	DB-D/256	AR
Heniger, Jacob	097	1867	WB-1/287	AR
Henkel, David	060	1831	WB-1/232	AR
Henkel, P. C.	021	1887	WB-2/475	AR
Henkle, Elizabeth	060	1875	WB-4/124	AR
Henkle, Hannah	040	1866	WB-1/189	
Henkle, Jacob	032	1826	WB-1/43	
Henkle, Osborne	040	1888	WB-2/321	AR
Henlen, Elizabeth	054	c1837	WB-2/173	AR
Henley, Anna	081	c1871	Orig. Only	AR-Copy
Henley, Anna	046	c1871	WB-E/95	AR
Henley, David V.	046	1893	WB-F/295	AR
Henley, Henry	081	1882	WB-15/397	AR
Henley, James A.	039	1873	WB-U/62	AR
Henley, James A.	039	1894	WB-V/37	AR
Henley, Jesse	081	1834	WB-6/396	AR
Henley, John	081	1815	WB-4/227	AR
Henley, John	038	1869	WB-2/12	AR
Henley, John	075	1728	SS 876/146	SS/AR
Henley, John	075	1754	Orig. Only	SS/AR
Henley, John	081	1834	WB-6/378	AR
Henley, John W.	018	1886	WB-E/159	AR
Henley, Joseph	075	1795	WB-L/26	
Henley, Mary	030	c1815	WB-3/60	
Henley, Peter	024	1758	SS 882/86	SS/AR
Henley, Stephen G.	081	1890	WB-16/179	AR
Henley, William	044	1808	WB-6/408	CTY
Henline, Hannah	033	1837	WB-1/3	
Henly, Darby	085	c1808	WB-G/108	AR
Henly, Darby	020	1786	RB-B/98	AR
Henly, James D.	078	1816	WI-7/129	AR
Henly, Lettis	078	1822	WI-9/325	AR
Henly, Washington	085	1883	WB-2/79	CTY
Hennan, Barbara	021	1856	WB-1/127	
Hennan, George	021	1850	WB-1/84	
Hennesa, John	017	c1844	WB-A/17	AR
Henness, Mildred	084	1855	WB-C/215	
Hennessee, Eliza W.	038	1855	WB-1/84	AR
Hennigan, Samuel	065	1835	WB-G/210	AR
Henning, John Adam	090	1824	WB-3/113	AR
Hennings, Demsey	075	1808	WB-M1/197	
Henniss, Mildred	084	1860	WB-C/347	CTY
Hennon, James	060	1786	Orig. Only	AR
Henry, Amelia	SC	c1806	Orig. Only	019 AR
Henry, Caroline	005	1875	Orig. Only	AR
Henry, Catharine	070	1864	WB-D/151	AR
Henry, Charles	FL	1860	070 WB-D/22	070 AR
Henry, Charles D.	070	1856	WB-C/615	AR
Henry, Dorcas	065	1827	WB-C/4	AR
Henry, Dorcas B.	013	1857	WB-A/187	
Henry, E. R.	065	1884	WB-L/113	AR
Henry, Elizabeth	022	1869	WB-E/92	AR
Henry, Elizabeth	028	1825	WB-C/256	AR
Henry, Emery M.	005	1896	WB-D/395	AR
Henry, Franklin	040	1891	WB-1/385	AR
Henry, George	022	1847	WB-C/201	AR
Henry, Hugh	028	1814	WB-C/78	AR
Henry, Hugh	053	1791	RW-1/204	
Henry, Isaac	040	1861	WB-1/131	AR
Henry, Jackson	070	1894	WB-G/173	AR
Henry, James	065	1817	WB-D/4	AR
Henry, James	070	1817	WB-C/163	AR
Henry, James	060	1841	WB-2/88	AR
Henry, James L.	013	1884	WB-B/337	AR
Henry, Joel	019	1804	Orig. Only	AR
Henry, John	VA	1868	Copy	047 AR
Henry, John	070	1818	WB-C/166	AR

Name	Co.	Date	Recorded Copy	Original
Henry, John A.	049	1883	WB-2/102	AR
Henry, John C.	005	1873	WB-D/24	AR
Henry, John H.	078	1895	WB-19/384	AR
Henry, Joseph N.	005	1887	WB-D/201	AR
Henry, Louis D.	099	1846	RB-26/177	AR
Henry, Martha	105	1887	WB-2/448	
Henry, Mary	040	1891	WB-2/408	AR
Henry, Neal	070	1812	WB-AB/172	AR
Henry, Neal	070	1862	WB-D/77	AR
Henry, Nehemiah	028	1777	Orig. Only	AR
Henry, Noah	050	1897	WB-2/267	CTY
Henry, P. T.	098	1893	WB-A/166	CTY
Henry, Philip	005	1847	WB-B/229	AR
Henry, R. F.	060	1856	WB-2/405	
Henry, Robert	053	1775	RW-1/73	AR
Henry, Robert	010	1806	WB-F/8	AR
Henry, Robert	013	1863	WB-C/114	AR
Henry, Robert	028	1819	WB-C/184	AR
Henry, Ruben	005	1880	WB-D/96	AR
Henry, Sarah	047	1820	WB-3/651	
Henry, Sarah	053	1869	WB-11/11	AR
Henry, Sarah	053	1842	WB-6/176	AR
Henry, Sarah C.	054	1888	Orig. Only	AR
Henry, Stephen	084	1846	WB-C/35	CTY
Henry, Thomas	060	1836	WB-1/381	AR
Henry, Thomas	085	c1777	WB-A/235	AR
Henry, William	028	1800	WB-B/109	
Henry, William	028	c1789	Orig. Only	AR
Henry, William	070	1833	WB-C/181	AR
Henry, William B.	050	1868	WB-1/101	CTY
Henry, William C.	070	1854	Orig. Only	AR
Henshaw, William	092	1833	WB-4/48	
Henslee, Amos	014	1828	Orig. Only	AR
Henslee, John	020	1816	RB-G/301	
Henslee, Macksfield	020	1801	RB-D/70	
Henslee, William	020	1793	RB-C/51	
Hensley, James A.	086	1886	WB-F/291	AR
Hensley, John	090	1825	WB-3/141	
Henslie, Spivey	073	1893	WB-I/13	CTY
Henson, Benjamin	086	1877	WB-F/94	AR
Henson, Jeremiah	065	1840	WB-H/20	AR
Henson, Joseph	081	1873	WB-15/122	AR
Henson, Joseph	081	1786	WB-1/34	AR
Henson, Philip	086	1832	WB-D/149	AR
Henson, Philip	086	1885	WB-F/260	AR
Henson, Reuben	086	1880	WB-F/158	AR
Henson, Thomas	055	c1867	WB-A/28	
Henson, William	086	1795	Orig. Only	AR
Henton, David	028	1870	WB-E/36	
Hepler, Christian	032	1846	WB-1/485	
Hepler, John	032	c1847	WB-2/17	
Hepler, Joseph	032	1878	WB-3/247	AR
Hepler, Noah	032	1865	WB-2/300	AR
Hepler, Thomas	032	1876	WB-3/187	AR
Hepthinstall, John W.	100	1890	WB-51/320	AR
Hepworth, John	065	1816	WB-D/75	AR
Herbart, William	047	1820	WB-3/659	
Herbert, Elles	028	1778	Orig. Only	AR
Herbert, George F.	070	1887	WB-F/123	AR
Herbert, Hillary	019	1767	RB-A/24	AR
Herbert, Hillary	019	c1797	WB-D/227	AR
Herbert, Ignatius	053	1798	RW-1/298	AR
Herbert, Jesse	047	1866	WB-5/142	
Herbert, John	047	1821	WB-3/663	
Herbert, T. J.	025	1894	WB-A/176	AR
Herbert, William	057	1799	WB-A/222	AR
Herbeson, Mary	021	1873	WB-2/92	AR
Herbin, Malinda	084	1854	WB-C/177	CTY
Herbin, Mary	046	1894	WB-F/368	AR
Herbin, William	084	1847	WB-C/65	CTY
Herbin, William	084	1879	WB-E/158	
Herbst, Jonas C.	090	N. D.	Orig. Only	AR
Herendon, Sarah	060	1841	WB-2/85	AR
Hering, William C.	070	1854	WB-C/565	
Herinton, James	009	1759	OWB/63	AR
Heriot, Henry F.	093	1890	WB-2/68	
Herman, Adelaide	038	1874	WB-2/185	AR
Herman, D. F.	003	1864	WB-A/9	AR
Herman, Elijah	021	c1898	WB-3/329	AR
Herman, Ephraim A.	021	1874	WB-2/102	AR
Herman, Frank L.	021	1900	WB-3/269	AR
Herman, Franklin	003	1897	WB-B/368	AR
Herman, George	060	c1841	Orig. Only	AR-Copy
Herman, George	003	1891	WB-B/293	AR
Herman, John	021	1886	WB-2/353	
Herman, John	003	c1877	Orig. Only	AR
Herman, John G.	038	1854	WB-1/63	AR
Herman, M. C.	102	1895	WB-A/101	AR
Herman, Peter, Sr.	021	1853	WB-1/105	AR
Hermon, George	081	1787	WB-1/45	AR
Hermon, Henry	084	1815	WB-A/186	CTY
Hermon, Sally M.	021	1875	WB-2/146	AR
Hern, James	037	1783	Orig. Only	AR
Herndon, Ann	073	1879	WB-H/212	CTY
Herndon, Bartlett	036	1889	WB-A/157	CTY
Herndon, D. E.	036	1885	WB-A/79	CTY
Herndon, David	073	c1812	WB-D/372	AR
Herndon, Duncan C.	044	1872	WB-23/59	CTY
Herndon, E. W.	013	1886	WB-B/375	AR
Herndon, Edmund	020	1840	RB-O/122	
Herndon, George	073	1796	WB-C/85	AR
Herndon, George	099	c1820	RB-20/127	
Herndon, James	073	1839	WB-F/31	AR
Herndon, John R.	044	1866	WB-22/409	CTY
Herndon, Lewis	073	1869	WB-H/7	CTY
Herndon, Lewis	073	1818	WB-D/518	AR
Herndon, Lydia	073	1836	Copy	099 AR
Herndon, Margaret	073	1847	WB-F/379	AR
Herndon, Mary	073	1844	WB-F/220	AR
Herndon, Pomphrett	073	1817	WB-D/515	AR
Herndon, Reuben	022	1855	WB-C/399	AR
Herndon, Rhodes N.	044	1863	WB-21/667	CTY
Herndon, Sarah	073	1802	WB-D/70	AR
Herndon, Stephen G.	044	1859	WB-21/154	CTY
Herndon, Thomas J.	022	1890	WB-E/444	AR
Herndon, Thomas S.	036	1883	WB-A/36	CTY
Heron, Alice	070	1813	WB-AB/198	AR
Heron, Benjamin	070	1771	WB-C/137	AR
Herr, Henry H.	PA	1890	Copy	074 AR
Herrenden, Hezekiah	010	1754	SS 879/147	SS/AR
Herrick, Edwin H.	013	1889	WB-B/504	AR
Herrin, Hezakiah	089	1858	WB-1/181	
Herring, Abel	099	1833	RB-22/376	AR
Herring, Abia	103	1884	WB-1/307	AR
Herring, Alexander	035	1819	WB-A/202	AR
Herring, Alice	059	1878	WB-A/162	CTY
Herring, Anthony	103	1784	Orig. Only	AR
Herring, B. M.	087	1863	WB-A/153	AR
Herring, Benajah	103	1896	WB-3/163	AR
Herring, Benajah	103	1859	RD-12/626	AR

Name	Co.	Date	Recorded Copy	Original
Herring, Benjamin	103	1844	RD-9/141	AR
Herring, Benjamin	070	1789	WB-C/155	AR
Herring, Benjamin	103	1815	RD-3/314	AR
Herring, Benjamin W.	103	1882	WB-1/240	AR
Herring, Catharine	035	1878	WB-4/128	AR
Herring, Celia	103	1848	RD-10/86	AR
Herring, Daniel	035	1865	WB-3/95	AR
Herring, Dorcas	070	1800	WB-C/158	AR
Herring, Edward	103	1899	WB-2/247	AR
Herring, Elisha	035	1858	WB-2/138	AR
Herring, Elizabeth	103	1842	RD-8/302	AR
Herring, Emily	059	1900	WB-B/286	CTY
Herring, Etheldred	103	1863	Orig. Only	AR
Herring, Everitt	035	1892	WB-4/417	AR
Herring, Fredrick	103	1789	Orig. Only	AR
Herring, Gabriel	087	1846	WB-1/303	AR
Herring, George W.	087	1893	WB-3/524	AR
Herring, Harding	092	1876	WB-6/89	AR
Herring, Jacob	103	1839	RD-7/533	AR
Herring, Jacob	087	c1796	WB-A/23	AR
Herring, James	103	1845	RD-9/273	AR
Herring, Joel	103	1812	RD-2/101	AR
Herring, Joel, Sr.	087	1832	WB-1/139	AR
Herring, John	070	1774	WB-C/143	AR
Herring, John I.	103	1889	WB-1/462	AR
Herring, John R.	047	1894	WB-7/117	AR
Herring, Julia	103	1875	WB-1/95	AR
Herring, Lewis	044	1807	WB-6/333	CTY
Herring, Lewis W.	050	1857	WB-1/52	CTY
Herring, Lucinda	035	1899	WB-4/550	
Herring, Mary	039	1885	WB-U/362	AR
Herring, Mary	011	c1834	WB-1/19	
Herring, Mary	103	1820	RD-4/366	AR
Herring, Mary W.	092	1855	WB-5/17	AR
Herring, Michael	103	1805	Orig. Only	AR
Herring, Nancy	059	1873	WB-A/67	
Herring, Nathan	087	1883	WB-3/274	AR
Herring, Nehemiah	087	1890	WB-3/468	AR
Herring, Oliver	059	1878	WB-A/154	CTY
Herring, Rachel	059	1873	WB-A/106	
Herring, Richard	087	c1802	WB-A/173	AR-Copy
Herring, Sallie F.	105	1893	WB-3/57	AR
Herring, Sally	103	1889	WB-1/495	AR
Herring, Sally	103	1796	WI-B/126	
Herring, Samll.	056	1750	028 DB-5/165	SS/AR
Herring, Samuel	035	1809	WB-A/208	AR
Herring, Samuel	070	1829	WB-C/179	AR
Herring, Sarah	103	1890	WB-1/512	AR
Herring, Simon	103	1819	RD-4/248	AR
Herring, Solomon	103	1789	WI-A/164	AR
Herring, Stephen	084	1823	WB-A/177	CTY
Herring, Stephen	035	1797	WB-A/209	AR
Herring, Stephen	087	1839	WB-1/214	AR
Herring, Stephen	087	c1817	WB-A/161	AR
Herring, Thomas U.	087	1852	WB-1/422	AR
Herring, Uzzill	087	c1803	WB-A/40	AR
Herring, William	070	1855	WB-C/594	AR
Herring, William	035	1873	WB-4/67	AR
Herring, William	018	1848	WB-C/341	
Herring, William	059	1883	WB-A/291	CTY
Herringg, Henry	092	1799	WB-3/33A	AR
Herrington, Charles	009	1828	OB-A/506	AR
Herrington, Elizabeth	011	1849	WB-1/171	
Herrington, Fanny	018	1829	WB-C/110	
Herrington, Joab	079	1864	WB-1/123	AR

Name	Co.	Date	Recorded Copy	Original
Herrington, John	009	1869	WB-1/6	CTY
Herritage, James S.	072	1885	WB-4/180	AR
Herritage, James S.	072	1885	057 WB-C/124	057 AR
Herritage, William	028	c1769	Orig. Only	SS/AR
Herritage, William M.	028	1843	WB-D/80	AR
Herritage, Wm. Martin	028	1808	Orig. Only	AR
Herron, David, Sr.	084	c1818	WB-A/185	CTY
Herron, Elizabeth	065	1821	WB-D/22	AR
Herron, Hugh	065	1805	WB-C/150	AR
Herron, James	065	1779	WB-C/135	AR
Herron, John	084	c1807	WB-A/88	CTY
Herron, John A.	065	1869	WB-K/29	AR
Herron, John T.	040	1886	WB-2/261	AR
Herron, John W.	065	1846	WB-I/45	AR
Herron, Thomas	065	1808	WB-D/67	AR
Herron, William M.	065	1896	WB-M/451	AR
Hervey, Gideon P.	047	1860	WB-5/89 & 92	
Hervey, Mary	030	1836	WB-4/15	
Hervey, Peyton P.	047	c1863	WB-5/125	
Hervey, Thomas	047	1806	WB-3/448	
Hess, Daniel	085	1848	WB-K/66	AR
Hess, Mary M.	085	1890	WB-2/421	CTY
Hesselbach, Henry J.	099	1876	RB-35/346	AR
Hessler, Abraham	090	1800	WB-1/168	AR
Hessler, Maria S.	090	1821	WB-3/64	AR
Hester, Aaron	011	1885	WB-3/80	
Hester, Alfred	044	1840	WB-14/532	CTY
Hester, Allafair F.	011	1893	WB-3/57	CTY
Hester, Ann	039	1817	WB-F/30	AR
Hester, B. B.	044	1892	WB-24/210	CTY
Hester, Barsheba	054	1854	WB-3/80	
Hester, Benjamin	044	1838	WB-14/250	CTY
Hester, Benjamin	044	1844	WB-16/63	CTY
Hester, Daniel	011	1896	WB 3/82	CTY
Hester, Daniel	011	1884	WB-2/185	
Hester, Drusilla	044	1863	WB-21/673	CTY
Hester, Elijah	039	1898	WB-4/84	AR
Hester, George	044	1892	WB-24/180	CTY
Hester, Hamilton	044	1860	WB-21/287	CTY
Hester, James	044	1848	WB-17/192	CTY
Hester, James	044	1832	WB-12/302	CTY
Hester, James	039	c1794	WB-A/157	AR
Hester, John	044	1818	WB-8/121	CTY
Hester, John	090	1819	WB-3/30	AR
Hester, John	044	1817	WB-7/637	CTY
Hester, John H.	099	1879	WB-A/70	AR
Hester, Joseph	044	1802	WB-5/284	CTY
Hester, Joseph P.	044	1893	WB-24/219	CTY
Hester, Martha Ann	099	1887	WB-B/210	AR
Hester, Mary	090	1808	WB-2/88	AR
Hester, Mary A.	098	1886	WB-A/73	CTY
Hester, Mary D.	044	1842	WB-15/299	CTY
Hester, Michael	086	1849	WB-E/188	AR
Hester, Moses B.	038	c1860	WB-1/172	AR
Hester, Nicholas	073	1875	WB-H/106	CTY
Hester, Robert	090	1843	WB-4/136	AR
Hester, Robert	090	1802	WB-2/30	AR
Hester, Robert	078	1827	WI-10/328	
Hester, Robert H.	078	1880	WB-19/107	AR
Hester, Thomas	044	1872	WB-23/91	CTY
Hester, Thomas	011	c1839	WB-1/59	
Hester, Thomas	054	c1828	WB-2/60	AR
Hester, William	044	1817	WB-8/19	CTY
Hester, William	083	c1822	WB-1/374	AR
Hester, William	047	1774	WB-1/96	CTY

Name	Co.	Date	Recorded Copy	Original
Hetchey, Solomon	085	1894	WB-3/62	
Hetfield, John C.	030	1857	WB-4/219	
Hethcock, Mary	089	1894	Orig. Only	AR
Hettrick, Philip	021	1866	WB-1/228	AR
Heugh, Timothy	085	c1789	WB-C/3	AR
Hewes, Joseph	024	1779	WB-A/8	AR
Hewet, Nancy	057	1812	WB-A/336	AR
Hewett, Charles	012	1884	WB-A/56	AR
Hewett, Edward	012	1878	WB-A/34	AR
Hewett, Isaac	012	1864	WB-B/49	AR
Hewett, Jeremiah	012	1880	WB-A/43	AR
Hewett, Joseph	012	c1794	Orig. Only	AR
Hewett, Josephus	071	1829	WB-4/64	AR
Hewett, Matthias	012	c1861	WB-B/40	
Hewett, Philip,Sr.	012	1823	WB-B/128	AR
Hewett, Robert	012	1879	WB-A/38	AR
Hewit, Ephraim	030	c1815	WB-3/62	
Hewit, John	072	1865	WB-3/9	AR
Hewit, John	072	1777	RW/L9	AR
Hewit, John C.	072	c1866	WB-4/195	AR
Hewit, Thomas	072	1778	RW/L5	AR
Hewit, William	021	1888	WB-2/425	AR
Hewitt, Barrilla	047	1777	WB-2/46	
Hewitt, Bartholomew	075	1720	SS 875/242	
Hewitt, John	012	1858	WB-B/12	AR
Hewitt, Joseph	012	1812	WB-B/102	AR
Hewitt, Rigdon P.	057	1893	WB-C/195	AR
Hewlett, Alexander	FL	1866	070 WB-D/191	070 AR
Hewlett, Almira	070	1898	WB-H/137	AR
Heyer, Barbara	070	1862	WB-D/100	AR
Heyer, William A.	070	1862	WB-D/99	AR
Hiaman (Hyman), Garrat	028	1768	Orig. Only	AR
Hiatt, Christopher	046	1849	WB-C/318	AR
Hiatt, Christopher	046	1793	WB-A/160	AR
Hiatt, Cuthbert	046	1862	WB-D/128	AR
Hiatt, George	046	1793	WB-A/184	AR
Hiatt, John	046	1849	WB-C/308	AR
Hiatt, Joseph	046	1843	WB-C/163	AR
Hiatt, Martin P.	092	1887	WB-6/265	AR
Hiatt, Mary Ann	046	1896	WB-F/519	AR
Hiatt, Nathan	046	1875	WB-E/146	AR
Hiatt, Nathan	046	c1786	WB-A/157	AR
Hiatt, William	046	1835	WB-B/531	AR
Hiatt, William	046	1814	WB-A/180	AR
Hiatt, Wilson	046	1891	WB-F/103	AR
Hibbits, Robert	054	c1835	WB-2/190	AR
Hibbs, John	019	1800	WB-D/231	AR
Hibbs, Jonathan	019	1825	WB-D/259	AR
Hibbs, Jonathan	075	1745	Orig. Only	SS/AR
Hibbs, Jonathan	072	1790	WB-A/58	AR
Hick, David	024	1732	SS 876/263	SS/AR
Hickerson, Mary	104	1794	WB-1/386	
Hickman, Agnes	100	1848	WB-39/458	
Hickman, James	017	1875	WB-B/51	AR
Hickman, Jesse	029	1807	WB-A/112	AR
Hickman, Joseph	092	c1825	WB-4/8	AR
Hickman, Nathaniel	037	1795	WB-C/341	AR
Hickman, Sarah	028	1818	WB-C/167	AR
Hicks, Absalom	044	1770	Orig. Only	CTY
Hicks, Africa	075	c1711	SS 874.1/37	
Hicks, Albert R.	103	1886	WB-1/373	AR
Hicks, Benjamin	044	1900	WB-24/466	CTY
Hicks, Benjamin	078	1869	Orig. Only	AR
Hicks, Benjamin	070	1760	DB-D/457	AR
Hicks, C. C.	054	1889	WB-5/302	CTY
Hicks, Daniel	072	c1762	RW/L43	AR
Hicks, Daniel	026	1876	WB-2/164 & 220	AR
Hicks, David	100	1889	WB-51/293	
Hicks, E. W.	098	1897	WB-A/289	CTY
Hicks, Edward B.	VA	c1852	Copy	047 AR
Hicks, Elijah	054	1866	WB-3/181	AR
Hicks, Elitha	071	1885	WB-6/459	AR
Hicks, Elizabeth	090	1896	WB-6/387	AR
Hicks, Elizabeth	046	1860	WB-D/61	AR
Hicks, Elizabeth	071	1862	WB-5/273	AR
Hicks, Eloner	054	1850	WB-3/43	AR
Hicks, Fannie	101	1900	WB-A/322	AR
Hicks, Frances	005	1867	WB-C/258	AR
Hicks, Francis	044	1847	WB-17/172	CTY
Hicks, George M.	039	c1862	WB-S/4	AR
Hicks, Henry	054	c1827	WB-2/172	AR
Hicks, Henry	054	1888	WB-5/207	CTY
Hicks, Henry	032	1890	WB-4/90	AR
Hicks, Henry C.	044	1877	WB-23/292	CTY
Hicks, Hiram	082	1881	WB-6/224	AR
Hicks, Isham J.	067	1866	WB-1/131	AR
Hicks, James	104	1829	WB-4/128	AR
Hicks, James	037	1841	WB-F/255	AR
Hicks, James	100	1797	WB-4/249	AR
Hicks, James	001	c1856	WB-1/106	AR
Hicks, James	064	c1858	Orig. Only	AR
Hicks, James	092	1848	WB-4/284	
Hicks, James H.	035	1874	WB-4/85	AR
Hicks, James M.	001	1862	WB-1/201	AR
Hicks, Jasper	044	1861	WB-21/495	CTY
Hicks, John	073	1832	WB-E/285	AR
Hicks, John	001	1874	WB-2/63	AR
Hicks, John	005	1761	WB-1/12	
Hicks, John	100	1877	WB-51/117	
Hicks, John	016	N.D.	WB-A/25	AR
Hicks, John	019	1749	SS 877/292	SS/AR
Hicks, John B.	044	1878	WB-23/315	CTY
Hicks, John R.	044	1877	WB-23/256	CTY
Hicks, Kaleb	057	1869	WB-C/3	AR
Hicks, Keturah	037	1883	WB-G/646	
Hicks, Lewis	099	1818	RB-12/146	AR
Hicks, Lucy F.	044	1890	WB-24/124	CTY
Hicks, Lydia	026	1885	WB-2/274	AR
Hicks, Malissa	067	1876	WB-2/66	AR
Hicks, Mary	103	1899	WB-2/242	AR
Hicks, Melissa A.	100	1894	WB-51/436	AR
Hicks, Miles	021	1892	WB-3/14	AR
Hicks, Moses	099	1810	RB-9/229	AR
Hicks, Moses	072	1786	WI/L2	AR
Hicks, Mourning	044	1823	WB-9/246	CTY
Hicks, Nancy E.	044	1899	WB-24/440	CTY
Hicks, Noah	047	1889	WB-6/531	AR
Hicks, Patrick	024	1793	WB-A/74	AR
Hicks, Richard	086	1812	WB-B/261	AR
Hicks, Richard H.	086	1864	WB-E/426	AR
Hicks, Robert	044	1829	WB-11/135	CTY
Hicks, Robert	071	1801	WB-2/215	AR
Hicks, Robert	024	1733	SS 876/297	AR
Hicks, Robert	044	1792	WB-2/290	CTY
Hicks, Robert A.	039	1888	WB-U/438	AR
Hicks, Samuel	044	1772	WB-1/4	CTY
Hicks, Samuel S.	098	1882	WB-A/10	CTY
Hicks, Sarah	044	1806	WB-6/294	CTY
Hicks, Sarah C.	069	1884	WB-5/201	AR

Name	Co.	Date	Recorded Copy	Original
Hicks, Sarah G.	039	1881	WB-U/250	AR
Hicks, Selas G.	100	1896	WB-51/453	AR
Hicks, Thankfull	035	1785	WB-A/185	AR-Copy
Hicks, Thomas	073	1880	WB-H/241	CTY
Hicks, Thomas	035	c1775	WB-A/186	AR-Copy
Hicks, Thomas	N	1724	SS 876/30	SS/AR
Hicks, Thomas J.	044	1864	WB-22/169	CTY
Hicks, William	100	1854	WB-43/194	AR
Hicks, William	064	1846	WB-1/17	AR
Hicks, William	044	1799	WB-4/346	CTY
Hicks, William	071	1834	WB-4/112	AR
Hicks, William R.	044	1874	WB-23/156	CTY
Hide, John	085	c1793	WB-D/177	AR
Hide, Margret	085	1850	WB-K/120	AR
Hiesley, Joachim	085	c1766	WB-A/256	AR
Hiett, Jesse	092	1835	WB-4/89	
Hiffines, Mary Ann	001	1900	WB-3/303	
Higgins, Alberto	064	1900	WB-2/482	AR
Higgins, Burr	046	1887	WB-E/494	AR
Higgins, Michael	028	1753	SS 879/84	SS/AR
Higgins, Michall	072	1777	RW/L15	AR
Higgins, Wiley F.	019	1876	WB-B/86	AR
Higgins, William	057	c1778	WB-A/196	AR
Higgins, William F.	064	1868	WB-1/98	AR
Higgs, Abraham	010	1782	WB-C/46	AR
Higgs, Jacob	047	1817	WB-3/602	
Higgs, John	010	1815	WB-F/295	AR
Higgs, Johnston	010	1839	WB-G/308	AR
Higgs, Judeth	010	1796	WB-D/340	AR
Higgs, Mary	010	1866	WB-H/171	AR
Higgs, Sally	047	1837	WB-4/151	
Higgs, Samuel	047	1838	WB-4/160	
Higgs, Samuel	069	1810	WB-1/213	AR
Higgs, Theophilus	047	1824	WB-3/707	
Higgs, Thomas	029	1770	Orig. Only	AR
High, Alsey	099	1822	RB-18/254	AR
High, Amelia	099	1789	RB-2/232	AR
High, Elizabeth	099	1862	RB-32/257	AR
High, Esau	027	1830	WB-A/14	AR
High, Isham E.	099	1835	RB-23/245	AR
High, Joel B.	069	1900	WB-6/113	AR
High, John	099	1777	RB-1/110	AR
High, Luke	027	c1845	WB-A/53	AR
High, Michal	027	1815	WB-A/10	AR-Nunc.
High, Middy	099	1816	RB-12/372	AR
High, Patsey	099	1804	RB-6/321	AR
High, Penina	105	1898	WB-3/306	AR
High, Rachel	099	1808	RB-7/313	AR
High, Samuel	099	1813	RB-11/27	AR
High, Sarah	039	1815	WB-D/171	AR
High, Sarah	071	1869	WB-6/9	AR
Highet, Thomas	041	1785	WB-1/50	
Highfill, Hezekiah	046	1818	WB-B/51	AR
Highfill, Hezekiah	046	1873	WB-E/109	AR
Highfill, John	046	1892	WB-F/191	AR
Highman, Rachel	028	1795	WB-A/326	AR
Highmiller, Conrad	054	c1818	WB-1A/93	AR
Highsmith, Daniel	070	1813	WB-AB/186	AR
Highsmith, Daniel	047	1772	WB-1/306	
Highsmith, Dorcas	070	1855	WB-C/584	AR
Highsmith, Jacob	087	1869	WB-3/16	AR
Highsmith, James	079	1861	WB-1/70	AR
Highsmith, John	035	1867	WB-3/125	AR
Highsmith, Lewis	087	1884	WB-3/287	AR
Highsmith, Mary	070	1829	WB-C/178	AR
Highsmith, Noah F.	087	1877	WB-3/142	AR
Highsmith, Sarah	035	1862	WB-3/57	AR
Highsmith, William	087	1890	WB-3/440	AR
Hight, Harbard H.	039	1861	WB-R/193	
Hight, Hartwell	098	1885	WB-A/53	CTY
Hight, John	039	c1795	WB-A/166	AR
Hight, Jonathan	068	1840	WB-B/128	
Hight, Nancy M.	039	1873	WB-U/70	AR
Hight, Nathaniel	039	c1849	WB-N/359	AR
Hight, Read	017	c1835	Orig. Only	AR
Hight, Richard	039	1881	WB-U/258	AR
Hight, William M.	098	1887	WB-A/83	CTY
Hightower, Agness	020	1853	RB-R/66	
Hightower, Austen	022	1784	RB-1/18	AR
Hightower, Catherine	020	1848	RB-Q/8	
Hightower, Charnal	020	1793	RB-C/37	
Hightower, Ephroditus	050	1853	WB-1/34	CTY
Hightower, Francis	020	1818	RB-H/188	AR
Hightower, Joshua	VA	c1770	Copy	044 CTY
Hightower, Joshua	020	1836	RB-M/537	
Hightower, Robert W.	100	1804	WB-12/273	AR
Hightower, William	020	1855	RB-R/321	AR
Higson, Nancy A.	009	1817	OB-A/269	AR
Higson, Willoughby	053	1826	WB-4/426	AR
Hildebrun, Sophia	085	1854	WB-K/176	AR
Hildreth, Charles F.	NH	1897	Copy	068 AR
Hilegh, Henry	085	1827	WB-H/381	AR
Hileman, Adam N.	016	1884	WB-3/422	
Hilick, John	085	1841	WB-I/88	AR
Hilker, Caroline	065	1887	WB-L/240	AR
Hill, Aaron	081	1863	WB-12/470	AR
Hill, Abraham	054	c1806	WB-1/109	AR
Hill, Abraham	005	1896	WB-D/386	AR
Hill, Abraham	019	1798	WB-D/228	AR
Hill, Abraham	024	c1760	WB-A/52	AR
Hill, Abraham	054	1842	WB-2/251	
Hill, Abram	085	1860	WB-K/283	AR
Hill, Ahambrick	045	1887	WB-1/146	AR
Hill, Alexander	016	1861	WB-2/73	AR
Hill, Alleyfore	028	1848	WB-D/151	AR
Hill, Ann	028	1800	WB-B/94	AR
Hill, Ann Ivie	070	1864	WB-D/145	AR
Hill, Anna Maria	103	1859	RD-12/674	AR
Hill, Anne	040	1851	WB-1/35	
Hill, Annie C.	005	1897	WB-D/427	AR
Hill, Asa	041	1859	WB-3/235	AR
Hill, Benjamin	047	1820	WB-3/657	
Hill, Benjamin	010	1753	SS 878/187	SS/AR
Hill, Benjamin	039	1790	WB-A/64	
Hill, Benjamine	039	c1802	WB-B/68	
Hill, Bennett	039	c1791	WB-A/167	AR
Hill, Boson	010	1817	WB-G/14	AR
Hill, Buckner H.	019	1845	WB-A/123	AR
Hill, Buckner L.	035	1861	WB-3/18	AR
Hill, Callier	100	c1799	Orig. Only	AR-Copy
Hill, Calyer	047	1799	WB-3/330	
Hill, Carson	080	1891	WB-1/160	AR
Hill, Catharine	022	1897	WB-F/42	AR
Hill, Catherine	041	1892	WB-4/349	AR
Hill, Chane	085	1858	WB-K/264	AR
Hill, Charles	022	1881	WB-E/232	AR
Hill, Charles A.	039	1831	WB-J/170	AR
Hill, Charles W.	092	1884	WB-6/211	AR
Hill, Charles W.	092	c1883	Copy	090 AR
Hill, Christopher	035	1874	WB-4/82	AR

Name	Co.	Date	Recorded Copy	Original
Hill, Cicero	019	1892	WB-B/224	AR
Hill, Clement	030	1826	WB-3/217	
Hill, D. H.	065	1889	WB-L/417	AR
Hill, Daniel	079	1868	WB-2/9	AR
Hill, Daniel	081	1875	WB:15/183	AR
Hill, Daniel S.	039	1873	WB-U/80	AR
Hill, David	085	c1774	WB-A/194	AR
Hill, David	006	1856	WB-D/17	AR
Hill, David	049	1895	WB-2/340	AR
Hill, David	028	1803	WB-B/189	AR
Hill, Delona	078	1895	WB-19/395	AR
Hill, Drewry	059	1870	WB-A/25	
Hill, Edward	087	1864	WB-2/58	
Hill, Edward	019	1866	WB-B/26	AR
Hill, Edward B.	019	1822	WB-D/255	AR
Hill, Edward H.	028	1888	WB-E/474	AR
Hill, Edwin G.	028	1899	WB-F/428	
Hill, Eliza Ann	099	1894	WB-C/239	AR
Hill, Eliza H.	099	1882	WB-A/357	AR
Hill, Eliza H.	099	1882	067 WB-2/250	067 AR
Hill, Elizabeth	096	1852	WB-3/29	AR
Hill, Elizabeth	051	1870	WB-C/30	AR
Hill, Elizabeth	006	c1872	Orig. Only	AR
Hill, Elizabeth	060	1879	WB-4/199	AR
Hill, Elizabeth	009	1813	OWB/450	AR
Hill, Elizabeth	019	1819	WB-D/253	AR
Hill, Erasmus	019	1833	WB-A/33	AR
Hill, Ezekiel L.	081	1894	WB-16/323	AR
Hill, F. G.	038	1899	WB-4/187	AR
Hill, Frances	VA	c1866	Copy	099 AR
Hill, Francis	087	c1800	Orig. Only	AR
Hill, Frederick	070	1861	WB-D/51	AR
Hill, George	073	1780	WB-A/210	
Hill, George	028	1823	WB-C/230	AR
Hill, George	009	1832	OWB/500	AR
Hill, George	008	1723	SS 876/26	SS/AR
Hill, Grace	015	1772	100 WB-1/247	AR
Hill, Green	071	1769	WB-1/172	
Hill, Green	071	1831	WB-4/74	AR
Hill, Green	016	1831	PQS.5/152	AR-Nunc.
Hill, Griffin	083	c1807	WB-1/107	AR
Hill, Guy, Sr.	024	c1775	WB-A/25	AR
Hill, Guy, Sr.	041	1787	WB-1/67	AR
Hill, Hardy	051	1854	WB-A/360	
Hill, Hardy	010	1777	WB-B/115	AR
Hill, Hardy	059	1881	WB-A/223	CTY
Hill, Harman	009	1755	Orig. Only	SS/AR
Hill, Harmon	071	1777	WB-1/20	AR
Hill, Harvey	009	1871	WB-1/81	CTY
Hill, Hatch	019	1816	Orig. Only	AR-Nunc.
Hill, Henry	071	1840	WB-4/296	AR
Hill, Henry	041	1781	WB-1/12	AR
Hill, Henry	085	c1799	WB-E/122	AR
Hill, Henry	085	1845	WB-I/251	AR
Hill, Henry J.	071	1875	WB-6/170	AR
Hill, Hermon	071	1823	WB-3/277	AR
Hill, Himrick	041	1809	WB-2/41	AR
Hill, Isaac	011	c1770	WB-1/504	
Hill, Isaac	072	c1866	Orig. Only	AR
Hill, Isaac	099	1790	RB-2/433	AR
Hill, Isaac	019	1817	WB-D/250	AR
Hill, Isaac	046	c1781	WB-A/154	AR
Hill, Isaac	090	1796	WB-1/82	
Hill, Isaac S.	019	1888	WB-B/163	AR
Hill, Isaac, Sr.	019	1815	WB-D/247	AR
Hill, Isaac, Sr.	019	1805	WB-D/237	AR
Hill, Isack	024	c1710	SS 875/33	
Hill, Ivey Hatch	019	c1825	WB-D/257	AR
Hill, Jacob	021	1855	WB-1/120	CTY
Hill, James	071	1819	WB-3/223	AR
Hill, James	057	1808	WB-A/310	AR
Hill, James	104	1828	WB-4/115	AR
Hill, James	085	1819	WB-H/9	AR
Hill, James	085	c1804	WB-D/181	AR
Hill, James	083	1855	WB-2/85	AR
Hill, James A.	054	1867	WB-3/197	AR
Hill, James L.	054	c1831	WB-2/131	AR
Hill, James M.	092	1892	WB-6/339	AR
Hill, James W.	041	1892	WB-4/343	AR
Hill, Jane	054	1875	WB-4/172	CTY
Hill, Jane	060	1838	WB-2/4	AR
Hill, Jesse	032	1882	WB-3/347	AR
Hill, Jessey	077	1808	Orig. Only	AR
Hill, Joel	092	1884	WB-6/192	AR
Hill, Joel	090	1857	WB-4/310	AR
Hill, John	078	1852	WB-17/83	AR
Hill, John	019	1808	WB-D/240	AR
Hill, John	054	c1805	WB-1/115	AR
Hill, John	045	1887	WB-1/160	AR
Hill, John	024	1777	WB-A/30	AR
Hill, John	047	1830	WB-4/59	
Hill, John	035	1807	WB-A/218	AR
Hill, John	010	1763	WB-A/85	AR
Hill, John	070	1847	WB-AB/467	AR
Hill, John	009	1731	SS 876/238	SS/AR
Hill, John	030	c1814	WB-3/31	
Hill, John	060	1797	Orig. Only	AR
Hill, John	047	1854	WB-4/372	
Hill, John	065	1838	WB-E/184	AR
Hill, John	071	1747	Orig. Only	SS/AR
Hill, John	009	1802	OWB/381	AR
Hill, John	026	1848	WB-1/87	AR
Hill, John	090	1861	WB-4/346	AR
Hill, John	070	1813	WB-C/160	AR
Hill, John	010	1802	WB-E/143	AR
Hill, John B.	059	1895	WB-B/140	CTY
Hill, John H.	019	1837	WB-A/67	AR
Hill, John H.	081	1889	WB-16/123	AR
Hill, John H.	028	1783	Orig. Only	AR
Hill, John L.	085	1864	WB-K/339	AR
Hill, John P.	050	1892	WB-2/160	CTY
Hill, John W.	072	1896	WB-4/327	AR
Hill, Jonathan	073	1799	WB-C/129	AR
Hill, Jonston	050	c1882	Orig. Only	AR
Hill, Joseph	071	1808	WB-3/11	
Hill, Joseph	057	1810	WB-A/326	AR
Hill, Joseph B.	063	1795	WB-1/219	
Hill, Joseph J.	047	1809	WB-3/524	
Hill, Joshua	009	c1785	OWB/205	AR
Hill, Joshua	009	1833	OB-B/295	AR
Hill, Joshua J.	070	1886	WB-F/36	AR
Hill, Lazarus	009	1817	OB-A/270	AR
Hill, Leah	106	c1875	WB-2/63	AR
Hill, Lemuel	103	1887	WB-1/405	AR
Hill, Levi	032	1881	WB-3/345	AR
Hill, Levi	028	1794	WB-A/311	AR
Hill, Levi	059	1893	WB-B/72	CTY
Hill, Lewis	050	1890	WB-2/61	CTY
Hill, Louisa M.	099	1882	067 WB-2/249	067 AR
Hill, Louisa M.	099	1882	WB-A/355	AR

Name	Co.	Date	Recorded Copy	Original
Hill, Louisa S.	079	1891	WB-2/567	AR
Hill, Lydia	085	1878	WB-1/468	CTY
Hill, M. E.	059	1887	WB-A/485	CTY
Hill, Margaret	081	1894	WB-16/288	AR
Hill, Margaret	032	1899	WB-4/411	AR
Hill, Maria	070	1897	WB-G/553	AR
Hill, Martha	081	1898	WB-16/475	AR
Hill, Martha	045	1889	WB-1/183	AR
Hill, Mary	081	1816	WB-4/289	AR
Hill, Mary	099	1793	RB-2/485	AR
Hill, Mary	009	1848	OB-F/521	AR
Hill, Mary	083	1856	WB-2/87	AR
Hill, Mary Ann	099	1878	RB-35/427	AR
Hill, Mary Ann	041	1852	WB-3/146	AR
Hill, Mary E.	047	1881	WB-6/246	AR
Hill, Mary McRae	070	1887	WB-F/87	AR
Hill, Matilda	046	1886	WB-E/438	AR
Hill, Matthew	090	1804	WB-2/48	AR
Hill, Merritt	071	1846	WB-5/56	AR
Hill, Micajah	027	1817	WB-A/12	AR
Hill, Micajah	081	1857	WB-10/497	AR
Hill, Moses	010	1763	WB-A/31	AR
Hill, Moses	024	1746	Orig. Only	SS/AR
Hill, Moses L.	054	c1825	WB-2/62	AR
Hill, Nancy	081	1840	WB-7/318	AR
Hill, Nathaniel	099	1795	RB-3/117	AR
Hill, Nathaniel	070	1842	WB-AB/361	AR
Hill, Nathaniel	022	1871	WB-E/60	AR
Hill, Nelson	099	1874	RB-35/246	AR
Hill, Noah	092	1887	WB-6/263	AR
Hill, Payne	022	c1895	Orig. Only	AR
Hill, Penelope	037	1826	WB-F/59	AR
Hill, Polly	070	1894	WB-G/257	AR
Hill, Rachel	028	1831	WB-C/335	AR
Hill, Rebecca	047	1845	WB-4/248	
Hill, Rebecca	039	1821	WB-G/9	
Hill, Richard	028	1729	SS 876/181	SS/AR
Hill, Richard	092	1845	WB-4/243	
Hill, Richard	090	1836	WB-3/306	
Hill, Robert	054	c1800	WB-1/1	AR
Hill, Robert	090	1834	WB-3/277	AR
Hill, Robert	039	c1802	WB-B/93 & 167	
Hill, Robert	047	1765	WB-1/159	
Hill, Robert	096	1735/6	Orig. Only	SS/AR
Hill, Robert	050	1863	WB-1/81	CTY
Hill, Robert	065	1786	WB-C/139	AR
Hill, Robert	039	1818	WB-F/67	AR
Hill, Robert	092	1895	WB-6/408	AR
Hill, Robert C.	071	1894	WB-7/208	AR
Hill, Robert R.	041	1862	WB-3/293	AR
Hill, Roland	071	1900	WB-7/454	AR
Hill, Samuel	057	c1772	Orig. Only	AR
Hill, Samuel	090	c1848	Orig. Only	AR-Copy
Hill, Samuel	084	1839	WB-B/200	
Hill, Sanford	092	1882	Orig. Only	AR
Hill, Sarah	085	1843	WB-I/163	AR
Hill, Sarah	047	1793	WB-3/213	
Hill, Sarah	103	1831	RD-6/280	AR
Hill, Sarah	026	1847	WB-1/58	AR
Hill, Sarah Julia	070	1855	WB-C/586	AR
Hill, Sion	099	1780	RB-1/155	AR
Hill, Slaughter	083	c1818	WB-1/242	AR
Hill, Stephen	054	c1829	WB-2/114	AR
Hill, Susan	028	1848	Orig. Only	AR
Hill, Susan P.	009	1888	028 WB-E/490	
Hill, Susan R.	092	1885	WB-6/222	AR
Hill, Susanna	103	1819	RD-4/220	AR
Hill, Susannah	022	1843	WB-C/152	AR
Hill, Thomas	070	1819	WB-C/167	AR
Hill, Thomas	035	1862	WB-3/48	AR
Hill, Thomas	047	1769	WB-1/236	
Hill, Thomas	079	1888	WB-2/433	AR
Hill, Thomas	081	1800	WB-2/68	AR
Hill, Thomas	047	1789	WB-3/173	
Hill, Thomas	092	1827	WB-3/165	AR
Hill, Thomas	022	c1867	Orig. Only	AR
Hill, Thomas	028	1760	Orig. Only	AR-Nunc.
Hill, Thomas	022	1883	WB-E/251	AR
Hill, Thomas	085	N. D.	WB-B/92	AR
Hill, Thomas C.	039	1814	WB-D/74	AR
Hill, Thomas M.	054	1878	WB-4/302	CTY
Hill, Thomas P.	059	1897	WB-B/182	CTY
Hill, W. A.	081	1899	WB-17/27	AR
Hill, W. H.	046	1899	WB-G/376	
Hill, W. H.	046	1899	104 WB-7/289	104 AR
Hill, W. L.	081	1862	WB-12/237	
Hill, W. R.	040	1889	WB-2/344	AR
Hill, Wade	086	1880	WB-F/145	AR
Hill, Whitmel J.	047	1873	WB-6/82	AR
Hill, Whitmell	063	c1797	WB-1/339	
Hill, Wiley	099	1835	RB-23/246	AR
Hill, William	024	1752	Orig. Only	SS/AR
Hill, William	081	c1803	WB-2/129	AR
Hill, William	015	1774	100 WB-1/272	AR
Hill, William	039	c1784	WB-A/24	
Hill, William	019	1802	WB-D/239	AR
Hill, William	072	c1765	WB-A/48	AR
Hill, William	072	1815	WB-A/48	AR
Hill, William	070	1860	047 WB-5/85	
Hill, William	030	1853	WB-4/170	
Hill, William	071	1748	Orig. Only	SS/AR
Hill, William	047	1798	WB-3/300	
Hill, William	092	1787	WB-2/73	AR
Hill, William	083	1833	Orig. Only	AR
Hill, William	019	1891	WB-B/212	AR
Hill, William	092	c1832	WB-4/158	AR
Hill, William	099	1857	RB-30/356	AR
Hill, William	070	1783	WB-C/147	AR
Hill, William	N	1758	SS 882/27	
Hill, William	081	1866	WB-13/435	AR
Hill, William	099	1857	067 WB-2/248	067 AR
Hill, William	028	1811	WB-C/40	AR
Hill, William B.	081	1878	WB-17/485	
Hill, William B.	099	1826	RB-20/71	AR
Hill, William C.	047	1803	WB-3/398	
Hill, William E.	035	1900	WB-4/570	AR
Hill, William G.	099	1877	RB-35/384	AR
Hill, William H.	044	1899	WB-24/442	CTY
Hill, William H.	028	1888	WB-E/478	AR
Hill, William L.	051	1843	WB-A/159	
Hill, William L.	035	1860	WB-3/9	
Hill, William R.	059	1877	WB-A/135	CTY
Hill, William W.	044	1899	Copy	078 AR
Hill, Winefred	063	c1799	WB-1/407	
Hill, Wm. Henry	070	1809	WB-AB/120	AR
Hill, Wylie	GA	1844	013 WB-C/340	013 AR
Hill, Zachariah	030	1833	WB-3/308	
Hill, Zephaniah	092	1838	WB-4/142	
Hillard, Joseph	033	1845	WB-1/67	
Hillhouse, Samuel	085	c1782	WB-B/138	AR

Name	Co.	Date	Recorded Copy	Original
Hilliard, Alfred	102	1900	WB-A/183	AR
Hilliard, Anne	071	1771	WB-1/204	
Hilliard, Benjamin	057	1828	WB-B/91	
Hilliard, Betsey	044	1847	WB-17/139	CTY
Hilliard, Dandridge	100	1896	WB-51/463	AR
Hilliard, Edward W.	099	1867	RB-34/333	AR
Hilliard, Elijah B.	069	1862	WB-1/582	AR
Hilliard, Elijah B.	069	1894	WB-5/458	AR
Hilliard, Ezekel	022	1877	WB-E/158	AR
Hilliard, Henry	071	1792	WB-2/15	AR
Hilliard, Isaac	047	1854	WB-4/364	
Hilliard, Isaac	069	1790	WB-1/67	AR
Hilliard, Jacob	037	1764	WB-A/125	AR
Hilliard, James	069	1832	WB-1/385	AR
Hilliard, James	071	1764	WB-1/109	
Hilliard, James C.	069	1860	WB-1/566	AR
Hilliard, John	070	1815	WB-AB/213	AR-Nunc.
Hilliard, John	071	1748	Orig. Only	SS/AR
Hilliard, John	071	1796	WB-2/125	AR
Hilliard, John T.	069	1837	WB-1/416	AR
Hilliard, Leah	069	1823	WB-1/318	AR-Nunc.
Hilliard, Louis	VA	1894	047 WB-7/152	
Hilliard, Lucy K.	019	1899	Copy	037 AR
Hilliard, Lucy K.	019	1899	WB-C/25	AR
Hilliard, Margaret	047	1787	WB-3/124	
Hilliard, Martha A.	069	1889	WB-5/323	AR
Hilliard, Mourning	069	1847	WB-1/503	AR
Hilliard, Robert	037	1751	Orig. Only	SS/AR
Hilliard, Robert C.	069	1828	WB-1/350	AR
Hilliard, Thomas	100	1852	WB-42/2	AR
Hilliard, Thomas D.	100	1888	WB-51/266	AR
Hilliard, Thomas, Jr.	100	1821	WB-23/315	AR
Hilliard, William	056	1898	WB-4/129	AR
Hilliard, William	071	1756	SS 880/52	SS/AR
Hills, Charles	086	1830	WB-D/132	AR
Hills, James	086	1862	WB-E/391	AR
Hills, Robert	086	1833	WB-D/160	AR
Hillsman, Bennett	039	1799	WB-A/127	
Hillyard, Elizabeth	044	1830	WB-11/525	CTY
Hillyard, Lucy	073	1823	WB-E/39	AR
Hilorey, Samuel	008	1712	Orig. Only	SS/AR
Hilsebeck, Frederik	090	1799	WB-1/137	AR
Hilsman, Patty	039	1816	WB-E/36	AR-
Hilton, James	046	1796	WB-A/164	AR
Hilton, John	081	1790	WB-1/80	AR
Hilton, Martha	046	1862	WB-D/133	AR
Hilton, William H.	038	1891	WB-3/208	AR
Hilyard, Gersham	070	c1797	Orig. Only	AR
Hinchey, George	104	1898	WB-7/59	AR
Hinchy, Elizabeth	005	1835	WB-B/53	AR
Hindricks, Joseph	081	1795	WB-2/15	
Hinds, John	077	1763	Orig. Only	AR
Hinds, Joseph	046	1772	WB-A/150	AR
Hinds, Sarah	075	1845	WB-N/193	AR
Hine, Cesar	038	1885	WB-2/564	AR
Hine, Jacob	090	1795	WB-1/78	
Hine, John	039	1858	WB-1/128	AR
Hine, John	090	1806	WB-2/69	AR
Hine, Julianna	090	1821	WB-3/62	
Hine, Peter	090	1819	WB-3/37	AR
Hine, Phillip	090	1815	WB-2/163	AR
Hine, Solomon	032	1864	WB-2/283	AR
Hine, Thomas L.	102	1889	WB-A/64	AR
Hines, A. D.	039	1886	WB-U/372	AR
Hines, Allen	039	1836	WB-K/94	AR

Name	Co.	Date	Recorded Copy	Original
Hines, Benjamin	047	1819	WB-3/637	
Hines, Benjamin	003	1894	WB-B/320	AR
Hines, Boling	022	c1812	WB-A/223	AR
Hines, Charles	103	1794	WI-A/467	AR
Hines, Daniel S.	040	1896	WB-2/497	AR
Hines, E.	044	1879	WB-23/354	CTY
Hines, E. F.	013	1896	WB-C/403	AR
Hines, Elias C.	024	1866	WB-D/38	AR
Hines, Elizabeth	003	c1858	Orig. Only	AR
Hines, Elizabeth	069	1864	WB-1/589	AR
Hines, Ellener	047	1823	WB-3/688	
Hines, Ezekial D.	046	1900	WB-G/187	AR
Hines, Fanny	105	1885	WB-2/363	AR
Hines, George	TN	1823	Copy	054 AR
Hines, Hartwell	069	1825	WB-1/329	AR
Hines, Ida E.	063	c1896	Orig. Only	AR
Hines, Isaac	070	1837	WB-AB/312	AR
Hines, Isaac W.	056	1890	WB-3/556	AR
Hines, James	087	1845	WB-1/299	AR
Hines, Joel	076	1881	WB-A1/15	AR
Hines, Joel	059	1846	WB-A/353	CTY-Copy
Hines, John	103	1869	WB-1/14	AR
Hines, John	063	1837	WB-2/227	
Hines, John L. B.	080	1874	WB-1/16	AR
Hines, Joseph	082	1805	WB-1/105	AR
Hines, Joseph	082	1865	WB-5/2	AR
Hines, Joshua	103	1823	RD-5/60	AR
Hines, Judith	039	1840	WB-L/2	AR
Hines, Kinchen	037	1830	WB-F/115	AR
Hines, Louisa R.	099	1891	WB-B/574	AR
Hines, Moses	041	1804	WB-1/213	AR
Hines, Nancy	059	1874	WB-A/79	CTY-Copy
Hines, Peter	103	1814	RD-3/105	AR
Hines, Peter R.	099	1880	WB-A/196	AR
Hines, Peter, Sr.	037	1805	WB-D/215	AR
Hines, Peter, Sr.	037	1783	WB-B/119	AR
Hines, Prudence	037	1855	WB-G/106	AR
Hines, Rachel	063	1819	WB-2/61	
Hines, Richard	037	1781	WB-B/67	AR
Hines, Richard	099	1851	RB-27/353	AR
Hines, Robert W.	037	1822	WB-E/305	AR
Hines, Sarah	103	1844	RD-9/117	AR
Hines, Sarah	039	1879	WB-U/216	AR
Hines, Susan Ann	028	1876	WB-E/151	AR
Hines, Susannah	069	1821	Orig. Only	AR
Hines, Thomas C.	098	1888	WB-A/104	CTY
Hines, William	070	1801	WB-AB/41	
Hines, William	077	1785	WB-C/288	AR
Hines, William	103	1860	RD-13/189	AR
Hines, William	003	1860	Orig. Only	AR
Hines, William H.	037	1854	WB-G/49 & 87	AR
Hines, Williams	037	1818	WB-E/205	AR
Hines, Wyatt E.	086	1841	WB-E/74	AR-Nunc.
Hinesley, Alfred	022	1893	Orig. Only	AR
Hingston, Richard	084	c1813	WB-A/187	CTY
Hinkle, Christian	032	1885	WB-3/489	AR
Hinkle, Cyrus	060	1887	WB-4/363	
Hinkle, Emanuel	032	1899	WB-4/402	AR
Hinkle, Jacob	085	1814	WB-G/327	AR
Hinkle, Matthias	032	1870	WB-3/14	
Hinkle, Peter	085	1775	WB-A/217	AR
Hinkle, Philip	085	1811	WB-G/204	AR
Hinkley, Eliphlet	070	1779	WB-C/147	AR

Name	Co.	Date	Recorded Copy	Original
Hinley, Jesse	081	1801	WB-2/80	
Hinnant, Ann	056	1847	WB-1/586	AR
Hinnant, Elizabeth	105	1858	WB-1/50	
Hinnant, Esther	056	1892	WB-3/586	AR
Hinnant, Henry	056	1887	WB-3/446	
Hinnant, Jacob	056	1890	WB-3/533	AR
Hinnant, James	056	1831	WB-1/423	AR
Hinnant, John	056	1829	Orig. Only	AR
Hinnant, John, Sr.	056	1768	WB-1/776	AR
Hinnant, Jonathan	056	N. D.	Orig. Only	AR
Hinnant, Josiah	056	1857	WB-1/713	AR
Hinnant, Josiah	056	1879	WB-3/224	AR
Hinnant, Josiah	056	1896	WB-4/33	AR
Hinnant, Lendy	105	1899	Orig. Only	AR
Hinnant, Martha	105	1865	WB-1/120	
Hinnant, Martha	056	1840	WB-1/525	AR
Hinnant, Mary	105	c1855	WB-1/23	AR
Hinnant, Patience	056	1820	WB-1/313	AR
Hinnant, Pollie A.	056	1900	WB-4/265	AR
Hinnant, Sarah	056	1837	WB-2/288	AR
Hinnant, William	056	1858	WB-1/715	AR
Hinnant, William	056	1801	WB-1/129	AR
Hinnant, William	056	1818	WB-1/292	AR
Hinnant, William	056	1818	WB-1/282	AR
Hinnant, William	056	1804	WB-1/167	AR
Hinsdale, Samuel J.	029	1894	WB-F/10	AR
Hinshaw, Aaron	081	1840	WB-7/304	AR
Hinshaw, Absolom	081	1830	WB-6/40	AR
Hinshaw, Benjamin	022	1840	WB-C/111	AR
Hinshaw, Benjamin	022	1866	WB-D/71	AR
Hinshaw, Benjamin	022	1842	WB-C/128	AR
Hinshaw, Benjamin	092	c1829	Orig. Only	AR
Hinshaw, Dorcas	022	1899	WB-F/79	AR
Hinshaw, Elizabeth	038	1890	WB-3/177	AR
Hinshaw, Enoch	081	1864	WB-13/141	AR
Hinshaw, Ferbe	022	1877	WB-E/137	AR
Hinshaw, Hannah	106	1887	WB-2/234	AR
Hinshaw, Hannah	081	1881	WB-15/339	AR
Hinshaw, Jacob	081	1796	WB-2/22	AR
Hinshaw, Jacob	092	1811	WB-3/98	
Hinshaw, Jacob	081	1848	Orig. Only	AR
Hinshaw, Jesse	022	1797	RB-2/126	AR
Hinshaw, Jesse G.	081	1875	WB-15/187	AR
Hinshaw, John	090	1800	WB-1/167	AR
Hinshaw, Joseph	022	1822	WB-B/99	AR
Hinshaw, Martha	081	1871	WB-15/45	AR
Hinshaw, Mary	022	1851	WB-C/292	AR
Hinshaw, Mary	081	1822	WB-5/76	AR
Hinshaw, Mebane	081	1900	WB-17/117	
Hinshaw, Nancy	022	1851	WB-C/290	AR
Hinshaw, Nancy A.	046	1898	WB-G/77	AR
Hinshaw, Rebecca	081	1849	WB-9/94	AR
Hinshaw, Rebecca	081	1873	WB-15/116	AR
Hinshaw, Sarah	081	1867	WB-14/188	AR
Hinshaw, Stephen	081	1877	WB-15/243	AR
Hinshaw, Thomas	081	c1826	Orig. Only	AR
Hinshaw, Thomas	022	1836	WB-C/28	AR
Hinshaw, Tristum	081	1871	WB-15/45	
Hinshaw, William	081	1818	WB-4/552	AR
Hinshaw, William	022	1854	WB-C/371	AR
Hinshaw, Zimri	001	1900	WB-3/346	AR
Hinshaw, Zimri	001	1900	022 WB-G/574	022 AR
Hinsley, Ann	024	1811	WB-B/315	AR
Hinsley, William	022	1823	WB-B/107	AR
Hinson, Bartlet	005	1839	WB-B/96	AR
Hinson, Benjamin	005	1816	WB-2/60	AR
Hinson, Charles	005	1847	WB-B/226	AR
Hinson, Elijah	103	1802	Orig. Only	AR
Hinson, Frederick	089	1859	WB-1/211	
Hinson, George	072	1805	WB-A/47	AR
Hinson, James, Sr.	054	c1829	WB-2/161	AR
Hinson, John	089	1890	WB-2/209	AR
Hinson, John W.	054	1877	WB-4/244	CTY
Hinson, Joseph	083	c1799	WB-1/57	
Hinson, Joseph	081	1786	WB-1/33	
Hinson, Joseph	081	1873	WB-15/122	
Hinson, Joshua	027	1866	WB-A/100	AR
Hinson, Lucy	027	1870	WB-2/3	AR
Hinson, Mourning	005	1847	WB-B/231	AR
Hinson, Nancy	054	1846	WB-3/10	
Hinson, Nancy M.	065	1896	WB-M/497	AR
Hinson, Pleasant	005	1854	WB-C/86	AR
Hinson, Richard D.	103	1874	WB-1/75	AR
Hinson, Tirsey	065	1897	WB-M/535	AR
Hinson, W. F.	089	1898	Orig. Only	AR
Hinson, William	060	1889	WB-4/397	AR
Hinston, Fannie	038	1895	WB-3/535	AR
Hinton, A. G.	022	1852	WB-C/337	
Hinton, Charles L.	099	1862	RB-32/126	AR
Hinton, David	099	1876	RB-35/329	AR
Hinton, David	099	1850	RB-27/138	AR
Hinton, Dempsey	009	c1808	OB-A/42	AR
Hinton, Elizabeth	099	1865	RB-33/484	AR
Hinton, Elizabeth	024	1777	WB-A/51	AR
Hinton, Esther	056	1854	WB-1/670	AR
Hinton, Grissy	099	1871	RB-35/107	AR
Hinton, Hardy	056	1760	WB-1/748	AR
Hinton, Henry	099	1812	RB-10/164	AR
Hinton, Hilliard	069	1881	WB-5/136	AR
Hinton, Isaac	056	c1795	WB-1/91	AR
Hinton, Jacob	024	c1760	Orig. Only	AR
Hinton, James	099	1842	RB-25/89	AR
Hinton, James	047	1781	WB-3/24	
Hinton, James	099	1842	SC/04965	AR-Copy
Hinton, James H.	037	1874	WB-G/439	AR
Hinton, Jane C.	099	1898	WB-D/128	AR
Hinton, John	010	1783	WB-C/51	AR
Hinton, John	024	1732	SS 876/240	SS/AR
Hinton, John	010	1791	WB-D/192	AR
Hinton, John	099	1845	RB-25/582	AR
Hinton, John	041	1857	WB-3/217	AR
Hinton, John	024	1778	WB-A/30	AR
Hinton, John, Sr.	099	1784	RB-2/16	AR
Hinton, John, Sr.	099	1818	RB-14/367	AR
Hinton, John, Sr.	056	1823	WB-1/352	AR
Hinton, Jonas	024	c1770	WB-A/34	AR
Hinton, Joseph	022	1809	WB-A/175	AR
Hinton, Joseph B.	009	1873	WB-1/109	AR
Hinton, Kitty	037	1873	WB-G/412	AR
Hinton, Laurens	099	1864	RB-33/330	AR
Hinton, Malachi	056	1808	WB-1/210	AR
Hinton, Margaret	099	1857	RB-30/357	AR
Hinton, Margaret	041	1859	WB-3/254	AR-Nunc.
Hinton, Martha	010	1774	WB-A/169	AR
Hinton, Mary	075	1838	WB-N/142	AR
Hinton, Micajah	010	1757	SS 880/254	SS/AR (N)
Hinton, Noah	010	1803	WB-E/223	AR
Hinton, Noah	010	1823	WB-G/104	
Hinton, Noah	041	1849	WB-3/122	AR

Name	Co.	Date	Recorded Copy	Original
Hinton, Penelope	041	1850	WB-3/130	AR
Hinton, Ransom	099	1838	RB-24/180	AR
Hinton, Rebecca	075	1762	WB-H/36	AR
Hinton, Reuben	041	1837	WB-2/392	AR
Hinton, Robert	GA	1798	Copy	069 AR
Hinton, Sarah	041	1825	WB-2/238	AR
Hinton, Sarah B.	099	1880	WB-A/126	AR
Hinton, Solomon	056	c1778	WB-1/775	AR
Hinton, Theophilus	099	1810	RB-9/317	AR
Hinton, Thomas	041	1844	WB-3/57	AR
Hinton, Thomas	020	1800	RB-D/1	AR
Hinton, William	041	1796	WB-1/147	AR
Hinton, William	099	1836	RB-23/494	AR
Hinton, William	056	1762	DB-D/L102	AR
Hinton, William	041	1806	WB-1/228	AR
Hinton, William	056	1833	WB-1/494	AR
Hinton, William	037	1841	WB-F/254	AR
Hinton, William L.	075	1828	WB-N/40	AR
Hinton, Willis	099	1806	RB-7/161	AR
Hinton, Z. R.	069	1887	WB-5/267	AR
Hip, Stephen	065	1782	WB-C/140	AR
Hipp, Gray P.	065	1860	WB-J/100	AR
Hipp, L. A.	065	1896	WB-M/462	AR
Hipp, Stephen	065	1828	Orig. Only	AR
Hipworth, John	020	1797	RB-C/229	AR
Hirst, William L.	PA	1895	016 WB-4/190	016 AR
Hise, Jacob, Sr.	049	1821	WB-2/205	AR
Hitchcock, Charles M.	CA	1885	023 WB-A/47	
Hitchcock, Isaac	085	c1793	WB-E/110	AR
Hitchcock, John	046	1832	WB-B/468	AR
Hitchcock, Martha T.	CA	1899	023 WB-A/154	
Hitchcock, Nancy	090	1825	WB-3/131	AR
Hitchcock, William	046	1811	WB-A/176	AR
Hitchcock, William	032	c1856	WB-2/135	
Hiter, Willis	018	1886	WB-E/140	AR
Hix, Betsey	056	1887	WB-3/436	AR
Hix, David	072	c1778	RW/L17	AR
Hix, Davis	104	1793	WB-1/365	AR
Hix, Elizabeth	078	1854	WB-17/304	
Hix, Joshua	067	1850	WB-1/55	AR
Hix, Patrick	024	1793	Copy	AR
Hix, R. D.	054	1894	WB-5/512	CTY
Hix, R. V.	055	1889	WB-A/90	
Hix, Stephen	056	1855	WB-1/671	
Hix, William	024	1825	WB-C/115	AR
Hix, William	071	1811	WB-3/41	AR
Hixon, Timothy	075	1774	Orig. Only	AR
Hixon, Timothy	075	1781	WB-K/66	AR
Hixt, John, Sr.	090	1807	WB-2/76	AR
Hoard, Mary	044	1806	WB-6/257	CTY
Hoard, Seth	070	1849	WB-C/497	AR
Hoat, Michael	060	1791	Orig. Only	AR
Hobbs, Abel	041	1894	WB-4/393	AR
Hobbs, Abraham	087	1860	WB-1/553	AR
Hobbs, Alfred H.	029	1896	WB-F/80	AR
Hobbs, Amos	041	1839	WB-3/14	AR
Hobbs, Augustus	030	c1811	WB-3/1	
Hobbs, Catharine	001	1858	WB-1/126	AR
Hobbs, David	041	1834	WB-2/347	AR
Hobbs, Edward	072	1832	WB-1/98	AR
Hobbs, Edward	041	1847	WB-3/91	AR
Hobbs, Elijah	072	1844	WB-2/52	AR
Hobbs, Elisha	081	1818	WB-4/626	AR
Hobbs, Elizabeth	087	1897	WB-4/41	AR
Hobbs, Emily	024	1833	WB-C/167	AR

Name	Co.	Date	Recorded Copy	Original
Hobbs, Gabriel	087	1858	WB-1/520	AR
Hobbs, Guy	041	1883	WB-1/185	AR
Hobbs, Guy	041	1786	WB-1/57	AR
Hobbs, Halsey	024	1869	WB-E/3	AR
Hobbs, Henry H.	024	1898	WB-E/290	AR
Hobbs, Henry H.	056	1860	WB-2/3	AR
Hobbs, James	072	1882	WB-4/148	AR
Hobbs, James	072	1801	Orig. Only	AR
Hobbs, James	054	c1801	WB-1/122	AR
Hobbs, Jesse	041	1855	WB-3/188	AR
Hobbs, Jesse	054	c1812	WB-1/352	AR
Hobbs, Jesse	054	1878	WB-4/336	CTY
Hobbs, John	065	1883	WB-K/565	AR
Hobbs, John, Sr.	024	c1768	WB-A/28	AR
Hobbs, Lizzie	103	1897	WB-2/199	AR
Hobbs, M. D.	054	1899	WB-6/275	CTY
Hobbs, Mary	037	1819	WB-E/222	AR
Hobbs, Mary A. R.	087	1875	WB-3/109	AR
Hobbs, Mary S.	046	1866	WB-D/315	AR
Hobbs, P. P.	072	1900	WB-4/424	AR
Hobbs, Samuel	099	1853	RB-28/318	AR
Hobbs, Seth	024	1838	WB-C/215	AR
Hobbs, Simon P.	087	1884	WB-3/290	AR
Hobbs, Thomas	041	1830	WB-2/284	AR
Hobbs, Walton	041	1845	WB-3/55	AR
Hobbs, William	087	1866	WB-2/107	AR
Hobbs, William	099	1788	RB-2/219	AR
Hobbs, William	027	1883	WB-2/50	AR
Hobbs, William	087	1836	WB-1/178	AR
Hobbs, William	073	1815	WB-D/421	AR
Hobbs, William B.	099	1839	RB-24/263	AR
Hobbs, William W.	099	1869	RB-35/37	AR
Hobby, Alexander	056	1804	WB-1/158	AR
Hobby, Jacob	037	1758	SS 811/218	SS/AR
Hobby, Lucy	022	1900	048 WB-1/115	048 CTY
Hobby, Lucy	022	1900	WB-F/156	AR
Hobby, Reuben	056	1815	WB-1/242	AR
Hobes, Simon, Sr.	072	1801	WB-A/53	AR
Hobgood, Henry	044	1888	WB-24/42	CTY
Hobgood, James B.	044	1885	WB-23/532	CTY
Hobgood, John	047	1783	WB-3/38	
Hobgood, Joseph D.	044	1862	WB-21/628	CTY
Hobgood, Micajah	047	1763	WB-1/106	
Hobgood, Rutha	047	1836	WB-4/137	
Hobgood, Samuel	044	1884	WB-23/506	CTY
Hobgood, Shelton	044	1828	WB-11/29	CTY
Hobgood, William	044	1876	WB-23/236	CTY
Hobgood, William	047	1762	WB-1/80	
Hobs, John	075	1729	Orig. Only	SS/AR
Hobson, Charles	073	1825	WB-E/90	AR
Hobson, David	106	c1850	WB-1/19	AR
Hobson, Francis	010	c1766	WB-A/93	AR
Hobson, Henry	084	1833	WB-B/68	CTY
Hobson, John P.	084	1840	WB-B/243	CTY
Hobson, Joseph	022	1850	WB-C/261	AR
Hobson, Stephen	022	1825	WB-B/94	AR
Hobson, Stephen	092	1803	WB-3/60	
Hobson, Thomas	028	1769	Orig. Only	AR
Hobson, William	022	1897	WB-F/60	AR
Hobson, Zeruah	073	1841	WB-F/84	AR
Hocaday, William	044	1830	WB-11/314	CTY
Hockaday, Edward	099	1894	WB-C/327	AR
Hockaday, Warwick	047	1851	WB-4/301	
Hockaday, William	044	1891	WB-24/147	CTY
Hockaday, William	029	1812	WB-A/183	AR

Name	Co.	Date	Recorded Copy	Original
Hockett, Isaac	081	1878	WB-15/280	AR
Hockett, Jesse D.	081	1898	WB-16/538	AR
Hockett, John	046	1874	WB-E/128	AR
Hockett, Susannah	046	1867	WB-D/337	AR
Hockett, William	046	1880	WB-E/280	AR
Hockett, William	046	1843	WB-C/158	AR
Hockings, John	035	1756	SS 880/173	SS/AR
Hocott, Richard	105	1855	WB-1/25	AR
Hocut, Benjamin	056	1858	WB-1/724	AR
Hocut, Eliza	056	1866	WB-2/78	AR
Hocut, William	056	1795	WB-1/40	AR
Hocutt, Benjamin	105	1857	WB-1/34	AR
Hocutt, Cynthia A.	056	1892	WB-2/122	AR
Hocutt, Edward	099	1792	RB-2/359	AR
Hocutt, Lucy O.	076	1891	WB-A1/127	AR
Hodge, Abraham	047	1805	WB-3/434	
Hodge, Charry	009	c1836	OWB/537	AR
Hodge, Elizabeth	083	1873	WB-3/51	AR
Hodge, Francis	065	1810	WB-D/21	AR
Hodge, George	014	1889	WB-2/374	CTY
Hodge, Henderson	099	1870	RB-35/97	AR
Hodge, John	073	1811	WB-D/320	AR
Hodge, John	073	1855	WB-G/94	AR
Hodge, Joseph	085	c1807	WB-G/43	AR
Hodge, Levina	065	1868	WB-J/247	AR
Hodge, M. C.	099	1885	WB-B/21	AR
Hodge, Richard	085	1892	WB-2/541	CTY
Hodge, Robert	011	c1797	WB-1/343	Nunc.
Hodge, Sarah	060	1804	Orig. Only	AR
Hodge, William T.	099	1853	RB-29/131	AR
Hodgens, Jesse H.	016	1866	WB-2/143	AR
Hodgeon, Henry	006	1866	WB-C/20	AR
Hodges, Anthony	037	1811	WB-E/17	AR
Hodges, Bartholomew	092	1832	WB-4/38	AR
Hodges, Benjamin	009	1822	OB-A/317	AR
Hodges, Benjamin	071	1893	WB-7/201	AR
Hodges, Benjamin	035	1824	WB-A/197	AR
Hodges, Charles	084	c1819	WB-A/188	CTY
Hodges, Daniel J.	056	1892	WB-2/140	AR
Hodges, Drury	092	1895	WB-6/402	AR
Hodges, Edward	102	1869	WB-A/37	
Hodges, Francis P.	009	1893	WB-1/569	
Hodges, Hollowell	035	1849	WB-2/40	AR
Hodges, James	075	1758	SS 881/170	SS/AR
Hodges, James	009	1835	OWB/521	AR
Hodges, James	024	1722	SS 875/343	SS/AR
Hodges, James A.	020	1889	WB-B/1	CTY
Hodges, Jesse	085	1864	WB-K/327	AR
Hodges, Joanna F.	104	1816	WB-3/128	AR
Hodges, John	010	1829	WB-G/184	AR
Hodges, John	009	1836	OWB/528	AR
Hodges, John	092	1893	WB-6/354	AR
Hodges, John	050	1849	WB-1/26	
Hodges, John T.	020	1898	WB-B/328	CTY
Hodges, John W.	056	1873	WB-3/103	AR
Hodges, Joseph	085	1850	WB-K/122	AR
Hodges, Joseph	092	1842	WB-4/181	
Hodges, Martha	047	c1867	Orig. Only	AR
Hodges, Mary E.	051	1892	WB-C/435	AR
Hodges, Matilda	092	1885	WB-6/223	AR
Hodges, Nancy	053	1868	WB-10/1	AR
Hodges, Olivia P.	009	1886	WB-1/394	CTY
Hodges, Rebecca	009	1826	OWB/483	AR
Hodges, Rebecca	009	1844	OB-E/381	AR
Hodges, Richard	009	1751	028 DB-5/200	SS/AR

Name	Co.	Date	Recorded Copy	Original
Hodges, Richard	030	1749	Orig. Only	SS/AR
Hodges, Richard	009	1827	OB-A/387	AR
Hodges, Sarah	037	1828	WB-F/88	AR
Hodges, Thomas	020	1858	RB-R/607	AR
Hodges, Thomas	037	1806	WB-D/244	AR
Hodges, Thomas J.	020	1897	WB-B/310	CTY
Hodges, Thomas R.	092	1864	WB-5/70	
Hodges, William	029	1830	WB-B/193	AR
Hodges, William	053	1899	WB-11/348	AR
Hodges, William	010	1889	WB-I/283	AR
Hodges, William	047	1896	WB-7/167	AR
Hodges, William	035	1845	Orig. Only	AR
Hodges, Winifred	029	1852	WB-C/223	AR
Hodgin, Absolom	046	1888	WB-E/547	AR
Hodgin, David	046	1882	WB-E/329	AR
Hodgin, Dorcas	046	1844	WB-C/180	AR
Hodgin, George	046	1878	WB-E/238	AR
Hodgin, Henry	046	1877	WB-E/179	AR
Hodgin, John	046	1886	WB-E/439	AR
Hodgin, Jonathan	046	1865	WB-D/273	AR
Hodgin, Joseph	081	1891	WB-16/204	
Hodgin, Joshua	046	1842	WB-C/124	AR
Hodgin, Louis John	061	1875	WB-2/21	AR
Hodgin, Micajah	047	1895	WB-F/469	AR
Hodgin, Thomas	081	1879	WB-15/313	AR
Hodgins, Joab	022	1844	WB-C/168	AR
Hodgins, John M.	085	1873	WB-1/164	CTY
Hodgison, Aron	035	1797	WB-A/217	AR
Hodgson, Anson	033	1859	WB-1/167	
Hodgson, Charles	010	1798	WB-E/41	AR
Hodgson, George	046	1774	WB-A/148	AR
Hodgson, John	N	c1712	SS 875/23	
Hodgson, John	046	1813	WB-A/170	AR
Hodgson, John	024	c1774	WB-A/44	AR
Hodgson, John	070	1738	SS 877/186	SS/AR
Hodgson, John Larkin	085	1816	WB-G/412	AR
Hodgson, Thomas	024	1772	WB-A/20	AR
Hodgton, John	081	1829	WB-5/465	AR
Hodnett, Philip	020	1897	WB-B/299	CTY
Hodson, David	046	1816	WB-A/186	AR
Hodson, George	046	1813	WB-A/178	AR
Hodson, Joseph	081	1829	WB-6/30	AR
Hodson, Robert	046	1813	WB-A/185	AR
Hodson, Robert	046	1844	WB-C/187	AR
Hoel, William H.	063	1893	WB-4/126	AR
Hoell, Elias	009	1819	OB-A/291	AR
Hoell, William H.	063	1836	WB-2/217	
Hoens, John Marks	090	1797	WB-1/100	AR
Hoey, John	065	1803	WB-D/66	AR
Hof, Hartman	SC	1890	044 WB-24/128	
Hoff, Francis W.	063	1845	WB-2/315	
Hoff, J. H.	101	1900	WB-A/318	AR
Hoffman, Catharine	046	1846	WB-C/253	AR
Hoffman, George	090	1807	WB-2/73	AR
Hoffman, James	039	1892	WB-3/324	AR
Hofheims, Jacob	046	1793	WB-A/161	AR
Hofler, Asa G.	041	1859	WB-3/244	AR
Hofler, Caroline	041	1893	WB-4/359	AR
Hofler, Garrett	041	1834	WB-2/344	AR
Hofler, Hance	041	1847	WB-3/221	AR
Hofler, Hance	024	1769	WB-A/46	AR
Hofler, Hanee	077	c1847	Orig. Only	AR-Copy
Hofler, James	041	1822	WB-2/183	AR
Hofler, Leah	041	1876	WB-4/69	AR
Hofler, Thomas	041	1817	WB-2/142	AR

Name	Co.	Date	Recorded Copy	Original
Hofman, Michael	085	1849	WB-K/88	AR
Hofner, Martin	085	1841	WB-I/118	
Hog, Richard	011	1769	Orig. Only	SS/AR
Hogan, Alexander	081	1852	WB-9/277	AR
Hogan, Daniel	073	1849	WB-F/443	AR
Hogan, Daniel	073	c1787	WB-B/2	AR
Hogan, Edward	086	1794	Orig. Only	AR
Hogan, Elizabeth	081	1857	WB-11/206	AR
Hogan, James	005	c1793	WB-A/22	AR
Hogan, James	047	1781	WB-3/22	
Hogan, Lemuel	047	1809	WB-3/485	
Hogan, Silence	005	1803	WB-2/62	AR
Hogan, Thomas	073	1858	WB-G/203	AR
Hogan, William	081	1837	WB-7/80	AR
Hogbin, William	002	1692	Orig. Only	SS/AR
Hogg, Gavin	099	1836	RB-23/491	AR
Hogg, Gideon	020	1793	RB-C/26	
Hogg, Grizza	071	1808	WB-3/5	AR-Nunc.
Hogg, James	008	1708/9	009 DB-1/98	
Hogg, James	073	1805	WB-D/146	AR
Hogg, John	039	c1795	WB-A/153	
Hogg, Sarah L.	099	1880	WB-A/150	AR
Hogg, Thomas	037	1789	WB-C/117	AR
Hoggard, Alonzo	010	1871	WB-I/39	AR
Hoggard, Armistead	010	1900	WB-K/63	
Hoggard, George	010	1866	WB-H/174	AR
Hoggard, Jesse H.	051	1893	WB-C/448	AR
Hoggard, Jessee G.	010	1900	WB-K/55	
Hoggard, Joseph	051	1875	WB-C/159	
Hoggard, Joseph B.	010	1899	WB-K/1	
Hoggard, Thomas	051	1881	WB-C/268	AR
Hoggard, Thomas W.	010	1893	WB-I/379	AR
Hoggard, William	010	1823	WB-G/100	AR
Hoggard, William H.	010	1886	WB-I/219	
Hoggard, Worley T.	010	1888	WB-I/256	AR
Hoggatt, Aaron	081	1804	WB-3/2	AR
Hoggatt, John	081	1816	WB-4/360	AR
Hoggatt, Joseph	046	1815	WB-A/181	AR
Hoggatt, Mohlan	046	1850	WB-C/322	AR
Hoggatt, Phillip	046	c1763	WB-A/155	AR
Hoggatt, William	046	1771	WB-A/153	AR
Hoggatt, William	081	1848	Orig. Only	AR
Hogges, Robert	010	1742	Orig. Only	SS/AR
Hogland, Eleazer	049	1852	Orig. Only	AR
Hogseid, Jason	023	1900	WB-A/195	AR
Hogshead, David	054	c1823	WB-2/81	AR
Hogshead, William H.	068	1855	WB-C/35	
Hogstead, Walter	065	c1766	WB-C/131	AR
Hogue, James L.	043	1893	WB-1/43	
Hogue, Louis	086	1819	WB-C/123	AR
Hogwood, Fannie	069	1889	Orig. Only	AR
Hogwood, John	039	c1858	WB-O/357	AR
Hogwood, Turner	039	1893	WB-V/14	AR
Hoicklefield, John	077	c1721	Copy	024 AR
Hoke, David R.	021	c1893	WB-3/335	AR
Hoke, Francis	060	1868	Orig. Only	AR
Hoke, Frederick	021	1844	WB-1/10	AR
Hoke, George M.	060	1867	WB-3/95	AR
Hoke, Harriet	021	c1888	Orig. Only	AR
Hoke, Henry	060	1836	WB-1/374	AR
Hoke, John	060	1845	WB-2/241	AR
Hoke, Marcus H.	060	1886	WB-4/321	AR
Hoke, Michael	060	1844	WB-2/230	AR
Hoke, N. C.	060	1893	WB-4/504	AR
Hoke, Rebecca	021	1863	WB-1/186	AR
Hoke, Sarah	054	1888	WB-5/178	CTY
Hoke, Sarah E.	060	1863	WB-3/56	AR
Hoke, William J.	060	1870	WB-4/64	AR
Holaday, Henry, Sr.	022	1800	WB-A/36	AR
Holaday, Samuel	022	1825	WB-B/114	AR
Holbrook, James	090	c1826	Orig. Only	AR
Holbrook, James M.	104	1887	WB-6/302	AR
Holbrook, Ralph	104	1808	WB-2/237	AR
Holbrook, Robert	092	1826	WB-3/171	AR
Holbrooks, Larkin	006	1840	WB-A/31	AR
Holbrooks, Sarah	004	1865	WB-1/13	AR
Holcomb, Anna	106	1880	WB-2/125	AR
Holcomb, George D.	092	c1844	Copy	106 AR
Holcomb, George D.	092	1845	Copy	054 AR
Holcomb, George D.	092	1845	WB-4/231	
Holcomb, John	092	1851	WB-4/316	
Holcomb, John	092	1781	WB-1/195	AR
Holcomb, Laurence	092	1827	WB-3/176	
Holcomb, Leroy	092	c1820	WB-3/146	AR
Holcomb, Thomas	092	1807	WB-3/82	
Holcombe, Obedeah	013	1843	WB-A/88	
Holcombe, Thomas	054	1893	WB-5/481	CTY
Holcrum, Sarah	020	1858	RB-S/28	AR
Holcum, Mary	020	1856	RB-R/439	AR
Holdbrooks, David G.	016	1894	WB-4/178	AR
Holdbrooks, Serena	060	1859	WB-3/25	AR
Holden, Elizabeth	073	1851	WB-F/495	AR
Holden, Frederick	065	1815	WB-C/157	AR
Holden, Isaac	073	1820	WB-D/585	AR
Holden, Louisa V.	099	1900	WB-D/363	AR
Holden, Richard	039	1889	WB-U/495	AR
Holden, Richard	025	1898	WB-A/223	
Holden, Samuel	099	1800	RB-5/61	AR
Holden, Thomas	012	1891	Orig. Only	AR
Holden, Thomas W.	073	1857	WB-G/158	AR
Holder, D. M.	092	1899	WB-6/494	AR
Holder, Elisha	010	1807	WB-F/57	AR
Holder, Elisha	010	1826	WB-G/140	AR
Holder, George	087	c1799	WB-A/29	AR
Holder, Henry	104	1873	WB-6/72	AR
Holder, Jesse	087	1848	WB-1/342	AR
Holder, Johanna	090	1821	WB-3/57	AR
Holder, John	087	c1790	WB-A/7	AR
Holder, John	073	1801	WB-D/55	AR
Holder, John	032	1869	WB-3/18	AR
Holder, John T.	038	1870	WB-2/37	AR
Holder, Lucinda	054	1878	WB-4/299	CTY
Holder, Martin	038	1872	WB-2/120	AR
Holder, Martin	038	c1863	WB-1/218	AR
Holder, Mary K.	090	1842	WB-4/99	AR
Holder, Thomas	010	1774	WB-B/4	AR
Holder, William	073	1825	WB-E/74	AR
Holder, Zachariah	056	1883	WB-3/334	AR
Holderby, Joseph	084	1875	WB-E/111	CTY
Holderby, Joseph, Sr.	084	1854	WB-C/192	CTY
Holderfield, Valentine	092	1820	WB-3/144	AR
Holdford, Little B.	047	1891	WB-6/576	AR
Holding, Benjamin	099	1845	RB-26/36	AR
Holding, Benjamin	012	c1778	DB-B/98	
Holding, Calvin	099	1883	WB-A/440	AR
Holding, Edwin	099	1814	RB-11/208	AR
Holding, Isaac	073	1767	WB-A/57	
Holding, Isham	099	1868	RB/35/9	AR
Holding, Joseph	099	1850	RB-27/135	AR
Holding, Nancy	039	1886	WB-U/378	AR

Name	Co.	Date	Recorded Copy	Original
Holding, Samuel	099	1800	RB-5/61	
Holding, Samuel	099	1803	RB-6/132	
Holdon, Jeremiah	035	c1774	WB-A/183	AR
Holdsclaw, James	060	1842	WB-2/116	AR
Holdsclaw, James	021	1844	WB-1/36	AR
Holdsclaw, John	021	1882	WB-2/247	
Holdsclaw, Lenna	021	1853	WB-1/104	AR
Holdsclaw, Moses	021	1855	WB-1/118	AR
Holdsclaw, Ruth	021	1853	WB-1/102	AR
Holdshouser, Ellen	085	1856	WB-K/227	AR
Holebrooks, Vechel	016	1831	PQS.5/152	AR
Holebrough, Joseph	009	c1711	SS 875/16	
Holeman, Charles	078	1815	WI-7/2	AR
Holeman, Isaac	085	c1807	WB-G/93	AR
Holeman, James	033	1839	WB-1/17	
Holeman, Orange	073	1892	WB-H/572	CTY
Holeman, Richard	078	1843	WI-15/176	AR
Holeman, Sarah	033	1840	WB-1/23	
Holeman, Thomas	104	1798	WB-1/487	
Holeman, William	085	1820	WB-H/27	AR
Holestine, Nicholas	044	1774	WB-1/40	CTY
Holey, John	016	1800	WB-A/46	AR
Holiday, Canada	096	1880	WB-4/54	
Holingsworth, Samuel	049	1810	WI-A/2	AR
Holladay, Hardy	063	1794	WB-1/200	
Holladay, John	010	1818	WB-G/31	AR
Holladay, Thomas	024	1744	Orig. Only	SS/AR
Holladay, William	096	1754	SS 879/124	SS/AR
Hollaman, Mary	100	1803	Orig. Only	AR
Hollaman, Mary	045	1889	WB-1/173	AR
Hollamon, Exum	071	1820	WB-3/237	AR
Hollamon, John	015	1770	100 WB-1/118	AR
Holland, Able	022	c1889	WB-E/436	
Holland, Amanda	001	1894	WB-3/7	AR
Holland, Bennett	099	1891	WB-B/534	AR
Holland, Burvin	022	1879	WB-E/169	AR
Holland, Catharine	054	1840	WB-2/214	AR
Holland, Charles	059	1871	WB-A/26	Nunc.
Holland, Daniel	028	1771	Orig. Only	SS/AR
Holland, Daniel	064	1891	WB-2/235	AR
Holland, David	037	1848	WB-F/394	AR
Holland, David C.	048	1893	099 WB-D/140	099 AR
Holland, David C.	048	1893	WB-1/21	CTY
Holland, E. B.	040	1896	WB-2/506	AR
Holland, Edward	068	1876	WB-D/83	
Holland, Elisha	103	1833	RD-6/475	AR
Holland, Elizabeth	009	1855	OB-K/22	AR
Holland, Esther	057	1831	WB-B/113	AR
Holland, Franklin	040	1857	WB-1/94	
Holland, Gray J.	056	1863	WB-2/45	AR
Holland, Isaac	040	1859	WB-1/107	AR
Holland, Isaac H.	040	1849	WB-1/16	
Holland, Isham	099	1862	RB-32/421	AR
Holland, J. C.	103	1898	WB-2/226	AR
Holland, J. R.	038	1866	WB-1/267	AR
Holland, Jacob	037	1799	WB-D/71	AR
Holland, Jacobine	090	c1815	Orig. Only	AR
Holland, James	060	1826	WB-1/44	
Holland, James	070	1831	WB-AB/273	AR
Holland, James. Sr.	099	1798	RB-4/133	AR
Holland, Jasper N.	040	c1859	WB-1/112	
Holland, John	090	1811	WB-2/124	AR
Holland, Joseph	010	1791	WB-D/168	AR
Holland, Julius	060	1813	Orig. Only	AR-Nunc.
Holland, Lavinia	041	1867	Orig. Only	AR

Name	Co.	Date	Recorded Copy	Original
Holland, M. D. S.	026	c1876	Orig. Only	AR
Holland, Marion L.	040	1864	WB-1/167	
Holland, Martha	040	1857	WB-1/91	
Holland, Mary	056	1889	WB-3/502	AR
Holland, Mary	060	c1816	Orig. Only	AR
Holland, Mary	038	1856	WB-1/76	AR
Holland, Mary	040	c1867	WB-1/198	AR
Holland, Mary C.	040	1865	WB-1/179	
Holland, Nathan	054	1849	WB-3/35	AR
Holland, Pasher	103	1859	RD-12/625	AR
Holland, Perry H.	064	1858	WB-1/57	AR
Holland, Philemon	029	1886	WB-E/386	AR
Holland, Philemon	028	1842	WB-D/49	AR
Holland, Richard	009	c1804	OWB/427	AR
Holland, Robert	040	1890	WB-2/373	AR
Holland, Sampson	022	1837	WB-C/46	AR
Holland, Simpson W.	099	1865	RB-33/351	AR
Holland, Summerset	054	1882	WB-5/198	CTY
Holland, Thomas	087	c1819	WB-A/99	AR
Holland, Thomas B.	072	1884	WB-4/161	AR
Holland, Warters	204	1868	WB-5/534	
Holland, Wiley	022	1848	WB-C/228	AR
Holland, William	056	1869	WB-3/28	AR
Holland, William	099	1810	RB-9/184	AR
Holland, William	026	1864	WB-1/334	AR
Holland, William	099	1889	WB-B/381	AR
Holland, William	028	1837	WB-C/396	AR
Holland, William G.	009	1867	OB-M/257	AR
Holland, William W.	056	1899	WB-4/165	AR
Holland, Woodard	103	1853	RD-11/340	AR
Hollard, Sarah H.	009	c1863	OB-M/147	AR
Hollbrook, John	010	1740	LGB-4/#126	SS/AR
Holleman, Anna	099	1862	RB-32/358	AR
Holleman, E. C.	099	1900	WB-D/421	AR
Holleman, Edward	100	1786	WB-4/187	AR
Holleman, Edwin	099	1889	WB-B/347	AR
Holleman, Frederick	056	1823	WB-1/355	AR
Holleman, James	005	1804	WB-2/64	AR
Holleman, John	099	1850	RB-27/88	AR
Holleman, Josiah	056	1845	WB-1/568	AR
Holleman, Laving	099	1856	RB-29/464	AR
Holleman, Nancy	099	1858	RB-30/534	AR
Holleman, W. H.	099	1894	WB-C/292	AR
Hollensworth, Elizabeth	092	1864	WB-5/72	
Holler, Andrew	021	1898	WB-3/211	AR
Hollery, Samuel	N	1713	Orig. Only	SS/AR (N)
Holley, Augustus	010	1882	WB-I/147	
Holley, Celia	010	1849	WB-G/437	AR
Holley, David A.	024	1868	WB-E/1	AR
Holley, Jacob	062	c1852	Orig. Only	AR
Holley, James	035	1761	087 DB-3/123	AR
Holley, James	010	1795	WB-D/288	AR
Holley, James	087	1831	WB-1/122	AR
Holley, Josiah	010	1846	WB-G/397	AR
Holley, Nancy	010	1829	WB-G/182	AR
Holley, Nathaniel	010	1784	WB-C/72	AR
Holley, Norfleet	024	1891	WB-E/199	AR
Holley, Sallie D.	010	1894	WB-I/395	AR
Holley, William	097	1882	WB-2/221	
Holley, William J.	024	1890	WB-E/177	AR
Holliday, James	047	1831	WB-4/81	
Holliday, Margaret	079	c1866	WB-1/182	
Holliday, Owen	001	1898	WB-3/235	AR
Hollifield, Elijah	086	1859	WB-E/361	AR

Name	Co.	Date	Recorded Copy	Original
Hollifield, Ralph	099	1790	RB-3/119	AR
Holliman, William	056	1819	WB-1/301	AR
Hollimon, Arthur	071	1796	WB-2/137	AR
Hollingsworth, A. J.	029	1896	WB-F/70	AR
Hollingsworth, Charles	009	1789	OWB/229	AR
Hollingsworth, Elizabeth	035	1788	WB-A/220	AR
Hollingsworth, Enoch	081	1784	WB-1/17	AR
Hollingsworth, Henry	035	1893	WB-4/433	AR
Hollingsworth, Henry	087	1840	WB-1/236	AR
Hollingsworth, Jacob	035	1790	WB-A/221	AR
Hollingsworth, John	103	1799	WI-B/305	
Hollingsworth, Louis	070	1899	WB-H/200	AR
Hollingsworth, Mary E.	076	1891	WB-A1/134	AR
Hollingsworth, Mary E.	076	1891	070 WB-G/65	070 AR
Hollingsworth, O. R.	076	1891	WB-A1/131	CTY
Hollingsworth, Stephen	011	c1840	WB-1/88	
Hollingsworth, Thomas	099	1803	RB-6/116	AR
Hollingsworth, William F.	069	1884	WB-5/192	AR
Hollingworth, Jacob, Sr.	087	1844	WB-1/281	AR
Hollins, Susan	070	c1878	Orig. Only	AR
Hollinsworth, Joseph	092	1887	WB-6/252	AR
Hollinsworth, William R.	092	1884	WB-6/207	AR
Hollis, Isaac	028	1815	WB-C/93	AR
Hollis, James	096	1735	SS 877/114	SS/AR
Hollis, William	028	1797	WB-B/28	AR
Hollister, Janet T.	028	1850	WB-D/169	AR
Hollister, Mary D.	099	1858	RB-30/639	AR
Hollman, Elizabeth	070	1828	WB-C/177	AR
Hollman, Peter A.	070	1827	WB-C/176	AR
Hollobock, George	085	c1804	WB-D/186	AR
Holloman, Celia	103	1866	RD-14/426	
Holloman, Christopher	103	1827	RD-5/389	
Holloman, James	041	1856	WB-A/385	
Holloman, Judah	051	1845	WB-A/242	
Holloman, Kindred	051	1895	WB-C/507	AR
Holloman, Rhoda	051	1899	WB-C/556	AR
Holloman, Sarah	051	1830	WB-A/1	
Hollomon, Abner	051	1882	WB-C/295	AR
Hollomon, Elizabeth	051	1892	WB-C/429	AR
Hollomon, George	051	1853	WB-A/356	
Hollomon, Jalon	051	1876	WB-C/170	AR
Hollomon, Josiah	051	1861	WB-B/42	AR
Hollomon, Priscilla	051	c1894	Orig. Only	AR
Hollomon, Roscius	010	1898	WB-I/559	
Hollomon, Susan J.	051	1881	WB-C/265	AR
Hollomon, William	100	1893	WB-51/323	AR
Holloway, Edward	100	1824	WB-27/48	AR
Holloway, Edward	030	1822	WB-3/128	
Holloway, Elizabeth	070	1892	WB-F/526	AR
Holloway, Elizabeth	099	1895	WB-C/425	AR
Holloway, Frances	028	1883	WB-E/341	AR
Holloway, George	017	c1843	WB-A/60	AR
Holloway, Hannah	077	1807	WB-E/273	AR
Holloway, Henry	030	1801	WB-2/168	
Holloway, James, Sr.	099	1858	RB-31/49	AR
Holloway, John	078	1840	WI-14/175	
Holloway, John	077	1812	WB-E/369	AR
Holloway, John	078	1799	WI-2/166	AR
Holloway, John	099	1828	RB-20/297	AR
Holloway, John	099	1857	RB-30/351	AR
Holloway, John	TN	c1855	Copy	078 AR
Holloway, John L.	073	1894	WB-I/53	CTY
Holloway, Malcom McN.	048	1897	WB-1/78	CTY
Holloway, Obadiah	020	1828	RB-L/272	AR
Holloway, Polly	030	1850	WB-4/154	

Name	Co.	Date	Recorded Copy	Original
Holloway, Richard B.	036	1895	WB-A/341	CTY
Holloway, Robert	017	1891	WB-B/199	AR
Holloway, Robert	073	1778	WB-A/205	
Holloway, Samuel	036	1887	WB-A/159	CTY
Holloway, Sarah	077	1816	WB-E/434	AR
Holloway, Thomas	073	1835	WB-E/355	AR
Holloway, Thomas	077	1750	Orig. Only	SS/AR
Holloway, Uferatha	077	1796	WB-E/73	
Holloway, William	085	c1815	Copy	032 AR
Holloway, William	099	1863	RB-32/608	AR
Holloway, William	030	c1808	WB-2/338	
Holloway, William D.	036	1894	WB-A/307	CTY
Holloway, William H.	099	1865	RB-33/483	AR
Hollowell, Aaron	077	c1830	WB-F/177	AR
Hollowell, Abner	024	1802	WB-B/192	AR
Hollowell, Arther	047	1804	WB-3/426	
Hollowell, Benjamin	053	1785	RW-1/131	AR
Hollowell, C. W.	075	1892	WB-O/355	AR
Hollowell, Catherine	103	1870	WB-1/20	AR
Hollowell, Edmond	077	1729	SS 876/208	SS/AR
Hollowell, Elizabeth	010	1814	WB-F/252	AR
Hollowell, Elizabeth	103	1841	RD-8/202	AR
Hollowell, Euridice	010	1822	WB-G/94	AR
Hollowell, Ezekiel	077	1794	WB-E/18	
Hollowell, Henry	077	1827	WB-F/128	AR
Hollowell, Henry	077	1833	WB-F/219	AR
Hollowell, Ira	053	c1825	WB-4/161	
Hollowell, Joel	077	1774	WB-C/147	AR
Hollowell, Joel	077	1808	WB-E/287	AR
Hollowell, John	075	1855	WB-M2/36	AR
Hollowell, John	077	1784	WB-C/273	AR
Hollowell, John	024	1824	WB-C/108	AR
Hollowell, Jordan	024	1885	WB-E/138	AR
Hollowell, Joseph	053	1771	RW-1/23	AR
Hollowell, Joseph	103	1820	RD-4/351	AR
Hollowell, Joseph	071	1768	WB-1/161	
Hollowell, Levi	063	c1798	WB-1/415	
Hollowell, Levi	103	1872	WB-1/57	AR
Hollowell, Luke	077	1735	SS 876/390	SS/AR
Hollowell, Luke	041	1832	WB-2/306	AR
Hollowell, Margaret	075	1864	WB-N/249	AR
Hollowell, Martha	103	1824	RD-5/97	AR
Hollowell, Martha	103	1836	RD-7/174	AR
Hollowell, Mary	009	1849	OB-G/124	AR
Hollowell, Nancy M.	103	1887	WB-1/400	AR
Hollowell, Nathan	077	1829	WB-F/166	AR
Hollowell, Noah	024	1865	WB-D/34	AR
Hollowell, Noah	075	c1854	WB-M2/28	AR
Hollowell, Reddick	077	1836	WB-F/251	AR
Hollowell, Reubin	022	1803	WB-A/51	AR
Hollowell, Rubin	077	1753	SS 878/223	SS/AR
Hollowell, Sally	009	1830	OWB/496	AR
Hollowell, Silas	103	1821	RD-4/378	AR
Hollowell, Susan	075	1898	WB-O/467	AR
Hollowell, Thomas	077	1806	WB-E/243	AR
Hollowell, Thomas	077	1772	WB-C/116	AR
Hollowell, Thomas	077	1791	WB-C/423	AR
Hollowell, Thomas	103	1865	RD-14/239	AR
Hollowell, Thomas F.	024	1881	WB-E/107	AR
Hollowell, William	010	1767	WB-A/27	AR
Hollowell, William	041	1893	WB-4/368	AR
Hollowell, William	103	1854	RD-11/543	AR
Holly, James	028	1810	WB-C/4	AR
Holly, John	010	1728	Orig. Only	SS/AR
Holly, Judith	028	1874	WB-E/107	AR

Name	Co.	Date	Recorded Copy	Original
Holly, Mary C.	073	1882	WB-H/318	CTY
Holly, Penelope	010	1853	WB-G/501	AR
Holly, Richard	028	1809	WB-B/336	AR
Holly, Thomas	010	1827	WB-G/164	AR
Hollyfield, Osborne R.	086	1854	WB-E/277	AR
Holman, Ebenezer	054	1879	WB-4/319	CTY
Holman, Isaac	033	1868	WB-1/207	
Holman, Lydia	033	1860	WB-1/170	
Holman, Manervas	033	1898	WB-2/236	
Holman, Mary	033	1877	WB-2/58	CTY
Holman, Mary E.	033	1893	WB-2/155	CTY
Holman, Samuel	033	1875	WB-2/49	CTY
Holman, Sarah	033	1847	WB-1/89	
Holman, Sarah	054	1881	WB-4/448	CTY
Holman, Sydney W.	036	1899	WB-A/473	CTY
Holman, Thomas	104	1833	WB-4/161	AR
Holman, Tilghman	054	1881	WB-4/448	CTY
Holman, Yancey	084	1854	WB-C/169	CTY
Holmes, Ann	087	1852	WB-1/409	AR
Holmes, Archibald	029	1862	WB-C/436	AR
Holmes, Delia	016	1879	WB-3/279	AR
Holmes, Ebenezer	072	1746	Orig. Only	SS/AR
Holmes, Edward	011	c1796	WB-1/344	
Holmes, Fredrick	103	1817	RD-4/97	AR
Holmes, George	029	1882	WB-E/274	AR
Holmes, George	025	1791	WB-A/222	AR
Holmes, George	029	1870	WB-E/25	AR
Holmes, Hardy	087	1852	WB-1/407	AR
Holmes, Henry	024	1829	WB-C/149	AR
Holmes, Hiram	056	1872	WB-3/77	AR
Holmes, James	081	1798	WB-2/33	AR
Holmes, James	054	1837	WB-2/169	AR
Holmes, James	029	1890	WB-E/493	AR
Holmes, James C.	087	1865	WB-2/90	AR
Holmes, Jane	081	1890	WB-16/93	AR
Holmes, Jesse	032	c1845	WB-2/123	
Holmes, John	073	1833	WB-E/307	AR
Holmes, John	085	1775	WB-A/189	AR
Holmes, John	072	c1760	RW/L53	AR
Holmes, John	030	1805	WB-2/269	
Holmes, John	009	1872	WB-1/104	AR
Holmes, John	037	1736	Orig. Only	SS/AR
Holmes, John H.	012	1839	WB-B/175	AR
Holmes, Louis L.	022	1854	WB-C/378	AR
Holmes, Maria J.	070	1848	WB-C/479	AR
Holmes, Mary	028	1824	Orig. Only	AR
Holmes, Mary	054	c1794	WB-1/11	AR
Holmes, Mary A.	TN	1851	022 WB-D/46	022 AR
Holmes, Moses	011	c1804	WB-1/346	
Holmes, Moses	032	c1852	WB-2/78	
Holmes, Nicholas	073	1889	WB-H/475	CTY
Holmes, Oliver	103	1867	RD-14/571	AR
Holmes, Owen	087	1840	WB-1/232	AR
Holmes, Reuben	032	c1830	Copy	085 AR
Holmes, Reuben J.	085	1899	WB-3/295	CTY
Holmes, Robert	054	1890	WB-5/316	CTY
Holmes, Susannah	085	1878	WB-1/472	CTY
Holmes, Theophilus	029	1885	WB-E/337	AR
Holmes, William	001	1886	WB-2/299	AR
Holmes, William S.	009	1842	OB-D/277	AR
Holmes. Reubin	032	1831	WB-1/161	
Holms, Archibald	029	1797	WB-A/1	AR
Holms, Esther	056	c1878	Orig. Only	AR
Holoman, Sally	051	1868	WB-C/8	AR
Holomon, Justin	051	1873	WB-C/86	AR

Name	Co.	Date	Recorded Copy	Original
Holsclaw, John	006	c1842	Copy	054 AR
Holshouser, Hannah	085	1847	WB-K/64	AR
Holshouser, Jacob	085	1845	WB-K/5	AR
Holshouser, Jacob	085	c1796	WB-G/91	AR
Holshouser, Michael	085	1810	WB-G/160	AR
Holsomback, Polly	078	1859	WB-18/71	AR
Holst, Louis	099	1859	RB-31/222	AR
Holstead, John	030	1793	WB-2/20	
Holstead, Lemuel	030	1786	WB-1/202	
Holstead, Malachi	030	c1814	WB-3/45	
Holstead, William	030	1816	WB-3/80	
Holsted, Mary	030	1835	WB-4/12	
Holstein, John	073	1790	WB-B/95	AR
Holston, Adam	090	1819	WB-3/30	AR
Holston, Jacob	044	1795	WB-3/170	CTY
Holt, Alexander	001	1892	WB-2/529	AR
Holt, Ausborn	099	1889	WB-B/334	AR
Holt, Charles T.	001	1900	WB-3/362	AR
Holt, Daniel C.	001	1892	WB-2/510	AR
Holt, David L.	NH	1894	068 WB-D/424	
Holt, E. M.	001	1884	065 WB-L/475	065 AR
Holt, Edwin M.	001	1884	WB-2/223	AR-Copy
Holt, Edwin M.	001	1888	032 WB-4/122	032 AR
Holt, Elizabeth	070	c1751	DB-C/328	AR
Holt, Elizabeth	072	1844	WB-2/46	AR
Holt, Elizabeth	020	1825	RB-I/343	AR
Holt, Elizabeth	047	1847	PQS.7/ November	
Holt, Emily	001	1900	WB-3/354	AR
Holt, Etheldred	056	1847	WB-1/597	AR
Holt, Frederick	029	1801	WB-A/49	AR
Holt, George	022	1893	WB-E/523	AR
Holt, George	073	c1839	Orig. Only	AR
Holt, George	073	1798	WB C/112	AR
Holt, Hamilton	046	1890	WB-F/63	AR
Holt, Hilliard	047	1855	WB-5/11	
Holt, Isaac	073	1823	WB-E/42	AR
Holt, Jacob	001	1883	WB-2/201	AR
Holt, James H.	001	1897	WB-3/180	AR
Holt, James H.	001	c1896	065 WB-N/85	065 AR
Holt, James, Sr.	056	1844	WB-1/560	AR
Holt, Jeremiah	001	1877	WB-2/103	AR
Holt, John	073	1824	WB-E/56	AR
Holt, John	001	1888	WB-2/353	AR
Holt, Joseph	047	1834	WB-4/107	
Holt, Mary	047	1852	WB-4/333	
Holt, Michael	073	1842	WB-F/126	AR
Holt, Michael	073	1799	WB-C/149	AR
Holt, Michael	073	1767	WB-A/76	
Holt, Michael W.	001	1858	WB-1/127	AR
Holt, Narcissa	072	1895	WB-4/315	AR
Holt, Nelly	001	c1844	WB-1/43	AR
Holt, Nicholas	073	c1787	WB-B/17	AR
Holt, Peter	001	1886	WB-2/277	AR
Holt, Peter F.	001	1888	WB-2/355	AR
Holt, Philemon	073	1836	WB-E/381	AR
Holt, Rebecah	029	1826	WB-B/144	AR
Holt, Richard	022	1840	WB-C/101	AR
Holt, Richard	022	1891	WB-E/458	AR
Holt, Samuel	077	1837	WB-F/268	AR
Holt, Samuel	071	1821	WB-3/251	AR
Holt, Sarah	001	c1832	WB-1/34	AR
Holt, Sidney B.	001	1895	WB-3/50	AR
Holt, Squire	022	1882	WB-E/262	AR
Holt, Thomas	001	1888	WB-2/415	AR

Name	Co.	Date	Recorded Copy	Original
Holt, Thomas	024	1778	WB-A/13	AR
Holt, Thomas	047	1794	WB-3/230	
Holt, Thomas M.	001	1897	WB-3/176	AR
Holt, Thomas M.	001	1896	WB-3/112	AR
Holt, Thomas M.	001	1896	032 WB-4/355	032 AR
Holt, W. P.	022	c1885	WB-F/570	AR
Holt, William	073	1846	WB-F/306	AR
Holt, William	001	1849	WB-1/15	AR
Holt, William D.	001	1896	WB-3/100	AR
Holt, William H.	047	1889	WB-6/551	AR
Holton, Abel	029	1792	Orig. Only	AR
Holton, Adaline N.	065	1889	WB-L/376	AR
Holton, Alexander	028	1888	WB-E/500	AR
Holton, Alfred	081	1884	WB-15/463	
Holton, Barzila	028	1841	WB-D/39	AR
Holton, Biggs	028	1839	WB-C/429	AR
Holton, Enoch	028	1865	WB-D/409	AR
Holton, George	028	1796	WB-B/8	AR
Holton, James	028	1822	WB-C/209	AR
Holton, Jeptha B.	074	1886	WB-1/86	
Holton, Jesse	009	c1772	OWB/113	AR
Holton, Jesse	028	1819	WB-C/183	AR
Holton, Lewis	046	1805	WB-A/171	AR
Holton, Martha	046	1887	WB-E/466	AR
Holton, Mary E.	079	1892	WB-3/20	AR
Holton, Matthew	028	1866	WB-D/424	AR
Holton, Nathaniel	029	1810	WB-A/148	AR
Holton, Peregin	009	c1779	OWB/144	AR
Holton, Thomas	074	1876	WB-1/29	AR
Holton, Thomas J.	065	1861	WB-J/107	AR
Holtsouser, Nancy	085	1850	WB-K/112	AR
Holycross, Robert	020	1871	WB-A/80	CTY
Holyfield, Joseph	049	1894	WB-2/320	AR
Holyfield, Nelly	092	1868	WB-5/98	
Holyfield, Purlina	092	1877	WB-6/95	AR
Holyfield, Samuel	049	1870	WB-2/4	AR
Holyfield, William	092	1846	WB-4/256	
Homan, Elizabeth	028	c1849	Orig. Only	AR
Homan, Wilhimina	038	c1858	WB-1/137	AR
Homans, Shepherd	NJ	1898	055 WB-A/142	
Homes, Edward	035	1761	087 DB-3/126	AR
Homes, Edward	010	1750	SS 879/9	SS/AR
Homes, Edward	077	1702	Orig. Only	SS/AR
Homes, Federick	044	1749	Orig. Only	CTY
Homes, George	065	1802	WB-D/65	AR
Homes, Solomon	071	1780	WB-1/233	
Homes, William	024	1791	WB-A/89	AR
Homesley, Joseph	060	1800	Orig. Only	AR
Homesley, Joseph	060	1799	Orig. Only	AR
Honbarger, William A.	085	1893	WB-3/10	
Hone, Edward	024	1757	SS 882/67	
Honey, Roben	005	1831	WB-B/7	AR
Honeycutt, Allen	099	1884	WB-A/522	AR
Honeycutt, Bolen	005	1811	WB-2/65	AR
Honeycutt, James	016	1885	WB-3/458	AR
Honeycutt, John A.	099	1899	WB-D/230	AR
Honeycutt, John H.	099	1865	RB-33/353	AR
Honeycutt, William	087	1876	WB-3/132	AR
Honeycutt, William B.	087	1891	WB-3/499	AR
Honeycutt, Willis	099	1875	RB-35/290	AR
Hood, Britton	103	1848	RD-10/84	
Hood, David	097	1884	WB-2/258	AR
Hood, Edward	103	1811	RD-1/338	AR
Hood, Edward B.	103	1899	WB-2/261	AR
Hood, Francis	MI	1898	013 WB-D/139	013 AR
Hood, James	065	1882	WB-K/467	AR
Hood, James H.	093	1888	WB-2/44	AR
Hood, James N.	061	1895	WB-2/166	AR
Hood, Jesse	020	1818	RB-H/189	AR
Hood, John	061	c1834	WB-1/8	AR
Hood, John H.	065	1840	WB-H/9	AR
Hood, John J.	103	1895	WB-2/102	AR
Hood, John R.	103	1883	WB-1/267	AR
Hood, Mack	017	1893	WB-B/236	AR
Hood, Patience	103	1834	RD-7/21	
Hood, Reuben	065	1856	WB-J/30	AR
Hood, Reuben	065	1845	WB-I/15	AR
Hood, Richard A.	065	1848	WB-I/136	AR
Hood, S. M.	098	1897	WB-A/299	CTY
Hood, Samuel	056	1894	WB-2/182	AR
Hood, Solomon P.	103	1893	WB-2/21	AR
Hood, Thomas	099	1818	RB-14/365	AR
Hood, Thomas	099	1783	RB-1/182	AR
Hood, Tunas	065	1801	WB-D/69	AR
Hood, Tunas, Sr.	065	1797	WB-D/16	AR
Hoof, John	039	1815	WB-E/12	AR
Hoofman, Lewis	090	1827	WB-3/169	AR
Hook, John	N	1734	Orig. Only	SS/AR
Hook, Thomas	090	c1821	Orig. Only	AR
Hooker, A. H.	085	1872	WB-1/111	CTY
Hooker, Benjamin	010	1774	WB-B/7	AR
Hooker, Eliza	096	1836	WB-2/129	AR
Hooker, Francis	075	1837	WB-N/132	AR
Hooker, Godphrey	010	1730	Orig. Only	SS/AR
Hooker, Hardy	005	1840	WB-B/105	AR
Hooker, Henry	009	c1894	Orig. Only	CTY
Hooker, Jacob	081	1828	WB-5/440	AR
Hooker, John	096	1790	WB-1/171	AR
Hooker, John	018	1835	WB-C/183	
Hooker, John	044	1800	WB-5/74	CTY-Nunc.
Hooker, John, Sr.	044	1791	WB-2/255	CTY
Hooker, Jordan	073	1894	WB-I/59	CTY
Hooker, Nancy	031	1899	WB-1/111	AR
Hooker, Nathan	073	1848	WB-F/398	AR
Hooker, Nathan	031	1883	WB-1/25	AR
Hooker, Nathan	096	1801	WB-2/49	AR
Hooker, Robin	081	1873	WB-15/125	AR
Hooker, Sarah B.	045	1871	WB-1/20	
Hooker, Sarah H.	045	1896	WB-1/309	AR
Hooker, Stephen	096	1767	Orig. Only	AR
Hooker, William	024	1717	SS 875/143	SS/AR
Hooker, William	010	1757	SS 880/241	SS/AR
Hooker, William	005	1875	WB-D/43	AR
Hooker, William B.	045	1889	WB-1/189	AR
Hooks, Albert	103	1862	RD-13/443	AR
Hooks, Ann M.	103	1870	WB-1/18	AR
Hooks, Ann W.	103	1865	RD-14/238	AR
Hooks, Bardin	103	1882	WB-1/248	AR
Hooks, Bennett	103	1897	WB-2/190	AR
Hooks, Boaz F.	103	1888	WB-1/444	AR
Hooks, Charles	063	c1800	WB-1/370	
Hooks, Curtis	103	1854	RD-11/540	AR
Hooks, David	032	c1855	WB-2/112	
Hooks, Elly	103	1850	RD-10/458	AR
Hooks, Ephraim	063	1787	WB-1/138	
Hooks, Hardy	103	1801	Orig. Only	AR
Hooks, Jacob	103	1855	RD-12/112	
Hooks, John	103	1825	RD-5/204	AR
Hooks, John	N	1734	SS 876/296	

Name	Co.	Date	Recorded Copy	Original
Hooks, John	063	1778	WB-1/53	
Hooks, Martha	103	1864	RD-13/739	AR
Hooks, Pressillah	103	1873	WB-1/55	AR
Hooks, Raiford	103	1854	RD-11/395	AR
Hooks, Robert	103	1900	WB-2/292 & 312	AR
Hooks, Robert	103	1793	WI-A/417	AR
Hooks, Simeon	103	1880	WB-1/188	AR
Hooks, Thomas	035	1803	WB-A/187	AR
Hooks, Whitmel	035	1796	WB-A/216	AR
Hooks, Whitmill	097	1862	WB-1/192	AR
Hooks, William	103	1820	RD-4/365	AR
Hooks, William	024	1751	Orig. Only	SS/AR
Hooks, William	063	1795	WB-1/213	
Hooper, Ann	073	1795	WB-C/56	AR
Hooper, Benjamin	020	1839	RB-N/377	AR
Hooper, Edward	PA	1891	069 WB-6/255	069 AR
Hooper, Elisha E.	020	1843	RB-P/1	AR
Hooper, Elizabeth	053	1857	WB-8/204	AR
Hooper, Elizabeth	020	1874	WB-A/154	CTY
Hooper, Enoc C.	043	1890	WB-1/1 & 96	
Hooper, George	070	1821	WB-C/170	AR
Hooper, Henry	020	1833	RB-M/353	
Hooper, J. DeB.	073	1886	WB-H/403	CTY
Hooper, James	104	1792	WB-1/338	AR
Hooper, James H.	029	1841	WB-B/353	AR
Hooper, Lydia	021	1866	WB-1/222	AR
Hooper, Margaret	029	1880	WB-E/208	AR
Hooper, Rebecca	069	c1883	Orig. Only	AR
Hooper, T. J.	043	1895	WB-1/47	
Hooper, Thomas E.	029	1828	WB-B/167	AR
Hooper, Thomas H.	012	1805	WB-B/78	
Hooper, William	073	c1788	Orig. Only	AR
Hooper, Woodlief	020	1853	RB-R/65	
Hooper, Zachariah	020	1868	RB-T/367	CTY
Hooten, Council	059	1891	WB-A/584	CTY
Hooten, John A.	009	1885	WB-1/361	CTY
Hooten, John Booth	029	1776	Orig. Only	AR
Hooten, William	063	c1801	WB-1/417	
Hooten, William	063	1794	WB-1/197	
Hoots, Daniel	092	1844	WB-4/215	
Hoots, Jacob	092	1801	WB-3/45	AR
Hoots, John, Sr.	106	1873	WB-2/32	AR
Hoots, Joseph	050	1866	WB-1/96	CTY
Hoots, W. F.	106	1894	WB-2/354	
Hoover, Adam	081	1883	WB-15/421	AR
Hoover, Adam E.	060	1895	WB-5/3	AR
Hoover, Alfred	081	1900	WB-17/121	
Hoover, Alfred	065	1898	WB-N/164	AR
Hoover, Andrew	081	1852	WB-9/420	AR
Hoover, C. A.	065	1886	WB-L/159	AR
Hoover, Daniel	060	1838	WB-1/420	AR
Hoover, David S.	060	1875	WB-4/128	AR
Hoover, Edmond	054	1880	WB-4/418	CTY
Hoover, George	081	1842	WB-7/410	
Hoover, Henry	060	1824	WB-1/3	AR
Hoover, Henry	065	1850	WB-I/167	AR
Hoover, Henry	028	1789	WB-A/209	
Hoover, Isaac	081	1890	WB-16/154	
Hoover, Jacob	060	1857	WB-3/2	AR
Hoover, Jacob	081	1821	Orig. Only	AR
Hoover, Jacob	014	1857	Orig. Only	AR-Copy
Hoover, Jacob	032	1832	WB-1/194	
Hoover, Jesse C.	028	1858	WB-D/299	AR
Hoover, John	060	1885	WB-4/302	AR
Hoover, John	054	1840	WB-2/212	AR
Hoover, Jonas	081	1828	WB-5/454	AR
Hoover, Levi	060	1885	WB-4/314	AR
Hoover, Mary	065	1856	WB-J/20	AR
Hoover, Mary J.	105	1889	WB-2/539	AR
Hoover, Mulvina	065	1897	WB-N/68	AR
Hoover, Nelson	085	1828	WB-H/417	AR
Hoover, Philip	060	1873	WB-4/105	AR
Hoover, Phillip	065	1849	WB-I/146	AR
Hoover, Polly	064	1886	Orig. Only	AR
Hoover, Robert L.	081	1899	WB-17/35	AR
Hoover, Samuel	028	1805	WB-B/222	
Hoover, Solomon	060	1847	WB-2/281	AR
Hoover, Thomas	060	1833	WB-1/280	AR
Hoover, Thomas B.	MS	1855	Copy	014 AR
Hoover, Valentine	032	1881	WB-3/314	AR
Hoover, William S.	028	1837	WB-C/405	AR
Hope, Benjamin	044	1834	WB-13/16	CTY
Hope, John H.	099	1866	RB-34/287	AR
Hope, Robert	016	1808	WB-A/64	AR
Hope, Thomas	065	1831	WB-E/121	AR
Hopkins, Alexander	044	1857	WB-20/227	CTY
Hopkins, Andrew	053	1774	RW-1/52	AR
Hopkins, B. C.	073	1873	WB-H/73	CTY
Hopkins, Bathsheba	079	1890	WB-2/496	AR
Hopkins, Benjamin	049	1885	WB-2/121	AR
Hopkins, Carmon	044	1896	WB-24/315	CTY
Hopkins, Charles	081	1816	WB-4/342	AR
Hopkins, Chuza	073	1844	WB-G/43	AR
Hopkins, Daniel	037	1846	WB-F/345	AR
Hopkins, Daniel	074	1889	Orig. Only	AR
Hopkins, David	069	1847	WB-1/504	AR
Hopkins, Edward B.	074	1891	WB-1/102	
Hopkins, Elender	081	1817	WB-4/433	AR
Hopkins, Elender	073	1840	WB-F/51	AR
Hopkins, Elizabeth	096	c1804	WB-2/29	AR
Hopkins, Elzy	073	1845	WB-F/260	AR
Hopkins, Emaline	099	1896	WB-C/531	AR
Hopkins, Isaac	070	1794	WB-C/157	AR-Nunc.
Hopkins, J. F.	099	1897	WB-D/33	
Hopkins, James	081	1872	WB-15/93	AR
Hopkins, James	065	1866	WB-J/219	AR
Hopkins, James	073	1759	SS 881/251	SS/AR
Hopkins, Jane	099	1859	RB-31/149	AR
Hopkins, John	070	c1870	WB-E/448	AR
Hopkins, John	096	c1783	WB-1/124	
Hopkins, John	073	1861	WB-G/369	CTY
Hopkins, John	010	1775	WB-B/24	AR
Hopkins, John	024	1754	SS 881/93	SS/AR
Hopkins, John, Sr.	099	1844	RB-25/500	AR
Hopkins, John, Sr.	002	1721	SS 875/301	SS/AR
Hopkins, Joseph	047	1804	WB-3/429	
Hopkins, Martha A.	036	1892	WB-A/244	CTY
Hopkins, Mary	024	c1771	Orig. Only	AR
Hopkins, Mary	073	1866	WB-G/487	CTY
Hopkins, Mary	037	1856	WB-G/138	AR
Hopkins, Mary S.	036	1892	WB-A/247	CTY
Hopkins, Neall	072	1794	Orig. Only	AR
Hopkins, Penelope	072	1810	WB-A/54	AR
Hopkins, Peter	069	1808	WB-1/183	AR
Hopkins, Robert	053	1836	WB-5/459	AR
Hopkins, Sally	063	1839	WB-2/259	
Hopkins, Sarah	073	1864	WB-G/424	CTY
Hopkins, Sarah	070	1868	WB-E/10	AR
Hopkins, Sarah Ann	084	1860	WB-C/316	CTY

Name	Co.	Date	Recorded Copy	Original
Hopkins, Savory	037	1853	WB-F/524	AR
Hopkins, Silas	073	1892	WB-H/560	CTY
Hopkins, Stephen	009	1817	OB-A/278	AR-Nunc.
Hopkins, Susan	036	1888	WB-A/138	CTY
Hopkins, Thomas	096	c1792	Orig. Only	AR
Hopkins, Thomas	084	1847	WB-C/63	CTY
Hopkins, William	079	1865	WB-1/104	AR
Hopkins, William T.	GA	1848	099 RB-26/415	099 AR
Hopper, George	092	1800	WB-3/39A	AR
Hopper, Haswell H.	086	1888	WB-F/330	AR
Hopper, Jeremiah	084	1851	WB-C/118	CTY
Hopper, John	024	c1761	WB-A/16	AR
Hopper, John	026	1862	WB-1/279	AR
Hopper, John A.	026	1893	WB-2/455	AR
Hopper, Joseph	084	1829	WB-A/327	CTY
Hopper, Joshua	084	1834	WB-B/99	CTY
Hopper, L. M.	026	1870	WB-2/38	AR
Hopper, Thomas	084	1870	WB-E/20	CTY
Hopper, Thomas	020	1777	RB-A/30	AR
Hopper, William	026	1854	WB-1/172	AR
Hoppers, Daniel	006	1816	WB-A/1	AR
Hoppers, Daniel	004	1899	WB-A/219	AR
Hoppers, Kesiah	004	1880	WB-A/39	AR
Hoppers, Kisiah	004	1891	WB-A/128	
Hopson, James	099	1866	RB-34/141	AR
Hopson, Richard	073	c1786	WB-B/15	AR
Hopson, Thomas	099	1805	RB-7/5	AR
Hopson, William	073	1845	WB-F/261	AR
Hopton, Charles	103	1842	RD-8/304	AR
Horacy, Peter	053	c1767	RW-1/10	
Horah, George	085	1864	WB-K/344	AR
Horah, Henry	085	c1789	WB-E/119	AR
Horah, Hugh	085	1822	WB-H/189	AR
Horah, William H.	085	1899	WB-3/264	CTY
Hord, F. M.	026	1875	WB-2/132	AR
Hord, John J.	026	1898	WB-3/17	AR
Hord, Richard T.	026	1888	WB-2/335	AR
Horlocker, Christopher	016	1800	WB-A/83	AR
Horn, Abel	103	c1808	RD-1/110	AR
Horn, Abishae	069	1814	WB-1/260	AR
Horn, Alfred	072	1858	WB-2/159	AR
Horn, Charity	071	1815	WB-3/154	AR
Horn, Elias	065	1822	WB-D/81	AR
Horn, Elijah	037	1815	WB-E/83	AR
Horn, Elisha	037	1765	WB-A/144	AR
Horn, Enoch	029	1788	Orig. Only	AR
Horn, Grantham	069	1820	Orig. Only	AR
Horn, Hardy	103	1839	RD-8/186	AR
Horn, Henry	037	1761	WB-A/52	AR
Horn, Henry	069	1857	WB-1/555	AR
Horn, Henry	072	c1810	WB-A/55	AR
Horn, Henry	103	1798	WI-B/198	AR
Horn, Howell	035	1890	WB-4/352	AR
Horn, Jacob	037	1827	WB-F/68	AR
Horn, James A.	097	1884	WB-2/245	AR
Horn, Jeremiah	103	1809	RD-1/168	
Horn, Jesse	086	1815	WB-C/22	AR
Horn, Joel	037	1785	WB-C/14	AR
Horn, Joel	069	1793	WB-1/85	AR
Horn, Jonathan	026	18864	WB-1/347	AR
Horn, L. G.	033	1864	WB-1/180	
Horn, Lewis	072	1868	WB-4/4	AR
Horn, Mary	037	1785	WB-B/155	AR
Horn, Michael	037	1814	WB-E/74	AR
Horn, Michael	029	1836	WB-B/272	AR
Horn, Michael	037	1796	WB-C/356	AR
Horn, Moses	071	1781	WB-1/242	
Horn, Plesant	005	1865	WB-C/230	AR
Horn, Richard	047	1783	WB-3/41	
Horn, Robert	085	1836	WB-H/670	AR
Horn, Ruth	037	1803	WB-D/187	AR
Horn, Ruth	037	1803	WB-D/171	AR
Horn, Sarah	037	1799	WB-D/78	AR
Horn, Thomas	035	1872	WB-4/61	AR
Horn, Thomas	092	1801	WB-3/43	AR
Horn, Thomas	103	1808	RD-1/82	AR
Horn, Thomas	069	1782	WB-1/226	AR
Horn, Thomas	073	1792	WB-B/183	AR
Horn, Thomas	071	1777	WB-1/288	
Horn, Thomas	103	1853	RD-11/355	
Horn, Thomas F.	054	c1863	Orig. Only	AR
Horn, Thomas, Sr.	069	1781	WB-1/22	AR
Horn, William	073	1812	WB-D/368	
Horn, William	037	1795	WB-C/323	AR
Horn, William	N	1759	SS 881/202	SS/AR
Horn, William E.	005	1882	WB-D/135	AR
Horn, Wright	072	1899	WB-4/408	AR
Hornaday, Balaam	001	1887	WB-2/325	AR
Hornaday, Christopher	073	1841	WB-F/104	AR
Hornaday, Lewis	073	1837	WB-E/500	AR
Hornaday, William	073	1839	WB-F/28	AR
Hornbee, William	077	1808	WB-E/328	AR
Hornbrey, John	085	1826	WB-H/357	AR
Hornbuckle, Dinah	055	1899	WB-A/180	
Hornbuckle, Richard	020	1806	RB-E/264	AR
Hornbuckle, Thomas	020	1799	RB-C/376	
Hornby, John C.	104	1857	WB-5/174	
Horne, Benejah	056	1878	WB-3/197	
Horne, Catherine	073	1843	WB-F/227	AR
Horne, Catherine	070	1889	WB-F/314	AR
Horne, James	071	1821	WB-3/253	AR
Horne, James I.	022	1844	WB-C/169	AR
Horne, Joel	029	1854	WB-C/320	AR
Horne, Joel	005	1841	WB-B/130	
Horne, Joseph	010	1829	WB-G/183	AR
Horne, Joshua	073	1829	WB-E/207	AR
Horne, Martin V.	005	1889	WB-D/264	AR
Horne, Mary	069	1840	WB-1/447	AR
Horne, Moses	071	c1781	Copy	010 AR
Horne, Sarah, Sr.	071	1823	WB-3/294	AR
Horne, William H.	071	1808	WB-2/367	AR
Horne, William T.	029	1865	WB-D/78	AR
Horner, Elenor	075	1720	SS 875/220	
Horner, Eliza	018	1857	WB-D/36	
Horner, James H.	044	1892	WB-24/197	CTY
Horner, Jefferson	044	1879	WB-23/331	CTY
Horner, Sarah	036	1885	WB-A/76	CTY
Horner, Sarah	073	1858	WB-G/198	AR
Horner, Sylvester	075	1794	WB-L/19	AR
Horner, Thomas	073	1844	WB-F/202	AR
Horner, William	044	1867	WB-22/655	CTY
Hornes, Mary	028	1824	WB-C/246	
Horney, Elizabeth	046	1861	WB-D/96	AR
Horney, Jason	081	1865	WB-13/352	AR
Horney, Jeffrey	046	1821	WB-B/119	AR
Horney, John	046	1821	WB-B/129	AR
Horney, Jonathan	046	1842	WB-C/114	AR
Horney, Margaret	046	1863	WB-D/166	AR
Horney, Phebe	046	1866	WB-D/311	AR
Horney, Philip	046	1820	WB-B/96	AR

Name	Co.	Date	Recorded Copy	Original
Horniblow, Elizabeth	024	1827	WB-C/141	AR
Horniblow, James	024	1828	WB-C/145	AR
Horniblow, James	024	c1820	Orig. Only	AR
Horniblow, Margaret	024	1826	WB-C/119	AR
Horniblow, Molly	024	1858	WB-C/431	AR
Horniblow, Thomas	024	1821	WB-C/97	AR
Hornine, Elizabeth	029	1898	WB-F/130	AR
Hornine, John T.	029	1885	WB-E/354	AR
Horscens, Richard	028	1808	WB-B/317	AR
Horsends, James	028	1792	WB-A/274	AR
Horsewell, Mary	063	1872	WB-3/20	
Horsford, James	084	c1790	OW/67	AR
Horsford, John	084	c1801	OW/70	AR
Horsley, Richard R.	040	1897	WB-2/558	AR
Horston, William	019	1761	SS 881/184	
Horswell, George	063	1857	WB-2/445	
Horton, Amos	099	1822	RB-17/397	AR
Horton, Angeline	036	1898	WB-A/426	CTY
Horton, Benjamin	022	1826	WB-B/90	AR
Horton, Bingham B.	005	1883	Orig. Only	AR
Horton, Calvin T.	099	1898	WB-D/181	AR
Horton, Candis R.	022	1881	WB-E/234	AR
Horton, Charles	099	1871	RB-35/144	AR
Horton, Charles H.	099	1864	RB-33/334	AR
Horton, Charles H.	099	c1864	Copy	039 AR
Horton, Cynthia	022	c1861	WB-D/115	AR
Horton, David	099	1816	RB-13/51	AR
Horton, David	099	1784	RB-2/18	AR
Horton, David J.	009	1882	WB-1/306	CTY
Horton, Elisha E.	051	1839	WB-A/135	
Horton, Francis	028	1788	WB-A/181	
Horton, Hartwell	099	1848	RB-26/365	AR
Horton, Henry	099	1897	WB-D/56	AR
Horton, Henry	073	1807	WB-D/214	AR
Horton, James	022	1841	WB-C/146	AR
Horton, James	009	c1799	OWB/353	AR
Horton, James C.	017	1896	WB-B/274	AR
Horton, Jesse	022	1833	WB-B/261	AR
Horton, John	022	1880	WB-E/212	AR
Horton, Jonathan	102	1896	WB-A/109	AR
Horton, Jordan J.	051	1892	WB-C/441	AR
Horton, Joseph	015	1768	100 WB-1/44	AR
Horton, Mary	100	1799	WB-10/91	
Horton, Nancy	099	1856	RB-29/463	AR
Horton, Parmenas	028	1772	Orig. Only	AR
Horton, Robert	071	1779	WB-1/320	
Horton, Sally	010	1847	WB-G/421	AR
Horton, Samuel	047	1795	WB-3/241	
Horton, William	022	1852	WB-C/306	AR
Horton, William	022	1820	WB-B/24	AR
Horton, William	104	1846	WB-4/316	
Horton, William	022	1888	WB-E/387	AR
Horton, William R.	099	1888	WB-B/281	AR
Horton, Willis	078	1845	Orig. Only	AR
Horton, Willis	039	1844	WB-M/32	
Hosea, Abram	075	1773	Orig. Only	SS/AR
Hosea, James	071	1814	WB-3/112	AR
Hosea, John	075	1792	WB-K/240	AR-Nunc.
Hosea, Joseph	077	1785	WB-C/329	AR
Hosea, Joseph	077	1753	SS 881/47	SS/AR
Hosea, Robert	075	1781	WB-K/61	AR
Hosea, Robert	077	1742	Orig. Only	SS/AR
Hosea, William	077	1782	WB-C/252	AR
Hosking, John	046	1857	WB-C/489	AR
Hoskins, Arnold	046	1799	WB-A/167	AR
Hoskins, Baker	024	1835	WB-C/184	AR
Hoskins, Charles	024	1855	WB-C/371	AR
Hoskins, Harriet W.	024	1858	WB-C/427	AR
Hoskins, Jesse F.	046	1900	WB-G/247	AR
Hoskins, John	024	1794	WB-A/3	AR
Hoskins, Joseph	046	1799	WB-A/165	AR
Hoskins, Luvina	063	1850	WB-2/368	
Hoskins, Margaret	041	1838	WB-3/5	AR
Hoskins, Mary	024	1792	WB-A/75	AR
Hoskins, Mary R.	024	1839	WB-C/222	AR
Hoskins, Richard	024	1800	WB-A/353	AR
Hoskins, Richard	024	1822	WB-C/100	AR
Hoskins, Sarah	096	1871	WB-4/18	
Hoskins, Thomas	024	c1781	WB-A/4	AR
Hoskins, Thomas	096	c1804	WB-2/14	AR
Hoskins, Thomas	024	1734	SS 876/304	SS/AR
Hoskins, Thomas	024	1762	WB-A/31	AR
Hoskins, William	002	c1693	Orig. Only	SS/AR
Hoskins, William	024	c1766	WB-A/36	AR
Hoskins, William	024	1818	WB-C/69	AR
Hoskins, Willis	041	1880	WB-4/132	AR
Hoskins, Winiford	096	1855	WB-3/40	AR
Hoskins, Winifred	024	1807	WB-B/182	AR
Hoslar, Henry	033	1882	WB-2/75	CTY
Hosmer, Hannah	072	1773	Orig. Only	SS/AR
Hostler, Alexander	070	N. D.	Orig. Only	AR-Nunc.
Hostler, James G.	070	1856	WB-C/614	AR
Hostler, Mary	070	1814	WB-AB/204	AR
Houch, John	032	1873	WB-3/90	AR
Houck, Barbary	104	1844	WB-4/296	AR
Houck, Elizabeth	085	1850	WB-K/122	AR
Houck, John	032	1897	WB-4/322	AR
Houck, Mary M.	085	1849	WB-K/86	AR
Houck, Sarah	032	1893	WB-4/191	AR
Houer, Mary M.	028	c1762	DB-8/176	AR
Hough, Amos	016	1876	WB-3/184	AR
Hough, Hekekiah	005	1817	WB-2/66	AR
Hough, James	005	1824	WB-A/108	AR
Hough, John	005	1847	WB-B/220	AR
Hough, Richard	005	c1754	WB-1/5	
Houghteling, William D.	013	1898	WB-D/169	AR
Houghton, George	024	1719	SS 875/171	
Houghton, James	077	1758	SS 882/64	SS/AR
Houghton, Thomas	024	1743	Orig. Only	SS/AR
Houghton, William	024	1745	Orig. Only	SS/AR
Houghton, William	024	c1749	Copy	ChM-5/66
Houie, John	016	1856	WB-1/283	AR
Houk, Calvin	014	1897	WB-3/33	CTY
Houk, David	104	1841	WB-4/257	AR
Houk, Henry	064	1892	WB-2/279	AR
Houlbrooke, Farmannes	002	c1683	Orig. Only	SS/AR
Houlder, James	056	1791	WB-1/42	AR
Houlshouser, Andrew	085	1811	WB-G/179	AR
Houlston, Thomas	046	1793	WB-A/160	AR
Houpe, Jacob	054	c1825	WB-2/33	
Houpe, John	054	1844	WB-2/290	AR
Houpt, Cathrine	054	c1812	WB-1/400	AR
Houre, Peter	002	1697	SS 874.2/76	
House, Benjamin	099	1846	RB-26/133	AR
House, Daniel	071	1796	WB-2/124	AR
House, David	079	1894	WB-3/47	AR
House, Dollie S.	087	1885	WB-3/305	AR
House, Dudley	044	1817	WB-8/17	CTY
House, Franky	070	1891	WB-F/470	AR

Name	Co.	Date	Recorded Copy	Original
House, George	010	1763	WB-A/24	AR
House, George	010	1771	Orig. Only	SS/AR
House, George	010	1796	WB-D/310	AR
House, Isaac	039	c1775	WB-A/102	
House, John	037	1791	WB-C/167	AR
House, John	010	1766	WB-A/78	AR
House, John	087	1849	WB-1/364	AR
House, John C.	087	1880	WB-3/207	AR
House, Joseph	099	1862	RB-32/357	AR
House, Joseph	099	1883	WB-A/479	AR
House, Mark	065	1789	WB-D/50	AR
House, Olive H.	072	1866	Orig. Only	AR
House, Patience	047	1871	WB-6/53	AR
House, Ransom	099	1830	RB-21/351	AR
House, Sally Ann	079	1878	WB-2/168	AR
House, Sarah	079	1866	WB-1/160	AR
House, Susan	099	1869	RB-35/55	AR
House, Thomas	100	1786	WB-4/153	AR
House, Thomas	024	1734	SS 876/299	SS/AR
House, Thomas	010	1795	WB-D/262	AR
House, Thomas	010	1803	WB-E/219	AR
House, William	099	1866	RB-34/146	AR
House, William	047	1763	WB-1/96	
House, Willie	099	1880	WB-A/146	AR
Houser, Adam	106	1895	WB-2/366	
Houser, Isaac	060	1866	WB-3/90	AR
Houser, Jacob	060	1857	WB-3/12	AR
Houser, Jacob	085	1823	WB-H/251	AR
Houser, Joseph	060	1896	WB-5/22 & 77	AR
Houser, Martha	060	1868	WB-3/106	AR
Houser, Martin	085	1762	WB-A/65	AR
Houser, Peter	060	1846	WB-2/246	AR
Houson, John	047	1842	WB-4/213	
Housten, Francis	028	1794	WB-A/315	
Houston, Aaron	065	c1777	WB-D/46	AR
Houston, Agness	016	c1824	WB-A/49	AR
Houston, Alexander	021	1900	WB-3/276	AR
Houston, Ann	054	c1828	Orig. Only	AR
Houston, Ann V. L.	021	1882	WB-2/245	
Houston, Anna	065	1892	WB-M/127	AR
Houston, Anna	046	1870	WB-E/46	AR
Houston, Archibald	016	1843	WB-1/20	AR
Houston, Archibald	016	c1800	Copy	065 AR
Houston, Archibald	016	1805	WB-A/51	AR
Houston, Asenath	021	1843	WB-1/8	AR
Houston, B. F.	097	1897	WB-2/520	AR
Houston, Calvin I.	035	1861	WB-3/35	AR
Houston, David	085	1762	WB-A/63	AR
Houston, David	054	c1826	WB-2/62	AR
Houston, David T.	016	1846	WB-1/100	AR
Houston, Elizabeth	085	1841	WB-I/117	AR
Houston, Franklin W.	060	1858	WB-3/18	AR
Houston, George	065	1839	WB-E/231	AR
Houston, George	065	c1778	WB-D/45	AR
Houston, George E.	035	1852	WB-2/70	AR
Houston, George S.	054	1869	WB-4/38	AR
Houston, George W.	065	1831	WB-G/197	
Houston, George W.	065	1835	WB-G/197	AR
Houston, Hugh	065	1801	WB-D/59	AR
Houston, James	035	1852	WB-2/69	AR
Houston, James	085	1839	WB-I/49	AR
Houston, James	097	1846	WB-1/34	AR
Houston, James	065	1802	WB-D/63	AR
Houston, James	054	c1818	WB-1A/78	AR
Houston, James H.	054	c1823	WB-2/36	AR
Houston, James M.M.	021	1867	WB-1/243	AR
Houston, James N.	065	1812	WB-D/1	AR
Houston, James N.	097	1853	WB-1/83	AR
Houston, Jane	016	1846	WB-1/93	AR
Houston, Jane	065	1854	WB-I/239	AR
Houston, Jane	054	1880	WB-4/391	CTY
Houston, Jane	054	c1827	WB-2/117	AR
Houston, Jane D.	065	1882	WB-K/479	AR
Houston, Joanna	085	1847	WB-K/55	AR
Houston, Joel B.	054	1856	WB-3/104	AR
Houston, John	097	1877	WB-2/135	AR
Houston, John	085	1839	WB-I/56	AR
Houston, John	065	1812	WB-C/154	AR
Houston, John	016	1829	WB-A/23	AR
Houston, John	065	1791	WB-D/52	AR
Houston, John B.	046	1861	WB-D/115	AR
Houston, John M.	065	1872	WB-K/101	AR
Houston, Joseph	054	c1831	WB-2/153	AR
Houston, Joseph A.	022	1891	WB-E/451	AR
Houston, Levi	046	1862	WB-D/156	AR
Houston, Levi	046	1888	WB-E/503	AR
Houston, Levinas	065	c1769	WB-D/9	AR
Houston, Margaret	016	1806	WB-A/89	AR
Houston, Margaret	054	1850	WB-3/48	AR
Houston, Mary	054	1888	WB-5/201	CTY
Houston, Mary	065	1885	WB-L/88	AR
Houston, Mary	085	c1781	WB-B/55	AR
Houston, Mary	054	c1833	WB-2/142	AR
Houston, Moses	019	1774	Orig. Only	SS/AR
Houston, Placebo	054	1859	WB-3/135	AR
Houston, Robert B.	021	1878	WB-2/190	AR
Houston, Samuel	054	1865	WB-3/174	AR
Houston, Samuel	054	c1814	WB-1/335	AR
Houston, Thomas	072	1733	LGB-4/#14	SS/AR
Houston, Thomas	065	1845	WB-I/27	AR
Houston, W. A.	059	1897	WB-B/169	CTY
Houston, William	016	1803	WB-A/50	AR
Houston, William	019	1761	Orig. Only	SS/AR
Houston, William	097	1870	WB-2/39	AR
Houston, William C.	054	c1830	WB-2/99	AR
Houston, William M.	046	1891	WB-F/138	AR
Houston, William W.	097	1895	WB-2/478	AR
Houze, Henry Y.	005	1873	WB-D/28	AR
Houze, William	039	c1787	WB-A/19	
Hover, John J.	028	1744	Orig. Only	SS/AR
Hover, Samuel	028	1798	WB-B/35	AR
Hovey, Margaret	053	1812	RW-1/461	AR
Hovey, Seth	053	c1815	WB-4/92	
Hovey, Seth	053	c1815	RW-1/503	
Hovis, Elizabeth	060	1833	WB-1/268	AR
Hovis, George	040	1859	WB-1/106	
Hovis, H. W.	060	1900	WB-5/153	AR
Hovis, Philip	060	1882	WB-4/262	AR
Hovis, Sarah	040	1877	WB-2/118	AR
Hovis, Solomon	060	1855	WB-2/399	AR
How, Alexander	010	1780	WB-B/150	AR-Nunc.
Howar, Job	070	c1748	DB-D/353	
Howard, Alanson	020	1875	WB-A/181	CTY
Howard, Alexander	044	1760	Orig. Only	CTY
Howard, Alice C.	037	1871	WB-G/370	AR
Howard, Allen	044	1835	WB-13/265	CTY
Howard, Alvin	054	1846	WB-3/4	AR
Howard, Ann	021	1873	WB-2/88	
Howard, Benjamin	096	1790	WB-1/165	AR
Howard, Benjamin	104	1828	WB-4/119	AR

Name	Co.	Date	Recorded Copy	Original
Howard, Benjamin	104	1825	WB-4/69	AR
Howard, Caleb D.	070	1803	WB-C/159	AR
Howard, Cary A.	020	1881	WB-A/301	CTY
Howard, Charles	028	1756	SS 880/33	SS/AR
Howard, Christopher	085	1815	WB-G/400	AR
Howard, Christopher	104	1879	WB-6/172	AR
Howard, Cornelius	053	1884	WB-11/141	AR
Howard, Dorcas	022	1826	WB-B/118	AR
Howard, Edmond	085	1821	WB-H/134	AR
Howard, Edmund	072	1882	WB-4/130	AR
Howard, Edmund	072	1796	Orig. Only	AR
Howard, Edney	037	1865	WB-G/260	AR
Howard, Edward	029	1793	Orig. Only	AR
Howard, Elias	037	1799	WB-D/74	AR
Howard, Elijah	010	1820	WB-G/75	AR
Howard, Eliza	020	1847	RB-P/522	
Howard, Elizabeth	103	1848	RD-10/2	AR
Howard, Elizabeth	073	1825	WB-E/80	AR
Howard, Evan	037	1847	WB-F/381	AR
Howard, Francis	020	1819	RB-H/286	
Howard, Francis	020	1785	RB-B/71	AR
Howard, Frank I.	021	c1892	WB-3/10	
Howard, Fred	044	1880	WB-23/374	CTY
Howard, Freeman	021	1887	WB-2/375	
Howard, George	019	1806	Orig. Only	AR-Nunc.
Howard, George	068	1871	WB-D/33	
Howard, George	037	1863	WB-G/231	AR
Howard, George	021	1857	WB-1/131	AR
Howard, George	030	1818	WB-3/101	
Howard, Groves	044	1807	WB-6/334	CTY
Howard, Henry A.	099	1887	WB-B/203	AR
Howard, Hester R.	070	c1889	Orig. Only	AR
Howard, Howell	089	1870	WB-2/3	
Howard, Israel	057	1846	WB-B/188	AR
Howard, J. H.	014	1893	WB-2/505	CTY
Howard, Jacob O.	097	1890	WB-2/392	AR
Howard, James	010	c1729	Orig. Only	SS/AR
Howard, James	031	1898	WB-1/107	AR
Howard, James	070	1817	WB-AB/250	AR
Howard, James	072	c1790	Orig. Only	AR
Howard, James	070	1802	Orig. Only	AR
Howard, James M.	070	1858	WB-C/666	AR
Howard, James M.	105	1889	WB-2/539	AR
Howard, James N.	105	1895	WB-3/161	
Howard, James, Sr.	029	1815	WB-A/216	AR
Howard, Jesse	092	c1835	WB-4/102	
Howard, John	085	c1781	WB-C/114	AR
Howard, John	019	1832	WB-A/19	AR
Howard, John	085	c1802	WB-D/184	AR
Howard, John	104	1811	WB-3/8	AR
Howard, John	085	1825	WB-H/316	AR
Howard, John	011	N. D.	WB-1/510	
Howard, John	015	1771	100 WB-1/157	AR
Howard, John	028	1780	Orig. Only	AR
Howard, John	070	1846	WB-AB/449	AR
Howard, John	070	c1862	Orig. Only	AR
Howard, John	044	1779	WB-1/212	CTY
Howard, John	068	1893	WB-D/365	CTY
Howard, John	033	1847	WB-1/91	
Howard, John	044	1829	WB-11/81	CTY
Howard, John D.	061	1885	WB-2/67	AR
Howard, John H.	028	1857	WB-D/278	AR
Howard, John H.	060	1887	WB-4/376	AR
Howard, Joseph	072	1788	Orig. Only	AR
Howard, Joseph	044	1875	WB-23/195	CTY

Name	Co.	Date	Recorded Copy	Original
Howard, Josiah	028	1822	WB-C/218	AR
Howard, Julia N.	057	1840	WB-B/144	AR
Howard, Julius	073	1867	WB-G/525	CTY
Howard, L.	061	1900	WB-2/261	AR
Howard, Larkin	106	c1866	WB-1/99	AR
Howard, Levina	085	c1829	WB-H/460	AR
Howard, Luke	051	1825	Copy	AR/CRX
Howard, Margaret	085	c1804	WB-E/114	AR
Howard, Margaret	097	1899	WB-3/3	AR
Howard, Mary	087	1883	WB-3/278	AR
Howard, Mary	104	c1836	Copy	006 AR
Howard, Mary	104	1836	WB-4/205	AR
Howard, Mary	085	1830	WB-H/474	AR
Howard, Mary D.	072	1888	WB-4/232	AR
Howard, Mary E.	053	1868	Orig. Only	AR
Howard, Mathew	085	1850	WB-K/108	AR
Howard, Milly	070	1881	WB-E/449	AR
Howard, Minson	087	1869	WB-3/8	AR
Howard, Philip	092	1809	WB-3/92	AR
Howard, Polly	060	1873	WB-4/98	AR
Howard, Rebekah	010	1819	WB-G/62	AR
Howard, Richard	073	1857	WB-G/172	AR
Howard, Robard	029	c1757	DB-1/180	
Howard, Robert	046	c1893	Orig. Only	AR
Howard, Robert	065	1799	WB-D/58	AR
Howard, Robert	028	c1760	Orig. Only	AR
Howard, Robert	078	1811	WI-6/29	AR
Howard, Robert G.	097	1862	WB-1/196	AR
Howard, Ruth	028	1790	WB-A/211	AR
Howard, Sallie H.	060	1894	WB-4/561	AR
Howard, Samuel	029	1761	Orig. Only	AR
Howard, Sephen	037	1788	WB-C/71	AR
Howard, Solomon	044	c1869	WB-23/21	CTY
Howard, Stephen	103	1843	RD-8/388	AR
Howard, Stephen	037	1838	WB-F/225	AR
Howard, Thomas	105	c1874	069 WB-5/73	069 AR
Howard, Thomas	073	1820	WB-D/577	AR
Howard, Thomas M.	087	1864	WB-A/151	AR
Howard, Titus	057	1796	WB-A/134	AR
Howard, William	072	1799	Orig. Only	AR
Howard, William	085	c1802	WB-D/5	AR
Howard, William	072	c1765	RW/L48	AR
Howard, William	KY	1849	084 WB-C/292	084 CTY
Howard, William	053	1851	WB-7/486	AR
Howard, William	053	1799	RW-1/311	
Howard, William	097	1843	WB-1/3	AR
Howard, William	092	1781	WB-1/153	AR
Howard, William	021	1887	WB-2/370	
Howard, William D.	097	1864	WB-1/241	AR
Howard, William H.	060	1878	WB-4/188	AR
Howard, William H.	TN	c1857	Copy	078 AR
Howard, Wilson	037	1865	WB-G/270	AR
Howard, Wilson	037	1841	Orig. Only	AR
Howcott, Charles R.	024	1845	WB-C/260	AR
Howcott, Edwd.	009	1750	SS 877/267	SS/AR
Howcott, Fred N.	024	1823	WB-C/101	AR
Howcott, John	010	1733	SS 876/283	SS/AR
Howcott, Nathaniel	024	1771	WB-A/11	AR
Howcutt, Nathaniel	024	1820	WB-C/86	AR
Howcutt, Sarah	024	1828	WB-C/150	AR
Howe, Alfred	070	1892	WB-G/80	AR
Howe, Elizabeth	070	1831	WB-AB/265	AR
Howe, Job	070	1803	WB-AB/70	AR
Howe, Joseph	028	1767	Orig. Only	AR
Howe, Margaret	070	1846	WB-AB/448	AR

Name	Co.	Date	Recorded Copy	Original
Howe, Mary	010	1814	WB-F/265	AR
Howe, Mary W.	070	1900	WB-H/273	AR
Howe, Robert	012	1829	WB-B/155	AR
Howe, Sarah	012	1804	WB-B/75	AR
Howe, Thomas C.	070	1811	WB-AB/160	AR
Howe, William	030	1792	WB-2/9	
Howel, Ellis	040	1857	WB-1/97	
Howel, John	044	1824	WB-9/313	CTY
Howel, John	060	c1828	SC/04600	AR-Copy
Howel, William	016	1810	WB-A/94	AR
Howell (Holmes), Sally	103	1847	RD-9/464	AR
Howell, Archibald	016	1894	WB-4/181	AR
Howell, Archilus	103	1812	RD-2/85	AR
Howell, Arthur	103	1825	RD-5/202	AR
Howell, Arthur	039	1791	WB-A/105	Nunc.
Howell, Baldy H.	099	1889	WB-B/331	AR
Howell, Benjamin	020	1828	RB-L/323	AR
Howell, Benjamin	103	c1828	SC/04087	AR-Copy
Howell, Benjamin	103	1829	RD-6/473	AR
Howell, Brittain	037	1867	WB-G/301	AR
Howell, Bythel	037	1888	WB-H/135	AR
Howell, Charles W.	033	1894	WB-2/165	CTY
Howell, Daniel	103	1800	WI-B/314	AR
Howell, Daniel	103	1853	RD-11/336	AR
Howell, David	103	1849	RD-10/310	AR
Howell, David	049	c1864	WB-1/5	AR
Howell, David	006	1889	WB-E/187	AR
Howell, Dicey	047	c1875	Orig. Only	AR-Copy
Howell, Dolly B.	063	1873	WB-3/50	
Howell, Edward A.	044	1878	WB-23/319	CTY-Nunc.
Howell, Elisha	056	c1792	WB-1/65	AR
Howell, Elizabeth	051	1886	WB-C/340	AR
Howell, Elizabeth	103	1821	RD-4/462	AR
Howell, Etheldred	071	1883	WB-6/418	
Howell, Fanny	071	1822	WB-3/262	AR
Howell, George	006	1886	WB-E/140	AR
Howell, Hamilton	103	1872	WB-1/48	AR
Howell, Helen P.	035	1882	WB-4/154	
Howell, Henry	103	c1828	Orig. Only	AR
Howell, Henry	099	1864	RB-33/330	AR
Howell, Henry	071	1794	WB-2/56	AR
Howell, Henry H.	099	1892	WB-C/560	AR
Howell, Hopkin	071	1770	WB-1/184	
Howell, Irving	047	1900	WB-7/266	AR
Howell, Isaac	041	1899	WB-4/476	AR
Howell, Isaac	016	1876	WB-3/154	AR
Howell, James	092	1847	WB-4/262	
Howell, James A.	103	1881	WB-1/223	AR
Howell, James D.	009	1850	037 WB-F/444	037 AR
Howell, James E.	041	1875	WB-4/65	AR
Howell, James M.	044	1890	WB-24/137	CTY
Howell, James M.	016	1895	WB-4/213	AR
Howell, James P.	051	1889	WB-C/397	AR
Howell, Jethro	063	1790	WB-1/158	
Howell, Jethro	103	1826	RD-5/217	AR
Howell, Jethro	103	1895	WB-2/124	AR
Howell, John	026	1864	WB-1/350	AR
Howell, John	103	1843	RD-8/451	AR
Howell, John	103	1793	Orig. Only	AR
Howell, John	071	1821	WB-3/259	AR
Howell, John	037	1847	WB-F/364	AR
Howell, John	049	1848	WB-2/214	AR
Howell, John	071	1819	WB-3/218	AR
Howell, John	060	1828	WB-1/90	AR
Howell, John	060	c1828	SC/03883	AR-Copy
Howell, John	010	1761	Orig. Only	AR
Howell, John	103	1836	RD-7/196	AR
Howell, John R.	089	1860	WB-1/218	
Howell, John W.	044	1888	WB-24/53	CTY
Howell, John W.	029	1835	WB-B/245	AR
Howell, Joseph	037	1750	Orig. Only	SS/AR
Howell, Joseph	085	c1807	WB-G/35	AR
Howell, Joseph	016	1867	WB-2/155	AR
Howell, Joshua	103	1799	WI-B/288	AR
Howell, Joshua P.	026	1864	WB-1/360	AR
Howell, Lazarus	103	1827	RD-5/325	
Howell, Levi	063	1860	WB-2/464	
Howell, Louisa C.	040	1900	WB-3/80	AR
Howell, Martha A.	037	1885	WB-H/1	
Howell, Mary L.	037	1893	WB-H/251	AR
Howell, Miles	041	1840	WB-3/21	AR
Howell, Mills	103	1878	WB-1/130	AR
Howell, Nancy	099	1883	WB-A/446	AR
Howell, Nancy	103	1858	RD-12/497	AR
Howell, Nancy J.	103	1900	WB-2/274	AR
Howell, Nancy T.	103	1897	WB-2/186	AR
Howell, Nathaniel	071	1762	WB-1/67	
Howell, Noel	103	1793	Orig. Only	AR
Howell, Rhody	103	1834	RD-7/21	
Howell, Richard	005	1802	WB-2/68	AR
Howell, Robert	022	c1803	WB-A/74	AR
Howell, Rowan	075	1800	WB-M1/44	AR
Howell, Sarah	071	1787	WB-1/386	AR
Howell, Sarah M.	103	c1889	Copy	056 AR
Howell, Silvanus	030	1788	WB-1/219	
Howell, Silvy	099	1854	RB-28/549	AR
Howell, Susana	051	1865	Orig. Only	AR
Howell, Susanna	037	1872	WB-G/399	AR
Howell, Thomas	092	1783	WB-2/3A	AR
Howell, Thomas	047	1796	WB-3/260	
Howell, Thomas	044	1791	WB-2/212	CTY
Howell, Thomas	047	1777	WB-2/65	
Howell, Thomas	066	1891	WB-1/121	AR
Howell, Whitney	063	c1832	WB-2/176	
Howell, William	103	1798	Orig. Only	AR
Howell, William	090	1804	WB-2/44	AR
Howell, William A.	033	1868	WB-2/1	
Howell, William E.	071	1879	WB-6/292	AR
Howe!l, William K.	071	1853	WB-5/113	AR
Howenton, Ezekiel	037	1828	WB-F/84	AR
Howenton, Thomas	037	1818	WB-E/189	AR
Howenton, William	037	1844	WB-F/301	AR
Howerton, Henrietta	069	1870	WB-1/602	AR
Howerton, Patrick	039	1875	WB-U/119	AR
Howett, Eliza A.	VA	1866	024 WB-D/48	024 AR
Howett, Richard	096	c1805	WB-2/24	AR
Howett, Richard	096	1847	WB-3/17	AR
Howett, Richard	024	1857	WB-C/405	AR
Howett, Silvanus	024	1825	WB-C/116	AR
Howett, Thomas B.	VA	1856	024 WB-D/55	024 AR
Howey, Aaron H.	097	1858	WB-1/141	AR
Howey, Anna	097	1869	WB-2/24	AR
Howey, David	097	1869	WB-2/19	AR
Howey, John	065	1807	WB-C/152	AR
Howey, John S.	065	1833	WB-G/122	AR
Howey, Nancy J.	097	1878	WB-2/138	AR
Howie, Athalinda	097	1850	WB-1/67	AR
Howie, Elizabeth	065	1884	WB-L/48	AR
Howie, George	097	1880	WB-2/180	

Name	Co.	Date	Recorded Copy	Original
Howie, Jeremiah	016	1858	WB-2/41	AR
Howie, John	065	1872	WB-K/106	AR
Howie, Margaret	029	1830	WB-B/184	AR
Howie, Nancy	065	1868	WB-J/258	AR
Howie, Samuel	029	1815	WB-A/219	AR
Howie, William	065	1818	WB-D/76	AR
Howington, N. J.	056	c1899	WB-4/281	AR
Howk, Daniel	104	1869	WB-6/7	AR
Howland, Samuel	019	1798	WB-D/229	AR
Howle, Malinda	099	1876	Orig. Only	AR
Howlet, Harmon	046	c1837	WB-B/580	AR
Howorth, Henry C.	061	c1841	WB-1/20	AR
Howren, John	009	1816	OB-A/255	AR
Howren, Rebecca	009	1816	OB-A/256	AR
Hows (House), James	072	1786	Orig. Only	AR
Hows, Job	070	1758	Orig. Only	028 AR
Howse, Buckner	072	1851	WB-2/116	AR
Howse, John	070	1790	WB-C/156	AR
Howser, Michael	090	1789	Orig. Only	AR-Copy
Howson, William	008	1715	Orig. Only	SS/AR
Howze, Isaac	039	1816	WB-E/65	AR
Howze, John	039	1808	WB-C/109	AR
Hoxie, Albert	028	1839	WB-C/433	AR
Hoye, Mary Ann	046	1844	WB-C/202	AR
Hoyl, Andrew	040	1857	WB-1/78	
Hoyl, Margaret	060	1827	WB-1/66	AR/CRX
Hoyle, Alsalom	014	1867	WB-1/23	AR
Hoyle, E. W.	065	1899	016 WB-4/336	016 AR
Hoyle, Eli	060	1844	WB-2/227	
Hoyle, Elizabeth	021	1889	WB-2/490	AR
Hoyle, Elizabeth	060	1856	WB-2/412	AR
Hoyle, Elizabeth	065	1899	WB-N/242	AR
Hoyle, Henry	026	1900	WB-3/89	AR
Hoyle, J. C.	026	1894	WB-2/490	AR
Hoyle, J. F.	014	1891	WB-2/463	CTY
Hoyle, Jacob	026	1848	WB-1/90	AR
Hoyle, John	026	1900	WB-3/74	
Hoyle, John D.	100	1864	WB-50/96	AR
Hoyle, Michael	060	1793	Orig. Only	AR
Hoyle, Peter	060	1827	WB-1/58	
Hoyle, S. V.	068	1892	032 WB-4/213	032 AR
Hoyle, S. V.	068	1892	WB-D/358	
Hoyle, Sarah	026	1900	WB-3/89	
Hoyle, Thomas L.	084	1888	WB-E/383	CTY
Hoyt, Andrew	040	c1856	Copy	065 AR
Hoyt, Goold	079	1862	WB-1/107	AR
Hoyt, Goold	NY	1842	097 WB-3/263	097 AR
Hoyt, Gould	NY	1883	Copy	050 AR
Hoyt, James	009	1808	OB-A/16	AR-Nunc.
Hoyt, Lydig M.	NY	1868	Copy	050 AR
Hoyt, Moses C.	072	1896	WB-4/339	AR
Hubank, Joseph	047	1795	WB-3/242	
Hubbard, Archibald	020	1879	WB-A/282	CTY
Hubbard, Benjamin	104	1823	WB-4/43	AR
Hubbard, Edwin R.	028	1883	WB-E/325	AR
Hubbard, Helen	010	1842	WB-G/341	AR
Hubbard, Henry	099	1813	RB-11/163	AR
Hubbard, James	061	1842	WB-1/22	AR
Hubbard, James	005	1881	WB-D/109	AR
Hubbard, John	046	1834	WB-B/507	AR
Hubbard, John L.	NH	1900	050 WB-2/344	050 CTY
Hubbard, Matthew	020	1819	RB-H/240	
Hubbard, Nathaniel	104	1816	WB-3/126	AR
Hubbard, Rane	N	c1714	Orig. Only	SS/AR
Hubbard, Thomas	024	1771	WB-A/17	AR

Name	Co.	Date	Recorded Copy	Original
Hubbard, Wade H.	005	1894	WB-D/348	AR
Hubbard, Zenas	023	1888	WB-A/66	AR
Hucabay, Samuel	044	1775	WB-1/117	CTY
Huckaba, John	086	1859	WB-E/365	AR
Huckabee, Allen	089	1857	WB-1/175	
Huckabee, John	068	1806	WB-A/247	
Huckabee, Richard	029	1833	WB-B/223	AR
Huckabee, Thomas	089	1844	WB-1/28	
Huckaby, Samuel	039	1792	WB-A/91	Nunc.
Huckins, Daniel	028	1733	Orig. Only	SS/AR
Hucks, Harriet C.	065	1896	WB-M/514	AR
Hudde, Christopher	008	1714	Orig. Only	SS/AR
Huddlestone, David	086	1786	WB-A/6	
Huddlestone, Hannah	086	1796	Orig. Only	AR
Huddlestone, Robert	044	1782	WB-1/349	
Huddlestone, Seth	046	1794	WB-A/163	AR
Hudgens, William	085	c1795	WB-D/172	AR
Hudgins, Elizabeth	077	c1842	Orig. Only	AR
Hudgins, Humphrey	041	1823	WB-2/191	AR
Hudgins, Josiah	050	1892	WB-2/154	CTY
Hudgins, Mary	041	1850	WB-3/126	AR
Hudgins, Mary	041	1853	WB-3/332	AR
Hudgins, Warner P.	041	1893	WB-4/364	AR
Hudgson, Abia	033	1842	WB-1/47	
Hudgson, Joseph	096	1744	Orig. Only	SS/AR
Hudler, Joseph	006	1892	WB-E/235	AR
Hudler, Whiteford	027	1879	WB-2/33	AR
Hudlow, Andrew	086	1894	WB-F/489	AR
Hudlow, Andrew	086	1856	WB-E/322	AR
Hudnall, Eliza	FL	1900	050 WB-2/363	050 CTY
Hudnall, John	020	1815	RB-G/77	
Hudnall, Robert	037	1763	WB-A/104	AR
Hudnall, Shapleigh	028	1777	Orig. Only	AR
Hudnall, William	063	c1784	WB-1/106	
Hudnell, Elisabeth	074	c1872	WB-1/67	AR-Copy
Hudnell, Nancy B.	009	1893	WB-1/571	CTY
Hudnell, Robert	009	1899	WB-2/191	CTY
Hudson, Charles	063	c1785	WB-1/124	
Hudson, Clarissa	103	1883	WB-1/261	AR
Hudson, Daniel	021	1848	WB-1/67	AR
Hudson, Daniel	021	1891	WB-2/517	
Hudson, Dicey	087	1900	WB-4/146	AR
Hudson, Edward	047	1811	WB-3/514	
Hudson, Ellen	016	1851	WB-1/190	AR
Hudson, Ezekiel	053	1857	WB-8/236	AR
Hudson, Fanny B.	016	c1856	WB-A/29	AR
Hudson, Hall	092	1799	WB-3/30A	AR
Hudson, Holley	087	1849	WB-1/358	AR
Hudson, J. J.	087	1899	WB-4/97	AR
Hudson, James	009	c1781	OWB/160	AR
Hudson, James	056	1882	WB-3/322	AR
Hudson, John	047	1857	WB-5/31	
Hudson, John	077	1772	WB-C/111	AR
Hudson, John	014	1886	WB-2/332	CTY
Hudson, Joseph	065	1845	Orig. Only	AR
Hudson, Joseph	027	1820	WB-A/28	AR
Hudson, Joseph R.	097	1879	WB-2/155	
Hudson, Joseph R.	097	1879	065 WB-L/335	065 AR
Hudson, Joshua	089	1896	WB-2/275	AR
Hudson, Mary	077	1771	Orig. Only	AR
Hudson, Mathew	021	c1851	Orig. Only	AR
Hudson, Richard	065	1791	WB-C/142	AR
Hudson, Robert	084	c1795	OW/25	AR
Hudson, Sarah M.	087	1893	WB-3/529	AR
Hudson, Seth	016	1822	WB-A/63	

Name	Co.	Date	Recorded Copy	Original
Hudson, Seth H.	016	1866	WB-2/136	AR
Hudson, Siddy Quin	059	1881	WB-A/227	CTY
Hudson, Thomas	047	1825	WB-4/7	
Hudson, Thomas	033	c1836	WB-1/43	
Hudson, Thomas I.	087	1884	WB-3/294	AR
Hudson, Uriah	077	c1760	Orig. Only	AR
Hudson, Uriah	077	1830	WB-F/175	AR
Hudson, William	087	1829	WB-1/96	AR
Hudson, William	067	1868	WB-2/1	
Hudson, William	071	1761	WB-1/55	
Hudson, William	056	1865	WB-2/72	AR
Hudson, William	067	1868	WB-1/166	AR
Hudson, William	084	1897	WB-F/95	CTY
Hudson, William H.	087	1900	WB-4/115	AR
Hudspeth, Benjamin	092	1792	WB-3/8A	AR
Hudspeth, Carter	092	1834	WB-4/64	AR
Hudspeth, Carter	044	1796	WB-3/242	CTY
Hudspeth, Elizabeth	092	1803	WB-3/56	AR
Hudspeth, Giles	092	1797	WB-3/25	Nunc.
Hudspeth, Jiles	044	1781	WB-1/323	CTY
Hudspeth, John	092	c1780	WB-1/142	
Hudspeth, Ralph	092	1777	WB-1/84	AR
Hudspeth, William	092	1778	WB-1/103	AR
Huett, Henry	075	c1854	WB-M2/25	AR
Huey, Solomon	030	N. D.	WB-2/325	
Huff, Daniel	090	1793	WB-1/46	
Huff, Jesse	032	1874	WB-3/115	AR
Huff, John	090	1842	WB-4/103	AR
Huff, Joshua	106	1881	WB-2/138	AR
Huff, Martha	070	1880	WB-E/394	AR
Huff, Richard	019	1791	WB-D/225	AR
Huffhind, John	073	1841	WB-F/238	AR
Huffhines, Daniel	073	1822	WB-E/15	AR
Huffhines, Lewis	001	1880	WB-2/176	AR
Huffines, Abel	046	1892	WB-F/182	AR
Huffines, Daniel	046	1865	WB-D/269	AR
Huffines, David	046	c1873	WB-E/141	
Huffines, George	046	1864	WB-D/220	AR
Huffines, Jacob	046	1883	WB-E/358	AR
Huffines, John	046	1900	WB-G/201	AR
Huffines, John	046	1864	WB-D/223	AR
Huffines, Mary Ann	001	1900	046 WB-I/249	
Huffines, Mary Ann	001	1900	WB-3/303	AR
Huffines, Peter	046	1894	WB-F/371	AR
Huffines, Phebe	001	1883	WB-2/197	AR
Huffines, Sarah	046	1886	WB-E/437	AR
Huffines, Simpson	001	1892	WB-2/508	AR
Huffines, William R.	046	1862	WB-D/161	AR
Huffman, Bryant H.	072	1900	WB-4/427	AR
Huffman, Christopher	072	1801	WB-A/56	AR
Huffman, Daniel	032	1823	WB-1/10	
Huffman, Daniel	073	1844	WB-F/222	AR
Huffman, David	032	c1846	WB-2/41	
Huffman, Davidson	021	1898	WB-3/205	AR
Huffman, Elijah	021	1884	WB-2/288	
Huffman, George	021	1849	WB-1/69	AR
Huffman, Heartwell	046	1833	Orig. Only	AR
Huffman, Henry	090	1828	WB-3/196	AR
Huffman, Henry W.	021	1854	WB-1/112	AR
Huffman, Jacob	060	1816	Orig. Only	AR
Huffman, Jacob	021	1891	WB-2/542	
Huffman, John	060	1832	WB-1/258	AR
Huffman, John P.	104	1889	WB-6/364	AR
Huffman, Jonas	060	1828	Orig. Only	AR
Huffman, Joseph W.	021	1866	WB-1/223	AR

Name	Co.	Date	Recorded Copy	Original
Huffman, Michael	014	1885	WB-2/285	CTY
Huffmon, George	021	1880	WB-2/228	
Huffstetler, Sarah	040	c1899	Orig. Only	AR
Hufham, John	035	1832	WB-1/32	AR
Hufman, Christian	073	1790	WB-B/93	AR
Hufman, Hudnal	011	c1790	WB-1/513	
Hufman, Solomon	011	c1810	WB-2/301	
Huggans, Edward	013	1835	WB-A/33	
Huggins, Alexander	054	1852	WB-3/58	
Huggins, Ann	072	1746	SS 877/41	SS/AR
Huggins, Charlotte	076	1898	WB-A1/243	AR
Huggins, Edmond	072	1737	SS 877/185	SS/AR
Huggins, Jacob	073	1813	WB-D/395	AR
Huggins, Jacob	072	c1789	WB-A/56	AR
Huggins, James	054	c1789	Orig. Only	AR
Huggins, James	057	1830	WB-B/105	AR
Huggins, John	060	1812	Orig. Only	AR
Huggins, John	072	1745	SS 878/98	SS/AR
Huggins, Louisa A.	061	c1864	WB-1/86	AR
Huggins, Luke	057	1784	WB-A/40	AR
Huggins, Luke	072	1835	WB-1/147	AR
Huggins, Narcissa	103	1882	WB-1/236	AR
Huggins, Rachel	054	1846	Orig. Only	AR
Huggins, Robert	054	1840	WB-2/210	AR
Huggins, William	060	1801	Orig. Only	AR
Hugh, Nancy	063	1836	WB-2/224	
Hughes (Huse), William	078	1816	WI-7/124	AR
Hughes, A. E.	073	1887	WB-H/438	CTY
Hughes, A. G.	001	1873	WB-2/35	AR
Hughes, Alexander	054	c1824	WB-2/14	AR
Hughes, Ann	010	1823	WB-G/126	AR
Hughes, Armstead	078	1881	WB-19/120	AR
Hughes, Barrott C.	044	1867	WB-22/705	
Hughes, Caroline A.	054	1870	WB-4/55	AR
Hughes, Christian	010	1900	WB-K/31	
Hughes, Cornelius	010	1823	WB-G/123	AR
Hughes, Daniel S.	013	1898	WB-D/130	AR
Hughes, Delia A.	065	1898	WB-N/108	AR
Hughes, George R.	010	1865	WB-H/153	AR
Hughes, Isaac W.	028	1881	WB-E/262	AR
Hughes, J. G.	018	1854	WB-D/4	
Hughes, James	054	c1801	WB-1/397	AR
Hughes, James	099	1846	RB-26/151	AR
Hughes, James	026	1882	WB-2/229	AR
Hughes, James B.	028	1900	WB-F/470	
Hughes, John	073	1836	WB-E/379	AR
Hughes, John	082	1870	WB-6/63	AR
Hughes, John	020	1855	RB-R/315	AR
Hughes, John	082	1881	WB-6/213	AR
Hughes, John	049	1813	Orig. Only	AR
Hughes, John	020	1799	RB-C/360	
Hughes, Joseph D.	073	1844	WB-F/193	AR
Hughes, Martha H.	044	1880	WB-23/359	CTY
Hughes, Mary	020	1879	WB-A/276	CTY
Hughes, Miles H.	024	1900	WB-E/327	AR
Hughes, Milton T.	046	1891.	WB-F/90	AR
Hughes, Nicholas C.	009	1893	WB-1/573	CTY
Hughes, S. R.	098	1890	WB-A/112	CTY
Hughes, Samuel	020	1866	RB-T/181	AR
Hughes, Sarah	020	1852	RB-Q/650	AR
Hughes, Sargent	085	c1802	WB-D/195	AR
Hughes, Temperance	022	c1848	Orig. Only	AR
Hughes, Thomas	071	1818	WB-3/209	AR
Hughes, Thomas H.	073	1892	WB-H/569	CTY
Hughes, Thomas J.	084	1885	WB-E/319	CTY

Name	Co.	Date	Recorded Copy	Original
Hughes, William C.	100	1829	WB-32/261	AR
Hughes, William H.	071	1896	WB-7/323	AR
Hughes, Williamson	073	1881	WB-H/287	CTY
Hughey, George C.	IN	1890	013 WB-C/38	
Hughey, Henry	085	1803	WB-D/190	AR
Hughey, Henry	085	c1790	WB-C/52	AR
Hughey, Jacob	085	c1792	WB-C/1	AR
Hughey, John, Sr.	054	c1793	WB-1/116	AR
Hughey, Nancy R.	090	1872	WB-6/24	AR
Hughey, Patrick	054	c1793	WB-1/111	AR
Hughey, Robert	085	c1793	WB-E/102	AR
Hughey, Samuel	085	c1780	WB-D/168	AR
Hughey, Samuel	085	1834	WB-H/623	AR
Hughlett, John	071	1767	WB-1/145	Nunc.
Hughs, Amanda E.	030	1838	WB-4/58	
Hughs, George	010	1764	WB-A/47	AR
Hughs, George	010	1802	WB-E/139	AR
Hughs, James	054	c1801	WB-1A/30	
Hughs, James	010	1805	WB-E/268	AR
Hughs, John	086	1803	WB-B/152	
Hughs, John	030	1772	WB-1/70	
Hughs, Margaret	079	1830	Orig. Only	AR
Hughs, Thomas	029	1797	Orig. Only	AR
Hughs, William	010	1823	WB-G/102	AR
Hughston, Robert	020	1781	RB-A/136	AR
Huie, Mary G.	016	1895	WB-4/216	AR
Huie, Peter	016	1819	WB-A/82	AR
Huie, Samuel	054	1857	WB-3/112	AR
Huie, Samuel	016	c1817	WB-A/70	AR
Huit, Ambrose M.	021	1865	WB-1/215	AR
Huit, John, Jr.	072	c1809	WB-A/59	AR
Huit, Lewis	060	1835	WB-1/359	AR
Huit, Lewis	060	1817	Orig. Only	AR
Huit, Moses M.	021	1880	WB-2/213	
Hukins, Ann	028	1796	WB-A/352	AR
Hukins, Hardy	028	1812	Orig. Only	AR
Hukits, Volantine	028	c1760	Orig. Only	AR
Hulbert, Eliza	Eng	1890	050 WB-2/63	050 CTY
Hulett, John	070	1849	WB-C/495	AR
Hulett, John	020	c1840	RB-0/318	AR
Hulgan, Rosannah	084	1860	WB-C/346	CTY
Hulgan, Thomas	073	1794	WB-C/19	AR
Hull, Benjamin	060	1864	WB-3/76	AR
Hull, Edward	070	1799	WB-C/157	AR
Hull, John	024	1752	SS 879/46	SS/AR
Hull, Major	060	1856	WB-3/1	AR
Hull, Moses	085	c1778	WB-B/112	AR
Hullen, Nicholas	070	1893	WB-G/157	AR
Hullender, C.	026	1898	WB-3/10	
Hulm, Anne	047	1805	WB-3/438	
Hulm, John	047	1789	WB-3/164	
Hulm, Mary	047	1789	WB-3/165	
Hulme, Robert	047	1789	WB-3/172	
Hulme, William	071	1777	WB-1/397	AR
Hulthin, Magnus	090	1843	WB-4/126	AR
Humble, Daniel	046	1855	WB-C/423	AR
Hume, Jane W.	093	1896	WB-2/150	AR
Hume, Robert W.	093	1880	WB-2/3	AR
Humell, Christian	090	1800	WB-1/157	AR
Humes, James	009	1745	SS 878/129	SS/AR
Humfreys, Thomas T.	020	1830	RB-L/441	AR
Humphers, John	030	1848	WB-4/129	
Humphers, William F.	030	1838	WB-4/59	
Humphrees, John	030	1796	WB-2/80	
Humphres, B.	086	1877	WB-F/97	AR
Humphres, James	064	1859	WB-1/61	AR
Humphrey, Chambers	083	c1788	WB-1/13	AR
Humphrey, David	024	1789	WB-A/6	AR
Humphrey, Edgar W.	072	1844	WB-2/53	AR
Humphrey, Eliza Jane	072	1873	WB-4/44	AR
Humphrey, Esther	072	1854	WB-2/133	AR
Humphrey, George F.	072	1891	WB-4/251	AR
Humphrey, Greene Ann	072	1877	WB-4/94	AR
Humphrey, Hustress	072	1791	Orig. Only	AR
Humphrey, Jacob	072	1791	Orig. Only	AR
Humphrey, Jacob	072	1817	Orig. Only	AR
Humphrey, James	083	1837	WB-1/310	AR
Humphrey, James P.	032	c1848	WB-2/20	
Humphrey, John	083	1847	WB-1/506	AR
Humphrey, John	072	c1864	WB-3/17	AR
Humphrey, John	083	1846	WB-1/477	
Humphrey, John	083	1884	WB-3/308	AR
Humphrey, Jonathan	075	1822	WB-M1/351	AR
Humphrey, Joseph	011	1752	Orig. Only	SS/AR
Humphrey, Lewis	072	c1854	Orig. Only	AR
Humphrey, Lott	072	1824	WB-2/30	AR
Humphrey, Mary	072	1829	WB-1/36	AR
Humphrey, Owen	104	1812	WB-3/36	
Humphrey, Robert	037	1785	WB-C/2	AR
Humphrey, Sally	072	1844	WB-2/56	AR
Humphrey, Samuel	092	1801	WB-3/40A	AR
Humphrey, Thomas	072	c1780	RW/L30	AR
Humphrey, Thomas	083	c1818	WB-1/336	AR
Humphrey, Whitehead	072	c1862	Orig. Only	AR
Humphrey, William	072	1807	Orig. Only	AR
Humphrey, William	072	1896	WB-4/324	AR
Humphrey, William	072	c1861	WB-3/1	
Humphrey, William	083	c1818	WB-1/239	AR
Humphreys, Absalom	046	1844	WB-C/200	AR
Humphreys, Elijah	047	1796	WB-3/271	
Humphreys, George	020	1804	RB-E/139	AR
Humphreys, Henry	046	1840	WB-C/55	AR
Humphreys, Henry	046	1840	SC/07008	AR-Copy
Humphreys, Johanna	085	1775	WB-A/213	AR
Humphreys, John	029	1820	WB-B/102	AR
Humphreys, Nathaniel	019	1799	WB-D/230	AR
Humphreys, Richard	024	1797	WB-A/283	AR
Humphreys, Robert	086	1844	WB-E/143	AR
Humphreys, Sally	006	1820	WB-A/77	AR
Humphreys, Sarah	084	1868	WB-D/97	CTY-Nunc.
Humphries, David	026	1844	WB-1/25	AR
Humphries, David	026	1842	WB-1/8	AR
Humphries, E. B.	026	1890	WB-2/409	AR
Humphries, Edmond F.	030	1897	WB-5/256	AR
Humphries, Elizabeth	026	1885	WB-2/279	AR
Humphries, James	078	1898	WB-19/451	AR
Humphries, John	026	1851	WB-1/128	AR
Humphries, John	018	1838	WB-C/230	
Humphries, John, Sr.	078	1801	WI-3/1	AR
Humphries, Lawson	026	1899	WB-3/22	AR
Humphries, Mary	030	1797	WB-2/110	
Humphries, Millicent	077	1885	WB-H/147	AR
Humphries, Ritchard	002	1688	Orig. Only	SS/AR
Humphries, Samuel	026	1849	WB-1/96	AR
Humphries, Thomas	075	1825	WB-N/9	AR
Humphries, W. W.	078	1897	WB-19/431	AR
Humphries, William	077	1798	WB-E/97	AR
Humphries, William	077	1833	WB-F/217	AR
Humphries, William	086	1825	WB-D/39	AR

Name	Co.	Date	Recorded Copy	Original
Humphries, Willis	026	1872	WB-2/70	AR
Humphris, Joseph	075	c1751	Orig. Only	AR
Humphry, Benjamin	083	1833	WB-1/283	AR
Humphry, John	075	c1708	Orig. Only	SS/AR
Hundel, Benjamin	077	1735	SS 876/417	
Huneycut, James	003	1885	WB-B/157	
Huneycutt, Demcey J.	097	1877	WB-2/111	AR
Huneycutt, Elizabeth	065	1885	WB-L/137	
Huneycutt, J. T.	089	1892	WB-2/408	AR
Huneycutt, John	089	1878	WB-2/59	AR
Huneycutt, Mary A.	065	1882	WB-K/481	AR
Hunley, Margaret	009	1819	OB-A/292	AR
Hunley, Mary	028	1777	Orig. Only	AR
Hunley, Richard	028	1800	WB-B/106	AR
Hunnewell, Louisa	MA	1891	Copy	050 AR
Hunnings, Phillip	096	1772	WB-1/75	AR
Hunnings, Thomas	096	c1815	Orig. Only	AR
Hunnings, William	030	1818	WB-2/102	
Hunnings, Zachariah	096	1791	Orig. Only	AR
Hunnycutt, Eli B.	089	1857	WB-1/157	
Hunsey, Jessie M.	037	1849	WB-F/434	AR
Hunsucker, Abram C.	067	1869	WB-2/5	AR
Hunsucker, Christian	021	1853	WB-1/103	
Hunsucker, David	021	1888	WB-2/417	AR
Hunsucker, Joseph	021	1875	WB-2/145	AR
Hunsucker, L. H.	021	c1890	WB-2/508	AR
Hunsucker, Mary	021	1888	WB-2/417	
Hunt, Absalom	086	1840	WB-E/72	AR
Hunt, Absalom	044	1866	WB-22/488	CTY
Hunt, Alexander	082	1846	WB-3/31	
Hunt, Andrew	085	c1801	WB-D/187	AR
Hunt, Ann	044	1835	WB-13/183	CTY
Hunt, Ann	044	1889	WB-24/95	CTY
Hunt, Anna S.	020	1900	WB-B/404	CTY
Hunt, Augustus	PA	1894	Copy	013 AR
Hunt, Braswell	083	c1787	WB-1/11	AR
Hunt, C. C.	068	1889	WB-D/320	CTY
Hunt, Charles	030	1804	WB-2/247	
Hunt, Daniel	092	1835	WB-4/116	AR
Hunt, Daniel	085	c1799	WB-E/115	AR
Hunt, David	085	1815	WB-G/342	AR
Hunt, David	044	1861	WB-21/368	CTY
Hunt, David	092	1829	WB-4/16	AR
Hunt, David A.	044	1891	WB-24/177	CTY
Hunt, David L.	032	1896	WB-4/310	AR
Hunt, Edward	044	1849	WB-17/450	CTY
Hunt, Eleazer	046	1841	WB-C/80	AR
Hunt, Elijah	032	1826	WB-1/49	
Hunt, Elizabeth	098	1900	WB-A/369	CTY
Hunt, Elizabeth	VA	1802	Copy	085 AR
Hunt, Enoch	085	1815	WB-G/344	AR
Hunt, Eunice	028	1822	WB-C/219	AR
Hunt, Eustace	VA	1892	020 WB-B/97	
Hunt, Frances C.	038	1881	WB-2/397	AR
Hunt, Frances C.	038	c1880	078 WB-19/376	
Hunt, George W.	044	1876	WB-23/228	CTY
Hunt, Gersham	085	1810	WB-G/149	AR
Hunt, Hannah	032	1871	WB-3/41	AR
Hunt, Henry	044	1750	Orig. Only	CTY
Hunt, Henry	068	1889	WB-D/317	CTY
Hunt, Isaiah	046	1822	WB-B/149	AR
Hunt, Ithamer	046	1869	WB-E/1	AR
Hunt, Jabez	046	1812	WB-A/177	AR
Hunt, Jacob	046	1830	WB-B/414	AR
Hunt, James	044	1791	WB-2/260	CTY

Name	Co.	Date	Recorded Copy	Original
Hunt, James	044	1848	WB-17/410	
Hunt, James	044	1798	WB-4/177	CTY
Hunt, James	086	c1862	Orig. Only	AR
Hunt, James C.	104	1872	WB-6/50	AR
Hunt, James C.	104	1847	Copy	004 AR
Hunt, James W.	019	1848	WB-A/133	AR
Hunt, John	N	1710	Orig. Only	SS/AR
Hunt, John	075	1710	Orig. Only	AR-Copy
Hunt, John	044	1789	WB-2/131	CTY
Hunt, John	039	1807	WB-C/85	
Hunt, John	046	1880	WB-E/274	AR
Hunt, John	046	c1809	WB-A/173	AR
Hunt, John Leigh	098	1890	WB-A/116	CTY
Hunt, John, Sr.	044	1818	WB-8/158	CTY
Hunt, Jonathan	085	c1782	WB-B/125	AR
Hunt, Joseph	067	1782	Orig. Only	SS/AR
Hunt, Joseph P.	044	1880	WB-23/371	CTY
Hunt, Laura E.	013	1900	WB-D/423	AR
Hunt, Lucy	069	1884	WB-5/190	AR
Hunt, Martha H.	032	1881	WB-3/340	AR
Hunt, Mary	039	1811	WB-C/232	AR
Hunt, Mary	081	1860	WB-11/423	AR
Hunt, Memucan	TX	1856	044 WB-21/165	
Hunt, Mimucan	044	1808	WB-7/1	CTY
Hunt, N. G.	106	1900	WB-2/469	
Hunt, Nathan D.	106	c1852	WB-1/11	AR
Hunt, Pleasant	106	1885	WB-2/210	
Hunt, Richard	106	1883	WB-2/161	AR
Hunt, Robert H.	039	1859	WB-0/376	Nunc.
Hunt, Robert L.	044	1883	WB-23/469	CTY
Hunt, Samuel	046	1888	WB-E/546	AR
Hunt, Samuel	044	1799	WB-4/272	CTY
Hunt, Samuel	044	1884	WB-23/500	CTY
Hunt, Sarah	069	1782	WB-1/87	AR
Hunt, T. P.	026	1863	WB-1/304	AR
Hunt, Thomas	039	1791	WB-A/76	
Hunt, Thomas	075	1696	Orig. Only	SS/AR
Hunt, Thomas	073	c1844	Orig. Only	AR
Hunt, Thomas	085	1763	WB-A/65	AR
Hunt, Tilman	046	1851	WB-C/358	AR
Hunt, William	044	1833	WB-12/467	CTY
Hunt, William	044	1786	WB-1/525	CTY
Hunt, William	030	1890	WB-5/177	AR
Hunt, William	044	1852	WB-19/132	CTY
Hunt, William	069	1884	WB-5/197	AR
Hunt, William	082	1807	WB-1/119	AR
Hunt, William A.	086	1884	WB-F/235	AR
Hunt, William L.	OH	1897	013 WB-D/355	013 AR
Hunt, Zebulun	032	1841	WB-1/373	
Hunter, Abner	065	1869	WB-K/22	AR
Hunter, Agnes	085	1760	WB-A/69	AR
Hunter, Alee	041	1781	WB-1/20	AR
Hunter, Alice	047	1804	WB-3/420	
Hunter, Andrew	073	1831	WB-E/253	AR
Hunter, Andrew	064	c1848	Orig. Only	AR
Hunter, Ann	024	1751	Orig. Only	SS/AR
Hunter, Ann	075	1893	WB-0/371	AR
Hunter, Anna B.	038	1863	WB-1/207	AR
Hunter, Archibald	069	1807	WB-1/171	AR
Hunter, Benjamin	047	1885	WB-6/387	AR
Hunter, Cader	010	1790	WB-D/134	AR
Hunter, Cader	010	1826	WB-G/143	AR
Hunter, Charles	085	c1803	WB-G/8	AR
Hunter, Cordal	069	1836	WB-1/414	
Hunter, David	063	1812	WB-2/7	

Name	Co.	Date	Recorded Copy	Original
Hunter, Dolly	099	1860	RB-31/488	
Hunter, Edward R.	041	1857	WB-3/213	AR
Hunter, Elisha	041	1786	WB-1/62	AR
Hunter, Elisha	022	1782	WB-A/35	AR
Hunter, Elizabeth	077	1853	WB-F/438	
Hunter, Elizabeth	041	1898	WB-4/466	AR
Hunter, Emily	041	1879	WB-4/128	AR
Hunter, Ephraim	005	1844	WB-B/177	AR
Hunter, Ezekiel	028	1811	Orig. Only	AR
Hunter, Ezekiel	072	c1773	RW/L20	AR
Hunter, Ezekiel	019	c1780	WB-D/220	AR
Hunter, H. H.	017	1885	WB-B/130	AR
Hunter, Hannah P.	065	1870	WB-K/32	AR
Hunter, Hardy	010	1794	WB-D/250	AR
Hunter, Henry	063	c1801	WB-1/384	
Hunter, Henry	037	1823	WB-F/14	AR
Hunter, Henry	065	1837	WB-E/181	AR
Hunter, Henry B.	063	1827	WB-2/125	
Hunter, Howel	035	1827	WB-A/204	AR
Hunter, Humphrey	065	1805	WB-C/151	AR
Hunter, Humphrey	060	1827	WB-1/74	AR
Hunter, Humphry	010	1805	WB-E/262	AR
Hunter, Isaac	035	1822	WB-A/199	AR
Hunter, Isaac	024	1753	SS 881/100	SS/AR
Hunter, Isaac	100	1815	WB-19/177	AR
Hunter, Isaac	099	1823	RB-18/120	AR
Hunter, Isaac	041	1816	WB-2/131	AR
Hunter, Isaac	099	1831	RB-22/144	AR
Hunter, Isaac	099	1885	WB-B/40	AR
Hunter, J. H.	069	1899	037 WB-H/455	037 AR
Hunter, J. H.	069	1899	WB-6/83	AR
Hunter, Jacob	099	1873	RB-35/242	AR
Hunter, Jacob	041	1784	WB-1/42	AR
Hunter, James	073	c1794	WB-B/249	AR
Hunter, James	047	1832	WB-4/83	
Hunter, James	084	c1817	WB-A/182	
Hunter, James Mc.	065	1879	WB-K/362	AR
Hunter, James S.	010	1816	WB-F/343	AR
Hunter, Jeremiah	038	1899	WB-4/178	AR
Hunter, Jesse	099	1786	RB-2/105	AR
Hunter, John	065	1800	WB-C/145	AR
Hunter, John	046	1778	WB-A/147	AR
Hunter, John	038	c1848	WB-1/5	AR
Hunter, John	085	c1786	WB-D/176	AR
Hunter, John	065	c1804	WB-D/17	AR
Hunter, John	024	c1771	WB-A/2	AR
Hunter, John	085	1795	WB-E/118	AR
Hunter, John	PA	1756	SS 880/131	SS/AR
Hunter, John	065	1890	WB-L/502	AR
Hunter, John	071	1884	WB-6/457	AR
Hunter, John B.	063	1810	WB-1/435	
Hunter, John M.	068	1889	WB-D/310	
Hunter, John S.	097	1889	WB-2/323	AR
Hunter, John, Sr.	065	1794	WB-D/53	AR
Hunter, John, Sr.	090	1803	WB-2/42	AR
Hunter, Joseph	065	1853	WB-I/212	AR
Hunter, Josiah	010	1812	WB-F/203	AR
Hunter, Leah H.	047	1896	WB-7/165	AR
Hunter, Lebbeus	019	1806	WB-D/242	AR
Hunter, Lorenzo	065	1893	WB-M/206	AR
Hunter, Lucy	029	1900	WB-F/185	AR
Hunter, Margaret	022	1791	RB-1/39	AR
Hunter, Martha	069	1859	WB-1/559	AR
Hunter, Mary	065	1811	WB-D/72	AR
Hunter, Mary	065	1841	WB-H/146	AR

Name	Co.	Date	Recorded Copy	Original
Hunter, Mary	041	1838	WB-3/3	AR
Hunter, Mary Eliza	041	1862	WB-3/283	AR
Hunter, Nancy	013	1900	WB-D/417	AR
Hunter, Nicholas	035	1791	WB-A/213	AR
Hunter, Nicholas	019	1749	SS 877/324	SS/AR
Hunter, Penny	099	1860	RB-31/488	
Hunter, Rachel	010	1807	WB-F/62	AR
Hunter, Rebcah	019	1785	Orig. Only	AR
Hunter, Rebeca	075	1762	WB-H/36	
Hunter, Richard	060	1821	Orig. Only	AR
Hunter, Robert	010	1753	SS 878/184	SS/AR
Hunter, Robert	073	1802	WB-D/76	AR
Hunter, Salley	099	1854	RB-28/588	AR
Hunter, Samuel	060	N. D.	Orig. Only	AR-Nunc.
Hunter, Samuel	082	1779	WB-1/1	AR
Hunter, Samuel H.	046	1877	WB-E/168	AR
Hunter, Sarah	099	1811	RB-10/61	AR
Hunter, Sarah H.	047	1888	WB-6/479	AR
Hunter, Sarah J.	099	1890	WB-B/426	AR
Hunter, Shadrack	028	1816	WB-C/128	
Hunter, Silas	065	1875	WB-K/169	AR
Hunter, Stephen	019	1808	WB-D/244	AR
Hunter, Theophilus	099	1840	RB-24/427	
Hunter, Theophilus	099	1798	RB-4/258	AR
Hunter, Thomas	041	1798	WB-1/156	AR
Hunter, Thomas	065	1871	WB-K/57	AR
Hunter, Thomas	065	1862	WB-J/127	AR
Hunter, Thomas	075	1760	WB-H/13	AR
Hunter, Thomas	063	c1800	WB-1/373	
Hunter, Thomas	090	1805	WB-2/63	AR
Hunter, Thomas C.	047	1883	WB-6/293	AR
Hunter, Thomas J.	065	1881	WB-K/431	AR
Hunter, Timothy	010	1823	WB-G/108	AR
Hunter, Timothy	075	1875	WB-O/60	AR
Hunter, W. J.	099	1864	RB-33/286	AR
Hunter, William	024	1750	Orig. Only	SS/AR
Hunter, William	082	c1800	WB-1/77	AR
Hunter, William	044	1893	WB-24/226	CTY
Hunter, William	041	1813	WB-2/79	AR
Hunter, William	038	1849	WB-1/10	AR
Hunter, William	024	1732	SS 876/265	SS/AR
Hunter, William C.	028	1837	WB-C/403	AR
Huntington, Olivia C.	028	1824	WB-C/254	AR
Huntington, Sarah	070	1812	WB-AB/170	AR
Huntington, Susan R.	072	1829	WB-1/33	AR
Huntley, Elijah	005	1839	WB-B/88	AR
Huntley, Elijah D.	005	1885	WB-D/188	AR
Huntley, Elizabeth	005	1854	WB-C/85	AR
Huntley, John W.	005	1843	WB-B/151	AR
Huntley, Robert	005	c1855	WB-2/71	AR
Huntley, Thomas	005	1863	WB-C/195	AR
Huntley, Thomas	005	1806	WB-2/70	AR
Huntley, Thomas	005	1802	WB-2/69	AR
Huntly, Robert S.	005	1887	WB-D/211	AR
Hurdle, Abraham	041	1836	WB-2/369	AR
Hurdle, Abraham	077	1849	WB-F/368	AR
Hurdle, Abram	041	1887	WB-4/257	AR
Hurdle, Bedford	078	1869	WB-19/8	AR
Hurdle, Benjamin	024	1802	WB-B/181	AR
Hurdle, Benjamin	077	1735	Orig. Only	SS/AR
Hurdle, Catharine	001	1876	WB-2/99	AR
Hurdle, Deborah	024	1822	WB-C/98	AR
Hurdle, Dickey	001	1852	WB-1/61	AR
Hurdle, Elizabeth	041	c1794	WB-1/238	AR
Hurdle, Hardy	073	1828	WB-E/164	AR

Name	Co.	Date	Recorded Copy	Original
Hurdle, Hardy, Sr.	024	1789	WB-A/48	AR
Hurdle, Harman	024	1838	WB-C/211	AR
Hurdle, Harmon	041	1820	WB-2/175	AR
Hurdle, James	001	1860	WB-1/176	AR
Hurdle, John	077	1828	WB-F/156	AR
Hurdle, Kader	024	1824	WB-C/111	AR
Hurdle, Martha	024	c1884	Orig. Only	AR
Hurdle, Martin	024	1797	WB-A/286	AR
Hurdle, Penelope	041	1885	WB-4/227	AR
Hurdle, Reuben	024	1853	WB-C/347	AR
Hurdle, Sarah	024	1834	WB-C/179	AR
Hurdle, Stephen	001	1900	WB-3/298	AR
Hurdle, Thomas	024	1770	WB-A/18	AR
Hurdle, William	024	1882	WB-E/117	AR
Hurley, Amos	022	1817	WB-A/304	AR
Hurley, Cornelius	067	c1854	WB-1/76	AR
Hurley, Harvey C.	006	1888	WB-E/163	AR
Hurley, James F.	006	1885	WB-E/124	AR
Hurley, Joshua	067	1896	WB-2/345	
Hurley, Thomas	006	1866	WB-C/21	AR
Hurley, Timothy	082	1783	WB-1/15	AR
Hurley, Timothy	082	1783	Orig. Only	SS/AR
Hurn, Edney	056	1866	WB-2/83	AR
Hurst, Catharine	035	1877	WB-4/118	AR
Hurst, Charles O.	019	1857	WB-A/214	AR
Hurst, George W.	035	1866	WB-3/106	AR
Hurst, Henry	036	1882	WB-A/22	CTY
Hurst, James	090	1795	WB-1/66	AR
Hurst, James	024	1772	WB-A/21	AR
Hurst, James R.	035	1879	Copy	072 AR
Hurst, James R.	035	1879	WB-4/139 & 191	AR
Hurst, John	010	1769	WB-A/103	AR
Hurst, John S.	078	1809	WI-5/135	AR
Hurst, Mary E.	072	1899	WB-4/412	AR
Hurst, Penelope	024	1832	WB-C/164	AR
Hurst, Phillip	047	1769	WB-1/234	
Hurst, Sarah B.	103	1844	SC/03859	AR-Copy
Hurst, Sarah B. B.	103	1849	RD-10/243	AR
Hurst, Spencer	047	1804	WB-3/430	
Hurst, William	063	c1784	WB-1/98	
Hurst, William B.	035	1826	WB-A/201	AR
Hurst, William B.	035	1858	WB-2/130	AR
Hurst, William H.	035	1837	Orig. Only	AR
Hurst, Williamson	070	1895	WB-G/418	AR
Hurt, Abel K.	014	1899	WB-3/91	CTY
Hurt, Albert P.	029	1883	WB-E/298	AR
Hurt, Dicy	092	1884	WB-6/199	AR
Hurt, Robert H.	092	c1831	WB-4/39	
Hurt, William	106	c1860	WB-1/82	AR
Hurtt, Catherine	028	1865	WB-D/399	AR
Hurtt, Sidney E.	028	1866	WB-D/441	
Husbands, John	005	1774	WB-1/19	
Husbands, Richard	070	1732	SS 876/263	SS/AR
Huske, Ann P.	029	1875	WB-E/150	AR
Huske, John	029	1848	WB-C/155	AR
Huske, John W.	029	1841	WB-B/356	AR
Husketh, Ann	044	1847	WB-17/37	CTY
Huskey, Isaac	044	1843	WB-15/507	CTY
Huskey, William	044	1843	Orig. Only	CTY
Huson, Mason	060	1817	Orig. Only	AR
Huson, Thomas	060	1813	Orig. Only	AR
Hussel, Caroline	SC	1899	070 WB-H/224	070 AR
Hussey, Beulah	046	1857	WB-C/486	AR
Hussey, Christopher	046	1774	WB-A/151	AR
Hussey, Emeliza	037	1854	WB-G/78	AR
Hussey, Henry	053	1774	RW-1/45	AR
Hussey, John	067	1874	WB-2/50	AR
Hussey, Mary	046	1821	WB-B/143	AR
Hussey, Mary	053	1786	RW-1/143	
Hussey, Robert	028	1894	WB-F/103	
Hussey, Simeon	072	c1781	Orig. Only	AR
Hussey, Toney	035	1893	WB-4/431	AR
Husted, Harriet	099	1875	RB-35/297	AR
Husted, Hiram W.	099	1869	RB-35/36	AR
Huston, Alexander	021	1900	WB-3/276	
Huston, Elisabeth	078	1842	WI-15/158	
Huston, George	020	1830	RB-L/443	AR
Huston, Grace	065	1802	WB-D/62	AR
Huston, James	085	1781	WB-C/220	AR
Huston, Mary Ann	020	1837	RB-N/11	AR
Huston, Robert	020	1781	RB-A/136	
Huston, Sarah A.	080	1894	WB-1/236	AR
Hutchens, Annis	030	1832	WB-3/323	
Hutchens, David	106	c1842	WB-1/48	AR
Hutchens, Frederick	090	1826	WB-3/153	AR
Hutchens, John	106	c1852	WB-1/26	AR
Hutchens, John, Sr.	092	c1824	WB-3/162	AR
Hutchens, Lewis	073	1865	WB-G/466	CTY
Hutchens, Rebecca	073	1860	WB-G/248	CTY
Hutchens, Sally	030	1825	WB-3/205	
Hutchens, Strangeman	092	1792	WB-3/5A	AR
Hutchens, Strangeman	092	1836	WB-4/95	
Hutchens, Susanna	092	1806	WB-3/76A	AR
Hutchens, Thoms	092	1802	WB-3/51A	
Hutcherson, James	073	1843	WB-F/160	AR
Hutcherson, John	084	1829	WB-B/24	CTY
Hutcherson, Joseph	090	1835	WB-3/299	AR
Hutcherson, Joshua	044	1832	WB-12/381	CTY
Hutcherson, Richard	044	1821	WB-8/431	CTY
Hutching, Thomas	030	c1779	WB-1/135	
Hutchings, Nathaniel	030	1824	WB-3/167	
Hutchings, William	051	c1831	WB-A/110	
Hutchins, Allen	073	1869	WB-H/20	CTY
Hutchins, Benjamin	092	1830	WB-4/23	AR
Hutchins, Elizabeth	099	1862	RB-32/359	AR
Hutchins, Isaac	099	1891	WB-C/15	
Hutchins, John	073	1880	WB-H/266	CTY
Hutchins, John	073	1824	WB-E/56	AR
Hutchins, John	099	1802	RB-6/77	AR
Hutchins, John	099	1863	RB-32/418	AR
Hutchins, John	086	1868	WB-F/2	AR
Hutchins, John, Sr.	099	1789	RB-2/221	AR
Hutchins, Josiah	092	1845	WB-4/240	
Hutchins, Katie	036	1890	WB-A/167	CTY
Hutchins, Louisa	099	1849	RB-26/615	AR
Hutchins, Lucinda E.	038	1885	WB-2/562	AR
Hutchins, Moses	099	1822	RB-17/398	AR
Hutchins, Moses	073	1822	WB-E/13	AR
Hutchins, Richard	030	1835	WB-4/7	
Hutchins, Ritchard	018	1850	WB-C/351	
Hutchins, Robert	090	1845	WB-4/206	AR
Hutchins, Tandy J.	090	1863	WB-4/355	AR
Hutchins, Thomas	086	1844	WB-E/121	AR
Hutchins, William	086	1858	WB-E/349	AR
Hutchinson, James	073	1796	WB-C/76	AR
Hutchinson, Peter	044	1846	WB-16/529	CTY
Hutchinson, Ruth A.	084	1899	WB-F/136	CTY
Hutchinson, Sarah E.	105	1891	WB-3/5	AR
Hutchinson, William	065	c1833	Orig. Only	AR

Name	Co.	Date	Recorded Copy	Original
Hutchinson, Willis	099	1883	WB-A/402	AR
Hutchison, Catherine	065	1845	WB-I/8	AR
Hutchison, Charles L.	040	1893	WB-2/448	AR
Hutchison, Cyrus N.	065	1879	WB-K/347	AR
Hutchison, David S.	065	1865	WB-J/203	AR
Hutchison, Dicy	065	1830	WB-E/81	AR
Hutchison, Esther Y.	065	1860	WB-J/74	AR
Hutchison, George	065	1810	WB-D/20	
Hutchison, Jacob	104	1867	WB-5/517	AR
Hutchison, James M.	065	1838	WB-E/190	AR
Hutchison, John	065	1777	WB-D/43	AR
Hutchison, Mathew H.	065	1892	WB-M/99	AR
Huthsteiner, Henry	064	1900	WB-2/494	AR
Hutsell, Eli K.	013	1852	WB-A/155	
Hutson, Eli	028	1789	WB-A/200	AR
Hutson, Lane A.	022	c1867	WB-D/172	AR
Hutson, Mary	010	1841	WB-G/339	AR
Hutson, Peter	099	1823	RB-18/252	AR
Hutson, William	028	1739	SS 877/137	SS/AR
Hutton, David K.	046	1856	WB-C/459	AR
Hutton, George	046	1810	WB-A/174	AR
Hutton, James	014	1877	WB-2/133	
Hutton, Polly	046	1866	WB-D/286	AR
Hux, Benjamin	047	1818	WB-3/619	
Hux, James	047	1885	WB-6/407	AR
Hux, William	047	1859	WB-5/66	
Hyat, Solomon	041	1786	WB-1/59	AR
Hyatt, Edward	049	c1817	WI-A/13	AR
Hyatt, Edward G.	055	1900	WB-A/188	
Hyatt, Elizabeth	009	1892	WB-1/532	CTY
Hyatt, Henry C.	049	1898	WB-2/409	AR
Hyatt, Lockwood	009	1892	WB-1/521	CTY
Hyatt, Nathan	055	c1868	ID/171	
Hyatt, P. Ann	013	1883	WB-B/300	AR
Hyatt, Shadrick	013	1845	WB-A/118	
Hybart, Thomas L.	029	1847	WB-C/142	AR
Hyde, Ann Porter	085	1885	WB-2/128	CTY
Hyde, Benjamin	086	1827	WB-D/64	
Hyde, Benjamin	085	1866	WB-K/379	AR
Hyde, David	071	1785	WB-1/348	AR
Hyde, James	085	1844	WB-I/220	AR
Hyde, James M.	085	1866	WB-K/378	AR
Hyde, Jane C.	085	1896	WB-3/124	CTY
Hyde, Lavina	085	1886	WB-2/193	
Hyde, Lydia	085	1850	WB-K/110	AR
Hyde, Richard	071	1763	WB-1/79	
Hyde, Richard	071	1784	WB-1/283	
Hyder, Catharine	086	1830	WB-D/133	AR
Hyer, Enoch	032	1835	WB-1/270	
Hyer, Rudy	085	1822	WB-H/147	AR
Hyett, Thomas	037	1783	WB-B/111	AR
Hyman, Ann G.	063	1865	WB-2/485	
Hyman, Aquilla	063	1849	WB-2/348	
Hyman, Catherine	063	1837	WB-2/222	
Hyman, Charlotte	047	1873	WB-6/87	AR
Hyman, Elizabeth	063	1852	WB-2/386	
Hyman, Elizabeth	037	1876	Orig. Only	AR
Hyman, Ella J.	100	1895	WB-51/426	AR
Hyman, Ellen P.	050	1887	WB-2/12	CTY
Hyman, Ellen P.	050	1888	013 WB-B/486	013 AR
Hyman, Emily	063	1898	WB-4/235	AR
Hyman, Emily	047	1891	WB-7/11	AR
Hyman, Gavin L.	047	1888	WB-6/506	AR
Hyman, Henry	037	1857	WB-G/140	AR
Hyman, Hugh	063	1844	WB-2/310	
Hyman, James	028	1803	WB-B/186	AR
Hyman, Joel	010	1817	WB-G/7	AR
Hyman, John	010	1794	WB-D/256	AR
Hyman, John D.	063	1844	WB-2/303	
Hyman, John H.	047	1868	WB-6/7	AR
Hyman, Kada	047	1887	WB-6/443	AR
Hyman, Kenneth	037	1834	WB-F/165	AR
Hyman, Mary Jane	047	1900	WB-7/295	
Hyman, Mary L.	037	1886	WB-H/43	
Hyman, Michael	028	1791	WB-A/237	AR
Hyman, Michael	028	1793	WB-A/294	AR
Hyman, Nancy D.	103	1883	WB-1/283	AR
Hyman, Nancy D.	063	1883	WB-3/238	
Hyman, Ned	063	1840	WB-2/276	
Hyman, Needham	063	1857	WB-2/432	
Hyman, Rosa	047	1873	WB-6/88	AR
Hyman, Samuel	028	1843	WB-D/91	AR
Hyman, Samuel	063	1829	WB-2/151	
Hyman, Samuel G.	010	1847	WB-G/418	AR
Hyman, Sarah	010	1797	WB-E/28	AR
Hyman, Susanah	063	c1823	WB-2/82	
Hyman, Theophilus	037	1841	WB-F/255	AR
Hyman, Thomas	028	1807	WB-B/287	AR
Hyman, Thomas	063	1820	WB-2/68	
Hyman, Thomas	037	1796	WB-C/350	AR
Hyman, Thomas	047	1774	063 WB-1/438	
Hyman, William	037	1862	WB-G/238	AR
Hyman, William	063	c1792	WB-1/189	
Hyman, William L.	037	1865	WB-G/259	AR
Hyman, William T.	063	1863	WB-2/514	
Hymen, Peter	028	1781	Orig. Only	AR
Hynes, John	063	1774	WB-1/437	
Hyrne, Edward	070	1755	DB-D/142	AR
Hyrne, Henry	070	1773	Orig. Only	SS/AR
Hyslip, Littleton	071	1835	WB-4/131	AR
Hysmith, Solomon	070	1815	WB-AB/223	AR
Hysmith, William	070	1838	WB-AB/317	AR
Hyson, Thomas J.	028	1866	WB-D/430	AR
Ibbeken, Henry E.	075	1803	WB-M1/83	AR
Icard, William	014	1882	WB-2/234	AR
Icehour, Michael	016	1843	WB-1/7	
Icenhour, Elizabeth	003	1857	WB-B/32	AR
Icenhour, Martin	003	1890	WB-B/286	AR
Icenhour, Mary A. S.	003	1890	WB-B/278	AR
Iddings, Joseph	046	1828	WB-B/371	AR
Iddings, M. F. C.	022	c1860	WB-D/136	AR
Iddings, Mark	046	1858	WB-C/301	AR
Iddings, Martha Ann	022	c1889	Orig. Only	AR
Iddings, Nancy	046	1900	WB-G/194	AR
Idle, Barnet	085	c1786	WB-C/145	AR
Idol, Charles E.	032	1888	WB-4/17	AR
Idol, Jacob	038	c1836	WB-1/24	AR
Idol, Jacob	032	1876	WB-3/189	AR
Idol, Matthias	032	1854	WB-2/102	AR
Idol, William	028	1880	WB-2/365	AR
Ihrie, Ross R.	022	1889	WB-E/411	AR
Ikard, Peter	060	1785	Orig. Only	AR
Iker, Henry	060	1800	Orig. Only	AR
Ikerd, G. A.	021	1881	WB-2/231	
Ikerd, George	021	1850	WB-1/82	AR
Ikner, George	011	c1774	WB-1/530	
Iknor, George	083	1830	Orig. Only	AR
Ilands, Richard	030	1735	SS 876/409	SS/AR
Ilar, Nicholas	060	1868	WB-3/112	AR
Iles, John	047	1817	WB-3/601	

Name	Co.	Date	Recorded Copy	Original
Iles, Susan	047	1841	WB-4/199	
Imbler, David	032	1888	WB-4/26	AR
Ing, Jacob	037	1869	WB-G/344	AR
Ing, Joseph	037	1774	WB-A/228	AR
Ing, Matthew	039	1814	WB-D/87	AR
Inge, Devereux	020	1800	RB-C/435	AR
Ingle, Andrew	060	1863	WB-3/49	AR
Ingle, Anthony	046	1897	WB-G/1	AR
Ingle, Barnett	046	1828	WB-B/373	AR
Ingle, David	046	1878	WB-E/219	AR
Ingle, Elizabeth	013	1842	WB-A/82	
Ingle, George	046	1801	WB-A/191	AR
Ingle, John	046	1853	WB-C/389	AR
Ingle, John C.	001	1897	WB-3/196	AR
Ingle, Michael	060	1812	Orig. Only	AR
Ingle, Michael	060	1831	WB-1/222	AR
Ingles, Courtney	044	1840	WB-14/562	CTY
Ingles, John	099	1816	RB-13/45	AR
Ingless, John	029	c1763	Orig. Only	AR
Inglis, Alexander	085	1797	WB-C/284	AR
Ingold, Dorothy	001	1864	WB-1/226	AR
Ingold, Eli	046	1865	WB-D/281	AR
Ingold, Elizabeth	046	1898	WB-G/90	AR
Ingold, Peter	073	1825	WB-E/89	AR
Ingold, Sarah	046	1890	WB-F/47	AR
Ingold, Solomon	046	1882	Orig. Only	AR
Ingram, Abner	035	1782	WB-A/225	AR
Ingram, Abner, Sr.	087	1844	WB-1/291	AR
Ingram, Abraham	072	1744	SS 877/334	SS/AR
Ingram, Anna E.	056	1890	WB-3/531	AR
Ingram, Archable	020	1858	RB-R/608	AR
Ingram, Barnaby	056	1833	WB-1/488	AR
Ingram, Benjamin	082	1803	WB-1/95	AR
Ingram, Benjamin	039	1822	WB-G/120	AR
Ingram, Brantley	054	1892	WB-5/441	CTY
Ingram, Charles	029	1834	WB-B/240	AR
Ingram, E. D.	082	1886	WB-6/334	AR
Ingram, Edith	056	1846	WB-2/281	AR
Ingram, Edwin	082	1843	WB-3/12	AR
Ingram, Elisha	054	1841	WB-2/229	AR
Ingram, Elizabeth	056	1871	WB-3/44	AR
Ingram, Field	003	1893	WB-B/312	AR
Ingram, George	005	1775	WB-1/23	AR
Ingram, George	089	1857	WB-1/172	
Ingram, Hugh M.	082	1831	WB-2/9	AR
Ingram, Isham	005	1851	WB-C/35	AR
Ingram, James	084	1865	WB-D/22	CTY
Ingram, James	020	1862	RB-S/524	AR
Ingram, James	020	1792	RB-C/18	AR
Ingram, Jeremiah	005	1856	WB-C/118	AR
Ingram, Jeremiah	039	1828	WB-H/201	
Ingram, Jesse	082	1835	WB-2/57	AR
Ingram, John	081	1857	WB-10/498	AR
Ingram, John	061	1898	WB-2/214	AR
Ingram, John	029	1797	WB-A/5	AR
Ingram, John	020	1822	RB-I/69	
Ingram, John	061	1898	107 WB-2/169	
Ingram, Joseph	005	c1828	WB-A/141	AR
Ingram, Joseph M.	082	1866	WB-5/9	AR
Ingram, Joshua	015	1772	100 WB-1/213	AR
Ingram, Lemuel	005	c1828	WB-A/145	AR
Ingram, Letici	039	1821	WB-G/58	
Ingram, Louis	013	1890	WB-B/562	AR
Ingram, Martha S.	016	1887	WB-3/555	
Ingram, Mary	005	1851	WB-C/33	AR
Ingram, Nancy	029	1850	WB-C/177	AR
Ingram, Richard	056	1781	WB-2/280	AR
Ingram, Sarah	054	1896	WB-6/22	CTY
Ingram, Sarah W.	100	1847	WB-39/370	AR
Ingram, Shadrach	056	1829	WB-1/465	AR
Ingram, Simeon	071	1860	WB-5/224	AR
Ingram, Thomas	039	c1795	WB-B/7	
Ingram, Thomas	013	1848	WB-A/129	
Ingram, William	056	c1771	WB-2/278	AR
Ingram, William	071	1820	WB-3/229	AR
Ingram, William P.	005	1844	WB-B/181	AR
Inlows, Mary	053		RW-1/86	
Inman, Alexander	083	1865	WB-2/218	AR
Inman, Elisabeth	083	c1799	WB-1/55	
Inman, Hardy	083	c1794	WB-1/38	
Inman, Henry	092	1886	WB-6/243	AR
Inman, Joel L.	083	1890	WB-3/492	
Inman, Lucy	092	1885	WB-6/226	AR
Inman, Martha A.	083	1874	WB-3/79	AR
Inman, Mooris	092	1868	WB-5/97	
Inman, Silas	012	1871	Orig. Only	AR
Innes, James	070	1759	DB-D/402	
Innes, James	070	1759	SS 881/191	SS/AR
Inness, Priscilla	085	1858	WB-K/269	AR
Inness, William	085	1837	WB-I/13	AR
Inness, William	085	1837	WB-I/15	AR
Innis, James	087	1898	WB-4/76	AR
Insco, Augustus	039	1861	WB-R/188	AR
Insco, Nancy	039	1873	WB-U/73	AR
Inscoe, Nancy	039	1887	WB-U/398	AR
Ipock, Elizabeth	057	1861	WB-B/253	AR
Ipock, Harriett	028	1897	WB-F/295	
Ipock, Henry	028	1849	WB-D/155	AR
Ipock, Jacob	057	c1780	WB-A/36	AR
Ipock, John	028	1815	WB-C/99	AR
Ipock, John	028	1854	WB-D/229	AR
Ipock, Pamelia	028	1892	WB-F/26	
Ipock, Peter	028	1802	WB-B/161	AR
Ipock, Sarah A.	028	1899	WB-F/438	
Irby, Elizabeth	047	1795	WB-3/243	
Irby, Henry	070	1734	SS 876/290	SS/AR
Irby, John	071	1760	WB-1/29	
Irby, William	044	1797	WB-4/114	CTY
Iredell, Hannah	024	1826	WB-C/125	AR
Iredell, Helen B.	065	1888	WB-L/342	AR
Iredell, James	024	1794	WB-B/142	AR
Irelan, David S.	099	1887	WB-B/212	AR
Ireland, Elizabeth	001	1888	WB-2/350	AR
Ireland, John	001	1879	WB-2/135	AR
Ireland, Judia	074	1885	WB-1/25	
Ireland, Louisa	051	1898	WB-C/549	AR
Ireland, R. L.	074	1900	WB-1/153	AR
Ireland, Samuel	073	1802	WB-D/82	
Ireland, Samuel R.	087	1888	WB-3/392	AR
Ireland, Sarah	054	c1800	WB-1/134	AR
Ireland, Sarah	051	1830	WB-A/4	
Ireland, William	054	c1796	WB-1/3	AR
Irvin, A. J.	026	1895	WB-2/513	AR
Irvin, Agness	104	c1824	WB-4/77	
Irvin, Andrew	085	c1801	WB-F/40	AR
Irvin, Ausea	026	1868	WB-1/427	AR
Irvin, Christopher	085	c1791	WB-C/7	AR
Irvin, Henry L	047	1813	WB-3/544	
Irvin, James	026	1845	WB-1/42	AR
Irvin, James	084	1844	WB-C/9	CTY

Name	Co.	Date	Recorded Copy	Original
Irvin, James	084	1836	WB-B/156	CTY
Irvin, James	028	1800	WB-B/100	AR
Irvin, James M.	016	1873	WB-3/87	AR
Irvin, John	085	c1809	WB-G/142	AR
Irvin, Joseph	085	1849	WB-K/91	AR
Irvin, Margaret	016	1896	WB-4/224	AR
Irvin, Margaret	085	1839	WB-I/55	AR
Irvin, Philip J.	084	c1784	Orig. Only	CTY
Irvin, Samuel	071	1811	WB-3/44	AR
Irvin, William	084	1862	WB-D/102	CTY
Irvine, Henry L.	047	1824	WB-3/711	
Irvine, Virginia	020	1883	WB-A/392	CTY
Irving, Robert	030	1737	LGB-4/#65	SS/AR
Irwin, Alexander	065	1863	WB-J/153	AR
Irwin, Andrew	065	1860	WB-J/108	AR
Irwin, Andrew	037	1772	WB-A/195	AR
Irwin, Anna M.	101	1894	WB-A/246	
Irwin, Catharine	054	c1805	WB-1/197	AR
Irwin, Charles	070	1757	DB-D/271	AR
Irwin, Christopher	065	1797	WB-D/95	AR
Irwin, Elizabeth	065	1852	WB-I/200	AR
Irwin, George C.	MD	1900	016 WB-4/382	016 AR
Irwin, Harriet M.	065	1897	WB-M/563	AR
Irwin, Henry	037	1778	WB-B/3	AR
Irwin, I. D.	065	1893	WB-M/154	AR
Irwin, James	GA	1828	054 WB-2/56	054 AR
Irwin, James	065	1845	Orig. Only	AR
Irwin, James A.	065	1885	WB-L/86	AR
Irwin, John	065	c1850	Orig. Only	AR
Irwin, John B.	086	1834	WB-E/6	
Irwin, John C.	065	c1845	WB-I/20	AR
Irwin, Joseph H.	065	1881	WB-K/475	AR
Irwin, Lydia	065	1834	WB-G/153	AR
Irwin, Margaret	065	1888	WB-L/320	AR
Irwin, Reuben M.	065	1849	WB-I/152	AR
Irwin, Robert	065	1801	Orig. Only	AR
Irwin, Robert	065	1851	WB-I/173	AR
Irwin, Robert	054	c1806	WB-1/129	AR
Irwin, Samuel	046	1820	WB-B/94	AR
Irwin, Samuel	016	1868	WB-2/166	
Irwin, Thomas	016	1843	WB-1/6	
Irwin, William	065	c1783	WB-D/91	AR
Irwin, William	054	c1795	WB-1/96	AR
Isaac, Jonathan	070	1784	WB-C/189	AR
Isaacs, James	006	1847	WB-A/71	
Isaacs, Richard	102	1898	WB-A/143	AR
Isbell, L.	092	c1832	WB-4/66	AR
Isbell, Thomas	104	1819	WB-3/208	AR
Isbey, Rosa	047	1866	WB-5/150	
Isbill, John	104	1827	WB-4/103	AR
Iseley, Alfred	001	1886	WB-2/312	AR
Iseley, Eli	046	c1846	WB-E/232	AR
Iseley, Eliza C.	046	1897	WB-F/591	AR
Iseley, Elizabeth	001	1883	WB-2/211	AR
Iseley, Emanual	046	1900	WB-G/226	AR
Iseley, George	046	c1846	WB-E/33	AR
Iseley, Hannah	046	1863	WB-D/162	AR
Iseley, Henry	001	1885	WB-2/266	AR
Iseley, Lodwick	046	c1788	WB-A/190	AR
Iseley, Martha	001	1891	WB-2/494	AR
Iseley, Mary	001	1862	WB-1/206	AR
Iseley, Peter R.	046	1890	WB-F/80	AR
Iseley, Philip	046	1865	WB-D/260	AR
Iseley, Polly	046	1884	WB-E/390	AR
Iseley, Rosey	046	1858	WB-C/521	AR
Iseley, Sarah	046	1852	WB-C/364	AR
Iseley, Susan	001	c1852	WB-1/66	AR
Isely, Austin	001	1878	WB-2/121	AR
Isenhour, George	060	1839	WB-2/23	AR
Isenhour, John Able	085	1897	WB-3/181	CTY
Isenhour, Leah	016	1897	WB-4/247	AR
Isenhour, Peter	016	1851	WB-1/185	
Isenhour, Valentine	060	1820	Orig. Only	AR
Isenhour, Valentine	060	c1820	Copy	049 AR
Isenhower, Joseph	021	1847	WB-1/50	AR
Isenhower, Joseph	016	1889	WB-4/37	AR
Isenhower, Margaret	021	1876	WB-2/154	AR
Isenhower, Margaret	021	1874	WB-2/118	AR
Isenhower, Sary	017	c1860	Orig. Only	AR
Isham, James	035	c1753	087 DB-2/188	
Isham, James	011	c1780	WB-1/518	
Isham, James	035	1753	SS 881/24	SS/AR
Isler, Barbara M.	103	1879	WB-1/153	AR
Isler, Christian	028	1747	SS 878/148	SS/AR
Isler, Edwin B.	057	1890	WB-C/164	AR
Isler, Frederick	057	1784	WB-A/38	AR
Isler, John	057	1823	WB-B/77	AR
Isler, Sarah	057	1786	WB-A/57	AR
Isler, Simmons	057	1839	WB-B/141	AR
Isler, William	057	1784	WB-A/42	AR
Isler, William	057	1834	WB-B/119	AR
Isler, William B.	057	1898	WB-C/239	AR
Isler, William P.	103	1879	WB-1/161	AR
Isley, Edwin	073	1847	WB-F/347	AR
Isley, George	073	1848	WB-F/419	AR
Isley, Jacob	001	1853	WB-1/75	AR
Isley, Levi	001	1876	WB-2/81	AR
Isley, Martin	001	1859	WB-1/160	AR
Isley, Rachael	001	N. D.	WB-1/103	AR
Ismay, John	024	1732	SS 876/312	SS/AR
Isom, Aaron	004	1880	WB-A/38	AR
Isom, Hugh	004	1899	WB-A/222	AR
Israel, David L.	050	1900	WB-2/370	
Israel, Lavina C.	013	1894	WB-C/330	AR
Isreal, John	083	1865	WB-2/219	AR
Ives, Durant	028	1830	WB-C/327	AR
Ives, Edwin	VA	1892	030 WB-5/197	030 AR
Ives, Elizabeth	028	1845	WB-D/111	AR
Ives, Henry	028	1844	WB-D/101	AR
Ives, Horace	079	1879	WB-2/174	AR
Ives, Jesse	046	1840	WB-C/48	AR
Ives, John	028	1813	WB-C/70	AR
Ives, John	028	1822	WB-C/222	AR
Ives, John	028	1752	DB-5/283	SS/AR
Ives, Lewis	028	1844	WB-D/97	AR
Ives, Margret	028	1796	WB-B/9	AR
Ives, Thomas	030	1834	WB-4/2	
Ives, Thomas	030	1751	SS 879/89	SS/AR
Ives, Timothy	047	1787	WB-3/131	
Ives, Timothy	030	1848	WB-4/136	
Ives, William	028	1781	Orig. Only	AR
Ives, William	030	1777	WB-1/118	
Ivester, Hugh	086	1792	Orig. Only	AR
Ivester, Isaac	026	1897	WB-2/545	AR
Ivester, Margaret	026	1868	WB-2/7	AR
Ivey, Adam	037	1762	WB-A/107	AR
Ivey, Alfred	099	1817	RB-13/210	AR
Ivey, Anna	038	1863	WB-1/208	AR
Ivey, Benjamin	047	1876	WB-6/157	AR
Ivey, Charles	011	1887	WB-2/215	

Name	Co.	Date	Recorded Copy	Original
Ivey, Charles	039	1796	WB-B/20	
Ivey, Elisabeth	047	1827	WB-4/35	
Ivey, Henry	099	1794	RB-3/50	AR
Ivey, Henry W.	071	1861	WB-5/247	AR
Ivey, Isabel	083	1890	WB-3/500	AR
Ivey, Jacob R.	GA	1822	083 WB-1/314	083 AR
Ivey, James	077	1892	WB-H/227	AR
Ivey, James, Sr.	056	1817	WB-1/258	AR
Ivey, John	047	1774	WB-1/361	
Ivey, John	047	1862	WB-5/102	
Ivey, John	073	1830	WB-E/215	AR
Ivey, John	103	1893	WB-1/15	AR
Ivey, John	035	1792	WB-A/224	AR
Ivey, John	011	1892	WB-2/243	
Ivey, John	075	1772	WB-I/121	AR
Ivey, John L.	047	1899	WB-7/279	AR
Ivey, John R.	089	1896	WB-2/320	AR
Ivey, Margaret	047	1891	WB-7/12	AR
Ivey, Nat	099	1887	WB-B/230	AR
Ivey, Richard	103	1832	RD-6/302	AR
Ivey, Richard A.	047	1882	WB-6/266	AR
Ivey, Robert	047	1814	WB-3/555	
Ivey, Robert W.	047	1893	WB-7/82	AR
Ivey, Rufus J.	099	1887	WB-B/173	AR
Ivey, Sarah	075	1805	WB-M1/104	AR
Ivey, Tabbitha	099	1844	RB-25/433	AR
Ivey, Thomas	087	c1796	WB-1/7	AR
Ivey, William	046	1841	WB-C/82	AR
Ivy, Benjamin	081	1802	WB-2/102	AR
Ivy, Joseph	073	1875	WB-H/127	CTY
Ivy, Mary A.	099	1862	RB-32/355	AR
Ivy, Peter, Sr.	099	1816	RB-13/53	AR
Ivy, Sarah H.	097	1895	WB-2/489	AR
Ivy, Temperance	099	1869	WB-35/32	AR
Izard, George	PA	1829	084 WB-B/129	084 CTY
Izard, James F.	PA	1836	084 WB-B/162	084 CTY
Jack, Patrick	065	1780	WB-D/93	
Jacken, David	009	1774	OWB/118	AR
Jacks, Job	022	c1854	WB-C/420	AR
Jacks, Richard	085	c1787	WB-C/69	AR
Jacks, Richard	006	1890	WB-E/200	AR
Jacks, Richard	092	1832	WB-4/38	
Jackson, Aaron	077	1772	WB-C/110	AR
Jackson, Ambrose	086	1898	WB-G/2	AR
Jackson, Amor	090	c1843	Orig. Only	AR
Jackson, Andrew	099	1890	WB-B/408	AR
Jackson, Ann	075	1845	WB-N/196	AR
Jackson, Ann	024	c1763	WB-B/81	AR
Jackson, Bailey	075	1815	WB-M1/268	AR
Jackson, Benjamin	037	1860	WB-G/211	AR
Jackson, Benjamin	073	1826	WB-E/122	AR
Jackson, Biggers	029	1853	WB-C/241	
Jackson, Burgess	068	1874	WB-D/58	
Jackson, Burton	079	1871	WB-2/53	AR
Jackson, C. P.	026	1883	WB-2/252	AR
Jackson, Christian	068	1812	WB-A/272	
Jackson, Cornelia	099	1894	WB-C/329	
Jackson, Courtney	075	1793	WB-L/4	AR
Jackson, Craft	046	1826	WB-B/346	AR
Jackson, Craft	046	1804	WB-A/202	
Jackson, Curtis	046	1829	WB-B/396	AR
Jackson, Daniel	085	c1797	WB-F/42	AR
Jackson, Daniel	020	1844	RB-P/160	
Jackson, Daniel	075	1762	WB-I/21	AR
Jackson, Daniel	028	1803	Orig. Only	AR
Jackson, Daniel	099	1894	WB-C/329	AR
Jackson, Daniel	075	1737	Orig. Only	SS/AR
Jackson, Daniel Loyd	071	1815	WB-3/140	AR
Jackson, David	028	1803	WB-B/165	
Jackson, David	046	1800	WB-A/201	AR
Jackson, David	N	1717	Orig. Only	SS/AR
Jackson, David	086	1832	WB-D/152	AR
Jackson, David	086	1832	WB-D/158	AR
Jackson, David R.	059	1892	WB-B/57	CTY
Jackson, Delia J.	MS	1873	022 WB-G/82	022 AR
Jackson, Dempsey	096	1793	Orig. Only	AR
Jackson, Eden	087	1872	WB-3/58	AR
Jackson, Edward	047	1762	WB-1/81	
Jackson, Edward	047	1803	WB-3/393	
Jackson, Eliza L.	071	1879	WB-6/300	AR
Jackson, Emiline	099	1897	WB-D/1	AR
Jackson, Emily	029	1847	WB-C/109	AR
Jackson, Francis	019	1818	WB-D/263	AR
Jackson, George	069	1795	WB-1/97	AR
Jackson, George W.	075	1870	WB-O/18	AR
Jackson, Hanah	090	1842	WB-4/104	AR
Jackson, Henderson	099	1864	RB-33/332	AR
Jackson, Henry	087	1877	WB-3/158	AR
Jackson, Hepsey	103	1896	WB-2/178	AR
Jackson, Hezekiah	075	1836	WB-N/123	AR
Jackson, Huldah	005	1804	WB-2/73	
Jackson, Irvin	087	1852	WB-1/412	AR
Jackson, Isaac	053	1717	009 DB-1/277	
Jackson, Isaac	073	1826	WB-E/117	AR
Jackson, Isaac	073	1814	WB-D/412	AR
Jackson, Isaac	020	1808	RB-E/420	AR
Jackson, Isaac	073	1820	WB-D/581	AR
Jackson, Isaac	047	1787	WB-3/133	
Jackson, Isaac	053	1717	SS 875/128	SS/AR
Jackson, Isham	028	1857	WB-D/287	AR
Jackson, J. Q.	059	1900	WB-B/270	CTY
Jackson, James	028	1850	WB-D/166	
Jackson, James	073	1829	WB-E/193	AR
Jackson, James	028	1816	WB-C/124	AR
Jackson, James	080	1895	WB-1/235	AR
Jackson, James	046	1789	WB-A/197	AR
Jackson, James	081	1832	WB-6/191	AR
Jackson, James	090	1797	WB-1/95	AR
Jackson, James	075	1817	WB-M1/303	AR
Jackson, James	073	1858	WB-G/210	CTY
Jackson, James	075	1818	WB-M1/318	AR
Jackson, James	029	1810	WB-A/146	AR
Jackson, James	073	1822	WB-E/22	AR
Jackson, James	056	1831	WB-1/422	AR
Jackson, James	006	1826	WB-A/82	AR
Jackson, James	087	c1825	WB-A/119	AR
Jackson, James E.	101	1883	WB-A/113	AR
Jackson, James H.	092	c1873	Orig. Only	AR
Jackson, James W.	GA	1855	026 WB-1/225	026 AR
Jackson, James W.	GA	1855	Copy	086 AR
Jackson, James, Sr.	047	1761	WB-1/45	
Jackson, Jane	075	1818	WB-M1/321	AR-Nunc.
Jackson, Joab	075	1807	WB-M1/138	AR
Jackson, John	046	1867	WB-D/362	AR
Jackson, John	005	c1794	WB-A/32	
Jackson, John	046	1881	WB-E/308	AR
Jackson, John	009	1728	Orig. Only	SS/AR
Jackson, John	009	c1732	OWB/12	AR
Jackson, John	005	1772	WB-1/66	AR
Jackson, John	087	1831	WB-1/126	AR

Name	Co.	Date	Recorded Copy	Original
Jackson, John	077	1774	WB-C/144	AR
Jackson, John	057	1798	WB-A/215	AR
Jackson, John H.	092	1886	WB-6/247	AR
Jackson, John J.	037	1799	WB-D/79	AR
Jackson, John R.	020	1867	RB-T/237	AR
Jackson, Jonathan	044	c1822	Orig. Only	CTY
Jackson, Joseph	092	1815	WB-3/117	AR
Jackson, Joshua	075	1884	WB-0/208	AR
Jackson, Joshua	075	1809	WB-M1/202	AR
Jackson, Josiah	039	1827	WB-H/183	AR
Jackson, Julious	GA	1808	039 WB-C/134	
Jackson, Leanna	029	1878	Orig. Only	AR
Jackson, Lemmon	087	1857	WB-1/504	AR
Jackson, Leroy	039	c1854	WB-0/326	AR
Jackson, Lewis	056	1824	WB-1/365	AR
Jackson, Loe	044	1846	WB-16/527	CTY
Jackson, Lucy W.	022	c1898	WB-F/555	AR
Jackson, Luther R.	029	1886	WB-E/390	AR
Jackson, M. O.	087	c1897	Orig. Only	AR
Jackson, Malachi	075	1849	WB-N/228	AR
Jackson, Margaret	029	1890	WB-E/488	AR
Jackson, Margaret	021	1844	WB-1/12	AR
Jackson, Margaret	105	1898	WB-3/302	AR
Jackson, Mary	024	1791	WB-A/88	AR-Nunc.
Jackson, Mary	075	1844	WB-N/187	
Jackson, Mary	075	c1863	WB-M2/78	
Jackson, Mary	073	1855	WB-G/84	AR
Jackson, Mary A.	075	1894	WB-0/413	AR
Jackson, Mary C.	083	1898	WB-4/226	AR
Jackson, Mary E.	075	1869	WB-0/3	AR
Jackson, Mathias	075	1774	WB-I/100	AR
Jackson, Matilda F.	098	c1890	WB-A/217	CTY
Jackson, Maxcy	075	1844	WB-N/188	AR
Jackson, Maxie	075	1863	WB-N/248	AR
Jackson, Mercy	029	1816	WB-A/236	
Jackson, Mordecai	075	1816	WB-M1/285	AR
Jackson, Moses	077	1793	WB-C/457	
Jackson, Nathan	092	1854	WB-5/4	AR
Jackson, Nemonia	073	1861	WB-G/358	CTY
Jackson, O. L.	037	c1890	Copy	069 AR
Jackson, O. L.	037	1890	WB-H/164	AR
Jackson, Peleg	075	1809	WB-M1/207	AR
Jackson, Pherobee	047	1854	WB-4/371	
Jackson, Phillip W.	020	1821	RB-H/404	
Jackson, Polly	080	1900	WB-1/334	AR
Jackson, Rachel	073	1848	WB-F/413	AR
Jackson, Ramson	044	1885	WB-23/537	CTY
Jackson, Reading	028	1815	WB-C/91	AR
Jackson, Rebecca	092	1899	WB-6/513	AR
Jackson, Rebecca N.	029	1876	WB-E/162	AR
Jackson, Rhoda	075	1849	WB-N/227	AR
Jackson, Richard	087	1822	WB-1/41	AR
Jackson, Robert	024	1757	SS 882/62	SS/AR
Jackson, Robertson	075	1891	WB-0/336	AR
Jackson, Sallie	059	1898	WB-B/211	CTY
Jackson, Samuel	SC	1867	080 WB-1/53	080 AR
Jackson, Samuel	075	1785	WB-K/130	AR
Jackson, Samuel	075	1750	Orig. Only	SS/AR
Jackson, Samuel	075	1748	Orig. Only	SS/AR
Jackson, Samuel	096	1808	WB-2/28	AR
Jackson, Samuel	075	1853	WB-M2/1	AR
Jackson, Samuel S.	022	1857	WB-C/449	AR
Jackson, Sarah	005	1814	WB-2/74	AR
Jackson, Sarah	024	1808	WB-B/244	AR
Jackson, Shadrick	065	c1795	WB-D/92	AR
Jackson, Simon	075	1775	WB-I/138	AR
Jackson, Simon Peter	075	1774	WB-I/87	AR
Jackson, Tamer	075	1889	WB-0/310	AR
Jackson, Thomas	081	1826	WB-5/309	AR
Jackson, Thomas	077	1854	WB-F/452	AR
Jackson, Thomas	010	1753	SS 878/217	SS/AR
Jackson, Thomas	047	1784	WB-3/62	
Jackson, Thomas	020	1809	RB-F/83	AR
Jackson, Thomas N.	087	1897	WB-4/51	AR
Jackson, W. M.	099	1894	WB-C/284	AR
Jackson, Wiley	097	1862	WB-1/193	AR
Jackson, William	046	1804	WB-A/202	AR
Jackson, William	024	1805	WB-B/233	AR
Jackson, William	087	1870	WB-3/53	AR
Jackson, William	075	1697	SS 874.2/90	SS/AR
Jackson, William	077	1735	LGB-4/#48	SS/AR
Jackson, William	047	1805	WB-3/441	
Jackson, William	024	1835	WB-C/181	AR
Jackson, William	071	1832	WB-4/92	AR
Jackson, William	077	1794	WB-E/14	
Jackson, William	075	1823	WB-M1/369	AR
Jackson, William	063	c1774	WB-1/96	
Jackson, William	092	1854	WB-5/5	AR
Jackson, William	075	1778	WB-K/11	AR
Jackson, William	090	1874	WB-6/64	AR
Jackson, William	039	1810	WB-C/191	AR
Jackson, William	046	1792	WB-A/198	AR
Jackson, William C.	070	1840	WB-AB/343	AR
Jackson, William C.	GA	c1892	068 WB-D/372	
Jackson, William H.	075	c1860	WB-M2/73	AR
Jackson, William R.	080	1897	WB-1/279	AR
Jackson, Willie B.	087	1860	WB-2/18	AR
Jackson, Willis	099	1867	RB-34/494	AR
Jackson, Wilson	073	1880	WB-H/263	CTY
Jackson, Zachariah	075	1806	WB-M1/124	AR
Jackson, Zacharias	075	1749	Orig. Only	SS/AR
Jackson, Zachary	075	1852	WB-N/247	AR
Jacob, Abraham	087	c1807	WB-A/49	AR
Jacob, Curtis W.	MD	1884	074 WB-1/17	
Jacob, Isaac	030	1714	Orig. Only	SS/AR
Jacob, Jeremiah	085	c1781	WB-C/165	AR
Jacobs, Benjamin	078	1815	WI-7/26	AR
Jacobs, Darcus	054	c1834	WB-2/187	AR
Jacobs, Edmund	071	1877	WB-6/210	AR
Jacobs, Elijah	078	1860	WB-18/152	AR
Jacobs, George	070	1788	WB-C/193	AR
Jacobs, Hughs	083	1884	Orig. Only	AR
Jacobs, Jacob	071	1799	WB-2/185	AR
Jacobs, Jacob	071	1831	WB-4/79	AR
Jacobs, John	018	1895	WB-E/234	AR
Jacobs, John C.	098	1886	WB-A/65	CTY
Jacobs, John C.	098	1886	071 WB-6/556	071 AR
Jacobs, Kindle	085	1850	WB-K/115	AR
Jacobs, Lewis	085	1858	WB-K/259	AR
Jacobs, Lucy	078	1872	WB-19/30	AR
Jacobs, Matthew	070	1791	WB-C/198	AR
Jacobs, Samuel	083	1885	WB-3/337	AR
Jacobs, Shadrach	011	c1818	WB-2/371	
Jacobs, Susannah	070	c1829	Orig. Only	AR
Jacobs, William H.	DE	1891	074 WB-1/97	074 AR
Jacobs, Zachariah	054	c1827	WB-2/77	AR
Jacocks, Charles W.	010	1777	WB-B/107	AR
Jacocks, Elizabeth	077	1853	WB-F/437	AR
Jacocks, Jonathan	010	1811	WB-F/181	AR
Jacocks, Jonathan	010	1892	WB-I/364	AR

Name	Co.	Date	Recorded Copy	Original
Jacocks, Jonathan	010	1787	WB-D/77	AR
Jacocks, Jonathan H.	077	1847	WB-F/330	AR
Jacocks, Thomas L.	077	1852	WB-F/402	AR
Jaecokes, Thomas	N	1692	Orig. Only	SS/AR
James, Alice	070	1835	WB-AB/305	AR
James, Andrew	032	1895	WB-4/253	AR
James, Armistead	099	1883	WB-A/475	AR
James, Benjamin	075	1807	WB-M1/140	AR
James, Charles	100	1794	WB-7/148	
James, Charles	028	1802	WB-B/162	AR
James, Comfort	028	1816	WB-C/115	AR
James, David	070	1792	WB-C/199	AR
James, Edward	075	1721	SS 875/321	SS/AR
James, Emma	037	1899	WB-H/458	AR
James, Enos	033	1872	WB-2/17	CTY
James, Franklin	038	1898	WB-4/121	AR
James, Frederick	010	1818	WB-G/45	AR
James, George	099	1805	RB-7/97	AR
James, Henry	005	c1818	WB-2/75	AR
James, Henry B.	079	1864	WB-1/120	AR
James, Hinton	046	1878	WB-E/249	AR
James, Hiram	003	1882	WB-B/138	
James, Isaac	076	1882	WB-A1/23	
James, Isaac	070	1813	WB-AB/196	AR-Copy
James, J. J.	020	1892	WB-B/108	CTY
James, Jacob	075	1765	WB-I/49	AR
James, James	085	1798	WB-C/313	AR
James, James	021	c1855	Copy	054 AR
James, James	035	1796	WB-A/227	AR
James, James	021	1873	WB-2/93	
James, James W.	020	1888	WB-A/535	CTY
James, Jane	075	1772	WB-H/160	AR
James, Jane	012	1817	WB-B/112	AR
James, Jesse	073	1841	WB-F/110	AR
James, Joel	079	1877	WB-2/148	AR
James, Joel, Sr.	079	1866	WB-1/161	AR
James, John	070	1799	WB-AB/25	AR
James, John	090	1821	WB-3/65	AR
James, John	082	1795	WB-1/57	AR
James, John, Sr.	082	1800	WB-1/79	AR
James, Joseph	035	1782	WB-A/246	AR
James, Joseph	028	1792	WB-A/262	AR
James, Joshua F.	070	1899	WB-H/249	AR
James, Lemuel	075	1807	WB-M1/156	AR
James, Lydia	079	1899	WB-3/186	AR
James, Margaret	070	1787	WB-C/190	AR
James, Martha	071	1869	WB-6/13	AR
James, Mary	032	1834	WB-1/245	AR
James, Mary M.	021	1877	WB-2/167	AR
James, Molon	071	1826	WB-4/16	AR-Nunc.
James, Rachel	070	1859	WB-D/8	AR
James, Rebecca	035	1824	WB-A/238	AR
James, Robert	082	1795	WB-1/55	AR
James, S. C.	038	1864	WB-1/246	AR
James, Samuel	068	1850	WB-B/208	
James, Silas	013	1887	WB-B/465	AR
James, Stephen	092	c1828	WB-4/9	
James, Susan	063	1866	WB-2/539	
James, Thomas	070	1819	WB-C/209	AR
James, Thomas	070	1761	DB-D/488	AR
James, Thomas	073	1832	WB-E/268	AR
James, Thomas	013	1840	WB-A/64	
James, Thomas	054	1854	WB-3/77	
James, Thomas	087	1835	WB-1/173	AR
James, Wiley	020	1856	RB-R/486	AR

Name	Co.	Date	Recorded Copy	Original
James, William	070	1826	WB-C/211	AR
James, William	073	1869	WB-H/19	CTY
James, William	075	1757	SS 882/145	SS/AR
James, William	075	1733	SS 876/313	SS/AR
James, William	075	1778	WB-K/8	AR
James, William	054	c1826	WB-2/34	AR
James, William C.	005	1892	WB-D/324	AR
James, Winneford	028	1802	WB-B/143	AR
Jameson, Polly	065	1812	WB-D/100	AR
Jameson, William	072	1783	RW/L42	AR
Jameson, William	072	c1785	WI/L32	AR
Jamesson, George	030	1784	WB-1/173	
Jamison, Arthur	065	1817	WB-D/102	AR
Jamison, Bond	024	1806	WB-B/213	AR
Jamison, George	046	1796	WB-A/200	AR
Jamison, James	085	c1778	WB-A/269	AR
Jamison, James	085	1847	WB-K/52	AR
Jamison, John E.	085	1900	WB-3/372	CTY
Jamison, John M.	085	1860	WB-K/283	AR
Jamison, Mary	065	1829	WB-E/70	AR
Jamison, R. M.	065	1887	WB-L/259	AR
Jamison, Robert	065	1832	WB-G/95	
Jamison, Samuel	065	1847	WB-I/4	AR
Jamison, Sarah	016	1855	WB-1/266	AR
Jamison, Sarah L.	065	1896	WB-M/458	AR
Jamison, Thomas	065	1809	WB-D/99	AR
Jamison, William	073	1793	WB-B/222	AR
Jamison, William	085	1842	WB-I/133	AR
Jane, Joseph	099	1798	RB-4/249	
Janes, Drury	026	1870	WB-2/40	
Janes, James	049	1847	WB-2/210	AR
Janes, John	086	1826	WB-D/58	AR
Jannet, John	096	1749	Orig. Only	SS/AR
Jaques, William	071	1789	WB-1/481	AR
Jarard, James	030	1857	WB-4/209	
Jarman, Benjamin	072	1837	WB-2/6	AR
Jarman, Emanuel	057	1843	WB-B/159	AR
Jarman, Hall	057	1794	WB-A/170	AR
Jarman, John	057	c1813	WB-B/20	AR
Jarman, John	072	1885	WB-4/173	AR
Jarman, John	072	1842	WB-2/41	AR
Jarman, John, Sr.	057	1840	WB-B/147	AR
Jarman, Jure	072	1899	WB-4/400	AR
Jarman, Lawrence	072	1807	WB-A/61	AR
Jarman, Mary	072	c1784	WI/L20	AR
Jarman, Rachael	057	1815	WB-B/6	AR
Jarman, Robert	028	c1761	SS 882/211	
Jarman, Robert	028	1761	Wills.7/211	AR
Jarman, Susan	072	c1848	Orig. Only	AR
Jarman, Thomas	072	1881	WB-4/137	AR
Jarman, Thomas	072	1760	SS 881/148	SS/AR
Jarman, William	057	1824	WB-B/185	AR
Jarman, Willis	005	1882	WB-D/128	AR
Jarnagan, Jacob	010	1795	WB-D/290	AR
Jarnagan, John	010	1733	SS 876/269	
Jarott, John	019	1745	SS 878/154	SS/AR
Jarratt, Fortunatus	VA	1795	Copy	099 AR
Jarratt, Isaac	106	1880	WB-2/123	AR
Jarratt, John C.	106	c1869	WB-2/3	AR
Jarratt, Nathaniel	039	c1799	WB-A/128	
Jarred, Thomas	030	1891	WB-5/184	AR
Jarrel, Rachel	030	1832	WB-3/327	
Jarrell, Coulby	084	1854	WB-C/188	CTY
Jarrell, John	099	1817	RB-13/360	AR
Jarrell, Mary D.	046	1892	WB-F/259	AR

Name	Co.	Date	Recorded Copy	Original
Jarrell, Thomas J.	020	1882	WB-A/342	CTY
Jarret, Samuel	060	1806	Orig. Only	AR
Jarrett, Fanny	013	c1860	WB-A/218	
Jarrett, John	085	1816	WB-G/449	AR
Jarrett, John	060	1829	WB-1/137	AR
Jarrett, Joshua	084	1808	WB-A/73	CTY
Jarrett, K. M.	064	1899	WB-2/470	AR
Jarrett, Mary	021	1890	WB-2/501	
Jarrett, Samuel	021	1889	WB-2/455	AR
Jarris, David	009	1888	Orig. Only	CTY
Jarrot, Enoch	029	1836	WB-B/254	
Jarrott, Abraham	072	c1785	WI/L61	AR
Jarrott, Elizabeth	072	c1789	WI/L13	AR
Jarrott, Isaac	072	1804	WB-A/73	AR
Jarrott, John	072	c1768	Orig. Only	AR
Jarrott, John	072	1804	WB-A/64	AR
Jarves, Edward S.	030	1845	WB-4/113	
Jarves, Thomas B.	030	1839	WB-4/65	
Jarvis, Agness	053	1814	RW-1/491	
Jarvis, Bannister	030	1878	WB-5/56	AR
Jarvis, Caroline M.	053	1884	WB-11/137	AR
Jarvis, Charles E.	009	1854	OB-I/339	AR
Jarvis, Daniel	092	1830	WB-4/24	
Jarvis, David	053	1814	RW-1/488	
Jarvis, Elizabeth	030	c1808	WB-2/340	
Jarvis, Emmy	053	1830	WB-5/23	AR
Jarvis, Ephraim	030	1816	WB-3/77	
Jarvis, Foster	053	c1813	WB-4/95	AR
Jarvis, Foster	030	1750	Orig. Only	SS/AR
Jarvis, Foster	053	1825	WB-7/172	AR
Jarvis, Foster	053	1854	WB-8/14	AR
Jarvis, Grace	030	1806	WB-2/287	
Jarvis, Ivey A.	030	1836	WB-4/23	
Jarvis, James	030	1788	WB-1/230	
Jarvis, James	053	1837	WB-5/480	AR
Jarvis, James N.	053	1892	WB-11/263	AR
Jarvis, Jesse	053	c1807	RW-1/416	
Jarvis, Jesse L.	009	1882	WB-1/318	CTY
Jarvis, John	030	1816	WB-3/82	
Jarvis, John	093	1860	WB-5/49	
Jarvis, John	104	1858	WB-5/182	
Jarvis, John M.	030	1876	WB-5/50	AR
Jarvis, John W.	053	1884	WB-11/150	AR
Jarvis, Jonathan	053	1829	WB-4/521	AR
Jarvis, Josiah	053	1803	RW-1/355	AR
Jarvis, Malan	030	1787	WB-1/210	
Jarvis, Mary M.	018	1900	WB-E/307	AR
Jarvis, Maxamilon	030	1791	WB-1/249	
Jarvis, Nathaniel	053	1896	WB-11/331	AR
Jarvis, Oliver	009	1883	WB-1/340	CTY
Jarvis, R. M.	106	1898	WB-2/429	
Jarvis, Samuel	030	1783	WB-1/162	
Jarvis, Samuel	085	1823	WB-H/207	AR
Jarvis, Sarah	030	1877	WB-5/54	AR
Jarvis, Sarah	090	1842	WB-4/108	AR
Jarvis, Silvester	053	1862	WB-9/114	AR
Jarvis, Solomon	030	c1814	WB-3/43	
Jarvis, Stephen	092	1829	WB-4/9	
Jarvis, Tennison	038	c1863	WB-1/214	AR
Jarvis, Thomas	030	1795	WB-2/59	
Jarvis, Thomas, Jr.	030	1836	WB-4/13	
Jarvis, Thomas, Sr.	030	1835	WB-4/11	
Jarvis, W. B.	079	1887	WB-2/410	AR
Jarvis, William	047	1785	WB-3/80	
Jarvis, William	030	1822	WB-3/131	

Name	Co.	Date	Recorded Copy	Original
Jarvis, William	104	1861	WB-5/284	
Jarvis, William	104	1876	WB-6/124	AR
Jarvis, William	030	1774	WB-1/93	
Jarvis, William A.	030	1870	WB-5/12	AR
Jarvis, Zachariah	053	1815	Orig. Only	AR
Jarvise, Jonathan	030	1776	WB-1/107	
Jasper, Dorcas	030	1823	WB-3/159	
Jasper, Elizabeth	053	1796	RW-1/267	AR
Jasper, Israel	009	1785	OWB/195	AR
Jasper, James	053	1796	RW-1/278	
Jasper, John	009	c1760	OWB/73	AR
Jasper, John	030	1805	WB-2/266	
Jasper, Jonathan	009	1779	OWB/140	AR
Jasper, Jonathan	053	1770	RW-1/16	
Jasper, Richard	009	1829	OB-B/5	AR
Jasper, Samuel	053	1753	SS 878/163	SS/AR
Jasper, Samuel	030	1801	WB-2/189	
Jasper, Seldon	053	1812	RW-1/464	
Jasper, William	009	c1811	OWB/463	AR
Jasper, William	009	c1801	OWB/382	AR
Jasper, William R.	053	1794	RW-1/243	
Jay, Elizabeth	078	1839	WI-14/104	AR
Jay, James	078	c1833	Orig. Only	AR
Jay, John	078	1835	WI-12/330	
Jayne, Nathaniel	092	1793	WB-3/11	
Jean, Mary	071	1802	WB-2/230	AR
Jean, Philip	046	1847	WB-C/286	AR
Jean, William	090	1803	WB-2/41	AR
Jean, William	071	1800	WB-2/204	AR
Jean, William	044	1825	WB-10/13	CTY
Jeanerett, Elias	027	1834	WB-A/25	AR
Jeanes, William	012	c1767	DB-A/42	AR
Jeffers, Fanny	020	1826	RB-L/130	AR
Jeffers, Hawkins	099	1899	WB-D/279	AR
Jeffers, Peyton	028	1897	WB-F/305	
Jefferson, George	100	1873	WB-51/70	AR
Jefferson, George	082	1780	WB-1/4	AR
Jefferson, Simon	085	1889	WB-2/367	CTY
Jefferys, Evan	001	c1850	WB-1/32	AR
Jeffrass, Drury	073	1841	WB-F/87	AR
Jeffrass, Drury	073	1841	Copy	001 AR
Jeffres, Adcrson	001	1884	WB-3/67	AR
Jeffres, Andrew	001	1867	WB-1/290	AR
Jeffress, Hillary T.	100	1895	WB-51/423	AR
Jeffrey, James	100	1815	WB-19/168	AR
Jeffreys, Christopher	077	1736	LGB-4/#29	SS/AR
Jeffreys, David	039	1796	WB-A/155	AR
Jeffreys, Elizabeth	071	1743	LGB-4/#142	Codicil
Jeffreys, Elizabeth	071	1742	LGB-4/#151	SS/AR
Jeffreys, Elizabeth	024	1743	Orig. Only	AR-Nunc.
Jeffreys, George W.	078	1848	WB-13/78	AR
Jeffreys, Gilly	099	1871	RB-35/114	AR
Jeffreys, James G.	099	1854	RB-28/550	AR
Jeffreys, John	020	1836	RB-M/614	
Jeffreys, John G.	020	1871	WB-A/58	CTY
Jeffreys, John O.	099	1858	RB-31/48	
Jeffreys, Josiah R.	099	1861	RB-31/559	AR
Jeffreys, Liddie P.	037	1875	WB-G/466	
Jeffreys, Martha H.	099	1896	WB-D/73	AR
Jeffreys, Mary	039	1822	Copy	099 AR
Jeffreys, Mary	039	1827	WB-H/166	AR
Jeffreys, Norfleet	099	1899	WB-D/321	AR
Jeffreys, Osborn	039	1793	WB-A/95	
Jeffreys, Paul	078	1801	Orig. Only	AR
Jeffreys, Peter	073	1809	WB-D/244	AR

Name	Co.	Date	Recorded Copy	Original
Jeffreys, Robert G.	039	1862	WB-R/306	
Jeffreys, Robert J.	036	1892	WB-A/254	CTY
Jeffreys, Stephen	038	1898	WB-4/132	AR
Jeffreys, Thomas	020	1832	RB-M/162	AR
Jeffreys, W. B.	044	1884	WB-23/501	CTY
Jeffreys, William	039	c1802	WB-B/69	
Jeffreys, William	044	1829	WB-11/210	CTY
Jeffreys, William	039	1864	Copy	099 AR
Jeffreys, William	039	1864	WB-R/799	AR
Jeffries, Jacob	073	1818	WB-D/543	AR
Jeffrys, Sarah	044	1836	WB-13/431	CTY-Nunc.
Jefris, Lucy	073	1831	WB-E/257	AR
Jelks, Etheldred	047	1824	WB-3/699	
Jelks, Lemuel	056	1805	WB-2/279	AR
Jelks, Millican	069	c1804	WB-1/247	AR
Jelks, William	037	1782	WB-B/96	AR
Jenings, Thomas	104	1833	WB-4/161	AR
Jenings, William	006	1856	WB-D/33	
Jenins, John	075	1751	Orig. Only	SS/AR
Jenitt, Abraham	077	1742	Orig. Only	SS/AR
Jenkes, Charles	070	1795	WB-AB/11	
Jenkins, A. H.	010	1900	WB-K/44	
Jenkins, A. T.	069	c1889	WB-5/339	AR
Jenkins, Aaron	016	1861	WB-2/75	
Jenkins, Aaron	085	1834	WB-H/614	AR
Jenkins, Abram	010	1894	WB-I/407	AR
Jenkins, Alonzo T.	028	1895	WB-F/188	
Jenkins, Amerum	072	c1876	WB-4/85	
Jenkins, Amos	057	1894	WB-C/204	AR
Jenkins, Ann	029	1895	WB-F/60	AR
Jenkins, Ann	040	1857	WB-1/95	AR
Jenkins, Annie	029	1880	WB-E/236	AR
Jenkins, Ashley	073	1885	WB-H/368	CTY
Jenkins, Benjamin	072	1855	WB-2/147	AR
Jenkins, Benjamin	071	1823	WB-3/276	AR
Jenkins, Benjamin	047	1879	WB-6/218	AR
Jenkins, Benjamin W.	072	1892	WB-4/285	AR
Jenkins, Cannon	047	1826	WB-4/26	
Jenkins, Charity	024	c1791	WB-A/297	AR
Jenkins, Charles	051	1773	Orig. Only	SS/AR
Jenkins, Charles C.	051	1877	WB-C/180	AR
Jenkins, D. A.	040	1886	WB-2/264	AR
Jenkins, Daniel	072	1807	WB-A/65	AR
Jenkins, David	051	1894	WB-C/472	AR
Jenkins, Demcy	046	1818	WB-B/57	AR
Jenkins, Dempsey	037	1822	WB-E/295	AR
Jenkins, Edward	085	1823	WB-H/253	AR
Jenkins, Edward H.	026	1892	WB-2/457	AR
Jenkins, Elias	044	1807	WB-6/386	CTY
Jenkins, Elijah	060	1805	Orig. Only	AR
Jenkins, Elisha	030	1795	WB-2/33	
Jenkins, Elizabeth	010	1854	WB-G/507	AR
Jenkins, Elizabeth	010	1843	WB-G/359	AR
Jenkins, Elizabeth	006	1876	WB-E/22	AR
Jenkins, Elizabeth	026	1865	WB-1/380	AR
Jenkins, Emily	001	1862	WB-H/119	AR
Jenkins, Emmey	071	1797	WB-2/141	AR
Jenkins, Ephraim	046	1811	WB-A/204	AR
Jenkins, Fanny E.	026	1888	WB-2/352	AR
Jenkins, Fredrick	037	1862	WB-G/236	AR
Jenkins, George	063	1892	WB-4/77	AR
Jenkins, George	072	1791	Orig. Only	AR
Jenkins, George W.	071	1813	WB-3/98	AR
Jenkins, Harrison	040	1874	WB-2/72	AR
Jenkins, Henry	044	1855	WB-20/11	CTY
Jenkins, Henry	106	c1875	WB-2/61 & 70	AR
Jenkins, Henry	081	1841	WB-7/390	AR
Jenkins, Henry D.	051	1856	WB-A/395	
Jenkins, Hugh	060	1835	WB-1/354	AR
Jenkins, Hugh	085	c1800	WB-C/309	AR
Jenkins, Isaac	056	1862	WB-2/37	AR
Jenkins, J. A.	103	1897	WB-2/195	AR
Jenkins, J. C.	060	1880	WB-4/228	AR
Jenkins, James	044	1852	WB-19/98	CTY
Jenkins, James	072	1851	WB-2/111	AR
Jenkins, James	029	1873	WB-E/82	AR
Jenkins, James	063	1847	WB-2/334	
Jenkins, James	010	1820	WB-G/67	AR
Jenkins, James	044	1790	WB-2/162	CTY
Jenkins, James C.	051	1854	WB-A/370	
Jenkins, James F.	037	1873	WB-G/420	AR
Jenkins, James M.	010	1891	WB-I/333	AR
Jenkins, Jenny	079	1883	WB-2/287	AR
Jenkins, Joel H.	085	1860	WB-K/279	AR
Jenkins, John	085	1890	WB-2/397	CTY
Jenkins, John	010	1779	WB-B/137	AR
Jenkins, John	082	1808	WB-1/128	AR
Jenkins, John L.	051	1893	WB-C/468	AR
Jenkins, John, Sr.	010	1829	WB-G/186	AR
Jenkins, Jonathan	073	1805	WB-D/150	AR
Jenkins, Jonathan	072	c1783	RW/L62	AR
Jenkins, Joseph	060	1821	Orig. Only	AR
Jenkins, Joseph D.	037	1878	WB-G/520	AR
Jenkins, Josiah	013	1842	WB-A/86	
Jenkins, Josiah	010	1823	WB-G/99	AR
Jenkins, Julia A.	044	1895	WB-24/281	CTY
Jenkins, L. G.	026	1887	WB-2/327	AR
Jenkins, Lavina	051	1867	WB-B/94	AR
Jenkins, Leonidas	044	1899	WB-24/444	CTY
Jenkins, Lettice	081	1866	WB-14/2	AR
Jenkins, Lewis	072	c1763	RW/L36	AR
Jenkins, Lodawick	010	1863	WB-H/132	AR
Jenkins, Lodema	040	1881	WB-2/178	AR
Jenkins, Lodema	065	1894	WB-M/266	AR
Jenkins, Mansfield	044	1819	WB-8/295	CTY
Jenkins, Martha	081	1841	WB-7/375	AR
Jenkins, Martha	044	1850	WB-18/134	CTY
Jenkins, Martha	100	1867	WB-50/235	AR
Jenkins, Martha	010	1824	WB-G/118	AR
Jenkins, Martha J.	100	1869	WB-51/10	AR
Jenkins, Mary L.	103	1898	WB-2/224	AR
Jenkins, Mourning	092	1849	WB-4/292	
Jenkins, Noah	037	1812	WB-E/30	AR
Jenkins, Patience	100	1780	WB-3/73	015 AR
Jenkins, Philmon	100	1858	WB-49/191	AR
Jenkins, Randal	063	1868	WB-2/503	
Jenkins, Roberson	079	1863	WB-1/89	AR
Jenkins, Rosa B.	044	1881	WB-23/399	CTY
Jenkins, Samuel P.	037	1868	WB-G/327	AR
Jenkins, Sarah	072	c1796	Orig. Only	AR
Jenkins, Sarah	072	c1817	WB-A/65	AR
Jenkins, Sarah	037	1856	WB-G/139	AR
Jenkins, Selina	099	1899	WB-D/325	AR
Jenkins, Smith	040	1877	WB-2/114	AR
Jenkins, Stephen	051	1882	WB-C/293	AR
Jenkins, Susie	051	1898	WB-C/547	
Jenkins, Thomas	044	1822	WB-9/95	CTY
Jenkins, Thomas	081	1807	WB-3/75	AR
Jenkins, Thomas	072	1864	Orig. Only	AR

Name	Co.	Date	Recorded Copy	Original
Jenkins, Thomas	046	1771	WB-A/193	AR
Jenkins, Thomas D.	051	1853	WB-A/351	
Jenkins, Thomas S.	044	1885	WB-23/526	CTY
Jenkins, Thomas W.N.	051	1883	WB-C/30	AR
Jenkins, Timothy P.	089	c1864	WB-1/293	
Jenkins, W. A.	092	1897	WB-6/472	AR
Jenkins, William	105	1870	WB-2/31	
Jenkins, William	063	1791	WB-1/176	
Jenkins, William	063	1894	WB-4/133	AR
Jenkins, William F.	047	1846	WB-4/252	
Jenkins, William P.	051	1886	WB-C/344	AR
Jenkins, Winborn	071	1814	WB-3/113	AR
Jenkins, Winborn	071	1793	WB-2/40	AR
Jenkins, Winborn	041	1815	WB-2/97	AR
Jenkins, Wineford	010	1828	WB-G/176	AR
Jenkins, Zady	073	1885	WB-H/369	CTY
Jenneret, Elias	012	1765	DB-A/15	
Jennet, Joseph	053	1795	RW-1/264	
Jennett, Elizabeth	053	1870	WB-11/22	AR
Jennett, James	070	1815	WB-AB/228	AR
Jennett, Jesse	030	1796	WB-2/78	
Jennett, Jesse W.	070	1853	WB-C/562	AR
Jennett, John	053	1774	RW-1/58	
Jennett, John	096	1749	Orig. Only	SS/AR
Jennett, Jones S.	053	1894	WB-11/315	AR
Jennett, Joseph	053	1813	RW-1/484	AR
Jennett, Robert	053	1857	WB-8/249	AR
Jennett, Thomas	053	1879	Orig. Only	AR
Jennett, Thomas G.	053	1821	WB-4/212	
Jennings, Ann	075	1720	SS 875/224	
Jennings, Ann P.	026	1888	WB-2/357	AR
Jennings, Arthur	075	1791	WB-K/221	AR
Jennings, Benjamin	075	1774	WB-I/83	AR
Jennings, Caleb	075	1761	WB-I/22	AR
Jennings, Charles B.	075	1889	WB-O/309	AR
Jennings, David	075	1835	WB-N/117	AR
Jennings, David	075	1768	WB-H/101	AR
Jennings, Delia A.	103	1887	WB-1/416	AR
Jennings, Demsey	075	1808	WB-M1/197	AR
Jennings, Edmund	075	1897	WB-O/449	AR
Jennings, Elijah	104	1874	WB-6/82	AR
Jennings, Elisabeth	075	1837	WB-N/140	AR
Jennings, Elizabeth	026	1850	WB-1/108	AR
Jennings, Elizabeth	075	1884	WB-O/218	AR
Jennings, Frederick	075	1889	WB-O/300	AR
Jennings, Frederick	072	1815	WB-A/62	AR-Nunc.
Jennings, George	070	1805	WB-AB/96	AR
Jennings, Isaac	075	1789	WB-L/33	AR
Jennings, Isaac	075	1797	WB-L/99	
Jennings, J. K.	SC	1899	Copy	086 AR
Jennings, James	075	1900	WB-O/514	AR
Jennings, Jesse	075	1791	WB-K/219	AR
Jennings, John	054	1883	WB-5/53	CTY
Jennings, John	075	1720	SS 875/223	
Jennings, John	075	1808	WB-M1/178	AR
Jennings, John	075	1840	WB-N/163	AR
Jennings, Jonathan	070	1800	WB-AB/39	AR
Jennings, Lemuel	075	1798	WB-M1/6	AR
Jennings, Margaret	075	1855	WB-M2/35	AR
Jennings, Martha	075	1877	WB-O/92	AR
Jennings, Samuel	075	1808	WB-M1/178	AR
Jennings, Samuel B.	027	1878	WB-2/26	
Jennings, Thomas	070	1809	WB-AB/126	AR
Jennings, Thomas	070	c1744	028 DB-3/29	
Jennings, Thomas	070	1744	SS 878/92	SS/AR
Jennings, Thomas	061	1845	WB-1/29	AR
Jennings, William	104	1838	WB-4/227	
Jennings, William	075	c1854	WB-M2/15	AR
Jennings, William	N	1687	Orig. Only	SS/AR
Jennings, William	030	1729	Orig. Only	SS/AR
Jennins, Mary	030	1729	Orig. Only	SS/AR
Jenoure, Joseph	N	1732	SS 876/265	SS/AR
Jenson, Anna M.	013	1899	WB-D/332	AR
Jerkins, Sarah	001	1874	WB-2/100	AR
Jerkins, Thomas	028	1856	WB-D/253	AR
Jernagan, Godwin	010	1820	WB-G/76	AR
Jernagan, John	010	1733	Orig. Only	SS/AR
Jernigan, Ann	056	1793	WB-1/68	AR
Jernigan, Benjamin	010	1800	WB-E/112	AR
Jernigan, David	103	1793	WI-A/539	AR
Jernigan, David	103	1791	WI-A/215	AR
Jernigan, Ferney	087	1867	WB-2/120	AR
Jernigan, Furnifold	103	1853	RD-11/294	AR
Jernigan, George	010	1874	WB-I/58	AR
Jernigan, George	103	1792	Orig. Only	AR
Jernigan, Henry	056	c1781	WB-2/275	AR
Jernigan, Isbel	103	1783	WI-A/25	AR
Jernigan, Jasper	056	1787	WB-1/8	AR
Jernigan, Jerusha	056	1868	WB-3/1	AR
Jernigan, Jesse	010	1785	WB-D/37	AR
Jernigan, Joseph J.	056	1868	WB-2/113	AR
Jernigan, Kador	103	1844	RD-9/60	AR
Jernigan, Lemuel R.	051	1867	WB-B/108	AR
Jernigan, Lydda	103	1798	Orig. Only	AR
Jernigan, Miles H.	051	1843	WB-A/192	
Jernigan, Nathaniel	010	c1866	WB-I/10	AR
Jernigan, Phereby	010	1804	WB-E/252	AR
Jernigan, Sally	051	1882	WB-C/285	AR
Jernigan, Sarah	105	1858	WB-1/48	AR
Jernigan, Sarah	010	1868	WB-H/208	AR
Jernigan, Thomas	035	1788	WB-A/244	AR
Jernigan, Watson	035	1853	WB-2/77	AR
Jernigan, Whitmel	011	c1804	WB-1/347	
Jernigan, William	056	c1762	WB-2/274	AR
Jernigan, William	056	1784	WB-2/272	AR
Jernigan, William J.	010	1890	WB-I/300	AR
Jernigan, Worley M.	010	1893	WB-I/374	AR
Jernigin, Henry	010	1736	LGB-4/#40	SS/AR
Jernignan, Josiah	103	1805	Orig. Only	AR
Jerrey, John	029	1800	WB-A/33	
Jervis, Jabez	107	1840	WB-1/40	
Jervis, James	092	1841	WB-4/183	
Jesop, Rachel	077	1824	WB-F/72	
Jesper, Richard	N	1723	SS 876/28	SS/AR
Jesse, Henry	020	1781	RB-A/165	AR
Jessip, John	011	c1786	WB-1/534	
Jessop, Caleb	046	1833	WB-B/472	AR
Jessop, Isaac	029	1811	WB-A/167	
Jessop, Joseph	077	1735	LGB-4/#46	SS/AR
Jessop, Joseph	092	1796	WB-3/22A	AR
Jessop, Joseph	090	1820	WB-3/50	AR
Jessop, Priscilla	092	1819	WB-3/137	AR
Jessop, Thomas	077	1819	WB-F/15	AR
Jessop, Timothy	077	1805	WB-E/223	AR
Jessup, Caleb	090	1874	WB-4/56	AR
Jessup, Eli	092	1871	WB-6/15	
Jessup, Eli	092	1871	Copy	090 AR
Jessup, Hiram	092	1889	WB-6/302	AR
Jessup, Isaac	011	c1852	SC/06279	AR-Copy
Jessup, Isaac	011	1852	WB-1/201	

Name	Co.	Date	Recorded Copy	Original
Jessup, Jesse	077	1874	WB-H/58	AR
Jessup, Mary Ann	092	1900	WB-6/547	AR
Jessup, Mary E.	077	1890	WB-H/190	AR
Jessup, William	077	c1711	Orig. Only	AR
Jessup, William	092	1890	WB-6/324	AR
Jester, John	106	1875	WB-2/68	
Jester, Maskill	046	1822	WB-B/148	AR
Jeter, Caleb	099	1819	RB-15/238	AR
Jeter, Edmund	085	1819	WB-H/2	AR
Jeter, James	072	c1765	RW/L55	AR
Jethro, Martha	101	1898	WB-A/304	AR
Jetton, Abraham	065	1800	WB-D/97	AR
Jetton, Abram	085	1786	WB-C/89	AR
Jetton, Elizabeth	065	1876	WB-K/236	AR
Jetton, Elizabeth	065	1817	WB-D/101	AR
Jetton, Ezekiel	065	1823	WB-D/105	AR
Jetton, John	065	1790	Orig. Only	AR
Jetton, Lewis	065	1826	WB-D/107	AR
Jetton, Priscilla	065	1838	WB-E/210	AR
Jevins, Elizabeth	075	1735	SS 876/404	SS/AR
Jevins, John	075	1735	Orig. Only	SS/AR
Jewel, Benjamin	053	1785	RW-1/134	
Jewel, Mary	053	1792	RW-1/220	AR
Jewel, Thomas	009	1735	LGB-4/#57	SS/AR
Jewell, B. H.	099	1877	RB-35/399	AR
Jewell, John	009	1744	Orig. Only	SS/AR
Jewell, John W.	099	1899	WB-D/262	AR
Jewell, Thomas	009	c1769	OWB/104	AR
Jewett, Lucy O.	070	1896	WB-G/474	AR
Jimison, James	050	1883	WB-1/245	CTY
Jinings, Cloe	075	1848	WB-N/224	AR
Jinings, Jaka	075	1845	WB-N/193	AR
Jinings, Lemuel	075	1833	WB-N/83	AR
Jinkens, Jesse	085	1803	WB-D/15	AR
Jinkins, Ephraim	010	1784	WB-C/80	AR
Jinkins, J. J.	022	1886	WB-E/339	AR
Jinkins, Jesse	026	1847	WB-1/68	AR
Jinkins, John	037	1808	WB-D/321	AR
Jinkins, John	073	1790	WB-B/105	AR
Jinkins, Joseph	092	c1835	Orig. Only	AR
Jinkins, Mary	010	1802	WB-E/177	AR
Jinkins, Mary	044	1836	WB-13/421	CTY
Jinkins, Rebecah	044	1848	WB-17/185	CTY
Jinkins, Samuel	099	1797	RB-3/326	AR
Jinkins, Sanford	022	1853	WB-C/352	AR
Jinkins, Sanford	022	1837	WB-C/63	AR
Jinkins, Simon	030	1837	WB-4/39	
Jinkins, Thomas	044	1828	WB-10/452	
Jinkins, Willis	083	1849	WB-2/12	AR
Jinkins, Winborn	010	1811	WB-F/184	AR
Jinkins, Winburn	005	1831	WB-B/15	AR
Jinks, Joseph	022	1811	WB-A/193	AR
Jinney, Thomas	005	1791	Orig. Only	AR
Jinnings, Thomas	075	1822	WB-M1/358	AR
Joanes, John	024	1736	Orig. Only	SS/AR
Job, James F.	046	1894	WB-F/316	AR
Job, Samuel	085	c1803	WB-C/312	AR
Job, Thomas	085	1787	WB-F/39	AR
John, James	070	1747	DB-C/172	AR
John, Lewis	009	c1805	OWB/430	AR
John, Mary	065	c1777	WB-D/90	AR
John, Mary	082	1896	WB-6/530	AR
John, Thomas	035	1762	WB-A/240	AR
Johnagan, William	041	1877	WB-4/96	AR
Johnes, Arthur	011	1750	SS 878/13	SS/AR
Johns, Alexander	084	1837	WB-B/181	CTY
Johns, Annie E.	084	1890	WB-E/455	CTY
Johns, Anthony B.	084	1876	WB-E/209	CTY
Johns, C. F.	099	1873	RB-35/198	AR
Johns, Isabel	070	1794	WB-C/201	AR
Johns, John	086	1878	WB-F/114	AR
Johns, John	073	1801	WB-D/42	AR
Johns, John B.	099	1862	RB-32/249	AR
Johns, Martha	084	1854	WB-C/182	CTY
Johns, Zacheriah	086	1857	WB-E/325	AR
Johnsen, John	077	1737	LGB-4/#101	
Johnson, A. H.	013	1868	WB-B/7	
Johnson, A. L.	033	1893	WB-2/139	
Johnson, Aaron	099	1810	RB-9/190	AR
Johnson, Aaron	006	1879	WB-E/55	AR
Johnson, Abel	056	1820	WB-1/317	AR
Johnson, Abram	009	c1800	OWB/374	AR
Johnson, Adeline	096	c1860	WB-3/77	AR
Johnson, Albert	070	1887	WB-E/115	AR
Johnson, Alexander	038	1871	WB-2/51	AR
Johnson, Alexander	029	1881	WB-E/269	AR
Johnson, Alexander	046	1816	WB-B/32	AR
Johnson, Alexander	083	1861	WB-2/175	AR
Johnson, Alexander	029	1804	WB-A/68	AR-Copy
Johnson, Alexander	005	1864	WB-C/225	AR
Johnson, Alexander	046	1793	WB-A/199	AR
Johnson, Alexander	083	1867	WB-2/238	AR
Johnson, Alfred L.	085	1898	WB-3/230	CTY
Johnson, Alice	044	1826	WB-10/185	CTY-Nunc.
Johnson, Allen	056	1871	WB-1/62	AR
Johnson, Allen D.	056	1854	WB-1/681	AR
Johnson, Alson G.	081	1877	WB-15/263	AR
Johnson, Ambrose	104	1858	WB-5/198	
Johnson, Amos	063	1848	WB-2/343	
Johnson, Amos	056	1873	WB-3/93	AR
Johnson, Amos	035	1802	WB-A/229	AR
Johnson, Amos	087	1871	WB-3/44	AR
Johnson, Anderson	054	1857	WB-3/125	AR
Johnson, Andrew W.	071	1865	WB-5/309	AR
Johnson, Anna	022	1863	WB-D/117	AR
Johnson, Anna C.	079	1888	WB-2/439	AR
Johnson, Archer	044	1813	WB-7/280	CTY
Johnson, Ary	056	1896	WB-2/228	AR
Johnson, Asa	054	1846	WB-3/1	AR
Johnson, Ashley	090	1820	WB-3/42	
Johnson, Athenson	100	1850	WB-40/249	
Johnson, Azeail	096	1823	WB-2/92	AR
Johnson, B. F.	056	1880	WB-3/253	AR
Johnson, Barnabas	029	1854	WB-C/317	
Johnson, Barnabas	099	1871	RB-35/110	AR
Johnson, Barnaby	071	1807	WB-2/340	AR
Johnson, Benjamin	029	1834	WB-B/231	
Johnson, Benjamin	035	1849	WB-2/45	AR
Johnson, Benjamin	061	c1848	WB-1/55	AR
Johnson, Benjamin	071	1806	WB-2/321	AR
Johnson, Benjamin	092	1843	WB-4/201	
Johnson, Benjamin	104	1859	WB-5/221	
Johnson, Benjamin	092	c1830	WB-4/33	
Johnson, Benjamin	054	1846	WB-3/13	AR
Johnson, Benjamin	071	1788	WB-1/391	AR
Johnson, Benjamin	022	1877	WB-E/133	AR
Johnson, Benjamin	037	1763	WB-A/123	AR
Johnson, Benjamin	029	1836	WB-B/264	
Johnson, Benjamin	044	1802	WB-5/227	CTY

Name	Co.	Date	Recorded Copy	Original
Johnson, Benjamin	047	1882	WB-6/262	AR
Johnson, Benjamin	054	c1812	WB-1/354	AR
Johnson, Bettie J.	105	1895	WB-3/15	AR
Johnson, Bizzell	035	1895	WB-4/472	AR
Johnson, Braxton	102	1890	WB-A/75	AR
Johnson, Bright	087	1866	WB-2/98	AR
Johnson, Britton	071	1837	WB-4/166	AR
Johnson, Caleb	038	1893	WB-3/358	AR
Johnson, Caleb W.	085	1899	WB-3/339	CTY
Johnson, Calvin	083	1895	WB-4/62	AR
Johnson, Campbell	006	1877	WB-E/25	AR
Johnson, Cary	083	1900	WB-4/293	AR
Johnson, Celia	099	1838	RB-24/171	AR
Johnson, Celie	004	1883	WB-A/62	AR
Johnson, Charles	028	1795	WB-A/347	AR
Johnson, Charles	104	1820	WB-3/220	AR
Johnson, Charles	024	1802	WB-B/270	AR
Johnson, Charles	024	c1802	Copy	101 AR
Johnson, Charles E.	024	1850	WB-C/302	AR
Johnson, Christian	029	1840	WB-B/333	
Johnson, Christopher	071	1879	WB-6/289	AR
Johnson, Collinson	057	1795	WB-A/161	AR
Johnson, Crumford W.	054	1876	WB-4/216	CTY
Johnson, D. H.	014	1867	WB-1/19	AR
Johnson, D. W. C.	032	1886	WB-3/500	AR
Johnson, Daniel	086	1813	WB-B/272	AR
Johnson, Daniel	046	1885	WB-E/421	AR
Johnson, Daniel	022	1853	WB-C/359	AR
Johnson, Daniel	011	1880	WB-2/102	
Johnson, Daniel	083	1851	WB-2/32	AR
Johnson, Daniel M.	029	1864	WB-D/63	
Johnson, Daniel P.	014	1896	WB-2/565	CTY
Johnson, Daniel P.	005	1892	WB-D/308	AR
Johnson, Darden	071	1815	WB-3/157	AR
Johnson, David	090	1798	WB-1/108	AR
Johnson, David	022	1897	WB-F/64	AR
Johnson, David B.	054	1877	WB-4/251	CTY
Johnson, Delilah	022	1898	WB-F/86	AR
Johnson, Dempsey	022	c1867	WB-D/177	AR
Johnson, Dougan C.	081	1878	WB-15/297	AR
Johnson, Dudley B.	044	1898	WB-24/401	CTY
Johnson, Duncan	029	1826	WB-B/142	AR
Johnson, Duncan B.	057	1857	WB-B/239	AR
Johnson, E. D.	083	1893	WB-4/6	
Johnson, E.Franklin	003	1900	WB-B/414	AR
Johnson, Edward	022	1893	WB-E/544	AR
Johnson, Edward A.	100	1895	WB-51/415	AR
Johnson, Edward, Sr.	077	1856	WB-F/478	AR
Johnson, Elias	047	1857	WB-5/46	
Johnson, Elijah	071	1807	WB-2/339	AR
Johnson, Elijah	061	1841	WB-1/18	AR
Johnson, Elisabeth	071	1789	WB-1/483	AR
Johnson, Elizabeth	037	1862	WB-G/224	AR
Johnson, Elizabeth	028	1881	WB-E/259	
Johnson, Elizabeth	009	1818	OB-A/285	AR
Johnson, Elizabeth	046	1832	WB-B/452	AR
Johnson, Elizabeth	071	1854	WB-5/118	AR
Johnson, Elizabeth	047	1892	WB-7/70	AR
Johnson, Elizabeth	056	1790	WB-2/277	AR
Johnson, Elizabeth	001	1872	WB-2/51	AR
Johnson, Elizabeth	069	c1850	Orig. Only	AR
Johnson, Emma	070	1895	WB-G/325	AR
Johnson, Emma	070	1895	056 WB-2/193	056 AR
Johnson, Enoch	092	1896	WB-6/431	AR
Johnson, Ephraim	087	c1818	WB-A/87	AR

Name	Co.	Date	Recorded Copy	Original
Johnson, Esther	056	1823	WB-1/456	AR
Johnson, Fannie S.	046	1900	WB-G/191	AR
Johnson, Felix	092	1894	WB-6/384	AR
Johnson, Fleet	028	1900	WB-F/468	
Johnson, Frank	009	1895	WB-2/54	
Johnson, Frederick	086	1852	WB-E/229	AR
Johnson, Frederick	028	1819	WB-C/176	AR
Johnson, Garret	072	c1771	RW/L50	AR
Johnson, George	046	1824	WB-B/193	AR
Johnson, George	038	1883	WB-2/467	AR
Johnson, George D.	037	1864	WB-G/249	AR
Johnson, George W.	033	1889	WB-2/105	CTY
Johnson, Gideon	084	1807	WB-A/68 & 193	CTY
Johnson, Gilley	056	1894	WB-2/185	AR
Johnson, Gustavus	024	1843	WB-C/237	AR
Johnson, H. F.	050	1899	WB-2/332	CTY
Johnson, Hadley	022	1884	WB-E/299	AR
Johnson, Hamilton	024	1894	WB-E/230	AR
Johnson, Hardy	079	1888	WB-2/448	AR
Johnson, Harriet	083	1856	WB-2/82	AR
Johnson, Harriett	063	1873	WB-3/56	
Johnson, Harry	056	1900	WB-4/253	AR
Johnson, Hattie G.	029	1895	WB-F/58	AR
Johnson, Henry	056	1807	WB-1/205	AR
Johnson, Henry	049	1882	WB-2/94	AR
Johnson, Henry	012	1878	WB-A/36	AR-Nunc.
Johnson, Henry	028	1811	WB-C/39	AR
Johnson, Henry	103	1852	RD-11/184	
Johnson, Henry J.	MD	1886	Copy	013 AR
Johnson, Henry L.	010	1870	WB-I/25	AR
Johnson, Henry W.	103	1899	WB-2/256	AR
Johnson, Henry W.	009	1900	WB-2/240	CTY
Johnson, Hezekiah	106	c1853	WB-1/16	AR
Johnson, Hugh	050	1874	WB-1/141	CTY
Johnson, Ira	046	1889	WB-F/3	AR
Johnson, Isaac	056	1823	WB-1/359	AR
Johnson, Isabella	083	1869	WB-2/246	AR
Johnson, Isahiah	028	1784	Orig. Only	AR
Johnson, Israel	046	1893	WB-F/298	AR
Johnson, Israel	071	1867	WB-5/347	AR
Johnson, Jacob	099	1889	WB-B/372	AR
Johnson, Jacob	028	1806	WB-B/256	AR
Johnson, Jacob	073	1822	WB-E/20	AR
Johnson, Jacob W.	028	1859	WB-D/319	
Johnson, James	070	1846	WB-AB/440	AR
Johnson, James	100	1808	WB-14/211	AR
Johnson, James	032	1830	WB-1/149	AR
Johnson, James	044	1795	WB-3/222	CTY-Copy
Johnson, James	063	1877	WB-3/131	
Johnson, James	056	1839	WB-1/510	AR
Johnson, James	077	1694	SS 874.2/62	SS/AR
Johnson, James	071	1895	WB-7/230	AR
Johnson, James	046	1809	WB-A/203	AR
Johnson, James	039	1819	Orig. Only	AR-Nunc.
Johnson, James A.	104	1893	WB-6/470	AR
Johnson, James H.	056	1890	WB-3/538	AR
Johnson, James M.	033	1892	WB-2/130	CTY
Johnson, James M. W.	104	1882	WB-6/222	AR
Johnson, James T.	106	1873	WB-2/36	AR
Johnson, Jane	070	1871	WB-E/229	AR
Johnson, Jane	083	1875	WB-3/125	AR
Johnson, Jane C.	VA	1900	099 WB-D/341	099 AR
Johnson, Jeffery	104	1789	WB-1/251	AR
Johnson, Jemima	092	1837	WB-4/131	AR

Name	Co.	Date	Recorded Copy	Original
Johnson, Jennet	083	1886	WB-3/127	AR
Johnson, Jesse	006	1838	WB-A/74	AR
Johnson, Jesse	022	1880	WB-E/207	AR
Johnson, Jesse	022	1831	WB-B/211	AR
Johnson, Joab	087	1842	WB-1/262	AR
Johnson, Joab	037	1860	WB-G/194	AR
Johnson, Joel	046	1834	WB-B/511	AR
Johnson, Joel	063	1847	WB-2/331	
Johnson, Joel	011	1861	WB-1/329	
Johnson, John	044	1894	WB-24/237	CTY
Johnson, John	039	1829	WB-J/37	AR
Johnson, John	037	1752	Orig. Only	SS/AR
Johnson, John	085	1797	WB-C/315	AR
Johnson, John	077	1694	SS 874.2/44	SS/AR
Johnson, John	077	1822	WB-F/49	AR
Johnson, John	062	1860	WB-A/27	AR
Johnson, John	062	1894	WB-B/162	AR
Johnson, John	059	1869	WB-A/8	
Johnson, John	046	1816	WB-B/31	AR
Johnson, John	071	1753	SS 879/189	SS/AR
Johnson, John	050	c1848	Orig. Only	AR
Johnson, John	065	c1827	Orig. Only	AR
Johnson, John	020	1781	RB-A/140	AR
Johnson, John	049	c1824	WI-A/20	AR
Johnson, John	071	1795	WB-2/91	AR
Johnson, John	016	1845	WB-1/73	
Johnson, John	053	1757	SS 880/141	SS/AR
Johnson, John	056	1780	Orig. Only	AR
Johnson, John	087	1860	WB-2/16	AR
Johnson, John	087	1875	WB-3/110	AR
Johnson, John C.	100	1855	WB-44/32	AR
Johnson, John C.	006	1896	WB-E/300	AR
Johnson, John H.	025	1889	WB-A/94	AR
Johnson, John J.	103	1877	WB-1/139	AR
Johnson, John R.	010	1899	WB-I/577	
Johnson, John R.	100	1890	WB-51/312	AR
Johnson, John S.	104	1873	WB-6/68	AR
Johnson, John W.	065	1865	WB-J/204	AR
Johnson, John, Sr.	085	c1807	WB-G/101	AR
Johnson, John, Sr.	022	1848	WB-C/212	AR
Johnson, Jonathan	070	1853	WB-C/558	AR
Johnson, Jonathan	096	1792	Orig. Only	AR
Johnson, Joseph	070	1745	DB-C/83	AR
Johnson, Joseph	081	c1834	Orig. Only	032 AR
Johnson, Joseph	039	1880	WB-U/232	AR
Johnson, Joseph	046	1859	Orig. Only	AR
Johnson, Joseph	049	c1828	WI-A/28	AR
Johnson, Joseph A.	003	1874	Orig. Only	AR
Johnson, Joshua	046	1829	WB-B/389	AR
Johnson, Joshua	063	1795	WB-1/217	
Johnson, Joshua	031	1896	WB-1/99	AR
Johnson, Joshua	073	1840	WB-F/68	AR
Johnson, Josiah	056	c1852	Orig. Only	AR
Johnson, Julia Ann	046	1880	WB-E/282	AR
Johnson, Julyan G.	079	1885	WB-2/330	AR
Johnson, Kindrick	099	1875	RB-35/281	AR
Johnson, L. D.	047	1900	WB-7/283	
Johnson, Lazarus	071	1850	WB-5/85	AR
Johnson, Leander	104	1861	WB-5/280	
Johnson, Levi	106	1880	WB-2/120	AR
Johnson, Lewis	084	1864	WB-D/9	CTY
Johnson, Lewis	008	c1711	SS 875/53	
Johnson, Lewis	104	1852	WB-5/70	AR
Johnson, Lilith	086	c1791	Orig. Only	AR
Johnson, Littleberry	039	c1857	WB-0/379	AR
Johnson, Littleton	056	1821	WB-1/433	AR
Johnson, Lucy	026	1842	WB-1/7	AR
Johnson, Lucy	056	1862	WB-2/33	AR
Johnson, Lucy	026	1853	WB-1/155	AR
Johnson, Lucy A.	099	1890	WB-B/403	AR
Johnson, Lucy C.	056	1893	WB-2/146	AR
Johnson, Lydia	032	1845	WB-1/464	AR
Johnson, Lytle	081	1853	WB-9/521	AR
Johnson, Maleca	029	1835	WB-B/246	
Johnson, Margaret	003	1896	WB-B/356	AR
Johnson, Marinda	070	1884	WB-E/534	AR
Johnson, Marioh	025	c1880	Orig. Only	AR
Johnson, Martha	047	1880	WB-6/240	AR
Johnson, Martha	099	1887	WB-B/168	AR
Johnson, Martha C.	075	1848	WB-N/223	AR
Johnson, Martha W.	033	1893	WB-2/144	CTY
Johnson, Mary	054	1888	WB-5/223	CTY
Johnson, Mary	085	1828	WB-H/417	AR
Johnson, Mary	028	1818	WB-C/166	AR
Johnson, Mary	100	1814	WB-19/17	AR
Johnson, Mary	085	1812	WB-G/236	AR
Johnson, Mary Eliz.	028	1881	Orig. Only	AR
Johnson, Mary H.	092	1880	WB-6/151	AR
Johnson, Mary P.	100	1896	WB-51/457	AR
Johnson, Mary R.	047	1857	WB-5/33	
Johnson, Mathew	044	1780	WB-1/274	CTY
Johnson, Mathias	071	1871	WB-6/70	AR
Johnson, Matthew	087	1852	WB-1/417	AR
Johnson, Matthew	069	1812	WB-1/256	AR
Johnson, Michael	081	1847	WB-8/456	AR
Johnson, Michael	022	c1831	WB-C/12	AR
Johnson, Mildred	039	1881	WB-U/254	AR
Johnson, Mollie	070	1889	WB-F/278	AR
Johnson, Moses	104	1855	WB-5/113	
Johnson, Moses	056	1804	WB-2/273	AR
Johnson, Moses	069	1848	WB-1/509	AR
Johnson, Nancy	087	1888	WB-3/400	AR
Johnson, Nancy	083	1859	WB-2/141	AR
Johnson, Nancy	032	1895	WB-4/250	AR
Johnson, Nancy	056	1885	WB-3/377	AR
Johnson, Nancy	018	1832	WB-C/135	
Johnson, Nancy C.	085	1889	WB-2/364	CTY
Johnson, Nathan	087	1854	WB-1/457	AR
Johnson, Nathan	045	1884	WB-1/116	AR
Johnson, Nathan	037	1829	WB-F/100	AR
Johnson, Nicholas	104	1898	WB-7/65	AR
Johnson, Nicholas E.	073	1899	WB-I/148	CTY
Johnson, P. H.	009	1895	WB-2/81	CTY
Johnson, Peter	047	1765	WB-1/152	Nunc.
Johnson, Philip	092	1868	WB-5/95	AR
Johnson, Philip A.	044	1823	WB-9/233	CTY-Nunc.
Johnson, Pleasant	046	c1787	WB-A/197	AR
Johnson, Polly J.	056	1826	WB-1/459	AR
Johnson, R. A.	048	1893	WB-1/10	CTY
Johnson, Rachel	081	1857	WB-10/504	AR
Johnson, Rachel G.	099	1900	WB-D/409	AR
Johnson, Randall	029	1814	WB-A/202	
Johnson, Rebecca	071	1890	WB-7/55	AR
Johnson, Reuben	050	c1840	Orig. Only	AR-Copy
Johnson, Reubin	084	1856	WB-C/230	CTY
Johnson, Richard	011	1881	WB-2/136	
Johnson, Richard	060	1826	WB-1/42	AR
Johnson, Richard	028	1796	WB-B/13	AR
Johnson, Richard M.	038	1896	WB-3/561	AR

Name	Co.	Date	Recorded Copy	Original
Johnson, Rigdon	099	1854	RB-28/589	AR
Johnson, Robert	060	1831	WB-1/227	AR
Johnson, Robert	090	1808	WB-2/93	AR
Johnson, Robert	020	1783	RB-B/1	AR
Johnson, Robert	099	1798	RB-4/215	AR
Johnson, Robert	085	1757	WB-A/70	AR
Johnson, Robert	063	1790	WB-1/165	
Johnson, Robert C.	070	1871	WB-E/231	AR
Johnson, Robert G.	065	1827	WB-D/108	AR
Johnson, Roena	039	1889	WB-U/467	AR
Johnson, Sally	022	1863	WB-D/116	AR
Johnson, Samuel	068	1820	WB-B/5	
Johnson, Samuel	065	1825	WB-D/106	AR
Johnson, Samuel	106	1869	WB-2/5	AR
Johnson, Samuel	063	1815	WB-2/38	
Johnson, Samuel	071	1858	WB-5/209	AR
Johnson, Samuel H.	036	1894	WB-A/310	CTY
Johnson, Sarah	041	1847	WB-3/93	AR
Johnson, Sarah	022	1859	WB-D/29	AR
Johnson, Sarah	071	1789	WB-1/482	AR
Johnson, Sarah A.	068	1896	WB-D/520	
Johnson, Sarah E.	099	c1897	Orig. Only	AR
Johnson, Sill	056	1763	WB-1/783	AR
Johnson, Sill	056	1832	WB-1/484	AR
Johnson, Simon	037	1789	WB-C/101	AR
Johnson, Soasbe	087	1822	WB-1/40	AR
Johnson, Solomon	056	1812	WB-1/384	AR
Johnson, Solomon	087	1832	WB-1/130	
Johnson, Solomon	011	c1831	WB-2/396	
Johnson, Stephen	044	1858	WB-20/432	CTY
Johnson, Stephen	022	1890	WB-E/422 & 428	AR
Johnson, Stephen	044	1829	WB-11/213	CTY
Johnson, Sterling	047	1774	WB-1/352	
Johnson, Sterling	100	1843	WB-38/168	AR
Johnson, Sugar	100	1815	WB-19/125	AR
Johnson, Susan Jane	038	1892	WB-3/302	AR
Johnson, Susanah	024	1718	SS 875/166	SS/AR
Johnson, Tapley	029	1823	WB-B/110	
Johnson, Tarlton	022	1879	WB-E/170	AR
Johnson, Tarlton	046	1821	WB-B/131	AR
Johnson, Tarlton	044	1878	WB-23/313	CTY
Johnson, Taylor	029	1885	WB-E/360	AR
Johnson, Telitha	065	1857	WB-J/38	AR
Johnson, Temperance	071	1869	WB-6/6	AR
Johnson, Thenny	056	1824	WB-1/370	AR
Johnson, Thomas	105	c1854	WB-1/127	AR
Johnson, Thomas	085	c1783	WB-C/218	AR
Johnson, Thomas	044	1824	WB-9/375	CTY
Johnson, Thomas	035	1814	WB-A/234	AR
Johnson, Thomas	056	1829	WB-1/471	AR
Johnson, Thomas	056	c1781	Orig. Only	AR
Johnson, Thomas	104	1786	WB-1/190	AR
Johnson, Travis	056	1790	WB-1/32	AR
Johnson, Trecy	069	1835	WB-1/412	AR
Johnson, U. S.	046	1881	WB-E/307	AR
Johnson, V. Q.	060	1887	013 WB-B/530	
Johnson, Virginia A.	071	1873	WB-6/107	AR
Johnson, W. K.	087	1898	WB-4/86	
Johnson, Walter	084	1830	WB-B/30	CTY
Johnson, Warren	087	1895	WB-3/562	
Johnson, Washington	010	1889	WB-I/261	AR
Johnson, William	071	1777	WB-1/290	
Johnson, William	065	1823	WB-D/106	AR
Johnson, William	001	1861	WB-1/187	AR
Johnson, William	005	1844	WB-B/176	AR
Johnson, William	013	1895	055 WB-A/128	
Johnson, William	005	c1786	WB-1/58	
Johnson, William	065	1847	WB-I/86	
Johnson, William	082	1825	WB-1/263	AR
Johnson, William	047	1817	WB-3/605	
Johnson, William	005	1806	WB-2/76	AR
Johnson, William	072	c1772	Orig. Only	AR
Johnson, William	011	N. D.	WB-1/78	
Johnson, William	090	1883	WB-6/133	AR
Johnson, William	002	1689	Orig. Only	SS/AR
Johnson, William	100	1804	WB-15/20	AR
Johnson, William	044	1816	WB-7/527	CTY
Johnson, William	056	1865	WB-2/53	AR
Johnson, William	092	1869	WB-6/1	
Johnson, William	092	1821	WB-3/148	AR
Johnson, William	081	1850	WB-9/145	AR
Johnson, William	079	1885	WB-2/328	AR
Johnson, William	070	c1825	Orig. Only	AR
Johnson, William	039	1852	WB-N/302	AR
Johnson, William	044	1863	WB-21/741	CTY
Johnson, William	082	1813	WB-1/159	AR
Johnson, William	019	1728	SS 876/140	SS/AR
Johnson, William	085	c1792	WB-C/50	
Johnson, William	099	1880	WB-A/96	AR
Johnson, William	068	1886	WB-D/210	
Johnson, William	087	N. D.	WB-A/48	AR
Johnson, William B.	006	1856	WB-D/12	AR
Johnson, William B.	029	1850	WB-C/163	AR
Johnson, William C.	087	1875	WB-3/103	AR
Johnson, William H.	096	1893	WB-4/146	AR
Johnson, William J.	071	1887	WB-6/566	AR
Johnson, William M.	001	1858	WB-1/145	AR
Johnson, William S.	099	1841	RB-24/527	AR
Johnson, William S.	035	1863	WB-3/71	AR
Johnson, William T.	050	1889	WB-2/55	CTY
Johnson, William W.	099	1896	WB-C/515	AR
Johnson, Willie	056	1855	WB-1/686	AR
Johnson, Willis	026	1860	WB-1/261	AR
Johnson, Willis R.	047	1886	WB-6/421	AR
Johnson, Wood T.	039	1862	WB-R/345	AR
Johnson, Wright	092	1867	WB-5/86	
Johnson, Zacheriah	082	1790	WB-1/36	AR
Johnson, Zebedee	032	1845	WB-1/460	
Johnston, Abraham	028	1844	WB-D/105	AR
Johnston, Abraham	047	1791	WB-3/193	Nunc.
Johnston, Adelia W.	084	1897	WB-F/78	CTY
Johnston, Adeline	084	1893	WB-E/542	CTY
Johnston, Amos	056	1824	WB-1/371	AR
Johnston, Amos	056	c1797	WB-1/112	
Johnston, Amos	037	1816	WB-E/133	AR
Johnston, Andrew	020	1839	RB-N/342	AR
Johnston, Andrew D.	065	1814	WB-D/101	AR
Johnston, Andrew H.	013	1894	WB-C/335	AR
Johnston, Andrew J.	100	1855	WB-44/124	AR
Johnston, Ann	070	1769	WB-C/183	AR
Johnston, Anthony M.	100	1874	WB-51/73	AR
Johnston, Asa M.	101	1897	WB-A/296	AR
Johnston, Benjamin	035	1828	WB-A/239	AR
Johnston, Benjamin	072	c1779	RW/L23	AR
Johnston, Benjamin	020	1847	RB-P/388	
Johnston, Berray	069	c1846	WB-1/542	AR
Johnston, Buck	073	c1891	Orig. Only	AR
Johnston, Burwell	010	1796	WB-D/356	AR
Johnston, Caleb	013	1899	WB-D/323	AR

Name	Co.	Date	Recorded Copy	Original
Johnston, Caroline	010	1793	WB-D/223	AR
Johnston, Catherine	037	1842	WB-F/268	AR
Johnston, Cecilia L.	065	1891	WB-L/562	AR
Johnston, Charles	073	c1789	WB-B/74	AR
Johnston, Charles	028	1788	WB-A/186	AR
Johnston, Charles W.	073	1855	WB-G/82	AR
Johnston, Cyrus	065	1855	WB-J/7	AR
Johnston, D. S.	001	1898	WB-3/247	AR
Johnston, David	016	1855	WB-1/260	
Johnston, David	037	1782	WB-B/101	
Johnston, Edward	037	1778	Orig. Only	AR
Johnston, Elisha	037	1800	WB-D/115	AR
Johnston, Elizabeth	078	1840	WI-14/227	AR
Johnston, Elizabeth	010	1875	WB-I/71	AR
Johnston, Elizabeth	037	1888	WB-H/123	AR
Johnston, Elizabeth	047	1785	WB-3/86	
Johnston, Elizabeth	065	1875	WB-K/218	AR
Johnston, Emily	037	1841	WB-F/264	AR
Johnston, Esther	028	1818	WB-C/170	AR
Johnston, Esther	037	1841	WB-F/249	AR
Johnston, Ezekiel	016	1874	WB-3/111	AR
Johnston, G. W.	079	1892	WB-3/5	AR
Johnston, Gabriel	010	1753	SS 879/153	
Johnston, Gedion	044	1797	WB-4/65	CTY
Johnston, Hannah	035	1783	WB-A/235	AR
Johnston, Henry	086	1823	WB-D/18	AR
Johnston, Henry J.	MD	1886	013 WB-B/382	
Johnston, Hugh	100	1810	WB-15/229	AR
Johnston, Hugh	013	1884	WB-B/321	AR
Johnston, Isabel	073	1836	WB-E/393	AR
Johnston, J. A.	020	1898	WB-B/333	CTY
Johnston, Jacob	100	1870	WB-51/90	AR
Johnston, Jacob	037	1782	Orig. Only	AR
Johnston, Jacob	057	1808	WB-A/311	AR
Johnston, Jacob	037	1808	WB-D/330	AR
Johnston, James	073	c1841	Orig. Only	AR
Johnston, James	001	c1857	WB-1/114	AR
Johnston, James	054	1855	WB-3/94	AR
Johnston, James	065	1819	WB-D/103	AR
Johnston, James	054	c1840	WB-2/227	AR
Johnston, James	060	1805	Orig. Only	AR
Johnston, James	009	1818	OB-A/285	AR
Johnston, James	035	1802	WB-A/249	AR
Johnston, James C.	024	c1863	Copy	047 AR
Johnston, James C.	024	1867	WB-D/57	AR-Copy
Johnston, James J.	020	1895	WB-B/176	CTY
Johnston, James J.	084	1895	WB-F/22	CTY
Johnston, James S.	065	1867	Orig. Only	AR
Johnston, James, Sr.	079	c1817	Orig. Only	AR-Copy
Johnston, Jane	047	1840	WB-4/188	
Johnston, Jennie E.	040	1896	WB-2/500	
Johnston, Jennie E.	065	c1892	060 WB-5/20	060 AR
Johnston, Jennie E.	065	1896	WB-M/445	AR
Johnston, Jesse	047	1836	WB-4/125	
Johnston, John	010	1791	WB-D/158	AR
Johnston, John	035	1845	WB-2/1	AR
Johnston, John	072	1792	Orig. Only	AR
Johnston, John	073	1818	WB-D/549	AR
Johnston, John	081	1810	WB-3/189	AR
Johnston, John	087	c1814	WB-A/77	AR
Johnston, John	085	1816	WB-G/445	AR
Johnston, John	035	1795	WB-A/233	AR-Nunc.
Johnston, John	081	1806	WB-3/37	AR
Johnston, John	010	1801	WB-E/127	AR
Johnston, John	020	1856	RB-R/438	AR
Johnston, John	084	1804	WB-A/14	CTY
Johnston, John	035	1840	Orig. Only	AR
Johnston, John C.	016	1864	WB-2/103	
Johnston, John H.	065	1886	WB-L/151	AR
Johnston, John P.	100	1874	WB-51/193	AR
Johnston, John W.	022	1857	WB-C/453	AR
Johnston, John, Sr.	020	1797	RB-C/232	AR
Johnston, Jonas	037	1779	WB-B/25	AR
Johnston, Jonathan	044	1797	WB-4/160	CTY
Johnston, Joseph	078	1794	WI-1/150	AR
Johnston, Joseph	070	1745	DB-C/83	
Johnston, Joseph	035	1802	WB-A/247	AR
Johnston, Joseph	071	1789	WB-1/480	AR
Johnston, Joseph	024	1790	WB-A/80	AR
Johnston, Joshua	078	1795	WI-1/166	AR
Johnston, Josiah	047	1819	WB-3/643	
Johnston, Josiah	065	1887	WB-L/197	AR
Johnston, Julius	013	1893	WB-C/235	AR
Johnston, Lancelot	020	1832	RB-M/223	AR
Johnston, Lancelot	020	1867	RB-T/243	AR
Johnston, Latta C.	065	1892	WB-M/59	AR
Johnston, Lelah	011	c1789	WB-1/511	
Johnston, Lemuel D.	085	1849	WB-K/90	AR
Johnston, Lemuel M.	020	1878	WB-A/234	
Johnston, Margaret	001	1882	WB-2/190	AR
Johnston, Martha	071	1815	WB-3/144	AR
Johnston, Mary	044	1803	WB-5/330	CTY
Johnston, Mary E.	065	1879	WB-K/321	AR
Johnston, Matthew	070	1857	WB-C/655	AR
Johnston, Matthew	070	1799	WB-AB/31	AR
Johnston, Milas W.	016	1897	WB-4/258	AR
Johnston, Moses	103	1788	WI-A/152	AR
Johnston, Mrs. A. B.	065	1885	WB-L/52	AR
Johnston, Nathaniel	016	1884	WB-3/416	AR
Johnston, Patrick	065	1845	Orig. Only	AR
Johnston, Peter	060	c1786	Orig. Only	AR
Johnston, Polly	020	1880	WB-A/291	CTY
Johnston, R. C.	065	1887	WB-L/194	AR
Johnston, R. H.	065	1867	WB-J/240	AR
Johnston, Rebecca	071	1822	WB-3/262	AR
Johnston, Richard	037	c1814	Orig. Only	AR
Johnston, Richard B.	084	1858	WB-C/269	CTY
Johnston, Richard W.	070	1857	WB-C/631	AR
Johnston, Robert	040	1854	WB-1/60	
Johnston, Robert	060	1815	Orig. Only	AR
Johnston, Robert	085	1841	WB-I/121	AR
Johnston, Robert	085	1815	WB-G/391	AR
Johnston, Robert	047	1823	WB-3/689	
Johnston, Robert	085	c1776	WB-B/22	AR
Johnston, Robert D.	038	1899	WB-4/166	AR
Johnston, Ross	PA	1885	Copy	075 AR
Johnston, Rufus	065	1869	013 WB-B/437	013 AR
Johnston, Rufus D.	085	1863	WB-K/313	AR
Johnston, Rufus M.	065	1869	WB-K/4	AR
Johnston, Sally	100	1848	WB-39/406	AR
Johnston, Saml.	016	1879	WB-3/267	AR
Johnston, Samuel	072	c1756	SS 881/133	
Johnston, Samuel	063	1816	WB-2/38	
Johnston, Samuel	020	1816	RB-G/216	
Johnston, Samuel	078	1874	WB-19/38	AR
Johnston, Samuel I.	024	1866	WB-D/42	AR
Johnston, Samuel N.	016	1897	WB-4/292	AR
Johnston, Samuel W.	010	1807	WB-F/59	AR
Johnston, Samuel W.	078	1865	WB-18/393	AR
Johnston, Sarah	100	1781	WB-3/79	AR

Name	Co.	Date	Recorded Copy	Original
Johnston, Sarah J.	065	1887	WB-L/234	AR
Johnston, Sidney H.	040	1885	WB-2/236	AR
Johnston, Stephen F.	079	1861	WB-1/53	AR
Johnston, Thomas	072	1805	WB-A/63	AR
Johnston, Thomas	072	1752	028 DB-5/260	SS/AR
Johnston, Thomas	082	1795	WB-1/60	AR
Johnston, Thomas	085	1767	WB-A/71	AR
Johnston, Thomas	020	1866	RB-T/180	AR
Johnston, Thomas T.	065	1880	WB-K/395	AR
Johnston, Thompson	010	1826	WB-G/142	AR
Johnston, V. Q.	065	1887	WB-L/236	AR
Johnston, W. D.	105	1873	WB-2/134	AR
Johnston, W. F.	025	1893	Orig. Only	AR
Johnston, W. H.	037	1899	WB-H/451	AR
Johnston, William	013	1890	062 WB-B/118	
Johnston, William	013	1890	WB-C/47	AR
Johnston, William	028	1811	WB-C/25	AR
Johnston, William	085	1798	WB-C/302	AR
Johnston, William	020	1815	RB-G/79	AR
Johnston, William	073	1785	WB-A/333	AR
Johnston, William	065	1813	WB-D/97	AR
Johnston, William	060	1854	WB-2/385	AR
Johnston, William	013	1890	107 WB-2/61	
Johnston, William	020	c1790	Copy	078 AR
Johnston, William	054	c1807	WB-1/33	AR
Johnston, William	DC	c1890	091 WB-1/144	
Johnston, William C.	001	1898	WB-3/211	AR
Johnston, William E.	100	1809	WB-12/340	AR
Johnston, William R.	065	1896	WB-M/454	AR
Johnston, William W.	010	1819	WB-G/51	AR
Joice, Alexander	013	1858	WB-A/191	
Joice, Margaret	013	1852	WB-A/153	
Joiner, David	054	1883	WB-4/576	CTY
Joiner, David	092	1837	WB-4/137	
Joiner, Drewry	069	1828	WB-1/357	AR
Joiner, Drewry	037	1821	WB-E/274	AR
Joiner, Elizabeth	069	1846	WB-1/489	
Joiner, Hardy	069	c1819	Orig. Only	AR
Joiner, Jenny	087	c1805	WB-A/45	AR
Joiner, John	069	1811	WB-1/214	AR
Joiner, John	092	1802	WB-3/50	AR
Joiner, Jordan	069	1847	WB-1/507	AR
Joiner, Joseph	054	N. D.	WB-1A/50	AR
Joiner, Lewis	069	1825	WB-1/326	AR
Joiner, Lucy	071	1770	WB-1/181	
Joiner, Moses	069	1873	WB-1/618	AR
Joiner, Nathan	069	1825	WB-1/332	AR
Joiner, Nathan	069	1840	WB-1/449	AR
Joiner, Patience	099	1811	RB-10/60	AR
Joiner, William	069	1831	WB-1/418	AR
Joiner, William	054	1876	WB-4/229	CTY
Joiner, William	090	1796	WB-1/86	AR-Nunc.
Joines, Ezekiel	104	1803	WB-2/95	AR
Joins, Thomas	004	1868	Orig. Only	AR
Joliff, Asael	047	1852	WB-4/328	
Joliff, Joshua G.	077	1840	WB-F/294	
Jolley, James	026	1853	WB-1/150 & 159	AR
Jolley, Jesse	063	1834	WB-2/197	
Jolley, Jonathan	063	c1820	WB-2/73	
Jolley, Meridith	086	1874	WB-F/51	AR
Jolley, Phillip	053	1774	RW-1/44	AR
Jolley, Terrel	026	1876	WB-2/143	AR
Jolliff, John M.	010	1847	WB-G/417	AR
Jolly, J. E.	099	1890	WB-B/450	AR

Name	Co.	Date	Recorded Copy	Original
Jolly, James	069	1799	WB-1/127	AR
Jolly, Jane	003	1899	WB-B/383	
Jolly, Peter	079	1871	WB-2/52	AR
Jolly, William	086	1838	WB-E/47	AR
Jonacre, Samuel C.	006	c1861	Orig. Only	AR
Jonakin, Elizabeth	039	c1793	WB-A/111	
Jonas, John	060	1863	WB-3/70	
Jones (Pitts), Hagar	028	1898	WB-F/337	
Jones, Aaron	081	1852	Orig. Only	AR
Jones, Aaron	022	1792	RB-1/42	AR
Jones, Abigail	028	1840	WB-D/7	AR
Jones, Abner	044	1862	WB-21/564	CTY
Jones, Abner N.	044	1865	WB-22/328	CTY
Jones, Abraham	053	1788	RW-1/173	
Jones, Abraham	005	1805	WB-2/77	AR
Jones, Abraham	092	1777	WB-1/69	AR
Jones, Aden	019	1808	Orig. Only	AR
Jones, Albridgton	099	1829	RB-21/131	AR
Jones, Albridgton	099	1788	RB-2/156	AR
Jones, Albrittian	047	1845	WB-4/239	
Jones, Alfred	099	1866	RB-34/152	AR
Jones, Alfred	070	1898	WB-H/125	AR
Jones, Alfred D.	099	1894	WB-C/197	AR
Jones, Allen	071	1807	WB-2/354	AR
Jones, Allen	029	1897	WB-F/94	AR
Jones, Allen	069	1797	WB-1/229	AR
Jones, Allen	069	1867	WB-1/599	AR
Jones, Allen	028	1887	WB-E/465	
Jones, Allen B.	071	1828	WB-4/46	AR
Jones, Allen B.	072	1874	WB-4/76	
Jones, Alpheus	099	1854	RB-28/591	AR
Jones, Alsey	099	1854	RB-28/591	AR
Jones, Alston A.	022	1856	WB-C/404	AR
Jones, Alvin	029	1834	WB-B/230	AR
Jones, Alvin	099	1879	WB-A/405	AR
Jones, Amanda M.	037	1884	WB-G/653	
Jones, Ambrose	078	1806	WI-4/137	AR
Jones, Ambrose	078	1858	WB-18/7	AR
Jones, Ambrose	019	c1787	Orig. Only	AR
Jones, Ambrose	044	1792	WB-2/320	CTY
Jones, Ambrose	019	1866	WB-B/12	AR
Jones, Ambrose	092	1881	WB-6/154	AR
Jones, America	044	1854	WB-19/461	CTY
Jones, Amos	070	1819	WB-C/210	AR
Jones, Amos	039	1849	WB-N/323	AR
Jones, Amy Ann	099	1892	WB-C/57	AR
Jones, Andes	069	1822	WB-1/306	AR
Jones, Ann	028	1843	WB-D/73	AR
Jones, Ann A.	044	1844	WB-16/71	CTY
Jones, Anna	038	1872	WB-1/115	AR
Jones, Annie	070	1882	WB-E/478	AR
Jones, Annie	065	1891	WB-L/515	AR
Jones, Annie E.	056	1894	WB-2/187	AR
Jones, Aquilla	073	1846	WB-F/309	AR
Jones, Aquilla	081	1797	WB-2/30	AR
Jones, Aquilla	073	1804	WB-D/119	AR
Jones, Archibald	022	1894	WB-F/94	AR
Jones, Arctus	059	1874	WB-A/71	
Jones, Arpie	099	1886	WB-B/157	AR
Jones, Arthur	103	1829	Orig. Only	AR
Jones, Asa	038	1890	WB-3/171	AR
Jones, Asa	103	1815	RD-3/201	AR
Jones, Asa	028	1840	WB-D/2	AR
Jones, Aseneth	028	1865	WB-D/398	
Jones, Asha	010	1805	WB-E/257	AR

Name	Co.	Date	Recorded Copy	Original
Jones, Atlas	099	1867	RB-34/482	AR
Jones, Augustus	041	c1851	WB-3/144	AR
Jones, Austin	099	1861	RB-31/607	
Jones, Austin	099	1861	SC/05451	AR-Copy
Jones, Austin C.	047	1809	WB-3/484	
Jones, Bailurn C.	028	1866	WB-D/467	
Jones, Barnabas	099	1843	RB-25/345	AR
Jones, Barsheba	056	c1772	WB-2/273	AR
Jones, Bartholomew	053	1800	RW-1/315	AR
Jones, Bartlett	096	1878	WB-4/38	
Jones, Bazzel	057	1845	WB-B/178	AR
Jones, Benjamin	096	1774	WB-1/85	AR
Jones, Benjamin	086	1809	WB-B/227	AR
Jones, Benjamin	015	1777	100 WB-2/122	AR
Jones, Benjamin	104	1821	WB-3/251	AR
Jones, Benjamin	041	1826	WB-2/253	AR
Jones, Benjamin	079	1819	Orig. Only	AR
Jones, Betsey	099	1845	RB-25/576	AR
Jones, Blake	041	1882	WB-4/171	AR
Jones, Brackell	047	1804	WB-3/424	
Jones, Brereton	044	1811	WB-7/154	CTY
Jones, Britain	075	1870	WB-0/8	AR
Jones, Buckner	084	1840	WB-B/232	CTY
Jones, Burrel	056	1804	WB-1/165	AR
Jones, Burrel	056	1820	WB-1/316	AR
Jones, Cadwallader	073	1860	WB-G/251	AR
Jones, Cadwalleder	090	1826	WB-3/153	AR
Jones, Calvert D.	VA	1860	103 RD-13/191	103 AR
Jones, Calvin	011	1885	WB-2/201	
Jones, Candace	099	1896	WB-C/518	AR
Jones, Cassie	078	1871	WB-19/18	AR
Jones, Catharine	073	c1850	Orig. Only	AR
Jones, Catherine	086	1888	Orig. Only	AR
Jones, Catherine	030	1801	WB-2/173	
Jones, Celia	044	1873	WB-23/111	CTY
Jones, Celia	010	1880	WB-I/117	
Jones, Charity	011	1878	WB-2/120	
Jones, Charles	041	1898	WB-4/448	AR
Jones, Charles	099	1842	RB-25/79	AR
Jones, Charles	019	1805	Orig. Only	AR
Jones, Charles	077	1695	SS 874.2/60	SS/AR
Jones, Charles R.	054	1857	WB-3/120	AR
Jones, Charlotte	028	1886	WB-E/453	
Jones, Charlotte	096	1783	WB-1/132	
Jones, Chesley	036	1882	WB-A/31	CTY
Jones, Clem	009	1838	OB-C2/78	AR
Jones, Cloe	028	1839	WB-C/431	AR
Jones, Colen	024	1863	WB-D/14	AR
Jones, Cooper	069	1800	WB-1/251	AR
Jones, Corbon	096	1818	Orig. Only	AR
Jones, Cornelius	075	1715	SS 875/93	SS/AR
Jones, Cornelius	030	1750	Orig. Only	SS/AR
Jones, Council	039	1805	WB-C/21	
Jones, Daniel	014	1832	Orig. Only	AR-Copy
Jones, Daniel	077	1714/5	SS 875/15	SS/AR
Jones, Daniel	014	1832	Copy	099 AR
Jones, Daniel	006	1857	Copy	004 AR
Jones, Daniel	014	1832	Copy	060 AR
Jones, Daniel	006	1857	WB-D/40	
Jones, Daniel	099	c1823	Orig. Only	AR
Jones, David	030	1852	WB-4/167	
Jones, David	085	1795	WB-D/7	AR
Jones, David	070	1793	WB-C/200	AR
Jones, David	041	1854	WB-3/178	AR
Jones, David	041	1798	WB-1/159	AR

Name	Co.	Date	Recorded Copy	Original
Jones, David	030	1775	WB-1/102	
Jones, David	081	1835	WB-6/458	AR
Jones, David	030	1823	WB-3/141	
Jones, David	047	1785	WB-3/88	
Jones, David	053	1753	Orig. Only	SS/AR
Jones, David	044	1866	WB-22/408	CTY
Jones, David	028	1810	WB-C/21	AR
Jones, David, Sr.	053	1757	SS 880/139	SS/AR
Jones, Delia	056	1889	WB-3/504	AR
Jones, Delilah	071	1838	WB-4/172	AR
Jones, Dempsey	041	1825	WB-2/232	AR
Jones, Demsy	041	1808	WB-2/20	AR
Jones, Dorothy	018	1830	WB-C/114	
Jones, Drury	026	1870	Orig. Only	AR
Jones, Drury	039	1847	WB-M/126	AR
Jones, E. H.	056	1896	WB-2/236	AR
Jones, E. P.	026	1862	WB-1/294	AR
Jones, Eady	028	1834	WB-C/373	
Jones, Ebed	013	1849	WB-A/133	
Jones, Ebenezer	083	1880	WB-3/209	AR
Jones, Edmond	022	1834	WB-C/13	AR
Jones, Edmund	071	1859	WB-5/221	AR
Jones, Edmund	044	1782	WB-1/351	CTY
Jones, Edmund	024	1816	WB-C/48	AR
Jones, Edmund W.	030	1875	WB-5/48	AR
Jones, Edmund W.	017	1876	WB-B/62	AR
Jones, Edward	044	c1750	Orig. Only	CTY
Jones, Edward	100	1799	WB-10/148	AR
Jones, Edward	011	1742	Orig. Only	SS/AR
Jones, Edward	041	1881	WB-4/160	AR
Jones, Edward	044	1841	WB-15/105	CTY
Jones, Edward	009	1857	OB-K/276	AR
Jones, Edward	075	1720	SS 875/245	
Jones, Edward D.	028	1880	WB-E/229	
Jones, Edward J.	100	1817	WB-21/5	AR
Jones, Edward S.	AL	1858	072 WB-2/166	
Jones, Edwin	041	1893	WB-4/352	AR
Jones, Eli	105	1875	WB-2/176	AR
Jones, Elias	082	1832	WB-2/22	AR
Jones, Elijah	035	1863	WB-3/69	
Jones, Elinah	084	1852	WB-C/130	CTY
Jones, Elisha	035	1840	Orig. Only	AR
Jones, Eliza	070	1883	Orig. Only	AR
Jones, Elizabeth	073	1864	WB-G/427	CTY
Jones, Elizabeth	050	1897	WB-2/275	CTY
Jones, Elizabeth	022	c1807	WB-A/136	AR
Jones, Elizabeth	056	1848	WB-1/611	AR
Jones, Elizabeth	056	1848	Copy	092 AR
Jones, Elizabeth	045	c1874	WB-1/28	AR
Jones, Elizabeth	003	1878	WB-B/96	AR
Jones, Elizabeth	039	1861	WB-R/15	AR
Jones, Elizabeth	047	1851	WB-4/308	
Jones, Elizabeth	039	1863	WB-R/568	AR
Jones, Elizabeth	070	1857	WB-C/645	AR
Jones, Elizabeth	054	c1807	WB-1A/65	AR
Jones, Elizabeth	039	1814	WB-D/106	AR
Jones, Elizabeth	056	1861	WB-2/17	AR
Jones, Elizabeth	100	1887	WB-51/264	AR
Jones, Elizabeth	054	1852	WB-3/61	AR
Jones, Elizabeth	099	1853	RB-28/222	AR
Jones, Elizabeth	099	1864	RB-33/337	AR
Jones, Elizabeth	053	1765	RW-1/3	AR-Nunc.
Jones, Elizabeth	078	1890	WB-19/271	AR
Jones, Elizabeth	069	1846	Orig. Only	AR
Jones, Ella	038	1897	WB-4/56	AR

Name	Co.	Date	Recorded Copy	Original
Jones, Ellen	054	1898	WB-6/162	CTY
Jones, Emanuel	060	1893	WB-G/119	AR
Jones, Emanuel	072	1789	WI/L14	AR
Jones, Emeline F.	099	1895	WB-C/472	AR
Jones, Emily	051	1842	WB-A/157	
Jones, Emma T.	044	1877	WB-23/244	CTY
Jones, Epaphroditus	051	1768	024 WB-1/28	024 AR
Jones, Ernest H.	019	1890	WB-B/195	AR
Jones, Evan	030	1786	WB-1/204	
Jones, Evan	028	1751	DB-5/268	SS/AR
Jones, Evan	047	1810	WB-3/492	
Jones, Evan	070	1756	DB-D/187	AR
Jones, Evan	028	1753	DB-5/286	SS/AR
Jones, Evan	077	1764	WB-C/40	AR
Jones, Ezekiel	084	1825	WB-A/215	CTY
Jones, Ezekiel	070	1866	WB-D/198	AR
Jones, Fabius H.	099	1864	RB-33/172	AR
Jones, Fedrick	039	N. D.	WB-B/44	
Jones, Ferebe	075	1847	WB-N/206	AR
Jones, Fereby	051	1862	WB-B/45	AR
Jones, Frances	030	1774	WB-1/81	
Jones, Frances	028	1852	WB-D/186	
Jones, Frances A.	069	1788	WB-1/45	AR
Jones, Francis	073	1844	WB-F/198	AR
Jones, Francis	047	1851	WB-4/316	
Jones, Francis	077	1791	WB-C/424	AR
Jones, Francis	071	1784	WB-1/333	AR
Jones, Francis	073	1888	022 WB-E/372	
Jones, Francis	037	1755	Orig. Only	SS/AR
Jones, Frederick	024	1723	SS 876/115	SS/AR
Jones, Frederick	024	c1722	HiDSC	AR-Copy
Jones, Frederick	083	1884	WB-3/317	AR
Jones, Frederick	041	1838	WB-3/4	AR
Jones, Frederick	028	1830	WB-C/322	AR
Jones, Frederick	070	1791	WB-C/196 & 202	AR
Jones, Frederick	028	1880	WB-E/241	
Jones, Frederick	037	1808	WB-D/334	AR
Jones, Frederick	028	1759	SS 882/53	SS/AR
Jones, Fredrick	071	1807	WB-2/344	AR
Jones, G. W.	003	1877	WB-B/84	AR
Jones, G. Wilson	021	1889	WB-2/478	AR
Jones, Gabriel	090	1808	WB-2/101	AR
Jones, Gabriel	082	1794	WB-1/54	AR-Nunc.
Jones, George	104	1830	WB-4/138	
Jones, George	086	1843	WB-E/105	
Jones, George	060	1830	WB-1/163	AR
Jones, George	086	c1842	Copy	050 AR
Jones, George	024	1791	WB-A/87	AR
Jones, George F.	100	1890	WB-51/318	AR
Jones, George H.	028	1900	WB-F/498	
Jones, George W.	013	1859	WB-A/194	
Jones, George W.	084	1837	WB-B/166	CTY
Jones, Gilbert A.	035	1887	WB-4/299	AR
Jones, Gilley Ann	099	1879	WB-A/76	AR
Jones, Gray	099	1889	WB-B/363	AR
Jones, Griffin	078	1861	WB-18/228	AR
Jones, Griffith	011	1782	WB-1/514	
Jones, Griffith	075	1776	WB-I/144	AR
Jones, Hamilton C.	085	1869	WB-1/19	CTY
Jones, Hancy	028	1868	WB-E/11	
Jones, Hannah	070	1810	WB-AB/157	AR
Jones, Hannah	046	1897	WB-F/581	AR
Jones, Harda M.	047	1873	WB-6/80	AR
Jones, Harding	028	1760	DB-8/221	AR
Jones, Hardy	086	1811	WB-C/10	AR
Jones, Hardy	009	c1800	OWB/378	
Jones, Hardy	037	1796	WB-D/3	AR
Jones, Hardy	057	1792	WB-A/163	AR
Jones, Hardy	092	1819	Orig. Only	AR
Jones, Harriet	039	1888	WB-U/463	AR
Jones, Harriet E.	039	1886	WB-U/370	AR
Jones, Harwood	071	1798	WB-2/169	AR
Jones, Harwood	071	1789	WB-1/484	AR
Jones, Henry	099	1893	WB-C/177	AR
Jones, Henry	028	1854	WB-D/234	AR
Jones, Henry	041	1831	WBV-2/293	AR
Jones, Henry	100	1886	WB-51/225	AR
Jones, Henry	047	1808	WB-3/474	
Jones, Henry	053	1900	WB-11/366	AR
Jones, Henry	071	1752	Orig. Only	SS/AR
Jones, Henry	099	1891	Orig. Only	AR-Copy
Jones, Henry	024	1754	Orig. Only	SS/AR
Jones, Henry	070	1870	WB-E/188	AR
Jones, Henry R.	047	1801	WB-3/367	
Jones, Henry W.	044	c1868	WB-23/34	CTY
Jones, Henry, Sr.	037	1757	Orig. Only	SS/AR
Jones, Henry, Sr.	053	1782	RW-1/103	
Jones, Hesekiah	038	c1855	WB-1/132	AR
Jones, Hezekiah	072	1827	WB-1/2	AR
Jones, Hiram	102	1899	WB-A/175	AR
Jones, Holla	044	1860	WB-21/249	CTY
Jones, Holland	009	c1797	OWB/340	AR
Jones, Hugh	053	1826	WB-5/73	
Jones, Hull	072	1796	Orig. Only	AR
Jones, Isaac	075	1776	WB-I/164	AR
Jones, Isaac	073	1831	WB-E/261	AR
Jones, Isaac	011	c1783	WB-1/525	
Jones, Isaac	075	1734	SS 876/349	SS/AR
Jones, Isaac	056	c1817	WB-1/273	AR
Jones, Isaac W.	056	c1895	Orig. Only	AR
Jones, Isam	037	1753	SS 881/50	SS/AR
Jones, Isham	083	1881	WB-3/248	AR
Jones, J. A.	099	1897	WB-D/82	AR
Jones, J. J.	039	1882	WB-U/296	AR
Jones, Jacob	039	1851	WB-N/341	AR
Jones, Jacob	039	1818	WB-F/103	
Jones, Jacob	029	1882	WB-E/279	
Jones, Jacob B.	041	1839	WB-3/15	AR
Jones, James	028	1804	WB-B/206	AR
Jones, James	051	1771	Copy	024 AR
Jones, James	096	c1797	Orig. Only	AR
Jones, James	039	1823	WB-G/173	
Jones, James	041	1824	WB-2/216	AR
Jones, James	073	1891	WB-H/547	CTY
Jones, James	057	1846	WB-B/186	
Jones, James	103	1827	RD-5/363	
Jones, James	010	1868	WB-H/212	AR
Jones, James	096	1754	Orig. Only	AR
Jones, James	057	1802	WB-A/258	AR
Jones, James	096	c1750	SS 879/126	SS/AR
Jones, James	022	1832	WB-B/237	AR
Jones, James	051	1783	Orig. Only	AR-Copy
Jones, James	024	1812	WB-C/16	AR
Jones, James	010	1797	WB-D/369	AR
Jones, James	009	c1796	OWB/327	AR
Jones, James	100	1872	WB-51/41	AR
Jones, James	099	1807	RB-7/214	AR
Jones, James	024	c1765	WB-B/78	AR
Jones, James	028	1801	WB-B/122	AR

Name	Co.	Date	Recorded Copy	Original
Jones, James	092	1815	WB-3/114	AR-Nunc.
Jones, James	057	1796	WB-A/104	AR
Jones, James	099	1777	RB-1/113	AR
Jones, James	041	1836	WB-2/372 & 387	AR
Jones, James	047	1778	WB-2/86	
Jones, James A.	056	1882	WB-3/325	AR
Jones, James A.	022	1890	WB-E/418	AR
Jones, James G.	037	1861	WB-G/215	AR
Jones, James G.	047	1844	WB-4/233	
Jones, James H.	032	1884	WB-3/421	AR
Jones, James H.	082	1897	083 WB-4/241	
Jones, James H.	082	1897	WB-6/558	AR
Jones, James M.	099	1898	WB-D/175	AR
Jones, James, Sr.	028	1833	WB-C/362	AR
Jones, James, Sr.	092	1792	WB-3/6A	AR
Jones, James, Sr.	099	1811	RB-10/6	AR
Jones, Jane	070	1855	WB-C/585	AR
Jones, Jane	065	1890	WB-L/443	AR
Jones, Jane	070	1801	WB-AB/41	AR
Jones, Jarves	046	1837	WB-B/579	AR
Jones, Jeremiah	018	1851	WB-C/352	
Jones, Jesse	103	1847	RD-9/534	AR
Jones, Jesse	028	1890	WB-E/531	
Jones, Jesse	010	1806	WB-F/19	AR
Jones, Jesse	035	1815	WB-A/237	AR-Nunc.
Jones, Jesse	099	1833	RB-22/518	AR
Jones, Jesse	020	1780	RB-A/104	AR
Jones, Jesse	099	1830	RB-21/346	AR
Jones, Jesse	028	1859	WB-D/324	
Jones, Jesse	028	1817	WB-C/146	AR
Jones, Jesse F.	063	c1830	WB-2/180	
Jones, Joel	029	1882	Orig. Only	AR
Jones, Joel	099	1854	RB-28/590	AR
Jones, John	057	1855	WB-B/228	AR
Jones, John	084	1840	WB-B/242	CTY
Jones, John	024	1727	SS 876/98	SS/AR
Jones, John	075	1723	SS 876/193	SS/AR
Jones, John	084	1854	WB-C/187	CTY
Jones, John	024	1755	SS 880/112	SS/AR
Jones, John	047	1810	WB-3/505	
Jones, John	028	1840	WB-D/1	AR
Jones, John	035	1758	SS 882/137	SS/AR
Jones, John	087	c1824	WB-A/114	AR
Jones, John	100	1794	WB-7/208	AR
Jones, John	063	c1790	WB-1/185	
Jones, John	035	1759	087 DB-2/441	
Jones, John	070	1770	WB-C/184	AR
Jones, John	035	1796	WB-A/231	AR
Jones, John	069	1860	WB-1/567	AR
Jones, John	070	1812	WB-AB/177	AR
Jones, John	071	1759	Orig. Only	SS/AR
Jones, John	010	1751	SS 879/14	SS/AR
Jones, John	077	1856	WB-F/480	AR
Jones, John	096	1794	Orig. Only	AR
Jones, John	004	1865	WB-1/15	
Jones, John	044	1860	WB-21/210	CTY
Jones, John	037	1758	SS 882/158	SS/AR
Jones, John	103	1839	RD-7/443	AR
Jones, John	006	1869	WB-D/79	AR
Jones, John	086	1821	WB-C/159	AR
Jones, John	012	1892	WB-A/90	AR
Jones, John	019	1879	WB-B/114	AR
Jones, John	104	1813	WB-3/55	AR
Jones, John	009	1859	OB-L/30	AR
Jones, John	092	1876	WB-6/75	AR
Jones, John	081	1822	WB-5/75	AR
Jones, John	009	1817	OB-A/267	AR
Jones, John	079	c1793	Orig. Only	028 AR
Jones, John	063	1837	WB-2/233	
Jones, John	N	c1712	SS 875/21	
Jones, John	073	1847	WB-F/340	AR
Jones, John	056	1850	Orig. Only	AR
Jones, John	099	1849	RB-26/534	AR
Jones, John	047	1794	WB-3/226	
Jones, John	020	1811	RB-F/173	AR
Jones, John	024	1744	Orig. Only	SS/AR
Jones, John	084	c1799	OW/58a	AR
Jones, John	075	1729	Orig. Only	SS/AR
Jones, John	075	1707/8	Orig. Only	SS/AR
Jones, John	072	1803	WB-A/68	AR
Jones, John A.	106	1900	WB-2/472	
Jones, John A.	004	1876	WB-A/19	AR
Jones, John A.	028	1897	WB-F/303	
Jones, John B.	030	1865	WB-4/253	
Jones, John B.	103	1851	RD-10/474	AR
Jones, John B. W.	100	1898	WB-51/505	AR
Jones, John C.	099	1810	RB-9/224	AR
Jones, John D.	070	1855	WB-C/597	AR
Jones, John E.	020	1862	RB-S/521	AR
Jones, John E.	069	1900	WB-6/100	AR
Jones, John G.	092	1891	WB-6/329	AR
Jones, John G.	057	1883	WB-C/96	AR
Jones, John H.	086	1880	WB-F/156	AR
Jones, John H.	028	1833	WB-C/356	AR
Jones, John H.	099	1880	WB-A/123	AR
Jones, John J.	020	1885	WB-A/457	CTY
Jones, John M.	024	1879	WB-E/76	AR
Jones, John M.	054	1832	Orig. Only	AR
Jones, John S.	038	c1859	WB-1/151	AR
Jones, John V.	084	1854	WB-C/190	CTY
Jones, John W.	006	1873	WB-E/5	AR
Jones, John W.	073	1878	WB-H/193	CTY
Jones, John W.	084	1866	WB-D/73	CTY
Jones, John W.	100	1870	WB-51/17	AR
Jones, John W.	046	1817	WB-B/38	AR
Jones, John Wesley	075	c1857	WB-M2/46	AR
Jones, John, Sr.	099	1846	RB-26/148	AR
Jones, John, Sr.	070	1847	WB-AB/456	AR
Jones, John, Sr.	086	1825	WB-D/40	AR
Jones, John, Sr.	010	1736	LGB-4/#42	SS/AR
Jones, Johnson M.	021	1868	WB-2/3	
Jones, Jonas	028	1810	WB-C/7	
Jones, Jonas	028	1817	WB-C/142	
Jones, Jonas	057	1850	WB-B/205	AR
Jones, Jonas	057	1839	WB-B/139	AR
Jones, Jonathan	073	1866	WB-G/506	CTY
Jones, Jonathan	075	1740	LGB-4/#108	SS/AR
Jones, Jonathan	106	c1855	WB-1/33	AR
Jones, Jonathan	011	1873	WB-2/67	
Jones, Joseph	077	1793	WB-C/449	
Jones, Joseph	018	1835	WB-C/186	
Jones, Joseph	077	1809	WB-E/330	AR
Jones, Joseph	032	1833	WB-1/202	AR
Jones, Joseph	070	1756	DB-D/235	
Jones, Joseph	063	c1797	WB-1/323	
Jones, Joseph	030	1799	WB-2/137	
Jones, Joseph	N	c1756	Orig. Only	SS/AR
Jones, Joseph	077	1819	WB-F/16	AR
Jones, Joseph	018	1803	Orig. Only	AR-Copy

Name	Co.	Date	Recorded Copy	Original
Jones, Joseph	041	1785	WB-1/49	AR
Jones, Joseph	012	1805	WB-B/77	AR
Jones, Joseph S.	024	1864	WB-D/27	AR
Jones, Joseph S.	075	1879	WB-O/113	AR
Jones, Joshua	047	1802	WB-3/374	
Jones, Joshua	028	1847	WB-D/138	AR
Jones, Joshua	050	1873	WB-1/135	CTY
Jones, Joshua	056	1869	WB-3/12	AR
Jones, Joshua	099	1844	RB-25/456	AR
Jones, Joshua	038	1888	WB-3/75	AR
Jones, Joshua	077	1814	WB-E/406	AR
Jones, Joshua	041	1866	WB-3/337	AR
Jones, Josiah	099	1850	RB-27/136	AR
Jones, Josiah	028	1817	Orig. Only	AR
Jones, Josiah	041	1845	WB-3/59	AR
Jones, Josiah	028	1810	Orig. Only	AR
Jones, Josiah	018	1850	WB-C/346	
Jones, Josiah H.	024	1871	WB-E/21	AR
Jones, Josias	009	c1760	OWB/76	AR
Jones, Jubilee R.	044	1879	WB-23/328	CTY
Jones, Julan	069	1800	WB-1/131	AR
Jones, Julia A.	106	1883	WB-2/172	AR
Jones, Julia W.	106	1879	WB-2/150	
Jones, Katharine	032	1867	WB-2/352	AR
Jones, Keziah	028	1801	WB-B/130	AR
Jones, Kilby	057	1814	WB-B/128	AR
Jones, Kimbrough	099	1866	RB-34/149	AR
Jones, L. C.	068	1889	WB-D/314	
Jones, L. W.	106	1895	WB-2/363	
Jones, Lafayette	013	1896	WB-C/496	
Jones, Lancelot	087	1862	WB-2/38	AR
Jones, Lazarus	069	1810	WB-1/204	AR
Jones, Lemuel	018	1825	WB-C/44	
Jones, Leroy	099	1865	RB-33/355	AR
Jones, Letitia L.	099	1892	WB-C/52	AR
Jones, Levi	092	1814	WB-3/109	AR
Jones, Levi	011	1849	WB-1/178	
Jones, Lewellen	044	1840	WB-14/604	CTY
Jones, Lewelling	039	c1794	WB-A/208	
Jones, Lewis	009	1871	WB-1/88	CTY
Jones, Lewis	059	1869	WB-A/1	
Jones, Lewis	024	1763	WB B/79	AR
Jones, Lewis	022	1863	WB-D/101	AR
Jones, Lewis	099	1839	RB-24/257	AR
Jones, Lewis, Sr.	099	1815	RB-12/9	AR
Jones, Littleton	044	1898	WB-24/395	CTY
Jones, Louis	069	1899	WB-6/78	AR
Jones, Lovick	028	1817	WB-C/156	AR
Jones, Loyd	072	1777	RW/L12	AR
Jones, Lucinda	098	1896	WB-A/257	CTY
Jones, Lucretia	028	1860	WB-D/339	
Jones, Lucy	047	1881	WB-6/276	AR
Jones, Lucy	044	1843	WB-15/487	CTY
Jones, Lucy F.	046	1893	WB-E/554	AR
Jones, Lura Ann	059	1876	WB-A/102	
Jones, Lydia	030	1826	WB-3/215	
Jones, Madison	099	1876	RB-35/357	AR
Jones, Major	079	1886	WB-2/359	AR
Jones, Malachi	030	1822	WB-3/121	
Jones, Malachi	077	1777	WB-C/190	AR
Jones, Malachi	030	1880	WB-5/73	AR
Jones, Malachi	030	1838	WB-4/43	
Jones, Margaret	050	1883	WB-1/247	CTY
Jones, Margaret	047	1870	WB-6/32	AR
Jones, Margaret	070	1791	WB-C/197	AR

Name	Co.	Date	Recorded Copy	Original
Jones, Maria	047	1861	WB-5/99	AR-Copy
Jones, Marmaduke	070	1788	WB-C/178	AR
Jones, Martha	003	1863	Orig. Only	AR
Jones, Martha	083	1876	WB-3/122	AR
Jones, Martha	044	1851	WB-18/270	CTY
Jones, Martha	084	1891	WB-E/478	CTY
Jones, Martha	063	1821	WB-2/74	
Jones, Martha	035	1831	WB-1/9	AR
Jones, Martha Ann	100	1838	WB-37/39	AR
Jones, Martha E.	059	1888	WB-A/513	CTY
Jones, Marthy	010	1840	Orig. Only	AR
Jones, Martin	044	1884	WB-23/491	CTY
Jones, Martin	099	1859	RB-31/258	AR
Jones, Martin	053	1853	WB-7/551	AR
Jones, Mary	100	1785	WB-4/145	AR
Jones, Mary	010	1748	Orig. Only	SS/AR
Jones, Mary	092	1832	WB-4/50	
Jones, Mary	030	1823	WB-3/156	
Jones, Mary	069	1851	WB-1/526	AR
Jones, Mary	073	1844	WB-F/187	AR
Jones, Mary	071	1842	WB-4/246	AR
Jones, Mary	028	1806	WB-B/240	AR
Jones, Mary	044	1841	WB-15/107	CTY
Jones, Mary Ann	028	1787	Orig. Only	AR
Jones, Mary C.	032	1859	WB-2/167	AR
Jones, Mary E.	022	1837	WB-C/55	AR
Jones, Mary E.	030	1898	WB-5/260	AR
Jones, Mary F.	099	1890	WB-B/443	AR
Jones, Mary H.	046	1890	WB-F/189	AR
Jones, Mary J.	SC	1898	013 WB-D/163	013 AR
Jones, Mary M.	100	1850	WB-40/316	AR
Jones, Mary M.	049	1892	WB-2/291	AR
Jones, Mary M.	019	1900	WB-C/27	AR
Jones, Mary N.	071	1886	WB-6/539	
Jones, Mary W.	099	1891	WB-B/505	AR
Jones, Matthew	022	1793	RB-2/6	AR
Jones, Matthew	083	1843	WB-1/428	AR
Jones, Maurice	053	1792	RW-1/219	AR
Jones, Maurice	053	c1819	WB-4/100	AR
Jones, Mc. G.	037	c1876	WB-G/596	
Jones, Michael	VA	1796	044 WB-4/49	044 CTY
Jones, Middleton	081	1889	WB-16/126	AR
Jones, Miles	075	1834	WB-N/107	AR
Jones, Miles	018	1858	WB-D/43	
Jones, Milly	105	1878	WB-2/221	AR
Jones, Miriam	077	1822	WB-F/47	AR
Jones, Moriss	053	1756	SS 880/83	SS/AR
Jones, Morris	028	1813	WB-C/64	AR
Jones, Moses	078	1854	WB-17/247	AR
Jones, Moses	073	1861	WB-G/368	CTY
Jones, Moses, Sr.	011	1846	WB-1/128	
Jones, Musgrove	011	1852	WB-1/205	
Jones, Musgrove	011	c1850	SC/06279	AR-Copy
Jones, Nancy	103	1858	RD-12/496	AR
Jones, Nancy	099	1891	WB-B/572	AR
Jones, Nancy	018	1859	WB-D/52	
Jones, Nancy	053	1842	WB-6/177	AR
Jones, Nancy	024	c1785	WB-B/76	AR-Nunc.
Jones, Nancy	071	1885	WB-6/451	AR
Jones, Nancy	037	1794	WB-C/295	AR
Jones, Nancy	047	1865	WB-5/131	
Jones, Nancy	041	1850	WB-3/136	AR
Jones, Nancy	079	1881	WB-2/232	AR
Jones, Nathan H.	029	1882	Orig. Only	AR
Jones, Nathaniel	071	1783	WB-1/335	AR

Name	Co.	Date	Recorded Copy	Original
Jones, Nathaniel	056	1829	WB-1/469	AR
Jones, Nathaniel	099	1810	RB-9/181	AR
Jones, Nathaniel	099	1815	RB-11/371	AR
Jones, Nathaniel	099	1828	RB-20/281	AR
Jones, Nathaniel	005	1895	WB-D/360	AR
Jones, Newsom	069	1797	WB-1/115	AR
Jones, Nice	009	1843	OB-E/182	AR
Jones, Nicholas	073	1830	WB-E/216	AR
Jones, Patience	065	1821	WB-D/104	AR
Jones, Penelope	099	1859	RB-31/221	AR
Jones, Peter	N	c1731	Orig. Only	SS/AR
Jones, Peter	100	1833	WB-34/53	AR
Jones, Peter	047	1760	WB-1/4	
Jones, Peter	077	1753	SS 881/42	SS/AR
Jones, Peter, Sr.	077	1752	Orig. Only	SS/AR
Jones, Philip	056	1761	WB-1/761	AR
Jones, Philip	070	1787	WB-C/191	AR
Jones, Pompey	047	1852	WB-4/324	
Jones, Pride	073	1889	WB-H/466	CTY
Jones, Priscilla	032	1844	WB-1/428	AR
Jones, Priscilla	053	1888	WB-11/202	AR
Jones, R. L. T.	013	1896	Orig. Only	AR
Jones, Rachel	087	1887	028 WB-E/460	
Jones, Rachel	077	1797	WB-E/87	
Jones, Randal	030	1799	WB-2/136	
Jones, Randolph	030	1799	WB-2/154	
Jones, Rebecca	026	1860	WB-1/250	AR
Jones, Rebecca J.	047	1886	100 WB-51/195	
Jones, Redding	099	1816	RB-12/267	AR
Jones, Redding H.	072	c1816	WB-A/61	AR
Jones, Reuben	044	1831	WB-12/39	CTY
Jones, Reuben	028	c1816	Orig. Only	AR-Copy
Jones, Rhody	010	1871	WB-I/33	AR
Jones, Rhody	083	1834	WB-1/285	AR
Jones, Richard	103	1783	WI-A/36	AR
Jones, Richard	039	1864	WB-R/752	AR
Jones, Richard	020	1861	RB-S/353	AR
Jones, Richard	099	1836	RB-23/546	AR
Jones, Richard	024	1848	WB-C/285	AR
Jones, Richard	100	1794	WB-7/206	AR
Jones, Richard	001	1862	WB-1/204	AR
Jones, Richard	045	1872	WB-1/22	
Jones, Richard	063	1815	WB-2/34	
Jones, Richard	078	1797	WI-2/62	AR
Jones, Richard H.	020	1891	WB-B/65	CTY
Jones, Richard M.	073	1899	WB-I/159	CTY
Jones, Richard M.	084	1897	WB-F/81	CTY
Jones, Richmond	103	1855	RD-12/19	AR
Jones, Riddick	041	1848	WB-3/104	AR
Jones, Ridley	047	1825	WB-4/14	
Jones, Ridley P.	056	1900	WB-4/237	AR
Jones, Robert	096	c1802	WB-2/12	AR
Jones, Robert	078	1840	WI-14/226	
Jones, Robert	071	1766	WB-1/135	
Jones, Robert	035	1828	WB-A/243	AR
Jones, Robert	047	1794	WB-3/237	
Jones, Robert	049	1809	WI-A/1	AR
Jones, Robert	078	1847	WB-13/2	AR
Jones, Robert	071	1795	WB-2/140	AR-Nunc.
Jones, Robert	100	1815	WB-19/121	AR
Jones, Robert	009	c1802	OWB/397	AR
Jones, Robert B.	099	c1867	Orig. Only	AR
Jones, Robert B.	044	1866	WB-22/458	CTY
Jones, Robert L.	100	1856	WB-49/1	AR

Name	Co.	Date	Recorded Copy	Original
Jones, Robert S.	100	1880	WB-51/181	AR
Jones, Roger	009	1741	Orig. Only	SS/AR
Jones, Roger	028	1801	WB-B/135	AR
Jones, Roger	028	1802	WB-B/142	AR
Jones, Roger	028	1830	WB-C/314 & 324	AR
Jones, Roland	LA	1869	085 WB-1/343	085 CTY
Jones, Rosamond	047	1810	WB-3/508	
Jones, Rowland	092	c1831	WB-4/32	
Jones, Russel R.	092	1858	WB-5/42	
Jones, Ruth	022	1881	WB-E/221	AR
Jones, Salley	071	1806	WB-2/317	AR
Jones, Sallie M.	039	1895	WB-V/68	AR
Jones, Sally Ann	079	1883	WB-2/272	AR
Jones, Sally K.	099	1874	RB-35/270	AR
Jones, Samuel	106	1869	WB-2/3	AR
Jones, Samuel	100	1793	Orig. Only	AR
Jones, Samuel	085	c1775	WB-A/202	AR
Jones, Samuel	037	1779	WB-B/34	AR
Jones, Samuel	044	1806	WB-6/289	CTY
Jones, Samuel	099	1894	WB-C/337	AR
Jones, Samuel	030	1726	SS 876/37	SS/AR
Jones, Samuel	056	1885	WB-3/385	AR
Jones, Samuel B.	SC	1894	080 WB-1/289	080 AR
Jones, Sarah	072	1845	WB-2/62	
Jones, Sarah	081	1836	WB-7/28	AR
Jones, Sarah	039	1863	WB-R/396	AR
Jones, Sarah	047	1792	WB-3/209	
Jones, Sarah	041	1845	WB-3/61	AR
Jones, Sarah	071	1832	WB-4/91	AR
Jones, Sarah	020	1845	RB-P/194	AR
Jones, Sarah	099	1857	RB-30/216	AR
Jones, Sarah	090	1824	WB-3/124	AR
Jones, Sarah	070	1798	WB-AB/16	AR
Jones, Sarah	008	1723	Orig. Only	SS/AR
Jones, Sarah	084	c1787	OW/26	AR
Jones, Sarah	071	1841	WB-4/234	AR
Jones, Sarah	084	c1787	Copy	090 AR
Jones, Sarah C. S.	041	1881	WB-4/153	
Jones, Sarah E.	051	1894	WB-C/484	AR
Jones, Sarah J.	028	1850	WB-D/163	
Jones, Sarah J.	011	1896	WB-3/77	CTY
Jones, Sarah L.	017	1878	WB-B/83	AR
Jones, Sarah M.	086	1900	WB-G/36	AR
Jones, Seburn	022	1884	WB-E/296	AR
Jones, Servan	071	1809	WB-3/15	AR
Jones, Seth	099	1866	RB-34/156	AR
Jones, Seth B.	099	1862	RB-32/337	AR
Jones, Shadrick	087	c1802	WB-A/36	AR
Jones, Silas	082	1852	WB-4/55	AR
Jones, Silas	092	c1840	WB-4/227	
Jones, Simon	045	1865	WB-1/54	AR
Jones, Simon	056	1878	WB-3/207	AR
Jones, Simon	039	c1833	Copy	099 AR
Jones, Simon J.	039	1837	WB-K/121	AR
Jones, Smith	075	1818	WB-M1/322	AR
Jones, Solomon	085	c1804	WB-C/307	AR
Jones, Solomon	035	1830	WB-1/4	AR
Jones, Solomon	050	1899	WB-2/313	
Jones, Solomon	053	1792	RW-1/217	AR
Jones, Solomon F.	054	1874	WB-4/156	CTY
Jones, Sophia H.	024	c1862	WB-E/93	AR
Jones, Spencer	038	1862	WB-G/226	AR
Jones, Starling	026	1864	WB-1/354	AR

Name	Co.	Date	Recorded Copy	Original
Jones, Stephen	078	1835	WI-13/17	AR
Jones, Stephen	035	1838	Orig. Only	AR
Jones, Sterling	086	1817	WB-C/81	AR
Jones, Sugar	022	1854	WB-C/367	AR
Jones, Sugar	044	1761	Orig. Only	CTY
Jones, Susan	028	1848	WB-D/142	
Jones, Susan J.	028	1899	WB-F/372	
Jones, Susanah	100	1815	WB-19/181	AR
Jones, Susannah	053	1797	RW-1/288	AR
Jones, Sylvia	098	1897	WB-A/271	CTY
Jones, Tabitha	103	1851	RD-10/479	AR
Jones, Tabitha	037	1863	WB-G/232	AR
Jones, Taylor,Sr.	030	1780	WB-1/142	
Jones, Temperance	099	1859	RB-31/154	
Jones, Tena	028	1895	WB-F/185	
Jones, Thamar	100	1824	WB-26/176	AR
Jones, Theophilus	103	1786	WI-A/73	AR
Jones, Thomas	029	1900	WB-F/212	AR
Jones, Thomas	081	1836	WB-7/1	AR
Jones, Thomas	024	1797	WB-A/281	AR
Jones, Thomas	029	1804	WB-A/66	
Jones, Thomas	009	c1781	OWB/165	AR
Jones, Thomas	090	1828	WB-3/178	
Jones, Thomas	024	c1763	WB-A/275	AR
Jones, Thomas	013	1832	WB-A/13	
Jones, Thomas	085	c1819	SC/03349	AR-Copy
Jones, Thomas	044	1837	WB-14/130	CTY
Jones, Thomas	032	1825	WB-1/40	AR
Jones, Thomas	053	1826	Orig. Only	AR
Jones, Thomas	047	1808	WB-3/478	
Jones, Thomas	063	1878	WB-3/155	AR-Copy
Jones, Thomas	024	c1775	WB-A/149	AR
Jones, Thomas	077	1788	WB-C/362	AR
Jones, Thomas	099	1779	RB-1/141	AR
Jones, Thomas	N	c1713	SS 875/29	
Jones, Thomas	070	1774	WB-C/185	
Jones, Thomas	028	1846	WB-D/122	AR
Jones, Thomas	047	1825	WB-4/13	
Jones, Thomas	053	1806	RW-1/396	
Jones, Thomas	029	1847	WB-C/154	
Jones, Thomas	017	c1854	WB-A/95	AR
Jones, Thomas	009	c1796	OWB/317	AR
Jones, Thomas	029	1813	WB-A/195	
Jones, Thomas	071	1765	WB-1/126	
Jones, Thomas	005	1866	WB-C/253	AR
Jones, Thomas	051	1839	WB-A/139	
Jones, Thomas	085	1819	Orig. Only	AR
Jones, Thomas	010	c1754	SS 879/173	SS/AR
Jones, Thomas B.	039	1865	WB-S/98	
Jones, Thomas C.	069	1810	WB-1/192	AR
Jones, Thomas D.	069	1895	WB-5/480	AR
Jones, Thomas L.	PA	1887	Copy	069 AR
Jones, Thomas W.	010	1875	WB-I/65	AR
Jones, Tignal	099	1850	RB-27/62	AR
Jones, Timothy	096	1831	WB-2/102	AR
Jones, Tingnall	099	1807	RB-7/295	AR
Jones, Tobias	103	1850	RD-10/401	AR
Jones, Tranquily	022	1900	WB-F/187	AR
Jones, Travis	046	1838	WB-C/17	AR
Jones, Turner M.	046	1890	WB-F/59	AR
Jones, Vinkler	044	c1817	WB-12/229	CTY
Jones, W. D.	099	1891	WB-B/553	AR
Jones, W. F., Sr.	001	1900	WB-3/308	AR
Jones, W. H.	084	c1862	WB-D/74	CTY
Jones, Walter	008	1728	009 OWB/6	009 AR
Jones, Walter	009	c1800	OWB/371	AR
Jones, Wendell	028	1888	WB-E/480	
Jones, Wesley	099	1865	RB-33/432	AR
Jones, Wesley T.	099	1887	WB-B/206	AR
Jones, Wiley	022	1879	WB-E/174	AR
Jones, Wiley	010	1898	WB-I/547	
Jones, Wiley	013	1864	WB-A/222	
Jones, Wiley	078	1826	WI-10/240	
Jones, Wilie	056	1869	WB-3/16	AR
Jones, Wilkerson	071	1876	WB-6/185	AR
Jones, William	044	1890	WB-24/110	CTY
Jones, William	024	1774	Orig. Only	SS/AR
Jones, William	096	1774	063 WB-1/436	
Jones, William	024	1817	WB-C/58	AR
Jones, William	078	1885	WB-19/185	
Jones, William	099	1859	RB-31/148	AR
Jones, William	075	1772	WB-H/162	AR
Jones, William	041	1881	WB-4/145	
Jones, William	077	1794	WB-E/16	
Jones, William	009	1742	Orig. Only	SS/AR
Jones, William	099	1800	RB-5/64	AR
Jones, William	051	1874	WB-C/134	AR
Jones, William	071	1766	WB-1/134	
Jones, William	044	1804	WB-6/129	CTY
Jones, William	078	1864	WB-18/389	
Jones, William	057	1795	WB-A/134	AR
Jones, William	018	1834	WB-C/162	
Jones, William	057	1842	WB-B/154	AR
Jones, William	099	1849	RB-26/588	AR
Jones, William	037	1750	Orig. Only	SS/AR
Jones, William	056	1844	WB-1/562	AR
Jones, William	078	1896	WB-19/400	AR
Jones, William	099	1796	RB-3/276	AR
Jones, William	072	1837	WB-2/4	
Jones, William	010	1736	LGB-4/#31	SS/AR
Jones, William	070	1802	WB-AB/65	AR
Jones, William	071	1807	WB-2/342	AR
Jones, William	028	1880	WB-E/231	
Jones, William	013	1845	WB-A/106	
Jones, William	082	1839	WB-2/88	AR
Jones, William	024	1723	SS 876/306	SS/AR
Jones, William	044	1829	WB-11/258	CTY
Jones, William	010	1790	WB-D/133	AR
Jones, William	022	1885	WB-E/313	AR
Jones, William	028	1838	WB-C/421	AR
Jones, William	072	c1780	RW/L31	AR
Jones, William	047	1759	SS 881/208	SS/AR
Jones, William	084	1813	WB-A/96	CTY
Jones, William	047	1762	WB-1/65	
Jones, William	024	1733	SS 876/308	SS/AR
Jones, William	071	c1784	WB-1/336	
Jones, William	028	1775	Orig. Only	AR
Jones, William	077	1752	Orig. Only	SS/AR
Jones, William	077	1836	WB-F/253	AR
Jones, William	028	1816	WB-C/130	AR
Jones, William	057	1868	WB-B/266	AR
Jones, William	099	1816	RB-12/365	AR
Jones, William	028	1829	WB-C/308	AR
Jones, William	047	1794	WB-3/236	
Jones, William	039	1848	WB-N/315	AR
Jones, William	047	1759	WB-3/209	
Jones, William	070	1790	WB-C/194	AR
Jones, William	070	1782	WB-C/188	AR

Name	Co.	Date	Recorded Copy	Original
Jones, William C.	073	1859	WB-G/222	AR
Jones, William E.	021	1900	WB-3/259	AR
Jones, William G.	100	1845	WB-38/393	AR
Jones, William H.	044	1880	WB-23/387	CTY-Nunc.
Jones, William H.	024	1732	SS 876/251	SS/AR
Jones, William H.	022	1865	WB-D/125	AR
Jones, William H.	099	1879	WB-A/93	AR
Jones, William J.	041	1888	WB-4/282	AR
Jones, William J.	078	1876	WB-19/55	
Jones, William M.	037	1884	WB-G/695	
Jones, William R.	041	1873	WB-4/32	AR
Jones, William T.	047	1772	WB-1/326	
Jones, William W.	039	1880	WB-U/218	AR
Jones, Willie	047	1801	WB-3/355	
Jones, Willie	099	1847	RB-26/194	AR
Jones, Willie W.	047	1837	WB-4/159 & 165	
Jones, Willis	099	1779	RB-1/143	AR
Jones, Willis	056	1818	WB-1/286	AR
Jones, Willis M.	060	1893	WB-4/517	AR
Jones, Willis S.	073	1857	WB-G/181	CTY
Jones, Willoughby	018	1822	WB-C/12	
Jones, Winiford	010	1871	WB-I/36	AR
Jones, Winnefred	099	1841	RB-24/493	AR
Jones, Yarberry N.	106	c1874	Orig. Only	AR
Jones, Zachariah	024	1803	WB-B/197	AR
Jonnesse, Samuel C.	006	c1861	WB-D/61	
Jons, Charles	010	1748	Orig. Only	SS/AR
Jonson, Arthur	009	c1773	OWB/116	AR
Jonson, Lewis	028	1712/3	PQS.1/10	
Jonston, Thomas	044	1806	WB-6/320	CTY
Joplin, Lyddea	099	1842	RB-25/127	AR
Joplin, Mark	099	1815	RB-12/8	AR
Jopling, Ralph	017	c1843	WB-A/11	AR
Jopling, Rebecca	014	c1852	Orig. Only	AR-Copy
Jordan, A. Smith	077	1897	WB-H/298	AR
Jordan, Abraham	028	1827	WB-C/291	AR
Jordan, Alfred	063	1891	WB-4/86	AR
Jordan, Amanda R.	105	1868	WB-1/135	AR
Jordan, Amos	099	1796	RB-3/264	AR
Jordan, Angelina	051	1890	WB-C/414	AR
Jordan, Ann	053	c1815	WB-4/86	
Jordan, Ann M.	044	c1869	WB-23/22	CTY
Jordan, Arthur	071	1755	SS 880/51	SS/AR
Jordan, Arthur	071	1840	WB-4/208	AR
Jordan, Arthur	071	1752	Orig. Only	SS/AR
Jordan, Arthur	044	1793	WB-3/63	CTY
Jordan, Beatrice	015	1774	100 WB-2/17	AR
Jordan, Benjamin	011	c1810	WB-2/303	
Jordan, Benjamin	071	1802	WB-2/211	AR
Jordan, Charles	024	1773	WB-B/145	AR
Jordan, Cornelias	037	1794	WB-C/261	AR
Jordan, Cornelius	037	1854	WB-G/83	AR
Jordan, Daniel P.	103	1890	WB-1/514	AR
Jordan, David W.	073	1896	WB-I/97	CTY
Jordan, Deborah	011	1770	Orig. Only	SS/AR
Jordan, Dinah	053	c1814	RW-1/515	
Jordan, Dovie D.	065	1895	WB-M/360	AR
Jordan, Eadath	037	1835	WB-F/180	AR
Jordan, Elijah	024	1897	WB-E/280	AR
Jordan, Eliza	077	1864	WB-F/552	AR
Jordan, Elizabeth	009	1891	WB-2/39	CTY
Jordan, Emma C.	010	1878	WB-I/96	
Jordan, Esther	024	1836	WB-C/192	AR
Jordan, Eugene L.	105	1896	WB-3/214	AR
Jordan, Frederick	103	1795	WI-A/541	
Jordan, George	001	c1855	WB-1/84	AR
Jordan, George	065	1899	WB-N/233	AR
Jordan, George	071	1792	WB-2/9	
Jordan, George	071	1840	WB-4/213	AR
Jordan, George	044	1761	Orig. Only	CTY
Jordan, Gray	037	1841	WB-F/263	AR
Jordan, Green D.	046	1891	WB-F/82	AR
Jordan, Hannah R.	093	1876	WB-1/175	
Jordan, Henry	071	1780	WB-1/232	
Jordan, Henry	056	1820	WB-1/308	AR
Jordan, Henry	037	1837	WB-F/210	AR
Jordan, Henry C.	079	1860	WB-1/39	AR
Jordan, Horace H.	022	1878	WB-E/152	AR
Jordan, Ichabod	077	1820	WB-F/31	AR
Jordan, Isaac	024	1864	WB-D/22	AR
Jordan, Isaac	010	1790	WB-D/118	AR
Jordan, Isaac	010	1790	Copy	024 AR
Jordan, Jacob	024	c1795	WB-B/102	AR
Jordan, Jacob	024	1826	WB-C/126	AR
Jordan, James	010	1836	WB-G/254	AR
Jordan, James	103	1782	WI-A/13	AR
Jordan, James B.	010	1804	WB-E/241	AR
Jordan, James W.	071	1888	WB-7/26	AR
Jordan, James, Sr.	099	1785	RB-2/79	AR
Jordan, James, Sr.	099	1796	RB-3/253	
Jordan, Jesse N.	010	1888	WB-I/249	AR
Jordan, John	053	1775	RW-1/62	
Jordan, John	096	c1780	Orig. Only	AR
Jordan, John	009	c1774	OWB/119	AR
Jordan, John	099	1799	RB-5/5	AR
Jordan, John	053	1720	SS 875/219	
Jordan, John B.	071	1836	WB-4/139	AR
Jordan, John C.	099	1898	WB-D/162	AR
Jordan, John S.	099	1815	RB-12/230	AR
Jordan, John S.	009	1847	OWB/545	AR
Jordan, John V.	028	1895	WB-F/194	
Jordan, Johnathan	051	1820	WB-A/18	
Jordan, Jonathan	073	1825	WB-E/94	AR
Jordan, Joseph	077	1817	WB-E/471	AR
Jordan, Joseph	010	1864	WB-H/138	AR
Jordan, Joseph	093	1864	WB-1/34	
Jordan, Joseph	010	1776	WB-B/55	AR
Jordan, Joseph	024	1800	WB-B/222	AR
Jordan, Joseph	010	1786	WB-D/50	AR
Jordan, Joseph	075	1752	SS 881/26	SS/AR
Jordan, Joseph	099	c1874	Orig. Only	AR
Jordan, Joseph	075	1762	WB-H/29	AR
Jordan, Joshaway	037	1791	WB-C/175	AR
Jordan, Joshua	037	1842	WB-F/275	AR
Jordan, Josiah	037	1848	WB-F/388	AR
Jordan, Josiah	077	1789	WB-C/393	AR
Jordan, Judith M.	071	1884	WB-6/435	AR
Jordan, Julia A.	077	1885	WB-H/146	AR
Jordan, Julia L.	028	1896	WB-F/227	AR
Jordan, Marcellus	046	1861	WB-D/73	AR
Jordan, Margaret	100	1833	WB-34/290	AR
Jordan, Margaret	081	1828	WB-5/427	AR
Jordan, Martha	100	1832	WB-33/374	AR
Jordan, Mary	053	1821	WB-4/211	AR
Jordan, Mary	075	1768	WB-H/78	
Jordan, Mary	010	1888	WB-I/251	AR
Jordan, Mary	010	1849	WB-G/445	AR
Jordan, Mary J.	105	1900	WB-3/444	

Name	Co.	Date	Recorded Copy	Original
Jordan, Mathew	077	1763	WB-C/42	AR
Jordan, Mathias	075	1762	WB-H/30	
Jordan, Matilda	068	1900	WB-E/37	
Jordan, Matthew M.	056	1849	WB-1/620	AR
Jordan, Micajah	075	1769	WB-H/93	
Jordan, Micajah	071	1864	WB-5/291	AR
Jordan, Michael	046	1775	WB-A/194	AR
Jordan, Mourning	024	1819	WB-C/78	AR
Jordan, Nancy	071	1849	WB-5/73	AR
Jordan, Naomi	046	1895	WB-F/463	AR
Jordan, Nevil	075	1779	WB-K/35	
Jordan, Nicholas	056	1841	WB-1/536	AR
Jordan, Over	071	1771	WB-1/203	
Jordan, Ovid	036	1893	WB-A/296	CTY
Jordan, Pantha R.	071	1838	WB-4/178	AR
Jordan, Peter H.	071	1885	WB-6/478	AR
Jordan, R. A.	001	1891	WB-2/492	AR
Jordan, Richard	053	1811	RW-1/451	
Jordan, River	011	1862	WB-1/300	
Jordan, Roanna	071	1877	WB-6/218	AR
Jordan, Robert	093	c1863	WB-1/41	
Jordan, Robert	051	1839	WB-A/136	
Jordan, Robert	075	1765	WB-H/68	AR
Jordan, Rotheas	009	1836	OWB/529	AR
Jordan, Rothias	053	1819	WB-4/1	
Jordan, Ruth	010	1777	WB-B/95	AR
Jordan, Sally	069	1830	WB-1/370	AR
Jordan, Sally L.	009	1860	OB-L/146	
Jordan, Samuel H.	073	1891	WB-H/546	CTY
Jordan, Sarah A.	103	1895	WB-2/122	AR
Jordan, Sary Ann	067	c1895	Orig. Only	AR
Jordan, Seth	100	1812	WB-16/315	AR
Jordan, Susan	051	1868	WB-B/102	AR
Jordan, Tabitha	100	1855	WB-44/33	AR
Jordan, Thomas	075	1840	Copy	096 AR
Jordan, Thomas	009	1820	OB-A/303	AR
Jordan, Thomas	071	1769	WB-1/175	
Jordan, Thomas	071	1815	WB-3/143	AR
Jordan, Thomas	075	1840	WB-N/164	AR
Jordan, Thomas B.	009	1837	OB-B/540	AR
Jordan, Thomas P.	093	1896	050 WB-2/236	050 CTY
Jordan, Thomas P.	093	1896	WB-2/143	AR
Jordan, Thomas S.	073	1867	WB-G/528	
Jordan, Turner	044	1781	WB-1/311	CTY-Copy
Jordan, Valentine	079	1852	WB-1/22	AR-Copy
Jordan, W. B.	069	1896	WB-5/525	AR
Jordan, W. Henry	045	1885	WB-1/111	AR
Jordan, W. S.	093	1893	WB-2/125	AR
Jordan, Welse	024	1899	WB-E/298	AR
Jordan, William	010	1790	WB-D/179 & 184	AR
Jordan, William	054	1891	WB-5/396	CTY
Jordan, William	010	1790	024 WB-A/95	024 AR
Jordan, William	009	1842	OB-D/197	AR
Jordan, William	028	1792	WB-A/273	AR
Jordan, William	010	1786	WB-D/63	AR
Jordan, William	022	c1855	WB-C/406	AR
Jordan, William	096	1732	SS 876/257	SS/AR
Jordan, William C.	071	1861	WB-5/251	AR
Jordan, William H.	073	1892	WB-H/558	CTY
Jordan, William H.	044	1883	WB-23/486	CTY
Jordan, William H.	077	1897	WB-H/308	AR
Jordan, William H.	105	1870	WB-2/24	AR
Jordan, William T.	075	1897	WB-O/444	AR

Name	Co.	Date	Recorded Copy	Original
Jordan, Willis	024	1892	WB-E/208	AR
Jordan, Winiford	051	1849	WB-A/302	
Jordan, Zachariah	009	1830	OB-B/46	AR
Jorden, Caswell	028	1877	WB-E/183	AR
Jorden, Richard	087	1864	WB-2/68	
Jorden, Sarah	044	1762	Orig. Only	CTY
Jorden, Thomas	028	1796	WB-A/355	AR
Jordian, Sollomon	N	1722	SS 875/296	SS/AR
Jordon, James	051	1863	WB-B/54	AR
Jordon, Kinchen G.	074	1875	WB-1/12	
Jordon, Thomas	053	1786	RW-1/155	
Jorksey, Elezebeth	075	1758	SS 882/139	
Jornagan, George	010	1778	WB-B/119	AR
Jornagan, Samuel	010	1825	WB-G/133	AR
Joseph, Euphane A.	009	1842	OB-D/359	AR
Josey, James	047	1787	WB-3/134	
Josey, James	047	1795	WB-3/250	
Josey, John	047	1802	WB-3/380	
Josey, John	085	c1805	WB-G/36	AR
Josey, Martha	071	1870	WB-6/59	AR
Josey, Stephen	071	1823	WB-3/295	AR
Josey, William	085	1844	WB-I/234	AR
Jouett, Matthew	020	1779	RB-A/80	AR
Journey, Lucy	054	1846	WB-3/12	AR
Journey, Nathaniel	054	1842	WB-2/253	
Journey, Nathaniel	054	c1827	WB-2/51	AR
Journey, R. A.	054	1863	Orig. Only	AR
Jowers, Thomas	005	1806	WB-2/79	AR
Joy, William	075	1725	SS 876/39	SS/AR
Joyce, Absolem	084	1842	WB-B/280	CTY-Nunc.
Joyce, Alexander	046	1778	WB-A/195	AR
Joyce, Alexander	090	1819	WB-3/29	AR
Joyce, Elizabeth	084	1873	WB E/49	CTY
Joyce, Elizabeth	090	c1854	Orig. Only	AR
Joyce, Elizabeth	063	c1804	WB-1/431	
Joyce, Elizabeth	063	1827	WB-2/133	
Joyce, Franklin	092	1888	WB-6/279	AR
Joyce, George D.	084	1850	WB-C/105	CTY
Joyce, Harrison	090	1887	WB-6/182	AR
Joyce, Jency	084	c1799	OW/59	AR
Joyce, John	063	1789	WB-1/161	
Joyce, John	090	1859	WB-4/334	AR
Joyce, John	084	1880	WB-E/197	CTY
Joyce, John	084	1866	WB-D/49	
Joyce, Joseph T.	090	1865	WB-5/26	
Joyce, Martin	063	c1812	WB-2/86	
Joyce, Minerva	084	1833	WB-B/81	CTY
Joyce, Robert	090	1863	WB-4/363	AR
Joyce, Thomas	090	1855	WB-4/294	AR
Joyce, Thomas	084	1843	WB-B/283	CTY
Joyce, W. A.	106	c1866	WB-1/113	AR
Joyce, William	090	1883	WB-6/138	AR
Joyce, William B.	090	1836	WB-3/315	
Joyce, William T.	090	1861	WB-4/344	AR
Joyes, Felix G.	084	1864	WB-C/397	CTY
Joyner, Abraham	071	1793	WB-2/29	AR
Joyner, Abraham	071	1850	WB-5/87	AR
Joyner, Abram	079	c1866	WB-1/164	AR
Joyner, Abram	079	1864	WB-1/118	AR
Joyner, Absalom	071	1800	WB-2/200	AR
Joyner, Alford	069	1876	WB-5/48	
Joyner, Alfred T.	071	1891	WB-7/84	AR
Joyner, Amos	079	1868	WB-2/1	AR
Joyner, Andrew	047	1856	WB-5/26	

Name	Co.	Date	Recorded Copy	Original
Joyner, Aron	079	1858	WB-1/16	AR
Joyner, Bardin	071	1845	WB-5/22	AR
Joyner, Blount	047	1834	WB-4/113	
Joyner, Bridgeman	047	1795	WB-3/259	
Joyner, Charles	037	1867	WB-G/294	AR
Joyner, Daniel	070	1840	WB-AB/341	AR
Joyner, Drewry	105	1889	WB-2/545	AR
Joyner, Elisha	051	1880	WB-C/254	AR
Joyner, Eliza D.	069	1888	WB-5/276	AR
Joyner, Elizabeth	069	1875	WB-5/41	AR
Joyner, Elizabeth	056	1896	WB-4/21	AR
Joyner, Elizabeth	047	1846	WB-4/253	
Joyner, Everitt	103	1877	WB-1/118	AR
Joyner, Gilbert	028	1894	WB-F/124	
Joyner, Harriet	079	1869	WB-2/13	AR
Joyner, Henry	047	1803	WB-3/386	
Joyner, Honour	069	1817	WB-1/293	AR
Joyner, Israell	N	c1739	009 OWB/31	009 AR
Joyner, Joel	047	1794	WB-3/231	
Joyner, John	047	1770	WB-1/273	
Joyner, John	056	1849	WB-1/623	AR
Joyner, John F.	051	1881	WB-C/271	AR
Joyner, John J.	056	1865	WB-2/73	AR
Joyner, Jonas	069	1864	WB-1/588	AR
Joyner, Joseph	047	1774	WB-1/369	
Joyner, Joshua	047	1771	WB-1/268	
Joyner, Lucy	099	1842	RB-25/31	AR
Joyner, Margaret	084	1886	WB-E/364	CTY
Joyner, Mary	039	1879	WB-U/210	AR
Joyner, Mary A.	079	1887	WB-2/401	AR
Joyner, Matthew	099	1832	RB-22/317	AR
Joyner, Moses	063	1816	WB-2/36	
Joyner, Mourning	069	1879	WB-5/95	AR
Joyner, Nancey	069	1815	WB-1/268	AR
Joyner, Nancy	069	1861	WB-1/577	AR
Joyner, Nathan	047	1770	WB-1/269	
Joyner, Nathan G.	069	1871	WB-1/611	AR
Joyner, Nelson	051	1850	WB-A/306	
Joyner, P. H.	046	1890	WB-F/70	AR
Joyner, Patience	047	1785	WB-3/075	
Joyner, Priscilla	039	1870	WB-U/20	AR
Joyner, Rebecca	071	1864	WB-5/299	AR
Joyner, Rosa	063	1868	WB-2/503	
Joyner, Rusia	051	1855	WB-A/377	
Joyner, Samuel R.	071	1892	WB-7/180	AR
Joyner, Susanna	079	1873	WB-2/83	AR
Joyner, Theophilus	047	1796	WB-3/264	
Joyner, Thomas	079	1857	WB-1/31	AR-Copy
Joyner, Thomas	071	1857	WB-5/173	AR
Joyner, Thomas	063	1790	WB-1/168	
Joyner, Whitney	063	1845	WB-2/316	
Joyner, William	054	1856	WB-3/107	AR
Joyner, William	069	1785	WB-1/37	AR
Joyner, William	079	1882	WB-2/258	AR
Joyner, William	103	1881	WB-1/214	
Joyner, William A.	VA	1882	071 WB-6/430	
Joyner, Zachariah	106	1885	WB-2/192	AR
Juckins, Daniel	028	1733	SS 876/407	
Judd, Henderson	068	1871	WB-D/42	Nunc.
Judd, J. W.	099	1863	RB-32/429	AR
Judd, William	068	1839	WB-B/124	
Judge, Christian	047	1816	WB-3/592	
Judge, Israel	070	1818	WB-C/208	AR
Judge, James	047	1813	WB-3/541	
Judkins, Gray	009	1841	OB-D/168	
Judkins, John E.	037	1802	WB-D/138	AR
Judkins, Lavinia	100	1826	WB-30/45	
Judkins, Nathaniel	047	1815	WB-3/572	
Judkins, Nicholas	071	1783	WB-1/255	AR
Judkins, Rebeccah	047	1823	WB-3/693	
Judy, James	047	1761	WB-1/30	
Julian, David	017	c1841	WB-A/32	AR
Julian, Eleanor	081	1849	WB-9/111	AR
Julian, Henry M.	003	1897	WB-B/359	AR
Julian, Jacob	065	1827	WB-B/11	AR
Julian, James	054	c1824	WB-2/15	AR
Julian, Jesse	081	1846	WB-8/317	AR
Julian, Jesse	081	1896	WB-16/390	AR
Julian, Jesse	046	1890	WB-F/66	AR
Julian, John	085	1886	WB-2/183	CTY
Julian, Tobias	081	1852	WB-9/376	AR
Julin, Rachel	065	1839	WB-H/69	AR
Jump, Nathan	028	1781	Orig. Only	AR
Jump, William	013	1875	WB-B/106	AR
Jurnigan, Anna	041	1879	WB-4/116	AR
Justice, Alexander	028	1879	WB-E/202	
Justice, Ann Maria	028	1843	WB-D/84	AR
Justice, Benjamin W.	084	1860	WB-C/340	CTY
Justice, D. M.	050	1892	WB-2/157	CTY
Justice, David	022	1832	WB-B/216	AR
Justice, David	099	1880	WB-A/198	AR
Justice, David	099	c1832	RB-22/455	AR
Justice, Elias	028	1784	WB-D/240	AR
Justice, Elijah	072	1854	WB-2/140	AR
Justice, Elijah	072	1870	WB-4/34	AR
Justice, Elizabeth	028	1894	WB-F/116	
Justice, Henry	081	1815	WB-4/248	AR
Justice, John	022	1794	RB-2/19	AR
Justice, Laben	072	1847	WB-2/81	AR
Justice, Martha A.	099	1880	WB-A/134	AR
Justice, Richard R.	099	1881	WB-A/251	AR
Justice, Sidney E.	028	1879	WB-E/206	AR
Justice, Susannah	022	1850	WB-C/267	AR
Justis, Joseph	028	1768	Orig. Only	AR
Justis, Mary	071	1791	WB-1/432	AR
Justis, Selvenus	028	1774	Orig. Only	AR
Justus, Stephen	073	1840	WB-F/52	AR
Jutson, Jean	054	c1801	WB-1/126	AR
Kacley, James	026	1883	WB-2/240	
Kail, John	010	1805	WB-E/272	AR
Kalbin, John	002	c1765	Orig. Only	SS/AR
Kaldison, George	085	c1803	Orig. Only	AR
Kale, Alanson	021	1887	WB-2/391	
Kale, Balser	060	1832	WB-1/255	AR
Kale, Elisha	021	1850	WB-1/80	AR
Kale, Ephraim	021	1853	WB-1/106	AR
Kale, Logan L.	021	1897	WB-3/150	AR
Kale, Loranza D.	021	1892	WB-3/21	AR
Kale, Nancy	021	1872	WB-2/68	AR
Kale, William	060	1786	Orig. Only	AR
Kallam, Benjamin	030	1833	WB-3/331	
Kallam, David	084	1865	WB-D/44	CTY
Kallam, James B.	030	1834	WB-3/332	
Kallam, Nancy	084	1894	WB-F/17	CTY
Kallam, Nancy	030	1833	WB-3/332	
Kallam, Spencer	084	1884	WB-E/280	CTY
Kallam, Spencer	084	1857	WB-C/246	CTY
Kallam, Theophilus	030	1804	WB-2/255	
Kallam, Winston	084	1893	WB-E/540	CTY
Kalley (Calley), Mathew	002	1699	Orig. Only	SS/AR

Name	Co.	Date	Recorded Copy	Original
Kanady, Samuel	083	c1800	WB-1/63	AR
Kane, Geraldine	NY	1894	Copy	050 AR
Kane, Peter	085	c1791	WB-C/235	AR
Kanipe, Ellen J.	021	c1900	WB-3/321	AR
Kannady, Elender	068	1801	WB-A/213	
Kannedy, Aaron	092	1845	WB-4/228	
Kapp, J. H.	038	1896	WB-4/15	AR
Kapp, Jacob	090	1807	WB-2/86	AR
Karn, John, Jr.	085	c1794	WB-C/228	AR
Karr, Adam	065	1847	WB-I/81	AR
Karr, Ann	024	1777	WB-A/147	AR
Karrer, Jacob	099	1872	RB-35/171	AR
Kasky, Frederick	090	1829	WB-3/198	AR
Kasner (Casner), Andon	090	1817	WB-3/10	AR
Kasowell, Francis	075	c1713	SS 875/41	
Katteiser, Henry	016	1835	PQS.5/353	
Katz, Morris M.	070	1894	WB-G/240	AR
Kay, Elizabeth	028	1856	WB-D/268	AR
Kay, James	019	c1766	RB-A/19	
Kay, Jonathan	072	c1778	RW/L28	AR
Kay, Richard	047	1794	WB-3/237	
Kaylor, Lewis	085	1815	WB-G/354	AR
Kaylor, Mary A.	064	1891	WB-2/224	AR
Kea, Faithy	037	1815	WB-E/88	AR
Kea, Henry	037	1842	WB-F/272	AR
Kea, James B.	071	1827	WB-4/36	AR
Kea, John	037	1878	WB-G/482	AR
Kea, John	011	1834	WB-1/18	
Kea, Sarah	037	1850	WB-F/438	AR
Kea, William	037	1804	WB-D/193	AR
Keach, Jasper	009	1833	OB-B/236	
Keachey, Samuel	083	1834	WB-1/288	AR
Keahey, George	082	1808	WB-1/122	AR
Keahey, William J.	065	1843	WB-H/128	AR
Keais, Nathan	009	c1788	OWB/225	AR
Keais, Sarah H.	009	1818	OB-A/287	AR
Keais, William	009	1809	OB-A/26	AR
Keane, Christian	070	1771	WB-C/213	AR
Kearby, Jesse	056	1804	WB-1/168	AR
Kearne, Shimuel	039	1808	WB-C/114	AR
Kearney, Crafford	039	c1843	WB-M/22	AR
Kearney, F. W.	038	1887	WB-3/73	AR
Kearney, Henry	039	1893	WB-V/2	AR
Kearney, John	039	1863	WB-R/614	AR
Kearney, Thomas	047	1764	WB-1/146	
Kearns, C. S.	081	1897	WB-16/454	AR
Kearns, C. S.	081	c1897	067 WB-2/384	
Kearns, Clarkston	081	1887	WB-16/40	AR
Kearns, Columbus D.	081	1877	WB-15/252	AR
Kearns, Mary	067	c1887	WB-2/418	
Kearns, Silas	081	1885	WB-15/518	AR
Kearns, Silas K.	081	1890	WB-16/163	AR
Kearny, Edmond	100	1794	WB-7/179	AR
Kearny, Edward	100	1868	WB-50/266	AR
Kearny, Philip	100	1794	WB-7/175	AR
Kearny, Sarah	100	1814	WB-19/40	AR
Kearny, Thomas	100	1797	WB-9/165	AR
Kearny, Thomas	100	1897	WB-51/481	
Kearny, William K.	100	1869	WB-51/4	AR
Keas, Nancy	009	1856	OB-K/71	AR
Keasler, Nancy	085	1858	WB-K/260	AR
Keathley, F. M.	035	1898	WB-4/516	AR
Keathley, James M.	035	1899	WB-4/543	AR
Keathley, Jonathan	035	1822	WB-A/271	AR
Keathley, Mark	035	1873	WB-4/75	AR
Keating, Jane	028	1883	WB-E/332	
Keaton, Edmund	075	1810	WB-M1/213	AR
Keaton, Grizell	075	1834	WB-N/98	AR
Keaton, Henry	075	1806	WB-M1/126	AR
Keaton, Joseph	075	1784	WB-K/104	AR
Keaton, Joseph	077	1824	WB-F/59	AR
Keaton, Silas	018	1862	WB-C/363	
Keator, Nathan	018	1831	WB-C/122	
Keatten, John	077	1735	SS 876/412	
Keck, George	073	1840	WB-F/75	AR
Keck, Henry	073	1820	WB-D/579	AR
Keddie, William	070	1809	WB-AB/122	AR
Kee, Charles R.	071	1845	WB-5/31	AR
Kee, Elizabeth	071	1842	WB-4/251	AR
Kee, James R.	071	1882	WB-6/372	AR
Kee, William	071	1819	WB-3/211	AR
Keeble, William S.	044	1827	WB-10/371	CTY
Keech, Benjamin	009	1866	OB-M/256	AR
Keech, Bryan	009	1826	OB-A/370	AR
Keech, Jasper	009	1833	OB-B/236	AR
Keech, John	009	c1759	OWB/66	AR
Keech, Levi S.	009	1898	WB-2/140	CTY
Keef, Edmund	028	1799	WB-B/86	AR
Keefe, Patrick	037	1809	WB-D/345	AR
Keefe, Tredell	010	1723	SS 876/102	SS/AR
Keehen, Christian	038	1859	WB-1/152	AR
Keehler, Theo. F.	038	1877	WB-2/316	AR
Keel, Irvin N.	079	1886	WB-2/377	AR
Keel, John	072	c1736	SS 877/76	SS/AR
Keel, Jonathan C.	079	1875	WB-2/112	AR
Keel, Lemuel	075	1748	Orig. Only	SS/AR
Keel, Simon	079	1842	WB-1/43	AR-Copy
Keel, Tamar	075	1748	Orig. Only	SS/AR
Keeland, John	037	1752	Orig. Only	SS/AR (N)
Keeler, Charles B.	019	1900	WB-B/30	AR
Keeler, Lucy S.	005	1890	WB-D/275	AR
Keeley, John	070	1788	Orig. Only	AR-Nunc.
Keeling, George	047	1759	WB-1/1	
Keeling, Osburn	104	1791	WB-1/301	AR
Keeling, William	073	1823	WB-E/37	AR
Keell, Charles	075	c1748	Orig. Only	AR
Keell, Robert	075	c1745	Orig. Only	AR
Keen, George W.	056	1895	WB-2/198	AR
Keen, Gideon	056	1896	WB-2/211	AR
Keen, Isaac	056	c1814	WB-1/241	AR
Keen, James R.	087	1890	WB-3/448	AR
Keen, Jesse	051	1892	WB-C/443	AR
Keen, John	020	1815	RB-G/111	
Keen, John, Sr.	087	c1803	WB-A/42	AR
Keen, Sasser	056	1822	WB-1/444	AR
Keen, Thomas	020	1849	RB-Q/180	AR
Keen, Wiley	103	1882	WB-1/242	AR
Keenan, Hugh	065	1868	WB-J/247	AR
Keene, Mournen	005	1882	WB-D/117	AR
Keener, Adam	060	1856	WB-2/410	AR
Keener, Daniel	MO	1873	021 WB-2/126	021 A
Keener, Jacob	060	1807	Orig. Only	AR
Keener, John	060	1823	Orig. Only	AR
Keenlee, Andreas	NJ	1897	013 WB-D/62	
Keerl, Thomas M.	MD	1888	093 WB-2/128	093 AR
Keerl, Thomas M.	MD	1888	091 WB-1/140	
Keerl, Thomas M.	MD	1888	055 WB-A/122	
Keeter, Caroline	010	1891	WB-I/322	AR
Keeter, Elizabeth	086	1879	WB-F/142	AR

Name	Co.	Date	Recorded Copy	Original
Keeter, Henry	086	1848	WB-E/178	AR
Keeter, J. M.	086	1899	WB-G/32	AR
Keeter, Lemuel	010	1850	WB-G/465	AR
Keeth, Mariah H.	099	1892	WB-C/106	AR
Keeton, Henry	075	1715	Orig. Only	SS/AR
Keeton, John	VA	1702	Copy	024 AR
Keeton, Zachariah	075	1743	Orig. Only	SS/AR
Keeton, Zachariah	075	1785	WB-K/132	AR
Keetor, Jesse	092	1824	WB-3/160	AR
Keever, Aaron	060	1895	WB-4/571	AR
Keever, Henry	060	1885	WB-4/327	AR
Keever, James	021	1888	WB-2/435	AR
Keever, Thomas	060	1863	WB-3/71	AR
Keil, Samuel	100	1796	WB-9/49	AR
Keile, Thomas	002	1682/3	Orig. Only	SS/AR
Keims, Phillip	046	1836	WB-B/544	AR
Keisler, John, Sr.	085	1841	WB-I/113	AR
Keith, Anna	099	1884	WB-A/516	AR
Keith, Christian	068	1891	WB-D/344	CTY-Nunc.
Keith, Daniel	099	1871	RB-35/150	AR
Keith, Duncan	068	1893	WB-D/389	CTY
Keith, Elizabeth	099	1866	RB-34/286	AR
Keith, Euphemia	029	1892	WB-E/545	AR
Keith, Frances	070	1886	WB-F/38	AR
Keith, George	099	1858	RB-30/530	AR
Keith, George A.	099	1885	WB-B/53	AR
Keith, Israel F.	076	1898	WB-A1/241	
Keith, James	028	c1762	Orig. Only	AR
Keith, James	028	1740	Deeds.1/L106	
Keith, James	069	1806	WB-1/168	AR
Keith, John	062	1871	WB-B/1	
Keith, John	062	1854	WB-A/14	AR
Keith, Lemuel	099	1899	WB-D/254	AR
Keith, Martha E.	099	1898	WB-D/171	AR
Keith, Mary	068	1871	WB-D/30	
Keith, Wesley	099	1891	WB-B/498	AR
Keith, William	062	1853	WB-A/10	AR
Keith, William	012	1810	WB-B/86	AR
Kell, John	073	1801	WB-D/28	AR
Kell, Samuel	100	1797	WB-9/136	AR
Kell, Thomas	073	1824	WB-E/58	AR
Kell, William	073	1836	WB-E/382	AR
Kellam, John	090	1816	WB-2/183	AR
Kellam, John	046	1805	WB-A/209	AR
Kellam, Mary	057	1811	WB-A/329	AR
Kellen, Adam	068	1803	WB-A/230	
Kellen, Sarah	068	1809	WB-A/263	
Keller, Barbary	033	1841	WB-1/37	AR
Keller, Henry	033	1891	WB-2/111	CTY
Keller, Henry	003	1884	WB-B/144	AR
Keller, Isaac	033	1853	WB-1/108	AR
Keller, John	033	1857	WB-1/136	AR
Keller, John, Sr.	085	c1803	WB-C/238	AR
Keller, Martin	021	c1854	WB-1/135	AR
Keller, Peter	021	1889	WB-2/472	AR
Keller, Peter, Sr.	021	1854	WB-1/109	AR
Keller, Susannah	033	1865	WB-1/189	AR
Kelley (Calley), John	030	1764	024 WB-1/14	024 AR
Kelley (Celley), Grigry	056	1762	WB-1/782	AR
Kelley (Celley), John	056	1791	WB-2/271	AR
Kelley (Celley), Smith	077	1734	Orig. Only	SS/AR
Kelley, Alexander	037	1765	WB-A/145	AR
Kelley, Benjamin	090	1823	WB-3/97	AR
Kelley, Charles	028	1867	WB-D/457	

Name	Co.	Date	Recorded Copy	Original
Kelley, Curtis	009	1826	OB-A/367	AR
Kelley, Daniel	005	1820	WB-2/80	AR
Kelley, Elizabeth	092	1858	WB-5/25	
Kelley, Gatsie	037	1881	WB-G/594	AR
Kelley, Henry	022	1796	RB-2/80	AR
Kelley, James	047	1802	WB-3/373	
Kelley, James, Sr.	011	c1835	WB-1/29	
Kelley, Jane	018	c1833	WB-C/174	
Kelley, Jesse J.	044	1867	WB-22/540	CTY
Kelley, John	037	1783	WB-B/124	AR
Kelley, John	075	1758	Orig. Only	SS/AR
Kelley, Joseph	022	1861	WB-D/11	AR
Kelley, Joseph	099	1887	WB-B/224	AR
Kelley, Marklin	106	1892	WB-2/314	
Kelley, Mary	009	1836	OWB/504	AR
Kelley, Mary Jane	106	1892	WB-2/320	AR
Kelley, Matthew	009	1752	OWB/46	AR
Kelley, Nancy	018	1838	WB-C/227	
Kelley, Rachel	009	c1797	OWB/332	AR
Kelley, Richard W.	103	1863	RD-13/685	AR
Kelley, Sarah	002	1700	SS 874.2/127	SS/AR
Kelley, Tulley	009	c1795	OWB/305	AR
Kellihan, Pinckney	027	1885	WB-2/58	AR
Kello, Isaac	084	1794	OW/49 & 61	AR
Kello, William	084	c1805	OW/55	AR
Kellogg, Martin	041	1879	WB-4/119	AR
Kellum, Ann	090	1822	WB-3/77	
Kellum, Elizabeth	IN	1875	067 WB-2/137	067 AR
Kelly, Abner B.	068	1885	WB-D/224	
Kelly, Alexander	068	1872	WB-D/39	
Kelly, Angus	029	1843	WB-C/53	AR
Kelly, Anne	073	1866	WB-G/499	CTY
Kelly, Arch D.	054	1879	WB-4/355	CTY
Kelly, Archibald	011	c1813	WB-2/316	
Kelly, Archibald	011	c1861	WB-1/333	
Kelly, Charles	056	1804	WB-1/156	AR
Kelly, Christian	068	1855	WB-C/32	
Kelly, Daniel	068	1892	WB-D/361	CTY
Kelly, Duncan	083	1861	WB-2/176	AR
Kelly, Edwin B.	018	1857	WB-D/34	
Kelly, Elizabeth	073	1871	WB-H/53	CTY
Kelly, Elizabeth	085	1845	WB-I/256	AR
Kelly, Felix	087	1864	WB-2/82	AR
Kelly, Hugh	029	1863	WB-D/50	AR
Kelly, Hugh	068	1851	WB-B/216	
Kelly, Hugh	054	1885	WB-5/47	CTY
Kelly, Hugh	068	1800	WB-A/207	
Kelly, James	018	1830	WB-C/118	
Kelly, James	083	1839	WB-1/382	AR
Kelly, James	056	1822	WB-1/448	AR
Kelly, James	068	1825	WB-B/39	
Kelly, James	103	1878	WB-1/131	AR
Kelly, James E.	011	c1878	WB-2/124	
Kelly, James H.	011	1892	WB-2/256	
Kelly, John	073	1826	WB-E/115	AR
Kelly, John	073	1851	WB-G/10	AR
Kelly, John	018	1822	WB-C/13	
Kelly, John	029	1842	WB-C/1	AR
Kelly, Joseph	099	1874	RB-35/238	AR
Kelly, Joseph	087	c1795	WB-A/22	AR
Kelly, Julia A.	070	1899	WB-H/187	AR
Kelly, Kesiah	AL	1868	097 WB-2/167	
Kelly, Lucinda	022	1882	WB-E/248	AR
Kelly, Margaret	083	1845	WB-1/455	AR
Kelly, Mary	011	c1847	WB-1/196	

Name	Co.	Date	Recorded Copy	Original
Kelly, Mary	073	1830	WB-E/213	AR
Kelly, Mary A.	065	1898	WB-N/111	AR
Kelly, Mary L.	009	1876	WB-1/150	
Kelly, Matthew	011	c1806	WB-1/351	
Kelly, Matthew	083	1849	WB-2/6	
Kelly, Neill	083	1869	WB-3/5	AR
Kelly, Neill	011	1864	WB-1/327	
Kelly, Patrick	083	c1808	WB-1/361	AR
Kelly, Richard	070	1802	WB-C/218	AR
Kelly, Sarah	056	c1896	WB-4/309	AR
Kelly, Susan	044	c1868	WB-23/3	CTY
Kelly, Sylvester	087	c1864	Orig. Only	AR
Kelly, Thomas	028	1791	WB-A/257	
Kelly, W. M.	011	c1892	Orig. Only	CTY
Kelly, William	103	1858	RD-12/597	AR
Kelly, William	024	1815	WB-C/37	AR
Kelly, William D.	092	1853	WB-4/328	
Kelly, William J.	029	1892	WB-E/543	AR
Kelly, William L.	027	1859	WB-A/73	AR
Keloin, Leonard	060	1795	Orig. Only	AR
Kelpen, Isaac	072	c1784	WI/L50	AR
Kemp, A. S.	011	1885	WB-2/191	
Kemp, George	075	1724	SS 876/29	SS/AR
Kemp, John	099	1806	RB-7/157	AR
Kemp, John W.	044	1887	WB-24/12 & 55	CTY
Kemp, Joseph	022	1847	WB-C/197	AR
Kemp, Joseph	022	1832	WB-B/218	AR
Kemp, Joseph	011	c1805	WB-1/349	
Kemp, Joseph R.	011	1883	WB-2/161	
Kemp, Josiah	022	1830	WB-B/193	AR
Kemp, Mathias	028	1767	Orig. Only	AR
Kemp, Nancy	054	c1810	WB-1/272	AR
Kemp, Richard	022	1789	RB-1/34	AR
Kemp, Squire	054	1865	WB-3/180	AR
Kemp, Susannah	022	1847	WB-C/202	AR
Kemp, William	005	1753	SS 879/136	SS/AR
Kemp, William	027	1837	WB-A/50	AR
Kemp, William J.	011	1866	WB-2/25	
Kemp, Zebulon	096	1837	WB-2/135	AR
Kempe, Amia G.	101	1871	Orig. Only	AR
Kenaday, David	035	1848	WB-2/39	AR
Kenaday, John	018	1834	WB-C/157	
Kenaday, Lydia	018	1838	WB-C/228	
Kenan, Elizabeth	035	1790	WB-A/259	AR/CRX
Kenan, George	083	c1829	WB-1/192	
Kenan, James	035	1810	Copy	103 AR
Kenan, James	035	1810	WB-A/257	AR/CRX
Kenan, Sarah	035	1819	WB-A/255	AR/CRX
Kenan, Thomas	035	c1762	WB-A/253	AR/CRX
Kendal, John	081	1821	WB-5/42	AR
Kendall, Benjamin	090	1868	WB-5/60	AR
Kendall, Benjamin	046	1832	WB-B/453	AR
Kendall, Catharine	032	1873	WB-3/79	AR
Kendall, Frances S.	089	1887	WB-2/146	AR
Kendall, Henderson	089	1881	WB-2/88	AR
Kendall, Jay O.	005	1894	WB-D/350	AR
Kendall, John P.	005	1865	WB-C/207	AR
Kendall, Nathan	032	1862	WB-2/226	AR
Kendall, Reuben	089	1855	WB-1/139	
Kendall, Solomon	046	1857	WB-C/483	AR
Kendall, Susannah	032	1876	WB-3/174	AR
Kendrick, John	065	1823	WB-D/147	AR
Kendrick, John	026	1878	WB-2/172	AR
Kendrick, William	015	1777	100 WB-2/119	AR
Keneday, James	078	1829	Orig. Only	AR

Name	Co.	Date	Recorded Copy	Original
Keneday, Prudence	078	1836	WI-13/105	AR
Keneday, Thomas	035	1851	WB-2/64	AR
Kenedy, Demsey	035	1784	WB-A/262	AR
Kenerly, Robert C.	085	1881	WB-1/561	CTY
Kenley, Charles	016	1845	WB-1/54	
Kennard, Martha	103	1822	RD-4/472	
Kenneday, Epeproditus	032	1875	WB-3/162	AR
Kenneday, John H.	056	1863	WB-2/42	AR
Kenneday, Robert	078	1852	WB-13/93	
Kenneday, Sherwood	032	1841	WB-1/363	
Kenneday, William B.	104	1874	WB-6/98	AR
Kennedy, Alexander	026	1892	WB-2/447	AR
Kennedy, Alpheus T.	059	1892	WB-B/36	CTY
Kennedy, Ann	024	1777	WB-A/302	AR
Kennedy, Bettie	068	1888	WB-D/255	
Kennedy, Bryan	035	1888	WB-4/312	AR
Kennedy, Catherine	070	1890	WB-F/352	AR
Kennedy, Claudius M.	059	1880	WB-A/206	
Kennedy, E. B.	059	1883	WB-A/360	CTY
Kennedy, Eleanor	065	1846	WB-I/53	AR
Kennedy, Elizabeth	065	1890	WB-L/466	AR
Kennedy, Francis M.	065	1843	WB-H/136	AR
Kennedy, Huldah J.	059	1882	WB-A/337	CTY
Kennedy, James	072	1781	Orig. Only	AR
Kennedy, Jesse	038	1876	WB-2/244	AR
Kennedy, John	035	1867	WB-3/115	AR
Kennedy, John	081	1788	WB-1/59	AR
Kennedy, John	104	1883	WB-6/227	AR
Kennedy, John	103	1823	RD-5/25	AR
Kennedy, John	009	1826	OB-A/363	AR
Kennedy, John	009	c1801	OWB/386	AR
Kennedy, John	092	1799	WB-3/31A	AR
Kennedy, John P.	TN	1872	013 WB-B/58	013 AR
Kennedy, Joseph	065	1778	WB-D/123	AR
Kennedy, Leroy	065	1894	WB-M/292	AR
Kennedy, Marcus T.	065	c1842	WB-H/98	AR
Kennedy, Margaret	065	1873	WB-K/139	AR
Kennedy, Margaret	085	1890	WB-2/404	CTY
Kennedy, Oscar H.	059	1882	WB-A/273	CTY
Kennedy, Ruth	063	1822	WB-2/79	
Kennedy, Samuel	029	1767	Orig. Only	AR
Kennedy, Thomas	032	1899	WB-4/395	AR
Kennedy, Thomas	065	1827	WB-B/7	AR
Kennedy, Thompson	004	1900	WB-A/242	AR
Kennedy, Victoria L.	059	1881	WB-A/333	CTY
Kennedy, Walter	059	1876	WB-A/111	
Kennedy, Walter	056	1751	028 DB-5/198	SS/AR
Kennedy, William	029	1804	WB-A/69	AR
Kennedy, William	096	1761	WB-1/21	AR
Kennedy, William	009	1834	OWB/507	AR
Kennemur, Plesant H.	GA	1869	Copy	093 AR
Kennerly, William	054	1871	WB-4/101	CTY
Kenney, Isaac	032	1874	WB-3/118	AR
Kennion, Lusanna	030	1804	WB-2/251	Nunc.
Kennon, Charles	099	1820	RB-16/226	AR
Kennon, Elizabeth	099	1799	RB-4/336	AR
Kennon, John	020	1856	RB-R/489	AR
Kennon, Mary	099	1848	RB-26/311	AR
Kennon, Thomas	084	1872	WB-E/40	CTY
Kent, Archelous	017	c1851	WB-A/80	AR
Kent, John	085	1822	WB-H/150	AR
Kent, John	009	1719	SS 875/219	
Kent, Joseph	010	1789	WB-D/103	AR
Kent, Levi	028	1819	WB-C/182	AR
Kent, Mourning	069	1851	WB-1/525	

Name	Co.	Date	Recorded Copy	Original
Kent, Samuel	028	1803	WB-B/173	AR
Kent, Thomas	028	1833	WB-C/351	AR
Kenutt, Jacob	046	1845	WB-C/235	AR
Kenutt, James	046	1860	WB-D/39	AR
Kenutt, John	046	1861	WB-D/92	AR
Kenyon, David H.	075	c1853	WB-M2/8	AR
Kenyon, John	077	1752	SS 878/227	SS/AR
Kepley, Matthias	032	1888	WB-4/4	AR
Kepley, Rachel	085	1859	WB-K/271	AR
Kerby, Henry	090	1790	WB-1/6	AR
Kerby, Jesse	006	1852	WB-A/45	AR
Kerby, John	017	c1830	Orig. Only	AR
Kerby, John	017	c1849	WB-A/49	
Kerby, Samuel	085	1824	WB-H/272	AR
Kerby, Thomas	024	1719	SS 875/173	
Kerchner, Lydia C.	070	1894	WB-G/249	AR
Kerfees, Caleb F.	033	1857	WB-1/134	AR
Kerlee, Elisha R.	013	1899	WB-D/328	AR
Kerlee, Larkin H.	003	1876	WB-B/95	AR
Kerley, Aaron	014	1894	WB-2/523	AR
Kerley, Elisha	003	1890	WB-B/288	AR
Kerley, Isom	003	1892	WB-B/304	AR
Kern, Conrad	085	1812	WB-G/238	AR
Kern, John	085	1823	WB-H/248	AR
Kern, Julius L.	038	1860	WB-1/154	AR
Kern, Leonhard	085	1790	WB-C/231	AR
Kern, Peter	085	1855	WB-K/186	AR
Kerner, Clara	038	1897	WB-4/30	AR
Kerner, Joseph	090	1830	WB-3/213	AR
Kerner, Nathaniel	038	1891	WB-3/196	AR
Kerner, Phillip	038	1875	WB-2/207	AR
Kerner, W. G.	038	1883	WB-2/436	AR
Kernodle, John R.	046	1888	WB-E/501	AR
Kernodle, R. B.	046	1897	WB-F/595	AR
Kerns, Mary	054	1899	WB-6/228	CTY
Kerns, Nancy A.	065	1896	WB-M/519	AR
Kerr, Absalom	092	1844	WB-4/212	
Kerr, Alexander	020	1814	RB-F/387	AR
Kerr, Alfred	085	1829	WB-H/452	AR
Kerr, Andrew	085	c1781	WB-B/42	AR
Kerr, Andrew	054	c1792	WB-1/128	AR
Kerr, Cathrine	046	1816	WB-A/211	AR
Kerr, Charlotte	013	1897	WB-D/33	AR
Kerr, Daniel	070	1821	WB-C/219	AR
Kerr, Daniel W.	022	1850	WB-C/259	AR
Kerr, David	046	1804	WB-A/207	AR
Kerr, David	085	c1803	WB-C/229	AR
Kerr, David	054	1895	WB-5/539	CTY
Kerr, David W.	001	1879	WB-2/147	AR
Kerr, Donald	070	1799	WB-AB/29	AR
Kerr, Elenor	054	c1828	WB-2/105	AR
Kerr, Elizabeth	054	1846	WB-3/4	AR
Kerr, Elizabeth	046	c1809	WB-A/210	AR
Kerr, Euphence	073	1840	WB-F/50	AR
Kerr, George S.	054	1876	WB-4/202	CTY
Kerr, Hannah	046	1831	WB-B/439	AR
Kerr, Henry	092	1887	WB-6/257	AR
Kerr, Hugh	026	1859	WB-1/238	AR
Kerr, Isaac	001	1900	WB-3/323	AR
Kerr, Jacob	087	1895	WB-3/581	AR
Kerr, James	065	1882	Orig. Only	AR
Kerr, James	054	c1814	WB-1/392	AR
Kerr, James	087	1872	WB-3/60	AR
Kerr, James	085	1844	WB-I/245	AR
Kerr, James	065	1866	WB-J/221	AR

Name	Co.	Date	Recorded Copy	Original
Kerr, John	085	c1804	WB-F/66	AR
Kerr, John	020	c1810	Orig. Only	AR
Kerr, John	065	1789	WB-D/133	AR
Kerr, John	090	1803	WB-2/39	AR
Kerr, John N.	065	1886	WB-L/164	
Kerr, John W.	046	1897	WB-G/21	AR
Kerr, Joseph	065	1772	WB-D/121	AR
Kerr, Joseph	085	1829	WB-H/461	AR
Kerr, Joseph	065	1822	WB-D/147	AR
Kerr, Joseph	081	1784	WB-1/2	AR
Kerr, Margaret	085	1848	WB-K/64	AR
Kerr, Margaret	073	1848	WB-F/410	AR
Kerr, Mary	085	1840	WB-I/72	AR
Kerr, Mary	065	1806	WB-D/143	AR
Kerr, Mary	085	1805	WB-C/234	AR
Kerr, Mary	020	1831	RB-L/626	AR
Kerr, Nancy	054	1850	WB-3/40	AR
Kerr, Nathaniel	046	1826	WB-B/222	AR
Kerr, Nathaniel	046	1830	WB-B/417	AR
Kerr, Nathaniel	054	c1806	WB-1/130	AR
Kerr, Robert	065	1784	WB-D/129	
Kerr, Robert	065	1843	WB-H/126	AR
Kerr, Robert M.	065	1855	WB-J/6	AR
Kerr, Samuel	065	1847	WB-I/109	AR
Kerr, Samuel	085	1865	WB-K/360	AR
Kerr, Samuel M.	046	1860	WB-D/65	AR
Kerr, Washington	099	1885	WB-B/82	AR
Kerr, William H.	085	1844	WB-I/232	AR
Kerr, William K.	086	1831	WB-D/135	AR
Kerr, William M.	065	1892	WB-M/49	
Kerşey, Agnes	071	1824	WB-3/296	
Kersey, Alexander	020	1852	RB-Q/633	AR
Kersey, Amos	046	1831	WB-B/437	AR
Kersey, Baldy	044	1899	WB-24/464	CTY
Kersey, Eleazer	046	1816	WB-B/20	AR
Kersey, Elizabeth	046	1835	WB-B/530	AR
Kersey, Jesse	046	1822	WB-B/156	AR
Kersey, John	VA	1786	020 RB-B/426	
Kersey, John	020	1812	RB-F/303	
Kersey, Martha	020	1822	RB-I/148	AR
Kersey, Sally	020	1815	RB-G/76	AR
Kersey, Samuel	046	1837	WB-B/572	AR
Kesler, C. C. R.	085	1892	WB-2/494	CTY
Kesler, Tobias	085	1897	WB-3/172	CTY
Kesler, Tobias	085	c1894	Copy	016 AR
Kesler, William A.	085	c1868	WB-1/8	CTY
Kester, Samuel	054	1869	WB-4/11	AR
Kestler, Henry	085	1845	WB-K/13	
Kestler, Mary	085	1890	WB-2/425	CTY
Kestler, Peter	033	1893	WB-2/150	CTY
Ketchey, John	085	1872	WB-1/133	CTY
Ketchey, Peter	085	1877	WB-1/358	CTY
Ketchie, Rineholdt	085	1858	WB-K/257	AR
Ketchum, A. K.	006	1900	WB-E/418	AR
Ketchum, G. W.	006	1897	WB-E/320	AR
Ketchum, Jonathan	072	1818	WB-A/72	AR
Keter, James, Sr.	086	1802	WB-B/134	AR
Kethley, John	103	1794	WI-A/459	AR
Kethley, Richard	103	1808	RD-1/90	AR
Ketner, Dawalt	085	1853	WB-K/155	AR
Ketner, Francis	090	1831	WB-3/223	AR
Ketner, Frederic	090	1843	WB-4/116	AR
Ketner, George	085	1824	WB-H/270	AR
Ketner, George M.	085	1899	WB-3/275	CTY
Ketner, Matthew	090	1842	WB-4/106	AR

Name	Co.	Date	Recorded Copy	Original
Ketner. Leonard	038	1896	WB-4/7	AR
Keton, Abel	018	1852	WB-C/364	
Keton, John	077	1735	Orig. Only	SS/AR
Ketron, Elizabeth	025	1897	WB-A/217	
Kever, Sally Ann	021	1885	WB-2/310	
Kewell, Charles S.	009	1840	OB-C2/363	AR
Kewell, John, Sr.	009	c1809	OB-A/79	AR
Kewell, Mary A.	009	1862	OB-L/395	AR
Key, Garland	084	c1816	OW/60	AR
Key, George	071	1815	WB-3/165	AR
Key, Joseph	057	1829	WB-B/102	AR
Key, Kilis	092	c1834	WB-4/67	
Key, Nancy	092	1867	WB-5/90	
Key, Philip B.	054	1896	098 WB-A/282	098 CTY
Key, Philip B.	054	1896	WB-6/58	CTY
Key, Rice	092	c1828	WB-4/44	
Key, Russel R.	092	1896	WB-6/454	AR
Key, Samuel	071	1824	WB-3/304	AR
Keys, James H.	100	1821	WB-23/306	AR
Keys, Joseph	092	1808	WB-3/86	AR
Keziah, Charity	016	1882	WB-3/356	AR
Keziah, Susanna	097	1867	WB-1/288	AR
Kibb, Jesse	063	1863	WB-2/516	
Kibble, Abraham	072	1751	028 DB-5/185	SS/AR
Kibble, James	072	1787	WI/L42	AR
Kibbles, Edith	072	c1772	RW/L38	AR
Kibler, Michael	021	1849	WB-1/78	AR
Kidd, Benjamin	092	1847	WB-4/267	
Kidd, Charlie L.	092	1899	WB-6/505	AR
Kidd, Joseph	009	c1786	OWB/209	AR
Kidd, Martha B.	068	1885	WB-D/217	
Kidd, Moses	068	1843	WB-B/140	
Kidd, William	060	1841	WB-2/113	AR
Kidder, Edward	070	1885	WB-E/556	AR
Kiernan, Emily Jane	075	1885	WB-O/230	AR
Kienle, Andreas	NJ	1897	Copy	013 AR
Kiester, Mary B.	085	1856	WB-K/213	AR
Kiestler, Joseph	060	1898	WB-5/92	AR
Kiger, Jacob	038	c1848	WB-1/26	AR
Kight, Japtha	018	1884	WB-E/124	AR
Kiker, Edmund	097	1855	WB-1/109	AR
Kilbee, Christopher	071	1752	Orig. Only	SS/AR
Kilbee, John	070	1760	DB-D/458	AR
Kilbey, Abraham	104	1816	WB-3/126	AR
Kilbey, Elizabeth	100	1795	WB-8/20	AR-Nunc.
Kilby, Ann	104	1872	WB-6/61	AR
Kilby, Emily	104	1892	WB-6/433	AR
Kilby, John	091	1885	WB-1/11	
Kilgore, W. C.	SC	1867	055 ID/169	
Kilgroe, William	099	1813	RB-11/164	AR
Kilingsworth, Francis	056	1752	028 DB-5/274	SS/AR
Killan, Jesse	021	1892	WB-3/18	
Killebrew, Berthula	037	1898	WB-H/412	AR
Killebrew, C. B.	037	1889	WB-H/157	AR
Killebrew, John I.	037	1897	WB-H/386	AR
Killebrew, Joshua	037	1793	WB-C/221	AR
Killebrew, Mary	037	1865	WB-G/257	AR
Killebrew, Rebecah	037	1839	WB-F/238	AR
Killen, Thomas	029	1798	WB-A/13	AR
Killett, Alexander	087	1849	WB-1/351	AR
Killett, William	103	1785	Orig. Only	AR
Killette, Julian A.	087	1891	WB-3/479	AR
Killgo, John	056	1761	WB-2/270	AR
Killiam, William W.	013	1860	WB-A/210	
Killian, Andrew	060	1862	WB-3/42	AR
Killian, Barbara	021	1847	WB-1/51	AR
Killian, Elizabeth	060	1802	Orig. Only	AR
Killian, Frederick	021	1879	WB-2/207	AR
Killian, Harriet C.	021	1896	WB-3/119	AR
Killian, Jacob	060	1830	WB-1/196	AR
Killian, Jacob	060	1860	WB-3/30	AR
Killian, John	021	1884	WB-2/279	
Killian, Joseph	021	1889	WB-2/465	AR
Killian, L. S.	060	1897	WB-5/44	AR
Killian, L. S.	021	1897	WB-3/155	AR
Killian, Margaret	060	1810	Orig. Only	AR
Killian, Noah W.	021	1866	WB-1/217	AR
Killian, Ruthey	020	1875	WB-A/183	CTY
Killingsworth, Elizabeth	057	1886	WB-C/144	AR
Killingsworth, Nicholas	084	c1841	WB-B/518	CTY
Killingsworth, Richard	037	c1733	Orig. Only	SS/AR
Killinsworth, William	047	1811	WB-3/516	
Killion, Andrew	060	1788	Orig. Only	AR
Killough, Samuel	016	1835	PQS.5/331	
Killough, Samuel S.	016	1867	WB-2/151	
Killpatrick, Elizabeth	085	1829	WB-H/455	AR
Killpatrick, John	034	1760	Orig. Only	028 AR
Kilough, Margaret	065	c1868	Orig. Only	AR-Copy
Kilpatrick, Alexander	054	1853	WB-3/74	AR
Kilpatrick, Andrew	054	c1810	WB-1/324	AR
Kilpatrick, Darlie	059	1900	WB-B/247	CTY
Kilpatrick, David	085	1869	WB-1/47	CTY
Kilpatrick, Elias M.	023	1881	WB-A/24	AR
Kilpatrick, Elizabeth	054	c1827	WB-2/88	AR
Kilpatrick, J. D.	085	c1829	WB-H/470	AR
Kilpatrick, John	085	c1804	WB-C/232	AR
Kilpatrick, Moses	085	1855	Orig. Only	AR
Kilpatrick, Rachel	085	1871	WB-1/82	CTY
Kilpatrick, Sarah	079	1860	WB-1/54	AR
Kilpatrick, Simon B.	079	1890	WB-2/521	AR
Kilpatrick, William	085	1843	WB-I/149	AR
Kilpatrick, Worry	028	1821	WB-C/206	AR
Kilpattrick, Sally	039	1842	WB-L/93	
Kimball, Peter	100	1779	WB-3/25	015 AR
Kimball, Sarah	044	1861	WB-21/485	CTY
Kimbell, Benjamin	100	1794	WB-7/213	AR
Kimberley, Bettie M.	013	1876	WB-B/121	AR
Kimbro, Elizabeth	020	1861	RB-S/450	AR
Kimbrough, Cathorine	020	1855	RB-R/343	AR
Kimbrough, Elijah W.	099	1830	RB-21/350	AR
Kimbrough, Elizabeth	020	1828	RB-L/266	AR
Kimbrough, George	092	1846	WB-4/251	
Kimbrough, George	092	1823	WB-3/155	AR
Kimbrough, John	020	1823	RB-I/205	AR
Kimbrough, John	106	c1866	Orig. Only	AR
Kimbrough, Marma Duke	085	1769	WB-B/159	AR
Kimbrough, Mary	020	1841	RB-O/194	AR
Kimbrough, Nathaniel	099	1781	RB-1/147	AR
Kimbrough, William	020	1856	RB-R/366	AR
Kimbrow, Thomas	020	1777	RB-A/25	AR
Kime, David	081	1834	WB-6/337	AR
Kime, Frances L.	001	1896	WB-3/143	AR
Kime, Henderson	081	1896	WB-16/376	AR
Kime, Henry	046	1874	WB-E/123	AR
Kimel, Barny	038	1870	WB-2/19	AR
Kimel, Jacob	032	1865	WB-2/321	AR
Kimel, Noah L.	032	1893	WB-4/178	AR
Kimimon, James	100	1812	WB-17/3	AR
Kimmons, Elias W.	016	1888	WB-4/6	AR
Kimmons, Elizabeth	016	1850	WB-1/180	

Name	Co.	Date	Recorded Copy	Original
Kimmons, W. W. P.	016	1885	WB-3/470	AR
Kimra, Henry	089	1845	WB-1/36	
Kimra, Jacob	089	1893	WB-2/339	AR
Kincaid, Anna	040	c1868	WB-1/204	
Kincaid, David	060	1863	WB-3/66	AR
Kincaid, E. P.	025	1900	WB-A/184	AR
Kincaid, Eleanor	085	1849	WB-K/97	AR
Kincaid, Hannah	085	1873	WB-1/154	CTY
Kincaid, James	085	1827	WB-H/378	AR
Kincaid, James	060	1863	WB-3/55	AR
Kincaid, James R.	014	1891	WB-2/434	CTY
Kincaid, Jesse	085	1855	WB-K/204	AR
Kincaid, John	085	1816	WB-G/420	AR
Kincaid, John	014	1873	WB-2/80	
Kincaid, John	014	1863	WB-1/21	
Kincaid, Mary	085	1842	WB-I/140	AR
Kincaid, Milton W.	014	1869	WB-2/22	AR
Kincaid, Thomas	060	1800	Orig. Only	AR
Kincaid, William W.	014	c1864	WB-1/2	AR
Kince, Christan	N	1762	SS 881/215	SS/AR
Kincey, John	057	c1815	WB-B/5	AR
Kinchen, Alexander	022	1806	WB-A/122	AR
Kinchen, Cheatham	104	1834	WB-4/174	
Kinchen, Henry M.	039	1808	WB-C/113	AR
Kinchen, John	039	c1793	WB-A/116	AR
Kinchen, William	037	1779	WB-B/26	AR
Kinchen, William	037	1758	SS 881/197	SS/AR
Kindall, Henderson	089	1881	WB-2/88	
Kindall, John	104	1841	WB-4/264	AR
Kindall, Sarah	104	1830	WB-4/136	
Kindall, William	104	1840	WB-4/255	AR
Kindar, Casper	085	c1785	WB-C/194	AR
Kinder, Casper	054	1898	WB-6/136	CTY
Kinder, George	085	c1793	WB-C/242	AR
Kindley, John	032	1826	WB-1/67	AR-Copy
Kindley, John	033	1873	WB-2/31	CTY
Kindred, Elisha	005	c1823	WB-A/90	AR
Kindrick, Sarah	100	1796	WB-8/236	AR
Kindrick, Thomas	026	1855	WB-1/191	AR
King, Abbey	100	1844	WB-38/316	AR
King, Addison F.	046	1863	WB-D/186	AR
King, Alexander	011	1868	WB-2/29	
King, Alexander	011	c1846	WB-1/294	
King, Alexander	100	1857	WB-49/108	AR
King, Allen	046	1863	WB-D/181	AR
King, Allen	100	1860	WB-49/284	AR
King, Allen	099	1881	WB-A/238	AR
King, Alvis	001	1883	WB-2/203	AR
King, Amasa	001	1875	WB-2/87	AR
King, Amistead	100	1900	WB-51/544	
King, Andrew J.	073	1883	WB-H/328	CTY
King, Anna L.	039	1891	WB-U/516	AR
King, Anny	073	1844	WB-F/235	
King, Anthony	100	1823	WB-25/174	AR
King, Arenton	028	1798	WB-B/42	AR
King, Armour	073	c1834	Orig. Only	AR
King, B. B.	001	1896	WB-3/198	AR
King, Barney	056	1897	WB-4/49	AR
King, Baxter	073	1801	WB-D/34	AR
King, Benaja	090	c1790	Orig. Only	AR
King, Benjamin	099	1896	WB-C/489	AR
King, Benjamin	069	1891	WB-5/334	AR
King, Bettie A.	100	1877	WB-51/123	AR
King, Brittain	028	1798	WB-B/43	AR
King, Bryan	087	1835	WB-1/165	AR
King, Cader	010	1815	WB-F/279	AR
King, Charles	073	1864	WB-G/460	CTY
King, Charles	100	1822	WB-24/172	AR
King, Charles	047	1826	WB-4/27	
King, Charles	073	1811	WB-D/282	AR
King, Charles	010	1819	WB-G/62	AR
King, Charles	028	1797	Orig. Only	AR-Copy
King, Charles	028	1759	Orig. Only	AR
King, Charles	010	1818	WB-G/38	AR
King, Coffield	037	1877	WB-G/522	AR
King, Cynthia	065	1870	WB-K/52	AR
King, Daniel	013	1867	Orig. Only	AR
King, Daniel	050	1873	Orig. Only	CTY
King, Daniel C.	056	1894	WB-2/180	AR
King, David	063	1812	WB-2/13	
King, David C.	087	1872	WB-3/38	AR
King, Dorothy	084	1873	WB-E/65	CTY
King, Duncan	011	c1793	WB-1/536	
King, Eddela R.	019	1895	WB-B/272	AR
King, Edmund	087	1863	WB-2/45	AR
King, Edward	001	1873	WB-2/47	AR
King, Edward	047	1843	WB-4/219	
King, Edward	047	1798	WB-3/303	
King, Edwin	044	1842	WB-15/304	CTY
King, Elendor	020	1829	RB-L/394	AR
King, Elenor	097	1899	WB-2/582	AR
King, Elihu S.	054	1841	WB-2/220	AR
King, Elizabeth	103	1889	WB-1/480	AR
King, Elizabeth	050	1896	WB-2/231	CTY
King, Elizabeth	010	1821	WB-G/86	AR
King, Elizabeth	073	1836	WB-E/385	AR
King, Elizabeth	072	1797	Orig. Only	AR
King, Elizabeth	099	1872	RB-35/193	AR
King, Elizabeth	024	1816	WB-C/47	AR
King, Enoch	072	1890	WB-4/246	AR
King, Felix	057	1885	WB-C/131	AR
King, Fountain D.	084	1883	WB-E/270	CTY
King, Frederick	072	1892	WB-4/280	AR
King, George	047	1839	WB-4/177	
King, George	099	1864	RB-33/173	AR
King, George	047	1848	WB-4/264	
King, George W.	001	1884	WB-2/235	AR
King, George W.	065	1847	WB-I/102	AR
King, Hardy	037	1865	WB-G/266	AR
King, Henry	010	1751	SS 879/17	SS/AR
King, Henry	035	c1762	WB-A/260	AR
King, Henry	029	1822	WB-B/71	AR
King, Henry	024	1714	SS 875/100	SS/AR
King, Henry	024	1824	WB-C/106	AR
King, Henry	087	1880	WB-3/202	AR
King, Henry	041	1782	WB-1/31	AR
King, Henry	099	1793	RB-2/487	
King, Henry	084	1853	WB-C/158	CTY
King, Henry	084	1840	WB-B/233	CTY
King, Higason	063	c1786	WB-1/117	
King, Higason	096	1760	WB-1/11	AR
King, Hill	072	1892	WB-4/278	AR
King, Hiram	050	1891	WB-2/141	CTY
King, Irvin	103	1881	WB-1/204	AR
King, Irvin W.	001	1876	WB-2/86	AR
King, Isabella	029	1849	WB-C/164	AR
King, Ivy	057	1872	WB-C/28	AR
King, James	054	c1814	WB-1/373	AR
King, James	060	1832	WB-1/247	AR
King, James	072	1838	WB-2/11	AR

Name	Co.	Date	Recorded Copy	Original
King, James	099	1799	RB-4/337	AR
King, James	029	1852	WB-C/233	AR
King, James A.	LA	1855	Copy	065 AR
King, Jane	020	1837	RB-N/58	
King, Jeremiah	075	1842	WB-N/167	AR
King, Jeremiah	028	1793	WB-A/290	AR
King, Jeremiah	070	1870	WB-E/215	AR
King, Jethro	087	1823	WB-1/44 & 150	AR
King, Jinny	087	1856	WB-1/491	AR
King, Joel	028	1798	WB-B/63	AR
King, Joel	039	1864	WB-R/782	AR
King, John	001	c1857	WB-1/46	AR
King, John	054	c1806	WB-1/135	AR
King, John	073	1797	WB-C/94	AR
King, John	029	1838	WB-B/292	AR
King, John	073	1782	WB-A/255	AR
King, John	085	c1803	WB-C/236	AR
King, John	046	1894	WB-F/328	AR
King, John	103	c1813	SC/03438	AR-Copy
King, John	099	1800	RB-5/124	
King, John	103	1813	RD-3/6	AR
King, John	072	1749	SS 877/312	SS/AR
King, John	090	c1822	Orig. Only	AR
King, John	099	1795	RB-3/177	AR
King, John	071	1786	WB-1/369	AR
King, John	072	1793	WB-A/70	AR
King, John	073	1805	WB-D/153	AR
King, John	090	1835	WB-3/287	AR
King, John	073	1807	WB-D/186	AR
King, John	041	1849	WB-3/124	AR
King, John G.	039	1880	WB-U/238	AR
King, John G.	029	1866	WB-D/88	AR
King, John I.	065	1857	WB-J/42	AR
King, John Q. A.	090	1882	WB-6/129	AR
King, John W.	036	1897	WB-A/416	CTY
King, Johnson	081	1886	WB-16/9	AR
King, Jonathan	013	1866	WB-A/241	AR
King, Jonathan	080	1859	Copy	013 AR
King, Jonathan	080	1859	WB-1/180	AR
King, Joseph	050	c1845	Orig. Only	AR
King, Joseph	006	1879	WB-E/51	AR
King, Joseph A.	006	c1859	Orig. Only	AR
King, Joseph J.	022	1874	WB-E/96	AR
King, Joshua	047	1882	WB-6/282	AR
King, Josiah	099	1894	WB-C/376	AR
King, Julia F.	FL	1884	080 WB-1/92	080 AR
King, Julius A.	065	1898	WB-N/140	AR
King, Katie	084	1892	WB-E/528	CTY
King, Keturah	019	1860	WB-A/253	AR
King, Levi	084	1811	WB-A/227	CTY
King, Lewis	080	1862	WB-1/182	AR
King, Little	028	1804	WB-B/192	AR
King, Louisa	037	1878	WB-G/492	AR
King, Louisa	037	1878	103 WB-2/286	103 AR
King, Lydia A.	046	1896	WB-F/533	AR
King, Mangum	001	1859	WB-1/151	AR
King, Martha R.	001	1871	WB-2/58	AR
King, Mary	103	1882	WB-1/239	AR
King, Mary	071	1821	WB-3/257	AR
King, Mary	057	1782	WB-A/19	AR
King, Mary	103	1896	WB-2/157	AR
King, Mary	010	1824	WB-G/115	AR
King, Mary A.	054	1878	WB-4/300	CTY
King, Mary J.	099	1876	RB-35/353	AR
King, Mattie	097	1900	WB-3/67	AR
King, Maxmillan	SC	1882	050 WB-1/168	050 CTY
King, Meritt L.	071	1837	WB-4/161	AR
King, Micajah	072	1831	WB-1/72	AR
King, Michael	063	1811	WB-2/2	
King, Michael	010	1741	Orig. Only	SS/AR
King, Michael	029	c1783	Orig. Only	AR
King, Mima	099	1893	WB-C/145	AR
King, Mitchell	SC	1862	050 WB-1/64	
King, Nancy	083	1892	WB-3/567	AR
King, Nancy	084	1885	WB-E/306	CTY
King, Nasim S.	090	1864	WB-4/366	AR
King, Nathan	029	1834	WB-B/235	AR
King, Nathaniel	073	1824	WB-E/61	AR
King, Olly	050	1899	WB-2/317	CTY
King, Paul H.	060	1885	WB-4/319	AR
King, Penzy	047	1887	WB-6/467	AR
King, Peter	085	c1763	WB-B/24	AR
King, Polly P.	038	1855	WB-1/72	AR
King, Polly W.	100	1883	WB-51/168	AR
King, Presley	099	1827	RB-20/104	AR
King, Rebecca	071	1828	WB-4/44	AR
King, Reuben	083	1869	WB-3/1	AR
King, Richard	010	1825	WB-G/137	AR
King, Richard	085	c1779	WB-B/19	AR
King, Richard	065	1854	WB-I/242	AR
King, Richard F.	054	1877	WB-4/282	CTY
King, Richard J.	087	1864	WB-2/71	AR
King, Richard W.	059	1883	WB-A/300	
King, Robbin	020	1817	RB-H/43	AR
King, Robert	104	1799	WB-1/523	
King, Robert	063	1836	WB-2/218	
King, Robert	073	1837	WB-E/420	AR
King, Robert W.	029	1849	WB-C/166	AR
King, S. A.	011	1899	Orig. Only	CTY
King, Sally	069	1841	WB-1/452	AR
King, Samuel	054	1842	WB-2/247	AR
King, Samuel	057	1807	WB-A/290	AR
King, Sarah	054	c1820	Orig. Only	AR
King, Sarah	028	1855	WB-D/243	AR
King, Sarah A.	019	1885	WB-B/152	AR
King, Seney	087	1844	WB-1/285	AR
King, Sewell	099	1900	WB-D/368	AR
King, Simon	041	1818	WB-2/148	AR
King, Simon	041	1899	WB-4/497	AR
King, Solomon	041	1795	WB-1/136	AR
King, Solomon	099	1882	WB-A/346	AR
King, Thomas	090	1850	WB-4/264	AR
King, Thomas	024	1789	WB-A/148	AR
King, Thomas	028	1835	WB-C/379	AR
King, Thomas	054	c1812	WB-1/297	
King, Thomas	047	1858	WB-5/50	
King, Thomas	084	1817	WB-A/217	CTY
King, Thomas	024	1842	WB-C/230	AR
King, Thomas	079	1864	WB-1/136	AR
King, Thomas	073	1834	WB-E/315	AR
King, Thomas	084	c1819	WB-A/192	CTY
King, Thomas	VA	1883	Copy	078 AR
King, Thomas C.	010	1828	WB-G/174	AR
King, Thomas J.	041	1853	WB-3/166	
King, Turner	073	1894	WB-I/45	CTY
King, Vincent	099	1836	RB-23/554	AR
King, Washington	010	1890	WB-I/295	AR
King, Washington	039	1873	WB-U/88	AR
King, William	090	1898	WB-6/447	AR
King, William	073	1860	WB-G/242	AR

Name	Co.	Date	Recorded Copy	Original
King, William	054	1869	WB-4/19	AR
King, William	087	c1816	Orig. Only	AR
King, William	060	1892	WB-4/479	AR
King, William	011	1883	WB-2/166	
King, William	099	1860	RB-31/434	AR
King, William	010	1778	WB-B/126	AR
King, William	010	1790	WB-D/132	AR
King, William	084	1851	WB-C/119	CTY
King, William	073	1820	WB-D/571	AR
King, William	084	1849	WB-C/103	CTY
King, William	081	1827	WB-5/378	AR
King, William	060	1866	WB-3/88	AR
King, William	037	c1759	WB-A/158	AR
King, William	065	1798	WB-D/137	AR
King, William	041	1832	WB-2/307	AR
King, William	072	1786	WI/L51	AR
King, William	001	1866	WB-1/280	AR
King, William A.	029	1895	WB-F/37	AR
King, William C.	001	1865	WB-1/230	AR
King, William C.	037	1818	WB-E/208	AR
King, William D.	020	1891	WB-B/55	CTY
King, William J.	072	1879	WB-4/106	AR
King, William R.	039	1888	WB-U/428	
King, William T.	AL	1853	Copy	087 AR
Kingsbury, Augustus	029	1884	WB-E/325	AR
Kingsbury, Gabriel	070	1794	WB-C/215	AR
Kingsbury, Henry	070	c1796	Orig. Only	AR
Kingsbury, John	070	1791	WB-C/214	AR
Kingsbury, Russell	044	1856	WB-20/129	CTY
Kingsley, Isabella	070	1816	WB-AB/248	AR
Kingsmore, Ann	105	1889	WB-2/514	
Kingston, James	070	1748	SS 878/3	SS/AR
Kington, Bethiah	010	1815	WB-F/299	AR
Kinlaw, John C.	083	1873	WB-3/68	AR
Kinlaw, Sary	083	1832	WB-1/271	AR
Kinnamon, John	090	1831	WB-3/224	AR
Kinnebrugh, James	020	c1842	RB-0/439	
Kinnemon, Philip	100	1809	WB-15/112	AR
Kinney, Elizabeth	075	1884	WB-0/220	AR
Kinney, Lenard	085	1864	WB-K/326	AR
Kinnier, John	065	1816	WB-D/145	AR
Kinnin, Anthony	009	c1791	OWB/260	AR
Kinnon, Benjamin	075	1785	WB-K/127	AR
Kinny, C. R.	075	1845	WB-N/196	AR
Kinny, Isaac	081	1885	WB-15/553	AR
Kinny, John	068	1816	WB-A/293	
Kinsaul, Cornelius	079	1897	WB-3/131	AR
Kinsey, Ebenezer	OH	1900	023 WB-A/190	023 AR
Kinsey, Henry	030	1807	WB-2/319	
Kinsey, John	028	1752	DB-5/254	SS/AR
Kinsey, John	028	1772	Orig. Only	AR
Kinsey, John	077	1719	Orig. Only	SS/AR
Kinsey, Joseph	057	1816	WB-A/33	AR
Kinsey, Joseph	057	1858	WB-B/246	AR
Kinsey, Laura A.	059	1894	WB-B/89	CTY
Kinsey, Lewis	072	1847	WB-2/86	AR
Kinsey, Mary	057	1854	WB-B/218	AR
Kinsey, William	030	1868	WB-4/270	AR
Kinsland, Jesse	049	1850	WB-2/181	AR
Kinton, Kedar	041	c1806	Orig. Only	AR
Kinyon, Ann Marwood	077	1805	WB-E/225	AR
Kinyon, Duke	077	1788	WB-C/360	AR
Kinyon, Joab	077	1797	WB-E/84	AR
Kinyon, Levi	077	1833	WB-F/220	AR
Kinyon, Roger	077	1777	WB-C/199	AR
Kinyoun, Joel	085	1822	WB-H/170	AR
Kippen, Martha A.	024	c1758	Orig. Only	AR
Kipper, Mary S.	082	1879	WB-6/173	
Kipps, Seth	053	1811	RW-1/450	AR
Kirby (Cerbey), Absalom	056	1795	WB-1/795	AR
Kirby, Abraham	075	1799	WB-M1/33	AR
Kirby, Cynthia	017	c1851	WB-A/64	AR
Kirby, Elijah	017	1897	WB-B/287	AR
Kirby, Enoch	017	1876	WB-B/59	AR
Kirby, Henry	105	1878	WB-2/227	
Kirby, James	022	1816	WB-A/284	AR
Kirby, Jesse, Sr.	056	1850	WB-1/625	AR
Kirby, Lizzie	073	1900	WB-I/174	CTY
Kirby, P. Brison	004	1896	WB-A/174	AR
Kirby, Pitts	105	1876	WB-2/186	AR
Kirby, Samuel H.	077	1847	WB-F/335	AR
Kirby, Temperance	056	1889	WB-3/517	AR
Kirby, Thomas	073	1887	WB-H/441	CTY
Kirby, Thomas	024	1719	Orig. Only	SS/AR
Kirby, William	087	1843	WB-1/271	AR
Kirk, Ann J.	089	1887	WB-2/148	
Kirk, Daniel	089	1846	WB-1/49	
Kirk, David F.	076	1899	WB-A1/241	
Kirk, George	022	c1811	WB-A/194	AR
Kirk, James	084	c1801	OW/57	AR
Kirk, James	085	1864	WB-K/348	AR
Kirk, James C.	089	1890	WB-2/199	AR
Kirk, Jason	PA	1880	075 WB-0/214	
Kirk, John S.	106	1883	WB-2/174	
Kirk, Lewis	073	1808	WB-D/290	AR
Kirk, Mary A. L.	085	1895	WB-3/89	CTY
Kirk, Parham	089	1887	WB-2/144	AR
Kirk, Parham	089	1854	WB-1/123	
Kirk, Samuel	PA	c1883	075 WB-0/211	
Kirk, Stephen	089	1852	WB-1/88	
Kirk, W. M.	089	1864	WB-1/254	AR
Kirk, Wm. Porter	013	1897	WB-D/1 & 89	AR
Kirkby, H. James	070	1795	WB-C/216	AR
Kirkconell, John	009	c1783	OWB/183	AR
Kirkland, Elizabeth	073	1888	WB-H/457	CTY
Kirkland, Elizabeth	073	1882	WB-H/307	CTY
Kirkland, Elizabeth	073	1866	WB-G/488	CTY
Kirkland, Isabella	073	1887	WB-H/423	CTY
Kirkland, James	073	1882	WB-H/308	AR
Kirkland, John	073	1892	WB-H/575	CTY
Kirkland, Joseph	073	1841	WB-F/89	AR
Kirkland, Mary	073	1888	WB-H/450	CTY
Kirkland, William	073	1835	WB-E/388	AR
Kirkman, Amelia	028	1893	WB-F/63	
Kirkman, Elisha	046	1841	WB-C/81	AR
Kirkman, Esther A.	046	1861	WB-D/117	AR
Kirkman, James	046	1791	WB-A/205	AR
Kirkman, John W.	046	1889	WB-F/5	AR
Kirkman, Joseph	046	1886	WB-E/447	AR
Kirkman, Leven	046	1858	WB-C/517	AR
Kirkman, Leven	046	1858	WB-C/505	AR
Kirkman, Peter	046	1801	WB-A/207	AR
Kirkman, Roger, Sr.	046	1862	WB-D/148	AR
Kirkman, Thomas	081	1852	WB-9/278	AR
Kirkman, Virgil N.	046	1855	WB-C/444	AR
Kirkman, W. L.	046	1891	WB-F/95	AR
Kirkpatrick, Alexander	001	1874	WB-2/84	AR
Kirkpatrick, Hannah	073	1841	WB-F/112	AR
Kirkpatrick, Hugh	073	1883	WB-H/329	CTY
Kirkpatrick, Hugh	065	1827	WB-D/150	AR

Name	Co.	Date	Recorded Copy	Original
Kirkpatrick, John	065	1808	WB-D/144	AR
Kirkpatrick, John M.	065	1898	WB-N/121	AR
Kirkpatrick, Joseph	046	1859	WB-D/26	AR
Kirkpatrick, Josiah	029	1830	WB-B/200	AR
Kirkpatrick, Robert	016	1869	WB-3/48	
Kirkpatrick, Sarah P.	065	1893	WB-M/286	AR
Kirkpatrick, Thomas	065	1819	WB-D/146	AR
Kirkpatrick, Thomas	065	1846	WB-I/74	AR
Kirkpatrick, Thomas A.	065	1895	WB-M/409	AR
Kirkpatrick, Valentine	016	1830	PQS.5/135	
Kirkpatrick, W. L.	065	1872	WB-K/92	AR
Kirkpatrick, William	001	1865	WB-1/242	AR
Kirksey, Gideon	022	1801	WB-A/65	AR
Kirksey, Isaac	022	1779	Orig. Only	AR
Kirksey, James S.	065	1885	WB-L/62	AR
Kirkwood, Margaret	070	1790	Orig. Only	AR-Nunc.
Kirschbaum, L.	047	1874	WB-6/102	AR
Kirven, Thomas	029	1795	Orig. Only	AR-Nunc.
Kiser, Adam	060	1833	WB-1/285	AR
Kiser, Barbara	090	1835	WB-3/288	AR
Kiser, Clarissa	040	1891	WB-2/387	AR
Kiser, George	016	1830	PQS.5/107	
Kiser, Jacob	040	1893	WB-2/425	AR
Kiser, James M.	090	1898	WB-6/465	AR
Kiser, John	026	1848	WB-1/85	AR
Kiser, John	090	1886	WB-6/169	AR
Kiser, John, Sr.	038	1873	WB-2/133	AR
Kiser, Joseph	040	1863	WB-1/155	AR
Kiser, Juda	090	1881	WB-6/122	AR
Kiser, Lawrence	060	1786	Orig. Only	AR
Kiser, Levi	040	1876	WB-2/103	AR
Kiser, Mary M.	040	1865	WB-1/175	
Kiser, Michael	090	1881	WB-6/122	AR
Kiser, Michael	090	1864	WB-4/373	AR
Kiser, Susannah	040	1877	WB-2/121	AR
Kiser, William	090	1890	WB-6/234	AR
Kisible, Michael	028	1728	Orig. Only	SS/AR
Kisor, Ervin	016	1877	WB-3/212	AR
Kissee, John	020	1848	RB-Q/29	
Kistler, Catherine	054	1896	WB-6/32	CTY
Kistler, Catherine	085	1895	WB-3/81	CTY
Kistler, Elizabeth	060	1869	WB-4/30	AR
Kistler, Henry	060	1857	WB-3/15	AR
Kistler, Henry	085	1846	WB-K/68	AR
Kistler, Lawson H.	060	1869	WB-4/27	AR
Kistler, Paul	060	1848	WB-2/305	AR
Kistler, Susannah	060	1885	WB-4/317	AR
Kistler, Susannah	060	1891	WB-4/461	AR
Kistler, Susannah	060	1839	WB-2/15	AR
Kitchen, Elizabeth	037	1825	WB-F/44	AR
Kitchen, James	020	1808	RB-E/379	AR
Kitching, Booz	037	1772	WB-A/202	AR
Kitching, Mary	037	1785	WB-C/11	AR
Kitching, William	077	1736	LGB-4/#32	SS/AR
Kites, Charles	075	1768	WB-H/82	AR
Kits, Francis	086	1807	WB-B/208	AR
Kittle, J. B.	044	1864	WB-22/96	CTY
Kittle, Lewis H.	098	1885	WB-A/39	
Kittrell, Demsey	010	1797	WB-D/367	AR
Kittrell, Eliza T.	039	1843	WB-L/106	
Kittrell, Elizabeth	044	1821	WB-9/40	CTY
Kittrell, Elizabeth	041	1823	WB-2/196	AR
Kittrell, Fielding	044	1838	WB-14/324	CTY
Kittrell, George	041	1832	WB-2/312	AR
Kittrell, Jethro	079	c1856	WB-1/56	AR-Copy

Name	Co.	Date	Recorded Copy	Original
Kittrell, John	010	1793	WB-D/209	AR
Kittrell, John	010	1801	WB-E/133	AR
Kittrell, Jonathan	044	1812	Orig. Only	CTY
Kittrell, Jonathan	079	1860	WB-1/58	AR-Copy
Kittrell, Martha B.	044	1871	WB-23/39	CTY
Kittrell, Samuel	044	1808	WB-7/4	CTY
Kittrell, Samuel A.	079	1890	WB-2/525	AR
Kittrell, Sarah	010	1797	WB-E/6	AR
Kittrell, Simon W.	044	1879	WB-23/335	CTY
Kittrell, Tabitha	044	1872	WB-23/56	CTY
Kittrell, Thomas G.	069	c1893	Orig. Only	AR
Kittrell, William	044	1843	WB-15/504	CTY
Kivett, Daniel	081	1892	WB-16/228	
Kivett, Henry	081	1882	WB-15/374	AR
Kivett, John	081	1843	WB-7/480	AR
Kivett, Peter	081	1794	WB-2/7	AR
Kivett, Solomon	081	1880	WB-15/318	AR
Kivett, Zimri	081	1841	WB-7/375	AR
Kizer, William L.	097	1862	WB-1/201	AR
Kizor, Rachel	016	1872	WB-3/80	AR
Klapp, Caroline	001	1885	WB-2/243	AR
Klapp, Elizabeth	001	1885	WB-2/243	
Klapp, L. W.	046	1899	WB-G/165	AR
Klett, Frederick	PA	1859	103 WB-1/24	103 AR
Kline, Abraham	099	1868	RB-35/1	AR
Kline, Michael	065	1783	WB-D/126	AR
Klopp, Eliz. Ann	001	1879	WB-2/144	
Klotz, Conrad	085	c1807	WB-F/65	AR
Klutts, George	016	1870	WB-3/24	
Klutts, George	016	1840	PQS.6/102	
Klutts, Henry	085	1883	WB-2/67	CTY
Klutts, Jacob	085	1828	WB-H/414	AR
Klutts, L. J.	016	1886	WB-3/484	AR
Klutts, Leonard	085	1853	WB-K/159	AR
Klutts, Leonard	085	1867	WB-L/14	
Klutts, Marthy	085	1852	WB-K/147	AR
Klutts, Mary C.	016	1895	WB-4/209	AR
Klutts, Paul	016	1848	WB-1/146	
Klutts, Sophia	016	1882	WB-3/352	AR
Klutts, Tobias	085	1863	WB-K/312	AR
Klutts, Tobias Sr.	016	1839	PQS.6/17	
Klutts, William B.	085	1881	WB-1/576	CTY
Knibloe, Peter	075	1774	WB-I/77	AR
Knight, Abel	046	1810	WB-A/210	AR
Knight, Ann	037	1820	WB-E/247	AR
Knight, Arthur	037	1834	WB-F/160	AR
Knight, Asa	046	1890	WB-F/72	AR
Knight, B. F.	037	1854	WB-G/56	AR
Knight, Charles C.	037	1839	Orig. Only	AR
Knight, Clarrendy	018	1869	WB-E/5	AR
Knight, Demsey	041	1852	WB-3/151	AR
Knight, Edith	037	1875	WB-G/471	
Knight, Elizabeth	037	1897	WB-H/378	AR
Knight, Ephraim	047	1800	WB-3/345	
Knight, Esther	041	1862	WB-3/288	AR
Knight, Evans	020	1858	RB-S/87	AR
Knight, Francis	037	1808	WB-D/324	AR
Knight, Francis H.	037	1875	WB-G/464	
Knight, Frederick	047	1775	WB-2/4	
Knight, George	069	1785	WB-1/35	AR
Knight, Isaac	085	1835	WB-H/659	AR
Knight, J. L.	079	1891	WB-2/553	AR
Knight, James	041	1808	WB-2/9	AR
Knight, James	037	1794	WB-C/268	AR
Knight, James	037	1847	WB-F/384	AR

Name	Co.	Date	Recorded Copy	Original
Knight, James C.	037	1870	WB-G/350	AR
Knight, Jesse	037	1816	WB-E/122	AR
Knight, Jesse C.	037	1860	WB-G/176	AR
Knight, John	047	1818	WB-3/629	
Knight, John	047	1834	WB-4/105	
Knight, John	085	1832	WB-H/541	AR
Knight, John	037	1770	WB-A/184	AR
Knight, John	054	c1831	Orig. Only	AR
Knight, John	069	1783	WB-1/26	AR
Knight, John A.	041	1898	WB-4/460	AR
Knight, Jonas	037	1816	WB-E/125	
Knight, Jonathan	044	1809	WB-7/80	CTY
Knight, Jordan	037	1881	WB-G/601	AR
Knight, Joseph	063	1861	WB-2/481	
Knight, Kader	057	1822	WB-B/70	AR
Knight, Lavinia	099	1849	RB-26/543	AR
Knight, Lewis A.	075	1732	SS 876/246	SS/AR
Knight, Martha A.	037	1898	WB-H/419	AR
Knight, Mary	079	c1864	WB-1/162	AR
Knight, Moses	037	1781	WB-B/88	AR
Knight, Noel	099	1852	RB-28/103	AR
Knight, Peter	037	1811	WB-E/25	AR
Knight, Peter E.	037	1864	WB-G/244	AR
Knight, Peter H.	099	1895	WB-C/365	AR
Knight, Pinkney	084	1892	WB-E/526	CTY
Knight, Robert	037	1761	WB-A/54	AR
Knight, Sally	037	1887	WB-H/91	AR
Knight, Sally	037	1847	WB-F/368	AR
Knight, Sarah	051	1831	WB-A/111	
Knight, Stephen	044	1802	WB-5/281	CTY
Knight, Thomas	084	1856	WB-C/221	CTY
Knight, Thomas J.	041	1853	WB-3/166	AR
Knight, Tobias	008	1719	SS 875/147	SS/AR
Knight, Walker	037	1833	WB-F/143	AR
Knight, William	010	1752	SS 879/40	SS/AR
Knight, William	085	1831	WB-H/512	AR
Knight, Willis	037	1846	WB-F/343	AR
Knighten, Thomas	065	1776	WB-B/56	AR
Knighton, Elenor	020	1849	RB-Q/140	
Knohl, Frederick	070	1866	WB-D/174	AR
Knoles, Robert	035	1855	WB-2/93	AR
Knoles, Robert	035	1792	WB-A/264	AR
Knols, John	035	1804	WB-A/268	AR
Knoot, Thomas	022	1779	Orig. Only	AR
Knott, Absalom	010	1784	WB-C/81	AR
Knott, Caleb	044	1855	WB-20/15	CTY
Knott, David W.	098	1899	WB-A/315	CTY
Knott, Fielding	044	c1893	Copy	099 AR
Knott, Henry	046	1843	WB-C/152	AR
Knott, James	044	1801	WB-5/179	CTY
Knott, James	044	1783	WB-1/379	CTY
Knott, John	044	1799	WB-4/267	CTY
Knott, Joseph	010	1776	WB-B/53	AR
Knott, Joseph	010	1781	WB-C/4	AR
Knott, Risdom	044	1863	WB-21/675	CTY
Knott, William	010	1781	WB-C/27	AR
Knott, William	090	1844	WB-4/145	AR
Knott, William	010	1786	WB-D/66	AR
Knott, William M.	044	1864	WB-22/250	CTY
Knotts, Absolem	005	1855	WB-C/124	AR
Knotts, John	005	1824	WB-A/96	AR
Knotts, John	005	1897	WB-D/413	AR
Knotts, John	005	c1854	WB-2/83	AR
Knotts, John B.	005	1839	WB-B/93	AR

Name	Co.	Date	Recorded Copy	Original
Knotts, John, Sr.	005	1799	WB-2/81	AR
Knotts, Mary C.	005	1898	WB-D/433	AR
Knotts, William	070	1771	WB-C/212	AR
Knoure, Joseph	032	1826	WB-1/55	
Knouse, Mary E.	038	1898	WB-4/110	AR
Knowis, Rhoda	009	1817	OB-A/275	AR
Knowis, Sidney	009	1816	OB-A/261	AR-Nunc.
Knowis, Willowby	009	c1796	OWB/319	AR
Knowland, Edward	044	1796	WB-3/252	CTY
Knowles, David	060	1841	WB-2/94	AR
Knowls, Edward	015	1765	RB-1/27	AR
Knowls, Elizabeth	077	c1824	WB-F/147	AR
Knowls, Robert	035	1762	Orig. Only	AR
Knox, Ambrose	075	1796	WB-L/51	AR
Knox, Andrew	054	c1815	WB-1/358	AR
Knox, Andrew	077	1776	WB-C/179	AR
Knox, Andrew	075	1816	WB-M1/293	AR
Knox, Arseny	079	1885	WB-2/343	AR
Knox, Ashley	079	1886	WB-2/368	AR
Knox, Benjamin	054	1843	WB-2/280	AR
Knox, Celia	065	1829	WB-E/73	AR
Knox, Eliza H.	099	1890	WB-B/473	AR
Knox, George	085	1869	WB-1/36	CTY
Knox, Hannah	065	1847	WB-I/101	AR
Knox, Hardy	086	1814	WB-C/10	
Knox, Haywood	079	1899	WB-3/173	AR
Knox, Hugh	075	1818	WB-M1/316	AR
Knox, James	065	1794	WB-D/135	AR
Knox, James	065	1842	WB-H/113	AR
Knox, James G.	085	1849	WB-K/98	AR
Knox, Jane	065	1840	WB-H/11	AR
Knox, Jean	085	1772	WB-A/72	AR
Knox, John	028	1817	WB-C/151	AR
Knox, John	065	1860	WB-J/89	AR
Knox, John	054	c1801	Orig. Only	AR
Knox, John	085	1811	WB-G/192	AR
Knox, John	060	1830	WB-1/187	AR
Knox, John	028	1805	WB-B/217	AR
Knox, John	024	1730	Orig. Only	SS/AR
Knox, John	065	1792	WB-D/134	AR
Knox, John	065	1829	WB-E/71	AR
Knox, John	040	1857	WB-1/93	
Knox, John, Sr.	065	1777	WB-D/122	AR
Knox, Lorena A.	065	1889	WB-L/400	
Knox, Mary	054	c1812	WB-1/369	
Knox, Mary	028	1823	WB-C/229	AR
Knox, Mary	054	c1812	WB-1A/100	
Knox, Matthew	065	1803	WB-D/141	AR
Knox, Nancy	065	1840	WB-H/6	AR
Knox, Nansey J.	065	1895	WB-M/392	AR
Knox, R. J. W.	065	1899	WB-N/182	
Knox, Robert	060	1833	WB-1/288	AR
Knox, Robert	085	1885	WB-2/142	CTY
Knox, Samuel	065	1800	WB-D/138	AR
Knox, Samuel	065	1839	WB-G/118	AR
Knox, Samuel	085	1868	WB-1/4	
Knox, Samuel B.	065	1875	WB-K/198	AR
Knox, Samuel W.	065	1898	WB-N/95	AR
Knox, Sarah	037	11858	WB-G/162	AR
Knox, William	063	1837	WB-2/238	
Knox, William	054	1868	WB-4/7	
Knox, Zelote E.	079	c1874	WB-2/111	AR
Knoy, Molly	032	c1857	WB-2/151	
Knoy, Philip	032	1834	WB-1/250	

Name	Co.	Date	Recorded Copy	Original
Knup, John	085	1817	WB-G/489	AR
Knupp (Canup), Louisa C.	085	1899	WB-3/345	CTY
Koen, John	075	1840	WB-N/159	AR
Koen, William R.	075	1830	WB-N/60	AR
Kohler, Conrad	016	1861	WB-2/74	
Kook, John	065	1786	WB-B/21	AR
Kook, Thomas	090	1823	WB-3/96	
Koonce, Abraham	072	1830	WB-1/62	AR
Koonce, Amos I.	057	1857	WB-B/234	AR
Koonce, Beneter	057	1838	WB-B/135	
Koonce, Benjamin	028	1859	WB-D/317	AR
Koonce, Benjamin	057	1827	WB-B/89	AR
Koonce, Bryan S.	070	1852	WB-C/544	AR
Koonce, Christian	057	1791	WB-A/186	AR
Koonce, Daniel	057	1820	WB-B/58	AR
Koonce, Daniel	072	1823	WB-A/70	AR
Koonce, Edward B.	072	1873	Orig. Only	AR-Nunc.
Koonce, George	028	c1772	Orig. Only	AR
Koonce, Jacob	057	1784	WB-A/32	AR
Koonce, John	057	1791	WB-A/118	AR
Koonce, Lenas	057	1823	WB-B/79	AR
Koonce, Lewis	057	1881	WB-C/81	AR
Koonce, Lyda	057	1824	WB-B/82	AR
Koonce, Michael	057	1782	WB-A/15	AR
Koonce, Philpiny	057	1827	WB-B/95	AR
Koonce, Richard	057	1830	WB-B/104	AR
Koonce, Richard	059	1881	WB-A/234	CTY-Copy
Koonce, Simon E.	057	1844	WB-B/167	AR
Koonce, Tobias	072	c1771	RW/L52	AR
Koonce, Tobias	057	1834	WB-B/121	AR
Koonce, William	057	1825	WB-B/84	AR
Koone, George W.	086	1862	WB-E/405	AR
Koone, Madison	086	1891	WB-F/421	AR
Koone, Marion	086	1895	WB-F/493	AR
Koone, Susan	086	1884	WB-F/225	AR
Koons, George	006	1856	WB-D/20	AR
Koons, Jacob	006	1885	WB-E/129	AR
Koonts, Adeline	032	1877	WB-3/218	AR
Koonts, Andrew	032	1862	WB-2/231	AR
Koonts, David	032	1879	WB-3/275	AR
Koonts, George	032	1880	WB-3/298	AR
Koonts, Jacob	032	1833	WB-1/234	
Koonts, John, Sr.	032	1866	WB-2/342	AR
Koontz, John, Sr.	032	1842	WB-1/396	
Koonz, George	006	1803	Orig. Only	AR
Koonz, George	006	1870	WB-D/107	AR
Korb, Katy	103	1888	WB-1/438	AR
Korf, Henry	085	1848	WB-K/68	AR
Korn, Thomas	092	1801	WB-3/43	
Kornegay, A. G.	035	1880	WB-4/170	AR
Kornegay, Abraham	028	1810	WB-C/5	AR
Kornegay, Abram	035	1825	WB-A/263	AR
Kornegay, Abram	057	1811	WB-A/328	AR
Kornegay, Daniel	057	1802	WB-A/265	AR
Kornegay, Daniel	103	1843	RD-8/391	AR
Kornegay, Daniel	103	1844	RD-9/1	AR
Kornegay, David	057	1784	WB-A/34	AR
Kornegay, David	087	c1821	WB-1/36	AR
Kornegay, George	035	1808	WB-A/266	AR
Kornegay, George	028	1773	Orig. Only	SS/AR
Kornegay, H. R.	035	1898	WB-4/513	AR
Kornegay, Harget	035	1875	WB-4/99	AR

Name	Co.	Date	Recorded Copy	Original
Kornegay, Henry C.	035	1894	WB-4/444	AR
Kornegay, Isaac	035	1838	Orig. Only	AR
Kornegay, James F.	103	1883	WB-1/287	AR
Kornegay, John	057	1800	WB-A/242	AR
Kornegay, L. W.	103	1875	WB-1/93	AR
Kornegay, Letti	057	1785	WB-A/49	AR
Kornegay, Luke	035	1819	WB-A/251 & 269	
Kornegay, Margaret	103	1866	RD-14/336	
Kornegay, Margaret	035	1840	Orig. Only	AR-Nunc.
Kornegay, Mary	035	1826	WB-A/265	AR
Kornegay, Nancy O.	035	1888	WB-4/329	AR
Kornegay, Rebecca W.	059	1896	WB-B/155	CTY
Kornegay, Sarah	035	1859	WB-3/2	AR
Kornegay, Thomas H.	035	1854	WB-2/91	AR-Nunc.
Kornegay, W. F.	103	1894	WB-2/81	AR
Kornegay, William	035	1837	Orig. Only	AR
Kornegay, William W.	103	1879	WB-1/175	AR
Kortjohann, Catherine	070	1886	WB-F/77	AR
Kortjohann, Diedrich	070	1895	WB-G/366	AR
Kosht, Margaret	068	1814	WB-A/285	
Kramsch, Samuel	090	1833	WB-3/251	AR-Nunc.
Krause, John	090	1831	WB-3/226	AR
Krause, John Edwin	090	1842	WB-4/97	AR
Krause, Samuel	090	1835	WB-3/300	AR
Krauss, Gottlob	090	1802	WB-2/31	AR
Kreegar, John	090	1819	WB-3/37	AR
Kreeger, George	090	1841	WB-4/83	AR
Kreeger, Henry	090	1828	WB-3/179	
Kreeger, Isaac N.	090	1892	WB-6/290	AR
Kreeger, Jacob	090	1824	WB-3/130	AR
Kreeger, John H.	090	1900	WB-6/541	AR
Kreeger, Sarah	038	c1860	WB-1/163	AR
Kreger, Fredrick	090	1820	WB-3/53	AR
Kregger, Timothy	038	1893	WB-3/385	AR
Kreiger, Nacalaus	090	c1785	Orig. Only	AR
Kremer, Charles	038	c1849	WB-1/32	AR
Kress, Cattarina	065	1785	WB-D/132	AR
Kress, Nicholas	065	1784	WB-A/193	AR
Kreth, Philip J.	099	1886	WB-B/124	AR
Kreuser, Conrad	090	1845	WB-4/188	
Krider, Barnabas	085	1823	WB-H/192	AR
Krider, Henry	085	1820	WB-H/25	AR
Krider, Jacob	085	1874	WB-1/265	CTY
Krieger, Anna M.	090	1842	WB-4/101	AR
Kriminger, L. B.	016	1866	WB-2/140	
Krimmenger, Frederick	016	1861	WB-2/78	
Krimminger, Nathan	016	1877	WB-3/195	AR
Kritzphezer, John	032	1885	WB-3/492	AR
Kroehn (Green), Elizabeth	090	1834	WB-3/269	AR
Kron, George	067	1872	WB-2/29	
Krows, Reves	004	1865	WB-1/7	AR
Kuck, A. E. W.	065	1898	WB-N/106	AR
Kuck, Bertha	065	1870	WB-K/56	AR
Kuester, Ferdinan	065	1882	WB-K/484	AR
Kugler, George W.	009	1899	WB-2/170	CTY
Kuinzell, Frederick	090	1802	WB-2/21	
Kunsell, Salome	090	1816	WB-2/177	AR
Kurfees, J. P.	033	1898	WB-2/241	CTY
Kushke, John F.	090	1831	WB-3/222	AR
Kyle, Elizabeth	044	1883	WB-23/468	CTY
Kyle, James	029	1881	WB-E/251	AR
Kyle, Jemima	092	1861	WB-5/51	
Kyle, John	047	1886	WB-6/428	AR

Name	Co.	Date	Recorded Copy	Original
Kyles, Mary M.	054	1898	WB-6/134	CTY
Kyzer, Peetter	065	1780	WB-D/127	AR
LaBoyteaux, Mary Boggs	075	1898	WB-0/476	AR
Lacey, Drury	099	1885	068 WB-D/192	
Lacey, John	077	1786	WB-C/336	AR
Lacey, Joseph	077	1809	WB-E/339	AR
Lacey, Joseph	077	1837	WB-F/257	
Lacey, Nathan	077	1798	WB-E/95	AR
Lacey, Parker	053	c1788	RW-1/170	
Lacey, William	077	1734	SS 876/346	SS/AR
Laciter, John	024	c1759	WB-1/35	AR
Lackey, Abner H.	003	1898	WB-B/374	AR
Lackey, Alexander	003	1869	WB-B/5	AR
Lackey, F. M.	054	1891	WB-5/388	CTY
Lackey, George H.	003	1889	WB-B/274	AR
Lackey, George H.	003	1866	WB-A/13	AR
Lackey, George S.	054	1867	WB-3/199	AR
Lackey, J. C.	026	1895	WB-2/515	AR
Lackey, James	026	1883	Orig. Only	AR
Lackey, Jane	021	1888	WB-2/433	AR
Lackey, Jane	054	c1822	Orig. Only	AR
Lackey, Jane	026	1850	WB-1/106	AR
Lackey, John	060	1891	WB-4/455	AR
Lackey, John	073	1796	WB-C/81	AR
Lackey, John	013	1835	WB-A/37	
Lackey, Margaret	003	c1853	Orig. Only	AR
Lackey, Mary	024	1823	WB-C/103	AR
Lackey, Mary E.	003	1893	WB-B/319	AR
Lackey, R. C.	003	1888	WB-B/248	AR
Lackey, Reuben L.	003	1889	WB-B/267	AR
Lackey, S. C.	003	1898	WB-B/378	
Lackey, Samuel	003	1852	Orig. Only	AR
Lackey, Thomas	054	c1841	WB-2/289	AR
Lackey, Thomas J.	026	1871	WB-2/56	AR
Lackey, William	001	c1851	WB-1/47	AR
Lackey, William	054	c1820	WB-1/430	AR
Lacky, Martha	046	1820	WB-B/98	AR
Lacy, Anne	022	1811	WB-A/189	AR
Lacy, Daniel	010	1771	WB-A/138	AR
Lacy, Drury, Jr.	099	1869	RB-35/45	AR
Lacy, John	002	c1682	Orig. Only	SS/AR
Lacy, Nathan	077	1837	WB-F/269	AR
Lacy, Thomas	005	c1793	WB-A/25	AR
Lacy, William	077	1704	SS 874.1/22	
Lacy, William S.	099	1899	WB-D/313	AR
Ladd, Aaron	104	1893	WB-6/480	AR
Ladd, Constantine	090	1801	WB-2/8	
Ladd, Noble	092	1782	WB-1/172	AR
Ladd, Theadotia	090	1797	WB-1/90	AR-Nunc.
Ladd, William	090	1796	WB-1/89	AR
Ladson, Mary F.	SC	1886	050 WB-1/269	050 CTY
Lael, Jacob	003	1894	WB-B/321	
Lafater, W. W.	039	1887	WB-U/394	AR
Lafferty, R. H.	065	1864	WB-J/189	AR
Laffitte, Timothy	024	1742	Orig. Only	SS/AR
Laffoon, Matthew	092	1852	WB-4/295	AR
Lagenauer, George	090	1834	WB-3/270	AR
Lagenauer, George	038	c1850	WB-1/26	AR
Lagenauer, Phillip	090	1808	WB-2/96	AR
Lail, Jacob	014	1872	Orig. Only	AR
Lain, Fountain	029	1841	WB-B/359	
Lain, William	077	1804	WB-E/222	AR
Lainey, Emanuel	028	1786	WB-A/153	AR
Laird, John	054	c1806	WB-1/137	AR
Laka, James	104	1843	WB-4/287	AR
Lakar, Benjamin	077	1701	SS 874.1/8	SS/AR
Lake, Mary	068	1805	WB-A/258	
Laker, Juliana	077	1738	SS 877/81	SS/AR
Lakey, J. B.	061	1894	091 WB-1/156	
Lakey, J. B.	061	1894	WB-2/148	AR
Lakey, John	046	1794	WB-A/215	AR
Lakey, Richard	037	1777	WB-A/254	AR
Lakey, William	010	1768	WB-A/119	AR
Lam, Joshua	103	1845	RD-9/242	AR
Laman, John	083	c1796	WB-1/45	AR
Lamar, Osburn	081	1840	WB-7/338	AR
Lamay, John C.	044	1875	WB-23/171	CTY
Lamb, Abner	018	1847	WB-C/326	
Lamb, Abner M.	018	1852	WB-C/367	
Lamb, Algernon	030	1859	WB-4/232	AR
Lamb, Armijah	077	1819	WB-F/24	AR
Lamb, Benjamin	081	1845	WB-8/153	AR
Lamb, Chloe	018	1871	WB-E/29	AR
Lamb, Dinah	018	1855	WB-D/18	
Lamb, Elias	083	1850	WB-2/27	
Lamb, Elisha	077	1892	WB-H/239	AR
Lamb, Eliza	101	1891	WB-A/198	AR
Lamb, Elizabeth	046	1844	WB-C/201	AR
Lamb, Ephraim	083	1850	WB-2/28	
Lamb, Esau	081	1790	WB-1/80	AR
Lamb, Everett	069	1862	WB-1/580	AR
Lamb, Gabriel	081	1849	WB-9/119	AR
Lamb, George W.	035	1897	WB-4/493	AR
Lamb, Hardy	103	1810	RD-1/216	
Lamb, Isaac	018	1825	WB-C/47	AR-Copy
Lamb, Isaac	077	1782	Orig. Only	AR
Lamb, Isaac C.	070	1866	WB-D/184	AR
Lamb, Jacob	103	1795	WI-A/569	AR
Lamb, Jacob	081	1806	WB-3/38	AR
Lamb, James H.	087	1889	WB-3/432	AR
Lamb, Joab	081	1860	WB-11/487	AR
Lamb, John	077	1835	WB-F/243	AR
Lamb, John	018	1843	WB-C/286	
Lamb, John	077	1870	WB-H/36	AR
Lamb, Joseph	081	1813	WB-5/11	AR
Lamb, Joseph	077	1803	WB-E/201	AR
Lamb, Lemuel W.	018	1892	WB-E/213	AR
Lamb, Luke	018	1822	WB-C/6	
Lamb, Luke L.	018	1887	WB-E/162	AR
Lamb, Mary	085	c1831	WB-H/524	AR
Lamb, Mary	018	1888	WB-E/177	AR
Lamb, Mary	011	c1769	WB-1/527	
Lamb, Medy	083	c1804	WB-1/91	AR
Lamb, Michael	083	1900	WB-4/260	AR
Lamb, Nancey	083	c1822	WB-1/3331	AR
Lamb, Nancy	081	1869	WB-15/28	AR
Lamb, Nancy	061	c1858	WB-1/76	AR
Lamb, Nathan	081	1845	WB-8/122	AR
Lamb, Oliver	022	c1875	WB-F/207	AR
Lamb, Penny Elen	056	c1900	WB-4/337	AR
Lamb, Phinehas	077	1809	WB-E/331	AR
Lamb, Rebecca	087	1861	WB-2/22	AR
Lamb, Restore	077	1823	WB-F/53	AR
Lamb, Richard	081	1845	WB-8/150	AR
Lamb, Robert	046	c1814	WB-A/224	AR
Lamb, Samuel D.	018	1851	WB-C/354	
Lamb, Stephen	083	1859	WB-2/151	AR
Lamb, Thomas	077	1882	WB-H/130	AR
Lamb, Thomas	030	1879	WB-5/62	AR
Lamb, Thomas	018	1825	WB-C/51	

Name	Co.	Date	Recorded Copy	Original
Lamb, William	077	1758	SS 882/118	SS/AR
Lamb, Zachariah	077	1804	WB-E/208	AR
Lambe, Henry	085	1761	WB-A/81	AR
Lamberson, Henry	009	1744	SS 877/18	SS/AR
Lambert, Enoch	070	1789	WB-C/229	AR
Lambert, Jehu	022	1847	WB-C/199	AR
Lambert, John	081	1840	WB-7/333	AR
Lambert, John B.	081	1860	WB-12/3	
Lambert, John H.	046	1888	WB-E/514	AR
Lambert, Martha	022	c1863	WB-D/155	AR
Lambert, Thomas	089	1888	WB-2/179	AR
Lambert, William	046	1831	WB-B/435	AR
Lamberth, Samuel	102	1900	Orig. Only	AR
Lamberth. Joseph H.	078	1899	WB-19/476	AR
Lambertson, Andrew	071	1885	WB-6/502	AR
Lambertson, James T.	071	1872	WB-6/100	AR
Lambertson, James, Sr.	071	1814	WB-3/130	AR
Lambertson, Margaret	071	1855	WB-5/147	AR
Lambertson, William A.	071	1888	WB-7/5	AR
Lambeth, Charlotte	005	1891	WB-D/295	AR
Lambeth, David T.	032	1899	WB-4/422	AR
Lambeth, Dudley M.	032	1862	WB-2/230	AR
Lambeth, E. T.	046	1897	WB-F/559	AR
Lambeth, John	046	1846	WB-C/258	AR
Lambeth, Josiah	046	1851	WB-C/357	AR
Lambeth, Martha Ann	032	1899	WB-4/434	AR
Lambeth, R. S.	081	1866	WB-13/443	AR
Lambeth, Richardson	022	c1846	WB-C/258	AR
Lambeth, Shadrack	032	1853	WB-2/82	AR
Lambeth, Silas	032	1874	WB-3/116	AR
Lambeth, Thomas	022	c1836	WB-C/38	
Lambeth, William	085	1895	WB-3/75	CTY
Lambethson, John	012	1819	WB-B/120	AR
Lambly, George	085	1769	WB-A/79	AR
Lamborough, Austin	030	1803	WB-2/226	
Lambucht, Theodore	099	1868	RB-35/16	AR
Lamkin, Alice	100	1850	WB-41/35	AR
Lamkin, James	020	1820	RB-H/358	
Lamkin, William F.	100	1866	WB-50/181	AR-Copy
Lamm, Abraham	069	1871	WB-1/601	AR
Lamm, Abraham	103	1828	RD-5/452	AR
Lamm, Christian	105	1890	WB-2/527	AR
Lamm, Davis	105	1879	WB-2/248	AR
Lamm, Elias W.	105	1891	WB-2/574	AR
Lamm, Hewel	069	1894	WB-5/465	AR
Lamm, Isaac	105	c1856	WB-1/122	
Lamm, Isaac	105	1898	WB-3/308	AR
Lamm, Jackson	069	1900	WB-6/118	AR
Lamm, James	085	1823	WB-H/217	AR
Lamm, Jane	105	1892	WB-3/40	AR
Lamm, Jonas	105	1899	WB-3/372	AR
Lamm, Jonathan	103	1844	RD-9/138	AR
Lamm, Needham	103	1844	RD-9/139	AR
Lamm, Patience	105	1872	WB-2/53	AR
Lamm, Solomon	105	1891	WB-3/1	AR
Lamm, Stephen	105	1861	WB-1/63	AR
Lamm, Temperance	105	c1862	WB-1/86	AR
Lamm, Thomas	105	1899	WB-3/349	
Lamm, Thomas J.	105	1893	WB-3/80	AR
Lamm, William	105	1880	WB-2/244	AR
Lamm, Willie	105	1883	WB-2/296	AR
Lammond, Angus	011	c1815	WB-2/332	
Lammonds, Anguish	067	1872	WB-2/27	AR
Lamon, Alexander	011	c1824	WB-2/358	
Lamon, Duncan	039	c1810	WB-C/192	AR
Lamon, Henry	083	1872	WB-3/47	AR
Lamon, Kenneth	082	1829	WB-1/306	AR
Lamon, Martha	071	1771	WB-1/206	
Lamont, Duncan	011	c1798	WB-1/348	
Lamotte, Francis	028	1842	WB-D/64	AR
Lampkin, Grief L.	020	1830	RB-L/513	Nunc.
Lampley, Benjamin	082	c1816	WB-1/178	AR
Lancaster, Abraham	080	1885	WB-1/102	AR
Lancaster, Allen	086	1874	WB-F/53	AR
Lancaster, Amy	039	1874	WB-U/109	AR
Lancaster, Benjamin	037	1793	WB-C/235	AR
Lancaster, Coor P.	103	1889	WB-1/451	AR
Lancaster, David W.	037	1892	WB-H/199	AR
Lancaster, Elijah	056	1857	WB-1/703	AR
Lancaster, J. T.	028	1899	WB-F/446	
Lancaster, James G.	080	1900	WB-1/324	AR
Lancaster, John	039	1866	WB-S/331	AR
Lancaster, John	037	1898	WB-H/434	AR
Lancaster, John	083	1869	WB-3/16	AR
Lancaster, John	075	1786	WB-K/143	AR
Lancaster, John	100	1814	WB-18/122	AR
Lancaster, Joseph	039	1867	WB-S/507	AR
Lancaster, Joseph	039	1862	WB-R/227	
Lancaster, Lawrence	100	1792	WB-6/142	AR
Lancaster, Lawrence	100	1821	WB-23/159	AR
Lancaster, Levi	103	1826	RD-5/291	AR
Lancaster, Lucas	100	1871	WB-51/65	AR
Lancaster, Lucy B.	100	1895	WB-51/413	
Lancaster, Martha	100	1798	WB-9/307	AR
Lancaster, Mary	010	1794	WB-D/240	
Lancaster, Mary	075	1791	WB-K/215	AR
Lancaster, Munroe	045	1899	WB-1/385	AR
Lancaster, Robert W.	083	1866	WB-2/230	AR
Lancaster, Samuel B.	069	1878	WB-5/66	AR
Lancaster, Sarah J.	083	1894	WB-4/37	AR
Lancaster, William	100	1840	WB-37/395	AR
Lancaster, William	039	1826	WB-H/156	AR
Lancaster, William	103	1799	WI-B/304	
Lancaster, Willie	039	c1861	WB-U/11	AR
Lance, Jerusha	050	1882	WB-1/238	CTY
Lance, M. W.	062	1900	WB-B/229	AR
Lance, Rosanna	005	1835	Orig. Only	AR
Lance, Samuel J.	050	1877	WB-1/143	CTY
Lance, Samuel R.	025	1887	WB-A/67	AR
Lance, Sarah Ann	013	1860	WB-A/200	
Land, Charles	037	1838	WB-F/223	AR
Land, Daniel	105	1857	WB-1/42	AR
Land, Jane	104	1871	WB-6/34	AR
Land, Jeremiah	030	1836	WB-4/20	
Land, Littleberry	037	1829	WB-F/102	AR
Land, Margaret	104	c1869	Orig. Only	AR
Land, Renates	035	1798	WB-A/273	AR
Land, Richard	030	1784	WB-1/169	
Land, Robert	035	1782	WB-A/275	AR
Land, Thomas	104	1871	WB-6/34	AR
Land, V. W.	047	1899	Copy	037 AR
Land, V. W.	047	1899	WB-7/199	AR
Landen, Asa	072	1802	WB-A/74	AR
Landen, Atha	072	1854	WB-2/142	AR
Landen, James	072	1812	WB-A/78	AR
Landen, Phebe	072	1806	WB-A/76	AR
Lander, Samuel	060	1865	WB-3/83	AR
Lander, William	060	1868	Orig. Only	AR
Landers, John	044	1825	WB-10/15	CTY
Landers, Larkin A.	054	1842	WB-2/234	AR

Name	Co.	Date	Recorded Copy	Original
Landess, John	044	1868	WB-22/717	CTY
Landing, Elzy	072	1849	Orig. Only	AR
Landing, Henry	009	c1802	OWB/405	AR
Landing, Martha Ann	037	1855	WB-G/109	AR
Landing, Rachel	041	1846	WB-3/80	AR
Landing, Richard	009	1815	OB-A/247	AR
Landing, Stephen	072	1803	WB-A/77	AR
Landis, Emmer	099	1900	Orig. Only	AR-Nunc.
Landman, Henry	090	1823	WB-3/93	AR
Landmond, Mary	047	1860	WB-5/83	
Landress, Frances	044	1770	Orig. Only	CTY
Landreth, Asa	046	1845	WB-C/215	AR
Landreth, Edward T.	004	1863	WB-1/5	AR
Landreth, Isaac W.	004	1897	WB-A/184	AR
Landreth, Nathaniel	006	c1833	WB-B/71	AR
Landreth, Stephen	006	1857	WB-D/47	AR
Landreth, Thomas	046	1800	WB-A/218	AR
Landreth, Wagner	006	1869	WB-D/82	AR
Landreth, William	006	1801	WB-A/96	AR
Lane, A. C.	028	1888	WB-E/507	
Lane, Alexander	101	1892	WB-A/222	
Lane, Anna	028	1824	WB-C/241	AR
Lane, Annie B.	028	1875	WB-E/116	
Lane, Barnabas	047	1762	WB-1/83	
Lane, Brinkley	077	1874	WB-H/64	AR
Lane, Bryant	103	1863	RD-13/733	AR
Lane, Bryant H.	103	1884	WB-1/310	AR
Lane, Catharine	010	c1873	WB-I/170	
Lane, Christian	037	1748	Orig. Only	SS/AR
Lane, Daniel	028	1836	WB-C/392	AR
Lane, David	VA	1898	092 WB-6/534	092 AR
Lane, David	047	1790	WB-3/183	
Lane, David P.	047	1856	WB-5/21	
Lane, Elizabeth	070	1844	WB-AB/436	AR
Lane, Elsberry	024	1893	WB-E/213	AR
Lane, Epraham	028	1774	Orig. Only	SS/AR
Lane, Eve	081	1881	WB-15/342	AR
Lane, Everett	103	1895	WB-2/133	AR
Lane, Ezekiel	070	1834	WB-AB/295	AR
Lane, Ezekiel E.	070	1859	WB-D/5	AR
Lane, Francis	028	1892	WB-F/32	
Lane, Frederick	028	1798	WB-B/56	AR
Lane, Gabriel	103	1872	WB-1/65	AR
Lane, George	028	1770	Orig. Only	AR
Lane, George	028	1771	Orig. Only	AR
Lane, George	028	1808	WB-B/302	AR
Lane, Gera	022	1857	WB-C/436	AR
Lane, Hardy B.	028	1856	WB-D/261	AR
Lane, Harvey	024	1852	WB-C/331	AR
Lane, Henry	056	1861	WB-1/16	AR
Lane, Isaac	046	1883	Orig. Only	AR
Lane, Isaac	047	1807	WB-3/464	
Lane, Jacob	077	1836	WB-F/252	aR
Lane, James	099	1805	RB-7/3	AR
Lane, James	072	1810	WB-A/76	AR
Lane, James	010	1820	WB-G/71	AR
Lane, James S.	074	1893	WB-1/131	AR
Lane, James, Sr.	037	1789	WB-C/103	AR
Lane, Joel	099	1795	RB-4/54	AR
Lane, John	047	1766	WB-1/204	
Lane, John	028	1801	WB-B/113	AR
Lane, John	077	1848	WB-F/354	
Lane, John	047	1776	WB-2/32	
Lane, John	045	1868	WB-1/1	
Lane, John A.	105	1895	WB-3/123	AR

Name	Co.	Date	Recorded Copy	Original
Lane, John D.	081	1897	WB-16/441	
Lane, John, Sr.	046	1826	WB-B/340	AR
Lane, Joseph	099	1798	RB-4/249	AR
Lane, Joseph	081	1805	WB-3/40	AR
Lane, Joseph	037	1758	SS 882/143	SS/AR
Lane, Joseph	047	1777	WB-2/35	
Lane, Josiah	082	1825	WB-1/259	AR
Lane, Julia	099	1900	WB-D/382	AR
Lane, Leven	057	1823	WB-B/75	AR
Lane, Levi	047	1798	WB-3/304	
Lane, Levin	028	1775	Orig. Only	AR
Lane, Levin	070	1863	WB-D/131	AR
Lane, Lucy	071	1872	WB-6/102	AR
Lane, Lucy M.	104	1874	WB-6/84	AR
Lane, Margaret	059	1885	WB-A/436	CTY
Lane, Martha	047	1817	WB-3/611	
Lane, Mary	045	1887	WB-1/154	AR
Lane, Mary	059	1883	WB-A/267	CTY
Lane, Mary A.	028	1834	WB-C/374	AR
Lane, Mary Ann	103	1883	WB-1/272	AR
Lane, Nancy	024	1853	WB-C/338	AR
Lane, Nancy	046	1876	WB-E/172	AR
Lane, Nancy	028	1809	WB-B/330	AR
Lane, Nancy B.	069	1874	WB-5/7	AR
Lane, Narcissa	056	1881	WB-3/286	AR
Lane, Penelope	103	1887	WB-1/388	AR
Lane, Peter J.	070	1899	WB-H/203	AR
Lane, Polly	099	1813	RB-11/97	AR
Lane, Rebecca	056	c1900	WB-4/305	AR
Lane, Rhoda	032	c1860	WB-2/203	
Lane, Sallie Ann	024	1893	WB-E/213	AR
Lane, Samson	103	1848	RD-10/156	AR
Lane, Samuel	024	1894	WB-E/236	AR
Lane, Samuel	084	1832	WB-B/53	CTY
Lane, Samuell	009	1859	OB-L/25	AR
Lane, Sarah	046	1835	WB-B/523	AR
Lane, Temperance	099	1874	RB-35/258	AR
Lane, Thomas	010	1754	Orig. Only	SS/AR
Lane, Thomas W.	026	1885	WB-2/273	
Lane, Walter	028	1752	Orig. Only	SS/AR
Lane, William	075	1761	WB-I/18	AR
Lane, William	071	1865	WB-5/305	AR
Lane, William	047	1786	WB-3/106	
Lane, William C.	047	1858	WB-5/61	
Lane, Willis	077	1880	WB-H/96	AR
Lane, Winnefred	028	1860	WB-D/341	AR
Lanear, Thomas	071	1861	WB-5/253	AR
Laney, Burton	097	1875	WB-2/76	
Laney, George	065	1826	WB-B/45	AR
Laney, Mary	065	1821	WB-B/43	AR
Lang, Elisha	079	1854	WB-1/33	AR-Copy
Lang, James	051	1851	WB-A/333	
Lang, John W.	081	c1863	Copy	046 AR
Lang, Joshua J.	051	1851	WB-a/325	
Langdale, George	010	1882	WB-I/136	
Langdale, Sarah	010	1843	WB-G/357	AR
Langdon, Britton	056	1876	WB-3/152	AR
Langdon, Carroll	056	1898	WB-4/133	AR
Langdon, Caswell	056	1876	WB-3/164	AR
Langdon, Elizabeth	056	c1888	WB-4/521	AR
Langdon, Mary J.	070	1883	WB-E/496	AR
Langdon, Richard	070	1811	WB-AB/158	AR
Langdon, Richard F.	070	1895	WB-G/444	AR
Langford, David	071	1864	WB-5/297	AR
Langford, Edward	028	1762	Wills.7/329	AR

Name	Co.	Date	Recorded Copy	Original
Langford, Elias	071	1834	WB-4/114	AR
Langford, John	100	1828	WB-32/18	
Langford, John D.	100	1879	WB-51/136	AR
Langhorne, William B.	020	1841	RB-O/221	
Langler, George W.	028	1860	WB-D/344	AR
Langley, Arthur	056	c1898	WB-4/433	AR
Langley, Elizabeth	079	1875	WB-2/140	AR
Langley, Francis	056	1867	WB-2/98	AR
Langley, Godfrey	079	1860	WB-1/48	AR
Langley, Isaac	056	1879	WB-3/243	AR
Langley, James	056	1823	WB-1/455	AR
Langley, Jehu	037	1830	WB-F/113	AR
Langley, John	079	1890	WB-2/508	AR
Langley, John	072	1859	WB-2/173	AR
Langley, Joseph	020	1862	RB-S/573	AR
Langley, Levi	074	1880	WB-1/71	AR
Langley, Sarah	099	1833	RB-22/527	AR
Langley, Stephen	009	1818	OB-A/281	AR
Langley, Stephen	009	1819	OB-A/293	AR
Langley, Thomas	047	1764	WB-1/135	
Langley, William	037	1790	WB-C/142	AR
Langley, William J.	037	1892	WB-H/224	AR
Langmire, William	044	1816	WB-7/640	
Langston, Ann	037	1789	WB-C/84	AR
Langston, B. J.	103	1893	WB-2/36	AR
Langston, Cheley	103	1884	WB-1/334	AR
Langston, Furney	056	1867	WB-2/92	AR
Langston, Isaac	041	1803	WB-1/200	AR
Langston, Isaac	056	1852	WB-1/661	AR
Langston, Isaac	056	1881	WB-3/300	
Langston, J. T.	056	1899	WB-4/181	AR
Langston, Jacob	103	c1784	Orig. Only	AR
Langston, Joseph	056	1812	WB-1/386	AR
Langston, Joseph	056	1810	WB-1/223	AR
Langston, Leanard	037	1780	WB-B/59	AR
Langston, Levy	103	1819	RD-4/295	AR
Langston, Mary	103	1844	RD-9/140	AR
Langston, P. B.	056	1900	WB-4/245	AR
Langston, Robert	103	1838	RD-11/337	AR
Langston, Simon	103	1846	RD-9/417	AR
Langston, Thomas	103	1882	WB-1/257	AR
Langston, Uriah	041	1816	WB-2/137	AR
Langston, Uriah	103	1838	RD-7/385	AR
Langston, Westbrook	056	1858	WB-1/721	AR
Langstun, Thomas B.	041	1876	WB-4/74	AR
Lanham, John	094	c1765	094.901.1	AR
Lanier, Adams	063	1821	WB-2/76	
Lanier, Allen	035	1870	WB-4/30	AR
Lanier, Axem	009	1840	OB-C2/365	AR
Lanier, Benjamin	081	1893	WB-16/258	AR
Lanier, Benjamin	070	1829	WB-C/240	AR
Lanier, Buckner	029	1839	WB-B/377	AR
Lanier, Clement	085	1820	WB-H/72	AR
Lanier, Clement	005	1809	WB-2/86	AR
Lanier, Clement	085	1819	WB-H/7	AR
Lanier, Dennis	035	1871	WB-4/54	AR
Lanier, Drury	009	1843	OB-E/67	AR
Lanier, Edith	009	1840	OB-C2/371	AR
Lanier, Elizabeth	044	1853	WB-19/244	CTY
Lanier, Henry, Sr.	009	1894	WB-2/75	CTY
Lanier, Holden	035	1869	WB-4/16	AR
Lanier, Hosea G.	035	1885	WB-4/259	AR
Lanier, Isham	035	1844	Orig. Only	AR
Lanier, Jesse	035	1829	WB-A/277	AR
Lanier, John	035	1799	WB-A/272	AR
Lanier, John	009	c1794	Copy	SS/AR
Lanier, John	009	c1794	OWB/296	AR
Lanier, John	039	1821	WB-G/32	AR
Lanier, John	063	c1803	WB-1/419	
Lanier, John R.	063	1793	WB-1/194	
Lanier, Lucinda	039	1844	WB-L/215	AR
Lanier, Mary	005	1823	WB-A/79	AR
Lanier, Mary E.	063	1898	WB-4/216	AR
Lanier, Rachel	035	1879	WB-4/141	AR
Lanier, Robert	044	1835	WB-13/339	CTY
Lanier, Robert	092	1786	WB-2/67	
Lanier, Robert	096	1744	Orig. Only	SS/AR
Lanier, Sally	039	1850	WB-N/320	AR
Lanier, Sampson	084	1823	WB-A/218	CTY
Lanier, Sampson	005	1789	WB-1/70	AR
Lanier, Sarah K.	071	1873	WB-6/118	AR
Lanier, Seth	085	1821	WB-H/111	AR
Lanier, Thomas	035	1787	WB-A/274	AR
Lanier, Thomas	044	1805	WB-6/205	CTY
Lanier, Thomas	035	1884	WB-4/223	AR
Lanier, Thomas	092	1801	WB-3/42	AR
Lanier, William J.	063	1887	WB-4/20	AR
Lanier, Zilpha	035	1832	WB-1/20	AR
Lanius, Johanas	090	1837	WB-4/12	AR
Lank, Thomas	041	1829	WB-2/279	AR
Lankester, Henry	075	1796	WB-L/55	
Lankford, Braxton C.	093	1895	WB-2/135	
Lankford, George	100	1782	WB-3/143	
Lankford, James	092	1778	WB-1/90	AR
Lankford, James	056	1777	WB-2/269	AR
Lankford, Josiah E.	039	1879	WB-U/190	AR
Lankford, Martha	056	c1779	WB-2/267	AR
Lankford, Nathan	086	1826	WB-D/49	AR
Lankford, Robert	086	1831	WB-D/138	AR
Lankton, Thomas	N	1696	SS 874.2/86	SS/AR
Lanmon, John	005	1817	WB-2/85	AR
Lanning, Enos, Sr.	032	1844	WB-1/435	AR
Lanning, James	032	1877	WB-3/209	AR
Lanning, John	013	1871	WB-B/46	AR
Lanning, Margaret	050	1873	WB-1/130	CTY
Lanning, Rebecca	013	1886	WB-B/391	AR
Lanss, Richard	047	1769	WB-1/239	
Lantz, Jacob	021	1849	WB-1/74	AR
Lapell, Mary	077	1856	WB-F/475	AR
Lapish, George	033	1900	WB-2/254	CTY
Lappin, Elizabeth	084	1855	WB-C/218	CTY
Lapslee, James	073	1821	WB-D/588	AR
Lapslie, Thomas	073	1781	WB-A/220	AR
Larance, James	037	c1784	Orig. Only	AR
Larance, William	077	1694	SS 874.2/47	SS/AR
Lard, Nathaniel	085	1769	WB-A/87	AR
Lard, Patsey	085	1825	WB-H/320	AR
Laremore, Phillip	084	c1800	OW/95	AR
Larence, John	019	1772	RB-A/41	AR
Largeant, Edward J.	014	1884	WB-2/277	CTY
Largent, James	086	1858	WB-E/347	AR
Larimer, William	Eng	c1758	070 DB-E/172	
Larimore, James	090	1842	WB-4/105	AR
Larkin, Thomas	084	1818	WB-A/234	CTY
Larkins, Benjamin	070	1843	WB-AB/385	AR
Larkins, Benjamin	070	1833	WB-C/242	AR
Larkins, Evan	070	1869	WB-E/29	AR
Larkins, I. Robert	070	1869	WB-E/163	AR
Larkins, James	070	1822	WB-C/237	AR
Larkins, John	070	1782	WB-C/221	AR

Name	Co.	Date	Recorded Copy	Original
Larkins, John	070	1738	SS 877/212	SS/AR
Larkins, Robert	070	1836	WB-AB/308	AR
Larkins, Susannah	070	1833	WB-C/243	AR
Larkins, Thomas	070	1819	WB-C/234	AR
Larkins, William	070	1807	WB-AB/101	AR
Larkins, William	070	1891	WB-F/427	AR
Laroche, John	009	1824	OB-A/342	AR
Laroque, James	070	1817	WB-C/234	AR
Larrence, John	081	1800	WB-2/69	AR
Lary, James	096	1777	WB-1/97	AR
Lasater, Burnett	022	1849	WB-C/236	
Lasater, Hardy	022	c1861	WB-D/81	AR
Lasater, Thomas	022	1857	WB-C/447	AR
Lasater, William	022	1845	WB-C/177	AR
Lasater, William	022	1784	RB-1/16	AR
Lasater, William B.	022	1896	WB-F/20	AR
Laseter, Elizabeth	099	1867	RB-34/390	AR
Laseter, Hardy	037	1853	WB-F/502	AR
Lash, Ann P.	090	1888	WB-6/204	AR
Lash, Christian	090	1844	WB-4/142	AR
Lash, George	092	c1819	WB-3/143	AR
Lash, Isaac C.	038	c1863	WB-1/218	AR
Lash, Jacob	029	1822	WB-B/69	AR
Lash, Jacob	PA	1782	092 WB-2/8A	
Lash, Nathaniel	090	1828	WB-3/176	AR
Lash, Sandy	038	1892	WB-3/295	AR
Lash, Sarah	054	c1821	WB-1A/134	AR
Lash, Thomas B.	038	1888	WB-3/105	AR
Lashley, David W.	073	1862	WB-G/391	CTY
Lashley, Howell	068	1836	WB-B/99	
Lashley, Thomas	073	1824	WB-E/50	
Lashley, William	099	1844	RB-25/390	AR
Lashly, John	071	1778	WB-1/298	
Lashly, Lewis	099	1815	RB-12/224	AR
Lashly, Patrick	044	1759	SS 881/154	SS/AR
Lashmit, Elias	038	c1852	WB-1/8	AR
Lasiter, Jesse	071	1784	WB-1/330	AR
Lasiter, John	010	1868	WB-H/206	AR
Lasiter, Jotham	099	1810	RB-9/232	AR
Lasiter, Luke	099	1804	RB-6/321	AR
Lasiter, Martha A.	010	1898	WB-I/565	
Lasiter, Reuben	024	1855	WB-C/380	AR
Lasker, William	068	1900	WB-E/89	
Lasley, C. M.	090	1890	WB-6/226	AR
Lasley, Elijah	073	1852	WB-G/16	AR
Lasley, Johnson	073	1894	WB-I/54	CTY
Lasley, Joseph	090	1844	WB-4/154	AR
Lasley, William H.	001	1900	WB-3/327	AR
Lasly, Joseph	084	1866	WB-D/75	CTY
Laspeyre, Harriett	070	1853	WB-C/557	AR
Laspyre, Anne Eliza	012	1841	Orig. Only	AR
Lasseter, Moses	099	1849	RB-26/614	AR
Lasseter, Moses	024	c1767	WB-A/255	AR
Lassiter, Aaron	081	1897	WB-16/432	AR
Lassiter, Aaron	041	1781	WB-1/11	AR
Lassiter, Aaron	024	1804	WB-B/195	AR
Lassiter, Abigail	071	1835	WB-4/125	AR
Lassiter, B. A.	041	1900	WB-4/508	AR
Lassiter, Blake	047	1812	WB-3/528	
Lassiter, Bryant	071	1878	WB-6/244	AR
Lassiter, Bryant	071	1871	WB-5/365	AR
Lassiter, Calvin	056	1880	WB-3/262	AR
Lassiter, Charles	071	1803	WB-2/240	AR
Lassiter, Charlotte	099	1859	RB-31/257	AR
Lassiter, Daniel	082	1897	WB-6/567	AR

Name	Co.	Date	Recorded Copy	Original
Lassiter, Elijah	056	1848	WB-1/607	AR
Lassiter, Elizabeth	104	1873	WB-6/73	AR
Lassiter, Elizabeth	099	1894	WB-C/280	AR
Lassiter, Elizabeth	009	1885	WB-1/365	CTY
Lassiter, Elizabeth	081	1882	WB-15/403	AR
Lassiter, Everitt	071	1827	WB-4/29	AR
Lassiter, Ezekiel	081	1865	WB-13/257	AR
Lassiter, Fedrick	041	1810	WB-2/56	AR
Lassiter, Frederick	010	1787	WB-D/72	AR
Lassiter, Gabriel	024	1769	WB-A/260	AR
Lassiter, Garrison	041	1888	WB-4/271	AR
Lassiter, George	024	1764	WB-A/256	AR
Lassiter, George	041	1796	WB-1/142	AR
Lassiter, Green	071	1813	WB-3/105	AR
Lassiter, Harrison	071	1867	WB-5/352	AR
Lassiter, Harrison	044	1880	WB-23/376	CTY
Lassiter, Harrison C.	051	1877	WB-C/178	AR
Lassiter, Henry	099	1867	RB-34/478	AR
Lassiter, Hill	081	1857	WB-11/139	AR
Lassiter, Jacob	071	1761	WB-1/38	
Lassiter, James	071	1816	WB-3/177	AR
Lassiter, James	041	1835	WB-2/366	AR
Lassiter, James, Sr.	071	1813	WB-3/107	AR
Lassiter, John B.	041	1894	WB-4/390	AR
Lassiter, John H.	070	1856	WB-C/610	AR
Lassiter, Jonas	099	1814	RB-11/314	AR
Lassiter, Jonathan	081	1887	WB-16/62	AR
Lassiter, Joseph	071	1822	WB-3/270	AR
Lassiter, Joseph	071	1792	WB-2/22	AR
Lassiter, Joseph	082	c1803	WB-1/93	AR
Lassiter, Josiah	104	1860	WB-5/246	
Lassiter, Josiah	104	c1860	Copy	081 AR
Lassiter, Josiah C.	081	1892	WB-16/207	AR
Lassiter, Kilbee	087	1882	WB-3/232	AR
Lassiter, Leroy	051	1885	WB-C/336	AR
Lassiter, Louisa	099	1886	WB-B/160	AR
Lassiter, Love A.	098	1893	WB-A/183	CTY
Lassiter, Martha A.	071	1873	WB-6/129	
Lassiter, Mary Ann	071	1899	WB-7/435	AR
Lassiter, Micajah	081	1890	WB-16/168	AR
Lassiter, Michel	041	1794	WB-1/121	AR
Lassiter, Parthena	051	1870	WB-C/34	AR
Lassiter, Patience	087	1899	Orig. Only	AR
Lassiter, Penelope	071	1897	WB-7/352	AR
Lassiter, Penelope	071	1854	WB-5/121	AR
Lassiter, Reuben	041	1842	WB-3/43	AR
Lassiter, Reuben	041	1800	WB-1/174	AR
Lassiter, Robert	041	1780	WB-1/6	AR
Lassiter, Robert	087	c1813	Orig. Only	AR
Lassiter, Robert	071	1778	WB-1/311	
Lassiter, Sally	071	1818	WB-3/200	AR
Lassiter, Sarah	041	1795	WB-1/132	AR
Lassiter, Silas	071	1841	WB-4/240	AR
Lassiter, Terrisa E.	045	1893	WB-1/271	AR
Lassiter, Thaney	041	1801	WB-1/186	AR
Lassiter, Thomas W.	047	1833	WB-4/102	
Lassiter, Timothy	041	1897	WB-4/426	AR
Lassiter, Wilburn	GA	1888	067 WB-2/375	
Lassiter, William	069	1778	WB-1/1	AR
Lassiter, William	051	1867	WB-B/93	AR
Lassiter, William	071	1828	WB-4/41	AR
Lassiter, William	041	1805	WB-1/217	AR
Lassiter, William	056	1875	WB-3/132	
Lassiter, William	044	1846	WB-16/512	CTY
Lassiter, William D.	071	1859	WB-5/212	AR

Name	Co.	Date	Recorded Copy	Original
Lassiter, William F.	081	1885	WB-15/511	
Lassiter, William H.	099	1851	WB-27/351	AR
Lassiter, Willie	071	1875	WB-6/176	AR
Lasster, John	041	1881	WB-4/147	AR
Lastley, Elizabeth	020	1895	WB-B/202	CTY
Latham, Ann	009	1829	OB-B/26	AR
Latham, Ann E.	063	1874	WB-3/70	
Latham, Charles	101	1893	WB-A/232	AR
Latham, Cornelia Ann	009	1855	OB-I/344	AR
Latham, David	063	1834	WB-2/194	
Latham, Elizabeth	063	1844	WB-2/306	
Latham, Frederick	028	1866	WB-D/437	AR
Latham, James	081	1821	WB-5/14	AR
Latham, James	081	1897	WB-16/432	AR
Latham, James F.	009	1889	WB-1/457	CTY
Latham, James, Sr.	009	1834	OB-B/402	AR
Latham, Jasper	009	1826	OB-A/363	AR
Latham, John	081	1818	WB-4/537	AR
Latham, John	009	1859	OB-L/45	AR
Latham, John B.	053	1813	RW-1/480	
Latham, John D.	063	1860	WB-2/473	
Latham, John W.	101	1884	WB-A/122	AR
Latham, Livey E.	079	1891	WB-2/563	AR
Latham, Louis C.	079	1895	101 WB-A/277	101 AR
Latham, Louis C.	079	1895	WB-3/74	AR
Latham, Louisa J.	009	1897	WB-2/108	CTY
Latham, Rothears	053	1784	RW-1/121	
Latham, Samuel W.	101	1882	WB-A/91	AR
Latham, Sarah	053	1794	RW-1/247	AR
Latham, Sarah	009	c1831	OB-B/151	AR
Latham, Sarah	053	1805	RW-1/386	AR
Latham, Sarah	028	1856	WB-D/251	
Latham, Silas	006	1878	WB-E/41	AR
Latham, Thomas	009	1854	OB-I/263	AR
Latham, Thomas J.	009	1865	OB-M/249	AR
Lathem, Alexander	006	c1833	WB-B/67	AR
Lathem, Samuel	097	1849	WB-1/62	AR
Lathum, Paul	002	1693	Orig. Only	SS/AR
Latimer, Charles M.	073	1875	WB-H/94	CTY
Latimer, Elizabeth	DE	1895	Copy	075 AR
Latimer, George	PA	1825	093 WB-2/64	
Latimer, George	PA	1825	066 WB-1/75	
Latimer, George	PA	1825	013 WB-A/207	
Latimer, Herbert R.	070	1887	WB-F/103	AR
Latimer, Margaret	PA	1865	Copy	075 AR
Latta, Amelia	073	1867	WB-G/511	CTY
Latta, Arrena	073	1898	WB-I/135	CTY
Latta, Asahel M.	021	1877	WB-2/169	AR
Latta, Caroline	073	1884	WB-H/340	CTY
Latta, Elizabeth	073	1884	WB-H/339	CTY
Latta, Elizabeth	073	1898	WB-I/135	CTY
Latta, Henderson	044	1895	WB-24/275	CTY
Latta, James	065	1839	Orig. Only	AR
Latta, James C.	036	1886	WB-A/86	CTY
Latta, James M.	073	1892	WB-H/557	CTY
Latta, Jane	054	c1860	Orig. Only	AR
Latta, John	073	1818	WB-D/525	AR
Latta, John	073	1824	WB-E/67	AR
Latta, John C.	073	1868	WB-G/536	CTY
Latta, John W.	073	1899	WB-I/158	CTY
Latta, Joseph	073	1824	WB-E/66	AR
Latta, Maria C.	070	1900	WB-H/264	AR
Latta, Nancy J.	073	1893	WB-I/6	CTY
Latta, Priscilla	070	1894	WB-G/245	AR
Latta, Rachel	073	1898	WB-I/137	CTY

Name	Co.	Date	Recorded Copy	Original
Latta, Robert	085	c1780	WB-B/171	
Latta, Sarah	073	1861	WB-G/254	AR
Latta, Simpson	078	1863	WB-18/311	AR
Latta, Thomas	073	1842	WB-F/121	AR
Lattemore, Elizabeth	010	1753	SS 878/204	SS/AR
Lattimer, William	010	1750	SS 879/10	SS/AR
Lattimore, Daniel	086	1834	WB-E/2	AR
Lattimore, Elisha	NY	1813	028 WB-C/72	028 AR
Lattimore, Francis	026	1857	WB-1/212	AR
Lattimore, J. C., Jr.	026	1871	WB-2/51	AR
Lattimore, Mary	047	1764	WB-1/119	
Lattimore, Mary L.	026	1894	WB-2/485	AR
Lattimore, Samuel	026	1846	WB-1/51	AR
Lattimore, Samuel	026	1897	WB-2/540	AR
Lattimore, Ulysses	026	1892	WB-2/442	AR
Lattrell, Elizabeth	046	1825	WB-B/203	AR
Latty, William	N	1704	Orig. Only	SS/AR
Laugenour, Lewis C.	038	1893	WB-3/375	AR
Laughinghouse, Alice	009	1869	WB-1/31	CTY
Laughinghouse, Edward	079	c1851	Orig. Only	AR-Copy
Laughinghouse, Foreman M.	079	1899	WB-3/193	AR
Laughinghouse, J. A.	079	1875	WB-2/116	AR
Laughinghouse, Joseph H.	079	1863	WB-1/82	AR
Laughinghouse, Richard R.	028	1821	WB-C/198	AR
Laughinghouse, Thomas	009	c1788	OWB/227	AR
Laughlin, Chesley	081	1900	WB-17/138	
Laughlin, Chester	081	1900	WB-17/138	
Laughlin, Cornelius	081	1838	WB-7/216	
Laughlin, D. F.	081	1888	WB-16/114	AR
Laughlin, Hugh B.	073	1765	WB-A/39	
Laughlin, Iredell	081	1853	WB-9/499	AR
Laughlin, Richard	081	1803	WB-2/113	AR
Laughlin, Robert	081	1883	WB-15/417	AR
Laughlin, Robert	081	1827	WB-5/354	AR
Laughray, William	054	1816	WB-1/367	AR
Laughter, John	100	1817	WB-21/43	AR
Laughter, Joseph W.	080	1867	WB-1/200	AR
Laughton, James	010	1813	WB-F/228	AR
Laurence, Abraham	044	1839	WB-14/456	CTY
Laurence, John	071	1796	WB-2/135	AR
Laurence, John V.	051	1868	WB-C/3	AR
Laurence, Joseph	099	1801	RB-5/328	AR
Laurence, Joshua	071	1826	WB-4/7	AR
Laurence, Lemuel	071	1811	WB-3/47	AR
Laurence, Mary E. W.	029	1900	WB-F/179	AR
Laurence, Solomon	037	1804	WB-D/199	AR
Laurence, Thomas	037	1794	WB-C/285	AR
Laurence, Thomas	028	1784	WB-A/80	AR
Laurence, Thomas D.	047	1863	WB-5/108	
Laurence, William	044	1840	WB-14/572	CTY
Laurence, William G.	071	1831	WB-4/84	AR
Lautenschlager, John Jacob	084	1885	WB-E/326	CTY
Lavender, Benjamin	047	1892	WB-7/45	AR
Lavender, Clarissa	009	1815	OWB/474	AR
Lavender, Margaret	NY	1859	047 WB-6/184	047 AR
Lavender, William	057	1802	WB-A/263	AR
Lavender, William	057	1798	WB-A/202	AR
Law, Andrew	046	1807	WB-A/221	AR
Law, Burwell	VA	1845	Copy	084 AR
Law, Robert	046	1851	WB-C/352	AR
Lawed, Mary	010	1826	WB-G/146	AR

Name	Co.	Date	Recorded Copy	Original
Lawhon, Joel	056	1886	WB-3/427	AR
Lawhon, Jonie	056	1899	WB-4/149	AR
Lawhorn, Phereby	103	1817	RD-4/34	AR
Lawhorn, Sally	103	1813	RD-3/67	AR
Lawhorn, William	103	1813	RD-3/80	AR
Lawing, Biddy	065	1846	WB-I/64	AR
Lawing, C. G.	065	1886	WB-L/161	AR
Lawing, Jane C.	065	1866	WB-J/227	AR
Lawing, John M.	065	1866	WB-J/223	AR
Lawler, David	024	1734	SS 876/332	SS/AR
Lawler, John	068	1800	WB-A/211	
Lawler, Patrick	024	1728	Orig. Only	SS/AR
Lawly, Nickless	028	1777	Orig. Only	AR
Lawns, Burket	020	1897	WB-B/305	CTY
Lawrance, Carlos C.	021	1864	WB-1/191	
Lawrance, Ephraim	037	1777	WB-A/259	AR
Lawrance, George	010	1756	SS 880/160	SS/AR
Lawrance, Thomas	010	1763	WB-A/33	AR
Lawrance, William	073	1886	WB-H/409	CTY
Lawrence, Abraham	044	c1865	WB-23/23	CTY
Lawrence, Adam	054	c1816	WB-1/409	
Lawrence, Alexander	099	1880	WB-A/186	AR
Lawrence, Alphius	010	1844	WB-G/364	AR
Lawrence, B. D.	041	1898	WB-4/451	AR
Lawrence, Catherine	028	1844	WB-D/100	
Lawrence, Elisha	051	1832	WB-A/33	
Lawrence, Elizabeth	069	1830	WB-1/370	AR
Lawrence, Frederick	010	1823	WB-G/125	AR
Lawrence, Harriet P.	037	1874	WB-G/441	AR
Lawrence, Henry	090	1896	WB-6/402	AR
Lawrence, Humphrey	010	1772	WB-A/156	AR
Lawrence, James	037	1884	WB-G/683	AR
Lawrence, James M.	037	1866	WB-G/276	AR
Lawrence, John	037	1880	WB-G/577	AR
Lawrence, John	037	1844	WB-F/310	AR
Lawrence, John	028	1870	WB-E/33	
Lawrence, John	046	1804	WB-A/220	AR
Lawrence, John	010	1788	WB-D/88	AR
Lawrence, John	037	1795	WB-C/332	AR
Lawrence, John	037	1805	WB-D/218	AR
Lawrence, John H.	022	1896	WB-F/25	
Lawrence, John W.	037	1890	WB-H/162	AR
Lawrence, Jonathan	010	1824	WB-G/113	AR
Lawrence, Joseph	075	1883	WB-O/164	AR
Lawrence, Joseph J.	037	1861	WB-G/201	AR
Lawrence, Josephus D.	071	1835	WB-4/126	AR
Lawrence, Joshua	037	1843	WB-F/282	AR
Lawrence, Joshua L.	037	1867	WB-G/289	AR
Lawrence, Josiah	037	1870	WB-G/340	AR
Lawrence, Leanah	044	1857	WB-20/230	CTY
Lawrence, Marmaduke	041	1892	WB-4/335	AR
Lawrence, Mary	024	1799	WB-A/324	AR
Lawrence, Mary	051	1855	WB-A/379	
Lawrence, Mary	071	1817	WB-3/197	AR
Lawrence, Mary	051	1868	WB-B/99	AR
Lawrence, Mary G.	022	1893	WB-E/551	AR
Lawrence, Nathaniel	044	c1860	WB-22/373	CTY
Lawrence, Needham	022	1890	WB-E/439	AR
Lawrence, Peter P.	037	1855	WB-G/101	AR
Lawrence, R. B.	044	1881	WB-23/404	CTY
Lawrence, Rachel	041	1792	WB-1/101	AR
Lawrence, Robert	010	1808	WB-F/88	AR
Lawrence, Samuel	037	1838	WB-F/219	AR
Lawrence, Sarah	037	1870	WB-G/357	AR
Lawrence, Stewart	037	1899	WB-H/436	AR
Lawrence, Thomas	069	1813	WB-1/257	AR
Lawrence, Thomas	010	1790	WB-D/116	AR
Lawrence, Thomas J.	AR	1890	062 WB-B/111	
Lawrence, Thompson	068	1887	WB-D/236	
Lawrence, W. J.	037	1897	WB-H/375	AR
Lawrence, Watson	019	1866	WB-B/16	AR
Lawrence, William	010	1816	WB-F/317	AR
Lawrence, William	069	1816	WB-1/272	AR
Lawrence, William	044	1766	Orig. Only	CTY
Lawrence, William T.	044	1832	WB-12/383	CTY
Lawrence, William W.	010	1862	WB-H/112	AR
Lawrence, Williamson	063	c1796	WB-1/329	
Lawrey, Edward	071	1805	WB-2/277	AR
Lawrey, Mildred	071	1807	Orig. Only	AR
Laws, A. B.	104	1892	WB-6/436	AR
Laws, Allen F.	104	1900	Orig. Only	AR
Laws, Elizabeth	073	1833	WB-E/302	AR
Laws, Elizabeth	104	1897	WB-7/31	AR
Laws, Ezekiel	073	1856	WB-G/154	AR
Laws, George	073	1800	WB-D/20	AR
Laws, George	073	1815	WB-D/454	AR
Laws, George	073	1881	WB-H/285	CTY
Laws, John	104	c1819	Orig. Only	AR
Laws, John	104	1850	WB-5/38	AR
Laws, Leonard	099	1847	RB-26/193	AR
Laws, Mary	104	1900	WB-7/275	
Laws, Robert	073	1894	WB-I/54	CTY
Laws, Robert H.	064	1898	WB-2/439	AR
Laws, Thomas	078	1826	Orig. Only	AR
Laws, William	073	1817	WB-D/512	AR
Laws, William	099	1871	RB-35/120	AR
Laws, William	104	1780	WB-1/38	AR
Laws, William	044	1802	WB-5/283	CTY
Lawson, Adaline	062	1888	WB-B/89	
Lawson, Alva	083	1900	WB-4/263	AR
Lawson, Anthony	054	c1810	WB-1/141	AR
Lawson, Charles H.	100	1888	WB-51/291	AR
Lawson, Charlotte	084	1886	WB-E/341	CTY
Lawson, Christopher	035	1881	WB-4/157	AR
Lawson, David	054	c1799	Orig. Only	AR
Lawson, Elias	028	1828	WB-C/300	AR
Lawson, Elisha	090	1834	WB-3/265	AR
Lawson, F. M.	062	1897	WB-B/203	
Lawson, Frances Ann	084	1867	WB-D/79	CTY
Lawson, Francis I.	084	1845	WB-C/31	CTY
Lawson, George	020	1888	WB-A/526	CTY
Lawson, Henry	028	1816	WB-C/125	AR
Lawson, Hugh	004	1882	WB-A/55	AR
Lawson, Hugh, Jr.	085	1772	WB-A/87	
Lawson, John	078	1852	WB-17/82	AR
Lawson, John	078	1806	WI-4/91	AR
Lawson, John	008	c1708	SS 875/39 & 98	
Lawson, John	090	1813	WB-2/144	AR-Nunc.
Lawson, Jonas	090	1816	WB-2/174	
Lawson, Mary	065	1801	WB-B/32	AR-Nunc.
Lawson, Mary	062	1888	WB-B/89	
Lawson, Mary	054	1854	WB-3/76	AR
Lawson, Mary S.	078	1858	WB-18/6	AR
Lawson, Samuel	028	1799	WB-B/72	AR
Lawson, Samuel	028	1758	SS 881/137	SS/AR
Lawson, Thomas	078	1857	WB-17/450	AR
Lawson, Thomas T.	084	1835	WB-B/115	CTY
Lawson, Vianna	062	1888	WB-B/89	
Lawson, Winifred	045	1877	Orig. Only	AR
Lawter, Henry	015	1771	100 WB-1/177	AR

Name	Co.	Date	Recorded Copy	Original
Lawton, Matthew	070	1866	WB-D/182	
Lawton, Peleg	075	1796	WB-L/63	AR-Nunc.
Lawyer, Elizabeth	073	1821	WB-D/592	
Lax, Sarah E.	081	1877	WB-15/257	
Lax, William	081	c1825	Orig. Only	AR
Laxton, Elbert	017	1900	WB-B/326	AR
Laxton, Levi	017	1845	WB-A/21	AR
Laxton, Lewis	017	1892	WB-B/211	AR
Lay, Martin	073	1779	WB-A/207	
Laycock, Joseph	073	1829	WB-E/204	AR
Layden, Francis	077	1728	SS 876/183	SS/AR
Layden, Francis	077	1807	WB-E/305	AR
Layden, George	077	1761	WB-C/49	AR
Layden, Isaac	077	1786	WB-C/337	AR
Layden, William	077	1835	WB-F/238	AR
Layden, William	077	c1834	SC/01872	AR-Copy
Layne, William	092	1791	WB-3/4	AR
Layrle, Christopher	085	c1784	WB-E/129	
Layton, Roger	046	1838	WB-C/7	AR
Layton, Samuel	010	1791	WB-D/164	AR
Layton, Shadrack	046	1866	WB-D/293	AR
Lazarus, Rachel A.	NY	1883	070 WB-E/514	070 AR
Lazenby, E. E.	054	1889	WB-5/285	CTY
Lazenby, Elizabeth	054	1900	WB-6/278	CTY
Lazenby, Henry	054	1860	WB-3/155	AR
Lazenby, James S.	054	1868	WB-3/207	
Lazenby, John M.	054	1859	WB-3/138	AR
Lazenby, Joshua	054	1840	WB-2/215	AR
Lazenby, M. O.	054	1865	WB-3/170	AR
Lazenby, Robert	054	c1828	WB-2/65	AR
Lazenby, Ross M.	054	1874	WB-4/167	CTY
Lazenby, Thomas	054	c1835	WB-2/209	AR
LeGrand, Hampton	082	1885	WB-6/319	AR
LeGrand, Harriet	082	1827	WB-1/287	AR
LeGrand, Lucy	070	1896	WB-G/514	AR
LeGrand, Nash	082	1890	WB-6/417	AR
LeGrand, Wade	082	1858	WB-4/110	AR
LeGrand, William	082	1871	WB-6/72	AR
LeGros, Mary M. C.	070	1802	WB-C/132	AR
LeMay, Samuel	099	1823	RB-18/284	AR
LeMay, Thomas J.	056	c1863	099 WB-B/567	099 AR
LePartee, George	085	1835	WB-H/668	Nunc.
Lea, Carter	078	1859	WB-18/73	AR
Lea, Eunice	020	1826	RB-L/1	AR
Lea, Frances	078	c1866	Orig. Only	AR
Lea, Gabriel	020	c1826	RB-M/433	
Lea, Gabriel B.	001	1871	WB-2/31	AR
Lea, George	020	1830	RB-L/511	
Lea, Henry	073	1774	WB-A/168	
Lea, Ira	078	1825	WI-10/131	AR
Lea, James	020	1819	RB-H/285	
Lea, James	022	1883	WB-E/272	AR
Lea, James	020	1792	RB-B/455	AR
Lea, James	078	1816	WI-7/79	AR
Lea, James, Sr.	020	1835	RB-M/507	
Lea, John	020	1832	RB-M/160	
Lea, John	020	1781	RB-A/166	AR
Lea, John C.	020	1839	RB-N/337	AR
Lea, John G.	020	1862	RB-S/500	AR
Lea, John, Sr.	020	1803	RB-E/5	AR
Lea, Joseph	022	1805	WB-A/111	AR
Lea, Julia	022	c1861	WB-D/110	AR
Lea, Laurence	020	1808	RB-E/418	AR
Lea, Lucy A.	078	c1880	Orig. Only	AR
Lea, Mary	020	1785	RB-B/78	AR
Lea, Nancy	078	c1857	Orig. Only	AR
Lea, Nathaniel	020	1855	RB-R/352	AR
Lea, Patsey	078	1831	WI-12/50	AR
Lea, Richard	078	1835	WI-13/19	AR
Lea, Richard	078	1839	WI-14/102	
Lea, Rucker T.	020	1839	RB-N/344	AR
Lea, Sidney S.	020	1892	WB-B/111	CTY
Lea, Solomon	020	1897	WB-B/301	CTY
Lea, Thomas	020	1845	RB-P/190	AR
Lea, William	020	1885	WB-A/426	CTY
Lea, William	020	1873	WB-A/110	CTY
Lea, William	078	1804	WI-3/243	AR
Lea, William	020	1806	RB-E/288	AR
Lea, William M.	073	1879	WB-H/219	CTY
Lea, Woodson	022	c1866	WB-D/164	AR
Lea, Zachariah	020	1792	RB-B/441	AR
Leach, Alexander	029	1887	WB-E/417	AR
Leach, Angus	083	1877	WB-3/133	AR
Leach, Angus	082	1881	WB-6/205	AR
Leach, Claudia S.	099	1899	WB-D/272	AR
Leach, Cornelia	081	1898	WB-16/511	AR
Leach, Daniel	082	1888	WB-6/371	AR
Leach, Duncan	029	1851	WB-C/196	
Leach, Hugh	083	1877	WB-3/128	AR
Leach, Hugh	081	1882	WB-15/399	AR
Leach, James A.	032	1897	WB-4/327	AR
Leach, Jane	083	1862	WB-2/183	AR
Leach, John	081	1857	WB-10/503	AR
Leach, Julian E.	081	1844	WB-8/81	AR
Leach, Martin W.	081	1869	WB-15/10	AR
Leach, Mary	083	1848	WB-1/504	
Leach, Neil	029	1795	Orig. Only	AR
Leach, Richard	033	1842	WB-1/38	AR
Leach, T. E.	081	1844	WB-8/81	
Leach, Thomas C.	054	1845	WB-2/320	AR
Leach, Zadock	033	1844	WB-1/58	AR
Leachman, Thomas	020	1816	RB-G/153	
Leak, Ann C.	082	1895	WB-6/518	AR
Leak, Ann Eliza	005	1897	WB-D/408	AR
Leak, Ann P.	005	1856	WB-C/102	AR
Leak, Celestia	069	1874	WB-5/1	AR
Leak, Columbia	038	1891	WB-3/219	AR
Leak, Esau	082	1889	WB-6/584	AR
Leak, Francis	075	1763	WB-I/31	AR
Leak, Francis	082	1789	WB-1/28	AR
Leak, Jermiah	075	1781	WB-K/62	AR
Leak, Joel	075	1822	WB-M1/360	AR
Leak, John	084	1807	WB-A/40	CTY
Leak, John W.	082	1876	WB-6/136	AR
Leak, Maxy	075	1785	WB-K/139	AR
Leak, Moreau P.	005	1887	WB-D/215	AR
Leak, Richard	073	1784	WB-A/311	AR
Leak, Robert S.	082	1869	WB-6/43	AR
Leak, Sarah	075	1806	WB-M1/137	AR
Leak, Walter	082	1844	WB-3/16	AR
Leak, Walter F.	082	1880	WB-6/186	
Leak, William	071	1761	WB-1/47	
Leak, William P.	082	1827	WB-1/279	AR
Leak, Wyatt	005	1876	WB-D/51	
Lean, William	085	1820	WB-H/63	AR
Lear, John	VA	1695	Orig. Only	SS/AR
Leare, James W.	089	1894	WB-2/281	
Learge, Jacob	028	1732	SS 876/261	
Learge, Jacob	028	c1731	Deeds.1/118	
Leary, Cornelius	024	c1762	WB-A/262	AR

Name	Co.	Date	Recorded Copy	Original
Leary, Cornelius	096	1742	Orig. Only	SS/AR
Leary, Derby	010	1789	WB-D/110	AR
Leary, Elizabeth	010	1872	WB-I/42	AR
Leary, Esther	101	1855	WB-A/110	AR
Leary, Job	057	1898	WB-C/236	AR
Leary, Job	024	c1799	WB-B/317	AR
Leary, John O.	VA	1868	084 WB-E/14	084 CTY
Leary, John, Sr.	024	1807	WB-B/259	AR
Leary, Joseph	010	1886	WB-I/221	
Leary, Julia A.	029	1889	WB-E/459	AR
Leary, M. L., Sr.	029	1880	WB-E/227	AR
Leary, Martha F.	024	1898	WB-E/284	AR
Leary, Matthew N.	029	1892	WB-E/525	AR
Leary, Rachel	010	1839	WB-G/319	AR
Leary, Richard	096	1738	LGB-4/#85	SS/AR
Leary, Sarah	024	1833	WB-C/167	AR
Leary, Thomas	010	1815	WB-F/290	AR
Leary, Thomas	096	1780	WB-1/111	AR
Leary, Thomas H.	024	1862	WB-D/13	AR
Leary, Thomas H.	024	1891	WB-E/193	AR
Leary, Walter J.	024	1897	WB-E/269	AR
Leary, West	024	1881	WB-E/104	AR
Leary, William	010	1822	WB-G/90	AR
Leaser, Martin	085	1857	WB-K/237	AR
Leasey, Francis	077	1739	Orig. Only	SS/AR
Leath, Freeman	020	1855	RB-R/242	AR
Leath, John	053	1752	028 DB-5/228	SS/AR
Leath, John, Sr.	053	1751	028 DB-5/181	SS/AR
Leath, Mary E.	001	1873	WB-2/34	AR
Leath, Richard	053	1749	SS 877/296	SS/AR
Leath, Susannah	020	1811	RB-F/242	AR
Leatherman, Christian	085	1819	WB-H/18	AR
Leatherman, Nicholas	085	c1782	WB-C/150	AR
Leathers, Anderson	036	1896	WB-A/375	CTY
Leathers, Fielding	073	1856	WB-G/135	AR
Leathers, James	073	1845	WB-F/253	AR
Leathers, Levinah	032	1852	WB-2/72	AR
Leathers, Moses	073	c1841	Orig. Only	AR
Leathers, Oliver	036	1892	WB-A/252	CTY
Leathers, Sandy	036	1890	WB-A/184	
Leathers, Travis	084	1850	WB-C/112	CTY
Leathers, William	073	1825	WB-E/87	AR
Leatherwood, John	049	c1845	WB-2/280	AR
Leatherwood, William	025	1884	WB-A/47	AR
Leaton, Hugh	082	1784	WB-1/50	AR
Leaton, Hugh	082	1784	Copy	SS/AR
Leavistor, George	044	1787	WB-2/4	CTY
Leazar, Henry	085	1872	WB-1/101	CTY
Leazar, John	054	1887	WB-5/162	CTY
Leazar, John	085	1867	WB-L/13	AR
Lebon, Benedict	063	1795	WB-1/321	
Lecerf, Henry	024	c1780	WB-A/258	AR
Lecky, Adam	046	1801	WB-A/219	AR
Lecky, Martha	046	1820	WB-B/98	
Ledbetter, A. F.	046	1862	WB-D/152	AR
Ledbetter, A. L.	029	1893	WB-F/1	AR
Ledbetter, Alfred	089	1886	WB-2/124	AR
Ledbetter, Alfred	104	1892	WB-6/441	AR
Ledbetter, Anamus	026	1863	Orig. Only	AR-Nunc.
Ledbetter, Barzilla	086	1875	WB-F/78	AR
Ledbetter, Calvin	022	1895	WB-F/10	AR
Ledbetter, Ephraim	090	1878	WB-6/93	AR
Ledbetter, Henry	005	1852	WB-C/44	AR
Ledbetter, Henry	026	1885	WB-2/280	AR
Ledbetter, Henry W.	067	1892	WB-2/313	AR
Ledbetter, Isaac	086	1837	WB-E/37	AR
Ledbetter, Isaac	014	c1837	Copy	064 AR
Ledbetter, J. H.	064	1856	WB-1/51	AR
Ledbetter, Joel	089	1843	WB-1/26	AR
Ledbetter, John	022	1786	RB-1/26	AR
Ledbetter, John	022	1792	RB-1/46	AR
Ledbetter, John	086	1892	WB-F/439	AR
Ledbetter, John	086	1818	WB-C/84	
Ledbetter, John W.	086	1864	WB-E/439	AR
Ledbetter, Jonathan	064	1886	Orig. Only	AR
Ledbetter, Jonathan	049	1890	WB-2/251	AR
Ledbetter, Martha Jane	082	1896	WB-6/544	AR
Ledbetter, Mary B.	064	1888	WB-2/189	AR
Ledbetter, R. E.	064	1897	WB-2/409	AR
Ledbetter, R. O.	086	1890	WB-F/376	AR
Ledbetter, Rebecca	064	c1900	Orig. Only	AR
Ledbetter, Robert S.	082	1896	WB-6/548	AR
Ledbetter, Sarah	089	1868	WB-1/311	
Ledbetter, Temperance	089	1896	WB-2/304	AR
Ledbetter, William	022	1818	WB-A/299	AR
Ledford, Catharine	032	1871	WB-3/46	AR
Ledford, E. M.	025	1896	WB-A/196	AR
Ledford, Elias	107	c1856	WB-1/110	
Ledford, Elizabeth	086	1885	WB-F/262	AR
Ledford, Frederick	107	c1835	WB-1/8	
Ledford, George T.	061	1857	WB-1/66	AR
Ledford, H. W.	023	1879	WB-A/20	
Ledford, Hiram	026	1859	WB-1/244	AR
Ledford, Hiram	023	1887	WB-A/61	AR
Ledford, Hugh	066	c1882	Orig. Only	AR
Ledford, John	090	1826	WB-3/145	AR
Ledford, John	090	c1825	Copy	092 AR
Ledford, John	026	1864	WB-1/355	AR
Ledford, John Macon	013	1897	WB-D/72	AR
Ledford, Joseph	026	1885	Orig. Only	AR
Ledford, Julius	026	1884	Orig. Only	AR
Ledford, L. M.	026	1884	WB-2/163	
Ledford, Lewis	026	1862	WB-1/277	AR
Ledford, Mary A.	061	1895	WB-2/156	AR
Ledford, Rachel	026	1859	WB-1/237	AR
Ledford, Rebecca	026	1870	Orig. Only	AR
Ledford, Samuel	026	1863	WB-1/327	AR
Ledford, William	085	c1796	WB-E/150	AR
Ledford, William	032	1842	WB-1/394	AR
Lednum, Asa	046	1859	WB-C/533	AR
Lednum, Damarcus	046	1862	WB-D/143	AR
Lednum, Ebin	046	1846	WB-C/249	AR
Lednum, William	032	1855	WB-2/104	AR
Ledwell, Elizabeth	081	1892	WB-16/237	AR
Ledwell, John C.	081	1885	WB-15/559	AR
Ledwell, Thomas W.	081	1885	WB-15/550	AR
Ledwill, William	085	1821	WB-H/108	AR
Lee, Ann Rebecca	041	1873	WB-4/40	AR
Lee, Anna	010	1855	WB-H/19	AR
Lee, Asa	030	1799	WB-2/152	
Lee, Batt	087	1834	WB-1/156	
Lee, Batt	087	1871	WB-3/47	AR
Lee, Benjamin	028	1852	WB-D/197	
Lee, Benjamin	009	1829	OB-B/27	AR
Lee, Bethany	087	1890	WB-3/442	AR
Lee, Bethier	009	c1786	OWB/211	AR
Lee, Bettie D.	071	1889	WB-7/49	AR
Lee, Blackman	087	1877	WB-3/151	AR
Lee, Burchet	087	1824	WB-1/55	
Lee, Calvin	089	1897	WB-2/316	AR

Name	Co.	Date	Recorded Copy	Original
Lee, Charles W.	056	1862	WB-2/24	AR
Lee, Curtis	087	1864	Orig. Only	AR
Lee, Curtis	087	1859	WB-1/547	AR
Lee, Daniel	030	1823	WB-3/153	
Lee, Daniel	030	1776	WB-1/110	
Lee, David	010	1888	WB-I/248	AR
Lee, David	048	1895	WB-1/43	CTY
Lee, David	051	1838	WB-A/133	
Lee, David	056	1833	WB-2/266	AR
Lee, David M.	065	1873	WB-K/115	AR
Lee, Dempsey	030	1822	WB-3/134	
Lee, Drury	071	1805	WB-2/286	AR
Lee, Edward	056	1821	WB-1/430	AR
Lee, Edward	056	1775	Orig. Only	AR
Lee, Elizabeth	028	1869	WB-E/16	
Lee, Elizabeth	041	1839	WB-3/16	AR
Lee, Elizabeth	084	1808	OW/96	AR
Lee, Elizabeth	030	1847	WB-4/127	
Lee, Elizabeth	030	1816	WB-3/74	
Lee, Elizabeth	056	1900	WB-4/201	AR
Lee, Erasmus	029	1898	WB-F/132	AR
Lee, Frances	047	1856	WB-5/25	
Lee, Francis	096	1772	WB-1/76	AR
Lee, Gardner	087	1894	WB-3/548	AR
Lee, George	075	1735	Orig. Only	SS/AR
Lee, Green H.	032	1882	WB-3/375	AR
Lee, Henry	010	1856	WB-H/27	AR
Lee, Henry	010	1822	WB-G/93	AR
Lee, Henry	046	1808	WB-A/222	AR
Lee, Henry, Sr.	037	1812	WB-E/42	AR
Lee, Hugh	056	1844	WB-1/558	AR
Lee, Isaac N.	063	1787	WB-3/148	
Lee, James	010	1732	Orig. Only	SS/AR
Lee, James	037	1777	WB-A/256	AR
Lee, James	069	1811	WB-1/212	AR
Lee, James	060	1827	WB-1/67	AR
Lee, James	030	c1808	WB-2/341	
Lee, James	070	1844	WB-AB/413	AR
Lee, James H.	047	1864	WB-5/120	
Lee, James M.	065	1838	WB-E/171	AR
Lee, James M.	056	1878	WB-3/200	AR
Lee, James, Sr.	005	1847	WB-2/91	AR
Lee, Jane	070	1864	WB-D/141	AR
Lee, Jane	030	1801	WB-2/167	
Lee, Jebal	073	1880	WB-H/232	CTY
Lee, Jeremiah	056	1824	WB-1/367	AR
Lee, Jeremiah	056	1898	WB-3/81	AR
Lee, Jesse	083	1816	WB-1/175	
Lee, Jesse	005	1804	WB-2/87	AR
Lee, Jesse, Sr.	087	1831	WB-1/123	AR
Lee, Joab, Sr.	087	1860	WB-1/549	AR
Lee, John	083	c1792	WB-1/28	AR
Lee, John	056	1793	WB-2/267	AR
Lee, John	020	1832	RB-M/160	AR
Lee, John	047	1860	WB-5/75	
Lee, John	056	1836	Orig. Only	AR
Lee, John	072	1789	WI/L12	AR
Lee, John	041	1866	WB-3/339	AR
Lee, John	028	1768	Orig. Only	AR
Lee, John Burton	057	1800	WB-A/246	AR
Lee, John F.	010	1847	WB-G/416	AR
Lee, John J.	099	1862	RB-32/338	AR
Lcc, John W.	099	1900	WB-D/366	AR
Lee, John W.	084	1804	WB-A/157	CTY
Lee, John W.	028	c1841	Orig. Only	AR
Lee, John, Sr.	056	1768	WB-2/268	AR
Lee, Joseph	087	c1819	Orig. Only	AR
Lee, Joseph B.	010	1861	Copy	051 AR
Lee, Joseph B.	010	1861	WB-H/109	AR
Lee, Joseph T.	050	1898	WB-2/284	CTY
Lee, Joshua	037	1774	WB-A/215	AR
Lee, Joshua	032	1846	WB-1/482	AR
Lee, Josiah	035	1807	WB-A/245	AR
Lee, Josiah	030	1785	WB-1/189	
Lee, Josiah	051	1851	WB-A/331	
Lee, Kitsy	056	c1899	WB-4/301	AR
Lee, Larkin	086	1824	WB-D/25	AR
Lee, Leanna	056	1868	WB-3/8	AR
Lee, Lemuel	010	1799	WB-E/74	AR
Lee, Lewis	056	1827	WB-1/332	AR
Lee, Lovey	030	1840	WB-4/67	
Lee, Lucy	071	1838	WB-4/177	AR
Lee, Mabel	030	1848	WB-4/137	
Lee, Margery	099	1829	RB-20/311	AR
Lee, Martha	056	1816	WB-1/270	AR
Lee, Martha A.	053	1874	WB-11/45	AR-Nunc.
Lee, Mary	101	1869	Orig. Only	AR
Lee, Mary	016	1875	WB-3/114	AR
Lee, Mary	024	1716	Orig. Only	SS/AR
Lee, Mary	086	1898	WB-F/567	AR
Lee, Monroe	056	1900	WB-4/277	AR
Lee, Moses	012	1895	WB-A/94	AR
Lee, Nancy A. R.	105	1893	WB-3/77	AR
Lee, Osborn	026	1864	WB-1/336	AR
Lee, Owen	026	1854	WB-1/176	AR
Lee, Owin	086	1817	WB-C/78	AR
Lee, Peter	087	1846	WB-1/322	
Lee, Pharoah	087	1875	WB-3/101	AR
Lee, Philip	030	c1810	WB-2/363	
Lee, Rachel	072	1800	WB-A/76	AR-Nunc.
Lee, Ransom	056	1883	WB-3/330	AR
Lee, Reuben	021	1850	WB-1/88	AR
Lee, Richard	037	1756	SS 880/157	SS/AR
Lee, Richard	005	1802	WB-2/88	AR
Lee, Richard	059	1900	WB-B/276	CTY
Lee, Robert	005	1808	WB-2/89	AR
Lee, Robert	005	c1766	WB-1/14	
Lee, Robert	056	1788	WB-1/15	AR
Lee, Rufus	056	1864	WB-2/45	AR
Lee, Sally	099	1828	RB-20/292	AR
Lee, Sally	030	1825	WB-3/194	
Lee, Saml.	030	1804	WB-2/241	
Lee, Samuel	056	1831	WB-1/420	AR
Lee, Samuel	009	1853	OB-I/64	AR
Lee, Sarah	030	1801	WB-2/181	Nunc.
Lee, Sarah B.	099	1890	WB-B/410	AR
Lee, Sarah Rose	013	1877	WB-B/148	AR
Lee, Shepherd	005	1894	WB-D/346	AR
Lee, Sidney E.	028	1900	WB-F/460	
Lee, Solomon	037	1762	WB-A/89	AR
Lee, Stephen	072	1773	Orig. Only	SS/AR
Lee, Stephen	072	c1764	RW/L35	AR
Lee, Stephen	056	1840	WB-1/522	AR
Lee, Stephen	013	1879	WB-B/182	AR
Lee, Stevens	096	1750	Orig. Only	SS/AR
Lee, Stevens	096	c1779	WB-1/107	
Lee, Susan S.	028	1869	WB-E/15	
Lee, Thomas	024	1719	SS 875/161	SS/AR
Lee, Thomas	096	1753	Orig. Only	SS/AR
Lee, Thomas	030	1783	WB-1/162	

Name	Co.	Date	Recorded Copy	Original
Lee, Thomas	010	1752	SS 879/39	SS/AR
Lee, Thomas	N	1722	SS 875/343	SS/AR
Lee, Thomas	083	1895	WB-4/48	AR
Lee, Thomas	030	1835	WB-4/8	
Lee, Thomas M.	087	1881	WB-3/217	AR
Lee, Thomas N.	097	1900	WB-3/37	AR
Lee, Titus J.	041	1866	WB-3/338	AR
Lee, Tulie A.	010	1878	WB-I/98	
Lee, W. H.	041	1870	WB-4/16	AR-Nunc.
Lee, Walter A.	056	1900	WB-4/257	AR
Lee, Westbrook	056	1880	WB-3/255	
Lee, Westbrook	087	1880	Orig. Only	AR-Copy
Lee, William	070	1764	WB-C/220	AR
Lee, William	099	1794	RB-3/31	AR
Lee, William	030	c1779	WB-1/155	
Lee, William	005	1857	WB-C/122	AR
Lee, William	099	1861	RB-32/76	AR
Lee, William	087	1883	WB-3/259	AR
Lee, William	030	1781	WB-1/154	
Lee, William R.	056	1848	WB-1/604	AR
Lee, William W.	071	1875	WB-6/178	AR
Lee, Willoughby	084	1824	WB-A/230	CTY
Lee, Winney	005	1856	WB-C/107	AR
Lee, Zorel	074	1877	WB-1/48	AR
Leech, William	081	1805	WB-3/19	AR
Leechman, John	084	1801	WB-A/224	CTY
Leecraft, Lafayette	019	1866	WB-B/25	AR
Leecraft, Mary	019	1878	WB-B/100	AR
Leecraft, Susannah	019	1818	WB-D/272	AR
Leek, Henry	071	1833	WB-4/100	AR
Leek, Josiah	047	1788	WB-3/151	
Leeke, Josiah	071	c1837	Orig. Only	AR
Leeman, Christopher	086	1818	WB-C/87	AR
Leeman, Joseph	039	1817	WB-E/129	AR
Leemon, Temperance	044	1833	WB-12/522	CTY
Leeper, Andrew A.	040	1870	WB-2/10	AR
Leeper, James	060	1840	WB-2/49	AR
Leeper, John	060	1796	Orig. Only	AR
Leeper, Margaret	040	c1859	WB-1/103	
Leeper, Matthew	040	1849	WB-1/17	
Lees, Hannah M.	100	1828	WB-32/16	
Lees, James	065	1807	WB-B/36	AR
Lees, Jane	065	1827	WB-B/46	AR
Leete, Sarah A.	029	1871	WB-E/35	AR
Leeth, John	005	c1757	Orig. Only	SS/AR
Leffers, Samuel	019	1875	WB-B/82	AR
Lefler, Elizabeth	032	1876	WB-3/182	AR
Lefler, Jane	089	1878	WB-2/61	AR
Lefler, Thomas	016	1867	WB-2/150	Nunc.
Legett, Alexander	010	1814	WB-F/246	AR
Legett, Clarisa	010	1842	WB-G/340	AR
Legett, Elizabeth	010	1795	WB-D/274	AR
Legett, Elizabeth	083	1830	WB-1/252	AR
Legett, James	010	1797	WB-E/1	AR
Legett, James	010	1764	WB-A/41	AR
Legett, John	010	1817	WB-G/46	AR
Legett, Jonathan	010	1814	WB-F/245	AR
Legett, Thomas	010	1799	WB-E/72	AR
Legett, Thomas B.	010	1816	WB-F/325	AR
Legett, Titus	010	c1762	WB-A/50	AR
Legg, Humphrey	008	1709	009 DB-1/113	
Legget, Ann P.	101	1884	WB-A/127	AR
Legget, Noah	037	1825	WB-F/33	AR
Leggett, David	063	1822	WB-2/86	
Leggett, Elias	096	1762	WB-1/22	AR
Leggett, Elizabeth	024	1893	WB-E/224	AR
Leggett, Ezekial	009	c1804	OB-A/67	AR
Leggett, James R.	079	1881	WB-2/227	AR
Leggett, John	083	1877	Orig. Only	AR
Leggett, John A.	009	1869	WB-1/3	CTY
Leggett, Levin	037	1855	WB-G/102	AR
Leggett, Louisa	009	1887	WB-1/421	CTY
Leggett, Patience	009	1857	OB-K/231	AR
Leggett, William R.	083	1850	WB-2/26	
Leggette, Bryant	083	1890	WB-3/502	AR
Leggitt, Benjamin	063	1864	WB-2/522	
Leggitt, Elisha	063	1838	WB-2/245	
Leggitt, James, Sr.	063	c1785	WB-1/128	
Leggitt, John	063	1791	WB-1/175	
Legitt, Thomas	030	1749	Orig. Only	SS/AR
Legrand, Elizabeth	084	1846	WB-C/42	CTY
Legrand, Homer	082	1869	WB-6/37	AR
Legwin, Mathew	070	1798	WB-AB/14	
Lehew, Eliza	012	1874	WB-A/28	AR
Lehman, Adolph	103	1898	WB-2/212	AR
Lehman, Francis J.	060	1866	WB-3/86	AR
Lehman, Henry R.	038	1890	WB-3/146	AR
Lehman, Robert F.	028	1876	WB-E/135	
Lehmans, William	060	1883	WB-4/274	AR
Lehr, Bartholomew	060	1807	Orig. Only	AR
Leib, Godfrey	016	1849	WB-1/164	
Leib, Jonas	054	1843	WB-2/272	AR
Leicester, Jonathan	010	c1878	WB-I/168	
Leich, Lawson H.	017	1893	WB-B/230	
Leigh, Ann	009	1733	SS 876/270	SS/AR
Leigh, Betsey	073	1833	WB-E/292	AR
Leigh, Clayton	099	1861	RB-27/255	AR
Leigh, Francis	037	1798	WB-D/60	AR
Leigh, Gilbert	077	1793	WB-C/459	AR-Copy
Leigh, James	008	c1738	009 OWB/26	009 AR
Leigh, James	053	1728	Orig. Only	SS/AR
Leigh, James	077	c1854	Orig. Only	AR
Leigh, John	073	1821	WB-D/593	AR
Leigh, John	009	c1782	OWB/176	AR
Leigh, Joseph	028	1813	WB-C/76	AR
Leigh, Moor	069	1838	WB-1/421	AR
Leigh, Richard S.	036	1898	WB-A/451	CTY
Leigh, Sarah	077	1833	WB-F/214	AR
Leigh, Sullivan	073	1854	WB-G/49	AR
Leigh, Thomas	096	1822	WB-2/90	AR
Leigh, Thomas J.	036	1890	WB-A/186	CTY
Leigh, William	028	1831	WB-C/337	AR
Leigh, William	100	1898	WB-51/518	
Leigh, William	073	1841	WB-F/93	AR
Leigh, William C.	037	1855	WB-G/103	AR
Leigh, William H.	010	1897	WB-I/527	AR
Leinbach, Barbara	090	1847	WB-4/243	AR
Leinbach, Benjamin	038	1864	WB-1/236	AR
Leinbach, Fredrick	090	c1820	Orig. Only	AR
Leinbach, Johannes	085	1766	WB-A/79	AR
Leinbach, Joseph	038	1860	WB-1/160	AR
Leinbach, Josiah	038	1885	WB-2/529	AR
Leinbach, Lewis	038	1895	WB-3/528	AR
Leinbach, Lewis	090	1800	WB-1/164	AR
Leinbach, Mary C.	038	1896	WB-3/554	AR
Leinbach, Mary E.	038	1900	WB-4/255	AR
Leinbach, R. P.	038	1892	WB-3/332	AR
Leinbach, Sallie	038	1897	WB-4/25	AR
Leinbach, Simon P.	038	1862	WB-1/203	AR-Copy
Leinback, Jonas	038	1888	WB-3/82	AR

Name	Co.	Date	Recorded Copy	Original
Leinbauch, Peter	038	c1850	WB-1/49	AR
Leinster, Frederick	054	1895	WB-5/548	CTY
Leirmont, Richard	053	1752	028 DB-5/244	SS/AR
Leitch, Angus	VA	1870	099 WB-A/314	099 AR
Leitch, Christian	083	1864	WB-2/210	AR
Leitch, John	083	1865	WB-2/212	AR
Leith, Charles	009	c1779	OWB/148	AR
Leith, Charles J.	028	1845	WB-D/112	AR
Leith, Elizabeth	009	c1795	OWB/316	AR
Leith, Freeman	020	1792	RB-B/440	AR
Leith, James	053	1846	WB-7/31	AR
Leith, Sally R.	028	1845	WB-D/111	
Leith, Samuel	053	c1816	RW-1/528	AR
Leith, Sarah	044	1779	WB-1/247	CTY
Lekies, John B.	VA	1890	077 WB-H/202	077 AR
Lekies, John B.	VA	1890	071 WB-7/113	071 AR
Lekies, John B.	VA	1890	024 WB-E/195	024 AR
Lelly, John	077	1753	SS 881/7	SS/AR
Lemay, John	044	1834	WB-13/14	CTY
Lemay, Lewis	044	1810	WB-7/125	CTY
Lemay, Samuel	044	1852	WB-19/65	CTY
Lemay, Temperance	044	1878	WB-23/294	CTY
Lemay, Thomas J.	056	1868	WB-2/107	AR
Lembty, Hening	047	1771	WB-1/294	
Lemly, Henry	085	c1804	WB-E/149	AR
Lemly, Henry A.	038	1886	WB-2/569	AR
Lemly, John	085	c1806	WB-E/192	AR
Lemly, Joseph	085	c1804	WB-E/147	AR
Lemly, Nancy M.	085	1881	WB-1/582	CTY
Lemly, Phillip	085	1809	WB-G/142	AR
Lemmond, James M.	065	1824	WB-B/44	AR
Lemmond, Robert	065	1818	WB-B/37	AR
Lemmons, James	084	1858	WB-C/275	CTY
Lemond, John	065	1806	WB-B/34	AR
Lemons, Alexander	084	1859	WB-C/284	CTY
Lemons, Joseph	084	1824	WB-A/225	CTY
Lemons, Zaza D.	084	1849	WB-C/83	CTY
Lemount, Arther	030	1799	WB-2/147	
Lence, Christena	085	1848	WB-K/79	AR
Lenderman, Mary	104	1890	Orig. Only	AR
Lennard, Scota	039	1816	WB-E/109	AR
Lennin, George	011	c1822	WB-2/342	
Lennon, Dennis	027	1842	WB-A/21	
Lennon, John	011	1757	Orig. Only	SS/AR
Lennon, John E.	011	1900	WB-3/114	CTY
Lennon, John M.	011	1875	WB-2/89 & 95	
Lenoir, Betsey	TN	1856	013 WB-B/473	013 AR
Lenoir, Isaac T.	TN	1877	Copy	023 AR
Lenoir, Sarah J.	017	1899	WB-B/312	AR
Lenoir, Selina L.	017	c1863	WB-A/154	AR
Lenoir, Thomas	017	c1854	WB-A/125	AR
Lenoir, Thomas	037	1765	WB-A/147	AR
Lenoir, Walter W.	017	1890	WB-B/195	
Lenoir, Walter W.	102	1890	WB-A/72	
Lenoir, Walter W.	017	1890	Copy	049 AR
Lenoir, Walter W.	021	1890	WB-2/504	
Lenoir, William	104	1839	WB-4/240	
Lenton, Benjamin	030	1798	WB-2/124	
Lenton, William	028	1727	SS 876/97	
Lentz, Bostian	085	c1807	WB-F/62	AR
Lentz, Bostian	085	1854	WB-K/171	AR
Lentz, Davalt	054	1843	WB-2/268	AR
Lentz, Dewalt	085	1812	WB-G/251	AR
Lentz, Henry	085	1878	WB-1/432	CTY
Lentz, Mary A.	016	1886	WB-3/485	AR
Lentz, Peter	085	1815	WB-G/350	AR
Lentz, Peter J.	016	1881	WB-3/304	AR
Lentz, R. W.	085	1874	WB-1/221	CTY
Lentz, Rachel	054	1872	WB-4/94	CTY
Leonard, Alfred	046	1894	WB-F/334	AR
Leonard, Alice	032	1897	WB-4/312	AR
Leonard, Calvin D.	097	1863	WB-1/209	AR-Nunc.
Leonard, Charles S.	046	c1880	WB-E/278	AR
Leonard, Daniel	032	1866	WB-2/340	AR
Leonard, Daniel	021	1866	WB-1/219	AR
Leonard, David H.	032	1866	Orig. Only	AR
Leonard, Elizabeth	039	1864	WB-R/717	AR
Leonard, Elizabeth	085	c1803	WB-G/124	
Leonard, Febby	039	1899	WB-V/195	AR
Leonard, Frederick	039	1816	WB-E/68	AR
Leonard, George	032	1844	WB-1/427	AR
Leonard, George H.	032	1900	WB-4/458	AR
Leonard, Henry	085	c1803	WB-E/145	AR
Leonard, Henry	012	1774	DB-A/183	AR
Leonard, Jacob	032	1846	WB-1/479	AR
Leonard, Jacob	032	1886	WB-3/526	AR
Leonard, Jacob	060	1878	WB-4/184	AR
Leonard, Jacob W.	012	1825	WB-B/136	AR
Leonard, Jacob, Sr.	032	1835	WB-1/259	AR
Leonard, James	075	1795	WB-L/28	AR
Leonard, James	029	1801	Orig. Only	AR
Leonard, James H.	046	1887	WB-E/461	AR
Leonard, John	032	1847	WB-2/7	AR
Leonard, John	039	1817	WB-E/130	AR
Leonard, John	056	1849	WB-1/614	AR
Leonard, John	032	1866	WB-2/335	AR
Leonard, John P.	039	1852	WB-N/331	AR-Nunc.
Leonard, Joseph	046	1853	WB-C/402	AR
Leonard, Larkin	039	1885	WB-U/366	AR
Leonard, Louisa	106	1881	WB-2/132	AR
Leonard, Martha	046	1857	WB-C/488	AR
Leonard, Mary	032	1898	WB-4/352	AR
Leonard, Mary	039	1827	WB-H/191	AR
Leonard, Michael	032	1827	WB-1/84	AR
Leonard, Peter	032	1840	WB-1/343	AR
Leonard, Phebe	032	1879	WB-3/272	AR
Leonard, Philip	032	1830	WB-1/134	AR
Leonard, Pricilla	039	1877	WB-U/143	AR
Leonard, Robert	097	1879	WB-2/163	
Leonard, Sacky	039	1869	WB-U/8	
Leonard, Samuel	012	1810	WB-B/84	AR
Leonard, Samuel	012	c1782	DB-B/153	
Leonard, Samuel	077	1807	WB-E/277	AR
Leonard, Serophena	039	1899	WB-V/161	AR
Leonard, Theophilus	024	1764	WB-1/10	AR
Leonard, Valintine	085	1814	Orig. Only	AR
Leonard, Van	039	c1815	Orig. Only	AR
Leonard, Volentine	085	c1779	WB-B/6	
Leonard, William	039	1852	WB-N/339	AR
Leonard, William	005	1866	WB-C/239	AR
Leonhardt, J. W.	060	1898	WB-5/96 & 155	AR
Leonhardt, Jacob M.	060	1863	WB-3/65	AR
Leonhardt, Joseph	060	1855	WB-2/400	
Leonhardt, Sarah	060	1898	WB-5/98	AR
Leopard, John	099	1853	RB-28/279	AR
Lepper, Thomas	028	1719	SS 875/163	SS/AR
Leroy, Helen	009	1860	OB-L/208	AR
Lesley, Thomas	073	c1823	Orig. Only	AR
Leslie, Catherine	029	1873	WB-E/107	AR
Leslie, Daniel	029	1830	WB-B/198	AR

Name	Co.	Date	Recorded Copy	Original
Leslie, Daniel	029	1860	WB-C/412	AR
Leslie, James	047	1781	WB-3/3	
Lessman, August	070	1888	WB-F/181	AR
Lessman, Helena M.	070	1889	WB-F/388	AR
Lester, Banister	072	1827	WB-1/14	AR
Lester, Elizabeth	072	1840	WB-2/26	AR
Lester, Fridk.	085	1767	WB-A/87	
Lester, Jacob	075	1823	WB-M1/381	AR
Lester, Mary	092	1828	Copy	090 AR
Lester, Mary	092	1828	WB-4/13	AR
Lester, Moses	037	1825	WB-F/38	AR
Lester, Winefred	075	1814	WB-M1/270	AR
Lesueur, John L.	084	1859	WB-C/299	CTY
Letchfield, Jacob	030	1805	WB-2/267	
Letchworth, Joseph	028	1775	Orig. Only	AR
Letellier, Sarah	010	1882	WB-I/144	
Lethco, Eliza	046	1897	WB-F/576	AR
Lethco, Levinah	032	c1841	WB-2/72	
Letherman, Noah	107	1894	WB-2/77	
Letson, Johnson	NJ	1885	065 WB-N/1	065 AR
Letson, Johnson	NJ	1885	097 WB-3/199	097 AR
Lett, A. J.	022	1895	WB-F/3	
Lett, John	068	1846	WB-B/155	
Lett, John W.	029	1875	WB-E/147	AR
Lett, William	100	1895	WB-51/432	
Lettijohn, Job	024	1824	WB-C/106	AR
Leuerton, Mary	075	c1741	Orig. Only	AR
Leutz, Barbara	016	1900	WB-4/363	AR
Leventhorpe, Collett	017	1889	WB-B/166	AR
Leventhrope, Clarica	086	1894	WB-F/486	AR
Leversage, Sarah	028	1796	WB-B/3	AR
Leveton, Abner	030	1788	WB-1/225 & 229	
Levister, Davis	044	1852	WB-19/160	CTY
Levister, William R.	044	1867	WB-22/653	CTY
Levy, Alexander	029	1825	WB-B/136	AR
Lewallen, Catherine	006	1873	WB-E/6	AR
Lewallen, Jane	081	1850	WB-11/173	AR
Lewallen, Jonathan	081	1848	WB-9/22	AR
Lewallen, McLaren	081	1861	WB-12/7	
Lewellen, Dorcas	005	1842	WB-B/146	AR
Lewellen, Thomas	084	1861	WB-C/357	CTY
Lewellin, John A.	071	1833	WB-4/99	AR
Lewellin, Martha H.	001	1900	WB-3/343	AR
Lewellin, Obedients	071	1828	WB-4/39	AR
Lewellin, Samuel	084	1854	WB-C/181	CTY
Lewelling, Alexander	037	1792	WB-C/182	AR
Lewelling, John	037	1794	WB-C/279	AR
Lewelling, William	081	1799	WB-2/69	AR
Lewellyn, John	084	1886	WB-E/352	CTY
Lewerton, Epharim	024	c1713	SS 875/30	
Lewerton, William	024	1697	Orig. Only	SS/AR
Lewey, Jacob	046	1874	WB-E/131	AR
Lewey, John	046	1860	WB-D/60	AR
Lewis, A. J.	006	1867	WB-D/75	AR
Lewis, Aaron	076	1899	WB-A1/237	AR
Lewis, Alexander	065	1785	WB-D/156	AR
Lewis, Alfred	054	1881	WB-4/416	CTY
Lewis, Andrew	001	1889	WB-2/423	AR
Lewis, Angellica	071	1783	WB-1/271	
Lewis, Ann	037	1844	WB-F/300	AR
Lewis, Anne	024	1771	WB-A/254	AR-Nunc.
Lewis, Archabell	009	c1803	OWB/412	AR
Lewis, Argulon G.	092	1869	WB-6/11	
Lewis, Benjamin	104	1837	WB-4/223	AR
Lewis, Benjamin	099	1887	WB-B/195	
Lewis, Benjamin	009	1817	OB-A/270	AR
Lewis, Benjamin	083	c1821	WB-1/194	AR
Lewis, Betsey	047	c1893	WB-7/191	AR
Lewis, C. A.	046	1887	WB-E/463	AR
Lewis, Charles	044	1793	WB-3/60	CTY
Lewis, Charles	VA	1817	020 RB-H/133	020 AR
Lewis, Charles	086	1834	WB-E/4	AR
Lewis, Charles	046	1895	WB-F/445	AR
Lewis, Charles	084	1891	WB-E/481	CTY
Lewis, Charles	044	1821	WB-9/49	CTY
Lewis, Charles D.	044	1850	WB-18/134	CTY
Lewis, Christopher	028	1806	WB-B/234	AR
Lewis, Council	083	1895	WB-4/68	AR
Lewis, Cullin	047	1847	WB-4/258	AR-Copy
Lewis, Daniel	085	c1801	WB-E/141	AR
Lewis, Daniel	009	1836	OWB/531	AR
Lewis, Daniel	054	c1833	WB-2/159	AR
Lewis, Daniel	029	1811	WB-A/164	AR
Lewis, David	102	1877	WB-A/9	AR
Lewis, David	028	1772	Orig. Only	AR
Lewis, David	019	1773	Orig. Only	SS/AR
Lewis, David	041	1833	WB-2/325	AR
Lewis, David M.	039	1857	WB-S/458	AR
Lewis, E. F. M.	026	1880	WB-2/199	AR
Lewis, Edmond	078	1792	WI-1/28	AR
Lewis, Edward	083	1857	WB-2/119	AR
Lewis, Edward	026	1853	WB-1/152	AR
Lewis, Edward W.	028	1898	WB-F/358	
Lewis, Eliphas	071	1808	WB-3/9	AR
Lewis, Elizabeth	044	1872	WB-23/50	CTY
Lewis, Elizabeth	047	1867	WB-5/155	
Lewis, Ellen	028	1803	WB-B/186	AR
Lewis, Emily E.	054	1890	WB-5/358	CTY
Lewis, Emily E.	054	1890	079 WB-2/514	079 AR
Lewis, Enoch	073	1799	WB-C/156	AR
Lewis, Evan	N	1714	Orig. Only	SS/AR
Lewis, Evin	081	1799	WB-2/51	AR
Lewis, Exum	037	1796	WB-D/7	AR
Lewis, Exum	037	1839	WB-F/226	AR
Lewis, Exum	047	1888	WB-6/518	AR
Lewis, Fielding	073	1848	WB-F/401	AR
Lewis, Franklin	011	c1850	WB-1/188	
Lewis, Green	037	1814	WB-E/64	AR
Lewis, Griffin	103	1788	WI-A/142	AR
Lewis, Griffith	008	c1733	009 OWB/15	009 AR
Lewis, Henry	069	c1802	Orig. Only	AR
Lewis, Henry G.	101	1880	WB-A/41	AR
Lewis, Henry R.	103	1883	WB-1/264	AR
Lewis, Holden M.	076	1885	WB-A1/49	AR
Lewis, Holey	102	1899	WB-A/156	AR
Lewis, Howell	044	1814	WB-7/350	CTY
Lewis, Howell	044	1790	WB-2/150	CTY
Lewis, Isaac	028	1898	WB-F/362	
Lewis, J. Reece	049	1898	WB-2/417	AR
Lewis, Jacob	028	1796	WB-B/17	AR
Lewis, Jacob	039	1883	WB-U/306	AR
Lewis, Jacob	054	1845	WB-2/317	AR
Lewis, Jacob	090	1835	WB-3/295	AR
Lewis, James	071	1815	WB-3/153	AR
Lewis, James	037	1846	WB-F/350	AR
Lewis, James M.	054	1887	WB-5/150	CTY
Lewis, James W.	028	1887	WB-E/457	AR
Lewis, James, Sr.	044	1826	WB-10/93	CTY
Lewis, Jean	071	1794	WB-2/51	AR

Name	Co.	Date	Recorded Copy	Original
Lewis, Jeremiah	005	c1794	WB-A/30	AR
Lewis, John	046	1864	WB-D/201	AR
Lewis, John	047	1791	WB-3/199	Nunc.
Lewis, John	024	c1776	WB-A/247	AR
Lewis, John	086	1782	WB-A/2	
Lewis, John	083	1843	WB-1/418	AR
Lewis, John	041	1815	WB-2/78	AR
Lewis, John	022	1894	WB-E/549	AR
Lewis, John	020	1790	RB-B/340	AR
Lewis, John	104	1879	WB-6/170	AR
Lewis, John	081	1802	WB-2/100	AR
Lewis, John	016	1862	WB-2/82	
Lewis, John	103	1897	WB-2/182	AR
Lewis, John	VA	1866	044 WB-24/368	044 CTY
Lewis, John	084	c1802	OW/27	AR
Lewis, John	083	1817	WB-1/180	
Lewis, John	085	c1804	WB-G/11	AR
Lewis, John B.	065	1858	WB-J/50	AR
Lewis, John H.	085	1885	WB-2/127	CTY
Lewis, John R.	047	1877	WB-6/168	AR
Lewis, John W.	032	1886	WB-3/515	AR
Lewis, John W.	099	1842	RB-25/148	AR
Lewis, John, Jr.	028	1810	WB-C/20	AR
Lewis, John, Sr.	024	1765	WB-1/16	AR
Lewis, Joseph	028	1800	WB-B/107	AR
Lewis, Joseph	028	1774	Orig. Only	AR
Lewis, Joseph	009	1825	OB-A/344	AR
Lewis, Joseph	044	1844	WB-16/75	CTY
Lewis, Joseph	009	1876	WB-1/166	CTY
Lewis, Josephus	019	1874	WB-B/75	AR
Lewis, Joshua	VA	1760	Copy	071 AR
Lewis, Joshua	104	1864	WB-5/375	
Lewis, Josiah	011	c1808	WB-2/335	
Lewis, Kinchen C.	037	1894	WB-H/299	AR
Lewis, Lazarus	047	1852	WB-4/331	
Lewis, Leonard	103	c1888	WB-1/540	AR
Lewis, Lewis	047	1810	WB-3/497	
Lewis, Lucinda	092	1842	WB-4/187	
Lewis, Luke	086	1891	WB-F/412	AR
Lewis, Luten	041	1815	WB-2/103	AR
Lewis, Luten	041	1811	WB-2/69	AR
Lewis, Lyman	038	1875	WB-2/232	AR
Lewis, Magor	028	1803	WB-B/167	AR
Lewis, Marcus A.	053	1874	WB-11/51	AR
Lewis, Margaret	047	1888	WB-6/520	AR
Lewis, Maria J.	039	1897	WB-V/154	AR
Lewis, Martha E.	099	1897	WB-D/18	AR
Lewis, Mary	041	c1850	WB-3/143	AR
Lewis, Mary	044	1814	WB-7/357	CTY
Lewis, Mary	037	1862	WB-G/216	AR
Lewis, Mary	103	1893	WB-2/55	AR
Lewis, Mary	047	1824	WB-3/708	
Lewis, Mary	060	1817	Orig. Only	AR
Lewis, Mary	103	1848	RD-10/157	AR
Lewis, Mary	047	1834	WB-4/107	
Lewis, Mary A.	003	1885	WB-B/149	AR
Lewis, Mary A.	047	1849	WB-4/274	
Lewis, Mary A.	044	1859	WB-20/705	CTY
Lewis, Mary Ann	009	1874	WB-1/136	CTY
Lewis, Mary E.	038	1892	WB-3/316	AR
Lewis, Mason	028	1794	WB-A/316	AR
Lewis, Mattie E.	093	1882	WB-2/8	AR
Lewis, Molly	041	1822	WB-2/182	AR
Lewis, Morgan	047	1789	WB-3/162	
Lewis, Mullington	070	1850	WB-C/507	AR
Lewis, Nancy C.	006	1892	WB-E/226	AR
Lewis, Nathaniel	073	c1788	WB-B/50	AR
Lewis, Nathaniel	028	1816	WB-C/117	AR
Lewis, Nehemiah	028	1802	WB-B/139	AR
Lewis, Nicholas M.	020	1889	WB-B/89	CTY
Lewis, Oliver	009	1878	WB-1/227	CTY
Lewis, Olivia	047	1827	WB-4/30	
Lewis, Ollen M.	087	1890	WB-3/461	AR
Lewis, P. H.	004	1895	WB-A/170	AR
Lewis, Patience	085	1842	WB-I/141	AR
Lewis, Pattie A.	098	1900	WB-A/376	CTY
Lewis, Patty	028	1815	WB-C/102	AR
Lewis, Penina	103	1884	WB-1/300	AR
Lewis, Peter	085	c1803	WB-E/143	AR
Lewis, Peter	028	1772	Orig. Only	AR
Lewis, Philip	041	1800	WB-1/173	AR
Lewis, Phillip	046	1797	WB-A/214	AR
Lewis, Pitman	086	1858	WB-E/341	AR
Lewis, R. B.	027	1896	WB-2/123	AR
Lewis, Rebecca	084	1849	WB-C/93	CTY
Lewis, Richard	047	1760	WB-1/6	
Lewis, Richard	054	c1806	WB-1/138	AR
Lewis, Richard C.	076	1879	WB-A1/6	AR
Lewis, Richard H.	079	1857	WB-1/3	AR-Copy
Lewis, Richard M.	011	1856	WB-1/254	
Lewis, Richard M.	011	1845	WB-1/121	
Lewis, Riley	019	1878	WB-B/104	AR
Lewis, Robert	044	1781	WB-1/296	CTY
Lewis, Robert H.	020	1860	RB-S/323	AR
Lewis, Samuel	081	1826	WB-5/299	AR
Lewis, Samuel D.	022	1879	WB-E/189	AR
Lewis, Sarah	054	1851	WB-3/51	AR
Lewis, Selah	083	c1822	WB-1/373	AR
Lewis, Sirls	022	1863	WB-D/109	AR
Lewis, Stephen	081	1792	WB-1/112	AR
Lewis, Stephen	083	c1800	WB-1/62	
Lewis, Stephen	DE	1781	092 WB-3/61A	092 AR
Lewis, Susannah	005	1840	WB-B/111	AR
Lewis, Tabitha	087	1891	WB-3/493	AR
Lewis, Thomas	047	1859	WB-5/71	
Lewis, Thomas	005	1836	WB-B/61	AR
Lewis, Thomas	069	1789	WB-1/57	AR
Lewis, Thomas	054	c1823	Orig. Only	AR
Lewis, Thomas	096	1853	WB-3/37	AR
Lewis, Thomas	065	1834	WB-G/164	AR
Lewis, Thomas	012	1895	WB-A/100	AR
Lewis, Thomas	075	1720	SS 875/237	
Lewis, Thomas	019	1795	WB = D/267	AR
Lewis, Thomas	069	1865	WB-1/592	AR
Lewis, Thomas	073	1805	WB-D/151	AR
Lewis, Thomas	065	c1883	097 WB-2/357	
Lewis, Thomas B.	044	1851	WB-18/237	CTY
Lewis, Urban	103	1847	RD-9/460	AR
Lewis, Wallis	072	1886	WB-4/197	AR
Lewis, William	019	1809	WB-D/270	AR
Lewis, William	046	1831	WB-B/434	AR
Lewis, William	101	c1862	Orig. Only	AR
Lewis, William	070	1755	DB-D/137	AR
Lewis, William	104	1795	WB-1/453	AR
Lewis, William	041	1796	WB-1/141	AR
Lewis, William	008	1732	SS 876/252	SS/AR
Lewis, William	028	1838	WB-C/415	AR
Lewis, William	079	1867	WB-1/170	AR
Lewis, William	104	1820	WB-3/229	AR
Lewis, William	090	1793	WB-1/36	AR

Name	Co.	Date	Recorded Copy	Original
Lewis, William	073	1793	WB-B/237	AR
Lewis, William	044	1854	WB-19/492	CTY
Lewis, William A.	054	1884	WB-5/37	CTY
Lewis, William C.	097	1895	WB-2/535	AR
Lewis, William F.	070	1848	WB-C/485	AR
Lewis, William H.	098	1894	WB-A/208	CTY
Lewis, William J.	073	1818	WB-D/539	AR
Lewis, William J.	019	1855	WB-A/183	AR
Lewis, William K.	009	c1836	OB-F/198	AR
Lewis, William W.	101	1895	WB-A/273	AR
Lewman, Aaron	054	c1824	WB-2/49	AR
Lewter, Barbary	022	1861	WB-D/76	AR
Lewter, Barbee	099	1888	WB-B/300	AR
Lewter, Elias	071	1809	WB-3/20	AR
Lewter, Giles	071	1819	WB-3/224	AR
Lewter, Henry	022	1828	WB-B/142	AR
Lewter, John T.	051	1887	WB-C/359	AR
Lewter, M. C.	022	1885	WB-E/306	AR
Lewter, Wiley	022	c1842	WB-D/154	AR
Lewter, Willie	071	1836	WB-4/145	AR
Lewton, Mary	071	1827	WB-4/20	AR
Lewtor, Mary	022	1878	WB-E/161	AR
Lick, Christina	038	1865	WB-1/254	AR
Liddell, W. J. F.	065	1889	WB-L/381	AR
Lidell, John G.	040	c1853	WB-1/54	
Liderker, John	085	1822	WB-H/148	AR
Liggett, Michael	065	1781	WB-B/28	AR
Liggett, Robert	065	1816	WB-B/37	AR
Light, Jeremiah	047	1822	WB-3/677	
Light, John S.	038	1861	WB-1/190	AR
Lightell, Benjamin	085	1844	WB-I/209	AR
Lightell, Thomas	054	1892	WB-5/414	CTY
Lightfoot, Margaret	PA	1893	063 WB-4/111	063 AR
Lightfoot, Martha	099	1818	RB-14/253	AR
Lightfoot, Sally	029	1868	WB-E/1	AR
Lightfoot, William	PA	1876	063 WB-3/99	
Lightfoot, William	071	1834	WB-4/111	AR
Lightfoot, William T.	AR	c1867	Copy	099 AR
Ligon, Abraham	099	1879	WB-A/64	AR
Ligon, David P.	VA	1877	065 WB-K/273	065 AR
Ligon, John	099	1832	RB-22/311	
Ligon, John	099	1859	RB-31/255	AR
Ligon, Richard	099	1815	RB-12/212	AR
Likens, Jacob	085	1767	WB-A/85	
Lile, William	044	1805	WB-6/203	CTY
Liles, Benjamin	012	1828	WB-B/153	AR
Liles, Benjamin	071	1797	WB-2/144	AR
Liles, David N.	097	1897	WB-2/545	AR
Liles, George	024	c1758	Orig. Only	AR
Liles, Harris	099	1851	RB-27/207	AR
Liles, Jacob	099	1825	RB-19/193	AR
Liles, James A.	005	1889	WB-D/262	AR
Liles, James D.	005	1893	WB-D/333	AR
Liles, Mark	071	1838	WB-4/171	AR
Liles, Martha	071	1850	WB-5/91	AR
Liles, Nelson P.	005	1859	WB-C/150	AR
Liles, Rufus S.	005	1880	WB-D/94	AR
Liles, Sanford	005	1885	WB-D/173	AR
Liles, Thomas	071	1786	WB-1/358	AR
Liles, Thomas	086	1835	WB-E/24	AR
Liles, Thomas	044	1828	WB-10/448	CTY
Liles, Vernon B.	005	1882	WB-D/144	AR
Liles, William	024	c1774	WB-A/346	AR
Liles, William D.	005	1850	WB-C/17	
Liles, Wrightman	099	1881	WB-A/294	AR
Liley, Elizabeth	041	1850	WB-3/129	AR
Lillard, Moses	084	1813	WB-A/104	CTY
Lilley, Joseph	063	c1796	WB-1/330	
Lilley, Kedar	063	1816	WB-2/37	
Lilley, Kelly	009	c1881	Orig. Only	CTY
Lilley, Thomas	077	1736	LGB-4/#52	SS/AR
Lilley, Timothy	063	c1797	WB-1/348	
Lilliebridge, Joseph	072	1802	WB-A/75	AR
Lillington, Alexander	077	1697	SS 874.2/78	SS/AR
Lillington, Alexander	070	1784	WB-C/223	AR
Lillington, Ann	024	1725	SS 876/47	SS/AR
Lillington, Eliezer	019	1729	Orig. Only	SS/AR
Lillington, Eliza Ann	070	1850	WB-C/508	AR
Lillington, Elizabeth	053	1741	LGB-4/#154	SS/AR
Lillington, George	028	1742	Deeds.21/L22	
Lillington, George	070	1795	WB-C/231	AR
Lillington, John	070	1785	WB-C/232	AR
Lillington, John	008	1723	Orig. Only	SS/AR
Lillington, Richard	076	1896	WB-A1/207	AR
Lillington, Sarah Ann	070	1839	WB-AB/324	AR
Lilly, David C.	005	1849	WB-C/15	AR
Lilly, E. J.	029	1890	WB-E/480	AR
Lilly, Elizabeth	063	1885	WB-3/276	AR
Lilly, Frederick	056	1866	WB-2/86	AR
Lilly, Hannah B.	089	1876	Orig. Only	AR
Lilly, Harmon	063	1880	WB-3/190	
Lilly, John	063	1882	WB-3/228	
Lilly, John A.	089	1888	WB-2/167	AR
Lilly, Joseph	063	c1784	WB-1/100	
Lilly, Mark	099	1820	RB-16/292	AR
Lilly, Mary	067	c1854	Orig. Only	AR
Lilly, McGilbert	009	1888	WB-1/434	CTY
Lilly, Nebucadneezer	063	1880	WB-3/187	
Lilly, Sarah	077	1827	WB-F/140	AR
Lilly, Sarah A.	063	1862	WB-2/489	
Lilly, William	077	1809	WB-E/337	AR
Lilse, Rebecca	024	1849	WB-C/292	AR
Limon, Joanna	084	c1860	Orig. Only	CTY
Limons, Alexander	084	1858	WB-C/284	
Limore, Ephraim M.	092	1799	WB-3/31	
Lin, James, Sr.	099	1797	RB-4/89	AR
Linch (Lynch), James	056	1790	WB-1/28	AR
Linch, Anna	060	1824	WB-1/6	AR
Linch, Dannel	085	1814	WB-G/330	AR
Linch, Elias	086	1863	WB-E/423	AR
Linch, George	037	1810	WB-D/354	AR
Linch, James	073	1803	WB-D/130	AR
Linch, John	073	1813	WB-D/392	AR
Linch, John	100	1779	WB-3/8	015 AR
Linch, Olive, Sr.	037	1825	WB-F/36	AR
Linch, Orren	037	1822	WB-E/312	AR
Lind, Thomas	009	c1787	OWB/215	AR
Linder, Margaret	077	1814	WB-E/400	AR
Linder, Sally	084	1865	Orig. Only	CTY
Linders, Angeline	084	c1842	WB-B/288	CTY
Lindley, James	022	1852	WB-C/332	AR
Lindley, Jonathan	073	1828	WB-E/167	AR
Lindley, Joshua	046	1881	WB-E/303	AR
Lindley, Joshua	022	1851	WB-C/296	AR
Lindley, Oliver L.	022	1891	WB-E/465	AR
Lindley, Owen	022	1887	WB-E/355	AR
Lindley, Thomas	022	1833	WB-B/247	AR
Lindley, William T.	022	1884	WB-E/288	AR
Lindlum, Nicholas	068	1900	WB-E/85	
Lindly, Thomas	073	1782	WB-A/252	AR

Name	Co.	Date	Recorded Copy	Original
Lindly, William	073	1784	WB-A/311	AR
Lindsay, Andrew	046	1844	WB-C/208	AR
Lindsay, Ann	046	1832	WB-B/469	AR
Lindsay, Colin	082	1817	WB-1/185	AR
Lindsay, Daniel	030	1775	WB-1/96	
Lindsay, David	046	1860	WB-D/41	AR
Lindsay, David	070	1756	DB-D/168	AR
Lindsay, Edward	047	1836	WB-4/128	
Lindsay, Eliza J.	032	1875	WB-3/133	AR
Lindsay, Elizabeth	038	1871	WB-2/49	AR
Lindsay, Elizabeth	032	1847	WB-2/11	AR
Lindsay, Emily P.	046	1879	WB-E/258	AR
Lindsay, Eveline	017	1894	WB-B/254	AR
Lindsay, Isaac	082	1820	WB-1/213	AR
Lindsay, James	034	1770	Orig. Only	SS/AR
Lindsay, Jed H.	046	1881	WB-E/315	AR
Lindsay, Jesse H.	046	1887	WB-E/455	AR
Lindsay, John	029	1885	WB-E/333	AR
Lindsay, John	047	1801	WB-3/349	
Lindsay, John	084	1851	WB-C/115	CTY
Lindsay, John	084	1839	WB-B/217	CTY
Lindsay, John	032	1828	WB-1/103	AR
Lindsay, John W.	026	1865	WB-1/374	AR
Lindsay, John W.	032	1855	WB-2/109	AR
Lindsay, Johnson	106	c1851	Orig. Only	AR
Lindsay, Johnson J.	073	1897	WB-I/105	CTY
Lindsay, Joseph P.	090	1864	WB-4/368	
Lindsay, Josephus	009	c1890	Orig. Only	CTY
Lindsay, Josiah	047	1812	Copy	071 AR
Lindsay, Josiah	047	1812	WB-3/528	
Lindsay, Judah	047	1818	WB-3/614	
Lindsay, R. G.	046	1886	WB-E/445	AR
Lindsay, Reuben	084	c1814	OW/30	AR
Lindsay, Robert	046	1818	WB-B/66	AR
Lindsay, Robert	046	1801	WB-A/428	AR
Lindsay, Robert	065	1830	WB-E/83	AR
Lindsay, Samuel W.	026	1889	WB-2/394	AR
Lindsay, Sarah	046	1897	WB-G/34	AR
Lindsay, Selina P.	074	1892	Orig. Only	AR
Lindsay, Sherwood C.	GA	1879	097 WB-2/189	
Lindsay, William	046	1841	WB-C/103	AR
Lindsay, William	084	1889	WB-E/421	CTY
Lindsey, Andrew J.	013	1891	WB-C/227	AR
Lindsey, Caleb	022	1785	RB-1/21	AR
Lindsey, Charity	106	1870	WB-2/39	AR
Lindsey, Charles	030	c1809	WB-3/54	
Lindsey, Daniel	030	1837	WB-4/40	
Lindsey, Daniel	030	1839	WB-4/62	Nunc.
Lindsey, Edmund L.	075	1827	WB-N/38	AR
Lindsey, Eli	073	1816	WB-D/483	AR
Lindsey, Elisha	044	i792	WB-2/301	CTY
Lindsey, James	073	1847	WB-F/354	AR
Lindsey, Jane	073	c1816	Orig. Only	AR
Lindsey, Jane B.	030	1859	WB-4/230	
Lindsey, Jeptha	069	1877	WB-5/60	AR
Lindsey, John	073	1794	WB-B/275	AR
Lindsey, John	030	1799	WB-2/148	
Lindsey, John E.	069	1883	WB-5/172	AR
Lindsey, Joseph	100	1794	WB-7/203	AR
Lindsey, Labon	092	1840	WB-4/169	
Lindsey, Mary Ann	028	1870	WB-E/31	
Lindsey, Mary Jane	005	1895	WB-D/372	AR
Lindsey, Sarah A.	084	1900	WB-F/165	CTY
Lindsey, Susan	069	1883	WB-5/187	AR
Lindsey, Thomas	030	1857	WB-4/208	
Lindsey, Thomas	030	1790	WB-1/246	
Lindsey, Timothy	061	c1863	WB-1/80	AR
Lindsey, William	005	1801	WB-2/94	AR
Lindsey, William	069	1817	WB-1/289	AR
Lindsley, Silas C.	005	1866	WB-C/254	AR
Lindsy, Evelina	054	c1861	WB-3/164	AR
Linear, John	087	c1820	WB-1/25	AR
Linebach, Rosana S.	092	1898	WB-6/474	AR
Linebarger, Ephraim	040	1863	WB-1/150	
Linebarger, H. H.	021	1892	WB-3/1	
Linebarger, John	040	c1852	WB-1/65	
Linebeck, Abraham	090	1791	WB-1/16	
Lineberger, David	040	1887	WB-2/285	AR
Lineberger, Lewis	040	1880	WB-2/167	AR
Lineberger, Martin	021	1866	WB-1/227	AR
Lineberger, Pater, Sr.	060	1803	Orig. Only	AR
Lineberger, Peter, Jr.	060	1803	Orig. Only	AR
Lineberry, A. W.	046	1899	WB-G/119	AR
Lineberry, Archibald	001	1890	WB-2/462	
Lineberry, Catherine	046	1867	WB-D/329	AR
Lineberry, George	046	1826	WB-B/219	AR
Lineberry, Jacob	081	1821	WB-5/43	AR
Lineberry, Rebecca	001	1892	WB-2/527	AR
Linefield, Daniel	060	1828	WB-1/115	AR
Linegar, Elizabeth	046	1825	WB-B/215	AR
Lines, Charles M.	032	1877	WB-3/221	AR
Lines, George	032	1867	WB-2/353	AR
Lines, George	032	1896	WB-4/290	AR
Linfield, John	028	1766	Orig. Only	AR
Lingerfelt, John	060	1851	WB-2/358	AR
Lingerfelt, John	060	1828	WB-1/78	AR
Lingle, Casper	085	1828	WB-H/412	AR
Lingle, Catharine	085	c1868	WB-1/14	CTY
Lingle, Francis	085	1847	WB-K/63	AR
Lingle, Jacob	085	1882	WB-2/5	CTY
Lingle, John	085	1874	WB-1/278	
Lingle, Lawrence	085	1885	WB-2/105	CTY
Lingle, Lorens	085	1775	WB-A/213	AR
Lingle, Moses	085	1887	WB-2/224	CTY
Lingle, Nancy C.	085	1893	WB-3/5	
Linhardt, Larance	060	1833	WB-1/271	AR
Linheard, Daniel	060	1860	WB-3/32	AR
Linieer, Richard	022	1900	WB-F/159	AR
Linigar, Isaac	046	1818	WB-B/58	AR
Linigar, Rosannah	046	1821	WB-B/132	AR
Linington, Edward	028	1736	Orig. Only	SS/AR
Linington, George	028	1742	Orig. Only	SS/AR
Link, Jacob	085	c1800	WB-E/137	
Link, Jacob	085	c1807	WB-G/12	AR
Link, Jacob	032	1873	WB-3/76	AR
Link, Johannes	085	c1792	WB-D/82	AR
Link, John	073	1829	WB-E/185	AR
Link, Mary	016	1869	WB-3/17	
Link, Michael	021	1878	WB-2/186	AR
Link, Silas M.	073	1876	WB-H/134	CTY
Link, William	032	1844	WB-1/425	AR
Linke, John	085	c1794	WB-E/182	AR
Linker, M. A.	016	1894	WB-4/173	AR
Linker, William	085	1811	WB-G/209	AR
Linn, Catharine	033	1862	WB-1/171	AR
Linn, David	085	1854	WB-K/164	AR
Linn, Hugh	085	c1785	WB-C/183	
Linn, James	073	1822	WB-E/7	AR
Linn, James	065	1779	WB-D/153	AR
Linn, John	073	1807	WB-D/203	AR

Name	Co.	Date	Recorded Copy	Original
Linn, Mary	021	1867	WB-1/246	AR
Linn, Robert	085	c1869	WB-1/77	CTY
Linney, Martha	003	1886	WB-B/178	
Linney, Nancy	054	c1822	WB-1A/4	AR
Linney, William	054	c1821	WB-1A/113	AR
Linning, James	055	1855	ID/8	
Linow, Hugh	073	1766	WB-A/49	
Linsey, Daniel	030	1720/1	Orig. Only	SS/AR
Linsey, David	030	1750	Orig. Only	SS/AR
Linsey, Dennis	044	1762	Orig. Only	CTY
Linsey, George	005	1808	WB-2/95	AR
Linsey, Leonard	044	1785	WB-1/438	CTY
Linsey, Robert	002	1689	Orig. Only	SS/AR
Linster, Goodwin	085	1871	WB-1/119	CTY
Linster, Moses	085	1817	WB-G/482	AR
Linthicum, Richard	046	1819	WB-B/83	AR
Linton, Augustus	030	1829	WB-3/245	
Linton, Burriage H.	053	1833	WB-5/188	AR
Linton, Dorcas	009	1850	OB-G/302	AR
Linton, Edward	065	1777	WB-D/151	AR
Linton, James	074	c1888	Orig. Only	AR
Linton, John	053	1794	RW-1/241	AR
Linton, John	047	1764	WB-1/148	
Linton, John	035	1842	Orig. Only	AR
Linton, John W.	009	1900	WB-2/200	CTY
Linton, Julia	010	1824	WB-G/119	AR
Linton, Lazarus	030	1801	WB-2/169	
Linton, Lemuel	096	1764	WB-1/50	AR
Linton, Lovey	030	1839	WB-4/65	
Linton, Luke	009	1840	OB-C2/360	AR
Linton, Mary	053	c1855	Orig. Only	AR
Linton, Mary	053	1870	WB-11/19	AR
Linton, Nancy	018	1828	WB-C/98	
Linton, Rachel	010	1882	WB-I/156	
Linton, Thomas	081	1805	WB-3/35	AR-Nunc.
Linton, William	028	1727	Orig. Only	SS/AR
Linvill, David	092	1787	WB-2/72	AR
Linville, Benjamin	038	1887	WB-3/68	AR
Linville, David	090	1811	WB-2/123	AR
Linville, David, Sr.	090	1843	WB-4/138	AR
Linville, Lucy T.	038	1887	WB-3/26	
Linville, Milton H.	038	1876	WB-2/251	AR
Linville, Robert	038	c1848	WB-1/166	AR
Linville, Robert F.	038	1892	WB-3/319	AR
Lion, Martha	020	1831	RB-M/14	AR
Lipe, Alexander	054	1859	WB-3/142	AR
Lipe, E. F.	085	1889	WB-2/392	CTY
Lipe, Elias	054	1876	WB-4/221	CTY
Lipe, George	085	1843	WB-I/151	AR
Lipe, Moses	016	1877	WB-3/207	
Lipe, William L.	085	1894	WB-3/50	CTY
Lipford, William A.	069	1819	WB-1/303	AR
Lippard, Elizabeth	016	1830	PQS.5/94	
Lippard, Henry	085	c1833	Orig. Only	AR
Lippard, John	054	c1811	WB-1A/130	AR
Lippard, John	016	1865	WB-2/129	
Lippard, Margaret	085	1873	WB-1/182	CTY
Lippard, Mary M.	054	1877	WB-4/247	CTY
Lippard, Peter	016	1835	PQS.5/332	
Lippard, Solomon	054	1877	WB-4/278	CTY
Lippard, William	054	1859	WB-3/142	AR
Lipperd, William	065	c1781	WB-D/154	AR
Lippet, Philip	047	1772	WB-1/319	
Lippincott, David	077	1780	Orig. Only	AR
Lippman, Moses	070	1863	WB-D/114	AR
Lipscomb, Ann	073	1879	WB-H/215	CTY
Lipscomb, Archibald	078	1837	WI-13/193	AR
Lipscomb, Becky	073	1898	WB-I/152	CTY
Lipscomb, Celia R.	063	1873	WB-3/59	
Lipscomb, Clement	020	1850	RB-Q/353	
Lipscomb, William	073	1865	WB-G/469	CTY
Lipsey, Arthur	057	1795	WB-A/92	AR
Lipsey, Fanny	028	1795	WB-A/340	AR
Lipsey, Isaac	072	1821	WB-A/79	AR
Lipsey, James	057	1794	WB-A/96	AR
Lipsey, Rasco	057	1808	WB-A/300	AR
Lipsey, Sarah	057	1835	WB-B/127	AR
Lipsey, Timothy	057	1794	WB-A/174	AR
Lipsey, William	057	1792	WB-A/207	AR
Liscomb, John	009	1832	OWB/484	AR
Liscomb, Joseph G.	010	1870	WB-I/26	AR
Liscomb, Nancy	010	1887	WB-I/222	AR
Liscomb, Sally	009	1852	OB-H/134	AR
Lisk, Clinton	082	1860	WB-4/143	AR
Lisk, W. J.	089	1883	WB-2/112	AR
Lister, Elisha	075	1801	WB-M1/54	AR
Lister, Milly	046	1837	WB-B/577	AR
Lister, Susannah	075	1832	WB-N/79	AR
Litaker, Daniel	016	1867	WB-2/154	
Litaker, George	016	1862	WB-2/85	AR
Litaker, John W.	016	1864	WB-2/113	
Litaker, Mary M.	085	1871	WB-1/85	CTY
Litch, Dugald	083	1826	WB-1/365	AR
Litch, John	083	1835	WB-1/290	AR
Litchfield, Abraham	030	1795	WB-2/47	
Litchfield, Abram D.	096	1886	WB-4/125	AR
Litchfield, Jacob	030	1792	WB-1/267	
Litchfield, Jacob	030	1775	WB-1/100	
Litchfield, John	030	1795	WB-2/46	
Litchfield, Peter	030	1800	WB-2/156	
Litman, Samuel	073	1767	WB-A/63	
Littel, John	085	1772	WB-A/84	AR
Littell, Jonas	085	c1797	WB-E/180	AR
Littell, Thomas	028	c1761	Orig. Only	AR
Litten, H. P.	021	1891	WB-2/551	
Litten, James, Jr.	060	1826	Orig. Only	AR
Litten, Wesley W.	021	1847	WB-1/54	AR
Litten, William	021	1863	WB-1/185	AR
Little, Aaron	097	1870	WB-2/38	AR
Little, Abraham	037	1789	WB-C/85	AR
Little, Alexander	083	1815	WB-1/160	AR
Little, Alexander	060	1783	Orig. Only	AR
Little, Alexander	083	1870	WB-3/23	AR
Little, Andrew	024	1777	WB-A/250	AR
Little, Ann	100	1846	WB-39/236	AR
Little, Ann	005	1900	WB-D/473	AR
Little, Archibald	083	c1797	WB-1/47	AR
Little, Archibald	083	1812	WB-1/141	AR
Little, Benjamin	082	c1878	005 WB-D/478	005 AR
Little, Benjamin	082	1879	WB-6/175	AR
Little, Benjamin	063	1788	WB-1/142	
Little, Benjamin	082	1879	065 WB-N/371	065 AR
Little, Benjamin	082	1879	Copy	067 AR
Little, Benjamin	037	1847	WB-F/367	AR
Little, Calvin M.	005	1898	WB-D/428	AR
Little, Catharine	083	1884	WB-3/311	AR
Little, Catherine	060	1899	WB-5/116	AR
Little, Cornelia	005	1885	WB-D/186	AR
Little, Daniel	085	c1775	WB-A/223	
Little, Daniel	021	1875	WB-2/131	AR

Name	Co.	Date	Recorded Copy	Original
Little, Daniel	016	1870	WB-3/19	
Little, David A.	003	1886	WB-B/181	
Little, Devalt	003	1875	WB-B/54	AR
Little, E. R.	005	1899	WB-D/441	AR
Little, Elizabeth	005	1859	WB-C/154	AR
Little, Elizabeth	060	1898	WB-5/75	AR
Little, G. E.	079	1898	WB-3/165	AR
Little, George	097	1853	WB-1/92	AR
Little, George	051	c1752	Orig. Only	SS/AR
Little, George	060	1870	WB-4/70	AR
Little, George	099	1876	RB-35/380	AR
Little, George K.	005	1895	WB-D/378	AR
Little, George W.	097	1862	WB-1/201	AR
Little, George W.	005	1878	WB-D/60	AR
Little, Gilbert G.	083	c1862	WB-3/156	AR
Little, Hosea	097	1850	WB-1/70	AR
Little, Isaac	006	1893	WB-E/253	AR
Little, Isaac	100	1860	WB-49/281	AR
Little, J. C. R.	099	1899	WB-D/223	AR
Little, Jacob	003	1897	WB-B/361	
Little, Jacob	005	1838	WB-B/79	AR
Little, Jacob	037	1791	WB-C/157	AR
Little, Jacob	021	c1889	WB-2/481	AR
Little, Jacob W.	089	1859	WB-1/197	
Little, James	060	1814	Orig. Only	AR
Little, James	021	1862	WB-1/165	AR
Little, James	089	1842	WB-1/7	
Little, James	005	1792	WB-2/93	AR
Little, James B.	037	1858	WB-G/167	AR
Little, James H.	097	1881	WB-2/184	
Little, James H.	097	1881	Copy	089 AR
Little, Jane	037	c1833	WB-F/236	AR
Little, Jesse	037	1825	WB-F/42	AR
Little, Jesse C.	037	1886	WB-H/35	
Little, John	005	c1755	SS 880/127	SS/AR
Little, John	024	1824	WB-C/112	AR
Little, John F.	065	1894	WB-M/303	AR
Little, John N.	083	1847	WB-1/502	AR
Little, John S.	005	1880	WB-D/100	AR
Little, John, Sr.	085	1820	WB-H/49	AR
Little, Lafayette	003	1885	WB-B/162	
Little, Louis	047	c1892	WB-7/150 & 206	
Little, Louisa	060	1890	WB-4/422	AR
Little, Lydia	037	1877	WB-G/534	AR
Little, Margaret	099	1898	WB-D/132	AR
Little, Margaret	083	1885	WB-3/334	AR
Little, Martha H.	005	1881	WB-D/107	
Little, Mary	005	1886	WB-D/192	AR
Little, Mary	083	1869	WB-3/21	AR
Little, Mary Ann	051	c1813	WB-A/46	
Little, Michael	099	c1858	Orig. Only	AR
Little, Michael	037	1826	WB-F/51	AR
Little, Michael H.	028	1851	WB-D/181	
Little, Nancy	084	c1806	OW/5	
Little, Nathaniel	012	1895	WB-A/102	AR
Little, Noah	009	1900	WB-2/234	CTY
Little, Peter	060	1822	Orig. Only	AR
Little, Peter	021	c1892	Orig. Only	AR
Little, Pleasant	005	1832	WB-B/18	AR
Little, Polly	060	1869	WB-4/41	AR
Little, Robert	083	1813	WB-1/162	
Little, Romeo	009	1888	WB-1/442	CTY
Little, S. C.	060	1864	WB-3/75	AR
Little, Sallie W.	100	1863	WB-50/32	AR

Name	Co.	Date	Recorded Copy	Original
Little, Sally	083	c1819	WB-1/358	AR
Little, Samuel	085	c1830	WB-H/476	AR
Little, Sarah	060	1824	WB-1/1	AR
Little, Sarah E.	005	1895	WB-D/364	AR
Little, Sherod	060	1889	WB-4/405	
Little, Sherod S.	060	1852	WB-2/367	AR
Little, Susan B.	005	1894	WB-D/354	AR
Little, Sylvia	037	1831	WB-F/124	AR
Little, Thomas	060	1791	Orig. Only	AR
Little, Thomas	082	1855	Copy	067 AR
Little, Thomas	082	1855	WB-4/87	AR
Little, Thomas P.	100	1856	WB-49/63	AR
Little, Thomas S.	005	1882	WB-D/122	AR
Little, Walter S.	005	1892	WB-D/323	AR
Little, William	060	1833	WB-1/289	AR
Little, William	094	1772	Orig. Only	060 AR
Little, William	100	1869	WB-51/9	AR
Little, William	005	1892	WB-D/319	AR
Little, William	060	1880	WB-4/219	AR
Little, William	N	1734	Orig. Only	SS/AR
Little, William	005	1848	WB-B/237	AR-Copy
Little, William	019	1758	Orig. Only	SS/AR
Little, William	079	1860	WB-1/55	AR
Little, William	037	1794	WB-C/293	AR
Little, William P.	100	1829	WB-32/218	AR
Littlejohn, John	080	1889	WB-1/141	AR
Littlejohn, Thomas B.	100	1854	WB-43/185	AR
Littlejohn, William	024	1817	WB-C/56	AR
Littlejohn, William A.	024	1811	WB-B/309	AR
Littler, Jeremiah	081	1846	WB-8/342	AR
Littler, Joel	081	1893	WB-16/254	AR
Littler, John W.	081	1893	WB-16/255	
Littler, Mincher	085	1819	WB-G/536	AR
Littleton, Dellia	056	1882	WB-3/303	AR
Littleton, Enoch A.	089	1888	WB-2/163	AR
Littleton, Ivy	072	c1862	WB-A/74	AR
Littleton, Joel	056	1856	WB-2/265	AR
Littleton, Mary	057	1806	WB-A/283	AR
Littleton, Thomas	072	1832	WB-1/106	AR
Littleton, Thomas	057	1792	WB-A/190	AR
Littleton, Thomas	057	1785	WB-A/47	AR
Littleton, Zachariah	072	1832	WB-1/96	AR
Litzler, Anna	085	c1769	WB-B/159	AR
Litzler, Fredrick	085	c1767	WB-E/145	AR
Livengood, Christian	032	1823	WB-1/8	AR
Livengood, Christian	032	1850	WB-2/49	AR
Livengood, John	038	1890	WB-3/168	AR
Livengood, John	016	1846	WB-1/109	
Livengood, John	033	1869	WB-2/8	CTY
Livengood, John H.	038	1878	WB-2/332	AR
Livengood, Sallie E.	032	1897	WB-4/332	AR
Liverett, William	050	1897	WB-2/273	CTY
Liverman, A. J.	010	1892	WB-I/352	AR
Liverman, Asa D.	051	1861	WB-B/31	
Liverman, Dempsey	096	1838	WB-2/142	AR
Liverman, Elias	096	1839	WB-2/149	AR
Liverman, Hardy H.	096	1875	WB-4/30	AR
Liverman, Hartwell	010	1886	WB-I/208	
Liverman, Isaac	096	1822	WB-2/85	AR
Liverman, J. P.	051	1898	WB-C/546	AR
Liverman, James M.	096	1882	WB-4/89	
Liverman, John	096	c1808	Orig. Only	AR
Liverman, John W.	096	1784	WB-1/138	AR
Liverman, Justice B.	096	1812	WB-2/42	AR
Liverman, Martha A.	010	1897	WB-I/522	AR

Name	Co.	Date	Recorded Copy	Original
Liverman, Martha D.	051	1882	WB-C/291	AR
Liverman, Martha E.	051	1883	WB-C/307	AR
Liverman, Mary	096	1833	WB-2/118	AR
Liverman, Mary	096	1855	WB-3/41	AR
Liverman, Sarah	096	1822	WB-2/89	AR
Liverman, Sarah D.	051	1883	WB-C/309	AR
Liverman, Thomas	096	c1808	WB-2/39	AR
Liverman, Thomas	096	1818	Orig. Only	AR
Liverman, William	096	1806	WB-2/21	AR
Liverman, William E.	071	1878	WB-6/253	AR
Liverton, Daniel	092	1824	WB-3/161	AR
Liverton, Jane	092	c1830	WB-4/29	AR
Livingston, Angus M.	005	1885	WB-D/190	AR
Livingston, Catharine	029	1827	WB-B/154	AR
Livingston, Charles	082	1838	WB-2/71	AR
Livingston, Duncan	005	1861	WB-C/170	AR
Livingston, E. T. R.	067	1897	WB-2/353	AR
Livingston, George H.	046	1870	WB-E/23	AR
Livingston, Henry P.	028	1803	WB-B/166	AR
Livingston, John	070	1800	WB-AB/37	AR
Livingston, John Orrill	104	1824	WB-4/54	AR
Livingston, John, Sr.	013	1840	WB-A/65	
Livingston, Joseph	029	1762	Orig. Only	AR
Livingston, Madison	104	1895	WB-6/538	AR
Livingston, Maria M.	NY	1884	Copy	050 AR
Livingston, Martin	017	c1854	WB-A/79	AR
Livingston, Nancy	017	1890	WB-B/176	AR
Livingston, Robert C.	NY	1896	Copy	050 AR
Lloyd, Alfred	076	1900	WB-A1/258	
Lloyd, Anna	011	c1770	WB-1/509	
Lloyd, Fredrick	073	1804	WB-D/142	AR
Lloyd, Henrietta	063	1895	WB-4/185	AR
Lloyd, Henry S.	037	1860	WB-G/181	AR
Lloyd, Henry S.	037	1860	SC/08502	AR-Copy
Lloyd, James	029	1774	Orig. Only	AR
Lloyd, John D.	027	1884	WB-2/56	AR
Lloyd, Joseph R.	037	1841	WB-F/251	AR
Lloyd, L. J.	073	1889	WB-H/459	CTY
Lloyd, Nancy	011	c1801	WB-1/361	
Lloyd, Nicholas	037	1781	WB-B/91	AR
Lloyd, Richard	070	1830	WB-AB/260	AR
Lloyd, Sarah E.	037	1893	WB-H/272	AR
Lloyd, Sidney	073	1880	WB-H/273	CTY
Lloyd, Stephen	073	1864	WB-G/435	CTY
Lloyd, Thomas	073	1792	WB-B/170	AR
Lloyd, Thomas	073	1839	WB-F/38	AR
Lloyd, Thomas T.	073	1871	WB-H/49	CTY
Lloyd, William	046	1877	WB-E/198	AR
Lloyd, William	073	1887	WB-H/423	CTY
Lluellin, Samuel	070	1732	Orig. Only	AR
Loadman, James	077	1695	SS 874.2/59	
Localair, Molly	082	1879	Orig. Only	AR
Lochry, Jaramia	060	1807	Orig. Only	AR
Lock, Benjamin	011	1757	Orig. Only	SS/AR
Lock, David	011	c1812	WB-2/314	
Lock, Elizabeth	011	c1836	WB-1/42	
Lock, James	047	1842	WB-4/202	
Lock, John	047	1789	WB-3/166	
Lock, John	029	1815	WB-A/215	AR-Nunc.
Lock, John	011	c1782	WB-1/541	
Lock, Jonathan	044	1823	WB-9/167	CTY
Lock, Joseph	011	1781	WB-1/523	
Lock, Leonard	011	c1783	WB-1/539	
Lock, Maryann	047	1888	WB-6/492	AR
Lock, Primie A.	069	1900	WB-6/93	AR
Lock, Susannah	047	1823	WB-3/684	
Lock, Thomas	011	1739	SS 877/122	
Lock, William	044	1803	WB-6/4	CTY
Lockard, Hiram	020	1855	RB-R/296	AR
Lockart, Edith	099	c1866	Orig. Only	AR
Locke, Alexander	085	c1824	WB-H/490	AR
Locke, Ann	033	1849	Orig. Only	AR
Locke, Cecelia A.	054	1878	WB-4/292	CTY
Locke, Elizabeth	047	1876	WB-6/141	AR
Locke, Francis	085	1823	WB-H/194	AR
Locke, George	054	c1804	WB-1/378	AR
Locke, George	085	1816	WB-G/443	AR
Locke, George A.	085	1864	WB-K/324	AR
Locke, James	054	1845	WB-2/306	AR
Locke, James	085	1813	WB-G/296	AR
Locke, John	085	c1832	WB-H/522	AR
Locke, John F.	085	1850	WB-K/102	AR
Locke, Mary	085	1835	WB-H/651	AR
Locke, Mary	085	1855	WB-K/181	AR
Locke, Matthew	085	1801	WB-E/188	AR
Locke, Richard	085	1819	WB-G/528	AR
Locke, Robert	085	1818	WB-G/501	AR
Locke, Sarah F.	085	1882	WB-2/34	CTY
Lockemy, Joseph	029	1874	WB-E/126	AR
Locker, Joseph	085	1809	WB-G/130	AR
Lockerler, John	083	c1784	WB-1/8	AR
Lockerman, Jacob	087	1846	WB-1/315	AR
Lockett, Ann	020	1885	WB-A/467	CTY
Lockey, Cele	009	1774	OWB/121	AR
Lockey, Joseph	009	1746	SS 877/361	SS/AR
Lockhart, Adam	005	1833	WB-B/24	AR
Lockhart, Cary	056	1864	WB-2/49	AR
Lockhart, Catherine	099	1816	RB-13/49	AR
Lockhart, Cathrine	073	1792	WB-B/194	AR
Lockhart, Elizabeth	071	1832	WB-4/86	AR
Lockhart, Elizabeth	010	1796	WB-D/324	AR
Lockhart, George	010	1791	WB-D/171	AR
Lockhart, Handy	099	1884	WB-A/537	AR
Lockhart, Hannah H.	056	1821	WB-1/319	AR
Lockhart, James	010	1754	SS 879/149	SS/AR
Lockhart, James	056	1800	WB-1/117	AR
Lockhart, James	010	1754	Orig. Only	AR-Copy
Lockhart, John	053	1783	RW-1/108	
Lockhart, John J.	MS	1852	071 WB-5/177	071 AR
Lockhart, Lucy	056	1868	WB-2/105	AR
Lockhart, Rosenia	099	1884	WB-A/544	AR
Lockhart, Sarah	071	1855	WB-5/130	AR
Lockhart, William B.	071	1841	WB-4/226	AR
Locklair, Wiley	083	1866	WB-2/235	AR
Locklear, Godfrey	083	1894	WB-4/24	AR
Locklear, John	083	1874	Orig. Only	AR
Locklear, Rachel	083	1880	WB-3/195	AR
Lockler, Winslow	083	1897	Orig. Only	AR
Lockler, Zack	083	1892	WB-3/573	AR
Locklier, Maria	047	1832	WB-4/90	
Lockman, David	060	1883	WB-4/268	AR
Lockman, Elihu	060	1872	WB-4/93	AR
Lockman, James	087	N. D.	Orig. Only	AR
Lockman, John	060	1834	WB-1/323	AR
Lockman, John A.	060	1863	WB-3/61	AR
Lockwood, Holland	075	1803	WB-M1/84	AR
Lockwood, James C.	075	c1822	Copy	041 AR
Lockwood, James C.	075	1822	WB-M1/361	AR
Locus, Rachel	099	1852	RB-28/107	AR
Locus, Valentine	099	1812	RB-10/169	

Name	Co.	Date	Recorded Copy	Original
Lodge, Euphemia	NY	1881	028 WB-E/295	028 AR
Lodge, Gray	105	1881	WB-2/263	AR
Lodge, John	037	1804	WB-D/214	AR
Lodge, Luis	037	1794	WB-C/266	AR
Lodge, Nancy	037	1848	Orig. Only	AR
Lodge, Rebecca	105	1885	WB-2/342	AR
Lodge, Silvey	037	1864	WB-G/247	AR
Lodman, James	N	1695	Orig. Only	SS/AR
Loe, Daniel	083	c1822	WB-1/357	AR
Loe, George	075	c1729	SS 876/420	
Loe, William	005	1796	WB-A/45	AR
Loesch, Jacob	PA	1782	092 WB-2/8	092 AR
Loffman, Maria Lobre	070	1818	WB-C/233	AR
Lofin, John	032	1899	WB-4/389	AR
Lofin, John, Sr.	032	1867	WB-2/357	AR
Lofley, Daniel	103	1801	Orig. Only	AR
Loflin, Cornelius	081	1838	WB-4/216	AR
Loflin, John	032	1840	Orig. Only	AR
Loflin, John	085	1812	WB-G/225	AR
Loflin, William	032	1899	WB-4/430	AR
Loften, Martha	090	1823	WB-3/104	AR
Loftin, Ann	028	1890	WB-E/550	AR
Loftin, Cornelus	028	c1762	Orig. Only	AR
Loftin, Eldridge	060	1842	WB-2/137	AR
Loftin, Elijah	059	1893	WB-B/60	CTY
Loftin, Giles T.	103	1891	WB-1/546	AR
Loftin, James	060	1837	WB-1/393	AR
Loftin, James P.	021	1869	WB-2/23	
Loftin, John	032	1850	WB-2/51	AR
Loftin, John	059	1891	WB-B/16	CTY
Loftin, John L.	057	1844	WB-B/171	AR
Loftin, John L.	028	c1876	059 WB-B/137	
Loftin, John L.	028	1877	WB-E/157	
Loftin, Joseph	073	1809	WB-D/205	AR
Loftin, Julia	103	1867	RD = 14/555	
Loftin, Leonard	028	1774	Orig. Only	AR
Loftin, Leonard	028	1721	SS 875/317	SS/AR
Loftin, Mary	032	1842	WB-1/399	AR
Loftin, Mary	103	1852	RD-11/84	AR
Loftin, Samuel	103	1879	WB-1/167	AR
Loftin, Sarah A.	035	1884	WB-4/232	AR
Loftin, Sary	032	1835	WB-1/264	AR
Loftin, Shadrack	028	1812	WB-C/63	AR
Loftin, Susannah	021	1843	WB-1/7	AR
Loftin, Thomas	028	1794	WB-A/317	AR
Loftin, Thomas	032	1892	WB-4/166	AR
Loftin, Thomas J.	032	1894	WB-4/215	AR
Loftin, William F.	059	1882	WB-A/245	CTY
Loftis, Reuben J.	044	1853	WB-19/293	CTY
Loftis, William	044	1857	WB-20/232	CTY
Loftis, William R.	044	1859	WB-20/707	CTY
Lofton, Rachel	070	1825	WB-C/239	AR
Logan, Alexander	N	1739	SS 877/139	SS/AR
Logan, Catherine	086	1810	WB-B/246	AR
Logan, Felix	086	1870	WB-F/11	AR
Logan, George	070	c1802	WB-AB/58	AR
Logan, George W.	026	1889	Copy	086 AR
Logan, George W.	026	1889	WB-2/405	AR
Logan, Hugh	092	1817	WB-3/127	AR
Logan, James	086	1800	Orig. Only	AR
Logan, James	003	1866	WB-A/8	AR
Logan, John	092	c1835	Orig. Only	AR
Logan, John R.	026	1885	WB-2/265	AR
Logan, John, Sr.	086	1842	WB-E/92	AR
Logan, Larkin	086	1824	WB-D/31	AR

Name	Co.	Date	Recorded Copy	Original
Logan, Mariam	106	c1849	WB-1/30	AR
Logan, Mary	086	1813	WB-C/30	AR
Logan, Moses	086	1865	WB-E/461	AR
Logan, Nancy B.	086	1883	WB-F/216	AR
Logan, Patrick	092	1790	WB-2/168A	AR
Logan, Philip	026	c1863	Orig. Only	AR
Logan, Rachel	086	1808	WB-B/213	AR
Logan, Ransom P.	054	1892	WB-5/474	CTY
Logan, Rebecca	064	1855	WB-1/40	AR
Logan, Steven D.	086	1895	Orig. Only	aR
Logan, William	026	1892	WB-2/474	AR
Logan, William	073	1788	WB-B/43	AR
Logan, Winston	106	1895	WB-2/373	
Logue, Ephraim	020	1780	Copy	073 AR
Logue, Ephraim	020	1780	RB-A/116	AR
Lohon, Elizabeth	037	1791	WB-C/160	AR
Loles, Thomas	071	1800	WB-2/201	
Lollar, Archibald	086	1854	WB-E/265	AR
Lollar, Henry E.	054	1876	WB-4/237	CTY
Lollar, Mary	086	1897	WB-F/548	AR
Loller, Isaac	086	1810	WB-B/237	AR
Loman, Adam, Sr.	046	1814	WB-A/223	AR
Lomax, Albert	046	1878	WB-H/370	
Lomax, Albert	084	1878	WB-E/155	CTY
Lomax, Hezekiah	032	1882	WB-3/384	AR
Lomax, John	067	1872	Orig. Only	AR
Lomax, Lydia	046	1836	WB-B/550	AR
Lomax, Moses	084	1842	WB-B/266	CTY
Lomax, Susan	084	1853	WB-C/162	CTY
Lomax, William	046	1773	WB-A/212	AR
Lomax, William C.	032	1877	WB-3/224	AR
Lombrousyer, John	075	1744	Orig. Only	SS/AR
Lomison, H. G.	081	1895	WB-17/537	
London, Amos	092	1807	WB-3/77A	AR
London, Ann	022	c1842	WB-D/10	AR
London, Anonamus	026	1865	WB-1/368	AR
London, Catherine	022	1896	WB-F/34	AR
London, Chandler	026	1883	WB-2/239	AR
London, Henry	026	1850	WB-1/110	AR
London, Henry A.	022	1882	WB-E/267	AR
London, Henry A.	022	c1888	Orig. Only	AR
London, James	084	1858	WB-C/273	CTY
London, John L.	070	1842	WB-AB/371	AR
London, John Mack	070	c1873	WB-E/485	AR
London, John R.	070	1833	WB-C/241	AR
London, Marcus R.	014	1871	WB-2/68	AR-Copy
London, Robert	070	1893	WB-G/115	AR
London, Sarah E.	070	1865	WB-D/164	AR
Londonderry, (a slave)	011	c1818	WB-2/348	
Lonergan, Edward	065	1856	WB-J/27	AR
Lonergan, Edward	040	c1867	WB-1/198	
Loney, Edward	046	1795	WB-A/21	AR
Long, Adam	097	1849	WB-1/63	AR
Long, Agnes	065	1802	WB-B/33	AR
Long, Alexander	085	1877	WB-1/413	CTY
Long, Alexander	085	1824	WB-H/274	AR
Long, Ambrose	020	1791	RB-B/389	
Long, Andrew	096	1785	WB-1/145	AR
Long, Andrew G.	032	1886	WB-3/502	AR
Long, Andrew M.	086	c1886	Orig. Only	AR
Long, Andrew M.	006	1888	WB-E/165	AR
Long, Ann	073	1830	WB-E/212	AR
Long, Ann Eliza	012	1845	WB-B/185	AR
Long, Annis	037	1864	WB-G/242	AR
Long, Augustine	038	1865	WB-1/249	AR

Name	Co.	Date	Recorded Copy	Original
Long, Basheba	101	1890	WB-A/192	AR
Long, Benjamin	082	1815	WB-1/168	AR
Long, Benjamin	020	1786	RB-B/134	AR
Long, Britain	071	1792	WB-2/16	AR
Long, Catharine	065	1824	WB-B/43	AR
Long, Claudius	086	1807	WB-B/195	AR
Long, Conrad	073	1797	WB-C/103	AR
Long, Daniel	032	1890	WB-4/87	AR
Long, Drew	047	1893	WB-7/74	
Long, Drury	015	1778	100 WB-2/246	AR
Long, Elender	054	1842	WB-2/243	AR
Long, Elizabeth	077	1885	WB-H/152	AR
Long, Elizabeth	020	1816	RB-G/158	
Long, Elizabeth	047	1831	WB-4/69	
Long, Elizabeth	039	1866	WB-S/330	
Long, Felix	032	1832	WB-1/179	AR
Long, Francis H.	065	1888	WB-L/296	AR
Long, Frederick	071	1826	WB-3/336	AR
Long, Frederick	090	1829	WB-3/207	AR
Long, Frederik	106	1884	WB-2/181	AR
Long, Fredrick	085	c1794	WB-E/177	AR
Long, Gabriel	012	1889	Orig. Only	AR
Long, George	032	1853	WB-2/86	AR
Long, George	092	1805	WB-3/66	
Long, George	032	1828	WB-1/110	AR
Long, George H.	047	1808	WB-3/477	
Long, George R.	073	1883	WB-H/326	CTY
Long, Giles	047	1788	WB-3/159	
Long, Giles	N	1691/2	Orig. Only	SS/AR (N)
Long, Giles, Sr.	096	1785	WB-1/148	AR
Long, Gland	086	1801	WB-B/121	AR
Long, Gland	086	c1820	Copy	064 AR
Long, Gland	086	1820	WB-C/145	
Long, Hannah	001	1868	WB-2/2	AR
Long, Henry	097	1891	WB-2/416	AR
Long, Henry A.	077	1842	024 WB-C/235	024 AR
Long, Henry H.	103	1894	WB-2/87	AR
Long, Henry H.	038	1898	WB-4/126	AR
Long, Henry T.	097	1875	WB-2/86	
Long, Isaiah	006	1900	WB-E/424	AR
Long, Israel	092	1822	WB-3/152	AR
Long, Jacob	097	1852	WB-1/75	AR
Long, Jacob	001	1894	WB-3/13	AR
Long, Jacob	038	1879	WB-2/335	AR
Long, Jacob	001	1849	WB-1/13	AR
Long, Jacob	032	1855	WB-2/149	AR
Long, Jacob, Sr.	032	1824	WB-1/30	AR
Long, James	001	1874	WB-2/61	AR
Long, James	078	1851	WB-13/445	AR
Long, James	024	1712	SS 875/51	SS/AR
Long, James	064	1843	WB-1/6	AR
Long, James	026	1896	WB-2/508	AR
Long, James	086	1813	WB-C/3	AR
Long, James	024	1734	SS 876/350	SS/AR
Long, James	020	1796	RB-C/169	AR
Long, James	096	1753	WB-1/52	AR
Long, James	002	1682	Orig. Only	SS/AR
Long, James B.	022	1894	WB-E/561	AR
Long, James D.	023	c1858	Orig. Only	AR-Copy
Long, James R.	049	1899	WB-2/431	AR
Long, James S.	037	1880	WB-G/569	AR
Long, James T.	086	1884	WB-F/249	AR
Long, James, Sr.	096	1787	WB-1/156	AR
Long, Jane	001	1895	WB-3/69	AR
Long, Jane M.	097	c1886	Orig. Only	AR
Long, Jesse	038	1895	WB-3/565	AR
Long, Jesse	078	1880	WB-19/101	AR
Long, John	100	1796	WB-8/352	AR
Long, John	071	1782	WB-1/247	
Long, John	073	1836	WB-E/400	AR
Long, John	096	1757	WB-1/6	AR
Long, John	054	c1802	WB-1/139	AR
Long, John	047	1760	WB-1/16	
Long, John	086	1843	WB-E/110	AR
Long, John	073	1824	WB-E/65	AR
Long, John	032	c1854	WB-2/137	AR
Long, John	004	c1863	Orig. Only	AR
Long, John E.	097	1871	Orig. Only	AR
Long, John F.	049	1880	WB-2/91	AR
Long, John L. W.	071	1844	WB-5/2	AR
Long, John M.	085	1843	WB-I/177	AR
Long, John M.	016	1888	WB-3/581	AR
Long, John S.	085	1861	WB-K/287	AR
Long, John S.	036	1893	WB-A/277	CTY
Long, John W.	097	1846	WB-1/31	AR
Long, John W.	081	1863	WB-12/408	AR
Long, John, Sr.	060	1822	Orig. Only	AR
Long, John, Sr.	096	1790	WB-1/173	AR
Long, Jonathan	060	1835	WB-1/331	AR
Long, Jonathan	070	1817	WB-C/233	AR
Long, Jonathan	032	1858	WB-2/163	AR
Long, Joseph	027	1855	WB-A/64	AR
Long, Joseph	047	1775	WB-2/14	
Long, Joseph A.	001	1898	WB-3/213	AR
Long, Joshua	077	1791	WB-C/425	AR
Long, Joshua	077	1741	Orig. Only	SS/AR
Long, Joshua	096	1754	SS 881/117	SS/AR
Long, Josiah	077	1808	WB-E/288	AR
Long, Joyce	071	1818	WB-3/203	AR
Long, Lemuel Mc.	047	1849	WB-4/274	
Long, Leonard	060	1841	WB-2/91	AR
Long, Littleberry	071	1782	WB-1/250	
Long, Littleberry	071	1826	WB-4/10	AR
Long, Lunsfort	047	1810	WB-3/495	
Long, Margaret	016	1860	WB-2/64	
Long, Maria M.	047	1887	WB-6/455	AR
Long, Martha	077	1841	WB-F/297	
Long, Mary	001	c1852	WB-1/64	AR
Long, Mary	047	1822	WB-3/666	
Long, Mary	071	1779	WB-1/324	
Long, Mary A.	061	1892	WB-2/116	AR
Long, Mary L.	047	1811	WB-3/522	
Long, Matthias	032	1881	WB-3/337	AR
Long, Mattie R.	063	1894	WB-4/139	AR
Long, McKinnie	047	1804	WB-3/433	
Long, Micajah	027	1856	WB-A/68	AR
Long, Michael	049	1852	WB-2/184	AR
Long, Nancy	073	1890	WB-H/485	CTY
Long, Nancy	022	1887	WB-E/359	AR
Long, Nathan	077	1816	WB-E/457	AR
Long, Nathan	077	1841	WB-F/301	AR
Long, Nehemiah	071	1787	WB-1/387	
Long, Nellie Ann	085	1899	WB-3/293	CTY
Long, Newsom	037	1871	WB-G/367	AR
Long, Newton J.	026	1895	WB-2/500	AR
Long, Nicholas	047	1798	WB-3/292	
Long, Nicholas	047	1882	WB-6/285	
Long, Nicholas	071	1787	Orig. Only	AR
Long, Nicholas	039	1825	WB-H/107	AR

Name	Co.	Date	Recorded Copy	Original
Long, Noah	004	1894	WB-A/154	
Long, Osmond F.	073	1864	WB-G/458	CTY
Long, Pansie S.	020	c1886	WB-A/529	CTY
Long, Paul	078	1878	Orig. Only	AR
Long, Peninah	077	1817	WB-F/1	AR
Long, Peter	085	1900	WB-3/360	CTY
Long, Prissia	084	c1807	WB-A/70	CTY
Long, Rachel	060	1814	Orig. Only	AR
Long, Ratliff	078	1866	WB-18/409	AR
Long, Reubin	077	1814	WB-E/407	AR
Long, Reubin	078	1866	WB-18/412	AR
Long, Richard	071	1827	WB-4/33	AR
Long, Richard D.	037	1878	WB-G/484	AR
Long, Richard H.	047	1810	WB-3/499	
Long, Roseanna	021	1884	WB-2/295	
Long, Sallie F.	101	1881	WB-A/53	AR
Long, Samuel	063	1777	WB-1/45	
Long, Samuel	006	1842	WB-A/17	AR
Long, Samuel	065	1802	WB-B/33	AR
Long, Sandford A.	053	1900	WB-11/359	AR
Long, Sarah	077	1719	SS 875/160	SS/AR
Long, Sarah	024	1863	WB-D/15	AR
Long, Sarah	077	1847	WB-F/394	AR
Long, Sarah	071	1825	WB-3/326	AR
Long, Sarah	001	1879	WB-2/150	AR
Long, Sarah L.	061	1899	WB-2/226	AR
Long, Sidney Ann	009	1870	WB-1/56	CTY
Long, Simeon	061	1893	WB-2/121	AR
Long, Simeon P.	077	1850	WB-F/391	AR
Long, Stephen	063	1848	WB-2/341	
Long, Stephen	096	c1792	Orig. Only	AR
Long, Thomas	077	1817	WB-F/4	AR
Long, Thomas	038	1894	WB-3/446	AR
Long, Thomas	032	1899	WB-4/399	AR
Long, Thomas	077	1781	WB-C/326	AR
Long, Thomas	085	c1797	WB-E/178	AR
Long, Thomas	077	1754	SS 881/48	SS/AR
Long, Thomas	089	1843	WB-1/23	
Long, Thomas	077	1721	SS 876/136	SS/AR
Long, Thomas H.	001	1892	WB-2/547	AR
Long, Thomas S.	086	1887	WB-F/306	AR
Long, Thomas W.	061	1890	WB-2/101	AR
Long, Tobias	104	1862	WB-5/306	AR
Long, W. A.	016	1845	WB-1/68	
Long, W. H.	078	1884	WB-19/158	AR
Long, Wealthy A.	037	1878	WB-G/489	AR
Long, William	047	1777	WB-2/55	
Long, William	002	1712	Orig. Only	SS/AR
Long, William	020	1876	WB-A/217	CTY
Long, William	001	1888	WB-2/407	AR
Long, William	096	1790	Orig. Only	AR
Long, William	077	c1708	SS 875/54	
Long, William	038	1891	WB-3/234	AR
Long, William	106	1897	WB-2/413	
Long, William	077	1759	SS 881/233	SS/AR
Long, William	086	1854	WB-E/258	AR
Long, William	077	1795	WB-E/61	
Long, William J.	046	1883	WB-E/344	AR
Long, William R.	037	1849	WB-F/432	AR
Long, William S.	037	1895	WB-H/313	AR
Longest, James	019	1866	WB-B/4	AR
Longest, Joshua	019	1780	WB-D/266	AR
Longino, John Thomas	092	1796	WB-3/24	AR
Longlather, Daniel	077	1715/6	SS 875/105	SS/AR
Longman, Julia	009	1871	WB-1/74	CTY
Longmire, Lucy Ann	044	1848	WB-17/183	CTY
Longmire, Martha A.	044	1847	WB-17/173	CTY
Longmire, Robert	044	1847	WB-17/135	CTY
Longmire, Sarah H.	044	1848	WB-17/356	CTY
Longmire, William	044	1816	WB-7/640	CTY
Longworth, Fleat	038	1875	WB-2/237	AR
Longworth, Martin	038	1881	WB-2/407	AR
Lookadoo, Daniel	086	1890	WB-F/400	AR
Lookadoo, Jesse	086	1862	WB-E/391	
Lookinber, David	032	1838	WB-1/313	AR
Loomis, Nathaniel	072	1816	WB-A/78	AR
Loomiss, Jonathan	009	1794	OWB/291	AR
Loomiss, Jonathan	009	c1793	Copy	010 AR
Loop, John, Sr.	085	1801	WB-E/194	AR
Looper, William M.	003	1887	WB-B/210	AR
Loops, Amanda F.	059	1883	WB-A/282	CTY
Lopp, Jacob	032	1823	WB-1/3	AR
Lopp, Jacob	085	c1791	WB-C/32	AR
Lopp, Jacob	032	c1866	Orig. Only	AR
Lopp, Peter	032	1827	WB-1/78	AR
Lopp, Phillip	032	1895	WB-4/260 & 269	AR
Lorance, Jason	023	1894	WB-A/113	AR
Lord, Eliza	070	1847	WB-AB/461	AR
Lord, Eliza H.	070	1875	WB-E/301	AR
Lord, John	070	c1822	WB-AB/284	AR
Lord, Lord	078	1828	WI-11/59	AR
Lord, William	070	1780	WB-C/223	AR
Lord, William	070	1749	SS 877/85	SS/AR
Lord, William	070	c1748	DB-C/176 & 197	
Lord, William	029	1832	WB-B/209	
Lord, William C.	070	1878	WB-E/347	AR
Lord, William E.	012	N. D.	WB-B/64	
Lorde, John B.	085	1851	WB-K/134	AR
Lore, Andrew	021	1896	WB-3/124	AR
Loretz, Eliza	021	1865	WB-1/207	AR
Lorimer, Samuel	046	1774	WB-A/213	AR
Lorimer, Sarah J.	028	1871	WB-E/43	
Loring, Josiah	012	c1769	DB-A/128	AR
Lorrence, Barnabas	054	1840	WB-2/211	
Lorrence, Margaret	054	1841	WB-2/231	
Lorton, Thomas	047	1807	WB-3/469	
Louder, P. A.	016	1891	WB-4/74	
Loudermilk, Z. H.	081	1897	082 WB-6/577	082 AR
Lougee, Caroline	099	1895	WB-C/349	AR
Lougee, Weston G.	099	1876	RB-35/340	AR
Loughanor, G. Peter	060	1842	WB-2/134	AR
Loughton, Andrew	047	1766	WB-1/202	
Louper, John	054	c1834	WB-2/157	AR
Lourance, Emeline	021	1868	WB-2/11	
Lourance, J. M.	021	1867	WB-1/238	AR
Louther, Elizabeth	024	1866	WB-D/49	AR
Love, Amos	072	1798	Orig. Only	AR
Love, Amos	N	1773	Orig. Only	SS/AR
Love, Andrew	040	c1855	WB-1/74	
Love, Angus	083	1855	WB-2/65	AR
Love, Daniel	035	c1752	087 DB-2/189	
Love, Daniel	035	1753	SS 877/92	SS/AR
Love, Daniel	092	1879	WB-6/131	AR
Love, Daniel	083	1854	WB-2/53	AR
Love, Daniel	068	c1835	WB-B/157	
Love, Dillard	061	1872	WB-2/14	AR
Love, Effy	029	c1820	WB-B/51	
Love, Gaston	001	1899	WB-3/281	AR
Love, Henry A.	065	1858	WB-J/51	AR

Name	Co.	Date	Recorded Copy	Original
Love, Hiram	073	1816	WB-D/458	AR
Love, James	086	1803	WB-B/153	AR
Love, James	090	1800	WB-1/160	AR
Love, James R.	049	c1858	WB-1/7	AR
Love, James W.	089	1894	WB-2/281	AR
Love, Jennet	040	1883	WB-2/197	AR
Love, John	065	1791	WB-B/31	AR
Love, John	081	1819	WB-4/696	AR
Love, John	097	1898	WB-2/568	AR
Love, John A.	083	1866	WB-2/225	AR
Love, John B.	055	1870	WB-A/11 & 46	
Love, John C.	090	1827	WB-3/168	AR
Love, John C.	020	1889	WB-B/13	CTY
Love, John S.	065	1872	WB-K/83	AR
Love, John, Sr.	020	1844	RB-P/110	AR-Copy
Love, Jonah	089	1865	WB-1/276	
Love, Kenan	070	1803	WB-AB/72	AR
Love, Lorenzo	013	1872	WB-B/65	AR
Love, Mary	040	c1854	WB-1/66	
Love, Mary	071	1806	WB-2/315	AR
Love, Matthias	089	1898	WB-2/344	AR
Love, Michael G.	089	1865	WB-1/273	
Love, Miranda R.	020	1895	WB-B/191	CTY
Love, Naomi E.	040	1883	WB-2/195	AR
Love, Polley	073	c1808	Orig. Only	AR
Love, Robert	049	c1842	Orig. Only	AR-Copy
Love, S. W.	040	1862	WB-1/147	
Love, Samuel	020	1829	RB-L/393	AR
Love, Sarah	040	1900	WB-3/83	AR
Love, Susan L.	026	1886	WB-2/307	AR
Love, T. W.	026	1885	Orig. Only	AR
Love, Thomas	071	1790	WB-1/402	AR
Love, Thomas	073	1791	WB-B/154	AR
Love, Thomas	082	1847	WB-3/41	AR
Love, Thomas	102	1894	WB-A/95	AR
Love, William	029	1899	WB-F/163	AR
Love, William	005	c1753	WB-1/20	
Love, William	082	1793	082.801.1/1	AR
Love, William	082	1831	WB-2/14	AR
Love, William	071	1800	WB-2/190	AR
Love, William	047	1888	WB-7/116	AR
Love, William A.	092	1862	WB-5/61	
Love, William J.	070	1862	WB-D/81	AR
Lovelace, Archibald	104	1845	WB-4/306	
Lovelace, Asa	026	1887	WB-2/311	AR
Lovelace, Casander	054	c1811	WB-1/288	AR
Lovelace, Charles	054	c1796	WB-1/5	AR
Lovelace, Elam	054	c1837	WB-2/180	AR
Lovelace, Elizabeth	086	1893	WB-F/465	AR
Lovelace, James	086	1893	WB-F/458	AR
Lovelace, James	026	1896	WB-2/527	AR
Lovelace, Jane	104	1851	WB-5/50	
Lovelace, Nathan	026	1868	WB-2/9	AR
Lovelace, Nicholas	020	1884	WB-A/412	CTY
Lovelace, Thomas	054	c1829	WB-2/87	AR
Lovelace, Thomas	086	1887	WB-F/298	AR
Loveless, Josiah	092	1803	WB-3/58A	
Lovell, Hester E.	092	1854	WB-5/6	AR
Lovell, James	047	1762	WB-1/75	
Lovell, William	047	1803	WB-3/408	
Loveness, Henry	081	1824	WB-5/138	
Lovet, Elijah	057	1861	WB-B/254	AR
Lovet, John	072	1828	WB-1/30	AR
Lovett (Lovick), Richard	028	1801	WB-B/133	AR
Lovett, David	057	1833	WB-B/114	AR
Lovewater, Josef	085	1772	WB-A/89	AR
Lovey, Dinah	030	1832	WB-3/305	
Lovick, Alfred	059	1898	WB-B/232	CTY
Lovick, James	028	1831	WB-C/339	AR
Lovick, John	024	1733	LGB-4/#39	SS/AR
Lovick, John	024	1733	Orig. Only	AR-Copy
Lovick, Thomas	019	1759	SS 882/50	SS/AR
Lovin, Mahala J.	082	1893	WB-6/471	AR
Lovin, Sandefer	082	1830	WB-2/7	AR
Lovin, William R.	082	1882	WB-6/236	AR
Loving, F. J.	070	1856	WB-C/621	AR
Lovis, Thomas	028	c1730	Deeds.1/63	
Lovitt, Elizabeth	028	1810	WB-C/16	AR
Lovitt, Sarah	046	1836	WB-B/554	AR
Low, Alexander	010	1793	WB-D/213	AR
Low, Conrad	085	c1796	WB-E/185	AR
Low, David	046	1794	WB-A/215	AR
Low, Elizabeth	075	1770	WB-H/137	AR
Low, Emanuel	075	1727	SS 876/156	SS/A
Low, George	075	1786	WB-K/141	AR
Low, George R.	046	1892	WB-F/220	AR
Low, Hannah	075	1801	WB-M1/50	AR
Low, James	071	1769	WB-1/174	
Low, John	075	1759	SS 881/173	SS/AR
Low, John B.	046	c1846	Orig. Only	AR
Low, John, Sr.	075	1793	WB-L/12	AR
Low, Joshua	104	1841	WB-4/267	AR
Low, Lewis	046	1857	WB-C/474	AR
Low, Milisent	075	1809	WB-M1/204	AR
Low, Nathan	077	1832	WB-F/196	AR
Low, Nelly	046	1867	WB-D/354	AR
Low, Orpah	075	1823	WB-M1/372	AR
Low, Samuel	071	1780	WB-1/234	
Low, Solomon	001	1865	WB-1/244	AR
Low, Stephen	013	1843	WB-A/92	
Low, Thomas	081	1799	WB-2/43	AR
Low, Thomas	060	1829	WB-1/154	AR
Low, Thomas	075	1762	WB-I/13	AR
Low, William	075	1788	WB-K/161	AR
Low, William	104	1780	WB-1/44	AR
Lowasser, John	085	c1794	WB-E/135	AR
Lowber, Michaell	070	1756	DB-D/172	AR
Lowdemilk, Jacob	023	1874	WB-A/9	AR
Lowden, John	075	1719	SS 875/171	SS/AR
Lowder, John	089	1872	WB-2/19	AR
Lowder, Jonathan	038	1875	WB-2/224	AR
Lowder, M. Jane	089	1898	WB-2/332	AR
Lowdermilk, Jacob	054	1843	WB-2/266	AR
Lowdermilk, Stephen	081	1892	WB-16/233	
Lowdermilk, William	081	1867	WB-14/185	
Lowdermilk, Z. H.	081	1895	WB-16/366	AR
Lowe, Aaron	075	1803	WB-M1/87	AR
Lowe, Alfred	047	1885	WB-6/356	AR
Lowe, Ann	005	1867	WB-C/257	AR
Lowe, Anne	075	1731	Orig. Only	SS/AR
Lowe, Bird	084	1848	WB-C/74	CTY
Lowe, Eve	032	1840	WB-1/349	AR
Lowe, Exum L.	063	1835	WB-2/202	
Lowe, George W.	099	1896	WB-C/512	AR
Lowe, Isaac	060	1879	WB-4/197	AR
Lowe, Isaac	084	c1793	OW/32	AR
Lowe, Isaac	084	1807	WB-A/66	CTY
Lowe, J. W.	060	1882	WB-4/259	AR
Lowe, James	081	1858	WB-11/209	
Lowe, James, Sr.	032	1828	WB-1/94	AR

Name	Co.	Date	Recorded Copy	Original
Lowe, John	084	1831	WB-B/21	CTY
Lowe, John	071	1761	WB-1/41	
Lowe, John W. S.	084	1859	WB-C/306	CTY
Lowe, Joseph	081	1805	WB-3/40	
Lowe, L. L.	084	1891	WB-E/487	CTY
Lowe, Madison	081	1835	WB-6/485	AR
Lowe, Maria J.	047	1882	Copy	019 AR
Lowe, Maria J.	047	1882	WB-6/268	AR
Lowe, Penelope	036	1894	WB-A/319	CTY
Lowe, Priscilla	075	1871	WB-O/22	AR
Lowe, Samuel	081	1799	WB-2/45	AR
Lowe, Samuel	032	1879	WB-3/285	AR
Lowe, Sidney H.	060	1891	WB-4/467	AR
Lowe, Stephen	099	1796	RB-3/256	AR
Lowe, T. G.	047	1869	WB-6/17	AR
Lowe, T. L.	021	1862	WB-1/170	AR
Lowe, Thomas	071	1783	WB-1/274	
Lowe, Thomas	011	c1779	WB-1/521	
Lowe, Thomas	047	1839	WB-4/182	
Lowe, Thomas	047	1823	WB-3/682	
Lowe, Thomas W.	084	1863	WB-C/377	CTY
Lowe, Weston	081	1845	WB-8/183	AR
Lowe, William	060	1899	WB-5/103	AR
Lowe, William	047	1818	WB-3/613	
Lowe, William	047	1793	WB-3/213	
Lowe, William	024	1722	SS 875/336	SS/AR
Lowell, Charles	010	1738	LGB-4/#80	
Lowell, D. H.	VT	1897	068 WB-D/507	
Lowell, Edmond	072	1744	SS 878/96	SS/AR
Lowell, Hannah	019	c1779	WB-D/265	AR-Nunc.
Lowenburg, Charles	070	1892	WB-F/512	AR
Lowerance, Caney M.	021	1885	WB-2/338	
Lowerby, Henry	071	1805	WB-2/301	AR
Lowery, Alexander	064	1890	WB-2/206	AR
Lowery, Barbra	066	1888	WB-1/33	AR
Lowery, Francis S.	097	1880	WB-2/182	
Lowery, Green	099	1872	RB-35/178	AR
Lowery, Henry A.	099	1897	WB-D/52	AR
Lowery, James	013	1857	WB-A/184	
Lowery, James A.	059	1900	WB-B/273	CTY
Lowery, Jehu	099	1850	RB-27/134	AR
Lowery, Jesse	099	1840	RB-24/443	AR
Lowery, Mary F.	099	1892	WB-C/103	
Lowery, W. T.	099	1892	WB-C/101	AR
Lowery, William	075	1896	WB-O/430	AR
Lowery, William	026	1886	WB-2/298	AR
Lowman, Louisa	014	1883	WB-2/247	CTY
Lowndes, Charles T.	SC	1884	093 WB-2/21 &99	093 AR
Lowndes, Thomas	SC	1894	050 WB-2/198	050 CTY
Lowndes, William P.	NY	1887	050 WB-2/19	050 CTY
Lowrance, A. J.	085	1893	WB-3/13	CTY
Lowrance, Abraham	054	c1826	WB-2/66	AR
Lowrance, Alexander	085	1868	WB-1/12	CTY
Lowrance, Ann	054	1844	WB-2/293	AR
Lowrance, D. S.	021	c1884	WB-2/285	
Lowrance, Isaac	021	1843	WB-1/3	AR
Lowrance, Isaac	060	1837	WB-1/397	AR
Lowrance, Jane Eliza	085	1866	WB-K/381	AR
Lowrance, John	085	1781	WB-B/128	AR
Lowrance, John	054	1835	WB-2/129	AR
Lowrance, John	085	c1800	WB-E/183	AR
Lowrance, John A.	085	1875	WB-1/317	CTY
Lowrance, John N.	054	1885	WB-5/19	CTY
Lowrance, Joseph	085	1778	WB-B/113	AR-Nunc.
Lowrance, Joseph	085	c1776	WB-C/169	AR
Lowrance, Laura E.	085	1888	WB-2/299	CTY
Lowrance, Lydia A.	085	1894	WB-3/22	CTY
Lowrance, Milis	054	1846	WB-3/3	AR
Lowrance, Peter	085	1772	WB-A/76	AR
Lowrance, William	073	1886	WB-H/409	
Lowray, Issable	090	1812	WB-2/133	AR
Lowrence, Peter	085	1768	WB-A/82	AR
Lowrey, Allen	046	1882	WB-E/341	AR
Lowrey, Hugh	046	1861	WB-D/83	AR
Lowrey, James G.	046	1864	WB-D/238	AR
Lowrey, John	026	1866	WB-1/403	AR
Lowrey, Margaret	097	1875	WB-2/87	AR-Nunc.
Lowrey, Mildred	071	1807	WB-2/338	
Lowrey, Thomas	026	1874	WB-2/102	AR
Lowrie, Calvin C.	083	1892	WB-4/14	AR
Lowrie, P. P.	083	1893	WB-4/3	AR
Lowrie, Patrick J.	065	1862	WB-J/156	AR
Lowrie, Samuel	065	1818	WB-B/38	AR
Lowrie, William H.	070	1813	WB-AB/187	AR
Lowry, Arthur	099	1797	RB-4/15	AR
Lowry, Benjamin B.	075	1846	WB-N/205	AR
Lowry, Elizabeth	099	1870	RB-35/91	AR
Lowry, Elizabeth	085	1881	WB-1/571	CTY
Lowry, George	075	1753	Orig. Only	AR
Lowry, George	075	1753	Orig. Only	SS/AR
Lowry, James	083	c1810	WB-1/121	AR
Lowry, James T.	005	1885	WB-D/177	AR
Lowry, John	038	c1836	WB-1/3	AR
Lowry, John	073	1799	WB-C/134	AR
Lowry, John	075	1779	WB-K/32	AR
Lowry, Joseph	075	1812	WB-M1/245	AR
Lowry, Joseph	075	1754	Orig. Only	SS/AR
Lowry, Margrate	070	1842	WB-AB/356	AR
Lowry, Peter	005	1797	WB-A/47	AR
Lowry, Richard	085	1854	WB-K/178	AR
Lowry, Robert	037	1774	WB-A/208	AR
Lowry, Robert	075	1752	Orig. Only	SS/AR
Lowry, Robert	075	1805	WB-M1/105	AR
Lowry, Sandford R.	039	1900	WB-V/201	AR
Lowry, Telitha	099	1900	WB-D/429	AR
Lowry, Thomas	047	1789	WB-3/171	
Lowry, William	085	1812	WB-G/241	AR
Lows, James	072	c1779	WI/L39	
Lowther, Tristram	010	c1790	024 WB-A/348	024 AR
Lowther, Tristrim	071	1759	Orig. Only	SS/AR
Lowther, William	NY	c1782	024 WB-A/208	024 AR
Lowthrop, Sallie C.	028	1877	WB-E/165	
Loy, George	073	1799	WB-C/157	AR
Loy, Jacob	001	1857	WB-1/116	AR
Loy, Milton	001	1892	WB-2/534	AR
Loyd, Catharine	039	c1889	Orig. Only	AR
Loyd, Edward	044	1791	WB-2/215	CTY
Loyd, George W.	100	1864	WB-50/122	AR
Loyd, Joseph	072	c1794	Orig. Only	AR
Loyd, Joseph	072	c1781	WB-A/81	AR
Loyd, Marget	044	1806	WB-6/312	CTY
Loyd, Mary	044	1793	WB-3/33	CTY
Loyd, Robert	024	1728	SS 876/150	SS/AR
Loyd, Sarah	022	1866	WB-D/158	AR
Loyd, William	072	c1787	WI/L9	AR
Loyd, William	073	1835	WB-E/342	AR
Loyd, William	044	1803	WB-6/39	CTY
Loyd, Willis	100	1869	WB-51/14	
Loyde (Lide), John	071	1742	Orig. Only	SS/AR

Name	Co.	Date	Recorded Copy	Original
Luarton, John	053	1723	Orig. Only	SS/AR
Luby, Moses	065	1825	WB-E/93	
Lucas, Apsy	048	1899	WB-1/89	CTY
Lucas, Blackwell	070	1894	WB-H/166	AR
Lucas, Daniel	103	1849	RD-10/308	AR
Lucas, Frances	011	c1784	WB-1/520	
Lucas, George	022	c1807	WB-A/149	AR
Lucas, George A.	087	1887	WB-3/368	AR
Lucas, George D.	024	1786	WB-A/249	AR
Lucas, Henderson	029	1862	WB-C/452	AR-Nunc.
Lucas, Henry	105	1859	WB-1/56	AR
Lucas, Henry	011	c1839	WB-1/74	
Lucas, Henry L.	011	1859	WB-1/265	
Lucas, J. J. D.	011	1884	WB-2/178	
Lucas, James	026	1842	WB-1/7	AR
Lucas, John	105	1887	WB-2/446	AR
Lucas, John	026	1873	WB-2/79	AR
Lucas, John F.	009	1838	OB-B/501	AR
Lucas, Lewis	087	c1806	Orig. Only	AR
Lucas, Louisa	067	1898	WB-2/369	AR
Lucas, Mary	028	1761	Orig. Only	SS/AR
Lucas, Mary	022	1833	WB-B/264	AR
Lucas, Mary Eliza	070	1883	WB-E/472	AR
Lucas, Phillip	064	1850	WB-1/26	AR
Lucas, Polley	081	1851	WB-9/307	AR
Lucas, Rebecca	047	1803	WB-3/385	
Lucas, Rhoda	105	1858	WB-1/51	AR
Lucas, Samuel	009	c1782	OWB/173	AR
Lucas, Sarah	105	1858	WB-1/43	AR
Lucas, Silas	105	1893	WB-3/63	AR
Lucas, Tabitha	081	1891	WB-16/168	AR
Lucas, Thomas	011	c1792	WB-1/507	
Lucas, Thomas	081	1838	WB-7/217	AR
Lucas, Thomas	011	c1772	WB-1/340	
Lucas, William	022	c1805	WB-A/53	AR
Lucas, William	046	1824	WB-B/186	AR
Luche, Spencer	081	1884	WB-15/437	AR
Luck, Edmund	081	1847	WB-8/533	
Luck, Emsley	081	1887	WB-16/57	AR
Luck, John	054	1842	WB-2/242	AR
Luckey, David	060	1866	WB-3/93	AR
Luckey, Francis N.	085	1878	WB-1/454	CTY
Luckey, James	060	1861	WB-3/39	AR
Luckey, James	060	1799	Orig. Only	AR
Luckey, John	085	1789	WB-C/41	AR
Luckey, John	085	1882	WB-2/11	CTY
Luckey, Robert	065	1900	WB-N/386	AR
Luckey, Samuel	085	c1801	WB-E/136	AR
Luckey, Samuel	085	1866	WB-K/374	AR
Luckey, Sarah M.	060	1895	WB-4/577	AR
Luckey, William	060	1895	WB-4/582	AR
Luckey, William	085	1836	WB-H/671	AR
Luckie, James	085	1840	WB-I/83	AR
Luckie, Robert	085	1772	WB-A/77	AR
Luckie, Samuel	085	c1797	WB-E/132	AR
Lucky, Harriet	065	1845	WB-I/100	AR
Lucky, Robert	065	1864	WB-J/179	AR
Lucky, Sarah M.	065	1896	WB-M/430	AR
Lucus, Joseph	103	1817	RD-4/58	AR
Lucus, William	086	1839	WB-E/54	
Ludford, John	096	1737	LGB-4/#90	SS/AR
Ludford, Thomas	096	N. D.	WB-1/50	AR
Ludford, William	075	1733	SS 876/275	SS/AR
Ludford, William	N	c1702	Orig. Only	SS/AR
Ludlam, Cramford	012	c1782	DB-B/172	
Ludlam, Isaac	012	1769	DB-A/134	
Ludwick, Elizabeth	016	1855	WB-1/257	
Ludwick, Margret	046	1845	WB-C/234	AR
Ludwick, Martha M.	067	1885	WB-2/219	AR
Ludwick, Peter	090	1807	WB-2/87	AR
Ludwig, Nicholas	065	1781	WB-B/29	AR
Luerton, John	009	c1781	OWB/170	AR
Lueston, John	010	1742	LGB-4/#166	SS/AR
Luffman, Daniel	030	1789	WB-1/238	
Luffman, Owen	075	1801	WB-M1/46	AR
Luffman, Thomas	030	1825	WB-3/202	
Luffman, William	075	1798	WB-M1/19	AR
Luffman, William	075	1799	WB-M1/25	AR
Luffman, William	030	1728	SS 876/134	SS/AR
Luffman, William, Jr.	030	1728	SS 876/147	SS/AR
Lufman, Jonathan	030	1796	WB-2/76	
Luie, Michael	032	1825	WB-1/42	AR
Luis, Richard	024	1719	SS 875/176	
Lukber, John	085	c1803	WB-E/142	AR
Luky, Alexander	073	c1772	WB-A/117	
Lum, Elizabeth	051	1832	WB-A/50A	
Lumley, Elizabeth	036	1894	WB-A/330	CTY
Lumpkin, Anthony	044	1811	WB-7/171	CTY
Lumpkin, Joseph	044	1841	WB-15/22	CTY
Lumpkin, Sarah	044	1822	WB-9/123	CTY
Lumpkins, Fleming	044	1835	WB-13/264	CTY
Lumsden, Sarah E.	029	1872	WB-E/59	AR
Lunceford, David	056	1860	WB-2/4	AR
Lunceford, Emily	056	1888	WB-3/479	AR
Lunceford, John	077	1797	WB-E/86	
Lunceford, Mary	077	1806	WB-E/248	AR
Lund, Oliver	024	1857	WB-C/396	AR
Lunn, Rachel M.	033	1900	WB-2/252	CTY
Lunn, William	033	1837	WB-1/1	AR
Lunsford, Allen	054	1851	WB-3/50	AR
Lunsford, Allen H.	078	1881	WB-19/118	
Lunsford, David	036	1893	WB-A/294	CTY
Lunsford, Elizabeth	054	1852	WB-3/62	AR
Lunsford, John	078	1872	WB-19/20	AR
Lunsford, Joseph	036	1895	WB-A/360	CTY
Lunsford, Joseph	078	1856	WB-17/396	AR
Lunsford, Laura E.	036	1896	WB-A/394	CTY
Lunsford, Nimrod	003	1847	Orig. Only	AR
Lunsford, W. D.	036	1894	WB-A/316	CTY
Luntsford, Linom	039	c1793	WB-B/8	
Luper, Lindsey C.	038	1896	WB-3/590	AR
Luper, Mariah	037	1898	WB-H/430	AR
Luper, Mariah	037	1887	WB-H/106	AR
Lupo, James	037	1811	WB-E/20	AR
Lupo, Zachariah	037	1821	WB-E/281	AR
Lupton, Allen	019	1859	WB-A/233	AR
Lupton, Asenath	019	1881	WB-B/127	AR
Lupton, Christopher	019	1802	WB-D/268	AR
Lupton, Christopher	074	1891	WB-1/105	
Lupton, Dempsey G.	074	1894	WB-1/125	
Lupton, John	019	1840	WB-A/87	AR
Lupton, Joseph	019	1900	WB-C/33	AR
Lupton, Josiah	053	1870	WB-11/20	AR
Lupton, Robinson	074	1877	WB-1/73	
Lupton, Silas	019	1869	WB-B/49	AR
Lupton, Silas L.	053	1862	WB-9/126	AR
Lupton, Wilson	019	1878	WB-B/103	AR
Lurry, Anny	018	1838	WB-C/241	

Name	Co.	Date	Recorded Copy	Original
Lurry, Chloe	018	1843	WB-C/289	
Lurry, Demsey	018	1840	WB-C/257	
Lurry, John	018	1827	WB-C/77	
Lurry, Nathan	018	1830	WB-C/116	
Lurry, Polly	018	1829	WB-C/110	
Lurry, William	030	1817	WB-3/91	
Lurry, William	030	1746	Orig. Only	SS/AR
Lurry, Wilson	018	1852	WB-C/363	
Lusk, John	065	1778	WB-D/152	AR
Lusk, Samuel	085	c1773	WB-A/193	AR
Luten, Anne	024	1815	WB-C/35	AR
Luten, Henry	075	c1814	Orig. Only	AR
Luten, James	024	c1766	WB-A/252	AR
Luten, John	024	c1784	WB-A/248	AR
Luten, Thomas	024	c1766	WB-A/259	AR
Lutes, Jacob S.	021	1849	WB-1/71	AR
Luther, Altha V.	068	1891	WB-C/166	CTY
Luther, Arminta	061	1898	WB-2/211	AR
Luther, David	016	1843	WB-1/9	
Luther, George	081	1862	WB-12/238	AR
Luther, Jacob	081	1866	WB-13/439	AR
Luther, Jonathan	081	1895	WB-16/343	AR
Luther, Laura E.	013	1885	WB-B/366	AR
Luther, Martin	081	1883	WB-15/459	
Luther, Michael	081	1834	WB-6/396	AR
Luther, Nancy A.	061	1898	WB-2/232	AR
Luther, Solomon	013	1884	WB-B/308	AR
Luton, Adam	072	1746	Orig. Only	SS/AR
Luton, Adam	072	1746	Orig. Only	AR-Copy
Luton, Frederick	024	1816	WB-C/43	AR
Luton, Henderson	024	c1791	WB-A/79	AR
Luton, Polly	030	1883	Orig. Only	AR-Nunc.
Lutterloh, Charles	022	1858	WB-D/14	AR
Lutterloh, Elizabeth	022	1875	WB-E/106	AR
Lutterloh, Elizabeth	022	1812	WB-A/209	AR
Lutterloh, H. Lewis	022	1797	RB-2/100	AR
Lutterloh, Thomas S.	029	1900	WB-F/199	AR
Lutterloh, Thomas S.	029	1900	070 WB-L/106	070 AR
Luttrell, John	073	1820	WB-A/240	
Luttrell, John	073	1782	WB-A/240	AR
Lutz, Daniel	060	1861	WB-3/36	AR
Lutz, Daniel A.	060	1865	WB-3/84	AR
Lutz, Daniel A.	021	c1897	WB-3/333	AR
Lutz, Jacob	060	1808	Orig. Only	AR
Lutz, Jacob	021	1888	WB-2/446	AR
Lutz, John W.	026	1892	WB-2/439	AR
Lutz, Laban	021	1899	WB-3/234	AR
Lutz, Samuel	060	1886	WB-4/346	AR
Lyall, Thomas	085	c1781	WB-B/46	AR
Lyall, Thomas	085	c1781	WB-E/133	
Lyans, John	085	c1784	WB-B/73	AR
Lybass, David	084	1840	WB-B/237	CTY
Lyda, Anna	050	1894	WB-2/194	CTY
Lyda, Jacob	050	1860	WB-1/62	
Lyday, Adam	093	c1872	WB-1/109	
Lyerlee, David	089	1890	WB-2/183	AR
Lyerly, George	085	1893	WB-2/572	CTY
Lyerly, Jacob	085	1846	WB-K/21	AR
Lyerly, Jacob	085	1843	WB-I/181	AR
Lyerly, Jacob	085	1864	WB-K/339	AR
Lyerly, Margaret	085	1851	WB-K/138	AR
Lyerly, Margaret	085	1879	WB-1/501	CTY
Lyerly, Moses	085	1886	WB-2/200	CTY
Lyerly, Nancy	085	1872	WB-1/135	
Lyerly, Zachariah	085	1882	WB-2/31	CTY
Lyle, John	086	1851	WB-E/216	AR
Lyle, William	044	1825	WB-10/18	CTY-Nunc.
Lyles, Cynthia	084	1861	WB-C/361	CTY
Lyles, George	024	1753	Orig. Only	SS/AR
Lyles, James	006	1844	WB-A/87	AR
Lyles, Julia A.	071	1890	WB-7/78	AR
Lyles, Robert S.	047	1884	WB-6/322	AR
Lyman, Theodore	099	1893	Copy	061 AR
Lyman, Theodore	099	1893	WB-C/193	AR
Lynam, Charles	071	1785	WB-1/354	AR
Lynch (Linch), James	056	1790	WB-1/28	AR
Lynch, Andrew J.	099	1866	RB-33/489	AR
Lynch, Charles H.	VA	1875	084 WB-F/113	084 CTY
Lynch, Daniel	073	1833	WB-E/265	AR
Lynch, Dinah	084	1863	WB-C/374	CTY
Lynch, Eaton	037	1851	WB-F/460	AR
Lynch, Edison	086	1890	Orig. Only	AR
Lynch, Elizabeth	106	c1876	WB-2/110	
Lynch, Elizabeth	103	1801	Orig. Only	AR
Lynch, Francis	086	1887	WB-F/320	AR
Lynch, Francis S.	090	1892	WB-6/276	AR
Lynch, Frederick	086	1798	Orig. Only	AR
Lynch, George G.	047	1887	WB-6/450	AR
Lynch, H. P.	086	1898	WB-F/565	AR
Lynch, Hugh	084	1820	WB-A/222	CTY
Lynch, James W.	047	1883	WB-6/294	AR
Lynch, John	092	1800	WB-3/38	
Lynch, John	086	1879	WB-F/134	AR
Lynch, John, Sr.	044	1757	SS 881/162	SS/AR
Lynch, Lemuel	073	1893	WB-I/10	CTY
Lynch, Littleberry	024	1832	WB-C/162	AR
Lynch, Martha J.	013	1883	WB-B/302	AR
Lynch, Mary	073	1880	WB-H/261	CTY
Lynch, Mary S.	073	1878	WB-H/183	CTY
Lynch, Milly	037	1860	WB-G/181	AR
Lynch, Philip	005	c1807	WB-2/97	AR
Lynch, Robert	084	1831	WB-B/33	CTY
Lynch, Susan	073	1897	WB-I/121	CTY
Lynch, Thomas	073	1815	WB-D/438	
Lynch, Thomas	073	1869	WB-H/11	CTY
Lynch, William	037	1788	WB-C/61	AR
Lynd, John	085	c1781	WB-B/67	
Lyndon, Henry	081	1795	WB-2/10	AR
Lyndon, J. W.	081	1894	WB-16/326	
Lyne, Fanny B.	044	1826	WB-10/256	CTY
Lyne, Henry	044	1816	WB-7/635	CTY
Lyne, Henry	044	1798	WB-4/205	CTY
Lyne, James	044	1816	WB-7/578	CTY
Lynn, Alexander	084	1854	WB-C/179	CTY
Lynn, Jackson	084	1829	WB-A/331	
Lynn, John	060	1829	WB-1/143	AR
Lynn, John	099	1808	RB-8/18	AR
Lynn, Joseph	056	1800	WB-2/266	
Lynn, Thornton	084	1883	WB-E/263	CTY
Lynn, William	036	1882	WB-A/28	CTY
Lynn, William	085	c1784	WB-C/12	
Lyon, Bryson	104	1867	WB-5/514	AR
Lyon, Clement B.	044	1848	WB-17/186	CTY
Lyon, Dora	036	1894	WB-A/328	CTY
Lyon, Eleanor	011	1846	WB-1/141	
Lyon, Elijah	085	c1800	WB-E/138	AR
Lyon, Elkanah	044	1847	WB-17/175	CTY

Name	Co.	Date	Recorded Copy	Original
Lyon, Eneas	077	c1780	024 WB-A/261	024 AR
Lyon, Jacob	104	1840	WB-4/254	AR
Lyon, James	011	1752	SS 877/367	SS/AR
Lyon, James	090	1858	WB-4/319	AR
Lyon, James	104	1859	WB-5/238	
Lyon, John	044	1829	WB-11/215	CTY
Lyon, John	020	1784	RB-B/39	AR
Lyon, John	070	1782	WB-C/222	AR
Lyon, John	044	1813	WB-7/314	CTY
Lyon, John E.	044	1881	WB-23/393	CTY
Lyon, John W.	044	1879	WB-23/324	CTY
Lyon, M. S.	036	1900	WB-A/481	CTY
Lyon, Mary E.	036	1893	WB-A/287	CTY
Lyon, Mildred	070	1788	WB-C/228	AR
Lyon, Nancy	037	1879	WB-G/504	AR
Lyon, Nicholas	020	1870	WB-A/44	CTY
Lyon, R. Benjamin	036	1900	WB-A/504	CTY
Lyon, Rhesa	104	1899	WB-7/94	AR
Lyon, Robert	020	1804	RB-E/136	AR
Lyon, Robert H.	011	1895	WB-2/417	CTY
Lyon, Thomas	037	1836	WB-F/185	AR
Lyon, William M.	044	1876	WB-23/224	CTY
Lyon, Woodson	078	1891	036 WB-A/236	036 CTY
Lyon, Woodson	078	1891	WB-19/309	AR
Lyon, Zachariah	044	1815	WB-7/552	CTY
Lyons, Emily	045	1892	WB-1/225	AR
Lyons, James	092	1883	WB-6/194	AR
Lysinger, John	032	1897	WB-4/319	
Lytch, Archibald	082	1848	WB-4/16	AR
Lytch, James	082	1890	WB-6/419	AR
Lytle, Archibald	073	N. D.	WB-B/283	AR
Lytle, George	064	1858	WB-1/56	AR
Lytle, Susanah	064	1866	WB-1/97	AR
Lytle, Thomas	081	1794	WB-2/2	AR
Lytle, Thomas	064	1883	WB-2/127	AR
Maas, Henry	090	1822	WB-3/86	AR
Mabe, John	090	c1836	Orig. Only	AR
Mabe, Reuben	090	1856	WB-4/298	AR
Maben, Robert	044	1851	WB-18/287	CTY
Maberry, Alexander	104	1866	WB-5/425	AR
Maberry, John	054	1831	Orig. Only	AR
Maberry, Nancy	104	1869	WB-6/13	AR
Maberry, Randolph	104	1857	WB-5/167	
Mabin, John	050	1853	WB-1/35	CTY
Mabine, James	075	1778	WB-K/9	AR
Mabrey, Baker W.	037	1862	WB-G/225	AR
Mabrey, Charles D.	037	1864	WB-G/251	AR
Mabrey, M. L.	037	1895	WB-H/311	AR
Mabry, Aseneth C.	026	1868	WB-1/425	AR
Mabry, Charles	100	1844	WB-38/319	AR
Mabry, Darling	047	1821	WB-4/6	AR
Mabry, David	099	1834	RB-23/209	AR
Mabry, Eleanor	100	1845	WB-38/396	AR
Mabry, Francis	100	1784	WB-4/101	AR
Mabry, George	085	1771	WB-A/101	AR
Mabry, Jessey	039	c1791	WB-A/62	
Mabry, John H.	032	1879	WB-3/287	AR
Mabry, Jones	100	1850	WB-40/260	AR
Mabry, Joshua	100	1791	WB-5/249	AR
Mabry, Mary J.	047	1879	WB-6/216	AR
Mabry, Mary T.	099	1883	WB-A/464	AR
Mabry, Nancy	100	1873	WB-51/64	AR
Mabry, Penelope	037	1881	WB-G/609	AR
Mabry, Repps	100	1819	WB-22/119	AR
Mabry, Temperance	047	1850	WB-4/295	AR
Mabry, Wilkinson	037	c1833	WB-F/231	AR
Mabry, William	100	1825	WB-28/234	AR
Mabson, Arthur	070	1778	WB-C/258	AR
Mabson, Arthur	019	1748	SS 878/40	SS/AR
Mabson, Kate	070	1890	WB-F/408	AR
Mabson, Mary	070	1812	WB-AB/185	AR
MacAlpin, Neill	083	1857	WB-2/118	AR
MacArthur, Peter	083	c1798	WB-1/50 & 242	AR
MacBride, John	092	1838	WB-4/141	
MacCrary, Robert	010	1740	LGB-4/#115	SS/AR
MacCulloch, Margaret	073	1847	WB-F/343	AR
MacDonald, William	024	c1780	WB-B/155	AR
MacDowell, John	070	1763	DB-E/129	AR
MacKay, William	070	1823	WB-C/295	AR
MacKellar, Duncan	029	1812	WB-A/178	AR
MacKelroy, James	009	1773	Orig. Only	SS/AR
MacKilwean, Francis	034	1774	Orig. Only	SS/AR
MacKinnon, Charles	068	1816	WB-A/292	
MacKlemore, Abraham	010	1736	Orig. Only	SS/AR
MacKlemore, James	N	c1733	Orig. Only	SS/AR
MacLean, Hector	083	1814	WB-1/149	AR
MacLearan, Archibald	011	1751	Orig. Only	SS/AR
MacLeran, John	029	1817	WB-A/241	AR
MacMurphy, Agatha	070	c1796	Orig. Only	AR
MacNair, Edmund D.	039	c1855	Orig. Only	AR
MacNair, Thomas A.	009	1892	WB-1/547	CTY
MacNaughten, Ranald	011	1752	Orig. Only	SS/AR
MacNaughton, Caroline	NY	1886	Copy	050 AR
MacNeill, Alexander	020	1808	RB-F/4	AR
MacNeill, Alexander	083	1832	WB-1/264	AR
MacNeill, Hector	083	c1803	WB-1/77	AR
MacPherson, Martin	068	1821	WB-B/14	
MacRae, Caroline A.	070	1875	WB-E/305	AR
MacRae, Donald	070	1892	WB-G/75	AR
MacRae, Duncan	085	1889	WB-2/377	CTY
MacRae, John C.	070	1878	WB-E/349	AR
MacRae, Mary S.	070	1896	WB-G/496	AR
MacRae, Roderick	070	1900	WB-H/334	AR
MacRae, Sallie N.	070	1900	WB-H/329	AR
Macay, Alfred	085	1827	WB-H/399	AR
Macay, Elizabeth	085	1817	WB-G/462	AR
Macay, James	085	1847	WB-K/49	AR
Macay, James	085	1800	WB-E/88	AR
Macay, Jane	085	1857	WB-K/253	AR
Macay, Spruce	085	1810	WB-G/165	AR
Macay, William S.	085	1856	WB-K/218	AR
Macbride, John	092	c1833	WB-4/63	AR
Macdade, Willis	037	1823	WB-F/8	AR
Macdonnack, Andrew	009	c1787	OWB/218	AR
Mace, James	019	1810	WB-D/289	AR
Mace, William	N	c1757	Orig. Only	SS/AR
Mace, William	019	1831	WB-A/11	AR
Mace, William, Jr.	019	1831	WB-A/10	AR
Macey, Joseph	081	1810	WB-3/178	AR
Macguire, Samuel	024	c1789	WB-A/166	AR
Machaffe, John	054	1843	WB-2/266	AR
Machen, Thomas	100	1782	WB-3/136	AR
Mack, Lucy	038	1895	WB-3/521	AR
MackBride, Truman	075	1726/7	Orig. Only	AR-Nunc.
Mackane, George	019	1758	SS 881/140	SS/AR
Mackarty, Timothy	024	1718	SS 875/157	SS/AR
Mackay, William	070	1745	SS 878/25	SS/AR
Mackbride, John	075	1766	Copy	018 AR
Mackclenden, Deborah	077	1732	Orig. Only	SS/AR
Mackdaniel, James	028	c1759	Wills.7/268	

Name	Co.	Date	Recorded Copy	Original
Mackdaniel, James	028	c1759	SS 882/268	SS/AR
Mackdaniell, Owen	010	1743	Orig. Only	SS/AR
Mackdowell, Thomas	096	1786	WB-1/150	AR
Mackeel, Anthony	008	1723/4	Orig. Only	SS/AR
Mackeel, Rebacca	053	1729	Orig. Only	SS/AR
Mackeel, Thomas Sr.	075	1754	Orig. Only	SS/AR
Mackeele, Benjamin	075	1754	SS 881/80	SS/AR
Mackey, Alexander	086	1793	Orig. Only	AR
Mackey, Charles	064	1895	WB-2/352	AR
Mackey, Isaac	057	c1781	WB-A/76	AR
Mackey, Joseph	077	1802	WB-E/146	AR
Mackey, William	096	1786	WB-1/63	AR
Mackferrell, John	N	N.D.	SS 877/17	SS/AR (N)
Mackgue, Lawrance	010	1740	LGB-4/#118	SS/AR
Mackhoney, Thomas	030	1832	WB-3/316	
Mackie, John	030	1823	WB-3/142	
Mackie, Nathan	106	c1864	WB-1/92	
Mackie, R. W.	106	1892	WB-2/327	AR
Mackie, Robert	106	1872	Orig. Only	AR
Mackie, Solomon	106	c1864	WB-1/94	AR
Mackie, William	085	1753	DB-3/19	
Mackie, William	092	1850	WB-4/334	
Mackinne, Barnaby	037	1736	LGB-4/#58	
Mackinne, John	037	1753	SS 878/214	SS/AR
Mackinne, Richard	037	1755	Orig. Only	SS/AR
Mackinney, Sarah	047	1782	WB-3/26	AR
Macklemore, West	087	c1818	WB-A/93	AR
Mackleroy, Archibald	056	1761	WB-1/751	AR
Mackley, Henry	075	1721	SS 875/323	SS/AR
Macklin, Gray	099	1882	WB-A/408	AR
Macklin, Jane L.	069	c1889	Orig. Only	AR
Mackorrney, John	030	1805	WB-2/268	
Mackubin, Samuel	028	1766	Orig. Only	AR
Macky, William	010	1740/1	Orig. Only	SS/AR
Maclaine, Archibald	070	1791	WB-C/276	AR
Maclanen, James	030	1798	WB-2/114	
Maclanin, Mary	030	1798	WB-2/126	
Maclean, Thomas	040	c1854	WB-1/72	
Maclellan, John	047	1797	WB-3/290	AR
Maclennan, William	029	1813	WB-A/199	AR
Maclin, Mary E.	VA	1868	Copy	071 AR
Macmiel, John	010	1730	Orig. Only	SS/AR
Macnair, Altimare	037	c1877	WB-G/537	AR
Macnair, E. Duncan	037	1896	WB-H/363	AR
Macnair, Edmund D.	037	1843	WB-F/274	AR
Macnair, Thomas A.	100	1878	WB-51/29	AR
Macneill, John L.	070	1830	WB-AB/255	AR
Macon, Catherine	019	1842	WB-A/100	AR
Macon, Gideon	044	1762	Orig. Only	CTY
Macon, Gideon H.	100	1809	WB-15/6	AR
Macon, Gideon H.	047	1877	WB-6/175	AR
Macon, Gideon H.	039	1847	WB-M/192	AR
Macon, James E.	081	1882	WB-15/383	AR
Macon, John	067	1870	WB-2/10	AR
Macon, Lydia	081	1891	WB-16/234	AR
Macon, Margaretta	039	1847	WB-M/222	AR
Macon, N. T.	039	1888	WB-U/419	AR
Macon, Nathaniel	100	1837	WB-36/168	AR
Macon, Nathaniel	039	c1843	WB-L/181	AR
Macon, Rebecca	081	1860	WB-11/514	AR
Macon, Thomas	081	1882	WB-15/388	AR
Macon, William	081	1871	WB-15/62	
Macoy, John	030	c1813	WB-3/22	
Macy, Asa	046	1859	WB-D/30	AR
Macy, Dinah	046	1797	WB-A/227	AR
Macy, Enoch	046	1806	WB-A/239	AR
Macy, Henry	046	1900	WB-G/238	AR
Macy, Henry	046	1816	Orig. Only	AR
Macy, Matthew	046	1804	WB-A/235	AR
Macy, Matthew	032	1842	WB-1/385	
Macy, Uriah	046	1879	WB-E/261	AR
Madden, Mary	086	1816	WB-C/43	AR
Madding, Robert	020	1854	RB-R/168	AR
Madditt, Thomas	029	1863	WB-C/447	
Maddox, David	022	1795	RB-2/34	AR
Maddox, John B.	022	1866	WB-D/157	AR
Maddox, Samantha	022	1892	WB-E/490	AR
Maddox, Samuel	005	c1840	Orig. Only	AR
Maddrey, Anderson J.	071	1888	WB-7/33	AR
Maddrey, Elizabeth	071	1885	WB-6/500	AR
Maddrey, H. C.	051	1893	WB-C/450	AR
Maddrey, James	071	1819	WB-3/212	AR
Maddrey, Mary	071	1831	WB-4/85	AR
Maddrey, Nancy	071	1883	WB-6/412	AR
Maddrey, Nathaniel	071	1866	WB-5/338	AR
Maddrey, Peter	071	1786	WB-1/361	AR
Maddrey, Sally	071	c1842	WB-5/245	AR
Maddrey, William	071	1826	WB-4/13	AR
Maddry, Abel	073	1892	WB-H/565	CTY
Maddux, John	019	1774	Orig. Only	SS/AR
Maden, Andrew	085	1772	WB-A/90	AR
Maden, James E.	056	1899	WB-4/173	AR
Maderey, Moses	015	1777	100 WB-2/108	
Madge, Rebecca	019	1852	WB-A/157	AR
Madison, John	106	1899	WB-2/460	
Madison, John H.	054	1880	WB-4/397	CTY
Madkins, Richard	075	1847	WB-N/217	
Madren, Dorcas	075	1809	WB-M1/206	AR
Madren, Goldsmith	075	c1858	WB-M2/59	AR
Madren, Jacob	075	1770	WB-H/110	AR
Madren, Joseph	075	1786	WB-K/142	AR
Madren, Matthias	075	1807	WB-M1/148	AR
Madren, Reuben	075	1798	WB-M1/3	AR
Madren, Richard	075	1755	Orig. Only	SS/AR
Madren, Thomas	075	1796	WB-L/71	AR
Madrey, James	071	1783	WB-1/266	
Maer, Abraham	010	1783	WB-C/56	AR
Maer, Samuel	010	1802	WB-E/146	AR
Mafet, Charles	065	c1782	WB-B/126	AR
Maffoot, David	065	c1778	WB-B/115	AR
Magee, Green	038	c1861	WB-1/190	AR
Magee, Mary	046	1838	WB-B/593	AR
Magee, William R.	071	1875	WB-6/181	AR
Maget, Ann E.	071	1894	WB-7/225	AR
Maget, Samuel	071	1847	WB-5/61	AR
Maget, William	071	1829	WB-4/52	AR
Magette, Everitte E.	071	1873	WB-6/123	AR
Magnenate, Charles L.	030	1866	WB-4/260	AR
Magness, Benjamin	086	1828	WB-D/81	AR
Magness, Jacob	086	1855	WB-E/305	AR
Magoune, William	096	1782	WB-1/119	AR
Mahafey, William	049	c1843	WI-1-2/19	
Mahaffey, John	104	1866	WB-5/427	AR
Mahaffey, Joseph	GA	1854	Copy	065 AR
Mahaffey, Thomas	104	1870	WB-6/24	AR
Mahaffey, William	104	1864	WB-5/391	
Mahaines, Raiford	056	1872	WB-3/73	AR
Mahaly, Susan	085	1895	WB-3/109	CTY
Mahan, Dennis	085	c1804	WB-E/90	AR

Name	Co.	Date	Recorded Copy	Original
Mahan, John E.	016	1830	PQS.5/137	AR
Mahan, Julius	016	1898	WB-4/297	AR
Mahler, Henry	099	1895	WB-C/467	AR
Mahoney, Elizabeth	071	1847	WB-5/57	AR
Mahoney, William	047	1795	WB-3/254	AR
Mailey, Owen	085	1797	WB-E/80	AR
Main, Henry H.	102	1898	WB-A/150	AR
Mainard, John, Sr.	099	1883	WB-A/467	AR
Mainard, William	099	1816	RB-14/248	AR
Mainer, Rebecca E.	087	1888	WB-3/382	AR
Mainor, F. D.	087	1890	WB-3/459	AR
Mainord, George	056	1834	WB-1/499	AR
Mains, Matthew	020	1782	RB-A/189	AR
Mair, Robert F.	090	1900	WB-6/544	AR
Maison, Margret	028	c1769	Orig. Only	AR-Copy
Majett, James	VA	1862	051 WB-C/191	051 AR
Majette, William J.	051	1885	WB-C/334	AR
Major, Thomas	046	c1789	WB-A/234	AR
Major, William	099	1787	RB-2/150	AR
Majors, John, Sr.	090	1802	WB-2/19	AR
Makains, Stephen	028	1805	WB-B/218	
Makee, Daniell	N	1695	Orig. Only	SS/AR
Makepeace, George H.	081	1898	WB-16/514	
Malarkey, Maria	070	1895	WB-G/334	AR
Malbe, George	024	1719	SS 874/164	
Malding, Henrey	057	1800	WB-A/230	AR
Malesson, Elijah	020	1782	WB-1/159	
Maley, Hugh	032	1839	WB-1/327	
Maley, Jesse H.	032	1897	WB-4/330	AR
Maley, Nancy	032	1845	WB-1/456	
Mallard, Asa	035	1861	WB-3/31	AR
Mallard, Charles	070	c1735	SS 877/218	
Mallard, Daniel	057	1831	WB-B/107	AR
Mallard, George	035	1798	WB-A/332	AR
Mallard, James	035	1856	WB-2/100	AR
Mallard, John	057	1853	WB-B/216	AR
Mallard, John	047	1765	WB-3/100	AR
Mallard, John	047	1805	WB-3/443	AR
Mallard, John	035	1812	WB-A/319	AR
Mallard, John	035	1855	WB-2/92	AR
Mallard, Joseph	035	1827	WB-A/327	AR
Mallard, Keziah	057	1858	WB-B/245	AR
Mallard, Lawson	057	1839	WB-B/142	AR
Mallard, Liston Lee	035	1897	WB-4/510	AR
Mallard, Peter	028	1741	Wills.6/L32	
Mallard, Shaderach	057	1838	WB-B/134	AR
Mallard, W. H.	057	1891	WB-C/177	AR
Mallard, William	035	1827	WB-A/294	AR
Mallett, C. deB.	073	1900	WB-I/178	CTY
Mallett, E. S.	029	1899	WB-F/171	AR
Mallett, Lovedy	029	1894	WB-F/19	
Mallett, Lovedy	029	1871	WB-E/31	AR
Mallett, Mary	070	1808	WB-AB/116	AR
Mallett, Peter	029	1805	WB-A/72	AR
Mallett, Peter J.	029	1830	WB-B/189	AR
Mallett, Sally S.	029	1872	WB-E/57	AR
Mallett, Sarah	029	1835	WB-B/257	AR
Mallett, William P.	073	1889	WB-H/481	CTY
Mallison, Christopher	009	1827	OB-A/433	AR
Mallison, Franklin	009	1852	OB-H/80	AR
Mallison, Gidion	053	1809	RW-1/422	AR
Mallison, John	053	1771	RW-1/21	AR
Mallison, Mary	009	1846	OB-F/242	AR
Mallison, Sally	009	1834	OWB/516	AR
Mallison, Thomas	053	1805	RW-1/380	AR
Mallison, William	053	1812	RW-1/457	
Mallory, Charles	044	1849	WB-17/507	CTY
Mallory, Elizabeth	047	1884	WB-6/405	AR
Mallory, Francis	047	1798	WB-3/306	AR
Mallory, Polly	044	1842	WB-15/339	CTY
Mallory, William	044	1836	WB-13/336	CTY
Mallory, William	104	1779	WB-1/20	AR
Malloy, Charles	082	1829	WB-1/314	AR
Malloy, Charles	082	1891	WB-6/425	AR
Malloy, Duncan	083	1871	WB-3/36	AR
Malone, Bartlett Y.	020	1890	WB-B/51	CTY
Malone, Caleb	099	1849	RB-26/540	AR
Malone, Daniel	020	c1826	RB-L/131	AR
Malone, Elizabeth	020	1835	RB-M/464	
Malone, Ellis	039	1877	WB-U/146	AR
Malone, G. W.	078	1884	WB-19/151	AR
Malone, Henry	073	1886	WB-H/404	CTY
Malone, Huldah J.	078	1877	WB-19/72	
Malone, Isham, Sr.	044	1775	WB-1/109	
Malone, James	020	1873	WB-A/127	CTY
Malone, James A.	036	1898	WB-A/463	CTY
Malone, John	073	1896	WB-I/80	CTY
Malone, Lewis	020	1813	RB-F/363	AR
Malone, Lizzie C.	073	1887	WB-H/426	CTY
Malone, Nancey	078	1874	WB-19/36	AR
Malone, Robert	078	1861	WB-18/241	AR
Malone, Robert	071	1791	WB-1/441	AR
Malone, Wood	015	1774	100 WB-1/294	AR
Malpass, Simon	070	1806	WB-AB/97	AR
Mamor (Manor), Gasper	028	c1777	Orig. Only	AR
Man, John	096	1744	Orig. Only	SS/AR
Man, John	071	1757	SS 882/31	SS/AR
Man, Thomas	078	1834	WI-12/24	AR
Man, Thomas	010	1735	LGB-4/#7	SS/AR
Manard, James	099	1827	RB-20/104	AR
Mancreef, Thomas	030	1794	WB-2/24	
Manden, Thomas	010	1736	LGB-4/#45	SS/AR
Mandewell, David	053	c1806	RW-1/415	
Mandewell, Elizabeth	053	1813	RW-1/481	
Mandewell, Mary	053	1810	Orig. Only	AR
Mandewell, Samuel	053	1804	RW-1/364	AR
Mandovell, John	053	1752	028 DB-5/150	SS/AR
Maneas, John E.	068	1896	WB-D/472	
Maner, Aaron	037	1826	WB-F/57	AR
Maner, John	010	1729	Orig. Only	SS/AR
Maner, Penelope	037	1858	Copy	105 AR
Maner, Penelope	037	1858	WB-G/161	AR
Manes, Matthew	020	1782	RB-A/189	
Maness, Amos	005	1852	WB-2/99	AR
Maney, James	071	1752	Orig. Only	SS/AR
Mangram, James	047	1803	WB-3/405	AR
Mangum, Adolphus	073	1890	WB-H/494	CTY
Mangum, Arthur	073	1793	WB-B/100	AR
Mangum, Easley W.	036	1882	WB-A/12	CTY
Mangum, Ellison	073	1865	WB-G/509	AR
Mangum, Henry	047	1819	WB-3/633	AR
Mangum, James	036	1883	WB-A/40	CTY
Mangum, James M.	099	1854	RB-29/129	AR
Mangum, John	047	1794	WB-3/222	AR
Mangum, John	044	1846	WB-16/527	CTY
Mangum, Lucy	099	1896	WB-C/492	AR
Mangum, Nancy	071	1869	WB-6/20	AR
Mangum, Person	078	1866	WB-18/411	AR
Mangum, Reeves	073	1844	WB-F/214	AR
Mangum, Samuel	099	1865	RB-33/350	AR

Name	Co.	Date	Recorded Copy	Original
Mangum, Simpson	044	1845	WB-16/414	CTY
Mangum, T. A.	036	1900	WB-A/498	CTY
Mangum, William	044	1817	WB-8/42	CTY
Mangum, William	044	1848	WB-17/179	CTY
Mangum, William	073	1871	WB-H/57	CTY
Mangum, Willie Person	099	1881	WB-A/319	AR
Mangum, Willy P.	036	1899	WB-A/470	CTY
Maning, Moses	072	1791	Orig. Only	AR
Maning, Richard	069	1794	WB-1/93	AR
Maning, Willibough	069	1806	WB-1/167	AR
Manius, Andrew	085	1847	WB-K/50	AR
Mankins, James	092	1870	WB-6/13	
Manley, James	103	1858	RD-12/616	AR
Manley, Lydia	011	c1809	WB-2/300	
Manly, Aaron	103	1823	RD-5/61	AR
Manly, Basil	022	1824	WB-B/82	AR
Manly, Charles	099	1871	RB-35/134	AR
Manly, Furnifold	103	1856	RD-12/190	AR
Manly, John R.	103	1889	WB-1/472	AR
Manly, Martha D.	020	1889	WB-A/575	CTY
Manly, Matthias	028	1881	WB-E/270	
Manly, Sarah C.	099	1881	WB-A/267	AR
Manly, Sarah L.	028	1898	WB-F/342	
Mann, Ann H.	078	1900	WB-19/497	AR
Mann, Arnold	029	1819	WB-B/19	
Mann, Caroline M.	069	1900	100 WB-51/548	100 AR
Mann, Caroline M.	069	1900	WB-6/89	AR
Mann, Charlotte	071	1886	WB-6/528	AR
Mann, D. F.	089	1877	WB-2/51	AR
Mann, Edward	096	1876	WB-4/32	
Mann, Edward, Sr.	096	1865	WB-3/91	AR
Mann, Elizabeth	089	1883	WB-2/97	AR
Mann, Elizabeth	031	c1895	Orig. Only	AR
Mann, Isham	098	1891	WB-A/134	CTY
Mann, Isham	022	1838	WB-C/86	AR
Mann, James G.	022	1889	WB-E/424	AR
Mann, James N.	069	1853	WB-1/536	AR
Mann, Jane Grant	046	1895	WB-F/405	AR
Mann, John	078	1843	WI-15/227	AR
Mann, John	096	1778	Orig. Only	AR
Mann, John	078	1793	WI-1/68	AR
Mann, John	069	1781	WB-1/16	AR
Mann, John	099	1787	RB-2/129	AR
Mann, Johnathan	089	1891	WB-2/206	AR
Mann, Joseph	075	1783	WB-K/90	AR
Mann, Joseph	096	1770	Orig. Only	AR
Mann, Joseph B.	039	c1860	WB-S/3	AR
Mann, Joseph S.	053	1890	WB-11/226	AR
Mann, Leonard	019	1834	WB-A/40	AR
Mann, Martha	039	1884	WB-U/331	AR
Mann, Martha B.	089	1879	WB-2/63	AR
Mann, Martha M.	038	1895	WB-3/540	AR
Mann, Mary	089	1869	WB-2/2	
Mann, Mary C.	096	1885	WB-4/120	AR
Mann, Mary E.	063	1886	WB-3/286	AR
Mann, Nathan	073	1844	WB-F/215	AR
Mann, Rebecca L.	089	1883	WB-2/101	AR
Mann, Richard	099	1801	RB-5/329	AR
Mann, Roland T.	022	1842	WB-C/125	AR
Mann, Samuel	096	1827	Orig. Only	AR
Mann, Samuel	096	1801	WB-2/4	AR
Mann, Samuel	053	1889	WB-11/219	AR
Mann, Samuel	031	1888	WB-1/52	AR
Mann, Samuel M.	053	1893	WB-11/282	AR
Mann, Solomon	096	c1827	WB-2/101	AR
Mann, Stephen	099	1815	RB-12/11	AR
Mann, Theoderick	071	1825	WB-3/332	AR
Mann, Thomas	053	1894	WB-11/292	AR
Mann, Thomas	022	1830	WB-B/194	AR
Mann, Thomas	096	1767	Orig. Only	AR
Mann, Thomas	096	1802	WB-2/13	AR
Mann, Thomas	053	1805	RW-1/385	AR
Mann, Thomas	069	1792	WB-1/83	AR
Mann, Thomas	071	1792	WB-2/17	AR
Mann, Thomas E.	096	1840	WB-2/151	AR
Mann, Thomas N.	069	1824	WB-1/321	AR
Mann, Wesley	022	1863	WB-D/98	AR
Mann, William	049	c1837	WI-1-2/13	AR
Mann, William	031	1894	WB-1/89	AR
Mann, William	071	1820	WB-3/233	AR
Mann, William	071	1844	WB-4/278	AR
Manney, Caleb	040	1882	WB-2/188	
Manning, Ann G.	063	1825	WB-2/105	
Manning, Barbra	063	1874	WB-3/61	
Manning, Benjamin	010	1785	WB-D/11	AR
Manning, Bettie Ann	069	1892	WB-5/385	AR
Manning, Caroline	047	1889	WB-6/532	AR
Manning, Charles G.	024	1880	WB-E/89	
Manning, Diannie	069	1895	WB-5/501	AR
Manning, Edwin	063	1897	WB-4/207	AR
Manning, James	063	1873	WB-3/53	
Manning, John	073	1899	047 WB-7/211	
Manning, John	073	1899	WB-I/150	CTY
Manning, John A.	063	1881	WB-3/212	
Manning, John A.	079	1890	WB-2/510	AR
Manning, John R.	063	1852	WB-2/379	
Manning, Joseph	024	1836	SC/02653	AR-Copy
Manning, Joseph	024	1836	WB-C/168	AR
Manning, Julia	105	1885	WB-2/341	AR
Manning, Lecey A.	069	1881	WB-5/132	AR
Manning, Levy	069	1795	WB-1/95	AR
Manning, Marcom	063	c1792	WB-1/188	
Manning, Marcum	063	1856	WB-2/420	
Manning, Mary A.	079	1891	WB-2/561	AR
Manning, Mathias	069	1789	WB-1/59	AR
Manning, Mc. E.	051	1880	WB-C/256	AR
Manning, P. B.	070	1900	WB-H/257	AR
Manning, Pencillana	069	1889	WB-5/284	AR
Manning, Pierce	028	1804	WB-B/194	AR
Manning, Reuben	063	1829	WB-2/156	
Manning, Ruben, Sr.	063	c1831	WB-2/174	
Manning, Sally	047	1826	WB-4/19	AR
Manning, Samuel	100	1792	WB-6/101	AR
Manning, Sarah	024	c1840	WB-C/245	AR
Manning, Susannah	099	1825	RB-19/443	AR
Manning, Thomas	037	1823	WB-F/1	AR
Manning, W. D.	063	1866	WB-2/528	
Manning, William	069	c1791	WB-1/248	AR
Manor, John	099	1871	Orig. Only	AR
Manor, William	099	1859	RB-31/258	AR
Manring, Christian	090	1877	WB-6/84	AR
Mansell, Robert	090	1819	WB-3/33	AR
Mansfield, Barney	024	1812	WB-C/6	AR
Mansfield, Riddick	024	1865	WB-D/33	AR
Manship, Elijah	046	1831	WB-B/436	AR
Manson, Darcas	065	1831	WB-G/67	AR
Manson, Stephen D.	065	1839	WB-H/13	AR
Manson, William	065	1824	WB-B/103	AR
Manuel, Gilson	090	1865	WB-5/27	
Manuel, Ishmael	087	1853	WB-1/427	AR

Name	Co.	Date	Recorded Copy	Original
Manuel, John	089	1857	WB-1/168	
Manuel, John	099	1880	WB-A/165	AR
Manuel, Owen	011	1900	WB-3/118	CTY
Maple, Thomas	068	1831	WB-B/78	
Marable, Edward T.	044	1858	WB-20/410	CTY
Marable, Mary S.	044	1861	WB-21//494	CTY
Maran, John	067	1869	WB-2/3	AR
March, Benjamin	085	1832	WB-H/571	AR
March, David	026	1894	WB-2/493	AR
March, Elizabeth	033	1874	WB-2/47	CTY
March, Frederick	086	1806	WB-B/192	AR
March, John	041	1821	WB-2/176	AR
March, Mary	033	1839	WB-1/13	AR
March, Susan E.	032	1896	WB-4/284	AR
March, William	033	c1855	Orig. Only	AR
Marchadant, John	016	1798	WB-A/66	AR
Marchall, Joseph	072	1817	WB-A/95	AR
Marchant, Catherine	030	1797	WB-2/107	
Marchant, Gideon	030	1774	WB-1/94	
Marchant, Gideon C.	030	1861	WB-4/241	
Marchant, Johnson	030	1846	WB-4/120	
Marchant, Malachi	030	1785	WB-1/190	
Marckham, Anthony	002	c1710	Orig. Only	SS/AR
Marcom, Cynthia	099	1900	WB-G/258	AR
Marcom, Elizabeth	099	1847	RB-26/269	AR
Marcom, Isaiah	073	c1863	Orig. Only	AR
Marcom, James T.	099	1886	WB-B/111	AR
Marcom, Sarah	073	1880	WB-H/268	CTY
Marcom, Thomas	073	1839	WB-F/17	AR
Marcom, Thomas	073	1879	WB-H/224	CTY
Marcom, Wesley	099	1869	RB-25/47	AR
Marcom, William	099	1833	RB-22/526	AR
Marcom, William A.	022	1895	WB-F/7	AR
Marcom, Willis	073	1869	WB-H/8	CTY
Marcum, Richard	073	1829	WB-E/205	AR
Marcus, Fanny	070	1873	WB-E/262	AR
Marcus, Jane	022	c1835	WB-C/32	AR
Mardin, Mary Ann	006	1887	WB-E/150	
Mardre, Elizabeth	010	1832	WB-G/218	
Mardre, Elizabeth	010	1877	WB-I/85	
Mardre, George S.	010	1866	WB-H/174	AR
Mardre, James	010	1809	WB-F/108	AR
Mardre, John	077	1850	WB-F/376	AR
Mardre, John, Sr.	077	1832	WB-F/201	AR
Mardre, Joseph	077	1822	WB-F/48	AR
Mardre, Margaret	077	1839	WB-F/284	AR
Mardre, Mary	077	1837	WB-F/257	AR
Mareddy, Obed, Sr.	035	1888	WB-4/320	AR
Maremoon, John	071	1808	WB-3/1	AR
Maremoon, John	071	1785	WB-1/356	AR
Maremoon, Peter	071	1805	WB-2/289	AR
Marine, Zorobabel	072	1868	WB-3/17	AR
Mariner, Elizabeth	063	1879	WB-3/158	
Marion, Adam	092	1890	WB-6/327	AR
Marion, Christina	092	1892	WB-6/346	AR
Marion, Jeremiah	092	1893	WB-6/363	AR
Marion, William	092	1883	WB-6/187	AR
Maris, William	073	1864	WB-G/447	AR
Market, Elizabeth	057	1844	WB-B/168	AR
Markett, Frederick	019	1880	WB-B/115	AR
Markham, Aaron	036	1884	WB-A/57	CTY
Markham, Anthony	075	1761	WB-H/14	AR
Markham, C. G.	036	1891	WB-A/225	CTY
Markham, Charles	075	1810	WB-M1/220	AR
Markham, James C.	075	1893	WB-O/396	AR
Markham, John L.	036	1898	WB-A/438	CTY
Markham, Joshua	075	1747	Orig. Only	SS/AR
Markham, Joshua	075	1798	WB-M1/12	AR
Markham, Levi	075	1744	Orig. Only	SS/AR
Markham, Mary	036	1883	WB-A/47	CTY
Markham, Matthew	073	1862	WB-G/399	CTY
Markham, Thomas	075	1807	WB-M1/145	AR
Markham, Thomas	075	1828	WB-N/47	AR
Markham, Thomas	075	1815	WB-M1/279	AR-Nunc.
Markland, Jonathan	085	c1804	WB-E/50	AR
Markland, Matthew	090	1796	WB-1/81	
Marks, James	092	1772	WB-1/13	AR
Marks, Margaret	022	1848	WB-C/211	AR
Marks, Rebecca A.	065	1880	WB-K/418	AR
Marks, Richard S.	022	1869	WB-E/33	AR
Marks, Susannah	070	1875	WB-E/307	AR
Marks, Thomas E.	065	1864	WB-J/177	AR
Marley, Adam	073	c1789	WB-B/66	AR
Marley, Ann	037	1799	WB-D/88	AR
Marley, Benjamin	022	1815	WB-A/230	AR
Marley, Benjamin	022	1875	WB-E/101	AR
Marley, Francis	087	c1824	WB-A/117	AR
Marley, Jesse	022	c1859	WB-D/50	AR
Marley, N. G. S.	068	1898	WB-D/552	CTY
Marley, Nathan	037	1831	WB-F/124	AR
Marley, Robert	087	1837	WB-A/140	AR
Marlin, James	085	1817	WB-G/492	AR
Marlin, John	085	1847	WB-K/51	AR
Marlin, Mary	085	1869	WB-1/21	CTY
Marlin, Nancy	085	c1803	WB-E/52	AR
Marlin, Samuel	085	1848	WB-K/78	AR
Marlow, Charles	037	1784	WB-B/136	AR
Marlow, E. W.	064	1896	WB-2/368	AR
Marlow, Elijah	054	1842	WB-2/252	AR
Marlow, Elizabeth	105	1898	WB-3/313	
Marlow, James	104	1850	WB-5/37	AR
Marlow, Mark	054	c1818	WB-2/7	AR
Marlow, Mildred	100	1826	WB-30/44	AR
Marlow, P. B.	105	1898	WB-3/286	
Marlow, Thomas	054	c1804	WB-1/285	AR
Marlow, Wily	054	1841	WB-2/230	AR
Maroney, Martha	041	1814	WB-2/93	AR
Maroney, William A.	046	c1786	WB-A/233	AR
Marr, John	099	1821	RB-17/157	AR
Marr, Joseph	028	1745	SS 877/336	SS/AR
Marrett, James, Jr.	028	1848	WB-D/145	
Marrett, John	096	1775	WB-1/90	AR
Marriner, Ann	096	1826	Orig. Only	AR
Marriner, John	096	1772	WB-1/78	AR
Marriner, Robinson	096	c1773	WB-1/86	
Marring, Robert	020	1854	RB-R/168	
Marriott, Benjamin	099	1863	RB-32/615	AR
Marriott, James T.	099	1857	RB-30/258	AR
Marriott, John C.	099	1863	RB-32/614	AR
Marriott, Robert H.	069	1873	WB-1/619	AR
Marrow, Aaron	044	1873	WB-23/88	CTY
Marrow, Alexander	044	1864	WB-22/248	CTY
Marrow, Daniel	044	1817	WB-8/43	CTY
Marrow, Drury S.	044	1864	WB-22/100	CTY
Marrow, Elizabeth	044	1861	WB-21/363	CTY
Marrow, John	098	1894	WB-A/210	CTY
Marrow, Thomas F.	044	1846	SC/05871	AR-Copy
Marrow, Thomas F.	044	1846	WB-17/4	CTY
Mars, Richard	020	c1856	RB-R/500	AR
Marsden, Alice	070	1759	SS 882/23	SS/AR

Name	Co.	Date	Recorded Copy	Original
Marsden, Rufus	070	1751	DB-C/233	AR
Marsden, Thomas	070	c1739	SS 877/126	SS/AR
Marsh, Ann	009	1852	OB-H/126	AR
Marsh, Benjamin	085	1900	WB-3/367	CTY
Marsh, Edmond	081	1779	Orig. Only	AR
Marsh, Edmond	081	1779	Orig. Only	SS/AR
Marsh, Hannah	029	1854	WB-C/294	
Marsh, James	029	1824	WB-B/126	AR
Marsh, James B.	009	1855	OB-I/380	AR
Marsh, Jesse E.	005	1865	WB-C/223	AR
Marsh, John	092	1809	WB-3/90	AR
Marsh, John S.	097	1864	WB-1/238	AR
Marsh, Lucy	022	1868	WB-E/16	AR
Marsh, Lurenda	051	1899	WB-C/561	AR
Marsh, Matilda Smith	009	1874	WB-1/134	AR
Marsh, Nancy E.	009	1882	WB-1/298	CTY
Marsh, Rebecca	081	c1900	Orig. Only	AR
Marsh, Robert	022	1865	WB-D/128	AR
Marsh, Robert	022	c1801	WB-A/59	AR
Marsh, Sarah	081	1873	WB-15/107	AR
Marsh, Sarah R.	065	1900	WB-N/328	AR
Marsh, Simeon	097	1864	WB-1/229	AR
Marsh, Solomon	097	1848	WB-1/51	AR
Marsh, Solomon B.	097	1863	WB-1/210	AR
Marsh, Susan E.	097	1880	WB-2/187	
Marsh, Susan H.	022	1850	WB-C/278	AR
Marsh, Thomas L.	097	1868	WB-2/1	AR
Marsh, William	022	1856	Orig. Only	AR
Marsh, William	092	1855	WB-5/18	AR
Marsh, William T.	079	1863	WB-1/134	AR
Marshal, David	072	1863	Orig. Only	AR
Marshal, William	064	1873	Orig. Only	AR
Marshall, A. J.	028	1899	WB-F/407	
Marshall, Aaron	099	1866	RB-33/488	AR
Marshall, Alexander	047	1886	WB-6/434	AR
Marshall, Allen	047	1810	WB-3/505	AR
Marshall, Amos	090	1845	WB-4/197	AR
Marshall, Benjamin	022	1812	WB-A/196	AR
Marshall, Benjamin	047	1803	WB-3/390	AR
Marshall, Charles	100	1831	WB-33/311	AR
Marshall, Charles	100	1809	WB-15/110	AR
Marshall, Charles	028	1792	WB-A/265	
Marshall, Clement	005	1847	WB-B/222	AR
Marshall, David	024	1766	WB-1/18	AR
Marshall, David	047	1785	WB-3/82	AR
Marshall, Elizabeth	028	1866	WB-D/415	AR
Marshall, F. P.	028	1893	WB-F/74	
Marshall, F. S.	047	1858	WB-5/49	
Marshall, Frederic W.	090	1802	WB-2/15	AR
Marshall, Gabriel	021	1893	WB-3/29	
Marshall, Haly	044	1880	WB-23/383	CTY
Marshall, Henry	038	1892	WB-3/259	AR
Marshall, Henry	089	1866	WB-1/299	
Marshall, Henry	005	1875	WB-D/34	AR
Marshall, Isaac	071	1791	WB-1/431	AR
Marshall, Isaac	054	c1839	WB-2/194	AR
Marshall, Jacob	073	1818	WB-D/533	AR
Marshall, James	090	1893	WB-6/312	AR
Marshall, James	005	1818	WB-2/101	AR
Marshall, James	028	1846	WB-D/127	
Marshall, James	065	1864	WB-J/188	AR
Marshall, Jessee	100	1885	WB-51/189	AR
Marshall, John	099	1820	RB-16/1	AR
Marshall, John	047	1799	WB-3/326	AR
Marshall, John	099	1859	RB-31/305	AR
Marshall, John	037	1758	SS 882/141	SS/AR
Marshall, John	019	1807	WB-D/284	AR
Marshall, John G.	099	1841	RB-24/499	AR
Marshall, John H.	072	1866	WB-3/11	AR
Marshall, John M.	070	1864	WB-D/150	AR
Marshall, Jonathan	022	1887	WB-E/366	AR
Marshall, Joseph	036	1888	WB-A/117	CTY
Marshall, Joseph	092	1805	WB-3/68	AR
Marshall, Joseph	089	1884	WB-2/120	AR
Marshall, Lucy	100	1853	WB-42/238	AR
Marshall, Lucy T.	038	1887	WB-3/26	AR
Marshall, Margaret	065	1896	WB-M/516	AR
Marshall, Martha M.	047	1866	WB-5/143	
Marshall, Martin	090	1824	WB-3/128	AR
Marshall, Mary	070	1867	WB-D/234	AR
Marshall, Mary	028	1823	WB-C/232	AR
Marshall, Mary	054	1850	WB-3/38	AR
Marshall, Nancy Jane	001	1900	WB-3/349	AR
Marshall, Rachel	089	c1850	WB-1/129	
Marshall, Rebecca	047	1803	Copy	099 AR
Marshall, Rebeccah	047	1803	WB-3/416	AR
Marshall, Sarah	100	1821	WB-23/221	AR
Marshall, Sarah J.	028	1893	WB-F/77	
Marshall, Starling	047	1803	WB-3/395	AR
Marshall, Starling	047	1803	Copy	099 AR
Marshall, Stephen	100	1833	WB-34/54	AR
Marshall, Tabitha	100	1822	WB-23/310	AR
Marshall, Thomas	085	1811	WB-G/201	AR
Marshall, Thomas	019	1867	WB-B/30	AR
Marshall, Thomas	047	1782	WB-3/32	AR
Marshall, Washington	036	1893	WB-A/274	CTY
Marshall, William	038	1889	WB-3/122	AR
Marshall, William	070	1857	WB-C/647	AR
Marshall, William	065	1884	WB-L/15	AR
Marshall, William	005	1830	WB-B/6	AR
Marshall, William	010	1739	Orig. Only	SS/AR
Marshall, William P.	019	1866	WB-A/287	AR
Marshall, William S.	078	1878	WB-19/80	AR
Marshall, William S.	038	1850	WB-1/19	AR
Marshborn, Henry	072	1801	WB-A/91	AR
Marshborn, William	099	1885	WB-B/92	AR
Marshburn, Daniel H.	011	1874	WB-2/75	
Marshburn, Obed	001	1900	WB-3/313	AR
Marshill, John	085	1812	WB-G/234	AR
Marshill, John	022	1815	WB-A/244	AR
Marshill, John	022	1787	RB-1/31	AR
Marshill, William	073	1824	WB-E/60	AR
Marshill, William	022	1803	WB-A/80	AR
Marsilliott, Peter	084	1829	WB-A/333	CTY
Marston, Elizabeth	008	1733	SS 876/274	SS/AR
Marten, Joel	008	1716	009 DB-1/269	
Marten, William	010	1736	LGB-4/#55	SS/AR
Martenleer, John	029	1775	Orig. Only	AR
Martin, Aaron	103	1795	WI-A/555	AR
Martin, Aaron	106	1897	WB-2/411	
Martin, Abel	041	c1778	Orig. Only	AR
Martin, Abigail	084	1839	WB-B/220	CTY
Martin, Abraham	090	1815	WB-2/173	
Martin, Abram	090	1900	WB-6/532	AR
Martin, Alexander	084	1807	WB-A/44	
Martin, Allen	068	1816	WB-A/292	
Martin, Ambrose	047	1777	WB-2/38	
Martin, Andrew	084	1856	WB-C/228	CTY
Martin, Andrew	084	c1792	OW/150	AR
Martin, Andrew	084	1805	WB-A/21	CTY

Name	Co.	Date	Recorded Copy	Original
Martin, Angus	067	1863	WB-1/102	AR
Martin, Angus	067	1877	WB-2/88	AR
Martin, Angus	067	1862	WB-1/94	
Martin, Asa	085	c1805	WB-E/49	AR
Martin, Augustus	104	1866	WB-5/455	AR
Martin, Barnabas	017	1887	WB-B/150	AR
Martin, Benjamin	033	1839	WB-1/18	AR
Martin, Benjamin	104	1810	WB-2/280 & 290	AR
Martin, Benjamin	104	1821	WB-4/12	AR
Martin, Benjamin	053	1783	RW-1/112	
Martin, Betheny	103	1898	WB-2/228	AR
Martin, Charles	065	1772	WB-B/47	AR
Martin, Clementine	022	1799	WB-A/16	AR
Martin, Crisp	063	1865	WB-2/536	
Martin, Daniel	009	1886	WB-1/383	CTY
Martin, Daniel	082	1833	WB-2/35	AR
Martin, Daniel	067	1886	WB-2/232	AR
Martin, Daniel W.	053	1830	WB-5/30	AR
Martin, David	084	c1815	WB-A/249	CTY
Martin, David M.	035	1899	WB-4/538	
Martin, Edward B.	005	1824	WB-A/110	AR
Martin, Edwin	009	1880	WB-1/267	
Martin, Elias	071	1859	WB-5/219	AR
Martin, Elizabeth	040	1865	WB-1/163	AR
Martin, Elizabeth	077	1900	070 WB-H/337	
Martin, Elizabeth	087	1871	Orig. Only	AR-Nunc.
Martin, Elizabeth	028	c1767	Orig. Only	SS/AR
Martin, Ellener	065	1825	WB-B/105	AR
Martin, Elvira	104	1863	WB-5/360	
Martin, Emory A.	071	1878	WB-6/255	AR
Martin, Etheldred	071	1822	WB-3/265	AR
Martin, Flora	082	1887	WB-6/349	AR
Martin, George	022	1807	WB-A/54	AR
Martin, George	099	1808	RB-8/136	AR
Martin, George	024	1734	SS 876/288	SS/AR
Martin, George W.	020	1872	Orig. Only	CTY
Martin, Gibson	015	1775	100 WB-2/45	AR
Martin, Harriet	065	1892	WB-M/57	AR
Martin, Henderson	103	1877	WB-1/117	AR
Martin, Henderson	071	1856	WB-5/150	AR
Martin, Henry	073	1815	WB-D/431	AR
Martin, Henry D.	100	1879	WB-51/143	AR
Martin, Hetty	013	1898	WB-D/132	AR
Martin, Isaac	104	1858	WB-5/190	
Martin, Isaac	104	1798	WB-1/490	AR
Martin, Isabell	084	1820	WB-A/243	CTY
Martin, J. J.	071	1892	WB-7/169	AR
Martin, Jacob	013	1845	WB-A/104	
Martin, James	038	1871	WB-2/65	AR
Martin, James	046	1796	WB-A/231	AR
Martin, James	090	1834	WB-3/279	AR
Martin, James	040	c1851	WB-1/38	
Martin, James	104	1846	WB-4/320	
Martin, James	100	1785	WB-4/125	AR
Martin, James	084	1804	WB-A/2	CTY
Martin, James	084	c1799	OW/151	AR
Martin, James	016	c1825	WB-A/18	AR
Martin, James	065	1810	WB-B/88	AR
Martin, James	099	1778	RB-1/133	AR
Martin, James	022	1826	WB-B/116	AR
Martin, James	047	1788	WB-3/146	AR-Nunc.
Martin, James	085	1846	WB-K/26	AR
Martin, James	047	1764	WB-1/121	
Martin, James	104	1865	WB-5/417	
Martin, James	065	1787	WB-B/129	AR
Martin, James C.	046	1840	WB-C/51	AR
Martin, James C.	028	1841	WB-D/40	
Martin, James H.	005	c1832	SC/04047	AR-Copy
Martin, James H.	005	1836	WB-B/63	AR
Martin, Jemima	022	1871	WB-E/68	AR
Martin, Jesse	103	1862	RD-13/462	AR
Martin, Joell	008	1716	SS 875/131	SS/AR
Martin, John	075	1741/2	LGB-4/#157	SS/AR
Martin, John	047	1771	WB-1/280	
Martin, John	039	c1794	WB-A/115	AR
Martin, John	084	1837	WB-B/170	CTY
Martin, John	082	1820	WB-1/210	AR
Martin, John	026	1854	WB-1/174	AR
Martin, John	026	1856	WB-1/206	AR
Martin, John	068	1824	WB-B/34	
Martin, John	090	1895	WB-6/364	AR
Martin, John	099	1795	RB-3/94	
Martin, John	065	1828	WB-B/105	AR
Martin, John	090	c1821	WB-3/80	AR-Copy
Martin, John	104	1810	WB-2/296	AR
Martin, John	028	1785	WB-A/104	AR
Martin, John	028	1836	WB-C/386	
Martin, John	092	1844	WB-4/221	
Martin, John	010	1819	WB-G/57	AR
Martin, John	039	1805	WB-C/20	
Martin, John A.	071	1884	WB-6/445	AR
Martin, John P.	082	1863	WB-4/160	
Martin, John S.	087	1900	WB-4/122	AR
Martin, John W.	006	1877	WB-E/28	AR
Martin, John, Sr.	092	c1831	WB-4/103	
Martin, John, Sr.	090	1829	WB-3/197	
Martin, Jordon	078	1900	WB-19/487	AR
Martin, Joseph	005	c1787	WB-1/56	
Martin, Joseph	044	1795	WB-3/199	CTY
Martin, Joseph	028	1866	WB-D/417	AR
Martin, Joseph	075	1817	WB-M1/308	AR
Martin, Joseph	103	1835	RD-7/106	AR
Martin, Joseph B.	073	1898	WB-I/131	CTY
Martin, Joseph D.	003	1888	WB-B/234	AR
Martin, Joshua	046	1828	WB-B/375	AR
Martin, Louisa E.	022	1890	WB-E/437	AR
Martin, Lucy	071	1816	WB-3/183	AR
Martin, Lydia	084	1841	WB-B/254	CTY
Martin, Margaret	029	1880	WB-E/224	AR
Martin, Martha	090	c1857	WB-4/347	AR
Martin, Martha	104	1836	WB-4/206	AR
Martin, Martha	016	1850	WB-1/171	AR
Martin, Martha	060	1830	WB-1/192	AR
Martin, Martin	068	c1830	WB-B/136	
Martin, Mary	009	1826	OB-A/360	AR
Martin, Mary	104	1857	WB-5/161	
Martin, Mary	090	1846	WB-4/227	AR
Martin, Mary	084	1860	WB-C/334	CTY
Martin, Mary H.	019	1891	AR	
Martin, Mathew	099	1896	WB-C/533	AR
Martin, Moses	090	1793	WB-1/37	
Martin, Nancy	009	c1809	OB-A/44	AR
Martin, Nathan G.	104	1863	WB-5/359	
Martin, Nathaniel	075	1743	Orig. Only	SS/AR
Martin, Obediah	092	1826	WB-3/168	AR
Martin, P. W.	063	1879	WB-3/175	
Martin, Patrick	047	1803	WB-3/416	AR
Martin, Patrick H.	047	1810	WB-3/491	AR
Martin, Peter	071	1874	WB-6/154	AR

Name	Co.	Date	Recorded Copy	Original
Martin, Pleasant	084	1865	Orig. Only	CTY
Martin, Rachel	015	1777	100 WB-2/130	AR
Martin, Reuben	026	1858	WB-1/223	AR
Martin, Richard	020	c1841	RB-0/317	AR
Martin, Richard	087	c1810	WB-A/61	AR
Martin, Richard	016	1856	WB-1/287	AR
Martin, Richard	103	1786	WI-A/232	
Martin, Richard	090	1895	Orig. Only	AR
Martin, Robert	020	1837	RB-N/115	AR
Martin, Robert	104	1842	WB-4/279	AR
Martin, Robert	084	1848	WB-C/69	CTY
Martin, Robert	025	1877	WB-A/33	AR
Martin, Robert	084	1822	WB-A/240	CTY
Martin, Robert	090	1898	WB-6/471	AR
Martin, Robert	060	1823	Orig. Only	AR
Martin, Robert	071	c1776	Orig. Only	AR-Copy
Martin, Robert C.	104	1850	WB-5/30	AR
Martin, Robert G.	003	1877	WB-B/81	AR
Martin, Rothias	053	1818	RW-1/516	
Martin, Sallie J.	019	1889	WB-B/187	AR
Martin, Samuel	046	1900	WB-G/175	AR
Martin, Samuel	104	1887	WB-6/295	AR
Martin, Samuel	081	1826	WB-5/297	AR
Martin, Sarah	071	1866	WB-5/324	AR
Martin, Sarah	084	1845	WB-C/20	CTY
Martin, Sarah	104	1793	WB-1/361	AR
Martin, Sarah E.	100	1893	WB-51/367	
Martin, Silas N.	070	1877	WB-E/327	AR
Martin, Simon H.	106	c1854	WB-1/25	AR
Martin, Stevenson	071	1858	WB-5/202	AR
Martin, Susan	053	1846	WB-7/73	AR
Martin, Susannah	060	1829	WB-1/141	AR
Martin, Tennessee	073	c1860	Orig. Only	AR
Martin, Thomas	092	1869	WB-6/3	
Martin, Thomas	026	1854	WB-1/173	AR
Martin, Thomas	065	1796	Orig. Only	AR
Martin, Thomas	071	1829	WB-4/57	AR
Martin, Thomas	010	1780	WB-B/147	AR
Martin, Thomas	063	1789	WB-1/147	
Martin, Thomas	028	1766	Orig. Only	AR
Martin, Thomas	028	1758	Orig. Only	SS/AR
Martin, Thomas	047	1760	WB-1/2	
Martin, Thomas	090	1894	WB-6/325	AR
Martin, Thomas D.	099	1900	WB-D/416	AR
Martin, Thomas D.	075	1821	WB-M1/338	AR
Martin, Unicy	026	1877	WB-2/161	AR
Martin, W. A.	046	1892	WB-F/237	AR
Martin, W. J.	065	1896	WB-M/440	AR
Martin, Walter	084	1817	WB-A/245	CTY
Martin, Walter	084	1792	OW/278a	AR-Nunc.
Martin, William	022	1818	WB-A/302	AR
Martin, William	092	c1809	Orig. Only	AR
Martin, William	047	1788	WB-3/147	AR
Martin, William	099	1811	RB-10/157	AR
Martin, William	090	1808	WB-2/89	AR
Martin, William	009	c1769	Orig. Only	SS/AR
Martin, William	068	1819	WB-B/1	
Martin, William	005	1793	WB-A/19	AR
Martin, William	014	1899	WB-3/84	CTY
Martin, William	090	1812	WB-2/135	AR
Martin, William	018	1897	WB-E/276	AR
Martin, William	053	1744	Orig. Only	SS/AR
Martin, William	047	1800	WB-3/346	AR
Martin, William	075	1834	WB-N/102	AR
Martin, William	009	1745	SS 878/114	SS/AR

Name	Co.	Date	Recorded Copy	Original
Martin, William C.	092	c1836	Orig. Only	AR
Martin, William F.	100	1851	WB-41/187	AR
Martin, William F.	075	1880	WB-0/121	AR
Martin, William H.	063	c1822	WB-2/87	
Martin, William K.	039	1892	WB-U/544	AR
Martin, William M.	006	1887	WB-E/148	AR
Martin, William T.	009	1817	OB-A/278	AR
Martin, William W.	104	1824	WB-4/49	AR
Martin, Zaccheus	071	1831	WB-4/78	AR
Martin, Zachariah	022	1808	WB-A/103	AR
Martindale, Henry	070	1874	WB-E/266	AR
Martindale, John	070	1753	DB-D/49	AR
Martindale, Susanah	070	1762	DB-E/16	AR
Martine, Hester	029	1868	WB-D/100	AR
Marvis, John	046	1818	WB-B/55	AR
Mase, Francis	075	1749	Orig. Only	SS/AR
Mase, Polly	085	1846	WB-K/42	AR
Masey, Sally	022	1844	WB-C/167	AR
Mash, James	006	1894	WB-E/273	AR
Mash, William	006	1886	WB-E/138	AR
Mashbern, James	057	1817	WB-B/41	AR
Mashborn, Joseph	072	1869	WB-4/26	AR
Mashborne, Jethro	072	1753	Orig. Only	SS/AR
Mashborne, Joseph	072	1816	WB-2/48	AR
Mashborne, Mathew	071	1761	WB-1/40	
Mashburn, Benjamin	072	c1824	Orig. Only	AR
Mashburn, Benjamin	070	1815	WB-AB/214	AR
Mashburn, Daniel	072	c1783	RW/L59	AR
Mashburn, James	035	1840	Orig. Only	AR
Mashburn, James	072	1841	WB-2/38	AR
Mashburn, John	064	1861	WB-1/76	AR
Mashburn, Seney	072	1847	WB-2/83	AR
Mashburn, Tamer	072	1824	WB-A/89	AR
Mashburn, Thomas	072	1827	WB-1/8	
Masimore, John	085	c1804	WB-E/98	AR
Mask, John	082	1813	WB-1/164	AR
Mask, John	082	1781	WB-1/6	AR
Mask, John M.	067	1887	WB-2/246	AR
Mask, Lucy	082	1814	WB-1/166	AR
Mask, Pleasant	082	1829	WB-1/317	AR
Mask, Rebecca	067	c1860	Orig. Only	AR
Maske, Miles W.	005	1871	WB-D/16	AR
Maskil, William	028	1753	SS 877/80	SS/AR
Mason, Abraham	046	c1814	WB-A/244	AR
Mason, Adam	073	1763	WB-A/25	
Mason, Agness	053	1803	RW-1/363	AR
Mason, Alexander	028	1859	WB-D/313	AR
Mason, Armsted	044	c1851	Orig. Only	CTY
Mason, Ausbond Foy	053	1841	WB-6/135	AR
Mason, Ausbond Foy	053	1841	SC/08536	AR-Copy
Mason, Benjamin	028	1805	WB-B/223	
Mason, Benjamin	053	1772	RW-1/30	AR
Mason, Benjamin	053	1871	WB-11/23	AR
Mason, Caleb	070	1771	WB-C/253	AR
Mason, Caroline	049	1891	WB-2/272	AR
Mason, Catherine	033	1900	WB-2/245	CTY
Mason, Charles	065	1774	WB-B/48	AR
Mason, Dorothy	029	1852	WB-C/353	AR
Mason, Eleanor P.	019	1874	WB-B/80	AR
Mason, Elizabeth	047	1784	WB-3/70	AR
Mason, Elizabeth	065	1847	WB-I/83	AR
Mason, Elizabeth	022	1883	WB-E/272	AR
Mason, Elizabeth	069	1812	WB-1/244A	AR
Mason, Foster	029	1843	WB-C/35	AR
Mason, Francis	028	1858	WB-D/307	AR

Name	Co.	Date	Recorded Copy	Original
Mason, Francis	100	1824	WB-26/178	AR
Mason, Francis	028	1858	Copy	019 AR
Mason, G. G.	033	c1895	WB-2/169	CTY
Mason, Henry	071	1784	WB-1/343	AR
Mason, Henry	Sco	1841	047 WB-4/205	047 AR
Mason, Henry	075	1793	WB-L/9	AR
Mason, Hosea B.	030	1895	WB-5/308	
Mason, Isaac	065	1897	WB-M/574	AR
Mason, Isaac	082	1862	WB-4/154	AR
Mason, Isaac	082	1877	WB-6/147	AR
Mason, J. P.	033	1886	WB-2/90	CTY
Mason, James	065	1824	WB-B/102	AR
Mason, James	025	1900	WB-A/264	AR
Mason, James P.	073	1894	WB-I/36	CTY
Mason, James, Jr.	053	c1811	RW-1/517	AR
Mason, James, Sr.	053	1830	Orig. Only	AR
Mason, Jemimah	071	1807	WB-2/344	AR
Mason, John	053	1752	028 DB-5/233	SS/AR
Mason, John	072	1815	WB-A/87	AR
Mason, John	053	1824	Orig. Only	AR
Mason, John	030	1720/1	Orig. Only	SS/AR
Mason, John	028	1748	SS 877/57	SS/AR
Mason, John G.	079	1893	WB-3/38	AR
Mason, John, Sr.	053	1791	RW-1/216	AR
Mason, John, Sr.	053	1741	LGB-4/#155	SS/AR
Mason, Lavinia T.	NJ	1894	013 WB-C/501	013 AR
Mason, Littleton	071	1840	WB-4/214	AR
Mason, Littleton	028	1877	WB-E/168	
Mason, Malichi	053	1800	RW-1/319	AR
Mason, Maneau W.	019	1883	WB-B/144	AR
Mason, Margaret	072	c1823	WB-A/86	AR
Mason, Mark	069	1793	WB-1/86	AR
Mason, Mary	070	1772	Orig. Only	SS/AR
Mason, Mary	053	1806	RW-1/401	AR
Mason, Mary	065	1898	WB-N/157	AR
Mason, Mary A.	099	1881	WB-A/293	AR
Mason, Mary E.	073	1894	WB-I/38	CTY
Mason, Mary M.	054	1881	WB-4/446	CTY
Mason, Matthew	019	1862	WB-A/259	AR
Mason, Milas	033	1864	WB-1/181	
Mason, Moses	028	1887	WB-E/428 & 437	AR
Mason, Nancy J.	085	1877	WB-1/378	CTY
Mason, P. R.	082	1899	WB-7/39	AR
Mason, Polly	072	1860	WB-2/181	AR
Mason, Prudence	078	1853	WB-17/177	
Mason, R. P.	033	1890	WB-2/110	CTY
Mason, Richard	065	1800	WB-B/81	
Mason, Richard	072	1802	Orig. Only	AR
Mason, Richard S.	099	1874	RB-35/254	AR
Mason, Rocksalana	053	1829	WB-4/610	AR
Mason, Roger, Jr.	053	1752	SS 878/90	SS/AR
Mason, Roger, Sr.	053	1756	SS 880/39	SS/AR
Mason, Salley	030	1774	WB-1/80	
Mason, Samuel	053	1795	RW-1/265	AR
Mason, Sarah	070	1850	WB-C/509	AR
Mason, Thomas	047	1807	WB-3/461	AR
Mason, Thomas	053	1767	Orig. Only	AR
Mason, Thomas	060	1824	WB-1/2	AR
Mason, Thomas	053	1811	RW-1/449	AR
Mason, Vicey	099	1856	RB-29/558	AR
Mason, William	019	1895	WB-B/280	AR
Mason, William	022	1842	WB-C/135	AR
Maspern, Salley	056	1842	WB-1/542	AR
Massalon, Mary E.	070	1855	WB-C/603	AR

Name	Co.	Date	Recorded Copy	Original
Massenburg, A. C.	039	1864	WB-R/795	AR
Massenburg, Cargill	099	1809	RB-9/130	AR
Massenburg, Lucie C.	039	1896	WB-V/98	AR
Massenburg, Lucy H.	039	1896	WB-V/107	AR
Massenburg, Mary A.	099	1889	WB-B/306	AR
Massengale, Massa	069	1815	WB-1/265	AR
Massengill, Aaron, Sr.	056	1850	WB-1/637	AR
Massengill, Walker	069	1816	WB-1/281	AR
Masset, Hezekiah	100	1792	WB-6/113	AR
Massey, Abijah	073	1798	Orig. Only	AR
Massey, Abner	073	1841	WB-F/83	AR
Massey, Abraham	073	1799	WB-D/132	AR
Massey, Adkins	096	c1806	WB-2/3	
Massey, Benjamin	060	1816	Orig. Only	AR
Massey, Drury	029	1843	WB-C/42	AR-Copy
Massey, Ebenezer	054	1876	WB-4/67	AR
Massey, Fredrick	096	1818	WB-2/81	
Massey, Hardy	036	1885	WB-A/68	CTY
Massey, Henry	SC	1836	065 WB-E/165	065 AR
Massey, Hesekiah	099	1826	RB-20/125	AR
Massey, Hezekiah	039	c1791	WB-A/87	
Massey, Hezekiah	010	1727	SS 876/128	SS/AR
Massey, James	022	1818	WB-A/291	AR
Massey, John	049	c1819	WI-1-2/7	AR
Massey, John	060	1788	Orig. Only	AR
Massey, John	056	1899	WB-4/157	AR
Massey, John L.	005	1864	WB-C/201	AR
Massey, John, Sr.	015	1777	100 WB-2/124	AR
Massey, Levina	049	1894	WB-2/304	AR
Massey, Lucy	099	1855	RB-28/330	AR
Massey, Mary E.	SC	1891	097 WB-2/450	097 AR
Massey, Nathan	084	c1849	WB-C/134	CTY
Massey, Nathan J.	084	1860	WB-C/322	CTY
Massey, Patrick T.	056	1900	WB-4/217	AR
Massey, Patsey	099	1848	RB-26/364	AR
Massey, Peleg	056	1870	WB-3/31	AR
Massey, Pettepool	039	c1794	WB-B/13	AR
Massey, Pleasant C.	020	1885	WB-A/449	CTY
Massey, Ralph	056	1836	WB-2/264	AR
Massey, Richard	099	1803	RB-6/89	AR
Massey, Richard	099	1812	RB-10/167	AR
Massey, Richard	039	1815	WB-D/170	AR
Massey, Sallie	054	1894	WB-5/524	CTY
Massey, Tents	073	1795	WB-C/67	AR
Massey, Thomas	084	1817	WB-A/258	CTY
Massey, William	039	1814	WB-D/105	AR
Massey, William	020	1848	RB-P/523	
Massey, William	056	1845	WB-1/575	AR
Massey, William	056	1880	WB-3/246	AR
Massey, William	056	1891	WB-3/569	AR
Massey, Zilpha	099	1824	RB-18/345	AR
Massie, Drewry W.	029	1851	WB-C/207	
Massie, William H.	020	1890	WB-B/34	CTY
Massingae, Joseph	011	c1804	WB-1/427	
Massingail, George	056	1807	Orig. Only	AR
Massingale, Abraham	071	1793	WB-2/28	AR
Massingale, Kessiah	069	1853	WB-1/535	AR
Massingill, Henry	056	1827	WB-1/327	AR
Masson, Nancy	073	1817	WB-D/500	AR
Massy, Villiers T.	009	1881	WB-1/290	CTY
Mast, John A.	102	1896	WB-A/120	
Masten, Antoinette	038	1900	WB-4/220	AR
Masten, James	104	1895	WB-6/546	AR
Masten, John	038	1885	WB-2/549	AR
Masten, John, Sr.	090	1829	WB-3/197	AR

Name	Co.	Date	Recorded Copy	Original
Masten, Joseph	038	1876	WB-2/289	AR
Masten, Mathias	038	1873	WB-2/135	AR
Masten, Thomas	104	1830	WB-4/143	AR
Masten, William	038	c1860	WB-1/167	AR
Masten, William	054	1878	WB-4/288	CTY
Masters, Enoch	028	1849	Orig. Only	AR
Masters, James	028	1852	WB-D/197	
Masters, James	092	c1837	Orig. Only	AR
Masters, John	028	1773	Orig. Only	SS/AR
Masters, Joseph	028	1799	WB-B/82	
Masters, Joseph	028	1760	Orig. Only	SS/AR
Masters, Joseph	092	1781	WB-1/152	AR
Masters, Sarah	028	1854	WB-D/237	
Masters, Thomas	028	1749	Orig. Only	SS/AR
Masters, William	092	1793	WB-3/11A	
Mastin, Thomas	104	1829	WB-4/126	AR
Mastin, Thomas J.	104	1896	WB-7/292	
Matchet, John	035	1774	WB-A/324	AR
Matchet, Sarah	035	1790	WB-A/308	AR
Mateer, Andrew	084	1860	WB-C/312	CTY
Mateer, James	084	1845	WB-C/27	CTY
Mateer, John	084	1854	WB-C/195	CTY
Matham, Ralph	030	1750	Orig. Only	SS/AR
Matheny, John	026	1888	WB-2/338	AR
Mathers, Edward	028	c1753	Orig. Only	SS/AR
Matherson, John H.	037	1868	079 WB-2/4	079 AR
Mathes, Josiah	069	1861	WB-1/574	AR
Matheson, Alexander	054	c1818	WB-2/4	AR
Mathew, Andrew	033	1857	WB-1/158	AR
Mathews, Alexander	083	1836	WB-1/298	AR
Mathews, Allen	079	c1853	WB-2/163	AR
Mathews, Charity	096	1772	Orig. Only	SS/AR
Mathews, Frederick	075	1847	WB-N/211	AR
Mathews, Frederick	099	1867	RB-34/330	AR
Mathews, George W.	014	c1863	WB-1/4	AR
Mathews, Gideon	047	1815	WB-3/567	AR
Mathews, Hugh	068	c1878	WB-D/268	
Mathews, Jacob	035	1852	WB-2/74	AR
Mathews, Jacob O.	010	1887	WB-I/227	AR
Mathews, James	063	1777	WB-1/44	
Mathews, James	035	1822	WB-A/304	AR
Mathews, James	VA	1857	038 WB-1/146	038 AR
Mathews, James	047	1775	WB-2/1	
Mathews, Jane	054	c1863	Orig. Only	AR
Mathews, Jarrett	012	1898	WB-A/135	AR
Mathews, Jennett	048	1896	WB-1/53	
Mathews, Joel	087	c1821	WB-1/33	
Mathews, Joel	069	1882	WB-5/150	AR
Mathews, John	065	1835	WB-G/221	AR
Mathews, Luke	063	1831	WB-2/172	
Mathews, Molly	075	1837	WB-N/141	AR
Mathews, Redmond	099	1796	RB-3/214	AR
Mathews, Richmond	063	1887	WB-4/7	AR
Mathews, Samuel	075	1845	WB-N/190	AR
Mathews, Thomas	022	1785	RB-1/20	AR
Mathews, Thomas	024	1732	SS 876/233	SS/AR
Mathews, Thomas C.	075	1835	WB-N/113	AR
Mathews, William	046	1844	WB-C/210	AR
Mathews, William	104	1834	WB-4/174	AR
Mathews, William	047	1812	WB-3/535	AR
Mathews, William A.	063	1864	WB-2/518	
Mathewson, Nathan	037	1832	WB-F/133	AR
Mathewson, Sarah M.	037	1866	WB-G/274	AR
Mathias, Chloe	030	1822	WB-3/133	
Mathias, Elizabeth	030	1832	WB-3/314	
Mathias, Isaiah	077	c1780	Orig. Only	AR
Mathias, John	041	1819	WB-2/154	AR
Mathias, John	077	1748	Orig. Only	SS/AR
Mathias, John	030	1872	WB-5/24	
Mathias, Mathew	030	1795	WB-2/43	
Mathias, Olive	030	1882	WB-5/84	AR
Mathias, William	041	1799	WB-1/161	AR
Mathis, Allen	026	1844	WB-1/23	AR
Mathis, Clyborn	022	1806	WB-A/98	AR
Mathis, Coleman	082	1865	WB-4/177	AR
Mathis, Elizabeth	035	1899	WB-4/530	AR
Mathis, Frederick	087	1890	WB-3/456	AR
Mathis, Isaac	047	1768	WB-1/225	
Mathis, Jesse	064	1869	WB-2/22	AR
Mathis, Joel	087	c1821	WB-A/107	AR
Mathis, John	086	1830	WB-D/119	AR
Mathis, Mary	087	1864	WB-2/80	AR
Mathis, Rebeca	086	1860	WB-E/375	AR
Mathis, Thomas	047	1765	WB-1/156	
Mathus, David	038	1849	WB-1/7	AR
Matkins, William	001	1859	WB-1/159	
Matlock, Charlotte	084	1896	WB-F/73	CTY
Matlock, John	020	1900	WB-B/385	CTY
Matlock, Nicholas	020	1824	RB-I/329	
Matlock, William	001	1873	WB-2/37	AR
Mattherson, Clifton	047	1896	WB-7/175	AR
Matthews, Amos	029	1837	WB-B/276	AR
Matthews, Amos	029	1853	WB-C/274	AR
Matthews, Andrew	041	1823	WB-2/194	AR
Matthews, Anne	047	1806	WB-3/459	AR
Matthews, Arnette	079	1882	WB-2/247	AR
Matthews, Caleb H.	090	1885	WB-6/159	AR
Matthews, Caswell D.	069	1895	WB-5/508	AR
Matthews, D. L.	048	1897	WB-1/62	CTY
Matthews, Daniel	083	c1822	WB-1/360	AR
Matthews, Eliza M.	029	1851	WB-C/190	AR
Matthews, Elizabeth	065	1862	WB-J/145	AR
Matthews, Frank M.	084	1894	WB-E/567	CTY
Matthews, Hardy	029	1842	WB-B/375	AR
Matthews, Harmon	063	1892	WB-4/84	AR
Matthews, Harmon	079	1888	WB-2/435	AR
Matthews, Isaac	097	1854	WB-1/97	AR
Matthews, Isham	047	1847	WB-4/259	AR
Matthews, Israel	099	1864	RB-33/171	AR
Matthews, J. D.	069	1875	WB-5/46	AR
Matthews, Jacob	068	1855	WB-C/39	
Matthews, James	106	c1850	WB-1/5	AR
Matthews, James	090	1806	WB-2/70	AR
Matthews, James R.	069	1897	WB-6/7	AR
Matthews, Jethro P.	010	1882	WB-I/141	
Matthews, John	060	1816	Orig. Only	AR
Matthews, John	041	1836	WB-2/378	AR
Matthews, John E.	069	1885	WB-5/227	AR
Matthews, John G.	069	1898	WB-6/42	AR
Matthews, John W.	041	1833	WB-2/323	AR
Matthews, Joseph	029	1791	Orig. Only	AR
Matthews, Lucy R.	069	1896	WB-5/546	AR
Matthews, Mary	047	1819	WB-3/634	AR
Matthews, Mary	105	N. D.	WB-4/28	
Matthews, Mary	069	1891	WB-5/364	AR
Matthews, Mary E.	069	c1884	WB-5/316	AR
Matthews, Mary S.	090	1861	WB-4/350	AR
Matthews, Messendine	054	c1825	WB-2/97	AR
Matthews, Moses	047	1815	WB-3/562	AR
Matthews, Noel	105	1894	WB-3/117	AR

Name	Co.	Date	Recorded Copy	Original
Matthews, Robert	054	c1819	WB-2/88	AR
Matthews, Ross	047	1782	WB-3/30	AR
Matthews, Sallie	069	1888	WB-5/300	AR
Matthews, Simon	029	1853	WB-C/266	AR
Matthews, Stephen	104	1812	WB-3/19	
Matthews, Tandy	090	1842	Orig. Only	AR-Nunc.
Matthews, Thomas	048	1893	WB-1/27	CTY
Matthews, Thomas	071	1770	WB-1/177	
Matthews, Vines	020	1807	RB-E/296	AR
Matthews, William	065	1832	WB-G/90	AR
Matthews, William	081	1813	WB-4/44	AR
Matthews, William A.	041	1846	WB-3/72	AR
Matthews, William H.	069	1865	WB-1/590	AR
Matthews, William H.	038	1864	WB-1/243	AR
Matthias, Burroughs	030	1819	WB-3/109	
Matthias, Simon	030	c1815	WB-3/67	
Matthis, Abram N.	087	1876	WB-3/135	AR
Matthis, Charles	022	c1777	Orig. Only	AR
Matthis, Cornelius	085	1820	WB-H/71	AR
Matthis, Edmond	035	1783	WB-A/315	AR
Matthis, James	087	1851	WB-1/380	AR
Matthis, Marshal H.	087	1887	WB-3/349	AR
Matthis, Mary Ann	087	1864	WB-2/76	AR
Matthis, Thomas	047	1762	WB-1/62	
Matthis, Zacheous	087	1843	WB-A/143	AR
Matticks, Allen B.	072	1857	WB-2/153	AR
Matticks, Francis A.	072	1843	WB-2/44	AR
Matticks, John	072	1842	WB-2/40	AR
Matticks, John	072	1828	WB-1/25	AR
Matticks, William B.	072	1832	WB-1/90	AR
Mattocks, John	008	1733	SS 876/282	SS/AR
Mattocks, William G.	057	1871	WB-C/18	AR
Maudlin, Ezekiel	077	1732	SS 876/248	SS/AR
Maudlin, Gideon	077	1777	WB-C/189	AR
Maudlin, James	077	1802	WB-E/147	AR
Maudlin, John, Sr.	077	c1780	Orig. Only	AR
Maudlin, Thomas	077	1759	SS 881/230	SS/AR
Maudlin, William	077	1774	WB-C/166	AR
Maughon, William	071	1795	WB-2/65	AR
Maulbin, Lamuel	019	c1791	WB-D/278	AR
Maulden, A. C.	089	1857	WB-1/163	
Maulden, Benjamin	089	1878	WB-2/67	AR
Mauldin, Sarah	089	1892	WB-2/237	AR
Maule, John	009	1774	Orig. Only	SS/AR
Maule, Moses	009	c1799	OWB/360	AR
Maule, Patrick	009	1736	Orig. Only	SS/AR
Maule, William	010	1726	SS 876/34	SS/AR
Maulsbey, Thomas	072	c1762	RW/L41	AR
Mault, William	085	1848	WB-K/65	AR
Maultsby, Anthony	011	c1800	WB-1/441	
Maultsby, John	070	1757	DB-D/290	
Maultsby, John	011	1758	Orig. Only	SS/AR
Maultsby, John	070	1757	SS 882/38	SS/AR
Maultsby, Samuel	011	1892	WB-2/252	
Maultsby, Thomas	011	c1812	WB-2/312	
Maund, Mary	037	1795	WB-C/343	AR
Maund, Noah	037	1752	Orig. Only	SS/AR (N)
Maund, William	037	1761	WB-A/68	AR
Maunder, John	070	1897	WB-G/574	AR
Mauney, Anna	040	1897	WB-2/550	AR
Mauney, Caleb	040	1882	WB-2/188	AR
Mauney, Catharine	060	1844	WB-2/225	AR
Mauney, Catherine	060	1809	Orig. Only	AR
Mauney, Christian	060	1843	WB-2/186	AR

Name	Co.	Date	Recorded Copy	Original
Mauney, Christian	060	1815	Orig. Only	AR
Mauney, Daniel	026	1900	WB-3/61	AR
Mauney, David	040	1900	WB-3/76	AR
Mauney, E. A.	040	1896	WB-2/526	AR
Mauney, Eli	040	1861	WB-1/128	
Mauney, George	060	1842	WB-2/147	
Mauney, Isaac	023	1875	WB-A/12	AR
Mauney, J. W.	085	c1892	Copy	089 AR
Mauney, Jacob	060	1813	Orig. Only	AR
Mauney, John W.	085	1892	WB-2/522	
Mauney, Michael	040	1871	WB-2/30	AR
Mauney, Peter	060	1842	WB-2/135	AR
Mauney, Valentine	060	1806	Orig. Only	AR
Mauney, William P.	021	1900	WB-3/315	AR-Nunc.
Maurice, Francis B.	046	c1870	WB-E/54	AR
Maury, Richmond	105	1899	WB-3/336	AR
Mavis, George	046	1899	WB-G/152	AR
Maxfield, Mary	011	c1778	WB-1/557	
Maxley, Alfred	004	1888	WB-A/92 & 167	
Maxwell, Alexander	046	1849	WB-C/310	AR
Maxwell, Ann	065	1814	WB-B/95	AR
Maxwell, Ann	065	1873	WB-K/141	AR
Maxwell, Catherine	012	1886	WB-B/189	AR
Maxwell, Catherine	006	c1860	Orig. Only	AR
Maxwell, David	085	1832	WB-H/562	AR
Maxwell, David	004	1867	WB-1/24	AR
Maxwell, Deborah	046	1857	WB-C/492	AR
Maxwell, Eleanor	035	1833	WB-1/35	AR
Maxwell, Elizabeth	065	1843	WB-I/28	AR
Maxwell, Guy	065	1837	WB-E/135	AR
Maxwell, Houston	035	1866	WB-3/107	AR
Maxwell, James	006	1843	WB-A/43	AR
Maxwell, James	050	1874	WB-1/139	CTY
Maxwell, James	006	1843	Copy	004 AR
Maxwell, James	039	c1830	WB-J/123	AR
Maxwell, James	100	1839	WB-37/172	AR
Maxwell, James	046	1847	WB-C/262	AR
Maxwell, James	035	1811	WB-A/346	AR
Maxwell, James V.	046	1883	Orig. Only	AR
Maxwell, James W.	043	1898	WB-1/65	
Maxwell, John	046	1818	WB-B/69	AR
Maxwell, John	035	1814	WB-A/341	AR
Maxwell, John	035	1886	WB-4/277	AR
Maxwell, John L.	029	1884	WB-E/320	AR
Maxwell, Margaret	035	1890	WB-4/359	AR
Maxwell, Mary	039	1834	WB-K/26	
Maxwell, Nancy A.	065	1895	WB-M/348	AR
Maxwell, Peter	070	1814	WB-AB/209	AR
Maxwell, Rebecca	070	1810	WB-AB/137	AR
Maxwell, Robert	065	1785	WB-B/65	
Maxwell, Sarah	046	1852	WB-C/376	AR
Maxwell, Sidnia	006	1856	WB-D/34	AR
Maxwell, Thomas	029	1827	WB-B/156	
Maxwell, Thomas	085	c1800	WB-D/202	AR
Maxwell, Thomas T.	033	1879	WB-2/68	CTY
Maxwell, Virginia	100	1894	WB-51/362	AR
Maxwell, William	065	1890	WB-L/498	AR
Maxwell, William	046	c1837	WB-B/588	AR
May, A. D.	069	1896	WB-5/557	AR
May, A. J.	069	1884	WB-5/194	AR
May, Abner	085	c1801	WB-E/83	AR
May, Benjamin	039	1814	WB-D/87	AR
May, Benjamin	079	c1805	Orig. Only	AR
May, Catharine	070	1900	WB-H/260	AR
May, Daniel	073	1823	WB-E/36	AR

Name	Co.	Date	Recorded Copy	Original
May, George	030	1785	WB-1/184	
May, George	046	1850	WB-C/321	AR
May, Grove W.	097	1860	WB-1/186	AR
May, Indiana A.	VA	1892	039 WB-U/554	039 AR
May, Jacob	001	1869	WB-2/29	AR
May, James	044	1778	WB-1/160	CTY
May, James A.	046	1862	WB-D/154	AR
May, Jane	022	1867	WB-D/168	AR
May, Jesse	005	1831	WB-2/102	AR
May, John	079	1863	WB-1/94	AR
May, John	085	1844	WB-I/242	AR
May, John	006	1872	WB-D/114	AR
May, John A.	046	1884	WB-E/400	AR
May, John T.	039	1857	WB-0/385	AR
May, Joseph	030	1795	WB-2/53	
May, Joseph	022	1808	WB-A/99	AR
May, Levi	046	1891	WB-F/159	AR
May, Mark	061	1885	WB-2/72	AR
May, Martha	079	c1850	WB-1/29	AR-Copy
May, Martha J	036	1892	WB-A/233	CTY
May, Mary	046	1879	WB-E/250	AR
May, Mary	085	1861	WB-K/296	AR
May, Mary A. E.	079	1888	WB-2/422	AR
May, Nancy	006	1869	WB-D/92	AR
May, Nathan	039	1889	WB-U/488	AR
May, Peter	SC	1838	005 WB-B/85	
May, Peter	009	1882	WB-1/312	CTY
May, Peter	005	c1866	WB-D/2	AR
May, Robert C.	032	1898	WB-4/336	AR
May, Robert S.	079	1865	WB-1/115	AR
May, Sally M.	039	1888	WB-U/445	AR
May, Tabitha	079	1891	WB-2/533	AR
May, Tabitha	105	1891	WB-3/10	AR
May, Thomas	030	1782	WB-1/157	
May, Tobias	001	1886	WB-2/280	AR
May, William	106	1885	WB-2/205	AR
May, William	039	1834	WB-J/272	AR
May, William	079	N. D.	WB-1/66	AR-Copy
May, Willie	039	1868	WB-U/10	
Mayben, David	046	1821	WB-B/109	AR
Mayben, Matthew	050	c1842	WB-1/4	
Mayben, Robert	046	1834	WB-B/497	AR
Maybin, George V.	050	1859	WB-1/61	CTY
Maybin, Mathew	050	1863	WB-1/82	CTY
Mayer, Henry	085	1828	WB-H/419	AR
Mayer, Jacob	090	1801	WB-1/173	AR
Mayes, Stith	086	1827	WB-D/76	AR
Mayes, Thomas P.	071	1857	WB-5/172	AR
Mayfeild, Peter	002	1687	Orig. Only	SS/AR
Mayfield, Abraham	044	1778	WB-1/168	CTY
Mayfield, Abraham	100	1809	WB-15/14	AR
Mayfield, Abraham	100	1797	Orig. Only	AR
Mayfield, Edmond	100	1831	WB-33/338	AR
Mayfield, James O. K.	100	1875	WB-51/74	AR
Mayfield, Mary	044	1859	WB-20/711	CTY
Mayfield, Mary	100	1835	WB-35/52	AR
Mayfield, Thomas	100	1832	WB-34/1	AR
Mayfield, Valentine	044	1791	WB-2/233	CTY
Mayhew, Aaron	054	1845	WB-2/310	AR
Mayhew, B. F.	103	1889	WB-1/477	AR
Mayhew, Caroline	028	1897	WB-F/263	
Mayhew, John	054	c1838	WB-2/185	AR
Mayhew, Margaret	054	1883	WB-4/590	CTY
Mayhew, Mary E.	028	1889	WB-E/519	AR
Mayhew, McMillan	026	1863	WB-1/329	AR
Mayhew, William	054	1870	WB-4/73	AR
Mayho, James	039	c1785	WB-A/1	
Maynard, Allen	099	1891	WB-B/531	AR
Maynard, Amos	099	1886	WB-B/116	AR
Maynard, Ann	VA	1797	Copy	044 CTY
Maynard, Anna J.	099	1900	056 WB-6/205	056 AR
Maynard, Anna J.	099	1900	WB-D/391	AR
Maynard, Gibson	104	1802	WB-2/73	
Maynard, Joseph	099	1895	WB-C/408	AR
Maynard, Josiah	099	1869	RB-35/51	AR
Maynard, Martha	099	1857	RB-30/349	AR
Maynard, Richard	001	1849	WB-1/11	AR
Maynard, Richard	020	1893	WB-B/162	CTY
Maynard, Robert C.	044	1864	WB-22/98	CTY
Maynard, Sallie P.	044	1882	WB-23/440	CTY
Maynard, William	065	1792	Copy	044 CTY
Mayner, Henry	073	1760	WB-A/12	
Maynor, Eddie	099	1879	WB-A/15	AR
Maynor, William M.	036	1892	WB-A/258	CTY
Mayo, Alfred	009	1890	WB-1/497	CTY
Mayo, Ann Ramsey	024	1890	WB-E/179	AR
Mayo, Celia	103	1885	WB-1/339	AR
Mayo, Celia	105	1884	WB-5/90	
Mayo, Cuffee	044	1896	WB-24/302	CTY
Mayo, David	037	1834	WB-F/154	AR
Mayo, Dorcas E.	009	1899	WB-2/196	CTY
Mayo, Edward	075	1724	SS 876/17	SS/AR
Mayo, Edward	075	1734	SS 876/365	SS/AR
Mayo, Edward	103	1833	RD-6/405	AR
Mayo, James	063	1780	WB-1/60	
Mayo, John	009	1827	OB-A/447	AR
Mayo, John	037	1856	WB-G/119	AR
Mayo, John W.	037	1825	WB-F/26	AR
Mayo, Joseph	103	1813	RD-3/53	AR
Mayo, Mariah	037	1888	WB-H/113	AR
Mayo, Nathan	037	1811	WB-E/11	
Mayo, Rebecca	037	1847	WB-F/369	AR
Mayo, Reuben	037	1877	WB-G/510	AR
Mayo, Rowland	009	1843	OB-E/203	
Mayo, Solomon	009	c1796	OWB/320	AR
Mayo, William	009	1866	OB-M/88	
Mayo, William	009	c1759	OWB/67	AR
Mayo, William	037	1854	WB-G/53	AR
Mayo, William H.	037	1848	WB-F/389	
Mays, Absalem	054	1865	Orig. Only	AR
Mays, James C.	054	1868	WB-4/17	AR
Mays, John	099	1777	RB-1/102	AR
Mays, John J.	092	1898	WB-6/492	AR
Mays, Milas M.	054	1889	WB-5/260	CTY
Mays, Rhoda D.	054	1880	WB-4/364	CTY
Mays, Tabitha	081	1837	WB-7/129	AR
Mayton, John E.	099	1846	RB-26/107	AR
Mayzck, Thomas	014	c1876	Orig. Only	CTY
Mazey, John	022	1823	WB-B/101	AR
McAbee, Isaac	049	c1858	WB-1/25	AR
McAboy, Mary A.	080	1893	WB-1/226	AR
McAdam, James	075	1742	Orig. Only	SS/AR
McAdam, Joseph	077	c1792	Copy	075 AR
McAdam, Mary	075	1822	WB-M1/352	AR
McAdams, Elexena	001	1900	WB-3/335	AR
McAdams, Harriet	001	1877	WB-2/111	AR
McAdams, Isaac	073	1828	WB-E/161	AR
McAdams, James	073	c1806	Orig. Only	AR
McAdams, Jane	001	1858	WB-1/137	AR
McAdams, John	073	1864	WB-G/430	AR

Name	Co.	Date	Recorded Copy	Original
McAdams, Joseph	001	1897	WB-3/170	AR
McAdams, Margaret	001	1863	WB-1/218	AR
McAdams, Rebecca	073	1809	WB-D/250	AR
McAdams, Richard	046	1893	WB-F/277	AR
McAdams, Samuel	073	1790	WB-B/99	AR
McAdams, Sarah	075	1744	Orig. Only	SS/AR
McAdams, Tinnin	073	1822	WB-E/9	AR
McAdams, William	073	1834	WB-E/318	AR
McAdams, William B.	001	1889	021 WB-2/483	021 AR
McAdams, William W.	001	1866	WB-1/276	AR
McAdamson, George	072	1796	Orig. Only	AR
McAden, J. H.	065	c1894	Copy	040 AR
McAden, John H.	020	1827	RB-L/198	AR
McAden, Margarett	020	1828	RB-L/322	AR
McAden, R. Y.	065	c1900	043 WB-1/74	
McAden, Rufus Y.	065	1889	040 WB-2/332	040 AR
McAden, Rufus Y.	065	1889	023 WB-A/88	
McAden, Rufus Y.	065	c1888	026 WB-2/423	026 AR
McAden, Rufus Y.	065	1889	WB-L/349	
McAden, Rufus Y.	065	1889	091 WB-1/118	
McAdow, James	046	1805	WB-A/267	AR
McAdow, James	046	1800	WB-A/260	AR
McAfee, A. A.	026	N. D.	WB-2/59	AR
McAfee, Abner	026	1847	WB-1/72 & 80	AR
McAfee, Addie W.	026	1888	WB-2/378	AR
McAfee, James	033	1848	WB-1/93	AR
McAirn, John	082	1819	WB-1/204	AR
McAlester, Garland	099	1785	RB-2/43	AR
McAlester, Jennet	029	1824	WB-B/122	AR
McAlester, John	029	1761	Orig. Only	AR
McAlester, Mary	012	1795	Copy	070 AR
McAlister, Alexander	029	1858	WB-C/414	AR
McAlister, Alexander	029	1797	WB-E/158	AR
McAlister, Angus	082	1809	WB-1/129	AR
McAlister, Daniel	076	1885	WB-A1/63	AR
McAlister, Elisha C.	040	1887	WB-2/281	AR
McAlister, Hector	029	1810	WB-A/153	
McAlister, John	029	1835	WB-B/242	AR
McAlister, John H.	029	1890	Orig. Only	AR
McAlister, Sarah	082	1860	WB-4/145	AR
McAllister, Charles	029	1840	WB-B/319	AR
McAllister, Edith I.	029	1873	WB-E/87	AR
McAllister, Flora	029	1880	WB-E/245	AR
McAllister, John	073	1768	WB-A/84	
McAllister, Martha	068	c1870	WB-D/26	
McAllister, William B.	029	1872	WB-E/67	AR
McAllum, Archibald	029	1800	WB-A/35	AR
McAlpin, Alexander	020	1867	RB-T/307	AR
McAlpin, Jane W.	020	1893	WB-B/132	CTY
McAlpin, Malcom	029	1831	WB-B/207	AR
McAlpin, William	028	1747	SS 877/299	SS/AR
McAnally, Charles	090	1810	WB-2/113	AR
McAnally, Elizabeth	090	c1843	WB-4/168	AR
McAnulty, James W.	016	1880	WB-3/308	
McAnulty, Joseph	016	1834	PQS.5/318	AR
McAnulty, William	016	1808	WB-A/40	AR
McArn, Archibald	082	1830	WB-1/319	AR
McArn, Daniel	083	1859	WB-2/147	AR
McArn, Hugh	082	1883	WB-6/241	AR
McArn, Hugh	082	1830	WB-2/1	AR
McArn, Sarah	082	1857	WB-4/104	AR
McArthur, Alexander	083	1873	WB-3/66	AR
McArthur, Alexander	083	1832	WB-1/266	AR
McArthur, Catharine	SC	1884	083 WB-3/327	083 AR
McArthur, Catharine	082	1851	WB-4/68	AR
McArthur, Catharine	083	1851	WB-1/39	AR
McArthur, Christian	083	1880	WB-3/170	AR
McArthur, Colin	082	1849	WB-4/29	AR
McArthur, Colin	082	1811	WB-1/147	AR
McArthur, Daniel	083	1889	WB-3/465	AR
McArthur, Donald	029	1883	WB-E/304	AR
McArthur, Duncan	029	1886	WB-E/396	AR
McArthur, Eleazer	086	1888	WB-F/335	AR
McArthur, Jane	083	1858	WB-2/128	AR
McArthur, Jannet	SC	1891	083 WB-3/559	083 AR
McArthur, John	068	c1810	WB-A/270	
McArthur, John	SC	1881	083 WB-3/274	AR
McArthur, John A.	087	1848	WB-1/334	AR
McArthur, Juke	083	1889	WB-3/444	AR
McArthur, Margaret	083	1880	WB-3/206	AR
McArthur, Martha	059	1895	Orig. Only	CTY
McArthur, Martha	067	1847	WB-1/31	
McArthur, Mary	082	1894	WB-6/506	AR
McArthur, Neill	083	1835	WB-1/294	AR
McArthur, Neill	083	1897	WB-4/148	AR
McArthur, Peter	083	c1848	Orig. Only	AR
McArthur, Peter	029	1829	WB-B/177	AR
McArthur, Roseanna	083	1882	WB-3/280	AR
McAulay, Dewit C.	067	1882	WB-2/131	AR
McAulay, John	067	1864	WB-1/114	
McAuley, Daniel	065	1841	WB-H/27	AR
McAuley, Hugh	065	c1841	WB-J/148	AR
McAuley, John B.	054	1865	WB-3/175	AR
McAuley, Kenneth	067	1864	WB-1/117	AR
McAuley, Mary M.	065	1900	WB-N/346	
McAuley, Melvina	054	1875	WB-4/174	CTY
McAuley, Roderick	065	1886	WB-L/122	
McAuley, Rodrick	065	1844	WB-H/180	AR
McAuley, William	068	1838	WB-B/109	
McAuslan, Jane	029	1814	WB-A/203	AR
McAuslin, C. M.	070	c1884	WB-E/532	AR
McBee, Mary	064	1891	WB-2/267	AR
McBee, Mathew	064	1859	WB-1/68	AR
McBee, Sarah	040	1893	WB-2/456	AR
McBrawley, Neil	054	1884	WB-4/578	CTY
McBrayer, A. H.	086	1879	WB-F/146	AR-Nunc.
McBrayer, David	026	1843	WB-1/13	AR
McBrayer, Dobbins	026	1867	WB-1/415	AR
McBrayer, James	013	1851	WB-A/150	
McBrayer, R. H.	026	1896	WB-2/521	AR
McBrayer, Robert	026	1888	WB-2/341	AR
McBrayer, Samuel	026	1869	WB-2/14	AR
McBrayer, William	013	1887	WB-B/463	AR
McBride, Ailsa	046	1869	WB-E/8	AR
McBride, Alsey	046	1858	WB-C/528	AR
McBride, Andrew	073	1779	WB-A/206	
McBride, Daniel	092	1822	WB-3/151	AR
McBride, Edward	092	1899	WB-6/525	AR
McBride, Elisha	018	1803	Orig. Only	AR-Copy
McBride, Elizabeth	104	1863	WB-5/358	
McBride, Isaiah	046	1832	WB-B/466	AR
McBride, James	104	1808	WB-2/230	AR
McBride, John	092	c1821	WB-4/155	
McBride, John	075	1766	WB-H/71	AR
McBride, John	046	1806	WB-A/268	AR
McBride, John	054	c1829	Orig. Only	AR
McBride, John	099	1794	RB-3/24	AR
McBride, Richard	005	1883	WB-D/152	AR
McBride, Sarah	046	1858	WB-C/528	
McBride, William	054	c1822	WB-2/35	AR

Name	Co.	Date	Recorded Copy	Original
McBride, William	092	1818	WB-3/133	AR
McBride, William	106	1894	WB-2/352	
McBroom, Andrew	073	1851	WB-F/483	AR
McBroom, Andrew	073	1784	WB-A/294	AR
McBroom, Elizabeth	085	1770	WB-A/98	AR
McBroom, James	085	1799	WB-D/211	AR
McBroom, John	085	1843	WB-I/160	AR
McBroom, Margaret	073	1866	WB-G/486	CTY
McBroom, Martha	073	1867	WB-G/515	CTY
McBryde, Alexander	083	1876	WB-3/116	AR
McBryde, Alexander	083	1862	WB-2/181	AR
McBryde, Angus	083	1875	WB-3/106	AR
McBryde, Archibald	068	1837	022 WB-C/67	022 AR
McBryde, Archibald	083	1865	WB-2/224	AR
McBryde, Daniel	082	1872	WB-6/79	AR
McBryde, Duncan	082	c1812	WB-1/156	AR
McBryde, Margaret	083	1887	WB-3/401	AR
McBryde, Mathew	011	1880	WB-2/133	
McBryde, Sarah	083	1872	WB-3/48	AR
McBryde, Sarah M.	082	1878	WB-6/151	AR
McCabe, Henry H.	009	1827	OB-A/378	AR
McCabe, James	009	1807	OWB/449	AR
McCabe, James	101	1871	Orig. Only	AR
McCabe, Rachel	028	1825	WB-C/267	
McCabe, William	096	1869	WB-4/9	
McCabe, William	009	c1788	OWB/225	AR
McCabee, Demaris	096	1835	WB-2/129	AR
McCaddams, Hugh	073	1809	WB-D/248	
McCaddams, James	073	1807	WB-D/187	
McCaddams, Robert	073	c1846	Orig. Only	AR
McCadden, Hugh	044	1881	WB-23/407	CTY
McCaden, John	020	1846	RB-P/291	
McCafferty, James	028	1796	WB-A/350	
McCafferty, Jeremiah	065	1778	WB-B/114	AR
McCafferty, John	085	1786	WB-B/58	AR
McCain, Alexander	020	c1846	Orig. Only	AR
McCain, Andrew	097	1845	WB-1/19	AR
McCain, Daniel	082	1799	WB-1/66	AR
McCain, Elizabeth	078	1892	WB-19/333	AR
McCain, Hance	046	1824	WB-B/194	AR
McCain, Hugh	065	1821	WB-B/98	AR
McCain, Hugh	065	1832	WB-G/87	AR
McCain, Hugh B.	097	1874	WB-2/70	AR
McCain, Hugh H.	097	1845	WB-1/20	AR
McCain, James W.	020	1867	RB-T/239	AR
McCain, Jane T.	097	1896	WB-3/15	AR
McCain, John	020	1856	RB-R/398	AR
McCain, John	081	1834	WB-6/399	AR
McCain, John	065	1835	WB-G/212	AR
McCain, John C.	089	1863	WB-1/250	
McCain, John J.	097	1863	WB-1/208	AR
McCain, Joseph	065	1797	WB-B/77	AR
McCain, Robert	020	1846	RB-P/298	AR
McCain, William E.	097	1866	WB-1/284	AR
McCaleb, Archibald	070	1857	WB-C/643	AR
McCaleb, James	016	1827	WB-A/56	AR
McCalister, Grizzel	073	1794	WB-C/2	AR
McCall, Catherine	082	1888	WB-6/373	AR
McCall, Daniel	029	1830	WB-B/199	AR
McCall, Duncan	011	c1841	WB-1/73	
McCall, Francis	065	1794	WB-B/74	AR
McCall, Harriet	011	1884	WB-2/170	
McCall, Hugh	082	1884	WB-6/271	AR
McCall, James	065	1774	WB-B/49	AR
McCall, James F.	017	1871	WB-B/30	AR
McCall, John	046	1796	WB-A/255	AR
McCall, John	060	1812	Orig. Only	AR
McCall, John	011	1877	WB-2/107	
McCall, John Colton	082	1898	WB-6/576	
McCall, John J.	082	1885	WB-6/312	AR
McCall, Martha	065	1895	WB-M/351	
McCall, Mary E.	065	1880	WB-K/406	
McCall, Rena	054	1895	WB-5/555	CTY
McCall, Robert	064	1848	WB-1/20	AR
McCall, Robert A.	093	1897	WB-2/158	AR
McCall, Timothy	046	1774	WB-A/252	AR
McCall, William	065	1828	WB-A/164	AR
McCallom, Daniel	083	c1804	WB-1/87	AR
McCallum, Angus	083	1849	WB-2/10	AR
McCallum, Archibald	083	1850	WB-2/15	AR
McCallum, Charles	073	1866	WB-G/505	CTY
McCallum, Danel	068	1886	WB-D/158	
McCallum, Dugald	083	1881	WB-3/246	AR
McCallum, Duncan	068	1801	WB-A/218	
McCallum, Edward	067	1847	WB-1/39	AR
McCallum, Edward	067	1881	WB-2/122	AR
McCallum, Isabel	083	1871	WB-3/30	AR
McCallum, James T.	082	1893	WB-6/467	AR
McCallum, James T.	082	1893	070 WB-G/124	070 AR
McCallum, John	083	1866	WB-2/228	AR
McCallum, John	083	1873	WB-3/63	AR
McCallum, Malcom	067	1866	WB-1/132	
McCallum, Margaret	083	1861	WB-2/170	AR
McCallum, Mary	083	c1860	WB-2/162	AR
McCallum, Rhoda	083	1896	WB-4/152	AR
McCallum, William	067	1846	WB-1/18	
McCan, Mary	022	1824	WB-B/78	AR
McCanles, James	073	1784	WB-A/295	AR
McCanless, Jean	073	1807	WB-D/197	AR
McCann, Hugh	035	1796	WB-A/321	AR
McCann, William	035	1832	WB-A/313	
McCanne, Mary	035	1853	WB-2/76	AR
McCanne, William	035	1793	WB-A/543	AR
McCarn, Michael	032	1823	WB-1/11	
McCarrell, John	084	c1797	OW/246	AR
McCarrihan, William	054	c1831	WB-2/128	AR
McCarrol, Nathaniel	092	1780	WB-1/137	AR
McCarter, Aaron	090	1820	WB-3/56	AR
McCarter, Aholibamah	026	1900	WB-3/72	AR
McCarthy, J. W.	084	1898	WB-F/110	CTY
McCartney, James	070	1900	WB-H/262	AR
McCartney, Thomas	085	c1785	WB-C/86	AR
McCarty, Archibald	053	c1801	RW-1/373	
McCarty, Baily	053	1751	028 DB-5/202	SS/AR
McCarty, Dennis	053	1759	SS 882/131	SS/AR
McCarty, Sarah	053	1837	WB-6/5	AR
McCarver, John	060	1830	WB-1/178	AR
McCaskey, John	096	1760	WB-1/12	AR
McCaskey, Mary	063	c1778	WB-1/88	
McCaskill, Alexander	082	1886	WB-6/331	AR
McCaskill, Daniel	TX	1861	Copy	082 AR
McCaskill, Effy	083	1836	WB-1/301	AR
McCaskill, Hugh	067	1894	WB-2/330	
McCaskill, Isaac	082	1858	WB-4/124	AR
McCaskill, Kinneth	068	c1843	WB-B/142	
McCaskill, Norman	029	1880	WB-E/218	AR
McCaskill, R.	082	1897	Copy	070 AR
McCaskill, R.	082	1897	WB-6/565	AR
McCaskill, Sarah	067	1874	WB-2/61	AR
McCasland, Robert	060	1804	Orig. Only	AR

Name	Co.	Date	Recorded Copy	Original
McCaslin, Mathew	021	1889	WB-2/458	AR
McCaul, Bedice	021	1875	WB-2/136	AR
McCaul, Felix G.	021	1896	WB-3/107	CTY
McCauley, Andrew	073	1844	WB-F/186	AR
McCauley, Andrew	073	1839	WB-F/23	AR
McCauley, Charles	073	1837	WB-E/404	AR
McCauley, Charles	073	1864	WB-G/420	CTY
McCauley, Charles	073	1829	WB-E/183	AR
McCauley, Elizabeth	073	1891	WB-H/551	CTY
McCauley, George J.	067	1867	073 WB-H/78	073 CTY
McCauley, Gilbert	020	1891	WB-B/68	CTY
McCauley, J. A.	001	1888	WB-2/410	Nunc.
McCauley, James W.	073	1847	WB-F/383	AR
McCauley, John	073	1832	WB-E/283	AR
McCauley, John	073	1824	WB-E/53	AR
McCauley, John W.	001	1898	WB-3/227	AR
McCauley, Johnston	001	1889	WB-2/449	AR
McCauley, Martha	073	1846	WB-F/319	AR
McCauley, Matthew	073	1821	WB-D/610	AR
McCauley, Sarah J.	099	1859	RB-31/220	AR
McCauley, Thomas D.	097	1896	WB-2/499	AR
McCauley, William	073	1826	WB-E/97	AR
McCauley, William	073	1862	WB-G/386	AR
McCaulley, Roderick	065	1887	016 WB-3/567	016 AR
McCauslin, Isabella	070	1748	WB-C/244	AR-Nunc.
McCausten, John	070	1747	DB-C/171	
McCawey, Ward	072	c1786	Orig. Only	AR
McCendrick, Patrick	065	1761	WB-B/106	AR
McClain, Alexander	075	1789	WB-K/180	AR
McClain, Daniel	080	1884	WB-1/81	AR
McClain, James	030	1797	WB-2/109	
McClain, Jane	097	1897	WB-2/523	AR
McClain, John	GA	1844	050 WB-1/5	
McClain, John H.	SC	1891	080 WB-1/260	080 AR
McClain, Joseph	084	1805	WB-A/29	CTY
McClain, Martha	SC	1895	080 WB-1/264	080 AR
McClain, Mira A. C.	050	1866	WB-1/95	
McClain, Robert	SC	1892	080 WB-1/257	080 AR
McClalland, Andrew	011	1752	SS 878/100	SS/AR
McClam, Rose	103	1886	WB-1/372	AR
McClammy, Luke	070	1792	WB-C/278	AR
McClammy, Mark	070	1803	WB-C/286	AR
McClammy, Peter	070	1782	WB-C/265	AR
McClammy, Thomas	070	1773	Orig. Only	SS/AR
McClammy, William	070	1772	WB-C/254	AR
McClamrock, George	033	1846	WB-1/76	AR
McClamrock, John M.	033	1895	WB-2/178	CTY
McClanahan, Cornelius	044	1861	WB-21/462	CTY
McClanahan, Susan M.	044	1877	WB-23/252	CTY
McClanen, Elinor D.	030	1885	WB-5/124	AR
McClaney, William T.	101	1888	WB-A/161	AR
McClannahan, Mary	077	1813	WB-E/392	AR
McClannahan, Moses	030	1782	WB-1/149	
McClarney, Henry	020	1825	RB-K/63	AR
McClarney, Rosannah	020	1808	RB-E/392	AR
McClatchey, John	054	c1797	WB-1/170	AR
McClean, Alexander	075	1786	WB-K/145	AR
McCleary, Abigail	065	1805	WB-E/6	AR
McCleary, Deborah	065	c1811	WB-E/17	AR
McCleary, Samuel	065	1797	WB-B/143	AR
McCleary, William	065	1814	WB-E/20	AR
McClees, E. A.	097	1873	WB-4/23	AR
McClees, Joseph	096	1856	WB-3/43	AR
McClees, Lola O.	096	1896	WB-4/163	AR
McClees, William	096	1894	WB-4/153	

Name	Co.	Date	Recorded Copy	Original
McCleland, Nicolas	085	c1777	WB-A/242	AR
McClellan, James H.	016	1868	WB-2/161	AR
McClellan, Joseph	016	1811	WB-A/4	AR
McClellan, Robert P.	016	1888	WB-4/10	AR
McClellan, Thomas	016	1808	WB-A/4	AR
McClelland, Joseph	003	1864	Orig. Only	AR
McClelland, Margaret	065	1834	WB-G/187	AR
McClelland, Nat E.	054	c1834	WB-2/138	AR
McClelland, William	054	1802	WB-1/167	AR
McClellen, William	085	c1778	WB-A/267	AR
McClenachan, William	047	1786	WB-3/110	AR
McClenahan, John	044	1827	Orig. Only	CTY
McClenahan, Robert	065	c1767	WB-B/109	AR
McClenahan, Sallie	022	c1867	WB-D/169	AR
McClendon, Dennis	010	1725/6	Orig. Only	SS/AR
McClendon, John	070	1847	WB-AB/469	AR
McClendon, John	005	1784	WB-1/44	
McClenney, James	056	1793	WB-1/73	AR
McClenny, Joseph	024	1849	WB-C/291	AR
McClintock, George S.	046	1865	WB-D/270	AR
McClintock, John	046	1807	WB-A/269	AR
McClintock, Samuel	046	1834	WB-B/514	AR
McClintock, Sarah	046	1878	WB-E/277	AR
McClintock, William	046	1830	WB-B/410	AR
McClintock, William	046	1870	WB-E/36	AR
McCloud, Hiram G.	053	1885	WB-11/162	AR
McCloud, James	053	1847	WB-7/110	AR
McCloud, James C.	053	1881	WB-11/107	AR
McCloure, Elezar	006	1881	WB-E/86	AR
McCluer, Mary T.	009	1884	WB-1/350	CTY
McCluer, Richard	086	1835	WB-E/21	AR
McClur, Arthur	086	1823	WB-D/13	AR
McClur, John	086	1808	WB-B/218	AR
McClure, Ann	085	1822	WB-H/188	AR
McClure, Elizabeth	060	1821	Orig. Only	AR
McClure, Henry	073	1805	WB-D/156	AR
McClure, Isaac D.	086	1889	WB-F/346	AR
McClure, Jacob	028	1837	WB-C/404	
McClure, James A.	086	1893	WB-F/449	AR
McClure, John	060	1819	Orig. Only	AR
McClure, John	065	c1778	WB-B/57	AR
McClure, John	065	1817	WB-E/21	AR
McClure, Rachel	060	1840	WB-2/50	AR
McClure, William	028	1804	WB-B/207	
McClurg, Elizabeth	060	1849	WB-2/304	AR
McClurg, Nathaniel	060	1828	WB-1/111	
McCoad, Elizabeth	065	1860	WB-J/83	AR
McCoard, James	065	1782	WB-B/126	AR
McCoard, Robert C.	065	1838	WB-E/198	AR
McCobins, Samuel	057	1794	WB-A/162	AR
McColeman, Nelson E.	082	1892	WB-6/455	AR
McColister, Levin	084	1850	WB-C/111	
McColl, Christian	082	1790	WB-1/34	AR
McColl, Dugald	029	1816	WB-A/235	AR
McColl, Duncan	082	1823	WB-1/237	AR
McColl, Hugh	029	1822	WB-B/98	AR
McColl, John	082	1831	WB-2/12	AR
McColl, Mary	083	1823	WB-1/214	AR
McColloch, James	054	c1791	WB-1/164	AR
McColloch, Margaret	054	c1816	WB-1/388	AR
McCollom, John	047	1815	WB-3/559	AR
McCollom, John	085	1774	WB-A/175	AR
McCollum, Andrew	085	c1807	WB-G/33	AR
McCollum, Christian	068	1869	WB-D/3	
McCollum, Daniel	097	1865	WB-1/259	AR

Name	Co.	Date	Recorded Copy	Original
McCollum, Daniel	005	c1824	WB-A/115	AR
McCollum, Daniel	084	1868	WB-E/4	CTY
McCollum, David	084	1834	WB-B/91	CTY
McCollum, Duncan	082	1806	WB-1/109	AR
McCollum, Duncan	029	1846	WB-C/132	AR
McCollum, Duncan	068	1824	WB-B/33	
McCollum, Duncan	081	1784	WB-1/1	AR
McCollum, Elizabeth	085	c1776	WB-B/68	AR
McCollum, Elizabeth	085	1846	WB-K/41	AR
McCollum, James	097	1883	WB-2/226	AR
McCollum, James	084	1857	WB-C/266	CTY
McCollum, James	054	1846	WB-3/6	AR
McCollum, John	081	1843	WB-8/16	AR
McCollum, Ned	084	1897	WB-F/98	CTY
McCollum, Powhatan	084	1890	WB-E/434	CTY
McCollum, William	084	1882	WB-E/251	CTY
McColman, James A.	082	1885	WB-6/302	AR
McColough, Mary Ann	026	1896	WB-2/509	AR
McColskey, George	027	1889	WB-2/89	AR
McColskey, James	027	c1870	WB-2/21	AR
McColter, Hezekiah	028	1792	WB-A/271	
McComb, John	073	1769	WB-A/94	
McComb, Mary	065	1824	WB-B/101	AR
McCombs, Amy	065	1884	WB-L/1	
McCombs, James	065	1813	WB-B/93	AR
McCombs, James	065	1878	WB-K/305	
McCombs, James	065	c1812	SC/03914	AR-Copy
McCombs, Leannah	065	1861	WB-J/110	AR
McCombs, Major	026	1867	WB-1/409	AR
McCombs, Mary M.	085	1887	WB-2/286	CTY
McCombs, Samuel	065	1810	WB-E/12	AR
McCombs, Samuel B.	065	1842	WB-H/79	AR
McComis, William	035	1832	WB-1/30	
McCommon, Charles	016	1799	WB-A/60	AR
McCommon, Julia	097	1863	WB-1/206	AR
McCommon, William	097	1847	WB-1/47	AR
McConaughey, Hugh	085	c1798	WB-D/210	AR
McCondichea, John	056	1777	WB-2/262	AR
McConel, John	054	c1808	WB-1/176	
McConesky, Duncan	011	c1807	WB-1/446	
McConey, Robert	009	c1790	OWB/252	AR
McConkey, Robert	011	c1790	WB-1/551	
McConnal, Mary	024	c1779	WB-A/167	AR
McConnaughey, James	085	1825	WB-H/306	AR
McConnaughey, Joseph	085	c1804	WB-E/76	AR
McConnaughy, Ann	085	c1829	WB-H/468	AR
McConneghey, Joseph	085	1787	WB-E/64	AR
McConnel, Andrew	085	1760	WB-A/108	AR
McConnel, Elizabeth	054	1857	WB-3/124	AR
McConnel, John	085	c1791	WB-B/200	
McConnel, John	054	c1808	WB-1/50	AR
McConnel, John, Sr.	054	c1801	WB-1/180	
McConnel, Margaret	054	1859	WB-3/137	AR
McConnel, Robert	065	1883	WB-K/560	
McConnell, Alexander	005	1760	WB-1/7	
McConnell, James	054	c1810	WB-1/293	
McConnell, Jean	054	c1820	WB-2/89	AR
McConnell, John	065	1881	WB-K/436	
McConnell, John	054	c1822	WB-1/429	AR
McConnell, Mary	054	c1812	WB-1/314	AR
McConnell, Mary	046	1796	WB-A/256	AR
McConnell, Mary	054	1852	WB-3/56	AR
McConnell, Walter	046	1855	WB-C/427	AR
McConnell, William	054	c1811	WB-1A/104	AR
McConnell, William	065	1863	WB-J/163	AR
McCord, John	065	1787	WB-B/127	AR
McCord, John	065	1809	WB-E/10	AR
McCord, Thomas	065	1833	WB-G/106	AR
McCorkall, Margaret	070	1764	012 DB-A/35	
McCorkel, John	065	1811	WB-B/92	AR
McCorkel, Robert	005	N. D.	Orig. Only	SS/AR
McCorkle, Alexander	021	1854	WB-1/110	AR
McCorkle, Alexander	054	c1800	WB-1/158	AR
McCorkle, Andrew	065	c1781	WB-B/121	AR
McCorkle, Elias	097	1860	WB-1/172	AR
McCorkle, Elizbeth	021	1877	WB-2/163	AR
McCorkle, Francis	021	1853	WB-1/108	AR
McCorkle, J. A.	054	1897	WB-6/54	CTY
McCorkle, James	065	1795	WB-B/140	AR
McCorkle, James	097	1854	WB-1/101	AR
McCorkle, James M.	085	1885	WB-2/121	CTY
McCorkle, Joel	085	1818	WB-G/513	AR
McCorkle, John	085	c1797	WB-D/217	AR
McCorkle, John	097	1854	WB-1/98	AR
McCorkle, John Macon	021	1895	WB-3/98	AR
McCorkle, Margaret	085	1823	WB-H/245	AR
McCorkle, Matt	021	1844	WB-1/25	AR
McCorkle, Matthew L.	021	1899	WB-3/236	AR
McCorkle, Rebeca	054	c1802	WB-1/177	AR
McCorkle, Rosa L.	085	1895	WB-3/78	CTY
McCorkle, Samuel E.	085	1811	WB-G/187	AR
McCorkle, Susannah	065	1824	WB-E/34	AR
McCorkle, William	021	1857	WB-1/132	AR
McCormac, Neill	005	1890	WB-D/274	AR
McCormack, Archibald	082	1874	WB-6/123	AR
McCormack, John	082	1831	Orig. Only	AR
McCormack, John, Sr.	082	1831	Orig. Only	AR
McCormaig, John	083	1814	WB-1/151	
McCormick, Andrew	060	1795	Orig. Only	AR
McCormick, Ann	029	1895	WB-F/61	AR
McCormick, Archibald	082	1890	WB-6/399	AR-Nunc.
McCormick, Cathrine	029	1886	WB-E/401	AR
McCormick, Dinis	065	1783	WB-B/62	AR
McCormick, Duncan	024	c1788	WB-A/161	AR
McCormick, Duncan	029	1873	WB-E/102	AR
McCormick, John	094	1770	Orig. Only	060 AR
McCormick, John	083	1850	WB-2/23	AR
McCormick, John	029	1836	WB-B/268	AR
McCormick, Margaret	029	1889	WB-E/446	AR
McCormick, Mary	029	1890	WB-E/467	AR
McCormick, Peter	092	1886	WB-6/233	AR
McCormick, Robert W.	044	1863	WB-21/750	CTY
McCormick, Sarah	085	1895	WB-3/92	CTY
McCormick, William	065	1794	WB-B/73	AR
McCorquodale, John	029	1886	Orig. Only	AR
McCorrey, Finlah	083	c1803	WB-1/184	
McCotter, Archibald	028	1834	WB-C/368	
McCotter, Emeline	059	1887	WB-A/508	CTY
McCotter, Jacob	059	1887	WB-A/490	CTY
McCotter, Jesse	028	1829	WB-C/304	AR
McCotter, R. D.	074	1892	WB-1/107	
McCotter, Robert B.	079	1890	WB-2/517	AR
McCoulloch, John	073	1785	WB-A/355	AR
McCoulskey, Flora	083	1838	WB-1/313	AR
McCowen, James	060	1863	WB-3/51	AR
McCoy, Abner	060	1876	WB-4/152	AR
McCoy, Alexander	054	c1830	WB-2/102	AR
McCoy, Ann	085	1810	WB-G/156	AR
McCoy, D.	061	1882	WB-2/45	AR
McCoy, Daniell	030	1735	SS 876/411	SS/AR

Name	Co.	Date	Recorded Copy	Original
McCoy, Dely	085	1887	WB-2/215	CTY
McCoy, Dorcas	065	1855	WB-J/8	AR
McCoy, Edwin A.	065	1852	WB-I/191	AR
McCoy, Frederick	028	1826	WB-C/279	
McCoy, Hardey	028	1843	WB-D/79	
McCoy, Harriett	028	1859	WB-D/322	AR-Nunc.
McCoy, James	024	1892	WB-E/207	AR
McCoy, James	065	1818	WB-E/28	AR
McCoy, Jane	072	1785	WI/L31	AR
McCoy, Jesse	018	1874	WB-E/48	AR
McCoy, John	073	1768	WB-A/92	
McCoy, John	065	1839	WB-H/14	AR
McCoy, John	056	c1781	WB-2/265	AR
McCoy, John	018	1839	WB-C/246	
McCoy, John F.	065	1865	WB-J/203	AR
McCoy, Joshua	018	1837	WB-C/226	
McCoy, Joshua	077	1821	WB-F/33	AR
McCoy, Julia	077	1802	WB-E/179	AR-Nunc.
McCoy, Nancy	059	1893	WB-B/81	CTY
McCoy, Paschal	081	1885	WB-15/536	AR
McCoy, Permelia	081	1900	WB-17/129	
McCoy, Polly	018	1828	WB-C/101	
McCoy, R. Ada	064	1890	WB-2/214	AR
McCoy, Redden	028	1844	WB-D/108	
McCoy, W. A.	059	1887	WB-A/498	CTY
McCoy, William	030	1795	WB-2/63	
McCoy, William	077	1795	WB-E/46	
McCoy, William C.	028	1851	WB-D/178	AR
McCracken, Abigail	073	1858	WB-G/358	CTY
McCracken, Clark L.	098	1898	WB-A/311	CTY
McCracken, D. V.	049	1897	WB-2/387	AR
McCracken, James	085	1814	WB-G/341	AR
McCracken, Jeremiah	073	1802	WB-D/66	AR
McCracken, John	085	c1792	WB-B/205	
McCracken, John	049	1890	WB-2/247	AR
McCracken, John	001	c1856	WB-1/102	AR
McCracken, Joseph	049	1848	WB-2/178	
McCracken, Polly	085	1841	WB-I/92	AR
McCracken, Samuel	073	1838	WB-F/8	AR
McCracken, Sarah	073	1804	WB-D/138	AR
McCracken, Thomas	073	1845	WB-F/264	
McCracken, Thomas	073	1835	WB-E/339	AR
McCracken, Thomas	073	1892	WB-H/561	CTY
McCrackin, Robert	070	1766	WB-C/246	AR
McCrain, Hugh	083	1788	WB-1/6	AR
McCraine, Archibald	029	1819	WB-B/25	AR
McCraine, Hugh	029	1846	WB-C/137	AR
McCraine, Neal	029	1818	WB-B/9	AR
McCraney, John	068	1864	WB-C/99	
McCranie, Nancy	029	1851	WB-C/200	AR
McCrary, Elizabeth	054	1839	WB-2/189	AR
McCrary, Hugh	032	1830	WB-1/154	
McCrary, John	032	1830	WB-1/158	
McCrary, T. F.	054	1897	WB-6/90	CTY
McCrary, W. F.	038	1873	WB-2/130	AR
McCrary, William	038	c1847	WB-1/92	AR
McCrary, William	032	1892	WB-4/138	AR
McCraw, A. B.	026	c1894	Orig. Only	AR
McCraw, Adam I.	092	1853	WB-4/331	AR
McCraw, Beard	026	1861	WB-1/264	AR
McCraw, Benjamin	092	1813	WB-3/107	AR
McCraw, Francis M.	092	1897	WB-6/436	AR
McCraw, J. B.	026	1864	WB-1/331 & 333	AR
McCraw, Jacob	092	1815	WB-3/114	AR
McCraw, Jacob W.	092	1883	WB-6/181	AR
McCraw, Jessie E.	080	1892	WB-1/166	AR
McCraw, Linda	026	1890	WB-2/414	AR
McCraw, Nancy	026	1862	WB-1/281	AR-Nunc.
McCraw, Samuel	086	1840	WB-E/64	AR
McCraw, William	026	1863	WB-1/318	AR
McCray, James	001	c1855	WB-1/104	AR
McCray, John	001	c1854	WB-1/88	AR
McCray, Nancy	084	1857	WB-C/240	CTY
McCrearey, Hugh	085	c1785	WB-C/18	AR
McCreary, Margaret	054	1845	WB-2/312	AR
McCree, Hugh	016	1808	WB-A/97	AR
McCree, William	016	1815	WB-A/60	AR
McCreedy, James	040	1888	WB-2/304	
McCreedy, William	040	1886	WB-2/259	
McCrery, Samuel	054	c1814	WB-1/320	AR
McCrohon, John	028	1789	WB-A/188 & 363	
McCrorey, David	073	1832	WB-E/415	AR
McCrorey, David	073	1840	WB-F/62	AR
McCrorey, John	073	c1813	WB-D/367	AR
McCrory, George	073	c1806	Orig. Only	AR
McCrory, Martha	073	1890	WB-H/495	CTY
McCrow, K. J.	086	1892	WB-F/433	AR
McCrum, Samuel	065	1778	WB-B/119	AR
McCrummon, Margaret	029	1846	WB-C/104	AR
McCubbins, John	084	1809	WB-A/84	CTY
McCuiston, Isabella	046	1846	WB-C/250	AR
McCuiston, James	085	1766	WB-A/122	AR
McCuiston, Moses	046	1800	WB-A/261	AR
McCuiston, Robert	085	1766	WB-A/112	AR
McCuiston, Thomas	046	1853	WB-C/383	AR
McCuiston, Walte	046	1825	WB-B/212	AR
McCullah, James	065	1842	WB-H/81	AR
McCullen, George	056	1854	WB-1/677	AR
McCullen, Jane	056	1867	WB-2/93	AR
McCullen, William H.	056	1898	WB-4/69	AR
McCullers, John	056	c1767	WB-1/413	AR
McCullers, John, Sr.	056	1822	WB-1/453	AR
McCullers, Sarah	099	1844	RB-25/359	AR
McCulley, Sally	001	1859	WB-1/153	AR
McCulloch, Alexander	070	1822	WB-C/294	AR
McCulloch, Alexander	047	1798	WB-3/313	AR
McCulloch, Alfred	033	1865	WB-1/186	AR
McCulloch, Andrew	073	1835	WB-E/345	AR
McCulloch, Elisabeth	065	1802	WB-B/83	AR
McCulloch, Elizabeth	033	1841	WB-1/32	
McCulloch, Elizabeth	085	1836	WB-H/705	AR
McCulloch, Henry	N	1755	SS 880/24	SS/AR
McCulloch, James	085	1758	WB-A/113	AR
McCulloch, James	085	1812	WB-G/227	AR
McCulloch, John	054	1857	WB-3/118	AR
McCulloch, John	065	1845	WB-I/30	AR
McCulloch, John	065	1848	WB-I/144	AR
McCulloch, John	065	c1823	Orig. Only	AR
McCulloch, Joseph	073	1817	WB-D/503	AR
McCulloch, Joseph	073	1884	WB-H/356	CTY
McCulloch, Josiah	065	1864	WB-J/193	AR
McCulloch, Mary	060	1809	Orig. Only	AR
McCulloch, Robert	060	1819	Orig. Only	AR
McCulloch, Robert M.	011	c1808	WB-1/426	Nunc.
McCulloch, Thomas	046	1861	WB-D/90	AR
McCulloch, William	078	1867	WB-18/480	AR
McCulloch, William	073	1842	WB-F/143	AR
McCullock, James	060	1843	WB-2/167	AR

Name	Co	Date	Recorded Copy	Original
McCulloh, Charlotte	033	1896	WB-2/193	CTY
McCulloh, Elizabeth	033	1853	WB-1/107	AR
McCulloh, Elizabeth	033	1841	Orig. Only	AR
McCulloh, James	085	1816	WB-G/410	AR
McCulloh, Mary	065	1797	WB-B/83	
McCullough, Barnett	084	c1796	OW/244	AR
McCullough, David	SC	1866	040 WB-2/66	040 AR
McCullough, Ellen	009	1900	WB-2/261	CTY
McCullough, Hugh	009	1828	OB-A/507	AR
McCullough, James H.	054	1889	WB-5/308	CTY
McCullough, John	072	1800	Orig. Only	AR
McCullough, Lenny	050	1899	WB-2/330	
McCullough, Margaret	009	1892	WB-1/539	CTY
McCullough, Robert	040	c1857	WB-1/99	AR
McCully, Lettice	073	1830	WB-E/213	AR
McCully, Robert	073	1820	WB-D/574	AR
McCurdy, Archibald	016	1844	WB-1/38	AR
McCurdy, William	035	1838	Orig. Only	AR
McCurdy, William	003	1892	Orig. Only	AR
McCurdy, William	035	1806	WB-A/297	AR
McCurrey, William	060	1790	Orig. Only	AR
McCurry, Abraham	060	1800	Orig. Only	AR
McCurry, John W.	064	1890	WB-2/208	AR
McCurry, Joshua C.	014	1897	064 WB-2/384	064 AR
McCurry, Joshua C.	014	1897	WB-3/13	CTY
McCurry, K. J.	086	1865	WB-E/453	AR
McCurry, M. S.	086	1899	WB-G/30	AR
McCurry, Sarah E.	038	1900	WB-4/226	AR
McCurry, William	086	1828	WB-D/98	AR
McCutchan, John S.	054	1848	WB-3/30	AR
McCutchin, John	065	1786	WB-B/70	AR
McDade, A. J.	073	1900	WB-I/169	
McDade, Albritan	099	1868	Orig. Only	AR
McDade, Edward	073	1830	WB-E/229	AR
McDade, John	069	1828	WB-1/360	AR
McDade, John	073	1844	WB-F/208	AR
McDade, Margaret	073	1841	WB-F/96	AR
McDade, Mary	037	1833	WB-F/148	AR
McDade, Willis	099	1838	RB-24/226	AR
McDade, Willis R.	099	1897	WB-D/61	AR
McDaniel, A. H.	081	1897	WB-16/460	AR
McDaniel, Absalom	029	1798	WB-A/16	AR
McDaniel, Allen	085	1833	WB-H/605	AR
McDaniel, Amelia	104	1860	WB-5/264	
McDaniel, Arthur	047	1874	WB-6/111	AR
McDaniel, Campbell	037	1808	WB-D/302	AR
McDaniel, Cason	001	1859	WB-1/167	AR
McDaniel, Cornelia J.	081	1896	WB-16/393	AR
McDaniel, Daniel	037	1792	WB-C/205	AR
McDaniel, Daniel	029	1801	WB-A/38	AR
McDaniel, Daniel	037	1769	WB-A/169	AR
McDaniel, Durant	057	1828	WB-B/88	AR
McDaniel, E. G.	057	1896	WB-C/219	AR
McDaniel, E. J.	048	1899	WB-1/91	CTY
McDaniel, Eli	073	1809	WB-D/241	AR
McDaniel, Eli	073	c1789	WB-B/63	AR
McDaniel, Elisha	071	1839	WB-4/187	AR
McDaniel, George	086	1884	WB-F/238	AR
McDaniel, H. P.	092	1887	WB-6/268	AR
McDaniel, Henry	092	1825	WB-3/166	AR
McDaniel, James	057	1809	WB-A/317	AR
McDaniel, James	075	1780	WB-K/51	AR
McDaniel, James	057	1854	WB-B/219	AR
McDaniel, James	047	1854	WB-4/374	AR
McDaniel, James	011	c1779	WB-1/569	
McDaniel, James	103	1789	WI-A/159	AR
McDaniel, James	085	c1813	Orig. Only	AR
McDaniel, James	022	1821	WB-B/36	AR
McDaniel, James	071	1860	WB-5/228	AR
McDaniel, James	082	1821	WB-1/222	AR
McDaniel, Jane	020	N. D.	Orig. Only	AR
McDaniel, Jane T.	001	1860	WB-1/173	AR
McDaniel, John	022	1813	WB-A/229	AR
McDaniel, John	029	1874	WB-E/120	AR
McDaniel, John	011	N. D.	WB-2/327	
McDaniel, John	073	1851	WB-F/490	AR
McDaniel, John	073	1824	WB-E/62	AR
McDaniel, John	029	1836	WB-B/270	AR
McDaniel, John	057	1817	WB-B/42	AR
McDaniel, Jonas	028	1893	WB-F/86	
McDaniel, July An	086	1880	WB-F/155	AR
McDaniel, Lewis	057	1888	WB-C/150	AR
McDaniel, Lydia	086	1891	WB-F/406	AR
McDaniel, Mariam	037	1793	WB-C/237	AR
McDaniel, Mary M.	020	1858	RB-S/9	
McDaniel, Melchie	073	1780	WB-A/211	
McDaniel, Moses	086	1879	WB-F/136	AR
McDaniel, Mulchi	073	1830	WB-E/209	AR
McDaniel, Nathan	086	1842	WB-E/99	AR
McDaniel, Patrick	047	1842	WB-4/209	AR
McDaniel, Peter	071	1827	WB-4/21	AR
McDaniel, Rachel	075	1797	WB-L/114	AR
McDaniel, Rebecca	061	1843	WB-1/28	AR
McDaniel, Reuben	086	1862	WB-E/398	AR
McDaniel, Risdon	057	1828	WB-B/89	AR
McDaniel, Risdon	057	1831	WB-B/112	AR
McDaniel, Sampson	086	1879	WB-F/137	AR
McDaniel, Samuel	073	1845	WB-F/256	AR
McDaniel, Sarah	086	1878	WB-F/125	AR
McDaniel, Starling	085	1853	WB-K/158	AR
McDaniel, Thomas	029	1890	WB-E/473	AR
McDaniel, Thomas	057	1856	WB-B/230	AR
McDaniel, William	070	1789	WB-C/274	AR
McDaniel, William	020	1831	RB-L/604	
McDaniel, William C.	029	1870	WB-E/17	AR
McDaniel, William P.	001	1899	WB-3/249	AR
McDaniel, Zachariah	082	1795	WB-1/58	AR
McDaniell, Daniel	010	1734	SS 876/295	SS/AR
McDarmon, Charles	046	1799	WB-A/259	AR
McDearmid, John	083	1845	WB-1/456	AR
McDearmid, Mary	005	1867	WB-C/261	AR
McDiarmid, Daniel	029	1874	WB-E/122	AR
McDiarmid, Elizabeth	083	1891	WB-3/557	AR
McDiarmid, Mary R.	029	1882	WB-E/280	AR
McDiarmid, N. Lovely	083	1890	WB-3/487	AR
McDiarmid, W. W.	083	1897	WB-4/133	AR
McDiarmid, William L.	029	c1875	Orig. Only	AR
McDiffie, Daniel	011	c1828	WB-2/376	
McDill, Samuel	046	1811	WB-A/273	AR
McDivitt, Emily M.	013	1899	WB-D/345	AR
McDonald, A. L.	068	c1893	WB-D/402	
McDonald, Alexander	054	c1813	WB-1/307	AR
McDonald, Alexander	082	1861	WB-4/147	AR
McDonald, Allan	068	1828	WB-B/57	
McDonald, Angus	068	1857	WB-C/48	
McDonald, Angus	083	1878	WB-3/160	AR
McDonald, Archibald	068	1847	WB-B/200	
McDonald, Archibald	029	c1781	Orig. Only	AR
McDonald, Archibald	083	1855	WB-2/203	AR
McDonald, Archibald	029	1818	WB-B/10	AR

Name	Co.	Date	Recorded Copy	Original
McDonald, Archibald	029	1900	WB-F/196	AR
McDonald, Caroline	016	1899	WB-4/323	AR
McDonald, Christian	082	1849	WB-4/28	AR
McDonald, Coleman	086	1858	WB-E/339	AR
McDonald, Daniel	068	c1856	WB-C/73	
McDonald, Daniel	082	1843	WB-3/5	AR
McDonald, Daniel	082	1826	WB-1/274	AR
McDonald, Daniel	068	1850	WB-B/210	
McDonald, Daniel	068	1844	WB-B/146	
McDonald, Daniel	083	1862	WB-2/186	AR
McDonald, David	065	1838	WB-E/214	AR
McDonald, Donald	068	1825	WB-B/40	
McDonald, Donald	029	1840	WB-B/310	AR
McDonald, Donald	082	1810	WB-1/141	AR
McDonald, Duncan	029	1784	Orig. Only	AR
McDonald, Duncan	024	1861	WB-D/8	AR
McDonald, Elizabeth	024	1861	WB-D/11	AR
McDonald, Flora	082	1899	WB-7/11	AR
McDonald, G. W.	065	1895	WB-M/381	
McDonald, George	085	1769	WB-A/121	AR
McDonald, Henry	029	1880	WB-E/220	AR
McDonald, Isaac	012	1821	WB-B/123	AR
McDonald, James	016	1849	WB-1/158	AR
McDonald, Janet	084	1857	WB-C/254	CTY
McDonald, John	068	1809	WB-A/267	
McDonald, John	009	1890	WB-1/471	CTY
McDonald, John	029	1893	WB-E/574	AR
McDonald, John	083	1840	WB-1/390	AR
McDonald, John	029	1849	WB-C/168	AR
McDonald, John S.	083	1883	WB-3/293	AR
McDonald, Joseph B.	065	1874	WB-K/151	
McDonald, K. M.	068	1899	WB-E/11	
McDonald, Kenneth	068	1801	WB-A/243	
McDonald, Malcom	029	1870	WB-E/21	AR
McDonald, Margaret	029	1857	WB-C/359	AR
McDonald, Margaret	083	1865	WB-2/215	AR
McDonald, Martha	039	1895	WB-V/54	AR
McDonald, Mary	086	1801	WB-B/126	
McDonald, Mary	068	1861	WB-C/85	
McDonald, Mary	068	1900	WB-E/74	
McDonald, Mary	068	N. D.	Orig. Only	AR
McDonald, Mary A.	011	1894	WB-3/64	CTY
McDonald, Nancy	068	1886	WB-D/220	
McDonald, Neill	068	1887	WB-D/246	
McDonald, Roderick	029	c1825	WB-B/134	AR
McDonald, Ronald	084	1834	WB-B/108	CTY
McDonald, Sarah	068	c1883	WB-D/166	
McDonald, Sarah	087	1848	WB-1/340	AR
McDonald, Sarah	029	c1856	Orig. Only	AR
McDonald, William G.	029	1863	WB-D/56	AR
McDonald, William J.	029	1889	WB-E/448	AR
McDonnel, Duncan	020	1779	RB-A/68	AR
McDonnell, Thomas H.	061	c1866	WB-1/83	AR
McDonnell, William	013	1841	WB-A/68	
McDougal, Allen	011	c1771	WB-1/588	
McDougal, Daniel	068	1873	WB-D/43	
McDougal, Ronald	070	1856	WB-C/618	AR
McDougald, A. C.	083	1899	WB-4/235	AR
McDougald, Alexander	083	1848	WB-2/35	AR
McDougald, Allen	029	1844	WB-C/76	AR
McDougald, Annabella	029	1884	WB-E/316	AR
McDougald, Archibald	005	1885	WB-D/180	AR
McDougald, Daniel	029	1820	WB-B/47	AR
McDougald, Hugh W.	083	1863	WB-2/197	AR
McDougald, John	048	1899	WB-1/102	CTY

Name	Co.	Date	Recorded Copy	Original
McDougald, Maggie J.	064	c1897	Orig. Only	AR
McDougald, Mary	029	1845	WB-C/86	AR
McDougald, Nancy	029	1848	WB-C/153	AR
McDougall, James	047	1794	WB-3/225	AR
McDougall, John	029	1795	Orig. Only	AR
McDow, David	086	1809	WB-B/223	AR
McDowall, James	010	1752	SS 879/44	SS/AR
McDowall, William	029	1767	Orig. Only	AR
McDowel, Athan A.	013	1832	WB-A/15	
McDowell, Alexander	011	c1846	WB-1/133	
McDowell, Archibald	051	1881	WB-C/266	AR
McDowell, Charles	005	c1754	WB-1/2	AR-Copy
McDowell, Charles	014	1879	WB-2/186	
McDowell, Charlotte	050	1899	WB-2/310	
McDowell, Daniel	100	1885	WB-51/203	AR
McDowell, Elizabeth	010	1849	WB-G/444	AR
McDowell, Elizabeth	037	1835	WB-F/177	AR
McDowell, Esther	065	1804	WB-B/85	AR
McDowell, George B.	024	1882	WB-E/113	AR
McDowell, Henry	060	1895	WB-4/574	AR
McDowell, Hugh	065	1835	WB-G/219	AR
McDowell, James C.	081	1895	WB-16/355	AR
McDowell, John	037	1829	WB-F/98	AR
McDowell, John	070	1735	SS 877/200	SS/AR
McDowell, John	065	1795	WB-B/139	AR
McDowell, John	065	1844	WB-H/148	AR
McDowell, John	014	1803	Orig. Only	AR
McDowell, Joseph	014	c1795	Orig. Only	CTY-Copy
McDowell, Joseph	020	1837	RB-N/49	AR
McDowell, Joseph	046	1797	WB-A/257	AR
McDowell, Joseph	014	c1795	Orig. Only	AR-Copy
McDowell, Joseph	014	c1801	Orig. Only	AR-Copy
McDowell, Joseph	085	1771	WB-A/99	AR
McDowell, Mary M.	086	1872	WB-F/39	AR
McDowell, Mary S.	037	1881	WB-G/605	AR
McDowell, Nina	098	1890	WB-A/114	CTY
McDowell, R. I.	065	1886	WB-L/115	
McDowell, R. W.	065	1889	WB-L/406	
McDowell, Robert	065	1780	WB-B/61	
McDowell, Robert	065	1771	WB-B/47	AR
McDowell, Stephen	037	1899	WB-H/442	AR
McDowell, Stephen	010	1816	WB-F/332	AR
McDowell, Thomas D.	011	1898	WB-3/98	CTY
McDowell, W. B.	047	1900	WB-7/287	
McDowell, William	082	1811	WB-1/146	AR
McDowell, William	065	1782	WB-B/61	AR
McDowell, William	086	1818	WB-C/112	AR
McDowell, William R.	061	1887	WB-2/85	AR
McDuffee, Margaret	070	1848	WB-C/487	AR
McDuffie, Alexander	083	1880	WB-3/212	AR
McDuffie, Archibald	029	1805	WB-A/80	AR
McDuffie, Catharine	087	1877	WB-3/161	AR
McDuffie, Daniel	029	1789	Orig. Only	AR
McDuffie, Duncan	029	1827	WB-B/153	AR
McDuffie, Eliza A.	070	1897	WB-H/85	AR
McDuffie, James	070	1869	WB-E/161	AR
McDuffie, James M.	103	1862	RD-13/462	AR
McDuffie, John	029	1782	Orig. Only	AR
McDuffie, John	011	c1774	WB-1/548	Nunc.
McDuffie, Mary Jane	029	1853	WB-C/251	AR
McDuffie, Murdock	029	1866	WB-D/89	AR
McDuffie, Sarah	029	c1784	Orig. Only	AR
McDuffie, Sarah	082	1830	WB-2/1	AR
McDuffie, W. C.	029	1899	WB-F/179	AR

Name	Co.	Date	Recorded Copy	Original
McDuffie, W. C., Jr.	029	1897	WB-F/97	AR
McDuffie, William A.	087	1893	WB-3/535	AR
McDugald, Ann	011	c1825	WB-2/363	
McDugald, Archibald	068	1835	WB-B/92	
McDugald, Archibald	083	c1818	WB-1/324	AR
McDugald, Donald	068	1817	WB-A/296	
McDugald, Duncan	082	1828	WB-1/290	AR
McDugald, Margaret	011	1862	WB-1/280	
McEacharn, Peter R.	016	1852	WB-1/214	AR
McEachen, John	083	1815	WB-1/163	
McEachern, Angus	083	1866	WB-2/225	AR
McEachern, Archibald	083	c1866	Copy	082 AR
McEachern, Archibald	083	1874	WB-3/69	AR
McEachern, Catherine	016	1858	WB-2/45	AR
McEachern, Daniel	083	1871	WB-3/25	AR
McEachern, Duncan	083	1816	WB-1/167	
McEachern, Hector	083	1857	WB-2/114	AR
McEachern, Jenat	083	1828	WB-1/331	AR
McEachern, John S.	070	1889	WB-F/310	AR
McEachern, Robert M.	016	1887	WB-3/546	AR
McEachern, Thomas	016	1845	WB-1/55	AR
McEachin, Archibald	083	1837	WB-1/306	AR
McEachin, Evander	083	1869	WB-3/27	AR
McEachin, James C.	082	1890	WB-6/413	AR
McEachin, Patrick	083	1829	WB-1/189	AR
McEachran, John M. W.	016	1857	WB-2/31	AR
McEachron, Dion C.	016	1836	PQS.5/395	AR
McEachron, Hector	016	1836	PQS.5/394	AR
McEachron, John	016	1837	PQS.5/422	AR
McEatman, William	105	1897	WB-3/249	AR
McElrath, Frank	014	1873	WB-1/53	
McElrath, John	014	1870	WB-2/52	
McElrath, Mary	014	1884	WB-2/281	CTY
McElrath, Mary	014	1870	Orig. Only	CTY
McElroy, Margaret	084	1857	WB-C/264	CTY
McEntire, Aaron	086	1827	WB-D/73	AR
McEntire, Caroline	086	1894	WB-F/477	AR
McEntire, Ellinder	026	1858	WB-1/223	AR
McEntire, Henry	065	1826	WB-E/35	AR
McEntire, James	065	1802	WB-B/156	AR
McEntire, James	086	1818	WB-C/98	AR
McEntire, John	065	1797	WB-B/74	AR
McEntire, John	086	1857	Copy	064 AR
McEntire, John M.	086	1857	WB-E/327	AR
McEntire, M. J.	086	1894	WB-F/484	AR
McEntire, Rachel	086	1823	WB-D/12	AR
McEntire, Samuel	086	1822	WB-D/5	AR
McEntire, Thomas L.	086	1846	WB-E/158	AR
McEntire, William	026	1889	WB-2/381	AR
McEntire, William	086	1897	WB-F/560	AR
McEntire, William	086	1832	WB-D/150	AR
McEntire, William	026	1877	WB-2/166	AR
McEvoy, Alice	070	1900	WB-H/323	AR
McEwen, Elizabeth	016	1803	WB-A/33	AR
McEwen, Hugh	065	1792	WB-B/131	AR
McEwen, James	054	1840	WB-2/207	AR
McEwen, John	011	c1786	WB-1/559	
McEwen, Mary	065	1807	WB-E/10	AR
McEwen, Mary Grace	054	1876	WB-4/204	CTY
McEwen, Robert	011	c1804	WB-1/428	
McEwen, Thomas	016	1846	WB-1/101	AR
McEwen, William	054	1851	WB-3/54	AR
McEwen, William H.	054	1877	WB-4/240	CTY
McFadden, Cynthia	086	1894	WB-F/474	AR
McFadden, James T.	086	1887	WB-F/301	AR

Name	Co.	Date	Recorded Copy	Original
McFadden, John	086	1853	WB-E/242	AR
McFaddon, Thomas	016	1799	WB-A/79	AR
McFadin, John	094	1777	Orig. Only	AR
McFadyen, Angus	011	1896	WB-3/84	CTY
McFadyen, Archibald	029	1830	WB-B/187	AR
McFadyen, Henrietta	029	1874	WB-E/135	AR
McFarland, Aaron D.	080	1884	WB-1/78	AR
McFarland, Daniel	068	1881	WB-D/140	
McFarland, Flora	082	1889	WB-6/388	AR
McFarland, George E.	086	1883	WB-F/218	AR
McFarland, James	054	c1806	WB-1/357	AR
McFarland, John	082	1820	WB-1/212	AR-Nunc.
McFarland, John	029	1767	Orig. Only	AR
McFarland, Margaret	082	1848	WB-3/45	AR
McFarland, Neil	082	c1807	WB-1/115	AR
McFarland, Parland	068	1814	WB-A/281	
McFarland, Patrick	086	1810	WB-B/247	AR
McFarland, Patrick	086	1870	WB-F/15	
McFarland, Robert	080	1884	WB-1/96	
McFarland, Robert	020	1780	RB-A/111	AR
McFarland, Samuel	054	1857	WB-3/127	AR
McFarland, W. J.	086	1896	WB-F/515	AR
McFarland, William	070	1744	DB-C/20	
McFarland, William	086	1880	Orig. Only	AR
McFayden, John	082	1863	WB-4/167	AR
McFee, John	013	1850	WB-A/144	
McFeeters, Daniel	085	c1793	WB-D/218	AR
McGaha, James	093	1877	WB-1/211	
McGeachy, Alexander	083	1844	WB-1/441	AR
McGeachy, Neill	083	1861	WB-2/177	AR
McGee, Ann	035	1863	WB-3/74	AR
McGee, Betsy Ann	087	1877	Orig. Only	AR
McGee, Daniel	060	1805	Orig. Only	AR
McGee, E. C.	038	1882	WB-2/420	AR
McGee, Esther	046	1851	WB-C/339	AR
McGee, George	029	1863	WB-C/446	
McGee, Jane	099	1848	RB-26/406	AR
McGee, John	046	1774	Orig. Only	SS/AR
McGee, John	049	c1856	WB-1/21	AR
McGee, Joseph	068	1794	WB-A/173	
McGee, Rachel	046	1880	WB-E/283	AR
McGee, Richard J.	056	1894	WB-2/173	AR
McGee, Samuel	081	1809	WB-3/162	
McGee, Thomas	060	1822	Orig. Only	AR
McGee, William	035	1827	WB-A/320	AR
McGehee, Benjamin	044	1816	WB-7/636	CTY
McGehee, Charles A.	084	1896	WB-F/41	CTY
McGehee, Henrietta	033	1866	WB-1/203	
McGehee, Henry	099	1896	WB-C/566	
McGehee, Jack K.	099	1872	RB-35/73	AR
McGehee, Joseph	044	1889	WB-24/64	CTY
McGehee, Lemuel	044	1846	WB-16/510	CTY
McGehee, Mumford	078	1816	WI-7/82	AR
McGehee, Nathan	044	1871	WB-23/46	CTY
McGehee, Thomas	078	1867	WB-18/464	
McGehee, Thomas I.	078	1853	WB-17/130	AR
McGibboney, David	046	1850	WB-C/331	AR
McGibboney, Patrick	046	1804	WB-A/263	AR
McGibony, Nancy	084	1873	WB-E/45	CTY
McGill, Allen	082	1828	WB-1/296	AR
McGill, Archibald	083	c1821	WB-1/131	
McGill, Daniel	029	1865	WB-D/82	AR
McGill, James	065	1792	WB-B/132	AR
McGill, John	060	1819	Orig. Only	AR
McGill, John	029	c1829	WB-B/291	AR

Name	Co.	Date	Recorded Copy	Original
McGill, Neal	082	1837	WB-2/66	AR
McGill, Neill	083	c1812	WB-1/126	AR
McGill, Rodger	83	c1800	WB-1/183	
McGill, Thomas P.	040	1878	WB-2/123	AR
McGill, Wardlaw	013	1888	WB-B/495	AR
McGilvary, Archibald	068	c1851	WB-B/231	
McGilvary, Evander	068	1898	WB-D/535	
McGimsey, A. J.	014	1869	WB-2/25	AR
McGinn, James	065	1844	WB-H/179	AR
McGinn, Robert A.	065	1863	WB-J/167	AR
McGinn, W. A.	065	1863	WB-J/174	AR
McGinnis, Charles	016	1816	WB-A/47	AR
McGinnis, Charles B.	065	1862	WB-J/142	AR
McGinnis, Edward	060	1852	WB-2/364	
McGinnis, Joseph	065	1848	WB-I/130	AR
McGinnis, William	065	1869	WB-K/10	
McGinty, Alexander	065	1803	WB-E/1	AR
McGinty, Hannah	065	1803	Orig. Only	AR
McGinty, Mary A.	065	1804	WB-E/2	AR
McGirt, Duncan	083	1858	WB-2/138	AR
McGirt, James	083	1895	WB-4/118	AR
McGirt, Susan	083	1882	WB-3/283	AR
McGlamery, Andrew	026	1873	WB-2/82	AR
McGlamery, Ann	026	1850	WB-1/113	AR
McGlamery, George	104	1886	WB-6/276	AR
McGlaughlen, James	085	c1779	WB-B/114	AR
McGlauhon, William F.	010	1892	WB-I/335	AR
McGlawhon, James	010	1829	WB-G/195	AR
McGlawhon, William	010	1826	WB-G/139	AR
McGlawhon, William	056	1810	WB-1/225	AR
McGlawhorn, Joseph	079	1881	WB-2/213	AR
McGlawhorn, Meriear	079	1877	WB-2/153	AR
McGlohon, Luke	051	1858	WB-B/9	
McGoogan, Catharine	083	1866	WB-2/237	AR
McGoogan, Hugh	083	1836	Orig. Only	AR
McGoogan, John	083	1880	WB-3/188	
McGoone, Hugh	085	1817	WB-G/481	AR
McGough, Robert	065	c1778	WB-B/57	AR
McGowan, Esther	105	1897	WB-3/269	AR
McGowan, J. Q.	035	1890	WB-4/361	AR
McGowan, Joseph	009	1866	OB-M/243	AR
McGowan, Margaret A.	079	1883	WB-2/262	AR
McGowan, Martha	009	1866	OB-M/244	AR
McGowan, Patrick	099	1893	WB-C/148	AR
McGowan, W. C.	079	1900	WB-3/233	
McGowan, W. K.	079	1900	WB-3/216	AR
McGowen, John	079	1868	WB-1/177	AR
McGowen, William	035	1860	WB-3/13	AR
McGowen, William	035	1792	WB-A/309	AR
McGown, Hannah	096	1814	WB-2/38	AR
McGown, James	073	1770	WB-A/116	
McGrady, Elizabeth	104	1892	WB-6/429	AR
McGrady, James F.	046	1865	WB-D/278	AR
McGrady, Patrick R.	104	1884	WB-6/255	AR
McGrain, John	072	c1792	RW/L54	AR
McGraw, Alfred	016	1875	WB-3/122	AR
McGraw, Benjamin	016	1814	WB-A/9	
McGraw, James	016	1811	WB-A/5	AR
McGraw, John	028	1806	WB-B/250	
McGready, James	046	1800	WB-A/262	AR
McGready, Moses	046	1859	WB-C/535	AR
McGreger, Cloe	047	1815	WB-3/577	AR
McGregor, Anthony	005	1824	WB-A/104	
McGregor, Hugh	075	c1703	Orig. Only	SS/AR
McGregor, John	005	1797	WB-A/68	AR
McGregor, William	071	1815	WB-3/168	AR
McGrogan, Sarah	083	1846	WB-1/490	
McGroves, William	086	1883	WB-F/184	AR
McGufford, Nathaniel	070	1795	WB-C/280	AR
McGugan, Daniel	083	1858	WB-2/130	AR
McGugan, Duncan	083	1819	WB-1/369	AR
McGuin, James	065	1770	WB-B/110	
McGuire, Edward	085	1785	WB-C/64	AR
McGuire, Henry	032	1835	WB-1/257	
McGuire, Hugh	005	1818	WB-2/112	AR
McGuire, Issabel	085	1812	WB-G/250	AR
McGuire, James	085	1826	WB-H/338	AR
McGuire, John	054	c1818	WB-1A/95	AR
McGuire, John	085	1762	WB-A/123	AR
McGuire, John	024	1807	WB-B/209	AR
McGuire, John K.	029	1873	WB-E/84	AR
McGuire, John K.	029	1849	WB-C/161	
McGuire, Polly	033	1853	WB-1/109	AR
McGuire, Robert	006	1888	WB-E/179	AR
McGuire, Sarah	024	1820	WB-C/89	AR
McGuire, Thomas	054	c1799	WB-1/183	
McGuire, William	082	1790	WB-1/33	AR
McGwigan, John A.	047	1892	WB-7/30	AR
McGwinn, Daniel	086	1830	WB-D/121	AR
McHargue, James	054	c1823	WB-2/70	AR
McHargue, James	054	1856	WB-3/100	AR
McHargue, James A.	054	1866	WB-3/182	AR
McHargue, John	085	c1780	WB-B/44	AR
McHargue, Nancy E.	054	1885	WB-5/60	CTY
McHargue, Rhoda	054	1894	WB-6/48	CTY
McHargue, Samuel	054	1861	Orig. Only	AR
McHarney, Willoughby	085	1823	WB-H/200	AR
McHarry, James	065	1778	WB-B/48	AR-Nunc.
McHemphill, William	013	1892	WB-C/187	AR
McHenrey, Henrey	085	1771	WB-A/103	AR
McHenry, Elinor	085	1793	WB-B/203	AR
McHenry, Henry	085	1838	WB-I/35	AR
McHon, Elijah	086	1830	WB-D/115	AR
McHorney, Samuel	030	1866	WB-4/261	
McHorney, Samuel	030	1836	WB-4/18	
McIlhenny, Elizabeth	070	1831	WB-AB/264	AR
McIlhenny, John	070	1804	WB-AB/88	AR
McIlvean, Francis N.	028	1868	WB-E/9	
McIlwain, Levicy	097	1897	WB-2/547	AR
McIlwaine, A. G.	VA	1878	047 WB-6/191	
McIlwinen, John	087	c1792	WB-A/37	AR
McInis, John	082	1859	WB-4/136	AR
McInnis, Catherine	082	1873	WB-6/103	AR
McInnis, Duncan	011	1822	WB-2/342	
McInnis, Elizabeth	082	1886	WB-6/328	AR
McInnis, James	082	1848	WB-4/15	AR
McInnis, John	029	1821	WB-B/57	AR
McInnis, Malcom	011	1882	WB-2/152	
McInnis, Margaret	029	1873	WB-E/118	AR
McInnis, Miles	022	1833	WB-B/256	AR
McInnis, Murdock	083	1842	WB-1/409	AR
McInnish, Donald	029	1811	WB-A/171	AR
McIntire, Andrew	035	1784	WB-A/342	AR
McIntire, Sarah	065	1823	WB-B/99	AR
McIntosh, Alexander	068	1851	WB-B/218	
McIntosh, Alexander	065	1884	WB-L/12	
McIntosh, Alexander	068	1812	WB-A/274	
McIntosh, Angus	068	1862	WB-C/89	
McIntosh, Angus	082	1821	WB-1/228	AR
McIntosh, Daniel	082	1851	WB-4/52	AR

Name	Co.	Date	Recorded Copy	Original
McIntosh, Daniel	054	1851	WB-3/50	AR
McIntosh, Donald M.	049	1899	025 WB-A/245	025 AR
McIntosh, Duncn	068	1799	WB-A/201	
McIntosh, George	082	1848	WB-4/21	AR
McIntosh, Margaret	054	1846	WB-3/13	AR
McIntosh, Nancy	068	c1856	WB-C/156	
McIntosh, Rachel	107	c1846	WB-1/344	
McIntosh, Richard H.	075	1890	WB-0/323	AR
McIntyre, Alexander	083	1895	WB-4/77	AR
McIntyre, Archibald	082	1859	WB-4/133	AR
McIntyre, Archie	022	1900	WB-F/136	AR
McIntyre, Daniel	082	1900	WB-7/48	AR
McIntyre, Daniel	029	1816	WB-A/231	AR
McIntyre, Duncan	082	1888	WB-6/364	AR
McIntyre, Duncan	082	1831	WB-2/6	AR
McIntyre, Duncan	029	1795	Orig. Only	AR
McIntyre, Duncan	082	1832	WB-2/25	AR
McIntyre, Ellen	029	1864	WB-D/63	AR
McIntyre, Gilbert	029	1805	WB-A/70	AR
McIntyre, James	029	1820	WB-B/37	AR
McIntyre, John	083	1853	WB-2/45	
McIntyre, John	082	1885	WB-6/308	AR
McIntyre, John	082	c1803	WB-1/80	AR
McIntyre, John	083	c1819	WB-1/324	AR
McIntyre, John	082	1854	WB-4/72	
McIntyre, Malcom	029	1822	WB-B/64	AR
McIntyre, Margaret	082	1860	WB-4/144	AR
McIntyre, Nancy	082	1859	WB-4/134	AR
McIntyre, Nicoll	029	1830	WB-B/186	AR
McIver, Charles	068	1882	WB-D/149	
McIver, Colin	029	1850	Orig. Only	AR
McIver, Daniel	068	1848	WB-B/188	
McIver, Daniel	068	1845	WB-B/152	
McIver, Donald J.	MS	1869	022 WB-E/52	022 AR
McIver, Duncan	022	1808	WB-A/96	AR
McIver, Duncan	068	1812	WB-A/274	
McIver, Duncan	068	1876	WB-D/88	
McIver, Effie	068	1867	WB-C/153	AR-Copy
McIver, Evander	022	1866	WB-D/161	AR
McIver, Evander	022	1826	WB-B/117	AR
McIver, James	054	c1830	WB-2/101	AR
McIver, James	046	1857	WB-C/461	AR
McIver, John	029	1894	WB-F/27	AR
McIver, John	029	1894	037 WB-H/570	037 AR
McIver, John	022	1820	WB-B/41	AR
McIver, Kenneth	029	1822	WB-B/82	AR
McIver, M. S.	068	1894	WB-D/430	
McIver, Polly	046	1867	WB-D/344	AR
McKagg, James	028	1786	WB-A/142	AR
McKane, Lizzie	020	1900	WB-B/402	CTY
McKaskel, Allen	029	1879	WB-E/185	AR
McKaskel, Catharine	083	1847	WB-1/503	AR
McKaskill, John	082	1843	WB-3/10	AR
McKaughan, Forester	046	1888	WB-E/544	AR
McKay, Alexander	083	1859	WB-2/148	AR
McKay, Alexander	067	1883	Orig. Only	AR
McKay, Alexander	029	1769	Orig. Only	AR
McKay, Alexander	082	1862	WB-4/153	AR
McKay, Angus	054	1867	WB-3/202	AR
McKay, Ann	029	1844	WB-C/65	AR
McKay, Ann	054	1853	WB-3/56	AR
McKay, Ann	029	c1822	WB-B/99	
McKay, Ann	011	1862	WB-1/273	
McKay, Ann Eliza	011	1879	WB-2/127	
McKay, Archibald	029	1797	WB-A/2	AR
McKay, Archibald	082	c1804	WB-1/101	AR
McKay, Archibald	082	1860	WB-4/139	AR
McKay, Archibald	083	1829	WB-1/372	AR
McKay, Charles	054	1803	WB-1/165	AR
McKay, Daniel	083	c1802	WB-1/73	AR
McKay, Daniel	054	1818	WB-1A/6	AR
McKay, Donald	083	1787	WB-1/3	AR
McKay, Duncan	005	1833	WB-B/31	AR
McKay, Duncan	082	1822	WB-1/236	AR
McKay, Elizabeth	082	1869	WB-6/15	AR
McKay, George	054	c1793	WB-1/162	AR
McKay, George	054	c1813	WB-1/326	AR
McKay, Harrison	082	1894	WB-6/492	AR
McKay, Hector	083	1900	WB-4/306	AR
McKay, Hector	085	c1784	WB-C/147	AR
McKay, Hugh	082	1854	WB-4/75	AR
McKay, Iver	011	c1785	WB-1/566	
McKay, Jabez	027	1874	WB-2/23	AR
McKay, James I.	011	N. D.	WB-1/219	
McKay, Jane	070	1847	WB-AB/465	AR
McKay, Jefferson	068	1897	WB-D/504	
McKay, Jennet	083	1859	WB-2/153	AR
McKay, John	083	1845	WB-1/456	AR
McKay, John	011	c1820	WB-2/354	
McKay, John	005	1808	WB-2/103	AR
McKay, Margaret	083	1845	WB-1/471	AR
McKay, Mary	083	1845	WB-1/470	AR
McKay, Mary	082	1817	WB-1/193	AR
McKay, Mary Ann	082	1899	WB-7/35	AR
McKay, Mary, Sr.	005	1842	WB-B/147	AR
McKay, Neill	048	1893	WB-1/24	CTY
McKay, Neill	048	c1891	099 WB-D/525	099 AR
McKay, Neill	029	1830	Copy	046 AR
McKay, Neill	029	1830	WB-B/197	
McKay, Ralph	011	c1790	WB-1/437	
McKay, Robert	054	c1789	WB-1/168	AR
McKay, William	082	1813	WB-1/159	AR
McKee, Alexander	054	c1837	WB-2/183	AR
McKee, Alexander	065	1798	WB-B/77	AR
McKee, Ambrose	065	c1779	WB-B/116	AR
McKee, C. E.	013	1893	WB-C/260	AR
McKee, David	073	1882	WB-H/309	CTY
McKee, David B.	073	1871	WB-H/51	CTY
McKee, Eliza	065	1857	WB-J/36	AR
McKee, Isabella	065	1846	WB-I/43	AR
McKee, James	099	1823	RB-18/119	AR
McKee, James	060	1821	Orig. Only	AR
McKee, James	060	1832	WB-1/261	AR
McKee, James A.	073	1891	WB-H/542	CTY
McKee, Jane	073	1861	WB-G/378	CTY
McKee, John	073	1805	WB-D/160	AR
McKee, John H.	054	1870	WB-4/57	AR
McKee, Joseph W.	073	1880	WB-H/254	CTY
McKee, Margaret	054	c1790	WB-1/172	AR
McKee, Mille	085	1817	WB-G/476	AR
McKee, Nancy	054	c1861	Orig. Only	AR
McKee, Pira S.	040	1897	WB-2/535	AR
McKee, Prudence	065	1863	WB-H/108	AR
McKee, Sarah J.	040	1899	WB-3/53	AR-Nunc.
McKee, Susan R.	065	1844	WB-H/189	AR
McKee, William	073	1823	WB-E/32	AR
McKee, William	065	1832	WB-G/111	
McKee, William	054	c1819	WB-1A/125	AR
McKee, William	020	1801	RB-D/19	
McKee, William	099	1875	RB-35/294	AR

Name	Co.	Date	Recorded Copy	Original
McKee, William A.	073	1854	WB-G/68	AR
McKeel, John	075	1793	WB-L/11	AR
McKeel, John	075	1707	Orig. Only	SS/AR
McKeel, John	009	c1782	OWB/175	AR
McKeel, John, Sr.	075	1750	Orig. Only	SS/AR
McKeel, Patsey	009	1872	WB-1/98	CTY
McKeel, Thomas	009	1761	OWB/85	AR
McKeel, Thomas	075	1729/0	SS 876/196	SS/AR
McKeel, Thomas Sr.	075	1753	SS 881/78	SS/AR
McKeen, Hugh	020	1784	RB-B/42	AR
McKeil, Michael	077	1802	WB-E/177	AR
McKeithan, Daniel	068	1866	WB-C/128	
McKeithan, James G.	012	c1883	Orig. Only	AR
McKeithan, Neill	068	1835	WB-B/97	
McKeithan, Wm. James	011	1883	WB-2/163	
McKellar, Archibald	029	1832	WB-B/214	AR
McKellar, John	070	1809	WB-C/288	AR
McKellar, Peter	029	1846	WB-C/102	AR
McKemma, Gideon	046	1809	WB-A/272	AR
McKemmen, Daniel	065	1786	WB-B/69	AR
McKeney, George	046	1801	WB-A/274	AR
McKenney, Mathew	029	1793	Orig. Only	AR
McKennie, Barnaby	047	1761	WB-1/47	
McKennon, John	083	c1801	WB-1/67	
McKenny, Elizabeth	072	1825	WB-A/98	AR
McKenzie, Charles C.	085	1813	WB-G/280	AR
McKenzie, Daniel	029	1811	WB-A/166	AR
McKenzie, Daniel	029	1828	WB-B/164	AR
McKenzie, Duncan	005	1843	WB-B/155	AR
McKenzie, George	012	1813	WB-B/105	AR
McKenzie, George	012	1812	WB-B/103	AR
McKenzie, Hannah	085	1891	WB-2/460	CTY
McKenzie, John	082	1834	WB-2/37	AR
McKenzie, John	012	1898	WB-A/129	AR
McKenzie, John	029	c1846	WB-C/134	AR
McKenzie, Kenneth	063	c1784	WB-1/106	
McKenzie, Kenneth	082	1841	WB-2/532	AR
McKenzie, M. S.	085	1871	WB-1/88	CTY
McKenzie, Mary	029	1894	WB-F/8	AR
McKenzie, Murdoch	068	1852	WB-B/232	
McKenzie, Murdock	022	1823	WB-B/111	AR
McKenzie, Murdock	083	1894	WB-4/26	AR
McKenzie, R. M.	021	1895	WB-3/90	AR
McKenzie, Sarah	029	1842	WB-B/373	
McKenzie, William	063	1810	WB-2/1	
McKenzie, William	082	1878	WB-6/153	Nunc.
McKesson, Anna M.	014	c1865	WB-1/14	AR
McKethan, Alfred A.	029	1890	WB-E/475	AR
McKethan, Daniel T.	011	1863	WB-1/308	
McKethan, Duncan	011	c1774	WB-1/568	
McKethan, James	029	1794	Orig. Only	AR
McKethan, John	029	1818	WB-B/1	AR
McKethan, John C.	029	1864	WB-D/59	AR
McKethan, Mary	099	1823	RB-18/15	
McKethan, Mary	029	1826	WB-B/147	AR
McKever, Elihu	046	1830	WB-B/427	AR
McKey, John	084	1823	WB-A/255	CTY
McKey, Thomas F.	054	1865	WB-3/176	AR
McKibben, Frankey	065	1802	WB-B/153	AR
McKie, Robert	085	c1803	WB-E/95	AR
McKiechan, Dugald	011	1750	028 DB-5/203	SS/AR
McKildos, John	096	1772	024 WB-1/50	024 AR
McKillip, Andrew	090	1810	WB-2/112	AR
McKillip, Hugh	090	1802	WB-2/24	AR
McKilroy, James	028	1830	WB-C/330	
McKimmon, James	099	1866	RB-34/300	AR
McKimmon, Joseph	083	1863	WB-2/202	AR
McKimmon, Neill	083	1863	WB-2/203	AR
McKindley, Charles	016	1808	WB-A/32	AR
McKindley, John	016	c1827	WB-A/20	AR
McKindly, David B.	016	1872	WB-2/79	AR
McKiney, William	107	1837	WB-1/27	
McKinley, Charles D.	016	1890	WB-4/57	AR
McKinley, Charles M.	016	1859	WB-2/60	AR
McKinley, David	016	1843	WB-1/5	AR
McKinley, James	028	1819	WB-C/171	
McKinley, John	016	1853	WB-1/222	AR
McKinley, M. E.	016	1885	WB-3/463	AR
McKinley, Mary	028	1840	WB-D/13	
McKinley, Robert	065	c1775	WB-B/50	AR
McKinley, William	065	1815	WB-E/27	AR
McKinly, Frances	016	1851	WB-1/195	AR
McKinne, Barnaby	103	1816	RD-4/16	AR
McKinne, David	103	1800	Orig. Only	AR
McKinne, David F.	103	1868	RD-14/675	AR
McKinne, John	103	1804	Orig. Only	AR
McKinne, Joseph	028	1781	Orig. Only	AR
McKinne, Madelina R.	056	1889	WB-3/511	AR
McKinne, Mary	103	1838	RD-7/400	AR
McKinne, Mary	103	1814	RD-3/156	AR
McKinne, Richard	103	1800	WI-B/332	AR
McKinne, Sarah	103	1837	RD-7/307	AR
McKinne, William	103	1793	Orig. Only	AR
McKinne, Zilpha	056	1860	WB-1/741	AR
McKinney, A.	090	1894	WB-6/334	AR
McKinney, Barnaby	047	1761	WB-1/31	
McKinney, G.E.	092	1891	WB-6/349	AR
McKinney, Henry	086	1837	WB-E/39	AR
McKinney, Hezekiah	084	1882	WB-E/260	CTY
McKinney, James	086	1841	WB-E/75	AR
McKinney, James	092	1825	WB-3/161	AR
McKinney, Jesse	090	1866	WB-5/30	
McKinney, John	013	1852	WB-A/151	
McKinney, John	084	c1791	OW/264	AR
McKinney, John	086	1804	WB-B/179	AR
McKinney, John M.	028	1854	WB-D/230	AR
McKinney, Mary	037	1754	Orig. Only	SS/AR
McKinney, Miller	086	1896	WB-F/500	AR
McKinney, Nathaniel	084	1893	WB-E/535	CTY
McKinney, Rail W.	046	1890	WB-F/74	AR
McKinney, Samuel	065	c1843	Orig. Only	AR
McKinney, Sarah	065	1870	WB-K/39	
McKinney, Sarah E.	065	1898	WB-N/175	
McKinney, Stephen	053	1867	WB-10/48	AR
McKinney, Thomas	066	1892	Orig. Only	AR
McKinney, William	086	1857	WB-E/333	AR
McKinney, William	020	1843	RB-P/20	
McKinney, Willis M.	086	1874	WB-F/49	AR
McKinnon, A. P.	083	1863	WB-2/196	AR
McKinnon, Alexander	082	1850	WB-4/42	AR
McKinnon, Alexander	082	1857	WB-4/108	AR
McKinnon, Angus	029	1810	WB-A/158	
McKinnon, Archibald	027	1896	WB-2/126	AR
McKinnon, Charles	067	1890	WB-2/281	
McKinnon, Charles	083	1829	WB-1/187	AR
McKinnon, D. P.	083	1897	WB-4/143	AR
McKinnon, Daniel	082	1825	WB-1/262	AR
McKinnon, Gilbert	082	1862	WB-4/151	AR
McKinnon, Hector	029	1799	WB-A/21	
McKinnon, John	083	c1801	WB-1/247	

Name	Co.	Date	Recorded Copy	Original
McKinnon, John	003	1813	WB-1/180	Nunc.
McKinnon, John T.	067	1888	WB-2/266	
McKinnon, K. B.	083	1866	WB-2/233	AR
McKinnon, Kenneth	083	1848	WB-2/2	
McKinnon, Mary	082	1829	WB-1/310	AR
McKinnon, Murdock	082	1879	WB-6/166	AR
McKinnon, Neil	082	1817	WB-1/188	AR
McKinnon, Norman	068	1858	WB-C/60	
McKinnon, Rodrick	029	1824	WB-B/115	AR
McKinny, Brooks	019	1808	WB-D/285	AR
McKinny, George	086	1853	WB-E/247	AR
McKinsey, William	046	c1839	WB-C/85	AR-Copy
McKiny, Margaret	084	c1799	OW/156	AR
McKiny, Samuel	107	c1851	WB-1/64	
McKinzie, John	VA	1754	Copy	SS/AR
McKinzie, Kenneth	054	c1821	WB-1A/7	AR
McKinzie, Kenneth	029	1799	WB-A/22	AR
McKissock, John	078	1800	WI-2/281	AR
McKnight, Alexander	046	1775	WB-A/253	AR
McKnight, Alexander	039	1867	WB-S/428	AR
McKnight, Anderson	065	1894	WB-M/251	
McKnight, G. G.	054	1894	WB-5/529	CTY
McKnight, George	054	c1814	WB-1/319	
McKnight, George	090	1847	WB-4/238	AR
McKnight, George	038	1851	WB-1/33	AR
McKnight, Gilbraith	065	1838	WB-E/194	AR
McKnight, Hugh	085	1847	WB-K/59	AR
McKnight, Hugh, Sr.	054	c1810	WB-1/280	AR
McKnight, James	039	c1847	WB-N/360	AR
McKnight, James	065	1826	WB-B/8	AR
McKnight, James	054	c1822	WB-2/27	AR
McKnight, John	046	1771	WB-A/250	AR
McKnight, John	046	1876	WB-E/164	AR
McKnight, John	085	1825	WB-H/326	AR
McKnight, Joseph	054	1845	WB-2/313	AR
McKnight, Joseph	021	1889	WB-2/463	AR
McKnight, Margaret	054	1896	WB-6/25	CTY
McKnight, Margaret	085	1864	WB-K/336	AR
McKnight, Marshal D.	054	1891	WB-5/386	CTY
McKnight, Martha	046	1856	WB-C/450	AR
McKnight, Robert	046	1841	WB-C/84	AR
McKnight, Robert	065	1814	WB-B/95	AR
McKnight, Robert	065	1833	WB-G/116	AR
McKnight, Sarah	054	c1825	WB-2/17	AR
McKnight, Sarah	085	1826	WB-H/362	AR
McKnight, William	085	1760	WB-A/114	AR
McKnight, William	046	1842	WB-C/127	AR
McKnight, William	085	1811	WB-G/202	AR
McKoun, John	085	1772	WB-A/106	AR
McKown, Janet	073	c1785	Orig. Only	AR
McKoy, Allmand A.	087	1885	WB-3/328	AR
McKoy, Amy	027	1894	WB-2/108	AR
McKoy, Jacob	027	1891	WB-2/91	AR
McKoy, James	005	1888	WB-D/235	AR
McKoy, John	070	1796	WB-C/274	AR
McKoy, Mrs. F. E.	070	1889	WB-F/296	AR
McKoy, William H.	070	1858	WB-C/671	AR
McLain, Archibald	083	1864	WB-2/207	AR
McLain, Benjamin	060	c1884	Orig. Only	AR
McLain, Elizabeth	065	1884	WB-L/9	
McLain, Hugh, Sr.	065	1831	WB-G/87	
McLain, James S.	003	1897	WB-B/357	AR
McLain, Mary A. J.	099	1894	Orig. Only	AR
McLamb, Persis	087	1874	WB-3/79	AR
McLamb, Phebe	056	1857	WB-1/701	AR
McLamb, William	087	1896	WB-4/21	
McLane, Mary D.	040	1862	WB-1/140	
McLane, William	056	1887	WB-3/438	AR
McLannan, James	082	1830	Orig. Only	AR
McLarty, Alexander	016	1851	WB-1/188	AR
McLarty, Alexander	065	1824	WB-E/32	AR
McLarty, Archibald	097	1875	WB-2/97	
McLarty, Barbara	065	1811	WB-E/16	AR
McLarty, Ellen B.	097	1892	WB-2/433	AR
McLauchlan, Dugald	083	c1828	WB-1/353	AR
McLauchlan, Margaret	083	1851	WB-2/40	AR
McLauchlan, Nicholas	083	1826	WB-1/316	AR
McLauchlan, Nicholas	083	1880	Orig. Only	AR
McLauchlin, Archibald	029	1869	WB-E/8	AR
McLauchlin, Archibald	082	1850	Copy	083 AR
McLauchlin, Archibald	082	1850	WB-4/36	AR
McLauchlin, Archibald	083	1831	WB-1/258	AR
McLauchlin, Catharine	082	1869	WB-6/39	AR
McLauchlin, Catherine	029	1895	WB-F/42	AR
McLauchlin, Daniel	082	1873	WB-6/107	AR
McLauchlin, Dougald	083	1829	WB-1/398	
McLauchlin, Dugald	083	1832	WB-1/263	AR
McLauchlin, Duncan	029	1872	WB-E/64	AR
McLauchlin, Jane Ann	082	1869	WB-6/41	AR
McLauchlin, John	083	1817	WB-1/178	AR
McLauchlin, John	082	1847	WB-3/40	AR
McLauchlin, John	029	1873	WB-E/88	AR
McLauchlin, Malcom	083	c1827	WB-1/331	AR
McLauchlin, Margaret	083	1842	WB-1/408	AR
McLauchlin, Margaret	083	1869	WB-3/18	AR
McLauchlin, Mary	083	c1821	WB-1/206	AR
McLauchlin, Mary	083	1840	WB-1/386	AR
McLauchlin, Nelly	083	1855	Orig. Only	AR
McLauchlin, Robert	083	1816	WB-1/168	AR
McLauchlin, Sallie	083	1885	WB-3/325	AR
McLaughlin, Anny R.	065	1845	WB-I/18	
McLaughlin, Eli C.	085	1891	WB-2/484	CTY
McLaughlin, John H.	054	1872	WB-4/105	CTY
McLaughlin, Joseph	065	1893	WB-M/176	
McLaughlin, Joseph	065	1893	Copy	097 AR
McLaughlin, M. C.	065	1890	WB-L/451	
McLaughlin, Margrct	065	1862	WB-J/137	AR
McLaughlin, Mary	085	1860	WB-K/284	AR
McLaughlin, Robert	085	1864	WB-K/346	AR
McLaughlin, S. B.	065	1885	WB-L/130	
McLaughlin, Samuel	065	1875	WB-K/171	
McLaughlin, Samuel	085	1843	WB-I/178	AR
McLaughlin, Samuel W.	085	1897	WB-3/202	CTY
McLaurin, Catharine	082	1859	WB-4/131	AR
McLaurin, Christian	005	1856	WB-C/109	AR
McLaurin, Daniel	082	1844	WB-3/23	AR
McLaurin, Daniel	029	1817	WB-A/246	AR
McLaurin, Duncan	082	1825	WB-1/250	AR
McLaurin, Duncan	082	1828	WB-1/298	AR
McLaurin, Duncan	082	1872	WB-6/108	AR
McLaurin, Effy Ann	082	1846	WB-3/30	AR
McLaurin, Elizabeth	029	1898	WB-F/157	AR
McLaurin, Emily	SC	1894	083 WB-4/31	AR
McLaurin, Hugh	082	1817	WB-1/193	AR
McLaurin, Hugh	082	1846	WB-3/32	AR
McLaurin, Hugh	005	1889	WB-D/252	AR
McLaurin, L. W.	082	1893	WB-6/477	AR
McLaurin, Lauchlin	082	1837	WB-2/68	
McLaurin, Lauchlin B.	082	1898	WB-7/7	AR
McLaurin, Laura D.	082	1897	WB-6/555	AR

Name	Co.	Date	Recorded Copy	Original
McLaurin, Margaret	005	1896	WB-D/383	AR
McLaurin, Mary	082	1869	WB-6/33	AR
McLaurin, Nancy	082	1893	WB-6/477	AR
McLaurin, Nancy	082	1866	WB-5/13	AR
McLaurin, Owen	082	1869	WB-6/45	AR
McLaurin, Penelope	082	1884	WB-6/274	AR
McLawhorn, Warren	079	1899	WB-3/188	AR
McLean, A. Murphy	083	1888	WB-3/409	AR
McLean, A. Murphy	083	1888	Copy	029 AR
McLean, Alexander	060	1789	Orig. Only	AR
McLean, Alexander	083	1856	WB-2/76	AR
McLean, Alexander	029	1850	WB-C/167	AR
McLean, Alexander	083	1870	WB-2/248	AR
McLean, Allen	029	1825	WB-B/127	AR
McLean, Allen	083	1889	WB-3/454	AR
McLean, Amelia	054	1870	WB-4/64	AR
McLean, Angus	083	1845	WB-1/465	AR
McLean, Angus	083	1854	WB-2/89	AR
McLean, Angus	083	c1810	WB-1/117	AR
McLean, Angus	029	1895	WB-F/34	AR
McLean, Angus D.	083	1869	WB-3/11	AR
McLean, Angus M.	083	1886	WB-3/342	AR
McLean, Archibald	029	1822	WB-B/79	AR
McLean, Archibald	029	1835	WB-B/248	AR
McLean, Archibald	083	1844	WB-1/436	AR
McLean, Charles	099	1897	WB-D/9	AR
McLean, Cornelia	085	1884	WB-2/84	CTY
McLean, Daniel	054	1830	WB-2/96	AR
McLean, Daniel	029	1840	WB-B/321 & 379	AR
McLean, Daniel	054	1850	WB-3/47	AR
McLean, Daniel	083	1813	WB-1/143	AR
McLean, Duncan	082	1858	WB-4/109	AR
McLean, Effy	029	1831	WB-B/203	AR
McLean, Effy	083	1850	WB-2/18	AR
McLean, Effy	083	1878	WB-3/136	AR
McLean, Elizabeth	085	1892	WB-2/500	CTY
McLean, Elizabeth	046	1845	WB-C/219	AR
McLean, Ellen F.	083	1890	WB-3/473	AR
McLean, Fannie J.	046	1896	WB-F/543	AR
McLean, Flora	082	1899	WB-7/37	AR
McLean, Fountain	046	1891	WB-F/108	AR
McLean, Frank W.	OH	c1895	Copy	049 AR
McLean, Gilbert	083	1860	WB-2/161	
McLean, Hannah	046	c1866	WB-E/140	AR
McLean, Hector	083	1846	WB-1/484	
McLean, Hector	029	1807	WB-A/98	AR
McLean, Hector	029	1825	WB-B/131	
McLean, Hugh	029	1776	Orig. Only	AR
McLean, Hugh	082	1889	WB-6/394	AR
McLean, Hugh	029	1852	WB-C/221	AR
McLean, Hugh	029	1820	WB-B/42	AR
McLean, Isabella	083	1887	WB-3/391	AR
McLean, J. L.	060	1885	WB-4/310	AR
McLean, James C.	083	1886	WB-3/374	AR
McLean, James R.	046	1870	WB-E/28	AR
McLean, Jennette	083	1900	WB-4/288	AR
McLean, John	054	1817	WB-1/403	AR
McLean, John	054	c1818	WB-1/426	AR
McLean, John	083	1856	WB-2/70	AR
McLean, John	083	c1801	WB-1/66	AR-Copy
McLean, John	054	1873	WB-4/138	CTY
McLean, John	083	1861	WB-2/165	AR
McLean, John	083	1816	WB-1/169	
McLean, John	046	1807	WB-A/270	AR
McLean, John	083	1846	WB-1/493	
McLean, John	083	1833	WB-1/268	AR
McLean, John	029	1794	Orig. Only	AR
McLean, John	056	1858	WB-1/717	AR
McLean, John	082	1859	WB-4/137	AR
McLean, John D.	040	1880	WB-2/157	AR
McLean, John M.	046	1892	WB-F/198	AR
McLean, Joseph	046	1833	WB-B/473	AR
McLean, Katherine	029	1830	WB-B/197	AR
McLean, Margaret	060	1806	Orig. Only	AR
McLean, Margaret	083	1850	WB-2/23	AR
McLean, Margaret	083	1857	WB-2/112	
McLean, Margaret	SC	1858	040 WB-2/98	040 AR
McLean, Margaret	083	1835	WB-1/297	AR
McLean, Marshall	046	1834	WB-B/503	AR
McLean, Mary	029	c1737	Orig. Only	AR
McLean, Mary	029	1835	WB-B/243	AR
McLean, Mary	083	1863	WB-2/204	AR
McLean, Mary Ann	083	1883	WB-3/295	AR
McLean, Nancy	083	1823	Copy	082 AR
McLean, Nancy	083	1823	WB-1/323	AR
McLean, Nancy	068	1866	WB-C/143	
McLean, Narcissa	046	1873	WB-E/100	AR
McLean, Neill	083	1853	WB-2/62	AR
McLean, Neill	083	c1820	WB-1/216	
McLean, Neill	083	1857	WB-2/111	AR
McLean, Neill	029	1827	WB-B/153	AR
McLean, Neill	048	1858	SC/07977	
McLean, Niell	068	1814	WB-A/284	
McLean, Penelope	083	1878	WB-3/161	AR
McLean, Sally	083	1849	WB-2/4	
McLean, Sarah	083	1891	WB-3/584	AR
McLean, Sarah	029	1843	WB-C/44	
McLean, Washington	083	1876	WB-3/118	AR
McLean, William	060	1829	WB-1/127	AR
McLean, William	016	1839	PQS.6/1	
McLean, William	085	1863	WB-K/311	AR
McLean, William B.	054	1899	WB-6/222	CTY
McLeane, Archibald	083	c1794	WB-1/32	AR
McLearn, John	011	c1801	WB-1/435	
McLearty, Archibald	016	1815	WB-A/16	AR
McLeary, Elizabeth	060	1848	WB-2/304	
McLeary, Michael	065	c1844	Orig. Only	AR
McLeary, William H.	065	1846	WB-I/67	AR
McLeland, Martha	065	1840	WB-H/38	AR
McLellan, Angus	070	1827	WB-C/303	AR
McLellan, Elias	016	1879	WB-3/275	AR
McLellan, Isaac	016	1840	PQS.6/120	AR
McLellan, Robert P.	065	1892	WB-M/571	
McLelland, Andrew	011	1846	WB-1/136	
McLelland, James	054	c1837	WB-2/171	AR
McLelland, Jane	054	1842	WB-2/235	AR
McLelland, John	054	1843	WB-2/275	AR
McLelland, John	054	c1826	WB-2/53	AR
McLelland, John	054	c1811	WB-1/283	AR
McLelland, John	054	1892	WB-5/437	CTY
McLelland, Joseph	054	c1831	WB-2/114	
McLelland, Margaret	054	1843	WB-2/263	AR
McLelland, Margaret	054	c1832	WB-2/113	AR
McLelland, Margaret	054	c1831	WB-2/154	AR
McLelland, Mary	054	c1779	WB-1/174	
McLelland, Mary	054	c1853	WB-3/64	AR
McLelland, Mary	065	1840	WB-H/66	AR
McLelland, Mary	054	1869	WB-4/27	AR
McLelland, Milas	054	1846	WB-3/11	AR

Name	Co.	Date	Recorded Copy	Original
McLelland, N. R.	025	1895	WB-A/115	AR
McLelland, Samuel	011	1886	WB-2/204	
McLelland, Sarah L.	054	1879	WB-4/349	
McLelland, William L.	054	c1835	WB-2/127	AR
McLemore, Atkins	100	1791	WB-5/239	AR
McLemore, Ephraim	092	1799	WB-3/31	
McLemore, Harry	047	1900	WB-7/239	AR
McLemore, Joel H.	047	1835	WB-4/116	AR
McLemore, John Henry	068	1881	WB-D/174 & 186	
McLendon, Isaac	082	1882	WB-6/299	AR
McLendon, Jesse	035	1782	WB-A/317	
McLendon, Lewis	087	c1778	WB-A/11	AR
McLendon, Nancy	005	1883	WB-D/158	AR
McLennan, Ann	029	1833	WB-B/225	AR
McLennan, Daniel	029	1849	Orig. Only	AR
McLennan, Kenneth	067	1851	WB-1/57	
McLennan, Sarah	029	1846	WB-C/107	AR
McLennon, Rodrick	067	1857	WB-1/89	AR
McLeod, Alexander	083	1895	WB-4/64	AR
McLeod, Alexander	068	1815	WB-A/291	
McLeod, Angus	083	1845	WB-1/459	AR
McLeod, Anna	068	1894	WB-D/422	CTY
McLeod, Christian	067	1844	WB-1/13	AR
McLeod, Daniel	054	c1804	WB-1/161	AR
McLeod, Daniel	029	c1838	WB-B/295	AR
McLeod, Daniel	070	1791	WB-C/277	AR
McLeod, Daniel	068	c1852	WB-B/251	
McLeod, Donald	068	1803	WB-A/227	
McLeod, Donald	029	1813	WB-A/201	AR
McLeod, Donald	029	1806	WB-A/84	AR
McLeod, Duncan	068	1885	WB-D/196	
McLeod, Duncan	068	1838	WB-B/116	
McLeod, Duncan	082	1852	WB-4/58	AR
McLeod, Effie J.	068	1895	WB-D/401	
McLeod, Flora	068	1883	WB-D/168	
McLeod, James	083	1900	WB-4/319	AR
McLeod, Jennett	005	c1773	WB-1/17	
McLeod, John	056	1850	WB-1/626	AR
McLeod, John	068	1853	WB-C/11	
McLeod, John	068	1857	WB-C/51	
McLeod, John	082	1848	WB-4/18	AR
McLeod, John	068	1886	WB-D/228	
McLeod, John	017	1862	WB-A/136	AR
McLeod, John	068	1863	WB-C/94	
McLeod, John	067	1886	WB-2/229	AR
McLeod, John, Sr.	082	1816	WB-1/179	AR
McLeod, Katherine	083	1859	WB-2/144	AR
McLeod, Lauchlin	011	c1849	WB-1/185	
McLeod, Malcom	011	1878	WB-2/99	
McLeod, Margaret	065	1875	WB-K/193	
McLeod, Margaret	083	1859	WB-2/112	AR
McLeod, Murdoch	082	1845	WB-3/25	AR
McLeod, Murdoch	068	c1876	WB-D/80	
McLeod, Murdock	083	1843	WB-1/429	AR
McLeod, Murdock	029	1843	WB-C/30	AR
McLeod, Murdock	029	1846	WB-C/88	AR
McLeod, Murdock	083	c1810	WB-1/116	
McLeod, Nancy	068	1812	WB-A/273	
McLeod, Neill	068	1814	WB-A/283	
McLeod, Neill	068	1860	WB-C/80	
McLeod, Neill	068	1814	WB-A/286	Nunc.
McLeod, Neill	068	1840	WB-B/126	
McLeod, Neill	083	c1827	WB-1/338	AR
McLeod, Neill	087	c1818	WB-A/88	AR
McLeod, Norman	005	1842	WB-B/142	AR
McLeod, Norman	082	1893	WB-6/460	AR
McLeod, Sarah	068	1845	WB-B/151	
McLeod, Virgil	068	1884	WB-D/179	
McLeod, William	082	1852	WB-4/61	AR
McLeod, William	068	1896	WB-D/468	
McLeod, William	029	1813	WB-A/192	AR
McLeran, Archibald	029	1851	WB-C/230	AR
McLeran, Christian	029	1847	WB-C/150	AR
McLeran, Duncan	029	1822	WB-B/65	AR
McLeran, Elizabeth	029	1858	WB-C/375	AR
McLeran, Mary	029	1900	WB-F/193	AR
McLeran, N. H.	029	c1861	WB-C/441	
McLeran, Neill	029	1842	WB-B/369	AR
McLeran, Thomas	029	1860	WB-C/417	AR
McLerran, Daniel	029	1820	WB-B/50	AR
McLerran, Duncan	029	1795	Orig. Only	AR
McLester, Alexander	089	1891	WB-2/222	AR
McLester, Daniel	089	1870	WB-2/6	AR
McLester, Lydia	089	1892	WB-2/230	AR
McLin, Henry	070	1870	WB-E/192	AR
McLin, Thomas	028	1861	WB-D/350	AR
McLochlon, Hugh	029	1809	WB-A/135	AR
McLorinan, Henry	070	1785	WB-C/271	
McLoud, C. M.	061	1876	WB-2/26	AR
McLucas, Archibald	082	1825	WB-1/246	AR
McLucas, Nancy	SC	1837	Copy	082 AR
McLughan, Jane	065	1871	WB-K/64	
McLughen, Anny R.	065	1845	WB-I/18	AR
McLurd, R. L.	040	1880	WB-2/151	AR
McLure, George C.	016	1876	WB-3/167	AR
McLure, Hugh	065	1840	WB-H/74	AR
McLure, James	040	1854	WB-1/64	
McLure, James H.	060	1875	WB-4/174	AR
McLure, Matthew	065	1805	WB-E/4	
McLuse, William	061	1857	WB-1/68	AR
McMachen, John	085	1824	WB-H/284	AR
McMackin, David	016	c1858	Copy	089 AR
McMackin, David	016	1858	WB-2/49	
McMackin, James	016	c1822	WB-A/13	AR
McMackon, Andrew	085	1768	WB-A/109	AR
McMahan, B.	086	1896	WB-F/497	AR
McMahan, James	086	1866	WB-E/468	AR
McMahan, John	085	c1776	WB-A/238	
McMahan, Mary	085	1829	WB-H/454	AR
McMahan, R. A.	055	1887	WB-A/81	
McMahon, Patrick	009	c1803	OWB/420	AR
McMannen, Bettie A.	073	1880	WB-H/237	CTY
McMannen, Jannett	048	1893	WB-1/17	CTY
McManus, David	022	1888	WB-E/383	AR
McManus, George	097	1881	WB-2/199	AR
McManus, John H.	097	1863	WB-1/223	AR
McManus, Larance	022	1813	WB-A/234	AR
McManus, Nathan	022	1899	WB-F/75	AR
McMaster, Felix	011	c1793	WB-1/550	
McMasters, Anderson	081	1895	WB-16/357	AR
McMasters, Andrew	081	1833	WB-6/307	AR
McMasters, Andrew	081	1868	WB-14/237	
McMasters, David	081	1890	WB-16/173	AR
McMasters, E. J.	081	1896	WB-17/32	AR
McMasters, Elisha	081	1870	WB-15/34	AR
McMasters, James	022	1792	RB-1/46	AR
McMasters, Lewis	081	1839	WB-7/270	AR
McMasters, Mary	081	1853	WB-9/532	AR
McMasters, Nancey	081	1853	WB-11/214	

Name	Co.	Date	Recorded Copy	Original
McMasters, Simeon	081	1841	WB-7/342	AR
McMasters, William	022	1836	WB-C/30	AR
McMath, Robert	009	c1770	OWB/106	AR
McMerrill, John	013	1891	050 WB-2/143	050 CTY
McMerrill, John	013	1891	WB-C/167	AR
McMicann, David	065	1777	WB-B/111	AR
McMichael, Sarah	046	1898	WB-G/87	AR
McMichal, Charity	046	1829	Orig. Only	AR
McMickle, Cinclare	092	1856	WB-5/19	AR
McMickle, John	092	1806	WB-3/75A	AR
McMickle, John J.	092	1897	WB-6/450	AR
McMickle, Mary	092	1867	WB-5/94	AR
McMikell, Archabal	046	1818	Orig. Only	AR
McMillan, Alexander	044	1761	Orig. Only	CTY
McMillan, Alexander	082	1860	WB-4/146	AR
McMillan, Andrew	082	1897	WB-6/563	AR
McMillan, Andrew	006	1877	WB-E/43	AR
McMillan, Angus	067	1876	WB-2/70	
McMillan, Ann	029	1861	WB-C/430	AR
McMillan, Archibald	083	1875	WB-3/148	AR
McMillan, Archibald	083	1825	WB-1/244	AR
McMillan, Archibald	083	1900	WB-4/281	AR
McMillan, Archibald	083	1824	WB-1/248	AR
McMillan, Archibald	068	1814	WB-A/287	
McMillan, Archibald	083	c1820	WB-1/224	AR
McMillan, Catharine	082	1858	WB-4/125	AR
McMillan, Catherine	029	1889	WB-E/452	AR
McMillan, Christian	029	1880	WB-E/230	AR
McMillan, Daniel	083	c1811	WB-1/124	AR
McMillan, Daniel	029	1885	WB-E/356	AR
McMillan, Daniel	083	1839	WB-1/379	AR
McMillan, Daniel	027	1861	WB-A/77	
McMillan, Dugald	083	1856	WB-2/80	AR
McMillan, Dugald	011	c1835	WB-1/31	
McMillan, Duncan	011	c1806	WB-1/433	
McMillan, Duncan	083	1890	WB-3/495	AR
McMillan, Duncan	082	1846	WB-3/32	AR
McMillan, Duncan	083	1814	WB-1/148	AR
McMillan, Edward	029	1803	WB-A/60	AR
McMillan, Edward	011	c1778	WB-1/572	
McMillan, George H.	072	1854	WB-2/139	
McMillan, George J.	035	1900	WB-5/4	AR
McMillan, Gilbert	083	1849	WB-2/8	AR
McMillan, Gilbert	082	1832	WB-2/23	AR
McMillan, Hector	082	1862	WB-4/152	AR
McMillan, Iredell	006	1899	WB-E/398	AR
McMillan, Iver	011	c1839	WB-1/94	
McMillan, Jannett	011	c1833	WB-1/1	
McMillan, John	006	1855	WB-D/30	AR
McMillan, John	083	c1807	WB-1/104	AR
McMillan, John	011	c1820	WB-2/364	
McMillan, John	083	1874	WB-3/75	AR
McMillan, John	011	c1801	WB-1/419	
McMillan, John	083	1816	WB-1/174	AR
McMillan, John, Sr.	006	1844	WB-A/33	AR
McMillan, Joseph	082	1889	WB-6/384	AR
McMillan, Maggie	065	1897	WB-N/41	
McMillan, Malcolm	068	1822	WB-B/26	
McMillan, Malcolm	082	1825	WB-1/247	AR
McMillan, Malcom	083	1852	WB-2/102	AR
McMillan, Malcom	083	1843	WB-1/423	AR
McMillan, Malcom	082	1869	WB-6/5	
McMillan, Malcom	029	1877	WB-E/164	AR
McMillan, Margaret	082	1844	WB-3/20	AR
McMillan, Margaret	083	1821	WB-1/234	AR
McMillan, Margaret	083	1832	WB-1/267	AR
McMillan, Margaret J.	083	1893	WB-4/20	AR
McMillan, Mary	083	c1821	WB-1/195	AR
McMillan, Mary	083	1856	WB-2/88	AR
McMillan, Mary	029	1825	WB-B/139	AR
McMillan, Mary	083	1823	WB-1/322	AR
McMillan, Mary	029	1877	WB-E/165	AR
McMillan, Nancy	029	1855	WB-C/328	AR
McMillan, Nancy	029	1890	WB-E/490	AR
McMillan, Neill	082	1813	WB-1/160	AR
McMillan, Neill	083	1835	WB-1/296	AR
McMillan, Neill	083	1862	WB-2/185	AR
McMillan, Peter	083	1842	WB-1/411	AR
McMillan, Peter	082	1849	WB-4/26	AR
McMillan, Peter	083	c1817	WB-1/209	AR
McMillan, Sarah	083	1890	WB-3/497	AR
McMillen, William	037	1784	WB-B/141	AR
McMillin, Nathan	039	1821	WB-G/11	
McMillion, James	020	1811	RB-F/174	AR
McMin, Rachel	060	1829	WB-1/124	AR
McMinamy, John	020	1801	RB-D/18	
McMinn, Daniel	060	1871	WB-4/73	AR
McMinn, Robert	086	1802	WB-B/129	AR
McMinn, Samuel	060	1816	Orig. Only	AR
McMorine, John	075	1842	WB-N/168	AR
McMorine, Martha	075	c1848	WB-M2/40	AR
McMorine, Phoebe	075	c1887	Orig. Only	AR
McMorrow, William	086	1812	WB-B/263	AR
McMullan, Archibald	083	c1804	WB-1/89	AR
McMullen, James	077	1775	WB-C/172	AR
McMullen, James	020	1860	RB-S/180	AR
McMullen, Samuel	073	1802	WB-D/64	AR
McMullin, William	039	c1898	Orig. Only	AR
McMunn, James	073	c1802	Orig. Only	AR
McMunn, Mary	073	1820	WB-D/573	AR
McMurray, James	046	1805	WB-A/265	AR
McMurray, John	046	c1789	WB-A/254	AR
McMurray, John	046	1852	WB-C/375	AR
McMurray, Sarah	065	1785	WB-B/68	AR
McMurrey, Robert	016	1800	WB-A/35	AR
McMurry, Harvey M.	078	1847	WB-13/7	AR
McMurry, John	020	1836	RB-M/613	
McMurry, John	046	1798	WB-A/258	AR
McMurry, John	026	1855	WB-1/185	AR
McMurry, Mary	086	1833	WB-D/161	aR
McMurry, Robert	090	1795	WB-1/65	AR
McMurry, Samuel	078	1802	WI-3/93	AR
McMurry, Samuel	086	1803	WB-B/155	AR
McMurry, William	046	1871	WB-E/60	AR
McNabb, James	029	c1794	WB-A/89	AR
McNabb, Robert	068	1851	WB-B/227	
McNail, James	104	1834	WB-4/179	AR
McNair, Annabella	083	1891	WB-3/551	AR
McNair, Archibald	082	1839	WB-2/89	AR
McNair, Catharine	082	1883	WB-6/246	AR
McNair, Catherine	082	1882	WB-6/293 & 297	Nunc.
McNair, Daniel P.	083	1865	WB-2/221	AR
McNair, Duncan	083	c1853	Orig. Only	AR
McNair, Edward	082	1789	WB-1/30	
McNair, Edward	082	c1812	WB-1/153	AR
McNair, Edward	083	1825	WB-1/218	AR
McNair, Effy	083	1874	WB-3/83	AR
McNair, Enock	040	1863	WB-1/153	
McNair, Gilbert	082	1819	WB-1/205	AR

Name	Co.	Date	Recorded Copy	Original
McNair, James	080	1821	Orig. Only	AR
McNair, Jane	082	1875	WB-6/125	AR
McNair, John	083	1890	WB-3/480	AR
McNair, John	082	1835	WB-2/55	AR
McNair, John	082	c1808	WB-1/123	AR
McNair, John Calvin	083	1858	WB-2/125	AR
McNair, Malcom	083	c1822	WB-1/317	AR
McNair, Malcom	082	1813	WB-1/165	AR
McNair, Margaret	082	1880	WB-6/195	AR
McNair, Murphy C.	083	1881	WB-3/219	AR
McNair, Nancy	040	1896	WB-2/532	AR
McNair, Neil	082	1808	WB-1/124	AR
McNair, Neill	082	1858	WB-4/121	AR
McNair, Rodrick	083	1839	WB-1/377	AR
McNair, Roger	082	1796	WB-1/70	AR
McNair, Simon	083	1889	WB-3/504	AR
McNair, Turner	029	c1894	Orig. Only	AR
McNaire, Charles	009	1762	OWB/89	AR
McNairy, J. D. W.	046	1900	WB-G/235	AR
McNairy, James	046	1840	WB-C/74	AR
McNairy, Wyatt H.	046	1890	WB-F/23	AR
McNary, Gilbert	053	1747	SS 878/81	SS/AR
McNatt, Ann	083	1862	WB-2/178	AR
McNatt, John	083	1843	WB-1/416	AR
McNatt, John	083	1845	WB-1/460	AR
McNaught, William	046	1772	WB-A/251	AR
McNaughton, James	NY	1874	Copy	050 AR
McNaughton, John	011	1853	WB-1/210	
McNeal, Florella	013	c1894	WB-C/309	AR
McNeal, Martha	065	1775	WB-B/54	AR
McNear, Edward	082	1789	WB-1/30	AR
McNeeley, Isaac	085	1775	WB-A/205	AR
McNeeley, Lucinda	046	c1900	Orig. Only	AR
McNeelly, Adam	085	1767	WB-A/131	AR
McNeely, Adam	054	c1828	WB-2/85	AR
McNeely, Andrew	065	1828	WB-C/5	AR
McNeely, Ann	085	1887	WB-2/222	CTY
McNeely, Archibald	085	1825	WB-H/314	AR
McNeely, Archibald	085	c1801	WB-E/57	AR
McNeely, David	085	c1801	WB-E/77	AR
McNeely, David	054	1852	WB-3/57	
McNeely, Ebenezer	054	1887	WB-5/164	CTY
McNeely, Elizabeth	046	1848	WB-C/298	AR
McNeely, Elizabeth	054	1877	WB-4/263	CTY
McNeely, Harriet E.	054	1877	WB-4/280	CTY
McNeely, J. W.	065	1842	WB-H/93	AR
McNeely, James	085	1834	WB-H/626	AR
McNeely, James	054	1853	WB-3/68	AR
McNeely, James A.	065	1885	WB-L/93	
McNeely, Jesse	054	1872	WB-4/128	CTY
McNeely, John	085	1809	WB-G/146	AR
McNeely, John	085	1846	WB-K/43	AR
McNeely, John	085	1801	WB-E/60	AR
McNeely, John	085	1843	WB-I/180	AR
McNeely, John	065	1835	WB-G/216	AR
McNeely, John F.	065	1865	WB-J/208	AR
McNeely, John, Sr.	065	1800	WB-B/82	AR
McNeely, Joseph	054	c1861	Orig. Only	AR
McNeely, Lattice	054	1846	WB-3/10	AR
McNeely, Martha L.	065	1886	WB-L/124	
McNeely, Mary	054	1885	WB-5/65	CTY
McNeely, Mary B.	085	1855	WB-K/182	AR
McNeely, Nancy	054	c1853	WB-3/167	AR
McNeely, Rachel	065	1833	WB-G/140	AR
McNeely, Robert A.	065	1892	WB-M/64	
McNeely, Robert Y.	054	1865	WB-3/179	AR
McNeely, Samuel	085	1843	WB-I/176	AR
McNeely, Samuel	084	1855	WB-C/212	CTY
McNeely, Timothy	085	1839	WB-I/60	AR
McNeil, Hector	082	1812	WB-1/154	AR
McNeil, James	104	1880	WB-6/189	AR
McNeil, Larkin	104	1824	WB-4/51	AR
McNeil, Simon P.	054	1880	WB-4/381	CTY
McNeil, William S.	104	1876	WB-6/125	AR
McNeill, Agness	029	1819	WB-B/29	AR
McNeill, Alexander	083	1832	WB-1/264	
McNeill, Angus	082	1835	WB-2/56	AR
McNeill, Archibald	029	c1778	Orig. Only	AR
McNeill, Archibald	029	1807	WB-A/97	AR
McNeill, Archibald	029	c1801	WB-B/75	AR
McNeill, Archibald	082	1829	WB-1/308	AR
McNeill, Archibald	029	1812	WB-A/182	AR
McNeill, Archibald	083	1835	WB-1/292	AR
McNeill, Archibald	083	1881	WB-3/237	AR
McNeill, Archibald	083	1834	WB-1/289	AR
McNeill, Archibald	083	1862	WB-2/191	AR
McNeill, Caroline	083	1900	WB-4/322	AR
McNeill, Catharine	083	1866	WB-2/227	AR
McNeill, Daniel	082	1829	WB-1/307	AR
McNeill, Daniel	083	1853	WB-2/104	AR
McNeill, Daniel	029	1828	WB-B/168	AR
McNeill, Daniel	029	1808	WB-A/117	AR
McNeill, Daniel	068	c1827	WB-B/67	
McNeill, Daniel	068	1859	WB-C/70	
McNeill, Daniel	029	1816	WB-A/225	AR
McNeill, Daniel	083	1837	WB-1/312	AR
McNeill, Daniel	083	1813	WB-1/144	AR
McNeill, Dansey D.	083	1893	WB-4/17	AR
McNeill, David T.	083	1897	WB-4/170	AR
McNeill, Donald	083	c1792	WB-1/25	AR
McNeill, Dublin	029	1891	WB-E/522	AR
McNeill, Duncan	029	1793	Orig. Only	AR
McNeill, Duncan	083	1833	WB-1/272	AR
McNeill, Elizabeth	083	1820	WB-1/375	AR
McNeill, Flora	082	1899	WB-7/12	AR
McNeill, Flora	083	c1818	WB-1/232	
McNeill, Flora	048	1893	WB-1/19	CTY
McNeill, Flora	083	1839	WB-1/316	AR
McNeill, Flora	083	1875	WB-3/114	AR
McNeill, Frank	065	1895	WB-M/160	
McNeill, George	029	1865	WB-D/74	AR
McNeill, Godfrey	083	c1806	WB-1/97	AR
McNeill, Gripilla	029	1843	WB-C/38	AR
McNeill, Hector	029	1853	WB-C/237	AR
McNeill, Hector	082	1854	WB-4/80	AR
McNeill, Hector	082	1854	Copy	083 AR
McNeill, Hector	029	1768	Orig. Only	AR
McNeill, Hector	029	1840	WB-B/330	AR
McNeill, Hector	068	1900	WB-E/81	
McNeill, Hector	029	1833	WB-B/218	AR
McNeill, Hector	068	1843	WB-B/154	
McNeill, Hector	029	1848	WB-C/151	AR
McNeill, Hector	068	1824	WB-B/35	
McNeill, Hector	083	1895	WB-4/72	AR
McNeill, Hector	011	c1778	WB-1/574	
McNeill, Henry	029	1800	Orig. Only	AR
McNeill, Hosea	020	1857	RB-R/557	AR
McNeill, Isabella	029	1854	WB-C/301	AR
McNeill, Isabella	048	1900	WB-1/124	
McNeill, James	029	1805	WB-A/79	AR

Name	Co.	Date	Recorded Copy	Original
McNeill, Jane	083	1867	WB-2/239	AR
McNeill, Jane C.	083	1897	WB-4/174	AR
McNeill, Jennet	029	1823	WB-B/112	AR
McNeill, John	029	1844	WB-C/46	AR
McNeill, John	068	1820	WB-B/8	
McNeill, John	068	1845	WB-B/158	
McNeill, John	029	1809	WB-A/140	AR
McNeill, John	029	1875	WB-E/139	AR
McNeill, John	083	1851	WB-2/29	AR
McNeill, John	029	1850	WB-C/169	AR
McNeill, John	068	1871	WB-D/24	
McNeill, John	011	c1833	WB-1/5	
McNeill, John	068	1817	WB-A/296	
McNeill, John	029	1799	WB-A/24	AR
McNeill, John	082	1880	WB-6/193	AR
McNeill, John	029	1826	WB-B/148	
McNeill, John	083	c1809	WB-1/114	AR
McNeill, John A. D.	068	1838	WB-B/121	
McNeill, John D.	029	1892	WB-E/555	AR
McNeill, Lauchlin	082	1838	WB-2/81	AR
McNeill, Lochland	029	1796	Orig. Only	AR-Nunc.
McNeill, M.S.L.Jane	029	1837	WB-B/280	AR
McNeill, Malcom	083	1839	WB-1/384	AR
McNeill, Malcom	083	c1822	WB-1/317	
McNeill, Malcom	083	1833	WB-1/281	AR
McNeill, Malcom T.	068	1829	WB-B/69	
McNeill, Margaret	029	1829	WB-B/173	AR
McNeill, Margaret	029	1853	WB-C/249	AR
McNeill, Margaret	048	1900	WB-1/122	
McNeill, Margaret	083	1839	WB-1/379	AR
McNeill, Margaret	083	c1818	WB-1/193	AR
McNeill, Margaret	029	1822	WB-B/80	AR
McNeill, Martha	068	1884	WB-D/171	
McNeill, Martin V.B.	048	c1883	WB-1/46	
McNeill, Mary	011	c1841	WB-1/105	
McNeill, Mary	083	c1790	WB-1/21	AR
McNeill, Mary	083	1844	WB-1/448	AR
McNeill, Mary	029	1841	WB-B/351	AR
McNeill, Mary	029	1841	WB-B/340	AR
McNeill, Mary	083	1819	WB-1/227	AR
McNeill, Neill	029	1812	WB-A/180	AR
McNeill, Neill	083	1831	WB-1/261	AR
McNeill, Neill	029	1764	Orig. Only	AR
McNeill, Neill	083	1837	WB-1/304	AR
McNeill, Neill	083	1892	WB-3/570	AR
McNeill, Neill	082	1826	Orig. Only	AR
McNeill, Neill	029	1766	Orig. Only	AR
McNeill, Neill	029	1857	WB-C/370	AR
McNeill, Neill	083	N. D.	WB-1/111	AR
McNeill, Neill	029	1858	WB-C/384	AR
McNeill, Neill T.	083	1882	WB-3/269	AR
McNeill, Sarah	082	1816	WB-1/174	AR
McNeill, Thomas	020	1781	RB-A/173	AR
McNeill, Turquill	083	c1792	WB-1/27	AR
McNeill, William	083	1891	WB-3/547	AR
McNeill, William C.	083	1875	WB-3/108	AR
McNeilly, Robert	054	c1825	WB-2/39	
McNeily, George W.	084	1875	WB-E/100	
McNeley, David	085	c1776	WB-A/236	AR
McNesh, Nancy	029	1850	WB-C/171	AR
McNider, Sarah	024	1866	WB-D/47	AR
McNorton, John	011	1873	WB-2/65	
McNott, Nancy	068	1887	WB-D/242	
McPalmer, D.	017	c1863	WB-A/141	
McPhail, Duncan	087	1841	WB-1/237	AR

Name	Co.	Date	Recorded Copy	Original
McPhail, Malcom	029	1851	WB-C/181	AR
McPhail, Malcom	029	1828	WB-B/163	AR
McPhail, Thomas	065	1781	WB-B/123	
McPhail, William J.	029	1897	WB-F/86	AR
McPhaill, Dugald	029	c1793	Orig. Only	AR
McPhatter, Ann	083	1852	WB-2/103	AR
McPhatter, Annabella	083	1851	WB-2/31	
McPhatter, Archibald	083	1831	WB-1/259	AR
McPhatter, Archibald	083	1851	WB-2/43	
McPhatter, Duncan	083	1870	WB-2/248	AR
McPhatter, Eliza	083	1885	WB-3/359	aR
McPhaul, Daniel	082	c1833	Orig. Only	AR
McPhaul, Daniel	083	1849	WB-2/5	
McPhaul, Gilbert	083	1891	WB-3/521	AR
McPhaul, Margaret	083	1834	WB-1/287	AR
McPhaul, Mary	083	1816	WB-1/164	AR
McPhaul, Neill	027	1897	WB-2/137	AR
McPhaul, Neill	083	1859	WB-2/145	AR
McPheeters, Margaret	099	1862	RB-32/256	AR
McPheeters, Susan T.	099	1874	RB-35/256	AR
McPheeters, William	099	1842	RB-25/149	AR
McPherson, Alston	075	c1854	WB-M2/24	AR
McPherson, Andrew	030	1893	WB-5/215	AR
McPherson, Archibald	005	1852	WB-C/38	AR
McPherson, Colin A.	083	1879	WB-3/166	AR
McPherson, Daniel	030	1798	WB-2/113	
McPherson, Daniel	018	1836	WB-C/195	
McPherson, Daniel	075	1826	WB-N/28	AR-Nunc.
McPherson, Demsey	018	1825	WB-C/57	
McPherson, Duncan	082	1833	WB-2/28	AR
McPherson, Eli	001	1885	WB-2/244	AR
McPherson, Enoch	073	1837	WB-E/428	AR
McPherson, Flora	029	1873	WB-E/77	AR
McPherson, George	018	1858	WB-D/47	
McPherson, Hugh	029	1854	WB-C/308	AR
McPherson, Ira	VA	1839	018 WB-C/309	
McPherson, Isabel	083	1888	WB-3/438	AR
McPherson, James	082	1881	WB-6/216	AR
McPherson, James A.	018	1900	WB-E/316	AR
McPherson, James N.	018	1840	WB-C/259	
McPherson, Jane E.	054	1896	WB-5/565	CTY
McPherson, Jesse	018	1848	WB-C/339	
McPherson, Jesse	075	1807	WB-M1/142	AR
McPherson, John	082	1839	WB-2/86	AR
McPherson, John	083	c1789	WB-1/363	AR
McPherson, John	054	1843	WB-2/279	AR
McPherson, John Q.	029	1870	WB-E/13	AR
McPherson, Kiddy	018	1891	WB-E/200	AR
McPherson, Malachi	018	1842	WB-C/265	
McPherson, Martin	029	1852	WB-C/262	AR
McPherson, Mary	029	1873	WB-E/73	AR
McPherson, Matthew	054	1843	WB-2/278	AR
McPherson, Nancy	018	1837	WB-C/215	
McPherson, Nancy	029	1854	WB-C/286	
McPherson, Nancy	018	1897	WB-E/279	AR
McPherson, Noah	075	1840	WB-N/158	AR
McPherson, Oliver	018	1838	WB-C/236	
McPherson, Priscillah	005	c1778	WB-1/31	
McPherson, Robert	054	c1801	WB-1/171	AR
McPherson, Salley	018	1838	WB-C/143	
McPherson, Susanah	075	1877	WB-O/70	AR
McPherson, William	001	1867	WB-1/282	AR
McPherson, William	001	1871	WB-2/33	AR
McPherson, William	085	c1777	WB-A/249	AR
McPherson, William	018	1873	WB-E/42	AR

Name	Co.	Date	Recorded Copy	Original
McPherson, William	073	1818	WB-D/517	AR
McPherson, William	001	1879	WB-2/139	AR
McPhetters, John	085	1771	WB-A/102	AR
McPhoil, Marrion	083	c1783	WB-1/7	AR
McPhydon, Hector	083	1840	WB-1/392	AR
McQuaig, Alexander	029	1822	WB-B/68	AR
McQuaig, L. A.	065	1889	WB-L/400	
McQueen, Alexander	067	1879	WB-2/100	AR
McQueen, Archibald	022	1827	WB-B/141	AR
McQueen, Archibald	083	1896	WB-4/99	AR
McQueen, Archibald	083	1851	WB-2/37	
McQueen, Daniel	029	1815	WB-A/218	AR
McQueen, J. S.	082	1895	WB-6/515	AR
McQueen, Murdo	022	1828	WB-B/152	AR
McQueen, Nancy	083	1855	WB-2/79	AR
McQueen, Neill	029	1842	WB-C/28	AR
McQueen, Neill	029	1887	WB-E/422	AR
McQuien, Murdach	029	1774	Orig. Only	AR
McQuillin, Alexander	057	1783	WB-A/23	AR
McQuillin, Thomas	057	1815	WB-B/28	AR
McQuin, Norman	087	c1797	Orig. Only	AR
McQuown, Thomas	065	c1781	WB-B/123	AR
McRackan, Mary Ann	029	c1822	WB-B/91	AR
McRacken, James	029	1816	WB-A/238	AR
McRacken, Robert M.	027	1883	WB-2/51	AR
McRae, Alexander	083	1873	WB-3/64	AR
McRae, Alexander	082	1844	WB-3/15	AR
McRae, Alexander	067	1833	WB-1/53	AR
McRae, Alexander	029	1810	WB-A/155	AR
McRae, Alexander	083	1881	WB-3/264	AR
McRae, Alexander	082	1808	WB-1/125	AR
McRae, Archibald	082	1878	WB-6/149	AR
McRae, Archibald	005	1836	WB-B/62	AR
McRae, Cameron F.	100	1872	WB-51/99	AR
McRae, Catharine	082	1847	WB-3/43	AR
McRae, Christopher	029	1818	WB-B/7	AR
McRae, Christopher	005	1837	WB-B/71	AR
McRae, Colin	067	1863	WB-1/104	
McRae, Daniel	083	1854	WB-2/55	AR
McRae, Daniel	005	1841	WB-B/134	AR
McRae, Daniel	082	1850	WB-4/40	AR
McRae, Daniel	082	1843	WB-3/11	AR
McRae, Daniel	029	1822	WB-B/84	AR
McRae, Daniel	082	1864	WB-4/181	AR
McRae, Duncan	029	1837	WB-B/273	AR
McRae, Farquar	082	1800	WB-1/75	AR
McRae, Farquhard	005	1841	WB-B/132	AR
McRae, Finley	067	1817	WB-1/56	AR
McRae, Flora	029	1880	WB-E/215	AR
McRae, Frederick	067	1897	WB-2/360	
McRae, James	082	1866	WB-5/14	AR
McRae, James M.	067	1867	WB-1/146	AR
McRae, James Q. R.	082	1874	WB-6/120	AR
McRae, Jane	067	1870	WB-2/8	
McRae, Jason	103	1895	WB-2/109	AR
McRae, John	083	1844	WB-1/438	AR
McRae, John	070	1883	Copy	012 AR
McRae, John	082	1821	WB-1/224	AR
McRae, John	070	1883	WB-E/500	AR
McRae, John	083	c1827	WB-1/342	AR
McRae, John B.	082	c1826	WB-1/275	AR
McRae, John L.	083	1881	WB-3/240	AR
McRae, John W.	029	1880	WB-E/222	AR
McRae, M.	083	1899	WB-4/252	AR
McRae, Malcom	083	c1825	WB-1/329	AR
McRae, Margaret	SC	1897	083 WB-4/166	083 AR
McRae, Martha	005	1858	WB-C/130	AR
McRae, Martha B.	082	1878	Orig. Only	AR
McRae, Mary	082	1856	WB-4/99	AR
McRae, Murdock	005	1851	WB-C/32	AR
McRae, Norman	082	1851	WB-4/51	AR
McRae, Peter	082	1825	WB-1/245	AR
McRae, Philip	005	c1825	WB-A/122	
McRae, Rhoda	029	1854	WB-C/279	AR
McRae, Sarah M.	082	1886	WB-6/322	AR
McRae, Susan	100	1873	WB-51/101	AR
McRae, W. H.	067	1893	WB-2/317	AR
McRae, William	035	c1751	087 DB-2/85	
McRae, William	083	1881	WB-3/228	AR
McRaney, James	081	1867	WB-14/92	
McRary, David	054	1855	WB-3/99	AR
McRary, Henry	032	c1851	WB-2/162	
McRary, John	054	1870	WB-4/77	AR
McRary, Nancy	032	c1860	WB-2/214	AR
McRary, William H.	070	1886	WB-F/16	AR
McRary, William H.	070	1886	032 WB-3/559	
McRary, Wilson	032	c1851	WB-2/61	AR-Copy
McRaven, D. O.	065	1899	WB-N/190	
McRavin, John	065	1813	WB-E/19	AR
McRay, George	073	1807	WB-D/211	
McRee, A. C.	016	1879	WB-3/259	AR
McRee, Andrew	065	c1801	WB-B/154	AR
McRee, Ann	011	c1828	WB-1/72	
McRee, David	016	c1827	WB-A/21	AR
McRee, James C.	054	c1810	WB-2/107	AR
McRee, James F.	070	1869	WB-E/171	AR
McRee, James Iver	011	1854	WB-1/238	
McRee, Jane	065	1869	WB-K/12	
McRee, Jane	016	1850	WB-1/172	AR
McRee, John	065	1795	WB-B/137	AR
McRee, Margaret	065	c1803	WB-E/1	AR
McRee, Mary M.	014	1887	WB-2/340	CTY
McRee, Nancy	054	c1861	WB-3/159	
McRee, Richard	016	1829	WB-A/22	AR
McRee, Robert	065	1776	WB-B/55	AR
McRee, Robert	065	1802	Orig. Only	AR
McRee, Robert	011	c1793	WB-1/543	
McRee, Samuel	011	c1798	WB-1/423	
McRee, William	065	1788	WB-B/72	AR
McRee, William	035	1751	SS 879/64	SS/AR
McRee, William	011	c1789	WB-1/579	
McRee, William L.	014	c1855	Orig. Only	AR-Copy
McRine, William	019	1817	WB-D/294	AR
McRorie, Frank	054	1897	WB-6/95	CTY
McRum, Matilda H.	065	1859	WB-J/65	AR
McRum, Rachel	065	1822	WB-B/100	AR
McRum, S. T.	065	1862	WB-J/140	AR
McSheea, Mary	086	1844	WB-E/139	AR
McSorley, John	028	1897	WB-F/255	
McSuine, Donald	029	1809	WB-A/144	AR
McSwain, A. A.	026	1885	WB-2/290	
McSwain, Donald	083	1787	WB-1/4	AR
McSwain, Drury D.	086	1898	WB-F/575	AR
McSwain, Edward	053	1772	RW-1/35	AR
McSwain, Flora	083	1839	WB-1/316	AR
McSwain, George	026	1862	WB-1/292	AR
McSwain, H. K.	026	1899	WB-3/38	AR
McSwain, James	026	1854	WB-1/179	AR
McSwain, Roger	083	1816	WB-1/165	
McSwain, William	086	1868	WB-E/489	AR

Name	Co.	Date	Recorded Copy	Original
McSwain, William	026	1881	WB-2/217	AR
McSwain, William	026	1870	WB-2/48	AR
McSwane, John	022	1799	WB-A/12	
McSwean, Angus	082	1818	WB-1/195	AR
McSween, Alexander	082	1808	WB-1/120	AR
McSween, Finlay	082	1828	WB-1/300	AR
McSween, Sarah	082	1881	WB-6/227	AR
McTygart, Samuel	025	1871	WB-A/14	AR
McVay, John	078	1833	WI-12/156	AR
McVicar, Patrick	070	1753	DB-D/50	AR
McWhorter, Aaron	065	1799	WB-B/144	AR
McWhorter, George	065	1841	WB-H/52	AR
McWhorter, George	065	1806	WB-E/8	AR
McWhorter, Henry M.	065	1824	WB-F/30	AR
McWilliams, Clemon	047	1814	WB-3/549	AR
McWilliams, Jane	070	1895	WB-G/403	AR
McWilliams, John	009	c1836	OB-B/474	AR
McWilliams, Mary	037	1848	WB-F/396	AR
McWilliams, Nancy	009	1838	OB-C2/88	AR
Meacham, Banks	065	1820	WB-E/25	AR
Meacham, Henry	071	1809	WB-3/19	AR
Meacham, Thomas J.	059	1900	WB-B/255	CTY
Meacham, Washington	032	1878	WB-3/254	AR
Meacham, William	022	1808	WB-A/101	
Meachum, Martha	005	1871	WB-D/5	AR
Meachum, William S.	005	c1869	WB-D/3	AR
Mead, Rachel	057	c1798	WB-A/221	AR
Mead, Thomas	057	1794	WB-A/119	AR
Meades, Timothy	002	1686	Orig. Only	SS/AR
Meador, John	084	1844	WB-C/13	CTY
Meador, Thomas C.	084	1890	WB-E/471	CTY
Meadors, Jason	005	c1774	WB-1/16	AR-Copy
Meadors, John	005	1861	WB-C/169	AR
Meadors, Peter	005	1887	WB-D/206	AR
Meadows, Abraham	057	c1795	WB-A/162	AR
Meadows, Bettie	044	1898	WB-24/383	CTY
Meadows, Brody	044	1890	WB-24/105	CTY
Meadows, Deberry B.	044	1874	WB-23/134	CTY
Meadows, Elijah	044	1874	WB-23/135	CTY
Meadows, Gillom	054	1835	WB-2/152	AR-Nunc.
Meadows, Harvey	003	1897	WB-B/363	AR
Meadows, Hawkins	044	1875	WB-23/202	CTY
Meadows, Henry	084	1890	WB-E/446	CTY
Meadows, Isaac	019	1816	WB-D/293	AR
Meadows, James	044	1815	WB-7/508	CTY
Meadows, Jeason	019	1826	WB-D/297	AR
Meadows, Jesse	044	1883	WB-23/476	CTY
Meadows, John	015	1774	100 WB-2/22	AR
Meadows, John A.	028	1865	WB-D/368	AR
Meadows, John J.	044	1896	WB-24/319	CTY
Meadows, Millington	057	1866	WB-B/260	AR
Meadows, Pinkney	044	1896	WB-24/304	CTY
Meadows, Seth	044	1886	WB-23/559	CTY
Meadows, Simion	057	1842	WB-B/147	AR
Meadows, Squire	078	1889	WB-19/251	AR
Meadows, Thomas	044	1865	WB-22/332	CTY
Meadows, Thomas H.	028	c1877	Orig. Only	AR
Meadows, Vilater	057	1807	WB-A/299	AR-Nunc.
Mealer, James	100	1819	WB-22/185	AR
Meanas, Frederick	085	1835	WB-H/661	AR
Means, Benjamin	081	1832	WB-6/266	AR
Means, Camaline	016	c1892	Orig. Only	AR
Means, John S.	065	1900	WB-N/360	AR
Means, John S.	065	1877	WB-K/256	AR
Means, Robert	084	1822	WB-A/259	CTY

Name	Co.	Date	Recorded Copy	Original
Means, Susannah	016	1855	WB-1/258	AR
Meara, Martha	077	1883	WB-H/137	AR
Meares, Mark	028	1762	SS 881/228	SS/AR
Meares, Noah	083	1855	WB-2/59	AR
Meares, William B.	070	1841	WB-AB/350	AR
Mearns, William	030	1771	024 WB-1/41	024 AR
Mears, Elihue	011	1871	WB-2/49	
Mears, James	054	1881	WB-4/434	CTY
Mears, James	083	1856	WB-2/81	
Mears, Joab	083	1860	WB-2/164	AR
Mears, Martha L.	054	1896	WB-5/576	CTY
Mears, William	054	1856	WB-3/108	AR
Mears, William	054	1892	WB-5/426	CTY
Mears, Zadock	046	1790	WB-A/232	AR
Mebane, Alexander	073	1793	WB-B/216	AR
Mebane, Alexander	001	1866	WB-1/251	AR
Mebane, Alexander	010	c1846	Copy	077 AR
Mebane, Alexander	010	1847	WB-G/412	AR
Mebane, Alexander	073	1795	WB-C/53	AR
Mebane, Alexander	010	1871	WB-I/40	AR
Mebane, David	073	1843	WB-F/144	AR
Mebane, Elizabeth	073	1851	WB-G/1	AR
Mebane, George A.	073	1877	WB-H/166	CTY
Mebane, Giles	001	1899	WB-3/273	AR
Mebane, Hettie J.	084	1898	WB-F/106	CTY
Mebane, James	073	1807	WB-D/201	AR
Mebane, James	020	1858	RB-R/598	AR
Mebane, Jane A.	001	1886	WB-2/310	
Mebane, John	022	1837	WB-C/77	
Mebane, John A.	046	1864	WB-D/215	AR
Mebane, Samuel	TN	1855	078 WB-17/421	
Mebane, William	073	1856	WB-G/150	CTY
Mebane, William	073	1803	WB-D/101	AR
Mebane, William	022	c1820	WB-B/32	
Mebane, William N.	084	1860	WB-C/303	CTY
Mecholester, Levin	084	1850	Orig. Only	CTY
Meckdendal, Deborah	077	1732	SS 876/257	
Mecom, Ellen	069	1866	WB-1/599	AR
Mecom, Matthew	047	1817	WB-3/609	AR
Mecom, Samuel	071	1794	WB-2/45	AR-Nunc.
Mecoy, Hardy	028	1843	Orig. Only	AR
Mecoy, William	028	1802	WB-B/160	
Mecoy, Willis	028	1801	WB-B/112	AR
Mecraken, Alexander	073	1795	WB-C/65	AR
Mecum, Nancy	090	1815	WB-2/169	Nunc.
Medaris, Abraham	078	1827	Orig. Only	AR
Medcalf, William	005	1798	WB-2/104	AR
Medearis, Charles	046	1793	WB-A/227	AR
Medearis, Massey C.	046	1843	WB-C/155	AR
Medford, E. B.	049	1889	WB-2/171	AR
Medford, Henry	047	1774	Orig. Only	SS/AR
Medford, Henry	063	1819	WB-2/64	
Medford, James	063	1834	WB-2/190	
Medford, Rubin E.	049	1895	WB-2/350	AR
Medford, Stephen	063	1855	WB-2/423	
Medlen, Bartlet	039	1884	WB-U/333	AR
Medley, Bryant	090	c1833	Orig. Only	AR
Medley, Joseph	005	1869	WB-D/9	AR
Medley, Martha F.	044	c1857	Orig. Only	CTY
Medley, Nancy	097	1893	WB-2/447	AR
Medley, Reuben	005	1823	WB-A/80	AR
Medlin, Bartlette	039	1875	WB-U/133	AR
Medlin, Benjamin	099	1805	RB-7/96	AR
Medlin, Elizabeth	056	c1894	105 WB-3/469	105 AR
Medlin, Elizabeth	056	c1894	WB-4/313	AR

Name	Co.	Date	Recorded Copy	Original
Medlin, John	066	[illegible]	WB-4/309	AR
Medlin, John	047	1852	WB-4/328	AR
Medlin, Mathew	099	1883	WB-A/498	AR
Medlin, Mathew	039	c1837	WB-M/59	AR
Medlin, Michael	022	1806	WB-A/167	AR
Medlin, Rebecca	068	c1851	WB-C/30	
Medlin, Reubin	099	1840	RB-24/423	AR
Meeds, Benjamin	075	1824	WB-M1/392	AR
Meeds, Benjamin	075	1766	Orig. Only	AR
Meeds, Joseph	075	1775	WB-I/136	AR
Meeds, Susannah	075	1755	Orig. Only	SS/AR
Meeds, Thomas	075	c1751	Copy	024 AR
Meeds, Thomas	075	1751	Orig. Only	SS/AR
Meeds, Thomas	075	1785	WB-K/134	AR
Meeds, Timothy	075	1759	WB-H/4	AR
Meeds, Timothy	075	1751	SS 881/87	SS/AR
Meek, Adam, Sr.	065	1817	WB-E/29	
Meek, George	070	1788	Orig. Only	AR-Copy
Meek, George	011	c1789	WB-1/549	
Meek, James	065	1807	WB-E/15	AR
Meek, Margaret	016	1847	WB-1/138	AR
Meek, Mary	070	c1806	Orig. Only	AR
Meekens, James H.	009	1883	WB-1/328	CTY-Nunc.
Meekins, Adin	096	1842	WB-3/3	AR
Meekins, Agnes	053	1835	WB-5/354	AR
Meekins, Enoch J.	083	1878	WB-3/144	AR
Meekins, Esther	030	1861	WB-4/245	AR
Meekins, Isaac	096	c1769	Orig. Only	AR
Meekins, Isaac C.	031	1885	WB-1/29	AR
Meekins, Jonathan	096	1895	WB-4/159	AR
Meekins, Joseph	096	1833	WB-2/114	AR
Meekins, Martha A.	030	1900	WB-5/292	AR
Meekins, William	096	1836	WB-2/131	
Meeks, Benjamin	070	1848	WB-AB/480	AR
Meeks, John	079	1884	WB-2/308	AR
Meeks, Staten	070	1848	WB-AB/482	AR
Meenan, Hugh	065	1831	WB-G/67	AR
Meers, Thomas	092	1800	WB-3/34	AR
Meezell, Aaron	010	1809	WB-F/113	AR
Megee, Bluford	104	1849	WB-5/14	AR
Megee, Bluford B.	104	1887	WB-6/287	AR
Megee, David	104	1815	WB-3/92	AR
Megehee, Henry	099	1840	RB-24/437	AR
Megehee, Henry	099	1896	WB-C/566	AR
Meginney, Levin	070	1881	WB-E/418	AR
Meglohon, James	010	1750	Orig. Only	SS/AR
Mehaffey, James	104	1838	WB-4/230	AR
Mehaffey, Joseph	060	1836	WB-1/371	AR
Mehaffey, Thomas	104	1796	WB-1/484	
Mehaffey, William L.	021	1875	WB-2/142	AR
Mehoons, James	096	1772	WB-1/80	AR
Mehrekens, John Henry	070	1900	WB-H/253	
Meinung, Edwin A.	038	1891	WB-3/212	AR
Meinung, Frederic	038	1851	WB-1/28	AR
Meisenheimer, Mary M.	003	1897	WB-B/369	AR
Meissenheimer, Jacob	016	1801	WB-A/102	AR
Meizelle, Isam	063	1815	WB-2/30	
Melchor, Christopher	016	1871	WB-3/66	AR
Melchor, Elizabeth	016	1877	WB-3/227	AR
Melchor, John	016	1881	WB-3/312	AR
Melchor, John	016	1824	WB-A/13	AR
Melchor, L. E.	089	1897	WB-2/298	AR
Melchor, Sophia	089	1859	WB-1/208	
Meley, Peter	016	1820	WB-A/12	AR
Melton, John	069	c1823	Orig. Only	AR
Melke, Arthur C.	083	1891	WB-3/524	AR
Melke, Arthur C.	083	1891	013 WB-C/152	
Meller, Jacob	032	1844	WB-1/430	
Mellon, Edward	060	1828	WB-1/79	AR
Mellon, Johnathan	040	1850	WB-1/32	
Mellyne, Robert	008	1708/9	009 DB-1/98	
Melone, Daniel	078	1815	WI-7/28	AR
Melone, John	015	1774	100 WB-1/293	AR
Melone, Robert	071	1779	WB-1/209	
Melson, Edward	019	1800	WB-D/281	AR
Melson, Elijah P.	096	1867	WB-3/81	AR
Melson, James	030	1849	WB-4/140	
Melson, John	019	1802	WB-D/282	AR
Melson, John A.	096	1809	Orig. Only	AR
Melson, John A. P.	070	1857	WB-C/656	AR
Melson, Taylor	019	1827	WB-D/298	AR
Melten, Martha A.	038	1853	WB-1/42	AR
Melton, Alfred Webb	086	1883	WB-F/176	AR
Melton, Amon	092	1878	WB-6/112	AR
Melton, Andrew	069	1824	WB-1/321	AR
Melton, B. J.	086	1888	WB-F/358	AR
Melton, Benjamin	072	1803	WB-A/90	AR
Melton, Bolin	069	1871	WB-1/610	AR
Melton, Cornelius	086	1821	WB-C/151	AR
Melton, Daniel	086	1849	WB-E/193	AR
Melton, David	092	1787	WB-2/73A	AR
Melton, Edward	072	1823	WB-A/87	AR
Melton, Elizabeth	044	1853	WB-19/290	CTY
Melton, Elizabeth	071	1779	WB-1/219	
Melton, Esther	072	1860	WB-2/182	AR
Melton, Frany	086	1860	WB-E/382	AR
Melton, Henry	044	1794	WB-3/106	CTY
Melton, Isaiah W.	086	1865	WB-E/450	AR
Melton, James	057	1806	WB-A/282	AR
Melton, Jerry	010	1887	WB-I/226	AR
Melton, Jesse	005	1833	WB-B/32	AR
Melton, Jesse B.	097	1890	WB-2/366	AR
Melton, John	086	1813	WB-B/274	AR
Melton, John	069	1800	WB-1/133	AR
Melton, John	071	1796	WB-2/107	AR
Melton, John M.	086	1877	WB-F/98	AR
Melton, Jonathan	072	1758	SS 879/264	SS/AR
Melton, Joshua	086	1828	WB-D/91	AR
Melton, Mary	072	1864	WB-3/5	AR
Melton, Mary	071	1806	WB-2/326	AR
Melton, Mary M.	086	1898	WB-F/563	AR
Melton, Meady	051	1880	WB-C/258	AR
Melton, Nathan	069	1804	WB-1/152	AR
Melton, Richard	072	c1763	RW/L51	AR
Melton, Robert	069	1861	WB-1/578	AR
Melton, Robert	072	1785	WI/L23	AR
Melton, Robert	073	1759	SS 881/254	SS/AR
Melton, Sarah	086	1880	WB-F/152	AR
Melton, Solomon	072	1832	WB-1/107	AR
Melton, Stephen	044	1828	Orig. Only	CTY
Melton, Thomas	072	1831	WB-1/84	AR
Melton, William	072	1780	RW/L44	AR
Melton, William	106	1897	WB-2/396	
Melton, William T.	078	1899	WB-19/485	AR
Melton, Zackariah	069	1792	WB-1/77	AR
Melvill, Solomon	072	1831	WB-1/79	AR
Melvin, Barbara A.	029	1882	WB-E/288	AR
Melvin, Daniel	011	1846	WB-1/142	
Melvin, Daniel	087	1876	WB-3/115	AR

Name	Co.	Date	Recorded Copy	Original
Melvin, Demaris	011	1882	WB-2/154	
Melvin, Dorcas	029	1874	WB-E/141	AR
Melvin, George W.	011	1847	WB-1/152	
Melvin, Isaac C.	029	1880	WB-E/206	AR
Melvin, James	073	1836	WB-E/395	AR
Melvin, James	011	1881	WB-2/140	
Melvin, John	011	1853	WB-1/212	
Melvin, John	011	c1839	WB-1/97	
Melvin, Jonathan	011	1875	WB-2/84	
Melvin, Joshua	LA	1856	011 WB-1/285	
Melvin, Lula B.	029	1892	WB-E/530	AR
Melvin, Robert	072	1811	WB-A/82	AR
Melvin, Robert	011	1846	WB-1/154	
Melvin, Rosana J.	011	1882	WB-2/154	
Melvin, Solomon	072	c1780	RW/L29	AR
Memminger, C. G.	SC	1888	050 WB-2/35	050 CTY
Memory, G. W.	029	1900	WB-F/187	AR
Memory, George	011	c1806	WB-2/304	
Memory, T. S.	027	1896	WB-2/120	AR
Mendenhall, Aaron	046	1794	WB-A/230	AR
Mendenhall, Cyrus P.	046	1884	WB-E/394	AR
Mendenhall, Daniel	046	1817	WB-B/45	AR
Mendenhall, David	046	1832	WB-B/462	AR
Mendenhall, Delphina	046	1881	WB-E/318	AR
Mendenhall, Edwin B.	040	1863	WB-1/152	
Mendenhall, Eleazar	046	1887	WB-E/490	AR
Mendenhall, Elisha	046	1836	WB-B/555	AR
Mendenhall, Enoch	081	1869	WB-15/6	AR
Mendenhall, George	046	1805	WB-A/242	AR
Mendenhall, George C.	046	1860	WB-D/45	AR
Mendenhall, Hannah	081	1876	WB-15/230	AR
Mendenhall, Isaac	046	1833	WB-B/480	AR
Mendenhall, Isaac	046	1857	WB-C/482	AR
Mendenhall, Jabez H.	032	1844	WB-1/438	
Mendenhall, James	046	1861	WB-D/79	AR
Mendenhall, James	046	1811	WB-A/246	AR
Mendenhall, John	081	1886	WB-15/574	AR
Mendenhall, John	046	1800	WB-A/236	AR
Mendenhall, John	046	1877	WB-E/191	AR
Mendenhall, John	046	1831	WB-B/433	AR
Mendenhall, John J.	040	1891	WB-2/403	AR
Mendenhall, Joseph	090	1823	WB-3/94	AR
Mendenhall, Joseph	081	1842	WB-7/411	AR
Mendenhall, Judith J.	046	1896	WB-F/540	AR
Mendenhall, Margaret	040	1870	WB-2/9	AR
Mendenhall, Mary	046	1867	WB-D/342	AR
Mendenhall, Mary	005	1862	WB-C/180	AR
Mendenhall, Minerva	046	1900	WB-G/180	AR
Mendenhall, Mordecai	046	1803	WB-A/239	AR
Mendenhall, Mordecai	046	1879	WB-E/254	AR
Mendenhall, Mordecai	046	1850	WB-C/323	AR
Mendenhall, Moses	046	1805	WB-A/244	AR
Mendenhall, Moses	046	1847	WB-C/277	AR
Mendenhall, Moses H.	046	1860	WB-D/62	AR
Mendenhall, Nathan	046	1841	WB-C/97	AR
Mendenhall, Phebe	046	1852	WB-C/362	AR
Mendenhall, Phebe	046	1826	WB-B/220	AR
Mendenhall, Richard	046	1851	WB-C/346	AR
Mendenhall, Robert	040	c1858	WB-1/101	
Mendenhall, Sarah	081	1884	WB-15/472	AR
Mendenhall, Seth	046	1834	WB-B/508	AR
Mendenhall, Susannah	046	1844	WB-C/212	AR
Mendenhall, Thomas	046	c1782	WB-A/233	AR
Mendenhall, Tomsy	046	1899	WB-G/116	AR
Mendenhall, William	046	1829	Orig. Only	AR-Nunc.
Mendenhall, William	005	1846	WB-B/210	AR
Meng, William	029	1821	WB-B/60	AR
Menis, George W.	016	1877	WB-3/206	AR
Menner, John	073	1836	WB-E/394	
Menninger, Henry J.	099	1893	WB-C/151	AR
Menshaw, John	044	1763	Orig. Only	CTY
Menshew, Maxey	041	1789	WB-1/82	
Menster, John	054	1836	WB-2/159	AR
Menzies, John	084	1819	WB-A/253	CTY
Meradith, Joseph	035	1751	087 DB-2/83	
Mercer, Betsy	045	1893	WB-1/338	AR
Mercer, Bettie	037	1895	WB-H/335	AR
Mercer, Edward J.	030	1866	WB-4/258	AR-Nunc.
Mercer, Eli	069	1832	WB-1/389	AR
Mercer, Furnifold	057	1899	WB-C/242	AR
Mercer, Jeremiah	030	1797	WB-2/104	
Mercer, Jeremiah	030	c1814	WB-3/44	
Mercer, Jesse	018	1891	WB-E/192	AR
Mercer, Jesse	037	1892	WB-H/207	AR
Mercer, John	030	1788	WB-1/218	
Mercer, John	035	1781	WB-A/290	AR
Mercer, John	012	1861	WB-B/48	AR
Mercer, John R.	037	1894	105 WB-4/192	105 AR
Mercer, John R.	037	1894	WB-H/304	AR
Mercer, Mager	030	1900	WB-5/288	AR
Mercer, Malachi	030	c1805	WB-2/344	
Mercer, Margaret	069	1848	WB-1/510	AR
Mercer, Margaret	037	1852	WB-F/491	AR
Mercer, Nancy	075	c1854	WB-M2/10	AR
Mercer, Noah	083	1886	WB-3/381	AR
Mercer, Rowland	083	1863	WB-2/192	AR
Mercer, Rowland	083	1881	WB-3/37 & 234	AR
Mercer, Solomon	083	c1788	WB-1/12	AR
Mercer, Thomas	018	1825	WB-C/60	
Mercer, William	018	1830	WB-C/117	
Mercer, Wilson	018	1853	WB-C/379	
Merchant, Caleph	096	1808	WB-2/26	AR
Merchant, Christopher	028	1799	WB-B/75	
Merchant, Elizabeth	096	1831	WB-2/103	AR
Merchant, William	065	1801	WB-B/152	AR
Mercingale, James, Sr.	069	1785	WB-1/38	AR
Merck, Joseph	086	1894	WB-F/487	AR
Mercy, Abigail	073	1798	WB-C/120	
Meredett, Sarah	024	1825	WB-C/117	AR
Meredette, John	024	1821	WB-C/93	AR
Meredith, David	010	1791	WB-D/187	AR
Meredith, David	010	c1791	024 WB-A/168	024 AR
Meredith, Elisha	090	1848	WB-4/256	AR
Meredith, Elizabeth	051	1832	WB-A/62	
Meredith, James	011	1863	WB-1/310	
Meredith, James	005	c1785	WB-1/49	
Meredith, Lewis	051	c1798	WB-A/49	
Meredith, Mary	038	1893	WB-3/400	AR
Meredith, Sarah	038	1862	WB-1/192	AR
Meredith, Thomas	099	1850	RB-27/135	AR
Meredith, William	070	1799	WB-AB/32	AR
Meredith, William	010	1780	WB-B/153	AR
Merel, Joseph	035	1795	WB-A/307	AR
Meremoon, Jesse	071	1806	WB-2/324	AR
Meret, Charles	024	1718	Orig. Only	SS/AR
Merett, John	037	1757	SS 882/133	SS/AR
Merideth, William	010	c1780	EdDSC	AR-Copy
Meridith, Davis	010	1796	WB-D/344	AR
Meridith, James	092	1790	WB-2/165	
Meridith, Mildred	092	1796	WB-3/21A	AR

Name	Co	Date	Recorded Copy	Original
Merine, John	019	1820	WB-D/295	AR
Meritt, Nathaniel	037	1735	Orig. Only	SS/AR
Meritt, Phebe	047	1837	WB-4/150	AR
Meritt, Shadrach	047	1836	WB-4/130	AR
Meroney, John A.	033	1837	WB-1/5	AR
Meroney, Martha	033	1893	WB-2/229	CTY
Merreday, Thomas	075	1741	LGB-4/#158	SS/AR
Merrel, Margaret	032	1837	WB-1/294	
Merrel, William	050	1857	WB-1/50	CTY
Merrell, Anna	032	1900	WB-4/449	AR
Merrell, Benjamin	013	1836	WB-A/41	
Merrell, Ebenezer	032	1884	WB-3/434	AR
Merrell, Ebenezer	032	1898	WB-4/387	
Merrell, Jesse	013	1834	WB-A/31	
Merrell, John	013	1834	WB-A/28	
Merrell, John, Sr.	013	1877	WB-B/145	AR
Merrell, Samuel	085	N. D.	WB-G/5	AR
Merrell, William	050	c1857	WB-1/84	
Merret, Hezekiah	057	1805	WB-A/276	AR
Merret, Mary	047	1777	WB-2/66	
Merrett, James	068	1797	WB-A/194	
Merrett, Unity	087	c1873	WB-A/158	AR
Merriam, Charles R.	099	1837	RB-24/55	AR
Merriam, William R.	NY	1870	009 WB-1/157	
Merrian, Barthelomew	015	1777	100 WB-2/148	
Merrick, Frederick	MA	1888	070 WB-G/565	070 AR
Merrick, George	070	1806	WB-AB/139	AR
Merrick, Harry	070	1885	WB-E/446	AR
Merrick, John	070	1756	DB-D/190	AR
Merrick, Margaret	070	1882	WB-E/480	AR
Merrick, Sarah	070	c1892	Orig. Only	AR
Merrick, Thomas	070	1767	WB-C/250	AR
Merrill, Arter	019	1834	WB-A/42	AR
Merriman, Augustus	099	1892	WB-C/93	AR
Merrimon, Branch H.	013	1881	WB-B/254	AR
Merrit, Absolum	035	1803	WB-A/306	AR
Merrit, Benjamin	047	1761	WB-1/44	
Merrit, Mary	047	1765	WB-1/177	
Merrit, Thomas	047	1794	WB-3/224	AR
Merrit, William	047	1813	WB-3/544	AR
Merritt, Benajah C.	087	1863	WB-2/56	AR
Merritt, Benjamin	044	1840	WB-14/605	CTY
Merritt, Benjamin	044	1777	WB-1/205	CTY
Merritt, Benjamin	069	1779	WB-1/3	AR
Merritt, Charles D.	TN	1889	062 WB-B/165	062 AR
Merritt, Daniel	087	c1841	Orig. Only	AR
Merritt, Elizabeth	087	1864	WB-2/61	AR
Merritt, Ephraim	047	1789	WB-3/160	AR
Merritt, Ephraim	047	1801	WB-3/364	AR
Merritt, Frederick	039	1818	WB-F/66	AR
Merritt, Gabriel	087	c1820	WB-1/2	AR
Merritt, George	022	1819	WB-B/16	AR
Merritt, George W.	090	1898	WB-6/454	AR
Merritt, George W.	096	1900	WB-4/177	AR
Merritt, Green	044	1817	WB-8/78	CTY
Merritt, Hartwell	047	1843	WB-4/215	AR
Merritt, Henry	039	1861	WB-R/158	AR
Merritt, John	019	1845	WB-A/121	AR
Merritt, John	039	1805	WB-C/24	AR
Merritt, John	039	1846	WB-M/115	AR
Merritt, Joseph	100	1791	WB-6/22	AR
Merritt, Mary	037	1778	WB-B/1	AR-Nunc.
Merritt, Mary	087	1868	WB-2/123	AR
Merritt, Morris M.	039	1885	WB-U/348	AR
Merritt, Nathial	087	c1819	WB-A/95	AR

Name	Co.	Date	Recorded Copy	Original
Merritt, Richard	047	1781	WB-3/5	AR
Merritt, Sally	067	1863	WB-1/108	
Merritt, Stepney	073	1877	WB-H/156	CTY
Merritt, Thomas	047	1811	WB-3/521	AR
Merritt, Thomas	100	1786	WB-4/170	AR
Merritt, Thomas	037	1768	WB-A/159	AR
Merritt, William	047	1784	WB-3/54	AR
Merritt, William	022	c1829	WB-B/171	
Merritt, William	047	1892	WB-7/26	AR
Merritt, William H.	073	1850	WB-F/458	AR
Merry, William	018	1837	WB-C/210	
Merryman, Benjamin	047	1774	WB-1/374	
Merryman, Charles	044	1789	WB-2/100	CTY
Merton, Nancy	078	1877	WB-19/122	
Merwin, John W.	063	1810	WB-2/1	
Mesler, Cearsmer	024	1696	SS 874.2/82	SS/AR
Mesmer, Diana	085	1890	WB-2/441	CTY
Messamer, Peter	085	1805	WB-E/79	AR
Messe, Joseph	072	1754	SS 881/131	SS/AR
Messer, Benjamin	057	1793	WB-A/148	AR-Nunc.
Messer, Henry	083	c1791	WB-1/24	AR
Messer, James	057	1878	WB-C/63	AR
Messer, John	057	1891	WB-C/181	AR
Messer, John	055	1894	WB-A/120	
Messer, Solomon	049	c1824	WI-A/19	AR
Messer, William	056	c1800	Orig. Only	AR
Messer, William O.	049	1894	WB-2/317	AR
Messersmith, Conrod	073	1799	Orig. Only	AR
Messick, Elevin	070	1799	WB-AB/36	AR
Messick, George	092	1846	WB-4/248	
Messick, John M.	106	c1860	WB-1/71	AR
Messick, John N.	106	1885	WB-2/207	AR
Messick, John R.	009	1891	WB-1/509	CTY
Messick, Leonard	106	c1853	WB-2/64	AR
Metcalf, Caleb	028	1736	SS 877/219	SS/AR (N)
Metcalf, George	077	1795	WB-E/33	
Metcalf, J.	062	1883	Orig. Only	AR
Metcalf, James	062	1896	WB-B/194	AR
Metcalf, William	080	1900	WB-1/331	AR
Mets, George	028	1727	SS 876/133	SS/AR
Metts, Eliza	028	1875	WB-E/160	AR
Metts, George	057	1794	WB-A/172	AR
Meuse, Joshua	009	1842	OB-D/357	AR
Mew, Philip	057	1791	WB-A/188	AR
Mewboorn, Thomas	010	1749	SS 878/196	SS/AR
Mewborn, Ann	077	1848	WB-F/359	AR
Mewborn, George B.	077	1826	WB-F/123	AR
Mewborn, John M.	045	1900	WB-1/400	
Mewborn, Moses	010	1767	WB-A/79	AR
Mewborn, Sallie E.	059	1885	WB-A/383	CTY
Mewborn, Thomas	037	1782	WB-B/105	AR
Mewburn, Nicholas	010	1774	WB-B/9	AR
Meyer, John G.	085	c1799	WB-E/39	AR
Meyers, Sarah E.	VA	1893	013 WB-C/268	013 AR
Mezell, Jeremiah	010	1816	WB-F/328	
Mezger, C. A.	065	1899	WB-N/203	AR
Mezill, Hardy, Sr.	063	c1833	WB-2/186	
Mhoon, Mary	010	1839	WB-G/291	AR
Mhoon, William S.	AL	1845	010 WB-G/401	010 AR
Mial, Alonza T.	099	1898	009 WB-2/136	009 CTY
Mial, Alonzo T.	099	1898	WB-D/136	AR
Mial, Alonzo T.	099	1898	056 WB-4/97	056 AR
Mial, John	037	1778	WB-A/262	AR
Mial, Thomas	099	1811	RB-10/161	AR

Name	Co.	Date	Recorded Copy	Original
Mial, Thomas	099	1831	RB-21/383	AR
Miars, Mithias	044	1770	Orig. Only	CTY
Michael, Aaron	046	1864	WB-D/226	AR
Michael, Asa T.	102	1898	WB-A/148	AR
Michael, Catharine	032	c1858	WB-2/260	AR
Michael, David	001	1878	WB-2/133	AR
Michael, David L.	032	1886	WB-3/507	AR
Michael, Delila	032	1857	WB-2/149	AR
Michael, Eady	032	1874	WB-3/103	AR
Michael, Henry	032	c1852	WB-2/65	
Michael, Jacob	032	1885	WB-3/458	
Michael, Jacob, Sr.	032	c1846	WB-2/3	
Michael, John	032	c1848	WB-2/22	
Michael, Nancy	032	1875	WB-3/145	AR
Michael, Nicholas	032	1837	WB-1/301	
Michael, Sarah	032	1860	WB-2/184	AR
Michael, Sarah	023	1866	Orig. Only	AR
Michael, Susanna	032	1874	WB-3/101	AR
Michael, Warren	071	1817	WB-3/192	
Michael, William H.	060	1894	WB-4/539	AR
Michaely, William	085	1827	WB-H/384	AR
Michaux, Susan F.P.	014	1900	WB-3/114	CTY
Michel, David	044	1781	WB-1/307	CTY
Mickens, William	030	1775	WB-1/101	
Mickey, John	038	1884	WB-2/493	AR
Mickey, John	090	1807	WB-2/74	AR
Mickey, Solomon	038	1880	WB-2/384	AR
Micks, Eliza J.	087	1895	WB-3/572	AR
Micks, William G.	087	1876	WB-3/112	AR
Middellton, John	N	1718	Orig. Only	SS/AR
Middleton, Amos	035	1830	WB-1/3	AR
Middleton, Bazil	035	1886	WB-4/273	AR
Middleton, Cato	035	1874	WB-4/87	AR-Nunc.
Middleton, Clarissa	035	1884	WB-4/266	AR
Middleton, Daniel W.	082	1893	WB-6/480	AR
Middleton, David	035	1819	WB-A/349	AR
Middleton, Elizabeth	046	1842	WB-C/133	AR
Middleton, Henry	096	1739	LGB-4/#89	SS/AR
Middleton, Henry	013	1876	WB-B/130	AR
Middleton, Hugh	082	1899	WB-7/31	AR
Middleton, Isaac, Sr.	035	1820	WB-A/299	AR
Middleton, James	035	1805	WB-A/278	AR
Middleton, James M.	035	1869	WB-4/11	AR
Middleton, James, Jr.	035	1801	WB-A/292	AR
Middleton, John	046	1841	WB-C/102	AR
Middleton, John	024	1798	WB-A/340	AR
Middleton, John	072	1744	SS 878/33	SS/AR
Middleton, John	037	1750	Orig. Only	SS/AR
Middleton, Lebbens	035	1854	WB-2/85	AR
Middleton, Mary	035	1832	WB-1/24	AR
Middleton, Ruth	024	c1814	WB-C/31	AR
Middleton, Susannah	035	1802	WB-A/298	AR
Midelton, James	096	c1767	WB-1/68	AR
Midget, William	030	c1807	WB-3/28	
Midgett, Bethany	030	1795	WB-2/50	
Midgett, Daniel	030	c1809	WB-2/352	
Midgett, E. B.	030	1885	WB-5/114	AR
Midgett, F. S.	031	1888	WB-1/45	
Midgett, Fannie	031	1898	WB-1/104	AR
Midgett, John	030	1792	WB-1/255	
Midgett, Joseph	030	1778	WB-1/134	
Midgett, L. N.	031	1896	Orig. Only	AR
Midgett, Levi	019	c1878	Orig. Only	AR
Midgett, Little B.	031	1895	WB-1/96	
Midgett, Marcus L.	031	1889	WB-1/50	AR
Midgett, Samuel	030	c1808	WB-2/326	
Midgett, Samuel N.	031	1872	WB-1/4	AR
Midgget, Christopher	053	1806	RW-1/403	AR
Midlin, John	047	1852	WB-4/328	
Midyett, Ann	096	1818	WB-2/74	AR
Midyett, Benjamin	053	c1847	Orig. Only	AR
Midyett, Benjamin	053	1862	WB-10/17	AR
Midyett, Elizabeth	053	1884	WB-11/139	AR
Midyett, Jesse	053	1806	RW-1/402	AR
Midyett, John	053	1873	WB-11/36	AR
Midyett, John	096	1839	WB-2/148	AR
Midyett, John C.	075	1869	WB-0/6	AR
Midyett, Little John	053	1846	WB-6/74	AR
Midyett, Mathew	030	1735	SS 876/426	SS/AR
Midyett, Samuel	096	1833	WB-2/120	AR
Midyett, Thomas M.	096	1856	WB-3/45	AR
Midyette, J. S.	AR	1887	103 WB-1/424	103 AR
Mier, Christopher	073	1775	WB-A/194	
Miers, Ann	077	1816	WB-E/436	AR
Miers, Caty	085	1813	WB-G/255	AR
Miers, David	085	1821	WB-H/115	AR
Miers, Nathan	010	1839	WB-G/313	AR
Miers, Nathan	010	1800	WB-E/105	AR
Miers, Samuel	010	1834	WB-G/238	AR
Miers, Thomas	077	1815	WB-E/424	AR
Miers, William	010	1866	WB-H/169	AR
Mikel, Daniel	006	c1823	WB-A/10	AR
Mikel, David	104	1841	WB-4/260	AR
Mikle, Frederick	032	1831	WB-1/174	
Milam, Adam	100	1789	WB-5/102	AR
Milam, Elizabeth	100	1884	WB-51/330	AR
Milam, John	100	1816	WB-20/89	AR
Milam, Mary	006	c1862	Orig. Only	AR
Milam, Rebecca	039	1881	WB-U/278	AR
Milam, Tabitha	100	1870	WB-51/19	AR
Milam, William	006	1849	WB-A/57	
Milburn, Alexander	010	1806	WB-F/3	AR
Milburn, Henry Clay	010	1797	WB-E/14	AR
Milburn, Samuel	010	1796	WB-D/341	AR
Milburn, Sarah	010	1820	WB-G/69	AR
Milburn, Stephen E.	079	1867	WB-1/174	
Milby, Zadock	075	1799	WB-M1/22	AR
Mileham, Samuel	046	1795	WB-A/225	AR
Mileham, Walter	046	1798	WB-A/238	AR
Milen, William	060	1834	WB-1/317	
Miles, Alexander	020	1785	RB-B/80	AR
Miles, Alexander	020	1844	RB-P/131	
Miles, Jacob	020	1804	RB-E/139	AR
Miles, James	073	1839	WB-F/41	AR
Miles, John	020	1857	RB-R/573	AR
Miles, John	073	c1769	WB-A/119	
Miles, John S.	020	1885	WB-A/429	CTY
Miles, Levi	013	1880	WB-B/224	AR
Miles, Mary	047	1846	WB-4/249	AR
Miles, Mary	071	1830	WB-4/69	AR
Miles, Nancy	020	1858	RB-S/38	AR
Miles, Thomas	047	1796	WB-3/273	AR
Miles, Thomas	073	1766	WB-A/48	
Miles, William	071	1869	WB-6/1	AR
Miles, William C.	071	1891	WB-7/92	AR
Milholen, Thomas B.	003	1888	WB-B/221	AR
Miligan, Robert	085	c1777	WB-A/249	AR
Milikin, Joseph	085	1757	WB-A/119	AR
Mill, John	028	1764	DB-11/446	
Millakin, Charles	022	1785	RB-1/24	AR

Name	Co.	Date	Recorded Copy	Original
Millar, James	029	1840	WB-B/313	AR
Millar, Mary	029	1847	WB-C/122	AR
Millar, Mary	010	1800	WB-E/104	AR
Millar, Solomon	010	1802	WB-E/160	AR
Millar, Stephen	037	1803	WB-D/162	AR
Millard, Bethany	087	1830	WB-1/106	AR
Millard, Charles	070	1735	Orig. Only	SS/AR
Millard, Elizabeth	035	1840	Orig. Only	AR
Millard, Felix B.	087	1873	WB-3/73	AR
Millard, Jesse	035	1822	WB-A/302	AR
Millard, John	086	1880	WB-F/159	AR
Millard, Kenan	035	1848	WB-2/24	AR
Millen, John P.	065	1887	WB-L/184	AR
Millenton, Mary	001	1884	WB-2/219	AR
Millenton, Rebecca	001	1884	WB-2/222	AR
Miller, Aaron Wiley	089	1895	WB-2/278	AR
Miller, Abel	024	c1784	WB-A/266	AR
Miller, Abraham	085	1844	WB-I/197	AR
Miller, Abraham	065	1806	WB-B/87	AR
Miller, Adam	021	1868	WB-1/254	AR
Miller, Agnes	086	1829	WB-D/100	AR
Miller, Agness	085	1838	WB-I/33	AR
Miller, Alexander	056	1873	WB-3/83	AR
Miller, Alexander	024	1807	WB-B/247	AR
Miller, Ambrose	021	1858	WB-1/140	AR
Miller, Amelia B.	065	1881	WB-K/442	AR
Miller, Andrew	086	1835	WB-E/19	AR
Miller, Andrew	065	1776	WB-B/52	AR
Miller, Andrew	054	1873	WB-4/141	CTY
Miller, Andrew	085	1779	WB-B/32	AR
Miller, Andrew B.	062	1892	WB-B/156	AR
Miller, Ann	016	1845	WB-1/66	AR
Miller, Ann	085	1882	WB-2/27	CTY
Miller, Anne	021	c1899	Orig. Only	AR
Miller, Auguste S.	011	1885	WB-2/198	
Miller, Barbara	032	1863	WB-2/251	AR
Miller, Caleb	030	1846	WB-4/123	
Miller, Campbell	019	c1783	Orig. Only	AR
Miller, Catharine	021	1894	WB-3/65	
Miller, Catharine	089	1858	WB-1/193	
Miller, Catharine	010	1893	WB-I/392	AR
Miller, Charity	041	1836	WB-2/374	AR
Miller, Charles A.	085	c1867	WB-L/31	
Miller, Christian	092	1795	WB-3/18A	AR
Miller, Christiana	085	1814	WB-G/317	AR
Miller, Christina	084	1896	WB-F/58	CTY
Miller, Christopher	075	1882	WB-O/136	AR
Miller, Conrad	085	1886	WB-2/209	CTY
Miller, D. W.	026	1889	WB-2/375	AR
Miller, Daniel	057	1781	Orig. Only	AR-Nunc.
Miller, Daniel	085	1887	WB-2/266	CTY
Miller, Daniel	021	1863	WB-1/174	AR
Miller, Daniel	016	1876	WB-3/178	AR
Miller, Daniel	006	1898	WB-E/333	AR
Miller, David	086	1857	WB-E/334	AR
Miller, David	021	1874	WB-2/97	AR
Miller, David	065	1819	WB-E/24	AR
Miller, David	066	1892	WB-1/104	AR
Miller, David	086	1804	WB-B/162	AR
Miller, David B.	050	1859	WB-1/55	CTY
Miller, David D.	089	1882	WB-2/93	AR
Miller, David M.	065	1894	WB-M/283	AR
Miller, David, Sr.	065	1856	WB-J/21	AR
Miller, Elisha P.	017	c1861	WB-A/133	AR
Miller, Eliza	085	1846	WB-K/33	AR-Nunc.
Miller, Elizabeth	032	c1848	WB-2/39	
Miller, Elizabeth	065	1898	WB-N/160	AR
Miller, Elizabeth	065	1898	026 WB-3/12	026 AR
Miller, Ely	006	1886	WB-E/145	AR
Miller, Emilia	016	1840	PQS.6/88	AR
Miller, Ephraim	010	1826	WB-G/144	AR
Miller, Ervin S.	038	1896	WB-3/567	AR
Miller, Evan	030	1790	WB-1/242	Nunc.
Miller, Evan L.	070	1861	WB-D/56	AR
Miller, Fanny	021	1863	WB-1/180	AR
Miller, Frances A.	081	1892	WB-16/241	AR
Miller, Frances E.	010	1858	WB-H/64	AR
Miller, Frances J.	099	1881	WB-A/424	AR
Miller, Francis	016	1865	WB-2/118	AR
Miller, Francis	092	1897	WB-6/463	AR
Miller, Frederick	053	1800	RW-1/325	
Miller, Frederick	021	1854	WB-1/113	AR
Miller, Frederick	090	1818	WB-3/19	AR
Miller, Frederick	084	1865	WB-D/61	CTY
Miller, Frederick	010	1892	WB-I/347	AR
Miller, Frederick	011	c1834	WB-1/20	
Miller, George	073	1795	WB-B/290	AR
Miller, George	085	c1785	WB-C/34	
Miller, George	045	1878	WB-1/39	AR
Miller, George	085	1845	WB-K/10	AR
Miller, George	016	1836	PQS.5/372	AR
Miller, George	085	1834	WB-H/644	AR
Miller, George	057	1801	WB-A/257	AR
Miller, George W.	013	1894	WB-C/276	AR
Miller, Haman	081	1897	WB-16/438	AR
Miller, Haman	081	1814	WB-4/83	AR
Miller, Hamon	081	1858	WB-11/213	
Miller, Hamon	081	c1837	Copy	032 AR
Miller, Harmon	090	1818	WB-3/15	AR
Miller, Henry	038	c1863	WB-1/233	AR
Miller, Henry	013	1878	WB-B/163	AR
Miller, Henry	085	1857	WB-K/250	AR
Miller, Henry	016	1820	WB-A/12	AR-Nunc.
Miller, Henry	060	1814	Orig. Only	AR
Miller, Henry	085	c1809	WB-G/129	AR
Miller, Henry A.	085	1895	WB-3/100	CTY
Miller, Henry M.	099	1833	RB-23/451	AR
Miller, Henry W.	099	1862	RB-32/354	AR
Miller, Hezekiah	083	1880	WB-3/183	AR
Miller, Hillery	041	1838	WB-2/398	
Miller, Isaac	041	1810	WB-2/51	AR
Miller, Isaac, Sr.	032	1871	WB-3/38	AR
Miller, Isabella	099	1842	RB-25/24	AR
Miller, J. F.	021	1900	WB-3/257	AR
Miller, J. Jacob	085	1887	WB-2/249	CTY
Miller, Jacob	054	1885	WB-5/21	CTY
Miller, Jacob	032	1883	WB-3/391	
Miller, Jacob	060	1808	Orig. Only	AR
Miller, Jacob	028	c1732	Deeds.1/145	
Miller, Jacob	085	1870	WB-1/49	CTY
Miller, Jacob	016	1840	PQS.6/101	AR
Miller, Jacob	090	1803	WB-2/35	AR
Miller, Jacob	090	1798	WB-1/104	AR
Miller, Jacob	085	1842	WB-I/142	AR
Miller, James	096	1790	WB-1/168	AR
Miller, James	065	c1806	WB-B/86	AR
Miller, James	016	1844	WB-1/28	AR
Miller, James	073	1821	WB-D/594	AR
Miller, James	028	1816	WB-C/121	
Miller, James	085	1864	WB-K/341	AR

Name	Co.	Date	Recorded Copy	Original
Miller, James	070	1808	WB-C/287	AR-Nunc.
Miller, James E.	050	1897	WB-2/271	CTY
Miller, James H.	099	1898	WB-D/191	AR
Miller, James M.	065	1892	WB-M/112	AR
Miller, James P.	078	1813	WI-6/191	AR
Miller, James R.	073	1885	WB-H/363	
Miller, James T.	010	1861	WB-H/104	AR
Miller, James T.	070	1862	WB-D/87	AR
Miller, Jane	085	1790	WB-C/62	AR
Miller, Jane	085	1818	WB-G/509	AR
Miller, Jane	085	1839	WB-I/54	AR
Miller, Jane B.	032	1889	WB-4/43	AR
Miller, Jesse	073	1840	WB-F/46	AR
Miller, Jesse W.	085	1897	WB-3/184	CTY
Miller, Jessee	021	1885	WB-2/317	
Miller, John	038	1878	WB-2/326	AR
Miller, John	085	1870	Orig. Only	CTY
Miller, John	086	1807	WB-B/196	AR
Miller, John	032	1837	WB-1/305	
Miller, John	086	1788	Orig. Only	AR
Miller, John	090	1826	WB-3/143	AR
Miller, John	077	1822	WB-F/44	AR
Miller, John	010	1815	WB-F/292	AR
Miller, John	041	1787	WB-1/63	AR
Miller, John	026	1867	WB-1/420	AR
Miller, John	070	1816	WB-AB/246	AR
Miller, John	028	1839	WB-C/438	
Miller, John	060	1835	WB-1/341	AR
Miller, John	092	1799	WB-3/33	AR
Miller, John	054	1868	WB-3/207	AR
Miller, John	037	1823	WB-F/10	AR
Miller, John	060	1830	WB-1/179	AR
Miller, John	062	1891	WB-B/127	AR
Miller, John	085	c1780	WB-B/124	AR
Miller, John B.	086	1878	WB-F/116	AR
Miller, John C.	085	1893	WB-3/7	CTY
Miller, John D.	085	1864	WB-K/345	AR
Miller, John J.	085	1857	WB-K/231	AR
Miller, John S.	038	1894	WB-3/503	AR
Miller, John W.	016	1851	WB-1/199	AR
Miller, John, Sr.	085	1842	WB-I/137	AR
Miller, Jonathan	085	1835	WB-H/702	AR
Miller, Jonathan	010	1817	WB-G/8	AR
Miller, Jonathan	006	c1862	Orig. Only	AR
Miller, Jonathan	038	1888	WB-3/116	AR
Miller, Jonathan	006	1854	WB-D/6	
Miller, Jones	003	1867	WB-A/20	AR
Miller, Joseph	085	1882	WB-2/9	CTY
Miller, Joseph	090	1804	WB-2/52	AR
Miller, Joseph	028	1788	WB-A/175	
Miller, Joseph M.	013	1890	WB-C/59	AR
Miller, Joseph S.	070	1854	WB-C/581	AR
Miller, Joshua	037	1806	WB-D/249	AR
Miller, Julian	021	1897	WB-3/186	AR
Miller, L. K.	021	1851	WB-1/93	AR
Miller, Lee A.	013	1897	Orig. Only	AR
Miller, Letta C.	062	1897	WB-B/201	AR
Miller, Levi C.	102	1892	Orig. Only	AR
Miller, Lewis	072	c1796	Orig. Only	AR
Miller, Maggie E.	054	1894	WB-5/507	CTY
Miller, Malachi	010	1815	WB-F/285	AR
Miller, Margaret	099	1871	RB-35/148	
Miller, Margaret	090	1846	WB-4/211	AR
Miller, Martha	081	1883	WB-15/453	
Miller, Martha	021	c1896	Orig. Only	AR
Miller, Martha Ann	084	1896	WB-F/60	CTY
Miller, Martin	057	1843	WB-B/163	AR
Miller, Mary	028	1804	WB-B/204	
Miller, Mary	037	1802	WB-D/151	AR
Miller, Mary	085	1865	WB-K/366	AR
Miller, Mary A.	044	1867	WB-22/644	CTY
Miller, Mary A.	086	1886	WB-F/268	AR
Miller, Mary B.	075	1818	WB-M1/324	
Miller, Mary F.	010	1851	WB-G/481	AR
Miller, Mary M.	054	1873	WB-4/130	CTY
Miller, Mason	024	1803	WB-B/184	AR
Miller, Matie D.	054	1893	WB-5/487	CTY
Miller, Matthias	033	1891	WB-2/113	CTY
Miller, Maxamilian	030	1824	WB-3/168	
Miller, Michael	060	1796	Orig. Only	AR
Miller, Moses	085	c1778	WB-E/86	AR
Miller, Nancy	006	1893	WB-E/240	AR
Miller, Nancy W.	086	1900	WB-G/57	AR
Miller, Nannie E.	054	1894	WB-5/505	CTY
Miller, Nathaniel	086	1865	WB-E/449	AR
Miller, Nathl.	009	c1775	OWB/127	AR
Miller, Nelly	045	1878	WB-1/41	AR
Miller, Nicholas	085	c1807	WB-E/23	AR
Miller, P. W. Azel	085	1900	WB-3/370	CTY
Miller, Paul	016	1867	WB-2/159	AR
Miller, Peter	013	1881	WB-B/236	AR
Miller, Peter	085	1872	WB-1/109	CTY
Miller, Peter	085	1896	WB-3/158	CTY
Miller, Phillip	038	c1860	WB-1/169	AR
Miller, Phillip	065	1797	WB-B/142	AR
Miller, Priscilla	070	1897	WB-G/583	AR
Miller, Rachel	073	1824	WB-E/52	AR
Miller, Rebecca B.	054	c1833	WB-2/139	AR
Miller, Richard	035	1850	WB-2/53	AR
Miller, Robert	065	c1765	WB-B/107	AR
Miller, Robert	099	1858	RB-30/491	AR
Miller, Sallie	060	1895	WB-5/1	AR
Miller, Samuel	085	1842	WB-I/128	AR
Miller, Samuel	065	1812	WB-E/18	AR
Miller, Samuel	085	1772	WB-A/91	AR
Miller, Samuel	085	1857	WB-K/236	AR
Miller, Samuel	085	1835	WB-H/663	AR
Miller, Sarah	056	1883	WB-3/332	AR
Miller, Sarah	081	1820	WB-5/11	AR
Miller, Sarah	010	1855	WB-H/17	AR
Miller, Sarah	035	c1766	WB-A/317	AR
Miller, Sarah H.	065	1893	WB-M/187	AR
Miller, Solomon	030	c1815	WB-3/59	
Miller, Solomon	010	1885	WB-I/189	
Miller, Susan	057	1889	WB-C/161	AR
Miller, Susanna	086	1825	WB-D/37	AR
Miller, Thomas	075	1727	SS 876/104	SS/AR
Miller, Thomas	N	1694	Orig. Only	SS/AR
Miller, Thomas	100	1792	WB-6/123	AR
Miller, Thomas	092	1815	WB-3/112	AR
Miller, Thomas	100	1784	WB-4/51	AR
Miller, Thomas	003	1864	WB-A/24	AR
Miller, Thomas	030	1785	WB-1/195	
Miller, Thomas	085	1832	WB-H/545	AR
Miller, Thomas C.	070	1866	SC/09071	AR-Copy
Miller, Thomas C.	070	1866	WB-D/179	
Miller, Thomas L.	100	1806	WB-13/272	AR
Miller, Tobias	057	1789	WB-A/180	AR
Miller, Tobias	016	1863	WB-2/97	AR
Miller, Wendle	085	c1804	WB-D/203	AR

Name	Co.	Date	Recorded Copy	Original
Miller, Will	030	1805	WB-2/277	
Miller, William	085	1818	WB-G/526	AR
Miller, William	006	1893	WB-E/260	AR
Miller, William	085	1844	WB-I/202	AR
Miller, William	085	1819	WB-G/546	AR-Nunc.
Miller, William	062	1854	WB-A/12	AR
Miller, William	030	1795	WB-2/45	
Miller, William	073	1830	WB-E/227	AR
Miller, William	085	1824	WB-H/298	AR
Miller, William	084	1824	WB-A/261	CTY
Miller, William	070	1777	Orig. Only	SS/AR
Miller, William A.	102	1899	Orig. Only	AR
Miller, William C.	065	1843	WB-I/17	AR
Miller, William H.	086	1886	WB-F/294	AR
Miller, William K.	010	1816	WB-F/326	AR
Miller, William R.	099	1871	RB-35/147	AR
Miller, Winiford	010	1873	WB-I/45	AR
Miller, Wisdom	032	1900	WB-4/442	AR
Milles, James	100	1795	WB-8/143	AR
Milles, Thomas E.	100	1795	WB-8/154	AR
Millican, William	065	1797	WB-B/76	AR
Milligan, Alexander	054	c1820	WB-1A/41	AR
Milligan, Amy	026	1897	WB-2/536	AR
Milligan, Forgus	054	c1820	WB-1A/17	AR
Milligan, Hiram P.	026	1864	WB-1/353	AR
Milligan, Rebecca	021	1864	WB-1/189	AR
Millikan, Benjamin	081	1842	WB-7/433	
Millikan, Benjamin	081	1836	WB-7/30	AR
Millikan, Benjamin	081	1857	WB-10/505	AR
Millikan, Mildred	041	1843	WB-3/52	Nunc.
Millikan, Samuel	081	1871	WB-15/48	AR
Millikan, Samuel	081	1818	WB-4/534	AR
Milliken, James	073	1806	WB-D/167	AR
Milliken, Quainton	022	1816	WB-A/280	AR
Milliken, Robert	073	1813	WB-D/390	AR
Milliken, Samuel	012	c1821	WB-B/125	AR
Millikin, John	071	1816	WB-3/181	AR
Milling, Lucretia	040	c1896	Orig. Only	AR
Millis, Amanda	070	1891	WB-F/417	AR
Millis, Benjamin	072	1889	WB-4/241	AR
Millis, Edward	046	1817	WB-B/42	AR
Millis, James	046	1849	WB-C/330	AR
Millis, James N.	046	c1876	WB-E/196	AR
Millis, John W.	070	1899	WB-H/219	AR
Millon, Edward	070	1855	WB-C/591	AR
Milloway, Andrew	046	1865	WB-D/281	AR
Mills, A. Jackson	097	1897	WB-2/517	AR
Mills, Allin	079	1893	WB-3/42	AR
Mills, Ambrose	080	1873	WB-1/14	AR
Mills, Ambrose	086	1849	WB-E/182	AR
Mills, Amos	046	1826	WB-B/226	AR
Mills, Ann	035	1837	Orig. Only	AR
Mills, Anthony	028	1808	WB-B/311	
Mills, Bithian	099	1793	RB-2/408	AR
Mills, Bryan	072	c1825	Orig. Only	AR
Mills, Catharine	070	1855	WB-C/594	AR
Mills, Cornelius	097	1884	WB-2/242	AR
Mills, David	069	1891	WB-5/351	AR
Mills, Dorcas M.	065	1894	WB-M/272	AR
Mills, E. L.	099	1882	WB-A/308	AR
Mills, Elisabeth	079	1883	WB-2/268	AR
Mills, Elizabeth	054	1884	WB-5/5	CTY
Mills, Elizabeth	035	1822	WB-A/296	AR
Mills, Evelina	054	c1864	Orig. Only	AR
Mills, Francis M.	097	1854	WB-1/104	AR
Mills, George	081	1808	WB-3/96	AR
Mills, George	N	1689	Orig. Only	SS/AR
Mills, George J.	080	1891	WB-1/158	AR
Mills, Henry	084	1856	WB-C/220	CTY
Mills, Hur	085	1762	WB-A/125	AR
Mills, J. H.	032	1899	WB-4/421	AR
Mills, James	070	1795	WB-C/283	AR
Mills, James	072	c1823	WB-1/137	AR
Mills, James	097	1891	WB-1/418	AR
Mills, Jemima	028	1816	WB-C/127	
Mills, John	086	1842	WB-E/87	
Mills, John	005	1802	WB-2/105	AR
Mills, John, Sr.	085	1761	WB-A/124	AR
Mills, John, Sr.	009	c1739	OWB/28	AR-Copy
Mills, Jonathan	032	1841	WB-1/380	
Mills, Ladson A.	086	1883	WB-F/192	AR
Mills, London	072	1871	WB-4/37	AR
Mills, Louis	079	1887	WB-2/396	AR
Mills, Lucy A.	100	1897	WB-51/500	
Mills, Luiza J.	069	1900	WB-6/121	AR
Mills, Margaret	099	1888	WB-B/291	AR
Mills, Maria	054	1852	WB-3/58	AR
Mills, Nancy	072	1826	WB-A/86	AR
Mills, Nancy R.	065	1870	WB-K/46	AR
Mills, Nathan	099	1875	RB-35/302	AR
Mills, Otis P.	014	c1844	SC/03179	AR-Copy
Mills, Pheriby	099	1888	WB-B/238	AR
Mills, Rebeccah	047	1849	WB-4/281	AR
Mills, Richard H.	080	1870	WB-1/8	AR
Mills, Sally	079	1883	WB-2/270	AR
Mills, Sarah	054	1856	WB-3/102	AR
Mills, Sarah	084	1821	WB-A/214	CTY
Mills, Sarah	084	1854	WB-C/200	CTY
Mills, Sarah	084	1839	WB-B/207	CTY
Mills, Sarah A.	054	1896	WB-5/561	CTY
Mills, Synthia	029	c1840	WB-B/327	AR
Mills, Thomas	069	1885	WB-5/225	AR
Mills, Thomas J.	020	1874	WB-A/135	CTY
Mills, Tom	047	1892	WB-7/55	AR
Mills, Uzza	072	1889	WB-4/234	AR
Mills, W. A.	054	1890	WB-5/356	CTY
Mills, W. M.	065	1889	WB-L/353	AR
Mills, William	099	1874	RB-35/277	AR
Mills, William	054	1893	WB-5/468	CTY
Mills, William	046	1804	WB-A/241	AR
Mills, William	072	1845	WB-2/59	AR
Mills, William E.	086	1850	WB-E/202	AR
Mills, William H.	054	1876	WB-4/235	CTY
Mills, William S.	080	c1876	Orig. Only	AR
Millsaps, J. L.	102	1899	WB-A/162	AR
Millsaps, Jesse	043	1886	WB-1/37	
Millsaps, John A.	091	1885	WB-1/17	
Millsaps, Joseph	054	c1821	WB-1A/132	AR
Millsaps, Litten	003	1895	WB-B/337	
Millsaps, Richard J.	083	1875	WB-3/105	AR
Millwood, James	090	1792	WB-1/31	AR
Milne, Walter	098	1896	WB-A/241	CTY
Milner, James	047	1773	Orig. Only	SS/AR
Milner, Patewells	039	1788	WB-A/33	AR
Milnster, Dorothy	016	1838	PQS.5/471	AR
Milsap, Robert	081	1793	WB-1/126	AR
Milstead, John W.	003	1900	WB-B/392	
Miltaner, Ephram W.	047	1860	WB-5/73	
Miltear, Jethro	041	1804	WB-1/214	AR
Milton, David	022	1828	WB-B/156	AR

Name	Co.	Date	Recorded Copy	Original
Mimbs, Thomas	082	1809	WB-1/133	AR
Mims, Benjamin	082	1788	WB-1/18	AR
Mims, Catherine	029	1826	WB-B/146	AR
Mims, David J.	027	1823	WB-A/36	AR-Nunc.
Mims, John	020	1836	RB-M/535	AR
Mims, John W.	020	1895	WB-B/213	CTY
Mims, Margart W.	020	1862	RB-S/549	CTY
Mims, Sarah	020	1886	WB-A/490	CTY
Minachen, James	085	1799	WB-D/220	AR
Minatree, Mary	100	1889	WB-51/271	AR
Mincey, Richard	020	1789	RB-B/294	
Minchee, Michael	096	1869	WB-4/7	
Minchew, Bond	041	1815	WB-2/106	AR
Minchew, Judith	078	1807	WI-4/215	AR
Minchew, Maxey	041	1789	WB-1/82	AR
Minchew, Richard	078	1804	WI-3/276	AR
Mindel, August E.	070	1869	WB-E/155	AR
Miner, James	046	1881	WB-E/312	AR
Miner, Sallie	044	1874	WB-23/152	CTY
Ming, Francis	077	1842	WB-F/303	AR
Ming, Joseph	024	1751	Orig. Only	SS/AR
Ming, Michael	010	1741	LGB-4/#160	
Ming, Thomas	024	c1798	WB-B/130	AR
Minga, Dudley	100	1857	WB-49/131	AR
Mingea, Lydia	100	1882	WB-51/170	AR
Minges, Conrad	060	1809	Orig. Only	AR
Minges, Conrad	021	1869	WB-2/25	AR
Mingo, William T.	039	1890	WB-U/503	
Mingus, C. B.	049	1890	WB-2/255	AR
Mingus, Joseph H.	085	1881	WB-1/553	CTY
Minitree, J. J.	039	1875	WB-U/122	AR
Minnes, John	073	c1836	Orig. Only	AR
Minnis, James M.	073	1854	WB-G/48	AR
Minor, John	037	1869	WB-G/336	AR
Minor, John	033	1856	WB-1/129	AR
Minor, John, Sr.	044	1842	WB-15/287	CTY
Minor, Joseph	044	c1863	WB-23/29	CTY
Minor, Julia A.	044	1888	WB-24/21	CTY
Minor, Levina	037	1871	WB-G/361	AR
Minor, Mary	044	1818	WB-8/176	CTY
Minor, Massy	044	1859	WB-21/31	CTY
Minor, Meers	046	1816	WB-B/21	AR
Minor, Minerva A.	046	1896	WB-F/528	AR
Minor, Rachel	044	1896	WB-24/322	CTY
Minor, William	041	1857	WB-3/219	AR
Minor, William H.	044	1848	WB-17/353	CTY
Minshew, Celia	103	1893	WB-2/18	AR
Minshew, John	103	1793	Orig. Only	AR
Minshew, John	103	1878	WB-1/140	AR
Minshew, John	103	1853	RD-11/339	AR
Minshew, Nathan	103	1818	RD-4/185	AR
Minshew, Polly	103	1859	RD-13/22	AR
Minshew, Richard	024	c1778	WB-B/48	AR
Minshew, Winefred	103	1878	WB-1/144	AR
Minter, Cary	022	1782	Orig. Only	AR
Minter, John, Sr.	022	c1797	WB-A/50	AR
Minter, Joseph	022	1823	WB-B/108	AR-Copy
Minter, Phillip	022	1796	RB-2/79	AR
Minter, William	022	1796	RB-2/77	AR
Minton, Elizabeth	104	1897	WB-7/15	AR
Minton, Elmira	104	1872	WB-6/51	AR
Minton, Jesse	104	1849	WB-5/22	AR
Minton, Martha	010	1858	WB-H/60	AR
Minton, Mary	010	1853	WB-G/504	AR
Minton, Thomas	010	1804	WB-E/238	AR
Minton, Violet	104	1860	WB-5/265	
Mints, Elizabeth	029	1884	WB-E/313	AR
Mints, Emaline	029	1900	WB-F/191	AR
Mints, Jonas	012	1830	WB-B/169	AR
Mints, Lucy A.	029	1886	WB-E/408	AR
Minung, William L.	038	c1863	WB-1/235	AR
Mirritt, Kisiah	028	1811	WB-C/42	AR
Misenheimer, George	089	1859	WB-1/206	
Misenheimer, Lawson A.	065	1895	WB-M/356	AR
Misenheimer, M.	054	1894	WB-5/503	CTY
Misenheimer, Rosanna	016	1870	WB-3/18	AR
Misenheimer, Sophia C.	016	1893	WB-4/157	AR
Misenhimer, Abraham	016	1811	WB-A/30	AR
Misenhimer, Elizabeth	016	1832	PQS.5/237	
Misenhimer, George Sr.	016	1824	WB-A/62	AR
Misenhimer, Jacob	016	1821	WB-A/88	AR
Misenhimer, John	016	1831	PQS.5/167	AR
Miskell, Martha	099	1876	RB-35/333	AR
Misler, F. M.	016	1899	WB-4/318	
Missildine, Oscar S.	080	1895	WB-1/254	AR
Misswarf, William E.	084	1816	WB-A/242	CTY
Mitcalf, J.	062	1883	WB-B/72	
Mitchael, Thomas	030	1817	WB-3/89	
Mitchel, Andrew	054	c1790	WB-1/149	AR
Mitchel, David	044	1790	WB-2/185	CTY
Mitchel, George	103	1833	RD-6/405	AR
Mitchel, Ginney	044	1811	WB-7/205	CTY
Mitchel, Henry	065	1790	WB-B/129	AR
Mitchel, Jacob	060	1812	Orig. Only	AR
Mitchel, John	071	1777	WB-1/296	
Mitchel, John	020	1785	RB-B/87	AR
Mitchel, Joseph	065	1781	WB-B/122	AR
Mitchel, Mary	VA	1797	071 WB-2/142	071 AR
Mitchel, Mary	060	1828	WB-1/89	AR
Mitchel, Nancey	099	1849	RB-26/590	AR
Mitchel, Peter	037	c1770	Orig. Only	AR
Mitchel, Phillis	044	1792	WB-2/318	CTY
Mitchel, Randal	037	1758	SS 882/135	SS/AR
Mitchel, Robert	104	1859	WB-5/213	AR
Mitchel, Rubin	103	1832	RD-6/303	AR
Mitchel, Sarah	045	1877	Orig. Only	AR-Copy
Mitchel, William	016	1801	WB-A/36	AR
Mitchel, William	VA	c1763	HaDSC(M)/122	
Mitchell, Abba	039	c1817	Orig. Only	AR
Mitchell, Abraham	019	1746	SS 878/141	SS/AR
Mitchell, Abraham	019	1778	WB-D/275	AR
Mitchell, Abram	072	1747	SS 877/53	SS/AR
Mitchell, Abram	047	1790	WB-3/192	AR
Mitchell, Adam	046	1842	WB-C/118	AR
Mitchell, Adam	090	1855	WB-4/287	AR
Mitchell, Alexander	028	1876	Copy	009 AR
Mitchell, Alexander	028	1876	WB-E/145	
Mitchell, Anderson	001	1900	WB-3/300	AR
Mitchell, Andrew	073	1795	WB-B/279	AR
Mitchell, Andrew	086	1805	WB-B/182	AR
Mitchell, Andrew J.	020	1874	WB-A/165	CTY
Mitchell, Barbara	003	1887	WB-B/206	AR
Mitchell, Benjamin	028	1817	WB-C/157	
Mitchell, Betsy Ann	044	c1877	Orig. Only	CTY
Mitchell, Cader	010	1813	WB-F/239	AR
Mitchell, Catharine	070	1826	WB-C/298	AR
Mitchell, Celia B.	051	1868	WB-C/1	AR
Mitchell, Celia M.	051	1882	WB-C/283	AR
Mitchell, Charles	084	c1787	Orig. Only	CTY
Mitchell, Charlotte	010	1870	WB-I/27	AR

Name	Co.	Date	Recorded Copy	Original
Mitchell, Clarissa	072	c1809	WB-A/93	AR
Mitchell, Clarkey	101	c1892	Orig. Only	AR
Mitchell, David	072	1809	WB-A/90	
Mitchell, David	078	1795	WI-1/165	AR
Mitchell, David	020	1831	RB-M/89	AR
Mitchell, Dawson N.	065	1896	WB-M/523	AR
Mitchell, E.	073	1857	WB-G/176	CTY
Mitchell, Edmond	028	1765	DB-12&13/288	
Mitchell, Edward	078	1820	WI-8/330	AR
Mitchell, Elijah	099	1816	RB-12/298	AR
Mitchell, Elisha	010	1827	WB-G/160	AR
Mitchell, Elizabeth	020	1857	RB-R/559	AR
Mitchell, Elizabeth	010	1895	WB-I/444	AR
Mitchell, Elizabeth	047	1800	WB-3/342	AR
Mitchell, Elizabeth	046	1853	WB-C/387	AR
Mitchell, Elizabeth	099	1887	WB-B/208	AR
Mitchell, Ephraim	073	1809	WB-D/181	AR
Mitchell, Frances	010	1888	WB-I/253	AR
Mitchell, Gabriel	099	c1795	RB-3/167	AR
Mitchell, Gatsey	099	1889	WB-B/337	AR
Mitchell, George	056	1838	WB-2/261	AR
Mitchell, George	072	N. D.	WB-A/81	AR
Mitchell, Gideon	018	1882	WB-E/105	AR
Mitchell, Giles	010	1861	WB-H/105	AR
Mitchell, Henry	027	c1876	WB-2/52	
Mitchell, Henry	051	c1854	WB-A/369	
Mitchell, Henry	069	1852	WB-1/529	AR
Mitchell, Henry	018	1855	WB-D/26	
Mitchell, Jack	022	1896	WB-F/36	AR
Mitchell, James	084	1864	WB-C/390	
Mitchell, James	071	1813	WB-3/94	AR
Mitchell, James	010	c1801	Orig. Only	AR
Mitchell, James	024	1745	Orig. Only	SS/AR
Mitchell, James	028	1815	WB-C/95	
Mitchell, James	044	1779	WB-1/213	CTY
Mitchell, James	051	1876	WB-C/165	AR
Mitchell, James E.	003	1871	WB-B/19	AR
Mitchell, James H.	090	1873	WB-6/45	AR
Mitchell, James S.	010	1869	WB-I/14	AR
Mitchell, John	003	1879	WB-B/118	AR
Mitchell, John	046	1841	WB-C/98	AR
Mitchell, John	046	1841	SC/06007	AR-Copy
Mitchell, John	044	1787	WB-2/13	CTY
Mitchell, John	020	1838	RB-N/148	
Mitchell, John	039	1793	WB-A/112	
Mitchell, John	010	1796	WB-D/315	AR
Mitchell, John	024	1847	WB-C/277	AR
Mitchell, John	039	c1857	WB-O/380	AR
Mitchell, John E.	044	1888	WB-24/51	CTY
Mitchell, John H.	010	1874	WB-I/60	AR
Mitchell, John, Sr.	024	1821	WB-C/96	AR
Mitchell, John, Sr.	039	1849	WB-N/343	AR
Mitchell, Josiah	041	1898	WB-4/437	AR
Mitchell, Josiah	010	1866	WB-H/168	AR
Mitchell, King	010	1849	WB-G/458	AR
Mitchell, Lemuel	044	1879	WB-23/333	CTY
Mitchell, Lemuel R.	001	1881	WB-2/179	AR
Mitchell, Lon	013	1900	WB-D/367	AR
Mitchell, Lucy	078	1872	WB-19/23	AR
Mitchell, Lucy B.	071	1872	WB-6/90	AR
Mitchell, M. E.	099	1889	WB-B/395	AR
Mitchell, Major	029	1869	WB-E/6	AR
Mitchell, Maria N.	054	1877	WB-4/256	CTY
Mitchell, Martha Ann	024	c1874	Orig. Only	AR
Mitchell, Mary	010	1833	WB-G/226	AR
Mitchell, Mary	001	1899	WB-3/286	AR
Mitchell, Mary A.	051	1899	WB-C/558	AR
Mitchell, Mary E.	039	1894	WB-V/35	AR
Mitchell, Mary H.	010	1887	WB-I/231	AR
Mitchell, Miles	051	1879	WB-C/212	AR
Mitchell, Miles N.	083	1886	WB-3/385	AR
Mitchell, Minerva R.	020	1895	WB-B/194	CTY
Mitchell, Molly	104	1834	WB-4/169	AR
Mitchell, Moses	054	1853	WB-3/72	AR
Mitchell, Mourning	039	1828	WB-H/201	
Mitchell, Nancy	001	1880	WB-2/172	AR
Mitchell, Nancy	072	1812	WB-A/92	AR
Mitchell, Nathan	029	1844	WB-C/63	AR
Mitchell, Nazareth	083	1846	WB-1/476	AR
Mitchell, Noah	001	1860	WB-1/178	AR
Mitchell, Paulina J.	084	1891	WB-E/484	CTY
Mitchell, Pennie S.	024	1888	WB-E/164	AR
Mitchell, Perry	073	1823	WB-E/48	AR
Mitchell, Peter	100	1847	WB-39/310	AR
Mitchell, Phillip	046	1847	WB-C/269	AR
Mitchell, Pinkney	084	c1863	WB-D/52	CTY
Mitchell, Polly	001	c1854	WB-1/85	AR
Mitchell, R. J.	051	1887	WB-C/365	AR
Mitchell, Rachel	063	1788	WB-1/141	
Mitchell, Rachel	010	1847	WB-G/420	AR
Mitchell, Rebecca	001	1887	WB-2/328	AR
Mitchell, Rebecca	010	1873	WB-I/47	AR
Mitchell, Richard	041	1820	WB-2/160	
Mitchell, Robert	104	1828	WB-4/121	
Mitchell, Robert	071	1834	WB-4/116	AR
Mitchell, Robert	078	1891	WB-19/284	AR
Mitchell, Robert	046	1775	WB-A/229	AR
Mitchell, Robert	046	1832	WB-B/164	AR
Mitchell, Robert	044	1751	Orig. Only	CTY
Mitchell, Sally	010	1849	WB-G/441	AR
Mitchell, Sally	073	1837	WB-E/418	AR
Mitchell, Samuel	046	1839	WB-C/37	AR
Mitchell, Samuel	046	1841	WB-C/348	AR
Mitchell, Samuel P.	084	1875	WB-E/98	CTY
Mitchell, Sarah	001	1899	WB-3/288	AR
Mitchell, Sewell	099	1897	WB-D/36	AR
Mitchell, Solomon	051	1881	WB C/259	
Mitchell, Susan	099	1873	RB-35/227	AR
Mitchell, Susan A.	001	1866	WB-1/263	AR
Mitchell, Thomas	039	c1802	WB-B/92 & 168	
Mitchell, Thomas F.	013	1900	WB-D/455	AR
Mitchell, Thomas J.	028	1871	WB-E/48	AR
Mitchell, Wiley	039	1878	WB-U/184	AR
Mitchell, William	020	1795	RB-C/109	AR
Mitchell, William	010	1796	WB-D/321	AR
Mitchell, William	029	1875	WB-E/152	AR
Mitchell, William	099	1895	WB-C/418	AR
Mitchell, William	039	c1851	WB-O/338	AR
Mitchell, William	072	1830	WB-1/68	AR
Mitchell, William	020	1855	RB-R/285	AR
Mitchell, William	010	1854	WB-G/515	AR
Mitchell, William A.	099	1888	WB-B/243	AR
Mitchell, William C.	077	1848	WB-F/366	AR
Mitchell, William J.	021	1866	WB-1/217	AR
Mitchell, William J.	010	1866	WB-H/164	AR
Mitchell, William W.	051	1897	WB-C/534	
Mitchell, Zadock	010	1834	WB-G/234	AR
Mitchell, Zepheniah	046	1881	WB-E/305	AR
Mitchener, Agrippa	056	1860	WB-2/6	AR
Mitchener, James	056	1880	WB-3/269	

Name	Co.	Date	Recorded Copy	Original
Mitchenor, Luke	085	c1787	WB-D/214	
Mitchiner, Eliza W.	056	1888	WB-3/464	AR
Mitchler, Matthias	016	1811	WB-A/3	AR
Mitchner, Samuel	056	1836	WB-2/261	AR
Mitchum, Eliza	047	1883	WB-6/296	AR
Mitchum, Jeremiah	005	1865	WB-C/232	AR
Mitton, Henry	044	1794	WB-3/106	
Mixon, David	009	1859	OB-L/26	AR
Mixon, Elijah	009	1817	OB-A/266	AR
Mixon, Elizabeth	009	1865	OB-M/246	AR
Mixon, George	009	c1779	OWB/149	
Mixon, James	009	1840	OB-C2/357	AR
Mixon, James	009	1817	OB-A/268	AR
Mixon, Michael	070	1836	WB-C/305	AR
Mixon, Sally L.	009	1866	OB-M/245	AR
Mixon, Zedekiah	009	c1807	OB-A/181	AR
Mixson, Jeremiah	024	1828	WB-C/153	AR
Mixson, Jeremiah	024	1783	WB-B/24	AR
Mixson, Jeremiah	096	1828	Orig. Only	AR
Mize, Joshua	104	1790	WB-1/277	
Mizell, Alfred	063	1885	WB-3/267	AR
Mizell, Cleopatra	010	1896	WB-I/475	AR
Mizell, Cynthia A.	010	1892	WB-I/363	AR
Mizell, Eli H.	063	1874	WB-3/72	
Mizell, Elizabeth	010	1880	WB-I/116	
Mizell, George W.	010	1898	WB-I/543	
Mizell, Hanner	010	1823	WB-G/103	AR
Mizell, James	063	1894	WB-4/148	AR
Mizell, James	063	c1802	WB-1/405	
Mizell, James	063	1881	WB-3/193	
Mizell, Jeremiah	010	1816	WB-F/328	AR
Mizell, John	010	1854	WB-G/506	AR
Mizell, John	010	1803	WB-E/222	AR
Mizell, John B.	010	1890	WB-I/299	AR
Mizell, John G.	010	1863	WB-H/126	AR
Mizell, John R.	063	1879	WB-3/172	
Mizell, Jonathan	010	1892	WB-I/354	AR
Mizell, Jonathan	010	1883	WB-I/157	
Mizell, Joseph A.	051	1887	WB-C/363	AR
Mizell, Joseph J.	010	1898	WB-I/539	
Mizell, Josiah	010	1896	WB-I/478	AR
Mizell, Lawrence	010	1847	WB-G/415	AR
Mizell, Luke, Sr.	063	1826	WB-2/116	
Mizell, Martha	063	1860	WB-2/466	
Mizell, Martha	063	1892	WB-4/98	AR
Mizell, Mary	063	1847	WB-2/329	
Mizell, Moses	010	1845	WB-G/382	AR
Mizell, Moses	071	1781	WB-1/237	
Mizell, Timothy	010	1794	WB-D/236	AR
Mizell, William	010	1793	WB-D/224	AR
Mizell, William L.	063	1852	WB-2/377	
Mobley, Alexander	063	1842	WB-2/291	
Mobley, Alexander	056	1802	WB-1/135	AR
Mobley, Biggars	087	c1802	WB-A/38	AR
Mobley, Charity	063	1822	WB-2/82	
Mobley, Dorcas	099	1808	RB-7/311	AR
Mobley, Edward	099	1778	RB-1/136	
Mobley, Edward	099	1777	RB-1/92	AR
Mobley, John	037	1753	SS 878/202	SS/AR
Mobley, McG.	063	1900	WB-4/260	AR
Mobley, Middleton	063	1841	WB-2/285	
Mobley, Mordecai	099	1792	RB-2/386	AR
Mobley, Nathan	084	1894	WB-F/8	CTY
Mobley, Ollen	087	1841	WB-1/244	AR
Mobly, Frederick	079	1859	WB-1/27	AR
Mobly, Ollen	035	1860	WB-3/11	AR
Mock, Adam	032	c1850	WB-2/127	
Mock, Barbra	003	1888	WB-B/232	AR
Mock, Charles H.	MO	c1856	032 WB-2/141	
Mock, Devault	085	1798	WB-E/54	AR
Mock, Jacob	032	1842	WB-1/382	
Mock, Jesse	038	1886	WB-3/4	AR
Mock, Margaret	065	1883	WB-K/540	AR
Mock, Peter W.	032	1899	WB-4/393	AR
Mock, Philip	085	c1819	Orig. Only	AR
Mock, Phillip	038	1895	WB-3/514	AR
Mock, Regina	038	1892	WB-3/293	AR
Mode, William	086	1810	WB-B/236	AR
Moderwell, Libby	046	c1884	Orig. Only	AR
Moderwell, Martha	046	1867	WB-D/347	AR
Moderwell, Robert	046	1836	WB-B/556	AR
Moderwill, Martha	046	c1859	Copy	073 AR
Modkins, Richard	075	c1843	Orig. Only	AR
Modlin, Lovie	063	1881	WB-3/210	
Modlin, Peter	077	1878	WB-H/82	AR
Moffet, John	065	c1775	WB-B/51	AR
Moffet, Robert	065	1778	WB-B/59	AR
Moffett, William	065	1800	WB-B/151	AR
Moffitt, Aaron	081	1866	WB-13/445	
Moffitt, Adam	081	1809	WB-3/144	AR
Moffitt, Charles	081	1818	Orig. Only	AR
Moffitt, Dolly	081	1824	WB-5/170	AR
Moffitt, E. N.	081	1886	WB-16/1	AR
Moffitt, E. N.	068	1886	WB-D/207	
Moffitt, Elizabeth	064	1873	WB-2/32	AR
Moffitt, Hugh	022	1801	WB-A/52	AR
Moffitt, Jacob	081	1857	WB-10/500	AR
Moffitt, James	081	1827	WB-5/379	AR
Moffitt, James	081	1879	WB-15/300	AR
Moffitt, Jesse H.	081	1897	WB-16/457	AR
Moffitt, Logan Mc.	081	1892	WB-16/222	
Moffitt, Mary	081	1822	WB-5/56	AR
Moffitt, Peggy	081	1868	WB-15/1	AR
Moffitt, Samuel	081	1847	WB-8/516	AR
Moffitt, Sephen	081	1865	WB-13/349	
Moffitt, T. J.	081	1895	WB-16/363	AR
Moffitt, William	081	1797	WB-2/30	AR
Moffitt, William	081	1843	WB-7/448	AR
Moffitt, William C.	081	1884	WB-15/456	AR
Mohn, William	076	1889	WB-A1/99	AR
Mohoon, Josiah	047	1774	Orig. Only	SS/AR
Moignard, John L. B.	009	1805	OWB/393	AR
Moir, John	084	1886	WB-E/361	CTY
Moize, Henry	073	c1831	Orig. Only	AR
Moize, Johnathan	073	1854	WB-G/59	AR
Moldersly, John	015	1766	RB-1/58	
Moles, Sarah A.	065	1889	WB-L/373	AR
Moll, Conrad	085	1761	WB-A/119	AR
Mollison, John	053	1771	RW-1/21	
Mollison, Thomas H.	028	1900	WB-F/453	
Molloy, Daniel	083	c1800	WB-1/100	AR
Molloy, Duncan	029	1817	WB-A/244	
Molloy, John	083	c1804	WB-1/83	AR
Molloy, John T.	084	1863	WB-C/389	CTY
Molten, Abraham	035	1791	WB-A/335	AR
Molten, John	035	1790	WB-A/287	AR
Molten, Tamer	035	1762	WB-A/286	AR
Molton, John T.	087	1882	WB-3/238	AR
Molyneux, Edmund	Eng	1865	050 WB-1/160	050 CTY
Molyneux, Eliza H.	Eng	1882	050 WB-1/118	050 CTY

Name	Co.	Date	Recorded Copy	Original
Monaghan, Catharine	029	1881	WB-E/264	AR
Moncreif, John	N	1713	SS 875/43	SS/AR
Monday, James	023	1872	WB-A/4	AR
Mondle, Mary	071	1867	WB-5/348	AR
Monds, William	024	1816	WB-C/47	AR
Moneroytly, Jemmiah	030	1782	WB-1/151	
Money, Amelia	027	1872	WB-2/12	AR
Money, Hardy	106	c1867	Orig. Only	AR
Money, Joseph	078	1840	WI-14/177	AR
Monford, Martha E.	047	1836	WB-4/141	AR
Monger, Mary A.	068	1897	WB-D/485	
Monger, Nicholas	071	1767	WB-1/152	
Monger, Spell	039	1844	WB-L/214	
Monica, Manuel	071	1890	WB-7/62	AR
Monie, Maggie D.	099	1892	WB-C/84	AR
Monk, Archibald	087	1869	WB-3/12	AR
Monk, B. R.	087	1879	WB-3/192	AR
Monk, Christopher	070	1747	DB-C/126	AR
Monk, Elizabeth	099	1780	RB-1/151	
Monk, Elizabeth	035	1847	WB-2/15	AR
Monk, J. G.	078	1899	WB-19/463	AR
Monk, Jacob	035	1831	WB-1/12	AR
Monk, James	068	1854	WB-C/17	
Monk, John	056	1761	WB-1/769	AR
Monk, John C.	087	1877	WB-3/156	AR
Monk, John W.	035	1846	WB-2/6	AR
Monk, Thomas	063	1818	WB-2/52	
Monk, Willis	073	1824	WB-E/51	AR
Monroe, Archibald	082	1867	WB-5/18	AR
Monroe, Archibald	011	c1832	WB-2/397	
Monroe, Colin	011	1868	WB-2/35	
Monroe, Daniel	067	1848	WB-1/41	AR
Monroe, Daniel	011	1900	WB-3/116	CTY
Monroe, Daniel	082	1867	WB-5/21	AR
Monroe, Duncan	011	c1777	WB-1/589	
Monroe, Flora	083	1865	WB-2/216	AR
Monroe, Flora	082	1887	WB-6/354	AR
Monroe, George	086	1784	Orig. Only	AR
Monroe, George	085	1837	WB-I/22	AR
Monroe, John	032	1832	WB-1/181	
Monroe, John	011	1878	WB-2/125	
Monroe, John	085	1876	WB-1/345	CTY
Monroe, Malcom	029	1898	WB-F/140	AR
Monroe, Margaret	083	1852	WB-2/44	AR
Monroe, Nancy	011	c1859	WB-1/269	
Monroe, Nancy	082	1887	WB-6/352	AR
Monroe, Peter	083	1875	WB-3/112	AR
Monroe, Robert	029	1855	WB-C/351	AR
Monroe, Sarah Ann	029	1895	WB-F/49	AR
Monroe, Sarah J.	011	1883	WB-2/168	
Monroe, William	085	1814	WB-G/316	AR
Mons, Thomas	024	c1693	Orig. Only	SS/AR
Montague, A. E.	099	1893	WB-C/157	
Montague, Alexander	099	1866	RB-34/156	AR
Montague, Alfred K.	044	1880	WB-23/369	CTY
Montague, Elijah C.	044	1895	WB-24/262	CTY
Montague, H. W.	099	1887	WB-B/234	AR
Montague, Henry	086	1831	WB-D/139	AR
Montague, James P.	044	1886	WB-23/567	CTY
Montague, Janna E.	044	1900	WB-24/472	CTY
Montague, John	044	1877	WB-23/280	CTY
Montague, Lataney	044	1811	WB-7/211	CTY
Montague, Lewis	099	1863	RB-32/421	AR
Montague, Lewis	044	1885	WB-23/543	CTY
Montague, Mary	044	1876	WB-23/239	CTY
Montague, Samuel	044	1873	WB-23/94	CTY
Montague, William	044	1845	WB-16/245	CTY-Nunc.
Montague, Young	044	1846	WB-17/2	CTY
Montague, Zollie	038	1895	WB-3/582	AR
Monteeth, Nathaniel	016	1844	WB-1/33	AR
Montford, Donnen	028	1838	WB-C/423	
Montfort, Edward	047	1802	WB-3/377	AR
Montfort, Edward	072	c1813	WB-A/83	AR
Montfort, Frances	072	1851	WB-2/106	AR
Montfort, Joseph	047	1777	WB-2/40	AR
Montgomery, A. D.	084	1881	WB-E/193	CTY
Montgomery, Alexander	073	1768	WB-A/82	
Montgomery, Alpha R.	062	1896	WB-B/185	AR
Montgomery, Calvin	016	1899	WB-4/347	AR
Montgomery, David	097	1900	WB-3/30	AR
Montgomery, David	020	1847	RB-P/483	AR
Montgomery, Eliza C.	100	1847	WB-39/356	AR
Montgomery, Georgenia	098	1887	WB-A/87	CTY
Montgomery, Hugh	073	1830	WB-E/226	
Montgomery, Hugh	085	1780	WB-E/41	AR
Montgomery, James	020	1838	RB-N/198	AR
Montgomery, James	046	1797	WB-A/226	AR
Montgomery, James	100	1877	WB-51/130	AR
Montgomery, James	060	1829	WB-1/159	AR
Montgomery, James C.	065	1841	WB-H/75	AR
Montgomery, John	065	1778	WB-B/112	AR
Montgomery, John	065	1795	WB-B/135	AR
Montgomery, John	024	1744	Orig. Only	SS/AR
Montgomery, John	022	c1818	WB-A/300	AR
Montgomery, Joseph	060	1842	WB-2/158	AR
Montgomery, Josiah	065	1857	WB-J/44	AR
Montgomery, Lizzie A.	084	1864	WB-D/12	CTY
Montgomery, Margaret	084	1881	WB-E/195	CTY
Montgomery, Mary	020	1791	RB-B/429	
Montgomery, Mary	068	c1824	WB-B/37	
Montgomery, Nicholas	054	c1862	Orig. Only	AR
Montgomery, Rebecca	073	1839	WB-F/22	AR
Montgomery, Robert	065	1834	WB-G/169	AR
Montgomery, Robert A.	084	1873	WB-E/55	CTY
Montgomery, Sarah	073	1844	WB-F/233	AR
Montgomery, Thomas A.	AL	1874	Copy	100 AR
Montgomery, William	100	1849	WB-40/237	AR
Montgomery, William	046	1796	WB-A/229	AR
Montgomery, William	073	1815	WB-D/434	AR
Montgomery, William	046	1811	WB-A/246	AR
Montgomery, William P.	084	1859	WB-C/308	CTY
Montgomery, Wyatt	067	1888	WB-2/270	AR
Montgumery, Ann	024	1744	Orig. Only	SS/AR
Montieth, Franklin	065	1855	WB-J/4	AR
Montieth, James	054	1879	WB-4/311	CTY
Montieth, John	065	1856	WB-J/15	AR
Montieth, Nathaniel	065	1805	WB-E/8	AR
Monts, Christian	065	1777	WB-B/119	
Moody, Alexander	090	1826	WB-3/154	AR
Moody, Benjamin	022	1854	WB-C/369	AR
Moody, Hinchey G.	071	1871	Orig. Only	AR
Moody, Hinchey G.	071	1796	WB-2/104	AR
Moody, James	035	1859	WB-3/4	AR
Moody, John	060	1832	WB-1/239	AR
Moody, Joseph	071	1788	WB-1/475	AR
Moody, Joseph	071	1866	WB-5/328	AR
Moody, Kervy	010	1785	WB-D/2	AR
Moody, M. W.	VA	1885	071 WB-6/536	071 AR
Moody, Mariam	049	1880	WB-2/81	AR

Name	Co.	Date	Recorded Copy	Original
Moody, Mary	035	1867	WB-3/121	AR
Moody, Mary Janet	013	1889	WB-B/544	AR
Moody, Nancy A.	103	1882	WB-1/234	AR
Moody, Nathaniel	090	1864	WB-4/372	AR
Moody, Samuel	022	1867	WB-D/175	AR
Moody, Slomon	100	1851	WB-41/185	AR
Moody, Surrell	071	1829	WB-4/61	AR
Moody, Thomas	100	1819	WB-22/164	AR
Moody, William A.	071	1871	WB-6/76	AR
Moody, Wincey J.	071	1862	WB-5/269	AR
Moon, H. H.	081	1898	WB-16/504	AR
Moon, James	022	1807	WB-A/55	AR
Moon, John	022	1813	WB-A/226	AR
Mooney, A. H.	026	1894	WB-2/480	AR
Mooney, Anne	029	1851	WB-C/183	AR
Mooney, Charles	084	1885	WB-E/331	CTY
Mooney, Hugh	030	1801	WB-2/198	Nunc.
Mooney, Jacob	086	1827	WB-D/80	AR
Mooney, James C.	029	1857	WB-C/364	
Mooney, John Peter	086	1865	WB-E/456	
Mooney, Susanah	026	1842	WB-1/5	AR
Mooney, Willey	086	1871	WB-F/28	AR
Mooney, William D.	046	1864	WB-D/208	AR
Moony, Adam	086	1818	WB-C/92	AR
Moonyhan, Thomas	069	1804	WB-1/145	AR
Moor, Amos	037	1789	WB-C/99	AR
Moor, Ann	039	1842	WB-L/78	AR
Moor, George	085	c1807	WB-G/9	AR
Moor, Jane	061	c1854	WB-1/57	AR
Moor, John	020	1777	RB-A/8	AR
Moor, John	035	c1771	WB-A/338	AR
Moor, John	077	1748	Orig. Only	SS/AR
Moor, John	083	c1793	WB-1/31	AR
Moor, John	077	1755	SS 880/35	SS/AR
Moor, Levi	063	c1800	WB-1/421	
Moor, Martha A.	039	1874	WB-U/102	AR
Moor, Moses	063	1817	WB-2/49	
Moor, Samuel	072	1751	028 DB-5/167	SS/AR
Moor, Susanna	085	c1804	WB-E/97	AR-Nunc.
Moor, Thomas	070	1755	SS 879/179	SS/AR
Moorcock, Edward	047	1856	WB-5/20	
Moore, A. S.	077	1881	WB-H/112	AR
Moore, Aaron	051	1813	WB-A/35	
Moore, Aaron	017	c1883	Orig. Only	AR
Moore, Aaron	086	1782	WB-A/5	
Moore, Abraham	078	1831	WI-12/84	AR
Moore, Adam	060	1830	Orig. Only	AR
Moore, Adam	028	1741	Deeds.21/L7	
Moore, Adam	054	c1830	WB-2/119	AR
Moore, Adolphus	001	1876	WB-2/75	AR
Moore, Alexander	070	1892	WB-F/538	AR
Moore, Alexander	020	1855	RB-R/248	
Moore, Alexander	105	1895	WB-3/131	AR
Moore, Alexander	090	1803	WB-2/40	AR
Moore, Alexander	021	1885	WB-2/306	
Moore, Alexander	060	1838	WB-1/426	
Moore, Alexander	070	1858	WB-D/2	AR
Moore, Alfred	054	1869	WB-4/25	AR
Moore, Alfred	070	1877	WB-E/325	AR
Moore, Alfred	073	1837	WB-E/503	AR
Moore, Alfred	014	1895	WB-2/551	CTY
Moore, Alfred W.	047	1867	WB-5/168	
Moore, Alfred, Sr.	012	1811	WB-B/87	
Moore, Allen	051	1838	WB-A/198	
Moore, Allen	063	1858	WB-2/449	

Name	Co.	Date	Recorded Copy	Original
Moore, Amy	039	1838	WB-K/172	AR
Moore, Andrew	001	1862	WB1-1/207	AR
Moore, Andrew	065	1843	WB-I/35	AR
Moore, Andrew	097	1886	WB-2/288	AR
Moore, Ann	070	1835	WB-C/304	AR
Moore, Ann E.	077	1839	WB-F/286	AR
Moore, Ansalem L.	046	1884	WB-E/413	AR
Moore, Anthony	071	1804	WB-2/260	AR
Moore, Anthony	028	1788	WB-A/170	AR
Moore, Archibald	054	1877	WB-4/241	CTY
Moore, Arden	079	c1861	WB-1/80	AR
Moore, Augustus	024	1851	WB-C/319	AR
Moore, Austin	054	c1810	WB-1/197	AR
Moore, B. F.	099	1890	WB-B/462	AR
Moore, B. S.	026	1865	WB-1/377	AR
Moore, Babel	014	1874	WB-2/82	
Moore, Ballard	071	1872	WB-6/87	AR
Moore, Barnett	084	1823	WB-A/236	CTY
Moore, Bartholomew F.	099	1878	WB-A/18	AR
Moore, Baxter H.	065	1895	WB-M/353	AR
Moore, Benjamin	070	1834	WB-AB/290	AR
Moore, Benjamin	083	c1806	WB-1/133	AR
Moore, Benjamin	070	1851	WB-C/533	AR
Moore, Benjamin	010	1780	WB-B/163	AR
Moore, Berenger	011	c1775	WB-1/554	
Moore, Bitha	005	1849	WB-C/3	AR
Moore, Brittain	020	1820	RB-H/331	
Moore, C. P.	103	1889	WB-1/476	AR
Moore, Callum	097	1857	WB-1/136	AR-NUNC.
Moore, Calvin J.	090	1866	WB-5/37	
Moore, Camm	046	1845	WB-C/236	AR
Moore, Celia	063	1837	WB-2/239	
Moore, Charity	083	1874	WB-3/85	AR
Moore, Charles	063	1861	WB-2/484	
Moore, Charles	077	1790	WB-C/398	AR
Moore, Charles	047	1794	WB-3/217	AR
Moore, Charles	077	1806	WB-E/229	AR
Moore, Charles	084	1825	WB-A/250	
Moore, Charles E.	038	1889	WB-3/120	AR
Moore, Charles R.	072	1820	WB-A/93	AR
Moore, Cicero A.	054	1879	WB-4/316	CTY
Moore, Clayton	063	1882	WB-3/222	
Moore, Cornelius	028	1899	WB-F/373	
Moore, Cubid	065	1892	WB-M/39	AR
Moore, Cyntha	065	1857	WB-J/40	AR
Moore, Daniel	017	c1843	WB-A/31	
Moore, Daniel	063	1898	WB-4/224	AR
Moore, Daniel	048	1893	WB-1/7	CTY
Moore, Daniel C.	035	1864	WB-3/85	AR
Moore, David	N	1670	Orig. Only	SS/AR
Moore, David	065	1779	WB-B/60	AR
Moore, David, Sr.	065	1794	WB-B/133	AR
Moore, Dianna	073	1835	WB-E/344	AR
Moore, Dickinson	005	1840	WB-B/106	AR
Moore, Dock	079	1881	WB-2/242	AR
Moore, Dorothy A.	035	1875	WB-4/102	AR
Moore, Ebenezer	032	1843	WB-1/413	
Moore, Edith	032	1879	WB-3/292	AR
Moore, Edward	069	1785	WB-1/24	AR
Moore, Edward	044	1774	WB-1/26	CTY
Moore, Edward	045	1893	Orig. Only	AR
Moore, Edward	100	1813	WB-17/332	AR
Moore, Edward	092	1826	WB-3/173	AR
Moore, Edward	068	1803	WB-A/228	

Name	Co.	Date	Recorded Copy	Original
Moore, Edy	070	1802	WB-2/254	AR
Moore, Elam	065	1840	WB-E/240	AR
Moore, Elenor	020	1864	RB-T/44	
Moore, Eli	032	c1847	WB-2/16	
Moore, Elijah	063	1894	WB-4/136	AR
Moore, Elijah	037	1833	WB-F/140	AR
Moore, Elijah	037	1866	WB-G/274	AR
Moore, Elisha	056	c1781	WB-2/263	AR
Moore, Eliza	079	1871	WB-2/50	AR
Moore, Eliza	078	1872	WB-19/29	AR
Moore, Eliza E.	039	1881	WB-U/246	AR
Moore, Elizabeth	060	1839	WB-2/10	
Moore, Elizabeth	077	1885	WB-H/160	AR
Moore, Elizabeth	014	1899	WB-3/82	CTY
Moore, Elizabeth	092	1861	WB-5/53	
Moore, Elizabeth	009	1885	WB-1/373	CTY
Moore, Elizabeth	037	1852	WB-F/469	AR
Moore, Elizabeth	071	1818	WB-3/206	AR
Moore, Elizabeth	078	1852	WB-17/1	AR
Moore, Elizabeth	079	1866	WB-1/157	AR
Moore, Elizabeth	047	1825	WB-4/4	AR
Moore, Elizabeth	086	1820	WB-C/137	AR
Moore, Elizabeth	070	1764	WB-C/245	
Moore, Elizabeth	054	1900	WB-6/280	CTY
Moore, Ellen	093	1881	WB-2/6	
Moore, Ellen M.	071	1893	WB-7/183	AR
Moore, Ellon	001	c1836	WB-1/97	AR
Moore, Epaphras	010	1789	WB-D/102	AR
Moore, Epaphroditus	010	1757	SS 882/96	SS/AR
Moore, Esther	054	1846	WB-3/3	AR
Moore, Esther	010	1837	WB-G/289	AR
Moore, Etheldred	037	1840	WB-F/245	AR
Moore, Eve	078	1823	WI-10/22	AR
Moore, Ezekiel	063	1780	WB-1/63	
Moore, Fanny R.	039	1891	WB-U/523	AR
Moore, Francis	030	1806	WB-2/293	
Moore, Francis B.	084	1868	WB-D/94	CTY
Moore, Frank	001	1886	WB-2/320	AR
Moore, Gabriel B.	090	1891	WB-6/256	AR
Moore, George	070	1869	WB-E/186	AR
Moore, George	079	1887	WB-2/392	AR
Moore, George	070	1778	WB-C/260	AR
Moore, George	089	1864	WB-1/261	
Moore, George	086	1860	WB-E/377	
Moore, George	005	1871	WB-D/20	AR
Moore, George	086	1817	WB-C/65	AR
Moore, George A.	VA	1855	041 WB-3/193	041 AR
Moore, George B.	099	1895	WB-C/132	AR
Moore, George I.	070	1860	WB-D/34	AR
Moore, George J.	073	1879	WB-H/207	CTY
Moore, George L.	044	1818	WB-8/123	CTY
Moore, George M.	026	1895	WB-2/499	AR
Moore, George W.	051	1845	WB-A/239	
Moore, Gideon	090	1894	WB-6/329	AR
Moore, Gideon	077	1762	WB-C/17	AR
Moore, Godwin C.	051	1880	WB-C/250	AR
Moore, Goodrich	054	1850	WB-3/46	AR
Moore, Gregory	047	1816	WB-3/590	AR
Moore, Guilford	037	1895	WB-H/323	AR
Moore, Hannah	077	1802	WB-E/173	AR
Moore, Hannah	054	c1835	WB-2/176	AR
Moore, Hannah	077	1801	WB-E/141	AR
Moore, Harden F.	092	1897	WB-6/447	AR
Moore, Harriet	039	c1859	WB-Q/564	AR
Moore, Harriett	077	1881	WB-H/118	AR

Name	Co.	Date	Recorded Copy	Original
Moore, Henry	073	1831	WB-E/258	
Moore, Henry	084	1843	WB-B/285	CTY
Moore, Henry	079	1868	WB-1/176	
Moore, Henry G.	084	1896	WB-F/44	CTY
Moore, Henry H.	059	1886	WB-A/452	CTY
Moore, Hester	044	1855	WB-20/12	CTY
Moore, Higdon	100	1826	WB-30/1	AR
Moore, Hix	084	1865	WB-D/39	CTY
Moore, Hodges	063	c1795	WB-1/322	
Moore, Ichabod	079	1857	WB-1/12	AR-Copy
Moore, Ida N.	059	1885	WB-A/425	
Moore, Isaac	099	1895	WB-C/342	AR
Moore, Isaac	046	1836	WB-B/541	AR
Moore, Isaac	105	1890	WB-2/521	AR
Moore, Isabella	040	1888	WB-2/323	AR
Moore, J. Hutson	065	1863	WB-J/163	AR
Moore, J. M.	026	1881	WB-2/221	AR
Moore, James	VA	1848	084 WB-C/127	084 CTY
Moore, James	010	1798	WB-E/52	AR
Moore, James	087	1899	WB-4/109	AR
Moore, James	045	1882	WB-1/91	AR
Moore, James	070	1848	WB-C/474	AR
Moore, James	104	1893	WB-6/473	AR
Moore, James	073	1878	WB-H/186	CTY
Moore, James	001	1857	WB-1/121	AR
Moore, James	070	1778	Orig. Only	AR
Moore, James	010	1735	LGB-4/#24	SS/AR
Moore, James	022	1890	WB-E/440	AR
Moore, James	071	1800	WB-2/203	AR
Moore, James	001	1849	WB-1/3	AR
Moore, James	010	1790	WB-D/152	AR
Moore, James	054	c1793	WB-1/144	AR
Moore, James	047	1789	WB-3/168	AR
Moore, James	087	1846	WB-1/307	AR
Moore, James	021	1859	WB-1/149	AR
Moore, James	065	1834	WB-G/172	AR
Moore, James	086	1827	WB-D/66	AR
Moore, James	060	1864	WB-3/71	AR
Moore, James	083	1856	WB-2/81	AR
Moore, James	026	1869	WB-2/29	AR
Moore, James	073	1836	WB-E/388 & 402	AR
Moore, James	011	c1793	WB-1/546	
Moore, James	047	1852	WB-4/320	AR
Moore, James C.	079	1879	WB-2/172	AR
Moore, James H.	054	c1861	Orig. Only	AR
Moore, James R.	005	1900	WB-D/462	AR
Moore, Jane	054	c1836	WB-2/168	AR
Moore, Jesse	028	1796	WB-B/10	AR
Moore, Jesse	Ant	1769	077 WB-C/86	077 AR
Moore, Jesse	071	1843	WB-4/271	AR
Moore, Jesse	046	1855	WB-C/440	AR
Moore, Jesse J.	097	1863	WB-1/204	AR
Moore, Jessee	017	c1845	Orig. Only	AR-Copy
Moore, Job, Sr.	017	1885	WB-B/128	AR
Moore, Joel L.	070	1871	WB-E/225	AR
Moore, John	073	1795	WB-C/59	AR
Moore, John	020	1785	RB-B/68	AR
Moore, John	060	1836	WB-1/369	AR
Moore, John	044	1796	WB-3/253	CTY
Moore, John	044	1832	WB-12/357	CTY
Moore, John	005	c1760	WB-1/7	Nunc.
Moore, John	046	1848	WB-C/291	AR
Moore, John	010	1754	SS 879/167	SS/AR
Moore, John	028	1816	WB-C/120	

Name	Co.	Date	Recorded Copy	Original
Moore, John	070	1761	DB-E/12	AR
Moore, John	073	1816	WB-D/471	AR
Moore, John	051	1829	WB-A/22	
Moore, John	073	1799	WB-D/147	AR
Moore, John	084	1829	WB-A/338	CTY
Moore, John	086	1841	WB-E/79	AR
Moore, John	009	c1802	OWB/403	AR
Moore, John	092	c1866	WB-6/63	
Moore, John	073	1794	WB-B/264	AR
Moore, John	073	1801	WB-D/27	AR
Moore, John	064	1887	WB-2/186	AR
Moore, John	071	1753	SS 879/192	SS/AR
Moore, John	084	1858	WB-C/280	CTY
Moore, John	010	1754	SS 879/159	SS/AR
Moore, John	014	1877	WB-2/131	
Moore, John	085	c1795	WB-E/84	AR
Moore, John	099	1802	RB-6/3	AR
Moore, John	086	1844	WB-E/143	AR
Moore, John	046	1892	WB-F/233	AR
Moore, John	028	1768	Orig. Only	AR
Moore, John	057	1792	WB-A/183	AR
Moore, John	103	1812	RD-2/206	AR
Moore, John	022	1843	WB-C/149	AR
Moore, John	012	1821	WB-B/124	AR
Moore, John	020	1781	RB-A/174	AR
Moore, John	056	1777	Orig. Only	AR-Nunc.
Moore, John A.	009	1890	WB-1/463	CTY
Moore, John A.	054	c1844	WB-2/298	AR
Moore, John A.	047	1888	Copy	024 AR
Moore, John A.	022	1888	WB-E/394	AR
Moore, John A.	047	1888	010 WB-I/289	010 AR
Moore, John A.	047	1888	WB-6/482	AR
Moore, John Adam	028	1763	DB-8/91	
Moore, John D.	071	1881	WB-6/368	AR
Moore, John E.	105	1893	WB-3/70	AR
Moore, John F.	084	1852	WB-C/142	CTY
Moore, John F.	054	1877	WB-4/260	CTY
Moore, John H.	022	1888	068 WB-D/465	
Moore, John J.	060	1795	Orig. Only	AR
Moore, John J.	085	1894	WB-3/24	CTY
Moore, John K.	099	1879	WB-A/80	AR
Moore, John R.	047	1883	WB-6/290	AR
Moore, John S.	071	1842	WB-4/259	AR
Moore, John T.	070	1867	WB-D/231	AR
Moore, John, Sr.	099	1803	RB-6/111	AR
Moore, Jonathan	075	1776	WB-I/162	AR
Moore, Joseph	073	1831	WB-E/247	AR
Moore, Joseph	020	1885	WB-A/434	CTY
Moore, Joseph	065	1798	WB-B/79	AR
Moore, Joseph	010	1822	WB-G/89	AR
Moore, Joseph	037	1776	WB-A/240	AR
Moore, Joseph	037	1778	Orig. Only	AR-Nunc.
Moore, Joseph	073	1813	WB-D/383	AR
Moore, Joseph	079	c1863	WB-1/118	AR
Moore, Joseph	028	1814	WB-C/77	AR
Moore, Joseph	037	1757	SS 879/211	SS/AR
Moore, Joseph	065	c1769	WB-B/110	AR
Moore, Joseph F.	045	1899	WB-1/365	AR
Moore, Joseph H.	021	1894	WB-3/48	AR
Moore, Josephus	105	1895	WB-3/148	AR
Moore, Joshua	077	1734	SS 876/374	SS/AR
Moore, Joshua	077	1791	WB-C/420	AR
Moore, Julia A.	022	1878	WB-E/172	AR
Moore, Julius C.	076	1879	WB-A1/12	AR
Moore, Latham	028	1829	WB-C/310	
Moore, Laurence	005	1817	WB-A/77	AR
Moore, Lawrence H.	078	1866	WB-18/410	AR
Moore, Lear	014	1899	WB-3/82	CTY
Moore, Lee A.	040	1860	WB-1/115	
Moore, Lemuel J.	079	1891	WB-2/579	AR
Moore, Letissia A.	079	1884	WB-2/322	AR
Moore, Levin	084	1854	WB-C/171	CTY
Moore, Lizzie	078	1873	WB-19/44	AR
Moore, Lloyd	073	1853	WB-G/29	AR
Moore, Louis R.	077	1899	WB-H/319	
Moore, Louisa S.	071	1865	WB-5/301	AR
Moore, Lucinda B.	028	1881	WB-E/272	AR
Moore, Lucy W.	099	1887	WB-B/170	AR
Moore, Lydia A.	005	1891	WB-D/304	AR
Moore, M. M.	030	1884	WB-5/297	AR
Moore, Mahala	069	1877	WB-5/58	AR
Moore, Malachi	010	1796	WB-D/350	AR
Moore, Marcellus	079	1888	WB-2/415	
Moore, Margaret	049	1872	WB-1/263	AR
Moore, Margaret	028	1841	WB-D/27	AR
Moore, Mark	099	1837	RB-24/54	
Moore, Mark	100	1794	WB-7/217	AR
Moore, Marmaduke	071	1810	WB-3/29	AR
Moore, Martha	085	c1806	WB-E/51	AR
Moore, Martha	037	1853	WB-F/518	AR
Moore, Martha	051	1842	WB-A/152	
Moore, Martha	060	1880	WB-4/231	AR
Moore, Martha	079	1883	WB-2/290	AR
Moore, Martha C.	060	1863	WB-3/50	AR
Moore, Martha E.	105	1865	WB-1/117	AR
Moore, Mary	028	1855	WB-D/245	
Moore, Mary	028	1766	Orig. Only	AR
Moore, Mary	047	1803	WB-3/396	AR
Moore, Mary	077	1756	SS 880/114	SS/AR
Moore, Mary	044	1821	WB-8/427	CTY
Moore, Mary	028	1765	Wills.9/80	AR
Moore, Mary	047	1829	WB-4/53	AR
Moore, Mary	087	1874	WB-3/77	AR
Moore, Mary A.	001	c1885	084 WB-E/411	084 CTY
Moore, Mary A.	001	1888	WB-2/379	AR
Moore, Mary E.	022	1883	WB-E/269	AR
Moore, Mary H.	054	1883	WB-4/496	CTY
Moore, Mary L.	076	1892	WB-A1/157	CTY
Moore, Mary L.	076	1892	026 WB-2/533	026 AR
Moore, Mary L.	047	1886	WB-6/419	AR
Moore, Mary V.	030	1886	WB-5/143	AR
Moore, Matthew	057	1788	WB-A/68	AR
Moore, Matthew	090	1801	WB-2/9a	
Moore, Matthew	029	1825	WB-B/138	AR
Moore, Maurice	070	1754	DB-D/123	
Moore, Maurice	011	c1832	WB-1/3	
Moore, Michael	085	c1784	WB-B/162	AR
Moore, Michael M.	065	1887	WB-L/250	AR
Moore, Milly	105	1895	WB-3/156	AR
Moore, Moses	010	1818	WB-G/36	AR
Moore, Moses	065	1785	WB-B/66	
Moore, Moses	037	1802	WB-D/143	AR
Moore, Moses	069	1890	WB-5/291	AR
Moore, N. W.	02	51889	WB-A/108	AR
Moore, Nancey	078	1874	WB-19/32	AR
Moore, Nancy	073	1842	WB-F/142	AR
Moore, Nancy B.	014	1887	WB-2/355	CTY
Moore, Nathan	020	c1828	Copy	073 AR
Moore, Nathan	020	1828	RB-L/279	AR
Moore, Nathan	077	1831	WB-F/186	AR

Name	Co.	Date	Recorded Copy	Original
Moore, Nathaniel	085	1708	WB-E/60	AR
Moore, Needham	059	1880	WB-A/198	CTY
Moore, Noah	009	1882	WB-1/311	CTY
Moore, Patsy A.	079	1897	WB-3/102	AR
Moore, Pearson	084	1857	WB-C/244	CTY
Moore, Peter Cox	100	1790	WB-5/191	AR
Moore, Pettigrew	070	1802	WB-AB/66	AR
Moore, Pheriby	022	1854	WB-C/376	AR
Moore, Pleasant	097	1897	WB-2/539	AR
Moore, Polly	079	1873	WB-2/80	AR
Moore, Polly P.	105	1899	WB-3/377	AR
Moore, R. H.	064	1896	WB-2/373	AR
Moore, Rachel	035	1863	WB-3/82	AR
Moore, Rebecca	022	1846	WB-C/194	AR
Moore, Redding	079	1892	WB-3/12	AR
Moore, Reuben	090	1817	WB-3/8	AR
Moore, Reuben	047	1822	WB-3/673	AR
Moore, Reuben	030	1804	WB-2/250	
Moore, Richard	020	1857	RB-R/500	
Moore, Richard	010	1748	Orig. Only	SS/AR
Moore, Richard	071	1765	WB-1/130	
Moore, Richard	071	1787	WB-1/373	AR
Moore, Richard	078	1837	WI-13/192	AR
Moore, Richard F.	084	c1847	WB-C/66	CTY
Moore, Richard H.	078	1850	WB-13/400	
Moore, Robbin	104	1870	WB-6/23	AR
Moore, Robert	073	1830	WB-E/224	AR
Moore, Robert	054	1883	WB-4/586	CTY
Moore, Robert	077	1750	Orig. Only	SS/AR
Moore, Robert	054	c1792	Orig. Only	AR
Moore, Robert	073	1836	WB-E/371	AR
Moore, Robert	VA	1808	077 WB-E/313	077 AR
Moore, Robert	078	1817	WI-7/290	AR
Moore, Robert	085	1828	WB-H/424	AR
Moore, Robert	085	c1779	WB-B/117	
Moore, Robert G.	028	1844	WB-D/96	
Moore, Robert W.	076	1895	WB-A1/188	AR
Moore, Roger	070	1900	Copy	027 AR
Moore, Roger	070	1900	WB-H/284	
Moore, Roger	070	c1750	DB-C/288	
Moore, Roger	012	1782	070 WB-C/267	070 AR
Moore, Roger	070	1751	SS 881/62	SS/AR
Moore, Rosannah	005	1860	WB-C/166	AR
Moore, Rutha	037	1850	WB-F/449	AR
Moore, Sallie	103	1898	WB-2/230	AR
Moore, Samuel	084	1855	WB-C/217	CTY
Moore, Samuel	037	1794	WB-C/300	AR
Moore, Samuel	075	1694	Orig. Only	SS/AR
Moore, Samuel	077	1752	Orig. Only	SS/AR
Moore, Samuel	077	1811	WB-E/361	AR
Moore, Samuel	077	1756	SS 880/116	SS/AR
Moore, Samuel	084	1825	WB-A/246	CTY
Moore, Samuel	084	1864	WB-D/10	CTY
Moore, Samuel W.	063	1850	WB-2/354	
Moore, Sarah	010	1817	WB-G/48	AR
Moore, Sarah	084	c1809	WB-A/85	CTY
Moore, Sarah	071	1816	WB-3/183	AR
Moore, Sarah	077	c1885	Orig. Only	AR
Moore, Sarah E.	103	1881	079 WB-2/215	079 AR
Moore, Shadrach	010	1864	WB-H/140	AR
Moore, Sidney	078	1838	WI-14/73	
Moore, Simion	028	1819	WB-C/189	
Moore, Smith, Sr.	084	1867	WB-D/88	CTY
Moore, Solomon	070	1897	WB-G/578	AR
Moore, Sophronia	051	1900	WB-C/577	AR
Moore, Stanley	079	1886	WB-2/354	AR
Moore, Stephen	078	1800	WI-2/242	AR
Moore, Stephen S.	071	1833	WB-4/106	AR
Moore, Susan J.	024	1885	WB-E/140	AR
Moore, Susannah C.	090	1857	WB-4/300	AR
Moore, Theophilus	037	1859	WB-G/172	AR
Moore, Thomas	070	1755	DB-D/132	
Moore, Thomas	001	1880	WB-2/162	AR
Moore, Thomas	084	1865	WB-D/23	CTY
Moore, Thomas	086	1810	WB-B/238	AR
Moore, Thomas	084	1805	WB-A/27	CTY
Moore, Thomas	086	1893	WB-F/454	AR
Moore, Thomas	092	1889	WB-6/296	AR
Moore, Thomas	073	1819	WB-D/563	AR
Moore, Thomas	030	c1809	WB-2/347	
Moore, Thomas	070	1798	WB-AB/1	AR
Moore, Thomas A.	059	1885	WB-A/393	CTY
Moore, Thomas C.	084	1890	WB-E/440	CTY
Moore, Thomas C.	084	c1830	WB-B/67	CTY
Moore, Thomas J.	065	1898	WB-N/114	AR
Moore, Titus	010	1757	SS 880/245	SS/AR
Moore, Toms R.	077	1899	WB-H/319	AR
Moore, Truman	077	1753	SS 881/37	SS/AR
Moore, Tucker W.	090	1816	Orig. Only	AR-Nunc.
Moore, Vashte	084	1843	WB-B/294	CTY
Moore, W. B.	084	1894	WB-F/10	CTY
Moore, W. G.	006	1889	WB-E/190	AR
Moore, W. M.	107	1899	WB-2/101	AR
Moore, Warren	079	1868	WB-2/11	AR
Moore, William	099	1781	RB-1/152	AR
Moore, William	078	1813	WI-6/192	AR
Moore, William	054	1842	WB-2/256	AR
Moore, William	085	c1801	WB-E/58	AR
Moore, William	077	1808	WB-E/278	AR
Moore, William	032	1871	WB-3/48	AR
Moore, William	054	c1820	WB-2/41	AR
Moore, William	084	1839	WB-B/210	CTY
Moore, William	070	c1754	DB-D/134	AR
Moore, William	092	1853	WB-5/2	
Moore, William	053	1781	RW-1/99	
Moore, William	083	c1821	WB-1/351	AR
Moore, William	044	1761	Orig. Only	CTY
Moore, William	083	c1822	WB-1/352	AR
Moore, William	020	1850	RB-Q/403	
Moore, William	079	1877	WB-2/136	AR
Moore, William	083	c1809	WB-1/239	AR
Moore, William	022	1886	WB-E/340	AR
Moore, William	011	1768	WB-1/556	
Moore, William	078	1885	WB-19/179	AR
Moore, William	039	1829	WB-J/41	AR
Moore, William	028	1842	WB-D/45	
Moore, William	011	1774	WB-1/558	
Moore, William	079	1886	WB-2/362	AR
Moore, William	020	1851	RB-Q/524	
Moore, William	094	1771	Orig. Only	060 AR
Moore, William	046	1825	WB-B/201	AR
Moore, William	077	1842	WB-F/303	AR
Moore, William A.	005	1884	WB-D/171	AR
Moore, William A.	024	c1884	010 WB-I/292	010 AR
Moore, William A.	024	1884	WB-E/136	AR
Moore, William A.	009	1890	WB-1/461	CTY
Moore, William C.	016	1868	WB-2/164	AR
Moore, William C.	090	1863	WB-4/353	AR
Moore, William E.	071	1821	WB-3/248	AR
Moore, William F.	090	1866	WB-5/31	

Name	Co.	Date	Recorded Copy	Original
Moore, William H.	087	1889	WB-3/428	AR
Moore, William J.	041	1864	WB-3/311	AR
Moore, William J.	063	1886	WB-3/282	AR
Moore, William J.	090	1897	WB-6/439	AR
Moore, William K.	041	1850	WB-3/132	
Moore, William L.	044	1873	WB-23/104	CTY
Moore, William M.	090	1898	WB-6/461	AR
Moore, William P.	032	1896	WB-4/276	AR
Moore, William P.	097	1865	WB-1/257	AR
Moore, William P.	028	1880	WB-E/249	AR
Moore, William P.	028	1865	WB-D/369	AR
Moore, William R.	078	1886	WB-19/200	AR
Moore, William R.	060	1837	WB-1/413	AR
Moore, William Y.	037	1878	WB-G/518	AR
Moore, Wilson	009	c1789	OWB/242	AR
Moore, Zilly Ann	079	1896	WB-3/86	AR
Moorhead, James	011	c1807	WB-1/438	
Moorhead, James	011	1759	Orig. Only	SS/AR
Moorhead, Mary	011	c1787	WB-1/548	
Mooring, Arthur S.	063	1855	WB-2/417	
Mooring, Rebecca B.	047	1825	WB-4/1	AR
Mooring, Wiley	103	1880	WB-1/195	AR
Moorman, Benjamin	082	1782	WB-1/13	AR
Moorman, Benjamin	005	1798	WB-2/109	AR
Moorman, Lemuel	060	1828	WB-1/117	AR
Moorman, Thomas	082	1782	WB-1/11	AR
Moose, Alexander	089	1862	WB-1/238	
Moose, Barbara	016	1848	WB-1/153	AR
Moose, George	016	1852	WB-1/203	AR
Moose, Jacob W.	016	1896	WB-4/239	AR
Moose, John	016	1888	WB-3/578	AR
Moose, John G.	003	1886	WB-B/191	AR
Moose, Joseph	003	1886	WB-B/193	AR
Moose, Mariah	016	1893	WB-4/168	AR
Moose, Mary	016	1872	WB-3/64	AR
Moose, Noah A.	003	1874	WB-B/46	AR
Moose, Wellington	016	1897	WB-4/262	AR
Moose, Wiley	101	1883	WB-A/118	AR
Moran, Isaac	077	1869	WB-H/32	AR
Moran, James	070	1775	WB-C/255	AR
Moran, Joseph L.	024	1895	WB-E/243	AR
Moran, William	047	1797	WB-3/276	AR
Moran, William	022	1830	WB-B/191	AR
Mordagh, John	073	c1771	WB-A/137	
Mordah, Agness	054	c1828	WB-2/80	AR
Mordah, James	085	1775	WB-A/191	AR
Mordah, James	054	c1817	WB-1A/2	AR
Mordah, Jean	054	c1819	WB-2/146	AR
Mordah, Robert	054	c1824	WB-2/52	AR
Mordah, William	054	c1818	WB-2/148	AR
Mordak, James	073	1799	WB-D/139	AR
Mordak, John	073	1782	WB-A/248	AR
Mordecai, Ann W.	099	1854	RB-28/467	AR
Mordecai, Ellen	099	1884	WB-A/572	AR
Mordecai, George W.	099	1871	RB-35/117	AR
Mordecai, George W.	099	1871	013 WB-B/524	013 AR
Mordecai, Henry	099	1875	RB-35/309	AR
Mordecai, Jacob	099	1867	RB-34/447	AR
Mordecai, Moses	099	1824	RB-19/132	AR
Mordecai, Samuel	099	1865	RB-33/478	AR
Mordick, Benjamin	053	1777	RW-1/481	
Mordick, Levi	053	1771	RW-1/25	AR
Mordoh, Darcus	054	1857	WB-3/108	AR
Mordoh, Samuel	054	c1830	WB-2/103	AR
More, Benja	056	c1881	Orig. Only	AR
More, Charles	044	1801	WB-5/144	CTY
More, Elijah	097	1845	WB-1/25	AR
More, Henry	009	1824	OB-A/342	AR
More, James	021	c1859	WB-1/150	AR
More, Starling	104	1837	WB-4/215	AR
More, Thomas	009	1752	OWB/49	AR
More, Wilabey	009	1824	OB-A/331	AR
More, William	077	1732	SS 876/253	SS/AR
More, William	077	1752	Orig. Only	SS/AR
Morefield, Fannie	054	1900	WB-6/312	CTY
Morefield, Henderson	090	1900	WB-6/553	AR
Morehead, Ann E.	046	1868	WB-D/378	AR
Morehead, Eugene	046	1893	WB-F/283	AR
Morehead, Eugene	036	1889	WB-A/145	CTY
Morehead, James	086	1840	WB-E/65	AR
Morehead, James	082	1815	WB-1/170	AR
Morehead, John F.	086	1882	WB-F/171	AR
Morehead, John H.	046	1865	WB-D/255	AR
Morehead, Joseph	082	1806	WB-1/107	AR
Morehead, Mary Ann	099	c1863	WB-C/9	
Morehead, Obedience	084	1863	WB-C/379	CTY
Morehead, Robert L.	084	1876	WB-E/121	CTY
Morehead, Sidney	046	1895	WB-F/381	AR
Morehead, Thomas	046	1891	WB-F/144	AR
Morehead, Thomas	038	1891	WB-3/230	AR
Moreing, Henry	099	1884	WB-A/524	AR
Moreland, Edward	047	1806	WB-3/456	AR
Moreland, Francis	073	1802	WB-D/75	AR
Moreland, John	047	1766	WB-1/206	
Moreland, Joseph	092	1819	WB-3/137	AR
Moreland, Joseph	060	1789	Orig. Only	AR
Moreland, Thomas	046	1793	WB-A/275	AR
Morgain, Elizabeth	069	1790	WB-1/70	AR
Morgan, Aldis S.	056	1891	WB-3/567	AR
Morgan, Alexander	022	c1865	WB-D/127	AR
Morgan, Ally	085	1881	WB-1/564	CTY-Nunc.
Morgan, Andrew	046	1887	WB-E/477	AR
Morgan, Ann	075	1775	WB-I/130	AR
Morgan, Ann E.	100	1843	WB-38/230	AR
Morgan, Ann E.	075	1874	WB-O/56	AR
Morgan, Arnold	071	1807	WB-2/334	AR
Morgan, Asa	075	1801	WB-M1/49	AR
Morgan, B. A.	081	1867	WB-14/91	
Morgan, Benjamin	039	1830	WB-J/81	AR
Morgan, Benjamin	070	1802	WB-AB/63	AR
Morgan, Benjamin	075	1815	WB-M1/276	AR
Morgan, Bennet	075	1758	WB-H/6	AR
Morgan, Cader	075	1835	WB-N/118	AR
Morgan, Charity	041	1825	WB-2/237	AR
Morgan, Charles	022	1788	RB-1/32	AR
Morgan, Charles	075	1816	WB-M1/292	AR
Morgan, Charles	075	1795	WB-L/45	AR
Morgan, Claudius	075	1823	WB-M1/383	AR
Morgan, Daniel	013	1881	WB-B/241	
Morgan, Daniel	070	1782	WB-C/268	AR
Morgan, Daniel D.	014	1891	WB-2/426	CTY
Morgan, Daniel J.	070	1874	WB-E/271	AR
Morgan, David	034	1781	Copy	028 AR
Morgan, David	070	1790	WB-C/275	AR
Morgan, David J.	070	1891	076 WB-A1/146	
Morgan, Davis	086	1867	WB-E/484	AR
Morgan, E. P.	086	1864	WB-E/432	AR
Morgan, Edmon	075	1873	WB-O/47	AR
Morgan, Elijah	099	18770	RB-35/82	AR

Name	Co.	Date	Recorded Copy	Original
Morgan, Elijah	064	1869	WB-2/24	AR
Morgan, Elizabeth	075	1879	WB-0/110	AR
Morgan, Elizabeth	010	1866	WB-H/154	AR
Morgan, Enoch	016	c1826	WB-A/19	AR
Morgan, Ezekiel	070	1784	WB-C/270	AR-Nunc.
Morgan, Fereby	022	1844	WB-C/163	AR
Morgan, George W.	020	1895	WB-B/197	CTY
Morgan, Habikkuk	046	1816	WB-A/248	AR
Morgan, Hannah	070	1769	WB-C/273	AR
Morgan, Hardy	073	1797	WB-C/98	AR
Morgan, Henry	099	1882	WB-A/340	AR
Morgan, J. H.	093	1897	WB-2/160	AR
Morgan, J. P.	050	1887	WB-2/30	CTY
Morgan, James	097	1860	WB-1/165	AR
Morgan, James	069	1781	WB-1/19	AR
Morgan, James	075	1799	WB-M1/29	AR
Morgan, James	084	1894	WB-F/14	CTY
Morgan, James	013	c1853	WB-A/165	
Morgan, James	077	1745	Orig. Only	SS/AR
Morgan, James	041	1838	WB-2/396	AR
Morgan, James	075	1771	WB-H/132	AR
Morgan, James S.	037	1849	WB-F/419	AR
Morgan, James W.	016	1842	PQS.6/226	AR
Morgan, Jane, Sr.	077	1742	Orig. Only	SS/AR
Morgan, Jethro	064	1899	WB-2/455	AR
Morgan, John	019	1810	WB-D/286	AR
Morgan, John	068	1800	WB-A/209	
Morgan, John	028	1805	WB-B/230	
Morgan, John	044	1786	WB-1/488	CTY
Morgan, John	069	1840	WB-1/440	AR
Morgan, John	010	1827	WB-G/154	AR
Morgan, John	075	1873	WB-0/50	AR
Morgan, John	075	c1741	Orig. Only	AR
Morgan, John L.	064	1894	WB-2/333	AR
Morgan, John W.	041	1898	WB-4/463	AR
Morgan, John W.	016	1845	WB-1/70	AR
Morgan, John, Sr.	075	1755	Orig. Only	SS/AR
Morgan, John, Sr.	071	1821	WB-3/250	AR
Morgan, Jonathan	075	1846	WB-N/206	AR
Morgan, Jones	073	1862	WB-G/381	CTY
Morgan, Joseph	037	1792	WB-C/210	AR
Morgan, Joseph	022	1806	WB-A/91	AR
Morgan, Joseph	075	1777	WB I/139	AR
Morgan, Joseph	018	1830	WB-C/120	
Morgan, Joseph B.	030	1885	WB-5/126	AR
Morgan, Joshua	104	1811	WB-3/9	AR
Morgan, Josiah	077	1892	WB-H/223	AR
Morgan, Lewis	081	1802	WB-2/96	AR
Morgan, Lucy	069	c1897	Orig. Only	AR
Morgan, Lydia	099	1892	WB-C/91	
Morgan, Lydia	077	1802	WB-E/170	AR
Morgan, M. G.	085	1879	WB-1/503	CTY
Morgan, Madorah A.	069	1900	WB-6/106	AR
Morgan, Malinda	046	1900	WB-G/253	AR
Morgan, Martha V.	075	1892	WB-0/349	AR
Morgan, Mary	013	c1870	Orig. Only	AR
Morgan, Mary	075	1875	WB-0/58	AR
Morgan, Mary	033	1840	WB-1/29	
Morgan, Mary	077	1850	WB-F/378	AR
Morgan, Mary	077	1787	WB-C/352	AR
Morgan, Mathew	077	1764	WB-C/40	AR
Morgan, Mathew	071	1876	WB-6/198	AR
Morgan, Mathias	041	1832	WB-2/301	AR
Morgan, McCaney W.	016	1837	PQS.5/436	Nunc.
Morgan, Miles	075	1878	WB-0/93	AR
Morgan, Miloo	010	1037	WB-C/203	
Morgan, Nathan	068	1846	WB-B/159	
Morgan, Nathan	072	1750	028 DB-5/132	SS/AR
Morgan, Newell R.	046	1896	WB-F/549	AR
Morgan, Noah	013	1870	WB-B/29	AR
Morgan, Paul	073	1814	WB-D/411	AR
Morgan, Peter	047	1784	WB-3/52	AR
Morgan, Peter	047	1809	WB-3/492	AR
Morgan, Reese	065	1776	WB-B/55	AR
Morgan, Reuben	099	1892	WB-C/82	AR
Morgan, Reubin J.	069	1879	WB-5/90	AR
Morgan, Richard	082	1836	WB-2/58	AR
Morgan, Robert	075	1857	WB-M2/46	AR
Morgan, Robert	075	1730	Orig. Only	SS/AR
Morgan, Robert	075	1774	WB-I/73	AR
Morgan, Sallie H.	084	1900	WB-F/178	CTY
Morgan, Sampson	071	c1799	Orig. Only	AR
Morgan, Samuel	039	1860	WB-Q/673	
Morgan, Samuel W.	100	1864	WB-50/74	AR
Morgan, Sarah	073	1827	WB-E/152	AR
Morgan, Sarah	073	c1785	WB-B/3	AR
Morgan, Sarah	075	c1857	WB-M2/50	AR
Morgan, Sarah Ann	089	1880	WB-2/81	AR
Morgan, Sarah E.	024	1866	WB-D/40	AR
Morgan, Seth	075	1895	WB-0/419	AR
Morgan, Seth R.	041	1866	WB-3/349	AR
Morgan, Solomon	099	1875	RB-35/287	AR
Morgan, Solomon	099	1795	RB-3/122	AR
Morgan, Stephen	086	1858	WB-E/348	AR
Morgan, Stephen	064	1856	WB-1/46	AR
Morgan, Tabitha	044	1871	WB-23/47	CTY
Morgan, Theophilus	054	c1807	WB-1/143	AR
Morgan, Thomas	010	1816	WB-F/348	AR
Morgan, Timothy	046	1818	WB-B/64	AR
Morgan, Tirra H.	016	1857	WB-2/27	AR
Morgan, W. H.	075	1895	WB-0/416	AR
Morgan, W. M.	036	c1892	Orig. Only	029 AR
Morgan, William	020	1863	RB-S/613	AR
Morgan, William	011	c1823	WB-2/357	Nunc.
Morgan, William	071	1826	WB-3/339	AR
Morgan, William	071	1765	WB-1/129	
Morgan, William	005	1860	WB-C/164	AR
Morgan, William	037	1795	WB-C/309	AR
Morgan, William	085	1772	WB-A/93	AR
Morgan, William B.	069	c1851	Orig. Only	AR
Morgan, Wilson	064	1860	WB-1/69	AR
Morgan, Winfield	044	1853	WB-19/262	CTY
Morgin, Hardy	069	1811	WB-1/218	AR
Morgin, John	019	c1766	WB-D/274	AR
Morgin, William	037	c1837	WB-F/212	AR
Morice, Charles	005	c1774	WB-1/22	AR
Moring, Christian	010	1816	WB-F/346	AR
Moring, Eliza C.	099	1884	WB-A/524	AR
Moring, Fielding	099	1889	WB-B/340	AR
Moring, William	103	1795	WI-A/567	AR
Moring, William	010	1866	WB-H/166	AR
Moris, Joseph	018	1825	WB-C/45	
Morisey, James K.	087	1882	WB-3/246	AR
Morisey, Richard B.	087	1853	WB-1/440	AR
Morisey, William	087	1885	WB-3/325	AR
Morison, Benjamin	070	1760	SS 881/150	SS/AR
Morison, Catherine	029	1845	WB-C/78	AR
Morison, Christian	083	1842	WB-1/413	AR
Morison, John	065	c1777	WB-B/117	AR
Morison, Kean	029	1814	WB-A/206	AR

Name	Co.	Date	Recorded Copy	Original
Morison, Mary	085	c1784	WB-B/85	AR
Morison, Norman	082	1843	WB-3/7	AR
Morison, Roderick	029	1824	WB-B/115	
Morison, William	085	1771	WB-A/105	AR
Morisson, Andrew	085	1770	WB-A/94	AR
Morley, Robert	087	1837	WB-1/181	
Morning, Margaret	070	1779	WB-C/264	AR
Morning, Phoebe T.	056	1900	WB-4/269	AR
Morphy, Timothy	022	1783	Orig. Only	AR
Morpos, James	099	1820	RB-16/110	AR
Morras, Henry	073	1801	WB-D/50	AR
Morray, James	073	1806	WB-D/175	AR
Morrel, Humphry	N	1733	Orig. Only	SS/AR
Morrell, Benjamin	071	1761	WB-1/43	
Morrell, William	072	1831	WB-1/88	
Morres, Joseph	032	1823	WB-1/25	
Morress, John	041	1859	WB-3/238	AR
Morril, William H.	079	1887	WB-2/403	AR
Morris, Aaron	075	1770	WB-H/115	
Morris, Aaron	028	1810	WB-C/13	
Morris, Aaron	075	1796	WB-L/79	
Morris, Aaron, Sr.	075	1815	WB-M1/271	
Morris, Allen	010	1871	WB-I/35	AR
Morris, Allison L.	086	1899	WB-G/21	AR
Morris, Azile	105	1860	WB-1/60	AR
Morris, Benjamin	085	c1808	WB-G/30	AR
Morris, Benjamin	105	1885	WB-2/352	AR
Morris, Benjamin	075	1823	WB-M1/362	AR
Morris, Betsey	047	1850	WB-4/292	AR
Morris, Catharine	100	1837	WB-35/374	AR
Morris, Catharine	068	1892	WB-D/383	
Morris, Charity	075	1817	WB-M1/306	AR
Morris, Chislon	071	1803	WB-2/251	AR
Morris, Cornelius	096	c1795	Orig. Only	AR
Morris, D. E.	084	1891	WB-F/196	CTY
Morris, E. L.	064	1895	WB-2/355	AR
Morris, Edmund	063	c1784	WB-1/101	
Morris, Effy	083	1840	WB-1/387	AR
Morris, Elisabeth	070	c1764	WB-C/245	AR
Morris, Elisha	009	c1797	OWB/339	AR
Morris, Elizabeth	039	1859	WB-O/379	AR
Morris, Emanuel	070	1824	WB-C/296	AR
Morris, Francis	MD	1886	070 WB-G/90	070 AR
Morris, Francis	053	1809	RW-1/424	
Morris, Frederick	038	1875	WB-2/218	AR
Morris, George	086	1837	WB-E/33	
Morris, George W.	085	1860	WB-K/276	AR
Morris, Griffin	047	1783	WB-3/37	AR
Morris, Griffin	016	1806	WB-A/2	AR
Morris, Griffith	016	1815	WB-A/8	AR
Morris, Hammond	090	1810	WB-2/117	AR
Morris, Harriet	010	1877	WB-I/91	
Morris, Henry	064	1844	WB-1/7	AR
Morris, Henry C.	016	1895	WB-4/220	AR
Morris, Henry G.	099	1892	WB-C/112	AR
Morris, Henry R.	047	1839	WB-4/184	AR
Morris, Isaac	064	1859	WB-1/64	AR
Morris, Jacob	028	1799	WB-B/72	
Morris, James B.	086	1893	WB-F/456	AR
Morris, James B.	065	1894	WB-M/299	AR
Morris, James E.	028	1887	WB-E/463	AR
Morris, James, Sr.	086	1855	WB-E/292	AR
Morris, Jane A.	026	1883	WB-2/242	AR
Morris, Jeremiah	099	1856	RB-29/559	AR
Morris, Jeremiah	103	1828	RD-5/433	AR

Name	Co.	Date	Recorded Copy	Original
Morris, Jesse	105	1873	WB-2/110	AR
Morris, Jesse	037	1778	WB-B/9	AR
Morris, John	037	1838	Orig. Only	AR
Morris, John	068	1887	WB-D/234	
Morris, John	030	1803	WB-2/231	
Morris, John	089	1879	WB-2/75	AR
Morris, John	037	1800	WB-D/110	AR
Morris, John	075	1739	LGB-4/#103B	SS/AR
Morris, John	077	1774	WB-C/164	AR
Morris, John	100	1830	WB-33/140	AR
Morris, John	071	1764	WB-1/102	
Morris, John	067	1891	WB-2/324	AR
Morris, John	075	1778	WB-K/26	
Morris, John	050	1877	WB-1/145	CTY
Morris, John	075	1777	WB-I/126	
Morris, John	050	1859	Orig. Only	CTY
Morris, John	075	1798	WB-M1/7	AR
Morris, John	064	1866	Orig. Only	AR
Morris, John H.	064	1876	WB-2/53	AR
Morris, Jonathan	077	1796	WB-E/63	
Morris, Joseph	060	1847	WB-2/273	AR
Morris, Joseph	010	1891	WB-I/312	AR
Morris, Joseph	075	1798	WB-M1/18	AR
Morris, Joseph	075	1819	WB-M1/330	AR
Morris, Joseph H.	010	1864	WB-H/142	AR
Morris, Joshua	077	1777	WB-C/202	AR
Morris, Joshua	075	1824	WB-M1/400	AR
Morris, Josiah	028	1816	WB-C/123	
Morris, Lemuel H.	047	1875	WB-6/120	AR-Copy
Morris, Lewis W.	054	1896	WB-6/45	CTY
Morris, Locky	068	1864	WB-C/100	
Morris, Lydia	075	1807	WB-M1/144	AR
Morris, Marchan	099	1851	RB-29/353	AR
Morris, Marchelandess	047	c1865	WB-5/131	
Morris, Margaret	075	1845	WB-N/194	AR
Morris, Martha	065	1891	WB-L/558	AR
Morris, Mary	PA	1827	064 WB-2/245	
Morris, Mary	028	1817	WB-C/147	AR
Morris, Mary	PA	1827	107 WB-2/197	
Morris, Mary	100	1838	WB-36/196	AR
Morris, Mary	039	1861	WB-R/189	AR
Morris, Mary	PA	1827	014 WB-2/445	
Morris, Mary T.	028	1879	WB-E/218	AR
Morris, Matthew	010	1849	WB-G/449	AR
Morris, Matthew H.	010	1863	WB-H/128	AR
Morris, Mordecai	075	1831	WB-N/69	AR
Morris, Moses	028	1812	WB-C/52	
Morris, Moses	016	1813	WB-A/6	AR
Morris, Nancy	068	1855	WB-C/43	
Morris, Nancy	016	c1815	WB-A/7	AR
Morris, Nathan	075	1823	WB-M1/365	AR
Morris, Nathan	037	1829	WB-F/107	AR
Morris, Nathan	075	1830	WB-N/58	AR
Morris, Nathan	028	1801	WB-B/138	AR
Morris, Nathan C.	075	1823	WB-M1/367	AR
Morris, Oney B.	044	1884	WB-23/488	CTY
Morris, Peter	068	1882	WB-D/145	
Morris, Peter W.	068	c1873	WB-D/125	
Morris, Phereby T.	097	1859	WB-1/152	AR
Morris, Philemon	072	c1760	Copy	057 AR
Morris, Philemon	065	1860	WB-J/91	AR
Morris, Philemon	072	c1760	RW/L37	AR
Morris, Phoebe	044	1874	WB-23/124	CTY
Morris, Pritchard	077	1838	WB-F/274	AR
Morris, Reddick	035	1872	WB-4/64	AR

Name	Co.	Date	Recorded Copy	Original
Morris, Richard P.	075	1806	WB-M1/125	
Morris, Robert	PA	1806	014 WB-2/440	
Morris, Robert	PA	1806	064 WB-2/241	
Morris, Robert	PA	1806	107 WB-2/192	
Morris, Rutha	099	1866	RB-33/425	AR
Morris, Sallie	099	1888	WB-B/266	AR
Morris, Samson	028	1797	WB-B/30	
Morris, Samuel	016	c1815	WB-A/7	AR
Morris, Samuel	030	1816	WB-3/74	
Morris, Sarah	057	1818	WB-B/51	AR
Morris, Sarah	068	1868	WB-D/1	
Morris, Sarah	064	1887	WB-2/162	AR
Morris, Sollomon	070	1779	Orig. Only	AR
Morris, Stephen	105	1868	WB-1/137	AR
Morris, Thomas	073	1870	WB-H/24	CTY
Morris, Thomas	070	1744	SS 878/23	SS/AR
Morris, Thomas	086	1862	WB-E/396	AR
Morris, Thomas	069	1807	WB-1/178	AR
Morris, Thomas	072	1793	Orig. Only	AR
Morris, Thomas	099	1806	RB-7/202	AR
Morris, Thomas	MS	1859	044 WB-21/111	044 CTY
Morris, Thomas	028	1843	WB-D/73	AR
Morris, Thomas	070	1744	DB-C/43	
Morris, Thomas	028	1793	WB-A/297	
Morris, Thomas	028	1824	WB-C/254	AR
Morris, W. C.	038	1898	WB-4/117	AR
Morris, W. L.	093	1898	WB-2/166	
Morris, W. W.	024	1900	WB-E/317	AR
Morris, William	014	c1837	Copy	064 AR
Morris, William	069	1894	WB-4/461	AR
Morris, William	037	1838	WB-F/212	
Morris, William	010	1900	WB-K/6	
Morris, William	065	1804	WB-B/84	AR
Morris, William	096	1767	Orig. Only	AR
Morris, William	057	1786	WB-A/53	AR
Morris, William	064	1849	WB-1/23	
Morris, William	083	1846	WB-1/495	
Morris, William	028	1889	WB-E/505	AR
Morris, William	005	1804	WB-2/106	AR
Morris, William	070	1767	WB-C/247	AR
Morris, William	086	1821	WB-C/167	AR
Morris, William A.	005	1844	WB-B/186	AR
Morris, William A.	064	1869	WB-2/18	AR
Morris, William H.	VA	1881	099 WB-A/222	099 AR
Morris, William H.	VA	1896	047 WB-7/180	047 AR
Morris, William J.	028	1848	SC/06180	AR-Copy
Morris, William S.	028	1848	WB-D/153	AR
Morris, William S.	010	1864	WB-H/144	AR
Morris, Zachariah	103	1809	RD-1/205	
Morris, Zebulon	065	1872	WB-K/97	AR
Morriset, Peter	030	1803	WB-2/230	
Morrisett, A. D.	018	1891	WB-E/203	AR
Morrisett, John	030	1871	WB-5/14	
Morrisett, Malachi J.	018	1859	WB-D/55	
Morrisett, Monford S.	018	1895	WB-E/240	AR
Morrisett, P. G.	018	1899	WB-E/295	AR
Morrisey, Owen C.	103	1850	RD-10/323	AR
Morrison, Alexander	083	1882	WB-3/285	AR
Morrison, Alfred	054	1873	WB-4/124	CTY
Morrison, Alfred J.	065	1877	WB-K/246	AR
Morrison, Andrew	054	c1828	WB-2/59	AR
Morrison, Andrew	054	1866	WB-3/194	AR
Morrison, Andrew R.	054	1885	WB-5/26	CTY
Morrison, Andrew W.	054	1892	WB-5/428	CTY
Morrison, Ann	054	c1835	Orig. Only	AR
Morrison, Annabella	065	1818	WB-B/97	AR
Morrison, Archibald	085	1769	WB-A/97	AR
Morrison, Catharine	083	1869	WB-3/17	AR
Morrison, Columbus	016	1863	WB-2/93	AR
Morrison, Daniel	029	1841	WB-B/344	AR
Morrison, Daniel	057	1794	WB-A/87	AR
Morrison, David	085	c1800	WB-D/213	AR
Morrison, Donald	029	c1796	Orig. Only	AR
Morrison, Effy	083	1857	WB-2/113	AR
Morrison, Elizabeth	054	c1830	WB-2/110	AR
Morrison, Elizabeth	029	1840	WB-B/329	AR
Morrison, F. M.	064	1895	WB-2/350	AR
Morrison, Francis	064	1846	WB-1/19	AR
Morrison, G. L.	016	c1856	WB-2/69	AR
Morrison, J. S.	029	1894	WB-F/23	AR
Morrison, James	054	c1820	WB-2/93	AR
Morrison, James	065	1824	WB-E/31	AR
Morrison, James	014	c1790	Orig. Only	AR-Copy
Morrison, James	065	1847	WB-I/90	AR
Morrison, James	065	1805	WB-E/7	AR
Morrison, James	085	c1779	WB-B/95	AR
Morrison, James E.	005	1892	WB-D/314	AR
Morrison, James H.	054	1846	WB-3/16	AR
Morrison, James T.	080	1898	WB-1/306	AR
Morrison, Jane	083	1826	WB-1/355	AR
Morrison, John	065	1845	WB-I/10	AR
Morrison, John	082	1843	WB-3/3	AR
Morrison, John	013	1834	WB-A/29	
Morrison, John	082	1839	WB-2/82	AR
Morrison, John	054	c1831	Orig. Only	AR
Morrison, John	011	c1801	WB-1/434	
Morrison, John	085	c1790	WB-D/207	
Morrison, John	016	1846	WB-1/91	AR
Morrison, John	086	1827	WB-D/67	AR
Morrison, John	083	1832	WB-1/274	AR
Morrison, John A.	082	1869	WB-6/26	AR
Morrison, John D.	016	1890	WB-4/53	AR
Morrison, John L.	085	1883	WB-2/45	CTY
Morrison, John, Sr.	054	c1828	WB-2/153	AR
Morrison, Jonathan	077	1764	WB-C/48	AR
Morrison, Magnolia	054	1899	080 WB-1/351	080 AR
Morrison, Magnolia	054	1899	WB-6/240	CTY
Morrison, Malcom	046	1828	WB-B/364	AR
Morrison, Malcom	068	c1827	WB-B/66	
Morrison, Malcom	082	1831	WB-2/18	AR
Morrison, Margaret	054	1873	WB-4/140	CTY
Morrison, Mary	065	c1781	WB-B/120	AR
Morrison, Mary	065	1877	WB-K/269	AR
Morrison, Mary	054	1881	WB-4/432	CTY
Morrison, Neill	065	1784	WB-B/64	AR
Morrison, Norman	083	1829	WB-1/370	AR
Morrison, Norman	029	1815	WB-A/222	AR
Morrison, Pinkney	016	1884	WB-3/443	AR
Morrison, R. H.	060	1889	WB-4/399	AR
Morrison, Rachel	082	1832	WB-2/26	AR
Morrison, Rachel	014	1880	WB-2/211	AR
Morrison, Robert	065	1810	WB-B/90	AR
Morrison, Samuel	016	1872	WB-3/61	AR
Morrison, Sancho	054	1880	WB-4/362	CTY
Morrison, Sarah	054	1846	WB-3/2	AR
Morrison, Sarah	054	c1836	WB-2/152	AR
Morrison, Sarah	054	c1848	WB-3/146	AR
Morrison, Sarrah	029	1830	WB-B/202	AR
Morrison, Thomas	054	c1814	WB-1/322	
Morrison, Thomas	054	1887	WB-5/185	CTY

Name	Co.	Date	Recorded Copy	Original
Morrison, Thomas	054	1861	WB-3/161	AR
Morrison, W. H.	054	1888	WB-5/215	CTY
Morrison, Washington	065	1836	WB-E/154	AR
Morrison, William	060	1831	WB-1/200	AR
Morrison, William	005	1853	WB-C/64	AR
Morrison, William	054	c1822	WB-2/10	AR
Morrison, William	054	c1810	WB-2/18	AR
Morrison, William C.	054	c1864	Orig. Only	AR
Morriss (Moris), John	028	1742	Deeds.21/L25	SS/AR
Morriss, Benjamin	051	1884	WB-C/331	AR
Morriss, Daniel	051	1865	WB-B/60	AR
Morriss, Edward	039	c1854	WB-0/348	AR
Morriss, Elizabeth	047	1813	WB-3/544	AR
Morriss, Gideon W.	099	1900	WB-D/405	AR
Morriss, Hezekiah	047	1799	WB-3/330	AR
Morriss, John	010	1759	SS 881/213	SS/AR
Morriss, John	044	1815	WB-7/550	CTY
Morriss, Lewis	028	1820	WB-C/194	
Morriss, Nancy	103	1883	WB-1/265	AR
Morriss, Philemon	047	1818	WB-3/612	AR
Morriss, Phillis	051	1888	WB-C/389	AR-Nunc.
Morriss, Pressley	090	1815	WB-2/172	AR
Morriss, Thomas	047	1777	WB-2/37	
Morriss, W. W.	026	1866	WB-1/391	AR
Morriss, William	047	1814	WB-3/548	AR
Morriss, William	010	1807	WB-F/55	AR
Morriss, Zadock	010	1838	WB-G/305	AR
Morrisson, Robert	073	1808	WB-D/227	AR
Morrow, Alexander	073	1856	WB-G/146	AR
Morrow, Alfred	086	1878	WB-F/131	AR
Morrow, Benjamin	065	1875	WB-K/195	AR
Morrow, Charles	073	1768	WB-A/80	
Morrow, David	065	1811	WB-E/15	AR
Morrow, David P.	040	1895	WB-2/491	AR
Morrow, E. Graham	073	1863	WB-G/408	CTY
Morrow, Ebenezer	013	1878	WB-B/155	AR
Morrow, Elizabeth	065	1832	WB-G/110	AR
Morrow, Elizabeth	044	1840	WB-114/564	
Morrow, George	054	1870	WB-4/81	CTY
Morrow, George W.	060	1835	WB-1/353	AR
Morrow, Hugh	073	1783	WB-A/268	AR
Morrow, James	086	1870	WB-F/18	AR
Morrow, James S.	073	1863	WB-G/409	AR
Morrow, John	049	1826	WB-2/224	AR
Morrow, John	085	1815	WB-G/397	AR
Morrow, John	065	1795	WB-B/134	AR
Morrow, John	073	1846	WB-F/303	AR
Morrow, Joseph	085	1816	WB-G/423	AR
Morrow, Levi N.	001	1891	WB-2/489	AR
Morrow, Martha	065	1833	WB-G/109	AR
Morrow, Robert	065	1800	WB-B/145	AR
Morrow, Robert	073	1845	WB-F/269	AR
Morrow, Robert B.	054	1888	WB-5/213	CTY
Morrow, Sarah L.	040	1863	WB-1/158	
Morrow, William	078	1815	WI-7/4	AR
Morrow, William	001	c1845	WB-1/67	AR
Morrow, William	049	1827	WB-2/226	AR
Morrow, William	073	1807	WB-D/189	AR
Morrow, William P.	001	1877	WB-2/115	AR
Morse, Abigirl	019	1814	WB-D/292	AR
Morse, Archibald	030	1794	WB-2/29	
Morse, Arthur	030	1834	WB-4/3	
Morse, C. C.	070	1892	WB-F/509	AR
Morse, Caleb	030	1794	WB-2/29	
Morse, Davis B.	030	1868	WB-4/274	AR
Morse, Elizabeth	019	1814	WB-D/291	AR
Morse, Elizabeth	019	1831	WB-A/7	AR
Morse, Francis	030	1821	WB-3/151	
Morse, James	019	1811	WB-D/290	AR
Morse, John	030	1838	WB-4/45	
Morse, Joseph	019	c1784	WB-D/276	AR
Morse, Joseph	072	1841	WB-2/35	AR
Morse, Joshua	019	1793	WB-D/280	AR
Morse, Richardson	030	1782	WB-1/150	
Morse, Samuel	044	1792	WB-2/280	CTY
Morse, Samuel	044	1788	WB-2/67	CTY
Morse, Theodore	019	1821	WB-D/296	AR
Morse, Thomas	030	1824	WB-3/166	
Morse, Willis	099	1872	RB-35/177	AR
Morse, Zachariah	030	1817	WB-3/90	
Mortimer, John	070	1766	Orig. Only	SS/AR
Mortise, Thomas	073	1794	WB-C/1	AR
Morton, Anderson	020	1827	RB-L/195	AR
Morton, Ann	024	1797	WB-A/279	AR
Morton, Bryan	072	1899	WB-4/416	AR-Nunc.
Morton, Carey	078	1882	WB-19/127	AR
Morton, David W.	028	1892	WB-F/14	
Morton, Edward C.	005	1866	WB-C/245	AR
Morton, Edward T.	090	1861	WB-4/349	AR
Morton, Elijah	020	1875	WB-A/175	CTY
Morton, Eugene	096	1880	WB-4/63	AR
Morton, Ezekiel R.	089	1863	WB-1/245	
Morton, James	054	1803	WB-1/148	AR
Morton, James R.	067	1899	WB-2/387	AR
Morton, John	089	1895	WB-2/257	AR
Morton, John	054	c1824	WB-2/11	AR
Morton, John	022	c1773	Orig. Only	AR
Morton, John, Sr.	054	c1803	WB-1/147	AR
Morton, Joseph	044	1864	WB-22/184	CTY
Morton, Joseph	072	1801	WB-A/88	AR
Morton, Lewis S.	078	1896	WB-19/409	AR
Morton, Little Joe	VA	1808	044 WB-7/9	044 CTY
Morton, Litty	020	1845	RB-P/236 & 267	
Morton, Mary	005	1826	WB-2/107	AR-Nunc.
Morton, Mary	020	1818	RB-H/171	AR
Morton, Meltin	072	1887	WB-4/227	AR
Morton, Mettiah	072	1809	WB-A/90	AR
Morton, Nancy	020	1852	RB-Q/648	AR
Morton, Patrick	092	1815	WB-3/117	AR
Morton, Peter	072	1796	Orig. Only	AR
Morton, Peter C.	072	1879	WB-4/121	AR
Morton, Richard	092	1806	WB-3/74	
Morton, Robert	065	1778	WB-B/58	AR
Morton, Samuel	016	1799	WB-A/34	AR
Morton, Samuel V.	044	1859	WB-21/46	CTY
Morton, Stephen H.	070	1886	WB-F/33	AR
Morton, Virginia T.	IL	1892	080 WB-1/204	080 AR
Morton, West	072	1871	WB-4/65	AR
Morton, William	073	1840	WB-F/72	AR
Morton, William	054	1865	WB-3/183	AR
Morton, William	005	1808	WB-2/108	AR
Morton, William A.	089	1872	WB-2/23	AR
Mosby, Richard H.	VA	1849	047 WB-4/287	047 AR
Mosby, Samuel	092	1787	WB-2/74A	AR
Mosby, William	092	c1827	WB-4/12	AR
Moseley, Bassett	047	1812	WB-3/535	AR
Moseley, Dan	046	1839	WB-C/34	AR
Moseley, Daniel H.	084	1890	WB-E/449	CTY
Moseley, Edward	070	1749	SS 877/1	SS/AR
Moseley, Elsie	070	1894	WB-G/317	AR

Name	Co.	Date	Recorded Copy	Original
Moseley, James H.	105	1863	WB-1/97	AR
Moseley, John	100	1795	WB-8/9	AR
Moseley, Richard D.	087	1896	WB-4/18	AR
Moseley, Robert A.	087	c1863	WB-2/114	
Moseley, Thomas	070	1789	WB-C/272	AR
Moseley, William	070	1798	WB-AB/17	AR
Mosely, Adeline	070	1899	WB-H/209	AR
Mosely, John W.	100	1828	WB-31/146	AR
Mosely, Martha	087	1897	WB-4/37	AR
Mosely, Martha	028	1899	WB-F/375	
Mosely, West	092	1821	WB-3/149	
Mosely, Wylie T.	059	1897	WB-B/176	CTY
Moser, Boston	001	1850	WB-1/33	AR
Moser, Henry	097	1863	WB-1/212	AR
Moser, Henry	003	c1864	WB-A/17	
Moser, Israel	092	1898	WB-6/470	AR
Moser, Leonard	092	1782	WB-1/166	AR
Moser, Mary	001	1891	WB-2/493	AR
Moser, Mary M.	081	1844	WB-8/66	AR
Moser, Peter	073	1843	WB-F/162	AR
Moser, Peter	090	1821	WB-3/58	AR
Moses, A. F.	103	1869	WB-1/8	
Moses, Abraham	065	1821	WB-E/26	AR
Moses, Abram	039	1846	WB-M/109	AR
Moses, Ann B.	103	1884	WB-1/337	AR
Moses, David	061	1895	WB-2/162	AR
Moses, John S.	029	1880	WB-E/204	AR
Mosick, Jacob	011	c1788	WB-1/547	
Mosier, Frederic	073	1800	WB-D/3	AR
Mosier, William	022	1888	WB-E/367	AR
Mosley, David	086	1867	WB-E/482	AR
Mosley, David	086	1897	WB-F/527	AR
Mosley, Henry	092	1867	WB-5/91	
Mosley, John	072	c1865	Orig. Only	AR
Mosley, Nickles	028	1877	WB-E/177	
Moss, A. H.	016	1883	WB-3/378	AR
Moss, Abraham	039	1805	WB-C/24	AR
Moss, Celia	023	1896	WB-A/127	AR
Moss, Elizabeth	089	1857	WB-1/170	
Moss, Grace	028	1771	Orig. Only	SS/AR
Moss, Henry	023	1879	WB-A/18	
Moss, Howell	044	1825	WB-9/393	CTY
Moss, Howell	025	1887	WB-A/62	AR
Moss, Howell C.	105	1899	WB-3/381	AR
Moss, James	100	1809	WB-15/80	AR
Moss, James	099	1794	RB-3/17	AR
Moss, John	022	1831	WB-B/215	AR
Moss, John B.	081	1836	WB-7/2	AR
Moss, John B.	016	1888	WB-3/572	AR
Moss, John D.	044	1881	WB-23/419	CTY
Moss, Jordan D.	044	1873	WB-23/75	CTY
Moss, Joseph W.	065	1893	WB-M/147	AR
Moss, Martin	026	1895	WB-2/494	AR
Moss, Michael	005	1809	WB-2/110	AR
Moss, Reuben	044	1819	WB-8/230	CTY
Moss, Richard	047	1817	WB-3/597	AR
Moss, Richard A.	044	1861	WB-21/365	CTY
Moss, Samuel	044	1844	WB-16/66	CTY
Moss, Sarah P.	044	c1858	WB-23/18	CTY
Moss, Thomas	098	1887	WB-A/28	CTY
Moss, Thomas	092	1828	WB-4/13	AR
Moss, Thomas H.	039	1863	WB-R/397	AR
Moss, Wiley	099	1893	WB-C/190	AR
Moss, William	044	1762	Orig. Only	CTY
Moss, William	054	c1826	WB-2/48	
Mosteller, Harriet	021	1899	WB-3/253	AR
Mosteller, John	021	1891	WB-2/514	AR
Mosteller, Jonas	060	1879	WB-4/207	AR
Mosteller, Peter	060	1814	Orig. Only	AR
Mostiller, Daniel	064	1891	WB-2/272	AR
Mostiller, Jacob	021	c1885	WB-2/393	AR
Motheral, Robert	065	1818	WB-E/22	AR
Motherel, Robert	073	1770	WB-A/109	
Motherly, Isaac	032	1862	WB-2/219	AR
Motley, Jordan L.	020	1885	WB-A/460	CTY
Motley, Paschall W.	100	1860	WB-49/283	AR
Motley, Ransom	089	1885	WB-2/122	AR
Motley, Robert	016	1854	WB-1/236	AR
Motley, Robert	047	1795	WB-3/254	AR
Motley, Tabitha	047	1827	WB-4/30	AR
Motly, Thomas	067	1832	089 WB-1/75	
Moton, Nancy M.	078	1877	WB-19/122	AR
Motsinger, Christina	032	1895	WB-4/256	AR
Mott, Benjamin	070	1796	WB-C/274	AR
Mott, Benjamin	070	1850	WB-C/505	AR
Mott, Ruth	070	1824	WB-C/296	AR
Mott, Thomas S.W.	060	c1865	Orig. Only	AR-Copy
Mott, Thomas S.W.	054	1898	WB-6/148	CTY
Mott, Willett	031	1870	WB-1/3	
Motz, Caleb	060	1896	WB-5/14	AR
Motz, Jacob	085	c1793	WB-E/62	AR
Motz, John M.	060	1840	WB-2/52	AR
Motzinger, Filex	085	1791	WB-C/21	AR
Moughom, Sarah	071	1837	WB-4/150	AR
Moughon, Peyton	071	1822	WB-3/267	AR
Moules, Charles	009	1841	OB-D/171	AR
Moulton, Abraham	029	1821	WB-B/63	
Mound, Will	030	1803	WB-2/221	
Mounteague, Elizabeth	077	1757	SS 879/224	SS/AR
Mounticue, Thomas	077	c1750	Orig. Only	SS/AR
Mouser, Fed	021	1881	WB-2/238	Nunc.
Mowbry, William H.	054	1858	WB-3/127	AR
Mowery, Alexander	085	1895	WB-3/85	CTY
Mowery, Frederick	085	1855	WB-K/206	AR
Mowery, Margaret	085	1861	WB-K/285	AR
Mowery, Peter	085	1852	WB-K/144	AR
Mowra, John	085	1819	WB-H/5	AR
Mowre, Frederick	085	1814	WB-G/334	AR
Mowre, Rudolph	085	1811	WB-G/174	AR
Moxley, Alfred	004	1888	Orig. Only	AR
Moxley, Nathaniel	004	1898	WB-A/200	AR
Moxley, Zachriah	004	1873	Orig. Only	AR
Moy, John	030	1735	LGB-4/#9	SS/AR
Moye, Abraham D.	079	1861	WB-1/74	AR
Moye, Alfred	079	c1859	WB-1/85	AR
Moye, George	028	1823	WB-C/239	
Moye, Irwin	037	1832	WB-F/137	AR
Moye, James W.	079	c1855	Orig. Only	AR-Copy
Moye, John	028	1812	WB-C/45	
Moye, Joseph	085	c1799	WB-D/209	AR
Moye, M. T.	105	1900	WB-3/401	AR
Moye, Marmaduke	028	1843	WB-D/74	AR
Moye, Thomas	047	1786	WB-3/102	AR
Moye, Thomas	024	1723	SS 876/103	SS/AR
Moye, William	037	1848	WB-F/389	AR
Moyers, Philip	085	c1789	WB-D/216	AR
Mozingo, John	103	1886	WB-1/381	AR
Mozingo, Lelia	056	1842	WB-1/543	AR
Mozingo, Mark, Jr.	103	1894	WB-2/85	AR
Muckleroy, Adam	009	1862	OB-L/430	AR

Name	Co.	Date	Recorded Copy	Original
Muir, Robert	047	1803	WB-3/391	AR
Muir, William	047	1795	WB-3/243	AR
Muirhead, Claud	020	1782	RB-A/192	AR
Mukel, Rebecca	008	1729	LGB-4/#15	
Mulder, Griffin	030	1820	WB-3/293	
Mulford, David	065	1841	WB-H/30	AR
Mulford, Elizabeth	011	c1798	WB-1/414	
Mulford, Ephraim	011	c1805	WB-1/432	
Mulford, Sarah	011	c1824	WB-2/384	
Mulhollan, Martha	073	1836	WB-E/378	AR
Mulhollan, Thomas	073	1796	WB-C/80	AR
Mulinix, Jesse M.	067	1885	WB-2/202	AR
Mulkey, Philip	037	1737	Orig. Only	SS/AR
Mull, Ezra	021	1866	WB-1/224	AR
Mull, Jeremiah	049	1894	WB-2/312	AR
Mull, John	060	1839	WB-2/17	AR
Mull, John	060	1831	WB-1/214	AR
Mull, Margaret	026	1897	WB-2/544	AR
Mull, Mary	060	1841	WB-2/93	AR
Mull, Sarah	014	1890	WB-2/405	CTY
Mull, Thomas	085	1835	WB-H/660	AR
Mullen, Abraham	010	1780	WB-B/156	AR
Mullen, Ann	075	1844	WB-N/185	AR
Mullen, Augustus L.	077	1847	WB-F/328	AR
Mullen, Benjamin	077	1859	WB-F/505	AR
Mullen, Caroline	006	1875	Orig. Only	AR
Mullen, Charles	081	1822	WB-5/96	AR
Mullen, Edwin	060	1861	WB-3/40	AR
Mullen, Elizabeth	018	1897	WB-E/255	AR
Mullen, Francis N.	018	1897	WB-E/257	AR
Mullen, Greenberry	010	1811	WB-F/189	AR
Mullen, Hugh	081	1841	WB-7/387	AR
Mullen, Isaac	077	1743	Orig. Only	SS/AR
Mullen, Jacob	077	1758	SS 880/222	SS/AR
Mullen, James	077	1796	WB-E/69	
Mullen, James Henry	060	1864	WB-3/69	AR
Mullen, James L.	075	c1854	WB-M2/12	AR
Mullen, John F.	060	1888	WB-4/383	AR
Mullen, Joseph	077	1791	WB-C/430	AR
Mullen, Mary Susan	077	1877	WB-H/67	AR
Mullen, Otelia F.	065	1870	WB-K/41	AR
Mullen, Thomas	077	1786	WB-C/330	AR
Mullen, William	060	1883	WB-4/280	AR
Mullen, William A.	075	c1854	WB-M2/54	AR
Mullen, Zadock	077	1813	WB-E/387	AR
Muller, Martin	070	1895	WB-G/391	AR
Mullican, Lewis	032	1836	WB-1/273	
Mullican, Lewis	085	c1796	WB-D/206	AR
Mullin, Nancy	054	c1829	WB-2/91	AR
Mullinax, Brison	026	1899	WB-3/51	AR
Mullington, Richard	011	c1776	WB-1/586	
Mullinix, Jonathan	081	1800	WB-2/61	AR
Mullins, Burges	039	1884	WB-U/327	AR
Mullins, Charles	086	1815	WB-C/21	AR
Mullins, Henry	029	c1861	WB-C/451	
Mullins, James	073	1782	WB-A/249	
Mullins, John	039	c1784	WB-C/87	
Mullins, John	029	1846	WB-C/100	
Mullins, Martin	026	1866	WB-1/393	AR
Mullins, Susan A.	084	1896	WB-F/66	CTY
Mullins, Thomas	084	1817	WB-A/237	CTY
Mullins, Thomas	084	1859	WB-C/291	CTY
Mullins, William	006	1810	WB-A/49	AR
Mullis, Calvin	097	1883	WB-2/230	AR
Mullis, Frances	097	1898	WB-2/556	AR

Name	Co.	Date	Recorded Copy	Original
Mullis, George	054	1889	WB-5/262	CTY
Mullis, George	092	c1832	WB-4/47	
Mullis, James	006	1869	WB-D/86	
Mullis, Stephen	054	1899	WB-6/260	CTY
Mulloy, Edward	046	1801	WB-A/236	AR
Mulloy, James	084	c1790	OW/222	AR
Mumford, Edward	057	1821	WB-B/60	AR
Mumford, James	072	1793	Orig. Only	AR
Mumford, James H.	072	1843	Orig. Only	AR
Mumford, Janet	029	1824	WB-B/124	AR
Mumford, Jehew	072	c1770	RW/L66	AR
Mumford, John	072	1820	WB-A/97	AR
Mumford, Joseph	072	c1778	Orig. Only	AR
Mumford, Joseph	070	1832	WB-AB/288	AR
Mumford, Joseph	072	1732	SS 876/408	SS/AR
Mumford, Lewis	072	1792	Orig. Only	AR
Mumford, Mills	028	1804	WB-B/198	
Mumford, Robinson	029	1817	WB-A/240	AR
Mumford, Robinson	085	1819	WB-H/682	AR
Mumford, Zadock	072	N. D.	WB-A/97	AR-Nunc.
Munce, Ann	070	1857	WB-C/639	AR
Munce, Matthew	070	1855	WB-C/592	AR
Muncrief, William	047	1795	WB-3/242	AR
Muncus, William	092	1806	WB-3/73	AR
Munday, B. J.	054	1887	WB-5/147	CTY
Munday, Eliza	060	1875	WB-4/126	AR
Munday, J. S.	021	1896	WB-3/142	
Munday, Jeremiah	060	1835	WB-1/352	AR
Munday, Jesse	078	1875	WB-19/40	AR
Munday, Joseph M.	021	1887	WB-2/371	
Munday, Samuel	003	1882	WB-B/140	AR
Munden, Ann	077	c1828	WB-F/187	AR
Munden, Benjamin	077	1760	Orig. Only	AR
Munden, Elisha	077	1821	WB-F/39	AR
Munden, John B.	077	1845	WB-F/318	AR
Munden, Stephen	030	1800	WB-2/165	Nunc.
Munden, William	077	1793	WB-C/464	AR-Copy
Mundine, Francis	057	1835	WB-B/126	AR
Mundine, John	057	1792	WB-A/151	AR
Mundine, Kittrel	057	c1791	WB-A/189	AR
Mundine, Mary M.	057	1797	WB-A/165	AR
Mundine, Sarah	057	1799	WB-A/226	AR
Munds, Joseph	077	1832	WB-F/204	
Mundy, William	002	c1688	Orig. Only	SS/AR
Munford, Richard	047	1796	WB-3/268	AR
Mungar, William	071	1797	WB-2/160	AR
Munger, John	071	1849	WB-5/77	AR
Munger, Samuel	071	1801	WB-2/228	AR
Mungo, T. A.	065	1893	WB-M/233	AR
Mungumrey, George	008	1723	Orig. Only	SS/AR
Munn, Edward	067	1877	WB-2/85	AR
Munn, Malinda	029	1886	Orig. Only	AR
Munn, Mary	011	1895	WB-3/69	CTY
Munn, Niell	029	1818	WB-A/247	AR
Munro, Hugh	070	1779	WB-C/263	AR
Munro, Revell	012	c1764	DB-A/33	
Munroe, Archibald	068	1847	WB-B/170	
Munroe, Barbara	029	1830	WB-B/188	AR
Munroe, Francis	068	1865	WB-C/121	
Munroe, James T.	085	c1805	WB-E/94	
Munroe, John	029	1827	WB-B/155	AR
Munroe, John	029	1841	WB-B/357	AR
Munroe, Neill	029	1851	WB-C/193	AR
Munroe, Patrick	029	1797	WB-A/8	AR
Munroe, Peter	029	1888	WB-E/430	AR

Name	Co.	Date	Recorded Copy	Original
Muns, Thomas	024	1694	SS 874.2/42	
Munson, Horace H.	070	1900	WB-H/312	AR
Muntz, Christien	065	c1777	WB-B/119	AR
Munzler, Margaret	065	1900	WB-N/305	AR
Murcheson, Duncan	068	1840	WB-B/130	
Murchinson, Hannah	029	1860	WB-C/424	AR
Murchison, Barbara C.	054	1877	WB-4/243	CTY
Murchison, D. C.	022	1898	WB-F/67	AR
Murchison, Duncan	029	1870	WB-E/15	AR
Murchison, Duncan	068	c1853	WB-C/75	
Murchison, Ida F.	029	1885	011 WB-2/202	
Murchison, Isaac T.	048	1900	WB-1/120	CTY
Murchison, John A.	054	1873	WB-4/107	CTY
Murchison, Kineth	029	1836	WB-B/262	AR
Murchison, Kinnith	068	1834	WB-B/88	
Murchison, Rebecca	068	1899	WB-E/22	
Murchison, Roderick	038	1860	WB-1/158	AR
Murchison, Sarah	054	1898	WB-6/168	CTY
Murdah, John	054	1836	WB-2/158	AR
Murdah, John	054	c1806	Orig. Only	AR
Murdah, John	054	1811	WB-1/276	AR
Murdaugh, Joseph	077	1768	WB-C/64	AR
Murdaugh, Samuel	077	1788	WB-C/377	AR
Murden, David	022	1873	WB-E/84	AR
Murden, L. Uphan	099	1857	RB-30/355	AR
Murden, Robert	075	1759	WB-H/1	AR
Murdin, Jeremiah	075	1750	Orig. Only	SS/AR
Murdoch, Agness	054	1845	WB-2/319	AR
Murdoch, Alexander	003	1866	WB-A/10	AR
Murdoch, David	013	1891	WB-C/108	AR
Murdoch, Elizabeth	073	1814	WB-D/399	AR
Murdoch, James	054	c1827	WB-2/147	AR
Murdoch, John	073	1796	WB-C/84	AR
Murdoch, Margaret	SC	1883	013 WB-B/470	013 AR
Murdoch, Sarah S.	085	1895	WB-3/68	CTY
Murdoch, William	013	1865	WB-A/240	AR
Murdock, Andrew	073	1817	WB-D/498	
Murdock, Andrew C.	073	1876	WB-H/137	CTY
Murdock, David	028	1795	WB-A/345	
Murdock, Eleanor	054	c1859	Orig. Only	AR
Murdock, Isaac R.	003	1881	WB-B/132	
Murdock, James H.	073	1900	WB-I/168	CTY
Murdock, Joseph W.	054	1855	WB-3/89	AR
Murdock, Margaret	073	c1837	Orig. Only	AR
Murdock, Thomas C.	054	1898	WB-6/138	CTY
Murdock, W. M.	054	1894	WB-5/527	CTY
Murfey, Bridget	028	1775	Orig. Only	AR
Murford, William	070	1782	WB-C/269	AR
Murley, Ann	029	1845	WB-C/81	AR
Murph, Elizabeth	016	1873	WB-3/86	AR
Murph, Jacob B.	089	1895	WB-2/260	AR
Murphey, Alethhea	028	1796	WB-B/6	
Murphey, Alexander	020	1823	RB-I/197	AR
Murphey, Archibald	020	1818	RB-H/126	AR
Murphey, Archibald	020	c1816	SC/02641	AR-Copy
Murphey, Arthur	039	c1803	WB-B/162	
Murphey, Daniel	085	1813	WB-G/292	AR
Murphey, Edmond	028	c1745	SS 877/34	SS/AR
Murphey, Elizabeth	032	c1858	WB-2/161	
Murphey, Guilford	028	1849	WB-D/160	AR
Murphey, James	054	1838	WB-2/182	AR
Murphey, James Gray	039	1864	WB-R/716	AR
Murphey, Joseph	092	1816	WB-3/121	AR
Murphey, M. M.	056	1866	WB-2/77	AR
Murphey, Martha E.H.	039	1891	WB-U/537	AR
Murphey, Moses	028	1798	WB-B/39	
Murphey, Nicholas	039	1817	WB-F/44	AR
Murphey, Timmothy	035	1787	WB-A/325	AR
Murphey, William	028	1794	WB-A/312	
Murphey, William	037	1737	Orig. Only	SS/AR
Murphey, William	075	1846	WB-N/197	AR
Murphree, Daniel	022	1771	Orig. Only	AR
Murphree, James	039	1826	WB-H/144	AR
Murphrey, Joseth H.	056	1899	WB-4/177	AR
Murphy, Anne M.	085	1896	WB-3/138	CTY
Murphy, Archibald	083	1837	WB-1/305	AR
Murphy, Barbara	035	1802	WB-A/331	AR
Murphy, Barbara	083	1860	WB-2/160	AR
Murphy, Byrd	039	1871	WB-U/51	AR
Murphy, Caroline	099	1883	WB-A/418	AR
Murphy, Caroline W.	099	c1883	Copy	047 AR
Murphy, Clara P.	013	1897	WB-D/30	AR
Murphy, Cornelius	070	1857	WB-C/649	AR
Murphy, David	029	1885	076 WB-D/351	076 AR
Murphy, David	029	1885	WB-E/350	AR
Murphy, Duncan	083	c1802	WB-1/74	AR
Murphy, Eliza F.	035	1900	WB-5/12	AR
Murphy, Elizabeth	085	1868	WB-L/32	AR
Murphy, Esther	054	c1862	Orig. Only	AR
Murphy, Grizella	029	1881	WB-E/243	AR
Murphy, H. J.	073	1899	WB-I/162	CTY
Murphy, Hugh	011	c1835	WB-1/25	
Murphy, Isabella	029	1890	WB-E/495	AR
Murphy, Isabella	085	1868	WB-L/30	CTY
Murphy, James	021	1887	WB-2/386	
Murphy, James	060	1785	Orig. Only	AR
Murphy, James	039	c1860	WB-Q/698	
Murphy, James A.	070	1870	WB-E/208	AR
Murphy, James, Sr.	020	1861	RB-S/415	AR
Murphy, Jane E.	085	1872	WB-1/96	CTY
Murphy, Jeremiah	028	1752	DB-5/273	SS/AR
Murphy, Jeremiah H.	IA	1894	078 WB-19/504	
Murphy, John	045	1889	WB-1/201	AR
Murphy, John	082	c1801	WB-1/84	AR
Murphy, John	070	1819	WB-C/290	AR
Murphy, John	029	1816	WB-A/231	AR
Murphy, John	029	1845	WB-C/85	
Murphy, John	039	1885	WB-U/356	AR
Murphy, John	085	1848	WB-K/69	AR
Murphy, John	029	1800	WB-A/37	AR
Murphy, John A.	011	1893	WB-3/53	CTY
Murphy, John H.	047	1882	WB-6/287	AR
Murphy, John L.	046	1894	WB-F/311	AR
Murphy, John S.	001	1898	WB-3/200	AR
Murphy, Jonathan	046	1867	WB-D/356	AR
Murphy, Joseph S.	070	1881	WB-E/424	AR
Murphy, Josiah T.H.	103	c1873	WB-1/58	AR
Murphy, Laura	013	1888	WB-B/492	AR
Murphy, Lee	004	1897	WB-A/196	AR
Murphy, Malachi C.	024	1895	WB-E/241	AR
Murphy, Martin	073	1849	WB-F/432	AR
Murphy, Mary	057	1831	WB-B/111	AR
Murphy, Mary	070	1853	WB-C/556	AR
Murphy, Mary Ann	070	1889	WB-F/305	AR
Murphy, Miles	084	1821	WB-A/257	CTY
Murphy, Murdoch	083	c1820	WB-1/205	AR
Murphy, Nancy	083	1850	WB-2/22	AR
Murphy, Nicey	020	1889	WB-B/41	CTY
Murphy, Nottingham	PA	1883	014 WB-2/241	014 CTY
Murphy, Owen	094	1776	Orig. Only	060 AR

Name	Co.	Date	Recorded Copy	Original
Murphy, Patrick	070	1874	WB-E/287	AR
Murphy, Robert	070	1819	WB-C/291	AR
Murphy, Robert	070	1840	WB-AB/338	AR
Murphy, Robert	085	1892	WB-2/531	CTY
Murphy, Robert C.	070	1867	WB-D/224	AR
Murphy, Samuel	035	1886	WB-4/186	AR
Murphy, Thomas	057	1826	WB-B/98	AR
Murphy, Thomas	028	1746	SS 877/327	SS/AR
Murphy, Thomas K.	035	1899	WB-4/546	AR
Murphy, Timothy	035	1827	WB-A/328	AR
Murphy, Tunnal	045	1894	WB-1/321	AR
Murphy, William	106	c1877	WB-2/77	
Murphy, William	060	1779	Orig. Only	AR
Murphy, William	100	1785	WB-4/136	AR
Murphy, William	085	1867	WB-L/24	AR
Murphy, William	070	1869	WB-E/167	AR
Murr, Catie S.	016	1897	WB-4/251	AR
Murray, Aaron W.	076	1885	WB-A1/58	AR
Murray, Andrew	072	1746	SS 878/74	SS/AR
Murray, Arthur	035	1814	WB-A/344	AR
Murray, Asa	070	1827	WB-C/301	AR
Murray, Caroline	NY	1890	Copy	050 AR
Murray, Daniel	053	c1817	RW-1/524	
Murray, Daniel	035	1865	WB-3/94	AR
Murray, Daniel	053	1866	WB-10/20	AR
Murray, Edmund	089	1886	WB-2/170	AR
Murray, Eli	001	1870	WB-2/6	AR
Murray, Guilford	035	1889	WB-4/347	AR
Murray, Hiram	035	1877	WB-4/119	AR
Murray, Hosea	035	1861	WB-3/36	AR
Murray, J. L.	013	1895	WB-C/463	AR
Murray, James	073	1821	WB-D/597	AR
Murray, James	035	1797	WB-A/333	AR
Murray, James	035	1860	WB-3/15	AR
Murray, James	073	1884	WB-H/347	CTY
Murray, James	035	1828	WB-A/304	AR
Murray, James	072	1838	Orig. Only	AR
Murray, James	001	1894	WB-2/584	AR
Murray, James	050	1847	WB-1/21	CTY
Murray, Jane	035	1874	WB-4/84	AR
Murray, Jane	022	1798	RB-2/131	AR
Murray, John	070	1895	WB-G/417	AR
Murray, John	073	1800	WB-D/12	AR
Murray, John	073	c1837	Orig. Only	AR
Murray, John B.	NY	1890	Copy	050 AR
Murray, John W.	035	1889	WB-4/342	AR
Murray, Jonathan	072	c1808	WB-A/96	AR
Murray, Joseph L.	038	1900	WB-4/237	AR
Murray, Margaret	100	1825	WB-28/139	AR
Murray, Maria	NY	1852	Copy	050 AR
Murray, Maria F.	073	1873	WB-H/75	CTY
Murray, Mary	085	1757	WB-A/118	AR
Murray, Nancy	001	1874	WB-2/96	AR
Murray, Nathan	035	1886	WB-4/289	AR
Murray, Nathan	035	1864	WB-3/87	AR
Murray, Nicanor	070	1856	WB-C/611	AR
Murray, Patience	013	1882	WB-B/274 & 297	AR
Murray, Robert A.	013	1876	WB-B/133	AR
Murray, Sarah	053	1820	WB-4/85	
Murray, Sophronia	050	1900	WB-2/354	
Murray, Susan M.	076	1897	WB-A1/214	AR
Murray, Thomas	070	1812	WB-AB/183	AR
Murray, Thomas	044	1851	WB-18/241	CTY
Murray, Thomas	085	c1809	WB-G/121	AR

Name	Co.	Date	Recorded Copy	Original
Murray, Thomas	072	c1785	WI/L31	AR
Murray, Thomas	070	1864	WB-D/155	AR
Murray, Timothy	053	c1803	RW-1/366	AR
Murray, W. G.	053	1888	WB-11/217	AR
Murray, Wallis B.	086	1866	WB-E/469	AR
Murray, Washington	NY	1867	Copy	050 AR
Murray, William	069	1846	WB-1/494	AR
Murray, William	010	1806	WB-F/23	AR
Murray, William	053	c1825	Orig. Only	AR
Murray, William	001	1865	WB-1/249	AR
Murray, William	086	1832	WB-D/147	AR
Murray, William	073	1805	WB-D/143	AR
Murray, William H.	069	1864	039 WB-R/751	039 AR
Murray, William S.	013	1871	WB-B/42	AR
Murrel, George	032	1842	WB-1/388	
Murrel, Judah	005	1816	WB-2/113	AR
Murrell, Barnaby	071	1791	WB-1/426	AR
Murrell, Benjamin	071	1794	WB-2/63	AR
Murrell, Elijah	072	1865	WB-3/9	AR
Murrell, John	030	1816	WB-3/85	
Murrell, Mark	071	1807	WB-2/349	AR
Murrell, Robert	100	1893	Orig. Only	AR-Copy
Murrell, Robert M.	017	c1859	WB-A/120	AR
Murrell, Zachariah	011	c1807	WB-1/440	
Murrey, John, Sr.	069	1845	WB-1/474	AR
Murrie, James	020	1870	WB-A/56	CTY
Murrill, Alford	072	1900	WB-4/420	AR
Murrill, Ann	057	1886	WB-C/140	AR
Murrill, Elijah	072	1893	WB-4/293	AR
Murrill, John	072	1800	WB-A/84	AR
Murrill, John F.	021	1891	WB-2/559	AR
Murrill, Martin	072	1896	WB-4/321	AR
Murrill, Timothy	072	c1760	RW/L52	AR
Murrill, William	072	1831	WB-1/88	AR
Murrun, John	086	1812	WB-B/267	AR
Murry, Dominique	024	1806	WB-B/224	AR
Murry, Jacob	073	1882	WB-H/306	CTY
Murry, James	039	1807	WB-C/62	
Murry, Lucy	047	1816	WB-3/587	AR
Murry, William B.	073	18719	WB-H/47	CTY
Murtaugh, Margaret	070	1807	WB-AB/99	AR
Murtland, Robert	065	1793	WB-B/133	AR
Mury, Betholemy	035	1781	WB-A/330	AR
Musclewhite, Milbea	083	c1831	WB-1/302	
Muse, Daniel H.	068	1866	WB-C/138	
Muse, James	029	c1758	DB-1/241	
Muse, James	028	1860	WB-D/329	AR
Muse, James	029	c1780	Orig. Only	AR
Muse, James B.	068	1865	WB-C/114	
Muse, John	028	1803	WB-B/170	
Muse, John	028	1793	WB-A/292	
Muse, L. L.	068	1883	WB-D/170	
Muse, Levi	028	1816	WB-C/130	
Muse, Malachi	028	1838	WB-C/416	
Muse, William	028	1843	Orig. Only	AR
Muse, William T.	075	1823	WB-M1/375	AR
Musgrave, Caleb	103	1791	WI-A/237	AR
Musgrave, Charity	103	1827	RD-5/382	
Musgrave, Doctor H.	056	1856	WB-1/694	AR
Musgrave, Elisabeth	103	1828	RD-5/455	AR
Musgrave, G. John	075	c1854	WB-M2/18	AR
Musgrave, Isabella	103	1820	RD-4/304	
Musgrave, James	103	1824	RD-5/124	AR
Musgrave, Jesse	103	1808	WI-B/403	AR
Musgrave, John	103	1824	RD-5/95	AR

Name	Co.	Date	Recorded Copy	Original
Musgrave, Nancy	103	1830	RD-6/94	AR
Musgrave, Richard	103	1826	RD-5/262	AR
Musgrave, Thomas	103	1794	WI-A/461	AR
Musgrave, William H.	103	1864	RD-13/747	AR
Musgrove, John	070	1747	DB-C/127	
Musick, George	086	1809	WB-B/225	AR
Muslewhite, Dorcas	005	1868	WB-C/263	AR
Muslewhite, Elender S.	029	1897	WB-F/118	AR
Musselwhite, Alfred	083	1881	WB-3/222	AR
Musselwhite, Jesse	083	c1821	WB-1/368	AR
Mussgenug, Jacob	016	1803	WB-A/47	AR
Musslewhite, Leonard	097	1849	WB-1/55	AR
Mustin, John	038	1874	WB-2/165	AR
Mustion, John	005	1809	WB-2/111	AR
Mustlewhite, Thomas	011	c1770	WB-1/553	
Muter, Margaret	070	1810	WB-AB/132	AR
Mutor, Robert	070	1806	WB-AB/95	AR
Mutter, Thomas	044	c1799	WB-4/353	CTY
Myatt, Isaac B.	099	1891	WB-B/501	AR
Myatt, Mark	099	1821	RB-17/227	AR
Myatt, Mary	099	1879	WB-A/46	AR
Myatt, Nathan I.	099	1859	RB-31/257	AR
Myatt, W. Alfred	099	1879	WB-D/78	AR
Myers, Annie E.	077	1887	WB-H/164	AR
Myers, B. C.	106	1885	WB-2/216	AR
Myers, Benjamin	032	c1867	Orig. Only	AR
Myers, Christian	085	1812	WB-G/237	AR
Myers, David	032	1892	WB-4/163	AR
Myers, David	005	1847	WB-B/224	AR
Myers, David	SC	1835	050 WB-1/38	050 CTY
Myers, Elias	060	1805	Orig. Only	AR
Myers, Elizabeth	054	1876	WB-4/224	CTY
Myers, Eveline J.	059	1894	WB-B/104	
Myers, Jane M.	009	1876	WB-1/168	CTY
Myers, Joel G.	097	1864	WB-1/232	AR
Myers, John	060	1822	Orig. Only	AR
Myers, John	032	c1844	WB-2/37	
Myers, John G.	010	1899	WB-I/580	
Myers, John G. B.	009	1896	WB-2/87	CTY
Myers, Margaret	054	1886	WB-5/114	CTY
Myers, Marmaduke	005	1831	WB-B/16	AR
Myers, Mary	085	1872	WB-1/115	
Myers, Mary	085	c1784	WB-B/157	AR
Myers, Mary H.	009	1871	WB-1/76	AR
Myers, Michael	085	1801	WB-E/59	AR
Myers, Michal	085	1771	WB-A/110	AR
Myers, Nathan	010	1877	WB-I/83	
Myers, Near	005	1886	Orig. Only	AR
Myers, Peter	060	1794	Orig. Only	AR
Myers, Shepard	005	1884	WB-D/166	AR
Myers, Thomas	032	1893	WB-4/198	AR
Myers, W. R.	009	1895	WB-2/85	CTY
Myers, Whitaker	077	1897	WB-H/302	AR
Myers, William B.	009	1886	WB-1/404	CTY
Myers, William J.	047	1895	WB-7/143	AR
Myers, William J.	032	1898	WB-4/347	AR
Myers, William J.	010	1895	WB-I/422	AR
Myrick, Ben R.	051	1892	WB-C/431	AR
Myrick, Charles	100	1852	WB-42/9	AR
Myrick, Edmund	047	1834	WB-4/106	AR
Myrick, Francis	015	1777	100 WB-2/100	AR
Myrick, G. W.	100	1882	WB-51/171	AR
Myrick, George	100	1805	WB-13/68	
Myrick, Hardy	100	1853	WB-42/121	AR
Myrick, Jesse	100	1848	WB-40/47	AR
Myrick, Owen F.	039	1886	WB-U/382	AR
Myrick, Polly	039	1874	WB-U/132	AR
Myrick, Walter	051	1871	WB-C/46	AR
Myrick, William	100	1795	WB-8/86	
Myrover, Henry	029	1872	WB-E/56	AR
Nabb, James W.	068	1819	WB-A/299	Nunc.
Nadal, Edward M.	105	1896	WB-3/184	AR
Nading, John	038	1870	WB-2/30	AR
Nading, Joseph	038	1883	WB-2/461	AR
Nail, Margaret	085	c1802	WB-C/255	AR
Nails, Silas	009	1803	OWB/421	AR-Nunc.
Nall, Frederick	073	1768	WB-A/79	
Nall, John	022	1782	Orig. Only	AR
Nall, John	099	1828	RB-20/181	AR
Nall, Mary	068	1847	WB-B/163	
Nall, Nicholas	068	1833	WB-B/83	
Nall, Richard	099	1796	RB-3/269	AR
Nance, Anne	099	1857	RB-30/301	AR
Nance, Buckner	005	1813	WB-2/114	AR
Nance, Daniel	081	1784	WB-1/13	AR
Nance, Daniel	011	c1802	WB-1/436	
Nance, Edward J.	083	1878	WB-3/153	AR
Nance, Edward W.	027	1819	WB-A/3	AR
Nance, Elizabeth	081	1860	WB-11/525	AR
Nance, Frances	097	c1875	Orig. Only	AR
Nance, George	099	1844	RB-25/457	AR
Nance, Giles	099	1811	RB-10/9	AR
Nance, Hubbard	081	1892	WB-16/246	
Nance, John	044	1880	WB-23/378	CTY
Nance, John	065	1838	WB-E/168	AR
Nance, John A.	097	1870	WB-2/45	AR
Nance, Joseph	011	c1820	WB-1/23	
Nance, Joshua L.	083	1874	WB-3/80	AR
Nance, Jourdan	081	1843	WB-8/17	AR
Nance, Marshall	081	1859	WB-11/305	
Nance, Polly	097	1870	WB-2/34	AR
Nance, Robert	044	1816	WB-7/590	CTY
Nance, Sarah	099	1828	RB-20/290	AR
Nance, Thomas	081	1811	WB-3/293	AR
Nance, Thomas W.	001	1898	WB-3/225	AR
Nance, William	060	1854	WB-2/375	AR
Nance, William	104	c1826	WB-4/114	AR
Nanney, James	086	1859	WB-E/368	AR
Nanney, John	086	1887	WB-F/314	AR
Nanney, Martin	064	1864	WB-1/90	AR
Nanney, Mary	086	1878	WB-F/118	AR
Nanney, Nancy Jane	086	1899	WB-G/14	AR
Nanney, Samuel	086	1876	WB-F/87	AR
Nanney, Thomas	086	1856	WB-E/320	AR
Nansworthy, William	037	1781	WB-B/83	AR
Nantz, Clement R.	065	1863	WB-J/151	AR
Nantz, William J.	040	1877	WB-2/120	AR
Napier, Moses C.	084	1855	WB-C/210	CTY
Naron, Elizabeth	085	1830	WB-H/486	AR-Nunc.
Narron, Gilly	056	1844	WB-1/561	AR
Narsworthy, John	071	1789	WB-2/69	
Nash, Abner	NY	1786	028 WB-A/146	
Nash, Anna	028	1817	WB-C/140	AR
Nash, Caroline	099	1885	WB-B/60	
Nash, Chloe	018	1866	WB-D/81	AR
Nash, Demsey	075	1802	WB-M1/63	AR
Nash, E. B.	089	c1876	Orig. Only	AR
Nash, Elizabeth	018	1869	WB-E/3	AR
Nash, Flora	070	1900	WB-H/287	AR
Nash, Francis	012	1777	DB-B/98	

Name	Co.	Date	Recorded Copy	Original
Nash, Frederick	073	1859	WB-G/213	AR
Nash, George	099	1850	RB-27/115	AR
Nash, Griffin	005	1846	WB-B/209	AR
Nash, J. B.	099	1885	WB-B/59	AR
Nash, James	018	18854	WB-D/1	
Nash, John	099	1817	RB-13/323	AR
Nash, John C.	018	1871	WB-E/33	AR
Nash, John W.	070	1874	WB-E/268	AR-Nunc.
Nash, Joseph	097	1900	WB-3/55	AR
Nash, Josiah	018	1852	WB-C/359	
Nash, Josiah	075	1771	WB-H/128	AR
Nash, Lydia	075	1829	WB-N/56	AR
Nash, Margaret	020	1850	RB-Q/453	AR
Nash, Mary G.	073	1864	WB-G/422	CTY
Nash, Michael	005	1842	WB-B/140	AR
Nash, Nancy	097	1850	WB-1/69	AR
Nash, Richard	097	1858	WB-1/144	AR
Nash, Sallie	030	c1863	WB-5/10	AR
Nash, Sally K.	073	1894	WB-I/16	CTY
Nash, Samuel	018	1891	WB-E/205	AR
Nash, Solly	018	1834	WB-C/153	
Nash, Solomon W.	070	1846	WB-AB/451	AR
Nash, Thomas	024	1769	WB-1/30	
Nash, Thomas S.	018	1872	WB-E/40	AR
Nash, William	020	1808	RB-F/1	AR
Nasworthy, Issabel	071	1781	WB-1/236	
Nasworthy, William	071	1780	WB-1/222	
Nation, Christopher	081	1801	WB-2/84	AR
Nation, John	046	1774	WB-A/277	AR
Nation, John H.	092	1898	WB-6/485	AR
Nation, Thomas	092	1865	WB-5/78	AR
Naugle, Sylvanus	021	1887	WB-2/389	
Naule, Patrick	009	c1736	SS 877/238	
Nayler, Richard	002	1696	Orig. Only	SS/AR
Naylor, Benjamin	092	1850	WB-4/306	AR
Naylor, John	033	1844	WB-1/60	AR
Neagle, Andrew	040	1865	WB-1/178	
Neagle, John	060	1829	WB-1/150	AR
Neagle, John	060	1834	WB-1/296	AR
Neal, Asa	090	1889	WB-6/219	AR
Neal, Barre	028	1792	WB-A/264	AR
Neal, Benedick	053	1829	WB-4/520	AR
Neal, Benjamin	053	1793	RW-1/227	AR
Neal, Charles E.	037	1887	WB-H/89	AR
Neal, Chloe C.	039	N. D.	WB-N/355	AR
Neal, Conrad	090	1841	WB-4/78	AR
Neal, Edward	100	1821	WB-23/213	AR
Neal, Edward S.	041	051	WB-A/270	
Neal, Elizabeth	039	c1827	WB-L/193	AR
Neal, Ervin	050	1894	WB-2/195	CTY
Neal, Henry	073	1826	WB-E/112	AR
Neal, Henry	036	1897	WB-A/410	CTY
Neal, Henry	012	1783	DB-B/171	AR
Neal, Jaby H.	009	1871	WB-1/92	CTY
Neal, Jacob	070	1764	WB-C/307	AR
Neal, James	022	1834	WB-C/5	AR
Neal, Jeremiah	039	c1796	WB-B/31	
Neal, John	038	c1853	WB-1/70	AR
Neal, John	086	1848	Orig. Only	AR
Neal, John	039	1861	WB-R/191	AR
Neal, John	100	1827	WB-31/69	AR
Neal, John D.	086	1824	WB-D/26	AR
Neal, John P.	020	1858	RB-S/66	AR
Neal, John W.	026	1894	WB-2/479	AR
Neal, John, Sr.	035	1805	WB-A/366	AR
Neal, Joseph W.	084	1863	WB-C/373	CTY
Neal, Leacy	100	1867	WB-50/240	AR
Neal, Leonidas	039	c1855	WB-0/345	
Neal, Martha	073	c1797	Orig. Only	AR
Neal, Mary T.	084	1896	WB-F/51	CTY
Neal, Moses	039	1826	WB-H/153	AR
Neal, Nancy	084	1857	WB-C/256	CTY
Neal, Nancy	084	1899	WB-F/162	CTY
Neal, Nasa J.	068	c1893	022 WB-F/226	022 AR
Neal, Nasa J.	068	1893	WB-D/393	CTY
Neal, Philemon H.	084	1883	WB-E/267	CTY
Neal, Quincy F.	006	1893	WB-E/259	AR
Neal, Ralph	100	1804	WB-12/336	AR
Neal, Samuel J.	064	1889	WB-2/199	AR
Neal, Sarah	040	1896	WB-2/503	AR
Neal, Thomas	090	1832	WB-3/240	AR
Neal, Toney	064	1878	WB-2/68	AR
Neal, William	084	1887	WB-E/372	CTY
Neal, William D.	038	1876	WB-2/240	AR
Neal, Zachariah	020	1850	RB-Q/370	AR
Neale, Abner	028	1772	Orig. Only	SS/AR
Neale, Abner	028	1783	Orig. Only	AR
Neale, Abner P.	009	1850	OB-G/221	AR
Neale, Ann G.	009	1859	OB-K/520	AR
Neale, Charles	002	c1699	SS 874.2/126	SS/AR
Neale, Christopher	028	1784	WB-A/75	AR
Neale, Henry	N	1735	SS 877/196	SS/AR
Neale, Henry H.	012	1824	WB-B/132	AR-Nunc.
Neale, Nancy	012	c1790	Orig. Only	AR
Neale, Phillip	028	1818	WB-C/159	AR
Neale, Samuel	012	c1773	DB-B/6	
Neale, Thomas	012	1797	WB-B/57	AR
Neale, Thomas	012	1790	Orig. Only	AR-Nunc.
Nealey, Wesley	036	1898	WB-A/445	CTY
Nealy, John	073	1815	WB-D/455	AR
Nealy, Peggy	020	1820	RB-H/359	AR
Nealy, Sarah L.	040	1897	WB-2/542	AR
Near, Arques	028	1877	WB-E/154	
Nease, George	073	1840	WB-F/60	AR
Nease, Jacob	001	1863	WB-1/210	AR
Neathercut, Lofton	035	1844	Orig. Only	AR
Neathery, John B.	099	1894	WB-C/268	AR
Neazey, Ezekiel	073	1838	WB-F/14	
Neding, Mathew	090	1807	WB-2/78	AR
Neece, Felty	073	1839	WB-F/21	AR
Needham, Angeline	036	1891	WB-A/197	CTY
Needham, Ferebee	018	1895	WB-E/243	AR
Needham, Franky	081	1828	WB-5/426	AR
Needham, James	092	1899	WB-6/507	AR
Needham, James H.	092	1899	WB-6/523	AR
Needham, John	081	c1798	Orig. Only	AR
Needham, John	018	1878	WB-E/57	AR
Needham, Margaret	081	1892	WB-16/244	
Needham, Margret	075	1730	Orig. Only	AR
Needham, Sallie	018	1898	WB-E/284	AR
Needham, Thomas	075	1743	Orig. Only	SS/AR
Needham, Thomas	081	1808	WB-3/86	
Needham, Thomas	018	1835	WB-C/181	
Neel, Andrew	065	1796	WB-E/43	AR
Neel, Andrew M.	085	1862	WB-K/297	AR
Neel, Elam	054	1882	WB-4/478	CTY
Neel, Elizabeth	016	1866	WB-2/135	
Neel, George C.	065	1898	WB-N/101	AR
Neel, James	065	1792	WB-E/39	AR
Neel, James	085	1861	WB-K/288	AR

Name	Co.	Date	Recorded Copy	Original
Neel, James M.	085	1880	WB-1/550	CTY
Neel, John	016	1848	WB-1/155	
Neel, John, Sr.	016	1835	PQS.5/329	
Neel, Joseph	060	1823	Orig. Only	AR
Neel, Louisa	TN	1879	065 WB-K/358	065 AR
Neel, Mary	065	1840	WB-H/63	AR
Neel, Robert	016	1845	WB-1/60	
Neel, Sally M.	085	1896	WB-3/117	CTY
Neel, Samuel	065	1803	WB-E/46	AR
Neel, Samuel	065	1828	Orig. Only	AR
Neel, Thomas	065	1768	WB-E/35	AR
Neel, William	096	1791	Orig. Only	AR
Neel, William H.	065	1889	WB-L/345	AR
Neeley, John	090	1799	WB-1/135	AR
Neelley, Robert	046	c1787	WB-A/278	AR
Neely, Alexander	085	1832	WB-H/542	AR
Neely, Ann	065	1798	WB-E/45	AR
Neely, Catherine	085	1849	WB-K/101	AR
Neely, Francis	085	1829	WB-H/472	AR
Neely, Franklin	085	1858	WB-K/262	AR
Neely, Holeman	085	1823	WB-H/200	AR
Neely, J. S.	065	1887	WB-L/227	AR
Neely, James	046	1845	WB-C/216	AR
Neely, John	073	1855	WB-G/120	AR
Neely, John	040	1865	WB-1/183	AR
Neely, Margaret	085	1847	WB-K/51	AR
Neely, Martha M.	065	1854	WB-I/231	AR
Neely, Mary	065	1864	WB-J/187	AR
Neely, Mary A.	038	1900	WB-4/240	AR
Neely, Mary S.	016	1857	WB-2/30	
Neely, Moses	065	1837	WB-E/136	AR
Neely, Nathan	085	1828	WB-H/421	AR
Neely, Thomas	065	1794	WB-E/40	AR
Neely, Thomas	065	1796	WB-E/42	AR
Neese, George	046	1842	WB-C/111	AR
Neff, Henry	060	1818	Orig. Only	AR
Negus, William	103	1814	RD-3/111	AR
Neighbors, John H.	056	1899	WB-4/153	AR
Neil, Martha	054	1843	WB-2/284	AR
Neil, Thomas	090	1808	WB-2/93	AR
Neil, William	028	1814	WB-C/83	AR
Neill, Adam	060	1834	WB-1/321	AR
Neill, Agness	054	c1793	WB-1/153	AR
Neill, Andrew	054	c1808	WB-1/339	AR
Neill, Ann	054	1860	Orig. Only	AR
Neill, Gilbraith	054	c1832	WB-2/135	AR
Neill, James	083	1855	WB-2/83	
Neill, James	054	c1793	WB-1/154	AR
Neill, John	054	1866	WB-3/185	AR
Neill, Mary	083	1856	WB-2/87	
Neill, William	060	1829	WB-1/156	AR
Neilson, Alexander	072	1833	WB-1/112	AR
Neilson, Elaxander	070	1785	WB-C/313	AR
Neilson, M. L.	013	1894	WB-C/295	AR
Neilson, Thomas	070	1758	DB-D/355	AR
Neilson, William	013	1832	WB-A/9	
Neisler, Daniel	016	1830	PQS.5/95	
Neisler, Nicholas	016	1855	WB-1/251	
Neithercut, William	072	1790	Orig. Only	AR
Neley, William	020	1783	RB-A/235	AR-Nunc.
Nelloms, Meredith	047	1799	WB-3/329	
Nelms, Eben	039	1839	WB-K/190	
Nelms, Elizabeth	047	1848	WB-4/264	
Nelms, Jeremiah	057	1796	WB-A/153	AR
Nelms, Joshua	047	1769	WB-1/249	

Name	Co.	Date	Recorded Copy	Original
Nelms, Joshua	047	1768	WB-1/227	
Nelms, Josiah	047	1812	WB-3/529	
Nelms, Presley	005	1841	WB-B/128	AR
Nelms, Presly	039	c1797	WB-B/93	
Nelms, Prismus	047	1774	WB-1/365	
Nelms, William	072	c1778	WI/L33	AR
Nelsen, Caroline	028	1897	WB-F/250	
Nelson, Abraham	071	1816	WB-3/174	AR
Nelson, Agnes	084	1822	WB-A/284	CTY
Nelson, Alexander	046	1799	WB-A/280	AR
Nelson, Ann T.	038	1886	WB-2/578	AR
Nelson, Arthur	028	1778	Orig. Only	AR
Nelson, Austin R.	090	1893	WB-6/322	AR
Nelson, Azariah	020	1864	RB-T/24	CTY
Nelson, Benjamin	028	1801	WB-B/126	AR
Nelson, Benjamin	009	1814	OWB/473	AR
Nelson, Caleb	079	1862	WB-1/88	AR
Nelson, D. B.	050	1895	WB-2/227	CTY
Nelson, David	073	1825	WB-E/91	AR
Nelson, Edward	028	1839	WB-C/439	AR
Nelson, Edward	028	1842	WB-D/46	
Nelson, Eli	028	1785	WB-A/98	AR
Nelson, Elizabeth	054	c1790	WB-1/150	AR
Nelson, Elizabeth	054	c1815	WB-1/393	AR
Nelson, Francis	028	1891	WB-E/563	
Nelson, Francis	028	1799	WB-B/89	AR
Nelson, Garrett	009	1856	OB-K/183	AR
Nelson, George	046	1802	WB-A/282	AR
Nelson, George	085	c1809	WB-G/125	
Nelson, George	028	1825	WB-C/264	AR
Nelson, Isaac	090	1829	WB-3/202	
Nelson, James	037	1767	WB-A/152	AR
Nelson, James	047	1872	WB-6/68	AR
Nelson, James	046	1844	WB-C/173	AR
Nelson, James	020	1832	RB-M/84	AR
Nelson, James	028	1827	WB-C/294	AR
Nelson, James	037	1797	WB-D/17	AR
Nelson, James	073	1799	WB-C/140	AR
Nelson, Jane	073	1864	WB-G/464	CTY
Nelson, John	073	1822	WB-E/21	AR
Nelson, John	028	1821	WB-C/203	AR
Nelson, John	028	1783	Orig. Only	AR
Nelson, John	011	c1779	WB-1/545	Nunc.
Nelson, John H.	019	1876	028 WB-F/288	
Nelson, John H.	019	1876	WB-B/92	AR
Nelson, John S.	028	1833	WB-C/360	AR
Nelson, John W.	079	1888	WB-2/425	AR
Nelson, Joseph	090	1810	WB-2/108	AR
Nelson, Joseph	038	1849	WB-1/21	AR-Copy
Nelson, Josephus	028	1838	WB-C/419	AR
Nelson, Kinchen	063	1881	WB-3/207	
Nelson, Leroy	090	1873	WB-6/35	AR
Nelson, Lucy M.	084	1852	WB-C/139	CTY
Nelson, M. A.	044	1863	WB-22/26	CTY
Nelson, Margaret	046	1821	WB-B/133	AR
Nelson, Mary	029	1897	WB-F/89	AR
Nelson, Mary	019	1799	WB-D/300	AR
Nelson, Mary	028	1866	WB-D/422	AR
Nelson, Matthew	078	1849	WB-13/221	AR
Nelson, Moses	085	1770	WB-A/129	AR
Nelson, Nathan	009	c1822	OWB/480	AR
Nelson, Nimrod	079	1870	WB-2/32	AR
Nelson, Paisley	073	1855	WB-G/119	AR
Nelson, Rebekah	028	1801	WB-B/129	AR
Nelson, Rial	090	1885	WB-6/156	AR

Name	Co.	Date	Recorded Copy	Original
Nelson, Robert	019	1797	WB-D/299	AR
Nelson, Robert	084	c1792	OW/190	AR
Nelson, Robert	073	1790	WB-B/90	AR
Nelson, Sallie T.	078	1884	WB-19/155	AR
Nelson, Samuel	028	1881	WB-E/274	
Nelson, Samuel	022	1871	WB-E/58	AR
Nelson, Samuel	073	1837	WB-E/426	AR
Nelson, Samuel	085	1765	WB-A/133	AR
Nelson, Sarah	028	1895	WB-F/199	
Nelson, Sarah M.	028	1867	WB-D/453	AR
Nelson, Solomon	092	1786	WB-2/66A	
Nelson, Thomas	028	1802	Orig. Only	AR
Nelson, Thomas H.	028	1857	WB-D/286	AR
Nelson, Wiley M.	028	1856	WB-D/257	AR
Nelson, William	085	1818	WB-G/501	AR
Nelson, William	073	1786	WB-A/358	AR
Nelson, William	090	1893	WB-6/315	AR
Nelson, William	019	1824	WB-D/301	AR
Nesbet, John	085	1757	WB-A/130	AR
Nesbet, Milus	054	c1814	WB-1A/144	AR
Nesbett, Joseph	041	1784	WB-1/43	AR
Nesbit, Alexander	054	1861	WB-3/159	AR
Nesbit, Amelia Belk	097	1898	WB-2/531	AR
Nesbit, Millie	097	1891	WB-2/395	AR
Nesbit, William	085	c1799	WB-C/256	AR
Nesbitt, James	SC	c1875	003 WB-B/252	003 AR
Nesbitt, James R.	054	1885	WB-5/56	CTY
Nesbitt, Moses	085	c1778	WB-C/154	AR
Nessfield, John	011	1764	SS 881/280	SS/AR
Nethercut, Nancy	059	1874	WB-A/83	
Nettle, Allen	037	1860	WB-G/184	AR
Nettle, John	037	1830	WB-F/114	AR
Nettle, Mourning	037	1865	WB-G/264	AR
Nettles, Clodisha	079	1854	Orig. Only	AR-Copy
Nettles, Jacob	037	1838	WB-F/216	AR
Nevell, Francis	N	1735	SS 876/106	SS/AR
Nevill, Benjamin	047	1832	WB-4/87	
Nevill, Goodman	073	1871	WB-H/74	CTY
Nevill, Goodman	047	1837	WB-4/154	
Nevill, Hardy	047	1823	WB-3/693	
Nevill, Jesse	073	1810	WB-D/264	AR
Nevill, Jesse, Sr.	047	1819	WB-3/643	
Nevill, Samuel	073	1854	WB-G/73	AR
Neville, A. H.	047	1866	WB-5/152	
Neville, Benjamin	047	1759	SS 881/189	SS/AR
Neville, Charles	073	1893	WB-I/4	CTY
Neville, Lucy A.	047	1874	WB-6/104	AR
Neville, Patrick H.	047	1856	WB-5/15	
Neville, Sarah T.	047	1883	WB-6/305	AR
Nevills, John	044	1785	WB-1/424	CTY
Nevins, Mary	085	1843	WB-I/160	AR
Nevins, Robert	085	1816	WB-G/419	AR
Nevins, William	085	c1800	WB-C/252	AR
New, John	035	1780	WB-A/357	AR
New, John F.	090	1877	WB-6/90	AR
Newall, Sullivan	030	1818	WB-3/99	
Newbell, Richard A.	020	1876	WB-A/204	CTY
Newbern, Hunter	010	1878	WB-I/98	
Newbern, John	010	1899	WB-K/4	
Newberry, Alexander	085	1770	WB-A/127	AR
Newberry, Jeremiah	101	1883	WB-A/104	AR
Newberry, John	101	1881	WB-A/68	
Newberry, John	082	1793	WB-1/39	AR
Newberry, Jonathan	082	1838	WB-2/77	AR
Newberry, Joseph D.	101	1891	WB-A/196	AR
Newberry, William	082	c1789	WB-1/52	AR
Newbery, Jesse	029	1792	Orig. Only	AR
Newbery, John	029	1807	WB-A/115	AR
Newbey, Thomas	044	1798	WB-4/262	CTY
Newbold, Elisha	072	1816	WB-A/100	AR-Nunc.
Newbold, Elizabeth	075	1834	WB-N/96	AR
Newbold, James	077	1881	WB-H/100	AR
Newbold, Leah	072	1804	WB-A/99	AR
Newbold, Levi	072	1857	WB-A/98	AR
Newbold, Levi	072	1802	WB-A/98	AR-Nunc.
Newbold, Levi	072	1871	WB-4/32	AR
Newbold, Miriam	072	1849	WB-2/102	AR
Newborn, Elizabeth	010	1823	WB-G/111	AR
Newborn, Thomas	010	c1813	Orig. Only	AR
Newbould, William	077	1779	WB-C/230	AR
Newbury, Franklin A.	070	1894	WB-G/177	AR
Newby, Benjamin	075	1739	LGB-4/#102	SS/AR
Newby, Benjamin	075	1779	WB-K/29	
Newby, Edward	077	1720	SS 875/270	
Newby, Elizabeth	020	c1848	Copy	071 AR
Newby, Elizabeth	077	1855	WB-F/454	AR
Newby, Elizabeth	077	1824	WB-F/71	AR
Newby, Exum	077	1846	WB-F/324	AR
Newby, Francis	077	1807	WB-E/259	AR
Newby, Francis	077	1744	Orig. Only	SS/AR
Newby, Francis	077	1752	Orig. Only	SS/AR
Newby, Frederick	081	1833	WB-6/327	AR
Newby, Gabriel	077	1824	WB-F/74	AR
Newby, Gabriel	N	1735	SS 876/416	SS/AR
Newby, James	075	1743	Orig. Only	SS/AR
Newby, Jesse	077	1765	WB-C/54	AR
Newby, Jordan	077	1825	WB-F/105	AR
Newby, Joseph	077	1752	Orig. Only	SS/AR
Newby, Joseph	077	1814	WB-E/409	AR
Newby, Joseph	077	1768	WB-C/61	AR
Newby, Joseph	077	1735	SS 876/405	SS/AR
Newby, Joseph	081	1860	WB-11/476	AR
Newby, Joshua	081	1860	WB-11/441	AR
Newby, M. E.	010	1881	WB-I/134	
Newby, Mark	077	1785	WB-C/301	AR
Newby, Martha	077	1877	WB-H/69	AR
Newby, Mary	077	1739	LGB-4/#99	SS/AR
Newby, Mary	077	1822	WB-F/46	AR
Newby, Mordecai	075	1782	WB-K/78	
Newby, Nathan	077	1762	WB-C/13	AR
Newby, Nathan	077	1735	SS 876/401	SS/AR
Newby, Robert	077	1790	WB-C/407	AR
Newby, Robert B.	077	1848	WB-F/353	AR
Newby, Samuel	081	1820	WB-4/737	AR
Newby, Samuel	077	1737	SS 877/215	SS/AR
Newby, Samuel	077	1777	WB-C/192	AR
Newby, Thomas	077	1797	WB-E/80	
Newby, Thomas	075	1778	WB-K/23	
Newby, Thomas	099	1800	RB-5/96	AR
Newby, Thomas	077	1861	WB-F/516	AR
Newby, Thomas	077	1863	WB-F/543	AR
Newby, Thomas	077	1793	WB-C/445	
Newby, William	077	1836	WB-F/251	AR
Newby, William	077	1784	WB-C/248	AR
Newby, William	077	1720	SS 875/279	
Newby, Willis	077	1807	WB-E/254	AR
Newby, Wyke	024	1798	WB-A/333	AR
Newby, Zachariah	077	1794	WB-E/4	AR
Newell, Arrabella	100	1836	WB-35/341	
Newell, David H.	100	1821	WB-23/224	AR

Name	Co.	Date	Recorded Copy	Original
Newell, Dempsey	103	1883	WB-1/255	AR
Newell, John C.	065	1883	WB-K/534	AR
Newell, John H.	016	1899	WB-4/321	
Newell, John, Sr.	100	1796	WB-8/238	AR
Newell, Nancy S.	100	1846	WB-39/237	AR
Newell, Peter	065	1817	WB-E/48	AR
Newell, Samuel W.	065	1894	WB-M/259	AR
Newell, Thomas	046	1892	WB-F/218	AR
Newell, William	016	1849	WB-1/161	
Newfang, Martin	085	1775	WB-A/210	AR
Newheart, Sidney	065	1879	WB-K/316	AR
Newkirk, Abraham	070	1823	WB-C/320	AR
Newkirk, Bryan	070	1863	WB-D/128	AR
Newkirk, Joseph	070	1856	WB-C/622	AR
Newkirk, Timothy	035	1859	WB-3/5	AR
Newland, Benjamin	003	1850	Orig. Only	AR
Newland, J. C.	017	1893	WB-B/238	
Newlen, Joseph	081	1865	WB-13/356	AR
Newlin, James	073	1814	WB-D/401	AR
Newlin, John	001	1867	WB-1/284	AR
Newlin, John	073	1805	WB-D/162	AR
Newlin, Nathaniel	022	1882	WB-E/241	AR
Newlin, Ruth	022	1889	WB-E/421	AR
Newlin, William	001	1896	WB-3/137	AR
Newman, Anthony	085	1805	WB-F/57	AR
Newman, Austin	100	1887	WB-51/269	AR
Newman, Charles	090	1817	WB-3/1	AR-Nunc.
Newman, Daniel	100	1849	WB-40/180	AR
Newman, Henry	009	c1801	OWB/388	AR
Newman, Jacob	087	1869	WB-3/6	AR
Newman, Joel	078	1838	WI-14/32	AR
Newman, John	VA	1873	051 WB-C/109	
Newman, John	009	c1781	OWB/162	AR
Newman, Joseph J.	085	1900	WB-3/363	CTY
Newman, Kinchen	078	1874	WB-19/33	AR
Newman, Malachi	080	c1889	Orig. Only	AR
Newman, Mary	046	c1810	WB-A/281	AR
Newman, Michael	060	1795	Orig. Only	AR
Newman, Stephen	070	1785	WB-C/312	AR
Newman, Thomas	100	1791	WB-5/203	AR
Newman, Thomas	100	1828	WB-32/53	
Newman, William	084	1859	WB-C/297	CTY
Newnam, Thomas	024	1723	Orig. Only	SS/AR
Newnan, Ira T.	054	c1863	Orig. Only	AR
Newnan, Mary	085	1778	WB-A/254	AR-Nunc.
Newport, Peter	044	1783	WB-1/372	CTY
Newsom, Charles	051	1825	WB-A/84	
Newsom, Charles B.	051	c1884	WB-C/314	AR
Newsom, Daniel	010	1811	WB-F/178	AR
Newsom, David	103	1816	RD-3/339	
Newsom, Eleanor	103	1887	WB-1/393	AR
Newsom, Ely	051	1865	WB-B/61	
Newsom, Etheldred	083	c1820	WB-1/325	AR
Newsom, Henry	037	1863	WB-G/229	AR
Newsom, James M.	047	1890	WB-6/562	AR
Newsom, Joel	103	1837	RD-7/304	AR
Newsom, Joel	103	1820	RD-4/306	AR
Newsom, John	056	c1790	WB-1/24	AR
Newsom, Joseph	051	1886	WB-C/350	AR
Newsom, Louisa R.	071	1888	WB-7/19	AR
Newsom, Martha	071	1818	WB-3/208	AR
Newsom, Mary	103	1822	RD-5/20	AR
Newsom, Matilda C.	099	1884	WB-B/102	AR
Newsom, Michael E.	051	1882	WB-C/278	AR
Newsom, Moses	071	1846	WB-5/48	AR
Newsom, Moses	071	1805	WB-2/297	AR
Newsom, Nathaniel	071	1835	WB-4/137	AR
Newsom, Patience	071	1877	WB-6/226	AR
Newsom, Ruthy	051	1870	WB-C/38	AR
Newsom, Sampson	032	1889	WB-4/59	AR
Newsom, Sarah	051	1836	WB-A/99	
Newsom, Susan	028	1899	WB-4/181	AR
Newsom, Tabbitha	047	1863	WB-5/105	
Newsom, Thomas	037	1779	WB-B/12	AR
Newsom, Thomas	VA	1849	051 WB-A/316	
Newsom, William B.	045	1878	Orig. Only	AR
Newsom, William S.	045	1891	WB-1/287	AR
Newsom, Winborn	071	1812	WB-3/76	AR
Newsom, Winifred	071	1807	WB-2/353	AR
Newsome, Caroline	051	1892	WB-C/426	AR
Newsome, Cherry	051	1889	WB-C/399	AR
Newsome, Isaac	105	c1862	WB-1/88	
Newsome, Larry	105	1881	WB-2/269	AR
Newsome, Mary	103	1861	RD-13/344	
Newsome, Nancy	105	1884	WB-2/330	AR
Newsome, William	051	1858	WB-B/7	
Newsome, William	097	c1863	WB-2/10	AR
Newsome, William B.	045	1878	103 WB-3/413	103 AR
Newsum, Joel	071	1752	Orig. Only	SS/AR
Newton, Amy	044	1864	WB-22/176	CTY
Newton, B. B.	026	1892	WB-2/451	AR
Newton, Benjamin	072	1795	Orig. Only	AR
Newton, Benjamin	026	1845	WB-1/44	AR
Newton, Benjamin	026	1880	WB-2/207	AR
Newton, Chloe	032	c1850	WB-2/69	
Newton, Christofer	077	1759	SS 881/236	SS/AR
Newton, Daniel	072	1832	WB-1/100	AR
Newton, Daniel B.	035	c1888	Orig. Only	AR
Newton, E. F.	026	c1893	Orig. Only	AR
Newton, E. G.	026	1878	WB-2/171	AR
Newton, Ebe	055	1860	ID/63	
Newton, Ebenezer	086	1812	WB-B/266	AR
Newton, Edward	070	1844	WB-AB/411	AR
Newton, Edward	070	1837	WB-AB/287	AR
Newton, Elijah	072	1794	Orig. Only	AR
Newton, Elizabeth	044	1881	WB-23/410	CTY
Newton, Francis	008	c1734	009 OWB/19	009 AR
Newton, George	073	1801	WB-D/44	AR
Newton, Isaac	035	1799	WB-A/358	AR
Newton, Isaac	070	1826	WB-C/322	AR
Newton, James	070	1857	WB-C/630	AR
Newton, James	044	1874	WB-23/154	CTY
Newton, Jesse	053	c1815	WB-4/86	AR
Newton, John	072	1777	RW/L2	AR
Newton, John	044	c1812	Orig. Only	CTY
Newton, John	079	c1858	WB-1/109	AR
Newton, John	005	1810	WB-2/115	AR
Newton, John	026	1845	WB-1/40	AR
Newton, John I.	070	1851	WB-C/534	AR
Newton, Joseph	070	1833	WB-C/323	AR
Newton, Margaret	072	1836	WB-1/149	AR
Newton, Mary	070	1863	WB-D/115	AR
Newton, Mary	035	1823	WB-A/353	
Newton, Mary	070	1774	WB-C/307	AR
Newton, Nicholas	068	1796	WB-A/187	
Newton, Patrick	035	1793	WB-A/355	AR
Newton, Robert	086	1864	WB-E/429	
Newton, Robert	026	1871	WB-2/60	AR
Newton, Sarah	035	1821	WB-A/364	AR
Newton, Thomas	011	c1765	Orig. Only	SS/AR

Name	Co.	Date	Recorded Copy	Original
Newton, Thomas	028	1826	WB-C/280	AR
Newton, Thomas	100	1872	WB-51/185	AR
Newton, William	086	1824	WB-D/22	AR
Newton, William P.	036	1893	WB-A/281	CTY
Newton, William R.	026	1870	WB-2/32	AR
Niblack, George	085	1815	WB-G/348	AR
Niblock, John	085	1845	WB-K/2	AR
Niblock, Levi	085	1880	WB-1/534	CTY
Nice, William	070	1758	DB-D/342	SS/AR
Nichelson, Abel	104	1832	WB-4/153	AR
Nichelson, Ephraim	106	c1850	WB-1/17	AR
Nicholas, George	070	1756	DB-D/187	AR
Nicholas, John	071	1816	WB-3/179	AR
Nicholas, Nathaniel	010	1755	SS 880/159	SS/AR
Nicholls, Anna	010	1849	WB-G/442	AR
Nicholls, Benajah	010	1835	WB-G/242	AR
Nicholls, Fannie M.	047	1898	WB-7/214	AR
Nicholls, Humphrey	010	1791	WB-D/161	AR
Nicholls, James	047	1803	WB-3/417	
Nicholls, Jehu	010	1838	WB-G/302	AR
Nicholls, John	010	1800	WB-E/118	AR
Nicholls, John	104	1833	WB-4/162	AR
Nicholls, John	010	1791	WB-D/177	AR
Nicholls, Margaret	010	1843	WB-G/348	AR
Nicholls, Sarah	010	1797	WB-E/11	AR
Nicholls, Thomas	010	1812	WB-F/197	AR
Nicholls, Thomas B.	101	1868	Orig. Only	AR
Nichols, Alves	073	1845	WB-F/257	AR
Nichols, Ann	070	1891	WB-F/502	AR
Nichols, Arnold	105	1892	WB-3/28	AR
Nichols, Beathiar W.	036	1885	WB-A/72	CTY
Nichols, Caleb	070	1803	WB-C/318	AR
Nichols, Candis B.	036	1883	WB-A/33	CTY
Nichols, Catharine	070	1795	WB-C/315	AR-Nunc.
Nichols, Catherine	047	1879	WB-6/201	AR
Nichols, David	075	1779	WB-K/43	AR
Nichols, Delia	099	1848	RB-26/390	AR
Nichols, Elijah	104	1856	WB-5/148	
Nichols, Emaline	079	1884	WB-2/318	AR
Nichols, Esther	054	1856	WB-3/106	AR
Nichols, Frankey	030	1797	WB-2/99	
Nichols, George W.	004	1896	WB-A/178	AR
Nichols, Henry	075	1775	WB-I/137	AR
Nichols, Jabez	075	1792	WB-K/236	AR
Nichols, James	030	1797	WB-2/98	
Nichols, Jeremiah	069	1834	WB-1/401	AR
Nichols, Jeremiah	075	1778	WB-K/22	AR
Nichols, John	092	1894	WB-6/382	AR
Nichols, John	084	1788	OW/196	AR
Nichols, John	101	1889	WB-A/170	AR
Nichols, John	070	1802	WB-AB/59	AR
Nichols, John	096	1867	WB-3/78	AR
Nichols, John	070	1808	WB-C/319	AR
Nichols, John	047	1872	WB-6/75	AR
Nichols, John C.	082	1888	WB-6/376	AR
Nichols, Jonathan	073	1807	WB-D/190	AR
Nichols, Jonathan	041	1801	WB-1/187	AR
Nichols, Jonathan	073	1808	WB-D/227	AR
Nichols, Joseph	070	1786	WB-C/314	AR
Nichols, Joshua	054	c1793	WB-1/152	AR
Nichols, Josiah	099	1823	RB-18/244	AR
Nichols, Lemuel	051	1881	WB-C/274	AR
Nichols, Levi	081	1878	WB-15/283	AR
Nichols, Lizzie	054	c1864	Orig. Only	AR
Nichols, Luke	047	1790	WB-3/187	
Nichols, Maria	073	1858	WB-G/196	AR
Nichols, Martha	047	1858	WB-5/64	
Nichols, Micajah	078	1812	WI-6/114	AR
Nichols, Neal	051	1852	WB-A/345	
Nichols, Passun	039	1864	WB-R/783	AR
Nichols, Richison	073	1858	WB-G/206	CTY
Nichols, Sarah	099	1800	RB-5/171	AR
Nichols, Stephen	047	1854	WB-4/373	
Nichols, Stephen J.	099	1893	WB-C/136	AR
Nichols, Thomas	047	1815	WB-3/568	
Nichols, Thomas	099	1829	RB-21/171	AR
Nichols, Thomas	073	1828	WB-E/153	AR
Nichols, Thomas	075	1796	WB-L/65	AR
Nichols, William	015	1774	100 WB-2/7	AR
Nichols, William	070	1775	WB-C/309	AR
Nichols, William	075	1804	WB-M1/89	AR
Nichols, William	070	1757	DB-D/259	AR
Nichols, William	099	1795	RB-3/92	AR
Nichols, William	075	1769	WB-H/102	AR
Nichols, William	075	1783	WB-K/84	AR
Nichols, William	078	1869	WB-19/5	AR
Nichols, William A.	010	1898	WB-I/572	
Nichols, William A.	103	1875	WB-1/85	AR
Nichols, William R.	099	1897	WB-D/25	AR
Nichols, William S.	070	1816	WB-AB/242	AR
Nichols, William W.	064	1897	WB-2/417	AR
Nichols, Willie	099	1847	RB-26/210	AR
Nichols, Wright	051	1846	WB-A/255	
Nicholson, Abigail	039	1828	WB-J/9	
Nicholson, Alexander	082	1836	WB-2/62	AR
Nicholson, Anderson	038	1880	WB-2/362	AR
Nicholson, Ann	047	c1779	WB-2/101	
Nicholson, Archibald	073	1821	WB-D/612	AR
Nicholson, Benjamin	N	c1712	SS 875/15	
Nicholson, Caleb Ward	030	1880	WB-5/67	AR
Nicholson, Catherine	016	1867	WB-2/147	
Nicholson, Christopher	075	1793	WB-L/10	AR
Nicholson, D. B.	035	1866	WB-3/113	AR
Nicholson, Edward	069	1800	WB-1/129	AR
Nicholson, Eliza E.	047	1842	WB-4/211	
Nicholson, Elizabeth	032	c1857	WB-2/147	
Nicholson, Frances C.	103	1880	WB-1/191	AR
Nicholson, George	100	1799	WB-10/133	AR
Nicholson, George	069	1780	WB-1/12	AR
Nicholson, George	100	1818	WB-21/211	AR
Nicholson, George H.	075	1826	WB-N/29	AR
Nicholson, Gerusha	075	1825	WB-N/14	AR
Nicholson, Guilford	047	1836	WB-4/143	
Nicholson, Harriet	065	1874	WB-K/155	AR
Nicholson, Harriet A.	077	1888	WB-H/173	AR
Nicholson, James	039	1812	WB-C/297	
Nicholson, James M.	069	1809	WB-1/201	AR
Nicholson, John	054	1868	WB-4/9	AR
Nicholson, John	037	1799	WB-D/81	AR
Nicholson, John	039	1847	WB-M/223	AR
Nicholson, John	063	1854	WB-2/405	
Nicholson, John	063	1831	WB-2/170	
Nicholson, John A.	082	1892	WB-6/458	AR
Nicholson, John J.	100	1870	WB-51/24	
Nicholson, Joseph	075	1772	WB-I/120	
Nicholson, Joseph	077	1698	SS 874.2/95	SS/AR
Nicholson, Josiah	030	1818	WB-3/106	
Nicholson, Josiah	077	1852	WB-F/409	AR
Nicholson, Josiah	030	1807	WB-2/298	
Nicholson, Lemuel	047	1775	WB-2/10	

Name	Co.	Date	Recorded Copy	Original
Nicholson, Lucinda T.	039	1880	WB-U/226	AR
Nicholson, Lydia	069	1789	WB-1/58	AR
Nicholson, Malcom	082	1840	WB-2/93	AR
Nicholson, Martha	039	1838	WB-K/163	AR
Nicholson, Mary	100	1847	WB-39/339	AR
Nicholson, Mary G.	082	1849	WB-4/24	AR-Nunc.
Nicholson, Micajah	092	1884	WB-6/213	AR
Nicholson, Mildred	100	1877	WB-51/114	AR
Nicholson, Nancy D.	001	c1834	WB-1/93	AR
Nicholson, Nathaniel	100	1790	WB-5/172	AR
Nicholson, Nathaniel	077	1737	LGB-4/#66	SS/AR
Nicholson, Penelope	037	1820	WB-E/238	AR
Nicholson, Peter	083	1842	WB-1/414	AR
Nicholson, Priscilla	039	1846	WB-M/141	
Nicholson, Robert	039	1823	WB-G/184	Nunc.
Nicholson, Roderick	082	1798	WB-1/65	AR
Nicholson, Samuel	N	1727	SS 876/119	SS/AR
Nicholson, Samuel	051	1828	WB-A/9	
Nicholson, Samuel	104	1835	WB-4/196	AR
Nicholson, Sarah	077	1787	WB-C/350	AR
Nicholson, Thomas	077	1780	Orig. Only	AR
Nicholson, Timothy M.	069	1808	WB-1/188	AR
Nicholson, Urbane	100	1811	WB-16/28	AR
Nicholson, William	030	1723	Orig. Only	SS/AR
Nicholson, Winefreed	047	1849	WB-4/273	
Nickel, Thomas	065	1787	WB-E/37	AR
Nickells, James	084	c1796	OW/194	AR
Nickels, John	084	1816	WB-A/280	CTY
Nickens, Richard	030	1774	WB-1/89	
Nickolls, James	030	1742	Orig. Only	SS/AR
Nickols, Benjamin	075	1801	WB-M1/47	AR
Nickols, Catherine	099	1896	WB-C/542	AR
Nickols, Mathew G.	072	1779	RW/L13	AR
Nickols, Nickolas	030	1785	WB-1/192	
Nickolson, Christofer	030	1723	Orig. Only	SS/AR
Nickolson, Josiah	030	1750	Orig. Only	SS/AR
Nicks, Benjamin C.	020	1895	WB-B/220	CTY
Nicks, George	046	1838	WB-C/13	AR
Nickson, Thomas	071	1753	SS 880/22	SS/AR
Nicolls, John	010	c1762	WB-A/49	AR
Nicolls, Sarah	010	1793	WB-D/216	AR
Nicols, John	N	1712	Orig. Only	SS/AR
Niefong, George	085	c1797	WB-C/254	AR
Niel, Honore	024	1810	WB-B/302	AR
Nifong, James A.	032	1892	WB-4/193	AR
Nigh, Christian	060	1796	Orig. Only	AR
Night, Amy	099	1842	RB-25/76	AR
Night, Emanuel	075	c1765	WB-I/114	AR
Night, Mary	022	1859	WB-D/45	AR
Niler, William	028	1799	WB-B/85	AR
Nilor, William S.	028	1788	WB-A/169	AR
Nimson, Hannah	PA	1897	066 WB-1/170	
Nipper, Jacob	099	1897	WB-C/579	AR
Nipper, Josiah	099	1890	WB-B/441	AR
Nipper, Lucy	099	1888	WB-B/288	AR
Nisbet, Sarah	097	1844	WB-1/6	AR
Nisbet, W. B.	065	1892	WB-M/67	AR
Nisbett, John	054	c1815	Orig. Only	AR
Nison, John	029	1793	Orig. Only	AR
Nissen, Charles	038	c1853	WB-1/43	AR
Nissen, Loretta L.	038	1887	WB-3/49	AR
Nissen, Mary E.	038	1884	WB-2/502	AR
Nissen, Sophia E.	038	1887	WB-3/52	AR
Nithercut, Nancy	035	1853	WB-2/78	AR
Niven, Duncan	005	1863	WB-C/191	AR
Niven, John	029	1810	WB-A/150	AR
Nix, Elanor P.	064	1898	WB-2/450	AR
Nix, William	086	1837	WB-E/35	AR
Nixon, A. C.	077	1900	WB-H/327	AR
Nixon, Alexander	077	1900	WB-H/333	AR
Nixon, Barnabas	081	1858	WB-11/228	AR-Copy
Nixon, Charles D.	029	1892	WB-E/559	AR
Nixon, Christian	070	c1831	WB-AB/273	AR
Nixon, Daniel	072	1834	WB-1/132	AR
Nixon, David	024	1897	WB-E/272	AR
Nixon, Delight	077	1801	WB-E/127	AR
Nixon, Elenor B.	077	1894	WB-H/259	AR
Nixon, Eliza	103	1886	WB-1/366	AR
Nixon, Elizabeth	077	1769	WB-C/85	AR
Nixon, Elizabeth	077	1748	Orig. Only	SS/AR
Nixon, Francis	077	1887	WB-H/168	AR
Nixon, Francis	065	1788	WB-E/38	AR
Nixon, Francis	077	1773	WB-C/128	AR
Nixon, George W.	018	1890	WB-E/183	AR
Nixon, Hannah	077	1793	WB-C/453	
Nixon, Henry D.	077	1837	WB-F/264	AR
Nixon, Hetty	PA	1856	064 WB-2/249	
Nixon, Hetty	PA	1856	014 WB-2/457	
Nixon, Jack	070	1898	Orig. Only	AR
Nixon, James	060	1828	WB-1/92	AR
Nixon, James	075	1806	WB-M1/118	AR
Nixon, James	060	1861	WB-3/40	AR
Nixon, James	070	1842	WB-AB/359	AR
Nixon, Jane	092	1857	WB-5/24	
Nixon, John	077	1763	WB-C/26	AR
Nixon, John	060	1808	Orig. Only	AR
Nixon, John	060	1864	WB-3/64	AR
Nixon, John	077	1785	WB-C/323	AR
Nixon, John	103	1805	Orig. Only	AR
Nixon, John	060	c1865	WB-3/77	AR
Nixon, John	075	1692	Orig. Only	SS/AR
Nixon, John	024	1838	WB-C/212	AR
Nixon, John W.	077	1859	WB-F/499	AR
Nixon, Joseph	077	1789	WB-C/392	
Nixon, Joshua	060	1849	WB-2/328	AR
Nixon, Lavinia S.	075	1834	WB-N/99	AR
Nixon, Maria	PA	1852	014 WB-2/450	
Nixon, Maria	PA	1852	107 WB-2/202	
Nixon, Maria	PA	1852	064 WB-2/261	
Nixon, Mary	103	1893	WB-2/62	AR
Nixon, Matilda	060	1877	WB-4/165	AR
Nixon, Millicent	081	1851	WB-9/275	AR
Nixon, Morris	075	1825	WB-N/11	AR
Nixon, Nathan	077	1831	WB-F/181	AR
Nixon, Nathan	092	1891	WB-6/336	AR
Nixon, Nathan	077	1810	WB-E/344	AR
Nixon, Nicholas	070	1843	WB-AB/380	AR
Nixon, Nicholas	070	1869	WB-E/13	AR
Nixon, Ostain	041	1801	WB-1/188	AR
Nixon, Phineas	077	1813	WB-E/386	AR
Nixon, Phineas	081	1838	WB-7/144	AR
Nixon, Phineas	077	1772	WB-C/105	AR
Nixon, Richard	028	1799	WB-B/89	AR
Nixon, Richard W.	072	1894	WB-4/309	AR
Nixon, Robert	070	1777	WB-C/310	AR
Nixon, Robert	024	1836	WB-C/201	AR
Nixon, Robert	072	1795	Orig. Only	AR
Nixon, Robert	070	1808	WB-AB/105	AR
Nixon, Robert A.	060	1835	WB-1/350	AR
Nixon, Robert C.	076	1891	WB-A1/151	AR

Name	Co.	Date	Recorded Copy	Original
Nixon, Robert J.	076	1890	WB-A1/112	AR
Nixon, Robert J.	076	1890	072 WB-4/268	
Nixon, Samuel	070	1862	WB-D/92	AR
Nixon, Samuel	070	1877	WB-E/346	AR
Nixon, Samuel	005	1807	WB-2/116	AR
Nixon, Samuel	075	1824	WB-M1/402	AR
Nixon, Samuel	077	1815	WB-E/427	AR
Nixon, Sarah	077	1818	WB-F/11	AR
Nixon, Smith	077	1886	WB-H/161	AR
Nixon, Thomas	070	1801	WB-AB/53	AR
Nixon, Thomas	077	1794	WB-E/30	Nunc.
Nixon, Thomas	077	1895	WB-H/266	AR
Nixon, Thomas	070	1782	WB-C/316	AR
Nixon, Thomas	077	1772	WB-C/108	AR
Nixon, Timothy	075	1774	WB-I/97	
Nixon, William	077	1897	WB-H/300	AR
Nixon, William	060	1801	Orig. Only	AR
Nixon, William H.	070	1841	WB-AB/346	AR
Nixon, William P.	092	1897	WB-6/469	AR
Nixon, Zachariah	077	1752	Orig. Only	SS/AR
Nixon, Zachariah	077	1776	WB-C/244	AR
Nixon, Zachariah	077	1739	SS 877/133	SS/AR
Nixson, Richard	028	1746	SS 877/357	SS/AR
Noah, Henry M.	001	1865	WB-1/229	
Noah, Isaiah	001	1894	WB-3/27	AR
Noah, Sally	001	c1854	WB-1/86	AR
Nobbin, William	047	1796	WB-3/260	
Nobeland, John	037	1755	SS 880/155	SS/AR
Noble, Catharine	059	1892	WB-B/40	CTY
Noble, Celina	079	1897	WB-3/104	AR
Noble, Daniel	057	1810	WB-A/321	AR
Noble, Duncan	054	c1795	WB-1/156	AR
Noble, Frank H.	085	1900	WB-3/390	CTY
Noble, Hardy	027	1864	WB-A/88	AR
Noble, Martin M.	057	1900	WB-C/254	AR
Noble, Mary	057	1885	WB-C/120	AR
Noble, Samuel	019	1776	Orig. Only	SS/AR
Noble, Samuel	019	1776	RB-A/59	SS/AR
Noble, William	008	1724	Orig. Only	SS/AR
Noble, William M.	028	1891	WB-F/12	
Nobles, Blount	079	1864	WB-1/141	AR
Nobles, John	009	1834	OB-B/471	AR
Nobles, Johnson	079	1864	WB-1/138	AR
Nobles, Nathaniel	079	1868	WB-2/6	AR
Nobles, Simon J.	079	1891	WB-2/551	AR
Nobles, Thomas	079	1885	WB-2/348	AR
Nobles, Wilie	079	1861	WB-1/165	AR
Noblet, John	092	1791	WB-3/2	AR
Noblett, Ira	064	1870	WB-2/15	AR
Noblett, M. L.	064	1899	WB-2/461	AR
Noblett, William	064	1883	WB-2/141	AR
Nodin, Charles	071	1765	WB-1/120	
Noe, Isaac	019	1898	WB-B/335	AR
Noe, John	073	1846	WB-F/277	AR
Noe, Peter	073	1782	WB-A/237	AR
Noe, Peter, Sr.	019	1828	WB-D/302	AR
Noe, Thomas	099	1800	RB-5/91	AR
Noel, Edward	020	1802	RB-D/120	
Noland, Peter	104	1796	WB-1/485	
Noland, Stephen	085	c1791	WB-B/187	AR
Nolen, W. M.	040	1897	WB-2/536	AR
Noles, J. S.	065	1877	WB-K/254	AR
Noles, James	065	1887	WB-L/243	AR
Noles, William	100	1794	WB-7/242	AR
Noll, John	060	1832	WB-1/241	AR
Nolms, Ebenezer	072	c1745	SS 878/138	
Non (Nunn), Henry	099	1900	Orig. Only	AR
Nooe, John	104	1873	WB-6/75	AR
Norcom, Benjamin	024	1813	WB-C/18	AR
Norcom, Charles	024	c1806	WB-B/243	AR
Norcom, Cornelus	N	c1740	Orig. Only	SS/AR
Norcom, Edmund	024	1810	WB-B/311	AR
Norcom, Frederick	024	1812	WB-C/8	AR
Norcom, Frederick	024	1795	WB-B/165	AR
Norcom, John	024	1728	SS 876/139	SS/AR
Norcom, John	024	1746	Orig. Only	SS/AR
Norcom, John	024	c1813	WB-C/29	AR
Norcom, John	024	1746	Orig. Only	AR-Copy
Norcom, John	024	c1802	WB-B/3	AR
Norcom, Mary	077	1721	SS 875/313	SS/AR
Norcom, Mary M.	024	1869	WB-E/5	AR
Norcom, Thomas	077	1748	Orig. Only	SS/AR
Norcom, Thomas	077	1707	Orig. Only	SS/AR
Norcom, Thomas	077	1744	Orig. Only	SS/AR
Norcom, William A.	024	1881	WB-E/99	AR
Norcott, Hosea	097	1864	WB-1/236	AR
Norden, John	029	1824	WB-B/127	
Norden, Robert	029	1816	WB-A/237	AR
Norfleet, Abraham	024	1785	WB-A/84	AR
Norfleet, Benjamin	037	1896	WB-H/355	AR
Norfleet, Christiana	037	1853	WB-F/509	AR
Norfleet, Elisha	024	1811	WB-C/1	AR
Norfleet, Jacob	024	1780	041 WB-1/7	041 AR
Norfleet, James	024	1815	WB-C/34	AR
Norfleet, James	041	1796	WB-1/144	AR
Norfleet, James	077	1732/3	SS 876/281	SS/AR
Norfleet, John	037	1880	WB-G/551	AR
Norfleet, John	024	1754	Orig. Only	SS/AR
Norfleet, Kinchen	041	1849	WB-3/120	AR
Norfleet, Margaret	010	1858	WB-H/63	AR
Norfleet, Marmaduke	047	1762	SS 881/267	SS/AR
Norfleet, Marmaduke	071	1775	WB-2/120	
Norfleet, Marmaduke	047	1818	WB-3/626.	
Norfleet, Marmaduke	047	1830	WB-4/60	
Norfleet, Martha E.	041	1885	WB-4/230	AR
Norfleet, Mary	024	1816	WB-C/47	AR
Norfleet, Mary	077	1742	Orig. Only	SS/AR
Norfleet, Nathaniel	078	1836	WI-13/82	AR
Norfleet, Reuben	010	1801	WB-E/120	AR
Norfleet, Robert	037	1871	WB-G/365	AR
Norfleet, Seth R.	041	1882	WB-4/173	AR
Norfleet, Thomas	037	1746	Orig. Only	SS/AR
Norfleet, Thomas F.	010	1838	WB-G/299	AR
Norfleet, William	037	1872	WB-G/373	AR
Norman, Alfred	020	1874	WB-A/150	CTY
Norman, Benjamin	020	1820	RB-H/395	AR
Norman, Daniel	104	1875	WB-6/119	AR
Norman, David	065	1891	WB-M/27	AR
Norman, David W.	106	1900	WB-2/477	
Norman, George	044	1829	WB-11/136	CTY
Norman, Henry	092	1808	WB-3/87	AR
Norman, Henry	044	1831	WB-12/159	CTY
Norman, Henry	096	c1797	Orig. Only	024 AR
Norman, Henry	096	1808	WB-2/34	
Norman, Henry	096	c1804	WB-2/33	
Norman, Henry	096	1857	WB-3/50	
Norman, Ira E.	096	1858	WB-3/53	AR
Norman, Isaac	092	1894	WB-6/374	AR
Norman, Isaac	104	1816	WB-3/116	AR
Norman, James	104	1828	WB-4/110	AR

Name	Co.	Date	Recorded Copy	Original
Norman, James F.	101	1896	WB-A/281	AR
Norman, James Isaac	055	1900	WB-A/200	
Norman, Jeremiah	011	c1840	WB-1/96	
Norman, Jeremiah	096	1767	Orig. Only	AR
Norman, Jesse	101	1885	WB-A/134	AR
Norman, John	072	1753	SS 877/87	SS/AR
Norman, John	044	1802	WB-5/225	CTY
Norman, John	072	1806	WB-A/99	AR
Norman, John	072	1790	Orig. Only	AR
Norman, John W.	096	c1861	Orig. Only	AR
Norman, Joseph	092	1853	WB-5/1	
Norman, Martha	092	1899	WB-6/521	AR
Norman, Mary	096	1790	WB-1/164	AR
Norman, Mary	092	1898	WB-6/489	AR
Norman, Millie	106	1894	WB-2/346	AR
Norman, Nathan D.	065	1898	WB-N/127	AR
Norman, Nathan D.	065	c1888	Copy	101 AR
Norman, Nehemiah	096	1786	WB-1/150	AR
Norman, Rachel	096	1796	Orig. Only	AR
Norman, Richard	035	1807	WB-A/360	AR
Norman, Sarah	044	1833	WB-12/429	Nunc.
Norman, Sarah M.	038	1896	WB-3/551	AR
Norman, Thomas	044	1818	WB-8/176	CTY
Norman, Thomas	026	1852	WB-1/138	AR
Norman, Thomas W.	044	1853	WB-19/199	CTY
Norman, William	072	1808	WB-A/99	AR
Norman, William B.	044	1847	WB-17/174	
Norman, Wilson W.	009	1858	OB-K/347	AR
Norment, Charles T.	065	c1863	WB-J/195	AR
Norment, Samuel	VA	1810	Copy	032 AR
Norment, Thomas	035	1799	WB-A/362	AR
Norment, William S.	065	1882	WB-K/451	AR
Norris, Charity	037	1808	WB-D/310	AR
Norris, Daniel	073	1765	WB-A/37	
Norris, George	035	c1766	087 DB-1/230	
Norris, Hezekiah	054	1889	WB-5/252	CTY
Norris, Isaac	061	c1858	WB-1/75	AR
Norris, Isom	035	1817	WB-A/354	AR
Norris, James	065	1771	WB-E/36	AR
Norris, Jane	021	1846	WB-1/41	AR
Norris, Jesse	103	1834	RD-6/517	
Norris, Jessy	035	1807	WB-A/363	AR
Norris, John	065	1831	WB-G/68	AR
Norris, John	037	1801	WB-D/127	AR
Norris, John	056	1792	WB-1/63	AR
Norris, John	021	1845	WB-1/32	AR
Norris, Mary	078	1840	WI-14/195	
Norris, Mathew	103	1866	RD-14/262	AR
Norris, Samuel P.	099	1856	RB-29/461	AR
Norris, William	075	1774	WB-I/101	AR
Norris, William	075	1725	SS 876/6	SS/AR
Norris, Wright	027	c1873	WB-2/37	AR
Norriss, Joseph	039	1810	WB-C/193	
Norriss, Nahor	056	1801	WB-1/124	AR
Norsford, Susanah	047	1763	WB-1/107	
Norsworthy, John	100	1811	WB-16/30	AR
Norsworthy, William N.	100	1802	WB-11/354	AR
North, Ann	106	1891	WB-2/312	AR
North, John	084	1862	WB-C/362	CTY
North, John	092	c1827	WB-4/50	
North, Jonathan	106	1889	WB-2/282	AR
North, Joseph	010	1798	WB-E/43	AR
North, Richard	010	1805	WB-E/264	AR
North, Thomas	024	1735	LGB-4/#28	
North, Thomas	084	c1814	WB-A/106	CTY
Northam, Daniel T.	082	1881	WB-6/209	AR
Northam, George	082	1875	WB-6/133	AR
Northam, George	082	1820	WB-1/214	AR
Northam, Thomas	046	1864	WB-D/219	AR
Northam, Zilpha	103	1854	RD-11/394	AR
Northan, Philip	030	1837	WB-4/27	
Northan, William	028	1774	Orig. Only	AR
Northcott, Andrew	010	1872	WB-I/43	AR
Northcott, Elizabeth	051	1834	WB-A/69	
Northcraft, Virlinder	054	c1822	WB-1/428	AR
Northen, John, Sr.	030	1714	Orig. Only	SS/AR
Northen, William	037	1793	WB-C/218	AR
Northern, Dorotha	030	1819	WB-3/114	
Northern, Edmund	104	1788	WB-1/233	AR
Northern, John	030	1803	WB-2/213	
Northern, Polly	030	1838	WB-4/57	
Northey, James	065	1890	WB-L/469	
Northington, Jesse	029	1828	WB-B/161	AR
Northington, John	068	1802	WB-A/220	
Northington, Samuel	029	1792	Orig. Only	AR
Northrop, Edwin A.	070	1894	WB-G/280	AR
Northrop, Henry F.	082	1884	WB-6/269	AR
Northrop, Isaac	070	1862	WB-D/97	AR
Northumb, Solomon	028	1780	Orig. Only	AR
Norton, C. C.	082	1891	WB-6/429	AR
Norton, Edward	081	c1876	Orig. Only	AR
Norton, Eliza	016	1898	WB-4/304	
Norton, Fielder	064	1853	WB-1/33	AR
Norton, James	082	1813	WB-1/163	AR
Norton, John	030	1745	Orig. Only	SS/AR
Norton, John	016	1853	WB-1/228	
Norton, Nicholass	003	1864	Orig. Only	AR
Norton, Norman	054	1854	WB-3/75	AR
Norton, Stephen	073	1774	WB-A/179	
Norton, William	011	1751	SS 878/136	SS/AR
Norvel, Chapman	037	1850	WB-F/441	AR
Norvill, Ruel	037	1848	WB-F/401	AR
Norvill, Wiley J.	086	1874	WB-F/55	AR
Norville, Hardy	037	1881	WB-G/607	AR
Norville, Hyman	037	1893	WB-H/245	AR
Norville, James	037	1867	WB-G/293	AR
Norward, George	071	1807	WB-2/336	AR
Norwood, Augustin	099	1836	RB-23/548	AR
Norwood, Benjamin	044	1847	WB-17/133	CTY
Norwood, David	099	1863	RB-32/619	AR
Norwood, Elizabeth	098	1887	WB-A/121	CTY
Norwood, George	071	1749	Orig. Only	SS/AR
Norwood, George W.	099	1884	WB-A/531	AR
Norwood, Jane	089	1859	016 WB-2/57	
Norwood, John	039	c1800	WB-B/168	
Norwood, John A.	044	1842	WB-15/337	CTY
Norwood, John W.	073	1885	WB-H/377	CTY
Norwood, Jordan	044	1826	WB-10/233	CTY
Norwood, Joseph A.	044	1875	WB-23/161	CTY
Norwood, Laura C.	TN	1894	017 WB-B/241	017 AR
Norwood, Leah	039	1831	WB-J/176	
Norwood, Littleton	071	1883	WB-6/414	AR
Norwood, Milly	071	1857	WB-5/173	AR
Norwood, Moses	071	1837	WB-4/156	AR
Norwood, Nathaniel	044	1784	WB-1/385	CTY
Norwood, Richard	047	1795	WB-3/256	
Norwood, Sallie A.	071	1885	WB-6/464	AR
Norwood, Samuel	047	1795	WB-3/257	
Norwood, Susannah	054	1848	WB-3/28	AR
Norwood, Tabitha	071	1841	WB-4/231	AR

Name	Co.	Date	Recorded Copy	Original
Norwood, Thomas	028	1758	SS 880/206	SS/AR
Norwood, Washington	017	1896	WB-B/269	AR
Norwood, William	073	1842	WB-F/116	AR
Norwood, William	028	1748	SS 877/51	SS/AR
Norwood, William	022	c1803	WB-A/82	AR
Norwood, William	028	1762	DB-8/267	AR
Norwood, William	028	1762	SS 882/444	
Norwood, William	022	1894	WB-E/560	AR
Norwood, William E.	097	1866	WB-1/269	AR
Norwood, Zilly	099	1869	RB-35/92	AR
Norworthy, John	071	1789	WB-2/69	AR
Notz, John	046	1775	WB-A/278	AR
Novey, Yelinda L.	036	1900	WB-A/520	CTY
Nowel, David	005	1837	WB-B/77	AR
Nowell, Berry	099	1882	WB-A/330	AR
Nowell, Isaac	051	1833	WB-A/55	
Nowell, J. R.	099	1897	WB-D/68	AR
Nowell, Jasper	099	1882	WB-A/387	AR
Nowell, John	056	1793	WB-1/74	AR
Nowell, John	010	1885	WB-I/201	
Nowell, John, Sr.	099	1860	RB-31/489	AR
Nowell, Lemuel	063	1837	WB-2/241	
Nowell, Mark	099	1872	RB-35/205	AR
Nowell, W. W.	099	1891	WB-B/489	AR
Nowlan, Michael	065	c1830	Orig. Only	AR
Noyes, McWalter B.	NY	1886	070 WB-F/47	070 AR
Nuckels, James H.	098	1893	WB-A/164	CTY
Null, Daniel	021	1865	WB-1/214	AR
Null, Frederick	038	1865	WB-1/248	AR
Null, Jacob	090	1811	WB-2/130	AR
Null, John	021	1880	WB-2/229	
Null, John	090	1844	WB-4/155	AR
Null, Margaret	021	1851	WB-1/91	AR
Nunally, Elizabeth	020	1847	RB-P/407	
Nungesser, Adam	085	c1808	WB-G/99	AR
Nunn (Non), Henry	099	1900	Orig. Only	AR
Nunn, Carlton	020	1823	RB-I/236	AR
Nunn, David H.	073	1814	WB-D/407	AR
Nunn, Elizabeth	073	1852	WB-G/15	AR
Nunn, Henry S.	028	1890	WB-E/525	AR
Nunn, James D.	099	1875	RB-35/318	AR
Nunn, John	090	1884	WB-6/149	AR
Nunnally, James W.	020	1897	WB-B/288	CTY
Nunnally, Leander W.	084	1849	WB-C/89	CTY
Nunnally, Maria T.	020	1900	WB-B/407	CTY
Nunnally, Obediah	020	1822	RB-I/73	AR
Nunnally, Obediah	020	1846	RB-P/317	AR
Nunnery, Alexander	029	1895	WB-F/56	AR
Nunnery, Amos	029	c1838	WB-B/296	AR
Nunney, Mary	041	1845	WB-3/66	AR
Nunnnally, Elisha	032	c1847	WB = 2/99	
Nunns, Elizabeth	090	1829	WB-3/204	AR
Nunns, John	090	1806	WB-2/64	AR
Nuns, William	090	1828	WB-3/173	AR
Nusiman, Paul	016	1851	WB-1/193	
Nusum, Richard	010	1753	SS 878/182	SS/AR
Nutall, Sarah E.	046	1877	WB-E/181	AR
Nutt, Benjamin	092	c1867	Orig. Only	AR
Nutt, Hagar	070	1868	WB-E/11	AR
Nutt, John	099	1819	RB-15/161	AR
Nutt, John	070	1811	WB-AB/158	AR
Nutt, Richard T.	092	1895	WB-6/407	AR
Nutt, Robert	099	1795	RB-2/39	AR
Nutt, Susanna	099	1832	RB-22/283	AR
Nutt, William	099	c1808	RB-7/318	AR
Nutt, William	070	1812	WB-AB/176	AR
Nuttall, George A.	044	1836	WB-13/459	CTY
Nuttall, John	044	1832	WB-12/354	CTY
Nye, Edgar W.	050	1896	WB-2/233	CTY
Nye, George A.	006	1879	Orig. Only	AR
Nye, Josiah	027	1867	WB-A/101	AR
Nye, Parker	083	1863	WB-2/200	AR
Nye, R. R.	083	1896	WB-4/128	AR
O'Brian, Darbe	077	1725	SS 876/31	SS/AR
O'Briant, Alexander	078	1898	WB-19/459	AR
O'Briant, Denis	078	1817	WI-7/267	AR
O'Briant, Elijah	078	1878	WB-19/76	AR
O'Briant, John	044	1867	WB-22/652	CTY
O'Briant, Ransom	036	1896	WB-A/390	CTY
O'Briant, Rebecca	078	1837	WI-13/212	AR
O'Briant, Sidney	078	1896	WB-19/398	AR
O'Brien, Elizabeth	044	1850	WB-18/43	CTY
O'Brien, John	044	1851	WB-18/289	CTY
O'Brien, John	019	1874	WB-B/74	AR
O'Bryan, Dennis	082	1800	WB-1/74	AR
O'Bryan, Dennis	100	1843	WB-38/229	AR
O'Bryan, Elizabeth	037	1811	WB-E/9	AR
O'Bryant, John D.	044	1866	WB-22/490	CTY
O'Connell, Jeremiah	040	1894	WB-2/478	AR
O'Connell, John	022	1889	WB-E/400	AR
O'Connell, Lawrence	065	1891	WB-L/586	
O'Daniel, Alexdr.	036	1816	WB-A/370	AR
O'Daniel, Alonza	103	1895	035 WB-4/466	035 AR
O'Daniel, Alonzo	103	1895	WB-2/101	AR
O'Daniel, Archelaus	035	1864	WB-3/90	AR
O'Daniel, Henry	073	1847	WB-F/336	AR
O'Daniel, Henry	073	1829	WB-E/208	AR
O'Daniel, Henry	073	1813	WB-D/377	AR
O'Daniel, Jesse	073	1843	WB-F/175	AR
O'Daniel, John	073	1825	WB-C/78	AR
O'Daniel, John	073	1836	WB-E/369	AR
O'Daniel, John	073	1857	WB-G/175	CTY
O'Daniel, Martha	073	1855	WB-G/98	AR
O'Daniel, Mary	022	1847	WB-C/203	AR
O'Daniel, Owan	028	1736	SS 877/23	SS/AR
O'Daniel, Owen	035	1835	WB-1/54	AR
O'Daniel, William	073	1858	WB-G/202	AR
O'Daniel, William	073	1844	WB-F/227	AR
O'Daniel, William J.	040	1865	WB-1/171	
O'Donoghue, B. Agnes	065	1889	WB-L/369	
O'Dwyer, Thomas	051	1834	WB-A/106	
O'Fairhill, Barnabas	073	1831	WB-E/245	AR
O'Flaherty, J. Bernard	027	c1833	WB-A/3	AR
O'Hagan, Elvira L.	079	1889	WB-2/461	AR
O'Hagan, Sarah J.	105	1888	WB-2/487	AR
O'Kelly, Eliza	022	1890	WB-E/433	AR
O'Kelly, Eliza	036	1890	WB-A/196	
O'Kelly, Elizabeth	022	1833	WB-B/249	AR
O'Kelly, J. F.	022	1894	WB-F/557	AR
O'Kelly, James	022	1826	WB-B/125	AR
O'Kelly, John	099	c1892	Orig. Only	AR
O'Kelly, John	027	1837	WB-A/22	AR
O'Kelly, Leslie	073	1825	WB-E/75	AR
O'Kelly, Mary E.	022	1853	WB-C/344	AR
O'Kelly, Patsey A.	022	c1855	WB-D/13	AR
O'Kelly, William	022	1821	WB-B/34	AR
O'Leary, William D.	028	1865	WB-D/373	AR
O'Neal, Alonzo	053	1898	WB-11/336	AR
O'Neal, Anna	056	1835	WB-1/506	AR
O'Neal, Bateman	019	1837	WB-A/66	AR

Name	Co	Date	Recorded Copy	Original
O'Neal, Benjamin	053	1854	WB-8/68	AR
O'Neal, Charity	053	1824	Orig. Only	AR
O'Neal, Christopher	030	1817	WB-3/96	
O'Neal, Christopher	060	1812	Orig. Only	AR
O'Neal, Christopher	053	1869	WB-11/6	
O'Neal, Condary	069	1832	WB-1/391	AR
O'Neal, Edmon	037	1844	WB-F/309	AR
O'Neal, Edward	030	1831	WB-3/262	
O'Neal, Elisha	037	1855	WB-G/95	AR
O'Neal, Ephraim	053	1865	WB-10/23	AR
O'Neal, Francis	019	1825	WB-D/312	AR
O'Neal, Francis	037	1854	WB-G/74	AR
O'Neal, James	085	1823	WB-H/232	AR
O'Neal, James	056	1819	WB-1/297	AR
O'Neal, James	092	1877	Orig. Only	AR
O'Neal, James B.	056	1868	WB-2/115	AR
O'Neal, John	053	1795	RW-1/252	AR
O'Neal, Joseph	031	1893	WB-1/84	AR
O'Neal, Kiddy	056	1832	WB-1/481	AR
O'Neal, Micajah	069	1861	WB-1/579	AR
O'Neal, Moses	056	1813	WB-1/393	AR
O'Neal, Nathan	030	1821	WB-3/119	
O'Neal, Peter	084	c1789	OW/184	AR
O'Neal, Peter	024	1803	WB-B/232	AR
O'Neal, Sally	030	1840	WB-4/68	
O'Neal, Samuel	030	1850	WB-4/155	
O'Neal, Sarah	030	1871	WB-5/15	AR
O'Neal, William	053	1854	WB-8/42	AR
O'Neal, William	099	1883	WB-A/493	AR
O'Neal, William	019	1828	WB-D/313	AR
O'Neal, William	073	1797	WB-C/101	AR
O'Neal, William	053	c1817	RW-1/523	AR
O'Neal, William H.	056	1888	WB-3/475	AR
O'Neal, Wyatt	037	1888	WB-H/129	AR
O'Neel, Elizabeth	077	1807	WB-E/292	AR
O'Neel, Honour	060	1816	Orig. Only	AR
O'Neel, Isham	037	1811	WB-E/7	AR
O'Neil, Mickil	030	1797	WB-2/111	
O'Quin, Daniel	071	1781	WB-1/238	
Oakes, George W.	038	c1863	WB-1/217	AR
Oakes, Isaac	046	1894	WB-F/308	AR
Oakley, Elizabeth	084	1896	WB-F/55	CTY
Oakley, James	044	1834	WB-13/150	CTY
Oakley, Julia E.	070	1895	WB-G/310	AR
Oakley, Louisa	079	1891	WB-2/531	AR
Oakley, Mark	078	1872	WB-19/27	AR
Oakley, Martha	078	1863	WB-18/312	AR
Oakley, McFarling	078	1861	WB-18/217	AR
Oakley, Peter	084	1863	WB-C/388	CTY
Oakley, Rebecca	078	1888	WB-19/227	AR
Oakley, Sarah	078	1874	WB-19/35	AR
Oakley, Sterling	078	1873	WB-19/116	AR
Oakley, Susan	020	1899	WB-B/363	CTY
Oakley, Thomas	020	1856	RB-R/425	AR
Oakley, Thomas D.	078	1862	WB-18/275	AR
Oakley, William	046	1861	WB-D/85	AR
Oakley, William E.	078	1876	WB-19/59	
Oakly, Nathan	078	1892	WB-19/320	AR
Oaks, John	094	1774	Orig. Only	060 AR
Oaks, Mary	032	1845	WB-2/44	AR
Oaks, Ruth	038	c1860	WB-1/177	AR
Oaksmith, Appleton	019	1890	WB-B/203	AR
Oates, David	087	1875	WB-3/106	AR
Oates, Elizabeth	087	1839	WB-1/212	AR
Oates, George P.	046	1881	WB-E/298	AR
Oates, James	077	1703	SS 874.1/20 &27	
Oates, James	087	1877	WB-3/164	AR
Oates, James P.	040	1886	WB-2/272	AR
Oates, James S.	026	1874	WB-2/127	AR
Oates, Jethro	035	1781	WB-A/374	AR
Oates, Jethro	087	1823	WB-1/45	
Oates, John	026	1849	WB-1/98	AR
Oates, John E.	065	1897	WB-N/35	
Oates, Mary Ann	087	c1821	WB-1/33	
Oates, Robert	065	1897	WB-N/77	
Oates, Stephen	087	1835	WB-1/168	AR
Oates, Stephen	087	c1816	WB-A/82	AR
Oates, Susannah	035	1861	WB-3/43	AR
Oates, Thomas	040	c1855	WB-1/100	
Oates, Thomas D.	037	1893	WB-H/340	AR-Nunc.
Oates, William	026	1856	WB-1/194	AR
Oats, Jane	060	1819	Orig. Only	AR
Oats, John	060	1830	WB-1/183	AR
Oats, Mary	060	1842	WB-2/416	AR
Oats, Robert	060	1846	WB-2/267	AR
Oats, Scotland	053	1879	WB-11/86	AR
Oats, William	060	1819	Orig. Only	AR
Oberhauser, Fred	068	1894	WB-D/403	
Ochiltree, Ann Eliza	029	1885	WB-E/363	AR
Ochiltree, Lucy Ann	029	1873	WB-E/76	AR
Odean, Thomas	022	c1805	WB-A/93	AR
Odeer, Osten	064	1886	Orig. Only	AR
Odell, D. W.	023	1888	WB-A/68	AR
Odell, James	081	1886	WB-16/18	AR
Odell, Nehemiah	081	1791	WB-1/98	Nunc.
Oden, A. T.	009	1886	WB-1/402	CTY
Oden, Allen G.	028	1894	WB-F/145	
Oden, Charles	009	1824	OB-A/340	AR
Oden, George W.	009	1879	WB-1/233	CTY
Oden, Luveny	009	1899	WB-2/194	CTY
Oden, Richard	008	1708/9	009 DB-1/97	
Oden, Richard	009	1825	OB-A/351	AR
Oden, Richard	009	1825	OB-A/352	AR
Oden, Richard	009	c1789	OWB/232	AR
Oden, Robert	053	1815	Orig. Only	AR
Oden, Thomas	009	1850	OB-G/217	AR
Oden, William	009	1817	OB-A/271	AR
Oden, William H.	009	1859	OB-L/69	AR
Odeneal, John	084	1833	WB-B/76	CTY
Odeon, Charles	009	c1759	OWB/65	AR
Odeon, Charles	009	1736	LGB-4/#49	SS/AR
Odeon, Elizabeth	009	c1770	OWB/109	AR
Odeon, John	009	c1760	OWB/81	AR
Odeon, John	009	1741	LGB-4/#165	SS/AR
Odeon, Robert	010	1778	WB-B/118	AR
Odling, Charles	070	1818	WB-C/327	AR
Odom, Aaron	071	1791	WB-1/424	AR
Odom, Abraham	037	1827	WB-F/66	AR
Odom, Barshaba	051	1850	WB-A/308	
Odom, Benjamin	041	1822	WB-2/179	AR
Odom, Brittan	060	1900	WB-5/164	AR
Odom, Demsey	041	1808	WB-2/33	AR
Odom, Jacob	041	1835	WB-2/365	AR
Odom, Jacob	010	1736	Orig. Only	SS/AR
Odom, Jacob	051	1762	Copy	041 AR
Odom, Jacob	071	1805	WB-2/292	AR
Odom, Jacob	041	1841	WB-A/148	
Odom, James	103	1873	WB-1/60	AR
Odom, James F.	069	1879	WB-5/80	AR

Name	Co.	Date	Recorded Copy	Original
Odom, John	051	1777	Copy	024 AR
Odom, John	041	1815	WB-2/98	AR
Odom, John W.	041	1852	WB-3/154	AR
Odom, John W.	069	1882	WB-5/148	AR
Odom, Mary H.	037	1895	WB-H/321	AR
Odom, Michael	056	1821	WB-1/437	AR
Odom, Moses	071	1792	WB-2/21	AR
Odom, Nancy	056	1844	WB-1/564	AR
Odom, Peter	103	1899	WB-2/245	AR
Odom, Rachel	071	1801	WB-2/218	AR
Odom, Richard	005	c1797	WB-2/118	AR
Odom, Richard	024	1728	Orig. Only	SS/AR
Odom, Sarah	051	1837	WB-A/97	
Odom, Sarah	087	c1787	WB-A/159	AR
Odom, Susan	051	1889	WB-C/393	AR
Odom, Tabitha	071	1844	WB-4/277	AR
Odom, William	041	1794	WB-1/128	AR
Odom, Winborn	071	1869	WB-6/15	AR
Odowdee, William	030	1777	WB-1/112	
Odum, Dicy	087	1890	WB-3/437	AR
Odum, Jacob	069	1841	WB-1/455	AR
Odum, Sally	039	1869	Orig. Only	AR
Odyer, Dennis	056	1747	Orig. Only	SS/AR
Oehler, George M.	065	1872	WB-K/95	
Oehler, John	065	1895	WB-M/329	
Oen, Ralph	085	c1785	WB-C/67	CTY
Oettinger, David	105	1899	WB-3/353	AR
Ofeye, Danell	075	1708	Orig. Only	SS/AR
Ofray, Maturen	028	1798	WB-B/54	AR
Ogburn, John	056	1841	WB-1/576	AR
Ogburn, Stephen	022	1798	RB-2/132	AR
Ogburn, Stephenson	056	1895	WB-2/203	AR
Ogburn, William	046	1828	Orig. Only	AR
Ogden, Isaac	072	c1776	RW/L6	AR
Ogden, Josiah	056	1852	Est-23/282	
Ogden, Tabitha	072	c1784	WI/L40	AR
Ogden, Titus	028	1794	WB-A/308	AR
Ogelsbe, John	028	1797	WB-B/32	AR
Ogelsbee, John	019	c1760	Orig. Only	AR
Ogg, George	037	1800	WB-D/108	AR
Oggs, John	075	1771	WB-H/126	AR
Oggs, Prudence	018	1828	WB-C/103	
Ogilvia, Margarett	061	c1850	WB-1/44	
Ogilvy, William	075	1774	WB-I/81	AR
Ogleby, Patrick	024	1726/7	SS 876/108	
Oglesbee, Thomas	019	1796	WB-D/305	AR
Oglesby, John	019	1815	WB-D/307	AR
Oglesby, Levi	019	1866	WB-A/291	AR
Oglesby, Micajah	092	c1828	WB-4/31	
Oglesby, Micajah	104	1846	WB-4/319	
Oglesby, Thomas	019	1825	WB-D/311	AR
Oglesby, William T.	028	1838	WB-C/416	AR
Oglesby, Zemeriah	019	1870	WB-B/57	
Okey, Joseph	044	1805	WB-6/201	CTY
Old, William	018	1854	WB-D/7	
Oldfeld, Richard	072	1773	Orig. Only	SS/AR
Oldfield, Pitts	072	1809	WB-A/101	AR
Oldfield, Rebecca C.	057	1900	WB-C/256	AR
Oldham, Elizabeth	011	1853	WB-1/208	
Oldham, John, Sr.	022	1832	WB-B/226	AR
Oldham, Thomas D.	073	1886	WB-H/411	CTY
Oldham, Wesley	022	1892	WB-E/505	AR
Oldham, Young	022	1892	WB-E/489	AR
Oldredge, Hannah	060	1830	WB-1/199	AR
Olds, Keziah	030	1857	WB-4/210	
Oldy, Elizabeth	028	1786	WB-A/109	AR
Oliphant, Euphemia	012	1817	WB-B/117	AR
Oliphant, John	085	1785	WB-B/194	AR
Oliphant, John	054	c1798	WB-1/184	AR
Olive, A. J.	099	1897	WB-D/8	AR
Olive, Abel	099	1847	RB-26/238	AR
Olive, Anderson	099	1897	WB-D/38	AR
Olive, D. H.	099	1899	WB-D/295	AR
Olive, Henderson	099	1865	RB-33/431	AR
Olive, Jesse, Sr.	099	1829	RB-21/94	AR
Olive, Mary	099	1860	RB-31/490	AR
Olive, Nancy	099	1845	RB-26/11	AR
Olive, Sarah	056	1900	WB-4/193	AR
Olive, William, Sr.	099	1827	RB-20/126	AR
Oliver, Alexander	096	c1781	WB-1/131	AR
Oliver, Alida J.	065	1893	WB-M/143	
Oliver, Andrew	010	1746/7	Orig. Only	024 AR
Oliver, Andrew	065	1820	WB-E/62	AR
Oliver, Andrew	010	1793	WB-D/221	AR
Oliver, Asa	056	1852	WB-1/664	AR
Oliver, Benjamin	072	1802	WB-A/100	AR
Oliver, Benjamin	035	1881	WB-4/212	AR
Oliver, Elizabeth	028	1865	WB-D/402	AR
Oliver, Everit	071	1840	WB-4/213	AR
Oliver, Frances	024	1756	SS 880/71	SS/AR
Oliver, Francis	035	1808	WB-A/371	AR
Oliver, Hannah T.	028	1882	WB-E/308	AR
Oliver, Henry	056	1819	WB-1/298	AR
Oliver, James	006	1887	WB-E/152	AR
Oliver, James	084	1840	WB-B/229	CTY
Oliver, James	072	1781	RW/L46	AR
Oliver, James L.	084	c1847	WB-C/44	
Oliver, John	056	1792	WB-1/58	AR
Oliver, John	010	1797	WB-D/365	AR
Oliver, John	071	1810	WB-3/33	AR
Oliver, John	010	1816	WB-F/312	AR
Oliver, John	035	1844	Orig. Only	AR
Oliver, John	028	1777	Orig. Only	AR
Oliver, John	010	1774	WB-B/11	AR
Oliver, John	057	1787	WB-A/64	AR
Oliver, John	070	1794	WB-C/324	AR
Oliver, John	028	1776	Orig. Only	AR
Oliver, John	035	1863	WB-3/83	AR
Oliver, John	056	1803	WB-1/152	AR
Oliver, John S.	070	1813	WB-AB/201	AR
Oliver, Joseph	N	1737	Orig. Only	SS/AR
Oliver, Joseph	028	1817	WB-C/158	AR
Oliver, Joseph J.	057	1864	WB-B/257	AR
Oliver, Joseph W.	038	1891	WB-3/193	AR
Oliver, Joseph W.	090	1891	WB-6/250	AR
Oliver, Louisa A.	009	1852	OB-H/111	AR
Oliver, Mary	044	1805	WB-6/169	CTY
Oliver, Mary	028	1794	WB-A/318	AR
Oliver, Mary	010	1808	WB-F/75	AR
Oliver, Mary	006	c1858	WB-D/52	
Oliver, Moses	024	1728	SS 876/169	SS/AR
Oliver, Penelope B.	057	1872	WB-C/24	AR
Oliver, Peter	090	1810	WB-2/115	AR
Oliver, Phillip H.	056	1872	WB-3/80	AR
Oliver, Richard P.	028	1840	WB-D/8	AR
Oliver, Robert	078	1847	WB-13/5	AR
Oliver, Sarah	035	1838	Orig. Only	AR
Oliver, Stephen	078	1828	SC/06770	AR-Copy
Oliver, Stephen	078	1828	WI-11/80	AR
Oliver, Thomas	010	1765	WB-A/73	AR

Name	Co.	Date	Recorded Copy	Original
Oliver, Thomas	030	1745	Orig. Only	SS/AR
Oliver, Thomas	065	1836	WB-E/145	AR
Oliver, Thomas	056	1799	WB-1/115	AR
Oliver, Thomas	028	1811	WB-C/38	AR
Oliver, William	010	1816	WB-F/311	AR
Oliver, William	028	1779	Orig. Only	AR
Oliver, William	044	1762	Orig. Only	CTY
Oliver, William	056	1777	WB-2/260	AR
Oliver, Winnifred	099	1858	RB-30/519	AR
Olphin, William	072	c1773	RW/L10	AR
Oneal, Benjamin	005	1840	WB-2/117	AR
Oneal, Michael	030	1721/2	SS 876/153	SS/AR
Oneal, Michael	030	1723	SS 876/52	SS/AR
Oneal, William	005	1867	WB-C/255	AR
Oneale, Zacharias	056	1796	WB-1/100	AR
Oneil, Elizabeth	037	1827	WB-F/71	AR
Oneil, Henry M.	014	1861	WB-1/10	AR
Oneil, William	030	1799	WB-2/146	
Onley, Edward	051	1842	WB-A/155	
Onley, Penelope	041	1807	Orig. Only	AR-Nunc.
Onstott, George	081	1805	WB-3/10	AR
Oquin, Patrick	071	1752	Orig. Only	SS/AR
Oram, Benjamin	070	1749	DB-C/171	AR
Oram, Robert F.	NJ	1900	055 WB-A/192	
Orbison, Margaret	054	1841	WB-2/233	
Orders, Carter	014	1866	WB-1/16	AR
Ore, William	090	1819	WB-3/31	AR
Orindell, Edward	024	1732	SS 876/271	SS/AR
Orindell, Edward	024	c1762	WB-A/195	AR
Orkney, John	009	1872	WB-1/102	CTY
Orman, Michael	081	1818	WB-4/551	
Ormand, Benjamin	060	1829	WB-1/157	AR
Ormand, Benjamin	040	1853	WB-1/42	
Ormand, Henry	009	1875	WB-1/144	AR
Ormand, John J.	040	1889	WB-2/336	AR
Ormand, William	059	1872	WB-A/43	
Ormand, Zenas S.	040	1878	WB-2/132	AR
Orme, James	070	1818	WB-C/328	AR
Orme, Mary L.	070	1858	WB-C/658	AR
Orme, Robert	057	1779	WB-A/234	AR
Ormond, Elizabeth	065	1820	WB-E/61	AR
Ormond, Gatlin	045	1893	WB-1/318	AR
Ormond, Jacob	065	1810	WB-E/57	AR
Ormond, James	065	1770	WB-E/48	AR
Ormond, John J.	045	1895	WB-1/354	AR
Ormond, Nicey	045	1900	WB-1/406	
Ormond, Thomas B.	009	1838	OB-C2/79	AR
Ormond, Wilber E.	045	1895	WB-1/316	AR
Ormond, Wyriott	009	1773	Orig. Only	SS/AR
Ormsbee, Susan	028	1856	WB-D/269	
Orr, C. C.	093	c1863	WB-1/39	
Orr, George	093	1877	WB-1/197	
Orr, George	065	1792	WB-E/52	AR
Orr, James	065	1778	WB-E/48	
Orr, James	065	1808	WB-E/56	AR
Orr, James	020	1820	RB-H/295	AR
Orr, James R.	065	1856	WB-J/19	AR
Orr, James T.	065	1842	WB-H/67	AR
Orr, Joab L. A.	065	1847	WB-I/92	AR
Orr, John	060	1807	Orig. Only	AR
Orr, John	099	1779	RB-1/164	AR
Orr, John	065	1855	WB-J/2	AR
Orr, John	050	1849	WB-1/24	CTY
Orr, John P.	013	1882	WB-B/264	AR
Orr, Mary	065	1813	WB-E/58	AR
Orr, Mary	086	1822	WB-D/1	AR
Orr, Mathew	070	1791	WB-C/325	AR
Orr, Mildridge	065	1800	WB-E/54	AR
Orr, Nathan	065	1849	WB-I/161	AR
Orr, Nathan	065	1779	WB-E/59	AR
Orr, Nathan F.	065	1864	WB-J/195	AR
Orr, Nathan R.	065	1859	WB-J/59	AR
Orr, Robert	099	1780	RB-1/166	AR
Orr, Robert	065	1791	WB-E/51	AR
Orr, William	009	1811	096 WB-4/173	096 AR
Orr, William	009	1811	WB-2/203	AR
Orr, William	009	1811	Copy	101 AR
Orr, William W.	065	1855	WB-J/12	AR
Orrell, Daniel	085	c1830	WB-H/502	AR
Orrell, Franklin	009	1837	OWB/534	AR
Orrell, Nancy	085	1835	WB-H/649	AR
Orrell, R. M.	029	1892	WB-E/550	AR
Orrell, Stephen	009	c1803	OWB/418	AR
Orrell, William	009	1818	OB-A/279	AR
Orrell, William A.	009	1847	OB-F/391	AR
Orrenton, Charles	005	c1796	Orig. Only	AR
Orrill, L. D.	046	c1862	WB-E/15	AR
Orsborn, Lutitia	081	1889	WB-16136	AR
Orsburn, Obediah	072	1758	SS 882/55	SS/AR
Orten, James	054	c1825	WB-2/145	AR
Orton, James	085	c1776	WB-A/230	AR
Orton, Joseph	085	c1807	WB-C/289	AR
Osbern, Mary, Sr.	006	1838	WB-A/76	AR
Osbon, William	104	1836	WB-4/200	AR
Osborn, Adlai	054	c1814	WB-1/347	AR
Osborn, Alexander	085	1777	WB-A/224	AR
Osborn, Alfred	006	1876	WB-E/17	AR
Osborn, Caleb	089	1877	WB-2/45	AR
Osborn, Christopher	065	1789	WB-E/49	AR
Osborn, David	046	1842	WB-C/122	AR
Osborn, Enoch	006	1893	WB-E/163	AR
Osborn, Ephraim	049	1875	WB-2/6	AR
Osborn, Jeremiah	081	1845	WB-8/120	AR
Osborn, Jesse	081	1828	WB-5/428	AR
Osborn, John	065	1802	WB-E/55	AR
Osborn, Jonathan	044	1877	WB-23/248	CTY
Osborn, Joshua	089	1888	WB-2/212	AR
Osborn, Judson P.	049	1876	WB-2/28	AR
Osborn, Nathan	081	1836	WB-7/27	AR
Osborn, Obed	081	1890	WB-16/149	AR
Osborn, Peter	046	1843	WB-C/159	AR
Osborn, Stephen	032	c1860	WB-2/291	
Osborn, William	081	1850	WB-9/197	AR
Osborne, Eli	004	1864	WB-1/10	
Osborne, James	071	1789	WB-1/387	AR
Osborne, James W.	065	1869	WB-K/11	
Osborne, Jeremiah	093	1890	WB-2/70	AR
Osborne, John G.	049	1859	WB-2/217	AR
Osborne, Judson P.	049	c1876	Copy	013 AR
Osborne, Michael	097	1890	WB-2/350	AR
Osborne, Milton	065	1885	WB-L/109	
Osborne, Sarah	097	1867	WB-1/286	AR
Osborne, Stephen	006	1893	WB-E/242	AR
Osbourn, Jesse	099	1839	RB-24/260	AR
Osbun, Jonathan	049	c1805	WI-A/26	AR
Osburn, Alexander	097	1843	WB-1/1	AR
Osgood, Franklin	NY	1888	046 WB-H/471	
Osgood, Franklin	NY	1888	022 WB-F/114	
Osteen, Luke	093	1899	WB-2/170	AR
Ostwalt, J. H.	054	1891	WB-5/394	CTY

Name	Co.	Date	Recorded Copy	Original
Otrich, Charles A.	003	1893	WB-B/317	AR
Ott, George	VA	1831	075 WB-N/71	075 AR
Ott, V. G.	065	1896	WB-M/506	
Ottaway, Abram	012	1890	WB-A/86	
Otterbourg, Helena	070	1889	WB-F/249	AR
Otterson, Malichi	028	1803	WB-B/191	AR
Ottinger, Catherine	062	1899	WB-B/218	
Ottoson, Caleb	028	1804	WB-B/210	AR
Ottrich, Margaret	033	1866	WB-1/202	
Ottwell, Isaac	008	1733	SS 876/285	SS/AR
Otwell, James	046	1828	WB-B/359	AR
Otwell, Shadrack	046	1837	WB-B/588	AR
Ousby, Thomas	047	1857	WB-5/47	AR-Copy
Outerbridge, Drussila	063	1826	WB-2/109	
Outerbridge, Mary	063	1791	WB-1/177	
Outerbridge, Stephen	039	c1824	SC/01874	AR-Copy
Outland, Cornelius	071	1873	WB-6/115	AR
Outland, Cornelius	103	1810	RD-1/334	AR
Outland, Elijah	071	1897	WB-7/359	AR
Outland, Exum	071	1841	WB-4/241	AR
Outland, Exum J.	071	1893	WB-7/206	AR
Outland, Isaac O.	071	1891	WB-7/122	AR
Outland, Jeremiah	071	1824	WB-3/306	AR
Outland, Jesse	103	1832	RD-6/352	AR
Outland, John	071	1846	WB-5/41	AR
Outland, Jonathan	103	1827	RD-5/362	
Outland, Joseph	077	1790	WB-C/413	AR
Outland, Josiah	071	1831	WB-4/74	AR
Outland, Josiah	071	1873	WB-6/125	AR
Outland, Sarah J.	103	1896	WB-2/155	AR
Outland, Thomas	103	1850	RD-10/460	AR
Outland, Thomas	103	1883	WB-1/296	AR
Outland, Thomas	071	1855	WB-5/144	AR
Outland, Thomas	103	1801	Orig. Only	AR
Outland, William J.	103	1890	WB-1/537	AR
Outlar, Ann	070	1899	Orig. Only	AR
Outlaw, Aaron	010	1815	WB-F/281	AR
Outlaw, Agens	010	1795	WB-D/287	AR
Outlaw, Alexander	035	1862	WB-3/52	AR
Outlaw, David	039	c1848	WB-O/153	AR
Outlaw, Edward	035	1857	WB-2/118	AR
Outlaw, Edward	010	1808	WB-F/72	AR
Outlaw, Edward	035	c1759	WB-A/369	
Outlaw, Elizabeth	035	1830	WB-1/7	AR
Outlaw, George	041	1801	WB-1/191	AR
Outlaw, George	010	1825	WB-G/131	AR
Outlaw, George	010	1795	WB-D/278	AR
Outlaw, George	001	1854	WB-1/90	AR
Outlaw, George	035	1878	WB-4/134	AR
Outlaw, Harget K.	035	1890	WB-4/366	AR
Outlaw, Harriet	010	1900	WB-K/35	
Outlaw, Jacob	041	1808	WB-2/12	AR
Outlaw, James	041	1796	WB-1/139	AR
Outlaw, James	035	1827	WB-A/367	AR
Outlaw, James	010	1808	WB-F/78	AR
Outlaw, Jeremiah	010	1890	WB-I/287	AR
Outlaw, John	041	1823	WB-2/209	AR
Outlaw, John	010	1780	WB-B/155	AR
Outlaw, Joseph B.	028	1860	WB-D/330	AR
Outlaw, Joseph W.	010	1895	WB-I/449	AR
Outlaw, Noah	035	1893	WB-4/439	AR
Outlaw, Rachel	035	1876	WB-4/104	AR
Outlaw, Ralph	010	1790	WB-D/146	AR
Outlaw, Sally	035	1866	WB-3/109	AR
Outlaw, Sarah	010	1882	WB-I/143	
Outlaw, Thomas	010	1782	WB-C/47	AR
Outlaw, Timothy	010	1814	WB-F/268	AR
Outlaw, William	035	1868	WB-3/132	AR
Outlaw, William	009	1853	OB-I/108	
Outlaw, William T.	099	1855	RB-29/318	AR
Outler, Ralph	024	c1756	Orig. Only	AR
Outten, Abraham	028	1801	WB-B/115	AR
Outten, Macy	028	1866	WB-D/413	AR
Outten, Matthew A.	028	1857	WB-D/289	AR
Outterbridge, Burr	063	1819	WB-2/66	
Outterbridge, George T.	063	1860	WB-2/472	
Outterbridge, Stephen	063	1848	WB-2/341	
Outterbridge, Stephen	039	1824	WB-H/51	AR
Outterbridge, William	063	1794	WB-1/212	
Overby, Ann E.	099	1896	WB-C/545	AR
Overby, David	044	1881	WB-23/430	CTY
Overby, J. J.	099	1873	RB-35/212	AR
Overby, James	090	1900	WB-6/529	AR
Overby, John G.	051	1879	WB-C/227	AR
Overby, Mahala J.	020	1874	WB-A/158	CTY
Overby, Martin	099	1857	RB-30/300	AR
Overby, Mary	098	1899	WB-A/328	CTY
Overby, Mary Ann	056	1896	WB-4/25	AR
Overby, William	029	1885	WB-E/341	AR
Overcash, Catherine	054	1900	WB-6/315	CTY
Overcash, Christopher	085	1890	WB-2/418	CTY
Overcash, Daniel	085	1856	WB-K/216	AR
Overcash, Elizabeth	054	1873	WB-4/126	CTY
Overcash, Emeline	085	1891	WB-2/488	CTY
Overcash, Francis	085	c1865	WB-L/38	AR
Overcash, Henry	054	1846	WB-3/15	AR
Overcash, Jacob	085	1851	WB-K/126	AR
Overcash, Jacob	085	1833	WB-H/591	AR
Overcash, James	054	c1863	WB-3/177	AR
Overcash, John	085	1872	WB-1/137	CTY
Overcash, John	054	1846	WB-3/7	AR
Overcash, John A.	016	1874	WB-3/104	
Overcash, John J.	054	1864	WB-3/209	AR
Overcash, Leonard	085	1851	WB-K/138	AR
Overcash, Leonard	085	1895	WB-3/86	CTY
Overcash, Michal	003	1862	Orig. Only	AR
Overcash, Solomon	085	1865	WB-K/366	AR
Overcash, Solomon	054	1884	WB-5/445	CTY
Overcash, Sophia	003	1866	WB-A/5	AR
Overcash, Sophia	085	1893	WB-2/559	CTY
Overcash, Susannah	085	1841	WB-I/111	AR
Overcash, William	054	1893	WB-5/462	CTY
Overcast, George	016	1832	PQS.5/235	
Overcast, Peter	016	1847	WB-1/136	
Overhisen, John	070	1785	WB-C/324	AR
Overman, Aaron	103	1830	RD-6/94	AR
Overman, Anias	075	1794	WB-L/20	AR
Overman, Ann	075	1763	WB-H/48	
Overman, Charles	075	1898	WB-O/478	AR
Overman, Charles	077	1845	WB-F/319	AR
Overman, Charles	077	1774	WB-C/162	AR
Overman, Charles	075	1756	Orig. Only	SS/AR
Overman, Charles	075	1806	WB-M1/132	AR
Overman, Christopher	075	1762	WB-I/28	AR
Overman, Cornelius	103	1847	RD-9/513	AR
Overman, Elizabeth	075	1889	WB-O/313	AR
Overman, Enoch	075	1773	WB-I/129	AR
Overman, Enoch	075	1792	WB-K/234	AR
Overman, Ephraim	075	1785	WB-K/114	AR
Overman, Ephraim	075	1796	WB-L/57	AR

Name	Co.	Date	Recorded Copy	Original
Overman, Exum	103	1853	RD-11/296	AR
Overman, Henry P.	075	1822	WB-M1/349	AR
Overman, Isaac	075	1784	WB-K/96	AR
Overman, Jacob	077	1786	WB-C/331	AR
Overman, Jacob, Sr.	N	c1715	Orig. Only	SS/AR
Overman, James	075	1746	Orig. Only	SS/AR
Overman, James	075	1823	WB-M1/370	AR
Overman, Jesse	103	1828	RD-5/464	AR
Overman, John	103	1802	Orig. Only	AR
Overman, John	077	1832	WB-F/197	AR
Overman, John	075	c1779	Orig. Only	AR
Overman, John	103	1811	RD-2/30	AR
Overman, John	075	1745	Orig. Only	SS/AR
Overman, Joseph	075	1739	LGB-4/#107	SS/AR
Overman, Laura M.	085	1875	WB-1/291	CTY
Overman, Mary	075	1838	WB-N/144	AR
Overman, Mary E.	075	1891	WB-O/341	AR
Overman, Nathan	075	1779	WB-K/39	AR
Overman, Nathan	075	1823	WB-M1/373	AR
Overman, Nathan	075	1877	WB-O/90	AR
Overman, Penelope	075	1839	WB-N/146a	AR
Overman, R. F.	075	1895	WB-O/421	AR
Overman, Reuben	075	1785	WB-K/135	AR
Overman, Reuben	075	1851	WB-N/238	AR
Overman, Sarah	103	1840	RD-8/29	AR
Overman, Thomas	075	1789	WB-K/182	AR
Overman, Thomas	075	1784	WB-K/97	AR
Overman, Thomas	075	1761	WB-H/26	AR
Overman, Thomas	075	1789	WB-K/176	AR
Overman, Thomas	103	1845	RD-9/274	AR
Overman, Thomas	075	1816	WB-M1/280	AR
Overman, Thomas	075	1797	WB-L/109	AR
Overman, Thomas C.	103	1883	WB-1/291	AR
Overman, William	075	1774	WB-I/102	AR
Overstreet, Henry	047	1795	WB-3/252	AR
Overstreet, James	047	1826	WB-4/24	AR
Overstreet, John	047	1876	WB-6/143	AR
Overton, A. A.	044	1888	WB-24/48	CTY
Overton, Ann Booker	084	1814	WB-A/103	CTY
Overton, Aron	039	1824	WB-H/28	AR
Overton, Bailey J.	018	1884	WB-E/131	AR
Overton, Benjamin	018	1826	WB-C/67	
Overton, Charles	018	1846	WB-C/314	
Overton, Christopher	010	1819	WB-G/61	AR
Overton, Cornelius	051	1855	WB-A/374	
Overton, D. D.	098	1897	WB-A/304	CTY
Overton, Edward	096	1808	WB-2/27	AR
Overton, Elie	077	1848	WB-/361	AR
Overton, Elizabeth	018	1841	WB-C/263	
Overton, Furny	057	1895	WB-C/215	AR
Overton, Isom	029	1807	WB-A/109	AR
Overton, James	010	1870	WB-I/20	AR
Overton, James	051	c1826	WB-A/130	
Overton, James N.	018	1876	WB-E/62	AR
Overton, Jesse	077	c1853	WB-F/436	AR
Overton, Jesse	018	1834	WB-C/169	
Overton, Joab	018	1866	WB-D/82	AR
Overton, Joab	018	1859	WB-D/56	AR
Overton, John	039	1878	WB-U/173	AR
Overton, John	072	1739	SS 877/77	SS/AR
Overton, John	084	c1786	OW/186	AR
Overton, John R.	063	1895	WB-4/176	AR
Overton, Martha A.	098	1898	WB-A/305	CTY
Overton, Nancy	018	1860	WB-D/59	
Overton, Nancy	018	1881	WB-E/99	AR
Overton, Nancy Ann	037	1900	WB-H/474	AR
Overton, Ollie	018	1842	WB-C/269	
Overton, Penelopy	077	1842	WB-F/304	AR
Overton, Penelopy	051	1878	WB-C/187	AR
Overton, Priscilla	096	1835	WB-2/124	AR
Overton, Rachel	096	c1779	WB-1/109	
Overton, Robert	030	1753	SS 881/86	SS/AR
Overton, Rodah	018	1824	WB-C/36	
Overton, Rosanne	077	1880	WB-H/105	AR
Overton, Samuel	051	1872	WB-C/80	AR
Overton, Sarah	018	1880	WB-E/78	
Overton, William	051	1860	WB-B/29	
Overton, Willis	018	1857	WB-D/33	
Owen, Aaron	100	1893	WB-51/354	
Owen, Alfred	032	1823	WB-1/5	AR
Owen, Ambrose	085	1821	WB-H/106	AR
Owen, Benjamin	032	1827	WB-1/75	AR
Owen, Casper	032	1851	WB-2/55	AR
Owen, Daniel	022	c1802	WB-A/64	AR
Owen, David	062	1857	WB-A/18	AR
Owen, David S.	032	1890	WB-4/84	AR
Owen, Eliza	081	1887	WB-16/24	
Owen, Elizabeth	032	c1854	WB-2/200	
Owen, Henry	085	c1794	WB-C/287	AR
Owen, Hezekiah	032	1832	WB-1/191	AR
Owen, Humphrey	032	1843	WB-1/418	AR
Owen, J. F.	049	1890	WB-2/243	AR
Owen, Jacob	032	1900	WB-4/451	AR
Owen, James	070	1867	WB-D/230	AR
Owen, Jesse	090	1846	WB-4/217	AR
Owen, Jesse	032	1894	WB-4/233	AR
Owen, Joel	032	1838	WB-1/311	AR
Owen, John	087	1859	WB-1/538	AR
Owen, John	085	c1787	WB-B/108	AR
Owen, John	010	1779	WB-B/133	AR
Owen, John	044	1804	WB-6/133	CTY
Owen, John	011	c1841	WB-1/71	
Owen, John A.	103	1872	WB-1/40	AR
Owen, John H.	044	1858	WB-20/488	CTY
Owen, Joseph	071	1861	WB-5/257	AR-Nunc.
Owen, Louisa	081	c1886	Orig. Only	AR
Owen, Luke	032	1891	WB-4/95	AR
Owen, Martha Jane	070	1845	WB-AB/432	AR
Owen, Mary	020	1858	RB-S/79	AR
Owen, Mary	032	1852	WB-2/74	AR
Owen, Miles P.	087	1880	WB-3/208	AR
Owen, Millicent	100	1887	WB-51/257	AR
Owen, Murphy	092	1900	WB-6/529	AR
Owen, Peter	032	1865	WB-2/301	AR
Owen, Peter	032	1830	WB-1/144	AR
Owen, Ralph	085	1810	WB-G/153	AR
Owen, Redin	087	1866	WB-2/109	AR
Owen, Richard	032	1844	WB-1/423	AR
Owen, Richard	032	1834	WB-1/252	AR
Owen, Richard	061	1891	WB-2/108	AR
Owen, Samuel	046	1802	WB-A/284	AR
Owen, Sarah	026	1864	WB-1/360	AR
Owen, Thomas	011	c1799	WB-1/418	
Owen, Thomas M.	046	1878	WB-E/234	AR
Owen, William	104	1801	WB-2/37	AR
Owen, William	104	1788	WB-1/228	AR
Owen, William	032	1823	WB-1/16	AR
Owen, William	020	1820	RB-H/301	
Owen, William	019	1822	WB-D/310	AR
Owen, Winnifred	022	1834	WB-C/4	AR

Name	Co.	Date	Recorded Copy	Original
Owenley, Ambrose	050	1864	WB-1/88	
Owens, Abraham	031	1891	WB-1/70	AR
Owens, Adam	096	c1802	WB-2/11	AR
Owens, Alice	010	1814	WB-F/269	AR
Owens, Ann Eliza	096	1868	WB-3/89	
Owens, Charlotte	057	1855	WB-B/225	AR
Owens, Christina	085	1894	WB-3/36	CTY
Owens, Daniel	069	1801	WB-1/138	AR
Owens, David	031	1889	WB-1/67	AR
Owens, Delia	104	1855	WB-5/129	
Owens, Delitha	105	1888	WB-2/470	
Owens, Elisha	037	1817	WB-E/156	AR
Owens, Elizabeth	085	1824	WB-H/301	AR
Owens, Frances L.	009	c1863	OB-M/145	AR
Owens, Fredick	030	1839	WB-4/64	
Owens, George E.	037	1895	WB-H/333	AR
Owens, George W.	047	1850	WB-4/297	AR
Owens, George W.	071	1879	047 WB-6/208	047 AR
Owens, H. C.	085	1895	WB-3/73	CTY
Owens, Hansen	090	1888	WB-6/210	AR
Owens, Isaac	030	1849	WB-4/142	
Owens, Isabella M.	096	1881	WB-4/67	
Owens, Isham	090	1861	WB-4/341	AR
Owens, James	030	1854	WB-4/194	AR
Owens, James	044	1795	WB-3/206	
Owens, James H.	065	1866	WB-J/225	AR
Owens, Jane E.	065	1867	WB-J/238	AR
Owens, John	105	1877	WB-2/211	AR
Owens, John	096	1750	SS 879/5	SS/AR
Owens, John	096	1872	Orig. Only	AR
Owens, John M.	013	1856	WB-A/170	
Owens, John S.	104	1876	WB-6/130	AR
Owens, John, Sr.	090	1886	WB-6/173	AR
Owens, Joseph	085	1825	WB-H/310	AR
Owens, Kinchen	105	c1855	WB-1/94	
Owens, Lucinda	030	1899	WB-5/272	AR
Owens, Margaret	085	1899	WB-3/302	CTY
Owens, Martha	020	1873	WB-A/120	CTY
Owens, Moses	046	1865	WB-D/275	AR
Owens, Nancy	085	1799	WB-C/288	AR
Owens, Only	073	1810	WB-D/257	AR
Owens, Owen, Sr.	087	1838	WB-1/202	AR
Owens, Philip	085	1886	WB-2/196	CTY
Owens, Polly	030	1851	WB-4/158	
Owens, Polly	030	1897	WB-5/242	AR
Owens, Sarah	065	1869	WB-K/15	
Owens, Silas, Jr.	MS	1889	047 WB-6/556	047 AR
Owens, Sir Peyton	092	1896	WB-6/429	AR
Owens, Stephen	053	1835	WB-5/259	AR
Owens, Thomas	070	1898	WB-H/145	AR
Owens, Thomas	085	1756	WB-A/134	AR
Owens, Thomas	096	1818	WB-2/72	AR
Owens, Thomas W.	019	1896	WB-B/313	AR
Owens, William	096	1847	WB-3/14	AR
Owens, William	105	1878	WB-2/234	AR
Owens, William	044	1794	WB-3/146 & 169	CTY
Owens, William	019	1766	RB-A/16	AR
Owens, William C.	032	1855	Orig. Only	AR-Nunc.
Owens, Zachariah	030	1855	WB-4/198	AR
Owings, Bazaleel	085	1826	WB-H/364	AR
Owings, Elijah	085	c1804	WB-C/285	AR
Owings, Fannie T.	104	1899	WB-7/84	AR
Owings, Henry	085	1815	WB-G/394	AR
Owings, Norman	085	1831	WB-H/515	AR
Ownbey, Uriah	064	1892	WB-2/287	AR
Ownby, Daniel R.	064	1898	WB-2/451	AR
Ownby, Thomas	039	c1796	WB-A/203	
Ownell, John	037	1784	WB-B/144	AR
Ownley, Elizabeth	077	1879	WB-H/89	AR
Oxendine, Bryant	083	1836	WB-1/300	Nunc.
Oxendine, Charles	083	c1808	WB-1/206	AR
Oxendine, Moses	083	1857	WB-2/122	AR
Oxenwall, Peter	028	1730	Deeds.1/98	SS/AR
Oxford, E. C.	003	1890	WB-B/270	AR
Oxford, Isaac	017	1899	WB-B/304	
Oxford, Samuel	060	1811	Orig. Only	AR
Oxley, Elizabeth	010	1840	WB-G/326	AR
Oxley, Hardy	010	1826	WB-G/152	AR
Oxley, John	010	1805	WB-E/262	AR
Oxley, John, Sr.	010	1767	WB-A/81	AR
Oxley, Sarah	010	1830	WB-G/193	AR
Ozben, William	085	1768	WB-A/135	AR
Ozbun, Mathew	081	1816	WB-4/292	AR
Ozburn, Joseph	046	1833	WB-B/484	AR
Ozburn, Thomas	046	1825	WB-B/214	AR
Ozment, Charles	046	c1845	Orig. Only	AR
Ozment, Malinda	046	1888	WB-E/497	AR
Ozment, Richard	046	1817	WB-B/40	AR
Ozment, Samuel	046	1819	WB-B/80	AR
Ozment, Thomas	046	1850	WB-C/328	AR
Pace, Daniel	050	1871	WB-1/111	CTY
Pace, George	047	c1773	WB-2/103	
Pace, George	071	1789	WB-1/477	AR
Pace, Hardy	071	1792	WB-2/7	AR
Pace, J. B.	050	1890	WB-2/62	CTY
Pace, James	099	1880	WB-A/216	AR
Pace, James	099	1815	RB-12/6	
Pace, John	010	1727	SS 876/126	SS/AR
Pace, John	056	1875	WB-3/135	AR
Pace, Joseph B.	001	1885	WB-2/247	AR
Pace, Leander J.	050	1893	WB-2/173	CTY
Pace, Louisa	039	1862	WB-R/227	AR
Pace, Margaret	099	1879	WB-A/44	AR
Pace, Nancy	065	1888	WB-M/125	AR
Pace, Reubin	092	1846	WB-4/256	AR
Pace, Richard	010	1738	Orig. Only	SS/AR
Pace, Solomon	071	1795	WB-2/99	AR
Pace, Thomas	071	1805	WB-2/290	AR
Pace, Thomas	071	1765	WB-1/115	
Pace, William	069	1892	WB-5/377	AR
Pace, William	071	1775	WB-1/17	AR
Pace, William	071	1793	WB-2/26	AR
Pace, William	071	1791	WB-1/423	AR
Pace, William H.	099	1893	WB-C/164	AR
Pack, Richard	085	c1804	WB-C/299	AR
Pack, William	085	c1800	WB-F/30	AR
Pack, William	032	1835	WB-1/262	
Packer, Micajah	103	1793	Orig. Only	AR
Paddrick, Henry	030	1788	WB-1/228	
Padget, John	024	1806	WB-B/217	AR
Padget, Selvey	072	c1876	WB-4/199	AR
Padgett, Alanson	080	1878	WB-1/38	AR
Padgett, Daniel M.	072	c1865	Orig. Only	AR
Padgett, Ephraim	092	1826	WB-3/167	AR
Padgett, Isaac S.	076	1884	WB-A1/42	AR
Padgett, James	072	1758	Orig. Only	028 AR
Padgett, John	009	c1785	OWB/197	AR
Padgett, Jones	072	1758	SS 882/35	
Padgett, Spicer	076	1881	WB-A1/20	CTY

Name	Co.	Date	Recorded Copy	Original
Padgett, William	104	c1865	Orig. Only	AR
Padgett, William	086	1854	WB-E/284	AR
Padrick, Abigail	072	c1802	WB-A/107	AR
Padrick, Jacob	018	1828	WB-C/108	
Padrick, Peter	030	1800	WB-2/160	
Padrick, Peter	072	1796	Orig. Only	AR
Padrick, Sarey	030	c1812	WB-3/55	
Pady, Joseph	028	1789	WB-A/208	
Page, A. F.	099	c1899	Copy	068 AR
Page, Abram	011	1891	WB-2/238	
Page, Albert M.	020	1896	WB-B/265	CTY
Page, Alley	105	1896	WB-3/194	AR
Page, Allison F.	099	1899	WB-D/307	AR
Page, Anderson	099	1861	RB-32/86	AR
Page, Anne C.	024	1866	WB-D/42	AR
Page, Anthony	017	1873	WB-B/39	AR
Page, Augustus	083	1879	WB-3/168	AR
Page, Bartholomew	079	1886	WB-2/375	AR
Page, Bentley W.	020	1896	WB-B/286	
Page, Charles	035	1883	WB-4/221	AR
Page, Dempsy	085	1879	WB-1/481	CTY
Page, Edward	099	1806	RB-7/162	AR
Page, Elijah	014	1886	WB-2/336	CTY
Page, Elizabeth	099	1867	RB-34/329	AR
Page, Elizabeth	CT	1873	105 WB-2/155	
Page, Elizabeth	105	1869	WB-2/16	AR
Page, Henrietta	024	1868	WB-E/2	AR
Page, Henry	010	1861	WB-H/107	AR
Page, Humphry	085	1772	WB-A/138	AR
Page, Jacob	103	1789	WI-A/177	AR
Page, James	020	1878	WB-A/232	CTY
Page, James	020	1862	RB-S/574	
Page, John	099	1854	RB-28/546	AR
Page, John A.	063	1866	WB-2/530	
Page, John, Sr.	063	1838	WB-2/242	
Page, Lucy	070	1895	WB-G/329	AR
Page, Matthew	024	c1853	WB-C/355	AR
Page, Molly	010	1814	WB-F/258	AR
Page, Obadiah	099	1862	RB-32/339	AR
Page, Samuel	020	1846	RB-P/365	AR
Page, Sarah	022	c1851	WB-C/311	AR
Page, Sherwood	089	1846	WB-1/47	AR
Page, Sion	089	1887	WB-2/154	AR
Page, Stephen	020	1893	WB-B/139	CTY
Page, Thomas	020	1838	RB-N/149	
Page, Thomas	010	1786	WB-D/52	AR
Page, Washington	046	1877	WB-E/205	AR
Page, Whitehead	020	1853	RB-R/59	
Page, William	020	1806	RB-E/265	AR
Page, William A.	001	c1890	WB-2/509	AR
Page, Williamson	099	1881	WB-A/505	AR
Page, Zachariah	020	1896	WB-B/246	CTY
Page, Zachariah	020	c1864	Orig. Only	AR
Page, Zenith	020	1874	WB-A/131	CTY
Paget, Edward	024	1728	SS 876/137	
Paget, Louis	070	1839	WB-C/350	AR
Pagett, Thomas	028	1795	WB-A/339	AR
Paige, Anna	MA	1703	Copy	CCR 187
Paige, Nicholas	MA	1703	Copy	CCR 187
Pailin, John	075	1888	WB-O/294	AR
Pain, Barnabas	032	1827	WB-1/73	
Pain, Enoch	030	N. D.	WB-2/323	
Pain, Henry	017	c1854	WB-A/76	AR
Pain, John	085	c1784	WB-B/83	AR
Pain, John	086	1782	WB-A/12	
Pain, Lewis	017	1843	Orig. Only	AR
Pain, William	068	1799	WB-A/200	
Paine, Charles C.	PA	1886	028 WB-F/390	
Paine, Daniel	062	1889	WB-B/93	AR
Paine, Isaac E.	060	1894	WB-4/544	AR
Paine, J. W. A.	060	1892	WB-4/501	AR
Paine, James	100	1808	WB-14/273	AR
Paine, James	020	1783	RB-B/18	AR
Paine, James	085	c1810	WB-G/147	AR
Paine, John	099	1797	RB-4/87	AR
Paine, John	070	1767	SS 881/298	SS/AR
Paine, John	028	1754	SS 878/167	SS/AR
Paine, Margaret	030	c1857	WB-4/225	
Paine, Robert	078	1808	WI-5/27a	AR
Paine, Samuel	030	1715	Copy	SS/AR
Paine, Thomas	030	1804	WB-2/242	
Paine, Thomas	053	1837	WB-5/456	AR
Paine, Thomas	053	1826	WB-4/110	
Painter, Catharine	032	1871	WB-3/52	AR
Painter, George	086	1844	WB-E/130	AR
Painter, Jacob	032	1868	WB-2/360	AR
Painter, Leonard	086	1807	WB-B/205	AR
Painter, Spain	086	1897	WB-F/532	AR
Pair, Bythel	047	1811	WB-3/517	
Pair, John	065	1827	WB-A/155	AR
Pair, John, Sr.	099	1855	RB-28/404	AR
Pair, Nelson D.	099	1883	WB-A/384	AR
Paire, Edward M.	028	1891	WB-E/576	
Paisley, George	073	1845	WB-F/262	AR
Paisley, James	046	1869	WB-E/10	AR
Paisley, John	046	1845	WB-C/237	AR
Paisley, John	046	1811	WB-A/296	AR
Paisley, John	068	1866	WB-C/124	
Paisley, Preston	046	1836	WB-B/558	AR
Paisley, William	046	1822	WB-B/158	AR
Paisley, William A.	046	1893	WB-F/280	AR
Paisley, William D.	046	1857	WB-C/480	AR
Palin, Harriett	075	1882	WB-0/157	AR
Palin, Henry	075	1788	WB-K/163	AR
Palin, Henry	075	1768	WB-H/98	AR
Palin, Henry, Jr.	075	1700	SS 874.2/127	SS/AR
Palin, John	075	1755	Orig. Only	SS/AR
Palin, John	075	1784	WB-K/100	AR
Palin, John	075	1737	Orig. Only	SS/AR
Palin, Joseph	075	1802	WB-M1/74	
Palin, Thomas	075	1751	Orig. Only	SS/AR
Palin, Thomas	075	1734	SS 876/342	SS/AR
Palin, Thomas	075	1802	WB-M1/74	AR
Palmer, Arthur	028	1809	WB-B/341	
Palmer, Benjamin	075	1768	024 WB-1/22	024 AR
Palmer, C. B.	013	1877	WB-B/154	AR
Palmer, D. A. G.	054	1875	WB-4/176	CTY
Palmer, D. M.	017	1863	Orig. Only	AR
Palmer, Dabney	AL	1858	Copy	071 AR
Palmer, Edmond	085	1820	WB-H/33	AR
Palmer, Evelina	070	1899	WB-H/189	
Palmer, Frank	099	1895	WB-C/405	AR
Palmer, George	049	c1858	WB-1/27	AR
Palmer, Green	089	1875	WB-2/32	AR
Palmer, Harriett	046	1889	WB-F/12	AR
Palmer, Henry	NY	1893	067 WB-2/319	067 AR
Palmer, James	032	1845	WB-1/474	
Palmer, Jeremiah	075	1834	WB-N/104	AR
Palmer, Jesse	013	1850	WB-A/145	
Palmer, John	009	1761	OWB/87	AR

Name	Co.	Date	Recorded Copy	Original
Palmer, John F.	013	1867	WB-A/251	AR
Palmer, John W.	071	1872	Orig. Only	AR
Palmer, Joseph	075	1744	Orig. Only	SS/AR
Palmer, Lucy	089	1845	WB-1/33	AR
Palmer, Luke	084	c1852	WB-C/145	CTY
Palmer, Martin	073	1835	WB-E/358	AR
Palmer, Mary	049	1876	WB-2/26	
Palmer, Mary	073	1840	WB-F/47	AR
Palmer, Mary	028	c1860	Orig. Only	AR
Palmer, Nancy	084	1853	WB-C/161	CTY
Palmer, Nathaniel	020	1855	RB-R/264	AR
Palmer, Obid	028	1856	WB-D/258	AR
Palmer, Robert	022	1850	WB-C/271	AR
Palmer, Robert	075	1784	WB-K/122	AR
Palmer, Robert	075	1740	LGB-4/#125	SS/AR
Palmer, T. W.	026	1880	WB-2/215	AR
Palmer, Thomas	N	1721	SS 875/325	SS/AR
Palmer, Thomas	071	1854	WB-5/123	AR
Palmer, Thomas	001	1858	WB-1/132	
Palmer, Thomas	020	1791	RB-B/409	
Palmer, Thomas A.	089	1873	WB-2/25	
Palmer, Thomas A.G.	100	1841	WB-37/449	AR
Palmer, Walter	046	1883	WB-E/354	AR
Palmer, William	028	c1761	DB-11/197	
Palmer, William	009	c1786	OWB/208	
Pamplin, Agnes	046	1836	WB-B/549	AR
Pane, Isaac E.	060	1894	054 WB-6/189	054 CTY
Paniel, Benjamin	092	1778	WB-1/122	AR
Pankey, Auzy	082	1846	WB-3/37	AR
Pankey, Stephen	082	1863	WB-4/164	AR
Pannell, Martin	026	1888	WB-2/380	AR
Pansonby, John B.	020	1829	RB-L/396	AR
Panther, William	090	1833	WB-3/250	
Paquinet, Michael	019	1772	Orig. Only	SS/AR
Paquinet, Michael	019	1747	SS 877/49	SS/AR
Paquinett, John	019	1825	WB-D/324	AR
Paramore, James	079	1885	WB-2/324	AR
Pardin, Sallie	046	c1900	Orig. Only	AR
Pardue, Bevelly	106	1881	WB-2/148	
Pardue, Joseph	100	1790	WB-5/175	AR
Pardue, Patram	100	1822	WB-24/171	AR
Pardue, Robert H.	097	1887	WB-2/301	AR
Pardue, Thomas	104	1839	WB-4/235	AR
Pardue, William	100	1813	WB-17/263	AR
Parey, John	070	c1747	Orig. Only	AR
Parham, Cannon	044	1843	WB-15/503	CTY
Parham, David	022	1792	RB-1/43	AR
Parham, Elizabeth	086	1864	WB-E/436	AR
Parham, Gilly	099	1854	RB-28/593	AR
Parham, Isham	044	1807	WB-6/362	CTY
Parham, James	022	c1774	Orig. Only	AR
Parham, Jane	044	1882	WB-23/465	CTY
Parham, Jasper H.	098	1898	WB-A/301	CTY
Parham, John	022	1775	Orig. Only	AR
Parham, Joseph	022	1876	WB-E/115	AR
Parham, Joseph B.	044	1897	WB-24/338	CTY
Parham, Lewis I.	099	1851	RB-27/280	AR
Parham, Lucy	044	1837	WB-14/53	CTY
Parham, William	049	c1821	WI-A/17	AR
Parham, William A.	044	1893	WB-24/220	CTY
Parham, Williamson	044	1865	WB-22/377	CTY
Parham, Willie J.	044	1875	WB-23/167	CTY
Pariot, Jacob	010	1738	LGB-4/#84	
Paris, John	047	1764	WB-1/134	
Parish, Brissy	046	1847	WB-C/279	AR
Parish, Calvin E.	073	1899	WB-I/153	CTY
Parish, Charles	099	1833	RB-22/522	AR
Parish, Daniel	037	1848	063 WB-2/338	
Parish, Daniel	037	1848	WB-2/38	
Parish, David	022	1806	WB-A/126	AR
Parish, Edmond	024	1873	WB-E/45	AR
Parish, George W.	024	1872	WB-E/26	AR
Parish, Henry	073	1799	WB-C/131	AR
Parish, Humphrey	086	1840	WB-E/69	AR
Parish, James	020	1880	WB-A/289	CTY
Parish, James	024	1825	WB-C/118	AR
Parish, Joel	070	1817	WB-C/345	AR
Parish, John	024	c1772	WB-A/230	
Parish, John	056	1822	WB-1/443	AR
Parish, John	100	1828	WB-31/288	AR
Parish, John	084	1849	WB-C/98	CTY
Parish, John B.	024	1825	WB-C/118	AR
Parish, Johnson	056	1857	WB-1/704	AR
Parish, Justus	056	1808	WB-1/214	AR
Parish, Nathan	024	1818	WB-C/65	AR
Parish, Paty	056	1827	WB-1/343	AR
Parish, Reuben	046	1861	WB-D/75	AR
Parish, Robert	099	1825	RB-19/444	AR
Parish, Robert	022	1811	WB-A/195	AR
Parish, S. M.	099	1895	WB-C/373	AR
Parish, Sally	068	1793	WB-A/260	Nunc.
Parish, Susan	056	1861	WB-2/11	
Parish, William	035	1761	087 DB-3/125	AR
Parisher, Austin	096	1889	WB-4/139	AR
Park, B. F.	099	1898	WB-D/188	AR
Park, Betty	100	1804	WB-12/274	AR
Park, Humphrey	077	1803	WB-E/182	AR
Park, John	039	c1780	Orig. Only	AR
Park, John	032	1827	WB-1/69	
Park, Joseph	077	1821	WB-F/37	AR
Park, Nathan	077	1796	WB-E/65	
Park, William	100	1781	WB-3/87	AR
Parke, George	085	c1782	WB-B/165	AR
Parke, Hervey C.	MI	1899	021 WB-3/246	021 AR
Parke, James M.	104	1853	WB-5/79	
Parke, John	047	1766	WB-1/189	
Parke, Margaret	051	1835	WB-A/83	
Parke, Nathan	085	c1784	WB-B/62	AR
Parke, Robert	071	1803	WB-2/253	AR
Parke, Samuel	081	1801	WB-2/82	AR
Parke, Samuel	081	1802	WB-2/97	AR
Parke, Solomon	081	1810	WB-3/202	AR
Parker, Aaron	071	1831	WB-4/82	AR
Parker, Abner	044	1817	WB-8/86	CTY
Parker, Abram	041	1860	WB-3/259	AR
Parker, Abram W.	041	1842	WB-3/40	AR
Parker, Airland	071	1803	WB-2/249	AR-Nunc.
Parker, Amanda S.	099	1879	WB-A/84	AR
Parker, Amelia	010	1816	WB-G/1	AR
Parker, Amos	071	1800	WB-2/196	AR
Parker, Andrew	026	1857	WB-1/221	AR
Parker, Ann	087	1837	WB-1/179	
Parker, Ann	069	c1795	WB-1/233	AR
Parker, Ann	010	1852	WB-G/485	AR
Parker, Archibald	072	1839	WB-2/13	AR
Parker, Arthur	103	1816	RD-4/8	AR
Parker, Azarium	030	1789	WB-1/239	
Parker, Azricom	030	1738	SS 877/241	SS/AR
Parker, Barbara	054	1853	WB-3/71	
Parker, Barham	085	1840	WB-I/81	AR

Name	Co.	Date	Recorded Copy	Original
Parker, Bazwell	104	1887	WB-6/290	AR
Parker, Benjamin	051	1893	WB-C/463	AR
Parker, Britton	097	1890	WB-2/361	AR
Parker, Buckner	035	1879	WB-4/147	AR
Parker, Cader	044	1780	WB-1/292	CTY
Parker, Caleb	105	1870	WB-2/21	AR
Parker, Charity M.	087	1887	WB-3/346	AR
Parker, D. S.	033	1858	WB-1/164	AR
Parker, Daniel	041	1781	WB-1/17	AR
Parker, Daniel	041	1837	WB-2/387	AR
Parker, David	072	c1761	WB-A/101	AR
Parker, David	041	1875	WB-4/61	
Parker, David	051	1878	WB-C/208	AR
Parker, David	044	1834	WB-13/148	CTY
Parker, David	073	1850	WB-F/462	AR
Parker, Deberry	010	1900	WB-K/33	
Parker, Demsey	041	1808	WB-2/6	AR
Parker, Denison W.	071	1895	WB-7/254	AR
Parker, Dinah	059	1888	WB-A/537	CTY
Parker, Edmond	104	1868	WB-5/537	
Parker, Edward	085	1821	WB-H/112	AR
Parker, Edward	041	1885	WB-4/216	AR
Parker, Elijah	086	1894	WB-F/480	AR
Parker, Elijah	029	1883	WB-E/295	AR
Parker, Elijah	097	1899	WB-2/562	AR
Parker, Elisha	024	1830	WB-C/151	
Parker, Elisha	103	1821	RD-4/463	AR
Parker, Elisha	041	1806	WB-1/232	AR
Parker, Elisha	082	1805	WB-1/118	AR
Parker, Elisha	041	1793	WB-1/119	AR
Parker, Elisha	051	1869	WB-C/19	AR
Parker, Elisha	041	1881	WB-4/157	AR
Parker, Eliza J.	037	1887	WB-H/97	AR
Parker, Elizabeth	041	1800	WB-1/172	AR
Parker, Elizabeth	047	1840	WB-4/186	
Parker, Elizabeth	081	1843	WB-8/292	AR
Parker, Elizabeth	071	1868	WB-5/353	AR
Parker, Else	054	c1811	Orig. Only	AR
Parker, Ezekiel	083	1818	WB-1/327	AR-Nunc.
Parker, F. S.	079	1893	WB-3/18	AR
Parker, Feriba	041	1807	WB-2/4	AR
Parker, Francis	071	1827	WB-4/31	AR
Parker, Francis	071	1799	WB-2/186	AR
Parker, Francis	037	1757	SS 879/196	SS/AR
Parker, Francis	037	1774	WB-A/217	AR
Parker, Francis	083	1830	WB-1/253	AR
Parker, Francis	041	1791	WB-1/100	AR
Parker, Francis	069	1797	WB-1/111	AR
Parker, Garrott	067	1829	WB-1/88	AR
Parker, George	106	1880	WB-2/144	
Parker, George	027	1861	WB-A/59	AR
Parker, George W.	041	1883	WB-4/193	AR
Parker, Hardy	037	1854	WB-G/78	AR
Parker, Hardy D.	041	1869	WB-4/4	AR
Parker, Hardy W.	041	1862	WB-3/292	AR
Parker, Harriet	087	1866	WB-2/96	
Parker, Harrison	073	1864	WB-G/450	CTY
Parker, Henrietta	071	1882	WB-6/382	AR
Parker, Hester A.	010	1892	WB-I/343	AR
Parker, Isaac	071	1779	WB-1/318	
Parker, Isaac	051	1888	WB-C/377	AR
Parker, Isaac	085	1815	WB-G/370	AR
Parker, Isaac	041	1802	WB-1/196	AR
Parker, J. W.	054	1888	WB-5/238	CTY
Parker, Jacob	041	1839	WB-3/15	
Parker, Jacob N.	024	1842	WB-C/230	AR
Parker, James	047	1851	WB-4/309	
Parker, James	047	1790	WB-3/178	
Parker, James	010	1805	WB-E/248	
Parker, James	103	1819	RD-4/281	AR
Parker, James	047	1805	WB-3/445	
Parker, James	085	1873	WB-1/185	CTY
Parker, James	027	1885	WB-2/60	AR
Parker, James B.	047	1851	WB-4/318	
Parker, James B.	041	1895	WB-4/397	AR
Parker, James C.	075	1872	WB-0/28	AR
Parker, James H.	047	1899	WB-7/216	
Parker, James R.	103	1894	WB-2/75	AR
Parker, Jane	036	1886	WB-A/88	CTY
Parker, Jemima	087	1843	WB-1/269	
Parker, Jemmima	030	1792	WB-1/261	
Parker, Jesse	041	1800	WB-1/177	AR
Parker, Jesse S.	079	1863	WB-1/105	AR
Parker, Jesse W.	073	1871	WB-H/46	CTY
Parker, Jethro	041	1877	WB-4/98	AR
Parker, Jethro	047	1855	WB-5/13	
Parker, Job	024	1812	WB-C/11	AR
Parker, Joe A.	103	1892	WB-2/8	AR
Parker, Joel	077	1814	WB-E/405	AR
Parker, John	041	1826	WB-2/227	AR
Parker, John	087	1859	WB-1/534	AR
Parker, John	103	1795	WI-A/563	AR
Parker, John	035	1788	WB-A/382	AR
Parker, John	087	c1800	Orig. Only	AR
Parker, John	104	1791	WB-1/318	AR
Parker, John	037	1761	WB-A/80	AR
Parker, John	071	1808	WB-3/2	
Parker, John	037	1836	WB-F/196	AR
Parker, John	070	1834	WB-AB/293	AR
Parker, John	075	1809	WB-M1/204	AR
Parker, John A.	026	1889	WB-2/385	AR
Parker, John J.	079	c1862	WB-1/87	AR
Parker, John J.	051	1877	WB-C/176	AR
Parker, John James	047	1823	WB-3/683	
Parker, John W.	046	1869	WB-E/13	AR
Parker, John Y.	078	1852	WB-17/84	AR
Parker, John, Sr.	099	1806	RB-7/108	AR
Parker, John, Sr.	077	1803	WB-E/185	AR
Parker, Jonas	037	1808	WB-D/311	AR
Parker, Jonathan	092	1808	WB-3/87	AR
Parker, Jonathan	046	1843	WB-C/162	AR
Parker, Jonathan	023	1867	Orig. Only	AR
Parker, Jonathan	087	c1806	WB-A/163	
Parker, Jonathan	044	1788	WB-2/61	CTY
Parker, Jordan H.	041	1893	WB-4/375	AR
Parker, Joseph	103	1813	RD-3/27	AR
Parker, Joseph	024	1764	WB-B/98	AR
Parker, Joseph	071	1792	WB-2/11	AR
Parker, Joseph	077	1865	WB-F/555	AR
Parker, Joseph	041	1789	WB-1/83	AR
Parker, Joseph	060	1875	WB-4/131	AR
Parker, Joseph	041	1820	WB-2/173	AR
Parker, Joseph	024	1749	Orig. Only	SS/AR
Parker, Joseph	064	1884	WB-2/154	AR
Parker, Joseph	073	1775	WB-A/191	
Parker, Joseph	010	1803	WB-E/184	AR
Parker, Joseph D.	087	1890	WB-3/464	AR
Parker, Joseph S.	071	1877	WB-6/238	AR
Parker, Josiah	071	1833	WB-4/108	AR
Parker, Kedar	041	1837	WB-2/391	AR

Name	Co.	Date	Recorded Copy	Original
Parker, Kindred	041	1852	WB-3/156	AR
Parker, Lauretter	071	1888	WB-7/39	AR
Parker, Lemuel	071	1819	WB-3/225	AR
Parker, Lewis	071	1844	WB-5/1	AR
Parker, Lucy	044	1836	WB-13/460	CTY
Parker, Martha	071	1854	WB-5/119	AR
Parker, Martha	077	1855	WB-F/455	AR
Parker, Martha	071	1862	WB-5/268	AR
Parker, Martin	023	1897	WB-A/131	AR
Parker, Mary	037	1754	Orig. Only	SS/AR
Parker, Mary	037	1817	WB-E/151	AR
Parker, Mary	041	1882	WB-4/166	AR
Parker, Mary	041	1806	WB-1/234	AR
Parker, Mary	067	c1849	WB-1/79	AR
Parker, Mary	041	1856	WB-3/201	AR
Parker, Mary	078	1850	WB-13/401	
Parker, Mary Ann	037	1880	WB-G/558	AR
Parker, Mary E.	033	1898	WB-2/238	CTY
Parker, Mary Eliza	037	1899	WB-H/438	AR
Parker, Mason	099	1836	RB-23/566	
Parker, Mason	067	1881	WB-2/118	AR
Parker, Mathew	056	1850	WB-1/635	AR
Parker, Mathew	051	1874	WB-C/129 & 200	AR
Parker, Miles	041	1848	WB-3/98	AR
Parker, Nancy	026	1879	WB-2/193	AR
Parker, Nathan	024	1797	WB-A/284	AR
Parker, Needham	056	1847	WB-1/603	AR
Parker, Newton H.	046	1876	WB-E/165	AR
Parker, Patience	056	1829	WB-1/351	AR
Parker, Peggy	018	1837	WB-C/223	
Parker, Penelope	041	1865	WB-3/324	AR
Parker, Peter	024	1720	SS 875/229	
Parker, Peter	030	1750	Orig. Only	SS/AR (N)
Parker, Peter	030	1826	WB-3/218	
Parker, Peter	030	1722	Orig. Only	SS/AR
Parker, Peter	097	1881	WB-2/201	
Parker, Peter	030	1869	WB-5/4	AR
Parker, Peter	054	c1796	WB-1/188	AR
Parker, Peter	024	1789	WB-B/99	AR
Parker, Peter, Sr.	097	1860	WB-1/176	AR
Parker, Powell	056	1863	WB-2/57	AR
Parker, Priscilla	041	1866	WB-3/341	
Parker, Rachel	046	1886	WB-E/439	AR
Parker, Reuben	019	c1760	Orig. Only	AR
Parker, Reuben	010	1850	WB-G/464	AR
Parker, Reuben	041	1836	WB-2/367	AR
Parker, Rhodey	009	1828	OB-B/2	AR
Parker, Richard	037	1858	WB-G/169	AR
Parker, Richard	024	1752	Orig. Only	SS/AR
Parker, Richard	071	1800	WB-2/210	AR
Parker, Richard	085	c1830	Orig. Only	AR
Parker, Richard B.	047	1869	WB-6/13	AR
Parker, Robert	022	c1804	WB-A/108	AR
Parker, Robert	041	1823	WB-2/201	AR
Parker, Robert	044	1761	Orig. Only	CTY
Parker, Robert S.	051	1875	WB-C/136	AR
Parker, Roden	100	1894	WB-51/388	AR
Parker, Rosanna	041	1800	WB-1/181	AR
Parker, S. H.	097	1885	Orig. Only	AR
Parker, Sabra J.	037	c1859	Copy	105 AR
Parker, Sallie	054	1894	WB-5/515	CTY
Parker, Samuel	071	1799	WB-2/189	AR
Parker, Samuel	024	1811	WB-B/304	AR
Parker, Samuel	103	1791	WI-A/236	AR
Parker, Samuel J.	087	1897	WB-4/34	AR
Parker, Sarah A.	024	1860	WB-D/1	AR
Parker, Sarah Jane	071	1896	WB-7/316	AR
Parker, Sarah W.	051	1888	WB-C/388	AR
Parker, Sealy	071	1813	WB-3/104	AR
Parker, Seth	041	1879	WB-4/124	AR
Parker, Seth B.	024	1899	WB-E/291	AR
Parker, Seth, Sr.	024	1820	WB-C/91	AR
Parker, Sevility	030	1886	WB-5/138	AR
Parker, Silas	051	1849	WB-A/304	
Parker, Simmons B.	037	1846	WB-F/340	AR
Parker, Simon	037	1759	SS 881/200	SS/AR
Parker, Simon	037	1781	WB-B/84	AR
Parker, Solomon D.	069	1840	WB-1/448	AR
Parker, Stephen	054	1849	WB-3/34	AR
Parker, Stephen	018	1827	WB-C/85	
Parker, Stephen	046	1849	WB-C/307	AR
Parker, Susan	089	1887	WB-2/158	AR
Parker, Susan A.	063	1872	WB-3/32	
Parker, Theophilus	037	1849	WB-F/414	AR
Parker, Thomas	087	1861	WB-2/23	
Parker, Thomas	085	1812	WB-G/217	AR
Parker, Thomas	071	1797	WB-2/162	AR
Parker, Thomas	030	1755	SS 880/20	SS/AR
Parker, Thomas	059	1893	WB-B/69	CTY
Parker, Thomas	070	1782	WB-C/335	AR
Parker, Thomas	010	1762	WB-A/16	AR
Parker, Thomas	041	1825	WB-2/240	AR
Parker, Thomas	024	c1762	WB-A/220	AR
Parker, Thomas	030	1795	WB-2/62	
Parker, Thomas	065	1771	WB-F/34	AR
Parker, Thomas	024	1717	Orig. Only	SS/AR
Parker, Thomas	010	1807	WB-F/67	AR
Parker, Thomas L.	080	1886	WB-1/111	AR
Parker, W. N.	005	1899	Copy	097 AR
Parker, Weeks, Sr.	037	1844	WB-F/303	AR
Parker, William	069	1817	WB-1/292	AR
Parker, William	041	1835	WB-2/362	AR
Parker, William	047	1815	WB-3/560	
Parker, William	020	1840	RB-0/79	AR
Parker, William	024	1751	Orig. Only	SS/AR
Parker, William	035	1780	WB-A/375	AR
Parker, William	041	1789	WB-1/80	AR
Parker, William	011	c1802	WB-1/424	
Parker, William	086	1854	WB-E/263	AR
Parker, William	073	1836	WB-E/380	AR
Parker, William G.	010	1863	WB-H/128	AR
Parker, William H.	071	1885	WB-6/482	AR
Parker, William L.	085	1882	WB-2/1	CTY
Parker, William N.	005	1899	WB-D/445	AR
Parker, William T.	041	1864	WB-3/307	AR
Parker, Willie	099	1836	RB-23/566	AR
Parker, Willis	024	c1842	WB-C/278	AR
Parker, Winifred A.	100	1894	WB-51/384	
Parkes, Alfred	020	c1842	RB-0/474	AR
Parkes, Daniel	077	1809	WB-E/330	AR
Parkes, Henry	028	1734	LGB-4/#21	SS/AR
Parkes, Jane	032	1843	WB-1/420	
Parkes, Jane	085	1834	WB-H/642	AR
Parkes, John	099	1795	RB-3/207	AR
Parkes, John	103	1831	RD-6/262	AR
Parkes, Molly	103	1852	RD-11/148	AR
Parkes, Robert	071	1784	WB-1/345	AR
Parkes, Robert	071	1804	WB-2/253	

Name	Co.	Date	Recorded Copy	Original
Parkhill, William	046	c1789	WB-A/290	AR
Parkins, William	047	1771	WB-1/282	
Parkinson, Mary	044	1837	WB-14/255	CTY
Parks, Andrew D.	065	1839	WB-E/219	AR
Parks, Ann C.	065	1890	WB-L/446	AR
Parks, Barbara	065	1850	WB-I/166	AR
Parks, Chaney	071	1793	WB-2/35	AR
Parks, Dabney W.	104	c1862	Orig. Only	AR
Parks, David	065	1873	WB-K/125	AR
Parks, David, Sr.	065	1813	WB-F/81	AR
Parks, Elisabeth	071	1872	WB-6/95	AR
Parks, Elizabeth	065	1876	WB-K/224	AR
Parks, Elizabeth	085	1877	WB-1/362	CTY
Parks, Elmira	104	1899	WB-7/81	AR
Parks, Esther J.	065	1896	WB-M/470	AR
Parks, Faithy	085	1833	WB-H/608	AR
Parks, G. D.	065	1894	WB-M/254	AR
Parks, George	065	1827	WB-F/108	AR
Parks, George	104	1898	WB-7/68	AR
Parks, Harriett	105	1896	WB-3/238	AR
Parks, Hugh	065	1830	WB-F/31	AR
Parks, Hugh	085	N. D.	WB-B/123	AR
Parks, Hugh	085	1890	WB-2/448	CTY
Parks, Hugh M.	065	1895	WB-M/377	AR
Parks, James	071	1791	WB-1/421	AR
Parks, James	103	1864	RD-13/749	
Parks, James	049	1897	WB-2/377	AR
Parks, James	071	1888	WB-1/21	AR
Parks, James E.	004	1898	WB-A/198	AR
Parks, John	046	1868	WB-D/373	AR
Parks, John	104	1793	WB-1/357	AR
Parks, John	085	c1795	WB-F/33	AR
Parks, John	065	1813	WB-F/83	AR
Parks, John	104	1836	WB-4/199	AR
Parks, John	065	1810	WB-F/19	AR
Parks, John	104	1784	WB-1/126	
Parks, John M.	065	1849	WB-I/159	AR
Parks, John S.	014	1872	066 WB-1/52	066 AR
Parks, John S.	014	1873	WB-2/75	
Parks, Jonathan	104	1807	WB-2/207	
Parks, Joseph	103	1878	WB-1/134	AR
Parks, Lucy	071	1823	WB-3/294	AR
Parks, Major	103	1842	RD-8/310	AR
Parks, Margaret	085	c1787	WB-C/123	AR
Parks, Mary	016	1846	WB-1/90	
Parks, Mary	020	1816	RB-G/306	
Parks, Mary H.	020	1853	RB-R/59	
Parks, Mildred	071	1872	WB-6/92	AR
Parks, Moses	065	1828	WB-C/9	AR
Parks, Moses	039	1797	WB-A/206	
Parks, Noah	085	1815	WB-G/381	AR
Parks, Noah	085	1829	WB-H/459	AR
Parks, Olive	071	1850	WB-5/86	AR
Parks, R. H.	054	1877	WB-4/268	CTY
Parks, Robert	065	1841	WB-H/48	AR
Parks, Robert	020	1815	RB-G/108	AR
Parks, Robert B.	065	c1843	WB-I/56	AR
Parks, Robert W.	065	1845	WB-I/5	AR
Parks, Samuel	024	c1769	WB-B/124	
Parks, Samuel	073	N. D.	WB-B/37	
Parks, Solomon	020	1824	RB-I/326	
Parks, Thomas	104	1791	WB-1/296	AR
Parks, William B.	016	1868	WB-2/167	
Parks, William H.	081	1900	WB-17/42	
Parks, Wilson	065	1868	WB-J/254	AR
Parlen, E. A.	104	1862	WB-5/313	
Parlepough, Henry	028	1735/6	Orig. Only	SS/AR
Parlier, J. J.	104	1874	WB-6/88	AR
Parlier, James	104	1878	WB-6/159	AR
Parlier, Jonathan	104	1845	WB-4/313	AR
Parlier, Mary E.	104	1900	WB-7/108	AR
Parlier, Thomas	104	c1898	WB-7/192	AR
Parmell, Amos T.	067	1884	WB-2/188	AR
Parmelle, William	053	1814	RW-1/490	
Parmerle, Harriet M.	101	1873	WB-A/6	AR
Parmerle, William	053	1814	SC/02762	AR-Copy
Parmerlee, Arnold	053	1803	RW-1/356	AR-Nunc.
Parmily, Sylvia	070	1888	WB-F/274	AR
Parmle, Benjamin	009	1865	OB-L/476	AR
Parnel, Melvinie	056	1889	WB-3/500	AR
Parnell, John	083	c1798	WB-1/53	AR-Nunc.
Parnell, Rosanna	085	1897	WB-3/217	CTY
Parot, John	072	1782	RW/L34	AR
Parr, Daniel	030	1801	WB-2/196	
Parr, Elizabeth	018	1834	WB-C/147	
Parr, James	030	1845	WB-4/112	
Parr, Jessee	030	c1811	WB-3/26	
Parr, Richard	030	1825	WB-3/184	
Parr, Thaney	030	1832	WB-3/321	
Parr, William	030	c1800	WB-2/343	
Parr, William	030	1777	WB-1/122	
Parr, William, Sr.	020	1788	RB-B/254	AR
Parrack, Thomas	085	1816	WB-G/433	AR
Parratt, Joseph	069	1845	WB-1/477	AR
Parrey, Anne	072	1822	WB-A/105	AR
Parris, George	028	1803	WB-B/183	
Parris, John	028	1819	WB-C/186	AR
Parris, Thomas	024	1728	SS 876/155	
Parris, W. W.	091	1900	WB-1/174	
Parris, Zadock	028	1831	WB-C/337	AR
Parrish, Ailsy	084	1854	WB-C/166	CTY
Parrish, Bettie M.	024	1900	WB-E/315	
Parrish, Brissy	044	1791	WB-2/211	CTY
Parrish, Charles	044	1801	WB-5/166	CTY
Parrish, Claborn	044	1836	WB-13/419	CTY
Parrish, David	044	1792	WB-2/306	CTY
Parrish, Elijah	044	1794	WB-3/105	CTY
Parrish, Elizabeth	044	1868	WB-22/769	CTY
Parrish, Elizabeth	044	1816	WB-7/528	CTY
Parrish, James	073	1874	WB-H/86	CTY
Parrish, Joel	070	c1789	Orig. Only	AR
Parrish, John	024	c1772	Orig. Only	AR
Parrish, John	046	1883	WB-E/365	AR
Parrish, John	077	1738	LGB-4/#91	SS/AR
Parrish, Jones	084	c1844	WB-C/148	CTY
Parrish, Justus	099	1877	WB-A/58	AR
Parrish, Leah	024	1881	WB-E/106	AR
Parrish, W. N.	040	1884	WB-2/214	AR
Parrish, William	037	1736	LGB-4/#139	SS/AR
Parrish, Williamson	073	1862	WB-G/400	CTY
Parrish, Willis	084	1860	WB-C/326	CTY
Parrot, Jacob	010	1738	Orig. Only	SS/AR
Parrott, Abner	084	c1797	OW/185	AR
Parrott, Nancy	044	1873	WB-23/123	CTY
Parry, Daniel	057	1806	WB-A/279	AR
Parry, Hannah	057	1844	WB-B/169	AR
Parry, John, Sr.	057	1800	WB-A/250	AR
Parry, Mary	077	1797	WB-E/85	
Parry, Waxel	057	1800	WB-A/241	AR
Parry, William	086	1813	Orig. Only	AR

Name	Co.	Date	Recorded Copy	Original
Parry, William	057	1795	WB-A/94	AR
Parsins, Sarah	028	1873	WB-E/75	
Parsley, Anna M.	070	1889	WB-F/266	AR
Parsley, Oscar G.	070	1885	WB-E/582	AR
Parsley, Oscar G.	070	1896	WB-G/459	AR
Parson, William R.	104	1882	WB-6/214	AR
Parsons, Asa	077	1826	WB-F/114	AR
Parsons, Catherine	006	1882	WB-E/93	AR
Parsons, Charlotte	005	1858	WB-C/138	AR
Parsons, Francis	005	1801	WB-2/120	AR
Parsons, George	046	1843	WB-C/168	AR
Parsons, George	046	1833	WB-B/471	AR
Parsons, George	104	1863	WB-5/339	
Parsons, Hilliard	005	1866	WB-C/241	AR
Parsons, James	028	1809	WB-B/331	AR
Parsons, James	046	1857	WB-C/471	AR
Parsons, James N.	047	1778	WB-2/83	
Parsons, Jeremiah	028	1807	WB-B/291	AR
Parsons, John	077	1867	WB-H/21	AR
Parsons, John	028	1797	WB-B/22	AR
Parsons, John	028	1826	WB-C/272	AR
Parsons, Martin	104	1899	WB-7/100	
Parsons, Nancy	067	1849	WB-1/50	AR
Parsons, Phoebe	057	1893	WB-C/190	AR
Parsons, Robert H.	005	1845	WB-B/192	AR
Parsons, Samuel	096	c1778	WB-1/104	
Parsons, Samuell	077	1745	Orig. Only	SS/AR
Parsons, Sarah	028	1842	WB-D/66	AR
Parsons, Thomas	046	1841	WB-C/96	AR
Parsons, Thomas	028	1795	WB-A/336	AR
Parsons, Thomas	028	1799	WB-B/78	AR
Parsons, Thomas	028	1749	SS 877/304	SS/AR
Parsons, Vincent	005	1889	WB-D/253	
Parsons, W. C.	107	1899	WB-2/105	
Parsons, William	046	1814	WB-A/301	AR
Partee, George S.	085	1835	WB-H/704	AR-Nunc.
Partee, Noah	085	1841	WB-I/106	AR
Partie, Benjamin	044	1764	Orig. Only	CTY
Partin, Henry	071	1805	WB-2/274	AR
Partin, James	047	1862	WB-5/101	
Partin, Jesse	047	1804	WB-3/425	
Partin, Jessee	047	1855	WB-5/12	
Partin, John	047	1795	WB-3/256	
Partin, Pinkney	099	1886	WB-B/166	AR
Partin, W. R.	038	1894	WB-3/485	AR
Partin, William	073	1804	WB-D/120	AR
Partin, William	099	1822	RB-17/385	AR
Partin, William	047	1819	WB-3/635	
Partlow, Nancy	065	1818	WB-F/89	AR
Parton, G. W.	061	1896	WB-2/186	AR
Parton, Harbert	086	1867	WB-E/480	
Partree, Esther	053	c1811	RW-1/520	
Partree, Holmes	053	1810	RW-1/440	AR
Partree, James	009	1858	OB-K/460	
Partree, John	009	1832	OB-B/224	AR
Partree, Margrett	009	1836	OWB/520	AR
Partridge, E. R.	068	1900	WB-E/42	CTY-Copy
Partridge, John	022	1860	WB-D/66	AR
Partridge, Nicholas	022	1780	WB-A/315	AR
Partridge, Sarah	022	c1812	WB-A/214	AR
Partridge, Sophia A.	099	1881	WB-A/233	AR
Paryer, John	028	1738	LGB-4/#73	SS/AR
Paschal, D. F.	084	1897	WB-F/90	CTY
Paschal, Elisha	020	c1857	Orig. Only	AR
Paschal, Isiah	039	c1795	WB-A/169	AR
Paschal, James	100	1792	WB-6/115	AR
Paschal, Jessie D.	020	1886	WB-A/508	CTY
Paschal, Mariah A.	084	1900	WB-F/167	CTY
Paschal, Parthenia	084	1893	WB-E/545	CTY
Paschal, William	015	1774	100 WB-2/30	AR
Paschall, Anderson	044	1839	WB-14/441	CTY
Paschall, Dennis	100	1816	WB-20/140	AR
Paschall, Eleanor	098	1886	WB-A/61	CTY
Paschall, John	020	1827	RB-L/195	AR
Paschall, John	044	1878	WB-23/299	CTY
Paschall, John	100	1840	WB-37/390	AR
Paschall, John	044	1848	WB-17/446	CTY
Paschall, Lunsford	044	1879	WB-23/341	
Paschall, Phenavil J.	100	1892	WB-51/336	AR
Paschall, Thomas	100	1846	WB-39/173	AR
Paschall, Thomas P.	100	1895	WB-51/401	
Paschall, William	100	1852	WB-42/54	AR
Paschall, Z. M.	044	1880	WB-23/385	CTY
Pasinger, John	085	c1773	WB-A/170	AR
Pasley, Nancy	004	1894	WB-A/151	AR
Pasmore, John	037	1754	Orig. Only	SS/AR
Pasmore, Robert	047	1785	WB-3/77	
Pasour, Daniel	040	1862	WB-1/136	
Pasour, David	040	1860	WB-1/111	AR
Pasour, George J.	040	1884	WB-2/229	AR
Pasour, Jacob	040	c1861	WB-1/157	
Pass, Elizabeth	078	1885	WB-19/169	AR
Pass, Holloway	046	1846	WB-C/246	AR
Pass, James C.	035	1882	WB-4/168	AR
Pass, Nathaniel	020	1816	RB-G/131	
Pass, Richard S.	025	1891	WB-A/144	AR
Pass, Thomas C.	020	1876	WB-A/201	CTY
Pass, William	047	1785	WB-3/92	
Pass, William H.	078	1864	WB-18/374	AR
Passen, Ann Maria	028	1832	WB-C/348	
Passmore, Bennett	099	1883	WB-A/464	AR
Passmore, William	099	1816	RB-13/28	AR
Passmore, William	099	1813	RB-11/150 & 456	AR
Pasteur, Charles	047	1794	WB-3/220	
Pasteur, Edward	028	1823	WB-C/236	AR
Pasteur, Elizabeth	028	1884	WB-E/343	
Pasteur, James	047	1791	WB-3/193	
Pasteur, Martha	047	1810	WB-3/506	
Pasture, Ann M.	047	1837	WB-4/154	
Pat, (fwc)	081	1811	WB-3/292	AR
Patchitt, John	024	c1711	SS 875/36	
Pate, Bryan H.	103	1856	RD-12/133	AR
Pate, Christian	103	1873	WB-1/62	AR
Pate, Daniel	103	1791	WI-A/258	
Pate, Dicy	103	1838	RD-11/338	AR
Pate, Drusilla	027	1836	WB-A/42	AR-Nunc.
Pate, Edmund	057	1779	WB-A/195	AR-Nunc.
Pate, Elijah	103	1862	RD-13/475	AR
Pate, Elizabeth	103	1885	WB-1/357	AR
Pate, Elizabeth	103	1882	WB-1/244	AR
Pate, Gatlin	045	1899	WB-1/378	AR
Pate, James, Sr.	103	1826	RD-5/260	AR
Pate, John	103	1862	RD-13/444	AR
Pate, Joseph	103	1847	RD-9/531	AR
Pate, Joseph	028	1885	WB-E/514	AR
Pate, Lewis	103	1864	RD-13/740	AR
Pate, Martha	028	1891	WB-E/578	
Pate, Nancy	103	1895	WB-2/107	AR

Name	Co.	Date	Recorded Copy	Original
Pate, Nancy	071	1870	WB-6/56	AR
Pate, Ransom	048	1893	WB-1/30	CTY
Pate, Sally	009	1866	OB-M/320	AR
Pate, Samuel	082	1850	WB-4/39	AR
Pate, Shadrach	103	1837	RD-7/255	AR
Pate, Shadrack	103	1854	RD-11/559	AR
Pate, Silas	103	1858	RD-12/617	AR
Pate, Travis	056	1818	WB-1/290	AR
Pate, Travis	056	1808	WB-1/210	AR
Pate, W. W.	056	1896	WB-2/218	
Pate, William	057	1812	WB-A/333	AR
Pateman, Hopkins	028	1803	WB-B/165	
Paten, Elinor	085	c1790	WB-B/199	AR
Paterson, Archibald	068	1810	WB-A/268	
Paterson, Daniel	068	1793	WB-A/171	
Paterson, Daniel	068	1794	WB-A/171	
Paterson, John	090	1809	WB-2/103	AR
Paterson, John	068	1820	WB-B/7	
Paterson, John	068	c1802	SC/02434	AR-Copy
Paterson, John	068	1813	WB-A/276	
Paterson, Robert	024	1721	SS 875/330	SS/AR
Paterson, William	068	c1812	WB-A/275	
Paterson, William	012	1803	WB-B/74	AR
Patillo, Jackson	001	1891	WB-2/488	AR
Patison, Andrew	090	1799	WB-1/134	AR
Patnal, John	008	c1712	SS 875/24	
Paton, John	085	c1800	WB-F/68	AR
Paton, Robert	022	1883	WB-E/282	AR
Patrick, Ann	009	1849	OB-G/141	AR
Patrick, Cornelius	009	c1804	OWB/428	AR
Patrick, E. L.	027	1900	Orig. Only	AR
Patrick, Edward F.	028	1785	WB-A/99	
Patrick, Eliakim	009	1852	OB-H/202	AR
Patrick, Hugh	084	1828	WB B/28	CTY
Patrick, Hugh L.	084	1893	WB-E/551	CTY
Patrick, James	084	1835	WB-B/115	CTY
Patrick, James M.	059	1898	WB-B/223	CTY
Patrick, Jehoda	096	c1850	WB-3/32	AR
Patrick, Jerrymire	006	1889	WB-E/168	AR
Patrick, John	045	1896	WB-1/311	AR
Patrick, John	047	1826	WB-4/20	
Patrick, John A.	096	1837	WB-2/135	
Patrick, Lewis	100	1816	WB-19/219	AR
Patrick, Mary	084	1808	WB-A/16	CTY
Patrick, Thomas J.	046	1891	WB-I/233	
Patrick, Virginia	009	1883	WB-1/324	CTY
Patrick, William	084	c1783	OW/200	AR
Patrick, William	085	1818	WB-G/526	AR
Patrick, William	022	1841	WB-C/117	AR
Patrick, William H.	099	1889	WB-B/369	AR
Patrick, William M.	101	1889	WB-A/185	AR
Patridge, Jessee	030	c1808	WB-3/3	
Pattason, Francis	044	1753	Orig. Only	CTY
Patte, Charles	083	c1824	WB-1/237	
Patten, Elijah	086	1828	WB-D/86	AR
Patten, John	009	c1779	OWB/151	AR
Patten, John	009	c1779	Copy	028 AR
Pattenson, Henery	070	1751	Orig. Only	SS/AR
Patterson (Patton), Gideon	020	1803	RB-E/8	AR
Patterson, Adaline A.	068	1892	WB-D/355	
Patterson, Alexander	081	1797	WB-2/26	AR
Patterson, Alexander	082	1819	WB-1/202	AR
Patterson, Alexander	016	1851	WB-1/184	
Patterson, Angus R.	082	1870	WB-6/55	AR
Patterson, Ann C.	068	1831	WB-B/76	
Patterson, Anna	054	1884	WB-5/103	CTY
Patterson, Archibald	082	1869	WB-6/20	AR
Patterson, Arthur	026	1856	WB-1/201	AR
Patterson, Arthur	060	1803	Orig. Only	AR
Patterson, Arthur	026	1873	WB-2/109	AR
Patterson, Benjamin	071	1782	WB-1/257	AR
Patterson, Caroline	022	1890	WB-E/503	AR
Patterson, Caroline	028	1892	WB-F/28	
Patterson, Celia	084	1854	WB-C/199	CTY
Patterson, Charles	065	1777	WB-F/5	AR
Patterson, Charles	082	1848	WB-4/13	AR
Patterson, Clarissa	026	1900	WB-3/108	AR
Patterson, D. H.	085	c1870	Copy	054 AR
Patterson, Daniel	068	c1848	WB-C/8	
Patterson, Daniel	083	c1808	WB-1/112	AR
Patterson, Daniel	029	1819	WB-B/17	AR
Patterson, Daniel	011	c1832	WB-1/6	
Patterson, Daniel	082	1864	WB-4/178	AR
Patterson, David	073	1865	WB-G/472	CTY
Patterson, David	073	1847	WB-F/386	AR
Patterson, David	022	1863	WB-D/99	AR
Patterson, David H.	085	1873	WB-1/172	AR
Patterson, Duncan	082	1827	WB-1/284	AR
Patterson, Duncan	029	1794	Orig. Only	AR
Patterson, Effy	082	1861	WB-4/149	AR
Patterson, Eleasaph	003	1873	Orig. Only	AR
Patterson, Eliza Ann	022	1890	WB-E/416	AR
Patterson, Elizabeth	092	1893	WB-6/375	AR
Patterson, Elizabeth	016	1864	WB-2/114	
Patterson, George	046	1817	WB-B/41	AR
Patterson, Giles J.	SC	c1887	026 WB-3/20	026 AR
Patterson, Gorge	010	1749	Orig. Only	SS/AR
Patterson, Hannah	085	1873	WB-1/176	CTY
Patterson, Hugh	065	1834	WB-H/142	AR
Patterson, Hugh L.	082	1870	WB-6/61	AR
Patterson, I. Frank	085	1896	WB-3/120	CTY
Patterson, Isaac	022	1886	WB-E/330	AR
Patterson, Isaac	028	1889	WB-E/511	AR
Patterson, Isabella	054	1860	WB-3/148	AR
Patterson, J. C.	036	1900	WB-A/493	CTY
Patterson, James	060	1780	Orig. Only	AR
Patterson, James	081	1871	WB-15/65	AR
Patterson, James	082	1819	WB-1/207	AR
Patterson, James	060	1840	WB-2/38	AR
Patterson, James	085	1838	WB-I/45	AR
Patterson, James	054	c1814	WB-1/360	AR
Patterson, James	054	c1856	WB-3/133	AR
Patterson, James N.	065	1829	WB-E/68	AR
Patterson, Jemime	065	1834	WB-G/156	AR
Patterson, John	054	1855	WB-3/91	AR
Patterson, John	046	1857	WB-C/498	AR
Patterson, John	054	1891	WB-5/379	CTY
Patterson, John	068	c1842	WB-B/132	
Patterson, John	083	1846	WB-1/487	
Patterson, John	029	1769	Orig. Only	AR
Patterson, John	065	1786	WB-F/8	AR
Patterson, John	028	1879	WB-E/214	
Patterson, John	081	1851	WB-9/308	AR
Patterson, John	082	1848	WB-4/23	AR
Patterson, John K.	054	1868	WB-3/205	AR
Patterson, John R.	092	1891	WB-6/352	AR
Patterson, John S.	054	1887	WB-5/170	CTY
Patterson, John T.	073	1781	WB-A/233	AR
Patterson, John, Sr.	065	1831	WB-E/122	AR

Name	Co.	Date	Recorded Copy	Original
Patterson, John, Sr.	073	1791	WB-B/128	AR
Patterson, Jonathan	071	1805	WB-2/304	AR
Patterson, Jordan	054	c1827	WB-2/106	AR
Patterson, Joseph A.	016	1863	WB-2/95	
Patterson, Julia	026	1898	WB-2/562	AR
Patterson, Leah	020	1856	RB-R/406	AR
Patterson, Lizzie C.	068	1898	WB-D/543	
Patterson, Louis M.	038	1886	WB-2/581	AR
Patterson, Malcolm	068	1795	WB-A/184	
Patterson, Mann	073	1835	WB-E/353	AR
Patterson, Margaret	065	1840	WB-H/133	AR
Patterson, Margaret	065	1824	WB-F/101	AR
Patterson, Margaret	016	1894	WB-4/185	AR
Patterson, Mark	022	1809	WB-A/179	AR
Patterson, Mary	082	1863	WB-4/168	AR
Patterson, Mary	106	1887	WB-2/237	AR
Patterson, Mary	073	1796	WB-C/79	AR
Patterson, Mary	081	1851	Orig. Only	AR
Patterson, Mary	081	1818	WB-4/605	AR
Patterson, Mary C.	036	1888	WB-A/135	CTY
Patterson, Miriam	106	c1854	WB-1/44	AR
Patterson, Moses W.	010	1825	WB-G/135	AR
Patterson, Nancy E.	001	1875	WB-2/95	AR
Patterson, Nathan	039	1847	WB-M/247	
Patterson, Nathaniel	073	1791	WB-B/132	AR
Patterson, Neill C.	083	1894	WB-4/185	AR
Patterson, Peter	029	1890	WB-E/505	AR
Patterson, Peter	082	1872	WB-6/76	AR
Patterson, Richard A.	073	1885	WB-H/392	CTY
Patterson, Robert	060	1819	Orig. Only	AR
Patterson, Robert	026	1854	WB-1/177	AR
Patterson, Robert	PA	1899	014 WB-3/58	
Patterson, Sallie	083	1898	WB-4/188	AR
Patterson, Samuel	049	c1813	WI-A/8	AR
Patterson, Sarah	082	1839	WB-2/85	AR
Patterson, Thomas	026	1844	WB-1/34	AR
Patterson, Thomas	106	1885	WB-2/213	AR
Patterson, Thomas	060	1806	Orig. Only	AR
Patterson, Turner	084	1825	WB-A/263	CTY
Patterson, William	081	1846	WB-8/252	AR
Patterson, William	040	1871	WB-2/20	AR
Patterson, William	022	1877	WB-E/148	AR
Patterson, William	085	c1790	WB-C/297	AR
Patterson, William	083	1886	WB-3/371	AR
Patterson, William	046	1820	WB-B/100	AR
Patterson, William	065	1886	WB-L/173	AR
Patterson, William	065	1821	WB-F/91	AR
Patterson, William	092	1818	WB-3/132	AR
Patterson, William B.	020	1852	RB-Q/663	AR
Patterson, William G.	026	1899	WB-3/43 & 96	AR
Patterson, William H.	003	1866	WB-A/16	AR
Patterson, Young	046	1822	WB-B/157	AR
Pattillo, Anderson	100	1894	WB-51/382	
Pattillo, Ann W.	100	1814	WB-19/58	AR
Pattillo, Edward	065	1822	Copy	100 AR
Pattillo, Edward	100	1825	WB-28/232	AR
Pattillo, Mary L.	020	1877	WB-A/222	CTY
Pattillo, Mary M.	100	1871	WB-51/51	AR
Pattillo, William	020	1820	RB-H/296	AR
Pattillo, Zachariah	020	1825	RB-K/61	AR
Pattillo, Zachariah	020	1852	RB-Q/663	AR
Pattinson, Henry	070	c1751	DB-C/271	
Pattishall, Benjamin	022	1863	WB-D/104	AR
Pattishall, John	022	1847	WB-C/196	AR
Pattishall, John	022	1782	Orig. Only	AR

Name	Co.	Date	Recorded Copy	Original
Pattishall, Joshua	100	1782	WB-3/160	AR
Pattishall, Manly	022	1863	WB-D/118	AR
Pattishall, Pleasant	022	1873	WB-E/87	AR
Pattishell, William	022	c1818	WB-B/8	AR
Pattison, Joseph	090	1809	WB-2/105	AR
Patton, Alexander	001	1861	WB-1/183	AR
Patton, Alis	019	1865	WB-A/278	AR
Patton, Andrew	073	1790	WB-B/97	AR
Patton, Ann	013	1855	WB-A/168	
Patton, Charles	093	1898	WB-2/162	
Patton, Charles	065	1811	WB-F/21	AR
Patton, Eliza	013	1878	WB-B/210	AR
Patton, Elizabeth	064	1844	WB-1/10	AR
Patton, Elizur	093	1885	WB-2/18	AR
Patton, James	013	c1845	WB-A/108	
Patton, James	049	c1848	WB-1/18	AR
Patton, James	073	1840	WB-F/45	AR
Patton, James A.	013	1864	WB-A/225	
Patton, James C.	001	1894	WB-3/38	AR
Patton, James W.	013	c1861	WB-A/213b	
Patton, James W.	013	c1861	Copy	062 AR
Patton, John	013	1831	WB-A/1	
Patton, John	073	1828	WB-E/158	AR
Patton, John	073	1799	WB-C/128	AR
Patton, John	073	1838	WB-F/16	AR
Patton, Johnston	001	1863	WB-1/215	AR
Patton, Margaret	073	1847	WB-F/365	AR
Patton, Mary	061	1853	WB-1/52	AR
Patton, Mary	014	c1860	WB-1/5	AR
Patton, Prudence	065	1829	WB-D/39	AR
Patton, Robert	064	1853	WB-1/35	AR
Patton, Robert V.	014	1871	WB-2/58	
Patton, Samuel	001	1862	WB-1/205	AR
Patton, Samuel	073	1846	WB-F/283	
Patton, Samuel	073	1846	Copy	001 AR
Patton, Thomas	065	1767	WB-F/2	AR
Patton, William	001	1880	WB-2/164	AR
Patton, William	084	c1786	OW/214	AR
Patton, William B.	014	1882	WB-2/238	AR
Patton, William L.	065	1833	WB-E/200	AR
Paul (Poll), Abraham	083	c1801	Orig. Only	AR
Paul, Amanda	078	1892	WB-19/326	AR
Paul, Elias	083	1887	WB-3/404	AR
Paul, Elisabeth	073	1792	WB-B/160	AR
Paul, George	028	1792	WB-A/284	
Paul, Hiram	028	1866	WB-D/419	AR
Paul, Jacob	028	1812	WB-C/46	
Paul, James A.	009	1885	WB-1/356	CTY
Paul, Jesse	074	1886	WB-1/88	
Paul, John	028	1796	WB-B/8	
Paul, John	030	1803	WB-2/225	
Paul, John	071	1762	WB-1/73	
Paul, John	073	1851	WB-G/6	AR
Paul, John M.	073	1878	WB-H/190	CTY
Paul, Martha G.	073	1897	WB-F/124	CTY
Paul, Mary	028	1802	WB-B/153	
Paul, Robert	009	1762	Orig. Only	AR
Paul, Robert	028	1815	WB-C/94	
Paul, Samuel	065	1855	WB-J/14	AR
Paul, Sarah A.	001	1870	WB-2/10	AR
Paul, Stephen	083	1849	WB-2/7	
Paul, Thomas P.	073	1854	WB-G/64	AR
Paul, William	083	c1820	WB-1/247	
Paul, William G.	074	1888	WB-1/92	
Paul, Zacheus	074	1877	WB-1/45	AR

Name	Co.	Date	Recorded Copy	Original
Pauley, Agnes	086	1818	WB-C/100	AR
Pauley, James	086	1809	WB-B/230	AR
Paull, James	073	c1785	WB-B/54	AR
Paull, Joshua	070	1753	DB-D/49	AR
Paull, William	071	c1744	Orig. Only	SS/AR
Paullin, William T.	106	c1855	WB-1/43	AR
Pavey, Sarah	075	1791	WB-K/209	AR
Paw, William	039	1789	WB-A/48	
Pawlus, Adam	085	1834	WB-H/630	AR
Paxton, Harriet H.	064	1898	WB-2/426	AR
Paxton, James	065	1781	WB-F/36	AR
Paxton, Richard	024	1824	WB-C/110	AR
Paxton, Richard	024	1865	WB-D/31	AR
Paxton, Thomas N.	064	1883	Orig. Only	AR
Paydon, Martha J.	047	c1883	WB-6/330	AR
Paylet, Robert	022	1784	RB-1/18	AR
Paylor, Annie	078	1889	WB-19/265	AR
Paylor, James W.	078	1898	WB-19/439	AR
Paylor, John	078	1858	WB-18/26	AR
Paylor, Margaret	046	1895	WB-F/384	AR
Paylor, Richard	078	1849	WB-13/139	
Payn, George	104	1801	WB-2/30	AR
Payne, Abel	029	1879	WB-E/183	AR
Payne, Abner	017	1845	WB-A/29	AR
Payne, Charles	085	c1803	WB-F/29	AR
Payne, Charles	032	1879	WB-3/269	AR
Payne, Charles M.	009	1900	WB-2/254	CTY
Payne, Elizabeth	038	1899	WB-4/194	AR
Payne, Elizabeth	032	c1856	WB-2/145	
Payne, Henry	003	1888	WB-B/229	
Payne, Huldah	003	1877	WB-B/79	AR
Payne, Isaac	038	1860	WB-1/165	AR
Payne, James	046	1890	WB-F/45	AR
Payne, James F.	083	1898	WB-4/203	AR
Payne, John W.	046	1892	WB-F/173	AR
Payne, Joseph	020	1821	RB-I/1	AR
Payne, Judy	070	c1877	WB-E/323	AR
Payne, Martin	092	1893	WB-6/371	AR
Payne, Peter	024	1755	SS 880/95	SS/AR
Payne, Richard	030	1803	WB-2/237	
Payne, Robert	090	1873	WB-6/47	AR
Payne, Robert Lee	032	1895	WB-4/242	AR
Payne, Solomon	003	1879	WB-B/112	AR
Payne, Thomas	071	1874	WB-6/147	
Payne, Thomas	084	1891	WB-F/1	
Payne, Thomas	003	1899	WB-B/385	AR
Payne, W. L.	017	1899	WB-B/309	AR
Payne, Washington	038	1884	WB-2/517	AR
Payne, William M.	059	1899	WB-B/236	CTY
Payton, Benjamin	009	1748	OWB/35	AR
Payton, Robert	010	c1739	LGB-4/#121	
Payton, Robert	039	1785	WB-A/2	Nunc.
Peace, Catharine	044	1859	WB-21/105	CTY
Peace, Elizabeth	044	1841	WB-15/68	CTY
Peace, Emily	044	c1875	WB-23/218	CTY
Peace, Frances A.	044	1897	WB-24/343	CTY
Peace, Jane W.	044	1827	WB-10/284	CTY
Peace, John C.	044	c1865	WB-23/7	CTY
Peace, Josiah	044	1864	WB-22/177	
Peace, Margaret	044	c1868	WB-23/8	CTY
Peace, Mary R.	044	1881	WB-23/416	CTY
Peace, Susanna M.	044	1858	WB-20/485	CTY
Peace, Thomas	044	1854	WB-19/462	
Peace, William	099	1865	RB-33/429	AR
Peacock, Asel	032	1865	WB-2/324	AR
Peacock, Burden	103	1883	WB-1/276	AR
Peacock, E. G.	101	1890	WB-A/193	AR
Peacock, Elizabeth	070	1868	WB-E/1	AR
Peacock, Iredell	105	1869	WB-2/17	
Peacock, Isaac	009	1817	OB-A/276	AR
Peacock, Jesse	029	1797	Orig. Only	AR
Peacock, John	103	1829	RD-6/3	AR
Peacock, John A.	032	1893	WB-4/195	AR
Peacock, John, Sr.	103	1829	RD-6/78	AR
Peacock, Lawrence	056	1855	WB-1/684	AR
Peacock, Lovet	027	1863	WB-A/83	AR
Peacock, Martha	103	c1853	Orig. Only	AR
Peacock, Nancy	009	1838	OB-C2/57	AR
Peacock, Nancy	103	1878	WB-1/127	
Peacock, Noah	056	1824	WB-1/375	AR
Peacock, Peter L.	103	1861	RD-13/328	
Peacock, Samuel	032	1830	WB-1/153	
Peacock, Samuel	056	1793	WB-1/77	AR
Peacock, Simon	103	1831	RD-6/278	AR
Peacock, Stephen	103	1820	RD-4/305	AR
Peacock, William	032	1884	WB-3/438	AR
Peacock, William	056	1862	WB-2/26	AR
Peacock, Z. M. L.	103	1886	WB-1/374	AR
Peacock, Zadock	039	c1854	WB-O/324	AR
Peacock, Zadock	037	1852	WB-F/479	AR
Peak, Leonard	044	1784	WB-1/413	CTY
Peal, Abram	063	1862	WB-2/491	
Peal, Henry	063	1841	WB-2/281	
Peal, James	103	1848	RD-10/1	AR
Peal, James	063	1825	WB-2/107	
Peal, John	103	1848	RD-10/158	AR
Peal, John	063	1896	WB-4/188	AR
Peal, John, Sr.	063	1836	WB-2/223	
Peal, Joseph B.	063	1877	WB-3/121	
Peal, Martha	041	1860	WB-3/252	AR
Peal, Noah	063	1896	WB-4/195	AR
Peal, Thomas	063	1824	WB-2/101	
Peal, Thomas	063	1855	WB-2/419	
Peal, William	041	1864	WB-3/313	AR
Peale, John	071	1760	WB-1/32	
Pearam, William	029	1842	WB-B/382	
Pearce, Aaron	041	1849	WB-3/109	AR
Pearce, Abigail	009	1813	OWB/470	AR
Pearce, Abraham	041	1834	WB-2/342	AR
Pearce, Amelia	056	1847	WB-1/744	AR
Pearce, Ann Maria	029	1879	WB-E/199	AR
Pearce, Annie	039	1873	WB-U/76	AR
Pearce, Ansel	081	1861	WB-12/4	
Pearce, Arthur	056	1792	WB-1/60	AR
Pearce, Arthur	056	1887	WB-3/429	
Pearce, Asa	005	1822	WB-A/75	AR
Pearce, Barbara L.	009	1860	OB-L/218	AR
Pearce, Benjamin	047	1812	WB-3/530	
Pearce, Benjamin	009	c1778	OWB/138	AR
Pearce, Brinkley	081	1883	WB-15/414	AR
Pearce, Christopher	041	1801	WB-1/182	AR
Pearce, Cincinnatus	051	1897	WB-C/525	AR
Pearce, Clarkey	056	c1851	WB-1/666	AR
Pearce, David	028	1814	WB-C/79	
Pearce, Edmond	009	c1758	OWB/52	AR
Pearce, Elizabeth	028	1894	WB-F/105	
Pearce, Enoch	039	1878	WB-U/158	AR
Pearce, Evaline	056	1889	WB-4/197	
Pearce, Everitt	056	1807	WB-1/203	AR
Pearce, Ezra	081	1878	WB-15/274	AR

Name	Co.	Date	Recorded Copy	Original
Pearce, Frances	032	1834	WB-1/249	
Pearce, Frances	047	1821	WB-3/661	
Pearce, Francis B.	029	1890	WB-E/507	AR
Pearce, Haly	039	1833	WB-J/244	AR
Pearce, Henry	051	1847	WB-A/267	
Pearce, Henry	039	1887	WB-U/402	AR
Pearce, Henry	010	1881	WB-I/126	
Pearce, Isaac	041	1834	WB-2/350	AR
Pearce, Isaac	041	1843	WB-A/161	
Pearce, Isaac	041	1863	WB-3/300	AR
Pearce, Jacob	041	1802	WB-1/197	AR
Pearce, Jacob	090	1830	WB-3/211	AR
Pearce, James	051	1843	WB-A/221	
Pearce, James	028	1793	WB-A/286	
Pearce, Jeffrey	039	1863	WB-R/399	AR
Pearce, Jeremiah	010	1801	WB-E/126	AR
Pearce, Jesse	056	1807	WB-1/197	AR
Pearce, Jesse	081	1883	WB-15/409	AR
Pearce, Jesse	028	1829	WB-C/306	
Pearce, John	099	1892	WB-C/43	AR
Pearce, John	077	1682	Orig. Only	SS/AR
Pearce, John C.	024	1899	WB-E/300	AR
Pearce, John L.	065	1862	WB-J/125	AR
Pearce, Joseph	047	1816	WB-3/581	
Pearce, Joseph	009	1827	OB-A/386	
Pearce, Lazarus	009	c1801	OWB/407	AR
Pearce, Lazarus	009	1802	OWB/366	AR
Pearce, M. T.	039	1892	WB-U/549	AR
Pearce, Margaret	029	1829	WB-B/178	AR
Pearce, Martha	065	1900	WB-N/365	AR
Pearce, Mary	047	1798	WB-3/312	
Pearce, Mary	056	1816	WB-1/266	AR
Pearce, Miles	009	c1804	OWB/424	AR
Pearce, Obediah	078	1856	WB-17/398	
Pearce, Orran	065	1856	WB-J/23	AR
Pearce, Parthena	041	1838	WB-3/8	AR
Pearce, Paul	039	1900	WB-V/197	AR
Pearce, Rachel	028	c1785	WB-A/144	
Pearce, Rebecca Ann	081	c1867	Orig. Only	AR
Pearce, Reuben	081	1888	WB-16/117	
Pearce, Richard	022	1799	WB-A/6	AR
Pearce, Richard	056	1790	WB-1/29	AR
Pearce, Richard	077	1762	WB-C/3	AR
Pearce, Richardson	010	1892	WB-I/360	AR
Pearce, Robert	024	1729	SS 876/212	SS/AR
Pearce, Samuel	081	1860	WB-11/509	AR
Pearce, Sarah	009	c1798	OWB/349	AR
Pearce, Sarah	035	1791	WB-A/397	AR
Pearce, Sarah	009	c1801	OWB/388	AR
Pearce, Sarah	056	1796	WB-1/106	AR
Pearce, Simon	056	1827	WB-1/338	AR
Pearce, Simon	056	1826	WB-1/461	AR
Pearce, Slade	009	1821	OB-A/311	AR
Pearce, Snodan	035	1821	WB-A/391	AR
Pearce, Stephen	099	1831	RB-22/121	AR
Pearce, Stephen J.	028	1849	WB-D/156	AR
Pearce, Susan C.	010	1900	WB-K/46	
Pearce, Thomas	009	c1777	OWB/132	AR
Pearce, Walter P.	047	1819	WB-3/632	
Pearce, William	078	1862	WB-18/246	AR
Pearce, William	047	1797	WB-3/274	
Pearce, William	090	1881	WB-6/124	AR
Pearce, William	010	1775	WB-B/26	AR
Pearce, William	041	1842	WB-3/35	AR
Pearce, Windsor	081	1823	WB-5/122	AR
Pearce, Zebedee	081	1875	WB-15/195	AR
Pearcy, Lazarus	028	c1760	Orig. Only	SS/AR
Pearman, Richard	084	1843	WB-B/299	CTY-Nunc.
Pearman, William	047	1800	WB-3/342	
Pearsall, Ann	035	1865	WB-3/97	AR
Pearsall, David M.	035	1894	WB-4/455	AR
Pearsall, Edward	070	1762	DB-E/20	AR
Pearsall, Edward	035	1837	Orig. Only	AR
Pearsall, Edward O.	103	1877	WB-1/115	AR
Pearsall, Eva H.	104	1898	WB-7/46	AR
Pearsall, Hugh	035	1839	Orig. Only	AR
Pearsall, J. R.	014	1891	WB-2/477	CTY
Pearsall, James	035	1859	WB-2/141	
Pearsall, James	035	1813	WB-A/379	AR
Pearsall, James D.	035	1863	WB-3/84	AR
Pearsall, Jeremiah	035	1871	WB-4/47	AR
Pearsall, Joseph D.	035	1828	WB-A/379	AR
Pearsall, Mary E. W.	103	1899	WB-2/272	AR
Pearson, Eliazor	077	1795	WB-E/42	
Pearson, Elizabeth	085	1886	WB-2/177	CTY
Pearson, Giles W.	029	1847	WB-C/139	AR
Pearson, Harriet S.	014	1893	WB-2/502	CTY
Pearson, Henderson	099	1883	WB-A/457	AR
Pearson, Ichabod	103	1845	RD-9/210	AR
Pearson, Isaac	046	1835	WB-B/533	AR
Pearson, James	072	1782	RW/L39	AR
Pearson, James M.	099	1863	RB-32/427	AR
Pearson, James S.	047	1872	WB-6/76	
Pearson, Jane S.	014	1883	WB-2/259	CTY
Pearson, Jeremiah	046	1853	WB-C/386	AR
Pearson, Jeremiah	084	1844	WB-C/1	CTY
Pearson, Joel	104	1872	WB-6/57	AR
Pearson, John	075	1755	Orig. Only	SS/AR
Pearson, John	084	1838	WB-B/193	CTY
Pearson, John	010	1777	WB-B/77	AR
Pearson, John	100	1851	WB-41/159	AR
Pearson, John H.	014	1871	WB-2/61	
Pearson, John S.	011	1849	029 WB-C/159	029 AR
Pearson, John T.	103	1877	WB-1/124	AR
Pearson, Jonathan	103	1896	WB-2/151	AR
Pearson, Joseph	DC	1835	Copy	032 AR
Pearson, Joseph	077	1785	WB-C/287	AR
Pearson, Larrance	104	1808	WB-2/227	AR
Pearson, Lemuel	026	1863	WB-1/313	AR
Pearson, Louisa	104	1877	WB-6/145	AR
Pearson, Lucas	026	1860	WB-1/256	AR
Pearson, Margaret	010	1785	WB-D/16	AR
Pearson, Martha Ann	005	1856	WB-C/95	AR
Pearson, Mary Ann	077	1781	Orig. Only	AR
Pearson, Mary L.	014	1886	WB-2/316	CTY
Pearson, Paris	073	1832	WB-E/273	AR
Pearson, Peter	077	1735	SS 876/398	SS/AR
Pearson, Peter	103	1787	WI-A/127	AR
Pearson, Peter	077	c1779	Orig. Only	AR
Pearson, R. M.	106	1878	Copy	013 AR
Pearson, Rachel	077	1750	Orig. Only	SS/AR
Pearson, Rachel W.	014	1880	WB-2/200	
Pearson, Rheuben	020	1863	WB-1/315	AR
Pearson, Richard	085	c1789	WB-C/5	AR
Pearson, Richmond	085	1819	WB-H/13	AR
Pearson, Richmond M.	106	1878	WB-2/92	AR
Pearson, Samuel	099	1802	RB-6/1	AR
Pearson, Samuel	028	1846	WB-D/123	
Pearson, Sarah	103	1872	WB-1/39	AR

Name	Co.	Date	Recorded Copy	Original
Pearson, Sarah E.	014	1891	WB-2/470	CTY
Pearson, Stephen	070	1854	WB-C/579	AR
Pearson, Sullivan	084	c1797	OW/250	AR
Pearson, Thomas	028	1748	SS 877/277	SS/AR
Pearson, Thomas E.	087	1864	WB-2/72	
Pearson, Thomas W.	028	1791	WB-A/235	
Pearson, William	077	1807	WB-E/252	AR
Pearson, William	073	1862	WB-G/389	AR
Pearson, William	040	1876	WB-2/106	AR
Pearson, William	022	1806	WB-A/73	AR
Peartin, James	009	1858	OB-K/460	AR
Pearve, Mary	028	1802	WB-B/141	
Pease, Lewis M.	013	1897	WB-D/37	AR
Peasley, John C.	004	1873	WB-A/11	AR
Peay, Agnes	084	1847	WB-C/49	CTY
Peay, Elizabeth	084	1830	WB-B/15	CTY-Nunc.
Peay, George	084	1804	WB-A/12	CTY
Peay, John	084	c1793	OW/277	
Peay, Mary H.	084	1830	WB-B/5	CTY
Pechel, Franklin	085	1863	WB-K/321	AR
Peck, Ann	099	1856	RB-29/618	AR
Peck, George A.	070	1891	WB-F/506	AR
Peck, Henry	016	1854	WB-1/241	
Peck, John, Sr.	016	1843	WB-1/12	
Peck, Margaret	016	1839	PQS.6/1	
Peck, Mary B.	099	1877	RB-35/380	AR
Peck, Samuel	085	c1807	WB-G/41	AR
Peck, Will	099	1851	RB-27/303	AR
Peck, William A.	107	c1848	WB-1/365	
Pecklen, Joseph	089	1877	WB-2/66	
Pedder, Elizabeth	084	c1797	OW/272	AR
Peddicord, Margaret	038	1898	WB-4/143	AR
Peddy, Andrew	099	1888	WB-B/250	AR
Peddycoart, Sarah	090	1791	WB-1/20	AR
Peddycoart, William B.	090	1807	WB-2/85	AR
Peddycord, Grissilla	038	1864	WB-1/241	
Peden, Alexander	070	1830	WB-AB/257	AR
Peebles, Ann	047	1833	WB-4/96	
Peebles, Elisha	099	1795	RB-3/333	AR
Peebles, Etheldred	071	1865	WB-5/308	AR
Peebles, Etheldred	071	1853	WB-5/108	AR
Peebles, George	047	1832	WB-4/86	
Peebles, H. W.	046	1893	WB-H/261	
Peebles, Harriet E.	059	1898	WB-B/214	CTY
Peebles, Herbert	046	1820	WB-B/87	AR
Peebles, Hubbard	046	1821	WB-B/145	AR
Peebles, James M.	047	1858	WB-5/51	
Peebles, John	099	1825	RB-17/194	AR
Peebles, John	071	1825	WB-3/328	AR
Peebles, John	032	1833	WB-1/235	
Peebles, John H.	059	1864	WB-A/400	CTY
Peebles, John, Sr.	099	1790	RB-2/302	AR
Peebles, Lucy	071	1852	WB-5/103	AR
Peebles, Mary	071	1824	WB-3/299	AR
Peebles, Mary C.	047	1877	WB-6/164	AR
Peebles, Mary F.	071	1886	WB-6/543	AR
Peebles, Nathaniel	015	1775	100 WB-2/66	AR
Peebles, Nathaniel	032	1832	WB-1/186	
Peebles, Nicholas	071	1893	WB-7/190	AR
Peebles, Rebecca M.	071	1898	WB-7/393	AR
Peebles, Rebekah	071	1807	WB-2/350	AR
Peebles, Robert	071	1807	WB-2/342	AR
Peebles, Robert	071	1795	WB-1/22	AR
Peebles, Seth	071	1812	WB-3/89	AR
Peebles, Sterling	071	1811	WB-3/54	AR
Peebles, Turner	071	1825	WB-3/327	AR
Peed, Cyrus	021	1859	WB-1/142	AR
Peed, Elizabeth	009	1845	OB-E/409	AR
Peed, Gain	009	1851	OB-G/375	AR
Peed, George	085	1860	Copy	032 AR
Peed, George W.	009	1860	OB-L/233	AR
Peed, Henry	009	c1792	OWB/271	AR
Peed, John	044	1876	Orig. Only	CTY
Peed, John S.	009	1844	OB-E/208	AR
Peed, Jordan W.	009	1840	OB-C2/364	AR
Peed, Martha	077	1845	WB-F/319	AR
Peed, Martin	009	c1793	OWB/380	AR
Peed, Patience	077	1831	WB-F/187	AR
Peed, William	N	1773	Orig. Only	028 AR
Peed, William	009	1837	OWB/537	AR
Peed, William H.	044	1878	WB-23/297	CTY
Peede, Leroy	078	1848	WB-13/79	AR
Peeden, Handy	056	1879	WB-3/234	AR
Peeden, Newet	056	1867	WB-2/94	AR
Peeden, Sarah B.	056	1899	WB-4/169	
Peedin, James, Sr.	056	1846	WB-1/579	AR
Peedin, Kathaline	056	1894	WB-2/176	AR
Peek, Jesse	013	1839	WB-A/58	
Peek, Samuel	099	1801	RB-5/240	AR
Peeke, James	010	1728	Orig. Only	SS/AR
Peel, Alexander	010	c1882	WB-I/142	
Peel, Amos	010	c1882	WB-I/159	
Peel, George M.	103	1883	WB-1/290	AR
Peel, Hillary	037	1853	WB-F/500	AR
Peel, J. Edwin	063	1900	WB-4/266	AR
Peel, James, Sr.	065	1803	WB-F/44	AR
Peel, John, Sr.	037	1847	WB-F/355	AR
Peel, Mary E.	103	1887	WB-1/399	AR
Peel, Owen	103	1882	WB-1/251	AR
Peel, Robert	103	1885	WB-1/348	AR
Peel, Robert P.	103	1886	WB-1/369	AR
Peel, William	010	1829	WB-G/188	AR
Peel, William	037	1873	Orig. Only	AR
Peele, Amos R.	071	1873	Orig. Only	AR
Peele, David	103	c1800	WI-B/416	AR
Peele, Elizabeth	071	1884	WB-6/433	AR
Peele, Elizabeth	082	1900	WB-7/51	AR
Peele, Hannen	105	1873	WB-2/125	
Peele, Henry	069	1894	WB-5/425	AR
Peele, James	071	1863	WB-5/283	AR
Peele, Jarred	010	1894	WB-I/415	AR
Peele, Jesse	056	1818	WB-1/280	AR
Peele, Jesse H.	105	1893	WB-3/65	AR
Peele, John	071	1845	WB-5/38	AR
Peele, John	071	1869	WB-6/11	AR
Peele, John	037	1818	Orig. Only	AR
Peele, John	105	1888	WB-2/459	AR
Peele, John	071	1804	WB-2/255	AR
Peele, Lydia	071	1843	WB-4/270	AR
Peele, Martha	105	1869	WB-2/3	
Peele, Mathew	105	1861	WB-1/64	AR
Peele, Pascho	082	1807	WB-1/114	AR
Peele, Peggy	037	1870	WB-G/355	AR
Peele, R. E.	010	1900	WB-K/21	
Peele, Robert	082	1864	WB-4/180	AR
Peele, Sally	105	1883	WB-2/303	
Peele, Samuel	047	1794	WB-3/229	
Peele, Stephen J.	105	1870	Orig. Only	AR
Peele, Thomas	071	1873	WB-6/113	AR

Name	Co.	Date	Recorded Copy	Original
Peele, William T.	071	1890	WB-7/64	AR
Peeler, A. G.	026	1899	WB-3/28	AR
Peeler, Andrew	086	1839	WB-E/61	AR
Peeler, Anthony	085	c1828	WB-H/434	AR
Peeler, Any	085	1859	WB-K/273	AR
Peeler, Cordova	026	1898	WB-3/15	AR
Peeler, David	085	1894	WB-3/58	CTY
Peeler, Jane	026	1894	WB-2/484	AR
Peeler, John	026	1893	WB-2/468	AR
Peeler, Paul	085	1834	WB-H/648	AR
Peeler, Peter	086	1813	WB-B/269	AR
Peeler, S. D.	038	1898	WB-4/77	AR
Peeler, Sally	089	1843	WB-1/22	
Peeler, Sarah	085	1869	WB-1/37	CTY
Peelle, Abner	037	1798	WB-D/68	AR
Peelle, Anna	071	1830	WB-4/65	AR
Peelle, Catharine	037	1814	WB-E/71	AR
Peelle, Exum	010	1857	WB-H/43	AR
Peelle, John	069	1847	WB-1/502	AR
Peelle, Josiah	010	1843	WB-G/355	AR
Peelle, Josiah	010	1857	WB-H/52	AR
Peelle, Judith	071	1756	SS 880/120	SS/AR
Peelle, Pricilla	103	1808	RD-1/88	AR
Peelle, Robert	037	1808	WB-D/332	AR
Peelle, Robert	037	1803	WB-D/159	AR
Peelle, Robert	071	1782	WB-1/253	AR
Peelle, William A.	010	1859	WB-H/87	AR
Peelle, Willis	103	1833	RD-6/477	AR
Peelor, Benjamin	073	1800	WB-C/166	AR
Peelor, Samuel	073	1823	WB-E/35	AR
Peeples, A. H.	064	1897	WB-2/395	AR
Peeples, H. W.	038	1893	WB-3/361	AR
Peeples, Jehu	046	1813	WB-A/299	AR
Peeples, Lewis	084	1835	WB-B/135	CTY
Peeples, Lucy	046	1825	Orig. Only	AR
Peerson, Frankey	080	1865	WB-1/187	AR
Peerson, John	060	1831	WB-1/236	AR
Peet, William	N	1722/3	Orig. Only	SS/AR
Peete, Mark T.	071	1861	WB-5/239	AR
Peete, Mary	071	1794	WB-2/57	AR
Peete, Samuel	071	1780	WB-1/229	
Peete, William	071	1788	WB-1/391	AR
Pegg, William	046	1888	WB-E/496	AR
Peggs, John	075	1755	Orig. Only	SS/AR
Peggs, Margaret	075	1729	Orig. Only	SS/AR
Pegram, Daniel	015	1777	100 WB-2/170	AR
Pegram, Edward	046	1802	WB-A/293	AR
Pegram, George	046	1867	WB-E/251	AR
Pegram, George	100	1825	WB-28/319	AR
Pegram, George W.	048	1896	WB-1/50	CTY
Pegram, Gideon	100	1825	WB-25/226	AR
Pegram, James A.	053	1884	WB-11/135	AR
Pegram, Margaret	065	1896	WB-M/491	AR
Pegram, Margaret E.	103	1896	WB-2/165	AR
Pegram, Martha	100	1854	WB-43/4	AR
Pegram, Mary	040	c1866	WB-1/193	
Pegram, Parthena	046	1851	WB-C/344	AR
Pegram, Stephen	029	1854	WB-C/297	AR
Pegram, William	029	1842	WB-B/383	AR
Pegram, William	029	1813	Orig. Only	AR
Pegram, Winchester	040	1862	WB-1/134	
Peine, Joseph	N	1736	LGB-4/#43	
Peirce, James	077	1762	WB-C/23	AR
Peirce, John	077	1726	SS 876/100	SS/AR
Peirce, Joseph	077	1736	Orig. Only	SS/AR
Peirce, Joseph	047	1763	WB-1/116	
Peirce, Thomas	077	1772	WB-C/124	AR
Peirce, Thomas	077	1732	SS 876/234	SS/AR
Peirson, John	072	1829	WB-1/35	AR
Peirson, John	072	1812	WB-2/134	AR
Peirson, Salisbury	072	c1777	RW/L19	AR
Peirson, Samul	028	c1774	Orig. Only	AR-Copy
Pelcher, Daniel	092	c1830	WB-4/30	
Pell, A. J.	030	1898	WB-5/262	AR
Pell, Elizabeth	090	1885	WB-6/154	AR
Pell, Henry	090	1861	WB-4/342	
Pell, John	075	1770	WB-H/117	AR
Pell, William	092	1890	WB-6/311	AR
Pelletier, Edward W.	019	1899	WB-C/17	AR
Pelletier, Jerome	019	1801	WB-D/318	AR
Pelletier, Lamar	019	1842	WB-A/98	AR
Pelletier, Peter W.F.	019	1841	WB-A/92	AR
Pelletier, Sarah	019	1865	WB-A/281	AR
Pelley, James	085	1821	WB-H/88	AR
Pelt, Simon V.	060	1870	WB-4/291	AR
Pelton, F. Alaric	013	1897	WB-D/28	AR
Pemberton, E. L.	029	1883	WB-E/301	AR
Pemberton, Elizabeth	011	c1821	WB-2/339	
Pemberton, Emma L.	029	1892	WB-E/554	AR
Pemberton, James D.	082	1870	WB-6/48	AR
Pemberton, John	082	1812	WB-1/151	AR
Pemberton, John D.	005	1887	WB-D/219	AR
Pemberton, Mary E.	029	1884	WB-E/331	AR
Pemberton, Richard	047	1784	WB-3/64	
Pemberton, Thomas H.	029	1859	WB-C/398	AR
Pemberton, William	082	1819	WB-1/201	AR
Pemberton, William S.	029	1871	WB-E/46	AR
Penberthy, Henry	Eng	1846	Copy	065 AR
Penberthy, John	Eng	1845	Copy	065 AR
Pence, Abraham	049	1827	WB-2/230	AR
Pendar, Harday	056	1804	WB-1/161	AR
Pender(Searles), Mary	028	1899	WB-F/400	
Pender, Celia	037	1821	WB-E/267	AR
Pender, Drewry	047	1857	WB-5/44	
Pender, Elisha	010	1830	WB-G/197	AR
Pender, Elizabeth	103	1891	WB-1/548	AR
Pender, Elizabeth	069	1872	WB-1/614	AR
Pender, Elizabeth	103	1815	RD-3/236	AR
Pender, Elizabeth	103	c1808	RD-1/111	AR
Pender, James	037	1873	WB-G/445	AR
Pender, John	037	1818	WB-E/186	AR
Pender, John	010	1805	WB-E/254	AR
Pender, John C.	103	1816	RD-4/6	AR
Pender, Joseph	037	c1799	Orig. Only	AR
Pender, Joseph J.	105	1882	WB-2/320	AR
Pender, Joseph J.	037	1868	WB-G/315	AR
Pender, Josiah	037	1823	WB-E/329	AR
Pender, K. L.	105	1897	WB-3/265	AR
Pender, Lawrence	047	1871	WB-6/51	
Pender, Littleton	037	1892	WB-H/230	AR
Pender, Margaret	037	1864	WB-G/240	AR
Pender, Martha	037	1854	WB-G/82	AR
Pender, Nellie	037	1885	WB-H/59	
Pender, Nelly	037	1877	WB-G/514	AR
Pender, Patience	010	1797	WB-E/39	AR
Pender, Paul	010	1743	Orig. Only	SS/AR
Pender, R. H.	100	1881	WB-51/154	AR
Pender, Sarah	037	1836	WB-F/187	AR
Pender, Solomon	037	1783	WB-B/107	AR
Pender, Solomon	010	1800	WB-E/99	AR

Name	Co.	Date	Recorded Copy	Original
Pender, Stephen	010	1813	WB-F/224	AR
Pender, William	037	1852	WB-F/479a	AR
Pendergras, Alexander	006	c1863	Orig. Only	AR
Pendergrass, Alston	073	1892	WB-H/578	CTY
Pendergrass, Catherine	073	1878	WB-H/192	CTY
Pendergrass, Edward	073	1860	WB-G/240	AR
Pendergrass, James	073	1876	WB-H/139	CTY
Pendergrass, John	099	1794	RB-3/32	AR
Pendergrass, Julius R.	064	1855	WB-1/39	AR
Pendergrass, Miles H.	061	1873	WB-2/18	AR
Pendergrass, Richard	020	1818	RB-H/132	AR-Nunc.
Pendergrass, Warren	054	1843	WB-2/270	AR
Pendexter, John	073	c1772	WB-A/127	
Pendexter, Samuel	075	1815	WB-M1/270	
Pendland, Harvey M.	025	1889	WB-A/100	AR
Pendleton, Anne	075	1808	WB-M1/193	AR
Pendleton, Benjamin	075	1807	WB-M1/163	AR
Pendleton, Caleb	075	1797	WB-L/92	AR
Pendleton, Charles B.	075	1899	WB-O/487	AR
Pendleton, Frederick	075	1797	WB-L/94	AR
Pendleton, George	075	1774	WB-I/76	AR
Pendleton, George W.	075	c1857	WB-M2/45	AR
Pendleton, Henry	075	1784	WB-K/101	AR
Pendleton, Henry	075	1740	LGB-4/#105	SS/AR
Pendleton, Jesse	075	1795	WB-L/37	AR
Pendleton, John	075	1778	WB-K/15	AR
Pendleton, Joseph	075	1791	WB-K/213	AR
Pendleton, Joseph	075	1798	WB-M1/16	AR
Pendleton, Lemuel	075	1821	WB-M1/345	AR
Pendleton, Martha	075	1807	WB-M1/159	AR
Pendleton, Miles	075	1797	WB-L/97	AR
Pendleton, Mourning	075	1822	WB-M1/355	AR
Pendleton, Nehemiah	075	1835	WB-N/112	AR
Pendleton, Robert	075	c1855	WB-M2/55	AR
Pendleton, Sam	075	1825	WB-N/21	AR
Pendleton, Samuel	075	1815	WB-M1/270	AR
Pendleton, Sarah	075	1840	WB-N/150	AR
Pendleton, Sarah	075	1763	WB-H/49	AR
Pendleton, Sarah	075	1802	WB-M1/60	AR
Pendleton, Simeon	028	1818	WB-C/167	
Pendleton, T. D.	075	1897	WB-O/442	AR
Pendleton, Thomas	075	1750	Orig. Only	SS/AR
Pendleton, Thomas	075	1781	WB-K/65	AR
Pendleton, Thomas	075	1751	Orig. Only	SS/AR
Pendleton, Thomas	075	1732	SS 876/245	SS/AR
Pendleton, Timothy	075	1774	WB-I/85	AR
Pendleton, William B.	075	1826	WB-N/25	AR
Pendleton, William J.	054	1879	WB-4/327	CTY
Pendley, William	017	c1848	WB-A/50	AR
Pendrey, Aaron Read	099	1788	RB-2/161	AR
Pendry, James	085	c1796	WB-F/36	AR
Pendry, Patty	092	c1818	Orig. Only	AR
Pendry, Polly	106	c1858	WB-1/65	AR
Penelton, Hiram	060	1833	WB-1/291	AR
Penery, James, Sr.	033	1854	WB-1/116	AR
Penick, Agnes A.	016	1885	WB-3/481	AR
Penick, Agnes A.	054	1884	WB-5/2	CTY
Penick, Branch	020	1879	WB-A/268	CTY
Penick, Catharine	020	1889	WB-A/571	CTY
Penick, Daniel A.	016	1870	WB-3/14	
Penick, Nathaniel	016	1849	WB-1/157	
Penick, P. T.	054	1886	WB-5/112	CTY
Penick, Peter A.	084	1895	WB-F/25	CTY
Penick, William	020	1828	RB-L/320	AR
Penicks, Mary	100	1784	WB-4/60	AR
Peninger, Jacob	097	1883	WB-2/229	AR
Peninger, John	097	1898	WB-2/565	AR
Penix, John	020	1816	RB-G/156	
Penland, George	061	1877	WB-2/32	AR
Penland, James T.	049	1845	Orig. Only	AR-Nunc.
Penland, John	013	c1852	WB-A/166	
Penland, M. P.	013	1880	066 WB-1/108	
Penland, M. P.	013	1880	064 WB-2/261	
Penland, M. P.	013	1898	WB-2/108	
Penland, M. P.	013	1880	WB-B/204	AR
Penland, Manson	066	c1878	Orig. Only	AR
Penland, Robert	049	c1856	WB-1/27	AR
Penland, Robert	014	1828	Orig. Only	CTY-Copy
Penland, William M.	013	1893	WB-C/241	AR
Penland, William M.	061	1896	WB-2/188	AR
Penley, Thomas	086	1810	WB-B/242	
Penn, John	044	1788	WB-2/81	CTY
Penn, Mary	046	1844	WB-C/195	AR
Pennel, Joseph	003	1895	WB-B/330	AR
Pennel, Samuel	104	1863	WB-5/349	
Pennell, Elizabeth	072	c1874	Orig. Only	AR
Pennell, Larkin	017	1892	WB-B/213	AR
Pennell, Thomas	017	1889	WB-B/164	AR
Pennels, Joshua	104	1856	WB-5/141	
Penney, Edward	056	c1779	WB-2/256	AR
Penney, James	010	1792	WB-D/197	AR
Penney, John	072	c1770	RW/L50	AR
Penney, Thomas	037	1780	WB-B/51	AR
Penney, Thomas	010	1795	WB-D/296	AR
Penney, William	024	1767	WB-B/92	AR
Penning, Jacob	085	c1829	WB-H/467	
Penninger, Daniel	085	1900	WB-3/404	CTY
Penninger, Elizabeth	085	1827	WB-H/411	AR
Penninger, Moses	016	1864	WB-2/106	
Pennington, Charles H.	099	1894	WB-C/302	AR
Pennington, David	089	1851	WB-1/80	AR
Pennington, David	067	c1850	Orig. Only	AR
Pennington, Emma C.	067	1887	WB-2/251	AR
Pennington, George H.	099	1876	RB-35/344	AR
Pennington, Howell	099	1811	RB-10/107	AR
Pennington, James	103	1848	RD-10/83	AR
Pennington, John	099	1852	RB-27/459	AR
Pennington, Joseph	VA	1768	HiDSC	AR-Copy
Pennington, Kinchen	103	1890	WB-1/534	AR
Pennington, Levi	073	1813	WB-D/451	AR
Pennington, Levi	081	1790	WB-1/79	AR
Pennington, Melvina	089	1861	WB-1/225	
Pennington, Nancy	089	c1863	WB-1/264	
Pennington, Stephen	006	1890	WB-E/202	AR
Pennington, Thomas	047	1763	Orig. Only	AR
Pennington, Thomas	047	1763	010 WB-A/70	
Pennington, Whitson C.	089	1863	WB-1/252	
Pennix, John	065	1793	WB-F/40	AR
Pennoyer, S. L.	010	1868	WB-H/208	AR
Penny, Alexander	099	1845	RB-26/61	AR
Penny, Asbury	056	1898	WB-4/85	AR
Penny, Caleb	056	1802	WB-1/139	AR
Penny, Charles	022	1820	WB-B/22	AR
Penny, David	056	1864	WB-2/62	AR
Penny, Elizabeth	065	1775	WB-F/35	AR
Penny, James	099	1803	RB-6/61	AR
Penny, Jesse	099	1888	WB-B/252	AR
Penny, Margaret	085	1858	WB-K/261	AR
Penny, Patsy	028	1806	WB-B/258	

Name	Co.	Date	Recorded Copy	Original
Penny, Penuel	056	1806	WB-1/190	AR
Penny, Sarah R.	099	1884	WB-A/564	
Penny, William	060	1818	Orig. Only	AR
Penny, William D.	099	c1897	056 WB-4/373	056 AR
Penny, William J.	070	1900	WB-H/275	AR
Penny, Young	099	1884	WB-A/562	AR
Pennypacker, Enos J.	070	1890	WB-F/391	AR
Penrice, Elizabeth	024	c1785	WB-B/101	AR
Penrice, Francis	024	1760	WB-1/1	AR
Penrice, Francis	071	1790	WB-1/412	AR
Penrice, Francis	077	1758	SS 882/80	SS/AR
Penrice, Samuel	024	c1783	WB-A/207	AR
Penrice, Thomas	024	1739	Orig. Only	SS/AR
Penry, James	085	1816	WB-G/452	AR
Penry, John	033	1858	WB-1/165	AR
Penry, S. E.	032	1888	WB-4/22	AR
Penry, Thomas	085	c1825	WB-H/432	AR
Penson, Elizabeth	044	1876	WB-23/235	CTY
Penuel, John	057	1842	WB-B/155	AR
Peoples, Hugh	022	1799	WB-A/10	AR
Peoples, Jehu	022	1837	WB-C/57	AR
Peoples, John	065	1827	WB-F/95	AR
Peoples, John, Jr.	065	1827	WB-A/157	AR
Peoples, Richard	065	1870	WB-K/53	AR
Peppenger, Abraham	032	1833	WB-1/230	
Pepper, C. M.	046	1896	WB-F/504	AR
Pepper, James A.	090	1898	WB-6/475	AR
Pepper, Joseph	037	1833	WB-F/146	
Pepper, Sanford	047	1892	WB-7/22	AR
Pepper, Stephen	047	1850	WB-4/290	
Pepper, Stephen	047	1814	WB-3/546	
Pepper, Thomas	071	1856	WB-5/156	AR
Pepper, William	037	1852	WB-F/473	
Pepper, William R.	099	1879	WB-A/61	AR
Peppers, Wilson	029	1879	WB-E/190	AR
Peques, Edward W.	SC	1895	005 WB-D/366	
Perce, Ephriam	056	1826	WB-1/463	AR
Percey, Ephraim	107	1878	WB-2/19	
Percy, William	015	1776	100 WB-2/80	AR
Perdew, James	028	c1766	Orig. Only	AR
Perdue, James	039	c1859	WB-Q/565	AR
Perdue, John	015	1769	100 WB-1/52	AR
Perdue, Mary	046	1870	WB-E/42	AR
Perdue, Mary	039	1866	WB-S/160	AR
Perdue, Prudence	100	1840	WB-37/376	AR
Perdue, Solomon	100	1869	WB-51/6	AR
Peresho, James	096	1777	WB-1/99	AR
Pergason, John H.	084	1860	WB-C/317	CTY
Perisho, Benjamin	077	1804	WB-E/206	AR
Perisho, Elizabeth	077	1785	WB-C/289	AR
Perisho, John	077	1759	SS 881/261	SS/AR
Perisho, Joseph	077	1801	WB-E/135	AR
Perisho, Joseph	077	1763	WB-C/43	AR
Perisho, Joseph	077	1784	WB-C/269	AR
Perisho, Joseph	077	1802	WB-E/167	AR
Perisho, Sarah	077	1760	Orig. Only	SS/AR
Perkins, Abram, Sr.	020	1793	RB-C/50	
Perkins, Alexander	017	c1856	WB-A/98	AR
Perkins, Alfred	030	1857	WB-4/214	
Perkins, Allen	006	1867	WB-D/72	
Perkins, Bartlett	105	1890	WB-2/524	
Perkins, Betsy	046	c1841	Orig. Only	AR
Perkins, Caleb	046	c1788	WB-A/289	AR
Perkins, Catherine	060	1820	Orig. Only	AR
Perkins, Churchill	079	1868	WB-1/175	AR

Name	Co.	Date	Recorded Copy	Original
Perkins, Constant	084	1822	WB-A/286	CTY
Perkins, Constantine	084	1889	WB-E/427	CTY
Perkins, David	008	1734	SS 876/292	
Perkins, Edmund H.	075	1877	WB-O/74	AR
Perkins, Edny	030	1824	WB-3/168	
Perkins, George	030	1862	WB-4/246	AR
Perkins, Henry	047	1801	WB-3/353	
Perkins, Henry	047	1797	WB-3/281	
Perkins, Henry	030	1715	Orig. Only	SS/AR
Perkins, Henry	030	1796	WB-2/64	
Perkins, Ichabod	024	c1780	WB-A/128	AR
Perkins, Isaac	040	1889	WB-2/339	AR
Perkins, Isaac	028	1830	WB-C/326	
Perkins, Isaac	092	1883	WB-6/190	AR
Perkins, Jacob	030	1817	WB-3/99	
Perkins, James	022	1873	WB-E/89	AR
Perkins, James	009	c1760	OWB/78	AR
Perkins, James W.	092	1893	WB-6/359	AR
Perkins, Jared	046	1858	WB-C/516	AR
Perkins, John	075	1876	WB-O/67	AR
Perkins, John	046	1825	Orig. Only	AR
Perkins, John	020	1791	RB-B/428	
Perkins, John	060	1804	Orig. Only	AR
Perkins, Johnson	006	1884	WB-E/100	AR
Perkins, Jonathan	028	1826	WB-C/284	AR
Perkins, Joseph	046	1807	WB-A/295	AR
Perkins, Joseph	075	1823	WB-M1/367	AR
Perkins, Leah	018	1891	WB-E/207	AR
Perkins, Leveney	030	1783	WB-1/173	Nunc.
Perkins, Luther	006	c1854	WB-D/53	AR
Perkins, Mary T.	047	1894	WB-7/101	AR
Perkins, Moses	105	1870	WB-2/35	AR
Perkins, Pleasant	020	1795	RB-C/145	
Perkins, Robert	024	1810	WB-B/303	AR
Perkins, Robert B.	060	1824	Orig. Only	AR
Perkins, Robert B.	060	1820	Orig. Only	AR
Perkins, Sally	020	1800	RB-C/439	AR
Perkins, Samuel	071	1765	WB-1/118	
Perkins, Solomon	018	1839	WB-C/247	
Perkins, Thomas	092	1819	WB-3/138	AR
Perkins, Thomas F.	084	1864	WB-C/397	CTY
Perkins, W. E.	006	1898	WB-E/348	AR
Perkins, W. M.	047	c1898	Orig. Only	AR
Perkins, William	009	c1825	OWB/484	AR
Perkins, William	047	1834	WB-4/109	
Perkins, William	047	1801	WB-3/353	
Perkins, William A.	014	1891	WB-2/474	CTY
Perkins, William B.	028	1853	WB-D/205	AR
Perkins, William F.	006	c1870	WB-D/105	AR
Perkinson, Jesse C.	100	1881	WB-51/220	AR
Perkinson, John M.	099	1885	WB-B/23	AR
Perkinson, Julia	099	1884	WB-A/581	AR
Perkinson, Page	100	1834	WB-35/1	AR
Perkinson, R. J.	100	1896	WB-51/468	
Perkinson, Ransom	098	1895	WB-A/220	CTY
Perkinson, Seth	044	1819	WB-8/246	CTY
Permenter, James	037	1789	WB-C/106	AR
Permenter, John	005	1821	WB-A/111	AR
Perow, William	080	c1860	Orig. Only	AR
Perril, Joseph	032	c1861	WB-2/212	
Perriman, Isaac	084	c1795	OW/270	AR
Perrit, Priscilla	037	1761	WB-A/50	AR
Perritt, Ann	037	1796	WB-C/365	AR
Perritt, Lewis	037	1786	WB-C/30	AR
Perry, A. L.	039	1873	WB-U/55	AR

Name	Co.	Date	Recorded Copy	Original
Perry, Abner	051	c1810	WB-A/75	
Perry, Agness	044	1878	WB-23/301	CTY
Perry, Amanda	010	1891	WB-I/310	AR
Perry, Amanda	039	1890	WB-U/499	
Perry, Amos	024	1805	WB-B/211	AR
Perry, Amos	063	1842	WB-2/294	
Perry, Ann	070	1763	DB-E/31	AR
Perry, Ann C.	069	1856	WB-1/550	AR
Perry, Anny	039	1838	WB-K/154	
Perry, Augustus	024	1891	WB-E/182	AR
Perry, Basel	006	c1863	Orig. Only	AR
Perry, Beeze	029	1858	WB-C/381	AR
Perry, Benjamin	072	1812	WB-A/104	AR
Perry, Benjamin	099	1881	WB-A/228	AR
Perry, Benjamin	019	1870	028 WB-E/28	
Perry, Benjamin	019	1870	WB-B/59	AR
Perry, Benjamin	077	c1779	Orig. Only	AR
Perry, Bennet	039	c1847	WB-N/356	AR
Perry, Bennett	039	1841	WB-L/15	
Perry, Bryant	099	1873	RB-35/229	AR
Perry, Burell	039	c1816	SC/01656	AR-Copy
Perry, Burrel	039	1862	WB-R/322	AR
Perry, Burrell	039	1801	WB-B/118	
Perry, Burrell	039	1816	WB-E/123	AR
Perry, Bynum	001	1885	WB-2/250	AR
Perry, Cader	075	1882	WB-O/159	AR
Perry, Cader	075	1818	WB-M1/311	AR
Perry, Clary	099	1847	RB-26/294	AR
Perry, Cynthia	039	1893	WB-V/16	AR
Perry, David B.	009	c1866	OB-M/309	AR
Perry, Dempsey	056	1813	WB-1/395	AR
Perry, Doctrin R.	075	1873	WB-O/42	AR
Perry, Dorothy	071	1833	WB-4/103	AR
Perry, Eaton	069	1893	WB-5/403	AR
Perry, Ebenezer	046	1842	WB-C/129	AR
Perry, Elijah B.	039	c1844	WB-M/75	AR
Perry, Elisabeth	056	1815	WB-1/240	AR
Perry, Elisha	039	1892	WB-U/547	AR
Perry, Elisha	077	1853	WB-F/422	AR
Perry, Eliza C.	022	1899	WB-F/83	AR
Perry, Elizabeth	075	1824	WB-M1/395	AR
Perry, Elizabeth	022	1886	WB-E/332	AR
Perry, Elizabeth	077	1848	WB-F/343	AR
Perry, Elizabeth	039	1838	WB-K/164	
Perry, Elizabeth	039	1828	WB-H/200	
Perry, Elizabeth	010	1859	WB-H/85	AR
Perry, Elizabeth	039	1874	WB-U/96	AR
Perry, Elizabeth	010	N. D.	WB-I/167	
Perry, Elizabeth	056	1824	WB-1/378	AR
Perry, Ellie N.	WV	1895	064 WB-2/375	
Perry, Elliott	077	1839	WB-F/280	AR
Perry, Francis F.	099	1814	RB-11/315	
Perry, George W.	010	1869	WB-I/9	AR
Perry, Harbert	039	1823	WB-G/166	
Perry, Hardy	089	1881	WB-2/87	AR
Perry, Hardy	075	1823	WB-M1/363	AR
Perry, Hartsfield	039	1886	WB-U/380	
Perry, Henry H.	075	1892	WB-O/358	AR
Perry, Hester	024	1850	WB-C/312	AR
Perry, Howard L.	056	1855	WB-1/683	AR
Perry, Howell Y.	039	1870	WB-U/25	AR
Perry, Hubbard	047	1793	WB-3/215	
Perry, Hymrick	010	1857	WB-H/51	AR
Perry, Isaac	010	1834	WB-G/239	AR
Perry, Isaac	077	1835	WB-F/240	AR
Perry, Isaac	039	1870	WB-U/59	
Perry, Isaac	010	1866	WB-H/167	AR
Perry, Israel	077	1779	WB-C/224	AR
Perry, J. T.	099	1887	WB-B/390	AR
Perry, Jackson H.	005	1887	WB-D/221	AR
Perry, Jacob	077	1790	WB-C/414	AR
Perry, Jacob	039	1879	WB-U/200	AR
Perry, Jacob	077	1818	WB-F/5	AR
Perry, Jacob	077	1807	WB-E/269	AR
Perry, Jacob	063	1811	WB-2/2	
Perry, Jacob	077	1777	WB-C/234	AR
Perry, James	099	1841	Orig. Only	AR
Perry, James	039	c1844	WB-L/251	
Perry, James	077	1861	WB-F/527	AR
Perry, James	047	1771	WB-1/286	
Perry, James	039	1814	WB-D/103	AR
Perry, James	047	1837	WB-4/148	
Perry, James	083	1819	WB-1/217	
Perry, James A.	024	1881	WB-E/102	AR
Perry, James D.	075	1899	WB-O/483	AR
Perry, James M.	010	1863	WB-H/134	AR
Perry, James S.	003	1892	WB-B/306	
Perry, Jane	099	1889	WB-B/392	
Perry, Jane	022	1894	WB-E/569	AR
Perry, Jepthah	039	1853	WB-N/332	AR
Perry, Jere	039	1895	WB-V/51	AR
Perry, Jeremiah	039	1846	WB-M/122	AR
Perry, Jeremiah	039	1839	WB-K/179	AR
Perry, Jeremiah	024	1695	SS 874.2/65	SS/AR
Perry, Jesse	077	1801	WB-E/143	AR
Perry, Jesse	077	1807	WB-E/272	AR
Perry, Jesse J.	106	1891	WB-2/298	AR
Perry, John	010	1864	WB-H/148	AR
Perry, John	039	1877	WB-U/153	AR
Perry, John	070	1740	Orig. Only	AR
Perry, John	103	1796	WI-B/114	
Perry, John	077	1829	WB-F/165	AR
Perry, John	063	1789	WB-1/153	
Perry, John	072	1792	Orig. Only	AR
Perry, John	011	1871	WB-2/51	
Perry, John	039	1830	WB-J/99	
Perry, John	047	1783	WB-3/43	
Perry, John	044	1897	WB-24/358	CTY
Perry, John	047	1758	WB-1/1	
Perry, John	022	1845	WB-C/173	AR
Perry, John	099	1852	RB-28/87	AR
Perry, John	092	1843	WB-4/203	
Perry, John B.	077	1896	WB-H/281	AR
Perry, John H.	075	1891	WB-O/328	AR
Perry, John H.	024	1893	WB-E/222	AR
Perry, John W.	069	1857	WB-1/552	AR
Perry, John, Sr.	039	1829	WB-J/24	AR
Perry, John, Sr.	039	c1790	WB-B/75	
Perry, Jonathan	090	1814	WB-2/150	AR
Perry, Joseph	077	1801	WB-E/131	AR
Perry, Joseph	028	1816	WB-C/126	
Perry, Joseph J.	010	1896	WB-I/481 & 497	AR
Perry, Josephine	039	1887	WB-U/431	AR
Perry, Joshua	039	1811	WB-C/216	AR
Perry, Joshua	039	c1819	WB-F/221	AR
Perry, Joshua	039	1828	WB-J/14	
Perry, Joshua	039	1894	WB-V/26	AR
Perry, Joshua	100	1792	WB-6/225	AR
Perry, Josiah	010	1893	WB-I/370	AR
Perry, Josiah	010	1821	WB-G/81	AR

Name	Co.	Date	Recorded Copy	Original
Perry, Josiah	030	1839	WB-4/63	
Perry, Josiah H.	024	1900	WB-E/313	AR
Perry, Lavinia	075	1881	WB-0/127	AR
Perry, Lawrence	077	1826	WB-F/121	AR
Perry, Lucinda	001	1888	WB-2/348	AR
Perry, M. L.	039	1892	WB-U/577	AR
Perry, Maria	039	1890	WB-U/509	
Perry, Maria Jones	039	1896	WB-V/94	AR
Perry, Mark P.	100	1875	WB-51/105	AR-Nunc.
Perry, Martha	039	1849	WB-N/322	AR
Perry, Martha	010	1890	WB-I/308	AR
Perry, Martha A.	010	1899	WB-K/2	
Perry, Martha J.	099	1892	WB-C/61	AR
Perry, Mary	009	c1859	OB-M/146	AR
Perry, Mary	010	1861	WB-H/111	AR
Perry, Mary H.	099	1884	WB-A/550	AR
Perry, Mary J.	057	1851	WB-B/211	AR
Perry, Milicent	010	1823	WB-G/110	AR
Perry, Millicent	077	1837	WB-F/268	AR
Perry, Minton L.	039	1900	WB-V/182	AR
Perry, Nathan	039	1880	WB-U/228	AR
Perry, Nathan	039	1833	WB-J/254	AR
Perry, Nathaniel	099	1837	RB-24/26	AR
Perry, Nathaniel	039	c1790	WB-A/71	
Perry, Nathaniel	039	1790	WB-A/72	
Perry, Noah	063	1824	WB-2/98	
Perry, Norfleet	039	c1857	WB-O/375	
Perry, Patience	047	1771	WB-1/297	
Perry, Peter	029	1820	WB-B/48	AR
Perry, Peter	073	1843	WB-F/155	AR
Perry, Pherebee	075	1882	Orig. Only	AR
Perry, Philip	077	1809	WB-E/333	AR
Perry, Philip	083	c1805	WB-1/93	
Perry, Phillip	077	1751	Orig. Only	SS/AR
Perry, Polly	039	1855	WB-Q/563	AR
Perry, Randal	099	1845	RB-26/82	
Perry, Redding	039	c1850	WB-N/356	AR
Perry, Redding	098	1896	WB-A/334	CTY
Perry, Reuben	077	1845	WB-F/315	AR
Perry, Reuben	056	c1813	WB-1/274	AR
Perry, Reubin	103	1875	WB-1/87	AR
Perry, Robert	099	1837	RB-24/25	AR
Perry, Rosanna W.	099	1882	WB-A/371	AR
Perry, Rutherford	039	1891	WB-U/535	AR
Perry, Salley	099	1899	WB-D/298	AR
Perry, Sally	099	1824	RB-18/352	AR
Perry, Samuel	024	1760	WB-A/218	AR
Perry, Samuel	024	c1842	WB-C/253	AR
Perry, Samuel	039	1898	WB-V/150	AR
Perry, Samuel P.	099	1853	RB-28/378	AR
Perry, Sarah	063	1793	WB-1/195	
Perry, Silas J.	057	1846	WB-B/182	AR
Perry, Solomon	044	1843	WB-15/414	
Perry, Solomon	039	1815	WB-D/176	AR
Perry, Susan	075	1896	WB-0/425	AR
Perry, Susan A.	024	1891	WB-E/197	AR
Perry, Susan E.	059	1897	057 WB-C/231	057 AR
Perry, Susan E.	059	1898	WB-B/202	CTY
Perry, Temperance	039	1850	WB-N/301	AR
Perry, Thomas	077	1814	WB-E/402	AR
Perry, Thomas L.	009	1867	OB-M/235	AR
Perry, Timothy	077	1850	WB-F/387	AR
Perry, Turner	022	1854	WB-C/373	AR
Perry, Warren	098	1889	WB-A/110	CTY
Perry, Wesley W.	075	1881	WB-0/122	AR
Perry, Wilie	039	1859	WB-Q/562	AR
Perry, William	072	1796	Orig. Only	AR
Perry, William	039	1830	WB-J/114	
Perry, William	024	1886	WB-E/158	AR
Perry, William	022	1869	WB-E/27	AR
Perry, William	097	1870	WB-2/28	AR
Perry, William	022	1854	Orig. Only	AR
Perry, William	063	1829	WB-2/158	
Perry, William	039	1861	WB-R/16	AR
Perry, William	083	1895	WB-4/106	AR
Perry, William	075	1823	WB-M1/364	AR
Perry, William D.	010	1888	WB-I/259	AR
Perry, William E.	069	1893	WB-5/394	AR
Perry, William G.	022	1885	WB-E/321	AR
Perry, William J.	051	1862	WB-B/49	AR
Perry, Willie	099	1870	RB-35/63	AR
Perry, Willie	039	1865	WB-S/95	
Perry, Winnifred	056	1821	WB-1/322	AR
Perry, Wiston	039	1873	WB-U/82	AR
Perryman, Isaac K.	032	1867	WB-2/356	AR
Perryman, Melton	005	c1793	WB-A/21	AR
Persey, William	010	1782	WB-C/42	AR
Person, Abiah W.	039	1893	WB-V/8	AR
Person, Amy	039	1831	WB-J/171	AR
Person, Ann	100	1781	WB-3/94	AR
Person, Anthony A.	039	1878	WB-U/178	AR
Person, Benjamin	071	1826	WB-4/2	AR
Person, Francis	039	1815	WB-D/172	AR
Person, Harriett M.	071	1887	WB-6/574	AR
Person, Jesse	039	1872	WB-U/53	AR
Person, John	039	1841	WB-L/27	
Person, Joseph	015	1772	100 WB-1/208	AR
Person, Mary	022	c1866	WB-D/174	AR
Person, Mary	044	1761	Orig. Only	CTY
Person, Matthew P.	039	1898	WB-V/130	AR
Person, Murdoch B.	068	1851	WB-B/219	
Person, Presly C.	039	1845	WB-M/17	AR
Person, Rebecca	071	1845	WB-5/36	AR
Person, Sallie	039	1881	WB-U/286	AR
Person, Samuel	068	1801	WB-A/214	
Person, Samuel J.	070	1870	WB-E/191	AR
Person, Thomas H.	100	1831	WB-33/342	AR
Person, William	015	1771	100 WB-1/171	AR
Person, William	TN	1865	100 WB-50/189	100 AR
Person, William	015	1778	100 WB-2/224	
Person, William	100	1856	WB-49/54	AR
Person, William	039	1778	SC/01850	AR-Copy
Person, Willie M.	039	1884	WB-U/336	AR
Person, Zilpha	103	1881	WB-1/208	AR
Personett, John	092	1813	WB-3/109	AR
Persons, John	077	1754	Orig. Only	SS/AR
Persons, John	092	1802	WB-3/49A	AR
Persons, Richard	092	1820	WB-3/145	AR
Pescud, P. F., Sr.	099	1884	WB-A/534	AR
Petegrew, Stanford	044	1888	WB-24/39	CTY
Petegrew, William	044	1853	WB-19/245	CTY
Peter, Simon	090	1819	WB-3/36	AR
Peters, Henry	071	1819	WB-3/219	AR
Peters, Samuel	087	1851	WB-1/387	AR
Peters, Samuel	035	1784	WB-A/395	AR
Peters, Theodore	LA	1834	010 WB-G/455	010 AR
Peters, William	028	c1760	DB-8/227	
Peterson, Aaron	087	1823	WB-1/53	
Peterson, Catherine	056	1897	WB-4/61	AR
Peterson, Catherine	038	1885	WB-2/544	AR

Name	Co.	Date	Recorded Copy	Original
Peterson, Charles	087	1869	WB-3/10	AR
Peterson, Edwin R.	009	c1898	WB-2/146	
Peterson, Elisha	087	1849	WB-1/362	AR
Peterson, Elizabeth	020	1858	RB-S/76	AR
Peterson, Elizabeth	028	1881	WB-E/256	
Peterson, Elizabeth	087	1863	WB-2/52	
Peterson, Emma	070	1851	WB-C/521	AR
Peterson, Enoch	070	1859	Copy	087 AR
Peterson, Enoch	070	1859	WB-D/13	AR
Peterson, G. S.	056	1896	WB-4/17	
Peterson, Henry K.	010	1811	WB-F/192	AR
Peterson, Hiram	087	1881	WB-3/229	AR
Peterson, Jinnet	068	1827	WB-B/48	
Peterson, John	020	1802	RB-D/97	
Peterson, John	029	1809	WB-A/140	AR
Peterson, John	021	1891	WB-2/552	AR
Peterson, John G.	071	1826	WB-4/11	AR-Nunc.
Peterson, John W.	010	1854	WB-G/514	AR
Peterson, John W.	035	1874	WB-4/79	AR
Peterson, Kinchen	071	1799	WB-2/180	AR
Peterson, Labon	070	1851	WB-C/526	AR
Peterson, M. N.	038	1888	WB-3/86	
Peterson, Martha	010	1808	WB-F/116	AR
Peterson, Robert	010	1848	WB-G/430	AR
Peterson, Ross	087	1876	WB-3/123 & 127	
Peterson, Sousanah	107	1896	WB-2/86	
Peterson, Stephen	087	1895	WB-3/567	AR
Peterson, Susan A.	010	1858	WB-H/69	AR
Peterson, Thomas	087	1838	WB-1/194	
Peterson, Thomas	020	1851	RB-Q/483	AR
Peterson, Wiley R.	087	1896	WB-4/7	AR
Peterson, William D.	087	1881	WB-3/234	AR
Peteway, Robert	072	1825	WB-A/104	AR
Pethal, Annie	085	1894	WB-3/55	CTY
Petipher, Right	028	1870	WB-E/38	AR
Petit, Francis	024	1712	Orig. Only	SS/AR
Petorson, Jacob	002	1697	SS 874.2/88	SS/AR (N)
Petorson, Jacob	077	1698	SS 874.2/98	SS/AR
Petrea, Matthew	016	1892	WB-4/136	AR
Petree, Abraham	038	1899	WB 4/160	AR
Petree, Henry	090	1804	WB-2/47	
Petree, Henry	090	1868	WB-5/46	AR
Petree, Isaac	038	1894	WB-3/517	AR
Petree, Sarah	090	1878	WB-6/99	AR
Petree, William W.	038	1894	WB-3/496	AR
Petry, Jacob	090	1804	WB-2/54	
Petteford, William	099	1837	RB-24/28	AR
Petteway, William	037	1787	WB-C/43	AR
Pettifer, Rose	028	1854	WB-D/223	
Pettiford, Archibald	069	1899	WB-6/57	AR
Pettiford, Delila	044	1891	WB-24/149	CTY
Pettiford, Drury	099	1838	RB-24/225	AR
Pettiford, Tharrington	044	1899	WB-24/419	CTY
Pettiford, William	078	1888	WB-19/220	AR
Pettigrew, Charles	073	1847	WB-F/350	AR
Pettigrew, Ebenezer	096	1848	WB-3/19	
Pettigrew, Mary	001	1880	WB-2/161	AR
Pettijohn, Abraham	024	1818	WB-C/72	AR
Pettijohn, Abraham	024	1817	WB-C/51	AR
Pettijohn, Elizabeth	024	1844	WB-C/258	AR
Pettijohn, Frances	024	1845	WB-C/263	AR
Pettijohn, James L.	024	1849	WB-C/293	AR
Pettijohn, Job	024	1824	Orig. Only	AR
Pettijohn, Job	024	c1822	Copy	077 AR
Pettijohn, John	024	1833	WB-C/163	AR
Pettijohn, Rachel	024	1869	WB-E/10	AR
Pettijohn, Sarah	024	1855	WB-C/385	AR
Pettijohn, Thomas	024	c1767	WB-A/124	AR
Pettillo, William	020	1820	RB-H/296	
Pettipher, Alonzo T.	028	1895	WB-F/161	
Pettit, Benjamin	092	1786	WB-2/64A	AR
Pettit, Henry	086	1838	WB-E/52	AR
Pettit, Nathaniel	070	1865	WB-D/161	AR
Pettit, Thomas	092	1786	WB-2/64	AR
Pettit, Thomas	092	1789	WB-2/87	AR
Pettiway, John	072	1818	WB-A/102	AR
Pettus, John D.	SC	c1819	065 WB-F/106	065 AR
Pettus, Violet	065	1829	WB-D/36	AR
Pettway, John	100	1795	WB-8/166	AR
Pettway, John	044	1803	WB-6/1	CTY
Pettway, Martha	100	1796	WB-9/50	AR
Petty, Charles C.	028	1900	WB-F/506	
Petty, Charles C.	028	c1896	104 WB-7/188	104 AR
Petty, Charles Q.	040	1898	WB-3/2	AR
Petty, Elias	046	1825	WB-B/209	AR
Petty, George	086	1801	WB-B/120	AR
Petty, James	046	1827	WB-B/354	AR
Petty, Reuben	060	1794	Orig. Only	AR
Petty, Stephen B.	073	1891	WB-H/539	CTY
Petty, William	022	c1864	WB-D/140	AR
Petty, William C.	081	1885	WB-15/564	AR
Petty, William L.	080	1881	WB-1/66	AR
Pettyfort, Jessy	099	1870	RB-35/60	AR
Pettyjohn, Hannah F.	101	1884	WB-A/128	AR
Pettypool, Seth	044	1789	WB-2/124	CTY
Pew, William	028	1806	WB-B/231	
Pewett, William	017	c1842	WB A/6	
Peyton, A. M.	046	1876	WB-E/178	AR
Peyton, Charlotte	046	1877	WB-E/185	AR
Peyton, Elenor	009	1753	OWB/43	AR
Peyton, Henry	027	1899	WB-2/151	AR
Peyton, Mary	079	1896	WB-2/88	AR
Peyton, Robert	008	1754	SS 881/104	SS/AR
Peyton, Robert	009	c1759	OWB/65	AR
Peyton, Thomas	029	1846	WB-C/95	AR
Pfaff, Isaac	090	1832	WB-3/238	AR
Pfaff, Joseph	090	1815	WB-2/162	
Pfaff, Nathaniel	038	1890	WB-3/162	AR
Pfaff, Peter	038	1865	WB-1/257	AR
Pfifer, John	065	1777	Orig. Only	SS/AR
Pfohl, Anna E.	038	1876	WB-2/262	AR
Pfohl, Christian	090	1838	WB-4/25	AR
Pfohl, Dorothea	090	1844	WB-4/169	AR
Pfohl, Edward A.	038	1896	WB-3/584	AR
Pfohl, S. Thomas	038	1874	WB-2/174	AR
Pfohl, Theodore	038	1871	WB-2/73	AR
Phane, Elizabeth	078	1879	WB-19/82	AR
Phares, Samuel	011	c1837	WB-1/36	
Pharr, Bettie Y.	065	1899	WB-N/185	AR
Pharr, Catherine	016	1849	WB-1/166	AR
Pharr, Henry	016	1885	WB-3/465	
Pharr, Hugh S.	065	1880	WB-K/398	AR
Pharr, Hugh S.	065	1880	016 WB-3/511	
Pharr, Jane	016	1868	WB-2/163	
Pharr, Margaret	016	1885	WB-3/461	
Pharr, Rachel	016	1867	WB-2/149	
Pharr, W. R.	016	1864	WB-2/101	
Pharr, Walter F.	016	1854	WB-1/233	

Name	Co.	Date	Recorded Copy	Original
Pharr, Walter S.	065	1867	WB-J/231	AR
Pharr, Walter W.	065	1886	WB-L/167	AR
Pharr, William R.	016	1831	PQS.5/181	AR
Phelps, Asa	010	1897	WB-I/493	AR
Phelps, Baley	101	1895	WB-A/270	AR
Phelps, Benjamin	077	1785	WB-C/293	AR
Phelps, Benjamin	096	c1807	WB-2/55	AR
Phelps, Charles	101	1872	Orig. Only	AR
Phelps, Delila	032	1900	WB-4/463	AR
Phelps, Edmund	096	c1787	WB-1/159	
Phelps, Edward	096	1796	Orig. Only	AR
Phelps, Edward	028	1806	WB-B/250	Nunc.
Phelps, Ezekiel	085	1821	WB-H/134	AR
Phelps, Ezekiel	033	1892	WB-2/135	CTY
Phelps, Godfrey	096	1807	WB-2/53	AR
Phelps, Godfry	096	1751	Orig. Only	SS/AR
Phelps, Henry	010	1818	WB-G/20	AR
Phelps, Henry	077	1752	Orig. Only	SS/AR
Phelps, Horace F.	101	1895	WB-A/261	AR
Phelps, James	041	1794	WB-1/123	AR
Phelps, James	020	1788	RB-B/155	AR
Phelps, James	041	1834	WB-2/346	AR
Phelps, James	010	1849	WB-G/454	AR
Phelps, Jeremiah H.	096	1836	WB-2/133	AR
Phelps, John	101	1867	Orig. Only	AR
Phelps, John	096	1779	WB-1/102	AR
Phelps, John A.	010	1879	WB-I/107	
Phelps, John D.	010	1877	WB-I/89	
Phelps, John J.	047	1888	WB-6/476	AR
Phelps, Johnathon	077	1689	Orig. Only	SS/AR
Phelps, Jonathan	077	1732	SS 876/266	SS/AR
Phelps, Jordan H.	101	1878	WB-A/25	AR
Phelps, Joseph	086	1758	WB-1/8	Nunc.
Phelps, Joseph	101	N. D.	WB-A/148	
Phelps, Joseph, Sr.	096	c1787	WB-1/160	
Phelps, Joshua	096	1850	WB-3/25	AR
Phelps, Judah	041	1809	WB-2/44	AR
Phelps, Lewis	028	1860	WB-D/348	AR
Phelps, Mary	096	1854	WB-3/44	AR
Phelps, Micagy	101	1879	WB-A/35	AR
Phelps, Micajah	010	1816	WB-G/5	AR
Phelps, Nathan A.	096	1832	WB-2/111	AR
Phelps, Nehemiah	101	1871	Orig. Only	AR
Phelps, R. P.	010	1887	WB-I/228	AR
Phelps, Robert C.	020	1884	WB-A/414	CTY
Phelps, Samuel	077	1728	SS 876/145	SS/AR
Phelps, Sarah	077	1787	WB-C/359	AR
Phelps, Seth, Sr.	096	1823	WB-2/93	AR
Phelps, Susannah	106	1888	Orig. Only	AR
Phelps, Thomas	078	1849	WB-13/163	
Phelps, Thomas	020	1823	RB-I/247	AR
Phelps, William	077	1752	Orig. Only	SS/AR
Phelps, William A.	098	1886	WB-A/63	CTY
Phelpts, Gidan	041	1854	WB-3/177	AR
Phenney, George	N	1737	LGB-4/#68	SS/AR
Phibbs, James	046	1873	WB-E/112	AR
Phibbs, Robert J.	046	1865	WB-D/267	AR
Phibbs, Samuel M.	084	1863	WB-C/378	CTY
Phibbs, William	046	1871	Orig. Only	AR
Phibbs, Willie	046	1888	WB-E/500	AR
Phifer, Charles H.	016	1897	WB-4/270	AR
Phifer, David	065	1841	WB-H/71	AR
Phifer, David	097	1853	WB-1/85	AR
Phifer, Drucilla	097	1859	WB-1/155	AR
Phifer, Esther	016	1846	WB-1/84	
Phifer, George	016	1835	PQS.5/361	
Phifer, George L.	016	c1854	WB-A/28	
Phifer, Henry	065	1841	WB-H/69	AR
Phifer, Henry	085	1801	WB-F/31	AR
Phifer, J. Cowan	085	1863	WB-K/318	AR
Phifer, Jacob	054	1891	WB-5/374	CTY
Phifer, John	065	c1775	WB-F/2	AR
Phifer, John	016	1845	WB-1/71	
Phifer, John	085	1853	WB-K/152	AR
Phifer, John F.	060	1886	WB-4/350	AR
Phifer, John Locke	016	1880	WB-3/283	AR
Phifer, Margaret	054	1897	WB-6/71	CTY
Phifer, Martin	016	1838	PQS.5/465	
Phifer, Martin, Sr.	065	1791	WB-F/37	AR
Phifer, Mary M.	065	1880	WB-K/377	AR
Phifer, Matthew	097	1847	WB-1/39	AR
Phifer, Matthias	085	1852	WB-K/146	AR
Phifer, Nancy	097	1900	WB-3/47	AR
Phifer, Silas	085	1887	WB-2/279	CTY
Phifer, Tirza	054	1896	WB-6/9	CTY
Philbeck, George	086	1885	WB-F/272	AR
Philbeck, John	026	1877	WB-2/151	AR
Philbeck, Richard	026	1895	WB-2/516	AR
Philhour, Katherin	085	1847	WB-K/58	AR
Philip, George P.	NY	1891	047 WB-7/5	047 AR
Philipie, John	046	1863	WB-D/167	AR
Philips, Abraham	084	1836	Orig. Only	CTY
Philips, Bedder	085	1812	WB-G/248	AR
Philips, Elijah	085	c1806	WB-F/19	AR
Philips, Etheldred	037	1795	WB-C/329	
Philips, Exum	037	1802	WB-D/152	
Philips, Gilbry	084	1849	WB-C/101	CTY
Philips, Harriet C.	043	1886	WB-1/6	AR
Philips, Hartwell	037	1801	WB-D/133	AR
Philips, Hugh	090	1871	WB-6/13	AR
Philips, James J.	037	1874	WB-G/454	AR
Philips, Jane	037	1804	WB-D/195	
Philips, Jane	037	1816	WB-E/129	
Philips, John	037	1784	WB-B/156	AR
Philips, John	037	1810	WB-D/358	
Philips, John	028	1793	WB-A/277	AR
Philips, Joseph	037	1784	WB-B/147	AR
Philips, Mark	071	1778	WB-1/300	
Philips, Mary F.	037	1892	WB-H/239	AR
Philips, Nathan	006	1836	WB-B/72	AR
Philips, Phereby	037	1880	WB-G/587	AR
Philips, Richard F.	090	1816	WB-2/183	AR
Philips, Solomon	060	1836	WB-1/384	AR
Philips, Thomas	071	1778	WB-1/306	
Philips, Thomas	028	1743	Wills.6/L67	SS/AR
Philips, William	072	1840	WB-2/24	AR
Phillipie, John, Sr.	046	1888	WB-E/540	AR
Phillippy, John	046	1833	WB-B/492	AR
Phillips, Aaron	009	1892	WB-1/534	CTY
Phillips, Abner	092	1813	WB-3/103	AR
Phillips, Abner	022	1867	WB-D/162	AR
Phillips, Abraham	084	1836	WB-B/150	
Phillips, Amanda	037	1895	WB-H/339	AR
Phillips, Ann	073	1838	WB-F/4	AR
Phillips, Ann H.	082	1899	WB-7/17	AR
Phillips, Arthor	037	1790	WB-C/150	AR
Phillips, Barney	045	1888	WB-1/157	AR
Phillips, Benjamin	077	1839	WB-F/278	AR
Phillips, Benjamin	059	1893	WB-B/75	CTY
Phillips, Benjamin	075	1774	WB-I/106	AR

Name	Co.	Date	Recorded Copy	Original
Phillips, Bennett	092	1777	WB-1/81	AR
Phillips, Blake	066	1896	WB-1/147	AR
Phillips, Bryant G.	009	1842	OB-D/273	AR
Phillips, Caroline	047	1897	WB-7/184	AR
Phillips, Caroline E.	051	1888	WB-C/372	AR
Phillips, Catherine	038	1863	WB-1/209	AR
Phillips, Channie W.	038	1898	WB-4/92	AR
Phillips, Channie W.	046	1898	WB-G/63	AR
Phillips, Charles	046	1895	WB-F/410	AR
Phillips, Charles	085	1822	WB-H/142	AR
Phillips, Charlotte	083	1881	WB-3/226	AR
Phillips, Colley	090	1835	WB-3/285	AR
Phillips, Council	059	1882	WB-A/255	CTY
Phillips, Curtis	059	1877	WB-A/138	
Phillips, Daniel	075	1821	WB-M1/342	AR
Phillips, Daniel	030	1726	SS 876/55	SS/AR
Phillips, Dickson	056	1864	WB-2/50	AR
Phillips, Diley	099	1857	RB-30/298	AR
Phillips, Drewry	059	1871	WB-A/20	
Phillips, Edmond H.	081	1876	WB-15/205	AR
Phillips, Edward	099	1900	WB-D/380	AR
Phillips, Edwin W.	022	1900	WB-F/143	AR
Phillips, Eli	068	1848	WB-B/173	
Phillips, Elisha	049	1891	WB-2/263	AR
Phillips, Eliza W.	029	1869	WB-E/9	AR
Phillips, Elizabeth	079	1856	WB-1/56	AR-Copy
Phillips, Elizabeth	059	1889	WB-A/574	CTY
Phillips, Elizabeth	038	1880	WB-2/368	AR
Phillips, Elizabeth	037	1858	WB-G/154	AR
Phillips, Emma	028	1891	WB-E/570	AR
Phillips, Ephraim	092	1827	WB-3/177	AR
Phillips, Esther	038	1875	WB-2/229	AR
Phillips, F. M.	033	1897	WB-2/225	CTY
Phillips, Francis	032	1832	WB-1/185	
Phillips, Garland	039	1828	WB-J/1	
Phillips, George M.	047	1889	WB-6/539	AR
Phillips, George W.	083	1874	WB-3/82 & 123	AR
Phillips, H. P.	047	1878	WB-6/196	AR
Phillips, Henry	071	1859	WB-5/210	AR
Phillips, Irby	022	1894	WB-E/577	AR
Phillips, Jacob	005	1859	WB-C/156	AR
Phillips, James	073	1847	WB F/371	AR
Phillips, James	082	1785	WB-1/20	AR
Phillips, James A.	044	1895	WB-24/272	CTY
Phillips, James H.	059	1892	WB-B/45	CTY
Phillips, Jamima	075	1782	WB-K/76	AR
Phillips, Jane	065	c1793	WB-F/11	AR
Phillips, Jeremiah	022	1805	WB-A/116	AR-Nunc.
Phillips, Jesse	071	1822	WB-3/272	AR
Phillips, Joab	022	1875	WB-E/100	AR
Phillips, John	081	1884	WB-15/494	AR
Phillips, John	039	1876	WB-U/135	AR
Phillips, John	090	1827	WB-3/158	AR
Phillips, John	047	1804	WB-3/420	
Phillips, John	085	1801	WB-F/43	AR
Phillips, John	035	1795	WB-A/392	AR
Phillips, John	092	1845	WB-4/226	
Phillips, John	068	1799	WB-A/204	
Phillips, John	078	1836	WI-13/153	
Phillips, John E.	071	1880	WB-6/309	AR
Phillips, John, Sr.	056	1839	WB-1/512	AR
Phillips, Joseph	092	1865	WB-5/77	AR
Phillips, Joseph	038	1853	WB-1/46	AR
Phillips, Joseph M.	071	1881	WB-6/348	AR
Phillips, Joshua	085	1889	WB-2/333	CTY
Phillips, Joshua	016	1890	WB-4/65	AR
Phillips, Josiah T.	068	1864	WB-C/102	
Phillips, Lazarus	066	1868	Orig. Only	AR
Phillips, Lindsay	104	1869	WB-6/1	AR
Phillips, Liney	022	1851	Orig. Only	AR
Phillips, Margaret	059	1879	WB-A/177	CTY
Phillips, Margarette	071	1868	WB-5/360	AR
Phillips, Mark	029	1830	WB-B/193	AR
Phillips, Martha R.	044	1863	WB-22/77	CTY
Phillips, Mary	060	1845	WB-2/234	AR
Phillips, Mary	006	1844	WB-A/67	AR
Phillips, Mary E.	071	1879	WB-6/295	AR
Phillips, Micajah	104	1855	WB-5/137	
Phillips, Milton P.	066	1900	WB-1/195	
Phillips, N. M.	059	1894	WB-B/101	CTY
Phillips, Nancy	099	1863	RB-32/618	AR
Phillips, Nancy	006	1894	WB-E/278	AR
Phillips, Nathan	016	1844	WB-1/34	
Phillips, Olivia C.	059	1886	WB-A/445	CTY
Phillips, Pattie A.	010	1890	WB-I/305	AR
Phillips, Paul	028	1751	DB-5/176	SS/AR
Phillips, Philip	092	c1828	WB-4/15	AR
Phillips, Primas	059	1894	Orig. Only	CTY
Phillips, R. A.	061	1894	WB-2/152	AR
Phillips, R. P.	092	1896	WB-6/428	AR
Phillips, Rainey	073	1798	WB-C/116	AR
Phillips, Renchall	099	1808	RB-7/317	AR
Phillips, Reuben	104	1815	WB-3/94	AR
Phillips, Richard	092	c1834	WB-4/73	
Phillips, Robert	065	1797	WB-F/40	AR
Phillips, Robert	049	1823	WB-2/220	AR
Phillips, Robert H.	068	1889	WB-D/288	
Phillips, Robert L.	084	1863	WB-C/381	CTY
Phillips, S. C.	066	1888	WB-1/41	AR
Phillips, Samuel	018	1825	WB-C/62	
Phillips, Samuel	087	1832	WB-1/142	
Phillips, Sophia	068	1854	WB-C/14	
Phillips, Stephen	081	1855	WB-10/251	AR
Phillips, Susan	044	1839	WB-14/459	CTY
Phillips, Susan F.	001	1877	WB-2/108	AR
Phillips, Susan W.	037	1886	WB-H/31	
Phillips, Susannah	085	1844	WB-I/229	AR
Phillips, Thomas	071	1751	Orig. Only	SS/AR
Phillips, Thomas	028	1792	WB-A/263	AR
Phillips, Thomas	079	1880	WB-2/187	AR
Phillips, Thomas	005	1887	WB-D/223	AR
Phillips, Thomas	035	1889	WB-4/338	AR
Phillips, Thomas E.	029	1893	WB-E/576	AR
Phillips, Thomas H.	063	1839	WB-2/265	
Phillips, Thomas L.	071	1858	WB-5/200	AR
Phillips, Thomas M.	022	1876	WB-E/119	AR
Phillips, Thomas S.	059	1887	WB-A/464	CTY
Phillips, W. A.	059	1885	WB-A/412	CTY
Phillips, Wiley	023	1900	WB-A/180	AR
Phillips, William	073	c1794	Orig. Only	AR
Phillips, William	106	c1852	WB-1/38	AR
Phillips, William	022	1832	WB-B/225	AR
Phillips, William	099	1825	RB-19/199	AR
Phillips, William	071	1841	WB-4/230	AR
Phillips, William	106	1894	WB-2/360	
Phillips, William	009	1751	028 DB-5/237	SS/AR
Phillips, William	092	1826	WB-3/170	AR
Phillips, William	009	c1769	OWB/105	AR
Phillips, William	022	1862	WB-D/85	AR
Phillips, William	083	1875	WB-3/98	AR

Name	Co.	Date	Recorded Copy	Original
Phillips, William	065	1815	WB-F/26	AR
Phillips, William	097	1849	WB-1/65	AR
Phillips, William E.	037	1878	WB-G/516	AR
Phillips, William M.	038	1898	WB-4/113	AR
Phillips, Wright	059	1873	WB-A/88	
Philllips, John	029	1761	Orig. Only	AR
Philpot, John	063	1853	WB-2/389	
Philpot, Thomas	044	1787	WB-2/46	CTY
Philpot, Wiley	036	1898	WB-A/430	CTY
Philpott, Benja.	044	c1852	WB-19/448	
Philpott, Charles	063	1852	WB-2/376	
Philpott, Charles	063	1789	WB-1/162	
Philpott, David	046	c1781	WB-A/287	AR
Philpott, John	075	c1694	SS 874.2/104	SS/AR
Philpott, Micajah M.	063	1841	WB-2/284	
Philpott, Mills E.M.	063	1858	WB-2/448	
Philpott, Mimey	044	1850	WB-18/43	CTY
Philpott, Nannie O.	044	1897	WB-24/362	CTY
Philpott, Reuben W.	063	1860	WB-2/468	
Philpott, Samuel	044	1857	WB-20/238	CTY
Philpott, Thomas T.	078	1860	WB-18/162	AR
Philpott, William	044	1820	WB-8/359	CTY
Philpott, William A.	044	1874	WB-23/148	CTY
Philpott, William W.	063	1861	WB-2/493	
Philyaw, James	072	1847	Orig. Only	AR
Philyaw, James	057	c1885	Orig. Only	AR
Philyaw, Nancy	072	1848	Orig. Only	AR-Nunc.
Phipps, Greenberry	006	1889	WB-E/185	AR
Phipps, Isaiah	044	1766	Orig. Only	CTY
Phipps, James	046	1829	WB-B/395	AR
Phipps, John A.	004	1898	WB-A/210	
Phipps, Nathaniel	028	1803	WB-B/180	
Phipps, Nathaniel	028	1834	WB-C/366	
Phipps, Ransom	038	1893	WB-3/404	AR
Phipps, Samuel	006	1851	WB-A/70	AR
Phipps, Samuel	006	1854	WB-D/11	
Phipps, William C.	006	1894	WB-E/269	AR
Phips, Samuel	006	1837	WB-A/37	AR
Physic, George	028	1900	WB-F/493	
Physioc, Thomas J.	028	1853	WB-D/200	AR
Physive, Joseph	028	1842	WB-D/51	
Piat, James	064	1852	WB-1/32	AR
Pickard, Henry	022	1790	RB-1/38	AR
Pickard, J. O.	081	1900	WB-17/45	
Pickard, Jane	073	1881	WB-H/271	CTY
Pickard, John	073	c1812	WB-D/351	AR
Pickard, John H.	020	1858	RB-S/68	AR
Pickens, Andrew	N	c1756	Orig. Only	SS/AR
Pickens, Elisabeth	065	1825	WB-F/87	AR
Pickens, William	065	1809	WB-F/18	AR
Pickens, William	065	1822	WB-F/99	AR
Pickerin, Richard	010	1739	LGB-4/#109	SS/AR
Pickering, Phineas	070	1819	WB-C/348	AR
Picket, Charles	032	c1816	Orig. Only	AR-Copy
Picket, Hannah	022	1841	WB-C/124	AR
Picket, Ralph	085	1796	WB-C/296	AR
Picket, Ruth	070	c1796	Orig. Only	AR
Pickett, Alfred M.	081	1899	022 WB-F/92	022 AR
Pickett, Catharine	073	1868	WB-G/553	CTY
Pickett, Charles	085	c1816	Orig. Only	AR
Pickett, D. W.	032	1899	WB-4/409	AR
Pickett, Dawson	035	1829	WB-A/383	AR
Pickett, Edward	073	1819	WB-D/561	AR
Pickett, Elizabeth	001	1868	WB-2/4	AR
Pickett, Flora	005	1835	WB-B/43	AR

Name	Co.	Date	Recorded Copy	Original
Pickett, Francis	022	1860	WB-D/68	AR
Pickett, Frederick	035	1893	WB-4/436	AR
Pickett, Henry	070	1801	WB-AB/55	AR
Pickett, Henry	073	1809	WB-D/254	AR
Pickett, Hester	076	1879	WB-A1/9	AR
Pickett, Hosea	070	1843	WB-AB/378	AR
Pickett, Isaac	070	1867	WB-D/236	AR
Pickett, James	005	1798	WB-2/128	AR
Pickett, John	073	1844	WB-F/188	AR
Pickett, Joseph	005	1828	WB-A/155	AR
Pickett, Joseph	073	1823	WB-E/31	AR
Pickett, Martha	005	1809	WB-2/127	AR
Pickett, Martin	005	1834	WB-B/39	AR
Pickett, Martin J.	005	1852	WB-C/55	AR
Pickett, Mourning	082	1803	WB-1/97	AR
Pickett, Nathan	081	1835	WB-6/459	AR
Pickett, Pleasant	073	1863	WB-G/413	AR
Pickett, Simeon	022	1845	WB-C/179	AR
Pickett, Susan M.	076	1889	WB-A1/101	AR
Pickett, Theophilus	032	1887	WB-3/573	AR
Pickett, Thomas	032	1870	WB-3/27	AR
Pickett, Thomas	070	1805	WB-C/344	AR
Pickett, William	022	1881	WB-E/226	AR
Pickett, William	073	1809	WB-D/192	AR
Pickett, William	073	1824	WB-E/54	AR
Pickett, William	035	1840	Orig. Only	AR
Pickett, William W.	073	1874	WB-H/91	CTY
Picklar, Jane	089	1879	WB-2/76	AR
Picklar, Joseph	089	1877	WB-2/66	AR
Pickler, Joseph	033	1840	WB-1/28	AR
Pickrall, Elizabeth	100	1795	WB-8/39	AR-Nunc.
Pickren, Richard	057	1789	WB-A/187	AR
Pickrin, Moses	057	1782	WB-A/13	AR
Pidgeon, William	085	1770	WB-A/137	AR
Pierce, Chloe	039	1879	WB-U/198	AR
Pierce, David	051	1861	WB-B/35	AR
Pierce, Dempsey	051	1845	WB-A/243	
Pierce, Dorothy	018	1869	WB-E/8	
Pierce, Edward R.	047	1845	WB-4/241	
Pierce, Elisha	018	1853	WB-C/376	
Pierce, Elizabeth	051	1869	WB-C/15	AR
Pierce, Elizabeth	063	c1793	WB-1/386	
Pierce, George W.	010	1844	WB-G/370	AR
Pierce, Herod	054	c1828	WB-2/65	AR
Pierce, Israel A.	PA	1898	028 WB-F/385	
Pierce, J. C.	027	1884	WB-2/54	AR
Pierce, James	039	c1794	WB-A/113	AR
Pierce, Jehu	063	1826	WB-2/118 & 270	
Pierce, Job	051	1836	WB-A/89	
Pierce, Joel	071	1849	WB-5/78	AR
Pierce, John	071	1798	WB-2/171	AR
Pierce, John	099	1844	RB-25/496	AR
Pierce, John	054	c1820	WB-1/434	
Pierce, John W.	047	1854	WB-4/369	
Pierce, Joseph	077	1700	Orig. Only	SS/AR
Pierce, Joshua	069	1789	WB-1/60	AR
Pierce, Mariah	063	1893	WB-4/124	AR
Pierce, Mary	041	1871	WB-4/25	AR
Pierce, Mary	099	1810	RB-8/226	AR
Pierce, Matthew	047	1843	WB-4/220	
Pierce, Mourning	010	1807	WB-F/65	AR
Pierce, Narcissa	010	1891	WB-I/323	AR
Pierce, Philip	060	1807	Orig. Only	AR
Pierce, Priscilla	047	1854	WB-4/360	

Name	Co.	Date	Recorded Copy	Original
Pierce, R. K.	006	1898	WB-E/337	AR
Pierce, Solomon	044	1787	WB-2/45	CTY
Pierce, Tamer	063	1840	WB-2/266	
Pierce, Thomas	028	1798	WB-B/57	
Pierce, Thomas	096	1795	Orig. Only	AR
Pierce, Thomas	024	1756	SS 880/75	SS/AR
Pierce, William	063	1818	WB-2/55	
Pierce, William	005	1808	WB-2/125	AR
Pierce, William	063	1779	WB-1/54	
Pierce, William A.	039	1895	WB-V/65	AR
Pierce, Wm. F. G.	010	c1849	WB-G/451	AR
Piercy, J. W. C.	023	c1869	WB-A/1	AR
Pierse, Elisha	071	1821	WB-3/252	AR
Pierse, John	010	1799	WB-E/76	AR
Pierson, Martha A.	099	1895	Orig. Only	AR
Pigford, Edward	070	1863	WB-D/134	AR
Pigford, Edward T.	035	1900	WB-5/8	AR
Pigford, James B.	070	1865	WB-D/172	AR
Pigford, Timothy	035	1823	WB-A/387	AR
Pigford, William	070	1851	WB-C/528	AR
Pigford, William	070	1803	WB-C/343	AR
Piggat, John	081	1817	WB-4/416	AR
Piggot, Allen	019	1827	WB-D/325	AR
Piggott, Benjamin	073	1818	WB-D/529	AR
Piggott, Jeremiah	022	1779	Orig. Only	AR
Piggott, Jeremiah	081	1880	WB-15/323	AR
Piggott, John	019	1762	WB-D/314	AR
Piggott, John	022	1815	WB-A/274	AR
Piggott, Oliver	019	1809	WB-D/323	AR
Piggott, William	073	1770	WB-A/111	
Pigot, Elijah	019	1789	WB-D/316	AR
Pigot, Levi	019	1829	WB-D/328	AR
Pigott, Abram	019	1849	WB-A/137	AR
Pigott, Anna E.	019	1898	WB-C/1	AR
Pigott, Bernice	028	1885	WB-E/386	AR
Pigott, Culpepper	019	1833	WB-A/22	
Pigott, David W.	019	1854	WB-A/175	AR
Pigott, Elijah	019	1860	WB-A/246	AR
Pigott, Eliza	019	1889	WB-B/180	
Pigott, Jechonias	019	1856	WB-A/192	AR
Pigott, Jennings	019	1882	WB-B/131	AR
Pigott, John F.	012	1882	WB-A/50	AR
Pigott, Margarett	019	1836	WB-A/62	
Pigott, Maria Ann	019	1837	WB-A/74	AR
Pigott, Mary J.	019	1890	WB-B/193	AR
Pigott, Simeon	019	1881	WB-B/125	AR
Pigott, William H.	019	1866	WB-B/4	AR
Pigott, William S.	019	1856	WB-A/185	AR
Pike, Benjamin	075	1785	WB-K/117	AR
Pike, David	103	1823	RD-5/45	AR
Pike, Emma Eliza	103	1899	WB-2/234	AR
Pike, Jesse	022	1897	WB-F/50	AR
Pike, John	073	1774	WB-A/176	
Pike, John	009	1860	OB-L/210	AR
Pike, John, Sr.	075	1812	WB-M1/242	AR
Pike, Jonathan	056	1879	WB-3/214	AR
Pike, Mark	103	1850	RD-10/325	AR
Pike, Micajah	001	1890	WB-2/474	
Pike, Nathan	103	1844	RD-9/115	AR
Pike, Nathan R.	103	1862	RD-13/537	AR
Pike, Rachel	103	1850	RD-10/432	AR
Pike, Sallie A.	103	1887	WB-1/406	AR
Pike, Samuel	100	1870	WB-51/22	AR
Pike, Samuel	075	1719	SS 875/150	SS/AR
Pike, Samuel	073	1824	WB-E/59	AR
Pike, William	073	1829	WB-E/203	AR
Pike, William	IN	1844	Copy	073 AR
Piland, Celia	051	1897	WB-C/524	AR
Piland, Edward	041	1816	WB-2/135	AR
Piland, George	041	1796	WB-1/145	AR
Piland, James	041	1787	WB-1/64	AR
Piland, Jesse	041	1851	WB-3/140	AR
Piland, Mary	051	1894	WB-C/499	
Piland, Mary	041	1890	WB-4/304	AR
Piland, Milley	041	1832	WB-2/302	AR
Piland, Phillip	071	1864	WB-5/290	AR
Piland, Shadrack	041	1870	WB-4/10	AR
Piland, Susanna	041	1844	WB-3/56	AR
Piland, Thomas	041	1789	WB-1/84	AR
Pilcher, Daniel	092	c1830	WB-4/30	AR
Pilent, James	051	1884	WB-C/329	AR
Pilkenton, Samuel	022	1847	WB-C/198	AR
Pilkenton, Sarah	102	1894	WB-A/94	AR
Pilkington, Abram	022	1869	WB-E/1	AR
Pilkington, Seth	009	1754	SS 879/103	SS/AR
Pilkinton, John W.	099	1866	RB-34/143	AR
Pilkinton, Richard	022	1852	WB-C/317	
Pillard, Samuel	020	1820	RB-H/330	
Pilley, Ivey H.	009	1886	WB-1/377	CTY
Pilley, John	009	c1794	OWB/300	AR
Pilley, John	009	1836	OWB/530	AR
Pilly, William	009	1833	OB-B/231	AR
Pilson, Grace	028	1743	Orig. Only	SS/AR
Pilson, Nancy Jane	092	1900	Orig. Only	AR-Nunc.
Pilson, Richard T.	092	1898	WB-6/487	AR
Pilson, Thomas	028	1742/3	Wills.6/L56	SS/AR
Pimbrow, Daniell	N	1688	Orig. Only	SS/AR
Pinchback, Loving	078	1849	WB-13/226	
Pinckney, C. C., Sr.	SC	1866	050 WB-1/98	
Pindar, William	009	1775	OWB/125	AR
Pinell, J. J. P.	099	1891	WB-B/515	AR
Piner, John W.	019	1885	WB-B/149	AR
Piner, Vesty	019	1843	WB-A/105	AR
Pinkard, Thomas	104	1826	WB-4/90	AR
Pinkerton, David	073	1772	WB-A/164	
Pinkerton, James	013	1893	WB-C/262	AR
Pinkett, Elinor	009	1758	SS 882/13	SS/AR
Pinkham, George W.	009	1893	WB-1/557	CTY
Pinkham, James	009	c1808	OWB/454	AR
Pinkham, Rhoda	009	1824	OB-A/337	AR
Pinkston, Elizabeth	032	c1853	WB-2/89	
Pinkston, Meshack	032	c1858	WB-2/208	
Pinkston, Meshack	085	1824	WB-H/286	AR
Pinkston, Nancy	085	1866	WB-K/384	AR
Pinkston, Richard	085	c1782	WB-B/74	AR
Pinkston, Thomas	085	1823	WB-H/241	AR
Pinkston, William	085	1830	WB-H/489	AR
Pinkston, William	085	1815	WB-G/395	AR
Pinnegar, Petter	090	1795	WB-1/70	AR
Pinnell, Jackson	100	1865	WB-50/162	
Pinnell, John	039	1814	WB-D/72	AR
Pinnell, Levi	039	c1801	WB-B/76	
Pinnell, Lucy Ann	039	1889	WB-U/478	AR
Pinnell, Mary Ann	039	1873	WB-U/78	AR-Nunc.
Pinnell, Pegga N.	039	c1856	WB-O/362	AR
Pinnell, Rial	039	1852	WB-N/347	AR
Pinner, Burrell	013	1847	WB-A/124	
Pinner, Hugh	013	c1869	WB-B/33	AR
Pinner, Leander	013	1896	WB-C/514	AR
Pinnex, Overton	092	c1838	WB-4/145	

Name	Co.	Date	Recorded Copy	Original
Pinnix, Cornelia	032	1890	WB-4/80	AR
Pinnix, Elizabeth	020	1864	RB-T/25	CTY
Pinnix, John	020	1856	RB-R/404	AR
Pinnix, M. H.	032	1897	WB-4/314	AR
Pinnix, Mary F.	001	1873	WB-2/53	AR
Pinnix, Nancy	020	1865	RB-T/108	AR
Pinnix, William G.	020	1857	RB-R/560	AR
Pinson, Aron	044	1801	WB-5/143	CTY
Pinson, Joseph W.	020	1861	RB-S/439	AR
Pinson, Thomas	012	c1764	DB-A/31	AR
Pinyan, Reuben	089	1843	Orig. Only	AR
Piper, Elizabeth	073	1859	WB-G/225	AR
Piper, John	073	1798	WB-C/122	AR
Piper, Katherine	073	1871	WB-H/56	CTY
Piper, Samuel	073	1867	WB-G/520	CTY
Piper, Sarah	073	1861	WB-G/356	CTY
Piper, William	044	1863	WB-21/676	CTY
Pipkin, Charles	051	1900	WB-C/582	AR
Pipkin, Constant	028	1838	Orig. Only	AR
Pipkin, Edith	056	1827	WB-1/331	
Pipkin, Isaac	041	1839	WB-3/9	AR
Pipkin, Isaac	041	1814	WB-2/91	AR
Pipkin, Isaac	028	1839	WB-C/430	
Pipkin, John	024	1745	Orig. Only	SS/AR
Pipkin, Joseph	103	1789	Orig. Only	AR
Pipkin, Steward	071	1795	WB-2/75	AR
Pipkin, Tabitha	071	1811	WB-3/43	AR
Pippen, John	039	1838	WB-K/147	
Pippen, John W.	037	1880	WB-G/556	AR
Pippen, Joseph	037	1833	WB-F/146	AR
Pippen, Joseph	037	1791	WB-C/170	AR
Pippen, Joseph J.	037	1900	WB-H/489	AR
Pippen, Joseph J.	037	1853	WB-F/519	AR
Pippen, Mary	037	1805	WB-D/235	AR
Pippen, Mary H.	037	1897	WB-H/369	AR
Pippen, Pattie	037	1899	WB-H/449	AR
Pippen, Spicy	037	1853	WB-F/518	AR
Pippen, William	037	1852	WB-F/473	AR
Pippen, William M.	037	1889	WB-H/144	AR
Pippin, Temperance	037	1854	WB-G/84	AR
Pippins, R. B.	065	1892	WB-M/104	AR
Pirce, Jonathan	044	1763	Orig. Only	CTY
Pirent, James	037	1757	SS 879/201	SS/AR
Pirvis, John	103	c1809	RD-1/193	
Pistole, Robertson	005	1853	WB-C/58	AR
Pitcher, Sarah	084	1823	WB-A/283	CTY
Pitchford, Daniel	100	1822	WB-24/214	AR
Pitchford, Elijah	100	1826	WB-29/32	AR
Pitchford, Miles	046	1853	WB-C/402	AR
Pitchford, Samuel	100	1802	WB-11/307	AR
Pitchford, Thomas J.	100	1883	WB-51/205	AR
Pitchford, Wesley B.	100	1852	WB-42/33	AR
Pitkin, Horace W.	PA	1889	013 WB-C/27	013 AR
Pitman, Ambrose	047	1787	WB-3/122	
Pitman, Amey	037	1791	WB-C/165	AR
Pitman, Ann	027	1837	WB-A/39	AR
Pitman, Benjamin	037	1756	SS 880/154	SS/AR
Pitman, Blake	047	1822	WB-3/671	
Pitman, Blake	047	1822	WB-3/676	
Pitman, Dempsey	047	1824	WB-3/709	
Pitman, Duncan S.	076	1885	WB-A1/70	AR
Pitman, Elias	083	1859	WB-2/149	AR
Pitman, Elijah	037	1799	WB-D/93	AR
Pitman, Elisha	047	1803	WB-3/414	
Pitman, Elisha	056	1862	WB-2/22	AR
Pitman, Harrod	037	1836	WB-F/197	AR
Pitman, Henry	083	1868	WB-2/242	AR
Pitman, Henry	047	1811	WB-3/523	
Pitman, Isham	083	1825	WB-1/332	AR
Pitman, Jacob	011	c1779	WB-1/575	
Pitman, Jesse	037	1793	WB-C/248	AR
Pitman, Jesse	083	1846	WB-1/498	
Pitman, John	069	c1848	WB-1/545	AR
Pitman, John	047	1823	WB-3/686	
Pitman, Joseph	037	1787	WB-C/42	AR
Pitman, Joseph	037	1755	Orig. Only	SS/AR
Pitman, Joseph	028	1752	DB-5/281	
Pitman, Martha	047	1782	WB-3/34	
Pitman, Mary White	069	1839	WB-1/435	AR
Pitman, Milley	047	1799	WB-3/322	
Pitman, Moses	037	1760	WB-A/16	AR
Pitman, Nancy	037	1842	WB-F/271	AR
Pitman, Nathan	083	c1799	WB-1/59	
Pitman, Newell	083	1830	WB-1/251	AR
Pitman, Newit	083	1787	WB-1/4	AR
Pitman, Rachael	083	1816	WB-1/173	
Pitman, S. D.	083	1874	WB-3/77	AR
Pitman, Sally	037	1834	WB-F/156	AR
Pitman, Samuel	047	1812	WB-3/531	
Pitman, Sion	083	1825	WB-1/367	AR
Pitman, Stephen	083	1875	WB-3/95	AR
Pitman, William	047	1817	WB-3/600	
Pitman, William	069	1828	WB-1/355	AR
Pitman, Zilphia	047	1803	WB-3/389	
Pitmon, Thomas	013	1816	WB-A/158	
Pitt, Ann	037	1821	WB-E/264	AR
Pitt, B. C.	037	1897	WB-H/381	AR
Pitt, Bennett P.	037	1880	WB-G/571	AR
Pitt, Calvin	037	1886	WB-H/27	
Pitt, Catherine	037	1838	WB-F/217	AR
Pitt, Etheldred	037	1799	WB-D/77	AR
Pitt, James	037	1850	WB-F/443	AR
Pitt, James	037	1797	WB-D/21	AR
Pitt, James, Sr.	037	1831	WB-F/121	AR
Pitt, Joab P.	037	1854	WB-G/80	AR
Pitt, John R.	037	1871	WB-G/372	AR
Pitt, Joseph	071	1808	WB-3/12	AR
Pitt, Nancy	037	1898	WB-H/407	AR
Pitt, Rebecca	037	1856	WB-G/124	AR
Pitt, Thomas	037	1820	WB-E/243	AR
Pitt, Walter	047	1770	WB-1/264	
Pitt, William	084	1820	WB-A/107	CTY
Pittard, Anne S.	044	1840	WB-14/496	CTY
Pittard, Eliza	047	1883	WB-6/317	AR
Pittard, Howell G.	044	1840	WB-14/568	CTY
Pittard, John	020	1857	RB-R/556	AR
Pittard, John	044	1821	WB-9/7	CTY
Pittard, John W.	044	1898	WB-24/416	CTY
Pittard, Letty	044	1862	WB-21/570	CTY
Pittard, Martha	020	1875	WB-A/196	CTY
Pittard, Rebeccah	044	1840	WB-14/497	CTY
Pittard, Samuel	078	c1820	Orig. Only	AR
Pittard, Samuel	020	1846	RB-P/337	AR
Pittard, Thomas	044	1866	WB-22/415	CTY
Pittman, Ann	047	1858	WB-5/60	
Pittman, Arraminta	047	1893	WB-7/78	AR
Pittman, Arthur	047	1837	WB-4/153	
Pittman, Caroline	047	1856	WB-5/25	
Pittman, Clear	028	1866	WB-D/428	
Pittman, Eliza	047	1894	WB-7/113	AR

Name	Co.	Date	Recorded Copy	Original
Pittman, Elizabeth	028	1866	WB-D/415	
Pittman, Frederick	047	1851	WB-4/303	
Pittman, Grisham C.	037	1853	WB-F/496	AR
Pittman, Harrison	056	1900	WB-4/229	
Pittman, Harrison	037	1859	WB-G/171	AR
Pittman, Henry W.	047	1885	WB-6/403	AR
Pittman, James	105	1888	WB-2/477	AR
Pittman, John	047	1846	WB-4/254	
Pittman, Joseph	028	1867	WB-D/444	
Pittman, Joseph	037	1763	WB-A/122	AR
Pittman, Margaret	047	1854	WB-4/365	
Pittman, Martha	047	1867	WB-5/154	
Pittman, Mary	047	1839	WB-4/181	
Pittman, Newsom J.	037	1893	WB-H/254	AR
Pittman, Polly Jane	056	1881	WB-3/289	AR
Pittman, Reddin	037	1854	WB-G/59	AR
Pittman, Robert	069	1896	WB-5/551 & 559	AR
Pittman, Robert W.	047	1884	WB-6/319	AR
Pittman, Rosina	079	1888	WB-2/437	AR
Pittman, Ruffin	047	c1900	Orig. Only	AR
Pittman, Sallie	079	1897	WB-3/128	AR
Pittman, Thomas	056	1896	WB-2/234	
Pittman, William	037	1873	WB-G/418	AR
Pitts (Jones), Hagar	028	1898	WB-F/337	
Pitts, Ann	047	1830	WB-4/63	
Pitts, Aquilla	038	1893	WB-3/378	AR
Pitts, John	047	1862	WB-5/99	
Pitts, John	014	1898	WB-3/37	CTY
Pitts, John	022	c1780	Orig. Only	AR
Pitts, John	090	1823	WB-3/133	AR
Pitts, L. D.	046	1890	WB-F/40	AR
Pitts, Mary	072	1801	WB-A/110	AR
Pitts, Mary B.	MD	1881	070 WB-E/509	
Pitts, Matthew	047	1809	WB-3/488	
Pitts, Nancy	047	1884	WB-6/335	AR
Pitts, Nancy	072	1860	Orig. Only	AR
Pitts, Rebeckah	072	N. D.	Orig. Only	AR
Pitts, Richard	072	1766	RW/L48	Nunc.
Pitts, Rigdon	072	1825	WB-A/108	AR
Pitts, Robert	072	1830	WB-1/61	
Pitts, Robert	028	1741	Deeds.21/L77	
Pitts, Sally	059	1887	016 WB-4/46	016 AR
Pitts, Sally	059	1887	WB-A/522	CTY
Pitts, Samuel	090	1813	WB-2/140	AR
Pitts, Samuel P.	047	1867	WB-5/153	
Pitts, Thomas	072	1820	WB-A/102	AR
Pitts, Thomas	047	1826	WB-4/20	
Pitts, Walter	069	c1849	Orig. Only	AR
Piver, Clarissa	105	1899	WB-3/335	
Piver, Daniel	019	1836	WB-A/54	AR
Piver, Nathan	010	1836	WB-A/63	AR
Piver, William H.	019	1868	WB-B/38	AR
Place, Rufus J.	039	1877	WB-U/151	AR
Plagaman, Barbary	054	1838	WB-2/183	AR
Planing, Hugh	011	1752	028 DB-5/247	
Plaster, John	085	1812	WB-G/246	AR
Plaster, Mary	085	1877	WB-1/419	CTY
Plaster, William T.	085	1896	WB-3/155	CTY
Plato, Thomas	075	1736	LGB-4/#26	SS/AR
Plator, Richard	075	1705/6	Orig. Only	SS/AR
Platt, Amos	049	c1863	WB-1/15	AR
Platt, Ellen	065	1886	WB-L/162	AR
Platt, Enos	049	1875	WB-1/266	AR
Platt, Henry L.	012	1891	WB-A/81	AR
Player, John	070	1803	WB-AB/70	AR
Player, Mary	070	1791	WB-C/339	AR
Player, Richard	070	1754	DB-D/104	AR
Player, Richard	070	1785	WB-C/337	AR
Player, Samuel	076	1893	WB-A1/168	AR
Player, Stephen	070	1778	WB-C/333	AR
Player, Thomas	070	1795	WB-C/341	AR
Player, Thomas	070	1840	WB-AB/336	AR
Player, William	070	1783	WB-C/336	AR
Pleasant, John	020	1805	RB-E/202	AR
Pleasant, Lois	046	1876	WB-E/206	AR
Pleasant, Micajah	020	1835	RB-M/527	AR
Pleasant, Sarah	020	1852	RB-Q/644	
Pleasant, William	020	1836	RB-M/614	
Pleasants, James	044	1892	WB-24/182	CTY
Pleasants, Robert	039	1847	WB-M/221	AR
Pleasants, Robert C.	036	1900	WB-A/511	CTY
Pleasants, Thomas M.	044	1864	WB-22/208	CTY
Pleasants, William	044	1893	WB-24/216	CTY
Pledger, Anna	096	1894	WB-4/151	
Pledger, John, Sr.	071	1837	WB-4/163	AR
Pledger, Joseph	096	c1807	WB-2/22	AR
Pledger, Robert L.	096	1854	WB-3/38	AR
Pledger, Selby	096	1832	WB-2/104	AR
Pledger, Zellah	096	c1825	Orig. Only	AR
Plemmons, A. D.	062	1900	WB-B/232	AR
Plemons, Peter	013	1838	WB-A/54	
Pless, Henry, Sr.	016	1835	PQS.5/328	
Pless, Isaac	049	1883	WB-2/108	AR
Pless, Peter	089	1858	WB-1/188	
Plomer, Samuel S.	024	1755	SS 880/99	SS/AR
Plonk, David	060	1899	WB-5/120	AR
Plonk, Peter	060	1791	Orig. Only	AR
Plonk, Peter	060	1824	Orig. Only	AR
Plot, George	060	1815	Orig. Only	AR
Plott, Charity H.	049	1899	WB-2/435	AR
Plott, Elias	054	1845	WB-2/316	AR
Plott, Henry	049	c1837	WI-1-2/10	
Plott, John	016	1871	WB-3/34	AR
Plott, John	049	1876	WB-2/22	AR
Plott, Jonathan	049	1886	WB 2/130	AR
Plott, Wiley	049	1894	WB-2/309	AR
Plowman, John	024	1721	SS 875/301	SS/AR
Plowman, John	019	c1805	Orig. Only	AR
Plumblee, Mary D.	050	1874	WB-1/138	CTY
Plummer, Alfred	098	1892	WB-A/145	CTY
Plummer, Ann	011	c1798	WB-1/445	
Plummer, Asia M.	100	1896	WB-51/448	
Plummer, Harry H.	100	1887	Orig. Only	AR/CRX
Plummer, Henry L.	100	1864	WB-50/72	AR
Plummer, James	011	c1838	WB-1/86	
Plummer, John	032	1836	WB-1/274	
Plummer, Joseph	006	1841	WB-A/25	AR
Plummer, Kemp	100	1862	WB-49/413	AR
Plummer, Kemp	100	1826	WB-29/36	AR
Plummer, Kemp	100	1862	Copy	047 AR
Plummer, Matthew	085	1883	WB-2/71	CTY
Plummer, Nancy	006	1897	WB-E/322	AR
Plummer, Nannie	100	1894	WB-51/373	AR
Plummer, Richard	029	1838	WB-B/288	AR
Plummer, Samuel	006	1879	WB-E/65	AR
Plummer, Sprig	100	1886	WB-51/217	AR
Plummer, Susanna	100	1838	WB-36/301	AR
Plummer, Thomas	084	c1804	WB-A/1	CTY
Plummer, Thomas	098	1892	WB-A/155	CTY

Name	Co.	Date	Recorded Copy	Original
Plummer, Thomas C.	090	1843	WB-4/117	AR
Plummer, Thomas G.	100	1866	WB-50/170	AR
Plummer, Thornton H.	090	1866	WB-5/36	
Plummer, William	100	1859	WB-49/237	AR
Plummer, William G.	NJ	1872	013 WB-B/89	013 AR
Plunket, Catharine	046	1801	WB-A/292	AR
Plunket, William	046	1801	WB-A/292	AR
Plunkett, Achilles	100	1824	WB-26/34	AR
Plunkett, Thomas J.	046	1826	WB-B/343	AR
Plyler, C. A.	SC	1899	097 WB-3/9	097 AR
Plyler, Ellen	SC	1889	054 WB-5/257	054 CTY
Plyler, Frederick	054	1888	WB-5/195	CTY
Pobason, Sarah	063	1834	WB-2/193	
Pocock, Abel	073	1785	WB-A/321	AR
Poe, Jaine	006	1869	WB-D/94	
Poe, James	046	1812	WB-A/298	AR
Poe, Janett	092	1860	WB-5/47	
Poe, Jesse	022	1897	WB-F/44	AR
Poe, Jesse, Sr.	022	1860	WB-D/58	AR
Poe, John T.	046	1888	WB-E/498	AR
Poe, Joseph W.	022	1891	WB-E/463	AR
Poe, Ransom C.	022	1880	WB-E/198	AR
Poe, Reuben C.	022	1849	WB-C/242	AR
Poe, Robert	022	1814	WB-A/248	AR
Poe, Rolly	092	c1854	Orig. Only	AR
Poe, Simon	022	1793	RB-1/47	AR
Poe, Stephen	022	1824	WB-B/86	AR
Poe, William	046	1832	WB-B/460	AR
Poe, William	006	1868	Orig. Only	AR
Poe, Willis	022	1883	WB-E/371	AR
Poer, Salon D.	107	1873	WB-2/14	
Poff, Andrew	083	1826	WB-1/316	AR
Pogue, Joseph	020	1788	RB-B/233	AR
Pohlman, Frederick	009	1886	WB-1/408	CTY
Poindexter, Francis A.	092	1844	WB-4/220	
Poindexter, Gabriel	090	1842	WB-4/93	AR
Poindexter, Peter	106	1891	WB-2/304	AR
Poindexter, Setta	038	1893	WB-3/365	AR
Poindexter, W. A.	106	1882	WB-2/158	AR
Poiner, William	030	1755	Orig. Only	SS/AR
Pointer, Henry	077	1800	WB-E/123	AR
Pointer, John	011	N. D.	WB-1/419	
Pointer, Joseph	078	1879	WB-19/90	AR
Pointer, Matthew	075	1789	WB-K/178	AR
Poisson, DuBrutz	070	1891	WB-F/490	AR
Poisson, Jehu D.	070	1873	WB-E/264	AR
Poisson, John J.	012	1812	WB-B/101	AR
Poisson, Louis J.	070	1843	WB-AB/399	AR
Poisson, Louis J.	070	1891	WB-F/467	AR
Poisson, Mary	070	1818	WB-C/346	AR
Poisson, William M.	070	1900	WB-H/310	AR
Poitevent, James	070	1762	DB-E/16	AR-Copy
Poitevent, Jane	070	1805	WB-AB/92	AR
Poitevent, Joseph	070	1756	DB-D/165	AR
Poitevent, Ruth	070	c1743	Orig. Only	AR
Poitevent, Samuel	070	1741	DB-AB/488	
Poling, Hannah	028	1808	WB-B/318	
Polk, Andrew	097	1893	WB-2/448	AR
Polk, Charles	065	1821	WB-F/97	AR
Polk, Hugh	060	1806	Orig. Only	AR
Polk, John	065	1809	WB-F/19	AR
Polk, Marshall T.	065	1831	WB-G/66	AR
Polk, Sarah	097	1881	WB-2/208	
Polk, Sarah	010	1835	WB-G/249	
Polk, Sarah	099	1844	RB-25/363	AR
Polk, Thomas J.	005	1885	013 WB-B/353	013 AR
Polk, William	099	1834	RB-23/46	AR
Polk, William H.	097	1884	WB-2/243	AR
Polk, William H.	100	1863	WB-50/11	
Poll (Paul), Abraham	083	c1801	Orig. Only	AR
Pollard, Benjamin	079	1877	WB-2/150	AR
Pollard, Cynthia	079	1873	WB-2/81	AR
Pollard, Elizabeth	099	1843	RB-25/343	AR
Pollard, Jacob	028	1833	WB-C/359	AR
Pollard, James	070	1745	DB-C/83	AR
Pollard, John D.	045	1894	079 WB-3/50	
Pollard, John O.	045	1894	WB-1/391	AR
Pollard, Joseph	028	1843	WB-D/92	AR
Pollard, Patsey	079	1870	Orig. Only	AR
Pollard, Penelope	028	1866	WB-D/470	
Pollard, Reddick	079	1861	WB-1/67	AR
Pollard, Smithy Ann	079	1885	WB-2/332	AR
Pollard, Susan	028	1822	WB-C/221	AR
Pollard, Thomas	028	1791	WB-A/255	AR
Pollard, Turner	079	1880	WB-2/203	AR
Pollard, Walter	VA	1769	Copy	060 AR
Pollard, William B.	038	1900	WB-4/232	AR
Pollard, William L.	079	1863	WB-1/92	AR
Pollock, Amy	057	1821	WB-B/62	AR
Pollock, Cullen	096	1751	Copy	028 AR
Pollock, Cullen	096	1751	SS 879/23	
Pollock, Elijah	072	1807	WB-A/103	AR
Pollock, Esther	024	1723	Orig. Only	SS/AR
Pollock, George	096	1764	Copy	024 AR
Pollock, George	N	1738	LGB-4/#82	024 AR
Pollock, Hannah	072	c1807	WB-A/106	AR
Pollock, Hester	024	1723	SS 876/152	
Pollock, James	024	1701	SS 874.2/173	SS/AR
Pollock, John	072	1771	Copy	028 AR
Pollock, John	072	1771	WB-A/106	AR-Copy
Pollock, John	057	1851	WB-B/210	AR
Pollock, Mary	057	1858	WB-B/241	AR
Pollock, Quincey A.	072	1859	WB-2/174	AR
Pollock, Thomas	010	1732	SS 876/309	SS/AR
Pollock, Thomas	010	1753	SS 877/66	
Pollock, Thomas	NJ	c1777	028 WB-A/267	028 AR
Pollock, Thomas, Sr.	024	1722	Orig. Only	SS/AR
Pollock, William	072	c1800	WB-A/109	AR
Pollok, Cullen	010	1795	024 WB-A/231	024 AR
Polvogt, Charles C.	070	1866	WB-D/176	AR
Pond, Richard	037	1852	WB-F/478	AR
Pond, Stephen	037	1806	WB-D/251	AR
Ponder, Ransom	080	1899	WB-1/315	AR
Pons, John	047	1797	WB-3/275	
Ponsonby, John B.	020	c1827	Copy	078 AR
Ponsonby, John B.	020	1829	RB-L/396	
Ponton, Harriet	047	1844	WB-4/234	
Ponton, Lucie B.	047	1885	WB-6/390	AR
Ponton, Mungo T.	047	1874	WB-6/109	AR
Ponton, Rebecca E.	047	1860	WB-5/86	
Pool, Alexander	085	1894	WB-3/52	CTY
Pool, Alexander	086	1821	WB-C/150	AR
Pool, Charity	067	1880	WB-2/115	AR
Pool, Colwell	067	1858	WB-1/86	AR
Pool, David	067	1888	WB-2/256	AR
Pool, Debora	056	1896	WB-2/216	
Pool, E. M.	085	1855	WB-K/204	AR
Pool, E. R.	029	1894	WB-F/21	AR
Pool, Elijah	078	c1859	Orig. Only	AR
Pool, Elisabeth	075	1790	WB-K/195	AR

Name	Co	Date	Recorded Copy	Original
Pool, Elizabeth	078	1860	WB-18/113	
Pool, Elizabeth	075	c1857	WB-M2/49	AR
Pool, Elizabeth	075	1830	WB-N/61	AR
Pool, Elizabeth	056	1887	WB-3/441	AR
Pool, George	099	1773	RB-1/30	AR
Pool, Green P.	105	1896	WB-3/170	AR
Pool, Hardy	099	1813	RB-11/151	AR
Pool, Isaac	073	1873	WB-H/64	CTY
Pool, James	056	1816	WB-1/263	AR
Pool, James	081	1860	WB-11/440	AR
Pool, James	003	1890	WB-B/284	
Pool, James	075	1821	WB-M1/340	AR
Pool, James M.	099	1883	WB-A/489	AR
Pool, John	075	1774	WB-I/127	AR
Pool, John	036	1889	WB-A/161	CTY
Pool, John	075	1843	WB-N/180	AR
Pool, John	085	1832	WB-H/559	AR
Pool, John	056	1796	WB-1/103	AR
Pool, John	073	1840	WB-F/58	AR
Pool, John S.	067	1883	WB-2/161	AR
Pool, John T.	020	1864	RB-T/24	
Pool, John W.	056	1884	WB-3/349	AR
Pool, Joseph	075	1771	WB-H/123	AR
Pool, Joseph	085	c1829	WB-H/472	AR
Pool, Joseph H.	075	1866	WB-M2/96 & 107	AR
Pool, Joshua	081	1855	WB-10/280	AR
Pool, Lee	044	1900	WB-24/482	CTY
Pool, Lewis	099	1809	RB-9/69	
Pool, Lovey S.	075	1866	WB-M2/87	AR
Pool, Lucy A.	020	1897	WB-B/297	CTY
Pool, Miles	026	1874	WB-2/129	AR
Pool, N. A.	044	1889	WB-24/84	CTY
Pool, Nancy	056	1864	WB-2/51	AR
Pool, Patrick	075	1796	WB-L/59	AR
Pool, Patrick	075	1794	WB-L/23	AR
Pool, Rebecca	075	1881	Orig. Only	AR
Pool, Rebecca	075	1858	WB-M2/58	AR
Pool, Richard	075	1782	WB-K/79	AR
Pool, Richard V.	075	1852	WB-N/245	AR
Pool, Samuel	036	1883	WB-A/45	CTY
Pool, Sarah	056	1768	WB-2/255	AR
Pool, Seth	082	1883	WB-6/250	AR
Pool, Seth P.	044	1867	WB-22/707	
Pool, Seth Petty	044	1843	WB-15/506	CTY
Pool, Solomon	075	1739	LGB-4/#98	SS/AR
Pool, Solomon	075	1832	WB-N/72	AR
Pool, Solomon	075	1778	WB-L/88	AR
Pool, Solomon	075	1761	WB-H/25	
Pool, Solomon	075	1829	WB-N/49	AR
Pool, Theophilus	099	1859	RB-31/152	
Pool, Thomas	026	1871	WB-2/66	AR
Pool, Thomas	020	1848	RB-Q/91	AR
Pool, Thomas	044	1799	WB-5/22	CTY
Pool, Thomas	075	1838	WB-N/146	AR
Pool, Thomas J.	056	1856	WB-1/691	AR
Pool, W. G.	075	1887	WB-O/276	AR
Pool, William	054	1898	WB-6/165	CTY
Pool, William	003	1882	WB-B/142	AR
Pool, William	075	1781	WB-K/72	AR
Pool, William	060	1880	WB-4/235	AR
Pool, William	056	1763	WB-1/780	AR
Pool, William R.	068	1900	WB-E/63	
Poole, David L.	085	1861	WB-K/292	AR
Poole, Elizabeth	099	1870	RB-35/96	AR

Name	Co	Date	Recorded Copy	Original
Poole, Green	020	1873	WB-A/106	CTY
Poole, John	096	1795	Orig. Only	AR
Poole, Lewis	056	1879	WB-3/211	AR
Poole, Micajah	020	1795	RB-C/113	AR
Poole, Sallie	099	1899	WB-D/301	AR
Poole, Theophilus	099	1859	RB-31/152	
Poole, Theophilus	099	1847	RB-26/263	AR
Poole, Thomas	053	1772	RW-1/29	AR
Poole, William R.	099	1889	WB-B/315	AR
Poor, Hannah	090	1840	WB-4/68	AR
Poor, Isaac L.	013	1842	WB-A/84	
Poor, Peter	073	1768	WB-A/68	
Pope, Amey	011	c1805	WB-1/416	
Pope, Aseneth	016	1892	WB-4/146	AR
Pope, Benjamin	047	1823	WB-3/684	
Pope, Benjamin	047	1843	WB-4/225	
Pope, Benjamin E.	VA	1880	071 WB-6/357	071 AR
Pope, Charity	105	1860	WB-1/59	
Pope, Charles L.	032	1896	WB-4/305	AR
Pope, Dempsey	069	1835	WB-1/411	AR
Pope, Edward	075	1722	SS 875/337	SS/AR
Pope, Elijah	071	1781	WB-1/239	
Pope, Elijah	047	1859	WB-5/67	
Pope, Elijah	047	1798	WB-3/305	
Pope, Elijah	047	1849	WB-4/285	
Pope, Elijah	071	1842	WB-4/249	AR
Pope, Elijah	006	1890	WB-E/216	AR
Pope, Elisha	099	1838	RB-24/196	AR
Pope, Eliza H.	033	1894	WB-2/162	CTY
Pope, Emily	059	1886	WB-A/439	CTY
Pope, H. J.	047	1893	WB-7/92	
Pope, Hardie	047	1799	WB-3/323	
Pope, Hardyman	069	c1789	WB-1/231	AR
Pope, Henry	103	1810	RD-1/217	
Pope, Henry	047	1764	WB-1/144	
Pope, Jacob	037	1772	WB-A/189	AR
Pope, Jacob	047	1834	WB-4/112	
Pope, James	085	1823	WB-H/229	AR
Pope, James W.	083	1866	WB-2/226	AR
Pope, John	051	1889	WB-C/391	AR
Pope, John	VA	1896	098 WB-A/247	098 CTY
Pope, John	071	1831	WB-4/83	AR
Pope, John	039	c1785	WB-B/3	
Pope, John C.	071	1863	WB-5/282	AR
Pope, John, Sr.	086	1834	WB-E/7	AR
Pope, Jonas	071	1899	WB-7/415	AR
Pope, Jonathan	071	1801	WB-2/212	AR
Pope, Josiah	099	1806	RB-7/158	AR
Pope, K. C.	037	1869	WB-G/325	
Pope, Kinchen	071	1848	WB-5/69	AR
Pope, Kindred C.	037	1892	WB-H/222	AR
Pope, Kirby	016	1883	WB-3/405	
Pope, Lazarus	069	1789	WB-1/61	AR
Pope, Lazarus	071	1881	WB-6/336	AR
Pope, Lemuel	103	1844	RD-9/142	AR
Pope, Maria F.	047	1894	WB-7/138	AR
Pope, Mary	037	1864	WB-G/241	AR
Pope, Mary	037	1844	WB-F/313	AR
Pope, Mary	047	1855	WB-5/1	
Pope, Mary M.	087	c1897	Orig. Only	AR
Pope, Mathew	103	1898	WB-2/216	AR
Pope, Nicholas	071	1835	WB-4/129	AR
Pope, Osborn	044	1812	WB-7/229	CTY
Pope, Reddick	071	1896	WB-7/304	AR
Pope, Richard	047	1763	WB-1/111	

Name	Co.	Date	Recorded Copy	Original
Pope, Richard	075	1701	SS 874.1/15	SS/AR
Pope, Rosa	047	1874	WB-6/116	AR
Pope, Sally	047	1807	WB-3/464	
Pope, Samuel	028	1758	SS 880/230	SS/AR
Pope, Simon	099	1858	RB-31/51	
Pope, Stephen	103	1858	RD-12/615	AR
Pope, Stephen	029	1825	WB-B/137	AR
Pope, Susan	060	1896	WB-5/7	AR
Pope, Thomas	047	1762	WB-1/64	
Pope, Thomas	035	1762	WB-A/380	AR
Pope, Thomas	073	1858	WB-G/202	AR
Pope, Thomas	047	1762	WB-1/78	
Pope, Wiley	097	1882	WB-2/210	
Pope, William	099	1852	RB-28/92	AR
Pope, William	071	1809	WB-3/17	AR
Pope, William	047	1772	WB-1/320	
Pope, William	069	1842	WB-1/458	AR
Pope, William	099	1818	RB-14/327	AR
Pope, William	037	1749	Orig. Only	SS/AR
Pope, William	047	1799	WB-3/329	
Pope, William	103	1808	RD-1/80	AR
Pope, William	021	1862	WB-1/166	AR
Pope, William A.	069	1848	WB-1/513	AR
Pope, William B.	047	1869	WB-6/15	AR
Pope, William E.	037	1865	WB-G/268	AR
Pope, Willie	099	1854	RB-31/51	AR
Pope, Willis	083	1829	WB-1/190	AR
Pope, Winefred	047	1762	WB-1/85	
Popleston, Samuel	024	1789	WB-A/122	AR
Poplin, Georg	022	c1775	Orig. Only	AR
Poplin, Judith	089	1855	WB-1/131	
Poplin, Nancy	089	c1871	Orig. Only	AR
Popplein, Nicholas	MD	1885	Copy	046 AR
Popplein, Susanna	MD	1895	Copy	046 AR
Popplewell, William	030	1777	WB-1/115	
Porcupine, John	072	1796	Orig. Only	AR
Porham, James	009	1789	Orig. Only	AR
Porsell, Garitt	002	1729	Orig. Only	SS/AR
Portawint, Peter	N	1730	Orig. Only	SS/AR
Porter, Alexander	065	1833	WB-G/148	AR
Porter, Charles	037	1794	WB-C/298	AR
Porter, David	020	1795	RB-C/112	AR
Porter, David	086	1812	WB-B/265	AR
Porter, Edmund	024	c1739	Orig. Only	AR
Porter, Elisha	072	1857	WB-2/157	AR
Porter, Elizabeth	037	1831	WB-F/130	AR
Porter, Ely	037	1843	WB-F/279	AR
Porter, Gerald Lee	093	1873	WB-1/146	
Porter, Henry	046	1816	WB-A/301	AR
Porter, Hugh	065	1813	WB-F/23	AR
Porter, James	046	1812	WB-A/298	AR
Porter, James	041	1853	WB-3/164	AR
Porter, James	065	1859	WB-J/66	AR
Porter, James	065	1824	WB-F/47	AR
Porter, James	046	1778	WB-A/287	AR
Porter, James	085	c1789	WB-C/55	AR
Porter, James G.	065	1843	WB-H/122	AR
Porter, Jane	086	1819	WB-C/121	AR
Porter, John	087	c1796	WB-A/24	AR
Porter, John	011	c1773	WB-1/567	
Porter, John	002	1713	SS 875/5 & 46	
Porter, John	053	1751	028 DB-5/243	SS/AR
Porter, John	070	1728	Orig. Only	SS/AR
Porter, John	068	1815	WB-A/278	
Porter, John	046	1817	WB-B/47	AR
Porter, John A.	054	1879	WB-4/324	CTY
Porter, John C.	011	1845	WB-1/119	
Porter, John M.	065	1858	WB-J/49	AR
Porter, John P.	009	1755	Orig. Only	SS/AR
Porter, John S.	065	1859	WB-J/70	AR
Porter, John Swann	070	c1770	Copy	SS/AR
Porter, John, Sr.	065	1821	WB-F/91	AR
Porter, John, Sr.	SC	1872	097 WB-2/58	097 AR
Porter, Joseph J.	037	1888	WB-H/115	AR
Porter, Joshua	008	1734	SS 876/329	
Porter, Joshua	008	1734	Copy	024 AR
Porter, Lina	046	1897	WB-G/28	AR
Porter, Margaret	065	1867	WB-J/242	AR
Porter, Martha	037	1845	WB-F/330	AR
Porter, Mary	024	1717	SS 875/139	SS/AR
Porter, Mary Eliza	037	1892	WB-H/202	AR
Porter, Nancy	037	1881	WB-G/621	AR
Porter, Nancy	103	1895	WB-2/111	AR
Porter, Nicoless	056	1749	SS 877/314	SS/AR
Porter, Patience	037	1897	WB-H/400	AR
Porter, Rhoda	051	1848	WB-A/293	
Porter, Robert	086	1811	WB-B/256	AR
Porter, Robert	065	1847	WB-I/98	AR
Porter, Robert J.	039	1890	WB-U/497	AR
Porter, Ruth	065	1829	WB-B/149	AR
Porter, Samuel	047	1810	WB-3/502	
Porter, Samuel	011	1757	Orig. Only	SS/AR
Porter, Samuel	046	1806	WB-A/294	AR
Porter, Sarah	070	1753	DB-D/51	AR
Porter, Sarah	065	1846	WB-I/66	AR
Porter, Thomas	054	c1797	WB-1/193	AR
Porter, Wiley	029	1878	WB-E/177	AR
Porter, William	085	1761	WB-A/136	AR
Porter, William	028	1790	WB-A/223	
Porter, William	029	1853	WB-C/257	
Porter, William	065	1823	WB-F/13	AR
Porter, William	013	1835	WB-A/38	
Porter, William	065	1823	WB-F/100	AR
Porter, William	051	1865	WB-B/68	AR
Porter, William	053	1824	Orig. Only	AR
Porter, William	065	1810	WB-F/46	AR
Porter, William	053	1795	RW-1/255	AR
Porterfield, James	073	1890	WB-H/535	
Porterfield, John	029	1796	Orig. Only	AR
Portevint, Peter	027	1820	WB-A/47	AR
Portis, Abigail	016	1866	WB-2/142	AR
Portis, George	037	1776	WB-A/244	AR
Portis, George	069	1795	WB-1/97	AR
Portis, John	N	1794	HaDSC(M)/194	
Portlock, Polly	077	1815	WB-E/419	AR
Portlock, Thomas	077	1789	WB-C/388	AR
Portus, Delphy	060	1811	Orig. Only	AR
Portwood, Benjamin	030	1801	WB-2/182	
Portwood, Gilbert	030	1774	WB-1/86	
Posten, Daniel	060	1807	Orig. Only	AR
Postley, Charles T.	036	1899	WB-A/484	CTY
Poston, Benjamin	085	1802	WB-F/28	AR
Poston, D. P.	026	1897	WB-3/1	AR
Poston, Daniel	026	1895	WB-2/502	AR
Poston, Elizabeth	020	1803	RB-E/26	AR
Poston, James	026	1879	WB-2/184	AR
Poston, Jeremiah	020	1795	RB-C/114	AR
Poston, John	026	1862	WB-1/300	AR
Poston, John	085	c1784	WB-B/64	AR
Poston, Nora J.	054	1890	WB-5/325	CTY

Name	Co.	Date	Recorded Copy	Original
Poston, Rachel	026	1853	WB-1/166	AR
Poston, Samuel	086	1819	WB-C/127	AR
Poston, Sarah	054	c1831	WB-2/131	AR
Poston, Susanna	085	1853	WB-K/160	AR
Poteat, Eliza R.	020	1886	WB-A/499	CTY
Poteat, James	020	1889	WB-A/568	CTY
Poteet, Benjamin	016	1896	WB-4/237	AR
Poteet, John	020	1853	RB-R/27	AR
Poteete, John	020	1788	RB-B/238	
Potice, Isaac	039	1894	WB-V/50	AR
Potis, Mary	047	c1813	WB-3/545	
Pottel, Joseph	077	1749	Orig. Only	SS/AR
Potter, Ann	028	1814	WB-C/82	
Potter, Ann	028	1841	WB-D/23	AR
Potter, Corrina	046	1891	WB-F/154	AR
Potter, Daniel	035	1831	WB-1/8	
Potter, Ephriam	046	1775	WB-A/286	AR
Potter, Frederick	035	1870	WB-4/29	AR
Potter, Gilbert	070	1862	WB-D/78	AR
Potter, Henry	029	1858	WB-C/377	AR
Potter, Isaac	046	1864	WB-D/217	AR
Potter, James	028	1802	WB-B/171	
Potter, John	065	1849	Orig. Only	AR
Potter, John	084	1837	WB-B/167	CTY
Potter, John, Sr.	012	1828	WB-B/153	AR
Potter, Kitty	045	1886	WB-1/150	AR
Potter, Littleton	009	1817	OB-A/277	AR
Potter, Mary	028	1825	WB-C/266	AR
Potter, Miles	012	c1798	WB-B/62	AR
Potter, Miles	012	c1857	WB-B/10	AR
Potter, Miles, Sr.	012	1827	WB-B/151	AR
Potter, Richard	077	1832	WB-F/206	AR
Potter, Robert	070	1757	DB-D/247	AR
Potter, Samuel	028	1839	WB-C/433	AR
Potter, Samuel P.	012	1882	WB-A/53	AR
Potter, Sarah Jane	012	1834	WB-B/170	
Potter, Sylvia	029	1853	Orig. Only	AR
Potter, William	060	1835	WB-1/348	AR
Potter, William	044	1778	WB-1/172	CTY
Potter, William F.	070	1878	WB-E/359	AR
Potts, Agnes	065	1830	WB-F/53	AR
Potts, Dovie	054	1867	WB-3/196	AR
Potts, Edwin	065	1854	WB-I/250	AR
Potts, Eli	054	1866	WB-3/192	AR
Potts, Elisabeth	065	1834	WB-G/176	AR
Potts, Elizabeth	065	1860	WB-J/80	AR
Potts, Elizabeth	033	1869	WB-2/6	CTY
Potts, George	085	1826	WB-H/328	AR
Potts, Henry	085	1775	WB-A/197	AR
Potts, Hiram	054	1841	WB-2/219	
Potts, James	065	1781	WB-F/6	AR
Potts, James	065	1821	WB-F/94	AR
Potts, James	065	1827	WB-A/158	AR
Potts, James	054	c1819	WB-2/26	AR
Potts, James	054	c1826	WB-2/26	
Potts, James M.	054	1869	WB-4/44	AR
Potts, James, Sr.	054	c1810	WB-1/302	AR
Potts, Jeremiah	085	1823	WB-H/220	AR
Potts, John	065	1787	WB-F/10	AR
Potts, John	094	1771	094.901.1	AR
Potts, John M.	065	1875	WB-K/180	AR
Potts, Kesiah A.	065	1863	WB-J/168	AR
Potts, L. B.	055	1899	WB-A/170	
Potts, Maggie	065	1881	WB-K/445	AR
Potts, Margret	054	c1820	WB-2/5	AR

Name	Co.	Date	Recorded Copy	Original
Potts, Mary	065	1840	WB-H/1	AR
Potts, Newmon	103	1884	WB-1/319	AR
Potts, Pamelia	054	1850	WB-3/43	AR
Potts, Peter	033	1842	WB-1/45	AR
Potts, R. C.	065	1880	WB-K/371	AR
Potts, R. E.	046	1896	WB-F/485	AR
Potts, Ralph	009	1816	OB-A/257	AR
Potts, Richard	072	1766	Orig. Only	AR-Nunc.
Potts, Robert	065	1860	WB-J/76	AR
Potts, Robert	065	1821	WB-F/96	AR
Potts, Robert	054	1842	WB-2/243	AR
Potts, Sarah	054	1842	WB-2/234	AR
Potts, William	097	1856	WB-1/128	AR
Potts, William	065	1802	WB-F/12	AR
Potts, William	054	c1810	WB-1/191	AR
Poulan, John	069	1784	WB-1/26	AR
Poulan, John, Sr.	069	1829	WB-1/361	AR
Poulas, William	085	c1784	WB-B/137	AR
Pounce, Elizabeth	086	1821	WB-C/160	AR
Pouncey, Nathaniel	070	1793	WB-C/341	AR
Pound, John	072	c1770	RW/L45	AR
Pound, Mary	072	1782	RW/L32	AR
Pourter, Joseph	104	1820	WB-3/242	AR
Pouts, John	081	1802	WB-2/103	AR
Povey, Conrod	065	1767	WB-F/1	AR
Powe, Martha A.	085	1875	WB-1/322	CTY
Powel, Benjamin	037	1824	WB-F/17	AR
Powel, Charles	022	1777	Orig. Only	AR
Powel, John	073	1802	WB-D/80	AR
Powel, Robert	024	1778	WB-B/64	AR
Powel, Roderick	028	c1849	Orig. Only	AR
Powel, Stanford	073	1861	WB-G/355	AR
Powel, William	081	1816	WB-4/362	AR
Powel, William	039	1864	WB-R/719	AR
Powell, A. B.	VA	1876	084 WB-E/126	
Powell, A. F., Sr.	027	1873	WB-2/15	AR
Powell, Absalom	027	c1834	WB-A/35	AR
Powell, Albert H.	028	1896	WB-F/240	
Powell, Ann	070	1843	WB-AB/377	AR
Powell, Ann E.	046	1886	WB-E/429	AR
Powell, Arabella	099	1885	WB-B/75	AR
Powell, Asa	047	1844	WB-4/228	
Powell, Ashley G.	056	1889	WB-3/492	AR
Powell, Augustine	010	1884	WB-I/181	
Powell, Benjamin	100	1869	WB-51/2	AR
Powell, Brittain	035	1838	Orig. Only	AR
Powell, C. Y.	083	1895	WB-4/56	AR
Powell, Cader	051	1831	WB-A/8	
Powell, Carter	020	1858	RB-R/593	AR
Powell, Caswell	099	1814	RB-11/209	AR
Powell, Charles	051	1843	WB-A/162	
Powell, Charles	041	c1842	Orig. Only	AR
Powell, Charlotte	069	1894	WB-5/431	AR
Powell, Daniel	041	1826	WB-2/250	AR
Powell, Dempsey	099	1831	RB-22/117	AR
Powell, Douglas	083	1842	WB-1/406	AR
Powell, E. P.	047	1882	WB-6/279	AR
Powell, Edmond	100	1795	WB-8/178	AR
Powell, Edward	084	1808	WB-A/77	CTY
Powell, Edwin	039	1832	WB-J/194	
Powell, Eli K.	063	1895	WB-4/150	AR
Powell, Eliakim	056	1887	WB-3/455	AR
Powell, Elias	071	1833	WB-4/104	AR
Powell, Eliga	022	1832	WB-B/233	AR
Powell, Eliza B.	028	1833	WB-C/356	

Name	Co.	Date	Recorded Copy	Original
Powell, Elizabeth	039	c1841	Orig. Only	AR
Powell, Enoch	098	1890	WB-A/124	CTY
Powell, Esquire	046	1896	WB-H/185	
Powell, Feilder	028	1784	Orig. Only	AR
Powell, Ferabay	035	1845	Orig. Only	AR
Powell, Frances	047	1846	WB-4/251	
Powell, George	017	1875	WB-B/52	AR
Powell, George	010	1736	LGB-4/#53	SS/AR
Powell, George	047	1841	WB-4/195	
Powell, Henrietta	028	1884	WB-E/338	
Powell, Henry	010	1868	WB-H/211	AR
Powell, Henry	103	c1784	Orig. Only	AR
Powell, Henry A.	020	1867	RB-T/206	AR
Powell, Henry H.	026	1877	WB-2/159	AR
Powell, J. C.	047	1867	WB-5/160	
Powell, Jackson	084	1882	WB-E/246	CTY
Powell, Jacob	071	1791	WB-1/420	AR
Powell, Jacob	099	1856	RB-29/558	AR
Powell, Jacob	070	1823	WB-C/349	AR
Powell, Jacob	041	1788	WB-1/77	AR
Powell, Jacob S.	041	1816	WB-2/134	AR
Powell, Jacob, Sr.	027	1827	WB-A/31	AR
Powell, James	044	1840	WB-14/493	CTY
Powell, James	047	1819	WB-3/644	
Powell, James	041	1862	WB-3/279	AR
Powell, James C.	071	1898	WB-7/390	AR
Powell, James J.	099	1879	WB-A/28	AR
Powell, Jarratt	020	1838	RB-N/203	
Powell, Jesse	099	1842	RB-25/125	AR
Powell, Jesse	047	1860	WB-5/79	
Powell, Jesse	056	1777	WB-2/255	AR
Powell, Jesse A.	010	1864	WB-H/145	AR
Powell, Jesse H.	037	1879	WB-G/496	AR
Powell, John	020	1874	WB-A/139	CTY
Powell, John	083	1851	WB-2/149	AR
Powell, John	011	c1789	WB-1/583	
Powell, John	047	1785	WB-3/101	
Powell, John	020	1787	RB-B/168	AR
Powell, John	092	1818	WB-3/136	
Powell, John	047	1798	WB-3/301	
Powell, John	047	1838	WB-4/173	
Powell, John	002	1724	SS 876/23	SS/AR
Powell, John	104	1893	WB-6/484	AR
Powell, John	041	1804	WB-1/206	AR
Powell, John B.	017	1882	WB-B/102	AR
Powell, John B.	020	1878	WB-A/257	CTY
Powell, John B.	100	1858	WB-49/165	AR
Powell, John D.	099	1851	RB-29/331	AR
Powell, John H.	047	1825	WB-4/17	
Powell, John R.	047	1881	WB-6/254	AR
Powell, John W.	083	1873	WB-3/52	AR
Powell, John W.	047	1868	WB-6/9	AR
Powell, Jordan	047	1783	WB-3/36	
Powell, Joseph J.	037	1861	WB-G/213	AR
Powell, Kedar	056	c1786	WB-2/257	AR
Powell, Lemuel	077	1760	Orig. Only	AR
Powell, Louisa	100	1843	WB-38/134	AR
Powell, Lucy	099	1890	WB-B/413	AR
Powell, Lucy	047	1805	WB-3/444	
Powell, Luke	087	1842	WB-1/257	
Powell, Lydia	009	1847	OB-F/289	AR
Powell, Mark	087	1836	WB-1/174	
Powell, Martha J.	100	1892	013 WB-C/194	013 AR
Powell, Mary	100	1841	WB-38/10	AR
Powell, Mary	047	1838	WB-4/161	
Powell, Mary	010	1833	WB-G/233	AR
Powell, Mary	035	1847	WB-2/13	AR
Powell, Mary A.	069	1897	WB-6/1	AR
Powell, Mary A.	005	c1881	WB-D/120	
Powell, Mary E.	037	1897	WB-H/371	AR
Powell, Mary J.	082	1885	WB-6/315	AR
Powell, Mary W.	047	1875	WB-6/172	AR
Powell, Mathew	071	1829	WB-4/54	AR
Powell, Metilda	028	1890	WB-E/552	AR
Powell, Moses, Sr.	099	1799	RB-5/27	AR
Powell, Nancy	037	1809	WB-D/348	AR
Powell, Nathan	047	1763	WB-1/109	
Powell, Nathan	047	1761	WB-1/35	
Powell, Nathaniel	037	1777	WB-A/250	AR
Powell, Ozbern	028	1780	Orig. Only	AR
Powell, Patrick	035	1769	WB-A/388	AR
Powell, Penelope	063	1898	WB-4/229	AR
Powell, Priscilla	051	1833	WB-A/57	
Powell, Prudence	099	1814	RB-11/207	AR
Powell, Rachel	070	1860	WB-D/31	AR
Powell, Richard	047	1767	WB-1/214	
Powell, Robert	070	1888	WB-F/228	AR
Powell, Robert	044	1829	WB-11/250	CTY
Powell, Robert	096	1772	WB-1/77	AR
Powell, Robert	082	1842	WB-2/533	AR
Powell, Sarah	047	1845	WB-4/248	
Powell, Sarah	070	1889	WB-F/260	AR
Powell, Sarah B.	020	1878	WB-A/249	CTY
Powell, Solomon	047	1770	WB-1/271	
Powell, Solomon	047	1858	WB-5/63	
Powell, Stapleton	063	1851	WB-2/371	
Powell, Stephen	056	c1780	Orig. Only	AR
Powell, Sterling	103	1813	Orig. Only	AR
Powell, Thomas	039	1839	WB-K/191	
Powell, Thomas	022	1824	WB-B/75	AR
Powell, Thomas	027	c1832	WB-A/26	AR
Powell, Thomas	020	1886	WB-A/501	CTY
Powell, Thomas	071	1754	SS 879/183	SS/AR
Powell, Thomas B.	020	1864	RB-T/79	AR
Powell, Thomas B.	100	1864	WB-50/75	AR
Powell, William	037	1793	WB-C/249	AR
Powell, William	069	1815	WB-1/269	AR
Powell, William	041	1782	WB-1/24	AR
Powell, William	028	1765	DB-12&13/313	
Powell, William	008	1703	009 DB-1/41	
Powell, William	100	1791	WB-6/38	AR
Powell, William	047	1814	WB-3/557	
Powell, William	028	1748	SS 877/59	SS/AR
Powell, William	044	1848	WB-17/354	CTY
Powell, William M.	100	1889	WB-51/304	AR
Powell, William W.	071	1865	WB-5/303	AR
Powell, Willie	069	1860	WB-1/570	AR
Powell, Willis	047	1811	WB-3/519	
Powell, Zachariah	047	1806	WB-3/451	
Powell, Zachariah	047	1888	WB-6/488	AR
Powell, Zilpha	011	c1794	WB-1/585	
Power, Charles	010	1789	WB-D/105	AR
Power, John	100	1822	WB-24/211	AR
Power, William	100	1791	WB-5/227	AR
Power, William	024	1748	Orig. Only	SS/AR
Powers, Bradly	013	1842	WB-A/87	
Powers, Curiff	030	1796	WB-2/95	
Powers, David	099	1866	RB-34/148	AR
Powers, E. S.	068	1898	WB-D/532	
Powers, Edward	056	1761	WB-1/743	AR

Name	Co.	Date	Recorded Copy	Original
Powers, Frederick	028	1817	WB-C/142	AR
Powers, George	030	1795	WB-2/42	
Powers, George	N	1695/6	Orig. Only	ChM-1/4
Powers, George	030	1753	Orig. Only	SS/AR
Powers, Henry	047	1824	WB-3/694	
Powers, Henry	010	1816	WB-F/316	AR
Powers, Isobell	030	1757	SS 880/233	SS/AR
Powers, J. S. D.	030	1825	WB-3/189	
Powers, James	063	c1798	WB-1/346	
Powers, John	047	1787	WB-3/125	
Powers, John, Sr.	096	1784	WB-1/139	AR
Powers, Joshua	096	1818	Orig. Only	AR
Powers, Kinchen	070	1868	WB-E/6	AR
Powers, Magor	006	c1845	WB-A/11	AR
Powers, Martha A.	030	1889	WB-5/165	
Powers, Matthew	083	1858	WB-2/135	AR
Powers, Moses B.	030	1866	WB-4/261	AR
Powers, Rebecca	047	1835	WB-4/118	
Powers, Samuel	010	1774	WB-A/167	AR
Powers, Sandford	030	1859	WB-4/231	AR
Powers, William	030	1796	WB-2/65	
Powers, William	076	1898	WB-A1/233	AR
Powlas, Charles	016	1897	WB-4/283	
Powless, Henry	085	1833	WB-H/581	AR
Poyer, Dennis	056	c1746	SS 877/252	
Poyner, Adam	030	1798	WB-2/125	
Poyner, Anne	030	1777	WB-1/117	
Poyner, Dinah	030	1830	WB-3/255	
Poyner, Edward	009	c1787	OWB/217	AR
Poyner, George	030	1817	WB-3/92	
Poyner, Griffin	030	1851	WB-4/162	
Poyner, Humphrey	030	1791	WB-1/250	
Poyner, Isable	030	c1807	WB-2/339	
Poyner, Isaiah	030	1827	WB-3/234	
Poyner, James	009	c1787	OWB/213	AR
Poyner, James	030	1755	Orig. Only	SS/AR
Poyner, James	030	1825	WB-3/192	
Poyner, James	030	1776	WB-1/105	
Poyner, Jod	030	1804	WB-2/252	
Poyner, Jonathan	030	1793	WB-2/18	
Poyner, Jos	030	c1712	Orig. Only	SS/AR
Poyner, Joseph	030	1774	WB-1/83	
Poyner, Joseph	030	1721	SS 876/46	
Poyner, Joseph	030	1799	WB-2/130	
Poyner, Levi	030	1831	WB-3/283	
Poyner, Lydia	030	1845	WB-4/113	
Poyner, Mary	030	1816	WB-3/83	
Poyner, Nathan	030	1868	WB-4/271	AR
Poyner, Nathaniel	030	1777	WB-1/120	
Poyner, Nelson	030	1893	WB-5/208	AR
Poyner, Peter	030	1796	WB-2/92	
Poyner, Peter	N	1715	Orig. Only	SS/AR
Poyner, Peter	030	1758	SS 881/168	SS/AR
Poyner, Powers	030	1838	WB-4/49	
Poyner, Robert	030	1857	WB-4/213	
Poyner, Robert	030	c1804	WB-3/58	
Poyner, Robert M.	030	1854	WB-4/182	AR
Poyner, Sarah	030	1874	WB-5/45	AR
Poyner, Thomas	030	1798	WB-2/126	
Poyner, William	030	1723	Orig. Only	SS/AR
Poyner, William	030	c1809	WB-2/341	
Poyner, William	030	1790	WB-1/243	
Poynter, John	075	1774	WB-I/69	AR
Poynter, Samuel	075	1784	WB-K/103	AR
Poythress, John	019	1813	Orig. Only	AR

Name	Co.	Date	Recorded Copy	Original
Prather, Charity	092	1897	WB-6/467	AR
Prather, M. R.	092	1896	WB-6/413	AR
Prather, R. R.	046	1882	Orig. Only	AR
Prather, T. F.	092	1889	WB-6/308	AR
Prather, W. S.	065	1864	WB-J/185	AR
Pratt, Agnes	084	c1811	WB-A/92	CTY
Pratt, Alfred	084	1830	WB-B/5	CTY
Pratt, Benjamin	005	1835	WB-B/57	AR
Pratt, Eady	005	1843	WB-B/175	AR
Pratt, George	073	1862	WB-G/383	CTY
Pratt, James H.	073	1885	WB-H/388	CTY
Pratt, Jeremiah	077	1772	WB-C/121	AR
Pratt, Job	077	1736	LGB-4/#62	SS/AR
Pratt, John	024	1743	Orig. Only	SS/AR
Pratt, John	010	1742	LGB-4/#167	SS/AR
Pratt, Joseph	077	1737	Orig. Only	SS/AR
Pratt, Lewis	073	1873	WB-H/70	CTY
Pratt, Loftin K.	073	1846	WB-F/297	AR
Pratt, Mary	073	1815	WB-D/446	AR
Pratt, Samuel	005	1845	WB-B/197	AR
Pratt, Samuel	104	1847	WB-4/338	AR
Pratt, Thomas	073	1791	WB-B/29	AR
Pratt, W. F.	084	1897	WB-F/75	CTY
Pratt, William	005	1843	WB-B/158	AR
Pratt, William	028	1766	Orig. Only	AR-Nunc.
Pratt, William	005	1818	WB-2/121	AR
Pratt, William N.	073	1867	WB-G/521	CTY
Prempert, Henry C.	070	1890	WB-F/395	AR
Prendergast, George	020	1853	RB-R/67	
Prendergast, George W.	020	c1879	WB-A/287	CTY
Prendergast, Luke	020	1831	RB-L/632	AR
Prendergast, Thomas	020	1843	RB-P/17	
Prescoat, William	028	1745	SS 878/151	SS/AR
Prescoate, John	009	1773	Orig. Only	SS/AR
Prescoate, John	009	1778	OWB/134	AR
Prescoatt, Aaron	019	1801	WB-D/320	AR
Prescoatt, Willough	019	1829	WB-D/326	AR
Prescot, John	009	c1796	OWB/321	AR
Prescott, Austin	028	1838	WB-C/418	
Prescott, Benjamin	072	1861	WB-2/186	AR
Prescott, Moses	057	1791	WB-A/176	AR
Prescott, Moses	009	c1777	OWB/133	AR
Prescott, Moses	019	1751	028 DB-5/219	SS/AR
Prescott, Sallie L.	047	1899	WB-7/230	AR
Prescott, Thomas	057	c1780	WB-A/193	AR
Prescott, William	009	1756	SS 879/236	SS/AR
Preslar, Alvin	097	1857	WB-1/131	AR
Preslar, Elias	005	1835	WB-B/48	AR
Preslar, Elias	097	1855	WB-1/111	AR
Preslar, Joshua	005	1868	WB-D/1	AR
Preslar, Leo	065	1840	WB-E/237	AR
Presley, Peter	005	1829	WB-B/4	AR
Presley, Thomas	005	1808	WB-2/124	AR
Presnall, Stephen	081	1822	WB-5/76	AR
Presnell, Daniel	017	c1869	WB-B/15	AR
Presnell, Elizabeth	017	c1895	WB-B/257	AR
Presnell, Martha J.	064	1894	WB-2/331	AR
Presnell, William	081	1823	WB-5/107	
Pressgraves, George	047	1764	WB-1/132	
Pressler, John	005	1778	WB-1/29	
Pressley, W. B.	054	1884	WB-4/573	CTY
Pressly, John E.	016	1897	WB-4/265	AR
Presson, Jeames	005	1819	WB-2/123	AR
Presson, Samuel	097	1876	WB-2/117	AR
Preston, John	090	1874	WB-6/61	AR

Name	Co.	Date	Recorded Copy	Original
Preston, John A.	065	1896	WB-M/500	AR
Preston, Nathaniel	090	1841	WB-4/89	AR
Preston, Wetherenton	090	1826	WB-3/148	AR
Preswood, Johnathan	013	1839	WB-A/59	
Prevatt, Archibald	083	1895	WB-4/84	AR
Prevatt, Edith	083	1897	WB-4/160	AR
Prevatt, Elias W.	083	1886	WB-3/378	AR
Prevatt, Furney	083	1895	Orig. Only	AR
Prevatt, Holland	083	c1889	Orig. Only	AR
Prevatt, James	083	1862	WB-2/188	AR
Prevatt, P. P.	083	1897	WB-4/136	AR
Prevatt, William	083	1877	WB-3/130	AR
Prevett, Cader	054	1841	WB-2/230	AR
Prevett, Milly	054	1876	Orig. Only	AR
Prevette, Iredell T.	104	1899	WB-7/71	AR
Prewett, Marthy	044	1873	WB-23/116	CTY
Prewit, Newberry	026	1895	WB-2/504	AR
Prewit, Newberry	026	1895	014 WB-2/544	014 CTY
Prewit, Spencer	026	1865	WB-1/381	AR
Price, Absolem	003	c1862	WB-B/269	
Price, Alfred L.	070	1872	WB-E/240	AR
Price, Benjamin	077	1802	WB-E/166	AR
Price, Catharine	070	1853	WB-C/560	AR
Price, Charity	037	1826	WB-F/55	AR
Price, Daniel M.	097	1873	WB-2/67	
Price, Delilah	056	1866	WB-2/87	AR
Price, Doctor	024	1815	WB-C/36	AR
Price, Drury	084	1857	WB-C/248	CTY
Price, E. A.	026	1883	WB-2/238	AR
Price, Edward	056	1789	WB-1/17	AR
Price, Edward	056	1835	Orig. Only	AR
Price, Elijah	037	1792	WB-C/203	AR
Price, Elijah	063	1794	WB-1/198	
Price, Elijah	003	c1874	WB-B/49	
Price, Elizabeth	103	1855	RD-11/576	AR
Price, Elizabeth	065	1829	WB-B/149	AR
Price, Esther	065	1815	WB-F/24	AR
Price, Etheldred	056	1810	WB-1/226	AR
Price, Ezekiel	026	1864	WB-1/341	AR
Price, Fannie Watt	084	1884	WB-E/289	CTY
Price, Fuller	012	1900	WB-A/155	AR
Price, G. W.	086	1900	WB-G/73	AR
Price, George	VA	1880	020 WB-A/311	020 CTY
Price, George W.	020	1887	WB-A/514	CTY
Price, Gilliam G.	086	1887	WB-F/323	AR
Price, Isaac	065	1833	WB-G/130	AR
Price, Isabella	VA	1892	020 WB-B/141	020 CTY
Price, J. Allison	097	1887	WB-2/318	AR
Price, J. C.	085	1893	WB-3/17	CTY
Price, J. T.	026	1879	Copy	086 AR
Price, J. T.	026	1879	WB-2/182	AR
Price, Jacob A.S.	012	1869	WB-A/13	AR
Price, James	024	c1788	WB-A/76	AR
Price, James	070	1766	WB-C/331	AR
Price, James	086	1855	WB-E/286	AR
Price, James	024	1786	WB-B/31	AR
Price, James	028	1798	WB-B/48	AR
Price, James M.	084	1888	WB-E/381	CTY
Price, James P.	097	1866	WB-1/279	AR
Price, Jeremiah	084	1848	WB-C/76	CTY
Price, Jesse	037	1812	WB-E/47	AR
Price, Jesse	073	1803	WB-D/111	
Price, John	022	1895	WB-E/572	
Price, John	103	1865	RD-13/766	AR
Price, John	063	c1800	WB-1/378	
Price, John	086	1881	WB-F/163	AR
Price, John	063	1817	WB-2/41	
Price, John	065	c1749	WB-F/27	AR
Price, John	065	1814	WB-F/87	AR
Price, John	075	1800	WB-M1/41	AR
Price, John	009	c1806	OWB/439	AR
Price, John C.	097	1864	WB-1/234	AR
Price, John O.	020	1894	WB-B/164	CTY
Price, John, Sr.	065	1803	WB-F/16	AR
Price, Joseph	063	1789	WB-1/148	
Price, Joseph	070	1895	WB-G/356	AR
Price, Joseph	075	1893	WB-O/394	AR
Price, Joseph	005	1837	WB-B/76	AR
Price, Joseph	037	1815	WB-E/78	AR
Price, Joseph G.	086	1862	WB-E/404	AR
Price, Josiah L.	047	1892	WB-7/41	AR
Price, Linus M.	NJ	1893	013 WB-C/299	013 AR
Price, Louiza E.	037	1868	WB-G/312	AR
Price, Mannering	003	1877	WB-B/76	
Price, Martha	073	c1836	Orig. Only	AR
Price, Martha W.	097	1891	WB-2/420	AR
Price, Mary	065	1855	WB-I/255	AR
Price, Mary	065	1804	WB-F/43	AR
Price, Mary	103	1854	RD-11/557	AR
Price, Mary	020	1858	RB-R/592	AR
Price, Mary C.	047	c1861	WB-5/126	
Price, Mary J.	103	1896	WB-2/143	AR
Price, Mary M.	103	1886	WB-1/380	AR
Price, Matilda	097	1884	WB-2/246	AR
Price, Moses W. H.	097	1864	WB-1/232	AR
Price, Mountsier	005	1819	WB-2/129	AR
Price, Mycajah	010	1783	WB-C/61	AR
Price, Nancy	065	1855	WB-I/240	AR
Price, Nancy	099	1874	RB-35/262	AR
Price, Nancy S.	063	1889	WB-4/36	AR
Price, Needham	099	1870	RB-35/75	AR
Price, Noah	024	c1791	WB-A/77	AR
Price, Penelope	063	1830	WB-2/159	
Price, Peter	009	1734	Orig. Only	SS/AR
Price, Priscilla	063	1887	Orig. Only	AR
Price, R. T.	086	1853	WB-E/251	AR
Price, Redin J.	029	1889	WB-E/444	AR
Price, Reece	065	c1834	Copy	060 AR
Price, Reece	065	1834	WB-E/142	AR
Price, Reese	065	1811	WB-F/22	AR
Price, Reese	084	1830	WB-B/2	CTY
Price, Rice	070	c1756	SS 882/22	SS/AR
Price, Rice	070	1758	DB-D/319	
Price, Richard	070	1791	WB-C/340	AR
Price, Richard A.	070	1895	WB-G/449	AR
Price, Robert	086	1877	WB-E/149	AR
Price, Samuel B.	012	1900	WB-A/120 & 146	AR
Price, Saphronia	071	1879	WB-6/303	AR
Price, Sawney	084	1886	WB-E/345	CTY
Price, Simon T.	063	1872	WB-3/40	
Price, Susan Ann	070	1854	WB-C/580	AR
Price, Susan B.	020	1864	RB-T/63	CTY
Price, Thomas	056	c1781	WB-1/800	AR
Price, Thomas	037	1751	Orig. Only	SS/AR (N)
Price, Thomas	075	1696	SS 874.2/87	SS/AR
Price, Thomas	037	1781	WB-B/79	AR
Price, Thomas	071	1777	WB-1/297	
Price, Thomas	063	1835	WB-2/205	

Name	Co.	Date	Recorded Copy	Original
Price, Thomas W.	060	1831	WB-1/209	AR
Price, William	009	c1793	OWB/284	AR
Price, William	006	1874	WB-E/11	AR
Price, William	063	c1800	WB-1/378	
Price, William	077	1757	SS 880/180	SS/AR
Price, William	103	1818	RD-4/121	AR
Price, William	037	1793	WB-C/229	AR
Price, William	047	1832	WB-4/92	
Price, William	086	1870	WB-F/17	
Price, William	060	1835	WB-1/333	AR
Price, William	006	1892	WB-E/229	AR
Price, William G.	086	1886	WB-F/289	AR
Price, William H.	084	1860	WB-C/318	CTY
Price, William L.	104	1897	WB-7/27	AR
Price, William R.	097	1866	WB-1/280	AR
Price, William W.	020	1860	RB-S/282	AR
Price, Willie	056	1864	WB-2/68	AR
Price, Zachariah	056	1838	WB-2/259	AR
Prichard, Ann	073	1855	WB-G/105	
Prichard, Bannon	075	1772	WB-I/119	
Prichard, Caleb	057	1782	WB-A/20	AR
Prichard, David, Sr.	N	1697	Orig. Only	SS/AR
Prichard, Herbert	010	1738	LGB-4/#95	SS/AR
Prichard, James	075	1800	WB-M1/39	AR
Prichard, Jeremiah	057	1789	WB-A/2	AR
Prichard, Joseph	018	1848	WB-C/338	
Prichard, Joseph	075	1762	WB-H/27	
Prichard, Mary	075	1777	WB-K/2	
Prichard, Sarah	075	1857	WB-M2/50	AR
Prichard, Thomas	075	1760	WB-H/11	
Prichard, Thomas	075	1772	WB-H/155	
Prichard, William	073	1834	WB-E/313	
Prichard, William	073	1834	WB-E/313	AR
Prichett, Asa	096	1836	WB-2/127	
Pricklove, Elisabeth	077	1728	Orig. Only	SS/AR
Pricklove, Samuel	N	1702/3	SS 874.1/27	SS/AR
Priddey, Robert	044	1761	Orig. Only	CTY
Priddon, John	071	1850	WB-5/92	AR
Priddy, Elizabeth	044	1820	WB-8/335	CTY
Priddy, George	090	1830	WB-3/218	AR
Priddy, George	044	1821	WB-9/42	CTY
Priddy, Joseph	044	1835	WB-13/184	CTY
Priddy, Robert	044	1759	Orig. Only	CTY
Priddy, S. S.	090	1894	WB-6/343	AR
Pride, Halcott B.	071	1795	WB-2/86	AR
Pridgen, Abijah	069	1842	WB-1/459	AR
Pridgen, David	069	1813	WB-1/275	AR
Pridgen, Drewery	069	1835	WB-1/409	AR
Pridgen, Edwin G.	045	1892	WB-1/284	
Pridgen, Etheldred	027	1852	WB-A/66	AR
Pridgen, Glasgow	027	1879	WB-2/35	AR
Pridgen, Hannah	069	1894	WB-5/421	AR
Pridgen, Henry	011	1866	WB-2/20	
Pridgen, Isaiah	070	c1860	WB-E/183	AR
Pridgen, Jesse	069	1823	WB-1/312	AR
Pridgen, M. C.	105	1895	WB-3/140	AR
Pridgen, Margaret	069	1895	WB-5/469	AR
Pridgen, Margaret	070	1898	WB-H/122	AR
Pridgen, Mary Ann	059	1889	WB-A/556	CTY
Pridgen, Matthew	011	c1818	WB-1/11	
Pridgen, Robert	035	1869	WB-4/9	AR
Pridgen, William A.	069	1875	WB-5/37	AR
Pridgen, William H.	011	1885	WB-2/197	
Pridgeon, Gray R.	045	1866	WB-1/124	
Pridgeon, Mathew	087	c1820	WB-1/27	
Pridgeon, William	037	1762	WB-A/98	AR
Pridgeon, William E.	087	1882	WB-3/236	AR
Pridham, Noah	071	1770	WB-1/178	
Priech, Benedict	NJ	1879	039 WB-U/292	
Priest, Angus	082	1840	WB-2/529	AR
Priest, Mary	029	1856	WB-C/347	AR
Priest, Nelly	082	1898	WB-6/579	AR
Prieves, Abraham	030	1807	WB-2/308	
Prim, James	065	1892	WB-M/115	AR
Prim, Kitchen	065	1806	WB-F/45	AR
Prim, Mary	106	1889	WB-2/279	AR
Primm, Hessa	092	1848	Orig. Only	AR-Nunc.
Primrose, Ann	028	1865	WB-D/407	
Primrose, Ciciro	028	1868	WB-D/461	
Primrose, Temperance	073	1836	WB-E/368	AR
Prince, John	029	1782	Orig. Only	AR
Prince, Joseph	086	1792	Orig. Only	AR
Prince, Mary	099	1830	RB-21/194	
Prince, Miles H.	048	1882	WB-1/128	
Prince, Nathan	029	1821	WB-B/62	AR
Prince, Nicholas	022	c1812	WB-A/210	AR
Prince, Ruffin	022	1890	WB-E/447	AR
Prince, Theron E.	080	1893	WB-1/222	AR
Prince, William	022	1821	Orig. Only	AR
Prince, William L.	080	1878	WB-1/46	AR
Pringle, Alexander	028	1739/0	SS 877/170	SS/AR
Pringle, James	065	1818	WB-F/90	AR
Prior, Eleanor	046	1804	WB-A/294	AR
Prior, W. A.	026	1900	WB-3/104	AR
Prior, William	065	1830	WB-E/87	AR
Pritchard, Alsey	010	1852	WB-G/488	AR
Pritchard, Ann	073	c1855	Orig. Only	AR
Pritchard, Anna	075	1846	WB-N/199	AR
Pritchard, Arthur	102	1880	WB-A/16	AR
Pritchard, Arthur	075	1851	WB-N/237	AR
Pritchard, Benjamin	075	1821	WB-M1/336	AR
Pritchard, Benjamin	075	1752	Orig. Only	SS/AR
Pritchard, Benjamin	075	1791	WB-K/220	
Pritchard, Buckner	066	1884	Orig. Only	AR
Pritchard, Daniel	065	1764	WB-F/33	AR
Pritchard, David	075	1707	Orig. Only	SS/AR
Pritchard, David	075	1816	WB-M1/288	
Pritchard, David L.	018	1886	WB-E/142	AR
Pritchard, Delitha	010	1833	WB-G/221	AR
Pritchard, Elisha	075	1806	WB-M1/119	AR
Pritchard, H. M.	065	1872	Orig. Only	AR
Pritchard, Hannah	024	1838	WB-C/215	AR
Pritchard, Herbert	010	1799	WB-E/15	AR
Pritchard, Hugh	075	1823	WB-M1/389	AR
Pritchard, Isaac	075	1872	WB-O/37	AR
Pritchard, J. W.	073	1894	WB-I/21	CTY
Pritchard, James	010	1867	WB-H/197	AR
Pritchard, James	010	1786	WB-D/56	AR
Pritchard, James	075	1755	Orig. Only	SS/AR
Pritchard, James	010	1807	WB-F/69	AR
Pritchard, James B.	075	1883	WB-O/179	AR
Pritchard, Jessee	075	1881	WB-O/129	AR
Pritchard, Joane	075	1707/8	Orig. Only	SS/AR
Pritchard, John	075	1798	WB-M1/6	AR
Pritchard, John	018	1834	WB-C/168	
Pritchard, John	071	1777	WB-1/26	AR
Pritchard, John	081	1844	WB-8/81	AR
Pritchard, Jonathan	010	1838	WB-G/286	AR
Pritchard, Joseph	075	1825	WB-N/19	AR
Pritchard, Joseph	075	1816	WB-M1/279	

Name	Co.	Date	Recorded Copy	Original
Pritchard, Joshua	071	1815	WB-3/138	AR
Pritchard, Judith	071	1806	WB-2/328	AR
Pritchard, Lemuel	075	1850	WB-N/235	AR
Pritchard, Martha	075	1809	WB-M1/201	AR
Pritchard, Mary	075	1879	WB-O/111	AR
Pritchard, Mary W.	010	1892	WB-I/358	AR
Pritchard, Miles R.	075	1882	WB-O/151	AR
Pritchard, Pernecia	010	1890	WB-I/296	AR
Pritchard, Peter	075	1867	WB-M2/102	AR
Pritchard, Redden	010	1847	WB-G/421	AR
Pritchard, Rigdon	010	1810	WB-F/152	AR
Pritchard, Samuel	075	1795	WB-L/43	
Pritchard, Sarah	010	1888	WB-I/255	AR
Pritchard, Swan	071	1790	WB-1/395	AR
Pritchard, Thomas	075	1791	WB-K/232	
Pritchard, Thomas	075	1804	WB-M1/97	AR
Pritchard, Thomas H.	070	1896	WB-G/505	AR
Pritchard, Thomas H. H.	071	1840	WB-4/213	AR
Pritchard, William	010	1775	WB-B/21	AR
Pritchard, William B.	075	1890	WB-O/318	AR
Pritcher, Mary	077	1765	WB-C/55	AR
Pritchet, Thomas	022	1814	WB-A/249	AR
Pritchet, William	056	c1779	WB-2/258	AR
Pritchett, Abisha	009	1845	OB-E/475	AR
Pritchett, Abraham	009	c1809	OB-A/57	AR
Pritchett, Abraham	009	1750	SS 877/352	SS/AR
Pritchett, Christopher	047	1808	WB-3/480	
Pritchett, David	096	1867	WB-3/79	AR
Pritchett, Elizabeth	084	1863	WB-C/375	CTY
Pritchett, Ezekiel	046	1796	WB-A/291	AR
Pritchett, Franklin	046	1880	WB-E/279	AR
Pritchett, Isaac	084	1841	WB-B/261	CTY
Pritchett, Jacob	009	c1802	OWB/398	AR
Pritchett, James	009	c1772	OWB/111	AR
Pritchett, James C.	028	1890	WB-E/547	
Pritchett, Jenkins	046	1866	WB-D/296	AR
Pritchett, Jeptha	047	1848	WB-4/267	
Pritchett, Jeremiah	046	1840	WB-C/58	AR
Pritchett, John	047	1783	WB-3/45	
Pritchett, John M.	009	1847	OB-F/329	AR
Pritchett, John W.	096	1899	WB-4/167	AR
Pritchett, Joseph	084	c1788	OW/252	AR
Pritchett, Joshua	004	1895	WB-A/172	AR
Pritchett, Marget	009	1756	SS 880/200	SS/AR
Pritchett, Mary E.	057	1883	WB-C/99	AR
Pritchett, Penelope	009	c1798	OWB/344	AR
Pritchett, Peter	009	1772	OWB/110	AR
Pritchett, Polly	009	1837	OB-C2/1	AR
Pritchett, Priscilla	047	1834	WB-4/111	
Pritchett, Sary	009	c1734	Orig. Only	AR
Pritchett, Thomas	047	1851	WB-4/302	
Pritchett, Thomas	047	1796	WB-3/265	
Pritchett, Williams	047	1826	WB-4/22	
Pritchett, Zebulon	046	1842	WB-C/120	AR
Pritlow, Keziah	077	1791	WB-C/422	AR
Pritlowe, John	077	1728	Orig. Only	SS/AR
Prittyman, Mary	018	1826	WB-C/64	
Privatt, Jacob	099	1795	RB-3/145	AR
Privatt, Miles	099	1809	RB-8/437	AR
Privett, James	069	1895	WB-5/488	AR
Privett, James	054	c1809	WB-1/41	
Privett, John	039	1836	WB-K/106	AR
Privett, Jordan	054	c1805	WB-1/187	AR
Privett, Lida	054	1887	WB-5/180	CTY
Privett, Olive	099	1815	RB-12/114	AR
Privett, Stephen	105	1873	WB-2/136	AR
Privett, William	039	1873	WB-U/72	AR
Privett, William	024	1864	WB-D/24	AR
Privett, William C.	054	1897	WB-6/120	CTY
Privit, Noah	103	1832	RD-6/370	AR
Privit, William	099	1794	RB-3/64	AR
Privitt, Mary	099	1796	RB-3/220	AR
Privitt, Samuel	024	1838	WB-C/224	AR
Privitt, Wilie W.	103	1857	RD-12/324	AR
Privitt, Zachariah	099	1845	RB-26/4	AR
Probat, Mary	014	c1809	Orig. Only	AR-Copy
Proby, Sarah	075	1802	WB-M1/59	AR
Proby, William	075	1802	WB-M1/59	AR
Procter, Aaron	037	1821	WB-E/272	AR
Procter, John	005	1790	WB-A/5	AR
Proctor, Absalom	074	1875	WB-1/15 & 42	AR
Proctor, Absolum	037	1858	WB-G/165	AR
Proctor, Ambrose	077	1895	WB-H/274	AR
Proctor, Benjamin	060	1841	WB-2/114	AR
Proctor, Celia	105	1890	WB-2/556	AR
Proctor, Cherry	100	1786	WB-4/197	AR
Proctor, Elisabeth	037	1883	WB-G/649	
Proctor, Elizabeth	026	1860	WB-1/253	AR
Proctor, Elizabeth	018	1831	WB-C/126	
Proctor, F. M.	036	1895	WB-A/364	CTY
Proctor, Frederick	037	1881	WB-G/597	AR
Proctor, Hartwell S.	060	1893	WB-4/520	AR
Proctor, Jacob	037	1860	WB-G/195	AR
Proctor, John	105	1884	WB-2/374	AR
Proctor, John	099	1797	RB-3/285	AR
Proctor, John	008	1731/2	009 OWB/24	009 AR
Proctor, John	037	1794	WB-C/258	AR
Proctor, John	024	1834	WB-C/174	AR
Proctor, John	037	1772	WB-A/192	AR
Proctor, John S.	036	1891	WB-A/222	CTY
Proctor, Joseph	073	1860	WB-G/243	CTY
Proctor, Joseph	036	1898	WB-A/455	CTY
Proctor, Joseph	073	1860	WB-G/248	CTY
Proctor, Joseph	044	1843	WB-15/486	CTY
Proctor, Joshua	037	1785	WB-C/21	AR
Proctor, Lewey E.	037	1881	WB-G/589	AR
Proctor, Richard	073	1864	WB-G/462	CTY
Proctor, Samuel	018	1831	WB-C/123	
Proctor, Sterling	073	1877	WB-H/163	CTY
Proctor, Thomas	099	1797	RB-3/381	AR
Proctor, W. G.	037	1896	WB-H/352	AR
Proctor, William	026	1851	WB-1/123	AR
Proctor, William	037	1780	WB-B/48	AR
Proctor, William	036	1882	WB-A/7	CTY
Proctor, William B.	036	1883	WB-A/42	CTY
Profit, John	104	1814	WB-3/72	AR
Profitt, James C.	107	1871	WB-2/4	
Propst, Absalom	021	1897	WB-3/157	AR
Propst, Catherine	016	1846	WB-1/107	
Propst, Henry	016	1863	WB-2/94	AR
Propst, Henry	060	1799	Orig. Only	AR
Propst, Jane M.	021	1891	WB-2/525	
Propst, Lewis	060	1799	Orig. Only	AR
Propst, Mary M.	021	1894	WB-3/69	
Propst, Rhoda L.	021	1891	WB-2/530	AR
Propst, Valentine	085	1874	WB-1/253	CTY
Prother, Neamiah	006	1870	WB-D/109	AR
Prouse, Ane	N	c1682	Orig. Only	SS/AR
Provo, Benjamin	072	c1817	WB-A/109	AR
Provow, Isaiah M.	072	1875	WB-4/83	AR

Name	Co	Date	Recorded Copy	Original
Prowse, John	035	1791	WB-A/398	AR
Pruden, Anny	010	1831	WB-G/198	AR
Pruden, Celia	041	1893	WB-4/356	AR
Pruden, Esther	041	1824	WB-2/212	AR
Pruden, Henry	071	1878	WB-6/270	AR
Pruden, James	041	1823	WB-2/202	AR
Pruden, Lodowick	010	1815	WB-F/296	AR
Pruden, Lodowick	010	1815	Copy	041 AR
Pruden, Martha	010	1839	WB-G/312	AR
Pruden, Martha S.	051	1872	WB-C/72	AR
Pruden, William S.	010	1863	WB-H/124	AR
Pruett, John	044	1815	WB-7/516	CTY
Pruett, William	044	1837	WB-13/524	CTY-Nunc.
Pruit, Elizabeth	085	1818	WB-G/511	AR
Pruitt, Burell H.	092	1814	WB-3/110	AR
Pruitt, Elizabeth	103	1890	WB-1/526	AR
Pryor, Ezra	047	1830	WB-4/66	
Pryor, John	047	1770	WB-1/262	
Pryor, John	073	1772	WB-A/160	
Pryor, Mildred E.	047	1834	WB-4/112	
Pryor, Wiley	040	1889	WB-2/348	AR
Pryor, William	047	1836	WB-4/139	
Puce, Thomas	047	1795	WB-3/246	
Pucket, Eli	054	c1839	WB-2/211	AR
Pucket, Nancy	054	1842	WB-2/245	AR
Puckett, James	054	1821	Orig. Only	AR-Nunc.
Puckett, Jane	065	1890	WB-L/432	AR
Puckett, John H.	070	1866	WB-D/185	AR-Nunc.
Puckett, Shippe A..	100	1782	WB-4/150	AR-Nunc.
Puckette, Shippey A.	044	1888	WB-24/44	CTY
Puckit, William C.	096	1881	WB-4/91	
Puett, John	017	1872	Orig. Only	AR
Puett, W. I.	017	1884	WB-B/115	AR
Puett, William	017	1843	Orig. Only	AR
Puett, William	017	c1842	066 WB-1/46	066 AR
Pugh, Ann	047	1797	WB-3/277	
Pugh, Arnold	056	1824	WB-1/373	AR
Pugh, Christian	010	1881	WB-I/131	
Pugh, Crecy	087	1884	Orig. Only	AR
Pugh, Dameron	053	1838	WB-6/34	AR
Pugh, David	047	1791	WB-3/196	
Pugh, Eaton	071	1821	WB-3/259	AR
Pugh, Elizabeth	001	1879	WB-2/140	AR
Pugh, Elizabeth	010	1818	WB-G/34	AR
Pugh, Frances S.	010	1845	WB-G/375	AR
Pugh, Francis	010	1736	LGB-4/#34	SS/AR
Pugh, Francis	010	1807	WB-F/51	AR
Pugh, Frank P.	046	1894	WB-F/322	AR
Pugh, Henry	041	1833	WB-2/315	AR
Pugh, J. M.	099	1892	Copy	022 AR
Pugh, J. M.	099	1892	WB/115	AR
Pugh, James	081	1810	WB-3/176	AR
Pugh, John	N	1740	LGB-4/#112	SS/AR
Pugh, John	019	1842	WB-A/102	AR
Pugh, John A.	022	1892	WB-E/483	AR
Pugh, John Hill	063	1817	WB-2/44	
Pugh, John R.	001	1877	WB-2/118	AR
Pugh, John W.	071	1900	WB-7/463	AR
Pugh, Joseph H.	010	1807	WB-F/38	AR
Pugh, Joseph S.	010	1827	WB-G/157	AR
Pugh, Julias	006	1845	WB-A/24	AR
Pugh, Lewis B.	079	c1855	WB-1/19	AR
Pugh, Little J.	030	1845	WB-4/114	
Pugh, Margaret A.	059	1887	WB-A/501	CTY

Name	Co	Date	Recorded Copy	Original
Pugh, Margaret A.	059	1887	Copy	079 AR
Pugh, Martha D.	039	1822	WB-G/90	
Pugh, Marthy D.	063	c1821	WB-2/104	
Pugh, Rachel	022	1862	WB-D/93	AR
Pugh, S. M.	031	1881	WB-1/20	AR
Pugh, Thomas	081	1798	WB-2/34	AR
Pugh, Thomas	063	1836	WB-2/220	
Pugh, Thomas	010	1806	WB-F/26	AR
Pugh, Thomas	022	1846	WB-C/190	AR
Pugh, Thomas	030	1784	WB-1/177	
Pugh, Thomas	081	1846	WB-8/337	AR
Pugh, Thomas W.	010	1802	WB-E/179	AR
Pugh, Tignal	056	1818	WB-1/296	AR
Pugh, Whitmel S.	010	1869	WB-H/202	AR
Pugh, William	010	1809	WB-F/101	AR
Pugh, William	004	1881	WB-A/49	AR
Pugh, William	069	1798	Orig. Only	AR
Pulham, Thomas	086	1790	Orig. Only	AR
Pulle, Martha	105	1869	WB-2/3	
Pullen, Jeremiah	099	1857	RB-30/299	AR
Pullen, John	099	1852	RB-28/146	AR
Pullen, John, Sr.	099	1809	RB-8/461	AR
Pullen, Mrs. N. A.	099	1888	WB-B/294	AR
Pullen, R. S.	099	1895	WB-C/412	AR
Pullen, Roderick	047	1873	WB-6/89	AR
Pullen, Turner	099	1868	RB-35/2	AR
Pullen, Willie	069	1860	WB-1/565	AR
Pulley, Elizabeth	047	1811	WB-3/522	
Pulley, Thomas	099	1816	RB-12/265	AR
Pulliam, Ann	099	1849	RB-26/556	AR
Pulliam, B. G.	020	1878	WB-A/245	CTY
Pulliam, Barnet	044	1813	WB-7/342	CTY
Pulliam, Benjamin W.	090	1875	WB-6/68	AR
Pulliam, Byrd	078	1836	WI-13/151	
Pulliam, Elizabeth	044	1824	WB-9/347	CTY
Pulliam, Elizabeth	099	1860	RB-31/433	
Pulliam, Elizabeth	078	1819	WI-8/247	
Pulliam, James	078	1799	WI-2/173	
Pulliam, James H.	084	1863	WB-C/380	CTY
Pulliam, John	044	1810	WB-7/114	CTY
Pulliam, John	039	1816	WB-E/35	AR
Pulliam, John	044	1810	Copy	073 AR
Pulliam, Joseph	020	1844	RB-P/109	
Pulliam, Joseph	020	1822	RB-I/147	AR
Pulliam, Mary	099	1852	RB-28/155	AR
Pulliam, R. W.	013	1886	WB-B/369	AR
Pulliam, Sarah S.	099	1843	RB-25/157	AR
Pulliam, William P.	090	1874	WB-6/58	
Pullin, William	047	1795	WB-3/240	
Pumphrey, Silvenus	035	1778	WB-A/399	AR
Purcell, Alexander	083	1882	WB-3/277	AR
Purcell, Clarkie S.	083	1889	WB-3/441	AR
Purcell, Harriet	083	1896	WB-4/111	AR
Purcell, Malcom	083	1878	WB-3/141 & 215	AR
Purcell, Neall	028	1753	SS 877/14	SS/AR
Purdam, Benjamin	085	1811	WB-G/212	AR
Purdey, Mary	030	1827	WB-3/230	
Purdie, Ann M.	011	1878	WB-2/111	
Purdie, James B.	011	c1834	WB-1/17	
Purdie, James S.	011	c1817	WB-2/323	
Purdie, John W.	011	1884	WB-2/179	
Purdie, Sarah	051	1850	WB-A/310	
Purdy, George	N	1733	SS 876/276	SS/AR
Purdy, Mary	030	1826	WB-3/216	

Name	Co.	Date	Recorded Copy	Original
Purdy, Sarah	071	1820	WB-3/228	AR
Purdy, William	071	1762	WB-1/68	
Purefoy, Ellen	073	c1881	WB-H/313	AR
Purefoy, George W.	073	1880	WB-H/242	CTY
Purefoy, James S.	099	1889	WB-B/324	
Purefoy, Nead	073	1880	WB-H/268	CTY
Purguson, Martha E.	084	1900	WB-F/169	CTY
Purify, David	028	1785	WB-A/96	AR
Purify, Nicholas	028	1776	Orig. Only	AR
Purify, Thomas	028	1827	WB-C/288	AR
Purington, Robert F.	047	1837	WB-4/151	
Purkins, David	008	1733	Orig. Only	SS/AR
Purnal, John	047	1796	WB-3/265	
Purnell, Henry	047	1816	WB-3/591	
Purnell, Mary	047	1838	WB-4/175	
Purnell, William	047	1829	WB-4/51	
Purnell, William D.	047	1844	WB-4/227	
Pursel, William	024	c1778	WB-A/210	AR
Pursell, David	084	c1788	OW/274	AR
Pursell, George	084	1860	WB-C/349	CTY
Pursell, John	009	c1793	OWB/295	AR
Pursell, Noah	084	1838	WB-B/184	CTY
Purser, Ann Maria	028	1832	Orig. Only	AR
Purser, Coventer	028	1819	Copy	073 AR
Purser, Coventer	028	1819	WB-C/187	AR
Purser, John	065	1826	WB-F/102	AR
Purser, Robert	008	1733	SS 876/287	SS/AR
Purser, Robert	009	1821	OB-A/310	AR
Purser, Robert	009	c1807	OWB/446	AR
Pursley, Nathan	075	1761	WB-I/4	AR
Purviance, David	016	1839	PQS.6/49	
Purviance, David C.	016	1870	WB-3/21	
Purvis, Eliza Jane	019	1890	WB-B/200	AR
Purvis, Elizabeth	063	1866	WB-2/545	
Purvis, Elizabeth	063	1854	WB-2/408	
Purvis, George	022	1821	WB-B/38	AR
Purvis, James	104	1857	WB-5/175	
Purvis, James	010	1785	WB-D/39	AR
Purvis, James R.	063	1866	WB-2/496	
Purvis, Jason	063	1851	WB-2/374	
Purvis, John W.	063	1880	WB-3/184	
Purvis, Lewis	037	1851	WB-F/454	AR
Purvis, Lewis, Sr.	063	1826	WB-2/117	
Purvis, Mildred	039	1861	WB-R/119	AR
Purvis, Moses	010	1812	WB-F/206	AR
Purvis, Robert	022	1818	WB-A/297 & 313	
Purvis, Robert L.	068	1882	WB-D/184	
Purvis, Roderick	063	1858	WB-2/453	
Purvis, William	063	c1798	WB-1/344	
Puryear, James	044	1826	WB-10/240	CTY
Puryear, John	044	1835	WB-13/263	CTY
Puryear, John	090	1809	WB-2/103	AR
Puryear, John	046	1894	WB-F/322	AR
Puryear, Robert	037	1759	SS 881/204	SS/AR
Puryear, Robert D.	044	1863	WB-21/671	CTY
Puryear, Seymour	001	1880	WB-2/155	
Puryear, William	044	1838	WB-14/322	CTY
Pussell, Edward	069	1790	WB-1/63	AR
Pusser, Hugh	097	1864	WB-1/242	AR
Putman, Barnet	026	1860	WB-1/248	AR
Putman, David	026	1890	WB-2/421	AR
Putman, Griggs	026	1850	WB-1/114	AR
Putman, Jenila	026	1855	WB-1/189	AR
Putman, Sarah Ann	026	1867	WB-1/413	AR
Putman, T. J.	026	1870	WB-2/26	AR
Putman, Ursula	026	1897	WB-2/546	AR
Putman, William	026	1899	WB-3/57	AR
Putman, Willis	026	1846	WB-1/56	AR
Putnell, John	009	c1782	OWB/171	AR
Putnell, John	009	c1789	OWB/236	AR
Putnell, Stephen	009	c1798	OWB/348	AR
Putnell, William	008	1733	SS 876/291	SS/AR
Putney, Catharine	100	1836	WB-35/233	AR
Putney, John B.	071	1870	WB-6/54	AR
Putney, Richard	099	1814	RB-11/239	AR
Putney, Richard	071	1819	WB-3/220	AR
Putney, Sarah L. D.	071	1886	WB-6/532	AR
Pyatt, John D.	064	1870	WB-2/3	AR
Pyatt, Joseph	066	1865	Orig. Only	AR
Pybas, Henry	057	c1782	WB-A/55	AR
Pyle, James	073	1823	WB-E/40	AR
Pyle, James F.	073	1819	WB-D/562	AR
Pyle, John	022	c1799	WB-A/49	AR
Pyle, Samuel	073	1802	WB-D/73	AR
Pyler, Rebecca S.	066	1900	Orig. Only	AR
Pyles, Joseph	046	1839	WB-C/41	AR
Pyron, John M.	065	1882	WB-K/457	AR
Pyron, Mary Ann	065	1883	WB-K/512	AR
Pyron, Samuel	097	1869	WB-2/12	
Pyron, Sarah A.	097	1887	WB-2/316	AR
Quackenbush, Henry M.	001	1897	WB-3/185	AR
Quait, William	046	1805	WB-A/304	
Quakenbush, Henry	022	1823	WB-B/102	AR
Quakenbush, Peter, Sr.	022	c1793	RB-1/47	
Qualls, Chesley	044	1875	WB-23/169	CTY
Qualls, Elizabeth	044	c1858	WB-23/11	CTY
Qualls, James	047	1795	WB-3/240	AR
Qualls, Mary	047	1808	WB-3/478	AR
Qualls, Peter	047	1794	WB-3/220	AR
Qualls, William	044	1865	WB-22/374	CTY
Quay, Jane	016	1859	WB-2/56	
Queen, Francies	054	1803	Orig. Only	AR
Queen, Henson	086	1826	WQB-D/53	AR
Queen, James	086	1845	WB-E/151	AR
Queen, James A.	026	1883	WB-2/254	AR
Queen, James S.	055	1893	WB-A/117	
Queen, Jesse	003	1870	WB-B/13	AR
Queen, John	049	1852	WB-2/191	AR
Queen, John B.	055	1862	PQS.2/466	
Queen, Joseph	104	1827	WB-4/109	AR
Queen, Margaret	054	c1831	WB-2/119	AR
Queen, Mitchel	033	1897	WB-2/222	CTY
Query, Alexander	016	1803	WB-A/114	
Query, Cyrus	065	1846	WB-I/50	AR
Query, Elizabeth	065	1864	WB-J/176	AR
Query, H. A.	065	1888	WB-L/314	AR
Query, Henderson	065	1877	WB-K/278	AR
Query, J. L.	016	1898	WB-4/317	AR
Query, James	016	1844	WB-1/35	
Query, James A.	065	1869	WB-K/13	AR
Query, Jane P.	016	1854	WB-1/235	
Query, John G.	065	1860	WB-J/78	AR
Query, Lester H.	016	1886	WB-3/499	AR
Query, Robert	065	1847	WB-I/111	AR
Queslin, Henry	NY	1890	068 WB-D/339	
Quickle, Elizabeth	060	1860	WB-3/28	AR
Quickle, Michael	060	1850	WB-2/333	AR
Quickle, Michael	060	1818	Orig. Only	AR
Quidley, Nathaniel	030	1818	WB-3/104	

Name	Co.	Date	Recorded Copy	Original
Quidley, Thomas	030	1799	WB-2/132	
Quidley, William	030	1807	WB-2/310	
Quidly, Elizabeth	053	1828	WB-4/358	AR
Quilling, Daniel	057	1785	WB-A/48	AR
Quimby, George H.	MA	1896	068 WB-D/479	068 CTY
Quin, Edward	009	1834	OWB/514	AR
Quin, Hugh	051	1871	WB-C/44	AR
Quin, William	037	1790	WB-C/153	AR
Quinby, Abraham	071	1806	WB-2/322	
Quince, Ann	070	1818	WB-C/354	AR
Quince, John	070	1776	WB-C/352	AR
Quince, Nancy	070	1866	WB-D/178	AR
Quince, Richard	070	1809	WB-AB/130	AR
Quince, Richard	070	1778	WB-C/354	AR
Quince, Susannah	070	1812	WB-AB/180	AR
Quince, Thomas	022	1894	WB-E/571	AR
Quince, William	028	1802	WB-B/155	AR
Quine, Henry	020	1816	RB-G/130	
Quine, William	020	1792	RB-B/457	AR
Quinerly, John R.	079	1872	WB-2/74	AR
Quinerly, S. S.	059	1895	WB-B/143	CTY
Quinn, Aaron	026	1867	WB-1/414	AR
Quinn, Easter	035	1844	Orig. Only	AR
Quinn, Eliza E.	040	1892	WB-2/413	AR
Quinn, Ichabod	035	1862	WB-3/60	AR
Quinn, James	040	1878	WB-2/134	AR
Quinn, Jesse	035	1860	WB-3/12	AR
Quinn, John W.	040	1876	WB-2/101	AR
Quinn, Loftin	019	1774	Orig. Only	SS/AR
Quinn, Thomas F.	040	c1863	WB-1/162	
Rabb, John	093	1874	WB-1/142	
Rabb, Judith	060	1840	WB-2/59	
Rabb, Thomas	030	1784	WB-1/175	
Raborn, William B.	065	1874	WB-K/135	AR
Raburn, James M.	064	1897	WB-2/392	AR
Raby, Adam	010	1766	WB-A/66	AR
Raby, Blake	010	1825	WB-G/136	AR
Raby, Blake D.	010	1841	WB-G/331	AR
Raby, Luke	010	1789	WB-D/111	AR
Rachels, Starling	082	1849	WB-4/25	AR
Rachels, Starling	082	1864	WB-4/190	AR
Rachley, John H.	069	1882	WB-5/121	AR
Rackley, Cherry	069	1858	WB-1/558	AR
Rackley, Francis	069	1837	WB-1/416	AR
Rackley, Francis	069	1888	WB-5/305	AR
Rackley, John	015	1769	100 WB-1/86	AR
Rackley, Nancy	087	1835	WB-1/167	AR
Rackley, Persons	069	1814	WB-1/261	AR
Rackley, W. S.	029	1890	WB-E/503	AR
Rackly, Margaret	069	1896	WB-5/573	AR
Racksaker, Daniel	075	1733	SS 876/279	SS/AR
Radcliffe, Robert S.	070	1884	WB-E/538	AR
Radcliffe, Thomas R.	070	1892	WB-F/522	AR
Rader, Adam	060	1818	Orig. Only	AR
Rader, Caleb	021	1856	WB-1/123	AR
Rader, Daniel	021	1876	WB-2/156	AR
Radford, Bettie E.	056	1898	WB-4/89	AR
Radford, John	062	1852	WB-A/5	
Radford, Mary	103	1839	RD-7/442	AR
Rae, William	039	1896	WB-V/80	
Rafield, Fresvan	060	1871	WB-4/80	
Ragan, Charles	081	1900	WB-17/114	
Ragan, John	099	1858	RB-31/49	AR
Ragan, Nannie E.	046	1892	WB-F/209	AR
Ragan, Thomas	046	1882	WB-E/332	AR

Name	Co.	Date	Recorded Copy	Original
Ragans, Jacob J.	032	1899	WB-4/405	AR
Ragland, Amey	044	1790	WB-2/151	CTY
Ragland, Evan	044	1778	WB-1/199	
Ragland, Frederick	071	1758	SS 882/25	SS/AR
Ragland, George	071	1771	WB-1/195	
Ragland, Hudson	044	1820	WB-8/334	CTY
Ragland, John D.	VA	1872	Copy	099 AR
Ragland, Reuben	044	1805	WB-6/226	CTY
Ragland, Sallie A.	099	1875	RB-35/299	AR
Ragland, Stephen	071	1747	Orig. Only	SS/AR
Ragland, William	022	1789	RB-1/35	AR
Ragland, William	071	1783	WB-1/270	
Ragland, William	044	1825	WB-9/397	CTY
Raglin, George W.	029	c1835	Orig. Only	AR
Raiborn, William	099	1813	RB-11/100	AR
Raiford, James	082	1830	WB-2/4	AR
Raiford, Matthew	011	1758	Orig. Only	SS/AR
Raiford, Philip	056	1808	WB-1/208	AR
Raiford, Phillip	056	1844	WB-1/565	AR
Raiford, Sarah	056	1821	WB-1/434	AR
Raiford, William	103	1798	WI-B/196	AR
Railey, Abner	084	1817	WB-A/277	CTY
Railey, Susan	051	c1886	Orig. Only	AR
Railsback, Henry	085	1816	WB-G/405	AR
Raine, R. K.	084	1869	WB-E/13	CTY
Rainer, Amey	087	1834	WB-1/153	AR
Rainer, Stephen	035	1842	Orig. Only	AR
Rainey, Bartlet	071	1869	WB-6/43	AR
Rainey, Beckham	100	1791	WB-5/217	AR
Rainey, Benjamin	073	1811	WB-D/286	
Rainey, David	073	1802	WB-D/68	AR
Rainey, George	020	1781	RB-A/168	AR
Rainey, James	020	1841	RB-O/254	AR
Rainey, John	020	1782	RB-A/183	AR-Nunc.
Rainey, John G.	084	1885	WB-E/312	CTY
Rainey, Tabitha E.	084	1895	WB-F/34	CTY
Rainey, William	071	1799	WB-2/187	AR
Rains, Ishmael	081	1790	WB-1/99	AR
Rains, Mary	081	1847	WB-8/367	AR
Rains, Robert	081	1794	WB-2/6	AR
Rains, Robert	081	1829	WB-6/31	AR
Rains, William	081	1864	WB-13/1	AR
Rainwater, John	092	1777	WB-1/72	AR
Raley, Sarah	084	1827	WB-B/49	CTY
Ralston, J. Grier	PA	1880	065 WB-K/575	065 AR
Ralston, Samuel	079	c1829	SC/02913	AR-Copy
Raman, William	002	c1713	Orig. Only	SS/AR
Ramcke, Frederick	024	1800	WB-B/246	AR
Ramer, Daniel W.	085	1864	WB-K/347	AR
Ramer, Margaret	085	1872	WB-1/107	CTY
Ramer, Michael	085	1858	WB-K/269	AR
Ramey, Joseph	092	1859	WB-5/30	
Ramey, William	065	1796	WB-F/126	AR
Raminger, Mary	090	1848	WB-4/255	
Rammage, Darias	068	1809	WB-A/265	
Ramsay, Allen	024	c1799	WB-A/326	AR
Ramsay, Arnetta E.	071	1883	WB-6/405	AR
Ramsay, Francis	029	1793	Orig. Only	AR
Ramsay, George A.	076	1890	WB-A1/110	AR
Ramsay, J. Alston	021	1900	WB-3/262	AR
Ramsay, Jacob S.	054	1892	WB-5/431	CTY
Ramsay, John	071	1882	WB-6/395	AR
Ramsay, Lydia C.	085	1900	WB-3/375	CTY
Ramsay, Sarah Jane	085	1896	WB-3/127	CTY
Ramsay, W. C.	097	1892	WB-2/435	AR

Name	Co.	Date	Recorded Copy	Original
Ramsay, William T.	013	1863	WB-A/219	
Ramseur, Frederick	026	1891	WB-2/419	AR
Ramsey, Ambrose	022	c1803	WB-B/3	AR
Ramsey, Andrew	054	1844	WB-2/301	AR
Ramsey, Artemesea	075	1846	WB-N/201	
Ramsey, Catherine	014	1869	WB-2/48	AR
Ramsey, David	054	1857	WB-3/112	AR
Ramsey, David	054	c1815	WB-1/386	AR
Ramsey, Edmond	078	1883	WB-19/147	AR
Ramsey, Eliza	022	1824	WB-B/80	AR
Ramsey, Henry	051	1827	WB-A/28	
Ramsey, James	068	1823	WB-B/31	
Ramsey, James	060	1840	WB-2/45	AR
Ramsey, Jane K.	054	1860	WB-3/156	AR
Ramsey, Jasper N.	062	1900	WB-B/222	AR
Ramsey, Jean	054	c1790	WB-1/203	
Ramsey, John	022	c1801	WB-B/1	AR
Ramsey, John	022	c1815	Orig. Only	AR
Ramsey, John	010	1806	WB-F/4	AR
Ramsey, John	065	1776	WB-F/113	AR
Ramsey, John	060	1790	Orig. Only	AR
Ramsey, Mary	054	1847	WB-3/17	AR
Ramsey, Mary	078	1863	WB-18/336	AR
Ramsey, R. V.	062	1896	WB-B/189	AR
Ramsey, Robert	060	1834	WB-1/314	AR
Ramsey, Robert	046	1799	WB-A/317	AR
Ramsey, Robert	054	c1823	WB-2/74	AR
Ramsey, Robert	085	c1783	WB-C/162	AR
Ramsey, Robert G.	060	1869	WB-4/17	AR
Ramsey, Sally	010	1825	WB-G/132	AR
Ramsey, Samuel	072	c1768	RW/L36	AR
Ramsey, Thomas	070	1815	WB-AB/218	AR
Ramsey, W. W.	078	1897	WB-19/436	AR
Ramsey, William	060	1828	WB-1/93	AR
Ramsey, William	078	1852	WB-17/3	AR
Ramsey, William	022	1803	WB-A/78	AR
Ramsour, Alfred A.	060	1864	WB-3/63 & 81	AR
Ramsour, Caleb H.	060	1863	WB-3/62	AR
Ramsour, David	060	1786	Orig. Only	AR
Ramsour, David	060	1842	WB-2/162	AR
Ramsour, David	060	1844	WB-2/124	AR
Ramsour, David J.	021	1864	WB-1/196	AR
Ramsour, E. G.	060	1885	WB-4/332	AR
Ramsour, Eli	054	c1838	WB-2/191	AR
Ramsour, Elisha J.	021	1871	WB-2/50	AR
Ramsour, Franklin	060	1884	WB-4/289	AR
Ramsour, George M.	060	1856	WB-2/411	AR
Ramsour, Henry	060	1828	WB-1/99	AR
Ramsour, Henry	065	c1764	WB-F/109	AR
Ramsour, Jacob	060	1787	Orig. Only	AR-Nunc.
Ramsour, Jacob	060	1863	WB-3/48	AR
Ramsour, John	060	1857	WB-3/6	AR
Ramsour, John	065	c1764	WB-F/59	AR
Ramsour, John	060	1842	WB-2/151	AR
Ramsour, John	021	1844	WB-1/19	AR
Ramsour, Malvina	060	1890	WB-4/440	AR
Ramsour, Mary	060	1818	Orig. Only	AR
Ramsour, S. D.	060	1865	WB-3/85	
Ramsour, Solomon	021	1845	WB-1/34	AR
Ran, Mike	047	1850	WB-4/295	AR
Rand, Betsey	030	1843	WB-4/98	
Rand, Harrison	099	1861	RB-32/73	AR
Rand, John	099	1783	RB-1/158	
Rand, Lucy B.	099	1893	WB-C/199	AR
Rand, Lucy B.	099	1874	RB-35/245	
Rand, Walter	099	1813	RB-11/22	AR
Rand, William	099	1874	RB-35/244	
Randal, Blewford	026	1846	WB-1/50	AR
Randall, Esther	037	1894	WB-H/275	AR
Randall, James M.	013	1893	WB-C/252	AR
Randall, Payton	100	1799	WB-10/147	AR-Nunc.
Randall, William	086	1864	WB-E/447	AR
Randalll, Andrass	073	c1777	WB-B/20	AR
Randel, Francis	024	c1795	WB-A/292	
Randel, Kissiah	026	1853	WB-1/154	AR
Randel, William	054	c1821	WB-1A/36	AR
Randel, William	057	1793	WB-A/154	AR
Randell, Ann	028	1805	WB-B/227	AR
Randle, Mary A.	085	1894	WB-3/30	
Randleman, John H.	038	1865	WB-1/250	AR
Randleman, Julia E.	081	1888	WB-16/76	AR
Randolph, Bryan	071	1838	WB-4/175	AR
Randolph, David	037	1829	WB-F/101	AR
Randolph, Edward H.	085	1827	WB-H/386	AR
Randolph, Elizabeth	071	1808	WB-3/3	AR
Randolph, F. J.	045	1893	WB-1/240	AR
Randolph, Giles	071	1792	WB-2/2	AR
Randolph, James, Sr.	020	1797	RB-C/251	AR
Randolph, John	071	1866	WB-5/333	AR
Randolph, John	028	1885	WB-E/417	
Randolph, John	079	1890	WB-2/523	AR
Randolph, Louisa	079	c1857	WB-1/103	AR
Randolph, Mary	079	1881	WB-2/234	AR
Randolph, Mary V.	013	1890	WB-B/583	AR
Randolph, Penelope	071	1799	Orig. Only	AR
Randolph, Phebe	107	1892	WB-2/72	
Randolph, Prudence	079	1900	WB-3/213	AR
Randolph, Reuben	066	1895	WB-1/141	AR
Randolph, William	092	1848	WB-4/283	
Raney, David	005	1808	WB-2/131	AR
Raney, Mary	073	1821	WB-D/590	AR
Raney, Thomas H.	071	1826	WB-4/18	AR
Rank, Charles B.	038	1897	WB-4/28	AR
Rank, Elizabeth	090	1829	WB-3/206	AR
Rank, Gottlob	090	1822	WB-3/74	AR
Rank, John, Sr.	038	1848	WB-1/17	AR
Rank, Michael	090	1813	WB-2/147	AR
Rankhorn, Sarah	075	1832	WB-N/75	AR
Rankin, Alexander	040	1849	WB-1/14	
Rankin, Ann	070	1843	WB-AB/394	AR
Rankin, David	054	c1781	WB-1/200	AR
Rankin, George	085	1760	WB-A/141	AR
Rankin, Hannah	046	1814	WB-A/325	AR
Rankin, James	060	1833	WB-1/273	AR
Rankin, James	054	c1854	WB-3/91	AR
Rankin, Jane	046	1826	WB-B/239	AR
Rankin, Jesse	017	1876	WB-B/64	AR
Rankin, John	085	1859	WB-K/265	AR
Rankin, John	046	1814	WB-A/324	AR
Rankin, John	040	1876	WB-2/107	AR
Rankin, John C.	046	1881	WB-E/309	AR
Rankin, John D.	040	1871	WB-2/27	AR
Rankin, John M.	060	1884	WB-4/298	AR
Rankin, Leven	046	1897	WB-F/574	AR
Rankin, Louisa M.	017	1896	WB-B/265	AR
Rankin, Martha J.	065	1899	WB-N/209	AR
Rankin, Mary	046	c1897	Orig. Only	AR
Rankin, Mildred J.	046	1891	WB-F/165	AR
Rankin, Owen H.	070	1852	WB-C/538	AR
Rankin, Richard	040	1899	WB-3/55	

Name	Co.	Date	Recorded Copy	Original	Name	Co.	Date	Recorded Copy	Original
Rankin, Robert	016	1866	WB-D/299	AR	Rascoe, William M.	084	1892	WB-E/522	CTY
Rankin, Robert	046	1795	WB-A/316	AR	Rash, Asa	104	1829	WB-4/127	AR
Rankin, Samuel	060	1826	WB-1/37	AR	Rash, Charles	054	c1831	WB-2/105	AR
Rankin, Samuel D.	085	1860	WB-K/278	AR	Rash, Daniel A.	054	1877	WB-4/347	
Rankin, Samuel N.	065	1899	WB-N/209	AR	Rash, Henry	104	1874	WB-6/90	AR
Rankin, Sarah	054	1843	WB-2/274	AR	Rash, Levi	104	1869	WB-6/11	AR
Rankin, Thomas	046	1853	WB-C/397	AR	Rash, Luke	104	1843	WB-4/286	AR
Rankin, Thomas	046	1899	WB-G/150	AR	Rash, Mary B.	104	1886	WB-6/267	AR
Rankin, Watson W.	016	c1858	WB-2/36		Rash, Milley	104	1829	WB-4/133	
Rankin, William	046	1829	WB-B/397	AR	Rash, Nancy	104	1897	WB-7/36	AR
Rankin, William	046	1804	WB-A/318	AR	Rash, Sally M.	103	1873	WB-6/80	AR
Rankin, William	021	1860	WB-1/154	AR	Rash, W. G.	054	1884	WB-5/12	CTY
Rankin, William D.	013	1880	WB-B/220	AR	Rash, William B.	106	c1857	WB-1/60	AR
Ransdell, Emily F.	069	1887	WB-5/260	AR	Rasor, Edward	010	1776	WB-B/48	AR
Ransom, Amy	039	1807	WB-C/86		Rasor, Frances	010	1748	Orig. Only	SS/AR
Ransom, John	039	c1790	WB-A/114	AR	Ratchford, Esther	040	1885	WB-2/238	AR
Ransom, Joseph	090	1826	WB-3/146	AR-Nunc.	Ratchford, George J.	040	1884	WB-2/227	
Ransom, Joseph	009	1812	OB-A/229	AR	Ratchford, John	040	1888	WB-2/302	
Ransom, Martin	083	1894	WB-4/59	AR	Ratchford, Joseph	040	1870	WB-2/16	AR
Ransom, Priscilla	100	1827	WB-31/116	AR	Ratchford, Mary	060	1830	WB-1/161	AR
Ransom, Sarah	009	1840	OB-C2/369	AR	Ratchford, Moses	060	1822	Orig. Only	AR
Ransom, Seymour	100	1820	WB-22/458	AR	Ratchford, Robert C.	040	1884	WB-2/227	AR
Ransom, Thomas	038	1868	WB-2/2	AR	Ratcliff, Eveline	009	1874	WB-1/130	
Ransom, William	039	1841	WB-L/35		Ratcliff, James	070	1782	WB-C/364	AR-Nunc.
Ransom, William T.	100	1846	WB-39/196	AR	Ratcliff, Jeremiah	049	1890	WB-2/240	AR
Rantleman, Christopher	085	N. D.	WB-A/254		Ratcliff, John	022	c1796	WB-A/48	AR
Rany, William	073	1813	WB-D/378	AR	Ratcliff, Louisa J.	049	1900	WB-2/441	AR
Rapalje, Williamson	NY	1897	072 WB-4/354	072 AR	Ratcliff, Mary	070	1803	WB-C/378	AR
Rape, Peter	065	1832	WB-G/78	AR	Ratcliff, Thomas	022	1787	WB-B/268	AR
Rape, Peter, Sr.	065	1825	WB-F/138	AR	Rathbone, Edith	049	1899	WB-2/439	AR
Rape, Susannah	097	c1869	WB-2/4		Rathbun, Jacob	028	1794	WB-A/311	AR
Raper, Caleb	075	1844	WB-N/185	AR	Ratledge, Thomas	033	1841	WB-1/36	AR
Raper, Cornelius	075	1813	WB-M1/249	AR	Ratley, Benjamin	060	1791	Orig. Only	AR
Raper, Davis	038	1852	WB-1/37	AR	Ratlif, Damaris	N	1734	SS 876/373	SS/AR
Raper, Enoch	077	1789	WB-C/395	AR	Ratlif, Samuel	N	1733	SS 876/318	SS/AR
Raper, John	077	1791	WB-C/417	AR	Ratliff, Charles H.	009	1869	WB-1/27	AR
Raper, Joseph	077	1802	WB-E/168	AR	Ratliff, Elijah	005	1865	WB-C/208	AR
Raper, Josiah	075	1762	WB-H/31	AR	Ratliff, Ephraim	009	1869	WB-1/9	CTY
Raper, Manlove R.	046	1899	WB-G/128	AR	Ratliff, James	005	1833	WB-B/36	AR
Raper, Mary	075	1816	WB-M1/287	AR	Ratliff, James H.	005	1849	WB-C/9	AR
Raper, Robert	046	1872	Orig. Only	AR	Ratliff, Jesse	081	1797	WB-1/44	AR-=Nunc.
Raper, Thomas	090	1808	WB-2/94	AR					
Raper, William	046	1859	WB-C/540	AR	Ratliff, Joseph	077	1787	WB-C/349	AR
Raper, William	046	1795	WB-A/313	AR	Ratliff, Mary Jane	005	1878	WB-D/72	AR
Rapheld, William	096	1757	SS 882/70	SS/AR	Ratliff, Peninah	075	1807	WB-M1/170	AR-Nunc.
Rasberry, Anna Maria	070	1897	WB-H/94	AR	Ratliff, Rebecca	005	1866	WB-C/235	AR
Rasberry, John	051	1860	WB-B/27		Ratliff, Richard	077	1724	Orig. Only	SS/AR
Rasberry, Margaret	079	1900	WB-3/224	AR	Ratliff, Susannah	005	1865	WB-C/222	AR
Rasberry, Mourning	051	1868	WB-B/100	AR	Ratliff, Will	005	1887	WB-D/205	AR
Rasbuary, John	010	1749	Orig. Only	SS/AR	Ratliff, William	005	c1777	WB-1/26	
Rasche, Daniel	053	c1806	RW-1/427		Ratliff, William	005	1840	WB-B/112	AR
Rasco, Aquilla	082	c1872	Orig. Only	AR	Ratliff, William	009	c1843	OB-E/205	AR
Rascoe, Arthur	020	1874	WB-A/152	CTY	Ratliff, William H.	005	1865	WB-C/231	AR
Rascoe, Arthur	010	1796	WB-D/326	AR	Ratliffe, Pendleton	084	1871	WB-E/31	CTY
Rascoe, Granville	010	1896	WB-I/487	AR	Rattes, Godfrey	085	c1803	WB-D/97	AR
Rascoe, Jacob D.	024	1832	WB-C/161	AR	Ratts, Valentine	032	1886	WB-3/522	AR
Rascoe, John K.	053	1868	WB-10/34	AR	Rauseau, E. A.	104	1890	WB-6/393	
Rascoe, John P.	010	1888	WB-I/252	AR	Raven, John	078	1821	WI-9/226	AR
Rascoe, John T.	010	1863	WB-H/122	AR	Ravenscroft, John S.	099	1831	RB-21/385	AR
Rascoe, Joseph J.	010	1854	WB-H/4	AR	Ravin, Abraham	009	1826	OB-A/368	AR
Rascoe, Peter	010	1844	WB-G/360	AR	Rawdon, Benjamin	065	1798	WB-F/68	AR
Rascoe, Tamar	010	1802	WB-E/166	AR	Rawles, Jesse	071	1761	WB-1/50	
Rascoe, Thomas	010	1807	WB-F/44	AR	Rawles, William	047	1760	WB-1/8	
Rascoe, William	010	1891	WB-I/316	AR	Rawley, David J.	084	1863	WB-C/386	CTY
Rascoe, William D.	024	1846	WB-C/268	AR	Rawley, James	084	1853	WB-C/147	CTY

Name	Co.	Date	Recorded Copy	Original
Rawlings, Benjamin	037	1738	SS 877/63	SS/AR
Rawlings, John	071	1747	Orig. Only	SS/AR
Rawlins, Edward A.	100	1873	WB-51/95	AR
Rawls, David	069	1850	WB-1/523	AR
Rawls, Eli J.	079	1883	WB-2/280	AR
Rawls, Francis	063	c1789	009 OWB/235	009 AR
Rawls, Frusanah	010	1858	WB-H/67	AR
Rawls, Hosea	010	1800	WB-E/116	AR
Rawls, J. J.	079	1900	WB-3/231	AR
Rawls, James	063	1819	WB-2/61	
Rawls, Jesse	063	1820	WB-2/69	
Rawls, Josiah	010	1871	WB-I/41	AR
Rawls, Killey	069	1848	WB-1/512	AR
Rawls, Lydia	051	1882	WB-C/299	AR
Rawls, Martha	051	1897	WB-C/531	
Rawls, Micajah	047	1778	WB-2/72	
Rawls, Moore	010	1879	WB-I/108	
Rawls, Philip	010	1794	WB-D/260	AR
Rawls, Randol	051	1832	WB-A/35	
Rawls, Randolph	047	1849	WB-4/282	AR
Rawls, Sarah	063	1847	WB-2/328	
Rawls, Washington	047	1893	WB-7/100	AR
Rawls, William	010	1772	WB-A/164	AR
Rawson, John	060	1828	WB-1/111	AR
Ray, Albert H.	099	1888	WB-B/264	AR
Ray, Alexander	010	1769	WB-A/113	AR
Ray, Angus	029	1808	WB-A/130	AR
Ray, Ann	029	1829	WB-B/181	AR
Ray, Ann	100	1796	WB-8/336	AR
Ray, Annie E.	063	1888	WB-4/22	AR
Ray, Archibald	083	1839	WB-1/378	AR
Ray, Asher H.	039	c1856	WB-0/352	AR
Ray, Buckner	099	1881	WB-A/244	AR
Ray, C. W.	092	1893	WB-6/360	AR
Ray, Caroline	029	1892	WB-E/552	
Ray, Catharine	022	c1865	WB-D/149	AR
Ray, Catherine	029	1859	WB-C/409	AR
Ray, Clara J.	099	1885	WB-B/46	AR
Ray, Daniel	029	c1761	Orig. Only	AR
Ray, David	044	1781	WB-1/308	CTY
Ray, David	073	1808	WB-D/231	AR
Ray, David	073	1833	WB-E/297	AR
Ray, David	073	1821	WB-D/607	AR
Ray, David A.	029	1887	WB-E/410	
Ray, Dugald	011	1848	WB-1/165	
Ray, Duncan	029	1851	WB-C/216	AR
Ray, Duncan	029	1822	WB-B/81	AR
Ray, Elizabeth	073	1864	WB-G/421	CTY
Ray, Elizabeth	099	1900	WB-D/384	AR
Ray, Flora	029	1873	WB-E/80	AR
Ray, Franklin	080	1863	WB-1/191	AR
Ray, George	090	1829	WB-3/201	AR
Ray, George	073	1814	WB-D/414	AR
Ray, Hannah	073	1847	WB-D/510	AR
Ray, Harriet	010	1878	WB-I/94	
Ray, Henry	010	1885	WB-I/187	
Ray, Henry	010	1830	WB-G/194	AR
Ray, Henry	099	1872	RB-35/189	AR
Ray, Hiram	107	1840	WB-1/51	
Ray, Isaac	011	c1780	WB-1/563	
Ray, James	068	1813	WB-A/280	
Ray, James	084	1806	WB-A/38	CTY
Ray, James	073	1837	WB-E/408	AR
Ray, James	099	1862	RB-32/257	AR
Ray, James McD.	001	c1854	WB-1/85	AR

Name	Co.	Date	Recorded Copy	Original
Ray, James, Jr.	006	c1842	WB-B/106	AR
Ray, Jane	029	1875	WB-E/142	AR
Ray, Jane R.	065	1900	WB-N/362	AR
Ray, Jennet	029	1880	WB-E/238	AR
Ray, Jesse	006	1900	WB-E/413	AR
Ray, Jesse	107	1855	WB-1/397	
Ray, John	010	1801	WB-E/131	AR
Ray, John	073	1829	WB-E/175	AR
Ray, John	029	1811	WB-A/169	AR
Ray, John	029	1805	WB-A/77	AR
Ray, John	063	c1802	WB-1/401	
Ray, John	073	1856	WB-G/123	CTY
Ray, John	006	1868	WB-C/22	
Ray, John	063	1818	WB-2/54	
Ray, John	021	1862	WB-1/167	AR
Ray, John	027	c1829	WB-A/32	AR
Ray, John	029	1808	WB-A/118	AR
Ray, John	068	1821	WB-B/17	
Ray, Jordan	081	1875	WB-15/208	AR
Ray, Joseph	099	1805	RB-7/91	AR
Ray, Joseph	104	1856	WB-5/153	
Ray, Joseph B.	107	c1857	WB-1/394	
Ray, Margaret	068	1848	WB-B/175	
Ray, Martha	073	1838	WB-F/11	AR
Ray, Martha	081	1892	WB-16/225	AR
Ray, Mary	073	1857	WB-G/162	CTY
Ray, Mary	096	1782	WB-1/132	AR
Ray, Mary	090	1837	WB-4/11	AR
Ray, Matthew	073	1880	WB-H/257	CTY
Ray, Neill	083	c1808	WB-1/107	AR
Ray, Neill W.	029	1899	WB-F/167	
Ray, Neill, Sr.	029	1883	WB-E/308	AR
Ray, Octavia	084	1880	WB-E/190	CTY
Ray, Peter L.	073	1830	WB-E/232	AR
Ray, Pleasant	084	1846	WB-C/44	CTY
Ray, Rachel	099	1826	RB-20/44	AR
Ray, Robert	099	1845	RB-26/35	AR
Ray, Robert	020	1786	RB-B/138	AR
Ray, Robert	073	1793	WB-B/219	AR
Ray, Sarah C.	073	1892	WB-H/556	CTY
Ray, Sarah M.	073	1854	WB-G/58	AR
Ray, Susan	099	1897	WB-D/49	AR
Ray, Susana	073	c1794	Orig. Only	AR
Ray, Susannah	073	1831	WB-E/248	AR
Ray, Thomas	020	1883	WB-A/401	CTY
Ray, Thomas	022	1854	WB-C/360	AR
Ray, Thomas, Sr.	107	1843	WB-1/69	
Ray, William	073	1834	WB-E/316	AR
Ray, William	010	1834	WB-G/237	AR
Ray, William	073	c1794	Orig. Only	AR
Ray, William	107	c1879	Copy	013 AR
Ray, William	073	1813	WB-D/366	AR
Ray, William	022	1792	RB-1/41	AR
Ray, William	107	1883	WB-2/24	
Ray, Z. D.	099	1878	RB-35/422	AR
Rayborn, Henry	099	1881	WB-A/260	AR
Rayborn, William	099	1813	RB-11/100	
Raye, Fanney	096	1812	WB-2/54	AR
Rayfield, Trusvan	060	1871	WB-4/80	AR
Rayford, Mathew	029	c1752	DB-1/228	
Rayl, Caleb	046	1873	WB-E/120	AR
Rayl, William	046	1842	WB-C/121	AR
Raymond, Thomas	N	1730	SS 876/199	SS/AR
Raynard, James	092	1839	WB-4/158	AR
Rayner, Amos	051	1843	WB-A/222	

Name	Co.	Date	Recorded Copy	Original
Rayner, Enoch	010	1824	WB-G/116	AR
Rayner, Henry A.	010	1841	WB-G/337	AR
Rayner, James R.	010	1853	WB-G/498	AR
Rayner, Joel	010	1818	WB-G/21	AR
Rayner, John	010	1796	WB-D/343	AR
Rayner, Mary E. C.	010	1855	WB-H/20	AR
Rayner, Miles	010	1819	WB-G/56	AR
Rayner, Richard	010	1785	WB-D/29	AR
Rayner, Samuel	010	1817	WB-G/47	AR
Rayner, Sarah	010	1828	WB-G/181	AR
Rayner, Thomas J.	010	1838	WB-G/287	AR
Rayner, William	010	1860	WB-H/91	AR
Rayner, William	010	1827	WB-G/170	AR
Raynor, Martha	029	1894	WB-F/32	AR
Razor, China	099	1898	WB-D/168	AR
Rea, Andrew	065	1801	WB-F/69	AR
Rea, Avery S.	065	1843	WB-H/139	AR
Rea, David	065	1839	WB-E/238	AR
Rea, Elizabeth	065	1886	WB-L/171	AR
Rea, Green L.	065	1890	WB-L/434	AR
Rea, Green L.	065	c1888	Copy	097 AR
Rea, James	024	1829	WB-C/148	AR
Rea, James M.	065	1847	WB-I/106	AR
Rea, John M.	065	1859	WB-J/64	AR
Rea, John M.	065	c1859	097 WB-2/248	
Rea, John, Sr.	097	1844	WB-1/9	AR
Rea, Joseph G.	051	1851	WB-A/329	
Rea, M. A.	065	1897	WB-N/72	AR
Rea, Martha	024	1851	WB-C/315	AR
Rea, Mary	065	1875	WB-K/201	AR
Rea, Mary	097	1863	WB-1/224	AR
Rea, Millicent	077	1823	WB-F/54	AR
Rea, Nancy	051	1875	WB-C/150	AR
Rea, Sarah	071	1838	WB-4/169	AR
Rea, Silas	065	1852	WB-I/189	AR
Rea, Thomas	077	1798	Orig. Only	AR
Rea, Thomas S.	065	1831	WB-G/70	AR
Rea, William	073	1774	WB-A/154	
Rea, William	046	1789	WB-A/306	AR
Reach, Delia	099	1836	RB-23/565	
Reach, James	028	1866	009 WB-2/294	009 CTY
Read, Andrew	012	1817	WB-B/111	AR
Read, Arminty	001	1879	WB-2/146	AR
Read, Charity	019	1898	WB-C/4	AR
Read, Charles	053	1771	RW-1/17	AR
Read, Florence	054	c1834	WB-2/149	AR
Read, George	019	1755	SS 880/57	SS/AR
Read, George	019	1755	WB-D/331	AR-Copy
Read, Irvin	104	1890	WB-6/390	AR
Read, James	012	1805	WB-B/76	AR
Read, James	028	1819	WB-C/186	AR
Read, Jesse	047	1820	WB-3/654	AR
Read, Jesse	099	1817	RB-13/354	AR
Read, John	047	1820	WB-3/656	AR
Read, John S.	084	1826	WB-A/276	CTY
Read, Joseph E.	030	1899	WB-5/270	AR
Read, Malachi	030	1805	WB-2/272	
Read, Mary	047	1781	WB-3/15	AR
Read, Rhesa	047	1824	WB-3/697	AR
Read, Robert	019	1794	WB-D/338	AR
Read, Robert R.	078	1816	WI-7/131	
Read, Thomas A.	064	c1843	Orig. Only	AR
Read, Thomas H.	044	1833	WB-12/518	CTY
Read, William	057	1819	WB-B/53	AR
Read, Willis	100	1857	WB-49/129	AR

Name	Co.	Date	Recorded Copy	Original
Readdick, Monicha	024	1848	WB-C/286	AR
Reade, Edwin G.	099	1894	WB-C/306	AR
Reade, Edwin G.	078	1897	WB-19/416	AR
Reade, Harmon	047	1767	WB-1/216	
Reade, Mary E.	099	1896	WB-C/501	AR
Reader, Thomas	086	1819	WB-C/120	AR
Reading, Churchill	008	1734	SS 876/363	SS/AR
Reading, Jonathan	081	1844	WB-8/48	AR
Reading, Joseph	075	1731	Orig. Only	SS/AR
Reading, Lionel	008	1725	SS 876/41	SS/AR
Reading, Thomas	009	1748	SS 877/120	SS/AR
Readling, John W.	065	1877	WB-K/308	AR
Reagan, John	084	1826	WB-A/281	CTY
Real, Mary	064	1845	WB-1/9	AR
Real, Mary	072	1803	WB-A/112	AR
Real, Peter	028	1770	Orig. Only	AR
Real, Peter	028	1792	WB-A/286	AR
Reames, Jeremiah	071	1789	WB-1/478	AR
Reames, William	071	1794	WB-2/46	AR
Reap, Daniel	089	1892	WB-2/243	AR
Reape, Peter	065	c1787	WB-F/121	AR
Reardon, Jacob	029	1888	WB-E/435	AR
Reardon, James, Sr.	029	1836	WB-B/260	AR
Rease, George	060	1792	Orig. Only	AR
Reasonover, Elizabeth	028	1791	WB-A/247	AR
Reasons, Rawley	037	1841	WB-F/261	AR
Reasons, Richard	028	1775	Orig. Only	AR
Reasons, Thomas	010	1769	WB-A/105	AR
Reaves, Adam	103	1831	RD-6/227	AR
Reaves, Ann Jane	035	1892	WB-4/405	AR
Reaves, Catharine	087	1844	Orig. Only	AR
Reaves, David	035	1883	WB-4/219	AR
Reaves, Edal	068	1849	WB-B/201	
Reaves, Elijah	056	1781	Orig. Only	AR-Nunc.
Reaves, Isaac	104	1808	WB-2/229	
Reaves, James	086	1803	WB-B/157	AR
Reaves, Jerry	001	1897	WB-3/164	AR
Reaves, Joel	012	c1858	WB-B/36	AR
Reaves, John	103	1835	RD-7/32	AR
Reaves, Joseph	092	1804	WB-3/64A	AR
Reaves, Kizziah	056	1848	WB-1/799	AR
Reaves, Mabane	022	1900	WB-F/168	AR
Reaves, Malachi	013	1834	WB-A/32	
Reaves, Sally L.	073	1827	WB-E/147	
Reaves, Seley	022	1806	WB-A/125	AR
Reaves, Solomon	027	1836	WB-A/20	AR
Reaves, William	103	1793	Orig. Only	AR
Reavil, Humphree	071	1799	WB-2/183	AR
Reavis, Edward	071	1752	Orig. Only	SS/AR
Reavis, George B.	044	1898	WB-24/408	CTY
Reavis, George W.	100	1862	WB-49/401	AR
Reavis, Isaac	099	1789	RB-2/235	AR
Reavis, Lewis	098	1883	WB-A/26	CTY
Reavis, Samuel	099	1815	RB-12/111	AR
Reavis, Sarah	044	1850	WB-18/132	CTY
Reavis, William	071	c1784	WB-1/339	AR
Reavis, William	106	c1863	WB-1/122	AR
Reavis, William W.	106	1891	WB-2/306	AR
Record, John	073	1769	WB-A/97	
Record, John	022	1871	WB-E/73	
Records, Annanias	046	1807	WB-A/321	AR
Recton, John	056	1761	WB-1/763	
Rector, Catherine	014	1885	WB-2/303	CTY
Rector, Daniel	003	1863	Orig. Only	AR
Rector, Elihu F.	003	1888	WB-B/237	AR

Name	Co.	Date	Recorded Copy	Original
Rector, Elizabeth	003	1875	WB-B/57	AR
Rector, Martha	014	c1841	WB-2/47	
Rector, Peter	085	1822	WB-H/140	AR
Rector, Polly	003	1877	WB-B/86	AR
Rector, Thomas J.	062	1890	WB-B/106	AR
Reddick, Charity	063	1837	WB-2/240	
Reddick, David	063	c1804	WB-1/423	
Reddick, Hardy	090	1798	WB-1/106	AR
Reddick, Hardy	063	1895	WB-4/156	AR
Reddick, Henry E.	010	1851	WB-G/473	AR
Reddick, James	063	1826	WB-2/119	
Reddick, John	045	1826	WB-1/127	
Reddick, John, Sr.	063	1823	WB-2/93	
Reddick, Joseph	063	1827	WB-2/123	
Reddick, Martha	010	1832	WB-G/216	AR
Reddick, Mary	028	1900	WB-F/508	
Reddick, Noah	LA	1883	063 WB-4/251	063 AR
Reddick, Samuel	075	1810	WB-M1/219	
Reddick, Thomas	063	c1783	WB-1/104	
Reddick, Thomas	063	c1832	WB-2/184	
Reddick, Thomas W.	010	1863	WB-H/123	AR
Reddick, William	063	1830	WB-2/164	
Reddick, Willis	063	1829	WB-2/157	
Redding, Anex	081	1900	WB-17/125	
Redding, Jeremiah	028	1800	WB-B/99	AR
Redding, Jesse	081	1859	WB-11/159	AR
Redding, John	104	1869	WB-6/38	AR
Redding, John	077	1754	SS 879/74	SS/AR
Redding, John F.	068	1896	WB-D/470	
Redding, Martin	104	1866	WB-5/461	AR
Redding, Sarah C.	009	1891	WB-1/560	CTY
Redding, William	047	1774	Orig. Only	SS/AR
Redding, William	104	1853	WB-5/92	
Redditt, Alexander	009	1816	OB-A/254	AR
Redditt, James	009	1840	OB-C2/264	AR
Redditt, John	009	c1826	OWB/489	AR
Redditt, Josiah	010	1811	WB-F/193	AR
Redditt, Lewis	009	c1811	OB-A/179	AR
Redditt, Lodowick	009	1845	OB-D/274	AR
Redditt, Thomas	010	1855	WB-H/23	AR
Redditt, William	010	1739	LGB-4/#116	SS/AR
Redfearn, Alfred S.	005	1853	WB-C/69	AR
Redfearn, Isaac	081	1832	WB-6/252	AR
Redfearn, Malaci G.	005	1879	WB-D/86	AR
Redfearn, Nimrod	005	1830	WB-B/5	AR
Redfearn, Wilson	005	1853	WB-C/59	AR
Redford, Council	103	1877	WB-1/122	
Redford, John	065	1823	WB-F/137	AR
Reding, Benjamin	075	1780	WB-K/49	AR
Reding, Jeremiah	075	1761	WB-I/6	AR
Reding, Jonathan	075	1766	WB-H/72	AR
Reding, Joseph	077	1753	SS 881/22	SS/AR
Reding, Joseph	081	1815	WB-4/267	AR
Reding, Mary	099	1844	RB-25/432	AR
Reding, Milicent	075	1807	WB-M1/165	AR
Reding, Miriam	075	1807	WB-M1/164	AR
Reding, Robert	073	1890	WB-H/505	CTY
Reding, Samuel	075	1762	WB-I/10	AR
Reding, Sarah	075	1775	WB-I/141	AR
Reding, Thomas	075	1795	WB-L/31	AR
Reding, Thomas	075	1801	WB-M1/48	AR
Reding, Thomas	075	1762	WB-H/33	AR
Reding, Thomas	073	1821	WB-D/591	AR
Reding, Timothy	029	1799	WB-A/16	AR
Reding, Trimagin	075	1778	WB-K/36	AR
Redman, Absalom	054	1893	WB-5/450	CTY
Redman, Darnadus	054	1888	WB-5/189	CTY
Redman, Erastus	054	1894	WB-5/545	CTY
Redman, Franklin	090	1899	WB-6/520	AR
Redman, Hosea	054	1865	WB-3/170	AR
Redman, John	073	1834	WB-E/317	AR
Redman, John	054	N. D.	WB-2/174	
Redman, John T.	054	1886	WB-5/136	CTY
Redman, T. W.	054	1886	WB-5/125	CTY
Redman, Thomas	054	c1830	WB-2/160	AR
Redman, Thomas	054	1881	Orig. Only	AR
Redmon, Caty	090	1835	WB-3/286	Nunc.
Redmon, Harmon	090	1847	WB-4/240	AR
Redmond, Eliza M.	009	1819	OB-A/294	AR
Redmond, Mary	NY	1880	Copy	050 AR
Redmond, Phoebe	009	1881	WB-1/280	CTY
Redmond, Sabina	NY	1870	Copy	050 AR
Redmond, William	RI	1899	Copy	050 AR
Redwine, J. T.	089	1884	WB-2/118	AR
Redwine, Jacob	085	1833	WB-H/584	AR
Redwine, Jesse	032	1837	WB-1/309	AR
Redwine, Margaret	032	c1897	Orig. Only	AR
Redwine, Pleasant	085	1845	Orig. Only	AR-Nunc.
Reece, Abraham	092	1822	WB-3/154	AR
Reece, Abraham	106	c1852	WB-1/9	AR
Reece, Alvis	106	1889	WB-2/271	AR
Reece, Daniel	092	1822	WB-3/153	AR
Reece, James	013	1866	WB-A/242	AR
Reece, Jesse	106	c1861	WB-1/111	
Reece, Joel	092	1817	WB-3/123	AR
Reece, John	106	N.D.	WB-2/88	AR
Reece, John	106	c1877	WB-2/86	AR
Reece, John	006	1840	WB-A/85	AR
Reece, John M.	046	1870	WB-E/40	AR
Reece, Joseph L.	081	1874	WB-15/143	AR
Reece, Marcus E.	085	1874	WB-1/234	CTY
Reece, Noah	106	c1858	WB-1/59	AR
Reece, Thomas H.	106	c1860	WB-1/89	AR
Reed, Alexander	085	c1775	WB-A/243	AR
Reed, Alfred	084	1873	WB-E/67	CTY
Reed, Allen	065	1814	WB-F/75	AR
Reed, Andrew	003	1856	Orig. Only	AR
Reed, Andrew	077	1728	SS 876/151	SS/AR
Reed, Andrew	077	1728	Copy	CCR 187
Reed, Annie G.	046	1890	WB-F/49	AR
Reed, Anselom	038	1895	WB-3/546	AR
Reed, Augustinus	065	1781	WB-F/117	AR
Reed, Benjamin	077	1795	WB-E/53	
Reed, Christian	038	1894	WB-3/454	AR
Reed, David	085	1843	WB-I/161	AR
Reed, Durant	077	1767	WB-C/71	AR
Reed, Eldad, Sr.	013	1849	WB-A/137	
Reed, Elizabeth	084	1885	WB-E/339	
Reed, Elizabeth	003	1878	WB-B/104	AR
Reed, Ellen	016	1852	WB-1/208	
Reed, Frederick	073	1821	WB-D/606	AR
Reed, George	085	c1784	WB-B/154	AR
Reed, George	085	1815	WB-G/357	AR
Reed, George D.	010	1809	WB-F/122	AR
Reed, George W.	077	1853	WB-F/421	AR
Reed, Hannah	028	1784	WB-A/72	AR
Reed, Henry	046	1789	WB-A/307	AR
Reed, Henry	032	1893	WB-4/202	AR
Reed, Hugh	065	1778	WB-F/116	AR
Reed, J. F.	075	1887	WB-O/285	AR

Name	Co.	Date	Recorded Copy	Original
Reed, Jacob	013	1876	WB-B/117	AR
Reed, Jacob	090	1819	WB-3/35	AR
Reed, James	028	1799	WB-B/78	AR
Reed, James	028	1782	Orig. Only	AR
Reed, James	021	1857	WB-1/136	AR
Reed, Jane	086	1829	WB-D/111	AR
Reed, Jane	013	1853	WB-A/157	
Reed, Jesse	038	1892	WB-3/340	AR
Reed, Jesse	003	1870	WB-B/9	AR
Reed, John	075	1808	WB-M1/188	AR
Reed, John	073	c1786	WB-B/35	AR
Reed, John	084	c1844	WB-C/7	CTY
Reed, John	065	1811	WB-F/135	AR
Reed, John	085	c1805	WB-G/32	AR
Reed, John	054	1816	WB-1/401	AR
Reed, John H.	062	1898	WB-B/209	AR
Reed, John T.	032	1845	WB-1/457	AR
Reed, John, Sr.	086	1825	WB-D/42	AR
Reed, John, Sr.	016	1845	WB-1/64	
Reed, John, Sr.	013	1896	WB-C/568	AR
Reed, Joseph	077	1774	WB-C/155	AR
Reed, Joseph	005	1751	Orig. Only	SS/AR
Reed, Joseph	077	1765	WB-C/49	AR
Reed, Joseph B.	075	c1860	WB-M2/68	AR
Reed, Joshua	009	c1803	OWB/417	AR
Reed, Lemuel P.	077	1816	WB-E/432	AR
Reed, Lettis	060	1816	Orig. Only	AR
Reed, Margaret	010	1804	WB-E/251	AR
Reed, Margery	054	1854	WB-3/80	AR
Reed, Martha S.	075	1873	WB-0/46	AR
Reed, Mary	033	1847	WB-1/86	AR
Reed, Mary	065	1796	WB-F/66	AR
Reed, Mary	085	1831	WB-H/502	AR
Reed, Mary C.	065	1826	WB-F/104	AR
Reed, Mary C.	077	1867	WB-H/18	AR
Reed, Nancy	038	1881	WB-2/417	AR
Reed, Peter	013	1849	WB-A/132	
Reed, Robert	023	1885	WB-A/35	
Reed, Roda	103	1873	WB-1/71	AR
Reed, Ruth	016	1837	PQS.5/422	
Reed, Samuel	003	1876	WB-B/74	AR
Reed, Samuel	073	1769	WB-A/102	
Reed, Samuel	086	1803	WB-B/149	AR
Reed, Sarah E.	077	1873	WB-H/48	AR
Reed, Susanna	047	1771	WB-1/293	
Reed, Thomas	077	1837	WB-F/263	AR
Reed, Thomas	020	1847	RB-P/502	
Reed, Thomas P.	070	1892	WB-G/68	AR
Reed, Tulle W.	077	1802	WB-E/136	AR
Reed, William	077	1800	WB-E/107	AR
Reed, William	072	c1822	WB-1/144	AR
Reed, William	017	1846	WB-A/38	AR
Reed, William	041	1859	WB-3/239	AR
Reed, William D.	064	1858	WB-1/60	AR
Reed, William R.	013	1868	WB-B/10	AR
Reed, Wilson	077	1860	WB-F/512	AR
Reedy, A. W.	060	1897	WB-5/55	AR
Reedy, Andrew	060	1827	WB-1/68	
Reel, Catherine	085	1822	WB-H/179	AR
Reel, George	064	1867	Orig. Only	AR
Reel, Joshua	028	1768	Orig. Only	AR
Reel, Mary	028	1800	WB-B/91	AR
Reel, Nancy	028	1846	WB-D/126	AR
Reel, Peter	028	1739	SS 878/47	SS/AR
Reel, Rosey E.	064	1893	WB-2/311	AR
Reep, Adam	060	1837	WB-1/403	AR
Reep, David	060	1882	WB-4/265	AR
Reep, J. M.	060	1897	WB-5/40	AR
Reep, Jonas	060	1892	WB-4/473	AR
Reep, Michael	060	1852	WB-2/361	AR
Reep, Peter	060	1853	WB-2/373	AR
Reep, Susannah	060	1843	WB-2/188	AR
Rees, Enoch	020	1824	RB-I/309	
Rees, Jacob	085	1772	WB-A/142	AR
Rees, Sabra	070	1895	WB-G/361	AR
Reese, Charity	071	1864	WB-5/287	AR
Reese, David	065	1787	WB-F/62	AR
Reese, David	085	1827	WB-H/376	AR
Reese, John	071	1854	WB-5/115	AR
Reese, John T.	046	1875	WB-E/138	AR-Nunc.
Reese, Owen	075	1745	Orig. Only	SS/AR
Reese, Randolph H.	071	1863	WB-5/284	AR
Reese, Richard W.	071	1862	WB-5/265	AR
Reese, Rivers	071	1870	WB-6/48	AR
Reeve, George	073	1821	WB-D/605	AR
Reeves, Bettie	089	1893	WB-2/311	AR
Reeves, Charles	090	1833	WB-3/261	AR
Reeves, D. M.	085	1892	WB-2/496	CTY
Reeves, D. U.	085	1892	Copy	067 AR
Reeves, Delilah	001	1890	WB-2/484	AR
Reeves, Enoch	004	1871	WB-A/8	AR
Reeves, Evan	011	c1823	WB-2/356	
Reeves, Frederick	056	1791	WB-1/50	AR
Reeves, George T.	004	1881	WB-A/46	AR
Reeves, George W.	006	1899	WB-E/359	AR
Reeves, Harris	067	1866	WB-1/134	AR
Reeves, Hugh C.	073	1864	WB-G/442	CTY
Reeves, James	012	1890	WB-A/83	AR
Reeves, James	046	1781	WB-A/306	AR
Reeves, James S.	092	1894	WB-6/388	AR
Reeves, Jeremiah	092	1866	WB-5/81	
Reeves, Jesse A.	004	1865	WB-1/21	AR
Reeves, Jesse F.	004	1865	WB-1/18	AR
Reeves, John	028	1790	WB-A/229	AR
Reeves, John	013	1895	WB-C/348	AR
Reeves, John	073	c1832	Orig. Only	AR
Reeves, John	073	1854	WB-G/75	AR
Reeves, John C.	004	1881	WB-A/42	AR
Reeves, John M.	011	1894	WB-3/62	CTY
Reeves, Kindred	049	1887	WB-2/140	AR
Reeves, L. C.	102	1899	WB-A/167	AR
Reeves, Martha	073	1877	WB-H/169	CTY
Reeves, Micajah	092	1849	WB-4/290	
Reeves, Nancy	004	1887	WB-A/90	AR
Reeves, Nathaniel	029	c1792	WB-C/259	
Reeves, Priscilla	001	1888	WB-2/366	AR
Reeves, Rebecca	085	1900	WB-3/357	CTY
Reeves, Sally Lewis	073	1827	WB-E/147	AR
Reeves, Samuel	085	1873	WB-1/199	
Reeves, Samuel	085	c1801	WB-D/101	AR
Reeves, William	015	1778	100 WB-2/189	AR
Reeves, William D.	073	1885	WB-H/372	CTY
Refild, William	075	1731	SS 876/231	SS/AR
Regan, Alford	011	1894	WB-3/68	CTY
Regan, Ann	083	c1796	WB-1/44	AR
Regan, Daniel	N	c1727	Orig. Only	SS/AR
Regan, John	083	1814	WB-1/154	
Regan, John	100	1847	WB-39/323	AR
Regan, Joseph	011	c1773	WB-1/578	
Regan, Joseph	083	1843	WB-1/430	AR

Name	Co.	Date	Recorded Copy	Original
Regan, Mildred	100	1870	WB-51/21	AR
Regan, P. G.	060	1888	WB-4/389	AR
Regan, Ralph	083	1862	WB-2/180	AR
Regan, Ralph	083	c1795	WB-1/39	AR
Regan, Rhoda	083	1869	WB-3/20	AR
Regan, Susan	100	1850	WB-40/279	
Regan, William	083	c1806	WB-1/98	
Reggons, Joseph	010	1727	SS 876/127	SS/AR
Register, Allen	087	1872	Orig. Only	AR
Register, Benjamin	087	c1811	Orig. Only	AR
Register, Daniel	011	1885	WB-2/193	
Register, Gibson	087	1868	WB-2/125	AR
Register, Hamon H.	087	1878	WB-3/171	AR
Register, John	087	1832	WB-1/141	AR
Register, John J.	027	c1849	Orig. Only	AR
Register, Joseph	087	1823	WB-1/52	
Register, Mary	011	c1857	WB-1/264	
Register, William	011	c1802	WB-1/430	
Register, William	087	1851	WB-1/400	AR
Regon, William	022	1817	WB-A/290	AR
Reich, Anna Maria	032	1844	WB-1/439	AR
Reich, Catharina	090	1828	WB-3/188	AR
Reich, Christian	038	1864	WB-1/244	AR
Reich, Christopher	090	1824	WB-3/110	AR
Reich, Daniel	038	1876	WB-2/247	AR
Reich, Elizabeth	038	1859	WB-1/149	AR
Reich, Elizabeth	090	1830	WB-3/215	AR
Reich, Jacob	038	1876	Orig. Only	AR
Reich, John	038	1871	WB-2/53	AR
Reich, John H.	038	1894	WB-3/443	AR
Reich, John P.	038	1867	WB-1/286	AR
Reich, Lewis	090	1847	WB-4/246	AR
Reich, Matthew	090	1829	WB-3/199	AR
Reich, Naaman B.	038	1871	WB-2/43	AR
Reich, Samuel	038	1894	WB-3/508	AR
Reich, Thomas	038	1883	WB-2/469	AR
Reich, Thomas	038	1858	WB-1/133	AR
Reich, Verona	090	1838	WB-4/31	AR
Reichel, Benjamin	090	1834	WB-3/264	AR
Reid, Able	054	1900	WB-6/294	CTY
Reid, Alexander	054	1841	WB-2/229	AR
Reid, Amanda	065	1887	WB-L/246	AR
Reid, Amzi G.	065	1885	WB-L/57	AR
Reid, Ann	054	1889	WB-5/267	CTY
Reid, Bluford	046	1871	WB-E/59	AR
Reid, David	065	1842	WB-H/84	AR
Reid, David	TN	1858	087 WB-1/529	087 AR
Reid, David S.	084	1891	WB-E/498	CTY
Reid, Eliza	040	1876	WB-2/105	AR
Reid, Frank L.	099	1897	WB-D/47	AR
Reid, Frank L.	046	1894	WB-F/362	AR
Reid, George	070	1797	Orig. Only	AR-Nunc.
Reid, George V.	054	1882	WB-4/466	
Reid, Hugh K.	084	1897	WB-F/102	CTY
Reid, Isaac	065	1892	WB-M/125	AR
Reid, James	054	1897	WB-6/127	CTY
Reid, James	065	1900	WB-N/312	
Reid, James	054	1886	WB-5/118	CTY
Reid, James M.	085	1873	WB-1/156	CTY
Reid, James W.	020	1859	RB-S/164	AR
Reid, John	060	1821	Orig. Only	AR
Reid, John J.	084	1853	WB-C/156	CTY
Reid, Jonathan	065	1860	WB-J/84	AR
Reid, Joseph	064	1870	107 WB-2/165	
Reid, Joseph	064	1870	WB-2/113	AR
Reid, Joseph N.	065	1888	WB-L/274	AR
Reid, Lucy Ann	100	1895	WB-51/430	
Reid, Martha J.	078	1870	WB-19/11	AR
Reid, Mary	003	1879	WB-B/120	AR
Reid, Mary S.	022	1879	WB-E/173	AR
Reid, Noel	078	1867	WB-18/478	AR
Reid, Numa F.	084	1873	WB-E/63	
Reid, Preston	092	1894	WB-6/386	AR
Reid, Prudence M.	090	1864	WB-4/375	AR
Reid, R. James	065	1861	WB-J/113	AR
Reid, Robert	044	1805	WB-6/225	CTY
Reid, S. C.	065	1900	WB-N/362	AR
Reid, Sallie	038	1900	WB-4/245	AR
Reid, Sarah	054	c1830	WB-2/143	AR
Reid, Sarah A.	022	1860	WB-D/61	AR
Reid, Solomon	065	1863	WB-J/166	AR
Reid, Thomas	075	1827	WB-N/36	AR-Nunc.
Reid, William F.	046	1900	WB-G/198	AR
Reid, William K.	065	1867	WB-J/244	AR
Reid, William W.	030	1842	WB-4/87	
Reid, Zion	103	1890	WB-1/539	AR
Reigner, Richard	077	1762	WB-C/9	AR
Reinbach, Lewis	104	1865	WB-5/416	
Reinhardt, Christian	060	1818	Orig. Only	AR
Reinhardt, Conrad	060	1809	Orig. Only	AR
Reinhardt, F. M.	060	1869	WB-4/22	AR
Reinhardt, George	021	1866	WB-1/216	AR
Reinhardt, Jacob	060	1889	WB-4/371	AR
Reinhardt, Jacob	060	1833	WB-1/266	AR
Reinhardt, Jacob, Sr.	060	1800	Orig. Only	AR
Reinhardt, John J.	021	1900	WB-3/273	AR
Reinhardt, Sarah	060	1879	WB-4/205	AR
Reinhardt, William P.	021	1900	WB-3/282	AR
Reissig, Lydia	065	1900	WB-N/302	AR
Reitzel, Adam	046	1792	WB-A/311	AR
Reitzel, Christian	021	1870	WB-2/41	AR
Reitzel, F. A.	046	1895	WB-F/457	AR
Reives, John J.	068	1845	WB-B/166	
Relf, John	075	1742	Orig. Only	SS/AR
Relfe, John	075	1809	WB-M1/207	AR
Relfe, Josiah	075	1816	WB-M1/290	AR
Relfe, Mary	075	1725	Orig. Only	SS/AR
Relfe, Thomas	N	1720	SS 875/270	SS/AR
Relfe, William	075	1774	WB-I/89	AR
Relfe, William T.	075	1828	WB-N/43	AR
Relfe, William T.	075	1838	WB-N/145	AR
Remson, Charles P.	070	1892	WB-G/106	AR
Ren, Joseph	100	1833	WB-34/253	AR
Rench, John	099	1784	RB-2/33	AR
Rench, John Grant	099	1812	RB-10/234	AR
Rench, Rebeckah	099	1804	RB-6/334	AR
Rencher, Abram	022	1883	WB-E/278	AR
Rendleman, Henry	060	1859	WB-3/24	AR
Rendleman, Margaret	085	1816	WB-G/408	AR
Renear, Samuel	085	1832	WB-H/555	AR
Renegar, George	092	1794	WB-3/14	AR
Renegar, Joseph	038	1859	WB-1/186	AR
Renegar, Nathan	054	1900	WB-6/303	CTY
Reney, John	065	c1765	WB-F/111	AR
Renfrow, James	107	1852	WB-1/321	
Renfrow, John	037	1748	Orig. Only	SS/AR
Renn, James	037	1795	WB-C/311	AR
Renn, Thomas M.	039	1876	WB-U/137	AR
Renn, William	037	1792	Orig. Only	AR
Renno, David M.	PA	1890	064 WB-2/504	064 AR

Name	Co.	Date	Recorded Copy	Original
Reno, John	049	1888	WB-2/167	AR
Renshaw, Elijah	085	1854	WB-K/162	AR
Renshaw, Margaret	085	1896	WB-3/130	CTY
Renshaw, Mildred	033	1848	WB-1/96	AR
Renshaw, Thomas	085	1872	WB-1/117	CTY
Renshaw, William	085	1822	WB-H/173	AR
Rentfro, Jacob	103	1815	RD-3/273	AR
Rentfrow, Demaris	056	1843	WB-1/555	AR
Rentfrow, Jacob	105	1882	WB-2/279	
Rentfrow, Jacob	103	1825	RD-5/202	AR
Rentfrow, Mabary	105	1883	WB-2/292	AR
Rentfrow, Noel	056	1832	WB-1/464	AR
Rentfrow, Noel	056	1819	WB-1/299	AR
Rentfrow, Willey	105	1870	WB-2/42	AR
Rentfrow, William	056	1840	WB-1/515	AR
Repiton, Sarah Eliza	VA	1873	070 WB-E/332	070 AR
Repult, Joshua	085	1844	WB-I/200	AR
Resnig, Isaac	099	1789	RB-2/235	
Resonover, Clara	057	c1778	WB-A/193	AR
Respass, King	009	1898	WB-2/145	CTY
Respess, Henry	009	1845	OB-E/477	AR
Respess, Jeremiah	009	1858	OB-K/449	AR
Respess, Julia A.	009	1891	WB-1/512	CTY
Respess, Nancy	009	1871	WB-1/80	CTY
Respess, Richard	009	1837	OB-B/533	AR
Respess, Thomas	009	c1799	OWB/358	AR
Respess, Thomas H.	031	1887	WB-1/42	AR
Reston, Thomas	N	1724	SS 876/55	SS/AR
Reudasil, John	033	1862	WB-1/172	AR
Reusseum, Adoflus	104	1889	WB-6/372	
Revel, Elijah	069	1807	WB-1/173	AR
Revel, Humphrey	069	1832	WB-1/379	AR
Revell, James	071	1895	WB-7/284	AR
Revell, Lazarus	071	1808	WB-2/364	AR
Revell, Michael	103	1836	RD-7/173	AR
Revell, Patience	103	1839	RD-7/533	AR
Revelle, John	067	1864	WB-1/112	AR
Revels, James	029	1842	WB-C/21	AR
Revels, Nathaniel	083	1865	WB-2/214	AR
Reves, Jesse, Sr.	006	c1833	WB-B/53	AR
Reves, John	006	1885	WB-E/118	AR
Reves, John	033	1842	WB-1/42	AR
Revil, Joseph John	103	1784	Orig. Only	AR
Revill, Noah	067	1879	WB-2/109	AR
Revils, Benjamin	099	1835	RB-23/325	AR
Revis, W. C.	013	1879	WB-B/195	AR
Rew, Beverly	028	1782	Orig. Only	AR
Rew, Charles	028	1772	Orig. Only	AR
Rew, Demarius	053	c1814	RW-1/495	AR
Rew, Edward B.	053	1802	RW-1/360	AR
Rew, Elizabeth	053	1873	WB-11/39	AR
Rew, Frederick	009	1827	OB-A/387	AR
Rew, Frederick	028	1814	WB-C/91	AR
Rew, Mark	053	1786	RW-1/145	
Rew, Rachel	053	1788	RW-1/179	
Rew, Reuben	053	1807	RW-1/411	AR
Rew, Solomon	053	c1803	WB-4/91	AR
Rew, Southey B.	009	1827	OB-A/381	AR
Rew, Southy	028	1837	WB-C/399	AR
Rew, Southy	028	1754	SS 881/52	SS/AR
Rew, Southy	028	1799	WB-B/80	AR
Rew, Southy J.	028	1810	WB-C/9	AR
Rew, Thomas	053	1792	RW-1/221	AR
Rew, William	028	1806	Orig. Only	AR
Rex, John	099	1839	RB-24/261	AR
Reynaud, Benjamin	030	c1712	SS 875/24	
Reynolds, Alice G.	013	1895	WB-C/407	AR
Reynolds, Ann N.	046	c1842	Orig. Only	AR
Reynolds, Archibald	090	1824	WB-3/127	AR
Reynolds, Christopher	028	1808	WB-B/319	AR
Reynolds, David	046	1815	WB-A/326	AR
Reynolds, David, Sr.	047	1885	WB-6/354	AR
Reynolds, Delilah	046	1860	WB-D/56	AR
Reynolds, Dudley	092	c1878	Orig. Only	AR
Reynolds, E.	084	1833	Orig. Only	CTY
Reynolds, Elizabeth	096	1882	WB-4/80	AR
Reynolds, Elizabeth	057	1855	WB-B/226	AR
Reynolds, Emma T.	090	1900	WB-6/548	AR
Reynolds, Francis	104	1803	WB-2/99	AR
Reynolds, Hamilton	086	1815	WB-C/20	AR
Reynolds, Heusted	010	1837	WB-G/271	AR
Reynolds, Ignatius	SC	1855	099 RB-31/496	099 AR
Reynolds, Isaac	012	1870	WB-A/15	AR
Reynolds, James	057	1785	WB-A/43	AR
Reynolds, James M.	084	1884	WB-E/282	CTY
Reynolds, Jeremiah	046	1842	WB-C131	AR
Reynolds, Jeremiah	067	1876	WB-2/76	AR
Reynolds, Jeremiah	081	1815	WB-4/224	AR
Reynolds, John	013	1878	WB-B/169	AR
Reynolds, John D.	013	1880	WB-B/197	AR
Reynolds, John M.	084	1860	WB-C/335	CTY
Reynolds, John, Sr.	104	1860	WB-5/248	
Reynolds, Jonas	092	1812	WB-3/101	AR
Reynolds, Joseph	013	1867	WB-A/249	AR
Reynolds, Joshua	046	1883	WB-E/364	AR
Reynolds, Larkin C.	104	1872	WB-6/54	AR
Reynolds, Mark	012	1878	WB-A/32	AR
Reynolds, Mary	084	1842	WB-B/278	CTY
Reynolds, Nancy	014	1869	Orig. Only	AR
Reynolds, Nicholas	067	1857	WB-1/78	AR
Reynolds, Penelope	057	1809	WB-A/320	AR
Reynolds, Pennie	059	1891	WB-B/7	CTY
Reynolds, Pryor	084	1858	WB-C/282	CTY
Reynolds, Richard	011	c1804	WB-1/425	Nunc.
Reynolds, Richard	057	1843	WB-B/166	AR
Reynolds, Samuel T.	NY	1895	028 WB-F/169	
Reynolds, Sarah	081	1838	Orig. Only	AR
Reynolds, Terrissa	006	1892	WB-E/233	AR
Reynolds, Thomas	084	1872	WB-E/42	CTY
Reynolds, Thomas M.	068	1800	WB-A/210	
Reynolds, William	047	1885	WB-6/363	AR
Reynolds, William E.	104	1870	WB-6/40	AR
Rezan, James	070	1756	DB-D/166	
Rhea, John	010	1897	WB-I/524 & 531	AR
Rhea, Simon D.	VA	1883	047 WB-6/425	047 AR
Rheinstein, Frederick	070	1899	WB-H/192	AR
Rhem, John	028	1851	WB-D/177	
Rhem, Melcher	072	1857	WB-2/108	AR
Rhem, Melcher	028	1769	Orig. Only	AR
Rhem, William	057	1833	WB-B/116	AR
Rhew, Candis	036	1884	WB-A/61	CTY
Rhew, Frederick	070	1897	WB-G/591	AR
Rhew, Nelson	073	1878	WB-H/188	CTY
Rhew, Ruffin	078	1886	WB-19/191	
Rhew, Simpson	073	1848	WB-F/395	AR
Rheynolds, George D.	004	1876	WB-A/21	AR
Rhidenour, Nicholas	016	1855	WB-1/265	
Rhimer, Olitia	057	c1780	WB-A/194	AR
Rhoades, William	073	1791	WB-B/120	AR
Rhoads, Abraham	037	1821	WB-E/269	AR

Name	Co.	Date	Recorded Copy	Original
Rhoads, Elijah	104	1877	WB-6/143	AR
Rhoads, Levin	096	1818	Orig. Only	AR
Rhoads, William	096	1753	SS 881/75	SS/AR
Rhoda, Peter	024	1784	WB-A/99	AR
Rhodarmer, Noah	049	1895	WB-2/347	AR
Rhodes, Alexander	057	1889	WB-C/158	AR
Rhodes, Ambrose	099	1900	Orig. Only	AR
Rhodes, Anderson	073	1880	WB-H/238	CTY
Rhodes, Andrew	013	1856	WB-A/169	
Rhodes, Ann	037	1826	WB-F/54	AR
Rhodes, Ann	035	1848	WB-2/37	AR
Rhodes, Anthoney	037	1798	WB-D/39	AR
Rhodes, Anthony H.	072	1866	WB-3/12	AR
Rhodes, Benjamin	035	1805	WB-A/416	AR
Rhodes, Benjamin C.	083	1891	WB-3/541	AR
Rhodes, Burrelus	099	1888	WB-B/274	
Rhodes, Caleb	021	1896	WB-3/112	AR
Rhodes, David	018	1847	WB-C/322	
Rhodes, Delilah	073	1838	WB-F/6	AR
Rhodes, Durant H.	072	1874	WB-4/68	AR
Rhodes, Elizabeth	072	1829	WB-1/38	AR
Rhodes, Esther H.	072	c1875	WB-4/89	AR
Rhodes, George	073	1881	WB-H/298	CTY
Rhodes, George	ME	1839	075 WB-N/150	075 AR
Rhodes, H. W.	099	1888	WB-B/287	AR
Rhodes, Hannah	050	1882	WB-1/186	CTY
Rhodes, Henery	034	1774	Orig. Only	SS/AR
Rhodes, Henry	057	1849	WB-B/202	AR
Rhodes, Henry	060	1882	WB-4/255	AR
Rhodes, Henry	099	1824	RB-19/114	AR
Rhodes, Henry	010	1793	WB-D/225	AR
Rhodes, Henry	072	1751	028 DB-5/206	SS/AR
Rhodes, Henry	072	1781	RW/L68	AR
Rhodes, Hezekiah	046	1840	WB-C/217	AR
Rhodes, Hezekiah	073	1816	WB-D/494	AR
Rhodes, Hezekiah	092	1835	WB-4/87	
Rhodes, Jacob	083	1824	WB-1/198	AR-Copy
Rhodes, Jacob	099	1878	RB-35/424	AR
Rhodes, Jacob	085	c1782	WB-B/8	AR
Rhodes, Jacob	051	1819	WB-A/37	
Rhodes, James	103	1842	RD-8/156	
Rhodes, James	050	1889	WB-2/48	CTY
Rhodes, James	073	1868	WB-H/36	CTY
Rhodes, James	010	1800	WB-E/115	AR
Rhodes, James	103	1810	RD-1/218	
Rhodes, James	072	c1778	RW/L8	AR
Rhodes, James A.	099	1894	WB-C/209	AR
Rhodes, Jeremiah	099	1840	RB-24/377	AR
Rhodes, John	099	1874	RB-35/279	AR
Rhodes, John	103	1808	RD-1/47	AR
Rhodes, John	010	1826	WB-G/149	AR
Rhodes, John	096	1766	WB-1/39	AR
Rhodes, John	073	1824	WB-E/68	AR
Rhodes, John	010	1771	WB-A/152	AR
Rhodes, John	072	1786	WI/L11	AR
Rhodes, John	099	1882	WB-A/337	AR
Rhodes, John	104	1790	WB-1/295	AR
Rhodes, John	046	1792	WB-A/310	AR
Rhodes, John	099	1799	RB-5/1	AR
Rhodes, John Martin	057	1897	WB-C/227	AR
Rhodes, John, Sr.	099	1834	RB-23/212	AR
Rhodes, John, Sr.	010	1795	WB-D/299	AR
Rhodes, Joseph H.	063	1882	WB-3/230	
Rhodes, Joseph J.	099	1880	Orig. Only	AR
Rhodes, Joseph T.	035	1820	WB-A/421	
Rhodes, Joshua	010	1805	WB-E/260	AR
Rhodes, Mary	035	1836	Orig. Only	AR
Rhodes, Milley	010	1815	WB-F/294	AR
Rhodes, Pameli	046	1852	WB-C/377	AR
Rhodes, Polly	018	1848	WB-C/334	
Rhodes, Randolph	099	1792	RB-3/45	AR
Rhodes, Richard	002	c1693	Orig. Only	SS/AR
Rhodes, Robert	010	1808	WB-F/82	AR
Rhodes, Rudolph	060	1871	WB-4/78	AR
Rhodes, Samuel	049	c1825	WI-A/21	AR
Rhodes, Sarah	103	1794	WI-A/469	AR
Rhodes, Sarah	010	1803	WB-E/213	AR
Rhodes, Simeon	096	1870	WB-4/12	
Rhodes, Solomon	035	c1799	WB-A/407	AR
Rhodes, Thomas	010	1796	WB-D/317	AR
Rhodes, Thomas	010	1831	WB-G/212	AR
Rhodes, Thomas	073	1835	WB-E/351	AR
Rhodes, Wilie	036	1888	WB-A/142	CTY
Rhodes, William	096	1765	WB-1/32	AR
Rhodes, William	099	1864	RB-33/333	AR
Rhodes, William	073	1834	WB-E/329	AR
Rhodes, William	073	1804	WB-D/293	AR
Rhodes, William A.	099	1888	WB-B/272	AR
Rhodes, Woodhouse	072	1827	WB-1/4	AR
Rhoney, James	021	1869	WB-2/7	
Rhoney, John G.	021	1878	WB-2/188	AR
Rhoney, William	021	1900	WB-3/322	AR
Rhymes, Elizabeth	047	1826	WB-4/21	AR
Rhymes, Jesse	047	1822	WB-3/664	AR
Rhymes, Nicholas	085	1834	WB-H/615	AR
Rhyne, Adam A.	040	1891	WB-2/383	AR
Rhyne, Daniel	040	1878	WB-2/129	AR
Rhyne, Esli	040	1884	WB-2/231	AR
Rhyne, J. N.	065	1897	WB-M/560	AR
Rhyne, Jacob	040	1849	WB-1/28	
Rhyne, Jacob	060	1795	Orig. Only	AR
Rhyne, Jacob	040	1865	WB-1/177	
Rhyne, Jacob E.	040	1890	WB-2/368	AR
Rhyne, Jacob H.	040	1894	WB-2/481	AR
Rhyne, Jacob K.	040	1894	WB-2/473	AR
Rhyne, Jacob M.	040	c1857	WB-1/194	AR
Rhyne, John	040	1865	WB-1/181	AR-Copy
Rhyne, Jonas	060	1858	WB-3/16	AR
Rhyne, Lawson	060	1893	WB-4/524	AR
Rhyne, Micael	040	c1846	WB-1/55	
Rhyne, Moses H.	040	1888	WB-2/313	AR
Rhyne, Peter	060	1828	WB-1/96	AR
Rhyne, Philip	060	1797	Orig. Only	AR
Rhyne, Solomon	040	1866	WB-1/196	AR
Rhyne, Thomas	060	1837	WB-1/405	AR
Rialls, Stephen	011	c1825	WB-2/385	
Rials, Elizabeth	011	c1847	WB-1/138	
Ribelin, Jesse	085	1874	WB-1/275	CTY
Ribley, Martin	085	c1791	WB-C/57	AR
Rice, Benjamin	009	1746	SS 878/52	SS/AR
Rice, Betsy M.	084	1858	WB-C/274	CTY
Rice, Cathen	085	1883	WB-2/56	CTY
Rice, Celia	010	1900	WB-K/23	
Rice, Clarinda	097	1891	WB-2/396	AR
Rice, David	044	1856	WB-20/128	CTY
Rice, David	041	1804	WB-1/210	AR
Rice, Edmund	085	1891	WB-2/477	CTY
Rice, Edward	010	1867	WB-H/193	AR
Rice, Edward	010	1753	SS 878/212	SS/AR
Rice, Elizabeth	041	1801	WB-1/188	AR

Name	Co.	Date	Recorded Copy	Original
Rice, Elizabeth	047	1885	WB-6/395	
Rice, Enoch	085	1818	WB-G/521	AR
Rice, Ephriam	028	1788	WB-A/163	AR
Rice, Evan	028	1806	WB-B/253	AR
Rice, Fanny	085	c1806	WB-G/122	AR
Rice, Francis	085	1814	WB-G/332	AR
Rice, Francis	044	c1868	WB-23/9	CTY
Rice, Isaac C.	028	1880	WB-E/244	
Rice, James	028	1834	WB-C/369	AR
Rice, James	028	c1772	Orig. Only	AR
Rice, James C.	009	1890	WB-1/493	CTY
Rice, James Y.	046	1829	WB-B/386	AR
Rice, Jesse	073	c1798	Orig. Only	AR
Rice, John	069	1840	WB-1/443	AR
Rice, John	085	1878	WB-1/475	CTY
Rice, John	020	1797	RB-C/197	AR
Rice, John	054	c1791	WB-1/201	AR
Rice, John	073	1783	WB-A/262	AR
Rice, John	024	1753	Orig. Only	SS/AR
Rice, John	020	1794	RB-C/96	AR
Rice, John	024	c1764	WB-A/98	AR
Rice, John	041	1791	WB-1/94	AR
Rice, John B.	069	1865	WB-1/591	AR
Rice, John W.	098	1894	WB-A/192	CTY
Rice, John Y.	085	1886	WB-2/203	CTY
Rice, John, Sr.	069	1845	WB-1/480	AR
Rice, Joshua E.	047	1887	WB-6/469	
Rice, Judith	041	1808	WB-2/13	AR
Rice, Lucy	N	1720/1	SS 875/315	SS/AR (N)
Rice, Lucy Ann	032	1886	WB-3/511	AR
Rice, Martha	069	1861	WB-1/572	AR
Rice, Mary	010	1891	WB-I/326	AR
Rice, Mary	028	1819	WB-C/185	AR
Rice, Mary	070	1754	SS 878/192	SS/AR
Rice, Mary J.	100	1892	Orig. Only	AR
Rice, Morgin	N	c1684	Orig. Only	SS/AR
Rice, Napoleon	010	1864	WB-H/144	AR
Rice, Nathaniel	070	1753	028 DB-5/288	SS/AR
Rice, Phillip	085	1845	WB-I/252	AR
Rice, Rebacah	084	1820	WB-A/278	CTY
Rice, Reddin	083	1900	WB-4/256	AR
Rice, Sarah	010	1860	WB-H/90	AR
Rice, Sarah A.	009	1887	WB-1/432	CTY
Rice, Stephen A.	020	1899	WB-B/357	CTY
Rice, Thomas	044	1881	WB-23/427	CTY
Rice, Thomas	020	1804	RB-E/137	AR
Rice, Thomas	020	1800	RB-C/438	AR
Rice, William	024	c1759	Orig. Only	AR
Rice, William	085	c1806	WB-G/116	AR
Rice, William	010	1762	WB-A/39	AR
Rice, William	010	1853	WB-G/494	AR
Rice, William	083	1892	Orig. Only	AR
Rice, William	085	1837	WB-I/6	AR
Rice, William H.	084	1847	WB-C/61	CTY
Rice, Zadock	073	1866	WB-G/493	CTY
Rice, Zebulon	028	1788	WB-A/179	AR
Rich, Anthony F.	081	1894	WB-16/330	AR
Rich, Delaney S.	046	1896	WB-F/530	AR
Rich, Dicey	087	1864	Orig. Only	AR
Rich, Elizabeth	038	1887	WB-3/64	AR
Rich, Elizabeth	081	1897	WB-16/413	AR
Rich, Henry	085	c1793	WB-D/108	AR
Rich, Isaac	085	c1787	WB-D/107	AR
Rich, Jeremiah	099	1781	RB-1/174	AR
Rich, John	032	1851	WB-2/57	AR
Rich, John	033	1858	WB-1/162	AR
Rich, John	081	1798	WB-2/42	
Rich, Lott	087	1879	WB-3/199	AR
Rich, Moses	081	1850	WB-9/218	AR
Rich, Nancy	081	1870	WB-15/32	AR
Rich, Priscilla	035	1899	WB-4/554	
Rich, Samuel	090	1819	WB-3/32	AR
Rich, Thomas	038	1883	WB-2/469	
Richard, Jacob	085	c1795	WB-D/94	AR
Richards, Ann	009	1816	OB-A/250	AR
Richards, Charles B.	013	1881	WB-B/243	AR
Richards, Ezekiel	053	1790	Orig. Only	AR
Richards, George	039	1818	WB-F/123	
Richards, Henry	053	1795	RW-1/254	AR
Richards, John	075	1741	Orig. Only	SS/AR
Richards, John	039	c1796	WB-B/31	
Richards, John	071	1791	WB-1/439	AR
Richards, John	039	1888	WB-U/459	
Richards, John	085	1849	WB-K/83	AR
Richards, John, Sr.	057	1820	WB-B/57	AR
Richards, Joseph	085	1822	WB-H/153	AR
Richards, Mary	012	1827	WB-B/152	AR
Richards, Mary	024	1743	Orig. Only	SS/AR
Richards, Mary	039	c1854	WB-O/370	
Richards, Peter	028	1841	WB-D/28	AR
Richards, Ralph	009	c1796	OWB/329	AR
Richards, Richard	039	1795	WB-B/20	
Richards, Richard	037	1758	SS 881/219	SS/AR
Richards, Thomas	053	1790	RW-1/188	
Richards, Thomas Y.	039	1831	SC/09050	AR-Copy
Richards, Thomas Y.	039	1831	WB-J/167	AR
Richards, William	071	1820	WB-3/235	AR
Richards, William	039	c1795	WB-B/14	AR
Richards, Williamson	039	c1820	WB-G/36	AR
Richardson, A. W.	099	1891	WB-B/576	AR
Richardson, Abner	069	1896	WB-5/548	AR
Richardson, Adam	056	c1900	WB-4/331	
Richardson, Alexander	004	1889	WB-A/93	AR
Richardson, Alfred	047	1874	WB-6/106	AR
Richardson, Amanda M.	046	1882	WB-E/330	AR
Richardson, Andrew	054	c1797	WB-1/202	AR
Richardson, Annie	073	1894	WB-I/34	CTY
Richardson, Benjamin	075	1790	WB-K/184	AR
Richardson, Catherine	060	1835	WB-1/351	AR
Richardson, Charles	086	1823	WB-D/14	AR
Richardson, Clayborne	004	c1891	WB-A/124	AR
Richardson, Daniel	075	1723	SS 876/2	SS/AR
Richardson, Drewry	068	1811	WB-A/271	
Richardson, E. W.	097	1877	WB-2/124	AR
Richardson, Edith	099	1864	RB-33/331	AR
Richardson, Edward	065	1797	WB-F/127	AR
Richardson, Edward	084	1825	WB-A/266	CTY
Richardson, Edward A.	028	1896	WB-F/203	
Richardson, Eli D.	097	1889	WB-2/332	AR
Richardson, Elisha	006	1857	WB-D/45	AR
Richardson, Elizabeth	069	1883	WB-5/181	AR
Richardson, Fereby	075	1814	WB-M1/266	AR
Richardson, Frances	044	1826	WB-10/99	CTY
Richardson, George	070	1756	SS 882/6	SS/AR
Richardson, George	070	1756	DB-D/342	
Richardson, George A.	028	1899	WB-F/441	
Richardson, Gideon	069	1880	WB-5/108	AR
Richardson, Gideon	047	1880	WB-6/221	AR
Richardson, Green L.	090	1857	WB-4/304	AR

Name	Co.	Date	Recorded Copy	Original
Richardson, Hardy	047	1855	WB-5/7	
Richardson, Haynes	005	1847	WB-B/217	AR
Richardson, Henry T.	028	1900	WB-F/500	
Richardson, Isaac	022	1833	WB-B/242	AR
Richardson, Ivy	075	c1855	WB-M2/29	AR
Richardson, J. A.	099	1892	WB-C/46	AR
Richardson, J. H.	097	1886	WB-2/305	AR
Richardson, J. M.	060	1886	WB-4/344	AR
Richardson, Jacob	075	1829	WB-N/50	AR
Richardson, James	070	1864	WB-D/154	
Richardson, James	020	c1826	RB-L/112	AR
Richardson, Jesse	033	1844	WB-1/57	AR
Richardson, Jessee	022	1899	WB-F/97	AR
Richardson, John	006	1889	WB-E/183	AR
Richardson, John	072	1786	WI/L41	AR
Richardson, John	075	1761	WB-I/8	AR
Richardson, John	028	1773	Orig. Only	SS/AR
Richardson, John	077	1743	Orig. Only	SS/AR
Richardson, John W.	097	1865	WB-1/247	AR
Richardson, John, Sr.	096	1836	WB-2/118	AR
Richardson, Jonathan	056	1854	WB-1/672	AR
Richardson, Joseph	056	1840	WB-1/524	
Richardson, Joseph	075	1780	WB-K/47	AR
Richardson, Joseph	075	1876	WB-O/68	AR
Richardson, Josiah	075	1774	WB-I/93	AR
Richardson, Julia B.	005	1874	WB-D/29	AR
Richardson, Kiddy	075	1828	WB-N/46	AR
Richardson, Kindrick	097	1866	WB-1/265	AR
Richardson, Lebbeus	075	1778	WB-K/20	AR
Richardson, Margaret	028	1823	WB-C/233	AR
Richardson, Martha	078	1816	WI-7/78	AR
Richardson, Mary	075	1822	WB-M1/354	AR
Richardson, Mary A.	028	1854	WB-D/233	
Richardson, Miles	028	1889	WB-E/537	
Richardson, Nancy	056	1815	WB-1/244	AR
Richardson, Nancy	092	1888	WB-6/275	AR
Richardson, Nathaniel	011	N. D.	WB-1/544	
Richardson, Nathaniel	028	1896	WB-F/219	
Richardson, Perry R.	069	1897	WB-6/21	AR
Richardson, Purdie	005	1872	WB-D/22	AR
Richardson, Ransom	011	1892	WB-2/249	
Richardson, Richard	028	1855	WB-D/241	AR
Richardson, Richard	028	1835	WB-C/383	AR
Richardson, Sally	084	1847	WB-C/60	CTY
Richardson, Samuel N.	011	1851	WB-1/192	
Richardson, Samuel N.	011	c1836	WB-1/34	
Richardson, Sarah	085	1817	WB-G/489	AR
Richardson, Sarah	065	1865	WB-J/198	
Richardson, Sarah	097	1850	WB-1/78	AR
Richardson, Simon	028	1879	WB-E/198	AR
Richardson, Stephen	075	1723	Orig. Only	SS/AR
Richardson, Stephen	075	1802	WB-M1/57	AR
Richardson, Stephen	070	1881	WB-E/397	AR
Richardson, Thomas	029	1853	WB-C/247	AR-Nunc.
Richardson, Thomas	022	1803	WB-A/86	AR
Richardson, Valentine	028	1822	WB-C/214	AR
Richardson, Valentine	027	1864	WB-A/90	AR
Richardson, Vinton C.	103	c1871	WB-1/38	AR
Richardson, William	047	1798	WB-3/309	AR
Richardson, William	068	1805	WB-A/259	Nunc.
Richardson, William	020	1811	RB-F/243	AR
Richardson, William	081	1794	WB-2/3	AR
Richardson, William	069	1813	WB-1/254	AR
Richardson, William	056	1814	WB-1/231	AR
Richardson, William	075	1791	WB-K/222	AR
Richardson, William H.	099	1895	WB-C/353	AR
Richardson, William R.	027	1895	WB-2/113	AR
Richardson, William S.	046	1900	WB-G/209	
Richardson, William Z.	084	1885	WB-E/333	
Riche, Lewis	087	1824	Orig. Only	AR
Richerson, George	022	1801	WB-A/63	AR
Riches, Henry	085	c1793	WB-D/112	AR
Richie, John	085	1887	WB-2/257	CTY
Richmond, Ann	020	1816	RB-G/151	
Richmond, C. J.	020	1895	WB-B/206	CTY
Richmond, Caleb H.	020	1861	RB-S/416	AR
Richmond, D. W. K.	078	1889	WB-19/256	
Richmond, E. A.	020	1888	WB-A/532	CTY
Richmond, George T.	001	1898	WB-3/220	AR
Richmond, Henery	N	1714	Orig. Only	SS/AR
Richmond, John, Sr.	020	1841	RB-O/255	AR
Richmond, John, Sr.	020	1787	RB-B/164	AR
Richmond, Joshua	020	1807	RB-E/313	AR
Richmond, Rebecca	079	1893	WB-3/40	AR
Richmond, Skipwith	037	1774	WB-A/226	AR
Richmond, Stephen T.	020	1878	WB-A/238	CTY
Richmond, William	020	1832	RB-M/222	AR
Richson, Benjamin	047	1810	WB-3/506	AR
Rickard, Alex	032	1886	WB-3/524	
Rickard, Jacob	032	1877	WB-3/205	AR
Rickard, John, Sr.	032	1841	WB-1/375	AR
Rickerson, William	081	c1793	WB-2/3	AR
Rickert, Ann	054	c1883	Orig. Only	AR
Rickert, J. D.	054	1886	WB-5/100	CTY
Rickert, Michael	054	c1863	WB-4/232	CTY
Rickert, Michael	085	1822	WB-H/186	AR
Rickes, Henry	085	c1793	Orig. Only	AR-Copy
Rickets, John	005	1802	WB-2/132	AR
Ricketts, Alexander	005	1862	WB-C/178	AR
Ricketts, Bird	064	1899	WB-2/479	AR
Ricketts, William	005	1841	WB-B/137	AR
Rickitson, Gordius	028	1774	Orig. Only	SS/AR
Rickman, John	013	1897	WB-D/57	AR
Rickman, Robert	047	1777	WB-2/449	
Ricks, Abraham	069	1833	WB-1/394	AR
Ricks, Achsey	069	c1863	WB-1/604	AR
Ricks, Benjamin	024	1721	SS 875/344	SS/AR
Ricks, Benjamin	037	1775	WB-A/230	AR
Ricks, Catherine	046	1877	WB-E/194	AR
Ricks, D. A. T.	069	c1871	WB-1/608	AR
Ricks, David	071	1896	WB-7/313	AR
Ricks, Edwin	071	1821	WB-3/257	AR
Ricks, Francis A.	105	1897	WB-3/283	AR
Ricks, Isaac	037	1760	WB-A/9	AR
Ricks, Isaac	037	1748	SS 881/282	SS/AR
Ricks, Isaac	047	1820	WB-3/655	AR
Ricks, Isaac	037	1828	WB-F/90	AR
Ricks, Isbel	069	1841	WB-1/453	AR
Ricks, James	037	1792	WB-C/187	AR
Ricks, James C.	009	1898	WB-2/131	CTY
Ricks, James W.	037	1862	WB-G/221	AR
Ricks, John	046	1872	WB-E/93	AR
Ricks, John	047	1787	WB-3/143	AR
Ricks, John	069	1847	WB-1/504	AR
Ricks, John A.	069	1887	WB-5/233	AR
Ricks, John, Sr.	069	c1790	WB-1/245	AR
Ricks, Jonas	046	1821	WB-B/134	AR
Ricks, Louisianna	079	1899	WB-3/176	AR
Ricks, Lyda	069	1835	WB-1/411	AR
Ricks, Marmaduke	069	1890	WB-5/333	AR

Name	Co.	Date	Recorded Copy	Original
Ricks, Mary	071	1816	WB-3/171	AR
Ricks, Micajah	069	1848	WB-1/513	AR
Ricks, Michel	105	c1863	WB-1/113	
Ricks, Phebe	037	1812	WB-E/36	AR
Ricks, Rhoda	069	1834	WB-1/403	AR
Ricks, S. B.	069	1896	WB-5/567	AR
Ricks, Sarah	047	1778	WB-2/74	
Ricks, Sarah	044	1825	WB-10/16	CTY
Ricks, Thomas	069	1789	WB-1/247	AR-Nunc.
Ricks, Thomas	044	1803	WB-5/321	CTY
Ricks, William	071	1793	WB-2/38	AR
Ricks, William	037	c1771	Orig. Only	AR
Ricks, William	015	1893	WB-3/52	AR
Ricks, William	069	1832	WB-1/388	AR
Ricks, William	069	1888	WB-5/313	AR
Ricks, Willie	069	c1846	WB-1/545	AR
Riddick, Abram	051	1871	WB-C/40	AR
Riddick, Ann	041	1824	WB-2/221	AR
Riddick, Ann B.	024	1867	WB-D/52	AR
Riddick, Ann C.	077	1892	WB-H/214	AR
Riddick, Christen	041	1859	WB-3/242	AR
Riddick, Christopher	041	1798	WB-1/157	AR
Riddick, Clarissa	075	1893	WB-O/375	AR
Riddick, David	077	1781	Orig. Only	AR
Riddick, David	041	1849	WB-3/111	AR
Riddick, Docton	041	1861	WB-3/267	AR
Riddick, Edmund	077	1888	WB-H/179	AR
Riddick, Elbert T.	077	1863	WB-F/542	AR
Riddick, Elizabeth	041	1847	WB-3/85	AR
Riddick, Isaiah	041	1840	WB-3/21	AR
Riddick, Jacob	077	1798	WB-E/100	AR
Riddick, James	051	1865	WB-B/63	
Riddick, James	041	1786	WB-1/56	AR
Riddick, James C.	041	1863	WB-3/301	AR
Riddick, James R.	041	1866	WB-3/335	AR
Riddick, Jerry	101	1892	WB-A/208	
Riddick, John	041	1850	WB-3/137	AR
Riddick, John L.	077	1883	WB-H/139	AR
Riddick, Joseph	041	1818	WB-2/151	AR
Riddick, Joseph	077	1759	SS 881/239	SS/AR
Riddick, Josiah	VA	1838	041 WB-3/11	041 AR
Riddick, Keder	041	1785	WB-1/45	AR
Riddick, Lavina	077	1874	WB-H/60	AR
Riddick, Leah	041	1817	WB-2/139	AR
Riddick, Margaret A.	041	1890	WB-4/298	AR
Riddick, Margaret J.	041	1897	WB-4/433	AR
Riddick, Martha R.	077	1899	WB-H/321	AR
Riddick, Mary	041	1808	WB-2/16	AR
Riddick, Mary W.	077	1893	WB-H/245	AR
Riddick, Micajah	041	1832	WB-2/305	AR
Riddick, Micajah	041	1814	WB-2/86	AR
Riddick, Mills	VA	1844	Copy	009 CTY
Riddick, Mills	077	1777	WB-C/197	AR
Riddick, Nathan	041	1845	WB-3/67	AR
Riddick, Nathaniel	041	1799	WB-1/169	AR
Riddick, Richard H.	060	1863	WB-3/51	AR
Riddick, Robert	041	1806	WB-1/227	AR
Riddick, Robert	041	1845	WB-3/62	AR
Riddick, Samuel	075	1810	WB-M1/219	AR
Riddick, Seth	077	1825	WB-F/84	AR
Riddick, Solomon	077	1831	WB-F/187	AR-Nunc.
Riddick, Wilie	041	1885	WB-4/213	AR
Riddick, Willis	077	1832	WB-F/211	AR
Riddick, Willis	041	1850	WB-3/134	AR
Riddle, Arcenia	022	1874	WB-E/95	AR
Riddle, Cato	022	1849	WB-C/235	AR
Riddle, James	068	1802	WB-A/219	
Riddle, Jane	013	1890	WB-C/23	AR
Riddle, John	085	1826	WB-H/365	AR
Riddle, John	022	1822	WB-B/50	AR
Riddle, John W.	062	1859	WB-A/20	AR
Riddle, Julius	022	c1807	WB-A/47	AR
Riddle, Stephen	085	c1804	WB-F/69	AR
Ridenhower, John	089	1872	WB-2/14	AR
Ridenhower, Phillip	089	1896	Orig. Only	AR
Ridenhower, Wilson	016	1857	WB-2/34	
Rider, Adam	085	c1801	WB-D/96	AR
Ridge, Godfrey	081	1790	WB-1/85	AR
Ridge, John W.	081	1897	WB-17/10	AR
Ridge, Thomas	N	c1747	SS 881/35	SS/AR
Ridge, Thomas	081	1824	WB-5/131	AR
Ridge, William	081	1846	WB-8/251	AR
Ridgeway, Josiah	028	1775	Orig. Only	AR
Ridgway, Josiah	028	1779	Orig. Only	AR
Ridick, John	024	1853	WB-C/343	AR
Ridings, John	090	1828	WB-3/195	AR-Nunc.
Ridings, John D.	038	1865	WB-1/260	AR
Ridings, Joseph	080	1895	Copy	086 AR
Ridings, Joseph	080	1895	WB-1/251	AR
Ridley, Day	051	1777	Copy	024 AR
Ridley, Elizabeth	099	1850	RB-27/473	AR
Ridley, Frances	044	c1823	WB-9/248	CTY
Ridley, Howel L.	044	1827	WB-10/385	CTY
Ridley, James	044	1855	WB-19/540	CTY
Ridley, James D.	099	1820	RB-16/303	AR
Ridley, John C.	099	1837	RB-24/263	AR
Ridley, Thomas	VA	1875	071 WB-6/166	071 AR
Ridley, Thomas D.	044	1837	WB-13/522	CTY
Ridley, Timothy	051	1843	WB-A/164	
Ridley, William J.	099	1841	RB-24/528	AR
Ridout, James D.	044	1853	WB-19/294	CTY
Rielag, Eva V.	OH	1899	013 WB-D/275	013 AR
Rieley, Daniel	104	1818	WB-3/186	AR
Rieley, John	073	c1791	WB-B/152	AR
Rienssell, Petter	008	1734	SS 876/372	
Riethweil, Lewis	044	1772	Orig. Only	CTY
Rieusset, John	024	1763	WB-A/162	AR
Rieusset, John	N	1737	Orig. Only	SS/AR
Rieussett, Petter	008	1734	Orig. Only	SS/AR
Rieves, William	044	1751	Orig. Only	CTY
Rigby, William	070	1744	DB-C/26	
Rigby, William	070	1744	SS 878/21	SS/AR
Rigers, Durrell	099	1852	RB-27/470	
Riggan, Benjamin	100	1822	WB-24/122	AR
Riggan, Christopher	100	1852	WB-42/34	AR
Riggan, Francis	100	1846	WB-39/238	AR
Riggan, Francis	100	1818	WB-21/108	AR
Riggan, Hannah	100	1813	WB-17/148	AR
Riggan, Jacob	100	1816	WB-20/121	AR
Riggan, James	100	1867	WB-50/232	AR
Riggan, John	100	1803	WB-12/26	AR
Riggan, Littleton	099	1893	WB-C/125	AR
Riggan, Lucy	047	1843	WB-4/223	AR
Riggan, Sarah	100	1869	Orig. Only	AR
Riggan, William W.	100	1853	WB-43/394	AR
Riggins, Sarah	071	1815	WB-3/145	AR
Riggs, A. J.	103	1864	RD-13/751	AR
Riggs, Abraham	077	1761	Orig. Only	AR
Riggs, David	028	1796	WB-A/358	AR
Riggs, David	072	1837	WB-2/9	AR

Name	Co.	Date	Recorded Copy	Original
Riggs, Edward L.	101	c1849	024 WB-C/344	024 AR
Riggs, Frances	028	1852	WB-D/191	AR
Riggs, Francis T.	028	1866	WB-D/421	AR
Riggs, George	073	1798	WB-C/125	AR
Riggs, Giles	028	1785	WB-A/102	AR
Riggs, Isaac H.	018	1853	WB-C/372	
Riggs, James	028	1851	WB-D/172	AR
Riggs, James	073	1847	WB-F/389	AR
Riggs, James	028	1826	WB-C/281	AR
Riggs, James	028	1848	WB-D/150	AR
Riggs, John	028	1812	WB-C/56	AR
Riggs, John	028	1788	WB-A/167	AR
Riggs, John	073	1811	Orig. Only	AR
Riggs, John	073	c1803	Orig. Only	AR
Riggs, John	028	1810	WB-C/18	AR
Riggs, John H.	073	1865	WB-G/481	CTY
Riggs, Lemuel	018	1886	WB-E/138	AR
Riggs, Lott	092	1813	WB-3/106	AR
Riggs, Margaret	073	1849	WB-F/445	AR
Riggs, Mary	028	1858	WB-D/294	
Riggs, Mary J.	092	1885	WB-6/227	AR
Riggs, Nemiah	018	1845	WB-C/303	
Riggs, Noah	018	1826	WB-C/68	
Riggs, Samuel	092	1800	WB-3/36	
Riggs, Shadrack	028	1807	WB-B/299	AR
Riggs, Silas	030	1854	WB-4/184	AR
Riggs, Wiley	078	1892	WB-19/331	AR
Riggs, Wiley	028	1811	WB-C/41	AR
Riggs, William	073	1782	WB-A/270	AR
Riggsbee, Atlas J.	022	1894	WB-E/553	AR
Riggsbee, Lucian H.	022	1873	WB-E/91	AR
Riggsbee, Mark	022	1866	WB-D/149	AR
Riggsbee, Phebe P.	022	c1853	WB-C/432	AR
Riggsbee, Sarah M.	022	1881	WB-E/220	AR
Right, James	099	1824	RB-19/73	
Right, Zachariah	018	1835	WB-C/187	
Rightmyer, Fred O.	100	1871	WB-51/47	AR
Righton, William	024	c1835	WB-C/189	AR
Rights, Cornelia	038	1892	WB-3/326	AR
Rights, Elizabeth	038	1864	WB-1/245	AR
Rights, John	090	1810	WB-2/116	
Rights, Maria M.	090	1835	WB-3/283	AR
Rights, Matthew	090	1828	WB-3/182	AR
Rights, Zacharias	038	1867	WB-1/280	AR-Copy
Rightsell, Adam	046	1855	WB-C/431	AR
Rigin, William P.	015	1770	100 WB-1/123	AR
Rigler, D. M.	065	1900	WB-N/316	AR
Rigney, Benjamin	009	1750	028 DB-5/140	SS/AR
Rigney, Hanah	009	1766	OWB/101	AR
Rigney, James	009	1763	OWB/89	
Rigney, John	009	1726	SS 876/32	SS/AR
Rigoe, Elizabeth	070	1810	WB-AB/139	AR
Rigsbee, Frederick	099	1841	RB-24/528	AR
Rigsbee, James	099	1853	RB-28/319	AR
Rigsbee, Kerney	099	1882	WB-A/327	AR
Rigsbee, Leroy G.	073	1881	WB-H/278	CTY
Rigsbee, Mark	073	1876	WB-H/145	CTY
Rigsbee, Ruffin	073	1873	WB-H/68	CTY
Rigsby, Elizabeth	073	1851	WB-F/486	AR
Rigsby, Jesse	073	1827	WB-E/148	AR
Rike, Mary Ann	032	1880	WB-3/304	AR
Riles, John	072	1781	RW/L30	AR
Riley, Ezekiel A.	016	1897	WB-4/286	AR
Riley, Jacob	073	c1812	WB-D/365	AR
Riley, James	032	1843	WB-1/413	AR
Riley, James W.	073	1878	WB-H/194	CTY
Riley, John	032	1865	WB-2/309	AR
Riley, Nathan	032	1827	WB-1/87	AR
Riley, Peter	032	1842	WB-1/401	AR
Riley, Rhadias	032	1845	WB-1/455	AR
Riley, Sanders	073	1853	WB-G/30	AR
Riley, William	070	1744	WB-C/358	AR
Riley, William	073	1846	WB-F/238	AR
Riley, William A.	054	1866	WB-3/186	AR
Riley, William R.	DC	1893	061 WB-2/129	061 AR
Rilley, John	070	c1778	Orig. Only	AR
Rimer, Daniel	016	1889	WB-4/28	AR
Rimer, George	054	1872	WB-4/103	CTY
Rimer, Michael	054	1868	WB-3/208	AR
Rimer, Samuel M.	085	1863	WB-K/316	AR
Rimer, Thomas M.	016	1875	WB-3/143	AR
Rimmer, Samuel	078	1861	WB-18/239	AR
Rimmer, Sarah J.	078	1893	WB-19/346	AR
Rimmer, William	078	1896	WB-19/405	AR
Rinch, George	054	1874	Orig. Only	AR
Rinchey, Adem	035	1791	WB-A/404	AR
Rinck, Andrew	021	1866	WB-1/236	AR
Rinck, Ephriam	021	c1896	WB-3/338	AR
Rinck, Francis	060	1811	Orig. Only	AR
Rinehardt, Matthias	016	1895	WB-4/202	AR
Rineheardt, Christian	106	c1867	WB-1/125	
Ring, Leopold	092	1881	WB-6/158	AR
Ring, Sarah	038	1873	WB-2/143	AR
Ring, Thomas S.	038	1889	WB-3/139	AR
Ring, William J.	092	1900	WB-6/531	AR
Rinhart, Andrew	065	1785	WB-F/118	AR
Rintelman, John, Sr.	085	c1806	WB-G/119	AR-Copy
Rintels, Jacob	065	1876	WB-K/220	AR
Riordane, Denis	030	1724	Orig. Only	SS/AR
Ripley, Ann	075	1814	WB-M1/267	AR
Ripley, Spencer	075	1812	WB-M1/232	AR
Ripley, Valentine	050	1879	WB-1/148	CTY
Rippel, Henry	090	1836	WB-3/301	AR
Rippel, Martin	090	1846	WB-4/212	AR
Ripple, Christian	032	1869	WB-3/29	AR
Ripple, Elizabeth	038	1845	WB-1/52	AR
Rippy, Edward	026	1854	WB-1/168	AR
Rippy, Mary A.	001	1899	WB-3/251	AR
Rippy, Matthew	073	1817	WB-D/508	AR
Rippy, Thomas	001	c1844	WB-1/30	AR
Rish, George	061	1831	WB-1/3	AR
Rising, George W.	048	1897	WB-1/76	CTY
Risonouer, Mathew	028	1747	SS 877/29	SS/AR
Ristelubert, John B.	009	c1789	OWB/230	AR
Ritch, Edmond	097	1860	WB-1/162	
Ritch, Elijah	065	1870	WB-K/44	AR
Ritch, G. W.	097	1877	WB-2/114	AR
Ritch, Jacob	022	c1810	WB-A/181	AR
Ritch, James M.	097	1862	WB-1/195	
Ritch, John	065	1838	WB-E/189	AR
Ritch, Lott, Sr.	087	1846	WB-1/317	AR
Ritch, Octa M.	065	1897	WB-M/550	AR
Ritchardson, John	056	1802	WB-1/137	AR
Ritchey, John R.	085	1886	WB-2/191	CTY
Ritchey, William N.	016	1864	WB-2/114	
Ritchie, Jacob	054	1881	WB-4/443	CTY
Ritchie, Jacob M.	085	1889	WB-2/388	CTY
Ritchie, James	070	1809	WB-AB/117	AR
Ritchie, John	065	1788	WB-F/123	AR
Ritega, Jacob	075	1735	LGB-4/#12	SS/AR

Name	Co.	Date	Recorded Copy	Original
Ritsel, Henry	046	1836	WB-B/551	AR
Ritter, Alfred	030	1857	WB-4/210	
Ritter, James G.	029	1891	WB-E/531	
Ritter, James T.	029	1898	WB-F/146	AR
Ritter, Margaret	068	c1851	WB-B/222	
Ritter, Margret	068	1885	WB-D/181	
Ritter, William	072	1831	WB-1/83	AR
Rivenbark, David	070	1866	WB-D/192	AR
Rivenbark, David F.	087	1857	WB-1/517	AR
Rivenbark, Jerusha V.	076	1900	Orig. Only	AR
Rivenbark, Matthew J.	087	c1890	Orig. Only	AR
Rivenbark, Spicy	076	1895	WB-A1/209	AR
Rivera, Mary A.	MD	1870	070 WB-E/218	070 AR
Rivers, Aaron	028	1889	009 WB-1/514	009 CTY
Rivers, Aaron	028	1889	WB-E/535	
Rivers, Aaron	009	1879	WB-1/241	CTY
Rivers, Elizabeth	100	1895	WB-51/409	
Rivers, Fanny M.	100	1862	WB-49/421	AR
Rivers, Joshua, Sr.	100	1824	WB-26/37	AR
Rives, Clara	070	1875	Orig. Only	AR
Rives, Edwards	022	1840	WB-C/103	AR
Rives, Henry	071	c1834	Orig. Only	AR
Rives, James F.	022	1887	WB-E/344	AR
Rives, Levi	054	c1878	Orig. Only	AR
Rives, Lucy C.	071	1840	WB-4/205	AR
Rives, Thomas	022	c1807	WB-A/138	AR
Rives, Thomas	071	1816	WB-3/188	AR
Rives, William	100	1839	WB-37/244	AR
Rives, William	054	c1827	WB-2/83	AR
Rives, William A.	022	1883	WB-E/270	AR
Rivis, Elmina	079	1890	WB-2/491	AR
Roach, Charles	028	1821	WB-C/200	AR
Roach, David	028	1783	Orig. Only	AR
Roach, James	028	1866	Copy	009 AR
Roach, James	073	1792	WB-B/176	AR
Roach, James	028	1866	WB-D/435	AR
Roach, James, Sr.	084	1842	WB-B/268	
Roach, John	103	1790	Orig. Only	AR
Roach, John R.	079	c1863	WB-1/150	AR
Roach, Luke	084	1865	WB-D/31	CTY
Roach, Polly	028	1825	WB-C/265	AR
Roach, Rebecca	084	1838	WB-B/197	CTY
Roach, Sallie P.	084	1876	WB-E/104	CTY
Roach, Stephen H.	075	1849	WB-N/229	AR
Roach, Tabitha	084	1862	WB-C/366	CTY
Roach, Thomas	081	1832	WB-6/308	AR
Roach, William	009	1817	OB-A/274	AR
Roads, Joseph	019	1789	WB-D/337	AR
Roadsmith, Paul	085	1815	WB-G/380	AR
Roan, Felix	020	1891	WB-B/85	CTY
Roan, Mary B.	020	1896	WB-B/223	CTY
Roan, Milley	036	1899	WB-A/486	CTY
Roan, Nathaniel	020	1879	WB-A/264	CTY
Roan, Sarah	FL	c1850	Copy	020 AR
Roan, Thomas	020	1846	RB-P/265	AR
Roan, William	073	1856	WB-G/156	AR
Roark, Elijah	090	1808	WB-2/102	AR
Roark, Joshua	006	1893	WB-E/238	AR
Roark, Timothy	090	1839	WB-4/34	AR
Roark, William	006	1872	WB-E/8	AR
Robards, Allen	044	1861	WB-21/521	CTY
Robards, Andrew	028	1723	Orig. Only	SS/AR
Robards, H. J.	044	1879	WB-23/327	CTY
Robards, James	044	1804	WB-6/96	CTY
Robards, William	044	1842	WB-15/296	CTY
Robason, Amos	063	c1832	WB-2/182	
Robason, Daniel	063	1835	WB-2/209	
Robason, Elizabeth	063	1827	WB-2/129	
Robason, Harmon	063	1849	WB-2/351	
Robason, Henry	063	1829	WB-2/148	
Robason, Henry, Sr.	063	1828	WB-2/138	
Robason, Henry, Sr.	063	1794	WB-1/199	
Robason, James	063	1811	WB-2/6	
Robason, Jasper	009	c1823	OWB/480	AR
Robason, Jesse J.	009	1881	WB-1/270	CTY
Robason, Joshua	063	1829	WB-2/149	
Robason, Marme Duke	096	1762	WB-1/23	AR
Robason, Mary	063	1855	WB-2/410	
Robason, Sarah	013	1843	WB-A/89	
Robason, William	063	1830	WB-2/163	
Robason, William	063	1845	WB-2/320	
Robason, William	063	c1798	WB-1/346	
Robb, John	021	1865	WB-1/211	AR
Robb, Nancy	054	1883	WB-4/492	CTY
Robbens, William	037	1781	WB-B/90	AR
Robbin, Milly	010	1895	WB-I/439	AR
Robbins, A. S.	081	1894	WB-16/319	AR
Robbins, Amos	105	1885	WB-2/332	AR
Robbins, Arthur	105	c1867	WB-1/129	
Robbins, Ashbel W.	100	1826	WB-30/39	AR
Robbins, Frances A.	105	c1863	WB-1/98	
Robbins, Harriett	046	1899	WB-G/159	AR
Robbins, Isaac	037	1847	WB-F/370	AR
Robbins, Isaac	081	1808	WB-3/96	AR
Robbins, Isaac P.	038	1890	WB-3/153	AR
Robbins, Jacob	037	1861	WB-G/205	AR
Robbins, James	086	1884	WB-F/241	AR
Robbins, James	046	1867	WB-D/341	AR
Robbins, James	081	1799	WB-2/48	AR
Robbins, Jesse	081	1887	WB-16/51	AR
Robbins, John	081	c1892	Orig. Only	AR-Copy
Robbins, John	086	1893	WB-F/451	AR
Robbins, John	037	1819	WB-E/217	AR
Robbins, John	010	1846	WB-G/408	AR
Robbins, Jonathan	081	1834	WB-6/356	
Robbins, Joseph	081	1788	WB-1/61	AR
Robbins, Julius C.	009	1845	OB-F/90	AR
Robbins, L. H.	069	1899	WB-6/87	AR
Robbins, Leanna	081	1860	WB-11/369	AR
Robbins, Mary	100	1805	WB-13/9	AR
Robbins, Mary Ann	105	1890	WB-2/554	
Robbins, Mary E.	105	1898	WB-3/318	AR
Robbins, Mary E.	105	1898	037 WB-H/493	037 AR
Robbins, Michael	070	c1870	Orig. Only	AR
Robbins, Reubin	104	1833	WB-4/167	AR
Robbins, Roland	037	1832	WB-F/139	AR
Robbins, Sarah	009	1900	WB-2/237	CTY
Robbins, Sarah	037	1809	WB-D/346	AR
Robbins, Simon	037	1850	WB-F/439	AR
Robbins, Thomas	009	1843	OB-E/185	AR
Robbins, Thomas	086	1862	WB-E/400	AR
Robbins, William	037	1831	WB-F/120	AR
Robbinson, Alexander	073	1774	WB-A/147	
Robbs, Alexander	073	1807	WB-D/215	AR
Roberson, A. G.	022	1884	WB-E/298	AR
Roberson, Alexis	068	1877	WB-D/96	
Roberson, Alice	087	c1811	Orig. Only	AR
Roberson, Allen	019	1803	WB-D/342	AR
Roberson, Allison J.	073	1900	WB-I/176	CTY
Roberson, Amos	063	1893	WB-4/101	AR

Name	Co.	Date	Recorded Copy	Original
Roberson, Archalaus	037	1804	WB-D/203	AR
Roberson, Asa	077	1882	WB-H/189	AR
Roberson, Caroline	073	1863	WB-G/410	
Roberson, Catharine	072	1863	Orig. Only	AR
Roberson, Catherine	022	1883	WB-E/264	AR
Roberson, Christopher	100	1791	WB-5/245	AR
Roberson, David	073	1850	WB-F/467	AR
Roberson, Dennis	063	1889	WB-4/47	
Roberson, Dolph A.	046	1900	WB-G/232	AR
Roberson, Francis E.	063	1876	WB-3/109	
Roberson, George	107	1856	WB-1/65	
Roberson, George	044	1761	Orig. Only	CTY
Roberson, George	092	1785	WB-2/63A	AR
Roberson, Henry	106	1873	WB-2/29	
Roberson, Henry B.	063	1893	WB-4/103	AR
Roberson, Israel	044	1760	Orig. Only	CTY
Roberson, James	099	1823	RB-18/122	AR
Roberson, James A.	013	1886	WB-B/380	AR
Roberson, Jesse	063	1896	WB-4/192	AR
Roberson, John	104	1857	WB-5/179	
Roberson, John	044	1774	WB-1/36A	CTY
Roberson, John	092	c1836	WB-4/111	
Roberson, Josiah	077	1807	WB-E/289	
Roberson, Mary	104	1866	WB-5/449	AR
Roberson, Mary E.	086	1880	WB-F/148	AR
Roberson, Redden R.	063	1892	WB-4/88	AR
Roberson, Richard	049	1872	WB-2/12	AR
Roberson, Robert R.	019	1893	WB-B/229	AR
Roberson, Sally	019	1878	WB-B/106	AR
Roberson, Samuel	049	1872	WB-2/11	AR
Roberson, Sarah A.	063	1895	WB-4/173	AR
Roberson, Susan	045	1884	WB-1/125	AR
Roberson, Thomas	009	1836	OWB/519	AR
Roberson, William	092	1809	WB-3/91	AR
Roberson, William	001	1866	WB-1/269	AR
Roberson, William A.	063	c1894	Orig. Only	AR
Roberson, William J.	046	c1864	WB-E/148	AR
Roberson, William W.	063	1875	WB-3/88	
Roberts, Aaron	099	1849	RB-26/569	AR
Roberts, Abner	073	1842	WB-F/119	AR
Roberts, Abraham	026	1877	WB-2/154	AR
Roberts, Albert C.	036	1885	WB-A/67	CTY
Roberts, Ann	103	1866	RD-14/413	
Roberts, Ann	073	1877	WB-H/161	CTY
Roberts, B. B.	032	1894	WB-4/224	AR
Roberts, Benjamin	077	1804	WB-E/207	AR
Roberts, Betty	044	1804	WB-6/55	CTY
Roberts, Burwell S.	084	1885	WB-E/314	CTY
Roberts, Charles	024	c1766	WB-A/234	AR
Roberts, Charles	024	1807	WB-B/279	AR
Roberts, Chastin	084	1816	WB-A/270	CTY
Roberts, Curtis	099	1819	RB-15/241	
Roberts, Edward	072	c1776	RW/L13	AR
Roberts, Eleven	020	c1841	RB-O/485	AR
Roberts, Elisha	072	1811	WB-A/115	AR
Roberts, Eliza	032	1875	WB-3/151	AR-Nunc.
Roberts, Elizabeth	020	1847	RB-P/398	
Roberts, Elizabeth	029	1896	WB-F/78	AR
Roberts, Elizabeth	040	1886	WB-2/257	AR
Roberts, Elizabeth	028	1899	WB-F/370	
Roberts, Elizabeth	084	1854	WB-C/178	CTY
Roberts, Elizabeth McK.	028	1888	WB-E/483	AR
Roberts, Esther	071	1835	WB-4/130	AR
Roberts, Francis	073	1877	WB-H/157	CTY
Roberts, George	020	1833	RB-M/319	

Name	Co.	Date	Recorded Copy	Original
Roberts, George	028	1741	Deeds.21/L5	
Roberts, Henderson	026	1879	WB-2/195	AR
Roberts, Henry	084	1854	WB-C/175	CTY
Roberts, Houston	072	1823	WB-A/111	AR
Roberts, Houston	072	c1793	Orig. Only	AR
Roberts, Isaac	068	1847	WB-B/223	
Roberts, Ishmael	022	c1826	WB-B/149	AR
Roberts, James	084	c1784	OW/262	AR
Roberts, James	024	1825	WB-C/116	AR
Roberts, James	073	1821	WB-D/592	AR
Roberts, James	050	1847	WB-1/23	
Roberts, James	104	1800	WB-2/4	AR
Roberts, James	050	c1847		Copy
Roberts, James	028	1774	Orig. Only	SS/AR
Roberts, James	062	1900	WB-B/236	AR
Roberts, James	071	1809	WB-3/13	AR
Roberts, James	028	1764	DB-8/235	AR
Roberts, James	092	c1833	WB-4/71	
Roberts, James B.	028	1896	WB-F/205	
Roberts, James C.	073	1875	WB-H/109	CTY
Roberts, James D.	090	1806	WB-2/65	AR
Roberts, James H.	073	1883	WB-H/331	CTY
Roberts, James L.	024	1854	WB-C/351	AR
Roberts, James R.	013	1896	WB-C/550	
Roberts, James R.	013	1879	WB-B/179	AR
Roberts, James R.	105	1894	WB-3/95	AR
Roberts, James, Sr.	084	1867	WB-D/89	CTY
Roberts, Jane E.	032	1893	WB-4/204	AR
Roberts, Jeams	028	1745	Orig. Only	SS/AR (N)
Roberts, Jesse	044	1777	WB-1/149	CTY
Roberts, John	024	1878	WB-E/58	AR
Roberts, John	077	1803	WB-E/203	AR
Roberts, John	084	1862	WB-C/365	CTY
Roberts, John	025	1891	WB-A/149	AR
Roberts, John	062	1866	WB-A/42	
Roberts, John	084	1884	WB-E/293	CTY
Roberts, John	020	1852	RB-Q/649	AR
Roberts, John	104	1855	WB-5/112	
Roberts, John	104	1878	WB-6/156	AR
Roberts, John	041	1846	WB-3/75	AR
Roberts, John	013	1845	WB-A/103	
Roberts, John	026	1847	WB-1/64	
Roberts, John	073	1834	WB-E/315	AR
Roberts, John B.	073	1873	WB-H/74	CTY
Roberts, John G.	084	1881	WB-E/222	CTY
Roberts, John G.	019	1889	WB-B/175	AR
Roberts, John M.	028	1862	WB-D/362	
Roberts, Johnson	009	1899	WB-2/187	CTY
Roberts, Jonathan	071	1820	WB-3/241	AR
Roberts, Jonathan	041	1803	WB-1/202	AR
Roberts, Jonathan	092	1854	WB-5/9	
Roberts, Joseph	084	c1804	WB-A/19	CTY
Roberts, Joseph	028	1774	Orig. Only	SS/AR (N)
Roberts, Joseph	032	1882	WB-3/368	AR
Roberts, Joshua	013	1861	WB-B/434	AR-Copy
Roberts, Josiah	038	1867	WB-1/288	AR
Roberts, Layton T.	020	1883	WB-A/395	CTY
Roberts, Logan D.	092	1886	WB-6/239	AR
Roberts, Lucinda	013	c1869	Orig. Only	AR
Roberts, Lucy Ann	070	1891	WB-F/464	AR
Roberts, Malachi	104	1846	WB-4/323	
Roberts, Margaret	071	1794	WB-2/54	AR
Roberts, Marion	013	1883	WB-B/291	AR

Name	Co.	Date	Recorded Copy	Original
Roberts, Martin C.	026	1885	WB-2/269	AR
Roberts, Mary	077	1786	WB-C/339	AR
Roberts, Mary	092	1866	WB-5/84	
Roberts, Mary A.	084	c1812	WB-A/93	CTY
Roberts, Mary E.	073	1897	WB-I/123	CTY
Roberts, Mary E.	028	1874	WB-E/95	
Roberts, Matthew	036	1890	WB-A/181	CTY
Roberts, Morris	026	1876	WB-2/139	
Roberts, Mourning	084	1857	WB-C/263	CTY
Roberts, Nancy	084	1826	WB-A/267	CTY
Roberts, Nelly	024	1885	WB-E/150	AR
Roberts, Philip	029	1779	Orig. Only	AR
Roberts, Pleasant B.	092	1855	WB-5/15	AR
Roberts, Richard	044	1772	Orig. Only	CTY
Roberts, Richard	019	c1761	Orig. Only	AR
Roberts, Richard	057	1814	WB-B/8	AR
Roberts, Richard	084	1888	WB-E/396	CTY
Roberts, Richard	019	1870	WB-B/61	AR
Roberts, Samuel	085	1801	WB-D/90	AR
Roberts, Samuel	028	1782	Orig. Only	AR
Roberts, Sandy	039	1894	WB-V/33	AR
Roberts, Shadrack	073	1865	WB-G/477	CTY
Roberts, Stephen	085	c1802	WB-D/113	AR
Roberts, Susanna	092	c1830	WB-4/46	AR
Roberts, Thena	084	1873	WB-E/60	CTY
Roberts, Thomas	104	1843	WB-4/291	AR
Roberts, Thomas	104	1866	WB-5/454	AR
Roberts, Thomas	084	1818	WB-A/273	CTY
Roberts, Thomas	017	1872	WB-B/33	AR
Roberts, Thomas O.	013	1889	WB-B/498	AR
Roberts, Vinson	073	1816	WB-D/462	AR
Roberts, Wiley	068	c1849	WB-B/203	
Roberts, William	024	1807	WB-B/212	AR
Roberts, William	073	1837	WB-E/414	AR
Roberts, William	044	1799	WB-4/305	CTY
Roberts, William	024	1795	WB-A/351	AR
Roberts, William	104	1834	WB-4/169	AR
Roberts, William	081	1784	WB-1/15	
Roberts, William	070	1774	Orig. Only	AR-Nunc.
Roberts, William	092	1777	WB-1/84	AR
Roberts, William	077	1808	WB-E/325	AR
Roberts, William B.	024	1835	WB-C/186	AR
Roberts, William C.	024	1869	WB-E/13	AR
Roberts, William M.	044	1867	WB-22/657	CTY
Roberts, William R.	044	1821	WB-9/40	CTY
Roberts, William W.	028	1882	WB-E/303	
Roberts, Willis	073	1815	WB-D/436	AR
Roberts, Willis	073	1851	WB-F/493	AR
Roberts, Zephaniah	020	1868	WB-A/7	CTY
Robertson, Aaron P.	084	1864	WB-C/393	CTY
Robertson, Alexander	068	1851	WB-B/213	
Robertson, Andrew	029	1797	WB-A/4	
Robertson, Anne	047	1774	WB-1/363	
Robertson, Annie B.	084	1882	WB-E/249	CTY
Robertson, Athenatious	073	1795	WB-C/64	AR
Robertson, Betsy	067	1899	Orig. Only	AR
Robertson, Daniel	090	1899	WB-6/493	AR
Robertson, David	094	1771	094.901.1	AR-Copy
Robertson, Drury	005	1797	WB-2/134	AR
Robertson, Edward H.	020	1841	RB-O/218	AR
Robertson, Eli H.	063	1878	WB-3/152	
Robertson, Elijah	084	1843	WB-B/309	CTY
Robertson, Eliza C.	100	1880	WB-51/165	AR
Robertson, Elizabeth	036	1900	WB-A/525	
Robertson, Elizabeth	084	c1840	Orig. Only	CTY
Robertson, Elmera J.	020	1882	WB-A/345	CTY
Robertson, Eve	001	c1855	WB-1/98	AR
Robertson, Eveline P.	099	1897	WB-D/12	AR
Robertson, George	086	1815	WB-C/24	AR
Robertson, George	099	1835	RB-23/419	AR
Robertson, George	044	1826	WB-10/97	CTY
Robertson, Hardy	037	1795	WB-C/314	AR
Robertson, Henry	037	1752	Orig. Only	SS/AR
Robertson, Henry	047	1764	WB-1/125	
Robertson, Hugh	090	c1843	Orig. Only	AR
Robertson, James	085	1821	WB-H/139	AR
Robertson, James	075	1754	SS 881/121	SS/AR
Robertson, James B.	020	1846	RB-P/342	AR
Robertson, James G.	100	1866	WB-50/203	AR
Robertson, James P.	029	1900	WB-F/218	AR
Robertson, Jesse T.	084	1865	WB-D/34	CTY
Robertson, John	085	1810	WB-G/169	AR
Robertson, John	075	1802	WB-M1/61	AR
Robertson, John	056	1761	DB-D/L98	AR
Robertson, John	099	1803	RB-6/117	AR
Robertson, John	075	1809	WB-M1/211	AR
Robertson, John	073	1801	WB-D/46	AR
Robertson, John C.	075	1842	WB-N/169	AR
Robertson, John H.	099	1879	WB-A/52	AR
Robertson, Jonathan	086	1838	WB-E/43	AR
Robertson, Joseph D.	075	1898	WB-O/470	AR
Robertson, L. R.	086	1864	WB-E/431	AR
Robertson, Lewis	047	1774	WB-1/356	
Robertson, Little Bery	100	1876	WB-51/106	AR
Robertson, Lott	099	1827	RB-20/182	AR
Robertson, Luca	046	1797	WB-A/327	AR
Robertson, Malissa	057	1839	WB-B/140	AR
Robertson, Mark	084	1815	WB-A/113	CTY
Robertson, Mary	099	1852	RB-28/163	AR
Robertson, Mary	070	1828	WB-C/382	AR
Robertson, Mary	063	1842	WB-2/288	
Robertson, Mary M.	084	1881	WB-E/212	CTY
Robertson, Needam	099	1819	RB-20/101	AR
Robertson, Patsey	099	1830	RB-21/193	AR
Robertson, Peter	100	1837	WB-36/165	AR
Robertson, Peter	037	1824	WB-F/27	AR
Robertson, Rachel	PA	1876	053 WB-11/63	053 AR
Robertson, Randal	047	1794	WB-3/224	AR
Robertson, Richard	086	1853	WB-E/243	AR
Robertson, Sinny	018	1831	WB-C/122	
Robertson, Susannah	075	1812	WB-M1/243	AR
Robertson, T. C.	099	1896	WB-C/520	AR
Robertson, Thomas	073	c1804	WB-D/243	AR
Robertson, Thomas	047	1879	WB-6/219	AR
Robertson, Walter	028	1779	Orig. Only	AR
Robertson, William	086	1803	WB-B/158	AR
Robertson, William	033	1843	WB-1/49	AR
Robertson, William	038	1883	WB-2/439	AR
Robertson, William	038	1872	WB-2/77	AR
Robertson, William	081	1787	WB-1/69	AR
Robertson, William	032	1842	WB-1/393	AR
Robertson, William H.	090	1810	WB-2/107	AR
Robertson, William S.	086	1889	WB-F/361	AR
Robertson, William W.	084	1894	WB-E/583	CTY
Robertson, Willie	099	1839	RB-24/323	AR
Robeson, Alexander	011	1881	WB-2/144	
Robeson, Bartram	011	c1818	WB-2/372	
Robeson, Catharine	070	1865	WB-D/162	AR
Robeson, Eliza A.	011	1891	WB-2/240	
Robeson, Elizabeth	068	1801	WB-A/216	

Name	Co.	Date	Recorded Copy	Original
Robeson, James	011	1864	WB-1/325	
Robeson, Letitia K.	070	1849	WB-C/499	AR
Robeson, Margaret	011	c1830	WB-2/387	
Robeson, Peter	011	c1792	WB-1/420	
Robeson, Samuel	011	1846	WB-1/122	
Robeson, Sarah C.	083	1897	WB-4/212	AR
Robeson, Thomas	011	c1785	WB-1/565	Nunc.
Robeson, Thomas	070	1825	WB-C/379	AR
Robeson, Thomas	011	c1775	WB-1/562	Nunc.
Robeson, Thomas	011	c1780	WB-1/581	
Robeson, William	013	1837	WB-A/48	
Robeson, William	011	c1825	WB-2/360	
Robey, Eleanor	085	c1776	WB-A/233	AR
Robey, Thomas	085	1774	WB-A/179	AR
Robey, W. M.	103	1889	WB-1/486	AR
Robinett, George M.	003	1900	WB-B/411	
Robinett, M. A.	003	1896	WB-B/354	AR
Robinett, William F.	003	1890	WB-B/272	AR
Robins, Anne	104	1833	WB-4/163	AR
Robins, Christopher	Eng	c1888	Copy	014 AR
Robins, Cupid	010	1882	WB-I/145	
Robins, Frusa	051	1872	WB-C/70	AR
Robins, Isom	089	1843	WB-1/25	AR
Robins, James	008	1725	SS 876/33	SS/AR
Robins, Jane	014	1900	WB-3/123	CTY
Robins, John	077	1792	WB-C/440	AR
Robins, John	081	1827	WB-5/370	AR
Robins, Joseph	085	c1754	SS 880/134	SS/AR
Robins, Thomas	100	1780	WB-3/30	AR
Robins, Thomas	037	1776	WB-A/242	AR
Robins, William	086	1816	WB-C/40	AR
Robins, William	077	1817	WB-F/2	AR
Robinson, A. C.	013	1900	WB-D/464	AR
Robinson, A. Francis	019	1891	WB-B/209	AR
Robinson, Agnes J.	070	1894	WB-G/195	AR
Robinson, Alexander	065	1853	WB-I/208	AR
Robinson, Alexander	065	1805	WB-F/133	AR
Robinson, Alexander	060	1805	Orig. Only	AR
Robinson, Alexander	073	1851	WB-F/478	AR
Robinson, Alexander	073	1864	WB-G/446	CTY
Robinson, Ann	019	1787	WB-D/336	AR
Robinson, Annie G.	041	1896	WB-4/410	AR
Robinson, Arthur	082	1828	WB-1/291	AR
Robinson, Benjamin	021	1887	WB-2/359	
Robinson, Burwell	100	1816	WB-20/142	AR
Robinson, Caroline	073	c1863	Orig. Only	AR
Robinson, Catherine	060	1899	WB-5/140	AR
Robinson, Charles	059	1875	WB-A/98	
Robinson, Charles	005	c1754	SS 880/129	SS/AR
Robinson, Charles	082	1802	WB-1/88	AR
Robinson, Charles	082	1843	WB-3/9	AR
Robinson, Charles W.	016	1874	WB-3/105	AR
Robinson, Daniel	087	1897	WB-4/49	AR
Robinson, David	060	1801	Orig. Only	AR
Robinson, David	021	1850	WB-1/90	AR
Robinson, David S.	021	1865	WB-1/208	AR
Robinson, Delphia A.	037	1881	WB-G/610	AR
Robinson, Dennis	063	1889	Orig. Only	AR
Robinson, Dina	016	1878	WB-3/239	AR
Robinson, E. J.	040	1899	WB-3/42	AR
Robinson, Edmund R.	NY	1896	099 WB-D/142	099 AR
Robinson, Edward	029	1826	WB-B/149	AR
Robinson, Elizabeth	060	1829	WB-1/144	AR
Robinson, Elizabeth	014	1894	WB-2/540	CTY
Robinson, Ethered	030	c1812	WB-3/18	
Robinson, Ezekiel	065	1826	WB-F/105	AR
Robinson, Franklin	001	1900	WB-3/311	AR
Robinson, Froney	021	1887	WB-2/361	
Robinson, George	087	1865	WB-2/86	Ar-Nunc.
Robinson, George	054	c1833	WB-2/191	AR
Robinson, George R.	087	1874	WB-3/81	AR
Robinson, George W.	100	1860	WB-49/325	AR
Robinson, George W.	087	1882	WB-3/252	AR
Robinson, Harriet	024	1898	WB-E/283	AR
Robinson, Henry W.	021	c1875	WB-2/264	
Robinson, Humphry	024	1752	Orig. Only	SS/AR
Robinson, Isaac	021	1847	WB-1/53	AR
Robinson, Isaac	060	1808	Orig. Only	AR
Robinson, Isaac	049	1823	WB-2/222	AR
Robinson, Isaac V.	060	1860	WB-3/34	AR
Robinson, Israel	090	1819	WB-3/25	AR
Robinson, J. A.	060	1898	WB-5/100	AR
Robinson, J. L.	049	1896	WB-2/356	AR
Robinson, J. S.	049	1884	WB-2/111	AR
Robinson, Jacob	009	c1791	OWB/256	AR
Robinson, Jacob	090	1820	WB-3/43	
Robinson, Jacob, Sr.	020	1780	RB-A/103	AR
Robinson, James	037	1886	WB-H/62	
Robinson, James	070	1785	WB-C/370	AR-Nunc.
Robinson, James	065	1810	WB-F/73	AR
Robinson, James	097	1860	WB-1/174	AR
Robinson, James	087	1854	WB-1/449	AR
Robinson, James	087	c1846	Orig. Only	AR-Copy
Robinson, James A.	060	1846	WB-2/268	AR
Robinson, James B.	065	1883	WB-K/528	AR
Robinson, James L.	061	1887	WB-2/87	AR
Robinson, James, Sr.	060	c1786	Orig. Only	AR
Robinson, Jeffrey	029	1888	WB-E/428	AR
Robinson, Jethro	021	1864	WB-1/201	AR
Robinson, John	087	1868	WB-3/1	AR
Robinson, John	009	1779	OWB/140	AR
Robinson, John	024	c1756	WB-A/244	AR
Robinson, John	100	1831	WB-33/215	AR
Robinson, John	021	1847	WB-1/55	AR
Robinson, John	077	1764	WB-C/33	AR
Robinson, John	077	1758	SS 880/217	SS/AR
Robinson, John A.	011	1866	WB-2/22	
Robinson, John H.	100	1850	WB-41/50	AR
Robinson, John L.	097	1850	WB-1/68	AR
Robinson, John W.	087	1895	WB-3/578	AR
Robinson, John W.	021	c1899	Orig. Only	AR
Robinson, John, Rev.	016	1844	WB-1/26	
Robinson, John, Sr.	029	1798	WB-A/11	AR
Robinson, John, Sr.	060	1784	Orig. Only	AR
Robinson, Jonathan	024	1817	WB-C/53	AR
Robinson, Jonathan	037	1784	WB-B/139	AR
Robinson, Joseph	077	1717	Orig. Only	SS/AR
Robinson, Joseph	019	c1776	RB-A/45	AR
Robinson, Josiah	077	1803	WB-E/197	AR
Robinson, Judith	019	1853	WB-A/159	AR
Robinson, Kate M.	046	1897	WB-F/556	AR
Robinson, Kedar	087	1898	WB-4/67	
Robinson, L. D.	021	1896	WB-3/121	AR
Robinson, Lidia	009	1818	OB-A/283	AR
Robinson, Lucien W.	035	1900	WB-4/560	AR
Robinson, Ludyah	NY	1864	029 WB-E/27	
Robinson, Manuel	021	1898	WB-3/201	AR
Robinson, Margaret	070	1856	WB-C/609	AR
Robinson, Margaret	040	c1854	WB-1/80	AR
Robinson, Mary	029	1804	WB-A/34	AR

Name	Co.	Date	Recorded Copy	Original
Robinson, Mary	030	1785	WB-1/192	Nunc.
Robinson, Mary E. D.	076	1900	WB-A1/252	AR
Robinson, Mary M.	021	1886	WB-2/348	
Robinson, Michael	073	1807	WB-D/184	AR
Robinson, Michael	065	1853	WB-I/210	AR
Robinson, Milas J.	065	1825	WB-F/78	
Robinson, Milas J.	065	c1825	SC/06271	AR-Copy
Robinson, Mollie A.	089	1897	WB-2/284	AR
Robinson, Mourning	082	1871	WB-6/70	AR
Robinson, Nancy	073	1843	WB-F/158	AR
Robinson, Nathan	030	1831	WB-3/281	
Robinson, Oliver P.	087	1878	WB-3/168	AR
Robinson, Orpah	077	1819	WB-F/18	AR
Robinson, Pentecost	082	1833	WB-2/26	AR
Robinson, Phillip	029	c1791	Orig. Only	AR
Robinson, Richard B.	100	1877	WB-51/113	AR
Robinson, Samuel	040	c1856	WB-1/83	AR
Robinson, Samuel	030	1824	WB-3/176	
Robinson, Samuel C.	040	1875	WB-2/92	AR
Robinson, Sarah	060	1834	WB-1/316	AR
Robinson, Squire	082	1825	WB-1/266	AR
Robinson, Thomas	077	1787	WB-C/346	AR
Robinson, Thomas	020	1782	RB-A/191	AR
Robinson, Thomas	024	1755	SS 880/88	SS/AR
Robinson, Thomas	005	1877	WB-D/55	AR
Robinson, Thomas	019	1849	WB-A/135	AR
Robinson, Thomas	077	1820	WB-F/30	AR
Robinson, Thomas	077	1762	WB-C/22	AR
Robinson, Thomas	002	1719	SS 875/169	SS/AR
Robinson, Thomas	020	1783	RB-A/247	AR
Robinson, Wallace	065	1853	WB-I/226	AR
Robinson, William	009	1813	OWB/463	AR
Robinson, William	082	1799	WB-1/48	AR
Robinson, William	087	1843	WB-1/264	AR
Robinson, William	030	1783	WB-1/167	
Robinson, William	047	1771	WB-1/296	
Robinson, William	030	1799	WB-2/138	
Robinson, William	030	1807	WB-2/309	
Robinson, William	070	1816	WB-AB/243	AR
Robinson, William	077	1785	WB-C/321	AR
Robinson, William D.	087	1883	WB-3/262	AR
Robinson, William H.	073	1867	WB-G/527	CTY
Robinson, William H.	067	1894	WB-2/328	AR
Robinson, William H.	093	1896	WB-2/147	AR
Robinson, William L.	087	1870	WB-3/29	AR
Robinson, William P.	065	1875	WB-K/186	AR
Robinson, William P.	014	1886	WB-2/329	CTY
Robirds, Robird	013	1840	WB-A/66	
Robison, Alexander	065	1785	WB-F/61	AR
Robison, Ann	085	1821	WB-H/107	AR
Robison, Benjamin	085	c1790	WB-B/185	AR
Robison, Carnes H.	065	1845	WB-I/60	AR
Robison, Daniel	065	1826	WB-F/103	AR
Robison, David	065	1808	WB-F/134	AR
Robison, Elam	065	1888	WB-L/294	AR
Robison, George	085	c1785	WB-C/197	AR
Robison, George S.	054	1875	WB-4/190	CTY
Robison, Henry	085	1852	WB-K/140	AR
Robison, Hugh	085	1844	WB-I/215	AR
Robison, Hugh	085	c1802	WB-D/104	AR
Robison, Israel J.	055	c1873	WB-A/25	
Robison, James	075	c1700	SS 874.2/127	
Robison, James K.	085	1864	WB-K/330	AR
Robison, Jane	054	1857	WB-3/109	AR
Robison, John	075	1720	SS 875/238	
Robison, John	065	1808	WB-F/73	AR
Robison, Margery	085	1847	WB-K/61	AR
Robison, Mary	065	1830	WB-F/61	AR
Robison, Matthew	065	1825	WB-F/140	AR
Robison, Richard	065	1827	WB-F/141	AR
Robison, Richard	085	c1798	WB-D/91	AR
Robison, Robert	065	1804	WB-F/71	AR
Robison, William	085	1757	WB-A/143	AR
Robisson, Susanna	N	c1709	SS 875/13	
Robley, John	085	1823	WB-H/247	AR
Robly, Susannah	085	1848	WB-K/71	AR
Robson, James W.	073	1877	WB-H/170	CTY
Roby, Absalem	092	1857	WB-5/23	
Roby, John	054	c1804	WB-1/28	AR
Roby, John B.	054	c1820	WB-1A/61	AR
Roby, Martha	054	1854	WB-3/81	AR
Roby, Nathan	85c	1786	WB-C/93	AR
Roby, Tobias	054	c1802	WB-1/204	AR
Roch, Anderson	081	1814	WB-4/65	AR
Rochards, Ralph	009	c1796	OWB/329	
Rochel, Alsey	099	1867	RB-34/331	AR
Rochell, Benjamin	070	1826	WB-C/380	AR
Rochell, Christiana	046	1828	WB-B/361	AR
Rochell, Edward	099	1885	WB-B/37	AR
Rochell, George W.	099	1867	RB-34/479	AR
Rochell, Gilley	036	1884	WB-A/54	CTY
Rochell, Kinchen	051	1845	WB-A/244	
Rochell, Thomas	099	1849	RB-26/570	AR
Rochell, William	099	1818	RB-14/254	AR
Rochelle, Clement	VA	1846	WB-A/260	
Rockett, John R.	021	c1899	WB-3/346	AR
Rockett, Urban	021	1853	WB-1/101	AR
Rockwell, E. F.	054	1888	WB-5/232	CTY
Rockwell, Martin L.	PA	1898	028 WB-F/379	
Rodden, James L.	065	1865	WB-J/200	AR
Rodden, Thomas W.	065	1868	WB-J/252	AR
Roddick, Wilkin	070	1889	WB-F/271	AR
Rodes, William	022	1794	RB-2/18	AR
Rodes, William	075	1734	SS 876/353	SS/AR
Rodet, John	024	1804	WB-B/245	AR
Rodgers, Azny	016	1846	WB-1/118	
Rodgers, Benjamin	005	1866	WB-C/246	AR
Rodgers, Benjamin	041	1824	WB-2/218	AR
Rodgers, David	071	1785	WB-1/332	AR
Rodgers, Elisabeth	097	1862	WB-1/190	AR
Rodgers, Elizabeth	016	1845	WB-1/74	
Rodgers, Hugh	065	1841	WB-H/61	AR
Rodgers, Hugh	097	c1849	WB-1/166	AR
Rodgers, Hugh	065	1839	WB-E/218	AR
Rodgers, Isham	099	1804	RB-6/323	AR
Rodgers, Jacob	029	1774	Orig. Only	AR
Rodgers, James	073	1809	WB-D/194	AR
Rodgers, John	010	1726	SS 876/52	SS/AR
Rodgers, John	030	1831	WB-3/277	
Rodgers, John P.	079	1877	WB-2/143	AR
Rodgers, John R.	065	1863	WB-J/152	AR
Rodgers, Joseph	009	1704/5	DB-1/45	SS/AR
Rodgers, Martha	065	1785	WB-F/120	AR
Rodgers, Nancy	039	1884	WB-U/338	AR
Rodgers, Sarah D.	065	1862	WB-J/124	AR
Rodgers, Trustram	037	1799	WB-D/95	AR
Rodgers, William	063	1878	WB-3/145	
Rodgers, William	073	1797	WB-C/104	AR
Rodgers, William	073	c1813	Orig. Only	AR
Rodgers, William B.	070	1873	WB-E/258	AR

Name	Co.	Date	Recorded Copy	Original
Rodgerson, Daniel	077	1816	WB-E/447	AR
Rodgerson, Jane E.	010	1897	WB-I/530	AR
Rodman, Camilla D.	009	1887	WB-1/423	CTY
Rodman, Francis	054	c1819	WB-1A/103	AR
Rodman, William B.	009	1893	WB-1/575	CTY
Rodwell, Elizabeth	100	1864	WB-50/117	AR
Rodwell, Elizabeth	100	1896	WB-51/459	
Rodwell, James	100	1869	WB-51/1	AR
Rodwell, John	100	1822	WB-24/217	AR
Rodwell, John	100	1832	WB-33/507	AR
Rodwell, Robert	100	1859	WB-49/251	AR
Roe, Coleman	009	c1759	OWB/63	AR
Roe, Edmond	075	1696	SS 874.2/84	SS/AR
Roe, James	028	1737/8	LGB-4/#72	SS/AR
Roe, John	082	1783	Orig. Only	SS/AR
Roe, John	082	1783	WB-1/18	AR-Copy
Roe, Joseph	028	1888	WB-E/487	
Roe, Luke	028	1775	Orig. Only	SS/AR
Roe, Patsy	009	1866	OB-M/236	AR
Roe, Rachel	096	1835	WB-2/125	AR
Roe, Robert	009	1756	SS 879/240	SS/AR
Roe, Sarah	009	c1770	OWB/107	AR
Roe, Solomon	022	1827	WB-B/137	
Roe, Thomas	028	1841	WB-D/36	AR
Roe, Thomas	028	1781	Orig. Only	AR
Roe, Thomas	028	1765	DB-12&13/291	AR
Roebuck, William L.	063	1869	WB-3/4	
Roger, Adam	073	1767	WB-A/64	
Rogers, A. E.	041	1893	WB-4/370	AR
Rogers, Allen	032	1869	WB-3/26	AR
Rogers, Allen	099	1848	RB-26/384	AR
Rogers, Allen R.	099	1864	RB-33/280	AR
Rogers, Andrew	013	1860	WB-A/201	
Rogers, Andrew J.	001	1865	WB-1/240	AR
Rogers, Arthur W.	071	1850	WB-5/93	AR
Rogers, Belinda J.	097	1900	WB-3/44	AR
Rogers, Benjamin	016	1873	WB-3/96	AR
Rogers, Benjamin	099	1879	WB-A/42	AR
Rogers, Benjamin	099	1862	RB-32/120	AR
Rogers, Benjamin	105	1862	WB-1/67	AR
Rogers, Caroline	013	1886	WB-B/1886	AR
Rogers, Clark T.	GA	1896	Copy	025 AR
Rogers, Daniel	041	1785	WB-1/50	AR
Rogers, Daniel	072	1837	WB-1/157	AR
Rogers, Daniel	056	1807	WB-1/200	AR
Rogers, David	047	1764	WB-1/120	
Rogers, Dicy	044	1851	WB-18/286	CTY
Rogers, Durrell	099	1852	RB-27/470	
Rogers, Eleanor	073	1844	WB-F/217	AR
Rogers, Elizabeth	073	c1829	Orig. Only	AR
Rogers, Emanuell	010	1729	Orig. Only	SS/AR
Rogers, Ephraim	099	1802	RB-5/353	AR
Rogers, Esther Ann	099	1881	WB-A/284	AR
Rogers, Ezekiah	077	1787	WB-C/341	AR
Rogers, Francis	099	1846	RB-26/147	AR
Rogers, Frank C.	099	c1883	Orig. Only	AR
Rogers, George	099	1839	RB-24/300	AR
Rogers, George	022	1881	WB-E/222	AR
Rogers, George C.	078	1866	WB-18/407	
Rogers, Harriet	079	1890	WB-2/489	AR
Rogers, Harriet A.	065	c1843	WB-H/157	AR
Rogers, Henrietta	063	1894	WB-4/145	AR
Rogers, Hilliard	099	1898	WB-D/207	AR
Rogers, Hugh	055	1886	WB-A/73	
Rogers, Isaac H.	099	1890	WB-B/416	AR
Rogers, Isabella	036	1886	WB-A/83	CTY
Rogers, Jacob	046	1816	WB-B/23	AR
Rogers, James	099	1867	RB-34/446	AR
Rogers, James	100	1780	WB-3/91	AR
Rogers, Jane	046	1869	WB-E/11	AR
Rogers, Jennie	079	1871	WB-2/48	AR
Rogers, Jeremiah	023	1867	Orig. Only	AR
Rogers, Jesse	022	c1891	WB-E/528	AR
Rogers, Job	099	1772	RB-1/144	AR
Rogers, Job	005	1799	WB-2/136	AR
Rogers, John	049	1854	WB-2/197	AR
Rogers, John	065	1815	WB-F/76	AR
Rogers, John	078	1823	WI-9/435	AR
Rogers, John	099	1802	RB-6/73	AR
Rogers, John	047	1808	WB-3/477	AR
Rogers, John	065	1802	WB-F/131	AR
Rogers, John	016	1864	WB-2/115	
Rogers, John	035	1800	WB-A/419	AR
Rogers, John	099	1779	RB-1/144	AR
Rogers, John	065	1785	WB-F/64	AR
Rogers, John	078	1797	WI-2/18	AR
Rogers, John	001	1865	WB-1/228	AR
Rogers, John C.	093	1898	WB-2/164	AR
Rogers, John E.	071	1859	WB-5/216	AR
Rogers, John J.	078	c1874	WB-19/51	AR
Rogers, John R.	063	1893	WB-4/122	AR
Rogers, John W.	099	1880	WB-A/174	AR
Rogers, John, Sr.	037	1770	WB-A/183	AR
Rogers, Jonathan	041	1830	WB-2/288	AR
Rogers, Joseph	071	1752	Orig. Only	SS/AR
Rogers, Joseph	065	1806	WB-F/72	AR
Rogers, Joseph	099	1838	RB-24/225	AR
Rogers, Joseph	044	1813	WB-7/311	CTY
Rogers, Joseph	071	1791	WB-1/449	AR
Rogers, Joseph W.	016	1843	WB-1/23	
Rogers, Joshua	099	1850	RB-27/95	AR
Rogers, Josiah	037	1844	WB-F/316	AR
Rogers, Josiah	022	1813	WB-A/235	AR
Rogers, Lessey	073	1806	WB-D/180	AR
Rogers, Levi	041	1846	WB-3/74	AR
Rogers, Lula	099	1893	Orig. Only	AR
Rogers, M. L.	061	1889	WB-2/96	AR
Rogers, M. T.	099	1867	RB-34/389	AR
Rogers, Martha	016	1835	PQS.5/333	
Rogers, Mary	036	1846	WB-2/4	AR
Rogers, Mary	010	1777	WB-B/90	AR
Rogers, Mary Ann	099	1880	WB-A/137	AR
Rogers, Matthew	065	1796	WB-F/65	AR
Rogers, Michael	099	1795	RB-3/139	AR
Rogers, Nancy	001	1876	WB-2/82	AR
Rogers, Nathan	073	1815	WB-D/445	AR
Rogers, Orzeni	016	1875	WB-3/145	AR
Rogers, Peleg	044	1818	WB-8/156	CTY
Rogers, Peleg, Sr.	099	1816	RB-12/362	AR
Rogers, Philip	041	1821	WB-2/177	AR
Rogers, Randolph	032	1836	WB-1/277	AR
Rogers, Reubin	099	1811	RB-10/158	
Rogers, Richard	072	1749	SS 877/263	SS/AR
Rogers, Robert	069	1791	WB-1/227	AR
Rogers, Robert	049	c1819	WI-A/16	AR
Rogers, Robert	024	1739	LGB-4/#88	SS/AR
Rogers, Russell	097	1891	WB-2/403	AR
Rogers, Samuel	084	1794	OW/176	AR
Rogers, Samuel	063	1868	WB-2/511	
Rogers, Sarah	099	1848	RB-29/121	AR

Name	Co.	Date	Recorded Copy	Original
Rogers, Sarah	044	1850	WB-18/133	CTY
Rogers, Sarah	071	1827	WB-4/35	AR
Rogers, Sarah W.	020	1848	RB-P/524	
Rogers, Seth	016	1832	PQS.5/217	
Rogers, Shadrick	079	1859	WB-1/20	AR
Rogers, Silpha	041	1796	WB-1/140	AR
Rogers, Sion	099	1800	RB-5/172	AR
Rogers, Sion	022	c1779	Orig. Only	AR-Nunc.
Rogers, Stephen	099	1839	RB-24/324	AR
Rogers, Stephen	009	c1796	OWB/322	AR
Rogers, Stephen	035	1804	WB-A/408	AR
Rogers, Tammey	035	1829	WB-A/410	AR
Rogers, Thomas	069	1786	WB-1/42	AR
Rogers, Thomas	047	1790	WB-3/189	AR
Rogers, Thomas	096	1790	WB-1/166	AR
Rogers, Thomas	097	1856	WB-1/115	AR
Rogers, Thomas	010	1754	SS 879/141	SS/AR
Rogers, Thomas	039	1843	WB-L/159	AR
Rogers, Thomas	099	1847	RB-26/291	AR
Rogers, Thomas	010	1749	SS 879/169	SS/AR
Rogers, Thomas	070	1782	WB-C/366	AR
Rogers, William	073	1848	WB-F/414	AR
Rogers, William	082	1797	WB-1/64	AR
Rogers, William	002	c1690	Orig. Only	SS/AR
Rogers, William	035	c1775	WB-A/409	AR
Rogers, William M.	001	1873	WB-2/44	AR
Rogers, Willie	099	1803	RB-6/180	AR
Rogers, Willis	099	1822	RB-20/45	AR
Rogers, Zacariah	085	1837	WB-I/5	AR
Rogerson, Clara	063	1865	WB-2/548	
Rogerson, Daniel	077	1762	WB-C/15	AR
Rogerson, David	063	c1805	WB-1/429	
Rogerson, Eli	063	1885	WB-3/269	AR
Rogerson, Fannie	041	1875	WB-4/52	AR
Rogerson, Henry	063	1872	WB-3/29	
Rogerson, Josiah	077	1807	WB-E/264	AR
Rogerson, Levi	063	1894	WB-4/143	AR
Rogerson, Martha	075	1891	WB-O/333	AR
Rogerson, Mary	077	1803	WB-E/179	AR
Rogerson, Nancy	063	1838	WB-2/248	
Rogerson, Nancy	063	1854	WB-2/400	
Rogerson, Sarah	024	c1798	WB-A/357	AR
Rogerson, Simeon N.	075	1895	WB-O/422	AR
Rogerson, William A.	063	1878	WB-3/134	
Rogester, Daniel	063	1811	WB-2/4	
Roggers, Lydia Jane	016	1885	WB-3/452	AR
Rogsbey, Elizabeth	073	1851	WB-F/486	
Roland, David	006	1882	WB-E/91	AR
Roland, Elizabeth	071	1846	WB-5/43	AR
Roland, Elizabeth	083	1827	WB-1/318	AR
Roland, Isham	044	1794	WB-3/168	Nunc.
Rolands, Sukey	033	c1837	WB-1/10	AR
Roles, Alice	046	1895	WB-F/379	AR
Roles, Leonidas	099	1866	RB-34/300	AR
Roles, Richmond	099	1876	RB-35/414	AR
Rolf, Thomas	075	c1720	Orig. Only	AR
Rolfe, Thomas	N	1690/1	Orig. Only	SS/AR
Rolfe, Thomas	075	1772	WB-H/151	AR
Rollason, Benjamin	027	1900	WB-2/163	AR
Rollings, John	022	1821	WB-B/37	AR
Rollings, John S.	063	1839	WB-2/254	
Rollings, Jonathan	081	1834	WB-6/356	AR
Rollins, Burwell	099	1865	RB-33/426	AR
Rollins, Gaston	099	1897	WB-D/23	AR
Rollins, Gaston	022	1892	WB-E/482	AR

Name	Co.	Date	Recorded Copy	Original
Rollins, Gibson S.	029	1862	WB-C/442	AR
Rollins, Hebie	103	1900	WB-2/296	AR
Rollins, Henry	047	1857	WB-5/31	AR-Copy
Rollins, Hester	103	1897	WB-2/204	AR
Rollins, James J.	026	1895	WB-2/498	AR
Rollins, John	079	c1840	Orig. Only	AR
Rollins, John M.	096	1860	Copy	031 AR
Rollins, John M.	096	1860	WB-3/60	AR
Rollins, Jonas	026	1868	WB-2/6	AR
Rollins, Peyton P.	029	1880	WB-E/234	AR
Rollins, Rufus C.	079	1881	WB-2/244	AR
Rollins, W. C.	048	1894	WB-1/38	CTY
Rollinson, Christopher	030	1819	WB-3/110	
Rollison, Francis	030	1805	WB-2/274	
Rombough, Catherine	024	1808	WB-B/80	AR
Rombough, John	024	1784	WB-A/312	AR-Nunc.
Rombough, John	024	1778	WB-B/95	AR
Rombough, William	024	1808	WB-B/294	AR
Rominger, Cornelius	032	1825	WB-1/45	AR
Rominger, David	092	1777	WB-1/71	AR
Rominger, Edmund A.	038	1897	WB-4/141	AR
Rominger, Isabella	006	1899	WB-E/385	AR
Rominger, John B.	038	1892	WB-3/290	AR
Rominger, John M.	038	1868	WB-1/295	AR
Rominger, Mary	090	c1839	Orig. Only	AR
Rominger, Michael	090	1824	WB-3/125	AR
Rominger, Michael	090	1818	WB-3/17	AR
Rominger, Rosena	038	1854	WB-1/136	AR
Ronaldson, Andrew	070	1782	WB-C/365	AR
Ronard, Robert	047	1761	WB-1/41	
Rondel, Francois	024	1795	WB-A/292	AR
Rone, Benjamin	070	1895	WB-G/413	AR
Rone, Jesse	047	1794	WB-3/227	AR
Rone, William	047	1777	WB-2/55	
Roney, Benjamin	001	1895	WB-3/77	AR
Roney, Benjamin	073	1827	WB-E/143	AR
Roney, Elizabeth	036	1883	WB-A/38	CTY
Roney, John	001	1866	WB-1/255	AR
Roney, Polly	073	1843	WB-F/164	AR
Roney, Sarah	001	1879	WB-2/142	AR
Ronk, Caroline	038	1893	WB-3/439	AR
Rontree, Francis	056	1748	SS 877/116	
Rook, Benjamin	071	1829	WB-4/55	AR
Rook, John	071	1783	WB-1/272	AR
Rooke, Bartho.	028	1790	WB-A/216	AR-Copy
Rooker, John	SC	1840	065 WB-H/120	065 AR
Rooks, Ann	070	1874	WB-E/280	AR
Rooks, Elizabeth	051	1868	WB-B/106	AR
Rooks, Freddrick	041	1839	WB-3/10	AR
Rooks, Henry	070	1792	WB-C/373	AR
Rooks, James M.	070	1870	WB-E/213	AR
Rooks, Jesse	070	1828	WB-C/381	AR
Rooks, John	070	1868	WB-D/240	AR
Rooks, Joseph	070	1867	WB-D/232	AR
Rooks, Joseph	041	1810	WB-2/61	AR
Rooks, Lydia	071	1857	WB-5/193	AR
Rooks, Priscilla	051	1870	WB-C/36	AR
Rooks, Sarah	070	1830	WB-AB/255	AR
Rooks, Squire	071	1877	WB-6/241	AR
Rooney, James	073	1765	WB-A/42	
Roose, William	MA	1722	SS 875/342	SS/AR (N)
Root, William	ND	c1889	Copy	075 AR
Roots, John	070	c1779	Orig. Only	AR
Roots, Rodger	012	1787	Orig. Only	AR

Name	Co.	Date	Recorded Copy	Original
Roper, Ann	071	1818	WB-3/201	AR
Roper, Frederick	053	1856	WB-8/139	AR
Roper, Fredrick	053	1820	WB-4/142	
Roper, James	082	1833	WB-2/29	AR
Roper, James D.	047	1852	WB-4/327	AR
Roper, John	047	1797	WB-3/282	AR
Roper, Thomas	082	1858	WB-4/114	AR
Roper, William	024	1729/0	SS 876/213	SS/AR
Roper, William H.	020	1846	RB-P/363	AR
Rorie, Ann	005	c1798	WB-2/137	AR
Rorie, John, Sr.	047	1782	WB-3/31	AR
Rorie, William	005	c1802	WB-2/138	AR
Rorison, John S.	066	1900	Orig. Only	AR
Rorrie, James	005	1848	WB-B/234	AR
Rosbrough, George	020	1784	RB-B/26	AR
Roscoe, H. E.	MS	1885	041 WB-4/418	041 AR
Roscoe, Jane E.	MS	1899	041 WB-4/483	041 AR
Rose, (fwc)	065	1839	WB-E/224	AR
Rose, Alice L.	029	1892	WB-E/533	AR
Rose, Allen	085	1885	WB-2/130	CTY
Rose, Allen S.	054	1866	WB-3/187	AR
Rose, Anderson	078	1814	WI-6/218	AR
Rose, Ann	069	1825	WB-1/326	AR
Rose, B. F.	056	1882	WB-3/309	AR
Rose, Barney	105	1866	WB-1/123	AR
Rose, Benjamin	056	1836	WB-2/254	AR
Rose, Christian	037	1830	WB-F/116	AR
Rose, Clara L.	086	1889	WB-F/344	AR
Rose, Elisha	047	1795	Orig. Only	AR
Rose, Elizabeth	106	c1861	WB-1/80	AR
Rose, Elizabeth	069	1778	WB-1/1	AR
Rose, Emanuel	104	1796	WB-1/482	
Rose, Enos	069	1879	WB-5/87	AR
Rose, Francis	069	1796	WB-1/111	AR
Rose, Gardner	071	1813	WB-3/100	AR
Rose, George	015	1778	100 WB-2/247	AR
Rose, Harmon	072	c1786	WI/L13	AR
Rose, James	071	1888	WB-7/30	AR
Rose, James	071	1825	WB-3/320	AR
Rose, Jesse	071	1815	WB-3/156	AR
Rose, Joel	105	1875	WB-2/162	AR
Rose, John	009	c1797	OWB/331	AR
Rose, John	103	1882	WB-1/247	AR
Rose, John	072	1786	WI/L56	AR
Rose, John M.	029	1895	WB-F/46	AR
Rose, John P.	100	1869	Orig. Only	AR
Rose, John T.	023	c1882	Orig. Only	AR
Rose, Joseph G.	056	1887	WB-3/457	AR
Rose, L. R.	033	1855	WB-1/121	AR
Rose, Levi	103	1865	RD-14/237	AR
Rose, Lewis D.	100	1879	WB-51/143	AR
Rose, Martha	103	1892	WB-1/558	AR
Rose, Mary	086	1860	WB-E/382	AR
Rose, Mary	069	1890	WB-5/286	AR
Rose, Mary	103	1899	WB-2/240	AR
Rose, Mary J.	100	1894	098 WB-A/212	098 CTY
Rose, Mary J.	100	1894	WB-51/379	
Rose, Nicholas	056	1836	WB-2/253	AR
Rose, Robert	037	1820	WB-E/245	AR
Rose, Sally	103	1895	WB-2/129	AR
Rose, Sarah	105	1896	WB-3/204	AR
Rose, Sterling	104	1848	WB-4/347	AR
Rose, Tempie	069	c1884	Orig. Only	AR
Rose, Thomas	104	1900	WB-7/113	AR
Rose, Thomas	084	1822	WB-A/271	CTY
Rose, William	103	1843	RD-8/517	AR
Rose, William	037	1863	WB-G/234	AR
Rose, William	085	1858	WB-K/266	AR
Rose, William	044	1769	Orig. Only	CTY
Rose, William A.	005	1898	WB-D/434	
Rose, Willis	028	1891	WB-F/6	
Rosebro, John A.	054	1868	WB-4/2	AR
Rosebrough, James	085	1801	WB-D/103	AR
Rosebrough, John	085	1821	WB-H/101	AR
Rosebrough, John	085	c1777	WB-A/254	AR
Rosebrough, Margaret	085	c1785	WB-C/112	AR
Rosebrough, Samuel	085	1821	WB-H/128	AR
Rosebrough, Samuel	085	1775	WB-A/195	AR
Roseman, Daniel	021	1892	WB-2/571	AR
Roseman, David	085	1892	WB-2/533	CTY
Roseman, Ella Forney	060	1892	WB-4/488	AR
Roseman, George	085	1828	WB-H/528	AR
Roseman, Jane	054	1896	WB-6/28	
Roseman, John	085	1843	WB-I/164	AR
Roseman, Peter	085	1817	WB-G/478	AR
Roseman, T. D.	085	1899	WB-3/310	CTY
Rosenbacher, Sigmund	038	1893	WB-3/390	AR
Rosenthal, E.	103	1892	WB-2/12	AR
Rosenthal, George	029	1894	WB-F/6	AR
Rosenthal, L.	099	1896	WB-C/526	AR
Rosier, Nathl.	002	c1703	Orig. Only	SS/AR
Rosimon, Charles	060	c1885	Orig. Only	AR
Ross, A. D.	067	1886	WB-2/237	AR
Ross, Abel	075	c1760	Orig. Only	AR
Ross, Alexander	005	1890	WB-D/283	AR
Ross, Alexander	070	1767	WB-C/359	AR
Ross, Andrew	037	1761	WB-A/63	AR
Ross, Andrew	005	1803	WB-2/139	AR
Ross, Andrew D.	001	1882	WB-2/187	AR
Ross, Ann	070	1777	WB-C/360	AR
Ross, Anthony	065	1790	WB-F/60	AR
Ross, Benjamin	046	1867	WB-D/331	AR
Ross, Catharine	065	1839	WB-H/97	AR
Ross, Catherine	029	1867	WB-D/98	AR
Ross, Catherine	001	1887	WB-2/346	
Ross, Charles	044	1894	WB-24/241	CTY
Ross, Charles	012	c1765	DB-A/43	
Ross, Daniel	037	1761	WB-A/44	AR
Ross, Daniel	037	1781	WB-B/76	AR
Ross, David	VA	1817	027 WB-A/1	027 AR
Ross, Dorcas W.	065	1890	WB-L/448	AR
Ross, Dorris	099	1856	RB-29/459	AR
Ross, Dugal	097	1845	WB-1/24	AR
Ross, Elijah	009	1864	OB-L/441	AR
Ross, Elizabeth	064	1879	WB-2/77	AR
Ross, Esther E.	016	1851	WB-1/197	
Ross, Francis	016	1831	PQS.5/193	
Ross, George	065	1799	WB-F/128	AR
Ross, George W.	TN	1893	091 WB-1/24	
Ross, Green	039	1838	WB-K/168	AR
Ross, Hugh	005	c1793	WB-A/37	AR
Ross, Jacob	047	1802	WB-3/372	AR
Ross, James	085	1789	WB-D/89	AR
Ross, James	073	1793	WB-B/240	AR
Ross, James	073	1848	WB-F/392	AR
Ross, James	065	1809	WB-F/135	AR
Ross, James	010	1853	WB-G/495	AR
Ross, James R.	063	1900	WB-4/280	AR
Ross, John	085	1819	WB-G/530	AR
Ross, John	038	1857	WB-1/108	AR

Name	Co.	Date	Recorded Copy	Original
Ross, John	009	1855	OB-I/379	AR
Ross, John	051	1785	041 WB-1/46	041 AR
Ross, John	104	1792	WB-1/341	AR
Ross, John	085	1820	WB-H/35	AR
Ross, John	046	1802	WB-A/318	AR
Ross, John	046	1791	WB-A/318	AR
Ross, John C.	016	1883	WB-3/394	AR
Ross, John P.	065	1870	Orig. Only	AR
Ross, John S.	037	1828	WB-F/87	AR
Ross, John, Sr.	063	1794	WB-1/201	
Ross, Joseph	099	1832	RB-22/258	AR
Ross, Joseph A.	016	1837	PQS.5/406	
Ross, Joseph G.	001	1887	WB-2/347	AR
Ross, Joseph W.	065	1866	WB-J/223	AR
Ross, Joshua J. L.	103	1888	WB-1/422	
Ross, Kallum	037	1760	WB-A/7	AR
Ross, Kezia	065	1832	WB-G/80	AR
Ross, L. G.	046	1877	Orig. Only	AR
Ross, Lemuel	009	1836	OWB/526	AR
Ross, Levi	046	1856	WB-A/447	AR
Ross, Martha	016	1838	PQS.5/488	
Ross, Martha M.	097	1864	WB-1/227	AR
Ross, Martin	077	c1827	Copy	075 AR
Ross, Martin	077	1828	WB-F/155	AR
Ross, Mary	016	1837	PQS.5/423	
Ross, Moses	026	1878	WB-2/180	AR
Ross, Nichelson	065	c1767	WB-F/112	AR
Ross, Peter	070	1840	WB-AB/331	AR
Ross, Reuben	006	1820	WB-A/98	AR
Ross, Sarah	001	1886	WB-2/283	AR
Ross, Sherwood	097	1894	WB-2/471	AR
Ross, Stephen	014	1883	WB-2/255	CTY
Ross, Terza	016	1846	WB-1/94	
Ross, Thomas	099	1840	RB-24/424	AR
Ross, Thomas W.	036	1893	WB-A/299	CTY
Ross, Walter	070	1795	WB-C/374	AR
Ross, William	009	1859	OB-K/518	AR
Ross, William	063	c1801	WB-1/403	
Ross, William	070	1762	DB-E/11	AR
Ross, William	079	1859	WB-1/28	AR
Rossell, W. H.	013	1885	WB-B/360	
Rossen, Merritt	022	1886	WB-E/336	AR
Rossen, William M.	022	c1855	WB-D/106	AR
Rosser, Benjamon	022	1778	Orig. Only	AR
Rosser, James	056	1800	Orig. Only	AR
Rosser, Jesse	099	1876	RB-35/342	AR
Rosser, Joel	069	1850	WB-1/522	AR
Rosser, Joshua	099	1815	RB-12/215	AR
Rosser, Thomas C.	022	1875	WB-E/109	AR
Rotan, James	032	1837	WB-1/293	AR
Rotch, Breget	072	c1788	Orig. Only	AR
Rotchel, John	070	1784	WB-C/369	AR
Roten, David	102	1892	Orig. Only	AR
Roten, Larkin	006	1881	WB-E/74	AR
Roten, William	006	1875	WB-E/13	AR
Rothrock, George	038	c1850	WB-1/27	AR
Rothrock, Jacob	090	1807	WB-2/77	AR
Rothrock, John M.	032	1896	WB-4/278	AR
Rothrock, Joseph	038	1868	WB-2/24	AR
Rothrock, Martin	032	1864	WB-2/278	AR
Rothrock, Philip	090	1825	WB-3/142	AR
Rothrock, Samuel	085	1895	WB-3/71	CTY
Rothruck, Philip	032	1824	WB-1/36	AR
Rothwell, A. B.	070	1861	WB-D/45	AR
Rothwell, Jonathan	012	1847	WB-B/187	AR
Rothwell, Laura P.	070	1900	WB-H/306	AR
Rothwell, Mary	012	c1853	WB-B/5	AR
Rottenberry, John	100	1827	WB-30/157	AR
Rottenberry, Susan	100	1848	WB-40/18	AR
Rouch, Peter, Sr.	021	1856	WB-1/124	
Roughton, Agness	096	1815	WB-2/49	
Roughton, Daniel	096	c1809	WB-2/51	
Roughton, Josiah	092	c1837	WB-4/135	
Roulhac, Catharine	073	1880	WB-H/249	CTY
Roulhac, Frances	063	1826	WB-2/112	
Roulhac, Francis L.	010	1880	WB-I/111	
Roulhac, Gregoire	009	1807	OWB/440	AR
Roulhac, John B. G.	073	c1883	WB-H/323	CTY
Roulhac, John M.	009	1817	OB-A/265	AR
Roulhack, Elizabeth	053	1809	RW-1/432	AR
Round, George H.	017	1879	WB-B/88	AR
Round, Mary L.	017	1883	WB-B/106	AR
Roundtree, Elizabeth	103	1817	RD-4/57	AR
Roundtree, Ella G.	019	1894	WB-B/264	AR
Roundtree, Lemuel	009	c1809	OB-A/28	AR
Rounsaville, Benjamin	032	1832	WB-1/198	AR
Rountree, Abner	041	1816	WB-2/133	AR
Rountree, Alfred	024	1865	WB-D/28	AR
Rountree, C. J.	105	1881	WB-2/274	AR
Rountree, Cader	105	1858	WB-1/53	AR
Rountree, Charles	024	1760	WB-A/100	AR
Rountree, Charles	065	1896	WB-M/436	AR
Rountree, Charles	073	1816	WB-D/467	AR
Rountree, Charles	041	1816	WB-2/114	AR
Rountree, David R.	078	1851	WB-13/447	
Rountree, Elizabeth	077	1813	WB-E/394	AR
Rountree, F. M.	059	1888	WB-A/526	CTY
Rountree, Francis	028	1793	WB-A/276	AR
Rountree, Francis	056	1748	Orig. Only	SS/AR
Rountree, George	105	1872	WB-2/99	AR
Rountree, Hannah	077	1759	SS 882/116	SS/AR
Rountree, Harvey	073	1848	WB-F/402	AR
Rountree, Jason	041	1840	WB-3/26	AR
Rountree, Jesse	028	1777	Orig. Only	SS/AR
Rountree, John A.	041	1900	WB-4/523	AR
Rountree, John W.	073	1853	WB-G/36	AR
Rountree, Lewis	037	1850	WB-F/445	AR
Rountree, Malvina	105	1889	WB-2/499	AR
Rountree, Mary Ann	105	1873	WB-2/148	AR
Rountree, Mary D.	079	1876	WB-2/127	AR
Rountree, Monroe	028	1892	WB-F/30	
Rountree, Moses	105	1889	WB-2/549	AR
Rountree, Moses	077	1755	SS 880/37	SS/AR
Rountree, N. T.	105	1862	WB-1/69	AR
Rountree, Nancy	041	1892	WB-4/329	AR
Rountree, Nathan H.	037	1837	WB-F/209	AR
Rountree, Seth	041	1808	WB-2/14	
Rountree, Seth H.	041	1866	WB-3/342	AR
Rountree, Solomon	041	1871	WB-4/21	AR
Rountree, Thomas	073	1805	WB-D/148	AR
Rountree, Thomas	041	1832	WB-2/308	AR
Rountree, Thomas	073	1820	WB-D/580	AR
Rountree, Thomas	041	1781	WB-1/16	AR
Rountree, William	028	1791	WB-A/259	AR
Rountree, Willie	037	1847	WB-F/362	AR
Rourk, Edmund	011	1769	Orig. Only	SS/AR
Rourk, Joanna	MA	1891	070 WB-F/460	070 AR
Rourk, Peter	012	1881	WB-A/48	AR
Rourk, William A.	070	1858	WB-C/668	AR
Rouse, Alexander	070	c1780	WB-C/363	AR

Name	Co.	Date	Recorded Copy	Original
Rouse, Benjamin S.	103	1892	WB-1/564	AR
Rouse, Bennett	059	1898	WB-B/204	CTY
Rouse, Bythel	027	1860	WB-A/75	AR
Rouse, David	035	1885	WB-4/244	AR
Rouse, David	035	1870	WB-4/24	AR
Rouse, Elizabeth	070	1791	WB-C/371	AR
Rouse, Frances Ann	059	1876	WB-A/122	CTY-Copy
Rouse, George	035	1810	WB-A/418	AR
Rouse, Henry	035	1850	WB-2/55	AR
Rouse, Henry	103	1808	RD-1/81	
Rouse, Jessee	027	c1815	WB-A/46	AR
Rouse, Noah	059	1897	WB-B/166	CTY
Rouse, Phillip	035	1784	WB-A/415	AR
Rouse, Phineas	072	1834	WB-1/122	AR
Rouse, Solomon	103	1800	Orig. Only	AR
Rouse, Wiley	059	1883	WB-A/342	CTY
Rouse, William	103	1870	WB-1/157	AR
Rouse, William J.	103	1877	WB-1/107	AR
Rousham, Joseph	096	1783	WB-1/135	AR
Rousham, William	096	c1782	WB-1/129	AR
Rousseau, Adolphus	104	1889	WB-6/372	AR
Rousseau, Ann E.	044	1896	WB-24/296	CTY
Rousseau, Eddie A.	104	1890	WB-6/393	AR
Rousseau, John	104	1880	WB-6/194	AR
Roussom, Edward	096	1787	WB-1/157	AR
Routh, Aaron	081	1866	WB-14/42	AR
Routh, Henry	081	1851	Orig. Only	AR
Routh, Joshua	081	1872	WB-15/80	AR
Routh, William	037	1803	WB-D/163	AR
Routledge, Nicholas	035	c1765	WB-A/401	AR-Copy
Routledge, Thomas	035	1825	WB-A/406	AR
Routledge, Thomas	035	1801	WB-A/411	AR
Routledge, William	035	1795	WB-A/402	AR
Routon, Edward	096	c1797	Orig. Only	AR
Routon, John	096	1764	WB-1/58	AR
Routon, Richard	096	1817	Orig. Only	AR
Rovely, John	075	c1707	SS 875/41	
Rovers, Joshua	100	1824	WB-26/37	AR
Row, Ann	070	1808	WB-AB/103	AR
Row, Valentine	075	1740	Orig. Only	SS/AR
Row, William	069	1798	WB-1/123	AR
Row, William	037	1761	WB-A/48	AR
Rowan, Elizabeth	039	c1831	Orig. Only	AR
Rowan, Esther	070	1792	WB-C/372	AR
Rowan, Isaac H.	068	1874	WB-D/61	
Rowan, John	012	c1774	DB-B/117	
Rowan, Levicy	083	1893	WB-4/1	AR
Rowan, Matthew	070	1760	SS 881/151	SS/AR
Rowan, Robert	029	1799	WB-A/19	AR
Rowan, Thomas	068	c1831	WB-B/80	
Rowark, Elisha	020	1838	RB-N/275	AR
Rowark, Elizabeth	020	1846	RB-P/310	AR
Rowe, Benjamin	028	1825	WB-C/260	AR
Rowe, D. L.	021	1897	WB-3/180	AR
Rowe, David	105	1898	WB-3/289	AR
Rowe, Eli W.	003	1894	WB-B/328	
Rowe, Gaius	072	1813	WB-A/112	AR
Rowe, Harriot M.	072	c1813	WB-A/112	AR
Rowe, James M.	028	1853	WB-D/212	AR
Rowe, Jesse	028	1835	WB-C/378	AR
Rowe, John	022	1800	WB-A/23	AR
Rowe, John	070	1783	WB-C/368	AR
Rowe, John	075	1821	WB-M1/341	AR
Rowe, Joseph	020	c1836	RB-0/476	AR
Rowe, Joseph H.	021	1868	WB-1/253	AR
Rowe, Linnie L.	021	1899	WB-3/243	AR
Rowel, Elizabeth	071	1817	WB-3/189	AR
Rowell, Benjamin	012	1843	WB-B/178	AR
Rowell, Elizabeth	071	1746	Orig. Only	SS/AR
Rowell, Franklin	080	N. D.	Orig. Only	AR
Rowell, Samuel	012	c1859	WB-B/29	AR
Rowell, Samuel	071	1764	WB-1/106	
Rowland, A. J.	106	1883	WB-2/166	AR
Rowland, Alexander	083	1823	Orig. Only	AR
Rowland, Bennett	099	1881	WB-A/287	AR
Rowland, Candace	099	1876	RB-35/347	AR
Rowland, Eliza	044	1900	WB-24/492	CTY
Rowland, Flora A.	083	1878	WB-3/158	AR
Rowland, George	030	1815	WB-3/69	
Rowland, Henry	044	1857	WB-20/317	CTY
Rowland, Horace H.	098	1887	WB-A/81	CTY
Rowland, Isaac	099	1885	WB-B/50	AR
Rowland, James	107	c1854	WB-1/117	
Rowland, James	011	1782	WB-1/577	
Rowland, James	083	c1801	WB-1/68	AR
Rowland, John	083	c1803	WB-1/82	AR
Rowland, John A.	083	1872	WB-3/41	AR
Rowland, John H.	044	1877	WB-23/277	CTY
Rowland, John M.	099	1882	WB-A/332	AR
Rowland, John S.	083	1866	WB-2/234	AR
Rowland, Lewis	099	1842	RB-25/109	AR
Rowland, Mary E.	083	1858	WB-2/133	AR
Rowland, Meredith	044	1822	WB-9/142	CTY
Rowland, Noah	089	1865	WB-1/298	
Rowland, Pleasant	044	1867	WB-22/649	CTY
Rowland, Samuel	099	1883	WB-A/392	AR
Rowland, Sherod	097	1874	WB-2/72	AR
Rowland, Thomas	089	1862	WB-1/231	
Rowland, Thomas C.	097	1877	WB-2/131	AR-Nunc.
Rowland, Walter	099	1883	WB-A/393	
Rowland, William	099	1884	WB-B/9	AR
Rowland, William H.	069	1886	WB-5/216	AR
Rowland, William I.	099	1899	WB-D/245	AR
Rowlett, Margaret	039	1879	WB-U/212	AR
Rowlett, Thomas	084	1841	WB-B/263	CTY
Rowlett, Thomas W.	100	1877	WB-51/120	AR
Rowntree, Frances	103	1819	RD-4/220	AR
Rowntree, Francis	N	1734	SS 876/316	SS/AR
Rowntree, Moses	009	1841	OB-D/173	AR
Rowntree, Thomas	024	1748	Orig. Only	SS/AR
Rowntree, Thomas	024	1774	Orig. Only	SS/AR
Roy, James	071	1794	WB-2/58	AR
Royal, A.	087	1880	WB-3/201	AR
Royal, Catharine	087	1882	WB-3/250	AR
Royal, Hardy E.	087	1849	WB-1/367	AR
Royal, Hardy, Sr.	087	1832	WB-1/132	AR
Royal, Henry	092	c1828	WB-4/27	AR
Royal, James	028	1788	WB-A/174	AR
Royal, John	087	1862	WB-2/37	AR
Royal, Marmaduke	019	1835	WB-A/49	AR
Royal, Noah	087	1855	WB-1/474	AR
Royal, Ollen	087	1875	WB-3/90	AR
Royal, Owen	087	c1820	WB-1/23	
Royal, Rezin	087	1854	WB-1/470	AR
Royal, Sarah J.	087	1882	WB-3/240	AR
Royal, T. P.	087	1899	WB-4/100	AR
Royal, Thomas	028	1774	Orig. Only	AR
Royal, Whitney	087	1869	WB-3/18	AR
Royal, William	087	1833	WB-1/129	AR

Name	Co.	Date	Recorded Copy	Original
Royal, William	092	1826	WB-3/169	AR
Royal, Young	087	1894	WB-3/546	AR
Royal, Zachariah	087	1870	WB-3/24	AR
Royall, Isom	087	1833	WB-1/146	AR
Royall, John	092	1810	WB-3/95	AR
Royall, Samuel	072	c1772	RW/L38	AR
Royals, Barbara	029	1869	WB-E/11	AR
Royals, Mary M.	056	1895	WB-2/206	AR
Royals, R. D.	029	1884	Orig. Only	AR
Royse, Vere	075	1757	Orig. Only	AR
Royster, A. D.	099	1884	WB-A/560	AR
Royster, Abel	078	1837	WI-13/253	
Royster, Banister	044	1878	WB-23/307	CTY
Royster, Banister	044	1867	WB-22/658	CTY
Royster, Elizabeth	044	1842	WB-15/301	CTY
Royster, Francis	044	1820	WB-8/357	CTY
Royster, James	044	1879	WB-23/339	CTY
Royster, James A.	044	1889	WB-24/80	CTY
Royster, John	044	1845	WB-16/130	CTY
Royster, Joseph	078	1836	WI-13/152	
Royster, Madison B.	099	1890	WB-B/445	AR
Royster, Marcus D.	044	1878	WB-23/311	CTY
Royster, Mariah W.	078	1892	WB-19/322	AR
Royster, Moses	044	1879	WB-23/348	CTY
Royster, Rowena	044	1899	WB-24/452	CTY
Royster, Sally	044	1846	WB-16/514	CTY
Royster, Thomas S.	098	c1886	WB-A/314	CTY
Royster, Willey	044	1866	WB-22/577	CTY
Royster, William	044	1851	WB-18/277	CTY
Royster, William L.	044	1877	WB-23/254	CTY
Royster, Willis A.	044	1897	WB-24/354	CTY
Rozar, Reuben	083	c1798	WB-1/52	AR
Rozell, Pritchard	084	c1798	OW/121	AR
Rozier, Reuben	083	1870	WB-3/24	AR
Rozier, Simpson	083	1865	WB-2/220	AR
Rozzell, Richard	060	1826	WB-1/38	AR
Ruba, John C.	010	1869	WB-I/17	AR
Rucker, J. L.	086	1885	Orig. Only	AR
Rucker, Susannah	086	1833	WB-D/163	AR
Rucker, Thomas	024	1748	Orig. Only	SS/AR
Ruckman, Joseph	046	1792	WB-A/327	AR
Rudasall, Phillip	065	1764	WB-F/110	AR
Rudasill, Jonas E.	040	1897	WB-2/570	AR
Rudasill, Susannah	040	c1847	WB-1/40	
Rudd, Artelia	020	1890	WB-B/37	CTY
Rudd, Elijah W.	100	1853	WB-42/179	AR
Rudd, Hezekiah	046	1894	WB-F/325	AR
Rudd, Hezekiah	020	1803	RB-E/29	AR
Rudd, James G.	098	1891	WB-A/131	CTY
Rudd, Jeremiah	020	1863	RB-T/13	CTY
Rudd, Joshua	020	1849	RB-Q/159	
Rudd, William H.	100	1853	WB-42/240	AR
Rudduck, John	046	1790	WB-A/308	AR
Rudduck, Joseph	081	1800	WB-2/59	AR
Rudduck, William	046	1804	WB-A/320	AR
Rudisell, Fannie L.	021	1900	WB-3/271	AR
Rudisell, Marcus H.	021	1849	WB-1/79	AR
Rudisill, Emanuel A.	040	1896	WB-2/511	AR
Rudisill, J. F.	021	1894	WB-3/78	
Rudisill, Jacob M.	040	1864	WB-1/169	
Rudisill, John	060	1786	Orig. Only	AR
Rudisill, John	040	1848	WB-1/4	
Rudisill, Jonas	065	1830	WB-E/84	AR
Rudisill, Margaret	060	1859	WB-3/24	AR
Rudisill, Michael	060	1827	WB-1/72	AR
Rudisill, Michael	021	1867	WB-1/248	AR
Rudisill, Philip	060	1812	Orig. Only	AR
Rudisill, Philip	060	1795	Orig. Only	AR
Rudisill, Philip	021	1859	WB-1/147	CTY
Rudisill, Sallie	060	1889	WB-4/393	AR
Rudisill, Solomon	060	1896	WB-5/36	AR
Rudisill, Wiley	040	1899	WB-3/33	AR
Rudisill, William	060	1842	WB-2/77	AR
Rue, Bryan A.	053	1869	WB-11/14	AR
Rue, Elizabeth	047	1885	WB-6/395	AR
Rue, Joshua E.	047	1887	WB-6/469	AR
Ruff, Daniel	009	1837	OB-C2/3	AR
Ruff, Sarah	045	1869	WB-1/6	
Ruff, William	009	1827	OB-A/383	AR
Ruffin, Anne M.	073	1875	084 WB-E/460	
Ruffin, Anne M.	073	1875	090 WB-6/381	090 AR
Ruffin, Anne M.	073	1875	WB-H/121	CTY
Ruffin, Benjamin	037	1795	WB-C/320	AR
Ruffin, Duncan L.	105	1861	WB-1/62	AR
Ruffin, Elisabeth	037	c1881	WB-G/674	AR
Ruffin, Elizabeth	037	1851	WB-F/458	AR
Ruffin, Etheldred	071	1777	WB-1/13	AR
Ruffin, George W.	039	c1861	105 WB-1/92	
Ruffin, Henry J. G.	39	1854	WB-N/545	
Ruffin, John	071	1778	WB-1/316	
Ruffin, John	010	1845	WB-G/378	AR
Ruffin, John T.	010	1852	WB-G/484	AR
Ruffin, Joseph B.	010	1895	WB-I/426 & 433	AR
Ruffin, Lamon	037	1828	WB-F/93	AR
Ruffin, Lemon	105	c1862	WB-1/122	AR
Ruffin, Lucy	037	1838	WB-F/214	AR
Ruffin, Martha P.	073	1896	WB-I/90	CTY
Ruffin, Mary	037	1818	WB-E/203	AR
Ruffin, Mary	039	1879	WB-U/194	AR
Ruffin, Mary	037	1856	WB-G/117	AR
Ruffin, Mary R.	073	1879	WB-H/195	CTY
Ruffin, Mary R.	073	c1870	Copy	047 AR
Ruffin, P. B.	073	1900	WB-I/181	CTY
Ruffin, Pennina	105	1891	WB-2/579	AR
Ruffin, Pennina	105	1891	039 WB-U/526	039 AR
Ruffin, Pleasant	020	1865	WB-A/214	CTY
Ruffin, Richard	103	1783	WI-A/23	AR
Ruffin, Robert	071	c1767	WB-1/153	
Ruffin, Robert	071	1786	WB-1/357	AR
Ruffin, Samuel	037	1826	WB-F/60	AR
Ruffin, Samuel	037	1798	WB-D/63	AR
Ruffin, Sarah	037	1780	WB-B/44	AR
Ruffin, Starkey	063	1817	WB-2/42	
Ruffin, Sterling	020	1822	RB-I/92	
Ruffin, Thomas	010	1840	WB-G/324	AR
Ruffin, Thomas	073	1889	WB-H/470	CTY
Ruffin, Thomas	073	1870	WB-H/27	CTY
Ruffin, Thomas	073	1870	090 WB-6/378	090 AR
Ruffin, Thomas	103	c1863	RD-14/331	
Ruffin, William	037	1831	WB-F/126	AR
Ruffin, William	010	1808	WB-F/90	AR
Ruffin, William	010	1781	WB-C/28	AR
Ruffin, William	099	1825	RB-20/25	AR
Ruffin, William H.	099	1822	RB-17/433	AR
Ruffin, William K.	073	1880	WB-H/240	CTY
Ruffin, Zilpha Ann	037	1898	WB-H/403	AR
Rufty, Edward	085	1878	WB-1/440	
Rufty, George	003	c1850	Orig. Only	AR
Rufty, John	003	1895	WB-B/338	
Rumage, Nathan	089	1874	WB-2/35	AR

Name	Co.	Date	Recorded Copy	Original
Rumage, Sarah	089	1889	WB-2/181	AR
Rumbley, John	073	1844	WB-F/197	AR
Rumbly, Edgar	085	c1792	WB-D/109	AR
Rumbly, Edward	028	1788	WB-A/173	Nunc.
Rumley, Israel	046	1895	WB-F/402	AR
Rumley, Mary	046	1878	WB-E/225	AR
Rumley, Rachal	019	1866	WB-B/3	AR
Rummage, George	089	1856	WB-1/145	
Rumple, Daniel	054	1886	WB-5/126	AR-Copy
Rumple, J. W.	VA	1894	085 WB-3/44	
Rumple, John	016	1867	WB-2/156	
Rumple, Joseph	065	1893	WB-M/200	AR
Rumple, Mary	016	1860	WB-2/71	
Rumple, Mary Ann	016	1836	PQS.5/382	
Rumple, Peter	016	1857	WB-2/30	
Rumple, Peter A.	085	1864	WB-K/326	AR
Rumple, Philip	054	c1831	WB-2/124	AR
Rumple, Robert A.	013	1888	WB-B/490	AR
Runals, Sherod	099	1776	RB-1/172	AR
Runnells, Mary	028	1894	WB-F/122	
Runnels, Joice	056	1761	WB-1/798	AR
Runnels, Shadrach	035	1783	WB-A/414	AR
Runnyans, A. D.	026	1900	WB-3/106	AR
Runyon, Caroline	099	1863	RB-32/617	AR
Ruppe, Daniel	026	1900	WB-3/83	AR
Ruppe, Jacob	080	1894	WB-1/229	AR
Ruppe, William P.	086	1899	WB-G/23	AR
Rusal, Mary	085	c1787	WB-D/100	AR
Rush, Absalom	039	1807	WB-C/81	
Rush, Benjamin	081	1819	WB-4/713	AR
Rush, Benjamin	022	c1801	WB-A/70	AR
Rush, Benjamin	067	1864	WB-1/109	AR
Rush, Benjamin	VA	1767	015 RB-1/67	015 AR
Rush, Elizabeth	022	c1832	WB-C/118	AR
Rush, George N.	061	1898	WB-2/206	AR
Rush, Juliann	061	1869	WB-2/6	AR
Rush, Maria J.	067	1887	089 WB-2/150	089 AR
Rush, Maria J.	067	1887	WB-2/242	AR
Rush, Martin	067	c1877	089 WB-2/155	
Rush, Martin, Sr.	067	1883	WB-2/166	AR
Rush, Michael	081	1858	WB-11/221	AR
Rush, Reuben	081	1817	WB-4/713	AR
Rush, Sarah	039	c1790	WB-A/53	
Rush, Washington	081	1894	WB-16/305	
Rush, Zebedee	081	1872	WB-15/85	AR
Rushing, Abraham	005	1806	WB-2/141	AR
Rushing, Abraham D.	097	1866	WB-1/271	AR
Rushing, Darling	097	1897	WB-2/525	AR
Rushing, Solomon	005	1812	WB-2/140	AR
Rushing, William M.	097	1872	WB-2/63	AR
Russ, John	011	1838	WB-1/44	
Russ, John	082	1885	WB-6/325	AR
Russ, John	011	c1791	WB-1/564	
Russ, John D.	011	1879	WB-2/93	
Russ, Joseph	011	c1797	WB-1/429	
Russ, Mary	011	c1772	WB-1/560	
Russ, Simpronous	012	1817	WB-B/110	
Russ, Thomas	011	c1795	WB-1/443	
Russel, David M.	016	1861	WB-2/79	
Russel, John	072	1753	Orig. Only	SS/AR
Russel, Johnson	022	1876	WB-E/116	AR
Russel, Laura Jane	004	1876	WB-A/24	AR
Russel, Luke	057	c1780	Orig. Only	AR
Russel, Nancy H.	022	1882	WB-E/236	AR
Russel, Norval	100	1897	Orig. Only	AR
Russel, Rebecca	099	1850	RB-27/142	AR
Russel, Thomas	028	1744/5	DB-3/70	
Russel, Willis	030	1778	WB-1/128	
Russell, Aaron	089	1844	WB-1/30	
Russell, Alexander	073	1772	WB-A/158	
Russell, Alexander	073	1818	WB-D/550	AR
Russell, Andrew	046	1828	WB-B/369	AR
Russell, Ann	100	1796	WB-8/317	AR
Russell, Ann E.	070	1846	WB-AB/442	AR
Russell, B. B.	010	1868	WB-H/207	AR
Russell, Benjamin	053	1815	RW-1/492	AR
Russell, Benjamin	030	c1814	WB-3/42	
Russell, Catharine	020	1853	RB-R/78	
Russell, Clara T. W.	059	1900	WB-B/264	CTY
Russell, Daniel	081	1890	WB-16/181	AR
Russell, Daniel L.	070	1871	WB-E/232	AR
Russell, David	016	1834	PQS.5/302	
Russell, David	049	1850	WB-2/188	AR
Russell, David	065	1802	WB-F/129	AR
Russell, David	019	1813	WB-D/343	AR
Russell, David G.	097	1895	WB-2/486	AR
Russell, Elizabeth	016	1837	PQS.5/424	
Russell, Elizabeth	053	c1814	RW-1/514	AR
Russell, Fannie L.	100	N. D.	Orig. Only	AR
Russell, Gabriel	081	1857	WB-11/412	AR
Russell, George	024	c1781	WB-A/102	AR
Russell, George	028	1852	WB-D/188	AR
Russell, Habakkuk	019	1754	SS 879/68	SS/AR
Russell, Harris	081	1880	WB-15/325	AR
Russell, Henry	100	1889	WB-51/307	AR
Russell, Henry P.	070	1863	WB-D/142	AR
Russell, Isabella	044	1897	WB-24/350	CTY
Russell, Isaiah	081	1844	WB-8/63	AR
Russell, J. M.	081	1889	WB-16/86	
Russell, James	046	1812	WB-A/323	AR
Russell, James	065	1792	WB-F/125	AR
Russell, James	060	1805	Orig. Only	AR
Russell, James A.	044	1864	WB-22/172	CTY
Russell, James T.	100	1887	WB-51/249 & 263	
Russell, Jefery	047	1762	WB-1/81	
Russell, John	044	1812	WB-7/259	CTY
Russell, John	065	1790	WB-F/124	AR
Russell, John C.	044	1814	WB-7/464	CTY
Russell, Joseph	046	1830	WB-B/425	AR
Russell, Joseph	VA	1836	Copy	020 AR
Russell, Joseph	067	1864	WB-1/113	AR
Russell, Josiah	028	1786	WB-A/143	AR
Russell, L. W.	104	1873	WB-6/71	AR
Russell, Lemuel	030	1807	WB-2/300	
Russell, Linton	072	1800	WB-A/160	AR
Russell, Luke	028	1839	WB-C/434	AR
Russell, Luke	028	1780	Orig. Only	AR
Russell, Lydia	053	1804	RW-1/371	
Russell, Malichi	028	c1806	WB-B/232	
Russell, Mary	046	1848	WB-C/304	AR
Russell, Mary	090	1812	WB-2/139	AR
Russell, Nevil	019	1871	WB-B/66	AR
Russell, Obiah	072	1828	WB-1/27	
Russell, Ransom	081	c1844	Orig. Only	AR
Russell, Rebecca	010	1899	WB-I/579	
Russell, Richard	053	1790	Orig. Only	AR-Nunc.
Russell, Richard	005	1834	WB-B/34	AR
Russell, Robert	046	1804	WB-A/320	AR
Russell, Samantha	097	1898	WB-2/560	AR

Name	Co.	Date	Recorded Copy	Original
Russell, Sarah	072	1806	WB-A/114	AR-Nunc.
Russell, Sarah H.	065	1894	WB-M/257	AR
Russell, Sarah H.	065	1894	097 WB-2/467	097 AR
Russell, Thomas	075	1791	WB-K/218	AR
Russell, Thomas	072	c1813	WB-A/114	AR
Russell, Thomas	065	1871	WB-K/78	AR
Russell, Thomas	049	1891	WB-2/284	AR
Russell, Thomas	028	1744/5	SS 877/19	SS/AR
Russell, Thomas T.	041	1898	WB-4/457	AR
Russell, Thomas T.	039	1834	WB-K/27	AR
Russell, Timothy	046	1820	WB-B/91	AR
Russell, Twitty	100	1790	WB-5/161	AR-Nunc.
Russell, W. H.	013	1885	Orig. Only	AR
Russell, Whitson	081	1868	WB-14/209	AR
Russell, William	046	1810	WB-A/322	AR
Russell, William	084	c1790	OW/268	AR
Russell, William	046	1795	WB-A/314	AR
Russell, William	029	1823	WB-B/103	AR
Russell, William	067	1865	WB-1/129	AR
Russell, Wilson	081	1883	WB-15/425	
Russle, Matthew	061	1846	WB-1/30	AR
Rust, Henry	046	1898	WB-G/41	AR
Rust, Justin	099	1834	RB-23/213	AR
Rustell, John	019	1803	WB-D/340	AR
Rustell, Richard	019	1761	WB-D/333	AR
Rustull, John, Sr.	019	1861	WB-A/256	AR
Rustull, Richd.	019	1747	SS 877/259	SS/AR
Ruth, James B.	099	1838	RB-24/224	AR
Ruthera, David	085	1766	WB-A/139	AR
Rutherford, John	014	1900	WB-3/110	CTY
Rutherford, John	014	1880	WB-2/195	
Rutherford, John	014	1900	064 WB-2/489	064 AR
Rutherford, Martha C.	086	1871	WB-F/29	AR
Rutherford, Mary	073	1874	WB-H/88	CTY
Rutherford, Sophrona	064	1898	WB-2/444	AR
Rutherford, Sophronia	014	1898	WB-3/49	CTY
Rutherford, William	060	1809	Orig. Only	AR
Rutland, David	071	1860	WB-5/227	AR
Rutland, Drusilla	047	1831	WB-4/77	AR
Rutland, Elizabeth	047	1823	WB-3/691	AR
Rutland, Elizabeth	010	1836	WB-G/261	AR
Rutland, John	010	c1762	WB-A/52	
Rutland, John	010	1804	WB-E/231	AR
Rutland, Joseph	012	1829	WB-B/165	AR
Rutland, Martha	071	1792	WB-1/447	AR
Rutland, Martha	005	1826	WB-A/127	AR
Rutland, Rebecah	071	1805	WB-2/295	AR-Nunc.
Rutland, Redden	012	1834	WB-B/168	AR
Rutland, Shadrack	047	1797	WB-3/278	AR
Rutland, Sion	005	1805	WB-2/142	AR
Rutland, Thomas	071	1793	WB-2/33	AR
Rutland, Watson	071	1820	WB-3/231	AR
Rutland, William	071	1795	WB-2/71	AR
Rutland, Wilson	071	1802	WB-2/236	AR
Rutledge, Abel	085	1816	WB-G/415	AR
Rutledge, Alexander	040	1882	WB-2/182	AR
Rutledge, Belinda	040	1899	Copy	060 AR
Rutledge, Belinda	040	1899	WB-3/60	AR
Rutledge, Charles	060	1805	Orig. Only	AR
Rutledge, E.	092	1836	WB-4/91	
Rutledge, Elizabeth	028	1779	Orig. Only	AR
Rutledge, George	040	c1856	WB-1/82	AR
Rutledge, George	094	1779	094.901.1	AR
Rutledge, Isabella	090	1861	WB-4/339	AR
Rutledge, James	040	1883	WB-2/199	AR

Name	Co.	Date	Recorded Copy	Original
Rutledge, James	040	1883	Copy	060 AR
Rutledge, James	085	1813	WB-G/291	AR
Rutledge, Jean	060	1801	Orig. Only	AR
Rutledge, John	085	1805	WB-D/99	AR
Rutledge, John	085	1775	WB-A/196	AR
Rutledge, Sallie	060	1829	WB-1/150	AR
Rutledge, William	090	1804	WB-2/50	AR
Rutledge, William	092	1846	WB-4/253	
Rutledge, William G.	040	1864	WB-1/160	AR
Ryall, Charles	028	1755	SS 880/8	SS/AR
Ryall, William	087	c1794	Orig. Only	AR-Copy
Ryals, Richard	029	1816	WB-A/233	AR
Ryals, Right	056	1889	WB-3/520	AR
Ryan, David	010	1762	SS 881/272	SS/AR
Ryan, David	010	1897	WB-I/521	AR
Ryan, David	010	1802	WB-E/164	AR
Ryan, Elizabeth	010	1805	WB-E/258	AR
Ryan, Grisella	099	1868	Orig. Only	AR
Ryan, James	030	1784	WB-1/178	
Ryan, James	010	1777	WB-B/101	AR
Ryan, John	046	1794	WB-A/312	AR
Ryan, Malinda	046	1893	WB-F/305	AR
Ryan, Robert G.	046	1868	WB-D/366	AR
Ryan, Thadeus	024	1900	WB-E/310	AR
Ryan, William	046	1843	WB-C/150	AR
Ryburn, Andrew	040	1869	WB-2/6	AR
Ryding, Jonathan	010	1754	SS 879/145	SS/AR
Rye, John	082	1847	WB-3/44	AR
Ryin, Elijah	065	1789	WB-F/124	AR-Nunc.
Ryle, John	005	1778	WB-1/28	AR
Rylery, John	085	c1783	WB-C/162	AR
Rymer, Jacob	085	1843	WB-I/195	AR
Rymer, John P.	085	1897	WB-3/163	CTY
Rymer, Katherina	085	1833	WB-H/582	AR
Rymer, Nicholas	085	1834	WB-H/615	AR
Rymer, Sophia	085	1891	WB-2/472	CTY-Nunc.
Ryun, Thomas	010	1753	Orig. Only	SS/AR
Rzsau, James	070	1756	Orig. Only	AR
Sabiston, Love	019	1828	WB-D/386	AR
Sabiston, William	019	1894	WB = B/260	AR
Saddler, Sarah	084	1856	WB-C/233	CTY
Sadler, Ananias	053	1853	WB-7/552	AR
Sadler, Emery	028	1858	WB-D/301	AR
Sadler, Henry	060	1824	WB-1/4	
Sadler, J. A.	060	1899	WB-5/126	AR
Sadler, J. A.	060	1899	Copy	040 AR
Sadler, John R.	013	1835	WB-A/36	
Sadler, Martha	060	1803	Orig. Only	AR
Sadler, Phillip	065	1836	WB-E/146	AR
Sadler, Richard	024	1754	Orig. Only	SS/AR
Sadler, Richard	053	1857	WB-8/223	AR
Sadler, Richard	053	1815	RW-1/501	
Sadler, William	024	1727	Orig. Only	SS/AR
Sadler, William	002	c1711	SS 875/35	
Saffle, Virlinder	054	c1812	WB-1/296	AR
Safrit, Charles	085	1845	WB-K/7	AR
Safrit, George	085	1853	WB-K/150	AR
Safrit, Moses	085	c1863	Orig. Only	AR
Safrit, Sophia	016	1893	WB-4/153	AR
Sago, John	005	1785	WB-1/48	AR
Saillard, Francis	019	1805	WB-D/364	AR
Sailor, Clarissa	038	1886	WB-3/85	AR
Sain, George	085	1834	WB-H/619	AR
Sain, Jacob	060	1836	WB-1/378	AR

Name	Co.	Date	Recorded Copy	Original
Sain, John	060	1876	WB-4/145	AR
Sain, Joseph	085	1824	WB-H/260	AR
Sain, Samuel	060	1897	WB-5/48	AR
Sain, Samuel	026	1897	WB-2/554	AR
Saint, Daniel	077	1772	WB-C/115	AR
Saint, David	077	1793	WB-C/452	AR
Saint, Elizabeth	077	1779	WB-C/237	AR
Saintclair, John E.	104	1873	WB-6/78	AR
Sale, Cornelius	104	1811	WB-2/320	
Sale, Finley	106	c1862	WB-1/93	AR
Sale, John	104	1862	WB-5/302	
Sale, John	065	1806	WB-F/187	AR
Sale, Leonard	104	1824	WB-4/52	AR
Sale, Robert	104	1866	WB-5/452	AR
Sale, Robert	104	1890	WB-6/376	AR
Sale, Silas	104	1900	WB-7/103	
Sale, Thomas	065	1806	WB-F/187	
Sale, William	104	1788	WB-1/245	AR
Sale, William	104	1889	WB-6/360	
Sale, William	104	1883	WB-6/233	AR
Sales, Robert F.	013	1898	WB-D/110	AR
Saley, Elizabeth	081	1900	WB-17/100	AR
Salisbury, James	075	1758	SS 881/175	SS/AR
Salkeld, Isaac	087	c1795	011 WB-1/403	
Sallard, Charles	078	1843	WI-15/334	AR
Salmon, Avery G.	100	1878	WB-51/125	AR
Salmon, William	035	1818	Orig. Only	AR
Salmons, C. W.	054	1899	WB-6/236	CTY
Salmons, Enoch	106	1873	WB-2/44	AR
Salmons, Lucinda	090	1847	WB-4/232	AR
Salsbury, D'Alanson	064	1893	WB-3/306	AR
Salsbury, James	063	1864	WB-2/520	
Salsbury, Laura E.	063	1889	WB-4/32	AR
Salsbury, Richard B.	063	1889	WB-4/34	AR
Salsbury, Sallie E.	063	1899	WB-4/240	AR
Salt, Anthony	085	c1776	WB-B/109	AR
Salter, Edward	008	1734	SS 876/356	SS/AR
Salter, James	028	1841	WB-D/29	
Salter, John D.	011	1852	WB-1/203	
Salter, Margrett	009	1837	OWB/495	AR
Salter, Peter	077	1806	WB-C/232	AR
Salter, Richard	011	c1795	WB-1/406	
Salter, Richard	011	c1796	WB-1/413	
Salter, Robert	028	1842	WB-D/48	AR
Salter, Sarah	011	c1797	WB-1/402	
Salter, Tyson	019	1893	WB-B/231	AR
Salter, William	011	c1797	WB-1/448	
Salter, William	028	1881	WB-E/289	
Salter, William	011	c1836	WB-1/104	
Salter, William	019	1841	WB-A/95	AR
Saltonstall, William E.	075	c1858	WB-M2/58	AR
Salva, A. P.	070	1884	WB-E/542	AR
Salyear, Samuel	030	1822	WB-3/122	
Sample, Elizabeth	065	1822	WB-E/109	AR
Sample, James	065	1853	WB-I/205	AR
Sample, Joseph E.	065	1871	WB-K/70	AR
Sample, Joseph R.	065	c1826	WB-H/103	AR
Sample, Robert M.	065	1855	WB-J/11	AR
Sample, William	065	1892	WB-M/54	AR
Sample, William	065	1769	WB-F/143	AR
Sample, William A.	065	1877	WB-K/261	AR
Sampson, Aaron	070	1875	WB-E/313	AR
Sampson, Arvin	028	1803	WB-B/168	AR
Sampson, Caroline	070	1888	WB-F/224	AR
Sampson, Caroline	070	1873	WB-E/263	AR
Sampson, Cornelius	070	1890	WB-F/387	AR
Sampson, Fannie J.	070	1882	WB-E/468	AR
Sampson, Henry	070	1848	WB-C/477	AR
Sampson, Henry	070	1875	WB-E/311	AR
Sampson, James	070	1861	WB-D/49	AR
Sampson, John	028	c1806	Orig. Only	AR
Sampson, John	028	1811	WB-C/25	AR
Sampson, Joseph E.	070	1897	WB-G/66	AR
Sampson, Mary	070	1830	WB-AB/261	AR
Sampson, Stephen	047	1804	WB-3/426	
Sams, Charlotte	021	1888	WB-2/411	AR
Sams, Elijah	090	1864	WB-4/367	
Sams, J. C.	013	1897	WB-D/59	AR
Samson, Julius	NY	1890	070 WB-G/436	070 AR
Samson, Silva	019	1799	WB-D/358	AR
Samuel, Annen	020	1813	RB-F/374	AR
Samuel, Henry	090	1836	WB-3/308	
Samuel, James	020	1805	RB-E/179	AR
Samuel, Reuben	090	1831	WB-3/226	AR
Samuel, Thornton	092	1885	WB-6/229	AR
Sanday, Jarrad	099	1794	RB-3/59	AR
Sandbridge, Thomas I.	046	1872	WB-E/80	AR
Sandeford, Henry	069	1800	WB-1/235	AR-Nunc.
Sandeford, Tompkins	069	1783	WB-1/31	AR
Sandefur, Joseph	087	c1812	Orig. Only	AR
Sanderford, Alexander	099	1868	RB-35/6	AR
Sanderford, Elisha	099	1884	WB-A/579	AR
Sanderford, George A.	099	1873	RB-35/210	AR
Sanderford, Harriet	099	1868	RB-35/14	AR
Sanderford, Nancy	051	1869	WB-C/21	AR
Sanderford, Richard G.	051	1848	WB-A/280	
Sanderlain, Trimagen	018	1869	WB-E/1	AR
Sanderlan, Mary	009	1792	OWB/279	AR
Sanderlane, Milley	024	c1814	WB-C/39	AR
Sanderlin, Asa	075	1819	Orig. Only	AR
Sanderlin, Asa	010	1889	WB-I/265	AR
Sanderlin, Caleb	030	1873	WB-5/31	AR
Sanderlin, Chrissy	075	1886	WB-O/251	AR
Sanderlin, Dorsey	075	1881	WB-O/131	AR
Sanderlin, Dorsey	075	1881	Copy	041 AR
Sanderlin, Enoch	018	1840	WB-C/254	
Sanderlin, Isaac L.	018	1839	WB-C/248	AR-Copy
Sanderlin, John	010	1838	WB-G/307	AR
Sanderlin, Lemuel B.	018	1890	WB-E/187	AR
Sanderlin, Louisa	018	1874	WB-E/45	
Sanderlin, Mary	075	1765	WB-I/41	AR
Sanderlin, Maximilian	075	1781	WB-K/53	AR
Sanderlin, Sally	018	1823	WB-C/21	
Sanderlin, Thamer	018	1835	WB-C/182	
Sanderlin, William W.	018	1880	WB-E/75	AR
Sanderlin, Willis S.	018	1834	WB-C/159	
Sanderling, John	009	c1790	OWB/251	AR
Sanders, Abraham	077	c1835	WB-F/255	AR
Sanders, Abraham	077	1751	Orig. Only	SS/AR
Sanders, Abraham	077	c1802	Orig. Only	AR
Sanders, Abraham	024	1837	WB-C/195	AR
Sanders, Alexander	028	1884	WB-E/347	AR
Sanders, Alexander	056	1859	WB-1/732	AR
Sanders, Alexander	070	1814	WB-AB/208	AR
Sanders, Alsa	022	1819	WB-B/17	AR
Sanders, Ann	077	1752	Orig. Only	SS/AR
Sanders, Ann	077	1830	WB-F/179	AR
Sanders, Barbra	045	c1871	Orig. Only	AR-Copy
Sanders, Belinda	019	c1877	Orig. Only	AR
Sanders, Benjamin	077	1744	Orig. Only	SS/AR

Name	Co.	Date	Recorded Copy	Original
Sanders, Benjamin	077	1830	WB-F/179	AR
Sanders, Benjamin	077	1775	WB-C/171	AR
Sanders, Benjamin	022	c1822	WB-B/65	AR
Sanders, Benjamin	077	1795	WB-E/37	
Sanders, Benjamin	077	1800	WB-E/115	AR
Sanders, Brittiain	099	1798	RB-4/255	AR
Sanders, Cally	069	1886	WB-5/214	AR
Sanders, Celia	051	1870	WB-C/32	AR
Sanders, Charlotte	056	c1900	WB-4/541	AR
Sanders, Christopher	011	c1778	WB-2/259	
Sanders, Daniel	056	1873	WB-3/90	AR
Sanders, Daniel S.	070	1854	WB-C/563	AR
Sanders, David	046	1845	WB-C/240	AR
Sanders, David S.	072	1846	WB-2/72	AR
Sanders, David W.	072	1860	WB-2/184	AR
Sanders, Deborah	077	1823	WB-F/62	AR
Sanders, Edward W.	072	1854	WB-2/143	AR
Sanders, Edwin S.	056	1864	WB-2/51	AR
Sanders, Eli W.	019	1875	WB-B/85	AR
Sanders, Elisabeth	056	1867	WB-2/88	AR
Sanders, Elizabeth	060	1852	WB-C/539	AR
Sanders, Elizabeth	061	1847	WB-1/36	AR
Sanders, Elizabeth	005	1868	WB-C/262	AR
Sanders, Elleck	056	1815	WB-1/245	AR
Sanders, George	054	1874	WB-4/161	CTY
Sanders, Hardy, Jr.	099	1806	RB-7/116	AR
Sanders, Hezekiah	046	1863	WB-D/179	AR
Sanders, Hezekiah	046	1789	WB-A/378	AR
Sanders, Isaac	072	1821	WB-A/130	AR
Sanders, Isaac	077	1771	WB-C/95	AR
Sanders, Isaac A.	072	1866	WB-3/6	AR
Sanders, James	051	1900	WB-C/576	AR
Sanders, James	028	1785	WB-A/156	AR
Sanders, James	068	1866	WB-C/126	
Sanders, James, Sr.	020	1825	RB-K/93	AR
Sanders, James, Sr.	073	1776	WB-A/197	AR-Copy
Sanders, Jeffrey	026	1880	WB-2/198	AR
Sanders, Joel	046	1814	WB-A/374	AR
Sanders, John	077	1806	WB-E/228	AR
Sanders, John	072	1796	Orig. Only	AR
Sanders, John	024	1751	Orig. Only	SS/AR
Sanders, John	077	1818	WB-F/14	AR
Sanders, John	077	1805	WB-E/238	AR
Sanders, John	072	1733	SS 877/112	SS/AR
Sanders, John	019	c1768	Orig. Only	AR
Sanders, John	033	1866	WB-1/199	AR
Sanders, John	046	1793	WB-A/344	AR
Sanders, John	056	1830	WB-1/416	AR
Sanders, John	046	1809	WB-A/364	AR
Sanders, John	077	1777	WB-C/210	AR
Sanders, John	056	c1783	WB-1/416	AR
Sanders, John	019	1816	WB-D/376	AR
Sanders, Jordan	084	c1804	OW/133	AR
Sanders, Joseph	081	1805	WB-3/29	AR
Sanders, Julia	056	1867	WB-2/101	AR
Sanders, Letty	073	1827	WB-E/150	AR
Sanders, Levi	057	1797	WB-A/142	AR
Sanders, Margaret	041	1809	WB-2/43	AR
Sanders, Martha	046	1817	WB-B/50	AR
Sanders, Mary	028	1795	WB-A/348	AR
Sanders, Mary	010	1734	SS 876/287	SS/AR
Sanders, Mary	056	1800	WB-1/121	AR
Sanders, Mary	056	1843	WB-1/548	AR
Sanders, Mason	020	1837	RB-N/10	AR
Sanders, Miriam	077	1781	Orig. Only	AR
Sanders, Moses	057	c1799	WB-B/27	AR
Sanders, Nahum	090	1795	WB-1/76	AR
Sanders, Nancy	060	1800	Orig. Only	AR
Sanders, Nathan	077	c1831	WB-F/191	AR
Sanders, Peggy	051	1836	WB-A/87	
Sanders, Penelope	051	1875	WB-C/143	AR
Sanders, Primmy	069	c1869	WB-1/609	AR
Sanders, R. T.	092	1896	WB-6/416	AR
Sanders, Rachel	085	1823	WB-H/215	AR
Sanders, Rachel	099	1821	RB-17/1	AR
Sanders, Ransom	056	1844	WB-1/566	AR
Sanders, Reuben	056	1830	WB-1/404	AR
Sanders, Richard	075	1788	WB-K/226	AR
Sanders, Richard	006	1858	WB-D/48	AR
Sanders, Richard	099	1883	WB-A/462	AR
Sanders, Richard	077	1770	WB-C/88	AR
Sanders, Robert	085	c1804	WB-G/14	AR
Sanders, Robert	069	c1783	WB-1/29	AR
Sanders, Robert	072	1791	Orig. Only	AR
Sanders, Robert	100	1812	WB-16/353	AR
Sanders, Samantha	099	1894	WB-C/250	AR
Sanders, Samuel	019	1796	WB-D/354	AR
Sanders, Samuel	047	1794	WB-3/232	
Sanders, Sarah	028	1792	WB-A/270	AR
Sanders, Sary	024	1826	WB-C/127	AR-Nunc.
Sanders, Seth	096	1853	WB-3/37	AR
Sanders, Simion	072	1885	WB-4/189	AR
Sanders, Sion	069	1863	WB-1/586	AR
Sanders, Smith	020	1807	RB-E/321	AR
Sanders, Solomon	071	1778	WB-1/322	
Sanders, Stephen	077	1807	WB-E/251	AR
Sanders, Thomas	077	1828	WB-F/148	AR
Sanders, Thomas	037	1802	WB-D/141	AR
Sanders, Thomas	103	1789	Orig. Only	AR
Sanders, Thomas	077	1789	WB-C/387	AR
Sanders, Thomas	019	1795	WB-D/356	AR
Sanders, Thomas	027	1811	WB-A/31	AR-Nunc.
Sanders, Thomas	011	1776	DB-23/6	
Sanders, Vinson	039	1817	WB-E/131	AR
Sanders, Wealthy	056	1896	WB-2/214	AR
Sanders, William	104	1798	WB-1/492	AR
Sanders, William	103	1806	Orig. Only	AR
Sanders, William	037	1757	SS 879/207	SS/AR
Sanders, Winaford	039	1846	WB-M/108	AR
Sanders, Zebeah	096	1855	WB-3/44	AR
Sanderson, Bazil	024	1722	SS 875/339	SS/AR
Sanderson, Benjamin	028	1769	Orig. Only	AR
Sanderson, Benjamin	028	1758	Orig. Only	SS/AR
Sanderson, Caleb	075	1835	WB-N/105	AR
Sanderson, Daniel	030	1822	WB-3/136	
Sanderson, Eli	025	1876	WB-A/23	AR
Sanderson, Elijah	057	1814	WB-B/11	AR
Sanderson, James C.	030	c1806	WB-2/329	
Sanderson, Jesse	030	1792	WB-1/259	
Sanderson, Jesse	096	1858	WB-3/56	AR
Sanderson, John	030	1803	WB-2/216	
Sanderson, John	029	1830	WB-B/182	AR
Sanderson, John	030	1801	WB-2/176	
Sanderson, John	030	1825	WB-3/206	
Sanderson, Jonathan	028	1762	Deeds.15/L63	AR
Sanderson, Joseph	057	1810	WB-A/323	AR
Sanderson, Joseph	028	1774	Orig. Only	SS/AR
Sanderson, Joseph	030	1746	Orig. Only	SS/AR
Sanderson, Joseph	030	1758	SS 881/164	SS/AR
Sanderson, Joseph	030	1787	WB-1/212	

Name	Co.	Date	Recorded Copy	Original
Sanderson, Julia	030	1825	WB-3/203	
Sanderson, Julian	030	1752	Orig. Only	SS/AR
Sanderson, Richard	077	1733	SS 876/321	SS/AR
Sanderson, Richardson	077	1803	WB-E/192	AR
Sanderson, Ruth	002	1727	SS 876/120	SS/AR
Sanderson, Thomas	030	1816	WB-3/80	
Sanderson, Thomas	030	1778	WB-1/125	
Sanderson, Thomas	030	1821	WB-3/147 & 297	
Sanderson, Thomas	030	1784	WB-1/179	
Sanderson, Thomas	030	c1816	Copy	075 AR
Sandford, Robert	044	1823	WB-9/189	CTY
Sandifer, J. B.	092	1889	WB-6/294	AR
Sandifer, John	065	1895	WB-M/395	AR
Sandifer, John	071	1826	WB-4/7	AR
Sanding, Elzy	072	1849	WB-2/95	
Sandland, John	057	1805	WB-A/272	AR
Sandlin, David E.	072	1896	WB-4/335	AR
Sandlin, Jesse	072	1837	WB-1/154	AR
Sandlin, Mary E.	072	1897	WB-4/374	AR
Sandlin, Nichodemus	035	1877	WB-4/116	AR
Sandlin, R. E. L.	072	1895	WB-4/317	AR
Sands, Barham	047	1798	WB-3/316	
Sands, Samuel W.	047	1823	WB-3/685	
Sane, Peter	060	1846	WB-2/247	AR
Sanford, Darius	028	1786	WB-A/110	AR
Sanford, Lyman	065	1888	WB-L/327	AR
Sanford, Robert	044	1864	WB-22/105	CTY
Sanford, William H.	054	1862	WB-3/166	AR
Sapogh, Mary	021	1868	WB-2/5	
Sapp, A. J.	046	1892	WB-F/175	AR
Sapp, Newel	032	1826	WB-1/59	AR
Sapp, Robert	046	1810	WB-A/368	AR
Sargent, Joseph	020	1781	RB-A/138	AR
Sarker, Jacob	032	1837	WB-1/292	AR
Sarrat, Jane	017	c1841	WB-A/4	AR
Sarrat, Joseph	078	1801	WI-3/48	AR
Sarsnett, Henneritta	037	1820	WB-E/251	AR
Sarsnett, Richard	037	1795	WB-C/339	AR
Sarson, Laurence	010	1732	SS 876/232	SS/AR
Sartin, Elizabeth	020	1898	WB-B/318	CTY
Sartin, Ezekiel	073	1896	WB-I/98	CTY
Sarves, Thomas	040	1848	WB-1/9	
Sarvice, Annie	040	1890	WB-2/378	AR
Sarvice, Rachael W.	040	1878	WB-2/125	AR
Sasnett, Elizabeth	037	1858	WB-G/152	AR
Sasnett, Joshua	037	1834	WB-F/162	AR
Sasnett, Lucy	037	1854	WB-G/75	AR
Sasser, Arthur	056	1815	WB-1/246	AR
Sasser, Edith	056	1816	WB-1/255	AR
Sasser, Eli	103	1890	WB-1/502	AR
Sasser, Henry	103	1872	WB-1/46	AR
Sasser, James Henry	103	1880	WB-1/186	AR
Sasser, John, Sr.	103	1861	RD-13/334	
Sasser, Josiah	103	1782	WI-A/3	AR
Sasser, Lewis	103	1882	WB-1/228	AR
Sasser, Martha	103	1857	RD-12/247	AR
Sasser, Pherebah	103	1821	RD-4/418	AR
Sasser, Richard	005	c1818	WB-2/144	AR
Sasser, S. A.	103	1898	WB-2/232	AR
Sasser, Wiley B.	035	1893	WB-4/420	AR
Sasser, William	103	1858	RD-12/404	AR
Satchwell, James, Sr.	009	1838	OB-B/536	AR
Satchwell, John	009	1828	OB-A/455	AR
Satchwell, John	009	1887	WB-1/429	CTY

Name	Co.	Date	Recorded Copy	Original
Satchwell, John, Sr.	009	1820	OB-A/304	AR
Satchwell, Joseph D.	009	1847	OB-F/326	AR
Satchwell, Sarah Ann	009	c1850	Orig. Only	CTY
Sater, E. B.	099	1874	RB-35/268	AR
Sater, John	092	1820	WB-3/145	AR
Saton, John	089	1852	WB-1/91	
Satterfield, Alfred	024	1834	WB-C/179	AR
Satterfield, Elizabeth	024	1838	WB-C/214	AR
Satterfield, Henry	078	1869	WB-19/6	AR
Satterfield, Isaac	078	1862	WB-18/261	AR
Satterfield, James	078	1859	WB-18/72	
Satterfield, Jeremiah	078	1883	WB-19/141	AR
Satterfield, Jesse	061	c1859	WB-1/77	AR
Satterfield, John	078	1802	WI-3/139	AR
Satterfield, Nancey	078	1864	WB-18/354	
Satterfield, Naumah	078	c1847	Orig. Only	AR
Satterfield, Pattie	078	1885	WB-19/175	AR
Satterfield, William	078	c1833	Orig. Only	AR
Satterfield, William	024	1827	WB-C/128	AR
Satterthwait, Penelope	009	1834	OB-B/537	AR
Satterthwaite, Abraham	053	1776	RW-1/77	AR
Satterthwaite, Anna E.	009	1900	WB-2/271	CTY
Satterthwaite, Elizabeth	009	1825	OB-A/346	AR
Satterthwaite, Elizabeth	009	1877	WB-1/184	CTY
Satterthwaite, George H.	053	1894	WB-11/298	AR
Satterthwaite, James	009	1833	OB-B/229	AR
Satterthwaite, Jeremiah	053	c1811	Orig. Only	AR
Satterthwaite, Jonathan	053	1809	RW-1/425	AR
Satterthwaite, Lucretia	009	1890	WB-1/483	CTY
Satterthwaite, Sarah	053	c1788	RW-1/382	AR
Satterthwaite, William	053	c1810	Copy	009 AR/ CRX
Satterthwaite, William	053	1787	RW-1/160	
Satterthwaite, William	053	c1818	RW-1/521	
Satterthwaite, William	009	1820	OB-A/300	AR
Satterthwaite, William	053	1813	RW-1/472	AR
Satterwhite, Benjamin	070	1887	WB-F/113	AR
Satterwhite, Charles	017	1889	WB-B/167	AR
Satterwhite, Elijah	098	1886	WB-A/69	CTY
Satterwhite, Howel	044	c1873	Orig. Only	CTY
Satterwhite, James	044	1823	WB-9/164	CTY
Satterwhite, James F.	044	1876	WB-23/209	CTY
Satterwhite, John	044	1885	WB-23/539	CTY
Satterwhite, Martha M.	064	1898	WB-2/433	AR
Satterwhite, Michael	044	1868	WB-22/766	CTY
Satterwhite, Mitchel	044	1845	WB-16/243	CTY
Satterwhite, Solomon	044	1853	WB-19/261	
Satterwhite, Susan A.	044	1899	WB-24/461	CTY
Satterwhite, Thomas	044	1872	WB-23/73	CTY
Satwater, Wilson	073	1885	WB-H/381	CTY
Saul, Abraham	037	1772	WB-A/186	AR
Saul, James	065	1889	WB-L/390	AR
Saul, Mary	070	1840	WB-AB/332	AR
Saul, Miller	070	1814	WB-AB/205	AR
Saulman, John	014	1900	WB-3/100	CTY
Sauls, Benjamin	103	1887	WB-1/385	
Sauls, Benjamin	099	1831	RB-22/58	AR
Sauls, Britton	071	1806	WB-2/329	AR
Sauls, Ealy	103	c1850	Orig. Only	AR
Sauls, Eliza	103	1875	WB-1/82	AR
Sauls, Etheldred	103	1859	RD-13/38	AR
Sauls, Henry	103	1842	RD-8/307	AR
Sauls, John Hill	070	1860	WB-D/27	AR
Sauls, Julia A.	071	1874	WB-6/159	AR
Sauls, Lawrence J.	103	1866	RD-14/434	

Name	Co.	Date	Recorded Copy	Original
Sauls, Nancy	103	1854	RD-11/547	AR
Sauls, Nathan	045	1877	Orig. Only	AR
Sauls, Penelope	103	1877	WB-1/105	AR
Sauls, Phereby	056	1821	WB-1/320	AR
Sauls, Scipio	070	1893	WB-G/165	AR
Sauls, Thomas	071	1856	WB-5/168	AR
Sauls, Washington	071	1866	WB-5/339	AR
Sauls, William	100	1791	WB-6/53	AR
Sauls, Winnifred	103	1877	WB-1/125	AR
Saunders, Albert	077	1894	WB-H/256	AR
Saunders, Alice W.	010	1882	WB-I/157	
Saunders, Andrew	009	c1795	OWB/305	AR
Saunders, Anna H.	099	1871	RB-35/123	
Saunders, Benjamine	013	1868	WB-B/1	AR
Saunders, Catherine	024	1895	WB-E/249	AR
Saunders, Charles	028	1816	WB-C/118	AR
Saunders, Christian	077	1860	WB-F/510	
Saunders, Curtis	061	1885	WB-2/65	AR
Saunders, Edward	051	1873	WB-C/88	AR
Saunders, Edwin T.	099	1887	WB-B/197	AR
Saunders, Elizabeth	028	1839	WB-C/428	
Saunders, Elizabeth	020	1888	WB-A/540 & 559	CTY
Saunders, Francis	041	1785	WB-1/51	AR
Saunders, Frederick	077	1843	WB-F/309	AR
Saunders, Hardy	099	1812	RB-10/315	AR
Saunders, Henry	067	1895	WB-2/337	AR
Saunders, Henry	041	1808	WB-2/73	AR
Saunders, Hulda	047	1854	WB-4/370	
Saunders, James	028	1824	WB-C/241	AR
Saunders, James	033	1850	WB-1/100	AR
Saunders, Jesse	041	1813	WB-2/82	AR
Saunders, Jesse	046	1843	WB-C/143	AR
Saunders, Joel	046	1864	WB-D/239	AR
Saunders, John	038	1853	WB-1/54	AR
Saunders, John	073	1814	WB-D/412	AR
Saunders, John	041	1849	WB-3/118	AR
Saunders, John	077	1811	WB-E/362	AR
Saunders, John	041	1836	WB-2/375	AR
Saunders, Jonathan	077	1868	WB-H/33	AR
Saunders, Joseph	041	1808	WB-2/37	AR
Saunders, Joseph H.	079	1885	WB-2/350	AR
Saunders, Joshua	077	1819	WB-F/25	AR
Saunders, Josiah	077	c1824	WB-F/146	AR
Saunders, Julius S.	054	1855	WB-3/90	AR
Saunders, Lawrence	041	1815	WB-2/101	AR
Saunders, Margaret	054	c1833	WB-2/140	AR
Saunders, Mary	077	1846	WB-F/324	AR
Saunders, Mary	018	1845	WB-C/296	
Saunders, Nathaniel	051	1837	WB-A/184	
Saunders, Nettie	084	1894	WB-F/19	CTY
Saunders, Permelia F.	041	1885	WB-4/220	AR
Saunders, Robert P.	077	c1853	WB-F/472	AR
Saunders, Romulus M.	099	1867	RB-34/450	AR
Saunders, Sarah	041	1804	WB-1/203	AR
Saunders, Sarah A.	061	1898	Orig. Only	AR
Saunders, Stephen	024	1891	WB-E/190	AR
Saunders, Susanna	084	1807	WB-A/41	CTY
Saunders, Thaney	041	1822	WB-2/189	AR
Saunders, Thomas	046	1854	WB-C/414	AR
Saunders, W. P.	084	1888	WB-E/409	CTY
Saunders, William	051	1890	WB-C/409	AR
Saunders, William	033	1846	WB-1/79	AR
Saunders, William	009	c1800	OWB/374	AR
Saunderson, Benjamin	053	1846	WB-7/64	AR
Saunderson, John S.	053	1790	RW-1/202	AR
Saunderson, Mary	053	c1826	Orig. Only	AR
Saunderson, Richard	053	1788	RW-1/168	
Saunderson, Thomas	053	1843	WB-6/245	AR
Saunier, Francis	065	1836	Orig. Only	AR
Savage, Angelina	037	1894	WB-H/287	AR
Savage, Berry	037	1873	WB-G/433	AR
Savage, Caleb	041	1862	WB-3/286	AR
Savage, Charles	037	1794	WB-C/290	AR
Savage, Dolly	037	1866	WB-G/284	AR
Savage, Frances	037	1845	WB-F/328	AR
Savage, Francis	035	c1766	087 DB-1/279	
Savage, Granville	047	1894	WB-7/131	AR
Savage, Henry R.	070	1861	WB-D/62	AR
Savage, James	037	1834	WB-F/164	AR
Savage, Jesse	041	1834	WB-2/354	AR
Savage, John H.	070	1887	WB-F/84	AR
Savage, John P.	047	1889	WB-6/548	AR
Savage, Kate	070	1888	WB-F/234	AR
Savage, Lewis	037	1873	WB-G/429	AR
Savage, Loveless	037	1807	WB-D/274	AR
Savage, Mary C.	047	1886	WB-6/442	AR
Savage, N. Ellen	047	1899	WB-7/215	AR
Savage, Pryer	041	1838	WB-2/397	AR
Savage, Robert	063	1790	WB-1/163	
Savage, Robert R.	051	1892	WB-C/437	AR
Savage, Sarah	041	1865	WB-3/320	AR
Savage, Sarah A.	063	1897	WB-4/202	AR
Savage, Susan	037	1880	WB-G/584	AR
Savage, Suthe	030	1793	WB-2/13	
Savage, Tabitha	047	1883	WB-6/291	AR
Savage, Thomas	010	1762	WB-A/11	AR
Savage, Thomas	090	1881	Orig. Only	AR
Savage, Timothy	070	1864	WB-D/153	AR
Savage, William	024	1784	WB-B/148	AR
Savage, William B.	063	1894	WB-4/159	AR
Savidge, Absalom	037	1816	WB-E/119	AR
Savidge, Allen	037	1816	WB-E/128	AR
Savidge, Britton	063	1789	WB-1/155	
Savidge, Loveless	063	c1786	WB-1/126	
Savidge, Robert	037	1796	WB-C/364	AR
Savidge, Sterling	037	1794	WB-C/304	AR
Savills, Mary	018	1830	WB-C/119	
Savory, Robert	019	1784	WB-D/349	AR
Sawkill, John	010	1777	WB-B/81	AR
Sawney, William	073	1764	WB-A/36	
Sawrey, Henry, Sr.	071	c1775	011 WB-2/277	
Sawrey, John	071	1798	WB-2/178	AR
Sawton, Mathew	070	1866	WB-D/184	
Sawyer, Abel	075	1826	WB-N/27	AR
Sawyer, Ann	077	1807	WB-E/296	AR
Sawyer, Annis	018	1826	WB-C/69	
Sawyer, Benjamin	053	1881	WB-11/109	AR
Sawyer, Benjamin	075	1769	Orig. Only	AR
Sawyer, Caleb	075	1893	WB-O/377	AR
Sawyer, Catherine	077	1883	WB-H/141	aR
Sawyer, Charles	075	1750	Orig. Only	SS/AR
Sawyer, Daniel	075	1752	Orig. Only	SS/AR
Sawyer, Daniel	096	1819	WB-2/78	AR
Sawyer, Daniel	075	1882	WB-O/143	AR
Sawyer, David	075	1781	WB-K/58	AR
Sawyer, Dennis	096	1821	WB-2/84	AR
Sawyer, Ebenezer	075	1803	WB-M1/76	AR
Sawyer, Edmund	018	1842	WB-C/278	
Sawyer, Edmund	075	c1851	WB-M2/59	AR

Name	Co.	Date	Recorded Copy	Original
Sawyer, Edward	018	1887	WB-E/165	AR
Sawyer, Elisha	018	1842	WB-C/276	
Sawyer, Elisha	018	1823	WB-C/28	
Sawyer, Elizabeth	073	c1820	Orig. Only	AR
Sawyer, Elizabeth	009	1857	OB-K/267	AR
Sawyer, Elizabeth	030	1853	WB-4/172	
Sawyer, Elizabeth	028	1888	WB-E/498	AR
Sawyer, Enoch	018	1827	WB-C/82	
Sawyer, Ephriam	096	1790	WB-1/167	AR
Sawyer, Evan	018	1837	WB-C/208	
Sawyer, Ezekiel	096	c1850	WB-3/29	
Sawyer, Fanny	018	1870	WB-E/14	AR
Sawyer, Frederic	018	1894	WB-E/231	AR
Sawyer, Frederick	075	1825	WB-N/12	AR
Sawyer, Gardner	075	1870	WB-O/13	AR
Sawyer, Henry	075	1729	Orig. Only	SS/AR
Sawyer, Hollowell	018	1835	WB-C/180	
Sawyer, Hollowell	075	1807	WB-M1/150	AR
Sawyer, Isaac	075	1804	WB-M1/100	AR
Sawyer, Isaac S.	053	1869	WB-11/18	AR
Sawyer, Jabez	018	1837	WB-C/213	
Sawyer, Jacob	030	1827	WB-3/228	
Sawyer, James	018	1834	WB-C/160	
Sawyer, James	065	c1787	WB-F/166	AR
Sawyer, James A.	096	1882	WB-4/83	AR
Sawyer, Jenny	053	1831	WB-5/63	AR
Sawyer, Jeremiah	030	1828	WB-3/236	
Sawyer, Jeremiah	075	1756	Orig. Only	SS/AR
Sawyer, Jesse	101	1895	WB-A/263	
Sawyer, Joel	075	1836	WB-N/122	AR
Sawyer, John	020	1847	RB-P/482	AR
Sawyer, John	075	1743	Orig. Only	SS/AR
Sawyer, John	018	1839	WB-C/250	
Sawyer, John	075	c1854	WB-M2/20	AR
Sawyer, John	075	1772	WB-H/157	AR
Sawyer, John	075	1762	WB-I/20	AR
Sawyer, John	002	1713	Orig. Only	SS/AR
Sawyer, John	075	1824	WB-M1/393	AR
Sawyer, Jonathan	096	1801	WB-2/9	AR
Sawyer, Joseph	075	1797	WB-L/96	AR
Sawyer, Joseph	075	1777	WB-K/1	AR
Sawyer, Joshua	018	1827	WB-C/84	
Sawyer, Joshua	075	1753	SS 881/84	SS/AR
Sawyer, Kezziah	028	1874	WB-E/103	AR
Sawyer, Lavinia	075	1831	WB-N/65	AR
Sawyer, Lemuel	018	1884	WB-E/128	AR
Sawyer, Lott	075	1800	WB-M1/35	AR
Sawyer, Louisa A.	024	1865	WB-D/29	
Sawyer, Malachi	018	1824	WB-C/31	
Sawyer, Malachi	018	1885	WB-E/134	AR
Sawyer, Malachi	018	1840	WB-C/255	
Sawyer, Malachi G.	018	1859	WB-D/51	
Sawyer, Mark S.	075	c1860	WB-M2/74	AR
Sawyer, Mary V.	101	1880	WB-A/45	
Sawyer, Mathias	018	1833	WB-C/138	
Sawyer, Matthias	024	1835	WB-C/182	AR
Sawyer, Miles	075	1885	WB-O/228	AR
Sawyer, Miller	030	1837	WB-4/35	
Sawyer, Nancy	075	1898	WB-O/460	AR
Sawyer, Nancy	081	1862	WB-12/236	AR
Sawyer, Nathan G.	018	1888	WB-E/174	AR
Sawyer, Nelson	030	1897	WB-5/244	AR
Sawyer, Parthenia	075	1891	WB-O/338	AR
Sawyer, Penelope	018	1844	WB-C/302	
Sawyer, Peter C.	018	1900	WB-E/313	AR
Sawyer, Polly	075	1871	WB-O/17	AR
Sawyer, Rebecker	075	1867	WB-M2/105	AR
Sawyer, Rebekah	028	1827	WB-C/292	AR
Sawyer, Richard	030	c1810	WB-2/360	
Sawyer, Robert	075	1765	WB-I/40	AR
Sawyer, Robert	075	1735	Orig. Only	SS/AR
Sawyer, Robert	028	1825	WB-C/264	AR
Sawyer, Ruthy	075	1827	WB-N/45	AR
Sawyer, Sallie Ann	075	1893	WB-O/373	AR
Sawyer, Sally	075	c1855	WB-M2/29	AR
Sawyer, Samuel	081	1845	WB-8/151	AR
Sawyer, Samuel	075	1768	WB-H/83	AR
Sawyer, Sarah	077	1856	WB-F/469	AR
Sawyer, Sarah	075	1824	WB-N/2	AR
Sawyer, Simeon	030	c1814	WB-3/56	
Sawyer, Solomon	075	1742	Orig. Only	SS/AR
Sawyer, Susanah	018	1837	WB-C/207	
Sawyer, Thomas	081	1888	WB-16/112	AR
Sawyer, Thomas	075	1765	WB-H/63	AR
Sawyer, Thomas	075	1756	Orig. Only	SS/AR
Sawyer, Thomas	075	1750	Orig. Only	SS/AR
Sawyer, Thomas	096	1881	WB-4/69	AR
Sawyer, Tulle	030	1787	WB-1/209	
Sawyer, William	018	1823	WB-C/19	
Sawyer, William	020	1790	RB-B/359	AR
Sawyer, William	075	1784	WB-K/120	AR
Sawyer, William	020	1831	RB-M/1	AR
Sawyer, William	018	1847	WB-C/319	
Sawyer, William G.	009	1892	WB-1/549	CTY
Sawyer, William G.	018	1872	WB-E/38	AR
Sawyer, Willis	010	1808	WB-F/85	AR
Sawyer, Willis	053	1834	WB-5/210	AR
Sawyer, Willis	075	1753	SS 881/5	SS/AR
Sawyer, Willoughby	030	1832	WB-3/306	
Sawyer, Wilson	075	1823	WB-M1/387	AR
Sawyer, Zepheniah	053	c1817	RW-1/516	
Sawyers, Dicy	084	1859	WB-C/311	CTY
Saxon, Archelaus	047	1761	WB-1/20	
Saxon, Samuel	047	1766	WB-1/191	
Sayer, Thomas	075	1720	SS 875/233	
Sayles, Thomas	099	1881	WB-A/272	AR
Saylor, John	072	1845	WB-2/66	
Saymour, Hendry	054	c1805	WB-1/207	AR
Scales, Absalum	VA	1859	090 WB-4/335	090 AR
Scales, Alfred M.	046	1892	WB-F/178	AR
Scales, Elizabeth	084	1862	WB-C/372	CTY
Scales, Henry	084	c1818	WB-A/158	
Scales, J. Rawley	084	1896	WB-F/48	CTY
Scales, James	084	1860	WB-C/320	CTY
Scales, James M.	084	1861	WB-C/359	CTY
Scales, James R.	084	1896	090 WB-6/393	090 AR
Scales, Jane W.	084	1877	WB-E/136	CTY
Scales, John M.	082	1888	WB-6/366	AR
Scales, Joseph	046	1774	WB-A/337	
Scales, Joseph	090	1832	WB-3/235	AR
Scales, Joseph H.	090	c1846	Orig. Only	AR
Scales, Mary	084	c1803	WB-A/10	CTY
Scales, Mary	084	1831	WB-B/22	CTY
Scales, Nancy	084	1856	WB-C/225	CTY
Scales, Nancy	084	1840	WB-B/246	CTY
Scales, Nathaniel	084	1821	WB-A/311	CTY
Scales, Nathaniel	084	1828	WB-B/19	CTY
Scales, Nathaniel	084	1824	WB-A/289	CTY
Scales, Pleasant	084	1825	WB-A/300	CTY
Scales, Robert H.	084	1885	WB-E/317	

Name	Co.	Date	Recorded Copy	Original
Scales, Thomas	084	1819	WB-A/305	CTY
Scaner, Isaac	002	1693	Orig. Only	SS/AR
Scanlan, Eugene	098	1881	WB-A/9	CTY
Scarber, Salley	030	1838	WB-4/54	
Scarboro, Callie	099	1892	WB-C/40	AR
Scarboro, Tyranna A.	099	1890	WB-B/452	AR
Scarboro, Zillay	037	1856	WB-G/121	AR
Scarborough, Alexander	022	1886	WB-E/338	
Scarborough, David	037	1775	Orig. Only	AR
Scarborough, David	037	1774	WB-A/223	AR
Scarborough, Edward	030	1801	WB-2/193	
Scarborough, Edward	021	1845	WB-1/34	AR
Scarborough, George W.	099	1892	WB-C/48	AR
Scarborough, Gideon	071	1860	WB-5/223	AR
Scarborough, Ignatious	030	1801	WB-2/184	
Scarborough, Isaac	037	c1826	Orig. Only	AR
Scarborough, Isaac	105	1857	WB-1/37	AR
Scarborough, J. H.	057	1886	WB-C/138	AR
Scarborough, James	037	1836	WB-F/189	AR
Scarborough, Jesse B.	070	1855	WB-C/601	AR
Scarborough, John	099	1855	RB-29/23	AR
Scarborough, John A.	031	1888	WB-1/47	AR
Scarborough, Jonathan	037	1775	WB-A/233	AR
Scarborough, Miles	022	1825	WB-B/67	AR
Scarborough, Milly	099	1898	WB-D/178	AR
Scarborough, Nancey	030	1799	WB-2/145	
Scarborough, Nancy	105	c1863	WB-1/110	AR
Scarborough, Samuel	099	1841	RB-24/526	AR
Scarborough, Samuel	099	1804	RB-6/325	AR
Scarborough, Sarah	103	1884	WB-1/304	AR
Scarbrough, Ann	019	1843	WB-A/108	AR
Scarbrough, Charles	075	1751	Orig. Only	SS/AR
Scarbrough, Enos	010	1814	WB-F/259	AR
Scarbrough, John	075	1756	Orig. Only	SS/AR
Scarbrough, Macrora	077	1752	Orig. Only	SS/AR
Scarbrough, Thomas E.	067	1867	WB-1/151	AR
Scarbrough, William	019	1799	WB-D/362	AR
Scarbrough, William D.	019	1843	WB-A/107	AR
Scarf, John	075	1782	WB-K/67	AR
Scarfe, John	075	1751	SS 881/10	SS/AR
Scarlet, John	081	1808	WB-3/102	AR
Scarlett, Amanda E.	081	1893	WB-16/268	AR
Scarlett, John	073	1837	WB-E/412	AR
Scarlett, Maria	073	1873	WB-H/76	CTY
Scarlett, Stephen	073	1817	WB-D/511	AR
Scarlett, William	084	1856	WB-C/245	CTY
Scears, Abigal	030	1846	WB-4/121	
Scears, Henry Eborn	041	1806	WB-1/231	AR
Sceetor, Mary	103	1803	Orig. Only	AR
Schaaf, Christian	090	1841	WB-4/81	AR
Schaneywoolf, Charles	028	1780	Orig. Only	AR
Schatterly, John	046	1845	WB-C/243	AR
Schaub, Christophe	038	1857	WB-1/156	AR
Schaub, John Jacob	090	1837	WB-3/323	AR
Schaub, Maria S.	090	1858	WB-4/316	AR
Schaub, Thomas	092	1876	WB-6/91	
Schaub, William S.	090	1893	WB-6/296	AR
Schause, Anna	090	1845	WB-4/192	
Schaw, Alexander	070	c1802	WB-AB/62	AR
Schaw, Anne	070	1788	WB-C/396	AR
Schawitz, Andrew	090	1812	WB-2/134	AR
Schenck, David W.	060	1862	WB-3/41	AR
Schenck, David, Jr.	046	1899	WB-G/140	AR
Schenck, Elizabeth	060	1862	WB-3/46	AR
Schenck, Henry	026	1883	WB-2/231	AR
Schenck, Henry	060	1837	WB-1/390	AR
Schenck, John G. S.	037	1806	WB-D/256 & 271	AR
Schenck, Michael	060	1849	WB-2/318	AR
Schenck, Michael	060	1868	WB-3/113	
Schenck, W. H.	065	1897	WB-M/578	AR
Scheuermann, Henry	035	1868	WB-4/1	AR
Schieffelin, Charles	086	1835	Orig. Only	AR-Copy
Schiff, Phillip	065	1899	WB-N/246	AR
Schively, Annie M.	099	1895	WB-C/440	AR
Schively, David L.	099	1894	WB-C/257	AR
Schlarger, Charles	NY	1889	053 WB-11/256	053 AR
Schmidt, Johan C.	090	1822	WB-3/87	AR
Schnall, Henrietta	038	1866	WB-1/277	AR
Schneider, David	090	c1828	Orig. Only	AR
Schoaf, Henry	085	c1805	WB-G/25	
Schonwald, James T.	070	1882	WB-E/459	AR
Schoolfield, John	046	1839	WB-C/26	AR
Schools, Alexander	085	1824	WB-H/264	AR
Schorr, Johannes	085	1770	WB-A/153	AR
Schrober, J. Gottlob	090	1832	WB-3/237	AR
Schroebel, John	086	1826	WB-D/61	AR
Schulzer, Frederick	024	c1769	WB-A/193	AR
Schutt, George L.	070	1885	WB-F/1	AR
Schwanner, Mathias	096	1745	Orig. Only	SS/AR
Scobey, Mathew	073	1782	WB-A/273	AR
Scoby, Robert	073	c1795	Orig. Only	AR
Scofield, Ann H.	046	1887	WB-E/469	AR
Scoggin, Andrew J.	086	1888	WB-F/328	AR
Scoggins, John	068	1864	WB-C/104	
Scoggins, Johnson	020	1878	WB-A/240	CTY
Scollay, Elizabeth	010	1767	SS 881/295	SS/AR
Scollay, Elizabeth	010	1767	WB-A/90	AR-Copy
Scollay, Samuel	N	1752	SS 879/42	SS/AR
Scott, A. C.	016	1893	WB-4/162	
Scott, Abraham	047	1803	WB-3/400	
Scott, Adam	046	1838	WB-C/20	AR
Scott, Adam	072	1799	Orig. Only	AR
Scott, Adam	028	1824	WB-C/250	
Scott, Allen	071	1855	WB-5/129	AR
Scott, Amanda	045	1896	WB-1/341	AR
Scott, Andrew	009	1882	WB-1/294	CTY
Scott, Ann Radford	092	c1835	WB-4/82	
Scott, Benjamin	053	1761	OB-A/52	AR
Scott, Benjamin F.	092	1873	WB-6/42	
Scott, C. A.	103	1884	WB-1/313	AR
Scott, Cason	028	1842	WB-D/65	AR
Scott, Charles	103	1832	RD-6/350	AR
Scott, David	072	c1861	WB-A/162	AR
Scott, David	046	1875	WB-E/155	AR
Scott, David	084	1856	WB-C/235	CTY
Scott, Ebenezer	040	1876	WB-2/108	AR
Scott, Edward	075	1762	WB-H/39	
Scott, Eliza	014	1900	WB-3/112	CTY
Scott, Elizabeth	075	1870	WB-0/12	AR
Scott, Enoch	075	1823	WB-M1/374	AR
Scott, Fanny	001	1872	WB-2/54	AR
Scott, Francis	047	1774	WB-1/339	
Scott, George F.	013	1899	WB-D/264	AR
Scott, Green H.	056	1822	WB-1/449	AR
Scott, Henry	077	1817	WB-E/472	AR
Scott, Henry	092	1892	WB-6/344	AR
Scott, Henry	075	1840	WB-N/154	AR
Scott, Hillery	061	1851	WB-1/48	AR
Scott, Howard	047	1866	WB-5/141	

Name	Co.	Date	Recorded Copy	Original
Scott, Hugh	104	1787	WB-1/226	AR
Scott, James	082	1888	WB-6/380	AR
Scott, James	073	1864	WB-G/454	CTY
Scott, James	053	c1720	009 OWB/3	
Scott, James	030	1827	WB-3/227	
Scott, James	065	c1771	WB-F/145	AR
Scott, James	047	1785	WB-3/95	
Scott, James	078	1833	WI-12/159	AR
Scott, James G.	072	1884	WB-4/154	AR
Scott, James S.	001	1898	WB-3/203	AR
Scott, Jarret	092	1863	WB-5/66	AR
Scott, Jehu	099	1819	RB-15/347	AR
Scott, Jehu	057	1824	WB-B/80	AR
Scott, Jerutha	005	1806	WB-2/154	AR
Scott, John	072	1851	WB-2/112	AR
Scott, John	020	1798	RB-C/318	AR
Scott, John	099	1882	WB-A/352	AR
Scott, John	001	c1856	WB-1/108	AR
Scott, John	046	1774	WB-A/332	AR
Scott, John	075	1738	LGB-4/#96	SS/AR
Scott, John	085	1760	WB-A/148	AR
Scott, John	020	1781	RB-A/176	AR
Scott, John	028	1773	Orig. Only	SS/AR
Scott, John	054	1807	WB-1/210	AR
Scott, John	086	1817	WB-C/82	AR
Scott, Jonathan	087	1785	Orig. Only	AR
Scott, Joseph	N	c1685	Orig. Only	SS/AR
Scott, Joseph	024	1803	WB-B/176	AR
Scott, Joseph	035	1781	WB-A/445	AR
Scott, Joseph	020	1835	RB-M/532	AR
Scott, Joseph	075	1796	WB-M1/65	AR
Scott, Joseph	064	c1882	107 WB-2/117	
Scott, Joseph	064	1882	WB-2/106	AR
Scott, Joseph C.	041	1892	WB-4/340	AR
Scott, Joshua	002	c1686	Orig. Only	SS/AR
Scott, Joshua	074	1879	WB-1/32	
Scott, Leonard	092	1888	WB-6/285	AR
Scott, Leonard	090	1838	WB-4/17	AR
Scott, Letitia	086	1824	WB-D/24	AR
Scott, Louisa	075	1893	WB-0/406	AR
Scott, Lucretia	009	1831	OB-B/88	AR
Scott, Margaret	001	1893	WB-2/561	AR
Scott, Marmaduke	075	1813	WB-M1/253	AR
Scott, Mary	077	1692	Orig. Only	SS/AR
Scott, Mary	046	1856	WB-C/457	AR
Scott, Mary	075	1887	WB-0/262	AR
Scott, Mary E.	032	1883	WB-3/402	AR
Scott, Matthew	079	1771	Orig. Only	SS/AR
Scott, Mitchel	030	1833	WB-3/307	
Scott, Nathaniel	005	1801	WB-2/155	AR
Scott, O. M.	084	1853	WB-C/163	CTY
Scott, Obed	072	1827	Orig. Only	AR
Scott, Patsy	074	1881	WB-1/27	AR-Copy
Scott, Phoebe	075	1897	WB-0/440	AR
Scott, Rebecca	014	1866	WB-1/17	AR
Scott, Rebeckah	046	1806	WB-A/360	AR
Scott, Richard	070	1762	SS 881/257	SS/AR
Scott, Richard	047	1816	WB-3/590	
Scott, Robert	073	1784	WB-A/314	AR
Scott, Robert	046	1791	WB-A/340	AR
Scott, Robert	075	1821	WB-M1/348	AR
Scott, Rosanna	060	1837	WB-1/415	
Scott, S. G.	016	1866	WB-2/134	
Scott, Samuel	073	1841	WB-F/107	AR
Scott, Samuel	075	1770	WB-H/109	
Scott, Samuel	075	1807	WB-M1/171	AR
Scott, Sarah	054	1879	WB-4/322	CTY
Scott, Sarah	032	1830	WB-1/133	AR
Scott, Sarah M	075	1857	WB-M2/46	AR-Nunc.
Scott, Severn	077	1797	WB-E/83	
Scott, Simpson	075	1798	WB-M1/10	AR
Scott, Stephen	075	1816	WB-M1/300	AR
Scott, Stephen	075	1753	Orig. Only	SS/AR
Scott, Stephen	022	1851	WB-C/286	AR
Scott, Stephen	075	1716	SS 875/106	SS/AR
Scott, Stephen D.	075	1891	WB-0/344	AR
Scott, Susan	057	1899	WB-C/246	AR
Scott, Susan A.	099	1872	RB-35/376	AR
Scott, Susan M.	036	1890	WB-A/169	CTY
Scott, Thomas	075	1817	WB-M1/301	AR
Scott, Thomas B.	030	1884	WB-5/104	
Scott, Walter	001	1897	WB-3/195	AR
Scott, William	054	1843	WB-2/262	AR
Scott, William	049	1882	WB-2/99	AR
Scott, William	072	1853	WB-2/122	AR
Scott, William	073	1810	WB-D/271	AR
Scott, William	072	1799	WB-A/127	AR
Scott, William	075	1774	WB-I/111	
Scott, William	030	1805	WB-2/260	
Scott, William	075	1832	WB-N/80	AR
Scott, William	072	c1777	RW/L6	AR
Scott, William	046	1801	WB-A/352	AR
Scott, William	065	1836	Orig. Only	AR
Scott, William	060	1828	WB-1/119	
Scott, William	072	1868	WB-3/19	AR
Scott, William	096	1812	WB-2/27	AR-Nunc.
Scott, William A.	060	1839	WB-2/7	
Scott, William A.	065	1862	WB-J/141	AR
Scott, William C.	075	1844	WB-N/188	AR
Scott, William C.	016	1832	PQS.5/215	
Scott, William G.	078	1882	WB-19/129	AR
Scott, William R.	099	1854	RB-29/133	AR
Scottin, Lewis	001	1894	WB-3/2	AR
Scoville, E. Frank	009	1886	WB-1/389	CTY
Screws, Henry	069	1793	WB-1/87	AR-Copy
Screws, James	071	1835	WB-4/136	AR
Screws, John	071	1770	WB-1/182	
Screws, Joseph	072	c1798	Orig. Only	AR
Screws, Salley	069	1809	WB-1/197	AR
Scrivin, John	011	c1822	WB-2/345	
Scroggs, Abner	054	1889	WB-5/300	
Scroggs, Alexander	054	1856	WB-3/99	AR
Scroggs, David	054	1866	WB-3/189	AR
Scroggs, Esther	054	1891	WB-5/381	CTY
Scroggs, Esther	054	1867	WB-3/198	AR
Scroggs, Hiram	054	1881	WB-4/412	CTY
Scroggs, Jane	054	c1864	Orig. Only	AR
Scroggs, Jeremiah	054	1840	WB-2/203	AR
Scroggs, John	054	1842	WB-2/237	AR
Scroggs, John	054	1862	WB-3/168	AR
Scroggs, Mary A.	054	1899	WB-6/207	CTY
Scruggs, David	086	1874	WB-F/68	AR
Scruggs, Drury	086	1891	WB-F/414	AR
Scruggs, Richard	086	1819	WB-C/129	AR
Scruse, William	037	1761	WB-A/23	AR
Scudder, Matthias	085	1794	WB-D/20	AR
Scudder, Moses	092	1817	WB-3/131	AR
Scull, Alexander	029	1817	WB-A/242	AR
Scull, Celia	051	1836	WB-A/91	
Scull, Eleanor	012	1813	WB-B/104	AR

Name	Co.	Date	Recorded Copy	Original
Scull, Joseph J.	051	1888	WB-C/375	AR
Scull, William	071	1891	WB-7/116	AR
Scurlark, Cornelious	029	1883	Orig. Only	AR
Scurlock, Apphia	022	1852	WB-C/335	AR
Scurlock, Lucy	047	1843	WB-4/220	
Scurlock, Mial	022	1782	Orig. Only	AR
Scurlock, Thomas	047	1792	WB-3/208	
Scurry, Gidren	044	1775	WB-1/124	CTY
Seabolt, Willis	081	1866	WB-14/43	AR
Seaborn, William	029	1851	WB-C/198	AR
Seaford, Abraham	033	1842	WB-1/40	
Seaford, Daniel	016	1862	WB-2/87	
Seaford, John	085	1864	WB-K/346	AR
Seaford, Samuel	085	1877	WB-1/385	CTY
Seagle, Adam	060	1834	WB-1/305	AR
Seagle, Daniel	060	1885	WB-4/335	AR
Seagle, Jacob	014	1868	WB-1/48	AR
Seagle, John J.	060	1870	WB-4/52	AR
Seagle, Thomas J.	021	1898	WB-3/197	AR
Seago, Henderson	005	1857	WB-C/115	AR
Seago, Malachi G.	005	1854	WB-C/91	AR
Seagrove, Adam	030	1723/4	Orig. Only	SS/AR
Seagrove, John	092	c1830	WB-4/49	
Sealey, Joseph	083	c1822	WB-1/362	AR
Seals, James M.	083	1898	WB-4/200	AR
Seals, William	010	1786	WB-D/69	AR
Sealy, James	083	1863	WB-2/195	AR
Sealy, Sampson	083	1861	WB-2/166	
Seamann, John V.	100	1893	WB-51/341	AR
Seamon, Harriet N.	085	1891	WB-2/480	CTY
Seapaugh, Mary	026	1897	WB-2/556	AR
Searcey, William H.	044	1840	WB-14/606	CTY
Searcy, Bartlet	044	1784	WB-1/409	CTY
Searcy, Elizabeth	044	c1784	Orig. Only	CTY
Searcy, Finey	086	1890	WB-F/371	AR
Searcy, John	044	1787	WB-2/1	CTY
Searcy, Robert	084	1884	WB-E/295	CTY
Searcy, Sarah	086	1871	WB-F/31	AR
Searcy, Thomas	084	1894	WB-F/12	CTY
Searcy, Thomas	084	1841	WB-B/256	CTY
Searcy, William	046	1776	WB-A/333	AR
Seares, William	002	c1679	Orig. Only	SS/AR
Searles (Pender), Mary	028	1899	WB-F/400	
Searles, Coventon	009	1814	OWB/471	AR
Searles, Frances	028	1765	DB-12&13/294	AR
Searles, Thomas	073	1796	WB-C/91	AR
Searles, William	028	1826	WB-C/269	AR
Sears, Ann	077	1789	WB-C/392	AR
Sears, Barbee	022	1844	WB-C/166	AR
Sears, Beverly	017	1880	WB-B/90	AR
Sears, Caleb	030	1828	WB-3/235	
Sears, Charles	030	1826	WB-3/212	
Sears, Francis A.	051	1872	WB-C/84	AR
Sears, Henry	073	1774	WB-A/150	
Sears, James	041	1870	WB-4/13	AR
Sears, Jerry	041	1886	WB-4/255	AR
Sears, John	044	1857	WB-20/235	CTY
Sears, John	030	1801	WB-2/194	
Sears, John	051	1844	WB-A/212	
Sears, John A.	053	1837	WB-6/7	
Sears, John, Sr.	044	1823	WB-9/166	CTY
Sears, Nancy	009	1900	WB-2/266	CTY
Sears, R. T. D.	022	1888	WB-E/386	AR
Sears, Thomas	073	c1788	WB-B/40	AR
Sears, William	009	1855	OB-K/23	AR
Seat, Billison	071	1786	WB-1/372	AR
Seat, James	071	1845	WB-5/24	AR
Seat, Robert	078	1836	WI-13/106	AR
Seaton, Jane	065	1779	WB-F/153	AR
Seaton, Malachi	075	1797	WB-L/112	
Seaton, Willy	075	1810	WB-M1/218	
Seats, John Q.	021	1888	WB-2/407	AR
Seavey, Jeremiah	087	1881	WB-3/225	
Seawell, Benjamin	015	1778	100 WB-2/270	AR
Seawell, Grizzy	099	1863	RB-32/610	AR
Seawell, Henry	099	1858	RB-30/534	AR
Seawell, Henry	099	1835	RB-23/422	AR
Seawell, Mary	024	c1795	WB-A/280	
Seay, James	010	1774	Orig. Only	SS/AR
Sebaston, Benjamin	104	1819	WB-3/207	AR
Seboch, Jacob	060	1810	Orig. Only	AR
Seboch, Margaret	060	1848	WB-2/295	AR
Seboch, Peter	060	1866	WB-3/77	AR
Sebrell, Benjamin	VA	1879	069 WB-5/142	069 AR
Sechler, Abraham	085	1882	WB-2/22	CTY
Sechler, Barbara	085	1844	WB-I/233	AR
Sechler, Benjamin	085	1855	WB-K/190	AR
Sechler, Catherine	085	1899	WB-3/342	CTY
Sechler, G. A. J.	085	1899	WB-3/271	CTY
Sechler, Henry	085	1875	WB-1/310	CTY
Sechler, Jesse	085	1885	WB-2/116	CTY
Sechler, John F.	085	1862	WB-K/303	AR
Sechler, Rudolph	085	1895	WB-3/103	CTY
Sechler, Rudolph	085	1841	WB-I/108	AR
Sechler, Solomon	085	1858	WB-K/264	AR
Sechler, William A.	085	1900	WB-3/400	CTY
Sechrest, F. W.	046	1896	WB-F/475	AR
Sechrist, Christian	032	c1842	Orig. Only	AR
Sechrist, Solomon	032	c1864	WB-2/287	
Sechrist, Thomas	032	1844	WB-1/451	AR
Secrest, Abram J.	097	1883	WB-2/234	AR
Secrest, Andrew	097	1859	WB-1/156	AR
Secrest, Andrew J.	097	1867	WB-1/291	AR
Secrest, Barbara	065	1836	WB-E/144	AR
Secrest, Ephraim W.	097	1871	WB-2/47	AR
Secrest, J. P.	097	1886	WB-2/279	AR
Secrest, William	065	1817	WB-F/198	AR
Sedberry, Harrison T.	067	1891	WB-2/303	AR
Sedberry, John B.	067	1882	WB-2/134	AR
Sedgewicks (Sedgex), Ann	096	1786	WB-1/154	AR
Sedgewicks (Shegex), John	096	1769	Orig. Only	AR
Sedgex (Sedgewicks), Ann	096	1786	WB-1/154	AR
See, John	047	c1839	WB-4/216	
Seegraves, Feabuy	044	1834	WB-13/131	CTY
Seehorn, Charles E.	016	1850	WB-1/173	
Seemon, Solomon	054	1845	WB-2/311	AR
Segall, Umphrey	046	1883	WB-E/383	AR
Segla, Aaron	072	1802	WB-A/123	AR
Segler, Mathew	005	1808	WB-2/146	AR
Segraves, Wesley	099	1866	RB-34/162	AR
Seguine, Bornt	NY	1831	Copy	018 AR
Seguine, Henry S.	NY	1884	Copy	075 AR
Seguine, James S.	VA	1868	018 WB-D/87	018 AR
Seidel, Nathanael	PA	1782	092 WB-1/174	092 AR
Seigle, T. L.	065	1891	WB-L/539	AR
Seiler, John	090	1801	WB-2/5	AR
Seitz, George	060	1813	Orig. Only	AR

Name	Co.	Date	Recorded Copy	Original
Seitz, Jacob	060	1816	Orig. Only	AR
Seitz, John	060	1797	Orig. Only	AR
Selah, Joseph	069	1809	WB-1/200	AR
Selah, Joseph	069	1795	WB-1/99	AR
Selah, Rebecca	069	1803	WB-1/143	AR
Selby, Dorcas W.	053	1877	WB-11/75	AR
Selby, Elizabeth	009	1861	OB-L/267	AR
Selby, Henry	009	c1811	OWB/464	AR
Selby, Henry H.	009	1826	OB-A/354	AR
Selby, John	053	1789	RW-1/189	
Selby, John	053	c1823	Orig. Only	AR
Selby, John	009	1854	OB-I/269	
Selby, John H.	053	1830	WB-5/1	AR
Selby, Mary	053	1843	WB-6/246	AR
Selby, Milton	053	1886	WB-11/181	AR
Selby, Nathan	053	1805	RW-1/377	AR
Selby, Samuel	009	1825	OWB/486	AR
Selby, Samuel	053	1791	RW-1/206	
Selby, Sarah R.	099	1880	WB-A/144	AR
Selby, Talbot H.	099	1880	WB-A/101	AR
Selby, Tolbert	053	1799	RW-1/312	AR
Selby, William	053	1788	RW-1/166	AR
Selby, William	053	1859	WB-8/366	AR
Selby, William B.	053	1894	WB-11/313	AR
Seley, Rebecca	075	1810	WB-M1/214	AR
Seley, Tobias	083	c1803	WB-1/81	AR
Self, William	026	1878	WB-2/179	AR
Self, William	046	1883	WB-E/370	AR
Self, William	040	c1852	WB-1/49	
Self, William J.	026	1866	WB-1/395	AR
Sell, John	090	1836	WB-3/316	
Sell, Mary J.	097	1891	WB-2/414	AR
Sellars, B. A.	001	1896	WB-3/98	AR
Sellars, Barbara	070	1824	WB-C/409	AR
Sellars, Benjamin	037	1761	WB-A/25	AR
Sellars, John	070	1816	WB-A/421	
Sellars, Mary	083	c1823	WB-1/322	AR
Sellars, Peter L.	001	1895	WB-3/94	AR
Sellars, Phillip	026	1852	WB-1/132	AR
Sellars, Thomas	001	1892	WB-2/548	AR
Sellers, Archibald	083	c1804	WB-1/186	AR
Sellers, Benjamin	012	1817	WB-B/116	AR
Sellers, Catharine	083	1858	WB-2/134	AR
Sellers, Catharine	070	1790	WB-C/399	AR
Sellers, David	076	1900	WB-A1/272	AR
Sellers, Elisha	012	c1801	WB-B/69	AR
Sellers, Gilbert	083	c1832	WB-1/275	AR
Sellers, Harriet	083	1900	WB-4/272	AR
Sellers, James	022	1806	WB-A/129	AR
Sellers, Jeconias	012	c1813	WB-B/106	
Sellers, John	060	1814	Orig. Only	AR
Sellers, John J.	083	1872	WB-3/38	AR
Sellers, John W.	083	1896	WB-4/121	
Sellers, Mary	005	1875	WB-D/42	AR
Sellers, Mary B.	012	1893	WB-A/92	AR
Sellers, McKay	083	1900	WB-4/275	AR
Sellers, Samuel	087	c1784	Orig. Only	AR
Sellers, Simon, Sr.	012	1817	WB-B/115	AR
Sellers, William R.	012	1871	WB-A/21	AR
Scllew, Enos	OH	1876	091 WB-1/76	
Selph, Francis	029	1843	WB-C/37	AR
Semison, Samuel	065	1805	WB-F/188	
Sensing, James	015	1768	100 WB-1/33	AR
Sensing, Peter	100	1790	WB-5/189	AR
Senter, Nathaniel	006	1878	WB-E/34	AR
Sequad, John	024	c1796	Orig. Only	AR
Sequin, Mathew	070	1798	WB-AB/14	
Seraker, Jacob	032	1837	WB-1/292	
Sergant, Stephen	020	1864	RB-T/46	
Sergeant, J. T.	078	1893	WB-19/337	AR
Serjant, William	073	1768	WB-A/78	
Serman, Joseph	053	1814	RW-1/484	
Sermons, Susan	079	1873	WB-2/89	AR
Service, Joseph W.	040	1864	WB-1/164	
Servis, Jane	040	c1859	WB-1/102	
Serwin, James	103	1796	WI-B/93	
Session, Isaac	092	1792	WB-3/9	AR-Nunc.
Sessions, Richard	087	c1816	Orig. Only	AR
Sessoms, Daniel V.	051	1888	WB-C/384	AR
Sessoms, Elizabeth	051	1837	WB-A/93	
Sessoms, Henry, Sr.	029	1879	WB-E/194	AR
Sessoms, Mary	029	1898	WB-F/155	AR
Sessoms, Samuel H.	010	1837	WB-G/275	AR
Sessoms, William	051	1844	WB-A/166	
Sessums, Blake	087	1841	WB-1/250	AR
Sessums, Elizabeth	037	1798	WB-D/66	AR
Sessums, Elizabeth	037	1835	WB-F/173	AR
Sessums, Elmoor	047	1818	WB-3/618	
Sessums, Henry F.	037	1884	WB-G/690	AR
Sessums, Isaac	037	1785	WB-C/1	AR
Sessums, Jacob	037	1792	WB-C/191	AR
Sessums, Mary A.	037	1884	WB-G/637	
Sessums, Nancy	047	1857	WB-5/32	
Sessums, Nicholas	037	1764	WB-A/140	AR
Sessums, Richard	037	1769	WB-A/171	AR
Sessums, Solomon	037	1818	WB-E/173	AR
Sessums, Solomon	087	1832	WB-1/137	AR
Sessums, William	037	1864	WB-G/239	AR
Sessums, Wilson	037	1849	WB-F/423	AR
Seterson, Sarah Ann	024	c1877	WB-E/111	
Setliff, Abraham	084	1847	WB-C/47	CTY
Setliff, T. R.	092	1893	WB-6/376	AR
Setliffe, John	084	1856	WB-C/237	CTY
Setser, George	017	c1864	WB-A/166	AR
Setser, Jacob	017	c1861	WB-A/135	AR
Setser, Mathias	021	c1844	Orig. Only	AR
Setser, T. R.	025	1890	WB-A/109	
Settle, Benjamin	084	1843	WB-B/313	CTY
Settle, David	084	1833	WB-B/73	CTY
Settle, Hiram	104	1869	WB-6/36	AR
Settle, John	084	c1800	WB-A/97	CTY
Settle, Josiah	084	c1799	OW/127	AR
Settle, Nancy	084	c1806	Orig. Only	AR
Settle, Rhoda	084	1852	WB-C/144	CTY
Settle, Thomas	084	1857	WB-C/258	CTY
Settlemire, David	060	1840	WB-2/56	AR
Settlemire, Jacob	014	1813	WB-2/46	
Settlemyre, Henry H.	017	1888	WB-B/159	
Setton, Nathanel	077	1725	Orig. Only	SS/AR
Setzer, Caleb	085	1874	WB-1/270	CTY
Setzer, Daniel	021	c1854	Orig. Only	AR
Setzer, David	054	1884	WB-4/508	CTY
Setzer, Ephraim D.	017	1876	WB-B/59	AR
Setzer, George	021	1870	WB-2/30	
Setzer, Henry	054	1900	WB-6/286	CTY
Setzer, Jacob	085	1895	WB-3/65	CTY
Setzer, Jacob	021	1891	WB-2/566	AR
Setzer, John	021	1844	WB-1/23	
Setzer, John	054	1893	WB-5/479	CTY
Setzer, Mathias	021	N. D.	Orig. Only	AR

Name	Co.	Date	Recorded Copy	Original
Setzer, Melinda	021	1877	WB-2/176	AR
Setzer, Susan	017	1876	WB-B/58	AR
Setzer, Thomas W.	017	c1885	WB-B/254	AR
Setzer, William	017	1869	WB-B/19	AR
Setzer, William	060	1812	Orig. Only	AR
Sevenson, Elizabeth	077	1734	SS 876/331	
Severn, Isaiah	019	1834	WB-A/38	AR
Severs, H. H.	065	1878	WB-K/299	AR
Severt, Fredrick	006	1875	WB-E/15	AR
Sevier, Maggie P.	SC	1894	086 WB-G/27	
Seville, Stephen	028	1756	SS 880/32	
Sevinson, John	032	1833	WB-1/41	
Sevits, Catherine	085	1832	WB-H/545	AR
Sevitz, George	060	c1794	Orig. Only	AR
Sevitz, George	085	c1827	WB-H/495	
Seward, William A.	071	1841	WB-4/232	AR
Sewbridge, Caspar	028	1714	PQS.1/51	
Sewel, Daniel	072	1855	WB-2/144	AR
Sewel, Samuel	085	c1789	WB-D/73	AR
Sewell, Charity J.	019	1889	WB-B/185	AR
Sewell, Martha D.	051	1887	WB-C/362	AR
Sewell, Thomas	083	1814	WB-1/150	AR
Sewell, Unity	083	1815	WB-1/157	
Sexton, Ann	075	1833	WB-N/84	AR
Sexton, John	075	1829	WB-N/48	AR
Sexton, John T.	069	1896	WB-5/576	AR
Sexton, Malachi	075	1797	WB-L/113	AR
Sexton, Margaret	071	1816	WB-3/186	AR
Sexton, Mark	075	1812	WB-M1/235	AR
Sexton, Mary	009	1860	OWB/555	AR
Sexton, Obediah	099	1807	RB-7/282	
Sexton, Peter	022	1817	068 WB-A/294	
Sexton, William	075	1781	WB-K/56	AR
Sexton, William	009	1837	OB-B/541	AR
Sexton, Willis	075	1810	WB-M1/218	AR
Seymore, George W.	022	1893	WB-E/542	AR
Seymore, Miles	018	1841	WB-C/260	
Seymore, Mourning	018	1823	WB-C/21	AR-Copy
Seymore, Peter	018	1855	WB-D/20	
Seymore, Sarah	011	c1793	WB-2/281	
Seymore, Solomon	022	1876	WB-E/124	AR
Seymour, Augustus	028	1897	WB-F/257	
Seymour, Joseph	018	1845	WB-C/297	
Seymour, Penelopy	018	1845	WB-C/295	
Seymour, Philip D.	063	1837	WB-2/235	
Shackelford, Elisha	072	1841	WB-2/37	AR
Shackelford, Francis	020	1785	RB-B/86	AR
Shackelford, George	072	1802	WB-A/122	AR
Shackelford, Jesse	045	1892	Orig. Only	AR
Shackelford, John	019	1828	WB-D/347	AR
Shackelford, John	072	1778	RW/L20	AR
Shackelford, John	039	1865	WB-S/97	
Shackelford, John W.	072	1883	WB-4/151	AR
Shackelford, Kezia	019	1770	RB-A/36	AR
Shackelford, Mary	029	1846	WB-C/87	AR
Shackelford, Willoughby	072	1805	WB-A/118	AR
Shackleford, James	019	1759	SS 882/182	SS/AR
Shackleford, John	019	1734	LGB-4/#19	SS/AR
Shackleford, Kizia	019	1770	Copy	028 AR
Shackleford, P. C.	013	1889	WB-B/509	AR
Shadding, James	103	1805	Orig. Only	AR
Shaddy, John	073	1812	WB-D/331	AR
Shaefer, Johannes	085	c1805	WB-G/18	AR
Shaffer, Frederick	065	1804	WB-F/184	AR
Shaffer, Margaret	065	1855	WB-J/9	AR
Shaffner, Henry	038	1877	WB-2/307	AR
Shallington, Sallie	105	1893	WB-3/54	AR
Shallington, William B.	009	c1795	OWB/310	AR
Shamblee, John	099	1806	RB-7/201	AR
Shamborger, Henry	029	1767	Orig. Only	AR
Shamburger, Peter	068	1838	WB-B/112	
Shamel, Abraham	038	1876	WB-2/242	AR
Shamel, John	090	1827	WB-3/170	AR
Shamel, John	090	1813	WB-2/142	AR
Shane, William	022	1872	WB-E/81	AR
Shankle, Eliza	089	c1895	Orig. Only	AR
Shankle, George	089	1841	WB-1/1	AR
Shankle, Green	089	1866	WB-1/307	
Shankle, L. F.	089	1898	WB-2/329	
Shankle, Levi	089	c1862	WB-1/267	
Shanklen, John	001	1877	WB-2/128	AR
Shanklin, Andrew	AL	1870	053 WB-11/30	053 AR
Shanklin, Andrew	053	1847	WB-7/85	
Shanks, James	044	1863	WB-21/743	CTY
Shanks, James	020	1873	WB-A/104	CTY
Shannan, Joyner	030	1807	WB-2/318	
Shannon, Hugh	060	1787	Orig. Only	AR
Shannon, Hugh	040	1872	WB-2/43	AR
Shannon, James	060	1825	WB-1/23	AR
Shannon, James	030	1774	WB-1/92	
Shannon, James	040	1872	WB-2/52	AR
Shannon, William	073	1795	WB-B/289	AR
Shannon, William	046	1806	WB-A/361	AR
Shannon, William	040	c1860	WB-1/127	AR
Shannon, William J.	097	1864	WB-1/237	AR
Shannonhouse, B. J.	065	1889	WB-L/397	AR
Shannonhouse, Elizabeth	075	c1853	WB-M2/31	AR
Shannonhouse, James J.	077	1873	WB H/54	
Shannonhouse, James L.	075	1811	WB-M1/227	AR
Shannonhouse, Sarah	077	1891	WB-H/211	AR
Shannonhouse, Thomas L.	075	1842	WB-N/172	AR
Shannonhouse, Willie A.	065	1885	WB-L/60	AR
Shanon, Nathaniel	031	1896	Orig. Only	AR
Shapley, John	028	1790	WB-A/214	AR
Sharber, Joseph	075	1843	WB-N/182	AR
Sharbrough, Jonathan	075	c1771	Orig. Only	024 AR
Sharbrough, Joseph	046	1799	WB-A/351	AR
Sharp, Catherine	084	c1800	OW/123	AR
Sharp, Christian	001	1861	WB-1/185	AR
Sharp, Edward	081	1789	WB-1/10	AR
Sharp, Edward	065	1791	WB-F/170	AR
Sharp, Elizabeth	073	1800	WB-C/111	AR
Sharp, Henry	084	1816	WB-A/304	CTY
Sharp, Henry A.	046	c1863	WB-E/58	AR
Sharp, Isaac	073	1782	WB-A/241	AR
Sharp, Isaac	001	1877	WB-2/85	AR
Sharp, Jacob	010	1748	Orig. Only	SS/AR
Sharp, James	084	1852	WB-C/141	CTY
Sharp, James	071	1804	WB-2/271	AR
Sharp, Jenkins	051	c1882	WB-C/517	AR
Sharp, Jesse	073	1876	WB-H/130	CTY
Sharp, John	065	c1819	WB-E/118	AR
Sharp, John	046	1778	WB-A/335	AR
Sharp, John	037	1799	WB-D/102	AR
Sharp, John B.	051	1875	WB-C/146	AR
Sharp, Maria	046	1865	WB-D/274	AR
Sharp, Mary	065	1853	WB-I/211	AR
Sharp, Mary	084	1837	WB-B/176	CTY
Sharp, Nancy	071	1805	WB-2/275	AR

Name	Co.	Date	Recorded Copy	Original
Sharp, Peter	073	c1847	Orig. Only	AR
Sharp, Rhoda	013	1845	WB-A/102	
Sharp, Starkey	051	1833	WB-A/58	
Sharp, Thomas B.	051	1847	WB-A/272	
Sharp, Walter	085	c1779	WB-B/168	AR
Sharp, William W.	VA	1871	044 WB-23/48	044 CTY
Sharpe, A. P.	054	1891	WB-5/376	CTY
Sharpe, Abner	054	c1807	WB-1/21	AR
Sharpe, Alfred	054	1876	WB-4/226	
Sharpe, Asseaneth	003	c1856	Orig. Only	AR
Sharpe, Benjamin	105	1861	WB-1/141	AR
Sharpe, Bettie B.	054	1890	WB-5/353	
Sharpe, Carlos	054	c1820	WB-1A/55	AR
Sharpe, E. F.	054	1880	WB-4/369	CTY
Sharpe, James	054	c1825	WB-2/63	AR
Sharpe, Jane	054	1894	WB-5/517	CTY
Sharpe, John	054	c1810	WB-1/293	AR
Sharpe, John C.	054	1891	WB-5/392	CTY
Sharpe, John P.	037	1846	WB-F/336	AR
Sharpe, Joseph	054	c1839	WB-2/205	
Sharpe, Lilly	054	c1818	WB-1A/128	AR
Sharpe, Maranda	054	1885	WB-5/73	CTY
Sharpe, Mary	054	c1857	Orig. Only	AR
Sharpe, Silas	054	1851	WB-3/49	AR
Sharpe, Silas D.	054	1859	WB-3/137	AR
Sharpe, Thomas	054	c1814	WB-1/332	
Sharpe, William	054	c1818	WB-1A/13	
Sharpless, William E.	070	1835	WB-B/66	AR
Sharpley, William	065	1830	WB-F/55	AR
Sharranton, Thomas	039	1799	WB-A/127	
Sharrard, James	071	1818	WB-3/206	AR
Sharrock, David	010	1811	WB-F/174	AR
Sharrock, Elizabeth	010	1849	WB-G/447	AR
Sharrock, Mary	010	1848	WB-G/426	AR
Sharrock, Samuel	010	1819	WB-G/60	AR
Sharrock, Thomas	010	1802	WB-E/142	AR
Sharrock, Whitmel T.	010	1870	WB-I/31	AR
Sharrock, William	010	1799	WB-E/97	AR
Sharrock, Zadock	047	1816	WB-3/579	
Sharrod, Jonathan	077	1765	WB-C/53	AR
Sharwood, David	077	1723	Orig. Only	SS/AR
Shatterly, Andrew	104	1817	WB-3/153	
Shatterly, George	046	1864	WB-D/211	AR
Shatterly, Michael	046	1829	WB-B/382	AR
Shaub, Hanah	090	1833	WB-3/263	AR
Shaughan, David	VA	1763	047 WB-1/212	
Shaver, Abraham	085	1874	WB-1/237	CTY
Shaver, Amelia J.	085	1896	WB-3/147	CTY
Shaver, Ann	085	1867	WB-L/22	AR
Shaver, Caleb	085	1868	WB-L/27	CTY
Shaver, Daniel	085	1869	WB-1/16	CTY
Shaver, John	028	1730	LGB-4/#20	SS/AR
Shaver, John	085	1844	WB-I/238	AR
Shaver, John J.	085	1873	WB-1/189	CTY
Shaver, Margaret E.	085	1879	WB-1/506	CTY
Shaver, William	046	1801	WB-A/355	AR
Shavor, John	028	c1730	Deeds.1/55	
Shaw, Alexander	082	c1863	WB-4/169	AR
Shaw, Angus	029	1857	WB-C/348	AR
Shaw, Angus	082	1839	WB-2/84	AR
Shaw, Angus	029	1851	WB-C/212	AR
Shaw, Ann	029	1813	WB-A/190	AR
Shaw, Archibald	011	c1799	WB-1/387	
Shaw, Archibald	083	c1869	WB-3/100	AR
Shaw, Benjamin	046	1846	WB-C/245	AR

Name	Co.	Date	Recorded Copy	Original
Shaw, C. N.	099	1828	RB-20/183	AR
Shaw, Calvin C.	081	1870	WB-15/71	AR
Shaw, Catharine	083	1900	WB-4/278	AR
Shaw, Catharine	087	1897	WB-4/46	AR
Shaw, Catherine	029	1784	Orig. Only	AR-Nunc.
Shaw, Catherine	011	c1804	WB-1/397	
Shaw, Christian	029	1843	WB-C/31	AR
Shaw, Colin	029	1821	WB-B/58	AR
Shaw, Daniel	011	1870	WB-2/44	
Shaw, Daniel	011	1848	WB-1/168	
Shaw, Daniel	029	1829	WB-B/170	AR
Shaw, Daniel	083	1866	WB-2/228	
Shaw, Daniel	011	c1780	WB-2/283	
Shaw, Daniel	082	1800	WB-1/81	AR
Shaw, Daniel	053	1852	WB-7/527	AR
Shaw, David	047	1867	WB-5/157	
Shaw, Della M.	100	1897	WB-51/483	
Shaw, Duncan	029	1782	Orig. Only	AR
Shaw, Dushee	029	1765	Orig. Only	AR
Shaw, Edward	051	1850	WB-A/309	
Shaw, Eliza	099	1896	WB-C/555	AR
Shaw, Eliza Ann	046	1894	WB-F/375	AR
Shaw, Elizabeth	046	1828	WB-B/374	AR
Shaw, Ellet	047	1855	WB-5/2	
Shaw, Eugenia	024	1884	WB-E/133	AR
Shaw, Fanny	030	1837	WB-4/33	
Shaw, Finley	046	1871	WB-E/74	AR
Shaw, Frances	099	c1838	Orig. Only	AR
Shaw, Francis	075	1837	WB-N/136	AR
Shaw, Gardner	081	1846	WB-8/340	AR
Shaw, Gideon	047	1820	WB-3/659	
Shaw, Henry M.	030	1866	WB-4/258	
Shaw, Jack	039	1879	WB-U/192	AR
Shaw, James	073	1803	WB-D/100	AR
Shaw, James	047	1811	WB-3/517	
Shaw, James	047	1790	WB-3/186	
Shaw, James D.	099	1884	WB-A/512	AR
Shaw, Jane	001	1889	WB-2/430	AR
Shaw, John	081	1849	WB-9/117	AR
Shaw, John	068	1809	WB-A/264	
Shaw, John	099	1848	RB-26/387	AR
Shaw, John	019	c1760	RB-A/18	AR
Shaw, John	047	1832	WB-4/85	
Shaw, John	047	1796	WB-3/265	
Shaw, John	073	1838	WB-F/1	AR
Shaw, John	049	c1827	WB-2/228	AR
Shaw, John A.	075	1846	WB-N/200	AR
Shaw, John B.	099	1816	RB-12/237	AR
Shaw, John, Sr.	011	1847	WB-1/149	
Shaw, Joseph	073	1832	WB-E/277	AR
Shaw, Joseph B.	075	c1869	Orig. Only	AR
Shaw, Lovedy Jane	068	1888	WB-D/280	
Shaw, Malcom	083	1880	WB-3/180	
Shaw, Malcom	068	1846	WB-B/161	
Shaw, Marion	029	1813	WB-A/188	AR
Shaw, Mary	029	1815	WB-A/224	AR
Shaw, Matthew	099	1835	RB-23/417	AR
Shaw, Moses N.	001	1879	WB-2/143	AR
Shaw, Murdoch	083	1816	WB-1/170	
Shaw, Neill W.	068	c1891	WB-D/350	
Shaw, Noble	046	1856	WB-C/453	AR
Shaw, Norman	029	c1810	WB-A/160	
Shaw, Patrick	046	1802	WB-A/357	AR
Shaw, Penelope	011	c1849	WB-1/187	
Shaw, Polly	030	1832	WB-3/317	

Name	Co.	Date	Recorded Copy	Original
Shaw, Rachel	029	1826	WB-B/145	AR
Shaw, Robert J.	039	1865	WB-S/6	AR
Shaw, Samuel	029	1845	WB-C/84	AR
Shaw, Sarah E.	009	1885	WB-1/367	CTY
Shaw, Sarah H.	039	1888	WB-U/454	AR
Shaw, Stella V.	099	1891	WB-B/483	AR
Shaw, Thomas	009	1870	WB-1/64	CTY
Shaw, Torquil	048	1896	WB-A/47	CTY
Shaw, William	051	1863	WB-B/50	AR
Shaw, William	099	1828	RB-20/179	AR
Shaw, William	046	1793	WB-A/345	AR
Shaw, William	009	1890	WB-1/468	CTY
Shaw, William	068	1853	WB-B/253	
Shaw, William	099	1815	RB-12/110	AR
Shaw, William A.	RI	1895	062 WB-B/176	062 AR
Shaw, William V.	020	1872	WB-A/89	CTY
Shaw, Zilman J.	001	1899	WB-3/284	AR
Shean, Isaac	057	1797	WB-A/161	AR
Shearad, David	077	1740	LGB-4/#153	SS/AR
Shearen, Martha	047	1863	WB-5/104	
Shearer, James W.	025	1890	Orig. Only	AR
Shearer, Manerva	025	1897	WB-A/198	AR
Shearer, Robert	010	c1727	Orig. Only	SS/AR
Shearer, Robert	006	c1845	WB-A/8	AR
Shearer, Robert	102	1895	WB-A/105	AR
Sheargold, Tilley	030	1797	WB-2/112	
Shearin, Ann R.	100	1878	WB-51/124	AR
Shearin, Charlotte	100	1884	WB-51/187	AR
Shearin, Daniel	100	1846	WB-39/193	AR
Shearin, Dilly	100	1878	WB-51/132	AR
Shearin, Elizabeth	100	1854	WB-43/1	AR
Shearin, Ezekiel	100	1857	WB-41/188	AR
Shearin, Gardner	100	1842	WB-38/121	AR
Shearin, Gardner	100	1843	WB-38/168	AR
Shearin, Henry	100	1782	WB-3/133	AR-Nunc.
Shearin, Isham	100	1835	WB-35/58	AR
Shearin, Jacob J.	100	1892	WB-51/352	
Shearin, James	100	1862	WB-49/402	AR
Shearin, John	100	1795	WB-8/172	AR
Shearin, John Daniel	100	1889	WB-51/281	AR
Shearin, John R.	100	1871	047 WB-7/270	047 AR
Shearin, John R.	100	1871	WB-51/59	AR
Shearin, Joseph	100	1863	WB-50/8	AR
Shearin, Joseph	044	1752	Orig. Only	CTY
Shearin, Joseph H.	100	1895	WB-51/394	
Shearin, Leah W.	047	1845	WB-4/249	
Shearin, Martha	047	1831	WB-4/73	
Shearin, Micah	047	1846	WB-4/252	
Shearin, Nancy	100	1797	WB-9/246	AR-Nunc.
Shearin, Nelly	100	1852	WB-42/65	AR
Shearin, Silva G.	100	1879	WB-51/142	AR
Shearin, Tabitha	100	1898	WB-51/514	
Shearley, Richard	037	1823	WB-F/13	AR
Shearly, Delilah	037	1827	WB-F/70	AR
Shearman, Squire	078	1815	WI-7/43	
Shearmon, John, Sr.	044	1784	WB-1/402	CTY
Shearmon, Micheal	044	1804	WB-6/126	CTY
Shearon, William H.	099	1899	WB-D/282	AR
Shearrin, Lucy E.	047	1891	WB-7/20	AR
Sheborn, John	071	1868	WB-5/367	AR
Sheehan, John	070	1896	WB-G/509	AR
Sheek, Christian	106	c1867	WB-2/9	AR
Sheek, George	033	1867	WB-1/204	AR
Sheek, William	033	1840	WB-1/25	AR
Sheets, David	033	1837	WB-1/9	AR
Sheets, Jacob	085	1818	WB-G/528	AR
Sheets, John	085	1810	WB-G/159	AR
Sheets, John	073	1787	WB-B/26	AR
Sheets, Louis	081	1890	WB-16/145	
Sheetz, Silas	029	1890	WB-E/471	AR
Sheffield, John	068	1796	WB-A/186	
Sheffield, John	035	1831	WB-1/10	AR
Shegex (Sedgewicks), John	096	1769	Orig. Only	AR
Shehan, Miles	010	1779	WB-B/131	AR
Shehan, Miles M.	010	1774	WB-B/3	AR
Shehan, Thomas	010	1794	WB-D/246	AR
Shehane, Morris	065	1806	WB-F/187	AR
Sheils, John	073	1787	Orig. Only	AR-Copy
Shelby, Moses	065	c1776	WB-F/154	AR
Shelfer, John	057	1816	WB-B/24	AR
Shelhorn, Mary	032	1837	WB-1/303	AR
Shell, Casphor	060	1804	Orig. Only	AR
Shell, David	060	1877	WB-4/180	AR
Shell, Franklin	102	1893	WB-A/90	AR
Shell, Henry	097	1890	WB-2/374	AR
Shell, Solomon	021	1850	WB-1/85	AR
Shell, Stephen	100	1821	WB-23/39	AR
Shelley, John	075	1758	SS 881/177	
Shelley, John P.	037	1749	Orig. Only	SS/AR
Shelly, James	046	1798	WB-A/349	AR
Shelly, John	046	c1788	WB-A/340	AR
Shelly, Joseph	085	c1786	WB-C/110	AR
Shelly, Romulus W.	032	1867	WB-2/359	AR
Shelton, Alsey A.	054	1897	WB-6/86	CTY
Shelton, Benjamin	020	1799	RB-C/417	
Shelton, Charles W.	054	c1835	WB-2/155	AR-Copy
Shelton, David	020	1801	RB-D/12	
Shelton, David	062	1858	WB-A/19	AR
Shelton, David W.	021	1884	WB-2/286	
Shelton, Edward	092	1782	WB-2/23A	AR
Shelton, Ephram L.	049	1886	WB-2/136	AR
Shelton, Freeman	060	1869	WB-4/15	AR
Shelton, George	020	1838	RB-N/244	AR
Shelton, Giles F.	090	1892	WB-6/273	AR
Shelton, James W.	020	1875	WB-A/199	CTY
Shelton, John	092	1894	WB-6/399	AR
Shelton, John	084	1830	WB-B/1	CTY
Shelton, Joseph B.	060	1894	WB-4/557	AR
Shelton, Lademon	047	1786	WB-3/113	
Shelton, Mary W.	046	1891	WB-F/100	AR
Shelton, Meacon	060	1869	WB-4/13	AR
Shelton, Nathaniel	047	1831	WB-4/81	
Shelton, Nelson	060	1832	WB-1/260	AR
Shelton, Richard	046	1842	WB-C/126	AR
Shelton, Rutha	047	1825	WB-4/3	
Shelton, Squire	046	1897	WB-F/578	AR
Shelton, Thomas	073	1802	WB-D/71	AR
Shelton, William	037	1829	WB-F/107	AR
Shelton, William	090	1814	WB-2/155	AR-Nunc.
Shelton, William	092	1785	WB-2/61A	AR
Shelton, William R.	090	1897	WB-6/436	AR
Shelton, William T.	038	1884	WB-2/478	AR
Shelton, William V.	090	1892	WB-6/286	AR
Shemwell, James	044	1797	WB-4/133	CTY
Shemwell, Lorenzo D.	032	1874	WB-3/95	AR
Shemwell, William	086	1856	WB-E/323	AR
Shemwell, William T.	085	1852	WB-K/149	AR
Shenal, Margaret	084	1821	WB-A/310	CTY
Shepard, Alfred	070	1854	WB-C/570	AR

Name	Co.	Date	Recorded Copy	Original
Shepard, Benjamin	072	1805	WB-A/119	AR
Shepard, Benjamin	072	1791	Orig. Only	AR
Shepard, Charlotte	070	1872	WB-E/248	AR
Shepard, David	019	1801	WB-D/363	AR
Shepard, David	019	1775	Orig. Only	SS/AR
Shepard, Elizabeth	019	1818	WB-D/378	AR
Shepard, Gardner	072	1878	WB-4/102	AR
Shepard, George	072	1823	WB-A/122	AR
Shepard, Henry	070	1842	WB-B/129	AR
Shepard, Jacob	019	1773	RB-A/46	AR
Shepard, James B.	099	1872	RB-35/164	AR
Shepard, John	072	1809	WB-A/124	AR
Shepard, John	072	1812	WB-A/120	AR
Shepard, Mary	099	1864	RB-33/335	AR
Shepard, Mary S.	028	1883	WB-E/327	AR
Shepard, Matilda	072	1846	WB-2/74	AR
Shepard, Mitchell	070	1894	WB-G/270	AR
Shepard, Richard	099	1875	RB-35/323	AR
Shepard, Smith	072	1800	WB-A/117	AR
Shepard, Solomon	019	c1780	Orig. Only	AR
Shepard, Thomas	035	1851	WB-2/59	AR
Shepard, William	028	1819	WB-C/180	AR
Shepard, William	072	1895	WB-4/313	AR
Shepard, William B.	075	1852	WB-N/246	AR
Shepard, Williba	072	N. D.	Orig. Only	AR
Sheperd, Giles L.	090	1863	WB-4/359	AR
Shephard, George	102	1885	WB-A/48	AR
Shepheard, Mary	073	1761	WB-A/17	
Shepherd, Andrew	029	1774	Orig. Only	AR
Shepherd, Byrd	046	1873	WB-E/118	AR
Shepherd, Conrad	046	1843	WB-C/157	AR
Shepherd, Cyprian	075	1816	WB-M1/281	AR
Shepherd, David	081	1806	WB-3/43	AR
Shepherd, Elijah	029	1899	Orig. Only	AR
Shepherd, Elijah	083	1840	WB-1/388	AR
Shepherd, Emeline	036	1900	WB-A/500	CTY
Shepherd, Gardner	006	1880	WB-E/70	AR
Shepherd, J. W.	006	1899	WB-E/382	AR
Shepherd, Jacob	046	1850	WB-C/327	AR
Shepherd, John	104	1810	WB-2/300	AR
Shepherd, John	104	1812	WB-3/37	AR
Shepherd, Joseph	107	c1857	WB-1/417	
Shepherd, Larkin	104	1845	WB-5/20	AR
Shepherd, Mary Ann	005	1858	WB-C/134	AR
Shepherd, Melvin	006	1896	WB-E/307	AR
Shepherd, Sampson	047	c1778	WB-2/97	
Shepherd, Samuel S.	063	1875	WB-3/85	
Shepherd, Solomon	009	c1789	OWB/239	AR
Shepherd, Thomas	005	1810	WB-2/148	AR
Shepherd, Thomas	061	1842	WB-1/24	AR
Shepherd, Thomas R.	036	1896	WB-A/382	CTY
Shepherd, Valentine	056	c1842	WB-1/547	AR
Shepherd, William	005	1823	WB-A/88	AR
Shepherd, William	073	1826	WB-E/111	AR
Shepherd, William	005	1801	WB-2/149	AR
Shepherd, William	063	1892	WB-4/90	
Sheppard, Elijah	057	1792	WB-A/187	Nunc.
Sheppard, George	072	c1774	RW/L22	AR
Sheppard, Jane	084	1894	WB-E/573	CTY
Sheppard, John	068	1872	WB D/36	
Sheppard, Lewis	104	c1810	Orig. Only	AR
Sheppard, Mary	078	1829	WI-11/222	AR
Sheppard, Thomas J.	079	1900	WB-3/215	AR
Shepperd, Augustus	038	1864	WB-1/243	AR
Shepperd, Charles	081	1815	WB-4/229	AR

Name	Co.	Date	Recorded Copy	Original
Shepperd, Daniel	046	1856	WB-C/455	AR
Shepperd, Jacob	092	1808	WB-3/83	AR
Shepperd, James	092	1781	WB-1/150	AR
Shepperd, William	073	1822	WB-E/24	AR
Sherard, Dorothy	103	1839	RD-7/426	AR
Sherard, Elizabeth	103	1873	WB-1/67	AR
Sherard, James	071	1760	WB-1/34	
Sherard, John	071	1753	SS 879/188	SS/AR
Sherard, John V.	103	1897	WB-2/188	AR
Sherard, John, Sr.	103	1823	RD-5/26	AR
Sherard, William	103	1858	RD-12/406	AR
Sherard, William	103	1841	RD-8/243	AR
Sherbert, A. G. W.	065	1891	WB-M/204	AR
Shereman, Elizabeth	085	1799	WB-D/84	AR
Shergold, Thomas	030	1785	WB-1/187	
Sheridan, Thomas	011	1864	WB-1/317	
Sherlock, Mary W.	075	1846	WB-N/198	
Sherlock, Michael	070	1807	WB-AB/102	AR
Sherman, Margaret	092	1799	WB-3/30	AR
Sherman, Theodora	038	1870	WB-2/18	AR
Shermer, Peter	106	1881	WB-2/152	AR
Shermon, Peter	092	1794	WB-3/14A	
Sherod, Jonathan	077	1769	WB-C/84	AR
Sherod, Jordan	069	1843	WB-1/462	AR
Sherod, Robert	063	1779	WB-1/55	
Sheron, John, Sr.	099	1837	RB-24/27	AR
Sherrard, John	103	1795	WI-A/547	
Sherrard, William	071	1788	WB-1/383	AR
Sherrell, Babel	017	c1851	WB-A/53	
Sherril, Mary	021	1845	WB-1/30	
Sherrill, A. E.	085	1900	WB-3/354	CTY
Sherrill, Aaron	060	1829	WB-1/125	
Sherrill, Absa	021	1876	WB-2/159	AR
Sherrill, Absalom	054	1865	WB-3/174	AR
Sherrill, Adam	021	1844	WB-1/17	AR
Sherrill, Adam	085	1774	WB-A/167	AR
Sherrill, Alexander	060	1838	WB-2/6	AR
Sherrill, Alfred R.	003	1892	WB-B/300	AR
Sherrill, Aram	021	1861	WB-1/161	AR
Sherrill, David	017	1870	WB-B/22	AR
Sherrill, Elam A.	021	1868	WB-1/252	
Sherrill, Elisha	060	1832	WB-1/238	AR-Copy
Sherrill, Elitha	021	1893	WB-3/24	
Sherrill, Elizabeth	AR	1835	Copy	060 AR
Sherrill, Enos	060	1841	WB-2/96	AR
Sherrill, Francis	054	1845	WB-2/323	AR
Sherrill, Hiram	021	1860	WB-1/152	AR
Sherrill, Isaac	054	1856	WB-3/98	AR
Sherrill, Isaac	017	c1850	WB-A/127	
Sherrill, Jacob	060	1810	Orig. Only	AR
Sherrill, Jacob	017	1887	WB-B/147	
Sherrill, Jeptha	021	1850	WB-1/89	AR
Sherrill, John	021	1847	WB-1/60	AR
Sherrill, John H.	054	1858	WB-3/134	AR
Sherrill, Jonas B.	055	1877	WB-A/31	
Sherrill, Joseph	060	1831	WB-1/234	AR
Sherrill, Joseph	017	1897	WB-B/290	
Sherrill, Joshua	060	1817	Orig. Only	AR
Sherrill, Joshua	021	1850	WB-1/83	AR
Sherrill, Lawson L.	021	1850	WB-1/80	AR
Sherrill, Logan W.	060	1842	WB-2/144	AR
Sherrill, Lydia	016	1843	WB-1/3	
Sherrill, M. A.	060	1875	WB-4/123	AR
Sherrill, Mahala	021	1863	WB-1/183	AR
Sherrill, Margarett	021	1874	WB-2/124	AR

Name	Co.	Date	Recorded Copy	Original
Sherrill, Martha A.	060	1842	WB-2/121	AR
Sherrill, Mary	017	1899	WB-B/321	
Sherrill, Mary	021	c1844	WB-1/30	AR
Sherrill, Miles	021	1879	WB-2/212	
Sherrill, Moses	060	1829	WB-1/146	AR
Sherrill, Moses	060	1813	Orig. Only	AR
Sherrill, Nancy	021	1848	WB-1/68	AR
Sherrill, Reuben	021	1859	WB-1/151	AR
Sherrill, Rheuannah	021	1847	WB-1/49	AR
Sherrill, Sarah	021	1887	WB-2/373	
Sherrill, Sarah	021	1858	WB-1/141	AR
Sherrill, Sina	054	1846	WB-3/20	AR
Sherrill, Theophilus	060	1873	WB-4/103	AR
Sherrill, W. P.	021	1866	WB-1/221	AR
Sherrill, Wesley	021	1855	WB-1/121	AR
Sherrill, William	017	1887	WB-B/150	
Sherrill, William	017	1867	WB-A/178	
Sherrill, Zelie P.	054	1894	WB-5/494	CTY
Sherrin, John	099	c1832	RB-32/435	AR
Sherrod, Benjamin	047	1760	WB-1/9	
Sherrod, Benjamin	103	1826	RD-5/214	AR
Sherrod, Benjamin	071	1831	WB-4/82	AR
Sherrod, Dicy	069	1895	WB-5/486	AR
Sherrod, Elizabeth	037	1867	WB-G/287	AR
Sherrod, Elizabeth	039	1821	WB-G/36	AR
Sherrod, James	037	c1849	Orig. Only	AR
Sherrod, James	039	c1819	WB-F/217	AR
Sherrod, Jane F.	063	c1865	WB-2/535	
Sherrod, John	063	1843	WB-2/297	
Sherrod, John	071	1821	WB-3/247	AR
Sherrod, John	063	1780	WB-1/59	
Sherrod, John B.	071	1878	WB-6/247	AR
Sherrod, John J.	063	c1867	WB-2/500	
Sherrod, Lucian N.B.	039	1896	WB-V/71	AR
Sherrod, Lydia	063	1821	WB-2/73	
Sherrod, Martha	071	1860	WB-5/222	AR
Sherrod, R. W.	063	c1861	WB-2/510	
Sherrod, Rebecca	039	1824	WB-H/21	AR
Sherrod, Redden	037	1894	WB-H/281	AR
Sherrod, Robbert	063	c1800	WB-1/380	
Sherrod, Susan	051	1845	WB-A/233	
Sherrod, Thomas	039	1818	WB-F/122	AR
Sherrod, William	037	1778	WB-A/264	AR
Sherrod, William R.	063	1867	WB-2/544	
Sherrode, John J.	069	1848	WB-1/512	AR
Sherron, Aaron	044	1875	WB-23/179	
Sherron, John	099	c1832	SC/02219	AR-Copy
Sherron, John W.	044	1897	WB-24/328	CTY
Sherron, Lavina H.	044	1883	WB-23/478	CTY
Sherwood, Alsey	046	c1888	Orig. Only	AR
Sherwood, Annie M.	046	1897	WB-F/569	AR
Sherwood, Daniel	046	1838	WB-C/11	AR
Sherwood, Michael S.	046	1869	WB-E/5	AR
Sherwood, Robert	016	1832	PQS.5/236	
Sherwood, Thomas	002	1694	Orig. Only	SS/AR
Sherwood, William	103	1841	RD-8/243	
Shetts, Jacob	028	1752	DB-5/253	SS/AR
Shew, Phillip	104	1832	WB-4/159	AR
Shield, Abel	090	1833	WB-3/256	AR
Shield, Charles	047	1844	WB-4/232	
Shield, John	047	1836	WB-4/142	
Shield, Sarah	047	1831	WB-4/82	
Shield, Thomas	047	1836	WB-4/126	
Shields, A. C.	065	1899	WB-N/265	AR
Shields, Andrew	085	c1790	WB-D/47	AR

Name	Co.	Date	Recorded Copy	Original
Shields, Archibald	068	1837	WB-B/107	
Shields, Benjamin	068	1805	WB-A/242	Nunc.
Shields, Benjamin	068	c1867	WB-C/164	
Shields, Benjamin	068	c1851	WB-B/214	
Shields, Charles C.	047	1877	WB-6/161	AR
Shields, Charles W.	047	c1864	WB-5/134	
Shields, Cora	047	1896	WB-7/207	AR
Shields, D. P.	068	1900	WB-E/32	
Shields, E.	047	1871	WB-6/49	
Shields, Elizabeth	047	1875	WB-6/152	AR
Shields, Emma H.	047	c1895	WB-7/207	
Shields, Felicia N.	047	1879	WB-6/202	AR
Shields, James G.	047	1893	WB-7/88	AR
Shields, John	038	1884	WB-2/480	AR
Shields, John	038	1856	WB-1/90	AR
Shields, John W.	068	1900	WB-E/53	
Shields, Kisiah	043	1895	WB-1/51	
Shields, Lucy	086	1883	WB-F/210	AR
Shields, Martha J.	022	1871	WB-E/69	AR
Shields, Mary	065	1846	WB-I/55	AR
Shields, Mary E.	068	1871	WB-D/19	
Shields, Nancy C.	070	1881	WB-E/429	AR
Shields, Reuben	090	1837	WB-4/8	AR
Shields, Robert	022	1869	WB-E/50	AR
Shields, Thomas	047	1829	WB-4/50	
Shields, William	065	1847	WB-I/80	AR
Shields, William H.	047	1893	WB-7/98	AR
Shields, William H.	080	1898	WB-1/293	AR
Shimpock, Daniel F.	016	1886	WB-3/479	AR
Shimpock, John	016	1896	WB-4/242	AR
Shimpock, Moses	016	1877	WB-3/223	AR
Shimpock, William H.	016	1886	WB-3/493	AR
Shin, Levi	092	1837	WB-4/130	AR
Shinault, Daniel M.	092	1888	WB-6/273	AR
Shine, Daniel	039	1829	WB-J/25	AR
Shine, Daniel	028	1757	SS 880/191	SS/AR
Shine, Daniel	057	1801	WB-A/253	AR
Shine, Francis	028	1783	Orig. Only	AR
Shine, Francis	087	1831	WB-1/116	AR
Shine, James	028	c1761	Orig. Only	AR
Shine, James	047	1817	WB-3/605	
Shine, John	028	1851	WB-D/183	AR
Shine, Joseph A.	103	1887	WB-1/413	AR
Shine, Martha	035	1882	WB-4/152	AR
Shine, Mary W.	047	1860	WB-5/81	
Shine, Sarah	039	1846	WB-M/120	AR
Shine, William	047	1817	WB-3/604	
Shine, William	028	1869	WB-E/13	AR
Shine, William E.	047	1833	WB-4/93	
Shingleton, William	009	c1788	OWB/228	AR
Shinn, Isaac	054	1855	WB-3/91	AR
Shinn, Isaac	016	1846	WB-1/108	
Shinn, Mary	016	1858	WB-2/48	
Shinn, Mary A.	016	1892	WB-4/141	AR-Copy
Shinn, Samuel	085	1762	WB-A/144	AR
Shinpock, Michael	016	1851	WB-1/187	
Ship, Ann	087	1840	WB-1/230	AR
Ship, Michael	087	c1816	Orig. Only	AR
Ship, Richard	037	1778	WB-B/7	AR
Shipard, Thomas	030	1722	Orig. Only	SS/AR
Shipman, Daniel	011	c1772	WB-2/282	
Shipman, Daniel	011	c1799	WB-1/392	
Shipman, Daniel	011	c1844	WB-1/101	
Shipman, Edward	050	1865	WB-1/89	CTY
Shipman, Hayes F.	011	1844	WB-1/117	

Name	Co.	Date	Recorded Copy	Original
Shipman, Jacob	086	1795	Orig. Only	AR
Shipp, Bartlett	060	1869	WB-4/34	AR
Shipp, Elizabeth	040	1855	WB-1/63	AR
Shipp, John	099	1835	RB-23/244	AR
Shipp, John	075	1893	WB-0/402	AR
Shipp, R. J.	021	1895	WB-3/83	AR
Shipp, Susan F.	060	1880	WB-4/223	AR
Shipp, Thomas	090	1853	WB-4/284	AR
Shipp, William E.	099	1898	065 WB-N/197	065 AR
Shipp, William E.	099	1898	WB-D/200	AR
Shipp, Willis	028	1782	Orig. Only	AR
Shipplett, S. B.	032	1891	WB-4/137	AR
Shipwash, William	083	1842	WB-1/407	AR
Shireman, George	085	c1796	WB-D/52	AR
Shirlen, Bird	064	1896	WB-2/370	AR
Shirley, Eliza	046	1896	WB-F/541	AR
Shirley, James	070	1737/8	SS 877/172	SS/AR
Shirly, Elizabeth	037	1867	WB-G/297	AR
Shirly, James	037	c1817	Orig. Only	AR
Shirrard, Alexander	010	1734	SS 876/298	SS/AR
Shitle, John	060	1877	WB-4/167	AR
Shitle, John	026	1863	WB-1/311	AR
Shitle, Martin	060	1892	WB-4/492	AR
Shittle, Martin	060	1817	Orig. Only	AR
Shive, Katherine	016	1845	WB-1/62	
Shive, Ruben	016	1868	WB-3/12	
Shiver, David	076	c1891	Orig. Only	AR
Shivers, Martha	037	1893	WB-H/258	AR
Shivers, Sarah	009	c1780	OWB/154	AR
Shoaf, Henry	032	1881	WB-3/317	AR
Shoaf, Henry	085	1807	WB-G/25	AR
Shoaf, Henry L.	085	1856	WB-K/217	AR
Shober, Emanuel	090	1846	WB-4/217	AR
Shober, Gottleib	090	1838	WB-4/27	AR
Shober, Hetwig	038	1861	WB-1/187	AR
Shober, Nathaniel	090	1818	WB-3/26	AR
Shober, Rebecca	038	1853	WB-1/57	AR
Shoe, Henry	016	1860	WB-2/68	
Shoe, Jacob	085	1898	WB-3/229	CTY
Shoe, Jacob	016	1898	WB-4/299	AR
Shoe, John H.	016	1879	WB-3/247	AR
Shoemaker, Adam	092	1786	WB-2/70	
Shoemaker, Burrel	054	1887	WB-5/154	CTY
Shoemaker, Elizabeth	046	1839	WB-C/27	AR
Shoemaker, Joel A.	102	1892	WB-A/89	AR
Shoemaker, John, Sr.	054	c1797	WB-1/208	AR
Shoemaker, Randle	054	1880	WB-4/401	CTY
Shoemaker, Susannah	046	1813	WB-A/369	AR
Shoemaker, Wilborn	054	1875	WB-4/184	
Shoeman, John	085	c1814	Orig. Only	AR
Shofe, Henery	085	c1791	WB-B/175	AR
Shoffner, Frederick	073	1846	WB-F/279	AR
Shoffner, Henry	046	1863	WB-D/173	AR
Shofner, Michael	073	c1810	WB-D/342	AR
Sholar, David	035	1892	WB-4/399	AR
Sholar, John	010	1792	WB-D/200	AR
Sholar, Levi	035	1822	WB-A/454	AR
Sholar, Solomon	035	1828	WB-A/435	AR
Sholar, William	010	1776	WB-B/61	AR
Sholder, Sarah	010	1795	WB-D/276	AR
Shook, Abraham	054	c1832	WB-2/118	AR
Shook, Adam	021	1876	WB-2/150	AR
Shook, F. R.	054	1888	WB-5/248	CTY
Shook, Fredrick	060	1823	Orig. Only	AR
Shook, Henry	021	1870	WB-2/32	
Shook, Jacob	049	c1836	WI-1-2/16	
Shook, Mahala	049	1894	WB-2/314	AR
Shook, Martha	054	1846	WB-3/9	AR
Shook, Mary	021	1877	WB-2/172	AR
Shook, Susan E.	049	1892	WB-2/294	AR
Shope, Jacob	061	1876	WB-2/29	AR
Shorber, Jacob	055	1853	ID/2	
Shore, Elizabeth	038	1888	WB-3/102	AR
Shore, Frederick	092	1818	WB-3/135	
Shore, Frederick	092	1774	WB-1/17	AR
Shore, Henry	090	c1819	SC/04597	AR-Copy
Shore, Henry	090	1826	WB-3/151	
Shore, Henry	090	1839	WB-4/40	
Shore, Isaac	038	1865	WB-1/251	AR
Shore, Jacob	038	1850	WB-1/36	AR
Shore, Jacob	090	1843	WB-4/123	AR
Shore, Johannes	085	c1790	WB-D/80	
Shore, John	106	1867	WB-1/114	AR
Shore, John	092	1829	WB-4/17	
Shore, John H.	038	1890	WB-3/159	AR
Shore, John L.	038	1896	WB-3/587	AR
Shore, John, Sr.	090	1844	WB-4/176	AR
Shore, Leah	106	1884	WB-2/186	
Shore, Peter	090	1837	WB-3/320	AR
Shore, Samuel E.	038	1863	WB-1/209	AR
Shore, Saphrona	038	1862	WB-1/205	AR
Shore, William	038	1867	WB-1/291	AR
Shores, Jacob	092	1819	WB-3/141	AR
Shores, Margaret	106	c1867	Orig. Only	AR
Shores, Simeon	104	1837	WB-4/220	AR
Shores, Susannah	092	1806	WB-3/74A	
Short, Abraham	065	1782	WB-F/165	AR
Short, Eugene M.	009	1894	WB-2/51	AR-Copy
Short, Hennery	028	1780	Orig. Only	AR
Short, John	047	1819	WB-3/645	
Short, John	071	1792	WB-2/4	AR
Short, Jonathan	046	1847	WB-C/267	AR
Short, Judah	071	1797	WB-2/159	AR
Short, Julius A.	046	1885	WB-E/424	AR
Short, Margaret	068	1873	WB-D/45	
Short, Martha	100	1804	WB-12/339	AR
Short, Moses	084	c1809	WB-A/87	CTY
Short, Pleasant	068	1896	WB-D/462	
Short, Rebecah	071	1833	WB-4/107	AR
Short, Richard	069	1864	WB-1/594	AR
Short, Richard	100	1853	WB-42/214	AR
Short, Wiley	105	1895	WB-3/126	AR
Short, William	071	1764	WB-1/89	AR-Copy
Short, William	022	1796	RB-2/99	AR
Short, William	071	1801	WB-2/221	AR
Short, William D.	071	1823	WB-3/289	AR
Short, William O.	084	1815	WB-A/108	CTY
Shorte, Daniel	005	c1818	WB-2/156	AR
Shorter, Benjamin	071	1765	WB-1/114	
Shorter, William	071	1753	SS 879/186	SS/AR
Shott, Elisabeth	090	c1821	Orig. Only	AR
Shott, Eva Barbara	090	1841	WB-4/90	AR
Shotwell, Alexander	086	1863	WB-E/407	AR
Shoub, Levi H.	092	1863	WB-5/69	
Shouse, David	030	1893	WB-3/382	AR
Shouse, Harriet	038	1875	WB-2/213	AR
Shouse, Henry	038	1873	WB-2/152	AR
Shouse, Henry	090	1806	WB-2/72	AR
Shouse, John	090	1821	WB-3/68	AR
Shouse, John H.	038	1873	WB-2/156	AR

Name	Co.	Date	Recorded Copy	Original
Shouse, Lucinda A.	038	1894	WB-3/433	AR
Shouse, Phillip	090	1810	WB-2/115	AR
Shouse, William	038	1887	WB-3/58	AR
Shreyer, John Peter	090	1815	WB-2/171	
Shrock, Peter	010	1751	SS 879/29	SS/AR
Shrum, Daniel	060	1875	WB-4/135	AR
Shrum, Henry	060	1896	WB-5/33	AR
Shrum, Nicholas	060	1793	Orig. Only	AR
Shrum, Peter	060	1837	WB-1/389	
Shrum, Solomon	060	1894	WB-4/565	AR
Shubridge, William	072	1746	SS 878/65	SS/AR
Shuffield, Ephraim	071	1814	WB-3/129	AR
Shuffield, John	035	1791	WB-A/427	
Shuford, Alphonso	085	1863	WB-K/313	AR
Shuford, Andrew H.	021	1880	WB-2/226	
Shuford, Daniel	085	1839	WB-I/53	AR
Shuford, Daniel	060	1834	WB-1/312	
Shuford, David	060	1828	WB-1/107	AR
Shuford, E. P.	026	1899	WB-3/53	AR
Shuford, Elvira E.	021	1886	WB-2/340	
Shuford, George	065	c1762	WB-F/143	AR
Shuford, George	093	1891	WB-2/74	AR
Shuford, Jacob	021	1846	WB-1/43	AR
Shuford, Jacob H.	021	1874	WB-2/115	AR
Shuford, John	060	1790	Orig. Only	AR
Shuford, Julia A.	093	1896	WB-2/140	AR
Shuford, Macon	021	1899	WB-3/228	AR
Shuford, Sophia	085	1867	WB-L/15	AR
Shugart, Hannah	073	1815	WB-D/449	AR
Shugart, John W.	081	1879	WB-15/304	AR
Shugart, R. B.	106	c1858	WB-1/76	AR
Shuk, Millie	106	1895	WB-2/371	
Shulaberger, David	085	1838	WB-I/41	AR
Shular, James	032	1888	WB-4/9	AR
Shular, Michel	032	1830	WB-1/129	AR
Shuley, Nancey	075	1812	WB-M1/238	AR
Shuliberinger, Jacob	085	1878	WB-1/464	CTY
Shull, Anthony	060	1851	WB-2/346	AR
Shull, Charles	060	1840	WB-2/65	
Shull, Mary	006	N. D.	WB-A/13	AR
Shull, Simon	006	1813	WB-A/47	AR
Shultz, Anna M.	038	1855	WB-1/80	AR
Shultz, Christian	038	1882	WB-2/426	AR
Shultz, Christina	038	1874	WB-2/195	AR
Shultz, Edwin T.	032	1887	WB-3/550	AR
Shultz, Henry	090	1847	WB-4/247	AR
Shultz, Johanna E.	038	1874	WB-2/199	AR
Shultz, John Henry	038	1851	WB-1/31	AR
Shultz, John Henry	038	1895	WB-3/542	AR
Shultz, Mary	038	1885	WB-2/553	AR
Shultz, Samuel	038	1871	WB-2/56	AR
Shultz, Theodore	038	1844	WB-1/16	AR
Shultz, Thomas	090	1826	WB-3/150	AR
Shultz, William F.	038	1893	WB-3/371	AR
Shulur, George	049	c1803	WI-A/22	AR
Shulz, Dorothea	090	1828	WB-3/180	AR
Shuman, Christian	085	c1807	WB-G/26	AR
Shuman, Frederick	038	1862	WB-1/200	AR-Copy
Shuman, John	085	1874	WB-1/213	CTY
Shuman, John	085	1820	WB-H/48	AR
Shuman, Theodore	038	1870	WB-2/32	AR
Shuping, Caleb	014	1890	WB-2/380	CTY
Shuping, Jacob	085	1857	WB-K/244	AR
Shuping, Michael	085	1874	WB-1/224	CTY
Shuping, Michael	085	1852	WB-K/142	AR
Shuping, Michel	085	1892	WB-2/506	CTY
Shuping, Wiley M.	085	1865	WB-K/357	AR
Shuping, William A.	085	1900	WB-3/383	CTY
Shurley, Susan	037	1849	WB-F/413	AR
Shurly, Henry	037	c1849	Orig. Only	AR
Shuster, Elizabeth	038	1850	WB-1/44	AR
Shute, Gyles	008	1730	Orig. Only	SS/AR
Shute, John	097	1896	WB-2/505	AR
Shute, Joseph	009	1816	OB-A/251	AR
Shute, Phillip	009	c1762	OWB/88	AR
Shutes, Rebeca	Jam	1732	SS 876/261	SS/AR
Shutley, Jacob	060	1799	Orig. Only	AR
Shutt, Bettie S.	038	1900	WB-4/217	AR
Shutt, Charles	090	1845	WB-4/191	
Shutt, George	038	1850	WB-1/18	AR
Shutt, Henry	073	1811	WB-D/312	AR
Shutt, Louisa	038	1893	WB-3/388	AR
Shutt, Rudolph	038	1897	WB-4/39	AR
Shy, John	073	1795	WB-C/58	AR
Shy, Rachel	020	1804	RB-E/141	AR
Siball, Richard	024	c1695	SS 874.1/17	
Sibbet, Simon	027	1853	WB-A/58	AR
Sibley, Elijah	065	1831	WB-G/72	AR
Sibley, Elijah M.	005	1850	WB-C/18	AR
Sibley, Robert	065	1809	WB-F/193	AR
Sibrey, Moses	065	1825	WB-E/93	AR
Siceloff, Alexander	032	1896	WB-4/303	AR
Sickler, Elizabeth	054	1868	WB-3/209	AR
Sidberry, Seana	072	1845	WB-2/67	AR
Sidbury, James	070	1750	DB-C/248	AR
Sidbury, Rebecca	076	1886	WB-A1/84	AR
Sidbury, Stockley	070	1816	WB-AB/237	AR
Siddall, John	020	1798	RB-C/330	AR
Sidden, George	085	1822	WB-H/174	AR
Sidden, Nancy Ann	033	1895	WB-2/185	CTY
Siddle, C. G.	020	1883	WB-A/403	CTY
Siddle, Isaac B.	020	1982	WB-B/105	CTY
Siddle, Jesse	020	1862	RB-S/573	
Siddle, John	020	1886	WB-A/503	CTY
Siddle, W. W.	020	1895	WB-B/179	CTY
Sides, Daniel	054	1881	WB-4/421	CTY
Sides, Daniel A.	016	1894	WB-4/175	
Sides, Elizabeth	090	1820	WB-3/48	AR
Sides, J. S.	038	1893	WB-3/352	AR
Sides, John	016	1839	PQS.6/48	
Sides, John	085	1897	WB-3/211	CTY
Sides, John G.	038	1892	WB-3/337	AR
Sides, Katharine	089	1867	WB-1/308	
Sides, Lorentz	090	1824	WB-3/122	AR
Sides, M. S.	089	1900	Orig. Only	AR
Sides, Nelson	089	c1848	WB-1/74	AR
Sides, Phillip	090	1844	WB-4/180	AR
Sides, Sandford	038	1865	WB-1/262	AR
Siewers, Dorothy M.	038	1852	WB-1/87	AR
Siewers, John D.	038	1890	WB-3/174	AR
Siewers, Matilda A.	038	1900	WB-4/214	AR
Sifferd, Christina	085	1860	WB-K/277	AR
Sifferd, Paul A.	085	1893	WB-3/14	CTY
Sifford, G. Ludwig	085	c1789	WB-D/85	AR
Sifford, George	060	1816	Orig. Only	AR
Sifford, George	085	1813	WB-G/294	AR
Sifford, Mary	003	1894	WB-B/324	AR
Sifford, William	003	1878	WB-B/101	AR
Sifford, William A.	060	1879	WB-4/195	AR
Sigfred, Henerick	046	1802	WB-A/357	AR

Name	Co.	Date	Recorded Copy	Original
Sigler, Jacob	085	1817	WB-G/475	AR
Sigley, John	009	1754	SS 879/178	SS/AR
Sigman, Abel	021	1870	WB-2/34	AR
Sigman, Amon	021	1897	WB-3/182	AR
Sigman, Andrew M.	003	1891	WB-B/291	AR
Sigman, Anson	021	1864	WB-1/196	
Sigman, George H.	021	1861	WB-1/160	
Sigman, George Philip	021	1863	WB-1/182	
Sigman, George, Sr.	021	1848	WB-1/64	AR
Sigman, Jethro	021	1864	WB-1/197	AR
Sigman, Mary	021	1850	WB-1/81	AR
Sigman, Noah	021	c1863	Orig. Only	AR
Sigman, Polly	021	1864	WB-1/203	AR
Sigman, Rhoda C.	021	1896	WB-3/127	AR
Sigmon, Abel	021	1878	WB-2/182	AR
Sigmon, Barbara	021	1864	WB-1/206	AR
Sigmon, Barnet	060	1821	Orig. Only	AR
Sigmon, Christopher	060	1841	WB-2/86	AR
Sigmon, George	060	1834	WB-1/303	AR
Sigmon, George	060	1831	WB-1/211	AR
Sigmon, Jacob J.	021	1879	WB-2/209	
Sigmon, John	060	1811	Orig. Only	AR
Sigmon, Marcus L.	021	1891	WB-2/554	
Sikes, Abel	096	c1818	WB-2/71	
Sikes, Abraham	019	1835	WB-A/47	AR
Sikes, Alexander	011	1887	WB-2/218	
Sikes, Ann	071	1815	WB-3/164	AR
Sikes, Annie J.	027	1889	WB-2/77	AR
Sikes, Benjamin	030	c1810	WB-2/358	
Sikes, Briton	071	1815	WB-3/151	AR
Sikes, Caleb	075	1860	WB-M2/71	AR
Sikes, Caleb	075	1861	WB-M2/72	AR
Sikes, Daniel M.	087	1898	WB-4/83	AR
Sikes, David	011	1864	WB-1/315	
Sikes, Hannah	097	1853	WB-1/90	AR
Sikes, Henry	028	1788	Orig. Only	AR
Sikes, Isom	046	1838	WB-C/9	AR
Sikes, James	047	c1779	WB-2/105	
Sikes, James	075	1771	WB-H/135	AR
Sikes, James	012	1833	WB-B/164	AR
Sikes, James R.	046	1895	WB-F/392	AR
Sikes, Jesse	071	1842	WB-4/245	AR
Sikes, John	069	1797	WB-1/117	AR
Sikes, John	075	1757	Orig. Only	AR
Sikes, John	096	1827	Orig. Only	AR
Sikes, John	011	1868	WB-2/38	
Sikes, John	087	1849	WB-1/354	AR
Sikes, John, Sr.	070	1791	WB-C/400	AR
Sikes, Jonathan	011	c1818	WB-2/378	
Sikes, Joseph	071	1771	WB-1/192	
Sikes, Joshua	005	1840	WB-B/123	AR
Sikes, Josiah	011	c1812	WB-2/311	
Sikes, Kinchen	071	1865	WB-5/313	AR
Sikes, Lydia A.	005	1893	WB-D/327	AR
Sikes, Mary	071	1818	WB-3/205	AR
Sikes, Mary C.	096	1884	WB-4/109	AR
Sikes, Mary F.	027	1899	WB-2/152	AR
Sikes, Mourning	069	1852	WB-1/529	AR
Sikes, Murdock M.	087	1873	WB-3/69	AR
Sikes, Richmond	005	1890	WB-D/436	AR
Sikes, Sarah	071	1874	WB-6/139	AR
Sikes, Tempy	071	1812	WB-3/85	AR
Sikes, Thomas	071	1775	WB-1/24	AR
Sikes, Thomas	071	1829	WB-4/58	AR
Sikes, Thomas F.	097	1899	WB-3/11	AR

Name	Co.	Date	Recorded Copy	Original
Sikes, Willis	035	1817	WB-A/433	AR
Silberman, Simon	046	1883	WB-E/373	AR
Siler, Adam	022	1893	WB-E/522	AR
Siler, D. W.	TN	1886	061 WB-2/77	061 AR
Siler, Elizabeth	081	1878	WB-15/290	AR
Siler, J. D.	022	1888	WB-E/394	AR
Siler, Jacob	061	1871	WB-2/7	AR
Siler, Julius	061	c1866	WB-1/91	AR
Siler, Matthias	022	c1886	WB-E/357	
Siler, Philip	022	1834	WB-C/2	AR
Siler, Phillip	081	1859	WB-11/157	AR
Siler, Phillip	022	c1898	WB-F/272	AR
Siler, Samuel	022	1900	WB-F/170	AR
Siler, Solomon	022	1888	WB-E/388	AR
Silivant, Abner	045	1890	WB-1/204	AR
Sill, Edward	085	1856	WB-K/215	AR
Sillivan, Joel	046	c1842	WB-C/135	AR
Sillivan, Solomon	046	1821	WB-B/136	AR
Sillivant, Macey	009	1830	OB-B/85	AR
Sills, David	069	1833	WB-1/395	AR
Sills, Gray	069	1891	WB-5/345	AR
Sills, Isham	047	1802	WB-3/376	
Sills, John	047	1859	WB-5/66	
Sills, Lucy S.	069	1899	WB-6/74	AR
Sills, William	047	1761	WB-1/37	
Silvent, John	008	1735	009 OWB/19	009 AR
Silver, Levi	085	1800	WB-D/34	AR
Silverthorn, A. B.	053	1872	WB-11/27	AR-Nunc.
Silverthorn, Clarisa	028	1867	WB-D/448	
Silverthorn, Gilford	053	1737	LGB-4/#77	SS/AR
Silverthorn, Jordan	053	1869	WB-11/9	AR
Silverthorn, Scidney	053	1844	WB-6/310	AR
Silverthorn, Sebastin	053	1751	028 DB-5/230	SS/AR
Silverthorne, John	053	1775	RW-1/57	
Silvester, Richard	008	1729	SS 876/194	SS/AR
Silvester, Zachariah	077	1810	WB-E/343	AR
Simeral, Edward	009	c1790	OWB/254	AR
Simes, Christer	037	1833	WB-F/149	AR
Simeson, James	065	1782	WB-F/163	AR
Simeson, John	065	1825	WB-E/94	AR
Simeson, Samuel	065	1806	WB-F/188	
Simkins, Joseph	028	1811	WB-C/36	AR
Simmon, Daniel	021	1862	WB-1/168	AR
Simmonds, Henry	011	1758	Orig. Only	SS/AR
Simmonds, Jacob	070	1736	SS 877/223	SS/AR
Simmons, Abraham B.	057	1807	WB-A/285	AR
Simmons, Abram	020	1851	RB-Q/589	AR
Simmons, Abram	057	1893	WB-C/192	AR
Simmons, Alfred	047	1867	WB-5/159	
Simmons, Alonzo	070	1899	WB-H/206	AR
Simmons, Amos	057	1805	WB-A/273	AR
Simmons, Amos L.	057	1892	WB-C/185	AR
Simmons, Ann	030	1854	WB-4/181	AR
Simmons, Ann Maria	019	1897	WB-B/319	AR
Simmons, Anthony	030	c1815	WB-3/65	
Simmons, Anthony	030	1837	WB-4/30	
Simmons, Benjamin	030	1871	WB-5/18	AR
Simmons, Benjamin	028	1761	Wills.7/260	AR
Simmons, Benjamin	092	c1836	WB-4/118	AR
Simmons, Benjamin	072	1795	Orig. Only	AR
Simmons, Benjamin	032	1859	WB-2/135	AR
Simmons, Bullock	030	1746	Orig. Only	SS/AR
Simmons, Caleb	030	1804	WB-2/256	
Simmons, Charlotte	030	1838	WB-4/52	
Simmons, Daniel	057	1827	WB-B/94	AR

Name	Co.	Date	Recorded Copy	Original
Simmons, Daniel D.	063	1892	WB-4/96	AR
Simmons, Daniel D.	VA	1879	053 WB-11/90	053 AR
Simmons, Daniel H.	035	1888	WB-4/326	AR
Simmons, Dareus	030	1797	WB-2/103	
Simmons, David W.	072	1868	WB-4/7	AR
Simmons, Dianah	099	1790	RB-2/260	AR
Simmons, Edward	037	1735	LGB-4/#16	SS/AR
Simmons, Elijah	057	1851	WB-B/208	AR
Simmons, Elijah	072	1829	WB-1/46	AR
Simmons, Elizabeth	057	1826	WB-B/86	AR
Simmons, Emanuel	057	1807	WB-A/286	AR
Simmons, Ephraim	090	1880	WB-6/113	AR
Simmons, Eve	016	1865	WB-2/119	
Simmons, Everett	072	1840	WB-A/119	AR
Simmons, Frances	070	c1887	Orig. Only	AR
Simmons, Frances	030	1757	SS 880/231	SS/AR
Simmons, George	057	c1794	WB-A/120	AR
Simmons, George	020	c1855	RB-R/319	AR
Simmons, George T.	047	1870	WB-6/45	AR
Simmons, H. H.	030	1887	WB-5/150	AR
Simmons, Harriet K.	SC	1896	Copy	013 AR
Simmons, Henrietta	072	1880	WB-4/116	AR
Simmons, Henry	039	c1797	WB-A/210	
Simmons, Henry	030	1755	Orig. Only	SS/AR
Simmons, Henry	072	1774	Orig. Only	SS/AR
Simmons, Hillary	030	1788	WB-1/218	
Simmons, Hillary	030	c1797	WB-2/273	
Simmons, Isaac	028	1779	Orig. Only	AR
Simmons, Israel	064	1871	WB-2/12	AR
Simmons, Itey	103	1891	WB-1/555	AR
Simmons, J. H.	047	1840	WB-4/186	
Simmons, Jacob	019	c1888	Orig. Only	AR
Simmons, James	067	1844	WB-1/11	AR
Simmons, James	054	1826	WB-2/44	AR-Nunc.
Simmons, James	028	1796	WB-A/356	AR
Simmons, James	047	1836	WB-4/135	
Simmons, James	030	1755	Orig. Only	SS/AR
Simmons, James H.	086	1871	WB-F/58	AR
Simmons, James H.	053	1881	WB-11/117	AR
Simmons, James O.	009	1886	WB-1/375	CTY
Simmons, Jesse	047	1812	WB-3/524	
Simmons, Joel T.	090	1896	WB-6/390	AR
Simmons, John	056	1770	WB-1/787	AR
Simmons, John	057	1802	WB-A/264	AR
Simmons, John	063	1881	WB-3/196	
Simmons, John	030	1800	WB-2/161	
Simmons, John	030	1795	WB-2/51	
Simmons, John	030	1785	WB-1/188	
Simmons, John	065	1812	WB-F/194	AR
Simmons, John	086	1807	WB-B/193	AR
Simmons, John	028	1762	Deeds.15/L63	AR
Simmons, John	015	1773	100 WB-1/256	AR
Simmons, John	010	1781	WB-C/21	AR
Simmons, John	010	1818	WB-G/31	AR
Simmons, John	030	c1811	WB-3/4	
Simmons, John	087	c1887	Orig. Only	AR
Simmons, John	041	1808	WB-2/36	
Simmons, John B.	057	1875	WB-C/47	AR
Simmons, John W.	009	1856	OB-K/205	AR
Simmons, Jonas	092	1881	WB-6/156	AR
Simmons, Joseph	030	1824	WB-3/177	
Simmons, Joseph	072	1805	WB-A/120	AR
Simmons, Joseph T.	030	1850	WB-4/156	
Simmons, Lemuel	057	1846	WB-B/180	AR
Simmons, Lockey	099	1880	WB-A/108	AR
Simmons, Lockey	099	c1875	067 WB-2/221	067 AR
Simmons, Lucretia	038	1880	WB-2/375	AR
Simmons, Lucy	047	1789	WB-3/165	
Simmons, M. R.	047	1900	WB-7/277	AR
Simmons, M. T.	090	1899	WB-6/486	AR
Simmons, Martha	029	1888	WB-E/442	AR
Simmons, Mary	030	1804	WB-2/245	
Simmons, Mary	057	1849	WB-B/201	AR
Simmons, Mary	086	1878	WB-F/112	AR
Simmons, Mary	002	1724	SS 876/12	SS/AR
Simmons, Matthew	090	1864	WB-4/374	AR
Simmons, Mitchel	030	1832	WB-3/313	
Simmons, Mitchel	030	1824	WB-3/171	
Simmons, Needham	057	1822	WB-B/63	AR
Simmons, Nicholas	024	c1703	Orig. Only	SS/AR
Simmons, O. H.	090	1888	WB-6/199	AR
Simmons, P. H.	064	1895	WB-2/362	AR
Simmons, Pleasant	067	1864	WB-1/122	
Simmons, Preston	092	1896	WB-6/415	AR
Simmons, Rebeccah	030	1827	WB-3/231	
Simmons, Robert	030	1785	WB-1/182	
Simmons, S. S.	096	1888	WB-4/136	AR
Simmons, Sallie A.	009	1877	WB-1/202	CTY
Simmons, Sally	030	1855	WB-4/202	AR
Simmons, Samson	030	1785	WB-1/191	
Simmons, Samuel	051	c1894	Orig. Only	AR
Simmons, Samuel	046	1826	WB-B/224	
Simmons, Sanders	011	c1836	WB-1/46	
Simmons, Simeon	028	1817	WB-C/148	
Simmons, Simeon	059	1896	WB-B/163	CTY
Simmons, Susan D.	063	1887	WB-4/11	AR-Nunc.
Simmons, Thomas	030	1819	WB-3/106	
Simmons, Thomas	028	1781	Orig. Only	AR
Simmons, Thomas	070	1799	WB-AB/34	AR
Simmons, Thomas	030	1755	SS 880/64	SS/AR
Simmons, Thomas	020	1794	RB-C/97	AR
Simmons, Thomas M.	070	1894	WB-G/293	AR
Simmons, Will	030	1805	WB-2/278	
Simmons, William	028	1807	WB-B/276	AR
Simmons, William	028	1861	WB-D/348	AR
Simmons, William	039	c1795	WB-B/11	AR
Simmons, William	047	1819	WB-3/638	
Simmons, William	092	1889	WB-6/293	AR
Simmons, William	067	c1858	Orig. Only	AR
Simmons, William G.	099	1889	WB-B/311	AR
Simmons, Willis	099	1771	RB-1/2	AR
Simms, Anne	103	1820	RD-4/305	AR
Simms, Barnes	103	1805	Orig. Only	AR
Simms, Benjamin	105	1860	WB-1/58	AR
Simms, Benjamin	103	1827	RD-5/323	
Simms, Benjamin	037	c1846	SC/05922	AR-Copy
Simms, Benjamin	037	1815	WB-E/79	AR
Simms, Benjamin	105	1862	WB-1/89	AR
Simms, Benjamin	098	1896	WB-A/261	CTY
Simms, Briton	103	1826	RD-5/259	AR
Simms, Burwell	099	1835	RB-23/243	AR
Simms, Hezekiah	050	1890	WB-2/57	CTY
Simms, James	037	1847	WB-F/377	AR
Simms, Joseph	037	1795	WB-C/336	AR
Simms, Martha	103	c1821	Orig. Only	AR
Simms, Martha	098	1886	WB-A/35	
Simms, Martha	103	1848	RD-10/3	AR
Simms, Patrick H.	105	1864	WB-1/113	AR
Simms, Redding	005	c1823	WB-A/94	AR
Simms, Robert	103	1848	RD-10/110	

Name	Co.	Date	Recorded Copy	Original
Simms, Robert	103	1791	WI-A/244	AR
Simms, Tabitha	103	1862	RD-13/442	AR
Simms, William	037	1827	WB-F/78	AR
Simms, Willie	105	1876	WB-2/204	
Simms, Zilliah	037	1851	WB-F/459	AR
Simonds, A. Sena	041	1882	WB-4/180	AR
Simonds, Joel	023	1898	Orig. Only	AR
Simonds, John	012	1778	DB-B/95	AR
Simons, Andrew	009	1752	028 DB-5/246	SS/AR
Simons, Argell	024	1714	Orig. Only	SS/AR
Simons, George	077	1720	SS 875/238	
Simons, James	053	1828	Orig. Only	AR-Copy
Simons, James	077	1828	WB-F/150	AR
Simons, John	024	1732	Copy	CCR 187
Simons, John	024	1804	WB-B/230	AR
Simons, John	028	c1760	Orig. Only	SS/AR
Simons, John	024	c1772	WB-1/44	AR
Simons, John	028	1742	Orig. Only	SS/AR
Simons, John	024	1732	Orig. Only	SS/AR
Simons, John	085	c1796	WB-D/59	AR
Simons, John C.	077	1881	WB-H/106	AR
Simons, John, Jr.	024	c1803	WB-B/284	AR
Simons, Lydia	077	1857	WB-F/487	AR
Simons, Mathew	002	c1692	Orig. Only	SS/AR
Simons, Nancy M.	010	1896	WB-I/473	AR
Simons, Penelope	024	1825	WB-C/119	AR
Simons, Simeon	024	1822	WB-C/99	AR
Simons, W. J.	099	1892	WB-C/74	AR
Simonton, Adam R.	054	1874	WB-4/154	AR
Simonton, Margaret	054	1880	WB-4/409	
Simonton, Mary	054	c1814	Orig. Only	AR
Simonton, R. F.	054	1876	WB-4/206	CTY
Simonton, Robert	054	c1824	WB-2/19	
Simonton, W. Ross	054	1886	WB-5/97	CTY
Simonton, William	054	1811	WB-1/277	AR
Simontown, Marey	085	1767	WB-A/146	AR
Simontown, Theophilus	085	1757	WB-A/157	AR
Simpkin, Moore	084	1875	WB-E/108	
Simpkins, Thomas	099	1852	RB-28/99	AR
Simpson, Aaron	020	1833	RB-M/280	AR
Simpson, Aaron	020	1833	Copy	046 AR
Simpson, Alexander	N	1738	LGB-4/#75	SS/AR
Simpson, Ann	077	1837	WB-F/258	AR
Simpson, Benjamin	077	1762	Orig. Only	AR
Simpson, Benjamin	105	1875	WB-2/169	AR
Simpson, Caroline E.	080	1898	WB-1/298	AR
Simpson, Clifford	028	1871	WB-E/53	AR
Simpson, Comfort	019	1825	WB-D/382	AR
Simpson, David	097	1892	WB-2/422	AR
Simpson, David	065	1854	WB-I/234	AR
Simpson, Debroah	063	1853	WB-2/391	
Simpson, Edward	072	1782	RW/L33	AR
Simpson, Edward D.	030	1896	WB-5/238	AR
Simpson, Elizabeth	070	1866	WB-D/194	AR
Simpson, Elizabeth	028	1858	WB-D/306	AR
Simpson, Elizabeth	079	c1804	SC/05952	AR-Copy
Simpson, Elizabeth	077	1885	WB-H/154	AR
Simpson, Elizabeth	AR	1875	084 WB-E/123	084 CTY
Simpson, Elizabeth	070	1803	WB-AB/74	AR
Simpson, Exum	024	1844	WB-C/251	AR
Simpson, G. W.	089	1900	WB-2/359	AR
Simpson, George W.	077	1882	WB-H/121	AR
Simpson, Henderson	024	1884	WB-E/128	AR
Simpson, Irvin	097	1863	WB-1/207	AR
Simpson, Isaac	009	1882	WB-1/302	CTY
Simpson, Isaac	077	1837	WB-F/260	AR
Simpson, Isaiah	075	1881	WB-0/130	AR
Simpson, Jackson	097	1883	WB-2/227	AR
Simpson, James	030	1792	WB-1/256	
Simpson, James	070	1859	WB-D/9	AR
Simpson, James	020	1811	RB-F/158	
Simpson, James	092	1890	WB-6/314	AR
Simpson, James F.	076	1897	WB-A1/223	AR
Simpson, James T.	084	1892	WB-E/533	CTY
Simpson, Jemima	075	1806	WB-M1/130	AR
Simpson, Jessie	105	1857	WB-1/36	AR
Simpson, Jessie B.	083	1847	WB-1/492	
Simpson, John	012	1827	WB-B/146	AR
Simpson, John	070	1789	WB-C/398	AR
Simpson, John	011	c1838	WB-1/98	
Simpson, John	030	1804	WB-2/257	
Simpson, John	065	1893	WB-M/209	AR
Simpson, John	084	1869	WB-E/11	CTY
Simpson, John	024	1800	WB-B/69	AR
Simpson, John H.	020	1890	WB-B/22	
Simpson, John, Sr.	097	1845	WB-1/22	AR
Simpson, Jonathan	019	1764	RB-A/25	AR
Simpson, Joseph	014	1883	WB-2/251	CTY
Simpson, Joseph	101	1892	WB-A/219	
Simpson, Joseph	020	1855	RB-R/347	AR
Simpson, Joseph B.	009	1854	OB-I/341	AR
Simpson, Joshua	019	1809	WB-D/367	AR
Simpson, Joshua	030	N. D.	WB-2/323	
Simpson, Josiah	030	1801	WB-2/187	
Simpson, Margaret	105	1885	WB-2/389	AR
Simpson, Martha	070	1825	WB-C/413	AR
Simpson, Mary	063	1830	WB-2/166	
Simpson, Mary	020	1798	RB-C/331	AR
Simpson, Mary A. E.	046	1875	WB-E/161	AR
Simpson, Mary E.	024	1877	WB-E/56	AR
Simpson, Moses	020	1870	WB-A/37	CTY
Simpson, Moses	046	1844	WB-C/207	AR
Simpson, Nathaniel	046	1830	WB-B/415	AR
Simpson, Nellie	009	c1885	Orig. Only	CTY
Simpson, Penelope	077	1885	WB-H/149	AR
Simpson, Richard	046	1832	WB-B/451	AR
Simpson, Richard	046	1795	WB-A/347	AR
Simpson, Richard	072	1816	Orig. Only	AR
Simpson, Richard	046	1804	WB-A/379	AR
Simpson, Richard	070	1827	Orig. Only	AR
Simpson, Richard	020	1786	RB-B/103	AR
Simpson, Robert	075	1834	WB-N/101	AR
Simpson, Rosseter	019	1815	WB-D/372	AR
Simpson, Samuel	014	1899	WB-3/94	
Simpson, Samuel	028	1836	WB-C/389	AR
Simpson, Samuel	028	1856	WB-D/264	AR
Simpson, Samuel C.	072	1887	WB-4/223	AR
Simpson, Scarbar	019	1899	WB-C/14	AR
Simpson, W. P.	105	1896	047 WB-7/201	
Simpson, W. P.	105	1896	WB-3/199	AR
Simpson, Walter	070	1759	DB-D/372	
Simpson, Walter	070	1759	Orig. Only	SS/AR
Simpson, William	024	1799	WB-B/73	AR
Simpson, William	077	1853	WB-F/435	AR
Simpson, William	089	1887	WB-2/190	AR
Simpson, William	075	1798	WB-M1/17	AR
Simpson, William	084	1844	WB-C/3	CTY
Simpson, William	030	1787	WB-1/207	
Simpson, William	037	1823	WB-E/318	AR
Simpson, William C.	077	1881	WB-H/108	AR

Name	Co.	Date	Recorded Copy	Original
Simpson, William S.	020	1893	WB-B/134	CTY
Simpson, Willis	075	1820	WB-M1/332	AR
Simpson, Zachariah	030	1860	WB-4/239	
Simril, Eliza R.	065	c1865	WB-J/205	AR
Simril, F. G.	065	1875	WB-K/176	AR
Simril, Francis	065	1834	WB-G/160	AR
Simril, Thomas J.	065	1891	WB-L/523	AR
Sims, Adam	099	1826	RB-20/45	AR
Sims, Bennet	099	1836	RB-23/565	AR
Sims, Edward	100	1792	WB-6/72	AR
Sims, George	020	1809	RB-F/22	AR
Sims, Henry	069	1859	WB-1/560	AR
Sims, Isaac	029	1821	WB-B/54	AR
Sims, Isham	099	1791	RB-2/324	AR
Sims, James	044	1854	WB-19/452	CTY
Sims, Joel	099	1859	RB-31/148	AR
Sims, John	044	1766	Orig. Only	CTY
Sims, John Thomas	097	1877	WB-2/115	AR
Sims, Kezia	009	c1799	OWB/354	AR
Sims, Lennard	100	1804	WB-13/1	AR
Sims, Littleton	086	1845	WB-E/145	
Sims, Mark	029	c1785	Orig. Only	AR
Sims, Matthew	092	1796	WB-3/24A	Nunc.
Sims, R. E.	AR	1899	060 WB-5/132	060 AR
Sims, R.S.T.L.	065	1899	WB-N/268	AR
Sims, Robert	106	1869	WB-2/21	AR
Sims, Robert	010	1729	Orig. Only	SS/AR
Sims, Sarah	056	1771	Orig. Only	AR
Sims, Sarah	100	1811	WB-16/94	AR
Sims, Sherwood	100	1790	WB-5/151	AR
Sims, Thomas	084	1831	WB-B/40	CTY
Simson, Hanah	072	c1788	Orig. Only	AR
Simson, John	024	1764	WB-B/33	AR
Simson, John	072	c1774	RW/L58	AR
Simson, John	030	1754	SS 878/169	SS/AR
Simson, Robert	075	1787	WB-K/155	AR
Simson, William	002	1694	Orig. Only	SS/AR
Simson, William	075	1767	WB-H/79	AR
Sinchler, Peter	022	1782	Orig. Only	AR
Sinclair, Andrew	083	1831	WB-1/258	AR
Sinclair, Catharine	083	1882	WB-3/299	AR
Sinclair, Cherry	081	1881	WB-15/346	AR
Sinclair, D. A.	097	c1890	Orig. Only	AR
Sinclair, Duncan	083	1817	WB-1/177	Nunc.
Sinclair, Edward	028	1778	Orig. Only	AR
Sinclair, Elizabeth	068	1894	WB-D/434	
Sinclair, James	005	1824	WB-A/98	AR
Sinclair, John	068	1829	WB-B/64	
Sinclair, John	005	1827	WB-A/133	AR
Sinclair, John Calvin	083	1896	WB-4/115	AR
Sinclair, Lewellen	005	1889	WB-D/267	AR
Sinclair, Mahala	005	1897	WB-D/416	AR
Sinclair, Neill	083	1880	WB-3/204	AR
Sinclair, Neill	029	1867	WB-D/93	AR
Sinclair, Peter	068	1855	WB-C/26	
Sinclair, Peter	068	1846	WB-B/235	
Sinclair, Peter	068	1876	WB-D/109	
Sinclare, Robert	072	1799	Orig. Only	AR
Sinclare, Samuel	053	1755	SS 879/150	SS/AR
Sing, Milly	026	1843	WB-1/12	
Singeltary, John	009	1846	OB-F/117	AR
Singletary, Armistead	083	1888	WB-3/425	
Singletary, Benjamin	011	c1765	WB-1/596	
Singletary, Breyton	011	c1790	WB-2/270	
Singletary, Brister	011	1885	WB-2/188	
Singletary, David	011	1862	WB-1/338	
Singletary, Edward	011	1863	WB-1/312	
Singletary, Ithamar	011	c1773	WB-2/285	
Singletary, James, Sr.	011	c1810	WB-2/317	
Singletary, John	011	c1826	WB-1/10	
Singletary, Joseph	011	c1792	WB-2/271	
Singletary, Joshua	011	c1840	WB-1/70	
Singletary, Josiah	011	c1841	WB-1/92	
Singletary, Margaret	027	1895	WB-2/118	AR
Singletary, Mary	011	c1827	WB-2/375	
Singletary, Richard	011	1791	WB-2/274	
Singletary, Richard	011	N. D.	WB-1/2	
Singletary, Richard	011	N. D.	WB-2/392	
Singletary, Richard	011	c1773	WB-2/287	
Singletary, Thamar	083	c1822	WB-1/350	AR
Singletary, Thomas	011	c1823	WB-2/366	
Singletary, William	011	c1785	WB-2/262	
Singleton, David	009	1864	OB-L/448	AR
Singleton, John	071	1755	SS 880/49	SS/AR
Singleton, John	037	1763	WB-A/112	AR
Singleton, John C.	009	1888	WB-1/444	CTY
Singleton, Martha	028	1815	WB-C/92	AR
Singleton, Samuel	034	1762	SS 881/268	SS/AR
Singleton, Spyers	028	1814	WB-C/85	AR
Singleton, Thomas	099	1834	RB-23/27	AR
Singleton, Thomas S.	028	1856	WB-D/254	AR
Singleton, William	009	c1829	OWB/497	AR
Singleton, William A.	009	1888	WB-1/450	CTY
Singleton, William G.	028	1881	WB-E/266	AR
Sink, Adam	032	1887	WB-3/556	AR
Sink, Archibald	038	1873	WB-2/148	AR
Sink, Daniel	038	1884	WB-2/486	AR
Sink, Daniel	032	1891	WB-4/100	AR
Sink, Gideon	032	1864	WB-2/275	AR
Sink, Henry	032	1892	WB-4/153	AR
Sink, Jacob	032	1841	WB-1/356	AR
Sink, Jacob, Sr.	032	1866	WB-2/336	AR
Sink, Jesse	032	1870	WB-3/24	AR
Sink, John	032	1833	WB-1/200	AR
Sink, John	032	1842	WB-1/406	AR
Sink, Joseph	032	1892	WB-4/157	AR
Sink, Michael	032	1847	WB-2/9	AR
Sink, Michael	032	1889	WB-4/57	AR
Sink, Michael	032	1857	WB-2/139	AR
Sink, Philip	032	1829	WB-1/120	AR
Sink, Valentine	032	c1863	WB-2/293	
Sink, William	032	1892	WB-4/155	AR
Sink, William A.	032	c1862	WB-2/288	
Sinkler, Charles	073	1766	WB-A/45	
Sinkler, Elizabeth	024	1811	WB-B/318	AR
Sintas, Joseph A.	070	1852	WB-C/535	AR
Sipe, Daniel	003	1893	WB-B/316	
Sipe, Jacob	021	1843	WB-1/2	AR
Sipe, John	021	1877	WB-2/174	AR
Sipe, Noah	003	1900	WB-B/390	
Sirman, Peter	053	1775	RW-1/64	
Sirmon, Benjamin	009	c1797	OWB/335	AR
Sirmon, Brian	009	1827	OB-A/447	AR
Sirmon, Thomas	009	c1795	OWB/557	AR
Sirmon, William	009	c1793	OWB/283	AR
Siseloff, Arehart	032	1869	WB-3/3	AR
Sisk, Daniel	086	1851	WB-E/205	AR
Sisk, Littleberry	090	1868	WB-5/48	AR
Sisk, Micajah	064	1856	WB-1/48	AR
Sisk, Robert	086	1892	WB-F/423	AR

Name	Co.	Date	Recorded Copy	Original
Sisk, Salley	090	1822	WB-3/78	
Sisson, James	071	1779	WB-1/209	
Sitezen, Whary	024	1834	WB-C/173	AR
Sitgraves, John	047	1802	WB-3/372	
Sitgreaves, William	019	1747	SS 877/55	SS/AR
Sitlock, Mary	075	c1840	Orig. Only	AR
Sitten, James M.	093	1862	Copy	013 AR
Sitterson, Isaac	024	1817	WB-C/55	AR
Sitterson, James	077	1750	Orig. Only	SS/AR
Sitterson, Miles	101	1883	WB-A/98	
Sitterson, Penelope	024	1823	WB-C/105	AR
Sitteson, James	077	1768	WB-C/80	AR
Sitton, James M.	093	1862	WB-1/4	
Sitton, William	049	c1838	WI-1-2/14	AR
Sivill, Taylor	030	1849	WB-4/147	
Sizelove, Arehart	085	1819	WB-H/23	AR
Sizemore, Isham	106	1885	WB-2/196	AR
Skeen, Alexander	057	1798	WB-A/200	AR
Skeen, Betsy	057	1801	WB-A/251	AR-Nunc.
Skeen, Jacob T.	032	1861	WB-2/199	AR
Skeen, Jonathan	032	1865	WB-2/318	AR
Skeen, Martin N.	032	1891	WB-4/105	AR
Skeen, Mathew	081	1807	WB-3/77	AR
Skeen, Osborn	032	1887	WB-3/533	AR
Skeen, Rutha	032	1883	WB-3/387	AR
Skeen, Sarah	057	1796	WB-A/144	AR
Skenes, Henry	046	1887	WB-E/479	AR
Skenes, Milly	046	1894	WB-F/314	AR
Skibbons, Henry	072	c1762	Orig. Only	AR
Skibbow, Henry	072	N. D.	RW/L54	
Skidmore, Aley	106	1867	WB-1/120	AR
Skidmore, Henry	092	1775	WB-1/32	AR
Skiles, Harriet	010	1854	WB-H/8	AR
Skiles, John	085	1812	WB-G/231	AR
Skiles, John	010	1823	WB-G/107	AR
Skiles, Martha Ann	063	1863	WB-2/513	
Skiles, Mary	085	1815	WB-G/393	AR
Skiles, Richard	070	1870	WB-E/217	AR
Skiles, William	071	1841	WB-4/237	AR
Skiles, William	010	1820	WB-G/64	AR
Skilling, William	077	1789	WB-C/386	AR
Skindricks, Margaret	085	c1790	WB-C/6	AR
Skinner, B. S.	077	1864	WB-F/549	AR
Skinner, Benjamin	077	1839	WB-F/277	AR
Skinner, Benjamin S.	077	1861	WB-F/521 & 531	AR
Skinner, Charles	100	1863	WB-50/12	AR
Skinner, Dempsey	037	1827	WB-F/74	AR
Skinner, Edmund B.	077	1849	WB-F/372	AR
Skinner, Evan	024	c1789	WB-B/70	AR
Skinner, Fanny	024	1883	WB-E/119	AR
Skinner, Henry	037	1825	WB-F/49	AR
Skinner, Henry C.	047	1888	WB-7/24	AR
Skinner, James	077	1786	WB-C/334	AR
Skinner, Jerusha	024	1826	Orig. Only	AR
Skinner, John	010	1781	WB-C/1	AR
Skinner, John	024	1820	WB-C/80	AR
Skinner, John	077	1771	Orig. Only	SS/AR
Skinner, John	024	1861	WB-D/8	AR
Skinner, John	077	1866	WB-H/15	AR
Skinner, John B.	075	c1850	WB-M2/3	AR
Skinner, Joseph B.	024	1852	WB-C/327	AR
Skinner, Joshua	024	1826	WB-C/120	AR
Skinner, Joshua	077	1777	WB-C/215	AR
Skinner, Joshua	077	1829	WB-F/169	AR
Skinner, Joshua	024	1854	WB-C/361	AR
Skinner, Josiah	024	1832	WB-C/162	AR
Skinner, Josiah C.	077	1836	WB-F/248	AR
Skinner, Kindred	071	1795	WB-2/78	AR
Skinner, Lemuel	024	1833	WB-C/165	AR
Skinner, Lottie	079	1888	WB-2/431	AR
Skinner, M. L.	044	1863	WB-21/681	
Skinner, Nathan	077	1837	WB-F/262	AR
Skinner, Nathan	077	1855	WB-F/463	AR
Skinner, Rachel	077	1810	WB-E/354	AR
Skinner, Richard	077	1792	WB-C/435	AR
Skinner, Richard	024	1806	WB-B/301	AR
Skinner, Richard	077	1752	Orig. Only	SS/AR
Skinner, Richd, Jr.	077	1746	Orig. Only	SS/AR
Skinner, Samuel	077	1781	WB-C/316	AR
Skinner, Sarah	077	1851	WB-F/388	AR
Skinner, Sarah	024	1834	WB-C/178	AR
Skinner, Stephen	024	1838	WB-C/214	AR
Skinner, Stephen	077	1815	WB-E/412	AR
Skinner, Susan E.	100	1886	WB-51/223	AR
Skinner, T. L.	044	1863	WB-21/681	
Skinner, William	077	1798	WB-E/92	AR
Skinner, William	071	1771	WB-1/199	
Skinner, William	077	1798	Part Only	ChM-19/53
Skinner, William H.	105	1860	WB-1/61	
Skinner, William I.	024	1815	WB-C/67	AR
Skinner, William R.	024	1885	WB-E/147	AR
Skipper, Jacob	103	1805	Orig. Only	AR
Skipper, Joseph	072	1794	Orig. Only	AR
Skipper, Mary	082	1879	WB-6/171	AR
Skipper, Moses	012	1811	WB-B/85	AR
Skipper, Thomas	082	1815	WB-1/173	AR
Skirven, Thomas W.	010	1881	WB-I/132	
Slaback, Jacob	028	1765	Orig. Only	AR-Nunc.
Slaback, Nathan	028	1804	Orig. Only	AR
Slack, John	081	1827	WB-5/371	AR
Slack, Nancy	030	1828	WB-3/239	
Slade, Agnes	053	1800	RW-1/318	AR
Slade, Ann	053	1794	RW-1/233	
Slade, Ann	053	1846	WB-7/59	AR
Slade, Benjamin	053	1772	RW-1/33	AR
Slade, Catherine	028	1854	WB-D/222	AR
Slade, David Lot	053	1830	Orig. Only	AR
Slade, Ebenezer	028	c1801	WB-B/124	AR
Slade, Ebenezer	100	1818	WB-16/314	AR
Slade, Ebenezer, Jr.	063	c1787	WB-1/130	
Slade, Ebenezer, Sr.	063	1788	WB-1/138	
Slade, Edmond	053	1854	WB-8/66	AR
Slade, Elias D.	020	1875	WB-A/178	CTY
Slade, Euridice	009	c1807	OWB/447	AR
Slade, Furnifold	053	1813	RW-1/479	
Slade, George	024	c1710	SS 875/32	
Slade, Hannah	053	1782	RW-1/100	AR
Slade, Hannah	020	1813	RB-F/373	AR
Slade, Harry	070	1866	WB-D/202	AR
Slade, Helen B.	063	1881	WB-3/201	
Slade, Henry	009	c1799	OWB/363	AR
Slade, Henry	096	1766	WB-1/38	AR
Slade, Henry	063	1835	WB-2/210	
Slade, Henry	063	c1781	WB-1/87	
Slade, Henry	009	1822	OB-A/321	AR
Slade, Henry, Jr.	053	1721	009 DB-1/299	009 AR
Slade, Hezekiah	053	1787	RW-1/162	
Slade, Hezekiah	053	1752	028 DB-5/241	SS/AR

Name	Co.	Date	Recorded Copy	Original
Slade, Jeremiah	009	1815	OB-A/242	AR
Slade, Jeremiah	063	1824	WB-2/100	
Slade, John	009	c1760	OWB/72	AR
Slade, John	053	1743	SS 878/55	SS/AR
Slade, John	053	1763	OB-A/58	AR
Slade, John G.	053	c1832	WB-5/449	AR
Slade, John Gray	010	1797	WB-E/2	AR
Slade, Joseph	009	1764	OWB/95	AR
Slade, Lydia	053	1766	Orig. Only	AR
Slade, Martha	020	1850	RB-Q/395	
Slade, Mary	028	1812	WB-C/58	AR
Slade, Mary W.	063	1892	WB-4/73	AR
Slade, Nathan	020	1846	RB-P/366	AR
Slade, Reuben	053	1790	RW-1/197	AR
Slade, Reubin	028	1843	WB-D/72	AR
Slade, Robert	057	1882	WB-C/90	AR
Slade, Rutha	074	1886	Orig. Only	AR
Slade, Samuel	051	1796	WB-A/80	
Slade, Samuel	028	1789	WB-A/202	AR
Slade, Samuel	009	1746	SS 878/45	SS/AR
Slade, Samuel	028	1775	DB-22/536	AR
Slade, Sarah	009	1860	OB-L/145	AR
Slade, Thomas	020	1798	RB-C/303	AR
Slade, Thomas	020	1830	RB-L/560	AR
Slade, Thomas L.	020	1873	WB-A/124	CTY
Slade, Thomas T.	084	1864	WB-D/8	CTY
Slade, William	084	1866	WB-D/53	CTY
Slade, William	028	1794	WB-A/320	
Slade, William	063	1791	WB-1/172	
Slade, William	063	1853	WB-2/387	
Slade, Zaccheus	028	1876	WB-E/130	
Slagle, Elizabeth	066	1900	Orig. Only	AR-Nunc.
Slagle, James G.	013	1899	WB-D/256	AR
Slagle, Mary	093	1879	WB-2/1	
Slagle, Winnie	013	1896	WB-C/492	AR
Slate, Samuel	090	1883	WB-6/136	AR
Slater, Louisa	038	1897	WB-4/60	AR
Slatten, Anne K.	047	1843	WB-4/224	
Slatter, Elizabeth	047	1797	WB-3/291	
Slatter, James	047	1799	WB-3/325	
Slatter, Mary	047	1827	WB-4/29	
Slatter, Owen	010	1769	WB-A/111	AR
Slatter, Solomon	047	1850	WB-4/292	
Slaughter, Abraham	044	1840	WB-14/570	CTY
Slaughter, Abraham	044	1883	WB-23/480	CTY
Slaughter, Abraham R.	044	1895	WB-24/264	CTY
Slaughter, Abram S.	044	1852	WB-19/66	CTY
Slaughter, Ebenezer	010	1837	WB-G/277	
Slaughter, Isaac	044	1856	WB-20/153	CTY
Slaughter, Jacob	044	1824	WB-9/377	CTY
Slaughter, Jacob G.	078	1897	WB-19/424	
Slaughter, James	AL	1827	005 WB-A/135	005 AR
Slaughter, Joseph B.	051	1893	WB-C/466	AR
Slaughter, Michael	024	1741	Orig. Only	SS/AR
Slaughter, Owen, Sr.	082	1811	WB-1/149	AR
Slaughter, Theophilus	079	1860	WB-1/59	AR-Copy
Slector, Elizabeth	033	1837	WB-1/6	AR
Sledd, John	083	1833	WB-1/281	AR
Sledge, Archibald	047	1804	WB-3/422	
Sledge, Crafford	020	1897	WB-B/314	CTY
Sledge, Daniel	100	1793	WB-6/173	AR
Sledge, George R.	100	1883	WB-51/178	AR
Sledge, Hamblin	039	c1801	WB-B/88	
Sledge, Henry	047	1849	WB-4/271	
Sledge, Isham	039	c1793	WB-A/112	

Name	Co.	Date	Recorded Copy	Original
Sledge, James	100	1834	WB-34/476	AR
Sledge, Joel	039	1837	WB-K/134	AR
Sledge, John L.	047	1887	WB-6/445	AR
Sledge, Sherrod	039	1896	WB-V/75	AR
Sledge, Sherwood	100	1843	WB-38/136	AR
Sledge, Tabitha	100	1852	WB-42/51	AR
Sledge, Willis	047	1855	WB-5/4	
Sleight, Peter	101	1882	WB-A/81	
Slight, Henry	030	1794	WB-2/28	
Slimmons, George	099	1777	RB-1/94	AR
Slinkard, Henry	060	1823	Orig. Only	AR
Sloan, Alexander	022	1872	WB-E/79	AR
Sloan, Allan	070	1768	WB-C/385	AR
Sloan, Archibald	085	c1786	WB-C/70	AR
Sloan, Claborn	035	1897	Orig. Only	AR
Sloan, Cloey	022	c1860	WB-D/73	AR
Sloan, David	035	1785	WB-A/447	AR
Sloan, David	035	1820	WB-A/425	AR
Sloan, David	035	1801	WB-A/430	AR-Nunc.
Sloan, David A.	065	1891	WB-L/518	AR
Sloan, E. B. D.	065	1874	WB-K/147	AR
Sloan, Eliza J.	065	1889	WB-L/429	AR
Sloan, Ellen	035	1863	WB-3/81	AR
Sloan, Gibson	035	1868	WB-4/5	AR
Sloan, Henry A.	065	1853	Orig. Only	AR
Sloan, Horace	046	1897	WB-F/597	AR
Sloan, James	065	1844	WB-I/122	AR
Sloan, James	085	1846	WB-K/16	AR
Sloan, James	065	1862	WB-J/143	AR
Sloan, James	065	1772	WB-F/146	AR
Sloan, James	065	1796	WB-F/171	AR
Sloan, John	035	1827	WB-A/444	AR
Sloan, John	085	c1779	WB-C/212	AR
Sloan, John	065	1809	WB-F/192	AR
Sloan, John	065	1827	WB-C/2	AR
Sloan, John	085	N. D.	WB-D/78	AR
Sloan, Lettie N.	084	1893	WB-E/557	CTY
Sloan, Margaret	065	1815	WB-F/197	AR
Sloan, Mary	054	c1829	WB-2/90	AR
Sloan, Mary	054	c1803	WB-1/211	AR
Sloan, Nancy J.	065	1896	WB-M/509	AR
Sloan, R. M., Jr.	084	1888	WB-E/378	CTY
Sloan, Robert	035	1840	WB-A/547	AR
Sloan, Robert	065	1829	WB-D/37	
Sloan, Robert	065	1842	WB-H/77	AR
Sloan, Robert	065	1824	WB-E/113	AR
Sloan, Robert	054	c1793	WB-1/35	
Sloan, Sally	068	1898	WB-D/561	
Sloan, Samuel J.	065	1891	WB-L/555	AR
Sloan, Sara E.	085	1866	WB-K/386	AR
Sloan, Sarah	073	1825	WB-E/116	AR
Sloan, Sarah J.	046	1885	WB-E/409	AR
Sloan, Susan	035	1869	WB-4/20	AR
Sloan, T. A.	065	1879	WB-K/324	AR
Sloan, Thomas	104	1792	WB-1/327	AR
Sloan, William	072	1777	RW/L9	AR
Sloan, William B.	016	1872	WB-3/75	AR
Sloan, William L.	085	1899	WB-3/267	CTY
Sloane, William	TX	1862	091 WB-1/380	
Sloback, Nathan	028	1804	WB-B/203	
Slobock, Jacob	019	1756	SS 880/184	SS/AR
Slockum, Anthony	002	c1688	Orig. Only	SS/AR
Slocomb, John	028	c1759	Orig. Only	SS/AR
Slocomb, John	028	1722	Orig. Only	SS/AR
Slocomb, Samuel	008	1713	SS 875/8 & 53	SS/AR

Name	Co.	Date	Recorded Copy	Original
Slocum, Stephen	087	1828	WB-1/92	AR
Slocumb, J. C.	103	1881	WB-1/217	AR
Slocumb, Jesse	103	1821	RD-4/419	AR
Slocumb, Martha A.	087	1894	WB-3/556	AR
Slocumb, Samuel	035	c1767	WB-A/448	AR
Slocumb, William K.	087	1854	WB-1/446	AR
Slone, Anna	033	1858	WB-1/166	AR
Slone, John	104	1800	WB-2/29	AR
Sloop, Abraham	085	1897	WB-3/167	CTY
Sloop, Alex	054	1889	WB-5/292	CTY
Sloop, Caleb	003	1896	WB-B/344	AR
Sloop, Catharine	085	1867	WB-L/19	AR
Sloop, Conrad	085	1828	WB-H/429	AR
Sloop, John	085	1893	WB-2/549	CTY
Sloop, Peter	003	1863	Orig. Only	AR
Sloop, William	003	1889	WB-B/264	AR
Sloughter, Sarah	030	1801	WB-2/170	
Slover, Charles	028	1892	WB-F/37	
Slover, John	028	1843	WB-D/89	AR
Slover, Mary	028	1822	WB-C/2	
Sluder, E.	013	1885	WB-B/344	AR
Sluder, Elizabeth	085	1818	WB-G/527	AR
Sluder, Henry	085	c1799	WB-D/23	AR
Sluder, John	013	c1855	WB-A/166	
Sluder, John	013	1873	WB-B/71	AR
Sluder, William	102	1897	WB-A/124	AR
Slye, Susannah	028	1826	WB-C/274	
Small, Alonza F.	024	1885	WB-E/148	AR
Small, Amos	028	1767	Orig. Only	AR
Small, Benjamin	024	1839	WB-C/217	AR
Small, Benjamin	024	1821	WB-C/92	AR
Small, Benjamin	019	1756	SS 880/184	SS/AR
Small, Benjamin	019	1752	028 DB-5/257	
Small, Benjamin P.	074	1893	WB-1/120	
Small, Celah	077	1874	WB-H/56	AR
Small, David	024	1838	WB-C/213	AR
Small, Elizabeth	041	1864	WB-3/328	AR
Small, Elizabeth	024	1813	WB-C/20	AR
Small, Hannah	077	1853	WB-F/419	AR
Small, James	041	1800	WB-1/179	AR
Small, James A.	041	1860	WB-3/261	AR
Small, John	083	1863	WB-2/194	
Small, John	029	1844	WB-C/49	AR
Small, John	041	c1827	Orig. Only	AR
Small, Jonas	019	1820	WB-D/379	AR
Small, Joseph	019	1858	WB-A/223	AR
Small, Joseph	075	1812	WB-M1/239	AR
Small, Joseph	024	1755	WB-B/45	AR
Small, Joseph W.	022	1851	WB-C/289	AR
Small, Joshua	041	1790	WB-1/86	AR
Small, Lucinda	032	1900	WB-4/436	AR
Small, Obediah	075	1788	WB-K/169	AR
Small, Penelope	024	1873	WB-E/46	AR
Small, Reuben	057	1797	WB-A/167	AR
Small, Richard	081	1894	WB-16/317	AR
Small, Robert	084	1799	OW/142	AR
Small, Sally	070	c1874	WB-E/482	AR
Small, Stephen F.	019	1866	WB-B/21	AR
Small, William	077	1818	WB-F/7	AR
Small, William	077	1806	WB-E/240	AR
Small, William H.	075	1844	WB-N/184	AR
Smalledg, Ruth	072	1842	WB-2/40	AR
Smallwood, Charles	010	1880	WB-I/120	
Smallwood, Charles	010	1900	WB-K/14	
Smallwood, Edward F.	028	1881	WB-E/268	AR
Smallwood, Eli	028	1860	WB-D/331	AR
Smallwood, Elijah	092	1810	WB-3/96	AR
Smallwood, Harriet J.	010	1889	WB-I/276	AR
Smallwood, Julia O.	009	1886	WB-1/505	CTY
Smallwood, Lucy	028	1839	WB-C/432	AR
Smallwood, Mary	099	1826	RB-20/43	AR
Smallwood, Mary L.	010	1858	WB-H/68	AR
Smallwood, Orestes	084	1858	WB-C/286	CTY
Smallwood, Portia S.	009	1831	OB-B/91	AR
Smallwood, Robert W.	010	1891	WB-I/329	AR
Smallwood, William	044	1766	Orig. Only	CTY
Smally, Michal	047	1770	WB-1/254	
Smart, Andrew J.	065	1883	WB-K/515	AR
Smart, Elisha	065	1797	WB-F/168	AR
Smart, Joseph	086	1819	WB-C/115	AR
Smart, Mary	085	1816	WB-G/416	AR
Smart, Peter	022	1793	RB-1/139	AR
Smart, Susan	065	1852	WB-I/180	AR
Smart, Thomas	085	c1801	WB-D/71	AR
Smart, William	086	1828	WB-D/88	AR
Smart, William	086	1847	WB-E/175	AR
Smart, William	086	1893	WB-F/460	AR
Smartt, George A.	065	1827	WB-E/87	AR
Smartt, George W.	065	1809	WB-E/89	AR
Smartt, Mary	065	1833	WB-G/147	AR
Smartt, Mary	065	1796	WB-F/175	AR
Smartt, Thomas B.	065	1833	WB-G/142	AR
Smather, William	085	1823	WB-H/218	AR
Smathers, Levi	049	1896	WB-2/358	AR
Smaw, Elizabeth	009	1877	WB-1/180	CTY
Smaw, Henry	009	1795	OWB/308	AR
Smaw, Henry	009	1821	OB-A/305	AR
Smaw, Julett	009	1887	WB-1/415	CTY
Smaw, Mary	009	1853	OB-I/153	AR
Smaw, Mary	009	1815	OB-A/236	AR
Smaw, Mary	009	c1782	OWB/172	AR
Smaw, Rebecca	009	1845	OB-E/411	AR
Smaw, Sally	009	1858	OB-K/409	AR
Smaw, Thomas D.	009	1881	WB-1/283	CTY
Smedes, A. K.	103	1884	WB-1/298	AR
Smedes, Bennett	099	1899	WB-D/245	AR
Smedes, George	099	1867	RB-34/329	AR
Smedes, George M.	099	1885	WB-B/29	AR
Smedes, Sarah P.	099	1887	WB-B/188	AR
Smelly, Mary	100	1788	WB-5/13	AR
Smerdon, Catherine	098	1886	WB-A/46	CTY
Smewin, Herman	002	1673	Orig. Only	SS/AR
Smiley, James	029	1798	WB-A/10	AR
Smiley, Walter	065	1787	WB-F/161	AR
Smith, A. B.	081	1898	WB-16/526	AR
Smith, A. B.	046	1898	WB-G/61	AR
Smith, A. F.	032	1894	WB-4/235	AR
Smith, A. H.	096	1858	WB-3/54	AR
Smith, Abel	079	1893	WB-3/28	AR
Smith, Abner	099	1867	RB-34/328	AR
Smith, Abraham	096	c1799	Orig. Only	AR
Smith, Abraham	065	1871	WB-K/63	AR
Smith, Abraham	021	1864	WB-1/190	AR
Smith, Abram	010	1843	WB-G/358	AR
Smith, Absally N.	047	1822	WB-3/672	
Smith, Absalom P.	071	1834	WB-4/118	AR
Smith, Adam	073	1802	WB-D/59	AR
Smith, Adolphus	014	1876	WB-2/136	
Smith, Alethea	100	1881	WB-51/173	AR
Smith, Alexa. B.	005	1853	WB-C/67	AR

Name	Co.	Date	Recorded Copy	Original
Smith, Alexander	085	1831	WB-H/509	AR
Smith, Alexander	081	1829	WB-5/467	AR
Smith, Alexander	029	c1779	Orig. Only	AR
Smith, Alexander	083	c1811	WB-1/123	AR
Smith, Alexander	024	c1712	SS 875/54	
Smith, Alfred	027	1864	WB-A/93	AR
Smith, Alfred	032	c1843	WB-1/408	AR
Smith, Alfred	092	1874	WB-6/68	AR
Smith, Alvin L.	MS	1855	103 WB-1/324	103 AR
Smith, Ambrose	029	1789	Orig. Only	AR
Smith, Ambrose	022	1829	WB-B/160	AR
Smith, Amy	047	1784	WB-3/55	
Smith, Amy M.	044	1866	WB-22/553	CTY
Smith, Anderson	090	1897	WB-6/430	AR
Smith, Andrew	032	1884	WB-3/413	AR
Smith, Andrew	046	1872	WB-E/89	AR
Smith, Andrew	070	1760	SS 881/185	SS/AR
Smith, Andrew	085	1775	WB-A/204	AR
Smith, Andrew	040	c1863	Orig. Only	AR
Smith, Andrew T.	001	1897	WB-3/188	AR
Smith, Ann	047	1801	WB-3/362	
Smith, Ann	083	1864	WB-2/208	
Smith, Ann	032	1826	WB-1/62	AR
Smith, Ann	083	1847	WB-2/1	
Smith, Ann	044	1832	SC/03592	AR-Copy
Smith, Ann	070	1842	WB-AB/373	AR
Smith, Ann	028	1870	WB-E/34	AR
Smith, Ann B.	012	1846	WB-B/186	AR
Smith, Anna	077	1825	WB-F/100	AR-Nunc.
Smith, Anna P.	099	1896	WB-C/576	AR
Smith, Anne	044	1832	WB-12/352	CTY
Smith, Anne	020	1792	RB-B/438	AR
Smith, Annes P.	064	1894	WB-2/317	AR
Smith, Anthony	099	1881	WB-A/224	
Smith, Any	056	1797	WB-1/107	AR
Smith, Archibald	005	1862	WB-C/181	AR
Smith, Archibald	083	1871	WB-3/33	AR
Smith, Archibald	083	c1821	WB-1/197	AR
Smith, Archibald	029	1854	WB-C/292	AR
Smith, Archibald	016	1864	WB-2/100	
Smith, Archibald	029	1833	WB-B/218	AR
Smith, Archibald	083	1885	WB-3/344	
Smith, Aristides	047	1892	039 WB-U/559	039 AR
Smith, Aristides	047	1892	WB-7/49	AR
Smith, Arretta	037	1861	WB-G/210	AR
Smith, Arthur	103	1805	Orig. Only	AR
Smith, Arthur	028	1797	WB-B/25	AR
Smith, Arthur	047	1789	WB-3/169	
Smith, Arthur	103	1796	WI-B/188	AR
Smith, Asa	057	1835	WB-B/125	AR
Smith, B. J.	013	1886	WB-B/424	AR
Smith, Baily F.	089	1883	WB-2/95	AR
Smith, Barbara	083	1837	WB-1/312	AR
Smith, Barbary	099	1848	RB-26/355	AR
Smith, Barshaba	051	1856	WB-A/403	
Smith, Bazell	057	1812	WB-A/332	AR
Smith, Bazell	057	1812	Copy	028 AR
Smith, Benedicta	024	c1837	WB-C/199	AR
Smith, Benjamin	071	1841	WB-4/230	AR
Smith, Benjamin	056	1832	WB-1/482	AR
Smith, Benjamin	028	1800	WB-B/97	AR
Smith, Benjamin	005	1817	WB-2/151	AR
Smith, Benjamin	040	1883	WB-2/202	AR
Smith, Benjamin	012	1826	WB-B/137	AR
Smith, Benjamin	065	1866	WB-J/229	AR
Smith, Benjamin	103	1808	RD-1/80	AR
Smith, Benjamin	069	1799	WB-1/125	AR
Smith, Benjamin	103	1840	RD-8/28	AR
Smith, Benjamin H.	056	1845	Orig. Only	AR
Smith, Bennet	092	1816	WB-3/119	AR
Smith, Bennet	087	c1811	Orig. Only	AR
Smith, Bennett	069	1852	WB-1/527	AR
Smith, Betsey	020	1887	WB-A/521	CTY
Smith, Betty	100	1796	WB-9/24	AR
Smith, Britain	056	1793	WB-1/69	AR
Smith, Bryant	035	1882	WB-4/176	AR
Smith, Byrn	082	1841	WB-2/531	AR
Smith, C. A. V.	103	1879	WB-1/152	AR
Smith, C. C.	067	1878	WB-2/90	AR
Smith, Cain	070	1888	WB-F/175	AR
Smith, Caleb	072	1811	WB-A/121	AR
Smith, Callum	053	1858	WB-8/270	AR
Smith, Candis	022	1895	WB-F/1	AR
Smith, Caroline	099	1878	RB-35/416	AR
Smith, Casper	032	c1856	WB-2/168	AR
Smith, Casper	085	c1784	WB-D/60	
Smith, Casper M.	032	1855	WB-2/105	AR
Smith, Cassandra	028	1858	WB-D/303	AR
Smith, Catharine	085	1859	WB-K/273	AR
Smith, Catharine	082	1791	WB-1/38	AR
Smith, Catherin	044	1789	WB-2/120	CTY
Smith, Cattlet	092	1849	WB-4/302	
Smith, Charity	029	1818	WB-B/14	AR
Smith, Charity	069	c1836	Orig. Only	AR
Smith, Charles	092	c1827	Orig. Only	AR
Smith, Charles	041	1824	WB-2/223	AR
Smith, Charles	009	1735	OWB/30	AR
Smith, Charles	054	1840	WB-2/217	AR
Smith, Charles	032	1894	WB-4/230	AR
Smith, Charles	VA	1815	084 WB-B/44	084 CTY
Smith, Charles	024	1855	WB-C/381	AR
Smith, Charles C.	073	1857	WB-G/164	AR
Smith, Charles D.	085	1869	Orig. Only	CTY-Nunc.
Smith, Chauncy	035	1884	WB-4/233	AR
Smith, Chloe	047	1856	WB-5/24	
Smith, Christian	012	1834	Orig. Only	AR
Smith, Christian	090	1800	WB-1/158	AR
Smith, Christian	082	1883	WB-6/266	AR
Smith, Clara	085	1802	WB-D/42	AR
Smith, Clarky	103	1857	RD-12/359	AR
Smith, Clater	086	1822	WB-C/170	AR
Smith, Clement	046	1866	WB-D/305	AR
Smith, Conrad	073	1799	WB-C/155	
Smith, Cornelius	012	1898	WB-A/133	AR
Smith, Cullen	097	1858	WB-1/151	AR
Smith, Curtis	059	1882	WB-A/249	CTY
Smith, Cuthbert	VA	1780	Copy	085 AR
Smith, D. F.	060	1899	WB-5/106	AR
Smith, Daniel	029	1842	WB-B/364	AR
Smith, Daniel	005	1879	WB-D/81	AR
Smith, Daniel	028	1774	Orig. Only	AR
Smith, Daniel	085	c1807	WB-D/54	AR
Smith, Daniel	083	1832	WB-1/274	AR
Smith, Daniel	083	1825	WB-1/330	AR
Smith, Daniel	011	1878	WB-2/97	
Smith, Daniel H.	024	c1875	Orig. Only	AR
Smith, David	065	1823	WB-E/119	AR
Smith, David	085	c1784	WB-D/30	AR
Smith, David	087	1857	WB-1/506	AR

Name	Co.	Date	Recorded Copy	Original
Smith, David	032	1836	WB-1/281	AR
Smith, David	029	1758	DB-1/230	AR
Smith, David	029	c1775	Orig. Only	AR
Smith, David	089	1852	WB-1/98	
Smith, David	038	1890	WB-3/180	AR
Smith, David	032	1823	WB-1/13	AR
Smith, David	044	1788	WB-2/73	
Smith, David	040	1863	WB-1/151	AR
Smith, David	029	1849	WB-C/158	AR
Smith, David	032	1823	WB-1/18	AR
Smith, David	070	1828	WB-C/414	AR
Smith, David	040	1862	WB-1/146	
Smith, David	056	1806	WB-1/181	AR
Smith, David	029	1832	WB-B/217	AR
Smith, David	079	c1797	Orig. Only	AR-Copy
Smith, David	022	1793	RB-1/44	AR
Smith, David A.	005	1900	WB-D/470	AR
Smith, David J.	011	1855	WB-1/242	
Smith, Douglas M.	089	1877	WB-2/72	AR
Smith, Drew	033	1845	WB-1/65	AR
Smith, Drew	047	1762	WB-1/57	
Smith, Drew	047	1816	WB-3/594	
Smith, Drewry	029	1846	WB-C/92	AR
Smith, Drury	084	1822	WB-A/294	CTY
Smith, Dudley	030	1838	WB-4/44	
Smith, Duncan	029	1839	WB-B/299	AR
Smith, Duncan	029	1820	WB-B/33	AR
Smith, Duncan	083	1853	WB-2/61	
Smith, Eady	010	1898	WB-I/551	
Smith, Edmond	056	1760	WB-1/746	AR
Smith, Edmond	032	c1860	WB-2/201	
Smith, Edward	081	1899	WB-16/542	AR
Smith, Edward	N	1735	SS 877/170	SS/AR
Smith, Edward	075	c1690	Orig. Only	SS/AR
Smith, Edwin	099	1873	RB-35/202	AR
Smith, Effie C.	040	1890	WB-2/358	AR
Smith, Effy	083	1858	WB-2/123	AR
Smith, Eli	030	1792	WB-1/262	
Smith, Eli	046	1862	WB-D/139	AR
Smith, Eli	106	c1858	WB-1/62	AR
Smith, Elias	079	1895	WB-3/76	AR
Smith, Elias	079	1895	074 WB-1/158	074 AR
Smith, Elias	099	1860	Orig. Only	AR
Smith, Elijah	035	1831	WB-1/14	AR
Smith, Elijah	103	1844	RD-9/60	
Smith, Eliz. C.	016	1883	WB-3/391	AR
Smith, Eliza	103	1895	WB-2/104	AR
Smith, Elizabeth	028	1867	WB-D/455	AR
Smith, Elizabeth	077	1869	WB-H/35	AR
Smith, Elizabeth	028	1814	WB-C/88	
Smith, Elizabeth	057	1803	WB-A/270	AR
Smith, Elizabeth	032	1860	WB-2/178	AR
Smith, Elizabeth	071	1855	WB-5/139	AR
Smith, Elizabeth	065	1849	WB-I/153	AR
Smith, Elizabeth	071	1811	WB-3/41	AR-Nunc.
Smith, Elizabeth	077	1847	WB-F/336	AR
Smith, Elizabeth	085	1853	WB-K/151	AR
Smith, Elizabeth	084	1834	WB-B/98	CTY
Smith, Elizabeth	039	c1793	WB-A/114	AR
Smith, Elizabeth	099	1862	RB-32/429	AR
Smith, Elizabeth	099	1852	RB-22/468	AR
Smith, Elizabeth	045	1895	WB-1/380	AR
Smith, Elizabeth	041	1891	WB-4/318	AR
Smith, Elizabeth	041	1815	WB-2/109	AR
Smith, Elizabeth	079	1867	WB-1/168	AR

Name	Co.	Date	Recorded Copy	Original
Smith, Elizabeth	054	1845	WB-2/312	AR
Smith, Elizabeth	104	1896	WB-6/564	AR
Smith, Elizabeth	028	1840	WB-D/11	
Smith, Ellen	073	1866	WB-G/503	CTY
Smith, Emily C.	036	1898	WB-A/443	CTY
Smith, Ephraim	056	184	Est-23/580	
Smith, Ester	099	1821	RB-17/223	AR
Smith, Etheldred	056	1807	WB-1/207	AR
Smith, Eve	073	1818	WB-D/522	AR
Smith, Eveline	047	1891	WB-7/29	AR
Smith, Everett	082	1887	WB-6/356	AR
Smith, Ezekiel	103	1899	WB-2/238	AR
Smith, Ezekiel	103	1899	059 WB-B/249	059 CTY
Smith, Fannie E.	084	1882	WB-E/254	CTY
Smith, Fannie J.	001	1883	WB-2/216	AR
Smith, Fanny	065	c1861	WB-J/146	AR
Smith, Fanny I.	099	1863	RB-32/426	AR
Smith, Felix	020	1864	RB-T/46	
Smith, Flood	071	1798	WB-2/172	
Smith, Flora	083	1859	WB-2/146	AR
Smith, Francis	096	1842	WB-3/4	AR
Smith, Francis	005	1791	WB-A/7	
Smith, Francis J.	084	1864	WB-D/14	CTY
Smith, Frank	073	1900	WB-I/183	CTY
Smith, Frederick	081	1783	WB-1/7	
Smith, Frederick	046	1892	WB-F/185 & 215	AR
Smith, Frederick	046	1857	WB-C/491	AR
Smith, Frederick	032	c1862	WB-2/255	AR
Smith, Freeman	059	1897	WB-B/190	CTY
Smith, G. L.	054	1893	WB-5/465	CTY
Smith, Gasper	085	1834	WB-H/637	AR
Smith, Gasper	085	c1784	WB-B/59	AR
Smith, George	020	1880	WB-A/299	CTY
Smith, George	085	1866	WB-K/377	AR
Smith, George	085	1819	WB-G/518	AR
Smith, George	017	c1848	WB-A/57	AR
Smith, George	085	1814	WB-G/338	AR
Smith, George	020	1777	RB-A/23	AR
Smith, George	073	1842	WB-F/132	AR
Smith, George	035	1799	WB-A/437	AR
Smith, George	032	1849	WB-2/43	AR
Smith, George	020	1851	RB-Q/531	
Smith, George	010	1736	LGB-4/#63	SS/AR
Smith, George	047	1766	WB-1/182	
Smith, George	032	1844	WB-1/443	AR
Smith, George	071	1746	Orig. Only	SS/AR
Smith, George	060	1791	Orig. Only	AR
Smith, George	017	1878	WB-B/72	AR
Smith, George	090	1791	WB-1/19	
Smith, George A.	020	1860	RB-S/307	AR
Smith, George F.	032	1899	WB-4/418	AR
Smith, George F.	085	1875	WB-1/285	CTY
Smith, George F.	089	1870	WB-2/8	AR
Smith, George H.	SC	1849	040 WB-1/19	
Smith, George L.	085	1844	WB-I/207	AR
Smith, George M.	105	1894	WB-3/119	AR
Smith, George S.	046	1894	WB-F/337	AR
Smith, George W.	032	1879	WB-3/257	AR
Smith, Giles	103	1862	RD-13/508	AR
Smith, Gordon	084	1011	WB-A/89	CTY
Smith, Gulielmus	100	1814	WB-18/130	AR
Smith, Gustavus A.	084	1893	WB-E/586	CTY
Smith, Guy	044	1787	WB-2/12	CTY
Smith, Hardee J.	079	c1862	WB-1/152	AR

Name	Co.	Date	Recorded Copy	Original
Smith, Harriet C.	099	1857	RB-31/150	AR
Smith, Hellena	077	1880	WB-H/94	AR
Smith, Henry	VA	1813	071 WB-3/147	071 AR
Smith, Henry	079	1870	WB-2/39	AR
Smith, Henry	054	c1867	WB-4/1	AR
Smith, Henry	035	1845	Orig. Only	AR
Smith, Henry	017	1868	WB-B/1	AR
Smith, Henry	032	1866	WB-2/344	AR
Smith, Henry	060	1826	WB-1/34	AR
Smith, Henry	103	1835	RD-7/33	AR
Smith, Henry	041	1787	WB-1/65	AR
Smith, Henry	028	1748	SS 877/288	SS/AR
Smith, Henry	090	1813	WB-2/145	AR
Smith, Henry	045	1900	WB-1/405	
Smith, Henry D.	010	1816	WB-F/338	AR
Smith, Henry E.	087	1877	WB-3/153	AR
Smith, Henry M.	054	1857	WB-3/115	AR
Smith, Henry, Sr.	019	c1761	RB-A/10	
Smith, Hetty	060	1891	WB-4/458	AR
Smith, Hilliard	099	1882	WB-A/364	AR
Smith, Howard	029	1885	WB-E/374	AR
Smith, Hugh	006	c1863	WB-D/62	AR
Smith, Hugh	016	1832	PQS.5/203	
Smith, Hugh	065	1837	WB-E/174	AR
Smith, Hugh	104	1781	WB-1/70	AR
Smith, Huldah Ann	026	1878	WB-2/176	AR
Smith, Isaac	083	1857	WB-2/117	AR
Smith, Isaac	071	1892	WB-7/163	AR
Smith, Isaac J.	024	1885	WB-E/143	AR
Smith, Isabella	041	1882	WB-4/168	AR
Smith, Isaiah	059	1889	WB-A/548	CTY
Smith, Israel	077	1825	WB-F/80	AR
Smith, J. E. W.	097	1895	WB-2/500	AR
Smith, J. H.	013	1871	WB-B/40	AR
Smith, J. Henry	046	1900	WB-G/220	AR
Smith, J. M.	060	1874	WB-4/114	AR
Smith, J. W	040	1889	WB-2/331	AR
Smith, Jacob	051	1875	WB-C/156	AR
Smith, Jacob	046	1891	WB-F/85	AR
Smith, Jacob	092	c1827	WB-4/16	AR
Smith, Jacob	032	1894	WB-4/228	AR
Smith, Jacob	038	1883	WB-2/430	AR
Smith, Jacob	035	1897	WB-4/496	AR
Smith, Jacob	016	1883	WB-3/397	AR
Smith, Jacob	085	1847	Orig. Only	AR
Smith, Jacob G.	085	1855	WB-K/205	AR
Smith, James	104	1842	WB-4/268	AR
Smith, James	044	1833	WB-12/521	CTY
Smith, James	020	1878	WB-A/255	CTY
Smith, James	006	1870	WB-D/111	
Smith, James	028	1778	Orig. Only	AR
Smith, James	079	1877	WB-2/146	AR
Smith, James	044	1823	WB-9/188	
Smith, James	077	1784	096 WB-1/139	096 AR
Smith, James	099	1815	RB-15/221	
Smith, James	011	c1827	WB-1/49	
Smith, James	100	1784	WB-4/53	AR
Smith, James	083	1845	WB-1/449	AR
Smith, James	068	1848	WB-B/190	
Smith, James	065	1860	WB-J/79	AR
Smith, James	080	1863	WB-1/193	AR
Smith, James	028	1745	SS 877/24	SS/AR
Smith, James	099	1819	RB-15/3	AR
Smith, James	005	1852	WB-C/47	
Smith, James	077	1736	LGB-4/#51	SS/AR

Name	Co.	Date	Recorded Copy	Original
Smith, James	010	1882	WB-I/151	
Smith, James	005	1818	WB-2/152	AR
Smith, James	047	1762	WB-1/70	
Smith, James	039	1806	WB-C/46	
Smith, James	083	1855	WB-2/67	AR
Smith, James	032	1840	WB-1/338	AR
Smith, James	005	1835	WB-B/41	AR
Smith, James	047	1811	WB-3/514	
Smith, James	009	1749	SS 877/320	SS/AR
Smith, James	086	1818	WB-C/94	AR
Smith, James	075	1770	WB-H/112	AR
Smith, James	009	1834	OB-B/400	AR
Smith, James	028	1821	WB-C/197	
Smith, James	085	1844	WB-I/216	AR
Smith, James	085	1775	WB-A/215	AR
Smith, James	085	1826	WB-H/352	AR
Smith, James A.	104	1883	WB-6/225	AR
Smith, James A.	010	1893	WB-I/373	AR
Smith, James F.	103	1889	WB-1/466	AR
Smith, James G.	006	1872	WB-E/1	AR
Smith, James H.	103	1895	WB-2/91	AR
Smith, James M.	029	1886	WB-E/392	AR
Smith, James M.	087	1891	WB-3/485	AR
Smith, James M.	013	1856	WB-A/171	AR
Smith, James M.	013	1864	WB-A/234	
Smith, James McN.	082	1845	WB-3/27	AR
Smith, James R.	040	1891	WB-2/395	AR
Smith, James T.	077	1896	WB-H/291	AR
Smith, James T.	020	1877	WB-A/236	CTY
Smith, James T.	013	1887	WB-B/460	AR
Smith, James, Sr.	082	1791	WB-1/37	AR
Smith, Jane	099	1890	WB-B/481	AR
Smith, Jane	026	c1851	Orig. Only	AR
Smith, Jane	083	1826	WB-1/371	AR
Smith, Jane	071	1824	WB-3/310	AR
Smith, Jane	083	1864	WB-2/210	
Smith, Jane	065	1874	WB-K/161	AR
Smith, Jarvis	053	1802	RW-1/315	
Smith, Jarvis	104	c1809	WB-2/272	AR
Smith, Jennie L.	065	1898	WB-N/151	AR
Smith, Jeremiah	N	1720	Orig. Only	SS/AR
Smith, Jeremiah	083	1886	WB-3/387	AR
Smith, Jeremiah	005	1827	WB-A/131	AR
Smith, Jerry	079	1870	WB-2/27	AR
Smith, Jesse	103	1840	RD-8/83	AR
Smith, Jesse	028	1803	WB-B/177	AR
Smith, Jesse	005	1818	WB-2/153	AR-Nunc.
Smith, Jesse	046	1864	WB-D/199	AR
Smith, Jesse	032	1894	WB-4/207	AR
Smith, Jesse A.	056	1884	WB-3/365	AR
Smith, Jesse J.	063	1876	WB-3/106	
Smith, Jesse L.	079	1885	WB-2/339	AR
Smith, Joab	017	1859	WB-A/119	AR
Smith, Joab E.	017	1900	WB-B/328	AR
Smith, Joab P.	065	1864	WB-J/177	AR
Smith, Joanna	085	1827	WB-H/407	AR
Smith, Job	059	1879	WB-A/181	CTY
Smith, Joel L. G.	NY	1876	024 WB-E/82	024 AR
Smith, Joel, Sr.	047	1815	WB-3/564	
Smith, John	044	1833	WB-12/465	CTY
Smith, John	046	1872	WB-E/78	AR
Smith, John	028	1793	WB-A/290	AR-Nunc.
Smith, John	047	1801	WB-3/369	
Smith, John	065	1774	WB-F/151	AR
Smith, John	081	1796	WB-2/23	AR

Name	Co.	Date	Recorded Copy	Original
Smith, John	047	1784	WB-3/56	
Smith, John	044	1812	WB-7/250	
Smith, John	087	1834	WB-1/158	AR
Smith, John	029	1806	WB-A/86	AR
Smith, John	029	1871	Orig. Only	AR
Smith, John	005	1823	WB-A/82	AR
Smith, John	028	1840	WB-D/11	
Smith, John	046	1777	WB-A/339	AR
Smith, John	039	c1794	WB-A/122	
Smith, John	005	1854	WB-C/87	AR
Smith, John	029	c1816	Orig. Only	AR
Smith, John	003	1847	Orig. Only	AR
Smith, John	029	1859	WB-C/405	AR
Smith, John	044	1771	Orig. Only	CTY
Smith, John	053	c1772	Orig. Only	SS/AR
Smith, John	011	c1792	WB-1/401	
Smith, John	024	1734	SS 876/294	SS/AR
Smith, John	022	1815	WB-A/246	AR
Smith, John	024	1869	WB-E/7	AR
Smith, John	079	1886	WB-2/374	AR
Smith, John	063	1795	WB-1/214	
Smith, John	077	1798	WB-E/90	AR
Smith, John	039	c1787	WB-A/25	AR
Smith, John	029	1785	Orig. Only	AR
Smith, John	071	1801	WB-2/220	AR
Smith, John	046	1840	WB-C/53	AR
Smith, John	072	1804	WB-A/121	AR
Smith, John	011	1782	WB-2/294	
Smith, John	040	1848	WB-1/4	
Smith, John	024	1784	WB-B/41	AR
Smith, John	020	1779	RB-A/83	AR
Smith, John	044	1889	WB-24/67	CTY
Smith, John	010	1729	Orig. Only	SS/AR
Smith, John	029	1851	WB-C/185	AR
Smith, John	014	1890	WB-2/419	CTY
Smith, John	GA	c1798	063 WB-1/398	
Smith, John	084	1798	OW/16	AR
Smith, John	028	1770	Orig. Only	AR
Smith, John	077	1815	WB-E/417	AR
Smith, John	087	1881	WB-3/216	AR
Smith, John	083	1880	WB-3/199	AR
Smith, John	028	1770	Orig. Only	SS/AR
Smith, John	056	1829	WB-1/426	AR
Smith, John	032	1831	WB-1/164	AR
Smith, John	012	1794	Orig. Only	AR
Smith, John	005	1824	WB-A/103	AR
Smith, John	040	c1852	WB-1/52	AR
Smith, John	077	1835	WB-F/245	AR
Smith, John	029	1795	Orig. Only	AR
Smith, John	053	1774	RW-1/46	AR
Smith, John	009	1871	WB-1/90	AR
Smith, John	086	1814	WB-C/12	AR
Smith, John	047	1772	WB-1/324	
Smith, John	085	c1800	WB-D/63	AR
Smith, John	099	1843	RB-25/342	AR
Smith, John	087	1883	WB-3/267	AR
Smith, John	019	c1784	WB-D/350	AR
Smith, John A.	046	1847	WB-C/280	AR
Smith, John A.	022	1863	WB-D/101	AR
Smith, John B.	065	1868	WB-J/254	AR
Smith, John Blair	016	1846	WB-1/124	
Smith, John C.	029	1876	WB-E/155	AR
Smith, John C.	017	1895	WB-B/256	AR
Smith, John C.	020	1860	RB-S/181	AR
Smith, John C.	029	1891	WB-E/509	AR
Smith, John D.	020	1893	WB-B/144	CTY
Smith, John E.	103	1862	RD-13/463	AR
Smith, John F.	028	1831	WB-C/331	
Smith, John F.	038	1894	WB-3/458	AR
Smith, John G.	029	1871	WB-E/40	AR
Smith, John G.	044	c1828	SC/03069	AR-Copy
Smith, John G.	044	c1828	WB-14/356	CTY
Smith, John H. C.	069	1875	WB-5/9	AR
Smith, John J.	105	1890	WB-2/530	AR
Smith, John L.	004	1899	WB-A/225	AR
Smith, John M.	056	1815	WB-1/21	Nunc.
Smith, John M.	097	1863	WB-1/203	AR
Smith, John M.	073	1892	WB-H/573	CTY
Smith, John Pryor	044	1823	WB-9/185	CTY
Smith, John S.	028	1830	WB-C/329	AR
Smith, John W.	087	1891	WB-3/472	AR
Smith, John W.	105	1871	WB-2/83	AR
Smith, John, Sr.	053	1748	SS 877/153	SS/AR
Smith, John, Sr.	054	c1812	WB-1/300	AR
Smith, John, Sr.	010	1783	WB-C/54	AR
Smith, John, Sr.	021	1847	WB-1/61	AR
Smith, John, Sr.	090	1857	WB-4/308	
Smith, John, Sr.	056	1813	WB-1/349 & 408	AR
Smith, John, Sr.	011	c1845	WB-1/112	
Smith, John, Sr.	054	c1820	WB-1A/1	AR
Smith, John, Sr.	085	1854	WB-K/177	AR
Smith, Johnathan	024	1846	WB-C/272	AR
Smith, Jonathan	016	c1872	WB-3/59	
Smith, Jonathan	011	1823	WB-2/351	
Smith, Jonathan	103	1837	RD-7/205	AR
Smith, Jones	035	1832	WB-1/22	AR
Smith, Jones	035	1887	WB-4/305	AR
Smith, Joseph	092	1783	WB-2/4A	AR
Smith, Joseph	099	1873	RB-35/222	AR
Smith, Joseph	085	1801	WB-D/22	AR
Smith, Joseph	065	1803	WB-F/179	AR
Smith, Joseph	103	1785	Orig. Only	AR
Smith, Joseph	077	1733	SS 876/314	SS/AR
Smith, Joseph	075	c1857	WB-M2/44	AR
Smith, Joseph	037	1764	WB-A/132	AR
Smith, Joseph	016	1872	Orig. Only	AR-Nunc.
Smith, Joseph	077	1880	WB-H/97	AR
Smith, Joseph	046	1813	WB-A/371	AR
Smith, Joseph	028	1827	WB-C/294	AR
Smith, Joseph	024	c1783	WB-A/191	AR
Smith, Joseph	041	1829	WB-2/282	AR
Smith, Joseph	071	1817	WB-3/191	AR
Smith, Joseph M.	039	1841	WB-L/36	AR
Smith, Joseph M.	045	1895	WB-1/323	AR
Smith, Joseph P.	SC	1863	005 WB-C/188	005 AR
Smith, Joshua	079	1865	WB-1/127	AR
Smith, Josiah	077	1838	WB-F/273	AR
Smith, Josiah	012	c1859	WB-B/27	AR-Copy
Smith, Katherine	020	1884	WB-A/416	CTY
Smith, Keziah	063	1846	WB-2/324	
Smith, Kinchen	103	1862	RD-13/440	AR
Smith, L. Turner	036	1895	WB-A/338	CTY
Smith, Laben	030	1796	WB-2/72	
Smith, Larkin	092	1876	WB-6/83	AR
Smith, Larkin	099	1892	WB-C/76	AR
Smith, Laurence	071	1812	WB-3/70	AR
Smith, Lavinia	089	1862	WB-1/239	
Smith, Lazarus	079	c1858	Orig. Only	AR
Smith, Lemon	059	1893	WB-B/79	CTY

Name	Co.	Date	Recorded Copy	Original
Smith, Lemuel	044	1862	Copy	078 AR
Smith, Lemuel	044	1862	WB-21/560	CTY
Smith, Lemuel	022	1822	WB-B/43	AR
Smith, Leonard	090	1899	WB-6/508	AR
Smith, Leonard	085	c1818	Copy	032 AR
Smith, Leonard	081	1806	WB-3/46	AR
Smith, Leonard	073	1826	WB-E/121	AR
Smith, Leonard	085	1819	WB-G/531	AR
Smith, Leonard T.	073	1862	WB-G/401	CTY
Smith, Leroy	044	1857	WB-20/434	CTY
Smith, Levi	030	1715/6	Orig. Only	SS/AR
Smith, Levi	033	1840	WB-1/31	AR
Smith, Lewis	010	1866	WB-H/177	AR
Smith, Lewis F.	100	1836	WB-35/339	AR
Smith, Lewis G.	044	1891	WB-24/167	CTY
Smith, Lewis S.	049	1896	WB-2/370	AR
Smith, Lillian R.	065	1897	WB-N/75	AR
Smith, Louise M.	003	1896	WB-B/349	AR
Smith, Lovedy	029	1858	WB-C/395	AR
Smith, Lucinda	056	1857	WB-1/728	AR
Smith, Lucretia	009	1818	OB-A/283	AR
Smith, Lucritia	053	1801	RW-1/337	
Smith, Lucy	011	c1795	WB-1/399	
Smith, Lucy P.	099	1871	RB-35/143	AR
Smith, Lunsford	047	1838	WB-4/171	
Smith, M.	077	1828	WB-F/159	AR
Smith, M. M.	026	1891	WB-2/430	AR
Smith, M. T.	044	1864	WB-22/180	CTY
Smith, M. T. A.	103	1881	WB-1/215	AR
Smith, Malachi	063	1819	WB-2/65	
Smith, Malachi	018	1845	WB-C/306	
Smith, Malcom	082	1796	WB-1/62	AR
Smith, Mallory	092	c1838	WB-4/149	
Smith, Margaret	017	1874	WB-B/45	AR
Smith, Margaret	032	1831	WB-1/176	AR
Smith, Margaret	083	1855	WB-2/108	
Smith, Margaret	053	1809	RW-1/435	AR
Smith, Margaret	003	1887	WB-B/198	AR
Smith, Margaret	011	c1839	WB-1/80	
Smith, Margaret J.	083	1896	WB-4/95	
Smith, Mariah	104	1894	WB-6/515	AR
Smith, Mark	045	1893	WB-1/230	AR
Smith, Mark A.	090	1879	WB-6/108	AR
Smith, Mark N.	103	1886	WB-1/362	AR
Smith, Marmaduke	051	1859	WB-B/19	
Smith, Martha	047	1896	WB-7/205	AR
Smith, Martha	020	1868	RB-T/365	CTY
Smith, Martha	024	c1760	WB-B/21	AR
Smith, Martha	059	1881	WB-A/216	CTY
Smith, Martha	056	1849	WB-1/612	AR
Smith, Martha A.	105	1900	WB-3/394	AR
Smith, Martha I.	040	1887	WB-2/294	AR
Smith, Martin	022	1861	WB-D/74	AR
Smith, Mary	029	1886	WB-E/399	AR
Smith, Mary	038	1883	WB-2/464	AR
Smith, Mary	084	1826	WB-A/307	CTY
Smith, Mary	047	1890	WB-6/569	AR
Smith, Mary	083	1884	WB-3/319	AR
Smith, Mary	044	1828	WB-10/407	CTY
Smith, Mary	065	1817	WB-E/111	AR
Smith, Mary	024	1719	SS 875/225	
Smith, Mary	011	1871	WB-2/53	
Smith, Mary	009	c1787	OWB/215	AR
Smith, Mary	020	1884	WB-A/416	CTY
Smith, Mary	028	1822	WB-C/210	AR
Smith, Mary	090	1840	WB-4/62	AR
Smith, Mary	070	1829	WB-C/417	AR
Smith, Mary	077	1834	WB-F/228	AR
Smith, Mary	065	1835	WB-G/200	AR
Smith, Mary	083	1834	WB-1/286	AR
Smith, Mary	075	1797	Orig. Only	AR
Smith, Mary	024	1884	WB-E/132	AR
Smith, Mary	012	1787	WB-B/139	AR
Smith, Mary	032	1829	Orig. Only	AR
Smith, Mary	005	1859	WB-C/141	AR
Smith, Mary	053	1784	RW-1/124	AR
Smith, Mary	063	1785	WB-1/112	
Smith, Mary A.	103	1892	WB-1/566	AR
Smith, Mary A.	040	1891	WB-2/405	AR
Smith, Mary Ann	099	c1863	WB-C/9	AR
Smith, Mary C.	065	1863	WB-J/182	AR
Smith, Mary E.	056	1890	WB-3/522	AR
Smith, Mary F.	089	1892	WB-2/240	AR
Smith, Mary F.	090	1898	WB-6/480	AR
Smith, Mary H.	065	1852	WB-I/190	AR
Smith, Mary Jane	012	1858	WB-B/19	AR
Smith, Mary O.	099	1900	WB-D/347	AR
Smith, Mary R.	073	1885	022 WB-E/377	
Smith, Mary R.	073	1885	WB-H/394	CTY
Smith, Mary R.	073	c1881	Copy	099 AR
Smith, Mathias	016	1886	WB-3/488	AR
Smith, Matthew	065	1814	WB-F/195	AR
Smith, Michael	085	c1791	WB-C/24	AR
Smith, Michael	085	c1776	WB-A/241	AR
Smith, Michael	032	1842	WB-1/387	AR
Smith, Miles	047	1840	WB-4/189	
Smith, Milley	071	1813	WB-3/93	AR
Smith, Mills E.	051	c1855	WB-B/13	
Smith, Mimcy V.	059	1899	WB-B/234	CTY
Smith, Mordecai	075	1814	WB-M1/262	AR
Smith, Moses	047	1853	WB-4/352	
Smith, Moses	047	1864	WB-5/112	AR-Copy
Smith, Moses	021	1867	WB-1/251	AR
Smith, Moses	038	1869	WB-2/8	AR
Smith, Moses	032	1877	WB-3/226	AR
Smith, Mourning	069	1781	WB-1/8	AR
Smith, N. E.	072	N. D.	Orig. Only	AR
Smith, N. J.	091	1893	WB-1/31	CTY
Smith, N. J.	103	1900	WB-2/280	AR
Smith, N. J.	067	1890	WB-2/296	AR
Smith, Nancy	020	c1845	Orig. Only	AR
Smith, Nancy	022	1892	WB-E/509	AR
Smith, Nancy	024	1851	WB-C/317	AR
Smith, Nancy	047	1866	WB-5/144	
Smith, Nancy	085	1889	WB-2/349	CTY
Smith, Nancy	084	1846	WB-C/39	CTY
Smith, Nancy	028	1855	WB-D/244	AR
Smith, Nancy	056	1848	WB-1/606	AR
Smith, Nancy	056	1889	WB-3/495	
Smith, Nancy P.	081	1897	WB-16/425	
Smith, Nathan	028	1824	WB-C/226 & 255	AR
Smith, Nathan	056	1809	WB-1/217	AR
Smith, Nathan	085	c1803	WB-D/38	AR
Smith, Nathaniel	086	1820	WB-C/143	AR
Smith, Neill	068	1805	WB-A/244	
Smith, Neill	083	c1821	WB-1/233	AR
Smith, Nicholas	046	c1846	Orig. Only	AR
Smith, Nicholas	082	1828	WB-1/293	AR
Smith, Nicholes	009	1751	SS 879/35	SS/AR

Name	Co.	Date	Recorded Copy	Original
Smith, Obed	046	1864	WB-D/228	AR
Smith, Obediah M.	085	1844	WB-I/202	
Smith, Oliver	053	c1758	OB-A/36	
Smith, Oma	033	1849	WB-1/98	AR
Smith, Orrin A.	099	1891	WB-B/569	AR
Smith, Oswell A.	099	1886	WB-B/150	AR
Smith, Owen	013	1881	WB-B/252	AR
Smith, Owen	013	1881	027 WB-2/131	027 AR
Smith, P. H.	039	1857	WB-0/377	AR-Nunc.
Smith, Parham	089	1877	WB-2/55	
Smith, Parker	041	1881	WB-4/140	AR
Smith, Patrick	083	1816	WB-1/171	
Smith, Penelope	099	1870	RB-35/100	AR
Smith, Pennina	105	1899	WB-3/379	
Smith, Permenos	030	1787	WB-1/213	
Smith, Peter	073	c1812	WB-D/364	AR
Smith, Peter	081	1799	WB-2/44	AR
Smith, Peter	085	1767	WB-A/150	AR
Smith, Peter	054	1899	WB-6/256	CTY
Smith, Peter	090	1889	WB-6/217	AR
Smith, Peter	029	1824	WB-B/120	AR
Smith, Peter	032	1836	WB-1/271	AR
Smith, Peter	047	1805	WB-3/444	
Smith, Peter	020	1797	RB-C/249	AR
Smith, Peter	046	1813	WB-A/371	AR
Smith, Peter	047	1794	WB-3/233	
Smith, Peter	010	1791	WB-D/165	AR
Smith, Peter W.	032	1824	WB-1/32	AR
Smith, Phereby	103	1856	RD-12/189	AR
Smith, Polly	103	1864	RD-13/738	AR
Smith, Polly Ann	056	1892	WB-2/130	
Smith, Prier	103	1857	RD-12/245	AR
Smith, Priscilla	100	1792	WB-6/164	AR
Smith, Prudence	036	1889	WB-A/165	CTY
Smith, R. H.	056	1845	Est-20/179	
Smith, R. T.	071	1898	WB-7/376	AR
Smith, Rachel	032	1846	WB-1/483	AR
Smith, Rachel	071	1780	WB-1/235	
Smith, Rachel	103	1837	RD-7/286	AR
Smith, Rachel	026	1851	WB-1/129	AR
Smith, Randolph	100	1837	WB-36/73	AR
Smith, Rebecca	024	c1793	WB-A/293	AR
Smith, Reuben	044	1823	WB-9/220	CTY
Smith, Rhoda	044	c1850	Orig. Only	CTY
Smith, Richard	085	1841	WB-I/110	Nunc.
Smith, Richard	084	1866	WB-D/69	CTY
Smith, Richard	041	1835	WB-2/359	AR
Smith, Richard	037	1757	SS 879/199	SS/AR
Smith, Richard	047	1838	WB-4/168	AR-Copy
Smith, Richard	085	N. D.	Orig. Only	AR
Smith, Richard	090	1890	WB-6/238	AR
Smith, Richard	103	1829	RD-6/40	AR
Smith, Richard	099	1816	RB-12/269	AR
Smith, Richard	011	c1784	WB-2/268	
Smith, Richard	085	c1795	WB-D/55	AR
Smith, Richard	099	1852	RB-28/164	AR
Smith, Richard	099	1819	RB-15/243	AR
Smith, Richard	020	1859	RB-S/103	AR
Smith, Richard	075	1751	Orig. Only	SS/AR
Smith, Richard	028	1840	WB-D/10	
Smith, Richard	071	1756	SS 880/43	SS/AR
Smith, Richd.	028	1712/3	PQS.1/5	
Smith, Richmond	067	1881	WB-2/206	AR
Smith, Robert	077	1693	SS 874.2/38	SS/AR
Smith, Robert	070	1863	WB-D/112	AR

Name	Co.	Date	Recorded Copy	Original
Smith, Robert	085	c1785	WB-C/173	AR
Smith, Robert	024	c1782	WB-A/198	AR
Smith, Robert	041	1831	WB-2/296	AR
Smith, Robert	073	c1772	WB-A/121	
Smith, Robert	029	1813	WB-A/187	AR
Smith, Robert	090	1802	WB-2/32	AR
Smith, Robert	020	1870	WB-A/47	CTY
Smith, Robert	040	1851	WB-1/36	
Smith, Robert	046	1778	WB-A/336	AR
Smith, Robert	089	1848	WB-1/66	AR
Smith, Robert	010	1726	SS 876/53	SS/AR
Smith, Robert A.	047	1853	WB-4/335	
Smith, Robert H.	009	1841	OB-D/169	AR
Smith, Robert H.	085	1871	WB-1/79	CTY
Smith, Robert R.	047	1821	WB-3/662	
Smith, Robert W.	016	1836	PQS.5/393	
Smith, Robinson	011	1882	WB-2/150	
Smith, Roger	035	1795	WB-A/440	AR
Smith, Rosa	038	1895	WB-3/511	AR
Smith, Rosanna	096	1856	WB-3/42	AR
Smith, Rufus	103	1890	WB-1/541	AR
Smith, Rufus H.	084	1890	WB-E/431	CTY
Smith, Ruth	028	1815	WB-C/98	
Smith, S. A.	027	1890	WB-2/84	
Smith, Sallie	079	1888	WB-2/452	AR
Smith, Sally	044	1841	WB-15/109	CTY
Smith, Sally	103	1825	RD-5/206	AR
Smith, Sally	103	1839	RD-7/558	AR
Smith, Sampson	022	1895	WB-E/585	AR
Smith, Samuel	041	1800	WB-1/177	AR
Smith, Samuel	019	1813	WB-D/369	AR
Smith, Samuel	011	c1786	WB-1/594	
Smith, Samuel	020	1816	RB-G/303	
Smith, Samuel	077	1833	WB-F/216	AR
Smith, Samuel	053	1781	RW-1/97	
Smith, Samuel	019	1816	WB-D/377	AR
Smith, Samuel	056	c1795	WB-1/83	AR
Smith, Samuel	077	1789	WB-C/389	AR
Smith, Samuel	099	1815	Orig. Only	AR
Smith, Samuel	047	1797	WB-3/285	
Smith, Samuel	084	c1837	WB-B/223	CTY
Smith, Samuel	044	1800	WB-5/101	CTY
Smith, Samuel	100	1836	WB-35/311	AR
Smith, Samuel	044	1796	WB-4/20	
Smith, Samuel	056	c1779	WB-1/83	AR
Smith, Samuel	105	1882	WB-2/285	AR
Smith, Samuel	100	1821	WB-23/211	AR
Smith, Samuel	056	1809	WB-1/216	
Smith, Samuel	038	1876	WB-2/294	AR
Smith, Samuel	073	1858	WB-G/211	CTY
Smith, Samuel	085	c1826	WB-H/481	AR
Smith, Samuel E.	041	1886	WB-4/247	AR
Smith, Samuel H.	078	1843	WI-15/224	AR
Smith, Samuel W.	044	1884	WB-23/508	CTY
Smith, Samuel W.	027	1819	WB-A/43	AR-Nunc.
Smith, Sanders	103	1846	RD-9/308	AR
Smith, Sarah	100	1784	WB-4/63	AR
Smith, Sarah	070	1862	WB-D/88	AR
Smith, Sarah	005	1833	WB-B/30	AR
Smith, Sarah	103	1815	RD-3/291	AR
Smith, Sarah	099	1831	RB-22/120	AR
Smith, Sarah	040	1900	WB-3/79	AR
Smith, Sarah	050	1894	WB-2/196	
Smith, Sarah	030	1725	SS 876/33	SS/AR
Smith, Sarah	063	1825	WB-2/107	

Name	Co.	Date	Recorded Copy	Original
Smith, Sarah	030	1792	WB-2/8	
Smith, Sarah	029	1892	WB-E/527	AR
Smith, Sarah	045	1870	WB-1/8	
Smith, Sarah	005	1843	WB-B/165	AR
Smith, Sarah A.	013	1882	Orig. Only	AR
Smith, Sarah Ann	063	1884	WB-3/246	
Smith, Sarah Ann	099	1852	RB-27/399	AR
Smith, Sarah C.	064	1898	WB-2/447	AR
Smith, Sarah Dry	012	1822	WB-B/127	
Smith, Sarah E.	024	1886	WB-E/151	AR
Smith, Sarah E.	099	1894	WB-C/206	AR
Smith, Sarah Jane	083	1885	WB-3/350	
Smith, Sarah R.	029	1864	WB-D/71	AR
Smith, Sarah S.	020	1844	RB-P/132	
Smith, Sary	085	1844	WB-I/242	AR
Smith, Shadrick	047	c1865	WB-5/133	
Smith, Sidney	073	1867	WB-G/517	CTY
Smith, Sidney A.	056	1867	WB-2/97	AR
Smith, Silas	010	1829	WB-G/191	AR
Smith, Silla	099	1899	WB-D/252	AR
Smith, Solomon	017	c1860	WB-A/123	AR
Smith, Solomon	078	1888	WB-19/223	AR
Smith, Spias S.	103	1877	WB-1/112	AR
Smith, Stark B.	010	1867	WB-H/184	AR
Smith, Stephen	073	1828	WB-E/160	AR
Smith, Stephen	083	1892	WB-4/268	AR
Smith, Stephen	011	c1784	WB-2/274	
Smith, Sterling	047	1885	WB-6/415	AR
Smith, Sumner J.	GA	1869	Copy	026 AR
Smith, Susan	047	1895	WB-7/158	AR
Smith, Susan	003	1885	WB-B/166	AR
Smith, Susan Ann	054	1889	WB-5/305	CTY
Smith, Susanah	089	1885	WB-2/129	AR
Smith, Sylvester	099	1891	WB-B/563	AR
Smith, T. L.	083	1891	WB-3/544	
Smith, T. M.	027	c1895	Orig. Only	AR
Smith, Tabitha	103	1849	RD-10/224	AR
Smith, Tellitha	071	1842	WB-4/255	AR
Smith, Thomas	019	1787	WB-D/351	AR
Smith, Thomas	028	1808	WB-B/328	AR
Smith, Thomas	103	1850	RD-10/431	AR
Smith, Thomas	084	c1797	OW/15	AR-Copy
Smith, Thomas	009	1753	Copy	SS/AR
Smith, Thomas	020	1883	WB-A/398	CTY
Smith, Thomas	041	1820	WB-2/171	AR
Smith, Thomas	028	1781	Orig. Only	AR
Smith, Thomas	011	c1836	WB-1/50	
Smith, Thomas	005	c1751	WB-1/1	
Smith, Thomas	012	1830	WB-B/159	AR
Smith, Thomas	064	1889	WB-2/194	AR
Smith, Thomas	065	1812	Orig. Only	AR
Smith, Thomas	002	c1706	Orig. Only	SS/AR
Smith, Thomas	084	1854	WB-C/202	CTY
Smith, Thomas	096	c1763	WB-1/45	AR
Smith, Thomas	028	1853	WB-D/202	AR
Smith, Thomas	028	1806	WB-B/228	AR
Smith, Thomas	044	1790	WB-2/159	CTY
Smith, Thomas	047	1798	WB-3/317	
Smith, Thomas	073	1798	WB-C/124	AR
Smith, Thomas	037	1757	SS 879/205	SS/AR
Smith, Thomas	019	1796	WB-D/357	AR
Smith, Thomas	071	1809	WB-3/22	AR
Smith, Thomas	047	1784	WB-3/66	
Smith, Thomas C.	011	1874	WB-2/80	
Smith, Thomas C.	082	1838	WB-2/70	AR

Name	Co.	Date	Recorded Copy	Original
Smith, Thomas M.	020	1864	RB-T/61	CTY
Smith, Thomas R.	103	1870	WB-1/4	AR
Smith, Thompson	038	c1844	WB-1/78	AR
Smith, Thompson	090	1821	WB-3/73	AR
Smith, Toliver	080	1889	Orig. Only	AR
Smith, Treasy	010	1865	WB-H/151	AR
Smith, Turner	099	1808	RB-7/316	AR
Smith, Upchurch	099	1889	WB-B/367	AR
Smith, W. H.	099	1895	WB-C/422	AR
Smith, W. N. H.	099	1889	WB-B/387	AR
Smith, W. W.	084	1895	WB-F/28	CTY
Smith, Warner	020	1874	WB-A/172	CTY
Smith, Washington	079	1888	WB-2/455	AR
Smith, Wesley	014	1885	WB-2/306	CTY
Smith, Whitman H.	089	1892	WB-2/233	AR
Smith, Wilie	073	1886	WB-H/401	
Smith, Wilie	103	1887	WB-1/402	AR
Smith, William	085	1883	WB-2/82	CTY
Smith, William	054	1879	WB-4/308	CTY
Smith, William	046	1802	WB-A/358	AR
Smith, William	085	1851	WB-K/129	AR
Smith, William	075	1734	SS 876/299	SS/AR
Smith, William	079	1874	WB-2/99	AR
Smith, William	024	1743	SS 881/284	SS/AR
Smith, William	012	c1866	WB-B/21	AR
Smith, William	092	1818	WB-3/136	AR
Smith, William	065	1832	WB-G/100	AR
Smith, William	054	1867	WB-3/200	AR
Smith, William	047	1791	WB-3/197	
Smith, William	020	1831	RB-L/631	AR
Smith, William	083	c1882	Orig. Only	AR-Copy
Smith, William	086	1858	WB-E/352 & 473	AR
Smith, William	096	1742	Orig. Only	SS/AR
Smith, William	075	1724	SS 876/7	SS/AR
Smith, William	089	1845	WB-1/34	AR
Smith, William	051	1763	Orig. Only	AR-Copy
Smith, William	011	c1798	WB-1/396	
Smith, William	015	1765	RB-I/19	AR
Smith, William	085	1836	WB-H/673	AR
Smith, William	068	1826	WB-B/43	
Smith, William	047	1792	WB-3/206	
Smith, William	100	1818	WB-21/217	AR
Smith, William	057	1788	WB-A/73	AR
Smith, William	016	1852	WB-1/207	
Smith, William	065	1808	WB-F/191	AR
Smith, William	099	1821	RB-17/63	
Smith, William	065	1883	WB-K/548	AR
Smith, William	047	1777	WB-2/59	
Smith, William	046	1829	WB-C/25	AR
Smith, William	085	1801	WB-D/69	AR
Smith, William	024	1759	WB-B/59	AR
Smith, William	056	1851	WB-1/644	AR
Smith, William	072	1811	WB-A/129	AR
Smith, William	071	1761	WB-1/49	
Smith, William	024	1755	SS 880/92	SS/AR
Smith, William	103	1832	RD-6/300	AR
Smith, William	092	1781	WB-1/145	AR
Smith, William	020	1832	RB-M/86	AR
Smith, William	073	1820	WB-D/566	AR
Smith, William	029	1872	WB-E/66	AR
Smith, William	028	1769	Orig. Only	AR
Smith, William	099	1823	RB-18/117	AR
Smith, William	090	c1795	WB-2/43	AR
Smith, William	096	1791	Orig. Only	AR

Name	Co.	Date	Recorded Copy	Original
Smith, William	028	1749	SS 877/256	SS/AR
Smith, William	073	1783	WB-A/280	AR
Smith, William	046	1879	WB-E/262	AR
Smith, William	024	c1854	WB-C/369	AR
Smith, William	030	1865	WB-4/249	AR
Smith, William	003	1864	Orig. Only	AR
Smith, William	071	1786	WB-1/365	AR
Smith, William	022	1802	WB-A/72	AR
Smith, William	103	1877	WB-1/121	AR
Smith, William	028	1800	WB-B/107	AR
Smith, William A.	099	1823	RB-18/250	AR
Smith, William A.	099	1837	RB-24/49	AR
Smith, William B.	006	1864	WB-D/66	AR
Smith, William G.	044	1816	WB-7/665	CTY
Smith, William H.	069	1852	WB-1/528	AR
Smith, William H.	089	1873	WB-2/126	AR
Smith, William H.	087	1873	WB-3/66	
Smith, William H.	047	1895	WB-7/159	AR
Smith, William H.	020	1889	WB-A/551	CTY
Smith, William H.	009	1848	OB-F/500	AR
Smith, William J.	029	1877	WB-E/175	AR
Smith, William L.	101	1879	WB-A/31	
Smith, William P.	082	1851	WB-4/49	AR
Smith, William R.	046	c1896	Orig. Only	AR
Smith, William R.	047	1872	WB-6/70	AR
Smith, William R.	047	1845	WB-4/244	
Smith, William T.	029	1855	WB-C/330	AR
Smith, Willie	099	1881	WB-A/278	AR
Smith, Willis	073	1889	WB-H/463	CTY
Smith, Wincie J.	089	1889	WB-2/188	AR
Smith, Winifred	028	1878	WB-E/200	AR
Smith, Winnaford	011	1852	WB-1/199	
Smith, Wright	103	1872	WB-1/51	AR
Smith, Zaccheus	035	1863	WB-3/80	AR
Smith, Zachariah	084	c1796	OW/162	AR
Smith, Zacharias	047	1823	WB-3/681	
Smith, Zacheriah	099	1821	RB-17/223	AR
Smith, Zilpha	045	1879	WB-1/44	AR
Smith, Zilpha	103	1888	WB-1/439	AR
Smith, Zilpha	056	1813	WB-1/396	AR
Smith, Zion	001	1885	WB-2/251	AR
Smithdeal, Elizabeth	006	c1865	Orig. Only	AR
Smithdeal, Joseph	085	1861	WB-K/288	AR
Smithdeal, Tobias	006	1900	WB-E/416	AR
Smitherman, Clara	046	1895	WB-F/466	AR
Smitherman, Jesse	067	1883	WB-2/172	AR
Smitherman, Mary P.	106	1892	WB-2/317	AR
Smithey, Samuel	084	c1841	WB-B/260	CTY
Smithson, Barbara	081	1801	WB-2/83	AR
Smithson, John	075	1800	WB-M1/37	AR
Smithson, John	075	1808	WB-M1/180	AR
Smithson, Joseph	067	1846	WB-1/26	AR
Smithson, Malachi	075	1834	WB-N/93	AR
Smithson, Polly	075	1829	WB-N/50	AR
Smithson, Sarah	075	1793	WB-L/2	AR
Smithson, Thomas	075	1743	Orig. Only	SS/AR
Smithwick, Ann	008	c1711	Orig. Only	SS/AR
Smithwick, Ann	028	1712/3	PQS.1/14	
Smithwick, Edmason E.	063	c1801	WB-1/387	
Smithwick, Edmason J.	063	c1784	WB-1/371	
Smithwick, Edmond	063	1774	WB-1/440	
Smithwick, Edward	024	1716	Orig. Only	SS/AR
Smithwick, Hannah	063	1847	WB-2/330	
Smithwick, Henry	028	1867	WB-D/455	AR
Smithwick, Henry B.	063	1863	WB-2/515	

Name	Co.	Date	Recorded Copy	Original
Smithwick, James	100	1849	WB-40/191	AR
Smithwick, James M.	063	1845	WB-2/314	
Smithwick, James R.	100	1872	WB-51/43	AR
Smithwick, Jarrett	063	1900	WB-4/263	AR
Smithwick, Joel	063	1887	WB-4/13	AR
Smithwick, Joel	063	1839	WB-2/255	
Smithwick, John	009	1696	SS 874.2/93	SS/AR
Smithwick, John	010	1803	WB-E/203	AR
Smithwick, John	010	1797	WB-E/33	AR
Smithwick, John G.	063	1841	WB-2/278	
Smithwick, Luke	063	1806	WB-2/416	
Smithwick, Persey	074	1873	WB-1/69	AR
Smithwick, Samuel W.	010	1862	WB-H/114	AR
Smithwick, Sarah	010	1854	WB-H/1	AR
Smithwick, Stark W.	063	1835	WB-2/208	
Smithwick, Thomas	010	1864	WB-H/135	AR
Smithwick, Washington	063	1812	WB-2/7	
Smithwiock, Samuel S.	063	c1802	WB-1/413	
Smithy, Reuben	020	1874	WB-A/161	CTY
Smitson, Thomas	075	1792	WB-K/228	AR
Smokey, Andrew	046	1845	WB-C/228	AR
Smoot, Alexander	085	1826	WB-H/335	AR
Smoot, James	033	1837	WB-1/7	AR
Smoot, Samuel J.	033	1883	WB-2/80	CTY
Smoot, Temperance	033	1897	WB-2/218	CTY
Smoot, Thomas	085	c1824	WB-H/488	
Smoote, William	085	1815	WB-G/368	AR
Smothers, Thomas	073	1795	WB-C/57	AR
Smothers, Thomas	084	1881	WB-E/202	CTY
Smyer, Logan Q.	021	1865	WB-1/212	AR
Smyer, W. A.	021	c1900	WB-3/339	AR
Smyre, Daniel	021	1875	WB-2/148	AR
Smyre, Elias	021	1886	WB-2/367	
Smyth, James C.	085	1867	WB-L/16	AR
Smyth, Julia E. L.	085	1885	WB-2/123	CTY
Smythe, Charles W.	032	1864	WB-2/282	AR
Smythe, Elizabeth	020	1808	RB-E/380	AR
Snapp, Elizabeth	085	c1774	WB-A/188	AR
Snapp, Lawrence	085	1771	WB-A/154	AR
Snead, Catherine	082	1893	WB-6/485	AR
Snead, David	082	1787	WB-1/24	AR
Snead, David	081	1795	WB-1/56	AR
Snead, Elizabeth	084	1850	WB-C/105	CTY
Snead, Henly	082	1816	WB-1/184	AR
Snead, Isral, Sr.	082	1788	WB-1/28	AR
Snead, John	082	1826	WB-1/270	AR
Snead, John	028	1838	WB-C/414	AR
Snead, John	028	1756	SS 880/61	
Snead, Mary	028	1863	Copy from 059	028 AR
Snead, Nanney	082	1795	WB-1/43	AR
Snead, Robert	072	1802	WB-A/118	AR
Snead, Samuel	082	1846	WB-3/36	AR
Snead, Samuel	005	c1775	WB-1/24	AR-Copy
Snead, Samuel H.	082	1865	WB-5/1	AR
Snead, Shockley	082	1869	WB-6/1	AR
Snead, Solomon	082	1817	WB-1/187	AR
Snead, William	082	1803	WB-1/96	AR
Snead, Younger	082	1897	WB-6/569	AR
Snedeker, Garret	070	1770	Orig. Only	SS/AR
Snediker, William	NY	1868	009 OB-M/356	009 CTY
Sneed, Dudley	044	1831	WB-12/40	CTY
Sneed, Elizabeth	078	1835	WI-12/329	
Sneed, Jane	028	1774	Orig. Only	AR
Sneed, Jane	078	1823	WI-9/434	AR
Sneed, John R.	044	1838	WB-14/280	CTY

Name	Co.	Date	Recorded Copy	Original
Sneed, Julia A.	099	1900	Orig. Only	AR
Sneed, Robert	099	1846	RB-26/169	AR
Sneed, Sallie	044	1878	WB-23/296	CTY
Sneed, Samuel	078	1806	WI-4/174	AR
Sneed, Stephen	044	1821	WB-9/1	CTY
Sneed, William M.	TN	1895	098 WB-A/233	098 CTY
Sneeden, Hester	070	1892	WB-G/55	AR
Snell, Asa	101	1882	WB-A/84	
Snell, Azor	096	1879	WB-4/50	
Snell, Elias	016	1875	WB-3/147	AR
Snell, Holt	096	c1809	WB-2/40	AR
Snell, Holt	096	1769	WB-1/48	AR
Snell, James	035	1762	WB-A/455	AR
Snell, Jordan W.	101	1887	WB-A/156	
Snell, Robert L.	016	1893	WB-4/164	
Snell, Roger	096	1766	WB-1/41	AR
Snell, Roger	096	c1772	WB-1/87	
Snell, Roger	N	1708	Orig. Only	SS/AR
Snell, Roger	035	1759	SS 882/170	SS/AR
Snell, Roger	035	1759	087 DB-2/442	
Snell, Susan	096	1879	WB-4/52	
Snell, William	012	1814	WB-B/104	AR
Snellen, Israel	077	1700	SS 874.2/175	SS/AR
Snelling, Barnet	044	1812	WB-7/258	CTY
Snelling, Curtis	099	1898	Orig. Only	AR
Snelling, Curtis	099	1829	RB-21/167	AR
Snelling, Elichander	044	1778	WB-1/186	CTY
Snelling, Lettis	099	1814	RB-11/309	AR
Snider, George Z.	055	c1880	WB-A/42	
Snider, John Martin	085	c1806	WB-D/49	AR
Snider, Lewis	032	1848	WB-2/30	AR
Snider, Lewis, Sr.	032	1842	WB-1/386	AR
Snider, Mary	032	1875	WB-3/162	AR
Snider, Philip	090	1823	WB-3/100	AR
Snider, Philip	032	1875	WB-3/142	
Snider, Philip	032	1887	WB-3/553	AR
Snider, Solomon	097	1873	WB-2/65	AR
Snider, Solomon	032	1872	WB-3/50	AR
Snider, William	038	1898	WB-4/87	AR
Snider, William D.	033	1897	WB-2/203	CTY
Snipes, B. F.	022	1892	WB-E/493	AR
Snipes, Elizabeth	073	1837	WB-E/421	AR
Snipes, John	103	1891	WB-1/550	AR
Snipes, John	044	1816	WB-7/634	CTY
Snipes, John	022	1845	WB-C/174	AR
Snipes, Joseph J.	071	1778	WB-1/313	
Snipes, Nelson	022	1890	WB-E/448	AR
Snipes, Osborn	073	c1835	Orig. Only	AR
Snipes, Robert	071	1826	WB-3/338	AR
Snipes, Thomas	022	1844	WB-C/156	AR
Snipes, Thomas	078	c1842	Orig. Only	AR-Copy
Snipes, William	022	1787	RB-1/30	AR
Snipes, William	022	1882	WB-E/246	AR
Snipes, William	071	1820	WB-3/232	AR
Snoad, Henry	009	1752	Orig. Only	SS/AR
Snoad, John	009	1743	LGB-4/#145	SS/AR
Snoad, William	009	1747	Orig. Only	SS/AR
Snoddy, Elizabeth	054	1815	WB-1/418	AR
Snoddy, John	085	1775	WB-A/199	AR
Snoddy, Samuel	054	c1794	WB-1/215	AR
Snode, Susannah	010	1841	WB-G/334	
Snoden, Samuel	075	1753	SS 881/90	SS/AR
Snoden, Thomas	077	1736	LGB-4/#61	SS/AR
Snoterly, Philip	073	1793	WB-B/255	AR
Snourk, Daniel	077	c1712	SS 875/20	SS/AR

Name	Co.	Date	Recorded Copy	Original
Snow, Adam	066	1887	WB-1/21	AR
Snow, Alner L.	092	1897	WB-6/444	AR
Snow, Byrd	092	c1865	WB-5/76	
Snow, Fielding	092	c1824	WB-4/8	AR
Snow, Frost	092	1852	WB-4/325	
Snow, Ice	092	1899	WB-6/499	AR
Snow, Ice	092	1894	WB-6/396	
Snow, John	021	1850	WB-1/88	AR
Snow, John	100	1819	WB-22/97	AR
Snow, Richard	092	c1872	WB-6/26	
Snow, Robert	070	c1777	Orig. Only	AR
Snow, Samuel	VA	1833	100 WB-34/291	100 AR
Snow, Sarah	092	c1849	WB-4/294	AR
Snow, William	035	1762	WB-A/434	AR
Snowden, Elizabeth	077	1744	Orig. Only	SS/AR
Snowden, Elizabeth	030	1878	WB-5/42	AR
Snowden, Isaac	030	1852	WB-4/165	
Snowden, Isaac	030	1882	WB-5/86	AR
Snowden, Joseph	077	1740	LGB-4/#132B	SS/AR
Snowden, Lemuel	075	1831	WB-N/63	AR
Snowden, Martha	075	1831	WB-N/64	AR
Snowdon, Ann	075	1836	WB-N/120	AR
Snowton, William	075	1824	WB-M1/397	AR
Snuggs, John	089	1847	WB-1/57	
Snyder, J. B.	086	1897	WB-F/554	AR
Snyder, Phillip	081	1860	WB-11/471	
Soane, John	010	1733	SS 876/325	SS/AR
Soary, Andrew	037	1818	WB-E/185	AR
Sockment, Christopher	046	1807	Orig. Only	AR
Sockwell, John	046	1869	WB-E/17	AR
Sockwell, John	046	1862	WB-D/146	AR
Sockwell, Robert	046	1891	WB-F/123	AR
Sockwell, Thomas	046	1884	WB-E/405	AR
Soles, Armstead	030	1817	WB-3/95	
Solley, John	075	1752	Orig. Only	SS/AR
Solley, Joseph	075	1763	Orig. Only	AR
Sollis, Bryan	035	1857	WB-2/126	AR
Solms, Sidney J.	029	1893	WB-F/3	AR
Soloman, James	069	c1872	Copy	039 AR
Solomon, James	069	1873	WB-5/5	AR
Solomon, James	039	1826	WB-H/114	AR
Solomon, Jeremiah	039	1852	WB-N/330	AR
Solomon, William	039	1814	WB-D/88	AR
Somers, Elizabeth	001	1893	WB-2/552	AR
Somers, John	020	1803	RB-E/4	AR
Somers, William	054	c1799	WB-1A/28	
Somerset, Seymore	071	1752	Orig. Only	SS/AR
Somervell, Elizabeth	100	1867	WB-50/247	
Somervell, James	100	1854	WB-43/44	AR
Somervell, John	044	1807	WB-6/344	CTY
Somervell, Mary	044	1838	WB-14/277	CTY
Somervelle, John B.	100	1851	WB-41/175	
Sommers, John	020	1871	WB-A/75	CTY
Sommervill, John	VA	1831	Copy	044 CTY
Soots, Tobias	046	1863	WB-D/190	AR
Sorcy, Joab	030	1831	WB-3/264	
Sorels, W. F.	SC	1895	086 WB-F/551	086 AR
Soret, Thomas	071	1795	WB-2/67	AR
Sorey, Julia	047	1859	WB-5/72	AR-Copy
Sorey, Lucy	037	1842	WB-F/265	AR
Sorey, Robert	069	1857	WB-1/555	AR
Sorrel, Benjamin	010	1806	WB-F/5	AR
Sorrel, James	010	1802	WB-E/170	AR
Sorrel, John, Sr.	029	1812	WB-A/181	AR
Sorrell, Dempsey	099	1873	RB-35/204	AR

Name	Co.	Date	Recorded Copy	Original
Sorrell, Elizabeth	099	1864	RB-33/281	AR
Sorrell, Emily C.	099	1897	WB-D/96	AR
Sorrell, Jacob	099	1880	WB-A/208	AR
Sorrell, M. W.	022	1891	WB-E/461	AR
Sorrell, Micajah	099	1808	RB-8/365	AR
Sorrell, Penny	099	1846	RB-26/178	AR
Sorrell, Willis	099	1894	WB-C/236	AR
Sorrels, Isreal	086	1900	WB-G/51	AR
Sorrels, John	086	1813	WB-B/276	AR
Sorrels, Walter	086	1846	WB-E/155	AR
Sorrey, Willowby	047	1830	WB-4/65	
Sorsberry, Hartwell	029	1792	Orig. Only	AR
Sorsby, Alex	069	1818	WB-1/299	AR
Sorsby, Benjamin	069	1811	WB-1/221	AR
Sorsby, Benjamin	069	1870	WB-1/605	AR
Sorsby, Elizabeth	069	1800	WB-1/131	AR
Sorsby, Samuel	069	1791	WB-1/73	AR
Sorsby, Samuel D.	069	1823	WB-1/312	AR
Sory, Solomon	037	1855	WB-G/113	AR
Soseman, Henry	065	1789	WB-F/159	AR
Sosoman, Eleanor	016	1833	PQS.5/270	
Sothell, Seth	002	1693/4	SS 874.2/40	
Sotherland, James	100	1840	WB-37/374	AR
Sotherland, Simmons	100	1851	WB-41/111	AR
Sousabaugh, L. F.	055	c1869	WB-A/6	
Southall, John W.	051	1873	WB-C/101	AR
Southall, Mary A.	051	1900	WB-C/572	AR
Southard, Henry	092	1813	WB-3/104	AR
Southard, Isaac	092	1791	WB-3/2	AR
Souther, Jesse	064	1858	WB-1/58	AR
Souther, Joseph	013	1880	WB-B/201	AR
Souther, Lucinda	064	1882	WB-2/117	AR
Souther, Nancy	064	1883	WB-2/138	AR
Southerland, Alexander	035	1896	WB-4/489	AR
Southerland, Arkansas	087	1887	WB-3/352	AR
Southerland, David	035	1879	WB-4/208	AR
Southerland, Delilah	035	1866	WB-3/111	AR
Southerland, Elizabeth	073	1854	WB-G/79	AR
Southerland, James	035	1887	WB-4/297	AR
Southerland, James	100	1840	Copy	039 AR
Southerland, John	VA	1771	Orig. Only	SS/AR
Southerland, John	047	1794	WB-3/219	
Southerland, John	035	1881	WB-4/156	AR
Southerland, John, Sr.	037	1798	WB-D/44	AR
Southerland, Mary A.	019	1893	WB-B/248	AR
Southerland, Mary A.	047	1893	WB-7/95	AR
Southerland, Mary A.	047	1893	022 WB-E/533	022 AR
Southerland, Mary A.	047	1893	068 WB-D/397	
Southerland, Mordecai	073	1818	WB-D/530 & 535	AR
Southerland, Robert	035	1835	WB-A/541	AR
Southerland, Solon	098	1888	WB-A/92	CTY
Southerland, Thomas	035	1851	WB-2/67	AR
Southerland, Thomas J.	070	1891	WB-F/416	AR
Southerland, Thomas J.	070	1891	103 WB-2/331	103 AR
Southerlong, Fendal	073	1878	WB-H/181	CTY
Southern, Charlotte	090	1893	WB-6/309	AR
Southern, Reuben	090	1882	WB-6/132	AR
Southern, William	090	1794	WB-1/62	AR
Southward, John	073	1840	WB-F/65	AR
Soutz, Jacob	046	1800	WB-A/354	AR
Soward, Francis	024	c1777	WB-A/194	AR
Sowel, Samuel	072	1809	WB-A/126	AR
Sowell, Charles	010	1802	WB-E/183	AR
Sowell, Charles	010	1738	Orig. Only	SS/AR
Sowell, Charles	068	c1830	WB-B/76	
Sowell, Francis	010	1796	WB-D/307	AR
Sowell, Isaac	051	1856	WB-A/389	
Sowell, John	010	1755	Orig. Only	SS/AR
Sowell, Lavicy	063	1838	WB-2/251	
Sowell, Mary	024	1797	WB-A/280	
Sowell, Moses	063	1813	WB-2/18	
Sowell, Obediah	010	1803	WB-E/194	AR
Sowell, Richard	010	1751	SS 879/37	SS/AR
Sower, George	065	1785	WB-F/165	AR
Sower, Peter	085	c1802	WB-D/41	AR
Sower, Philip	085	c1784	WB-B/164	AR
Sowerby, Henry	071	1747	Orig. Only	SS/AR
Sowerby, John	071	1779	WB-1/211	
Sowers, Elizabeth	032	1893	WB-4/182	AR
Sowers, Elizabeth	085	1844	WB-I/205	AR
Sowers, Jacob	032	1846	WB-1/477	AR
Sowers, Jacob	032	1846	WB-1/490	AR
Sowers, Philip	032	1872	WB-3/54	AR
Spach, Adam, Sr.	085	1801	WB-D/29	AR
Spach, Christian	038	1886	WB-3/13	AR
Spach, Elizabeth	038	1877	WB-2/310	AR
Spach, Jacob	038	1898	WB-4/128	AR
Spach, Johanna	038	1855	WB-1/142	AR
Spach, John	038	1861	WB-1/181	AR
Spach, Jonas R.	038	1884	WB-2/510	AR
Spach, Jonathan	038	1864	WB-1/240	AR
Spaenhower, Henry	092	1788	WB-2/81A	AR
Spaight, Charles G.	028	1831	WB-C/340	AR
Spaight, Mary Jones	028	1810	WB-C/11	AR
Spaight, Richard Dobbs	028	1802	WB-B/155	
Spain, Abigail	099	1821	RB-17/176	AR
Spain, Charles H.	079	1864	WB-1/133	AR
Spain, D. O.	079	1865	WB-1/130	AR
Spain, Featherston	079	1890	WB-2/499	AR
Spain, Jacob R.	099	1865	RB-33/428	AR
Spain, James T.	079	c1857	WB-1/58	AR
Spain, Jearnbe B.	009	1871	WB-1/94	CTY
Spain, Susanna	060	1845	WB-2/237	AR
Spain, Thomas	029	1854	WB-C/311	AR
Spain, William G.	099	1854	RB-18/549	AR
Spainhaur, Henry	090	1821	WB-3/67	AR
Spainhour, Catharine	038	1891	WB-3/251	AR
Spainhour, Charles	038	1875	WB-2/216	AR
Spainhour, David	090	1845	WB-4/198	AR
Spainhour, John Jacob	090	1822	WB-3/89	AR
Spainhour, Joseph P.	017	1877	WB-B/69	
Spainhour, Michael	038	1862	WB-1/199	AR-Copy
Spainhour, Michael	014	1889	WB-2/371	CTY
Spainhour, Noah	017	1881	WB-B/95	
Spainhour, Thomas A.	017	1897	WB-B/293	
Spainhour, William W.	038	1899	WB-4/163	AR
Spainhower, John	090	1847	WB-4/241	AR
Spainhower, Michael	090	1827	WB-3/157	AR
Spainhower, Solomon	090	1868	WB-5/51	
Spake, Adam	026	1893	WB-2/476	AR
Spake, Phillip	026	1873	WB-2/123	AR
Spane, Fredrick	099	1798	RB-4/136	AR
Spangler, Abs.	026	1872	WB-2/91	AR
Spangler, J. W.	026	1878	WB-2/168	AR
Spangler, John	026	1868	WB-1/423	AR
Spanhouer, Anna J.	090	1843	WB-4/119	AR
Spann, Francis	028	c1730	Deeds.1/35	
Spann, Thomas	030	1825	WB-3/191	
Spann, Willis	047	1802	WB-3/374	

Name	Co.	Date	Recorded Copy	Original
Sparger, Murlin	092	1877	WB-6/100	AR
Sparkman, Charney	072	1839	WB-2/10	AR
Sparkman, Edward	010	1833	WB-G/227	AR
Sparkman, John	024	1728	Orig. Only	SS/AR
Sparkman, John	024	1739	Orig. Only	SS/AR
Sparkman, Lewis	041	1825	WB-2/229	AR
Sparkman, Lucretia	041	1857	WB-3/209	AR
Sparkman, Thomas	037	1808	WB-D/317	AR
Sparkman, William	010	1785	WB-D/22	AR
Sparkman, Zilpah	076	1891	WB-A1/255	AR
Sparks, A. J.	028	1884	WB-E/364	
Sparks, Allen	107	c1849	WB-1/352	
Sparks, Benjamin	106	c1872	WB-2/81	AR
Sparks, Benjamin	106	1900	WB-2/474	
Sparks, Charles	005	1798	WB-2/145	AR
Sparks, Colby	104	1869	WB-6/5	AR
Sparks, Elizabeth	039	1849	WB-N/315	AR
Sparks, George	092	1842	WB-4/191	
Sparks, Joel	104	1850	WB-5/29	AR
Sparks, John	004	1868	Orig. Only	AR
Sparks, Jonas	085	c1805	WB-D/50	AR
Sparks, L. M.	086	1864	WB-E/438	AR
Sparks, Lucy	099	1824	RB-19/74	AR
Sparks, Matthew	092	1819	WB-3/140	AR
Sparks, Nancy	004	1890	WB-A/111	AR
Sparks, Nancy C.	106	1886	WB-2/222	AR
Sparks, Reubin	104	1878	WB-6/153	AR
Sparks, Samuel	092	1811	WB-3/99	
Sparks, Samuel	104	1858	WB-5/189	AR
Sparks, Solomon	104	1818	WB-3/171	
Sparks, William	092	1802	WB-3/52A	AR
Sparnon, Joseph	075	1718	SS 875/155	SS/AR
Sparrow, Ann	028	1810	WB-C/8	AR
Sparrow, Dicy	073	1850	WB-F/470	AR
Sparrow, Francis	028	1786	WB-A/154	AR
Sparrow, H. W.	040	1889	WB-2/328	AR
Sparrow, Henrietta	046	1868	028 WB-E/7	028 AR
Sparrow, Henry	028	1797	WB-B/24	AR
Sparrow, Joshua	028	1806	WB-B/243	AR
Sparrow, Nancy	009	1883	WB-1/337	CTY
Sparrow, Paul	028	1798	WB-B/62	AR
Sparrow, Roderick	028	1781	Orig. Only	AR
Sparrow, Sally	028	1826	WB-C/280	
Sparrow, Samuel	028	1811	WB-C/24	AR
Sparrow, Sarah	028	1825	WB-C/258	AR
Sparrow, Stephen P.	053	1887	WB-11/189	AR
Sparrow, Thomas	N	1717	SS 875/120	SS/AR
Sparrow, Thomas	028	1823	WB-C/224	AR
Sparrow, Thomas	028	1852	WB-D/196	AR
Sparrow, William S.	028	1827	WB-C/284	AR
Spate, Edward	075	1878	WB-0/98	AR
Spauch, Fredrick	090	1846	WB-4/230	AR
Spaugh, Adam	085	1816	WB-G/441	AR
Spaugh, Benjamin	039	1871	WB-2/39	AR
Spaugh, David	038	1872	WB-2/113	AR
Spaugh, Elizabeth	038	1861	WB-1/182	AR
Spaugh, George	090	c1826	Orig. Only	AR-Copy
Spaugh, Jacob	039	c1898	WB-4/128	
Spaugh, James A.	038	1863	WB-1/232	AR
Spaugh, Levi	038	1876	WB-2/274	AR
Spaugh, Martin	038	1863	WB-1/231	AR
Spaugh, Phillip	038	1879	WB-2/356	AR
Spaugh, Sarah	038	c1848	WB-1/48	AR
Spaugh, Thomas	038	1892	WB-3/263	AR
Spaugh, Timothy S.	032	1900	WB-4/471	AR

Name	Co.	Date	Recorded Copy	Original
Spaulding, Benjamin	027	1862	WB-A/81	AR
Spaulding, Iver	027	c1887	WB-2/75	
Spaulding, Philip	070	1799	WB-AB/36	AR
Spawls, Thomas	071	1769	WB-1/177	
Speagle, David	021	1879	WB-2/202	
Speagle, Martin	060	1805	Orig. Only	AR
Speaks, Albert	054	1896	WB-6/130	CTY
Speaks, Messentine	054	1885	WB-5/26	CTY
Spear, Crawford	PA	1893	Copy	066 AR
Spear, Jacob	101	1882	WB-A/95	
Spear, Nathan	047	1790	WB-3/191	
Spear, William	005	c1821	WB-A/114	
Spearman, Dolly J.	087	1885	WB-3/312	AR
Spearman, Edward	029	1872	WB-E/71	AR
Spearman, Edward	070	1804	WB-AB/85	AR
Spearman, Edward	087	c1818	Orig. Only	AR
Spearman, Elizabeth	072	c1771	RW/L13	AR
Spears, Amy	016	1876	WB-3/160	AR
Spears, Christopher	099	1855	RB-29/403	AR
Spears, F. W.	080	1871	WB-1/10	AR
Spears, Hezekiah	047	1772	WB-1/322	
Spears, James G.	016	1836	PQS.5/393	
Spears, Jane	065	1834	WB-G/187	AR
Spears, Jane	065	1873	WB-K/132	AR
Spears, Margary	047	1816	WB-3/578	
Spears, Philip H.	044	1788	WB-2/76	CTY
Spears, Richard	065	1837	WB-E/179	
Spears, Wade H.	016	1887	WB-3/525	AR
Spears, William	065	1836	WB-G/233	AR
Spears, William	044	1790	WB-2/181	CTY
Spears, William	016	1856	WB-1/281	
Spears, William W.	016	1844	WB-1/31	
Speas, Catharine	038	1890	WB-3/166	AR
Speas, John H.	038	1880	WB-2/394	AR
Speas, John L.	106	1888	WB-2/255	AR
Speas, Jonathan	038	1894	WB-3/472	AR
Speas, Wesley O.	038	1896	WB-4/46	AR
Speas, William H.	038	1900	WB-4/234	AR
Spease, John	090	1841	WB-4/72	AR
Speck, Daywalt	016	1844	WB-1/49	
Speed, E. A.	078	1898	WB-19/442	AR
Speed, John J.	044	1882	WB-23/450	CTY
Speer, Aaron	092	1816	WB-3/122	AR
Speer, Alexander	030	1842	WB-4/89	
Speer, Aquila	106	1888	WB-2/268	
Speer, Jacob	092	1796	WB-3/20	AR
Speer, Jacob	092	1802	WB-3/48	AR
Speer, Lyda	106	1899	WB-2/448	
Speer, Samuel	106	c1864	WB-2/7	AR
Speer, Thomas	092	1797	WB-3/26	
Speight, Abigail	099	1781	RB-1/146	AR
Speight, Ann	041	1810	WB-2/50	AR
Speight, Anna	041	1843	WB-3/49	AR
Speight, Clio C.	037	1889	WB-H/142	AR
Speight, Edwin G.	099	1866	RB-34/144	AR
Speight, Francis	024	1749	Orig. Only	SS/AR
Speight, Henry	041	1827	WB-2/268	AR
Speight, James	099	1835	RB-23/418	AR
Speight, James P.	045	1891	WB-1/218	AR
Speight, John A.	077	1895	WB-H/268	AR
Speight, John F.	037	1860	Copy	028 AR
Speight, John F.	037	1860	WB-G/200	AR
Speight, John F.	037	1885	WB-H/74	
Speight, Joseph	041	1792	WB-1/105	AR
Speight, Joseph	041	1792	SC/01852	AR-Copy

Name	Co.	Date	Recorded Copy	Original
Speight, Josiah	024	c1783	WB-A/197	AR
Speight, Mary J.	099	1854	RB-28/594	AR
Speight, Mary S.	099	1895	WB-C/344	AR
Speight, Moses	041	1794	WB-1/130	AR
Speight, Nancy	077	1834	WB-F/225	AR
Speight, Peggy	103	1829	RD-6/5	AR
Speight, Penelope	099	1821	RB-18/191	AR
Speight, Thomas	010	1796	WB-D/312	AR
Speight, William	099	1774	RB-1/40	AR
Speight, William	099	1809	RB-9/45	AR
Speir, Elizabeth	079	1774	Orig. Only	SS/AR
Speir, James	037	1761	WB-A/38	AR
Speir, James	010	1731	SS 876/236	SS/AR
Speir, James E.	079	1899	WB-3/199	AR
Speir, John	028	1767	Orig. Only	SS/AR
Speir, John	037	1790	WB-C/129	AR
Speir, Martha	047	1891	WB-7/3	AR
Speir, R. M.	079	1898	WB-3/162	AR
Speir, Wright	037	1799	WB-D/97	AR
Spell, Drewry	037	1782	WB-B/102	AR
Spell, John, Sr	087	1854	WB-1/444	AR
Spell, John, Sr.	037	1784	WB-B/145	AR
Spell, Margaret	087	1886	WB-3/334	AR
Spell, Reddick	056	1855	WB-1/676	AR
Spell, Wiley D.	087	1893	WB-3/521	AR
Speller, Cullen C.	010	1895	WB-I/442	AR
Speller, David G.	010	1891	WB-I/327	AR
Speller, Elizabeth	010	1853	WB-G/496	AR
Speller, Henry	010	1727	SS 876/124	SS/AR
Speller, Henry, Sr.	010	1807	WB-F/60	AR
Speller, Patience	010	1738	LGB-4/#79	SS/AR
Speller, Thomas	010	1833	WB-G/231	AR
Speller, Thomas	063	1812	WB-2/11	
Spellings, Elizabeth	010	1864	WB-H/137	AR
Spellings, William	009	1817	OB-A/272	AR
Spelman, Boston	070	1896	WB-G/484	AR
Spence, Alexander	075	1735	LGB-4/#5	SS/AR
Spence, Courtney	018	1841	WB-C/264	
Spence, Daniel	075	1850	WB-N/232	AR
Spence, Esther	075	1785	WB-K/126	AR
Spence, G. W.	048	1900	WB-1/114	
Spence, Isaac	075	1806	WB-M1/128	AR
Spence, James	018	1828	WB-C/107	
Spence, James	075	1755	Orig. Only	SS/AR
Spence, James	075	1740	LGB-4/#129	SS/AR
Spence, John	075	1736	LGB-4/#60	SS/AR
Spence, John, Sr.	018	1837	WB-C/219	
Spence, Joseph	075	c1841	Orig. Only	AR
Spence, L. D.	056	1865	WB-2/65	AR
Spence, Levina	075	1888	WB-O/287	AR
Spence, Margaret	077	1820	WB-F/27	AR
Spence, Miles	018	1867	WB-D/84	AR
Spence, Noah	018	1822	WB-C/2	
Spence, Parthana	075	1825	WB-N/15	AR
Spence, Rencher	075	1796	WB-L/68	AR
Spence, Robert	032	1825	WB-1/39	AR
Spence, Sally	018	1844	WB-C/299	
Spence, Samuel	075	1805	WB-M1/107	AR
Spence, Sarah	018	1860	WB-D/57	
Spence, Sarah A.	075	1877	WB-O/88	AR
Spence, Thomas	018	1891	WB-E/190	AR
Spence, Thornton	075	1829	WB-N/52	AR
Spence, William	075	1785	WB-K/124	AR
Spence, William	077	1816	WB-E/432	AR
Spence, Wilson	075	1872	WB-O/30	AR
Spencer, A. P.	039	1865	WB-S/33	AR
Spencer, Benjamin	053	1829	WB-4/430	AR
Spencer, Benjamin	053	1813	RW-1/483	AR
Spencer, Britaney	053	1844	WB-6/270	AR
Spencer, Cason G.	053	1864	WB-10/26	AR
Spencer, Catharine	040	1897	WB-2/563	AR
Spencer, Council B.	053	1857	WB-8/222	AR
Spencer, David M.	009	1892	WB-1/585	CTY
Spencer, Edward	053	1795	RW-1/258	
Spencer, Eliza E.	017	1878	WB-B/75	AR
Spencer, Elizabeth	017	1880	WB-B/91	AR
Spencer, Frisbay	053	c1815	Orig. Only	AR
Spencer, Henry S.	053	1851	WB-7/450	AR
Spencer, James	103	1839	RD-7/441	AR
Spencer, James A.	039	1849	WB-N/316	AR
Spencer, Jane	053	1819	Orig. Only	AR
Spencer, Jane	040	1848	WB-1/10	
Spencer, Jesse	085	1825	WB-H/339	AR-Nunc.
Spencer, John	056	1829	WB-1/470	AR
Spencer, John	053	1790	RW-1/202	
Spencer, John	092	1840	WB-4/164	
Spencer, John	017	1869	WB-B/13	AR
Spencer, John	053	1783	RW-1/106	
Spencer, Johnson	081	c1852	Orig. Only	AR
Spencer, Jonathan	053	1824	WB-4/264	AR
Spencer, Joseph	081	1884	WB-15/450	
Spencer, Joseph	075	1783	WB-K/89	AR
Spencer, Joseph A.	018	1898	WB-E/287	AR
Spencer, Martha B.	044	1876	WB-23/210	CTY
Spencer, Mary Ann	039	1892	WB-U/566	AR
Spencer, Mary Jane	065	1887	WB-L/256	AR
Spencer, Nancy	053	1824	Orig. Only	AR
Spencer, Nancy	053	1836	WB-5/430	AR
Spencer, Nathan	081	1877	WB-15/232	AR
Spencer, Nathan	096	1817	Orig. Only	AR
Spencer, Nathan	053	1893	WB-11/306	AR
Spencer, Nathan, Sr.	053	c1815	RW-1/507 & 518	
Spencer, Peledge	053	c1810	RW-1/444	AR
Spencer, Peters P.	053	1880	WB-11/106	AR
Spencer, Rachel	103	1857	RD-12/254	
Spencer, Richard	028	1841	WB-D/25	AR
Spencer, Samuel	005	1860	WB-C/160	AR
Spencer, Samuel	053	1864	WB-9/146	AR
Spencer, Samuel	053	1829	WB-4/513	AR
Spencer, Samuel	074	1873	WB-1/61	AR
Spencer, Samuel P.	005	1889	WB-D/255	AR
Spencer, Sarah	065	1806	WB-F/186	AR
Spencer, Sarah Ann	053	1869	Orig. Only	AR
Spencer, Selby	053	1882	WB-11/122	AR
Spencer, Selby	053	1831	WB-5/69	AR
Spencer, Stephen B.	012	c1857	WB-B/51	AR
Spencer, Susan	053	1886	WB-11/169	AR
Spencer, T. S.	041	1849	WB-3/117	AR
Spencer, Thomas	020	1781	RB-A/163	AR
Spencer, William	053	1793	RW-1/224	AR
Spencer, William W.	053	1886	WB-11/171	AR
Spencer, Zachariah	060	1789	Orig. Only	AR
Sperlin, Daniel	004	1880	WB-A/40	AR
Spicer, Calvin W.	037	1860	WB-G/191	AR
Spicer, Delilah	037	1862	WB-G/217	AR
Spicer, Esther	070	1812	WB-AB/170	AR
Spicer, Evlina	037	1896	WB-H/358	AR
Spicer, Hardin	104	1897	WB-7/18	AR
Spicer, James	070	1788	WB-C/397	AR-Nunc.

Name	Co.	Date	Recorded Copy	Original
Spicer, Jane	104	1855	WB-5/123	
Spicer, Jeremiah	070	1808	WB-AB/104	AR
Spicer, John	072	1800	WB-A/128	AR
Spicer, Rebecca	070	1894	WB-G/218	AR
Spicer, S. L.	037	c1862	Orig. Only	AR
Spicer, William	037	1822	WB-E/308	AR
Spiers, Lewis T.	051	1879	WB-C/217	AR
Spiers, Mary A.	051	1881	WB-C/281	AR
Spiers, Susan O.	051	1873	WB-C/107	AR
Spight, Mary	010	1743	Orig. Only	SS/AR
Spight, Mary	057	1822	WB-B/74	AR
Spight, Sally	028	1868	WB-E/5	AR
Spight, Simon	057	1816	WB-B/1	AR
Spight, Thomas	028	1756	SS 880/126	SS/AR (N)
Spight, Thomas	077	1737	Orig. Only	SS/AR
Spight, William	028	1797	WB-B/49	AR
Spights, John	083	c1803	WB-1/79	AR
Spikes, Elisha	099	1864	RB-33/284	AR
Spiller, James	029	1799	WB-A/18	AR
Spiller, Margaret	029	1797	WB-A/9	AR-Nunc.
Spillman, Jasper	106	c1866	WB-1/106	
Spinks, Enoch	046	1772	WB-A/330	AR
Spinks, John	081	1862	WB-12/160	AR
Spinks, Louis	081	1871	WB-15/59	
Spirer, John	072	c1789	Orig. Only	AR
Spires, Robert	022	1789	RB-1/36	AR
Spivey, A. W.	025	1892	WB-A/155 & 208	AR
Spivey, Aaron	010	1822	WB-G/96	AR
Spivey, Aaron	056	1803	WB-1/154	AR
Spivey, Aaron J.	010	1855	WB-H/15	AR
Spivey, Abraham	041	1810	WB-2/57	AR
Spivey, B. F.	013	1891	WB-C/149	AR
Spivey, Benjamin	024	c1773	WB-B/29	AR
Spivey, Britton	071	1830	WB-4/72	AR
Spivey, Champion	024	c1787	WB-A/195	AR
Spivey, Charity	041	1847	WB-3/92	AR
Spivey, Cornelius	071	1865	WB-5/306	AR
Spivey, David W.	039	1881	WB-U/282	AR
Spivey, E. P.	039	1883	WB-U/303	AR
Spivey, Elijah	024	1781	041 WB-1/10	041 AR
Spivey, Elizabeth	013	1891	WB-C/149	AR
Spivey, Emily	071	1868	WB-5/363	AR
Spivey, Gabriel	022	1878	WB-E/164	AR
Spivey, George	010	1778	WB-B/129	AR
Spivey, George N.	039	1882	WB-U/288	AR
Spivey, Jacob	024	1887	WB-E/162	AR
Spivey, Jacob	041	1789	WB-1/83	AR
Spivey, Jacob	041	1877	WB-4/86	AR
Spivey, Jacob	024	c1776	WB-B/112	AR
Spivey, Jesse	041	1793	WB-1/110	AR
Spivey, John	103	1805	Orig. Only	AR
Spivey, John F.	010	1763	WB-A/30	AR
Spivey, Josiah	071	1878	WB-6/267	AR
Spivey, Julia	041	1884	WB-4/205	AR
Spivey, Littleton	044	1761	Orig. Only	CTY
Spivey, Louvey	041	1860	WB-3/265	AR
Spivey, Margaret	010	1867	WB-H/199	AR
Spivey, Marina	047	1859	WB-5/71	
Spivey, Martha	099	1880	WB-A/156	AR
Spivey, Moses	041	1792	WB-1/102	AR
Spivey, Moses	010	1771	WB-A/150	AR
Spivey, Nathanel	024	1759	WB-A/199	AR
Spivey, Nina R.	039	1898	WB-V/141	AR
Spivey, Phebe	099	1855	RB-29/348	AR
Spivey, Rachel	041	1816	WB-2/115	AR
Spivey, Sarah	071	1865	WB-5/300	AR
Spivey, Sarah	010	1848	WB-G/435	AR
Spivey, Scarborough	056	1864	WB-2/59	AR
Spivey, Susan	010	1838	WB-G/285	AR
Spivey, Thomas	024	1729/0	SS 876/195	SS/AR
Spivey, Timothy	041	1857	WB-3/277	AR
Spivey, W. Hill	010	1897	WB-I/517	AR
Spivey, William	041	1865	WB-3/319	AR
Spivey, William	010	1837	WB-G/296	AR
Spivy, Edmond	083	c1798	WB-1/52	AR
Spivy, Sceniah	041	1872	WB-4/27	AR
Splawn, Jane	080	1885	WB-1/106	AR
Splawn, William	080	1884	086 WB-F/243	
Splawn, William	080	1884	WB-1/84	AR
Spock, Morgan	028	1881	WB-E/277	
Sponhauer, Jacob	090	1814	WB-2/155	AR
Spoon, Adam	001	1849	WB-1/6	AR
Spoon, George	001	1876	WB-2/101	AR
Spoon, John	001	1849	WB-1/5	AR
Spoon, Joseph	081	1886	WB-16/4	AR
Spooner, John	072	1757	SS 880/172	
Spooner, John	072	1757	Copy	028 AR
Spoonhower, Catherine	038	1891	WB-3/251	AR
Spradlin, James	104	1806	WB-2/169	AR
Spraggins, R. G.	065	1891	WB-M/1	AR
Spraker, George	085	1818	WB-G/519	AR
Spratt, Charles E.	065	1861	WB-J/121	AR
Spratt, Hugh	060	1868	WB-3/107	AR
Spratt, James	065	1829	WB-E/101	AR
Spratt, James	065	1802	WB-F/178	
Spratt, James J.	030	1850	WB-4/159	
Spratt, James W.	065	1840	WB-H/25	AR
Spratt, Mary	065	1840	WB-H/12	AR
Spratt, Thomas	060	1868	WB-3/107	AR
Spratt, Thomas C.	065	1849	WB-I/158	AR
Spratten, Henry	030	1752	Orig. Only	SS/AR
Sprewell, Elisabeth	010	1788	WB-D/85	
Spriggs, Linda	070	1900	WB-H/290	AR
Sprincle, George	090	1810	WB-2/110	AR
Spring, Aaron	009	1818	OB-A/283	AR
Spring, Abraham	009	c1801	OWB/381	AR
Spring, Aron	009	1756	SS 879/250	SS/AR
Spring, Moses	053	1782	RW-1/101	AR
Spring, Robert	028	1762	Wills.8/407	AR
Spring, Robert	009	1817	OB-A/267	AR
Spring, Robert	028	1762	SS 882/407	
Spring, Turnis	053	1884	WB-11/148	AR
Springer, Adam	073	1825	WB-E/90	AR
Springer, Lewis	089	1863	WB-1/260	
Springer, Ruben	089	1889	WB-2/196	AR
Springer, Samuel	NJ	1877	009 WB-1/564	009 CTY
Springer, Silvy	089	1847	WB-1/59	AR
Springer, Uriah	073	1800	WB-D/5	AR
Springfield, John	022	1805	WB-A/117	AR
Springle, Charles	009	c1807	OWB/390	AR
Springs, Adam A.	060	1842	WB-2/192	AR
Springs, Andrew	065	1860	WB-J/94	AR
Springs, Eliza M.	065	1867	WB-J/232	AR
Springs, Elizabeth	065	1872	WB-K/99	AR
Springs, John	070	1767	WB-C/384	AR
Springs, John	SC	1853	065 WB-J/114	065 AR
Springs, John	065	1793	WB-F/171	AR
Springs, Margaret	065	1871	WB-K/75	AR

Name	Co.	Date	Recorded Copy	Original
Springs, Mary	065	1869	WB-K/20	AR
Springs, Richard	065	1879	WB-K/340	
Springs, Richard	065	1834	WB-G/158	AR
Springs, Richard A.	065	1884	WB-L/5	AR
Springs, Sarah	065	1832	WB-G/99	AR
Springs, Sedgwick	012	1837	WB-B/174	AR
Springs, Tirza B.	065	1855	WB-J/10	AR
Springs, William L.	065	1896	WB-M/431	AR
Sprinkle, Charity	106	1859	WB-1/46	AR
Sprinkle, Elizabeth	090	1831	WB-3/230	AR
Sprinkle, George	090	1821	WB-3/61	AR
Sprinkle, Stacy	092	c1827	WB-4/127	AR
Sprinkle, Thomas	038	1866	WB-1/272	AR
Sprot, Thomas	005	1757	Orig. Only	SS/AR
Sprouse, Vincent	080	1879	WB-1/59	AR
Sprout, William	084	c1793	OW/224	AR
Sprowl, William	029	1782	Orig. Only	AR
Spruce, Elizabeth	046	1821	WB-B/135	AR
Spruce, George	046	1847	WB-C/270	AR
Spruce, Nancy	046	1867	WB-D/327	AR
Spruce, Sarah	046	1819	WB-B/74	AR
Spruce, William	046	1808	WB-A/362	AR
Spruill, Benjamin	096	c1791	WB-2/6	
Spruill, Benjamin	101	1892	WB-A/214	
Spruill, Benjamin	096	1808	WB-2/21	AR
Spruill, Benjamin	096	1822	WB-2/88	AR
Spruill, Benjamin	096	1787	WB-1/157	AR
Spruill, Benjamin	096	1880	WB-4/56	
Spruill, Charles	096	1815	WB-2/69	AR
Spruill, Christian	071	1866	WB-5/327	AR
Spruill, Daniel N.	096	1837	WB-2/139	AR
Spruill, Dempsey	101	1852	WB-A/178	
Spruill, Dempsey	101	c1842	SC/08176	AR-Copy
Spruill, Esther	096	1818	Orig. Only	AR
Spruill, Frederick	101	1888	WB-A/163	
Spruill, George E.	100	1845	WB-38/355	AR
Spruill, Godfrey	024	1719	SS 875/271	
Spruill, Hezekiah	096	1804	WB-2/44	AR
Spruill, Hezikiah	096	1835	WB-2/126	AR
Spruill, James A.	096	c1866	WB-3/85	AR
Spruill, James B.	047	1899	WB-7/233	AR
Spruill, James T.	101	1893	WB-A/1893	
Spruill, Jeremiah	096	1786	WB-1/153	AR
Spruill, Jesse	096	c1804	WB-2/59	
Spruill, John	096	1899	WB-4/168	AR
Spruill, John	096	c1759	WB-1/46	AR
Spruill, Joseph	096	c1804	Orig. Only	AR
Spruill, Joseph	096	1764	WB-1/30	AR
Spruill, Joseph A.	096	1860	WB-3/63	AR
Spruill, Laura K.	047	1882	WB-6/284	AR
Spruill, Mary	096	c1818	Orig. Only	AR
Spruill, Mary	101	1873	WB-A/1	
Spruill, Milley	096	1852	WB-3/31	AR
Spruill, Peter E.	100	1862	WB-49/428	AR
Spruill, Richard	096	1841	WB-2/154	AR
Spruill, S. R.	047	1878	WB-6/179	AR
Spruill, Samuel	096	c1760	WB-1/8	AR
Spruill, Samuel	096	1805	WB-2/35	AR
Spruill, Samuel	096	1842	WB-3/6	AR
Spruill, Samuel	096	1766	WB-1/59	AR
Spruill, Samuel	096	1833	WB-2/115	AR
Spruill, Simeon	096	1796	Orig. Only	AR
Spruill, Theophilus	063	1844	WB-2/312	
Spruill, Thomas	096	1808	WB-2/52	
Spruill, Tully	074	1886	WB-1/83	
Spruill, Uri	096	1865	WB-3/83	AR
Spruill, W. A.	101	1890	Copy	096 AR
Spruill, W. A.	101	1890	WB-A/188	
Spruill, William	096	1841	WB-2/155	AR
Spruill, William	096	1847	WB-3/13	AR
Spruill, William N.	096	c1848	Orig. Only	AR
Sprunt, Alexander	070	1884	WB-E/528	AR
Sprunt, Jane	070	1893	WB-G/128	AR
Spry, Gemima	030	1833	WB-3/330	
Spry, James	030	1846	WB-4/120	
Spry, Spencer	030	1862	WB-4/247	AR
Spunhouer, Warner	092	1787	WB-2/75A	AR
Spurgin, John	032	1881	WB-3/328	AR
Spurgin, Joseph	032	1859	WB-2/172	AR
Spurgin, Sarah	032	1889	WB-4/66	AR
Spurgin, William	090	1837	WB-4/9	AR
Spurlin, Elijah	026	1845	WB-1/43	AR
Spurlin, Elizabeth	026	1846	WB-1/49	AR
Spurlin, Isaac	026	1854	WB-1/180	AR
Spurlin, John	060	1822	Orig. Only	AR
Spurlin, John	060	1822	Copy	026 AR
Spurlin, Miley	026	1845	WB-1/47	AR
Spurlin, Sarah	026	1883	WB-2/256	AR
Squire, John	053	c1723	009 OWB/4	009 AR
Squire, John G.	070	1764	WB-C/383	AR
Squire, John W.	071	1874	WB-6/134	AR
Squire, Roger	071	1830	WB-4/70	AR
Squire, Sebastian	071	1842	WB-4/251	AR
Squire, Sebastian	071	1764	WB-1/100	
Squires, Appleton	009	1822	OB-A/327	AR
Squires, Betsy	028	1896	WB-F/245	
Squires, Elizabeth	019	1827	WB-D/385	AR
Squires, John	075	1772	WB-I/117	AR
Squires, Jordan	009	c1804	OWB/429	AR
Squires, Meriam	075	1775	WB-I/125	AR
Squires, Polly	018	1866	WB-D/78	AR
Squires, Roger	028	1772	Orig. Only	AR
Squires, Roger	075	1783	WB-K/81	AR
Squires, Thomas	073	1865	WB-G/473	CTY
Squires, Thomas	073	1887	WB-H/425	CTY
Srote, Adam	085	1821	WB-H/110	AR
Srum, Peter	060	1837	Orig. Only	AR
St. George, Elijah	070	1798	WB-AB/2	AR
St. George, Elizabeth	070	1855	WB-C/590	AR
St. John, William	039	1806	WB-C/50	AR
St. Lawrence, Elizabeth	022	1823	WB-B/103	AR
Stacey, Charis	024	1725	Orig. Only	SS/AR
Stacey, Rachel	024	1802	WB-B/194	AR
Stacey, Sarah	077	1826	WB-F/115	AR
Stack, David	046	1885	WB-E/431	AR
Stack, Elijah	046	1791	WB-A/343	AR
Stack, Jackson	097	1862	WB-1/199	AR
Stacy, Buckner	067	1842	Orig. Only	AR-Copy
Stacy, Isaac S.	064	1892	WB-2/299	AR
Stacy, M. L.	104	1885	WB-6/265	AR
Stacy, Robert	077	1844	WB-F/312	AR
Stadder, Robert	022	c1776	Orig. Only	AR
Stadler, Barzlia G.	020	1864	RB-T/26	CTY
Stadler, John	020	1860	RB-S/228	AR
Stadler, Mary	020	1894	WB-B/160	CTY
Stadler, Melissa S.	020	1879	WB-A/280	CTY
Stafford, A. J.	038	1863	WB-1/210	AR
Stafford, Adam	020	1792	RB-B/456	AR
Stafford, Adam	075	1841	WB-N/167	AR
Stafford, Charles	028	1889	WB-E/502	AR

Name	Co.	Date	Recorded Copy	Original
Stafford, Cudbert	071	1804	WB-2/267	AR
Stafford, Cynthia M.	054	1881	WB-4/439	CTY
Stafford, E. J.	033	1892	WB-2/122	CTY
Stafford, E. J.	033	1892	038 WB-3/266	
Stafford, Eli	016	1846	WB-1/110	
Stafford, Elisha	057	1817	WB-B/45	AR
Stafford, Emma C.	081	1895	WB-16/352	AR
Stafford, Franklin	065	1872	WB-K/81	AR
Stafford, George	065	1824	WB-E/96	AR
Stafford, Henry	038	1888	WB-3/96	AR
Stafford, Hiram	032	1849	WB-2/44	AR
Stafford, J.	081	c1847	Orig. Only	AR
Stafford, J. W.	003	1897	WB-B/372	AR
Stafford, James	065	1813	WB-E/195	AR
Stafford, James	046	1816	WB-B/24	AR
Stafford, James	092	c1873	WB-6/67	
Stafford, Jane	081	1845	WB-8/203	AR
Stafford, John	077	1784	WB-C/267	AR
Stafford, John	001	1860	WB-1/177	AR
Stafford, John	075	1813	WB-M1/247	AR
Stafford, John	008	1735	SS 877/166	SS/AR
Stafford, John	075	1809	WB-M1/198	AR
Stafford, John M.	038	1877	WB-2/300	AR
Stafford, Joseph T.	075	1884	WB-0/223	AR
Stafford, Laban	020	1811	RB-F/204	AR
Stafford, Margaret	046	1858	WB-C/514	AR
Stafford, Mary	075	1823	WB-M1/385	AR
Stafford, Samuel	075	1774	WB-I/74	AR
Stafford, Sarah	046	1829	WB-B/389	AR
Stafford, Stephen	075	1847	WB-N/208	AR
Stafford, Stephen	075	1824	WB-M1/410	AR
Stafford, Thomas	001	1885	WB-2/241	AR
Stafford, Thomas	077	1793	WB-C/451	
Stafford, Thomas	020	1839	RB-N/287	AR
Stafford, Tirzah	065	1825	WB-E/98	AR
Stafford, William	075	1751	Orig. Only	SS/AR
Stafford, William	070	1765	Orig. Only	SS/AR
Stafford, William	030	1742	LGB-4/#169	SS/AR
Stafford, William	030	1728	SS 876/148	SS/AR
Stagg, Judith	073	1792	WB-B/190	AR
Stagg, Radford	036	1897	WB-A/418	CTY
Stagnor, John Barnet	085	c1775	WB-A/248	AR
Staiert, Sebastian	029	1828	WB-B/165	AR
Stainback, Forester	020	1858	RB-R/574	AR
Stainback, James	044	1778	WB-1/175	CTY
Stainback, Patsy	039	1881	WB-U/272	AR
Stainback, William H.	020	1891	WB-B/58	CTY
Staines, Daniel	097	1871	WB-2/49	
Staines, Jacob	013	1891	WB-C/98	
Stalcop, John	073	1804	WB-D/125	AR
Stalcup, Alston	020	1810	RB-F/116	
Stalcup, Peter S.	023	1900	WB-A/187	AR
Stalcup, William	020	1888	WB-A/527	CTY
Staley, Catharine	081	1867	WB-14/154	AR
Staley, Christian	022	1817	WB-A/287	
Staley, Conrad	081	1833	WB-6/293	AR
Staley, Daniel	081	1817	WB-4/417	AR
Staley, Henry	081	1871	WB-15/76	AR
Staley, John	081	1853	WB-9/519	AR
Staley, John H.	104	1885	WB-6/262	AR
Staley, Martin	081	1817	WB-4/413	AR
Staley, Martin	022	1859	WB-D/47	AR
Staley, William	081	1885	WB-15/529	AR
Stalings, Elijah	022	1818	WB-A/311	AR
Stalker, George	046	1790	WB-A/350	AR

Name	Co.	Date	Recorded Copy	Original
Stalker, John	081	1842	WB-7/405	AR
Stalker, Thomas	081	1841	WB-7/344	AR
Stallcup, Jesse R.	023	1893	WB-A/109	AR
Stallians, James	037	1764	WB-A/131	AR
Stallings, A. J.	099	1895	WB-C/449	AR
Stallings, Abram	037	1867	WB-G/286	AR
Stallings, Alexander	GA	c1893	039 WB-V/21	
Stallings, Alexander	039	1877	WB-U/164	AR
Stallings, Anne	056	1837	Orig. Only	AR
Stallings, Briant	099	1884	WB-B/4	AR
Stallings, Callin	056	1881	WB-3/297	AR
Stallings, Cornelius	039	1861	WB-R/188	AR
Stallings, Daniel	077	1837	WB-F/259	AR
Stallings, Daniel	077	1800	WB-E/116	AR
Stallings, Elias	010	1763	WB-A/23	AR
Stallings, Elias	024	1797	WB-A/289	AR
Stallings, Elias	039	c1795	WB-B/11	AR
Stallings, Elias	077	1785	WB-C/298	AR
Stallings, Elisha	037	1792	WB-C/180	AR
Stallings, Elizabeth	100	1860	WB-49/306	AR
Stallings, Emma Davis	100	1899	WB-51/531	
Stallings, Frusey	041	1860	WB-3/264	AR
Stallings, Hardy	063	1821	WB-2/72	
Stallings, Henry	077	1835	WB-F/242	AR
Stallings, Henry	041	1885	WB-4/224	AR
Stallings, Hilliard	039	c1856	WB-0/373	
Stallings, Isaac	056	1843	WB-1/550	AR
Stallings, James	099	1873	RB-35/219	AR
Stallings, James	056	1782	Orig. Only	AR
Stallings, James	037	1834	WB-F/157	AR
Stallings, James	039	1851	WB-N/345	AR-Nunc.
Stallings, James B.	056	c1885	WB-4/397	AR
Stallings, Jesse	077	1841	WB-F/299	AR
Stallings, Jesse S.	063	1890	WB-4/49	AR
Stallings, John	037	1780	WB-B/53	AR
Stallings, John	035	1815	WB-A/441	AR
Stallings, John	077	1818	WB-F/10	AR
Stallings, Joseph	037	1862	WB-G/237	AR
Stallings, Josiah	100	1886	WB-51/199	AR
Stallings, Josiah	010	1772	WB-A/157	AR
Stallings, Kenneth	063	1837	WB-2/225	
Stallings, Lena	009	1879	WB-1/231	CTY
Stallings, Lott	024	1749	Orig. Only	SS/AR
Stallings, Lou C.	098	1899	WB-A/330	CTY
Stallings, Luke	077	1799	WB-E/102	AR
Stallings, Martha	024	1839	WB-C/216	AR
Stallings, Meshack	035	1827	WB-A/450	AR
Stallings, Nancy	056	1878	WB-3/205	AR
Stallings, Nancy	039	c1800	WB-B/87	
Stallings, Nicholas	077	1767	WB-C/67 & 76	AR
Stallings, Noah	077	c1860	WB-F/556	AR
Stallings, Pallitiah	041	1808	WB-2/27	AR
Stallings, Pricilla	077	1860	WB-F/508	AR
Stallings, Reuben	039	1846	WB-M/119	AR
Stallings, Reubin	077	1825	WB-F/85	AR
Stallings, Sallie R.	100	1892	WB-51/371	
Stallings, Simon	041	1808	WB-2/18	AR
Stallings, Simon	077	1788	WB-C/381	AR
Stallings, Solomon	100	1877	WB-51/115	AR
Stallings, Sophia	077	1889	WB-H/185	AR
Stallings, Tempie	069	1893	WB-5/407	AR
Stallings, Whitmel	041	1858	WB-3/227	AR
Stallions, Griggre	037	1790	WB-C/138	AR
Stalls, Jesse	010	1875	WB-I/68	AR
Staly, William D.	001	1881	WB-2/459	AR

Name	Co.	Date	Recorded Copy	Original
Stamey, Alexander	092	1893	WB-6/364	AR
Stamey, Elizabeth	014	c1865	Orig. Only	CTY
Stamey, John R.	060	1844	WB-2/226	AR
Stamey, Joseph	060	1890	WB-4/442	AR
Stamier, George	070	1793	WB-C/401	AR
Stamp, Debrough	075	1781	WB-K/64	AR
Stamp, Richard	075	1722	SS 875/334	SS/AR
Stamp, Thomas	075	1729	Orig. Only	SS/AR
Stamper, Anna	004	1900	WB-A/230	AR
Stamper, Elizabeth	047	1786	WB-3/115	
Stamper, James	044	1874	WB-23/147	CTY
Stamper, John	006	1890	WB-E/196	AR
Stamper, Johnathan	004	c1822	Orig. Only	AR
Stamper, Jonathan	104	1799	WB-1/509	AR
Stamper, Jonathan	006	1831	WB-B/23	AR
Stamper, William	044	1831	WB-12/100	CTY
Stamps, E. R.	099	1891	WB-B/548	AR
Stamps, Joseph	084	1812	WB-A/95	CTY
Stamps, Thomas	020	1855	RB-R/287	AR
Stamps, William L.	020	1896	WB-B/232	CTY
Stanaland, Joseph	012	1897	WB-A/124	AR
Stanaland, Patrick	012	c1775	DB-B/82	
Stanard, Lou Belle	046	1898	WB-G/57	AR
Stanback, David	082	1833	WB-2/32	AR
Stanback, Elizabeth	082	1869	WB-6/22	AR
Stanback, George	082	1818	WB-1/209	AR
Stanback, M. C.	068	c1890	082 WB-7/55	
Stanback, M. C.	068	1899	WB-E/19	
Stanback, Mary	082	1836	WB-2/59	AR
Stanback, Phebe	082	1834	WB-2/45	AR
Stanback, Presley N.	082	1891	WB-6/436	AR
Stanbock, Christian	028	1745	DB-3/60	
Stancell, Everitt	071	1837	WB-4/151	AR
Stancell, Green	071	1862	WB-5/258	AR
Stancell, Mary E.	071	1873	Orig. Only	AR
Stancell, Nathan	071	1794	WB-2/50	AR
Stancell, Robert H.	071	1896	WB-7/329	AR
Stancell, Samuel	071	1817	WB-3/196	AR
Stancil, Jonathan	056	1847	WB-1/602	AR
Stancil, Joseph	056	1889	WB-3/508	AR
Stancill, Eliza E.	082	1899	WB-7/13	AR
Stancill, Godfrey	079	1868	WB-1/181	AR
Stancill, Godfrey	079	1866	WB-1/163	AR
Stancill, Jesse R.	079	1863	WB-1/91	AR
Standfield, Benjamin	020	1862	RB-S/577	
Standin, Edward	077	1766	WB-C/66	AR
Standin, Frances L.	024	1867	WB-D/53	AR
Standin, Henderson	024	c1781	WB-A/200	AR
Standin, Lemuel	024	1803	WB-B/199	AR
Standin, Mary	024	1857	WB-C/394	AR
Standin, Samuel	077	1752	Orig. Only	SS/AR
Standin, Samuel	077	1779	WB-C/231	AR
Standin, William	077	1760	Orig. Only	SS/AR
Standin, William	077	1815	WB-E/416	AR
Standing, Edward	024	1721	SS 875/311	SS/AR
Standley, Ann	010	1775	WB-B/38	AR
Standley, David	010	1795	WB-D/265	AR
Standley, James	057	1793	WB-A/107	AR
Standley, James	070	1804	WB-C/408	AR
Standley, James, Sr.	070	1793	WB-C/403	AR
Standley, Jonathan	010	1773	Orig. Only	SS/AR
Standley, Jonathan	010	1807	WB-F/40	AR
Standley, Lemuel	018	1824	WB-C/37	
Standley, Martha	010	1800	WB-E/117	
Standley, Sarah	010	1807	WB-F/49	AR
Stanfield, Elisabeth	078	1883	WB-19/150	AR
Stanfield, Eliza A.	078	c1884	Orig. Only	AR
Stanfield, Francis W.	078	c1853	Orig. Only	AR
Stanfield, Harrison	078	1858	WB-18/27	AR
Stanfield, J. E.	084	1899	WB-F/134	CTY
Stanfield, John	073	1755	Orig. Only	SS/AR
Stanfield, Joseph M.	078	1855	WB-17/343	AR
Stanfield, Josiah A.	020	1896	WB-B/228	CTY
Stanfield, Robert	078	1826	WI-10/255	AR
Stanfield, S. A.	078	1874	Orig. Only	AR
Stanfield, Sarah	020	1846	RB-P/350	AR
Stanford, Anthony	073	1790	WB-B/85	AR
Stanford, Hannah	065	1837	WB-E/164	AR
Stanford, James	073	1843	WB-F/152	AR
Stanford, Jonathan	035	1834	WB-1/52	AR
Stanford, Levin	009	1773	Orig. Only	SS/AR
Stanford, Margaret	035	1858	WB-2/133	AR
Stanford, Richard	073	1816	WB-D/486	AR
Stanford, Samuel	035	1833	WB-1/38	AR
Stanland, James C.	012	c1860	WB-B/34	
Stanland, William W.	012	1884	WB-A/59	AR
Stanley, Abigail	046	c1860	Orig. Only	AR
Stanley, Alfred	092	1843	WB-4/199	
Stanley, Archilus	092	1807	WB-3/82	AR
Stanley, Asa	046	1864	WB-D/203	AR
Stanley, Christopher	090	1837	WB-4/9	AR
Stanley, Elijah	072	1849	WB-2/93	AR
Stanley, Elizabeth	059	1894	WB-B/110	CTY
Stanley, Elwood	046	1885	WB-E/186	AR
Stanley, Gravener	046	1877	WB-E/186	AR
Stanley, Herod	036	1882	WB-A/26	CTY
Stanley, Isaac	046	1861	WB-D/88	AR
Stanley, J. E.	092	1897	WB-6/458	
Stanley, Jesse	046	1834	WB-B/559	AR
Stanley, John	092	1795	WB-3/18	AR
Stanley, John A.	070	1892	WB-F/534	AR
Stanley, John A.	025	1885	WB-A/38	
Stanley, John W.	071	1866	WB-5/336	AR
Stanley, Joseph	046	1840	Orig. Only	AR
Stanley, Joseph	085	c1804	WB-D/39	AR
Stanley, Joshua	046	1855	WB-C/443	AR
Stanley, Micajah	046	1819	WB-B/82	AR
Stanley, Milton M.	046	1900	WB-G/177	AR
Stanley, Moses	103	1812	RD-2/202	AR
Stanley, Nash	062	1893	WB-B/159	AR
Stanley, Richard	030	1793	WB-2/19	
Stanley, Samuel	046	1835	WB-B/527	AR
Stanley, Samuel	090	1846	WB-4/229	AR
Stanley, Sarah	046	1874	WB-E/132	AR
Stanley, Shadrack	046	1793	WB-A/346	AR
Stanley, Zimri	046	1841	WB-C/83	AR
Stanly, Barney	059	1867	WB-A/395	
Stanly, Benjamin G.	057	1885	WB-C/117	AR
Stanly, Catherine	028	1866	WB-D/431	
Stanly, Daniel	057	1835	WB-B/124	AR
Stanly, Edward	053	1891	WB-11/235	AR
Stanly, Edward R.	NJ	1883	028 WB-E/320	028 AR
Stanly, Elizabeth	099	1872	RB-35/182	AR
Stanly, Francis C.	028	1829	WB-C/302	AR
Stanly, J. E.	092	1897	WB-6/458	
Stanly, James G.	028	1858	WB-D/296	AR
Stanly, John	057	1837	WB-B/131	AR
Stanly, John W.	056	1862	WB-2/28	AR
Stanly, John Wright	028	1789	WB-A/198	AR
Stanly, Nathan	057	1855	WB-B/224	AR

Name	Co.	Date	Recorded Copy	Original
Stanly, Susan	092	1895	WB-6/405	AR
Stanly, Thomas T.	028	1813	WB-C/68	
Stanly, Wright	057	1856	WB-B/233	AR
Stansbury, Moses	104	c1833	Orig. Only	AR
Stansbury, Samuel	020	1779	RB-A/55	AR
Stansell, Godfrey	056	1855	WB-1/674	AR
Stansell, John	096	1750	SS 879/11	SS/AR
Stansell, John, Sr.	056	1795	WB-1/89	AR
Stansell, Willie P.	056	1878	WB-3/190	
Stantefar, Israel	073	1794	WB-B/267	AR
Stanton, Anna	019	1826	WB-D/384	AR
Stanton, Benjamin	019	1799	WB-D/360	
Stanton, David	081	1860	WB-11/370	AR
Stanton, Elijah	077	1779	WB-C/229	AR
Stanton, Frederick	071	1824	WB-3/316	AR
Stanton, George	062	1851	WB-A/1	AR
Stanton, Green	044	1861	WB-21/492	CTY
Stanton, Henry	019	1751	028 DB-5/187	SS/AR
Stanton, Henry	019	c1759	Orig. Only	AR
Stanton, Hope	019	1788	WB-D/352	AR
Stanton, James	019	1816	WB-D/375	AR
Stanton, John	077	1803	WB-E/184	AR
Stanton, John	028	1797	WB-B/26	AR
Stanton, John	081	1835	WB-6/483	AR
Stanton, John, Sr.	077	1799	WB-E/105	AR
Stanton, Jonathan	019	1883	WB-B/139	AR
Stanton, Lemon P.	037	1846	WB-F/334	AR
Stanton, Mary	N	1721	SS 875/309	SS/AR
Stanton, Michael	070	1760	Orig. Only	AR-Nunc.
Stanton, Nancy	077	1891	WB-H/209	AR
Stanton, Owen	019	1814	WB-D/371	AR
Stanton, Sally M.	047	1887	WB-6/444	AR
Stanton, Samuel	081	1821	WB-5/70	AR
Stanton, Thomas	077	1813	WB-E/381	AR
Stanton, Thomas	077	1784	WB-C/250	AR
Stanton, Thomas	075	1720	SS 875/308	SS/AR
Stanton, William	077	c1856	WB-F/494	AR
Stanton, William	057	1799	WB-A/229	AR
Stap, Joshua	071	1765	WB-1/126	
Staples, Henry	084	1893	WB-E/537	CTY
Staples, Thomas	018	1828	WB-C/98	
Staples, Walter R.	046	1898	WB-G/84	AR
Star (Stoehr), Henry	090	1812	WB-2/134	AR
Star, Christopher	054	c1823	Orig. Only	AR
Starbuck, D. H	038	1887	WB-3/36	AR
Starbuck, Elihu	046	1890	WB-F/33	AR
Starbuck, Gayer	046	1814	WB-A/373	AR
Starbuck, Junius S.	038	1900	WB-4/200	AR
Starbuck, Matthew	046	1816	WB-A/375	AR
Starbuck, Paul	090	1827	WB-3/160	AR
Starbuck, Rachel	046	1892	WB-F/246	AR
Starbuck, Reuben	046	1880	WB-E/288	AR
Starbuck, Thomas	046	1884	WB-E/398	AR
Starbuck, Thomas	046	1834	WB-B/501	AR
Starbuck, William	046	1837	WB-B/576	AR
Starcey, Willim	077	1765	Orig. Only	AR
Stark, James	044	1798	WB-4/220	CTY
Stark, Oliver P.	029	1861	WB-C/432	AR
Stark, Thomas	086	1817	WB-C/74	
Starkes, Kyzer J.	044	1872	WB-23/57	CTY
Starkey, Alice	072	1809	WB-A/126	AR
Starkey, Edward	057	1808	WB-A/305 & 314	AR
Starkey, Edward	072	c1781	Orig. Only	AR
Starkey, Henry	028	1888	WB-E/494	AR

Name	Co.	Date	Recorded Copy	Original
Starkey, Jonathan	020	1836	RB-M/560	
Starkey, Peter	072	c1766	RW/L63	AR
Starkey, Peter	072	1782	WB-A/128	AR
Starkey, William	072	c1766	RW/L41	AR
Starling, Adam	056	1805	WB-1/178	AR
Starling, Hilbard	056	1817	WB-1/260	AR
Starling, Isaac	056	1887	WB-3/443	AR
Starling, Isaac	071	1764	WB-1/95	
Starling, Jesse	056	1832	WB-1/480	AR
Starling, John	068	1885	WB-D/213	
Starling, William	056	1827	WB-1/329	AR
Starling, Willie	056	1866	WB-2/85	AR
Starnes, Elmira	097	1890	WB-2/382	AR
Starnes, J. Benson	097	1891	WB-2/413	AR
Starnes, Jacob	013	1891	Orig. Only	AR
Starnes, Valentine	097	1875	WB-2/101	
Starns, Jesse	003	1876	WB-B/82	AR
Starns, Molly	021	1861	WB-1/159	AR
Starns, Shubal	046	1772	WB-A/329	AR
Starr, Adam	046	1823	WB-B/162	AR
Starr, C. A.	046	1891	WB-F/148	AR
Starr, Catherine	021	1893	WB-3/33	
Starr, Eli	021	1885	WB-2/302	
Starr, Hanna	065	1800	WB-F/177	AR
Starr, Jacob	060	1833	WB-1/292	AR
Starr, John D.	029	1862	WB-C/453	AR
Starrat, James	046	1804	WB-A/359	AR
Starratt, Benjamin	046	1778	WB-A/359	AR
Starratt, William	046	1852	WB-C/366	AR
Stasey, Thomas	024	1697	SS 874.2/91	SS/AR
Staten, Ennis	097	1885	WB-2/265	AR
Staton, Alfred	051	1899	WB-C/550	AR
Staton, Arthur	037	1822	WB-E/300	AR
Staton, Baker	037	1866	WB-G/276	AR
Staton, Bennett	028	1866	WB-D/468	
Staton, Charlotte	063	c1832	WB-2/183	
Staton, Ezekiel	037	1815	WB-E/113	AR
Staton, Frederick	005	1866	WB-C/243	AR
Staton, Henry L.	037	1886	WB-H/79	
Staton, Henry M.	037	1893	WB-H/267	AR
Staton, James M.	005	1895	WB-D/376	
Staton, Jeanette	037	1875	WB-G/468	
Staton, Jesse	037	1813	WB-E/58	AR
Staton, John L.	020	1898	WB-B/336	CTY
Staton, Maggie	037	1894	WB-H/277	AR
Staton, Margaret	037	1892	WB-H/234	AR
Staton, Mary	037	1836	WB-F/192	AR
Staton, Nancy	037	1871	WB-G/364	AR
Staton, Nehemiah	037	1822	WB-E/297	AR
Staton, Pennina	037	1894	WB-H/309	AR
Staton, Rebacha	037	1830	WB-F/110	AR
Staton, Spencer	037	1879	WB-G/494	AR
Staton, Thomas	047	1770	WB-1/259	
Staton, Torry	097	1883	WB-2/236	
Staton, Uriah	005	1888	WB-D/249	AR
Staton, William	086	1846	WB-E/166	AR
Staton, Windfield	047	1855	WB-5/8	
Stats, Miles	063	1847	WB-2/334	
Staub, Augustus	038	1853	WB-1/113	AR
Stauber, Anna J.	038	1891	WB-3/203	AR
Stauber, Catherine	038	1876	WB-2/266	AR
Stauber, Lydia	038	1880	WB-2/371	AR
Stauber, Samuel B.	038	1884	WB-2/507	AR
Stavins, Samuel	085	c1781	WB-B/140	AR
Stawl, William	063	1856	WB-2/426	

Name	Co.	Date	Recorded Copy	Original
Steadman, Joseph	086	1857	WB-E/336	AR
Steadman, Margarett	086	1886	WB-F/274	AR
Stearnes, Jacob	SC	1868	026 WB-2/10	026 AR
Stearns, Catherine	080	1898	WB-1/302	AR
Stearns, William E.	068	1898	WB-D/550	
Stedham, John	006	c1864	Orig. Only	AR
Stedman, Elisha	029	1832	WB-B/215	AR
Stedman, Robert P.	022	1836	WB-C/42	AR
Stedman, Winship	022	1828	WB-B/147	AR
Steed, Abner	100	1871	WB-51/49	
Steed, Berrier	070	1785	WB-C/395	AR
Steed, Calier	081	1874	WB-15/159	AR
Steed, John	081	1810	WB-3/287	AR
Steed, Nathaniel	081	1805	WB-3/20	AR
Steel, A. W.	029	1873	WB-E/105	AR
Steel, Agness	054	c1793	WB-1/213	AR
Steel, Andrew	054	1877	WB-4/277	CTY
Steel, Andrew M.	001	1866	WB-1/267	AR
Steel, Elizabeth	085	1881	WB-1/580	CTY
Steel, Elizabeth	085	c1789	WB-B/188	AR
Steel, James	016	1835	PQS.5/353	
Steel, John	085	1815	WB-G/376	AR
Steel, John	085	1837	WB-I/7	AR
Steel, John	065	1821	WB-E/108	AR
Steel, John	073	1793	WB-B/251	AR
Steel, Josiah	065	1825	WB-E/93	AR
Steel, Martin	065	1830	WB-F/172	AR
Steel, Matthew	085	1846	WB-K/23	AR
Steel, Moses	065	1787	WB-F/164	AR
Steel, Peter	057	1792	WB-A/185	AR
Steel, Robert	085	c1781	WB-B/14	AR
Steel, Samuel	085	1790	WB-D/44	AR
Steel, Sarah	010	1832	WB-G/219	AR
Steel, Sarah	022	1840	WB-C/110	AR
Steel, Tabitha	047	1783	WB-3/40	
Steel, Thomas	047	1771	WB-1/284	
Steel, William	085	1774	WB-A/168	AR
Steel, William	065	1795	WB-F/170	AR
Steel, William	065	1827	WB-C/3	AR
Steel, William	010	1816	WB-F/344	AR
Steele, Abram C.	065	1863	WB-J/173	AR
Steele, Ambrose	008	1725	Orig. Only	SS/AR
Steele, Cornelia	046	1899	WB-G/161	AR
Steele, Henry	054	1853	WB-3/69	AR
Steele, John	065	1803	WB-F/181	AR
Steele, John	067	1844	WB-1/9	
Steele, John	024	1891	WB-E/203	AR
Steele, Margaret	090	1878	WB-6/95	AR
Steele, Mary B.	046	1892	WB-F/223	AR
Steele, Nancy	065	1895	WB-M/343	AR
Steele, Ninian	054	c1813	WB-1/318	AR
Steele, Ninian F.	054	1858	WB-3/129	AR
Steele, Peter	017	1866	WB-A/160	AR
Steele, R. L.	054	1890	WB-5/355	CTY
Steele, Richard W.	097	c1872	WB-2/93	
Steele, Robert J.	082	1887	WB-6/347	AR
Steele, Robert J.	082	c1856	WB-5/16	AR
Steele, Robert J.	082	1816	WB-1/181	AR
Steele, Robert L.	082	1896	WB-6/526	AR
Steele, Robert R.	065	1900	WB-N/322	AR
Steele, Samuel	054	c1811	WB-1/286	AR
Steele, Thomas	GA	1866	Copy	082 AR
Steele, Walter L.	082	1891	WB-6/440	AR
Steele, William	085	1816	WB-G/422	AR
Steele, William C.	097	1872	WB-2/62	AR

Name	Co.	Date	Recorded Copy	Original
Steele, William P.	090	1892	WB-6/283	AR
Steell, Alexander	072	1751	028 DB-5/218	SS/AR
Steell, Martin	065	1817	WB-E/110	AR
Steell, Moses	065	1827	WB-C/4	AR
Steelman, Almeda	106	1881	WB-2/146	AR
Steelman, Charles	092	1845	WB-4/242	
Steelman, Charles	106	c1855	WB-1/34	AR
Steelman, George	092	1800	WB-3/37	
Steelman, George	106	1893	WB-2/331	
Steelman, John	106	1859	Orig. Only	AR-Nunc.
Steelman, Matthias	092	1793	WB-3/12A	
Steelman, William	085	1836	WB-H/675	AR
Steely, Edmund	010	1841	WB-G/338	AR
Steely, Thomas	024	1719	SS 875/177	SS/AR
Stegall, George	097	1846	WB-1/31	AR
Stegall, George L.	097	1866	WB-1/285	AR
Stegall, Moses	005	1841	WB-B/126	AR
Stegall, Rebeccah	047	1823	WB-3/690	
Steiner, Abraham	090	1833	WB-3/253	AR
Steiner, Charles E.	038	1894	WB-3/451	AR
Steiner, Henry A.	038	1855	WB-1/66	AR
Steiner, Will W.	046	1890	WB-F/36	AR
Stell, Cory	099	1890	WB-B/459	AR
Stell, John	099	1852	RB-28/106	AR
Stell, W. R.	099	1898	WB-D/197	AR
Steller, Peter	085	1822	WB-H/604	AR
Stem, Alfred	044	1874	WB-23/153	CTY
Stem, George C.	044	1886	WB-23/586	CTY
Stem, Robert J.	044	1898	WB-24/397	CTY
Stem, William T.	044	1891	WB-24/175	CTY
Stem, Wm. Jacob	044	1828	WB-10/450	CTY
Stemmerman, Anna M.	070	1884	WB-E/433	AR
Stemmerman, Claus	070	1892	WB-F/519	AR
Stenberg, Peter A.	099	1876	RB-35/327	AR
Stendley, Henry	020	1892	WB-B/91	CTY
Step, Joshua	071	1781	WB-1/240	
Stephen, Martha	099	1873	RB-35/221	AR
Stephens, Albert G.	020	1891	WB-B/81	CTY
Stephens, Alexander	032	1824	WB-1/28	AR
Stephens, Alfred B.	083	1843	WB-1/435	AR
Stephens, Anthony	020	1846	RB-P/364	
Stephens, Anthony	020	1849	RB-Q/255	
Stephens, Arthur	073	1776	WB-A/200	
Stephens, Benjamin	020	1832	RB-M/191	
Stephens, Benjamin	030	c1815	WB-3/52	
Stephens, Charles	020	1793	RB-C/48	
Stephens, Charlotte	056	1824	WB-1/377	AR
Stephens, Christopher	072	1891	WB-4/257	AR
Stephens, Christopher	072	1891	035 WB-4/572	
Stephens, Edmund	099	1869	RB-35/25	AR
Stephens, Edward	056	1751	028 DB-5/275	SS/AR
Stephens, Esther	046	1864	WB-D/218	AR
Stephens, Evan	046	1830	WB-B/424	AR
Stephens, Grey	099	1874	RB-35/271	AR
Stephens, Henry	099	1885	WB-B/84	AR
Stephens, Iverson G.	020	1861	RB-S/444	AR
Stephens, J. T.	020	1893	WB-B/146	CTY
Stephens, Jacob	056	1781	Orig. Only	AR
Stephens, James	099	1873	RB-35/232	AR
Stephens, James M.	070	1792	WB-C/401	AR-Nunc.
Stephens, Jeremiah	069	1805	WB-1/159	AR
Stephens, John	056	c1898	WB-4/481	AR
Stephens, John	005	c1781	WB-1/42	
Stephens, John	083	c1804	WB-1/86	AR
Stephens, John	049	1881	Orig. Only	AR

Name	Co.	Date	Recorded Copy	Original
Stephens, John	057	1782	WB-A/8	AR
Stephens, John	030	1816	WB-3/86	
Stephens, John Allen	022	1881	WB-E/223	AR
Stephens, John F.	065	1899	WB-N/274	AR
Stephens, John W.	020	1898	WB-B/323	CTY
Stephens, John W.	020	1870	WB-A/51	CTY
Stephens, Lydia	030	1817	WB-3/92	
Stephens, Martha Ann	087	1897	WB-4/48	AR
Stephens, Martha F.	084	1891	WB-E/475	CTY
Stephens, Mary	020	1855	RB-R/322	AR
Stephens, Noah	027	1873	WB-2/14	AR
Stephens, Rachel	057	c1825	WB-B/101	AR
Stephens, Richard	009	1785	OWB/207	AR
Stephens, Shadrack	037	1790	WB-C/126	AR
Stephens, Thomas	020	1839	RB-N/341	AR
Stephens, William	085	1803	WB-D/43	AR
Stephens, William	020	1837	RB-N/14	AR
Stephens, Willoughby	072	1839	WB-2/14	AR
Stephenson, Abraham	071	1791	WB-1/427	
Stephenson, Amos	071	1862	WB-5/260	AR
Stephenson, Benjamin	071	1873	WB-6/127	AR
Stephenson, Clarisy	081	1898	WB-16/497	AR
Stephenson, David	071	1873	WB-6/120	AR
Stephenson, David	099	1830	RB-22/460	
Stephenson, David	099	1808	RB-8/9	AR
Stephenson, Edwin L.	047	1849	WB-4/274	
Stephenson, Emaline	071	1899	WB-7/428	AR
Stephenson, Emily	047	1885	WB-6/410	AR
Stephenson, George	056	1886	WB-3/410	AR
Stephenson, George	037	1754	SS 879/131	SS/AR
Stephenson, Henry	099	c1830	RB-22/460	AR
Stephenson, J. A. D.	054	1897	WB-6/80	
Stephenson, James	065	1824	WB-E/95	
Stephenson, James	071	1869	WB-6/39	AR
Stephenson, James A.	071	1865	WB-5/312	AR
Stephenson, James E.	099	1868	RB-35/57	AR
Stephenson, John	056	1829	WB-1/347	AR
Stephenson, John	065	1843	WB-H/132	AR
Stephenson, John W.	071	1878	WB-6/251	AR
Stephenson, L. B.	071	1895	WB-7/240	AR
Stephenson, Lavinera	047	1900	WB-7/275	AR
Stephenson, Louisa M.	099	1886	WB-B/114	AR
Stephenson, M. McC.	09	1887	WB-B/229	AR
Stephenson, M. W.	003	1897	WB-B/367	
Stephenson, Martha M.	071	1877	WB-6/223	AR
Stephenson, Martha W.	051	1899	WB-C/565	AR
Stephenson, Mary	018	1809	Orig. Only	AR-Copy
Stephenson, Matthew	046	c1788	WB-A/341	AR
Stephenson, Moore	056	1896	WB-4/9	
Stephenson, Nathaniel	071	1856	WB-5/167	AR
Stephenson, P. H.	071	1876	WB-6/192	AR
Stephenson, Quinton	056	1869	WB-3/23	AR
Stephenson, Robert P.	071	1897	WB-7/343	AR
Stephenson, Samuel B.	071	1900	WB-7/456	AR
Stephenson, Sarah	056	1892	WB-2/132	
Stephenson, Sarah L.A.	099	1885	WB-B/86	AR
Stephenson, Solomon	056	1861	WB-2/18	AR
Stephenson, Stephen	099	1863	RB-32/600	AR
Stephenson, William	071	1837	WB-4/158	AR
Stephenson, William	028	1807	WB-B/264	AR
Stephenson, William T.	071	1876	WB-6/188	AR
Stepney, John	077	1754	SS 881/30	SS/AR
Stepney, John	077	1750	Orig. Only	SS/AR
Stepney, Major	077	1855	WB-F/460	AR
Stepp, Henry	050	1893	WB-2/176	CTY
Stepp, James	071	1818	WB-3/208	AR
Stepp, Rachael	013	1876	WB-B/140	AR
Stepp, Silas H.	013	1866	WB-A/243	AR
Steptoe, Ann W.	047	1877	WB-6/165	AR
Sterling, Ann	065	1877	WB-K/280	
Sterling, John J.	027	1821	WB-A/45	AR
Sterling, Polley	103	1856	RD-12/188	AR
Stern, A. L.	079	1884	WB-2/306	AR
Stertsbach, Daniel	060	1823	Orig. Only	AR
Stevens, A. F.	097	1895	WB-2/475	AR
Stevens, Abraham	029	1822	WB-B/96	AR
Stevens, Alice	087	c1802	Orig. Only	AR
Stevens, Alsey	056	1838	WB-1/504	AR
Stevens, Amos	097	1855	WB-1/106	AR
Stevens, Barnabas	087	c1800	Orig. Only	AR
Stevens, Benjamin	056	1840	WB-1/520	AR
Stevens, Bryant	056	1895	WB-2/192	AR
Stevens, Charles	051	1837	WB-A/94	
Stevens, Edmund H.	037	1853	WB-F/507	AR
Stevens, Edward	103	1813	RD-3/76	AR
Stevens, Elizabeth	056	1855	WB-1/685	AR
Stevens, Everett P.	056	1878	WB-3/203	AR
Stevens, Irby	056	1867	WB-2/100	AR
Stevens, Isham	099	1823	RB-18/26	AR
Stevens, Jacob	056	1830	WB-1/409	AR
Stevens, James	083	c1804	WB-1/86	AR
Stevens, James	099	1885	WB-B/89	AR
Stevens, James	008	1739	SS 877/128	SS/AR
Stevens, James	103	1782	WI-A/1	AR
Stevens, Jane	073	1848	WB-F/425	AR
Stevens, Jemima	087	1831	WB-1/120	AR
Stevens, Jeremiah	030	1757	SS 882/185	SS/AR
Stevens, John	056	c1777	Orig. Only	AR
Stevens, John	029	1779	Orig. Only	AR
Stevens, John F.	026	1899	WB-3/55	AR
Stevens, John, Sr.	087	1784	Orig. Only	AR
Stevens, John, Sr.	087	1829	WB-1/100	AR
Stevens, Lewis	075	1812	WB-M1/244	AR-Nunc.
Stevens, Mary	099	1797	RB-4/31	AR
Stevens, Mary J.	087	1891	WB-3/476	AR
Stevens, Needham B.	103	1898	WB-2/214	AR
Stevens, Needham B.	056	1898	WB-4/101	AR
Stevens, Olivia R.	035	1887	WB-4/310	AR
Stevens, Rebeckah	056	1793	WB-1/76	AR
Stevens, Richard	072	c1784	WB-A/125	AR
Stevens, Sallie K.	056	1900	WB-4/249	AR
Stevens, Sally K.	103	1900	WB-2/314	AR
Stevens, Squire, Sr.	097	1844	WB-1/13	AR
Stevens, Thomas	028	1751	DB-5/174	SS/AR
Stevens, Thomasen	030	1748	Orig. Only	SS/AR
Stevens, William	024	1698	SS 874.2/92	SS/AR
Stevens, William	087	1841	WB-1/252	AR
Stevens, William	009	1750	028 DB-5/169	SS/AR
Stevens, Zachariah	099	1832	RB-22/314	AR
Stevenson, Abraham	013	1888	WB-B/529	AR
Stevenson, Andrew	065	1868	WB-K/51	AR
Stevenson, Ann	046	1797	WB-A/348	AR
Stevenson, Arthur	071	1789	WB-2/20	AR
Stevenson, Arthur	071	1823	WB-3/285	AR
Stevenson, Charles	057	1794	WB-A/173	AR
Stevenson, Charles	071	1751	Orig. Only	SS/AR
Stevenson, Elizabeth	077	1800	WB-E/113	AR
Stevenson, George S.	028	1861	WB-D/356	AR
Stevenson, J. Austin	054	1900	WB-6/306	CTY
Stevenson, J. H.	054	1897	WB-6/101	CTY

Name	Co.	Date	Recorded Copy	Original
Stevenson, James	056	1848	WB-1/609	AR
Stevenson, James	028	1784	Orig. Only	AR
Stevenson, James	054	c1817	WB-1A/101	
Stevenson, James	054	c1828	WB-2/59	AR
Stevenson, John	075	N. D.	Orig. Only	AR
Stevenson, John	028	1756	SS 880/26	
Stevenson, John F.	054	1886	WB-5/139	CTY
Stevenson, John H.	059	1889	WB-A/560	CTY
Stevenson, Joseph	047	1769	WB-1/242	
Stevenson, Lemuel B.	051	1839	WB-A/142	
Stevenson, Lydia	054	1857	WB-3/126	
Stevenson, Martin	028	1849	WB-D/163	
Stevenson, Mary	028	1802	WB-B/139	AR
Stevenson, Prudence	054	1851	WB-3/51	AR
Stevenson, Richard	100	1898	WB-51/511	
Stevenson, Sebert W.	046	1870	WB-E/31	AR
Stevenson, Sollomon	056	1794	WB-1/78	AR
Stevenson, Thomas	077	1774	WB-C/131	AR
Stevenson, Thomas	077	1802	WB-E/154	AR
Stevenson, William	071	1761	WB-1/59	
Stevenson, William	054	1841	WB-2/224	AR
Stevenson, William	077	1739	LGB-4/#93	SS/AR
Stevenson, William	054	c1803	WB-1/37	AR
Stevenson, William R.	054	1874	WB-4/164	CTY
Stevenson, William S.	054	1900	WB-6/297	CTY
Stevenson, Winbern	071	1847	WB-5/65	AR
Steward, Charles	070	1777	WB-C/394	AR
Steward, N. T.	026	1897	WB-2/541	AR
Steward, William	077	1711/2	SS 874.1/46	SS/AR
Stewart (Stuart), John A.	097	1848	WB-1/50	AR
Stewart, A. J.	016	1837	PQS.5/460	
Stewart, Abner	054	1885	WB-5/62	CTY
Stewart, Affish	030	1804	WB-2/239	
Stewart, Alexander	081	1870	WB-15/42	
Stewart, Alexander	028	1798	WB-B/61	AR
Stewart, Andrew	065	1834	WB-G/179	AR
Stewart, Andrew	028	1826	WB-C/277	AR
Stewart, Charles	019	1844	WB-A/110	AR
Stewart, Charles	022	1782	Orig. Only	AR
Stewart, Culpeper P.	097	1898	WB-2/570	AR
Stewart, Daniel	048	1900	WB-1/111	CTY
Stewart, Daniel	087	1875	WB-3/99	AR
Stewart, David	085	c1829	WB-H/481	AR
Stewart, David	048	1900	WB-1/141	CTY
Stewart, Donald	046	1830	WB-B/413	AR
Stewart, Dugal	087	c1805	Orig. Only	AR
Stewart, Dugald	029	1818	WB-B/12	AR
Stewart, Effie	029	1886	WB-E/380	AR
Stewart, Eldridge	048	1893	WB-1/3	CTY-Copy
Stewart, Eli	065	1865	WB-L/99	AR
Stewart, Eli	097	1866	WB-1/273	AR
Stewart, Elizabeth	029	1815	WB-A/210	
Stewart, Elizabeth	097	1877	WB-2/109	AR
Stewart, Elizabeth	098	1889	WB-A/106	CTY
Stewart, Elizabeth	085	c1792	WB-D/65	AR
Stewart, Everet	067	N. D.	WB-1/77	AR
Stewart, Finley	046	1809	WB-A/363	AR
Stewart, Francis	019	1820	Orig. Only	AR
Stewart, George	068	1874	WB-D/53	
Stewart, Harriet	065	1897	WB-N/27	AR
Stewart, Harriet E.	097	1897	WB-2/513	AR
Stewart, Hector	029	1842	WB-C/22	AR
Stewart, Henry	082	1894	WB-6/489	AR
Stewart, Hugh	097	1848	WB-1/53	AR
Stewart, Hugh	017	c1858	WB-A/111	AR
Stewart, Hugh	011	c1771	WB-2/269	
Stewart, James	046	1840	WB-C/50	AR
Stewart, James	082	1899	WB-7/32	AR
Stewart, James	022	1889	WB-E/397	AR
Stewart, James	099	1867	RB-34/445	AR
Stewart, James	022	1794	RB-2/16	AR
Stewart, James	028	1795	WB-A/343	AR
Stewart, James	079	1802	Orig. Only	028 AR
Stewart, James	085	c1778	WB-C/204	AR
Stewart, James	054	c1793	WB-1/208	AR
Stewart, James	085	1823	WB-H/208	AR
Stewart, James	028	1805	WB-B/221	AR
Stewart, James	022	c1775	Orig. Only	AR
Stewart, James	020	1783	RB-A/246	AR
Stewart, James	082	1822	WB-1/218	AR
Stewart, James D.	VA	1883	Copy	078 AR
Stewart, James R.	054	1899	WB-6/244	CTY
Stewart, James, Sr.	054	c1812	WB-1/344	AR
Stewart, Jane A.	065	1891	WB-M/20	AR
Stewart, John	030	c1803	WB-2/338	
Stewart, John	028	1881	WB-E/283	AR
Stewart, John	083	1821	WB-1/319 & 400	AR
Stewart, John	029	c1793	Orig. Only	AR
Stewart, John	065	1826	WB-E/105	AR
Stewart, John	029	1844	WB-C/75	
Stewart, John	087	1846	WB-1/313	AR
Stewart, John	070	1793	WB-C/402	AR
Stewart, John	010	1774	Orig. Only	SS/AR
Stewart, John	048	c1873	WB-1/16	CTY-Copy
Stewart, John	085	1832	WB-H/558	AR
Stewart, John	028	1742	Deeds.21/L22	SS/AR
Stewart, John	090	1877	WB-6/92	AR
Stewart, John	005	1783	WB-1/65	
Stewart, John C.	013	1873	WB-B/68	AR
Stewart, John D.	097	1884	WB-2/250	AR
Stewart, John T.	085	1873	WB-1/194	AR
Stewart, Jonathan	038	c1858	WB-1/183	
Stewart, Joseph	097	1866	WB-1/277	AR
Stewart, Joseph	030	1786	WB-1/206	
Stewart, Joseph	068	1867	WB-C/162	
Stewart, Joshua	075	1877	WB-O/78	AR
Stewart, Kinnon	099	1815	RB-12/191	
Stewart, Levi	030	1753	Orig. Only	SS/AR
Stewart, Lydia	028	1822	WB-C/220	AR
Stewart, Lydia	092	1772	WB-1/13	AR
Stewart, Manson	044	1899	WB-24/435	CTY
Stewart, Margaret	082	1823	WB-1/241	AR
Stewart, Margaret	029	1886	WB-E/380	AR
Stewart, Martha	054	1844	WB-2/285	AR
Stewart, Martha A.	090	1891	WB-6/259	AR
Stewart, Mary	029	1857	WB-C/372	
Stewart, Matthew	065	1808	WB-F/190	AR
Stewart, Nancy	017	1871	WB-B/31	AR
Stewart, Nathaniel	028	1796	WB-B/7	AR
Stewart, Nelson	099	1884	WB-A/583	AR
Stewart, Oliver	019	1869	WB-B/54	AR
Stewart, Patrick	011	c1777	WB-2/284	
Stewart, Penelope E.	009	1886	WB-1/381	CTY
Stewart, Rachael	016	1877	WB-3/209	AR
Stewart, Reuben	097	1847	WB-1/46	AR
Stewart, Robert	065	1777	WB-F/158	AR
Stewart, Robert	046	1833	WB-B/481	AR

Name	Co.	Date	Recorded Copy	Original
Stewart, Robert A.	054	1892	WB-5/443	CTY
Stewart, Sallie	084	1891	WB-E/489	CTY
Stewart, Sampson	046	1832	WB-B/454	AR
Stewart, Samuel	073	1827	WB-E/145	AR
Stewart, Samuel	085	1770	WB-A/153	AR
Stewart, Samuel	046	1833	WB-B/493	AR
Stewart, Samuel	081	1869	WB-15/39	
Stewart, Samuel S.	065	1872	WB-K/104	AR
Stewart, Sarah	028	1823	WB-C/240	AR
Stewart, Silas P.	097	1852	WB-1/80	AR
Stewart, Susan	065	1879	WB-K/334	AR
Stewart, T. J.	054	1893	WB-5/484	CTY
Stewart, Thomas	096	1792	Orig. Only	AR
Stewart, Thomas	078	1818	WI-8/77	AR
Stewart, William	011	c1778	WB-2/296	
Stewart, William	086	1832	WB-D/144	AR
Stewart, William	099	1884	WB-A/545	AR
Stewart, William	086	1838	WB-E/50	AR
Stewart, William C.	098	1885	WB-A/37	CTY
Stewart, William M.	038	1899	WB-4/147	AR
Stewart, William R.	066	1897	WB-1/157	AR
Stewart, William W.	038	1900	WB-4/272	
Stewartt, David	090	1807	WB-2/84	AR
Sthudards, William	092	1809	WB-3/94	AR
Stiball, Richard	002	c1695	Orig. Only	SS/AR
Stigerwalt, Peter	085	c1795	WB-D/25	AR
Stigerwatt, John	085	1800	WB-D/56	AR
Stigleather, John G.	065	c1780	WB-D/33	AR
Stikeleather, George	085	1824	WB-H/290	AR
Stikeleather, Nicholas	054	1885	WB-5/41	AR-Copy
Stikeleather, Susan	054	1886	WB-5/108	CTY
Stiles, Anna E.	100	1895	WB-51/434	
Stiles, James W.	072	c1869	WB-A/162	AR
Stiles, John	049	c1833	WI-1-2/2	AR
Stiles, Lemuel	072	1884	Orig. Only	AR
Stiles, William	021	c1888	WB-2/422	AR
Stiles, William	039	c1790	WB-A/80	
Stiley, Sarah	057	1821	WB-B/59	AR
Still, John	016	1844	WB-1/52	
Stilley, Ephram	028	1812	WB-C/50	AR
Stilley, Ishmail	028	1836	WB-C/386	AR
Stilley, William	009	1882	WB-1/316	
Stillwell, Ephraim P.	055	1888	WB-A/84	
Stillwell, Thomas	085	1774	WB-A/184	AR
Stilly, Earl R.	059	1878	Orig. Only	CTY
Stilly, Fountain	028	1826	WB-C/269	AR
Stilly, Levi	009	1854	OB-I/172	AR
Stilman, Samuel	037	1827	WB-F/81	AR
Stilwell, Jacob	061	1849	WB-1/39	AR
Stilwell, John	065	1849	WB-I/148	AR
Stilwell, John F.	097	1886	WB-2/296	AR
Stilwell, Mary M.	065	1898	WB-N/82	AR
Stilwell, Middleton	014	1894	WB-2/528	CTY
Stilwell, Sarah M.	065	1884	WB-K/583	AR
Stilwell, Silas N.	065	1884	WB-K/588	AR
Stimpson, Solomon	054	1888	WB-5/234	CTY
Stimson, Daniel	ME	1890	028 WB-E/544	028 AR
Stimson, E. B.	054	1898	WB-6/150	CTY
Stimson, F. W.	038	1855	WB-1/68	AR
Stimson, Jane	054	1848	WB-3/28	AR
Stine, A. J.	021	1898	WB-3/216	AR
Stine, Catharine	021	1851	WB-1/92	AR
Stine, John	003	1878	WB-B/103	AR
Stines, Walton	049	1898	WB-2/411	AR
Stinson, Aaron	022	1799	WB-A/15	AR

Name	Co.	Date	Recorded Copy	Original
Stinson, Alexander	020	1781	RB-A/182	AR
Stinson, Andrew	065	c1779	WB-F/150	AR
Stinson, B. B.	022	1891	WB-E/460	AR
Stinson, Cyrus	065	1894	WB-M/262	AR
Stinson, David	065	1856	WB-J/34	AR
Stinson, George W.	054	1883	WB-4/511	CTY
Stinson, Hugh	065	1778	WB-F/157	AR
Stinson, Hugh	065	1827	WB-E/91	AR
Stinson, James	065	1824	WB-E/94	AR
Stinson, John	065	1837	WB-E/156	AR
Stinson, Jonathan	065	1881	WB-K/448	AR
Stinson, Lovel	099	1880	WB-A/99	AR
Stinson, Nancy	065	1837	WB-E/133	AR
Stinson, Robert	022	1850	WB-C/265	AR
Stinson, William R.	067	1874	WB-2/40	AR
Stion, Millie	051	c1896	WB-D/2	AR
Stirewalt, Allison	085	1866	WB-K/376	AR
Stirewalt, Anah Mariah	054	c1858	Orig. Only	AR
Stirewalt, Caleb	085	1886	WB-2/212	CTY
Stirewalt, Catherine	016	1866	WB-2/130	
Stirewalt, Charles	085	1836	WB-H/681	AR
Stirewalt, Daniel	085	c1868	WB-1/18	CTY
Stirewalt, Emeline	021	c1900	WB-3/293	AR
Stirewalt, Frederick	085	1889	WB-2/381	CTY
Stirewalt, Henry	085	1861	WB-K/292	AR
Stirewalt, Jacob	054	1869	WB-4/40	AR
Stirewalt, Jacob	016	1855	WB-1/261	
Stirewalt, Jacob	016	1889	WB-4/34	AR
Stirewalt, John	085	1828	WB-H/436	AR
Stirewalt, John N.	085	1836	WB-H/705	AR
Stirewalt, Michael	085	1833	WB-H/599	AR
Stirewalt, Tobias	016	1853	WB-1/225	
Stiring, George	019	1745	SS 877/47	SS/AR
Stiron, John	019	1823	WB-D/380	AR
Stiron, John, Sr.	019	1793	WB-D/353	AR
Stiron, Richard	019	1806	WB-D/365	AR
Stiron, Samuel	019	1798	WB-D/359	AR
Stirring, George	019	1745	Orig. Only	AR
Stith, A. B.	032	1873	WB-3/84	AR
Stith, Bassett	047	1817	WB-3/607	
Stith, Lucy	100	1815	WB-19/116	AR
Stith, Nicholas	032	1886	WB-3/517	AR
Stith, Nicholas	022	1878	WB-E/177	AR
Stitt, Ann	065	1848	WB-I/116	AR
Stitt, Edward	065	1828	WB-C/8	AR
Stitt, James M.	097	1865	WB-1/262	AR
Stitt, Jane	097	1844	WB-1/7	AR
Stitt, John	065	1847	WB-I/112	AR
Stitt, John, Sr.	065	1843	WB-H/109	AR
Stitt, Neil M.	065	1865	WB-J/211	AR
Stitt, Susannah	097	1853	WB-1/84	AR
Stitt, William	065	1816	WB-F/199	AR
Stitt, William M.	065	1839	WB-E/233	AR
Stoakes, John	077	1772	WB-C/120	AR
Stoakes, William	035	1833	WB-1/43	AR
Stoakes, William	072	1787	WI/L43	AR
Stoakley, Joseph	075	1729/0	SS 876/210	SS/AR
Stockard, James G.	001	1871	WB-2/26	AR
Stockard, John	001	1861	WB-1/191	AR
Stockard, Julia Ann	001	1888	WB-2/372	AR
Stockard, Samuel S.	001	1873	WB-2/56	AR
Stockburger, Elizabeth	038	1862	WB-1/212	AR
Stockburger, Johanna J.	038	1877	WB-2/323	AR
Stockburger, Sarah	038	1869	WB-2/6	AR
Stockburger, Sarah	090	1843	WB-4/122	AR

Name	Co.	Date	Recorded Copy	Original
Stockdale, James	037	1790	WB-C/139	AR
Stockdale, John	037	1774	WB-A/221	AR
Stockham, Alonzo	PA	1900	Copy	025 AR
Stockinger, Lewis	085	c1806	WB-G/6	AR
Stockley, John	070	1756	DB-D/206	
Stockley, Thomas	070	1758	SS 882/48	SS/AR
Stockly, Thomas, Sr.	070	c1749	DB-D/320	AR
Stocks, John	079	1866	WB-1/159	
Stocks, Louvenia	079	1891	WB-2/578	AR
Stocks, Susan	079	1861	WB-1/65	AR
Stocks, Wiley	045	1879	WB-1/51	AR
Stockton, Daniel	090	1804	WB-2/51	AR
Stockton, Daughty	038	1855	WB-1/81	AR
Stockton, John B.	038	1884	WB-2/483	AR
Stockton, Joseph H.	038	1900	WB-4/203	AR
Stockton, Joseph W.	054	1881	WB-4/451	CTY
Stockton, Margaret	054	1877	WB-4/275	CTY
Stockton, Mary M.	038	1897	WB-4/58	AR
Stockton, Reitta C.	038	1898	WB-4/119	AR
Stockton, Richard	013	1840	WB-A/74	
Stockton, Richard	NJ	c1826	049 WB-2/70	
Stockton, Samuel	086	1807	WB-B/211	AR
Stoehr (Star), Henry	090	1812	WB-2/134	AR
Stoehr, Casper	085	1814	WB-G/311	AR
Stogdill, Thomas	085	1797	WB-D/68	AR
Stokely, Isaac	075	1811	WB-M1/223	AR
Stokely, Lydia	075	c1857	WB-M2/51	AR
Stokely, Martha	075	1852	WB-N/239	AR
Stokely, Murden	075	1875	WB-O/62	AR
Stokely, Penelope	075	1889	WB-O/307	AR
Stoker, Mary Ann	089	1888	WB-2/173	AR
Stoker, Sarah	089	1858	WB-1/195	
Stokes, Amace	020	1817	RB-H/85	AR
Stokes, Andrew	035	1838	Orig. Only	AR
Stokes, Bathenia	039	c1856	WB-O/355	AR
Stokes, Calvin	079	1891	WB-2/571	AR
Stokes, Christopher	085	1822	WB-H/182	AR
Stokes, David	039	1789	WB-A/42	
Stokes, David	017	1873	WB-B/40	AR
Stokes, Elisabeth	085	1791	WB-B/173	AR-Nunc.
Stokes, Exum	077	1882	WB-H/116	AR
Stokes, Fanny	077	1833	WB-F/219	AR
Stokes, Guilford	079	1881	WB-2/230	AR
Stokes, Henry C.	077	1885	WB-C/159	AR
Stokes, J. J. F.	037	1847	WB-F/361	AR
Stokes, James G.	035	1882	WB-4/194	AR
Stokes, John	037	1784	WB-B/132	AR
Stokes, John	075	1801	WB-M1/51	AR
Stokes, John	075	1882	WB-O/155	AR
Stokes, John A.	053	1862	WB-9/127	
Stokes, Malinda	086	1900	WB-G/34	AR
Stokes, Marcus	037	1784	WB-B/142	AR
Stokes, Mary	100	1784	WB-4/46	AR
Stokes, Rachel	104	1861	WB-5/270 & 393	AR
Stokes, Rebecca	039	1832	WB-J/191	AR
Stokes, Richard	089	1853	WB-1/115	
Stokes, Robert M.	065	1899	WB-N/432	AR
Stokes, Samuel	106	1897	WB-2/408	
Stokes, Silvanus	020	1847	RB-P/427	
Stokes, Stadrack	037	1784	WB-B/142	AR-Nunc.
Stokes, Thomas	078	1881	WB-19/125	
Stokes, Thomas	039	1850	WB-N/300	AR
Stokes, William	085	1864	WB-K/331	AR
Stokes, William	047	1897	WB-7/212	AR
Stokes, William	079	1885	WB-2/352	AR
Stokes, William	039	c1843	WB-O/392	AR
Stokes, William	022	c1860	WB-D/71	AR
Stokes, William Y.	084	1882	WB-E/232	CTY
Stokesberry, John A.	053	1862	WB-9/127	AR
Stokesbury, John P.	009	1847	OB-F/383	AR
Stokley, James	070	1869	WB-E/158	AR
Stokley, Joseph	075	1805	Orig. Only	AR
Stolkup, Austen	020	1810	RB-F/116	AR
Stolts, Gertrude	038	1857	WB-1/131	AR
Stoltz, Alice W.	038	1887	WB-3/66	AR
Stoltz, Casper	090	1842	WB-4/95	AR
Stoltz, Daniel	092	1886	WB-6/250	AR
Stoltz, Joel T.	038	1863	WB-1/206	AR
Stoltz, John	090	1837	WB-3/318	AR
Stoltz, Sally	092	1899	WB-6/514	AR
Stoltz, Simon	090	1843	WB-4/141	AR
Stoltz, Thomas S.	038	1891	WB-3/244	AR
Stone, Abraham	092	1846	WB-4/249	
Stone, Angelo	070	c1789	Orig. Only	AR
Stone, Ann	022	1831	WB-B/199	AR
Stone, Augustin	092	1892	WB-6/341	AR
Stone, Benjamin	011	c1780	WB-1/399	
Stone, Benjamin	010	1812	WB-F/212	AR
Stone, Daniel	098	1886	WB-A/48	CTY
Stone, David W.	099	1848	RB-26/415	AR
Stone, Elijah	054	c1882	WB-4/476	CTY
Stone, Elisha	077	1808	WB-E/310	AR
Stone, Elizabeth	078	1811	WI-5/253	AR
Stone, Ellen M.	092	1900	WB-6/527	AR
Stone, Enoch	099	1862	RB-32/603	AR
Stone, Eproditus	020	1811	RB-F/204	AR
Stone, Francis	022	1817	WB-A/288	AR
Stone, Happy	039	1853	WB-N/330	AR
Stone, Hezekiah	078	1798	WI-2/68	AR
Stone, James R.	083	1890	WB-3/478	AR
Stone, John	046	1812	WB-A/369	AR
Stone, John	022	1847	WB-C/206	AR
Stone, John	039	1833	WB-J/245	AR
Stone, John	077	1744	Orig. Only	SS/AR
Stone, John S.	022	c1861	WB-D/83	AR
Stone, John W.	VA	1880	030 WB-5/225	030 AR
Stone, Jonathan	069	1877	WB-5/62	AR
Stone, Jonathan	044	1837	WB-13/523	CTY
Stone, Joseph B.	022	1879	WB-E/176	AR
Stone, Joshua	022	1876	WB-E/110	AR
Stone, Lemuel	075	1800	WB-M1/43	AR
Stone, Lemuel W.	068	c1855	WB-C/84	
Stone, Lucy A.	092	1896	WB-6/434	AR
Stone, Lydia	077	1793	WB-C/467	AR-Copy
Stone, McCullan	069	1862	WB-1/583	AR
Stone, Moses	077	1791	WB-C/427	AR
Stone, Moses	077	1802	WB-E/158	AR
Stone, Nancy	075	1867	WB-M2/101	AR
Stone, Pinkney M.	084	1874	WB-E/80	CTY
Stone, Polly	084	1845	WB-C/29	CTY
Stone, Rachel	010	1846	WB-G/411	AR
Stone, Richard	030	1749	Orig. Only	SS/AR
Stone, Samuel	083	1885	Orig. Only	AR
Stone, Sarah	099	1838	RB-24/195	AR
Stone, Sarah A.	099	1897	WB-D/16	AR
Stone, Thomas	022	1827	WB-B/140	AR
Stone, Thomas R.	GA	1860	084 WB-C/327	084 CTY
Stone, W. A.	092	1889	WB-6/290	AR-Nunc.
Stone, William	020	1843	RB-P/20	

Name	Co.	Date	Recorded Copy	Original
Stone, William	010	1873	WB-I/46	AR
Stone, William	028	1720	SS 875/277	
Stone, William	104	1825	WB-4/60	AR
Stone, William	092	1821	WB-3/147	AR
Stone, William	092	1858	WB-5/36	
Stone, Zedekiah	010	1797	WB-E/4	AR
Stoner, Barbara	085	1850	WB-K/114	AR
Stoner, Jacob	032	1841	WB-1/364	AR
Stoner, John M.	085	1875	WB-1/306	CTY
Stoner, Jonathan	085	1879	WB-1/486	CTY
Stoner, Margaret	032	1860	WB-2/217	AR
Stoner, Peter	085	1846	WB-K/16	AR
Stoner, Samuel	085	1857	Orig. Only	AR
Stonesipher, John Henry	104	1818	WB-3/184	AR
Storey, James	085	1762	WB-A/148	AR
Stork, Charles A.	085	c1830	WB-H/507	AR
Storm, Jamima	083	1828	WB-1/341	AR
Storm, Mary	011	c1803	WB-1/398	
Storm, Wandal	011	c1770	WB-2/289	
Story, Benjamin	071	1895	WB-7/278	AR
Story, Elizabeth	071	1895	WB-7/251	AR
Story, James	047	1777	WB-2/60	
Story, Rachel	029	1831	WB-B/205	AR
Story, Samuel	071	1866	WB-5/323	AR
Story, Sarah	047	1796	WB-3/269	
Stots, Samuel	090	1820	WB-3/46	
Stoudivant, Sarah	047	1783	WB-3/37	
Stough, Andrew	067	1839	PQS.2/224	
Stough, Martin	016	1842	PQS.6/168	
Stough, Mary A.	065	1883	WB-K/545	AR
Stout, Charles	072	1780	RW/L15	AR
Stout, Eliza E.	081	1891	WB-16/210	AR
Stout, Hannah	081	1894	WB-16/307	
Stout, Joseph	081	1831	WB-6/14	AR
Stout, Joseph	081	1866	WB-14/1	AR
Stout, Nancy J.	081	1881	WB-15/364	AR
Stout, Permelia L.	081	1898	WB-16/493	AR
Stout, Peter	001	1859	WB-1/169	AR
Stout, Samuel	081	1801	WB-2/75	AR
Stout, William	022	1843	WB-C/137	AR
Stout, Zemri	081	1894	WB-16/278	AR
Stovall, Bartholomew	073	1803	WB-D/91	AR
Stovall, John	044	1820	WB-8/412	CTY
Stovall, John	044	1781	WB-1/313	CTY
Stovall, John W.	044	1899	WB-24/421	CTY
Stovall, William	044	1803	WB-5/301	CTY
Stover, Jeremiah	104	1808	WB-2/226	AR
Stover, John Jacob	028	1744	SS 877/331	
Stow, George	030	1850	WB-4/156	
Stow, Joseph	030	1795	WB-2/48	
Stow, Mariam	030	1790	WB-1/247	
Stowe, Abram	060	1841	WB-2/107	AR/CRX
Stowe, Elizabeth	040	1871	WB-2/26	AR
Stowe, Jacob	060	1831	WB-1/207	
Stowe, Jemima P.	065	1885	WB-L/55	AR
Stowe, Joseph	016	1886	WB-3/495	AR
Stowe, Larkin	040	1857	WB-1/89	
Stowe, Lemuel	060	1841	WB-2/79	AR
Stowe, Matilda	016	1884	WB-3/473	AR
Strader, Adam M.	001	1892	WB-2/502	AR
Strader, Conrad	020	1808	RB-F/19	AR
Strader, David	020	1826	RB-L/80	AR
Strader, Henry	001	1861	WB-1/186	AR
Strader, Jonathan	046	1877	WB-E/208	AR
Strader, Michael	001	1874	WB-2/91	AR
Strader, Sarah T.	084	1886	WB-E/356	CTY
Stradford, Elias	083	c1800	WB-1/60	
Strain, David	073	1837	WB-E/402	AR
Strain, Jane	073	1855	WB-G/100	AR
Strain, John	073	1826	WB-E/99	AR
Strain, Miriam	073	1869	WB-H/17	CTY
Strain, Miriam	073	1843	WB-F/163	AR
Strain, Miriam	073	1830	WB-E/219	AR
Strain, Sarah	073	1830	WB-E/221	AR
Strait, David	099	1792	RB-2/379	
Strane, Andrew	014	c1825	049 WI-A/24	049 AR
Strange, Abraham	104	1815	WB-3/103	AR
Strange, Abraham A.	104	c1814	Copy	017 AR
Strange, Abraham A.	104	1815	SC/03797	AR-Copy
Strange, James	039	1892	WB-U/575	AR
Strange, James	065	1863	WB-J/167	AR
Strange, James W.	029	1892	WB-E/566	AR
Strange, John	085	c1782	WB-B/2	AR
Strange, Mary T.	099	1863	RB-32/604	AR
Strange, Robert	029	1854	WB-C/277	AR
Strange, Ruth	072	c1798	WB-A/125	AR
Strange, Thomas W.	070	1899	WB-H/236	AR
Strange, William	032	1823	WB-1/22	AR
Strange, William F.	065	1868	WB-J/232	AR
Stratton, William	084	1842	WB-B/275	CTY
Straughan, Richard	022	1805	WB-A/118	AR
Straughan, Wiley B.	022	1843	WB-C/140	AR
Straughn, Alston	022	1853	WB-C/353	AR
Strauss, Joseph	103	1899	WB-2/263	AR
Strauss, Mary E.	103	1899	WB-2/236	AR
Strauss, William H.	070	1896	WB-G/518	AR
Strayhorn, Charles	073	1855	WB-G/112	AR
Strayhorn, Elizabeth	073	1837	WB-E/410	AR
Strayhorn, Gilbert	073	1803	WB-D/87	AR
Strayhorn, Harriet H.	073	1881	WB-H/293	CTY
Strayhorn, James	073	1852	Orig. Only	AR
Strayhorn, James	073	1833	WB-E/287	AR
Strayhorn, John	073	1843	WB-F/165	AR
Strayhorn, Mary	073	1888	WB-H/581	CTY
Strayhorn, Parthenia	036	1898	WB-A/422	CTY
Strayhorn, Rachel	073	1837	WB-E/406	AR
Strayhorn, Sally	073	1888	WB-H/446	CTY
Strayhorn, Samuel	073	1821	WB-D/600	AR
Strayhorn, Thomas J.	073	1864	WB-G/459	CTY
Strayhorn, Thomas N.	073	1852	WB-G/26	
Strayhorn, William	073	1837	WB-E/424	AR
Streater, Edward	005	c1820	WB-2/150	AR
Streater, Emeline	005	1865	WB-C/221	AR
Streater, William K.	005	1884	WB-D/169	AR
Streator, Thomas	024	1765	WB-B/44	AR
Street, Ann	068	1858	WB-C/78	
Street, Anthony	086	1841	WB-E/76	AR
Street, Elizabeth	028	1861	WB-D/345	AR
Street, George W.	028	1866	WB-D/440	AR
Street, John J.	046	1871	WB-E/71	AR
Street, Moses	078	1815	WI-7/27	AR
Street, Nathaniel	028	1825	WB-C/262	AR
Street, Richard	068	1826	WB-B/45	
Street, Richard	068	1804	WB-A/231	
Street, Susan W.	078	1868	WB-19/2	
Street, Thomas	086	1800	WB-B/106	AR
Street, William	078	1847	WB-13/1	
Street, William J.	066	1887	WB-1/17	AR
Street, William R.	028	1853	WB-D/199	AR
Strehle, Gottlieb	090	1817	WB-3/5	AR

Name	Co.	Date	Recorded Copy	Original
Stricker, C. Ann	016	1856	WB-1/280	
Stricker, Daniel	016	c1836	WB-A/27	AR
Stricker, Eve	016	1863	WB-2/96	
Stricker, Susannah	016	1856	WB-1/279	
Stricklain, Burrell	082	1787	WB-1/23	AR-Nunc.
Strickland, Abel	039	1892	WB-U/538	AR
Strickland, Allison	069	1891	WB-5/340	AR
Strickland, Arnold	069	c1859	WB-1/585	AR
Strickland, Benjamin	056	1821	WB-1/324	AR
Strickland, Britton	103	1807	Orig. Only	AR
Strickland, C. B.	105	1886	WB-2/414	AR
Strickland, Calvin	069	1891	WB-5/336	
Strickland, Clara A.	099	1897	WB-C/588	AR
Strickland, Davis	056	1806	WB-1/192	AR
Strickland, Dinah	069	1835	WB-1/408	AR
Strickland, Drewry	071	1867	WB-5/345	AR
Strickland, Elisha	099	1795	RB-3/173	AR
Strickland, Elizabeth	035	1891	WB-4/390	AR
Strickland, Elvira	083	c1890	Orig. Only	AR
Strickland, Hardy	035	1880	WB-4/183	AR
Strickland, Harmon	047	1797	WB-3/276	
Strickland, Henry Right	056	1898	WB-4/117	AR
Strickland, Holley	087	1822	WB-1/42	AR
Strickland, Isaac	069	1882	WB-5/174	AR
Strickland, Jacob	069	1790	WB-1/66	AR
Strickland, Jacob	069	1858	WB-1/559	AR
Strickland, Jeremiah	103	1878	WB-1/145	AR
Strickland, Jesse	035	1872	WB-4/56	AR
Strickland, John	056	1886	WB-3/402	AR
Strickland, Joseph	069	1781	WB-1/17	AR
Strickland, Joseph	083	c1789	WB-1/17	AR
Strickland, Joseph	071	1755	SS 880/50	SS/AR
Strickland, Lot	099	1785	RB-2/45	AR
Strickland, M. W.	VA	1900	092 WB-6/556	092 AR
Strickland, Major	035	1887	WB-4/308	AR
Strickland, Mark	069	1811	WB-1/218	AR
Strickland, Mary	099	1845	RB-25/576	AR
Strickland, Mary	039	1874	WB-U/94	AR
Strickland, Matthew	099	1829	RB-21/107	AR
Strickland, Matthew	029	1892	WB-E/548	AR
Strickland, Moses	047	1765	WB-1/162	
Strickland, Nancy	069	1886	WB-5/237	AR
Strickland, Nancy	069	1835	WB-1/407	AR
Strickland, Nancy	047	1885	WB-6/397	AR
Strickland, Noah	069	1813	WB-1/277	AR
Strickland, Osborn	069	c1850	WB-1/534	
Strickland, Richardson	029	1886	WB-E/382	AR
Strickland, Samuel	056	1859	WB-1/730	AR
Strickland, Simon K.	099	1855	RB-29/403	AR
Strickland, Susan	047	1878	WB-6/195	AR
Strickland, Susan M. B.	105	1887	WB-2/425	
Strickland, Telitha	099	18878	RB-35/425	AR
Strickland, Uriah	056	1812	WB-1/387	AR
Strickland, William	071	1789	WB-1/388	AR
Strickland, William	N	1728	SS 876/145	SS/AR
Strickland, Wright	069	1868	WB-5/106	
Strickland, Zadok	069	1861	WB-1/578	AR
Stricklen, Benjamin	071	1805	WB-2/279	AR
Stricklen, Mathew	029	1829	WB-B/177	AR
Strickler, Daniel	016	1843	WB-1/4	
Stricklin, Abel	039	c1801	WB-B/77	
Stricklin, Benjamin	103	1863	RD-13/509	AR
Stricklin, Feraba	057	1865	WB-B/261	AR
Stricklin, Francis L.	005	1876	WB-D/50	AR
Stricklin, Lucy L.	005	1888	WB-D/248	AR
Stricklin, William	082	1850	WB-4/32	AR
Strickling, Nathan	071	1816	WB-3/182	AR
Strickling, Samuel	056	c1784	Orig. Only	AR
Strider, Abraham	081	1894	WB-16/274	AR
Strider, Mary	081	1828	WB-5/428	AR
Stringer, Edward	020	1779	RB-A/76	AR
Stringer, Francis	028	1753	Orig. Only	SS/AR
Stringer, Mary	024	1746	Orig. Only	SS/AR
Stringer, William	028	1857	WB-D/275	AR
Stringfellow, William	082	1825	WB-1/268	AR
Stringfield, Richard	071	1747	Orig. Only	SS/AR
Strohle, Catherine	038	1843	WB-1/41	AR
Strom, Christian	044	1812	WB-7/261	CTY
Stronach, George T.	099	1887	WB-B/178	AR
Stronach, William	099	1857	RB-30/258	AR
Strong, Anna E.	099	1897	WB-D/85	AR
Strong, Elizabeth	044	c1834	Orig. Only	CTY
Strong, Guernsey	039	1826	WB-H/155	AR
Strong, James P.	065	1899	WB-N/291	AR
Strong, Joel	044	1857	WB-20/467	CTY
Strong, John	084	1811	WB-A/313	CTY
Strong, John	057	1822	WB-B/71	AR
Strong, John	084	1873	WB-E/59	CTY
Strong, Robert	084	1848	WB-C/79	CTY
Strong, Ruth	084	1853	WB-C/159	CTY
Strong, Salmon	087	1848	WB-1/346	AR
Strother, John	TN	1816	093 WB-2/14	
Strother, John	TN	1816	062 WB-B/75	
Strother, John	TN	1816	107 WB-2/124	
Strother, John	TN	1816	055 WB-A/58	
Strother, John	TN	1816	049 WB-2/84	049 AR
Strother, Solomon	082	1790	WB-1/35	AR
Strothers, James	039	1843	WB-L/120	AR
Strothers, William H.	039	1862	WB-R/304	
Stroud, Andrew	073	1864	WB-G/444	CTY
Stroud, Bryant	073	1875	WB-H/95	CTY
Stroud, Charles P.	073	1888	WB-H/454	CTY
Stroud, Edwin A.	073	1885	WB-H/390	CTY
Stroud, Elizabeth	073	1800	WB-D/9	AR
Stroud, Ginsey	059	1900	WB-B/253	CTY
Stroud, Isaac	059	1871	WB-A/40	
Stroud, Lutson	035	1798	WB-A/429	AR
Stroud, Pheribee	103	1815	RD-3/236	AR
Stroud, Ransom	044	1877	WB-23/259	CTY
Stroud, William	073	1787	Copy	090 AR
Stroud, William	073	c1786	WB-B/6	AR
Stroud, William	035	1890	WB-4/355	
Stroude, Logan	065	1893	WB-M/173	AR
Stroup, Andrew J.	040	1898	WB-2/28	AR
Stroup, Caleb	040	1873	WB-2/53	AR
Stroup, Daniel	060	1825	WB-1/12	AR
Stroup, Hosea	040	1865	WB-1/186	AR-Copy
Stroup, Jacob	060	1805	Orig Only	AR
Stroup, Jacob	040	c1859	WB-1/110	
Stroup, John D.	040	1875	WB-2/86	AR
Stroup, Jonas	040	1853	WB-1/47	
Stroup, Lawson	040	1854	WB-1/62	
Stroup, Moses	060	1877	WB-4/160	AR
Stroup, Moses, Sr.	040	1887	WB-2/287	AR
Stroup, Nancy	013	1883	WB-B/288	AR
Stroup, Phillip	060	1837	WB-1/408	AR
Stroup, Solomon	040	1869	WB-1/203	AR
Stroup, Solomon	040	c1868	Copy	013 AR
Strowd, John S.	022	1891	WB-E/476	AR
Strowde, John	030	1703/4	Orig. Only	SS/AR

Name	Co.	Date	Recorded Copy	Original
Strub, John	092	1789	WB-2/90	AR
Strudwick, Elsie	036	1889	WB-A/143	CTY
Strudwick, Martha	073	1805	WB-D/154	AR
Strudwick, Samuel	070	1794	WB-C/404	AR
Struill, Daniel N.	074	1897	WB-1/139	
Struill, M. F.	101	1881	WB-A/60	
Strum, Sarah H.	044	1852	WB-19/130	CTY
Strup, Ephraim	090	1845	WB-4/200	AR
Strupe, Samuel	038	1885	WB-2/526	AR
Strutt, George	060	1875	WB-4/133	AR
Stuart, Alexander	065	1789	WB-F/182	AR
Stuart, Alexander	022	1848	WB-C/224	AR
Stuart, Alexander	081	1870	WB-15/42	AR
Stuart, Alexander	VA	c1832	Copy	092 AR
Stuart, Alexander	073	1767	WB-A/60	
Stuart, Benjamin	022	1880	WB-E/205	AR
Stuart, Daniel	083	1861	WB-2/171	AR
Stuart, Duncan	054	c1820	Orig. Only	AR
Stuart, George	029	1831	WB-B/204	
Stuart, James	044	1835	WB-13/281	CTY
Stuart, James	099	1824	RB-19/130	AR
Stuart, James	020	1855	SC/05677	AR-Copy
Stuart, James	020	1855	RB-R/259	AR
Stuart, Jehu	046	1827	WB-B/352	AR
Stuart, John	070	1736	SS 877/179	SS/AR
Stuart, John	046	1844	WB-C/181	AR
Stuart, John	024	1706/7	Orig. Only	SS/AR
Stuart, Mary	071	1778	WB-1/309	
Stuart, Mary	099	1900	WB-D/331	
Stuart, Mary	075	1798	WB-M1/9	AR-Nunc.
Stuart, Mary	047	1811	WB-3/518	Nunc.
Stuart, Nancy	046	1844	WB-C/192	AR
Stuart, Peter	071	1805	WB-2/309	AR
Stuart, Prudence	046	1821	WB-B/120	AR
Stuart, Samuel	081	1869	WB-15/39	AR
Stuart, Synthia	099	1889	WB-B/303	AR
Stuart, Thomas	065	c1778	WB-F/148	AR
Stuart, William	085	c1781	WB-C/186	AR
Stuart, William	005	1817	WB-2/157	AR
Stuart, William A.	VA	1892	106 WB-2/343	
Stubbins, Samuel	073	1883	WB-H/335	CTY
Stubblefield, Carter	084	1829	WB-A/340	CTY
Stubblefield, Hugh C.	084	1821	WB-A/298	CTY
Stubblefield, Richard	084	1847	WB-C/52	CTY
Stubblefield, Sarah	084	1853	WB-C/155	CTY
Stubblefield, William	020	1860	RB-S/321 & 348	AR
Stubbs, Everett	096	c1793	Orig. Only	AR
Stubbs, George	011	c1845	WB-1/108	
Stubbs, John	096	1790	WB-1/169	AR
Stubbs, John B.	009	1887	WB-1/495	CTY
Stubbs, Richard	096	1754	SS 881/73	SS/AR
Stubbs, Thomas	096	c1795	Orig. Only	AR
Stubbs, Thomas	008	1737	LGB-4/#83	SS/AR
Stubbs, William	063	c1795	009 OWB/311	009 AR
Stubbs, William	009	1757	SS 879/234	SS/AR
Stubbs, Wm. Fuller	005	1897	WB-D/420	AR
Stubs, William	053	c1816	RW-1/518	AR
Stucky, John	056	1820	WB-1/307	AR
Studivant, Anderson	047	1815	WB-3/577	
Studivent, Biggins	047	1771	WB-1/298	
Stultz, Henry	090	1822	WB-3/76	AR
Stultz, John	090	1841	WB-4/88	AR
Stump, Christopher	006	1880	WB-E/88	AR
Sturdevant, Mary A. E.	029	1864	WB-D/66	
Sturdie, William	104	1791	WB-1/297	
Sturdivant, Allen	099	1889	WB-B/360	AR
Sturdivant, Elizabeth	099	1846	RB-26/149	AR
Sturdivant, Hollom	099	1795	RB-3/153	AR
Sturdivant, Hollum	099	1845	RB-25/577	AR
Sturdivant, Jesse	047	1802	WB-3/370	
Sturdivant, John, Sr.	005	1862	WB-C/172	AR
Sturdivant, Lucy	099	1832	RB-22/147	AR
Sturdivant, Nancy	099	1879	WB-A/30	AR
Sturdivant, Sidney	005	1891	WB-D/299	AR
Sturdivant, W. A.	099	1889	WB-B/361	
Sturdivant, William	071	1790	WB-1/400	AR
Stureon, Samuel T.	070	1751	DB-D/64	AR
Sturgeon, John	065	1824	WB-E/106	AR
Sturgeon, Lettie	065	1856	WB-J/28	AR
Sturgeon, Mary	065	1845	WB-I/29	AR
Sturgill, David	004	1891	WB-A/131	AR
Sturgill, Francis	006	1842	WB-A/62	AR
Sturgis, Martha	100	1835	WB-35/177	AR
Sturts, John	068	1889	WB-D/332	
Stuts, John	022	1875	WB-E/103	AR
Stutts, Abram	068	1866	WB-C/140	
Stutts, Jacob	068	1796	WB-A/189	
Styers, Abram	032	1889	WB-4/41	AR
Styers, Jane	032	1885	WB-3/473	AR
Styers, John A.	038	1892	WB-3/272	AR
Styles, John	072	c1790	Orig. Only	AR
Styron, David	028	1900	WB-F/462	
Styron, Wallace H.	009	1862	OB-L/427	AR
Styron, Wallace W.	028	1856	WB-D/246	AR
Styron, Willis W.	009	1856	OB-K/196	AR
Sudderth, A. A.	017	1898	WB-B/299	AR
Sudderth, A. H.	023	1896	WB-A/120	AR
Sudderth, James	017	1870	WB-B/25	AR
Sudderth, John	023	1868	WB-A/70	
Sudderth, John	014	1865	WB-1/26	
Sueringen, Green H.	016	1859	WB-2/52	
Sugg, Aquilla H.	045	1888	WB-1/177	AR
Sugg, Britton	099	1892	WB-C/66	AR
Sugg, D. A.	045	1894	WB-1/306	AR
Sugg, Easter	045	1889	WB-1/185	AR
Sugg, Fannie	045	1890	WB-1/192	AR
Sugg, George	009	1758	SS 882/120	SS/AR
Sugg, Henry	045	c1862	WB-1/121	
Sugg, Joel	099	1818	RB-14/252	AR
Sugg, John	099	1842	RB-25/12	AR
Sugg, Joseph E.	098	1900	WB-A/365	CTY
Sugg, Joshua	099	1828	RB-20/283	AR
Sugg, Joshua	099	1819	RB-15/314	AR
Sugg, L. T.	045	1882	WB-1/93	AR
Sugg, Lemuel	037	1780	WB-B/56	AR
Sugg, Lemuel	045	1870	WB-1/10	
Sugg, Lucinda	037	1876	WB-G/480	
Sugg, Marritt	045	1895	WB-1/299	AR
Sugg, Moses	099	1819	RB-15/312	AR
Sugg, Nancy	037	1892	WB-H/212	AR
Sugg, Noah	037	1804	WB-D/207	AR
Sugg, R. M.	081	1867	WB-14/190	AR
Sugg, Reading	037	1841	WB-F/257	AR
Sugg, Warren	099	1882	WB-A/334	AR
Sugg, William	099	1820	RB-19/525	AR
Sugg, William	037	1788	WB-C/57	AR
Sugg, Winefred	045	1900	WB-1/408	
Suggs, Isaac	CA	1896	067 WB-2/364	067 AR
Suggs, John H.	059	1899	WB-B/241	CTY
Suggs, M. A.	081	1885	WB-15/524	

Name	Co.	Date	Recorded Copy	Original
Suggs, M. I.	040	1885	WB-2/248	AR
Suggs, Nancy	103	1847	RD-9/533	AR
Suggs, William	011	1874	WB-2/73	
Suing, Daniel	032	1882	WB-3/378	
Suit, Elijah	038	1898	WB-4/75	AR
Suit, Henry	100	1810	WB-15/141	AR
Suit, John	044	1840	WB-14/495	
Suit, Mary	100	1855	WB-44/264	AR
Suit, William	044	1859	WB-21/102	CTY
Suit, William H.	100	1871	WB-51/56	AR
Suite, Richard	047	1801	WB-3/354	
Suiter, J. L.	071	1896	WB-7/319	AR
Suiter, William E.	084	1832	WB-B/60	CTY
Suitts, Adam	084	1829	WB-A/337	CTY
Sulavint, John	029	1793	Orig. Only	AR
Sulivan, Thomas	038	1873	WB-2/127	AR
Sulivan, Thomas	081	1805	WB-3/35	AR
Sulivane, Daniel	073	1792	WB-B/162	AR
Sullavant, Owen	069	1839	WB-1/433	AR
Sullen, John	046	1809	WB-A/365	AR
Sullins, Zachariah	086	1823	WB-D/6	AR
Sullivan, Daniel	046	1809	WB-A/366	AR
Sullivan, Daniel	032	c1846	Orig. Only	AR
Sullivan, Daniel	046	1821	WB-B/136	
Sullivan, Daniel	035	1778	WB-A/451	AR
Sullivan, Daniel	060	1831	WB-1/237	AR
Sullivan, Drury	039	1812	WB-C/300	
Sullivan, Frederick	012	1818	WB-B/119	AR-Nunc.
Sullivan, Insil	035	1891	WB-4/372	AR
Sullivan, James	035	1848	WB-2/28	AR
Sullivan, James	060	1826	WB-1/27	AR
Sullivan, James J.	054	1899	WB-6/198	CTY
Sullivan, John R.	046	1850	WB-C/325	AR
Sullivan, Jordan	009	1900	WB-2/268	CTY
Sullivan, Lemuel	105	1896	WB-3/242	AR
Sullivan, Margaret	021	1862	WB-1/163	AR
Sullivan, Martha	IN	c1883	054 WB-5/536	054 AR
Sullivan, Samuel	035	1896	WB-4/482	AR
Sullivan, William	032	1838	WB-1/315	AR
Sullivan, William	032	1848	WB-2/23	AR
Sullivant, James	069	1851	WB-1/525	AR
Sullivant, Rachal	020	1808	RB-E/222	AR
Sullivant, Timothy	024	c1762	Orig. Only	AR
Sumerow, B. F.	054	1898	WB-6/171	CTY
Sumerset, Seymore	027	1846	WB-A/44	AR
Sumerville, Robert	065	1800	WB-F/176	AR
Sumey, Peter	060	1787	Orig. Only	AR
Summer, John	060	1805	Orig. Only	AR
Summerell, George M.	070	1900	027 WB-2/166	027 AR
Summerell, Jacob	037	1762	WB-A/93	AR
Summerell, John	071	c1859	Copy	085 AR
Summerell, John	071	1877	WB-6/230	AR
Summerell, Mary	079	1880	WB-2/207	AR
Summerlin, Barnes	037	1817	WB-E/162	AR
Summerow, Daniel	060	1866	WB-3/87	AR
Summerow, Daniel	060	1855	WB-2/403	AR
Summerow, Henry	060	1836	WB-1/367	AR
Summerow, Michael	060	1848	WB-2/296	AR
Summerow, Peter	060	1841	WB-2/110	AR
Summerow, Susan	040	1893	WB-2/445	AR
Summerrell, George M.	070	1900	WB-H/301	AR
Summerrow, Noah	021	1891	WB-2/556	
Summers, Alwin	054	c1829	WB-2/86	AR
Summers, Andrew	001	1900	WB-3/329	AR
Summers, Andrew	084	1855	WB-C/214	CTY
Summers, Basil	054	1860	WB-3/155	AR
Summers, Basil	054	c1824	WB-2/17	AR
Summers, Benjamin	054	c1829	WB-2/77	AR
Summers, Elizabeth	046	1886	WB-E/448	AR
Summers, Emmiline	054	1885	WB-5/39	CTY
Summers, George	020	1855	RB-R/319	
Summers, George W.	001	1900	WB-3/319	AR
Summers, Harper	046	1865	WB-D/279	AR
Summers, Hezekiah	020	1865	RB-T/147	AR
Summers, Jaazaniah	046	1865	WB-D/279	AR
Summers, John	085	1823	WB-H/254	AR
Summers, John	046	1836	WB-B/561	AR
Summers, John	054	c1808	WB-1/17	AR
Summers, John, Sr.	092	1810	WB-3/94	AR
Summers, Johnson	092	1807	WB-3/82	
Summers, Joseph	054	1850	WB-3/41	AR
Summers, Joshua	073	1846	WB-F/314	AR
Summers, Lucy	054	1896	WB-6/3	CTY
Summers, Ludwick W.	046	1871	WB-E/47	AR
Summers, Margaret	065	1895	WB-M/401	AR
Summers, Margaret	013	1895	WB-C/376	AR
Summers, Martha	054	1896	WB-6/5	CTY
Summers, Mary Ann	054	1896	WB-6/18	CTY
Summers, Moseheim	046	1873	WB-E/97	AR
Summers, Peter	046	c1837	WB-C/1	AR
Summers, Peter R.	046	1863	WB-D/178	AR
Summers, R. H.	054	1894	WB-5/563	CTY
Summers, Robert	092	1785	WB-2/62	AR
Summers, Salome	054	1829	WB-2/92	AR-Nunc.
Summers, Sarah E.	054	1894	WB-6/1	CTY
Summers, Solomon	054	c1860	Orig. Only	AR
Summers, Valentine	046	1853	WB-C/404	AR
Summers, William	054	c1799	WB-1/205	AR
Summers, William I.	054	c1836	WB-2/162	AR
Summersett, Stafford	027	1868	WB-2/1	AR
Summersill, Harriett	072	1890	WB-4/248	AR
Summersill, R. N.	072	1898	WB-4/394	AR
Summerskill, John	086	1817	WB-C/57	
Summerville, Aretus	072	c1872	WB-4/177	AR
Summerville, William	065	1868	WB-J/257	AR
Summey, Jacob	050	1841	WB-1/11	CTY
Summey, Margaret	060	1825	WB-1/11	AR
Summey, Peter	060	1864	WB-3/73	AR
Summey, S. Rose	013	1898	WB-D/117	AR
Summit, John	021	c1879	WB-2/355	
Summy, Jacob	032	1838	WB-1/318	AR
Summy, Judge	032	1893	WB-4/186	AR
Summy, Peter	085	c1804	WB-D/36	AR
Sumner, Benjamin	085	c1863	WB-L/34	AR
Sumner, Charles E.	041	1829	WB-2/283	AR
Sumner, David	047	c1774	WB-2/94	
Sumner, Demsey	041	1779	WB-1/4	AR
Sumner, Demsey	071	1808	WB-2/366	AR
Sumner, Edith	035	1896	WB-4/487	AR
Sumner, Edward E.	060	1884	WB-4/296	AR
Sumner, Edwin	041	1793	WB-1/117	AR-Nunc.
Sumner, Edwin	069	1840	WB-1/446	AR
Sumner, James	077	1750	Orig. Only	SS/AR
Sumner, James	041	1787	WB-1/68	AR
Sumner, James	013	1846	WB-A/123	
Sumner, James	077	1824	WB-F/63	AR
Sumner, James D.	071	1842	WB-4/248	AR
Sumner, Jethro	041	1833	WB-2/331	AR
Sumner, Jethro	100	1785	WB-4/87	AR
Sumner, John	041	1809	WB-2/36	AR

Name	Co.	Date	Recorded Copy	Original
Sumner, John	037	1797	WB-D/26	AR
Sumner, John	024	1755	SS 880/2	SS/AR
Sumner, John V.	041	1843	WB-3/51	AR
Sumner, Joseph	071	1872	WB-6/79	AR
Sumner, Joseph	037	1785	WB-C/12	AR
Sumner, Joseph	037	1795	WB-C/326	AR
Sumner, Joseph	072	c1784	WI/L31	AR
Sumner, Laura	085	1892	WB-2/515	CTY
Sumner, Richard	013	1852	WB-A/152	AR
Sumner, Richard	010	1729	Orig. Only	SS/AR
Sumner, Richard	013	1893	WB-C/255	
Sumner, Richard	071	1785	WB-1/351	AR
Sumner, Samuel	024	c1765	WB-B/107	AR
Sumner, Seth	077	1787	WB-C/344	AR
Sumner, Solomon	071	1812	WB-3/91	AR
Sumner, Thomas J.	085	1890	WB-2/437	CTY
Sumner, William	VA	1785	047 WB-3/84	
Sumners, Jacob	037	1815	WB-E/104	
Sumpter, Henry	017	1862	WB-A/138	AR
Sumpter, John M.	054	1899	WB-6/273	CTY
Sumpter, William R.	054	1854	WB-3/82	AR
Suratt, John	032	1830	WB-1/148	AR
Surbastin, Isaac	073	1792	WB-B/193	AR
Suree, Simeon	085	c1804	WB-D/77	AR
Surgener, Robert	037	1778	WB-B/2	AR
Surles, Major	056	1891	WB-3/563	AR
Surles, Mattie E.	056	1890	WB-3/542	AR
Surles, Robert	083	1884	WB-3/313	
Surls, Berry	099	1845	Orig. Only	AR
Surratt, Lewis S.	032	1884	WB-3/418	AR
Susong, Mary M.	TN	1894	062 WB-B/264	
Sussdorff, Christian	038	1886	WB-3/1	AR
Suter, Arthur	071	1830	WB-4/66	AR
Suter, Henry	071	1804	WB-2/264	AR
Suter, Henry B.	071	1824	WB-3/319	AR
Suter, John	071	1805	WB-2/306	AR
Suter, Lucretia	071	1862	WB-5/267	AR
Suter, Sally	071	1829	WB-4/59	AR
Suther, Amelia	016	1882	WB-3/375	AR
Suther, Cornelia	016	1886	WB-3/501	AR
Suther, Harriet S.	016	1892	WB-4/128	AR
Suther, Mary M.	016	1886	WB-3/502	AR
Sutherland, Alexander	082	1843	WB-3/2	AR
Sutherland, Daniel	037	1792	WB-C/214	AR
Sutherland, John	039	1815	WB-D/174	AR
Sutherland, John	VA	1771	019 RB-A/43	
Sutherland, Mary	029	1851	WB-C/204	AR
Sutherland, Mary	082	1863	WB-4/162	AR
Sutherland, Neill	082	1883	WB-6/263	AR
Sutherland, Ransom	099	1823	RB-18/286	AR
Sutherland, Solomon A.	099	1818	RB-14/328	AR
Sutherland, William R.	073	1838	WB-F/9	AR
Sutlive, Joseph	090	1824	WB-3/128	AR
Suton, Adam	072	1746	SS 877/248	
Suton, Polly	030	1883	WB-5/97	Nunc.
Sutten, William	011	c1804	WB-2/307	
Suttenson, Margaret	073	1900	WB-I/173	
Suttle, B. F.	086	1859	WB-E/363	AR
Suttle, George	086	1816	WB-C/44	AR
Suttle, Joseph	026	1861	WB-1/270	AR
Suttle, Reuben	104	1832	WB-4/155	AR
Suttle, Susannah	086	1817	WB-C/55	AR
Suttle, William B.	086	1890	WB-F/398	AR
Suttlemoyer, Henry H.	017	c1887	Orig. Only	AR
Suttles, Mary	064	1890	WB-2/211	AR
Sutton, Ashbury	075	1822	WB-M1/357	AR
Sutton, Ashbury	077	1793	WB-C/443	
Sutton, B. Frank	059	1887	WB-A/468	CTY
Sutton, Barnabas	087	1879	WB-3/182	AR
Sutton, Benajob	103	1890	WB-1/497	AR-Nunc.
Sutton, Benjamin	009	1843	OB-E/64	AR
Sutton, Benjamin	059	1864	Orig. Only	CTY-Copy
Sutton, Benjamin	077	1772	WB-1/53	AR
Sutton, Benjamin F.	059	1897	WB-B/192	CTY
Sutton, Edmond	087	1864	WB-2/62	AR
Sutton, Elizabeth	087	1885	WB-3/298	AR
Sutton, Elizabeth	077	1891	WB-H/200	AR
Sutton, Geo.	N	c1699	SS 874.2/122	SS/AR
Sutton, George	041	1827	WB-2/272	AR
Sutton, Greenbury	077	1795	WB-E/34	AR
Sutton, Hardy	059	1861	WB-B/398	CTY-Copy
Sutton, Henrietta	059	1878	WB-A/157	CTY
Sutton, India P.	059	1898	WB-B/227	CTY
Sutton, J. M.	046	1896	WB-F/538	AR
Sutton, James	087	1889	WB-3/408	AR
Sutton, Jasper	010	1772	WB-A/154	AR
Sutton, Jeremiah	077	1825	WB-F/89	AR
Sutton, Jeremiah	059	1900	WB-B/279	CTY
Sutton, John	077	1777	Orig. Only	AR-Nunc.
Sutton, John	077	1826	WB-F/115	AR
Sutton, John	086	1817	WB-C/69	AR
Sutton, John	011	c1806	WB-2/337	
Sutton, John B.	087	1891	WB-3/496	AR
Sutton, John R.	069	1887	WB-5/251	AR
Sutton, Joseph	073	c1775	WB-A/184	
Sutton, Joseph	077	1724	Orig. Only	SS/AR
Sutton, Joseph	087	1835	WB-1/160	AR
Sutton, Joseph	077	1817	WB-E/470	AR
Sutton, Joseph	077	1763	WB-C/30	AR
Sutton, Joseph	077	1723	SS 876/19	SS/AR
Sutton, Joseph	077	1773	WB-C/129	AR
Sutton, Joseph	077	1794	WB-E/1	
Sutton, Joseph	077	1696	SS 874.2/66	SS/AR
Sutton, Joseph	077	1771	WB-C/99	AR
Sutton, Joshua	070	1796	WB-C/405	AR
Sutton, Josiah	059	1898	WB-B/221	CTY
Sutton, Julia A.	059	1889	WB-A/552	CTY
Sutton, Keziah	077	1818	WB-F/7	AR
Sutton, Luke W.	087	1837	WB-1/189	AR
Sutton, Margaret	011	c1822	WB-2/341	
Sutton, Martha	070	1838	WB-AB/320	AR
Sutton, Mary	077	1738	SS 877/221	SS/AR
Sutton, Mary	077	1774	WB-C/158	AR
Sutton, Matilda	087	1877	WB-3/145	AR
Sutton, Nathaniel	N	1682	Orig. Only	SS/AR
Sutton, Nathaniel	077	1725	SS 876/35	
Sutton, Nicholas	075	1832	WB-N/82	AR
Sutton, Noah H.	059	1875	WB-A/95	
Sutton, Robert B.	099	1896	WB-C/504	AR
Sutton, Samuel	077	1840	WB-F/290	AR-Copy
Sutton, Samuel	077	1764	WB-C/36	AR
Sutton, Samuel M.	077	1892	WB-H/234	AR
Sutton, Sarah	077	1772	WB-C/112	AR
Sutton, Sarah	077	1777	WB-C/201	AR
Sutton, Sarah, Sr.	011	c1823	WB-2/357	
Sutton, Seline	075	1884	WB-O/253	AR
Sutton, Stark A.	010	1866	WB-H/173	AR
Sutton, Theophilus	087	1893	WB-3/517	AR

Name	Co.	Date	Recorded Copy	Original
Sutton, Thomas	069	1807	WB-1/179	AR
Sutton, Thomas	010	1779	WB-B/141	AR
Sutton, Thomas	077	1825	WB-F/98	AR
Sutton, Thomas	077	1872	WB-H/40	AR
Sutton, Thomas	103	1894	WB-2/73	
Sutton, Thomas	010	1750	SS 879/12	SS/AR
Sutton, Thomas J.	101	c1880	074 WB-1/130	074 AR
Sutton, Thomas J.	101	1885	WB-A/138	
Sutton, Thomas J.	077	1892	WB-H/220	AR
Sutton, William	059	1884	WB-A/374	CTY
Sutton, William	011	c1841	WB-1/110	
Sutton, William C.	083	1869	WB-2/247	AR
Sutton, William R.	077	1818	WB-F/8	AR
Swafford, William	081	1831	WB-6/128	AR
Swafford, William	026	1858	WB-1/230	AR
Swaim, Amiel G.	046	1847	WB-C/271	AR
Swaim, Franklin	106	1877	WB-2/83	Nunc.
Swaim, Jesse	038	1873	WB-2/140	AR
Swaim, John	104	c1832	Orig. Only	AR
Swaim, Jonathan	090	1844	WB-4/183	AR
Swaim, Jonathan	038	1886	WB-3/10	AR
Swaim, Louisa	032	1898	WB-4/378	AR
Swaim, Lyndon	046	1893	WB-F/256	AR
Swaim, Mary M.	090	1841	WB-4/80	AR
Swaim, Michael	092	1840	WB-4/172	
Swaim, Peter D.	001	1887	WB-2/345	AR
Swaim, Solomon D.	106	c1865	WB-1/102	AR
Swaim, William	090	1813	WB-2/141	AR
Swaim, William	081	1850	WB-9/216	AR
Swain, Abigail	096	1849	WB-3/21	AR
Swain, Abram J.	096	1849	WB-3/23	
Swain, Bryant	010	1898	WB-I/549	
Swain, David L.	073	1868	WB-G/539	CTY
Swain, David L.	073	1868	099 WB-B/121	099 AR
Swain, David L.	073	1868	013 WB-C/90	
Swain, Eleanor H.	099	1883	WB-A/396	AR
Swain, Eleanor H.	099	1883	091 WB-1/320	091 CTY
Swain, Eleanor H.	099	1883	013 WB-C/173	013 AR
Swain, Eliakim	096	1813	WB-2/61	AR
Swain, Elizabeth	063	1777	WB-1/38	
Swain, Elizabeth	010	1794	WB-D/239	AR
Swain, Elizabeth	063	c1800	WB-1/372	
Swain, George W.	012	1890	WB-A/79	AR
Swain, Hannah	012	1899	WB-A/143	AR
Swain, James	010	1817	WB-G/6	AR
Swain, James	077	1887	WB-H/166	AR
Swain, James	010	1817	WB-G/11	AR
Swain, James	096	1806	WB-2/68	AR
Swain, James	096	1837	WB-2/134	AR
Swain, James	096	1763	WB-1/47	AR
Swain, James, Sr.	063	1819	WB-2/63	
Swain, Jehu	063	c1799	WB-1/364	
Swain, Jeremiah	096	1747	Orig. Only	SS/AR
Swain, Jeremiah	096	1791	Orig. Only	AR
Swain, Jesse	096	1833	WB-2/122	AR
Swain, Job	096	1884	Orig. Only	AR
Swain, John	096	1749	Orig. Only	SS/AR
Swain, John	010	1845	WB-G/391	AR
Swain, John	010	1785	WB-D/15	AR
Swain, John	096	1790	WB-1/171	AR
Swain, John	106	c1872	WB-2/47	
Swain, John	063	1779	WB-1/57	
Swain, John, Sr.	096	1766	WB-1/62	AR
Swain, John, Sr.	096	1789	WB-1/161	AR
Swain, Joseph	046	1829	WB-B/383	AR

Name	Co.	Date	Recorded Copy	Original
Swain, Joseph	096	1834	WB-2/121	AR
Swain, Joseph W.	046	1840	WB-C/47	AR
Swain, Letchworth	010	1792	WB-D/208	AR
Swain, Lewis M.	089	1853	WB-1/102	
Swain, Mary	096	1774	WB-1/85	AR
Swain, Nancy Ann	101	1884	WB-A/123	
Swain, Paul	046	1884	WB-E/430	AR
Swain, Preson	010	1802	WB-E/167	AR
Swain, Rachel	096	1817	Orig. Only	AR
Swain, Richard	010	1782	WB-C/35	AR
Swain, Richard	010	1812	WB-F/209	AR
Swain, Silvanus	046	1824	WB-B/191	AR
Swain, Starkey	063	1866	WB-2/531	
Swain, Stephen	096	1819	WB-2/77	
Swain, William	010	1779	WB-B/123	AR
Swain, William	096	1784	WB-1/143	AR
Swain, William	010	1810	WB-F/157	AR
Swain, William	096	1753	SS 881/115	SS/AR
Swain, William B.	096	1874	WB-4/28	
Swain, Zachius	046	1829	WB-B/228	
Swaine, Stephen	024	c1712	SS 875/57	SS/AR
Swales, Mary	037	1800	WB-D/111	AR
Swan, Agness	020	1856	RB-R/421	AR
Swan, Constantine	028	1861	WB-D/349	AR
Swan, Dorcus	065	1842	WB-H/86	AR
Swan, Even	028	1793	WB-A/306	AR
Swan, Ezra	054	c1808	WB-1/16	AR
Swan, Henry	077	1801	WB-E/127	AR
Swan, Thomas	020	1832	RB-M/190	
Swancy, John Wilson	071	1804	WB-2/258	AR
Swaner, Lemuel	096	1759	WB-1/14	AR-Nunc.
Swann, Ann Sophia	070	1866	WB-D/181	AR
Swann, Aquilla	064	1878	WB-2/314	AR
Swann, Aurilia	070	1838	WB-C/419	AR
Swann, E. K.	065	1886	WB-L/154	AR
Swann, Elizabeth	070	1840	WB-AB/329	AR
Swann, Enas	054	c1858	WB-3/165	AR
Swann, Fannie T.	020	1896	WB-B/236	CTY
Swann, Frances	020	1876	WB-A/220	CTY
Swann, John	065	1817	WB-F/189	AR
Swann, John	070	1762	DB-E/13	AR
Swann, John	070	1824	WB-C/411	AR
Swann, John	012	c1856	Copy	070 AR
Swann, John	012	1857	WB-B/7	AR
Swann, John C.	064	1884	WB-2/148	AR
Swann, John, Sr.	075	1789	WB-K/172	AR
Swann, Joseph	020	1861	RB-S/417	AR
Swann, Joseph	020	1823	RB-I/239	AR
Swann, Joseph	065	c1829	Orig. Only	AR
Swann, Joseph	075	1781	WB-K/58	AR
Swann, Mary	077	1771	WB-C/96	AR
Swann, Mrs. F. M.	068	1882	WB-D/159	
Swann, Rebecca	065	1847	WB-I/95	AR
Swann, Samuel	075	1787	WB-K/148	AR
Swann, Samuel	077	1753	SS 881/2	SS/AR
Swann, Samuel	075	1772	WB-H/150	
Swann, Samuel	070	1774	WB-C/386	AR
Swann, Samuel	077	1708	Orig. Only	SS/AR
Swann, Samuel	086	1817	WB-C/67	AR
Swann, Samuel	075	1768	WB-I/56	SS/AR
Swann, Sarah	022	1845	WB-C/182	AR
Swann, Thomas	085	1811	WB-G/176	AR
Swann, Thomas	085	c1795	WB-D/27	AR
Swann, Thomas	075	1733	SS 876/319	SS/AR
Swann, William	075	1766	WB-I/51	AR

Name	Co.	Date	Recorded Copy	Original
Swann, William B.	020	1891	WB-B/75	CTY
Swann, William M.	070	1888	WB-F/194	AR
Swanner, Eli H.	009	1873	WB-1/114	CTY
Swanner, Richardson	022	1792	RB-1/41	AR
Swanner, Sally	009	1845	OB-E/410	AR
Swanner, Thomas	063	1789	WB-1/153	
Swanner, U. W.	101	1881	WB-A/64	
Swanner, William	063	1822	WB-2/81	
Swanner, William	063	1834	WB-2/191	
Swanner, William	063	1777	WB-1/33	
Swanson, James	104	1861	WB-5/285	
Swanson, John	104	1851	WB-5/48	
Swanson, Richard	039	1809	WB-C/157	
Swanson, Sallie	039	1888	WB-U/415	AR
Swaringen, J. F.	033	1863	WB-1/177	AR
Swaringen, William	089	1861	WB-1/223	
Swaringer, Samuel	060	1819	Orig. Only	AR
Swaringgame, Samuel	049	1811	WB-2/202	AR
Swazy, Annie	070	1896	WB-G/534	AR
Sweaney, Patience	046	1888	WB-E/507	AR
Sweaney, Tirza	073	1846	WB-F/276	AR
Swearingen, E. G.	089	1864	WB-1/285	
Sweatt, Edward	092	1812	WB-3/102	AR
Sweeney, Lydia	081	1850	WB-11/415	AR
Swene, Joseph	081	1806	WB-3/58	AR
Swepson, George	099	c1882	Copy	001 AR
Swepson, George W.	099	1883	091 WB-1/212	
Swepson, George W.	099	1883	WB-A/422	AR
Swepson, George W.	099	c1882	073 WB-H/387	073 CTY
Swepson, George W.	099	1883	043 WB-1/78	
Swett, Abraham	047	1820	WB-3/653	
Swett, Isham	070	1897	WB-G/70	AR
Swezey, Rachel	086	1815	WB-C/26	AR
Swicegood, Adam	032	1833	WB-1/236	AR
Swicegood, Andrew	032	1862	WB-2/215	AR
Swicegood, Catherine	032	1859	WB-2/174	AR
Swicegood, George	032	1886	WB-3/497	AR
Swicegood, John	032	1870	WB-3/20	AR
Swicegood, Mary	032	1866	WB-2/345	AR
Swicegood, Philip	032	1877	WB-3/199 & 214	AR
Swicegood, Philip	032	1865	WB-2/295	AR
Swicegood, Sarah C.	032	1899	WB-4/432	AR
Swift, Anthony	020	1811	RB-F/210	AR
Swift, Elizabeth	020	1817	RB-G/350	AR
Swift, Elizabeth	102	1897	WB-A/127	AR
Swift, Ephraim	072	c1744	SS 877/301	SS/AR
Swift, Frances	020	1821	RB-I/17	
Swift, George A.	020	1839	RB-N/375	
Swift, Joseph	096	1792	Orig. Only	AR
Swift, Robert	020	1853	RB-R/86	
Swift, Thomas	081	1807	WB-3/69	AR
Swift, Thomas	081	1816	WB-4/291	AR
Swift, Thomas	020	1816	RB-G/148	
Swift, Thomas S.	046	1865	WB-D/262	AR
Swift, Wesley	020	1858	RB-S/70	AR
Swift, William	020	1808	RB-E/429	AR
Swift, William P.	020	1809	RB-F/69	AR
Swiggett, Nancy Ann	046	1880	WB-E/270	AR
Swindal, Samuel	011	c1841	WB-1/61	
Swindal, Willis	027	1824	WB-A/4	AR
Swindall, Samuel	011	c1841	SC/06484	AR-Copy
Swindell, Ann L.	009	1867	OB-M/143	AR
Swindell, Annmariah	053	1879	WB-11/99	AR
Swindell, C. A.	079	1884	WB-2/302	AR

Name	Co.	Date	Recorded Copy	Original
Swindell, Caleb	053	1805	RW-1/383	AR
Swindell, Caleb	053	1791	RW-1/210	
Swindell, Cornelius	053	1886	WB-11/174	AR
Swindell, David T.	099	1895	WB-C/451	AR
Swindell, Dorcas	053	1857	WB-8/205	AR
Swindell, Elizabeth	019	1889	WB-B/172	AR
Swindell, Elizabeth	053	1864	WB-10/21	AR
Swindell, Emery	009	1843	OB-E/204	AR
Swindell, F. R.	009	1898	WB-2/154	CTY
Swindell, Harriet	053	1894	WB-11/310	
Swindell, Isaac	028	1869	WB-E/12	AR
Swindell, Isaac	053	1799	RW-1/305	AR
Swindell, Jennie	028	1892	WB-F/58	
Swindell, Joel	053	1814	RW-1/489	
Swindell, John	053	1775	RW-1/68	
Swindell, John	053	1828	Orig. Only	AR
Swindell, Johnathan	009	1847	OB-F/396	AR
Swindell, Joseph	053	1869	WB-11/3	AR
Swindell, Joseph	053	1824	WB-4/284	AR
Swindell, Josiah	053	1790	RW-1/191	AR
Swindell, Josiah	053	1806	RW-1/400	AR
Swindell, Leroy M.	053	1876	WB-11/59	AR
Swindell, Marcus	053	1864	WB-10/36	AR
Swindell, Mary	053	1828	WB-4/385	AR
Swindell, Megatling	074	1876	WB-1/41	AR
Swindell, Recy	053	1835	Orig. Only	AR
Swindell, Robert	053	1823	WB-5/447	AR
Swindell, Salinea E.	009	1883	WB-1/339	CTY
Swindell, Valentine	053	1835	WB-5/260	AR
Swindell, W. H.	009	1891	WB-1/507	CTY
Swindell, Wade	053	1893	WB-11/268	AR
Swindell, Wade	053	1882	WB-11/120	AR
Swindell, William	053	1837	WB-5/437	AR
Swindell, Zedekiah	053	1795	RW-1/256	AR
Swing, Abram	032	1875	WB-3/167	AR
Swing, Daniel	032	1882	WB-3/378	AR
Swing, David	032	1884	WB-3/425	AR
Swing, Henry	032	1900	WB-4/465	AR
Swing, Ludovick	046	c1790	WB-A/342	AR
Swing, Mathias	046	1840	WB-C/69	AR
Swing, William	032	1885	WB-3/447	AR
Swink, Adam W.	032	1900	WB-4/444	AR
Swink, George	085	1816	WB-G/437	AR
Swink, George	085	1867	WB-L/12	
Swink, Henry	085	1876	WB-1/325	CTY
Swink, Michael	085	c1781	WB-B/3	AR
Swink, Samuel	085	1867	WB-L/23	AR
Swinney, Darby	082	1821	WB-1/230	AR
Swinney, Robert R.	044	1848	WB-17/189	CTY
Swinny, Nancy	037	1817	WB-E/150	AR
Swinson, B. F.	035	1863	WB-3/69	AR
Swinson, Birchy	045	1876	WB-1/36	AR
Swinson, Daniel	035	1864	WB-3/92	AR
Swinson, John	063	1888	WB-4/42	AR
Swinson, John	035	1857	WB-2/122	AR
Swinson, John	035	1866	WB-3/104	AR
Swinson, John A.	035	1833	Orig. Only	AR
Swinson, Levi	063	1791	WB-1/178	
Swinson, Major	035	1886	WB-4/275	AR
Swinson, Polly	035	1873	WB-4/77	AR
Swinson, Richard	024	1716	Orig. Only	SS/AR
Swinson, Sharlotte	035	1875	WB-4/92	AR
Swinson, Theophilus	035	1835	WB-1/66	AR
Swinson, Tilda	103	1891	WB-1/547	AR
Swinson, William	096	1758	WB-1/7	AR

Name	Co.	Date	Recorded Copy	Original
Swisher, Mathew L.	033	1866	WB-1/196	AR
Swisher, Mathias	033	1870	WB-2/10	CTY
Sybery, Christopher	085	c1785	WB-C/92	AR
Syers, Gerrard	070	1755	SS 880/1	SS/AR
Sykes, Abel	030	1784	WB-1/181	
Sykes, Benjamin	071	1898	WB-7/403	AR
Sykes, Edmond	039	1900	WB-V/184	AR
Sykes, Edward	047	1890	WB-6/572	AR
Sykes, Emily J.	073	1879	WB-H/202	CTY
Sykes, Henry	044	1872	WB-23/80	CTY
Sykes, Henry	073	1863	WB-G/416	CTY
Sykes, J. Anderson	073	1864	WB-G/453	CTY
Sykes, James	073	1882	WB-H/320	CTY
Sykes, James H.	036	1897	WB-A/418	CTY
Sykes, John C.	073	1900	WB-I/187	CTY
Sykes, John F.	071	1874	WB-6/144	AR
Sykes, John H.	073	1895	WB-I/62	CTY
Sykes, Levi	077	1809	WB-E/338	AR
Sykes, Martha A.	071	1893	WB-7/195	AR
Sykes, Mary E.	071	1899	WB-7/423	AR
Sykes, Nedum	087	c1806	Orig. Only	AR
Sykes, Sarah	073	1876	WB-H/141	CTY
Sykes, Thomas	096	c1824	Orig. Only	AR
Sykes, Walter	030	1790	WB-1/247	
Sykes, William	047	1848	WB-4/262	
Sylevan, Lambeth	009	c1792	OWB/269	AR
Sylvester, James	077	1855	WB-F/456	AR
Sylvester, William	077	1860	WB-F/511	AR
Symington, William N.	093	1900	WB-2/178	AR
Symmons, Benjamin	032	c1856	WB-2/133	
Symms, Martha	099	1829	RB-21/88	AR
Symons, Abraham	075	1789	WB-K/173	
Symons, Amaritta	075	1825	WB-N/8	AR
Symons, Benjamin	075	1748	Orig. Only	SS/AR
Symons, Benjamin	075	1776	WB-I/161	
Symons, David	075	1802	WB-M1/62	AR
Symons, Jehoshaphat	075	1768	WB-H/81	
Symons, Jeremiah	075	1740	LGB-4/#132A	SS/AR
Symons, Jerremiah	075	1715	Orig. Only	SS/AR
Symons, John	075	1748	Orig. Only	SS/AR
Symons, John	024	1732	SS 876/250	
Symons, John	075	1741	LGB-4/#159	SS/AR
Symons, John	075	1788	WB-K/159	
Symons, Martha	075	1838	WB-N/142	AR
Symons, Mary Ann	075	c1853	WB-M2/43	AR
Symons, Penelope	075	1855	WB-M2/39	AR
Symons, Peter	075	1755	Copy	028 AR
Symons, Rachael	075	1749	Orig. Only	SS/AR
Symons, Samuel	075	1777	WB-K/4	
Symons, Thomas	075	1706	Orig. Only	SS/AR
Symons, Thomas	075	1769	WB-H/89	
Symons, Thomas	075	1758	SS 882/153	SS/AR
Symons, William	075	1761	WB-H/21	
Syms, Joseph	056	1800	WB-1/116	AR
Syms, William	037	c1755	SS 880/152	SS/AR
Synnott, Michael	073	1781	WB-A/219	AR
Tabb, Diana	039	1818	WB-F/66	AR
Tabb, Elizabeth	015	1769	100 WB-1/101	AR
Tabb, Thomas	047	1791	WB-3/200	
Tabb, Thomas J.	018	1855	WB-D/24	
Tabb, William	015	1778	100 WB-2/276	AR
Taber, Allen	050	1882	Orig. Only	AR
Tabor, John	086	1806	WB-B/188	AR
Tabor, Nathan	061	1851	WB-1/47	AR
Tabor, Thomas	022	1798	WB-A/3	AR-Nunc.
Taburn, Nathan	071	1833	WB-4/97	AR
Tacker, Seaborn	085	c1805	WB-G/96	AR
Tadlock, Absolum	010	1816	WB-F/309	AR
Tadlock, John W.	081	1899	WB-17/7	AR
Tadlock, Joshua	103	1899	WB-2/269	AR
Tadlock, Mary C.	010	1875	WB-I/69	AR
Tadlock, Sumner	103	1805	Orig. Only	AR
Tadlock, Thomas	071	1795	WB-2/96	AR
Taft, Godfrey E.	079	1894	WB-3/58	AR
Taft, James Henry	079	1873	WB-2/88	AR
Taft, William S.	009	1877	WB-1/199	CTY
Taggart, Elizabeth	065	1888	WB-L/299	AR
Taggart, John	065	1886	WB-L/131	AR
Tague, Michael	090	1816	WB-2/177	AR
Taillade, Louis F.	009	1820	OB-A/299	
Tailor, George W.	038	1861	WB-1/179	AR
Tainter, Dean W.	062	1896	WB-B/187	AR
Tait, Simpson	073	1804	WB-D/129	AR
Talbert, James	073	1770	WB-A/112	
Talbert, John	078	1794	WI-1/152	AR
Talbert, Josiah	081	1855	WB-11/189	
Talbert, Wesley	085	1880	WB-1/541	CTY
Talent, Aaron	014	c1895	Orig. Only	CTY
Talka, John	028	1832	WB-C/350	AR
Tallent, John H.	061	1899	WB-2/229	AR
Tallent, Josiah	092	c1826	WB-3/174	
Taller, Silas	071	1891	WB-7/139	AR
Talley, Frederik	100	1818	WB-21/219	AR
Talley, Joel	100	1854	WB-43/5	AR
Talley, John	078	c1870	Orig. Only	AR
Talley, Nancy	100	1846	WB-39/197	AR
Talley, Nicholas	046	1795	WB-A/386	AR
Talley, Rahab	100	1824	WB-26/258	AR
Talley, Ransom	100	1838	WB-37/40	AR
Talley, Robert	100	1808	WB-14/164	AR
Talley, Samuel	073	1791	WB-B/136	AR
Talley, Travis	100	1855	WB-44/128	AR
Tallor, Abraham	057	c1811	WB-B/2	AR
Tally, Daniel	020	1877	WB-A/224	CTY
Tally, Reubin	044	1812	WB-7/263	CTY
Talman, John	072	1833	WB-1/118	AR
Talton, Asa	056	1871	WB-3/51	AR
Talton, Hardy	056	1822	WB-1/447	AR
Talton, Lewis	056	1880	WB-3/260	AR
Talton, Needham	056	1814	WB-1/233	AR
Talton, William	056	1791	WB-1/47	AR
Talton, William	056	1841	WB-1/537	AR
Taner, Benjamin	072	1807	WB-A/132	AR
Taner, Peter	104	1860	WB-5/249	
Tankard, George	009	1815	OB-A/244	AR
Tankard, Martha	009	c1830	OWB/498	AR
Tankersley, Felix	073	1866	WB-G/504	CTY
Tann, Benjamin	069	1806	WB-1/171	AR
Tannahill, Susan M.	100	1898	WB-51/498	
Tannahill, William	009	1845	OB-E/412	AR
Tanner, Dorcas	100	1811	WB-16/213	AR
Tanner, James	065	1778	WB-F/201	
Tanner, John	100	1806	WB-13/197	AR
Tanner, Joseph	065	1779	WB-D/32	AR
Tanner, Joseph	005	1830	WB-A/167	AR
Tanner, Margaret	085	1848	WB-K/76	AR
Tanner, Mary W.	020	1860	RB-S/346	AR
Tanner, Michael	086	1807	WB-B/205	AR
Tanner, Silvy	071	1812	WB-3/60	AR
Tanner, Susan	080	1895	Orig. Only	AR

Name	Co.	Date	Recorded Copy	Original
Tanner, Thomas	065	1820	WB-D/114	AR
Tanner, Walter	077	c1713	SS 875/18	
Tanner, Wilford	054	1893	WB-5/490	CTY
Tanner, Zilla	080	c1881	Orig. Only	AR
Tant, William	039	1790	WB-A/74	
Tapley, Elizabeth	001	1860	WB-1/171	AR
Tapley, Hosea	020	1781	RB-A/139	AR
Tapley, Hosea, Jr.	073	1770	WB-A/125	
Tapp, Abner	073	1810	WB-D/273	AR
Tapp, George	078	1853	WB-17/128	
Tapp, James E.	073	1865	WB-G/476	CTY
Tapp, Ruffin R.	073	1881	WB-H/289	CTY
Tapp, William	078	1808	WI-5/53	AR
Tapp, William H.	073	1892	WB-H/567	CTY
Tappey, W. H.	065	1899	WB-N/279	AR
Tappey, William H.	VA	1890	047 WB-7/83	047 AR
Tapscott, Elizabeth	020	1828	RB-N/201	AR
Tapscott, Henry	020	1832	RB-M/188	
Tapscott, Henry C.	001	1858	WB-1/123	AR
Tapscott, John	020	1840	RB-O/1	
Tapscott, Mary	001	1857	WB-1/119	AR
Tapscott, Samuel	001	1859	WB-1/154	
Tapscott, Winifred	020	1828	RB-L/278	
Tarbe, Peter A.	011	c1822	WB-2/346	
Tarkenton, James	101	1885	WB-A/136	
Tarkenton, John	096	c1809	WB-2/41	
Tarkenton, Joseph	096	1804	WB-2/17	AR
Tarkenton, Levi N.	096	1897	WB-4/165	AR
Tarkenton, Sarah Jane	101	1880	WB-A/47	
Tarkenton, Thomas G.	010	1895	WB-I/456	AR
Tarkington, John	N	1716	Orig. Only	SS/AR
Tarkington, William	096	1748	SS 878/4	SS/AR
Tarlton, Willis R.	005	1900	WB-D/453	AR
Tarpley, Henry	001	1878	WB-2/127	AR
Tarpley, Margaret	001	1894	WB-3/17	AR
Tarpley, Mason	073	1826	WB-E/118	AR
Tarpley, William C.	001	1883	WB-2/233	AR
Tarr, Samuel	054	c1813	WB-1/315	AR
Tarrington, Southy	087	c1810	Orig. Only	AR
Tarry, Stephen	VA	1897	100 WB-51/521	
Tart, Elnathan	037	1796	WB-C/360	AR
Tart, John	087	c1795	Orig. Only	AR
Tart, Jonathan	037	1789	WB-C/87	AR
Tart, Joseph	053	1748	Orig. Only	SS/AR
Tart, Mary	010	1850	WB-G/469	AR
Tart, Nathan	056	1882	WB-3/306	AR
Tart, Thomas	087	1850	WB-1/369	AR
Tart, William	056	1885	WB-3/382	AR
Tart, William C.	071	1794	WB-2/42	AR-Nunc.
Tart, William R.	056	1886	WB-3/424	AR
Tarte, Nathan	010	1826	WB-G/153	AR
Tartt, Enos	037	1817	WB-E/153	
Tartt, Margaret	105	1866	WB-1/123	
Tarver, Andrew	071	1780	WB-1/220	
Tarver, Frederic	056	1772	WB-1/793	AR
Tarver, Frederick	071	1794	WB-2/55	AR
Tarver, Harmon	071	c1776	WB-1/11	AR
Tarver, James	071	1777	WB-1/7	AR
Tarver, Samuel	071	1778	WB-1/315	
Tarver, Thomas	071	1787	WB-1/353	AR
Tate, A.	001	1897	WB-3/166	AR
Tate, Abner	073	1841	WB-F/101	AR
Tate, Anthony	046	1830	WB-B/426	AR
Tate, Asa	086	1876	WB-F/95	AR
Tate, Ernest W.	046	1893	WB-F/302	AR
Tate, Francis	047	1812	WB-3/533	
Tate, George	073	1774	WB-A/144	
Tate, George J.	064	1900	WB-2/492	AR
Tate, Henrietta	001	1868	WB-2/92	AR
Tate, Hugh A.	064	1877	WB-2/63	AR
Tate, James	099	1782	RB-1/178 & 184	AR
Tate, James	073	1838	WB-F/8	AR
Tate, James	070	1795	WB-AB/12	AR
Tate, James	073	1816	WB-D/459	AR
Tate, James S.	001	1880	WB-2/160	AR
Tate, Jennet	073	1786	WB-A/359	AR
Tate, Jessa	001	1884	WB-2/217	AR
Tate, Jesse	086	1806	WB-B/190	AR
Tate, John	001	1866	WB-1/259	AR
Tate, Joseph	001	1883	WB-2/197	AR
Tate, Joseph	073	1826	WB-E/153	
Tate, Joseph	078	1880	WB-19/103	AR
Tate, Joseph	046	1779	084 OW/236	084 AR
Tate, Joseph	001	c1849	WB-1/40	AR
Tate, Margaret	001	1883	WB-2/210	AR
Tate, Mark A.	099	1832	RB-22/297	AR
Tate, Mary	014	1825	Orig. Only	AR-Copy
Tate, Mary	001	1895	WB-3/63	AR
Tate, Mary A.	046	1872	WB-E/92	AR
Tate, Rachel	090	1797	WB-1/93	AR
Tate, Robert	085	c1776	WB-B/93	AR
Tate, Robert	070	1866	WB-D/200	AR
Tate, Robert B.	046	1864	WB-D/222	AR
Tate, Rowan	001	1871	WB-2/28	AR
Tate, S. C. W.	014	1892	WB-2/480	CTY
Tate, Samuel	001	c1855	WB-1/95	AR
Tate, Samuel N.	073	1856	WB-G/128	AR
Tate, Thomas	073	1841	WB-F/100	AR
Tate, Thomas R.	040	1871	WB-2/32	AR
Tate, Waddy	020	1789	RB-B/275	
Tate, William	099	1832	RB-22/297	AR
Tate, William	073	1828	WB-E/153	AR
Tate, William C.	014	1869	WB-2/17	AR
Tate, William S.	001	1882	WB-2/189	AR
Tate, Zacheus	073	1798	WB-C/118	AR
Tate, Zephariah	073	1816	WB-D/461	AR
Tatem, Benjamin	030	1843	WB-4/94 & 99	
Tatem, Thomas	030	1844	WB-4/108	
Tathem, J. W.	023	1891	WB-A/102	
Tatlock, Edward	075	1762	WB-H/38	AR
Tatlock, John	075	1792	WB-K/229	AR
Tatlock, Susannah	075	1811	WB-M1/230	AR
Tatom, Absalom	073	1803	WB-D/94	AR
Tatom, J. H.	011	1899	WB-3/107	CTY
Tatom, Joseph	078	1808	WI-5/77	AR
Tatom, Joshua	087	1834	WB-1/151	AR
Tatom, Laban	087	1835	WB-1/170	AR
Tatom, M. W.	011	1889	WB-2/226	
Tatom, Stephen	073	c1788	WB-B/73	AR
Tatom, Theophilus	011	1863	WB-1/306	
Tatscott, William	020	1847	RB-P/394	
Tatum, Asenath	054	1891	WB-5/372	CTY
Tatum, Benjamin	075	1900	WB-O/512	AR
Tatum, Chadwick	030	1899	WB-5/282	AR
Tatum, Edward	046	1811	WB-A/390	AR
Tatum, Halen	085	1820	Orig. Only	AR-Copy
Tatum, Henry	046	1858	WB-C/524	AR
Tatum, James	006	1828	WB-B/24	AR
Tatum, Jesse	033	1856	WB-1/126	AR
Tatum, John	090	1803	WB-2/38	AR

Name	Co.	Date	Recorded Copy	Original
Tatum, John	030	N. D.	WB-2/321	
Tatum, John	030	c1815	WB-3/53	
Tatum, Joseph	006	1889	WB-E/194	AR
Tatum, Joseph	030	1832	WB-3/315	
Tatum, Joshua	047	1765	WB-1/166	
Tatum, Love A.	087	1866	WB-2/103	AR
Tatum, Nathaniell	037	1750	Orig. Only	SS/AR
Tatum, Osborne	054	1887	WB-5/157	CTY
Tatum, Osburn	054	c1803	WB-1/219	AR
Tatum, Phebe	084	1807	WB-A/39	CTY
Tatum, Samuel	075	c1858	WB-M2/65	AR
Tatum, Sihon	038	1833	WB-1/150	AR
Tatum, Susan	030	1852	WB-4/166	
Tatum, William	030	1817	WB-3/93	
Tatum, William C.	030	1882	WB-5/92	AR
Tavis, John D.	038	1889	WB-3/112	AR
Tavis, William	038	1900	WB-4/196	AR
Tayler, Isaac	009	1893	WB-1/562	CTY
Tayler, Kinchen	063	1837	WB-2/230	
Tayler, Peggy	063	1835	WB-2/207	
Tayloe, Abraham	010	1802	WB-E/135	AR
Tayloe, Benjamin	010	1810	WB-F/146	AR
Tayloe, Benjamin	010	1892	WB-I/338	AR
Tayloe, James	010	1833	WB-G/223	AR
Tayloe, Leander	051	1846	WB-A/250	
Tayloe, Margaret	010	1845	WB-G/374	AR
Tayloe, Richard	010	1795	WB-D/302	AR
Tayloe, William H.	010	1894	WB-I/413	AR
Taylor, A. D.	070	1899	WB-H/230	AR
Taylor, Abraham	065	1778	WB-D/30	AR
Taylor, Abraham	056	1751	028 DB-5/262	SS/AR
Taylor, Absalom	070	1841	WB-AB/349	AR
Taylor, Absalom	028	1791	WB-A/246	AR
Taylor, Alexander	099	1858	RB-30/53	AR
Taylor, Amos	018	1841	WB-C/261	
Taylor, Amy	070	1890	WB-F/361	AR
Taylor, Andrew	071	1759	Orig. Only	SS/AR
Taylor, Andrew	086	1809	WB-B/222	AR
Taylor, Ann	N	1764	SS 881/279	SS/AR (N)
Taylor, Ann	071	1800	WB-2/202	AR
Taylor, Ann	070	1849	WB-C/493	AR
Taylor, Ann	099	1899	028 WB-F/403	
Taylor, Archibald	044	1885	WB-23/524	CTY
Taylor, Arden B.	009	1894	WB-2/49	CTY
Taylor, Arthur	037	1765	WB-A/163	AR
Taylor, Arthur	069	1823	WB-1/319	AR
Taylor, Asa	028	1852	WB-D/184	AR
Taylor, B. F.	019	1897	WB-B/325	AR
Taylor, Babel	VA	1886	010 WB-I/215	
Taylor, Benjamin	030	1853	WB-4/172	
Taylor, Benjamin	103	1847	RD-9/516	AR
Taylor, Benjamin	103	1854	RD-11/548	AR
Taylor, Benjamin	092	1853	WB-5/3	
Taylor, Benjamin	029	1900	WB-F/21	AR
Taylor, Benjamin	030	c1810	WB-2/362	
Taylor, Bennett	039	c1856	WB-O/383	
Taylor, Burket	037	1864	WB-G/248	AR
Taylor, Catherine	028	1888	WB-E/496	AR
Taylor, Catherine	070	1878	Copy	012 AR
Taylor, Catherine	035	1801	WB-A/465	AR
Taylor, Celicia	103	1897	WB-2/193	AR
Taylor, Charity	083	c1813	WB-1/220	
Taylor, Charles	006	1887	WB-E/154	AR
Taylor, Charles	078	1797	WI-2/8	AR

Name	Co.	Date	Recorded Copy	Original
Taylor, Charles	020	1863	RB-S/612	AR
Taylor, Chloe	018	1845	WB-C/295	
Taylor, Christopher	069	1822	WB-1/310	AR
Taylor, Cornelius	057	1791	WB-A/143	AR
Taylor, Daniel	011	c1830	WB-1/8	
Taylor, Daniel	090	1873	WB-6/54	AR
Taylor, Daniel D.	004	1883	WB-A/64	AR
Taylor, David	030	c1812	WB-3/15	
Taylor, David W.	033	1837	WB-1/2	AR
Taylor, Davis	028	1801	WB-B/128	AR
Taylor, Dawson	037	1877	WB-G/524	AR
Taylor, Dempsey	071	1851	WB-5/99	AR
Taylor, Dempsey	069	1845	WB-1/477	AR
Taylor, Dempsey	069	c1822	Orig. Only	AR
Taylor, Dexter	103	1870	WB-1/16	AR
Taylor, Drury	069	1809	WB-1/198	AR
Taylor, Earl J.	023	1872	WB-A/6	
Taylor, Ebenezer	N	c1711	SS 875/273	
Taylor, Ebenezer	030	1798	WB-2/116	
Taylor, Edmond	044	1808	WB-6/423	CTY
Taylor, Edward	032	1833	WB-1/203	AR
Taylor, Edward	030	c1809	WB-2/342	
Taylor, Edward	N	1711/2	SS 874.1/42	
Taylor, Edwin	059	1876	WB-A/118	
Taylor, Eleanor	028	1900	WB-F/496	
Taylor, Eleanor M.	054	1857	WB-3/124	AR
Taylor, Eli	017	c1860	WB-A/118	AR
Taylor, Elijah	028	1873	WB-E/81	AR
Taylor, Elisabeth	075	1840	WB-N/153	AR
Taylor, Elisabeth	086	1895	WB-F/495	AR
Taylor, Eliza C.	028	1894	WB-F/154	
Taylor, Eliza L.	099	1881	WB-A/301	AR
Taylor, Elizabeth	100	1821	WB-23/49	AR
Taylor, Elizabeth	056	1885	WB-3/390	AR
Taylor, Elizabeth	073	1860	WB-G/236	CTY
Taylor, Elizabeth	057	1881	WB-C/76	AR
Taylor, Elizabeth	029	1887	WB-E/414	AR
Taylor, Elizabeth	044	1798	WB-4/208	CTY
Taylor, Elizabeth	041	1891	WB-4/315	AR
Taylor, Elizabeth	100	1881	WB-51/159	AR
Taylor, Esdrass	018	1832	WB-C/130	
Taylor, Ethelred	039	1792	WB-A/101	
Taylor, Evaline	071	c1873	Orig. Only	AR
Taylor, Fannie M.	059	1888	WB-A/532	CTY
Taylor, Fisher	046	1861	WB-D/86	AR
Taylor, Frances	028	1898	WB-F/348	
Taylor, Frances	030	c1829	WB-3/325	
Taylor, Francis	044	1816	WB-7/666	CTY
Taylor, Francis	039	1816	WB-E/69	AR
Taylor, Franklin D.	080	1878	WB-1/56	AR
Taylor, Frederick	NY	1899	091 WB-1/217	
Taylor, Frederick	063	1868	WB-2/497	
Taylor, Frederick	057	1855	WB-B/225	AR
Taylor, George	090	1832	WB-3/233	AR
Taylor, George	038	1898	WB-4/98	AR
Taylor, George	028	1897	WB-F/329	
Taylor, George W.	022	1833	WB-B/254	AR
Taylor, H. D.	TX	1894	063 WB-4/163	063 AR
Taylor, Hannah	028	1853	WB-D/217	
Taylor, Hardy	069	1809	WB-1/203	AR
Taylor, Harriet E.	065	1845	WB-I/33	AR
Taylor, Harriett	105	1898	WB-3/295	AR
Taylor, Harry	069	1788	WB-1/46	AR
Taylor, Helen N.	006	1900	WB-E/411	AR
Taylor, Henry	012	c1799	WB-B/61	AR

Name	Co.	Date	Recorded Copy	Original
Taylor, Henry	070	1813	WB-AB/194	AR-Nunc.
Taylor, Henry	083	1828	WB-1/335	AR
Taylor, Henry	102	1899	WB-A/160	AR
Taylor, Henry A.	044	1898	WB-24/414	CTY
Taylor, Hugh	014	1882	WB-2/227	AR
Taylor, Hugh S.	065	1900	WB-N/309	AR
Taylor, Irvin	037	1857	WB-G/150	AR
Taylor, Isaac	081	1788	WB-1/49	AR
Taylor, Isaac	019	1865	WB-A/269	AR
Taylor, Isaac	028	1846	WB-D/125	AR
Taylor, Isaac	072	1879	WB-4/118	AR
Taylor, Isaac	019	1808	WB-D/396	AR
Taylor, Isaac, Sr.	051	1835	WB-A/78	
Taylor, Isham U.	035	1894	WB-4/448	AR
Taylor, Isiah	099	1862	RB-34/477	AR
Taylor, J.J.D.W.	069	1897	WB-6/16	AR
Taylor, Jacob	035	1788	WB-A/472	AR
Taylor, Jacob	028	c1770	Orig. Only	AR
Taylor, Jacob	105	1863	WB-1/94	AR
Taylor, Jacob C.	099	1855	RB-29/323	AR
Taylor, James	069	1796	WB-1/110	AR
Taylor, James	092	1872	WB-6/32	
Taylor, James	073	1812	WB-D/333	AR
Taylor, James	022	1830	WB-B/183	AR
Taylor, James	030	1846	WB-4/126	
Taylor, James	047	1772	WB-1/304	
Taylor, James	059	1882	WB-A/270	CTY
Taylor, James	037	1783	WB-B/114	AR
Taylor, James	070	1805	WB-C/422	AR-Nunc.
Taylor, James	084	1815	WB-A/117	CTY
Taylor, James	092	1837	Orig. Only	AR-Nunc.
Taylor, James B.	063	1889	WB-4/38	AR
Taylor, James G.	028	1811	WB-C/28	AR
Taylor, James J.	105	1887	WB-2/474	AR
Taylor, James L.	086	1863	WB-E/413	AR
Taylor, Jane	044	1823	WB-9/245	CTY
Taylor, Jane	019	1734	SS 876/30l	SS/AR (N)
Taylor, Jesse	041	1825	WB-2/239	AR
Taylor, Jesse F.	099	1894	WB-C/277	AR
Taylor, Jethro	071	1867	WB-5/344	AR
Taylor, Joel	045	1888	WB-1/168	AR
Taylor, John	044	1787	WB-2/48	CTY
Taylor, John	024	c1763	WB-A/309	AR
Taylor, John	069	1796	WB-1/106	AR
Taylor, John	030	1805	WB-2/261	
Taylor, John	039	c1785	WB-A/27	
Taylor, John	028	1772	Orig. Only	SS/AR
Taylor, John	011	c1832	WB-2/399	
Taylor, John	082	1828	WB-1/297	
Taylor, John	077	1791	WB-C/429	AR
Taylor, John	037	1825	WB-F/40	AR
Taylor, John	073	1847	WB-F/388	AR
Taylor, John	073	1813	WB-D/380	AR
Taylor, John	022	1881	WB-E/218	AR
Taylor, John	063	1842	WB-2/295	
Taylor, John	099	1824	RB-19/111	AR
Taylor, John	029	1894	WB-F/26	AR
Taylor, John	065	1800	WB-D/109	AR
Taylor, John	063	1828	WB-2/140	
Taylor, John	065	1777	WB-D/29	AR
Taylor, John	039	1808	WB-C/112	AR
Taylor, John	103	1881	WB-1/200	AR
Taylor, John	047	1820	WB-3/653	
Taylor, John	022	1792	RB-1/44	AR

Name	Co.	Date	Recorded Copy	Original
Taylor, John	082	1820	WB-1/221	AR
Taylor, John	072	1845	WB-2/45	AR
Taylor, John	065	1830	WB-F/28	AR
Taylor, John	047	1770	WB-1/276	
Taylor, John	033	1843	WB-1/48	AR
Taylor, John	044	1780	WB-1/275	CTY
Taylor, John	024	1716	SS 875/99	SS/AR
Taylor, John	071	1762	WB-1/72	
Taylor, John A.	070	1873	WB-E/260	AR
Taylor, John A.	092	1887	WB-6/255	AR
Taylor, John B.	018	1842	WB-C/267	
Taylor, John B.	051	1867	WB-B/91	AR
Taylor, John B.	046	1890	WB-F/68	AR
Taylor, John C.	044	1873	WB-23/114	CTY
Taylor, John C.	069	1888	WB-5/297	AR
Taylor, John H.	071	1895	WB-7/235	AR
Taylor, John Henry	076	1877	WB-A1/3	AR
Taylor, John W.	070	1865	WB-D/170	AR
Taylor, John, Sr.	044	1837	WB-13/519	CTY
Taylor, John, Sr.	063	1824	WB-2/96	
Taylor, Jonathan	010	1885	WB-I/190	
Taylor, Jonathan	030	1849	WB-4/141	
Taylor, Jonathan	030	1807	WB-2/314	
Taylor, Jonathan	103	1819	RD-4/294	AR
Taylor, Joseph	086	1878	WB-F/122	
Taylor, Joseph	071	1788	WB-1/479	AR
Taylor, Joseph	019	1860	WB-A/248	AR
Taylor, Joseph	047	1784	WB-3/63	
Taylor, Joseph	019	c1815	Orig. Only	AR
Taylor, Joseph	041	1827	WB-2/270	AR
Taylor, Joseph	044	1815	WB-7/513	CTY
Taylor, Joseph D.	065	1877	WB-K/266	AR
Taylor, Joshua	086	1830	WB-D/122	AR
Taylor, Joshua	086	1855	WB-E/303	AR
Taylor, Joshua	019	1840	WB-A/89	
Taylor, Joshua	009	1861	OB-L/307	AR
Taylor, Joshua	063	1868	WB-2/526	
Taylor, Joshua	063	1884	WB-3/253	
Taylor, Joshua	028	1870	WB-E/44	AR
Taylor, Joshua	086	1855	Copy	080 AR
Taylor, Joshua	063	1883	WB-3/242	
Taylor, Josiah	090	1863	WB-4/364	AR
Taylor, Josiah	069	1847	WB-1/497	AR
Taylor, Josiah	079	1875	WB-2/117	AR
Taylor, Josiah F.	084	1876	WB-E/113	CTY
Taylor, Kinchin	069	c1851	WB-1/544	AR
Taylor, Lemuel	077	1720	SS 876/29	SS/AR
Taylor, Lemuel	083	1881	WB-3/258	AR
Taylor, Leroy	099	1856	RB-29/461	
Taylor, Lewis	044	1880	WB-23/364	CTY
Taylor, Lewis, Sr.	044	1820	WB-8/384	CTY
Taylor, Louis	009	1879	WB-1/239	CTY
Taylor, Lovey	030	1858	WB-4/224	
Taylor, Lucrecy	037	1869	WB-G/338	AR
Taylor, Luke	024	1774	Orig. Only	SS/AR
Taylor, Lydia	041	1830	Orig. Only	AR
Taylor, Lydia	018	1870	WB-E/16	AR
Taylor, M. B.	033	1875	WB-2/51	CTY
Taylor, Major J.	035	1865	WB-3/102	AR
Taylor, Marenda	069	1854	WB-1/543	AR
Taylor, Margaret	099	1891	009 WB-1/554	009 CTY
Taylor, Margaret	099	1891	WB-C/23	AR
Taylor, Margaret	028	1866	WB-D/426	AR
Taylor, Margaret	073	1885	WB-H/364	CTY
Taylor, Mark P.	045	1890	WB-1/197	AR

Name	Co.	Date	Recorded Copy	Original
Taylor, Martha	037	1828	WB-F/85	AR
Taylor, Martha	086	1864	WB-E/435	AR
Taylor, Martha	005	1890	WB-D/279	AR
Taylor, Martha B.	044	1896	WB-24/291	CTY
Taylor, Martha J.	020	1888	WB-A/524	CTY
Taylor, Martin	081	1885	WB-15/557	AR
Taylor, Mary	063	1834	WB-2/199	
Taylor, Mary	065	1833	WB-G/138	AR
Taylor, Mary	046	1806	WB-A/389	AR
Taylor, Mary	051	1868	WB-B/103	AR
Taylor, Mary	071	1801	WB-2/226	AR
Taylor, Mary	022	1860	WB-D/53	AR
Taylor, Mary	047	1792	WB-3/201	
Taylor, Mary	073	1865	WB-G/480	CTY
Taylor, Mary B.	044	1889	WB-24/89	CTY
Taylor, Mary C.	020	c1896	Orig. Only	AR
Taylor, Mary E.	045	1875	WB-1/30	AR
Taylor, Mary E.	037	1843	WB-F/294	AR
Taylor, Mary T.	071	1854	WB-5/124	AR
Taylor, Mary W.	071	1888	WB-6/585	AR
Taylor, Maxey	085	1820	WB-H/30	AR
Taylor, Mildred L.	044	1863	WB-21/679	CTY
Taylor, Miller E.	086	1887	WB-F/312	AR
Taylor, Moses	072	1822	WB-A/132	AR
Taylor, Nancy	041	1875	WB-4/51	AR
Taylor, Nancy	032	1889	WB-4/64	AR
Taylor, Nancy	085	1832	WB-H/553	AR
Taylor, Nancy	020	1837	RB-N/63	
Taylor, Nathaniel	041	1826	WB-2/249	AR
Taylor, Nathaniel	019	1734	SS 876/300	SS/AR
Taylor, Nehemiah	072	1829	WB-1/39	AR
Taylor, Neil	029	1807	WB-A/114	AR
Taylor, Newton	037	1848	WB-F/398	AR
Taylor, Norfleet	071	1853	WB-5/114	AR
Taylor, Patience	103	1877	WB-1/120	AR
Taylor, Penny	103	1843	RD-8/504	AR
Taylor, Phebe	028	1881	WB-E/255	AR
Taylor, Philip	022	1795	RB-2/45	AR
Taylor, Philip	044	1766	Orig. Only	CTY
Taylor, Polley	041	1826	WB-2/265	AR
Taylor, Pollie	046	1900	WB-G/257	AR
Taylor, Polly	032	1889	WB-4/62	AR
Taylor, Primus	022	1886	WB-E/334	AR
Taylor, Rachel	057	c1779	WB-A/195	AR
Taylor, Ralph	070	1758	SS 882/1	SS/AR
Taylor, Ralph	070	1758	DB-D/317	
Taylor, Ransom	087	1886	WB-3/332	AR
Taylor, Reuben	030	c1810	WB-3/1	
Taylor, Reuben	069	1822	Orig. Only	037 AR
Taylor, Reubin	020	1830	RB-L/510	
Taylor, Richard	044	1826	WB-10/257	CTY
Taylor, Richard	072	c1891	Orig. Only	AR
Taylor, Richard B.	059	1899	WB-B/243	CTY
Taylor, Richard P.	044	c1870	WB-23/24	CTY
Taylor, Robert	037	1758	SS 881/217	SS/AR
Taylor, Robert	086	1835	WB-E/12	
Taylor, Robert	086	1807	WB-B/199	AR
Taylor, Robert	041	1832	WB-2/297	AR
Taylor, Robert	086	c1832	Copy	080 AR
Taylor, Robert	075	c1700	SS 874.1/13	
Taylor, Robert	041	1862	WB-3/298	AR
Taylor, Robert	041	1792	WB-1/93	AR
Taylor, Robert	044	1847	WB-17/127	CTY
Taylor, Robert J.	013	1881	WB-B/233	AR
Taylor, Roger	047	1763	WB-1/113	

Name	Co.	Date	Recorded Copy	Original
Taylor, Rosaman	069	1829	Orig. Only	AR
Taylor, Rubin	069	1822	WB-1/307	
Taylor, Sally	038	1891	WB-3/238	AR
Taylor, Sally Ann	009	1866	OB-M/242	AR
Taylor, Samuel	039	1831	WB-J/124	AR
Taylor, Samuel	071	1834	WB-4/114	AR
Taylor, Samuel	100	1802	WB-11/349	AR
Taylor, Samuel	071	1746	Orig. Only	SS/AR
Taylor, Samuel	041	1806	WB-1/230	AR
Taylor, Samuel	029	c1840	WB-B/325	AR
Taylor, Samuel	104	1874	WB-6/101	AR
Taylor, Samuel G.	009	1764	OWB/94	AR
Taylor, Samuel H.	092	1893	WB-6/361	AR
Taylor, Sarah	022	c1837	Copy	099 AR
Taylor, Sarah	075	1824	WB-N/4	AR
Taylor, Sarah	086	1887	WB-F/303	AR
Taylor, Sarah	022	1837	WB-C/53	AR
Taylor, Sarah A.	073	1900	WB-I/183	CTY
Taylor, Shelton	039	1831	Copy	090 AR
Taylor, Sidney A.	019	1883	WB-B/137	AR
Taylor, Silas	030	1870	WB-5/8	
Taylor, Simeon	046	1774	WB-A/381	AR
Taylor, Solomon	019	1799	WB-D/389	AR
Taylor, Stacy	086	1862	WB-E/401	AR
Taylor, Starlin	092	1869	WB-6/4	
Taylor, Stephen	005	1825	WB-A/120	AR
Taylor, Stephen	073	1862	WB-G/394	CTY
Taylor, Stephen	037	1848	WB-F/391	AR
Taylor, Susan	073	1862	WB-G/393	CTY
Taylor, Susan	045	1883	WB-1/109	AR
Taylor, Tabitha	103	1837	RD-7/206	AR
Taylor, Teagle	037	1826	WB-F/64	AR
Taylor, Thomas	044	1825	WB-10/9	CTY
Taylor, Thomas	037	1774	WB-A/222	AR
Taylor, Thomas	030	1798	WB-2/119	
Taylor, Thomas	005	1879	WB-D/88	AR
Taylor, Thomas	037	1802	Orig. Only	AR-Nunc.
Taylor, Thomas	030	1818	WB-3/100	
Taylor, Thomas	067	1867	WB-1/149	
Taylor, Thomas	030	1736	LGB-4/#47	SS/AR
Taylor, Thomas	083	c1800	WB-1/51	AR
Taylor, Thomas	046	1802	WB-A/388	
Taylor, Thomas	022	1881	WB-E/215	AR
Taylor, Thomas	075	1771	024 WB-1/42	024 AR
Taylor, Thomas A.	097	1889	WB-2/343	AR
Taylor, Thomas B.	047	1871	WB-6/62	AR
Taylor, Thomas P.	078	1872	WB-19/26	AR
Taylor, Timothy G.	019	1871	WB-B/64	AR
Taylor, Turner S.	071	1861	WB-5/246	
Taylor, Turner S.	071	1890	WB-7/81	AR
Taylor, Walter C.	033	1874	WB-2/42	CTY
Taylor, William	075	1771	WB-H/125	AR
Taylor, William	075	1814	WB-M1/264	AR
Taylor, William	047	1825	WB-4/12	
Taylor, William	044	1803	WB-6/44	CTY
Taylor, William	103	1819	RD-4/246	AR
Taylor, William	037	1833	WB-F/142	AR
Taylor, William	047	1762	WB-1/72	
Taylor, William	070	1788	WB-C/420	AR
Taylor, William	037	1786	WB-C/33	AR
Taylor, William	075	1773	Orig. Only	SS/AR
Taylor, William	019	1854	WB-A/171	AR
Taylor, William	073	1839	WB-F/33	AR
Taylor, William	006	1893	WB-E/246	AR
Taylor, William	090	1803	WB-2/36	AR

Name	Co.	Date	Recorded Copy	Original
Taylor, William	006	1823	WB-A/40	AR
Taylor, William	033	1843	WB-1/52	AR
Taylor, William	047	1785	WB-3/99	
Taylor, William	075	1773	Orig. Only	AR-Copy
Taylor, William B.	090	1890	WB-6/240	AR
Taylor, William B.	100	1821	WB-23/44	AR
Taylor, William F.	016	1854	WB-1/232	
Taylor, William J.	037	1881	WB-G/590	AR
Taylor, William L.	044	1897	WB-24/374	CTY
Taylor, William T.	057	1888	WB-C/155	AR
Taylor, William W.	086	1883	WB-F/212	AR
Taylor, Willie S.	028	1898	WB-F/354	
Taylor, Wilson	069	1827	WB-1/346	AR
Taylor, Winifred	045	1887	WB-1/139	AR
Taylor, Zachariah	030	1816	WB-3/84	
Tays, S. L.	054	1895	WB-5/550	CTY
Teabo, Adam	012	1827	WB-B/147	AR
Teaboe, John	012	1843	WB-B/183	AR
Teacher, Seny M.	103	1893	WB-2/51	AR
Teachey, Arnold	076	1893	Copy	035 AR
Teachey, Arnold	076	1893	WB-A1/174	AR
Teachey, Daniel	035	1794	WB-A/460	AR
Teachey, Daniel	035	1826	WB-A/470	AR
Teachey, Flora	070	1837	WB-AB/313	AR
Teachey, Jacob	035	1829	WB-A/463	AR
Teachey, Mary	035	1858	WB-2/134	AR
Teachey, Timothy	035	1828	WB-A/479	AR
Teachey, Wiley	035	1887	WB-4/294	AR
Teague, Aaron	032	1844	WB-1/452	AR
Teague, Chris.	001	1900	WB-3/316	AR
Teague, David	022	1830	WB-B/180	
Teague, E. B.	038	1874	WB-2/191	AR
Teague, Elender	054	1802	WB-1/219	AR-Nunc.
Teague, Ezekiel	032	1832	WB-1/199	AR
Teague, Francis	054	c1816	WB-1A/4	AR
Teague, Henry	003	1890	WB-B/276	
Teague, Isaac	068	c1824	WB-B/36	
Teague, Isaac	032	1856	WB-2/119	AR
Teague, James	032	c1830	Orig. Only	AR
Teague, James	032	1865	WB-2/326	AR
Teague, James E.	022	1891	WB-E/456	AR
Teague, Joab	038	1856	WB-1/91	AR
Teague, John	032	1899	WB-4/416	AR
Teague, John	022	1860	WB-D/65	AR
Teague, John	085	1814	Orig. Only	AR-Nunc.
Teague, John	090	1823	WB-3/108	AR
Teague, Magnus	003	1869	WB-B/7	AR
Teague, Malissa E.	003	1879	WB-B/116	AR
Teague, Margaret	022	1881	WB-E/224	AR
Teague, Martha	003	1863	Orig. Only	AR
Teague, Martin	061	1884	WB-2/63	AR
Teague, Mary B.	003	1878	WB-B/106	AR
Teague, Moses	022	1799	WB-A/7	AR
Teague, Moses	085	c1793	WB-E/72	AR
Teague, Moses	006	1881	WB-E/72	AR
Teague, Thomas	003	1897	WB-B/371	AR
Teague, Vandover	003	1872	WB-B/29	AR
Teague, William	090	1839	WB-4/35	AR
Teague, William	054	1806	WB-1/216	AR
Teague, William	003	1894	WB-B/325	AR
Teague, William	092	1889	WB-6/306	AR
Teague, William S.	003	1896	WB-B/352	AR
Teal, Isham	005	1888	WB-D/246	AR
Teal, Samuel	005	1852	WB-C/51	AR
Teal, Thomas	005	1895	WB-D/374	AR

Name	Co.	Date	Recorded Copy	Original
Teaster, Celie	051	1894	WB-C/480	AR
Teaster, David	085	1859	WB-K/269	AR
Teaster, Joseph	051	1883	WB-C/303	AR
Teaster, Thomas	051	1878	WB-C/194	AR
Tedder, George	011	c1795	WB-1/391	
Tedder, George	022	1863	WB-D/109	AR
Tedder, George, Sr.	011	c1796	WB-1/389	
Tedder, Thomas	029	1800	WB-A/32	AR
Tedder, William	104	1864	WB-5/377	
Teel, Agnes H.	037	1880	WB-G/586	AR
Teel, James A.	079	c1862	WB-1/119	AR
Teel, Joseph	079	c1862	WB-1/113	AR
Teel, Mary Jane	079	1899	WB-3/171	AR
Teel, Moses	079	1890	WB-2/528	AR
Teel, Rachel	079	1881	WB-2/220	AR
Teel, Richard	079	1897	WB-3/100	AR
Teel, Thomas	079	1874	WB-2/102	AR
Teel, W. J.	079	1884	WB-2/310	AR
Teel, William	005	c1816	WB-2/158	AR
Teel, William E.	079	c1864	WB-1/151	AR
Teer, Haywood	001	1884	WB-2/236	AR
Teer, Luke	001	c1842	WB-1/16	
Teer, Luke	073	1858	WB-G/192	AR
Teeter, James M.	016	1889	WB-4/22	AR-Copy
Teeter, Joshua	016	1873	WB-3/89	
Teeter, M. H.	016	1883	WB-3/384	AR
Teeter, Martin T.	016	1876	WB-3/182	AR
Telfair, Eliza V.	FL	1873	009 WB-1/123	009 CTY
Telfair, Eliza V.	FL	1873	Copy	028 AR
Telfair, John	070	1801	WB-C/421	AR
Telfair, John	037	1870	WB-G/354	AR
Telfair, Pauline D.	009	1876	WB-1/172	CTY
Telford, Thomas	073	1785	WB-A/325	AR
Temple, Almon	075	1832	WB-N/74	AR
Temple, Burwell	099	1873	RB-35/214	AR
Temple, Hattie H.	059	1894	WB-B/87	CTY
Temple, Henry	099	1820	RB-16/229	AR
Temple, James	075	1847	WB-N/215	AR
Temple, James	075	1837	WB-N/135	AR
Temple, Joseph	075	1795	WB-L/39	
Temple, Joseph	075	1804	WB-M1/90	AR
Temple, Martha	099	1899	WB-D/317	AR
Temple, Mary	099	1835	RB-23/421	AR
Temple, Mary	075	1879	WB-O/108	AR
Temple, Nancy	099	1873	RB-35/217	
Temple, Nancy	075	1837	WB-N/134	AR
Temple, Nancy T.	099	1880	WB-A/176	AR
Temple, Robert	075	1836	WB-N/129	AR
Temple, Samuel	022	1785	RB-1/22	AR
Temple, Starling	056	1847	WB-1/582	AR
Temple, Thomas	075	1791	WB-K/223	AR
Temple, Thomas	075	1833	WB-N/92	AR
Temple, William	019	1816	WB-D/397	AR
Templeman, Mary	075	1797	Orig. Only	AR
Temples, Henry	099	1799	RB-5/30	AR
Temples, Needham	032	1877	WB-3/202	AR
Templeton, David G.	054	1851	WB-3/54	AR
Templeton, George	054	c1820	WB-1A/44	AR
Templeton, John Gracy	054	1882	WB-4/471	CTY
Templeton, Joseph	054	1856	WB-3/97	AR
Templeton, Martha	054	c1832	WB-2/146	AR
Templeton, Rachel W.	099	1886	Orig. Only	AR
Templeton, Samuel D.	054	c1829	WB-2/75	AR
Templeton, Thomas	054	1898	WB-6/177	
Templeton, Wiley	003	1861	Orig. Only	AR

Name	Co.	Date	Recorded Copy	Original
Teneson, John	020	1808	RB-E/422	AR
Tennent, Charles	013	1892	WB-C/218	AR
Tennent, John F.	013	1897	WB-D/26	AR
Tennent, Marianne	013	1892	WB-C/208	AR
Tennent, Roswell A.	032	1875	WB-3/151	AR
Termend, Theresa K.	032	1883	WB-3/397	AR
Ternell, John	028	1713/4	PQS.1/30	SS/AR
Terrel, Thomas J.	078	1843	WI-15/332	
Terrell, Ann K.	039	1882	WB-U/329	AR
Terrell, Charles A.	099	1878	WB-A/4	AR
Terrell, Eliza	073	1885	WB-H/383	CTY
Terrell, Elizabeth	099	1861	RB-32/91	AR
Terrell, Francis	020	1832	RB-M/88	AR
Terrell, James	020	1851	RB-Q/485	AR
Terrell, James S.	099	1857	RB-32/354	AR
Terrell, Jephthah	044	1811	WB-7/147	CTY
Terrell, Jephthah	099	1815	RB-12/112	AR
Terrell, Joel	086	1820	WB-C/130	AR
Terrell, Joel	069	1820	WB-1/305	AR
Terrell, Joel	086	c1819	SC/02522	AR-Copy
Terrell, John	020	1814	RB-G/21	AR
Terrell, John	039	c1783	Copy	104 AR
Terrell, John C.	078	1897	WB-19/420	
Terrell, Marion	020	1866	RB-T/148	AR
Terrell, Martha	078	1866	WB-18/432	AR
Terrell, Martha E.	099	1861	RB-32/90	AR
Terrell, Susan W.	020	1886	WB-A/506	CTY
Terrell, Thomas J.	039	1864	WB-R/719	AR
Terrell, Timothy	073	1763	WB-A/29	
Terrell, Toliver	039	1863	WB-R/566	
Terrell, W. L.	099	1895	WB-C/434	AR
Terrell, William	020	1886	WB-A/481	CTY
Terrell, Zachary T.	039	1888	WB-U/451	AR
Terrence, Ann	054	c1802	WB-1/224	AR
Terrence, Hugh	054	c1792	WB-1/223	AR
Terrence, Sarah	054	c1832	WB-2/126	AR
Terril, M. C.	099	1870	RB-35/67	AR
Terry, Champ	082	1821	WB-1/216	AR
Terry, Champ G.	082	1893	WB-6/483	AR
Terry, Dabney	020	1862	RB-S/568	
Terry, Eli	082	1866	WB-5/6	AR
Terry, Hannah	022	1840	WB-C/109	AR
Terry, Henry	046	1859	WB-C/542	AR
Terry, James	083	1819	WB-1/217	AR
Terry, James	022	1834	WB-C/14	AR
Terry, James	020	1779	RB-A/54 & 71	AR
Terry, James F.	078	1889	WB-19/236	AR
Terry, James L.	082	1866	WB-5/4	AR
Terry, James T.	073	1880	WB-H/252	CTY
Terry, James, Sr.	044	1848	WB-17/187	CTY
Terry, James, Sr.	044	1799	WB-4/265	CTY
Terry, John	082	1854	WB-4/71	AR
Terry, Joseph S.	020	1848	RB-Q/31	
Terry, Kimbro	099	c1876	Orig. Only	AR
Terry, Matthew	082	1831	WB-2/8	AR
Terry, Rowland	044	1824	WB-9/285	CTY
Terry, Samuel	082	1874	WB-6/117	AR
Terry, Tarsle M.	082	1844	WB-3/14	AR
Terry, Thomas	092	1814	WB-3/111	AR
Terry, Thornton	084	1894	WB-E/564	CTY
Terry, William	082	1805	WB-1/104	AR
Terry, William	005	c1755	WB-1/37	
Terry, William	082	1837	WB-2/67	AR
Terry, William W.	038	1879	WB-2/349	AR
Tesenear, Nicholas	086	1877	WB-F/88	AR
Tesh, Emma	032	1898	WB-4/385	AR
Tesh, George	038	1860	WB-1/176	AR
Tesh, Henry	085	c1803	WB-E/8	AR
Tesh, Mary L.	032	1881	WB-3/312	AR
Tessinear, George	026	1900	WB-3/77	AR
Tessinear, George	026	c1897	086 WB-G/68	086 AR
Tester, Robert	077	1695/6	SS 874.2/63	SS/AR (N)
Testerman, Peter	006	1879	WB-E/48	AR
Tetterton, Benjamin	101	1883	WB-A/92	AR
Tetterton, Charles	009	1871	WB-1/70	CTY
Tetterton, Charles E.	009	1897	WB-2/106	CTY
Tetterton, William	096	1762	WB-1/24	AR
Tevepaugh, John	065	c1849	MD-3/339	
Tevepaugh, W. D.	065	1868	WB-J/251	AR
Tew, Alexander	087	1868	Orig. Only	AR
Tew, Daniel	087	1860	WB-2/21	AR
Tew, Emily Jane	087	1893	WB-3/515	AR
Tew, Holley	087	1853	WB-1/434	AR
Tew, Holly J.	029	1890	WB-E/491	AR
Tew, Lewis, Sr.	087	1857	WB-1/510	AR
Tew, Phillip	087	1831	WB-1/114	AR
Thach, Green	077	1782	WB-C/253	AR
Thach, John	077	c1777	Orig. Only	AR
Thach, Leaven	077	1803	WB-E/202	AR
Thach, Mary Ann	051	1852	WB-A/335	
Thach, Nathan	077	1832	WB-F/202	AR
Thach, Rosannah	077	1848	WB-F/348	AR
Thach, Thomas	077	1792	WB-C/439	AR
Thacker, Abner	084	1887	WB-E/369	CTY
Thacker, Charles	020	1845	RB-P/219	AR
Thacker, Isaac	046	1883	WB-E/380	AR
Thacker, Isaac G.	084	1866	WB-G/64	CTY
Thacker, James M.	FL	c1856	Orig. Only	046 AR
Thacker, Nancy	084	1884	WB-E/291	
Thacker, William	084	1849	WB-C/84	
Thacker, William	020	1876	WB-A/206	CTY
Thackray, John	075	1771	WB-H/143	AR
Thackrey, Joseph	075	1775	WB-I/140	AR
Thaggard, Isaac	011	1846	WB-1/131	
Thaggard, James B.	029	1866	Orig. Only	AR
Thain, Samuel B.	056	c1899	WB-4/341	AR
Thally, Andrew	035	1816	WB-A/481	AR
Thally, John	070	1847	WB-AB/455	AR
Thames, Joseph	029	1819	Orig. Only	AR
Thames, Joseph	029	1881	WB-E/267	AR
Thames, Martha	029	1815	WB-A/218	AR
Thames, William	029	1813	Orig. Only	AR-Nunc.
Tharington, Eldred	106	1875	WB-2/49	
Tharp, Henry H.	056	1860	WB-2/1	AR
Tharp, Jane	039	1837	WB-K/122	AR
Tharp, Jeremiah	039	1837	WB-K/145	AR
Tharp, Joshua	039	1823	WB-G/178	
Tharp, Mable	075	1722/3	Orig. Only	AR
Tharp, Mary	056	1845	WB-1/571	AR
Tharp, Paul	096	1756	WB-1/4	AR
Tharp, Richard	030	1720	SS 875/239	
Tharp, Solomon	037	1793	WB-C/247	AR
Tharp, Thomas	056	1804	WB-1/160	
Tharp, Thomas P.	056	1821	WB-1/321	
Tharpe, Eda	054	1893	WB-5/472	CTY
Tharpe, Esther	054	1859	WB-3/139	AR
Tharpe, Hetta E.	054	1896	WB-5/580	CTY
Tharpe, Joseph	054	1840	WB-2/205	AR
Tharpe, Lurania	054	1885	WB-5/76	CTY

Name	Co.	Date	Recorded Copy	Original
Tharpe, William	054	1850	WB-3/38	AR
Tharpe, William	054	c1807	WB-1/220	AR
Tharpe, William	054	1844	WB-2/300	AR
Tharranton, John	039	1825	Orig. Only	AR
Tharrenton, William	039	1887	WB-U/386	AR
Tharrington, Allen P.	100	1887	WB-51/253	AR
Tharrington, Sally	039	1813	WB-D/3	AR
Thatch, Stephen	051	1836	WB-A/86	
Thayer, Abner	081	1859	WB-11/149	AR
Thayer, Cassandra	067	1899	WB-2/397	AR
Thayer, Sarah A.	013	1894	WB-C/293	AR
Thedford, Walter	073	1767	WB-A/70	
Themes, Sarah	029	1816	WB-A/229	AR
Thems, Thoma	011	1750	Orig. Only	SS/AR
Therrell, Francis	065	1842	WB-H/94	AR
Therrill, William	002	1682	Orig. Only	SS/AR
Thigpen, Allen	035	1885	WB-4/255	AR
Thigpen, Gilead	037	1838	WB-F/215	AR
Thigpen, Irvin	037	1870	WB-G/349	AR
Thigpen, James	037	1849	WB-F/420	AR
Thigpen, James R.	037	1886	WB-H/22 & 47	
Thigpen, John	035	1818	WB-A/473	AR
Thigpen, Jordan	037	1876	WB-G/475	AR
Thigpen, Joshua	072	1803	WB-A/132	AR
Thigpen, Littleberry	079	1863	WB-1/121	AR
Thigpen, Patience	037	1888	WB-H/126	AR
Thigpen, Patsie	037	1872	WB-G/382	AR
Thigpen, Samuel	037	1841	WB-F/256	AR
Thigpen, Susan F.	037	1881	WB-G/595	AR
Thigpen, William	037	1886	WB-H/55	
Thom, David C.	054	1876	Orig. Only	AR
Thom, John	046	1824	WB-B/183	AR
Thom, John W.	046	1883	WB-E/369	AR
Thomas, Aaron	048	1889	WB-1/33	CTY
Thomas, Aaron	061	1847	WB-1/34	AR
Thomas, Abner	028	1796	WB-A/351	AR
Thomas, Abraham	051	1879	WB-C/219	AR
Thomas, Abraham	010	1864	WB-H/143	AR
Thomas, Ada W.	036	1887	WB-A/100	CTY
Thomas, Addison M.	032	1851	WB-2/57	AR
Thomas, Admiral	103	1878	WB-1/136	AR
Thomas, Alexander	032	1842	WB-1/392	AR
Thomas, Alexander	022	1875	WB-E/113	AR
Thomas, Alexander	056	1814	WB-1/401	AR
Thomas, Alfred S.	102	1882	WB-A/30	AR
Thomas, Amanda A.	032	1850	WB-2/52	AR
Thomas, Ann	085	1770	WB-A/158	AR
Thomas, Annanias	097	1862	WB-1/200	AR
Thomas, Annie B.	098	1897	WB-A/269	CTY
Thomas, Asenath	065	1893	WB-M/222	AR
Thomas, Athenatious	039	1832	WB-J/179	AR
Thomas, B. N.	001	1897	WB-3/192	AR
Thomas, Badsell	099	1857	RB-30/257	AR
Thomas, Barnabas	029	1852	WB-C/305	AR
Thomas, Barnabee	N	1735	LGB-4/#23	SS/AR
Thomas, Benjamin	039	c1793	WB-A/202	
Thomas, Benjamin	022	1857	WB-C/443	AR
Thomas, Benjamin	005	1858	WB-C/128	AR
Thomas, Benjamin	065	1794	WB-C/143	AR
Thomas, Benjamin	005	1836	WB-B/60	AR
Thomas, Benjamin	045	1866	WB-1/123	
Thomas, C. W.	053	1884	WB-11/133	AR
Thomas, Charles R.	028	1891	019 WB-B/205	019 AR
Thomas, Charles R.	028	1891	WB-E/559	
Thomas, Christo.	028	1830	WB-C/316	AR

Name	Co.	Date	Recorded Copy	Original
Thomas, Daniel	082	1810	WB-1/144	AR
Thomas, David	046	1840	WB-C/63	AR
Thomas, David	AL	c1853	Copy	020 AR
Thomas, David	039	1864	WB-R/796	AR
Thomas, David	092	1784	WB-2/30	AR-Nunc.
Thomas, E. J.	071	1895	WB-7/244	AR
Thomas, Ebenezer	097	1882	WB-2/220	
Thomas, Edward	073	1836	WB-E/387	AR
Thomas, Elijah	099	1809	RB-8/426	AR
Thomas, Elisabeth	071	1776	WB-1/9	AR
Thomas, Elisabeth	072	1899	WB-4/397	AR
Thomas, Elisha	056	1803	WB-1/144	AR
Thomas, Elisha	010	1826	WB-G/141	AR
Thomas, Elizabeth	072	1820	WB-A/133	AR
Thomas, Elizabeth	001	1874	WB-2/79	AR
Thomas, Elizabeth	079	1890	WB-2/506	AR
Thomas, Elizabeth	001	1889	WB-2/446	AR
Thomas, Eugene B.	080	1896	WB-1/274	AR
Thomas, Ezekiel	005	1839	WB-B/94	AR
Thomas, Frances	024	1739	Orig. Only	SS/AR
Thomas, Francis	011	c1756	Orig. Only	SS/AR
Thomas, Fredrick	TX	1896	048 WB-1/57	
Thomas, G. B.	078	1899	WB-19/468	AR
Thomas, George	073	1837	WB-E/511	AR
Thomas, George	011	c1796	WB-1/411	
Thomas, George	010	1834	WB-G/236	AR
Thomas, George F.	084	c1866	WB-D/77	CTY
Thomas, Gregory	035	1869	WB-4/13	AR
Thomas, Hannah	015	1766	RB-1/42	
Thomas, Hannah	032	1850	WB-2/96	AR
Thomas, Headly	097	1862	WB-1/194	AR
Thomas, Henry	104	1899	WB-7/96	AR
Thomas, Henry	039	1818	WB-F/65	AR
Thomas, Hezekiah	059	1883	WB-A/278	CTY
Thomas, Howell	079	1880	WB-2/185	AR
Thomas, Isaac	035	1803	WB-A/467	AR
Thomas, Isaac	054	1845	WB-2/310	AR
Thomas, Isaac, Sr.	TN	1877	023 WB-A/15	
Thomas, Isabella	032	c1854	WB-2/116	AR
Thomas, Isaiah	010	1854	WB-H/2	AR
Thomas, J. S.	022	c1819	Orig. Only	AR
Thomas, J. Y.	020	1900	WB-B/389	
Thomas, Jacob	097	1887	WB-2/314	AR
Thomas, Jacob	085	c1778	WB-B/148	AR
Thomas, Jacob	020	1855	RB-R/325	AR
Thomas, Jacob	037	1840	WB-F/243	AR
Thomas, Jacob	054	c1864	Orig. Only	AR
Thomas, James	084	1890	WB-E/495	CTY
Thomas, James	067	1874	WB-2/45	AR
Thomas, James	037	1777	WB-A/261	AR
Thomas, James	030	c1811	WB-3/17	
Thomas, James	009	c1783	OWB/181	AR
Thomas, James	046	c1788	WB-A/384	AR
Thomas, James B.	054	1873	WB-4/117	CTY
Thomas, James E.	010	1780	WB-B/158	AR
Thomas, James J.	039	1875	WB-U/120	AR
Thomas, James M.	022	1893	WB-E/525	AR
Thomas, James, Jr.	VA	1898	013 WB-D/83	013 AR
Thomas, Jane F.	078	1887	WB-19/203	
Thomas, Jehu	001	1900	WB-3/332	AR
Thomas, Jesse	069	1804	WB-1/147	AR
Thomas, Jesse	073	1827	WB-E/139	AR
Thomas, Jesse	079	c1865	WB-1/126	AR
Thomas, Jesse	085	1815	WB-G/392	AR
Thomas, Jethro	069	1803	WB-1/144	AR

Name	Co.	Date	Recorded Copy	Original
Thomas, John	102	1899	WB-A/165	AR
Thomas, John	054	c1829	Orig. Only	AR
Thomas, John	029	1790	Orig. Only	AR
Thomas, John	011	c1811	WB-2/315	
Thomas, John	028	1809	WB-B/321	AR
Thomas, John	054	1840	WB-2/204	AR
Thomas, John	037	1789	WB-C/80	AR
Thomas, John	039	1823	WB-G/175	
Thomas, John	073	1818	WB-D/550	AR
Thomas, John	071	1746	Orig. Only	SS/AR
Thomas, John	068	1850	WB-B/207	
Thomas, John	073	1766	WB-A/41	
Thomas, John	037	1777	WB-A/248	AR
Thomas, John	039	1806	WB-C/51	AR
Thomas, John	084	1826	WB-A/301	CTY
Thomas, John	056	1818	WB-1/291	AR
Thomas, John E.	039	1888	WB-U/442	AR
Thomas, John F.	098	1888	WB-A/97	
Thomas, John Giles	099	1785	RB-2/41	AR
Thomas, John R.	097	1857	WB-1/137	AR
Thomas, John R.	022	c1863	WB-D/150	AR
Thomas, John R.	037	1826	WB-F/51	AR
Thomas, Jonathan	FL	1832	076 WB-A1/77	076 AR
Thomas, Jonathan	037	1775	Orig. Only	AR
Thomas, Jonathan	070	1761	Orig. Only	AR-Nunc.
Thomas, Jordan	047	1763	WB-1/92	
Thomas, Joseph	065	1782	WB-C/137	AR
Thomas, Joseph	029	c1818	WB-B/20	
Thomas, Joseph	010	1758	SS 882/92	SS/AR
Thomas, Joseph	037	1758	SS 882/165	SS/AR
Thomas, Joseph	056	1764	WB-1/791	AR
Thomas, Joseph	011	c1780	WB-2/275	
Thomas, Joseph	032	1892	WB-4/148	AR
Thomas, Joseph	010	1735	LGB-4/#37	SS/AR
Thomas, Joseph J.	100	1886	WB-51/210	AR
Thomas, Josiah	039	1830	WB-J/101	
Thomas, Josiah	070	1752	SS 878/127	SS/AR
Thomas, Josiah	010	1866	WB-H/178	AR
Thomas, Josiah	070	1752	DB-C/326	
Thomas, Lewis	083	1814	WB-1/150	
Thomas, Louis	028	1730/1	SS 877/168	SS/AR
Thomas, Louis R.	067	1894	WB-2/326	AR
Thomas, Louisa	009	1897	WB-2/111	CTY
Thomas, Luke	087	c1801	Orig. Only	AR
Thomas, Luke	037	1757	Orig. Only	SS/AR
Thomas, M. G.	078	1863	WB-18/313	AR
Thomas, Malcom	048	1895	WB-1/40	CTY
Thomas, Marcus C.	019	1854	WB-A/169	AR
Thomas, Martha A.	039	1881	WB-U/276	AR
Thomas, Mary	037	1802	WB-D/148	AR
Thomas, Mary	037	1880	WB-G/570	AR
Thomas, Mary	032	1885	WB-3/484	AR
Thomas, Mary	001	c1839	WB-2/48	AR
Thomas, Mary	056	c1779	WB-1/793	AR
Thomas, Mary	037	1810	WB-D/363	AR
Thomas, Mary W.	VA	1898	013 WB-D/106	013 AR
Thomas, Massa	032	1835	WB-1/266	AR
Thomas, Micajah	069	1788	WB-1/49	AR
Thomas, Micajah	037	1770	WB-A/178	AR
Thomas, Michael	084	1817	WB-A/308	CTY
Thomas, Michael	011	c1807	WB-1/404	
Thomas, Michel	010	c1766	WB-A/59	AR
Thomas, Morgan	075	c1709	Orig. Only	AR-Copy
Thomas, Morgan	075	1713	SS 875/3	SS/AR
Thomas, Nancy	068	c1838	WB-B/135	
Thomas, Nancy	075	1836	WB-N/125	AR
Thomas, Nancy Ann	084	1882	WB-E/233	AR-Copy
Thomas, Nancy P.	082	1866	WB-5/9	AR
Thomas, Nathaniel	020	c1851	SC/07676	AR-Copy
Thomas, Nathaniel	020	1851	RB-Q/565	AR
Thomas, Osborne	097	1863	WB-1/205	AR
Thomas, Owen	073	1769	WB-A/96	
Thomas, Phebe	084	1894	WB-E/559	CTY
Thomas, Philemon	082	1797	WB-1/47	AR
Thomas, Philip	037	1788	WB-C/74	AR
Thomas, Philip H.	044	1854	WB-19/494	CTY
Thomas, Phillip	029	1819	WB-B/27	AR
Thomas, Polly W.	032	1875	WB-3/158	AR
Thomas, Rebecca	065	1794	WB-D/27	AR
Thomas, Rebecca	069	1800	WB-1/132	AR
Thomas, Rebecca	040	1872	WB-2/44	AR
Thomas, Remus	070	1886	WB-F/29	AR
Thomas, Richard	069	c1784	WB-1/28	AR
Thomas, Richard	083	c1792	WB-1/30	AR
Thomas, Robert	039	1871	WB-U/33	
Thomas, Robert	060	1842	WB-2/157	AR
Thomas, Robert	046	1887	WB-E/473	AR
Thomas, Robert	044	1807	WB-6/325	CTY
Thomas, Sallie	022	1872	WB-E/85	AR
Thomas, Samuel	039	1833	WB-J/246	AR
Thomas, Samuel	040	1882	WB-2/191	AR
Thomas, Sarah	011	1846	WB-1/123	
Thomas, Sarah	029	1840	WB-B/309	AR
Thomas, Sarah Ann	079	1891	WB-2/541	AR
Thomas, Serry	018	c1853	WB-E/7	
Thomas, Simon	082	1815	WB-1/167	AR
Thomas, Stanhope	054	1899	WB-6/211	CTY
Thomas, Stephen	005	1809	WB-2/162	AR
Thomas, Stephen	041	1787	WB-1/66	AR
Thomas, Susie	062	1895	WB-B/171	AR
Thomas, Temperance	055	c1873	WB-A/32	
Thomas, Tena	032	1893	WB-4/200	AR
Thomas, Theophilus	037	1803	WB-D/172	AR
Thomas, Thomas K.	039	1880	WB-U/244	AR
Thomas, Tillman	068	1885	WB-D/203	
Thomas, Vine	028	1892	WB-F/56	
Thomas, W. N.	032	1898	WB-4/334	AR
Thomas, W. P.	006	1886	WB-E/142	
Thomas, William	037	1777	WB-A/251	AR
Thomas, William	020	1799	RB-C/411	
Thomas, William	038	1888	WB-3/88	AR
Thomas, William	032	1884	WB-3/427	AR
Thomas, William	028	1874	Orig. Only	AR
Thomas, William	035	1782	WB-A/477	AR-Copy
Thomas, William	082	1800	WB-1/80	AR
Thomas, William C.	022	1900	WB-F/147	AR
Thomas, William D.	032	1899	WB-4/430	AR
Thomas, William E.	082	1834	WB-2/43	AR
Thomas, William G.	070	1890	WB-F/365	AR
Thomas, William G.	044	1875	WB-23/186	CTY
Thomas, Winney	097	1894	WB-2/465	AR
Thomason, Adeline	032	1887	WB-3/530	AR
Thomason, Arnold	082	1821	WB-1/226	AR
Thomason, George	032	1850	WB-2/46	AR
Thomason, George B.	064	1899	WB-2/464	AR
Thomason, James	085	1857	WB-K/246	AR
Thomason, Lucy	082	1830	WB-2/6	AR
Thomason, Susan	032	1900	WB-4/471	AR
Thomason, Turner P.	085	1899	WB-3/306	CTY
Thomason, William	085	1848	WB-K/72	AR

Name	Co.	Date	Recorded Copy	Original
Thomasson, A. H.	106	1880	WB-2/130	AR
Thomasson, David T.	065	1890	WB-L/493	AR
Thomasson, Fleming	046	c1872	WB-E/107	AR
Thomasson, George	090	1814	WB-2/158	AR
Thomasson, George	085	c1792	WB-C/49	AR
Thomasson, George	044	1836	WB-13/421	CTY
Thomasson, John	090	1827	WB-3/162	AR
Thomasson, John	009	1846	OWB/543	AR
Thomasson, Lidia	044	1849	WB-18/1	CTY
Thomasson, Richard	044	1808	WB-6/424	CTY
Thomasson, Richard	085	1824	WB-H/288	AR
Thomasson, Thomas	044	1820	WB-8/333	CTY
Thomasson, William H.	044	1887	WB-24/10	CTY
Thomerson, Terecy	044	1859	WB-21/152	CTY
Thomes, Joseph	077	1727	SS 876/121	SS/AR
Thomes, M. S.	093	1883	WB-2/11	
Thomeson, Sarah	090	1835	WB-3/297	AR
Thomlinson, Elisabeth	075	1792	WB-K/231	
Thomlinson, Elizabeth	028	1802	WB-B/151	AR
Thomlinson, Thomas	028	1802	WB-B/157	AR
Thomly, Thomas	028	1789	WB-A/204	AR
Thompson, A. J.	092	1891	WB-6/335	AR
Thompson, Alafare	032	1887	WB-3/537	AR
Thompson, Alaxander	004	1885	006 WB-E/109	
Thompson, Alexander	083	1831	WB-1/256	AR
Thompson, Alfred	001	1894	WB-3/10	AR
Thompson, Alfred	105	1896	WB-3/177	AR
Thompson, Alfred S.	099	1871	RB-35/136	AR
Thompson, Alice A.	028	1842	WB-D/57	AR
Thompson, Amos	073	1782	WB-A/257	AR
Thompson, Andrew	081	1811	WB-3/305	AR
Thompson, Ann	060	1847	WB-2/286	AR
Thompson, Ann	001	1859	WB-1/156	AR
Thompson, Ann R.	073	1894	WB-I/25	CTY
Thompson, Anna	NY	c1748	Copy	070 AR
Thompson, Anna	080	1899	WB-1/320	AR
Thompson, Anthony	073	1836	WB-E/396	AR
Thompson, Archibald	083	1900	WB-4/301	AR
Thompson, Arena	100	1892	WB-51/397	AR
Thompson, Arthur	105	1873	WB-2/113	AR
Thompson, Ave	092	1784	WB-2/36A	
Thompson, Azariah A.	065	1865	WB-J/199	AR
Thompson, Basil M.	082	1855	WB-4/95	AR
Thompson, Ben	022	1897	Orig. Only	AR
Thompson, Benjamin	015	1771	100 WB-1/183	AR
Thompson, Benjamin	011	1874	WB-2/69	
Thompson, Benjamin	073	1795	WB-C/62	AR
Thompson, Benjamin W.	100	1891	WB-51/332	AR
Thompson, C. H.	092	1858	WB-5/34	
Thompson, Cador	083	1793	WB-1/30	Nunc.
Thompson, Charles	083	c1821	WB-1/230	AR
Thompson, Charles	060	1837	WB-1/386	AR
Thompson, Charles	071	1808	WB-2/365	AR
Thompson, Charles	083	c1811	WB-1/122	
Thompson, Charles A.	083	1873	WB-3/59	AR
Thompson, D. S.	001	1893	WB-2/559	AR
Thompson, Daniel	070	1803	WB-AB/83	AR
Thompson, Daniel	072	1846	WB-2/76	AR
Thompson, Daniel W.	073	1868	WB-G/547	CTY
Thompson, David	086	1801	WB-B/122	AR
Thompson, David	080	1872	WB-1/11	AR
Thompson, David A.	003	1865	WB-A/2	AR
Thompson, Deborah	024	1785	WB-A/203	AR
Thompson, Delia	099	1885	WB-B/73	AR
Thompson, Dugald	029	1783	Orig. Only	AR
Thompson, Easther	030	1840	WB-4/76	
Thompson, Edmond	020	1874	WB-A/142	CTY
Thompson, Edward	072	c1760	RW/L39	AR
Thompson, Edwin G.	073	1841	WB-F/106	AR
Thompson, Eldridge	047	1857	WB-5/42	
Thompson, Elijah	086	1840	WB-E/63	AR
Thompson, Elijah	080	1896	WB-1/271	AR
Thompson, Elijah	092	1872	WB-6/29	
Thompson, Elisha	067	1848	WB-1/45	
Thompson, Elizabeth	032	1875	WB-3/164	AR
Thompson, Elizabeth	092	1872	WB-6/37	
Thompson, Elizabeth	073	1848	WB-F/412	AR
Thompson, Elizabeth	075	c1853	WB-M2/12	AR
Thompson, Elizabeth	037	1792	WB-C/216	AR
Thompson, Elizabeth	100	1813	WB-17/335	AR
Thompson, Enoch	072	1823	WB-A/131	AR
Thompson, Even	030	1793	WB-2/11	
Thompson, Fanny	073	1853	WB-G/31	AR
Thompson, Frances	073	1870	WB-H/25	CTY
Thompson, Frances	073	1799	WB-C/146	AR
Thompson, Franklin	072	1886	WB-4/214	
Thompson, G. T.	026	1865	WB-1/375	AR
Thompson, George	105	1885	WB-2/381	AR
Thompson, George N.	020	1891	WB-B/73	CTY
Thompson, George W.	099	1892	WB-C/25	AR
Thompson, George W.	022	1852	WB-C/328	AR
Thompson, Gidion	065	1796	WB-D/35	AR
Thompson, Grant B.	075	1892	WB-O/369	AR
Thompson, Hannah	073	1859	WB-G/223	CTY
Thompson, Hannah	022	1788	RB-1/34	AR
Thompson, Helen M.	010	1893	WB-I/371	AR
Thompson, Henery	046	1771	WB-A/380	AR
Thompson, Henry	073	1825	WB-E/71	AR
Thompson, Henry	071	1818	WB-3/202	AR
Thompson, Henry	024	1777	WB-A/237	AR
Thompson, Henry M.	105	1896	WB-3/217	AR
Thompson, Hezekiah	010	1820	WB-G/70	AR
Thompson, Hezekiah	010	1869	WB-I/13	AR
Thompson, Hezekiah	010	1771	WB-A/132	AR
Thompson, Hillary	099	1872	RB-35/173	AR
Thompson, Hugh	072	c1825	WB-A/131	AR
Thompson, Hugh	083	1871	WB-3/28	AR
Thompson, Isaac	103	1877	WB-1/126	AR
Thompson, Isaac	103	c1825	Orig. Only	AR
Thompson, Isley E.	099	1884	WB-A/567	AR
Thompson, James	010	1854	WB-G/509	AR
Thompson, James	005	1819	WB-2/165	AR
Thompson, James	072	c1786	WI/L53	AR
Thompson, James	073	1846	WB-F/294	AR
Thompson, James	073	1812	WB-D/335	AR
Thompson, James	024	c1764	WB-A/355	AR
Thompson, James	100	1804	WB-12/282	AR
Thompson, James	073	1794	WB-C/21	AR
Thompson, James	003	1886	WB-B/170	AR
Thompson, James	001	1888	WB-2/369	AR
Thompson, James	103	1895	WB-2/97	AR
Thompson, James	072	c1792	Orig. Only	AR
Thompson, James	086	1820	WB-C/135	AR
Thompson, James	103	1839	RD-7/557	AR
Thompson, James	097	1890	WB-2/376	AR
Thompson, James	010	1824	WB-G/118	AR
Thompson, James	085	1814	WB-G/331	AR
Thompson, James	001	1858	WB-1/141	AR
Thompson, James	092	c1847	WB-4/265	
Thompson, James A.	027	1897	WB/2/135	AR

Name	Co.	Date	Recorded Copy	Original
Thompson, James H.	073	1889	WB-H/483	CTY
Thompson, Jane	081	1868	WB-14/208	AR
Thompson, Jason H.	046	1887	WB-E/488	AR
Thompson, Jehu	037	1791	WB-C/174	AR
Thompson, Jennins	065	1791	WB-D/26	AR
Thompson, Jethro	103	1821	RD-4/460	AR
Thompson, John	047	1881	WB-6/278	AR
Thompson, John	085	1774	WB-A/177	AR
Thompson, John	028	1738	SS 877/230	SS/AR
Thompson, John	092	1786	WB-2/65A	AR
Thompson, John	046	1830	WB-B/407	AR
Thompson, John	073	1884	WB-H/360	CTY
Thompson, John	103	1784	WI-A/41	AR
Thompson, John	054	c1798	WB-1/221	AR
Thompson, John	104	1805	WB-2/174	
Thompson, John	029	1813	WB-A/186	
Thompson, John	075	c1858	WB-M2/60	AR
Thompson, John	022	1811	WB-A/161	AR
Thompson, John	029	1842	WB-C/27	AR
Thompson, John	103	1825	RD-5/192	AR
Thompson, John	073	1847	WB-F/357	AR
Thompson, John	075	1810	WB-M1/216	AR
Thompson, John	065	1822	WB-D/115	AR
Thompson, John	024	1755	SS 880/100	SS/AR
Thompson, John	072	1831	WB-1/77	AR
Thompson, John	081	1804	WB-2/131	AR
Thompson, John	054	1853	WB-3/73	
Thompson, John	046	1794	WB-A/385	AR
Thompson, John	073	1820	WB-D/568	AR
Thompson, John	024	1884	Orig. Only	AR
Thompson, John	065	1800	WB-D/109	AR
Thompson, John	065	1814	WB-D/112	AR
Thompson, John	103	1808	RD-1/88	AR
Thompson, John A.	099	1883	WB-A/484	AR
Thompson, John B.	083	1868	WB-2/243	AR
Thompson, John C.	082	1895	WB-6/522	AR
Thompson, John C.	044	1841	WB-15/104	CTY
Thompson, John G.	036	1881	WB-A/3	CTY
Thompson, John N.	065	1892	WB-M/35	
Thompson, John W.	103	1889	WB-1/473	AR
Thompson, John, Sr.	054	c1814	WB-1/342	AR
Thompson, Joseph	073	1842	WB-F/134	AR
Thompson, Joseph	092	1852	WB-4/322	AR
Thompson, Joseph	083	1883	WB-3/363	AR
Thompson, Joseph	003	c1869	WB-A/21	AR
Thompson, Joseph	083	c1865	Orig. Only	AR
Thompson, Joseph	073	1832	WB-E/269	AR
Thompson, Joseph S.	020	1890	Copy	078 AR
Thompson, Joseph S.	020	1891	WB-B/71	CTY
Thompson, Joshua	073	1837	WB-E/425	AR
Thompson, L. B.	097	1875	WB-2/82	
Thompson, L. W.	083	1893	WB-3/586	AR
Thompson, Leah	072	c1885	WB-4/220	
Thompson, Lemuel	083	1820	WB-1/228	
Thompson, Lewis	056	1900	WB-4/209	AR
Thompson, Lewis	010	1814	WB-F/255	AR
Thompson, Lewis	010	1868	WB-H/205	AR
Thompson, Lewis	011	1864	WB-1/323	
Thompson, Lorell	071	1817	WB-3/198	AR
Thompson, Louisa	099	1881	WB-A/248	AR
Thompson, Margaret	073	1884	WB-H/359	CTY
Thompson, Margaret	063	1899	WB-4/243	AR
Thompson, Margaret	010	1881	WB-I/127	
Thompson, Margaret	026	1863	WB-1/329	AR
Thompson, Martha A.	100	1853	WB-42/236	AR
Thompson, Mary	010	1807	WB-F/39	AR
Thompson, Mary	073	1830	WB-E/227	AR
Thompson, Mary	071	1827	WB-4/22	AR
Thompson, Mary Ann	072	1858	WB-2/157	AR
Thompson, Mary Eliza	010	1858	WB-H/75	
Thompson, Mary Ellen	083	1897	WB-4/157	AR
Thompson, Mary L.	046	1850	WB-C/519	AR
Thompson, Mehitable	028	1819	WB-C/190	
Thompson, Michael	099	1877	RB-35/397	AR
Thompson, Nancy	083	1837	WB-1/303	AR
Thompson, Nancy	028	1854	WB-D/236	
Thompson, Nancy	071	1830	WB-4/74	AR
Thompson, Nancy	099	1873	RB-35/197	AR
Thompson, Nancy	072	c1816	WB-A/134	AR
Thompson, Nathan	083	1825	WB-1/328	AR
Thompson, Nellie	103	1895	WB-2/138	AR
Thompson, Nicholas	020	1857	RB-R/564	AR
Thompson, Noah	010	1827	WB-G/163	AR
Thompson, Noah	010	1799	WB-E/85	AR
Thompson, Patrick	067	1878	WB-2/93	AR
Thompson, Patterson	001	1892	WB-2/504	AR
Thompson, Peter	073	1883	WB-H/410	CTY
Thompson, Porter	073	1853	WB-G/42	AR
Thompson, Providence	085	1850	WB-K/105	AR
Thompson, Reuben	010	1780	WB-B/151	AR
Thompson, Richard	082	1782	WB-1/14	AR
Thompson, Richard	072	c1790	Orig. Only	AR
Thompson, Richard T.	073	1894	WB-I/17	CTY
Thompson, Robert	VA	1788	Copy	092 AR
Thompson, Robert	001	1849	WB-1/20	AR
Thompson, Robert	046	1839	WB-C/32	AR
Thompson, Rosannah	073	1875	WB-H/110	CTY
Thompson, Samantha A.	103	1896	WB-2/153	
Thompson, Samuel	083	1882	WB-3/272	AR
Thompson, Samuel	081	1859	WB-11/250	AR
Thompson, Samuel	073	1829	WB-E/195	AR
Thompson, Samuel	001	1893	WB-2/555	AR
Thompson, Samuel	073	c1800	Orig. Only	AR
Thompson, Samuel	092	1792	WB-3/7	AR
Thompson, Samuel	046	1801	WB-A/394	AR
Thompson, Samuel	073	1837	WB-E/505	AR
Thompson, Samuel	073	1821	WB-D/599	AR
Thompson, Samuel	099	1801	RB-5/218	AR
Thompson, Samuel	001	1874	WB-2/89	AR
Thompson, Samuel G.	046	1865	WB-D/242	AR
Thompson, Samuel L.	001	1898	WB-3/243	AR
Thompson, Sarah	073	1860	WB-G/247	AR
Thompson, Sarah	100	1782	WB-3/129	AR
Thompson, Sarah	046	1866	WB-D/285	AR
Thompson, Sarah	073	1831	WB-E/262	AR
Thompson, Sarah	010	1825	WB-G/127	AR
Thompson, Sarah	010	1828	WB-G/174	AR
Thompson, Sarah	072	1839	WB-2/20	AR
Thompson, Solomon	073	1868	WB-G/551	CTY
Thompson, Solomon	099	1847	RB-26/256	AR
Thompson, Stephen	083	1826	WB-1/314	AR
Thompson, Susan	073	1880	WB-H/251	CTY
Thompson, Swan	099	1801	RB-5/236	AR
Thompson, Tabitha	072	1802	WB-A/134	AR
Thompson, Tarlton	009	1872	WB-1/100	CTY
Thompson, Thomas	065	c1781	WB-D/120	AR
Thompson, Thomas	073	1841	WB-F/102	AR
Thompson, Thomas	073	1796	WB-C/70	AR
Thompson, Thomas	010	1827	WB-G/167	AR
Thompson, Thomas	085	c1793	WB-E/34	AR

Name	Co.	Date	Recorded Copy	Original
Thompson, Thomas	046	1853	WB-C/406	AR
Thompson, Thomas	103	1830	RD-6/181	AR
Thompson, Thomas	028	1816	WB-C/138	AR
Thompson, Thomas W.	075	1837	WB-N/136	AR
Thompson, Thomas W.	010	1894	WB-I/403	AR
Thompson, Trimigan	083	1873	WB-3/56	AR
Thompson, W. C .	089	1890	WB-2/186	AR
Thompson, Wesley	006	1891	WB-E/219	AR
Thompson, William	092	1782	Orig. Only	AR
Thompson, William	083	1856	WB-2/90	AR
Thompson, William	085	c1830	Orig. Only	AR
Thompson, William	099	1869	RB-35/33	AR
Thompson, William	081	1837	WB-7/94	AR
Thompson, William	024	1822	WB-C/99	AR
Thompson, William	086	1844	WB-E/116	AR
Thompson, William	056	1769	WB-1/789	AR
Thompson, William	070	1856	WB-C/616	AR
Thompson, William	030	1790	WB-1/244	
Thompson, William	085	1843	WB-I/148	AR
Thompson, William	083	1813	WB-1/128	AR
Thompson, William	072	1844	WB-2/51	AR
Thompson, William	010	1799	WB-E/67	AR
Thompson, William	071	1792	WB-2/18	AR
Thompson, William A.	001	1886	WB-2/317	AR
Thompson, William B.	083	1857	WB-2/116	AR
Thompson, William C.	010	1895	WB-I/451	AR
Thompson, William F.	010	1813	WB-F/226	AR
Thompson, William H.	073	1861	WB-G/372	CTY
Thompson, William P.	001	1871	WB-2/39	AR
Thompson, William R.	047	1771	WB-1/288	
Thompson, Willis	010	1834	WB-G/241	AR
Thompson, Zachariah	099	1800	RB-5/122	AR
Thompson, Zilpha	105	c1899	Orig. Only	AR
Thomson, Audry	030	1805	WB-2/262	
Thomson, Charles	071	1790	WB-1/411	AR
Thomson, Daniel	029	1784	Orig. Only	AR
Thomson, David	035	1773	Orig. Only	AR-Copy
Thomson, David	028	1781	Orig. Only	AR
Thomson, David	035	1773	Orig. Only	SS/AR
Thomson, Ella N.	029	1891	WB-E/517	AR
Thomson, Isbell	073	1841	WB-F/86	AR
Thomson, James W.	099	1816	028 WB-C/139	028 AR
Thomson, Jane	019	1803	WB-D/390	AR
Thomson, Jane	081	1799	WB-2/45	AR
Thomson, John	030	1783	WB-1/161	
Thomson, John	085	1760	WB-A/159	AR
Thomson, John	010	1798	WB-E/55	AR
Thomson, John	071	1778	WB-1/307	
Thomson, John	035	1786	WB-A/464	
Thomson, John C.	029	1897	WB-F/126	AR
Thomson, Malcolm	029	1792	Orig. Only	AR
Thomson, Mary	037	1853	WB-F/495	AR
Thomson, Mehetable	028	1819	Orig. Only	AR
Thomson, Moses	085	c1802	WB-E/31	AR
Thomson, Richard	072	1795	Orig. Only	AR-Nunc.
Thomson, Sarah	065	1828	WB-A/160	AR
Thomson, Thomas	082	c1804	WB-1/100	AR
Thomson, Thomas	029	1774	Orig. Only	AR
Thomson, William	019	1803	WB-D/393	AR
Thomson, William	024	c1795	WB-B/221	AR
Thomson, William	085	c1810	WB-G/151	AR
Thomson, William	035	1785	WB-A/456	Nunc.
Thoragood, Francis	008	1716	SS 875/129	SS/AR
Thorington, Jesse	106	c1858	WB-1/57	AR
Thorinton, William	009	1818	OB-A/288	AR

Name	Co.	Date	Recorded Copy	Original
Thorn, Nicholas	037	1789	WB-C/95	AR
Thorn, Taylor	069	1854	WB-1/536	AR
Thorn, Thomas	051	1833	WB-A/60	
Thorn, William W.	047	1838	WB-4/170	
Thornbery, Edward	081	1791	WB-1/90	AR
Thornborough, Mary	081	1818	Orig. Only	AR
Thornbrough, William	081	1786	WB-1/26	AR
Thornburg, Jacob	060	1844	WB-2/222	AR
Thornburg, James	046	1814	WB-A/391	AR
Thornburg, Joseph	046	1877	WB-E/193	AR
Thornburg, Joseph	046	1800	WB-A/387	AR
Thornburg, Mary A.	040	1897	WB-2/555	AR
Thornburg, Samuel L.	065	1863	WB-J/173	AR
Thornburg, Thomas	046	1797	WB-A/382	AR
Thornburg, Thomas	046	1833	WB-B/478	AR
Thornburgh, Martha	081	1814	WB-4/77	AR
Thornburgh, Thomas	046	c1787	WB-A/383	AR
Thornburgh, Thomas	081	1833	WB-6/329	AR
Thorne, Abram	105	1879	WB-2/242	AR
Thorne, Leah	099	1828	RB-20/224	AR
Thorne, Martin	105	1870	WB-2/103	
Thorne, Samuel	047	1838	WB-4/172	
Thorne, William	099	1812	RB-10/165	AR
Thorne, William H.	057	1890	WB-C/167	AR
Thornel, Benjamin	037	1810	WB-D/365	AR
Thornton, Benjamin	087	1823	WB-1/48	AR
Thornton, Benjamin	087	1848	WB-1/347	AR
Thornton, Eldridge	056	1849	WB-1/621	AR
Thornton, Elenor	053	1824	WB-4/284	AR
Thornton, Frances	100	1797	WB-9/111	AR
Thornton, James	029	1763	Orig. Only	AR
Thornton, John	039	1787	WB-A/22	AR
Thornton, John	070	c1879	WB-E/420	AR
Thornton, John	044	1755	Orig. Only	SS/AR
Thornton, John J.	046	1899	WB-G/143	AR
Thornton, Joseph A.	046	1888	WB-E/516	AR
Thornton, L. J. A.	070	1881	WB-E/438	AR
Thornton, Malinda	060	1867	WB-3/98	AR
Thornton, Margaret	075	1873	WB-0/55	AR
Thornton, Nancy	104	1848	WB-4/347	AR
Thornton, Nathaniel	087	c1821	WB-1/29	AR
Thornton, Rosa A. M.	070	1896	WB-G/455	
Thornton, Sara T.	044	1887	WB-24/14	CTY
Thornton, Suzy	087	1830	WB-1/109	AR
Thornton, Thomas	053	1794	RW-1/238	
Thornton, Thomas	087	c1801	Orig. Only	AR
Thornton, William	DC	1828	089 WB-1/107	
Thornton, William	075	1835	WB-N/110	AR
Thornton, William	075	1840	WB-N/161	AR
Thornton, Willie	047	1807	WB-3/467	
Thornton, Y. N.	056	1876	WB-3/159	AR
Thorntown, Mary	077	1777	WB-C/194	AR
Thorough, Arquil	053	c1768	RW-1/9	AR
Thoroughgood, Amos	096	1837	WB-2/138	AR
Thoroughgood, John	096	c1825	Orig. Only	AR
Thoroughgood, Paul	096	1835	WB-2/122	AR
Thorp, Benjamin	044	1858	WB-20/567	CTY
Thorp, Haywood	044	1897	WB-24/335	CTY
Thorp, Jane	044	1859	WB-20/703	CTY
Thorp, John	069	1883	WB-5/170	AR
Thorp, M. E.	069	1883	WB-5/170	AR
Thorp, Peterson	044	1887	WB-24/7	CTY
Thorp, Priscilla	069	1814	WB-1/258	AR
Thorp, Richard	044	1889	WB-24/86	CTY
Thorp, Richard	044	1889	Copy	078 AR

Name	Co.	Date	Recorded Copy	Original
Thorp, Thomas	056	1804	WB-1/160	AR
Thorp, Thomas P.	056	1821	WB-1/321	AR
Thorp, Timothy	039	1821	WB-G/67	AR
Thorpe, Frank	037	1897	WB-H/398	AR
Thorpe, Lewis, Sr.	044	1888	WB-24/46	CTY
Thorpe, Lucy	044	1890	WB-24/103	CTY
Thorpe, Sidney A.	028	1857	WB-D/284	AR
Thralkill, Michael	022	1880	WB-E/194	AR
Thrash, Valentine	013	1835	WB-A/35	
Thrasher, Joseph C.	GA	1807	Copy	085 AR
Threadgill, Elizabeth	089	1900	Orig. Only	AR
Threadgill, George R.	005	1844	WB-B/188	AR
Threadgill, George W.	005	1891	WB-D/297	AR
Threadgill, John C.	005	1826	WB-A/126	AR
Threadgill, John H.	005	1880	WB-D/93	AR
Threadgill, Randall	005	1811	WB-2/159	AR
Threadgill, Sidney	089	1900	WB-2/356	AR
Threadgill, Thomas	005	c1835	SC/08059	AR-Copy
Threadgill, Thomas	005	1843	WB-B/167	AR
Threadgill, Thomas H.	005	1889	WB-D/257	AR
Threadgill, William	005	1820	WB-2/160	AR
Threatt, Frederick	097	1898	WB-2/558	AR
Threatt, Joseph S.	065	1869	WB-K/28	AR
Threwitts, Frederick	047	1820	WB-3/648	
Thrift, Allen	026	1900	WB-3/79	AR
Thrift, Annie E.	081	1888	WB-16/79	AR
Thrift, Isham	073	c1812	WB-D/344	AR
Thrift, Mary	073	1835	WB-E/334	AR
Thrift, Nathaniel	071	1814	WB-3/120	AR
Thrift, Sally	100	1847	WB-39/322	AR
Thrift, William	071	1790	WB-1/413	AR
Throneburg, A. M.	021	1863	WB-1/178	AR
Throughgood, Francis	008	1716	009 DB-1/170	
Thrower, Eldridge	047	1870	WB-6/30	AR
Thrower, Harriet	100	1895	WB-51/420	
Thrower, Lafayette	010	1890	WB-I/303	AR
Thrower, Oliver P.	047	1891	WB-7/15	AR
Thrower, Sarah	047	1836	WB-4/124	
Thrower, Thomas	047	1787	WB-3/120	
Thrower, W. N.	029	1897	WB-F/124	AR
Thrower, William E.	100	1853	WB-42/170	AR
Thurston, Gaston E.	VA	1899	103 WB-2/249	103 AR
Thurston, Zilpha	056	1895	WB-2/220	AR
Thurston, Zilpha	056	1895	Copy	070 AR
Thuston, John	002	c1692	Orig. Only	SS/AR
Tibbet, John	019	1755	SS 880/28	SS/AR (N)
Tice, Abram	063	c1820	WB-2/67	
Tice, Alfred T.	063	1882	WB-3/220	
Tice, Thomas	063	1854	WB-2/401	
Tickel, George	001	1880	WB-2/173	AR
Tickle, Conrod	073	c1825	Orig. Only	AR
Tickle, Daniel	001	1888	WB-2/391	AR
Tickle, Eli	001	1892	WB-2/496	AR
Tickle, Joel	001	1888	WB-2/399	AR
Tickle, John	073	1822	WB-E/19	AR
Tickle, John W.	001	1900	WB-3/320	AR
Tickle, Lewis	001	1880	WB-2/153	AR
Tickle, Peter	073	1823	WB-E/33	AR
Tickle, Rankin S.	046	1863	WB-D/193	AR
Tickle, Simeon	001	1865	WB-1/247	AR
Tickle, Solomon	092	1888	WB-6/281	AR
Tiddy, William	065	1895	WB-M/346	AR
Tienken, Claus	070	1870	WB-E/211	AR
Tienken, Sallie J.	070	1889	WB-F/322	AR
Tiernan, James M.	085	1898	WB-3/223	CTY
Tighe, John	099	1871	RB-35/161	AR
Tighlman, Joshua	022	1828	WB-B/145	AR
Tigner, James	028	1749	SS 877/286	SS/AR
Tignor, James	028	1787	WB-A/152	AR
Tignor, Mary	028	1829	WB-C/312	AR
Tignor, William	028	1809	WB-B/342	AR
Tiler, Silvia	028	1883	WB-E/318	AR
Tilghman, Margaret	028	1893	WB-F/71	
Tilghman, Wilson	059	1880	WB-A/192	CTY
Tiller, Major	022	1780	Orig. Only	AR
Tillery, Alice B.	047	1860	WB-5/77	
Tillery, Eppy	047	1798	WB-3/310	
Tillery, George	046	1801	WB-A/388	AR-Nunc.
Tillery, John	047	1795	WB-3/245	
Tillery, John P.	037	1900	WB-H/468	AR
Tillery, John P.	069	1900	WB-6/103	AR
Tillery, Parasmus	047	1842	WB-4/204	
Tillett, James W.	001	1889	078 WB-27/327	078 AR
Tillett, James W.	001	1896	WB-3/160	AR
Tillett, John	065	1890	WB-L/489	AR
Tillett, John B.	018	1878	WB-E/55	AR
Tillett, Samuel	030	c1812	WB-3/13	
Tillett, Samuel	031	1876	WB-1/9	AR
Tillett, William	075	1775	WB-I/124	AR
Tillett, William T.	018	1853	WB-C/383	
Tilley, Aaron B.	090	1880	WB-6/119	AR
Tilley, Brice P.	090	1896	WB-6/399	AR
Tilley, David	090	1863	WB-4/365	AR
Tilley, Dennis	036	1900	WB-A/491	CTY
Tilley, Edmond	036	1886	WB-A/91	CTY
Tilley, Edmund	090	1870	WB-6/8	AR
Tilley, Edmund	090	1835	WB-3/294	AR
Tilley, Edmund	104	1800	WB-2/11	
Tilley, Elisha	036	1896	WB-A/378	CTY
Tilley, George	036	1892	WB-A/230	CTY
Tilley, George	036	c1887	078 WB-19/319	078 AR
Tilley, Henderson	036	1896	WB-A/368	CTY
Tilley, Henry	092	1790	WB-3/1	
Tilley, James	073	1879	WB-H/210	CTY
Tilley, Joel	090	1847	WB-4/233	AR
Tilley, John F.	090	1888	WB-6/196	AR
Tilley, John, Sr.	073	N. D.	Orig. Only	AR
Tilley, Lazarus	073	1841	WB-F/92	AR
Tilley, Lewis	017	1860	WB-A/164	AR
Tilley, Martin	090	1872	WB-6/29	
Tilley, Minerva	073	1895	WB-I/66	CTY
Tilley, Sarah	017	c1861	WB-A/143	AR
Tilley, William	036	1888	WB-A/131	CTY
Tillinghast, Cyrus P.	029	1827	WB-B/155	AR
Tillinghast, Paris J.	029	1822	WB-B/93	AR
Tillinghast, Samuel M.	029	1861	WB-C/440	AR
Tillinghim, Benjamin	028	1803	WB-B/190	
Tillitt, Thomas	030	1797	WB-2/100	
Tillman, Alfred	047	1856	WB-5/24	
Tillman, Benjamin	028	1827	WB-C/296	AR
Tillman, Clara	028	1831	WB-C/345	AR
Tillman, Cornelia	005	1900	WB-D/466	AR
Tillman, David	005	1859	WB-C/147	AR
Tillman, George	044	1780	WB-1/292	CTY
Tillman, Henry	028	1813	WB-C/74	
Tillman, Mary	028	1815	WB-C/96	AR
Tillman, Mary	028	1830	WB-C/328	
Tillman, Mary C.	022	1878	WB-E/157	AR
Tillman, Richard H.	005	1865	WB-C/217	AR

Name	Co.	Date	Recorded Copy	Original
Tillman, Sarah G.	028	1869	WB-E/18	AR
Tillory, Thomas	047	1844	WB-4/237	
Tillotson, Parthenia	090	1899	WB-6/490	AR
Tillson, Edmund	100	1872	WB-51/44	AR
Tilly, Durell	073	1867	WB-G/538	CTY
Tilly, Earl R.	059	1878	WB-A/150	AR
Tilly, John, Sr.	036	1885	WB-A/64	CTY
Tilman, Mary	078	1889	WB-19/241	AR
Tilmun, William	010	1808	WB-F/95	AR
Tilton, John	103	1783	WI-A/24	AR
Tilton, Leathy N.	103	1883	WB-1/274	AR
Timberlake, Augustine	020	1853	RB-R/73	
Timberlake, F. J.	039	1865	WB-S/96	AR
Timberlake, James	039	1847	WB-M/228	AR
Timberlake, Joseph P.	039	1861	WB-R/160	
Timberlake, Luedna	039	1886	WB-U/374	AR
Timberlake, Mary W.	084	1865	WB-D/29	CTY
Timberlake, Temperance	039	c1856	WB-O/367	AR
Timison, Jeremiah	068	1894	WB-D/411	
Timmerman, John G.	028	1722	Orig. Only	SS/AR
Timmons, S. M.	065	1891	WB-M/12	AR
Tims, John	015	1774	100 WB-2/23	AR
Tindal, Joshua	087	1883	WB-3/264	AR
Tindall, Henry K.	074	1888	WB-1/90	AR
Tindall, Julia	045	c1857	WB-1/203	
Tindel, John	009	c1767	OWB/102	AR
Tindol, Nancy	005	1811	WB-2/161	AR
Tindsley, Isaac	104	1803	WB-2/84	AR
Tiner, Jesse	056	1818	WB-1/288	AR
Tiner, John	056	1780	WB-1/790	AR
Tingen, Joanna	078	1854	WB-17/236	AR
Tingle, David	028	1824	WB-C/248	AR
Tingle, Hugh	028	1765	Wills.9/294	AR
Tingle, Jacob	028	1767	Orig. Only	AR
Tingle, James	028	1774	Orig. Only	AR
Tingle, James	028	1824	WB-C/252	AR-Nunc.
Tingle, Joseph	028	1793	WB-A/292	AR
Tingle, Mary	028	1769	Orig. Only	AR
Tingle, Silvester	028	1842	WB-D/71	AR
Tingle, Solomon	028	1795	WB-A/330	AR
Tinker, Euphamia	028	1818	WB-C/161	AR
Tinker, Judith	028	1817	WB-C/145	AR
Tinker, Stephen	028	1795	WB-A/362	AR
Tinnen, Carns	044	1816	WB-7/662	CTY
Tinnin, Catlett C.	073	1877	WB-H/160	CTY
Tinnin, David	073	1861	WB-G/375	CTY
Tinnin, David	073	1851	WB-F/488	AR
Tinnin, Elizabeth	001	1866	WB-1/266	AR
Tinnin, James	073	1798	WB-C/114	AR
Tinnin, John W.	022	1865	WB-D/126	AR
Tinnin, Robert	073	1836	WB-E/375	AR
Tinning, Elizabeth	073	1801	WB-D/53	AR
Tinsbloom, J. C. W.	044	1879	WB-23/346	CTY
Tinsley, Balus	050	1900	WB-2/373	CTY
Tinsley, Bob	084	1875	WB-E/89	CTY
Tipet, John	085	c1796	WB-E/73	AR
Tipkin, Edith	056	1827	WB-1/787	AR
Tippler, Mary	070	c1832	WB-AB/294	AR
Tippong, Conrad	060	1838	WB-2/2	AR
Tipton, Jonathan	107	c1850	WB-1/375	
Tiry, John	104	1793	WB-1/369	AR
Tisdal, Renison	037	1811	WB-E/2	AR
Tisdale, Elizabeth	069	c1865	WB-1/602	
Tisdale, Maria	075	1871	WB-O/26	AR
Tisdale, Mary	037	1820	WB-E/234	AR
Tisdale, Renison	037	c1808	Copy	069 AR
Tison, Elizabeth	079	c1846	Orig. Only	AR-Copy
Tison, Samuel	009	1736	SS 877/209	SS/AR
Tisson, Mathias	008	c1710	Orig. Only	SS/AR
Titcombe, Margarett	013	1890	WB-B/584	AR
Titman, Philip	060	1841	WB-2/112	AR
Titsworth, Marshall	061	1893	WB-2/123	AR
Tizdel, Henry	069	1808	WB-1/193	AR
Tod, Sarah	070	c1814	WB-AB/206	AR
Todd, A. H.	065	1890	WB-L/457	AR
Todd, Adam	065	1879	WB-K/326	AR
Todd, Caleb	085	c1795	WB-E/30	AR
Todd, Fruzy	010	1898	WB-I/553	
Todd, James	085	1814	WB-G/336	AR
Todd, James	099	1857	RB-30/299	
Todd, James E.	099	1892	WB-C/120	AR
Todd, John	065	1813	WB-D/111	AR
Todd, John	085	1800	WB-E/47	AR
Todd, John	065	1799	WB-D/36	AR
Todd, John	065	1861	WB-J/112	AR
Todd, John	100	1781	WB-3/117	AR
Todd, John A.	065	1851	WB-I/174	AR
Todd, Joseph	065	1825	WB-D/7	AR
Todd, Lavinia	010	1884	WB-I/180	
Todd, Mary	085	1846	WB-K/18	AR
Todd, Mary E.	010	1877	WB-I/84	
Todd, Mary Y.	065	1853	WB-I/224	AR
Todd, Moses	099	1841	RB-24/517	AR
Todd, Moses	099	1816	RB-13/48	AR
Todd, Nancy A.	004	1885	WB-A/74	AR
Todd, Penelope	010	1889	WB-I/263	AR
Todd, S. H.	065	1889	WB-L/402	AR
Todd, Sarah	065	1890	WB-M/70	AR
Todd, Sarah C.	065	1889	WB-L/427	AR
Todd, Solomon	099	1838	RB-24/224	AR
Todd, Thomas	085	1869	WB-1/29	CTY
Todd, Thomas	085	1778	WB-A/259	AR
Todd, William	010	1795	WB-D/294	AR
Todd, William	010	1769	WB-A/114	AR
Todd, William	065	1829	WB-D/36	AR
Todd, William	065	1892	WB-M/81	AR
Todd, William H.	010	1896	WB-I/479	AR
Todd, William M.	065	1825	WB-D/116	AR
Todd, Wilson	105	1896	WB-3/203	AR
Tolar, Hardy	029	1889	Orig. Only	AR
Tolar, John	029	1828	WB-B/159	AR
Tolar, Judy	029	1886	WB-E/403	AR
Tolar, Matthias	030	1807	WB-2/317	
Tolar, Winniford	103	1817	RD-4/98	AR
Tolbert, Josiah	081	1855	WB-11/189	AR
Tolbert, William	016	1884	WB-3/432	AR
Toleferro, Diannah	092	1847	WB-4/261	
Toler, America	103	1843	RD-8/390	AR
Toler, James, Sr.	028	1871	WB-E/51	AR
Toler, Mary A.	056	1865	WB-2/64	AR
Toler, Mathias	030	1842	WB-4/91	
Toler, Matthias	030	c1812	WB-3/17	
Toler, Robert	103	1787	Orig. Only	AR
Toler, Sarah	030	c1814	WB-3/67	
Toler, Thomas	103	1813	RD-3/7	AR
Toler, Thomas	103	1818	RD-4/196	AR
Toler, William	103	1786	WI-A/72	AR
Tolio, Charles	092	c1837	WB-4/152	
Toliver, Jacob	004	1887	WB-A/77 & 82	AR
Toliver, Patience	004	1891	WB-A/129	AR

Name	Co.	Date	Recorded Copy	Original
Toliver, Susan	004	1893	WB-A/142	AR
Toliver, William	004	1874	WB-A/13	AR
Tollar, William	020	1854	RB-R/110	AR
Tolley, Joseph	075	1763	WB-H/46	AR
Tolly, Sousanah	066	c1879	Orig. Only	AR
Tolson, Benjamin	028	1808	WB-B/301	
Tolson, Benjamin	028	1798	WB-B/45	AR
Tolson, Daniel	030	1819	WB--3/107	
Tolson, Elizabeth	077	1900	WB-H/340	AR
Tolson, Elizabeth	077	1900	070 WB-H/337	070 AR
Tolson, George	019	1825	WB-D/399	AR
Tolson, James H.	028	1875	WB-E/124	AR
Tolson, John	028	1817	WB-C/144	AR
Tolson, Sidney	019	1856	WB-A/189	AR
Tolson, Thomas	019	c1812	Orig. Only	AR
Tolson, William	019	1796	WB-D/387	AR
Tolson, Winder	037	c1837	WB-F/228	AR
Tolson, Winna	028	1805	WB-B/219	
Tomberlinson, Isaac	069	1804	WB-1/146	AR
Tomblin, Hugh	085	1786	WB-C/143	AR
Tomblin, William H.	054	c1832	WB-2/137	AR
Tomes, Francis	077	1729	SS 875/55	SS/AR
Tomes, Joshua	077	1732	SS 876/247	SS/AR
Tomkins, Moses	104	1809	WB-2/253	AR
Tomlin, A. N.	106	1897	WB-2/398	
Tomlin, Andrew J.	054	1853	WB-3/73	AR
Tomlin, Elisabeth	084	1810	WB-A/42	
Tomlin, Elizabeth	084	1807	WB-A/312	CTY
Tomlin, John	077	c1715	SS 875/212	SS/AR
Tomlinson, B. H.	056	1863	WB-2/46	AR
Tomlinson, Basil	054	1865	WB-3/173	AR
Tomlinson, Clarkson	046	1865	WB-D/245	AR
Tomlinson, Edith	099	1867	RB-34/481	AR
Tomlinson, English	032	1891	046 WB-G/38	046 AR
Tomlinson, English	032	1891	WB-4/133	AR
Tomlinson, Humphry B.	054	c1825	WB-2/25	
Tomlinson, John	077	1697	SS 874.2/94	
Tomlinson, John	085	1809	WB-G/128	AR
Tomlinson, John	054	1848	WB-3/24	AR
Tomlinson, Josiah	046	1843	WB-C/147	AR
Tomlinson, L. D.	105	1896	WB-3/211	AR
Tomlinson, Mary	105	c1855	WB-1/46	
Tomlinson, Moses	032	1827	WB-1/70	AR
Tomlinson, Sallie	105	1897	WB-3/263	AR
Tomlinson, Samuel	085	1803	WB-E/70	AR
Tomlinson, Sarah	054	1865	Orig. Only	AR
Tomlinson, Thomas	056	c1780	WB-1/792	AR
Tomlinson, Warren	105	1893	WB-3/74	AR
Tomlinson, William	022	1859	WB-D/40	AR
Tomlinson, William	103	1817	RD-4/96	AR
Tomlinson, William	081	1874	WB-15/167	AR
Tomlinson, William	081	1813	WB-4/46	AR
Tomlinson, William H.	022	1864	WB-D/131	AR
Tomlinson, William H.	029	1885	WB-E/344	AR
Tommas, Thomas	005	1807	WB-2/164	AR
Tommasson, John	086	1794	Orig. Only	AR
Tommison, Simon	022	1784	RB-1/20	AR
Tomoson, John	047	1760	WB-1/12	
Tomosson, Mathias	009	c1799	OWB/352	AR
Tompkins, Fred M.	013	1893	WB-C/253	AR
Tompkins, Hannah	085	1811	WB-G/199	AR
Tompkins, John S.	037	1824	WB-F/21	AR
Tompkins, Rosannah	069	1849	WB-1/518	AR
Tompson, Sarah	056	1898	WB-4/73	AR
Toms, Benjamin	077	1839	WB-F/282	AR

Name	Co.	Date	Recorded Copy	Original
Toms, Foster	077	1808	WB-E/282	AR
Toms, Foster	077	1779	WB-C/221	AR
Toms, Foster	077	1794	WB-E/12	
Toms, Francis	077	1729	SS 876/201	
Toms, Francis	077	1861	WB-F/515	AR
Toms, Francis	077	1771	WB-C/97	AR
Toms, John	075	1798	WB-M1/8	AR
Toms, John	077	1807	WB-E/301	AR
Toms, Joseph	077	c1839	WB-F/295	
Toms, Joseph	075	1801	WB-M1/53	AR
Toms, Martha	077	1794	WB-E/9	
Toms, Mary	077	1717/8	SS 875/156	SS/AR
Toms, Mary	077	1816	WB-E/454	AR
Toms, Rodney	086	1844	WB-E/125	AR
Toms, Samuel	077	c1809	WB-E/355	AR
Toms, Thomas	086	1892	WB-F/435	AR
Toms, William	086	1861	WB-E/389	AR
Toms, Zachariah	077	1774	WB-C/149	AR
Tomson, Jacob	056	1750	028 DB-5/152	SS/AR
Tomson, Mary	028	1774	Orig. Only	AR
Tomson, Sarah	010	1762	WB-A/72	AR
Tomson, William	N	1736	SS 877/188	SS/AR
Toney, James	086	1851	WB-E/209	AR
Toney, Jefferson	014	1884	WB-2/269	CTY
Toney, John	047	1825	WB-4/1	
Toney, Robert P.	039	1859	WB-O/377	AR
Toney, William	086	1855	WB-E/291	AR
Tonkin, John	KS	1899	055 WB-A/175	
Tooke, James	075	1720	SS 875/228	SS/AR
Tooke, John	028	1805	WB-B/216	AR
Tooke, Joseph	028	1806	WB-B/235	AR
Tooks, Joseph	028	1802	WB-B/172	
Tool, Edward	087	1785	Orig. Only	AR
Tool, Edward	010	c1772	WB-A/149	AR
Toole, Elizabeth	039	c1853	WB-O/358	AR
Toole, Elizabeth	037	1832	WB-F/136	AR
Toole, Geraldus	037	1834	WB-F/166	AR
Toole, Henry J.	037	1816	WB-E/147	AR
Toole, Henry J.	079	1851	070 WB-C/522	070 AR
Toole, Jonathan	010	1783	WB-C/63	AR
Toole, Laurence	037	1761	WB-A/82	AR
Tooley, Abel	053	1847	WB-7/90	AR
Tooley, Henry	053	1811	RW-1/447	AR
Tooley, Henry Gibbs	053	1827	Orig. Only	AR
Tooley, Jacob	053	1834	WB-5/200	AR
Tooley, Jeremiah	053	1819	WB-4/1	AR
Tooley, Job	053	1850	WB-7/268	AR
Tooley, John	053	1794	RW-1/235	AR
Tooley, Major	053	1842	WB-6/201	AR
Tooley, Mary	028	1796	WB-A/357	
Tooley, Nathaniel	053	1803	RW-1/354	AR
Tooley, Ormond	053	1836	WB-5/340	AR
Tooley, Solomon	053	1842	WB-6/188	AR
Tooly, Elizabeth	053	1821	WB-4/210	
Tooly, Jacob	053	1772	RW-1/24	
Tooly, James	053	c1817	RW-1/512	
Toomer, Anthony B.	070	1805	WB-AB/94	AR
Toomer, Henry	070	1799	WB-AB/23	AR
Toomer, John D.	022	N. D.	WB-C/422	AR
Toomer, Joshua	070	1762	DB-E/119	AR
Toomer, M. M.	070	1825	WB-C/423	AR
Toomer, Mary J.	070	1891	WB-F/459	AR
Toomey, Patrick	085	1825	WB-H/319	AR
Toon, Anthony F.	027	1853	WB-A/61	AR
Toon, Frances M.	027	1873	WB-2/19	AR

Name	Co.	Date	Recorded Copy	Original
Toops, Joseph	N	c1755	Orig. Only	SS/AR
Topping, Evelina B.	009	1883	WB-1/329	CTY
Topping, Nancy	053	1866	WB-10/46	AR
Topping, Samuel	024	1816	WB-C/48	AR
Topping, Samuel	053	1866	WB-10/43	AR
Topping, Samuel	053	1866	009 WB-1/475	009 AR
Topping, William	024	c1773	WB-A/245	AR
Torian, Nathaniel	078	1873	WB-19/31	AR
Torksey, Benjamin	075	1776	WB-I/145	AR
Torksey, Elizabeth	075	1758	Orig. Only	SS/AR
Torksey, Henry	018	1865	WB-D/73	AR
Torksey, John	075	1747	Orig. Only	SS/AR
Torksey, John N.	018	1881	WB-E/87	AR
Torksey, John W.	018	1855	WB-D/19	
Torksey, John, Sr.	018	1846	WB-C/318	
Torksey, Noah	018	1856	WB-D/30	
Torksey, Phillip	075	1755	Orig. Only	SS/AR
Torksey, Phillip	075	1727	Orig. Only	SS/AR
Torksey, Thomas	075	1765	WB-H/67	AR
Torrance, David	029	1866	WB-D/90	AR
Torrance, Ephraim	040	1850	WB-1/31	AR
Torrance, Hugh	060	1813	Orig. Only	AR
Torrance, Hugh	040	1849	WB-1/25	
Torrance, John	040	1849	WB-1/27	
Torrans, Elizabeth	087	1827	Orig. Only	AR
Torrans, Martha	087	1839	WB-1/221	AR
Torrans, Samuel	028	1812	Orig. Only	AR
Torrans, Thomas K.	087	c1820	WB-1/20	AR
Torrence, Abraham	065	1769	WB-D/26	AR
Torrence, Adam	054	1844	WB-2/299	AR
Torrence, Albert	085	1826	WB-H/341	AR
Torrence, Alexander	054	1845	WB-2/308	AR
Torrence, Barnabas	054	c1840	Orig. Only	AR
Torrence, Charles L.	065	1866	WB-J/213	AR
Torrence, Edwin B.	026	1885	WB-2/288	AR
Torrence, Elizabeth	085	1870	WB-1/59	CTY
Torrence, Elizabeth	085	1837	WB-I/24	AR
Torrence, George	065	1843	WB-H/128	
Torrence, Harrison	040	1894	WB-2/468	AR
Torrence, J. L.	040	1900	WB-3/73	AR
Torrence, James G.	065	1845	WB-I/117	AR
Torrence, Jamison F.	040	c1856	WB-1/81	AR
Torrence, Margaret	065	1880	WB-K/382	AR
Torrence, Margaret	054	c1841	WB-2/231	AR
Torrence, Nancy	054	1847	WB-3/19	
Torrence, Robert	040	1888	WB-2/298	AR
Torrence, Robert	085	1816	WB-G/454	AR-Copy
Torrence, Samuel A.	040	1886	WB-2/267	AR
Torrence, Sarah Ann	022	1857	WB-C/457	AR
Torrence, William L.	054	1865	WB-3/179	AR
Torrentine, Robert	054	c1862	Orig. Only	AR
Torverson, James	002	c1675	Orig. Only	SS/AR
Totewine, William	028	1777	Orig. Only	SS/AR
Totten, Jeannie L.	PA	1885	080 WB-1/108	080 AR
Totten, Joseph S.	020	1862	RB-S/471	AR
Totten, William R.	084	1864	WB-C/396	CTY
Tottey, Francis	047	1808	WB-3/480	
Tottey, Priscilla	047	1816	WB-3/578	
Touchstone, Jonas	046	1815	WB-A/392	AR
Touchstone, Richard	028	c1757	Orig. Only	AR
Towe, Joseph	077	1834	WB-F/226	AR
Towe, Martin	077	1866	WB-H/10	AR
Towe, Mary	077	1848	WB-F/357	AR
Towe, Thomas O.	075	c1875	WB-O/80	AR
Towell, John C.	085	1874	WB-1/259	CTY
Towne, Trueman B.	MA	1896	040 WB-2/574	040 AR
Townes, Charmer	098	1889	WB-A/108	CTY
Townes, Edmund	044	1861	WB-21/370	
Townes, Elizabeth	044	1865	WB-22/333	CTY
Townes, Janette	098	1883	WB-A/33	CTY
Townes, William	VA	1879	078 WB-19/96	078 AR
Towns, David	015	1777	100 WB-2/121	AR
Towns, John	100	1788	WB-5/5	AR
Towns, Joice	100	1815	WB-19/145	AR
Towns, Richard	100	1809	WB-15/73	AR
Townsen, William	077	1766	WB-C/56	AR
Townsend, Aaron, Sr.	016	1843	WB-1/10	
Townsend, Abitha	005	1843	WB-B/161	AR
Townsend, Alexander	083	c1827	WB-1/346	AR
Townsend, C. W.	077	1882	WB-H/120	AR
Townsend, David	005	1845	WB-B/160	AR
Townsend, David	083	1887	WB-3/396	AR
Townsend, E. B.	083	1891	WB-3/511	AR
Townsend, Jackson	083	1892	WB-3/564	
Townsend, Jacob	030	1780	WB-1/146	
Townsend, James H.	016	1882	WB-3/370	AR
Townsend, Jane	016	1886	WB-3/504	AR
Townsend, John	030	1787	WB-1/214	
Townsend, Josiah	077	1827	WB-F/141	
Townsend, Mary Jane	070	1879	WB-E/379	AR
Townsend, Richard	083	1900	WB-4/310	AR
Townsend, Robert R.	050	1886	WB-1/261	CTY
Townsend, Sarah	077	1832	WB-F/197	AR
Townsend, Thomas	029	1796	Orig. Only	AR
Townsend, Thomas	083	c1828	WB-1/320	AR
Townsend, William	077	1785	WB-C/311	AR
Townsend, William	083	1830	WB-1/253	AR
Townson, John	077	1739	Orig. Only	SS/AR
Towrey, George	081	1794	WB-2/6	AR
Towson, Mary	028	1757	Orig. Only	AR
Tracy, James W.	026	1896	WB-2/531	AR
Tradaway, Richard	029	c1774	Orig. Only	AR
Tradenick, Nicholas	065	1856	WB-J/17	
Trader, James M.	051	1882	WB-C/287	AR
Trader, Sallie R.	051	1890	WB-C/413	AR
Trafenstet, William	054	1878	WB-4/297	CTY
Traffenstate, Elizabeth	054	1894	WB-5/522	CTY
Trafton, Gardner	018	1848	WB-C/335	
Trainer, John	001	1858	WB-1/130	AR
Transon, Solomon	038	1873	Copy	032 AR
Transou, A. C.	038	1864	WB-1/246	AR
Transou, Abraham	090	1833	WB-3/257	AR
Transou, Ephraim	038	1883	WB-2/453	AR
Transou, Lydia S.	038	1871	WB-2/46	AR
Transou, Maria E.C.	038	1888	WB-3/86	AR
Transou, Mary M.	038	1872	WB-2/102	AR
Transou, Solomon	038	1873	WB-2/159	AR
Transu, Maria C.	090	1819	WB-3/34	AR
Transu, Philip	090	1793	WB-1/41	AR
Tranter, John	008	1727	Orig. Only	SS/AR
Trantham, A. J.	032	1891	WB-4/97	AR
Trantham, Daniel	032	c1863	WB-2/249	AR
Trantham, Joseph	013	1850	WB-A/142	
Trapier, Richard S.	SC	1895	061 WB-2/192	061 AR
Trapier, Sarah R.	DC	1890	013 WB-C/1	013 AR
Trausau, James W.	104	1893	WB-6/498	AR
Travelstreet, Barbara	060	1793	Orig. Only	AR
Travis, Edward	009	1740	Orig. Only	SS/AR
Travis, Isaac	020	1890	WB-B/31	
Travis, John	020	1864	RB-T/47	

Name	Co.	Date	Recorded Copy	Original
Travis, Levi T.	021	1900	WB-3/308	AR
Tray, Rosa	005	1835	WB-B/47	
Traylor, William	044	1777	WB-1/150	CTY
Traynham, Jeffrey P.	032	1884	WB-3/415	AR
Traywick, Asa	005	1883	WB-D/154	AR
Traywick, Parthenia	099	1892	WB-C/71	AR
Treadwell, Adoniram	035	1782	WB-A/475	AR
Treadwell, James P.	087	1867	WB-2/122	AR
Treadwell, John	087	1822	WB-1/17	AR
Treadwell, Rachel Ann	011	1891	WB-2/237	
Treaweek, Orthneel	083	1801	WB-1/65 & 202	AR-Nunc.
Tredway, Robert	006	1820	WB-A/29	AR
Tredwell, Margaret	099	1849	RB-26/567	AR
Tredwell, Samuel	024	1827	WB-C/135	AR
Treece, George	089	1865	WB-1/280	AR
Trees, Henry	085	c1803	WB-E/76	AR
Treese, Jacob	085	1811	WB-G/181	AR
Treloar, John	065	1871	WB-K/61	AR
Tremain, Jonathan	072	1742	Orig. Only	SS/AR
Trenholm, Edward L.	SC	1893	050 WB-2/182	
Trentham, Martin	085	c1783	WB-B/120	AR
Trentham, Martin	032	1824	WB-1/33	AR
Treuhitt, Levi	028	1812	Orig. Only	AR
Trevathan, Robert	037	1791	WB-C/171	AR
Trevathan, Robert	037	1824	WB-F/24	AR
Trevathan, Trecy	105	1894	WB-3/109	
Trevathan, Willis	069	1815	WB-1/264	AR
Trewit, Willis	073	1829	WB-E/190	AR
Trexler, Caleb	085	1865	WB-K/352	AR
Trexler, Harriet M.	085	1872	WB-1/122	CTY
Trice, Edward	073	1800	WB-D/7	AR
Trice, George W.	099	1871	RB-35/132	AR
Trice, Henry	073	1840	WB-F/48	AR
Trice, James	073	1781	WB-A/223	AR
Trice, Thomas	073	1803	WB-D/115	AR
Trice, William	073	1839	WB-F/19	AR
Trice, Zilpha	099	1880	WB-A/119	AR
Trickey, Giles	078	1802	WI-3/70	AR
Triece, Peter	089	1855	WB-1/133	
Trimm, R. B.	078	1877	WB-19/67	AR
Triplet, Austin P.	017	1844	WB-A/13	AR
Triplett, Annie	066	1898	WB-1/169	AR
Triplett, Joel	104	1864	WB-5/376	
Triplett, John J.	104	1891	WB-6/414	AR
Triplett, Thomas	104	1850	WB-5/41	AR
Triplett, Thomas	104	1877	WB-6/147	AR
Triplett, William	104	1873	WB-6/76	AR
Tripp, Arthur	079	1858	WB-1/1	AR
Tripp, Charles	009	1862	OB-L/396	AR
Tripp, James	009	c1799	OWB/351	AR
Tripp, John	022	1805	WB-A/119	AR
Tripp, John	009	1761	OWB/50	AR
Tripp, Robert	009	c1800	OWB/375	AR
Tripp, Robert	009	1857	OB-K/256	AR
Tripp, Sarah	009	1864	OB-L/459	AR
Tripp, William	028	1843	WB-D/89	
Tripp, William H.	009	1881	WB-1/289	CTY
Trippe, John	009	c1766	OWB/99	AR
Trippe, Nevile	009	c1765	OWB/74	AR
Trippe, William	009	c1780	OWB/153	AR
Tritt, Balber	060	1794	Orig. Only	AR
Tritt, James B.	049	1853	WB-2/192	AR
Trogdon, Emsley	081	1877	WB-15/255	AR
Trogdon, Henderson	081	1877	WB-15/265	AR
Trogdon, Joel F.	081	1898	WB-16/478	
Trogdon, Reuben F.	084	1885	081 WB-15/531	081 AR
Trogdon, Reuben F.	084	1885	WB-E/308	CTY
Trogdon, William	081	1805	WB-3/26	AR
Trogdon, William	081	1865	WB-13/255	AR
Trolinger, Henry	073	1844	WB-F/181	AR
Trolinger, Henry	001	1899	WB-3/257	AR
Trolinger, Jacob T.	001	1879	WB-2/152	AR
Trolinger, John	001	c1867	082 WB-7/26	
Trolinger, John	001	1870	WB-2/14	AR
Trollinger, Frederick	046	1818	WB-B/56	AR
Trotman, Amos	041	1790	WB-1/85	AR
Trotman, Demcy	041	1795	WB-1/136	AR
Trotman, Edward	041	1809	WB-2/38	AR
Trotman, Edward	024	N. D.	WB-B/117	
Trotman, Elisha	041	1809	WB-2/42	AR
Trotman, Elizabeth	041	1781	WB-1/13	AR
Trotman, Ezekiel	041	1807	WB-1/235	AR
Trotman, Ezekiel	018	1826	WB-C/65	
Trotman, Ezekiel H.	041	1880	WB-4/134	AR
Trotman, John M.	041	1899	WB-4/472	AR
Trotman, Moses R.	041	1869	WB-4/1	AR
Trotman, Noah	041	1817	WB-2/144	AR
Trotman, Penelope	041	1822	WB-2/190	AR
Trotman, Quintin H.	041	1862	WB-3/280	AR
Trotman, Rachel	041	1793	WB-1/109	AR
Trotman, Seth	041	1808	WB-2/28	AR
Trotman, Thomas	041	1791	WB-1/97	AR
Trotman, Timothy G.	041	1846	WB-3/79	AR
Trott, Brice	072	1879	WB-4/124	AR
Trott, Henry	085	c1802	WB-E/74	AR
Trott, James	085	c1802	WB-E/66	AR
Trott, John, Sr.	072	1823	WB-A/134	AR
Trott, S. S.	085	1876	WB-1/341	CTY
Trotter, Ephriam	046	1819	WB-B/79	AR
Trotter, Frances	078	1866	WB-18/433	AR
Trotter, George	046	1821	WB-B/112	AR
Trotter, Jane	085	1838	WB-H/711	AR
Trotter, John	046	1853	WB-C/396	AR
Trotter, John	077	1768	WB-C/65	AR
Trotter, Josiah	046	1792	Orig. Only	AR
Trotter, Moses	061	1887	WB-2/81	AR
Trotter, Shadrack	046	1846	WB-C/257	AR
Trotter, Thomas	009	c1832	OWB/502	AR
Trotter, Thomas	065	1865	WB-J/201	AR
Trotter, William	078	1824	WI-10/79	AR
Trotter, William	077	1729	SS 876/204	SS/AR
Trouberil, Walter	047	1764	WB-1/143	
Troublefield, Peter B.	087	1873	WB-3/64	AR
Troughton, Mary	047	1783	WB-3/46	
Trousdale, John	073	1784	WB-A/293	AR
Trout, Benjamin F.	086	1883	WB-F/214	AR
Troutman, Adam	085	1837	WB-I/18	AR
Troutman, Adam	085	1820	WB-H/66	AR
Troutman, Andrew	089	1883	WB-2/109	AR
Troutman, Elizabeth	085	1859	WB-K/274	AR
Troutman, Ellen Jane	054	1888	WB-5/245	CTY
Troutman, George	016	1865	WB-2/128	
Troutman, Henry	016	1880	WB-3/292	AR
Troutman, Jacob	085	1861	WB-K/294	AR
Troutman, Jacob	054	1846	WB-3/14	AR
Troutman, John	085	1849	WB-K/97	AR
Troutman, Peter	016	1861	WB-2/80	AR
Troutman, Peter, Sr.	085	1799	WB-E/36	AR
Troutman, Sarah	016	1878	WB-3/246	AR
Troutman, Solomon	016	1866	WB-2/133	

Name	Co.	Date	Recorded Copy	Original
Trowell, Joseph	077	1736	Orig. Only	SS/AR
Troxler, Barnett	084	1886	WB-E/347	CTY
Troxler, Barney	073	1817	WB-D/507	AR
Troxler, George	073	1826	WB-E/101	AR
Troxler, John	046	1849	WB-C/318	AR
Troxler, John C.	001	1894	WB-3/22	AR
Troxler, Powel	001	c1851	WB-1/71	AR
Troy, Frances E.	027	1863	WB-A/85	AR
Troy, John B.	081	1864	WB-13/108	AR
Troy, Rachel	027	1867	WB-A/102	AR
Troy, Robert	005	1807	WB-2/166	AR
Troy, Robert E.	083	1862	011 WB-1/297	
Troy, Rosa Anna	005	1838	WB-B/81	AR
Truax, John	029	1820	WB-B/32	AR
Trublood, John	002	1692	Orig. Only	SS/AR
Trublood, John	075	1734	LGB-4/#6	SS/AR
Trueblood, Abel	075	1807	WB-M1/166	AR
Trueblood, Agnes	075	1692	Orig. Only	SS/AR
Trueblood, Amos	075	1759	WB-H/7	AR
Trueblood, Ann	075	1805	WB-M1/110	AR-Nunc.
Trueblood, Caleb	075	1822	WB-M1/352	AR
Trueblood, Caleb	075	1804	WB-M1/93	AR
Trueblood, Daniel	075	1795	WB-L/49	
Trueblood, Elisabeth	075	1804	WB-M1/96	AR
Trueblood, Ephraim	075	1795	WB-L/48	
Trueblood, Jane Louisa	075	1883	WB-O/177	AR
Trueblood, Jesse	046	1877	WB-E/227	AR
Trueblood, John	075	1796	WB-L/83	
Trueblood, Joseph	075	1807	WB-M1/168	
Trueblood, Joshua	077	1859	WB-F/497	AR
Trueblood, Joshua	075	1762	WB-I/24	
Trueblood, Josiah	075	1803	WB-M1/77	AR
Truelove, William	039	1821	Orig. Only	AR
Trueman, Windsor	099	1809	RB-8/136	AR
Truet, Levi	061	1830	WB-1/2	AR
Truett, Millicent	077	c1864	WB-F/546	AR
Truett, Samuel A.	077	1880	WB-H/93	AR
Truhitt, William	028	1793	WB-A/296	AR
Truitt, Joseph	028	1756	SS 880/60	SS/AR
Truitt, Levi	001	1872	WB-2/42	AR
Truitt, Samuel	092	1801	WB-3/42A	AR
Truitt, Solomon	061	c1858	WB-1/70	AR
Truitt, William	004	1894	WB-A/156	AR
Trull, Solomon	005	1820	WB-2/172	AR
Trumball, William	077	1781	Orig. Only	AR
Trumbel, Thomas	N	1733	SS 876/338	SS/AR
Trummell, Reuben	051	1847	WB-A/279	
Tubbs, Elisha	075	1819	WB-M1/328	AR
Tubbs, Lemuel	075	1818	WB-M1/313	AR
Tubbs, William	075	1818	WB-M1/314	AR
Tubbs, William D.	075	1840	WB-N/162	AR
Tuck, L. R.	054	1881	WB-4/414	CTY
Tucker, Alsa H.	099	1850	RB-27/134	AR
Tucker, Ann	060	1814	Orig. Only	AR-Nunc.
Tucker, Annie E.	046	1894	WB-F/359	AR
Tucker, Anthony	071	1821	WB-3/267	AR
Tucker, Benjamin	069	1830	WB-1/367	AR
Tucker, Benjamin	028	1858	WB-D/305	AR
Tucker, Binion	104	1879	WB-6/175	AR
Tucker, Branch	092	1832	WB-4/42	
Tucker, Calvin	079	1869	WB-2/21	AR
Tucker, Curle	071	c1788	WB-1/347	
Tucker, Daniel	005	1863	WB-C/199	AR
Tucker, Daniel	100	1841	WB-37/479	AR
Tucker, Daniel	084	1813	WB-A/119	CTY
Tucker, Daniel	099	1792	RB-2/389	
Tucker, David	092	1863	WB-5/65	AR
Tucker, David	054	c1820	WB-1A/63	AR
Tucker, David	092	1880	WB-6/135	AR
Tucker, Dinah	069	1810	WB-1/208	AR
Tucker, Easter	069	1836	WB-1/401	AR
Tucker, Edward	099	1775	RB-1/59	AR
Tucker, Elizabeth	079	1875	WB-2/122	AR
Tucker, Elizabeth	104	1836	WB-4/203	AR
Tucker, Fannie S.	021	c1894	WB-3/292	AR
Tucker, Francis	092	1867	WB-5/89	
Tucker, George	081	1801	WB-2/85	AR
Tucker, George	015	1778	100 WB-2/186	AR
Tucker, James	069	1797	WB-1/228	AR
Tucker, James M.	084	1885	WB-E/336	CTY
Tucker, Joel	VA	1853	090 WB-4/286	
Tucker, John	069	1872	WB-1/620	AR
Tucker, John	060	1800	Orig. Only	AR
Tucker, John	028	1740	Deeds.1/L106	
Tucker, John	100	1814	WB-19/16	AR
Tucker, John B.	039	1864	WB-R/798	AR
Tucker, John C.	079	1878	WB-2/161	AR
Tucker, John H.	098	1900	WB-A/344	CTY
Tucker, John W.	100	1799	Orig. Only	AR
Tucker, Joshua	092	1897	WB-6/449	AR
Tucker, Judy	059	1897	WB-B/185	CTY
Tucker, Laura E.	079	1897	WB-3/141	AR
Tucker, Levi	016	1858	WB-2/46	
Tucker, Levi	046	1816	WB-A/395	AR
Tucker, Levy C.	089	1895	WB-2/267	
Tucker, Lewis B.	069	1840	WB-1/439	AR
Tucker, Martha A.	100	1882	WB-51/176	AR
Tucker, Mary E.	039	1900	WB-V/188	
Tucker, Mason W.	079	1865	WB-1/130	AR
Tucker, McLendon	099	1883	WB-A/379	AR
Tucker, Nancy C.	079	1891	WB-2/575	AR
Tucker, Nathaniel	072	1751	028 DB-5/160	SS/AR
Tucker, Nathaniel	081	1846	WB-8/320	AR
Tucker, Pascal G.	084	1848	WB-C/67	CTY
Tucker, Rebecca	069	1877	WB-5/65	AR
Tucker, Robert	090	1844	Orig. Only	AR
Tucker, Robert	030	1720	SS 875/249	
Tucker, Robey	054	1885	WB-5/58	CTY
Tucker, Robey	054	1842	WB-2/236	AR
Tucker, Rufus S.	099	c1880	Copy	022 AR
Tucker, Rufus S.	099	1894	079 WB-3/60	
Tucker, Rufus S.	099	1894	WB-C/259	AR
Tucker, Russell	069	1883	WB-5/178	AR
Tucker, Shadrach	084	1834	WB-B/93	CTY
Tucker, Silas	090	1884	WB-6/140	AR
Tucker, Symon	099	1872	RB-35/159	AR
Tucker, Thomas	092	1863	WB-5/68	
Tucker, Thomas	054	c1803	WB-1/218	AR
Tucker, Thomas	005	1886	WB-D/194	AR
Tucker, Thomas	069	c1778	WB-1/16	AF
Tucker, Thomas G.	071	1888	WB-7/8	A
Tucker, Thomas L.	054	c1858	WB-3/148	A
Tucker, Warren	079	1895	WB-3/68	/
Tucker, William	092	1825	WB-3/165	
Tucker, William	081	1896	WB-16/372	
Tucker, William	056	1799	WB-1/114	
Tucker, William C.	099	1860	RB-31/430	
Tucker, William G.	046	1892	WB-F/195	
Tucker, Wilson	060	1874	WB-4/354	
Tucker, Wright	069	c1890	Orig. Only	

Name	Co.	Date	Recorded Copy	Original
Tucker, Wyatt	046	1893	WB-F/265	AR
Tudor, John	044	1782	WB-1/338	CTY
Tuggle, Francis	020	1819	RB-H/283	
Tuggle, Griffin	020	1807	RB-E/322	AR
Tugman, William	104	1875	WB-6/113	AR
Tugmon, James	104	1862	WB-5/62	AR
Tugwell, Joseph	041	1779	WB-1/3	AR
Tugwell, Robert	079	c1862	WB-1/93	AR
Tulbert, Henry	106	c1868	WB-2/58	
Tulbert, James	092	c1836	WB-4/107	
Tulbert, Joshua	092	c1826	WB-3/174	AR
Tuley, Cornelus	053	1798	RW-1/299	AR
Tuley, Hannah	053	c1825	Orig. Only	AR
Tuley, Jacob	053	1815	RW-1/499	AR
Tuley, Jeremiah	053	1798	RW-1/302	AR
Tuley, Levi	053	1798	RW-1/293	AR
Tuley, Levi	053	1802	RW-1/338	AR
Tuley, Major	053	1812	RW-1/463	
Tuley, Nathaniel	053	1776	RW-1/74	
Tuley, Richard	053	c1803	RW-1/399	
Tuley, Thomas	053	1798	RW-1/291	AR
Tullas, Richard	029	1771	Orig. Only	AR
Tulley, Jane	075	1732	SS 876/259	SS/AR
Tulloch, Thomas	047	1785	WB-3/78	
Tully, Cornelius	075	1709	Orig. Only	CCR 187
Tuly, Thomas	053	1741	Orig. Only	SS/AR
Tumblin, Samuel	075	1776	WB-I/153	
Tuncil, Jackson	009	1892	WB-1/550	CTY
Tunks, Thomas	020	1790	RB-B/323	AR
Tunnel, Samuel	047	1807	WB-3/466	
Tunnell, Byrd B.	069	1864	WB-1/587	AR
Tunnell, Easter	053	1865	WB-10/41	AR
Tunnell, Joseph	053	1843	WB-6/231	AR
Tunnell, Joseph C.	053	1869	WB-11/3	
Tunnell, Samuel T.	053	1852	WB-7/494	AR
Tunsell, Jincy	100	1831	WB-33/341	AR
Tunstall, Elizabeth	010	1803	WB-E/218	AR
Tunstall, George	039	1828	WB-J/19	
Tunstall, George D.	039	1867	WB-S/460	AR
Tunstall, George W.	100	1866	WB-50/184	AR
Tunstall, Patrick A.	044	1881	WB-23/425	CTY
Tunstall, Thomas P.	009	1883	WB-1/334	CTY-Nunc.
Tupper, Henry M.	099	1893	WB-C/185	AR
Turbavell, Richard	010	1726	SS 876/51	SS/AR
Turbevill, Joseph	087	c1794	Orig. Only	AR
Turbevill, Sampson	087	c1797	Orig. Only	AR
Turbiville, C. W.	054	1900	WB-6/309	CTY
Turkinett, Henry	046	1852	WB-C/365	AR
Turley, Candis H.	056	1864	WB-2/56	AR
Turley, Thomas	056	1862	WB-2/37	AR
Turlington, Andrew J.	048	1897	WB-1/71	CTY
Turlington, Cader	029	c1850	WB-C/304	
Turlington, Eastwood	070	1893	WB-G/148	AR
Turlington, J. D.	056	1900	WB-4/221	AR
Turlington, John	069	1784	WB-1/27	AR
Turlington, Mary J.	070	1891	WB-F/487	AR
Turlington, Philicia	087	1812	Orig. Only	AR
Turlington, William	063	1795	WB-1/215	
Turnage, Cader	035	1825	WB-A/476	AR
Turnage, James	057	1843	WB-B/165	AR
Turnage, Nancy	087	c1872	Orig. Only	AR
Turnage, Nancy	045	1892	WB-1/290	AR
Turnage, Travis	068	1846	SC/06994	AR-Copy
Turnage, William	087	c1848	Orig. Only	AR
Turnbull, James	096	1754	SS 881/123	SS/AR
Turner, Abraham	077	1774	WB-C/159	AR
Turner, Ambrose N.	077	1851	WB-F/401	AR
Turner, Amey	070	1815	WB-AB/224	AR
Turner, Andrew	006	c1848	WB-D/65	AR
Turner, Andrew	060	1794	Orig. Only	AR
Turner, Andrew	036	1881	WB-A/1	CTY
Turner, Ann	099	1820	RB-16/8	AR
Turner, Ann	077	1800	WB-E/112	AR
Turner, Ann	010	1822	WB-G/92	AR
Turner, Anna	080	1864	WB-1/184	AR
Turner, Augustin	099	1860	RB-31/435	AR
Turner, Augustin	099	c1859	SC/08458	AR-Copy
Turner, Austuern	005	1851	WB-C/34	
Turner, Bannister	049	c1875	Orig. Only	AR-Copy
Turner, Belt	054	c1862	Orig. Only	AR
Turner, Benaiah	010	1777	WB-B/75	AR
Turner, Benjamin	071	1896	WB-7/331	AR
Turner, Betsy	100	1830	WB-33/141	AR
Turner, Bryan	057	1872	WB-C/15	AR
Turner, Charles	077	1840	WB-F/292	
Turner, Charles E.	036	1900	WB-A/507	CTY
Turner, Chasey	020	1895	WB-B/185	CTY
Turner, Comfort	077	1805	WB-E/223	AR
Turner, Daniel	100	1862	WB-49/536	AR
Turner, David	001	1864	WB-1/225	AR
Turner, David	022	1892	WB-E/495	AR
Turner, David	056	1822	WB-1/454	AR
Turner, David C.	085	1877	WB-1/381	CTY
Turner, David W.	035	1894	WB-4/441	AR
Turner, Demsey	077	1784	WB-C/260	AR
Turner, Dilly	005	1864	WB-C/203	AR
Turner, Edith	099	1895	WB-D/470	AR
Turner, Edith C.	099	1895	WB-D/470	AR
Turner, Edmund	071	1837	WB-4/153	AR
Turner, Edward	010	1791	WB-D/190	AR
Turner, Edwin	047	1795	WB-3/249	
Turner, Edwin	047	1789	WB-3/162	
Turner, Edwin W.	047	1819	WB-3/642	
Turner, Elias	092	c1769	WB-2/59A	AR
Turner, Elijah	026	1879	WB-2/189	AR
Turner, Elisha M.	079	1900	WB-3/203	AR
Turner, Eliza	099	1883	WB-A/414	AR
Turner, Elizabeth	020	1878	WB-A/243	CTY
Turner, Elizabeth	054	1887	WB-5/172	CTY
Turner, Elizabeth	085	1854	WB-K/169	AR
Turner, Elizabeth	001	1899	WB-3/260	AR
Turner, Elizabeth	087	1837	WB-1/187	AR
Turner, Elizabeth	081	1817	WB-4/415	AR
Turner, Elsberry	077	1827	WB-F/144	AR
Turner, Ezekiel	046	1836	WB-B/540	AR
Turner, Fielding	047	1788	WB-3/150	
Turner, Frances A.	070	1876	WB-E/329	AR
Turner, Gaston T.	099	1879	WB-A/50	AR
Turner, George	047	1777	WB-2/62	
Turner, George	005	1878	WB-D/63	AR
Turner, Hareson	077	1815	WB-E/410	AR
Turner, Henley	100	1830	WB-32/293	AR
Turner, Henry	037	1748	Orig. Only	SS/AR
Turner, Henry	070	1897	WB-H/80	AR
Turner, Henry	VA	c1713	SS 875/26	SS/AR
Turner, Henry	020	1809	RB-F/82	AR
Turner, Henry	020	1876	WB-A/193	CTY
Turner, Henry	037	1819	WB-E/227	AR
Turner, Henry C.	089	1892	WB-2/251	AR

Name	Co.	Date	Recorded Copy	Original
Turner, Henry D.	099	1866	RB-34/289	AR
Turner, Israel	073	1893	WB-I/1	CTY
Turner, Jacob	077	1872	WB-H/42	
Turner, James	021	1862	WB-1/167	AR
Turner, James	073	1818	WB-D/527	AR
Turner, James	100	1824	WB-26/54	AR
Turner, James	069	1796	WB-1/102	AR
Turner, James	005	1812	WB-2/170	AR
Turner, James	005	1843	WB-B/162	AR
Turner, James	071	1768	WB-1/168	
Turner, James A.	044	1862	WB-21/629	CTY
Turner, James H.	035	1884	WB-4/412	AR
Turner, James, Sr.	001	c1841	WB-1/99	AR
Turner, Jane	071	1835	WB-4/132	AR
Turner, Jane	001	1859	WB-1/158	AR
Turner, Jason	026	1859	WB-1/246	AR
Turner, Jasper	005	1828	WB-A/149	AR
Turner, Jesse	047	1796	WB-3/263	
Turner, John	N	1716	Orig. Only	SS/AR
Turner, John	056	1864	WB-2/48	AR
Turner, John	071	1771	WB-1/196	
Turner, John	087	c1883	Orig. Only	AR
Turner, John	077	1718	Orig. Only	SS/AR
Turner, John	077	1770	WB-C/91	AR
Turner, John	044	1854	WB-19/441	CTY
Turner, John	073	1870	WB-H/38	CTY
Turner, John B.	057	1884	WB-C/102	AR
Turner, John D.	080	1859	WB-1/179	AR
Turner, John M.	026	1864	WB-1/357	AR
Turner, Joseph	063	1893	WB-4/119	AR
Turner, Joseph L.	071	1832	WB-4/87	AR
Turner, Joshua	077	1795	WB-E/60	
Turner, Joshua	096	1755	WB-1/3	AR
Turner, Laza	069	1853	WB-1/532	AR
Turner, Leah	099	1863	RB-32/606	AR
Turner, Leah M.	021	1890	WB-2/502	AR
Turner, Lewis	100	1846	WB-39/233	AR
Turner, Lewis C.	106	1885	WB-2/200	AR
Turner, Louisa	100	1859	WB-49/236	AR
Turner, Louiza J.	026	1878	WB-2/165	AR
Turner, Lucinda	036	1887	WB-A/113	CTY
Turner, Lucy	020	1860	RB-S/183	AR
Turner, Lucy	020	1892	WB-B/121	CTY
Turner, Lucy B.	020	1898	WB-B/331	CTY
Turner, Lyttleton	087	1854	WB-1/467	AR
Turner, Margaret	001	1879	WB-2/148	AR
Turner, Mariah	026	1870	WB-2/44	AR
Turner, Mariah L.	100	1896	WB-51/441	
Turner, Mark G.	100	1865	WB-50/163	AR
Turner, Martha	077	1818	WB-F/12	AR
Turner, Martha A.	077	1853	WB-F/424	
Turner, Martha B.	047	1849	WB-4/282	
Turner, Martha N.	077	1852	WB-F/414	AR
Turner, Martial	054	1859	WB-3/138	AR
Turner, Martin	020	1829	RB-L/325	
Turner, Mary	046	1823	WB-B/169	AR
Turner, Mary	005	1878	WB-D/70	AR
Turner, Mary	099	1891	WB-C/6	AR
Turner, Mary	100	1853	WB-42/241	AR
Turner, Mary M.	020	1899	WB-B/361	CTY
Turner, Mathew	010	1794	WB-D/259	AR
Turner, Matthew	103	1801	Orig. Only	AR
Turner, Matthew R.	099	1847	RB-26/290	AR
Turner, Matthias	026	1851	WB-1/124	AR
Turner, Matthias	026	1864	WB-1/343	AR
Turner, Myles	077	1817	WB-F/2	AR
Turner, Nathan	077	1849	WB-F/370	AR
Turner, Nathan	047	1783	WB-3/42	
Turner, Paul	032	1873	WB-3/81	AR
Turner, Peter	047	1806	WB-3/447	
Turner, Peterson	047	1813	WB-3/536	
Turner, Phebe E.	038	1890	WB-3/155	AR
Turner, Phillip	028	1801	WB-B/123	AR
Turner, Rebecca	001	1862	WB-1/197	AR
Turner, Rebecca	001	1872	WB-2/52	AR
Turner, Rhody	010	1800	WB-E/98	AR
Turner, Richard	077	1719	SS 875/175	SS/AR
Turner, Richard	077	1871	WB-H/39	AR
Turner, Richard	077	1834	WB-F/230	AR
Turner, Richard A.	071	1825	WB-3/323	AR
Turner, Robert	009	1745	SS 878/105	SS/AR
Turner, Robert	077	1743	Orig. Only	SS/AR
Turner, Robert	073	1800	WB-D/6	AR
Turner, Roger R.	092	1778	WB-1/121	AR
Turner, Ross B.	026	1867	WB-1/419	AR
Turner, Sampson	030	1792	WB-2/2	
Turner, Samuel	001	1877	WB-2/117	AR
Turner, Samuel	054	1857	WB-3/110	
Turner, Sarah	077	c1827	WB-F/157	AR
Turner, Sarah	071	1855	WB-5/141	AR
Turner, Sarah	011	c1819	WB-2/333	
Turner, Sarah	029	1815	WB-A/211	AR
Turner, Simon	010	1800	WB-E/102	AR
Turner, Simon	099	1783	RB-1/161	AR
Turner, Sion	069	1885	WB-5/210	AR
Turner, Solomon	100	1884	WB-51/200	AR
Turner, Solomon	047	1807	WB-3/465	
Turner, Solomon	035	1871	WB-4/52	AR
Turner, Sophia B.	085	1845	Orig. Only	AR-Nunc.
Turner, Standiford	006	1885	WB-E/132	AR
Turner, Stephen	100	1799	WB-10/193	AR
Turner, Stephen	100	1841	WB-37/532	
Turner, Susan G.	047	1857	WB-5/48	
Turner, Susannah	047	1818	WB-3/628	
Turner, Temperance	069	c1880	Orig. Only	AR
Turner, Thamer	075	1801	WB-M1/56	AR
Turner, Thomas	100	1788	WB-5/36	AR
Turner, Thomas	071	1826	WB-4/4	AR
Turner, Thomas	010	1776	WB-B/64	AR
Turner, Thomas	047	1790	WB-3/185	
Turner, Thomas	010	1810	WB-F/159	AR
Turner, Thomas D.	073	1898	WB-I/140	CTY
Turner, Thomas D.	099	1899	WB-D/235	
Turner, Thomas H.	101	1870	WB-A/570	
Turner, Thomas H.	073	1879	WB-H/197	CTY
Turner, Trecy	005	1852	WB-C/54	AR
Turner, William	020	1853	RB-R/84	AR
Turner, William	002	1698	SS 874.2/102	SS/AR
Turner, William	047	1789	WB-3/164	
Turner, William	006	1885	WB-E/122	AR
Turner, William	038	1889	WB-3/142	AR
Turner, William	047	1786	WB-3/115	
Turner, William	075	1704	Orig. Only	SS/AR
Turner, William	075	1753	SS 881/15	SS/AR
Turner, William	054	1890	WB-5/366	CTY
Turner, William	100	1856	WB-49/62	AR
Turner, William	075	1750	Orig. Only	SS/AR
Turner, William	010	1770	WB-A/127	AR
Turner, William	099	1809	RB-9/116	AR
Turner, William	069	1843	WB-1/467	AR

Name	Co.	Date	Recorded Copy	Original
Turner, William	002	c1696	Orig. Only	SS/AR
Turner, William	075	1884	WB-0/201	AR
Turner, William A.	010	1854	WB-H/5	AR
Turner, William L.	029	1813	WB-A/199	AR
Turner, Wilson	033	1842	WB-1/46	AR
Turner, Winifred	071	1873	WB-6/109	AR
Turney, Thomas	070	1892	WB-G/112	AR
Turpin, John	049	1896	WB-2/363	AR
Turrentine, Absalom	073	1856	WB-G/145	AR
Turrentine, Daniel	073	1856	WB-G/130	AR
Turrentine, Deborah	073	1800	WB-D/4	AR
Turrentine, John S.	001	1871	WB-2/32	AR
Turrentine, Nancy	073	1857	WB-G/188	AR
Turrentine, Samuel	073	1845	WB-F/266	AR
Turrentine, Samuel	073	1801	WB-D/38	AR
Turtne, Archelus	030	1802	WB-2/202	
Tussey, Catharine	032	1881	WB-3/342	AR
Tussey, Gersham	032	c1859	WB-2/245	AR
Tuten, Amos	009	c1834	OWB/513	AR
Tuten, Elizabeth	009	1835	OWB/523	AR
Tuten, John	028	1775	Orig. Only	AR
Tuten, Noah	009	1834	OWB/511	AR
Tuten, Noah B.	009	1891	WB-1/504	CTY
Tuten, Redding	009	1877	WB-1/204	CTY
Tuten, Thomas	009	1892	WB-1/529	CTY
Tuten, Thomas	009	c1796	OWB/321	AR
Tuten, William	009	1846	OB-F/127	AR
Tutenton, Margaret	073	1900	WB-I/173	CTY
Tutherow, George	060	1873	WB-4/111	AR
Tutherow, Susan	060	1899	WB-5/118	AR
Tutherton, Benjamin	073	1835	WB-E/366	
Tutington, Barrington	073	1881	WB-H/300	CTY
Tutle, Ann	035	1844	WB-A/546	AR
Tutle, Hephzibah	035	1848	WB-2/27	AR
Tuton, William	087	c1815	Orig. Only	AR
Tutor, Martha	014	c1841	Orig. Only	AR
Tutor, William	048	1892	WB-1/1	CTY
Tutterow, David	033	1882	WB-2/76	CTY
Tutterow, William W.	033	1897	WB-2/212	CTY
Tuttle, Andrew H.	017	c1843	WB-A/24	AR
Tuttle, Asa	018	1824	WB-C/34	
Tuttle, Barbara	090	1895	WB-6/361	AR
Tuttle, Daniel	075	1832	WB-N/76	AR
Tuttle, John	090	1840	WB-4/69	AR
Tuttle, Lucinda L.	017	1887	WB-B/140	AR
Tuttle, Lucius M.	017	1894	WB-B/252	
Tuttle, Marcus A.	066	1885	Orig. Only	AR
Tuttle, Peter	090	1885	WB-6/151	AR
Tuttle, Robert G.	017	1884	WB-B/112	AR
Tuttle, Thomas	090	1838	WB-4/15	AR
Tweed, Gilbert W.	062	1892	WB-B/150	AR
Tweed, Reuben	062	1900	WB-B/240	AR
Tweede, Thomas	075	1706	Orig. Only	SS/AR
Tweedy, Benjamin	096	1817	Orig. Only	AR
Tweedy, David, Sr.	096	1845	WB-3/11	AR
Twiddy, Jesse	057	1824	WB-B/83	AR
Twidy, Devotion	096	1814	WB-2/63	
Twidy, Levi	096	1882	WB-4/78	
Twidy, Saley	096	c1867	WB-3/83	AR
Twidy, Thomas	096	1878	WB-4/45	
Twiford, George	046	1837	WB-B/568	AR
Twiford, Jonathan	046	1821	WB-B/138	AR
Twiford, Nancy A.	030	1885	WB-5/116	AR
Twiford, William	030	c1812	WB-3/55	
Twig, Nancy	029	1833	WB-B/220	AR
Twigg, William	024	1741	Orig. Only	SS/AR
Twigg, Winnie	029	1868	WB-E/3	AR
Twilley, Ann	070	1819	WB-C/423	AR
Twine, Abraham	077	1801	WB-E/125	AR
Twine, James	077	1829	WB-F/164	AR
Twine, James B.	030	1866	WB-4/262	
Twine, John	024	1826	WB-C/120	AR
Twine, John	077	1783	WB-C/262	AR
Twine, Lemuel	077	1839	WB-F/279	AR
Twine, Prudence	077	1838	WB-F/276	AR
Twine, Thomas	077	1824	WB-F/64	AR
Twine, William	075	1827	WB-N/35	AR
Twisdale, Green	098	1892	WB-A/146	CTY
Twisdale, James H.	100	1898	WB-51/515	
Twisdale, Sally	100	1876	WB-51/107	AR
Twitty, Ann S.	100	1853	WB-42/237	AR
Twitty, Caroline	100	1886	WB-51/209	AR
Twitty, Elizabeth	086	1885	Orig. Only	AR
Twitty, John E.	100	1864	WB-50/135	AR
Twitty, Mary S.	100	1852	WB-42/78	AR
Twitty, Robert G.	086	1864	WB-E/440	AR
Twitty, Russell	086	1841	WB-E/84	AR
Twitty, W. L.	086	1898	WB-G/6	AR
Twitty, William	100	1817	WB-20/226	AR
Twitty, William	094	1775	094.901.1	AR-Nunc.
Twitty, William E.	100	1852	WB-42/254	AR
Twox, James	N	c1711	SS 874.1/40	
Tyer, W. P.	046	1878	WB-E/213	AR
Tyer, William L.	009	c1885	Orig. Only	CTY
Tyler, Alfred	044	1874	WB-23/126	CTY
Tyler, Amelia	009	1867	OB-M/258	AR
Tyler, C. A.	065	1899	WB-0/101	AR
Tyler, Celia	010	1892	WB-I/353	AR
Tyler, Johnson	047	1863	WB-5/106	
Tyler, Moses	011	1762	SS 881/259	SS/AR
Tyler, Perry	010	1799	WB-E/91	AR
Tyler, Perry C.	010	1866	WB-H/158	AR
Tyler, Reuben	084	1832	WB-B/62	CTY
Tyler, Richard	010	1831	WB-G/213	AR
Tyler, Thomas	008	1722	SS 875/346	SS/AR
Tyler, William	044	c1870	WB-23/30	CTY
Tyler, William M.	044	1898	WB-24/411	CTY
Tyner, Arthur	071	1782	WB-1/249	
Tyner, Crofford	071	1836	WB-4/143	AR
Tyner, Dew	071	1823	WB-3/278	AR
Tyner, Etheldred	103	1837	RD-7/256	AR
Tyner, James	071	1846	WB-5/39	AR
Tyner, John	071	1815	WB-3/141	AR
Tyner, John, Sr.	063	1887	WB-4/1	AR
Tyner, Nicholas	071	1753	SS 879/195	SS/AR
Tyner, Nicholas	071	1850	WB-5/88	AR
Tyner, William	071	1779	WB-1/325	
Tyner, William R.	071	1849	WB-5/75	AR
Tynes, Joel A.	105	1891	WB-2/576	AR
Tynes, West	010	1841	WB-G/328	AR
Tyre, Elizabeth	046	1886	WB-E/435	AR
Tyre, William	028	1813	WB-C/73	AR
Tysinger, Adam	085	1822	WB-H/144	AR
Tysinger, John	032	1897	WB-4/319	AR
Tysinger, Peter	032	1876	WB-3/195	AR
Tyson, Aaron	081	1852	WB-9/377	AR
Tyson, Aaron	053	1781	RW-1/96	
Tyson, Ann	053	1813	RW-1/478	AR
Tyson, Aron	053	c1815	RW-1/500	
Tyson, Aron	068	1805	WB-A/249	

Name	Co.	Date	Recorded Copy	Original
Tyson, Charlotte	079	1860	WB-1/48	AR
Tyson, Cornelius	068	1795	WB-A/180	
Tyson, Cornelius	022	1822	WB-B/56	AR
Tyson, Cornelius	068	1867	WB-C/150	
Tyson, Daniel	053	1786	RW-1/148	
Tyson, Elizabeth	053	1871	WB-11/24	
Tyson, George W.	069	1887	WB-5/263	AR
Tyson, Green D.	067	1883	WB-2/163	AR
Tyson, Hosea	009	1831	053 WB-5/77	053 AR
Tyson, James A.	079	1873	WB-2/86	AR
Tyson, Jane	068	1797	WB-A/190	
Tyson, Jehu	005	1800	WB-2/173	AR
Tyson, Joel, Sr.	005	1865	WB-C/204	AR
Tyson, John	068	1827	WB-B/52	
Tyson, John	068	c1851	WB-B/234	
Tyson, John	005	1885	WB-D/174	AR
Tyson, John O.	053	1871	WB-11/25	AR
Tyson, Jordan	022	1895	WB-E/581	AR
Tyson, Lydia	068	1828	WB-B/62	
Tyson, Nannie L.	009	1888	WB-1/436	CTY
Tyson, Samuel	005	1851	WB-C/31	AR
Tyson, Sarah	053	1837	WB-6/6	AR
Tyson, Seth H.	009	1880	WB-1/257	AR
Tyson, Sherrod	079	1867	WB-1/169	AR
Tyson, Thomas	053	1843	WB-6/212	AR
Tyson, Thomas	068	1813	WB-A/278	
Tyson, Thomas B.	068	1893	WB-D/377	
Tyson, Thomas O.	009	1878	053 WB-11/343	053 AR
Tyson, Thomas O.	009	1878	WB-1/229	
Tyson, William	037	1828	WB-F/82	AR
Tyson, William	068	1820	WB-B/11	AR
Tyson, William W.	053	1835	WB-5/284	AR
Udy, Jacob	016	1852	WB-1/216	
Ulrich, Ferdinand	028	1871	WB-E/56	AR
Umelage, Edward	072	1745	SS 878/19	SS/AR
Umflet, Job	103	1806	Orig. Only	AR
Umflet, William	041	1784	WB-1/41	AR
Umphlet, William	041	1833	WB-2/329	AR
Umphlett, Mary	041	1893	WB-4/361	AR
Umphlett, Thomas	041	1893	WB-4/372	AR
Umphrey, Robert	037	1761	WB-A/66	AR
Umphries, Judith	047	1801	WB-3/350	
Umphries, William	020	1815	RB-G/88	AR
Umstead, John	073	1829	WB-E/182	AR
Umstead, Sabrina	036	1895	WB-A/348	CTY
Umsted, Elisha	073	1854	WB-G/66	AR
Umsted, Jacob	073	1816	WB-D/495	AR
Unday, Thomas	008	1725	SS 876/47	SS/AR
Underdown, Stephen	KY	c1828	017 WB-A/22	017 AR
Underhill, Henry	047	1826	WB-4/24	AR
Underhill, Joseph	024	1815	WB-C/32	AR
Underhill, Joseph	024	c1789	WB-A/83	AR
Underhill, Joseph S.	077	1871	WB-H/45	AR
Underhill, William	099	1890	WB-B/438	AR
Underhill, William	035	1802	WB-A/457	AR
Underhill, William	103	1849	RD-10/244	AR
Underwood, Alexander	081	1874	WB-15/136	AR
Underwood, Anna	081	1896	WB-16/396	AR
Underwood, Henry	081	1826	WB-5/280	AR
Underwood, Jacob	087	1896	WB-4/25	AR
Underwood, Jacob	069	1798	WB-1/120	AR
Underwood, Jesse	071	1795	WB-2/93	AR
Underwood, Jesse	071	1831	WB-4/80	AR
Underwood, John	081	1900	WB-17/61	
Underwood, John	071	1805	WB-2/299	AR
Underwood, John	092	1811	WB-3/97	
Underwood, John	087	1860	WB-2/1	AR
Underwood, John	071	1792	WB-1/446	AR
Underwood, Joshua	046	1837	WB-B/564	AR
Underwood, Josiah	087	1854	WB-1/464	
Underwood, Matilda B.	051	1880	WB-C/252	AR
Underwood, Samuel	073	1774	WB-A/148	
Underwood, Sarah	087	1849	WB-1/360	AR
Underwood, Sarah	037	1776	WB-A/246	
Underwood, Thomas	008	1735	009 OWB/16	009 AR
Underwood, Thomas	056	1875	WB-3/142	
Underwood, William	071	1854	WB-5/120	AR
Underwood, Wright L.	087	1859	WB-1/536	AR
Unthank, Allen	046	1822	WB-B/155	AR
Unthank, Jasper	046	1896	WB-F/481	AR
Unthank, Jemima	046	1840	WB-C/76	AR
Unthank, John	046	c1780	WB-A/398	AR
Unthank, Joseph	046	1823	WB-B/159	AR
Unthank, Joseph	046	c1780	WB-A/397	AR
Upchurch, A. J.	105	1873	WB-2/116	
Upchurch, Alfred A.	069	1892	WB-5/374	
Upchurch, Allen	089	1848	WB-1/64	
Upchurch, Benton A.	099	1872	RB-35/190	AR
Upchurch, Calvin	039	1844	WB-M/25	AR
Upchurch, Elias	086	1844	WB-E/133	AR
Upchurch, Esther	099	1864	RB-33/284	AR
Upchurch, Gilbert	099	1895	WB-C/464	AR
Upchurch, Golden A.	099	1893	WB-C/182	AR
Upchurch, Howell	089	1846	WB-1/53	AR
Upchurch, Hubbard	099	1859	RB-31/223	AR
Upchurch, J. H.	022	c1862	WB-D/151	AR
Upchurch, James	039	1850	WB-N/318	AR
Upchurch, Kearney	099	1882	WB-A/342	AR-Copy
Upchurch, Lindemond	099	1866	RB-34/286	AR
Upchurch, Murry	022	1872	WB-E/74	AR
Upchurch, Nancy T.	022	1870	WB-E/45	AR
Upchurch, Nathan	099	1825	RB-23/323	AR
Upchurch, Parker	099	1864	RB-33/282	AR
Upchurch, Ruffin	099	1866	RB-34/160	AR
Upchurch, Tabitha	099	1855	RB-29/230	AR
Upchurch, William	104	1787	WB-1/221	AR
Upchurch, William G.	099	1895	WB-C/458	AR
Upperman, Bettie A.	039	1899	WB-V/150	AR
Upright, David	085	1856	WB-K/225	AR
Upright, Peter	085	1865	WB-K/352	AR
Upright, William J.	054	1896	WB-6/37	CTY
Upston, Thomas	075	1750	Orig. Only	SS/AR
Uptegrove, Isaac	092	1817	WB-3/130	AR
Upton, Edward	o75	1755	Orig. Only	SS/AR
Upton, Elizabeth	064	1852	WB-1/30	AR
Upton, John	075	c1715	SS 875/326	SS/AR
Upton, John	018	1892	WB-E/210	AR
Upton, John	018	1855	WB-D/25	
Upton, John	075	1720	SS 875/241	
Upton, Joseph	075	1767	WB-H/77	AR
Upton, Latimore	018	1829	WB-C/109	
Upton, Margaret	018	1900	Orig. Only	AR
Upton, Mark	018	1839	WB-C/253	
Upton, Quenton	018	1853	WB-C/371	
Upton, Richard	068	1828	WB-B/58	
Upton, Robert	083	c1819	WB-1/211	AR
Upton, Thomas	086	1841	WB-E/78	AR
Upton, Thomas	077	1804	WB-E/217	AR
Ure, Andrew	070	1804	WB-AB/90	AR
Urich, Elizabeth	060	1828	WB-1/94	AR

Name	Co.	Date	Recorded Copy	Original
Urich, George	065	1774	Orig. Only	AR
Urquhart, Alexander	010	1804	WB-E/246	AR
Urquhart, Anna	070	1845	WB-AB/422	AR
Urquhart, Charles F.	VA	1868	071 WB-6/29	071 AR
Urquhart, Eliza B.	VA	1869	071 WB-6/27	071 AR
Urquhart, Henrietta	070	1862	WB-D/107	AR
Urquhart, James B.	VA	1850	010 WB-G/470	010 AR
Urquhart, John	028	1818	WB-C/168	AR
Urquhart, Richard A.	VA	1857	010 WB-H/44	010 AR
Urquhart, Whitmell	038	1856	010 WB-H/48	010 AR
Urquhart, William	024	1738	Orig. Only	SS/AR
Ury, Mary	016	1856	WB-1/285	
Usher, John	070	1812	WB-AB/173	AR
Usher, Thomas	082	1825	WB-1/265	AR
Usher, William	035	1867	WB-3/124	
Usher, William	010	1780	WB-C/5	AR-Nunc.
Usry, Dardie N.	044	1898	WB-24/404	CTY-Nunc.
Usry, Thomas H.	044	1863	WB-21/744	CTY
Ussery, William D.	082	1892	WB-6/444	AR
Utley, Asa	022	1866	WB-D/163	AR
Utley, Britain	099	1813	RB-11/168	AR
Utley, Briton	099	1880	WB-A/162	AR
Utley, Burwell	099	1852	RB-27/401	AR
Utley, Eliza J.	099	1875	RB-35/305	AR
Utley, Foster	073	1894	WB-I/41	CTY
Utley, Gabriel	022	1850	WB-C/275	AR
Utley, Grey	065	1872	WB-K/94	AR
Utley, Jacob	099	1796	RB-3/261	AR
Utley, John	099	1853	RB-28/275	AR
Utley, Jonathan	099	1862	RB-32/251	AR
Utley, Joseph	029	1877	WB-E/170	AR
Utley, Mariah	056	1889	WB-3/553	
Utley, Pheby	099	1805	RB-7/1	AR
Utley, Samuel M.	009	1891	WB-B/550	AR
Utley, Simeon J.	099	1880	WB-A/180	AR
Utley, William	099	1893	WB-C/175	AR
Utley, William	099	1794	RB-3/62	AR
Utley, Young	099	1849	RB-26/586	AR
Utzman, John	085	1851	WB-K/137	AR
Uzzel, Elisha	103	1798	WI-B/243	AR
Uzzell, Elizabeth	103	1884	WB-1/335	AR
Uzzell, John M.	103	1893	WB-2/47	AR
Uzzell, Joshua	103	c1876	WB-1/98	AR
Uzzell, Lewis	TX	1879	103 WB-1/170	103 AR
Uzzell, Major	103	1841	RD-8/151	AR
Uzzell, Rebecca	103	1878	WB-1/133	AR
Uzzell, William B.	039	1892	WB-U/551	AR
Vaden, George	047	1822	WB-3/671	
Vaden, Mary	099	1863	RB-32/612	AR
Vaden, William	099	1823	RB-18/296	AR
Vail, A. N.	101	1896	WB-A/283	
Vail, David	009	1818	OB-A/282	AR
Vail, David	103	1887	WB-1/387	AR
Vail, Edward	024	1777	WB-A/320	AR
Vail, Edward	009	c1865	OB-M/316	AR
Vail, Eliza	028	1853	WB-D/214	AR
Vail, Elizabeth	028	1806	WB-B/252	
Vail, Frederick	024	c1778	WB-A/317	AR
Vail, Harriet C.	101	1897	WB-A/302	
Vail, Jeremiah	009	c1779	OWB/150	AR
Vail, John	024	1765	WB-1/19	AR
Vail, Mary	009	1816	OB-A/261	AR
Vail, Thomas O.	101	1891	WB-A/201	
Vainright, Pricilla E.	079	1874	WB-2/95	AR

Name	Co.	Date	Recorded Copy	Original
Valentine, Daniel	047	1782	WB-3/29	
Valentine, David	051	c1839	WB-A/258	
Valentine, Fannie B.	069	1897	WB-6/23	AR
Valentine, James H.	069	1896	WB-5/520	AR
Valentine, John	051	1857	WB-B/1	
Valentine, John B.	074	c1886	Orig. Only	AR
Valentine, Lemuel	051	1861	WB-B/33	
Valentine, Martha	051	1869	WB-C/24	
Valentine, Mary A. E.	029	1864	WB-D/66	
Valentine, Mary J.	010	1900	WB-K/30 & 37	
Valentine, Rigdon	044	1844	WB-16/67	CTY
Valient, Ancel	046	1816	WB-A/27	AR
Vallentine, Alexander	071	1796	WB-2/101	AR
Vallentine, Richard	070	1731	SS 877/108	SS/AR
Vallette, Francis	024	1806	WB-B/236	AR
Van Amringe, Cyrus S.	070	1862	WB-D/103	AR
Van Amringe, George O.	070	c1866	Orig. Only	AR
Van Amringe, Stacy	070	1897	WB-G/549	AR
Van Bokkelen, Adrian H.	070	1891	WB-F/480	AR
Van Bokkelen, Evalina	070	1896	WB-G/527	
Van Bokkelen, Libertus	NY	1889	070 WB-F/435	070 AR
Van Clief, John M.	070	1827	WB-C/427	AR
Van Dike, Joseph	096	1791	Orig. Only	AR
Van Eaton, Barcina	033	1864	WB-1/197	AR
Van Eaton, Samuel	033	1846	WB-1/82	AR
Van Etten, John	085	c1786	WB-C/181	AR
Van Hook, Lawrence	020	1801	RB-D/16	
Van Nest, Margaret	NY	1890	Copy	050 AR
Van Pelt, John	NY	1748	Orig. Only	SS/AR
Van Pelt, Simon	065	c1799	WB-F/42	AR
Van Pelt, Simon	065	1857	WB-I/175	AR
Van Pool, John	085	1827	WB-H/401	AR
Van Poole, Jacob	085	1795	WB-F/37	AR
Van Sickle, Anna H.	070	1870	WB-E/200	AR
Van Sickle, John	070	1869	WB-E/205	AR
Van Slyck, George S.	030	1875	WB-5/46	AR
Van Vleck, Charles A.	TN	1846	090 WB-4/223	090 AR
Van Vleck, Christiana	038	1877	WB-2/303	AR
Van, Bedieth	056	1862	WB-2/30	
VanBokkelen, Adrian H.	028	1846	WB-D/129	AR
Vance, Harriet	013	c1886	Orig. Only	AR
Vance, James L.	065	1832	WB-G/103	AR
Vance, John	038	1883	WB-2/443	AR
Vance, John	090	1839	WB-4/48	AR
Vance, Mary	038	1883	WB-2/445	AR
Vance, Mira M.	062	1878	WB-B/56	AR
Vance, Priscilla	013	1835	WB-A/38	
Vance, Robert B.	013	1900	WB-D/387	AR
Vance, Samuel	092	1789	WB-2/88A	AR
Vance, Thomas	107	1851	WB-1/63	
Vance, William	065	1817	WB-F/207	AR
Vance, William H.	065	c1862	WB-J/162	AR
Vandeford, John	022	1792	RB-1/40	AR
Vandemerck, Jacobus	092	1773	WB-1/13	AR
Vanderburg, Julia A. E.	054	1883	WB-4/481	
Vandergriff, Jesse	099	1884	WB-A/514	AR
Vandermulen, Thomas	030	1720	SS 875/234	
Vanderpool, Abraham	092	1795	WB-3/17	
Vanderveer, Jacob	009	1864	079 WB-1/145	079 AR
Vandike, William	102	1885	WB-A/46	AR
Vandyke, James	026	1863	WB-1/305	AR
Vandyke, Lydda	044	1778	WB-1/188	
Vandyke, Margaret	060	1837	WB-1/387	AR
Vandyke, William R.	026	1864	WB-1/344	AR
Vanhook, Aaron	073	1760	WB-A/9	

Name	Co.	Date	Recorded Copy	Original
Vanhook, Alfred	078	1810	WI-5/177	AR
Vanhook, David	078	1795	WI-1/209	AR
Vanhook, David	020	1785	RB-B/66	AR
Vanhook, Isaac	061	1849	WB-1/40	AR
Vanhook, Isaac	078	1802	WI-3/97	AR
Vanhook, Kindle	078	1854	WB-17/303	AR
Vanhook, Sarah	078	1816	WI-7/129	AR
Vanhook, Thomas C.	061	1894	WB-2/142	AR
Vanhorn, John	014	c1842	Orig. Only	AR
Vanhosen, John	005	c1762	WB-1/13	
Vanhoy, Clayton	106	1876	WB-2/71	AR
Vanhoy, James	089	1879	WB-2/74	
Vanhoy, John	090	1798	WB-1/114	AR
Vanhoy, Nancy	106	1891	WB-2/302	
Vanhoy, Richard	038	1891	WB-3/255	AR
Vanlandingham, Dawson	100	1802	WB-11/257	AR
Vanlandingham, John	015	1774	100 WB-2/21	AR
Vanlandingham, Mary R.	100	1875	WB-51/84	AR
Vanlandingham, Richard	100	1866	WB-50/200	AR
Vanlandingham, Richard	084	1811	WB-A/116	CTY
Vanluvan, Henry	010	1764	WB-A/39	AR
Vanluven, Christopher	010	1732	SS 876/256	SS/AR
Vann, A. R.	099	1892	WB-C/90	AR
Vann, Annie G.	051	1891	WB-C/420	AR
Vann, Darkes	041	1793	WB-1/116	AR
Vann, Edward	024	1752	Orig. Only	SS/AR
Vann, Edward	010	1770	WB-A/130	AR
Vann, Enoch	087	1847	WB-1/328	AR
Vann, Ezekiel	029	c1840	WB-B/361	AR
Vann, Henry	087	1887	WB-3/364	AR
Vann, J. J.	097	1894	WB-2/463	AR
Vann, James	051	1843	WB-A/226	
Vann, James	087	1866	WB-2/107	AR
Vann, John	051	1851	WB-A/327	
Vann, John	087	1842	WB-1/259	AR
Vann, John	071	1859	WB-5/215	AR
Vann, John R.	035	1804	WB-4/234	AR
Vann, Joseph	024	1753	Orig. Only	SS/AR
Vann, Mills L.	041	1883	WB-4/190	AR
Vann, Needam	087	1833	WB-1/148	AR
Vann, Owen	087	1858	WB-1/526	AR
Vann, Susan A.	087	1875	WB-3/87	AR
Vann, Temperance	071	1899	WB-7/458	AR
Vann, Thomas	087	1838	WB-1/209	AR
Vann, Valentine	087	1888	WB-3/379	AR
Vann, William	024	1740	LGB-4/#119	SS/AR
Vann, William	041	1788	WB-1/76	AR
Vann, William H.	087	1864	WB-2/79	AR
Vann, William H.	070	1849	WB-C/489	AR
Vannoe, Neil C.	104	1863	WB-5/342	
Vannoy, Cornelius	032	c1828	Orig. Only	AR
Vannoy, Enoch	104	1880	WB-6/201	AR
Vannoy, James	104	1857	WB-5/169	
Vannoy, James H.	104	1898	WB-7/40	AR
Vannoy, Jesse	104	1875	WB-6/115	AR
Vannoy, Joel	104	1858	WB-5/202	
Vannoy, John H.	006	c1885	WB-E/199	AR
Vanover, Cornelius	006	1817	WB-A/52	
Vanover, Henry	004	1875	Orig. Only	AR
Vanstorie, Catherine	046	1839	WB-C/29	AR
Vanstorre, John	046	1863	WB-D/176	AR
Vanstorre, John, Jr.	046	1831	WB-B/441	AR
Vanzant, Garrett	086	1788	Orig. Only	AR
Vanzant, Mary	086	1796	Orig. Only	AR
Varden, Joseph	075	1838	WB-N/143	AR
Varden, Tuley	075	1823	WB-M1/386	AR
Vardin, Moses	075	1810	WB-M1/217	AR
Varnell, Richard	092	1780	WB-1/143	
Varnell, William	037	1898	WB-H/415 & 424	AR
Varner, Elizabeth	060	1811	Orig. Only	AR
Varner, Jacob	085	1814	WB-G/328	AR
Varner, James	065	1778	WB-F/201	AR
Varner, John	032	1828	WB-1/92	AR
Varner, John	065	1806	WB-F/206	AR
Varner, John	081	1829	WB-5/466	AR
Varner, Mathew	032	1882	WB-3/359	AR
Varner, W. A.	081	1896	WB-16/381	AR
Varnon, Jonathan	090	1805	WB-2/62	AR
Varnor, Henry	065	1784	WB-F/202	AR
Varnor, Robert	065	1800	WB-F/202	AR
Varnum, Jacob	MA	1716	Orig. Only	SS/AR
Vasor, James	071	1838	WB-4/170	AR
Vass, Caty	078	1797	WI-1/307	AR
Vass, Fanny	044	1799	WB-4/304	CTY
Vass, Reuben	044	1827	WB-10/386	CTY
Vass, Robert H.	044	1867	WB-22/706	CTY
Vass, Thomas	044	1818	WB-8/107	CTY
Vass, Thomas	044	1857	WB-20/224	CTY
Vass, W. W.	099	1896	WB-C/573	AR
Vassen, Temperance	037	1840	WB-F/245	AR
Vasser, Joseph	071	1827	WB-4/28	AR
Vasser, Joseph	071	1796	WB-2/108	AR
Vasser, Martha	105	1871	WB-2/70	AR
Vasser, Winifred	071	1866	WB-5/341	AR
Vassor, Henry	071	1892	WB-7/151	AR
Vassor, James	071	1897	WB-7/339	AR
Vassor, John W.	071	1859	WB-5/213	AR
Vassor, Nancy	071	1855	WB-5/138	AR
Vaugh, Sampson	072	1872	WB-H/62	CTY
Vaughan, Anne	044	1833	WB-12/427	CTY
Vaughan, Burwell	100	1827	WB-30/267	AR
Vaughan, Charlotte	071	1852	WB-5/101	AR
Vaughan, Demcy	069	1790	WB-1/70	AR
Vaughan, E. L.	004	1889	WB-A/100	
Vaughan, Elijah	051	1897	WB-C/522	AR
Vaughan, Elisha	051	1855	WB-A/375	
Vaughan, Ephram	069	1797	WB-1/128	AR
Vaughan, Harris	099	1886	WB-B/108	AR
Vaughan, James	044	1816	WB-7/606	CTY
Vaughan, James	073	c1788	WB-B/36	AR
Vaughan, James	071	1843	WB-4/265	AR
Vaughan, Jeremiah	047	1832	WB-4/88	
Vaughan, Jesse	051	1837	WB-A/104	
Vaughan, John	073	1786	WB-A/357	AR
Vaughan, John	051	1864	WB-B/56	AR
Vaughan, John	071	1750	Orig. Only	SS/AR
Vaughan, John	071	1812	WB-3/81	AR
Vaughan, John	051	1845	WB-A/237	
Vaughan, John	044	1853	WB-19/201	CTY
Vaughan, John	020	1805	RB-E/204	AR
Vaughan, John D. L.	071	1861	WB-5/243	AR
Vaughan, Joseph E.	051	1861	WB-B/47	AR
Vaughan, Lemanther	047	1807	WB-3/467	Nunc.
Vaughan, Martha	044	1846	WB-16/530	CTY
Vaughan, Martha E.	100	1872	WB-51/42	AR
Vaughan, Matthias	051	1879	WB-C/229	AR
Vaughan, Nancy	051	1892	WB-C/424	AR
Vaughan, Rebecca	071	1823	WB-3/282	AR
Vaughan, Salley	071	1842	WB-4/257	AR

Name	Co.	Date	Recorded Copy	Original
Vaughan, Thomas	020	1835	RB-M/475	AR
Vaughan, Thomas J.	051	c1895	Orig. Only	AR
Vaughan, Uriah	071	1890	WB-7/67	AR
Vaughan, Uriah	051	1890	WB-C/401	AR
Vaughan, Vincent	044	1838	WB-14/134	CTY
Vaughan, Vinson	071	1749	SS 879/229	SS/AR
Vaughan, Vinson	071	1765	WB-1/127	
Vaughan, Wiley E.	045	1886	WB-1/134	AR
Vaughan, William	051	1874	WB-C/120	AR
Vaughan, William	071	1794	WB-2/60	
Vaughan, William	047	1806	WB-3/455	
Vaughan, William	071	1780	WB-1/219	AR
Vaughan, William	051	1861	WB-B/38	AR
Vaughan, William	051	1884	WB-C/324	AR
Vaughan, William T.	100	1867	WB-50/236	AR
Vaughn, Amos	039	c1815	WB-D/173	AR
Vaughn, Ann	090	1859	WB-4/333	AR
Vaughn, Bently	078	1892	WB-19/335	AR
Vaughn, David	103	1877	WB-1/115	AR
Vaughn, Harriss	051	1850	WB-A/324	
Vaughn, J. A. J.	026	1863	WB-1/321	AR
Vaughn, James	045	c1875	Orig. Only	AR-Copy
Vaughn, Jason	069	1883	WB-5/154	AR
Vaughn, John	MD	1814	019 WB-E/24	019 AR
Vaughn, John W.	090	1885	WB-6/162	
Vaughn, John W.	064	1895	WB-2/347	AR
Vaughn, Josiah	091	1884	WB-1/73	
Vaughn, Lucy S.	020	1889	WB-A/573	CTY
Vaughn, Mary D.	069	1877	WB-5/64	AR
Vaughn, Stephen	005	c1785	WB-1/48	
Vaughn, Sterling	054	1846	WB-3/14	AR
Vaughn, Steven	099	1832	RB-22/313	AR
Vaughn, Thomas	071	1797	WB-2/143	AR
Vaughn, Uriah	051	c1880	092 WB-6/316	092 AR
Vaughn, Vicy	045	c1886	Orig. Only	AR
Vaughn, William	020	1856	RB-R/362	AR
Vaughn, Zebulun	090	1831	WB-3/220	AR
Vaulks, James	047	1761	WB-1/32	
Vawter, Alexander	038	1861	WB-1/188	AR
Vawter, Chadwell	090	1843	WB-4/128	AR-Nunc.
Vawter, John	090	1844	WB-4/158	AR
Vawter, John M.	038	1874	WB-2/203	AR
Vawter, Josiah C.	038	1863	WB-1/233	AR
Veach, John, Sr.	032	1826	WB-1/54	AR
Veach, Rachel	032	1860	WB-2/184	AR
Veal, Richard	071	1781	WB-1/245	
Veale, Bond	028	c1764	Orig. Only	AR
Veale, Burthany	053	c1819	Orig. Only	AR
Veale, Francis	070	1748	DB-C/174	
Veale, John	028	1787	WB-A/151	AR
Veale, Morris	071	1766	WB-1/142	
Veale, Richard	010	1820	WB-G/72	AR
Veale, Thomas	010	1806	WB-F/20	AR
Veale, Thomas	010	1824	WB-G/120	AR
Veale, William	070	1760	SS 881/274	SS/AR
Veanel, George	032	1845	WB-1/459	
Vears, Susannah	104	1815	WB-3/107	
Veasey, Frances	044	1817	WB-8/85	CTY
Veatch, John	085	1819	Orig. Only	AR
Veazey, Abner	044	1880	WB-23/373	CTY
Veazey, Alfred M.	044	1895	WB-24/284	CTY
Veazey, Edward	044	1771	Orig. Only	CTY
Veazey, Elijah	044	1801	WB-5/163	CTY
Veazey, Ezekiel	044	c1834	Copy	073 AR
Veazey, Joseph H.	044	1880	WB-23/389	CTY

Name	Co.	Date	Recorded Copy	Original
Veazey, Mark	044	1830	WB-11/309	CTY
Veazey, Martha	036	1898	WB-A/448	CTY
Veazey, Rebecca	044	1891	WB-24/169	CTY
Veazey, William	044	1845	WB-16/246	CTY
Veillard, Gabriel	072	1792	Orig. Only	AR
Venable, Haywood	090	1899	WB-6/504 & 569	AR
Venable, Haywood	090	1899	SC/20203	AR-Copy
Venable, Isabella	044	1876	Copy	047 AR
Venable, Isabella	044	1876	WB-23/226	CTY
Venable, Jesse	092	1882	WB-6/166	AR
Venable, Martha R.	084	1894	WB-E/576	CTY
Venable, Richard	060	1800	Orig. Only	AR
Venable, William	092	c1822	WB-3/157	AR
Vendrick, Abraham	028	1812	WB-C/51	AR
Vendrick, Bryan	028	1811	WB-C/29	AR
Vendrick, Churchill	028	1822	WB-C/217	
Vendrick, Daniel	028	1780	Orig. Only	AR
Vendrick, Francis	028	1815	WB-C/108	AR
Vendrick, James	028	1845	WB-D/115	
Vendrick, Jesse	028	1820	WB-C/192	AR
Vendrick, Joanna	028	1804	WB-B/199	AR
Vendrick, John	028	1804	WB-B/211	AR
Vendrick, John	028	1785	WB-A/157	AR
Vendrick, John	028	1789	WB-A/196	AR
Vendrick, Peter	028	1834	WB-C/364	AR
Vendrick, Rebecca J.	074	1892	WB-1/118	AR
Venters, Slade	079	1879	WB-2/200	AR
Ventress, William	057	1795	WB-A/136	AR
Verble, Catharine	085	1853	WB-K/157	AR
Verble, Daniel	085	c1778	WB-B/174	AR
Verble, Daniel	085	1834	WB-H/610	AR
Verble, Eve Ann	085	1875	WB-1/315	CTY
Verble, John H.	085	1898	WB-3/245	CTY
Verble, Nancy	085	1898	WB-3/254	CTY
Vernal, Richard	092	1780	WB-1/143	AR
Vernon, Alexander	084	N. D.	Orig. Only	CTY-Nunc.
Vernon, Alexander	046	1778	WB-A/195	
Vernon, Alfred M.	083	1876	WB-3/119	AR
Vernon, Anne	011	c1760	WB-1/597	
Vernon, Ephraim	070	1761	DB-D/469	AR
Vernon, Isaac	084	c1787	OW/230	AR
Vernon, James A.	084	1900	WB-F/175	CTY
Vernon, John	012	1798	WB-B/60	Nunc.
Vernon, Richard	084	1878	WB-E/151	CTY
Vernon, Richard	084	1855	WB-C/206	CTY
Vernon, William A.	020	1857	RB-R/526	AR
Verser, Elizabeth	100	1854	WB-49/156	AR
Verser, Francis	100	1830	WB-32/292	
Verser, John, Sr.	100	1856	WB-49/79	AR
Verser, William	100	1825	WB-28/312	AR
Verser, William	100	1825	WB-28/310	
Vest, Charles	038	1860	WB-1/155	AR
Vest, John	090	1833	WB-3/251	AR-Nunc.
Vest, Johnson	038	1896	WB-3/592	AR
Vest, Lecresesa	090	c1813	Orig. Only	AR
Vest, Sallie	038	1892	WB-3/310	AR
Vest, William	090	1812	WB-2/138	AR
Vestal, Alexander	106	1899	WB-2/450	
Vestal, Benjamin	022	1828	WB-B/157	AR
Vestal, Daniel	106	c1866	WB-2/90	AR
Vestal, David	022	1855	WB-C/395	AR
Vestal, David	022	1828	WB-B/159	AR
Vestal, Eliza	022	1891	WB-E/453	AR

Name	Co.	Date	Recorded Copy	Original
Vestal, James	092	1793	WB-3/10	
Vestal, Jesse	081	1883	WB-15/448	AR
Vestal, Jesse	106	c1857	WB-1/66	AR
Vestal, Martha	106	c1863	WB-2/56 & 80	
Vestal, Rebecca	022	1859	WB-D/33	AR
Vestal, S. M.	106	1898	WB-2/431	
Vestal, Sarah A.	106	1892	WB-2/322	AR
Vestal, Simpson F.	001	1896	WB-3/154	AR
Vestal, Sina	106	1888	WB-2/243	AR
Vestal, Solomon	032	1862	WB-2/225	AR
Vestal, Thomas	022	1813	WB-A/237	AR
Vestal, William	081	1888	WB-16/107	AR
Vestal, William	022	c1787	WB-A/47	AR
Vester, B. H.	069	1890	WB-5/325	AR
Vester, Benjamin	069	1844	WB-1/472	AR
Vester, William	069	1804	WB-1/145	AR
Vester, William	069	1801	WB-1/137	AR
Vestle, Emeline	081	1888	WB-16/109	AR
Viars, Robert	104	1821	WB-3/250	AR
Vick, Asael	069	c1850	WB-1/551	AR
Vick, B. S.	069	1862	WB-1/585	AR
Vick, Benjamin	069	1804	WB-1/152	AR
Vick, Benjamin	069	1808	WB-1/186	AR
Vick, Benjamin	047	1783	WB-3/48	
Vick, Council	071	1849	WB-5/79	AR
Vick, Edmund	005	1853	WB-C/62	AR
Vick, Elisha	071	1833	WB-4/105	AR
Vick, Elizabeth	069	1830	WB-1/368	AR
Vick, Elizabeth	069	1866	WB-1/597	AR
Vick, Francis A.	068	1895	WB-D/447	
Vick, Hudson	069	c1884	Orig. Only	AR
Vick, Isaac	069	1832	WB-1/380	AR
Vick, Jesse W.	069	1887	WB-5/258	AR
Vick, John	069	1831	WB-1/374	AR
Vick, John	047	1876	WB-6/148	AR
Vick, John	069	1834	WB-1/402	AR
Vick, John Henry	069	1859	WB-1/563	AR
Vick, John N.	069	1881	WB-5/140	AR
Vick, Joseph	069	1816	WB-1/282	AR
Vick, Josiah	069	1886	WB-5/218	AR
Vick, Lawrence W.	079	1885	WB-2/334	AR
Vick, Lewis	069	1806	WB-1/230	AR
Vick, Lewis	069	1860	WB-1/568	AR
Vick, Margaret	069	1865	WB-1/593	AR
Vick, Martha	069	1885	WB-5/230	AR
Vick, Mary	069	1834	WB-1/399	AR
Vick, Mary Eliza	068	1895	WB=D/437	
Vick, Matthew	069	1882	WB-5/129	AR
Vick, Nathan	069	1835	WB-1/408	AR
Vick, Pennina	037	1873	WB-G/430	AR
Vick, Pitie	069	1899	WB-6/72	AR
Vick, Robert	069	1796	WB-1/108	AR
Vick, Ruffin	069	1882	WB-5/146	AR
Vick, Sallie E.	079	1890	WB-2/481	AR
Vick, Sarah	071	1858	WB-5/205	AR
Vick, Susanah	069	1842	WB-1/471	AR
Vickers, David	073	1875	WB-H/120	CTY
Vickers, George W.	036	1885	WB-A/77	CTY
Vickers, James	073	1862	WB-G/392	AR
Vickers, John	037	1784	WB-B/152	AR
Vickers, Mary	070	1797	WB-C/426	AR
Vickers, Rachel J.	036	1897	WB-A/414	CTY
Vickers, Ralph	037	1762	WB-A/110	AR
Vickers, Sarah	037	1783	WB-B/117	AR
Vickers, Sarah	104	1854	WB-5/100	
Vickers, Thomas	070	1795	WB-C/423	AR
Vickers, William	060	1831	WB-1/217	AR
Vickery, John W.	054	1883	WB-4/588	CTY
Vickory, Abiathar	046	1881	WB-E/311	AR
Vickray, Christopher	081	1841	WB-7/389	AR
Vickray, Marmaduke	081	1788	WB-1/66	AR
Vickry, J. C.	054	1880	WB-4/368	
Vierling, Martha E.	090	1844	WB-4/147	AR
Villines, D. D.	078	1876	WB-19/56	
Vince, Humphry	030	1739	SS 877/205	SS/AR
Vince, Thomas	030	1721	Orig. Only	SS/AR
Vincent, Ann	020	1820	RB-H/328	
Vincent, Jacob	044	1840	WB-14/530	CTY
Vincent, James	069	1875	WB-5/14	AR
Vincent, John	047	1798	WB-3/298	
Vincent, John B.	073	1825	WB-E/95	AR
Vincent, Joshua	071	1812	WB-3/99	AR
Vincent, Levi A.	001	1895	WB-3/92	AR
Vincent, Levi A.	001	1895	073 WB-I/73	073 CTY
Vincent, Lucy	071	1832	WB-4/88	AR
Vincent, Michael	047	1833	WB-4/103	
Vincent, Peter	085	c1803	WB-D/247	AR
Vincent, Stephen	N	1698	Orig. Only	SS/AR
Vincent, Thomas	073	1825	WB-E/84	AR
Vincent, Thomas L.	001	1852	WB-1/59	AR
Vincent, William B.	001	1867	WB-1/296	
Viner, John	082	1802	WB-1/87	AR
Vines, Charles	037	1823	WB-E/324	AR
Vines, Prudence S.	105	1881	WB-2/267	
Vines, Samuel	079	c1859	WB-1/90	AR
Vines, Samuel	100	1854	WB-43/49	AR
Vines, Samuel	012	1831	WB-B/157	AR
Vines, Samuell	009	1741	Orig. Only	SS/AR
Vines, Sidney C.	009	1866	OB-M/317	AR
Vines, Thomas	009	1836	OWB/527	AR
Vines, Thomson	009	c1799	OWB/354	AR
Vines, William	009	1830	OB-B/82	AR
Vinniner, Hezekiah	VA	1784	SC/02013	AR-Copy
Vinson, Abner	056	1832	Est-18/86	
Vinson, Andrew J.	051	1876	WB-C/162	AR
Vinson, Carolina	056	1888	WB-3/481	
Vinson, Clarky	103	1860	RD-13/222	AR
Vinson, Daniel	071	1854	WB-5/117	AR
Vinson, Drewry	051	1803	WB-A/81	
Vinson, Elijah	051	1896	WB-C/516	AR
Vinson, George H.	103	1887	WB-1/404	AR
Vinson, James	071	1797	WB-2/164	AR
Vinson, James	103	1850	RD-10/328	AR
Vinson, James W.	071	1895	WB-7/281	AR
Vinson, Joseph	099	1806	RB-7/159	AR
Vinson, Lawrence	051	1873	WB-C/82	AR
Vinson, Littleberry	047	1887	WB-6/441	AR
Vinson, Martha A.	051	1894	WB-C/496	AR
Vinson, Philipp	047	1808	WB-3/479	
Vinson, Robert J.	047	1872	WB-6/77	AR
Vinson, Rutha	056	1859	WB-1/731	
Vinson, Sallie	069	1868	WB-1/620	AR
Vinson, Sarah A.	051	1884	WB-C/327	AR
Vinson, Thomas	071	1797	WB-2/164	
Vinson, Thomas	071	1764	WB-1/86	
Vinson, William	065	1797	WB-F/204	AR
Vinters, Rebecca	009	1837	OWB/519	AR
Vipon, Elizabeth	028	1859	WB-D/321	AR
Virgin, Mary	063	c1801	WB-1/385	
Virgin, Prudence	039	1856	WB-0/335	AR

Name	Co.	Date	Recorded Copy	Original
Virgin, Samuel	063	1795	WB-1/217	
Viverett, Andrew J.	069	1894	WB-5/444	AR
Viverett, Martha	069	1896	WB-5/564	AR
Vivrett, Thomas	069	1792	WB-1/78	AR
Vogler, Anna J.	038	1870	WB-2/34	AR
Vogler, Charlotte	038	1900	WB-4/230	AR
Vogler, Christopher	090	1827	WB-3/172	AR
Vogler, E. A.	038	1876	WB-2/291	
Vogler, Hannah C.	038	1876	WB-2/282	AR
Vogler, John	038	1881	WB-2/404	AR
Vogler, Julius R.	038	1886	WB-2/575	AR
Vogler, Martha	106	1878	WB-2/95	
Vogler, Martha M.	038	1890	WB-3/186	AR
Vogler, Nathaniel	038	1872	WB-2/107	AR
Vogler, Paulina E.	038	1893	WB-3/429	AR
Vogler, Peter	038	1880	WB-2/391	AR
Vogler, Timothy	038	1896	WB-3/563	AR
Vokes, George	100	1836	WB-35/338	AR
Vokes, Thomas	100	1838	WB-36/255	AR
Volckmann, Henry	NY	1884	071 WB-6/468	071 AR
Volivo, Esther C.	028	1897	WB-F/236	
Vollers, Luhr	070	1895	WB-G/397	AR
Volloway, Joseph	096	c1804	WB-2/15	AR
Volviva, John	053	1840	WB-6/80	AR
Von Eberstein, Annis	009	c1891	Orig. Only	CTY
Von Eberstein, William H.	009	1890	WB-1/489	CTY
Von Schweinitz, Lewis David	PA	1834	090 WB-3/272	
Voss, E. R.	038	1858	WB-1/139	AR
Voss, Lydia A.M.	038	1869	WB-2/1	AR
Voss, Thomas	038	1855	WB-1/118	AR
Voss, Thomas	009	c1784	OWB/186	AR
Vreeland, Henry	029	1820	WB-B/38	AR
Vuncannon, Olive	081	1885	WB-15/555	
Vuncannon, Shadrach	081	1848	Orig. Only	AR
Vyne, Gerrit	104	1898	WB-7/64	AR
Waad, Edward	024	1691	Orig. Only	SS/AR
Waddail, Frances	039	1847	WB-M/187	AR
Waddell, Annie Lee	056	1899	WB-4/77	
Waddell, Claudia E.	070	1880	Orig. Only	AR
Waddell, David	054	1873	WB-4/144	CTY
Waddell, Edmund B.	012	1830	WB-B/161	AR
Waddell, Edward	056	1812	WB-1/389	AR
Waddell, Elizabeth	103	1832	RD-6/389	AR
Waddell, Ellen S.	070	1895	WB-G/422	AR
Waddell, Everett	056	1866	WB-2/77	AR
Waddell, Harris	103	c1887	WB-1/500	AR
Waddell, Hugh	011	1823	012 WB-B/129	012 AR
Waddell, Hugh	011	c1772	WB-2/291	
Waddell, James	046	1796	WB-A/406	AR
Waddell, John A.	056	1892	WB-2/124	AR
Waddell, John, Sr.	012	1831	WB-B/160	AR
Waddell, Mary	011	c1766	WB-1/598	
Waddell, Mary H.	070	1880	WB-E/381	AR
Waddell, Richard	103	1832	RD-6/371	AR
Waddell, Sarah	022	1837	WB-C/59	AR
Waddell, T. D.	056	1898	WB-4/113	AR
Waddell, William H.	065	1847	WB-I/99	AR
Waddey, Spence	039	1826	WB-H/155	AR
Waddill, Burgess	004	1884	WB-A/69	AR
Waddill, Edmund	081	1815	WB-4/108	AR
Waddill, Elizabeth	051	1837	WB-A/95	
Waddill, James M.	005	1854	WB-C/78	AR
Waddill, John	081	1860	WB-11/409	AR
Waddill, John D.	038	1887	WB-3/43	AR
Waddill, Lucy	005	1846	WB-B/203	AR
Waddill, M. T.	089	c1882	Orig. Only	AR
Waddill, Marseline	029	1874	WB-E/137	AR
Waddill, Mary E.	089	1891	WB-2/202	AR
Waddill, Thomas	029	1863	Orig. Only	AR
Waddill, Turner	071	1776	WB-1/12	
Waddill, William T.	081	1887	WB-16/53	AR
Waddington, William	065	1771	WB-G/25	
Waddle, Archibald	065	1864	WB-J/192	AR
Waddle, David	054	c1805	WB-1/247	AR
Waddle, Henry	092	1843	WB-4/197	
Waddle, Jacob	039	1815	WB-D/175	AR
Wade, Amos	028	1879	Copy	074 AR
Wade, Amos	028	1879	WB-E/210	AR
Wade, Amos	018	c1879	Copy	009 AR
Wade, Amos	028	1801	WB-B/134	AR
Wade, Andrew	092	1838	WB-4/144	
Wade, Benjamin	044	1782	WB-1/456	CTY
Wade, Benjamin	019	1873	WB-B/72	
Wade, Benjamin	099	1803	RB-6/134	AR
Wade, C. B.	106	1898	WB-2/421	
Wade, Caleb	019	1851	WB-A/153	AR
Wade, Charlotte	028	1837	WB-C/400	AR
Wade, Edwin	082	1863	WB-4/163	AR
Wade, Elizabeth	028	1830	WB-C/315	AR
Wade, Elizabeth	019	1815	WB-E/26	AR
Wade, Gholson	106	1898	WB-2/438	
Wade, Grief B.	084	1877	WB-E/149	CTY
Wade, Hannah	028	1819	WB-C/179	AR
Wade, Henry	005	c1775	Copy	081 AR
Wade, Horatio	082	1816	WB-1/176	AR
Wade, Hulda	049	1887	WB-2/146	AR
Wade, Isaac	019	1808	WB-E/21	AR
Wade, Jacob	019	1797	Orig. Only	AR
Wade, Jane	005	1808	WB-2/174	AR
Wade, Jedidah	019	1820	WB-E/28	AR
Wade, John	081	1808	WB-3/94	
Wade, John	075	1750	Orig. Only	SS/AR
Wade, John C.	020	1865	RB-T/99	AR
Wade, Jonadab	084	1835	WB-B/132	CTY
Wade, Joseph	028	1808	WB-B/307	AR
Wade, Joseph	073	1757	SS 880/193	SS/AR
Wade, Joseph	019	1865	WB-A/285	AR
Wade, Joseph	073	c1757	WB-A/67	
Wade, Joseph	035	1795	WB-A/530	AR
Wade, Kezia	028	1857	WB-D/276	AR
Wade, L. F.	009	N. D.	OWB/561	
Wade, Laura E.	082	1899	WB-7/10	
Wade, Levi C.	029	1863	WB-D/53	AR
Wade, Lucy J.	067	1898	WB-2/381	AR
Wade, Lydia	005	1815	WB-2/175	AR
Wade, Margaret	070	1857	WB-C/631	AR
Wade, Martha	086	1835	WB-E/16	AR
Wade, Mary	075	1736	LGB-4/#137	SS/AR
Wade, Robert	078	1815	WI-6/269	CTY
Wade, Robert	019	1745	WB-E/3	Nunc.
Wade, Sarah A.	029	1898	WB-F/152	AR
Wade, Thomas	005	1786	WB-1/52	AR
Wade, Thomas	005	c1792	WB-A/53	AR
Wade, William	071	1829	WB-4/62	AR
Wade, William	086	1829	WB-D/103	AR
Wade, William	071	1864	WB-5/294	AR
Wade, William H.	098	1899	WB-A/320	CTY
Wade, Windsor	019	1816	WB-E/27	AR

Name	Co.	Date	Recorded Copy	Original
Wadkins, Andrew	091	1876	WB-1/3	
Wadkins, John	100	1842	WB-38/35	AR
Wadle, Elizabeth	085	c1828	WB-H/418	AR
Wadsworth, Adrian R.	MD	1891	050 WB-2/148	
Wadsworth, Ann	028	1836	WB-C/388	AR
Wadsworth, Christiana	028	1879	WB-E/204	AR
Wadsworth, Dennis	028	1897	WB-F/317	
Wadsworth, Flora	068	1871	WB-D/17	
Wadsworth, Helen McM.	075	1880	WB-O/118	AR
Wadsworth, Hiram	068	1887	WB-D/250	
Wadsworth, Ignatious	028	1806	WB-B/246	AR
Wadsworth, John	068	1826	WB-B/44	
Wadsworth, Mary A.	050	1897	WB-2/262	CTY
Wadsworth, Rigdon	085	1875	WB-1/297	CTY
Wadsworth, Sarah	028	1834	WB-C/370	AR
Wadsworth, William B.	028	1868	WB-E/6	AR
Waff, Joseph T.	041	1895	WB-4/403	AR
Waff, Thomas	024	c1803	WB-B/178	AR
Waff, William W.	024	1873	WB-E/44	AR
Wafford, John	084	1809	WB-A/315	CTY
Wagg, John	006	c1838	WB-A/5	AR
Waggoner, Adam	090	1832	WB-3/233	AR
Waggoner, Adam	092	1850	WB-4/304	AR
Waggoner, David	106	c1867	Orig. Only	AR
Waggoner, Gabriel	090	1824	WB-3/123	AR
Waggoner, George	073	1781	WB-A/231	AR
Waggoner, Henry	073	1785	WB-A/330	AR
Waggoner, Henry	006	1885	WB-E/120	AR
Waggoner, Jacob	085	1846	WB-K/38	AR
Waggoner, John	092	1851	WB-4/311	
Waggoner, Joseph	090	c1843	Orig. Only	AR
Waggoner, Joseph	085	1791	WB-C/40	AR
Waggoner, Lewis	090	1838	WB-4/23	AR
Waggoner, Lewis P.	038	1885	WB-1/559	AR
Waggoner, Lucy Ann	073	c1885	Orig. Only	AR
Waggoner, Mary	085	1819	WB-G/537	AR
Waggoner, Peter	073	1835	WB-E/367	AR
Waggoner, Philip	092	1782	WB-1/161	AR
Waggoner, Samuel	090	1805	WB-2/60	AR
Waggoner, William	016	1821	WB-A/52	AR
Waggoner, William	009	c1755	OWB/562	AR
Waggoner, William	090	1804	WB-2/45	
Wagner, Aaron	090	1888	WB-6/202	AR
Wagner, Allison	014	1898	WB-3/42	CTY
Wagner, Annie	013	1899	WB-D/261	AR
Wagner, Henry	104	1880	WB-6/191	AR
Wagner, J. L.	054	1894	Orig. Only	AR
Wagner, James L.	078	1883	WB-19/133	AR
Wagner, Moses	033	1875	WB-2/50A	CTY
Wagner, Peter R.	046	1865	WB-D/249	AR
Wagner, William	033	1853	WB-1/110	AR
Wagoner, Catharine	106	1900	WB-2/464	
Wagoner, Conrad	060	1796	Orig. Only	AR
Wagoner, Daniel	004	c1863	WB-A/32	AR
Wagoner, Daniel	106	c1867	WB-1/121	
Wagoner, Jacob	085	1799	WB-D/248	AR
Wagoner, Jacob	004	1882	WB-A/58	AR
Wagoner, Jacob	085	c1812	Orig. Only	AR
Wagoner, Jacob	085	1822	WB-H/222	AR
Wagoner, James J.	054	1892	WB-5/415	CTY
Wagoner, John	106	1889	WB-2/285	AR
Wagoner, John H.	073	1888	WB-H/579	CTY
Wagoner, Johnathan	106	1897	WB-2/394	
Wagoner, Joseph	032	c1858	WB-2/186	AR
Wagoner, Rebecca	046	1892	WB-F/206	AR
Wagoner, William	046	1884	WB-E/387	AR
Wagoner, William	106	1894	WB-2/358	
Wagoner, Wirey	032	1845	WB-1/473	
Wagstaff, Britain	060	1817	Orig. Only	AR
Wagstaff, Britton	078	1862	WB-18/276	AR
Wagstaff, Eliza J.	078	1889	WB-19/239	
Wagstaff, James B.	078	1883	WB-19/144	AR
Wahab, Ann F.	028	1900	WB-F/489	
Wahab, James	030	1798	WB-2/127	
Wahab, James	030	1774	Orig. Only	SS/AR
Wahab, William	030	1784	WB-1/171	
Waide, Alice	024	c1701	SS 874.2/172	SS/AR
Waills, Joshua	030	1745	Orig. Only	SS/AR
Wain, Thomas Sr.	009	1747/8	SS 877/303	SS/AR
Wainright, R. J.	105	1895	100 WB-51/488	100 AR
Wainright, T. A.	105	1883	100 WB-51/490	100 AR
Wainwright, Kinchen	045	1876	WB-1/33	AR
Wainwright, R. J.	105	1895	WB-3/134	AR
Wainwright, R. J.	105	1895	100 WB-51/488	
Wainwright, T. A.	105	1883	WB-2/301	AR
Wair, Martha	010	1815	WB-F/301	AR
Wait, Samuel	099	1867	RB-34/445	AR
Waite, John	075	1804	WB-M1/95	AR
Waitman, David	032	1894	WB-4/209	AR
Wakefield, Rachael	017	1879	WB-B/86	AR
Wakeley, George	070	1765	WB-C/429	AR
Wakeley, Robert	070	1756	DB-D/234	
Walbridge, Heman D.	065	1899	WB-N/218	
Walbridge, Hiram	065	1885	WB-L/103	
Walbridge, Hiram	NY	1873	049 WB-2/16	049 AR
Walbutton, Robert	010	1733	SS 876/274	SS/AR
Walcher, Michael	085	1838	WB-I/37	AR
Walck, Martin	085	c1791	WB-C/44	AR
Walden, Bartlett	001	c1852	WB-1/75	AR
Walden, Drury	071	1834	WB-4/117	AR
Walden, Edmond	022	1885	WB-E/312	AR
Walden, John	005	1817	WB-2/176	AR
Walden, John	022	1897	WB-F/57	AR
Walden, John C.	022	1829	WB-B/170	AR
Walden, Martha	071	1808	WB-2/361	AR
Walden, Mike	071	1806	WB-2/330	AR
Walden, William	071	1778	WB-1/302	
Waldin, Ada C.	098	1897	WB-A/273	CTY
Walding, Benjamin	103	1795	WI-A/545	
Waldo, Catherine	063	1868	WB-3/95	
Waldo, Francis L.	NJ	1898	043 WB-1/55	
Waldo, S. P.	099	1892	WB-C/30	AR
Waldriven, Ursula S.	038	1880	WB-2/379	AR
Waldron, Jacob	070	1765	Orig. Only	SS/AR
Waldron, William	072	1799	WB-A/135	AR
Waldrop, Edmund	086	1846	WB-E/162	AR
Waldrop, Jechonias	086	1826	WB-D/57	AR
Waldrop, Jeconias	080	1856	WB-1/173	AR
Waldrop, Luke	086	1854	WB-E/260	AR
Waldrop, Luke	086	1829	WB-D/102	AR
Waldrop, Michal	071	1791	WB-1/438	AR
Waldrop, Rebecca	086	1839	WB-E/57	AR
Waldrop, Theron D.	080	1864	WB-1/186	AR
Waldson, John	072	1791	Orig. Only	AR
Walk, Joseph J.	032	1874	WB-3/98	AR
Walker, Aaron	073	1833	WB-E/289	AR
Walker, Abner	020	1850	RB-Q/357	
Walker, Abner	020	1898	WB-B/320	CTY
Walker, Abram E.	097	c1870	WB-2/44	AR
Walker, Ajax J.	020	1850	RB-Q/398	

Name	Co.	Date	Recorded Copy	Original
Walker, Albert H.	099	1881	WB-A/274	
Walker, Alcy	104	1889	WB-6/353	AR
Walker, Alexander	073	1835	WB-E/331	AR
Walker, Alexander	029	1871	WB-E/44	AR
Walker, Alice	084	1899	WB-F/145	CTY
Walker, Andrew	016	c1853	WB-A/28	AR
Walker, Ann	084	1848	WB-C/81	CTY
Walker, Ann	070	1788	WB-C/452	AR
Walker, Ann	001	1872	WB-2/50	AR
Walker, Ann E.	075	1866	WB-M2/95	AR
Walker, Anna M.	081	1885	WB-15/515	
Walker, Appeline S.	070	1846	WB-AB/453	AR
Walker, Benjamin	104	1899	WB-7/91	
Walker, C. W.	101	1889	WB-A/176	
Walker, Caleb	030	1838	WB-4/53	
Walker, Caleb	030	1793	WB-2/12	
Walker, Carlton	070	1844	WB-AB/415	AR
Walker, Caroline	070	1873	WB-E/263	AR
Walker, Charles	104	1859	WB-5/222	AR
Walker, Charles	083	c1818	WB-1/343	AR
Walker, Conley	073	1845	WB-F/267	AR
Walker, Dannel	078	1822	WI-9/381	AR
Walker, David	020	1890	WB-B/78	CTY
Walker, Davidson	086	1863	WB-E/410	AR
Walker, Dempsey	030	1891	WB-5/190	AR
Walker, Diana	084	1843	WB-B/290	CTY
Walker, Dicy	104	1891	WB-6/423	AR
Walker, E. H.	030	1874	WB-5/32	AR
Walker, Edward	030	c1811	WB-3/10	
Walker, Edward	096	c1797	Orig. Only	AR
Walker, Elijah	086	1863	WB-E/418	AR
Walker, Elijah M.	097	1875	WB-2/88	AR
Walker, Eliza	030	1867	WB-4/266	AR
Walker, Eliza C.	101	1882	WB-A/88	
Walker, Elizabeth	044	1900	WB-24/477	CTY
Walker, Elizabeth	086	c1805	WB-B/215	AR
Walker, Elizabeth	030	1854	WB-4/193	AR
Walker, Elizabeth	073	1830	WB-E/211	AR
Walker, Ellis	044	1853	WB-19/259	CTY
Walker, Ellis	044	1888	WB-24/37	CTY
Walker, Elmira	023	1898	WB-A/135	AR
Walker, Emiline	009	1875	WB-1/146	AR
Walker, Erasmas	092	1875	WB-6/81	
Walker, Esther	065	1850	WB-I/168	AR
Walker, Faithy	029	1839	WB-B/302	AR
Walker, Felix	049	c1826	WI-A/30	AR
Walker, Francis	029	1823	WB-B/109	AR
Walker, Francis	029	1837	WB-B/283	AR
Walker, Francis	029	1763	Orig. Only	AR
Walker, Frederick	085	1872	WB-1/129	CTY
Walker, Garrison	001	1891	WB-2/491	AR
Walker, George	104	1851	WB-5/55	
Walker, George	019	c1877	Orig. Only	AR
Walker, George E.	070	1859	WB-D/4	AR
Walker, George W.	104	1882	WB-6/217	AR
Walker, Golden	084	1899	WB-F/143	CTY
Walker, Grizzey	099	1899	Orig. Only	AR
Walker, Hardwick	100	1796	WB-8/212	AR
Walker, Harry	083	1815	WB-1/156	
Walker, Henderson	N	1704	Orig. Only	SS/AR
Walker, Henry	065	1823	WB-G/12	
Walker, Henry	024	1899	WB-E/296	AR
Walker, Henry	016	1887	WB-3/528	AR
Walker, Henry J.	001	1883	WB-2/207	AR
Walker, Hiram	003	1873	WB-B/37	AR
Walker, Howard	104	1808	WB-2/236	AR
Walker, Hugh	065	1818	WB-G/14	AR
Walker, Hugh	020	1845	RB-P/188	AR
Walker, Hugh	081	1896	WB-16/385	
Walker, Irena	044	1849	WB-18/3	CTY
Walker, J. Green	100	1861	WB-49/385	AR
Walker, J. W.	030	1890	WB-5/171	
Walker, J. Wilson	104	1897	WB-7/12	AR
Walker, Jacob	090	c1845	Orig. Only	AR
Walker, Jacob	086	1842	WB-E/102	AR
Walker, James	065	1794	WB-F/227	AR
Walker, James	084	1806	WB-A/31	
Walker, James	070	1808	WB-AB/111	AR
Walker, James	100	1832	WB-33/526	AR
Walker, James	065	1782	WB-F/221	AR
Walker, James	078	1873	WB-19/92	AR
Walker, James	047	1819	WB-3/631	
Walker, James	020	1864	RB-T/62	CTY
Walker, James	073	1855	WB-G/115	AR
Walker, James	073	1793	WB-B/229	AR
Walker, James	084	c1803	OW/226	AR
Walker, James E.	084	1895	WB-F/23	CTY
Walker, James S.	100	1886	WB-51/211	AR
Walker, Jane	105	1898	WB-3/304	
Walker, Jerusha A.	029	1900	WB-F/183	AR
Walker, Jesse	070	1862	WB-D/82	AR
Walker, Jesse	086	1891	WB-F/429	AR
Walker, Jesse	086	1784	WB-A/17	
Walker, Joel	069	1886	WB-5/247	AR
Walker, Joel	069	1815	WB-1/267	AR
Walker, Joel	026	1866	WB-1/405	AR
Walker, Joel	047	1795	WB-3/248	
Walker, Joel R.	044	1860	WB-21/332	CTY
Walker, John	086	1820	WB-C/132	AR
Walker, John	065	1804	WB-G/1	AR
Walker, John	070	1756	DB-D/165	AR
Walker, John	012	1775	DB-B/55	AR
Walker, John	030	1793	WB-2/16	Nunc.
Walker, John	019	1811	WB-E/22	AR
Walker, John	086	1820	WB-C/142	AR
Walker, John	086	1826	WB-D/52	AR
Walker, John	084	1821	WB-A/318	CTY
Walker, John	070	1862	WB-D/72	AR
Walker, John	097	c1857	Orig. Only	AR
Walker, John	020	1790	RB-B/310	AR
Walker, John	073	1812	WB-D/336	AR
Walker, John	002	c1709	SS 875/37	
Walker, John	078	1795	WI-1/208	AR
Walker, John	073	1846	WB-F/288	AR
Walker, John	073	1818	WB-D/523	AR
Walker, John	085	c1803	WB-E/22	AR
Walker, John	073	1843	WB-F/172	AR
Walker, John	046	1823	WB-B/167	AR
Walker, John	070	1813	WB-C/455	AR
Walker, John	065	1872	WB-K/108	
Walker, John	070	1827	WB-C/466	AR
Walker, John	096	c1766	WB-1/112	AR
Walker, John	078	1795	Copy	044 CTY
Walker, John A.	068	1897	WB-D/522	
Walker, John B.	065	1862	WB-J/144	AR
Walker, John David	084	1887	WB-E/376	CTY
Walker, John E.	100	1843	WB-38/135	AR
Walker, John G.	001	1888	WB-2/363	AR
Walker, John G.	073	1879	WB-H/228	CTY
Walker, John M.	070	1825	WB-C/463	AR

Name	Co.	Date	Recorded Copy	Original
Walker, John M.	VA	1827	100 WB-31/175	100 AR
Walker, John, Sr.	065	1837	WB-E/185	AR
Walker, John, Sr.	099	1842	RB-25/42	AR
Walker, John, Sr.	084	c1851	WB-C/127	CTY
Walker, Joseph	047	1872	WB-6/81	AR
Walker, Julia C.	029	1900	WB-F/181	AR
Walker, Julius H.	070	1823	WB-C/468	AR
Walker, Levi	030	1860	WB-4/237	
Walker, Levi	020	1844	RB-P/161	
Walker, Lucretia	037	1855	047 WB-5/6	
Walker, Magdaline	070	1828	WB-C/470	AR
Walker, Margaret	083	1858	WB-2/127	AR
Walker, Martha A.	100	1857	WB-49/134	AR
Walker, Martha J.	021	1900	WB-3/266	AR
Walker, Martin W.	009	1899	WB-2/218	CTY
Walker, Mary	013	1898	WB-D/187	AR
Walker, Mary	086	1836	WB-E/29	AR
Walker, Mary	065	1836	WB-E/235	AR
Walker, Mary	084	1813	WB-A/98	CTY
Walker, Mary	084	1851	WB-C/114	CTY
Walker, Mary Ann	065	1897	WB-M/566	AR
Walker, Mary H.	100	1845	WB-38/357	AR
Walker, Mary Vance	070	1900	WB-H/298	AR
Walker, Mitchell	020	1890	WB-B/32	CTY
Walker, Morgan A.	016	1865	WB-2/127	AR
Walker, Moses	078	1806	WI-4/138	AR
Walker, Nancy	065	1854	WB-I/244	AR
Walker, Nancy	033	1855	WB-1/124	AR
Walker, Nancy	099	1881	WB-A/289	AR
Walker, Nancy	030	1823	WB-3/162	
Walker, Nancy B.	078	1854	WB-17/230	AR
Walker, Nathan	075	1900	WB-O/504	AR
Walker, Nicholas	020	1861	RB-S/438	AR
Walker, O'Neil	030	1798	WB-2/122	
Walker, Peter	073	1824	WB-E/64	AR
Walker, Philip	073	1895	WB-I/71	CTY
Walker, Philip	073	1795	WB-C/62	AR
Walker, Phillip	001	1878	WB-2/123	AR
Walker, Phillip	073	1826	WB-E/109	AR
Walker, Phillip	104	1795	WB-1/453	AR
Walker, Pruella	030	1802	WB-2/200	
Walker, Prussia	047	c1860	WB-5/116	
Walker, Rachel	029	1852	WB-C/236	AR
Walker, Rachiel E.	001	1892	WB-2/496	AR
Walker, Ransom	100	1831	WB-33/344	AR
Walker, Rebecca	039	1825	WB-H/107	
Walker, Richard	046	1802	WB-A/408	AR
Walker, Richard	070	1879	WB-E/445	AR
Walker, Richard	070	1894	WB-G/209	AR
Walker, Richard	044	1875	WB-23/197	CTY
Walker, Richmond	069	1875	WB-5/24	AR
Walker, Robert	092	1786	WB-2/68	
Walker, Robert	073	1826	WB-E/107	AR
Walker, Robert	080	c1876	Orig. Only	AR
Walker, Robert	090	1848	WB-4/249	AR
Walker, Robert	065	1827	WB-B/12	AR
Walker, Robert	084	1863	WB-C/376	CTY
Walker, Robert	070	1746	DB-C/123	AR
Walker, Robert F.	073	1870	WB-H/37	CTY
Walker, Sally	036	1890	WB-A/173	CTY
Walker, Samuel	044	1807	WB-6/365	CTY
Walker, Samuel	030	c1810	WB-3/4 & 7	
Walker, Samuel	030	1795	WB-2/58	
Walker, Samuel	081	1783	WB-1/1	
Walker, Samuel	072	1797	Orig. Only	AR
Walker, Samuel	020	1798	RB-C/320	AR
Walker, Samuel	081	1828	WB-5/453	
Walker, Samuel	092	1858	WB-5/39	
Walker, Sarah	068	1843	WB-B/138	
Walker, Sarah	073	1843	WB-F/170	AR
Walker, Sarah	030	1854	WB-4/179	AR
Walker, Solomon	044	1791	WB-2/214	CTY
Walker, Susan M.	084	1896	WB-F/42	CTY
Walker, Susannah	019	1786	Orig. Only	AR
Walker, Susannah	069	1876	WB-5/50	AR
Walker, Thomas	009	1821	OB-A/307	AR
Walker, Thomas	065	1828	WB-C/88	AR
Walker, Thomas	028	1753	SS 877/284	SS/AR
Walker, Thomas	SC	1796	086 WB-B/103	086 AR
Walker, Thomas	030	1807	WB-2/307	
Walker, Thomas D.	070	1865	WB-D/157	AR
Walker, Thomas, Sr.	009	1822	OB-A/323	AR
Walker, Virginia	044	1888	WB-24/57	CTY
Walker, W. T.	046	1895	WB-F/436	AR
Walker, W. W.	096	1885	WB-4/110	AR
Walker, Warren	092	1781	WB-1/144	AR
Walker, Watt	100	1887	WB-51/234	AR
Walker, William	070	1851	WB-C/532	AR
Walker, William	092	1880	WB-6/144	AR
Walker, William	030	1829	WB-3/250	
Walker, William	009	1840	OB-C2/359	AR
Walker, William	084	1801	OW/258	AR
Walker, William	104	1880	WB-6/185	AR
Walker, William	070	1808	WB-AB/113	AR
Walker, William	001	1874	WB-2/70	AR
Walker, William	090	1814	WB-2/156	AR
Walker, William	073	1769	WB-A/101	
Walker, William	104	1830	WB-4/141	
Walker, William	020	1854	RB-R/109	AR
Walker, William	047	1772	WB-1/327	
Walker, William A.	001	1879	WB-2/138	
Walker, William E.	065	1870	WB-K/48	AR
Walker, William E.	084	1862	WB-C/371	CTY
Walker, William J.	030	1890	WB-5/173	AR
Walker, William J.	073	1890	WB-H/488	CTY
Walker, William L.	084	1896	020 WB-B/340	020 CTY
Walker, William L.	029	1847	Orig. Only	AR
Walker, William L.	084	1896	WB-F/63	CTY
Walker, William P.	046	1824	WB-B/197	AR
Walker, William R.	073	1881	WB-H/292	CTY
Walker, William S.	020	1896	WB-B/281	CTY
Walker, Willis	044	1892	WB-24/195	CTY
Walker, Willis	030	1801	WB-2/185	
Walker, Willis	104	1870	WB-6/42	AR
Walker, Willy S.	080	1878	WB-1/34	AR
Walkup, E. J.	097	c1892	WB-2/444	AR
Walkup, James A.	065	1874	WB-K/154	AR
Walkup, Pamelia R.	097	1880	WB-2/178	
Walkup, Robert	097	1846	WB-1/32	AR
Walkup, Samuel H.	097	1876	WB-2/104	AR
Walkup, Samuel P.	097	1885	WB-2/273	AR
Wall, Abraham	092	1807	WB-3/79	AR
Wall, Adam	090	1886	WB-6/167	AR
Wall, Alexander	084	1866	WB-D/58	CTY
Wall, Bennett	056	1861	WB-2/19	AR
Wall, Burrell	099	1834	RB-23/214	AR
Wall, C. J.	086	1898	WB-F/572	AR
Wall, Claybourn	084	c1802	OW/1	AR
Wall, Daniel	084	1846	WB-C/33	CTY
Wall, Delaney	051	1894	WB-C/489	AR

Name	Co.	Date	Recorded Copy	Original
Wall, Dorcit	037	1761	WB-A/55	AR
Wall, Edward F.	071	1892	WB-7/174	AR
Wall, Elijah	037	1761	WB-A/34	AR
Wall, Eliza H.	005	1889	WB-D/254	AR
Wall, Elizabeth	056	1857	WB-1/698	AR
Wall, Elizabeth	099	1834	RB-23/215	
Wall, Eveline R.	071	1892	WB-7/144	AR
Wall, George W.	084	1852	WB-C/138	CTY
Wall, Gerrird	037	1761	WB-A/19	AR
Wall, Henry	099	1866	RB-33/491	AR
Wall, Henry	084	1845	WB-C/29	CTY
Wall, Henry	065	1777	WB-F/216	AR
Wall, Henry	047	1817	WB-3/599	
Wall, Henry C.	082	1899	WB-7/23	AR
Wall, Irene	086	1887	WB-F/296	AR
Wall, Isaac	056	1884	WB-3/359	AR
Wall, James	069	1780	WB-1/10	AR
Wall, James	079	1895	WB-3/72	AR
Wall, James	009	1758	OWB/57	AR
Wall, James, Sr.	005	1854	WB-C/80	AR
Wall, Jeptha A.	026	1886	WB-2/300	AR
Wall, Jesse, Sr.	056	1842	WB-1/541	AR
Wall, John	037	1779	WB-B/15	AR
Wall, John	071	1793	WB-2/31	AR
Wall, John	099	1861	RB-32/86	AR
Wall, John	082	1831	WB-2/10	AR
Wall, John	VA	1808	Copy	071 AR
Wall, John	084	1846	WB-C/36	CTY
Wall, John	086	1832	WB-D/153	AR
Wall, John, Sr.	084	1842	WB-B/269	CTY
Wall, Joseph	009	c1791	OWB/259	AR
Wall, Joseph	009	1756	Orig. Only	SS/AR
Wall, Joseph M.	084	1863	WB-D/36	CTY
Wall, Joshua S.	084	1883	WB-E/273	CTY
Wall, Lucinda	102	1899	WB-A/173	AR
Wall, Margaret	073	1846	WB-F/301	AR
Wall, Mary	084	1860	WB-C/344	CTY
Wall, Mary E.	084	1888	WB-E/420	CTY
Wall, Mastin	090	1894	WB-6/352	AR
Wall, Mial	082	1868	WB-5/21	AR
Wall, Mildred J.	051	1887	WB-C/352	AR
Wall, Molly	056	1851	WB-1/643	AR
Wall, Nelson	081	1894	WB-16/335	AR
Wall, Perry	056	1836	WB-1/789	AR
Wall, R. M.	089	1895	WB-2/263	AR
Wall, Rebecca S.	099	1883	WB-A/420	AR
Wall, Richard	071	1755	SS 880/45	SS/AR
Wall, Robert	084	1844	WB-C/9	CTY
Wall, Robert	047	1799	WB-3/333	
Wall, Sallie S.	084	1885	WB-E/321	CTY
Wall, Samuel	081	1823	WB-5/130	AR
Wall, Samuel S.	090	1888	WB-6/187	AR
Wall, Sarah	037	1758	SS 882/150	SS/AR
Wall, Solomon	081	1864	WB-13/110	AR
Wall, Stephen	082	1846	WB-3/28	AR
Wall, Susan	084	1860	WB-C/343	CTY
Wall, Tabitha	038	1880	WB-2/381	AR
Wall, Wiley	099	1890	WB-B/448	AR
Wall, William	089	1854	WB-1/118	
Wall, William	089	c1851	WB-1/164	
Wall, William	082	1801	WB-1/83	AR
Wall, William	071	1841	WB-4/238	AR
Wall, William	056	1835	WB-1/507	AR
Wall, William M.	090	1886	WB-6/171	AR
Wall, Zachariah	084	1816	WB-A/321	CTY
Wall, Zachariah	084	1851	WB-C/120	CTY
Wallace, Aaron	016	1822	WB-A/80	AR
Wallace, Alexander	065	1808	WB-G/42	AR
Wallace, Alice	070	1893	WB-G/152	AR
Wallace, Archabald	028	1807	Orig. Only	AR
Wallace, Archibald	028	1856	WB-D/270	AR
Wallace, Benjamin	028	1821	WB-C/204	AR
Wallace, Catharine	065	1823	WB-G/13	AR
Wallace, Easter M.	059	1892	WB-B/33	CTY
Wallace, Frances	104	1873	WB-6/69	AR
Wallace, George	065	1803	WB-G/1	AR
Wallace, George F.	VA	1891	077 WB-H/328	
Wallace, Hannah B.	065	1856	WB-J/26	AR
Wallace, Hannah W.	032	1883	WB-3/405	AR
Wallace, I. N.	065	1887	WB-L/191	AR
Wallace, James	016	1795	WB-A/78	AR
Wallace, James	065	1874	WB-K/158	AR
Wallace, James A.	067	1870	WB-2/12	AR
Wallace, James B.	065	1867	WB-J/232	AR-Nunc.
Wallace, James H.	028	1810	WB-C/16	AR
Wallace, Jane	079	1876	WB-2/141	AR
Wallace, Jane C.	065	1888	WB-L/305	AR
Wallace, Jannet	028	1852	WB-D/195	AR
Wallace, John	044	1762	Orig. Only	CTY
Wallace, John	009	1794	OWB/296	AR
Wallace, John	065	1812	WB-G/51	AR
Wallace, John C.	054	1896	WB-6/42	CTY
Wallace, John C.	019	c1840	Orig. Only	AR
Wallace, John M.	016	c1827	WB-A/21	AR
Wallace, John R.	035	1873	WB-4/73	AR
Wallace, John, Jr.	016	1795	WB-A/77	AR
Wallace, Joseph	019	1805	Orig. Only	AR
Wallace, Joseph	065	1783	WB-F/223	AR
Wallace, Joseph	028	1826	WB-C/274	AR
Wallace, Joseph S.	086	1869	WB-F/16	
Wallace, Lydia	065	1828	WB-A/163	AR
Wallace, M. A.	016	1864	WB-2/116	AR
Wallace, M. B.	065	1883	WB-K/552	AR
Wallace, Malinda	065	1874	WB-K/163	AR
Wallace, Malinda S.	001	1894	WB-2/580	AR
Wallace, Mary	024	c1792	WB-A/68	AR
Wallace, Mary	028	1817	WB-C/150	AR
Wallace, Mary E.	040	1880	WB-2/155	AR
Wallace, Matilda	065	1874	WB-K/160	AR
Wallace, Matthew	065	1838	WB-H/53	AR
Wallace, Matthew	065	1862	WB-J/135	AR
Wallace, Matthew	065	1824	WB-G/63	AR
Wallace, Matthew	065	1852	WB-I/246	AR
Wallace, Matthew	065	1851	WB-I/178	AR
Wallace, Matthew L.	065	1865	WB-J/197	AR
Wallace, Michael	047	1771	WB-1/291	
Wallace, Nancey	047	1835	WB-4/122	
Wallace, Nancy	079	1900	WB-3/211	AR
Wallace, Nathaniel	089	1900	WB-2/336	AR
Wallace, R. B.	065	1897	WB-M/538	AR
Wallace, Rebekah	019	1824	WB-E/29	AR
Wallace, Reuben	019	1804	WB-E/20	AR
Wallace, Reuel	054	1857	WB-3/117	AR
Wallace, Richard	072	1774	RW/L19	AR
Wallace, Robert	028	1824	WB-C/247	AR
Wallace, Robert	035	1893	WB-4/422	AR
Wallace, Robert, Sr.	028	1796	WB-B/1	AR
Wallace, Shadrach	077	1837	WB-F/270	AR
Wallace, Stephen	028	1791	WB-A/248	AR
Wallace, Stephen D.	070	1889	WB-F/254	AR

Name	Co.	Date	Recorded Copy	Original
Wallace, Susan	065	1880	WB-K/374	AR
Wallace, Thomas	030	1747	Orig. Only	SS/AR
Wallace, Thomas	028	1860	WB-D/331	AR
Wallace, Thomas	035	1892	WB-4/414	AR
Wallace, W. W.	019	c1796	Orig. Only	AR
Wallace, William	063	1775	Orig. Only	SS/AR
Wallace, William	054	c1824	WB-2/9	AR
Wallace, William	065	1824	WB-G/58	AR
Wallace, William	016	c1832	WB-A/26	AR
Wallace, William	082	1853	WB-4/63	AR
Wallace, Williamson	065	1869	WB-K/1	AR
Wallach, Isidor	NY	1887	013 WB-B/570	013 AR
Waller, Carter	044	1860	WB-21/245	CTY
Waller, Commilla	085	c1868	WB-1/10	CTY
Waller, Elizabeth	044	1898	WB-24/395	CTY
Waller, Eve	085	1870	WB-1/57	CTY
Waller, Henry	092	1783	WB-2/11A	AR
Waller, Henry	090	1839	WB-4/50	
Waller, James	037	1869	WB-G/324	AR
Waller, James	035	1823	WB-A/487	AR
Waller, James	037	1808	WB-D/315	AR
Waller, John	047	1762	WB-1/50	
Waller, John	044	1877	WB-23/289	CTY
Waller, Joseph	059	1879	WB-A/166	CTY
Waller, Margaret	037	1830	WB-F/109	AR
Waller, Mary	085	1896	WB-3/150	CTY
Waller, N. A.	044	1886	WB-23/555	CTY
Waller, Nancy	044	1858	WB-20/486	CTY
Waller, S. E.	044	1896	WB-24/324	CTY
Waller, Thomas	002	1687	Orig. Only	SS/AR
Waller, William	047	1804	WB-3/423	
Waller, Zepheniah	044	1797	WB-4/63	CTY
Walles, John	024	c1756	Orig. Only	AR
Walles, Mary	030	1832	WB-3/328	
Wallice, George	047	1787	WB-3/127	
Walling, Elizabeth	009	1895	WB-2/63	CTY
Wallis, Alexander	065	c1828	WB G/202	AR
Wallis, Andrew	028	1745	SS 877/33	SS/AR
Wallis, Charles	009	1867	OB-M/144	AR
Wallis, E. C.	065	1873	WB-K/118	AR
Wallis, Ezekiel	065	1813	WB-G/6	AR
Wallis, Hardy	009	1894	WB-2/33	CTY
Wallis, James	104	1818	WB-3/169	AR
Wallis, James	065	1820	WB-G/20	AR
Wallis, John	009	c1791	OWB/257	AR
Wallis, John	024	c1771	WB-B/57	AR
Wallis, John	019	1768	RB-A/30	AR
Wallis, Johnathan	009	c1773	OWB/117	AR
Wallis, Joseph G.	003	1870	WB-B/15	AR
Wallis, Mary	070	1811	WB-AB/162	AR
Wallis, Mary	065	1879	WB-K/313	AR
Wallis, Miles	001	c1844	WB-1/24	AR
Wallis, Miles	001	c1849	Orig. Only	AR
Wallis, Rebecca	001	c1850	WB-1/29	AR
Wallis, Sarah	019	1801	WB-E/17	AR
Wallis, Sarah	019	1785	WB-E/11	AR
Wallis, Stephen	028	1757	SS 880/190	SS/AR
Wallis, Thomas	024	1750	Orig. Only	SS/AR
Wallis, Thomas	009	1831	OB-B/131	AR
Wallis, Thomas	081	1800	WB-2/67	AR-Nunc.
Wallis, Thomas M.	028	1752	DB-5/278	
Wallis, William	065	1829	WB-D/118	AR
Wallis, William	009	1749	SS 877/264	SS/AR
Wallis, William C.	009	1895	WB-2/56	CTY
Walliss, John	072	1751	Orig. Only	SS/AR
Walliss, John	072	1751	028 DB-5/164	
Wallkings, W. C.	070	1856	WB-C/617	
Walls, George	038	1863	WB-1/216	AR
Walls, John	029	c1783	Orig. Only	AR
Walls, John	086	1792	Orig. Only	AR
Walls, Joshua	.053	1805	RW-1/387	AR
Walls, Joshua	030	1752	Orig. Only	SS/AR
Walls, Rachael	009	1847	OB-F/324	AR
Walmrley, John	030	1803	WB-3/221	
Walser, Elizabeth	032	1894	WB-4/211	AR
Walser, Frederic	032	1837	WB-1/296	
Walser, H. C.	032	1879	WB-3/262	AR
Walser, Jacob	032	1879	WB-3/289	AR
Walser, John	032	1888	WB-4/6	AR
Walser, Philip	032	c1859	WB-2/192	AR
Walser, Sarah C.	032	1897	WB-4/320	AR
Walser, William	032	1879	WB-3/259	AR
Walston, Ambrose	018	1871	WB-E/12	AR
Walston, Ambrose	018	1855	WB-D/22	
Walston, Ambrose	018	c1870	Copy	075 AR
Walston, Jeptha	079	1869	WB-2/16	AR
Walston, John	045	1891	WB-1/277	AR
Walston, John	037	1892	WB-H/226	AR
Walston, Jonas	037	1816	WB-E/125	AR
Walston, Josiah	047	1892	WB-7/36	AR
Walston, Littleton	037	1874	WB-G/461	AR
Walston, London	053	1728	SS 876/134	SS/AR
Walston, Margarett	018	1851	WB-C/356	
Walston, Mary	037	1898	WB-H/405	AR
Walston, Mary J.	079	1891	WB-2/558	AR
Walston, Noah	018	1866	WB-D/77	AR
Walston, Sarah	077	1821	WB-F/35	AR
Walston, Silas	037	1815	WB-E/109	AR
Walston, Thomas	018	1836	WB-C/198	
Walston, William	037	1880	WB-G/561	AR
Walston, William	105	1892	WB-3/23	
Walston, William C.	018	1837	WB-C/209	
Walter, Alfred	016	1891	WB-4/71	AR
Walter, James	056	c1816	WB-1/272	AR
Walter, Laurance	089	1863	WB-1/287	
Walter, Louis	NY	1895	071 WB-7/260	071 AR
Walter, Mary	047	1809	WB-3/488	
Walters, Azariah G.	VA	1899	020 WB-B/375	020 CTY
Walters, Celia	059	1886	WB-A/442	CTY
Walters, Daniel	078	1820	WI-8/309	AR
Walters, Dave	070	1900	WB-H/327	
Walters, Edward P.	078	1886	WB-19/196	AR
Walters, Elijah	097	1849	WB-1/56	AR
Walters, Elizabeth	041	1807	WB-2/3	AR
Walters, Haywood	059	1891	WB-B/30	CTY
Walters, Isaac	041	1816	WB-2/112	AR
Walters, Isaac	041	1801	WB-1/184	AR
Walters, Jacob	041	1794	WB-1/129	AR
Walters, James Bray	041	1784	WB-1/38	AR
Walters, Jeremiah	083	1853	WB-2/51	
Walters, Joel B.	020	1893	WB-B/148	CTY
Walters, John	082	1785	WB-1/22	AR
Walters, Joseph	070	1763	DB-E/33	
Walters, Lewis	041	1832	WB-2/310	AR
Walters, Paul, Sr.	016	1835	PQS.5/352	AR
Walters, Richard	092	1882	WB-6/172	AR
Walters, Sarah	070	1757	Orig. Only	SS/AR
Walters, Simon	041	1876	WB-4/81	AR
Walters, Speer	083	1873	WB-3/55	AR
Walters, William	041	1804	WB-1/212	AR

Name	Co.	Date	Recorded Copy	Original
Walters, William	083	1858	WB-2/142	AR
Walters, William T.	099	1877	RB-35/367	AR
Walthall, Branch	099	1828	RB-20/181	AR
Walthall, Judith	056	1847	WB-1/601	AR
Walthorp, John	071	1795	WB-2/68	AR
Walthrop, Mitcheil	071	1791	WB-1/438	
Waltis, Polley	078	1843	WI-15/174	AR
Walton, Alfred J.	041	1874	WB-4/48	AR
Walton, Alse	046	1791	WB-A/405	AR
Walton, Celia	010	1862	WB-H/116	AR
Walton, Conrad	085	1811	WB-G/205	AR
Walton, George	086	1835	WB-E/18	AR
Walton, George	024	1826	WB-C/124	AR
Walton, Henry, Sr.	041	1820	WB-2/166	AR
Walton, Hilda	078	1826	Orig. Only	AR
Walton, Jacob	041	1825	WB-2/234	AR
Walton, James	010	1841	WB-G/336	AR
Walton, James	072	c1813	WB-A/136	AR
Walton, James	072	c1773	RW/L43	AR
Walton, John	010	1828	WB-G/179	
Walton, John	024	1798	WB-A/342	AR
Walton, John	044	1811	WB-7/170	CTY
Walton, John	072	1885	WB-4/159	AR
Walton, John B.	041	1829	WB-2/280	AR
Walton, Jonathan	056	1806	WB-1/185	AR
Walton, Lewis	081	1864	WB-13/104	AR
Walton, Lewis	010	1895	WB-I/460	AR
Walton, Martha	014	1868	WB-1/50	AR
Walton, Mary	073	1792	WB-B/209	AR
Walton, Mary C.	099	1894	WB-C/271	AR
Walton, Nancy	078	1847	Orig. Only	AR
Walton, Nancy	086	1860	WB-E/373	AR
Walton, Nathaniel	073	c1771	WB-A/131	
Walton, Palatiah	024	c1776	WB-A/173	AR
Walton, Peter	085	1849	WB-K/80	AR
Walton, Rachel	024	1868	WB-D/63	AR
Walton, Richard	085	1814	WB-G/312	AR
Walton, Robert	020	1877	WB-A/228	CTY
Walton, Samuel	099	1850	RB-27/40	AR
Walton, Sarah	024	c1761	WB-A/182	AR
Walton, Thomas	041	1788	WB-1/74	AR
Walton, Thomas	072	1804	WB-A/141	AR
Walton, Thomas	024	1751	Orig. Only	SS/AR
Walton, Thomas	024	1719	SS 875/145	
Walton, Thomas R.	085	1876	WB-1/355	CTY
Walton, Timothy	024	c1770	WB-A/172	AR
Walton, Treacy	024	c1841	WB-C/262	AR
Walton, William	024	c1760	WB-A/183	AR
Walton, William	024	c1771	WB-A/177	AR
Waman, William	075	1721	SS 875/283	SS/AR
Waman, William	075	1740	Orig. Only	SS/AR
Wammack, Martha	047	1841	WB-4/197	
Wanick, Daniel	046	1822	WB-B/151	AR
Waples, Nathaniel	057	1852	WB-B/213	AR
War, William	071	1756	SS 880/44	SS/AR
Warbleton, Kisiah	069	1896	WB-5/554	AR
Warborton, James	010	1780	WB-B/161	AR
Warborton, John	010	1762	WB-A/64	AR
Warborton, Winifred	010	1785	WB-D/26	AR
Warburton, James W.	010	1818	WB-G/41	AR
Warburton, William	024	1799	WB-A/313	AR
Ward, Aaron	024	1832	WB-C/160	AR
Ward, Agnes	090	1894	WB-6/340	AR
Ward, Alfred	073	1887	WB-H/427	CTY
Ward, Alfred	035	1868	WB-4/3	AR

Name	Co.	Date	Recorded Copy	Original
Ward, Alsaly	077	1827	WB-F/132	AR
Ward, Amelia	063	c1856	WB-2/517	
Ward, Ann	046	1875	WB-E/136	AR
Ward, Ann	027	1848	WB-A/56	AR
Ward, Anthony	070	1779	WB-C/441	AR
Ward, Anthony	096	c1797	Orig. Only	AR
Ward, Arthur	027	1865	WB-A/99	AR
Ward, Asa	105	1882	WB-2/289	
Ward, Avis	019	1856	WB-A/186 & 201	AR
Ward, Benajah	056	1848	WB-1/610	AR
Ward, Benjamin	081	1818	WB-4/595	AR
Ward, Benjamin	072	c1767	RW/L64	AR
Ward, Benjamin	006	1820	WB-A/20	AR
Ward, Benjamin	072	1845	WB-2/69	AR
Ward, Benjamin	044	1774	WB-1/25	CTY
Ward, Benjamin	047	1827	WB-4/33	
Ward, Benjamin	100	1788	WB-5/40	AR
Ward, Caesar	072	1893	WB-4/297	AR
Ward, Catharine	037	1872	WB-G/409	AR
Ward, Celia	063	1853	WB-2/398	
Ward, Charles	060	1787	Orig. Only	AR
Ward, Charles	092	1780	WB-1/140	AR
Ward, Charlotte	037	1855	WB-G/111	AR
Ward, Comfort	070	1897	WB-G/558	AR
Ward, Conrad	021	1855	WB-1/121	AR
Ward, D. A.	103	1900	WB-2/305	AR
Ward, David	072	1801	WB-A/147	AR
Ward, David L.	085	c1808	Copy	033 AR
Ward, David L.	085	c1808	WB-G/113	
Ward, Demby	010	1858	WB-H/74	AR
Ward, Dorsey C.	024	1898	WB-E/285	AR
Ward, E. A.	105	1893	WB-3/142	AR
Ward, E. W.	060	1897	WB-5/66	AR
Ward, Eason	010	1860	WB-H/89	AR
Ward, Ebenezer	046	1863	WB-D/168	AR
Ward, Eber B.	MI	1875	061 WB-2/236	061 AR
Ward, Edward	072	c1765	Orig. Only	AR
Ward, Edward	073	1846	WB-F/286	AR
Ward, Edward	072	1812	WB-A/149	AR
Ward, Edward	072	1836	WB-A/156	AR
Ward, Edward H.	022	1896	WB-F/28	AR
Ward, Eli	067	1885	WB-2/198	AR
Ward, Elijah	081	1820	WB-4/735	AR
Ward, Elisha	010	1843	WB-G/350	AR
Ward, Elizabeth	072	c1767	RW/L49	AR
Ward, Elizabeth	077	c1840	Orig. Only	AR
Ward, Enoch	019	1750	028 DB-5/148	SS/AR
Ward, Enoch	083	1871	WB-3/35	AR
Ward, Enoch	050	1887	WB-2/8	CTY
Ward, Enoch	072	c1762	RW/L57	AR
Ward, Fannie G.	044	1889	WB-24/82	CTY
Ward, Frances	063	1798	WB-1/353	
Ward, Francis	069	1800	WB-1/133	AR
Ward, Francis	096	1772	WB-1/71	AR
Ward, Franklin	054	1862	WB-3/167	AR
Ward, G. W.	105	1892	WB-3/33	AR
Ward, George	072	1803	Orig. Only	AR
Ward, George J.	072	1860	WB-2/178	
Ward, George W.	010	c1881	WB-I/161	
Ward, Humphrey	024	1821	WB-C/94	AR
Ward, Humphrey	024	1884	WB-E/130	AR
Ward, James	073	1855	WB-G/102	AR
Ward, James	010	1843	WB-G/351	AR
Ward, James	010	1780	WB-B/165	

Name	Co.	Date	Recorded Copy	Original
Ward, James	024	1785	WB-A/294	AR
Ward, James	024	1745	Orig. Only	AR
Ward, James M.	046	1896	WB-F/553	AR
Ward, James W.	046	1891	WB-F/106	AR
Ward, James, Sr.	063	1825	WB-2/105	
Ward, Jane	019	1868	WB-B/41	AR
Ward, Jeremiah	024	1850	WB-C/313	AR
Ward, Jesse	027	1896	WB-2/121	AR
Ward, Jesse	019	1845	WB-A/124	AR
Ward, John	075	1806	WB-M1/123	AR
Ward, John	021	1879	WB-2/204	
Ward, John	027	c1859	WB-2/182	
Ward, John	090	1838	WB-4/32	AR
Ward, John	099	1787	RB-2/127	AR
Ward, John	024	1748	Orig. Only	SS/AR
Ward, John	035	1839	Orig. Only	AR
Ward, John	069	1870	Orig. Only	AR
Ward, John	096	1750	028 DB-5/138	SS/AR
Ward, John	063	1810	WB-1/433	
Ward, John D.	037	1823	WB-F/3	AR
Ward, John F.	083	1898	WB-4/178	AR
Ward, John L.	100	1836	WB-35/308	AR
Ward, John R.	073	1876	WB-H/149	CTY
Ward, John, Sr.	035	1777	WB-A/534	
Ward, John, Sr.	045	c1795	Copy	028 AR
Ward, Jonathan	024	1854	WB-C/358	AR
Ward, Jonathan	009	1887	WB-1/410	CTY
Ward, Joseph	047	1826	WB-4/25	
Ward, Joseph	072	c1760	RW/L49	AR
Ward, Joseph	071	1879	077 WB-H/90	077 AR
Ward, Joseph	077	1879	WB-H/90	AR
Ward, Joseph	073	1833	WB-E/296	AR
Ward, Joshua	SC	1869	093 WB-1/91	
Ward, Josiah	072	1849	WB-2/97	AR
Ward, Katherine	033	1897	WB-2/200	CTY
Ward, Lemuel	071	1889	WB-7/46	AR
Ward, Louisa	070	1845	WB-AB/434	AR
Ward, Louisa	063	1883	WB-3/237	
Ward, Louisa T.	079	1870	WB-2/44	AR
Ward, Luke	073	1878	WB-H/178	CTY
Ward, Luke	035	1796	WB-A/526	AR
Ward, Luke, Sr.	037	c1838	WB-F/234	AR
Ward, Margaret	024	1836	WB-C/191	AR
Ward, Maria	072	1834	WB-1/126	AR
Ward, Martha	022	c1833	Copy	081 AR
Ward, Martha	022	1834	WB-C/10	
Ward, Mary	079	1896	WB-3/99	AR
Ward, Mary	087	1885	WB-3/320	AR
Ward, Mary	053	1838	WB-6/35	
Ward, Mary A. M.	063	1891	WB-4/59	AR
Ward, Mary E.	063	1869	WB-3/1	
Ward, Matilda	090	1896	WB-6/406	AR
Ward, Michael	010	1803	WB-E/210	AR
Ward, Morris	057	1834	WB-B/122	AR
Ward, Nancy	037	1854	WB-G/57	AR
Ward, Nancy	073	1867	WB-G/518	CTY
Ward, Nancy	087	1888	WB-3/389	AR
Ward, Nancy	103	1864	RD-13/752	AR
Ward, Nancy	024	1895	WB-E/253	AR
Ward, Nancy	087	1888	035 WB-4/317	035 AR
Ward, Nathan	104	1873	WB-6/66	AR
Ward, Nathan	041	1858	WB-3/230	AR
Ward, Nathan	069	1823	WB-1/311	AR
Ward, Nathan	070	1796	WB-C/454	AR
Ward, Needham	105	1859	WB-1/57	AR
Ward, Needham	045	1831	Copy	037 AR
Ward, Olive	029	1828	WB-B/157	AR
Ward, Orren U.	022	1892	WB-E/478	AR
Ward, Permelia	020	1859	RB-S/159	AR
Ward, Peter	090	1871	WB-6/22	AR
Ward, Peter D.	032	c1862	WB-2/339	
Ward, Phillip	010	1777	WB-B/78	AR
Ward, Polser	060	1841	WB-2/74	AR
Ward, Priscilla	035	1828	WB-A/515	AR
Ward, Quinton H.	024	1891	WB-E/185	AR
Ward, Rachel	024	1794	WB-B/68	AR
Ward, Rachel	022	1804	WB-A/90	AR
Ward, Reddick	101	1897	WB-A/286	
Ward, Reuben	067	1889	WB-2/273	AR
Ward, Richard	100	1789	WB-5/29	AR
Ward, Richard	039	1850	WB-N/326	AR
Ward, Richard	072	c1774	RW/L1	AR
Ward, Richard	072	1825	WB-A/143	AR
Ward, Richard G.	072	1893	WB-4/289	AR
Ward, Robert	022	1833	WB-B/250	AR
Ward, Robert	092	1778	WB-1/104	AR
Ward, Rosana	028	1899	WB-F/413	
Ward, S. E.	083	1888	WB-3/418	AR
Ward, Sallie E.	010	1898	WB-I/558	
Ward, Sarah	028	1795	WB-A/337	AR
Ward, Seth	100	1820	WB-22/290	AR
Ward, Seth	072	1787	WI/L37	AR
Ward, Shadrick	073	c1880	WB-H/317	AR
Ward, Shadrick	024	1839	WB-C/271	AR
Ward, Silas	037	1832	WB-F/135	AR
Ward, Sollomon	037	1827	WB-F/67	AR
Ward, Solomon	037	1843	WB-F/293	AR
Ward, Solomon	072	1804	WB-A/140	AR
Ward, Spencer	047	1896	WB-7/162	AR
Ward, Spious	103	1847	RD-9/458	AR
Ward, Stephen	073	1837	WB-E/417	AR
Ward, Stewart	101	1889	WB-A/174	
Ward, Susannah	073	1822	WB-E/18	AR
Ward, Thomas	024	c1756	Orig. Only	AR
Ward, Thomas	081	1793	WB-1/125	AR
Ward, Thomas	024	c1798	WB-A/329	AR
Ward, Thomas	100	1880	WB-51/146	AR
Ward, Thomas	024	1751	Orig. Only	SS/AR
Ward, Thomas	024	c1793	WB-A/91	AR
Ward, Thomas	010	1790	WB-D/125	AR
Ward, Thomas	010	1796	WB-D/358	AR
Ward, Thomas	024	c1772	WB-A/188	AR
Ward, Thomas	087	1856	WB-1/484	AR
Ward, Thomas L.	102	1900	WB-A/181	AR
Ward, Thomas M.	069	1897	WB-6/10	AR
Ward, Timothy	024	1879	WB-E/288	AR
Ward, Timothy	081	1801	WB-2/77	AR
Ward, W. J.	099	1883	WB-A/477	AR
Ward, William	024	1827	WB-C/130	AR
Ward, William	063	c1793	WB-1/192	
Ward, William	075	1753	Orig. Only	AR
Ward, William	073	1889	WB-H/478	CTY
Ward, William	010	1842	WB-G/342	AR
Ward, William	100	1829	WB-32/86	AR
Ward, William	087	1836	WB-1/190	AR
Ward, William	081	c1801	WB-2/125	AR
Ward, William	024	1829	WB-C/155	AR
Ward, William	073	1884	WB-H/337	CTY
Ward, William	010	1858	WB-H/61	AR
Ward, William	070	1770	WB-C/433	AR-Nunc.

Name	Co.	Date	Recorded Copy	Original
Ward, William	099	1797	RB-3/412	AR
Ward, William	032	c1862	WB-2/285	
Ward, William	022	1832	WB-B/235	AR
Ward, William	073	1800	WB-C/164	AR
Ward, William	085	1818	WB-G/516	AR
Ward, William J.	090	1855	WB-4/292	AR
Ward, William N.	054	1886	WB-5/93	CTY
Ward, William R.	035	1892	WB-4/410	AR
Ward, William S.	019	1867	WB-B/33	AR
Ward, William S.	010	1810	WB-F/149	AR
Ward, William W.	063	1840	SC/05808	AR-Copy
Ward, William W.	063	1840	WB-2/267	
Ward, Willis	069	1859	WB-1/563	AR
Warden, Ann	029	1889	WB-E/463	AR
Warden, William	022	1894	WB-E/558	AR
Wardlaw, William	084	1880	WB-E/187	CTY
Wardlow, Ester	084	1838	WB-B/191	CTY
Wardlow, James	084	c1790	OW/216	AR
Wardlow, John	084	1831	WB-B/42	CTY
Wardlow, Patrick	084	1808	WB-A/129	CTY
Wardworth, Edward	075	1762	WB-H/35	AR
Ware, Alfred B.	026	1893	WB-2/472	AR
Ware, Ansel	020	1873	WB-A/102	CTY
Ware, Francis	020	1846	RB-P/340	AR
Ware, James T.	020	1891	WB-B/47	CTY
Ware, John Abel	026	1883	WB-2/248	AR
Ware, Martha	020	1799	RB-C/354	
Ware, Samuel	073	1831	WB-E/265	AR
Ware, Thomas	020	1845	RB-P/185	
Ware, Thomas	020	1886	WB-A/485	CTY
Ware, Thomas T.	044	1873	WB-23/118	CTY
Warford, Joseph	085	c1798	WB-D/229	AR
Warlick, Absalam	026	1873	WB-2/68	
Warlick, Andrew	026	1882	WB-2/236	AR
Warlick, Catharine	021	1873	WB-2/90	
Warlick, Daniel	026	1841	WB-1/2	AR
Warlick, David	026	1850	WB-1/111	AR
Warlick, David E.	021	1891	WB-2/536	AR
Warlick, John	040	1861	WB-1/130	
Warlick, John Lewis	014	c1865	WB-1/1	AR
Warlick, L. F.	014	1893	WB-2/508	CTY
Warlick, Lawson	040	1872	WB-2/45	AR
Warlick, Lyda	040	1884	WB-2/225	AR
Warlick, Lydia	040	1898	WB-3/12	AR
Warlick, Margaret	060	1872	WB-4/87	AR
Warlick, Maxwell	060	1894	WB-4/533	
Warlick, Peter	021	1878	WB-2/180	AR
Warlick, Phillip	014	1878	WB-2/157	
Warlick, R. F.	026	1891	WB-2/431	AR
Warlow, Peter	085	c1781	WB-B/139	AR
Warming, Abraham	024	N. D.	Orig. Only	SS/AR
Warmington, Britannia	053	c1796	RW-1/277	
Warmoth, John	039	1816	WB-E/123	AR
Warnack, Abraham	091	1894	WB-1/192	
Warner, Adam	009	1894	WB-2/42	CTY
Warner, Benjamin	038	1851	WB-1/61	AR
Warner, Benjamin	009	1873	WB-1/111	CTY
Warner, Elizabeth	032	1830	WB-1/151	
Warner, Francis	009	c1781	OWB/161	AR
Warner, Hardin	068	1877	WB-D/106	
Warner, James	053	c1802	RW-1/368	
Warner, James H.	053	1879	WB-11/88	AR
Warner, Rhoda	075	1795	WB-L/30	AR
Warner, William	085	c1804	WB-E/6	AR
Warnick, Moses	083	1846	WB-1/491	
Warnier, Deborah	024	1835	Orig. Only	AR
Warnock, Samuel	090	1798	WB-1/109	AR
Warr, James	071	1796	WB-2/118	AR
Warr, Joyce	071	1789	WB-1/386	AR
Warr, Millie	071	1801	WB-2/219	AR
Warren (Welch), Sarah	077	c1730	Orig. Only	SS/AR
Warren, A. E.	026	1880	WB-2/201	AR
Warren, Abraham	077	c1710	SS 875/19	
Warren, Alva D.	009	1842	OB-D/363	AR
Warren, America	051	1890	WB-C/415	AR
Warren, Ann	028	1810	WB-C/15	AR
Warren, Bartemeous	020	1899	WB-B/371	CTY
Warren, Bennett	087	1889	WB-3/418	AR
Warren, David	073	1857	WB-G/189	AR
Warren, Derry	009	1893	WB-1/556	CTY
Warren, Drew H.	009	1886	WB-1/400	CTY
Warren, Edward	041	1789	WB-1/81	AR
Warren, Edward J.	009	1877	WB-1/179	AR
Warren, Elizabeth	033	1856	WB-1/128	AR
Warren, Emma C.	068	1895	WB-D/451	
Warren, Everard	009	1889	WB-1/467	CTY
Warren, Frank L.	020	1882	WB-A/355	CTY
Warren, George	099	1807	RB-7/216 & 309	AR
Warren, Henry	008	1717	SS 875/123	SS/AR
Warren, Henry	099	1811	RB-10/62	AR
Warren, Henry	008	1717	009 DB-1/275	
Warren, Isaiah	087	1847	WB-1/326	AR
Warren, James	075	1869	WB-O/5	AR
Warren, James	020	1817	RB-G/351	AR
Warren, James	020	1894	WB-B/175	CTY
Warren, James A.	037	1863	WB-G/227	AR
Warren, Jesse	071	1786	WB-1/370	AR
Warren, John	073	1890	WB-H/498	CTY
Warren, John	020	1899	WB-B/369	CTY
Warren, John	020	1817	RB-G/351	
Warren, John R.	079	1898	WB-3/167	AR
Warren, Joseph	057	1790	WB-A/75	AR
Warren, Joseph H.	063	c1790	WB-1/169	
Warren, Joseph L.	NJ	1890	077 WB-H/196	077 AR
Warren, Julia Ann	036	1897	WB-A/420	CTY
Warren, Maria L.	024	c1870	Orig. Only	AR
Warren, Martha A.	020	1895	WB-B/189	CTY
Warren, Mary	069	1852	WB-1/528	AR
Warren, Mary A.	070	1848	WB-C/488	AR
Warren, Mary A.	003	1887	WB-B/202	AR
Warren, Michael	071	1817	WB-3/192	AR
Warren, Nathaniel	099	1849	RB-26/538	AR
Warren, Peter M.	006	1894	WB-E/280	AR
Warren, Priscilla	037	1820	WB-E/256	AR
Warren, Redding	009	1872	WB-1/103	AR
Warren, Richard	087	1851	WB-1/390	AR
Warren, Robert	013	1845	WB-A/101	
Warren, Robert	063	c1779	WB-1/86	
Warren, Robert	071	1795	WB-2/102	AR
Warren, Robert	051	1846	WB-A/248	
Warren, Sarah C.	051	1898	WB-C/545	AR
Warren, Solomon	046	c1855	WB-E/84	AR
Warren, Susan J.	046	1895	WB-F/429	AR
Warren, Thelma D.	024	1878	WB-E/59	AR
Warren, Thomas	047	1839	WB-4/185	
Warren, Thomas H.	009	1898	WB-2/152	CTY
Warren, Valentine	028	1891	WB-E/573	
Warren, Westley	020	1883	WB-A/385	CTY
Warren, William	081	1790	WB-1/84	AR
Warren, William	N	1723	Orig. Only	SS/AR

Name	Co.	Date	Recorded Copy	Original
Warren, William	020	1860	RB-S/294	AR
Warren, William	010	1788	WB-D/93	AR
Warren, William	041	1797	WB-1/150	AR
Warren, William	078	1857	WB-17/482	AR
Warren, William	078	1816	WI-7/86	AR
Warren, Willis	069	1886	WB-5/245	AR
Warrick, Andrew	020	1804	RB-E/125	AR
Warrick, Honer	029	1841	WB-B/350	
Warrick, Jacob	103	1794	WI-A/509	AR
Warrick, Jobe	103	1879	WB-1/172	AR
Warrick, John	020	1812	RB-F/251	AR
Warrick, John	029	1833	WB-B/224	AR
Warrin, Abraham	077	1740	LGB-4/#120	SS/AR
Warrin, Albert	078	1862	WB-18/276	AR
Warrin, John	078	1795	WI-1/162	AR
Warrin, Robert	047	1759	SS 881/226	SS/AR
Warrin, Robert, Sr.	073	1776	Nunc.	071 AR
Warrington, Elizabeth	075	1827	WB-N/40	AR
Warrington, John	096	1800	WB-2/1	AR
Warrock, John J.	071	1892	WB-7/157	AR
Warrock, William S.	070	1900	WB-H/269	AR
Warsden, Nelly	004	1881	WB-A/45	AR
Warsham, John	085	c1806	Orig. Only	AR
Warsharsky, Daniel	105	1879	WB-2/258	AR
Warterer, Thomas	059	1855	Copy	039 AR
Warters, Chelly	059	1879	WB-A/169	CTY
Warters, Delia F.	045	1882	WB-1/79	AR
Warters, Isaac	059	1873	WB-A/91	
Warters, Isaac	009	1843	OB-E/136	AR
Warters, Isaac, Sr.	009	c1808	OB-A/17	AR
Warters, James	059	1874	WB-A/74	
Warters, James L.	009	1870	WB-1/48	AR
Warters, James R.	045	1878	Orig. Only	AR
Warters, John	009	N. D.	OWB/560	AR
Warters, William	059	1896	WB-B/160	CTY
Warton, Abraham	057	1810	WB-A/323	AR-Nunc.
Warvil, Daniel	085	c1807	Orig. Only	AR
Warvil, Jacob	085	c1804	WB-E/2	AR
Warwick, Benjamin	087	c1797	Orig. Only	AR
Warwick, Charlotte	070	1822	WB-C/462	AR
Warwick, George	083	1860	WB-2/158	AR
Warwick, John	083	1888	WB-3/412	AR
Warwick, John	009	c1789	OWB/234	AR
Wasden, Elizabeth	VA	1898	071 WB-7/385	071 AR
Wasden, Uriah	071	1887	WB-6/572	AR
Wasdin, Jonathan	103	1795	WI-B/74	AR
Wasdit, James	071	1817	WB-3/198	AR
Washam, Alexander	065	1862	WB-J/140	AR
Washam, Alfred	065	1897	WB-N/37	AR
Washam, Sarah C.	065	1871	WB-K/72	AR
Washam, Thomas	065	1882	WB-K/531	AR
Washburn, Abraham	026	1874	WB-2/124	AR
Washburn, Gabriel	086	1826	WB-D/47	AR
Washington, Barbary	044	1836	WB-13/430	CTY
Washington, Elizabeth	073	1858	WB-G/200	AR
Washington, Elizabeth	044	1859	WB-21/48	CTY
Washington, Ephriam	044	1867	WB-22/538	CTY
Washington, Etheldred	071	1768	WB-1/163	
Washington, James	071	1766	WB-1/132	
Washington, James	071	1798	WB-2/167	AR
Washington, John	044	1826	WB-10/179	CTY
Washington, John	071	1768	WB-1/170	
Washington, John	044	1844	WB-16/77	CTY
Washington, Julia	VA	1895	013 WB-C/357	013 AR
Washington, Lansdon	056	1761	WB-1/749	AR
Washington, Richard	051	1765	Orig. Only	AR-Copy
Washington, Robert	071	1770	WB-1/183	
Washington, William	044	1840	WB-14/567	CTY
Washington, Woodson	044	1874	WB-23/192	CTY
Washington, Woodson	044	1881	WB-23/422	CTY
Washington, Zebadiah	071	1840	WB-4/212	AR
Wasner, John	085	1815	WB-G/365	AR
Wason, Archibald	085	c1785	WB-C/84	AR
Wasson, Joseph	054	c1794	WB-1/248	AR
Wasson, William	013	1856	WB-A/182	
Waterfield, Abraham	030	1830	WB-3/256	
Waterfield, Amy	030	1838	WB-4/45	
Waterfield, Ann B.	030	1898	WB-5/264	AR
Waterfield, Elizabeth	030	1877	WB-5/53	AR
Waterfield, John	030	1803	WB-2/224	
Waterfield, John	030	1875	WB-5/37 & 52	
Waterfield, John J.	030	1866	WB-4/256	AR
Waterfield, Johnson	030	1895	WB-5/225	AR
Waterfield, Lydia	030	1854	WB-4/184	AR
Waterfield, Lydia	030	1852	WB-4/166	
Waterfield, Lydia	030	1857	WB-4/212	
Waterfield, Malachi	030	1871	WB-5/13	
Waterfield, Mary	030	c1814	WB-3/36	
Waterfield, Mary Janet	030	1895	WB-5/223	AR
Waterfield, Michal	030	1856	WB-4/203	AR
Waterfield, Mikiel	030	1796	WB-2/87	
Waterfield, Samuel	030	1843	WB-4/97	
Waterfield, Samuel J.	030	1899	WB-5/276	
Waterfield, Sanders	030	1849	WB-4/140	
Waterfield, Sarah	030	1848	WB-4/131	
Waterfield, Southward	030	1816	WB-3/84	
Waterfield, William	030	1880	WB-5/74	
Waterfield, Zachariah	030	1865	WB-4/254	AR
Waterman, Eliza	010	1878	WB-I/102	
Waterman, William	035	1820	WB-A/508	AR
Waters, David	009	c1809	OB-A/51	AR
Waters, Eliza C.	101	1881	WB-A/77	
Waters, Everett	009	1882	WB-1/296	CTY
Waters, Hardy L.	009	1899	WB-2/202	CTY
Waters, Henry	019	1877	WB-B/96	AR
Waters, Hoyt N.	009	1888	WB-1/437	CTY
Waters, Jeremiah	009	1833	OB-B/233	AR
Waters, John	072	1805	WB-A/142	AR
Waters, John	086	1864	WB-E/428	AR
Waters, Jonathan	009	1858	OWB/554	AR
Waters, Jonathan	086	1870	WB-F/14	AR
Waters, Joseph	020	1797	RB-C/250	AR
Waters, Loyd	084	1846	WB-C/43	CTY
Waters, Martha	072	c1760	RW/L45	AR
Waters, Moses	104	1838	WB-4/234	AR
Waters, Nathan M.	035	1880	WB-4/159	AR
Waters, Oliver	086	1865	WB-E/460	
Waters, Ransom	009	1888	WB-1/440	CTY
Waters, Southey	072	1847	WB-2/85	AR
Waters, Stancil	009	1880	WB-1/254	CTY
Waters, Wilborn	006	1879	WB-E/53	AR
Waters, William	072	1754	SS 879/72	SS/AR
Waters, William	083	1841	WB-1/402	AR
Watford, Ann M.	010	1856	WB-H/31	AR
Watford, Elizabeth	010	1854	WB-H/12	AR
Watford, Hardy	010	1784	WB-D/1	AR
Watford, Joseph	010	1795	WB-D/280	AR
Watford, William	010	1846	WB-G/407	AR
Watkins, Abel	038	1872	WB-2/97	AR
Watkins, Abner	084	1861	WB-C/356	CTY

Name	Co.	Date	Recorded Copy	Original
Watkins, Ann	056	1803	WB-1/788	AR-Nunc.
Watkins, Archibald	084	1827	WB-A/213	CTY
Watkins, Becton	028	1841	WB-D/26	
Watkins, Benjamin	VA	1864	Copy	084 CTY
Watkins, C. J.	038	1900	WB-4/268	AR
Watkins, Charles	VA	1895	020 WB-B/276	
Watkins, Charles	VA	1895	098 WB-A/222	098 CTY
Watkins, Charles	VA	1895	044 WB-24/389	044 CTY
Watkins, Charles	VA	1895	036 WB-A/432	036 CTY
Watkins, Charles	VA	c1891	078 WB-19/449	078 AR
Watkins, Christopher	005	1871	WB-D/18	AR
Watkins, Daniel	086	1800	WB-B/111	AR
Watkins, David	029	1900	WB-F/233	AR
Watkins, E. F.	020	1896	WB-B/250	CTY
Watkins, Edmund W.	098	1882	WB-A/19	CTY
Watkins, Eliza J.	005	1897	WB-D/425	AR
Watkins, Francis	084	1875	WB-E/87	
Watkins, Henry	069	1804	WB-1/150	AR
Watkins, Henry T.	044	1871	WB-23/38	CTY
Watkins, Incel	056	1871	WB-3/70	AR
Watkins, Isaac	069	1822	WB-1/308	AR
Watkins, Israel	082	1831	WB-2/13	AR
Watkins, Jacob	082	1886	WB-6/344	AR
Watkins, James	056	1801	WB-1/127	AR
Watkins, James	056	1865	WB-2/70	
Watkins, James	005	1840	WB-B/100	AR
Watkins, Joel	046	1844	WB-C/186	AR
Watkins, John	076	1892	WB-A1/154	AR
Watkins, John	069	1808	WB-1/189	AR
Watkins, John	072	1807	WB-A/137	AR
Watkins, John	071	1801	WB-2/224	AR
Watkins, John	082	1832	WB-2/24	AR
Watkins, John	099	1836	RB-23/563	AR
Watkins, John	103	1796	WI-B/190	AR
Watkins, John D.	038	1896	WB-4/11	AR
Watkins, Lelia	072	1821	WB-A/135	AR-Nunc.
Watkins, Levis	035	1812	WB-A/518	AR
Watkins, Lucy	084	1869	WB-E/19	CTY
Watkins, Malachi	082	1845	WB-3/26	AR
Watkins, Mary	009	1832	OB-B/215	AR
Watkins, Mary S.	028	1855	WB-D/243	
Watkins, Mrs. T. M.	085	1892	WB-2/513	CTY
Watkins, Mumford	005	1849	WB-C/11	AR
Watkins, Nabby	022	c1866	WB-D/181	AR
Watkins, Peter	086	1801	WB-B/124	AR
Watkins, Philip	086	1866	WB-E/466	AR
Watkins, Samuel	020	1868	WB-A/3	CTY
Watkins, Sanders	100	1867	WB-50/248	AR
Watkins, Sarah Jane	020	1888	WB-A/544 & 564	CTY
Watkins, Silas	076	1889	WB-A1/105	AR
Watkins, Susannah	098	1891	WB-A/129	
Watkins, Thomas	077	1754	SS 878/225	SS/AR
Watkins, Thomas	085	1815	WB-G/360	AR
Watkins, W. H.	089	1886	WB-2/132	AR
Watkins, Warner M.	020	1894	036 WB-A/332	036 CTY
Watkins, Warner M.	020	1894	078 WB-19/368	078 AR
Watkins, Warner M.	020	1894	098 WB-A/206	
Watkins, Warner M.	020	1894	WB-B/167	CTY
Watkins, William	081	1816	Orig. Only	AR
Watkins, William	079	1773	Orig. Only	SS/AR
Watkins, William	001	c1848	WB-1/159	AR
Watkins, William	086	1851	WB-E/213	AR
Watkins, William	082	1790	WB-1/31	AR
Watkins, William D.	089	1878	WB-2/56	
Watkins, Willis	099	1832	RB-22/257	AR
Watkins, Winsor	056	1867	WB-2/90	AR
Watlington, E. L.	020	1885	WB-A/438	CTY
Watlington, Emanuel	020	1882	WB-A/351	CTY
Watlington, James	020	1885	WB-A/471	CTY
Watlington, Jonathan	046	1844	WB-C/189	AR
Watlington, Paul	020	1882	WB-A/358	CTY
Watlington, William	084	1870	WB-E/29	CTY
Watson, Abner	VA	1835	084 WB-B/140	084 CTY
Watson, Adam	049	1841	WI-1-2/18	AR
Watson, Alexander	083	1855	WB-2/185	AR
Watson, Amos	056	1850	WB-1/639	AR
Watson, Anderson	001	c1855	WB-1/86	AR
Watson, Andrew	073	1842	WB-F/137	AR
Watson, Ann L.	099	1880	WB-A/213	AR
Watson, Annie E.	068	1888	WB-D/264	
Watson, Arther	063	1826	WB-2/113	
Watson, Augustine	053	1884	WB-11/143	AR
Watson, Benjamin	022	1886	WB-E/327	AR
Watson, Benjamin	053	1835	WB-5/258	AR
Watson, Bridges	056	1876	WB-3/172	
Watson, Briton	103	1827	RD-5/391	
Watson, Catharine	072	1802	WB-A/139	AR
Watson, Catherine	028	1798	WB-B/53	AR
Watson, Christian	083	1861	WB-2/172	AR
Watson, Daniel	068	c1855	WB-C/50	
Watson, Daniel	086	1837	WB-E/33	AR
Watson, David	071	1808	WB-3/8	AR
Watson, David	010	1782	WB-C/49	AR
Watson, David	071	1845	WB-5/15	AR
Watson, David	104	1821	WB-4/15	AR
Watson, Dempsey	105	1876	WB-2/190	AR
Watson, Dinah B.	053	1857	WB-8/245	AR
Watson, Edward C.	010	1810	WB-F/161	AR
Watson, Elizabeth	068	1888	WB-D/266	
Watson, Elizabeth	063	1839	WB-2/260	
Watson, Elizabeth	051	1866	WB-B/79	AR
Watson, Elizabeth	022	c1853	WB-C/379	AR
Watson, Ephriam	056	1821	WB-1/435	AR
Watson, Flora	082	1883	WB-6/257	AR
Watson, Frances H.	070	1888	WB-F/201	AR
Watson, Francis	063	c1784	WB-1/102	
Watson, Frederic	009	1816	OB-A/263	AR
Watson, George	086	1831	WB-D/134	AR
Watson, George P.	086	1900	WB-F/70	AR
Watson, Gideon	105	1885	WB-2/372	AR
Watson, Hannibal	053	1884	WB-11/146	AR
Watson, Harriett	101	1884	WB-A/130	
Watson, Henry	048	1898	WB-1/84	CTY
Watson, Henry B.	046	1834	WB-B/509	AR
Watson, Hugh	068	1799	WB-A/206	
Watson, Hugh	086	1857	WB-E/326	AR
Watson, Israel, Sr.	053	1832	WB-5/118	AR
Watson, Jacob	005	1821	WB-2/179	AR
Watson, Jacob	063	c1791	WB-1/218	
Watson, Jacob	056	c1773	WB-1/788	AR
Watson, James	083	1817	WB-2/49	
Watson, James	083	1855	WB-2/152	AR
Watson, James	094	1771	Orig. Only	060 AR
Watson, James	082	1827	WB-1/283	AR
Watson, James	056	c1782	WB-1/336	AR
Watson, James	053	1826	WB-4/154	AR
Watson, James	056	1829	WB-1/336	AR
Watson, James	073	1777	WB-A/202	
Watson, James	056	c1775	Orig. Only	AR

Name	Co.	Date	Recorded Copy	Original
Watson, James	073	1813	WB-D/381	AR
Watson, James	082	1899	WB-7/15	AR
Watson, James	057	1793	WB-A/157	AR
Watson, James	083	1863	WB-2/205	AR
Watson, James	073	1801	WB-D/49	AR
Watson, James	101	1879	WB-A/37	
Watson, James M.	005	1899	WB-D/448	AR
Watson, James R.	073	1851	WB-G/4	AR
Watson, James S.	046	1853	WB-C/409	AR
Watson, Janet	082	1829	WB-1/305	AR-Nunc.
Watson, Jeremiah	057	1792	WB-A/100	AR
Watson, Jinnette	059	1895	WB-B/151	CTY
Watson, John	086	1813	WB-B/279	AR
Watson, John	086	1803	WB-B/148	AR
Watson, John	083	c1802	WB-1/241	AR
Watson, John	068	1880	WB-D/130	
Watson, John	009	1826	OB-A/355	AR
Watson, John	022	1840	WB-C/113	AR
Watson, John	098	1899	WB-A/340	
Watson, John	047	1791	WB-3/197	
Watson, John	100	1889	WB-51/277	AR
Watson, John	070	1774	Orig. Only	SS/AR
Watson, John	099	1856	RB-28/560	AR
Watson, John	010	1777	WB-B/85	AR
Watson, John	N	1743	SS 878/54	SS/AR
Watson, John	056	1815	WB-1/236	AR
Watson, John	082	1853	WB-4/64	AR
Watson, John	010	1838	WB-G/293	AR
Watson, John	070	1743	DB-C/13	
Watson, John	046	1835	WB-B/526	AR
Watson, John	068	1844	WB-B/143	
Watson, John W.	099	1889	WB-B/321	AR
Watson, John W.	074	1884	WB-1/50	AR
Watson, John W. B.	099	1897	056 WB-2/247	
Watson, John W. B.	099	1897	WB-C/582	AR
Watson, Jonathan	070	1772	WB-C/437	AR
Watson, Jordan	063	1833	WB-2/189	
Watson, Joseph	070	1774	WB-C/438	AR
Watson, Josiah O.	056	1852	099 WB-F/17	099 AR
Watson, Josiah O.	056	1852	WB-1/653	AR
Watson, Judith	046	1834	WB-B/510	AR
Watson, Julius	073	1859	WB-G/236	AR
Watson, L. P.	102	1899	WB-A/158	AR
Watson, Lewis	022	1898	WB-F/81	AR
Watson, Malcom	068	1888	WB-D/262	
Watson, Malcom B.	068	1896	WB-D/475	
Watson, Margaret	073	1831	WB-E/263	AR
Watson, Margaret	065	1871	WB-K/66	AR
Watson, Margaret	083	1832	WB-1/280	AR
Watson, Marion	083	c1820	WB-1/203	AR
Watson, Mark	085	1818	WB-G/515	AR
Watson, Martha E.	065	1893	WB-M/219	AR
Watson, Martha P.	044	1861	WB-21/487	CTY
Watson, Mary	084	1837	WB-B/179	CTY
Watson, Mary	086	1840	WB-E/66	AR
Watson, Mary	075	1754	Orig. Only	AR-Nunc.
Watson, Mary	010	1844	WB-G/366	AR
Watson, Mary A.	099	1894	WB-C/228	AR
Watson, Mary Allen	086	1849	WB-E/188	AR
Watson, Mary S.	016	1898	WB-4/301	AR
Watson, Matthew	083	1841	WB-1/397	AR
Watson, Michael	051	1819	WB-A/38	
Watson, Miles	010	1882	WB-I/151	
Watson, Nancy	053	1891	WB-11/239	AR
Watson, Neale	028	1793	WB-A/288	AR
Watson, Noah	105	1880	WB-2/250	AR
Watson, Patrick	086	1810	WB-B/232	AR
Watson, Prudence	009	1833	OWB/510	AR
Watson, Riddick	024	1861	WB-E/108	AR
Watson, Robert	068	1802	WB-A/222	
Watson, Robert	022	1823	WB-B/105	AR
Watson, Robert C.	010	1841	WB-G/330	AR
Watson, Robert F.	082	1890	WB-6/407	AR
Watson, Sally	053	1834	WB-5/239	AR
Watson, Samuel	029	1789	Orig. Only	AR
Watson, Samuel	103	1834	RD-7/8	
Watson, Samuel	083	1839	WB-1/380	AR
Watson, Samuel B.	065	1895	WB-M/389	
Watson, Sarah	073	1877	WB-H/177	CTY
Watson, Selby	053	1869	WB-11/16	AR
Watson, Solomon	056	1806	WB-1/194	AR
Watson, Stephen	105	1859	WB-1/44	AR
Watson, Susan	001	1887	WB-2/342	AR
Watson, Thomas	063	1776	WB-1/30	
Watson, Thomas	047	1827	WB-4/38	
Watson, Thomas	063	c1803	WB-1/412	
Watson, Thomas	016	1798	WB-A/57	AR
Watson, Thomas	047	1851	WB-4/317	
Watson, Thomas P.	083	1874	WB-3/71	AR
Watson, Watt	048	1887	WB-1/56	CTY
Watson, William	086	1854	WB-E/256	AR
Watson, William	063	c1799	WB-1/361	
Watson, William	084	c1791	OW/159	AR
Watson, William	068	1854	WB-C/15	
Watson, William	071	1827	WB-4/31	AR
Watson, William	012	1845	WB-B/184	AR
Watson, William	073	1785	WB-A/330	AR
Watson, William	068	1799	WB-A/197	
Watson, William	100	1863	WB-50/13	AR
Watson, William	047	1781	WB-3/8	
Watson, William	053	1801	RW-1/332	
Watson, William	011	N. D.	WB-2/331	Nunc.
Watson, William	053	1834	WB-5/253	AR
Watson, William	056	1765	WB-1/786	AR
Watson, William F.	047	1889	WB-6/546	AR
Watson, William H.	056	1863	WB-2/59	
Watson, William P.	TX	1867	056 WB-2/108	056 AR
Watson, William P.	072	1886	WB-4/203	AR
Watson, Willis	056	1815	WB-1/268	AR
Watson, Wilson	073	1854	WB-G/53	AR
Watt, Absalom	084	1834	WB-B/103	CTY
Watt, Ann S.	084	1841	WB-B/261	CTY
Watt, Elizabeth	084	1835	WB-B/110	CTY
Watt, James	084	1864	WB-C/391	CTY
Watt, Jane	084	1843	WB-B/301	CTY
Watt, John	084	1829	WB-B/16	CTY
Watt, John N.	084	1845	WB-C/21	CTY
Watt, Laura T.	065	1889	WB-L/363	AR
Watt, Lina B.	084	1865	WB-D/26	CTY
Watt, Margaret	084	1852	WB-C/136	CTY
Watt, Robert	084	1840	WB-B/227	CTY
Watt, Samuel	084	c1792	OW/164	
Watt, Samuel	084	c1802	OW/7	
Watt, William J.	065	1857	WB-J/39	AR
Watt, William P.	084	1877	WB-E/133	CTY
Watters, Dave	070	1900	WB-H/326	
Watters, Henry H.	012	1858	WB-B/15	AR
Watters, Joseph	070	1763	Orig. Only	AR
Watters, Joseph	012	1851	Orig. Only	AR
Watters, Samuel	012	1782	DB-B/240 & 242	

Name	Co.	Date	Recorded Copy	Original
Watters, Sarah	012	1826	WB-B/144	AR
Watters, Sarah	070	1756	SS 881/275	
Watters, William	070	1751	DB-C/323	
Watterson, Benjamin	026	1861	WB-1/274	AR
Watterson, Margaret	026	1862	WB-1/296	AR
Watterson, Nancy	026	1844	WB-1/36	AR
Watts, A. L.	065	1855	WB-J/1	AR
Watts, B. B.	063	1898	079 WB-3/139	079 AR
Watts, B. B.	063	1898	WB-4/214	AR
Watts, Benjamin	003	c1859	Orig. Only	AR
Watts, Berryman	027	c1811	WB-A/10	AR
Watts, Cora Z.	003	1900	WB-B/400	
Watts, Elizabeth	003	1867	WB-A/18	
Watts, Fannie	103	1897	WB-2/201	AR
Watts, Isaac	054	1868	WB-3/207	AR
Watts, J. Butler	003	1895	WB-B/342	
Watts, James	054	c1793	WB-1/261	AR
Watts, James	003	1880	WB-B/126	AR
Watts, Jean	054	1816	WB-1/391	AR
Watts, John	063	1892	WB-4/82	AR
Watts, John	063	1819	WB-2/59	
Watts, John	003	1895	WB-B/333	AR
Watts, John	054	c1818	WB-2/34	AR
Watts, John D.	054	1838	WB-2/181	AR
Watts, Josiah	073	1788	WB-B/38	AR
Watts, Magnus	003	1875	WB-B/60	AR
Watts, Malachi	005	1804	WB-2/177	AR
Watts, Rachel	054	1858	WB-3/132	AR
Watts, Spencer	099	1803	RB-6/135	AR
Watts, Thomas	054	1846	WB-3/8	AR
Watts, Thomas	005	1841	WB-B/138	AR
Watts, William	003	1863	WB-A/26	AR
Watts, William	063	1859	WB-2/461	
Watts, William	054	c1818	WB-1/416	AR
Watts, William	054	c1806	WB-1/237	AR
Watts, William	054	c1789	WB-1/240	AR
Watts, William F.	054	1874	WB-4/159	CTY
Waugh, David	104	1816	WB-3/117	
Waugh, Elizabeth	038	1854	WB-1/115	AR
Waugh, H. M.	092	1883	WB-6/177	AR
Waugh, James	VA	1875	Copy	006 AR
Waugh, James	090	1844	WB-4/181	AR
Waugh, James P.	006	1891	WB-E/218	AR
Waugh, Rebecca J.	054	1878	WB-4/286	CTY
Waugh, W. H.	104	1897	WB-7/3	AR
Waugh, W. M.	054	1878	WB-4/287	CTY
Waugh, Wallace	038	1870	WB-2/26	AR
Waugh, William P.	104	1852	WB-5/72	AR
Waughup, James	065	1795	WB-G/32	AR
Waxdale, John	028	1739	SS 877/174	SS/AR
Waxdale, John	028	1734	SS 876/351	SS/AR
Way, Calvin	022	1885	WB-E/317	AR
Way, James	065	1807	WB-G/43	AR
Way, Lydia	009	1897	WB-2/113	CTY
Wayman, Thomas	006	1876	WB-E/18	AR
Wayman, William	075	1765	WB-I/35	AR
Wayman, William	075	1788	WB-K/158	AR
Waymire, Rudolph	081	1801	WB-2/85	AR
Waynac, Tobias	046	1890	WB-F/25	AR
Wayne, Jane	059	1896	WB-B/153	CTY
Wayne, Levi	028	1835	WB-C/381	
Waynick, Jesse	084	1871	WB-E/36	CTY
Waynick, Philip	001	c1891	WB-2/514	AR
Wayrick, Ludwick	073	1823	WB-E/48	AR
Wayt, William M.	084	1899	WB-F/148	CTY
Weadon, Martha	084	1868	WB-D/96	CTY
Weadon, William	084	1857	WB-C/243	CTY
Weakes, John	037	1810	WB-D/367	AR
Weakley, Robert	028	1756	Copy	070 AR
Weaks, Benjamin	019	1745	SS 878/62	SS/AR
Weant, Catherine	085	1842	WB-I/134	AR
Weant, Jacob	085	1838	WB-I/47	AR
Weant, John	085	1822	WB-H/178	AR
Wear, Margaret	026	1864	WB-1/352	AR
Wear, William	032	1892	WB-4/171	AR
Weasner, David	032	1877	WB-3/239	AR
Weatherbee, Cade	011	c1793	WB-1/592	
Weatherford, Hiram	020	1851	RB-Q/571	
Weatherford, William	020	1827	RB-L/197	AR
Weatherington, William	031	1870	WB-1/1	
Weatherley, Isaiah	046	1818	Orig. Only	AR
Weatherly, Andrew	046	1877	WB-E/200	AR
Weatherly, Andrew	046	1853	WB-C/395	AR
Weatherly, Edward	046	1810	WB-A/415	AR
Weatherly, Elizabeth	046	1866	WB-D/294	AR
Weatherly, Isaac	046	1858	WB-C/509	AR
Weatherly, Isaiah	046	1847	WB-C/266	AR
Weatherly, James	046	1816	WB-B/26	AR
Weatherly, Jane	046	1853	WB-C/387	AR
Weatherly, Jane	046	1853	WB-C/401	AR
Weatherly, Martha	096	1844	WB-3/10	
Weatherly, Martin	046	1848	WB-C/305	AR
Weatherly, William	046	1824	WB-B/178	AR
Weatherly, William	046	1805	WB-A/411	AR
Weatherman, Christian	092	1801	WB-3/46	
Weatherman, Samuel	106	c1852	WB-1/13	AR
Weathers, C. M.	026	1899	WB-3/48	AR
Weathers, Edmund	099	1832	RB-22/458	AR
Weathers, Elisha	060	1841	WB-2/80	AR
Weathers, James	039	1887	WB-U/396	AR
Weathers, James	060	1810	Orig. Only	AR
Weathers, James	099	1863	RB-32/621	AR
Weathers, James	044	1843	WB-15/411	CTY
Weathers, John	100	1797	WB-9/137	AR
Weathers, Polly	065	1820	WB-G/19	AR
Weathers, Reuben	065	1806	Orig. Only	AR
Weathers, William	099	1860	RB-31/434	AR
Weathersbe, Thomas	063	1852	WB-2/380	
Weathersbe, Wyatt	047	1762	WB-1/76	
Weathersbee, Amanda M.	063	1895	WB-4/179	AR
Weathersbee, John	063	1811	WB-2/4	
Weathersbee, Joseph	047	1864	WB-5/121	
Weathersbee, Lydia A.	037	1880	WB-G/564	AR
Weathersbee, R. E.	063	1900	WB-4/278	AR
Weathersbee, Thomas	063	1774	WB-1/447	
Weathersbee, Thomas	063	1814	WB-2/23	
Weathersbee, Thomas H.	063	1828	WB-2/144	
Weatherspoon, John	104	1778	WB-1/16	AR
Weatherspoon, Robert T.	099	1872	RB-35/194	AR
Weatherspoon, Sarah Ann	036	1887	WB-A/107	CTY
Weatherspoon, William	099	1818	RB-18/121	AR
Weathington, Mary	069	1858	WB-1/557	AR
Weathington, Reuben	079	1859	WB-1/24	AR
Weathington, Willis	079	1880	WB-2/205	AR
Weavel, Catharine	032	1883	WB-3/411	AR
Weavel, John	032	1886	WB-3/507	AR
Weavel, John	032	1853	WB-2/81	AR
Weaver, Absalom	021	c1886	WB-2/363	
Weaver, B. M.	006	c1884	WB-E/104	AR

Name	Co.	Date	Recorded Copy	Original
Weaver, Benjamin	037	1815	WB-E/107	AR
Weaver, Conrad	060	1841	WB-2/82	AR
Weaver, Conrad	021	1845	WB-1/31	AR
Weaver, Cornelia	071	1880	WB-6/318	AR
Weaver, David H.	021	1863	WB-1/177	AR
Weaver, Edward	051	1816	WB-A/188	
Weaver, Edward	044	1806	WB-6/321	CTY
Weaver, Elizabeth	100	1823	WB-25/220	AR
Weaver, Esrom	016	1891	WB-4/114	AR
Weaver, Gideon	006	1882	WB-E/82	AR
Weaver, Henry	047	1808	WB-3/474	
Weaver, Hester	051	1883	WB-C/310	AR
Weaver, Hiram	006	1873	WB-E/7	AR
Weaver, J. T.	013	1867	WB-A/250	AR
Weaver, Jacob	013	1868	WB-A/252	
Weaver, Jacob	060	1788	Orig. Only	AR
Weaver, James	104	1887	WB-6/293	AR
Weaver, Jesse	051	1834	WB-A/65	
Weaver, Jesse R.	013	1869	WB-B/13	AR
Weaver, John	044	1795	WB-3/219	
Weaver, John	013	1831	WB-A/4	
Weaver, John	024	1750	Orig. Only	SS/AR
Weaver, John E.	022	1887	WB-E/360	
Weaver, John H.	073	1887	WB-H/429	CTY
Weaver, John M.	085	1893	WB-2/560	CTY
Weaver, John S.	013	1875	WB-B/113	AR
Weaver, John W.	044	1865	WB-22/329	CTY
Weaver, John W. F.	054	1896	WB-5/578	CTY
Weaver, Jonathan	037	1848	WB-F/389	AR
Weaver, Joseph	016	1859	WB-2/53	AR
Weaver, Lemuel H.	064	1880	WB-2/72	AR
Weaver, Lucinda	026	1891	WB-2/420	AR
Weaver, M. M.	013	1882	WB-B/283	AR
Weaver, Michael	090	1803	WB-2/33	AR
Weaver, Moses	048	1899	WB-1/98	CTY
Weaver, Nancy	060	1852	WB-2/370	AR
Weaver, Peter	071	1800	WB-2/205	AR
Weaver, Phillip	051	1881	WB-C/273	AR
Weaver, Robert A.	071	1878	WB-6/265	AR
Weaver, Samuel	026	1888	WB-2/354	AR
Weaver, Sarah P.	037	1900	WB-H/472	AR
Weaver, Sarah S.	071	1823	WB-3/280	AR
Weaver, Susan Ann	044	1891	WB-24/171	CTY
Weaver, Theophilus	048	1893	WB-1/5	CTY
Weaver, Thomas	073	1897	WB-I/126	CTY
Weaver, Thomas	073	1843	WB-F/168	AR
Weaver, William	036	1884	WB-A/52	CTY
Weaver, William	010	1735	LGB-4/#38	SS/AR
Weaver, William	051	1844	WB-A/219	
Weaver, William	004	1877	WB-A/33	AR
Weaver, William G.	073	1899	WB-I/156	CTY
Weaver, William G.	044	1882	WB-23/436	CTY
Weaver, William W.	069	1883	WB-5/183	AR
Weavil, William A.	038	1896	WB-3/578	AR
Webb, Alexander	001	1849	WB-1/1	AR
Webb, Amy B.	044	1853	WB-19/258	CTY
Webb, Andrew	054	c1819	WB-1A/9	AR
Webb, Angeletta	046	1890	WB-F/52	AR
Webb, Ann Celey	086	1855	WB-E/288	
Webb, Ann H.	078	1840	WI-14/225	AR
Webb, Anthony	010	1750	SS 879/7	SS/AR
Webb, Benjamin	084	1801	OW/135	AR
Webb, Briant	086	1863	WB-E/424	AR
Webb, Caleb	085	1822	WB-H/158	AR
Webb, Caleb	054	c1804	WB-1/267	
Webb, Cornelia	001	1892	WB-2/501	AR
Webb, Daniel	012	1845	WB-B/183	AR
Webb, Daniel	070	1769	WB-C/432	AR
Webb, Daniel	085	1827	WB-H/409	AR
Webb, Daniel	085	1839	WB-I/51	AR
Webb, Daniel	086	1864	WB-E/437	AR
Webb, Daniel	063	1860	WB-2/471	
Webb, David	085	1828	WB-H/422	AR
Webb, David	086	1829	WB-D/112	AR
Webb, David	026	1863	WB-1/316	
Webb, David	037	1872	WB-G/404	
Webb, David H.	084	1894	WB-E/580	CTY
Webb, David J.	105	1888	WB-2/501	AR
Webb, Easter	105	1888	WB-2/483	AR
Webb, Edmond	071	1853	WB-5/107	AR
Webb, Elias	086	1814	WB-C/6	AR
Webb, Elijah	090	1842	WB-4/98	AR
Webb, Elisha	071	1815	WB-3/147	AR-Nunc.
Webb, Eliza A.	019	c1891	Orig. Only	AR
Webb, Geneva M.	039	1873	WB-U/58	AR
Webb, George	082	1797	WB-1/63	AR
Webb, George	100	1808	WB-14/201	AR
Webb, George W.	039	c1854	WB-0/342	
Webb, Giles	063	1828	WB-2/136	
Webb, Gill Strap	084	1844	WB-C/1	CTY
Webb, Hailey	082	1850	WB-4/41	AR
Webb, Henry	071	1797	WB-2/158	AR
Webb, Henry	073	1759	SS 881/250	SS/AR
Webb, Isham	096	c1778	Orig. Only	AR
Webb, James	078	1827	WI-11/3	AR
Webb, James	073	1855	WB-G/86	AR
Webb, James M.	086	1854	WB-E/270	AR
Webb, James T.	069	1887	WB-5/265	AR
Webb, Jeptha F.	037	1870	WB-G/348	AR
Webb, Jeremiah	086	1862	WB-E/405	AR
Webb, Jesse	024	c1803	WB-B/194	AR
Webb, Jesse	071	1821	WB-3/254	AR
Webb, Jesse	039	1837	WB-K/141	AR
Webb, John	037	1853	Orig. Only	AR
Webb, John	082	1794	WB-1/42	AR
Webb, John	037	1869	WB-G/335	AR
Webb, John	044	1826	WB-10/254	CTY
Webb, John	071	1778	WB-1/305	
Webb, John	104	1785	WB-1/162	AR
Webb, John	071	1797	WB-2/148	AR
Webb, John	096	1790	063 WB-1/164	
Webb, John	044	1858	WB-20/482	CTY
Webb, John	037	1785	WB-C/19	AR
Webb, John	071	1848	WB-5/71	AR
Webb, John	071	1749	Orig. Only	SS/AR
Webb, John	085	1826	WB-H/345	AR
Webb, John Lewis	010	1849	WB-G/436	AR
Webb, John N.	010	1869	WB-I/18	AR
Webb, John P.	078	c1845	Orig. Only	AR
Webb, John T.	054	1895	WB-5/559	CTY
Webb, John, Sr.	037	1842	WB-F/271	AR
Webb, Joseph	063	1883	WB-3/235	
Webb, Joseph C.	073	1893	WB-I/3	CTY
Webb, Keziah	073	1886	WB-H/414	CTY
Webb, Laura C.	038	1891	WB-3/269	AR
Webb, Lavinia	010	1884	WB-I/175	
Webb, Lewis	086	1845	WB-E/148	AR
Webb, Loranzo	026	1893	WB-2/463	AR
Webb, Margaret	010	1854	WB-H/3	AR
Webb, Mary	024	1812	WB-C/4	AR

Name	Co.	Date	Recorded Copy	Original
Webb, Mary	044	1795	WB-3/175	CTY
Webb, Mary	063	1837	WB-2/232	
Webb, Mary A.	097	1879	WB-2/165	
Webb, Mary Ann	021	1849	WB-1/73	AR
Webb, Mary Jane	039	1890	WB-U/505	
Webb, Maurice G.	044	1866	WB-22/550	
Webb, Moses	077	1847	WB-F/339	AR
Webb, Moses	024	1779	WB-A/188	AR-Nunc.
Webb, Nathaniel	096	1785	WB-1/144	AR
Webb, Peter	071	1803	WB-2/246	AR-Nunc.
Webb, Rebecca	071	1879	WB-6/298	AR
Webb, Richard	077	1802	WB-E/145	AR
Webb, Robert	096	1772	WB-1/70	AR
Webb, Robert	086	1843	WB-E/113	AR
Webb, Robert	026	1862	WB-1/284	AR
Webb, Robert F.	036	1891	WB-A/191	CTY
Webb, Robert, Sr.	082	1817	WB-1/190	AR
Webb, Ruben	017	1848	WB-A/44	AR
Webb, Sally	071	1809	WB-3/20	AR-Nunc.
Webb, Samuel	072	c1764	RW/L38	
Webb, Samuel	010	1754	SS 879/158	SS/AR
Webb, Samuel	035	1816	WB-A/509	AR
Webb, Sarah	044	1856	WB-20/188	CTY
Webb, Sarah	085	1822	WB-H/141	AR
Webb, Sealy	086	1855	Orig. Only	AR
Webb, Selah	086	1858	WB-E/346	AR
Webb, Sewell R.	056	1894	WB-2/164	AR
Webb, Silas	019	1892	Orig. Only	AR
Webb, Stacy	013	c1826	049 WB-2/174	049 AR
Webb, Stephen	013	1895	WB-C/396	AR
Webb, Stephen	073	1889	WB-H/472	CTY
Webb, Susan	044	c1867	WB-23/31	CTY
Webb, Tempa	105	1861	WB-1/65	AR
Webb, Thomas	046	1830	WB-B/404	AR
Webb, Thomas	071	1797	WB-2/149	AR
Webb, Thomas	028	1788	WB-A/177	
Webb, Thomas	073	1894	WB-I/42	CTY
Webb, Thomas	071	1785	WB-1/342	AR
Webb, William	086	1806	WB-B/189	AR
Webb, William	072	c1769	RW/L50	AR
Webb, William	037	1848	WB-F/399	AR
Webb, William	072	1830	WB-1/71	AR
Webb, William	090	1800	WB-1/149	AR
Webb, William	044	1810	WB-7/86	CTY
Webb, William	005	1888	WB-D/238	AR
Webb, William	047	1827	WB-4/34	
Webb, Willis	047	1852	WB-4/330	
Webb, Wilson	077	1807	WB-E/250	AR
Webb, Young John	044	1864	WB-22/183	CTY
Webb, Zachariah	024	1812	WB-C/9	AR
Webb, Zachariah	077	1761	024 WB-1/4	024 AR
Webb, Zachariah	024	c1783	WB-B/16	AR
Webb, Zacheriah	077	1830	WB-F/178	AR
Webber, Catherine	028	1838	WB-C/426	AR
Webber, Eliza	026	1880	WB-2/212	AR
Webber, Sarah	028	1824	WB-C/253	AR
Webber, Thomas	028	1788	Orig. Only	AR
Weber, Adam	054	1897	WB-6/50	CTY
Weber, August	NY	1890	013 WB-C/66	013 AR
Weber, Jacob	037	1880	WB-G/559	AR
Weber, John G.	054	1890	WB-5/336	CTY
Weber, Nancy	103	1810	RD-1/307	AR
Webster, B. R.	084	1891	WB-E/504	CTY
Webster, E. P.	026	1878	WB-2/177	AR
Webster, Elisabeth	019	1754	SS 881/61	SS/AR

Name	Co.	Date	Recorded Copy	Original
Webster, Elizabeth	022	1852	WB-C/324	AR
Webster, Ellenner	096	1817	Orig. Only	AR
Webster, James	053	1801	RW-1/326	
Webster, James	084	1847	WB-C/45	CTY
Webster, James, Sr.	054	c1826	WB-2/102	AR
Webster, John	053	1774	Orig. Only	SS/AR
Webster, John	084	1833	WB-B/78	CTY
Webster, John	053	c1816	RW-1/522	AR
Webster, John	084	1827	WB-B/13	CTY
Webster, John	019	1746	SS 878/84	SS/AR
Webster, John H.	090	1898	WB-6/444	AR
Webster, Margaret	053	1836	WB-5/430	AR
Webster, Nancy A.	084	1881	WB-E/225	CTY
Webster, Pembrok	053	1774	RW-1/54	AR
Webster, Pleasent	090	1873	WB-6/42	AR
Webster, Richard	022	1842	WB-C/129	AR
Webster, Richard	053	1796	Orig. Only	AR
Webster, Richard	022	1893	WB-E/547	AR
Webster, Sarey	096	1834	WB-2/119	AR
Webster, Senna P.	003	1895	WB-B/340	AR
Webster, Solomon	084	c1796	OW/170	AR
Webster, Susan	090	1889	WB-6/222	AR
Webster, Thomas	038	1896	WB-3/596	AR
Webster, William	053	1770	RW-1/14	
Webster, William	053	1745	SS 878/93	SS/AR
Webster, William	084	1843	WB-B/311	CTY
Wechon, Frederick	085	c1800	WB-E/1	AR
Weddell, Matthew	037	1888	WB-H/138	AR
Wedding, Elizabeth	099	1875	RB-35/314	AR
Weddington, Isaac	065	1884	WB-K/567	AR
Weddington, Jane Y.	065	1840	WB-H/4	AR
Weddington, John R.	085	1891	WB-2/455	CTY
Weddington, Josiah W.	054	c1838	WB-2/184	AR
Weddington, Margaret	016	1891	WB-4/108	AR
Weddington, Samuel	016	1844	WB-1/45	
Weddington, William	065	1772	WB-G/25	AR
Weedon, Sarah	001	1876	WB-2/76	AR
Weekes, Benjamin	077	c1782	Orig. Only	AR
Weekes, James	077	1779	WB-C/239	AR
Weekes, John	077	1768	WB-C/77	AR
Weekes, Thomas	077	1763	WB-C/28	AR
Weekes, Thomas	077	1805	WB-E/224	AR
Weeks, Andrew	086	1894	WB-F/472	AR
Weeks, Archelaus	057	c1778	WB-A/195	AR
Weeks, Benajah C.	087	1888	WB-3/385	AR
Weeks, Benjamin	064	c1867	Orig. Only	AR
Weeks, Cely	037	1827	WB-F/77	AR
Weeks, Charles L.	075	1896	WB-O/427	AR
Weeks, Elijah	019	1859	WB-A/231	AR
Weeks, Elisabeth	077	1816	WB-E/445	AR
Weeks, Elizabeth	077	1793	WB-C/447	
Weeks, Isaac	019	1782	WB-E/10	AR
Weeks, J. R.	047	1898	WB-7/197	AR
Weeks, Jabez, Sr.	019	c1828	WB-E/33	AR
Weeks, James	037	1838	WB-F/211	AR
Weeks, James E.	075	1866	WB-M2/93	
Weeks, James, Sr.	037	1815	WB-E/93	AR
Weeks, John	065	1840	WB-H/38	
Weeks, John	075	1842	WB-N/170	AR
Weeks, John	065	1848	WB-I/128	AR
Weeks, John	019	1790	Orig. Only	AR
Weeks, John	087	1851	WB-1/393	AR
Weeks, John D.	047	1892	WB-7/27	AR
Weeks, Joseph	065	1844	WB-H/170	AR
Weeks, Kenan	087	1893	WB-3/532	AR

Name	Co.	Date	Recorded Copy	Original
Weeks, Lizzie J.	047	1897	WB-7/185	AR
Weeks, Mary	087	1895	WB-3/575	AR
Weeks, Noah	077	1836	Orig. Only	AR
Weeks, Phillip	065	1809	WB-G/39	AR
Weeks, Samuel	077	1815	WB-E/423	AR
Weeks, Sarah	037	c1792	WB-C/212	AR
Weeks, William	077	1816	WB-E/442	AR
Weeks, William	077	1832	WB-F/198	AR
Weer, Edward	032	1842	WB-1/395	
Weesner, Andrew	032	1823	WB-1/23	AR
Weesner, Daniel T.	032	1843	WB-1/414	
Weesner, Michael	085	1772	WB-A/160	AR
Wehunt, Caleb	060	1864	WB-3/72	AR
Wehunt, John	060	1886	WB-4/338	AR
Weidman, George	085	c1798	WB-D/244	AR
Weidner, Henry	060	c1790	WB-2/414	
Weil, Herman	103	1878	WB-1/141	AR
Weir, David P.	046	1865	WB-D/241	AR
Weir, Edward	065	c1841	WB-H/73	AR
Weir, John	060	1819	Orig. Only	AR
Weir, Thomas	065	1816	WB-G/10	AR
Welborn, Abigail	032	1877	WB-3/233	AR
Welborn, James	104	1855	WB-5/118	AR
Welborn, James M.	032	1882	WB-3/373	AR
Welborn, John	081	1805	WB-3/27	
Welborn, John	081	1831	WB-6/129	AR
Welborn, John H.	032	1887	WB-3/542	AR
Welborn, John T. M.	032	1874	WB-3/100	AR
Welborn, Maberry	104	1878	WB-6/150	AR
Welborn, Nancy	104	1888	WB-6/325	AR
Welborn, T. S.	081	1895	WB-16/360	AR
Welborn, T. W.	046	1896	WB-F/501	AR
Welborn, Thomas	046	1778	WB-A/400	AR
Welborn, William	038	1879	WB-2/342	AR
Welborn, William	046	1842	WB-C/116	AR
Welbourn, Daniel	104	1885	WB-6/261	AR
Welbourn, John	081	1830	WB-6/129	
Welch (Warren), John	077	c1730	Orig. Only	SS/AR
Welch, Abner	024	1825	WB-C/117	AR
Welch, Alvis	068	c1879	WB-D/117	
Welch, Baker F.	024	1864	WB-D/20	AR
Welch, David	090	1870	WB-6/15	AR
Welch, David	024	1788	WB-B/50	AR
Welch, E. A.	038	1865	WB-1/255	AR-Copy
Welch, Edward	024	1827	WB-C/138	AR
Welch, Eli	022	1896	WB-F/17	AR
Welch, Elizabeth	016	1831	PQS.5/151	AR
Welch, Franer	033	1845	WB-1/70	AR
Welch, Henry	022	1853	WB-C/346	AR
Welch, Isaac	024	1806	WB-B/247	AR-Nunc.
Welch, James	099	1871	RB-35/378	AR
Welch, James	006	1898	WB-E/354	AR
Welch, John	094	c1769	Orig. Only	060 AR
Welch, John	024	c1730	Orig. Only	SS/AR
Welch, Lemuel	024	1815	WB-C/38	AR
Welch, Loyd R.	023	1880	WB-A/22	
Welch, Luke	022	1772	Orig. Only	AR
Welch, Maria	041	1899	WB-4/495	AR
Welch, Mary E.	022	1900	WB-F/181	AR
Welch, Matthew	009	c1767	OWB/102	AR
Welch, Michael	024	c1768	WB-B/47	AR
Welch, Michael	022	1784	RB-1/19	AR
Welch, Miles	024	1837	WB-C/196	AR
Welch, Murphy S.	099	1865	RB-33/422	AR
Welch, Nathaniel	077	1789	WB-C/383	AR
Welch, Nathaniel	075	1735	Orig. Only	SS/AR
Welch, Sarah	024	1848	WB-C/284	AR
Welch, Thomas	086	1794	Orig. Only	AR
Welch, Thomas	024	c1711	SS 875/40	
Welch, Walter	022	1798	RB-2/133	AR
Welch, William	046	1848	WB-C/296	AR
Welch, William	SC	1853	Copy	054 AR
Welch, William	009	c1814	OWB/472	AR
Welch, William	049	1831	061 WB-1/6	061 AR
Welch, William	022	1854	WB-C/365	AR
Welch, William B.	099	1877	RB-35/412	
Weldon, Mary F.	100	1894	WB-51/386	
Weldon, Nancy	047	1843	WB-4/218	
Weldon, Sales	100	1868	WB-50/264	AR
Weldon, Samuel	047	1782	WB-3/33	
Weldon, William	047	1785	WB-3/97	
Weldon, William	100	1817	WB-20/194	AR
Welfare, Alanson E.	038	1883	WB-2/459	AR
Welfare, Daniel C.	090	1841	WB-4/79	AR
Welfare, Julia E.	038	1897	WB-4/70	AR
Welfare, Robert N.	032	1900	WB-4/455	AR
Welfare, T. S.	032	1882	WB-3/371	AR
Welker, George W.	046	1894	WB-F/340	AR
Wellborn, Abel R.	104	1855	WB-5/116	
Wellborn, Mary M.	104	1894	WB-6/517	AR
Wellborn, Rebecca	104	1861	WB-5/273	
Wellings, Robert	071	1852	WB-4/244	AR
Wellmon, E. R.	026	1897	WB-2/539	AR
Wellmon, John	026	1897	WB-2/558	AR
Wellmon, Wilkins	026	1852	WB-1/134	AR
Wellmon, William	026	1857	WB-1/218	
Wellmon, William	026	1859	WB-1/246	
Wellons, Erastus	056	1869	WB-3/25	AR
Wellons, Jesse	056	1868	WB-2/116	AR
Wellons, Kesiah	103	1869	WB-1/7	AR
Wellons, Louiza J.	056	1861	WB-2/8	AR
Wellons, Lucretia	056	1813	WB-1/399	AR
Wellons, Melissa	056	1879	WB-3/237	AR
Wellons, Willie H.	056	1868	WB-2/104	AR
Wells, Absalom	069	1796	WB-1/106	AR-Nunc.
Wells, Benjamin	020	1889	WB-B/15	CTY
Wells, Benson W.	061	1898	WB-2/220	AR
Wells, Betty	071	1815	WB-3/156	AR
Wells, Boney	035	1862	WB-3/50	AR
Wells, Boney	035	1890	WB-4/363	AR
Wells, Burrel F.	040	1887	WB-2/283	AR
Wells, Burwell	060	1828	WB-1/82	AR
Wells, David	040	1878	WB-2/126	AR
Wells, Dorothy	077	1788	WB-C/359	AR
Wells, Elizabeth	073	1854	WB-G/51	AR
Wells, Elizabeth	069	1810	WB-1/208	AR
Wells, Featherston	040	1856	WB-1/70	AR
Wells, Frederick	084	1838	WB-B/182	CTY
Wells, Fredrach	069	1779	WB-1/3	AR
Wells, George	024	1767	Orig. Only	AR
Wells, George H.	044	1875	WB-23/175	CTY
Wells, George T.	084	1862	WB-C/365	CTY
Wells, Isaac	026	1857	WB-1/214	AR
Wells, J. R.	013	1884	WB-B/328	AR
Wells, Jacob	035	1808	WB-A/516	AR
Wells, Jacob	035	1826	WB-A/495	AR
Wells, James	092	1810	WB-3/96	
Wells, James	060	1826	WB-1/26	
Wells, James	076	1890	WB-A1/108	AR
Wells, Jamima	026	1867	WB-1/416	AR

Name	Co.	Date	Recorded Copy	Original
Wells, Jessie R.	086	1900	WB-G/66	AR
Wells, Joel	069	1873	WB-1/618	AR
Wells, John	060	1819	Orig. Only	AR
Wells, John	069	1847	WB-1/498	AR
Wells, John	072	c1764	RW/L48	AR
Wells, John D.	105	1895	WB-3/146	AR
Wells, John L.	086	1858	WB-E/344	AR
Wells, Joseph	072	c1780	Orig. Only	AR
Wells, Joseph	073	1804	WB-D/140	AR
Wells, Joseph	077	1816	WB-E/449	AR
Wells, Leander J.	013	1849	WB-A/139	
Wells, M. L.	086	1887	WB-F/309	AR
Wells, Margarett	047	1835	WB-4/116	
Wells, Mary	087	1883	Orig. Only	AR
Wells, Matthew	037	1836	WB-F/194	AR
Wells, Miles	078	1829	WI-11/178	AR
Wells, Miles	092	1849	WB-4/298	
Wells, Phebe	092	1886	WB-6/241	AR
Wells, Richard	086	1866	WB-E/476	AR
Wells, Robert	026	1853	WB-1/163	AR
Wells, Silvey	064	1883	Orig. Only	AR
Wells, Solomon	069	1790	WB-1/64	AR
Wells, Stephen	069	1853	WB-1/533	AR
Wells, Stephen	037	1775	WB-A/238	AR
Wells, Stephen	069	1807	WB-1/171	AR
Wells, Stoaks	035	1889	WB-4/333	AR
Wells, Thomas	037	1801	WB-D/130	AR
Wells, Thomas	077	1834	WB-F/231	AR
Wells, Thomas	047	1820	WB-3/650	
Wells, Thomas	013	1834	WB-A/32	
Wells, William	072	1743	Orig. Only	SS/AR
Wells, William	001	1878	WB-2/124	AR
Wells, William	001	1858	WB-1/124	AR
Wells, William B.	035	1863	WB-3/78	AR
Wells, William C.	071	1815	WB-3/146	AR
Welman, John	085	1831	WB-H/548	AR
Welmon, Jeremiah	085	1834	WB-H/616	AR
Welsel, Hillery	075	1889	WB-O/315	AR
Welser, Ebenezer C.	051	1889	WB-C/396	AR
Welsh, James	019	1814	WB-E/25	AR
Welsh, Mary	019	1803	WB-E/19	AR
Welsh, Thomas	090	1864	WB-4/376	AR
Welts, Elizabeth	035	1817	WB-A/507	AR
Welty, Abraham	085	c1787	WB-D/233 & 258	AR
Welty, John A.	072	1840	WB-2/33	
Weltz, Joseph	035	1812	WB-A/484	AR
Wenham, Robert, Sr.	N	1735	SS 876/414	SS/AR
Wennam, Sarah	028	1813	Orig. Only	AR
Wensel, Henry	085	c1789	WB-E/14	AR
Wents, Andrew	065	1809	WB-G/40	AR
Wentz, James M.	097	1899	Orig. Only	AR
Wentz, Jeremiah	097	1895	WB-2/481	AR
Werden, John	009	c1764	OWB/304	AR
Werden, Samuel	009	c1795	OWB/310	AR
Werlow, Elizabeth	032	1825	WB-1/43	
Wescott, F. M.	012	1895	WB-A/96	AR
Wescott, John L.	012	1896	WB-A/111	AR
Wescott, John L.	012	c1893	Copy	070 AR
Weson, James	086	1826	WB-D/51	AR
Wessell, Albert C.	070	1897	WB-H/55	AR
Wessner, George C.	016	1795	WB-A/58	AR
Wesson, Amos, Sr.	037	1811	WB-E/28	AR
Wesson, Isaac	084	1857	WB-C/264	CTY
Wesson, Luke	026	1882	WB-2/233	AR

Name	Co.	Date	Recorded Copy	Original
Wesson, Oren	047	1887	WB-6/451	AR
Wesson, William	026	1874	WB-2/120	AR
Wesson, William	086	1812	WB-B/262	AR
West, Allen	096	1866	WB-3/71	AR
West, Arther	005	1803	WB-2/180	AR
West, Arthur	010	1730	Orig. Only	SS/AR
West, Barney	060	1828	WB-1/117	AR
West, Benjamin	020	1849	RB-Q/281	AR
West, Charles	005	1859	WB-C/144	AR
West, Charles	075	1785	WB-K/111	AR
West, Charles	075	1748	Orig. Only	SS/AR
West, Christina	085	1866	WB-K/382	AR
West, Cordelia	013	1900	049 WB-2/451	049 AR
West, Cordelia	013	1899	WB-D/337 & 401	AR-Copy
West, Council B.	028	1878	WB-E/192	AR
West, Cyrus W.	085	1854	WB-K/165	AR
West, Daniel	083	1866	WB-2/236	AR
West, Daniel	028	1809	Orig. Only	AR
West, David	028	1809	WB-B/334	
West, Edward	030	c1807	WB-2/345	
West, Eli	057	1797	WB-A/129	AR
West, Elizabeth	030	1836	WB-4/17	
West, Elizabeth	010	1863	WB-H/130	AR
West, Gabriel	096	1846	WB-3/16	AR
West, George Day	030	1789	WB-1/241	
West, George M.	096	1880	WB-4/52	
West, George W.	013	1896	WB-C/557	AR
West, Handy	087	1885	WB-3/307	AR
West, Henry	013	1849	WB-A/136	
West, Henry	009	c1752	Orig. Only	AR
West, Henry	009	1752	SS 878/194	CTY
West, Henry J.	029	1894	WB-F/29	AR
West, Ignatius	022	1831	WB-B/208	AR
West, Isaac	022	c1853	WB-D/100	AR
West, Israel	047	1789	WB-3/166	
West, J. H.	017	1893	WB-B/232	AR
West, James H.	085	1893	WB-2/562	CTY
West, James S.	099	1894	WB-C/362	AR
West, Jenkins	085	c1805	WB-E/2	AR
West, John	103	1794	WI-A/515	AR
West, John	030	1840	WB-4/75	
West, John	024	c1713	SS 875/27	
West, John	030	1854	WB-4/195	AR
West, John	087	1898	WB-4/72	AR
West, John	013	1864	WB-A/228	
West, John	061	1850	WB-1/41	AR
West, John	028	1800	WB-B/104	AR-Nunc.
West, John	028	1844	WB-D/105	AR
West, John	028	c1760	Wills.7/191	AR
West, John S.	028	1822	WB-C/223	AR
West, John S.	028	1818	WB-C/173	AR
West, John W.	TX	1870	070 WB-F/134	070 AR
West, Jonathan	075	1751	Orig. Only	SS/AR
West, Jonathan	073	1774	WB-A/181	
West, Joseph S.	054	1871	WB-4/90	CTY
West, Joshua	030	1803	WB-2/229	
West, Joshua	030	1835	WB-4/6	
West, Joshua	030	1774	WB-1/87	
West, Kinnian T.	028	1865	WB-D/395	AR
West, Levi	072	c1787	WI/L10	AR
West, Lewis	083	1878	WB-3/140	AR
West, Loyed, Sr.	087	1881	WB-3/214	AR
West, Lucy	056	1891	WB-3/579	AR
West, Margaret	085	1886	WB-2/207	CTY

Name	Co.	Date	Recorded Copy	Original
West, Martha E.	057	1900	WB-C/248	AR
West, Martin	065	1830	WB-F/173	AR
West, Mary	054	c1820	WB-1A/11	AR
West, Mary	016	1875	WB-3/150	AR
West, Mary Ann	030	1890	WB-5/182	AR
West, Milton C.	017	1880	WB-B/93	AR
West, Nathaniel	030	1780	WB-1/143	
West, Nelly	030	1847	WB-4/127	
West, Noah	035	1895	WB-4/475	
West, Noah F.	074	1892	WB-1/122	AR
West, Noel	056	1846	WB-1/577	AR
West, Obediah	030	1807	WB-2/299	
West, Penelope	010	1815	WB-F/274	AR
West, Peter	044	1841	WB-15/20	CTY
West, Peter	010	1751	SS 879/22	SS/AR
West, Peter	010	1769	WB-A/116	AR
West, Reading	028	1817	WB-C/156	AR
West, Remus J.	085	1886	WB-2/187	CTY
West, Richard	028	1809	WB-B/329	AR
West, Robert	030	c1813	WB-3/27	
West, Robert	024	1689	Copy	CCR 187
West, Robert	010	c1771	WB-A/159	AR
West, Robert	060	1834	WB-1/302	AR
West, Robert	024	1689	Orig. Only	SS/AR
West, Robert	056	1790	WB-1/26	AR
West, Sarah	030	c1809	WB-3/35	
West, Solomon	084	c1787	OW/212	AR
West, Stephen	009	c1887	Orig. Only	CTY
West, Susan	100	1871	WB-51/48	AR
West, Susana	010	1828	WB-G/174	AR
West, Thomas	022	1822	WB-B/49	AR
West, Thomas	017	1875	WB-B/49	AR
West, Thomas	010	1795	WB-D/272	AR
West, Thomas	010	1811	WB-F/176	AR
West, Thomas	086	1832	WB-D/145	AR
West, Thomas	010	1757	SS 880/256	SS/AR
West, Thomas	022	1808	WB-A/97	AR
West, Thomas S.	024	1896	WB-E/255	AR
West, Wade W.	047	1831	WB-4/80	
West, William	028	1750	Orig. Only	SS/AR
West, William	009	1745	SS 877/20	SS/AR
West, William	010	1735	LGB-4/#1	SS/AR
West, William	086	1848	WB-E/177	AR
West, William	037	1749	Orig. Only	SS/AR
West, William	040	1861	WB-1/122	
West, William	011	c1830	WB-2/390	
West, William	010	1810	WB-F/154	AR
West, William	028	1781	Orig. Only	AR
West, William	100	1821	WB-23/282	AR
West, William H.	059	1892	WB-B/51	CTY
West, William L.	010	1828	WB-G/179	AR
West, Willoughby	030	1840	WB-4/74	
Westbrook, Ann Maria	027	1891	WB-2/101	AR
Westbrook, Cathern	057	1852	WB-B/215	AR
Westbrook, Charles	029	1824	WB-B/113	AR
Westbrook, Elizabeth	029	1821	WB-B/53	AR
Westbrook, Fredrick	056	1883	Orig. Only	AR
Westbrook, Harman	057	1848	WB-B/197	AR
Westbrook, J. E.	035	1884	WB-4/225	AR
Westbrook, James	057	1829	WB-B/103	AR
Westbrook, James	087	c1817	Orig. Only	AR
Westbrook, James, Sr.	087	c1816	Orig. Only	AR
Westbrook, Jesse D.	070	1871	WB-E/246	AR
Westbrook, John	057	1846	WB-B/187	AR
Westbrook, John	057	1845	WB-B/173	AR
Westbrook, Thomas	071	1793	WB-2/36	AR
Westbrook, Thomas	078	1818	WI-8/163	AR
Westbrook, Thomas S.	086	1886	WB-F/276	AR
Westbrook, Uriah	056	1888	WB-3/472	AR
Westbrook, William	087	c1816	Orig. Only	AR
Westbrook, William	087	c1809	Orig. Only	AR
Westbrook, William	027	1886	WB-2/64	AR
Westbrooks, James	011	c1832	WB-1/30	
Westcott, Stephen	030	1807	WB-2/316	
Wester, Arthur	069	1792	WB-1/75	AR
Wester, Axum	039	c1854	Orig. Only	AR
Wester, Benjamin	039	1893	WB-V/4	AR
Wester, L. C.	039	1883	WB-U/308	AR
Wester, Lockey	039	1852	WB-N/336	AR
Wester, Martha	039	1881	WB-U/252	AR
Wester, Martha	039	1849	WB-N/306	AR-Nunc.
Wester, Miranda	039	1887	WB-U/400	AR
Wester, Patsy Ann	039	1898	WB-V/152	AR
Westermann, Heinrich	064	1895	WB-2/335	AR
Westery, William	069	1848	WB-1/514	AR
Westfeldt, George	AL	1878	050 WB-2/59	
Westfeldt, George	AL	1878	091 WB-1/60	091 CTY
Westfeldt, Jane	AL	1878	091 WB-1/178	091 CTY
Westfeldt, Jane	AL	1878	050 WB-2/322	
Westlock, James	104	1809	WB-2/252	AR
Westman, Gustaf	017	1885	WB-B/116	AR
Westmoreland, David	038	1861	WB-1/196	AR
Westmoreland, Thomas A.	065	1896	WB-M/466	
Westmoreland, William L.	054	1896	WB-6/35	CTY
Weston, Absalom	035	c1775	WB-A/510	AR
Weston, Benjamin	053	1847	WB-7/84	AR
Weston, Daniel	086	1892	WB-F/431	AR
Weston, Dartnis	072	c1782	RW/L61	AR
Weston, Edward	035	1798	WB-A/522	AR
Weston, Emeline	053	1896	WB-11/327	AR
Weston, Ephraim	010	1818	WB-G/22	AR
Weston, Ephriam	010	1801	WB-E/132	AR
Weston, James	041	1842	WB-A/150	
Weston, James	053	1878	WB-11/80	AR
Weston, John W. H.	053	1893	WB-11/272	AR
Weston, Martha M.	009	1899	053 WB-11/346	053 AR
Weston, Martha M.	009	1899	WB-2/189	CTY
Weston, Samuel	053	1826	WB-6/88	AR
Weston, Samuel	053	1840	WB-6/106	AR
Weston, Sarah	010	1820	WB-G/74	AR
Weston, Solomon	010	1814	WB-F/250	AR
Weston, Uriah	051	1847	WB-A/274	
Weston, William	010	1796	WB-D/323	AR
Weston, William	010	1748	Orig. Only	SS/AR
Westory, Elizabeth	022	1820	WB-B/30	AR
Westray, Benjamin	022	1817	WB-A/286	AR
Westray, S. E.	069	1894	WB-5/428	AR
Westray, Samuel	069	1828	WB-1/353	AR
Westray, Sarah B.	069	1839	WB-1/434	AR
Wetherington, Solomon	028	1840	WB-D/10	
Wetherman, Christian	092	1849	WB-4/288	
Wetherow, Ewalt	085	1814	WB-G/299	AR
Wetherspoon, Asgil	056	1867	WB-2/96	AR
Wetmore, Elizabeth	029	1866	WB-D/85	
Wetmore, George B.	085	1888	WB-2/311	CTY
Wetmore, Ichabod	029	1851	WB-C/203	AR
Wettenspoon, Mary	028	1800	WB-B/93	Nunc.
Wevel, Stephen	085	1822	WB-H/181	AR

Name	Co.	Date	Recorded Copy	Original
Wever, Adam	021	1885	WB-2/327	
Weymouth, Thomas	075	1817	WB-M1/307	AR
Whaley, Elizabeth	072	1875	WB-4/81	AR
Whaley, Joseph	054	1818	WB-1A/91	AR
Whaley, Kincey	035	1862	WB-3/56	AR
Whaley, Samuel	035	1857	WB-2/114	AR
Whaltone, Thomas	024	1719	Orig. Only	SS/AR
Wharey, James	VA	1842	086 WB-E/101	086 AR
Wharey, Thomas	086	1839	WB-E/58	AR
Wharrey, Anthony	077	1718	Orig. Only	SS/AR
Wharton, Abey	075	1787	WB-K/152	
Wharton, David	028	1784	Orig. Only	AR
Wharton, Edmund	057	1812	WB-A/331	AR
Wharton, Elam	046	1832	WB-B/456	AR
Wharton, Elisha	046	c1860	Orig. Only	AR
Wharton, Evans	046	1862	WB-D/121	AR
Wharton, Gideon	046	1847	WB-C/282	AR
Wharton, Green	046	1887	WB-E/487	AR
Wharton, Jesse	084	1871	WB-E/33	CTY
Wharton, John	046	1891	WB-F/120	AR
Wharton, Joseph	072	c1785	WI/L58	AR
Wharton, Lynn	072	1879	WB-4/127	AR
Wharton, Pinkney R.	084	1860	WB-C/315	CTY
Wharton, Rachel D.	046	1900	WB-G/189	AR
Wharton, Robert N.	046	1877	WB-E/188	AR
Wharton, Thomas	028	1789	WB-A/191	AR
Wharton, Thomas J.	SC	1899	049 WB-2/423	049 AR
Wharton, Watson	046	1813	WB-A/419	AR
Whary, Joshua	077	1730	Orig. Only	SS/AR
Whatley, Sherley	100	1783	WB-3/162	015 AR
Wheadon, John	028	1821	WB-C/196	AR
Whealer, John	071	1798	WB-2/179	AR
Wheat, J. T.	085	1888	WB-2/290	CTY
Wheat, Samuel C.	047	1854	WB-4/362	
Wheatfield, John	063	1823	WB-2/91	
Wheatley, Benjamin	063	c1791	WB-1/179	
Wheatley, John	030	1803	WB-2/218	
Wheatley, John	024	1706/7	Orig. Only	SS/AR
Wheatley, John	096	1770	Orig. Only	AR
Wheatley, John	030	1843	WB-4/96	
Wheatley, John	063	c1800	WB-1/365	
Wheatley, John	063	1814	WB-2/21	
Wheatley, Mary	063	c1792	WB-1/193	
Wheatley, Mason	104	1807	WB-2/208	AR
Wheatley, Samuel	063	1816	WB-2/35	
Wheatley, William	104	1860	WB-5/246	
Wheatly, George	037	1766	WB-A/150	AR
Wheaton, Elizabeth	028	1835	WB-C/380	AR
Wheaton, Mary R.	099	1863	RB-32/423	AR
Wheaton, Robert	077	1816	WB-E/459	AR
Wheaton, Sterling	099	1832	RB-22/344	AR
Wheaton, William	077	1800	WB-E/118	AR
Wheatton, Leven	028	1801	WB-B/137	AR
Whedbee, Addison	075	c1854	WB-M2/21	AR
Whedbee, Ann	077	1834	WB-F/227	AR
Whedbee, Elizabeth	MD	1896	028 WB-F/277	
Whedbee, George	077	1784	WB-C/264	AR
Whedbee, George	075	1749	Orig. Only	SS/AR
Whedbee, James	077	1831	WB-F/193	AR
Whedbee, James N.	077	1848	WB-F/342	AR
Whedbee, James N.	VA	1855	077 WB-F/482	077 AR
Whedbee, James P.	077	1853	WB-F/427	AR
Whedbee, James S.	MD	1891	028 WB-F/274	
Whedbee, James S.	MD	1891	Copy	063 AR
Whedbee, John	077	1784	WB-C/257	AR
Whedbee, Joseph	096	c1780	WB-1/116	
Whedbee, Joshua S.	041	1900	WB-4/526	AR
Whedbee, Mary	077	1795	WB-E/48	
Whedbee, Mary P.	075	1871	WB-O/16	AR
Whedbee, Matilda	077	1882	WB-H/127	AR
Whedbee, Richard	077	1788	WB-C/371	AR
Whedbee, Richard	077	1746	Orig. Only	SS/AR
Whedbee, Richard	077	1785	WB-C/303	AR
Whedbee, Samuel	075	1797	WB-L/91	AR
Whedbee, Seth	077	1798	WB-E/98	AR
Whedbee, Thomas	077	1808	WB-E/320	AR
Wheedbee, Ann	075	1750	Orig. Only	SS/AR
Wheelass, John	022	c1780	Orig. Only	AR
Wheeler, Amanda F.	038	1884	WB-2/496	AR
Wheeler, Benjamin	044	1883	WB-23/477	CTY
Wheeler, Burrett T.	065	1888	WB-L/279	AR
Wheeler, Celia	071	1830	WB-4/67	AR
Wheeler, Charles S.	038	1894	WB-3/488	AR
Wheeler, Cherry	071	1899	WB-7/419	AR
Wheeler, David R.	033	1874	WB-2/45	CTY
Wheeler, Elvirah	044	1885	WB-23/528	CTY
Wheeler, Ezekiel	044	1871	WB-23/41	CTY
Wheeler, Frusey	056	1887	WB-3/459	AR
Wheeler, Henry	071	1779	WB-1/217	
Wheeler, Henry	071	1840	WB-4/209	AR
Wheeler, Jacob	009	1828	OB-A/470	AR
Wheeler, John	046	1833	WB-B/490	AR
Wheeler, John	073	c1795	Orig. Only	AR-Copy
Wheeler, John	051	1832	WB-A/50A	
Wheeler, Junius B.	017	1886	WB-B/135	AR
Wheeler, Kezia	046	1858	WB-C/522	AR
Wheeler, Manlove	046	1826	WB-B/348	AR
Wheeler, Margaret	022	1846	WB-C/189	AR
Wheeler, Moses	044	1865	WB-22/372	CTY
Wheeler, Richard	046	1821	WB-B/112	AR
Wheeler, Sarah	051	1833	WB-A/56	
Wheeler, Sarah	071	1801	WB-2/223	AR
Wheeler, Sion	071	1839	WB-4/200	AR
Wheeler, Susan C.	056	1892	WB-2/120	AR
Wheeler, Thomas	015	1776	100 WB-2/83	AR
Wheeler, Thomas	060	1811	Orig. Only	AR
Wheeler, Thomas B.	084	1857	WB-C/252	CTY
Wheeler, Thomas B.	071	1820	WB-3/228	AR
Wheeler, William	046	1817	WB-B/43	AR
Wheeless, Benjamin	037	1772	WB-A/201	AR
Wheeless, Joiner	047	1834	WB-4/115	
Wheeless, Joseph	047	1787	WB-3/119	
Wheeless, Rhoda	047	1869	WB-6/34	
Wheeley, Benjamin	073	1829	WB-E/174	AR
Wheeley, Martha	073	1877	Orig. Only	AR
Whelar, Stanford	099	1883	WB-A/481	AR
Whelas, Joseph	047	1761	WB-1/38	
Wheless, Amos	069	1800	WB-1/130	AR
Wheless, Martha	069	1884	WB-5/208	AR
Wheless, William	069	1829	WB-1/365	AR
Wheless, William	069	1808	WB-1/186	AR
Wheller, Henry	010	1727	SS 876/124	SS/AR
Whelor, Samuel	078	1817	WI-7/293	AR
Wherry, Joseph	077	1730	SS 876/207	
Wheteley, William	030	c1810	WB-2/360	
Whetly, Samuell	096	1740	LGB-4/#117	SS/AR
Whichard, James	079	1896	WB-3/97	AR
Whichard, Lydia	079	1895	WB-3/84	AR
Whichard, W. R.	079	1900	WB-3/219	AR
Whichard, William J.	079	1866	WB-1/149	AR

Name	Co.	Date	Recorded Copy	Original
Whicker, James	090	1831	WB-3/221	AR
Whicker, Robert O.	038	1894	WB-3/469	AR
Whidbe, George	002	1723	Orig. Only	SS/AR
Whidbe, George	075	1717/8	SS 876/24	SS/AR
Whidbe, Richard	096	1740	LGB-4/#130	SS/AR
Whidbee, Benjamin	073	1819	WB-D/558	AR
Whidbee, Frances	024	1881	WB-E/96	AR
Whidbee, John	030	1792	WB-1/258	
Whidbee, John W.	024	1806	WB-B/229	AR
Whidbee, Mary	024	1811	WB-B/314	AR
Whiddon, Lott, Sr.	069	1785	WB-1/30	AR
Whinnery, Robert	022	1809	WB-A/164	AR
Whirlow, Joseph	032	1887	WB-3/547	AR
Whisanant, Phillip	060	1791	Orig. Only	AR
Whisant, George	060	c1833	Orig. Only	AR
Whisenhunt, Daniel	021	1881	WB-2/240	
Whisenhunt, David	081	1828	WB-5/427	AR
Whisenhunt, John	021	1843	WB-1/7	AR
Whisinant, Absalom	064	1893	WB-3/308	AR
Whisinant, Adam	060	1784	Orig. Only	AR
Whisnant, Adam, Sr.	026	1856	WB-1/198	AR
Whisnant, David	026	1880	WB-2/196	AR
Whisnant, Elisabeth	026	1878	WB-2/174	AR
Whisnant, George	026	1861	WB-1/266	AR
Whisnant, John	026	1865	WB-1/369	AR
Whisnant, Marthy	026	1842	WB-1/6	AR
Whisnant, Mary M.	026	1883	WB-2/250	AR
Whisnant, Susan	065	1895	WB-M/325	AR
Whisonant, Michael	SC	1885	026 WB-2/282	
Whitacer, William	009	1843	OB-E/201	AR
Whitaker, A. B.	047	1863	WB-5/107	
Whitaker, Aaron	092	1878	WB-6/110	AR
Whitaker, Aaron D. M.	092	1892	WB-6/343	AR
Whitaker, Abraham	073	1807	Orig. Only	AR
Whitaker, Abraham	092	1890	WB-6/313	
Whitaker, Abram	086	1867	WB-E/479	AR
Whitaker, Absolum B.	047	1845	WB-4/240	
Whitaker, Alice	047	1894	WB-7/124	AR
Whitaker, Benjamin	028	1784	WB-A/76	AR
Whitaker, Cary	047	1860	WB-5/78	
Whitaker, Cary	047	1816	WB-3/588	
Whitaker, Cary	047	1858	WB-5/57	
Whitaker, Cary	047	1865	WB-5/128	
Whitaker, Cyrus	099	1850	RB-27/91	AR
Whitaker, E. W.	009	1877	WB-1/187	CTY
Whitaker, Elizabeth	047	1893	WB-7/72	AR
Whitaker, Elizabeth	047	1819	WB-3/634	
Whitaker, Elizabeth	GA	1889	047 WB-7/250	047 AR
Whitaker, F. H.	047	1896	WB-7/172	AR
Whitaker, George W.	099	1888	WB-B/254	AR
Whitaker, Harriet	047	1877	WB-6/174	AR
Whitaker, Henry	013	1883	Orig. Only	AR
Whitaker, Henry H.	069	1882	WB-5/125	AR
Whitaker, James	023	1872	WB-A/2	AR
Whitaker, James	047	1825	WB-4/11	
Whitaker, Jane E.	009	1874	WB-1/132	CTY
Whitaker, Jesse	004	c1873	Orig. Only	AR-Copy
Whitaker, Jesse E.	047	1871	WB-6/66	AR
Whitaker, Jesse I.	023	1899	WB-A/138	AR
Whitaker, John	047	1784	WB-3/57	
Whitaker, John	047	1816	WB-3/584	
Whitaker, John	086	1838	WB-E/43	AR
Whitaker, John	013	1841	WB-A/73	
Whitaker, John	073	1885	WB-H/366	CTY
Whitaker, John	085	1800	WB-D/241	AR

Name	Co.	Date	Recorded Copy	Original
Whitaker, John Carey	047	1839	WB-4/184	
Whitaker, John H.	071	1863	WB-5/281	AR
Whitaker, L. H. B.	047	1865	WB-5/123	AR-Copy
Whitaker, Lewis H.	047	1859	WB-5/69	
Whitaker, Margaret	047	1868	WB-6/4	AR
Whitaker, Mary	099	1854	RB-28/594	AR
Whitaker, Mary E.	099	1880	WB-A/188	AR
Whitaker, Mary H.	099	1884	WB-A/547	AR
Whitaker, Mathew C.	047	1814	WB-3/551	
Whitaker, Nancy	092	1887	WB-6/267	AR
Whitaker, Nancy	047	1869	WB-6/27	AR
Whitaker, Patsy	073	1887	WB-H/431	CTY
Whitaker, Peter	006	1852	WB-A/58	AR
Whitaker, Richard	047	1794	WB-3/235	
Whitaker, Richard M.	069	1895	WB-5/481	AR
Whitaker, Robert	046	1765	WB-1/164	
Whitaker, Sarah	009	1849	OB-G/140	AR
Whitaker, Sarah E.	063	1885	WB-3/274	AR
Whitaker, Susan B.	099	1892	WB-C/37	AR
Whitaker, Thomas	085	1836	WB-H/680	AR
Whitaker, Wesley	099	1861	RB-32/75	AR
Whitaker, William	013	1860	WB-A/202	
Whitaker, William	013	1860	WB-A/211	
Whitaker, William	085	c1802	WB-E/5	AR
Whitaker, William	092	1898	WB-6/483	AR
Whitaker, William	085	c1799	WB-D/265	AR
Whitaker, William	063	1874	WB-3/75	
Whitaker, William	073	1832	WB-E/270	AR
Whitaker, Willis S.	099	1880	WB-A/115	AR
Whitaker, Wilson C.	047	1851	WB-4/304	
Whitaker, Wilson H.	047	1891	WB-7/17	AR
Whitaker, Wineford	063	1892	WB-4/75	AR
Whitaker, Young P.	073	1893	WB-I/9	CTY
Whitby, John	071	1818	WB-3/201	AR
Whitchard, Staton	037	1885	WB-G/704	
Whitcomb, Charlotte	030	1898	075 WB-O/462	075 AR
Whitcomb, M. P.	023	1892	WB-A/104	AR
Whitcomb, Theania R.	PA	1884	075 WB-O/205	075 AR
White, A. S.	016	1863	WB 2/96	AR
White, Abraham	075	1746	Orig. Only	SS/AR
White, Abraham	075	1796	WB-L/61	
White, Agnes	100	1830	WB-33/139	AR
White, Alexander	024	1849	WB-C/297	AR
White, Alexander	016	1881	WB-3/342	AR
White, Alfred	001	1883	WB-2/213	AR
White, Alfred	047	1891	WB-6/585	AR
White, Ambrose D.	077	1894	WB-H/250	AR
White, Angeline	099	1895	WB-C/340	AR
White, Ann	037	1810	WB-D/366	AR
White, Ann	013	1849	WB-A/140	
White, Ann	046	1860	WB-D/69	AR
White, Ann R.	077	1885	WB-H/157	AR
White, Anna	077	1796	WB-E/72	
White, Anna J.	011	c1819	WB-2/336	
White, Anna J.	011	c1819	SC/01657	AR-Copy
White, Aquinus	016	1883	WB-3/400	AR
White, Archibald	016	1801	WB-A/67	AR
White, Archibald	016	c1815	WB-A/10	AR
White, Archibald	037	1783	WB-B/110	AR
White, Arnold	077	1752	Orig. Only	SS/AR
White, Arnold	N	1690	Orig. Only	SS/AR
White, Arnold	075	1730	SS 876/205	
White, Benjamin	024	1847	WB-C/281	AR
White, Benjamin	037	1808	WB-D/313	AR
White, Benjamin	105	1860	WB-1/57	AR

Name	Co.	Date	Recorded Copy	Original
White, Benjamin	075	1785	WB-K/112	
White, Benjamin	075	1789	WB-K/192	
White, Benjamin	028	1814	WB-C/87	
White, Benjamin	077	1808	WB-E/322	AR
White, Benjamin	028	1842	WB-D/53	AR
White, Benjamin	075	1816	WB-M1/286	
White, Borden	046	1847	WB-C/276	AR
White, Bridget	030	1839	WB-4/66	
White, Caleb	030	1788	WB-1/224	
White, Caleb	053	c1789	RW-1/222	
White, Caleb	077	1795	WB-E/57	
White, Caleb	030	1872	WB-5/28	AR
White, Catharine	046	1887	WB-E/549	AR
White, Catharine	054	1868	WB-4/4	AR
White, Cealy	036	1885	WB-A/70	CTY
White, Celia	057	1873	WB-C/44	AR
White, Cely	026	1872	WB-2/74	AR
White, Charles	073	1883	WB-H/329	CTY
White, Charlotte	037	1899	WB-H/447	AR
White, Christian	075	1829	WB-N/51	AR
White, Coleman R.	044	1837	WB-14/16	CTY
White, Daniel	075	1846	WB-N/204	AR
White, David	016	1867	WB-2/158	AR
White, David	016	1816	WB-A/98	AR
White, David	018	1898	WB-E/289	AR
White, David	013	1879	WB-B/174	AR
White, David	046	1895	WB-F/397	AR
White, David	073	1837	WB-E/508	AR
White, David	077	1895	WB-H/264	AR
White, David	077	1864	WB-F/550	AR
White, David	054	c1831	Orig. Only	AR
White, David	054	1896	WB-5/570	CTY
White, David	010	1860	WB-H/92	AR
White, David B.	054	1893	WB-5/477	CTY
White, Davis	077	1852	WB-F/412	AR
White, Deborah	DE	1794	Copy	054 AR
White, Dempsy	077	1829	WB-F/167	AR
White, Doctrine	077	1883	WB-H/135	AR
White, Drusilla	039	1856	WB-Q/97	AR
White, Durent	010	1875	WB-I/70	AR
White, Edmond	100	1854	WB-43/184	AR
White, Edmund	077	1833	WB-F/221	AR
White, Edmund	001	1889	WB-2/434	AR
White, Edmund	075	1812	WB-M1/239	
White, Edward G.	054	1839	WB-2/193	AR
White, Edward S.	013	1891	WB-C/181	AR
White, Elam	065	1835	WB-E/193	AR
White, Elenor	054	1862	Orig. Only	AR
White, Elexander	077	1835	WB-F/239	AR
White, Elias	075	1833	WB-N/90	AR
White, Elihu A.	077	1900	WB-H/323	AR
White, Elisabeth	065	1845	WB-I/4	AR
White, Elisabeth	054	c1856	Orig. Only	AR
White, Eliza A.	010	1854	WB-G/505	AR
White, Elizabeth	040	1869	WB-2/2	AR
White, Elizabeth	054	1849	WB-3/33	AR
White, Elizabeth	100	1817	WB-21/4	AR
White, Elizabeth	077	1853	WB-F/418	AR
White, Elizabeth	024	1846	WB-C/264	AR
White, Elizabeth	069	1834	WB-1/404	AR
White, Elizabeth	010	1887	WB-I/223	AR
White, Elizabeth	041	1845	WB-3/66	AR
White, Elizabeth	010	1847	WB-G/413	AR
White, Emily	030	1889	WB-5/166	AR
White, Emma C.	099	1882	WB-A/367	AR

Name	Co.	Date	Recorded Copy	Original
White, Emma Jane	024	1886	WB-E/156	AR
White, Fanny	033	c1845	Orig. Only	AR
White, Francis	077	1813	WB-E/396	AR
White, Frederick	079	1892	WB-3/16	AR
White, Gabriel	077	1853	WB-F/413	AR
White, Gabriel	077	1824	WB-F/78	AR
White, George	044	1792	WB-2/297	CTY
White, George	037	1782	WB-B/97	AR
White, George	072	1830	WB-1/63	AR
White, George	054	c1826	WB-2/82	
White, George	028	1744	SS 878/20	SS/AR
White, George	024	1747	Orig. Only	SS/AR
White, George	028	1744	Deeds.21/L31	
White, George	024	1855	WB-C/376	AR
White, George W.	083	1875	Orig. Only	AR
White, Gulielmus	069	1804	WB-1/150	AR
White, H. A.	057	1897	WB-C/222	AR
White, Hedgepeth	084	c1798	OW/202	AR
White, Henrietta	011	c1785	WB-2/264	
White, Henry	085	1819	WB-G/534	
White, Henry	075	1739	SS 877/129	SS/AR
White, Henry	010	1866	WB-H/160	AR
White, Henry	030	1754	SS 878/171	SS/AR
White, Henry	030	1803	WB-2/234	
White, Henry P.	100	1864	WB-50/147	AR
White, Henry, Sr.	002	c1706	Orig. Only	SS/AR
White, Henry, Sr.	030	1794	WB-2/25	
White, Hillary	030	1839	WB-4/63	
White, Hugh	026	1891	WB-2/458	AR
White, Isaac	046	1811	WB-A/416	AR
White, J. B.	037	1891	WB-H/186	AR
White, J. Harvey	065	1864	WB-J/183	AR
White, J. O.	026	c1894	Orig. Only	AR
White, Jacob	077	1816	WB-E/462	AR
White, James	020	1862	RB-S/575	AR-Copy
White, James	060	1823	Orig. Only	AR
White, James	010	1854	WB-H/10	AR
White, James	077	1864	WB-F/554	AR
White, James	085	c1781	WB-B/17	AR
White, James	040	1851	WB-1/33	
White, James	024	1794	Orig. Only	AR-Nunc.
White, James	030	1897	WB-5/237	AR
White, James	072	c1874	WB-4/113	AR
White, James	075	1807	WB-M1/157	AR
White, James	070	1801	WB-AB/48	AR
White, James A.	038	1899	WB-4/146	AR
White, James B.	027	1820	WB-A/29	AR
White, James E.	054	1853	WB-3/69	AR
White, James F.	040	1874	WB-2/69	AR
White, James G.	026	1862	WB-1/276	AR
White, James H.	060	1884	WB-4/285	AR
White, James H.	040	1884	WB-2/212	AR
White, James W.	001	1887	WB-2/336	AR
White, James, Sr.	030	1831	WB-3/284	
White, Jane	016	1838	PQS.5/472	AR
White, Jane	016	1867	WB-2/157	AR
White, Jane	065	1844	WB-H/182	AR
White, Jane H.	016	1871	Orig. Only	AR
White, Jasper	030	1887	WB-5/148	AR
White, Jean	016	1807	WB-A/98	AR
White, Jeptha	077	1873	WB-H/49	AR
White, Jeremiah	041	1845	WB-3/60	AR
White, Jesse	077	1825	WB-F/87	AR
White, Jesse	077	1873	WB-H/43	AR
White, Jesse	075	1816	WB-M1/287	

Name	Co.	Date	Recorded Copy	Original
White, Jesse	077	1814	WB-E/404	AR
White, Jinnette	016	1861	WB-2/81	AR
White, John	077	1730	Orig. Only	SS/AR
White, John	041	1792	WB-1/103	AR
White, John	054	1819	WB-1A/32	AR
White, John	019	1746	SS 877/342	SS/AR
White, John	011	c1797	WB-1/389	
White, John	022	1829	WB-B/162	AR
White, John	075	1754	SS 881/77	SS/AR
White, John	053	1726	SS 876/53	SS/AR
White, John	046	c1787	WB-A/403	AR
White, John	022	1799	WB-A/4	AR
White, John	016	1805	WB-A/95	AR
White, John	077	1842	WB-F/306	AR
White, John	028	1812	WB-C/59	AR
White, John	044	1865	WB-22/381	CTY
White, John	011	c1770	WB-2/260	
White, John	037	1800	WB-D/109	AR
White, John	106	c1869	WB-2/19	AR
White, John	046	1812	WB-A/418	AR
White, John	037	1804	WB-D/198	AR
White, John	009	c1799	OWB/351	AR
White, John	010	1845	WB-G/389	AR
White, John	047	1880	WB-6/230	AR
White, John	077	1772	WB-C/109	AR
White, John	002	1692	Orig. Only	SS/AR
White, John	077	1774	WB-C/161	AR
White, John	016	1841	PQS.6/136	AR
White, John	089	1858	WB-1/184	
White, John	077	1848	WB-F/364	AR
White, John A.	054	1880	WB-4/379	CTY
White, John E.	026	1864	WB-1/332	AR
White, John H.	016	1857	WB-2/28	AR
White, John H.	038	1894	WB-3/426	AR
White, John M.	083	1886	WB-3/368	AR
White, John P.	045	1887	WB-1/143	AR
White, John R.	016	1822	WB-A/14	AR
White, Johnson L.	010	1890	WB-I/297	AR
White, Jonathan	044	1772	Orig. Only	CTY
White, Jonathan	077	1823	WB-F/56	AR
White, Jordan	075	1801	WB-M1/45	AR
White, Joseph	005	1807	WB-2/191	AR
White, Joseph	077	1808	WB-E/311	AR
White, Joseph	077	c1861	WB-F/535	AR
White, Joseph	011	c1784	WB-2/280	
White, Joseph	069	1795	WB-1/96	AR
White, Joseph	009	c1802	OWB/404	AR
White, Joseph	044	1829	WB-11/150	CTY
White, Joseph	028	1759	Orig. Only	AR
White, Joseph	073	1844	WB-F/195	AR
White, Joseph	077	1852	WB-F/411	AR
White, Joseph	075	1827	WB-N/34	AR
White, Joseph	028	1838	WB-C/409	AR
White, Joseph	073	1846	WB-F/312	AR
White, Joseph	077	1759	SS 882/105	
White, Joseph H.	077	1850	WB-F/380	AR
White, Joseph Sr.	016	1842	PQS.6/224	AR
White, Joseph W.	010	1889	WB-I/274	AR
White, Joseph, Sr.	005	1808	WB-2/190	AR
White, Joseph,Jr.	069	1795	WB-1/239	AR
White, Joshua	009	c1804	OWB/422	AR
White, Joshua	075	1779	WB-K/41	
White, Joshua	077	1865	WB-H/1	AR
White, Joshua	030	1777	WB-1/119	
White, Joshua	044	1826	WB-10/181	CTY

Name	Co.	Date	Recorded Copy	Original
White, Joshua	077	1831	WB-F/181	AR
White, Joshua	077	1784	WB-C/265	AR
White, Joshua J.	075	1867	WB-M2/104	AR
White, Josiah	005	1804	WB-2/193	AR
White, Josiah	010	1898	WB-I/575	
White, Josiah	077	1808	WB-E/279	AR
White, Josiah	077	1825	WB-F/91	AR
White, Josiah	010	1878	WB-I/103	
White, Josiah H.	077	1895	WB-H/271	AR
White, Judah	024	1798	WB-A/334	AR
White, Katherine	022	c1810	WB-A/191	AR
White, Leah	019	1813	WB-E/23	AR
White, Leah	077	1854	WB-F/445	AR
White, Lela	072	1873	WB-4/52	AR
White, Levenia	065	1887	WB-L/200	AR
White, Lewis	026	1891	WB-2/413	AR
White, Lewis	028	1851	WB-D/180	
White, Littleberry	069	1842	WB-1/469	AR
White, Lizzie	065	1876	WB-K/227	AR
White, Lorenzo	081	1869	WB-15/15	AR
White, Lucinda	010	1874	WB-I/56	AR
White, Luke	010	1837	WB-G/273	AR
White, Luke	010	1796	WB-D/331	AR
White, Luke	010	1858	WB-H/66	AR
White, Luke	024	1771	WB-A/184	AR
White, Luke	087	c1804	Orig. Only	AR
White, Luke	030	1758	SS 882/176	SS/AR
White, Lydia	077	1868	WB-H/23	AR
White, Marcus	065	1862	WB-J/147	
White, Margaret	083	1898	WB-4/229	AR
White, Margaret	075	1813	WB-M1/252	
White, Margaret	075	1822	WB-M1/353	AR
White, Margaret	028	1821	WB-C/202	
White, Margaret	077	1790	WB-C/403	AR
White, Margaret	016	1838	PQS.5/511	AR
White, Margeret	016	c1797	WB-A/2	
White, Mark	044	1793	WB-3/72	CTY
White, Martha	010	1833	WB-G/222	AR
White, Martha	037	1840	WB-F/244	AR
White, Martha	077	1859	WB-F/500	AR
White, Martha	105	c1860	WB-1/84	AR
White, Martha C.	016	1883	WB-3/382	AR-Nunc.
White, Martha S.	010	1900	WB-K/56	
White, Mary	016	1804	WB-A/72	AR
White, Mary	077	c1860	WB-F/520	AR
White, Mary	040	1871	WB-2/39	AR
White, Mary	030	c1804	WB-2/270	
White, Mary	MA	1895	028 WB-F/207	
White, Mary	030	1855	WB-4/197	AR
White, Mary	028	1800	WB-B/95	AR
White, Mary	054	c1830	WB-2/109	AR
White, Mary A.	077	1892	WB-H/243	AR
White, Mary A.	073	1872	WB-H/60	CTY
White, Mary A.	077	1899	WB-H/312	AR
White, Mary Ann	030	1795	WB-2/38	
White, Mary Ann	054	1845	WB-2/318	AR
White, Mary C.	040	1877	WB-2/118	AR
White, Mary E.	098	1882	WB-A/12	CTY
White, Mary H.	NY	1892	047 WB-7/103	047 AR
White, Mary P.	016	1881	WB-3/319	AR
White, Maryium	077	1824	WB-F/67	AR
White, Mathew R.	011	c1793	WB-1/395	
White, Matthew	077	1788	WB-C/372	AR
White, Matthew	077	1834	WB-F/225	AR
White, McAmy A.	016	1866	WB-2/145	AR

Name	Co.	Date	Recorded Copy	Original
White, Medey	010	1804	WB-E/244	AR
White, Media	024	1749	Orig. Only	SS/AR
White, Meedy	010	1850	WB-G/466	AR
White, Miles	077	1788	WB-C/361	AR
White, Miriam	077	1834	WB-F/232	AR
White, Miriam	075	1840	WB-N/152	AR
White, Mordeca	010	1779	WB-B/145	AR
White, Moses	085	c1783	WB-C/115	AR
White, Moses A.	054	1880	WB-4/406	CTY
White, Moses W.	024	c1878	WB-E/86	AR
White, Nancy	026	1889	WB-2/399	AR
White, Nancy	073	1877	WB-H/174	CTY
White, Nancy	010	1900	WB-K/17	
White, Nathan	075	1814	WB-M1/260	
White, Nathan	075	1824	WB-M1/407	AR
White, Nathan	077	1897	WB-H/294	AR
White, Nehemiah	075	1806	WB-M1/129	AR
White, Nehemiah	075	1751	Orig. Only	SS/AR
White, Nehemiah	075	1834	WB-N/100	AR
White, Norris T.	016	1876	WB-3/115	AR
White, Peggy	077	1840	WB-F/289	
White, Peter	010	1884	WB-I/171	
White, Peter	024	1860	WB-D/6	AR
White, Philip	044	1845	WB-16/335	CTY
White, Polley	010	1876	WB-I/79	AR
White, Polly	071	1796	WB-2/125	AR
White, Priscilla	100	1897	WB-51/477	
White, R. Benton	016	1900	WB-4/352	AR
White, Rachel	029	1808	WB-A/122	AR
White, Rachel	077	1835	WB-F/246	AR
White, Rachel	077	N.D.	Orig. Only	AR
White, Rachel R.	075	1808	WB-M1/182	AR
White, Reuben	053	1837	Orig. Only	AR
White, Reuben	037	1804	WB-D/196	AR
White, Richard	015	1775	100 WB-2/73	AR
White, Richard	044	1757	Orig. Only	CTY
White, Richard	015	1775	SC/04941	AR-Copy
White, Richardson	054	c1824	WB-2/22	AR
White, Riley	092	1869	WB-6/5	
White, Robert	075	1698	SS 874.2/96	SS/AR
White, Robert	065	1877	WB-K/250	AR
White, Robert	063	1894	WB-4/129	AR
White, Robert	065	1810	WB-G/3	AR
White, Robert	030	1837	WB-4/27	
White, Robert	075	1733	SS 876/324	SS/AR
White, Robert F.	001	1896	WB-3/147	AR
White, Robert J.	030	1893	WB-5/204	AR
White, Robert R.	054	1873	WB-4/111	CTY
White, Robert W.	016	1879	WB-3/251	AR
White, Roger	002	1686	Orig. Only	SS/AR
White, Ruth	075	1803	WB-M1/80	AR
White, Samuel	060	1793	Orig. Only	AR
White, Samuel	001	c1849	WB-1/53	AR
White, Samuel	077	1813	WB-E/390	AR
White, Samuel	016	1820	WB-A/53	AR
White, Samuel	077	1779	WB-C/227	AR
White, Samuel H.	016	1859	WB-2/54	AR
White, Samuel S.	077	1816	WB-E/446	AR
White, Sarah	010	1809	WB-F/126	AR
White, Sarah	077	1832	WB-F/208	AR
White, Sarah	016	1830	PQS.5/107	AR
White, Sarah	077	1821	WB-F/34	AR
White, Sarah	001	1852	WB-1/60	AR
White, Sarah	053	1727	SS 876/99	SS/AR
White, Sarah A.	VA	1894	030 WB-5/301	030 AR

Name	Co.	Date	Recorded Copy	Original
White, Sarah A.	040	c1866	WB-1/193	
White, Saul	056	1806	WB-1/191	AR
White, Seth	077	1826	WB-F/124	AR
White, Seth	075	1846	WB-N/200	AR-Nunc.
White, Silas	024	c1841	WB-C/232	AR
White, Silas	024	1797	WB-A/287	AR
White, Silas	022	1885	WB-E/318	AR
White, Simon	001	1866	WB-1/265	AR
White, Simon	022	1840	WB-C/102	AR
White, Solomon	009	c1809	OWB/458	AR
White, Solomon	051	1854	WB-A/362	
White, Stephen	026	c1869	WB-2/27	AR
White, Stephen	022	1829	WB-B/166	AR
White, Stephen	073	1818	WB-D/544	AR
White, Stephen	075	1816	WB-M1/296	
White, Susan	099	1882	WB-A/369	AR
White, Susan A.	026	1897	Orig. Only	AR
White, Susan E.	028	1880	WB-E/237	AR
White, Susan T.	020	1894	WB-B/169	CTY
White, Temperance	070	1825	WB-C/464	AR
White, Theophilus	077	1855	WB-F/457	AR
White, Thomas	077	1819	WB-F/19	AR
White, Thomas	024	1754	SS 881/118	SS/AR
White, Thomas	030	1823	WB-3/164	
White, Thomas	029	c1802	Orig. Only	AR
White, Thomas	046	1832	WB-B/458	AR
White, Thomas	077	1762	WB-C/1	
White, Thomas	002	c1695	Orig. Only	SS/AR
White, Thomas	075	1808	WB-M1/181	AR
White, Thomas	019	1757	SS 882/124	SS/AR
White, Thomas	024	1788	WB-A/182	AR
White, Thomas	005	c1785	WB-1/54	
White, Thomas	077	1823	WB-F/54	AR
White, Thomas	022	1812	WB-A/205	AR
White, Thomas	011	1768	WB-2/273	
White, Thomas	030	1819	WB-3/113	
White, Thomas	073	1856	WB-G/142	AR
White, Thomas	096	1883	WB-4/93	
White, Thomas	077	1835	WB-F/234	AR
White, Thomas	085	c1801	WB-D/271	AR
White, Thomas	024	1802	WB-B/202	AR
White, Thomas	016	1846	WB-1/104	AR
White, Thomas	016	1842	PQS.6/169	AR
White, Thomas	041	1813	WB-2/85	AR
White, Thomas	IN	1838	090 WB-4/58	090 AR
White, Thomas	010	1856	WB-H/38	AR
White, Thomas	077	1809	WB-E/336	AR
White, Thomas	077	1854	WB-F/446	AR
White, Thomas	028	1842	WB-D/43	AR
White, Thomas J.	077	1835	WB-F/240	AR
White, Thomas P.	089	1863	WB-1/249	
White, Toms	075	1813	WB-M1/248	AR
White, Turner D.	078	1865	WB-18/393	AR
White, Virgil	024	c1874	Orig. Only	AR
White, W. L.	065	1838	WB-E/193	
White, Warren W.	101	1893	WB-A/235	
White, Whichart	028	1869	WB-E/17	AR
White, Whichcoat	028	1819	WB-C/188	AR
White, William	046	1806	WB-A/412	AR
White, William	024	1849	WB-C/294	AR
White, William	070	1763	DB-C/15	AR
White, William	011	c1783	WB-1/591	
White, William	099	1812	RB-10/170	AR
White, William	028	1892	WB-F/21	AR
White, William	070	1784	WB-C/448	AR

Name	Co.	Date	Recorded Copy	Original
White, William	077	1772	WB-C/118	AR
White, William	010	1866	WB-H/178	AR
White, William	024	1724	SS 876/10	SS/AR
White, William	016	1854	WB-1/230	AR
White, William	077	1784	WB-C/252	AR
White, William	029	1798	WB-A/10	AR
White, William	086	1849	WB-E/198	AR-Nunc.
White, William	077	1796	WB-E/66	
White, William	024	1885	WB-E/141	AR
White, William	077	1811	WB-E/408	AR
White, William	010	1816	WB-F/305	AR
White, William	077	1795	WB-E/54	
White, William	100	1832	WB-33/373	AR
White, William	029	1774	Orig. Only	SS/AR
White, William	026	1879	WB-2/186	AR
White, William	030	1755	Orig. Only	SS/AR
White, William	016	1800	WB-A/71	AR
White, William E.	065	1866	WB-J/214	AR
White, William F.	077	1831	WB-F/182	AR
White, William H.	100	1896	WB-51/406	
White, William O.	077	1888	WB-H/176	AR
White, William P.	021	1897	WB-3/144	AR
White, William S.	016	c1822	WB-A/14	AR
White, William W.	075	1850	WB-N/234	AR
White, Willoughby	030	1825	WB-3/179	
White, Zachariah	077	1808	WB-E/326	AR
White, Zachariah	010	1866	WB-H/196	AR
White, Zachariah	005	1852	WB-C/40	AR
Whitead, Daniel	004	1876	WB-A/22	AR
Whitecar, Anne E.	009	1889	WB-1/502	CTY
Whitefield, James T.	078	1850	WB-13/338	AR
Whitefield, Thomas L.	078	1863	WB-18/311	AR
Whitefield, William	078	1857	WB-17/477	AR
Whitehall, Thomas	030	1828	WB-3/241	
Whitehall, Thomas	030	1892	WB-5/202	AR
Whitehead, Abi	030	1856	WB-4/206	AR
Whitehead, Abraham	047	1766	WB-1/187	
Whitehead, Alice	028	1743	LGB-4/#144	SS/AR
Whitehead, Alice	028	1742/3	Wills.6/L56	
Whitehead, Allen	047	1839	WB-4/183	
Whitehead, Arthur	069	1824	Orig. Only	AR
Whitehead, Arthur	022	1815	WB-A/264	AR
Whitehead, Arthur	022	1877	WB-E/135	AR
Whitehead, Augustin	037	1846	WB-F/357	AR
Whitehead, Benjamin	047	1831	WB-4/70	
Whitehead, Benjamin	069	c1794	WB-1/232	AR
Whitehead, Christopher	035	1859	WB-2/148	AR
Whitehead, Cordy	071	1877	WB-6/215	AR
Whitehead, Edwin M.	081	1863	WB-12/515	AR
Whitehead, Eliza D.	070	1888	WB-F/178	AR
Whitehead, Elizabeth	069	1832	WB-1/384	AR
Whitehead, Elizabeth	099	1852	RB-28/147	AR
Whitehead, Faithy	047	c1844	WB-4/243	
Whitehead, Henry	029	1897	WB-F/105	AR
Whitehead, Henry	037	1848	WB-F/400	AR
Whitehead, Howell G.	105	1887	WB-2/451	AR
Whitehead, J. R.	099	1897	WB-D/4	AR
Whitehead, James	081	1863	WB-12/368	AR
Whitehead, James	069	1854	WB-1/542	AR
Whitehead, James W.	047	1883	WB-6/298	AR
Whitehead, John	028	1832	WB-C/347	
Whitehead, John	022	1850	WB-C/281	AR
Whitehead, John	028	1822	WB-C/215	AR
Whitehead, John	035	c1838	Orig. Only	AR
Whitehead, John	035	1842	Orig. Only	AR
Whitehead, Joseph	047	1833	WB-4/101	
Whitehead, Joseph	047	1781	WB-3/1	
Whitehead, Joseph B.	047	1888	WB-6/508	AR
Whitehead, Joseph B.	047	c1867	Orig. Only	AR
Whitehead, Josiah	022	1809	WB-A/168	AR
Whitehead, Mary	069	1806	WB-1/169	AR
Whitehead, Mary	029	1900	WB-F/206	AR
Whitehead, Mary B.	028	1882	WB-E/305	AR
Whitehead, Mary E.	047	1897	WB-7/195	AR
Whitehead, Mary F.	047	1874	WB-6/107	AR
Whitehead, Matthew	037	1848	Orig. Only	AR
Whitehead, Nathan	053	1809	RW-1/434	AR
Whitehead, Nathan	069	1811	WB-1/222	AR
Whitehead, Nathan	069	1779	WB-1/4	AR
Whitehead, Nathaniel	071	1858	WB-5/208	AR
Whitehead, Quintina	047	1883	WB-6/299	AR
Whitehead, Rahab	099	1815	RB-12/214	AR
Whitehead, Samuel	078	1795	WI-1/213	AR
Whitehead, Sarah	037	1816	WB-E/120	AR
Whitehead, Susan	105	1883	WB-2/315	AR
Whitehead, Susan V.	045	1895	WB-1/250	AR
Whitehead, Thomas	069	1808	WB-1/180	AR
Whitehead, Thomas	022	1866	WB-D/62	AR
Whitehead, Tobias	047	1774	WB-1/334	
Whitehead, Turner	047	1847	WB-4/256	
Whitehead, W. J.	105	1890	WB-2/533	AR
Whitehead, Wiley	047	1865	WB-5/133	
Whitehead, William	047	1802	WB-3/380	
Whitehead, William	047	1765	WB-1/162	
Whitehead, William	092	1822	WB-3/151	AR
Whitehead, William B.	070	1877	WB-E/317	AR
Whitehead, William B.	037	1807	WB-D/286	AR
Whitehead, Williamson	029	1834	WB-B/237	AR
Whitehead, Willis	028	1826	WB-C/271	AR
Whitehead, Willis	077	1894	WB-H/261	AR
Whitehead, Willis	030	1855	WB-4/200	
Whitehouse, John	069	1810	WB-1/209	AR
Whitehouse, Kizier	030	1825	WB-3/185	
Whitehouse, Samuel	019	1756	SS 880/142	SS/AR
Whitehurst, C. L.	075	1879	WB-O/106	AR
Whitehurst, Christopher	018	1824	WB-C/43	
Whitehurst, David W.	019	1866	WB-B/13	AR
Whitehurst, Frederick	075	1843	WB-N/177	AR
Whitehurst, James	018	1853	WB-C/375	
Whitehurst, John	079	1883	WB-2/265	AR
Whitehurst, John	009	1848	OB-F/459	AR
Whitehurst, John	018	1822	WB-C/14	
Whitehurst, John	072	1860	WB-2/183	AR
Whitehurst, John	019	c1795	WB-E/12	AR
Whitehurst, John T.	072	1864	Orig. Only	AR
Whitehurst, Jonathan	018	1828	WB-C/97	
Whitehurst, Joseph	018	1844	WB-C/300	
Whitehurst, Josiah	030	1792	WB-1/251	
Whitehurst, Josias	009	c1734	OWB/23	AR
Whitehurst, Keeling	075	c1854	WB-M2/26	AR
Whitehurst, Levin	030	1884	WB-5/106	AR
Whitehurst, Louweza	079	1892	WB-3/10	AR
Whitehurst, Margaret	075	1860	WB-M2/65	AR
Whitehurst, Mary	072	1794	Orig. Only	AR
Whitehurst, Olly	018	1861	WB-D/64	AR
Whitehurst, Polly	030	1830	WB-3/261	
Whitehurst, Rachel	019	1895	WB-B/286	AR
Whitehurst, Richard	072	1777	RW/L7	AR
Whitehurst, Richard	072	c1765	RW/L54	AR
Whitehurst, Samuel	028	1850	WB-D/170	

Name	Co.	Date	Recorded Copy	Original
Whitehurst, Samuel	030	1814	WB-3/42	Nunc.
Whitehurst, Samuel, Sr.	030	c1814	WB-3/41	
Whitehurst, Shadrick	009	1818	OB-A/286	AR
Whitehurst, Simon	018	1826	WB-C/73	
Whitehurst, Thomas	072	1812	WB-A/138	AR
Whitehurst, Thomas	N	1766	Orig. Only	SS/AR
Whitehurst, William	028	1781	Orig. Only	AR
Whitehurst, William B.	018	1855	WB-D/14	AR-Copy
Whitehurst, William W.	075	c1861	WB-M2/74	AR
Whiteman, John	077	1831	WB-F/185	AR
Whiteman, Richard	024	1894	WB-E/226	AR
Whiten, George	NY	1880	028 WB-F/68	
Whitener, A. J.	021	1895	WB-3/94	AR
Whitener, Abel	021	c1896	Orig. Only	AR
Whitener, Andrew M.	021	1867	WB-1/249	AR
Whitener, Benjamin	060	1816	Orig. Only	AR
Whitener, Benjamin	021	1900	WB-3/310	AR
Whitener, Daniel	021	1868	WB-1/256	AR
Whitener, Daniel B.	021	1874	WB-2/104	AR
Whitener, David B.	021	1859	Orig. Only	AR
Whitener, David P.	021	1864	WB-1/198	AR
Whitener, Eli	021	1894	WB-3/46	
Whitener, Eliza	021	1892	WB-2/581	AR
Whitener, Henry	021	1847	WB-1/58	AR
Whitener, Hosea H.	021	c1892	WB-3/344	AR
Whitener, Jesse R.	021	1847	WB-1/52	AR
Whitener, John B.	021	1855	WB-1/117	AR
Whitener, Laban S.	021	1899	WB-3/230	AR
Whitener, Lafayette	017	1875	WB-B/47	AR
Whitener, Michael	060	1796	Orig. Only	AR
Whitener, Moses	021	1891	WB-2/562	AR
Whitener, Phillip	060	1833	WB-1/278	AR
Whitenton, L. B.	099	1888	WB-B/245	AR
Whitenton, Richard	056	1821	WB-1/431	AR
Whitesell, David	001	1885	WB-2/253	AR
Whitesell, Jose	001	1880	WB-2/158	AR
Whitesell, Sallie M.	001	1895	WB-3/46	AR
Whiteside, A. W.	086	1855	WB-E/295	AR
Whiteside, Elizabeth	086	1862	WB-E/403	AR
Whiteside, G. M.	086	1880	WB-F/154	AR
Whiteside, James	086	1790	Orig. Only	AR
Whiteside, Joseph	086	1879	WB-F/138	AR
Whiteside, Major	040	1864	WB-1/160	AR
Whiteside, Richard	080	1889	WB-1/138	AR
Whiteside, William	080	1869	WB-1/3	AR
Whitesides, Dorcas	065	1819	WB-F/224	AR
Whitesides, Edward	060	1832	WB-1/243	AR
Whitesides, Edward	040	1897	WB-2/552	AR
Whitesides, Elizabeth	065	1852	WB-I/187	AR
Whitesides, John	040	1847	WB-1/1	AR
Whitesides, John	065	1824	WB-G/61	AR
Whitesides, John B.	013	c1859	WB-A/213	
Whitesides, Major M.	040	1862	WB-1/143	AR
Whitesides, Margaret	040	1870	WB-2/11	AR
Whitesides, Mary	040	1875	WB-2/97	AR
Whitesides, Mary J.	065	1827	WB-A/156	AR
Whitesides, Wallace	040	c1852	WB-1/51	
Whitesides, William	094	1778	Orig. Only	060 AR
Whitesides, William	040	c1866	WB-1/192	
Whitesides, William T.	040	1882	WB-2/186	AR
Whitfeal, William	069	1828	WB-1/356	AR
Whitfield, Allen	103	1845	RD-9/241	AR
Whitfield, Arnold	063	1857	WB-2/429	
Whitfield, Benjamin	069	1808	WB-1/181	AR
Whitfield, Bettie G.	059	1896	WB-B/157	CTY
Whitfield, Charity	069	1854	WB-1/540	AR
Whitfield, Charlotte	035	1880	WB-4/164	AR
Whitfield, Constantine	028	1798	WB-B/46	AR
Whitfield, Delilah	069	1818	WB-1/300	AR
Whitfield, Demaris	059	1879	WB-A/185	CTY
Whitfield, Edwin	078	1885	WB-19/171	
Whitfield, Henry E.	069	1886	WB-5/240	AR
Whitfield, Isaac	069	c1796	WB-1/238	AR
Whitfield, James	020	1859	RB-S/85	AR
Whitfield, John	035	1825	WB-A/523	AR
Whitfield, John	044	1833	WB-12/426	CTY
Whitfield, John B.	103	1835	RD-7/69	AR
Whitfield, John G.	047	1879	WB-6/214	AR
Whitfield, John T.	035	1876	WB-4/106	AR
Whitfield, Joseph	035	1852	WB-2/68	AR
Whitfield, Joseph	035	1835	WB-1/64	AR
Whitfield, Kenneth B.	063	1864	WB-2/538	
Whitfield, Lewis	059	c1848	Copy	103 AR
Whitfield, Lewis	078	1884	WB-19/153	AR
Whitfield, Martha A.	078	1885	WB-19/173	AR
Whitfield, Mary	069	1844	WB-1/468	AR
Whitfield, Mary	103	1871	WB-1/22	AR
Whitfield, Mary	069	c1792	WB-1/239	AR
Whitfield, Mary L.	037	1879	WB-G/547	AR
Whitfield, Needham	103	1812	RD-2/153	AR
Whitfield, Penelope	069	1861	WB-1/576	AR
Whitfield, Penelope	103	1816	RD-3/380	AR
Whitfield, Reuben	069	1816	WB-1/272	AR
Whitfield, Sallie J.	073	1898	WB-I/137	CTY
Whitfield, Sally	035	1837	Orig. Only	AR
Whitfield, Sarah	069	1836	WB-1/413	AR
Whitfield, Sarah	038	1899	WB-4/191	AR
Whitfield, Sarah F.	020	1865	RB-T/109	AR
Whitfield, Solomon	069	1808	WB-1/194	AR
Whitfield, Tabithy	051	1867	WB-B/95	AR
Whitfield, Thomas	069	1781	WB-1/224	AR
Whitfield, Thomas	069	1800	WB-1/229	AR
Whitfield, W. L.	097	1897	WB-2/540	
Whitfield, William	047	1806	WB-3/446	
Whitfield, William	103	1817	RD-4/31	AR
Whitfield, William	070	1776	WB-C/440	AR-Nunc.
Whitfield, William	103	1795	WI-A/558	AR
Whitfield, William	096	1761	WB-1/21	AR
Whitfield, William	069	1826	WB-1/335	AR
Whitford, David R.	028	1866	WB-D/469	AR
Whitford, Edward	028	1894	WB-F/127	
Whitford, Hardy	028	1841	WB-D/31	
Whitford, Holton	028	1839	WB-C/432	
Whitford, John	028	1829	WB-C/311	AR
Whitford, Mary J.	028	1890	WB-F/2	
Whitford, Nathan	028	1867	WB-D/450	AR
Whitford, Nelson	028	1899	WB-F/416	
Whitford, Thomas	028	1781	Orig. Only	AR
Whitford, William C.	028	1899	WB-F/426	
Whithous, Gracey	030	c1809	WB-2/343	
Whithurst, Gideon	030	1790	WB-1/243	
Whithurst, Hillery	009	1834	OWB/517	AR
Whithurst, Nancy	030	1843	WB-4/95	
Whithurst, William	079	1876	WB-2/124	AR
Whitiker, William	092	1825	WB-3/164	
Whiting, James	028	1781	Orig. Only	AR
Whitington, Sarah	054	1866	WB-3/187	AR
Whitlet, Nancy	081	1834	WB-6/435	AR
Whitley, Adison	097	1866	WB-1/281	AR
Whitley, Alby J.	103	1890	WB-1/506	AR

Name	Co.	Date	Recorded Copy	Original
Whitley, Arthur	009	c1794	OWB/303	AR
Whitley, Arthur	009	1817	OB-A/269	AR
Whitley, Ashley	103	1876	WB-1/96	AR
Whitley, Daniel	009	1883	WB-1/325	CTY
Whitley, Elijah	087	c1825	Orig. Only	AR
Whitley, Elizabeth	056	1864	WB-2/54	AR
Whitley, Elizabeth	060	1813	Orig. Only	AR
Whitley, Enoch	056	1842	WB-1/545	AR
Whitley, Esther	056	1825	WB-1/458	AR
Whitley, Ezekiel S.	063	1849	WB-2/347	
Whitley, George	060	1798	Orig. Only	AR
Whitley, George	089	c1845	Orig. Only	AR
Whitley, H. M.	056	1879	WB-3/222	AR
Whitley, J. K.	105	1888	WB-2/490	AR
Whitley, Jane	103	1880	WB-1/180	AR
Whitley, Jesse	009	c1832	OWB/505	AR
Whitley, Jesse	VA	1861	051 WB-C/241	051 AR
Whitley, John	056	1819	Est-11/258	AR
Whitley, John D.	037	1866	WB-G/280	AR
Whitley, John R.	089	1863	WB-1/255	
Whitley, John, Sr.	056	1819	WB-1/302	
Whitley, Josiah	069	1831	WB-1/372	AR
Whitley, Judith J.	071	1883	WB-6/421	
Whitley, L. R.	069	c1886	Orig. Only	AR
Whitley, Leander	056	1863	WB-2/40	AR
Whitley, Lou Edney	VA	1879	051 WB-C/234	
Whitley, Marintha	089	1893	Orig. Only	AR
Whitley, Mary D.	063	1838	WB-2/249	
Whitley, Mary M.	069	1887	WB-5/249	AR
Whitley, Michael	099	1881	WB-A/254	AR
Whitley, Mills	069	1840	WB-1/450	AR
Whitley, Nancy	105	1866	WB-1/124	AR
Whitley, Nancy	024	1897	WB-E/267	AR
Whitley, Needham	056	1832	WB-1/476	AR
Whitley, Pierce	063	1841	WB-2/286	
Whitley, R. D.	065	1900	WB-N/332	
Whitley, Richard R.	069	c1862	Orig. Only	AR
Whitley, Sally	051	1856	WB-A/381	
Whitley, Sion	069	1840	WB-1/436	AR
Whitley, Thomas	069	c1800	WB-1/240	AR
Whitley, William	056	1833	WB-1/495	AR
Whitley, Willis	069	1861	WB-1/575	AR
Whitliff, John	056	1761	WB-1/770	AR
Whitlo, William	071	1759	Orig. Only	SS/AR
Whitlock, Charles	090	1814	WB-2/153	AR
Whitlock, Charles	092	1885	WB-6/215	AR
Whitlock, George	044	1774	WB-1/21	CTY
Whitlock, John	092	1833	WB-4/61	AR
Whitly, Alison	089	1896	WB-2/318	AR
Whitly, Elizabeth	009	1837	OB-C2/2	AR
Whitly, Nancy	037	1873	WB-G/431	AR
Whitly, Temple	089	1865	WB-1/272	
Whitman, John A.	085	1865	WB-K/370	AR
Whitmell, Thomas	063	c1779	WB-1/133	
Whitmell, Thomas	010	1735	LGB-4/#22	
Whitmell, Thomas	010	1779	WB-C/50	AR-Nunc.
Whitmell, Thomas B.	047	1798	WB-3/318	
Whitmire, Christopher	050	c1838	WB-1/13	
Whitmire, Christopher	013	1837	WB-A/47	
Whitmire, Christopher	050	c1838	Copy	093 AR
Whitmire, George W.	093	1888	WB-1/205	AR
Whitmire, S. D.	093	1892	WB-2/122	AR
Whitmire, William	093	1873	WB-1/129	AR-Nunc.
Whitmore, Elizabeth	047	1892	WB-7/52	AR
Whitmore, Henry B.	047	1876	WB-6/155	AR
Whitmore, P. H.	047	1883	WB-6/307	AR
Whitner, Betsey	021	1882	WB-2/246	
Whitner, George	021	1880	WB-2/218	
Whitner, Joseph	021	1873	WB-2/74	AR
Whitner, Joseph N.	SC	1864	061 WB-2/39	061 AR
Whitney, Abner	075	1810	WB-M1/221	AR
Whitney, James W.	037	1873	WB-G/422	AR
Whitney, Joshua	N	1735	LGB-4/#25	SS/AR
Whitney, Samuel	063	1794	WB-1/204	
Whitous, Anthony	076	1834	WB-N/95	AR
Whitridge, Thomas	065	1883	WB-L/28	AR
Whitsall, Adam	073	1822	WB-E/7	AR
Whitsel, Adam	073	1822	WB-E/1	AR
Whitsell, Jacob	001	c1848	WB-1/69	AR
Whitsell, James	084	c1839	Orig. Only	AR
Whitsell, Mary	001	1877	WB-2/114	AR
Whitsett, John	084	1806	WB-A/33	CTY
Whitson, J. C.	064	1900	WB-2/499	AR
Whitson, J. C.	064	1900	107 WB-2/214	
Whitt, James	036	1883	WB-A/49	CTY
Whittaker, Heny	013	1883	WB-B/304	
Whittaker, M. L.	013	1891	WB-C/184	
Whitted, Anderson	073	1880	WB-H/296	CTY
Whitted, Archa	011	1883	WB-2/157	
Whitted, James	073	c1817	Orig. Only	AR
Whitted, Jehu	073	1804	WB-D/132	AR
Whitted, Levi	073	1849	WB-F/439	AR
Whitted, Mary	073	1823	WB-E/34	AR
Whitted, S. E. Y.	050	1893	WB-2/178	CTY
Whitted, W. N.	011	1893	WB-3/55	CTY
Whitted, William	073	1816	WB-D/468	AR
Whitted, William	073	1822	WB-E/1	AR
Whitted, William H.	073	1825	WB-E/76	AR
Whitted, Wilson	073	1895	WB-I/64	CTY
Whittemore, J. B.	084	1890	WB-E/467	CTY
Whittemore, Nancy	020	1858	RB-S/71	AR
Whittemore, William W.	084	1860	WB-C/325	CTY
Whittenton, Richard	037	1761	WB-A/41	AR
Whitticor, Thomas	092	1787	WB-2/78A	AR
Whittier, Clarke	091	1887	WB-1/95	
Whittier, John	070	1843	WB-AB/392	AR
Whittington, A. G.	104	1891	WB-6/383	AR
Whittington, James	104	1886	WB-6/281	AR
Whittington, John	006	1802	WB-A/19	
Whittington, John W.	104	1888	WB-6/332	AR
Whittington, Joseph	046	1821	WB-B/138	AR
Whittington, Mary	092	1894	WB-6/395	AR
Whittington, Thomas	046	1877	WB-E/190	AR
Whittle, James	081	1824	WB-5/168	AR
Whittle, William	029	1761	Orig. Only	AR
Whittson, Michael	096	c1778	WB-1/149	
Whitty, Edward	057	1802	WB-A/259	AR
Whitty, Joseph	057	1843	WB-B/157	AR
Whitty, Mariah	028	1897	WB-F/253	
Whitty, William	028	1815	WB-C/100	AR
Whitworth, Isaac	084	1807	WB-A/63	CTY
Whitworth, John	084	1817	WB-A/128	CTY
Whitworth, Margaret	026	1892	WB-2/444	AR
Whorten, Abey	075	1787	WB-K/152	AR
Whorton, David	074	1872	WB-1/1	AR
Whorton, Edward	075	1771	WB-H/131	AR
Whyte, Solomon H.	010	1864	WB-H/137	AR
Whyte, William	073	1831	WB-E/251	AR
Wiant, Peter	104	1797	WB-1/460	AR
Wiat, John	077	1739	LGB-4/#97	SS/AR

Name	Co.	Date	Recorded Copy	Original
Wiat, John	015	1771	100 WB-1/159	AR
Wiat, Thomas	002	1735	SS 876/400	SS/AR
Wiate, John	047	1801	WB-3/351	
Wiatt, Frederick	001	1866	WB-1/264	AR
Wiatt, John	085	1816	WB-G/453	AR
Wicke, James	092	1889	WB-6/304	AR
Wicker, Benjamin	068	1809	WB-A/266	
Wicker, Benjamin	022	c1867	WB-D/173	AR
Wicker, David	068	1816	WB-A/292	
Wicker, Edward	068	c1876	WB-D/120	
Wicker, Elijah	030	1853	WB-4/171	
Wicker, Elijah	090	1821	WB-3/60	AR
Wicker, James	022	1794	RB-2/30	AR
Wicker, John	030	1792	WB-1/265	
Wicker, Milley	022	1839	WB-C/98	AR
Wicker, Richard	030	1699/0	Orig. Only	SS/AR
Wicker, Richard	030	1774	WB-1/85	
Wicker, Thomas	022	1784	RB-1/17	AR
Wicker, Thomas	022	1832	WB-B/229	AR
Wicker, William	030	1799	WB-2/142	
Wickliffe, William	028	1754	SS 881/127	SS/AR
Wickliffe, William	028	1775	Orig. Only	AR
Wicks, Prudence	028	1880	WB-E/226	AR
Wickstead, Pall	070	1738	SS 877/193	SS/AR (N)
Widdop, William	046	1820	WB-B/102	AR
Widdows, Jane	046	1893	WB-F/286	AR
Widdows, Mary E.	046	1898	WB-G/71	AR
Widop, Charles	046	c1876	WB-E/167	AR
Wier, Mary A.	100	1874	Orig. Only	AR
Wiers, Rachal	081	c1807	Orig. Only	AR
Wigenton, Robert	030	1865	WB-4/255	AR
Wiggens, Archerbald	039	1844	WB-L/210	AR
Wiggins, Abraham	043	c1879	WB-1/29	
Wiggins, Ambrose	041	1805	WB-1/219	AR
Wiggins, Andrew C.	091	c1896	WB-1/20	
Wiggins, Arthur	047	1812	WB-3/533	
Wiggins, Blake B.	063	1815	WB-2/29	
Wiggins, Blake H.	037	1828	WB-F/83	AR
Wiggins, Bridgitt	041	1798	WB-1/155	AR
Wiggins, David	099	1779	RB-1/150	AR
Wiggins, Edward	059	1882	WB-A/357	CTY
Wiggins, Eliza J.	051	c1900	WB-C/584	
Wiggins, Elizabeth	028	1829	WB-C/302	
Wiggins, Fanney	063	c1784	WB-1/109	
Wiggins, Fredrick	044	1836	WB-13/338	CTY
Wiggins, James	037	1823	WB-E/339	AR
Wiggins, Jesse	041	1826	WB-2/254	AR
Wiggins, Jesse B.	011	1870	WB-2/46	
Wiggins, John	063	c1783	WB-1/124	
Wiggins, John	041	1839	WB-3/19	AR
Wiggins, John	028	1803	WB-B/184	AR
Wiggins, John L.	037	1897	WB-H/390	AR
Wiggins, Lawrence	037	1847	WB-F/373	AR
Wiggins, Margaret	051	1847	WB-A/268	
Wiggins, Matthew	010	1820	WB-G/77	AR
Wiggins, Rebecca	051	1843	WB-A/348	
Wiggins, Richard	037	1774	WB-A/213	AR
Wiggins, Robert A.	037	1803	WB-D/168	AR
Wiggins, Rowland	105	1882	WB-2/281	AR
Wiggins, Salley	063	1810	WB-2/71	
Wiggins, Sally	045	c1875	Orig. Only	AR
Wiggins, Sampson	039	1816	WB-E/36	AR
Wiggins, Sarah	071	1858	WB-5/206	AR
Wiggins, Sarah	039	1856	WB-0/363	AR

Name	Co.	Date	Recorded Copy	Original
Wiggins, Solomon	099	1883	WB-A/491	AR
Wiggins, Thomas	044	1815	WB-7/514	CTY
Wiggins, Thomas	044	1799	WB-4/295	CTY
Wiggins, Thomas	024	1760	WB-A/187	AR
Wiggins, Thomas	063	c1779	WB-1/93	
Wiggins, Thomas	047	1774	WB-1/373	
Wiggins, Thomas M.	079	1868	WB-1/179	AR
Wiggins, Thoms	103	c1802	Orig. Only	AR
Wiggins, Wiley	041	1897	WB-4/412	AR
Wiggins, William	047	1791	WB-3/195	
Wiggins, William B.	019	1889	WB-B/174	AR
Wiggons, James	037	1794	WB-C/291	AR
Wiggs, Alexander	039	1888	WB-U/420	AR
Wiggs, Esther	039	c1844	WB-L/268	AR
Wiggs, Henry	103	1811	RD-1/336	AR
Wiggs, Henry	103	1860	RD-13/190	AR
Wiggs, J. T.	056	1896	WB-4/1	AR
Wiggs, James H.	099	1887	WB-B/227	AR
Wiggs, John	103	1827	RD-5/327	
Wiggs, John, Sr.	103	1828	RD-5/464	AR
Wiggs, John, Sr.	103	1830	RD-6/180	AR
Wiggs, Lucy J.	021	1900	WB-3/296	AR
Wiggs, Ralph	087	c1801	Orig. Only	AR
Wiggs, Susan	103	1858	RD-12/596	AR
Wiggs, William	099	1874	RB-35/251	AR
Wight, Edward	070	1760	DB-D/454	AR
Wight, Henry	N	1670	Orig. Only	SS/AR
Wigle, Mary M.	049	1810	WI-A/4	AR
Wigon, Cressey	039	1807	WB-C/128	
Wike, Andrew	055	c1882	WB-A/53	
Wike, Delilah	021	1891	WB-2/540	
Wike, Julius A.	021	1888	WB-2/428	
Wilbert, John	075	1816	WB-M1/280	AR
Wilborn, James	104	1871	WB-6/32	
Wilborn, John	073	1819	WB-D/553	AR
Wilborn, Levi	081	1859	WB-11/231	AR
Wilborn, Mary B.	075	1818	WB-M1/324	AR
Wilborn, Richard	092	1848	WB-4/276	
Wilborn, Sarah Jane	TN	1898	066 WB-1/173	
Wilborn, Temperance	044	1826	WB-10/236	CTY
Wilbourn, Edward	092	1806	WB-3/71	
Wilbourn, Mary	073	1840	WB-F/57	AR
Wilcock, James	028	1807	WB-B/285	AR
Wilcocks, John	028	1762	Wills.7/279	SS/AR
Wilcocks, John	028	1762	Wills.7/280	
Wilcott, Annah	019	1760	RB-A/29	AR
Wilcox, Adam	045	1883	WB-1/112	AR
Wilcox, Benjamin	057	1826	WB-B/92	AR
Wilcox, George	068	1857	WB-C/54	
Wilcox, L. N.	080	1900	WB-1/340	AR
Wilcox, Thomas	028	1865	WB-D/403	AR
Wilcoxen, Thomas L.	092	1893	WB-6/377	AR
Wildar, John	029	1800	WB-A/34	AR
Wilde, John	061	c1860	WB-1/88	AR
Wilder, Augustus	024	1851	WB-C/314	AR
Wilder, Celia	051	1847	WB-A/275	
Wilder, Elizabeth	024	1848	WB-C/288	AR
Wilder, Esther	099	1857	RB-30/350	AR
Wilder, Francis A.	009	1880	WB-1/266	CTY
Wilder, Gaston H.	099	1873	RB-35/84	AR
Wilder, Hopkins	072	1792	Orig. Only	AR
Wilder, Jackson	039	1879	WB-U/208	AR
Wilder, James	020	1861	RB-S/443	AR
Wilder, James	056	1815	WB-1/248	AR
Wilder, James W.	039	1887	WB-U/413	AR

Name	Co.	Date	Recorded Copy	Original
Wilder, Joel	072	1828	WB-1/23	AR
Wilder, John	024	1807	WB-B/292	AR
Wilder, John	056	1805	WB-1/175	AR
Wilder, Jonathan	072	1824	Orig. Only	AR
Wilder, Kerney	056	1887	WB-3/449	AR
Wilder, Louisa	039	1896	WB-V/97	AR
Wilder, Matthew	056	1806	WB-1/187	AR
Wilder, Matthew	069	1861	WB-1/576	AR
Wilder, Richard	024	1843	WB-C/240	AR
Wilder, Sampson	051	1836	WB-A/238	
Wilder, Samuel	099	1861	RB-32/89	AR
Wilder, Sophia	039	1874	WB-U/112	AR
Wilder, Thomas	024	1827	WB-C/132	AR
Wilder, Willis	024	1818	WB-C/72	AR
Wiles, Annis	051	1834	WB-A/64	
Wiles, James	004	1863	WB-1/2	AR
Wiles, Lucy	084	1892	WB-E/530	CTY
Wiles, Marthy	106	c1848	WB-1/47	AR
Wiles, Susan	084	1892	WB-E/510	CTY
Wiley, Alexander	020	1861	RB-S/440	AR
Wiley, B. F.	046	1897	WB-G/26	AR
Wiley, Betsey	046	1832	WB-B/465	AR
Wiley, David, Sr.	046	1816	WB-A/422	AR
Wiley, Hugh A.	046	1863	WB-D/187	AR
Wiley, Isabel	046	1817	WB-B/48	AR
Wiley, James	096	1771	Orig. Only	AR
Wiley, John M.	085	1898	WB-3/242	CTY
Wiley, Robert	046	1819	WB-B/84	AR
Wiley, Rufus	099	1848	RB-26/385	AR
Wiley, Samuel H.	085	1894	WB-3/38	CTY
Wiley, Samuel H.	085	c1891	Copy	013 AR
Wiley, Shannon	046	1868	WB-D/369	AR
Wiley, Thomas	046	1812	WB-A/417	AR
Wiley, Thomas	020	1825	RB-K/101	AR
Wiley, William	072	1801	WB-A/143	AR
Wiley, William T.	028	1887	WB-E/435	AR
Wilfong, B. E. L.	021	1888	WB-2/403	AR
Wilfong, George	060	1829	WB-1/148	AR
Wilfong, John	060	1838	WB-2/1	
Wilfong, John	021	1883	WB-2/251	AR
Wilfong, Peter	060	1842	WB-2/118	AR
Wilford, James	010	1825	WB-G/129	AR
Wilhelm, Anny	085	c1868	WB-1/1	CTY
Wilhelm, George	016	1797	WB-A/76	AR
Wilhelm, Mary	085	1857	WB-K/237	
Wilhite, Philip	039	c1801	WB-B/73	
Wilhite, William	039	1808	WB-C/120	
Wilie, Mary	016	1822	WB-A/84	AR
Wilkerson, Ann	073	1838	WB-F/7	AR
Wilkerson, Anna	009	1840	OB-C2/266	AR
Wilkerson, Catherine	073	1885	WB-H/384	CTY
Wilkerson, David	078	1844	Orig. Only	AR
Wilkerson, David	044	1819	WB-8/292	CTY
Wilkerson, David S.	044	1875	WB-23/206	CTY
Wilkerson, Elizabeth	073	1874	WB-H/93	CTY
Wilkerson, Elizabeth	009	c1840	OB-D/315	AR
Wilkerson, Elizabeth	073	1870	WB-H/34	CTY
Wilkerson, Harris	073	1879	WB-H/221	CTY
Wilkerson, Henrietta	078	1849	WB-13/217	AR
Wilkerson, James N.	044	1890	WB-24/134	CTY
Wilkerson, Jethro	086	1854	WB-E/280	AR
Wilkerson, John	078	1846	Orig. Only	AR
Wilkerson, John	044	1887	WB-24/3	CTY
Wilkerson, John	053	1780	RW-1/87	
Wilkerson, John	082	1831	WB-2/7	AR

Name	Co.	Date	Recorded Copy	Original
Wilkerson, John	022	1788	RB-1/33	AR
Wilkerson, John Y.	078	1865	WB-18/391	AR
Wilkerson, Joseph	073	1899	WB-I/154	CTY
Wilkerson, Joshua	056	1761	WB-1/768	AR
Wilkerson, Josiah L.	078	1899	WB-19/482	AR
Wilkerson, Kate	073	1895	WB-I/77	CTY
Wilkerson, Liddia	009	1845	OB-E/480	AR
Wilkerson, Marvel	053	1856	WB-8/180	
Wilkerson, Mary Jane	009	1826	OB-A/362	AR
Wilkerson, Mary W.	070	1877	WB-10/65	
Wilkerson, Mercy	090	1832	WB-3/234	AR
Wilkerson, Reuben	056	1809	Orig. Only	AR
Wilkerson, Susan	073	1895	WB-I/79	CTY
Wilkerson, Thomas	085	1797	WB-C/43	AR
Wilkerson, Thomas	020	1871	WB-A/71	CTY
Wilkes, Francis	099	1813	RB-11/101	AR
Wilkes, James	010	1831	WB-G/208	AR
Wilkes, John	047	1824	WB-3/696	
Wilkes, Micajah	010	1842	WB-G/345	AR
Wilkeson, Duncan	083	c1806	WB-1/96	AR
Wilkeson, Margaret	083	c1803	WB-1/78	AR
Wilkeson, Philip	011	1758	Orig. Only	SS/AR
Wilkeson, William	011	c1795	WB-1/408	
Wilkie, L. Thomas	060	1893	WB-4/514	AR
Wilkings, Winslow S.	070	1839	WB-AB/318	AR
Wilkins, Alexander	022	1812	WB-A/208	AR
Wilkins, Allen	099	1832	RB-22/315	AR
Wilkins, Benjamin	053	1796	RW-1/271	AR
Wilkins, Bennett R.	047	1860	WB-5/87	
Wilkins, Charles	024	1734	SS 876/366	SS/AR
Wilkins, Charles	075	N. D.	WB-M2/76	AR
Wilkins, Charles S.	086	1817	WB-C/59	AR
Wilkins, Clement	039	1850	WB-N/310	
Wilkins, E. W.	071	1899	WB-7/413	AR
Wilkins, Edmund	071	1867	WB-5/342	AR
Wilkins, Elijah	071	1852	WB-5/102	AR
Wilkins, Elijah	005	1829	WB-B/4	AR
Wilkins, Elisha	029	1830	WB-B/201	AR
Wilkins, Elizabeth	009	1840	OB-C2/267	AR
Wilkins, Esther	022	c1836	WB-C/43	
Wilkins, Esther Ann	037	1887	WB-H/102	AR
Wilkins, Etheldred	041	1871	WB-4/23	AR
Wilkins, F. H.	026	1865	WB-1/366	AR
Wilkins, Frances	053	1785	RW-1/137	
Wilkins, George	106	1893	WB-2/333	
Wilkins, George	090	c1874	WB-6/70	
Wilkins, George	024	1804	WB-B/35	AR
Wilkins, George T.	005	1890	WB-D/288	AR
Wilkins, Harriet A.	005	1892	WB-D/321	AR
Wilkins, Henry	001	c1885	WB-2/260	AR
Wilkins, Jacob	009	1822	OB-A/319	AR
Wilkins, John	090	1870	WB-6/20	AR
Wilkins, John	024	1774	Orig. Only	SS/AR
Wilkins, John	024	c1778	WB-A/176	AR
Wilkins, John	022	1796	RB-2/78	AR
Wilkins, John	053	1810	RW-1/446	
Wilkins, John	035	1791	WB-A/493	AR
Wilkins, John L.	VA	1845	071 WB-5/27	071 AR
Wilkins, John S.	072	c1880	WB-4/206	AR
Wilkins, John S.	VA	1843	071 WB-4/267	071 AR
Wilkins, John S.	009	1846	OB-F/251	AR
Wilkins, John, Sr.	090	1838	WB-4/24	AR
Wilkins, Littleton	053	1784	RW-1/113	
Wilkins, Louisa G.	VA	1891	071 WB-7/125	071 AR
Wilkins, Martha	047	1876	WB-6/150	AR

Name	Co.	Date	Recorded Copy	Original
Wilkins, Mary	037	1868	WB-G/320	AR
Wilkins, Mary	099	1843	RB-25/315	AR
Wilkins, Melissa	080	1890	WB-1/152	AR
Wilkins, Patrick	053	1807	RW-1/410	AR
Wilkins, Raeford B.	048	1900	WB-1/118	CTY
Wilkins, Robert	035	1857	WB-2/112	AR
Wilkins, Rosomond	072	1790	WI/L16	AR
Wilkins, Rotheas	053	c1816	RW-1/513	AR
Wilkins, Sallie Ann	087	1887	WB-3/373	AR
Wilkins, Samuel	065	c1763	WB-G/24	AR
Wilkins, Samuel	009	1840	OB-C2/329	AR
Wilkins, Samuel	018	1837	WB-C/201	
Wilkins, Sarah	024	1802	WB-B/226	AR
Wilkins, Terrell	086	1844	WB-E/137	AR
Wilkins, Thomas	026	1844	WB-1/35	AR
Wilkins, Thomas	026	1868	WB-1/426	AR
Wilkins, Thomas	090	1880	WB-6/115	AR
Wilkins, Thomas	053	1799	RW-1/308	AR
Wilkins, Thomas	047	1762	WB-1/53	
Wilkins, Thomas M.	037	1854	WB-G/69	AR
Wilkins, Violet	069	c1887	Orig. Only	AR
Wilkins, W. H.	010	1900	WB-K/20	
Wilkins, William	024	1777	WB-A/175	AR
Wilkins, William	037	1816	WB-E/144	AR
Wilkins, William	035	1876	WB-4/108	AR
Wilkins, William	071	1840	WB-4/222	AR
Wilkins, William A.	044	1882	WB-23/443	CTY
Wilkins, William B.	001	1872	WB-2/41	AR
Wilkinson, Aaron	009	c1791	OWB/261	AR
Wilkinson, Abner C.	037	1863	WB-G/228	AR
Wilkinson, Abraham	053	1762	OB-A/79	
Wilkinson, Abram	009	1830	OB-B/83	AR
Wilkinson, Angus	054	c1829	WB-2/99	AR
Wilkinson, Anna Jane	083	1889	Orig. Only	AR
Wilkinson, Barbara	035	1827	WB-A/488	AR
Wilkinson, Benjamin	037	1837	WB-F/203	AR
Wilkinson, Benoni M.	063	c1854	WB-2/413	
Wilkinson, Charles	056	1830	WB-1/413	AR
Wilkinson, Charles	005	1810	WB-2/181	AR
Wilkinson, Charles	056	1792	WB-1/53	AR
Wilkinson, Daniel	073	1842	WB-F/124	AR
Wilkinson, Francis	073	1806	WB-D/174	AR
Wilkinson, Francis T.	009	1900	WB-2/213	CTY
Wilkinson, Frederick	053	1801	RW-1/330	
Wilkinson, George M.	021	1887	WB-2/365	AR
Wilkinson, Henry H.	060	1885	WB-4/295	AR
Wilkinson, Isaac	053	1813	RW-1/474	
Wilkinson, Israel	009	1829	OB-B/28	AR
Wilkinson, Israel	053	1820	WB-4/138	
Wilkinson, Israel	009	1834	OWB/512	AR
Wilkinson, Israel	028	1780	Orig. Only	AR
Wilkinson, J. G.	065	1864	WB-J/186	AR
Wilkinson, J. J.	037	1878	WB-G/554	AR
Wilkinson, James	073	1818	WB-D/526	AR
Wilkinson, James	073	1814	WB-D/410	AR
Wilkinson, James	037	1855	WB-G/107	AR
Wilkinson, James	053	1783	RW-1/109	
Wilkinson, James	021	1846	WB-1/40	AR
Wilkinson, James R.	009	1870	WB-1/55	CTY
Wilkinson, Jesse	053	1786	RW-1/157	
Wilkinson, John	073	1814	WB-D/398	AR
Wilkinson, John	012	1772	WB-B/166	AR
Wilkinson, John	060	1835	WB-1/342	AR
Wilkinson, John	012	1833	WB-B/167	AR
Wilkinson, John	035	1837	Orig. Only	AR
Wilkinson, Joshua	037	1818	WB-E/194	AR
Wilkinson, Laban	009	1878	WB-1/219	CTY
Wilkinson, Letisha	021	1871	WB-2/58	
Wilkinson, Margaret	035	1761	WB-A/532	AR
Wilkinson, Martha A.	065	1891	WB-L/531	
Wilkinson, Marvel	053	1856	WB-8/180	AR
Wilkinson, Mary	009	1821	OB-A/308	AR
Wilkinson, Milly	037	1845	WB-F/325	AR
Wilkinson, Minerva V.	009	1898	WB-2/138	CTY
Wilkinson, Nancy	037	1893	WB-H/243	AR
Wilkinson, Nathan	056	1822	WB-1/452	AR
Wilkinson, Nathaniel	VA	1813	071 WB-3/108	071 AR
Wilkinson, Neill	029	1846	WB-C/136	AR
Wilkinson, Oden	009	1835	OWB/524	AR
Wilkinson, Patience	009	1856	OB-K/54	AR
Wilkinson, Recey	056	1824	WB-1/376	AR
Wilkinson, Samuel	020	1782	RB-A/185	AR
Wilkinson, Samuel J.	009	1866	OB-M/319	AR
Wilkinson, Samuel M.	073	1898	WB-I/144	CTY
Wilkinson, Sarah	053	c1814	RW-1/527	
Wilkinson, Wiley	009	1845	OB-F/37	AR
Wilkinson, William	073	1815	WB-D/451	AR
Wilkinson, William	070	1780	WB-C/444	AR
Wilkinson, William	073	1847	WB-F/349	AR
Wilkinson, William	053	c1768	RW-1/5	
Wilkinson, William	081	c1822	Orig. Only	AR
Wilkinson, William	082	1830	WB-2/3	AR
Wilkison, Archibald	083	c1808	WB-1/228	AR
Wilkison, Christian	083	c1820	WB-1/246	
Wilkison, Daniel	083	1854	WB-2/107	AR
Wilkison, Edward	082	1843	WB-3/13	AR
Wilkison, John	078	1821	WI-9/249	AR
Wilkison, Mary J.	056	1877	WB-3/180	AR
Wilkison, Neill	083	1834	WB-1/287	AR
Wilkison, Richard	083	c1799	WB-1/135	
Wilkison, Robert	083	c1799	WB-1/54	AR
Wilkison, Samuel	085	c1792	WB-D/234	
Wilkison, William	N	1706	Orig. Only	SS/AR
Wilks, Humphrey	028	1795	WB-A/327	AR
Wilks, James	010	1798	WB-E/59	AR
Wilks, James	079	1884	WB-2/300	AR
Wilks, Susan A.	029	1883	WB-E/306	AR
Will, Conrad	060	1807	Orig. Only	AR
Will, Gerhard	094	c1778	Orig. Only	060 AR
Willard, Alfred	009	1881	WB-1/278	CTY
Willard, Augustian	092	c1823	WB-3/156	AR
Willard, George	090	1822	WB-3/92	AR
Willard, John	075	1816	WB-M1/281	AR
Willard, W. H.	099	1898	WB-D/110	AR
Willbanks, Richard	104	1790	WB-1/293	AR
Willborn, Daniel	104	1834	WB-4/178	AR
Willcockson, George	085	1786	WB-C/104	AR
Willcox, Jeremiah	075	1754	Orig. Only	SS/AR
Willcox, Martha	047	1849	WB-4/275	
Willcox, Rebecca	022	1808	WB-A/158	AR
Willcox, Thomas	047	1877	WB-6/173	AR
Willeford, Eliza	016	1871	WB-3/56	AR
Willeford, Nathan	100	1780	WB-3/39	AR
Willet, James	022	c1818	WB-B/6	AR
Willets, Henry	090	1816	WB-2/175	
Willett, Caroline	NY	1853	Copy	050 AR
Willett, Marinus	NY	1881	Copy	050 AR
Willetts, Henry	012	1827	WB-B/150	AR-Copy
Willetts, Hope	012	1767	DB-A/30	AR
Willey, Edward W.	046	1793	WB-A/406	AR

Name	Co.	Date	Recorded Copy	Original
Willey, Frances	047	1853	WB-4/343	
Willey, Henry	041	1889	WB-4/290	AR
Willey, Henry W.	070	1858	WB-C/677	AR
Willey, Hillary	041	1838	WB-2/398	AR
Willey, James	068	1809	WB-A/265	
Willey, John A.	072	1840	Orig. Only	AR
Willey, John A.	072	1793	Orig. Only	AR
Willey, John, Sr.	041	1864	WB-3/308	AR
Willey, Matthias	010	1802	WB-E/141	AR
Willey, Polly	004	c1895	Orig. Only	AR-Copy
Willey, W. P.	046	1897	WB-F/572	AR
Willhalem, Lewis	085	1846	Orig. Only	AR-Nunc.
William, Edward	096	1765	WB-1/58	AR
Williams, A. D.	VA	1852	037 WB-F/515	037 AR
Williams, Aaron	084	c1794	OW/206	AR
Williams, Aaron	035	1808	Orig. Only	AR
Williams, Abel	097	1878	WB-2/147	
Williams, Abel L.	084	1892	WB-E/523	CTY
Williams, Abner	075	1839	WB-N/149	AR
Williams, Abner	063	1857	WB-2/443	
Williams, Absalom	083	1813	WB-1/145	AR
Williams, Absalom	037	1814	WB-E/63	AR
Williams, Adam	056	1873	WB-3/85	AR
Williams, Agnes	075	1845	WB-N/190	AR
Williams, Agnes	009	1859	OB-L/57	AR
Williams, Agness	044	1803	WB-5/324	
Williams, Alanson	100	1825	WB-27/81	AR
Williams, Alex	TN	1852	062 WB-B/143	
Williams, Alexander	054	1852	WB-3/59	AR
Williams, Alexander	003	1863	Orig. Only	AR
Williams, Alexander	087	1900	WB-4/112	AR
Williams, Alexander	054	1897	WB-6/55	CTY
Williams, Alexander	049	1893	WB-2/300	AR
Williams, Alfred	086	1862	WB-E/399	AR
Williams, Alfred	099	1896	WB-C/475	AR
Williams, Allen	099	1810	RB-9/189	AR
Williams, Allen	050	1887	WB-2/10	CTY
Williams, Allen G.	009	1888	WB-1/448	CTY
Williams, Alphonso	046	1897	WB-G/14	AR
Williams, Amandaline	104	1876	WB-6/135	AR
Williams, Amas	054	1878	WB-4/290	CTY
Williams, Amey	030	1822	WB-3/132	
Williams, Andrew	073	1837	WB-E/507	AR
Williams, Andrew C.	028	1859	WB-D/316	AR
Williams, Andrew J.	030	1892	WB-5/195	AR
Williams, Ann	047	1785	WB-3/98	
Williams, Ann	073	1900	WB-I/165	CTY
Williams, Ann	024	1798	WB-A/337	AR
Williams, Ann	100	1827	WB-31/78	AR
Williams, Ann	041	1822	WB-2/191	AR
Williams, Ann Mariah	057	1873	WB-C/21	AR
Williams, Ann Mary	072	c1792	Orig. Only	AR
Williams, Anna	100	1878	WB-51/260	AR
Williams, Anthony	035	1752	028 DB-5/248	SS/AR
Williams, Anthony	035	1752	087 DB-2/124	
Williams, Anthony	024	1718	Orig. Only	SS/AR
Williams, Anthony E.	071	1807	WB-2/332	AR
Williams, Arthor	037	1779	WB-B/28	AR
Williams, Arthur	010	1775	WB-B/30	AR
Williams, Arthur	010	1739	Orig. Only	SS/AR
Williams, Ashkenaz	022	c1810	WB-A/171	AR
Williams, Ausborne	067	1864	WB-1/125	AR
Williams, Austin	099	1849	RB-26/529	AR
Williams, Azariah	032	1865	WB-2/312	AR
Williams, B. S. D.	099	1870	RB-35/87	AR
Williams, Barbara	075	1873	WB-O/44	AR
Williams, Barden	069	1896	WB-5/541	AR
Williams, Barshaba	087	c1820	WB-1/19	AR
Williams, Benjamin	010	1824	WB-G/117	AR
Williams, Benjamin	VA	1879	092 WB-6/200	092 AR
Williams, Benjamin	069	1841	WB-1/451	AR
Williams, Benjamin	081	1825	WB-5/175	AR
Williams, Benjamin	010	1817	WB-F/320	AR
Williams, Benjamin	056	c1794	WB-1/96	AR
Williams, Benjamin	022	1807	WB-F/61	AR
Williams, Benjamin	037	1793	WB-C/238	AR
Williams, Benjamin	072	c1778	RW/L3	AR
Williams, Benjamin	039	c1794	WB-B/19	
Williams, Benjamin	068	1828	WB-B/56	
Williams, Benjamin	069	1818	WB-1/298	AR
Williams, Benjamin	028	1780	Orig. Only	AR
Williams, Bersada	037	1880	WB-G/582	AR
Williams, Billey	100	1800	WB-10/314	AR
Williams, Billey	069	1804	WB-1/148	AR
Williams, Blany	087	1852	WB-1/414	AR
Williams, Brice	019	c1779	Orig. Only	AR
Williams, Britton	063	1810	WB-1/434	
Williams, Bryan	072	c1790	Orig. Only	AR
Williams, Bryan	028	1861	WB-D/355	AR
Williams, Buckner	071	1836	WB-4/140	AR
Williams, Burrel	037	1811	WB-E/19	AR
Williams, Burwell	029	1841	WB-B/346	AR
Williams, Burwell	022	c1816	WB-A/278	AR
Williams, C. T.	030	1897	WB-5/240	
Williams, C. W.	106	c1874	WB-2/75	
Williams, Caleb	018	1828	WB-C/102	
Williams, Caroline	039	1889	WB-U/473	AR
Williams, Cary	078	1841	WI-15/5	AR
Williams, Catharine	TN	1870	062 WB-B/131	
Williams, Chaplain	057	1793	WB-A/166	AR
Williams, Charity	028	1875	WB-E/122	AR
Williams, Charity	063	1822	WB-2/83	
Williams, Charles	030	1799	WB-2/155	
Williams, Charles	060	1857	WB-3/15	AR
Williams, Charles	044	1819	WB-8/259	CTY
Williams, Charles	060	1802	Orig. Only	AR
Williams, Charles	047	1798	WB-3/315	
Williams, Charles J.	099	1859	RB-31/254	AR
Williams, Charlotta	079	1861	WB-1/65	
Williams, Charlotte	084	1870	WB-E/27	CTY
Williams, Christian	069	1816	WB-1/274	AR
Williams, Christopher	071	1786	WB-1/362	AR
Williams, Clement	054	1868	WB-4/13	AR
Williams, Daniel	044	1759	Orig. Only	CTY
Williams, Daniel	075	1801	WB-M1/48	AR
Williams, Daniel	083	1874	WB-3/74	AR
Williams, Daniel	081	1882	WB-15/379	AR
Williams, Daniel	072	c1813	WB-A/144	AR
Williams, Daniel	100	c1879	Orig. Only	AR
Williams, Daniel	075	1790	WB-K/187	AR
Williams, Daniel	075	1852	WB-N/244	AR
Williams, David	075	1806	WB-M1/121	AR
Williams, David	065	c1777	WB-F/215	AR
Williams, David	037	1881	WB-G/612	AR
Williams, David	070	1772	WB-C/436	AR
Williams, David	073	1850	WB-F/469	AR
Williams, David	060	1887	WB-4/373	AR
Williams, David	104	1855	WB-5/128	
Williams, Delphia	022	1850	WB-C/257	AR
Williams, Dempsey	063	1853	WB-2/395	

Name	Co.	Date	Recorded Copy	Original
Williams, Demsey	041	1804	WB-1/208	AR
Williams, Dixon	063	c1804	WB-1/420	
Williams, Dove M.	009	1775	OWB/126	AR
Williams, Drewry	037	1831	WB-F/125	AR
Williams, Dudley	005	1815	WB-2/182	AR
Williams, E. T.	068	1894	WB-D/415	
Williams, Edmund C.	030	1892	WB-5/200	AR
Williams, Edward	018	1826	WB-C/75	
Williams, Edward	075	1739	LGB-4/#103A	SS/AR
Williams, Edward	060	1814	Orig. Only	AR
Williams, Edward	028	1781	Orig. Only	AR
Williams, Edward	075	1790	WB-K/189	AR
Williams, Edward	082	1799	WB-1/67	AR
Williams, Edward	024	1714	SS 875/102	SS/AR
Williams, Edward	035	1826	WB-A/531	AR
Williams, Edward S.	072	1889	WB-4/243	AR
Williams, Edy	028	1877	WB-E/163	AR
Williams, Elias	030	1896	WB-5/235	
Williams, Elias	018	1843	WB-C/282	
Williams, Elias	085	1800	WB-D/246	AR
Williams, Elihu	075	c1852	WB-M2/6	AR
Williams, Elijah	081	1854	WB-10/92	AR
Williams, Elijah	044	1854	WB-19/453	CTY
Williams, Elisha	037	1755	Orig. Only	SS/AR
Williams, Elisha	075	1845	WB-N/189	AR
Williams, Eliza	068	1818	WB-A/366	
Williams, Eliza A.	054	1896	WB-6/15	CTY
Williams, Elizabeth	035	1821	WB-A/527	AR
Williams, Elizabeth	071	1891	WB-7/90	AR
Williams, Elizabeth	045	1898	WB-1/347	AR
Williams, Elizabeth	103	1892	WB-2/1	AR
Williams, Elizabeth	068	1898	WB-D/546	
Williams, Elizabeth	018	1894	WB-E/229	AR
Williams, Elizabeth	070	1898	Orig. Only	AR
Williams, Elizabeth	041	1900	WB-4/505	AR
Williams, Elizabeth	030	1896	WB-5/228	AR
Williams, Elizabeth	065	1873	WB-K/121	AR
Williams, Elizabeth	030	1836	WB-4/21	
Williams, Elizabeth	022	c1862	WB-D/102	AR
Williams, Elizabeth	099	1871	RB-35/146	AR
Williams, Elizabeth	063	1794	WB-1/205	
Williams, Elizabeth	044	1871	WB-23/40	CTY
Williams, Elizabeth	087	1876	WB-3/130	AR
Williams, Elizabeth	077	1745	Orig. Only	SS/AR
Williams, Elizabeth	030	1796	WB-2/86	
Williams, Elizabeth	100	1863	WB-50/31	AR
Williams, Elizabeth	100	1844	WB-38/251	AR
Williams, Elizabeth	035	1878	WB-4/126	AR
Williams, Ellen	098	1897	WB-A/288	CTY
Williams, Emily	028	1897	WB-F/327	
Williams, Emma W.	039	1881	WB-U/274	AR
Williams, Erwin	097	1861	WB-1/189	AR
Williams, Etheriel	010	1818	WB-G/28	AR
Williams, Evaline	045	1898	WB-1/336	AR
Williams, Ezekiel	022	1824	WB-B/74	AR
Williams, Ezekiel	010	1797	WB-E/17	AR
Williams, F. J.	056	1900	WB-4/261	AR
Williams, F. Victoria	078	1894	WB-19/370	AR
Williams, Fanny	018	1869	WB-E/2	AR
Williams, Fennettie	037	1896	WB-H/350	AR
Williams, Finettie	079	1871	WB-2/57	AR
Williams, Fleet	005	1843	WB-B/149	AR
Williams, Floyd	039	1832	WB-J/201	AR
Williams, Floyd	039	1896	WB-V/91	AR
Williams, Frances	067	c1839	Orig. Only	AR-Copy
Williams, Francis	047	1766	WB-1/179	
Williams, Francis	100	1793	WB-6/198	AR
Williams, Francis	010	1816	WB-F/323	AR
Williams, Francis	035	1868	WB-4/7	AR
Williams, Gabriel	100	1826	WB-29/40	AR
Williams, Gatsey	028	1893	WB-F/60	
Williams, George	037	1759	SS 881/190	SS/AR
Williams, George	035	1817	WB-A/520	AR
Williams, George	053	1837	WB-5/450	AR
Williams, George	071	1750	Orig. Only	SS/AR
Williams, George	010	1735	Copy	024 AR
Williams, George	068	1797	WB-A/192	
Williams, George	010	1735	LGB-4/#8	
Williams, George	022	1836	WB-C/40	AR
Williams, George	100	1886	WB-51/215	AR
Williams, George	041	1815	WB-2/104	AR
Williams, George H.	009	1887	Orig. Only	CTY
Williams, George M.	011	c1819	WB-2/386	
Williams, George W.	070	1899	WB-H/179	AR
Williams, George W.	046	1900	WB-G/222	AR
Williams, George W.	099	1884	WB-A/526	AR
Williams, George W.	070	1869	WB-E/157	AR
Williams, George W.	070	1899	029 WB-F/241	029 AR
Williams, George W.	070	1899	Copy	064 AR
Williams, Giles	083	1844	WB-1/440	AR
Williams, Giles	083	1894	WB-4/39	AR
Williams, Gray	063	1896	WB-4/190	AR
Williams, H. Clay	041	1900	WB-4/511	AR
Williams, Hamilton	022	c1863	WB-D/103	AR
Williams, Harrett	069	1895	WB-5/503	AR
Williams, Harry	012	1883	Orig. Only	AR
Williams, Harvy	075	1846	WB-N/198	AR
Williams, Hatten	024	c1779	WB-A/179	AR
Williams, Hearty H.	100	1868	WB-50/268	AR
Williams, Henry	100	1894	WB-51/380	AR
Williams, Henry	045	1842	Copy	028 AR
Williams, Henry	103	1847	RD-9/531	AR
Williams, Henry	022	1858	WB-D/7	AR
Williams, Henry	039	1852	WB-N/304	AR
Williams, Henry	045	1842	WB-1/75	AR-Copy
Williams, Henry	070	1840	WB-AB/335	AR
Williams, Henry	063	1861	WB-2/477	
Williams, Henry	039	1852	SC/05954	AR-Copy
Williams, Henry	020	1786	RB-B/92	AR
Williams, Henry C.	100	1828	WB-32/32	AR
Williams, Henry F.	081	1898	WB-16/499	AR
Williams, Henry G.	100	1835	WB-35/52	AR
Williams, Henry G.	041	1874	WB-4/45	AR
Williams, Henry S.	051	1846	WB-A/262	
Williams, Henry, Sr.	070	1809	WB-AB/119	AR
Williams, Herren	097	1870	WB-2/29	AR
Williams, Herren	097	1871	WB-2/53	AR
Williams, Hetty	073	1849	WB-F/427	AR
Williams, Hezekiah	072	1834	WB-1/135	AR
Williams, Hill	072	1840	WB-2/28	
Williams, Hill	072	1800	WB-A/145	AR
Williams, Hill	072	c1816	WB-A/146	AR
Williams, Hiram	054	1874	WB-4/186	CTY
Williams, Hollowell	030	1795	WB-2/31	
Williams, Hopkin	035	1866	WB-3/110	
Williams, Hugh R.	054	1870	WB-4/52	AR
Williams, Hugh, Sr.	040	1849	WB-1/25	
Williams, Hulda	070	1897	WB-G/597	AR
Williams, Isaac	056	1830	WB-1/402	AR
Williams, Isaac	056	1768	Orig. Only	AR

Name	Co.	Date	Recorded Copy	Original
Williams, Isaac	041	1876	WB-4/71	AR
Williams, Isaac	084	c1802	OW/13	AR
Williams, Isaac	106	c1860	WB-1/70	AR
Williams, Isaac	077	1881	WB-H/114	AR
Williams, Isaac	075	1822	WB-M1/355	AR
Williams, Isaac	106	c1865	WB-1/118	AR
Williams, Isaac H.	056	1861	WB-2/15	AR
Williams, Isaac M.	005	1897	WB-D/406	AR
Williams, Isaac M.	045	1896	WB-1/344	AR
Williams, Isaac W.	086	1849	WB-E/191	AR
Williams, J. Buxton	100	1887	WB-51/245	AR
Williams, J. M.	104	1899	WB-7/88	AR
Williams, Jackson	079	1897	WB-3/112	AR
Williams, Jacob	087	c1757	Orig. Only	AR
Williams, Jacob	005	1831	WB-B/8	AR
Williams, Jacob	079	1877	WB-2/160	AR
Williams, Jacob	033	1854	WB-1/111	AR
Williams, Jacob	047	1774	WB-1/359	
Williams, Jacob C.	026	1865	WB-1/382	AR
Williams, James	010	1807	WB-F/47	AR
Williams, James	057	1790	WB-A/205	AR-Nunc.
Williams, James	030	1793	WB-1/21	
Williams, James	019	1770	Orig. Only	SS/AR
Williams, James	044	1892	WB-24/193	CTY
Williams, James	VA	1800	037 WB-D/120	037 AR
Williams, James	072	1847	WB-2/78	AR
Williams, James	009	c1792	OWB/280	AR
Williams, James	036	1895	WB-A/358	CTY
Williams, James	041	c1854	WB-3/204	AR
Williams, James	037	1789	WB/C/91	AR
Williams, James	035	1856	WB-2/104	AR
Williams, James	035	1799	WB-A/536	AR
Williams, James	024	1828	WB-C/145	AR
Williams, James	035	1849	WB-2/43	AR
Williams, James	090	1844	WB-4/149	AR
Williams, James	056	1861	WB-1/20	AR
Williams, James	073	1888	WB-H/442	CTY
Williams, James	010	1803	WB-E/204	AR
Williams, James	010	1737	SS 877/225	SS/AR
Williams, James	077	1777	WB-C/207	AR
Williams, James C.	084	1865	WB-D/41	CTY
Williams, James N.	046	1891	WB-F/88	AR
Williams, Jane	071	1810	WB-3/25	AR
Williams, Jane	047	1764	WB-1/131	
Williams, Jane	075	c1854	WB-M2/20	AR
Williams, Jane	078	1849	WB-13/164	AR
Williams, Jane	073	1819	070 WB-C/458	070 AR
Williams, Jane	072	c1797	Orig. Only	AR
Williams, Jane	099	1870	RB-35/69	AR
Williams, Jesse	071	1782	WB-1/261	
Williams, Jesse	092	c1868	WB-6/20	AR
Williams, Jesse	072	1802	WB-A/145	AR
Williams, Jesse	072	1773	Orig. Only	SS/AR
Williams, Jesse	047	1796	WB-3/263	
Williams, Jesse	028	1781	Orig. Only	AR
Williams, Jesse	022	1862	WB-D/86	AR
Williams, Jesse	106	1878	WB-2/97	AR
Williams, Jesse	035	1857	WB-2/119	AR
Williams, Jethro	051	1831	WB-A/13	
Williams, Joab	010	1791	WB-D/183	AR
Williams, Joannah	010	1756	SS 880/163	SS/AR
Williams, Job	065	c1796	WB-G/29	AR-Copy
Williams, Joel	087	1841	WB-1/250	AR
Williams, Joel	069	c1809	Orig. Only	AR
Williams, Joel	056	1761	WB-1/754	AR
Williams, Joel	081	1877	WB-15/245	AR
Williams, Joel	060	1823	Orig. Only	AR
Williams, Joel, Jr.	029	1865	WB-D/72	AR
Williams, John	037	1849	WB-F/412	AR
Williams, John	085	1817	WB-G/464	AR
Williams, John	081	1869	WB-15/17	
Williams, John	070	1855	WB-C/599	AR
Williams, John	056	1833	WB-1/490	AR
Williams, John	077	c1836	WB-F/254	
Williams, John	092	1818	WB-3/132	
Williams, John	037	1737	LGB-4/#94	SS/AR
Williams, John	070	1769	WB-C/430	AR
Williams, John	N	1722	SS 875/306	SS/AR
Williams, John	005	1806	WB-2/183	AR
Williams, John	037	1817	WB-E/160	AR
Williams, John	010	1795	WB-D/284	AR
Williams, John	081	1830	WB-6/103	AR
Williams, John	019	c1787	Orig. Only	AR
Williams, John	028	1834	WB-C/376	AR
Williams, John	060	1867	WB-3/94	AR
Williams, John	035	1761	WB-A/497	AR
Williams, John	009	c1796	OWB/328	AR
Williams, John	028	1765	DB-12&13/292	
Williams, John	035	1840	Orig. Only	AR
Williams, John	047	1771	WB-1/299	
Williams, John	030	1798	WB-2/118	
Williams, John	072	1792	Orig. Only	AR
Williams, John	099	1845	RB-26/35	AR
Williams, John	037	1793	WB-C/254	AR
Williams, John	030	1835	WB-4/9	
Williams, John	047	1795	WB-3/246	
Williams, John	092	1798	WB-3/29	
Williams, John	022	1816	WB-A/282	AR
Williams, John	075	1843	WB-N/178	AR
Williams, John	063	c1805	WB-1/430	
Williams, John	047	1792	WB-3/202	
Williams, John	010	1758	SS 882/77	SS/AR
Williams, John	070	1787	WB-C/450	AR
Williams, John	039	1836	WB-K/28	AR
Williams, John	035	1803	WB-A/513	AR
Williams, John	002	1728	SS 876/119	SS/AR
Williams, John	077	1774	WB-C/132	AR
Williams, John	044	1799	WB-5/16	CTY
Williams, John	037	1819	WB-E/228	AR
Williams, John	020	1780	RB-A/113	AR
Williams, John	010	1894	WB I/410	AR
Williams, John	039	1815	WB-F/42	AR
Williams, John	081	1811	WB-3/235	
Williams, John	022	1900	WB-F/166	AR
Williams, John	035	1790	WB-A/503	AR
Williams, John	103	1827	RD-5/390	
Williams, John	078	1820	WI-8/332	AR
Williams, John	020	1804	RB-E/168	AR
Williams, John	030	c1813	WB-3/20	
Williams, John A.	100	1882	WB-51/166	AR
Williams, John A.	100	1895	WB-51/390	
Williams, John Beeke	009	1856	OB-K/212	AR
Williams, John C.	065	1874	WB-L/165	AR
Williams, John D.	005	1890	WB-D/280	AR
Williams, John D.	083	1868	WB-2/244	AR
Williams, John G.	099	1879	WB-A/32	AR
Williams, John M.	099	1865	RB-33/477	AR
Williams, John R.	026	1865	WB-1/373	AR
Williams, John W.	032	1886	WB-3/513	AR
Williams, John W.	069	1872	WB-1/617	AR

Name	Co.	Date	Recorded Copy	Original
Williams, John W.	078	1852	WB-17/20	AR
Williams, John W.	028	1880	WB-E/246	AR
Williams, John W.	009	c1847	OB-F/520	AR
Williams, John, Sr.	024	1798	WB-B/159	AR
Williams, John, Sr.	030	1886	WB-5/140	AR
Williams, Jonas	057	1878	WB-C/67	AR
Williams, Jonathan	041	1856	WB-3/198	AR
Williams, Jonathan	032	1845	WB-1/472	
Williams, Jonathan	041	1816	WB-2/116	AR
Williams, Joseph	077	1776	WB-C/184	AR
Williams, Joseph	084	c1788	OW/158	AR
Williams, Joseph	053	1845	WB-6/314	AR
Williams, Joseph	030	1776	WB-1/106	
Williams, Joseph	044	1774	WB-1/33	CTY
Williams, Joseph	030	1821	WB-3/255	Nunc.
Williams, Joseph	053	1773	RW-1/41	AR
Williams, Joseph	092	1827	WB-4/1	
Williams, Joseph	092	1840	WB-4/173	
Williams, Joseph	077	c1772	Orig. Only	SS/AR
Williams, Joseph	085	1811	WB-G/206	AR
Williams, Joseph	085	1880	WB-1/524	CTY
Williams, Joseph	106	1887	WB-2/240	AR
Williams, Joseph	005	1896	WB-D/384	AR
Williams, Joseph	002	1693	Orig. Only	SS/AR
Williams, Joseph	037	1808	WB-D/338	AR
Williams, Joseph	072	c1784	WI/L22 & L26	AR
Williams, Joseph	092	c1825	Copy	090 AR
Williams, Joseph	087	c1808	Orig. Only	AR
Williams, Joseph	047	1816	WB-3/581	
Williams, Joseph	005	1825	WB-A/118	AR
Williams, Joseph A.	079	c1861	WB-1/141	AR
Williams, Joseph J.	063	1866	WB-2/529	
Williams, Joseph J.	047	1808	WB-3/480	
Williams, Joseph J.	047	1818	WB-3/615	
Williams, Joseph J.	047	1833	WB-4/94	
Williams, Joseph J.	022	1887	WB-E/362	AR
Williams, Joseph S.	022	1861	WB-D/84	
Williams, Joseph T.	020	1856	RB-R/424	AR
Williams, Joshua	037	1798	WB-D/48	AR
Williams, Joshua	047	1761	WB-1/28	
Williams, Joshua	022	c1848	SC/07042	AR-Copy
Williams, Joshua	022	1849	WB-C/244	AR
Williams, Josiah	097	1871	WB-2/52	AR
Williams, Josiah	010	1780	WB-B/149	AR
Williams, Josie A.E.	045	1889	WB-1/187	AR
Williams, Joyce	035	1752	087 DB-2/124	
Williams, Kate A.	070	1892	WB-F/515	AR
Williams, Katie	054	1893	WB-5/466	CTY
Williams, Keelon	054	1892	WB-5/457	CTY
Williams, Laura S.	010	1894	WB-I/409	AR
Williams, Lavinia	038	1893	WB-3/416	AR
Williams, Lemuel S.	077	1851	WB-F/398	AR
Williams, Leon A.	037	1868	WB-G/313	AR
Williams, Levin	046	1845	WB-C/224	
Williams, Levina	041	1848	WB-3/96	AR
Williams, Lewis	024	1717	Orig. Only	SS/AR
Williams, Lewis	006	1849	WB-A/63	AR
Williams, Lewis	092	c1841	SC/09282	AR-Copy
Williams, Lewis	057	1858	WB-B/244	AR
Williams, Lewis	001	1896	WB-3/151	AR
Williams, Lewis	092	1842	WB-4/193	
Williams, Lewis	072	c1783	WI/L27	AR
Williams, Lewis A.	063	1837	WB-2/236	
Williams, Lewis P.	080	1878	Orig. Only	AR
Williams, Lightfoot	060	1832	WB-1/252	AR

Name	Co.	Date	Recorded Copy	Original
Williams, Lockhart	077	1797	WB-E/77	
Williams, Lodowick	075	1770	WB-H/120	AR
Williams, Lodwick	002	1684	Orig. Only	SS/AR
Williams, Lodwick	075	1847	WB-N/210	AR
Williams, Lodwick	075	1809	WB-M1/209	AR
Williams, Lott	072	1757	Orig. Only	SS/AR
Williams, Lott	072	1790	Orig. Only	AR
Williams, Lucias	030	1794	WB-2/23	
Williams, Lucie	103	1824	RD-5/96	AR
Williams, Lucy	100	1857	WB-49/109	AR
Williams, Lucy	047	1782	WB-3/35	
Williams, Lucy P.	041	1878	WB-4/113	AR
Williams, Lydda	039	1821	WB-G/58	AR
Williams, Lydia	075	1884	WB-O/187	AR
Williams, Lydia	018	1828	WB-C/105	
Williams, Lydia	047	1773	WB-1/330	
Williams, Lydia	030	1890	WB-5/175	AR
Williams, M. D.	022	c1891	Orig. Only	AR
Williams, M. D., Sr.	022	1881	WB-E/214	AR
Williams, M. S.	046	1900	WB-G/184	AR
Williams, Malvina	083	1894	WB-4/43	AR
Williams, Margaret	035	1861	WB-3/39	AR
Williams, Margaret	CT	1887	070 WB-F/91	070 AR
Williams, Maria A.	100	c1898	047 WB-7/268	047 AR
Williams, Maria A.	100	1899	WB-51/507	
Williams, Marion M.	028	1891	WB-E/566	
Williams, Marmaduke	081	1885	WB-15/479	
Williams, Martha	056	1761	WB-1/762	AR
Williams, Martha	100	1851	WB-41/183	AR
Williams, Martha	073	1806	WB-D/167	AR
Williams, Martha	035	1875	WB-4/97	AR
Williams, Martha	071	1866	WB-5/322	
Williams, Mary	010	1852	WB-G/486	AR
Williams, Mary	029	1837	WB-B/275	AR
Williams, Mary	081	1833	WB-6/330	AR
Williams, Mary	084	1819	WB-A/320	CTY
Williams, Mary	041	1817	WB-2/140	AR
Williams, Mary	099	1797	RB-4/88	AR-Nunc.
Williams, Mary	071	1845	WB-5/32	AR
Williams, Mary	075	1846	WB-N/198	AR
Williams, Mary	026	1852	WB-1/136	AR
Williams, Mary	082	1815	WB-1/172	AR
Williams, Mary	060	1839	WB-2/13	AR
Williams, Mary	083	1881	WB-3/255	AR
Williams, Mary	054	1897	Orig. Only	AR
Williams, Mary	077	1804	WB-E/210	AR
Williams, Mary	028	1774	Orig. Only	AR
Williams, Mary A.	084	1888	WB-E/404	CTY
Williams, Mary A. E.	079	1897	WB-3/133	AR
Williams, Mary B.	099	1865	RB-33/424	AR
Williams, Mary D.	044	1896	WB-24/323	CTY
Williams, Mary E.	077	1882	WB-H/133	AR
Williams, Mary H.	MD	1878	039 WB-U/206	
Williams, Mary J.	029	1900	WB-F/202	AR
Williams, Mary Jane	069	1889	WB-5/319	AR
Williams, Mary K.	100	1887	WB-51/238	AR
Williams, Mary W.	022	1887	WB-E/351	AR
Williams, Mason	100	1889	WB-51/299	AR
Williams, Mathew M.	100	c1889	Copy	AR/CRX
Williams, Mathias	006	1849	WB-A/46	AR
Williams, Matilda W.	099	1885	WB-B/13	AR
Williams, Matthew S.	039	1861	WB-R/118	AR
Williams, Mc.	103	1869	WB-1/1	AR
Williams, Micajah	065	1828	WB-A/160	AR
Williams, Michael	041	1884	WB-4/198	AR

Name	Co.	Date	Recorded Copy	Original
Williams, Michel	022	1779	Orig. Only	AR
Williams, Miles	082	1799	WB-1/73	AR
Williams, Moab	071	1752	Orig. Only	SS/AR
Williams, Mordecai	017	1876	WB-B/61	AR
Williams, Moses	041	1796	WB-1/140	AR
Williams, Mountain	022	1873	WB-E/105	AR
Williams, Nancy	039	1815	WB-D/187	AR
Williams, Nancy	030	1871	WB-5/21	
Williams, Nancy	092	1805	WB-C/200	AR
Williams, Nancy	MD	1899	006 WB-E/369	
Williams, Nancy Ellen	083	1897	WB-4/163	AR
Williams, Nancy K.	086	1880	WB-F/220	AR
Williams, Nancy M.	079	1858	WB-1/9	AR
Williams, Nanny	010	1818	WB-G/32	AR
Williams, Nathan	056	1867	WB-2/99	AR
Williams, Nathan	071	1758	SS 882/15	SS/AR
Williams, Nathaniel	077	1776	WB-C/177	
Williams, Nathaniel	044	1831	WB-12/41	CTY
Williams, Nathaniel	077	1789	WB-C/384	AR
Williams, Nathaniel	084	1805	WB-A/25	CTY
Williams, Nicholas	030	1787	WB-1/208	
Williams, Nicholas L.	106	1867	WB-1/105	
Williams, Nimrod	100	1790	WB-5/176	AR
Williams, Norwood	099	1878	WB-A/11	AR
Williams, Obed	072	1789	WI/L1	AR
Williams, Olive	103	1881	WB-1/212	AR
Williams, Oliver P.	064	1880	WB-2/87	AR
Williams, Olzie E.	105	1896	WB-3/206	AR
Williams, Orren, Jr.	037	1899	WB-H/453	AR
Williams, Orrin T.	099	1873	RB-35/234	AR
Williams, Owen	075	1834	WB-N/97	AR
Williams, Owen	075	1824	WB-M1/404	AR
Williams, Owen	090	1810	WB-2/109	AR
Williams, Parmilia	035	1887	WB-4/304	
Williams, Parthenia	077	1841	WB-F/296	
Williams, Paul	072	1792	Orig. Only	AR
Williams, Penny	022	1886	WB-E/326	AR
Williams, Permelia	026	1897	WB-2/561	AR
Williams, Phebe	035	1878	WB-4/124	AR
Williams, Philander	069	c1794	WB-1/242	AR
Williams, Philip	100	1898	WB-51/551	
Williams, Phillip	063	1887	WB-4/40	AR
Williams, Phillis	037	1760	WB-A/11	AR
Williams, Phineas	107	1886	WB-2/36	
Williams, Pilgrim	037	1764	WB-A/139	AR
Williams, Polly	039	1837	WB-K/134	AR
Williams, Presley	047	1879	WB-6/206	AR
Williams, Prudence	010	1800	Orig. Only	AR
Williams, R. E.	039	1852	WB-N/331	Nunc.
Williams, R. H.	041	1886	WB-4/239	AR
Williams, Rachel	106	1886	WB-2/223	AR
Williams, Rachel	077	1777	WB-C/238	AR
Williams, Ralph	078	1820	WI-8/341	AR
Williams, Ransom	066	1864	Orig. Only	AR
Williams, Rebecca	071	c1782	WB-1/286	AR
Williams, Rebeckah	092	c1831	WB-4/43	
Williams, Redding	035	1850	WB-2/54	AR
Williams, Reuben N.	100	1888	WB-51/285	AR
Williams, Rhoda H.	053	1871	WB-11/26	AR
Williams, Richard	022	1848	WB-C/215	AR
Williams, Richard	030	1803	WB-3/219	
Williams, Richard	100	1894	WB-51/429	
Williams, Richard	073	1802	WB-D/57	AR
Williams, Richard	035	1774	WB-A/490	AR
Williams, Richard	028	1816	WB-C/116	AR
Williams, Richard	010	1761	WB-A/1	AR
Williams, Richard	077	1785	WB-C/305	AR
Williams, Richard	063	1826	WB-2/110	
Williams, Richard	085	1823	WB-H/205	AR
Williams, Richard	010	1782	WB-C/44	AR
Williams, Richard J.	045	1884	Orig. Only	AR
Williams, Richard J.	045	1884	059 WB-A/370	059 CTY
Williams, Robert	099	1821	RB-17/187	AR
Williams, Robert	044	1822	WB-9/143	CTY
Williams, Robert	087	1831	WB-1/118	AR
Williams, Robert	030	1893	WB-5/213	AR
Williams, Robert	103	1844	RD-9/2	AR
Williams, Robert	TN	1815	078 WI-7/29	078 AR
Williams, Robert	087	1827	WB-1/80	AR
Williams, Robert	071	1842	WB-4/244	
Williams, Robert	018	1896	075 WB-0/432	075 AR
Williams, Robert	009	c1787	OWB/214	AR
Williams, Robert	029	1899	WB-F/165	AR
Williams, Robert	035	1819	WB-A/491	
Williams, Robert	018	1896	WB-E/250	
Williams, Robert	087	c1813	Orig. Only	AR
Williams, Robert	100	1786	WB-4/165	AR
Williams, Robert B.	099	1832	RB-22/318	AR
Williams, Robert P.	084	1861	WB-C/353	CTY
Williams, Robert, Sr.	015	1772	100 WB-1/241	AR
Williams, Roberta F.	100	1893	WB-51/349	
Williams, Roland	069	1816	WB-1/279	AR
Williams, Roland	005	1802	WB-2/184	AR
Williams, Roland	069	1816	SC/01445	AR-Copy
Williams, Rowland	071	1754	Orig. Only	SS/AR
Williams, Rowlin	084	1837	WB-B/174	CTY
Williams, Sallie	078	1871	WB-19/19	AR
Williams, Sallie	037	1894	WB-H/279	AR
Williams, Sally	053	1885	WB-11/157	AR
Williams, Sally	075	1817	WB-M1/305	AR
Williams, Sally	030	1826	WB-3/214	
Williams, Samual	072	1807	WB-A/162	AR
Williams, Samuel	069	1781	WB-1/17	AR
Williams, Samuel	018	1843	WB-C/280	
Williams, Samuel	100	1791	WB-5/213	AR
Williams, Samuel	079	1870	WB-2/42	AR
Williams, Samuel	100	1824	WB-27/9	AR
Williams, Samuel	037	1754	SS 881/109	SS/AR
Williams, Samuel	037	1748	Orig. Only	SS/AR
Williams, Samuel	029	1805	WB-A/76	AR
Williams, Samuel	075	1751	Orig. Only	SS/AR
Williams, Samuel	063	c1805	WB-1/426	
Williams, Samuel	063	1850	WB-2/356	
Williams, Samuel	077	1790	WB-C/410	AR
Williams, Samuel	069	1855	WB-1/547	AR
Williams, Samuel	041	1792	WB-1/90	
Williams, Samuel	099	1855	RB-29/349	AR
Williams, Samuel	054	c1811	WB-1/376	AR
Williams, Samuel	010	1736	Orig. Only	SS/AR
Williams, Samuel	010	1764	WB-A/54	AR
Williams, Samuel A.	100	1883	WB-51/177	AR
Williams, Samuel L.	053	1896	WB-11/329	AR
Williams, Samuel T.	100	1835	WB-35/214	AR
Williams, Sarah	070	1779	WB-C/441	AR-Nunc.
Williams, Sarah	060	1866	WB-3/92	AR
Williams, Sarah	056	1806	WB-1/131	AR
Williams, Sarah	069	1808	WB-1/190	AR
Williams, Sarah A.	099	1896	WB-C/495	AR
Williams, Sebrina	075	1853	WB-M2/4	AR
Williams, Seth	075	1900	WB-0/502	AR

Name	Co.	Date	Recorded Copy	Original
Williams, Seth	071	1826	WB-4/8	AR
Williams, Sharper	068	1897	WB-D/494	
Williams, Silvia	047	1818	WB-3/623	
Williams, Simon	099	1883	WB-A/389	AR
Williams, Simon	100	1831	WB-33/213	AR
Williams, Simon	100	1809	WB-14/304	AR
Williams, Simon	100	1809	Copy	032 AR
Williams, Simon	039	1823	WB-G/166	
Williams, Solomon	100	1871	WB-51/49	AR
Williams, Solomon	100	1873	WB-51/62	AR
Williams, Solomon	047	1770	WB-1/277	
Williams, Solomon	100	1794	WB-7/151	AR
Williams, Solomon	100	1871	047 WB-7/34	047 AR
Williams, Spencer	077	1793	WB-C/448	
Williams, Stephen	035	1841	WB-A/486	AR
Williams, Stephen	030	1767	Copy	SS/AR
Williams, Stephen	035	1849	WB-2/48	AR
Williams, Stephen	072	1788	WI/L3	AR
Williams, Stephen	012	1843	WB-B/182	AR
Williams, Stephen	082	1830	WB-2/2	AR
Williams, Susan	032	1891	WB-4/110	AR
Williams, Susan Jane	070	1873	WB-E/249	AR
Williams, Susannah	046	c1848	WB-E/29	AR
Williams, Susannah	005	1837	WB-B/78	AR
Williams, Sutton	065	1879	WB-K/351	AR
Williams, Talbot	028	1820	WB-C/192	AR
Williams, Theodore	059	1897	WB-B/174	CTY
Williams, Theophelous	085	1819	WB-H/1	AR
Williams, Thomas	039	c1864	WB-S/5	AR
Williams, Thomas	030	1807	WB-2/303	
Williams, Thomas	018	1855	WB-D/16	
Williams, Thomas	106	c1855	WB-1/84	AR
Williams, Thomas	030	1789	WB-1/231	
Williams, Thomas	TN	1843	071 WB-5/125	071 AR
Williams, Thomas	099	1898	WB-D/99	AR
Williams, Thomas	106	c1856	Copy	033 AR
Williams, Thomas	044	1825	WB-10/52	CTY
Williams, Thomas	009	c1796	OWB/324	AR
Williams, Thomas	044	1761	Orig. Only	CTY
Williams, Thomas	070	1867	WB-D/223	AR
Williams, Thomas	092	c1846	Copy	033 AR
Williams, Thomas	030	1733	SS 876/284	SS/AR
Williams, Thomas	009	1852	OB-H/81	AR
Williams, Thomas	009	1758	SS 881/142	SS/AR
Williams, Thomas	071	1815	WB-3/158	AR
Williams, Thomas	037	1827	WB-F/72	AR
Williams, Thomas	009	c1759	OWB/69	AR
Williams, Thomas	092	c1830	WB-4/28	AR
Williams, Thomas	057	1796	WB-A/128	AR
Williams, Thomas	039	c1855	WB-O/347	AR
Williams, Thomas	056	1761	WB-1/766	AR
Williams, Thomas	065	1874	WB-K/419	AR
Williams, Thomas	099	1896	WB-C/563	AR
Williams, Thomas	030	1801	WB-2/190	
Williams, Thomas	060	1858	WB-3/20	AR
Williams, Thomas	009	1753	SS 879/99	SS/AR
Williams, Thomas	009	c1793	OWB/283	AR
Williams, Thomas	035	1775	WB-A/532	AR
Williams, Thomas	035	1823	WB-A/539	AR
Williams, Thomas A.	100	1892	WB-51/334	AR
Williams, Thomas H.	035	1864	WB-3/91	AR
Williams, Thomas H.	070	1858	WB-C/674	AR
Williams, Thomas J.	100	1831	WB-33/214	AR
Williams, Thomas J.	092	1894	WB-6/380	AR
Williams, Thomas N.	078	1793	WI-1/75	AR
Williams, Thomas P.	030	1803	WB-2/233	
Williams, Thomas S.	009	c1790	OWB/252	AR
Williams, Thomas T.	063	1872	WB-3/36	
Williams, Thownie	030	1803	WB-2/227	
Williams, Tulle	077	1773	Orig. Only	AR
Williams, Tullie	075	1772	WB-I/116	AR
Williams, Unity	057	1822	WB-B/73	AR
Williams, Uriah	077	1815	WB-E/414	AR
Williams, W. H.	035	1889	WB-4/344	AR
Williams, Warren	051	1836	WB-A/88	
Williams, Wesley	060	1889	WB-4/407	AR
Williams, West	045	c1857	WB-1/396	
Williams, Weston	019	1788	WB-E/8	AR
Williams, Wiley	029	1898	WB-F/159	AR
Williams, William	044	1777	WB-1/144	CTY
Williams, William	086	1834	WB-E/8	AR
Williams, William	024	1809	WB-B/306	AR
Williams, William	100	1832	WB-33/443	AR
Williams, William	084	c1784	OW/183	AR
Williams, William	084	1835	WB-B/120	CTY
Williams, William	028	c1760	Orig. Only	SS/AR
Williams, William	026	1869	WB-2/34	AR
Williams, William	087	c1827	Orig. Only	AR
Williams, William	032	c1839	WB-2/354	
Williams, William	030	1817	WB-3/96	
Williams, William	037	1843	WB-F/294	AR
Williams, William	063	c1778	WB-1/90	
Williams, William	075	1881	WB-O/134	AR
Williams, William	087	c1826	Orig. Only	AR
Williams, William	100	1838	WB-37/20	AR
Williams, William	030	1724/5	SS 876/48	SS/AR
Williams, William	044	1765	Orig. Only	CTY
Williams, William	085	1783	WB-B/136	AR
Williams, William	081	1811	WB-3/235	AR
Williams, William	068	1842	WB-B/149	
Williams, William	073	c1787	WB-B/22	AR
Williams, William	077	1838	WB-F/272	AR
Williams, William	063	1829	WB-2/152	
Williams, William	084	1846	WB-C/41	CTY
Williams, William	024	1712	SS 875/38	SS/AR
Williams, William	005	1807	WB-2/185	AR
Williams, William	026	1847	WB-1/62	AR
Williams, William	010	1758	SS 882/57	
Williams, William	024	1732	SS 876/264	SS/AR
Williams, William	021	1897	WB-3/172	AR
Williams, William	020	1786	RB-B/133	AR
Williams, William	047	1806	WB-3/449	
Williams, William	022	1774	Orig. Only	AR
Williams, William B.	073	1875	WB-H/103	CTY
Williams, William B.	099	1899	WB-D/285	AR
Williams, William B.	069	1883	WB-5/163	AR
Williams, William C.	037	1872	WB-G/407	AR
Williams, William E.	047	1883	WB-6/302	AR
Williams, William H.	063	1844	WB-2/301	
Williams, William H.	080	1877	WB-1/29	AR
Williams, William H.	078	1893	WB-19/348	AR
Williams, William P.	039	1875	WB-U/128	AR
Williams, William R.	075	1876	WB-O/69	AR
Williams, William S.	100	1885	WB-51/201	AR
Williams, William S.	063	1864	WB-2/542	
Williams, William W.	030	1873	WB-5/47	AR
Williams, William W.	035	1859	WB-3/2	AR
Williams, Wilson	075	c1861	WB-M2/86	AR
Williams, Wilson	047	1774	WB-1/366	
Williams, Wilson H.	039	1871	WB-U/31	

Name	Co.	Date	Recorded Copy	Original
Williams, Winniford	037	1849	WB-F/416	AR
Williams, Wyatt	100	1820	WB-22/488	AR
Williams, Zephaniah	050	1893	WB-2/163	CTY
Williams, Zilpha	035	1878	WB-4/122	AR
Williamson, Albin	074	1894	WB-1/128	AR
Williamson, Allen	087	1877	WB-3/165	AR
Williamson, Anderson	026	1895	WB-2/496	AR
Williamson, Anderson	086	1803	WB-B/160	AR-Nunc.
Williamson, Ann	060	1823	Orig. Only	AR
Williamson, Benjamin	071	1819	WB-3/214	AR
Williamson, Betsey	047	1807	WB-3/463	
Williamson, Bluford	069	1880	WB-5/97	AR
Williamson, Burrell	087	1875	WB-3/95	AR
Williamson, Charles	072	1746	028 DB-5/145	SS/AR (N)
Williamson, Charlotte	079	1861	WB-1/65	AR
Williamson, Cloe	082	1866	WB-5/11	AR
Williamson, David	057	1793	WB-A/109	AR
Williamson, Dorothea	047	1814	WB-3/546	
Williamson, Elijah	013	1837	WB-A/50	
Williamson, Elizabeth	020	1809	RB-F/21	AR
Williamson, Elizabeth	030	1881	WB-5/78	AR
Williamson, Elizabeth	013	1858	WB-A/192	
Williamson, Francis	030	1802	WB-2/208	
Williamson, Francis	051	1833	WB-A/61	
Williamson, Francis	030	1785	WB-1/196	
Williamson, George	020	1856	RB-R/444	AR
Williamson, Godfrey	065	1836	WB-G/236	AR
Williamson, H. G.	087	1879	WB-3/190	AR
Williamson, Hannah	010	1781	WB-C/12	AR
Williamson, Hardy	056	1833	WB-1/492	AR
Williamson, Hardy	037	1761	WB-A/22	AR
Williamson, Henry	079	c1850	WB-1/34	
Williamson, Hugh	030	1846	WB-4/124	
Williamson, Isaac	082	1838	WB-2/74	AR
Williamson, Isaac	105	c1854	WB-1/24	AR
Williamson, James	078	1834	WI-12/321	
Williamson, James	087	c1825	Orig. Only	AR
Williamson, James E.	020	1867	RB-T/238	AR
Williamson, James G.	065	1863	WB-J/153	AR
Williamson, Jamima	047	1808	WB-3/473	
Williamson, Jesse A.	037	1878	WB-G/486	AR
Williamson, John	084	1863	WB-C/383	CTY
Williamson, John	047	1800	WB-3/339	
Williamson, John	065	1885	WB-K/84	AR
Williamson, John	077	c1836	WB-F/254	AR
Williamson, John	072	1734	SS 876/340	SS/AR
Williamson, John	065	1843	WB-H/102	AR
Williamson, John	029	c1791	Orig. Only	AR
Williamson, John P.	039	1881	WB-U/268	AR
Williamson, John, Sr.	029	1800	WB-A/35	AR
Williamson, John, Sr.	068	c1789	WB-A/240	
Williamson, Joseph	069	1797	WB-1/113	AR
Williamson, Josiah	029	c1782	Orig. Only	AR
Williamson, Latta	068	1900	WB-E/68	
Williamson, Lewis	011	c1795	WB-1/409	
Williamson, Mary	099	1870	RB-35/84	AR
Williamson, Mary	087	1831	WB-1/128	AR
Williamson, Mary E.	020	1881	WB-A/382	CTY
Williamson, Nathan	020	1839	RB-N/347	AR
Williamson, Nathan	020	1816	RB-G/133	
Williamson, Nathaniel	087	c1807	Orig. Only	AR
Williamson, Ollin	087	1861	WB-2/25	AR
Williamson, Patrick	105	1896	WB-3/196	AR
Williamson, Raiford	056	1873	WB-3/96	

Name	Co.	Date	Recorded Copy	Original
Williamson, Rebecca	065	1833	WB-G/108	AR
Williamson, Richard	030	1731	Orig. Only	SS/AR
Williamson, Richard	027	c1841	WB-A/52	AR
Williamson, Robert	060	1805	Orig. Only	AR
Williamson, Robert	013	c1851	WB-A/164	AR
Williamson, Robert	060	1854	WB-2/394	AR
Williamson, Robert	047	1764	WB-1/129	
Williamson, Robert P.	084	1849	WB-C/102	CTY
Williamson, Ruth	054	1887	Orig. Only	AR
Williamson, Sallie C.	002	1806	WB 6/513	AR
Williamson, Samuel	053	1821	WB-4/213	AR
Williamson, Sarah	056	1850	WB-1/634	AR
Williamson, Shadrack	035	1807	WB-A/514	AR
Williamson, Shadrick	082	1794	WB-1/54	AR-Nunc.
Williamson, Solon	080	1897	WB-1/286	AR
Williamson, Stephen	020	1787	RB-B/191	AR
Williamson, Stephen H.	087	1885	WB-3/296	AR
Williamson, Tabitha	070	1789	WB-C/453	AR
Williamson, Tempie	039	1880	WB-U/236	AR
Williamson, Thomas	020	1848	RB-Q/73	AR
Williamson, Thomas	105	1857	WB-1/39	AR
Williamson, Thomas	105	c1856	SC/08294	AR-Copy
Williamson, Tryal	105	1878	WB-2/230	AR
Williamson, Upton	065	1829	WB-E/64	AR
Williamson, William	030	1832	WB-3/1832	
Williamson, William	087	c1797	Orig. Only	AR
Williamson, William	030	1805	WB-2/259	
Williamson, William	030	1859	WB-4/229	AR
Williamson, William M.	035	1867	WB-3/119	AR
Williamson, Wright	087	c1820	WB-1/22	AR
Williard, Dianna	032	1895	WB-4/258	AR
Williard, Robert	038	1900	WB-4/249	AR
Willie, Lewis K.	044	1878	WB-23/308	CTY
Willie, Mary B.	099	1861	RB-32/72	AR
Williford, Abner	010	1812	WB-F/214	AR
Williford, Elizabeth	105	1889	WB-2/506	AR
Williford, James	010	1867	WB-H/196	AR
Williford, James	016	1867	WB-2/152	AR
Williford, Jason	087	1878	WB-3/177	AR
Williford, John	010	1833	WB-G/228	AR
Williford, Joseph W.	010	1892	WB-I/341	AR
Williford, Lewis D.	044	1892	WB-24/199	CTY
Williford, Martha A.	010	1878	WB-I/104	
Williford, Mary E.	087	1881	WB-3/220	AR
Williford, Meedy	069	1846	WB-1/490	AR
Williford, Meedy	069	1846	Copy	037 AR
Williford, Micajah	087	1833	WB-1/144	AR
Williford, Richard	010	1808	WB-F/80	AR
Williford, Sarah	070	1849	WB-C/500	AR
Williford, Sion	087	c1803	Orig. Only	AR
Williford, William	099	1880	WB-A/148	AR
Williford, Willis	037	1825	WB-F/50	AR
Williford, Winnifred	010	1867	WB-H/190	AR
Willis, Alfred P.	028	1866	WB-D/423	AR
Willis, Andrew	019	1828	WB-E/32	AR
Willis, Ann	047	1813	WB-3/543	
Willis, Asa	022	1877	WB-E/141	AR
Willis, Augustine	047	1799	WB-3/321	
Willis, Benjamin	019	1836	WB-A/55	AR
Willis, Billey	047	1771	WB-1/281	
Willis, Britten	019	1847	WB-A/131	AR
Willis, Daniel	011	c1800	Copy	039 AR
Willis, Daniel	011	c1800	WB-1/393	
Willis, Daniel	011	c1784	WB-2/265	
Willis, Daniel	019	1835	WB-A/45	AR

Name	Co.	Date	Recorded Copy	Original
Willis, David S.	028	1860	WB-D/325	AR
Willis, Edgar	019	1885	Orig. Only	AR
Willis, Elijah	028	1829	WB-C/305	
Willis, Elizabeth	011	c1792	WB-1/594	
Willis, Ephraim	028	1829	WB-C/305	AR
Willis, Ephraim F.	019	1896	WB-B/300	AR
Willis, Francis	022	c1831	WB-B/209	AR
Willis, Freeman	026	1864	WB-1/338	AR
Willis, George P.	028	1900	WB-F/491	
Willis, George S.	070	1889	WB-F/384	AR
Willis, Henry	020	1821	RB-H/405	AR-Copy
Willis, Henry S.	019	1895	WB-B/289	AR
Willis, Iola T.	019	1897	WB-B/329	AR
Willis, Isaac	028	1808	WB-B/309	
Willis, J. R.	026	1887	WB-2/322	AR
Willis, Jacob	086	1828	WB-D/94	AR
Willis, James	022	1796	RB-2/97	AR
Willis, James	028	1798	WB-B/59	AR
Willis, James	009	1842	OB-E/385	AR
Willis, Jane	038	1860	WB-1/159	AR
Willis, Jane	038	c1860	Copy	090 AR
Willis, Jemima	026	1860	WB-1/259	AR
Willis, Jeremiah	028	1806	WB-B/244	AR
Willis, John	011	c1844	WB-1/109	
Willis, John	013	1846	WB-A/122	
Willis, John T.	019	1897	WB-B/316	AR
Willis, Joseph	090	1878	WB-6/97	AR
Willis, Joseph	028	1784	Orig. Only	AR
Willis, Joseph	026	1891	WB-2/426	AR
Willis, Joseph H.	070	1889	WB-F/326	AR
Willis, Joshua	028	1808	WB-B/304	
Willis, Josiah	019	1866	WB-B/22	AR
Willis, Laney	028	1893	WB-F/82	
Willis, Leanar	006	1842	WB-A/53	AR
Willis, Lewis	047	1829	WB-4/48	
Willis, Lewis, Sr.	028	c1860	WB-D/445	
Willis, Littleton	019	1849	WB-A/139	AR
Willis, Louisa L.	099	1891	WB-B/555	AR
Willis, Major	028	1844	WB-D/106	AR
Willis, Marshall	028	1869	WB-E/22	AR
Willis, Mehala	019	1851	WB-A/152	AR
Willis, Nancy P.	028	1846	WB-D/120	AR
Willis, Norman	028	1842	WB-D/67	
Willis, Robert	011	c1787	WB-1/590	
Willis, Samuel	028	1806	WB-B/245	
Willis, Samuel	028	1782	Orig. Only	AR
Willis, Samuel	028	1845	WB-D/110	
Willis, Samuel S.	046	1879	WB-E/266	AR
Willis, Seth	019	1830	WB-A/5	AR
Willis, Susan	044	1844	WB-16/41	CTY
Willis, Thomas	019	1858	WB-A/227	AR
Willis, Thomas	085	1794	WB-E/19	AR
Willis, Thomas	028	1797	WB-B/33	AR
Willis, Thomas	069	c1777	WB-1/237	AR
Willis, Thomas H.	044	1859	WB-21/33	CTY
Willis, Tillman	028	1866	WB-D/427	AR
Willis, Tillman N.	028	1870	WB-E/26	AR
Willis, William	037	1776	WB-A/245	AR
Willis, William	022	1801	WB-A/58	AR
Willis, William	019	1855	WB-A/179	AR
Willis, William	009	1742	Orig. Only	SS/AR
Willis, William	086	1782	WB-A/1	
Willis, William	022	1826	WB-B/124	AR
Williston, George	019	1795	Orig. Only	AR-Nunc.
Williston, John	019	1785	WB-E/6	AR
Williston, John	019	c1771	RB-A/39	
Williston, Samuel	019	1798	WB-E/15	AR
Willkings, William C.	070	c1856	WB-C/617	AR
Willman, Jeremiah	085	1819	Orig. Only	AR
Willoughby, Adelia	030	1875	WB-5/49	AR
Willoughby, Eli	051	1880	WB-C/238	AR
Willoughby, Hancey	030	1825	WB-3/185	
Willoughby, Josiah G.	010	1896	WB-I/484	AR
Willoughby, Justin	051	1881	WB-C/277	AR
Willoughby, Richard	056	1780	Orig. Only	AR
Willoughby, Robert	079	1880	WB-2/196	AR
Willoughby, Thomas	075	1753	SS 881/9	SS/AR
Wills, Edward	047	1900	WB-7/247	AR
Wills, George	024	c1767	WB-A/172	
Wills, Henry	024	1827	WB-C/136	AR
Wills, James	024	1826	WB-C/123	AR
Wills, Mary	051	1856	WB-B/36	
Wills, Thomas	037	1766	WB-A/155	AR
Wills, William	072	1743	LGB-4/#152	
Wills, William H.	047	1889	WB-6/534	AR
Willson, Benjamin	085	1823	WB-H/233	AR
Willson, Edward	107	1862	WB-1A/15	
Willson, Elizabeth	020	1838	RB-N/286	AR
Willson, Elizabeth	077	1754	Orig. Only	SS/AR
Willson, George M.	020	1818	RB-H/169	AR
Willson, Isaac	077	1724	SS 876/35	SS/AR
Willson, James	020	1817	RB-H/1	
Willson, Jesse	084	1833	WB-B/64	CTY
Willson, Joel A.	046	1893	WB-F/249	AR
Willson, John	077	1760	Orig. Only	AR
Willson, John, Sr.	035	1829	WB-A/528	AR
Willson, Lucy G.	051	1875	WB-C/140	AR
Willson, Margaret	075	1706	Orig. Only	SS/AR
Willson, Pattison	075	1746	Orig. Only	SS/AR
Willson, Rebekah	077	1826	WB-F/121	
Willson, Robert	077	1696	SS 874.2/76	SS/AR
Willson, Robert	083	c1799	WB-1/219	
Willson, Samuel	072	1759	SS 882/56	SS/AR
Willson, Sarah	075	1754	Orig. Only	SS/AR
Willson, Seth P.	009	c1790	OWB/249	AR
Willson, William	071	c1745	Orig. Only	SS/AR
Willson, William	096	1741	Orig. Only	SS/AR
Willy, Henry W.	070	1858	Copy	072 AR
Wilmoth, Tyson S.	092	1889	WB-6/297	AR
Wilson, A. W.	014	1898	WB-3/56	CTY
Wilson, Abraham	077	1795	WB-E/43	
Wilson, Absalom	011	1868	WB-2/31	
Wilson, Absoly C.	059	1883	WB-A/328	CTY
Wilson, Albert	065	1873	WB-K/127	AR
Wilson, Albert G.	079	1860	WB-1/36	AR
Wilson, Albia A.	068	1900	WB-E/57	
Wilson, Alexander	001	1867	WB-1/288	AR
Wilson, Alexander	070	1821	WB-C/459	AR
Wilson, Alexander	070	1761	DB-E/15	AR
Wilson, Alexander	001	1880	WB-2/171	AR
Wilson, Alexander	026	1879	WB-2/187	AR
Wilson, Alfred	013	1894	WB-C/306	AR
Wilson, Allen	046	1792	WB-A/405	AR
Wilson, Allen	022	c1862	WB-D/97	AR
Wilson, Andrew	046	1834	WB-B/502	AR
Wilson, Andrew	021	1845	WB-1/27	
Wilson, Andrew	019	1826	WB-E/31	AR
Wilson, Andrew B.	065	1832	WB-G/111	
Wilson, Ann	073	1820	WB-D/586	AR
Wilson, Anna	035	1878	WB-4/132	AR

Name	Co.	Date	Recorded Copy	Original
Wilson, Anne	065	1819	WB-G/56	AR
Wilson, Aquilla	084	c1802	OW/172	AR
Wilson, Archibald	046	c1885	WB-E/433	AR
Wilson, Benjamin	093	1886	WB-2/33	
Wilson, Benjamin	065	1817	WB-G/55	AR
Wilson, Benjamin	103	1855	RD-12/38	AR
Wilson, Benjamin	065	1800	WB-F/232	AR
Wilson, Benjamin	050	1854	WB-1/36	CTY
Wilson, C. J.	026	1891	WB-2/432	AR
Wilson, C. O.	026	1883	WB-2/244	AR
Wilson, Caleb	073	1857	WB-G/167	AR
Wilson, Caleb	030	1754	SS 881/68	SS/AR
Wilson, Catherine	079	1861	WB-1/77	AR
Wilson, Charles	009	c1742	Orig. Only	SS/AR
Wilson, Charles	073	1802	WB-D/67	AR
Wilson, Charles B.	065	1880	WB-K/403	AR
Wilson, Charles C.	028	1848	WB-D/149	AR
Wilson, Charles R.	073	1896	WB-I/84	CTY
Wilson, Christopher	077	1824	WB-F/65	AR
Wilson, Cyntha	010	1840	WB-G/320	AR
Wilson, D. A.	026	1862	WB-1/298	AR
Wilson, Daniel	029	1882	WB-E/291	AR
Wilson, David	046	1856	WB-C/454	AR
Wilson, David	065	1820	WB-G/18	
Wilson, David	017	1877	WB-B/67	AR
Wilson, David	028	1801	WB-B/121	AR
Wilson, David	014	1875	WB-2/116	
Wilson, Delia M.	060	1880	WB-4/216	AR
Wilson, Dennis	099	1880	WB-A/190	AR
Wilson, Ebenezar	044	1767	Orig. Only	CTY
Wilson, Edward	073	c1812	WB-D/347	AR
Wilson, Edward	069	1799	WB-1/241	AR
Wilson, Eleanor	060	c1809	Orig. Only	AR
Wilson, Eleanor A.	065	1867	WB-J/242	AR
Wilson, Elisha M.	087	c1811	Orig. Only	AR
Wilson, Eliza H.	070	1897	WB-G/570	AR
Wilson, Elizabeth	046	1865	WB-D/264	AR
Wilson, Elizabeth	071	1860	WB-5/235	AR
Wilson, Elizabeth	026	1887	WB-2/329	AR
Wilson, Elizabeth	085	c1799	WB-E/10	AR
Wilson, Elizabeth	021	1855	WB-1/116	AR
Wilson, Elizabeth	060	1830	WB-1/181	AR
Wilson, Elizabeth	079	1880	WB-2/202	AR
Wilson, Elizabeth	021	1896	WB-3/178	AR
Wilson, Elvira	079	1893	WB-3/35	AR
Wilson, Ephraim	026	1887	WB-2/312	AR
Wilson, Ephraim	077	1781	Orig. Only	AR
Wilson, Ezra B.	040	1880	WB-2/152	AR
Wilson, F. A.	039	1889	WB-U/491	AR
Wilson, George	005	1783	WB-1/39	AR
Wilson, George	028	1844	WB-D/103	
Wilson, George	060	c1803	Orig. Only	AR
Wilson, H. B.	086	1890	WB-F/385	AR
Wilson, Hattie	026	1899	WB-3/41	AR
Wilson, Henderson	032	1891	WB-4/135	AR
Wilson, Henry B.	099	1890	WB-B/424	AR
Wilson, Hiram	081	1898	WB-16/531	AR
Wilson, Hugh	073	1857	WB-G/172	AR
Wilson, Hugh	065	1857	WB-J/43	AR
Wilson, Hugh	097	1863	WB-1/225	
Wilson, Isaac	077	1714	Orig. Only	SS/AR
Wilson, Isaac	065	1881	WB-K/413	AR
Wilson, Isaac	077	1816	WB-E/437	AR
Wilson, Isaac	077	1751	Orig. Only	SS/AR
Wilson, Isaac	037	1779	WB-B/18	AR
Wilson, Isham	087	1851	WB-1/403	AR
Wilson, J. A.	026	1861	WB-1/271	AR
Wilson, J. McCamie	065	1896	WB-M/478	
Wilson, Jacob	077	1793	WB-C/467	AR-Copy
Wilson, James	060	1796	Orig. Only	AR
Wilson, James	010	1819	WB-G/53	AR
Wilson, James	078	1837	WI-13/182	AR
Wilson, James	065	1777	WB-G/26	AR
Wilson, James	010	1837	WB-G/288	AR
Wilson, James	073	1818	WB-D/537	AR
Wilson, James	069	1797	WB-1/116	AR
Wilson, James	065	1844	WB-H/186	AR
Wilson, James	021	1851	WB-1/93	AR
Wilson, James	103	1832	RD-6/369	AR
Wilson, James	086	1888	WB-F/326	AR
Wilson, James	100	1800	WB-10/239	
Wilson, James	065	1820	WB-G/15	AR
Wilson, James	086	1829	WB-D/105	AR
Wilson, James	107	1897	WB-2/96	
Wilson, James	039	1872	WB-U/44	
Wilson, James	065	1815	WB-G/9	AR
Wilson, James	056	1896	WB-2/222	
Wilson, James	065	1872	WB-K/91	AR
Wilson, James	073	1825	WB-E/81	AR
Wilson, James	046	1828	WB-B/376	AR
Wilson, James	086	1860	WB-E/381	AR
Wilson, James A.	060	1881	WB-4/241	AR
Wilson, James D.	044	1882	WB-23/463	CTY
Wilson, James M.	065	1899	WB-N/271	
Wilson, James S.	032	1892	WB-4/150	AR
Wilson, Jane	073	1850	WB-F/453	AR
Wilson, Jane	097	1859	WB-1/160	AR
Wilson, Jane	029	1858	WB-C/374	AR
Wilson, Jane L.	065	1895	WB-M/511	AR
Wilson, Janet M.	099	1899	WB-D/323	AR
Wilson, Jemima	026	1860	WB-1/254	AR
Wilson, Jemima	046	1834	WB-B/549	AR
Wilson, Jesse	081	1814	WB-4/78	AR
Wilson, Job	072	1897	WB-4/371	AR
Wilson, Joel	054	1875	WB-4/195	CTY
Wilson, John	085	1802	WB-D/242	AR
Wilson, John	065	1782	WB-F/218	
Wilson, John	070	1785	WB-C/449	AR
Wilson, John	020	1875	WB-A/186	CTY
Wilson, John	026	1884	WB-2/258	AR
Wilson, John	029	1833	WB-B/222	AR
Wilson, John	013	1851	WB-A/149	
Wilson, John	077	1785	WB-C/306	AR
Wilson, John	073	c1812	WB-D/362	AR
Wilson, John	020	1854	RB-R/204	AR
Wilson, John	065	1782	WB-G/30	AR
Wilson, John	086	1822	WB-D/3	AR
Wilson, John	075	1778	WB-K/6	AR
Wilson, John	084	1843	WB-B/302	CTY
Wilson, John	046	1891	WB-F/171	AR
Wilson, John	044	1802	WB-5/247	CTY
Wilson, John	022	1866	WB-D/146	AR
Wilson, John	086	1808	WB-B/217	AR
Wilson, John	054	c1796	WB-1/243	AR
Wilson, John	065	c1795	WB-G/34	AR
Wilson, John	060	1831	WB-1/229	AR
Wilson, John	065	1837	WB-E/138	AR
Wilson, John	073	1829	WB-E/180	AR
Wilson, John	021	1867	WB-1/244	AR
Wilson, John	060	1797	Orig. Only	AR

Name	Co.	Date	Recorded Copy	Original
Wilson, John	028	1813	WB-C/70	AR
Wilson, John A.	060	1886	WB-4/352	AR
Wilson, John Dixon	087	1897	WB-4/58	AR
Wilson, John E.	021	c1891	WB-3/342	AR
Wilson, John G.	051	1874	WB-C/124	AR
Wilson, John H.	026	1855	WB-1/193	AR
Wilson, John M.	065	1831	WB-E/129	AR
Wilson, John M.	065	1900	WB-N/389	
Wilson, John T.	068	1898	WB-D/555	
Wilson, John W.	073	1852	WB-G/18	AR
Wilson, John W.	001	1881	WB-2/181	AR
Wilson, John, Sr.	014	1872	WB-2/69	
Wilson, Jonathan	046	1823	WB-B/168	AR
Wilson, Jonathan	046	1805	WB-A/410	AR
Wilson, Jordan	017	1892	WB-B/217	AR
Wilson, Joseph	065	1804	WB-B/146	AR
Wilson, Joseph	087	1881	WB-3/222	AR
Wilson, Joseph	067	1847	WB-1/27	AR
Wilson, Joseph	065	c1795	WB-G/36	AR
Wilson, Joseph	083	1835	WB-1/291	AR
Wilson, Joseph	081	1803	WB-2/123	AR
Wilson, Joseph	021	1853	WB-1/97	AR
Wilson, Joseph	077	1790	WB-C/402	AR
Wilson, Joseph	077	1752	Orig. Only	SS/AR
Wilson, Joseph	075	1763	WB-H/45	AR
Wilson, Joseph A.	021	1870	WB-2/38	AR
Wilson, Joseph C.	PA	1815	029 WB-A/213	029 AR
Wilson, Joseph H.	065	1884	WB-L/22	AR
Wilson, Joshua	021	1863	WB-1/173	AR
Wilson, Joshua	060	1819	Orig. Only	AR
Wilson, Joshua	072	1845	WB-2/63	AR
Wilson, Josiah	011	c1772	WB-2/266	
Wilson, Julia E.	038	1892	WB-3/306	AR
Wilson, Lafayette	060	1865	WB-3/85	AR
Wilson, Lavina	065	1865	WB-J/207	AR
Wilson, Leroy L.	060	1883	Copy	040 AR
Wilson, Leroy L.	060	1883	WB-4/272	AR
Wilson, Lewis	010	1844	WB-G/373	AR
Wilson, Lewis F.	054	c1804	WB-1/343	AR
Wilson, Lou	062	1900	WB-B/226	AR
Wilson, Louis D.	037	1847	WB-F/380	AR
Wilson, Lovey	079	1874	WB-2/97	AR
Wilson, Lucinda	032	1880	WB-3/310	AR
Wilson, Lucinda	022	c1864	WB-D/136	AR
Wilson, Lysander	021	1872	WB-2/64	AR
Wilson, M. A.	065	1883	WB-K/509	AR
Wilson, M. E.	001	1896	WB-3/159	AR
Wilson, Malachi	075	1795	WB-L/35	
Wilson, Marcus K.	054	1868	WB-3/206	AR
Wilson, Marcus R.	021	1900	WB-3/305	AR
Wilson, Margaret	032	1866	WB-2/346	AR
Wilson, Margaret	065	1843	WB-H/130	
Wilson, Margaret	065	1876	WB-K/239	AR
Wilson, Margaret	040	1857	WB-1/92	
Wilson, Margaret	073	1899	WB-I/151	CTY
Wilson, Margaret	065	1805	WB-G/47	AR
Wilson, Margaret	021	1844	WB-1/14	
Wilson, Margaret	065	1814	WB-G/5	AR
Wilson, Margaret M.	044	c1880	Orig. Only	CTY
Wilson, Martha	065	1836	WB-G/234	AR
Wilson, Martha R.	DC	1893	091 WB-1/132	
Wilson, Mary	032	1841	WB-1/378	
Wilson, Mary	073	1863	WB-G/414	CTY
Wilson, Mary	037	1855	WB-G/110	AR
Wilson, Mary A.	065	1888	WB-L/330	AR
Wilson, Mary A.	040	1857	WB-1/88	AR
Wilson, Mary Ann	028	1845	WB-D/116	
Wilson, Mary J.	046	1894	WB-F/319	AR
Wilson, Mary J.	051	1900	WB-C/583	AR
Wilson, Mary L.	054	1880	WB-4/375	CTY
Wilson, Mary M.	040	1893	WB-2/437	AR
Wilson, Mary V.	060	1891	WB-4/470	AR
Wilson, Mathew	060	1817	Orig. Only	AR
Wilson, Mathew	021	1874	WB-2/112	AR
Wilson, Mathew	050	1845	Orig. Only	CTY
Wilson, Mathias	073	1812	WB-D/324	AR
Wilson, Matilda	065	1893	WB-M/140	AR
Wilson, Matilda E.	046	c1862	WB-E/30	AR
Wilson, Matthew N.	065	1890	WB-L/463	AR
Wilson, Michael	046	1823	WB-B/171	AR
Wilson, Michael	022	c1800	WB-A/56	AR
Wilson, Milley	090	1837	WB-4/4	AR
Wilson, Miner	099	c1875	RB-35/312	AR
Wilson, Miriam	077	1855	WB-F/457	AR
Wilson, Mrs.	065	1804	WB-G/45	Nunc.
Wilson, N. H. D.	046	1888	WB-E/509	AR
Wilson, Nathaniel	021	1852	WB-1/96	AR
Wilson, Nathaniel	075	1767	WB-H/74	AR
Wilson, Peter	040	1872	WB-2/47	
Wilson, Peter	032	1839	WB-1/330	
Wilson, Phereba	077	1865	WB-H/5	AR
Wilson, Phillip	068	1813	WB-A/277	Nunc.
Wilson, Pridence	065	1895	WB-M/427	AR
Wilson, R. Adeline	060	1898	WB-5/85	AR
Wilson, R. D.	064	1883	WB-2/122	AR
Wilson, R. D.	064	1883	107 WB-2/218	
Wilson, Rebecca	084	1868	WB-E/16	CTY
Wilson, Rebekah	077	1795	WB-E/32	AR
Wilson, Rewben	077	1794	WB-E/26	
Wilson, Robert	065	1843	WB-I/47	AR
Wilson, Robert	040	1874	WB-2/76	AR
Wilson, Robert	087	1884	WB-3/280	AR
Wilson, Robert	041	1838	WB-3/7	AR
Wilson, Robert	032	1830	WB-1/156	AR
Wilson, Robert	046	1821	Orig. Only	AR
Wilson, Robert	046	1890	WB-F/78	AR
Wilson, Robert	075	1738	Orig. Only	SS/AR
Wilson, Robert	065	1829	WB-D/117	AR
Wilson, Robert	085	c1797	WB-D/239	
Wilson, Robert	065	1794	WB-F/225	AR
Wilson, Robert	046	1863	WB-D/182	AR
Wilson, Robert	VA	1873	Copy	047 AR
Wilson, Robert	046	c1833	Orig. Only	AR
Wilson, Robert C.	003	1877	WB-B/88	AR
Wilson, Robert F.	085	1850	WB-K/107	AR
Wilson, Robert H.	086	1871	WB-F/59	
Wilson, Robert L.	065	1865	WB-J/205	AR
Wilson, Robert M.	040	1880	WB-2/146	AR
Wilson, Robert W.	054	c1811	WB-1/279	AR
Wilson, Robert W.	001	1868	WB-2/1	
Wilson, Rocinda	065	1845	WB-I/2	AR
Wilson, Rosa P.	103	1895	WB-2/127	AR
Wilson, Ruffin	099	1863	RB-32/609	AR
Wilson, S. M.	065	1894	WB-M/243	AR
Wilson, S. N.	085	1898	WB-3/251	CTY
Wilson, Samuel	085	c1792	WB-B/201	AR
Wilson, Samuel	065	c1778	WB-F/211	AR
Wilson, Samuel	060	1854	WB-2/379	AR
Wilson, Samuel	022	1859	WB-D/43	AR
Wilson, Samuel	065	1821	WB-G/57	AR

Name	Co.	Date	Recorded Copy	Original
Wilson, Samuel	072	c1777	RW/L10	AR
Wilson, Samuel	016	1856	WB-1/289	AR
Wilson, Samuel	026	c1863	WB-1/406	AR
Wilson, Samuel	065	1841	WB-H/123	
Wilson, Samuel	075	1719/0	SS 875/240	
Wilson, Samuel	065	1794	WB-F/225	AR
Wilson, Samuel	073	1840	WB-F/63	AR
Wilson, Samuel	060	1804	Orig. Only	AR
Wilson, Samuel C.	020	1860	WB-1/242	AR
Wilson, Samuel K.	078	1865	WB-18/401	AR
Wilson, Samuel P.	098	1897	WB-A/255	CTY
Wilson, Sarah	060	1838	WB-1/416	AR
Wilson, Sarah	097	1844	WB-1/18	AR
Wilson, Sarah A.	065	1874	WB-K/157	
Wilson, Sarah Ann	028	1858	WB-D/302	AR
Wilson, Seth, Sr.	009	1826	OB-A/373	AR
Wilson, Sherod	044	1847	WB-17/132	CTY
Wilson, Sherwood	100	1844	WB-38/306	AR
Wilson, Silas	010	1868	WB-H/204	AR
Wilson, Silvanus	029	1785	Orig. Only	AR
Wilson, Solomon	010	1775	WB-B/18	AR
Wilson, Stephen	065	1883	WB-K/542	
Wilson, Stephen	022	1832	WB-B/221	AR
Wilson, Stephen	073	1803	WB-D/104	AR
Wilson, Sylvanus	060	1890	WB-4/428	AR
Wilson, Synthia	080	1884	Orig. Only	AR
Wilson, T. A.	065	1897	WB-M/586	
Wilson, Thomas	060	1832	WB-1/254	AR
Wilson, Thomas	065	1817	WB-G/22	
Wilson, Thomas	026	1852	WB-1/139	AR
Wilson, Thomas	026	1861	WB-1/267	AR
Wilson, Thomas	077	1785	WB-C/318	AR
Wilson, Thomas	065	1798	WB-F/230	AR
Wilson, Thomas	078	1897	WB-19/411	AR
Wilson, Thomas	085	1775	WB-A/208	AR
Wilson, Thomas	073	1829	WB-E/188	AR
Wilson, Thomas	072	1808	WB-A/138	AR
Wilson, Thomas	100	1814	WB-19/42	AR
Wilson, Thomas	020	1800	RB-C/473	AR
Wilson, Thomas A.	065	1863	WB-J/155	AR
Wilson, Thomas J.	038	1900	WB-4/262	AR
Wilson, Thomas M.	026	1865	WB-1/368	AR-Nunc.
Wilson, Unity	084	1852	WB-C/131	CTY
Wilson, Valentine	046	1895	WB-F/451	AR
Wilson, W. C.	022	1892	WB-F/508	AR
Wilson, W. G.	086	1898	WB-F/569	
Wilson, William	073	1781	WB-A/229	AR
Wilson, William	086	1807	WB-B/194	AR
Wilson, William	100	1799	WB-10/106	AR
Wilson, William	060	1837	WB-1/391	AR
Wilson, William	075	1772	WB-I/62	
Wilson, William	075	1829	WB-N/56	AR
Wilson, William	075	1835	WB-N/116	AR
Wilson, William	028	1744/5	DB-3/21	
Wilson, William	024	1771	WB-A/170	AR
Wilson, William	050	1858	WB-1/43	CTY
Wilson, William	032	1826	WB-1/66	
Wilson, William	107	1871	WB-2/11	
Wilson, William	077	1848	WB-F/350	
Wilson, William	028	c1744	DB-5/110	
Wilson, William	071	1843	WB-4/262	AR
Wilson, William	037	1807	WB-D/280	AR
Wilson, William	094	1778	094.901.1	AR
Wilson, William B.	022	c1899	WB-F/189	
Wilson, William D.	046	1886	WB-E/454	AR
Wilson, William D.	090	1872	WB-6/33	AR
Wilson, William E.	075	1862	WB-M2/78	AR
Wilson, William G.	086	1897	WB-F/545	AR
Wilson, William J.	065	1833	WB-G/135	AR
Wilson, William J.	040	1854	WB-1/56	AR
Wilson, William O.	066	1896	WB-1/191	AR
Wilson, Willis	028	1741/2	Deeds.21/L7	
Wilson, Willis	018	1828	WB-C/100	
Wilson, Willis	022	1862	WB-D/96	AR
Wilson, Winifred	009	c1783	OWD/100	AR
Wilsonn, Samuel	054	1803	WB-1/265	AR
Wilsson, William	086	1812	WB-B/262	
Wilton, Elizabeth	099	1891	WB-B/511	AR
Wilton, William	028	1773	Orig. Only	SS/AR
Wimberley, Benjamin	010	1811	WB-F/187	AR
Wimberley, Elizabeth	010	1845	WB-G/384	AR
Wimberley, George	037	1790	WB-C/132	AR
Wimberley, George	037	1768	WB-A/165	AR
Wimberley, James	005	1815	WB-2/187	AR
Wimberley, John	010	1749	Orig. Only	SS/AR
Wimberley, Malachi	056	1809	Orig. Only	AR
Wimberley, Robert D.	037	1872	WB-G/383	AR
Wimberly, George	056	1834	WB-1/500	AR
Wimberly, Jacob	022	1801	WB-A/60	AR
Wimberly, John L.	037	1893	WB-H/269	AR
Wimberly, Thomas	010	1752	SS 879/56	SS/AR
Wimberly, Zachariah	099	1856	RB-29/462	AR
Wimbish, Lewis W.	VA	1851	044 WB-18/373	044 CTY
Winants, Winant	010	1796	WB-D/346	AR
Winberly, Thomas	010	1732	SS 876/244	SS/AR
Winberry, John	075	1788	WB-K/157	AR
Winberry, John	063	1815	WB-2/31	
Winberry, Lydia	063	1869	WB-3/11	
Winbery, John	075	1753	Orig. Only	AR
Winborn, Henry	063	1818	WB-2/53	
Winborn, Josiah	069	1798	WB-1/121	AR
Winborn, Mary A.	010	1889	WB-I/279	AR
Winborn, Rowena	105	1874	Orig. Only	AR
Winborn, Thomas	047	1829	WB-4/52	
Winborne, David	069	1848	WB-1/511	AR
Winborne, David	071	1779	WB-1/208	
Winborne, David B.	069	1876	WB-5/45	AR
Winborne, Dempsey	071	1816	WB-3/170	AR
Winborne, Gilford J.	071	1827	WB-4/33	AR
Winborne, Henry	037	1899	WB-H/460	AR
Winborne, Mary H.	051	1900	WB-C/580	
Winborne, Nancy	051	1866	WB-B/75	
Winborne, Philip	071	1777	WB-1/155	
Winborne, Samuel D.	051	1895	WB-C/502	AR
Winborne, William	071	1807	WB-2/341	AR
Winborne, William	071	1761	WB-1/44	
Winbourne, Josiah	105	1883	WB-2/309	AR
Winbourne, Mary	069	1882	WB-5/127	AR
Winchester, Coleman	084	1835	WB-B/109	CTY
Winchester, Mary	097	1856	WB-1/117	AR
Winchester, Thomas	097	1864	WB-1/239	AR
Winchester, Thomas D.	097	1895	WB-2/492	AR
Winder, Adam	084	c1802	OW/125	AR
Winder, John C.	099	1896	098 WB-A/317	098 CTY
Winder, John C.	099	1896	WB-C/509	AR
Winder, John C.	099	1896	Copy	068 AR
Winder, John C.	099	1896	Copy	040 AR
Winders, D. J.	035	1862	WB-3/60	AR
Winders, Dollie	035	1900	WB-5/15	AR
Winders, Edward	035	1893	WB-4/425	AR

Name	Co.	Date	Recorded Copy	Original
Winders, Fanny	085	1843	WB-I/199	AR
Winders, Henry C.	085	1846	WB-K/44	AR
Winders, Pearcey	035	1894	WB-4/457	AR
Winders, W. H.	035	1900	WB-4/564	AR
Windfield, John	053	1788	RW-1/172	
Windham, Sarow	079	c1855	WB-1/38	AR
Windley, Aaron	009	1838	OB-B/502	AR
Windley, Aaron	009	c1800	OWB/365	AR
Windley, Barbara	053	1835	WB-5/338	AR
Windley, Elizabeth	053	c1767	RW-1/3	
Windley, Elizabeth	009	c1853	OWB/549	AR
Windley, Elvira	028	1872	WB-E/77	AR
Windley, Hannah	009	1845	OB-E/183	AR
Windley, Henry	009	1835	OWB/478	AR
Windley, Henry E.	009	1838	OB-C2/58	AR
Windley, Horace A.	009	1866	OB-M/250	AR
Windley, Israel	009	1825	OB-A/243	AR
Windley, Israel	053	1762	OB-A/78	
Windley, James	009	1871	WB-1/82	CTY
Windley, James R.	009	1828	OB-B/1	AR
Windley, John	053	c1764	RW-1/1	
Windley, John	009	1856	OB-K/181	AR
Windley, John	009	c1840	OB-E/30	AR
Windley, John L.	009	1836	OWB/512	AR
Windley, Joseph B.	009	1871	WB-1/85	CTY
Windley, Levi	009	1827	OB-A/389	AR
Windley, Mabell	053	1802	RW-1/349	AR
Windley, Margaret	009	1859	OB-K/512	AR
Windley, Moses	009	1828	OB-A/509	AR
Windley, Moses	009	1883	WB-1/335	CTY
Windley, Richard C.	009	1886	WB-1/396	CTY
Windley, Robert	002	1690	Orig. Only	SS/AR
Windley, Ruel	009	1854	OB-I/331	AR
Windley, Samuel, Sr.	009	1874	WB-1/137	CTY
Windley, Seth	009	1866	OB-M/252	AR
Windley, Thomas	009	1827	OB-A/382	AR
Windley, Thomas	053	c1813	RW-1/529	AR
Windley, William	009	1834	OB-B/464	AR
Windley, William B.	009	1878	WB-1/222	CTY
Windley, William D.	009	1892	WB-1/543	CTY
Windley, Wilson T.	009	c1854	OWB/551	AR
Windly, Israel	009	c1808	OWB/454	AR
Windly, Nancy	009	1831	OB-B/144	AR
Windly, Samuel H.	009	1852	OB-H/204	AR
Windly, Sarah	028	1843	WB-D/87	AR
Windson, Joseph	020	1867	RB-T/242	
Windsor, Ananias	019	1888	WB-B/165	AR
Windsor, Bennet	106	c1865	WB-1/98	AR
Windsor, Daniel	092	1844	WB-4/223	
Windsor, Elisha A.	106	1900	WB-2/466	
Windsor, Isaac	092	1821	WB-3/149	
Windsor, James R.	106	c1859	WB-1/91	AR
Windsor, Jesse	106	c1863	WB-1/96	AR
Windsor, John, Sr.	020	1818	RB-H/131	AR
Windsor, Joseph	020	c1866	Orig. Only	AR
Windsor, Richard	020	1793	Orig. Only	AR-Copy
Winecoff, Allison	016	1877	WB-3/199	AR
Winecoff, Daniel	085	1888	WB-2/294	CTY
Winecoff, David	016	1889	WB-4/43	AR
Winecoff, David	016	1855	WB-1/269	AR
Winecoff, Godfrey	016	1881	WB-3/331	AR
Winecoff, James B.	016	1895	WB-4/204	AR
Winecoff, John M.	016	1832	PQS.5/204	AR
Winecoff, Leah	016	1883	WB-3/403	AR
Winecoff, Mathias	016	1876	WB-3/191	AR

Name	Co.	Date	Recorded Copy	Original
Winecoff, Michael	016	1846	WB-1/81	AR
Winecoff, Ransom	016	1876	WB-3/172	AR
Winecoff, Simeon	016	1874	WB-3/108	AR
Winecoff, Valentine	016	1887	WB-3/552	AR
Winekauf, Michel	016	1802	WB-A/55	AR
Winfield, Bryan	053	1813	RW-1/470	AR
Winfield, Davis	009	1830	OB-B/48	AR
Winfield, Henry	009	1859	OB-L/13	AR
Winfield, John	009	1821	OB-A/314	AR
Winfield, John	053	1795	RW-1/249	
Winfield, Joseph	103	1794	WI-A/465	AR
Winfield, Penelope	009	1839	OB-C2/154	AR
Winfield, Richard	008	1733	SS 876/301	SS/AR
Winfield, Richard	053	1799	RW-1/310	
Winfield, Robert	053	c1808	RW-1/417	
Winfield, Robert	053	1784	RW-1/115	
Winfield, Samuel	009	c1836	OWB/536	AR
Winfield, Sophia	009	1833	OB-B/235	AR
Winfield, Thomas	028	1780	Orig. Only	AR
Winfree, Anney	005	1844	WB-B/189	AR
Winfree, Charles	005	c1827	WB-A/137	AR
Winfree, Charles B.	005	1857	WB-C/116	AR
Winfree, Gideon B.	005	1853	WB-C/60	AR
Winfree, Gideon E.	005	1866	WB-C/247	AR
Winfree, James	044	1864	WB-22/182	CTY
Winfree, Mollie F.	005	1867	WB-C/260	AR
Winfree, William W.	005	1882	WB-D/140	AR
Winfrey, Caleb	092	183(?)	Orig. Only	AR
Wingate, Ann	SC	c1763	011 WB-2/278	
Wingate, Isaac	028	1818	WB-C/162	
Wingate, Isabella	099	1887	WB-B/190	AR
Wingate, James	060	1848	WB-2/311	AR
Wingate, Jessie	060	1862	WB-3/43	AR
Wingate, John	011	1847	WB-1/146	
Wingate, Joseph	077	1837	WB-F/259	AR
Wingate, Mary	060	1815	Orig. Only	AR
Wingate, Needham	060	1859	WB-3/21	AR
Wingate, Neil	065	1863	WB-J/162	AR
Wingate, Peter	028	1848	WB-D/142	AR
Wingate, Samuel	070	1770	Orig. Only	SS/AR
Wingate, Thomas	028	1790	WB-A/222	AR
Wingate, W. M.	099	1879	WB-A/36	AR
Wingate, William	070	1821	WB-C/460	AR
Wingate, William	077	1774	WB-C/154	AR
Wingfield, Lawrence	047	1776	WB-2/27	
Wingler, H. W.	104	1894	WB-6/512	AR
Winham, Robert	028	1753	Orig. Only	SS/AR
Winingham, Shearwood	044	1788	WB-2/53	CTY
Winkler, Adam	085	1799	WB-D/261	AR
Winkler, Amelia R.	038	1898	WB-4/90	AR
Winkler, Anderson	104	1895	WB-6/549	AR
Winkler, Charles A.	038	1893	WB-3/368	AR
Winkler, Christian	090	1839	WB-4/37	AR
Winkler, Joshua	102	1896	WB-A/112	AR
Winkler, Lewis	085	1799	WB-E/13	AR
Winkler, Mary	017	1852	WB-A/62	AR
Winkler, William P.	038	1867	WB-1/282	AR
Winn, Caroline	099	1883	WB-A/434	AR
Winn, Charles	103	1892	WB-2/3	AR
Winn, James	028	c1756	DB-8/219	AR
Winn, John	075	1739	LGB-4/#104	SS/AR
Winn, Lucretia	099	1842	RB-25/29	AR
Winn, Martha	046	1828	WB-B/365	AR
Winn, Peter	100	1863	WB-50/34	AR
Winn, Rodiah	077	1821	WB-F/38	AR

Name	Co.	Date	Recorded Copy	Original
Winn, Stephen W.	028	1841	WB-D/34	AR
Winn, William	028	1801	WB-B/128	AR
Winn, William	026	1884	WB-2/255	AR
Winnam, Sarah	028	1813	WB-C/76	
Winright, James	019	1744	SS 878/158	SS/AR
Winship, Joseph	030	1746	Orig. Only	SS/AR
Winslow, Benjamin	024	1898	WB-E/281	AR
Winslow, Benjamin	077	1794	WB-E/23	
Winslow, Caleb	077	1831	WB-F/184	AR
Winslow, Caleb	MD	1895	077 WB-H/277	077 AR
Winslow, Caleb	077	1811	WB-E/356	AR
Winslow, Caroline	029	1863	WB-C/447	AR
Winslow, Eleazer	081	1857	WB-10/501	AR
Winslow, Elizabeth	077	c1893	Orig. Only	AR
Winslow, Elizabeth	077	1785	WB-C/285	AR
Winslow, Francis	024	1857	WB-C/411	AR
Winslow, Frank E.	077	1882	WB-H/126	AR
Winslow, Israel	077	1762	WB-C/5	AR
Winslow, Jacob	077	1774	WB-C/156	AR
Winslow, Jacob	077	1807	WB-E/270	AR
Winslow, Jacob	024	1857	WB-C/408	AR
Winslow, Jesse	077	1771	WB-C/92	AR
Winslow, Jesse	077	1806	WB-E/226	AR
Winslow, Jesse B.	077	1877	WB-H/72	AR
Winslow, Jesse T.	075	c1854	WB-M2/14	AR
Winslow, Job	024	1883	WB-E/125	AR
Winslow, Job	024	1839	WB-C/219	AR
Winslow, John	075	1833	WB-N/85	AR
Winslow, John	077	1822	WB-F/43	AR
Winslow, John	077	1755	Orig. Only	SS/AR
Winslow, John	029	1820	WB-B/49	AR
Winslow, John	077	1844	WB-F/310	AR
Winslow, John	077	1833	WB-F/222	AR
Winslow, John E.	077	1892	WB-H/229	AR
Winslow, John L.	024	1877	WB-E/91	AR
Winslow, John, Jr.	077	1754	SS 879/91	SS/AR
Winslow, Jordan	077	c1852	WB-F/437	AR
Winslow, Jordan H.	077	1852	WB-F/416	AR
Winslow, Joseph	077	1766	WB-C/68	AR
Winslow, Joseph	077	1750	Orig. Only	SS/AR
Winslow, Joseph	024	c1765	WB-A/186	AR
Winslow, Josiah	075	1785	WB-K/136	
Winslow, Lancelott	077	1856	WB-F/470	AR
Winslow, Mary	077	1777	WB-C/200	AR
Winslow, Moses	054	c1815	WB-1/383	AR
Winslow, Nancy	081	1859	WB-11/273	
Winslow, Nathan	081	1847	WB-8/369	AR
Winslow, Obed	077	1775	WB-C/168	AR
Winslow, Obed	024	1876	WB-E/54	AR
Winslow, Peggy	077	1822	WB-F/51	AR
Winslow, Pleasant	024	1836	Orig. Only	AR
Winslow, Rachel	077	1861	WB-F/529	AR
Winslow, Reubin	041	1883	WB-4/181	AR
Winslow, Samuel	075	1774	WB-I/88	
Winslow, Sarah S.	024	1876	WB-E/54	AR
Winslow, Thomas	077	1747	Orig. Only	SS/AR
Winslow, Thomas	081	c1825	Orig. Only	AR
Winslow, Thomas	077	1745	Orig. Only	SS/AR
Winslow, Thomas A.	077	1890	WB-H/193	AR
Winslow, Thomas E.	077	1891	WB-H/207	AR
Winslow, Timothy	077	1752	Orig. Only	SS/AR
Winslow, Timothy	077	1839	WB-F/285	AR
Winslow, Timothy A.	077	1892	WB-H/236	AR
Winslow, Uriah	077	1833	WB-F/216	AR
Winslow, William	024	1806	WB-B/204	AR

Name	Co.	Date	Recorded Copy	Original
Winslow, William H.	077	1830	WB-F/175	
Winslow, Wilson S.	075	1885	WB-O/237	AR
Winsly, Benjamin	085	1759	WB-A/164	AR
Winson, Lewis	071	1780	WB-1/224	
Winstand, Mary	075	1797	WB-M1/2	
Winstead, Alexander	020	1828	RB-L/276	AR
Winstead, B. L.	105	1895	WB-3/133	
Winstead, David	069	1848	WB-1/513	AR
Winstead, David W.	069	1883	WB-5/156	AR
Winstead, Duncan H.	069	c1882	Orig. Only	AR
Winstead, Elizabeth	069	1850	WB-1/523	AR
Winstead, Frank	105	1897	WB-3/261	AR
Winstead, Harris	105	1899	WB-3/383	
Winstead, James H.	105	1896	WB-3/186	AR
Winstead, Jeremiah	037	1851	WB-F/463	AR
Winstead, John H.	105	1876	WB-2/27	
Winstead, Joseph	069	1794	WB-1/88	AR
Winstead, Joseph	037	1823	WB-E/336	AR
Winstead, Louisa	105	1899	WB-3/368	
Winstead, Martha	078	c1872	Orig. Only	AR
Winstead, Richard	037	1792	WB-C/201	AR
Winstead, Salley	037	1838	WB-F/222	AR
Winstead, Samuel	078	1829	WI-11/181	AR
Winstead, Samuel	078	1806	WI-4/120	AR
Winstead, Sarah	078	1834	WI-12/327	AR
Winstead, Susan Ann	105	1895	WB-3/127	AR
Winstead, Thomas	069	1852	WB-1/526	AR
Winstead, W. R.	069	1894	WB-5/433	AR
Winstead, W. W.	105	1875	WB-2/166	
Winstead, William	078	1829	WI-11/150	AR
Winston, Anthony	039	c1786	WB-A/18	
Winston, B. T.	044	1898	WB-24/387	CTY
Winston, Benjamin	039	1835	WB-K/60	AR
Winston, Duncan C.	044	1851	WB-18/269	CTY
Winston, Elijah	044	1899	WB-24/454	CTY
Winston, George	039	c1810	WB-C/242	AR
Winston, George D.	084	1831	WB-B/37	CTY
Winston, George P.	084	1864	WB-C/398	CTY
Winston, Isaac	044	1761	Orig. Only	CTY
Winston, Isaac	039	1871	WB-U/35	
Winston, Isaac	039	c1843	WB-N/362	AR
Winston, John	039	1883	WB-U/320	AR
Winston, John	015	1768	100 WB-1/46	AR
Winston, John B.	039	1863	WB-R/401	AR
Winston, John R.	020	1888	WB-A/538 & 561	CTY
Winston, Joseph	090	1815	WB-2/168	
Winston, M. E.	010	1899	WB-I/578	
Winston, Mary	044	1877	WB-23/241	CTY
Winston, Moses	044	1851	WB-18/280	CTY
Winston, Orange	044	1882	WB-23/434	CTY
Winston, P. H.	010	1886	WB-I/212	
Winston, Samuel H.	039	1897	WB-V/119	AR
Winston, Thomas	039	1897	WB-V/109	AR
Winston, William	039	1815	WB-E/13	AR
Winston, Willie J.	039	1882	WB-U/290	AR
Winter, Daniel	022	1800	WB-A/23	AR
Winter, Joseph	047	1808	WB-3/482	
Winter, Joseph	047	1795	WB-3/239	
Winter, Mary	047	1824	WB-3/706	
Winter, Thomas	047	1788	WB-3/157	
Winterbottom, Joseph	008	1735	Orig. Only	SS/AR
Winters, Stephen W.	014	1896	WB-2/557	CTY
Winters, Temperance	014	1869	WB-2/21	AR
Winters, W. M.	014	1899	WB-3/97	CTY

Name	Co.	Date	Recorded Copy	Original
Winters, Watson	064	1857	WB-1/55	AR
Winthrop, Charlotte	NY	1872	Copy	050 AR
Winthrop, John S.	028	1860	WB-D/327	AR
Winwright, Ann	019	1751	028 DB-5/178	SS/AR
Wirick, Joel	046	1871	WB-E/43	AR
Wirick, Mary	046	1825	WB-B/202	AR
Wisdom, Abner	020	1854	RB-R/200	AR
Wisdom, Ann	104	1801	WB-2/49	AR
Wisdom, Ursilla	078	1868	WB-19/4	AR
Wisdom, William	005	1802	WB-2/189	AR
Wise, Barbara	060	1897	WB-5/61	AR
Wise, Barbara M.	060	1879	WB-4/193	
Wise, Edith	103	1826	RD-5/217	AR
Wise, Elizabeth	037	1862	WB-G/219	AR
Wise, Fredrick	060	1807	Orig. Only	AR
Wise, I. L.	060	1894	WB-4/530	AR
Wise, Isaac	103	1814	RD-3/169	AR
Wise, Jacob	060	1892	WB-4/476	AR
Wise, Jacob	060	1836	WB-1/377	AR
Wise, Jacob	070	c1876	WB-E/475	AR
Wise, James	103	1784	Orig. Only	AR
Wise, John	022	1787	RB-1/32	AR
Wise, John	060	1857	WB-3/3	AR
Wise, John	085	1880	WB-1/544	CTY
Wise, John	028	1854	WB-D/233	
Wise, Joseph	096	c1764	009 OWB/96	009 AR
Wise, Josiah	103	1803	Orig. Only	AR
Wise, Maple	028	1865	WB-D/404	AR
Wise, Mary	060	1875	WB-4/193	AR
Wise, Matilda	028	1795	WB-A/346	AR
Wise, Sarah	014	1894	WB-2/538	CTY
Wise, Selby H.	057	1822	WB-B/64	AR
Wise, Thomas	072	1807	WB-A/142	AR
Wise, William	028	1829	WB-C/307	
Wise, William B.	051	1865	WB-B/70	AR
Wiseman, A. N.	085	1865	WB-K/354	AR
Wiseman, Alexander	066	1878	WB-1/187	AR
Wiseman, Isaac	032	1835	WB-1/264	AR
Wiseman, Isaac	085	c1779	WB-C/185	AR
Wiseman, Isaac N.	032	1836	WB-1/276	AR
Wiseman, Jacob	085	c1807	WB-G/16	AR
Wiseman, Jesse P.	085	1887	WB-2/253	CTY
Wiseman, Josiah	064	1873	WB-2/35 & 425	AR
Wiseman, Mary	085	c1790	WB-B/179	AR
Wiseman, Peter	032	1889	WB-4/53	AR
Wiseman, Phebe A.	032	1889	WB-4/56	
Wiseman, William	085	c1805	WB-E/27	AR
Wiseman, William W.	032	1835	WB-1/269	AR
Wiser, Michael	016	1805	WB-A/91	AR
Wiser, Phillip	016	1798	WB-A/55	AR
Wishart, Elizabeth	083	c1790	WB-1/20	AR
Wishart, Giles E.	082	1890	WB-6/404	AR-Nunc.
Wishart, Jonathan	083	1819	WB-1/181	AR
Wishart, Margaret	065	1826	WB-G/65	AR
Wisheart, Joseph	065	1790	WB-G/37	AR
Wishon, Conrad	106	c1854	WB-1/21	AR
Wisson, Margaret	071	1881	WB-6/341	AR
Witcher, Ephraim	092	1820	WB-3/144	
Witherenton, Solomon	028	1766	Orig. Only	AR
Witherington, James	069	1829	WB-1/364	AR
Witherington, Joseph G.	045	1884	103 WB-1/329	103 AR
Witherington, Solomon	028	1840	Orig. Only	AR
Witherington, Susanna	028	1840	WB-D/21	AR
Witherington, William H.	028	1898	WB-F/346	
Witherington, Zebulon V.	079	1893	WB-3/23	AR
Withers, A. A.	090	1897	WB-6/434	AR
Withers, Benjamin	065	1841	WB-H/32	AR
Withers, Catharine	020	1843	RB-P/2	AR
Withers, Elijah K.	020	1870	WB-A/29	CTY
Withers, Jemima	065	1863	WB-J/157	AR
Withers, S. M.	065	1864	WB-J/193	
Witherspoon, David	028	1802	WB-B/144	AR
Witherspoon, Ezra B.	085	1872	WB-1/142	CTY
Witherspoon, Ezra B.	085	1872	065 WB-L/178	065 AR
Witherspoon, Henry	046	1897	WB-G/11	AR
Witherspoon, I. A.	054	1886	WB-5/131	CTY
Witherspoon, James	060	1838	WB-2/5	AR
Witherspoon, James	104	1790	WB-1/279	Nunc.
Witherspoon, John	017	c1863	WB-A/149	
Witherspoon, John	054	c1801	WB-1/269	AR
Witherspoon, John S.	016	1864	WB-2/105	AR
Witherspoon, John, Rev.	016	1846	WB-1/77	AR
Witherspoon, Mary	028	1800	Orig. Only	AR-Nunc.
Witherspoon, Susan D.	SC	1854	073 WB-G/69	
Witherspoon, Thomas	023	c1869	Orig. Only	AR
Witherspoon, Thomas	021	1856	WB-1/129	AR
Witherspoon, Thomas	104	1790	WB-1/280	
Witherspoon, William	065	1833	WB-G/144	AR
Withrow, James	086	1878	WB-F/111	AR
Withrow, John	086	c1792	Orig. Only	AR
Withrow, Margaret	086	1839	WB-E/56	AR
Witt, Hezekiah	023	1881	WB-A/27	AR
Witt, Michael	046	1795	WB-A/399	AR
Wittenberg, William	060	1800	Orig. Only	AR
Wittenburg, Daniel	003	1865	WB-A/1	AR
Wittenburg, David	003	1874	WB-B/40	AR
Witty, Cummings	084	1844	WB-B/314	CTY
Witty, Elijah	046	1844	Orig. Only	AR-Copy
Witty, Elijah	084	1847	WB-C/48	CTY
Witty, Elijah, Sr.	084	1844	WB-B/316	CTY
Witty, Levi R.	046	1871	WB-E/75	AR
Woddail, William	039	1832	WB-J/191	AR
Woff, Thomas	024	c1803	Orig. Only	AR-Copy
Wohlfahrt, Jacob	090	1807	WB-2/80	AR
Wolf, Charles	103	1831	RD-6/404	AR
Wolf, Edith	103	1832	RD-6/299	AR
Wolf, George	065	1825	WB-G/64	AR
Wolf, Jacob	097	1853	WB-1/88	AR
Wolf, Michall	100	1899	WB-51/530	
Wolf, Phillip	065	1814	WB-G/50	AR
Wolf, Richard	087	1848	WB-1/349	AR
Wolf, William	073	1808	WB-D/237	AR
Wolfe, F. L.	004	1881	WB-A/44	AR
Wolfe, John	065	1879	WB-K/330	AR
Wolfe, John W.	065	1900	WB-N/350	
Wolfe, Maria J.	065	1894	WB-M/316	AR
Wolfe, Samson	065	1885	WB-L/75	AR
Wolfe, W. H.	092	1898	WB-6/476	AR
Wolfenden, Ann E.	009	1893	WB-1/567	CTY
Wolfenden, John	010	1803	WB-E/207	AR
Wolfendon, John	077	1692	Orig. Only	SS/AR
Wolff, Ann Pines	090	1835	WB-3/289	AR
Wolff, Daniel	090	1831	WB-3/227	AR
Wolff, Jacob H.	038	1864	WB-1/238	AR
Wolff, Laurenz	090	1826	WB-3/147	AR
Wolff, Lewis	090	1842	WB-4/108	AR
Wolff, Lydia	038	1896	WB-4/10	AR
Wolff, William W.	092	1876	WB-6/71	AR
Wolfington, Jane	046	1823	WB-B/170	AR
Wolger, Adam	016	1801	WB-A/68	AR

Name	Co.	Date	Recorded Copy	Original
Wollard, David	063	1878	WB-3/142	
Wollard, Penelope	009	1855	OB-K/44	AR
Wollard, Sarah	009	1830	OB-B/79	AR
Wollard, Simon	009	1859	OB-L/64	AR
Wollard, Worden	009	1821	OB-A/309	AR
Woller, Elizabeth	060	1813	Orig. Only	AR
Womach, Thomas	085	c1799	WB-E/21	AR
Womack, Abraham	060	1803	Orig. Only	AR
Womack, Abraham	020	1800	RB-C/476	AR
Womack, Abram	084	1892	WB-E/512	CTY
Womack, Elizabeth	022	c1857	WB-D/148	AR
Womack, Green	022	1856	WB-C/414	AR
Womack, James	085	1820	WB-H/32	AR
Womack, John	078	1827	WI-10/323	AR
Womack, John	078	c1825	Copy	020 AR
Womack, John A.	022	1896	WB-F/14	AR
Womack, John, Sr.	022	1849	WB-C/243	AR
Womack, Joseph B.	020	1859	RB-S/84	AR
Womack, Josiah	020	1848	RB-Q/5	
Womack, Richard	085	1821	WB-H/118	AR
Womack, Sarah	VA	1860	Copy	084 CTY
Womack, Sarah M.	020	1867	RB-T/292	
Womack, Thomas J.	020	1889	WB-A/577	CTY
Womack, William	047	1778	WB-2/70	
Womack, Willie	099	1820	RB-16/6	AR
Womack, Willis	086	1884	WB-F/348	AR
Wombivell, Benjamin	009	1750	028 DB-5/172	SS/AR
Womble, Aaron T.	022	1862	WB-D/87	AR
Womble, Archibald	022	1893	WB-E/538	AR
Womble, Catharine	022	1840	WB-C/108	AR
Womble, Catharine	022	1878	WB-E/165	AR
Womble, Cornelius	022	1863	WB-D/108	AR
Womble, Edwin	010	1895	WB-I/446	AR
Womble, Eliza	022	1881	WB-E/245	AR
Womble, Emily	105	1896	WB-3/245	AR
Womble, Fannie R.	022	1891	WB-E/466	AR
Womble, Jehu J.	022	c1864	WB-D/144	AR
Womble, Jesse	068	c1854	WB-C/22	
Womble, John	099	1856	RB-29/463	AR
Womble, Jordan	099	1890	WB-B/477	AR
Womble, Julia	081	1887	WB-16/71	AR
Womble, Rufus H.	099	1894	WB-C/217	AR
Womble, Samuel	022	1814	WB-A/231	AR
Womble, Thomas	022	1807	WB-A/94	AR
Womble, Thomas C.	022	1874	WB-E/94	AR
Womble, Thomas W.	022	1883	WB-E/280	AR
Womble, Walter R.	099	1891	WB-B/582	AR
Womble, William	099	1852	RB-18/121	AR
Womble, William D.	100	1862	WB-49/532	AR
Womick, Isam	086	1883	WB-F/222	AR
Wommack, Carter	047	1822	WB-3/680	
Wommack, John, Sr.	022	1814	WB-A/242	AR
Wommack, Wilson	032	1845	WB-1/467	
Wood, A. H.	099	1889	WB-B/384	AR
Wood, Aaron	057	1811	WB-A/328	AR
Wood, Alex F.	044	1861	Orig. Only	CTY
Wood, Alexander	021	1896	WB-3/105	AR
Wood, Ann	077	1830	WB-F/173	AR
Wood, Anne	073	1818	WB-D/521	AR
Wood, Archibald	071	1803	WB-2/239	AR
Wood, Ashley	VA	1797	056 Est-3/192	
Wood, Augustus M.	071	1862	WB-5/271	AR
Wood, B. F.	047	1888	WB-6/500	AR
Wood, Benjamin	028	1808	WB-B/312	
Wood, Benjamin	071	1823	WB-3/280	AR
Wood, Britton	069	1874	WB-5/4	AR
Wood, Bryant C.	103	1865	RD-13/765	
Wood, Burrell	032	1847	WB-2/1	AR
Wood, Catherine	044	1857	WB-20/339	CTY
Wood, Cullin	071	1792	WB-2/1	AR
Wood, Daniel	085	1829	WB-H/464	AR
Wood, Edward	077	1827	WB-F/136	AR
Wood, Edward	070	1799	WB-AB/30	AR
Wood, Edward	072	1738	SS 878/72	SS/AR
Wood, Edward	024	1872	WB-E/33	AR
Wood, Elany	059	1898	WB-B/218	CTY
Wood, Elihu	073	1807	WB-D/208	AR
Wood, Elizabeth	077	1864	WB-F/553	AR
Wood, Elizabeth	078	1878	WB-19/50	AR
Wood, Elizabeth	077	1815	WB-E/425	AR
Wood, Elizabeth	044	1816	WB-7/590	CTY
Wood, Emma L.	103	1893	WB-2/57	AR
Wood, Evan	075	1790	WB-K/207	AR
Wood, Ezekael	044	1826	WB-10/234	CTY
Wood, Ezekiel	044	1826	Copy	078 AR
Wood, Fanny	018	1852	WB-C/361	
Wood, Garrett	085	c1795	WB-D/238	AR
Wood, George	075	1778	WB-K/17	
Wood, George	044	1841	WB-15/171	CTY
Wood, Gersham	057	1798	WB-A/219	AR
Wood, Handy	073	1846	WB-F/285	AR
Wood, Hardy	039	1870	WB-U/21	AR
Wood, Harriet	056	1884	WB-3/362	AR
Wood, Henrietta	103	1892	WB-1/568	AR
Wood, Henrietta	047	1899	WB-7/228	AR
Wood, Henry A.	071	1796	WB-2/116	AR
Wood, Henry B.	092	1895	WB-6/409	AR
Wood, Henry S.	026	1865	WB-1/367	AR-Nunc.
Wood, Isaac	053	1797	Orig. Only	AR
Wood, Isaiah	028	1892	WB-F/43	AR
Wood, Jackson	070	1880	WB-E/399	AR
Wood, James	096	c1824	Orig. Only	AR
Wood, James	071	1752	SS 879/48	SS/AR
Wood, James	077	1822	WB-F/68	AR
Wood, James	085	c1805	WB-D/269	AR
Wood, James	071	1797	WB-2/145	AR
Wood, James	032	c1856	WB-2/159	AR
Wood, James	071	1786	WB-1/363	AR
Wood, James	073	1819	WB-D/564	AR
Wood, James D.	071	1817	WB-3/194	AR
Wood, James H.	071	1840	WB-4/218	AR
Wood, James R.	009	1880	WB-1/251	CTY
Wood, Jeremiah	028	1793	WB-A/297	AR
Wood, Jesse	045	c1848	WB-1/120	
Wood, Jesse, Sr.	056	1822	WB-1/445	AR
Wood, Jesse, Sr.	072	c1770	RW/L47	
Wood, John	056	1750	SS 877/275	SS/AR
Wood, John	090	1861	WB-4/338	
Wood, John	075	1803	WB-M1/78	AR
Wood, John	057	1843	WB-B/156	AR
Wood, John	056	1778	Orig. Only	AR-Nunc.
Wood, John	085	c1781	WB-B/39	AR
Wood, John	071	1826	WB-4/16	AR
Wood, John	039	1875	WB-U/116	AR
Wood, John	024	c1767	WB-A/174	AR
Wood, John	077	1848	WB-F/345	AR
Wood, John	044	1761	Orig. Only	CTY
Wood, John H.	047	1888	WB-6/489	AR
Wood, John H.	060	1891	WB-4/464	AR
Wood, John L.	075	1893	WB-O/385	AR

Name	Co.	Date	Recorded Copy	Original
Wood, John W.	081	1890	WB-16/156	AR
Wood, John W.	GA	1898	025 WB-A/228	025 AR
Wood, Jonas	071	1790	WB-1/397	
Wood, Jonas	071	1804	WB-2/256	AR
Wood, Jonathan	029	1857	WB-C/357	AR
Wood, Joseph	071	1791	WB-1/416	
Wood, Joseph	075	1822	WB-M1/359	AR
Wood, Joseph	077	1802	WB-E/148	AR
Wood, Joseph	037	1785	WB-C/27	AR
Wood, Joseph	073	1833	WB-E/291	AR
Wood, Joseph	104	1824	WB-4/55	AR
Wood, Joseph L.	021	1896	WB-3/114	AR
Wood, Joshua	085	c1805	WB-D/6	AR
Wood, Josiah	037	1818	WB-E/183	AR
Wood, Kincheon	099	1836	RB-23/564	AR
Wood, Larkin H.	099	1900	WB-D/354	AR
Wood, Lucretia	086	1885	WB-F/255	AR
Wood, Marcum	099	1871	RB-35/137	AR
Wood, Margaret	032	1862	WB-2/216	AR
Wood, Margaret	104	1872	WB-6/53	AR
Wood, Mark	070	1788	WB-C/451	AR
Wood, Martha	071	1869	WB-6/45	AR
Wood, Mary	001	1863	WB-1/220	AR
Wood, Mary	073	1856	WB-G/127	AR
Wood, Mary A. E.	044	1892	WB-24/206	CTY
Wood, Mary M.	077	1876	WB-H/80	AR
Wood, Michael L.	081	1890	WB-16/184	AR
Wood, Moses	099	1804	RB-6/326	
Wood, Moses	010	1757	SS 880/258	SS/AR
Wood, Nathan	077	1844	WB-F/313	AR
Wood, Pennel	081	1841	WB-7/343	
Wood, Pernell S.	081	1895	WB-16/348	AR
Wood, Pincney V.	086	1896	WB-F/517	AR
Wood, Priscilla	039	1871	WB-U/36	
Wood, Rebecca	044	1859	WB-21/101	CTY
Wood, Reuben	081	1812	Orig. Only	AR
Wood, Richard	078	c1817	Orig. Only	AR
Wood, Richard	024	1837	WB-C/210	AR
Wood, Robert	085	1804	WB-D/222	AR
Wood, Sabret	073	1808	WB-D/220	AR
Wood, Sailey	069	1882	WB-5/145	AR
Wood, Sally	078	1843	WI-15/223	AR
Wood, Sarah	024	1833	WB-C/168	AR
Wood, Sarah	081	1885	WB-15/567	AR
Wood, Sarah	028	1847	WB-D/132	
Wood, Sarah B.	048	1896	WB-1/48	CTY
Wood, Sarah B.	039	c1889	Orig. Only	AR
Wood, Seth	024	1815	WB-C/33	AR
Wood, Solomon	073	1830	WB-E/231	AR
Wood, Spence	075	1883	WB-0/182	AR
Wood, Spencer	032	1887	WB-3/539	AR
Wood, Susan	096	1878	WB-4/48	
Wood, Susan C.	078	1893	WB-19/357	AR
Wood, Susanna	038	1856	WB-1/114	AR
Wood, Thomas	071	1751	Orig. Only	SS/AR
Wood, Thomas	053	1740	Orig. Only	SS/AR
Wood, Thomas	073	1800	WB-C/110	AR
Wood, Thomas F.	070	1892	WB-G/70	AR
Wood, Venters	028	1873	Orig. Only	AR
Wood, Vincent	032	1837	WB-1/295	
Wood, Vincent	060	1861	WB-3/38	AR
Wood, W. D.	056	1885	WB-3/379	
Wood, W. T.	047	1867	WB-5/156	
Wood, William	081	1801	WB-2/136	AR
Wood, William	015	1764	RB-1/9	AR

Name	Co.	Date	Recorded Copy	Original
Wood, William	086	1877	WB-F/90	AR
Wood, William	099	1844	RB-25/497	AR
Wood, William	085	1817	WB-G/479	AR
Wood, William	077	1824	WB-F/79	AR
Wood, William	103	1796	WI-B/124	
Wood, William	022	c1801	WB-A/61	AR
Wood, William	028	1789	WB-A/206	AR
Wood, William	044	1829	WB-11/216	CTY
Wood, William	090	1873	WB-6/36	AR
Wood, William	072	c1774	RW/L56	AR
Wood, William	075	1733	SS 876/325	SS/AR
Wood, William	086	1884	WB-F/251	AR
Wood, William	087	c1800	Orig. Only	AR
Wood, William K.	081	1844	WB-8/65	AR
Wood, William R.	047	1899	WB-7/229	AR
Wood, Williamson	086	1879	WB-F/143	AR
Wood, Wilmot	098	1893	WB-A/175	CTY
Wood, Zachariah	086	1825	WB-D/32	AR
Wood, Zebedee	081	1824	WB-5/159	AR
Woodall, B. A.	056	1894	WB-2/178	AR
Woodall, Berry	056	1855	Est-24/124	
Woodall, Jacob	056	1850	WB-1/631	AR
Woodall, James	056	1834	WB-1/501	AR
Woodall, James G.	056	1865	WB-2/71	AR
Woodall, Merrit	056	1881	WB-3/291	AR
Woodall, Pensa Villa	056	1869	WB-3/18	AR
Woodall, Seth	056	1900	WB-4/225	
Woodall, William W.	099	1875	RB-35/286	AR
Woodard, Amy Ann	087	1864	WB-2/74	AR
Woodard, Annie	056	1891	WB-3/577	AR
Woodard, Benjamin	056	1896	WB-2/230	
Woodard, C. W. W.	069	1870	WB-1/606	AR
Woodard, Catherine	082	1895	WB-6/509	AR
Woodard, Drucilla	103	1846	RD-9/309	AR
Woodard, Elisha	037	1798	WB-D/50	AR
Woodard, George A.	071	1862	WB-5/270	AR
Woodard, Hannah	103	1887	WB-1/411	AR
Woodard, Henry	009	c1815	OWB/475	AR
Woodard, Hillman	069	1883	WB-5/161	AR
Woodard, Irvin S.	056	1875	WB-3/149	AR
Woodard, Isaiah	009	1815	OB-A/248	AR
Woodard, James	103	1808	WI-B/406	AR
Woodard, James	039	1881	WB-U/260	AR
Woodard, James	069	c1808	WB-1/233	AR
Woodard, James	087	1840	WB-1/227	AR
Woodard, James A.	024	1889	WB-E/169	AR
Woodard, James B.	105	1863	WB-1/99	AR
Woodard, Jenney	024	1824	WB-C/109	AR
Woodard, Jethro	056	1820	WB-1/311	AR
Woodard, John	099	1782	RB-1/157	
Woodard, John	071	1834	WB-4/113	AR
Woodard, John	103	1821	RD-4/380	AR
Woodard, John	008	1734	SS 876/343	SS/AR
Woodard, John	009	c1785	OWB/198	AR
Woodard, John	037	1765	WB-A/146	AR
Woodard, Joseph	071	1791	WB-1/434	AR
Woodard, Joseph	056	1872	WB-3/67	AR
Woodard, Joshua	103	1798	WI-B/192	AR
Woodard, London	105	1870	WB-2/46	AR
Woodard, Luke	103	1808	RD-1/82	AR
Woodard, Mary	071	1866	WB-5/330	AR
Woodard, Mathew	056	1847	WB-1/587	AR
Woodard, Oliver	071	1816	WB-3/178	AR
Woodard, Peter	069	1888	WB-5/282	AR
Woodard, Sally	022	1871	WB-E/66	AR

Name	Co.	Date	Recorded Copy	Original
Woodard, Sarah A.	056	1884	WB-3/355	AR
Woodard, Stephen	105	1897	WB-3/257	AR
Woodard, Stephen	105	1864	WB-1/104	AR
Woodard, T. F.	074	1887	WB-1/94	AR
Woodard, Thomas	069	c1790	Orig. Only	AR
Woodard, William	107	1837	WB-1/24	
Woodard, William	107	c1842	WB-1/346	
Woodard, Willis	056	1862	WB-2/34	AR
Woodburn, Allen C.	046	1867	WB-D/33	AR
Woodburn, Arthur	046	1816	WB-A/425	AR
Woodburn, Eliel	005	1886	WB-D/196	AR
Woodburn, Thankful	046	1829	WB-B/390	AR
Woodburn, Thomas	046	1822	WB-B/152	AR
Woodburn, William	046	1806	WB-A/414	AR
Woodcock, J. A.	013	1889	WB-B/538 & 588	AR
Woodcock, John	065	1876	WB-K/235	AR
Woodell, Berry	056	1855	WB-1/688	AR
Woodfin, Eliza G.	013	1876	WB-B/518	AR
Woodfin, J. W.	013	1863	WB-A/221	
Woodfin, John W.	013	1863	Copy	093 AR
Woodfin, John W.	013	1894	055 WB-A/138	
Woodfin, Samuel	061	c1833	WB-1/11	AR
Woodford, Sarah N.	021	1879	WB-2/199	
Woodhouse, Edmond S.	030	1853	WB-4/175	AR
Woodhouse, Hadley	030	c1814	WB-3/46	
Woodhouse, Henry	030	1751	Orig. Only	SS/AR
Woodhouse, Hezekiah	030	c1821	WB-3/252	
Woodhouse, Horatio	072	1755	SS 880/19	SS/AR
Woodhouse, John	030	1772	WB-1/71	
Woodhouse, John	072	1776	RW/L16	AR
Woodhouse, John H.	030	1891	WB-5/193	AR
Woodhouse, Julia	030	1845	WB-4/112	
Woodhouse, Lancelott	030	1838	WB-4/55	
Woodhouse, Lem	030	1780	WB-1/137	
Woodhouse, Margret	030	1882	WB-5/94	AR
Woodhouse, Mary	030	1815	WB-3/72	
Woodhouse, Susan	030	1899	WB-5/278	AR
Woodhouse, William	030	1856	WB-4/207	AR
Woodhouse, William	030	1853	Orig. Only	AR
Woodhouse, Wilson	030	1817	WB-3/97	
Woodland, Mary	096	c1765	WB-1/35	AR
Woodland, Samuel	096	1777	WB-1/94	AR
Woodley, Balcy	101	1885	WB-A/145	
Woodley, Eli	096	1893	WB-4/149	AR
Woodley, Margaret	009	1817	OB-A/271	AR
Woodley, Mary I.	046	1897	WB-G/4	AR
Woodley, Mary I.	065	1895	010 WB-I/583	
Woodley, Mary I.	065	1895	WB-M/420	AR
Woodley, Mary I.	065	1895	024 WB-E/260	024 AR
Woodley, Samuel P.	101	1878	WB-A/22	
Woodley, Thomas	075	1752	Orig. Only	SS/AR
Woodley, Thomas	075	1753	WB-I/1	
Woodley, Willis	077	1849	WB-F/368	AR
Woodlief, Benjamin	039	1880	WB-U/248	AR
Woodlief, George	044	1766	Orig. Only	CTY
Woodlieff, Lucy	039	1888	WB-U/425	AR
Woodlieff, Mary	039	1888	WB-U/425	
Woodliff, Polly	098	1881	WB-A/7	CTY
Woodliff, Robbin	039	1877	WB-U/169	AR
Woodly, Daniel	096	1882	075 WB-O/291	075 AR
Woodly, Daniel	096	1882	WB-4/75	
Woodly, Hardy	096	1882	WB-4/85	
Woodman, Frances	RI	c1834	Copy	037 AR
Woodman, George W.	037	1833	WB-F/150	AR
Woodnot, Henry	024	1719	SS 875/176	SS/AR
Woodring, Daniel	060	1825	WB-1/14	AR
Woodring, Henry	054	1877	WB-4/272	CTY
Woodroffe, Thomas	092	1900	WB-6/541	AR
Woodroof, David	071	1810	WB-3/26	AR
Woodroof, Richard	071	1893	WB-7/203	AR
Woodroof, Roxie	071	1898	WB-7/374	AR
Woodroof, William L.	071	1878	WB-6/280	AR
Woodrow, Alexander	070	1759	DB-D/398	
Woodrow, Alexander	070	1759	SS 881/188	SS/AR
Woodruff, Aaron	106	c1860	WB-1/72	AR
Woodruff, Allen P.	106	c1851	WB-1/3	AR
Woodruff, Andrew J.	004	1890	WB-A/119	AR
Woodruff, Daniel D.	006	1899	WB-E/401	AR
Woodruff, Gideon	092	1821	WB-3/147	
Woodruff, James W.	069	1882	WB-5/152	AR
Woodruff, John	092	1812	WB-3/103	
Woodruff, John	092	1890	WB-6/397	
Woodruff, John Allen	006	1833	WB-B/36	AR
Woodruff, Moses	092	1817	WB-3/130	AR
Woodruff, William B.	092	1894	WB-6/389	AR
Woods, A. M.	020	1899	WB-B/354	CTY
Woods, A. S. G.	020	1895	WB-B/187	CTY
Woods, Eleanor	073	1843	WB-F/157	AR
Woods, Eli	073	1840	WB-F/42	AR
Woods, Elizabeth	085	1827	WB-H/377	AR
Woods, Elizabeth	085	1846	WB-K/41	AR
Woods, Elmore W.	073	1895	WB-I/74	CTY
Woods, Harris	036	1888	WB-A/128	CTY
Woods, Henry	073	1879	WB-H/230	CTY
Woods, Henry J.	092	1883	WB-6/183	AR
Woods, Hugh	073	1800	WB-D/1	AR
Woods, J. Milas	054	c1891	Orig. Only	AR
Woods, James	085	1781	WB-C/26	AR
Woods, James	054	c1793	WB-1/264	AR
Woods, John	073	1847	WB-F/334	AR
Woods, John	090	1799	WB-1/139	AR-Nunc.
Woods, John	020	1853	RB-R/56	
Woods, John	044	1836	WB-13/458	CTY
Woods, John	073	1813	WB-D/393	AR
Woods, John	073	1792	WB-B/197	AR
Woods, John	060	1804	Orig. Only	AR
Woods, John W.	073	1863	WB-G/402	CTY
Woods, Joseph	073	1852	WB-G/26	AR
Woods, Joseph F.	054	1890	WB-5/364	CTY
Woods, Lavinia	001	1874	WB-2/65	AR
Woods, Mary	073	1822	WB-E/26	AR
Woods, Mary	073	c1820	Orig. Only	AR
Woods, Mary	073	1817	WB-D/514	AR
Woods, Mary	085	1857	WB-K/237	AR
Woods, Matthew	085	1775	WB-A/190	AR
Woods, Matthew	065	1795	WB-F/231	
Woods, Matthew	085	c1801	WB-E/17	AR
Woods, Oliver	085	1760	WB-A/162	AR
Woods, Robert	085	1766	WB-A/163	AR
Woods, Samuel	078	1793	WI-1/80	
Woods, Samuel	085	c1772	WB-A/265	AR
Woods, Sarah	060	1842	WB-2/417	AR
Woods, Thomas	078	1878	WB-19/86	
Woods, Thomas	054	1874	WB-4/152	CTY
Woods, Trisey	085	1873	WB-1/250	CTY
Woods, William	073	1830	WB-E/236	AR
Woods, William	054	c1832	Orig. Only	AR
Woods, William	073	1819	WB-D/556	AR
Woods, William F.	085	1830	WB-H/476	AR-Nunc.

Name	Co.	Date	Recorded Copy	Original
Woodside, Cornelia	085	1850	WB-K/114	AR
Woodside, Jane	016	1857	WB-2/29	AR
Woodside, Janith	054	c1853	WB-3/64	AR
Woodside, John	046	1801	WB-A/407	AR
Woodside, John W.	012	1896	WB-A/107	AR
Woodside, Martha	085	1847	WB-K/53	AR-Nunc.
Woodside, Polly	085	1858	WB-K/270	AR
Woodside, Robert	054	c1805	WB-1/245	AR
Woodsides, Ephraim	054	1891	WB-5/492	CTY
Woodsides, Jane	054	1887	WB-5/158	CTY
Woodsides, Joseph	065	1897	WB-N/21	AR
Woodsides, Margaret	070	1801	WB-AB/49	AR
Woodson, Benjamin	084	1854	WB-C/167	CTY
Woodson, Martha	085	1827	WB-H/395	AR
Woodson, Obadiah	085	1873	WB-1/202	CTY
Woodward, Andrew	099	1862	RB-32/342	
Woodward, Christopher	099	1785	RB-2/66	AR
Woodward, David	037	c1798	Orig. Only	AR
Woodward, Edward	024	1822	WB-C/97	AR
Woodward, James	041	1886	WB-4/251	AR
Woodward, John	099	1799	RB-5/6	
Woodward, Samuel	N	1713	Orig. Only	SS/AR (N)
Woodward, Samuel	084	1813	WB-A/114	CTY
Woodward, Samuell	024	1752	Orig. Only	SS/AR
Woody, Allen	078	1839	WI-14/114	
Woody, David	078	1821	WI-9/230	AR
Woody, Francis E.	022	1868	WB-E/18	AR
Woody, Hugh	022	1826	WB-B/92	AR
Woody, James	078	1860	WB-18/163 & 214	AR
Woody, James	073	1792	WB-B/191	AR
Woody, James	073	1822	WB-E/28	AR
Woody, James	022	c1859	WB-D/49	AR
Woody, Joseph	073	1815	WB-D/425	AR
Woody, Mary	001	1873	WB-2/36	AR
Woody, Nancy H.	078	1866	WB-18/443	AR
Woody, Thomas	001	1886	WB-2/289	AR
Woody, Wyate	107	c1848	WB-1/377	
Woodyard, Abram	046	1864	WB-D/204	AR
Woodyard, Mary	046	1891	WB-F/151	AR
Woodyard, Susan	046	1848	Orig. Only	AR
Wooff, Henery	028	1775	Orig. Only	AR
Woolard, Almarina	009	1879	WB-1/243	CTY
Woolard, Ashley	009	1884	WB-1/346	CTY
Woolard, Harmon	009	1844	OB-E/352	AR
Woolard, Henry J.	009	1894	WB-1/37	CTY
Woolard, John	063	1873	WB-3/42	
Woolard, Martin	009	c1844	OB-F/443	
Woolard, Redding	009	1880	WB-1/264	CTY
Woolard, Richard	N	1707	Orig. Only	SS/AR
Woolard, Solomon	037	1889	WB-H/154	AR
Woolard, Wiley	009	c1890	Orig. Only	CTY
Woolard, William	024	1762	EdDSC	AR-Copy
Woolard, William	024	1762	WB-1/8	
Woolener, Mikel	081	1890	WB-16/199	AR
Wooley, A. C.	067	1892	WB-2/308	AR
Wooley, Robert R.	067	1840	WB-2/212	AR-Copy
Woolfolk, Richard	090	1808	WB-2/99	AR
Woolford, Charles D.	009	1821	OB-A/315	AR
Woollard, John	009	c1797	OWB/356	
Woollard, Mary	024	1789	WB-B/55	AR
Woollen, Leven	046	1832	WB-B/467	AR
Wools, Jacob	024	1900	WB-E/324	AR
Woolsey, Nancy	047	1819	WB-3/647	

Name	Co.	Date	Recorded Copy	Original
Woolvin, Joel W.	070	1889	WB-F/380	AR
Woolward, William	002	1691/2	Orig. Only	SS/AR
Woosley, William	032	1866	WB-2/341	AR
Wooster, John L.	070	1885	WB-F/8	AR
Wooten, Abraham	104	1855	WB-5/114	
Wooten, Absalom	037	1836	WB-F/193	AR
Wooten, Benjamin	047	1765	WB-1/151	
Wooten, Bryant	070	1856	WB-C/620	AR
Wooten, David A.	054	1866	WB-3/183	AR
Wooten, Edmund	079	1884	WB-2/326	AR
Wooten, Elizabeth	037	1885	WB-G/700	
Wooten, Emma Carr	045	1885	WB-1/107	AR
Wooten, James	037	1821	WB-E/265	AR
Wooten, James	049	c1862	WB-1/17	AR
Wooten, Jane H.	105	1893	WB-3/50	AR
Wooten, Jeremiah	092	1858	WB-5/29	
Wooten, Jesse	056	1812	WB-1/385	AR
Wooten, John	103	1835	RD-7/104	AR
Wooten, John	045	1887	WB-1/149	AR
Wooten, John A.	011	1859	WB-1/266	
Wooten, Josiah	059	1881	WB-B/21	CTY
Wooten, L. W.	054	1894	WB-5/510	CTY
Wooten, R. W.	104	1898	WB-7/61	AR
Wooten, Richard	092	1808	WB-3/85	
Wooten, Richard	027	1878	WB-2/24	
Wooten, Sarah	039	1789	WB-A/44	
Wooten, Shadrach	011	c1845	WB-1/114	
Wooten, Thomas	092	1796	WB-3/21	AR
Wooten, William	047	1835	WB-4/120	
Wooten, William	075	1767	WB-H/76	AR
Wooton, Thomas	106	1880	WB-2/127	AR
Wootten, Amos, Sr.	037	1812	WB-E/31	AR
Wootten, James	047	1810	WB-3/490	
Wootten, Jesse	037	1826	WB-F/62	AR
Wootten, John	047	1800	WB-3/338	
Wootten, John F.	084	1893	WB-E/547	CTY
Wootten, Priselah	037	1815	WB-E/101	AR-Nunc.
Wootten, William	037	1792	WB-C/197	AR
Wootten, William	047	1793	WB-3/211	
Wootton, Charles	075	1825	WB-N/13	AR
Wootton, Nathan	071	1839	WB-4/188	AR
Wootton, Sarah	103	1837	RD-7/306	AR
Word, Mary	053	1838	WB-6/35	AR
Worden, James	024	1755	SS 880/94	SS/AR
Work, Alexander	085	1778	WB-A/252	AR
Work, Alexander	054	N. D.	WB-1/250	AR-Copy
Work, Caroline	046	1893	WB-F/366	AR
Work, John	046	c1781	WB-A/409	AR
Work, John	046	1830	WB-B/407	AR
Work, John	046	1802	WB-A/421	AR
Work, William M.	046	1895	WB-F/416	AR
Worke, Robert	054	c1808	WB-2/1	AR
Workington, Samuel	053	c1786	RW-1/171	
Workman, Arthur	N	1697	SS 874.2/119	SS/AR
Workman, Henry	032	1876	WB-3/179	
Workman, John Alex	001	1881	WB-2/182	AR
Workman, Martha Ann	040	1898	WB-3/23	AR
Workman, Nancy M.	073	1896	WB-I/100	CTY
Workman, Reuben	032	c1852	WB-2/76	
Workman, Thomas	022	1857	WB-C/455	AR
World, Amanda J.	032	1894	WB-4/237	AR
Worley, Ann	035	1795	WB-A/499	AR
Worley, John	047	1795	WB-3/239	
Worley, John	096	1740	Orig. Only	SS/AR
Worley, Kezia	039	c1852	WB-O/325	AR

Name	Co.	Date	Recorded Copy	Original
Worley, Lovick	096	1754	SS 879/79	SS/AR
Worley, Mary	039	1846	WB-M/125	AR
Wormack, Benjamin	029	1791	Orig. Only	AR
Wormington, Britannia	053	1797	RW-1/277	AR
Wornum, Nancy	071	1810	WB-3/37	AR
Wornum, Samuel	071	1837	WB-4/168	AR
Worrell, Amos	047	1842	WB-4/210	
Worrell, Coley	103	c1843	Orig. Only	AR
Worrell, David	103	1789	WI-A/161	AR
Worrell, Francis	037	1875	WB-G/473	
Worrell, Henry	103	1854	RD-11/558	AR
Worrell, James	051	1846	WB-A/246	
Worrell, James	103	1838	RD-7/336	AR
Worrell, James A.	051	1874	WB-C/132	AR
Worrell, John	103	1820	RD-4/332	AR
Worrell, John	103	1789	WI-A/178	AR
Worrell, John	041	1856	WB-3/194	AR
Worrell, Richard	103	1808	RD-1/95	AR
Worrell, Suckey	103	1835	RD-7/103	AR
Worrell, William	103	1816	RD-3/340	AR
Worsham, Dicy	065	1859	WB-I/201	AR
Worsham, Dicy	065	1840	WB-H/5	AR
Worsham, Eliza A.	020	1892	WB-B/114	CTY
Worsham, John	065	1806	WB-G/44	AR
Worsham, John	020	1885	WB-A/436	CTY
Worsley, Becca	009	c1803	OWB/413	AR
Worsley, Benjamin	009	1821	OB-A/310	AR
Worsley, Dicy	037	1833	WB-F/148	AR
Worsley, Ethalia	037	1894	WB-H/288	AR
Worsley, James A.	037	1870	WB-G/352	AR
Worsley, John	009	1750	028 DB-5/130	SS/AR
Worsley, John	N	c1760	Orig. Only	SS/AR
Worsley, John	035	1796	WB-A/483	AR
Worsley, Littleberry	047	1888	WB-6/515	AR
Worsley, Littleberry	047	1888	037 WB-H/132	
Worsley, Lucrecia	010	1763	WB-A/76	AR
Worsley, Mary E.	037	1895	WB-H/337	AR
Worsley, Reddin	037	1888	WB-H/125	
Worsley, Thomas	009	1737	Orig. Only	SS/AR
Worsley, William	009	c1803	OWB/412	AR
Worsley, William	037	1884	WB-G/678	
Worth, David	006	1888	WB-E/175	AR
Worth, David G.	070	1897	WB-H/98	AR
Worth, Fatima	029	1898	WB-F/138	AR
Worth, Francis	046	1807	WB-A/413	AR
Worth, Frederick	013	1884	WB-B/313	AR
Worth, J. M.	081	1900	046 WB-H/536	
Worth, J. M.	081	1900	WB-17/65	
Worth, Job	092	1877	WB-6/105	AR
Worth, John	011	1743	LGB-4/#148	SS/AR
Worth, Jonathan	099	1869	RB-35/40	AR
Worth, Joseph	024	c1775	WB-A/181	AR
Worth, Joseph	081	1816	WB-4/342	AR
Worth, Pheba	046	1899	WB-G/126	AR
Worth, T. C.	046	1891	WB-F/131	AR
Worth, Thomas C.	070	1862	WB-D/93	AR
Wortham, Edward	073	1818	WB-D/538	AR
Wortham, Elizabeth	100	1826	WB-29/173	AR
Wortham, John	100	1839	WB-37/266	AR
Wortham, John	100	1866	WB-50/204	AR
Wortham, John, Sr.	100	1830	WB-33/65	AR
Wortham, Joseph	100	1853	WB-42/215	AR
Wortham, Martha W.	044	1876	WB-23/237	CTY
Wortham, Mary	073	1829	WB-E/174	
Wortham, William	100	1809	WB-14/296	AR
Wortham, William D.	044	1877	WB-23/285	CTY
Worthington, Charles S.	045	1889	WB-1/180	AR
Worthington, Ephraim	081	1877	WB-15/249	AR
Worthington, Ephraim	081	1834	WB-6/338	AR
Worthington, Louisa B.	070	1897	WB-G/587	AR
Worthington, Martha Ann	045	c1875	WB-1/62	
Worthington, Sarah	028	1861	WB-D/358	AR
Worthy, Anna	068	c1891	WB-D/353	
Worthy, Elizabeth	068	1843	WB-B/148	
Worthy, James	068	1864	WB-C/108	
Worthy, John	068	1828	WB-B/60	
Wortman, Daniel	086	1830	WB-D/117	AR
Wortman, Henry	026	c1842	WB-1/411	AR
Wortman, John	026	1872	Orig. Only	AR
Wortman, Jonathan	026	1887	WB-2/305	AR
Worton, Matix	019	1765	Orig. Only	AR
Wotsford, Joseph	010	1739	Orig. Only	SS/AR
Wray, Alec	046	1885	WB-E/408	AR
Wray, James	026	1851	WB-1/120	AR
Wray, Mary	084	1835	WB-B/145	CTY
Wray, Robert	084	1872	Orig. Only	AR
Wray, Robert	084	1829	WB-B/18	CTY
Wray, William	090	1825	WB-3/140	AR
Wray, William	026	1865	WB-1/362	AR
Wren, Angelina	081	1847	WB-8/368	AR
Wren, Elizabeth	081	1862	WB-12/235	AR
Wren, Harmon	100	1825	WB-27/269	AR
Wren, James	056	1794	Orig. Only	AR
Wren, John	081	1833	WB-6/294	AR
Wren, Mary P.	032	1889	WB-4/68	AR
Wren, Nancy	100	1847	WB-39/301	AR
Wren, William	072	1789	WI/L56	AR
Wrench, Jacky	099	1817	RB-13/361	AR
Wrench, James	087	1864	WB-2/66	AR
Wrench, Rebeckah	099	1804	RB-6/334	AR
Wrenn, Elizabeth	039	1837	WB-K/133	AR
Wrenn, Janette	078	1899	WB-19/474	AR
Wrenn, Mary A.	036	1900	WB-A/489	CTY
Wrenn, Sarah	039	1825	WB-H/91	AR
Wright, Aaron	067	1900	Orig. Only	AR
Wright, Aleaph	018	1824	WB-C/35	
Wright, Ann	028	1838	WB-C/423	AR
Wright, Anna P.	100	1862	WB-49/418	
Wright, Archibald	029	1897	WB-F/118	AR
Wright, Arthur	018	1824	WB-C/39	
Wright, Auston	075	1742	Orig. Only	SS/AR
Wright, Charles	075	1772	WB-H/146	AR
Wright, Cloe	069	1818	WB-1/296	AR
Wright, David	067	1886	WB-2/226	AR
Wright, David	035	1827	WB-A/500	AR
Wright, David	009	1856	OB-K/181	AR
Wright, Demsey	018	1880	WB-E/73	AR
Wright, Edmund	024	1868	WB-D/62	AR
Wright, Edward	067	c1842	WB-1/16	AR
Wright, Edward	084	1841	WB-B/259	CTY
Wright, Elisha A.	084	1858	WB-C/288	CTY
Wright, Eliza	087	1880	WB-3/211	AR
Wright, Eliza A.	070	1861	WB-D/43	AR
Wright, Eliza Ann	070	1895	WB-G/431	AR
Wright, Elizabeth	084	1841	WB-B/252	CTY
Wright, Elizabeth	084	1848	WB-C/82	CTY
Wright, Elizabeth	081	1812	WB-4/1	AR
Wright, Elizabeth	035	1841	Orig. Only	AR
Wright, Elizabeth	077	1785	WB-C/287	
Wright, Elizabeth	005	1830	WB-B/2	AR

Name	Co.	Date	Recorded Copy	Original
Wright, Eunice	032	1892	WB-4/143	AR
Wright, Francis	018	1826	WB-C/76	
Wright, Gamiel	030	1799	WB-2/131	
Wright, Gamiel W.	018	1842	WB-C/270	AR-Copy
Wright, George	039	c1851	Orig. Only	AR
Wright, George B.	037	1894	WB-H/295	AR
Wright, Griffin	039	1816	WB-E/110	AR
Wright, Hannah	044	1792	WB-2/283	CTY
Wright, Henry	100	1868	WB-51/7	AR
Wright, Henry	030	1784	WB-1/181	
Wright, Henry	060	1821	Orig. Only	AR
Wright, Hiram A.	020	1881	WB-A/334	CTY
Wright, Humphrey	024	c1850	WB-C/310	AR
Wright, Isaac	073	1774	WB-A/174	
Wright, Isaac	011	1866	WB-2/4	
Wright, Isaac	081	1862	WB-12/162	AR
Wright, Isaac	035	1861	WB-3/42	AR
Wright, Isaac C.	087	1873	WB-3/34	AR
Wright, Jacob	020	1820	RB-H/297	AR
Wright, James	067	1865	WB-1/127	AR
Wright, James	035	1840	Orig. Only	AR
Wright, James	053	1814	RW-1/488	
Wright, James	099	1824	RB-19/73	AR
Wright, James W.	104	1865	WB-5/421	
Wright, James, Jr.	046	c1784	WB-A/403	AR
Wright, Jane	081	1886	WB-15/575	AR
Wright, Jeptha	039	1829	WB-J/62	AR
Wright, Jeremiah	081	1900	WB-17/85	
Wright, Jeremiah	DE	c1783	009 OWB/182	009 AR
Wright, Jobe	026	1838	WB-1/149	AR
Wright, Jobe	086	1838	WB-E/45	AR
Wright, John	092	1790	WB-2/160A	
Wright, John	046	c1783	WB-A/402	AR
Wright, John	077	1797	WB-E/89	AR
Wright, John	015	1771	100 WB-1/192	AR
Wright, John	070	1749	DB-C/191	
Wright, John	035	1800	WB-A/511	AR
Wright, John	090	1836	WB-3/314	
Wright, John	100	1852	WB-42/70	AR
Wright, John	005	1807	SC/02820	AR-Copy
Wright, John	070	1749	SS 877/323	SS/AR
Wright, John	104	1861	WB-5/279	
Wright, John	106	c1852	WB-1/7	AR
Wright, John	075	1772	WB-I/122	AR
Wright, John	018	c1813	Orig. Only	AR-Copy
Wright, John B.	024	1857	WB-C/404	AR
Wright, John H.	044	1878	WB-23/322	CTY
Wright, John M.	046	1864	WB-D/205	AR
Wright, John P.	018	1895	WB-E/237	
Wright, John W.	029	1854	WB-C/282	AR
Wright, John, Jr.	005	1808	WB-2/194	AR
Wright, John, Sr.	087	1848	WB-1/344	AR
Wright, Joseph	044	1762	Orig. Only	CTY
Wright, Joseph	104	1888	WB-6/342	AR
Wright, Joseph	099	1796	RB-3/227	AR
Wright, Joseph M.	084	1875	WB-E/95	CTY
Wright, Joshua G.	070	c1863	WB-D/144	AR
Wright, Major	018	c1864	WB-E/36	
Wright, Marchus	011	1892	WB-2/247	
Wright, Martha	047	1787	WB-3/132	
Wright, Martin	084	1833	WB-B/69	CTY
Wright, Martin P.	084	1843	WB-B/292	CTY
Wright, Mary	070	1866	WB-D/206	AR
Wright, Mary	028	1785	WB-A/90	AR
Wright, Mary	071	1811	WB-3/57	AR
Wright, Mathias	018	1836	WB-C/192	AR-Copy
Wright, Micajah	046	1890	WB-F/76	AR
Wright, Nancy	047	1822	WB-3/670	
Wright, Nancy C.	065	1899	WB-N/231	AR
Wright, Nathan	084	1850	WB-C/104	CTY
Wright, Newton	026	1849	WB-1/97	AR
Wright, Owen	030	1826	WB-3/213	
Wright, Penelope	024	1889	WB-E/171	AR
Wright, Rachel	070	1869	WB-E/174	AR
Wright, Randleson	035	1891	WB-4/388	AR
Wright, Rebecca	082	1888	WB-6/397	AR-Nunc.
Wright, Richard	085	c1784	WB-C/207	AR
Wright, Richard	032	1833	WB-1/229	
Wright, Richard	086	1805	WB-B/187	AR
Wright, Richardson	032	c1852	WB-2/160	
Wright, Robert	026	1875	WB-2/137	AR
Wright, Robert	079	1774	035 WB-A/524	035 AR
Wright, Sabra	082	1846	WB-3/34	AR
Wright, Samuel	099	1805	RB-7/55	AR
Wright, Samuel	077	1754	SS 879/75	SS/AR
Wright, Samuell	077	1718	Orig. Only	SS/AR
Wright, Sarah	084	1854	WB-C/173	CTY
Wright, Sarah	017	1899	WB-B/315	
Wright, Sarah	018	1899	WB-E/298	AR
Wright, Stephen	005	1791	WB-A/16	AR
Wright, Stephen	028	1793	WB-A/287	AR
Wright, Susan	070	1842	WB-AB/366	AR
Wright, Thomas	035	1847	WB-2/9	AR
Wright, Thomas	077	1790	WB-C/405	AR
Wright, Thomas	053	1797	RW-1/287	AR
Wright, Thomas	046	c1816	SC/02062	AR-Copy
Wright, Thomas	046	1816	WB-A/424	AR
Wright, Thomas	018	1825	WB-C/45	
Wright, Thomas	070	1771	WB-C/434	AR
Wright, Thomas	092	c1838	WB-4/175	
Wright, Thomas	070	1813	WB-AB/200	AR
Wright, Thomas H.	070	1861	WB-D/58	AR
Wright, William	081	1893	WB-16/262	AR
Wright, William	037	1763	WB-A/116	
Wright, William	069	1814	WB-1/258	AR
Wright, William	100	1781	WB-3/100	AR
Wright, William	035	1881	WB-4/178	AR
Wright, William	044	1815	WB-7/556	CTY
Wright, William	053	c1786	RW-1/165	
Wright, William	068	1895	WB-D/439	
Wright, William	068	1822	WB-B/27	
Wright, William	075	1797	WB-L/111	AR
Wright, William	070	1843	WB-AB/390	AR
Wright, William	024	1841	WB-C/226	AR
Wright, William A.	070	1878	WB-E/356	AR
Wright, William B.	029	1880	WB-E/216	AR
Wright, William H.	070	1847	WB-AB/476	AR
Wright, William L.	067	1900	WB-2/425	AR
Wright, William P.	081	1898	WB-16/501	AR
Wright, Winfield	044	1783	WB-1/376	CTY
Wright, Wingfield	047	1775	WB-2/15	
Wriston, Miles L.	065	1876	WB-K/213	
Writesman, Christian	081	1825	WB-5/236	AR
Wroten, Thomas	038	1887	WB-3/61	AR
Wyatt, Ambrose K.	077	1826	WB-F/120	AR
Wyatt, Brantley	085	1863	WB-K/316	AR
Wyatt, D. C.	033	1892	WB-2/120	CTY
Wyatt, Elizabeth	073	c1815	Orig. Only	AR
Wyatt, Elizabeth	001	1882	WB-2/192	AR
Wyatt, Ezekiel	063	1843	WB-2/299	

Name	Co.	Date	Recorded Copy	Original
Wyatt, Hugh K.	077	1832	WB-F/207	AR
Wyatt, Jacob	077	1788	WB-C/378	AR
Wyatt, Jacob	047	1761	WB-1/40	
Wyatt, James	047	1785	WB-3/78	
Wyatt, James	047	1787	WB-3/129	
Wyatt, Jesse	047	1794	WB-3/224	
Wyatt, John	063	1836	WB-2/215	
Wyatt, John	065	1833	WB-G/139	AR
Wyatt, John	006	1895	WB-E/283	AR
Wyatt, Joseph	001	1890	WB-2/470	AR
Wyatt, Joshua	073	1799	WB-C/144	AR
Wyatt, Mary	004	1875	WB-A/18	AR
Wyatt, Mary	077	1825	WB-F/105	AR
Wyatt, Rebecca	104	c1891	Orig. Only	AR
Wyatt, Robert K.	077	1826	WB-F/119	AR
Wyatt, Solomon	063	1777	WB-1/32	
Wyatt, Vickery	104	1897	WB-7/8	AR
Wyatt, William	085	c1804	WB-D/268	AR
Wyatt, William	006	1858	WB-A/106	AR
Wyatt, Zebedee	006	1851	WB-A/73	AR
Wyche, James	044	1845	WB-16/240	CTY
Wyche, Mary	099	1890	WB-B/457	AR
Wyche, Mary V.	098	1897	WB-A/278	CTY
Wyke, Jacob	060	1835	WB-1/336	
Wyles, Thomas	092	1827	WB-3/173	
Wylie, James	065	1804	WB-G/46	AR
Wylie, James	065	1772	WB-F/208	AR
Wylie, John	065	1812	WB-G/53	AR
Wylie, John	065	c1784	WB-F/219	AR
Wylie, Oliver	067	1854	WB-1/64	AR
Wylie, William	065	1798	WB-F/228	AR
Wynants, Penelope	024	1804	WB-B/226	AR
Wynens, Peter	065	1800	WB-G/49	AR
Wynn, Benjamin	051	1857	WB-B/5	
Wynn, Daniel	010	1813	WB-F/236	AR
Wynn, George	022	1868	WB-D/176	AR
Wynn, George	063	1900	WB 4/273	AR
Wynn, George W.	063	1891	WB-4/65	
Wynn, Isiah H.	101	1876	WB-A/18	
Wynn, James D.	024	1866	WB-D/46	AR
Wynn, John M.	037	1848	WB-F/387	AR
Wynn, Thomas	044	1817	WB-7/637	CTY
Wynn, William	N	1717/8	009 DB-1/284	
Wynn, William B.	051	1840	WB-A/205	
Wynne, Catharine	020	1900	WB-B/374	CTY
Wynne, Charles	039	1826	WB-H/115	AR
Wynne, Elizabeth	028	1843	WB-D/71	AR
Wynne, Jeremiah	096	1832	WB-2/105	AR
Wynne, John	096	c1796	Orig. Only	AR
Wynne, John T.	096	1848	WB-3/17	AR
Wynne, Joseph	096	1849	WB-3/24	AR
Wynne, Mary	053	1850	WB-7/435	AR
Wynne, Peter	096	1782	WB-1/123	AR
Wynne, Robert	099	1848	RB-26/419	AR
Wynne, Robert	096	1853	WB-3/33	AR
Wynne, Sarah	096	1833	WB-2/113	AR
Wynne, Thomas	096	1757	WB-1/5	AR
Wynne, Thomas K.	039	c1794	WB-A/157	
Wynne, William	096	1850	WB-3/26	AR
Wynne, William	099	1831	RB-22/57	AR
Wynns, David	063	1841	WB-2/279	
Wynns, George	010	1751	SS 879/18	SS/AR
Wynns, George	010	1859	WB-H/82	AR
Wynns, John	010	1753	SS 878/208	SS/AR
Wynns, John	063	1848	WB-2/345	
Wynns, Joseph P.	051	1877	WB-C/183	AR
Wynns, Levina	010	1821	WB-G/79	AR
Wynns, Phoebe	010	1860	WB-H/99	AR
Wynns, Watkin W.	063	1812	WB-2/8	
Wynns, William	010	1758	Orig. Only	SS/AR
Wyre, Barnabas	032	1876	WB-3/169	AR
Wyrick, Absolom	046	1865	WB-D/282	AR
Wyrick, Alfred	046	c1877	WB-E/259	AR
Wyrick, Elizabeth	046	c1900	Orig. Only	AR
Wyrick, George	046	1883	WB-E/367	AR
Wyss, Ninian	028	1783	Orig. Only	AR
Wyttenback, John	050	1894	WB-2/187	CTY
Yancey, A. G.	020	1887	WB-A/512	CTY
Yancey, Ann	020	1818	RB-H/211	AR
Yancey, Anne	020	1855	RB-R/329	AR
Yancey, Charles	044	1858	WB-20/560	CTY
Yancey, James	044	1779	WB-1/252	CTY
Yancey, Jechonias	044	1828	WB-10/404	CTY
Yancey, Jeconias	047	1760	WB-1/13	
Yancey, John G.	098	1883	WB-A/30	CTY
Yancey, Lewis	044	1819	WB-8/245	CTY
Yancey, Richard E.	044	1898	WB-24/385	CTY
Yancey, Zilpah	020	c1843	RB-O/486	AR
Yancy, Algernon	020	c1846	Orig. Only	AR
Yancy, Charles	073	1860	WB-G/237	AR
Yandle, James	065	1797	Orig. Only	AR
Yandle, Samuel	065	1866	WB-J/220	AR
Yarboro, Sarah	026	1888	WB-2/308	AR
Yarborough, Agnes	039	c1861	WB-R/14	AR
Yarborough, Edward	099	1866	RB-34/298	AR
Yarborough, Eli	068	1897	WB-D/528	
Yarborough, Elizabeth	029	1806	WB-A/63	AR
Yarborough, Hannah H.	099	1883	WB-A/428	AR
Yarborough, James	078	1891	WB-19/281	
Yarborough, Joanna	067	c1854	WB-1/75	AR
Yarborough, Lewis	060	1821	Orig. Only	AR
Yarborough, Nancy	067	1878	WB-2/97	AR
Yarborough, Thomas	032	1833	WB-1/231	
Yarbrough, Archibald	039	1842	WB-L/91	AR
Yarbrough, Charles	039	c1801	Orig. Only	AR-Copy
Yarbrough, Charles	032	1879	WB-3/281	AR
Yarbrough, Edward	085	c1805	WB-D/267	AR
Yarbrough, Elizabeth	078	c1854	Orig. Only	AR
Yarbrough, George	047	1798	WB-3/308	AR
Yarbrough, Henry	039	1794	WB-A/122	
Yarbrough, J. J.	020	1896	WB-B/243	CTY
Yarbrough, James	039	1832	WB-J/196	AR
Yarbrough, James	078	1891	WB-19/281	AR
Yarbrough, James	039	1815	WB-E/14	AR
Yarbrough, James S.	039	1863	WB-R/398	AR
Yarbrough, John	099	1785	RB-2/68	AR
Yarbrough, John	078	1857	WB-17/471	
Yarbrough, John	078	1811	WI-6/12	AR
Yarbrough, John B.	039	1862	WB-R/323	
Yarbrough, Jonathan	005	1812	WB-2/197	AR
Yarbrough, Joseph	022	1885	WB-E/305	AR
Yarbrough, Martha	039	1817	WB-E/133	AR
Yarbrough, Richard T.	039	1851	WB-N/350	AR
Yarbrough, Sally	039	1863	WB-R/518	AR
Yarbrough, Samuel	078	c1845	Orig. Only	AR
Yarbrough, Samuel	073	1770	WB-A/107	
Yarbrough, Samuel	078	1820	WI-8/328	AR
Yarbrough, Susan	044	1852	WB-19/133	CTY
Yarbrough, William	078	1820	WI-8/324	AR
Yarbrough, William	100	1792	WB-7/5	AR

Name	Co.	Date	Recorded Copy	Original
Yarbrough, William	100	1803	WB-12/65	AR
Yarbrough, William J.	022	c1861	WB-D/91	AR
Yarbrough, Zachariah	032	1844	WB-1/434	
Yarrell, Peter	090	1800	WB-1/143	AR
Yates, Alvis	099	1871	RB-35/155	AR
Yates, Ann E.	020	1874	WB-A/156	CTY
Yates, B. M.	099	1879	WB-A/91	AR
Yates, Bazel	019	1795	WB-E/36	
Yates, Calvin	099	1887	WB-B/217	AR
Yates, Carlos	099	1882	WB-A/304	AR
Yates, Charles G.	046	1882	WB-E/336	AR
Yates, Clara	099	1897	WB-C/593	AR
Yates, David	028	1793	WB-A/299	
Yates, Delilia	071	1886	WB-6/551	AR
Yates, Eli	022	1857	WB-C/445	AR
Yates, Eli C.	006	1888	WB-E/158	AR
Yates, Elizabeth	082	1896	WB-6/550	AR
Yates, Gabrielle	099	1900	WB-D/411	AR
Yates, Hilliard	099	1884	WB-A/557	AR
Yates, Hinton	099	1891	WB-B/538	AR
Yates, James	019	1750	028 DB-5/146	SS/AR
Yates, John	020	1779	RB-A/64	AR
Yates, John	020	1798	RB-C/272	AR
Yates, Levi S.	079	1898	WB-3/152	AR
Yates, Levi S.	063	1898	WB-4/227	AR
Yates, Lewis	099	1895	WB-C/395	AR
Yates, Louisa	063	1897	WB-4/199	AR
Yates, Mary	038	1889	WB-3/145	AR
Yates, Mathew	099	1837	RB-24/92	AR
Yates, Melchisedick	028	1838	WB-C/410	AR
Yates, Peter R.	028	1836	WB-C/389	AR
Yates, Samuel	071	1864	WB-5/288	AR
Yates, Squire A.	006	1895	WB-E/285	AR
Yates, Stephen	057	1803	WB-A/269	AR
Yates, Tilmon	104	1856	WB-5/147	
Yates, Wesley M.	022	c1863	WB-D/147	AR
Yates, Western B.	065	1832	WB-G/89	AR
Yates, William	099	1866	RB-34/162	AR
Yates, William	019	1895	WB-B/274	AR
Yaudle, Jesse	097	1882	WB-2/212	
Yaudle, Sherod	097	1883	Orig. Only	AR
Yaunts, Peter	032	1838	WB-1/319	
Yeargain, Samuel	100	1785	WB-4/66	AR
Yeargan, Sarah	073	1825	WB-E/76	AR
Yeargan, Thomas	081	1839	WB-7/232	AR
Yeargin, Benjamin	073	1812	WB-D/338	AR
Yeargin, David	039	1896	WB-V/73	AR
Yeates, Benjamin	072	1802	WB-A/152	AR
Yeates, Daniel	072	1795	Orig. Only	AR
Yeates, David	057	1806	WB-A/284	AR
Yeates, James	010	1807	WB-F/31	AR
Yeates, John	037	1746	Orig. Only	SS/AR
Yeates, Peter G.	009	1852	OB-H/77	AR
Yeates, William	010	1826	WB-G/147	AR
Yeates, William	010	1752	SS 879/58	SS/AR
Yeates, William	019	c1777	Orig. Only	AR
Yeats, David	010	1795	WB-D/292	AR
Yeats, Elizabeth	010	1792	WB-D/207	AR
Yeats, John	010	1787	WB-D/76	AR
Yeats, John D.	104	1876	WB-6/129	AR
Yeats, John, Sr.	104	1875	WB-6/103	
Yeats, Peter	010	1795	WB-D/286	AR
Yeats, Thomas	009	1811	OWB/460	AR
Yeats, William	099	1808	RB-7/314	AR
Yeats, William	010	1789	WB-D/95	AR
Yellowley, Edward C.	079	1885	WB-2/347	AR
Yellowley, Harriet A.	079	1890	WB-2/484	AR
Yelton, Jacob	086	1900	WB-G/53	AR
Yelventon, Jacob	039	1884	WB-U/340	AR
Yelventon, John	103	1795	WI-B/70	AR
Yelverton, Bryant	103	1887	WB-1/383	AR
Yelverton, Delany	103	c1858	RD-14/335	
Yelverton, Elizabeth	103	1818	RD-4/153	AR
Yelverton, Etheldred	103	1851	RD-10/477	AR
Yelverton, Hardy	103	1887	WB-1/397	AR
Yelverton, Hardy	103	1829	RD-6/77	AR
Yelverton, Hyman	045	1887	WB-1/171	AR
Yelverton, Jason	103	1850	RD-10/433	AR
Yelverton, Mary	103	1898	WB-2/267	AR
Yelverton, Robert	103	1899	WB-2/258	AR
Yelverton, T. W.	103	1890	WB-1/517	AR
Yelvington, Eli	056	1837	Est-18/397	
Yelvington, Sarah Jane	056	1892	WB-2/118	
Yelvinton, Shadrick	056	1824	WB-1/364	AR
Yerton, Jacob	016	1861	WB-2/77	AR
Yewel, Samuel	047	1764	WB-1/141	Nunc.
Yoder, David	021	1863	WB-1/181	AR
Yoder, Elizabeth	021	1883	WB-2/263	
Yoder, Elizabeth	021	1867	WB-1/237	
Yoder, Fanny	021	1883	WB-2/263	
Yoder, Frances	021	1867	WB-1/237	
Yoder, Frances	021	1892	WB-2/578	
Yoder, Marcus	021	1880	WB-2/221	AR
Yoder, Michael	021	1874	WB-2/94	
Yoder, Sarah	021	1867	WB-1/237	
Yoder, Sarah	021	1883	WB-2/263	
Yoeman, Drury	084	c1794	OW/204	AR
Yoeman, Shadrach	084	c1802	OW/218	AR
Yoemans, Anna	024	1835	WB-C/183	AR
Yokeley, Hugh	032	1842	WB-1/402	
Yokely, David	032	1873	WB-3/88	AR
Yokely, Hannah	032	c1856	WB-2/123	
Yokley, J. M.	032	1875	WB-3/156	AR
Yokley, Jacob	032	1896	WB-4/288	AR
Yokley, John	032	c1848	Orig. Only	AR-Copy
Yokley, Samuel	032	1881	WB-3/330 & 463	AR
Yokley, Solomon	032	1894	WB-4/217	AR
Yonce, Rudolph	085	1815	WB-G/370	AR
Yonge, Catherina	016	1815	WB-A/9	AR
Yopp, Elizabeth	072	1895	WB-4/319	AR
Yopp, Jare W.	072	1892	WB-4/282	AR
Yopp, John	072	1803	WB-A/153	AR
Yopp, Winneford	072	1804	WB-A/153	AR
York, Aaron	081	1896	WB-16/388	AR
York, Abner	054	c1836	WB-2/166	AR
York, Amos	028	1885	WB-E/367	AR
York, Archibald	054	c1837	WB-2/175	AR
York, Bethany	081	1898	WB-16/534	AR
York, C. E.	092	1894	WB-6/397	AR-Nunc.
York, Delphina	081	1898	WB-16/523	AR
York, Edward	069	1818	WB-1/295	AR
York, Elinor	081	1795	WB-2/17	AR
York, Henry	104	1817	WB-3/147	AR
York, Isaac	081	1806	WB-3/57	AR
York, Jabez	081	1879	WB-15/307	
York, James B.	054	1888	WB-5/229	CTY
York, John	081	1827	WB-5/380	AR
York, John	081	1792	WB-1/109	AR
York, Lamon	069	c1820	Orig. Only	AR

Name	Co.	Date	Recorded Copy	Original
York, Margaret	054	1839	WB-2/195	AR
York, Mary Ann	086	1827	WB-D/62	AR
York, Nancy	092	1820	WB-3/144	
York, Nancy M.	081	1897	WB-16/451	AR
York, Nathaniel	081	1837	WB-7/114	AR
York, Semore	081	1783	WB-1/8	AR
York, Thomas	081	1790	WB-1/81	AR
York, W. R.	014	1892	WB-2/483	
Yorke, Margaret	016	1879	WB-3/272	AR
Yorrell, Thomas	072	1786	WI/L46	AR
Yost, Alexander	016	1899	WB-4/340	AR
Yost, Francis	065	c1774	Orig. Only	AR
Yost, Franklin	085	1862	WB-K/302	AR
Yost, Frederick	016	1853	WB-1/221	AR
Yost, George	085	1864	WB-K/330	AR
Yost, Jacob	085	1863	WB-K/319	AR
Yost, John	085	1887	WB-2/245	CTY
Yost, Levi	016	1884	WB-3/425	AR
Yost, Paul	085	1879	WB-1/490	CTY
Yost, Paul	085	1878	WB-1/450	CTY
Yost, Philip	085	1850	WB-K/103	AR
Yost, Phillip	085	1842	WB-I/126	AR
Youell, Henry	069	c1798	WB-1/248	AR
Youell, Mary W.	063	1838	WB-2/244	
Younce, Solomon	102	c1879	WB-A/12	AR
Young, A. D.	056	1898	WB-4/121	
Young, Adam	032	1866	WB-2/332	AR
Young, Alexander	085	1770	WB-A/166	AR
Young, Allen	022	1872	WB-E/77	AR
Young, Andrew	104	1837	WB-4/218	AR
Young, Andrew	086	1835	WB-E/18	AR
Young, Andrew	032	1877	WB-3/228	AR
Young, Ann	054	c1834	Orig. Only	AR
Young, Ann	054	1860	WB-3/153	AR
Young, Ann L.	044	1873	WB-23/138	CTY
Young, Benjamin	054	1877	WB-4/249	CTY
Young, Bryant	039	c1869	WB-U/16	AR
Young, C. A.	105	1896	WB-3/232	
Young, C. E.	021	1895	WB-3/88	
Young, Catharine	070	1794	WB-C/472	AR
Young, Christopher	092	c1853	Orig. Only	AR
Young, Creed F.	107	c1885	Copy	013 AR
Young, Creed F.	107	1887	WB-2/42	
Young, Daniel	010	1823	WB-G/109	AR
Young, Dauphin	047	1795	WB-3/251	AR
Young, David J.	044	1844	WB-16/101	CTY
Young, David S.	035	1895	WB-4/459	AR
Young, Edward	072	c1796	WB-A/151	AR
Young, Edward	092	1791	WB-3/3	AR
Young, Edward	072	1817	WB-A/152	AR
Young, Edward J.	053	1876	WB-11/67	AR
Young, Elizabeth	046	1873	WB-E/98	AR
Young, Emily	084	1868	WB-D/100	CTY
Young, Ezekiel	099	1872	RB-35/187	AR
Young, Fannie	099	1877	RB-35/407	AR
Young, Francis	054	1854	WB-3/88	
Young, Frederic	032	1840	WB-1/345	
Young, General	047	1867	WB-5/158	AR
Young, George	N	1698	Orig. Only	SS/AR
Young, George	047	1794	WB-3/221	AR
Young, George	032	1874	WB-3/112	AR
Young, Gerrard	071	1796	WB-2/105	AR
Young, Giffin	086	1827	WB-D/79	AR
Young, Henry	081	1838	WB-7/146	AR
Young, Isabell	084	1836	WB-B/154	CTY

Name	Co.	Date	Recorded Copy	Original
Young, Isham	099	1875	RB-35/312	AR
Young, James	039	1814	WB-D/72	AR
Young, James	086	1896	WB-F/505	AR
Young, James	065	1835	WB-G/192	AR
Young, James M.	044	1846	WB-16/530	CTY-Nunc.
Young, James, Sr.	090	1822	WB-3/79	
Young, Jarrod	010	1820	WB-G/73	AR
Young, John	054	1875	WB-4/188	CTY
Young, John	010	1836	WB-G/262	AR
Young, John	075	1803	WB-M1/86	AR
Young, John	032	1882	WB-3/356	AR
Young, John	044	1797	WB-4/156	CTY
Young, John	013	1850	WB-A/146	
Young, John	039	1887	WB-U/407	AR
Young, John	032	1877	WB-3/207	AR
Young, John	053	1763	OB-A/55	
Young, John	073	1822	WB-E/23	AR
Young, John	047	1781	WB-3/18	AR
Young, John	044	1827	WB-10/285	CTY
Young, John	047	1849	WB-4/270	AR
Young, John	026	1841	WB-1/3	AR
Young, John M.	054	1859	WB-3/140	AR
Young, John P.	107	1888	WB-2/47	
Young, John, Sr.	039	1837	WB-K/135	AR
Young, Joseph	096	1781	WB-1/126	AR
Young, Joseph	085	c1807	WB-G/23	AR
Young, Joseph	073	1781	WB-A/225	AR
Young, Joseph	084	1845	WB-C/24	CTY
Young, Joseph	016	c1816	WB-A/11	AR
Young, Joshua M.	093	1875	WB-1/161	
Young, Julia Ann	044	1851	WB-18/282	CTY
Young, Keziah	016	1833	PQS.5/256	AR
Young, Larry	032	1884	WB-3/443	AR
Young, Lewis	013	1887	WB-B/467	AR
Young, Lucy H.	099	1900	WB-D/389	AR
Young, M. J.	PA	1899	Copy	068 AR
Young, Malvina S.	065	1895	WB-M/418	AR
Young, Margaret	085	c1831	WB-H/513	AR
Young, Marmaduke	047	1795	WB-3/253	AR-Nunc.
Young, Martha	010	1849	WB-G/439	AR
Young, Martha M.	NY	1866	Copy	053 AR
Young, Mary	084	1879	WB-E/185	CTY
Young, Mary C.	047	1858	WB-5/52	
Young, Mary Jenny	022	c1881	Orig. Only	AR
Young, Matthew	011	1856	WB-1/248	
Young, Mourning	099	1898	WB-D/103	AR
Young, Nancy	016	1832	PQS.5/216	AR
Young, Nancy	085	1839	WB-I/48	AR
Young, Nathan	011	c1841	WB-1/91	
Young, Pattie H.	098	1892	WB-A/157	CTY
Young, Peter	035	1802	WB-A/458	AR
Young, Peter W.	044	1884	WB-23/492	CTY
Young, R. E.	098	1892	WB-A/150	CTY
Young, Rebecca	013	c1897	Orig. Only	AR
Young, Reuben	066	1864	Orig. Only	AR
Young, Richard H.	053	1841	WB-6/129	AR
Young, Robert	090	1855	WB-4/296	AR
Young, Robert	069	1781	WB-1/9	AR
Young, Robert C.	046	1865	WB-D/266	AR
Young, Robert S.	016	1864	WB-2/117	AR
Young, Robert T.	039	1852	WB-N/305	
Young, Rosanna N.	016	1899	WB-4/338	AR
Young, Rosannah	013	1851	WB-A/148	
Young, Ruth	016	1872	WB-3/70	AR

Name	Co.	Date	Recorded Copy	Original
Young, Samuel	009	1820	OB-A/301	AR
Young, Samuel	085	c1793	WB-D/250	AR
Young, Samuel	099	1810	RB-9/305	AR
Young, Samuel	084	c1798	OW/182	AR
Young, Samuel	054	1847	WB-3/20	AR
Young, Samuel	099	1846	RB-26/108	AR
Young, Sarah	090	1831	WB-3/236	AR
Young, Sarah	065	1868	WB-J/249	AR
Young, Sarah	047	1814	WB-3/554	AR
Young, Sarah	013	1854	WB-A/161	
Young, Silas	016	1858	WB-2/41	AR
Young, Solomon	026	1844	WB-1/30	AR
Young, Solomon	060	1892	WB-4/495	AR
Young, Thomas	054	c1818	Orig. Only	AR
Young, W. W.	098	c1888	WB-A/168	
Young, Wesley W.	044	1857	WB-20/236	CTY
Young, William	099	1878	RB-35/418	AR
Young, William	090	1882	WB-6/127	AR
Young, William	054	c1804	Orig. Only	AR
Young, William	090	1844	WB-4/156	AR
Young, William	016	1826	WB-A/15	AR
Young, William	085	1813	WB-G/264	AR
Young, William	009	c1797	OWB/341	AR
Young, William	011	1856	WB-1/256	
Young, Willie	039	1892	WB-U/545	AR
Youngblood, Budd	056	1858	WB-1/726	
Youngblood, Henry	056	1774	Orig. Only	AR
Youngblood, Richard C.	065	1872	WB-K/85	AR
Younger, Alice R.	054	1893	WB-5/456	CTY
Younger, Amelia	038	1900	WB-4/299	
Younger, David Lee	087	c1793	Orig. Only	AR
Younger, Joseph	020	1826	RB-L/79	AR
Younger, Joseph	104	1823	WB-4/41	AR
Younger, Mary	073	1851	WB-F/481	AR
Younger, P. P.	104	1893	WB-6/492	AR
Younger, Sarah	073	1836	WB-E/371	AR
Younghusband, Thomas	030	1792	WB-2/3	
Yount, Andrew	021	1894	WB-3/35	AR
Yount, Anna	021	1847	WB-1/63	AR
Yount, C. E.	021	1895	WB-3/88	AR
Yount, Catherine	060	1869	WB-4/38	AR
Yount, Cynthia A.	021	c1885	WB-3/71	
Yount, Elcanah	021	1864	WB-1/203	AR
Yount, Ephraim	021	1870	WB-2/36	AR
Yount, Henry	060	1807	Orig. Only	AR
Yount, J. H.	060	1888	WB-4/387	AR
Yount, J. H. A.	021	1889	WB-2/450	AR
Yount, John	060	1790	Orig. Only	AR
Yount, John	021	1844	Orig. Only	AR
Yount, John	021	1863	WB-1/187	AR
Yount, Noah	021	c1883	WB-2/319	
Yount, Noah	064	1894	WB-2/329	AR
Yount, P. L.	021	1884	WB-2/297	
Yours, William	084	c1796	OW/24	AR
Yow, Alfred L.	081	1899	WB-17/16	AR
Yow, Enoch S.	081	1894	WB-16/291	
Yow, Henry	081	1859	WB-11/265	AR
Yow, John	022	1891	WB-E/472	AR
Yure, Eliza	065	1891	WB-L/584	AR
Zachary, Anna	055	1883	WB-A/57	
Zachary, J. M.	055	1898	WB-A/149	
Zachary, M.	055	1898	WB-A/155	
Zachary, William	092	c1823	Orig. Only	AR
Zachary, Woodford	055	1885	WB-A/68	
Zachory, Jonathan	093	1899	WB-2/173	
Zachry, Jonathan	022	1795	RB-2/57	AR
Zager, B. M.	013	1898	WB-D/119	AR
Zearge, Jacob	028	1731	Orig. Only	SS/AR
Zeigler, John H.	075	1889	WB-0/302	AR
Zeraker, Samuel	032	1842	WB-1/398	
Zerker, John	085	c1803	WB-E/175	AR
Zevely, A. T.	038	1872	WB-2/89	
Zevely, Van N.	038	1863	WB-1/220	AR
Ziglar, Benjamin	090	1858	WB-4/315	AR
Ziglar, John	090	1867	WB-5/39	AR
Ziglar, Leonard	090	1845	WB-4/199	AR
Ziglar, Leonard	090	1850	WB-4/263	AR
Ziglar, William M.	090	1865	WB-6/231	
Zimmerman, Christian	085	c1790	WB-D/263	AR
Zimmerman, George	046	1812	WB-A/426	AR
Zimmerman, Jacob	060	c1803	Orig. Only	AR
Zimmerman, James	090	1843	WB-4/110	AR
Zimmerman, John	046	c1878	WB-E/231	AR
Zimmerman, John	038	1855	WB-1/86	AR
Zimmerman, John	028	1722	Orig. Only	SS/AR
Zimmerman, John	060	1831	WB-1/205	AR
Zimmerman, John	090	1808	WB-2/91	AR
Zimmerman, Peter	060	1845	WB-2/235	AR
Zimmerman, Reuben	090	1844	WB-4/171	AR
Zimmerman, Reuben	090	1843	WB-4/113	AR
Zinn, Margaretha	092	1774	WB-1/22	AR
Zoeller, Edward	037	1897	WB-H/373	AR
Zollicoffer, Ann	047	1834	WB-4/109	AR
Zollicoffer, George	047	1815	WB-3/569	AR
Zollicoffer, James	047	1836	WB-4/134	AR
Zollicoffer, Julius H.	047	c1853	Orig. Only	AR